European Americana

Volume II: 1601–1650

*Preparation of the present volume
has been made possible by
funds provided by the
Division of Research Programs of the
National Endowment for the Humanities
through its Research Materials
and Research Resources Programs
with the further assistance of
The Readex Microprint Corporation
and
Brown University*

The John Carter Brown Library

EUROPEAN AMERICANA

A Chronological Guide to Works Printed in
Europe Relating to the Americas,
1493–1776

Volume II: 1601–1650

Edited by

John Alden

and

Dennis C. Landis

New York
Readex Books
A Division of the Readex Microprint Corporation
1982

Copyright© 1982 by the

Readex Microprint Corporation

ISBN 0-918414-09-1

Library of Congress Card No. 80-51141

Printed in the United States of America

Table of Contents

Preface

Though the principles by which the present series has been developed were set forth in the preface to the previous volume, some consideration of the particular nature of that here offered is perhaps appropriate. For one thing, the closing years of the sixteenth century represented to a marked degree the end of an era, or rather, the opening of a new phase in the history of the Americas and their relation to Europe. Whereas the New World had previously been dominated by the Spanish, more determined effectors of that hegemony arose on all sides, from the Dutch, the English, and the French. Now to find realization were the efforts of those earlier constrained to view riches tantalizingly from afar, or to nibble precariously at them.

On one hand the exploits of Sir Walter Raleigh were to be echoed by those of the Dutch, their independence from Spain as the United Provinces enlarged by the secret treaty of 1609 with Philip III, permitting trade in Spanish waters. In France the Edict of Nantes in 1598 released energies previously dissipated in religious controversy and strife. And, on the other hand, the death of Philip II in that same year was to produce a pronounced shift in Spanish polity. Whereas he had kept affairs of state closely within his own control, his successor, Philip III, self-indulgent and indolent, was to delegate to subordinates the administration of a realm increasingly weakened economically from within and politically abroad.

In attempting to chart the consequences of the above factors in relation to the Americas as reflected in works published in Europe, a somewhat tighter definition of our scope than that previously set may now be valid. Should we consider as American, for instance, those works written in the New World which in no way draw upon American experience and might as readily have been produced in Europe itself? Though José Toribio Medina in his *Biblioteca Hispano-Americana* included all possible references to the Spanish in the New World, it should be borne in mind that his stated focus was indeed on the Spanish themselves.

This is a different emphasis from our own, which is the effect of the Americas upon Europe, and what the area offered as a field for conquest; the discovery and exploitation of resources; and an opportunity for missionary endeavour. On these grounds we have ventured to exclude those works which, though previously categorized as American, to our view cannot truly be characterized as such; these range from the numerous theological works composed by Spanish clerics as recorded by Medina, to comparable writings produced by New England divines that might as readily have been penned in an English study and were concerned primarily with religious controversy there.

In this context perhaps the most vexatious problem has been that of the multitudinous Spanish documents which, because they ap-

Preface

peared in printed form, Medina undertook, with varying degrees of success, to describe. That such proliferation reflects the altered nature of Spanish administration under Philip III and his successor Philip IV seems an inescapable conclusion, as is that these documents, howsoever widely scattered today, were intended not for general distribution but for internal use by the committees and councils concerned. Largely constituting petitions on behalf of private individuals or special interests, these documents accelerated in number to a dismaying degree during the years under review, with an added complication that, all too frequently, no date can be authoritatively assigned them. We have found ourselves constrained to be selective in including them, limiting ourselves chiefly to those of general significance, though we have thought it worthwhile to record those in the British Library which appear not to have come to the notice of Richard Garnett, Medina's source for its holdings. (Regrettably, Medina was apparently without comparable assistance for the Bibliothèque Nationale.)

If our treatment of the sixteenth century seemed overburdened with works relating to syphilis, introduced to Europe from Hispaniola, so the present volume reflects the extraordinary concern of its period with tobacco. True, the plant was early known to Spanish explorers, and in Spain (as later elsewhere) every effort was made to find in it therapeutic value. Now, however, the use of tobacco for purely personal pleasure takes on a major rôle, particularly in the British Isles where it was made fashionable, we are told, by Sir Walter Raleigh, to whom Sir Francis Drake and Sir Ralph Lane, first governor of Virginia, had introduced it. Though the individual references we report may not in themselves be significant, cumulatively they reveal the extent of the addiction, beyond that provided by those works lavishly described in the catalog of the collection formed by George Arents and now in the New York Public Library. Nor should it be forgotten that tobacco so caught the fancy of the British public as alone to make viable the settlement of Virginia, and that of Barbados prior to the introduction of sugar cane. The economic consequences of the tobacco plant should in no way be underestimated, and are accounted for by the hold it quickly gained upon its users.

That syphilis continues to figure in this volume will be apparent, despite our announced conclusion that by the year 1601 Europe had made the disease its own. But what we have found it necessary to include are not references to syphilis as such: they are confined to discussions of its American origins. We are confident that the significance of these discussions extends beyond that immediate question, in that they reveal a new approach to the nature of the New World. In his *The Old World and the New* (Cambridge, 1970), J. H. Elliott has pointed out that in the sixteenth century the European's interest in the Americas was inhibited by a deference to the classical tradition; that what was unknown to the ancients scarcely merited notice. Now in the seventeenth century we find a fresh recognition of far wider fields of knowledge to be confronted. In the wide acceptance of an American origin for syphilis it is possible to see symptoms of a new awareness on the part of Europeans that the ancients—in the persons of a Galen or a Hippocrates—were not omniscient, an awareness which liberated the Europeans to seek wider perceptions.

Of the approximately 7400 items contained in this volume, less than one third appear in Sabin. As noted in our first volume, an increase of this magnitude reflects a wider recognition, with the passage of time, of the multiple aspects of the Americas' impact on Europe. Ranging from literature to the natural sciences, the subjects newly introduced or more extensively examined constitute, we feel, an indispensable resource for the study of that impact.

Americana as found in this volume will fall into three of the categories defined by Henry Harrisse: 'obvious,' 'partial' and 'incidental' Americana. In 'obvious' Americana, embracing books entirely on America or American subjects, we would venture to hope that we have approached definitiveness. In 'partial' Americana, an area comprised of books containing substantial sections of American interest, we hope to have identified at least eighty percent of the existing items.

The concept of 'incidental' Americana involves books with one or more American references as an essential part of an author's immediate thought, but not necessarily as part of the work's overall purpose. Here it is not possible to estimate precisely what level of completeness has been achieved. We have endeavored to include all that has come to our attention, and have searched wherever we suspected more lay hidden. Nevertheless, this is a field of Americana which is still being actively collected and in which new material is constantly being identified.

The decision to prepare a bibliographic guide which offers reasonable definitiveness in two categories but with only partial coverage in the third is somewhat unconventional. We feel, however, that it is justified on the following grounds. First, the more generous approach is in the tradition of Harrisse and Sabin, and to attempt anything less would do violence to a concept proven by time and experience to be the most effective way of dealing with the matter at hand. Second, to restrict the guide to the first two categories would produce a static work which would fail to perform a basic function of a bibliography, that of offering new insights into its subject.

The reader should be reminded that our practice is to provide a descriptive note concerning American content only when such content is not obvious from the title, this practice being employed only for the earliest edition of each work; later editions and translations refer back to that edition. Exceptions will occur when subsequent editions have been enlarged or otherwise altered to include further American material. It will be noted that the guide largely excludes serials.

Once again it is necessary to emphasize how conscious we are of how much may have escaped our notice. Yet it can perhaps be said that here brought together is a new mosaic which more richly reveals

Preface

the complexity of its components as Europeans asserted themselves in the New World.

In our efforts, Dr Landis has taken on added responsibilities. For work in this period, he held chief responsibility for the German and Dutch items, but his efforts in compilation and description were by no means limited to those languages or geographical areas. In addition, he supervised the construction of the indexes, and is responsible for their form and content. Upon my retirement, Dr Landis assumed editorship of the project, overseeing the completion of this volume.

To Donald K. Moore fell the task of preparing the completed manuscript for the compositor. He improved the book's design and was responsible for the proofreading of its text. In addition to coordinating relations with the printer, he aided in the final stages of our research and was most helpful in detecting errors and inconsistencies we had overlooked. Mrs Leslie R. Patterson later assumed from Dr Moore the coordination of book design and completed the proofreading of the indexes and page proofs.

We are grateful for the patience and accuracy of Miss Lynne A. Southwick, who typed the manuscript and entered the computerized index, in addition to carrying out a large number of editorial tasks requested by us. Miss Ann P. Barry is to be thanked for her copious assistance in editing the indexes. We would also express our continuing gratitude to those colleagues who have replied to our queries, and to the libraries which have made available their collections for our examination.

John Alden

References

Aa   Aa, Abraham Jacob van der. *Biographisch woordenboek der Nederlanden . . .* uitgegeven onder hoofredactie van Dr. G. D. J. Schotel. Nieuwe uitgaaf. Haarlem: J. J. van Brederode [1863–78]. 12 v.

Abkoude   Abkoude, Johannes van. *Naamregister van de bekendste en meest in gebruik zynde Nederduitsche boeken welke sedert het jaar 1600 tot het jaar 1761 zyn uitgekomen . . .* Nu . . . vermeerderd door Reinier Arrenberg. Tweede druk. Rotterdam: G. A. Arrenberg. 1788. (Repr., Leyden: A. W. Sijthoff, 1965).

Alcocer (Valladolid)   Alcocer y Martínez, Mariano. *Catálogo razonado de obras impresas in Valladolid, 1481–1800.* Valladolid: Casa Social Católica, 1926.

Aldis   Aldis, Harry Gidney. *A list of books printed in Scotland before 1700, including those printed furth of the realm for Scottish booksellers.* Edinburgh: The Edinburgh Bibliographical Society, 1904.

Allison & Rogers   Allison, Antony Francis, & Rogers, David Morrison. *A catalogue of Catholic books in English . . . 1558–1640.* Bognor Regis: Arundel Press, 1913. 2 v. (Repr., London: Dawson, 1964).

Arents   Arents, George. *Tobacco, its history.* New York: Rosenbach Co., 1937–52. 5 v.

Arents (Add.)   New York. Public Library. Arents Tobacco Collection. *Tobacco; a catalogue.* New York: New York Public Library, 1958–69. 10 pts.

Asher   Asher, Georg Michael. *A bibliographical and historical essay on the Dutch books and pamphlets relating to New-Netherland.* Amsterdam: F. Muller, 1854–67. 2 pts.

Atkinson (Fr. Ren.)   Atkinson, Geoffroy. *La littérature géographique francaise de la Renaissance; répertoire bibliographique.* Paris: A. Picard, 1927. (Repr., Geneva: Slatkine Reprints, 1972).

BN (Hist. de France)   Paris. Bibliothèque Nationale. Département des imprimés. *Catalogue de l'histoire de France.* Paris: Firmin Didot frères, 1855–79. 11 v.

Backer   Backer, Augustin de. *Bibliothèque de la Compagnie de Jésus.* Bruxelles: O. Schepens; Paris: A. Picard, 1890–1932. 11 v.

References

Baer (Md)   Baer, Elizabeth. *Seventeenth century Maryland; a bibliography.* Baltimore: John Work Garret Library, 1949.

Baginsky (German Americana)   Baginsky, Paul. 'German works relating to America, 1493–1800; a list compiled from the collections of the New York Public Library'. *Bulletin of the New York Public Library,* XLII-XLIV (1938–40), *passim.*

Barrett (Baja Calif.)   Barrett, Ellen Catherine. *Baja California 1535–1956; a bibliography of historical, geographical, and scientific literature relating to . . . Baja California and to the adjacent islands.* Los Angeles: Bennett & Marshall, 1957–67. 2 v.

Baudrier (Lyons)   Baudrier, Henri Louis. *Bibliographie Lyonnaise; recherches sur les imprimeurs, libraires, relieurs et fondeurs de lettres de Lyon au XVI siècle.* Lyons: A. Brun, 1895–1921. 13 v. (Repr., Paris: F. De Nobele, 1964–65).

Baudrier (Lyons) Suppl.   *Supplément provisoire á la 'Bibliographie Lyonnaise' du president Baudrier.* Paris: Bibliothèque Nationale, 1967–.

Baumgartner (Fracastoro)   Baumgartner, Leona, & Fulton, John F. *A bibliography of the poem* Syphilis, sive Morbus gallicus *by Girolamo Fracastoro, of Verona.* New Haven: Yale University Press, 1935.

Bechtold   Bechtold, Arthur. *Kritisches Verzeichnis der Schriften Johann Michael Moscheroschs.* Munich: H. Stobbe Verlag, 1922. (Einzelschriften zur Bücher und Handscriften, hrsg. von Georg Leidinger und Ernst Schulte-Strathaus, II).

Becker   Becker, Carl. *Jobst Amman, Zeichner und Form-schneider, Kupferätzer und Stecher.* Leipzig: R. Weigel, 1854. (Repr., Nieuwkoop: B. de Graaf, 1961).

Bell (Jes.rel.)   Bell, James Ford. *Jesuit relations and other Americana in the library of James F. Bell;* a catalogue compiled by Frank K. Walter and Virginia Doneghy. Minneapolis: University of Minnesota Press, 1950.

Bell Catalogue   Minnesota. University. Library. James Ford Bell Collection. *The James Ford Bell collection; a list of additions. . . .* Comp. by John Parker [and Carol Urness]. Minneapolis: University of Minnesota Press, 1955–70; The James Ford Bell Library, 1975.

Berès (Pays-Bas anciens)	Berès, Pierre. *Pays-Bas anciens.* [Catalogue 71.] Paris: P. Berès, n.d.
Benzing	Benzing, Josef. *Die Buchdrucker des 16. und 17. Jahrhunderts im deutschen Sprachgebiet.* Wiesbaden: O. Harrassowitz, 1963. (Beiträge zum Buch- und Bibliothekswesen, XII).
Bibl. belg.	*Bibliotheca Belgica; bibliographie générale des Pays-Bas.* Ghent: Vanderpoorten (l.sér.: C.Vyt); The Hague: M. Nijhoff, 1880–1967. 240 pts.
Bibl. mar. esp.	Instituto nacional del libro español. *Ensayo de bibliografía marítima española.* Barcelona: Casa Provincial de Caridad, 1943.
Borba de Moraes	Moraes, Rubens Borba de. *Bibliographie Brasiliana; a bibliographical essay.* Amsterdam: Colibris Editora, 1958, 2 v.
Borsa	Borsa, Gedeon. 'Die Ausgaben der "Cosmographia" von Johannes Honter'. *Essays in honour of Victor Scholderer,* Mainz: K. Pressler, 1970, p. 90–105.
Bragge	Bragge, William. *Bibliotheca nicotiana; a catalogue of books about tobacco.* Birmingham: Priv. print., 1880.
Briels	Briels, J. G. C. A. *Zuidnederlandse boekdrukkers en boekverkopers in de republiek der Verenigde Nederlanden omstreeks 1570–1630.* Nieuwkoop: B. de Graaf, 1974. (Bibliotheca bibliographica Neerlandica, VI).
Brigham (Roy.procl.)	Great Britain. Sovereigns, etc. *British royal proclamations relating to America, 1603–1783.* Ed. by Clarence S. Brigham. Worcester, Mass.: American Antiquarian Society, 1911. (Transactions and collections of the American Antiquarian Society, XII).
Bruckner	Bruckner, J. *A bibliographical catalogue of seventeenth-century German books published in Holland.* The Hague: Mouton, 1971. (Anglia germanica; British studies in Germanic languages and literatures, XIII).
Brunet	Brunet, Jacques-Charles. *Manuel du libraire et de l'amateur de livres.* Paris: Firmin Didot frères, 1860–80. 9v. (Repr., Copenhagen: Rosenkilde & Bagger, 1966–67).
Brushfield (Raleigh)	Brushfield, Thomas Nadauld. *A bibliography of Sir Walter Raleigh.* 2nd edn., rev. & enl. Exeter: J. G. Commin, 1908.

References

Burmeister (Münster) Burmeister, Karl Heinz. *Sebastian Münster; eine Bibliographie.* Wiesbaden: G. Pressler, 1964.

Cartier (de Tournes) Cartier, Alfred. *Bibliographie des éditions des de Tournes, imprimeurs lyonnais.* Paris: Bibliothèques Nationales de France, 1937–38. 2 v. (Repr., Geneva: Slatkine Reprints, 1970).

Caspar (Kepler) Caspar, Max. *Bibliographia Kepleriana; ein Führer durch das gedruckte Schrifttum . . .* unter Mitarbeit von Ludwig Rothenfelder. Munich: C. H. Beck, 1936.

Catalogus van boeken Amsterdam. Nationale Tentoonstelling van het Boek, 1910. *Catalogus van boeken in Noord-Nederland verschenen van den vroegsten tijd tot op heden.* The Hague: M. Njihoff, 1911.

Church Church, Elihu Dwight. *A catalogue of books relating to the discovery and early history of North and South America, forming a part of the Library of E. D. Church [1482–1884].* New York: Dodd, Mead & Co., 1907. 5 v. (Repr., Gloucester, Mass.: P. Smith, 1951).

Church (Eng.lit.) ———. *A catalogue of books, consisting of English literature and miscellanea.* New York: Dodd, Mead & Co., 1902, 2 v.

Cioranescu (Bibl. francoespañola) Cioranescu, Alexandre. *Bibliografía francoespañola (1600–1715).* Madrid: Real Academia Española, 1977. (Anejos del Boletín de la Real Academia Española, XXXVI).

Cioranescu (XVI) ———. *Bibliographie de la littérature française du seizième siècle.* Paris: C. Klincksieck, 1959.

Cioranescu (XVII) ———. *Bibliographie de la littérature française du dix-septième siècle.* Paris: Centre National de la Recherche Scientifique, 1965–66. 3 v.

Clayton-Torrence Virginia. State Library, Richmond. Dept. of Bibliography. *A trial bibliography of Colonial Virginia . . .* William Clayton-Torrence, bibliographer. Richmond: D. Bottom, superintendent of public printing, 1908–10. 2 v. (Virginia. State Library, Richmond. 5th-6th annual report).

Coccia Coccia, Edmondo Maria. *Le edizioni delle opere del Mantovano.* Rome: Institutum Carmelitanum, 1960. (Collectanea bibliographica carmelitana, II).

Collijn (Sver.bibl.) Collijn, Isak G. A. *Sveriges bibliografi intil år 1600.* Uppsala: Svenska Litteratursällskapet, 1927–38. 3 v.

References

Colmeiro

Colmeiro, Manuel. 'Biblioteca de los economistas españoles de las siglos XVI, XVII, XVIII.' *In* Academia de Ciencias Morales y Politicas. *Memorias.* Tercera ed., Tomo 1. Madrid: Imprenta del Asilo de huérfanos, 1900.

Crawford (Roy. procl.)

Crawford, James Ludovic Lindsay, 26th earl of. *Bibliotheca Lindesiana . . . a bibliography of royal proclamations of the Tudor and Stuart sovereigns and of others published under authority, 1485–1714.* Oxford: Clarendon Press, 1910.

Cundall (WI)

Cundall, Frank. *Bibliography of the West Indies (excluding Jamaica).* Kingston, Jamaica: The Institute of Jamaica, 1909.

Cushing

Yale University. School of Medicine. Yale Medical Library. Historical Library. *The Harvey Cushing collection.* New York: Schuman's, 1943.

Dampierre

Dampierre, Jacques, marquis de. *Essai sur les sources le l'histoire des Antilles françaises (1492–1664).* Paris: A. Picard et fils, 1904. (Mémoires et documents publies par la Société de l'Ecole des chartes, VI).

Desgraves (Les Haultin)

Desgraves, Louis. *Les Haultin, 1571–1623.* Geneva: E. Droz. 1960. (L'imprimerie à La Rochelle, II).

Doe (Paré)

Doe, Janet. *A bibliography of the works of Ambroise Paré.* Chicago: University of Chicago Press, 1937.

Dr. Williams

Williams Library, London. *Early nonconformity, 1566–1800; a catalogue of books in Dr. Williams's Library, London.* Boston: G. K. Hall, 1968.

Dt. Ges. Kat.

Deutscher Gesamtkatalog . . . herausgegeben von der Preussischen Staatsbibliothek. Berlin: Preussische Druckerei- und Verlags-Aktiengesellschaft, 1931–39. 14 v. (A–Beethordnung).

Elst (Avontroot)

Elst, C. van den. 'Une dernière victime Belge du Saint-Office. 1632. J.-B. Avontroot'. *Revue Trimestrielle* (Brussels) XXIII (July 1859), 160–75.

Escudero (Seville)

Escudero y Perosso, Francisco. *Tipografía Hispalense; anales bibliográficos de la ciudad de Sevilla desde el establecimiento de la imprenta hasta fines del siglo XVIII.* Madrid: Sucesores de Rivadeneyra, 1894.

Faber du Faur

Yale University. Library. Yale Collection of German Literature. *German Baroque literature; a catalogue of the collection in the Yale University*

References

	Library, by Curt von Faber du Faur. New Haven: Yale University Press, 1958.
Ferguson (Bibl. chem.)	Glasgow. Royal Technical College. Library. Young Collection. *Bibliotheca chemica: a catalogue of the alchemical, chemical and pharmaceutical books in the collection of the late James Young of Kelly and Durris . . .* by John Ferguson. Glasgow: J. Maclehose and Sons, 1906. 2 v.
Firpo (Campanella)	Firpo, Luigi. *Bibliografia degli scritti di Tommaso Campanella.* Turin: V. Bona, 1940.
Firpo (Ragguagli)	———. *I 'Ragguagli di Parnaso' di Traiano Boccalini; bibliografia delle edizioni italiane.* Florence: Sansoni, 1955. (Biblioteca degli eruditi e dei bibliofili, XII).
Fleuret & Perceau	Esternod, Claude d'. *L'espadon satyrique de Claude d'Esternod. Première édition critique . . . avec . . . une bibliographie . . . et des notes par Fernand Fleuret et Louis Perceau.* Paris: J. Fort, 1922.
Garcia (Alcalá de Henares)	García López, Juan Catalina. *Ensayo de una tipografía Complutense.* Madrid: M. Tello, 1889.
Gibson (Bacon)	Gibson, Reginald Walter. *Francis Bacon: a bibliography of his works and of Baconiana to the year 1750.* Oxford: Scrivener Press, 1950.
Gibson (More)	———. *St. Thomas More: a preliminary bibliography of his works . . . With a bibliography of Utopiana;* compiled by R. W. Gibson and J. Max Patrick. New Haven: Yale University Press, 1961.
Goedeke	Goedeke, Karl. *Grundriss zur Geschichte der deutschen Dichtung aus den Quellen.* 2. ganz neubearb. Aufl. Dresden: Ehlermann, 1884–1966. 15 v.
Goldsmith (France)	British Museum. Dept. of Printed Books. *A short title catalogue of French books, 1601–1700, in the library of the British Museum,* by V. F. Goldsmith. Folkestone & London: Dawsons of Pall Mall, 1969–73. 7 pts.
Goldsmith (Spain)	———. *A short title catalogue of Spanish and Portuguese books, 1601–1700, in the library of the British Museum . . .* by V. F. Goldsmith. Folkestone & London: Dawsons of Pall Mall, 1974.
Goujet (Bibl. franç.)	Goujet, Claude Pierre. *Bibliotheque françoise, ou Histoire de la littérature françoise.* Paris: P. J. Mariette & H.-L. Guerin, 1741–56. 18 v.
Graesse	Grässe, Johann Georg Theodor. *Trésor de livres rares et précieux.* Dresden: R. Kuntze, 1859–69. 7 v. in 4. (Repr., Milan: G. Görlich, 1951).

Greg — Greg, Sir Walter Wilson. *A bibliography of the English printed drama to the Restoration.* London: The Bibliographical Society, 1939–59. 4 v.

Grolier Club (Langland to Wither) — Grolier Club, New York. *Catalogue of original and early editions of some of the poetical and prose works of English writers from Langland to Wither.* New York: Grolier Club, 1893.

Grolier Club (Wither to Prior) — ——. *Catalogue of original and early editions of some of the poetical and prose works of English writers from Wither to Prior.* New York: Grolier Club, 1905. 3 v.

Guerra (Monardes) — Guerra, Francisco. *Nicolás Bautista Monardes: su vida y su obra.* Mexico, D. F.: Comp. fundidora de Fierro y Acero de Monterrey, 1961. (Yale University. Dept. of the History of Medicine. Publication no. 41).

Handler (Barbados) — Handler, Jerome S. *A guide to source materials for the study of Barbados history, 1627–1834.* Carbondale: Southern Illinois University Press, 1971.

Hanke/ Giménez — Hanke, Lewis, & Giménez Fernández, Manuel. *Bartolomé de las Casas, 1474–1566; bibliografía crítica y cuerpo de materiales.* Santiago de Chile: Fondo José Toribio Medina, 1954.

Harrisse (NF) — Harrisse, Henry. *Notes pour servir à l'histoire, à la bibliographie et à la cartographie de la Nouvelle-France et des pays adjacents, 1545–1700.* Paris: Libr. Tross, 1872. (Repr., Dubuque, Ia.: Brown, 1964).

Henrey (Brit. bot.) — Henrey, Blanche. *British botanical and horticultural literature before 1800.* London: Oxford University Press, 1975. 3 v.

Hertzberger — Internationaal Antiquariaat (Menno Hertzberger & Co.) N.V., Amsterdam. *Catalogues.* Amsterdam: 1920–.

Hoe (English) — Hoe, Robert. *Catalogue of books by English authors who lived before the year 1700, forming a part of the library of Robert Hoe.* New York: Gillis Press, 1903–05. 5 v.

Hoe (Foreign, 1909) — ——. *Catalogue of books in foreign languages published after the year 1600 . . .* New York: Priv. print., 1909, 4 v.

Holmes (Du Bartas) — Du Bartas, Guillaume de Salluste, seigneur. *The works . . . a critical edition . . .* by Urban Tigner Holmes, Jr., John Coriden Lyons, Robert White

References

	Linker. Chapel Hill: University of North Carolina Press, 1935–40. 3 v. 'Bibliography': III:565–576.
Holmes (MM)	Holmes, Thomas James. *The minor Mathers; a list of their works.* Cambridge, Mass.: Harvard University Press, 1940.
Holzmann-Bohatta	Holzmann, Michael, & Bohatta, Hanns. *Deutsches Anonymen-Lexikon, 1501–1850.* Weimar: Gesellschaft der Bibliophilen, 1902–28. 7 v. (Repr., Hildesheim: G. Olms, 1961).
Horden (Quarles)	Horden, John. *Francis Quarles (1592–1644); a bibliography of his works to the year 1800.* Oxford: Oxford University Press, 1953. (Oxford Bibliographical Society. Publications, new ser., II [1948]).
Houzeau & Lancaster	Houzeau, Jean Charles, & Lancaster, Albert. *Bibliographie générale de l'astronomie jusqu'en 1880.* Nouv. éd. London: Holland Press, 1964. 2 v. in 3.
Hunt (Bot.)	Hunt, Rachel McM. M. *Catalogue of botanical books.* Pittsburgh: Hunt Botanical Library, 1958–61. 2 v. in 3.
Huth	Huth, Henry. *The Huth library; a catalogue.* London: Ellis & White, 1880. 5 v.
Ind. aur.	*Index Aureliensis; catalogus librorum sedecimo saeculo impressorum,* I–VI (A–Carr). Geneva: Fondation Index Aureliensis, 1962–. In progress.
Innocencio	Silva, Innocencio Francisco da. *Diccionario bibliografico portuguez.* Lisbon: Imprensa Nacional, 1858–1923. 22 v.
JCB AR	Brown University. John Carter Brown Library. *Annual report.* Providence: The Library, 1901–75. (Years 1901–1966, repr., with index, The Library, 1972).
JCB (101 Bks.)	——. *Rare Americana: a selection of one hundred & one books, maps & prints* not in the John Carter Brown Library. Providence: Associates of the John Carter Brown Library, 1974.
JCB (3)	——. *Bibliotheca Americana; catalogue of the John Carter Brown Library.* 3rd ed. Providence: The Library, 1919–31. 3 pts in 5 v.
JCB (STL)	——. *Bibliotheca Americana: catalogue of the John Carter Brown Library . . . Short-title list of additions, books printed 1471–1700.* Providence: Brown University Press, 1973.

Jameson (Usselinx) — Jameson, John Franklin. *Willem Usselinx, founder of the Dutch and Swedish West India Companies.* New York: G. P. Putnam's Sons, 1887.

Jantz (German Americana) — *The Harold Jantz collection at Duke University; a selected bibliography, with an introduction by Dr. Jantz.* Prepared for the 1979 Conference on German-American Literary Relations. [Durham, N.C.: 1979].

Jantz (German Baroque) — *German Baroque literature: a descriptive catalogue of the collection of Harold Jantz.* New Haven: Research Publications, 1974. 2 v.

Jiménez Catalán (Saragossa) — Jiménez Catalán, Manuel. *Ensayo de una tipografía zaragozana del siglo xvii.* Saragossa: Tipografía 'La Académica', 1925 [i.e., 1927].

Jöcher — Jöcher, Christian Gottlieb. *Allgemeines Gelehrten-Lexikon,* Leipzig: Gleditsch, 1750–51. 4 v.

——. ——. Fortsetzung und Ergänzungen. Leipzig, Bremen, Delmenhorst: 1784–97. 7 v. (Repr. with the preceding, Hildesheim: G. Olms, 1960–61).

Jördens — Jördens, Karl Heinrich. *Lexikon deutscher Dichter und Prosaisten.* Leipzig: Weidmann, 1806–11. 6 v. (Repr., Hildesheim: G. Olms, 1970).

Johnson (Spenser) — Johnson, Francis Rarick. *A critical bibliography of the works of Edmund Spenser.* Baltimore: Johns Hopkins Press, 1933.

Jones (Goulart) — Jones, Leonard Chester. *Simon Goulart, 1543–1628; étude biographique et bibliographique.* Geneva: Georg & cie, 1917.

Kebabian — Kebabian, John S. *The Henry C. Taylor Collection.* New Haven: Yale University Library, 1971.

Kelly (Calendar of Docs) — Kelly, Celsus, comp. *Calendar of documents: Spanish voyages in the South Pacific . . . 1567–1794.* Madrid: Franciscan Historical Studies (Australia), with Archivo Ibero-Americano (Madrid), 1965,

Keuning (Blaeu) — Keuning, Johannes, *Willem Jansz. Blaeu: A biography and history of his work as a cartographer and publisher . . .* Rev. & ed. by Marijke Donkersloot-De Vrij. Amsterdam: Theatrum Orbis Terrarum, [1973].

Keynes (Browne) — Keynes, Sir Geoffrey. *A bibliography of Sir Thomas Browne.* Oxford: Clarendon Press, 1968.

Keynes (Donne) — ——. *Bibliography of Dr. John Donne.* 3rd ed. Cambridge: Cambridge University Press, 1958.

References

Kleerkooper   Kleerkooper, M. M. *De boekhandel te Amsterdam voornamelijk in de 17e eeuw.* The Hague: M. Nijhoff, 1914–16. 2 v.

Knuttel   The Hague. Koninklijke Bibliotheek. *Catalogus van de pamfletten-verzameling berustende in de Koninklijke Bibliotheek,* berwerkt . . . door Dr. W. P. C. Knuttel. The Hague: Algemeene Landsdrukkerij, 1889–1920. 9 v.

Koeman (Bl)   'The Blaeus: Willem Janszoon, Cornelis & Joan'. In Koeman, Cornelis. *Atlantes Neerlandici; bibliography of terrestrial, maritime, and celestial atlases and pilot books, published in the Netherlands up to 1880.* Amsterdam: Theatrum Orbis Terrarum, 1967–71, I:68–294.

Koeman (Lan)   'Langenes, Barent'. As in the above, II: 252–261.

Koeman (M.Bl)   'Pilot guides published by Willem Janszoon Blaeu and his successors'. As in the above, IV:27–112.

Koeman (Me)   'Mercator-Hondius-Janssonius'. As in the above, II:281–549.

Koeman (Ort)   'Ortelius, Abraham'. As in the above, III:25–83.

Koeman (Wyt)   'Wytfliet, Cornelis van'. As in the above, III:219–220.

Kress   Harvard University. Kress Library of Business and Economics. *Catalogue.* Boston: Baker Library, Harvard Graduate School of Business Administration, 1940–67. 5 v.

Lande (Canadiana)   McGill University, Montreal. Library. *The Lawrence Lande collection of Canadiana in the Redpath Library of McGill University; a bibliography* . . . by Lawrence Lande. Montreal: Lawrence Lande Foundation for Canadian Historical Research, 1965.

Laurenti (Nov. pic. esp.)   Laurenti, Joseph Luciano. *Ensayo de una bibliografía de la novela picaresca española años 1554–1964.* Madrid: C.S.I.C., 1968. (Cuadernos bibliograficos XXIII).

Leclerc (1867)   Leclerc, Charles. *Bibliotheca Americana: Catalogue raisonné d'une très-précieuse collection de livres.* Paris: Maisonneuve & Cie., 1867.

Leclerc (1878)   ——. *Bibliotheca Americana: Histoire, géographie, voyages . . . des deux Amériques.* Paris: Maisonneuve & Cie., 1878.

Ledeboer   Ledeboer, Adrianus Marinus. *Alfabetische lijst der boekdrukkers, boekverkoopers en uitgevers in Noord-Nederland.* Utrecht: J. L. Beijers, 1876.

Leite   Leite, Serafim. *Historia da companhia de Jesus no Brasil.* Rio de Janeiro: Instituto Nacional do Livro, 1938–50. 9 v. 'Suplemento bio-bibliographico', v. 8–9.

Le Moine   Le Moine, Roger. *L'Amérique et les poètes français de la Renaissance.* Ottawa: Université d'Ottawa, 1972.

Libr. Vinciana   Libreria Vinciana. *Autori italiani del '600, a cura di Sandro Piantanida, Lamberto Diotallevi, Giancarlo Livraghi.* Milan: Libreria Vinciana, 1948–51. 4 v.

Lohmeier (Olearius)   Olearius, Adam. *Vermehrte newe Beschreibung der muscowitischen und persischen Reyse.* Hrsg. von Dieter Lohmeier. Tübingen: M. Niemeyer, 1971. 'Bibliographie', p. 63–77.

McAlpin   New York. Union Theological Seminary. Library. *Catalogue of the McAlpin collection of British history and theology.* Comp. & ed. by Charles Ripley Gillett. New York: 1927–30. 5 v.

McCoy   McCoy, James Comly. *Jesuit relations of Canada, 1632–1673; a bibliography.* Paris: A. Rau, 1937.

Madan (Oxford)   Madan, Falconer. *Oxford books; a bibliography of printed works relating to the university and city of Oxford or printed or published there.* Oxford: Clarendon Press, 1895–1931. 3 v.

Maggs   Maggs Bros., London. *Bibliotheca Americana et Philippina.* London: 1922–30. 9 v. in 8.

Maggs Cat. 412 (1921)   ——. *The voyages & discoveries of early travellers and missionaries. Part 1: America.* London: 1921. (*Its* Catalogue 412).

Maggs Cat. 465 (Americana IV)   ——. *Bibliotheca Americana et Philippina. Part IV.* London: 1925. (*Its* Catalogue 465).

Maggs Cat. 479 (Americana V)   ——. *Bibliotheca Americana. Part V.* London: 1926. (*Its* Catalogue 479).

Maggs Cat. 496 (Americana VI)   ——. *Bibliotheca Americana. Part VI. Books on America in Spanish.* London: 1927. (*Its* Catalogue 496).

Maggs Cat. 502 (Americana VII)   ——. *Bibliotheca Americana. Part VII.* London: 1928. (*Its* Catalogue 502).

Maggs. French ser., Cat. 8   ——. *The French colonisation of America as exemplified in a remarkable collection of French*

References

	administrative acts (1581–1791). Abbeville & Paris: F. Paillart, 1936.
Magne (Scarron)	Magne, Émile. *Bibliographie générale des oeuvres de Scarron, documents inédits.* Paris: L. Giraud-Badin, 1924. (Les bibliographies nouvelles [Collection du Bulletin du bibliophile], VI).
Medina (Arau.)	Ercilla y Zúñiga, Alonso de. *La Araucana . . . Edición del centenario, ilustrada con grabados . . . y bibliográficas y una biografía del autor.* La publica José Toribio Medina. Santiago de Chile: Impr. Elzeviriana, 1910–18. 5 v. 'Bibliografía de la Araucana': IV:1–60.
Medina (BHA)	Medina, José Toribio. *Biblioteca Hispano-Americana (1493–1810).* Santiago de Chile: The Author, 1898–1907. 7 v. (Repr.: Amsterdam: N. Israel, 1958–62).
Medina (BHA) (Ampl.)	'Ampliaciones'. In the preceding. VI:507–30.
Medina (Chile)	———. *Biblioteca Hispano-Chilena (1523–1817).* Santiago de Chile: The Author, 1897–99. 3 v.
Medina (Lima)	———. *La imprenta en Lima (1584–1824).* Santiago de Chile: The author, 1904–07. 4 v.
Medina (Phil.)	———. *Bibliografía española de las islas Filapinas (1523–1810).* Santiago de Chile: Imprenta Cervantes, 1897–98.
Mengel (Ellis)	Kansas. University. Libraries. *A catalogue of the Ellis Collection of ornithological books in the University of Kansas Libraries.* Comp. by Robert M. Mengel. Lawrence, 1972–. (University of Kansas publications. Library series. XXXIII).
Meulen/Diermanse	Meulen, Jacob ter, & Diermanse, Pieter J. J. *Bibliographie des écrits imprimés de Hugo Grotius.* The Hague: M. Nijhoff, 1950.
Meulman	Meulman, Isaac. *Catalogus van de tractaten, pamfletten, enz., over de geschiedenis van Nederland aanwezig in de bibliotheek van Isaac Meulman.* Bewerkt door J. K. van der Wulp. Amsterdam: Heirs of H. van Munster & Son, 1866–68. 3 v.
Michel (Répertoire)	Michel, Suzanne P. *Répertoire des ouvrages imprimés en langue italienne au XVIIe siècle conservés dans les bibliothèques de France.* Paris: Centre National de la Recherche Scientifique, 1967–. In progress.
Millares Carlo (Avontroot)	Millares Carlo, Agustin. 'Algunas noticias y documentos referentes a Juan Bartolomé Avontroot'. *El Museo Canario* III (5) 1–26.

Molhuysen	Molhuysen, Philip Christiaan, & Blok, Petrus Johannes, eds. *Nieuw Nederlandsch biografisch woordenboek.* Leiden: A. W. Sijthoff's Uitgevers-Maatschappij, 1911–37. 10 v.
Moranti (Urbino)	Moranti, Luigi. *Le cinquecentine della Biblioteca universitaria di Urbino.* Florence: L. S. Olschki, 1977. 3 v. (Biblioteca di bibliografia italiana, LXXX).
Moreau (Mazarinades)	Moreau, Celestine. *Bibliographie des Mazarinades.* Paris: J. Renouard & Cie, 1850–51. 3 v. (Sociéte de l'histoire de France. Publications in octavo, LXI, LXIII, LXVII).
Müller	Müller, Wolf. *Bibliographie des Kaffee, des Kakao, der Schokolade, des Tee und deren Surrogate, bis zum Jahre 1900.* Bad Bocklet: W. Krieg, 1960. (Bibliotheca bibliographica, XX).
Muller (1872)	Muller, Frederick. *Catalogue of books, maps, plates on America.* Amsterdam: F. Muller, 1872–75. 3 pts. (Repr., Amsterdam: N. Israel, 1966).
Muller III	——. ——. Part III. Amsterdam: F. Muller, 1875. (*In* the preceding).
Murphy (Engl. char.-bks)	Murphy, Gwendolen. *A bibliography of English character-books, 1608–1700.* Oxford: The Bibliographical Society, 1925. (Bibliographical Society. Transactions. Supplement IV).
Mus. Cats.	Jonge van Ellemeet, Willem Cornelis Mary de. *Museum Catsianum, 1837–1887.* 2. verm. uitgave. The Hague: M. Nijhoff, 1887.
Navarrete	Navarrete, Martín Fernández de. *Biblioteca marítima española.* Madrid: Viuda de Calero, 1851. 2 v.
Nijhoff (Noort)	Nijhoff, Wouter. *Bibliographie van de beschrijvinghe van de voyagie om den geheelen werelt cloot door O. van Noort.* The Hague: Linschoten-vereeniging, 1926.
Nissen (Birds)	Nissen, Claus. *Die illustrierten Vogelbücher, ihre Geschichte und Bibliographie.* Stuttgart: Hiersemann Verlag, 1953.
Nissen (Bot.)	——. *Die botanische Buchillustration, ihre Geschichte und Bibliographie.* Stuttgart: Hiersemann Verlags-Gesellschaft, 1951. 2 v.
Nissen (Zool.)	——. *Die zoologische Buchillustration, ihre Bibliographie und Geschichte.* Stuttgart: A. Hiersemann, 1966–69.

References

Ortroy (Apian)   Ortroy, Fernand Gratien van. *Bibliographie de l'oeuvre de Pierre Apian.* Besançon: P. Jacquin, 1902. (Repr., Amsterdam: Meridian, 1963).

Otto   Otto, Karl F. *Philipp von Zesen; a bibliographical catalogue.* Berne & Munich: Francke [1972]. (Bibliographien zur deutschen Barockliteratur, I).

Palha   Palha, Fernando. *Catalogue de la bibliothèque de m. Fernando Palha.* Lisbon: Libania da Silva, 1896. 4 v.

Palau   Palau y Dulcet, Antonio. *Manual del librero Hispano-Americano.* 2da ed. Barcelona: A. Palau, 1948–77. 28 v.

Palmer   Palmer, Philip Motley. *German works on America, 1492–1800.* Berkeley: University of California Press, 1952. (University of California Publications in modern philology, XXXVI (10):271–412).

Pardo de Tavera   U.S. Library of Congress. *Bibliography of the Philippine Islands.* Washington, D.C.: Govt. Print. Off., 1903. Pt 2: *Bibliotheca Filipina,* by T. H. Pardo de Tavera.

Peeters-Fontainas (Impr.esp.)   Peeters-Fontainas, Jean. *Bibliographie des impressions Espagnoles des Pays-Bas méridionaux.* Nieuwkoop: B. de Graaf, 1965. 2 v.

Pérez Pastor (Madrid)   Pérez Pastor, Cristóbal. *Bibliografía Madrileña; descripción de las obras impresas en Madrid.* Madrid: Tipografía de los Huérfanos, 1891–1907. 3 v.

Pérez Pastor (Medina del Campo)   ——. *La imprenta en Medina del Campo.* Madrid: Sucesores de Rivadeneyra, 1895.

Pérez Pastor (Toledo)   ——. *La imprenta en Toledo; descripción bibliográfica de las obras impresas en la imperial ciudad desde 1483 hasta nuestros días.* Madrid: M. Tello, 1887.

Petit   Leyden. Bibliotheca Thysiana. *Bibliotheek van Nederlandsche Pamfletten . . .* Bewerkt door Louis D. Petit. The Hague: M. Nijhoff, 1882–84. 2 v.

Pettersen (Before 1814)   Pettersen, Hjalmar Marius. *Norske forfattere før 1814.* Copenhagen: Rosenkilde & Bagger, 1973. (Bibliotheca norvegica, III).

Pforzheimer   Pforzheimer, Carl Howard. *The Carl H. Pforzheimer Library: English literature, 1475–1700.* New York: Priv. print., 1940. 3 v.

Philips (Atlases)   U.S. Library of Congress. Map Division. *A list of geographical atlases in the Library of Congress . . .* compiled under the direction of Philip Lee

Phillips. Washington, D. C.: Govt. Print. Off., 1909–20. 4 v.

Plan (Rabelais) — Plan, Pierre Paul. *Bibliographie Rabelaisienne: Les éditions de Rabelais de 1532 à 1711.* Paris: Imprimerie Nationale, 1904. (Repr., Nieuwkoop: B. de Graaf, 1965).

Poynter (Markham) — Poynter, Frederick Noël Lawrence. *A bibliography of Gervase Markham, 1568?–1637.* Oxford: Oxford Bibliographical Society, 1962. (Oxford Bibliographical Society Publications, new ser., XI).

Pritzel — Pritzel, Georg August. *Thesaurus literaturae botanicae.* Leipzig: F. A. Brockhaus, 1872–77. (Repr., Milan: G. Görlich, 1950).

Proksch — Proksch, Johann Karl. *Die Litteratur über die venerischen Krankheiten von den ersten Schriften über Syphilis aus dem Ende des fünfzehnten Jahrhunderts bis zum Jahre 1889.* Bonn P. Hanstein, 1889–91. 5 pts. (Repr., Nieuwkoop: B. de Graaf, 1966).

Puliatti (Tassoni) — Puliatti, Pietro. *Bibliografia di Alessandro Tassoni.* Florence: Sansoni, 1969–70. 2 v.

Racc. Tassiana — Bergamo. Biblioteca civica A. Mai. *La raccolta Tassiana della Biblioteca civica "A. Mai" di Bergamo.* Bergamo: Banca Piccolo Credito Bergamasco, 1960.

Rahir (Elzevier) — Rahir, Edouard. *Catalogue d'une collection unique de volumes imprimés par les Elzevier et divers typographes hollandais du XVIIᵉ siècle.* Paris: D. Morgand, 1896.

Rép. bibl. — *Répertoire bibliographique des libres imprimés en France au sezième siècle.* Baden-Baden: Libr. Heitz; V. Koerner, 1968–77. 22 v.

Retana (Filipinas) — Retana y Gamboa, Wenceslao Emilio. *Aparato bibliográfico de la historia general de Filipinas.* Madrid: Minuesa de los Rios, 1906. 3 v.

Riccardi — Riccardi, Pietro. *Bibliotheca matematica italiana, dalla origine della stampa ai primi anni del secolo XIX.* Modena: Tipografia Soliana, 1870–80. 2 v. (Repr., Milan: M. Görlich, 1952).

Ríus (Cervantes) — Ríus y de Llosellas, Leopoldo. *Bibliografía crítica de las obras de Miguel de Cervantes Saavedra.* Madrid: M. Murillo, 1895–1905. 3 v. (Repr., New York: B. Franklin, 1970).

Rodrigues — Rodrigues, José Carlos. *Bibliotheca brasiliense.* Rio de Janeiro: Typographia do 'Jornal do commercio', 1907.

References

Rodrigues (Dom. Hol.) — Rodrigues, José Honorio. *Historiografia e bibliografia do domínio holandês no Brasil.* Rio de Janeiro: Departamento de Imprensa Nacional, 1949.

Rothschild — Rothschild, Nathan James Edouard, baron de. *Catalogue des livres composant la bibliothèque de feu M. le baron James de Rothschild.* Paris: D. Morgand, 1884–1920. 5 v. (Repr., New York: B. Franklin, 1967).

STC — Pollard, Alfred William, & Redgrave, Gilbert Richard, comps. *A short-title catalogue of books printed in England, Scotland, & Ireland and of English books printed abroad, 1475–1640.* London: The Bibliographical Society, 1926. (Repr., Oxford: Oxford University Press, 1946). Refs for entries 14045.5 ff. are to the following edn.
——. ——. 2nd edn, rev. & enl., begun by W. A. Jackson & F. S. Ferguson, completed by Katharine F. Pantzer; v. 2, I-Z. London: The Bibliographical Society, 1976.

Sabin — Sabin, Joseph. *Bibliotheca Americana; a dictionary of books relating to America . . .* Begun by Joseph Sabin, continued by Wilberforce Eames and completed by R. W. G. Vail, for the Bibliographical Society of America. New York: Sabin, 1868–92; Bibliographical Society of America, 1928–36. 29 v. (Repr., Amsterdam: N. Israel; New York: Barnes & Noble, 1961–62).

Salvá — Salvá y Pérez, Vicente. *Cátalogo de la biblioteca de Salvá,* escrito por D. Pedro Salvá y Mallen. Valencia: Ferrer de Orga, 1872. 2 v. (Repr., Barcelona: Porter-Libros, 1963).

Scott (Naval) — Royal Institution of Naval Architects. *Catalogue of the Scott collection of books, manuscripts, prints and drawings,* compiled by Betty M. Cooper. London: 1954.

Shaaber — Shaaber, Matthias Adam. *Sixteenth-century imprints in the libraries of the University of Pennsylvania.* Philadelphia: University of Pennsylvania Press, 1976.

Shaaber (Brit. auth.) — ——. *Check-list of works of British authors printed abroad, in languages other than English, to 1641.* New York: The Bibliographical Society of America, 1975.

Sherrington (Fernel) — Sherrington, Sir Charles Scott. *The endeavour of Jean Fernel, with a list of the editions of his writings.* Cambridge: Cambridge University Press, 1946.

Silva (Camões)

Silva, Innocencio Francisco da. *Diccionario bibliographico portuguez*, XIV. Lisbon: Imprensa Nacional, 1886.

Simón Díaz (XVII)

Simón Díaz, Juan. *Impresos del siglo XVII*. Madrid: Consejo Superior de Investigaciones Científicas, 1972.

Skelton

Blaeu, Willem Janszoon. *The light of navigation, Amsterdam, 1612 . . .* With an introduction by R. A. Skelton. [Amsterdam: N. Israel, 1964].

Stevens (Ptolemy)

Stevens, Henry Newton. *Ptolemy's Geography; a brief account of all the printed editions down to 1730.* 2nd edn. London: H. Stevens, Sons & Stiles, 1908. (Repr., Amsterdam: Theatrum Orbis Terrarum, 1972).

Stokes (Manhattan)

Stokes, Isaac Newton Phelps. *The iconography of Manhattan island, 1498–1909.* New York: R. H. Dodd, 1915–28. 6 v. (Vol. 6 includes 'Bibliography' by Victor H. Paltsits.)

Streit

Streit, Robert. *Bibliotheca Missionum.* Münster i. W., Aachen: 1916–74. 30 v. (Veröffentlichungen des Internationalen Instituts für missionswissenschaftliche Forschung).

Sudhoff (Paracelsus)

Sudhoff, Karl. *Bibliographia Paracelsica; Besprechung der unter Hohenheims Namen 1527–1893 erschienenen Druckschriften.* Graz: Akademische Druck- und Verlagsanstalt, 1958.

Szabó

Szabó, Károly. *Régi Magyar Könyvtár.* Budapest: A Magyar Tudományos Akadémia Könyvkiadó Hivatala, 1879–98. 3 v.

Taylor (Regiment)

Bourne, William. *A regiment for the sea;* ed. by E. G. R. Taylor. Cambridge: Hakluyt Society, 1963. (Hakluyt Society Publications, 2nd ser., CXXI).

Tazbir

Tazbir, Janusz. 'La conquête de l'Amérique à la lumière de l'opinion Polonaise.' *Acta Poloniae historica*, XVII (1968) 5–22.

Tchémerzine

Tchémerzine, Avenir. *Bibliographie d'éditions originales et rares d'auteurs français des XVᵉ, XVIᵉ, XVIIᵉ, et XVIIᵉ siècles.* Paris: M. Plee, 1927–34. 10 v.

Ternaux

Ternaux-Compans, Henri. *Bibliothèque américaine.* Paris: Arthus-Bertrand, 1837.

Thickett (Pasquier)

Thickett, Dorothy. *Bibliographie des oeuvres d'Estienne Pasquier.* Geneva: E. Droz, 1956. (Travaux d'humanisme et renaissance, XXI).

References

Thiébaud (La chasse)   Thiébaud, Jules. *Bibliographie des ouvrages français sur la chasse.* Paris: E. Nourry, 1934.

Thomason   British Museum. Dept. of Printed Books. Thomason collection. *Catalogue of the pamphlets, books, newspapers and manuscripts relating to the Civil War, the Commonwealth, and Restoration, collected by George Thomason, 1640–1661.* London: 1908. 2 v.

Tiele   Tiele, Pieter Anton. *Nederlandsche bibliographie van land- en volkenkunde.* Amsterdam: F. Muller, 1884. (Repr., Amsterdam: Theatrum Orbis Terrarum, 1966).

Tiele (Pamfletten)   ——. *Bibliotheek van Nederlandsche pamfletten.* Amsterdam: F. Muller, 1858–61. 3 v.

Tiele-Muller   Muller, Frederik. *Mémoire bibliographique sur les journaux des navigateurs néerlandais . . . en la possession de Frederik Muller . . .* Rédigé par P. A. Tiele. Amsterdam: F. Muller, 1867. (Repr., Amsterdam: Theatrum Orbis Terrarum, 1969).

Toda y Güell (Bibl. esp. d'Italia)   Toda y Güell, Eduardo. *Bibliografia espanyola d'Italia dels origens de la imprenta fins a l'any 1900.* Barcelona: Vidal-Güell, 1927–31. 5 v.

Trömel   Brockhaus, firm, publishers, Leipzig. *Bibliothèque américaine . . .* Redigé par Paul Trömel. Leipzig: F. A. Brockhaus, 1861.

Tuttle (Cotton)   Tuttle, Julius Herbert. 'Writings of Rev. John Cotton.' *Bibliographical essays; a tribute to Wilberforce Eames.* Cambridge, Mass.: Harvard University Press, 1924, 363–80.

Unger (Vondel)   Unger, Johan Hendrick Willem. *Bibliographie van Vondels wercken.* Amsterdam: F. Muller & Co., 1888.

Vail (Frontier)   Vail, Robert W. G. *The voice of the old frontier.* Philadelphia: University of Pennsylvania Press, 1949.

Valdenebro (Cordoba)   Valdenebro y Cisneros, José María de. *La imprenta en Córdoba; ensayo bibliografico.* Madrid: Sucesores de Rivadeneyra, 1900.

Van Alphen   Groningen. Rijksuniversiteit. Bibliotheek. *Catalogus der pamfletten van de Bibliotheek der Rijksuniversiteit te Groningen 1542–1853 . . .* Bewerkt door Dr. G. van Alphen. Groningen: J. B. Wolters, 1944.

Van de Velde   Van de Velde, Albert J. J. 'Bio-bibliographische aanteekeningen over Johan van Beverwijck, 1594–1647.' *In* Vlaamsche Academie voor Taalen Letterkunde, Ghent. *Verslagen en mededeelingen*, (1933) 71–121; (1934) 35–47.

Van Rensselaer Bowier   New York (State). State Library, Albany. *Van Rensselaer Bowier manuscripts.* Albany: University of the State of New York, 1908.

Viñaza   Viñaza, Cipriano Muñoz y Manzano, conde de la. *Bibliografía española de lenguas indígenas de América.* Madrid: Sucesores de Rivadeneyra, 1892.

Vindel   Vindel, Francisco. *Manual gráfico-descriptivo del bibliófilo Hispano-Americano (1475–1850).* Madrid: Impr. Gógora, 1930–34. 12 v.

Vries   Vries, Anne Gerard Christiaan de. *De Nederlandsche emblemata.* Amsterdam: Ten Brink & de Vries, 1899.

Wagner (NW)   Wagner, Henry Raup. *The cartography of the northwest coast of America to the year 1800.* Berkeley, Calif.: University of California Press, 1937. 2 v. (Repr., Amsterdam: B. M. Israel, 1968).

Wagner (SW)   ——. *The Spanish Southwest, 1542–1794.* Albuquerque: The Quivira Society, 1937. 2 v.

Waller   Sallander, Hans. *Bibliotheca Walleriana; the books illustrating the history of medicine and science collected by Dr. Erik Waller and bequeathed to the Library of the Royal University of Uppsala. A catalogue.* Stockholm: Almquist & Wiksell, 1955. 2 v. (Repr., New York: Arno Press, 1967).

Waring   Waring, Edward John. *Bibliotheca therapeutica, or bibliography of therapeutics.* London: The New Sydenham Society, 1878–79. 2 v.

Weale/Bohatta   Weale, William Henry James. *Bibliographia liturgica: catalogus missalium ritus latini ab anno MCCCCLXXV impressorum; iterum edidit Hanns Bohatta.* London: B. Quaritch, 1928.

Wegelin (Poetry)   Wegelin, Oscar. *Early American poetry; a compilation of the titles of volumes of verse and broadsides by writers born or residing in North America, north of the Mexican border.* 2d. ed., rev. and enl. New York: P. Smith, 1930. 2 v.

Weller (Falsch. & fing. Druckorte)   Weller, Emil Ottokar. *Die falschen und fingierten Druckorte.* 2. verm. und verb. Aufl. Leipzig: W. Engelmann, 1864. 2 v. (Repr., Hildesheim: G. Olms, 1960).

Wieder (Mon. Cart.)   Wieder, Frederick Caspar, ed. *Monumenta cartographica; reproductions of unique and rare maps,*

References

plans and views. The Hague: M. Nijhoff, 1925–33. 5 v.

Willems (Elzevier)   Willems, Alphonse Charles Joseph. *Les Elzevier, histoire et annales typographiques.* Brussels: G.-A. van Trigt; Paris: A. Labitte; The Hague: M. Nijhoff, 1880.

Wing   Wing, Donald. *Short-title catalogue of books printed in England, Scotland, Ireland, Wales and British America, and of English books printed in other countries, 1641–1700.* New York: Printed for the Index Society by the Columbia University Press, 1945–51. 3 v. Refs through E2926 are to the following edition.
——. ——. 2d ed., rev. & enl. New York: Index Committee of the Modern Language Association of America, 1972–. In progress.

Winship (Cabot)   Winship, George Parker. *Cabot bibliography; with an introductory essay.* London: H. Stevens, Son & Stiles; New York: Dodd, Mead & Co., 1900. (Repr., New York: B. Franklin, 1967).

Wolfenbüttel   Wolfenbüttel. Herzog August Bibliothek. *Die Neue Welt in den Schätzen einer alten europäischen Bibliothek.* Wolfenbüttel: 1976.

Woodfield   Woodfield, Denis B. *Surreptitious printing in England, 1550–1640.* New York: Bibliographical Society of America, 1973.

Wroth & Annan   Wroth, Lawrence C., & Annan, Gertrude L. *Acts of the French royal administration concerning Canada, Guiana, the West Indies and Louisiana, prior to 1791.* New York: New York Public Library, 1930.

Locations

North America

Arizona

AzU	University of Arizona, Tucson

California

C	California State Library, Sacramento
CCB	Francis Bacon Foundation, Claremont
CCC	Claremont College, Claremont
CLL	Los Angeles County Law Library, Los Angeles
CLSU	University of Southern California, Los Angeles
CLU	University of California at Los Angeles
CLU-C	—William Andrews Clark Memorial Library
CLU-M	—Biomedical Library
CLgA	Alma College, Los Gatos
CSS	Sacramento State College, Sacramento
CSfU	University of San Francisco, San Francisco
CSmH	Henry E. Huntington Library, San Marino
CSt	Stanford University Libraries, Stanford
CU	University of California, Berkeley
CU-A	—University of California, Davis
CU-B	—Bancroft Library, Berkeley
CU-I	—University of California, Irvine
CU-L	—Law Library, Berkeley
CU-M	—University of California Medical Center, San Francisco
CU-S	—University of California, San Diego, La Jolla

Colorado

CoDU	University of Denver, Denver
CoU	University of Colorado, Boulder

Connecticut

CtHT	Trinity College, Hartford
CtU	University of Connecticut, Storrs
CtW	Wesleyan University, Middletown
CtY	Yale University, New Haven
CtY-D	—Divinity School
CtY-L	—Law School
CtY-M	—Medical School

Locations

District of Columbia

DCU	Catholic University of America Library
DCU-IA	—Ibero-American Collection
DDO	Dumbarton Oaks Research Library of Harvard University
DFC	University of the District of Columbia (Formerly Federal City College)
DFo	Folger Shakespeare Library
DGU	Georgetown University
DHN	Holy Name College. *Now merged into* Washington Theological Coalition Library, Silver Spring, Maryland
DLC	U.S. Library of Congress
DN	U.S. Department of the Navy Library, Washington
DN-MS	—Naval Medical School, Edward Rhodes Stitt Library, Bethesda, Maryland
DNAL	U.S. National Agricultural Library, Beltsville, Maryland
DNLM	U.S. National Library of Medicine, Bethesda, Maryland
DNW	U.S. National War College Library, Fort McNair, Washington
DPU	Organization of American States (Formerly Pan American Union Library)
DS	U.S. Department of State Library
DSI	Smithsonian Institution Library

Delaware

DeU	University of Delaware, Newark

Florida

FTaSU	Florida State University, Tallahassee
FU	University of Florida, Gainesville

Illinois

ICJ	John Crerar Library, Chicago
ICN	Newberry Library
ICU	University of Chicago
IEG	Garret Theological Seminary, Evanston
IEN	Northwestern University, Evanston
IEN-M	—Medical School Library, Chicago
IHi	Illinois State Historical Library, Springfield
IMunS	Saint Mary of the Lake Seminary, Mundelein
INS	Illinois State University, Normal
IU	University of Illinois, Urbana

Iowa

IaU   University of Iowa, Iowa City

Indiana

InNd   University of Notre Dame, Notre Dame

InStme   St. Meinrad's Archabbey, St. Meinrad

InU   Indiana University, Bloomington

InU-L   —Lilly Library

Kansas

KMK   Kansas State University, Manhattan

KStMC   Saint Mary's College, Saint Marys

KU   University of Kansas, Lawrence

KU-M   —Medical Center Library, Kansas City

Kentucky

KyLoS   Southern Baptist Theological Seminary, Louisville

KyU   University of Kentucky, Lexington

Louisiana

LNHT   Howard-Tilton Memorial Library of Tulane University, New Orleans

Massachusetts

MB   Boston Public Library

MBAt   Boston Athenaeum, Boston

MBCo   Countway Library of Medicine (Harvard Boston Medical Libraries)

MBH   Massachusetts Horticultural Society, Boston

MBrZ   Zion Research Library, Brookline

MBtS   St. John's Seminary Library, Brighton

MCM   Massachusetts Institute of Technology, Cambridge

MH   Harvard University, Cambridge

MH-A   —Arnold Arboretum (Early materials are largely on deposit in the Houghton Library)

MH-AH   —Andover-Harvard Theological School

MH-BA   —Graduate School of Business Administration

MH-GE   —Institute of Geographical Exploration Library (Collections dispersed; bulk of material in College Library)

MH-L   —Law School

MH-P   —Peabody Museum Library

MH-Z   —Museum of Comparative Zoology

MHi   Massachusetts Historical Society, Boston

MNS   Smith College, Northampton

Locations

MSaE	Essex Institute, Salem
MShM	Mount Holyoke College, South Hadley
MU	University of Massachusetts, Amherst
MWA	American Antiquarian Society, Worcester
MWalB	Brandeis University, Waltham
MWelC	Wellesley College, Wellesley
MWiW-C	Chapin Library, Williams College, Williamstown
Maryland	
MdAN	U.S. Naval Academy, Annapolis
MdBJ	Johns Hopkins University, Baltimore
MdBJ-G	—John Work Garret Library
MdBP	Peabody Institute. Now incorporated in Enoch Pratt Free Library.
MdE	Mount St. Mary's College, Emmitsburg
MdSsW	Washington Theological Coalition Library, Silver Spring
Maine	
MeB	Bowdoin College, Brunswick
Michigan	
MiAC	Alma College, Alma
MiD	Detroit Public Library
MiD-B	—Burton Historical Collection
MiDu	University of Detroit
MiDW	Wayne State University, Detroit
MiEM	Michigan State University, East Lansing
MiU	University of Michigan, Ann Arbor
MiU-C	—William L. Clements Library
MiU-L	—Law Library
Minnesota	
MnCS	St. John's University, Collegeville
MnHi	Minnesota Historical Society, St. Paul
MnS	St. Paul Public Library
MnU	University of Minnesota, Minneapolis
MnU-B	—James Ford Bell Collection
MnU-L	—Law Library
Missouri	
MoSB	Missouri Botanical Garden, St. Louis
MoSM	Mercantile Library Association, St. Louis
MoSMed	St. Louis Medical Society Library
MoSU	St. Louis University

MoSU-D	—School of Divinity
MoSW	Washington University
MoU	University of Missouri, Columbia

New York

N	New York State Library, Albany
NBC	Brooklyn College
NBu	Buffalo and Erie County Public Library, Buffalo
NBuU-L	State University of New York at Buffalo, Law Library
NCH	Hamilton College, Clinton
NHC	Colgate University, Hamilton
NHi	New York Historical Society, New York
NIC	Cornell University, Ithaca
NN	New York Public Library
NN-A	—Arents Collection
NN-RB	—Rare Book Division
NNAHI	*See* PVAHI
NNBG	New York Botanical Garden, Bronx Park, New York
NNC	Columbia University, New York
NNC-L	—Law Library
NNC-M	—Medical Library
NNCC	Chemists' Club, New York
NNE	Engineering Societies Library
NNG	General Theological Seminary of the Protestant Episcopal Church
NNH	Hispanic Society of America
NNJ	Jewish Theological Seminary of America
NNNAM	New York Academy of Medicine
NNPM	Pierpont Morgan Library
NNS	New York Society Library
NNU	New York University Libraries
NNU-H	—University Heights Library, Bronx
NNUT	Union Theological Seminary, New York
NNUT-Mc	—McAlpin Collection
NPV	Vassar College, Poughkeepsie
NSchU	Union College, Schenectady
NSyU	Syracuse University, Syracuse

North Carolina

NcD	Duke University, Durham
NcD-MC	—Medical Center

Locations

NcGuG	Guilford College, Guilford
NcU	University of North Carolina, Chapel Hill
New Jersey	
NjN	Newark Public Library
NjNbS	Gardner A. Sage Library, New Brunswick
NjP	Princeton University, Princeton
NjPT	Princeton Theological Seminary
NjR	Rutgers University, New Brunswick
Ohio	
OC	Public Library of Cincinnati and Hamilton County, Cincinnati
OCH	Hebrew Union College, Cincinnati
OCT	Cincinnati Technical College
OCU	University of Cincinnati
OCl	Cleveland Public Library
OClJC	John Carroll University, Cleveland
OClStM	St. Mary's Seminary, Cleveland
OClW	Case Western Reserve University
OClW-H	—Cleveland Health Sciences Library
OO	Oberlin College, Oberlin
OOxM	Miami University, Oxford
OU	Ohio State University, Columbus
Oklahoma	
OkTG	Thomas Gilcrease Foundation, Tulsa
OkU	University of Oklahoma, Norman
Oregon	
OrU	University of Oregon, Eugene
Pennsylvania	
PBL	Lehigh University, Bethlehem
PBa	Academy of the New Church, Bryn Athyn
PBm	Bryn Mawr College, Bryn Mawr
PCC	Crozer Theological Seminary, Chester
PCarlD	Dickinson College, Carlisle
PHC	Haverford College, Haverford
PHi	Historical Society of Pennsylvania, Philadelphia
PLatS	Saint Vincent College and Archabbey, Latrobe
PMA	Allegheny College, Meadville
PP	Free Library of Philadelphia
PPAN	Academy of Natural Sciences
PPAmP	American Philosophical Society

PPC	College of Physicians of Philadelphia
PPF	Franklin Institute
PPFr	Friends' Free Library of Germantown, Philadelphia
PPGenH	Philadelphia General Hospital Laboratories
PPHa	Hahnemann Medical College and Hospital
PPL	Library Company of Philadelphia
PPLT	Lutheran Theological Seminary
PPM	Mercantile Library, Philadelphia. No longer in existence.
PPPH	Pennsylvania Hospital Medical Library
PPPM	Philadelphia Museum of Art
PPPrHi	Presbyterian Historical Society, Philadelphia
PPRF	Rosenbach Foundation
PPT	Temple University
PPeSchw	Schwenckfelder Historical Library, Pennsburg
PPiD	Duquesne University, Pittsburgh
PPiHB	Rachel McMasters Miller Hunt Botanical Library, Carnegie-Mellon University
PPiPT	Pittsburgh Theological Seminary
PSC	Swarthmore College, Swarthmore
PSt	Pennsylvania State University, University Park
PU	University of Pennsylvania, Philadelphia
PU-B	—Biology Library
PU-D	—Evans Dental Library
PU-F	—H. H. Furness Memorial Library
PU-L	—Biddle Law Library
PU-Mus	—University Museum Library
PU-S	—Edgar Fahs Smith Memorial Library
PV	Villanova University, Villanova
PVAHI	Augustinian Historical Institute, Villanova

Rhode Island

RP	Providence Public Library
RPB	Brown University, Providence
RPJCB	John Carter Brown Library, Providence

Tennessee

TNJ	Joint University Libraries, Nashville
TU	University of Tennessee, Knoxville

Texas

TxDaM-P	Southern Methodist University, Perkins School of Theology Library, Dallas

Locations

TxHU	University of Houston
TxLT	Texas Technological College, Lubbock
TxU	University of Texas, Austin
TxU-L	—Law Library

Utah

UU	University of Utah, Salt Lake City

Virginia

ViHarEM	Eastern Mennonite College, Harrisonburg
ViN	Norfolk Public Library
ViRA	Richmond Academy of Medicine, Richmond
ViU	University of Virginia, Charlottesville
ViW	College of William and Mary, Williamsburg

Wisconsin

WU	University of Wisconsin, Madison
WU-M	—School of Medicine

Washington

Wa	Washington State Library, Olympia
WaSpG	Gonzaga University, Spokane
WaU	University of Washington, Seattle

Wyoming

WyU	Wyoming University, Laramie

Canada

CaBVaU	University of British Columbia, Vancouver
CaOHM	McMaster University, Hamilton, Ontario
CaOOA	Public Archives Library, Ottawa
CaOTU	University of Toronto, Toronto
CaQMM	McGill University, Montreal

Other Locations

Aberdeen: UL	University of Aberdeen, Scotland
Aberdeen: Marischal	Marischal College, Aberdeen
Aix-en-Provence: Bibl. Méjanes	Bibliothèque Municipale (Bibliothèque Méjanes), Aix-en-Provence, France

Ajaccio: BM	Bibliothèque Municipale, Ajaccio, France
Albi: BM	Bibliothèque Municipale, Albi, France
Amsterdam: E. R. Crone	E. R. Crone, Private Collection, Amsterdam
Amsterdam: KOG	Koninklijk Oudheidkundig Genootschap
Amsterdam: MBG	Koninklijke Nederlandse Maatschappij tot Bevordering der Geneeskunst
Amsterdam: NHSM	Nederlandsch Historisch Scheepvaart Museum
Amsterdam: UB	Universiteitsbibliotheek
Amsterdam: VBBB	Vereeniging ter Bevordering van de Belangen des Boekhandels
Antwerp: Plantin Mus.	Musée Plantin-Moretus, Antwerp
Auch: Archives	Archives, Auch, France
Avignon: Mus. Calvet	Muséum Calvet, Avignon, France
BL	British Library, London
BM (NH)	British Museum (Natural History)
BN	Bibliothèque Nationale, Paris
Barcelona: B. Central	Biblioteca Central de la Diputación, Barcelona
Barcelona: B. de Cataluña	
Basel: UB	Öffentliche Bibliothek der Universität, Basel, Switzerland
Berlin: StB	Staatsbibliothek. Now distributed between the Staatsbibliothek Preussischer Kulturbesitz, West Berlin, and the Deutsche Staatsbibliothek, East Berlin.
Berne: ML	Municipal Library, Berne, Switzerland
Berne: StB	Stadt- und Universitätsbibliothek, Berne
Besançon: BM	Bibliothèque Municipale, Besançon, France
Bethersden, Kent: Parish Church	Parish Church, Bethersden, Kent, England
Bologna: BC	Biblioteca Comunale dell'Archiginnasio, Bologna, Italy
Bonn: UB	Bibliothek der Rheinischen Universität, Bonn, Germany (West)
Bordeaux: BM	Bibliothèque Municipale, Bordeaux, France
Breda: MA	Municipal Archives, Breda, The Netherlands
Breslau: BU Breslau: StB	Staats- und Universitätsbibliothek, Breslau, Germany. Now Wrocław, Poland
Breslau: StB	Stadtbibliothek, Breslau, Germany. Now Wrocław, Poland
Brunswick: StAK	Stadtarchiv und Stadtbibliothek, Braunschweig, Germany (West)
Brussels: BR	Bibliothèque Royale Albert 1er, Brussels
Caen: BU	Bibliothèque de l'Université de Caen, France

Locations

Cambridge: Christ's	Christ's College, Cambridge
Cambridge: Emmanuel	Emmanuel College
Cambridge: King's	King's College
Cambridge: Magdalene	Magdalene College
Cambridge: Pembroke	Pembroke College
Cambridge: Pepys	Pepys Library, Magdalene College
Cambridge: Peterhouse	Peterhouse College
Cambridge: St. John's	St. John's College
Cambridge: Trinity	Trinity College
Cambridge: UL	Cambridge University Library
Chantilly: Mus. Condé	Bibliothèque du Musée Condé au Chateau de Chantilly, Oise, France
Chatsworth	The Duke of Devonshire, Private Collection, Chatsworth, Bakewell, Derbyshire, England
Cologne: StUB	Universitäts- und Stadt-bibliothek, Cologne, Germany (West)
Copenhagen: KB	Kongelige Bibliothek (The Royal Library), Copenhagen
Cracow: BCzart	Czartoryski Library and Archives, Cracow, Poland
Cracow: PAN	Polska Akademia Nauk (Polish Academy of Sciences), Cracow
Danzig: StB	Stadtbibliothek, Danzig. Now Gdansk, Poland.
Darmstadt: UB	Hessische Landes- und Hochschulbibliothek, Darmstadt, Germany (West)
Deventer: Athenaeum	Athenaeum (Stadsbibliotheek), Deventer, The Netherlands
Dublin: Marsh's Libr.	Narcissus Marsh's Library, Dublin, Ireland
Dublin: PRO	Public Record Office of Ireland, Dublin
Dublin: Trinity	Trinity College, University of Dublin
Durham: Cosin Libr.	Cosin Library. On deposit at University of Durham, England
Edinburgh: Advocates Edinburgh: NL	National Library of Scotland, Edinburgh
Edinburgh: UL	Edinburgh University, Scotland
Edwards	Edwards; listed in Koeman (M.Bl) 50A as purchaser from Sotheby catalogue of 20 April 1959, no. 91.
Erlangen: UB	Bibliothek der Universität Erlangen-Nürnberg, Erlangen, Germany (West)
Evora: BP	Biblioteca Pública e Arquivo Distrital de Evora, Portugal

Florence: B. Marucel	Biblioteca Marucelliana, Florence, Italy
Florence: BN	Biblioteca Nazionale Centrale, Florence
Frankfurt a.M.: StB Frankfurt a.M.: StUB	Stadt- und Universitätsbibliothek, Frankfurt a.M., Germany (West)
Freiburg i. Br.: UB	Universitätsbibliothek, Freiburg im Breisgau, Germany (West)
Fribourg: BC	Bibliothèque Cantonale et Universitaire, Fribourg, Switzerland
Fulda: B. Sem.	Bischöfliches Priesterseminar, Fulda, Germany (West)
Fulda: LB	Landesbibliothek, Fulda
Geneva: BP	Bibliothèque Publique et Universitaire, Geneva, Switzerland
Geneva: Bibl. Mus. de la Reformation	Bibliothèque de la Société du Musée Historique de la Réformation. Now housed in the Bibliothèque Publique et Universitaire, Geneva
Ghent: BU	Bibliotheek van de Rijksuniversiteit, Ghent, Belgium
Glasgow: Hunterian Mus.	Hunterian Museum, Glasgow, Scotland
Glasgow: UL	Library of the University of Glasgow
Göttingen: StUB Göttingen: UB	Niedersächsische Staats- und Universitätsbibliothek, Göttingen, Germany (West)
Gotha: HB	Herzogliche Bibliothek, now the Landesbibliothek, Schloss Friedenstein, Gotha, Germany (East)
Granada: BU	Biblioteca de la Universidad, Granada, Spain
Grantham: Belvoir	Duke of Rutland, Private Collection, Belvoir Castle, Grantham, Leicestershire, England
Greenwich: NMM	National Maritime Museum, Greenwich, England
Greifswald: UB	Bibliothek der Universität Greifswald, Germany (East)
Grenoble: BM	Bibliothèque Municipale, Grenoble, France
Groningen: UB	Rijksuniversiteit, Groningen, The Netherlands
Haarlem: MA	Municipal Archives (Archief der Gemeente), Haarlem, The Netherlands
The Hague: AR	Algemeen Rijksarchief, The Hague, The Netherlands
The Hague: KB	Koninklijke Bibliotheek
The Hague: PP	Peace Palace (Vredepaleis)
Halle: UB	Universitäts- und Landesbibliothek Sachsen-Anhalt, Halle, Germany (East)
Hamburg: PL Hamburg: StB, StUB	Staats- und Universitätsbibliothek, Hamburg, Germany (West)

Locations

Hannover: NLB	Niedersächsische Landesbibliothek, Hannover, Germany (West)
Hatfield: Hatfield House	The Marquess of Salisbury, Private Collection, Hatfield House, Hatfield, England
Horblit	Harrison D. Horblit, Private Collection
Innerpeffray Libr.	Innerpeffray Library, Perthshire, Scotland
Innsbruck: UB	Universitätsbibliothek, Innsbruck, Austria
Karlsruhe: BLB	Badische Landesbibliothek, Karlsruhe, Germany (West)
Kassel: LB	Landesbibliothek, Kassel, Germany (West)
Kew: BG	Royal Botanic Gardens, Kew, Surrey, England
Keynes, G.L.	Sir Geoffrey L. Keynes, Private Collection
Königsberg: StB	Staats- und Universitätsbibliothek, Königsberg, Germany. Now Kaliningrad, USSR.
Lamport	Lamport Hall, Northampton, England (the late Sir Gyles Isham, Bt)
Leeds: UL	University of Leeds, England
Leeuwarden: Buma	Buma-Bibliotheek, Leeuwarden, The Netherlands
Leeuwarden: PB Leeuwarden: PLF	Provinciale Bibliotheek van Friesland, Leeuwarden
Leipzig: StB	Stadtbibliothek, Leipzig, Germany (East)
Leipzig: UB	Universitätsbibliothek, Karl-Marx-Universität, Leipzig
Leningrad: Saltykov PL	Gosudarstvennaya Publichnaya Biblioteka imeni M.E. Saltykova-Shchedrina (Saltykov-Shchedrin State Public Library), Leningrad, USSR
León: BP	Biblioteca Provincial, León, Spain
Leyden: B. Thysiana	Bibliotheca Thysiana, Leyden, The Netherlands
Leyden: MNL	Maatschappij der Nederlandse Letterkunde, Leyden
Leyden: UB	Bibliotheek der Rijksuniversiteit, Leyden
Lille: BU	Bibliothèque de l'Université de Lille, France
Lima: BN	Biblioteca Nacional, Lima, Peru
Lincoln: Cathedral	Lincoln Cathedral, Lincoln, England
Lisbon: Ajuda	Biblioteca de Ajuda, Lisbon, Portugal
Lisbon: BN	Biblioteca Nacional, Lisbon
Loeb-Larocque	Private collection of bookseller Loeb-Larocque, Paris

London: Admiralty	Admiralty Centre for Scientific Information and Liaison, London
London: College of Surgeons	Royal College of Surgeons Library
London: Dulwich	Dulwich College
London: Dutch Church	Dutch Church
London: Dyce	Dyce Collection, Victoria & Albert Museum
London: Guildhall	Guildhall Library
London: Lambeth	Lambeth Palace Library
London: Law Soc.	Law Society's Library
London: Med. Soc.	Medical Society of London (Collection dispersed; some items now at London: Wellcome, others at Queen's University at Kingston)
London: PRO	Public Record Office
London: Privy Council	Privy Council Office
London: RGS	Royal Geographical Society Library
London: Royal Institution of Naval Architects	Royal Institution of Naval Architects
London: Roy. Soc. of Med.	Royal Society of Medicine
London: Sion College	Library of Sion College
London: Sir J. Soane's Mus.	Sir John Soane's Museum
London: Soc. Ant.	Society of Antiquaries
London: Trinity House	Trinity House
London: UC	University College Library, University of London
London: UL	University of London Library
London: V & A	Victoria and Albert Museum
London: Wellcome	Wellcome Historical Medical Library
London: Westminster School	Westminster School
Louvain: BU Louvain: UB	Bibliothèque Centrale de l'Université Catholique, Louvain, Belgium. Now distributed between French and Dutch units of the University
Lownes	A.E. Lownes Collection, Brown University Library, Providence, R.I.
Lucerne: ZB	Zentralbibliothek (Kantons- & Bürgerbibliothek), Lucerne, Switzerland
Lund: UB	Lunds Universitetsbibliotek, Lund, Sweden
Lyons: BM	Bibliothèque Municipale, Lyons, France
Madrid: Acad. de la Hist.	Biblioteca de la Real Academia de la Historia, Madrid
Madrid: Arch. hist. nac.	Archivo Histórico Nacional

Locations

Madrid: BN	Biblioteca Nacional
Madrid: BU	Biblioteca de la Universidad
Madrid: BU (S. Isidro)	—San Isidro Collection
Madrid: Bibl. Palacio	Biblioteca del Palacio de Oriente
Madrid: Fac. de Med.	Biblioteca de la Facultad de Medecina de la Universidad
Madrid: Ministerio del Ultramar	Museo Biblioteca de Ultramar, Ministerio del Ultramar, Madrid (Collections now distributed among the Museo Arqueológico Nacional, the Museo Naval, the Museo de Ciencias Naturales, the Biblioteca Nacional, etc.)
Madrid: Museo Naval	Biblioteca del Museo Naval
Maldon: Plume	Plume Library, Maldon, Essex, England
Manchester: PL	Manchester Public Library, Manchester, England
Manchester: Rylands Manchester: UL	John Rylands University Library, Manchester, (Combined in 1972)
Marburg: StB	Stiftung Preussischer Kulturbesitz. Staatsbibliothek (Westdeutsche Bibliothek), Marburg, Germany (West)
Marburg: UB	Bibliothek der Philipps Universität, Marburg
Mellon	Paul Mellon, Private Collection, Washington, D.C.
Middelburg: PL	Provinciale Bibliotheek van Zeeland, Middelburg, The Netherlands
Milan: BN	Biblioteca Nazionale Braidense, Milan, Italy
Montpellier: BM	Bibliothèque de la Ville et du Musée Fabre, Montpellier, France
Montpellier: Ecole de Médecine	Bibliothèque de la Faculté de Médecine de l'Université de Montpellier
Münster: UB	Westfälische Universitätsbibliothek, Münster, Germany (West)
Munich: StB	Bayerische Staatsbibliothek, Munich
Munich: UB	Universitätsbibliothek
Nancy: BM	Bibliothèque Municipale, Nancy, France
Nantes: BM	Bibliothèque Municipale, Nantes, France
Naples: BN	Biblioteca Nazionale Vittorio Emanuele III, Naples
Nice: BM	Bibliothèque Municipale, Nice, France
Nuremberg: Germ. Mus.	Germanisches Nationalmuseum, Nuremberg, Germany (West)
Orense: BP	Biblioteca Publica, Orense, Spain
Orléans: BM	Bibliothèque Municipale, Orléans, France

Oxford: Balliol	Balliol College, Oxford University
Oxford: Bodl.	Bodleian Library
Oxford: Chr. Ch.	Christ Church
Oxford: Corpus	Corpus Christi College
Oxford: Lincoln	Lincoln College
Oxford: Magdalen	Magdalen College
Oxford: Merton	Merton College
Oxford: Oriel	Oriel College
Oxford: Queen's	Queen's College
Oxford: Worcester	Worcester College
Palencia: Catedral	Catedral, Palencia, Spain
Palma: BP	Biblioteca Publica de Palma de Mallorca, Majorca, Spain
Paris: Arsenal	Bibliothèque de l'Arsenal, Paris
Paris: Bibl. du Prot. Franc.	Bibliothèque de la Société de l'Histoire du Protestantisme Français
Paris: CD	Chambre des Députés
Paris: DM	Depôt de la Marine
Paris: Inst. de France	Bibliothèque de l'Institut de France
Paris: Loeb-Larocque	Private collection of bookseller Loeb-Larocque, Paris
Paris: Mazarine	Bibliothèque Mazarine
Paris: Ste Geneviève	Bibliothèque Ste Geneviève
Paris: Sorbonne	Bibliothèque de la Sorbonne
Petworth	Lord Egremont, Private Collection, Petworth House, Petworth, Sussex, England
Pirie, Robert S.	Robert S. Pirie, Private Collection, Hamilton, Mass.
Puebla: B. Palafoxiana	Biblioteca Palafoxiana, Puebla, Mexico
Rennes: BM	Bibliothèque Municipale, Rennes, France
Rennes: BU	Bibliothèque de l'Université de Rennes, France
Rio de Janeiro: BN	Biblioteca Nacional, Rio de Janeiro, Brazil
Roanne: BM	Bibliothèque Municipale, Roanne, France
Rome: Accad. Lincei	Accademia Nazionale dei Lincei, Palazzo Corsini, Rome
Rome: BN	Biblioteca Nazionale Centrale Vittorio Emanuele II, Rome
Rome: B. Alessandrina	Biblioteca Universitaria Alessandrina
Rome: Bibl. Casanatense	Biblioteca Casanatense

Locations

Rome: Bibl. Palatinum	Biblioteca Palatina of the Biblioteca Apostolica Vaticana, Vatican City
Rome: Capuchins	Library of the Capuchin Order, Rome
Rome: OFM	Ordo Fratrum Minorum (Library of the Franciscan Order)
Rome: Vatican	Biblioteca Apostolica Vaticana, Vatican City
Rostock: UB	Bibliothek der Universität Rostock, Germany (East)
Rotterdam: MA	Municipal Archives, Rotterdam, The Netherlands
Rotterdam: ML	Municipal Library (Bibliotheek der Gemeente)
Rotterdam: Mar. Mus. Rotterdam: Prins Hendrik Maritime Museum	Maritiem Museum 'Prins Hendrik'
Rotterdam: WAE	W. A. Engelbrecht Collection, Maritiem Museum 'Prins Hendrik'
Rotterdam: W.A. Engelbrecht	W. A. Engelbrecht, Private Collection, Rotterdam (Now presumably transferred to Rotterdam: WAE)
Rouen: BM	Bibliothèque Municipale, Rouen, France
St Andrews: UL	Library of the University of St. Andrews, Scotland
Salamanca: BU	Biblioteca Universitaria, Salamanca, Spain
Santiago, Chile: BN	Biblioteca Nacional, Santiago, Chile
Santiago de Compostela: BU	Biblioteca Provincial y Universitaria, Santiago de Compostela, Spain
Santiago de Compostela: Colegio de Misiones	Colegio de Misiones
São Paulo: BM	Biblioteca Municipal Mário de Andrade, São Paulo, Brazil
Saragossa: BU	Biblioteca Provincial y Universitaria, Saragossa, Spain
Schwerin: MLB	Mecklenburgische Landesbibliothek, Schwerin, Germany (East)
Seville: Archivo de Indias	Archivo General de las Indias, Seville, Spain
Seville: B. Colombina	Biblioteca Colombina
Seville: BM	Biblioteca Municipal
Seville: BP	Biblioteca Provincial y Universitaria
Seville: BU	Biblioteca de la Universidad
Seville: Residencia de Jesuitas	Biblioteca de la Residencia de los Jesuitas
Seville: Seminario	Biblioteca del Seminario

Stockholm: KB	Kungliga Biblioteket, Stockholm, Sweden
Stourhead	Stourhead, near Mere, Wiltshire, England
Strasbourg: BN Strasbourg: BU	Bibliothèque Nationale et Universitaire, Strasbourg, France
Stuttgart: LB	Württembergische Landesbibliothek, Stuttgart, Germany (West)
Sutton, Coldfield: St Mary's Seminary	St Mary's Seminary, New Oscott, Sutton Coldfield, Warwickshire, England
Sydney: State Library	State Library of New South Wales, Sydney, Australia
Taylor, Robert	Robert Taylor, Private Collection, Princeton, N.J.
Torun: BU	Uniwersytet im. Mikołaja Kopernika (Copernicus University Library), Torun, Poland
Toulouse: BM	Bibliothèque Municipale, Toulouse, France
Tours: BM	Bibliothèque Municipale, Tours, France
T'Serclaes, Duque de	Duque de T'Serclaes, Private Collection, Spain
Tübingen: UB	Universitätsbibliothek, Tübingen, Germany (West)
Turin: BU	Biblioteca Nazionale Universitaria, Turin, Italy
Unger, J. H. W.	J. H. W. Unger, Private Collection, Rotterdam (ca. 1900)
Uppsala: UB	Uppsala Universitetsbiblioteket, Uppsala, Sweden
Urbino: BU	Biblioteca Universitaria, Urbino, Italy
Utrecht: Geog. Inst.	Geografisch Instituut, Rijksuniversiteit, Utrecht The Netherlands
Utrecht: UB	Bibliotheek der Rijksuniversiteit, Utrecht
Valencia: BU	Biblioteca de la Universidad, Valencia, Spain
Valladolid: Dominican Friary	Biblioteca de los Padres Dominicos de San Pablo de Valladolid, Spain
Versailles: BM	Bibliothèque Municipale, Versailles, France
Vienna: NB	Österreichische Nationalbibliothek, Vienna
Ware, Herts: St Edmunds College	St Edmund's College, Ware, Hertfordshire, England
Warsaw: BN	Biblioteka Narodowa, Warsaw, Poland
Warsaw: IG	Biblioteka Instytutu Geografii PAN, Warsaw
Wertheim: RL	Royal Library (Fürstl. Löwenstein-Wertheim Gemeinschaftliches Archiv), Wertheim, Germany (West)
White, W. A.	W. A. White, Private Collection, New York

Locations

Wiesbaden: NLB	Hessische (Nassauische) Landesbibliothek, Wiesbaden, Germany (West)
Winchester: Cathedral	Winchester Cathedral, Winchester, England
Winchester Coll.	Winchester College
Wolfenbüttel: HB	Herzog August Bibliothek, Wolfenbüttel, Germany (West)
Wrocław: BU	Biblioteka Uniwersytecka, Wrocław, Poland
Würzburg: UB	Universitätsbibliothek, Würzburg, Germany (West)
York: Minster	York Minster Dean & Chapter Library, York, England
Zurich: ZB	Zentralbibliothek Zürich, Kantons-, Stadt- und Universitätsbibliothek
Zutphen: Librye	Librye der St. Walburgskerk, Zutphen, The Netherlands

European Americana

European Americana

160–?

Vertooninghe aen de Vereenichde Provintien van Nederlandt. [*Amsterdam? 160–?*]. 11 p.; 4to. States that it is better for the Netherlands to obtain Peruvian gold by peaceful commerce than to force Spain into war, thereby disrupting trade. NN-RB.

60–/1

1601

Acosta, José de S.J. Neundter und letzter Theil Americae. *Frankfurt a. M.: W. Richter* (pt 1) *& M. Becker* (pt 2), 1601. 2 pts; illus.; fol. (Theodor de Bry's *America*. Pt 9. German). Pt 1 transl. by J. Humberger from Acosta's *Historie naturael ende morael van de Westersche Indien*, Haarlem, 1598; 1st publ., Seville, 1590, under title *Historia natural y moral de las Indias*. Pt 2, with special t.p., is Barent Janszoon Potgieter's *Historische Relation, oder Eygendtliche und warhafftige Beschreibung alles dess jenigen, so den 5 Schiffen, welche . . . durch das Fretum Magelanum . . . kommen,* transl. by G. Arthus from the author's *Wijdtloopigh Verhael van tgene de vijf schepen,* 1st publ., Amsterdam, 1600. Cf. Sabin 8784; Baginsky (German Americana) 114; Church 195; JCB (3) I:409. CSmH, CtY, ICN, NN, RPJCB; BL, BN.

601/1

Alemán, Mateo. Primera parte de Guzman de Alfarache. *Madrid: F. de Espino, for J. Martínez,* 1601. 278 numb. lvs; 8vo. 1st publ., Madrid, 1599. For the numerous scattered refs to America, see M. J. Gray, *An index to Guzmán de Alfarache* (New Brunswick, 1948). Medina (BHA) 450; Laurenti (Nov. pic. esp.) 545; Pérez Pastor (Madrid) 771. NNH; BL, BN.

601/2

Barrough, Philip. The method of phisick . . . The third [*sic*] edition, corrected and amended. *London: R. Field,* 1601. 476 p.; 4to. 1st publ., London, 1583. In bk vi introduction of syphilis into Europe is attributed to Columbus's crew; for treatment, guaiacum is recommended. STC 1511. CSmH, CtY, IaU, MBCo; London: Wellcome.

601/3

Bodin, Jean. De republica libri sex . . . Editio quarta. *Oberursel: C. Sutor, for J. Rose,* 1601. 1221 p.; 8vo. 1st publ. in Latin, Paris, 1586, as transl. by the author from the Paris, 1576, text. In bk 1, chapt. 5 mentions West Indian slavery; in bk 5, chapt. 1 refers to the New World as a whole. CtY, ICU, MH-L, PU; BL.

601/4

Botero, Giovanni. Della ragion di stato libri dieci . . . Di nuovo . . . mutati alcuni luoghi . . . & accresciuti di diversi discorsi. *Venice: The Giolitis,* 1601. 432 p.; 8vo. 1st publ., Venice, 1589. Included are refs to Jesuits in New World & to Spanish colonization there. Michel (Répertoire I:201. DLC, ICU; BL, BN.

601/5

——. I prencipi . . . con le Aggiunte alla Ragion di stato. *Venice: G. B. Ciotti,* 1601. 2 pts; 8vo. The *Aggiunte,* 1st publ., Rome, 1598, in the 'Relatione del mare' contain geographic refs to the New World. DLC, IU.

601/6

——. Relationi universali . . . Arricchite di molte cose rari. *Turin: G. D. Tarino,* 1601. 4 pts; 8vo. 1st publ., Rome, 1591–96. Contains substantial discussion of New World. Cf. Sabin 6805; Michel (Répertoire) I:202. London: Wellcome, Paris: Mazarine.

601/7

——. The travellers breviat, or An historical description of the most famous kingdomes in the world. *London: E. Bollifant, for J. Jaggard,* 1601. 179 p.; 4to. Transl. by Robert Johnson from Botero's *Delle relationi universali,* 1st publ., Rome, 1591–96. Sabin 36287; STC 3398. MH; BL.

601/8

3

—[Anr edn]. The worlde, or An historicall description of the most famous kingdomes. *London: E. Bollifant, for J. Jaggard,* 1601. 222 p.; 4to. A reissue of the preceding, with cancel t.p. & additional text. Sabin 105491; STC 3399; JCB (3) II:10. CSmH, DFo, RPJCB; BL. 601/9

Bourne, William. A regiment for the sea . . . Newly corrected and amended by Tho. Hood. *London: T. Wight,* 1601. 106 lvs; 4to. 1st publ., London, [1574], but here incorporating added navigational references to the Americas 1st publ., London, 1580. Taylor (Regiment) 453–54; cf. STC 3428. CtY; Amsterdam: E. R. Crone. 601/10

Camerarius, Philipp. Operae horarum subcisivarum, sive Meditationes historicae . . . Centuria altera. *Frankfurt a. M.: J. Saur, for P. Kopff,* 1601. 568 p.; 4to. Includes ref. to American Indian women, who go about nude without lascivious intent, as reported by Léry. For the 1st 'century' of Camerarius's work, see the year 1602; for the 3rd, see the year 1609. Jantz (German Baroque) 45; cf. Faber du Faur 1239. NcD, NjP, WU. 601/11

Clavius, Christoph. In Sphaeram Joannis de Sacro Bosco commentarius, nunc tertio ab ipso auctore recognitus. *Venice: G. B. Ciotti,* 1601. 483 p.; illus.; 4to. 1st publ., Rome, 1570; included are scattered refs to New World. Shaaber (Brit. auth.) H434. CSt, DLC; BN. 601/12

Coignet, Michiel. Epitome theatri orbis terrarum. *Antwerp:* 1601. *See* Ortelius, Abraham, *below.*

Columba, Gerardus. Disputationum medicarum de febris pestilentis cognitione et curatione, libri duo . . . Accessit . . . Nicolai Macchelli . . . de morbo gallico, eiusque curatione. *Frankfurt a. M.: Heirs of R. Beatus, G. Beatus & J. L. Bitsch,* 1601. 2 pts; 8vo. Macchelli's *Tractatus de morbo gallico,* 1st publ., Venice, 1555, discusses use of guaiacum for treatment of syphilis. DNLM; London: Wellcome, BN. 601/13

Conestaggio, Girolamo Franchi di. L'union du royaume de Portugal à la couronne de Castille . . . prise de l'italien . . . par m. Th. Nardin . . . Deuxième édition. *Besançon: N. de Moingesse,* 1601. 478 p.; 8vo. 1st publ. as here transl. from the author's

Dell' unione del regno di Portogallo alla corona di Castiglia (Genoa, 1585), Besançon, 1596. Included are refs to Columbus & Portuguese settlement of Brazil. Palau 313378. BN. 601/14

Cortés, Jerónimo. Libro de phisonomia natural y varios segretos de naturaleza. *Madrid: P. Madrigal, for M. Martínez,* 1601. 128 numb. lvs; 8vo. 1st publ., Valencia, 1597. Included are numerous refs to the New World, derived largely from José de Acosta's *Historia natural y moral de las Indias,* 1st publ., Seville, 1591. Palau 63297. NNH. 601/15

—[Anr edn]. *Cordova:* 1601. 8vo. Palau 63298. 601/16

—[Anr edn]. El curioso de varios secretos de naturaleza. *Lisbon: J. Rodríguez,* 1601. 8vo. Palau 63299. 601/17

—[Anr edn]. Phisonomia y varios secretos de naturaleza. *Saragossa:* 1601. 107 p.; 8vo. Palau 63300. 601/18

Daniel, Samuel. The works . . . newly augmented. *London: [V. Simmes,] for S. Waterson,* 1601. 3 pts; fol. In verse. Originally published, London, 1599, as Daniel's *Poeticall essayes.* Included is his 'Musophilus' with couplet 'What worlds in th'yet unformed Occident/May come refin'd with th'accents that are ours.' STC 6236; cf. Grolier Club (Langland to Wither) 60; Pforzheimer 248. CSmH, MH; BL. 601/19

Dickenson, John. Speculum tragicum. Regum, principum & magnatum superioris saeculi celebriorum ruinas exitusque calamitosos breviter complectens. *Delft: J. C. Vennecool,* 1601. 127 p.; 8vo. Includes passage on Montezuma & Atabalipa, referring to Cortés & Pizarro. BL, BN. 601/20

Dilich, Wilhelm Schäffer, called. Beschreibung und Abriss dero Ritterspiel, so . . . Herr Moritz . . . angeordnet. *Kassel: W. Wessel,* 1601. 2 pts; illus., port.; 4to. Includes allegorical representation of America with other continents in courtly procession. Wolfenbüttel 143. BL, Wolfenbüttel: HB. 601/21

Doglioni, Giovanni Nicolò. Compendio historico universale di tutte le cose notabili già successe nel mondo . . . riveduto, corretto & ampliato, con aggiunta sino all' anno 1600. *Venice: D. Zenaro,* 1601. 862 p.;

port.; 4to. Though not included in 1st volume, 1st publ., Venice, 1594; here enl. Includes refs to Columbus's discovery of America and Drake's sacking of Santo Domingo in 1585. Michel (Répertoire) II:177. ICN, IU; BN, Paris:Mazarine. 601/22

Dracht-thoneel waer op het fatsoen van meest alle de kleedren, soo wel der gener diemen nu ter tyt de gansche weirelt door dragende is . . . in rym beschreven. *Amsterdam: Z. Heyns* [1601]. 74 lvs.; illus.; 8vo. In verse. Apparently transl. from the *Recueil de la diversité des habits*, 1st publ., Paris, 1562, with illus. of Brazilian natives. For an earlier Dutch translation, see *Alderhande habijt ende cleedinge*, Antwerp, 1570. BL (Heyns). 601/23

Du Bartas, Guillaume de Salluste, seigneur. Les oeuvres poétiques. [*Geneva:*] *J. Chouët*, 1601. 3 v.; 12mo. In verse. Included are the author's *La sepmaine*, 1st publ. with commentaries by Simon Goulart, Paris, 1584, and his *La seconde sepmaine*, 1st publ. with Goulart's commentaries, Geneva, 1589. Included are numerous refs to America. Cf. Holmes (DuBartas) I:88 no. 15a; Jones (Goulart) 20p. BL, Paris:Arsenal. 601/24

——. La divina settimana, cioè I sette giorni della creazione del mondo . . . tradotta . . . in verso sciolto italiano, dal sig. Ferrante Guisone. *Venice: G. B. Ciotti*, 1601. 153 numb. lvs; illus.; 12mo. In verse. Transl. from author's *La seconde sepmaine*, 1st publ., Paris, 1584; 1st publ. in Italian, Tours, 1592. Included are numerous refs to New World. Holmes (Du Bartas) I:109 no. 19n; Michel (Répertoire) II:186. IU, NcD; Edinburgh:UL, Paris:Ste Geneviève. 601/25

——. La sepmaine ou Creation du monde . . . En ceste derniere edition ont esté adjoustez . . . explications des principales difficultez du texte, par S[imon]. G[oulart]. [*Geneva:*] *J. Chouët*, 1601. 3v.; 12mo. In verse. 1st publ. with Goulart's annotations, Geneva, 1581. Both these & the text itself (in verse) contain numerous refs to New World. Holmes (DuBartas) I:74 no. 26; Jones (Goulart) 20p; Goldsmith (France) S189. BL, Paris:Arsenal. 601/26

Du Périer, Anthoine, sieur de La Salargue. Les amours de Pistion et de Fortunée, tirees du voyage du Canada dicte France Nou-

velle. *Paris: T. de La Ruelle*, 1601. 381 p.; 12mo. LeMoine 41; Cioranescu (XVII) 27544. ICN. 601/27

Durante, Castore. Il tesoro della sanità. *Venice: L. Spineda*, 1601. 270 p.; 8vo. 1st publ., [Rome?], 1586. Includes discussion of therapeutic value of eating turkey. Michel (Répertoire) II:191. DLC, DNLM; BL, Avignon:BM. 601/28

Emili, Paolo. De rebus gestis Francorum . . . libri X. Arnoldi Ferroni . . . De rebus gestis Gallorum libri IX. *Basel: S. Henricpetri* [1601]. 4 pts; ports; fol. 1st publ. with Le Ferron's appendix, Paris, 1548–49. The latter work includes account of the appearance of syphilis at Naples, referring to Columbus & the use of guaiacum; bk 8 refers to the capture of a Spanish ship from the Indies. CtY, ICN, NNC. 601/29

Estienne, Charles. L'agriculture et maison rustique. [*Geneva:*] *C. La Fontaine*, 1601. 2 pts; illus.; 8vo. 1st publ. as here enl. by Jean Liébault, Paris, 1567. Included are refs to tobacco & the turkey. Thiébaud (La chasse) 351. BL. 601/30

——. Dictionarium historicum geographicum. *Oberursel: C. Sutor*, 1601. 1565 p.; 4to. 1st publ. in this enl. edn with descriptions of American areas, Lyons, 1595. ICN. 601/31

Fernel, Jean. Universa medicina. *Lyons: J. Veyrat & T. Soubron*, 1601–2. 4 pts; fol. 1st publ. as here constituted, Paris, 1567. Included in pt 2 is Fernel's *De luis venerae curatione perfectissima liber*, 1st publ., Antwerp, 1579, recommending use of guaiacum; pt 3 comprises his *De abditis rerum causis libri duo*, itself 1st publ., Paris, 1548, containing in addition to chapt. on syphilis, a discussion of the effect upon classical knowledge of the discovery of the New World. Sherrington (Fernel) 73.J17. DNLM; BN, Rome: Vatican. 601/32

Fragoso, Juan. Aromatum, fructuum et simplicium aliquot medicamentorum ex India utraque, et Orientali et Occidentali nunc latine edita opera . . . Israelis Spachii. *Strassburg: J. Martin*, 1601. 115 numb. lvs; 8vo. Transl. from Fragoso's *Discursos de las cosas aromaticas*, 1st publ., Madrid, 1572; here a reissue with altered imprint date of printer's 1600 edn? Cf. Sabin 25418 (&

26005); cf. Medina (BHA) 415; cf. Pritzel 3000n; Palau 94181n. DNLM, MoSB; BL, BN.   601/33

Galvão, António. The discoveries of the world . . . unto the yeere . . . 1555. Briefly written in the Portugall tongue . . . Corrected, quoted, and now published . . . by Richard Hakluyt. *London: G. Bishop,* 1601. 97 p.; 4to. Transl. from Galvão's *Tratados . . . dos diversos . . . caminhos,* 1st publ., Lisbon, 1563. 'The first beginning of the discoveries of the Spanyards . . .': p. 29–97. Sabin 26496; Borba de Moraes I:2, STC 11543; Church 323; JCB (3) II:9. CSmH, CtY, DLC, ICN, MB, MiU-C, MnU-B, NN-RB, RPJCB; BL, BN.   601/34

Garzoni, Tommaso. La piazza universale di tutte le professioni del mondo, nuovamente ristampata & posta in luce. *Venice: R. Meietti,* 1601. 958 p.; 4to. 1st publ., Venice, 1585. Includes, in chapt. on cosmographers, section on America. Michel (Répertoire) IV:25. BN, Paris:Arsenal.   601/35

Glen, Jean Baptiste de. Des habits, moeurs, ceremonies, façons de faire . . . du monde. *Liège: J. de Glen,* 1601. 218 numb. lvs; illus.; 8vo. On verso of lf [1] the gold of Peru is mentioned; on verso of lf 181, Columbus's discovery of America. DFo, ICN; BL, BN.   601/36

Gómara, Francisco López de. Histoire generalle des Indes Occidentales, et terres neuves . . . Augmentee en ceste cinquiesme edition de la description de la Nouvelle Espagne . . . Composee en espagnol . . . & traduite . . . par le s. de Genillé Mart. Fumee. *Paris: L. Sonnius,* 1601. 485 numb. lvs; 8vo. 1st publ. in French, Paris, 1568; transl. from the author's *Istoria de las Indias,* 1st publ., Saragossa, 1552. Cf. Sabin 27749; cf. Wagner (SW) 2mm. ICU.   601/37

Goulart, Simon. Deuxiesme[-troisiesme] partie, du premier livre des Histoires de nostre temps. *Paris: J. Houzé,* 1601. 2 pts; 12mo. Continues 1st pt, 1st publ., Paris, 1600. Includes scattered refs to New World, drawn from such sources as Benzoni & Monardes. Jones (Goulart) 54(a). BN.   601/38

Guzmán, Luis de, S.J. Historia de las missiones que han hechos los religiosos de la Compañia de Jesus . . . en la India Oriental. *Alcalá de Henares: Widow of J. Gracián,* 1601. 2 v.; fol. In bk 3, chapts 41–55 discuss early Jesuits in Brazil. Borba de Moraes I:326; Streit V:14; Backer III:1979; García (Alcalá de Henares) 761. CU, DLC, ICN, InU-L, MH, NN-RB, RPJCB; BL, BN.   601/39

Heresbach, Conrad. Foure bookes of husbandry . . . Newly Englished, and encreased by Barnaby Googe. *London: T. Wight,* 1601 [colophon: 1600]. 183 numb. lvs; 4to. Transl. from author's *Rei rusticae,* 1st publ., Cologne, 1570; 1st publ. in English, London, 1577. In bk iv, on poultry, turkeys are discussed. STC 13200; Hunt (Bot.) 178. CSmH, DLC, ICU, MH; BL.   601/40

Herrera y Tordesillas, Antonio de. Descripcion de las Indias Occidentales. *Madrid: J. Flamenco, for the Imprenta Real,* 1601. 96 p.; illus., maps; fol. Issued as supplement to author's *Historia general de los hechos de los Castellanos* of this year. Sabin 31539; cf. Medina (BHA) 455; Wagner (SW) 12n; Streit II:1332; Pérez Pastor (Madrid) 784n; Arents (Add.) 117. CtY, DNW, MH, NN-RB; BL, BN.   601/41

——. Historia general de los hechos de los Castellanos en las islas i tierra firme del mar Oceano . . . En quatro decadas desde el año de 1492. hasta el de 1531. *Madrid: J. Flamenco, for the Emprenta Real,* 1601. 4 v.; illus.; ports; fol. Four further *decadas* appeared in 1615. With v. 4 is bd the author's *Descripcion de las Indias Occidentales.* Sabin 31544; Medina (BHA) 455; Wagner (SW) 12; Streit II:1331; Pérez Pastor (Madrid) 784; JCB (3) II:9–10. CU, InU-L, MH, MiU-C, MnU-B, NN-RB, PBL, RPJCB; BL, BN.   601/42

——. Primera parte de la Historia general del mundo, de xvi años del tiempo del señor Rey don Felipe II . . . desde el año de M.D.LIX. hasta el de M.D.LXXIIII. *Madrid: L. Sánchez, for J. de Montoya,* 1601. 617 p.; fol. Includes numerous passages on New World. Subsequent pts were publ.: a 2nd, Valladolid, 1606, & 3rd, Madrid, 1612. Cf. Sabin 31559; Pérez Pastor (Madrid) 785; JCB (3) II:10. CU, DLC, ICN, NN-RB, PPL, RPJCB; BL, BN.   601/43

Heyns, Peeter. An epitome of Ortelius his Theatre of the world. [*Antwerp:* 1601?]. *See* Ortelius, Abraham, *below.*

Jack Drum's entertainment. Jacke Drums entertainment; or The comedie of Pasquill and Katherine. *London:* [*T. Creede,*] *for R. Olive,* 1601. [72] p.; 4to. On recto of lf B3, tobacco is mentioned. Written mainly by John Marston. STC 7243; Greg 177(a). CSmH, DLC, IEN, MH, NN-RB; BL.
601/44

Jesuits. Letters from missions. Annuae litterae (1593) 1601. Annuae litterae . . . anni MDXCII. *Florence: F. Giunta,* 1601. 450 p.; 8vo. Includes section on Mexican province. Streit I:249; Backer VIII:156. NNH, RPJCB.
601/45

Jonson, Ben. Every man in his humor. *London:* [*S. Stafford,*] *for W. Burre,* 1601. 44 lvs; 4to. Included is a discussion of tobacco; the character Musco mentions having been wounded in America. STC 14766; Greg 176(a); Pforzheimer 545; Arents (Add.) 118. CSmH, DFo, MH, NN-RB; BL.
601/46

——. The fountaine of selfe-love. or Cynthias revells. *London:* [*R. Read,*] *for W. Burre,* 1601. [92] p.; 4to. Comedy. Includes mention of potato. See Greg for variant issues. STC 14773; Greg 181 (aI & aII). CSmH, CtY, DLC, MH, NNPM; BL. 601/47

Khunrath, Conrad. Medulla destillatoria et medica. Das ist, Wahrhafftiger . . . Bericht, wie man den spiritum Vini . . . item die Perlen, Corallen, &c. Künstlich destilliren . . . soll. Item etzlicher herlicher Wundt Balsam [etc.]. *Hamburg: Froben Office,* 1601. 4to. 1st pub., Schleswig, [1594]. Treatise 'Von dem Frantzosen' discusses guaiacum at length & its discovery in Santo Domingo & Puerto Rico. BL. 601/48

L'Ecluse, Charles de. Rariorum plantarum historia. *Antwerp: Plantin Press,* 1601. 2 pts; illus.; fol. Included are descriptions of American plants. Pritzel 1759; Nissen (Bot.) 372. CSt, DLC, ICJ, InU-L, MH-A, MiU, MnU-B, NN-RB, PPL, RPB; BL, BN.
601/49

Le Paulmier de Grentemesnil, Julien. De morbis contagiosis libri septem. *Frankfurt a. M.: C. Marne & Heirs of J. Aubry,* 1601. 552 p.; 8vo. 1st publ., Paris, 1578. Discus-sion of syphilis describes its American origin, and that of guaiacum, while that of 'radix Chinae' (i.e., ginseng) refers to a variety found in Florida & elsewhere in America. Two chapts are devoted to sarsaparilla. Wellcome I:4857. CtY, DLC, MnU, PPC; London:Wellcome, BN. 601/50

Lerma, Francisco de Sandoval y Rojas, duque de. Señor. Por las razones que en este memorial se refieren a Vuestra Magestad parece cosa muy conveniente al servicio de Dios . . . y al V.M. y al bien del reyno del Peru perpetuar los repartimientos, y encomiendas que en al ay. [*Valladolid?* 1601?]. 8 p.; fol. Presented to the king at Valladolid, 28 June 1601. Medina (BHA) 454; Kress 227. MH-BA; Seville:Archivo de Indias.
601/51

Linschoten, Jan Huygen van. Tertia pars Indiae Orientalis. *Frankfurt a. M.: M. Becker, for J. T. & J. I. de Bry, Bros,* 1601. 170 p.; illus., maps; fol. (J. T. de Bry's *India Orientalis.* Pt 3. Latin). Transl from de Bry's German version, *Dritter Theil Indiae Orientalis,* Frankfurt a. M., 1599. Itself without Americana, contains also 1st pt of Willem Lodewijcksz's *Navigatio Hollandorum in insulas Orientales,* 1st publ., Amsterdam, 1598, under title *D'eerste boeck; Historie van Indien.* Includes refs to Brazil on p. 57. For variant issues see Church. Church 208–10; JCB (3) I:425. CSmH, DLC, ICN, NN-RB, PHi, RPJCB; BL, BN. 601/52

——. Voyagie, ofte Schip-vaert . . . van by noorden om langes Noorwegen de Noortcaep. *Franeker: G. Ketel, for J. H. van Linschoten, at Enkhuizen,* 1601. 38 numb. lvs.; illus., maps; fol. Prelim. lvs include refs to American exploration. Sabin 41357n; Tiele-Muller 155; Tiele 691; Muller (1872) 2064; Church 324; JCB (3) II:11. CSmH, DLC, MnU-B, NN-RB, RPJCB; BL. 601/53

Lobo Lasso de la Vega, Gabriel. Elogios en loor de los tres famosos varones, Don Jayme rey de Aragon, Don Fernando Cortes marques del Valle, y Don Alvaro de Baçan, marques de Santacruz. *Saragossa: A. Rodríguez,* 1601. 144 numb. lvs; 16mo. Sabin 39138; Medina (BHA) 456; Jiménez Catalán (Saragossa) 11; JCB (3) II:10. NN-RB, RPJCB, WU; BL, BN. 601/54

——. Manojuelo de romances nuevas. *Barce-*

lona: *S. de Cormellas*, 1601. 197 numb. lvs;
12mo. In verse. The 'romances' beginning
'Donde su crespa madeja' & 'El que de la
varia Diosa' describe Cortés in New World.
Palau 132560.   601/55
—[Anr edn]. *Saragossa: M. Fortuño Sánchez, for
F. Sanz,* 1601. 12mo. Jiménez Catalan (Sara-
gossa) 14; Palau 132561. Naples: BN.
                                           601/56
Mariana, Juan de.   Historia general de Es-
paña. *Toledo: P. Rodríguez,* 1601. 2 v.; fol.
Transl., rev., & augm. by the author from
his *Historiae de rebus Hispaniae,* 1st publ.,
Toledo, 1592.   Sabin 44546;   Backer
V:548–49; Pérez Pastor (Toledo) 442. CLU,
NNH, RPB; BL.   601/57
Massaria, Alessandro.   Practica medica, seu
Praelectiones academicae. *Frankfurt a. M.:
M. Hartmann, for N. Basse,* 1601. 968 p.; 4to.
In bk 6, the chapt. 'De morbo gallico' in-
cludes prescriptions for treating syphilis
containing guaiacum & sarsaparilla. DNLM,
ICJ; London:Wellcome.   601/58
Melich, Georg.   Dispensatorium medicum,
sive De recta medicamentorum . . . parandorum ratione, commentarii. . . in latinum
sermonem conversi a Sam. Keller. *Frankfurt
a. M.: Palthenius Office,* 1601. Transl. from
Melich's *Avertimenti nelle compositioni de' medicamenti,* 1st publ., Venice, 1575. Includes
description of tobacco & its use by Indians
of Mexico. DNLM, WU; BL.   601/59
Mercuriale, Girolamo.   Medicina practica,
seu De cognoscendis, discernendis, et curandis omnibus humani corporis affectibus
. . . libri v. *Frankfurt a. M.: J. T. Schönwetter,*
1601. 652 p.; fol. While believing that
syphilis was known to the ancient Greeks,
includes guaiacum & sarsaparilla in its treatment. Reprinted, 1603, under title *Praelectiones Patavinae.* DNLM; BN.   601/60
Meteren, Emanuel van.   Historia, oder Eigentliche und warhaffte Beschreibung aller
fürnehmen Kriegshändel . . . so sich in Ni-
derteutschlandt . . . zugetragen haben . . .
in 19. Bücher abgetheilet . . . gebessere
und verm. [*Hamburg?*] 1601. 824 p.; fol. 1st
publ. in German, Hamburg, 1596; transl.
from Dutch ms. Includes scattered American refs. DLC.   601/61
Molina, Luis de.   Disputationes de contractibus. *Venice: M. Collosini & B. Barezzi,* 1601.

880 p.; fol. 1st publ., Cuenca (Spain), 1597,
under title *De justitia, tomus secundus.* In disp.
398, 406, & 408, on monetary exchanges,
refs occur to the New World, citing Brazil
and Peru. Backer V:1176. DCU, MiU; BN.
                                           601/62
More, Sir Thomas, Saint.   De optimo reipublicae statu, deque nova insula Utopia,
libri duo. *Frankfurt a. M.: J. Sauer, for P. Kopff,*
1601. 299 p.; 12mo. 1st publ., Louvain,
1516. Set in New World, with ref. to Vespucci's voyages. Gibson (More) 8; Shaaber
(Brit. auth.) M237. CtY, MH; Oxford:Bodl.;
Brussels:BR.   601/63
Neck, Jacob Corneliszoon van.   Journal, was
sich von Tag zu Tag mit den holländischen
Schiffen so . . . Amsterdam ausgefahren.
Arnhem. J. Janszoon, 1601. 4to. Prob. transl.
from the author's *Het tweede boeck below,* the
translator being unknown. Tiele-Muller
127; Tiele 786n.   601/64
—[Anr edn]. Fünffter Theil der Orientalischen Indien; Eygentlicher Bericht . . . der
gantzen volkommenen Reyse oder Schiffart, so die Holländer mit acht Schiffen . . .
gethan haben . . . Auss niederländischer
Verzeichnuss . . . beschrieben durch M.
Gothart Artus. *Frankfurt a. M.: M. Becker,*
1601. 66 p.; illus., maps; fol. (J. T. de Bry's
India Orientalis. Pt 5. German). Transl., with
omissions, from Neck's *Het tweede boeck,* below. Tiele-Muller, p. 143; Church 234; JCB
(3) I:431–32. CSmH, DLC, MBAt, NN-RB,
RPJCB; BL, BN.   601/65
——. The journall, or dayly register, contayning a true manifestation and historicall declaration of the voyage. *London: [S. Stafford
& F. Kingston] for C. Burby & J. Flasket,* 1601.
58 lvs; 4to. Transl. by W. Walker from the
author's *Het tweede boeck,* below. Tiele-Muller, p. 144; STC 18417. CSmH, NN-RB;
BL.   601/66
——. Quinta pars Indiae Orientalis: quâ continetur Vera & accurata descriptio universae
navigationis illius, quam Hollandi cum oc-
tonis navibus in terras Orientales . . . susceperunt . . . Opus Belgica lingua primò
editum: postea Germanico idiomate puri-
ore redditum: & ex hoc iam Latio donatum
à Bilibaldo Strobaeo. *Frankfurt a. M.: M.
Becker,* 1601. 60 p.; illus., maps; fol. (J. T.
de Bry's *India Orientalis.* Pt 5. Latin). Transl.

from Neck's *Fünffter Theil der Orientalischen Indien,* above. For variant issue cf. Church. Tiele-Muller, p. 143; Church 212; JCB (3) I:430–31. CSmH, DLC, ICN, NN-RB, RPJCB; BL, BN. 601/67

———. Le second livre, Journal ou Comptoir . . . du voyage faict par les huict navires d'Amsterdam. *Amsterdam: C. Claeszoon, for B. Dacivelle, at Calais,* 1601. 2 pts; illus., maps; fol. Transl. from Neck's *Het tweede boeck, Journael oft Dagh-register,* below. Also issued with Lodewijcksz's *Premiere livre de l'Histoire de la navigation aux Indes Orientales,* Amsterdam, 1598. Tiele-Muller 126; Tiele 785; JCB (3) II:11. CSmH, CtY, MH-A, MnU-B, NN-RB, RPJCB; BL, BN. 601/68

———. Het tweede boeck, Journael oft Dagh-register, inhoudende een warachtich verhael ende historische vertellinghe vande reyse, gedaen door de acht schepen van Amstelredamme. *Amsterdam: C. Claeszoon,* 1601. 50 numb. lvs; illus., maps; obl. 4to. 1st publ., Amsterdam, [1600]. Includes refs to Brazil and tobacco from the West Indies. Also issued with W. Lodewijcksz's *D'eerste boeck; Historie van Indien,* Amsterdam, 1598. Tiele-Muller 124; Tiele 782. BL. 601/69

—[Anr issue]. [*Amsterdam: C. Claeszoon, for*] *B. Langenes, at Middelburg,* 1601. Tiele-Muller 125; Tiele 782n; Muller (1872) 2211; JCB (3) II:12. NN-RB, NIC, RPJCB; BN. 601/70

Noort, Olivier van. Beschryvinghe van de voyagie om den geheelen werelt cloot . . . door de Strate Magellanes. *Rotterdam: J. van Waesberghe; Amsterdam: C. Claeszoon* [1601]. 92 p.; illus., maps; obl. 4to. 1st publ. in extract at Rotterdam in this year; see the following item. Includes refs to Brazil, Chile, Peru, etc., & their natives. Sabin 55434; Tiele-Muller 15; Tiele 804; Nijhoff (Noort) c. NN-RB. 601/71

———. Extract oft Kort verhael wt het groote journael van de . . . reyse ghedaen door de Strate Magellana. *Rotterdam: J. van Waesberghe,* 1601. 16 lvs; obl. 4to. A brief extract from Noort's *Beschryvinghe van de voyagie om den geheelen werelt cloot,* publ. later this year at Rotterdam & Amsterdam. Sabin 55432; Tiele-Muller 14; Tiele 803; Nijhoff (Noort) a. NN-RB. 601/72

Ortelius, Abraham. Abrégé du Théâtre, contenant la description des principales parties & régions du monde . . . Dernière edition, corrigée en plusieurs lieux, & augmentée de quelques cartes nouvelles. *Antwerp:* [*H. Swingen, for*] *J. B. Vrients,* 1601. 135 lvs; maps; obl. 8vo. 1st publ. in French, Antwerp, 1577. Koeman (Ort) 59. Florence: BN. 601/73

———. An epitome of Ortelius his Theatre of the world. [*Antwerp:*] *H. Swingen, for J. Norton, at London* [1601?]. 110 numb. lvs; maps; obl. 8vo. Transl. from Antwerp, 1595, Latin text; without Favolius's Latin version of Heyns's verse. Koeman (Ort) 62; Phillips (Atlases) 418; STC 18857. CSmH, DLC, ICN, MH, NN-RB, RPJCB; BL. 601/74

———. Epitome theatri orbis terrarum . . . de novo recognita, aucta et geographica ratione restaurata à Michaele Coigneto. *Antwerp: J. van Keerberghen,* 1601. 2 pts; maps; obl. 8vo. In this edition the maps were newly engraved by the Brothers Arsenius with fresh descriptive text by Coignet. A rival edition to that described in the following entry. Cf. Sabin 57691; Koeman (Ort) 63; Phillips (Atlases) 3404. CtY, DLC, ICN, NNC; BN. 601/75

———. Epitome theatri Orteliani, praecipuarum orbis regionum delineationes . . . continens. *Antwerp: H. Swingen, for J. B. Vrients,* 1601. 138 lvs; maps; obl. 8vo. 1st publ. in Latin form with maps engraved by Philippe Galle, Antwerp, 1585. Here Favolius's Latin rendering of Peeter Heyns's text is not present. Sabin 57690n; Koeman (Ort) 58; Phillips (Atlases) 413; JCB (3) II:13. DLC, ICN, InU-L, MiU-C, NN-RB, RPJCB; BL, Brussels:BR. 601/76

———. Theatrum orbis terrarum . . . quod ante extremum vitae suae diem, postremum recensuit novis tabulis et commentariis auxit atque illustravit. *Antwerp: Plantin Press,* 1601. 3 pts; maps; fol. 1st publ., Antwerp, 1572. Koeman (Ort) 33; Phillips (Atlases) 412; JCB (3) II:12. DLC, MiU, NjP, RPJCB; BL, Brussels:BR. 601/77

Padovani, Fabrizio. Tractatus duo, alter de ventis, alter perbrevis de terraemotu. *Bologna: G. B. Bellagamba,* 1601. 163 p.; illus., maps; fol. Includes world map showing America. Riccardi 230–31. CtY, DFo, MH; BN. 601/78

Paré, Ambroise. Wundt Artzney oder Artzney spiegell . . . Von Petro Uffenbach . . . auss der lateinischen editio Jacobi Guillemeau . . . transferirt und gesetzt. *Frankfurt a. M.: Z. Palthenius, for P. Fischer,* 1601. 1239 p.; illus.; fol. Transl. from Paré's *Opera,* 1st publ., Paris, 1582, as transl. from his French text, 1st publ., Paris, 1575. Treatment of syphilis calls for use of guaiacum, while section on monsters & prodigies (derived from Jean de Léry & André Thevet) describes strange birds, fish, etc., in the New World— e.g., the toucan, flying fish, & crocodiles. In some copies the dedication is signed by Zacharias Palthenius, in others by Jonas Rose. Doe (Paré) 56. CtY-M, DNLM, ICJ, MBCo, MiU; Vienna: NB. 601/79

Potgieter, Barent Janszoon. Historische Relation, oder Eygendtliche und warhafftige Beschreibung alles dess jenigen, so den 5 Schiffen, welche . . . durch das Fretum Magelanum . . . kommen. *Frankfurt a. M.: M. Becker,* 1601. 72 p.; illus.; fol. (Theodor de Bry's *America.* Pt 9. German). Transl. from the author's *Wijdtloopigh verhael van tgene de viif schepen,* 1st publ., Amsterdam, 1600. Issued as pt 2 of José de Acosta, *Neundter und letzter Theil Americae,* above. Cf. Sabin 8784; Baginsky (German Americana) 114; Church 195; JCB (3) I:409. CSmH, CtY, ICN, NN-RB, RPJCB; BL, BN. 601/80

Raleigh, Sir Walter. Kurtze wunderbare Beschreibung dess goldreichen Königreichs Guianae in America oder newen Welt. *Nuremberg: C. Lochner, for L. Hulsius,* 1601. 17 p.; illus., map; 4to. (Levinus Hulsius's *Sammlung von . . . Schiffahrten.* Pt 5). 1st publ. in this version, Nuremberg, 1599; transl. from author's *Discoverie of . . . Guiana,* 1st publ., London, 1596. Sabin 67563 (& 33658); Baginsky (German Americana) 115; Shaaber (Brit. auth.) R14; Church 276; JCB (3) I:455–56. CSmH, NN-RB, RPJCB; BL, BN. 601/81

—[Anr issue]. *Nuremberg: C. Lochner, for L. Hulsius,* 1601. Sheet c reset; e.g., p. 13 has 36 lines, rather than 33. Baginsky (German Americana) 116; Shaaber (Brit. auth.) R15; Church 276. NN-RB. 601/82

A rich storehouse or treasury for the diseased . . . By A. T. And now newly corrected, augmented and inlarged by G. W. *London: R. Blower; sold by W. Barley,* 1601. 4to. 1st publ., London, 1596. In treatment of syphilis, use of guaiacum & sarsaparilla is discussed. STC 23606.5. DFo; BL(imp.). 601/83

Richeome, Louis, S.J. Trois discours pour la religion catholique. *Lyons: P. Rigaud,* 1601. 686 p.; 8vo. 1st publ., Bordeaux, 1597. In bk 1, chapt. 23 discusses Brazil, Peru, etc. Cf. Backer VI:1817; cf. Cioranescu (XVII) 59455. BN. 601/84

Rivadeneira, Pedro de, S.J. Tratado de la religion y virtudes que deve tener el prencipe christiano para governar y conservar sus estados. Contra lo que Nicolas Machiavelo y los politicos deste tiempo enseñan. *Madrid: L. Sánchez,* 1601. 656 p.; 8vo. 1st publ., Madrid, 1595. In bk ii are refs to the riches of the New World, citing José de Acosta, mentioning Cortés, etc. Pérez Pastor (Madrid) 792; Backer VI:1735; Palau 266335. PU; BN, Madrid: BU (S. Isidro). 601/85

Rondelet, Guillaume. Methodus curandorum omnium morborum corporis humani. *Lyons: J. Lertout,* 1601. 1277 p.; 8vo. 1st publ., [Paris? 1563?]. Section 'De morbo italico' mentions treatment of syphilis with guaiacum. DNLM; London:Wellcome, BN. 601/86

Sacro Bosco, Joannes de. Sphaera . . . emendata, aucta et illustrata. Eliae Vineti . . . nunc accessere r.p. Christoph. Clavii breve commentarius. *Cologne: G. Cholinus,* 1601. 213 p.; illus.; 8vo. 1st publ. with Vinet's *Scholia,* with refs to Spanish & Portuguese discoveries in West & East Indies, Paris, 1551; Clavius's *Commentarius,* with refs to New World, 1st publ., Rome, 1570— cf. separate 1601 edn. MiU, NN-RB, PPL; BN. 601/87

Scaliger, Julius Caesar. Exotericarum exercitationum liber xv. *Frankfurt a. M.: Wechel Office, for C. Marne & Heirs of J. Aubry,* 1601. 1129 p.; illus.; 8vo. 1st publ., Paris, 1557. In addition to guaiacum & sarsaparilla, the potato, maize, & the manatee are mentioned. CLSU, CtY-M, MH, NcU, PU. 601/88

Silvaticus, Joannes Baptista. Controversiae numero centum. *Frankfurt a. M.: Heirs of A.*

Wechel, for C. de Marne & Heirs of J. Aubry, 1601. 470 p.; fol. 'Controversiae' lxx–lxxiii discuss treatment of syphilis with guaiacum & sarsaparilla. DNLM, NNNAM, PPC; BL.
601/89

Sostmann, Johann. Indianische Reise. *Paderborn: M. Brückner,* 1601. 31 p.; 8vo. Relates experiences in West Indies, Mexico, Cartagena, etc. Sabin 87198; Palmer 391; JCB (3) II:13. RPJCB.
601/90

Spain. Sovereigns, etc., 1598–1621 (Philip III). Los que por mi mandado del rey nuestro señor se assienta y concierta con J. Rodriguez Cutinho . . . sobre el arrendamiento de la renta de los esclavos negros, que se llevan a las Indias Occidentales y islas dellas. [*Madrid?* 1601?]. 15 numb. lvs. fol. Decree of 26 March 1601. BL.
601/91

Stow, John. The annales of England . . . Untill 1601. *London: [Eliot's Court Press & F. Kingston for] R. Newbery* [1601]. 1312 p.; 4to. 1st publ. with accounts of Frobisher, Drake, Cavendish, etc., London, 1592; here a reissue of 1600 edn with altered t.p. STC 23336. CSmH, DFo, MH, OCU; London: Guildhall.
601/92

Tasso, Torquato. Il Goffredo, ò vero Gierusalemme liberata. *Rome: L. Zannetti, for G.A. Ruffinelli,* 1601 (Colophon: 1600). 1st publ. with American refs, Parma, 1581. Includes in canto 15, stanzas 30–32, discussion of Columbus. For the numerous edns of this work printed after 1600, see Racc. Tassiana. Racc. Tassiana 183. MH (imp.), PHC; BN.
601/93

Teixeira Pinto, Bento. Naufragio que passou Jorge Dalbuquerque Coelho, capitão, & governador de Pernambuco. *Lisbon: A. Alvarez, for A. Ribeiro,* 1601. 2 pts; illus., port.; 4to. Sabin 94595; Borba de Moraes II:296; Palau 328960. DCU.
601/94

Wecker, Johann Jakob. Antidotarium generale, et speciale. *Basel: C. Waldkirch, for the Episcopius Heirs,* 1601. 2 pts; illus.; 4to. 1st publ., Basel, 1574 & 1576. Formulas are provided employing guaiacum, tobacco (*Nicotiana*), mentioning its American origin, mechoacan, sarsaparilla, specified as American, & sassafras. DNLM, ICU, NNNAM; BL, BN.
601/95

Wirsung, Christoph. Medecyn boec . . . nu

uut de vierde editie . . . overgheset door d. Carolum Battum . . . De 3. verbeterde druck. *Dordrecht: I. J. Canin,* 1601. 676 p.; fol. Transl. from Wirsung's *New Artzney Buch,* 1st publ., Heidelberg, 1568; cf. 1605 edn. DNLM.
601/96

Wittich, Johann. Bericht von den wunderbaren Bezoardischen Steinen . . . welche . . . erst innerhalb 30 Jahren aus India orientali und occidentali durch Gartiam ab Horto und Nicolaum Monardum kündig gemacht worden seindt. [*Arnstadt:*] *Vögelin Press,* 1601. 120 p.; 4to. 1st publ., Leipzig, 1589. Cf. Sabin 104966. London:Wellcome.
601/97

Wright, Thomas. The passions of the minde. *London: V. S[immes]., for W. B[urre].,* 1601. 8vo. In bk iv, chapt. viii, the author's passion 'in taking Tabacco' is cited; in bk v, chapt. i, the 'people of Tangia in America'; in bk vi, chapt. i, the gold mines of the New World. STC 26039. CSmH, DFo, MiU; BL.
601/98

Zecchi, Giovanni. Liber primus Consultationum medicinalium. *Rome: G. Facciotti, for G. Martinelli,* 1601. 499 p.; 4to. 1st publ., Rome, 1599. Treatment of syphilis invokes use of guaiacum & sarsaparilla. DNLM.
601/99

1602

Acosta, José de, S.J. Americae nona & postrema pars . . . omnia e Germanico Latinitate donata. *Frankfurt a. M.: M. Becker,* 1602. 3 pts; illus., port., maps; fol. (Theodor de Bry's *America.* Pt 9. Latin). Pts 1 & 2 transl. from *Neundter und letzter Theil Americae,* Frankfurt a. M., 1601. Pt 1 1st publ., Seville, 1590, under title *Historia natural y moral de las Indias.* Pt 2 is Potgieter's *Relatio historica . . . navigationis, quam V naves . . . susceperunt,* 1st publ., Amsterdam, 1600, under title *Wijdtloopigh verhael van tgene de vijf schepen.* Pt 3 is Olivier van Noort's *Additamentum nonae partis Americae,* described separately. Cf. Sabin 8784; Streit II:1340; Church 168; JCB (3) I:406–8. CSmH, CtY, ICN, NN-RB, PHi, RPJCB; BL, BN.
602/1

Alemán, Mateo. Primera parte de Guzman de Alfarache. *Seville: J. de León,* 1602. 263

numb. lvs; 4to. 1st publ., Madrid, 1599; cf. 1601 edn. Laurenti (Nov. pic. esp.) 546; Palau 6682. BN. 602/2

Alfonce, Jean, i.e., Jean Fonteneau, known as. Les voyages avantureux . . . contenant les reigles & enseignemens necessaires à la bonne & seure navigation. Reveu et corrigé de nouveau. *Rouen: T. Reinsart,* 1602. 128 p.; 4to. 1st publ., Poitiers, [ca. 1558?]. Describes coasts of the Americas, from Labrador to the Strait of Magellan. Sabin 100834. NN-RB. 602/3

Arnauld, Antoine (1560–1619). Bedencken an die königliche May[estät]. in Franckreich uber der Jesuiter . . . aussöhnung . . . auss der frantz. . . . Sprach versetzet. *Heidelberg:* 1602. 189 p.; 8vo. Transl. from Arnauld's *Le franc et veritable discours,* below. Dt. Ges. Kat. 6.8997. Berlin:StB, Munich:StB. 602/4

——. Le franc discours. A discourse, presented of late to the French king . . . of the Jesuits . . . Written in French this present yeere 1602, and . . . Englished. [*London: W. Jaggard?*] 1602. 138 p.; 8vo. Transl. from the author's *Le franc et veritable discours,* below. STC 780. DFo; BL, Cambridge:Emmanuel. 602/5

——. Le franc et veritable discours au roy, sur le restablissement qui luy est demandé pour les Jésuites. [*Paris?*] 1602. 120 (i.e., 90) p.; 8vo. Includes ref. to Spanish control of East & West Indies, & to Jesuits' desire to Christianize the world. ICN, MnU, NNUT, WU; BN. 602/6

—[Anr edn]. [*Paris?*] 1602. 144 p.; 12mo. Dt. Ges. Kat. 6.8994. BL, BN. 602/7

——. Ingenua & vera oratio ad regem christianissimum perscripta. *Lyons:* 1602. 72 p.; 8vo. Transl. from Arnauld's *Le franc et veritable discours,* above. Dt. Ges. Kat. 6.8999. BN, Göttingen:UB. 602/8

Augenio, Orazio. Epistolarum et consultationum medicinalium . . . libri xii. *Venice: D. Zenari,* 1602. 2 v.; port.; fol. 1st publ. with American refs, Venice, 1592. Vol. 2 includes refs to guaiacum & tobacco. DNLM, MnU; BN, Munich:StB. 602/9

Avelar, André do. Chronographia ou Reportorio dos tempos . . . nesta quarta impressam reformada. *Lisbon: J. Rodriguez, for*

E. Lopez, 1602. 372 numb. lvs; illus.; 4to. 1st publ., Lisbon, 1585. 'De mundo novo': lf 54r–lf 55v. Elsewhere other refs to New World occur. BL. 602/10

Barco Centenera, Martín del. Argentina y conquista del río de La Plata, con otros acaecimientos de los reynos del Peru, Tucumán, y estado del Brasil. *Lisbon: P. Craesbeeck,* 1602. 230 p.; 4to. In verse. Sabin 3370; Medina (BHA) 459; Borba de Moraes I:64; Palau 24089; JCB (3) II:14. CtY, MH, NBC, RPJCB; BL. 602/11

Beaumont, Sir John. The metamorphosis of tabacco. *London: [F. Kingston] for J. Flasket,* 1602. [34] p.; 4to. In verse. Describes American origins of plant. STC 1695; Arents 63. CSmH, CtY, MH, NN-A; BL. 602/12

Bertius, Petrus. Tabularum geographicarum contractarum libri quinque, cum luculentis singularum tabularum explicationibus. Editio secunda. *Amsterdam: C. Claeszoon; for sale by J. Janszoon, at Arnhem,* 1602. 679 p.; maps; obl. 8vo. 1st publ., Amsterdam, 1600; incorporates maps 1st publ. in Barent Langenes's *Caert-thresoor,* 1st publ., Middelburg. [1598]. Cf. Sabin 5014; Koeman (Lan) 5; Phillips (Atlases) 414. DLC; Paris: Arsenal. 602/13

Botero, Giovanni. Mundus imperiorum, sive De mundi imperiis libri quatuor: das ist Beschreibung aller Keyserthumb und Königreich. *Oberursel: C. Sutor,* 1602. [120] p.; maps; 4to. 1st publ. as transl. by Johann von Brüssel from pt 2 of Botero's *Relationi universali* (1st publ., Rome, 1591), Cologne, 1596, under title *Theatrum, oder Schawspiel.* 602/14

——. Le relazioni universali . . . Nuovamente ristampate, & corrette. *Venice: N. Polo & Co.,* 1602. 4 pts; maps; 4to. 1st publ., Rome, 1591–96; cf. 1601 edn. Cf. Sabin 6805; Streit I:251; JCB (3) II:14. MiU-C, NN-RB, RPJCB (pt 4); BL, BN. 602/15

——. Tractatus duo: Prior: De illustrium statu & politia, libris x. Posterior: De origine urbium . . . Ex italico primum in germanicum, atque exinde in latinum . . . auctore m. Georgio Draudio. *Oberursel: C. Sutor, for L. Zetzner, at Strassburg,* 1602. 946 p.; 8vo. Transl. from Botero's *Della ragion di stato,*

1st publ., Venice, 1589, as transl. into German, Strassburg, 1596. Mentions Jesuits in New World & Spanish colonization there. JCB (3) II:14. ICN, RPJCB; BL. 602/16

Bozio, Tommaso. De signis ecclesiae Dei, libri xxiii. *Lyons:* 1602. 2 v.; 8vo. 1st publ., Rome, 1591. Includes, as 'Signum lxxxiv', discussion of the New World as evidence of superiority of Catholic faith. Streit I:252. 602/17

Brereton, John. A brief and true relation of the discoverie of the north part of Virginia. *London: G. Bishop,* 1602. 24 p.; 4to. Describes New England, not present-day Virginia. Vail (Frontier) 9; STC 3610; Church 325; JCB (3) II:15. CSmH, PP, RPJCB. 602/18

—[Anr edn]. . . . With divers instructions . . . newly added in this second impression. *London: G. Bishop,* 1602. 48 p.; 4to. Includes also extracts from Hakluyt, Laudonnière, & Hariot. Sabin 7730; Vail (Frontier) 10; STC 3611; Church 326; JCB (3) II:15. CSmH, CtY, ICN, MH, MiU-C, MnU-B, NN-RB, PP, RPJCB; BL. 602/19

Breton, Nicholas. A poste with a madde packet of letters. *London: [T. Creede,] for J. Smethwicke,* 1602. 23 lvs; 4to. Includes ref. to tobacco as purge for rheum. For a 2nd pt see the year 1605. STC 3684. CSmH, DFo. 602/20

——. Wonders worth the hearing. *London: J. Tapp,* 1602. [32] p.; 4to. A purse of gold said to be worth ten pipes of tobacco. STC 3714. BL. 602/21

Bruele, Gualtherus. Praxis medicinae theorica et empirica familiarissima. *Venice: Societas Venetas,* 1602. 196 numb. lvs; 8vo. 1st publ., Antwerp, 1579. Amongst ingredients recommended for therapeutic purposes are guaiacum, sarsaparilla, & the pineapple. BN. 602/22

Camerarius, Philipp. Operae horarum subcisivarum, sive Meditationes historicae . . . Centuria prima. *Frankfurt a. M.: J. Saur, for P. Kopff,* 1602. 474 p.; 4to. 1st publ., Altdorf, 1591. Includes ref. to new islands in the west, & to the swiftness of Indians chasing stags. Mention is also made of a place called 'Zauana' in 'Guaccaiarima', as reported by Peter Martyr d'Anghiera. For 2nd

'century', see the year 1601. Jantz (German Baroque) 45. CtY, ICU, NcD, NjP; BL, BN. 602/23

Canevari, Demetrio. De ligno sancto commentarium. *Rome: G. Facciotti,* 1602. 141 p.; 8vo. Discusses guaiacum, mentioning its sources and describing it as 'sanctissimum American lignum'. DNLM, MH-A, NNNAM; BL. 602/24

Catholic Church. Commisarius Generalis Cruciatae. Instruction y forma que se ha de tener en la publicación, administracion y cobranza de la Bula de la Santa Cruzada . . . que se ha de hacer del tercero assiento, en el arçobispado de Mexico y obispados de Taxcala, Guaxaca, Mechuacan y Nueva Galicia y Yucatan. *Valladolid:* 1602. 15 p.; fol. 1st (?) publ., [Barcelona? 1537?]; cf. Palau 120105. Included are instructions relating to Spanish America (cf. 1608 edn). Palau 120130; Maggs Cat. 479 (Americana V):4088. 602/25

Cesalpino, Andrea. Artis medicae pars prima[-II]. *Rome: A. Zanetti,* 1602–3. 3 v.; 8vo. In the 2nd pt, bk 4, on syphilis, discusses its transmission by Columbus & its treatment with guaiacum & sarsaparilla. For other edns under variant titles, see the years 1605 & 1606. CtY-M, NNNAM; BN. 602/26

Clavius, Christoph. In Sphaeram Joannis de Sacro Bosco commentarius nunc quarto ab ipso auctore recognitus. *St. Gervais: S. Crespin,* 1602. 551 p.; illus.; 4to. 1st publ., Rome, 1570; cf. 1601 edn. Shaaber (Brit. auth.) H435. BN. 602/27

—[Anr edn]. *Lyons: J. de Gabiano,* 1602. 551 p.; illus.; 4to. ICU, MB, NN-RB, PPL, RPB. 602/28

Coignet, Michiel. L'épitome du théâtre de l'univers. *Antwerp:* 1602. *See* Ortelius, Abraham, *below.*

Conestaggio, Girolamo Franchi di. De Portugalliae conjunctione cum regno Castellae. *Frankfurt a. M.: C. Marne & Heirs of J. Aubry,* 1602. 502 p.; illus.; 8vo. Transl. from the author's *Dell'unione del regno di Portogallo alla corona di Castiglia,* 1st publ., Genoa, 1585. Included are refs to Columbus & Portuguese settlement of Brazil. Palau 313383. NjP, CaBVaU; BL, BN. 602/29

Copley, Anthony. Another letter of Mr. A. C. to his dis-Jesuited kinsman. [*London?*] 1602. 46 lvs; 4to. Includes disparaging refs to tobacco. STC 5736. NN-A; BL.

602/30

Daniel, Samuel. The works . . . newly augmented. London: [*V. Simmes,*] *for S. Waterson,* 1602. 3 pts; fol. In verse. Originally published, London, 1599, under title *Poeticall essayes.* Cf. 1601 edn with above title of which this is a reissue with altered imprint date. STC 6237; Grolier Club (Langland to Wither) 60. CLU-C, CtY, DLC, ICN, MH, NjP; BL.

602/31

Dekker, Thomas. Satiro-mastix. or The untrussing of the humorous poet. *London: E. A[llde]. for E. White,* 1602. [93] p.; 4to. Drama. Includes refs to tobacco. STC 6521; Greg 195(A). Oxford:Worcester.

602/32

—[Anr issue]. *London:* [*E. Allde*] *for E. White,* 1602. Greg 195(A) variant; Arents 65. CSmH, CtY, DFo, IU, MH, NN-A; BL.

602/33

Dickenson, John. Speculum tragicum . . . Editio secunda. *Delft: J. C. Vennecool,* 1602. 136 p.; 8vo. BL (imp.).   602/34

—[Anr issue]. *Delft: J. C. Vennecool,* [*for*] *L. Elsevier* [*at Leyden*] 1602. Willems (Les Elzevier) 44; Rahir (Les Elzevier) 28. BL.

602/35

Du Bartas, Guillaume de Salluste, seigneur. Premiere sepmaine ou Creation du monde . . . La seconde sepmaine . . . En ceste derniere edition ont esté adjoustez . . . explications des principales difficultez du texte, par S[imon]. G[oulart]. *Rouen: R. Du Petit Val,* 1602. 4 v.; 12mo. In verse. 1st publ. with Goulart's annotations, Geneva, 1581, as *La sepmaine;* cf. 1601 edn. In verse. Holmes (DuBartas) I:74 no. 27; Jones (Goulart) 20q(n). BL, Nancy:BM.

602/36

—[Anr issue]. *Rouen:* [*R. Du Petit Val, for*] *T. Reinsart,* 1602. Holmes (DuBartas) I:74 no. 27n; Jones (Goulart) 20q. Cambridge:UL, Paris:Ste Geneviève.   602/37

——. La seconde sepmaine. *Rouen:* [*R. Du Petit Val, for*] *T. Reinsart,* 1602. 682 p.; 12mo. In verse. 1st publ., Paris, 1584, cf. 1601 edn of the author's *Oeuvres poétiques.* Included are commentaries by Simon Goulart

of 1589. Numerous refs to the New World appear, esp. in section 'Les colonies'. Holmes (DuBartas) I:87 no. 13a. TxU; BL, Auch:Archives.   602/38

Duchesne, Joseph. Opera medica. *Frankfurt a. M.: L. Albert,* 1602. 2 pts; 8vo. 1st publ. as here collected, Lyons, 1591. Included is Duchesne's *Sclopetarius* (1st publ., [Geneva?], 1576), with directions for therapeutic use of tobacco. WU; BN.   602/39

Du Périer, Anthoine, sieur de La Salargue. Les amours de Pistion. *Paris: T. de La Ruelle,* 1602. 381 p.; 16mo. 1st publ., Paris, 1601. Cf. Cioranescu (XVII) 27544. ICN; Paris: Arsenal.   602/40

Durante, Castore. Herbario novo . . . con figure che rappresentano le vive piante, che nascono in tutta Europa, & nell'Indie Orientali, & Occidentali. *Venice: The Sessas,* 1602. 492 p.; illus., port.; fol. 1st publ., Rome, 1585. Pritzel 2552n; Nissen (Bot.) 569n; Arents 66. DNLM, MH-A, NN-A, PPPH; BL, BN.   602/41

Estienne, Charles. L'agriculture et maison rustique. *Paris: J. & P. Mettayer,* 1602. 394 numb. lvs.; illus.; 4to. 1st publ. as here enl. by Jean Liébault, Paris, 1567; cf. 1601 edn. DNAL.   602/42

Fioravanti, Leonardo. De' capricci medicinali . . . libri quattro. *Venice: L. Spineda,* 1602. 267 numb. lvs; illus.; 8vo. 1st publ., Venice, 1561, under title *Capricci medicinali.* Included in discussion of syphilis are refs to its West Indian source & its treatment using sarsaparilla, etc. DNLM; BN.

602/43

——. Miroir universel des arts et des sciences en général . . . divisé en 3 livres . . . traduict d'italien . . . par Gabriel Chappuys . . . Seconde édition. *Paris: D. Douceur,* 1602. 525 p.; 8vo. 1st publ. in French, Paris, 1584. Transl. from the author's *Dello specchio di scientia universale,* 1st publ., Venice, 1564; cf. 1603 edn. BN.   602/44

Goulart, Simon, comp. Les memoires de la Ligue . . . Premier volume. [*Geneva?*] 1602. 340 (i.e., 540) p.; 8vo. 1st publ., [Geneva?], 1590, under title *Le premier recueil . . . ;* here a reissue, with cancel t.p., of that 1590 edn with above error in paging? Includes Walter Bigges's *Voyage de messire François Drake,* 1st publ. in French, Leyden, 1588, & the *Dis-*

cours au Roi Henri III, 1st publ., [Paris?], 1584. Jones (Goulart) 30(e). MiU-C; BL, BN.   602/45

——, comp. Le second recueil, contenant l'histoire des choses plus memorables advenues sous la Ligue. [*Geneva?*] 1602. 606 p.; 8vo. 1st publ., [Geneva?], 1590. Includes account of Sir Francis Drake's exploits in the West Indies. Jones (Goulart) 30(e) v. 2. BL, BN.   602/46

Heyns, Peeter. Abrégé du Théâtre. *Antwerp:* 1602. *See* Ortelius, Abraham, *below.*

——. Breve compendio dal Theatro Orteliano. *Antwerp:* 1502 [i.e., 1602]. *See* Ortelius, Abraham, *below.*

Honter, Johannes. Enchiridion cosmographiae; continens praecipuarum orbis regionum delineationes. *Zurich: J. Wolf,* 1602. [58] p.; illus., maps; 8vo. In verse. 1st publ. in this version, Kronstadt, 1542, under title *Rudimenta cosmographica.* Borsa 96; Szabo III:997; JCB (STL) 20. RPJCB.   602/47

Houtman, Cornelis de. Erste Schiffart. Inn die Orientalische Indien, so die holländischen Schiff . . . verricht . . . Tertia editio. *Nuremberg: L. Hulsius,* 1602. 76 p.; illus., maps; 4to. (Levinus Hulsius's *Sammlung von . . . Schiffahrten.* Pt 1). 1st publ. in this version, Nuremberg, 1598; transl. from the *Verhael vande reyse by de Hollandtsche schepen,* Middelburg, 1597; perhaps comp. by Barent Langenes. Includes mention of Brazil and the Strait of Magellan. Sabin 33653; Tiele-Muller p. 122; Church 258; JCB (3) I:450. CSmH, CtY, NN-RB, RPJCB; BL, BN.   602/48

Illescas, Gonzalo de. Segunda parte de la Historia pontifical y catholica. *Barcelona: S. de Cormellas, for J. de Bonilla,* 1602. fol. 1st publ. with material on missions to the Indians in America, Barcelona, 1596. BL.   602/49

Junius, Hadrianus. Nomenclator octilinguis, omnium rerum propria nomina continens. *Geneva: J. Stoer,* 1602. 634 p.; 8vo. 1st publ., Antwerp, 1577. Included is an entry for guaiacum as 'lignum Guaiacum'. Copies may occur without location in imprint. CU, DNLM, IU, NNNAM; BN.   602/50

—[Anr edn]. *Lyons: J. A. Gabiano & S. Girard,* 1602. 634 p.; 8vo. BN.   602/51

Keckermann, Bartholomaeus. Meditatio de insolito et stupendo illo terrae-motu quo, anno praeterito . . . tota pene Europa et Asiae . . . contremuit. *Heidelberg: G. Vögelin,* 1602. 28 lvs; 4to. Includes refs to American earthquakes. BN.   602/52

Langenes, Barent. Thrésor de chartes, contenant les tableaux de tous les pays du monde . . . Reveu et augmenté. *Leyden: C. Guyot, for C. Claeszoon, at Amsterdam,* 1602. 2 pts; illus., maps; obl. 8vo. 1st publ. in this version, The Hague [1600?]; transl. by Jean de La Haye from Langenes's *Caertthresoor,* 1st publ., Middelburg, [1598]. Sabin 95757n; cf. Atkinson (Fr. Ren.) 408; Koeman (Lan) 6; Tiele 225n; Phillips (Atlases) 428n. DLC, MH, MiU-C, NNH; Leningrad:Saltykov PL.   602/53

Marbecke, Roger. A defence of tobacco. *London: R. Field, for T. Man,* 1602. 55 lvs; 4to. STC 6468; Arents 62. CSmH, DFo, ICN, MH, MiU, NN-A; BL.   602/54

Marees, Pieter de. Beschryvinge ende historische verhael vant gout Koninckrijck van Gunea. *Amsterdam: C. Claeszoon,* 1602. 129 p.; obl. 4to. The 1st chapt. describes dangers in rounding tip of Brazil. Tiele-Muller 134; Tiele 715. NN-RB; BL.   602/55

Martí, Juan José, supposed author. Segunda parte de la vida del picaro Guzman de Alfarach, compuesta por Matheo Luxan de Sayavedra [pseud.]. *Valencia: P. P. Mey, for F. Miguel,* 1602. 443 p.; 8vo. Continues Mateo Alemán's 1st pt, 1st publ., Madrid, 1599, on which see the 1601 edn above. For Alemán's genuine continuation, see the year 1604. In bk i, chapt. 3, Hernando Cortés is mentioned; in bk ii, chapt. 3, Pizarro's conquest of Peru. Laurenti (Nov. pic. esp.) 787; Palau 6683.   602/56

—[Anr edn]. *Barcelona: J. Amello, for J. Simón,* 1602. 197 numb. lvs; 8vo. Medina (BHA) 471; Palau 6683n. Madrid:BN.   602/57

—[Anr issue of preceding]. *Barcelona: J. Amello, for A. Ribera,* 1602. Palau 6683n. DLC, NNH.   602/58

Martini, Lucas. Der christlichen Jungkfrawen Ehrenkräntzlein. Darinnen alle ihre Tugendten durch die gemeine Krätzblumlein abgebildet und erklärt werden. *Prague: W. Marino,* 1602. 12mo. 1st publ., Prague, 1585. Included is a description & illus. of the marigold. BL.   602/59

Medina, Pedro de. L'art de naviguer . . . traduit . . . par Nicolas de Nicolai. *Rouen: T. Reinsart,* 1602. 227 (i.e., 263) p.; illus., maps; 4to. 1st publ. as here transl., Lyons, 1553. Instructional manual for voyages to America. Palau 159675. DN, MH; Paris: Arsenal. 602/60

Mercuriale, Girolamo. Medicina practica . . . libri v. *Frankfurt a. M.: J. T. Schönwetter,* 1602. 594 p.; fol. 1st publ., Frankfurt a. M., 1601. Wellcome I:4251. DNLM, MBCo, PPL; BL, BN. 602/61

Meteren, Emanuel van. A true discourse historicall, of the succeeding governors in the Netherlands, and the civill warres . . . Translated and collected by T[homas]. C[hurchyard]. . . . and Ric. Ro[binson]. . . . out of the 15 bookes Historiae belgicae; and other collections added . . . perused and corrected. *London: [F. Kingston] for M. Lownes,* 1602. 154 p.; 4to. Transl. from van Meteren's *Historia belgica,* 1st publ. [Antwerp? 1598]. Includes scattered American refs. For variant issues see the STC. Palau 166946; STC 17846. CSmH, CtY, DLC, ICN, MH, MiU, NN-RB; BL, Madrid:BN. 602/62

Molina, Luis de. De justitia et jure tomi duo. *Mainz: B. Lipp, for A. Mylius,* 1602. 2 v.; fol. Vol. 1 1st publ., Cuenca (Spain), 1593, v. 2, in 1597; cf. the year 1601 & following item. Backer V:1176; Palau 174617:I–II. BL. 602/63

——. De justitia, tomus primus. *Venice: Society of Minims,* 1602. 1008 cols; fol. 1st publ., Cuenca (Spain), 1593. In tract. 2, disp. 33 discusses slavery, citing that in Peru. Backer V:1176; Palau 174616:In. DCU. 602/64

Montaigne, Michel Eyquem de. Les essais . . . Edition nouvelle prise sur l'exemplaire trouvé apres le deceds de l'autheur, reveu & augmente d'un tiers oultre les precedentes impressions. *Paris: A. L'Angelier,* 1602. 1165 p.; 8vo. 1st publ., Bordeaux, 1580. Includes scattered refs to the New World; chapt. on cannibals in bk 1 derives from description of Brazilian cannibals; in bk 3, 'Des coches' includes discussion of Spanish in Peru. Tchémerzine VIII:411; Rothschild 142. DLC, MH, NjP; BL, BN. 602/65

—[Anr edn]. *Leyden: J. Doreau,* 1602. 1031 p.; 8vo. Tchémerzine VIII:412. CSt, DLC, MH; BL, BN. 602/66

—[Anr issue]. *Cologny & Leyden: J. Doreau,* 1602. BN. 602/67

Montoya, Juan de. Relacion del descrubimiento [*sic*] del Nuovo Mexico: y de otras muchas provincias, y ciudades, halladas de nuevo; venida de las Indias, à España, y de alli mandada a Roma. *Rome: B. Bonfadino,* 1602. 59 p.; 8vo. Sabin 69210; Medina (BHA) 465; Palau 257304. NN-RB. 602/68

Mylius, Arnold, comp. De rebus hispanicis, lusitanicis, aragonicis, indicis, et aethiopicis, Damiani a Goes, Hieronymi Pauli, Hieronymi Blanchi, Jacobi Tevis opera. *Cologne: House of Birckmann,* 1602. 443 (i.e., 484) p.; port.; 8vo. Goes's contributions are derived from his *Hispania,* 1st publ., Louvain, 1542, with refs to Cortés, Pizarro, & Brazil, as well as from other works. Palau 69221; Maggs Cat. 502 (Americana VII):5001. DLC, MdBJ, MB; BL, BN. 602/69

Neck, Jacob Corneliszoon van. Ander Schiffart in die Orientalische Indien, so die holländischen Schiff . . . verricht. *Nuremberg: C. Lochner, for L. Hulsius,* 1602. 126 p.; illus., maps; 4to. (Levinus Hulsius's *Sammlung von . . . Schiffahrten.* Pt 2). Prob. transl. from Neck's *Het tweede boeck,* Amsterdam, 1601; cf. German edns of 1601. For variant issue cf. Church. Sabin 33654; Tiele-Muller, p. 144; Church 261 (& 262); JCB (3) I:451. CSmH, CtY, MnU-B, NN-RB, RPJCB, ViU; BL, BN. 602/70

Nederlandsche Oost-Indische Compagnie. Het out Oost-Indische octroy by de . . . Staten Generael . . . in . . . den jare 1602 verleent, ende wtgegeven. [*The Hague?* 1602?]. 20 p.; 4to. Includes refs to Strait of Magellan. Petit 763; cf. Tiele 490. Leyden:B. Thysiana. 602/71

Noort, Olivier van. Additamentum nonae partis Americae . . . e Germanico Latinitate donata. *Frankfurt a. M.: M. Becker,* 1602. 100 p.; illus., port.; maps; fol. (Theodor de Bry's *America.* Pt 9. Appendix. Latin). Transl. from *Additamentum oder Anhang dess neundten Theils Americae,* Frankfurt a. M., 1602; 1st publ., Rotterdam & Amsterdam, 1602, under title *Beschryvinghe van de voyagie om den geheelen werelt cloot.* Issued with José de Acosta's *Americae nona & postrema pars,* of this year. Cf. Sabin 8784; Church 168; JCB (3) I:407–8. CSmH, CtY, ICN, NN-RB, PHi, RPJCB; BL, BN. 602/72

——. Beschryvinghe van de voyagie om den geheelen werelt cloot. *Rotterdam: J. van Waesberghe; Amsterdam: C. Claeszoon,* 1602. 92 p.; illus., maps; obl. 4to. 1st publ., Rotterdam & Amsterdam, 1601. Sabin 55435; Tiele-Muller 16; Tiele 805; Nijhoff (Noort) e. NN-RB; BL, BN. 602/73

——. Description du penible voyage faict entour de l'univers ou globe terrestre . . . Le tout translaté du flamand. *Amsterdam: C. Claeszoon,* 1602. 61 p.; illus., maps; fol. Transl. from Noort's *Beschryvinghe van de voyagie,* 1st publ., Rotterdam & Amsterdam, 1601. Sabin 55436; Atkinson (Fr. Ren.) 428; Tiele 806; JCB (3) II:16. DLC, MnU-B, RPJCB; BL, BN. 602/74

——. Eigentliche und warhafftige Beschreibung der wunderbärlichen Schiffarth (der Hollander) rundtumbher dem gantzem Kreitz der Erden . . . aus der niederländischen Sprach . . . vertolmetschet durch Joannem Schäffer. *Amsterdam: C. Claeszoon,* 1602. 92 p.; illus., maps; obl. 4to. Transl. from Noort's *Beschryvinghe van de voyagie om den geheelen werelt cloot,* 1st publ., Rotterdam & Amsterdam, 1602. Sabin 55437; Palmer 367; Tiele-Muller 18; Tiele 807; Nijhoff (Noort) aa. NN-RB. 602/75

—[Anr edn]. Neue Schiffart; warhafftige und eygentliche Beschreibung der . . . Reyse . . . durch das gefehrliche Fretum Magellanum . . . aus niderländischer Verzeichnuss . . . beschrieben durch M. Gothardt Arthes. *Frankfurt a. M.: M. Becker,* 1602. 119 p.; illus., maps; 4to. Abridged version of the full Arthus translation publ. later this year. Sabin 55433; Palmer 367; Graesse VIII:131; Church 327; JCB (3) II:16. CSmH, CtY, InU, MiU-C, NN, NcU, RPJCB; BL, Munich:StB. 602/76

—[Anr edn]. Additamentum oder Anhang dess neundten Theils Americae . . . aus niderländischer Verzeichnuss . . . beschrieben durch M. Gothardt Artus. *Frankfurt a. M.: M. Becker* (text) *& W. Richter* (plates), 1602. 130 p.; illus., map; fol. (Theodor de Bry's *America.* Pt 9. Appendix. German). Cf.

Sabin 8784; Baginsky (German Americana) 117; Graesse VIII:131; Church 195; JCB (3) I:410–11. CSmH, CtY, ICN, NN, RPJCB; BL, BN. 602/77

Nueva instruction y ordenança para los que son . . . cofrades del Grilimon, o mal frances. *Cuenca: C. Bodan,* 1602. [7] p.; illus.; 4to. In verse. 'Romance de un cofrade viejo, que se yva a curar con el palo de las Indias [i.e., guaiacum]': p. [7]. BL. 602/78

Ojea, Hernando, O. P. La venida de Christo . . . Compuesta por fray Hernando Ojea gallego, de la Orden de Predicadores de la provincia de Mexico de la Nueva España. *Medina del Campo: C. Lasso Vaca,* 1602. 349 numb. lvs; fol. Included are refs to Mexico. Medina (BHA) 462; Pérez Pastor (Medina del Campo) 322; Palau 199768. DLC, InU-L; Seville:BU. 602/79

Orta, Garcia da. Histoire des drogues espiceries, et de certains medicamens simples, qui naissent és Indes . . . divisée en deux parties. La premiere composée de trois livres: les deux premiers de m. Garcie du Jardin, & le troisiesme de m. Christ. de la Coste. La seconde composée de deux livres de m. Nicolas Monard, traittant de ce qui nous est apporté des Indes Occidentales . . . Le tout fidelement translate . . . sur la traduction latine de Clusius: par Antoine Colin. *Lyons: J. Pillehotte,* 1602. 711 p.; illus.; 8vo. Transl. from L'Ecluse's Latin text, including also C. da Costa's *Aromatum et medicamentorum . . . liber,* & N. Monardes's *Simplicium medicamentorum . . . historia,* as publ., Antwerp, 1593. Sabin 115; Guerra (Monardes) 34; Atkinson (Fr. Ren.) 423; Arents (Add.) 68; JCB (3) II:17. CtY-M, DNLM, MH-A, NN-A, RPJCB, WU; London:Wellcome, BN. 602/80

Ortelius, Abraham. Abrégé du Théâtre, contenant la description des principales parties & régions du monde . . . Dernière édition, corrigée en plusieurs lieux, & augmentée de quelques cartes nouvelles. *Antwerp: J. B. Vrients,* 1602. 118 numb. lvs; maps; obl. 8vo. 1st publ. with French text, Antwerp, 1577; cf. 1601 edn, of which this is perhaps a reissue with altered imprint date. Koeman (Ort) 60; Phillips (Atlases) 416. DLC, MnU-B; BL, Brussels:BR. 602/81

——. Breve compendio dal Theatro Orteliano. Contenendo la delineatione de tutti li regioni principali . . . La postrema editione in molti luoghi emendata & con alcune tavole nuove augmentata. *Antwerp: J. B. Vrients,* 1502 [i.e., 1602]. 2 pts; maps; obl. 8vo. 1st publ. in Italian, Antwerp, 1593. Koeman (Ort) 61; JCB (3) II:18. MiU-C, RPJCB; Brussels:BR.   602/82

——. L'épitome du théâtre de l'univers . . . nouvellement recogneu, augmentè et restaurè . . . par Michel Coignet. *Antwerp: J. van Keerberghen,* 1602. 2 pts; maps; obl. 8vo. 1st publ. with text by Coignet, Antwerp, 1601. Sabin 57691; Atkinson (Fr. Ren.) 430; Koeman (Ort) 64; Phillips (Atlases) 417; JCB (3) II:18. DLC, InU-L, MiU-C, RPJCB; BN.   602/83

——. Theatro d'el orbe de la tierra. *Antwerp: Plantin Office, for J. B. Vrients,* 1602. 118 maps; fol. 1st publ. in Spanish, Antwerp, 1588. Medina (BHA) 464; Peeters-Fontainas (Impr. esp.) 991; Palau 205364. DLC; Antwerp:Plantin Mus., Brussels:BR.   602/84

Ovidius Naso, Publius. Amores. English. Ovids elegies: three bookes. By C. M[arlowe]. Epigrames by J. D[avies]. '*Middlebourgh*' [i.e., *London:* after 1602]. 8vo. Davies's epigrams (1st publ. separately 'Middlebrough', [1590?]) include: no. 22, 'In Ciprum', mentioning tobacco; no. 28, 'In Sistam', with passage 'He that dares take Tobacco on the Stage, Dares man a whore at Noone-day through the street'; no. 36, 'Of Tobacco'. STC 18931. Oxford:Bodl.   602/85

—[Anr edn]. All Ovids elegies. '*Middleborough*' [i.e., *London:* after 1602]. 8vo. STC 18931a. CSmH; London:V. & A, Oxford:Bodl.   602/86

Panciroli, Guido. Nova reperta, sive Rerum memorabilium recens inventarum . . . Liber secundus . . . ex italico . . . redditus, & commentariis illustratus ab Henrico Salmuth. *Amberg: M. Forster,* 1602. 719 p.; 8vo. Continues, 1st vol., publ., Amberg, 1599, with title *Rerum memorabilium . . . libri duo;* transl. from ms. of author's *Raccolta breve d'alcune cose più segnalate,* itself not publ. till 1612, at Venice. The 1st 'titulus' (p. 1–141) discusses the New World. Sabin 58413.

CSmH, DFo, ICU, InU-L, MH, NNC, RPJCB;BN.   602/87

Paschetti, Bartolomeo. Del Conservare la sanità, et del vivere de' Genovesi . . . libri tre. *Genoa: G. Pavoni,* 1602. 439 p.; 4to. 'Il gallo d'India presta ottimo, & abbondante nutrimento: ristora i corpi deboli: aumenta lo sperma: incita l'huomo a Venere'—p. 377. Wellcome I:4839. London:Wellcome.   602/88

Penot, Bernard Georges. Tractatus varii de vera praeparatione et usu medicamentorum chymicorum . . . Editio tertia . . . emendatior. *Oberursel: C. Sutor, for J. Rose,* 1602. 256 p.; 12mo. 1st publ., Frankfurt a. M., 1594. Includes description of a salt derived from guaiacum. Wellcome I:4891. DNLM, ICU; BL, BN.   602/89

Platter, Felix. Praxeos, seu De cognoscendis praedicendis, praecavendis, curandisque affectibus homini incommodantibus tractatus. *Basel: C. Waldkirch,* 1602–3. 2 v.; 8vo. Included are minor refs to guaiacum & sarsaparilla. Wellcome I:5086. DNLM; Wellcome (v. 1 only).   602/90

Potgieter, Barent Janszoon. Relatio historica, sive vera, et genuina consignatio ac descriptio illius navigationis, quam v. naves . . . fretum Magellanicum in Moluccanas insulas transmittendi instituto susceperunt. *Frankfurt a. M.: M. Becker,* 1602. 56 p.; illus., map; fol. (Theodor de Bry's *America.* Pt 9b. Latin). Transl. from the author's *Historische Relation . . . alles dess jenigen, so den 5 Schiffen, welche . . . durch das Fretum Magelanum . . . kommen,* Frankfurt a. M., 1601; 1st publ., Amsterdam, 1600, under title *Wijdtloopigh verhael van tgene de viif schepen.* Issued with José de Acosta's *Americae nona & postrema pars* of this year. Cf. Sabin 8784; Church 168; JCB (3) I:406–8. CSmH, CtY, ICN, NN-RB, PHi, RPJCB; BL, BN.   602/91

Richeome, Louis. Trois discours pour la religion catholique. *Rouen: J. Osmont,* 1602. 626 p.; 12mo. 1st publ., Bordeaux, 1597; cf. 1601 edn. Cf. Backer VI:1817; cf. Cioranescu (XVII) 59455. BL, BN.   602/92

—[Anr edn]. *Paris: J. Rèze,* 1602. 422 p.; 8vo. BL.   602/93

—[Anr issue]. *Paris: M. Verard,* 1602. Backer VI:1817.   602/94

Rivadeneira, Pedro de, S.J. Vita p. Ignatii

Loiolae . . . nunc denuo recognita & locupletata. *Cologne: House of Birckmann, for A. Mylius,* 1602. 689 p.; 8vo. 1st publ., Naples, 1572. Includes, as bk 2 chapt. 19, 'De fidei Christiane apud Indios propagatione', describing Jesuits in Brazil. Sabin 70784; Palau 266209. CtY, MB, WaSpG; BL, BN.
602/95

Romancero general. Romancero general, en que se contienen todos los romances . . . en las nueve partes de romanceros. *Medina del Campo: J. Godínez de Millis, for P. Ossete & A. Coello, at Valladolid,* 1602. 362 numb. lvs; 4to. 1st publ. under this title, Madrid, 1600. The 2 final 'romances' in the 6th pt refer to Chile; other scattered refs to the Indies occur. Pérez Pastor (Medina del Campo) 253; Palau 276979. MB, NNH, PU; BL.
602/96

Rosaccio, Giuseppe. Le sei eta del mondo. *Venice:* 1602. 48 p.; 16mo. 1st publ., Brescia, 1593. In chronology, Columbus is mentioned. Sabin 73197n. InU-L, NN-RB.
602/97

Rowlands, Samuel. Tis merrie when gossips meete. *London: W. W[hite].; sold by G. Loftus,* 1602. 4to. In verse. Includes mention of tobacco & turkey. STC 21409. CSmH (imp.)
602/98

Ryff, Walter Hermann. Newe aussgerüste deütsche Apoteck. *Strassburg: L. Zetzner,* 1602. 3 pts; illus.; fol. 1st publ., Strassburg, 1573, under title *Reformierte deutsche Apoteck.* Described are guaiacum, &, with illus., tobacco. Wellcome I:5681. DNLM, WU; London:Wellcome, BN.
602/99

Satyre Ménippée. English. Englands bright honour. *London: J. Deane,* 1602. 216 p.; 4to. A reissue, with cancel t.p., of the London, 1595, edn, transl. by T. W[ilcox?] from *Le Satyre Ménippée* as publ., [Paris? 1594], with 'Discours' in which French Leaguers are symbolized by the West Indian prickly pear (*Opuntia*). STC 15490. IU; BL.   602/100

Schmidel, Ulrich. Vierte Schiffart; warhafftige Historien einer wunderbaren Schiffart . . . von Anno 1534, biss Anno 1554, in Americam oder Neuwewelt, bey Brasilia und Rio della Plata gethan . . . editio secunda. *Nuremberg: L. Hulsius,* 1602. 103 p.; illus., maps, port.; 4to. (Levinus Hulsius's *Sammlung von . . . Schiffahrten.* Pt 4). 1st

publ. in this version, Nuremberg, 1599; 1st publ., Frankfurt a. M., 1567. Sabin 77681 (& 33656); Palmer 339; Church 272; JCB (3) I:454. CSmH, CtY, NN-RB, RPJCB; BL, BN.
602/101

Sepúlveda, Juan Ginés de. Opera, quae reperiri potuerunt omnia. *Cologne: House of Birckman, for A. Mylius,* 1602. 634 p.; 4to. Includes author's *Apologia pro libro de justis belli causis,* 1st publ., Rome, 1550, & including also (as then) the 'Decretum et indultum Alexandri sexti super expeditione in barbaros Novi Orbis quos Indos vocant'. Justifies, in controversy with Las Casas, waging war on Indians. Sabin 79179; Palau 309311. CU, MiU-C, PU, RPJCB; BL, BN.
602/102

Shakespeare, William. A most pleasaunt and excellent comedie, of syr John Falstaffe and the merrie wives of Windsor. *London: T. C[reede]., for A. Johnson,* 1602. 4to. In act 1, scene 3, Guiana & the West Indies are mentioned, as in act 5, scene 5, are potatoes. STC 22299; Greg 187(a). CSmH, DFo; BL.
602/103

Soto, Domingo de. De justitia et jure libri decem. *Venice: Heirs of G. A. Bertano,* 1602. 1006 p.; 4to. 1st publ., Salamanca, 1553. Refs to New World appear in bk 4, quaest. 4, art. 2, & in bk 5, quaest. 3, art. 5. Palau 320164.
602/104

Syria, Pedro de. Arte de la verdadera navegacion. En que se trata de la machina del mundo. *Valencia: J. C. Garriz, for F. Miguel,* 1602. 152 p.; illus.; 4to. Includes specific refs to the Americas. Sabin 94133; Medina (BHA) 466; Bibl. mar. esp. 223; JCB (3) II:19. CSmH, DSI, ICN, InU-L, MH, MnU-B, NN-RB, RPJCB; BL, BN.   602/105

Tapp, John. The seamans kalendar, or An ephemerides of the sun, moon and certaine stars. *London: E. Allde, for J. Tapp,* 1602. [100] p.; illus.; 4to. In tables of latitude & longitude, American locations are included, e.g., for 'Cuba', 'Brasill regnum', & 'Panama'. STC 23679. CtY; BL.   602/106

Teixeira, José. The true historie of . . . the late and lamentable adventures of Don Sebastian. *London: S. Stafford & [i.e., for] J. Shaw,* 1602. 28 p.; 4to. Includes ref. to strategic importance of Azores for American ships. STC 23865. BL.   602/107

Torres, Juan de, S.J. Philosophia moral de principes. *Burgos: J. B. Varesio, for D. Pérez,* 1602. 995 p.; fol. 1st publ., Burgos, 1596. Includes mention of Mexican Indians encountered by Cortés as possessing an idol in shape of crucifix. Backer VIII:126; Palau 336555. BN. 602/108

—[Anr edn]. *Lisbon: P. Craesbeeck,* 1602. 786 p.; fol. Palau 336556. MH-L; NcD; BL. 602/109

Vaughan, William. Naturall and artificial directions for health. *London: R. Bradock,* 1602. 8vo. 1st publ., London, 1600. Includes directions for therapeutic use of tobacco. STC 24613. BL. 602/110

—[Anr issue]. *London: R. Bradock; sold by J. Newbery,* 1602. STC 24613.5 Oxford:Bodl. (sheet A only). 602/111

Veer, Gerrit de. Dritte Theil, und warhafftige Relation der dreyen newen unerhörten, seltzamen Schiffart, so die holländischen und seeländischen Schiff gegen Mitternacht, drey jar nacheinander . . . verricht . . . aus der niderländischen Sprach . . . gebracht durch Levinum Hulsium. *Nuremberg: L. Hulsius,* 1602. 147 p.; illus., maps; 4to. (Levinus Hulsius's *Sammlung von . . . Schiffahrten.* Pt 3). 1st publ., Nuremberg, 1598; here a reissue of that edn. Transl. from *Waerachtighe beschryvinghe van drie seylagien.* 1st publ., Amsterdam, 1598. Preface by Hulsius includes refs to American exploration. Cf. Sabin 33655; Baginsky (German Americana) 118; Church 267. CSmH, NN-RB; BL, BN. 602/112

—[Anr edn]. Dritte Theil, warhafftige Relation der dreyen newen unerhörten seltzamen Schiffart . . . secunda editio. *Nuremberg: L. Hulsius,* 1602. 121 p.; illus., maps; 4to. Sabin 33655; Baginsky (German Americana) 119; Church 268; JCB (3) I:453. CSmH, MH, NN, RPJCB; BL, BN. 602/113

Vega Carpio, Lope Félix de. Arcadia, prosas y versos. *Barcelona: S. de Cormellas, for G. Aleu,* 1602. 312 numb. lvs; 8vo. 1st publ., Madrid, 1598. In bk iii a statue (with its inscription) of Hernando Cortés is described. Palau 356293. MnU, NNH; BL, Madrid:BN. 602/114

—[Anr edn]. *Madrid: P. Madrigal,* 1602. 312 numb. lvs; 8vo. NNH. 602/115

—[Anr edn?]. *Madrid: [L. Sánchez]; sold by J. de Montoya,* 1602. 312 numb. lvs; 8vo. NNH. 602/116

—[Anr edn]. *Valencia: J. C. Gárriz,* 1602. 252 numb. lvs; 8vo. Palau 356292. DFo, NNH. 602/117

—[Anr issue of preceding]. *Valencia: J. C. Gárriz, for F. Miguel, & R. Sonzonio,* 1602. Palau 356294. NNH; Madrid:BN. 602/118

——. La hermosura de Angelica, con otras diversas rimas. *Madrid: P. Madrigal,* 1602. 488 numb. lvs; port.; 8vo. Includes the author's poem, *La Dragontea,* 1st publ., Valencia, 1598, describing Sir Francis Drake's exploits in Spanish America. Sabin 98769; Medina (BHA) 467; Pérez Pastor (Madrid) 826; Palau 356330. CU, IU, MB, NNH, PU; BL, Madrid:BN. 602/119

Villifranchi, Giovanni. Copia del primo e del secondo canto del Colombo, poema eroico. *Florence: C. Giunta, for the Sermatellis,* 1602. 2 pts; 4to. Sabin 99744; Palau 369536; JCB AR66:20–21. MH, NN-RB, RPJCB. 602/120

Wecker, Johann Jakob. Practica medicinae generalis. *Treviso: F. Zanetti,* 1602. 542 p.; 16mo. 1st publ., Basel, 1585. Includes ref. to mechoacan. DNLM, WU-M. 602/121

Work for chimney-sweepers: or A warning for tobacconists. Describing the pernicious use of tobacco. *London: T. East, for T. Bushell,* 1602. [48] p.; 4to. Signed 'Philaretes'; authorship has been attributed to John Hind. Sabin 105468; STC 12571; Arents 61. CSmH, DFo, MH, NN-A; BL. 602/122

1603

Alemán, Mateo. Primera parte de la vida del picaro Guzman de Alfarache. *Saragossa: A. Tavanno,* 1603. 207 numb. lvs; 8vo. 1st publ., Madrid, 1599; cf. 1601 edn. Laurenti (Nov. pic. esp.) 551; Jiménez Catalan (Saragossa) 21; Palau 6691. NN-RB, NNH. 603/1

1602–1603—[Anr edn]. *Tarragona: F. Roberto, for H. Martín,* 1603. 207 numb. lvs; 8vo. Medina (BHA) 471; Laurenti (Nov. pic. esp.) 550; Palau 6690. DLC, NN-RB, PPL; Madrid:BN.

—[Anr edn]. De la vida del picaro Guzman de Alfarache. Primera parte. *Milan: G. Bordone & P. M. Locarno,* 1603. 411 p.; 8vo. Medina (BHA) 470; Laurenti (Nov. pic. esp.) 552; Palau 6689. IEN, MB, NNH; BL, Madrid:BN. 603/3

Arnauld, Antoine (1560–1619). Bedencken an die königliche Mayestat in Franckreich . . . auss der frantz. . . . Sprach versetzt. [*Heidelberg?*] 1603. 156 p.; 8vo. 1st publ. in German, Heidelberg, 1602. Dt. Ges. Kat. 6.8998. MH; Berlin:StB, Munich:StB. 603/4

——. Le franc et veritable discours au roy. [*Paris?*] 1603. 144 p.; 12mo. 1st publ., [Paris?] 1602. ICN, ICU; BN. 603/5

——. Ingenua & vera oratio ad regem christianissimum perscripta . . . Editio secunda. *Hanau:* 1603. 328 p.; 8vo. 1st publ. in Latin, Lyons, 1602; transl. from Arnauld's *Le franc et veritable discours* above. Dt. Ges. Kat. 6.9000. BN, Halle:UB. 603/6

—[Anr edn?]. Editio secunda. *Leyden:* 1603. 328 p.; 8vo. Dt. Ges. Kat. 6.9001. ICU, IaU, BN, Berlin:StB, Munich:StB. 603/7

Ayanz, Gerónimo de. Respuesta . . . a lo que el Reyno le preguntó acerca de las minas dest reyno, y del metal negrillo de Potosí. *Valladolid:* 1603. [8] p.; fol. Sabin 70095; Medina (BHA) 469; Palau 20779. CtY. 603/8

Baño, Pedro de. Yo Pedro de Baño escrivano publico . . . de Granada . . . Doy fé y verdadero testimonio. [*Granada?* 1603?]. [8] p.; fol. Dated at end, Granada, 1603. Deposition against one Bartolomé López Mellada, citing acts of piracy committed at Santo Domingo. RPJCB. 603/9

Bertonio, Ludovico. Arte breve dela lengua aymara. *Rome: A. Zannetti,* 1603. Sabin 5017; Medina (BHA) 472; Viñaza 106; Backer I:1392; Palau 28507. ICN; BL. 603/10

——. Arte y grammatica muy copiosa de la lengua aymara. *Rome: A. Zannetti,* 1603. 348 p.; 8vo. Cf. Sabin 5018; Medina (BHA) 473; Viñaza 105; Backer I:1392; Palau 28508; JCB (3) II:19. DLC, RPJCB; BL. 603/11

Boaistuau, Pierre. Historias prodigiosas y maravillosas . . . Escritas en lengua francesca por Pedro Bouistau, Claudio Tesserant, y Francisco Belleforest. Traducidas . . . por Andrea Pescioni. *Madrid: L. Sánchez, for B. López,* 1603. 402 numb. lvs; 8vo. 1st publ. in Spanish, Medina del Campo, 1586; 1st publ. in French, Paris, 1571, with Belleforest's brief allusion to West Indies. Pérez Pastor (Madrid) 832; Palau 34215. BL, BN. 603/12

Botero, Giovanni. Descripcion de todas las provincias y reynos del mundo, sacada de las Relaciones toscanas de Juan Botero . . . por f. Jayme Rebullosa. *Barcelona: G. Graells & G. Dotil,* 1603. 360 numb. lvs; 8vo. Extracted & transl. from Botero's *Relationi universali,* 1st publ., Rome, 1591–96. Cf. Sabin 68338 (& 6810); Medina (BHA) 485; Streit I:257; Palau 33705. BN. 603/13

——. An historicall description of the most famous kingdomes and common-weales in the worlde. *London: J. Jaggard,* 1603. 268 p.; 4to. Transl. by Robert Johnson from Botero's *Delle relationi universali,* 1st publ, Rome, 1591–92; cf. 1601 edns with alternate titles. Sabin 6811 (& 36282); STC 3400. CSmH, NN-RB, OCT; BL. 603/14

——. Mundus imperiorum, sive De mundis imperiis libri quatuor . . . a Guidone de Bruecqs, ex . . . italicis relationibus latine factum. *Oberursel: C. Sutor,* 1603. 2 pts; maps; 4to. 1st publ. as here extracted & transl. from Botero's *Delle relationi universali,* Cologne, 1598. BL, BN. 603/15

——. Razon d'estado . . . Traduzido de italiano . . . por Antonio de Herrera. *Burgos: S. de Cañas, for P. de Ossete; & A. Cuello, at Valladolid,* 1603. 175 numb. lvs; 8vo. 1st publ. in Spanish, Barcelona, 1598; transl. from Botero's *Della ragion di stato,* 1st publ., Venice, 1589. Mentioned are Jesuits in New World & Spanish colonization there. Palau 33702n. DLC, MB, NNH; BN. 603/16

——. Relaciones universales del mundo . . . Primera y segunda parte, traduzidas . . . por . . . Diego de Aguilar. *Valladolid: Heirs of D. Fernández de Córdova, for sale by M. de Córdova,* 1603. 2 pts; fol. 1st publ. in Italian, Rome, 1591–92; here a reissue with cancel t.p. of printer's 1599 edn. Sabin 6809; Medina (BHA) 468; Borba de Moraes I:100–101; Streit I:256; Palau 33704; JCB (3) II:20. ICN, MH, MnU-B, RPJCB; BL, Salamanca:BU. 603/17

Breton, Nicholas. A poste with a packet of madde letters. Newly inlarged. *London: [T. Creede?] for J. Smethwicke,* 1603. 4to. 1st publ., London, 1602. STC 3685. Edinburgh:NL (imp.).   603/18

Brito, Bernardo de. Elogios dos reis de Portugal com os mais verdadeiros retratos que se puderao achar. *Lisbon: P. Craesbeeck,* 1603. 112 p.; port.; 4to. Includes mention of the discovery of Brazil, and an account of the expulsion of the Dutch from Brazil. MH; BL, BN.   603/19

Camerarius, Philipp. Les meditations historiques . . . reduits en dix livres & nouvellement tournez de latin . . . par S[imon]. G[oulart]. *Lyons: A. de Harsy,* 1603. 2 v.; 4to. Transl. from the author's *Operae horarum subcisivarum,* pt 1 (1st publ., Altdorf, 1591) & 2 (1st publ., Frankfurt a. M., 1601); cf. 1602 Latin text above. Jones (Goulart) 57a. Paris: Bibl. du Protestantisme Français, Geneva:BP.   603/20

Capivaccio, Girolamo. Opera omnia. *Frankfurt a. M.: Palthenius Office, for J. Rosa,* 1603. 1051 p.; port.; fol. Includes as bk 5, 'De artritide, & Lues venerea', the author's *De lue venerea acroaseis,* 1st publ., Speyer, 1590. Discusses use of guaiacum & sarsaparilla for treatment of syphilis. DNLM, NIC, NNNAM; London:Wellcome, BN.   603/21

Caro, Annibale. De le lettere familiari . . . di nuovo . . . ristampata e da notabilissimi errori emendate. *Venice: P. Ugolino,* 1603. 2 pts; 4to. 1st publ., Venice, 1572. A letter of 10 May 1539 refers to 'legno d'India', i.e., guaiacum. Michel (Répertoire) II:49. BL, BN.   603/22

Champlain, Samuel de. Des sauvages, ou, Voyage . . . fait en la France nouvelle, l'an mil six cens trois. *Paris: C. de Monstr'oeil* [1603?]. 36 numb. lvs; 8vo. Sabin 11834; Harrisse (NF) 10; Atkinson (Fr. Ren.) 434; Bell (Jes. rel.) 225–26; Church 327A; JCB (3) II:20. CSmH, CtY, MnU-B, RPJCB; BL, BN.   603/23

Coignet, Michiel. Abraham Ortelius his Epitome. *[Antwerp:]* 1603. *See* Ortelius, Abraham, *below.*

Cortés, Jerónimo. Libro de phisonomia natural. *Alcalá de Henares: Heirs of J. Gracián,* 1603. 120 numb. lvs; 8vo. 1st publ.,

Valencia, 1597; cf. 1601 edn. Palau 63301.   603/24

Crosse, Henry. Vertues commonwealth. *London: J. Newbery,* 1603. 79 lvs; 4to. Description of gentleman includes need to 'take tabacco with a whiffe'. Reprinted, London, 1605, under title *The school of pollicie.* STC 6070; Arents (Add.) 121. CSmH, DFo, NN-A; BL, Dublin:Trinity.   603/25

Cueva, Juan de la. Conquista de la Betica, poema heroico. *Seville: F. Pérez,* 1603. 458 numb. lvs; port.; 8vo. Included are refs to Mexico. Medina (BHA) 476; Escudero (Seville) 872; Palau 66155. MH, NNH; BL.   603/26

Daniel, Samuel. A panegyricke congratulatorie delivered to the Kings . . . Majestie . . . also certaine Epistles. *London: V. S[immes]., for E. Blount,* 1603. [45] p.; fol. In stanza 35 of the 'Panegyricke' Daniel describes means by which England 'shall gaine much more/ Then by Peru, or all discoveries'; in the 'Epistles', on lf C2v, is a ref. to King Ferdinand's banning of migration by Spanish lawyers to 'th'Indian Colonies'. STC 6258. CSmH; BL.   603/27

—[Anr issue]. *London: V. S[immes]., for E. Blount,* 1603. [73] p.; fol. A reissue of the above with addition on t.p. of phrase 'With a Defence of ryme' & of the text of the latter, p. [47–73]. STC 6259; Grolier Club (Langland to Wither) 57. CSmH, CtY, DFo, MWiW-C; BL.   603/28

—[Anr edn]. *London: V. S[immes]., for E. Blount,* 1603. [128] p.; 8vo. STC 6260; Grolier Club (Langland to Wither) 58; Pforzheimer 244. CSmH, DLC, IU, MH; BL.   603/29

Dekker, Thomas. The pleasant comodie of Patient Grissill. *London: [E. Allde] for H. Rocket,* 1603. [84] p.; 4to. Includes refs to tobacco & to turkey. STC 6518; Greg 198. CSmH, DFo; BL.   603/30

——. The wonderfull yeare. wherein is shewed the picture of London, lying sicke of the plague. *London: T. Creede,* 1603. [47] p.; 4to. Included are refs to tobacco & West Indies. At head of title: 1603. STC 6535. Oxford:Bodl.   603/31

Del Rio, Martin Anton, S.J. Disquisitionum magicarum libri sex . . . Nunc secundis curis auctior. *Mainz: J. Albin,* 1603. 3 v.; fol.

1st publ., Louvain, 1599–1600. In v. 2 Cortés's conquest of Mexico is mentioned, citing López de Gómara, as are the volcanoes of Peru; in v. 3 supernatural remedies, based on Cieza de León's *Cronica del Peru*, are described at length. Backer II:1898. CU-S, DCU, MH, MiU, NNUT; BL. 603/32

Delle rime piacevoli del Berni, Casa, Mauro, Varchi, Dolce, et d'altri autori. *Vicenza: [P. Bertelli?] for B. Barezzi, at Venice,* 1603. 3 v.; 12mo. 1st publ., as here constituted, Venice, 1552–55, under title *Opere burlesche.* Included in bk 1 is Agnolo Firenzuola's 'In lode del Legno santo [i.e., guaiacum]', 1st publ., Florence, 1549, in his *Rime*. MH, NcD; BL (Berni, F.). 603/33

Dickenson, John. Speculum tragicum . . . Tertio editum . . . auctore J. D. [*Delft: J. C. Vennecool, for] L. Elsevier, at Leyden,* 1603. 148 p.; 8vo. 1st publ., Delft, 1601. Willems (Les Elzevier) 45; Rahir (Les Elzevier) 29. ICN, DFC; BL, BN. 603/34

Du Bartas, Guillaume de Salluste, seigneur. Les oeuvres poetiques . . . Derniere edition. *Lyons: P. Rigaud,* 1603. 394 p.; 8vo. Includes the author's *La sepmaine*, 1st publ., Paris, 1578, & *La seconde sepmaine*, 1st publ., Paris, 1584, both of which contain numerous refs to New World. Cf. 1601 edn. Holmes (DuBartas) I:75 no. 29. NIC; Grenoble:BM. 603/35

——. Premiere sepmaine ou Creation du monde . . . La seconde sepmaine . . . En ceste derniere edition ont esté adjoustez . . . explications des principales difficultez du texte, par S[imon]. G[oulart]. *Paris: A. Périer,* 1603. 781 p.; illus.; 8vo. In verse. 1st publ. with Goulart's annotations, Geneva, 1581, as *La sepmaine;* cf. 1601 edn, & that of 1602 with title as above. In verse. Holmes (DuBartas) I:74 no. 28. NcU; Paris:Arsenal. 603/36

——[Anr issue]. *Paris: J. Du Carroy,* 1603. Holmes (DuBartas) I:74 no. 28n; Jones (Goulart) 20(r). Rennes:BM. 603/37

——[Anr issue]. *Paris: J. Mettayer,* 1603. MdBP. 603/38

——[Anr edn]. *Paris: J. Houzé,* 1603. 947 p.; 8vo. DFo. 603/39

——[Anr edn?). *Paris: T. de La Ruelle,* 1603. ICU, MdBP, NcU. 603/40

——. The second day of the first weeke. Done out of French into English heroicall verse by Thomas Winter. *London: [R. Field, for] J. Shaw,* 1603. 4to. Extracted & transl. from author's *La sepmaine*, 1st publ., Paris, 1578. Includes ref. to manatee. STC 21659. CSmH, PU. 603/41

——. La seconde sepmaine. *Paris: P. Bertault,* 1603. 682 p.; 12mo. In verse. 1st publ., with commentary by Simon Goulart, Paris, 1584; cf. 1602 edn. Holmes (DuBartas) I:87 no. 13a(n). Lille:BU. 603/42

——[Anr issue]. *Paris: J. Du Carroy,* 1603. Holmes (DuBartas) I:87 no. 13a(n). NcD; Tours:BM. 603/43

——[Anr issue]. *Paris: J. Gesselin,* 1603. Holmes (DuBartas) I:87 no. 13a(n). DLC, MdBP. 603/44

——[Anr issue]. *Paris: A. Périer,* 1603. Holmes (DuBartas) I:87 no. 13a(n). Paris:Arsenal. 603/45

Duchesne, Joseph. Liber de priscorum philosophorum verae medicinae materia. *Saint Gervais: Heirs of E. Vignon,* 1603. 432 p.; 8vo. Includes discussion of guaiacum & the sunflower. Wellcome I:1882. DNLM, PPC; BL, BN. 603/46

Du Fail, Noël, seigneur de La Herissaye. Les contes et discours d'Eutrapel. *Rennes: N. Glamet,* 1603. 213 numb. lvs; 8vo. 1st publ., Rennes, 1585. In chapt. 'Musique d'Eurtapel' is a description of discovery of Canada by Bretons, citing Jacques Cartier; that 'De la verole' discusses its origins, mentioning guaiacum. CtY, MH; BN. 603/47

Du Hamel, Jacques. Acoubar, tragédie tiree des Amours de Pistion & Fortunie en leur voyage de Canada. *Rouen: R. Du Petit Val,* 1603. 71 p.; 12mo. Based on Anthoine Du Périer's *Les amours de Pistion*, 1st publ., Paris, 1601. Sabin 29939; Cioranescu (XVII) 2699. BL. 603/48

Durante, Castore. Il tesoro della sanità. *Venice: D. Farri,* 1603. 324 p.; illus.; fol. 1st publ., [Rome?], 1586; cf. 1601 edn. DNLM. 603/49

Estienne, Charles. Dictionarium historicum, geographicum, poeticum. [*Geneva:] J. Stoer,* 1603. 452 numb. lvs; 4to. 1st publ., Lyons, 1595, in this enl. edn; cf. 1601 edn. ICN, LNHT, PMA. 603/50

Figueiredo, Manuel de. Chronographia, reportorio dos tempos. *Lisbon: J. Rodriguez, for P. Ramiers,* 1603. 284 numb. lvs; illus., map; 4to. In pt 3, chapt. xi briefly describes America. Maggs Cat. 479 (Americana V):4090. MH. 603/51

Fioravanti, Leonardo. Della fisica . . . divisa in libri quattro . . . di nuovo posta in luce. *Venice: L. Spineda,* 1603. 390 p.; 8vo. 1st publ., Venice, 1582. Includes material on therapeutic uses of tobacco, Mexican opobalsam, guaiacum, sarsaparilla, etc. Michel (Répertoire) III:47. PPL; Paris:Faculté de médecine. 603/52

——. Dello specchio di scientia universale . . . libri tre. *Venice: L. Spineda,* 1603. 347 numb. lvs; 8vo. 1st publ., Venice, 1564. Section on agriculture mentions products of the Indies, e.g. guaiacum ('legno santo'), brazilwood, sarsaparilla; sect. on trade includes similar list of commodities from Indies. Section on navigation mentions Spain's crossing the Indies. Michel (Répertoire) III:48. DNLM, WU; Paris: Arsenal. 603/53

——. Il tesoro della vita humana . . . di nuovo posto in luce. *Venice: L. Spineda,* 1603. 327 numb. lvs; 8vo. 1st publ., Venice, 1570. Treatments for syphilis call for use of guaiacum. Michel (Répertoire) III:48. Paris:Arsenal. 603/54

Gabelkover, Oswald. Artzneybuch. *Tübingen: G. Gruppenbach,* 1603. 3 pts; 4to. 1st publ., Tübingen, 1589, under title *Nützlich Artzneybuch.* Describes embrocation employing tobacco. London:Wellcome. 603/55

Gallucci, Giovanni Paolo. Coelestium corporum et rerum . . . accurata explicatio. *Venice: R. Meietti,* 1603. 478 p.; illus., map; 4to. 1st publ., Venice, 1588, under title *Theatri mundi et temporis;* here a reissue of that edn with cancel t.p. BL, BN. 603/56

Gonzaga, Francisco, Bp. De origine seraphicae religionis franciscanae. *Venice: D. Imberti,* 1603. 1596 p.; 4to. 1st publ., Rome, 1583. Contains copious accounts of Franciscans in New World. Streit I:258. MdSsW; Milan:BN. 603/57

Goulart, Simon. Histoires admirables et memorables de nostre temps. Recueillies de plusieurs autheurs . . . Corrigé, & aug-

menté . . . en ceste seconde edition. *Paris: J. Houzé,* 1603. 206+ numb. lvs; 12mo. 1st publ., Paris, 1600–1601. DFo, MH (imp.). 603/58

Le grand dictionaire françois-latin, augmente en ceste edition, outre infinies dictions françoises . . . Recueilli des observations de plusieurs hommes doctes, entre autres de m. Nicod [i.e., Nicot]. [*Geneva:*] *J. Stoer,* 1603. 100026 (i.e., 1126) p.; 4to. 1st publ., Paris, 1573, under title *Dictionaire françois-latin.* Includes, as 'Nicotiane', description of tobacco. CU. 603/59

Great Britain. Sovereigns, etc., 1603–1625 (James I). A proclamation for the due and speedy execution of the statute against rogues. *London: R. Barker,* 1603. 2 lvs; fol. Among lands to which rogues are to be conveyed are the East & West Indies & Newfoundland. Crawford (Roy. procl.) 971; Brigham (Roy. procl.) 1–3; STC 8333. DFo; BL. 603/60

Heresbach, Conrad. Rei rusticae libri quatuor. [*Heidelberg:*] *Commelin Office,* 1603. 889 p.; 8vo. 1st publ., Cologne, 1570. In bk iv the turkey is discussed. Here a reissue with cancel t.p. of 1594, Speyer, edn? CU. 603/61

Hulsius, Levinus, ed. Sechste Theil, Kurtze, warhafftige Relation und Beschreibung der wunderbarsten vier Schiffarten . . . nemlich: Ferdinandi Magellani . . . mit Sebastiano de Cano, Francisci Draconis . . . Thomae Candisch . . . Olivarij von Noort . . . umb den gantzen Erdtkreiss . . . aus unterschiedenen Authoribus und Sprachen zusamen getragen. *Nuremberg: C. Lochner, for L. Hulsius,* 1603. 53 p.; illus., maps; 4to. (Levinus Hulsius's *Sammlung von . . . Schiffahrten.* Pt 6). Sabin 33660; Baginsky (German Americana) 121; Church 282; JCB (3) I:457. CSmH, CtY, NN-RB, RPJCB; BL, BN. 603/62

Laudonnière, René Goulaine de. Der ander Theil der newlich erfunden Landtschafft Americae, von dreyen Schiffahrten, so die Frantzosen in Floridam . . . gethan . . . Auss dem Frantzösischen in Latein beschrieben, durch C. C[lusius]. A. und jetzt auss dem Latein in Teutsch bracht durch . . . Oseam Halen. *Frankfurt a. M.: W. Richter, for Widow & Sons of T. de Bry,* 1603.

42 p.; illus., map; fol. (Theodor de Bry's *America*. Pt 2. German). 1st publ. in this version, Frankfurt a. M., 1591; transl. from Latin edn of that year; 1st publ., Paris, 1586, under title *L'histoire notable de la Floride*. Cf. Sabin 8784; Baginsky (German Americana) 120; Church 180; JCB (3) I:389. CSmH, ICN, NN, RPJCB; BL.   603/63

A letter written to the governours of the East Indian merchants. *London: [V. Simmes?] for T. Thorpe; sold by W. Aspley*, 1603. 9 p.; 4to. Mentioned is capture of ship *Vianna* en route to Brazil with cargo of wine, oil, & meal. STC 7448. NIC; Oxford:Bodl.
603/64

Libavius, Andreas. Alchymistische Practic. *Frankfurt a. M.: J. Sauer, for P. Kopff*, 1603. 293 p.; 4to. Described are two oils employing guaiacum. Ferguson (Bibl. chem.) II:32; Wellcome I:3774. NNE; BL.   603/65

Lima (Ecclesiastical Province). Council, 1583. Catecismo en la lengua española. y quichua del Piru. *Rome: A. Zannetti*, 1603. 126 p.; 12mo. Extracted from the Council's *Doctrina christiana*, 1st publ., Ciudad de Los Reyes (i.e., Lima, Peru), 1584. Sabin 67161; Medina (BHA) 474; Viñaza 104; Streit II:1072n; Palau 50151; JCB (3) II:20. RPJCB.   603/66

——. Confessario para los curas de Indios . . . Compuesto y traduzido en las lenguas quichua y aymara. *Seville: C. Hidalgo*, 1603. 3 pts; 4to. 1st publ., Ciudad de Los Reyes (i.e., Lima, Peru), 1585. Sabin 67163; Medina (BHA) 475; Streit II: 1072n; Palau 59200. NN-RB, RPJCB.   603/67

Lodge, Thomas. A treatise of the plague. *London: [T. Creede & V. Simmes] for E. White & N. L[ing]*., 1603. 44 lvs; 4to. Mentions Hispaniola and a disease 'not much unlike the French poxes', treated successfully with guaiacum. STC 16676; Pforzheimer 622; Wellcome I:3841. CSmH, DFo, MH (imp.); BL.   603/68

López de Castro, Baltasar. Baltasar Lopez de Castro, criado de su Magestad, y su juez de comission para el remedio de los resates con hereges en la isla Española. Presento en este Real Consejo dos memoriales. *Valladolid*: 1603. 24 p.; fol. Maggs Cat. 502 (Americana VII): 5005A. CtY.   603/69

Maffei, Giovanni Pietro, S.J. Histoire des Indes . . . ou il est traicté de leur descouverte, navigation et conqueste faicte tant par les Portugais que Castillans . . . traduit par f. A[rnault]. d[e]. L[a]. B[oerie]. *Lyons: J. Pillehotte*, 1603. 953 p.; 8vo. Transl. from Maffei's *Historiarum Indicarum libri iv*, 1st publ., Florence, 1588. Included are references to Brazil. Cf. Sabin 43782; cf. Borba de Moraes II:10; Atkinson (Fr. Ren.) 438. IaU; BL, BN.   603/70

Maffei, Raffaele. Commentariorum urbanorum libri octo et triginta. *Frankfurt a. M.: C. Marne, & Heirs of J. Aubry*, 1603. 1496 p.; fol. 1st publ., Rome, 1506. Includes ref. to Columbus. OC, NcD, OU; BL, BN.
603/71

Marees, Pieter de. Sechster Theil der Orientalischen Indien; warhafftige historische Beschreibung dess gewaltigen goltreichen Königreichs Guinea . . . aus niederländischer Verzeichnuss . . . beschrieben durch M. Gotthardt Arthus. *Frankfurt a. M.: W. Richter*, 1603. 154 p.; illus.; fol. (J. T. de Bry's *India Orientalis*. Pt 6. German). Transl. from author's *Beschryvinge ende historische verhael . . . van Gunea*, 1st publ., Amsterdam, 1602. Brunet I:1358; Church 236; JCB (3) 434–35. CSmH, DLC, MBAt, NN-RB, RPJCB; BL, BN.   603/72

—[Anr edn]. Siebende Schiffahrt in das goldreiche Königreich Guineam. *Frankfurt a. M.: W. Richter, for L. Hulsius*, 1603. 228 p.; illus., map; 4to. (Levinus Hulsius's *Sammlung von . . . Schiffahrten*. Pt 7). Sabin 33661; Church 285; JCB (3) I:458. CSmH, CtY, NN, RPJCB; BL, BN.   603/73

Martí, Juan José, supposed author. Segunda parte de la vida del picaro Guzman de Alfarache. Compuesta por Matheo Luxan de Sayavedra [pseud.]. *Barcelona: J. Cendrat*, 1603. 1st publ., Valencia, 1602. NNH.   603/74

—[Anr edn]. *Barcelona: S. de Cormellas, for G. Aleu*, 1603. 302 p.; 8vo. Laurenti (Nov. pic. esp.) 791; Palau 6685.   603/75

—[Anr edn]. *Lisbon: A. Alvarez*, 1603. NNH.
603/76

—[Anr edn]. *Lisbon: J. Rodríguez*, 1603. 220 numb. lvs; 8vo. Palau 6684. NNH.
603/77

—[Anr edn]. *Madrid: J. Flamenco, for F. López*, 1603. 437 p.; 8vo. Laurenti (Nov. pic. esp.)

789; Pérez Pastor (Madrid) 838; Palau 6688.
603/78

—[Anr edn]. De la vida del picaro Guzman de Alfarache. Segunda parte. *Milan: G. Bordone & P. M. Locarno*, 1603. 384 p.; 8vo. Laurenti (Nov. pic. esp.) 553 (& 788). IEN, MB, NNH; BL.
603/79

—[Anr edn]. *Salamanca: A. Renaut*, 1603. 586 p.; 8vo. Palau 6687.
603/80

—[Anr edn]. *Saragossa: A. Tavano*, 1603. 392 p.; 8vo. Laurenti (Nov. pic. esp.) 790; Jiménez Catalan (Saragossa) 22; Palau 6686. NNH.
603/81

Megiser, Hieronymus. Thesaurus polyglottus, vel Dictionarium multilingue, exquadringentis circiter tam veteris quam novi . . . orbis nationum. *Frankfurt a. M.: The author*, 1603. 2 pts; 8vo. Table 9 is devoted to America, table 10 to 'Novi orbis insula'. ICN; BL, BN.
603/82

Mercuriale, Girolamo. Praelectiones Patavinae. De cognoscendis, discernendis, et curandis omnibus humani corporis affectibus. *Venice: The Giuntas*, 1603. 656 p.; fol. 1st publ., Frankfurt a. M., 1601, under title *Medica practica*. Wellcome I:4252. DNLM, ICU; London: Wellcome.
603/83

Meteren, Emanuel van. Historia oder eigentliche und warhaffte Beschreibung aller Kriegshändel . . . in Niderlandt . . . Jetzo gebessert und vermehrt. [*Amsterdam or Dordrecht?*] 1603. 2 pts; illus., ports, map; fol. 1st publ. in German, Hamburg, 1596; cf. year 1601. Palau 166947.
603/84

Montaigne, Michel Eyquem de. The essayes . . . now done into English [by John Florio]. *London: V. Simmes, for E. Blount* [1603]. 664 p.; fol. 1st publ. in French, Bordeaux, but here perhaps transl. from the Paris, 1602, edn, q.v. STC 18041. CSmH, CtY, DLC, ICN, MH, MiU, PPRF; BL, BN.
603/85

Ortelius, Abraham. Abraham Ortelius his Epitome of the theater of the worlde . . . renewed and augmented, the mappes all new graven . . . by Micheal Coignet. [*Antwerp:*] *For J. Shaw, at London*, 1603. 134 lvs; maps; obl. 8vo. Transl. from Coignet's text, 1st publ., Antwerp, 1601. Koeman (Ort) 65; Phillips (Atlases) 3407; STC 18856; JCB (3) II:21–22. DLC, ICN, MH, MiU-C, MnU-B, NN-RB, RPJCB; BL.
603/86

——Theatrum orbis terrarum . . . Tabulis aliquot novis . . . illustratum. Editio ultima. *Antwerp: J. B. Vrients*, 1603. 118 numb. lvs; maps, port.; fol. 1st publ., Antwerp, 1570. Sabin 57700; Koeman (Ort) 36; Phillips (Atlases) 419; JCB (3) II:21. CSmH, DLC, ICN, InU-L, MH, MiU-C, NNH, PP, RPJCB; Oxford: Bodl., BN.
603/87

Ottsen, Hendrick. Journael oft Daghelijcxregister van de voyagie na Rio de Plata, ghedaen met het schip ghenoemt de Silveren Werelt. *Amsterdam: C. Claeszoon*, 1603. 49 p.; illus.; obl. 4to. Sabin 57901 (& 31228); Tiele-Muller 206; Tiele 835; cf. JCB (3) II:120. BL, BN.
603/88

Paracelsus. Erster[–zehender] Theil der Bücher und Schrifften . . . auffs trewlichst . . . an Tag geben: durch Joannem Huserum. *Frankfurt a. M.: Heirs of J. Wechel*, 1603. 3v.; illus.; 4to. 1st publ. as here constituted [Basel], 1589–90. Bk 1 includes the author's *Vom Holtz Guaiaco gründlicher heylung*, 1st publ., Nuremberg, 1529; bk 7 includes formula for an 'Oleum Guaici'. Sudhoff (Paracelsus) 254–55; Wellcome I:4806. DNLM, PPHa, WU; Wellcome (v. 2 only), Munich:StB.
603/89

—[Anr edn]. Opera. Bücher und Schrifften. *Strassburg: L. Zetzner*, 1603. 2 v.; illus.; fol. Sudhoff (Paracelsus) 256; Wellcome I:4807. CtY, DNLM, ICJ, MBCo, PPC; BL, Berlin: StB.
603/90

——La grande chirurgie . . . Traduite . . . de la version latine de Josquin d'Alhem . . . Par m. Claude Dariot . . . Seconde edition. *Lyons: A. de Harsy*, 1603. 3 pts; 4to. 1st publ. as here transl. from the author's *Chirurgia magna* ([Basel], 1573), itself transl. from his *Opus chyrurgicum* (Frankfurt a. M., 1565), Lyons, 1593. Included is discussion of guaiacum. Sudhoff (Paracelsus) 253. DNLM, MoSMed; BL, BN.
603/91

Porcacchi, Tommaso. L'isole piu famose del mondo descritte da Thomaso Porcacchi . . . e intagliate da Girolamo Porro. *Venice: Heirs of S. Galignani*, 1603. 211 p.; illus., maps; fol. 1st publ., Venice, 1572. Includes descriptions & maps of New World areas, from expanded Venice, 1575, edn. Cf. Sabin 64151. BL.
603/92

Possevino, Antonio. Biblioteca selecta. *Venice: A. Salicato*, 1603. 2 v.; fol. 1st publ.,

Rome, 1593. Includes substantial discussions of methods for proselytizing Indians. Streit I:262. WU; BL, BN.   603/93

Raleigh, Sir Walter. Die fünffte kurtze wunderbare Beschreibung dess goldreichen Königreichs Guianae in America oder neuen Welt. *Nuremberg: C. Lochner, for L. Hulsius, 1603.* 17 p.; illus., map; 4to. (Levinus Hulsius's *Sammlung von . . . Schiffahrten*, Pt 5). 1st publ. in this version, Nuremberg, 1599; cf. year 1601. Sabin 67564 (& 33658); Baginsky (German Americana) 122; Shaaber (Brit. auth.) R16; Church 277; JCB (3) I:456. CSmH, CtY, DLC, NN, RPJCB; BL, BN.   603/94

Ripa, Cesare. Iconologia, overo Descrittione di diverso imagini cavate dall'antichità, & di propria inventione. *Rome: L. Facio, 1603.* 523 p.; illus.; 4to. The earliest edn to contain, under entry for 'Mondo', emblematic representation, with explanatory text, of America, depicted as a woman. Included is a representation of an alligator, more authentically rendered in later edns. DFo, MH, NcD, PU; BN.   603/95

Rivadeneira, Pedro de, S.J. Princeps christianus adversus Nicolaum Machiavellum . . . nunc latine a p. Joanne Orano editus. *Antwerp: J. Trognaesius, 1603.* 376 p.; 4to. Transl. from author's *Tratado de la religion,* 1st publ., Madrid, 1595; cf. year 1601. Cf. Backer VI:1735; Palau 266342. DFo, PV; BN.   603/96

—[Anr edn]. *Mainz: C. Butgen, 1603.* 564 p.; 8vo. ICN, IaU; BL.   603/97

——. La vie du père François de Borja . . . tournee en nostre langue vulgaire par le seigneur [Michel d'Esne] de Betencourt. *Douai: B. Bellère, 1603.* 480 p.; 8vo. 1st publ. as here transl., Douai, 1596, from author's *Vida del padre Francisco de Borja,* 1st publ., Madrid, 1592. Includes refs to Jesuits in Florida, Peru, & Mexico. Backer VI:1734; Palau 266316; cf. Cioranescu (XVI) 9483. PLatS; BN.   603/98

——. Vita Francisci Borgiae . . . latine verò ab And. Schotto. *Mainz: B. Lipp, 1603.* 816 p.; 12mo. Transl. from author's *Vida del padre Francisco de Borja,* 1st publ., Madrid, 1592. Includes accounts of Jesuits in Florida, Peru, & Mexico. Palau 266312. MB, MnCS, NNUT; BL, BN.   603/99

San Román de Ribadeneyra, Antonio, O.S.B. Historia general de la Yndia Oriental; los descubrimientos, y conquistas, que han hecho las armas de Portugal, enel Brasil, y en otras partes de Africa, y de la Asia. *Valladolid: L. Sánchez, for D. Pérez, 1603.* 804 p.; fol. Sabin 76188; Medina (BHA) 488; Borba de Moraes II:229; Streit II:2363; Maggs Cat. 479 (Americana V):4092. CU, CtY, DLC, InU-L, MB, MiU-C, MnU-B, NN-RB, RPJCB; Rome: BN.   603/100

Santorio, Santorio. Methodi vitandorum errorum omnium, qui in arte medica contingunt libri quindecim. *Venice: F. Bariletti, 1603.* 230 numb. lvs; illus.; fol. Advances reasons why guaiacum cures syphilis. Wellcome I:5757. DNLM, MnU-B, PPC; London:Wellcome, BN.   603/101

Sassonia, Ercole. Pantheum medicinae selectum, sive Medicinae practicae templum. *Frankfurt a. M.: Palthenius Office* [1603?]. 1063 p.; fol. Included is the author's *De lue venerea,* 1st publ., Padua, 1597. DNLM, NNNAM; BL, BN.   603/102

Schottus, Andreas. Hispaniae illustratae, seu Rerum urbiumque Hispaniae, Lusitaniae, Aethiopiae, et Indiae scriptores varii. *Frankfurt a. M.: C. de Marne & Heirs of J. Aubry, 1603–8.* 4v.; illus., maps; fol. Vol. 2 contains (p. 1282–84) Columbus's letter *De insulis . . . nuper inventis,* 1st publ. in Latin, Rome, 1493, as well as (p. 1062–1220) Girolamo di Conestaggio, *De Portugaliae conjunctione cum regno Castellae,* 1st publ. as here transl., Frankfurt a. M., 1602. Sabin 77900–905 (& 32005); Backer VII:880; Palau 305068. CU, CtY, DLC, MH, MiU, MnU-B, NN-RB, RPJCB (v. 1–3); BL, BN.

603/103

Serres, Olivier de, seigneur du Pradel. Le théatre d'agriculture et mesnage des champs . . . Deuxieme edition, reveuë et augmentee par l'auteur. *Paris: A. Saugrain, 1603.* 907 p.; illus.; 4to. 1st publ., Paris, 1600. Included are sections on the turkey & tobacco. MB, MH, NNC.   603/104

Solinus, C. Julius. Memorabilia mundi . . . Nunc primum notos atque annotationibus, quibus multa quoque Memorabilia inserta sunt; itidemque iis quae Novus Orbis nostri seculo . . . exhibuit . . . aucta à m. Georgio Draudio. *Frankfurt a. M.: J. Sauer, for T.*

Schönwetter, 1603. 678 p.; 4to. Medina (BHA) 228n (I:379); Wellcome I:6011. CU, DLC, IEN; London:Wellcome, BN.

603/105

Spain. Audiencia territorial. Seville. Ordenanças de la Real Audiencia de Sevilla. *Seville: B. Gómez,* 1603. 461 numb. lvs; fol. Includes sections on 'Poliça general de yda a Indias' & 'Poliça general de venida de Indias'. ICU (imp.); BL.   603/106

Spain. Consejo de las Indias. Ordenanzas reales del Consejo de las Indias. *Valladolid: V. de Castro,* 1603. xxii lvs; fol. Promulgated 24 Sept. 1571; 1st publ. [Seville, 1571?]. Sabin 57483; Medina (BHA) 482; Palau 202818. CU-B; BL.   603/107

Spain. Laws, statutes, etc., 1516–1556 (Charles I). Leyes y ordenanças nuevamente hechas por su Magestad, para la governacion de las Indias, y buen tratamiento y conservacion de los Indios. *Valladolid: V. de Castro,* 1603. 13 numb. lvs; fol. 1st publ., Alcalá de Henares, 1543. Sabin 40904; Medina (BHA) 478; Streit I:263; Palau 137460; JCB (3) II:23. CU-B, RPJCB; BL.

603/108

Spain. Sovereigns, etc., 1598–1621 (Philip III). Este es un traslado . . . de una cedula de su Magestad . . . para que los . . . maravedis que estevan consignados en las rentas de los almoxarifazgos mayor y de Indias de la ciudad de Sevilla . . . se muden al servicio des los diez y ocho miliones. [*Valladolid:* 1603]. 2 lvs; fol. Decree of 6 Aug. 1603. BL.   603/109

——. Instrucion para el virrey del Piru. [*Madrid?*] 1603. 20 numb. lvs; fol. MiU-C.

603/110

——. El Rey. Lo que por mi mandado se assienta, y concierta con Juan Nuñez Correa portugues . . . se cobra de todo el oro, y plata, piedras, perlas, y joyas, y otras cosas que vienen de las Indias. [*Madrid?* 1603]. 15 numb. lvs; fol. Dated at end, Valladolid, 26 Sept. 1603. Sabin 16836; Medina (BHA) 484; Palau 87306; JCB (3) II:22. RPJCB.

603/111

Tabourot, Estienne. Les bigarrures et touches . . . Derniere edition, de nouveau et de beaucoup augmentée. *Paris: J. Richer,* 1603. 5 pts; illus., port.; 12mo. In verse.

1st publ., Paris, 1585. Includes sonnet addressed to Jacques Gohory, with refs to mechoacan & tobacco. Ciorenescu (XVI) 20921; Arents (Add.) 122. DFo, MH, NN-A; BN.   603/112

Thoelde, Johann. Haliographia, das ist, Gründliche und eigendliche Beschreibung aller Saltz Mineralien. *Eisleben: J. Gaubisch, for J. Apel,* 1603. 316 p.; 8vo. A salt of tobacco is described. NjP; BL.   603/113

Torres Bollo, Diego de, S.J. O rozszerzeniu wiary S. Chrzescianskiey Katholickiey w Americe na nowym swiecie, zwlaszcza w krolestwie Peru . . . Na koncu przydany iest list roczny wysep Philippinskich. Roku 1600. *Cracow: A. Piotrkowczyk,* 1603. 61 p.; 4to. Transl. from the author's *Relatione breve* of this year. Sabin 96258; Streit II:1351; Backer VIII:133.   603/114

——. Relatione breve del p. Diego de Torres della Compagnia di Giesù, procuratore della provincia del Perù, circa il frutto che si raccoglie con gli Indiani di quel regno . . . Al fine s'aggiunge la lettera annua dell'Isole Filippine del 1600. *Rome: A. Zannetti,* 1603. 92 p.; 8vo. Sabin 96253; Medina (BHA) 490n; Streit II:1349; Backer VIII:133; JCB (3) II:23. ICN, InU-L, NN-RB, RPJCB.   603/115

——[Anr edn]. *Milan: Heirs of P. da Ponte & G. B. Piccaglia,* 1603. 92 p.; 8vo. Sabin 96253n; cf. Medina (BHA) 490n; Streit II: 1350; Backer VIII:132. MH, NN-RB; BN.

603/116

Vega Carpio, Lope Félix de. Arcadia, prosas y versos. *Madrid: P. Madrigal, for J. de Montoya,* 1603. 312 numb. lvs; 8vo. 1st publ., Madrid, 1598; cf. 1602 edns. A reissue with altered imprint date on t.p. of Madrid, 1602 edn, with colophon dated 1602. Pérez Pastor (Madrid) 855; Palau 356295. NNH; BL.

603/117

——[Anr edn?]. *Madrid: P. Madrigal, for J. de Montoya,* 1603. 312 numb. lvs; 8vo. The colophon is dated 1603. NNH.   603/118

Wittich, Johann. Von dem Ligno Guayaco Wunderbawm, Res nova genannt, von der China ex occidentali India, von der Sarsaparilla, von dem Fenchelholtz Sassafras. [*Arnstadt:*] *Vögelin Press,* 1603. 18 numb. lvs; 8vo. 1st publ., Leipzig, 1589, as pt of Wittich's *Bericht von den . . . bezoardischen Steinen.* London:Wellcome.   603/119

Wytfliet, Corneille. Descriptionis Ptolemaicae augmentum, sive Occidentis notitia brevi commentario illustrata, et hac secunda [*sic*] editione magna sui parte aucta. *Douai: F. Fabri,* 1603. 191 p.; maps; fol. 1st publ., Louvain, 1597. Sabin 105698; Borba de Moraes II:38; Koeman (Wyt) 1C; Phillips (Atlases) 1148. CtY, DLC, MH, NN, PPL, RPJCB: BL.   603/120

—[Anr edn]. *Douai: F. Fabri,* 1603. 104 (i.e. 95) p.; maps; fol. DLC.   603/121

Zappullo, Michele. Historie di quattro principali città del mondo, Gerusalemme, Roma, Napoli, e Venetia . . . Aggiuntovi un compendio dell'istorie dell'Indie. *Vicenza: G. Greco,* 1603. 449 p.; 8vo. 'Parte quinta, dove si fa un discorso dell'Indie': p. 341–422. Sabin 106255. CtY, DLC, MH, MiU-C, RPJCB; BL.   603/122

1604

Acosta, José de, S. J. The naturall and morall historie of the East and West Indies . . . translated . . . by E. G[rimstone?]. *London: V. Simmes for E. Blount & W. Aspley,* 1604. 590 p.; 4to. Transl. from author's *Historia natural y moral de las Indias,* 1st publ., Seville, 1590. Sabin 131: Medina (BHA) 330n (I:503); Streit II:1357; STC 94; Arents 67; Church 328; JCB (3) II:24. CSmH, CtY, DLC, ICN, InU-L, MH, MiU-C, NN-RB, PU, RPJCB; BL.   604/1

Alemán, Mateo. Primera parte de la vida del picaro Guzman de Alfarache. *Brussels: J. Mommaert,* 1604. 215 (i.e., 198) numb. lvs; 8vo. 1st publ., Madrid, 1599; cf. 1601 edn. Medina (BHA) 491; Laurenti (Nov. pic. esp.) 554; Peeters-Fontainas (Impr. esp.) 33a; Palau 6692. CtY, NNC; BL, BN.   604/2

——. Segunda parte de la vida de Guzman de Alfarache. *Lisbon: P. Craesbeeck,* 1604. 3 pts; 4to. Continues Alemán's 1st pt, 1st publ., Madrid, 1599; cf. 1601 edn. Laurenti (Nov. pic. esp.) 555; Palau 6693. CtY.   604/3

Alfonso X, el Sabio, King of Castile & Leon.

Las quatro partes enteras de la Coronica de España. *Valladolid: S. de Cañas, for A. Cuello,* 1604. 2 v.; fol. 1st publ. as here ed. by Florian Ocampo with ref. to Spanish exploration of New World, Zamora, 1541. Cf. Sabin 56618; cf. Medina (BHA) 113; Alcocer (Valladolid) 452. ICN, MB, NNH; BL, BN.   604/4

Amaral, Melchior Estacio do. Tratado das batalhas, e successos do galeão Sanctiago com os Olandeses na ilha de Sancta Elena. *Lisbon: A. Alvarez,* 1604. 65 numb. lvs; illus., map; 4to. Describes capture by Dutch of Portuguese East India galleon, marooning of its crew on island of Fernando de Naronha off Brazil; also described is navigation to Brazil. For counterfeit 18th-century edns see C. R. Boxer, 'An introduction to the *História trágico-maritima*', *Miscelânea de estudos em honra do Prof. Hernâni Cidade* (Lisbon, 1957), p. [48]–[100]. Borba de Moraes I:26; Boxer (as cited above) p. 68–70; Maggs Cat. 479 (Americana V):4094 (cf. 4093, a counterfeit). BL.   1604/5

—[Anr edn]. Das batalhas do galeaom Sanctiago com Olandeses. *Lisbon: A. Alvarez,* 1604. 65 numb. lvs; illus., map; 4to. Boxer (as cited above) p. 70–71. Lisbon: Ajuda.   604/6

Beuter, Pedro Antonio. Primera parte de la Coronica general de toda España. *Valencia: P. P. Mey,* 1604. 2 pts.; port.; fol. 1st publ., Valencia, 1546. Records theory that following the Moorish invasion of Spain Spanish emigrés settled in Yucatan. Palau 28826–27. CU-S, InU-L, MH, MnU-B, NNH, PU; BL, BN.   604/7

Boemus, Johan. Mores, leges, et ritus omnium gentium . . . Itidem & ex Brasiliana J. Lerii historia. Fides, religio & mores Aethiopum . . . Damiano à Goës auctore. [*Geneva:*] *J. de Tournes,* 1604. 504 p.; 8vo. Léry's account of Brazil, transl. & expanded from the French, 1st publ. in Latin, Geneva, 1586; Goes's work, with ref. to Columbus, 1st publ., Louvain, 1540. Sabin 6117n; cf. Borba de Moraes I:96; Cartier (de Tournes) 719; JCB (3) II:25. CLU, MB, NN-RB, PPL, RPJCB; BL, Florence:BN.   604/8

Botero, Giovanni. Theatro de los mayores principes del mundo y causas de la grandeza de sus estados . . . con cinco tratados de razon de estado: por f. Jayme Rebullosa. *Barcelona: S. Matevad & H. Anglada,* 1604. 287 numb. lvs; 8vo. 1st publ. in this version, Barcelona, 1603, under title *Descripcion de todas las provincias . . . del mundo.* Cf. Palau 33706. MB.　　604/9

Buonfiglio Costanzo, Giuseppe. Prima [e secunda] parte dell'Historia siciliana. *Venice: B. Ciera,* 1604. 2 pts; port.; 4to. Includes an account of Columbus & his discoveries. Sabin 9193. CtY, DLC, MiU, MnU; BL, BN.　　604/10

Camerarius, Joachim, the Younger. Symbolorum et emblematum . . . centuria quarta. [*Nuremberg? P. Kaufmann?*] 1604. 100 numb. lvs; illus.; 4to. Continues 1st three centuries, 1st publ., Nuremberg, 1590–96; cf. 1605 edn below. Text for emblem vi mentions Pigafetta & Strait of Magellan. MBAt, NN-RB; BL.　　604/11

Champlain, Samuel de. Des sauvages, ou, Voyage . . . faict en la France nouvelle, l'an mil six cens trois. *Paris: C. de Monstr'oeil,* 1604. 36 numb. lvs; 8vo. 1st publ., Paris, [1603?]; here a reissue with t.p. reset & some paging errors corrected. Cf. Sabin 11834; Harrisse (NF) 11; Atkinson (Fr. Ren.) 441. MH, NNPM; BN.　　604/12

Coignet, Michiel. Ausszug auss des Abrahami Ortelÿ Theatro orbis. *Frankfurt a. M.:* 1604. *See* Ortelius, Abraham, *below.*

Cooke, Jo. Epigrames served out in 52 severall dishes. *London: G. Eld, for W. C[otton].,* [1604]. [54] p.; 8vo. The 10th epigram mentions Drake, Hawkins, & Frobisher; the 40th describes 'Seignior Tobacco'. Also attrib. to John Elsum. STC 5672 (& 7609?). Oxford:Bodl.　　604/13

Córdoba, Antonio de. Quaestionarium theologicum, sive Sylva amplissima decisionum . . . casuum conscientiae. *Venice: B. Barezzi,* 1604. 2 v.; fol. 1st publ., Venice, 1570, as the author's *Opera.* 'Quaestio 57' discusses 'De bello infidelium et insularum'. Streit I:266. Munich:StB.　　604/14

Dekker, Thomas. Newes from Graves-end: sent to nobody. *London: T. C[reede]., for T. Archer,* 1604. [90] p.; 8vo. Included is a ref. to Thomas Cavendish's & Sir Francis Drake's voyages. STC 12199. CSmH; Oxford:Bodl.　　604/15

——. The wonderfull year. 1603. *London: T. Creede* [1604?]. [47] p.; 4to. 1st publ., London, 1603. STC 6534. London: V. & A.　　604/16

Del Rio, Martin Anton, S. J. Disquisitionum magicarum libri sex . . . Nunc secundis curis auctior. *Lyons: J. Pillehotte,* 1604. 3 v.; 4to. 1st publ., Louvain, 1599–1600; cf. 1603 edn. Backer II:1898. MH, NNUT, TU.　　604/17

Drayton, Michael. The owle. *London: E. A[llde]., for E. White & N. Ling,* 1604. 4to. In verse. Includes mention of 'turckiecocke'. For full distinguishing features of the 3 edns dated '1604', see the Pforzheimer catalog. In the present the reading 'OVVLE' appears on the t.p.; see also the following item & that entered at '162–'. STC 2711; Pforzheimer 304A. CSmH, CtY, DFo, MH, NN-RB; BL.　　604/18

—[Anr edn]. *London: E. A[llde]., for E. White & N. Ling,* 1604. 4to. In the title the reading used is 'OWLE'. STC 2712; Pforzheimer 304B. CSmH, MH, NN-RB.　　604/19

Du Bartas, Guillaume de Salluste, seigneur. The third dayes creation . . . Done verse for verse out of the originall French by Thomas Winter. *London: [R. Field,] for T. Clarke,* 1604. 32 p.; 4to. In verse. Extracted from Du Bartas's *La sepmaine,* 1st publ., Paris, 1578. Included is mention of American rivers, Peru, Newfoundland, etc. STC 21660. CSmH; BL.　　604/20

Duchesne, Joseph. Ad veritatem hermeticae medicinae ex Hippocratis veterúmque decretis ac therapeusi. *Paris: A. Saugrain,* 1604. 312 p.; 8vo. Includes refs to guaiacum & marigolds. DNLM, WU; BL, BN.　　604/21

Eliseo, O. C. D. Aviendo representado el conde de Monterey a su Magestad los agravios y molestias, que los Indios de la Nueva España recibian . . . el padre Elisio . . . escrivio un papel . . . que es del tenor siguiente. [*Madrid?* 1604?]. 8 lvs; fol. Denounces conduct of judges in Mexico. Medina notwithstanding, the British Library assigns printing & date to Mexico and the year 1693. Medina (BHA) 6423; Streit I:267. BL.　　604/22

Eugalenus, Severinus. De scorbuto morbo liber . . . Nunc vero ordine meliore . . .

in lucem productus. *Leipzig: M. Lantzenberger, for B. Voigt,* 1604. 321 p.; 8vo. In discussing guaiacum as remedy for syphilis describes it as an example of Divine Providence. DNLM, NjP, WU; BL. 604/23

Fernel, Jean. De Abditis rerum causis libri duo. *Lyons: T. Soubron & J. Veyrat,* 1604. 8vo. 1st publ., Paris, 1548; cf. 1601–2 edn of Fernel's *Universa medicina.* Sherrington (Fernel) 34.F18. CtY-M, DNLM. 604/24

——. Universa medicina. *Orleans: P. de La Rovière,* 1604. 4 pts; fol. 1st publ. as here constituted, Paris, 1567; cf. 1601–2 edn. Sherrington (Fernel) 74.J18. CtY-M; London: Wellcome. 604/25

Fioravanti, Leonardo. Corona; oder, Kron der Artzney . . . Erstlich neuwlich in italiänischer Spraach . . . in Truck verfärtiget. Nunmehr aber in unsere hochteutsche Spraach . . . versetzt. *Frankfurt a. M.: N. Hoffmann, for J. Berner,* 1604. 507 p.; illus.; 8vo. Transl. from author's *Capricci medicinali,* 1st publ., Venice, 1561; cf. 1602 edn. DNLM. 604/26

——. Physica, das ist: Experientz und Naturkündigung . . . Jetzund auss dem Italiänischen . . . versetzt. *Frankfurt a. M.: N. Hoffmann, for J. Berner,* 1604. 8vo. Transl. from the author's *Della fisica,* 1st publ., Venice, 1582. Includes passages on American medical botany. NNE. 604/27

Francisco de Vitoria, O. P. Relectiones morales. *Antwerp:* 1604. 2 v.; 8vo. 1st publ., Lyons, 1557, under title *Relectiones theologicae.* Includes discussions of the West Indies, and theology of war on natives. Sabin 100620n; Streit I:269; Palau 371071. 604/28

Fregoso, Battista. Factorum et dictorum memorabilium lib. ix. a Camilo Galino latina facta. *Cologne: J. Mylius (House of Birckmann),* 1604. 380 p.; 8vo. 1st publ., Milan, 1509. Included is a ref. to Columbus. Sabin 26140n. InU-L; BL. 604/29

Gesner, Konrad. Historia animalium liber iii. qui est de avium natura . . . nunc denuo recognita. *Frankfurt a.M.: A.Cambier,* 1604. 806 p.; illus.; fol. 1st publ., Frankfurt a. M., 1555; here a reissue with cancel t.p. of 1585 edn. Includes descriptions & illus. of turkey & toucan. BL, BN. 604/30

Goulart, Simon. Histoires admirables et memorables de nostre temps. *Arras: G. de La Rivière,* 1604. 12mo. 1st publ., Paris, 1600–1601; cf. 1603 edn. Jones (Goulart) 54(b). Paris:Bibl. du Prot. Franç. 604/31

——, **comp.** Le quatriesme recueil, contenant l'histoire de la Ligue. *[Geneva?]* 1604. 768 p.; 8vo. 1st publ., [Geneva?], 1595; here a reissue of that 1595 edn similarly paged. Includes the *Response à un avis,* 1st publ., [Paris?], 1589, citing as examples of Spanish justice that accorded Atabalipa (last Inca ruler of Peru) & Temistitan (i.e., Mexico). Jones (Goulart) 30(e). BL, BN. 604/32

Gracián, Jerónimo. Lampara encendida. Compendio de la perfeccion. *Madrid: J. de la Cuesta,* 1604. 352 numb. lvs; 8vo. Includes (lvs. 246–312), with t.p. dated 1603, the author's *Estimulo de la propagacion de la fe,* 1st publ., Lisbon, 1586. Included are refs to proselytizing of Indians in Mexico. Streit I:271; Pérez Pastor (Madrid) 867; Palau 106781. 604/33

Guicciardini, Francesco. La historia d'Italia . . . divisa in venti libri. *Treviso: F. Zanetti,* 1604. 2 pts; 4to. 1st publ., Florence, 1561. In bk 6, chapt. 9 comprises an account of the discovery of America, mentioning Columbus & Vespucci. Michel (Répertoire) IV:101. ICU, MWelC, TNJ; Paris:Arsenal. 604/34

Guyon, Louis, sieur de la Nauche. Les diverses leçons . . . divisees en cinq livres. *Lyons: C. Morillon,* 1604. 910 p.; 8vo. Included are refs to the New World, incl. use there of poison for arrows. BL, BN. 604/35

Herring, Francis. A modest defence of the caveat given to the wearers of amulets. *London: A. Hatfield, for W. Jones,* 1604. 26 lvs; 4to. Praises King James's *Counterblaste to tobacco* of this year, described below. STC 13248; Arents (Add.) 123. DFo, MH, NN-A; BL. 604/36

Hieron, Samuel. An answer to a popish ryme. *London: S. Stafford,* 1604. 4to. Anti-Catholic verse, including couplet 'Indeede the Spaniards loving gold,/Have brought the Indians to your fold.' STC 13388. DFo; BL. 604/37

James I, King of Great Britain. A counterblaste to tobacco. *London: R. B[arker].,* 1604. 13 lvs; 4to. In attacking use of tobacco, acknowledges its merits for treatment of syphilis. Sabin 35675; STC 14363; Arents 68. CSmH, DFo, MH, NN-A, OCl; Oxford:Bodl.　　　　604/38

Jesuits. Letters from missions. Annuae litterae (1594–95) 1604. Litterae . . . annorum M.D.XCIIII. et M.D.XCV. *Naples: T. Longo,* 1604. 868 p.; 8vo. Includes accounts of Mexican, Peruvian, & Brazilian provinces. Streit I:275. NNH; BL.　　604/39

Libavius, Andreas. Praxis alchymiae, hoc est Doctrina de artificiosa praeparatione praecipuorum medicamentorum chymicorum, duobus libris explicata. *Frankfurt a. M.: J. Sauer, for P. Kopff,* 1604. 680 p.; illus.; 8vo. Transl. by Leonhardus Doldius from the author's *Alchymistische Practic,* 1st publ., Frankfurt a. M., 1603. Wellcome I:3775. CtY, DNLM, MB, NNE, PU-S, WU; BL, BN.
604/40

Lima (Ecclesiastical Province). Council, 1583. Catecismo en la lengua española, y aymara del Piru. *Seville: B. Gómez,* 1604. 49 numb. lvs; 8vo. Extracted from the council's *Doctrina christiana,* 1st publ., Ciudad de Los Leyes (i.e., Lima, Peru), 1584. Sabin 2520; Medina (BHA) 493; Viñaza 112; Streit II:1072n (dated '1608'). NNH.
604/41

Linschoten, Jan Huygen van. Reys-gheschrift van de navigatien der Portugaloysers in Orienten . . . Als oock van de gantsche custen van Brasilien, ende alle die havens van dien. Item van 't vaste landt ende die voor eylanden (Las Antilhas genaemt) van Spaenschs Indien. *Amsterdam: C. Claeszoon,* 1604. 147 p.; fol. 1st publ., Amsterdam, 1595 [i.e., 1596]. Ostensibly issued as a part of the author's *Itinerario,* Amsterdam, [1605], q.v. Sabin 41359; cf. Borba de Moraes I:420; Tiele-Muller 82.　　604/42

Maffei, Giovanni Pietro, S.J. Histoire des Indes . . . traduit par f. A[rnault]. d[e]. L[a]. B[oerie]. *Lyons: J. Pillehotte,* 1604. 953 p.; 8vo. Transl. from Maffei's *Historiarum Indicarum libri iv,* 1st publ., Florence, 1588; cf. 1603 edn of which this is perhaps a reissue with altered imprint date. Sabin 43782;

Borba de Moraes II:10; Streit V:50; Backer V:299. DLC, InU-L, MnU-B.　　604/43

Malvenda, Tommaso. De antichristo libri undecim. *Rome: C. Vullietto,* 1604. 548 p.; fol. Includes account of Columbus's discoveries, discussing possibility that a lost tribe of Israel may have settled in America. Sabin 44176; Graesse IV:356. IMunS, MH, NIC; BL, BN.　　604/44

Marcos da Lisboa, Bp, O.F.M. Troisieme partie des Chroniques des Frères mineurs . . . reduicte de castillan en italien par . . . Horace Diola . . . et nouvellement traduicte en françois par r.p.f. Jean Blancone. *Paris: Widow of G. Chaudière,* 1604. 774 p.; 4to. 1st publ. in Spanish, Salamanca, 1570; includes account of Franciscans in Mexico. Cioranescu (XVII) 12384. BL, BN.
604/45

Marees, Pieter de. Indiae Orientalis, pars vi; veram et historicam descriptionem auriferi Regni Guinea . . . Latinitate ex Germanico donata. *Frankfurt a. M.: W. Richter, for J. T. & J. I. de Bry,* 1604. 127 p.; illus.; fol. (J. T. de Bry's *India Orientalis.* Pt 6. Latin). Transl. from *Sechster Theil der Orientalischen Indien,* Frankfurt a. M., 1603; 1st publ., Amsterdam, 1602, under title *Beschryvinge ende historische verhael . . . van Gunea.* Tiele-Muller 134; Brunet I:1338; Church 213 & 214; JCB (3) I:433–34. CSmH, DLC, ICN, NN, RPJCB; BL, BN.　　604/46

Marlowe, Christopher. The tragicall historie of the life and death of Doctor Faustus. *London: V. S[immes]., for T. Bushell,* 1604. [45] p.; 4to. Drama. In opening scene, ref. is made to searching 'all corners of the new found World for pleasant fruits and princely delicates.' STC 17429; Greg 205(a). Oxford:Bodl.　　604/47

Marston, John. The malcontent. *London: V. S[immes]., for W. Aspley,* 1604. [64] p.; 4to. Drama. Included are refs to tobacco. STC 17479; Greg 203(a). CSmH, CtY, DFo, MH, NN-RB; BL.　　604/48

—[Anr edn]. *London: V. S[immes]., for W. Aspley,* 1604. [67] p.; 4to. STC 17480; Greg 203(b). CSmH, DLC(imp.), MB(imp.); BL.
604/49

—[Anr edn]. Augmented . . . With the additions . . . by Jhon Webster. *London: V. S[immes]., for W. Aspley,* 1604. [72] p.; 4to. STC 17481; Greg 203(c). CSmH, CtY, DFo, IU, MH, MiU, NN-A; BL. 604/50

Martí, Juan José, supposed author. Segunda parte de la vida del picaro Guzman de Alfarache. Compuesto por Matheo Luxan de Sayavedra [pseud.]. *Brussels: R. Velpius,* 1604. 382 p.; 8vo. 1st publ., Valencia, 1602. Laurenti (Nov. pic. esp.) 792; Peeters-Fontainas (Impr. esp.) 33b; Palau 6692. CtY, NIC, NNH; BL, BN. 604/51

Mattioli, Pietro Andrea. De i discorsi . . . nelli sei libri di Pedacio Dioscoride . . . della materia medicinale. *Venice: B. degli Alberti & D. Nicolino,* 1604. 1527 p.; illus., port.; fol. 1st publ. as here transl. from Latin, Venice, 1555. Includes discussion of medicinal uses of American plants. Pritzel 5988n; Nissen (Bot.) 1304n; Michel (Répertoire) V:152. DNLM, MH-A, N; London: Wellcome, BN. 604/52

Mayr, Johann. Epitome cronicorum seculi moderni . . . mit vilen Historien, sonderlich der Newen Welt Americae, und Ost-Indien vermehret. *Munich: N. Heinrich,* 1604. 339 numb. 1vs; 4to. 1st publ., Munich, 1598, under title *Compendium chronologicum.* Sabin 47110. CtY, DLC, NN-RB; BL. 604/53

Meteren, Emanuel van. Historia, oder Eigentliche und warhaffte beschreibung aller fürnehmen Kriegshändel . . . so sich in Niderlandt . . . bis in das jahr 99. zugetragen haben . . . Jetzo . . . bis an gegenwertiges jahr 1604. continuiert und gebessert. *Arnhem: J. Janszoon,* 1604. 2 pts; ports, map; fol. 1st publ. in German, Hamburg, 1596; cf. 1601 edn. Pt 2 has title: *Niderländische historia.* Palau 166953; Bruckner 4. ICU; BL. 604/54

Mexía, Pedro. Les diverses leçons . . . mises en françois par Claude Gruget . . . plus la suite de celles d'Antoine du Verdier. *Tournon: C. Michel & T. Soubron,* 1604. 738 p.; 8vo. 1st publ. in this version, with American refs in Du Verdier's continuation, Lyons, 1577. Included also are Mexía's dialogues, 1st publ. in Spanish, Seville, 1547, under title *Colóquios,* mentioning syphilis, Magel-

lan's circumnavigation, etc. Sabin 48245n; Palau 167322n. CtY-M, ICU, NjP; BL, BN. 604/55

——. The historie of all the Romane emperors . . . First collected in Spanish . . . since enlarged in Italian by Lodovico Dolce and Girolamo Bardi, and now englished by W. T[raheron]. *London: [F. Kingston, for] M. Lownes,* 1604. 890 p.; fol. Transl. from Mexía's *Le vite di tutti gl'imperadori,* 1st publ. in Italian with Dolce's life of Charles V, incl. ref. to Cortés & West Indies, Venice, 1561. STC 17851. CSmH, CtY, DLC, ICN, MH, MiU-C, NN-RB; BL. 604/56

Middleton, Thomas. The blacke booke. *London: T. C[reede]., for J. Chorlton,* 1604. 22 lvs; 4to. Includes refs to tobacco. STC 17875; Arents 70. CSmH, CtY, DFo, MH, NN-A; BL. 604/57

Monsalve, Miguel de, friar. Reducion universal de todo el Piru, y demas Indias, con ochos muchos avisos, par el bien de los naturales dellas, y en aumento de las reales rentas. *[Madrid? 1604].* 45 numb. 1vs; 4to. BL. 604/58

Montaigne, Michel Eyquem de. Essais. *Paris: A. L'Angelier,* 1604. 1165 p.; 8vo. 1st publ., Bordeaux, 1580; cf. 1602 edn. Tchémerzine VIII:413; Maggs Cat. 502 (Americana VII):5007. MH, NjP; BL, BN. 604/59

Ortelius, Abraham. Ausszug auss des Abrahami Ortelÿ Theatro orbis Teutsch beschriben durch Levinum Hulsium. *Frankfurt a. M.: L. Hulsius, & J. van Keerberghen, at Antwerp,* 1604. 135 numb. 1vs; maps; obl. 8vo. Based on van Keerberghen's Antwerp edn, 1st publ., 1601. Baginsky (German Americana) 123; Koeman (Ort) 66; Phillips (Atlases) 420. DLC, ICN, NN-RB; BN, Turin:BU. 604/60

Ottsen, Hendrick. Warhafftige Beschreibung der unglückhafften Schiffarht eines Schiffs von Ambsterdam, die Silberne Welt genannt . . . nach Rio de Plata . . . aus niederländischer Erzelung . . . in hochteutscher Sprach beschrieben durch M. Gotthart Arthus. *Frankfurt a. M.: W. Richter,* 1604. 62 p.; illus; 4to. Transl. from the author's *Journael oft Daghelijcxregister van de voy-*

agie na Rio de Plata, 1st publ., Amsterdam, 1603. Cf. Sabin 31228; Tiele 836n; JCB (3) II:26–27. MH, NN, RPJCB; BL, BN.
604/61

Paré, Ambroise. De chirurgie, ende alle de opera, ofte wercken . . . Nu eerst uut de fransoysche . . . overgheset: door d. Carolum Battum. *Leyden: J. Bouwenszoon, for C. Claeszoon, at Amsterdam,* 1604. 940 p.; illus.; fol. 1st publ. as here transl. from the Paris, 1585, 4th edn, Dordrecht, 1592; cf. the 1601 German edn. Doe (Paré) 59. CtY-M, MiU, NNNAM; Paris:Mazarine.   604/62

Pigray, Pierre. La chirurgie tant theorique que pratique . . . Revuee, corrigee et augmentee par l'autheur. Seconde edition. [*Paris:*] *M. Orry,* 1604. 712 p.; 8vo. 1st publ., Paris, 1600. Included is a prescription employing guaiacum & sarsaparilla. CtY-M, DNLM.   604/63

Porcacchi, Tommaso. L'isole piu famose del mondo descritte da Thomaso Porcacchi . . . e intagliate da Girolamo Porro. *Venice: Heirs of S. Galignani,* 1604. 211 p.; illus., maps; fol. 1st publ., Venice, 1572; cf. 1603 edn, of which this may be a reissue with altered imprint date. Sabin 64151; Phillips (Atlases) 168; Michel (Répertoire) VI:141. CtY, DLC, ICN, MWiW-C, MnU-B, NN-RB, PSt; Paris:Mazarine.   604/64

Quad, Matthias. Enchiridion cosmographicum: dass ist, Ein Handbüchlein . . . von newem gedruckt, vermehrt und gebessert. *Cologne: W. Lützenkirchen,* 1604. 427 p.; maps; 4to. 1st publ., Cologne, 1599. Pages 260–312 and a map relate to America. Sabin 66891. DLC.   604/65

Richeome, Louis, S.J. Trois discours pour la religion catholique. *Rouen: J. Osmont,* 1604. 626 p.; 12mo. 1st publ., Bordeaux, 1597; cf. 1601 edn. Cf. Backer VI:1817; cf. Cioranescu (XVII) 59455. RPJCB; BL, BN.
604/66

Rivadeneira, Pedro de, S.J. Princeps christianus, adversus Nicolaum Machiavellum. *Cologne: B. Wolter,* 1604. 492 p.; 8vo. 1st publ. as here transl., Antwerp, 1603; cf. year 1601. Palau 266343. BN.   604/67

—[Anr edn]. *Mainz: C. Butgen,* 1604. 596 p.; 8vo. Palau 266344. BN.   604/68

Romancero general. Romancero general, en que se contienen todos los romances que andan impressos. *Madrid: J. de la Cuesta, for F. López,* 1604. 499 numb. 1vs; 4to. 1st publ. under this title, Madrid, 1600; cf. 1602 edn. Here added are further pts, including in the 13th a 'romance' beginning 'Quiero descansar un poco' with ref. to Mexico, possibly written by Gabriel Lobo Lasso de la Vega. Other refs to the New World occur. Pérez Pastor (Madrid) 891; Palau 276981. CLU-C, NNH, PU; BL.
604/69

Rosaccio, Giuseppe. Mondo elementare, et celeste . . . nel quale si tratta de' moti, & ordini delle sfere; della grandezza della terra; dell'Europa, Africa, Asia, & America. *Treviso: E. Deuchino, for G. B. Ciotti, at Venice,* 1604. 243 p.; illus., maps; 8vo. Comprises Rosaccio's *Teatro del cielo e della terra,* 1st publ., Brescia, 1592, with addition of his *Sei età del mondo,* 1st publ., Brescia, 1593. Sabin 73196. DLC, MiU-C, NNH, RPJCB; BL, BN.   604/70

Rossi, Girolamo. De destillatione, sive De stillatitiorum liquorum . . . methodo . . . Quarta editione. *Venice: G. B. Ciotti,* 1604. 181 p.; illus.; 4to. 1st publ., Ravenna, 1582. Chapt. xvi describes a 'Guaiaci ligni oleum.' Wellcome I:5602. PPC; London:Wellcome, BN.   604/71

Rowlands, Samuel. Looke to it: for, Ile stabbe ye. *London: E. Allde for W. Ferbrand & G. Loftus,* 1604. 4to. Includes refs to tobacco. STC 21398. CSmH; Oxford:Bodl.
604/72

—[Anr edn]. *London: W. W[hite]. for W. Ferbrand; sold by W. F[erbrand]. & G. L[oftus].,* 1604. 4to. STC 21399; Arents 71. NN-A.
604/73

Sacro Bosco, Joannes de. Sfera . . . tradotta, e dichiarata da don Francesco Pifferi. *Siena: S. Marchetti,* 1604. 400 p.; illus., port.; 4to. In discussing eclipses (p. 105) Pifferi mentions Florida; in discussing cosmography (p. 339–40) he includes the Americas. Michel (Répertoire) IV:128. MiU-C, NN-RB, PU, RPJCB; BN.   604/74

San Antonio, Gabriel Quiroga de, O.P. Breve y verdadera relacion de los successos del reyno de Camboxa. Al Rey Don Philipe nuestro señor. *Valladolid: P. Lasso,* 1604. 85 numb. 1vs; fol. In addition to mentioning writer's arrival in the Philippines, advocates establishing Catholic faith in Southeast Asia as means of fostering commerce with South America. Medina (Philippines) 93; Alcocer (Valladolid) 456; Maggs Cat. 465 (Americana IV):2679. Madrid:BN. 604/75

Sandoval, Prudencio de, Bp of Pamplona. Primera [-segunda] parte de la Vida y hechos del emperador Carlos Quinto. *Valladolid: S. de Cañas,* 1604–6. 2 v.; fol. Includes accounts of conquest of Mexico & Peru. Sabin 76423; Alcocer (Valladolid) 481; Palau 297145 (cf. 297146). NNH; BN (v. 1), Salamanca:BU. 604/76

Satyre Ménippée. Satyre Menippee de la vertu de Catholicon d'Espagne . . . Augmenté outre les precedentes impressions tant de l'interpretation du mot du Higuero d'infierno . . . que du supplément . . . du Catholicon. [*Paris?*] 1604. [253] p.; 12mo. 1st publ. with added 'Discours . . . du mot Higuero d'infierno', comparing French Leaguers with the prickly pear, Paris, 1594. NIC. 604/77

Shakespeare, William. The history of Henrie the fourth [Pt 1]. *London: V. Simmes, for M. Law,* 1604. 40 lvs; 4to. 1st publ., London, 1598. In act 2, scene 1, turkeys are mentioned. STC 22282; Greg 145 (d). DFo; Oxford:Bodl. 604/78

Spain. Casa de Contratación de las Indias. Ordenanzas reales, para la Casa de la contratacion de Seville y para otras Casas de las Indias y de la navegacion y contratacion dellas. *Valladolid: Heirs of J. Iñiguez de Lequérica,* 1604. 84 lvs; fol. 1st publ., Seville, 1553, but here incorporating additions publ., Madrid, 1585. Sabin 57485; Medina (BHA) 495. CU-B, InU-L; BL. 604/79

Spain. Consejo de las Indias. Interrogatorio para todas la ciudades, villas y lugares de Españoles, y pueblos de naturales de las Indias Occidentales, islas y tierra firme: al qual se ha de satisfazer, conforme a las preguntas siguientes. [*Madrid:* 1604]. 8 numb. lvs; fol. Medina (BHA) 8465; Pérez Pastor (Madrid) 871; Palau 120871. Madrid:BN. 604/80

Suchten, Alexander von. Antinomii mysteria gemina . . . Das ist: Von den grossen Geheimnussen dess Antinomii. *Leipzig: J. Apel,* 1604. 530 p.; 8vo. 1st publ., 1570. Described is an 'aqua ligni Guaiaci'. Ferguson (Bibl. chem.) II:415; Wellcome I:6137. NjP, WU; BL. 604/81

Thou, Jacques Auguste de. Historiarum sui temporis pars prima. *Paris: Widow of M. Patisson,* 1604. 684 p.; fol. Contains bks i–xviii, covering years 1543–60 only. Included are substantial accounts of the discovery of the New World, Columbus, Cortés, Villegagnon's Brazilian venture, the introduction of syphilis by the Spanish, etc. For the complete work, see the year 1620. Copies occur on large paper. Renouard (Les Estienne) I:193–94; Brunet V:840. BL, BN. 604/82

—[Anr edn]. *Paris: Widow of M. Patisson,* 1604. 2 v.; 8vo. For subsequent vols in this format, see the year 1606. Copies occur on large paper. Renouard (Les Estienne) I:194; Brunet V:840. BN. 604/83

—[Anr issue]. *Paris: A. & H. Drouart,* 1604. 2 v.; 8vo. Renouard (Les Estienne) I:194. MH; BL. 604/84

Torquemada, Antonio de. Giardino di fiori curiosi . . . Tradotto di spagnuola . . . per Celio Malespina. *Venice: G. B. Ciotti,* 1604, 208 numb. lvs; 8vo. 1st publ. in Italian, Venice, 1590; transl. from the author's *Jardin de flores curiosas,* 1st publ., Salamanca, 1570. Included are numerous scattered refs to Spanish America. MH. 604/85

Torres Bollo, Diego de, S.J. Breve relatione del p. Diego de Torres della Compagnia di Giesu, procuratore della provincia del Perù, circa il frutto che si raccoglie con gli Indiani di quel regno . . . Al fine s'aggiunge la lettera annua dell'Isole Filippe del 1600. *Venice: G. B. Ciotti,* 1604. 101 p.; 8vo. 1st publ., Rome, 1603. Sabin 96253n; Medina (BHA) 490n; Streit II:1359; Backer VIII:132; JCB (3) II:28. CtY, DLC, InU-L, MH, NN-RB, RPJCB; BL, BN. 604/86

——. Brevis relatio historica in provincia Peruana apud Indos à patribus Societatis Jesu gestarum . . . Accessere annuae literae rerum ab iisdem gestarum in insulis Philippinis. Primum Roma italico idiomate excusae. *Mainz: B. Lipp,* 1604. 101 p.; 8vo. Transl. from author's *Relatione breve,* 1st publ., Rome, 1603. Sabin 96256; Medina (BHA) 496; Streit II:1360; Backer VIII:133; JCB (3) II:27. NN-RB, RPJCB; BL, Munich:StB. 604/87

——. De rebus Peruanis . . . commentarius, à Joanne Hayo Dalgattiensi ex italo in latinum conversus. *Antwerp: M. Nuyts,* 1604. 99 p.; 8vo. Transl. from author's *Relatione breve,* 1st publ., Rome, 1603. Sabin 96257; Medina (BHA) 497; Streit II:1362; Backer VIII:135; JCB (3) II:27. DLC, ICN, InU-L, NN-RB, RPJCB; BL, BN.　　604/88

——. Kurtzer Bericht was Gott, vermittelst der Societet Jesu, in den Peruanischen Ländern aussgericht . . . Sampt einem Jarschreiben auss den Philippinischen Insulen dess 1600 Jars. Erstlich in Italienischer Sprach zu Rom getruckt. *Würzburg: G. Fleischmann,* 1604. 154 p.; 8vo. Transl. from author's *Relatione breve,* 1st publ., Rome, 1603. Sabin 96255; Medina (BHA) 490n; Streit II:1361; Backer VIII:132–33. DGU, NNH; Munich:StB.　　604/89

——. La nouvelle histoire du Perou. *Paris: J. Richer,* 1604. 56 numb. 1vs; 8vo. Transl. by P. V. Palma Cayet from author's *Relatione breve,* 1st publ., Rome, 1603. Sabin 96254n; Atkinson (Fr. Ren.) 445n; Backer VIII:133; Cioranescu (XVI) 6071. NN-RB; BL, BN.　　604/90

—[Anr issue]. *Paris: [J. Richer] for Catherine Niverd, widow of C. de Monstr'oeil,* 1604. Sabin 96254; Medina (BHA) 490n; Atkinson (Fr. Ren.) 445; Streit II:1363; JCB (3) II:28. NN-RB, RPJCB; BN.　　604/91

Valori, Filippo. Termini di mezzo rilievo e d'intera dottrina tra gl'archi di casa Valori in Firenze. *Florence: C. Marescotti,* 1604. 38 p.; 4to. Includes discussion of Columbus. DFo; BN.　　604/92

Veer, Gerrit de. Vraye description de trois voyages de mer tres admirables. *Amsterdam: C. Claeszoon,* M.VI'C.IIII [1604]. 44 numb. 1vs.; illus., maps; fol. 1st publ. in this version, Amsterdam, 1598; transl. from de Veer's *Waerachtighe beschryvinghe* of that year, with its refs to Cortés, Magellan, the West Indies, & Brazil. Cf. Tiele 1131n; JCB (3) II:28–29. CtY, NN-RB, RPJCB.　　604/93

Vega Carpio, Lope Félix de. La hermosura de Angelica, con otras diversas rimas. *Barcelona: J. Amello, for M. Menescal,* 1604. 482 numb. 1vs; 8vo. Includes the author's *La Dragontea,* 1st publ., Valencia, 1598; cf. 1602 edn. Sabin 98769n; Medina (BHA)

499; Palau 356331. NNC, NNH; BL, Santiago(Chile):BN.　　604/94

Vergilius, Polydorus. De rerum inventoribus libri octo . . . Accesserunt C. Plinii, Alexandri Sardi, aliorumque de eadem materia collectanea. *Geneva: J. Stoer,* 1604. 2 pts; 8vo. In pt 2, the 'collectanea', is a poem, 'Nova reperta ix. ex imaginibus Philippi Gallaei', referring to America & naming it as the source of syphilis. BN.　　604/95

Verstegen, Richard. Theatrum crudelitatum haereticorum nostri temporis. Editio seconda emendatior. *Antwerp: A. Hubert,* 1604. 95 p.; illus.; 4to. 1st publ., Antwerp, 1587. Included is an account of the martyrdom of Inácio de Azevedo & fellow Jesuits en route to Brazil. CtY, DFo, IU, MH; BL.　　604/96

Wittich, Johann, ed. Nobiliss[imo]rum ac doctiss[imo]rum Germaniae medicorum Consilia, observationes atque epistola medicae, opera . . . J. Wittichi . . . collecta. Addita est methodus componendi theriacam . . . Johannis Pontani. *Leipzig: H. Gross,* 1604. 645 p.; illus., port.; 4to. The 'LXXIII. Consilium', on syphilis, refers to treatment with a decoction of guaiacum. CtY-M, DNLM, ICJ, PPC; BL, BN.　　604/97

Wright, Thomas. The passions of the minde. *London: V. Simmes [& A. Islip], for W. Burre,* 1604. 2 pts; 4to. 1st publ., London, 1601. Sabin 26040. CSmH, CtY, DFo, MH, PU-F; BL.　　604/98

1605

Abbot, George, Abp of Canterbury. A briefe description of the whole worlde. *London: J. Browne,* 1605. 82 lvs; 4to. 1st publ., London, 1599. Cf. Sabin 21; STC 26. CSmH, NN-RB, NNH; Cambridge:UL.　　605/1

Acosta, José de, S.J. America, oder wie mans zu Teutsch nennet, die Neuwe Welt, oder West India. *Oberursel: C. Sutor,* 1605. 266 p.; fol. Bks 1 & 2 1st publ., Cologne, 1598, under title *Geographische und historische Beschreibung der Landschafft America;* transl. from

Acosta's *De natura Novi Orbis*, 1st publ., Salamanca 1588. Sabin 130; Medina (BHA) 330 (I:503); Baginsky (German Americana) 124; Streit II:1365; Palau 1995n; JCB (3) II:29. ICN, NN, RPJCB; Berlin:StB. 605/2

Alemán, Mateo. Primera parte de la vida de Guzman de Alfarache. *Barcelona: S. de Cormellas,* 1605. 207 numb. lvs; 8vo. 1st publ., Madrid, 1599; cf. 1601 edn. Laurenti (Nov. pic. esp.) 559; Palau 6697. 605/3

—[Anr edn]. *Valencia: P. P. Mey, for R. Sonzoni,* 1605. 585 p.; 8vo. Medina (BHA) 500. NNH. 605/4

——. Segunda parte de la vida de Guzman de Alfarache. *Valencia: P. P. Mey, for R. Sonzoni,* 1605. 585 p.; 8vo. 1st publ., Lisbon, 1604. Laurenti (Nov. pic. esp.) 557; Palau 6694. MB, NN-RB, NcU. 605/5

—[Anr edn]. *Barcelona: S. Cormellas,* 1605. 264 numb. lvs; 8vo. Laurenti (Nov. pic. esp.) 559a; Palau 6695. NNH; BL. 605/6

—[Anr edn]. *Barcelona: H. Anglada, for M. Manescal,* 1605. 12mo. Laurenti (Nov. pic. esp.) 558; Palau 6697n. CtY, NNH. 605/7

—[Anr edn]. *Lisbon: P. Craesbeeck,* 1605. 768 p.; 8vo. Laurenti (Nov. pic. esp.) 556; Palau 6696. BN. 605/8

—[Anr edn]. *Lisbon: A. Alvarez,* 1605. 4to. BL. 605/9

Alfonce, Jean, i.e., Jean Fonteneau, known as. Les voyages avantureux . . . Contenant les reigles et enseignemens necessaires à la bonne et seure navigation. Reveu et corrige de nouveau. *La Rochelle: Heirs of J. Haultin,* 1605. 93 p.; 8vo. 1st publ., Poitiers, [ca. 1558?]; cf. year 1602. Sabin 100834; Atkinson (Fr. Ren.) 450; Borba de Moraes I:18; Desgraves (Les Haultin) 221. Paris: Ste Geneviève, Bordeaux:BM. 605/10

Bacon, Francis, viscount St Albans. The twoo bookes . . . of the proficience and advancement of learning. *London: [T. Purfoot,] for H. Tomes,* 1605. 2 pts; 4to. In pt 2, discussing 'Invention' attributes discovery of New World to 'discovery' of compass, while the rareness of flint in the West Indies as an instrument of fire is mentioned. For variants, see Gibson. Gibson (Bacon) 81; STC 1164; Pforzheimer 36. CSmH, CtY, DLC, ICN, MH, MWA, NN-RB; BL, BN. 605/11

Bertonio, Ludovico. Arte y grammatica muy copiosa de la lengua aymara. *Rome: A. Zannetti,* 1605. 348 p.; 8vo. 1st publ., Rome, 1603. With colophon dated 1603, ostensibly a reissue of that edn. Cf. Sabin 15018; Palau 28509. 605/12

Bodin, Jean. Universae naturae theatrum. In quo rerum omnium effectrices causae, et fines contemplantur. *Hanau: Wechel Press & C. Marne,* 1605. 633 p.; 8vo. 1st publ., Lyons, 1596. In bk 2 the mountains of Peru are mentioned. CU, DNAL, IaU, PPL; BN. 605/13

Botero, Giovanni. Theatro de los mayores principes del mundo, y causas de la grandeza de sus estados, sacado de la Relaciones toscanas . . . con cinco Tratados de razon de estado . . . por f. Jayme Rebullosa. *Barcelona: S. Matevad & H. Anglada,* 1605. 287 numb. lvs; 8vo. A reissue of printers' 1604 edn? Palau 33706. BL, BN. 605/14

Breton, Nicholas. An olde mans lesson, and a young mans love. *London: [E. Allde] for E. White,* 1605. 26 lvs; 4to. The 'most dogged bird in the world' said to be the 'turkey-cock, for he beates his hen when he hath troden her.' STC 3674. CSmH, CtY, DFo, ICN MH, PU; BL, Dublin:Marsh's Libr. 605/15

——. [A poste with a packet of madde letters. The first part. *London? T. Creede? for J. Smethwicke?* 1605?]. 30 lvs; 4to. 1st publ., London, 1602. Perhaps issued with Breton's pt 2, the following item. Cf. STC 3685. DFo (lacks t.p.). 605/16

——. A poste with a packet of madde letters. The second part. *London: T. Creede, for J. Browne & J. Smethwicke,* 1605. 30 lvs; 4to. Includes refs to tobacco & 'tobacco breath'. Perhaps issued with the author's pt 1, the preceding item. Cf. STC 3686. DFo. 605/17

Calvisius, Seth. Chronologia. *Leipzig: J. Apel,* 1605. 997 p.; 4to. Under year 1492, Columbus is mentioned; 1495, syphilis, as brought from New World; 1518, Magellan; 1577, Martin Frobisher; etc. Subsequent edns have title *Opus chronologicum.* MB, ICU; BL, BN. 605/18

Camerarius, Joachim, the Younger. Symbolorum & emblematum . . . centuriae tres . . . Editio secunda, auctior & accuratior. Accessit noviter centuria. [*Leipzig:*] *Vögelin Press,* 1605. 4 pts; illus.; 4to. Though not included in our prior volume, pts 1–3 were 1st publ. at Nuremberg, 1590–96 (cf. BN Catalogue). In pt 1 emblem xlix describes & illustrates a 'Chrysanthemum peruvianum' (sunflower); pt 2, emblem lxxxiii, an armadillo; pt 3, emblem xlvii, a turkey; in pt 4, 1st publ., [Nuremberg?], 1604, text for emblem vi mentions Pigafetta & the Strait of Magellan. Nissen (Bot.) 312; Hunt (Bot.) 181. CtY, DFo, ICN, MH-A, MiDW, NNC; BL, BN. 605/19

Cayet, Pierre Victor Palma. Chronologie septenaire de l'histoire de la paix entre les roys de France et d'Espagne . . . avec le succez de plusieurs navigations faictes aux Indes Orientales, Occidentales & Septentrionales, depuis le commencement de l'an 1598. jusques à la fin de l'an 1604. *Paris: J. Richer,* 1605. 498 numb. lvs; 8vo. In this version, lf 20 is unnumbered & lf 207 misnumbered '107'. Cf. Sabin 11627; Atkinson (Fr. Ren.) 456; cf. Cioranescu (XVI) 6012. BL, BN. 605/20

—[Anr issue]. *Paris: J. Richer,* 1605. Lf 20 is numbered, & lf 207 correctly foliated, while the placing of marginal notes differs. Atkinson (Fr. Ren.) 457, describing the above as differing 'impressions'. RPJCB; BN. Undifferentiated locations: CtY, DLC, ICN, InU-L, MH, MiU-C, MnU-B, NN-RB, PPL. 605/21

—[Anr edn]. Seconde edition. *Paris: J. Richer,* 1605. 506 numb. lvs; 8vo. InU-L, MH. 605/22

Cesalpino, Andrea. Κατοπτρον; sive, Speculum artis medicae Hippocraticum. *Frankfurt a. M.: M. Becker, for L. Zetzner,* 1605. 663 p.; 8vo. 1st publ., Rome, 1602–3, under title *Artis medicae pars prima* [-II]. CtY-M, DNLM, NNNAM, PU; BN. 605/23

Chapman, George. Al fooles, a comedy. *London: [G. Eld,] for T. Thorpe,* 1605. [72] p.; 4to. Includes refs to tobacco. Some copies have reading 'comody' in title. STC 4963; Greg 219; Arents 72, CSmH, CtY, DLC, ICN, MH, NN-RB; BL. 605/24

——. Eastward Hoe. *London: [G. Eld,] for W. Aspley,* 1605. [72] p.; 4to. Drama, written jointly by Chapman, Ben Jonson, & John Marston. Of the characters two are bound as colonists to Virginia, to which numerous refs appear. STC 4970; Greg 217 (aI). London:V. & A. 605/25

—[Anr issue]. *London: [G. Eld,] for W. Aspley,* 1605. Leaves E3 & E4 are cancels, deleting ref. to the Scots & one to Virginia. STC 4971; Greg 217 (aII). CSmH, CtY, DLC, MH; Oxford:Worcester. 605/26

—[Anr edn]. *London: [G. Eld,] for W. Aspley,* 1605. 32 lvs; 4to. In prologue, line 5 has reading 'opposde'. STC 4972; Greg 217 (b). DFo, IU, MH; BL. 605/27

—[Anr edn]. *London: [G. Eld,] for W. Aspley,* 1605. 32 lvs; 4to. In prologue, line 5 has reading 'opposd'. STC 4973; Greg 217 (c). CSmH, DFo, MH, WU; London:V. & A. 605/28

Chiabrera, Gabriello. Rime. *Venice: S. Combi,* 1605. 2 pts; 12mo. In author's *Canzoni eroiche* is a poem 'Per Cristoforo Colombo'. BL, BN. 605/29

Croce, Giovanni Andrea della. Cirugia universale e perfetta. *Venice: R. Meietti,* 1605. 319 numb. lvs; illus.; fol. 1st publ., as transl. from Croce's *Chirurgiae . . . libri septem* (Venice, 1573), Venice, 1574. In bk 5, the 12th treatise (lvs 225–38) discusses syphilis, attributing to Columbus's crew its introduction into Europe. For its treatment, guaiacum & sarsaparilla are recommended. Michel (Répertoire) II:148. DNLM; London:Wellcome, BN. 605/30

Crosse, Henry. The schoole of pollicie; or The arraignement of state abuses. *London: V. Simmes, for N. Butter,* 1605. 4to. 1st publ., London, 1607, under title *Vertues commonwealth.* STC 6071. DFo; Cambridge:UL. 605/31

Dekker, Thomas. The wonderfull year. 1603. *London: T. Creede* [ca. 1605?]. [47] p.; 4to. 1st publ., London, 1603. In this edn the text of verso of lf A4 is set in italic. Cf. STC 6534. DFo; BL. 605/32

Dickenson, John. Speculum tragicum . . . Editio quarta. [*Delft: J. C. Vennecool, for*] *L. Elsevier at Leyden,* 1605. 262 p.; 8vo. 1st publ., Delft, 1601. Willems (Les Elzevier) 47; Rahir (Les Elzevier) 31. NN; BL, BN. 605/33

Doglioni, Giovanni Nicolò. Compendio historico universale di tutte le cose notabili già successe nel mondo . . . con aggiunta sino all'anno 1605. *Venice: N. Misserini,* 1605. 960 p.; port.; 4to. 1st publ., Venice, 1594; cf. 1601 edn. ICN. 605/34

Drayton, Michael. Poems. *London: [V. Simmes,] for N. Ling,* 1605. 3 pts; 8vo. In 'The legend of Matilda' appears the couplet 'With much we surffet, plenty makes us poore,/The wretched Indian spurnes the golden ore.' STC 7216; Grolier Club (Langland to Wither) 87. CSmH, CtY, DLC, IU, MH, MiU, NNPM; BL. 605/35

Du Bartas, Guillaume de Salluste, seigneur. Bartas: his devine weekes and workes translated . . . by Josuah Sylvester. *London: H. Lownes,* 1605. 715 p.; illus.; 4to. In verse. Transl. from Du Bartas's *La sepmaine & La seconde sepmaine,* 1st publ., Paris, 1578 & 1588. Included are numerous refs to the New World, with 'American' defined in the 'Index of the hardest words' at end as 'the French disease brought first from the Indies to Naples, from thence to France, &c.' For variant issues or states, see the STC & also the year 1606. STC 21649–21649a; CSmH, CtY, DLC, IU, MH, MiU, NNPM, PPRF; BL. 605/36

Duchesne, Joseph. Ad veritatem hermeticae medicinae ex Hippocratis veterúmque decretis ac therapeusi. *Frankfurt a. M.: W. Richter, for C. Neben,* 1605. 300 p.; 8vo. 1st publ., Paris, 1604. DNLM, MiU, PPC; BL, BN. 605/37

——. The practise of chymicall, and hermeticall physicke . . . translated . . . by Thomas Timme. *London: T. Creede,* 1605. [204] p.; 4to. Transl. from Duchesne's *Ad veritatem hermeticae medecinae* above. STC 7276. CSt, CtY-M, DLC, MBCo, MiU, NN-RB, PPC; BL. 605/38

Duret, Claude. Histoire admirable des plantes et herbes esmerveillables & miraculeuses en nature. *Paris: N. Buon,* 1605. 341 p.; illus.; 8vo. Numerous American plants are described & identified as such, amongst them cacao & the pineapple. Pritzel 2553; Nissen (Bot.) 571. DNLM, MH, MoSB, NIC; BL, BN. 605/39

Espinosa, Pedro, comp. Primera parte de las Flores de poetas ilustres de España. *Valladolid: L. Sánchez,* 1605. 204 (i.e., 192)

numb. lvs; 4to. Included is a 'letrilla' of Quevedo y Villegas beginning 'Poderoso cavallero es don Dinero' referring to West Indian origins. No more published. Alcocer (Valladolid) 490; Palau 82752. MH, NNH; BL, BN. 605/40

Fernel, Jean. De abditis rerum causis libri duo. *Lyons: B. Vincent,* 1605. 264 p.; 8vo. 1st publ., Paris, 1548; cf. 1601–2 edn of Fernel's *Universa medicina.* Sherrington (Fernel) 36.F20. DNLM; BN. 605/41

——. Pharmacia Jo. Fernelii, cum Guilel. Planti & Franc. Saguyeri scholiis: in usum pharmacopoeorum nunc primum edita [a K. Bauhin]. *Hanau: Wechel Press, for C. Marne & Heirs of J. Aubry,* 1605. 348 p.; 12mo. A separate printing of bk vii of section on therapeutics in Fernel's *Universa medicina,* 1st publ., Paris, 1567; cf. also Fernel's *Therapeutices universalis,* Lyons, 1571. Includes refs to Brazil (p. 181) & tacamahac, citing Monardes (p. 227). Scattered refs to Indies & Indian medicines do not specify continent involved. Sherrington (Fernel) 124.U; Wellcome I:2218. CtY-M; BL, BN. 605/42

Foreest, Jan van. Idyllia sive Heroes, et alia poemata quaedam. *[Leyden:] Plantin Office (Raphelengius)* 1605. 78 (i.e., 87) p.; 4to. Portions in Greek & Latin. Includes ref. to gold mines of Indies on p. 47. CtY; BL, BN. 605/43

France. Sovereigns, etc., 1589–1610 (Henry IV). Commissions du Roy & de monseigneur l'Admiral, au sieur de Monts, pour l'habitation és terres de Lacadie, Canada, & autres endroits en la nouvelle France. *Paris: P. Patisson,* 1605. 39 p.; 8vo. Sabin 50223 (& 14991); Harrisse (NF) 14; Wroth & Annan 5; Church 330; JCB (3) II:33. CSmH, NN-RB, RPJCB. 605/44

Gallucci, Giovanni Paolo. Coelestium corporum et rerum . . . accurata explicatio. *Venice: G. A. Somasco,* 1605. 478 p.; illus., map; 4to. 1st publ., Venice, 1588, under title *Theatri mundi et temporis;* cf. 1603 edn. BN. 605/45

Garcilaso de la Vega, el Inca. La Florida del Ynca. Historia del adelantado Hernando de Soto, governador . . . del reyno de la Florida, y de otros heroicos cavalleros españoles è Indios. *Lisbon: P. Craesbeeck,* 1605. 351 numb. lvs; 4to. Sabin 98745; Medina (BHA) 502; Streit II:1370; Palau 354790; JCB (3) II:31. CU, CtY, DLC, ICJ, InU-L, MB, MiU-C, NN-RB, PPL, RPJCB; BL, BN.   605/46

Garzoni, Tommaso. La piazza universale di tutte le professioni del mondo, nuovamente ristampata. *Venice: M. Claseri, for R. Meietti,* 1605 [colophon: 1604]. 933 p.; 4to. 1st publ., Venice, 1585; cf. 1601 edn. Michel (Répertoire) IV:25. IU, PU, RPJCB; BN.   605/47

Gómara, Francisco López de. Histoire generalle des Indes Occidentales, et terres neuves . . . Augmentée en ceste cinquiesme edition de la description de la Nouvelle Espagne. *Paris: M. Sonnius,* 1605. 485 numb. lvs; 8vo. 1st publ. as transl. by Martin Fumée from pt 1 of Gómara's *Historia general de las Indias* (1st publ., Saragossa, 1552–53) with chapts from 2nd pt, Paris, 1584. Sabin 27748; Medina (BHA) 159n (I:272); Wagner (SW) 2mm; Atkinson (Fr. Ren.) 453n; Streit II:1367; Palau 141163; JCB (3) II:32. DLC, RPJCB; Lyons: BM.   605/48

Goulart, Simon. Le sage vieillard . . . par S.G.S. *Lyons:* 1605. 12mo. Includes remark that men aged 200 years have been found in East & West Indies. Possibly a ghost; cf. 1606 edn. Jones (Goulart) 60(a).   605/49

Great Britain. Treaties, etc., 1603–1625 (James I). Articles of peace, entercourse, and commerce concluded in the names of . . . Prince James . . . and Philip the third, King of Spaine . . . Translated out of Latine. *London: R. Barker,* 1605. [38] p.; 4to. Includes refs to commerce with 'the Kingdomes and Dominions of the . . . King of Spaine', i.e., including the New World. STC 9211; Kress 261. CSmH, CtY, DLC, MH-BA, MiU-L, MnU-B, NNC-L, RPJCB; BL.   605/50

——. Articulen van het contract ende accoort ghemaeckt tusschen Jacobus den eersten . . . ende Philips den derden . . . Uut het Enghels . . . overgheset. Nae de copie. *'London: R. Barker'* [i.e., *Middelburg:* 1605]. [13] p.; 4to. (Den Nederlandtschen byecorf, no. 20). Transl. from the *Articles of peace* of this year above. Knuttel 1253; Asher

28.21. CtY, MiU-C, MnU, NN-RB, RPJCB; The Hague: KB.   605/51

——[Anr edn]. De artijcken van den peys. [*The Hague?* 1605?]. [12] p.; 4to. Knuttel 1254. The Hague: KB.   605/52

——[Anr edn]. [*The Hague?* 1605?]. [8] p.; 4to. Knuttel 1255. The Hague:KB.   605/53

Guerreiro, Fernão, S.J. Relaçam anual das cousas que fezeram os padres da Companhia de Jesus nas partes da India Oriental, & no Brasil, Angola, Cabo Verde, Guine, nos annos de seiscentos & dous & seiscentos & tres . . . tirada das cartas dos mesmo padres . . . Pelo padre Fernam Gueirreiro. *Lisbon: J. Rodríguez,* 1605. 2 pts; 8vo. Sabin 29128; Borba de Moraes I:321; Streit II:2365. DLC, InU-L, NN-RB, RPJCB; Munich: UB, Rome:BN.   605/54

Guyon, Louis, sieur de la Nauche. Les diverses leçons. *Lyons: C. Morillon,* 1605. 910 p.; 8vo. 1st publ., Lyons, 1604; here a reissue of that edn with altered imprint date? BN.   605/55

Hall, Joseph, Bp of Norwich. Mundus alter et idem . . . Authore Mercurio Britannico. *'Frankfurt a. M.: Heirs of Ascanius de Rinialme'* [i.e., *London: H. Lownes,* 1605?]. 224 p.; illus., maps; 8vo. Imaginary voyage, the prefatory 'Itineris occasio' containing refs to explorers of New World, from Columbus to Drake. In this original issue, on the engraved t.p. the top of the pedestal base has mainly vertical if slightly diagonal hatching, while the prelim. leaves have catchwords on rectos as well as versos; cf. [Hanau? 1606?] issue. The locations given below may represent either or both of these issues. Sabin 29819; STC 12685; Arents (Add.) 124; JCB (3) II:31. CSmH, CtY, DFo, ICN, MH, MiU-C, MnU-B, NN-A, RPJCB; BL, BN.   605/56

Hay, John, S.J. De rebus Japonicis, Indicis, et Peruanis epistolae recentiores. *Antwerp: M. Nuyts, the Younger,* 1605. 968 p.; 8vo. Also issued as v. 2 of G. P. Maffei's *Historiarum Indicarum libri xvi* of this year, q.v. Sabin 31016 (& 68339); Medina (BHA) 498; Streit V:58; Backer IV:165; Palau 112581; JCB (3) II:31. DLC, RPJCB; London:Wellcome.   605/57

Hulsius, Levinus, comp. Achte Schiffart, kurtze Beschreibung, was sich mit den Holländern und Seeländern in den Ost Indien . . . zugetragen. *Frankfurt a. M.: W. Richter, for L. Hulsius,* 1605. 58 p.; illus., maps; 4to. (Levinus Hulsius's *Sammlung van . . . Schiffahrten.* Pt 8). Includes brief account of Olivier van Noort's voyage along the coast of South America. Sabin 33662; Church 288; JCB (3) I:459. CSmH, MnU, NN, RPJCB; BL, BN. 605/58

Hume, Tobias. The first part of Ayres, French, Pollish, and others. *London: J. Windet,* 1605. fol. Includes earliest known song on tobacco. STC 13958; Arents (Add.) 141n. BL, Manchester:PL. 605/59

Jesuits. Letters from missions. Annuae litterae (1596) 1605. Annuae litterae . . . anni M.D.XCVI. *Naples: T. Longo,* 1605. 1063 p.; 8vo. Includes chapts on Mexican & Peruvian provinces. Streit I:279; Backer I:1325. NNH; Fulda:B. Sem. 605/60

José de Sigüenza, O.S.H. Tercera parte de la Historia de la orden de San Geronimo. *Madrid: J. Flamenco, for the Imprenta Real,* 1605. 899 p.; fol. Chapts 25–26 discuss Hieronymite missions in Spanish America. The earlier pts, publ. 1595 & 1600, are without American relevance. Medina (BHA) 508; Streit I:277; Pérez Pastor (Madrid) II:924; Palau 312930. RPJCB; BL. 605/61

Khunrath, Conrad. Medulla destillatoria et medica, tertium aucta & renovata; das ist Gründliches und vielbewehrtes Destillier und Artzney Buch. *Hamburg: Froben Office,* 1605. 628 p.; 4to. 1st publ., Schleswig, [1594]; cf. 1601 edn. DNLM, OCU; BL. 605/62

Laffémas, Barthélemy, sieur de Bauthor. Instruction du plantage des meuriers . . . avec les figures pour apprendre à nourrir les vers, faire & tirer les soyes. *Paris: D. LeClerc,* 1605. 14, 8p.; illus.; 4to. Americana in recommending mulberry leaves for feeding turkeys! BN. 605/63

Lange, Johannes (1485–1565). Epistolarum medicinalium. *Hanau: Heirs of A. Wechel, for C. Marne & Heirs of J. Aubry,* 1605. 1020 p.; port.; 8vo. 1st publ., Basel, 1554. Letter lxiii (p. 304–16) treats 'De novis Americi orbis insulis'; elsewhere discovery of guaiacum is attrib. to King Ferdinand of Castile. Wellcome I:3656. DNLM, NNNAM, PPL; BL, BN. 605/64

L'Ecluse, Charles. Exoticorum libri decem: quibus animalium, plantarum, aromatum, aliorumque peregrinorum fructurum historiae describuntur. [*Leyden:*] *Plantin Office (Raphelengius),* 1605. 3 pts; illus.; fol. Includes also extracts from G. da Orta (bks 7–8); C. da Costa (bk 9); and N. Monardes (bk 10). Included are refs to America & American plants. Pritzel 1760; Nissen (Bot.) 369; Guerra (Monardes) 35; Bibl. belg., 1st ser., XIV:L94; Arents (Add.) 65. CU, DLC, MH, MiU, MnU, NN-RB, PPC, RPB; BL, BN. 605/65

Léon, Andrés de. Practico de morbo gallico. *Valladolid: L. Sánchez,* 1605. 126 numb. lvs; 4to. Attributes appearance of syphilis in Europe to Columbus, who brought Indian men & women from Santo Domingo first to Barcelona & thence to Naples. Chapt. xlvii, on guaiacum as a remedy, describes it at length, giving as its sources Santo Domingo & Puerto Rico. Medina (BHA) 503; Alcocer (Valladolid) 494; Palau 135082. DNLM, MoU, NNNAM, RPJCB; London:Wellcome, Seville:BU. 605/66

Linschoten, Jan Huygen van. Beschrijvinghe van de gantsche Custe van Guinea . . . ende teghen over de Cabo de S. Augustijn in Brasilien . . . Noch volght de beschrijvinghe van West-Indien int langhe. *Amsterdam: C. Claeszoon,* 1605. [82] p.; map; fol. 1st publ., Amsterdam, 1596. Ostensibly issued as pt of Linschoten's *Itinerario,* of this year below (q.v.), since the present item includes an index for all 3 pts. Sabin 41360; cf. Borba de Moraes I:420; Tiele-Muller 82. 605/67

——. Itinerario, voyage ofte Schipvaert . . . naer Oost ofte Portugaels Indien. *Amsterdam: C. Claeszoon,* 1605, '04. 3 pts; illus., port., maps; fol. 1st publ., Amsterdam, 1596; here ostensibly issued with Linschoten's *Reys-gheschrift,* Amsterdam, 1604, & his *Beschrijvinghe van . . . Guinea* of this year, the latter of which includes an index for all 3 pts. The American interest of the *Itinerario* is limited to a world map showing North & South America. Sabin 41358–60; cf. Borba de Moraes I:419–20; Tiele-Muller 82; Tiele 679. NN-RB; BL.   605/68

L'Obel, Matthias de. In G. Rondelletii . . . Pharmaceuticam officinam animadversiones . . . Accesserunt auctaria, in antidotaria vulgata censurae benevolae, et dilucidae simplicium medicamentorum explicationes. *London: T. Purfoot,* 1605. 2 pts; illus.; fol. Pt 2, with title *Dilucidae simplicium medicamentorum explicationes,* is a reissue with cancel t.p. of Pierre Pena's *Stirpium adversaria nova,* 1st publ., London, 1571. Includes descriptions of American plants. Pritzel 7029n; Nissen (Bot.) 1502n; STC 19595.5 (formerly 16650); Henrey (Brit. bot.) 232; Arents 74. CSmH, DLC, MH, MiU, NN-A, RPB; BL, BN.   605/69

Madrigal, Miguel de, comp. Segunda parte del Romancero general . . . recopilados por Miguel de Madrigal. *Valladolid: L. Sánchez, for A. García,* 1605. 214 numb. 1vs; 4to. Continues the *Romancero general* 1st publ., Madrid, 1600; cf. 1602 edn. Included are scattered refs to Potosí & the Indies. Alcocer (Valladolid) 496; Palau 276984. NNH; Madrid:BN.   605/70

Maffei, Giovanni Pietro, S.J. Historiarum Indicarum libri xvi . . . Accessit liber recentiorum epistolarum a Joanne Hayo . . . nunc primum excusus. *Antwerp: M. Nuyts, the Younger,* 1605. 2 v.; 8vo. Maffei's work with accounts of Azevedo & the Brazilian martyrs 1st publ., Florence, 1588. Sabin 43773; Borba de Moraes II:10; Streit V:59; Backer V:298; JCB (3) II:32. DLC, ICU, InU-L, MH, MnU-B, PU, RPJCB; BL (v. 1), BN.   605/71

Marcos da Lisboa, O.F.M., Bp. Delle croniche de gli ordini instituti dal p.s. Francisco, parte terza . . . composta . . . in lingua portoghese. Poi ridotta nella castigliana dal r.p.f. Diego Navarro; e tradotta . . . dal sig. Horatio Diola. *Milan: G. Bordoni & P. M. Locarno,* 1605. 576 p.; 4to. 1st publ. in Italian, Venice, 1591, as transl. from Salamanca, 1570, edn. Includes chapts on Franciscans in Mexico. Streit I:279. Rome: Capuchins.   605/72

Marees, Pieter de. Description et recit histo-

rial du riche royaume d'or de Gunea. *Amsterdam: C. Claeszoon,* 1605. 99 p.; illus.; fol. Transl. from the author's *Beschryvinghe . . . v. Gunea,* 1st publ., Amsterdam, 1602. Mentions dangers of rounding tip of Brazil. Tiele 717; Tiele-Muller 135; JCB (3) II:33. CSmH, CtY, MH, NN-RB, PBL, RPJCB, WU; BL.   605/73

Mariana, Juan de, S.J. Historiae de rebus Hispaniae libri xxx. *Mainz: B. Lipp, for Heirs of A. Wechel,* 1605. 2 v.; 4to. 1st publ., Toledo, 1592. Includes chapts on Spanish West Indies. Cf. Sabin 44543; Backer V:548; Palau 151662. IaU, MH, RPJCB, WU.   605/74

Matthieu, Pierre. Histoire de France et des choses memorables, advenues aux provinces estrangeres durant sept années de paix, du regne de Henry IIII. *Paris: J. Mettayer & M. Guillemot,* 1605. 2 v.; 4to. Included are numerous scattered refs to the New World, incl. one to syphilis (1f 63v), 'verole apportee d'Amerique par Americ Vespuce pilote tres-renommé'. NIC, OCl, WU; BL, BN.   605/75

Mattioli, Pietro Andrea. Les commentaires . . . sur les six livres de Pedacius Dioscoride . . . de la matiere medecinale, traduits de latin . . . par m. Antoine du Pinet . . . et augmentez . . . tant de plusieurs remèdes . . . comme aussi de distillations et de la cognoissance des simples. *Lyons: P. Rigaud,* 1605. 606 p.; illus., port.; fol. 1st publ. as here transl. from Jean Ruel's version of Mattioli's *Commentarii,* Lyons, 1561. Includes discussion of medicinal uses of American plants. Pritzel 5991n; Nissen (Bot.) 1312n. TxU; London:Wellcome, BN.   605/76

Melich, Georg. Avertimenti nelle compositioni de' medicamenti per uso della spetiaria, con una diligente esaminatione di molti simplici. *Venice: G. Vincenti* [1605]. 2 pts; 4to. 1st publ., Venice, 1575. A 'Descrittione e facolta della pianta Nicosiana' describes tobacco as long used by the Indians of New Spain. Wellcome I:4192. London:Wellcome.   605/77

Mercado, Luis. Tomus secundus Operum. *Valladolid: L. Sánchez,* 1605. 3 pts; fol. Included are Mercado's *Libri duo. De communi et peculiari praesidiorum artis medicae indicatione,*

1st publ., Valladolid, 1574, with description of therapeutic uses of tobacco; & also section on 'Morbi Gallici naturam et curationem', describing New World origins of syphilis & prescribing guaiacum & sarsaparilla for its treatment. Palau 164991.

605/78

Merula, Paulus. Cosmographiae generalis libri tres. Item geographiae particularis libri quatuor. [*Leyden:*] *Plantin Office (Raphelengius); sold by C. Claeszoon, at Amsterdam, 1605.* 1358 p.; maps; 4to. Scattered American refs include mention of Peru, Strait of Magellan, toucan, & 'Pica Brasilica'. Tiele 751; Maggs Cat. 465 (Americana IV):2684. DLC, InU, NN-RB; BL, BN. 605/79

Meteren, Emanuel van. Belgische ofte Nederlantsche historie van onsen tijden . . . tot . . . den uutgaenden jare 1598 . . . eensdeels int Latijn ende Hoochduytsch stuckwijs in druck uutghegaen, maer nu . . . verbetert en vermeerdert uutghegheven. *Delft: J. C. Vennecool,* 1605. 382 numb. 1vs; illus., ports, map; fol. 1st publ. in Dutch, Delft, 1599. Includes scattered American refs. MH; Amsterdam:NHSM. 605/80

——. Historia, oder Eigentliche und warhaffte Beschreibung aller fürnehmen Kriegshändel. *Arnhem: J. Janszoon,* 1605. 2 pts; fol. 1st publ. in German, Hamburg, 1596; cf. year 1601. Bruckner 4. WU; Oxford:Bodl. 605/81

Neck, Jacob Corneliszoon van. Ander Schiffart in die Orientalische Indien, so die holländische Schiff . . . verrichtet . . . Editio secunda. *Frankfurt a. M.: L. Hulsius,* 1605. 118 p.; illus., maps; 4to. (Levinus Hulsius's *Sammlung von . . . Schiffahrten.* Pt 2). 1st publ. in this version, Frankfurt a. M., 1602. Sabin 33654; Church 263; JCB (3) I:452. CSmH, MnU-B, NN-RB, RPJCB; BL. 605/82

Núñez, Pedro. Advertencias de Pedro Nuñez, satisfaziendo a las dificultades de su arbitrio puestas por los señores del Consejo de hazienda. [*Valladolid?* 1605]. [4] p.; fol. Subscribed at end: Valladolid y Julio. 7. de 1605. Memorial to king of Spain designed 'perpetuar las minas de plata y oro, y facilitar sus beneficios y labor, assi en las del Piru, como de la Nueva España, y sus

provincias, y en España'. Supplements memorial of 12 March below. Palau 196874n. MH-BA; BL. 605/83

——. Excellencias y calidades del arbitrio de Pedro Nuñez. [*Valladolid?* 1605]. bds.; fol. Relates to other memorials by Núñez of this year. Subscribed at end: Valladolid y de Julio. 27. de 1605. Cf. Palau 196874. BL.

605/84

——. Señor. Pedro Nuñez, vezino de la ciudad de Sevilla. [*Valladolid?* 1605]. [4] p.; fol. Memorial to king of Spain on working of mines of Spanish Indies. Subscribed at end: Valladolid, 12 March 1605. Palau 196874. BL. 605/85

Oña, Pedro de. Arauco domado. *Madrid: J. de la Cuesta, for F. López,* 1605. 342 numb. lvs; 8vo. 1st publ., Lima, Peru, 1596. A continuation in verse of Ercilla y Zúñiga's *La Araucana* on the conquest & settlement of Chile. Sabin 57301; Medina (Chile) 27; Pérez Pastor (Madrid) 913; Palau 201617. MH, NN-RB, RPJCB; BL, Madrid:BN. 605/86

Orta, Garcia da. Dell'historia de i semplici. Et altre cose che vengono portate dall'Indie Orientali pertinenti all'uso della medicina . . . Et due altri libri parimente di quelle cose che si portano dall'Indie Occidentali . . . Di Nicolò Monardes . . . Hora tradotti . . . da m. Annibale Briganti. *Venice: Heirs of G. Scoto,* 1605. 525 p.; illus.; 8vo. 1st publ. in Italian, Venice, 1576. Sabin 57670; Guerra (Monardes) 36; Michel (Répertoire) VI:41; Palau 99522. DNLM, MH-A, MiU, NNBG; Paris:Sorbonne. 605/87

Paracelsus. Chirurgische Bücher und Schrifften . . . an tag geben . . . Durch Johannem Huserum. *Strassburg: L. Zetzner,* 1605. 2 pts; fol. 1st publ. as here constituted, [Basel], 1589–90; cf. 1603 edn. Sudhoff (Paracelsus) 267; Wellcome I:4811. CtY, DNLM, ICU, PPPH; BL, Munich:StB. 605/88

Pena, Pierre. Dilucidae simplicium medicamentorum explicationes, & stirpium adversaria . . . authoribus Petro Pena & Matthia de L'Obel. *London: T. Purfoot,* 1605. In L'Obel, Matthias, *In G. Rondelletii . . . Pharmaceuticam officinam animadversiones* of this year, q.v.

Pisa, Francisco de. Descripcion de la imperial ciudad de Toledo . . . Primera parte. *Toledo: P. Rodríguez, 1605.* 277 numb. lvs; fol. Includes material on the impact of the discovery of the New World. No more published. Pérez Pastor (Toledo) 456; Palau 227400. CU, ICN, NNH; BL.　　605/89

Porcacchi, Tommaso. L'isole piu famose del mondo descritte da Thomaso Porcacchi . . . e intagliate da Girolamo Porro. *Venice: Heirs of S. Galignani, 1605.* 211 p.; illus., maps; fol. 1st publ., Venice, 1572; cf. 1603 edn above. Cf. Sabin 64151; Michel (Répertoire) VI:141. BN.　　605/90

Ptolemaeus, Claudius. Geographiae libri octo graeco-latini . . . recogniti & emendati, cum tabulis geographicis . . . restitutis per Gerardum Mercatorem . . . à Petro Montano iterum recogniti. *Amsterdam: [J. Theuniszoon?] for C. Claeszoon & J. Hondius, 1605.* 215 p.; maps; fol. 1st publ. as ed. & suppl. by Magini, Venice, 1596, but here with Greek text added. For variant forms of the imprint, see Sabin & Koeman. Sabin 66494; Stevens (Ptolemy) 57; Koeman (Me) 3; Phillips (Atlases) 421; JCB (3) II:35. CSmH, CtY, DLC, ICN, InU-L, MH, MiU-C,MnU-B,NN-RB,PU,RPJCB;London: Wellcome (imp.), Paris:Inst. de France.　　605/91

Rabelais, François. Oeuvres . . . contenant cinq livres de la vie, faits, & dits heroiques de Gargantua, & de son fils Pantagruel. *Antwerp: J. Fuet, 1605.* 3 pts; 12mo. Includes 'Le quart livre', 1st publ., Paris, 1552, describing a voyage perhaps inspired by that of Jacques Cartier, & interpreted as a search for a Northwest Passage. For the numerous edns of this work publ. after 1600, see Plan (Rabelais). Plan (Rabelais) 120. MH, MiU, NNC, RPB; BL, BN.　　605/92

Raleigh, Sir Walter. Warachtighe ende grondighe beschryvinghe van . . . Guiana . . . ende den vermaerden zeevaerder Capiteyn Laurens Keymis. *Amsterdam: C. Claeszoon, 1605.* 47 numb. lvs; obl. 4to. 1st publ. in Dutch, Amsterdam, 1598; transl. from Raleigh's *Discovery of . . . Guiana,* 1st publ., London, 1596. Includes, with special t.p., Lawrence Kemys's *Waerachtighe ende grondighe beschryvinghe vande tweede zeevaert . . . nae Guiana,* 1st publ. (in English) London, 1596. Sabin 67596 & 37689 (Keymis);

Tiele-Muller 286, Shaaber (Brit. auth.) R17. NN-RB; BL, Amsterdam:NHSM.　　605/93

Ribera, Juan de, S.J. Lettera annua della v. provincia delle Filippine dal giugno del 1602. al seguente giugno 1603. *Rome: L. Zannetti, 1605.* 84 p.; 12mo. The Jesuit author was Mexican born. Streit V:696; Backer VI:1767–68; Palau 266940. Rome:BN.　　605/94

——[Anr edn]. *Venice: G. B. Ciotti, 1605.* 69 p.; 12mo. Streit V:697; Backer VI:1767–68; Palau 266941. NN-RB, NNH, RPJCB; Göttingen:WB.　　605/95

——. Lettre annuelle de la province de Philippines. Du mois de juin 1602, jusques au mesme moi 1603. *Paris: Widow of G. de La Noue, 1605.* 103 p.; 12mo. Transl. from the Italian text above. Streit V:698; Backer VI:1767; Palau 266942.　　605/96

Rivadeneira, Pedro de, S.J. Las obras . . . agora de nuevo revistas y acrecentas. *Madrid: L. Sánchez, 1605.* 3 v.; port.; fol. 1st publ. in collective form, Madrid, 1595. Included in v. 1 are the author's lives of Ignatius Loyola & Francisco Borgia, with refs to Jesuit missions in New World, and in v. 3, the author's 'Libro de las virtudes del principe christiano' 1st publ., Madrid, 1595, with title *Tratado de la religion.* Sabin 70779; Backer VI:1736; Pérez Pastor (Madrid) 919; Palau 266196. BN.　　605/97

Roelofsz, Roelof. Zwo underschiedliche newe Schiffarten aus niederländischer Verzeichnus in hochteutscher Sprache beschrieben durch m. Gotthardt Artus. *Frankfurt a. M.: W. Richter, 1605.* 135 p.; illus.; 4to. The original Dutch text has not been traced. Includes Roelofsz's *Historische Beschreibung der Reyse, so der Admiral Jacob von Neck . . . gethan,* mentioning attempt to cure scurvy through use of tobacco. InU-L, NN-RB; BL.　　605/98

Rosier, James. A true relation of the most prosperous voyage made this present yeere 1605, by Captaine George Waymouth, in the discovery of the land of Virginia. *London: [Eliot's Court Press,] for G. Bishop, 1605.* [39] p.; 4to. Describes coast of Maine, rather than present-day Virginia. Sabin 73288; Vail (Frontier) 11; STC 21322; Arents 3273; Church 331; JCB (3) II:35.

CSmH, CtY, DFo, ICN, MiU-C, NN-RB, PP, RPJCB; BL.   605/99

Rowlands, Samuel. Humors antique faces. *London: [E. Allde,] for H. Rocket,* 1605. [31] p.; 4to. In verse. Epigram on lf B4v describes slavery to tobacco; that on lf C3r is on tobacco. STC 21385 (formerly 17133); Arents (Add.) 125. CSmH, DFo; Manchester:UL.   605/100

——. Humors ordinarie. *London: W. Ferbrand* [1605?]. 4to. 1st publ., London, 1600, under title *The letting of humors blood.* In verse. Contains adverse comments on tobacco. STC 21394. CSmH; BL.   605/101

Rubio, Antonio. Logica mexicana, sive Commentarii in universam Aristotelis Logicam. *Cologne: A. Mylius (House of Birckmann),* 1605. 2 v.; 4to. Written while author was resident in Mexico. Sabin 73860; Medina (BHA) 505; Backer VII:280; Palau 280352. IU; BL, BN.   605/102

Sande, Johan van den. Trouhertighe vermaninghe aen het vereenichde Nederlandt. *[Amsterdam? D. C. Troost?]* 1605. [21] p.; 4to. Mentioned are the Indies & Brazil. Foreword signed 'Ireneus Ammonius.' Knuttel 1300. MnU-B; BL (Ammonius), The Hague:KB.   605/103

—[Anr edn]. *[Amsterdam?]* 1605. 40 p.; 4to. Knuttel 1301. The Hague:KB.   605/104

—[Anr edn]. *[Amsterdam?]* 1605. 64 p.; 4to. Knuttel 1302. The Hague:KB.   605/105

Sandys, Sir Edwin. A relation of the state of religion. *London: V. Simmes, for S. Waterson,* 1605. 175 p.; 4to. In addition to mention of wealth of Spanish Indies, ref. is made (lf Q1r) to decline of Spain's manhood by war & migration to colonies. For reasons for assigning priority to this edn (publ. without author's consent), see James Ellison, 'The order of editions of Sir Edwin Sandys's Relation of the state of religion (1605)', *The Library,* 6th ser., II (1980), 208–11. For a piracy of this work, dated 1605, see the year 1622. STC 21717. CSmH, CtY, DFo, MH, NIC; BL.   605/106

—[Anr edn]. *London: [G. & L. Snowdon,] for S. Waterson,* 1605. 179 p.; 4to. STC 21716. DLC, MnU-B; BL.   605/107

Serres, Olivier de, seigneur du Pradel. Le theatre d'agriculture . . . Troisiesme edition, reveuë et augmentee par l'auteur.

Paris: A. Saugrain, 1605. 997 p.; illus.; 4to. 1st publ., Paris, 1600; cf. 1603 edn. BN.   605/108

Silvaticus, Joannes Baptista. De unicornu, lapide bezaar, smaragdo, & margaritis. *Bergamo: C. Ventura,* 1605. 160 p.; 4to. America is described as new source of bezoar stones, 'praesertim ad regionem Peru in qua abondant magis lapides isti'. Citing José de Acosta, emeralds of New World are mentioned, as are pearls, citing both Acosta & Vespucci. CtY, MH-Z; BL, BN.   605/109

Spain. Sovereigns, etc., 1598–1621 (Philip III). La orden e instruccion que su Magestad manda dar, para los quatro secretarios de las Indias, y el escrivano de camara de justicia dellas. *[Madrid? 1605?].* 4 numb. lvs; fol. Decree of 31 Dec. 1604. BL.   605/110

Spilbergen, Joris van. Het journael. *Delft: F. Balthasar,* 1605. 69 p.; illus., ports, maps; obl. 4to. 1st publ., Delft, 1601. Tiele-Muller 139; Tiele 1019. DLC; BL.   605/111

—[Anr edn]. *Delft: F. Balthasar,* 1605. 71 p.; illus., ports, maps; obl. 4to. Tiele-Muller 140; Tiele 1019n.   605/112

—[Anr edn]. t Historiael journael van tghene ghepasseert is van weghen drie schepen. *Delft: F. Balthasar,* 1605. 72 p.; illus., ports, maps; obl. 4to. Muller (1872) 2253; Tiele-Muller 141; Tiele 1020. NN-RB.   605/113

——. Siebender Theil der Orientalischen Indien . . . aus niderländischer . . . Spraach beschrieben durch M. Gothardt Arthus. *Frankfurt a. M.: M. Becker,* 1605. 2 pts; illus., maps; fol. (J. T. de Bry's *India Orientalis.* Pt 7. German). Spilbergen's voyage, transl. from *t'Historiael journael,* 1st publ., Delft, 1601. Church 237. CSmH, NN-RB.   605/114

—[Anr issue]. *Frankfurt a. M.: M. Becker,* 1605. Dedication omitted. Church 238; JCB (3) I:436. CSmH, DLC, IU, MBAt, NN-RB, RPJCB; BL, BN.   605/115

—[Anr edn]. Newe Schifffahrt einen dreyjährigen Reyse. *Frankfurt a. M.: M. Becker,* 1605. 78 p.; illus., maps; 4to. Church 237n; JCB (3) II:36. CSmH, InU-L, NN-RB, RPJCB.   605/116

Spinelli, Giovanni Paolo. Lectiones aureae

in omni quod pertinet ad artem pharmaco-poeam lucubratae. *Bari: G. C. Ventura*, 1605. 295 p.; illus.; 4to. Includes refs to guaiacum & sarsaparilla. BL.   605/117

Staden, Hans. Americae tertia pars memora-bilem provinciae Brasiliae historiam conti-nens, germanico primum sermone scriptam . . . nunc autem latinitate donatam à Teu-crio Annaeo Privato . . . Addita est Narra-tio profectionis Joannis Lerij in eandem provinciam, quam ille initio gallicè cons-cripsit . . . His accessit Descriptio morum & ferocitatis incolarum illius regionis. *Frankfurt a. M.: M. Becker, for T. de Bry*, 1605. 296 p.; illus., map; fol. (Theodor de Bry's *America*. Pt 3. Latin). 1st publ. in this ver-sion, Frankfurt a. M., 1592. Staden's work 1st publ., Marburg, 1557; that of Léry, La Rochelle, 1578; and the 'Descriptio', by Nicolas Barré, Paris, 1558. For variant issue see Church 151. Cf. Sabin 8784; Church 150; JCB (3) I:390. CSmH, DFo, ICN, NN, RPJCB; BL, BN.   605/118

Stow, John. The annales of England . . . Untill . . . 1605. *London: [Eliot's Court Press & F. Kingston, for]* G. Bishop & T. Adams [1605]. [1410] p.; 4to. 1st publ. with Ameri-can refs, London, 1592; cf. [1601] edn, of which this is a reissue with additions & can-cel t.p. STC 23337. CSmH, CtY, DLC (imp.), IU; BL.   605/119

Torres, Marcos de. El licenciado Marcos de Torres . . . contra Doña Francisca Colon y consortes. [*Madrid?* ca. 1605?]. 16 numb. lvs; fol. On rights of Columbus's descen-dants to revenues from Panama & other Spanish colonies in America. MH.
605/120

Veer, Gerrit de. Waerachtighe beschry-vinghe van drie seylagien. *Amsterdam: C. Claeszoon*, 1605. 61 numb. lvs; illus., maps; obl. 4to. 1st publ., Amsterdam, 1598; in-cludes refs to Cortés, Magellan, Brazil, the West Indies, etc. Muller (1872) 2076; Tiele-Muller 98; Tiele 1129n; JCB (3) II:36. NN-RB, RPJCB; BL.   605/121

Vega Carpio, Lope Félix de. Arcadia, prosas y versos. *Madrid: J. de la Cuesta, for J. de Mon-toya*, 1605. 312 numb. lvs; port.; 8vo. 1st publ., Madrid, 1598; cf. 1602 edns. Pérez Pastor (Madrid) 928; Palau 356296. BL, BN.   605/122

—[Anr edn]. *Antwerp: M. Nuyts*, 1605. 471 p.; 12mo. Peeters-Fontainas (Impr.esp.) 1342; Palau 356297. MH, NNH; BN, Madrid:BN.
605/123

——. La hermosura de Angelica, con otras diversas rimas. *Madrid: J. de la Cuesta*, 1605. 376 numb. lvs; 8vo. Includes the author's *La Dragontea*, 1st publ. Valencia, 1598; cf. 1602 edn. Sabin 98769n; Medina (BHA) 512; Pérez Pastor (Madrid) 929; Palau 356332. DFo, MH, PU; BL.   605/124

Wecker, Johann Jakob. Ein nutzliches Büchlein von mancherleyen künstlichen Wassern, Ölen unnd Weinen. *Basel: C. Waldkirch*, 1605. 86 p.; 8vo. Transl. from Wecker's *Antidotarium generale*, 1st publ., Ba-sel, 1576; cf. 1601 edn. Wellcome I:6705. CtU, DNLM; London:Wellcome. 605/125

Wirsung, Christoph. Medecyn boec . . . ende nu uut de vierde editie . . . overghe-sedt, door d. Carolum Battum . . . De vierde verbeterde druck. *Dordrecht: P. Verha-gen, & A. Canin*, 1605. 676 p.; fol. Transl. from Wirsung's *New Artzney Buch*, 1st publ., Heidelberg, 1568; cf. following entry. DNLM.   605/126

——. Ein new Artzney Buch. *Oberursel: C. Sutor*, 1605. 2 pts; fol. 1st publ., Heidelberg, 1568. Source of syphilis attributed to West Indies, & guaiacum specified for its treatment. Wellcome I:6757. DNLM; London:Well-come.   605/127

——. Praxis medicinae universalis; or A gene-rall practice of physicke . . . translated into English . . . by Jacob Mosan. *London: [R. Field,] for G. Bishop*, 1605. 790 p.; fol. 1st publ. as here transl. from Wirsung's *Artzney Buch* (Heidelberg, 1568), London, 1598; cf. preceding entry. STC 25864; Wellcome I:6759. CSmH, DFo, IU, MBCo, WU; BL.
605/128

Wytfliet, Corneille. Histoire universelle des Indes, Orientales et Occidentales. Divisée en deux livres, le premier par Corneille Wytfliet: le second par Ant. M[agini]. & au-tres historiens. *Douai: [J. Bogard, for] F. Fa-bri*, 1605. 2 pts; illus., maps; fol. The 1st pt is extracted & transl. from the author's *Descriptionis Ptolemaicae augmentum*, 1st publ., Louvain, 1597. Pt 2, with its mention of Cabral's discovery of Brazil, may owe some-thing to Magini's commentaries on Ptolemy's *Geographiae . . . libri octo* (1st publ., Venice, 1596), but the full range of sources here used awaits exploration. Sabin 105699; Borba de Moraes II:381; Atkinson (Fr. Ren.) 459; Streit V:63; Phillips (Atlases) 1143; JCB (3) II:36. CSmH, CtY, DLC, MnU-B, NN-RB, RPJCB; BL, BN.

605/129

1606

Acosta, José de, S.J. Histoire naturelle et moralle des Indes, tant Orientalles qu'Occidentalles . . . Composée en castillan . . . & traduite . . . par Robert Regnault . . . Derniere edition, reveuë & corrigée de nouveau. *Paris: M. Orry,* 1606. 352 numb. lvs; 8vo. 1st publ., Paris, 1598; transl. from Acosta's *Historia natural y moral de las Indias,* 1st publ., Seville, 1590. Sabin 125; Medina (BHA) 330n (I:501); Streit II:1374; Atkinson (Fr. Ren.) 465; Arents 51-b; JCB (3) II:37. DLC, MH, NNH, PU, RPJCB; BL, BN.

606/1

Alemán, Mateo. Vita del picaro Gusmano d'Alfarace . . . tradotta dalla lingua spagnuola . . . da Barezzo Barezzi. *Venice: B. Barezzi,* 1606. 454 p.; 8vo. 1st publ. in Spanish, Madrid, 1599; cf. 1601 edn. Contains 1st pt only; for translation of pt 2, see the year 1615. Laurenti (Nov. pic. esp.) 709; Palau 6776. OU; BN. 606/2

Alfaro, Francisco de. Tractatus de officio fiscalis. *Valladolid: L. Sánchez,* 1606. 362 p.; fol. The author, fiscal procurator in Peru, sets forth legal principles of his office, with scattered refs to the Indies. Medina (BHA) 514; Alcocer (Valladolid) 514: Palau 6983. RPJCB; Salamanca:BU, Santiago, Chile:BN.

606/3

Alonso y de los Ruyses de Fontecha, Juan. Diez previlegios para mugeres preñadas . . . Con un diccionario medico [de los nombres de piedras, plantas, fructos, yervas, flores, enfermedades, causas y accidentes]. *Alcalá de Henares: L. M. Grande,* 1606. 2 pts; 4to. The dictionary includes entries & descriptions for guaiacum, mechoacan, sassafras, etc. Palau 8542. DNLM, MiU, MnU, NNH, PU; BL.

606/4

The araignement and execution of the late traytors. *London: [J. Windet,] for J. Chorlton,* 1606. [30] p.; 4to. Describes Guy Fawkes & his fellow conspirators in the Gunpowder Plot as 'taking Tabacco' in quantities 'out of measure'. Signed at end: T.W. STC 24916 (& also formerly 784); Arents (Add.) 128. CtY, DFo, NN-A; BL (W., T.).

606/5

—[Anr issue with t.p. reset]. A true report of the imprisonment, the arraignement, and execution of the late traytors. *London: [J. Windet,] for J. Chorlton,* 1606. STC 24916.3. DFo; Sutton Coldfield: St Mary's Seminary.

606/6

Benzoni, Girolamo. Chronicon, das ist: Beschreibung der occidentalischen und indianischen Ländern . . . aus dem Latein ins Deutsche gebracht. *Wittenberg: Widow of Z. Lehmann, for C. Berger,* 1606. 527 p.; 4to. Transl. from Benzoni's *Historia Indiae Occidentalis,* Geneva, 1586, 1st publ., Venice, 1565, under title *Historia del Mondo Nuovo.* Sabin 12959; Medina (BHA) 250 (I:420); Palmer 290; Palau 27637; Streit II:1375; JCB (3) II:38. RPJCB; Berlin:StB.

606/7

Bertius, Petrus. Tabularum geographicarum contractarum libri quinque, cum luculentis singularum tabularum explicationibus. Editio tertia. *Amsterdam: C. Claeszoon,* 1606. 679 p.; maps; obl. 8vo. 1st publ., Amsterdam, 1600; cf. year 1602. Cf. Sabin 5014; Koeman (Lan) 7; Phillips (Atlases) 3409. DLC, ICN, MiU-C, NNH, PBL; BL, BN. 606/8

Blundeville, Thomas. M. Blundeville his Exercises . . . Third edition. *London: J. Windet,* 1606,'05. 392 numb. lvs; illus., map; 4to. 1st publ., London, 1594. Also included is John Blagrave's *A very brief . . . description of Master Blagrave his Astrolabe,* 1st publ., London, 1585, under title *The mathematical jewel.* Both contain scattered refs to the Americas, incl. guaiacum. Cf. Sabin 6023; STC 3148. DFo, MH, MnU-B, NN-RB; BL.

606/9

Bodin, Jean. Of the lawes and customes of a commonwealth . . . Out of the French and Latine copies . . . by Richard Knolles. *London: A. Islip, for G. Bishop,* 1606. 794 p.; fol. 1st publ. in French, Paris, 1576; in

Latin, Paris, 1586; cf. 1601 edn above.
CSmH, CtY, DLC, ICN, MH, MiU-C, NNC;
BL.   606/10

Botero, Giovanni. Aggiunte fatte . . . alla
sua Ragion di stato . . . Con una relatione
del mare. *Venice: N. Misserini,* 1606. 182 p.;
8vo. Here issued as pt 2 of Botero's *Della
ragion* below.   606/11

——. Della ragion di stato libri dieci. *Venice:
N. Miserini,* 1606. 2 pts; 8vo. 1st publ., Venice, 1589; cf. 1601 edn above. Pt 2, the *Aggiunte,* 1st publ., Rome, 1598, with refs to
New World. Michel (Répertoire) I:201. IU
(pt 2), RPB: BL, Paris:Arsenal.   606/12

——. Macht, Reichthum und Einkommen aller Keyser, Könige und fürnembsten Fur-
sten der gantzen Welt. *Cologne: W.
Lützenkirchen,* 1606. 119 p.; 4to. Extracted
& transl. by Mathias Quad from Botero's
Relationi universali, 1st publ., Rome, 1591–
95. RPJCB.   606/13

——. A treatise, concerning the causes of the
magnificencie and greatness of cities . . .
done into English by Robert Peterson. *London: T[homas]. P[urfoot]. for R. Ockould & H.
Tomes,* 1606. 108 p.; 4to. 1st publ. in Italian,
Rome, 1588, under title *Delle cause della grandezza delle città.* Contains numerous refs to
cities, rivers, & wealth of New World, incl.
Canada, Brazil, & Peru. STC 3405. CSmH,
DLC, ICU, MH, NN-RB; BL.   606/14

Bourne, William. [A regiment for the sea.
London: E. Weaver, 1606?]. Mentioned by
Anthony Linton in his *Newes of the complement
of the arte of navigation* (London, 1609), and
entered to Weaver in the Stationers' Register on 6 May 1605 & 2 March 1607. Cf.
1601 edn. Taylor (Regiment) 454.
                                       606/15

Breton, Nicholas. A poste with a packet of
madde letters. The second part. *London: R.
B[lower?]., for J. Browne & J. Smethwicke,* 1606.
4to. 1st publ., London, 1605. STC 3686.
CSmH.   606/16

Bry, Johann Theodor de. Achter Theil der
Orientalischen Indien. *Frankfurt a. M: W.
Richter,* 1606. 2 pts; illus.; fol. (J. T. de Bry's
India Orientalis. Pt 8. German). Includes R.
Roelofsz's *Historische Beschreibung der Schif-
fart, so der Admiral Jacob von Neck . . . gethan,*
1st publ., Frankfurt a. M., 1605, in *Zwo un-
derschiedliche newe Schiffarten.* The ref. to to-

bacco appears here on p. 2. Cf. Tiele, p.
162–66; Church 239; JCB (3) I:437–38.
CSmH, CtY, DLC, IU, MBAt, NN-RB,
RPJCB; BL, BN.   606/17

Calestani, Girolamo. Delle osservationi . . .
parte prima[-seconda]. *Venice: A. Angelieri,*
1606. 2 v.; 4to. 1st publ., Venice, 1564.
Medicinal uses of guaiacum & sarsaparilla
are described. DNLM.   606/18

Camerarius, Philipp. Operae horarum subcisivarum, sive Meditationes historicae . . .
Centuria et editio correctior, atque auctior
altera. *Frankfurt a. M.: J. Saur, for P. Kopff,*
1506 [i.e., 1606]. 391 p.; 4to. 1st publ., in
modified form, Frankfurt a. M., 1601. Ind.
aur. 130.591; Faber du Faur 1239. CtY,
ICU, MnU-B; BL, BN.   606/19

Capivaccio, Girolamo. Opera omnia. *Venice:
The Sessas,* 1606. 910 p.; fol. Includes the
author's *De lue venerea acroaseis,* 1st publ.,
Speyer, 1590; cf. 1603 edn. London:Well-
come.   606/20

Cayet, Pierre Victor Palma. Chronologie
septenaire de l'histoire de la paix entre les
roys de France et d'Espagne . . . avec le
succez de plusieurs navigations faictes aux
Indes Orientales, Occidentales & Septentrionales, depuis le commencement de l'an
1598. jusques à la fin de l'an 1604 . . . Seconde edition. *Paris: J. Richer,* 1606. 506
numb. lvs; illus.; 8vo. 1st publ., Paris, 1605.
A reissue of the 'Seconde edition' of 1605,
with altered imprint date? Cf. Sabin 11627;
Atkinson (Fr. Ren.) 473; Lande 113. BL.
                                       606/21

Cesalpino, Andrea. Praxis universae artis
medicae. *Treviso: R. Meietti, for E. Deuchino,*
1606. 715 p.; 8vo. 1st publ., Rome, 1602–
3, under title *Artis medicae pars prima [-II].*
CtY-M, DNLM, InU, MH-A, NNNAM; Lon-
don:Wellcome.   606/22

Chapman, George. Monsieur d'Olive. A comedie. *London: T. C[reede]., for W. Holmes,*
1606. [63] p.; 4to. Includes long passage
on tobacco. In this issue title statement is
in 8 lines. STC 4983; Greg 236; Arents 75.
CSmH, CtY, DFo, IU, MH, MiU, NN-RB;
BL.   606/23

—[Anr issue]. *London: T. C[reede]., for W.
Holmes,* 1606. Title statement comprises 7
lines. STC 4984; Greg 236. CSmH, DLC,
ICN; London:Dyce.   606/24

Chappuys, Gabriel. Histoire de nostre temps. Soubs les regnes de roys . . . Henry III . . . & Henry IIII. *Paris: G. Chaudière,* 1606. 335 numb. lvs; 8vo. In chapt. x the 1595 arrival of the Spanish silver fleet is mentioned; in chapt. xii, also covering year 1595, the defeat of British ships in the Caribbean under Drake & Hawkins is described at length. ICN; BL. 606/25

Chiabrera, Gabriello. Delle poesie . . . Parte seconda. *Genoa: G. Pavoni,* 1606. 159 p.; 8vo. 1st (?) publ., Venice, 1605, in author's *Rime.* 'Per Cristoforo Colombo': p. 125–27. MH. 606/26

Chytraeus, Nathan. Variorum in Europa itinerum deliciae . . . Editio tertia. [*Herborn:*] *C. Corvinus,* 1606. 655 p.; 8vo. 1st publ., Herborn, 1594. Includes legends of Sebastian Cabot's map of New World, 1st publ., [Antwerp? ca. 1544?] as *Declaratio chartae novae.* Sabin 13037n; Winship (Cabot) 75; JCB (3) II:38. ICN, MH, NN-RB, PPL, RPJCB; BL, BN. 606/27

Clavius, Christoph. In sphaeram Joannis de Sacro Bosco commentarius, nunc quinto ab ipso auctore . . . recognitus, *Rome: A. Zannetti, for G. P. Gelli,* 1606. 669 p.; 4to. 1st publ., Rome, 1570; cf. 1601 edn. Shaaber (Brit. auth.) H440. MB, NcD; BL. 606/28

Colonna, Fabio. Minus cognitarum stirpium aliquot. *Rome: G. Facciotti,* 1606. 2 pts; illus.; 4to. Includes comments on origins & use of tobacco, as well as on the 'aloe americanus'. Pritzel 1823n; Nissen (Bot.) 385. MH, NN-RB; BL, BN. 606/29

The copy of a letter . . . written by E. D. doctour of physicke. *London: M. Bradwood,* 1606. 27 lvs; 4to. Discusses medical use of tobacco. STC 6164; Arents 76-A. CSmH, NN-A; BL. 606/30

Cordus, Valerius. Dispensatorium, sive Pharmacorum conficiendorum ratio. *Lyons: J. A. Huguetan,* 1606. 468 p.; illus.; 8vo. 1st publ., Nuremberg, 1546. Includes ref. to American opobalsam. DNLM. 606/31

Crespin, Jean. Gross Martyrbuch und Kirchen-Historien . . . Anfänglich in frantzösischer Spraach beschrieben . . . jetzund aber . . . übergesetzt . . . durch Paulum Crocium. *Hanau: W. Antonius,* 1606. 1721 p.; fol. Transl. from Crespin's *Histoire des Martyrs,* 1st publ. with American material, Geneva, 1564. Includes section on Villegagnon's attempted Brazilian settlement, transl. from the anon. *Histoire des choses memorables advenues en . . . Bresil,* 1st publ., [Geneva], 1561. Cf. Borba de Moraes I:199; Jones (Goulart) 23(c); cf. JCB (3) II:117. NIC, NNUT, PU; Geneva:BP. 606/32

Daniel, Samuel. The queenes arcadia. A pastorall trage-comedie. *London: G. Eld, for S. Waterson,* 1606. [78] p.; 4to. In verse. Contains passage on tobacco. STC 6262; Greg 227(a); Arents 76. CSmH, DFo, MH, NN-A; BL. 606/33

Dekker, Thomas. Newes from hell; brought by the divells carrier. *London: R. B[radock]., for W. Ferbrand,* 1606. 4to. Included are refs to the Indies, Virginia, Peru, etc. For a subsequent version, see Dekker's *A knights conjuring* of 1607. STC 6514. CSmH; BL. 606/34

Del Rio, Martin Anton, S.J. Disquisitionum magicarum libri sex . . . Nunc secundis curis auctior. *Venice: G. A. & J. de Francisci,* 1606. 3 v.; 4to. 1st publ., Louvain, 1599–1600; cf. 1603 edn. Backer II:1898. ICU; London:Wellcome. 606/35

—[Anr edn]. Nunc tertiis curis auctior. *Mainz: J. König,* 1606. 3 v.; 8vo. Backer II:1898–99. DLC, MH, MiU, NNC; BN. 606/36

Doglioni, Giovanni Nicolò. Del theatro universale de' prencipi e di tutte l'historie del mondo. Volume primo [-secondo]. *Venice: N. Misserini,* 1606. 2 v.; illus.; 4to. Includes scattered American refs. Michel (Répertoire) II:178. NjP, NNC; BL, BN. 606/37

Drayton, Michael. Poemes lyrick and pastorall: odes, eglogs, the man in the moone. *London: R. B[radock]., for N. L[ing]. & J. Flasket* [1606?]. [120] p.; 8vo. The 11th Ode, entitled 'To the Virginian voyage', lauds the undertaking and its participants. STC 7217. CSmH, CtY, DFo, MiU, MH, NN-RB; BL. 606/38

Du Bartas, Guillaume de Salluste, seigneur. Les oeuvres poëtiques et chrestiennes. *Lyons: T. Ancelin,* 1606. 394 numb. lvs; 16mo. Includes the author's *La sepmaine,* 1st publ., Paris, 1578, & his *La seconde sepmaine,* 1st publ., Paris, 1584. Cf. 1603 edn. Holmes (DuBartas) I:75 no. 30. BN. 606/39

——. Bartas his devine weekes and workes translated . . . by Josuah Sylvester. [*London:*] *H. Lownes,* 1605 [i.e., 1606]. 2 pts; illus.; 4to. In verse. A reissue of Lownes's 1605 edn with addition of 'I Posthumous Bartas. The third day of his second weeke' dated '1606'. STC 21649a.5. CSmH, DFo, MH, NNPM, WU; BL.   606/40

Du Périer, Anthoine, sieur de La Salargue. Les amours de Pistion et de Fortunie. Tirees du voyage de Canada, dicte France nouvelle. *Paris: T. de La Ruelle,* 1606. 240 p.; 16mo. 1st publ., Paris, 1601. Cf. Cioranescu (XVII) 27544. DLC.   606/41

Dupleix, Scipion. La curiosite naturelle; redigée en questions selon l'ordre alphabétique. *Paris: L. Sonnius,* 1606. 312 numb. lvs; 12mo. Section on syphilis ('la verole') ascribes its introduction into Europe to the Spanish, who brought it from the Indies. The subsequent English translations are without this section. ICU, KU; BL, BN.
606/42

Durante, Castore. Il tesoro della sanità. *Venice: Heirs of D. Farri,* 1606. 324 p.; illus.; fol. 1st publ., [Rome?], 1586; cf. 1601 edn. DNLM, MH, PPC.   606/43

Estienne, Charles. Agricoltura nova, et casa de villa. *Venice: M. Valentin,* 1606. 510 p.; 4to. 1st publ. as here transl. by Ercole Cato from Estienne's *L'agriculture,* Venice, 1581. Arents (Add.) 39. ICN, MH, NN-A, RPB.
606/44

——. Dictionarium historicum, geographicum, poeticum. [*Geneva:*] *J. Stoer,* 1606. 452 numb. lvs; 4to. 1st publ. in this enl. edn, Lyons, 1595; cf. 1601 edn. CoU.
606/45

——. Maison rustique, or The countrie farme. Compiled in the French tongue by Charles Stevens and John Liebault . . . And translated . . . by Richard Surflet. *London: A. Hatfield, for J. Norton & J. Bill,* 1606. 901 p.; illus.; 4to. Transl. from *La maison rustique,* as publ., Paris, 1567; 1st publ. in English, London, 1600. Contains refs to tobacco, turkeys, etc. Thiébaud (La chasse) 357; STC 10548; Arents 76-B. CSmH, CtY, DFo, ICU, MH, NN-A; BL.   606/46

Foreest, Pieter van. Observationum et curationum medicinalium liber xxxii, De lue venerea. *Leyden: Plantin Press (Raphelengius),* 1606. 284 p.; 12mo. Includes statement that in treatment of syphilis, sarsaparilla, 'ex Peru', may be substituted for guaiacum. WU-M.   606/47

Gabelkover, Oswald. Artzneybuch. *Tübingen: G. Gruppenbach,* 1606. 434 p.; 4to. 1st publ., Tübingen, 1589, under title *Nützlich Artzneybuch;* cf. 1603 edn. BL.   606/48

Gallucci, Giovanni Paolo. Theatro del mundo y de el tiempo . . . Traducido de lengua latina . . . y añadido por Miguel Perez. *Granada: S. Múñoz,* 1606. 369 numb. lvs; illus., map; fol. Transl. from author's *Theatrum mundi,* 1st publ., Venice, 1588. Here newly included (lf 172 ff.) is a 'Catálogo de las ciudades y lugares de la América y las otras regiones de las Indias Occidentales de nuestra Castilla'. Medina (BHA) 517. NNH, UU; BL.   606/49

García de Céspedes, Andrés. Regimiento de navegacion mando hazer el Rei . . . por su Consejo real de las Indias. *Madrid: J. de la Cuesta,* 1606. 184 numb. lvs; illus., map; fol. Sabin 11718; Medina (BHA) 515; Scott (Naval) 54; Perez Pastor (Madrid) 936; JCB (3) II:39. CSmH, CtY, DLC, InU-L, MH, MnU-B, NNH, RPJCB; BL, BN.   606/50

Gesner, Konrad. Icones avium omnium, quae in Historia avium Conradi Gesneri describuntur . . . Editio tertia. *Heidelberg: J. Lancellot, for A. Cambier,* 1606. 237 (i.e., 137) p.; illus.; fol. 1st publ., Zurich, 1555; cf. 1560 edn. Includes illus. of turkey. Nissen (Birds) 352. IEN, MnU; BL.   606/51

——. Nomenclator aquatilium animantium. Icones animalium in mari et dulcibus aquis degentium . . . Editio tertia. *Heidelberg: J. Lancellot, for A. Cambier,* 1606. 374 p.; illus.; fol. 1st publ., Zurich, 1560. Described as American are the 'Ostracion Americae', a 'Hyperus homicida' & the 'Crocodilus terrestris' of Brazil. Nissen (Zool.) 1554. DLC, MnU (imp.); BL.   606/52

——. Thierbuch, das ist, Ausführliche beschreibung und lebendige ja auch eigentliche Contrafactur und Abmahlung aller Vierfüssigen thieren, so auff der Erden und in Wassern wohnen. *Heidelberg: J. Lancellot, for A. Cambier,* 1606. 172 p.; illus.; fol. 1st publ., Zurich, 1583. On lf 7r Peter Martyr

Anghiera is cited on animals, 'in der neüw gefundnen welt, umb die gegne der landtschafft Cariai'. NIC, OC1W; BL.   606/53

Gómara, Francisco López de. Histoire generalle des Indes Occidentalles, et terres neuves . . . Augmentée en ceste cinquiesme edition de la description de la nouvelle Espagne. *Paris: M. Sonnius,* 1606. 485 lvs; 8vo. A reissue, with altered imprint date, of Sonnius's 1605 edn, q.v. In the present issue, the imprint contains the phrase 'à l'enseigne de l'escu de Basle'. Sabin 27749; Wagner (SW) 2nn; Atkinson (Fr. Ren.) 453; Streit II:1376; JCB (3) II:40. MH, RPJCB.   606/54

—[Anr issue]. *Paris: M. Sonnius,* 1606. In this issue the imprint contains reading 'au Coq & Compas d'Or'. MiU-C, NN-RB; BN.   606/55

González de Mendoza, Juan, O.E.S.A., Bp. Histoire du grand royaume de la Chine . . . ensemble un Itineraire du nouveau monde, & le descouvrement du nouveau Mexique en l'an 1583 . . . Nouvellement traduite de latin en françois. [*Geneva:*] *J. Arnaud,* 1606. 419 p.; 8vo. 1st publ. in French, Paris, 1588; transl. from the author's *Historia . . . de la China,* 1st publ. with Antonio de Espejo's 'Itinerario', Madrid, 1586. Cf. Sabin 47829; Wagner (SW) 7gg; Atkinson (Fr. Ren.) 471; JCB (3) II:39. CU-B, DLC, InU-L, NN-RB, RPJCB; BN.   606/56

—[Anr issue]. *Geneva: J. Arnaud,* 1606. Atkinson (Fr. Ren.) 471n. Paris:Arsenal.   606/57

Goulart, Simon. Histoires admirables et memorables de nostre temps. *Paris: J. Houzé,* 1606. 2 v.; 12mo. 1st publ., Paris, 1600–1601; cf. 1603 edn. Jones (Goulart) 54c; Brunet (Suppl.) I:558.   606/58

—[Anr edn]. *Rouen: T. Daré,* 1606. 2 v.; 12mo. MH; BL.   606/59

——. Le sage vieillard, décrit de divers autheurs, par S.G.S. *Lyons:* [*J. Poyet,*] *for A. de Harsy,* 1606. 437 p.; 12mo. 1st publ., Lyons, 1605. Jones (Goulart) 60(b). BN, Berne:StB.   606/60

Hall, Joseph, Bp of Norwich. Mundus alter et idem . . . Authore Mercurio Britannico. '*Frankfurt a. M.: Heirs of Rinialme*' [i.e., *Hanau: W. Antonius,* 1606?]. 224 p.; illus., maps;

8vo. A reissue of the original [London? 1605?] edn, with new engraved t.p., on which the top of the pedestal base has strong crosshatching. Elsewhere, e.g., the prelim. leaves with catchwords on versos only and sheet D, settings of type of the Hanau, 1607, reprinting will be found supplied. Cf. years 1605 & 1607. The locations given for the [London, 1605?] edn may include copies of this reissue. Cf. Sabin 29819; cf. STC 12685; cf. Arents (Add.) 124. NN-RB.   606/61

Herrera y Tordesillas, Antonio de. Primera parte de la Historia general del mundo, de xvii. años del tiempo del señor Rey don Felipe II. *Valladolid: J. Godínez de Millis,* 1606. 820 p.; fol. 1st publ., Madrid, 1601. The 2nd pt follows; for the 3rd pt see the year 1612. Sabin 31559; Alcocer (Valladolid) 518; Palau 114318; JCB (3) II:39-40. CtY, NN-RB, PPL, RPJCB; BL.   606/62

——. Segunda parte de la Historia general del mundo, de xv. años del tiempo de señor Rey don Felipe II . . . desde el año de M.D.LXXI. *Valladolid: J. Godínez de Millis,* 1606. 630 p.; fol. Continues the preceding item. For a 3rd pt, see the year 1612. Sabin 31559; Alcocer (Valladolid) 518; Palau 114319; JCB (3) II:40. CtY, NN-RB, PPL, RPJCB; BL, BN.   606/63

Houtman, Cornelis de. Erste Schiffahrt in die Orientalische Indien, so die holländische Schiff . . . verricht . . . Editio quarta. *Frankfurt a. M.: W. Richter, for Heirs of L. Hulsius,* 1606. 68 p.; illus., maps; 4to. (Levinus Hulsius's *Sammlung von . . . Schifffahrten.* Pt 1). 1st publ. in this version, Nuremberg, 1598; cf. year 1602. Sabin 33653; Church 259; JCB (3) I:451. CSmH, MnU-B, NN-RB, RPJCB; BL, BN.   606/64

Hurault, Michel, sieur de Belesbat et du Fay. Le recueil des excellens et libres discours sur l'estat présent de la France. [*Paris?*] 1606. 3 pts; 12mo. 1st publ., [Paris?], 1593, under title *Quatre excellens discours;* cf. 1598 edn under present title. Includes Hurault's 'Discours sur l'estat present de la France', with ref. to Spanish control of Indian riches, & his 'Second discours', referring to Spanish treasures of the Indies, Antoine Arnauld's *La fleur de lys* (1st publ., [Paris?], 1593), with ref. to Spanish cruelties, & the latter's *Anti-Espagnol* (1st publ., Basel, 1590), referring to Spanish expulsion of French from Florida. CtY, ICN, MH; BL. 606/65

Illescas, Gonzalo de. Segunda parte de la Historia pontifical y catholica. *Barcelona: J. Cendrat,* 1606. 364 numb. lvs; fol. 1st publ. with American material, Barcelona, 1596; cf. 1602 edn. Palau 118424n. 606/66

Jacobi, Heyman. Den cleynen herbarius ofte Kruyt-boecxken. *Amsterdam: H. Barentszoon,* 1606. 192 p.; 8vo. Sections 181–83 discuss medical uses of mechoacan, sarsaparilla, & tobacco. MH-A. 606/67

Jesuits. Compendium privilegiorum. Compendium facultatum, et indulgentiarum, quae religiosis Societatis Jesu . . . in Indiarum Orientalium, & Occidentalium provinciis conceduntur. *Rome: Jesuit College,* 1606. 46 p.; 12mo. 1st publ., Rome, 1580. Streit I:285. CtY-D; Rome:BN. 606/68

—[Anr edn]. Literae apostolicae. *Rome: Jesuit College,* 1606. 147 p.; 12mo. Streit I:287. Rome:BN. 606/69

Junius, Hadrianus. Nomenclator octilinguis omnium rerum propria nomina continens. *Paris: D. Douceur,* 1606. 190 p.; 4to. 1st publ., Antwerp, 1577; cf. expanded 1602 edn. CtY, DLC, MH; BL, BN. 606/70

Lescarbot, Marc. [Adieu a la France sur l'embarquement du sieur de Poutrincourt et de son équipage faisant voile en la terre de Canadas, dicte la France Occidentalle, le 26e. de may 1606. *La Rochelle:* 1606]. Cf. following item. Sabin 40166; Harrisse (NF) 15. 606/71

—[Anr edn]. *Rouen: J. Petit,* 1606. 8 p.; 8vo. 'Imprimé . . . jouxte la copie imprimée à La Rochelle'. Desgraves (Les Haultin) 230. BN. 606/72

——. A Dieu aux François retournans de la Nouvelle France en la France gauloise. [*La Rochelle: Heirs of J. Haultin,* 1606?]. 6 p.; 4to. In verse. Desgraves (Les Haultin) 231. MH. 606/73

Libavius, Andreas. Alchymia . . . recognita, emendata, et aucta. *Frankfurt a. M.: J. Sauer, for P. Kopff,* 1606. 3 pts; illus.; fol. 1st publ. as here transl. from the author's *Alchymistische Practic* (Frankfurt a. M., 1603), Frank-

furt a. M., 1604, under title *Praxis alchymiae.* Ferguson (Bibl. chem.) II:31; Wellcome I:3776. CU-M, DLC, MiU, NNNAM, PBL; BL, BN. 606/74

Marcos de Lisboa, Bp. Delle croniche de gli ordini instituti dal p.s. Francisco, parte terza . . . Composta . . . in lingua portoghese. Poi ridotta nella castiglione dal r.p.f. Diego Navarro; e tradotta . . . dal sig. Horatio Diola. *Venice: E. Viotti,* 1606. 342 numb. lvs; 4to. 1st publ. in Italian, Venice, 1591, as transl. from Salamanca, 1570, edn; cf. 1605 edn above. Streit I:281; Michel (Répertoire) V:112. MB; BN. 606/75

Marees, Pieter de. Siebende Schiffart in das goldreiche Königreich Guineam. *Frankfurt a. M.: W. Richter, for Heirs of L. Hulsius,* 1606. 228 p.; illus., map; 4to. (Levinus Hulsius's *Sammlung von . . . Schiffahrten.* Pt 7). 1st publ. in this version, Frankfurt a. M., 1603. Sabin 33661; Church 286; JCB (3) I:459. CSmH, NN, RPJCB; BL. 606/76

Mariana, Juan de. Historiae hispanicae appendix. Liber scilicet xxi. & novem ceteri ad xxx. *Frankfurt a. M.: C. de Marne, & Heirs of J. Aubry,* 1606. 337 p.; fol. 1st publ., Madrid, 1592; cf. 1605 edn. Normally bound with, as issued, Andreas Schottus's *Hispaniae illustratae,* v. 4. Sabin 44545 (misdated 1616); Backer V:547; Palau 151663. CU, CtY, DLC, ICN, MiU, RPJCB; BN. 606/77

Matthieu, Pierre. Histoire de France et des choses memorables, advenues aux provinces estrangeres durant sept annees de paix, du regne du roy Henry IIII. *Paris: J. Mettayer & M. Guillemot,* 1606. 2 v.; 4to. 1st publ., Paris, 1605; here a reissue with altered imprint date of that edn? CSt, PU; BN (v.1). 606/78

Mercator, Gerardus. Atlas sive Cosmographicae meditationes de fabrici mundi et fabricata figura. Iam tandem . . . perductus, quamplurimus aeneis tabulis Hispaniae, Africae, Asiae & Americae auctus ac illustratus à Judoco Hondio. *Amsterdam: J. Hondius,* 1606. 354 p.; maps; fol. Includes 6 maps of America not found in earlier edns. Sabin 47882; Koeman (Me) 15. BL, Lucerne:ZB. 606/79

Mercuriale, Girolamo. Praelectiones Patavinae. *Venice: The Giuntas,* 1606. 644 p.; fol.

1st publ., Frankfurt a. M., 1601, under title *Medica practica.* DNLM, PPC. 606/80

Núñez, Pedro. Tassa y postura en el valor de las mercadurias de estos reynos. [*Valladolid:* 1606]. fol. Described are numerous products of the Spanish West Indies, Mexico, &c. Dated at end: Valladolid a 10. de Febrero de 1606. años. BL. 606/81

Oliveira, Simão d'. Arte de navegar. *Lisbon: P. Craesbeeck,* 1606. 170 p.; illus.; 4to. Includes navigational directions for voyage to Brazil & return. Innocencio VII:283; Palau 200533; Maggs Cat. 502 (Americana VII) 5012. InU-L; Madrid:BN. 606/82

Ortelius, Abraham. Theatrum orbis terrarum. *London:* 1606. *See the year* 1608.

Owen, John. Epigrammatum libri tres. *London: J. Windet, for S. Waterson,* 1606. 88 p.; 8vo. In bk 2, Epigram 38, on Francis Drake, refers to his voyages; also included is one on tobacco. STC 18984.5. MH; Winchester Coll. 606/83

—[Anr edn]. Secunda editio. *London: J. Windet, for S. Waterson,* 1606. 8vo. STC 18984.7. DFo; Oxford:Bodl. 606/84

Palmer, Sir Thomas. An essay of the means how to make our travailes, into forraine countries, the more profitable and honourable. *London: H. L[ownes]., for M. Lownes,* 1606. 131 p.; 4to. Includes incidental refs to New World, e.g. (p. 84), to ship masts of Newfoundland. STC 19156; JCB (3) II:41. CSmH, CtY, DLC, ICN, MH, MiU, NN-RB, PU, RPJCB; BL. 606/85

Ramusio, Giovanni Battista, comp. Delle navigationi et viaggi . . . Volume primo. *Venice: The Giuntas,* 1606. 394 numb. lvs; illus., maps; fol. 1st publ., Venice, 1550. For an analysis of the American content, see G. B. Parks, 'The contents and sources of Ramusio's *Navigationi', Bulletin of the New York Public Library,* L (1955) 279–313. Sabin 67734; Streit I:282; JCB (3) II:41–42. CtY, DLC, ICN, InU-L, MH, MiU-C, NN-RB, PPL, RPJCB; BL, BN. 606/86

——, **comp.** Delle navigationi et viaggi . . . Volume secondo. *Venice: The Giuntas,* 1606. 256 numb. lvs; illus., maps; fol. 1st publ. with American material, the 'Navigatione di Sebastiano Cabota' (lvs 211–19), Venice, 1583; here a reissue of that edn with cancel t.p. and certain leaves reset; the final leaf

& its conjugate are found as a cancel or in their original state with 1583 colophon. For contents, cf. Parks as cited for v. 1 of this year. Sabin 67739; Streit I:282; JCB (3) II:42. CtY, DLC, ICN, InU-L, MH, MiU-C, MnU-B, NN-RB, PPL, RPJCB; BN. 606/87

——, **comp.** Delle navigationi et viaggi . . . Volume terzo. *Venice: The Giuntas,* 1606. 430 numb. lvs; illus., maps; fol. 1st publ., Venice, 1556; to this edn is added Gerrit de Veer's 'Tre navigationi fatte da gli Olandese', with mention of Columbus, Cortés, Brazil, the West Indies, 1st publ. in Dutch, Amsterdam, 1598. For full contents, see the article by Parks cited for v. 1 above. Sabin 67742; Streit I:282; JCB (3) II:42–43. CtY, DLC, ICN, InU-L, MH, MiU-C, MnU-B, NN-RB, PPL, RPJCB; BL, BN. 606/88

Ranconet, Aimar de. Thresor de la langue françoyse . . . Reveu et augmenté . . . par Jean Nicot. *Paris: D. Douceur,* 1606. 666 p.; fol. 1st publ. with discussion of tobacco as 'Nicotiane', Paris, 1573, under title *Dictionaire françois-latin.* Arents (Add.) 56. CtY, DLC, ICN, MH, NN-A; BL, BN. 606/89

Relacion de lo que le sucedio a Don Luis Fajardo, Capitan general de la armada de sn [*sic*] Magestad, en la jornada que hizo, el año passado de seiscientos y cincos a las Indias, donde se dize los navios de enemigos olandeses, e ingleses, y franceses. *Málaga:* 1606. [4] p.; fol. Account of naval encounters off island of Dominica & elsewhere in Caribbean. Medina (BHA) 518; Palau 257347. NN-RB. 606/90

—[Anr edn]. Relacion de los sucesos que tuvo Don Luis Fajardo. *Madrid:* 1606. Sabin 69207; Pérez Pastor (Madrid) 947; Palau 257348. 606/91

Return from Parnassus. The returne from Pernassus. *London: G. Eld, for J. Wright,* 1606. [68] p.; 4to. Comedy. Includes refs to tobacco smoking. STC 19309; Greg 225(a); Arents (Add.) 127. CSmH, DFo, MH, NN-A; BL. 606/92

—[Anr edn]. *London: G. Eld, for J. Wright,* 1606. [64] p.; 4to. STC 19310; Greg 225(b); Arents 77. CSmH, CtY, DLC, MH, NN-A; BL. 606/93

Rich, Barnabe. Faultes faults. *London:* [*V.*

Simmes,] *for J. Chorleton,* 1606. 66 lvs; 4to. Attacks use of tobacco. STC 20983; Arents 78. CSmH, DFo, ICN, MH, NN-A; BL.

606/94

Rivadeneira, Pedro de, S.J. Catalogus quorundam e Societate Jesu qui pro fide vel pietate sunt interfecti ab anno 1540 ad annum 1603. *Naples: T. Longo,* 1606. 12 lvs; 12mo. Includes accounts of Jesuits martyred in New World. Streit I:283; Backer II:581; Palau 266539. Rome:BN.

606/95

—[Anr edn]. *Cracow: N. Lob,* 1606. [36] p.; 24mo. Streit I:284; Palau 266540. BL (Jesuits), Bologna:BC.

606/96

——. Vita del b.p. Ignatio Loiola . . . nuovamente tradotta dalla spagnuola . . . da d. Salustio Gratii. *Venice: G. B. Ciotti,* 1606. 188 p.; 8vo. 1st publ. in Italian, Venice, 1586. Includes refs to Jesuits in Brazil. Backer VI:1730; Palau 266241. NN-RB; Rome:BN.

606/97

Rodríguez de Robles, Antonio. Señor. Antonio Rodriguez de Robles dize, que ahora quarenta y cinquenta años, avia en los ciudades y sitios de minas de la Nueva España, gran suma de Indios, y muy pocos Españoles: y el dia de oy es por el contrario. [*Madrid?* 1606?]. 2 p.; fol. Memorial to king of Spain. Medina (BHA) 6829; Palau 274838. CU-B; Seville:Archivo de Indias.

606/98

——. Señor. Antonio Rodriguez de Robles dize, que assi como los mineros sacan la plata, la manifiestan a los alcaldes mayores de la minas, los quales cobrando lo que los tales mineros davan a V. Magestad del azogue que han recibido a rata, conforme a la cantidad de plata que sacan, los echan en cada plancha el hierno del diezmo. [*Madrid?* 1606?]. [3] p.; fol. Memorial to king of Spain. Medina (BHA) 6828. CU-B; Seville:Archivo de Indias.

606/99

——. Señor. Antonio Rodriguez de Robles dize, que aunque de algunos años a esta parte por V. Magestad y su Real Consejo de Indias està mandado, que las salinas de la governacion de la Nueva España se incorpore en el patrimonio real [etc.]. [*Madrid?* 1606?]. [4] p.; fol. Medina (BHA) 6827; Palau 274839 & 274840. CU-B; Seville:Archivo de Indias.

606/100

——. Señor. Antonio Rodriguez de Robles dize, que como a V. Magestad y a su Real Consejo de Indias es notorio, acabados los Indios de la Nueva España, no ay Indias en ella, ni podran tener tal nombre. [*Madrid?* 1606?]. [4] p.; fol. Memorial to king of Spain, opposing forced labor from Indians. Medina (BHA) 6830; Palau 274846. CU-B; Seville:Archivo de Indias.

606/101

——. Señor. Antonio Rodriguez de Robles dize, que de 9. años a esta parte que han residido en la ciudad de Mexico, ha visto, que cado año se han levantado desde .100. hasta .150. hombres de guerra para las islas Philippinas. [*Madrid?* 1606?]. [2] p.; fol. Memorial to king of Spain. Medina (BHA) 6825; Palau 274843. RPJCB; Seville:Archivo de Indias.

606/102

——. Señor. Antonio de Rodriguez de Robles dize, que quando la Nueva España se gano . . . avia en la provincia de Taxcala. 200 mil Indios tributarios. [*Madrid?* 1606?]. [2] p.; fol. Memorial to king of Spain on tribute exacted from Indians in Mexico. Medina (BHA) 6826; Palau 274844. Seville:Archivo de Indias.

606/103

Rowlands, Samuel. A terrible battell betweene the two consumers of the whole world: time, and death. *London: [W. Jaggard] for J. Deane* [1606?]. 4to. In verse. 'Potato pies' are mentioned. STC 21407. Oxford: Bodl.

606/104

Sacro Bosco, Joannes de. Sphaera . . . emendata. Eliae Vineti . . . scholia. *Lyons: H. Gazeau,* 1606. 174 p.; illus.; 8vo. 1st publ. with Vinet's *Scholia,* Paris, 1551; cf. 1601 cdn above. NN-RB, OkU.

606/105

Sandoval, Prudencio de, Bp of Pamplona. Primera[-segunda] parte de la Vida y hechos del emperador Carlos Quinto. *Valladolid: S. de Cañas,* 1606. 2 v.; fol. Vol. 1 1st publ., Valladolid, 1604; v. 2 here 1st publ. Cf. Sabin 76423n; Alcocer (Valladolid) 520; Palau 297146. Orense:BP.

606/106

Serres, Jean de. Inventaire general de l'histoire de France. [*Paris:*] *P. Marceau,* 1606. 2 v.; 8vo. 1st publ. with an American ref., Paris, 1600, not found in the Paris, 1603, edn. Here now introduced are refs to New France. BN.

606/107

Entry canceled.

606/108

Spain. Consejo de las Indias. Ordenanzas reales para el govierno de los tribunales de la contaduria mayor, que en los reynos de las Indias y ciudades de los reyes en el Piru, Mexico en la Nueva España, Santafe, en el nuevo reyno de Granada ha mandado fundar el Rey nuestro señor. *Valladolid: L. Sánchez,* 1606. 11 lvs; fol. Sabin 57484; Medina (BHA) 516; Palau 202829. CU-B; BL.
606/109

Spain. Sovereigns, etc., 1598–1621 (Philip III). El Rey [14 Dec. 1606]. [*Madrid:* 1606?]. 3 numb. lvs; fol. On the civil administration of Spanish America. BL.
606/110

Spiegel, Adriaan van de. Isagoges in rem herbariam. *Padua: L. Pasquato, for P. Meietti,* 1606. 138 p.; 4to. Described are the marigold ('Cariophyllis'), 'ex India defertur', and the yucca, identified as from the West Indies. Pritzel 8827; Hunt (Bot.) 184. CtY-M, DNLM, MB, PPC; BL, BN.
606/111

Spilbergen, Joris van. Indiae Orientalis, pars septima. *Frankfurt a. M.: W. Richter,* 1606. 126 p.; illus., maps; fol. (J. T. de Bry's *India Orientalis.* Pt 7. Latin). Spilbergen's voyage transl. from *Siebender Theil der Orientalischen Indien,* Frankfurt a. M., 1606; 1st publ., Delft, 1601, under title *t'Historiael journael.* For variant issues, see Church 217. Church 216; JCB (3) I:435. CSmH, DLC, ICN, MB, NN-RB, RPJCB; BL, BN.
606/112

Staden, Hans. Dritte Buch Americae, darinn Brasilia . . . auss eigener Erfahrung in Teutsch beschrieben. Item Historia der Schiffart Ioannis Lerij in Brasilien, welche er selbst publiciert hat, jetzt von newem verteutscht durch Teucrium Annaeum Privatum, C. Vom Wilden unerhörten Wesen der Innwoner von allerley frembden Gethieren und Gewächsen, sampt einen Colloquio in der wilden Sprach. *Frankfurt a. M.: T. de Bry,* 1593 [i.e., ca. 1606–12]. 285 p.; illus., map; fol. (Theodor de Bry's *America.* Pt 3. German). 1st publ. in this version, Frankfurt a. M., 1593. Cf. Sabin 8784; Church 182; JCB (3) I:393. CSmH, ICN, NN, RPJCB; BL.
606/113

Steeghius, Godefridius. Ars medica. *Frankfurt a. M.: C. Marne, & Heirs of J. Aubry,* 1606.

554 p.; port.; fol. Guaiacum, mechoacan, sarsaparilla, & tobacco are discussed. Wellcome I:6059. DNLM, NNNAM, PPC; BL, BN.
606/114

Thou, Jacques Auguste de. Historiarum sui temporis tomus primus[-tertius]. *Paris: A. & H. Drouart,* 1606–9. 4 v.; fol. Bks i–xxvi 1st publ. Paris, 1604, as xviii bks; here added are bks xxvii–xxxxi & lii–lxxx, covering years 1560–85. Here added are accounts of the French in Florida, and new discoveries in America. For the complete work, see the year 1620. Brunet V:840. DLC, NjP, PPL; BN (v. 1–3 only).
606/115

——. Historiarum sui temporis, tomi secundi. *Paris: A. & H. Drouart,* 1606–8. 3 v.; 8vo. Contains bks xxvii–lvii, here publ. to supplement earlier vols in this format, 1st publ., Paris, 1604. Cf. the folio edn of this year above. InStme, PSt; BL, BN.
606/116

A true report of the imprisonment . . . of the late traytors. *London:* 1606. See The araignement and execution of the late traytors *above.*

Ulloa, Alfonso de. Vita, et fatti dell'invitissimo imperatore Carlo Quinto, et historie universali del mondo. *Venice: A. Vecchi,* 1606. 255 numb. lvs; port.; 4to. 1st publ., Venice, 1560. Describes Spanish conquests in Mexico & Peru. Sabin 97682n; Palau 343397. DLC, ICN, MH, NN-RB, RPJCB; BN.
606/117

Vergilius, Polydorus. De rerum inventoribus libri octo . . . Accesserunt C. Plinii, Alexandri Sardi, aliorumque de eadem materia collectanea. *Strassburg: L. Zetzner,* 1606. 2 pts; 8vo. 1st publ. as here constituted, Geneva, 1604. IU, MH, PPL; BL.
606/118

Warner, William. A continuance of Albions England. *London: F. Kingston for G. Potter,* 1606. 4to. In verse. Contains ref. to tobacco as Indian weed. STC 25085; Arents 79. CSmH, CtY, DFo, ICN, MH, MiU; BL.
606/119

Wecker, Johann Jakob. Practica medicinae generalis. *Lyons: Heirs of G. Rouillé,* 1606. 593 p.; 16mo. 1st publ., Basel, 1585; cf. 1602 edn. Wellcome I:6720. London:Wellcome.
606/120

1607

Baeza, Pedro de. Este memorial es traslado de otro que di a Su Magestad en mano proprio quando le hable y le di cuenta deste negocio y asiento del azogue. [*Madrid:* 1607?]. 6 numb. lvs; fol. With ref. to transportation of mercury from China to Acapulco for use in Mexican mines. Subscribed: En Madrid a primero de octubre de mil y seiscientos y siete. Pérez Pastor (Madrid) 953; Maggs Cat. 496 (Americana VI):27. CtY, DLC, MH-BA; BL.   607/1

——. Traslado del memorial que se hizo con el licenciado Don Francisco de Tejada, oydor del Consejo real de las Indias . . . para tratar el assiento del açogue. [*Madrid:* 1607?]. 3 numb. lvs; fol. On implementation of preceding memorial. Pérez Pastor (Madrid) 959; Maggs Cat. 496 (Americana VI):28. DLC, MH-BA; BL.   607/2

Barclay, John. Euphormionis Lusinini Satyricon pars secunda. *Paris: F. Huby,* 1607. 130 numb. lvs; 12mo. Chapt. 31 includes an extended description, with poem, of postprandial smoking of tobacco. Shaaber (Brit. auth.) B156. BN, Paris:Arsenal.
                                                                 607/3

Bauderon, Brice. Paraphrase sur la Pharmacopoee . . . Quatrieme edition. *Lyons: P. Rigaud,* 1607. 721 p.; 12mo. 1st publ., Lyons, 1588. No copy of the 3rd edn has been located. In bk 2, sect. 1, 'Des huyles qui se font par descensoire en general', guaiacum is mentioned; in sect. 2, an unguent employing tobacco is described. BN.
                                                                 607/4

Blefken, Dithmar. Islandia, sive Populorum et mirabilium quae in ea insula reperiuntur accuratior descriptio, cui De Gronlandia sub finem quaedum adjecta. *Leyden: H. van Haestens,* 1607. 71 p.; 8vo. Sabin 5902; Tiele 143; JCB (3) II:43. DLC, MH, MnU-B, NN-RB, RPJCB; BL, BN.   607/5

Bodin, Jean. Methodus ad facilem historiarum cognitionem. *Strassburg: L. Zetzner,* 1607. 547 p.; 16mo. 1st publ., Paris, 1566. Included in chapt. 6 is a ref. to Spanish undertakings in Africa & America; in chapt. 10, historians of the Americas are named. MoSU; BN.   607/6

Botero, Giovanni. I capitani . . . con alcuni

discorsi curiosi . . . discorso dell'eccellenza della monarchia. *Turin: G. D. Tarino,* 1607. 250 p.; 8vo. The section on monarchy adverts to Spanish rule in New World. Michel (Répertoire)I:200. CtY, MH, NcD; BN.
                                                                 607/7

Breton, Nicholas. A poste with a packet of mad letters. The fourth time enlarged. *London: J. W[indet]., for J. Smethwicke & J. Browne,* 1607. 4to. 1st publ., London, 1602. STC 3687. CSmH.   607/8

Bry, Johann Theodor de. Indiae Orientalis, par octava. *Frankfurt a. M.: W. Richter,* 1607. 114 p.; illus.; fol. (J. T. de Bry's *India Orientalis.* Pt 8. Latin). Transl. (?) from de Bry's *Achter Theil der Orientalischen Indien,* Frankfurt a. M., 1606. Includes R. Roelofsz's *Historica descriptio navigationis, a Iacobo Neccio . . . susceptae,* 1st publ., Frankfurt a. M., 1605, in *Zwo underschiedliche newe Schiffarten.* For variant issue, see Church. Cf. Tiele, p. 162–66; Church 218 (& 219); JCB (3) I:437. CSmH, DLC, ICN, MB, NN, RPJCB; BL, BN.   607/9

Buchanan, George. Franciscanus & fratres. *Saumur: T. Portau,* 1607. 222 p.; 16mo. Includes Buchanan's poem 'Brasilia', 1st publ. in his *Franciscanus,* Basel, [1568?], & his 'In colonias Brasilienses vel Sodomitas', 1st publ., [Paris?], 1566. Shaaber (Brit. auth.) B701. MH.   607/10

Casas, Bartolomé de las, O.P., Bp of Chiapa. Spieghel der Spaenscher tyrannie, in West-Indien . . . *Amsterdam: C. Claeszoon,* 1607. [86] p.; 4to. 1st publ., [Antwerp?], 1578, under title *Seer cort verhael . . .* as transl. from the author's *Brevíssima relacion,* 1st publ., Seville, 1552; cf. [Antwerp?], 1579 edn with the present title. Sabin 11252; Medina (BHA) 1085n (II:476); Hanke/Giménez 501; Streit I:289; JCB (3) II:44. DLC, NN-RB, PHi, RPJCB; BL.
                                                                 607/11

Catholic Church. Liturgy and ritual. Ritual. Peru. Rituale, seu Manuale peruanum, et forma brevis administrandi apud Indos sacrosancta . . . sacramenta . . . et quae indigent versione, vulgaribus idiomatibus indicis, secundum diversos situs omnium provinciarum novi orbis Perù, aut per ipsum translata, aut eius industria elaborata, per p.f. Ludovicum Hieronymum Ore.

Naples: G. G. Carlino & C. Vitale, 1607. 418 p.; 4to. Text in Latin & Spanish, with translations into Kechua & Aymara. Sabin 57542; Medina (Chile) 30; Streit II:1423n; Viñaza 120; Palau 203693. DLC; BL, BN.

607/12

Cayet, Pierre Victor Palma. Chronologie septenaire de l'histoire de la paix entre les roys de France et d'Espagne . . . avec le succez de plusieurs navigations faictes aux Indes Orientales, Occidentales & Septentrionales, depuis le commencement de l'an 1598. jusques à la fin de l'an 1604 . . . Troisiesme edition. *Paris: J. Richer,* 1607. 506 numb. lvs; 8vo. 1st publ., Paris, 1605. Atkinson (Fr. Ren.) 483; JCB (3) II:47. CtY, MH, MiD-B, NNH, PU, RPJCB; BN. 607/13

Clavius, Christoph. In Sphaeram Joannis de Sacro Bosco commentarius, nunc quinto ab ipso auctore . . . recognitus. *Rome: A. Zannetti, for G. P. Gelli,* 1607. 669 p.; illus.; 4to. 1st publ., Rome, 1570; cf. 1601 edn. Here a reissue of Gelli's 1606 edn with altered imprint date. Shaaber (Brit. auth.) H441. DLC, IU, InU-L, MH, MiU, NN-RB; BL, BN. 607/14

—[Anr edn]. *Lyons: H. de La Porte, for J. de Gabiano,* 1607. 639 p.; illus.; 4to. Shaaber (Brit. auth.) H443. CtY, ICU, NN-RB; BL, BN. 607/15

—[Anr edn]. *St. Gervais: S. Crespin,* 1607. 4to. Shaaber (Brit. auth.) H444. BL. 607/16

Cortés, Jerónimo. Libro de phisonomia natural. *Alcalá de Henares: J. Gracián,* 1607. 120 numb. lvs; 8vo. 1st publ., Valencia, 1597; cf. 1601 edn & also Gracián's 1603 edn. Palau 63302. 607/17

Croce, Giovanni Andrea della. Officina aurea; das ist, Guldene Werckstatt der Chirurgy . . . Aus dem Italienischen . . . versetzt durch Petrum Uffenbachium. *Frankfurt a. M.: J. Sauer, for J. Rose,* 1607. 716 p.; illus.; fol. Transl. from Croce's *Cirugia universale,* 1st publ., Venice, 1583; as transl. from his *Chirurgiae . . . libri septem,* 1st publ., Venice, 1573. DNLM. 607/18

Daniel, Samuel. Certain small works. *London: J. W[indet]., for S. Waterson,* 1607. 8vo. Includes Daniel's *The queenes arcadia,* 1st publ., London, 1606. STC 6240; Greg 227 (b). CSmH, DFo, MH, NN-RB; BL. 607/19

——. A panegyrike congratulatorie, delivered to the Kings . . . Majestie. *London: [R. Read?] for M. Bradwood,* 1607. [94] p.; 8vo. 1st publ., London, 1603. CSmH. 607/20

Davys, John. The seamans secrets . . . wherein is taught three kindes of sayling . . . Newly corrected. *London: T. Dawson,* 1607. 2 pts; illus.; 4to. 1st publ., London, [1594?]. The dedication includes discussion of Thomas Cavendish's voyages, with mention of Brazil. STC 6369. BL. 607/21

Dekker, Thomas. Jests to make you merie. *London: N. O[kes]., for N. Butter,* 1607. 4to. Written jointly with George Wilkins. The 59th & 60th Jests relate to tobacco. STC 6541. CSmH: Oxford:Bodl. 607/22

——. A knights conjuring, done in earnest, discovered in jest. *London: T. C[reede]., for W. Barley,* 1607. 41 lvs; 4to. An altered version of Dekker's *Newes from hell,* 1st publ., London, 1606. Chapt. 2 contains mention of Virginia, Peru, &c. STC 6508. CSmH, DFo; BL. 607/23

——. North-ward hoe. *London: G. Eld,* 1607. [63] p.; 4to. Drama; John Webster, co-author. In act 5, scene 1, tobacco & Spanish voyages to Indies are mentioned. STC 6539; Greg 250; Arents (Add.) 129. CSmH, CtY, DLC, IU, MH, NN-A; BL. 607/24

——. West-ward hoe . . . by Tho: Dekker, and John Webster. *London: [W. Jaggard?] for J. Hodgets,* 1607. [68] p.; 4to. Drama. Includes ref. to tobacco as smoked by women. STC 6540; Greg 257; Arents 80. CSmH, CtY, DFo, ICN, MH, NN-A; BL. 607/25

——. The whore of Babylon. *London: N. Butter,* 1607. [81] p.; 4to. Drama. Included are numerous refs to tobacco. STC 6532; Greg 241; Arents 3274. CSmH, CtY, DLC, ICN, MH; BL. 607/26

Du Bartas, Guillaume de Salluste, seigneur. Les oeuvres poëtiques et chrestiennes. *Lyons: T. Ancelin,* 1607. 394 numb. lvs; 16mo. Includes the author's *La sepmaine,* 1st publ., Paris, 1578, & his *La seconde sepmaine,* 1st publ., Paris, 1584. Cf. Ancelin's 1606 edn of which this is perhaps a reissue with altered imprint date. Holmes (DuBartas) I:75 no. 30n. BN. 607/27

Duchesne, Joseph. Pharmacopoea dogmaticorum restituta. *Paris: C. Morel,* 1607. 630

p.; 4to. Included is chapt. 'Extractum sive gummi guaici ut appellant' (p. 568–78); elsewhere formulas employing mechoacan, sarsaparilla, & tobacco are described. BL.
607/28

—[Anr edn]. Secunda editio. *Paris: C. Morel*, 1607. 919 (i.e., 621) p.; 8vo. DNLM, MH, WU; BL.
607/29

Erastus, Thomas. Examen de simplicibus, quae ad compositionem theriacae Andromachi requiruntur. *Lyons:* 1607. 635 p.; 8vo. Includes (p. 323) ref. to guaiacum, 'durum & apprimè solidum.' BL, BN.
607/30

Estienne, Charles. XV. Bücher von dem Feldbaw . . . von Carolo Stephano und Joh. Libalto . . . vom Herrn Melchiore Sebizio . . . inn Teutsch gebracht. *Strassburg: L. Zetzner*, 1607. 761 p.; fol. 1st publ. in this enl. German version, Strassburg, 1587; transl. from Liebault's enl. version of Estienne's *L'agriculture*, 1st publ., Paris, 1567. Includes refs to tobacco & turkey. Goldsmith (France) E333. WU; BL.
607/31

Fernel, Jean. De abditis rerum causis libri duo. *Frankfurt a. M.: C. Marne & Heirs of J. Aubry*, 1607. 272 p.; port.; 8vo. 1st publ., Paris, 1548; also issued as pt 3 of Fernel's *Universa medicina* of this year below. Sherrington (Fernel) 37.F21. DNLM, NjP, InU-L; Aberdeen:UL, Paris:Faculté de Médecine.
607/32

——. Universa medicina . . . Editio sexta. *Frankfurt a. M.: C. Marne & Heirs of J. Aubry*, 1607. 4 pts; ports; 8vo. 1st publ. as here constituted, Paris, 1567; cf. 1601–2 edn. Sherrington (Fernel) 76.J20. DNLM, NjP; London:Wellcome, BN.
607/33

Fragoso, Juan. Cirugia universal, aora nuevamente emendada . . . Y mas otros quatro tratados . . . El quarto, de la naturaleza y calidades de los medicamentos simples. *Alcalá de Henares: J. Gracián*, 1607. 685 p.; fol. The 4th additional pt, 1st publ., Madrid, 1572, contains numerous refs, derived from Monardes, to American plants. García (Alcalá de Henares) 811; Palau 94186n. Madrid:BN.
607/34

García, Gregorio. Origen de los Indios de el Nuevo Mundo, e Indias Occidentales. *Valencia: P. P. Mey*, 1607. 535 p.; 8vo. Sabin

26566; Medina (BHA) 524; Streit II:1378; Palau 98007; JCB (3) II:44. CtY, DLC, InU-L, MH, MiU-C, NN-RB, RPJCB; BL, BN.
607/35

González de Nájera, Alonso. El quinto, y sexto punto de la relacion del desengaño de la guerra de Chile. [*Madrid?* ca. 1607?]. 16 numb. lvs; 4to. Medina (Chile) 201; Palau 105576. BL (dated '1640?').
607/36

Goulart, Simon. Admirable and memorable histories . . . Collected into French out of the best authors . . . and . . . into English. By Ed. Grimeston. *London: G. Eld*, 1607. 646 p.; 4to. Transl. from author's *Histoires admirables et memorables de nostre temps*, 1st publ., Paris, 1600–1601; cf. year 1603. Contains the 1st vol. only. Jones (Goulart) 54(d); STC 12135. CSmH, CtY, DFo, ICN, MH, MnU-B, PPL; BL.
607/37

——. Histoires admirables et memorables de nostre temps. *Paris: J. Houzé*, 1607. 398 p.; 12mo. 1st publ., Paris, 1600–1601; cf. year 1601. NjP.
607/38

Hall, Joseph, Bp of Norwich. Mundus alter et item. *Hanau: W. Antonius*, 1607. 224 p.; maps; 8vo. 1st publ., [London, 1605?]. For the bibliographical complexities of this work, see editions of 1605 & 1606. Sabin 29819; cf. STC 12685; Shaaber (Brit. auth.) H50; JCB (3) II:46. CtY, DLC, ICN, MiU-C, RPJCB; BL, BN.
607/39

Jesuits. Letters from missions. Annuae litterae (1597) 1607. Annuae litterae . . . anni M.D.XCVII. *Naples: T. Longo*, 1607. 610 p.; 8vo. Includes accounts of Brazilian & Mexican provinces. Streit I:293; Backer I:1325. BL, Rome:BN.
607/40

Jesuits. Letters from missions. Annuae litterae (1598) 1607. Annuae litterae . . . anni M.D.XCVIII. *Lyons: J. Roussin*, 1607. 559 p.; 8vo. Includes account of Mexican province. Streit I:294. BL, Rome:BN.
607/41

Jesuits. Letters from missions. Annuae litterae (1599) 1607. Annuae litterae . . . anni M.D.XCIX. *Lyons: J. Roussin*, 1607. 702 p.; 8vo. Includes account of Mexican province. Streit I:295. NNH.
607/42

Jonson, Ben. Volpone. *London: [G. Eld,] for T. Thorpe*, 1607. [118] p.; 4to. Includes refs to tobacco, sassafras, & guaiacum. STC 14783; Greg 259 (aI)–(aII). CSmH, CtY, DFo, InU-L, MH, NNPM; BL. 607/43

Kerkhove, Jan van. Nouvelles des choses qui se passent en diverses et loingtaines parties du monde: pour l'advancement de la saincte foy Catholique . . . Par la diligence des Peres Jesuites. *Paris: F. Bourriquant,* 1607. 16 p.; 8vo. Pages 14–16 treat 'l'Orient Occidental.' Atkinson (Fr. Ren.) 482; Streit I:296; Backer IX:1202. BN. 607/44

Libavius, Andreas. Alchymia triumphans. *Frankfurt a. M.: J. Sauer, for P, Kopff,* 1607. 926 p.; 8vo. 1st publ. as here transl. from the author's *Alchymistische Practic* (Frankfurt a. M., 1603), Frankfurt a. M., 1604, under title *Praxis alchymiae.* Wellcome I:3777. BL, BN. 607/45

Maiolo, Simeone, Bp of Volturara. Dies caniculares, hoc est Colloquia tria et viginti . . . Editio altera. *Mainz: J. Albin,* 1607. 780 p.; 4to. 1st publ., Rome, 1597. Included are numerous refs to natural history of New World. Cf. Sabin 44056. CU, NNC, NNH; BN. 607/46

Markham, Gervase. Cavelarice, or The English horseman. [*London: E. Allde & W. Jaggard,*] *for E. White,* 1607. 3 pts; 4to. Includes remedy for horses employing tobacco. Poynter (Markham) 19.1; STC 17334; Arents (Add.) 130. CLU-C, CtY, DFo, ICN, MH, NN-A, PU; BL. 607/47

Marston, John. What you will. *London: G. Eld, for T. Thorpe,* 1607. [62] p.; 4to. Comedy. Includes ref. to tobacco. STC 17487; Greg 252(a); Arents 81. CSmH, CtY, DLC, ICN, MH, MiU, NN-A; BL. 607/48

Massaria, Alessandro. Practica medica. *Treviso: E. Deuchino, for G. B. Pulciano,* 1607. 2 pts; fol. 1st publ., Frankfurt a. M., 1601. DNLM, ICU, MnU, NIC. 607/49

Medina, Pedro de. L'art de naviguer . . . traduit . . . par Nicolas de Nicolai. *Rouen: T. Reinsart,* 1607. 227 (i.e., 263) p.; illus., maps; 4to. 1st publ. as here transl., Lyons, 1553; cf. 1602 edn, of which this is a reissue. Palau 159675n. CtY-M, InU-L, NN-RB. 607/50

Mercator, Gerardus. Atlas minor . . . à J.

Hondius plurimis aeneis tabulis auctus atque illustratus. *Amsterdam: J. Hondius; sold also by C. Claeszoon & by J. Janszoon, at Arnhem,* 1607. 682 p.; maps; obl. 12mo. Included are 5 maps of the Americas. Cf. Sabin 47887; Koeman (Me) 186; Phillips (Atlases) 423. DLC, ICN, MnU-B, NNH; BL, BN. 607/51

——. Atlas, sive Cosmographicae meditationes de fabrica mundi et fabricata figura. Iam tandem . . . perductus, quamplurimis aeneis tabulis Hispaniae, Africae, Asiae & Americae auctus ac illustratus à Judoco Hondio . . . Editio secunda. *Amsterdam: C. Claeszoon & J. Hondius,* 1607. 355 p.; maps; fol. 1st publ., Amsterdam, 1606. Cf. Sabin 47882; Cf. Koeman (Me) 17. MiU-C, BN. 607/52

—[Anr issue]. *Amsterdam: J. Hondius,* 1607. Koeman (Me) 17. Leyden:UB. 607/53

—[Anr issue]. *Amsterdam: C. Claeszoon,* 1607. The imprint is a paste-on cancel of the preceding with Hondius's name alone in imprint. Koeman (Me) 16; Phillips (Atlases) 422. DLC. 607/54

Middleton, Thomas. The phoenix. *London: E. A[llde]., for A. J[ohnson].,* 1607. 38 lvs; 4to. Drama. Contains ref. to tobacco. STC 17892; Greg 243(a); Arents 82. CSmH, CtY, DFo, MH, MiU, NN-A, PU; BL. 607/55

Migoen, Jacob Willem. Eene treffelijcke tzamensprekinghe tusschen den Paus ende Koninck van Spaegnien, belangende den Peys met ons lieden aen te gaene. [*Netherlands:* ca. 1607?]. [8] p.; 4to. Includes refs to Panama, Gulf of Mexico, etc., on p. [7]. Cf. Knuttel 1398. RPJCB. 607/56

—[Anr edn]. Eene treffelijcke tzamensprekinghe tusschen den Paus ende Koninc van Spagnien. [*Netherlands:* ca. 1607?]. [8] p.; 4to. Signed (∴) (∴)ij, etc. Knuttel 1398. The Hague:KB. 607/57

—[Anr edn]. Eene treffelijcke t'zamensprekinghe tusschen den Paus ende Coninck van Spaengnien. [*Netherlands:* ca. 1607?]. [8] p.; 4to. Signed A, Aij, etc. Knuttel 1399. NN; The Hague:KB. 607/58

—[Anr edn]. Eene treffelijcke t'samensprekinge tusschen den Paus ende Coninck van

Spangien. [*Netherlands:* ca. 1607?]. [8] p.; 4to. Title in roman type. Knuttel 1400. CtY, MnU; BL (Paul V, Pope), The Hague:KB.
607/59

Netherlands (United Provinces, 1581–1795). Staten Generaal. Placcaet ende ordonnantie opte wapeninghe ende manninghe vande schepen. *The Hague: H. Jacobszoon van Wouw,* 1607. [18] p.; 4to. Includes ref. to shipping in West Indies. JCB (3) II:47. MnU-B, RPJCB.
607/60

Nicholl, John. An houre glasse of Indian news. Or, A true and tragicall discourse, showing the most lamentable miseries . . . indured by 67 Englishmen . . . sent for a supply to the planting in Guiana . . . 1605. who . . . were . . . left a shore in Saint Lucia. *London: [E. Allde,] for N. Butter,* 1607. [43] p.; 4to. Sabin 55183; STC 18532; Arents 82-A; Church 332; JCB (3) II:47. CSmH, MWiW-C, NN-RB, PP, RPJCB; BL.
607/61

Nierop, Adriaan van, supposed author. Echo ofte galm, dat is: Wederklinckende ghedicht van de teghenwoordighe vredehandelinghe. [*Amsterdam?*] 1607. [8] p.; 4to. Includes ref. to Spanish exploitation of Peru. Knuttel 1405. The Hague:KB.
607/62

Nieuwen, klaren astrologen-bril, tot verstercking van veel schemerende ooghen, die niet wel en connen sien, die duystere Jesuyten comeet-sterre. [*Amsterdam?* 1607?]. [64] p.; 8vo. Includes refs to economic potential of Indies & Spanish possessions there. Knuttel 1424. MnU, NN; The Hague:KB.
607/63

Owen, John. Epigrammatum . . . libri tres. *London: H. Lownes, for S. Waterson,* 1607. 2 pts; 12mo. 1st publ., London, 1606. STC 18986 (& formerly also 18985); Arents (Add.) 131. CSmH, CtY, DFo, ICU, MH, NN-A; Oxford:Bodl.
607/64

Panciroli, Guido. Rerum memorabilium libri duo . . . latiné redditi . . . ab Henrico Salmuth. Editio secunda. *Amberg: M. Forster,* 1607–8. 2 v.; 8vo. 1st publ., Amberg, 1599–1602; v. 2 has title *Nova reperta.* Both vols contain refs to the New World; cf. 1602 edn above. Sabin 58411 (& 58413n); JCB

(3) II:48 & 53. ICN, MnU-B, NN-RB, PPF, RPJCB; BL.
607/65

Paré, Ambroise. Les oeuvres . . . Sixiesme edition. *Paris: N. Buon,* 1607. 1228 p.; illus., port.; fol. 1st publ., Paris, 1575; cf. the 1601 German edn. Doe (Paré) 33. London:Med. Soc., Paris:Mazarine.
607/66

—[Anr issue]. *Paris: B. Macé,* 1607. Doe (Paré) 34. CtY-M, MiU, NNNAM; Cambridge:Peterhouse, BN.
607/67

Pasquier, Etienne. Les lettres. *Lyons: P. Frellon,* 1607. 438 numb. lvs; 16mo. 1st publ., Paris, 1586. In bk 3, letter 3 contains a description of customs of Brazilian natives. Thickett (Pasquier) 23n. ICN; Cambridge:UL, Avignon:Mus. Calvet.
607/68

—[Anr issue]. *Lyons: J. A. Huguetan,* 1607. Thickett (Pasquier) 23. NIC; BL, BN.
607/69

——. Les recherches de la France . . . Reveuës et augmentées d'un livre, & de plusieurs chapitres par le mesme autheur. *Paris: L. Sonnius,* 1607. 1175 p.; port.; 4to. 1st publ. with American content, Paris, 1596. In bk 4, chapt. xxv, syphilis is described as unknown till its appearance at Naples in 1494, with mention of Fracastoro's *Syphilis;* for its treatment guaiacum is lauded. Thickett (Pasquier) 12; Tchémerzine IX:83. CtY, RPB; BL, BN.
607/70

Penot, Bernard Georges. Theophrastisch Vade mecum. Das ist: Etliche sehr nützliche Tractat, von der warhafftigen Bereitung und rechtem Gebrauch der chymischen Medicamenten . . . erstlich in Latein herausz geben. Jetzo . . . in unsere . . . Muttersprache transferiret, durch Johannem Hippodamum [i.e., J. Lange]. *Magdeburg: J. Franck,* 1607. 215 p.; 4to. 1st publ. as transl. from the author's *Tractatus varii, de vera praeparatione . . . medicamentorum chymicorum,* (Frankfurt a. M., 1594) Eisleben, 1597. 'De sale Guaiaci': p. 168–69. Sudhoff (Paracelsus) 278; Wellcome I:4895. London: Wellcome.
607/71

Peucer, Kaspar. Commentarius, de praecipuis divinationum generibus . . . Recognitus ultimo . . . ab authore. *Frankfurt a. M.: C. de Marne & Heirs of J. Aubry,* 1607. 738

p.; 8vo. 1st (?) publ. in this version, Wittenberg, 1560. In section on astrology a passage mentions Columbus & contrasts time required for east & west voyages between Spain & West Indies. CtY, ICN, MH, NN-RB; BN. 607/72

—[Anr edn]. *Hanau: W. Antonius,* 1607. 8vo. BL. 607/73

Piò, Giovanni Michele, O.P. Delle vite de gli huomini illustri di S. Domenico. *Bologna: G. B. Bellagamba,* 1607. 2 pts; fol. In pt 2 are accounts of Dominican missions in Spanish America. A 2nd vol. was publ., 1613, at Pavia. Streit I:291; cf. Palau 227137. BL, BN. 607/74

Possevino, Antonio. Bibliotheca selecta. *Cologne: J. Gymnicus,* 1607. 2 v.; fol. 1st publ., Rome, 1593; cf. 1603 edn. Streit I:292. ICN, NN-RB, NcU: BL, BN. 607/75

Resende, Garcia de. Choronica que trata da vida . . . do christianissimo . . . Joao o segundo. *Lisbon: J. Rodriguez,* 1607. fol. 1st publ., Lisbon, 1545, under title *Lyvro . . . que trata da vida . . . de . . . rey don Joao o segundo;* includes account of encounter between John II of Portugal & Columbus. Cf. Sabin 70062. BL. 607/76

A rich storehouse, or Treasurie for the diseased . . . First set foorth . . . by A.T. and now fourthly corrected, augmented and inlarged, by G. W. *London: R. Blower,* 1607. 91 numb. lvs; 4to. 1st publ., London, 1596; cf. year 1601 above. STC 23607. DFo, MH; BL. 607/77

Richeome, Louis, S.J. Trois discours pour la religion catholique. *Lyons: P. Rigaud,* 1607. 686 p.; 12 mo. 1st publ., Bordeaux, 1597; cf. 1601 edn. Backer VI:1817–18; cf. Cioranescu (XVII) 59455. 607/78

Rivadeneira, Pedro de, S.J. Vita del b.p. Ignatio Loiola . . . nuovamente tradotta dalla spagnuola . . . da d. Salustio Gratii. *Naples: S. Bonino, for G. B. Sottile,* 1607. 182 p.; 12mo. 1st publ. in Italian, Venice, 1586; cf. year 1606. Backer VI:1730; Palau 266242. 607/79

Rowlands, Samuel. Democritus, or Doctor Merry-man his medicines. *London: [W. Jaggard,] for J. Deane,* 1607. 4to. In verse. In 2nd poem, beginning 'Two beggars', tobacco is mentioned. STC 21366. CSmH; BL. 607/80

——. Humors ordinarie. *London: E. Allde, for W. Ferbrand,* 1607. 4to. In verse. 1st publ., London, 1600, under title *The letting of humors blood;* cf. the year 1605. STC 21395; Arents 83. NN-A; BL. 607/81

Rubio, Antonio. Commentarii in universam Aristotelis Logicam. *Valencia:* 1607. 1st publ., Cologne, 1605, under title *Logica Mexicana.* Sabin 47860n; Medina (BHA) 525; Palau 280353. 607/82

Scaliger, Julius Caesar. Exotericarum exercitationum liber xv. *Frankfurt a. M.: [Wechel Office, for] C. Marne & Heirs of J. Aubry,* 1607. 1129 p.; 8vo. 1st publ., Paris, 1557; cf. 1601 edn. MH, MiU, NNE, PPAmP. 607/83

Serres, Jean de. A general inventorie of the history of France, from the beginning of that monarchie, unto . . . 1598 . . . And continued unto these times, out of the best authors [P. Matthieu, etc.] . . . Translated out of French . . . by Edward Grimeston. *London: G. Eld,* 1607. 2 pts; ports; fol. Transl. from the author's *Inventaire general de l'histoire de France* as publ., Paris, 1600, but here containing in the 'Continuation' under the year 1603 a substantial section on 'The navigation of the French to new France or Canada' transl. from P. V. P. Cayet's *Chronologie septenaire,* 1st publ., Paris, 1605. STC 22244; Arents (Add.) 134. CSmH, CtY, DFo, ICN, NN-RB, RPJCB; BL. 607/84

Serres, Olivier de, seigneur du Pradel. The perfect use of silk-wormes . . . Done out of the French originall . . . by Nicholas Geffe. *London: F. Kingston, for R. Sergier & C. Purset,* 1607. 2 pts; illus.; 4to. The 4th prelim. lf contains a poem by Michael Drayton to the translator comparing him to Columbus. For varying imprints, see the STC. STC 22249 & 22249.3; Arents (Add.) 134. CSmH, CtY, DFo, ICN, MH-A, NN-RB, RPJCB; BL. 607/85

Sharpham, Edward. Cupids whirligig. *London: E. Allde; sold by A. Johnson,* 1607. 42 lvs; 4to. Comedy. In act 3, scene 1, one 'Captain Tobacco Pipe' is mentioned. STC 22380; Greg 247(a); Arents (Add.) 136; Pforzheimer 921. CSmH, CtY, DFo, MH, MiU, NN-A; BL.   607/86

——. The fleire. *London:* [*E. Allde,*] *for F. B*[*ur-ton*]*.,* 1607. 30 lvs; 4to. Drama. Includes character symbolic of tobacco. STC 22384; Greg 255(a); Arents 84. CSmH, CtY, DFo, MH, NN-A; BL.   607/87

Spain. Consejo de las Indias. Memorial del pleyto sobre la sucession en possession del estado y mayorazgo de Veragua, marquesado de Jamayca, y almirantazgo de las Indias, que fundò don Christoval Colon. [*Madrid:* 1607]. 288 numb. lvs; fol. Cf. entry under Colón y Pravia, Francisca, under the year 1608. Medina (BHA) 8466; Pérez Pastor (Madrid) 971. NN-RB; Madrid: Acad. de la Hist.   607/88

Stafford, Robert. A geographicall and anthologicall description of all the empires and kingdomes in this globe. *London: T. C*[*reede*]*., for S. Waterson,* 1607. 67 p.; 4to. STC 23135. CSmH, DLC, MH, NN-RB; BL.   607/89

Stradling, Sir John. Epigrammatum libri quatuor. *London:* [*Eliot's Court Press, for*] *G. Bishop & J. Norton,* 1607. 176 p.; 8vo. In verse Bk 1 includes epigrams on Sir Francis Drake, John Hawkins, & John Norris. STC 23354. CSmH, CtY, DFo, ICN, MH, NNC; BL.   607/90

Tagault, Jean. Institutione di cirugia . . . Distinta in libri cinque. *Venice: L. Spineda,* 1607. 421 numb. lvs; illus.; 8vo. Transl. from Tagault's *De chirurgica institutione libri quinque,* 1st publ., Paris, 1543. Guaiacum is mentioned in treatment of syphilis. Wellcome I:6208. DNLM; London:Wellcome.
                                        607/91

Tomkis, Thomas. Lingua, or The combat of the tongue. *London: G. Eld, for S. Waterson,* 1607. [98] p.; 4to. Drama. In act 4, scene 4, a character named & representing tobacco appears in appropriate garb, speaking a purported Caribbean language. STC 24104; Greg 239 (a). CSmH, DFo, DLC; BL.   607/92

Topsell, Edward. The historie of fourefooted beastes . . . Collected out of all the volumes of Conradus Gesner, and all other writers to this present day. *London: W. Jaggard,* 1607. 757 p.; illus.; fol. On p. 660 is a description of Patagonian giants who

clothe themselves with skins of the 'Su', with illus. derived from Thevet's *Singularitez de la France antarctique,* chapt. lvi. For printing variants, see the STC. Sabin 27228; Nissen (Zool.) 4145; STC 24123. CSmH, CtY, DLC, ICN, MH, MiU, PU, RPB; BL.
                                        607/93

Valbuena, Bernardo de. Siglo de oro, en las selvas de Erifile. *Madrid: A. Martín, for A. Perérez,* 1607. *See the year* 1608.

Vaughan, William. Naturall and artificial directions for health . . . Third edition, newly corrected, revised and enlarged. *London:* [*R. Bradock,*] *for Roger Jackson,* 1607. 8vo. 1st publ., London, 1600; cf. 1602 edn. STC 24614. MH (imp.); BL.   607/94

Verstegen, Richard. Theatre des cruautez des hereticques de nostre temps. Traduit du latin . . . Seconde edition. *Antwerp: A. Hubert,* 1607. 95 p.; illus., port.; 4to. 1st publ. in French, Antwerp, 1588, as transl. from the author's *Theatrum crudelitatum haereticorum* (Antwerp, 1587). Included is an account of the martyrdom of Inácio de Azevedo & fellow Jesuits en route to Brazil. DFo, ICN, MWiW-C; BL.   607/95

Wake, Sir Isaac. Rex platonicus, sive De . . . Jacobi . . . Regis, ad . . . Academiam Oxoniensem adventu . . . 1605. narratio. *Oxford: J. Barnes,* 1607. 140 p.; 4to. In this account of the entertainment afforded James I during his visit to Oxford, p. 81–88 describe the discussion of the medicinal uses of tobacco. STC 24939; Madan (Oxford) 1607:10; Arents 85. CSmH, CtY, DLC, MH, NN-A; BL.   607/96

—[Anr edn]. Editio secunda. *Oxford: J. Barnes,* 1607. 224 p.; 12mo. STC 24939.5; Madan (Oxford) 1607:11. CSmH, DFo, CaOTU; BL.   607/97

Walkington, Thomas. The optick glasse of humors. *London: J. Windet, for M. Clarke,* 1607. 8vo. In chapt. ix, 'Of a cholericke complexion', tobacco is discussed, with mention of Peru, West Indies, etc. STC 24967. CSmH, DFo; BL.   607/98

Wilkins, George. The miseries of inforst marriage. *London:* [*W. Jaggard*] *for G. Vincent,* 1607. [78] p.; 4to. Drama. Includes ref. to tobacco. STC 25635; Greg 249 (a). CSmH, CtY, DFo, MH; BL.   607/99

Wytfliet, Corneille. Histoire universelle des

Indes Occidentales, divisée en deux livres, faicte en latin . . . nouvellement traduicte. *Douai: P. Auroy, for F. Fabri, 1607.* 3 pts; illus., maps; fol. 1st publ. in this version, 1605, under title *Histoire des Indes, Orientales et Occidentales.* Pt 2, with special t.p., comprises the *Histoire universelle des Indes Orientales* of G. A. Magini & others, here however supplemented by *La suite de l'Histoire des Indes Orientales.* Sabin 105700; Borba de Moraes II:381; Atkinson (Fr. Ren.) 489; Streit V:88; cf. Phillips (Atlases) 1143; JCB (3) II:48. DLC, ICN, InU-L, MH, NN, PPL, RPJCB; BL, BN. 607/100

1608

Abbot, George, Abp of Canterbury. A briefe description of the whole worlde . . . The third edition. *London: J. Browne, 1608.* [160] p.; 4to. 1st publ., London, 1599. Sabin 21n; STC 27; JCB (3) II:49. DFo, MH, NN-RB, RPJCB; BL. 608/1

Acosta, José de, S.J. Historia natural y moral de las Indias. *Madrid: A. Martín, for J. Berrillo, 1608.* 535 p.; 4to. 1st publ., Seville, 1590. Sabin 122; Medina (BHA) 529; Streit II:1387; Pérez Pastor (Madrid) 982; Arents 35-a; JCB (3) II:50. CtY, ICN, MH-A, NN-RB, RPJCB; BL. 608/2

Het af-scheidt vande edele moghende Heeren Staten vande Gheunieerde Provintien, gegeven aende Ghecommitteerde vanden Coninck van Spaengien. *Middelburg: S. Janszoon [1608].* [6] p.; 4to. Includes refs to West Indies. Knuttel 1529. NN-RB, RPJCB, WU; The Hague:KB. 608/3

Amelung, Peter. Tractatus nobilis secundus. *Leipzig: A. Lamberg, for J. Apel, 1608.* 356 p.; 8vo. In chapt. 2 mechoacan is mentioned. London:Wellcome, BN. 608/4

Antwoordt op het tweede refereyn by de overheerde Nederlantsche provintien aen Hollant gheschreven. *[Amsterdam? 1608?].* [28] p.; 4to. In verse. Includes ref. to West Indies. NN; BL (Netherlands). 608/5

Arthus, Gotthard. Historia Indiae Orientalis, ex variis auctoribus collecta. *Cologne: W. Lutzenkirchen, 1608.* 616 p.; 8vo. An abridgment of J. T. de Bry's collection, *India Orientalis.* In chapt. vi minor refs to Brazil

occur. Sabin 2139; Streit V:94; Muller 1866; JCB (3) II:50. C, DLC, NN-RB, OCl, PBL, RPJCB; BL, BN. 608/6

Avendaño y Villela, Pedro. Señor. Quien considerare la opulencia y grandeza a que ha llegado la poblacion de las Indias Occidentales de solos setenta años a esta parte, que los Españoles la dieron principio, y el aumento en que cada diava . . . *[Madrid? 1608?].* 7 numb. lvs; fol. Dated at end, Madrid, 14 April 1608. On the decline of Spanish American commerce. Medina (BHA) 532. BL, Santiago, Chile:BN. 608/7

Bertonio, Ludovico, S.J. Arte y grammatica muy copiosa de la lengua aymara. *Rome: A. Zannetti, 1608.* 8vo. 1st publ., Rome, 1603. Despite bibl. refs, perhaps a ghost created by a misreading of a '3' as '8'. Sabin 5018; Medina (BHA) 535; Viñaza 125; Backer I:1392. 608/8

Blaeu, Willem Janszoon. Het licht der zeevaert. *Amsterdam: W. J. Blaeu, 1608.* 2v.; illus., maps; obl. fol. Chapt. xxv in introduction discusses the use of maps in voyages to the West Indies and return, describing navigational problems and recommending the use of West Indian sea maps made by the publisher. Cf. Sabin 35775; Koeman (M.Bl) 1; cf. Tiele 121; Skelton, p. xii. Rotterdam:WAE, Madrid:Museo Naval. 608/9

Blefken, Dithmar. Een corte ende warachtige beschrijvinge der twee eylanden, Ijslandt ende Groen-landt. *Gorinchem: A. Helmichszoon, 1608.* 48 p.; 8vo. Transl. from the author's *Islandia,* 1st publ., Leyden, 1607. Sabin 5904; Tiele 144; JCB (3) II:50. RPJCB; BL. 608/10

Bodin, Jean. Discours . . . sur le rehaussement et dimunution tant d'or que d'argent. *[Geneva? G. Cartier?]* 1608. 8vo. 1st publ., Paris, 1578. Included is a discussion of economic effects of gold derived from Peru. BN. 608/11

——. Les six livres de la Republique. *[Geneva:]* G. Cartier, 1608. 1060 p.; 8vo. 1st publ., Paris, 1576. In bk 1, chapt. 5, are refs to West Indian slavery, in bk 5, chapt. 1, to the New World as a whole. ICU, MU, NN-RB; BL, BN. 608/12

Botero, Giovanni. I capitani . . . Con alcuni discorsi curiosi. *Turin: G. D. Tarino, 1608.*

250 p.; 8vo. A reissue with altered imprint date of printer's 1607 edn? WU.
608/13

——. Historia ecclesiástica y estado presente de la religion de todos los reynos de Europa, Asia, Africa, sacada de las Relaciones toscanas . . . por Jayme Rebullosa. *Barcelona: J. Cendrat, for J. Margarit,* 1608. 212 numb. lvs; 8vo. 1st publ. in this version, Barcelona, 1603, under title *Descripcion de todas las provincias . . . del mundo.* Palau 33707. MnU-B.
608/14

——. Relationi universali . . . Nuovamente ristampate, & corrette. *Venice: A. Angelieri,* 1608,'07. 5 pts; maps; 4to. 1st publ., Rome, 1591–96. MnU-B, OCU; BN.
608/15

——. Relations of the most famous kingdomes. *London: [W. Jaggard,] for J. Jaggard,* 1608. 330 p.; 4to. 1st publ. in English, London, 1601, under title *The travellers breviat & The worlde;* also publ., London, 1603, under title *An historicall description.* Sabin 36282n; STC 3401. DFo, ICN, MH; BL.
608/16

Bulle oft Mandaet des Paus van Roomen aende gheestelicheydt al om bevolen, om haer advijs te vernemen opt stuck van den vredehandel met de Hollantsche ketters. *[Amsterdam:* 1608]. [6] p.; 4to. (Den Nederlandtschen bye-corf, no. 2). Includes ref. to West Indies in 'Carmeliten' segment. Sometimes ascribed to Willem Usselinx. Asher 28.2; Knuttel 1444. MiU-C, NN-RB; The Hague:KB.
608/17

—[Anr edn]. Bulle oft Mandaet . . . aende gheestelicheyt. *[Amsterdam:* 1608]. [6] p.; 4to. Knuttel 1445. MiU-C, RPJCB; The Hague:KB.
608/18

—[Anr edn]. *[Amsterdam?* 1608?]. [6] p.; obl. 4to. Knuttel 1446. The Hague:KB.
608/19

Buyr-praetjen: ofte Tsamensprekinge ende discours op den brief vanden agent Aerssens uyt Vranckrijck. *[Amsterdam?* 1608]. [16] p.; 4to. (Den Nederlandtschen bye-corf, no. 35). Includes refs to West Indian commerce and Spanish tyranny over Indians. Asher 28.36; Knuttel 1525. The Hague:KB.
608/20

—[Anr edn]. Buyr-praetjen . . . op den brieff.

[Amsterdam? 1608]. [16] p.; 4to. DLC, MiU-C, NN, RPJCB; The Hague:KB.
608/21

Cambridge. University. Act verses. Anima unita corpori est perfectior, quam separata. *[Cambridge:* ca. 1608]. bds.; fol. In verse. Printed as 2nd col. is thesis 'Britannus Virginiae naturalis dominus'. STC (2) 4474.6. Oxford:Bodl.
608/22

Camerarius, Philipp. Les meditations historiques . . . reduits en dix livres & nouvellement tournez de latin . . . par S[imon]. G[oulart]. *Paris: J. Gesselin,* 1608. 2 v.; 8vo. 1st publ. in French, Lyons, 1603. Copies of v. 2 occur with imprint of J. Cottereau. Jones (Goulart) 57b. BN.
608/23

Catechismus ofte Tsamen-spreeckinghe, ghemaeckt op den vrede-handel . . . Overghezet uyt de Fransoysche. *[Amsterdam?]* 1608. [8] p.; 4to. Transl. from unpubl. French manuscript—Knuttel 1413. Includes ref. to West Indian shipping, & to Ferdinand & Isabella's discovery of New World. Knuttel 1414. MnU, NN; The Hague:KB.
608/24

—[Anr edn]. Dialogus oft Tsamensprekinge. *[Amsterdam?]* 1608. [16] p.; 8vo. Knuttel 1415. The Hague:KB.
608/25

—[Anr edn]. *[Amsterdam?]* 1608. [8] p.; 4to. Knuttel 1416. The Hague:KB.
608/26

—[Anr edn]. Dialogus oft Tzamensprekinge. *[Amsterdam?]* 1608. [6] p.; 4to. (Den Nederlandtschen bye-corf, no. 26). Knuttel 1417. CtY, MiU-C, NN-RB, RPJCB, WU; BL, The Hague:KB.
608/27

Catholic Church. Commisarius Generalis Cruciatae. Instrucion y forma que se ha de tener y guardar en la publicacion . . . y cobrança de la Bula de la Santa Cruzada, de la sexta predicacion . . . fecha por . . . Sixto .V. . . . confirmada . . . por . . . Paulo quinto . . . que se ha de hazer en el arcobispado de las Charcas Cuzco, Quito Tucuman, . . . Santiago de Chile, y la Assuncion, y provincias del Rio de la Plata, Panama, Carthagena, Santamarta: y ansi mismo en el arçobispado . . . de Granada, y obispados de Popayan y Venezuela. *[Madrid?* 1608?]. 13 numb. lvs; fol. 1st (?) publ., *[Barcelona?* 1537?]; cf. 1602 edn. Sub-

scribed: Dada en Madrid a veynte y cinco de Noviembre, de 1608. años. Medina (BHA) 8467; Pérez Pastor (Madrid) 1003; Palau 120136. Madrid: Acad. de la Hist.
608/28

Cayet, Pierre Victor Palma. Chronologie novenaire, contenant l'histoire de la guerre sous le regne du . . . roy . . . Henry IIII. *Paris: J. Richer,* 1608. 3 v.; 8vo. Under year 1595 is a section 'Ce que fit Drak en ceste annee, allant en devant de la flotte d'Espagne qui venait des Indes'. Sabin 47931n; Cioranescu (XVI) 6013. CtY, DLC, MH, NN-RB, RPB; BL, BN.
608/29

Clavius, Christoph. In Sphaeram Joannis de Sacro Bosco commentarius. *Geneva: S. Crespin,* 1608. 585 p.; illus.; 4to. 1st publ., Rome, 1570; cf. 1601 edn. Shaaber (Brit. auth.) H445. Edinburgh:UL, BN.
608/30

—[Anr issue]. *St. Gervais: S. Crespin,* 1608. CtY, IU, NN-RB.
608/31

Colón y Pravia, Francisca, plaintiff. Alegacion en derecho por Doña Francisca Colon de Toledo, sobre la sucession en possession del estado y ducado de Veragua. *Madrid: L. Sánchez,* 1608. 120 numb. lvs; fol. On succession as heiress to Columbus. Medina (BHA) 528; Pérez Pastor (Madrid) 984. Santiago, Chile:BN.
608/32

—[Anr edn]. Allegacion de derecho. Por parte de Doña Francisca Colon de Toledo, sobre la tenuta y possession de los estados de almirantazgo de las Indias. [*Madrid?* 1608?]. 92 numb. lvs; fol. DLC.
608/33

Consideratien vande vrede in Nederlandt gheconcipieert, Anno 1608. [*Netherlands:* 1608]. [4] p.; 4to. (Den Nederlandtschen bye-corf, no. 15). Includes refs to West Indian commerce. Sometimes attributed to Willem Usselinx. Asher 28.16; Knuttel 1447. MiU-C; The Hague:KB.
608/34

—[Anr edn]. [*Netherlands:* 1608]. Text begins 'DOorlogh' rather than 'DOorloch'. Knuttel 1448. DLC, MiU-C, RPJCB; The Hague:KB.
608/35

Coquerel, Nicolas de. Discours de la perte que les François reçoivent en la permission d'exposer les monnoyes estrangeres. *Paris: F. Jacquin,* 1608. 28 numb. lvs; 8vo. In-cluded are refs to gold & silver of Potosí, Peru, & Chile. MH-BA; BL, BN.
608/36

Cordus, Valerius. Dispensatorium, sive Pharmacorum conficiendorum ratio. [*Leyden:*] *Plantin Press (Raphelengius),* 1608. 467 p.; illus.; 16mo. 1st publ., Nuremberg, 1546; cf. 1606 edn. London: Wellcome.
608/37

Crespin, Jean. Histoire des martyres, persecutez et mis a mort pour la verité de l'evangile . . . Reveuë, & augmentée. [*Geneva: J. Vignon*] 1608. 765 numb. lvs; fol. 1st publ. as enl. by Goulart, [Geneva?], 1582. Includes account of Villegagnon's attempted colony in Brazil. Jones (Goulart) 23(d). ICN, NN-RB; Geneva:BP.
608/38

Day, John. Law-tricks, or, Who would have thought it. *London:* [*E. Allde?*] *for R. More,* 1608. [71] p.; 4to. Drama. Includes refs to tobacco. STC 6416; Greg 267; Arents 87. CSmH, CtY, DLC, MH, MiU-L, PU, TxU; BL.
608/39

Daza, Antonio, O.F.M. Delle chroniche dell'Ordine de' Frati minori . . . parte quarta, nuovamente datta in luce. *Venice: B. Barezzi,* 1608. 1287 p.; 4to. Continues Marcos da Lisboa's *Cronica general;* 1st publ. in Spanish, Salamanca, 1570. Described are Franciscan missionary activities in Spanish America. Streit I:298.
608/40

Dees wonder-maer end' prophetsije wis. [*Amsterdam?* 1608?]. [16] p.; 4to. (Den Nederlandtschen bye-corf, no. 34). Includes ref. to West Indies. Asher 28.35; Knuttel 1464. MiU-C, MnU, NN, RPJCB; BL, The Hague:KB.
608/41

Dekker, Thomas. The dead tearme. *London: J. Hodgets,* 1608. [54] p.; 4to. 'Going to law' is compared to a West Indian voyage. STC 6496. CSmH, DLC, MH; BL.
608/42

——. Lanthorne and candle-light, or The second part of the Belman. *London: J. Busby,* 1608. 39 lvs; 4to. Included are refs to tobacco. Reprinted, 1612, under title *O per se O;* 1616, as *Villainies discovered;* & 1632, as *English villanies.* STC 6485. DFo; BL, Oxford:Bodl.
608/43

Del Rio, Martin Antón, S.J. Disquisitionum magicarum libri sex. *Lyons: H. Cardon,* 1608.

1st publ., Louvain, 1599–1600; cf. 1603 edn. Backer II:1899. London:Wellcome, BN.   608/44

—[Anr issue]. *Lyons: J. Pillehotte, 1608.* Backer II:1899. NIC; BL, BN.   608/45

Descubrimiento de los terros y riquezas que tiene Dios escondidos en las Indias. *Barcelona: H. Anglada, 1608.* 2 v.; 8vo. Sabin 19730; Ternaux 313.   608/46

Ein Dialogus oder Gespräch, die noch wehrende niderländische Friedenstractation betreffendt. [*Germany?*] 1608. [36] p.; 4to. Transl. from *Schuyt-praetgens,* 1st publ., [*Amsterdam?* 1608]. Knuttel 1453. The Hague:KB.   608/47

Dialogus oft Tsamensprekinge. [*Amsterdam?*] 1608. *See the* Catechismus ofte Tsamen-spreeckinghe *above.*

Discours by forme van remonstrantie: vervatende de noodsaeckelickheyd vande Oos-Indische navigatie. [*Netherlands:*] 1608. [14] p.; 4to. 2nd leaf is signed 'Aij'. Includes refs to Strait of Magellan and Spanish control of West Indies. Also forms part of *Den Nederlandtschen bye-corf.* Sometimes attributed to Willem Usselinx. Sabin 98192; Knuttel 1428; Kress 287; JCB (3) II:56. DLC, MH-BA, NN-RB, RPJCB; BL, The Hague:KB.   608/48

—[Anr edn]. Discours by forme van remonstrantye: vervatende de nootsaeckelickheydt vande Oost-Indische navigatie. [*Netherlands:*] 1608. [14] p.; 4to. 2nd leaf unsigned. Sabin 98193; Asher 35; Knuttel 1429; JCB (3) II:55–56. RPJCB; The Hague:KB.   608/49

—[Anr edn]. Discours by forme van remonstrantie; vervatende de nootsakelijckheyt vande Oost-Indische navigatie. [*Netherlands: 1608?*]. [8] p.; 4to. Knuttel 1430. BN, The Hague:KB.   608/50

Discours van Pieter en Pauwels, op de handelinghe vanden vreede. Anno 1608. [*Amsterdam? 1608?*]. [8] p.; 4to. (Den Nederlandtschen bye-corf, no. 25). Includes refs to Spanish tyranny in Mexico, Peru, Florida, etc. Asher 28.26; Knuttel 1456. The Hague:KB.   608/51

—[Anr edn]. [*Amsterdam? 1608?*]. [3] p.; 4to. Sabin 20230. DLC, MiU-C, NN-RB, RPJCB; BL (Pieter).   608/52

Dodoens, Rembert. Cruydt-boeck . . . volgens sijne laetste verbeteringe . . . Met biivoegsels achter elck capittel, uut verscheyden cruydtbeschrijvers: item in't laetste een beschrijvinge vande Indiaensche gewassen, meest getrocken uut de schriften van Carolus Clusius. *Leyden: Plantin Press (Raphelengius), 1608.* 1580 p.; illus.; fol. Transl. & enl., possibly by Josse van Raphelengen, from author's *Stirpium historiae pemptades sex,* Antwerp, 1583. Pritzel 2345n; Nissen (Bot.) 518; Bibl. belg., 1st ser., IX, D118; Arents 88. DFo, MH-A, NN-A, OU; BL, BN.
608/53

Dominicans. Acta capituli generalis Romae . . . Ordinis Praedicatorum celebrati . . . xxv. Maij, anno Domini M DCVIII. *Rome: C. Vullietti, 1608.* 71 p.; 4to. Included are reports on order's provinces in Spanish America. RPJCB.   608/54

Drayton, Michael. Poems . . . Newly corrected. *London:* [*W. Stansby,*] for *J. Smethwick, 1608.* 3 pts; 8vo. 1st publ., London, 1605. STC 7218. CSmH, CtY, DFo, MiU, MH, NjP, PPRF; BL.   608/55

Du Bartas, Guillaume de Salluste, seigneur. Les oeuvres poétiques . . . avec argumens, sommaires & annotations augmentees par S[imon. G[oulart]. *Geneva: P. & J. Chouët, 1608.* 3 v.; 12mo. In verse. Included are the author's *La sepmaine,* 1st publ. with Goulart's commentaries, Paris, 1584, & his *La seconde sepmaine,* 1st publ. with Goulart's commentaries, Geneva, 1589. Cf. 1601 edn. Cf. Holmes (DuBartas) I:75–76 no. 33; Jones (Goulart) 20t. Geneva:BP.
608/56

—[Anr issue]. *Geneva: S. Crespin, 1608.* Holmes (DuBartas) I:76 no. 34 & I:89 no. 19abcd; Jones (Goulart) 20u. BN.   608/57

—[Anr issue]. [*Geneva:*] *Michelle Nicod, 1608.* Holmes (DuBartas) I:76 no. 34 & I:89 no. 19abcd. Grenoble:BM.   608/58

—[Anr edn]. *Geneva: G. Cartier, 1608.* 697 p.; 12mo. Holmes (DuBartas) I:76 no. 35. BN.
608/59

———. Bartas his devine weekes & workes translated . . . by Josuah Sylvester. *London: H. Lownes, 1608.* 2 pts; illus.; 4to. In verse. 1st publ. as here transl., London, 1605, with addition of Du Bartas's 'Historie of Judith'.

For variant state see the STC. STC 21650. CSmH, CtY, DFo, ICU, MH, NNC, PU; BL.
608/60

——. Premiere sepmaine ou Creation du monde . . . En ceste derniere edition ont esté adjoustez . . . explications des principales difficultez du texte, par S[imon]. G[oulart]. *Lyons: F. Arnoullet*, 1608. 12mo. In verse. 1st publ. with Goulart's annotations, Geneva, 1581, as *La sepmaine;* cf. 1601 edn & that of 1602 with title as above. Holmes (DuBartas) I:75 no. 31n; Jones (Goulart) 20v. BN.
608/61

—[Anr issue]. *Lyons: P. Rigaud*, 1608. Holmes (DuBartas) I:75 no. 31; Jones (Goulart) 20y. Montpellier:BM.
608/62

—[Anr edn]. *Rouen: R. Du Petit Val*, 1608. Holmes (DuBartas) I:75 no. 32; Jones (Goulart) 20r. BL, Paris:Arsenal.
608/63

——. La seconde sepmaine. [*Geneva:*] *P. & J. Chouët*, 1608. 12mo. In verse. 1st publ., Paris, 1584; cf. 1601 edn. Included are commentaries by Simon Goulart of 1589. Holmes (DuBartas) I:89 no. 18a. MdBP; Paris:Arsenal.
608/64

—[Anr edn]. *Lyons: F. Arnoullet*, 1608. 12mo. Holmes (DuBartas) I:90 no. 22a(n). BN.
608/65

—[Anr issue]. *Lyons: P. Rigaud*, 1608. 12mo. Holmes (DuBartas) I:90 no. 22a. BN.
608/66

—[Anr edn]. *Rouen: R. Du Petit Val*, 1608. 12mo. Holmes (DuBartas) I:89–90 no. 21a; Jones (Goulart) 20y. BN.
608/67

Duchesne, Joseph. Pharmacopoea dogmaticorum restituta. *Venice: G. A. & J. de Francisci*, 1608. 269 p.; 4to. 1st publ., Paris, 1607. DNLM, MH, WU; London:Wellcome.
608/68

Esquibel, Juan de. Copia de una carta que el maese de campo Juan de Esquibel escrivio de la isla de Terrenate . . . la qual carta se escrivio a la nueva España ala ciudad de Mexico a Diego de Ochandiano . . . paraque representasse . . . la necessidad en que quedava el y toda la gente que tenia a su cargo para guarda de aquella isla de Soquoro. [*Madrid?* 1608?]. [7] p.; fol. Dated at end: 'de Terrenate a 4. de Junio de 1605'. Medina (BHA) 6437; Kress 288. DLC, MH-BA, RPJCB.
608/69

Estienne, Charles. Dictionarium historicum, geographicum, poeticum. *Paris: P. Rèze*, 1608. 452 numb. lvs; 4to. 1st publ. in this enl. edn, Lyons, 1595; cf. 1601 edn. BN.
608/70

—[Anr issue]. *Paris: R. Fouët*, 1608. BN.
608/71

Figueiredo, Manuel de. Hydrographia, exame de pilotos. *Lisbon: V. Alvarez*, 1608. 3 pts; illus., map; 4to. Pt 2 has title *Roteiro de Portugal, para o Brasil, Rito de Prata, &c.* Borba de Moraes I:265. CtY.
608/72

Gesner, Konrad. Köstlicher Artzneyschatz dess wolerfarnen unnd weytberümpten Euonymi Philiatri [pseud.] . . . von Johan Rüdolph Landenberger . . . ubersetzt. *Zurich:* 1608. 2 pts; illus.; 4to. Pt 1 1st publ. in German, Zurich 1555; transl. from Gesner's *Thesaurus*, 1st publ., Zurich, 1552, Pt 2 1st publ. in German, St Gall, 1583, as transl. by J. J. Nüschler from Gesner's *Euonymus . . . pars secunda*, Zurich, 1569. Includes refs to guaiacum & syphilis, citing Monardes. MnU.
608/73

Ghetrouwen raedt ende goede waerschouwinghe. [*Amsterdam?* 1608]. *See* Een oud schipper van Monickendam *below.*

Giovio, Paolo, Bp of Nocera. Delle istorie del suo tempo . . . tradotte da m. Lodovico Domenichi. *Venice: Sign of Concordia*, 1608. 2 v.; 4to. 1st publ., as here transl. from Giovio's *Historiarum sui temporis* (Venice, 1550–52), Venice, 1551–54. Vol. 2 contains refs to American discovery, exploration, & conquest. Michel (Répertoire) IV:55. BL, BN.
608/74

González de Legaria, Juan. Aqui se contiene una obra nueva, graciosa . . . para reir . . . y es un cuento que le passó a un soldado con un gato. *Lisbon: V. Alvarez*, 1608. [8] p.; 4to. In verse. 'Tampoco de Terranuova bacallaos me han llegado'—Respuesta del gato. Palau 105415.
608/75

Greene, Robert. Greenes carde of fancie. *London: H. L[ownes]., for M. Lownes*, 1608. [151] p.; 4to. 1st publ., London, 1584, under title *Gwydonius*. On recto of lf Cl is a ref. to 'violets in America, which in sommer yeeld an odiferous smell, and in winter a most pestilent savour'. STC 12264. CSmH, DFo, MH; BL.
608/76

Grimestone, Edward. A generall historie of the Netherlands . . . Continued unto . . . 1608, out of the best authors that have written of that subject. *London: A. Islip & G. Eld,* 1608. 1415 p.; ports; fol. Section on the Netherlands' 1608 peace negotiations outlines Dutch demands for trade & navigation in East & West Indies. STC 12374. CSmH, CtY, DLC, ICN, MH, MnU-B; BL.
608/77

Hariot, Thomas. Admiranda narratio fida tamen, de commodis et incolarum ritibus Virginiae . . . Anglico scripta sermone . . . nunc autem primum Latio donata a C. C[lusius]. *Frankfurt a. M.: J. Wechel, for T. de Bry; to be sold by S. Feyerabend,* 1590 [i.e., ca. 1608]. 2 pts; illus., map; fol. (Theodor de Bry's *America.* Pt 1. Latin). 1st publ. in this version, Frankfurt a. M., 1590; transl. from Hariot's *A brief and true report of . . . Virginia,* 1st publ., London, 1588. For variant issue see Church. Cf. Sabin 8784; Church 143 (& 144); JCB (3) I:384. CSmH, NN, RPJCB; BL.
608/78

Hieron, Samuel. An answere to a popish ryme . . . The second edition. [*London:*] H. L[ownes]., for S. Macham, 1608. 37 p.; 4to. In verse. 1st publ., London, 1604. STC 13389. CSmH, DFo, MH, NNUT; BL.
608/79

Horst, Gregor. Problematum medicorum decades priorum quinque. *Wittenberg: Crato Press, for J. Gormann,* 1608. 12 lvs; 4to. Includes discussion of medicinal use of tobacco. Arents 86. DNLM, NN-A.
608/80

Hovt en beleght. [*Spa (?):* 1608]. *See* Een oud schipper van Monickendam *below.*

Hulsius, Levinus, comp. Achte Schiffart, oder Kurtze Beschreibung etlicher Reysen, so die Holländer . . . in die Ost Indien . . . gethan. *Frankfurt a. M.: M. Becker, for Widow of L. Hulsius,* 1608. 56 p.; illus., maps; 4to. (Levinus Hulsius's *Sammlung von . . . Schifffahrten.* Pt 8). 1st publ., Frankfurt a. M., 1605. Sabin 33662; Church 289; JCB (3) I:459. CSmH, CtY, ICN, MB, MnU-B, NN-RB, RPJCB; BL, BN.
608/81

Le Mire, Aubert. Rerum toto orbe gestarum chronica. *Antwerp: H. Verdussen,* 1608. 2 pts; fol. Included are numerous refs to discover-

ies & events in New World. JCB (3) II:51–52. ICN, InU-L, MH, RPJCB; BL, BN.
608/82

Lemos, Pedro Fernández de Castro, conde de. Relacion de la provincia de los Quixos en Indias. [*Madrid:* 1608]. 16 numb. lvs; map; 4to. The province in question is today part of Ecuador. Sabin 40013; Medina (BHA) 536; Pérez Pastor (Madrid) 1000; Palau 88258. NN-RB; Palencia:Catedral.
608/83

Lescarbot, Marc. La defaite des sauvages armouchiquois par le sagamos Membertou & ses alliez sauvages en la Nouvelle France, au mois de juillet dernier 1607. *Paris: J. Périer* [1608]. 12 numb. lvs; 8vo. Sabin 40168; Harrisse (NF) 18; JCB AR54:3–9. MH, RPJCB; BN.
608/84

Liddel, Duncan. Ars medica. *Hamburg: Froben Bookshop (P. Lang),* 1608. 868 p.; 8vo. Describes syphilis as endemic to America, whence it was introduced to Europe. Wellcome I:3795. DNLM, PPC; BL.
608/85

Lorenzini, Niccolò. Le lagrime del peccatore, poema eroico. *Venice: B. Giunta, & G. B. Ciotti & Co.,* 1608. 173 (i.e., 137) numb. lvs; illus.; 8vo. 1st publ., Venice, 1591, under title *Il peccator contrito;* here a probable reissue. Includes ref. to guaiacum & other treasures of the Indies. CtY, IU; BL.
608/86

Lyskander, Claus Christoffersen. DenGrønlandske chronica. *Copenhagen: B. Laurentz,* 1608. 96 lvs; 8vo. In verse. Sabin 42882; JCB (3) II:51. CSt, CtY, MH, RPJCB.
608/87

Macchelli, Niccolò. Tractatus methodicus . . . de lue venerea, ejusque natura et causis . . . nec non singulorum curatione. *Frankfurt a. M.: N. Hoffmann,* 1608. 2 pts; 8vo. 1st publ., Venice, 1555; cf. Gerardus Columba's *Disputationum medicarum . . . libri duo,* Frankfurt a. M., 1601. DNLM; BL, BN.
608/88

Mariana, Juan de, S.J. Historia general de España . . . segunda impression. *Madrid: L. Sánchez,* 1608. 2 v.; fol. Transl., rev. & augm. by the author from his *Historiae de rebus Hispaniae,* 1st publ., Toledo, 1592; cf. 1601 edn. Sabin 44546n; Backer V:549; Pérez Pastor (Madrid) 1010; Palau

151667n. DLC, ICU, MiU-C, NNH; BN.
608/89

Martini, Lucas. Christeliga jungfrwrs ärakrantz. *Rostock: S. Mölemann,* 1608. 355 p.; illus.; 12mo. Transl. from Martini's *Der christlichen Jungfrawen Ehrenkräntzlein,* 1st publ., Prague, 1585; cf. 1602 edn. Wellcome I:4090. London:Wellcome.
608/90

Matthieu, Pierre. Histoire de France et des choses memorables, advenues aux provinces estrangeres durant sept années de paix, du regne de Henry IIII. *Leyden: C. Bonaventure,* 1608–10. 2 v.; 8vo. 1st publ., Paris, 1605. BL. 608/91

Mayerne, Louis Turquet de. Histoire generale d'Espagne. *Paris: A. L'Angelier,* 1608. 1536 p.; fol. 1st publ., Geneva, 1587. Includes numerous refs to Spanish in New World. Cf. Sabin 47117. DLC; BL, BN.
608/92

Mendes de Vasconcelos, Luiz. Do sitio de Lisboa. *Lisbon: L. Estupiñán,* 1608. 242 p.; 16mo. On p. 23 is a ref. to the potential importance of Brazil. Palau 162884. DLC, InU-L, MH-BA, NN-RB, RPJCB; BN.
608/93

Mercado, Luis. Opera omnia in quatuor tomos divisa. *Frankfurt a. M. Z. Palthenius,* 1608. 4 v.; fol. Included is Mercado's *Tomus secundus Operum* as publ., Valladolid, 1605. Palau 164993. DNLM (v. 1–2 only); BL, BN.
608/94

——. Praxis medica . . . in quatuor partes divisa. *Venice: B. Giunta & G. B. Ciotti & Co.,* 1608. 624 p.; fol. 1st publ. as here constituted as the *Tomus secundus* of Mercado's *Operum,* Valladolid, 1605, q.v. Palau 165017. DNLM, MBCo, NIC. 608/95

Mercator, Gerardus. Atlas minor . . . Traduict de latin . . . par le sieur de la Popeliniere. *Amsterdam: J. Hondius; sold also by J. Janszoon, at Arnhem,* 1608. 655 p.; maps; obl. 12mo. Transl. from author's *Atlas minor,* Amsterdam, 1607. Cf. Sabin 47888; Koeman (Me) 187; Phillips (Atlases) 4253. DLC, MiU; Brussels:BR, Madrid:BN. 608/96

——. Atlas, sive Cosmographicae meditationes de fabrica mundi et fabricata figura. Iam tandem . . . perductus, quamplurimis aeneis tabulis Hispaniae, Africae, Asiae &

Americae auctus ac illustratus à Judoco Hondio . . . Editio secunda. *Amsterdam: C. Claeszoon,* 1608. 355 p.; maps; fol. 1st publ., Amsterdam, 1606; here a reissue of the Hondius 1607 edn with the present imprint a paste-on cancel. Cf. Sabin 47882; Koeman (Me) 18. Copenhagen:KB. 608/97

Middelgeest, Simon van, supposed author. Discours of t'samensprekinghe tusschen den Coning van Spaengien ende Jan Neyen, vanden vredehandel der Vereenichde Nederlanden. [*Amsterdam?* 1608?]. [8] p.; 4to. Includes ref. to West Indies. Knuttel 1418. The Hague:KB. 608/98

—[Anr edn]. Droom oft t'samensprekinge. [*Amsterdam?* 1608]. [8] p.; 4to. Knuttel 1419. InU-L, NN; The Hague:KB. 608/99

—[Anr edn]. Raedtsel. Ieghelijck doet geern wat. Naer dat verscheyden discoursen ende droomen op den handel vanden vrede . . . zijn uytgheghaen. [*Amsterdam?* 1608?]. [8] p.; 4to. (Den Nederlandtschen bye-corf, no. 5). Signed 'Yemant Adams'. Knuttel 1420; Asher 28.5. MiU-C; The Hague:KB.
608/100

—[Anr edn]. Raedtsel. Ieghelijck doet geern wat, naer dat discourssen ende verscheyden droomen. [*Amsterdam:* 1608]. [7] p.; 4to. Knuttel 1421. RPJCB; The Hague:KB.
608/101

—[Anr edn]. Raedtsel. Ieghelyck. [*Amsterdam?* 1608?]. [7] p.; 4to. Knuttel 1422. The Hague:KB. 608/102

—[Anr edn]. Raedtslagh, Iegelick. [*Amsterdam?* 1608?]. [7] p.; 4to. Knuttel 1423. The Hague:KB. 608/103

Middleton, Richard. Epigrams and satyres. *London: N. Okes, for J. Harrison,* 1608. 22 lvs; 4to. In verse. Section titled 'Times metamorphosis' includes passage on tobacco. STC 17874; Arents (Add.) 137. NN-A; Edinburgh:UL. 608/104

Middleton, Thomas. A mad world, my masters. *London: H. B[allard]., for W. Burre,* 1608. 34 lvs; 4to. Comedy. In opening scene a tobacco shop is mentioned. STC 17888; Greg 276(a); Arents (Add.) 138. CSmH, DFo, ICN, MH, NN-A; BL.
608/105

Migoen, Jacob Willem. Proeve des nu onlangs uyt-ghegheven drooms off t'samen-

spraack tusschen den Coning van His-
panien ende den Paus van Roomen.
[*Amsterdam?* 1608]. [8] p.; 4to. (Den Neder-
landtschen bye-corf, no. 33). 1st publ.,
[Netherlands, ca. 1607], under title *Eene
treffelijcke tzamensprekinghe;* here enlarged.
Asher 28.34; Knuttel 1401. NN-RB, RPJCB;
The Hague:KB. 608/106

Montaigne, Michel Eyquem de. Les essais
. . . Edition nouvelle enrichie d'annotations en marge. *Paris: J. Petit-Pas,* 1608. 1129
p.; port.; 8vo. 1st publ., Bordeaux, 1580;
cf. 1602 edn. Tchémerzine VIII:414. BL,
BN. 608/107

—[Anr issue]. *Paris: M. Nivelle,* 1608. Tchémerzine VIII:414. BN. 608/108

—[Anr issue]. *Paris: C. Sevestre,* 1608. Tchémerzine VIII:414. DFo, BN. 608/109

—[Anr issue]. *Paris: Widow D. Salis,* 1608.
Tchémerzine VIII:414. IU, MH; BN.
608/110

—[Anr issue]. *Paris: C. Rigaud,* 1608. Tchémerzine VIII:414. MH; BN. 608/111

—[Anr issue]. *Paris: F. Gueffier,* 1608. Tchémerzine VIII:414. 608/112

—[Anr issue]. *Antwerp: A. Maire* [1608?].
Tchémerzine VIII:414. MH, NjP; BN.
608/113

Murtola, Gasparo. Della creazione del
mundo, poema sacro. *Venice: E. Deuchino &
G. B. Pulciano,* 1608. 531 p.; 12mo. The 3rd
canto includes sections on 'Scoprimento
dell'Indie' & 'Viaggio del Colombo'. Michel
(Répertoire) V:208. IaU, MH, MiU; BL, BN.
608/114

Neck, Jacob Corneliszoon van. Het tweede
boeck, Journael oft Dagh-register. *Amsterdam: C. Claeszoon,* 1608. 50 numb. lvs; illus.,
maps; obl. 4to. 1st publ., Amsterdam,
[1600]; cf. 1601 edn. Tiele-Muller 128;
Tiele 783. 608/115

Den Nederlandtschen bye-corf: waer in ghy
beschreven vindt, al tghene dat nu wtghegaen is, op den stilstant ofte vrede. [*Amsterdam?* 1608]. [8] p.; 4to. (Den Nederlandtschen bye-corf, no. 1). Includes refs
to West Indies. Sabin 98201; Muller (1872)
418; Asher 26; Knuttel 1474. MiU-C, NN-
RB, NNC; The Hague:KB. 608/116

—[Anr edn]. Den Nederlandtschen bye-corf:
waer in ghy beschreven vint, al het gene
dat nu wtghegaen is. [*Amsterdam?* 1608]. [8]

p.; 4to. Sabin 98201n; Asher 27; Knuttel
1475. DLC; The Hague:KB. 608/117

—[Anr edn]. Den Nederlandtschen bye-corf:
waer ghy beschreven vint, al het gene dat
nu uytgegaen is. [*Amsterdam?* 1608]. [8] p.;
4to. Sabin 98201n; Asher 28.1; Knuttel
1476. NN-RB, RPJCB; The Hague:KB.
608/118

Den Nederlandtschen bye-korf. Stucken
gemencioneert in den Bycorff. *The Hague:
H. Jacobszoon van Wouw,* 1608. [49] p.; 4to.
A reprinting of pts 7, 22, 32, 17, 19, & 29
from the 3rd edn of *Den Nederlandtschen bye-
corf* of this year above. Sabin 98209; Knuttel
1477 (cf. 1476). DLC, NN-RB; The
Hague:KB. 608/119

Nierop, Adriaan van, supposed author.
Echo ofte galm, dat is Wederklinckende
gedichte. [*Amsterdam?*] 1608. [8] p.; 4to.
(Den Nederlandtschen bye-corf, no. 36). 1st
publ., [Amsterdam?] 1607. Here, 1st 4
words on t.p. appear in roman type. Locations cited may include copies of the following edn. Asher 28.37; Knuttel 1406. MnU,
RPJCB; BL, The Hague:KB. 608/120

—[Anr edn]. [*Amsterdam?*] 1608. [8] p.; 4to.
Here, 'Echo' & 'galm' appear in roman type;
'ofte' & 'dat is' appear in black letter. Knuttel 1407. The Hague:KB. 608/121

Nieuwen, klaren astrologen-bril. [*Amsterdam?* 1608?]. *See the year* 1607.

Ortelius, Abraham. Theatro del mondo . . .
Traslato . . . dal sigr. Filippo Pigafetta. *Antwerp: J. B. Vrients,* 1608. 3 pts; maps, port.;
fol. Transl. from Antwerp, 1603, edn of the
Theatrum orbis terrarum, including also the
author's *Parergon* & his *Nomenclator.* Sabin
57703; Koeman (Ort) 38; cf. Phillips (Atlases) 430; Michel (Répertoire) VI:42; JCB
(3) II:53. ICN, RPJCB; The Hague:KB,
Paris:Mazarine. 608/122

——. Theatrum orbis terrarum . . . The theatre of the whole world. *London: [Eliots Court
Press, for] J. Norton, & J. Bill,* 1606 [i.e.,
1608?]. 2 pts; maps; fol. Text transl. from
Antwerp, 1603, edn of the *Theatrum orbis
terrarum.* For the printing history of this
work, see the bibliographical note by R. A.
Skelton in the facsimile edn of this work
publ. by Theatrum Orbis Terrarum Ltd
(Amsterdam, 1968). Sabin 57708; Koeman
(Ort) 37; Phillips (Atlases) 3410; STC

18855 (with conjectured date); JCB (3)
II:41. CSmH, DLC, ICN, MiU-C, PBL,
RPJCB; BL. 608/123

Een oud schipper van Monickendam. [*Amsterdam? 1608?*]. [5] p.; illus.; 4to. (Den Nederlandtschen bye-corf, no. 37). Includes refs to Tierra del Fuego and West Indies. For variants see Knuttel. Asher 28.38; Knuttel 1466–72. MiU-C, RPJCB; BL, The Hague:KB. 608/124

—[Anr edn]. Hovt en beleght; een oud schipper van Monickendam . . . Ghedruckt te spae, buyten Altenae. [*Spa (?), outside Altena:* 1608]. [5] p.; illus., 4to. Knuttel 1472. NN, RPJCB; The Hague:KB. 608/125

—[Anr edn]. Ghetrouwen raedt ende goede waerschouwinghe eens ouden ervaren schippers. [*Amsterdam?* 1608]. [5] p.; illus.; 4to. Knuttel 1473. BL, The Hague:KB. 608/126

Ovidius Naso, Publius (Two or more works. Spanish). Primera parte del Parnaso antarctico, de obras amatorias. Con las 21. Epistolas de Ovidio . . . Por Diego Mexia, natural de la ciudad de Sevilla; y residente en la de los Reyes, en los riquissimos reynos del Peru. *Seville: A. Rodríguez Gamarra,* 1608. 268 numb. lvs; 4to. No more published. Sabin 48231; Medina (BHA) 538; Escudero (Seville) 917. ICN, MB, NNH, RPJCB; BL. 608/127

Owen, John. Epigrammatum libri tres. *Amberg: J. Schönfeld,* 1608. 12mo. 1st publ., London, 1606. Shaaber (Brit. auth.) O83. PPL. 608/128

Paracelsus. La grande chirurgie . . . Traduite . . . de la version latine de Josquin d'Alhem . . . Par m. Claude Dariot . . . Troisiesme edition. *Montbéliard: J. Foillet,* 1608. 3 pts; illus.; 8vo. 1st publ. as here transl., Lyons, 1593; cf. 1603 edn. Sudhoff (Paracelsus) 279; Wellcome I:4750. DNLM; BL, BN. 608/129

Peleus, Julien. Les questions illustres de m[aitre]. Julien Peleus, advocat en Parlement. *Paris: N. Buon,* 1608. 943 p.; 4to. Pages 910–23 relate to the Sieur de Monts's trading company in Acadia. MH-L, MiU-L, MnU-B. 608/130

Penot, Bernard Georges. Theophrastisch Vade mecum. Das ist: Etliche sehr nützliche Tractat, von der warhafftigen Bereitung . . . der chymischen Medicamenten. *Magdeburg: J. Franck,* 1608. 215 p.; 4to. 1st publ. as here transl., Eisleben, 1597; cf. 1607 edn, of which this is perhaps a reissue with altered imprint date. BN. 608/131

Porta, Giovanni Battista della. De distillatione lib. ix. *Rome: Apostolic Camera,* 1608. 154 p.; illus., port.; 4to. Described are ointments derived from guaiacum & opobalsam. Wellcome I:5211. The following locations may represent any one of the 4 edns here entered: CtY, DNLM, IEN, MH, NNE, RPB; BL, BN. 608/132

—[Anr edn]. *Rome: Apostolic Camera,* 1608. 154 p.; illus., port.; 4to. Printed on blue paper in a differing setting of type from above. Wellcome I:5211a. London:Wellcome, BN. 608/133

—[Anr edn]. *Rome: Apostolic Camera,* 1608. 154 p.; illus., port.; 4to. A differing setting of type from above. Wellcome I:5211b. London:Wellcome. 608/134

—[Anr edn]. *Rome: Apostolic Camera,* 1608. 154 p.; illus., port.; 4to. A differing setting of type from above. Wellcome I:5211c. London:Wellcome. 608/135

——. Phytognomonica . . . octo libris contenta. *Frankfurt a. M.: N. Hoffmann,* 1608. 539 p.; illus.; 8vo. 1st publ., Naples, 1588. Among plants described for medicinal uses are guaiacum & sarsaparilla. Pritzel 7273n; Nissen (Bot.) 463n. DNLM, MH, MiU, NNBG; BL, BN. 608/136

Ptolemaeus, Claudius. Geographiae universae tum veteris, tum novae absolutissimum opus . . . commentariis . . . illustratus est à Joan. Antonio Magini. *Cologne: P. Keschedt,* 1608. 2 v.; maps; 4to. 1st publ. as ed. & suppl. by Magini, Venice, 1596. Sabin 66495; Stevens (Ptolemy) 59; Phillips (Atlases) 5921; JCB (3) II:54. DLC, ICN, MH, NN-RB, RPJCB; BL, BN. 608/137

Quad, Matthias. Fasciculus geographicus complectens praecipuarum totius orbis regionum tabulas circiter centrum una cum earundem enarrationibus. *Cologne: J. Bussemacher,* 1608. 346 p.; fol. 1st publ. with German text, Cologne, 1600, under title *Geographisch Handtbuch.* Five maps relate to America. Sabin 66893; Phillips (Atlases) 4253a. DLC, ICN, MiU-C, MnU-B, NN-RB, PPL; BL, BN. 608/138

Relacion verdadera, y de mucho aprovachamiento para el Christiano, donde se declara lo que en la ciudad de Sevilla a un hombre . . . y de como se metio frayle en la Orden de San Francisco, y como passò a las Indias, y predicando alla suo martirizado . . . Compuesto por un padre de la mesma Orden. *Alcalá de Henares: Heirs of J. Gracián,* 1608. [8] p.; 4to. In verse. Palau 257370; JCB (3) II:54. RPJCB.
608/139

Renou, Jean de. Institutionum pharmaceuticarum libri quinque. *Paris: Widow of G. de La Nouë, & D. de La Nouë,* 1608. 3 pts; port.; 4to. In pt 2, 'De plantis,' bk 1, sect. 1, chapt. xvi speaks of opobalsam both of Peru & Tolu (Brazil); chapt. xxiii, 'De sassafras', describes it as grown in Florida. Elsewhere guaiacum, mechoacan, & tacamahac are discussed. Subsequent edns have title *Dispensatorium medicum.* Wellcome I:5428. CtY-M, DNLM (imp.), WU; London:Wellcome, BN.
608/140

Rivadeneira, Pedro de, S.J. Illustrium scriptorum religionis Societatis Jesu catalogus. *Antwerp: Plantin Office (J. Moretus),* 1608. 287 p.; 8vo. Includes biobibliographies of Jesuits who served in New World. Also included are accounts of Jesuits who had been martyred, some in the Americas, 1st publ. separately, Naples, 1606, under title *Catalogus quorundam e Societate Jesu qui . . . sunt interfecti.* Sabin 70778; Backer VI:1754. ICU, MnU-B, PV; BN.
608/141

———. La vie du b.p. Ignace de Loyola . . . Escrite premierement en espagnol . . . depuis mise en italien par d. Saluste Gratii de Sienne: et nouvellement traduite en françois par . . . Henry de Sponde. *Paris: C. Chappelet,* 1608. 214 p.; 8vo. Transl. from Italian version, 1st publ., Venice, 1606. Backer VI:1729; Palau 266249. BN.
608/142

—[Anr edn]. *Pont-à-Mousson: M. Bernard,* 1608. 239 p.; 8vo. Cioranescu (XVII) 63609; Palau 266250.
608/143

Roca, Balthasar Juan. Historia verdadera de la vida, y milagros del . . . padre S. Luys Bertran . . . . *Valencia: J. C. Gárriz,* 1608. 554 p.; port.; 8vo. In the 'Tratato I' chapts ix–xii describe Bertran's experiences in present-day Colombia. Medina (BHA) 541; Streit II:1390; Palau 27341. RPJCB.
608/144

Romanus, Adrianus. Parvum theatrum urbium, sive Urbium praecipuarum totius orbis brevis & methodica descriptio. *Frankfurt a. M.: W. Richter, for Heirs of N. Bassé,* 1608. 365 p.; illus.; 4to. A reissue with cancel t.p. of Frankfurt, 1595, edn. Based in part on Georg Braun's *Civitates orbis terrarum,* 1st publ., Cologne, 1572. 'De Novo orbe, sive India Occidentali': p. 359–65. Cf. Sabin 73000. NNH, RPJCB; BL, BN.
608/145

Rowlands, Samuel. Humors looking glasse. *London: E. Allde for W. Ferbrand,* 1608. 16 lvs; 4to. In verse. Describes use of tobacco. STC 21386; Arents 89. CSmH; BL.
608/146

Ruland, Martin (1569–1611). Propugnaculum chymiatriae: das ist, Beantwortung und beschützung der alchymischen Artzneyen. *Leipzig: M. Lantzenberger, for J. Apel,* 1608. 192 p.; 4to. Mentioned are guaiacum, mechoacan, sarsaparilla, & sassafras. MBCo; BL.
608/147

Sacro Bosco, Joannes de. Sphaera . . . emendata. Eliae Vineti . . . scholia. *Paris: H. de Marnef, for Denise Cavellat,* 1608. 190 p.; illus.; 8vo. 1st publ. with Vinet's *Scholia,* Paris, 1551; cf. 1601 edn above. MiU, NIC.
608/148

Schenck, Johann Georg. Hortus Patavinus. Cui accessêre vcl Melchioris Guilandi . . . Conjectanea synonymica plantarum eruditissima. *Frankfurt a. M.: Widow & Heirs of J. T. de Bry,* 1608. 93 p.; illus.; 8vo. Described are various American plants. The engraved title border includes the date '1600' but presumably comprises that of an earlier unidentified work. Pritzel 8151. MH, MoSB; BL.
608/149

Schottus, Andreas. Hispaniae bibliotheca, seu De academiis ac bibliothecis. *Frankfurt a. M.: C. de Marne & Heirs of J. Aubry,* 1608. 3 pts; 4to. Constitutes 3rd vol. of Schottus's *Hispaniae illustratae* of 1603, q.v. Sabin 77900.
608/150

Schuyt-praetgens op de vaert naer Amsterdam, tusschen een lantman, een hovelinck, een borger, ende schipper. [*Amsterdam?*

1608?]. [8] p.; 4to. (Den Nederlandtschen bye-corf, no. 23). Includes refs to Indies and Spanish mistreatment of Indians. In poem at end, line 2 ends 'vercelt'; line 3 includes reading 'in Druck'. Asher 28.24; Knuttel 1450. [Edns not differentiated:] MiU-C, NN; BL, The Hague:KB. 608/151

—[Anr edn]. [*Amsterdam? 1608?*]. [8] p.; 4to. Here, in poem at end, line 2 ends 'verteld' as corrected; line 3 includes reading 'inden Druck'. Knuttel 1451. MiU-C; The Hague:KB. 608/152

—[Anr edn]. Schuyt-praetgens . . . tusschen . . . een borgher ende schipper. [*Amsterdam? 1608*]. [8] p.; 4to. Knuttel 1452. RPJCB; The Hague:KB. 608/153

Het secreet des Conings van Spangien, Philippus den tweeden, achter-gelaten aen zijnen lieben zoone Philips de derde . . . In't licht gebracht door . . . Rodrigo D. A., ende nu over-gheset uyt den Spaenschen door P. A. P. [*Amsterdam? 1608*]. [5] p.; 4to. (Den Nederlandtschen bye-corf, no. 30). 1st publ., [Amsterdam?] 1599. Includes refs to Spanish control of West Indies. For variants see Knuttel 1059–63. Sometimes ascribed to Willem Usselinx, or to Philip of Spain, 1527–98. Asher 28.31; Knuttel 1060. RPJCB; BL, The Hague:KB. 608/154

Serres, Olivier de, seigneur du Pradel. Le theatre d'agriculture . . . Derniere edition, reveuë et augmentee par l'auteur. *Paris: A. Saugrain,* 1608. 907 p.; illus.; 8vo. 1st publ., Paris, 1600; cf. 1603 edn. MH; BL. 608/155

—[Anr edn]. Quatriesme edition. *Paris: J. Berjon,* 1608. 4to. Arents (Add.) 139. NN-A; BL. 608/156

Shakespeare, William. The historie of Henrie the fourth [Pt 1]. *London: [J. Windet] for M. Law,* 1608. 40 lvs; 4to. 1st publ., London, 1598; cf. 1604 edn. STC 22283; Greg 145(e). CSmH, DFo, MH; BL. 608/157

Smith, Capt. John. A true relation of such occurrences . . . as hath hapned in Virginia . . . Written by a gentleman of the said collony. *London: [E. Allde,] for J. Tapp, & sold by W. W[elby].,* 1608. [44] p.; 4to. For a full discussion of the variant issues of this work, see Wilberforce Eames's contributions in Sabin. Sabin 82844; Clayton-Torrence 1A; Vail (Frontier) 12; STC 22795. NHi, NN-RB, PP; Chatsworth. 608/158

—[Anr issue]. . . . Written by Th. Watson. *London: [E. Allde,] for J. Tapp, & sold by W. W[elby].,* 1608. Sabin 82845; Clayton-Torrence 1B; STC 22795.3; JCB (3) II:55. CSmH, NHi, RPJCB; BL. 608/159

—[Anr issue]. . . . Written by Captaine Smith Coronell of the said collony. *London: [E. Allde,] for J. Tapp, & sold by W. W[elby].,* 1608. Sabin 82846; Clayton-Torrence 1C; STC 22795.5; Church 333. CSmH, CtY, MB, MiU-C, NN-RB, RPJCB. 608/160

—[Anr issue]. . . . Written by Captaine Smith one of the said collony. *London: [E. Allde,] for J. Tapp, & sold by W. W[elby].,* 1608. Sabin 82847; Clayton-Torrence 1D; STC 22795.7; JCB AR28:15–19 & AR50:13–14. CSmH, CtY, NN-RB, RPJCB. 608/161

Soto, Domingo de. De justitia et jure libri decem. *Venice: P. M. Bertano,* 1608. 1006 p.; 4to. 1st publ., Salamanca, 1553; cf. year 1602. Perhaps a reissue of the latter edn. Palau 320164n. 608/162

Suárez de Argüelo, Francisco. Ephemerides generales . . . por doze años, desde el de M.DC.VII. hasta el de M.DC.XVIII . . . No solo anotados los eclypses . . . que en estos doze años occurren en nostro meridiano, sino tambien los que en todas las Indias Orientales y Ocidentales aurà. *Madrid: J. de la Cuesta,* 1608. 355 p.; fol. Sabin 93309; Medina (BHA) 542; Pérez Pastor (Madrid) 93309. InU-L; BL, Santiago, Chile:BN. 608/163

Tabourot, Estienne. Les bigarrures et touches. *Paris: J. Richer,* 1608. 5 pts; illus., ports; 12mo. In verse. 1st publ. in this collective edn, Paris, 1603. MH, MiU (imp.); BL, BN. 608/164

Tapp, John. The seamans kalendar . . . Third edition: newly corrected. *London: E. Allde, for J. Tapp,* 1608. 4to. 1st publ., London, 1602; no intervening 2nd edn has been traced. STC 23679.5. BL. 608/165

Topsell, Edward. The historie of serpents. *London: W. Jaggard,* 1608. 315 p.; illus.; fol. Continues the author's 1607 *Historie of foure-*

footed beastes. On p. 141, with illus., is a description of a Brazilian alligator. For printing variants, see the STC. Cf. Sabin 27228; Nissen (Zool.) 4146; STC 24124. CSmH, DLC, ICN, MH, MiU, PU, RPB; BL.
608/166

Usselinx, Willem, supposed author. Aussführung allerhand wolbedencklicher Argumenten, Anzeigungen, Umbstenden und Beweiss der Ursachen, warumb die Vereinigte Provintzen in Niderlandt . . . die Schiffarten ihn [!] Ost und West Indien nicht verlassen . . . Auss dem Latein . . . versetzt. [*Germany?*] 1608. [10] p.; 4to. Transl. from the author's *Waerschouwinghe vande ghewichtighe redenen* of this year below. Sabin 98190; Deutscher Gesamtkatalog 8.7687; Kress 282 (& 291). MH-BA; Berlin:StB.
608/167

——. Bedenckinghen over den staet vande vereenichde Nederlanden: nopende de zeevaert, coop-handel, ende de gemeyne neeringe inde selve. [*Amsterdam?*] 1608. [16] p.; 4to. Includes refs to commerce with the West & East Indies, and to Spanish power in the Indies. Also forms part of Den Nederlandtschen bye-corf, almost exclusively under title *Grondich discours.* Sabin 98191; Jameson (Usselinx) 1; Asher 29; Knuttel 1438; Kress 295; JCB (3) II:56. DLC, MH-BA, NN-RB, RPJCB; The Hague:KB.
608/168

—[Anr edn]. Grondich discours over desen aen-staenden vrede-handel. [*Amsterdam?* 1608]. [15] p.; 4to. In this edn, text begins 'Alzo ic dagelijcx'. Sabin 98195; Jameson (Usselinx) 2; Asher 30; Knuttel 1439; JCB (3) II:56. [Locations may include the following edn:] DLC, MH-BA, MnU-B, NN-RB, PHi, RPJCB; BL, The Hague:KB.
608/169

—[Anr edn]. [*Amsterdam?* 1608]. [15] p.; 4to. Text begins 'Alzoo ick daghelijcks'. Sabin 98195; Jameson (Usselinx) 3; Knuttel 1440. DS; The Hague:KB.
608/170

——. Naerder bedenckingen over de zeevaerdt, coop-handel ende neeringhe, als mede de versekeringhe van den staet deser vereenichde landen. [*Netherlands:*] 1608. [36] p.; 4to. Arguments advanced in favor of a West Indian trade company; refs to

Spanish power in Indies. In some copies, p. 36, line 7 includes reading 'verliezende' rather than the improved 'verkiesende'. Forms part of *Den Nederlandtschen bye-corf.* Sabin 98200; Asher 32; Knuttel 1441; Jameson (Usselinx) 4; Kress 297; JCB (3) II:57. DLC, InU-L, MH-BA, MiU-C, MnU-B, NN-RB, PHi, RPJCB; BL, The Hague:KB.
608/171

—[Anr edn]. [*Netherlands:*] 1608. [44] p.; 4to. Sabin 98200; Asher 31; Jameson (Usselinx) 5.
608/172

——, **supposed author.** Onpartydich discours opte handelinghe vande Indien. [*Amsterdam?* 1608?]. [7] p.; 4to. (Den Nederlandtschen bye-corf, no. 28). Transl. from an untraced French text reprinted in van Meteren IX:375–84 (Knuttel). Contains refs to commerce with West & East Indies; includes ref. to Spanish exploitation of Indians. Jameson disputes attribution to Usselinx. In this edn the penultimate line ends 'af te-'. Sabin 98206; cf. Jameson (Usselinx), p. 36n; Asher 36 & 28.29; Knuttel 1436; JCB (3) II:67. [Locations may include the following edn:] CtY, DLC, MH-BA, MiU-C, NN, PHi, RPJCB; BL, The Hague:KB.
608/173

—[Anr edn]. [*Amsterdam?* 1608?]. [7] p.; 4to. Here, the penultimate line of text ends 'af te wil-'. Sabin 98206; Knuttel 1437. The Hague:KB.
608/174

——, **supposed author.** Le plaidoyer de l'Indien hollandois. [*Antwerp?*] 1608. *See* Walerande, J. B. de, *below.*

——, **supposed author.** Sommaire recueil des raisons plus importantes, qui doyvent mouvoir messieurs des Estats des Provinces unies du Pays-bas, de ne quitter point les Indes. Traduit de flamand. [*Paris?*] 1608. 19 p.; 12mo. Transl. from the author's *Waerschouwinghe* of this year below, or from edn with title beginning 'Memorie'. Cf. Sabin 98208; Atkinson (Fr. Ren.) 496. MnU-B; BN.
608/175

—[Anr edn]. *La Rochelle: Heirs of J. Haultin,* 1608. 22 p.; 12mo. Sabin 98208; Atkinson (Fr. Ren.) 497; Desgraves (Les Haultin) 243; Knuttel 1434. CtY, NN-RB; BN, The Hague:KB.
608/176

—[Anr edn]. [*Rouen:*] *J. Petit,* 1608. 13 p.; 8vo.

Sabin 98208; Atkinson (Fr. Ren.) 498; Asher 39. DLC; BN. 608/177

——. Vertoogh, hoe nootwendich, nut ende profijtelick het sy voor de Vereenighde Nederlanden te behouden de vryheyt van te handelen op West-Indien inden vrede metten Coninck van Spaignen. [*Netherlands:* 1608]. [20] p.; 4to. For variant issue see JCB (3). Forms part 21 of *Den Neder-landtschen bye-corf.* Sabin 98212; Asher 33; Knuttel 1442; Jameson (Usselinx) 6; Church 334; Kress 298; JCB (3) II:57. CSmH, DLC, ICN, MH-BA, MiU-C, MnU-B, NN-RB, RPJCB; BL, The Hague:KB.

608/178

—[Anr edn]. [*Netherlands:* 1608]. [20] p.; 4to. 1st line of caption title in upper-case letters. Sabin 98213; Asher 34; Knuttel 1443; Jameson (Usselinx) 7. NN-RB; The Hague:KB.

608/179

——, **supposed author.** Waerschouwinghe van de ghewichtighe redenen, die de Heeren Staten Generael behoeren te beweghen, om gheensins te wijcken vande handelinghe en de vaert van Indien. [*Nether-lands:* 1608]. [8] p.; 4to. Sabin 98216; Asher 37. 608/180

—[Anr edn]. Memorie vande gewichtige rede-nen die de Heeren Staten Generael be-hooren te beweghen om gheensins te wijcken vande handelinghe ende vaert van Indien. [*Amsterdam?* 1608]. [7] p.; 4to. (Den Nederlandtschen bye-corf, no. 4). Sabin 98216n; cf. Asher 28.4; Knuttel 1431. MiU-C; The Hague:KB. 608/181

—[Anr edn]. Memorie vande ghewichtighe re-denen. [*Amsterdam?* 1608]. [7] p.; 4to. At end: 'In dese tweede editie verbetert'. Sabin 98216n; Asher 38; Knuttel 1532; JCB (3) II:57. MiU-C, RPJCB; BL, The Hague:KB.

608/182

—[Anr edn]. Memorie vande ghewichtighe re-denen. [*Amsterdam?* 1608]. [7] p.; 4to. At end: 'In dese derde editie verbetert'. Sabin 98216n; Knuttel 1433; Kress 291; JCB (3) II:56. DLC, MH-BA, MiU-C, NN-RB, RPJCB; The Hague:KB. 608/183

Valbuena, Bernardo de. Siglo de oro, en las selvas de Erifile. *Madrid: A. Martín, for A. Pérez,* 1608 [colophon: 1607]. 165 (i.e.,

175) numb. lvs; 8vo. In verse. Included in the 6th eclogue is a description of 'la grandeza Mexicana'. Cf. Sabin 2863; Me-dina (BHA) 534; Pérez Pastor (Madrid) 989. NNH; BL. 608/184

Vallet, Pierre. Le jardin du roy très chrestien Henry IV. [*Paris:*] 1608. 73 pls; illus.; fol. Among the plants illustrated are a few of American origin. Included is a '*Hyacinthus peruvianus*' (today designated *Scilla peru-vianus*); it is, however, not of American ori-gin but Southern European. Pritzel 9671; Nissen (Bot.) 2039; Hunt (Bot.) 187. DLC, MH-A, NNBG; BL, BN. 608/185

Vaughan, William. The golden-grove . . . a worke very necessary for all such, as would know how to governe themselves, their houses, or their countrey . . . The second edition . . . reviewed and enlarged by au-thour. *London: S. Stafford; sold by R. Sergier & J. Browne,* 1608. [430] p.; 8vo. 1st publ., London, 1600. In bk 3, chapt. 26, the Coun-cil of the Indies is mentioned; in chapt. 61, Spanish cruelty to Indians is cited. STC 24611. CU (imp.), CtY, DLC, ICU, MH; BL.

608/186

Verheiden, Willem. Nootelijcke considera-tien die alle goede liefhebbers des vader-landts behooren rijpelijc te overweghen op-ten voorgheslaghen tractate van peys met den Spagniaerden. [*Amsterdam?*] 1608. [16] p.; 4to. (Den Nederlandtschen bye-corf, no. 16). 1st publ., [Amsterdam?] 1587. In op-posing treaty, Spanish cruelty to Indians is cited. Sabin 55950; Asher 28.17; Knuttel 1449. MiU-C, RPJCB; The Hague:KB.

608/187

Virginia Company of London. Whereas [*blank*] hath paid in readie monie to Sir Thomas Smith knight, treasurer of Virginia, the somme of [*blank*] for his adventures to-wards the said voyage . . . [*London:* 1608]. 2 lvs; fol. Sabin 99854; STC 24830.4. CSmH. 608/188

Walerande, J. B. de. Le plaidoyer de l'Indien hollandois, contre le pretendu pacificateur espagnol. [*Antwerp?*] 1608. 4 lvs; 4to. Based on *Waerschouwinghe* of this year below as at-trib. to W. Usselinx. For anr French version, see Usselinx's *Sommaire recueil* above. Sabin 98208n (& 101026); Rothschild 2404;

Knuttel 1435. MnU-B, NN-RB; BL, BN.
608/189

—[Anr issue]. [*Antwerp?*] 1608. This issue has differing t.p. with woodcut border. BL.
608/190

Wecker, Johann Jakob. Antidotarium generale, et speciale. *Venice: G. Varisco,* 1608. 2 pts; illus.; 4to. 1st publ., Basel, 1574 & 1576; cf. 1601 edn. Wellcome I:6703. DNLM; London:Wellcome.
608/191

——. Practica medicinae generalis. *Venice: F. Bolzetta,* 1608. 337 (i.e., 437) p.; 16mo. 1st publ., Basel, 1585; cf. 1602 edn. DNLM, NNNAM.
608/192

Weelkes, Thomas. Cantus. Ayeres or phantasticke spirites for three voices. *London: [J. Windet, for]* W. Barley, 1608. 3 pts; music; 4to. Text of Cantus vi comprises poem praising tobacco 'that sweet of Trinidado'. STC 25202; Arents (Add.) 141. CSmH, DLC, INS, NN-A (pt 3 only); BL.
608/193

1609

Apianus, Petrus. Cosmographie, ofte Beschrijvinge der geheelder werelt. *Amsterdam: C. Claeszoon,* 1609. 121 numb. lvs; illus., maps; 4to. 1st publ. in this enl. version, Antwerp, 1592. Sabin 1755; Ortroy (Apian) 65; JCB (3) II:58. ICN, RPJCB; BL, BN.
609/1

Arias, Juan Luis. Señor. El doctor Juan Luis Arias, dize: Que por convenir tanto al servicio de V.M. [*Valladolid:* 1609]. 7 numb. lvs; fol. Memorial to king of Spain on conversion of Spanish American Indians. BL.
609/2

Avila, Esteban de, O.F.M. Tratado de domicilio. Compuesto por el p. Esteban de Avila . . . lector de teologia . . . en la Universidad de Lima, reyno de Peru. *Madrid: L. Sánchez,* 1609. 72 numb. lvs; 8vo. Includes (lf 18) comment on those coming to Peru to become rich. Pérez Pastor (Madrid) 1031; Palau 20364. MH-L; Madrid:BN.
609/3

Barclay, John. Euphormionis Lusinini Satyricon. Pars secunda. *Paris: F. Huby,* 1609. 130

numb. lvs; 12mo. 1st publ., Paris, 1607. The imprint date is in roman numerals. Shaaber (Brit. auth.) B157. BN.
609/4

—[Anr edn?]. [*Paris? F. Huby?*] 1609. 130 numb. lvs; 12mo. The imprint date is in arabic numerals. Shaaber (Brit. auth.) B158; Tchémerzine I:441. DFo; BN, Leipzig:UB.
609/5

Bembo, Pietro, Cardinal. Omnes . . . opera, in unum corpus collecta, & nunc demum ab C. Augustino Curione . . . collata. *Strassburg: L. Zetzner,* 1609. 2 v.; 8vo. Vol. 1 comprises Bembo's *Historiae Venetae,* 1st publ., Venice, 1551, with, in bk vi, an account of Portuguese & Spanish explorations, cited as a cause of the economic decline of Venice. CtY, NcU; BL.
609/6

Blagrave, John. The art of dyalling. *London: N. O[kes]., for S. Waterson,* 1609. 152 p.; illus.; 4to. On p. 126 lands to the west unknown to Ptolemy are mentioned. STC 3116. CSmH, DFo, MH; BL.
609/7

Bocchi, Francesco. Elogiorum, quibus viri clarissimi Florentiae decorantur, liber primus[-secundus]. *Florence: The Giuntas* (v. 1), *Sermatelli Press* (v. 2), 1609, '07. 2 v.; 4to. Those praised include Amerigo Vespucci. Sabin 6102. ICN; BL, BN.
609/8

Bodin, Jean. De republica libri sex . . . Editio quinque. *Frankfurt a. M.: N. Hoffmann,* 1609. 1221 p.; 8vo. 1st publ. as transl. from Bodin's French text of 1576, Paris, 1586; cf. 1601 edn above. DLC, MH, PPL; BN.
609/9

Boodt, Anselm Boèce de. Florum, herbarum, ac fructuum selectiorum icones. *Frankfurt a. M.: C. Marne,* 1609. Includes ref. to the marigold as *flos d'Inde;* cf. 1640 edn. Pritzel 989n; Nissen 208n.
609/10

Bourne, William. De conste der zee-vaert. *Amsterdam: C. Claeszoon,* 1609. 55 numb. lvs; 4to. 1st publ. in Dutch, Amsterdam, 1594, as freely transl. from London, 1592, edn of author's *A regiment for the sea.* Included are numerous navigational refs to the Americas. Taylor (Regiment) 453; Shaaber (Brit. auth.) B613. BL.
609/11

Breton, Nicholas. A poste with a packet of madde letters. The fourth time enlarged. *London: J. W[indet]., for J. Smethwicke & J.*

Browne, 1609. 2 pts; 4to. 1st publ., London, 1602–5. STC 3688; Hoe (English) V:194–96. CSmH; BL (pt 1). 609/12

Buchanan, George. Franciscanus et fratres. [*Heidelberg:*] *Commelin Office,* 1609. 272 p.; 8vo. In verse. 1st publ. as here constituted, Basel, [1568?]; cf. 1607, Saumur, edn. Shaaber (Brit. auth.) B702. CtY, MH, NNUT; London: Wellcome, BN. 609/13

Cabredo, Luis de, S.J. Historia insignis miraculi, quod Deus invocatione S. Ignatii . . . patravit Limae die novembris anno 1607. *Graz: G. Widmanstetter,* 1609. Possibly transl. from Spanish edn. publ. at Lima, 1609. Sabin 9810; Medina (BHA) 547; Medina (Peru) 41n; Backer IV:84. 609/14

Cabredo, Rodrigo de, S.J. Copia d'una lettera . . . al padre Alfonso Messia. *Palermo: G. A. di Franceschi,* 1609. 8 lvs; 4to. Transl. from the Spanish text below. Palau 38814. 609/15

——. Copia di una carta . . . para el padre Alonso Messia procurador general por la provincia del Peru. Escrita en . . . Lima en 29. de noviembre de MDCVII. en que se refiere un milagro . . . por intercession del b. padre Ignacio de Loyola. *Barcelona: S. Matevad & L. Déu,* 1609. 4 lvs; 4to. 1st publ., Lima, in this year. Palau 38812. NNH. 609/16

Camerarius, Philipp. Operae horarum subcisivarum, sive Meditationes historicae . . . Centuria tertia. *Frankfurt a. M.: N. Hoffmann, for P. Kopff,* 1609. 395 p.; 4to. Includes ref. to flora & fauna of West Indies as reported by Monardes. For Camerarius's 1st 'century', see the year 1602; for the 2nd, see the year 1601. Cf. Jantz (German Baroque) 45–46. NjP; BL. 609/17

Camões, Luiz de. Os Lusiadas. *Lisbon: P. Craesbeeck, for D. Fernandes,* 1609. 186 numb. lvs; 4to. 1st publ., Lisbon, 1572. In verse. In Canto X, the 1st stanza mentions 'Temistatão', i.e., Mexico; in 63rd stanza Brazil is mentioned. In this edn, amongst other differences, Canto i ends 'Fin'. Silva (Camões) 14. DLC, MH, NNH; BL, Lisbon:BN. 609/18

—[Anr edn]. *Lisbon: P. Craesbeeck, for D. Fernandes,* 1609. In this edn Canto i ends 'Fim.'

Silva (Camões) 15. DLC, MH; Lisbon:BN. 609/19

Casas, Bartolomé de las, O.P., Bp of Chiapa. Den spieghel vande Spaensche tyrannie beeldelijchen afgemaelt. *Amsterdam: C. Claeszoon,* 1609. xvii lvs; 4to. Comprises plates, with captions, copied in reverse from illustrations produced for T. de Bry's edns of Las Casas's work publ. at Frankfurt a. M., 1597–99. Sabin 11253; Medina (BHA) 1085n (II:476); Hanke/Giménez 502; Streit I:302; JCB (3) II:59. DLC, NN-RB, RPJCB; BL, Göttingen:UB. 609/20

Cayet, Pierre Victor Palma. Chronologie septenaire de l'histoire de la paix entre les roys de France et d'Espagne . . . avec le succez de plusieurs navigations faictes aux Indes Orientales, Occidentales & Septentrionales, depuis le commencement de l'an 1598. jusques à la fin de l'an 1604 . . . Derniere edition. *Paris: J. Richer,* 1609. 506 numb. lvs; 8vo. 1st publ., Paris, 1605. Sabin 11627 (& 32015); Atkinson (Fr. Ren.) 518; Palau 50667. ICN, InU-L, RPJCB; BL, BN. 609/21

Chaumette, Antoine. Enchiridion, ou Livret portatif pour les chirurgiens. *Lyons: A. Huguetan,* 1609. 540 p.; 8vo. 1st publ. as transl. from Chaumette's *Enchiridion chirurgicum* (Paris, 1560), Lyons, 1571. Use of guaiacum for treatment of syphilis is discussed. BN. 609/22

Coignet, Michiel. L'épitome du théâtre de l'univers. *Antwerp:* 1609. *See* Ortelius, Abraham, *below.*

——. Epitome theatri orbis terrarum. *Antwerp:* 1609. *See* Ortelius, Abraham, *below.*

Contant, Paul. Le jardin et cabinet poétique. *Poitiers: A. Mesnier,* 1609. 99 p.; illus.; 4to. Included are numerous refs to American topics, e.g., the (Brazilian) toucan, the canoe, & the armadillo. Hunt (Bot.) 188. PPiHB; BL, BN. 609/23

Cortés, Jerónimo. Libro de phisonomia natural. *Tarragona: F. Roberto,* 1609. 115 numb. lvs; 8vo. 1st publ., Valencia, 1597; cf. 1601 edn. Palau 63303. BL. 609/24

Cortés, Martín. The arte of navigation. First written in the Spanish tongue . . . From thence translated . . . by Richard Eden: and now newly corrected and inlarged . . . by John Tapp. *London:* [*F. Kingston?*] *for J. Tapp,* 1609. 157 p.; illus., map; 4to. Transl. from Cortés's *Breve compendio de la sphera,* 1st publ., Seville, 1551; 1st publ. as transl. by Eden, London, 1561; as enl. by Tapp, London, 1596. Sabin 16968; STC 5804. CSmH; BL. 609/25

Craig, Alexander. The poetical recreations. *Edinburgh: T. Finlason,* 1609. 16 lvs; 4to. Includes poem of 6 verses, 'Against the sellers of tobacco'. STC 5959. CSmH; BL. 609/26

Crakanthorpe, Richard. A sermon at the solemnizing of the happie inauguration of King James. *London: W. Jaggard, for T. Adams,* 1609. [54] p.; 4to. On recto of 1f D2 the intended expedition to Virginia is mentioned. STC 5979. DFo, IU, MH; BL. 609/27

Croll, Oswald. Basilicus chymica . . . Additus est . . . Tractatus novus de signaturis rerum internis. *Frankfurt a. M.: C. Marne & Heirs of J. Aubry,* 1609. 3 pts; illus.; 4to. In the 'Tractatus . . . de signaturis' the turkey is mentioned. CtY, DNLM, NNC; London: Wellcome, BN. 609/28

Dekker, Thomas. The guls horne-booke. *London:* [*N. Okes?*] *for R. Sergier,* 1609. 23 lvs; 4to. Includes refs to tobacco. STC 6500; Arents 90. CSmH, DLC, MH, NN-A; BL. 609/29

——. Lanthorne and candle-light . . . The second edition, newly corrected and amended. *London: J. Busby,* 1609. [86] p.; 4to. 1st publ., London, 1608. STC 6486; Pforzheimer 274. CSmH, DFo, MH (imp.); BL. 609/30

——. Worke for armorours. *London: N. Butter,* 1609. 4to. Ref. is made to the golden mines of the West Indies. STC 6536. CSmH; BL. 609/31

Delle rime piacevoli del Berni, Casa, Mauro, Varchi, Dolce et d'altri auttori. *Vicenza: F. Grossi,* 1609–10. 3 pts; 12mo. 1st publ. as here constituted, Venice, 1552–55; cf. 1603 edn. PU (pt 1 only); BL (Berni, F.). 609/32

Des Combes, ——, sieur. Coppie d'une lettre envoyée de Nouvelle France ou Canada, par le sier Cõbes, gentilhomme poictevin . . . en laquelle sont briefvement descrites les merveilles, excellences et richesses du pays. *Lyons: L. Savine,* 1609. 15 p.; 8vo. A work of fiction. Sabin 56083; Harrisse (NF) 20; Church 335. CSmH, NN-RB. 609/33

Donato d'Eremita. Il fiore della granadiglia, over Della passione di nuestro signore Giesù Christo, spiegato e lodato. *Bologna: B. Cocchi, for S. Pariasca,* 1609. 2 pts; 4to. On the passionflower, & the symbolism of its blossom. Michel (Répertoire) III:12. BN, Grenoble:BM. 609/34

Du Bartas, Guillaume de Salluste, seigneur. [De eerste weke der scheppinge der werelt, eerst ghevonden, ende in françoische dicht ghestelt . . . Vertaelt in nederlantschen ryme door T[heoderick]. v[an]. L[iefvelt]. *Brussels: R. Velpius,* 1609. 166 p.; 4to. In verse. Transl. from author's *La sepmaine,* 1st publ., Paris, 1578. Holmes (Du Bartas) I:108 no.11. MH; BL. 609/35

——. Hebdomas II, a Samuele Benedicto . . . latinitate donata. *Lyons: B. Vincent,* 1609. 162 p.; 12mo. In verse. Transl. from author's *La seconde sepmaine,* 1st publ., Paris, 1584. Included are numerous refs to New World. Holmes (Du Bartas) I:107 no. 7 (misdated 1619). ICU; BN. 609/36

Duchesne, Joseph. Liber de priscorum philosophorum verae medicinae materia. *Geneva: J. Vignon,* 1609. 432 p.; 8vo. 1st publ., St Gervais, 1603. DNLM, PPC; BN. 609/37

Durante, Castore. Hortulus sanitatis. Das ist Ein heylsam und nützliches Gährtlin der Gesundtheit . . . in hoch teutsche Sprach versetzt durch Petrum Uffenbachium. *Frankfurt a. M.: N. Hoffmann, for J. Rose,* 1609. 1081 p.; illus.; 4to. Transl. from author's *Herbario nuovo,* 1st publ., Rome, 1585; cf. year 1602. Nissen (Bot.) 570; Arents (Add.) 84. CtY-M, DNLM, MoSB, NN-A; BL. 609/38

Estienne, Charles. L'agricoltura, et casa di villa. *Turin: G. D. Tarino,* 1609. Cf. 1606 edn. DNLM, MH; Paris: Ste Geneviève. 609/39

——. Dictionarium historicum, geographicum, poeticum. [*Geneva:*] *J. Stoer,* 1609. 452 numb. lvs; 4to. 1st publ. in this enl. edn, Lyons, 1595; cf. 1601 edn. MnCS. 609/40

Everie woman in her humor. *London: E.*

A[*llde*]., *for T. Archer,* 1609. [64] p.; 4to. Drama. Includes mention of tobacco. STC 25948; Greg 283; Arents 91. CSmH, CtY, DLC, ICN, MH, NN-RB, PU-F; BL.
609/41

Figueiredo, Manuel de. Roteiro e navegação das Indias Occidentais ilhas, antilhas do mar Oceano occidental . . . Novamente ordenado segundo os pilotos antigos, modernos. *Lisbon: P. Craesbeeck,* 1609. 42 numb. lvs; 4to. Sabin 73433; Borba de Moraes I:265; JCB (3) II:59. CSmH, MnU-B, RPJCB.
609/42

Foreest, Pieter van. Observationum et curationum medicinalium . . . libri xxx. xxxi. & xxxii. De venenis, fucis & lue venerea. *Frankfurt a. M.: Palthenius Office,* 1609. 135 p.; fol. 1st publ., Leyden, 1606. Wellcome I:2374. DNLM; BL, BN.
609/43

Garcilaso de la Vega, el Inca. Primera parte de los Commentarios reales, que tratan del origen de los Yncas, reyes que fueron del Peru. *Lisbon: P. Craesbeeck,* 1609. 264 numb. lvs; fol. Colophon dated 1608. Continued by the author's *Historia general del Peru* of 1616. Sabin 98757; Medina (BHA) 549; Palau 354788; JCB (3) II:61. CSmH, CtY, DLC, IEN, InU-L, MH, MiU-C, NN-RB, RPJCB; BL, BN.
609/44

Gaultier, Jacques. Table chronologique de l'estat du christianisme depuis la naissance de Jésus-Christ jusques à l'année MDCVIII. *Lyons: J. Roussin,* 1609. 440 p.; fol. Under year 1555 Villegagnon's Brazilian venture is mentioned. Backer III:1274; Cioranescu (XVII) 32619. BL, BN.
609/45

Génebrard, Gilbert, Abp of Aix. Chronographiae libri quatuor. *Lyons: J. Pillehotte,* 1609, '08. 954 p.; fol. 1st publ., Paris, 1567. Included are numerous refs to America (e.g., Brazil & Peru), Columbus, etc. BL.
609/46

González de Mendoza, Juan, Bp. Histoire du grand royaume de la Chine . . . ensemble un Itineraire du nouveau Mexique en l'an 1583 . . . nouvellement traduite de latin en françois. *Lyons: F. Arnoullet,* 1509 [i.e., 1609]. 388p.; 8vo. 1st publ. in French, Paris, 1588; cf. 1606 edn above. Cf. Sabin 47829; Wagner (SW) 7hh; Atkinson (Fr. Ren.) 517; Baudrier (Lyons) X:170. ICN, NN-RB, RPJCB; BN.
609/47

Gracián, Jerónimo. Zelo de la propagacion de la fee. *Brussels: J. Mommaert,* 1609. 28 numb. lvs; 4to. 1st publ., Lisbon, 1586, under title *Estimulo de la propagacion de la fe;* cf. Gracián's *Lampara encendida,* Madrid, 1604. Streit I:301; Peeters-Fontainas (Impr. esp.) 537; Palau 106789. WU; BN, Madrid:BN.
609/48

Grahame, Simion. The anatomie of humors. *Edinburgh: T. Finlason,* 1609. 74 numb. lvs; 4to. Tobacco is mentioned on lvs 7v & 71v ('Indian hearbs which in black smok I spend'). STC 12168; Allis 412; Arents (Add.) 142. CSmH, DFo, ICN, MH, NN-A; BL.
609/49

Granado, Diego. Libro del arte de cozina. *Madrid: A. Martín,* 1609. 348 numb. lvs; 8vo. 1st publ., Madrid, 1599. Includes section on how to 'assare el gallo y gallina de las Indias', i.e., turkeys. BN.
609/50

Gray, Robert. A good speed to Virginia. *London: F. Kingston, for W. Welby,* 1609. [29] p.; 4to. Sabin 27837; Clayton-Torrence 2; Vail (Frontier) 14; STC 12204; Church 336; JCB (3) II:59. CSmH, DLC, ICN, MH, MiU-C, NN-RB, PP, RPJCB; BL.
609/51

Great Britain. Council for Virginia. Considering there is no publicke action, being honest and good in it selfe . . . but that the same is also beneficiall . . . we thought it therefore requisite, to import unto you . . . how many wayes it hath pleased God to encourage us to goe on, in that great worke and enterprize of planting colonies of our English nation, in those parts of America, which wee commonly call Virginia, or Nova Britannia . . . . [*London:* 1609?]. bds.; fol. Offer of stock in Virginia Company. Sabin 99855; Clayton-Torrence 7; STC 24830.9. NN-RB, PPRF, RPJCB.
609/52

Grégoire, Pierre. De republica libri sex et viginti. *Lyons: J. Pillehotte,* 1609. 2 v.; fol. 1st publ., Pont-à-Mousson, 1596. Includes mention of Spanish in Hispaniola. DLC, ICN, MH, NNC; BL, BN.
609/53

—[Anr edn]. *Frankfurt a. M.: N. Hoffmann,* 1609. 4to. BL.
609/54

——. Syntagma juris universi. *Lyons: J. Pillehotte,* 1609. 3 pts; fol. 1st publ., Lyons, 1582. Book xlii, chapt. viii, sect. 25—'Provinciae & civitates, quae habent in Gallia ius regni-

colarum'—includes ref. to America. BN.
609/55

Grimestone, Edward. A generall historie of the Netherlands. *London: A. Islip & G. Eld,* 1609. 1415 p.; ports; fol. 1st publ., London, 1608; here a reissue of that edn. STC 12375. CSmH, ICN, MiU, MWA, NjP; BL, Oxford:Bodl.
609/56

Grotius, Hugo. Mare liberum sive de jure quod Batavis competit ad Indicana commercia dissertatio. *Leyden: L. Elsevier,* M.DI.IX. [1609]. 42 (i.e., 66) p.; 8vo. Includes refs to Spanish West Indies. Meulen/ Diermanse 541; Willems (Les Elzevier) 56; Bibl. Belg. G331. RPB; BN, The Hague:PP.
609/57

—[Anr edn]. *Leyden: L. Elsevier,* M.DI.IX. [1609]. 70 p.; 8vo. An apparent piracy of the above. Meulen/Diermanse 542; Willems (Les Elzevier) 56n. The Hague:PP.
609/58

Guerreiro, Fernão, S.J. Relaçam anual das cousas que fezeram os padres da Companhia de Jesus . . . Vai dividada em quatro livros . . . O quarto de Guiné, & Brasil. *Lisbon: P. Craesbeeck,* 1609. 204 numb. lvs; 4to. Sabin 69162; Borba de Moraes I:321; Streit II:2369; Backer III:1914; JCB (3) II:60. InU-L, MH, NN-RB, RPJCB; BL, Rome:BN.
609/59

Hall, Joseph, Bp of Norwich. The discovery of a new world. *London: [G. Eld,] for E. Blount & W. Barrett* [1609?]. 244 p.; illus., maps; 8vo. Transl. by John Healey from author's *Mundus alter,* 1st publ., [London, 1605?]. Sabin 29820; STC 12686; JCB (3) II:60. CSmH, CtY, DFo, ICN, MH, NN-RB, RPJCB; BL.
609/60

Heurne, Johan van. Praxis medicinae nova ratio. *Leyden: Plantin Press (Raphelengius),* 1609. 376 p.; illus.; 8vo. 1st publ., Leyden, 1587. Included are instructions for therapeutic use of tobacco. Arents (Add.) 87. DNLM, NN-A; London:Wellcome.
609/61

Johnson, Robert. Nova Britannia. Offring most excellent fruites by planting in Virginia. *London: [J. Windet,] for S. Macham,* 1609. [36] p.; 4to. Of this work there exist two settings of type, the sheets being indiscriminately gathered, while of the t.p. there are three states—cf. Clayton-Torrence &

the STC as cited. Sabin 36284 & 56098; Clayton-Torrence 4A–4C; Vail (Frontier) 15; STC 14699–99.5; Church 338; JCB (3) II:60–61. CSmH, CtY, DLC, ICN, InU-L, MH, MiU-C, MnU-B, NN-RB, RPJCB; BL.
609/62

Langenes, Barent. Hand-boeck, of Cort begrijp der caerten ende beschrijvinghen van alle landen des werelds. Van nieuws oversien ende vermeerdert. *Amsterdam: C. Claeszoon,* 1609. 761 p.; illus., maps; obl. 8vo. 1st publ., Middelburg, [1598], under title *Caert-thresoor;* here rev. & enl. by Jacobus Viverius. Sabin 38881 (& 9839n); Koeman (Lan) 8; Phillips (Atlases) 424; JCB (3) II:61. DLC, MnU-B, PHi, RPJCB; BL, Amsterdam:UB.
609/63

Laudonnière, René Goulaine de. Brevis narratio eorum quae in Florida Americae provincia Gallis acciderunt . . . Latio verò donata a C. C[lusius]. *Frankfurt a. M.: J. Wechel, for T. de Bry; for sale by S. Feyerabend,* 1591 [i.e., 1609]. 30 p.; illus., map.; fol. (Theodor de Bry's *America.* Pt 2. Latin). 1st publ. in this version, Frankfurt a. M., 1591; transl. from author's *L'histoire notable de la Floride,* 1st publ., Paris 1586. Cf. Sabin 8784; Church 146; JCB (3) I:388. CSmH, NN-RB, RPJCB; BL, BN.
609/64

Leonardo y Argensola, Bartolomé Juan. Conquista de las islas Malucas. *Madrid: A. Martín,* 1609. 407 p.; fol. Included are numerous scattered refs to the Americas, e.g., to Columbus, Sir Francis Drake, Patagonian giants, Peru, the Strait of Magellan, etc. Sabin 1946; Medina (BHA) 551; Pérez Pastor (Madrid) 1046; Palau 16089; JCB (3) II:61. CSmH, CtY, DLC, ICU, InU-L, MnU-B, NNH, PU, RPJCB; BL, BN.
609/65

Lescarbot, Marc. Histoire de la Nouvelle France, contenant les navigations, découvertes, & habitations faites par les François és Indes Occidentales & Nouvelle-France. *Paris: J. Millot,* 1609. 888 p.; maps; 8vo. Includes in bk 1 account of Villegagnon's attempted settlement in Brazil, as well as of Huguenot colony in Florida. Sabin 40169; Harrisse (NF) 16; Borba de Moraes I:406–7; Atkinson (Fr. Ren.) 513; Church 399; JCB (3) II:62. CSmH, CtY, DLC, InU-L, MH, MiU-C, MnU-B, NN-RB, PPL, RPJCB; BL, BN.
609/66

——. Les muses de la Nouvelle France. *Paris: J. Millot*, 1609. 66 p.; 8vo. In verse. Sabin 40174; Harrisse (NF) 17; Church 340; JCB (3) II:62. DLC, InU-L, MH, MiU, MnU-B, PPL, RPJCB; BN. 609/67

——. Nova Francia, or The description of that part of New France, which is one continent with Virginia . . . Translated out of French . . . by P[ierre]. E[rondelle]. *London: [Eliot's Court Press,] for G. Bishop*, 1609. 307 p.; map; 4to. Transl. from author's *Histoire de la Nouvelle France* of this year. Sabin 40175; Harrisse (NF) 19; Vail (Frontier) 16; Borba de Moraes I:407; STC 15491; cf. Church 341. CSmH, CtY, DLC, MH, MiU-C, NN-RB, PPL: BL, BN. 609/68

Linton, Anthony. Newes of the complement of the arte of navigation, and of the mightie empire of Cataia. *London: F. Kingston*, 1609. 44 p.; 4to. Mentioned are English explorers who have visited America. Sabin 41385; STC 15692; Church 343; JCB (3) II:63. CSmH, DLC, MnU-B, NN-RB, RPJCB; BL. 609/69

Lodewijcksz, Willem. D'eerste boeck; Historie van Indien, waer inne verhaelt is de avontuere die de Hollandtsche schepen bejegent zijn . . . Door G.M.A.W.L. *Amsterdam: C. Claeszoon*, 1609. 70 lvs.; illus., maps; obl. 4to. 1st publ., Amsterdam, 1598. Includes mention of Brazil. Tiele 508; Tiele-Muller 114. CSmH, NN-RB. 609/70

——. Premier livre de l'Histoire de la navigation aux Indes Orientales, par les Hollandois . . . Par G.M.A.W.L. *Amsterdam: C. Claeszoon*, 1609. 53 numb. lvs; illus., maps; fol. 1st publ. in this version, Amsterdam, 1598. Atkinson (Fr. Ren.) 514; Tiele-Muller 115; JCB (3) II:63. CSmH, CtY, ICU, MH, NN-RB, RPJCB; BL, BN. 609/71

Lopes, Duarte. Regnum Congo, hoc est Warhaffte und eigentliche Beschreibung dess Königreichs Congo . . . in teutsche Spraach transferieret . . . durch Augustinum Cassiodorum. *Frankfurt a. M.: M. Becker, for J. T. & J. I. de Bry, Bros*, 1609. 74 p.; illus., maps; fol. (J. T. de Bry's *India Orientalis*. Pt 1. German). 1st publ. in this version, Frankfurt a. M., 1597; transl. from *Relatione del reame di Congo*, 1st publ., Rome, 1591. Includes refs to Brazilian cannibals, and to explorers Drake & Cavendish.

Church 227; JCB (3) I:421–22. CSmH, CtY, MBAt, NN, RPJCB; BL, BN. 609/72

Maiolo, Simeone, Bp of Volturara. Les jours caniculaires, c'est a dire Vingt et trois excellents discours des choses naturelles et surnaturelles . . . mis en françois par François de Rosset. *Paris: R. Fouët*, 1609. 1029 p.; 4to. Transl. from Maioli's *Dies caniculares*, 1st publ., Rome, 1597. Included are refs to natural history of New World. Cioranescu (XVII) 60184. BN. 609/73

The man in the moone . . . or, The English fortune-teller. *London: J. W[indet]., for N. Butter*, 1609. [48] p.; 4to. Lvs C1r–C2v describe a tobacconist. Signed: W. M. STC 17155; Murphy (Engl. char.-bks) 121. DFo; BL, Oxford:Bodl. 609/74

Marlowe, Christopher. The tragicall historie of the life and death of Doctor Faustus. *London: G. E[ld]., for J. Wright*, 1609. [45] p.; 4to. Drama. 1st publ., London, 1604. STC 17430; Greg 205 (b). CSmH; Petworth, Hamburg:PL. 609/75

Matthieu, Pierre. Histoire de France et des choses memorables advenues aux provinces estrangeres durant sept annees de paix du regne de Henry IIII roy de France. *Paris: J. Mettayer & M. Guillemot*, 1609. 2 v.; 8vo. 1st publ., Paris, 1605. CtY, MH; BL, BN. 609/76

Medina, Pedro de. Arte del navigare. *Venice: T. Baglioni*, 1609. 137 numb. lvs; illus., maps; 4to. 1st publ. as here transl. by Vicenzo Palatino da Corsula, Venice, 1555. Instructional manual for voyages to America. Palau 159680; Michel (Répertoire) V:160. MB, RPJCB; BL, BN. 609/77

Melton, Sir John. A sixe-folde politician. *London: E. A[llde]., for J. Busby*, 1609. 174 p.; 8vo. Includes comments on tobacco. STC 17805; Arents 93. CSmH, CtY, DLC, ICN, MH, NN-RB, RPB; BL. 609/78

Mercado, Luis. Opera omnia in tres tomos divisa. *Venice: B. Giunta & G. B. Ciotti & Co.*, 1609. 3 v.; fol. Included is Mercado's *Tomus secundus Operum*, 1st publ., Valladolid, 1605. Palau 164992; Wellcome I:4217. DNLM; London:Wellcome, BN. 609/79

Mercator, Gerardus. L'atlas, ou Méditations cosmographiques de la fabrique du monde et figure d'iceluy . . . Traduit . . . par le sieur de La P[opelinière]. Editio secunda.

Amsterdam: J. Hondius, 1609. 358 p.; maps; fol. Transl. from Mercator's Latin *Atlas*, 1st publ., Amsterdam, 1606. Cf. Sabin 47882; Koeman (Me) 19; Phillips (Atlases) 426. DLC; BN. 609/80

——. Atlas minor, das ist, Ein kurtze jedoch gründtliche Beschreibung der gantzen Welt. [*Amsterdam:*] *J. Hondius; sold also by C. Claeszoon & by J. Janszoon, at Arnhem* [1609]. 676 p.; maps; obl. 12mo. Transl. from author's Latin *Atlas minor*, 1st publ., Amsterdam, 1607. Cf. Sabin 47889; Koeman (Me) 188; Phillips (Atlases) 425. DLC, ICJ, MH; Brussels:BR. 609/81

——. Atlas minor . . . Traduict de latin . . . par le sieur de la Popeliniere. *Amsterdam: J. Hondius; sold also by J. Janszoon, at Arnhem*, 1609. 656 p.; maps; obl. 12mo. 1st publ. in French, Amsterdam, 1608; here a reissue of that edn with altered imprint date. Cf. Sabin 47888; Koeman (Me) 187n. BL. 609/82

Meteren, Emanuel van. Belgische ofte Nederlantsche oorlogen ende geschiedenissen beginnende van't jaer 1598 tot 1609. '*Schotland outside Danswijck*' [i.e., *The Hague?*]: *H. van Loven*, 1609. [632] p.; ports; 4to. 1st publ. in Dutch, Delft, 1599; cf. year 1605. Though the place of printing is often assumed to be Amsterdam, Utrecht, or Dordrecht, van Loven is recorded as active in The Hague from 1608 to 1610 (Ledeboer, p. 112). Amsterdam:NHSM. 609/83

—[Anr edn]. Commentarien ofte Memorien van-den Nederlandtschen staet, handel, oorloghen ende gheschiedenissen van onsen tyden . . . verbetert ende vermeerdert. '*Schotland, outside Danswijck*' [i.e., *The Hague?*]: *H. van Loven, for E. van Meteren, at London*, 1609. 4 pts; illus., ports, map; fol. Here enl. to include additional American material. Cf. Palau 166948; STC 17845.3. MH, MiU-C, MnU-B, NN-RB, RPJCB; London:Dutch Church. 609/84

——. Niderlendischer Historien ander Theil. [*Arnhem? J. Janszoon?*] 1609. fol. Continues the author's *Historia*, 1st publ. in German, Hamburg, 1596; cf. years 1601 & 1604. Issued as pt of the publisher's Arnhem, 1612, *Niederländische Historien oder Geschichten*, q.v.

Mexía, Pedro. Les diverses leçons . . . mises de castillan en françois, par Cl. Gruget . . .

avec sept dialogues . . . Plus la suite de celles d'Antoine Du Verdier. *Tournon: C. Michel*, 1609. 2 pts; 8vo. 1st publ. in this version with American refs in Du Verdier's continuation, Lyons, 1577; cf. 1604 edn. Palau 167322n. Paris:Arsenal. 609/85

Middelgeest, Simon van. Het testament ofte wtersten wille vande Nederlandsche oorloghe . . . door Yemand van Waermond [pseud.]. '*Franc end al: Frede-rijck de Vrije*' [i.e., *Amsterdam?* 1609]. [16] p.; 4to. In verse. Includes ref. to Las Casas's writings on West Indies. Sometimes attrib. to W. Usselinx. This edn has reading 'Ghelijc als sy, liggende' on t.p. Knuttel 1581. CtY, MiU-C, NN-RB; The Hague:KB. 609/86

—[Anr edn]. '*Franc end al: Frede-rijck de Vrije*' [i.e., *Amsterdam?* 1609]. [16] p.; 4to. T.p. has reading 'Ghelijck'; phrase 'Dies en attulit ultro' added at end of text. Knuttel 1582. MiU-C; The Hague:KB. 609/87

—[Anr edn]. '*Franc end al: Frede-rijck de Vrije*' [i.e., *Amsterdam?* 1609]. [16] p.; 4to. T.p. has reading 'Ghelijck, als sy, ligghende'. Knuttel 1583. The Hague:KB. 609/88

Montaigne, Michel Eyquem de. Essais. *Geneva: J. Can*, 1609. 1132 p.; 8vo. 1st publ., Bordeaux, 1580; cf. 1602 edn. Tchémerzine VIII:415. BN. 609/89

—[Anr edn]. *Leyden: J. Doreau*, 1609. 1132 p.; 8vo. Tchémerzine VIII:415. BN. 609/90

Entry canceled. 609/91

Morellas, Cosmé Gil, O.P. Compendiosa relatio vitae eximiae sanctitatis viri fr. Ludovici Bertrandi. *Cologne: A. Kempen*, 1609. 4to. Saint Luís Bertrán had been a Dominican missionary in Colombia & elsewhere. Streit II:1395; Palau 181654. 609/92

Neck, Jacob Corneliszoon van. Le second livre, Journal ou Comptoir. *Amsterdam: C. Claeszoon*, 1609. 2 pts; illus., maps; fol. 1st publ. in this version, Amsterdam, 1601. Also issued with W. Lodewijcksz's *Premiere livre de l'Histoire* of this year above. Tiele-Muller 129; Tiele 786; Muller (1872) 2216; JCB (3) II:64. MH, NN-RB, PP, RPJCB; BL, BN. 609/93

Ortelius, Abraham. L'épitome du théâtre de l'univers . . . nouvellement recogneu, augmenté et restauré . . . par Michel Coignet. *Antwerp: J. B. Vrients*, 1609. 148 lvs; maps; obl. 8vo. Though with French t.p., the text is that in Latin of Coignet, 1st publ., Antwerp, 1601. Koeman (Ort) 67A; Phillips (Atlases) 3411. DLC, MiU-C, NN-RB; Brussels:BR. 609/94

——. Epitome theatri orbis terrarum . . . de novo recognita, aucta, et geographica ratione restaurata, à Michaele Coigneto. *Antwerp: J. B. Vrients,* 1609. 295 p.; maps; obl. 8vo. 1st publ. with Coignet's text, Antwerp, 1601. Koeman (Ort) 67B; Phillips (Atlases) 5922. DLC; Antwerp: Plantin Mus. 609/95

——. Theatrum orbis terrarum. *Antwerp: J. B. Vrients,* 1609. 2 pts; maps; fol. 1st publ. in Latin, Antwerp, 1570; cf. year 1603. Cf. Sabin 57700; Koeman (Ort) 39; cf. Phillips (Atlases) 427. CtY, DLC; Groningen:UB. 609/96

Oviedo, Luís de. Methodo de la coleccion y reposicion de las medicinas simples . . . Va añadido . . . el tercer libro, y . . . el quarto . . . en que se trata de la composicion de los unguentos. *Madrid: L. Sánchez,* 1609. 1st publ., Madrid, 1581; in this enl. edn, Madrid, 1595. Includes formulas for 'Agua de palo de Indias' (guaiacum), 'Agua de çarçaparilla' (sarsaparilla) and a discussion of 'Balsamo dela Nueva España'. This edn is perhaps a ghost derived from Nic. Antonio. Pérez Pastor (Madrid) 1051; Palau 207730. No copy known; see 1622 edn. 609/97

Pigray, Pierre. Chirurgia cum aliis medicinae partibus juncta. *Paris: M. Orry,* 1609. 771 p.; port.; 8vo. Transl. from Pigray's *La chirurgie,* 1st publ., Paris, 1600; cf. 1604 edn. DNLM, PPL. 609/98

——. Epitome des preceptes de medecine et chirurgie. *Paris: M. Orry,* 1609. 764 p.; port.; 8vo. 1st publ., Paris, 1600, under title *La chirurgie;* cf. 1604 edn. DNLM; BN. 609/99

Platter, Felix. Praxeos. *Basel: C. Waldkirch,* 1609, '08. 3 v.; 8vo. Vols. 1–2, 1st publ., Basel, 1602–3. CtY-M, DNLM, WU-M; BN. 609/100

Porta, Giovanni Battista della. De distillatione lib. ix. *Strassburg: L. Zetzner,* 1609. 149 p.; illus., port.; 4to. 1st publ., Rome, 1608. Ferguson (Bibl. chem.) II:215; Wellcome I:5212. DNLM, OkU, PPC; BL, BN. 609/101

Price, Daniel. Sauls prohibition staide. Or, the apprehension . . . of Saule; . . . with a reproofe of those that traduce the honourable plantation of Virginia. Preached in a sermon. *London: [J. Windet,] for M. Law,* 1609. [46] p.; 4to. Sabin 65421; Clayton-Torrence 5; Vail (Frontier) 18; STC 20302; JCB (3) II:66. CSmH, DLC, ICN, MH, NjP, RPJCB; BL. 609/102

Queiros, Pedro Fernandes de. Copia de unos avisos muy notables dados a la . . . Real Magestad del Rey Don Felipe . . . y en un memorial presentados este año de 1609. *Barcelona: G. Graells & G. Dotil,* 1609. 2 lvs; 4to. Includes testimony taken in Mexico regarding recent voyage of exploration in South Pacific. Palau 89596. 609/103

Renou, Jean de. Dispensatorium medicum. *Frankfurt a. M.: J. T. Schönwetter,* 1609. 983 p.; 8vo. 1st publ., Paris, 1608, under title *Institutionum pharmaceuticarum, libri quinque.* Wellcome I:5429. London:Wellcome. 609/104

Rivadeneira, Pedro de, S.J. Illustrium scriptorum religionis Societatis Jesu catalogus . . . Hac secunda editione auctus. *Lyons: J. Pillehotte,* 1609. 304 p.; 8vo. 1st publ., Antwerp, 1608. Sabin 70778n; Backer VI:1754; Palau 266559. CtY, DCU, ICN, NNH, RPJCB; BL, BN. 609/105

——. Trattato della religione, e virtuti, che deve haver il principe christiano . . . tradotto per Scipioni Metelli. *Brescia: Comp. Bresciana,* 1609. 541 p.; 8vo. 1st publ. as transl. from author's *Tratado de la religion* (1st publ., Madrid, 1595), Genoa, 1598. Here a reissue of printers' 1599 edn? Backer VI:1736; Palau 266341. 609/106

——. La vie du b. p. Ignace de Loyola . . . Escrite premièrement en espagnol . . . depuis mise en françois [par Henry de Sponde], et nouvellement reveüe et corrigée. *Lyons: L. Savine, for P. Rigaud,* 1609. 262 p.; 12mo. 1st publ. as here transl., Paris(?), 1608. Backer VI:1755–56; Palau 266251. BN. 609/107

——. La vie du reverend père François de Borgia . . . 3me édition. *Lyons: L. Savine, for P. Rigaud,* 1609. 417 p.; 8vo. 1st publ. as here transl. by François Solier from au-

thor's *Vida del p. Francisco de Borja* (itself 1st publ., Madrid, 1592), Verdun, 1596. Includes refs to Jesuits in New World. The 2nd edn has not been identified. Palau 266316n; cf. Cioranescu (XVII) 63230. BN.
609/108

Rondelet, Guillaume. Methodus curandorum omnium morborum corporis humani. [*Geneva:*] *J. Stoër,* 1609. 1277 p.; 8vo. 1st publ., [Paris? 1563?]; cf. 1601 edn. DNLM; London:Wellcome, BN.
609/109

Rowlands, Samuel. Doctor Merrie-man, or Nothing but mirth. *London:* [*W. White?*] *for J. Deane,* 1609. 4to. In verse. 1st publ., London, 1607, under title *Democritus, or Doctor Merry-man his medicines.* STC 21367. MH.
609/110

——. The knave of clubbes. *London:* [*E. Allde*] *for W. Ferbrand,* 1609. 24 lvs; 4to. 1st publ., London, 1600, under title *A merry meeting.* In verse. Includes poem on tobacco, 'The devils health-drinker'. STC 21387; Arents 94. MH.
609/111

——. A whole crew of kind gossips. *London:* [*W. Jaggard,*] *for J. Deane,* 1609. 4to. In verse. 'The fift gossip' describes 'Such weeds, as Indians do Tobacco call'. Includes also the author's *Tis merrie,* 1st publ., London, 1602. STC 21413. Oxford:Bodl.
609/112

Schenck von Grafenberg, Johann. Παρατηρησεων, sive Observationum medicarum . . . volumen. *Frankfurt a. M.: N. Hoffmann, for J. Rose,* 1609. 1018 p.; port.; fol. 1st publ., Frankfurt a. M., 1600, under title *Observationum medicarum . . . tomus unus* [-alter]. While not stating syphilis to be American in origin, calls for use of sarsaparilla in its treatment, also mentioning guaiacum. Wellcome I:5827. DNLM, MnU, NNC, PPC; London:Wellcome.
609/113

Schyron, Jean. Methodi medendi, seu Institutionis medicinae faciendae . . . libri quatuor. *Montpellier: F. Chouët,* 1609. 542 p.; 16mo. In bk 3, chapts xxxix–xlii, on syphilis, call for use of guaiacum, sarsaparilla, & sassafras. DNLM; BL.
609/114

Spain. Laws, statutes, etc., 1598–1621 (Philip III). Este en em traslado bien y fielmente sacado . . . de una cedula de su Magestad . . . para que la plata que viniere de los Indias en las dos flotas primeras . . . se labre como en ella se dize. [*Madrid:* 1609?]. bds.; fol. Dated 22 Nov. 1608. BL.
609/115

——. Instruccion de la forma que se ha de tener en la provincias del Pirú, Tierra Firme, sobre las caxas de comunidades, en el entretanto que otra cosa por su Magestad se ordena y manda. [*Madrid:* 1609]. 3 lvs; fol. Dated 12 Nov. 1609. Palau 120138.
609/116

——. Lo que se ordena de nuevo para lo que toca el exercicio y jurisdicion de los oficios de contadores de quentas de los tribunales . . . en las Indias. [*Madrid?* 1609]. 8 numb. lvs; fol. Dated 17 May 1609. Maggs Cat. 479 (Americana V):4115. DLC; BL.
609/117

——. El Rey. Marques de Montes Claros . . . governador . . . del Piru, mande dar las ordenes que paracieron convenientes, sobre el servicio personal, alivio, y buen tratamiento de los Indios. [*Madrid?* 1609]. 3 numb. lvs; fol. Comprises nine edicts directed to governor of Peru. Maggs Cat. 479 (Americana V):4111. BL.
609/118

Spain. Sovereigns, etc., 1598–1621 (Philip III). El Rey [26 May 1609]. [*Madrid:* 1609]. 9 numb. lvs; fol. 'Al Virrey de la Nueva España, sobre lo que se le ordena, y provee acerca de los servicios personales de los Indios.' BL.
609/119

——. El Rey [26 May 1609]. [*Madrid:* 1609]. 3 numb. lvs; fol. 'Al Virrey de Nueva España, sobre que informe, si conserva moderar tributos de Indios.' BL.
609/120

Spenser, Edmund. The faerie queene. *London: H. L[ownes]., for M. Lownes,* 1609. 363 p.; fol. 1st publ., London, 1590. In the prologue to the 2nd bk refs to the New World, incl. 'fruitfellest Virginia', occur; in bk 3, canto v, stanzas xxxii–xxxiii, therapeutic use of tobacco is described. Johnson (Spenser) 12; STC 23083; Arents (Add.) 143; Pforzheimer 971. CSmH, CtY, ICN, MH, MiU, NN-RB, RPB; BL.
609/121

Symonds, William. Virginia. A sermon preached at White-Chappel, in the presence of many, honourable and worshipfull, the adventurers and planters for Virginia. 25. April. 1609. *London: J. Windet, for E. Edgar, & W. Welby,* 1609. 54 p.; 4to. Sabin 94125; Clayton-Torrence 6; Vail (Frontier) 19; STC 23594; Church 344; JCB (3) II:66.

CSmH, DLC, ICN, MB, MiU-C, NN-RB, RPJCB; BL. 609/122

Thou, Jacques Auguste de. Historiarum sui temporis. Opera. M.DC.IX. *Offenbach: C. Neben, the Younger* (v. 1); *Frankfurt a. M.: J. Saur, for P. Kopff* (v. 2–3), 1609–10. 3 v.; fol. 1st publ. as here constituted, Paris, 1606–9. CtY, MiU, NNC, PPL; BL. 609/123

——. Historiarum sui temporis libri cxxv. *Paris: A. & H. Drouart,* 1609–14. 11 v.; 12mo. The title statement notwithstanding, contains lxxx bks only as publ. in folio format, Paris, 1606–9. Brunet V:840. BL, BN. 609/124

Usselinx, Willem, supposed author. Onpartydich discours. [*Amsterdam? 1609?*]. *See the year 1608.*

Valdivia, Luis de. Copia de una carta del padre Luys de Valdivia para el señor conde de Lemos presidente de Indias, fecha en Lima á 4. de enero de 1607. en que da particular relacion de lo tocante á lo sucedido en la guerra, y pazes de la provincia de Chile. [*Madrid? 1609?*]. 6 numb. lvs; fol. Sabin 98327; Medina (Chile) 202; Palau 347839. BL, Santiago, Chile:BN. 609/125

——. Señor. El padre Luis de Valdivia . . . dize: que el Virrey de Pirù ha escrito á S.M. en esta flota de 1609 su paracer cerca de la guerra de Chile. [*Madrid? 1609?*]. 2 lvs; fol. Sabin 98332; Medina (Chile) 203; Streit II:1399; Backer VIII:380; Palau 347841. 609/126

Veer, Gerrit de. The true and perfect description of three voyages. *London: [W. White, for]* T. Pavier, 1609. 81 lvs.; 4to. Transl. by William Phillip from the author's *Waerachtighe beschryvinghe van drie seylagien,* 1st publ., Amsterdam, 1598; cf. 1605 edn. Sabin 98738; STC 24628; JCB (3) II:67–68. DLC (imp.), MWiW-C, MiU-C, MnU-B, NN-RB, RPJCB; BL, Rotterdam: Mar. Mus. 609/127

——. Vraye description de trois voyages de mer tres admirables. *Amsterdam: C. Claeszoon,* 1609. 44 numb. lvs; illus., maps; fol. 1st publ. in this version, Amsterdam, 1598; cf. 1604 edn. Muller (1872) 2085; Tiele-Muller 99; JCB (3) II:67. DLC, NN-RB, RPJCB, TxU; BL. 609/128

t'Vertoig der Zeeuscher nymphen. [*Middel-burg? 1609?*]. [15] p.; 4to. In verse. Includes ref. to murder of Indians (by Spaniards). Knuttel 1573. MnU-B, NN; BL (as [1607?]), The Hague:KB. 609/129

Virginia Company of London. For the plantation in Virginia or Nova Britannia. Whereas . . . for the better setling of the colony and plantation in Virginia. . . . *London: J. Windet,* 1609. bds.; fol. Sets forth terms whereby laborers may become colonists. Sabin 99856; Vail (Frontier) 21; STC 24831. BL. 609/130

Virginia richly valued, by the description of the maine land of Florida . . . out of the foure yeeres continual travell and discoverie . . . of Don Ferdinando de Soto . . . Written by a Portugall gentleman of Elvas . . . and translated . . . by Richard Hakluyt. *London: F. Kingston, for M. Lownes,* 1609. 180 p.; 4to. Transl. from the anon. *Relaçam verdadeira dos trabalhos que ho governador don Fernando d'Souto e certos fidalgos portugueses passarom,* Evora, 1557. Sabin 24896; Clayton-Torrence 3; Vail (Frontier) 13; STC 22938; Church 337; JCB (3) II:68. CSmH, CtY, DLC, ICN, MH, MiU-C, NN-RB, PPL, RPJCB; BL. 609/131

Wecker, Johann Jakob. Le grand dispensaire, ou Thresor general, et particulier des preservatifs . . . descouvert aux François et enrichi d'annotations . . . par Jean Du Val. *Geneva: E. Gamonet,* 1609–10. 2 pts; illus.; 4to. Transl. from Wecker's *Antidotarium,* 1st publ., Basel, 1574 & 1576; cf. 1601 edn. Wellcome I:6704. DNLM, WU-M; BL. 609/132

Wybarne, Joseph. The new age of old names. *London: [J. Windet,] for W. Barret & H. Fetherstone,* 1609. 133 p.; 4to. Includes mentions of Virginia, Montezuma 'a king in America', and the worship of devils there. STC 26055. CSmH, CtY, DFo, ICN, MH; BL. 609/133

Zapata y Sandoval, Juan, O.S.A. De justitia distributiva ac acceptione personarum ei apposita. Disceptio. Pro Novi Indiarum orbis rerum moderatoribus, summisque, & regalibus consiliariis, elaborata. *Valladolid: C. Laso Vaca,* 1609. 454 p.; 4to. Sabin 106252A; Medina (BHA) 555; Streit I:305; Alcocer (Valladolid) 551 (& 546). RPJCB; Granada:BU. 609/134

Zappullo, Michele. Sommario istorico . . . Ove con occasione di celebrare i successi di quattro gran città, cioè di Gerusalem, di Roma, di Napoli, e di Venetia, e dell'Indie. si viene atrattar dei regni del Giappone, dello Cina, dell'Egitto, e della Soria . . . terza impressione corretto, e migliorato. *Naples: G. G. Carlino & C. Vitale,* 1609. 587 p.; 4to. 1st publ., Vicenza, 1603, under title *Historie di quattro principali città del mondo*. The implied 2nd edn has not been traced. Sabin 106256; JCB (3) II:68. ICN, MH, NN-RB, RPJCB.   609/135

1610

Aguilar, Gaspar Honorato de. Expulsion de los Moros de España. *Valencia: P. P. Mey, for J. Ferrer,* 1610. 232 p.; 8vo. In verse. Includes refs to Potosí, Mexico, Indies, & 'untractable' Indians. Palau 3581. DLC, NNH; BL, Göttingen:UB.   610/1

Aldrovandi, Ulisse. Ornithologiae . . . libri xii[–xx]. *Frankfurt a. M.: W. Richter, for Heirs of N. Basse,* 1610–13. 3 v.; illus.; fol. 1st publ., Bologna, 1599–1603. Includes American birds, e.g. Brazilian magpie, cardinal, turkey. Nissen (Birds) 82; cf. Mengel (Ellis) 42; Dt. Ges. Kat. 3.498. DNAL (v. 1–2), NjP (v. 1–2), TxU (v. 1–2); BL (v. 1–2), BN, Munich:StB.   610/2

Arnauld, Antoine. Le franc et veritable discours au roy. [*Paris?*] 1610. 120 p.; 8vo. 1st publ., [Paris?], 1602. ICN; BN.   610/3

—[Anr edn]. [*Paris? after* 1610?]. 8vo. BN.   610/4

Barclay, John. Euphormio, seu Satyricon. *Paris:* 1610. 12mo. Includes pt 2, 1st publ., Paris, 1607. Shaaber B180. Oxford:Merton.   610/5

Barrough, Philip. The method of phisick . . . The fourth edition, corrected and amended. *London: R. Field,* 1610. 477 p.; 4to. 1st publ., London, 1583; cf. 1601 edn. STC 1512. DNLM, MiU, PPC; BL.   610/6

Baudart, Willem. Morghen-wecker der vrye Nederlantsche provintien, ofte Een cort verhael van de bloedighe vervolghinghen . . . door de Spaenjaerden. '*Danswick: C. Vermeulen de Jonge'* [i.e., *The Hague?*] 1610. [88] p.; 4to. Includes account of Indians rejecting Christian heaven if Spaniards are to be there; also cites Bodin on Indians. Signed 'G[uilielmus]. W. B[audartii]. F.V.D. T.p. has reading 'troublen'. Knuttel 1729; cf. Petit 897–98; Tiele (Pamfletten) 859 (cf. 860). [Edn uncertain: NN], WU; BL (D., G.W.B.F.V.), The Hague:KB.   610/7

—[Anr edn]. '*Danswick: C. Vermeulen de Jonge'* [i.e., *The Hague?*] 1610. 88 p.; 4to. T.p. has reading 'trublen' & 'op de leege zijde'. Knuttel 1730. The Hague:KB.   610/8

—[Anr edn]. '*Danswick: C. Vermeulen de Jonge'* [i.e., *The Hague?*] 1610. 88 p.; 4to. T.p. has reading 'op de leeghe zijde'. Knuttel 1731. The Hague:KB, Ghent:BU.   610/9

—[Anr edn]. *Amsterdam: J. E. Cloppenburg* [after 1610?]. 96 p.; 4to. Meulman 1210. Ghent: BU.   610/10

—[Anr edn]. De Spaensche tiranije. [n.p., n.d.]. *See the year* 1620.

Bauderon, Brice. Paraphrase sur la Pharmacopoee . . . Reveüe, corrigée et augmentée par l'auteur mesme. *Lyons: P. Rigaud,* 1610. 721 p.; 12mo. 1st publ., Lyons, 1588; cf. 1607 edn. London:Wellcome.   610/11

Bauhin, Kaspar. De compositione medicamentorum. *Offenbach: C. Neben, for Heirs of N. Basse* [*at Frankfurt a. M.*], 1610. 294 p.; 8vo. In chapt. 44 an 'oleum guaiacinum' is mentioned. DNLM; BL, BN.   610/12

Benzoni, Girolamo. De historie van de nieuwe weerelt, te weten, de beschrijvinghe van West-Indien . . . Wt het Italiaens overgheset . . . door Carel vander Mander Schilder. *Haarlem: H. P. van Wesbusch,* 1610. 404 p.; illus.; 8vo. Transl. from Benzoni's *Historia del Mondo Nuovo*, 1st publ., Venice, 1565. Sabin 4803; Tiele-Muller 276; Arents (Add.) 144-A; JCB (3) II:69. DLC, NN-RB, RPJCB; BL, Amsterdam:NHSM.   610/13

—[Anr issue]. De historie vande nieuwe weerelt. *Haarlem: H. P. van Wesbusch,* 1610. Sabin 4802; Streit II:1402.   610/14

Bertrand, ——. Lettre missive, touchant la conversion, et baptesme du grand sagamos de la nouvelle France, qui en estoit auparavant l'arrivée des François le chef & souverain . . . Envoyée du Port Royal . . . 28. juin 1610. *Paris: J. Regnoul,* 1610. [7] p.; 4to.

Sabin 40682 (& 5025); Harrisse (NF) 22. MH, NN-RB; BN.   610/15

Blaeu, Willem Janszoon. Het licht der zeevaert. *Amsterdam: W. J. Blaeu,* 1610. 1st publ., Amsterdam, 1608. Though no copy is known, that such an edn was publ. is inferred from the engraved Dutch t.p. with this date in a copy of the English edn of 1612, q.v. Koeman (M.Bl) 2.   610/16

Bodin, Jean. Methodus ad facilem historiarum cognitionem. *Geneva: J. Stoer,* 1610. 445 (i.e., 345) p.; 8vo. 1st publ., Paris, 1566; cf. 1607 edn. CU, DLC, PPL; BL, BN.
610/17

Boutrays, Raoul. De rebus in Gallia, & pené toto orbe gestis, commentariorum lib. xvi. *Paris: P. Chevalier,* 1610. 2 v.; 8vo. Covers years 1594–1609; under year 1595 is an account of Sir Francis Drake's Caribbean expedition of that year. ICU; BL, BN.
610/18

———. Historiopolitographia; sive, Opus historico-politicum duorum praeclarissimorum huius aetatis historicorum, Rodolphi Boteri . . . nec non Petri Matthaei . . . in quo res toto pene orbe hisce proximis annis gestae . . . illustrantur. *Frankfurt a. M.: M. Becker, for J. T. Schönwetter,* 1610. 4 pts; 4to. On Boutrays's work, see the preceding entry; on that of Matthieu, see his *Histoire de France . . . du regne de Henry IIII,* 1st publ., Paris, 1605, of which this is a translation. IaU; BL, BN.   610/19

Camerarius, Philipp. Les heures desrobees, ou Meditations historiques . . . Mis en françois par F[rançois]. d[e]. R[osset]. *Paris: J. Cottereau,* 1610. 687 p.; 8vo. Transl. from pt 3 of Camerarius's *Operae horarum subcisivarum,* 1st publ., Frankfurt a. M., 1609, to continue the two earlier vols. publ., Paris, 1608, under title *Les méditations historiques.* BL, BN.
610/20

———. Les meditations historiques . . . comprinses en trois volumes . . . tournez de Latin . . . par S[imon]. G[oulart]. . . . Nouvelle édition, reveuë . . . augmenté par l'auteur & enrichie d'un tiers par le translateur; outre la nouvelle & entiere version du troisiesme volume. *Lyons: Widow of A. de Harsy,* 1610. 3 v.; 4to. Pts 1 & 2 1st publ. in French, Lyons, 1603; pt 3 transl. from Camerarius's *Operae horarum subcisivarum*

. . . *Centuria tertia,* 1st publ., Frankfurt a. M., 1609. Jones (Goulart) 57c. ICN, MBtS; BL, BN.   610/21

Caro, Annibale. De le lettere familiari. *Venice: G. Alberti,* 1610. 2 pts; 4to. 1st publ., Venice, 1572; cf. 1603 edn. Michel (Répertoire) II:49. BL, Paris:Arsenal.   610/22

Casas, Bartolomé de las, O.P., Bp of Chiapa. Spieghel der Spaenscher tyrannye in West-Indien. *Amsterdam: Widow of C. Claeszoon,* 1610. 43 lvs; map; 4to. 1st publ. in Dutch, [Antwerp?] 1578, under title *Seer cort verhael vande destructie van d'Indien;* transl. from his *Brevissima relacion,* 1st publ., Seville, 1552. Sabin 11254; Medina (BHA) 1085 (II:476); Hanke/Giménez 503; Streit I:309; JCB (3) II:69. ICN, RPJCB.   610/23

Chiabrera, Gabriello. Rime . . . di nuovo in questa seconda impressione corrette et accresciute. *Venice: S. Combi,* 1610. 3 pts; 12mo. 1st publ., Venice, 1605. BN.
610/24

Colonna, Fabio. Minus cognitarum stirpium aliquot. *Rome: G. Facciotti,* 1610. 2 pts; illus., port.; 4to. 1st publ., Naples, 1606; here a reissue with new preliminary matter. Arents (Add.) 145. NN-A, PPAN.   610/25

Conestaggio, Girolamo Franchi di. Historia de la union del reyno de Portugal á la corona de Castilla . . . traduzida de lengua italiana . . . por . . . Luys de Bavia. *Barcelona: S. de Cormellas,* 1610. 227 numb. lvs; 4to. Transl. from the author's *Dell'unione del regno di Portogallo alla corona di Castiglia,* 1st publ., Genoa, 1585. Included are refs to Columbus & to Portuguese settlement of Brazil. Palau 313384. ICU, MH, NjP, PU; BN.   610/26

Cortés, Jerónimo. Phisonomia. *Barcelona: J. Margarit,* 1610. 120 numb. lvs; 8vo. 1st publ., Valencia, 1597; cf. 1601 edn. Palau 63304. NNH; BN.   610/27

Crashaw, William. A sermon preached in London, before the Right Honorable the Lord Lawarre, lord governour and captaine generall of Virginia . . . and the rest of the adventurers in that plantation. *London: W. Welby,* 1610 [91] p.; 4to. Sabin 17425; Vail (Frontier) 22; Clayton-Torrence 8; STC 6029; Church 345; JCB (3) II:67–70. CSmH, DLC, MHi, MiU-C, NN-RB, PPRF, RPJCB; BL.   610/28

Croll, Oswald. Basilica chymica . . . Additus est . . . Tractatus novus de signaturis rerum internis. *Geneva: Fabri Office,* 1610. 2 pts; illus.; 8vo. 1st publ., Frankfurt a. M., 1609. CtY-M, WU.   610/29

Dawson, Thomas. The good huswifes jewell. *London: E. A [llde]., for E. White,* 1610. 8vo. 1st publ., London, 1587. Includes mention of potato. STC 6393. CSmH.   610/30

Dessi, Juan. La divina semana, o Siete días de la creacion del mundo, en otava rima. *Barcelona: S. Matevad & L. Déu,* 1610. 248 numb. lvs; 8vo. Included are numerous refs, esp. in the 3rd day, to the New World, its discoverers, rivers, plants (incl. maize), etc. Cf. G. Salluste, seigneur Du Bartas's *La semaine,* on which this is modeled. Palau 71243; Salvá 562. NNH; BL (R. Southey copy).   610/31

Donne, John. Pseudo-martyr. Wherein out of certaine propositions . . . this conclusion is evicted. That those which are of the Romane religion in this kingdome, may and ought to take the oath of allegiance. *London: W. Stansby, for W. Burre,* 1610. 392 p.; 4to. Cites José de Acosta's *De natura Novi Orbis* (Salamanca, 1588) on missionary efforts there. Keynes (Donne) 1; STC 7048; Pforzheimer 298. CSmH, CtY, DFo, IU, MH, MiU-L, MnU, NNC, PU; BL.   610/32

Drayton, Michael. Poems . . . Newly corrected by the author. *London: [W. Stansby?] for J. Smethwick,* 1610. 3 pts; 8vo. 1st publ., London, 1605. STC 7220; Grolier Club (Langland to Wither) 89. CSmH, CtY, DFo, ICN, MH, NIC, PPRF; BL.   610/33

Du Bartas, Guillaume de Salluste, seigneur. Les oeuvres poétiques. *Rouen: P. Calles,* 1610. 2 v.; 12mo. In verse. Included are the author's *La sepmaine,* 1st publ., Paris, 1578, & his *La seconde sepmaine,* 1st publ., Paris, 1584; cf. 1601 edn. Holmes (DuBartas) I:77 no. 40 & I:90 no. 23abc; Tchémerzine X:197. Chantilly:Mus. Condé.   610/34

—[Anr issue]. *Rouen: A. Ouyn,* 1610. Holmes (DuBartas) I:77 no. 40n & I:90 no. 23abc. BN (imp.).   610/35

Du Jarric, Pierre, S.J. Seconde partie de l'Histoire des choses plus memorables ad-

venues tant ez Indes Orientales, que autres païs de la descouverte des Portugais, en l'etablissement & progrez de la foy chrestienne . . . et principalement de ce que les religieux de la Compagnie de Jesus y ont faict. *Bordeaux: S. Millanges,* 1610. 699 p.; 4to. Contains, p. 248–359, a substantial account of Jesuits in Brazil. The 1st part, publ. 1608, & a subsequent 3rd pt of 1614, are without American material. Sabin 35790; cf. Atkinson (Fr. Ren.) 501; Borba de Moraes I:358–59; Streit V:96; Backer IV:750–52. CU, ICN, MnU-B, NN-RB, RPJCB; BL, BN.   610/36

Ercilla y Zúñiga, Alonso de. Primera, segunda, y tercera parte de la Araucana. *Madrid: J. de la Cuesta, for M. Martínez,* 1610. 457 numb. lvs; 8vo. In verse. 1st publ. with all 3 pts, Madrid, 1590. On war with Araucanian Indians. Sabin 22724; Medina (Arau.) 18; Medina (Chile) 34. MB, MH, PU; BL, Madrid:BN.   610/37

Estienne, Charles. Dictionarium historicum, geographicum, poeticum. *Gex: B. L'Abbé,* 1610. 452 numb. lvs; 4to. 1st publ. in this enl. edn, Lyons, 1595; cf. 1601 edn. IU, TxU; BN.   610/38

Fernel, Jean. Universa medicina . . . Editio sexta. *Hanau: Heirs of C. Marne (J. & A. Marne & Co.),* 1610. 4 pts; port.; fol. 1st publ. as here constituted, Paris, 1567; cf. 1601–2 edn. Sherrington (Fernel) 77.J21. CLU-M, CtY-M, DNLM, PPC, WU-M; Cambridge:UL, BN.   610/39

Fioravanti, Leonardo. La cirugia . . . con una gionta de secreti nuovi. *Venice: L. Spineda,* 1610. 182 numb. lvs; 8vo. 1st publ., Venice, 1570. In bk 1, chapt. xxiv, on syphilis, recommends use of guaiacum & sarsaparilla; chapt. lxi discusses guaiacum at length. Michel (Répertoire) III:47. Paris: Mazarine.   610/40

Folkingham, William. Feudigraphia. The synopsis or epitome of surveying methodized . . . no less remarkable for all undertakers in the plantation of Ireland or Virginia. *London: R. More,* 1610. 88 p.; 4to. Sabin 24951; STC 11123. CSmH, DLC, NN-RB, RPJCB, WU; BL.   610/41

Gabelkover, Oswald. Artzneybuch. *Frankfurt a.M.: J. J. Porsch & J. Berner,* 1610. 2 pts; 4to. 1st publ., Tübingen, 1589, under title *Nützlich Artzneybuch;* cf. 1603 edn. DNLM, PPHa. 610/42

Gardiner, Edmund. The triall of tabacco. *London: H. L[ownes]., for M. Lownes,* 1610. 58 numb. lvs; 4to. Sabin 26614; STC 11564; Arents 96. CSmH, DNLM, MH, MiU, NN-RB; BL. 610/43

Garzoni, Tommaso. La piazza universale di tutte le professioni del mondo, nuovamente ristampata, & posta in luce. *Venice: T. Baglioni,* 1610. 403 numb. lvs; 4to. 1st publ., Venice, 1585; cf. 1601 edn. Michel (Répertoire) IV:25. NCorniG; BN. 610/44

Gerhard, Johann. Locorum theologicorum . . . tomus primus [–nonus]. *Jena:* 1610–22. 9 v.; 4to. For volumes containing Americana, see the years 1617 & 1619.

Gesner, Konrad. Mithridates Gesneri, exprimens differentias linguarum . . . per totum terrarum orbe . . . Editio altera. *Zurich: Wolf Press,* 1610. 140 numb. lvs; 8vo. 1st publ., Zurich, 1555, but here including commentary by Caspar Waser, with minor American refs. Gesner's text includes section on languages of New World, discussing those of Cuba & Hispaniola, & citing P. M. d'Anghiera as source. ICN, MnU, MdBP, NNC, PU; BL, BN. 610/45

Goulart, Simon. Thresor d'histoires admirables et memorables. *[Geneva:] P. Marceau,* 1610. 2 v.; 12mo. 1st publ., Paris, 1600, under title *Histoires admirables . . . de nostre temps.* Jones (Goulart) 54g. CSmH, CtY, DLC, ICN, MB, MiDW, NNC, PPL; Paris: Bibl. du Prot. Franç. 610/46

Gracián, Jerónimo. Zelo della propagazione della fede . . . Tradotto di lingua spagnuola. *Rome: S. Paolini,* 1610. 43 p.; 4to. Transl. from the author's *Stimulo dela propagacion dela fee,* 1st publ., Lisbon, 1586. Includes refs to evangelization of Indians in Mexico. Streit I:308. Rome:BN. 610/47

Great Britain. Council for Virginia. By the Counsell of Virginia. Whereas the good shippe, called the Hercules, is now preparing. . . . *[London: T. Haveland,* 1610]. bds.; obl. 4to. An appeal for laborers to emigrate. Sabin 99857; Clayton-Torrence 11; Vail (Frontier) 25; STC 24831.3. London:Soc. Ant. 610/48

—. A publication by the Counsell of Vir-

ginea, touching the plantation there. *London: T. Haveland, for W. Welby,* 1610. bds.; fol. A further appeal for laborers. Sabin 99858; Clayton-Torrence 12; Vail (Frontier) 26; STC 24831.7. London:Soc. Ant. 610/49

Grotius, Hugo. Liber de antiquitate reipublicae Batavicae. *Leyden: Plantin Office (Raphelengius),* 1610. lx p.; 4to. Includes ref. to Spanish garrisons in West Indies. Meulen/Diermanse 691; Bibl. Belg. G341. CtY, ICN, MH, NNC, WU; BL, BN. 610/50

—[Anr issue]. *[Leyden:] Plantin Office (Raphelengius),* 1610. Probably designed for distribution by the Plantin Office at Antwerp. Meulen/Diermanse 692. BL. 610/51

——. Tractaet vande oudtheyt vande Batavische nu Hollandsche republique; beschreven int Latijn . . . nae . . . overgestelt, ende by den autheur oversien. *The Hague: H. Jacobszoon van Wouw,* 1610. 52 p.; 4to. Transl. from Grotius's *Liber de antiquitate,* 1st publ., Leyden, 1610. Meulen/Diermanse 698; Bibl. Belg. G342. ICN, MdBP; BN, The Hague:PP. 610/52

Guarinoni, Cristoforo. Consilia medicinalia. *Venice: T. Baglioni,* 1610. 738 p.; fol. Numerous 'consilia' discuss syphilis, specifying guaiacum, sarsaparilla, or tobacco for its treatment. Wellcome I:2964. DNLM, NNNAM, PPC; BL, BN. 610/53

Guicciardini, Francesco. La historia d'Italia . . . divisa in venti libri. *Venice: N. Polo & F. Rampazetto,* 1610. 2 pts; 4to. 1st publ., Florence, 1561; cf. 1604 edn. Michel (Répertoire) IV:101. CtY; BN. 610/54

Guyon, Louis, Sieur de la Nauche. Les diverses leçons . . . Seconde edition. *Lyons: C. Morillon,* 1610. 913 p.; 8vo. 1st publ., Lyons, 1604. DNLM, MH, MnU-B; BN. 610/55

Heath, John. Two centuries of epigrammes. *London: J. Windet,* 1610. 46 lvs; 8vo. Includes verse epigram on tobacco. STC 13018; Arents 97. CSmH, MH, NN-A; BL. 610/56

Hobbes, Stephen. Margarita chyrurgica: containing a compendious practise of chyrurgerie. *London: T. C[reede]., for R. Bonion & H. Walley,* 1610. 2 pts; 12mo. The 4th bk, on the cure of syphilis, prescribes remedies using guaiacum & sassafras. STC

13538; Wellcome I:3254. BL, London: Wellcome.   610/57

Hollings, Edmund. Medicamentorum oeconomia nova. *Ingolstadt: Eder Press, for A. Angermaier,* 1610. 303 p.; 8vo. Chapts 7, 10, & 15 mention guaiacum, chapt. 10, sarsaparilla & sassafras. Shaaber (Brit. auth.) H241; Wellcome I:3286. BL, London:Wellcome.   610/58

Horst, Gregor. Centuria problematum medicorum. *Wittenberg: J. Schmidt, for C. Berger,* 1610. 404 p.; 8vo. In 2nd decade, quaestio x discusses guaiacum & its limitations; in 3rd decade, quaestio vii describes therapeutic uses of tobacco; in decade x, quaestio iii attributes source of syphilis to West Indies. Ferguson (Bibl. chem.) I:417–18; Arents (Add.) 147; Wellcome I:3309. DNLM, NN-A; London:Wellcome, BN.   610/59

Jesuits. Verzeichnuss alle Provintzen, Collegien und Heusser in welchen die Societet Jesu durch die Christenheit ihre Wohnung ha. *Cologne: J. Christoffel,* 1610. bds; fol. Includes lists for 5 American provinces. Streit I:314. Göttingen:UB.   610/60

Jourdain, Silvester. A discovery of the Barmudas, otherwise called the Ile of Divels. *London: J. Windet, sold by R. Barnes,* 1610. 24 p.; 4to. Sabin 100460; Clayton-Torrence 9; Vail (Frontier) 23; STC 14816. CSmH, DFo; BL.   610/61

Keckermann, Bartholomaeus. De natura et proprietatibus historiae, commentarius. *Hanau: W. Antonius,* 1610. 225 p.; 8vo. In chapt. iii, writings on the Americas are discussed. BL, BN.   610/62

La Faye, Antoine de. Emblemata et epigrammata miscellanea selecta. *Geneva: P. & J. Chouët,* 1610. 299 p.; 8vo. In verse. Includes (p. 121) poem 'Novi orbis repertores celebrati' mentioning Columbus, Vespucci, & Magellan. Wellcome I:3629. NcD; BL, BN.   610/63

Langenes, Barent. Trésor de chartes, contenant les tableaux de tous les pays du monde . . . reveu & augmente. [*Frankfurt a. M.:*] *M. Becker, for H. Laurenszoon, at Amsterdam* [ca. 1610?]. 2 pts; illus., maps; obl. 8vo. 1st publ., The Hague, [1600?]; transl. by Jean de La Haye from Langenes's *Caertthresor*, 1st publ., Middelburg, [1598]; cf. year 1602. Sabin 95757n; Koeman (Lan)

9; Phillips (Atlases) 428; Atkinson (Fr. Ren.) 435. DLC, MH, MiU-C; Paris:Arsenal.
                                              610/64

Lescarbot, Marc. La conversion des sauvages qui ont este baptizés en la Nouvelle France, cette annee 1610. Avec un bref recit, du voyage du sieur de Poutrincourt. *Paris: J. Millot* [1610]. 46 p.; 8vo. Sabin 16212; Streit II:2458; JCB (3) II:70. RPJCB; BN.   610/65

—[Anr edn]. *Paris: J. Millot* [1610]. 44 p.; 8vo. Sabin 40167; Harrisse (NF) 21. NN-RB.
                                              610/66

——. Les muses de la Nouvelle France. *Paris: J. Millot,* 1610. 66 p.; 8vo. 1st publ., Paris, 1609; here anr issue with altered imprint date. Cf. Sabin 40174, etc. MWiW-C.
                                              610/67

Linschoten, Jan Huygen van. Histoire de la navigation de Jean Hugues de Linscot hollandois et de son voyage es Indes Orientales . . . Avec annotations de Bernard Paludanus . . . Le tout recueilli et descript par le meme Linscot en bas alleman, & nouvellement traduict en françois. *Amsterdam: H. Laurenszoon,* 1610. 275 p.; illus., maps; fol. Transl. from the author's *Itinerario, voyagie ofte schipvaert,* 1st publ., Amsterdam, 1596. Shoals off Brazil are mentioned as a navigational hazard. Sabin 41368; Borba de Moraes I:419; Tiele 685; JCB (3) II:70. RPJCB; BL, BN.   610/68

—[Anr issue]. *Amsterdam: T. Pierre* [i.e., *D. P. Pers?*] 1610. Sabin 41369; Tiele-Muller 95(f); JCB (3) II:71. DLC, RPJCB; BL, BN.
                                              610/69

Maiolo, Simeone, Bp of Volturara. Dies caniculares, hoc est Colloquia tria et viginti . . . Editio nova. *Mainz: J. T. Schönwetter,* 1610. 558 p.; 4to. 1st publ., Rome, 1597; cf. 1607 edn. Cf. Sabin 44056. DNLM, MnCS; London:Wellcome, BN.   610/70

Marquardus, Joannes. Practica medicinalis . . . Huic in fine accesserunt Sebastiani Cortilionis . . . libri quinque Institutionum chirurgicarum. *Frankfurt a. M.: N. Hoffmann, for P. Musculus & R. Pistorius,* 1610. 705 p.; 8vo. 1st publ., Speyer, 1589. In Cortilio's 'De chirurgica lib. v', bk 3, on syphilis, includes chapts on guaiacum & sarsaparilla. DNLM; BL.   610/71

Mercado, Luis. Praxis medica . . . in

quatuor partes divisa. *Venice: B. Giunta,* 1610. 624 p.; fol. 1st publ. as here constituted as the *Tomus secundus* of Mercado's *Operum,* Valladolid, 1605, q.v.; cf. also the Venice, 1608, edn with above title. CtY-M.
610/72

Mercator, Gerardus. Atlas minor. *Dordrecht: A. Bot, for J. Hondius & C. Claeszoon, at Amsterdam, & J. Janszoon, at Arnhem,* 1610. 684 p.; maps; obl. 12mo. 1st publ., Amsterdam, 1607; here added is a map of Tierra del Fuego. Sabin 47887; Koeman (Me) 189A; Phillips (Atlases) 429. CtY, DLC, ICN, MB, NN-RB, PPL; BL, BN.
610/73

—[Anr edn]. *Dordrecht: A. Bot, for J. Hondius & C. Claeszoon, at Amsterdam, & J. Janszoon, at Arnhem,* 1610. 684 p.; maps; obl. 12mo. Differs from above in that p. 683–84 alone are numbered. Koeman (Me) 189B. Utrecht:UB.
610/74

Meteren, Emanuel van. Belli civilis in Belgio per quadraginta ferè continuos annos gesti historia, ad praesens usque tempus deducta . . . Opus novem è Belgicis . . . Meterani & aliorum commentariis concinnatum a Gaspare Ens. [*Arnhem? J. Janszoon?*] 1610. 502 p.; fol. Transl. from van Meteren's Dutch text, 1st publ., Delft, 1599. For an earlier Latin edn, see the year 1598. Palau 166957 (& 166950n). ICN; BL, BN.
610/75

——. Commentarien ofte Memoiren van den Nederlandtschen staet, handel, oorloghen ende gheschiedenissen van onsen tyden. *'Schotland, outside Danswijck'* [i.e., *The Hague?*]: *H. van Loven, for E. van Meteren, at London,* 1610. 4 pts; ports, map; fol. 1st publ. in Dutch, Delft, 1599; cf. years 1605 & 1609. Earliest edn to discuss Henry Hudson's discoveries (lf 629). Stokes (Manhattan) VI:256; STC 17845.7; Palau 166948. DLC (pt 2), ICN, NN-RB; BL, BN.
610/76

——. Historia oder Eigentliche vii [i.e., und] warhaffte Beschreibung aller fürnehmen Kriegshändel . . . so sich in Niderlandt . . . zugetragen haben . . . in 28. Bücher abgetheilt. *Frankfurt a. M.: N. Roht,* 1610. 3 pts; ports, map; fol. 1st publ. in German, Hamburg, 1596; cf. year 1601. NN-RB, BL.
610/77

Mexía, Pedro. Les diverses leçons . . . mises de castillan en françois, par Cl. Gruget . . . avec sept dialogues . . . Plus la suite de celles d'Antoine Du Verdier. *Tournon: C. Michel,* 1610. 2 pts; 8vo. 1st publ. in this version with American refs in Du Verdier's continuation, Lyons, 1577; cf. 1604 edn. Sabin 48245. DFo; BN.
610/78

Noort, Olivier van. Description du penible voyage fait entour de l'univers ou globe terrestre. *Amsterdam: Widow of C. Claeszoon,* 1610. 61 p.; illus., maps; fol. 1st publ. in French, Amsterdam, 1602. Sabin 55438; Borba de Moraes II:103; Tiele 806; JCB (3) II:71. CtY, DLC, InU-L, MH, NN-RB, RPJCB, TxU: BL.
610/79

Orlers, Jan Janszn. Beschrijvinghe ende afbeeldinge van alle de victorien . . . die Godt almachtich de . . . heeren Staten der Vereenichde Neder-landen verleent heeft, deur het . . . beleyt des . . . fursts Maurits van Nassau. *Leyden: J. J. Orlers & H. van Haestens,* 1610. 220 p.; illus., port., maps; fol. Includes scattered refs to European exploration of the Americas in context of Dutch history. Written jointly with Hendrick van Haestens. Sometimes referred to by its half title, 'Den Nassauschen lauren-crans'. For an expanded version covering later Dutch exploration, see the year 1651. Brunet IV:233, Molhuysen I:1392; Van der Aa V:60. CtY, NN-RB; Amsterdam:NHSM.
610/80

Ortelius, Abraham. Theatrum orbis terrarum . . . Tonneel des aert-bodems. *Antwerp:* [*J. B. Vrients, for the*] *Widow of C. Plantin & J. Mourentorff* [1610?]. 91 maps; fol. Partially reset from Antwerp, 1598, edn; 1st publ. in Dutch, Antwerp, 1571. Cf. Sabin 57705; Koeman (Ort) 40; Phillips (Atlases) 407. DLC, ICN; BL, Brussels:Plantin Mus.
610/81

Pasquier, Etienne. Les recherches de la France. *Paris: L. Sonnius,* 1610. 994 p.; port.; 4to. 1st publ. with American content, Paris, 1596; cf. 1607 edn. Thickett (Pasquier) 13n. ICN; Erlangen:UB.
610/82

Pérez de Lara, Alfonso. Compendio de las tres gracias de la Santa Cruzada . . . que su Santidad concede a la . . . Magestad del Rey Don Felipe III . . . para gastos de la guerra contra infideles. *Madrid: Imprenta Real,* 1610. 2 pts; fol. Included are numerous refs to Spanish America, e.g., pt 1, p. 148–205, 'Forma de los despachos que de su Magestad . . . se embian a las provincias de Nueva España, y sus partidos'; pt 1, p. 241–88, 'Instruccion para las Indias'; & pt 2, p. 97–102, 'Cedula . . . por la qual manda, que todo el dinero, oro, o plata . . . que viniero de . . . las Indias, se ponga en una arca a parte'. Medina (BHA) 561; Pérez Pastor (Madrid) 1110; Palau 221236. ICN, InU-L, MH, NNH, RPJCB; BL. 610/83

Perlinus, Hieronymus. De alexiteriis et alexipharmicis commentariolus. *Rome:* 1610. 4to. Mentioned is the bezoar stone as found in the West Indies as well as Asia. For subsequent appearance, see the author's *Binae historiae* of 1613. BL (imp.). 610/84

Pilletier, Casparus. Plantarum tum patriarum, tum exoticarum, in Walachria . . . nascentium synonymia. *Middelburg: R. Schilders,* 1610. 398 p.; 8vo. Includes discussion of tobacco & other American plants. Pritzel 7027; Arents (Add.) 148. DNAL, MH-A, MoSB, NN-A; BL, BN. 610/85

Possevino, Antonio, S. J. Cultura ingeniorum . . . Septima editio recognita & nunc primum in Germania separatim emissa . . . Accessit . . . Vera narratio fruticis, florum et fructuum novissime in Occidentalibus Indiis nascentur Eugenii Petrelli. *Cologne: J. Gymnicus,* 1610. 207 p.; 8vo. Petrelli's 'Vera narratio', here 1st publ., includes description of passionflower & symbolism of its blossom. Sabin 64450 (& 58989); Pritzel 7090; Backer VI:1078. ICN, MiU-C, NNBG; BL, BN. 610/86

Queiros, Pedro Fernandes de. Señor . . . con este son ocho los memoriales que a V.M. ha presentado, en razon de la poblacion que se deue hazer en las tierras que V.M. mandò que descubriesse en la parte austral incognita. [*Madrid:* 1610?]. 2 numb. lvs; fol. Seeks permission to establish colony in South Pacific, in part to provide market for products of Spanish America. Sabin 67353; Medina (BHA) 6456; Kelly (Calendar of Docs) 573; Pérez Pastor (Madrid) 1093. BL, Sydney:State Library. 610/87

—[Anr edn]. Relacion de un memorial que ha presentado a su Magestad . . . sobre la poblacion y descubrimiento de la quarta parte del mundo, australia incognita. *Pamplona: C. de Labayen,* 1610. 4 lvs; 4to. Sabin 67353n; Medina (BHA) 558; Palau 89604. Sydney:State Library. 610/88

—[Anr edn]. Relacion de un memorial que presento à su Magestad. *Seville: L. Estupiñán,* 1610. Sabin 67353n; Kelly (Calendar of Docs) 574 (and variant issues 574–78). 610/89

—[Anr issue]. Memorial que presento a su Magestad. *Seville: L. Estupiñán,* 1610. Kelly (Calendar of Docs) 574. 610/90

Rich, Richard. Newes from Virginia. The lost flocke triumphant. With the happy arrival of . . . Sr. Thomas Gates: and . . . Captaine Mr. Christopher Newporte, and others, into England. With the maner of their distresse in the Iland of Devils (otherwise called Bermoothawes). *London: E. Allde, to be sold by J. Wright,* 1610. [14] p.; illus.; 4to. In verse. Sabin 70889; Clayton-Torrence 10; Vail (Frontier) 24; STC 21005; Church 346. CSmH, DFo, NjP; BL. 610/91

Rivadeneira, Pedro de, S. J. Traité de la religion que doit suivre le prince chrestien . . . contre la doctrine de Nicolas Machiavel . . . traduit par le p. Antoine de Balinghem. *Douai: J. Bogard,* 1610. 519 p.; 8vo. Transl. from author's *Tratado de la religion,* 1st publ., Madrid, 1595; cf. year 1601. Backer VI: 1735; Palau 266347. BN. 610/92

——. La vie du bienheureux pere Ignace de Loyola . . . Traduite . . . par . . . Henry de Sponde. *Tournai: N. Laurent,* 1610. 276 p.; 16mo. 1st publ. as here transl., Paris (?) 1608. Backer VI:1729; Palau 266252. 610/93

Rowlands, Samuel Humors ordinarie. *London: [E. Allde,] for T. Archer,* 1610. 4to. In verse. 1st publ., London, 1600, under title *The letting of humors blood;* cf. year 1605. STC 21395.5. Stourhead. 610/94

Sacro Bosco, Joannes de. Sphaera . . . emendata . . . Eliae Vineti . . . scholia . . . Clavii breves commentarii. *Cologne: G. Cholinus,* 1610. 262 p.; illus.; 8vo. 1st publ. with Vinet's *Scholia,* Paris, 1551; Clavius's *Commentarius* 1st publ., Rome, 1570. Cf. Cholinus's 1601 edn above. NN-RB; BN. 610/95

Sandoval, Francisco de. Advertencia en fabor y defensa del arbitrio de Luys de Arratia y Guebara, y Christoval de Dueñas, sobre la remision del quinto de la plata. [*Madrid?* ca. 1610?]. 7 numb. lvs; fol. Memorial in part in behalf of 'las Indias, y particularmente el Piru, Cerro de Potosi, y demas assientos de minas'. Medina (BHA) 6873. BL, Seville:Archivo de Indias.   610/96

——. Señor. Por aver entendido quan del servicio de V. Mag. es la execucion deste arbitrio de la moneda. [*Madrid?* 1610?]. [3] p.; fol. Memorial to king of Spain on currency; included are refs to Peru & Potosí. BL.   610/97

——. Señor. Si conviniere al servicio de V.M. para algunos effectos juntar . . . cantidad de plata . . . el modo mas facil . . . es el siguiente. [*Madrid?* 1610?]. [4] p.; fol. Memorial to king of Spain, with refs to Mexico & Peru. BL.   610/98

Scholtz, Lorenz, ed. Consiliorum medicinalium. *Hanau: Heirs of A. Wechel, for Heirs of J. Aubry,* 1610. 1164 cols; fol. 1st publ., Frankfurt a. M., 1598. Ref. is made to mechoacan & sarsaparilla. Wellcome I:5851. DNLM, NcD-MC; London:Wellcome, BN.   610/99

——, **ed.** Epistolarum philosophicarum, medicinalium ac chymicarum . . . volumen. *Hanau: Heirs of A. Wechel, for Heirs of J. Aubry,* 1610. 536 cols; fol. 1st publ., Frankfurt a. M., 1598. Mentioned are mechoacan & sassafras, while Puerto Rico is named as source of guaiacum, distinguishing it as having two forms, guaiacum proper as a tree, 'lignum sanctum' as a shrub. Wellcome I:5852. DNLM, NcD-MC; London:Wellcome.   610/100

Sharpham, Edward. The fleire. *London: [T. Purfoot,] for N. Butter,* 1610. [60] p.; 4to. Drama. 1st publ., London, 1607. STC 22385; Greg 255(b). CSmH, DFo, ICU, MB; BL.   610/101

Sonnet, Thomas, sieur de Courval. Satyre contre les charlatans, et pseudomedecins empyriques. *Paris: J. Millot,* 1610. 335 p.; illus., port.; 8vo. Mentions charlatans who have been cured of syphilis by a 'decoction de Chine ou de Gaiag'. Wellcome I:6019. DLC, MH, NNNAM, WU; BL, BN.   610/102

Spain. Consejo de las Indias. El fiscal con doña Francisca Colon de Toledo, y don Francisco Pancheco de Cordova, y demas consortes. [*Madrid?* ca. 1610?]. 6 lvs; fol. NN-RB.   610/103

——. Memorial del pleyto que tratan en el Consejo real delas Indias, doña Francisca Colon de Toledo . . . sobre los frutos del estado de Veragua, y particularmente sobre el situado que tiene en la caxa de Panamà. [*Madrid?* ca. 1610?]. 24 numb. lvs; fol. NN-RB.   610/104

——. [Traslado del despacho del servicio personal de los Indios del Pirù y Nueva España. *Madrid: A. Martín,* 1610?]. Publication inferred from invoice submitted by Martín for payment. Sabin 96476; Medina (BHA) 8468; Pérez Pastor (Madrid) 1117.
     610/105

Spain. Laws, statutes, etc., 1598–1621 (Philip III). Este es un traslado bien y fielmente sacado . . . de una cedula del Rey . . . Para que no se tomen ningun dineros que vinieren de las Indias, de difuntos. [*Madrid:* 1610?]. bds.; fol. Dated 22 Nov. 1610. BL.   610/106

Suárez de Salazar, Juan Bautista. Grandezas y antiguedades de la isla y ciudad de Cadiz. *Cadiz: C. Hidalgo,* 1610. 317 p.; illus.; 4to. Included are numerous refs to Spanish America. Palau 324112; Maggs Cat. 479 (Americana V):4118. BL, BN.   610/107

Torquemada, Antonio de. Hexameron, ou, Six journees, contenans plusieurs doctes discours . . . mis en françois par Gabriel Chappuys. *Rouen: R. de Beauvais,* 1610. 561 p.; 12mo. 1st publ. in Spanish as the *Jardin de flores curiosas,* Salamanca, 1570; as here transl., Lyons, 1579. Included are numerous scattered refs to Spanish America. Palau 334920. MiU, PU, WU; BN.
     610/108

Uffenbach, Peter, comp. Thesaurus chirurgiae. *Frankfurt a. M.: N. Hoffmann, for J. Fischer,* 1610. 1164 p.; illus., ports; fol. Included are Ambroise Paré's *Opera* 1st publ. separately in Latin translation by Jacques Guillemeau, Paris, 1582; here reprinted from separate Frankfurt, 1594, text. Cf. the 1601 German edn. Doe (Paré) 49; Wellcome I:6389. DNLM, ICJ, MiU, MnU, PPC; BL, Paris:Mazarine.   610/109

Ulloa, Alfonso de. Historie ende het leven

van den . . . Keyser Caerle de vijfde . . .
oock de merckelijckste saken die over alle
de werelt, insonderheyt inde Oost ende
West-Indien geschiet zijn. *Dordrecht: I. J.
Canin,* 1510 [i.e., 1610]. 221 numb. lvs; fol.
1st publ. in Dutch, Antwerp, 1570; transl.
from Ulloa's *Vita dell'invittissimo Imperator
Carlo V.,* 1st publ., Venice, 1560. Sabin
97678; Muller (1872) 1540. RPJCB.
610/110

—[Anr issue?]. [*Dordrecht? I. J. Canin? for?] J.
P. Paets, at Amsterdam,* 1610. fol. Sabin
97678n.   610/111

—[Anr edn]. *Delft: A. Gerritszoon van Beyeren,*
1610. 457 p.; fol. Amsterdam:NHSM.
610/112

Valdivia, Luis de, S. J. Señor. El padre Luis
de Valdivia . . . digo, que siendo V.M. informado, de la importancia grande de cor-
tar la guerra de Chile . . . Cometio este
negocio el año passado de 608. [*Madrid?*
1610?] 24 numb. lvs; fol. Sabin 98331;
Medina (Chile) 204; Streit II:1400; Backer
VIII:380; Palau 347840. BL, Madrid:Acad.
de la Hist.   610/113

Veer, Gerrit de. Le trois navigations admirables . . . faictes trois ans continuels par les
Hollandois & Zelandois. *Paris: N. Buon,*
1610. 366 p.; 8vo. 1st publ. in this pirated
version, Paris, 1599, the sheets of that edn
being here reissued as p. 15–366; cf. de
Veer's *Vraye description,* Amsterdam, 1604.
Cf. Tiele-Muller 96. MH, NN-RB.
610/114

Victoria, Pedro Gobeo de, S. J. Naufragio
y peregrinacio de Pedro Gobeo de Vitoria
. . . escrito por él mismo. *Seville: C. Hidalgo,*
1610. 160 numb. lvs; 8vo. An account of
author's experiences in New World in
search of fortune & later as Jesuit in Peru.
Sabin 99445; Medina (BHA) 559; Backer
I:1515; Escudero (Seville) 930; Palau
102963.   610/115

Villagrá, Gaspar Pérez de. Historia de la
Nueva Mexico. *Alcalá de Henares: L. Martínez
Grande, for B. López,* 1610. 287 numb. lvs;
port.; 8vo. An epic poem. Sabin 99641;
Medina (BHA) 366; Wagner (SW) 14; Palau
366656; JCB (3) II:72; JCB AR40:15–16.
CSmH, CtY, DLC, ICN, InU-L, MH,
MiU-C, NN-RB, RPJCB; BL, BN. 610/116

Virginia Company of London. A true and

sincere declaration of the purpose and ends
of the plantation begun in Virginia. *London:
[G. Eld,] for J. Stepney* [i.e., *Stepneth*], 1610.
26 p.; 4to. Sabin 99859; Clayton-Torrence
13; Vail (Frontier) 27; STC 24832a. CSmH,
MH, PP, RPJCB; Durham:UL (Cosin).
610/117

—[Anr state]. *London: [G. Eld,] for J. Stepneth,*
1610. Sabin 99859; Vail (Frontier) 27n;
STC 24832. DLC, NjP, PPRF; BL.
610/118

——. A true declaration of the estate of the
colonie in Virginia, with a confutation of
such scandalous reports as have tended to
the disgrace of so worth an enterprise. *London: [Eliot's Court Press & W. Stansby] for W.
Barrett,* 1610. 68 p.; 4to. Sabin 99860; Clayton-Torrence 13A; Vail (Frontier) 28; STC
24833; Church 348; JCB (3) II:73. CSmH,
CtY, DLC, MH, MiU-C, NN-RB; PPL,
RPJCB; BL.   610/119

Wecker, Johann Jakob. Le grand thresor,
ou Dispensaire et antidotaire special ou
particulier . . . fait françois . . . par Jan
Du Val. *Geneva: E. Gamonet,* 1610. 2 pts;
illus.; 4to. Transl. from Wecker's *Antidotarium,* 1st publ., Basel, 1574 & 1576; cf. 1601
edn. Here a reissue of Gamonet's 1609–10
edn with cancel t.p. DNLM; BN.
610/120

Wright, Edward. Certaine errors in navigation . . . With many additions . . . not in
the former edition. *London: F. Kingston,*
1610. 2 pts; illus.; 4to. 1st publ., London,
1599. Included are numerous refs to the
Americas. Sabin 105573; STC 26020. CtY,
DLC, NN-RB; BL.   610/121

Zurita y Castro, Gerónimo. Anales de la corona de Aragon. *Saragossa: L. de Robles, in
College of St. Vincent Ferrer, for J. de Lanaja y
Quartanet,* 1610. 6 v.; fol. 1st publ., Saragossa, 1562–80. Vol. 5 (itself 1st publ.
1580), with its special t.p. with title *Historia
del Rey Don Hernando el Catholico,* includes
in bk 1, as chapt. xiii, 'Del descubrimiento
de las islas del Ocean Ocidental que lla-
maron Indias', describing Columbus's merits; and, in chapt. xxv, a discussion of the
demarcation line of Pope Alexander VI. Imprints of individual vols vary. Palau 381762.
CtY, DFo, ICU, MH, MiU, NNH, PU; BL.
610/122

1611

Alpini, Prosper. De medicina methodica libri tredecim. *Padua: L. Pasquato, for F. Bolzetta*, 1611. 424 p.; fol. In bk 3, chapt. 9, 'Mechoacan radix proximis annis ex orientalibus [*sic*] Indiis ad nos perlata' is discussed. DNLM, NcD-MC, PPL; BL, BN.
611/1

Bembo, Pietro, Cardinal. Venetae historiae . . . libri xii. *Strassburg: L. Zetzner*, 1611. 623 p.; 8vo. 1st publ., Venice, 1551. In bk vi is an account of Portuguese & Spanish explorations, cited as a cause of Venice's economic decline. Sabin 4619n. IU, RPB; BN.
611/2

Beringer, Joachim. Hispanicae Inquisitionis et carnificinae secretiora . . . Per Joachimum Ursinum [pseud.]. *Amberg: J. Schönfeld*, 1611. 334 p.; 8vo. Preface includes refs to Spanish cruelties toward Indians, noting the extinction of millions. Text compiled largely from the works of Gonsalvius, including account of Joannes Legionensis (Juan de León), formerly of Mexico, which 1st appeared in Gonsalvius's Heidelberg, 1567, *Sanctae Inquisitionis Hispanicae.* ICN, MH; BL (Ursinus), BN.
611/3

——. Der tyrannischen hispanischen Inquisition Heimligkeiten . . . offenbaret. *Amberg:* 1611. *See the year* 1612.

Boemus, Johann. The manners, lawes and customs of all nations . . . The like also out of the Historie of America or Brasill, written by John Lerius . . . Written in Latine, and now newly translated . . . By Ed. Aston. *London: G. Eld*, 1611. 589 p.; 4to. Léry's 'Historie' transl. from his *Historia navigationis in Brasiliam*, 1st publ. in Latin, Geneva, 1586. Sabin 6120; Borba de Moraes I:95–96; STC 3198; JCB (3) II:73. CSmH, DLC, ICN, MH, MnU-B, NN-RB, RPJCB; BL.
611/4

Bonardo, Giovanni Maria, conte. La minera del mondo . . . Mandata in luce . . . da Luigi Grotto. *Venice: A. Turino*, 1611. 112 numb. lvs; 8vo. 1st publ., Venice, 1585. Included are descriptions of American plants & trees & their uses. Michel (Répertoire) I:184; JCB (3) II:74. PU, RPJCB; Paris:Ste Geneviève.
611/5

Botero, Giovanni. Allgemeine historische Weltbeschreibung . . . in vier Bücher abgetheilt . . . Durch Aegidium Albertinum . . . auss dem Italienischen . . . ubersetzt. *Munich: N. Heinrich, for A. Hierat, at Cologne*, 1611. 471 p.; maps; fol. Bks 1–2 1st publ. in German, Cologne, 1596; here supplemented by bks 3–4; transl. from Botero's *Relationi universali*, 1st publ., Rome, 1591–96. Sabin 6808; Baginsky (German Americana) 125; Borba de Moraes I:100; Streit I:315; JCB (3) II:74. NN-RB, RPJCB; Fulda:LB.
611/6

——. Relations of the most famous kingdomes. *London: J. Jaggard*, 1611. 437 p.; 4to. 1st publ. in English, London, 1601, under title *The travellers breviat* & *The worlde;* also publ., London, 1603, under title *An historicall description.* Sabin 36283; STC 3402. CSmH, DLC, MiU-C, NN-RB; Oxford:Bodl.
611/7

Bourne, William. A regiment for the sea . . . Corrected and amended by Thomas Hood. *London: T. Snodham, for E. Weaver*, 1611. 95 numb. lvs; 8vo. 1st publ., London, [1574]; but cf. 1601 edn. Taylor (Regiment) 454–55; STC 3429. BL, Rotterdam:W. A. Engelbrecht.
611/8

Cano, Tomé. Arte para fabricar, fortificar, y apareiar naos de guerra, y merchante. *Seville: L. Estupiñán*, 1611. 59 numb. lvs; 8vo. In the form of dialogues, the 1st of which treats 'del antiguedad del navegar', mentioning Columbus's & Magellan's voyages. Elsewhere refs to New World occur. Escudero (Seville) 958; Palau 42342; Maggs Cat.502 (Americana VII):5019. MH, NN-RB, RPJCB; BL, BN.
611/9

Castile. Laws, statutes, etc., 1252–1284 (Alfonso X). Las siete partidas nuevamente glosadas por . . . Gregorio Lopez. *Mainz: B. Lipp, for J. Hasrey, at Madrid*, 1611,'10. 4 v.; fol. 1st publ. with López's annotations containing American refs, Salamanca, 1555. CU-A, DLC, MiU; BN.
611/10

Cayet, Pierre Victor Palma. Chronologie septenaire de l'histoire de la paix entre les roys de France et d'Espagne . . . avec le succez de plusieurs navigations faictes aux Indes Orientales, Occidentales & Septentrionales. *Paris: J. Richer*, 1611. 506 numb. lvs; 8vo. 1st publ., Paris, 1605. FTaSU; BN.
611/11

Cebà, Ansaldo. Rime. *Rome: B. Zannetti,* 1611. 713 p.; illus.; 8vo. Includes poem addressed to Columbus. Graesse II:95. ICN.
611/12

Clyte, Nicasius van der. Cort verhael der destructie van d'Indien vergadert door den Bisschop don fay Bertolome de las Casas . . . En nu in nederduytschen rym gestelt door N.V.C.C. *Flushing: B. Langenes* [1611]. A versification of B. de las Casas's *Brevissima relacion, de la destruycion de las Indias.* Hanke/ Giménez 504. CSmH
611/13

Codogno, Ottavio. Nuovo itinerario delle poste per tutto il mondo . . . Aggiuntovi il modo di scrivere à tutte le parti. *Venice:* 1611. 16mo. Included is a brief chapt. on the Americas. Sabin 14142.
611/14

Cortés, Jerónimo. Phisonomia y varios secretos de naturaleza. *Pamplona: C. Labáyen,* 1611. 107 numb. lvs; 8vo. 1st publ., Valencia, 1597; cf. 1601 edn. Palau 63305. London:Wellcome.
611/15

Coryat, Thomas. Coryats crudities. *London: W. S[tansby].,* 1611. 655p.; illus.; port.; 4to. Amongst the commendatory poems is one in Latin by Hugh Holland addressed to Sir John Harington adverting to latter's predilection for tobacco. STC 5808; Arents (Add.) 149; Pforzheimer 218. CSmH, CtY, DLC, ICN, MH, NN-RB, PPRF; BL.
611/16

Cotgrave, Randle. A dictionarie of the French and English tongues. *London: A. Islip,* 1611. [906] p.; fol. 'Ameriquain' is defined as 'The Neapolitaine, or French disease; called so, because it first came from America'. Also includes entries for 'Bois sainct', 'Callebasse', 'Maiz', 'Manat', 'Nicotiane', &c. STC 5830. CSmH, CtY, DLC, ICN, MH, MiU, NN-RB, PPL; BL.
611/17

Covarrubias Horozco, Sebastián de. Tesoro de la lengua castellana, o española. *Madrid: L. Sánchez,* 1611. 602 numb. lvs; fol. Certain of the articles refer to the New World. Sabin 57647; Pérez Pastor (Madrid) 1130. CU, DLC, MB, NNH, OU, PPL: BL, Madrid:BN.
611/18

Croll, Oswald. Basilica chymica . . . Additus est . . . Tractatus novus de signaturis rerum internis. *Frankfurt a. M.: J. F. Weiss, for G. Tampach* [1611]. 3 pts; illus.; 4to. 1st

publ., Frankfurt a. M., 1609. DLC, MH, NNNAM, PPC, WU; London:Wellcome, BN.
611/19

Daniel, Samuel. Certain small works . . . Corrected and augmented. *London: J. L[egat]. for S. Waterson,* 1611. 183 lvs; 12mo. 1st publ. as here collected, London, 1607; includes the author's *The queenes arcadia,* 1st publ. separately, London, 1606. STC 6243; Greg 227(c). CSmH, CtY, DFo, ICN, MH, NN-RB; BL.
611/20

Davies, John (1565?-1618). The scourge of folly. *London: E. A[llde]., for R. Redmer* [1611]. 264 p.; 8vo. In verse. Included are several poems on tobacco. STC 6341; Grolier Club (Langland to Wither) 69; Arents 98. CSmH, CtY, DFo, ICU, MWiW-C, NN-A; BL.
611/21

Daza, Antonio, O.F.M. Quarta parte de la Chronica general del nu[es]tro padre San Francisco. *Valladolid: J. Godínez de Millis & D. de Córdova,* 1611. 4 pts; fol. Transl. from Daza's *Delle chroniche delle Ordine de' Frati minori . . . parte quarta,* 1st publ., Venice, 1608. In bk 1 chapt. xii & all of bk 2 relate to Franciscans in New World. Continues Marcos da Lisboa's *Chronicas de la orden de los frayles menores del . . . padre sant Francisco,* Salamanca, 1570. Medina (BHA) 570; Streit I:316; Alcocer (Valladolid) 562; Palau 69040. BL, Madrid:BN.
611/22

De La Warr, Thomas West, 3rd baron. The relation of the Right Honourable the Lord De-La-Warre, lord governour and captaine generall of the colonie, planted in Virginia. *London: W. Hall, for W. Welby,* 1611. [17] p.; 4to. Sabin 102756; Clayton-Torrence 16; Vail (Frontier) 31; STC 25266; Church 349; JCB (3) II:79. CSmH, DLC, ICN, MH, MiU-C, NN-RB, PHi, RPJCB; BL.
611/23

Del Rio, Martin Anton, S.J. Les controverses et recherches magiques . . . Traduit et abregé du latin par André du Chesne. *Paris: J. Petit-Pas,* 1611. 1024 p.; 8vo. Transl. from the author's *Disquisitionum magicarum libri sex,* 1st publ., Louvain, 1599–1600; cf. 1603 edn. Backer II:1900. DLC, NIC; BN.
611/24

—[Anr issue]. *Paris: R. Chaudière,* 1611. Backer II:1900. BN.
611/25

Dickenson, John. Speculum tragicum. *Ley-*

den: L. Elsevier, 1611. 305 (i.e., 299) p.; 12mo. 1st publ., Delft, 1601. Willems (Les Elzevier) 69; Rahir (Les Elzevier) 51. NN.

611/26

Digges, Sir Dudley. Fata mihi totum mea sunt agitanda per orbem. [*London:*] *W. W[hite]., for J. Barnes,* 1611. 26 p.; 8vo. Text in English. Republished, 1612, under title *Of the circumference of the earth.* Included are numerous refs to the Americas as related to geographic measurements. STC 6846. CSmH; Oxford:Bodl. 611/27

Donne, John. An anatomy of the world. *London:* [*H. Lownes,*] *for S. Macham,* 1611. 16 lvs; 8vo. Comprises poem, later known as *The first anniversary,* in memory of Elizabeth Drury, in which she is said to have 'guilt the West-Indies', &c. STC 7022; Keynes (Donne) 74. CSmH; G. L. Keynes.

611/28

———. Conclave Ignatii: sive Eius in nuperis inferni comitiis inthronisatio. [*London: W. Burre,* 1611]. 94 p.; 12mo. Cited are Diego de Torres Bolo's *Brevis relatio historica rerum in provincia Peruana apud Indos* (Mainz, 1604); Jean Matal's preface to Jerónimo Osorio's *De rebus Emanuelis Regis Lusitaniae . . . gestis* (Cologne, 1576); inferentially Bartolomé de las Casas's *Brevissima relacion* (Seville, 1552); & José de Acosta's *De natura Novi Orbis* (Salamanca, 1588). For the publishing history of this work, see T. S. Healy's edition of Donne's *Ignatius his conclave* (Oxford, 1969). Keynes (Donne) 2; STC 7026; Grolier Club (Wither to Prior) 277n. CtY, MH; BL.

611/29

—[Anr edn]. [*Hanau?* 1611]. 35 p.; 4to. Keynes (Donne) 3. BL, Cambridge:UL, Breslau:StB. 611/30

———. Ignatius his conclave: or His inthronisation in a late election in hell. *London: N. O[kes]., for R. More,* 1611. 143 p.; 12mo Transl., prob. by Donne, from his *Conclave Ignatii* above. Keynes (Donne) 4, 5; STC 7027; Grolier Club (Wither to Prior) 277. CSmH, MH; BL. 611/31

Draud, Georg. Bibliotheca classica, sive, Catalogus officinalis, in quo singuli singularum facultatum ac professionum libri . . . recensentur. *Frankfurt a. M.: N. Hoffmann, for P. Kopff,* 1611. 1253 p.; 4to. In section 'Libri historici, geographici et politici' are

included categories for America, Florida, India Occidentalis, Insularum descriptio, Peruana, & Virginia. CtY, DLC, MiU, PPC, RPJCB, WU; BL, BN. 611/32

Du Bartas, Guillaume de Salluste, seigneur. Les oeuvres. *Paris: J. de Bordeaulx,* 1611,'10. 2 v.; illus.; fol. In verse. Included are the author's *La sepmaine,* 1st publ. with commentaries by Simon Goulart, Paris, 1584, & his *La seconde sepmaine,* 1st publ. also with Goulart's commentaries, Geneva, 1589. Cf. 1601 edn. Holmes (DuBartas) I:76 no. 36 & I:91 no. 24abc; Jones (Goulart) 20z(n); Tchémerzine X:197. BN. 611/33

—[Anr issue]. *Paris: T. Du Bray,* 1611,'10. Holmes (DuBartas) I:76 no. 36n & I:91 no. 24abc; Jones (Goulart) 20z; Tchémerzine X:197. CU, IaU; BL, BN. 611/34

—[Anr issue]. *Paris: C. Rigaud,* 1611,'10. Holmes (DuBartas) I:76 no. 36n & I:91 no. 24abc(n); Jones (Goulart) 20z(n); Tchémerzine X:197. LNHT, MH, NcU; BL, BN.

611/35

———. Du Bartas his devine weekes and workes translated by . . . Josuah Sylvester . . . Now thirdly corrected and augmented. *London: H. Lownes; sold by A. Johnson,* 1611. 819 p.; illus., port.; 4to. In verse. 1st publ. as here transl., London, 1605. STC 21651. CSmH, CtY, DLC, ICU, MH, NN-RB, PU; BL. 611/36

Du Hamel, Jacques. Acoubar, tragédie tiree des Amours de Pistion & Fortunie en leur voyage de Canada. *Rouen: R. Du Petit Val,* 1611. 71 p.; 12mo. 1st publ., Rouen, 1603. Cf. Cioranescu (XVII) 26999. RPJCB; BN. 611/37

Du Jarric, Pierre, S.J. L'histoire des choses plus memorables advenuës tant es Indes Orientales qu'autres pays de la descouverte des Portugais. *Arras: G. de La Rivière,* 1611. 977 p.; 4to. 1st publ., Bordeaux, as the *Seconde partie de l'Histoire* etc. Cf. Sabin 35790; Borba de Moraes I:358–59; Backer IV:751.

611/38

—[Anr issue]. *Arras: G. de La Rivière, for J. Vervliet, at Valenciennes,* 1611. Borba de Moraes I:360; Streit V:155; Backer IV:751. Munich:UB. 611/39

—[Anr issue]. *Arras: G. Bauduin,* 1611. BL. 611/40

Durante, Castore. Il tesoro della sanita. *Ven-*

ice: D. Imberti, 1611. 324 p.; illus.; fol. 1st publ., [Rome?], 1586; cf. 1601 edn. Michel (Répertoire) II:191. CU, DNLM; Paris:Ste Geneviève.　　　　　　　　　　　611/41

—[Anr issue?]. *Venice: G. Sarzina,* 1611. Michel (Répertoire) II:191. DNLM, WU; Paris:Sorbonne.　　　　　　　　　　　　　611/42

Fernández, Alonso, O.P. Historia eclesiastica de nuestros tiempos. *Toledo: Widow of P. Rodríguez,* 1611. 496 p.; fol. 'De la conversion del Nuevo mundo, o Indias Occidentales': libro 1. Sabin 24128; Medina (BHA) 571; Streit I:317; Pérez Pastor (Toledo) 469; JCB (3) II:75. CSmH, CtY, DLC, ICN, MH, MiU-C, NNH, PBL, RPJCB; BL, BN.　　　　　　　　　　　　　　611/43

Florio, John. Queen Anna's new world of words, or Dictionarie of the Italian and English tongues, collected, and newly much augmented. *London: M. Bradwood, for E. Blount & W. Barret,* 1611. 690 p.; fol. 1st publ., London, 1598, under title *A worlde of wordes.* Included are definitions of the word *tobacco.* STC 11099; Michel (Répertoire) III:52; Arents (Add.) 109. CSmH, CtY, DLC, ICN, InU-L, MH, MiU, NN-RB, PU-F; BL, BN.　　　　　611/44

Fontaine, Jacques. Practica curandorum morborum corporis humani. *Paris: A. Beys,* 'M.XC.XI' [i.e., 1611]. 2 pts; 8vo. Formulas included employ sarsaparilla (for gonorrhea) & mechoacan. DNLM, MBCo; BL.　　　　　　　　　　　　　611/45

Gallucci, Giovanni Paolo. Theatro del mundo y de el tiempo . . . traducido de lengua latina . . . y añadido por Miguel Pérez. *Granada: S. Múñoz,* 1611. 369 numb. lvs; illus., map; fol. A reissue with altered imprint date of 1606 edn. MB, MH.　　　　　　　　　　　　　　611/46

Gardiner, Edmund. Phisicall and approved medicines. *London: [H. Lownes,] for M. Lownes,* 1611. 4to. 1st publ., London, 1610, under title *The triall of tobacco,* here reissued with cancel t.p. STC 11563. Cambridge:UL.　　　　　　　　　　　　　611/47

Great Britain. Council for Virginia. By the Counsell of Virginia. Seeing it hath pleased God . . . that . . . by the wisdome . . . of the Governour . . . in Virginia . . . the English plantation there succeedeth . . . it

is resolved . . . to make a new supply of men. *London: [T. Haveland,] for W. Welby,* 1611. bds.; fol. A further appeal for laborers. Sabin 99861 (& Sabin 99863?); Clayton-Torrence 15A; Vail (Frontier) 30; STC 24833.2. London: Soc. Ant.　　　611/48

Grégoire, Pierre. Syntagma juris universi. *Frankfurt a. M.: N. Hoffmann,* 1611. 1104 p.; fol. 1st publ., Lyons, 1582; cf. 1609 edn. NCH.　　　　　　　　　　　　611/49

Gualterotti, Raffaello. L'America. *Florence: C. Giunta,* 1611. [46] p.; 12mo. Canto I (all publ.) of a poem on Amerigo Vespucci's 'scoprimento de le nuove Indie'. Sabin 29050; Palau 109367; JCB (3) II:75. DLC, RPJCB; BL.　　　　　　　　　611/50

Guidi, Guido (d. 1569). Ars medicinalis. *Venice: Giunta Office,* 1611. 3 v.; fol. 1st publ., Frankfurt a. M., 1596. Medicinal properties of guaiacum & sassafras are described; elsewhere, decoctions using sarsaparilla, guaiacum, & sassafras are mentioned. Wellcome I:6601. ICJ, ViRA; London:Wellcome, BN.　　　　　　　　　　　　　611/51

Guillaumet, Tannequin. Traicté de la maladie nouvellement appelee cristaline [i.e., syphilis]. *Lyons: P. Rigaud,* 1611. 104 p.; 12mo. For treatment guaiacum, sarsaparilla, & sassafras are prescribed. Wellcome I:2994. DNLM, NNNAM, PPC; BL, BN.　　　　　　　　　　　611/52

Heurne, Johan van. Opera omnia. [*Leyden:*] *Plantin Press (Raphelengius),* 1611,'09. 2 pts; 4to. Included is the author's *Praxis medicinae nova ratio,* 1st publ., Leyden, 1587; cf. 1609 edn. DNAL, NNNAM; BL.　　　611/53

Hues, Robert. Tractatus. de globis, coelesti, et terrestri. *Amsterdam: J. Hondius,* 1611. 92 p.; illus.; 8vo. 1st publ., London, 1594. Included are numerous refs to American geography. Shaaber (Brit. auth.) H478. DLC, MH; BL.　　　　　　　　　611/54

—[Anr edn]. *London: Norton Office,* 1611. 258 p.; 12mo. STC 13906a. DFo, MB, NN-RB.　　　　　　　　　　　　　611/55

Jesuits. Letters from missions. Drey newe Relationes; erste auss Japon . . . andere von Missionibus oder Reisen . . . im Jahr 1607, in das Königreich Mexico. *Augsburg: C. Dabertzhofer,* 1611. 170 p.; 4to. Sabin 54943; Palmer 315; Streit II:1417; Backer

VI:1972; JCB (3) II:75. DLC, NN-RB, RPJCB; BL, Munich:StB. 611/56

Junius, Hadrianus. Nomenclator octilinguis omnium rerum propria nomina continens. *Frankfurt a. M.: N. Hoffmann, 1611.* 8vo. 1st publ., Antwerp, 1577; cf. 1602 edn. BL. 611/57

Keckermann, Bartholomaeus. Systema astronomiae compendiosum. *Hanau: Heirs of W. Antonius, 1611.* 297 p.; 8vo. Includes minor ref. to American southern hemisphere. BN. 611/58

——. Systema geographicum duobus libris adornatum. *Hanau: Heirs of W. Antonius, 1611.* 2 pts; 8vo. Includes numerous scattered refs to America. CtY. 611/59

Kornmann, Heinrich. Templum naturae historicum. *Darmstadt: J. J. Porsch, 1611.* 334 p.; 8vo. On p. 234 the American (i.e., Mexican) province of Mechoacan is mentioned. Wellcome I:3581. CU, MH, NjP, PPC; BL, BN. 611/60

Entry canceled. 611/61

L'Ecluse, Charles de. Curae posteriores, seu Plurimarum non antè cognitarum, aut descriptarum stirpium, peregrinorumque aliquot animalium novae descriptiones. [*Leyden:*] *Plantin Press (Raphelengius), 1611.* 2 pts; illus.; fol. Comprises additions & corrections to author's earlier works. Pritzel 1761; Bibl. belg., 1st ser., XIV:L95; Arents 99. DLC, MH-A, MoSB, NN-A, PPC; BL, BN. 611/62

—[Anr edn]. [*Leyden:*] *Plantin Press (Raphelengius), 1611.* 2 pts; illus.; 4to. Pritzel 1761n; Nissen (Bot.) 368; Bibl. belg., 1st ser., XIV:L96. DFo, NN-RB, PPL, RPB; BL, BN. 611/63

Le Mire, Aubert. Notitia patriarchatuum et archiepiscopatuum orbis christiani. *Antwerp: D. Martin, 1611.* 144 p.; 8vo. Pages 129–30 describe bishoprics of New World. Streit I:320. NN-RB; BN. 611/64

Léry, Jean de. Histoire d'un voyage fait en la terre de Bresil . . . Cinquiesme edition. *Geneva: J. Vignon, 1611.* 489 p.; illus.; 8vo. 1st publ., La Rochelle, 1578. An account of Villegagnon's Brazilian settlement. Sabin 40152; Borba de Moraes II:404; JCB (3) II:76. DLC, MH, NN-RB, PBL, RPJCB; BN. 611/65

Lescarbot, Marc. Histoire de la Nouvelle-France. Contenant les navigations, découvertes, & habitations faites par les François és Indes Occidentales & Nouvelle-France . . . Seconde edition, reveuë, corrigée, & augmentée par l'autheur. *Paris: J. Millot, 1611.* 877 p.; maps; 8vo. 1st publ., Paris, 1609. Sabin 40170; Harrisse (NF) 23; Borba de Moraes I:407; Streit II:2463; Church 350; JCB (3) II:76–77. CSmH, DLC, MWiW-C, MiU-C, PHi, RPJCB; BL, BN. 611/66

Libavius, Andreas. Syntagma selectorum undiquaque et perspicue traditorum alchymiae arcanorum. *Frankfurt a. M.: N. Hoffmann, for P. Kopff, 1611–13.* 2 v.; illus.; fol. Includes descriptions of gums & liquids based on guaiacum, sassafras, & tobacco. Ferguson (Bibl. chem.) II:32; Wellcome I:3778. CtY, DNLM, ICU, MiU, NIC, PU; London:Wellcome. 611/67

L'Obel, Matthias de. Perfuming of tobacco, and the great abuse committed in it . . . Translated out of Latin by I. N[asmith]. G. *London: W. Stansby, 1611.* 10 lvs; 4to. Extracted & transl. from L'Obel's *In G. Rondeletii Pharmaceuticam officinam animadversiones,* London, 1605. STC 16650.5; Arents 99. NN-A. 611/68

Manardo, Giovanni. Ἰατρολογία ἐπιστολική, sive Curia medica . . . viginti libris epistolarum . . . adumbrata . . . tertio iam revisa. *Hanau: Heirs of A. Wechel, for Heirs of J. Aubry, 1611.* 432 p.; fol. 1st publ., Basel, 1540. In bk 19, epist. ii, guaiacum is discussed. Wellcome I:4003. DNLM; BL, BN. 611/69

Marlowe, Christopher. The tragicall historie of the life and death of Doctor Faustus. *London: G. E[ld]., for J. Wright, 1611.* [47] p.; 4to. Drama. 1st publ., London, 1604. STC 17431; Greg 205(c). CSmH. 611/70

Mattioli, Pietro Andrea. Kreutterbuch. *Frankfurt a. M.: N. Hoffman, for J. Fischer, 1611.* 460 p.; illus.; fol. 1st publ. as here ed. by Joachim Camerarius, Frankfurt a. M., 1586. Includes discussion of medicinal uses of American plants. Pritzel 5990n; Nissen (Bot.) 1311n. DNLM; London:Wellcome. 611/71

Mercado, Luis. Praxis medica . . . in quatuor partes divisa. *Venice: B. Giunta & G. B. Ciotti & Co.,* 1611. 624 p.; fol. 1st publ. as here constituted as the *Tomus secundus* of Mercado's *Operum,* Valladolid, 1605, q.v.; cf. also the Venice, 1608 edn with above title. Wellcome I:4218. London:Wellcome.
611/72

——. Tomus secundus Operum. *Venice: B. Giunta & G. B. Ciotti & Co.,* 1611. 624 p.; fol. 1st publ. as here constituted, Valladolid, 1605. The present edn represents a resetting of the printers' 1609 edn. Also issued independently under title *Praxis medica,* the preceding item. Wellcome I:4218. DNLM, NNNAM; London:Wellcome.
611/73

Mercator, Gerardus. Atlas sive Cosmographicae meditationes de fabrica mundi et fabricati figura. Denuò auctus. Editio quarta. *Amsterdam: J. Hondius,* 1611. 359 p.; maps; fol. 1st publ., Amsterdam, 1606. Koeman (Me) 20B describes a copy with minor variants. Cf. Sabin 47882; Koeman (Me) 20A; Phillips (Atlases) 3412. DLC, ICN; The Hague:KB.
611/74

Meteren, Emanuel van. Belgische ofte Nederlantsche oorlogen ende gheschiedenissen, beginnende van t'jaer 1595 tot 1611 . . . verbetert ende vermeerdert. *'Schotland, outside Danswijck'* [i.e., The Hague?]: *H. Van Loven, for E. van Meteren, [at London]* 1611. 360 lvs; 4to. 1st publ. in Dutch, Delft, 1599; cf. years 1605 & 1610. A pirated edn. Sabin 48175; Harrisse (BAV) p. xxxvii (n); Stokes (Manhattan) VI:256; cf. Palau 166949. NcU, NjP.
611/75

—[Anr edn]. Historie der Nederlandscher ende haerder naburen oorlogen ende geschiedenissen. *The Hague: H. Jacobszoon van Wouw,* 1611. 1 v.; ports, map; 4to. Palau 166951.
611/76

Mexía, Pedro. Selva di varia lettione . . . Coll'aggiunta della quarta e della quinta parte. *Venice: F. Baba,* 1611. 487 p.; 4to. 1st publ. with addition of Francesco Sansovino's 'Della grandezza dell'Indie, & chi le trovò, & perche furono chiamate Indie', Venice, 1559, under title *Della selva di varia lettione.* Palau 167301.
611/77

Middleton, Thomas. The roaring girle. *London: [N. Okes,] for T. Archer,* 1611. 48 lvs;

4to. Drama; written with Thomas Dekker. In act 1, scene 1, an apothecary shop is described as selling tobacco. STC 17908; Greg 298; Pforzheimer 703. CSmH, DFo, MB; BL.
611/78

Molina, Luis de. De justitia et jure tractatus. *Venice: The Sessas,* 1611. 1008 cols; fol. 1st publ., Cuenca (Spain), 1593; cf. the year 1602 above. Palau 174619:I. CU-L, DCU; Madrid:BN.
611/79

Montaigne, Michel Eyquem de. Essais. *Paris: F. Gueffier,* 1611. 1129 p.; port.; 8vo. 1st publ., Bordeaux, 1580; cf. 1602 edn. BN.
611/80

—[Anr issue]. *Paris: M. Nivelle,* 1611. CtY; BN.
611/81

—[Anr issue]. *Paris: J. Petit-Pas,* 1611. BN.
611/82

—[Anr issue]. *Paris: C. Rigaud,* 1611. Tchémerzine VIII:416. BL.
611/83

—[Anr issue]. *Paris: C. Sevestre,* 1611. MiU.
611/84

Müller, Philipp (1585–1659). Miracula chymica et misteria medica. [*Wittenberg:*] *L. Seuberlich, for C. Berger,* 1611. 189 p.; 12mo. Formulas for treatment of syphilis call for guaiacum, sarsaparilla, & sassafras. Wellcome I:4473. DFo, WU; BL.
611/85

Opmeer, Pieter van (1525–1595). Opus chronographicum orbis universi . . . usque ad annum M.D.C.XI. *Antwerp: H. Verdussen,* 1611. 2 v.; ports; fol. In v. 1, America, Columbus (with port.), Cortés, & Francis Drake are described; in v. 2, Francis Drake & Virginia, with special section on America. Reprinted, Cologne, 1625, under title *Chronographia mundi.* Wellcome I:4636. CtY, DLC, InU-L, MB, MnU-B, NN, PU; BL, BN.
611/86

Ortelius, Abraham. Thesaurus geographicus, recognitus et auctus. *Hanau: Heirs of W. Antonius,* 1611. 662 lvs; 4to. 1st publ., Antwerp, 1578, under title *Synonymia geographica;* cf. Antwerp, 1596, edn with above title. Sabin 57709n. MH, NNC, RPJCB, ViU; BN.
611/87

Owen, John. Epigrammatum libri tres. *Amberg: J. Schönfeld,* 1611. 8vo. 1st publ., London, 1606. Shaaber (Brit. auth.) O84. Oxford:Bodl.
611/88

Pasquier, Etienne. Les recherches de la France. *Paris: L. Sonnius,* 1611. 994 p.; port.;

4to. 1st publ. with American content, Paris, 1596; cf. 1607 edn; here another issue of Sonnius's 1610 edn with altered imprint date. Thickett (Pasquier) 13; Tchémerzine IX:84. BL, Munich:StB. 611/89

Polo, Gaspar Gil. Primera parte de Diana enamorada. *Paris: R. Estienne, 1611.* 116 numb. lvs; 12mo. 1st publ., Valencia, 1564. Included are numerous refs to the New World & its riches. Palau 102077. MB, NNH; BN. 611/90

Pontanus, Johannes Isaacus. Rerum et urbis Amstelodamensium historia. *Amsterdam: J. Hondius, 1611.* 292 p.; illus., maps; fol. Included are accounts of Dutch voyages to Greenland. Sabin 64002; Tiele 876; JCB (3) II:78. DLC, ICN, InU-L, MiU-C, NSchU, RPJCB; BL, BN. 611/91

Porta, Giovanni Battista della. Ars destillatoria; das ist, Die edele . . . Kunst zu destilliern. *Frankfurt a. M.: J. Bringer, for A. Humm, 1611.* 174 p.; illus.; 4to. Transl. by Peter Uffenbach from Porta's *De distillatione lib. ix,* 1st publ., Rome, 1608. DNLM; BN. 611/92

Pyrard, François. Discours du voyage des François aux Indes. *Paris: D. Le Clerc, 1611.* 292 p.; 8vo. 'Description du Bresil, des façons de faire des habitans': p. 279–92. Sabin 66879; Borba de Moraes II:168; JCB (3) II:78–79. MH, NN-RB, RPJCB; BL, BN. 611/93

Queiros, Pedro Fernandes de. Relacion de un memorial que ha presentado á su Magestad . . . sobre la poblacion, y descubrimiento de la quarta parte del mundo. *Valencia: 1611.* 8 p.; 4to. 1st publ., Madrid, 1610. Palau 89604; Kelly (Calendar of Docs) 580. 611/94

——. Relation . . . von dem new erfundnem vierten Theil der Welt . . . in spanischer Sprach zu Pampelona . . . getruckt jetzo aber . . . ins Teutsch gebracht. *Augsburg: C. Dabertzhofer, 1611.* 9 p.; 4to. Transl. from author's *Relacion de un memorial que ha presentado a su Magestad,* Pamplona, 1610; 1st publ., Madrid, 1610, with caption title beginning 'Señor'. Sabin 67354; Medina (BHA) 6456 (VI:82); Palmer 374; Church 352; JCB (3) II:75. CSmH, InU-L, NN-RB, RPJCB; BL, Munich:StB. 611/95

Reneaulme, Paul de. Specimen historiae plantarum. *Paris: H. Beys, 1611.* 152 p.; illus.; 4to. Included are descriptions of American plants, incl. tobacco. Pritzel 7542; Nissen (Bot.) 1621; Arents (Add.) 151; Hunt (Bot.) 192. DLC, ICJ, MH, NN-RB, PPL; BL, BN. 611/96

Rich, Richard, supposed author. [The last newes from Virginia, beinge an encouragemente to all others to followe the noble enterprise. *London: J. Wright, 1611.*] Ballad. Existence, description, & authorship conjectured from entry in Stationers' Register for 16 Aug. 1611 and ref. in Rich's *Newes from Virginia* of 1610. Sabin 100483; Clayton-Torrence 14. 611/97

Ripa, Cesare. Iconologia, overo Descrittione d'imagini delle virtù, vitii, affetti, passioni humane, corpi celesti, mondo e sue parti. *Padua: P. P. Tozzi, in Pasquato Office, 1611.* 552 p.; illus.; 4to. 1st publ. with American content, Rome, 1603. Wellcome I:5497. DLC, ICU, PSt, RPB, TxU: BL. 611/98

Röslin, Elisaeus. Mitternächtige Schiffarth, von den Herrn Staden inn Niderlanden vor xv. Jaren vergebenlich fürgenommen . . . vom indischen Paradeiss der gantzen Welt. *Oppenheim: H. Galler, for J. T. de Bry, 1611.* 175 p.; 8vo. Though concerned primarily with an arctic voyage, refers to America (p. 56) as a paradise. The constellation Cygnus is interpreted as a cross, with other stars representing heathens in America, India, etc. Sabin 73294; cf. Muller (1872) 3362. NN-RB; BL. 611/99

Rowlands, Samuel. The knave of clubbes. *London: E. A[llde]., 1611.* 4to. In verse. 1st publ., London, 1600, under title *A merry meeting;* cf. year 1609. STC 21388. CSmH; Oxford:Corpus. 611/100

——. The letting of humours blood. *London: W. White, 1611.* 8vo. 1st publ., London, 1600; intervening edns have title *Humors ordinarie,* etc.; cf. year 1605 above. STC 21396. BL. 611/101

Rubio, Antonio, S.J. Logica mexicana . . . Hoc est, Commentarii breviores . . . in Universam Aristotelis Dialecticam. *Lyons: J. Pillehotte, 1611.* 738 p.; 8vo. 1st publ., Cologne, 1605. Cf. Sabin 73860; Medina (BHA) 575; Backer VII:281; Palau 280354. Seville:BU, Santiago, Chile:BN. 611/102

Sennert, Daniel. Institutionum medicinae libri v. *Wittenberg: W. Meisner, for Z. Schürer, the Elder,* 1611. 1194 p.; illus., port.; 4to. Bks 4 & 5 discuss the turkey ('Gallus indicus'), mechoacan (& its related 'Jalapa'), guaiacum, sassafras, & sarsaparilla. DNLM.
611/103

Serres, Jean de. A generall historie of France . . . unto the yeare .1598. Much augmented and continued unto this present . . . By Ed: Grimeston. *London: G. Eld,* 1611. 1419 (i.e., 1343)p.; ports; fol. 1st publ. in English, London, 1607, under title *The general inventorie of France;* in pt transl. from author's *Inventaire general,* 1st publ. with American refs, Paris, 1600. STC 22245; Arents (Add.) 135. CSmH, CtY, DFo, IU, InU-L, MH, MiU, MnU-B, NN-RB, PBm; BL, BN.
611/104

Serres, Olivier de, seigneur du Pradel. Le théâtre d'agriculture . . . Derniere edition, reveuë & augmentee par l'autheur. *Geneva: M. Berjon,* 1611. 1198 p.; illus.; 8vo. 1st publ., Paris, 1600; cf. 1603 edn. MH-A.
611/105

Sharpham, Edward. Cupids whirligig. *London: T. C[reede].; sold by A. Johnson,* 1611. 40 lvs; 4to. Comedy. 1st publ., London, 1607. STC 22381; Greg 247(b); Arents (Add.) 136. DFo, ICN, MH, NN-A; BL.
611/106

Spain. Consejo de las Indias. Sentencias de revista . . . sobre la paga y consignacion de los frutos caydos de los estados de Beragua. *[Madrid?* 1611?]. 2 lvs; fol. On suit between Francisco Pacheco Córdoba & Carlos & D. F. Colón and Luisa Carvajal as heiress of Columbus. Palau 308799. CU-B, InU-L.
611/107

Spenser, Edmund. The faerie queene. *London: H. L[ownes]., for M. Lownes,* 1611. 363 p.; fol. 1st publ., London, 1590; here a reissue with cancel t.p. of 1609 edn, q.v. For the bibliographical complexities of this work, see Johnson as cited. Johnson (Spenser) 12; STC 23083.3. CU, ICU, MWelC, NNPM; London:UL.
611/108

Vaughan, William. Approved directions for health, both naturall and artificiall . . . Newly corrected and augmented . . . The

fourth edition. *London: T. S[nodham]., for Roger Jackson,* 1611. 8vo. 1st publ., London, 1600, under title *Naturall and artificial directions for health;* cf. 1602 edn. STC 24614.5; Arents (Add.) 153. NN-A.
611/109

——. The spirit of detraction conjured and convicted in seven circles. A worke both divine and morall. *London: W. Stansby [& T. Snodham,] for G. Norton,* 1611. 351 p.; 4to. Preface to reader mentions 'those stormy Heteroclites of the West Indies, called the Furicanoes', & declaims against tobacco. STC 24622. BL, Oxford:Bodl.
611/110

——[Anr issue]. *London: W. S[tansby & T. Snodham]., for G. Norton,* 1611. STC 24622.5; Arents (Add.) 152. DFo, MH, NN-A; London:Lambeth.
611/111

Vega Carpio, Lope Félix de. Arcadia, prosas y versos. *Madrid: A. Martín, for A. Pérez,* 1611. 308 numb. lvs; port.; 8vo. 1st publ., Madrid, 1598; cf. 1602 edns. Pérez Pastor (Madrid) 1158; Palau 356298. NNH; BL, BN.
611/112

La veritable response a l'anticipation sans falcification [*sic*] de son texte. [*Paris?*] M.C.D.XI [i.e., 1611]. 141 p.; 8vo. In passing, contrasts failure of Portuguese to dominate East Indies with Spanish successes in West Indies. Purportedly reprinted 'jouxte la copie imprimée à Nantes', that edn has not been traced. BL.
611/113

Virginia Company of London. Whereas [*blank*] hath paid in ready mony to Sir Thomas Smith knight, treasurer of Virginia. . . . [*London: W. Welby,* 1611?]. bds.; fol. 1st publ., London, 1608]. Line 6 ends 'shall have ra-'. Sabin 99862; STC 24830.6. CSmH: Hatfield:Hatfield House.
611/114

Wilkins, George. The miseries of inforst marriage. *London: [W. White,] for G. Vincent,* 1611. [78] p.; 4to. Drama. 1st publ., London, 1607. STC 25636; Greg 249 (b); Arents 100. CSmH, DFo, IU, MH, NN-A; BL.
611/115

The worthye and famous history, of the travailes, discovery, & conquest, of . . . Terra Florida. *London: [F. Kingston,] for M. Lownes,* 1611. 180 p.; 4to. Sheets of the 1609 edn above, with title *Virginia richly valued,* here reissued with cancel t.p. Sabin 24897; Vail (Frontier) 29; STC 22939. NN-RB; BL.

611/116

Wytfliet, Corneille. Histoire universelle des Indes Occidentales et Orientales, et de la conversion des Indiens. *Douai: F. Fabri,* 1611. 3 pts; maps; fol. Transl. from Wytfliet's *Descriptionum Ptolemaicae augmentum,* 1st publ., Douai, 1597; cf. 1605 edn above. Sabin 105701; cf. Borba de Moraes II:381; Streit V:158; Phillips (Atlases) 4459; JCB (3) II:80. CtY, DLC, MH, MiU-C, NN-RB, RPJCB; BL.

611/117

1612

Aldrovandi, Ulisse. De piscibus libri v. et de cetis lib. unus. *Bologna: G. B. Bellagamba, for G. Tamburini,* 1612. 372 (i.e., 732) p.; illus.; fol. In bk 1, chapt. xi, 'De cetis', the manatee is described & illustrated, and its West Indian habitat is mentioned. Nissen (Zool.) 70. MH-Z.

612/1

Alemán, Mateo. Vita del picaro Gusmano d'Alfarace . . . Tradotta . . . da Barezzo Barezzi. *Venice: B. Barezzi,* 1612. 12mo. 1st publ. as here transl., Venice, 1606. Laurenti (Nov. pic. esp.) 710.

612/2

Anghiera, Pietro Martire d'. De novo orbe, or The Historie of the West Indies . . . translated . . . by R. Eden, whereunto the other five are newly added by . . . M. Lok. *London: T. Adams,* 1612. 318 numb. lvs; 4to. Eden's incomplete version 1st publ., London, 1555. Sabin 1563; STC 650; Arents 5; Church 358; JCB (3) II:86. CSmH, CtY, DLC, ICN, MH, MiU-C, MnU-B, NN-RB, PU, RPJCB; BL.

612/3

Antidotario romano, tradotto da latino in volgare da Ippolito Ceccarelli . . . Con l'aggiunta dell'elettione de semplici. *Rome: B. Zannetti,* 1612. 2 pts; 4to. Mentioned in the text here added are various American products, identified as such, amongst them copal (a resin), balsam, guaiacum, mechoacan, sassafras, etc. London:Wellcome.

612/4

Bacon, Francis, viscount St Albans. The essaies. *London: J. Beale,* 1612. 241 p.; 8vo.

Here 1st publ. is 'Of atheisme' with statement that in West Indies gods have been given names but not God Himself. Gibson (Bacon) 6; STC 1141; Pforzheimer 28. CSmH, DLC, MH, NNPM; BL.

612/5

—[Anr edn]. *London: [W. Jaggard,] for J. Jaggard,* 1612. 2 pts; 8vo. An expanded version of Jaggard's earlier edns, now including 'Of atheisme'. Gibson (Bacon) 7; cf. STC 1140.

612/6

Bauderon, Brice. Paraphrase sur la Pharmacopoee. *Rouen: A. Ouyn,* 1612. 721 p.; 12mo. 1st publ., Lyons, 1588; cf. 1607 edn. DNLM; London:Wellcome.

612/7

Béguin, Jean. Tyrocinium chymicum. *Paris: M. Le Maître,* 1612. 188 p.; 8vo. In bk 2, chapt. ii includes formula for 'Aqua acida quercus, juniperi, Guaiaci'. On this work, see T. S. Patterson, 'Jean Beguin and his *Tyrocinium chymicum*', Annals of science, II (1937):243–98.

612/8

—[Anr edn]. Secunda editione. *Cologne: A. Boetzer,* 1612. 195 p.; 12mo. Ferguson (Bibl. chem.) I:93. CtY, WU; Glasgow:UL.

612/9

Beringer, Joachim. Der tyrannischen hispanischen Inquisition Heimligkeiten . . . offenbaret . . . In deutsche Sprach . . . mitgetheilt. *Amberg: J. Schönfeld,* 1611 (Colophon: 1612). 341 p.; 8vo. Transl. from Beringer's *Hispanicae Inquisitionis . . . secretiora,* 1st publ., Amberg, 1611. BL.

612/10

Bertaldi, Giovanni Lodovico. Medicamentorum apparatus, in quo remediorum omnium compositorum . . . disertissime enodantur. *Turin: Cavaleri Bros,* 1612. 973 (i.e., 873) p.; 4to. Decoctions descr., p. 374–75, employ guaiacum & sarsaparilla. DNLM, MiU (imp.); BL, BN.

612/11

Bertius, Petrus. Geographischer eyn oder zusammengezogener Tabeln fünff unterschiedliche Bücher. *Frankfurt a. M.: M. Becker, for H. Laurenszoon, at Amsterdam,* 1612. 830 p.; maps; obl. 8vo. Transl. by Peter Uffenbach from author's *Tabularum geographicarum . . . libri septem,* 1st publ., Amsterdam, 1600. Sabin 5014n; Koeman (Lan) 10; Phillips (Atlases) 3413. DLC, IU, NN-RB; Leningrad:Saltykov PL.

612/12

Bickerus, Johannes. Hermes redivivus, declarans hygieinam, de sanitate vel bona hominis conservanda, in qua omnia ex antiquae sapientiae fontibus . . . cum chymiatrom principiis & Paracelsi dogmatibus veris conjuguntur. *Giessen: C. Chemlin & A. Humm,* 1612. 480 p.; 8vo. Passage (p. 40), 'Oceani divisiones in homine' states that 'Caeterum vesica urinaria mare Oceanum Occidentis reptaelentat, abyssus splenis Oceanum Septentrionalem, abyssus renum Peruvianum . . .'. In pt 2, 'De diaeta speciali', chapt. xvii discusses the American climate. BL, London:Wellcome.   612/13

Blaeu, Willem Janszoon. The light of navigation wherein are declared . . . all the coasts and havens of the West, North and East Seas. *Amsterdam: W. J. Blaeu,* 1612. 2 v.; illus., maps; obl. fol. Transl. from Blaeu's *Het licht der zee-vaert,* 1st publ., Amsterdam, 1608. Title pasted on engr. t.p. of the 1610 Dutch edn. Koeman (M.Bl) 11; STC 3110. BL, Rotterdam:WAE.   612/14

Boccalini, Traiano. De' ragguagli di Parnaso . . . Centuria prima. *Venice: P. Farri,* 1612. 478 p.; 4to. Preface to reader mentions Columbus, Vespucci, & Magellan. For the 2nd Centuria, see the year 1613. Firpo (Ragguagli) 1; Michel (Répertoire) I:175. DFo, ICN, NIC; BL, Paris:Arsenal.   612/15

—[Anr edn]. Edizione sopra tutte le altre accuratissima. *Venice: P. Farri,* 1612. 478 p.; 4to. Firpo (Ragguagli) 2; Michel (Répertoire) I:175. Toulouse:BM.   612/16

Botero, Giovanni. Allgemeine historische Weltbeschreibung . . . in vier Bücher abgetheilt . . . Durch Aegidium Albertinum . . . auss dem Italianischen . . . ubersetzt. *Munich: N. Heinrich, for A. Hierat, at Cologne,* 1612. 471 p.; maps; fol. A reissue, with altered imprint date, of bookseller's 1611 edn above. Sabin 6808; Borba de Moraes I:100; JCB (3) II:82. DLC, RPJCB.   612/17

——. Le relationi universali . . . Nuovamente ristampate, & corrette. *Venice: A. Vecchi,* 1612. 8 pts; maps; 4to. 1st publ., Rome, 1591–96. Cf. Sabin 6806; Streit I:323; Michel (Répertoire) I:202. ICN, RPJCB, TxLT; Paris:Ste Geneviève, Madrid:BN.   612/18

Braun, Georg. Civitates orbis terrarum [Liber primus]. *Cologne: P. von Brachel, for the Author,* 1612. 59 double pls; fol. 1st publ., Cologne, 1572. Includes views of Mexico City & Cuzco as engraved by F. Hogenberg, with descriptions by Braun. Vols 2–6 are without Americana. Cf. Koeman (Braun & Hogenberg) 1; Phillips (Atlases) 3292. CtY, DLC (imp.); BL, BN.   612/19

Breton, Nicholas. Cornu-copiae. Pasquils night-cap: or Antidot for the head-ache. *London: T. Thorp.* 1612. 119 p.; 4to. In verse. In enumerating 'men of all countries', mentions 'new Virgineans'; an unmarried girl attributes her pregnancy to a 'Captaine Horner, before he travail'd to the Newfound land'. STC 3639. CSmH, DFo, MH, NN, OU, PU; London:V. & A.   612/20

——. Wits private wealth. London: E. Allde, for J. Tapp, 1612. 4to. Includes ref. to tobacco as purge for head & purse. STC 3708. CSmH; Oxford:Bodl.   612/21

Bruele, Gualtherus. Praxis medicinae theorica et empirica familiarissima. *Leyden: Plantin Press (Raphelengius),* 1612. 421 p.; 12mo. 1st publ., Antwerp, 1579; cf. 1602 edn. CtY-M, DNLM, MnU.   612/22

Bry, Johann Theodor de. Florilegium novum . . . New Blumenbuch. [*Oppenheim:*] *J. T. de Bry,* 1612[–14]. 78 pls; illus.; fol. Included are numerous plants of American origin. As initially issued in 1612 contained 54 unnumbered plates; subsequently the plates were foliated and reissued in 1613 with additional plates 55–78, to be followed in 1614 by other plates. For a later enl. edn with title *Anthologia magna,* see the year 1626. Pritzel 1299; Nissen (Bot.) 272; Hunt (Bot.) 197. DFo, MH-A, MoSB; BL, BN.   612/23

Bucholtzer, Abraham. Index chronologicus, monstrans annorum seriem a mundo condito usque ad annum nati Christi 1580. Tertia cura emendatus, & . . . continuatus. *Frankfurt a. M.: N. Hoffmann, the Elder, for J. Rose,* 1612. 792 p.; 8vo. 1st publ., Görlitz, 1584. Included are refs to America, Brazil, Columbus, Cortés, Magellan, Sir Francis Drake, etc. MiU; BN.   612/24

Camões, Luiz de. Os Lusiadas. Lisbon: V.

Alvares, for D. Fernandes, 1612. 186 numb. lvs; 4to. In verse. 1st publ., Lisbon, 1572; cf. 1609 edn above. Silva (Camões) 17. DLC, MH, NNH; BL, Lisbon:BN.

612/25

Casas, Bartolomé de las, O.P., Bp of Chiapa. Den spiegel der Spaensche tierannye-geschiet in Westindien. *Amsterdam: D. de Meyne, & D. P. Voskuyl,* 1612. 53 lvs; illus.; 4to. 1st publ. in Dutch, [Antwerp?], 1578; cf. 1607 edn above. Sabin 11255; Medina (BHA) 1085n (II:477); Hanke/Giménez 506; Streit I:325; Palau 46975. NN-RB.

612/26

—[Anr issue]. *Amsterdam: D. P. Voskuyl,* 1612. Hanke/Giménez 505. DLC, NN-RB.

612/27

Cayet, Pierre Victor Palma. Chronologie septenaire de l'histoire de la paix entre les roys de France et d'Espagne . . . avec le succez de plusieurs navigations faictes aux Indes Orientales, Occidentales & Septentrionales. Paris: J. Richer, 1612. 506 numb. lvs; 8vo. 1st publ., Paris, 1605. A reissue of an earlier edn with same foliation? ICN, MB.

612/28

—[Anr edn]. *Paris: J. Richer,* 1612. 498 numb. lvs; 8vo. A reissue of an earlier edn with same foliation? BN.

612/29

Chapman, George. An epicede or funerall song: on the . . . death of . . . Henry Prince of Wales. *London: T. S[nodham].,for J. Budge,* 1612. [32] p.; illus.; 4to. In verse. Includes a passage describing Sir Thomas Gates's 1609 shipwreck at Bermuda, en route from Virginia. STC 4974. CSmH, CtY, DLC, ICN, MH, PU; BL. 612/30

Claude d'Abbeville, O.F.M. Cap. L'arrivée des peres Capucins en l'Inde Nouvelle, appellée Maragnon, avec la reception que leur ont faict les sauvages de ce pays, & la conversion d'iceux à nostre saincte foy. *Paris: A. Le Fèvre.* 1612. 16 p.; 8vo. Borba de Moraes I:1; Streit II:2370. NN-RB; BN.

612/31

—[Anr edn]. Lettre d'un pere capucin s'estant acheminé . . . au fleuve de Maragnon & terres adjacentes en l'Inde Occidentale. *Paris: G. Blaizot,* 1612. 12 p.; 8vo. Borba de Moraes I:2. MnU-B; BN. 612/32

Coignet, Michiel. Epitome theatri orbis terrarum. *Antwerp:* 1612. *See* Ortelius, Abraham, *below.*

Contract d'association des Jesuites au trafique de Canada. Pour apprendre à Paul de Gimont, l'un des donneurs d'advis pour les Jesuites contre le Recteur et Université de Paris, et à ses semblables, pourquoi les Jesuites sont depuis peu arrivez en Canada. [*Paris?*] 1612. 8vo. Sabin 16176.

612/33

Coppino, Aquilino. De Hispanicae monarchiae amplitudine . . . oratio. *Milan: The Malatesti,* 1612. 4to. Included are refs to Spanish possessions in New World. Sabin 16714; Palau 61520. BL. 612/34

Cortés, Jerónimo. Phisonomia. *Alcalá de Henares: Heirs of J. Gracián,* 1612. 8vo. 1st publ., Valencia, 1597; cf. 1601 edn. Palau 63306. 612/35

Cotta, John. A short discoverie of the unobserved dangers of severall sorts of ignorant practisers of physicke in England. *London: [R. Field,] for W. Jones & R. Boyle,* 1612. 135 p.; 4to. Describes (p. 4–6) introduction of tobacco into England & its therapeutic use. STC 5833; Arents (Add.) 156. DFo, IEN-M, MH, NN-RB; BL. 612/36

Dekker, Thomas. If it be not good, the divel is in it; a new play. *London: [T. Creede,] for J. T[rundle].; sold by J. Marchant,* 1612. [92] p.; 4to. Included are refs to the Spanish Indies, tobacco, Indians, & the Bermudas. STC 6507; Greg 305; Arents 101. CSmH, CtY, DLC, MH, NN-A; BL. 612/37

——. O per se O, or A new cryer of lanthorne and candlelight. *London: J. Busby,* 1612. 2 pts; illus.; 4to. 1st publ., London, 1608, under title *Lanthorne and candle-light.* STC 6487. CSmH, DFo, MH; BL. 612/38

Del Rio, Martin Anton, S.J. Disquisitionum magicarum libri sex. *Lyons: H. Cardon,* 1612. 468 p.; fol. 1st publ., Louvain, 1599–1600; cf. 1603 edn. Backer II:1899. BN.

612/39

—[Anr issue]. *Lyons: J. Pillehotte,* 1612. BL, BN. 612/40

—[Anr edn]. *Mainz: J. Albin,* 1612. 1070 p.; 4to. Backer II:1899. OCl, MH, NcD, PU, TxU. 612/41

Digges, Sir Dudley. Of the circumference of the earth. *London: W. W[hite]., for J.*

Barnes, 1612. 26 p.; 8vo. 1st publ., London, 1611, under title *Fata mihi totum mea sunt agitanda per orbem.* Sabin 33388 (misdated 1632); STC 6847. CSmH, MHi; BL.

612/42

Donne, John. The first anniversarie. *London: M. Bradwood, for S. Macham,* 1612. 64 lvs; 8vo. In verse. 1st publ., London, 1611, under title *An anatomy of the world.* STC 7023; Keynes (Donne) 75. CSmH, CtY, DFo, MH, NN-RB; G. L. Keynes.   612/43

Drayton, Michael. Poly-Olbion. *London: [H. Lownes,] for M. Lownes, J. Browne, J. Helme, J. Busby* [1612]. 2 pts; illus., maps, port.; fol. In verse. 'A chorographicall description of Great Britain.' In the 9th Song, ref. is made (p. 140) to Madog's voyage to Florida, anticipating voyages of Columbus & Vespucci, explained further (p. 148) in commentary on passage. STC 7226; Grolier Club (Langland to Wither) 82. CSmH, DLC, IU, MH, NN-RB, PBm; BL. 612/44

Durante, Castore. Il tesoro della sanità. *Turin: G. D. Tarino,* 1612. 480 p.; 8vo. 1st publ., [Rome?], 1586; cf. 1601 edn. DNLM.

612/45

Ens, Gaspar. Indiae Occidentalis historia. *Cologne: G. Lützenkirchen,* 1612. 370 p.; 8vo. Sabin 22656; Palau 79881; JCB (3) II:83. CU, CtY, DLC, ICN, MH, MiU-C, NN-RB, RPJCB; BL, BN.   612/46

——. Mauritiados libri vi in quibus Belgica describitur, civilis belli caussae. *Cologne: W. Lützenkirchen,* 1612. 438 p.; 8vo. In bk 5, a chapt. 'Batavi orbem terrarum circumnavigant' describes earlier circumnavigators as well as Dutch enterprises in New World & passage of Strait of Magellan. Sabin 46956; Borba de Moraes I:244n. ICN, NN-RB, RPJCB; BN.   612/47

Fabronius, Hermann. Newe summarische Welt-Historia: uññd Beschreibung aller Keyserthumb, Königreiche, Fürstenthumb, unnd Völcker heutiges Tages auff Erden. *Schmalkalden: W. Ketzel,* 1612. 2 pts; illus., maps; 4to. Pt 2 has title *Der newen summarischen Welt Historia . . . Das ander Theil, von der Newen Welt.* Cf. Sabin 23605. CtY.

612/48

Floyd, John. The overthrow of the Protestants pulpit-babels. [*St Omer: English College Press*] 1612. 328 p.; 4to. In part a reply to

Wm Crashaw's *A sermon, preached . . . before . . . the Lord Lawarre, lord governour . . . of Virginia* (London, 1610). Included are refs to the Virginia colony. STC 11111; Allison/Rogers 326; Church 353; JCB (3) II:83. CsmH, DFo, MH, MiU-C, NN-RB, RPJCB; BL.   612/49

Fontaine, Jacques. Opera in quibus universae artis medicae secundum Hippocratis et Galeni doctrinam partes quatuor methodicae explicantur. *Paris: A. Périer,* 1612. 2 pts; 4to. Mentioned are formulas employing sarsaparilla & mechoacan. DNLM, ICJ.

612/50

Gallucci, Giovanni Paolo. Theatro del mundo y di el tiempo . . . traducido de latin . . . por Miguel Perez. *Granada: [S. Múñoz], for J. Castello,* 1612. 369 numb. lvs; illus., map; fol. 1st publ. in Spanish, Granada, 1606, BN.   612/51

Gerritsz, Hessel, ed. Beschryvinghe van der Samoyeden landt in Tatarien . . . Met een verhael van de opsoeckingh ende ontdeckinge van de nieuwe deurgang ofte straet int Noordwesten na de Rijcken van China ende Cathay; ende ein memorial gepresenteert aenden Coningh van Spaengien. *Amsterdam: H. Gerritsz,* 1612. [38] p.; maps; 4to. Includes Isaac Massa's *Beschryvinghe van der Samoyeden landt;* Queiros's *Memorial,* transl. from *Relacion de un memorial,* Pamplona, 1610; and original material by Gerritsz on Hudson's discoveries. Massa's work includes speculation on a land link between Asia and America, with resultant eastward migration of natives. Sabin 33489; Tiele 372; Tiele-Muller 149; Shaaber (Brit. auth.) H470; JCB AR32:20. RPJCB; BL, The Hague:KB.   612/52

—[Anr edn]. *Amsterdam: H. Gerritsz,* 1612. The preceding, with supplementary [3] p., *Verhael van d'ontdeckinghe van de nieughesochte strate int 't Noord-westen . . . ghedaen door Mr. Henry Hudson.* Tiele-Muller 150. BL.

612/53

——, ed. Descriptio ac delineatio geographica detectionis freti, sive, transitus ad occasum, supra terras Americanas, in Chinam atque Japonem ducturi, recens investigati ab M. Henrico Hudsono Anglo: item, Narratio sermo. Regi Hispaniae facta, super tractu, in quinta orbis terrarum parte . . .

recens detecto, per Capitaneum . . . de Quir; unà cum descriptione terrae Samoiedarum. *Amsterdam: H. Gerritsz,* 1612. [45] p.; illus., maps; 4to. Transl. from 2nd edn of *Beschryvinghe van der Samoyeden Landt,* 1st publ., Amsterdam, 1612. Sabin 33490; Medina (BHA) 6456n (VI:82), Tiele-Muller 151; Shaaber (Brit. auth.) H469; Church 354; JCB (3) II:83. CSmH, DLC, ICN, InU, MH, MnU, NN, RPJCB; BL, BN. 612/54

—[Anr issue]. Exemplar libelli supplicis potentissimo Hispaniarum Regi exhibiti à Capitaneo de Quir. *Amsterdam: H. Gerritsz,* 1612. Sheets of preceding with variant t.p. Sabin 33490 & 67355; Tiele 373n; Tiele-Muller 152; cf. Church 354. NN-RB, RPJCB; BL. 612/55

Great Britain. Council for Virginia. [The articles sett down for the second lottery. *London: W. Welby,* 1612.] Publication inferred from entry in Stationers' Register dated 17 July 1612. Cf. following entry. Sabin 99864. 612/56

——. By his Majesties Counsell for Virginea. Forasmuch as notwithstanding the late publication of our purpose to make use of the King his majesties most gratious grant of lotteries, for the advancement of . . . Virginea. . . . *London: F. Kingston, for W. Welby,* 1612. bds.; fol. On deferring of announced lottery. Entered in Stationers' Register 16 May 1612. Sabin 99865 (& 99869?); Clayton-Torrence 23; Vail (Frontier) 34; STC 24833.4; JCB (3) II:90. RPJCB. 612/57

——. [The lottery for Virginea opened the xxixth of June 1612 declaringe the names of suche as have prices or rewardes. *London: W. Welby,* 1612.] Publication inferred from entry in Stationers' Register dated 2 July 1612. Sabin 99867. 612/58

Guicciardini, Francesco. Histoire des guerres d'Italie. *Paris: P. LeMur,* 1612. 479 numb. lvs; fol. 1st publ. in this version, Paris, 1568. Transl. by Jérôme Chomeday from the author's *L'historia d'Italia,* 1st publ., Florence, 1561; cf. 1604 edn. NjP. 612/59

—[Anr issue?]. *Paris: J. Orry,* 1612. BN. 612/60

Hentzner, Paul. Itinerarium Germaniae, Galliae, Angliae, Italiae. *Nuremberg: A. Wagenmann, for the author,* 1612. 418 p.; 4to.

In describing London, ref. is made to American weed, tobacco. Arents 102. CU-S, CtY, DFo, ICN, MH, NN-A, PU; BL. 612/61

Herrera y Tordesillas, Antonio de. Tercera parte de la Historia general del mundo . . . desde el año de 1585. hasta el de 1598. *Madrid: A. Martín de Balboa, for A. Pérez,* 1612. 780 p.; fol. Continues 1st & 2nd pts, 1st publ. Madrid & Valladolid, 1601 & 1606. Sabin 31559; Pérez Pastor (Madrid) 1177; Palau 114317. CU, DLC, ICN, NN-RB, PPL, RPJCB; BL, BN. 612/62

——. Tratado, relación y discurso histórico de los movimientos de Aragón. *Madrid: Imprenta Real,* 1612. 140 p.; 4to. Includes ref. to Consejo de las Indias. Palau 114320. MH, PU. 612/63

—[Anr edn?]. *Madrid: Imprenta Real,* 1612. 236 p.; 4to. BN. 612/64

Hues, Robert. Tractaet ofte Handelinge van het gebruijck der hemelscher ende aertscher Globe . . . In't Latijn beschreven . . . nu . . . overgheset ende . . . vermeerdert . . . door I. Hondium. *Amsterdam: M. Colijn,* 1612. 67 p.; 4to. 1st publ. in Dutch, Amsterdam, 1597; transl. from author's *Tractatus de globis,* 1st publ., London, 1594. Includes description of America & Magellanica. The 1618 imprint date given by Shaaber is presumably an error. Cf. Sabin 33562; cf. Shaaber (Brit. auth.) H478a. BL. 612/65

Illescas, Gonzalo de. Segunda parte de la Historia pontifical y catholica. *Barcelona: S. de Cormellas,* 1612. fol. 1st publ. with American materials, Barcelona, 1596; cf. 1602 edn. BN. 612/66

Johnson, Robert. The new life of Virginea: declaring the former successe and present estate of that plantation, being the second part of Nova Britannia. *London: F. Kingston, for W. Welby,* 1612. [54] p.; 4to. The author's *Nova Britannia* had appeared in 1609. Sabin 53249 (& 36287); Clayton-Torrence 17; Vail (Frontier) 32; STC 14700; Church 355; JCB (3) II:85. CSmH, CtY, DLC, ICN, MH, MiU-C, MnU-B, NN-RB, PPL, RPJCB; BL. 612/67

Jonson, Ben. The alchemist. *London: T. Snodham, for W. Burre; sold by J. Stepneth,* 1612. [96] p.; 4to. Act 2 begins with refs to riches of New World & Ophir. STC 14755; Greg

303. CSmH, CtY, DFo, ICN, InU-L, MH, NNPM; BL.   612/68

Keckermann, Bartholomaeus. Systema geographicum duobis libris adornatum. *Hanau: Heirs of W. Antonius*, 1612. 2 pts; 8vo. 1st publ., Hanau, 1611; here a reissue of that edn? MnU-B; BN.   612/69

Lancre, Pierre de. Tableau de l'inconstance des mauvais anges et demons. *Paris: J. Berjon*, 1612. 571 p.; illus.; 4to. Included is passage describing use of tobacco by Indians of Hispaniola. ICN, MH, NN-RB; BL, BN.   612/70

La Noue, François de. Discours politiques et militaires. [*Basel? Geneva?*] 1612. 710 p.; 8vo. 1st publ., Basel, 1587. In discourse 8 is a ref to the mines of Peru. MiU.
                                        612/71

Le Mire, Aubert. Notitia episcopatuum Hispaniae et Indiarum. *Antwerp: D. Martin*, 1612. 4 lvs; 8vo. Extracted from the author's *Notitia patriarchatuum*, Antwerp, 1611. Streit I:327; Palau 171565. BN.   612/72

Lescarbot, Marc. Histoire de la Nouvelle-France. Contenant les navigations, découvertes, & habitations faites par les François és Indes Occidentales & Nouvelle-France . . . Seconde edition, reveuë, corrigée, & augmentée par l'autheur. *Paris: J. Millot*, 1612. 877 p.; maps; 8vo. 1st publ., Paris, 1609; here anr issue of the printer's 1611 edn with altered imprint date. Sabin 40171; Harrisse (NF) 25; Streit II:2468; Church 356; Rothschild 1964. CSmH, MH, MnU-B, NN-RB; BN.   612/73

———. Les muses de la Nouvelle France. *Paris: J. Millot*, 1612. 66 p.; 8vo. 1st publ., Paris, 1609. Normally bound with, as issued, the author's *Histoire de la Nouvelle France* of 1611. Sabin 40174n; Harrisse (NF) 24; Streit II:2463n; Church 357; Rothschild 1964n; JCB (3) II:86. CSmH, DLC, MH, MnU-B, NN-RB, PBL, RPJCB; BN.   612/74

———. Relation derniere de ce qui s'est passé au voyage du sieur de Poutrincourt en la Nouvelle-France depuis 20 mois ença. *Paris: J. Millot*, 1612. 39 p.; 8vo. Sabin 40178; Harrisse (NF) 26; Streit II:2469; JCB (3) II:85. CSmH, CtY, ICN, InU-L, MH, MiU-C, MnU-B, NN-RB, RPJCB; BN.   612/75

Leubelfing, Johann von. Ein schön lustig

Reissbuch vor niemals in Truck kommen darinnen begriffen in was Gestalt die Herren Staaden der Unirten Niderländischen Provincien, ein Armada zugericht und . . . West Indien besuchen lassen. *Ulm: J. Meder*, 1612. 23 lvs; 4to. Sabin 40727; Palmer 352; Palau 137010; JCB (3) II:86. NN-RB, RPJCB; BL, Berlin:StB.   612/76

Loubayssin de Lamarca, Francisco. Historia tragicomica de Don Henrique de Castro. *Paris: Widow of M. Guillemot*, 1612. 877 p.; 8vo. Picaresque novel, set in part in Chile. Medina (Chile) 36.   612/77

Lowe, Peter. A discourse of the whole art of chyrurgerie . . . second edition . . . enlarged by the author. *London: T. Purfoot*, 1612,'11. 2 pts; 4to. 1st publ., London, 1597, under title *The whole course of chirurgie*. Includes refs to guaiacum. STC 16870. DNLM, NNNAM; BL, Oxford:Christ Church.   612/78

Marcos da Lisboa, O.F.M., Bp. Delle chroniche de' Frati minori del . . . p.s. Francisco, parte terza . . . tradotta di lingua spagnuola . . . dal signor Horatio Diola . . . Quarta . . . impressione. *Venice: B. Barezzi*, 1612. 352 numb. lvs; 4to. 1st publ. as here transl. from Spanish text (1st publ., Salamanca, 1570), Venice, 1591. Includes account of Franciscan missions in Mexico. Streit I:326. Rome: Franciscans.
                                        612/79

Mayerne, Louis Turquet de. The generall historie of Spaine . . . Translated into English, and continued unto these times by Edward Grimeston. *London: A. Islip & G. Eld*, 1612. 1380 p.; fol. Transl. from author's *Histoire generale d'Espagne*, 1st publ., Geneva, 1587. Includes numerous refs to Spanish in New World. Sabin 47118; STC 17747; Palau 159015. CSmH, CtY, DLC, ICN, MH, MnU-B, NN-RB, PPAmP, RPJCB; BL.
                                        612/80

Mercator, Gerardus. Atlas, sive Cosmographicae meditationes de fabrica mundi et fabricati figura. Denuò auctus. Editio quarta. *Amsterdam: J. Hondius*, 1612. 1st publ., Amsterdam, 1606. Cf. Sabin 47882; Koeman (Me) 21. NjN; Louvain:BU.   612/81

Meteren, Emanuel van. Nederlantsche historien ofte geschiedenissen inhoudende den gantzen staet, handel . . . verbetert ende vermeerdert tot . . . 1611. [*Dordrecht?* 1612]. 2 pts; illus., ports, map; 4to. 1st publ. in Dutch, Delft, 1599; cf. years 1605 & 1611. Pt 2 has title: *Belgische ofte nederlantsche oorloghen ende gheschiedenissen beginnende van t'jaer 1598 tot 1611.* Cf. Stokes (Manhattan) 256. MiU-C, NjP. 612/82

———. Niederländische Historien oder Geschichten aller deren Händel . . . biss auf das Jahr 1611 . . . gemehret und gebessert und . . . ubergesetzt. [*Arnhem: J. Janszoon*] 1612,'09. 3 pts; illus., ports, map; fol. 1st publ. in German, Hamburg, 1596; cf. years 1601 & 1610. Pt 2, *Niderlendischer Historien ander Theil,* has imprint dated 1609. MnU, NjP, OU. 612/83

More, Sir Thomas, Saint. De optimo reipublicae statu . . . Ordentliche und aussführliche Beschreibung der . . . Insul Utopia. *Leipzig: M. Lantzenberger, for H. Gross, the Younger,* 1612. 211 p.; 8vo. Transl. by Gregor Wintermonat from Latin text, 1st publ., Louvain, 1516; cf. 1601 edn. Gibson (More) 35; Shaaber (Brit. auth.) M239. CSt, CtY, ICN, MH: BL, Jena:UB. 612/84

Núñez Correa, Juan. Resolucion y resumen del estado en que se hallava el averia antes del assiento que se tomò con Juan Nuñez Correa, y de los daños y quiebra que del resultaron a la dicha hazienda . . . conforme a quatro relaciones particulares, que firmadas de los contadores Francisco de Salazar y Juan de Sologuren, se embiaron a los señores Duque de Lerma y Marques de Salinas, presidente de Indias. [*Madrid?* 1612?]. fol. Cf. memorials of Sologuren of this year. BL. 612/85

Orlers, Jan Janszn. Description & representation de toutes de victoires . . . souz la conduite et gouvernement de son excellence . . . Maurice de Nassau. *Leyden: J. J. Orlers & H. v. Haestens,* 1612. 282 p.; illus., port., maps; fol. Transl. from Orlers's *Beschrijvinghe . . . van alle de victorien,* 1st publ., Leyden, 1610. Molhuysen I:1392. DFo, MH, MiU, NN-RB; BL (Maurice), BN. 612/86

Ortelius, Abraham. Epitome theatri orbis terrarum . . . de novo recognita, aucta, et geographica ratione restaurata, a Michaele

Coigneto. *Antwerp: Plantin Office,* 1612. 147 lvs; maps; obl. 8vo. 1st publ. with Coignet's text, Antwerp, 1601. Koeman (Ort) 68A; Phillips (Atlases) 431 & 3414. DLC, InU-L; Antwerp:Plantin Mus. 612/87

———. Theatro del mondo . . . Traslato . . . dal sigr. Filippo Pigafetta. *Antwerp: Plantin Office,* 1612. 2 pts; maps, port.; fol. A reissue, with fresh t.p., of the Antwerp, 1608, Italian edn above. Sabin 57703n; Koeman (Ort) 42; Phillips (Atlases) 430; Michel (Répertoire) VI:42. CSmH, DLC, InU-L; BL, Antwerp:Plantin Mus., Bordeaux:BM. 612/88

———. Theatro d'el orbe de la tierra. *Antwerp: Plantin Office,* 1612. 3 pts; maps; fol. 1st publ. in Spanish, Antwerp, 1588. Includes also, in Latin texts as earlier publ., the author's *Parergon* & his *Nomenclator Ptolemaicus.* Koeman (Ort) 43; Peeters-Fontainas (Impr. esp.) 992; Palau 205365. ICN, NN-RB; BL, Madrid:BN. 612/89

———. Theatrum orbis terrarum. *Antwerp: Plantin Office,* 1612. 3 pts; maps; fol. 1st publ. in Latin, Antwerp, 1570. Includes, as issued, the author's *Parergon* & his *Nomenclator Ptolemaicus.* Cf. Sabin 57700; Koeman (Ort) 41; Phillips (Atlases) 5923. DLC, MiU-C; Oxford:Bodl., Brussels:BR. 612/90

Owen, John. Epigrammatum . . . libri tres . . . Editio quarta. *London: J. Legat, for S. Waterson,* 1612. 12mo. 1st publ., London, 1606. Also issued as pt 1 of the following. STC 18987. CSmH, CtY, DFo, ICN, MH, NjP; BL. 612/91

—[Anr issue]. Epigrammatum libri decem . . . Editio quarta. *London: N. Okes, for S. Waterson,* 1612. 3 pts; 12mo. A reissue of the above containing also, with general t.p., two further pts. STC 18988.5. DFo; Oxford:Bodl. 612/92

Panciroli, Guido. Raccolta breve d'alcune cose piu segnalate c'hebbero gli antichi, e d'alcune altre trovate da moderni . . . con l'aggiunta d'alcune considerationi curiose . . . di Flavio Gualtieri. *Venice: B. Giunta, G. B. Ciotti & Co.,* 1612. 443 p.; 4to. 1st publ. in Latin translation, Amberg, 1599–1602. Included are refs to Columbus & to tobacco. Michel (Répertoire) VI:69; Arents

103; JCB (3) II:87. ICU, InU-L, MH, NN-A, RPJCB; BL, BN.   612/93

——. Rerum memorabilium libri duo . . . latine redditi . . . ab Henrico Salmuth. Editio tertia. *Amberg: M. Forster,* 1612–17. 2 v.; 8vo. 1st publ., Amberg, 1599–1602; v. 2 has title *Nova reperta;* cf. 1602 edn above. Sabin 58411 (misdated 1812; & 58413n). MH, MnU-B, NN-RB, RPJCB; London: Wellcome (v. 2), BN.   612/94

Paré, Ambroise. Opera chirurgica. *Frankfurt a. M.:* [*N. Hoffmann, for*] *J. Fischer,* 1612. 1164 p.; illus., ports; fol. A reissue, with cancel t.p. & additional prelim. lvs of Peter Uffenbach's *Thesaurus chirurgiae* of 1610. Cf. the 1601 German edn. Doe (Paré) 50. MBCo; Vienna:UB, Wolfenbüttel:HB.   612/95

Peleus, Julien. Les questions illustres de m[aitre]. Julien Peleus . . . Edition quatriesme, reveue et augmentee. *Paris: N. Buon,* 1612. 943 p.; 4to. 1st publ., Paris, 1608. The intervening 2nd & 3rd edns have not been traced. ICN, RPJCB.   612/96

Pico della Mirandola, Giovanni Francesco. Strix, sive De ludificatione daemonum diologi tres, nunc primùm in Germania eruti. *Strassburg: P. Ledertz,* 1612. 160 p.; 8vo. 1st publ., Bologna, 1523. 'Navigatio Indica tam incredibilis quam iter ad ludum Dianae': p. 124. ICU, MB, NIC, RPJCB; BL, BN.   612/97

Pigray, Pierre. Epitome praeceptorum medicinae chirurgiae. *Paris: Widow of M. Orry,* 1612. 771 p.; 8vo. Transl. from Pigray's *Epitome des preceptes de medecine,* 1st publ., Paris, 1600; cf. 1604 edn. DNLM, NNNAM; BL, BN.   612/98

Puteo, Zaccharias. Clavis medica rationalis, spagyrica, et chyrurgica. *Venice: L. Aureati,* 1612,'11. 3 pts; illus.; 4to. Section viii discusses mechoacan ('Micciocanis radix'). Wellcome I:5301. DNLM, WU; BL, BN.   612/99

Raleigh, Sir Walter. Die fünffte kurtze wunderbare Beschreibung dess goldreichen Königreichs Guianae in America oder newen Welt. *Frankfurt a. M.: E. Kempfer, for Widow of L. Hulsius,* 1612. 17 p.; illus., map; 4to. (Levinus Hulsius's *Sammlung von . . . Schiffahrten.* Pt 5). 1st publ. in this version, Nuremberg, 1599; cf. year 1603. Sabin

67565 (& 33658); Baginsky (German Americana) 126; Shaaber (Brit. auth.) R18; Church 278. CSmH, NN-RB; BL, BN.   612/100

—[Anr issue]. *Frankfurt a. M.: E. Kempfer, for Widow of L. Hulsius,* 1612. Sabin 67565n; Baginsky (German Americana) 127; Church 279; JCB (3) I:456–57. CSmH, NN-RB, RPJCB.   612/101

—[Anr issue]. *Frankfurt a. M.: E. Kempfer, for Widow of L. Hulsius,* 1612. Sabin 67565n; Baginsky (German Americana) 129; Church 278b. NN-RB.   612/102

Rauw, Johann. Weltbeschreibung: das ist Ein schöne richtige und volkomliche Cosmographie dess gantzen Umbkreiss der weiten Welt. *Frankfurt a. M.:* 1612. 1031? p.; illus., maps; fol. 1st publ., Frankfurt, 1597, under title *Cosmographia, das ist Eine . . . Beschreibung . . . ;* here a reissue of that edn with cancel t.p.? The final chapt. describes the New World. Sabin 67978.   612/103

Recentes Novi Orbis historiae, hoc est, I. Inquisitio navigationis septentrionalis . . . II. Relatio super detectione novi ad Caurum transitus ad terras Americanas in Chinam atque Japonem ducturi. III. Memorialis libellus . . . Hispaniarum Regi oblatus super detectione quartae orbis terrarum partis . . . IIII. Rerum ab Hispanis in India Occidentali hactenus gestarum, libri tres. *Geneva: P. de La Rovière,* 1612. 480 p.; maps; 8vo. 1st publ. in Latin, Geneva, 1578, as transl. from Benzoni's *Historia del Mondo Nuovo,* 1st publ., Venice, 1565, with addition of an account of Henry Hudson's voyage derived from Hessel Gerritsz's *Descriptio ac delineatio geographica* of this year. Sabin 68346; Medina (BHA) 579; Streit II:1419; Shaaber (Brit. auth.) H471; JCB (3) II:81. CU-M, DLC, NN-RB, RPJCB; BL, BN.   612/104

Rich, Barnabe. A true and a kinde excuse . . . in defence of that booke, intituled A new description of Irelande. *London:* [*T. Dawson,*] *for T. Adams,* 1612. 25 numb. lvs; 4to. Includes passing mentions of tobacco. STC 21003; Arents (Add.) 157. CSmH, DFo, MH, NN-A, WU; BL.   612/105

A rich storehouse or treasurie for the diseased. First set foorth . . . by G. W. and

now fifthly augmented . . . by A. T. *London: R. Blower,* 1612. 176 (i.e., 146) numb. lvs; 4to. 1st publ., London, 1596; cf. 1601 edn. STC 23608. CtY, MH, NNNAM; BL.
612/106

Rivadeneira, Pedro de, S.J. Vita beati patris Ignatii . . . A p. Gaspare Quartemont . . . latine conversa. *Ypres: F. Bellet,* 1612. 212 p.; port.; 12mo. Transl. from author's *Vida del p. Ignacio de Loyola,* 1st publ. in Spanish, Madrid, 1583. Includes refs to Jesuits in Brazil. Cf. Sabin 70783. MoSU-D; BL, BN.
612/107

—[Anr edn]. *Paris:* 1612. 4to. Sabin 70783.
612/108

Röslin, Elisaeus. Praematurae solis apparitionis in Nova Zembla . . . cum accurata instructione navigationis septentrionalis ad Indias Orientales. *Strassburg: K. Kieffer,* 1612. 12 lvs; map; 4to. On verso of t.p. is a map of the Arctic including parts of Greenland & North America. Discusses Northwest Passage. Sabin 73295. NN-RB; BL.
612/109

Rowlands, Samuel. The knave of clubbes. *London: E. A[llde].,* 161[2?]. 4to. In verse. 1st publ., London, 1600, under title *A merry meeting;* cf. year 1609. STC 21389. BL, Oxford:Bodl.
612/110

——. The knave of harts. Haile fellow well met. *London: T.S[nodham].; sold by G. Loftus,* 1612. 4to. In verse. 'A lying knave' mentions West Indies; 'A prodigall knave', tobacco. STC 21390. CSmH; Oxford:Bodl.
612/111

—[Anr. edn]. *London: [T. Snodham], for J. Bache,* 1612. STC 21390.5. Robt S. Pirie.
612/112

Salazar, Ambrosio de. Almoneda general de las mas curiosas recopilaciones de los reynos de España. *Paris: A. DuBreuil,* 1612. 210 numb. lvs; 8vo. Includes account of income derived from Indies by king of Spain. Palau 286462. DFo, NNH, WU; BL, BN.
612/113

——. Inventaire general des plus curieuses recherches des royaumes d'Espagne. *Paris: A. DuBreuil,* 1612. 178 numb. lvs; 8vo. Transl. by the author from the preceding item. Sabin 75557; Palau 286463. DFo, PU; BL, BN.
612/114

Salazar, Pedro de, O.F.M. Coronica y histo-ria de la fundacion y progresso de la provincia de Castilla, de la Orden del . . . padre san Francisco. *Madrid: J. Flamenco, for the Imprenta Real,* 1622 [i.e., 1612]. 546 p.; fol. Includes accounts of Franciscan missions in Indies & martyrdom of Diego de Landa in Yucatan. Medina (BHA) 585; Streit I:328; Pérez Pastor (Madrid) 1202; Palau 286714. Madrid:BU, Rome:BN.
612/115

Satyre Ménippée. Satyre Menippée de la vertu du Catholicon d'Espagne. *[Paris?]* 1612. [360] p.; illus.; 12mo. 1st publ. with added 'Discours . . . du mot de Higuiero d'infierno', Paris, 1594; cf. 1604 edn. CtY; BL (imp.).
612/116

Scaliger, Julius Caesar. Exotericarum exercitationum liber quintus decimus. *Frankfurt a. M.: [Wechel Office, for] Heirs of C. Marne, J. & A. Marne,* 1612. 1129 p.; illus.; 8vo. 1st publ., Paris, 1557; cf. 1601 edn. Wellcome I:5807. CU, DFo, MB, MnU-B, NNC, NcU; BL, BN.
612/117

Schmidel, Ulrich. Vierdte Schiffart; warhafftige Historien einer wunderbaren Schiffart . . . von Anno 1534 biss Anno 1554 in Americam oder Neuwewelt, bey Brasilia und Rio della Plata gethan . . . editio tertia. *Frankfurt a. M.: E. Kempfer, for Widow of L. Hulsius,* 1612. 104 p.; illus., maps, port.; 4to. (Levinus Hulsius's *Sammlung von . . . Schifffahrten.* Pt 4). 1st publ., Frankfurt a. M., 1567; cf. year 1602. Sabin 77682 (& 33656); Palmer 340; Church 273; JCB (3) I:454. CSmH, CtY, ICN, MB, NN-RB, RPJCB, ViU; BL, BN.
612/118

Smith, Capt. John. A map of Virginia. With a description of the countrey. *Oxford: J. Barnes,* 1612. 2 pts; map; 4to. The 2nd pt comprises William Symonds's *The proceedings of the English colonie.* For varying dedicatees, see the STC; for varying states of the map, see Sabin. Sabin 82832; Baer (Md) 1; Clayton-Torrence 19; Vail (Frontier) 33; STC 22791; Madan (Oxford) 1612:19–20; Arents 3275; Church 359; JCB (3) II:88. CSmH, CtY, DLC, ICN, InU-L, MH, MiU-C, NN-RB, PP, RPJCB; BL.
612/119

Sologuren, Juan de. Señor. Diferentes ministros han representado a V. Magestad los daños que la hazienda de averias recibe de la mucha que los Generales de la armada de galeones, y de las flotas gastan en las

Indias [etc.]. [*Madrid?* 1612?]. 5 numb. lvs; fol. Sabin 86508. BL.   612/120

——. Señor. Los sueldos y salarios ordinarios y tributos que la Avena paga en cada un año. [*Madrid?* 1612?]. 13 numb. lvs; fol. Memorial to king of Spain on naval affairs of Spanish Indies. Sabin 86509; Palau 318929. BL.   612/121

Spain. Casa de Contratación de las Indias. Relacion de las obligaciones que tiene el Contador de la Casa de la Contratacion de las Indias. [*Seville?* 1612?]. 12 numb. lvs; fol. Issued by Antonio López de Calatayd. Medina (BHA) 583. BL (López de Calatayd, A.).   612/122

Spenser, Edmund. The faerie queene. *London: H.L[ownes]., for M. Lownes,* 1611 [i.e., 1612]. 363 p.; fol. 1st publ., London, 1590; cf. 1609 edn. Anr issue of 1609 edn with subsidiary t.p. dated 1612. STC 23083.7. DFo, ICN, MB; Oxford:Bodl.   612/123

Strachey, William. For the colony in Virginea Britannia. Laws divine, morall and martiall. *London: [W. Stansby,] for W. Burre,* 1612. 89 p.; 4to. For variant dedicatory lvs, see the STC & Sabin. Sabin 99866; Clayton-Torrence 20; STC 23350; JCB (3) II:90. CSmH, DFo, MHi, PPL, RPJCB; BL.
612/124

Sweerts, Emanuel. Florilegium . . . tractans de variis floribus et aliis Indicis plantis. *Frankfurt a. M.: A. Kempner,* 1612–14. 2 v.; illus.; fol. Included are American plants. Pritzel 9073; Nissen (Bot.) 1920; Hunt (Bot.) 196; Arents (Add.) 158. DLC, MH-A, MoSB, NN-A; BL, BN.   612/125

Tassoni, Alessandro. Varietà di pensieri . . . divisa in ix parti. *Modena: Heirs of G. M. Verdi,* 1612. 592 p.; 4to. Bk 5, chapt. vi, mentions decline of male population in Spain 'per le navigazioni dell'Indie'. Pugliatti (Tassoni) 2. ICN; BL, BN.
612/126

Taylor, John, the Water-poet. Laugh, and be fat. [*London: W. Hall? for H. Gosson?* 1612]. 46 + p.; 8vo. In verse. In poem addressed to John Donne, tobacco is mentioned. STC 23769. BL (imp.).
612/127

——. The sculler, rowing from Tiber to Thames. *London: E. A[llde].; sold by [N. But-*

ter], 1612. 24 lvs; 4to. In verse. Epigram 32 cites the potato; tobacco is also mentioned. A 1614 edn has title *Taylors waterworke.* STC 23791. CSmH, MH; Oxford: Bodl. (imp.).   612/128

Thoelde, Johann. Haliographia, das ist, Gründliche und eigendliche Beschreibung aller Saltz Mineralien. *Leipzig: J. Apel,* 1612. 336 p.; 8vo. 1st publ., Eisleben, 1603. PPC; BL (imp.).   612/129

Thompson, Thomas. A diet for a drunkard. Delivered in two sermons in Bristoll, 1608. *London: [W. Stansby,] for R. Bankworth,* 1612. 82 p.; 4to. In 2nd sermon tobacco & its American origin are discussed (p. 58–59). STC 24027; Arents 103-A. CSmH, CtY, DFo, MWA, NN-A; BL.   612/130

Torquemada, Antonio de. Giardino di fiori curiosi. *Venice: P. Bertano,* 1612. 198 numb. lvs; 8vo. 1st publ. in Spanish, Salamanca, 1570, as here transl. by Celio Malespina, Venice, 1604, q.v. Palau 334924.
612/131

—[Anr edn]. *Venice: P. Bertano,* 1612. 182 numb. lvs; 8vo. Palau 334925. MB.
612/132

Urdiñola, Francisco de. Francisco de Urdinola, governador y capitan general de la Nueva Vizcaya por su Magestad, y teniente de capitan general por el Virrey de la Nueva España, del reyno de la Nueva Galicia. [*Madrid?* 1612?]. 7 lvs; fol. Memorial on writer's services in New Mexico. Sabin 98121; Medina (BHA) 6924; Wagner (SW) 15. Seville:Archivo de Indias.   612/133

Valderrama, Pedro de. Teatro de las religiones. *Seville: L. de Estupiñán,* 1612. 743 p.; fol. The birth in Brazil of a monster from intercourse of woman with an incubus is mentioned. Escudero (Seville) 967; Palau 347320. DLC; Seville:BP.   612/134

Vaughan, William. Approved directions for health, both naturall and artificiall . . . Newly corrected and augmented . . . The fourth edition. *London: T. S[nodham]., for Roger Jackson,* 1612. 150 p.; 8vo. 1st publ., London, 1600, under title *Naturall and artificial directions for health;* here a reissue with altered imprint date of 1611 edn. STC 24615. DFo; London:Wellcome.
612/135

Veer, Gerrit de. Dritter Theil, warhafftiger Relation der dreyen newen unerhörten seltzamen Schifffahrt . . . tertio editio. *Frankfurt a. M.: E. Kempfer, for Widow of L. Hulsius,* 1612. 95 p.; illus., maps; 4to. (Levinus Hulsius's *Sammlung von . . . Schiffahrten.* Pt 3). 1st publ. in this version, Nuremberg, 1598; cf. the year 1602. Sabin 33655; Baginsky (German Americana) 130; Church 269; JCB (3) I:453. CSmH, ICN, NN-RB, RPJCB, ViU; BL, BN. 612/136

Vega Carpio, Lope Félix de. Arcadia, prosas y versos. *Lérida: J. Margarit & L. Menescal, for M. Menescal,* 1612. 270 numb. lvs; 12mo. 1st publ., Madrid, 1598; cf. 1602 edns. Palau 356299. NNH; BN. 612/137

Villagrá, Gaspar Pérez de. El capitan Gaspar de Villagra para justificacion de las muertes, justicias, y castigos que el adelantado don Juan de Oñate dizen que hizo en la Nueva Mexico, como uno de sus soldados. [*Madrid?* 1612?]. 5 numb. lvs; fol. Sabin 99368; Medina (BHA) 6979; Wagner (SW) 16; JCB AR40:16–17. RPJCB. 612/138

—[Anr edn]. [*Madrid?* 1612?]. 6 numb. lvs; fol. Sabin 99369; Wagner (SW) 16. CSmH. 612/139

Vives, Juan Luis. Libri xii de disciplinis. [*London: W. Stansby*] 1612. 392 p.; 8vo. 1st publ., Antwerp, 1531. Includes ref. to P. M. d'Anghiera's writings on New World. Here, contents appear on verso of t.p. STC 24852. DFo; BL, Oxford:Bodl. 612/140

—[Anr issue]. [*London: W. Stansby*] 1612. Here, verso of t.p. is blank. STC 24852.3. London:Westminster School, Oxford:Bodl. 612/141

1613

Aldrovandi, Ulisse. De piscibus libri v. et de cetis lib. unus. *Bologna: G. B. Bellagamba, for G. Tamburini,* 1613. 732 p.; illus.; fol. 1st publ., Bologna, 1612; here a reissue with altered imprint date & with error in paging corrected. Nissen (Zool.) 70. CLU-C, DLC, ICJ, MH, MiU, MnU, NN-RB, PPAN; BL, BN. 613/1

Arsène de Paris, O.F.M. Cap. Derniere lettre du pere Arsene de Paris. au r. p. provincial des Capucins de . . . Paris. [*Paris:* 1613]. 7 p.; 8vo. Dated at end: Isle de Maragnon . . . 27 aoust, 1612. Borba de Moraes I:41; JCB (3) II:91. RPJCB. 613/2

—[Anr edn]. Derniere lettre du reverend pere Arsene de Paris estant de present en l'Inde Occidentale, en la coste du Bresil, en une isle appellé Marignon. *Paris: J. Nigaut,* 1613. 15 p.; 8vo. Borba de Moraes I:41; Streit II:2371. NN-RB; BN. 613/3

Aventrote, Juan. Sendbrief van Joan Aventroot tot den . . . Coninck van Spaengien. *Amsterdam: P. van Ravesteyn,* 1613. 54 p.; 8vo. Preface includes ref. to misery of workers in Indian [i.e., Peruvian] silver mines. Millares Carlo (Avontroot) 1; Molhuysen I:200–201; Knuttel 2035. The Hague:KB; Ghent:BU. 613/4

Avity, Pierre d', sieur de Montmartin. Les estats, empires et principautez du monde. *Paris: P. Chevalier,* 1613. 1396 p.; 4to. Includes section describing America. Cf. Sabin 2498. Munich:StB. 613/5

—[Anr issue]. *Paris: O. de Varennes,* 1613. NN-RB; Vienna:NB. 613/6

Bacon, Francis, viscount St Albans. The essaies. *London: [W. Jaggard,] for J. Jaggard,* 1613. 114 lvs; 8vo. 1st publ. with 'Of atheism', London, 1612. In this edn the t.p. has reading 'Atturny'. Gibson (Bacon) 8; STC 1142. CSmH, CtY, DFo, MH; BL. 613/7

—[Anr edn]. *London: [W. Jaggard,] for J. Jaggard,* 1613. 114 lvs; 8vo. This edn has reading 'Aturney'. Gibson (Bacon) 9; STC 1143; Pforzheimer 29. CSmH, DFo, MH, NNPM; BL. 613/8

—[Anr edn]. *London: [W. Jaggard,] for J. Jaggard,* 1613. 114 lvs; 8vo. This edn has reading 'Atturney'. Gibson (Bacon) 10; STC 1144. CSmH, DFo, NNPM; BL. 613/9

Barclay, John. Euphormionis Lusinini Satyricon. [*Frankfurt a. M.?*], 1613–15. 4 pts; 8vo. Includes pt 2, 1st publ., Paris, 1607, & pt 4, the *Icon animorum,* 1st publ., London, 1614. Shaaber B183 (&, pt 4, B165); Tchémerzine I:445. DFo (pt 4), NjPT (pt 4); Berlin:StB, Munich:StB, Wolfenbüttel:HB. 613/10

——. Euphormionis Lusinini Satyricon: pars ii. Nunc secundùm in lucem edita. [*Paris?*

F. Huby?] 1613. 240 p.; 12mo. 1st publ., Paris, 1607. Shaaber B159; Tchémerzine I:442. DFo; BL, BN.   613/11

Bauhin, Kaspar. De lapidis bezaar Orientalis et Occidentalis cervini. *Basel: C. Waldkirch,* 1613. 288 p.; illus.; 8vo. 'De lapide bezaar Occidentali sive Peruviano': chapt. xxxiix; 'De vicunnas [i.e., llamas] et teraguas in Peru': chapt. xxxix. CtY-M, DNLM, ICJ, MH, NN, PPC; BL, BN.   613/12

Beaumont, Francis. The knight of the burning pestle. *London: W. Burre,* 1613. 4to. Comedy, written jointly with John Fletcher. Included are refs to tobacco. STC 1674; Greg 316(a). CSmH, DFo, MH; BL.
                                               613/13

Benzoni, Girolamo. Americae, das fünffte Buch, vol schöner unerhörter Historien, auss dem andern Theil . . . gezogen: von der Spanier Wüten beyd wider ihre Knecht die Nigriten, unnd auch die arme Indianer . . . Sampt kurtzer und nützlicher Erklärung der Historien bey jedem Capitel. *Frankfurt a. M.: E. Kempfer,* 1613. 115 p.; illus., map; fol. (Theodor de Bry's *America.* Pt 5. German). 1st publ. in this version, Frankfurt, 1595; 1st publ. in this translation by Nicolaus Höniger as bk 2 of the Basel, 1579, *Der Newen Weldt . . . History* but here suppl. by annotations supplied by Urbain Chauveton in the Basel, 1598, Latin *Novae Novi Mundi historiae,* 1st transl. 1595; cf. earlier pt (bk 1) of 1594. Cf. Sabin 8784; Baginsky (German Americana) 131; Church 187; JCB (3) I:396. CSmH, NN-RB, RPJCB; BL.
                                               613/14

——. Das vierdte Buch von der neuwen Welt, oder Neuwe und gründtliche Historien von dem Nidergängischen Indien . . . Mit nützlichen Scholien und Ausslegungen fast auf jede Kapitel. *Frankfurt a. M.: Widow of M. Becker, for J. T. de Bry,* 1613. 141 p.; illus., map; fol. (Theodor de Bry's *America.* Pt 4. German). 1st publ. in this version, Frankfurt, 1594; 1st publ. in this translation by Nicolaus Höniger as bk 1 of the Basel, 1579, *Der Newen Weldt . . . History* but here suppl. by annotations supplied by Urbain Chauveton in the Basel, 1578, Latin *Novae Novi Mundi historiae,* 1st publ., 1594. Cf. Sabin 8784; Palmer 298; Church 184; JCB (3)

I:394. CSmH, ICN, NN-RB, RPJCB; BL, BN.   613/15

——[Anr state]. *Frankfurt a. M.: Widow of M. Becker, for J. T. de Bry,* 1613. Headpiece of 1st *Vorrede* depicts Noah's sacrifice, rather than Columbus. Church 185. CSmH, NN-RB.   613/16

Besler, Basilius. Hortus Eystettensis, sive Diligens et accurata omnium plantarum . . . que in . . . arcem episcopalem . . . conspiciuntur delineatio. [*Nuremberg:*] 1613. 2 v.; illus., port.; fol. Included are American plants, e.g., 'Alcea americana', 'Solanum americanum', etc. Pritzel 745; Nissen (Bot.) 158. DLC, MH-A, MiU, MnU, NN-RB, PPAmP, RPB; BL, BN.
                                               613/17

Blaeu, Willem Janszoon. Het licht der zeevaert. *Amsterdam: W. J. Blaeu,* 1613. 2 v.; illus., maps; obl. fol. 1st publ., Amsterdam, 1608. Koeman (M.Bl) 3. Amsterdam: NHSM, Rotterdam:Mar. Mus.   613/18

Blundeville, Thomas. M. Blundeville his Exercises . . . The fourth edition corrected and augmented. *London: W. Stansby,* 1613. 799 p.; illus., map; 4to. 1st publ., London, 1594; cf. 1606 edn. Also included is John Blagrave's *A very brief . . . description of Master Blagrave his Astrolabe,* 1st publ., London, 1585. Cf. Sabin 6023; STC 3149. CSmH, DFo, IU, MB, NN-RB; BL.   613/19

Boccalini, Traiano. De' ragguagli di Parnaso . . . Centuria prima. *Milan: Heirs of P. M. Locarno & G. B. Bidelli,* 1613. 452 p.; 8vo. 1st publ., Venice, 1612. Firpo (Ragguagli) 3; Michel (Répertoire) I:175. IMunS; BL, BN.   613/20

——. De' ragguagli di Parnaso . . . Centuria seconda. *Venice: B. Barezzi,* 1613. 453 p.; 4to. Continues the Centuria prima, Venice, 1612. In Ragguaglio iv the prestige of Spain is said to be due not to riches derived from New World; in Ragguaglio xxiii, named & discussed are famous navigators, amongst them Columbus, Vespucci, & Magellan; Ragguaglio xc discusses 'Cristofano Colombo e altri scopritori del mondo nuovo'. Firpo (Ragguagli) 5; Michel (Répertoire) I:175. DFo, ICN, NIC; BL, Paris:Arsenal.
                                               613/21

Breton, Nicholas. Wits private wealth. *Lon-*

don: *E. Allde, for J. Tapp,* 1613. 4to. 1st publ.,
London, 1612. STC 3709. CSmH.
                                        613/22

Camões, Luiz de. Os Lusiados . . . Com-
mentados pelo licendiado Manoel Correa.
Lisbon: P. Craesbeeck, for D. Fernandes, 1613.
308 numb. lvs; 4to. In verse. Text 1st publ.,
Lisbon, 1572. In addition to brief refs to
America (cf. 1609 edn above) Correa's commentary includes (lf 4r) an account of discovery of New World; on lf 53v is a ref.
to Magellan's voyage; elsewhere scattered
refs occur. In this issue the Portuguese coat
of arms appears on the t.p. Silva (Camões)
18. CtY, InU-L, MH, MiU-C, NNH, RPJCB;
BL, Lisbon:BN.   613/23
—[Anr issue]. *Lisbon: P. Crasbeeck, for D. Fernandes,* 1613. On t.p. is a vignette with ini-
tials 'D.F.D.F.'. Silva (Camões) 18. MH;
Lisbon:BN.   613/24

Canale, Floriano. De' secreti universali raccolti et sperimentati. *Brescia: B. Fontana,*
1613. 269 p.; illus.; 8vo. 'Descrittione del
Mechiocan', citing Mexican origin: p. 184–
87; 'Del Tabacco, ò herba regina': p. 189–
92; elsewhere use of guaiacum for treatment of syphilis is described. DLC, DNLM,
NcU; London:Wellcome.   613/25
—[Anr edn]. *Venice: P. Bertano,* 1613. 266 p.;
8vo. Michel (Répertoire) II:29. DNLM;
Paris:Ste Geneviève.   613/26

Canoniero, Pietro Andrea. Flores illustrium
epitaphiorum, ex praeclarissimarum totius
Europae civitatum et praestantissimorum
poëtarum monumentis. *Antwerp: J. Trognaesius,* 1613. 544 p.; 8vo. Includes epitaphs
on Columbus. Sabin 24830. MH, OrU; BL,
BN.   613/27

Casas, Bartolomé de las, O.P., Bp of Chiapa.
Warhafftiger und gründlicher Bericht, der
Hispanier grewlich: und abschewlichen
Tyranney von ihnen in den West Indien
die newe Welt genant begangen . . . uber-
gesezt. *Oppenheim: J. T. de Bry,* 1613. 178
p.; illus.; 4to. 1st publ. in this version,
Frankfurt a. M., 1597. Sabin 11280; Medina
(BHA) 1085n (II:479); Hanke/Giménez
507; Baginsky (German Americana) 133;
Streit I:332; JCB (3) II:93. N, NN, RPJCB;
Munich:StB.   613/28

Cervantes Saavedra, Miguel de. Novelas ex-

emplares. *Madrid: J. de la Cuesta, for F. de
Robles,* 1613. 274 numb. lvs; 4to. 'El licenciado Vidriera' mentions Columbus &
Cortés. In 'El celoso extremeño' the New
World is described as a refuge for the crimi-
nal & the incompetent. 'La española in-
glesa' also refers to the Indies in similar
terms. Ríus (Cervantes) 219; Palau 53399.
MH, NNH, PPRF; BL.   613/29

Champlain, Samuel de. Les voyages du sieur
de Champlain . . . ou, Journal tres-fidele
des observations faites és descouvertes de
la Nouvelle France. *Paris: J. Berjon,* 1613.
325 p.; illus., maps; 4to. Sabin 11835; Harrisse (NF) 27; Church 360; Lande 116; JCB
(3) II:93. CSmH, DLC, ICN, InU-L, MH,
MiU-C, MnU-B, NN-RB, RPJCB; BL, BN.
                                      613/30

Chapman, George. The memorable maske
of the two honorable houses or Inns of
Court . . . performd before the King . . .
15. of February. 1613. *London: G. Eld, for
G. Norton* [1613]. [97] p.; 4to. Described
are masquers garbed as Indian princes; the
text of the masque refers to them. Inigo
Jones's original designs for the costumes
are preserved at Chatsworth. Greg 310(b);
STC 4981. CSmH, DFo, IU, MH, NNPM,
RPJCB; BL.   613/31
—[Anr edn]. *London: F. K[ingston]., for G. Norton* [1613?]. [52] p.; 4to. Greg 310(a); STC
4982. CSmH, CtY, MH.   613/32

Claude d'Abbeville, O.F.M. Cap. Die An-
kunfft der Vätter Capuciner Ordens in die
newe Indien Maragnon genannt . . . Auss
der Frantzösischen . . . durch ein S. Fran-
cisci Ordens Liebhaber ubersetzt. *Augsburg:
C. Dabertzhofer,* 1613. 10 p.; 4to. 1st publ.
in French, Paris, 1612; here transl. from
J. Nigaut's Paris edn of this year. Borba de
Moraes I:3; Streit II:2373; JCB (3) II:91.
NN-RB, RPJCB; Munich:UB.   613/33
——. L'arrivee des peres Capucins en l'Inde
Nouvelle, appellée Maragnan. *Lyons: G.
Pailly,* 1613. 16 p.; 8vo. 1st publ., Paris,
1612. Sabin 13505; Borba de Moraes I:1–
2; Streit II:2372; JCB (3) II:91. NN-RB,
RPJCB.   613/34
—[Anr edn]. L'arrivee des peres Capucins,
& la conversion des sauvages. *Paris: J. Ni-
gaut,* 1613. 16 p.; 8vo. Sabin 5; Borba de

Moraes I:1; cf. Streit II:2370; JCB (3) II:91.
NN-RB, RPJCB; BN. 613/35
—[Anr edn]. *Paris: J. Nigaut,* 1613. 15 p.; 8vo.
BN. 613/36
—[Anr edn]. Discours et congratulation à la
France sur l'arrivée des peres Capucins en
l'Inde nouvelle. *Paris: D. Langlois,* 1613. 32
p.; 8vo. Borba de Moraes I:3–4; Streit
II:2375; JCB (3) II:91–92. MnU-B, NN-RB,
RPJCB. 613/37
—[Anr edn of preceding]. *Tournon: C. Michel,*
1613. 32 p.; 8vo. Borba de Moraes I:3–4;
Maggs Cat. 797 no. 2333. (Voyages & Trav-
els III pt 5). 613/38
——. [Relatione del viaggio, e sbaracamento
d'alcuni padri capuccini francesi nell' India
nuova chiamata Maragona, volgarizata so-
pra l'originale francese, stampato in Lione.
Bergamo: C. Ventura, 1613.] As indicated by
title, transl. from Pailly's Lyons edn of this
year described above. Of this edn no copy
is known; its existence is inferred from the
Treviso edn described below. Borba de
Moraes I:2n. 613/39
—[Anr edn]. *Treviso: A. Reghettini,* 1613. [8]
p.; 8vo. The imprint describes this as reprinted from the Bergamo edn above.
Borba de Moraes I:2; JCB AR52:26–31.
RPJCB. 613/40
Conestaggio, Girolamo Franchi di. L'union
du royaume de Portugal à la couronne de
Castille . . . prise de l'italien . . . par m.
Th. Nardin. *Arras: G. Bauduin,* 1613. 591
p.; 8vo. 1st publ. as here transl., Besançon,
1596; cf. 1601 edn. Palau 313379. BN.
613/41
Cortés, Jerónimo. Quinta, y ultima impression de la Phisonomia natural, y varios secretos de naturaleza . . . Revisto, y
mejorado por el mismo autor. *Valencia:
Widow of the author,* 1613. 256 p.; 8vo. 1st
publ., Valencia, 1597; cf. 1601 edn. NNC.
613/42
Dekker, Thomas. A strange horse-race . . .
The bankrouts banquet. *London: J. Hunt,*
1613. [51] p.; 4to. 'The bankrouts banquet'
mentions the Bermudas. STC 6528. CSmH,
DFo, ICU, MH; BL. 613/43
Deliciae lusitano-hispanicae: in quibus continentur De magnitudine Hispanici imperii
relatio: Novi orbis regionum à Lusitanis

subactarum brevis descriptio. *Cologne: G.
Greuenbruch,* 1613. 346 p.; 8vo. Borba de
Moraes II:199; Palau 262169; JCB (3) II:99.
DLC, RPJCB; BL. 613/44
Doglioni, Giovanni Nicolò. Le théâtre uni-
versel des princes, ou Histoire générale.
Paris: F. Huby, 1613. 2 v.; 4to. Transl. from
the author's *Del theatro universale de' prencipi,*
1st publ., Venice, 1606. MnU. 613/45
—[Anr edn]. *Paris: J. Gesselin,* 1613. 2 v.; 4to.
BN. 613/46
Donati, Marcello. De historia medica mira-
bili libri sex. Iam primum in Germania editi,
ab . . . opera . . . Gregor Horsti. *Frankfurt
a. M.: E. Kempfer, for J. J. Porsch,* 1613. 715
p.; 8vo. 1st publ., Mantua, 1588, under title
De medica historia mirabili. In bk 3, chapt. x
includes discussion of guaiacum. Wellcome
I:1839. CtY-M, DNLM, ICJ, N, PPL; BL,
BN. 613/47
Drayton, Michael. A chorographicall de-
scription of Great Britain. *London: [H.
Lownes,] for M. Lownes, J. Browne, J. Helme,
J. Busby,* 1613. 2 pts; illus., maps, port.; fol.
In verse. 1st publ., London, [1612], under
title *Poly-Olbion;* here a reissue with altered
t.p. STC 7228. CSmH, CtY, DFo, ICN, MH;
BL. 613/48
——. Poems . . . Collected into one volume.
London: W. Stansby, for J. Smethwick, 1613.
3 pts; 8vo. 1st publ., London, 1605. STC
7221; Pforzheimer 305. CSmH, CtY, DFo,
ICN, MH, NNC, PPRF; BL. 613/49
——. Poly-Olbion. *London: [H. Lownes,] for
M. Lownes, J. Browne, J. Helme, J. Busby,* 1613.
2 pts; illus., maps, port.; fol. In verse. 1st
publ., London, [1612]; here a reissue with
printed t.p. & with a dated imprint. STC
7227; Grolier Club (Langland to Wither)
83; Arents 104. CSmH, CtY, DFo, ICN,
MH, NN-RB; BL. 613/50
Du Bartas, Guillaume de Salluste, seigneur.
Du Bartas his devine weekes and workes
translated by . . . Josuah Sylvester . . .
Now fourthly corr: & augmented. *London:
H. Lownes,* 1613. 813 p.; illus., port.; 4to.
In verse. 1st publ. as here transl., London,
1605. STC 21652 (incl. 7291). CSmH, CtY,
DLC, ICN, MH, NN-RB; BL. 613/51
——. La divina settimana, cioè I sette giorni
della creazione del mondo . . . tradotta . . .

in verso sciolto italiano, dal sig. Ferrante Guisone. *Venice: G. B. Ciotti,* 1613. 122 numb. lvs; illus.; 12mo. Transl. from author's *La seconde sepmaine,* 1st publ., Paris, 1584; 1st publ. in Italian, Tours, 1592; cf. year 1601. Holmes (DuBartas) I:109 no. 19n; Michel (Répertoire) II:186. CU; Paris:Arsenal. 613/52

Duchesne, Joseph. Liber de priscorum philosophorum verae medicinae materia. *Leipzig: T. Schürer & B. Voigt,* 1613. 480 p.; 8vo. 1st publ., St Gervais, 1603. DNLM, WyU. 613/53

——. Pharmacopoea dogmaticorum restituta. *Leipzig: Heirs of M. Lantzenberger, for T. Schürer & B. Voigt,* 1613. 745 p.; 8vo. 1st publ., Paris, 1607. London:Wellcome. 613/54

Dupleix, Scipion. La curiosite naturelle. *Paris: F. Gueffier,* 1613. 312 p.; 12mo. 1st publ., Paris, 1606. CU. 613/55

Duport, François. Medica decas. *Paris: F. Jacquin, for M. Mondière,* 1613. 462 p.; 4to. In verse. 1st publ., Paris, 1584, under title *De signis morborum libri quatuor.* Therapeutic uses of guaiacum & sarsaparilla are discussed. DLC, DNLM; London:Wellcome, BN. 613/56

—[Anr issue]. *Paris: F. Jacquin, for A. Saugrain,* 1613. DNLM, ICN; BN. 613/57

Duret, Claude. Thresor de l'histoire des langues de cest univers. *Cologny: M. Bérion, for the Société Caldorienne,* 1613. 1030 p.; 4to. Includes accounts of West Indian & Canadian native languages. Cf. Sabin 21420. CLU, CtY, DLC, IEN, InU-L, MnU-B, NN-RB; BL, BN. 613/58

Estienne, Charles. L'agriculture et maison rustique. *Rouen: J. Osmont,* 1613. 672 p.; illus.; 4to. 1st publ. in this version, Paris, 1567; cf. 1601 edn. MH. 613/59

Fontaine, Jacques. Opera in quibus universae artis medicae secundum Hippocratis et Galeni doctrinam partes quatuor methodice explicantur. *Geneva: P. & J. Chouët,* 1613. 3 pts; 4to. 1st publ., Paris, 1612. Wellcome I:2348. London:Wellcome. 613/60

—[Anr issue]. *Cologny: P. & J. Chouët,* 1613. BN. 613/61

Gaultier, Jacques, S.J. Table chronologique de l'estat du christianisme . . . jusques à

l'année MDXII. *Lyons: J. Roussin,* 1613. 610 p.; fol. 1st publ., Lyons, 1609. Cf. Backer III:1274; Cioranescu (XVII) 32620. BL, BN. 613/62

Gerritsz, Hessel, ed. Descriptio ac delineatio geographica detectionis freti. *Amsterdam: H. Gerritsz,* 1613. [44] p.; illus., maps; 4to. 1st publ., Amsterdam, 1612; here a new translation. Sabin 33491; Tiele 374; Tiele-Muller 153; Church 354n. CtY, ICN, MH, MiU-C, NN-RB, ViU; BL, BN. 613/63

—[Anr edn]. *Amsterdam: H. Gerritsz,* 1613. The preceding, with supplementary 4p. Sabin 33491n; Tiele 374n; Tiele-Muller 154; JCB (3) II:95–96. RPJCB; BL. 613/64

——. Histoire du pays nomme Spitsberghe . . . La triste racompte des maux, que noz pecheurs, tant Basques que Flamens, ont eu a souffrir des Anglois, en l'esté passée. *Amsterdam: [H. Gerritsz]* 1613. 30 p.; illus., map; 4to. Sabin 32028; Tiele-Muller 158; Knuttel 2053; JCB (3) II:94. CtY, MnU-B, NN-RB, RPJCB; BL, The Hague:KB. 613/65

——, ed. Indiae Orientalis pars X. Qua continetur, Historica relatio sive Descriptio novi ad aquilonem transitus, supra terras americanas in Chinam atq; Japonem ducturi, quemadmodum is ab Henrico Hudsono Anglo nuper inventus . . . Item discursus ad Sereniss. Hispaniae Regem . . . à Capitaneo . . . de Quir. *Frankfurt a. M.: Widow of M. Becker,* 1613. 32 p.; illus., maps; fol. (J. T. de Bry's *India Orientalis.* Pt 10. Latin). Largely a reprint of the author's *Descriptio ac delineatio geographica detectionis freti,* 1st publ., Amsterdam, 1612. Includes extract from Linschoten's northern voyages, without Americana. Cf. Tiele-Muller 149–54; Brunet I:1341; Church 222; JCB (3) I:441–42. CSmH, DLC, ICN, MB, NN-RB, RPJCB; BL, BN. 613/66

——, ed. Zehender Theil der Orientalischen Indien, begreiffend eine kurtze Beschreibung der neuwen Schiffart gegan Nordt Osten uber die Amerische Inseln in Chinam und Iapponiam, von . . . Henrich Hudson newlich erfunden . . . Item ein Discurs an Ihr. Kön. Maj. in Spanien, wegen dess fünfften Theils der Welt . . . von . . . de Quir. . . . *Frankfurt a. M.: Widow of M.*

Becker, 1613. 37 p.; illus., maps; fol. (J. T. de Bry's *India Orientalis.* Pt 10. German). Transl. from author's *Descriptio ac delineatio geographica detectionis freti,* Amsterdam, 1612; 1st publ. in Dutch, Amsterdam, 1612; here enlarged to include extract from Linschoten's northern voyages. Cf. Tiele-Muller 149–54; Brunet I:1360; Shaaber (Brit. auth.) H474; Church 242; JCB (3) I:442. CSmH, CtY, DLC, NN-RB, PPAmP, RPJCB; BL, BN.   613/67

Goulart, Simon. Schatzkammer uber naturlicher, wunderbarer und woldenckwurdiger Geschichten. *Strassburg: P. Ledertz,* 1613–14. 3 v.; 8vo. Transl. from Goulart's *Histoires admirables et memorables de nostre temps.* Jones (Goulart) 54j. Basel:UB.   613/68

Great Britain. Council for Virginia. By his Majesties Councell for Virginia. Whereas sundrie the adventurers to Virginia . . . have published a little standing lotterie . . . we do purpose . . . to begin drawing of this lotterie the 10. day of May next. [*London:*] *F. Kingston, for W. Welby,* 1613. bds.; fol. Sabin 99870; Clayton-Torrence 25; Vail (Frontier) 36; STC 24833.6. London:Soc. Ant.   613/69

Guarguante, Orazio. Responsa varia, ad varias aegritudines. Et in primis tres tractatus, unus de dysenteria, alter de morbo gallico, et tertius de febre pestilentiali. *Venice: A. & B. Dei,* 1613. 295 p.; port.; 4to. Treatise on syphilis discusses its possible American origins. Wellcome I:2963. DNLM, KU-M, PPL; BL, BN.   613/70

Guyon, Louis, sieur de la Nauche. Les diverses leçons . . . Troisiesme édition. *Lyons: C. Morillon,* 1613. 3 v.; 8vo. 1st publ., Lyons, 1604. BN.   613/71

Hall, Joseph, Bp of Norwich. Mundus alter & idem . . . durch . . . Albericum . . . Gentilem [i.e., Gregor Wintermonat] . . . verteutscht. *Leipzig: J. Hermann, for H. Gross, the Younger,* 1613. 232 p.; illus., maps; 8vo. At head of title: Utopia pars II. Transl. from Hall's *Mundus alter & item,* 1st publ., [London, 1605?], q.v. Normally bound with, as issued, Sir Thomas More's *Utopia* of 1612 from the same press. Shaaber (Brit. auth.) H51. ICN, NNC; BL.   613/72

Harcourt, Robert. A relation of a voyage to Guiana. *London: J. Beale, for W. Welby,*

1613. 71 p.; 4to. Sabin 30296; STC 12754; Arents 105; Church 361; JCB (3) II:95. CSmH, CtY, DLC, ICN, InU-L, MH, MiU-C, MnU-B, NN-A, PPRF, RPJCB; BL.   613/73

Hieron, Samuel. An answere to a popish ryme . . . The third edition. *London: S. Waterson,* 1613. 4to. In verse. 1st publ., London, 1604. STC 13390. BL.   613/74

Hoby, Sir Edward. A counter-snarle for Ishmael Rabschacheh. *London:* [*T. Snodham,*] *for N. Butter,* 1613. 78 p.; 4to. The author admits (p. 40) to smoking tobacco. A reply to John Floyd's *The overthrow of the Protestants pulpit-babels,* [St Omer], 1612. The verso of the 2nd prelim. lf lacks errata note. STC 13539. CSmH, DFo; BL.   613/75

—[Anr issue]. *London:* [*T. Snodham*] *for N. Butter,* 1613. The verso of the 2nd prelim. lf contains an errata note. STC 13539a; Arents (Add.) 159-A; JCB (3) II:95. CSmH, NN-A, RPJCB.   613/76

Hues, Robert. Tractatus de globis, coelesti et terrestri. [*Heidelberg:*] *G. Vögelin* [1613?]. 258 p.; 12mo. 1st publ., London, 1594; cf. 1611 edn. Shaaber (Brit. auth.) H479. NN-RB; BL.   613/77

Illescas, Gonzalo de. Segunda parte de la Historia pontifical y catholica. *Barcelona: S. de Cormellas,* 1613. fol. 1st publ. with American material, Barcelona, 1596; cf. 1602 edn. Palau 118424n.   613/78

—[Anr edn]. *Madrid: Imprenta Real, for J. Hasrey,* 1613. 782 p.; fol. Streit I:331. BL.   613/79

—[Anr issue?]. *Madrid: Imprenta Real, for J. de la Cuesta,* 1613. Palau 118424n.   613/80

Jourdain, Silvester. A plaine description of the Barmudas, now called Sommer Ilands. With the manner of their discoverie anno 1609. *London: W. Stansby, for W. Welby,* 1613. [51] p.; 4to. 1st publ., London, 1610, under title *A discovery of the Barmudas.* Sabin 9759; Clayton-Torrence 24; Vail (Frontier) 35; STC 14817; Church 362; JCB (3) II:96. CSmH, CtY, DLC, MHi, NN-RB, PPL, RPJCB; BL.   613/81

Keckermann, Bartholomaeus. Systema astronomiae compendiosum. *Hanau: Heirs of W. Antonius,* 1613. 192 p.; 8vo. 1st publ., Hanau, 1611.   613/82

King, Humphrey. An halfe-penny-worth of

wit . . . The third impression. *London: T. Thorp, by assignement of E. Blount,* 1613. 24 lvs; 4to. In verse. No prior 'impression' has survived. Preface cites 'new wine of Peru, that is made of no grape'. STC 14973; Arents 106. CSmH, DFo, NN-A; BL.

613/83

Lancre, Pierre de. Tableau de l'inconstance des mauvais anges et demons . . . Reveu, corrige, & augmenté. *Paris: J. Berjon,* 1613. 590 p.; illus.; 4to. 1st publ., Paris, 1612. BN.

613/84

——[Anr issue]. *Paris: N. Buon,* 1613. Arents (Add.) 160. CSmH, IU, MdBP, NN-A, PU; BL, BN.

613/85

Le Mire, Aubert. Notitia episcopatuum orbis christiani. *Antwerp: Plantin Press,* 1613. 418 p.; 8vo. Chapt. xxvi treats of bishoprics of New World. Sabin 49404; Streit I:335; Palau 171564. DLC, InU-L, MB, MiU, NNC, PU; BL, BN.

613/86

——. Relacion de los arçobispados y obispados de España, y de las Indias Occidentales y Orientales. *Antwerp: D. Martin,* 1613. 8 lvs; 8vo. Transl. from the author's *Notitia episcopatuum Hispaniae et Indiarum,* 1st publ., Antwerp, 1612. Medina (BHA) 591; Streit I:334; Peeters-Fontainas (Impr. esp.) 692; Palau 171566. RPJCB; BL, BN.

613/87

Lescarbot, Marc. Nova Francia. Gründliche History von Erfündung der grossen Landschafft Nova Francia, oder New Frankreich . . . aus einem zu Pariss gedruckten französischen Buch summarischer weiss ins Teutsch gebracht. *Augsburg: C. Dabertzhofer,* 1613. 86 p.; 4to. Extracted and transl. from author's *Histoire de la Nouvelle France,* 1st publ., Paris, 1609. Sabin 40177; Harrisse (NF) 29; Palmer 352; Streit II:2472; Church 363; JCB (3) II:97. CSmH, DLC, InU-L, MnU-B, NN-RB, RPJCB; BL, Munich:StB.

613/88

Maffei, Giovanni Pietro, S.J. La vie du bienheureux p. Ignace de Loyola . . . et des peres Jacques Laynez, & François de Borja . . . La premiere faicte en latin par le p. Pierre Maffee, les autres en espagnol par le p. Pierre de Ribadeneyra . . . De la traduction de messire Michel Desne. *Tournai: C. Martin,* 1613. 536 p.; 4to. Rivadeneira's life of François de Borja (p. 289–536) transl. from his *Vida del p. Francisco de Borja,* 1st

publ., Madrid, 1592, contains in bk 3, chapts vi–vii, accounts of Jesuit missions in New World. Backer V:297 & VI:1729; Palau 146975. MoSU-D, RPJCB.

613/89

Massaria, Alessandro. Practica medica. *Venice: T. Bertolotti,* 1613. 3 pts; fol. 1st publ., Frankfurt a. M., 1601. DNLM.

613/90

Matienzo, Juan de. Commentaria Joannis Matienzo Regii senatoris in cancellaria argentina regni Peru. *Madrid: L. Sánchez, for J. Hasrey,* 1613. 485 numb. lvs; fol. 1st publ., Madrid, 1580. Medina (BHA) 590; Pérez Pastor (Madrid) 1237. CLL; Madrid:BU.

613/91

Megiser, Hieronymus. Septentrio novantiquus, oder Die newe nort Welt . . . zuvor in teutscher Sprach nie ausgangen, sondern an jetzo erst alles aus vielen . . . Schriften . . . zusammen verfasset, verdeutschet. *Leipzig: Heirs of N. Nerlich, by J. Hermann, for H. Gross, the Younger,* 1613. 473 p.; illus., maps; 8vo. Includes accounts of voyages to America, esp. Virginia. Sabin 47383 (& 5905n); Baginsky (German Americana) 134; JCB (3) II:97–98. CtY, DLC, ICN, NN-RB, RPJCB; BL, Munich:StB.

613/92

Mercator, Gerardus. Atlas minor . . . Traduict de latin . . . par le sieur de la Popeliniere . . . De nouveau revue, et augmente. *Amsterdam: J. Hondius; sold also by C. Claeszoon & by J. Janszoon, at Arnhem,* 1613. 656 p.; maps; obl. 12mo. 1st publ. in French, Amsterdam, 1608. Cf. Sabin 47888; Koeman (Me) 190; Phillips (Atlases) 3415. CU-B, DLC, NN-RB; BN.

613/93

——. L'atlas, ou Meditations cosmographiques de la fabrique du monde et figure diceluy. De nouveau reveu augmente. *Amsterdam: J. Hondius,* 1613. 5 pts; maps; ports; fol. 1st publ. in French, Amsterdam, 1609. Cf. Sabin 47882; Koeman (Me) 23A. InU-L, MiU-C; Amsterdam:NHSM.

613/94

——. Atlas, sive Cosmographicae meditationes de fabrica mundi et fabricati figura. Denuò auctus. Editio quarta. *Amsterdam: J. Hondius,* 1613. 356 p.; illus., maps; fol. 1st publ., Amsterdam, 1606. Sabin 47882; Koeman (Me) 22; Phillips (Atlases) 3416. DLC, ICU; BL, BN.

613/95

Molina, Luis de. De justitia et jure. Tomi

vi. *Mainz: B. Lipp, for H. Mylius, at Cologne,* 1613–14. 3 v.; fol. *See the year* 1614.

Montaigne, Michel Eyquem de. Essayes . . . Done into English . . . by John Florio. *London: M. Bradwood, for E. Blount & W. Barret,* 1613. 630 p.; port.; fol. 1st publ. as here transl., London, 1603. STC 18042. CSmH, CtY, DFo, ICN, InU-L, MH, NN-RB; BL, BN.   613/96

More, Sir Thomas, Saint. De optimo reipublicae statu, deque nova insula Utopia, libri duo. *Hanau: H. J. Henne, for P. Kopff,* 1613. 299 p.; 12mo. Gibson (More) 9; Shaaber (Brit. auth.) M240. CSmH, CtY, MH, MiU-C, NNUT, PPL, RPJCB; BL, BN.   613/97

Orlers, Jan Janszn. The triumphs of Nassau: or, a description of all the victories . . . granted by God to the . . . Estates Generall of the United Netherland Provinces. Under . . . Prince Maurice of Nassau. Translated out of the French by W. Schute. *London: A. Islip,* 1613. 392 p.; fol. Transl. from Orlers's *Description . . . de toutes de victoires,* 1st publ., Leyden, 1612, itself transl. from Orlers's *Beschrijvinghe,* 1st publ., Leyden, 1610. STC 17676. CSmH, DFo, ICN, MH, MnU-B, NNH, PPL; BL, Amsterdam: NHSM.   613/98

Owen, John. Eipgrammatum libri tres. *Die (France): J. R. Fabri,* 1613. [142] p.; 8vo. 1st publ., London, 1606. Brunet IV:300 (13110); Shaaber (Brit. auth.) O85. IU, MH; BN.   613/99

Perlinus, Hieronymus. Binae historiae, seu Instructiones medicae, physiologicae, pathologicae, et therapeuticae. *Hanau: Heirs of A. Wechel, for Heirs of J. Aubry,* 1613. 155 p.; 4to. Chapt. 'De alexiteriis' 1st publ., separately Rome, 1610. Wellcome I:4908. DNLM; BL, BN.   613/100

Pezieu, Louis de. Brief recueil des particularitez contenues aux lettres envoyées . . . de l'isle de Marignan au Brezil. *Lyons: J. Poyet,* 1613. 31 p.; 8vo. Borba de Moraes II:142–43; Cioranescu (XVII) 54635; JCB AR28:12. MH, RPJCB; BN.   613/101

Pharmacopoeia Augustana. Jussu et auctoritate . . . Senatus a Collegio Medico rursus recognita . . . nunc sextum in lucem emissa. *Augsburg: [C. Mang, for J. Kruger]* 1613. 4 pts; fol. Substantially enl. edn. of work

by Adolph Otto, 1st publ., Augsburg, [1564], under title *Enchiridion, sive . . . Dispensatorium,* here ed. by Raymund Minderer. Ingredients called for include bezoar stone (Peruvian as well as Asian), mechoacan, tobacco, & opobalsam, both Peruvian & of Tolu. Wellcome I:4978. DNLM, ICU, MBCo, NNNAM; London:Wellcome, BN.   613/102

Pió, Giovanni Michele, O.P. Delle vite de gli huomini illustri di S. Domenico. Seconda parte. *Pavia: G. Ardizzoni & G. B. de Rossi,* 1613. 2 pts; fol. Continues the 1st pt, publ., Bologna, 1607. Includes accounts of Dominicans in the New World. Streit I:292. BL, BN.   613/103

Polo, Gaspar Gil. Los cinco libros de la Diana enamorada. *Brussels: R. Velpius & H. Anthoine,* 1613. 172 numb. lvs; 12mo. 1st publ. with refs to New World & its riches in pt 1, Valencia, 1564; cf. 1611 edn. Peeters-Fontainas (Impr. esp.) 503; Palau 102078. MB, NNH; BN.   613/104

Potosí, Bolivia. Señor. Cinco cosas son las que la villa imperial de Potosi suplica à V[uestra]. M[agestad]. en este Memorial, por persona del licenciado Juan de Yvarra su Procurador general. [*Madrid?* ca. 1613]. 8 lvs; fol. Petition to king of Spain seeking economic concessions on behalf of Potosí. Medina (BHA) 6549. InU-L.   613/105

Purchas, Samuel. Purchas his Pilgrimage. Or Relations of the world and the religions in all ages and places discovered. *London: W. Stansby, for H. Fetherstone,* 1613. 752 p.; fol. The 8th & 9th bks (p. 601–752) describe the two Americas. Sabin 66678; Streit I:336; STC 20505; JCB (3) II:98. CSmH, CtY, DLC, ICN, InU-L, MH, MiU-C, MnU-B, NN-RB, RPJCB; BL.   613/106

Quervau, Vincent, sieur du Sollier. Epitome ou brief recueil de l'histoire universelle, depuis la creation du monde . . . Seconde edition. *Paris: F. Huby,* 1613. 380 p.; 12mo. Under year 1608 'navigations des François en Canada' are mentioned. The earlier edn implied by title has not been traced. BL.   613/107

Ramusio, Giovanni Battista. Delle navigationi et viaggi . . . in tre volumi divise . . . Volume primo. *Venice: The Giuntas,* 1613. 394 numb. lvs; illus., maps; fol. 1st publ.,

Venice, 1550; cf. 1606 edn above. Sabin 67735; Streit I:337. CSmH, MH, NN-RB, RPJCB; BL, BN. 613/108

Rich, Barnabe. Opinion diefied [*sic*], discovering the ingins, traps, and traynes that are set to catch opinion. *London: [T. Dawson,] for T. Adams,* 1613. 32 lvs; 4to. On p. 41 is the statement, '. . . there is nothing in better request then flattery and Tobacco: two smoakie vapours.' STC 20994. CSmH, CtY, DFo, NN-RB; BL. 613/109

Ridley, Mark. A short treatise of magneticall bodies and motions. *London: N. Okes,* 1613. 157 p.; illus., port., map; 4to. Included is a map showing Virginia & New England. No errata note appears on lf X3r. Sabin 71297; STC 21045. CtY, MH, NN-RB; BL. 613/110

—[Anr issue]. *London: N. Okes,* 1613. Lf X3 is a cancel with errata note on recto. STC 21045.5. CSmH, DLC, WU; Cambridge: Trinity. 613/111

Ripa, Cesare. Iconologia . . . nella quale si descrivono diverse imagini di virtù . . . tutte le parti del mondo. *Siena: Heirs of M. Florimi, for B. Ruoti, at Florence,* 1613. 2 pts; illus.; 4to. 1st publ. with American content, Rome, 1603. DFo, ICN, MH, NjP, RPB; BL, BN. 613/112

Rivadeneira, Pedro de, S.J. Catalogus scriptorum religionis Societatis Jesu . . . Secunda editio. *Antwerp: Plantin Office (Widow & Sons of J. Moretus),* 1613. 380 p.; 8vo. 1st publ., Antwerp, 1608, under title *Illustrium scriptorum religionis Societatis Jesu catalogus.* Sabin 70778n; Backer VI:1754. DGU, ICU, NNUT, PV; BL. 613/113

——. Leben Francisci Borgiae . . . in hispanischer Sprach beschrieben; von Andrea Scotto aber . . . in die lateinische, und anjetzo von Conrado Vettern in die teutsche Sprach gebract. *Ingolstadt: A. Angermaier,* 1613. 309 p.; port.; 4to. Transl. from Mainz, 1603, *Vita Francisci Borgiae.* Backer VI:1734; Palau 266322. CU, CtY, NN-RB. 613/114

——. La vie du bienheureux p. Ignace de Loyola . . . De la traduction de . . . Michel Desne, evesque de Tournay [i.e., Michel d'Esne, seigneur de Béthencourt]. *Tournai:* 1613. *See* Maffei, Giovanni Pietro, *above.* 613/115

Rowlands, Samuel. The knave of harts. *Lon-*

don: [T. Snodham], for J. Bache, 1613. 4to. In verse. 1st publ., London, 1612. STC 21391. BL. 613/116

——. The letting of humours blood. *London: W. W[hite].,* 1613. 8vo. 1st publ., London, 1600; intervening edns have title *Humors ordinarie,* etc.; cf. year 1605 above. CSmH. 613/117

——. More knaves yet? The knaves of spades and diamonds. *London: [E. Allde,] for J. Tapp* [1613]. 4to. In verse. In 'To smokey noses and stinking nostrils' & 'The picture of a swagerer' are refs to tobacco. 'To Maddam Maske and Francis Fan' describes American origins of syphilis. STC 21392. BL, Oxford: Bodl. 613/118

—[Anr edn]. With new additions. *London: [E. Allde, for J. Tapp,* 1613?]. 4to. STC 21392.3. CSmH; BL. 613/119

——. Tis merrie when gossips meete . . . Newly enlarged. *London: W. W[hite]., for J. Deane* [1613?]. 4to. In verse. 1st publ., London, 1602. STC 21410.5. DFo (imp.) 613/120

Shakespeare, William. The history of Henrie the fourth [Pt 1]. *London: W. W[hite]., for M. Law,* 1613. 4to. Drama. 1st publ., London, 1598; cf. 1604 edn. STC 22284; Greg 145(f). CSmH, DFo, NN-RB; BL. 613/121

Soto, Domingo de. De justitia et jure libri decem. *Douai: P. Boremann,* 1613. 1st publ., Salamanca, 1553; cf. year 1602. Palau 320164n. 613/122

Spain. Sovereigns, etc., 1598–1621 (Philip III). Cedula en que su Magestad reprehende gravemente a D. Francisco Balverdi de Mercado, presidente de la Audiencia Real de Panama. [*Madrid:* 1613]. [1] p.; fol. Dated at Madrid, 23 Nov. 1613. Palau 50890; JCB (3) II:99. RPJCB. 613/123

Spenser, Edmund. The faerie queene. *London: H. L[ownes]., for M. Lownes,* 1611 [i.e., 1613]. 363 p.; fol. 1st publ., London, 1590; cf. 1609 edn. Anr issue of 1609 edn with subsidiary t.p. dated 1613. STC 23083.7. CLU-C, DFo, RPB; London:UL.

613/124

Suárez de Figueroa, Cristóbal. Hechos de Don Garcia Hurtado de Mendoza, quarto marques de Cañete. *Madrid: Imprenta Real,* 1613. 324 p.; 4to. An account of Hurtado de Mendoza's career as governor of Chile during the Araucanian War, & of his administration in Peru, as well as encounters with Drake, Cavendish, & Hawkins. Sabin 93311 (& 24317); Medina (Chile) 39; Pérez Pastor (Madrid) 1253; JCB (3) II:100. CSmH, DLC, InU-L, MH, MiU-C, NN-RB, RPJCB; BL, BN.　　　　　613/125

Suchten, Alexander von. Antinomii mysteria gemina . . . Das ist: Von den grossen Geheimnussen dess Antinomii. *Leipzig: J. Apel*, 1613. 511 p.; 8vo. 1st publ., 1570; cf. 1604 edn. Wellcome I:6138. PU-S; London: Wellcome.　　　　　613/126

—[Anr issue?]. *Gera: J. Apel*, 1613. BL, BN.　　　　　613/127

Syreniusz Syrénski, Szymon. Zielnik, Herbarzem [który] z języka tacińskiego zowią [i.e., Viridiarium, herbarium latino sermone vocant]. *Cracow: B. Skalskus*, 1613. 1540 p.; illus.; fol. Described are maize ('Frumentum Turcicum . . . Maizum') & the marigold ('Othona lacunae . . . Flos Indicus'). Pritzel 9089; Wellcome I:6191. DDO (imp.); London:Wellcome (imp.), BN.　　　　　613/128

Tassoni, Alessandro. Varieta di pensieri. *Modena: Heirs of G. M. Verdi*, 1613. 396 p.; 4to. 1st publ., Modena, 1612. Puliatti (Tassoni) 3. DFo, NIC, NNC; Rome:BN, Leningrad:Saltykov.　　　　　613/129

Taylor, John, the Water-poet. Odcombs complaint . . . with his epitaph in the Barmuda [i.e., Bermuda], and Utopian tongues. *'Utopia'* [i.e., *London: G. Eld, for W. Burre?*] 1613. [26] p.; 8vo. STC 23780. BL, Manchester:Rylands.　　　　　613/130

Theatrum chemicum, praecipuae selectorum auctorum tractatus de chimiae et lapidis philosophici. *Strassburg: L. Zetzner*, 1613–22. 8vo. Included in v. 1 is Bernard George Penot's *Tractatus varii de vera praeparatione . . . medicamentorum* (1st publ., Frankfurt a. M., 1594); cf. 1602 edn. Ferguson (Bibl. chem.) II:436–39. CU, CtY, ICU, MH, NNC; BL (Zetzner, L.).　　　　　613/131

Theodorus, Jacobus. Neuw vollkommentlich Kreuterbuch . . . gemehret durch Casparum Bauhinum. *Frankfurt a. M.: N. Hoffmann, for J. Basse & J. Dreutel*, 1613. 3 pts; illus.; fol. 1st publ., Frankfurt a. M., 1588–91. Described are numerous American plants, in part identified as such. Bagin-

sky (German Americana) 135; Pritzel 9093n; Nissen (Bot.) 1931. DNLM, MoSB, NN-RB, PU; BL.　　　　　613/132

The treasurie of auncient and moderne times . . . Translated [by Thomas Milles] out of . . . Pedro Mexia and m. Francisco Sansovino. *London: W. Jaggard*, 1613. 965 p.; fol. Includes in bk 8, chapt. xxx, 'How mines of gold are known', describing those of the New World, referring to harsh usage of Indians by Spanish; and, bk 8, chapt. xxxix, 'Of the Indian beare' describing an anteater. Sabin 48247; STC 17936. CSmH, CtY, DLC, ICN, MH, MiU, MnU-B, NN-RB, PP; BL.　　　　　613/133

Vergilius, Polydorus. De rerum inventoribus libri octo . . . Accesserunt C. Plinii, Alexandri Sardi, aliorumque de eadem materia collectanea. *Strassburg: L. Zetzner*, 1613. 2 pts; 8vo. 1st publ. as here constituted, Geneva, 1604. CU, InU, MH, PV.　　　　　613/134

Verken, Johann. Continuatio oder Ergäntzung dess neundten Theils der Orientalischen Indien, das ist, kurtze Continuirung . . . der vorigen Reyse, so von den Holl- und Seeländern . . . unter . . . Verheiffen in die Orientalischen Indien von 1607. bis in das 1612. Jahr verrichtet worden . . . in hoch teutscher Sprach beschrieben durch M. Gothardt Arthussen. *Frankfurt a. M.: Widow of M. Becker, for J. T. de Bry*, 1613. 35 p.; illus., map; fol. (J. T. de Bry's *India Orientalis*. Pt 9. Appendix. German). Includes map on t.p. showing America. Brunet I:1360; Church 240; JCB (3) I:440. CSmH, CtY, DLC, NN-RB, RPJCB; BL, BN.　　　　　613/135

—[Anr issue]. *Frankfurt a. M.: Widow of M. Becker, for J. T. de Bry*, 1613. Plates re-engraved. Church 241. CSmH, NN-RB, RPJCB; BL.　　　　　613/136

Vicary, Thomas. The English-mans treasure . . . Now sixtly augmented and enlarged . . . by G. E. *London: T. Creede*, 1613. 224 p.; 4to. 1st publ., London, 1548, under title *A profitable treatise of . . . man's body*, but here enlarged to include, in pt ii, 'Of medicine', a potion for treatment of syphilis employing 'poxwood', i.e., guaiacum. STC 24710. CSmH, DFo (imp.), MBCo, NNNAM (imp.), WU; BL.　　　　　613/137

Villerias, Mateo de. El capitan Mateo de Villerias vezino de Mexico. pide seis mil ducados de renta, un abito de una de las tres Ordenes, algun oficio de governacion, o guerra. [*Madrid?* 1613]. 7 p.; fol. Petition based in part on wife's descent from Jorge Cerón, who had served in California and Florida. Sabin 99740; Wagner (SW) 17; Palau 369490. Seville:Archivo de Indias.
613/138

Le voyage de l'illustre seigneur et chevalier François Drach. *Paris: J. Gesselin,* 1613. 90 p.; 8vo. Transl. by François de Louvencourt, sieur de Vauchelles, from 'The famous voyage of Sir Francis Drake into the South Seas', inserted in Hakluyt's *Principall navigations,* as publ., London, 1589. Traditionally attributed to Francis Pretty, but according to H. R. Wagner in *Sir Francis Drake's voyage around the world* (San Francisco: 1926), p. 238, it is probably a compilation by Hakluyt himself from three or more sources; there is no evidence that Pretty was present on the voyage. Sabin 20844; Wagner (SW) 9b; Shaaber (Brit. auth.) H6; JCB AR29:16. MH, NN-RB, RPJCB; BL.
613/139

Whitaker, Alexander. Good newes from Virginia. Sent to the Counsell and Company of Virginia . . . Wherein also is a narration of the present state of that countrey. *London: F. Kingston, for W. Welby,* 1613. 44 p.; 4to. Sabin 103313, Clayton-Torrence 26; Vail (Frontier) 37; STC 25354; Church 364; JCB (3) II:100. CSmH, DLC, ICN, MiU-C, NN-RB, PPL, RPJCB; BL.
613/140

Wither, George. Abuses stript, and whipt. *London: G. Eld, for F. Burton,* 1613. 276 p.; 8vo. In verse. In bk 1, chapt. 4, in poem 'Of the passion of love', phrase 'The swart West Indian' appears; in bk 2, Satyr 1, on vanity, tobacco is discussed at length & 'potato pie' mentioned; in Epigram I, the 'Magalanick strands' are cited. To distinguish the various edns of this year, consult the STC. STC 25891. CSmH, DFo, MH; BL.
613/141

—[Anr edn]. *London: G. Eld, for F. Burton,* 1613. 8vo. STC 25891.5; Arents 108. CtY, NN-A; BL (imp.).
613/142

—[Anr edn]. *London: G. Eld, for F. Burton,*
1613. 8vo. STC 25893. CSmH, DFo, ICN, MH; BL.
613/143

—[Anr edn]. *London: G. Eld, for F. Burton* [i.e., *T. Creede*], 1613. 8vo. A piracy. STC 25893. CSmH, CtY, DFo, MH; BL.
613/144

—[Anr edn]. *London: G. Eld, for F. Burton,* 1613. 8vo. STC 25894. DFo, MH, NNPM; BL.
613/145

Zouch, Richard. The dove: or Passages of cosmography. *London:* [*T. Snodham,*] *for G. Norton,* 1613. [71] p.; 8vo. In verse. In prose epilogue, Sir Francis Drake's passage through the Strait of Magellan is mentioned. STC 26130. CSmH, DFo, NNPM; BL.
613/146

1614

Acosta, José de, S.J. Historia natural y moral de las Indias. *Madrid: L. Sánchez,* 1614. 1st publ., Seville, 1590; cf. 1608 edn. Backer I:34, Palau 1982n.
614/1

Aldrete, Bernardo José. Varias antiguedades de España, Africa y otras provincias. *Antwerp: G. van Wolsschaten & H. Aertssens, for J. Hasrey,* 1614. 640 p.; illus., maps; 4to. Aldrete, discussing Columbus's voyages, credits actual discovery of New World to Sánchez de Huelva, & objects to use of term *America* for the area. Peeters-Fontainas (Impr. esp.) 30; Palau 6391; Maggs Cat. 479 (Americana V):4129. CU, CtY, DLC, ICU, MH, NN-RB, PU, RPJCB; BL, BN.
614/2

Avity, Pierre d', sieur de Montmartin. Les estats, empires, et principautez du monde. *Paris: O. de Varennes,* 1614. 1467 p.; 4to. 1st publ., Paris, 1613. Cf. Sabin 2498; Cioranescu (XVII) 23601. Munich:StB.
614/3

—[Anr edn]. *St Omer: C. Boscard,* 1614. 1104 p.; 4to. DLC, ICN, NN-RB, PU.
614/4

—[Anr issue]. Les empires, royaumes, estats . . . et principautez du monde. *St Omer: C. Boscard,* 1614. BL.
614/5

Bacon, Francis, viscount St Albans. The essaies. *Edinburgh: A. Hart,* 1614. 78 lvs; 8vo. 1st publ. with 'Of atheisme', London, 1612. Gibson (Bacon) 11; STC 1145. MH, NNPM; BL, BN.
614/6

Barclay, John. Icon animorum. *London: B.*

Norton, for J. Bill, 1614. 356 p.; 8vo. Constitutes pt 4 of Barclay's *Euphormionis Lusinini Satyricon.* In chapt. ii Spanish domination of America is mentioned; in chapt. vii, 'Hispanorum genus, mores', Columbus's discovery of America is noted. Tchémerzine I:143; STC 1398. CSmH, CtY, DFo, MH, MnU; BL.   614/7

—[Anr edn]. *Paris: P. Mettayer,* 1614. 356 p.; 8vo. Shaaber (Brit. auth.) B164; Tchémerzine I:144. ViU; BN, Lübeck:StB.
                                             614/8

Barclay, William. Nepenthes, or The vertues of tabacco. *Edinburgh: A. Hart,* 1614. 16 lvs; 8vo. Includes refs to American origins of tobacco. STC 1406; Arents 109. CSmH; Oxford:Bodl.   614/9

Bauderon, Brice. Paraphrase sur la Pharmacopée . . . Sixiesme edition. *Lyons: P. Rigaud,* 1614. 2 pts; 8vo. 1st publ., Lyons, 1588; cf. 1607 edn. MBCo; London:Wellcome.   614/10

Béguin, Jean. Tyrocinium chymicum . . . ab ipsomet autore . . . recognitum. *Cologne: A. Boetzer,* 1614. 195 p.; 12mo. 1st publ., Paris, 1612. NIC; BL.   614/11

Boccalini, Traiano. De' ragguagli di Parnaso . . . Centuria prima . . . seconda impressione. *Venice: G. Guerigli,* 1614. 472 p.; 4to. 1st publ., Venice, 1612. Firpo (Ragguagli) 6; Michel (Répertoire) I:175. CLSU, ICU, MH, NN, NcU; BN.   614/12

—[Anr edn]. *Venice: G. Guerigli,* 1614. 478 p.; 4to. Firpo (Ragguagli) 7; Michel (Répertoire) I:175. BL, Versailles:BM.   614/13

——. De' ragguagli di Parnaso . . . Centuria seconda. *Milan: G. B. Bidelli,* 1614. 430 p.; 8vo. 1st publ., Venice, 1613; issued with Bidelli's Centuria prima of this year above. Firpo (Ragguagli) 6; Michel (Répertoire) I:175. BN.   614/14

—[Anr edn]. Seconda impressione. *Venice: G. Guerigli,* 1614. 453 p.; 4to. Firpo (Ragguagli) 7; Michel (Répertoire) I:175. CLSU, ICU, MH, NN, NcU; BL,Versailles:BM.
                                             614/15

Borough, William. A discours of the variation of the cumpas. *London: T. C[reede]., for J. Tapp,* 1614. 4to. 1st publ., London, 1582. Included are refs to marine plats for voyages to Newfoundland. Issued with Robert

Norman's *The newe attractive* of this year. STC 3392 (misdated 1611). CCC; BL.
                                             614/16

Brerewood, Edward. Enquiries touching the diversity of languages and religions. *London: [W. Stansby,] for J. Bill,* 1614. 198 p.; 4to. Includes reports on New World religious practices encountered by Spanish & Portuguese explorers. Cf. Sabin 7732; STC 3618. CSmH, CtY, DLC, ICN, MH, MiU, NN-RB, RPJCB; BL, BN.   614/17

Casas, Bartolomé de las, O.P., Bp of Chiapa. Narratio regionum Indicarum per Hispanos quosdam devastatarum verissima. *Oppenheim: H. Galler, for J. T. de Bry,* 1614. 138 p.; illus.; 4to. 138 p.; illus.; 4to. 1st publ. in Latin, 1598, as transl. from the 1579 French version of the author's *Brevíssima relación,* 1st publ., Seville, 1552. Sabin 11284; Medina (BHA) 604; Hanke/ Giménez 508; Streit I:343; JCB (3) II:101. DLC, RPJCB.   614/18

Catelan, Laurent. Discours et demonstration des ingrediens de la thériaque. *Lyons: J. Mallet,* 1614. 313 p.; 8vo. In the '9me journée' American opobalsam ('balsam de Tolu') is discussed. DNLM, MH, PPC; London:Wellcome, BN.   614/19

Cervantes Saavedra, Miguel de. Novelas exemplares. *Madrid: J. de la Cuesta, for F. de Robles,* 1614. 236 numb. lvs; 4to. 1st publ., Madrid, 1613. Ríus (Cervantes) 220; Palau 53400. MH, NNH; BL.   614/20

—[Anr edn]. *Pamplona: N. de Assiayn,* 1614. 391 numb. lvs; 8vo. Ríus (Cervantes) 221; Palau 53401. NNH, PU; BL, BN.   614/21

—[Anr edn]. *Brussels: R. Velpius & H. Anthoine,* 1614. 616 p.; 8vo. Ríus (Cervantes) 222; Palau 53402. CtY, DLC, MH, NNH, PU; BL, BN.   614/22

Claude d'Abbeville, O. F. M. Cap. Les fruicts de la mission des reverends peres Capucins en l'isle de Maragnan. *Lille: C. Beys,* 1614. 31 p.; 8vo. Borba de Moraes I:3; Streit II:2377; JCB (3) II:101. RPJCB.
                                             614/23

——. Histoire de la mission des peres Capucins en l'isle de Maragnan et terres convoisines. *Paris: F. Huby,* 1614. 395 numb. lvs; illus.; 8vo. Sabin 4; Borba de Moraes I:5– 7; Streit II:2376; JCB (3) II:100. CtY, DLC,

ICN, InU-L, MH, MnU-B, NN-RB, RPJCB; BL, BN. 614/24

—[Anr edn]. *Paris: F. Huby,* 1614. 394 numb. lvs; illus.; 8vo. InU-L; BL, BN. 614/25

Collibus, Hippolytus à. Fürstliche Tischreden, auss vielen vornehmen Scribenten zusammen gezogen durch Johann Werner Gebharten [pseud.]. Hie bevor in Truck aussgangen und an jetzo in bessere . . . Ordnung mit mercklicher Vermehrung abermals an Tag geben. *Frankfurt a. M.: J. Bringer, for J. Bassé,* 1614. 458 p.; 8vo. Though not entered in our 1st volume, 1st publ., Frankfurt a. M., 1597; here rev. & enl. by Georg Draud. Includes, in chapt. lxxxiii, suggestion that the discovery of the New World did more harm than good, citing specifically the effects of gold & silver. Cf. Jantz (German Baroque) 838. MH. 614/26

Colón, Fernando. Historie . . . Nelle quali s'ha particolare . . . della vita . . . dell'ammariglio Don Christoforo Colombo . . . Et dello scoprimento, ch'egli fece dell'Indie Occidentali, dette Mondo Nuova . . . Già tradotte di lingua spagnuola [da Alfonso Ulloa] . . . Con aggiunta di lettere & testamento dell'Ammiraglio . . . da Cesare Parona. *Milan: G. Bordone* [1614]. 494 p.; 8vo. 1st publ. as transl. by Ulloa, Venice, 1569. Included are letters, etc., not found in earlier edns. The Spanish text is unknown, & the authenticity of the work disputed: cf. Palau 57209 & 221828n. Sabin 14675; Streit II:1434; Palau 57210; Arents (Add.) 161-A; JCB (3) II:101. DLC, InU-L, MWA, MiU-C, NN-RB, RPJCB; BL. 614/27

Cooke, Jo. Greene's Tu quoque: or, The cittie gallant. *London: J. Trundle,* 1614. [87] p.; illus.; 4to. Drama. On verso of lf B3, Virginia is mentioned. STC 5673; Greg 323(a). CSmH, DLC, MH, NNPM; BL. 614/28

Cortés, Jerónimo. Phisonomia. *Barcelona: J. Margarit,* 1614. 115 numb. lvs; 8vo. 1st publ., Valencia, 1597; cf. 1601 edn. Salvá 2693; Palau 63307. BN. 614/29

Davies, William. A true relation of the travailes and most miserable captivitie of William Davies, barber-surgion of London. *London: N. Bourne,* 1614. [40] p.; 4to. Includes description of Amazon River & Indians of area. Sabin 18774; Borba de Moraes I:210; STC 6365; JCB (3) II:101. CSmH, DFo, NN-RB, RPJCB; BL. 614/30

Du Bartas, Guillaume de Salluste, seigneur. Les oeuvres. *Paris: T. Du Bray,* 1614. 2 v.; illus.; fol. In verse. Included, with Simon Goulart's annotations, are the author's *La sepmaine,* 1st thus publ., Paris, 1584, & his *La seconde sepmaine,* 1st publ. thus, Geneva, 1589. The present edn is a reissue of that of 1611, '10. Cf. 1601 edn. Holmes (DuBartas) I:76 no. 36n; Tchémerzine X:197. CSmH; BN. 614/31

—[Anr issue]. *Paris: C. Rigaud,* 1614. Holmes (DuBartas) I:76 no. 36n. 614/32

Duchesne, Joseph. Opera medica. *Leipzig: T. Schürer & B. Voigt,* 1614. 2 v.; 8vo. 1st publ. as here collected, Lyons, 1591; cf. 1602 edn. DNLM, WU; BL, BN. 614/33

——. Pharmacopoea dogmaticorum restituta. *Venice: J. de Francisci,* 1614. 2 pts; 4to. 1st publ., Paris, 1607. Arents (Add.) 162. NN-A; London:Wellcome. 614/34

Durante, Castore. Il tesoro della sanità. *Venice: L. Spineda,* 1614. 334 p.; 8vo. 1st publ., Rome, 1586; cf. 1601 edn. Michel (Répertoire) II:191. DNLM; Paris: Ste Geneviève. 614/35

Esternod, Claude d'. Les desirs amoureux de Dom Philippe prince d'Espagne. *Paris: P. Durand,* 1614. 24 p.; 8vo. In verse. Included is a litany of American place names for lands unknown to ancestors. Cf. Cioranescu (XVII) 28482. BN. 614/36

Fabronius, Hermann. Newe summarische Welt-Historia uñd Beschreibung aller Keyserthum, Königreiche, Fürstenthumb, und Völcker heutiges Tages auff Erden . . . Die ander Edition. *Schmalkaden: W. Ketzel,* 1614. 2 pts; illus., maps; 4to. 1st publ., Schmalkalden, 1612. Pt 2 has title *Der newen summarischen Welt . . . das ander Theil, von der newen Welt.* Though its t.p. is dated '1612', this date may represent a literal reprinting of the earlier edn, rather than the reissue of it. Cf. Sabin 23605. MnU-B, NNH, RPJCB. 614/37

Figueiredo, Manuel de. Hydrographia, exame de pilotos. *Lisbon: V. Alvarez,* 1614. 3

pts; illus., map; 4to. 1st publ., Lisbon, 1608. Sabin 24316; Borba de Moraes I:266; Palau 91333n. DLC, NN-RB.   614/38

Gallucci, Giovanni Paolo. Theatro, y descripcion del mundo, y del tiempo . . . Traduzido de latin . . . por Miguel Perez. *Granada: S. Múñoz*, 1614. 369 numb. lvs; illus., map; fol. 1st publ. in Spanish, Granada, 1606. NjP.   614/39

Gentleman, Tobias. Englands way to win wealth, and to employ ships and marriners. *London: N. Butler*, 1614. 46 p.; illus.; 4to. Concerned chiefly with the herring fishery in competition with the Dutch but with a ref. to Sebastian Cabot's offer to Henry VII 'for the discovery of the West Indies' in the dedication. STC 11745; Kress 330; JCB (3) II:102. CSmH, DFo, MH, MnU-B, PU, RPJCB; BL.   614/40

Gerritsz, Hessel, ed. Zwölffte Schiffahrt, oder Kurtze Beschreibung der newen Schiffahrt gegen Nord Osten, uber die Amerische Inseln in Chinam und Japponiam, von . . . Heinrich Hudson newlich erfunden, beneben einen Discurss an Ihr. Kön. Maj. in Spanien, wegen dess fünfften Theils der Welt . . . in hochteutscher Sprach beschrieben durch M. Gothardum Arthusen. *Oppenheim: H. Galler, for Widow of L. Hulsius*, 1614. 67 p.; illus., maps; 4to. (Levinus Hulsius's *Sammlung von . . . Schiffahrten.* Pt 12). 1st publ. in this translation as pt 10 of J. T. de Bry's *India Orientalis*, Frankfurt a. M., 1613. Sabin 33666; Baginsky (German Americana) 136; Church 300; JCB (3) I:462. CSmH, ICN, MH, MnU-B, NN-RB, RPJCB.   614/41

—[Anr issue]. *Oppenheim: H. Galler, for Widow of L. Hulsius*, 1614. Church 301; Baginsky (German Americana) 137. CSmH, CtY, NN-RB.   614/42

González de Mendoza, Juan, O. E. S. A., Bp. Histoire du grand royaume de la Chine . . . ensemble un Itineraire du nouveau monde & le descouvrement du Nouveau Mexique en l'an 1583 . . . nouvellement traduite de latin en françois. *Rouen: N. Angot*, 1614. 388 p.; 8vo. 1st publ. in French, Paris, 1588; cf. 1606 edn above. Sabin 27780; Wagner (SW) 7ii; Maggs Cat. 502 (Americana VII):5026A. DLC, InU-L, MiU, MnU-B, NN-RB, RPJCB; BL, BN.   614/43

Goulart, Simon. [Schat-camer der wonderbare ende gedencweerdige historien onses tijts . . . int françois uytghegheven; ende nu . . . overgheset door Johannem Lamotium.] *Delft: J. A. Cloeting*, 1614. 2 pts; 8vo. Transl. from Goulart's *Histoires admirables et memorables de nostre temps*, 1st publ., Paris, 1600–1601; cf. year 1601. Jones (Goulart) 54n. NjR (pt 2 only).   614/44

Granado, Diego. Libro del arte de cozina. *Lérida: L. Menescal*, 1614. 299 numb. lvs; 8vo. 1st publ., Madrid, 1599; cf. 1609 edn. Palau 108418n; Wellcome I:2902. London: Wellcome.   614/45

Le grand dictionnaire françois-latin, augmenté [par Guillaume Poille] . . . recueilli des observations de plusieurs hommes doctes, entre autres de m. Nicod [i.e., Nicot]. *Paris: N. Buon*, 1614. 284 lvs; 4to. 1st publ., Paris, 1573, under title *Dictionaire françois-latin*. Includes, as 'Nicotiane', description of tobacco. BN.   614/46

Grotius, Hugo. Vrye zeevaert, ofte Bewys van 'trecht dat den Hollanders toecompt over de Indische coophandel. Overghestelt uyt het Latynsche. *Leyden: J. Huybertszoon*, 1614. 85 p.; 8vo. Transl. from Grotius's *Mare liberum*, 1st publ., Leyden, 1609. For variants cf. Meulen/Diermanse. Meulen/Diermanse 552; Bibl. Belg. G332. NN-RB; The Hague:PP.   614/47

—[Anr edn]. Vrye zeevaert, ofte Bewys van 't recht dat de in-gesetenen deser geunieerde landen toecomt . . . Ten tweede mael oversien ende verbetert. *Leyden: J. Huybertszoon*, 1614. 85 p.; 8vo. Meulen/Diermanse 553. Leyden: B. Thysiana.   614/48

—[Anr edn]. . . . Wten Latijne vertaelt door P. B. *Leyden: J. Huybertszoon; sold by W. J. Blaeu, at Amsterdam*, 1614. 85 p.; 8vo. Meulen/Diermanse 554. Leyden:MNL. 614/49

Gruterus, Janus. Chronicon chronicorum ecclesiastico-politicum. *Frankfurt a. M.; Aubry Office*, 1614. 1641 p.; 8vo. Included is LeMire's *Notitia episcoporum orbis christiani*, 1st publ. as part of his *Notitia patriarchatum*, Antwerp, 1611. Streit I:342. OC; BL, BN.   614/50

Guibert, Nicolas. De interitu alchymiae. *Toul: S. Philippe*, 1614. 2 pts; 8vo. Mentioned is a form of orichalcum found in Mexico

& Darien. Wellcome I:2981. WU; London: Wellcome. 614/51

Guillaumet, Tannequin. Traicté second de la maladie appelee cristaline [i.e., syphilis]. *Nîmes: J. Vaguenar,* 1614. 174 p.; 12mo. Continues earlier *Traicté* of 1611. Includes account of introduction of syphilis from West Indies; describes guaiacum & its uses. Wellcome I:2995. London:Wellcome. 614/52

Heresbach, Conrad. The whole art and trade of husbandry . . . Enlarged by Barnaby Googe. *London: T. S[nodham]., for R. More,* 1614. 182 numb. lvs; 4to. Transl. from author's *Rei rusticae,* 1st publ., Cologne, 1570; cf. 1601 English edn, with title *Foure books of husbandry.* STC 13201. CSmH, CtY, DLC, ICN, IU, MH, NN-RB, PU-F; BL. 614/53

Keckermann, Bartholomaeus. Operum omnium quae extant tomus primus [-secundus]. *Geneva: P. Aubert,* 1614. 2 v.; illus.; fol. Included are the author's *Systema astronomiae compendiosum,* & his *Systema geographicum,* both 1st publ., Hanau, 1611; cf. his *Systema compendiosum totius mathematices,* Hanau, 1617. MH-AH, MdBJ, MoSU; BL, BN. 614/54

Krachteloose donder van den Helschen hondt . . . waer in vertoont wort al het principaelste dat in tsestich jaren ghepasseert is in desen . . . staet, ende . . . in . . . Bohemien, Moscovien, jae in Oost ende West-Indien selfs. [*Amsterdam?* 1614?]. [8] p.; illus.; 4to. Attacks Jesuits & Spain. Printer's mark on t.p. portrays warrior-angel slaying devil. Sabin 38293 (as [1615?]); Backer XI:1085–86; Knuttel 2136; JCB (3) II:103. RPJCB (imp.); The Hague:KB. 614/55

—[Anr edn]. [*Amsterdam?* 1614?]. [8] p.; illus.; 4to. Printer's mark on t.p. is design with two seahorses. RPJCB. 614/56

—[Anr edn?]. [*Amsterdam?* 1614?]. 4to. BL (as [1600?]). 614/57

La Noue, François de. Discours politiques et militaires. *Geneva: P. & J. Chouët,* 1614. 1019 p.; 16mo. 1st publ., Basel, 1587; cf. 1612 edn. OCU; BL, BN. 614/58

Lima (Ecclesiastical province). Council, 1567. Sumario del concilio provincial, que se celebro en la ciudad de los Reyes, el año de 1567. *Seville: M. Clavijo,* 1614. 231 p.; 4to. Sabin 93584; Medina (BHA) 611; Streit II:1446; Palau 325055; JCB (3) II:105. InU-L, MH, RPJCB; BL. 614/59

Lima (Ecclesiastical province). Council, 1583. Concilium Limense. Celebratum anno 1583. *Madrid: J. Sánchez,* 1614. 92 numb. lvs; 4to. 1st publ., Madrid, 1590. Authorship attrib. to José de Acosta. Sabin 41087; Medina (BHA) 605; Streit II:1443; Pérez Pastor (Madrid) 1274; JCB (3) II:110. RPJCB. 614/60

Linschoten, Jan Huygen van. Beschrijvinghe van de gantsche custe van Guinea . . . ende tegen over de Cabo de S. Augustijn in Brasilien. *Amsterdam: J. E. Cloppenburg,* 1614. [82] p.; fol. 1st publ., Amsterdam, 1596; cf. 1605 edn. Ostensibly issued as pt of Linschoten's *Itinerarium ofte Schipvaert* of this year below, q.v., since the present item includes an index for all 3 pts. Sabin 41361n; Tiele-Muller 86. 614/61

——. Itinerarium, ofte Schipvaert naer Oost ofte Portugaels Indien . . . Op't nieuwe gecorrigeert eñ verbetert. *Amsterdam: J. E. Cloppenburg,* 1614. 3 pts; illus., port., maps.; fol. 1st publ., Amsterdam, 1596 (cf. 1605 edn); here ostensibly issued with Linschoten's *Reys-gheschrift* & his *Beschrijvinghe van . . . Guinea* of this year, the latter including an index for all three pts. Sabin 41361; cf. Borba de Moraes I:419–20; Tiele-Muller 86; Tiele 680. NN-RB; BL. 614/62

——. Navigatio ac itinerarium . . . in Orientalem sive Lusitanorum Indiam. *Amsterdam: J. Walschaert,* 1614. 2 v.; illus., port., maps; fol. 1st publ., The Hague, 1599; here a reissue with cancel t.p. & preface to reader of that edn. Included here because under the above title, constituting v. 1, was also reissued, as v. 2 with its original t.p. uncanceled, Linschoten's *Descriptio totius Guineae,* 1st publ., The Hague, 1599. Sabin 41367; Tiele-Muller 85; JCB (3) II:104. DLC, NN-RB, RPJCB. 614/63

——. Reys-gheschrift van de navigatien der Portugaloysers in Orienten . . . Als oock van de gantsche custen van Brasilien. *Amsterdam: J. E. Cloppenburg,* 1614. 147 p.; fol. 1st publ., Amsterdam, 1595 [i.e., 1596]; cf. 1604 edn. Ostensibly issued as a pt of Linschoten's *Itinerarium ofte Schipvaert* of this year above, q.v. Sabin 41361n; Tiele-Muller 86.   614/64

Lithgow, William. A most delectable, and true discourse, of an admired and painefull peregrination in Europe, Asia and Affricke. *London: N. Okes, for T. Archer,* 1614. [152] p.; 4to. Included are refs to tobacco. Reprinted 1632 & 1640 under title *The totall discourse,* etc. STC 15710. CSmH, CtY, DFo, MH; BL.   614/65

Lodewijcksz, Willem. Pirma [i.e., Prima] pars Descriptionis itineris navalis in Indiam Orientalem . . . Authore G.M.A.W.L. *Amsterdam: J. Walschaert,* 1614. 51 numb. lvs; illus., maps; fol. 1st publ. in this version, Amsterdam, 1598; transl. from *D'eerste boeck; Historie van Indien,* 1st publ., Amsterdam, 1598; cf. year 1609. Tiele-Muller 116.
                                                     614/66

Maffei, Giovanni Pietro, S.J. Historiarum Indicarum libri xvi. *Caen: J. Mangeant,* 1614. 718 p.; 12mo. 1st publ. as here constituted, Florence, 1588; cf. 1605 edn. Sabin 43774; Borba de Moraes II:10; Streit V:181; Backer V:298–99. DLC, MSaE, NNH, OU; BL, BN.
                                                     614/67

—[Anr issue]. *Caen: [J. Mangeant, for] A. Cavalier,* 1614. Borba de Moraes II:10; Streit V:181n; Backer V:298–99. BN.   614/68

Maiolo, Simeone, Bp of Volturara. Dies caniculares . . . Opus hac tertia editione revisum. *Mainz: J. T. Schönwetter,* 1614. 1060 p.; fol. 1st publ., Rome, 1597; cf. 1607 edn. Sabin 44056n. NNUT; BL, BN.   614/69

Markham, Gervase. Cheape and good husbandry, for the well-ordering of all beasts, and fowles. *London: T. S[nodham]., for R. Jackson,* 1614. 4to. In the 2nd bk, 'Of poultry', the rearing & use of turkeys is discussed. Poynter (Markham) 22.1; STC 17336. CSmH; BL.   614/70

Martini, Lucas. Alle christelige oc dydelige jomfruers aerekrantz. *Copenhagen: H. Waldkirch,* 1614. 252 lvs; illus.; 12mo. Transl. from Martini's *Der christlichen Jungfrawen Ehrenkräntzlein,* 1st publ., Prague, 1585; cf. 1602 edn. BN.   614/71

The maske of flowers. Presented by the gentlemen of Graies-Inn. *London: N. O[kes]., for R. Wilson,* 1614. [33] p.; music; 4to. Performers include Kawasha and Florida na-

tives, dressed with tobacco leaves, carrying bows & arrows. STC 17625; Greg 320. CSmH, MH; BL.   614/72

Matthieu, Pierre. Histoire de France et des choses memorables advenues aux provinces estrangeres durant sept annees de paix du regne de Henry IIII roy de France. *Paris: J. Mettayer & M. Guillemot,* 1614. 2 v.; 8vo. 1st publ., Paris, 1605. DFo, MiU; BN.
                                                     614/73

Mercator, Gerardus. Atlas minor . . . Traduict de latin . . . par le sieur de la Popeliniere . . . De nouveau revue, et augmente. *Amsterdam: J. Hondius; sold also by C. Claeszoon, & by J. Janszoon, at Arnhem,* 1614. 656 p.; maps; obl. 12mo. 1st publ. in French, Amsterdam, 1608. Cf. Sabin 47888; Koeman (Me) 191. BL, BN.   614/74

Meteren, Emanuel van. Eigentlich und volkomene historische beschreibung des niderlendischen Kriegs . . . in hochteutsch ubergesetzt . . . nach der letzten edition ubersehen und verbessert, und biss auff diese zeit continuirt. *Arnhem: J. Janszoon,* 1614. 2 pts; illus., ports, map; fol. 1st publ. in German, Hamburg, 1596; cf. year 1601. For a supplement, see the year 1620. Bruckner 12. MB, MdAN, NNC; Leyden:UB.
                                                     614/75

——. Historie der Nederlandscher ende haerder naburen oorlogen ende geschiedenissen. Tot den jare M.VI.CXII. . . . verbetert in xxxii boecken voltrocken. *The Hague: H. Jacobszoon von Wouw,* 1614. 671 numb. lvs; illus., ports, map; fol. 1st publ. in Dutch, Delft, 1599; cf. years 1605 & 1610. Stokes (Manhattan) VI:256. CSmH, CtY, DLC, ICN, MiU-C, MnU-B, NN-RB, RPJCB (lacks map), WU; BL.   614/76

Molina, Luis de. De justitia et jure. Tomi vi. *Mainz: B. Lipp, for H. Mylius, at Cologne,* 1614. 6 v.; fol. Vols 1 & 2 1st publ., Cuenca (Spain), 1593 & 1597; cf. years 1601 & 1602 above. Vols 1 & 2 have added, engr. t.p. dated 1613. Backer V:1177; Palau 174620. MH-L, NSyU; BN.   614/77

—[Anr edn]. De justitia et jure opera omnia. *Venice: The Sessas,* 1614. 2 pts; fol. Backer V:1177; Palau 174622.   614/78

Müller, Philipp (1585–1659). Miracula et mysteria chymico-medica . . . Editio secunda. [*Wittenberg?*] *C. Berger*, 1614. 493 p.; illus.; 12mo. 1st publ., [Wittenberg], 1611. Wellcome I:4474. DNLM, NNNAM, PCarlD, WU; London:Wellcome. 614/79

Münster, Sebastian. Cosmographey: das ist Beschreibung aller Länder . . . Hernach . . . durch ihne selbs gebessert: jetzt aber letzlich . . . bis in M.DC.XIV. jahr gemehret. *Basel: S. Henricpetri*, 1614. 1575 p.; port., maps; fol. 1st publ., Basel, 1544. Burmeister (Münster) 84. CSmH, DLC, NN-RB, OCU; Basel:UB, Heidelberg:UB. 614/80

Norman, Robert. The new attractive, containing a short discourse of the magnes or loadstone. *London: T. C [reede]., for J. Tapp*, 1614. 3 pts; 4to. 1st publ., London, 1581. Includes discussion of effect of arctic pole on compass variation in voyages to Newfoundland, West Indies, &c. Issued with this was William Borough's *A discours of the variation of the cumpas*, described above. STC 18652. CCC; BL. 614/81

Ordóñez de Ceballos, Pedro. Viage del mundo. *Madrid: L. Sánchez*, 1614. 290 numb. lvs; port.; 4to. Largely concerned with Spanish America. Sabin 57524; Medina (BHA) 1874; Streit I:345; JCB (3) II:104–5. RPJCB; BL. 614/82

Oré, Luis Jerónimo de, O. F. M., Bp of Imperial, Chile. Relacion de la vida, y milagros del venerable padre f. Francisco Solano, de la orden de S. Francisco . . . Murió en la ciudad de Lima. [*Madrid*: 1614]. 62 numb. lvs; 4to. Medina (Chile) 40; Streit II:1437; Palau 203695; JCB (3) II:98. RPJCB; Madrid:BN. 614/83

Owen, John. Epigrammatum libri tres. *Die (France): J. R. Fabri*, 1614, '13. 2 pts; 8vo. 1st publ., London, 1606; here a reissue of printer's 1613 edn with altered imprint date on t.p. of pt 1. Brunet IV:300 (13110n); Shaaber (Brit. auth.) O86. BL, BN. 614/84

—[Anr edn]. *Frankfurt a. M.: J. Bringer*, 1614. 168 p.; 8vo. ICN, ICU. 614/85

Paré, Ambroise. Les oeuvres . . . Septiesme édition. *Paris: N. Buon*, 1614. 1228 p.; illus.; fol. 1st publ., Paris, 1575; cf. the 1601 German edn. Doe (Paré) 35. CtY-M, PPL; BN. 614/86

—[Anr issue]. *Paris: B. Macé*, 1614. Doe (Paré) 36. PPC; BN. 614/87

Passe, Crispijn van de. Den blomhof, inhoudende de rare oft onghemeene blommen. *Utrecht: C. van de Passe*, 1614. 2 pts; illus.; obl. 4to. 1st publ. in this year with Latin text, the following item. Nissen (Bot.) 1494n. Utrecht:UB. 614/88

——. Hortus floridus, in quo rariorum & minus vulgarium florum icones ad vivam veramque formam accuratissime delineatae. *Arnhem: J. Janszoon*, 1614[–17]. 2 pts; illus.; obl. 4to. Included are discussions with illus. of American plants. For a full discussion of the complex printing history of this work, see S. Savage, 'The Hortus Floridus of Crispijn vande Pas the Younger', *Transactions of the Bibliographical Society*, n.s., IV (1923), 181–206. Sabin 58996; Pritzel 6972; Nissen (Bot.) 1494; Hunt (Bot.) 199. DLC, MH-A, MoU, NN-RB, RPB; London:Wellcome, BN. 614/89

Platter, Felix. Observationum, in hominis affectibus . . . incommodantibus, libri tres. *Basel: C. Waldkirch, for L. König*, 1614. 845 p.; 8vo. Treatments for syphilis mention guaiacum. Wellcome I:5089. CtY-M, DNLM, NIC, WU; London:Wellcome, BN. 614/90

Pontanus, Johannes Isaacus. Historische beschrijvinghe der seer wijt beroemde coop-stadt Amsterdam . . . Eerst int latijn ghestelt . . . ende nu . . . overgheset door Petrum Montanum. *Amsterdam: J. Hondius*, 1614. 360 p.; illus., maps; 4to. Transl. from the author's *Rerum et urbis Amstelodamensium historia*, Amsterdam 1611. Sabin 64003; Tiele 877. DLC, ICJ, MnU-B, NNH; BL, BN. 614/91

Por los hijos, y nietos de conquistadores de Yucatan, sobre la confirmacion que piden de ayudas de costa que los governadores les han señalado en los tributos de los Indios [etc.]. [*Madrid?* 1614]. 4 numb. lvs; fol. BL (Yucatan). 614/92

Poutrincourt, Jean de Biencourt, sieur de, baron de Saint-Just. Factum du procez entre messire Jean de Biencourt . . . sieur de Poutrincourt . . . d'une part, et Pierre Biard, Evemond Massé & consorts, soy disans prestres de la Société de Jesus. [*Paris?*]

1614. 47 p.; 4to. On Jesuits in Canada. For a reply by Biard, see the year 1616. Cf. Harrisse (NF) 28 & 30; cf. Streit II:2476; Backer XI:1607; JCB AR51:29–31. MH, MiU-C, RPJCB; BL.   614/93

Purchas, Samuel. Purchas his Pilgrimage . . . The second edition, much enlarged with additions. *London: W. Stansby, for H. Fetherstone,* 1614. 918 p.; fol. 1st publ., London, 1613. For variant settings of the t.p., &c., see the STC. Sabin 66679 & 66680; Streit I:346; STC 20506; JCB (3) II:105. CSmH, CtY, DLC, ICN, MB, NN-RB, PU, RPJCB; BL.   614/94

Raleigh, Sir Walter. The history of the world. *London: W. Stansby, for W. Burre,* 1614. 2 v.; maps; fol. Included in pt 1 are scattered refs to Hispaniola, Peru, mangrove tree (termed 'ficus indica'), for which see the appended table of contents. Sabin 67560n; Brushfield (Raleigh) 223 (A); STC 20637. CSmH, CtY, DLC, ICN, InU-L, MH, NN-RB, RPB (imp.); BL.   614/95

Ravenscroft, Thomas. A briefe discourse of the true . . . use of charact'ring the degrees by their perfection, imperfection, and diminution in measurable musicke. *London: E. Allde, for T. Adams,* 1614. [108] p.; 4to. In discussion of musical notation, employs song on tobacco. STC 20756; Arents 110. CSmH, CtY, DLC, NN-A; BL.   614/96

Rich, Barnabe. The honestie of this age. *London: [T. Dawson] for T. A[dams].,* 1614. 4to. Includes diatribe condemning tobacco. STC 20986. CSmH, DFo; BL.   614/97

Rivadeneira, Pedro de, S.J. Leben dess seligen p. Ignatii [Loyolae]. *Ingolstadt: Elisabeth Angermaier,* 1614. 222 p.; 4to. Transl. from author's *Vita Ignatii Loiolae,* 1st publ., Naples, 1572. Includes refs to Jesuits in Brazil. InU-L.   614/98

Romancero general. Romancero general, en que se contiene todos los romances . . . aora nuevamente añadido, y enmendado por Pedro Flores. *Madrid: J. de la Cuesta, for M. Martínez,* 1614. 499 numb. lvs; 4to. 1st publ. in this version, Madrid, 1604. Pérez Pastor (Madrid) 1298; Palau 276982. MWiW-C, NNH; BL, BN.   614/99

Rowlands, Samuel. Doctor Merrie-man: or, Nothing but mirth. *London: [W. White,] for*

S. Rand, 1614. 4to. In verse. 1st publ., London, 1607, under title *Democritus, or Doctor Merry-man his medicines.* STC 21372.5. BL (t.p. only).   614/100

——. A fooles bolt is soon shot. *London: [E. Allde?] for G. Loftus, [sold by A. Johnson],* 1614. 4to. In verse. The West Indies & their gold are mentioned. STC 21381. Cambridge: Trinity.   614/101

Sandoval, Prudencio de, Bp of Pamplona. Historia de la vida y hechos del Emperador Carlos V. *Pamplona: B. Paris,* 1614. 2 v.; illus.; fol. 1st publ., Valladolid, 1604–6. Sabin 76424; Palau 297147. BN.   614/102

Settala, Lodovico. Animadversionum, & cautionum medicarum libri septem. *Milan: G. B. Bidelli,* 1614. 260 p.; port.; 8vo. In bk 7, paragraphs 199–204 & 211–13 describe use of guaiacum, mechoacan, & sarsaparilla for treatment of syphilis. CtY-M, DNLM.   614/103

Sosa, Pedro de, O. F. M. Señor. Fray Pedro de Sossa de la Orden de S. Francisco, guardian del convento de S. Francisco de la ciudad de Santiago en . . . Chile, dize, que el dicho reyno le embia a dar quenta a V. Magestad del trabajoso estado en que queda. *[Madrid? 1614?].* [4] p.; fol. Sabin 87186; Medina (Chile) 210; Streit II:1438. BL, Santiago, Chile:BN.   614/104

Tabourot, Estienne. Les bigarrures et touches. *Paris: J. Richer,* 1614. 4 pts; illus., ports; 12mo. In verse. 1st publ. in this collective edn, Paris, 1603, q.v. NN-RB; BN.
                              614/105

——. Le quatriesme des Bigarrures. *Paris: J. Richer,* 1614. 50 numb. lvs; 12mo. In verse. Issued as part of author's *Les bigarrures et touches,* Paris, 1615, q.v.

Tailor, Robert. The hogge hath lost his pearle. A comedy. *London: [J. Beale,] for R. Redmer,* 1614. [62] p.; 4to. Tobacco is in passing compared to vainglory; also cited are the 'Plantation in Virginia' & West Indies. STC 23658; Greg 321; Arents (Add.) 163. CSmH, CtY, DLC, MH, NN-A; BL.
                              614/106

Taylor, John, the Water-poet. The nipping or snipping of abuses. *London: E. Griffin, for N. Butter,* 1614. 52 lvs; 4to. In verse. Included are 'Plutoes proclamation concern-

ing his infernall pleasure for the propagation of tobaco' and 'A proclamation or
approbation from the King of execration,
to every nation, for tobaccoes propagation',
both mentioning America. STC 23779;
Arents 111. CSmH, CtY, DFo (imp.), NN-
RB; BL. 614/107

——. Taylors water-worke: or The scullers
travels. *London:* [*T. Snodham?*] *for N. Butter,*
1614. 4to. In verse. 1st publ., London,
1612, under title *The sculler.* STC 23792.
NN-RB, ViU; BL (imp.), Oxford:Bodl.
614/108

——. The watermens suit, concerning players. [*London: G. Eld,* 1614?]. 4+ p.; 4to. Tobacco and the Bermudas are mentioned.
STC 23813.3. DFo (imp.), MH (imp.).
614/109

Entry canceled. 614/110

Thou, Jacques Auguste de. Historiarum sui
temporis. *Frankfurt a. M.: N. Hoffmann, for
P. Kopff,* 1614–21. 5 v.; 4to. 1st publ. as
here constituted, Paris, 1606–9. CU-A, ICU,
MB, NjP. 614/111

Vega Carpio, Lope Félix de. Doze comedias
. . . Quarta parte. *Madrid: M. Serrano de Var-
gas, for M. de Siles,* 1614. 296 (i.e., 322)
numb. lvs; 4to. Included is 'El nuevo
mundo, descubierto por Cristoval Colon'.
For numerous scattered refs to the New
World in the author's works, see M. A. Mo-
rínigo, *América en el teatro de Lope de Vega* (Bue-
nos Aires, 1946); see also Lope de Vega,
El nuevo mundo, as adapted by Joaquín de
Entrambasaguas, 2da ed. (Madrid, 1963).
Sabin 98767; Pérez Pastor (Madrid) 1309;
Palau 355277. PU; BL. 614/112

—[Anr edn]. *Pamplona: N. de Assiayn,* 1614.
296 numb. lvs; 4to. Palau 355278. BN, Ma-
drid:BU. 614/113

—[Anr edn]. Comedias . . . quarta parte. *Barcelona: S. de Cormellas,* 1614. 312 numb. lvs;
4to. Palau 355279. BL, Madrid:BN.
614/114

—[Anr issue of preceding]. *Barcelona: S. de Cormellas, for J. Bonilla,* 1614. Palau 355279n.
Madrid:BN. 614/115

Virginia Company of London. [A declaration of the presente estate of the English
in Virginia with a finall resolucon concerning the great lotterye intended for there

supply. *London: F. Kingston,* 1614.] Known
only from entry in Stationers' Register for
9 March 1613, i.e., 1614. Sabin 99871.
614/116

Visscher, Roemer. Sinne-poppen. *Amsterdam: W. J. Blaeu,* 1614. 183 p.; illus.; obl.
4to. Included is an engraving, with supporting text, portraying a smoker. Vries 53; cf.
Arents (Add.) 196. CSmH. 614/117

Wither, George. Abuses stript, and whipt.
London: T. S[nodham]., for F. Burton, 1614.
[332] p.; 8vo. In verse. 1st publ., London,
1613. STC 25895. CSmH, CtY, DFo, MH;
BL. 614/118

1615

Abriss der Blü[men] und Frucht, die in den
nidergängien Indien wächst und newlichen
ubersandt worden ist ihrer päpst: heyl:
Paulo dem Fünfften zu praesentiren. *Augsburg: C. Mang, for D. Custos* [ca. 1615?]. bds.;
fol. ICN (as [1610?]); BL (West Indies; as
[1620?]). 615/1

An advice how to plant tobacco in England
. . . Written by C. T. *London: N. Okes, sold
by W. Burre,* 1615. [22] p.; 4to. STC 23612;
Arents 120. CSmH, DFo, NN-A; BL.
615/2

Alemán, Mateo. De la vida del picaro Guzman de Alfarache. *Milan: G. B. Bidelli,* 1615.
2 v.; 8vo. Contains both parts, the 1st having been 1st publ., Madrid, 1599, the 2nd,
Lisbon, 1604. Medina (BHA) 613; Laurenti
(Nov. pic. esp.) 560–61; Palau 6698. MH,
NNH, PU; BN. 615/3

——. Der Landtstörtzer: Gusman von Alfarche oder Picaro genant . . . Durch Aegidium Albertinum . . . auss dem Spanischen
verteutscht. *Munich: N. Heinrich,* 1615. 723
p.; 8vo. Transl. from Aleman's *Guzman de
Alfarache,* 1st publ., Madrid, 1599; cf. 1601
edn. Incorporates selections from Juan José
Martí's spurious continuation of 1602. Laurenti (Nov. pic. esp.) 603; Dt. Ges. Kat.
3:868; Faber du Faur 904. CtY:BL, Mu-
nich:StB. 615/4

——. Vita del picaro Gusmano d'Alfarace
. . . Tradotta . . . da Barezzo Barezzi. *Venice: B. Barezzi,* 1615. 2 v.; 8vo. Includes both

pts, the former 1st publ. Madrid, 1599 (cf. 1601 edn above), the 2nd, Lisbon, 1604. Pt 1 as here transl. 1st publ., Venice, 1606, with translation of pt 2 now added. Laurenti (Nov. pic. esp.) 711; Palau 6678. DLC, MiU; Munich:StB. 615/5

Amati, Scipione. Historia del regno di Voxu del Giapone. *Rome: G. Mascardi*, 1615. 76 p.; 4to. Included are refs to Franciscan missions in Mexico, etc. Streit V:1126. DLC, MiU, NN-RB, PHi; BL, BN. 615/6

Antist, Vincente Justiniano, O.P. Tratado de la immaculada concepcion de nuestra Señora; es parte del ultimo capitulo de las adiciones . . . a la historia del santo fray Luys Bertran. *Seville: G. R. Vejarano*, 1615. 22 lvs; 4to. 1st publ., Valencia, 1593, as *Adiciones a la historia del s.p.fr. Luis Beltran*. Medina (BHA) 615; Escudero (Seville) 1.006 & 1.011; Palau 13085. BL. 615/7

Aventrote, Juan. Epistola . . . ad . . . potentissimum regem Hispaniarum . . . In latinam linguam nunc conversa de exemplari Belgico. [Rotterdam?] 1615. 66 p.; 8vo. Transl. from Amsterdam, 1613, edn of Aventrote's *Sendbrief*, with preface referring to silver mines in Peru. Other edns & translations of this year have a differing preface, lacking Americana. Millares Carlo (Avontroot) 5; Knuttel 2037. The Hague:KB. 615/8

Entries canceled. 615/9–615/14

Avity, Pierre d', sieur de Montmartin. The estates, empires, and principallities of the world . . . Translated out of French by Edw: Grimstone. *London: A. Islip, for M. Lownes & J. Bill*, 1615. 1234 p.; fol. Transl. from Avity's *Les estates, empires et principautez du monde*, 1st publ., Paris, 1613. STC 988. CSmH, CtY, DLC, ICN, MiU, MnU-B, NN-RB; BL. 615/15

——. Les estats, empires, et principautez du monde. *Paris: P. Chevalier*, 1615. 1464 p.; 4to. 1st publ., Paris, 1613. Cf. Sabin 2498. Göttingen:UB. 615/16

Barros, João de. Quarta decada de Asia . . . Reformada, accrescentada e illustrada com notas e taboas geographicas por João Baptista Lavanha. *Madrid: A. Falorsi, for the Imprenta Real*, 1615. 711 p.; maps; fol. Continues earlier Decades 1st publ., Lisbon, 1552–53 & 1563. Covers period 1526–38. In bk 9, chapt. 20, citing Diogo do Couto, Grijalva's voyage from Peru to the Moluccas is described. Cf. Sabin 3646; Borba de Moraes I:71; Streit IV:667; Pérez Pastor (Madrid) 1318; JCB (3) II:106. DLC, ICN, MH, MnU-B, NN-RB, RPJCB; BL, BN. 615/17

Béguin, Jean. Les elemens de chymie. *Paris: M. Le Maître*, 1615. Transl. from Béguin's *Tyrocinium chymicum*, 1st publ., Paris, 1612. Glasgow:UL. 615/18

——. Tyrocinium chymicum. *Cologne: A. Boetzer*, 1615. 1st publ., Paris, 1612. Glasgow:UL. 615/19

Boccalini, Traiano. Les cent premieres nouvelles et advis de Parnasse . . . Le tout traduict d'italien . . . par Th. de Fougasses. *Paris: A. Périer*, 1615. 686 p.; 8vo. Transl. from the author's *De' ragguagli di Parnaso . . . Centuria prima*, 1st publ., Venice, 1612. Cioranescu (XVII) 31046. MH; BL, BN. 615/20

——. De' ragguagli di Parnaso . . . Centuria prima. *Milan: G. B. Bidelli*, 1615. 472 p.; 8vo. 1st publ., Venice, 1612. Firpo (Ragguagli) 9; Michel (Répertoire) I:175. BN. 615/21

——. De' ragguagli di Parnaso . . . Centuria seconda. *Milan: G. B. Bidelli*, 1615. 430 p.; 8vo. 1st publ., Venice, 1613; issued with Bidelli's Centuria prima of this year above. Firpo (Ragguagli) 9. BN. 615/22

——. Pietra del paragone politico tratta dal monte Parnaso. *'Cormopoli'* [i.e., *Venice*]: A. Teler, 1615. 138 p.; 4to. Continues Boccalini's *De' ragguagli di Parnaso*, Venice, 1612–13. A satire on the Spanish monarchy, with chapter 'Li cani delle Indie sono divenuti lupi', referring to Dutch intrusions in Spanish America. Michel (Répertoire) I:174. ICN, MiU; Albi:BM. 615/23

—[Anr edn]. *'Cormopoli'* [i.e., *Venice*]: Z. Teler, 1615. 51 lvs (A–N⁴); 4to. Michel (Répertoire) I:174. CU, CtY, DLC, IU, InU-L, MH, PU; Nantes:BM. 615/24

—[Anr edn]. *'Cormopoli'* [i.e., *Venice*]: Z. Teler, 1615. 56 lvs (A–O⁴); 4to. Michel (Répertoire) I:174. BN. 615/25

—[Anr edn]. *'Cormopoli'* [i.e., *Venice*]: Z. Teler, 1615. 38 lvs (A–K⁴); 4to. Michel (Répertoire) I:174. Aix-en-Provence:Bibl. Méjanes. 615/26

—[Anr edn]. *'Cormopoli'* [i.e., *Venice*]: *G. Teler,* 1615. 42 lvs (A–K⁴, A⁴); 4to. Michel (Répertoire) I:174. BN. 615/27

—[Anr edn]. *'Cormopoli'* [i.e., *Venice*]: *Z. Teler,* 1615. [83] p. (A–K⁴); 4to. Michel (Répertoire) I:174. Toulouse:BM. 615/28

—[Anr edn]. *'Cormopoli'* [i.e., *Venice*]: *G. Teler,* 1615. 40 lvs (A–K⁴); 4to. Michel (Répertoire) I:174. BN. 615/29

—[Anr edn]. *'Cormopoli'* [i.e., *Venice*]: *G. Teler,* 1615. 32 lvs (A–H⁴); 4to. Michel (Répertoire) I:174. BN. 615/30

—[Anr edn]. *'Cormopoli'* [i.e., *Venice*]: *G. Teler,* 1615. 38 lvs (A–I⁴, K²); 4to. MnU, NIC, OU. 615/31

Brathwait, Richard. A strappado for the divell. Epigrams and satyres. *London: J. B[eale]., for R. Redmer,* 1615. 2 pts; 8vo. In epigram 'The authors morall to his Civell Divell' is a ref. to smoking. STC 3588; Arents (Add.) 164. CSmH, DFo, IU, MH, NN-A, PBL; BL. 615/32

Breton, Nicholas. Wits private wealth. *London: T. Creede, for J. Tapp,* 1615. 4to. 1st publ., London, 1612. STC 3710. CSmH; Oxford:Bodl. 615/33

Buchanan, George. Poemata omnia. *Edinburgh: A. Hart,* 1615. 2 pts; 12mo. In addition to poems earlier publ. (cf. Saumur, 1607, edn), here included is one 'De Nicotiana falso nomine Medicea appellata'. To the title of the poem 'In colonias Brasilienses' is added the phrase 'A Lusitanis missis in Brasiliam'. STC 3990; cf. Arents 165. CSmH, MH; BL. 615/34

Camden, William. Annales rerum Anglicarum . . . ad annum salutis M. D. LXXXIX. *London: W. Stansby, for S. Waterson,* 1615. 499 p.; fol. Under years 1580, 1585, & 1587 are accounts of Sir Francis Drake's various voyages. For a continuation, see the year 1625. STC 4496; Arents (Add.) 165. CSmH, CtY, DLC, ICN, MH, PPL, NN-RB, RPJCB; BL. 615/35

Camerarius, Philipp. Operae horarum subcisivarum . . . Centuria prima. *Frankfurt a. M.: E. Emmel, for P. Kopff,* 1615. 474 p.; 4to. 1st publ., Altdorf, 1591; cf. 1602 edn. CtY, DLC, MnU-B; BN. 615/36

Cartari, Vincenzo. Le vere e nove imagini de gli dei delli antichi. *Padua: P. P. Tozzi,* 1615. 576 p.; illus.; 4to. Includes as pt 2 the 'Imagine de gli Indiani Orientali et Occidentali' of Lorenzo Pignoria, not found in earlier edns of Cartari's work. Sabin 11104; Michel (Répertoire) II:52. CU, DLC, MWiW-C, MnU-B, NPV, PPL; BL, BN. 615/37

Cervantes Saavedra, Miguel de. Les nouvelles . . . Traduites . . . les six premieres, par F. de Rosset, et les autres six, par le sr. d'Audiguier. *Paris: J. Richer,* 1615,'14. 3 pts; 8vo. Translated from the author's *Novelas exemplares,* Madrid, 1613. Ríus (Cervantes) 885; Palau 53520. MH, NNH; BN. 615/38

——. Novelas exemplares. *Pamplona: N. de Assiayn,* 1615. 391 numb. lvs; 8vo. 1st publ., Madrid, 1613. Ríus (Cervantes) 223; Palau 53403. NN-RB; BL. 615/39

—[Anr edn]. *Milan: G. B. Bidelli,* 1615. 763 p.; 12mo. Ríus (Cervantes) 224; Palau 53404. MB, NNH, PU; BL, BN. 615/40

——. Segunda parte del ingenioso cavallero Don Quixote de la Mancha. *Madrid: J. de la Cuesta, for F. de Robles,* 1615. 280 numb. lvs; 4to. In chapt. x, Sancho Panza mentions Mexico; in chapt. lxxi, Don Quixote tells Sancho that the mines of Potosí would be inadequate to reward him for his services. Ríus (Cervantes) 12; Pérez Pastor (Madrid) 1325; Rothschild 3069; Palau 51985. CSmH, CtY, MH, NN-RB, PU; BL, BN. 615/41

Clercq, Nikolaas de. Tooneel der keyseren eñ coningen van Christenryck sedert den onderganck van het Griecks keyserdom . . . Uyt de geloofsveerdigste schrijvers, door N. D. C. *Delft: N. de Clercq,* 1615. 213 lvs; ports; fol. Includes account of the discovery of America & description of the West Indies. For a 2nd pt, see Clercq's *Tooneel der beroemder hertogen,* Delft, 1617. Muller (1872) 363. NN, NNH, PBL. 615/42

Corbeius, Theodorus. Pathologia, sive Morborum et affectuum omnium praeter naturam . . . enumeratio. *Frankfurt a. M.: H. Palthenius,* 1615. 508 p.; 8vo. In bk 2, sect. 7, chapt. 2, 'De morbo gallico', the possible New World source of syphilis is discussed. BN. 615/43

Cortés, Martín. The arte of navigation. *London: W. Stansby, for J. Tapp,* 1615. 169 p.; illus., map; 4to. Transl. by Richard Eden from Cortés's *Breve compendio de la sphera*, 1st publ., Seville, 1551; cf. English edn, London, 1609, above. STC 5805. NN-RB; BL.   615/44

Dalechamps, Jacques. Histoire generale des plantes . . . Sortie latine de la bibliotheque de me Jaques Dalechamps, puis faite françoise par me Jean des Moulins. *Lyons: Heirs of G. Rouillé*, 1615. 2 v.; illus.; fol. Transl. from the author's *Historia generalis plantarum*, 1st publ., Lyons, 1586. Included are descriptions, & illus., of numerous American plants. Pritzel 2035n; Nissen (Bot.) 447. DNLM, MH-A, MoSB, RPB; BL, BN.
                                             615/45

—[Anr issue]. De l'histoire generale des plantes. *Lyons: Heirs of G. Rouillé*, 1615. Arents (Add.) 166. DLC, NN-A, OOxM.
                                             615/46

Digges, Sir Dudley. The defence of trade. In a letter to Sir Thomas Smith. *London: W. Stansby, for J. Barnes*, 1615. 50 p.; 4to. A reply to Robt Kayll's *The trades increase* of this year. Largely focused on East Indian commerce, but with mention of Virginia. STC 6845; Kress 341; JCB (3) II:107. CSmH, CtY, DLC, IU, InU-L, MH, MnU-B, NNC, RPJCB; BL.   615/47

Du Bartas, Guillaume de Salluste, seigneur. Les oeuvres poetiques et chrestiennes. *Geneva: P. & J. Chouët*, 1615. 3 v.; 12mo. In verse. Included are the author's *La sepmaine*, 1st publ., Paris, 1578, & his *La seconde sepmaine*, 1st publ., Paris, 1584; cf. 1603 edn. Holmes (DuBartas) I:77 no. 37. BN.
                                             615/48

—[Anr issue]. *Geneva: S. Crespin*, 1615. Holmes (DuBartas) I:77 no. 37n. NCH; BL, BN.   615/49

Du Jarric, Pierre, S.J. Thesaurus rerum Indicarum . . . Opus nunc primum Matthia Martinez e gallico . . . translatum. *Cologne: P. Henning*, 1615. 3 v.; 8vo. Transl. from author's *L'histoire des choses plus memorables*, 1st publ., Bordeaux, 1608–14; cf. year 1610. Contains in v. 2 description of Brazil & Jesuit missions there. Sabin 35791; Borba de Moraes I:358; Streit V:186; Backer IV:752. CU, CtY-D, DLC, MH, NN-RB; BL, BN.
                                             615/50

Fernel, Jean. Universa medicina. *Lyons: C. Morillon*, 1615. 4 pts; fol. 1st publ. as here

constituted, Paris, 1567; cf. 1601–2 edn. Sherrington (Fernel) 78.J22. Edinburgh:UL
                                             615/51

Fresneau, Jacques. A messieurs des estat en la Chambre de la noblesse. [*Paris?*] 1615. 8 p.; 16mo. Requests, *inter alia*, that French ambassador in London arrange sharing of whaling between France & England in Baltic & off Greenland. JCB (3) II:107. ICN, RPJCB; BN.   615/52

Fuchs, Samuel. Metoposcopia et ophthalmoscopia. *Strassburg: T. Glaser, for P. Ledertz*, 1615. 140 p.; illus.; 8vo. Included is a port. of Columbus. Sabin 26106. BL, BN.
                                             615/53

Goddard, William. A neaste of waspes. *Dort:* 1615. 4to. In verse. Includes ref. to use of tobacco as a dentifrice. STC 11929. CSmH, DFo; Oxford: Worcester.   615/54

González de Azevedo, Juan. Señor. El capitan Juan Goncalez de Azevedo. [*Madrid:* 1615?]. 9 numb. lvs; fol. Memorial to king of Spain defending Indians against tribute imposed on them. Medina (BHA) 6509. BL.
                                             615/55

——. Señor. El capitan Juan Gonçalez de Azevedo, por lo que toca al servício de Dios . . . y de V. Real Magestad. [*Madrid?* 1615?]. 4 numb. lvs; fol. Memorial to king of Spain on grievances of Peruvian natives. Medina (BHA) 6511. BL.   615/56

Greene, Robert. Philomela, the Lady Fitzwaters nightingale. *London: G. Purslowe*, 1615. [78] p.; 4to. 1st publ., London, 1592. On verso of lf D4 'most false Lutesio' is compared to 'the Hysop [i.e., tobacco?], growing in America, that is liked of strangers for the smell'. STC 12297. CSmH, DFo, MH; BL.   615/57

——. Theeves falling out. *London: T. G[ubbin].,* 1615. 4to. 1st publ., London, 1592, under title *A disputation betweene a hee conny-catcher, and a shee conny-catcher*. The potato is mentioned. STC 12235. Oxford:Bodl.
                                             615/58

Guerrero, Marcos. Por los herederos del doctor don Marcos Guerrero, oydor de la Real Audiencia di Mexico, difunto. Con el Señor fiscal. Sobre los cargos de su visita. [*Madrid:* 1615?]. 8 numb. lvs; fol. BL.
                                             615/59

Hamor, Ralph, the Younger. A true discourse of the present estate of Virginia. *London: J. Beale, for W. Welby,* 1615. 69 p.; 4to. For variance in issues see Vail as cited. Sabin 30120; Clayton-Torrence 27; Vail (Frontier) 38; STC 12736; Arents 112; Church 365; JCB (3) II:107. CSmH, CtY, DLC, ICN, InU-L, MH, MiU-C, MnU-B, NN-RB, PPL, RPJCB; BL. 615/60

Harington, Sir John. Epigrams both pleasant and serious. *London: J. Budge,* 1615. 24 lvs; 4to. Includes refs to tobacco & to Trinidad. STC 12775; Arents 113. CSmH, CtY, DFo, MH, NN-A; BL. 615/61

Histoire veritable de ce qui c'est passé de nouveau entre les François & Portugais en l'isle de Maragnan au pays de Toupinambous. *Paris: N. Rousset,* 1615. 21 p.; 8vo. Borba de Moraes I:343; JCB AR52:26–31. NN-RB, RPJCB; BL (French). 615/62

—[Anr edn]. Histoire veritable du combat, tant par mer que par terre . . . en l'isle de Maragnan. *Paris: Y. Du Guy,* 1615. 15 p.; 8vo. Describes Portuguese & French rivalry. MnU-B. 615/63

Hoby, Sir Edward. A curry-combe for a coxe-combe. *London: W. Stansby, for N. Butter,* 1615. 266 p.; 4to. Includes refs to tobacco. STC 13540; Arents 115. CSmH, CtY, DFo, ICN, MH, NN-A; BL. 615/64

Hollings, Edmund. Medicamentorum oeconomia nova. *Ingolstadt: Eder Press, for Elizabeth Angermaier,* 1615. 303 p.; 8vo. 1st publ., Ingolstadt, 1610; here a reissue of that edn with new t.p. & prelim. matter. Shaaber (Brit. auth.) H242. DNLM, MiU; Oxford: Merton. 615/65

Hues, Robert. Tractatus de globis. *[Heidelberg?] G. Vögelin* [1615?]. 258 p.; 12mo. 1st publ., London, 1594; cf. 1611 edn. Shaaber (Brit. auth.) H479. NN-RB; BL. 615/66

Hughes, Lewis. A letter, sent into England from the Summer Ilands. *London: J. B[eale]., for W. Welby,* 1615. [13] p.; 4to. STC 13919; Church 367A. CSmH, MiU-C, NN-RB; BL. 615/67

Jesuits. Historiae Societatis Jesu prima pars, autore Nicolao Orlandino. *Rome: B. Zannetti,* 1615. 578 p.; fol. Included are numerous refs to Brazil. Borba de Moraes II:119; Streit I:354; Backer V:1935 & VII:365:366; Palau 204235; JCB (3) II:109. CU-L, DLC, NNH, RPJCB; BN. 615/68

—[Anr edn]. *Cologne: A. Hierat,* 1615. 578 p.; fol. Borba de Moraes II:119; Streit I:355. Backer V:1935. BN. 615/69

Jesuits. Compendium privilegiorum. Compendium facultatum, et indulgentiarum, quae religiosis Societatis Jesu, & aliis Christi fidelibus in Indiarum Orientalium & Occidentalium provinciis conceduntur. *Rome: Jesuit College,* 1615. 62 p.; 12mo. 1st publ., Rome, 1580; cf. 1606 edn. Streit I:356. Madrid:BN. 615/70

Johnson, Jacob (fl. 1615). Schediasmata poetica: sive, Epigrammatum libellus. *London: J. Beale,* 1615. 32 lvs; 8vo. Includes discussion of tobacco. STC 14665; Arents 116. DFo, NN-A; Chatsworth. 615/71

—[Anr issue]. Epigrammatum libellus: sive Schediasmata poetica. *London: J. Beale, for R. Redmer,* 1115 [i.e., 1615]. The preceding item, here reissued with cancel t.p. STC 14666. NNC; BL. 615/72

Juan de Santa María, O.F.M. Chronica de la provincia de San Joseph de los Descalços de la orden de los Menores de . . . S. Francisco. *Madrid: Imprenta Real,* 1615–18. 2 v.; fol. In bk 4, chapts 14, 18, &c., describe establishment of Mexican province; chapt. 24 describes career of Luis Beltrán. Medina (BHA) 631; Streit I: 351; Pérez Pastor (Madrid) 1367 & 1571. RPJCB; BL, BN. 615/73

Kayll, Robert. The trades increase. *London: N. Okes, sold by W. Burre,* 1615. 56 p.; 4to. On the herring fishery, incl. refs to Newfoundland, Bermuda, & Virginia. On authorship, see William Foster, 'The author of "The trades increase",' *TLS,* 29 March 1934, p. 229. For printing variants see the revised STC. Sabin 71899; STC 20579 (rev. to 14894.7–9); Arents (Add.) 167; Kress 347; JCB (3) II:109. CSmH, CtY, DLC, ICU, MH, MiU-C, NN-RB, RPJCB; BL. 615/74

Krachteloose donder van den Helschen hondt. *[n.p., 1615?]. See the year* 1614.

Libavius, Andreas. Sintagmatis selectorum undiquaque et perspicue traditorum alchymiae arcanorum. *Frankfurt a. M.: N. Hoffmann, for P. Kopff,* 1615. 2 v.; illus.; fol. 1st publ., Frankfurt a. M., 1611–13. BN. 615/75

López, Juan, O.P., Bp of Monopoli. Quarta

parte de la Historia general de Santo Domingo, y de su Orden de Predicadores. *Valladolid: F. Fernández de Córdoba*, 1615. 1137 p.; fol. Included are accounts of Dominican missions in Spanish America. For a subsequent 5th part, see the year 1621. Medina (BHA) 623; Streit I:352; Alcocer (Valladolid) 614; Palau 14140. Rome:BN, Santiago, Chile:BN. 615/76

Losa, Francisco de. La vida, que hizo el siervo de Dios Gregorio Lopez, en algunos lugares de esta Nueva España. *Lisbon: P. Craesbeeck*, 1615. 107 numb. lvs; 8vo. 1st publ., Mexico, 1613. Cf. Sabin 42575; Medina (BHA) 624; Streit II:1449; Palau 142524n. DLC, MB, MnU-B, NNH; BL (imp.). 615/77

Maiolo, Simeone, Bp of Volturara. Dies caniculares . . . hoc est, Colloquia physica nova. *Mainz: J. T. Schönwetter*, 1615. 1248 p.; fol. 1st publ., Rome, 1597; cf. 1607 edn. ICN, NNH; BL. 615/78

Marcos da Lisboa, Bp, O.F.M. Primera [-tercera] parte das Chronicas da ordem dos Frades menores do . . . padre sam Francisco . . . Novamente empressa . . . por o padre frey Luis dos Anjos. *Lisbon: P. Craesbeeck, for T. do Valle*, 1615. 3 v.; fol. The 3rd pt, 1st publ. in Spanish, Salamanca, 1570, includes account of Franciscans in Mexico. Silva VI:131. MH; BN. 615/79

Marguérite d'Angoulême, Queen of Navarre. L'Heptameron. *Paris: J. Bessin*, 1615. 587 p.; 12mo. 1st publ., Paris, 1558, under title *Histoires des amans fortunez;* subsequently issued under above title. The 67th tale, naming Canada, recounts an episode from Cartier's voyage there in 1542–44. Tchémerzine VII:395. BN. 615/80

Markham, Gervase. Countrey contentments, in two bookes. *London: J. B[eale]., for R. Jackson*, 1615. 2 pts; 4to. The 2nd pt comprises *The English huswife*, in which, in bk 2, chapt. 2, instructions are included for the cooking of turkeys. Poynter (Markham) 23.1; STC 17342. CSmH, DFo, NN-RB (pt 2 only); BL. 615/81

Matthieu, Pierre. Histoire de France et des choses memorables, advenues aux provinces estrangeres durant sept années de paix, du regne de Henry IIII. *Rouen: J. Os-*

mont & T. Daré, 1615 (v. 1); *Paris: J. Bessin* [n.d.] (v. 2). 1st publ., Paris, 1605. ICN, WaU. 615/82

—[Anr edn]. *Paris: J. Mettayer & M. Guillemot*, 1615. 2 v.; 8vo. BN. 615/83

Medina, Pedro de. L'art de naviguer . . . traduit . . . par Nicolas de Nicolai . . . nouvellement reveu . . . par Jean de Séville, dit Le Souci. *La Rochelle: J. Brethommé, for A. de La Forge*, 1615. 273 p.; illus.; 4to. 1st publ. as here transl., Lyons, 1553; cf. 1607, Rouen, edn. Palau 159676. BL 615/84

Mexía, Pedro. Ragionamenti dottissimi et curiosi. *Venice: A. & B. Dei, bros*, 1615. 112 p.; 4to. 1st publ. as here transl. from Mexía's *Colóquios* (Seville, 1547), Venice, 1557, under title *Dialoghi*. The 1st dialogue, on physicians, includes a ref. to syphilis & its cure by guaiacum; the 3rd, on the sun, refers to the Magellan circumnavigation. Palau 167382. CaBVaU; Barcelona:BU. 615/85

Molina, Luis de. De justitia et jure tomi sex. *Antwerp: J. van Keerberghen*, 1615. 2 v.; fol. 1st publ., Cuenca (Spain); cf. years 1601 & 1602 above. Backer V:1177; Palau 174623. 615/86

Münster, Sebastian. Cosmographia, das ist, Ausführliche und eigentliche beschreibung aller Ländern . . . durch Joan. Jacobum Grasserum . . . gemehret und verbessert. *Basel: S. Henricpetri*, 1615. 1575 p.; ports, maps; fol. 1st publ., Basel, 1544; here anr issue of 1614 edn with added t.p. as above. Burmeister (Münster) 85. Copenhagen:KB, Freiburg i. Br:UB. 615/87

Neck, Jacob Corneliszoon van. Ander Schiffart in die Orientalische Indien, so die holländische Schieff . . . verrichtet . . . Editio tertia. *Frankfurt a. M.: Widow of L. Hulsius*, 1615. 118 p.; illus., maps; 4to. (Levinus Hulsius's *Sammlung von . . . Schiffahrten*. Pt 2). 1st publ. in this version, Frankfurt a. M., 1602. For variant issue see Church. Sabin 33654; Church 264 & 265; JCB (3) I:451. CSmH, ICN, NN-RB, RPJCB; BL, BN. 615/88

Orlandini, Nicolò, S.J. Historiae Societatis Jesu prima pars. *Rome: 1615. See* Jesuits *above.*

Overbury, Sir Thomas. New and choise characters, of several authors . . . sixt impression. *London: T. Creede, for L. Lisle*, 1615. [184] p.; 8vo. Here 1st publ. is a character of 'A Purveior of Tobacco'. Subsequent edns have title *Sir Thomas Overbury his wife.* STC 18908; Murphy (Engl. char.-bks) 17–18. DFo, NIC; BL.   615/89

Owen, John. Epigrammatum . . . libri decem. *Leipzig: Valentin Heirs, for T. Schürer*, 1615. 4 pts; 12mo. 1st publ., London, 1606. Shaaber (Brit. auth.) O87. NNC; BL.
615/90

Paré, Ambroise. De chirurgie, ende alle de opera, ofte wercken . . . Nu eerst uut de fransoysche . . . overgheset; door d. Carolum Battum. *Amsterdam: H. Laurenszoon*, 1615. 940 p.; illus.; fol. 1st publ. as here transl. from the Paris, 1585, 4th edn, Dordrecht, 1592; cf. the 1601 German edn. Doe (Paré) 60. CtY-M, DNLM, MiU; Paris:Mazarine.   615/91

Parrot, Henry. The mastive, or Young-whelpe of the olde-dogge. *London: T. Creede, for R. Meighen & T. Jones*, 1615. [69] p.; 4to. Included are several refs to tobacco. STC 19333; Arents (Add.) 168. CSmH, DFo, MH, NN-A; BL.   615/92

Passe, Crispijn van de. A garden of flowers . . . translated out of the Netherlandish. *Utrecht: S. de Roy, for C. van de Passe*, 1615. 2 pts; illus.; obl. 4to. 1st publ. with Latin text, Arnhem, 1614, under title *Hortus floridus.* Cf. Sabin 58996; Nissen (Bot.) 1494n; STC 19459. CSmH (imp.), DFo, WU; BL.
615/93

——. Jardin de fleurs. *Utrecht: C. van de Passe; & sold by J. Janszoon, at Arnhem* [1615?–1617]. 4 pts. illus.; obl. 4to. 1st publ. with Latin text, Arnhem, 1614, under title *Hortus floridus.* Nissen (Bot.) 1494n. DFo; BM(NH).
615/94

Petraeus, Henricus. Nosologia harmonica dogmatica et hermetica. *Marburg: P. Egenolff*, 1615–16. 2 v.; 4to. In v. 2, Dissertatio xlvi, 'De lue Venerea', ascribes the introduction of syphilis in Europe to Columbus & Vespucci. Wellcome I:4925. DNLM; London:Wellcome, BN.   615/95

—[Anr edn]. *Marburg: P. Egenolff*, 1615–23. 2 v. CtY-M, NNNAM.   615/96

Pigray, Pierre. Epitome des preceptes de médecine et chirurgie. *Rouen: A. Ouyn*, 1615. 764 p.; 8vo. 1st publ., Paris, 1600, under

title *La chirurgie;* cf. 1604 edn. CtY-M, DNLM; BL.   615/97

Pinon, Jacques. De anno romano carmen. *Paris: J. Libert*, 1615. 2 pts; 8vo. Included are refs to Columbus & America. Cioranescu (XVII) 55041. MH; BN.   615/98

Potier, Pierre. Insignes curationes, & singulares observationes centum. *Venice: G. B. Ciotti*, 1615. 111 p.; 8vo. Curatio xliii calls for use of sarsaparilla, xliv of guaiacum. MnU.   615/99

Praetorius, Michael. Syntagma musicum. *Wittenberg: J. Richter & Wolfenbüttel: E. Holwein*, 1615–20. 3 v.; illus.; 4to. In v. 2, following p. 236, is a section 'Theatrum instrumentorum, seu Sciagraphia' in which, on p. xxx, are illustrated American Indian woodwind & percussion instruments. CU, DLC, ICN, MH; BL (v. 2–3 only), BN.
615/100

Pyrard, François. Voyage de François Pyrard de Laval contenant sa navigation aux Indes Orientales, aux Moluques & au Bresil. *Paris: S. Thiboust, & R. Dallin*, 1615. 2 v.; 8vo. 1st publ., Paris, 1611, under title *Discours du voyage.* Sabin 66880; Borba de Moraes II:168–69. InU-L, MH, MnU-B, NNH; BN.   615/101

Renou, Jean de. Dispensatorium medicum. *Frankfurt a. M.: P. Jacobi, for J. T. Schönwetter*, 1615. 3 pts; 4to. Included also is Renou's *Institutionum pharmaceuticarum libri quinque*, 1st publ., Paris, 1608, as well as Joseph Duchesne's *Pharmacopoea dogmaticorum restituta*, 1st publ., Paris, 1607. DNLM, WU; London: Wellcome, BN.   615/102

Rich, Barnabe. The honestie of this age. *London: [J. Legat,] for T. A[dams].*, 1615. 28 lvs; 4to. 1st publ., London, 1614. In this edn, t.p. has reading 'Barnabe Rych'. STC 20987; Arents 117. CSmH, DFo, NN-A; Oxford: Bodl.   615/103

—[Anr edn]. *London: [J. Legat,] for T. A[dams].*, 1615. 28 lvs; 4to. The t.p. has reading 'Barnabe Rich'. STC 20987.5. BL.   615/104

Rivadeneira, Pedro de, S.J. Les vies des bienheureux peres de la Compagnie de Jesus, Ignace de Loyola, François Xavier, François Borgia [etc.] . . . Nouvellement traduictes d'espagnol . . . par M.I.G. *Arras: G. de LaRivière,* 1615. 461 p.; 8vo. Perhaps transl. from the author's *Obras*, 1st publ.

in collected form, Madrid, 1595; cf. year 1605 above. Backer VI:1756; Palau 266254.
615/105

Rosaccio, Giuseppe. Discorso della nobiltà ed eccellenza della terra rispetto a cieli ed altri elementi. *Florence: V. Tedesco* [1615?]. 12 lvs; map; fol. Sabin 73194.　615/106

Rowlands, Samuel. The melancholie knight. [*London:*] *R. B*[*lower*]. *sold by G. Loftus,* 1615. 4to. In verse Included are numerous refs to tobacco & the Indies. STC 21401. InU-L; Oxford: BL.　615/107

—[Anr edn]. *London: G. Loftus,* 1615. STC 21401.5. BL (t.p. only).　615/108

Rubio, Antonio. Logica mexicana . . . Hoc est Commentarii breviores . . . in Universam Aristotelis dialecticam. *Paris: J. Petit-Pas,* 1615. 738 p.; 8vo. 1st publ., Cologne, 1605. Cf. Sabin 73860; Medina (BHA) 629; Palau 280355. BL, BN.　615/109

Salazar, Ambrosio de. Almoneda general de las mas curiosas recopilaciones de los reynos de España. *Paris: T. DuBray,* 1615. 210 numb. lvs; 8vo. A reissue, with substitution of new prelim. lvs, of sheets of Paris, 1612, edn above. Cf. Palau 286462. BL.
615/110

——. Inventaire general des plus curieuses recherches des royaumes d'Espagne. *Paris: T. DuBray,* 1615. Like the preceding, a reissue, with substitution of new prelim. lvs, of sheets of Paris, 1612, edn above. Cf. Sabin 75557; Palau 286463n. BN.
615/111

Sandys, George. A relation of a journey . . . containing a description of the Turkish empire. *London:* [*R. Field,*] *for W. Barrett,* 1615. 310 p.; illus., maps; fol. Includes refs to Turks' use of tobacco. STC 21726; Arents 118. CSmH, CtY, DLC, ICN, MH, NN-RB; BL, BN.　615/112

Scaliger, Julius Caesar. Exotericarum exercitationum liber quintus decimus. *Lyons: Widow of A. Harsy,* 1615. 897 p.; illus.; 8vo. 1st publ., Paris, 1557; cf. 1601 edn. Wellcome I:5808. MH, PPiD, RPB; London: Wellcome, BN.　615/113

Segunda relacion la mas copiosa, y verdadera que ha salido. *Seville:* 1615. *See the year* 1625.

Serres, Olivier de, seigneur du Pradel. Le théatre d'agriculture. *Paris: A. Saugrain,* 1615. 907 p.; illus.; 4to. 1st publ., Paris, 1600; cf. 1603 edn. Arents (Add.) 140. DNAL, NN-A, WU.　615/114

Sharpe, Edward. Britaines busse. or A computation as well of the charge of busse of herring-fishing ship. *London: W. Jaggard.* 1615. [47] p.; 4to. Includes refs to timber from Virginia & the Bermudas.Occurs with or without errata note at end. STC 21846; Kress 348. CSmH, CtY, DFo, MH, NNC, RPJCB; BL.　615/115

Sharpham, Edward. The fleire. *London:* [*T. Snodham,*] *for N. Butter,* 1615. [58] p.; 4to. Drama. 1st publ., London, 1607. STC 22386; Greg 255(c). CSmH, CtY, DLC, MB; BL.　615/116

Sobrino, Gaspar, S.J. Señor, El padre Gaspar Sobrino de la Compañia de Jesus, (á quien el padre Luis de Valdivia ha embiado del reyno de Chile) propone á V. Magestad algunas razones, que prueven la eficacia de los medios resueltos cerca los negocios del dicho reyno. [*Madrid? ca.* 1615?]. 12 lvs; fol. Medina (BHA) 212; Streit II:1451; Backer VII:1342. Seville:Archivo de Indias.
615/117

Spain. Sovereigns, etc., 1598–1621 (Philip III). Cedula en que Su Magestad da licencia al doctor don Jorge Manrique de Lara, oydor de la Audiencia real de Panama. [*Madrid?* 1615?]. [2] p.; fol. Palau 50892; JCB (3) II:109. RPJCB.　615/118

Spenser, Edmund. The faerie queene. *London: H. L*[*ownes*]., *for M. Lownes,* 1611 [i.e., 1615?]. 363 p.; fol. 1st publ., London; cf. 1609 edn. Here a partially reset issue of 1609 edn. STC 23084. CSmH, DFo, MH, NNC; BL.　615/119

Stephens, John. Satyrical essayes, characters and others. *London: N. Okes, for R. Barnes,* 1615. 321 p.; 8vo. In bk i, characters of 'A coxcombe' & 'A drunkard' mention tobacco; that of 'An epicure', 'potato-rootes'. In bk ii, 'A common player' again mentions tobacco. STC 23249; Murphy (Engl. char.-bks)29; Arents 119. CSmH, DLC, ICN, MH, NN-A; BL.　615/120

—[Anr edn]. Essayes and characters . . . The second impression. *London: E. Allde, for P. Knight,* 1615. 434 p.; 8vo. STC 23250;

Arents (Add.) 169. CSmH, CtY, DFo, ICU, MH, MiU, NN-RB; BL. 615/121

Stow, John. The annales . . . of England . . . [Continued] unto . . . 1614. by Edmond Howes. *London: [T. Dawson,] for T. Adams,* 1615. 988 p.; fol. 1st publ. with American refs, London, 1592. In addition to those refs found in 1601 edn, English settlements in North America are described. STC 23338; Arents (Add.) 170. CSmH, CtY, DFo, ICN, MH, MnU, NN-RB; BL. 615/122

Suárez de Figueroa, Cristóbal. Plaza universal de todas ciencias y artes. Parte traducida de toscano, y parte compuesta por el doctor Christoval Suarez de Figueroa. *Madrid: L. Sánchez,* 1615. 368 numb. lvs; 4to. Transl. in part from Tommaso Garzoni's *La piazza universale,* 1st publ., Venice, 1585. Pérez Pastor (Madrid) 1370; Palau 323908. CtY, InU-L, MH, PU, RPJCB; BL, Madrid:BU. 615/123

Tabourot, Estienne. Les bigarrures et touches. *Paris: J. Richer,* 1615. 5 pts; illus., ports.; 12mo. In verse 1st publ., as here collected, Paris, 1603, q.v. Included, with imprint dated 1614, is *Le quatriesme des Bigarrures,* 1st publ., Paris, 1585; see also the printer's 1614 collective edn of which this is perhaps a reissue. Rothschild 1779. CLSU; BL, BN. 615/124

Tapp, John. The seamans kalendar . . . Fifth edition newly corrected and enlarged. *London: E. Allde, for J. Tapp,* 1615. 4to. 1st publ, London, 1602; no 4th edn has been traced. STC 23680. BL. 615/125

Taylor, John, the Water-poet. Faire and fowle weather: or A sea and land storme . . . With an apologie in defence of the painefull life and needful use of sailors. *London: [R. Blower, for] W. B[utler?].; sold by E. Wright,* 1615. 4to. In verse. 'An apologie for sea-men' mentions tobacco sellers. STC 23752. Oxford:Bodl. 615/126

Tomkis, Thomas. Albumazar. A comedy. *London: N. Okes, for W. Burre,* 1615. [81] p.; 4to. Includes ref. to tobacco shops. STC 24100; Greg 330 (a). CSmH, CtY, DFo, MH; BL. 615/127

——[Anr edn]. *London: N. Okes, for W. Burre,* 1615. [72] p.; 4to. STC 24101; Greg 330

(b); Arents (Add.) 171. CLU-C, DFo, IU, MH, NN-A; BL. 615/128

——. Lingua, or The combat of the tongue. *London: N. Okes, for S. Waterson* [ca. 1615]. 4to. Drama. 1st publ., London, 1607. STC 24105; Greg 239(b). CSmH; BL. 615/129

Torquemada, Juan de, O.F.M. Ia[-IIIa] parte de los veynte y un libros rituales y monarchia yndiána, con el origen y guerras de los Yndios Occidentales, de sus poblaciones, descubrimientos, conquistas, conversion y otras cosas maravillosas de la mesma tierra. *Seville: M. Clavijo,* 1615. 3 v.; fol. Sabin 96212; Medina (BHA) 634; Wagner (SW) 18; Streit II:1453; Escudero (Seville) 1.024; JCB (3) II:109–10. CtY, ICN, RPJCB; BL, BN. 615/130

Valderrama, Pedro de. Teatro de las religiones. *Barcelona: L. Déu, for M. Manescal,* 1615. 268 p.; fol. 1st publ., Seville, 1612. Palau 347321. MiU (imp.). 615/131

Valdivia, Luis de. Relacion de lo que sucedio en el reyno de Chile, despues que el padre Luys de Valdivia . . . entrò en el con sus ocho compañeros . . . el año de 1612. [*Madrid?* 1615?]. 22 numb. lvs; fol. Sabin 98330; Medina (Chile) 206; Palau 257417. BL. 615/132

Vaz Coutinho, Gonçalo. Copia de la carta que Gonzalo Vaz Coutiño . . . escribio a su Majestad, sobre la fabrica y sustento de la armada de Barlovento en las Indias. [*Madrid:* 1615?]. 24 numb. lvs; fol. Sabin 98711 (& 17201); Medina (BHA) 6940 & 8470; Pérez Pastor (Madrid) 1375; Palau 353567; JCB (3) II:110. RPJCB; BL. 615/133

Vega Carpio, Lope Félix de. Arcadia, prosas y versos. *Barcelona: S. de Cormellas,* 1615. 270 numb. lvs; 8vo. 1st publ., Madrid, 1598; cf. 1602 edns. Palau 356301. NNH; Madrid: BN. 615/134

Villagrá, Gaspar Pérez de. Servicios que a su Magestad hà hecho el capitan Gaspar de Villagra, para que V.m le haga merced. [*Madrid?* 1615?]. 4 numb. lvs; fol. Sabin 99642; Medina (BHA) 6980; Wagner (SW) 19; JCB AR40:16–17. ICN, RPJCB; Seville: Archivo de Indias. 615/135

Virginia Company of London. A declaration for the certaine time of drawing the

great standing lottery. *London: F. Kingston, for W. Welby,* 1615. bds.; illus.; fol. Sabin 99872; Clayton-Torrence 28; Vail (Frontier) 39; STC 24833.8. London:Soc. Ant.
615/136

Wake, Sir Isaac. Rex platonicus, sive De . . . Jacobi . . . Regis, ad . . . Academiam Oxoniensem adventu . . . 1605. narratio . . . Editio tertia. *Oxford: J. Barnes,* 1615. 224 p.; 12mo. 1st publ., Oxford, 1607. STC 24940; Madan (Oxford) 1615:18. CSmH, CtY, ICU, MWiW-C, NNUT; BL.
615/137

Wither, George. Abuses stript and whipt. *London: H. Lownes, for F. Burton,* 1615. 302 p.; port.; 8vo. In verse. 1st publ., London, 1613. STC 25896. CSmH, CtY, DFo, ICU, MH, MiU; BL.
615/138

Wytfliet, Corneille. Descriptionis Ptolemicae [*sic*] augmentum, sive Occidentis notitia . . . rev. & cor. *Arnhem: J. Janszoon,* 1615. 104 (i.e., 95) p.; maps; fol. 1st publ., Louvain, 1597; here a reissue of F. Fabri's 2nd 1603 edn with cancel t.p.? ICN. 615/139

Yves d'Evreux, O.F.M.Cap. Suitte de l'Histoire des choses plus memorables advenues en Maragnan es annees 1613. & 1614. Second traité. *Paris: F. Huby,* 1615. 384 numb. lvs; 8vo. A continuation of Claude d'Abbeville's *Histoire de la mission des peres Capucins en l'isle de Maragnan,* Paris, 1614. Suppressed in deference to France's political rapprochement with Spain, to which Portugal & its Brazilian colony were then subject. Sabin 106227; Borba de Moraes II:383–85; Streit II:2378–79. NN-RB (imp.); BN (imp.).
615/140

1616

Acosta, José de, S.J. Histoire naturelle et moralle des Indes, tant Orientalles qu'Occidentalles . . . Composée en castillan . . . & traduite . . . par Robert Regnault. Dernière édition, revue et corrigée de nouveau. *Paris: A. Tiffaine,* 1616. 375 numb. lvs; 8vo. 1st publ. in French, Paris, 1598; cf. year 1606. Sabin 125n; Medina (BHA) 330n (I:501–2); Streit II:1454; Palau 1989; JCB (3) II:110. NN-RB, RPJCB; London:Wellcome, BN.
616/1

Alemán, Mateo. Der Landstörtzer: Gusman von Alfarche . . . Durch Aegidium Albertinum . . . verteutscht. *Munich: N. Heinrich,* 1616. 544 p.; 8vo. 1st publ. in German, Munich, 1615; for Spanish text see 1601 edn. Laurenti (Nov. pic. esp.) 604; Dt. Ges. Kat. 3.869. MB; BL, Munich:StB.
616/2

—[Anr edn]. *Munich: N. Heinrich,* 1616. 723 p.; 8vo. Dt. Ges. Kat. 3.870. Berlin:StB.
616/3

Aubigné, Théodore Agrippa d'. L'histoire universelle. *Maillé: J. Moussat,* 1616–20. 3 v.; fol. In v.1 is an account, p. 40–42, of the Spanish in the New World, also mentioning Villegagnon's attempted colony in Brazil. In addition, p. 354–56 describe the massacre of a Spanish garrison in Florida by Dominique Gourgues to avenge murder of Ribaut. MiD, NNU, RPJCB; BL, BN.
616/4

Aventrote, Juan. Epistola . . . ad potentissimum regem Hispaniarum. [*Rotterdam?*] 1616. 66 p.; 8vo. 1st publ. in Latin, [Rotterdam?], 1615; here an apparent reissue with altered imprint date. Cf. Millares Carlo (Avontroot) 5; cf. Knuttel 2037; Dt. Ges. Kat. 8.11135. MHi; Königsberg:StUB.
616/5

Entry canceled.
616/6

Avity, Pierre d', sieur de Montmartin. Les estats, empires, et principautez du monde. *Cologny: P. Aubert,* 1616. 1464 p.; 8vo. 1st publ., Paris, 1613. Cf. Sabin 2498. RPJCB; Berlin:StB.
616/7

—[Anr issue?]. *Paris: P. Chevalier,* 1616. Berlin:StB.
616/8

Barclay, John. Euphormionis Lusinini Satyricon. [*Frankfurt a. M?*] 1616. 4 pts; 8vo. Includes pt 2, 1st publ., Paris, 1607, & pt 4, the *Icon animorum,* 1st publ., London, 1614. Shaaber (Brit. auth.) B184. Berlin:StB, Munich:StB.
616/9

Barlow, William (d. 1625). Magneticall advertisements. *London: E. Griffin, for T. Barlow,* 1616. 86 p.; illus.; 4to. In chapt. vii, use of magnetic compass on voyages to America is discussed. STC 1442. CSmH, CtY, DFo, MH, MiU, NNE, PU, WU; BL. 616/10

Barreiros, Gaspar. Commentarius de Ophyra regione. *Rotterdam: J. L. Berewout,* 1616. [82] p.; 8vo. In the *Novus orbis* of this year, which see *below.*

Beaumont, Francis. The scornful ladie. A

comedie . . . by Fra. Beaumont and Jo. Fletcher. *London: [R. Bradock] for M. Partridge,* 1616. 36 lvs; 4to. Amongst the characters is a 'tobacco-man'; in act 2, scene 1, tobacco & tobacco shops are mentioned. STC 1686; Greg 334(a) CSmH, MB, MH; BL. 616/11

Belmonte y Bermúdez, Luis de. La aurora de Cristo. *Seville: F. de Lyra,* 1616. 40 numb. lvs; 8vo. Prefatory note to reader mentions author's *Vida del padre maestro Ignacio de Loyola* as publ. in Mexico. Medina (BHA) 638; Escudero (Seville) 1.053; Palau 26622. Madrid:BN. 616/12

Bertius, Petrus. Tabularum geographicarum contractarum libri septem. *Amsterdam: J. Hondius,* 1616. 830 p.; maps; obl. 8vo. 1st publ., Amsterdam, 1600. Sabin 5014; Koeman (Lan) 11A; Phillips (Atlases) 5924. DLC, MiU-C, MnU-B, NNH, PBL; BL, BN. 616/13

Besler, Basilius. Fasciculus rariorum et aspectu dignorum varii generis. *[Nuremberg:] The author,* 1616. 25 lvs; illus.; obl. 4to. Includes depictions of alligator & Brazil nuts. Pritzel 746; Nissen (Zool.) 345. CtY, MH; BL, BN. 616/14

Biard, Pierre, S.J. Relation de la Nouvelle France. *Lyons: L. Muguet,* 1616. 338 p.; 12mo. The earliest of the Jesuit accounts devoted to Canada. For variant states, see Church. Sabin's 1612 edn is undoubtedly a ghost. Sabin 69268 (& 5136n); Harrisse (NF) 30; Church 368. CSmH, ICN, MH-GE, NN-RB; BN. 616/15

Boccalini, Traiano. De' ragguagli di Parnaso . . . Centuria prima . . . terza impressione. *Venice: G. Guerigli,* 1616. 478 p.; 8vo. 1st publ., Venice, 1612. Firpo (Ragguagli) 12; Michel (Répertoire) I:176. Paris: Ste Geneviève. 616/16

——. De' ragguagli di Parnaso . . . Centuria seconda . . . terza impressione. *Venice: G. Guerigli,* 1616. 448 p.; 8vo. 1st publ., Venice, 1613; issued with Guerigli's Centuria prima of this year above. Firpo (Ragguagli) 12; Michel I:176. BL, Paris:Ste Geneviève. 616/17

Botero, Giovanni. Relations, of the most famous kingdomes. *London: [W. Jaggard,] for J. Jaggard,* 1616. 437 p.; 4to. 1st publ. in English, London, 1601, under title *The trav-*

ellers breviat & The world; also publ, London,1603, under title *An historicall description.* Sabin 36283; STC 3403; JCB (3)II: 112. CSmH, CtY, DFo, ICN, MiU-C, NN-RB, RPJCB; Oxford:Bodl. 616/18

Breton, Nicholas. Crossing of proverbs. The second part . . . by B.N. *London: J. Wright,* 1616. 8vo. Tobacco is said to be the 'dearest herb in the world'. Breton's pt 1, also publ. this year, is without Americana. STC 3644. BL (N., B.; imp.). 616/19

——. The good and the badde, or Descriptions of the worthies and unworthies of this age. *London: G. Purslowe, for J. Budge,* 1616. 40 p.; 4to. The character of 'An effeminate foole' describes him as taking tobacco. STC 3656; Murphy (Engl. char.-bks) 27; Arents (Add.) 173. CSmH, DFo, MH, NN-A; BL. 616/20

Bucholtzer, Abraham. Index chronologicus, monstrans annorum seriem a mundo condito usque ad annum nati Christi 1616. *Frankfurt a. M.: N. Hoffmann, the Elder, for J. Rose,* 1616. 788 p.; 8vo. 1st publ., Görlitz, 1584; cf. 1612 edn. BL, BN. 616/21

Calestani, Girolamo. Delle osservationi . . . parte prima[-seconda]. *Venice: G. A. Giuliani,* 1616. 2 v.; 4to. 1st publ., Venice, 1564; cf. 1606 edn. BN. 616/22

Camden, William. Annales rerum anglicarum. *Frankfurt a. M. : J. Bringer, for the Rulands,* 1616. 2 v.; 8vo. Vol. 1 1st publ. London, 1615. Shaaber (Brit. auth.) C17. CtY, IU, NNUT, PU; BN. 616/23

Canterbury, Eng. (Province). Commissary General. To the minister and church-wardens of [blank. 15 Apr. 1616. *London: T. Snodham,* 1616]. bds.; fol. Brief authorized by James I, 28 Febr. 1616, for collections for conversion of Indians in Virginia. *Virginia Magazine of history and biography,* LXXX (1972): 258–66. STC 4587.7. Bethersden, Kent: Parish Church. 616/24

Carmelites. Chapter General. Constituciones pro regimine provinciae S. Alberti Novae Hispaniae, ordinis reformati b. Mariae de Monte Carmelo . . . 1616. *[Alcalá de Henares? 1616?].* 8 lvs; 8vo. Medina (BHA) 7757; Streit II:1462. 616/25

Carrasco del Saz, Francisco. Initium a Domino. Factum. El Rey nuestro señor. *[Ma-*

drid? 1616?]. [10] p.; fol. On the powers, privileges, and functions of the viceroys of Peru. Medina (BHA) 639; Pérez Pastor (Madrid) 1389; Palau 45120. BL.   616/26

Cervantes Saavedra, Miguel de. Segunda parte del ingenioso cavallero Don Quixote de la Mancha. *Brussels: H. Anthoine,* 1616. 687 p.; 8vo. 1st publ., Madrid, 1615. Ríus (Cervantes) 13; Peeters-Fontainas (Impr. esp.) 228; Palau 51986. CU, DLC, MH, NN-RB; BL, BN.   616/27

—[Anr edn]. *Valencia: P. P. Mey, for R. Sonzonio,* 1616. 766 p.; 8vo. Ríus (Cervantes) 14; Palau 51987. BL.   616/28

Codogno, Ottavio. Nuovo itinerario delle poste per tutto il mondo. *Milan: G. Bordone,* 1616. 299 p.; 16mo. 1st publ., Venice, 1611. Pages 178–79 give postal routings 'Da Siviglia alle Indie Occidentali; cioè Cuba'; p. 289, 'Da Siviglia alla Nuova Ispagna'. Cf. Sabin 14142. BL.   616/29

Colonna, Fabio. Minus cognitarum rariorumque nostro coelo orientium stirpium. *Rome: J. Mascardi,* 1616. 3 pts; illus.; 4to. 1st publ., Naples, 1606; here a reissue of 1610 edn with cancel t.p. & added text. Pritzel 1823; Nissen (Bot.) 385; Arents (Add.) 146. MH, NN-A, RPB; BL, BN.   616/30

Conestaggio, Girolamo Franchi di. Dell' unione del regno di Portugallo alla corona di Castiglia. *Milan: G. B. Bidelli,* 1616. 471 p.; 8vo. 1st publ., Genoa, 1585. Includes mentions of Columbus & Portuguese settlement of Brazil. Michel (Répertoire) II:123; Palau 313375n. CtY, MH, NNH; BN.   616/31

Corbeius, Theodorus. Pathologia. *Frankfurt a. M.: H. Palthenius,* 1616. 508 p.; 8vo. 1st publ., Frankfurt a. M., 1615; here a reissue of that edn with altered imprint date? London:Wellcome, BN.   616/32

Deacon, John. Tobacco tortured, or The filthie fume of tobacco refined. *London: R. Field,* 1616. 194 p.; 4to. STC 6436; Arents 122; Kress S.450. CSmH, DFo, MH, NN-A; BL.   616/33

Dekker, Thomas. Villanies discovered by lanthorne and candlelight. *London: J. Busby,* 1616. [119] p.; illus.; 4to. 1st publ., London, 1608, under title *Lanthorne and candlelight.* STC 6488. CSmH, CtY, DFo; Cambridge:UL.   616/34

Del Rio, Martin Anton, S.J. Disquisitionum magicarum libri sex. *Venice: V. Fiorini,* 1616. 3 v.; 4to. 1st publ., Louvain, 1599–1600; cf. 1603 edn. Backer II:1899. DLC, IEN, MH; BL.   616/35

Dodoens, Rembert. Stirpium historiae pemptades sex, sive libri xxx., variè ab auctore . . . aucti & emendati. *Antwerp: Plantin Press,* 1616. 872 p.; illus.; fol. 1st publ., Antwerp, 1583; here reprinted as revised & corrected by author. Included are numerous American plants. Pritzel 2350n; Nissen (Bot.) 517n; Bibl. belg., 1st ser., IX, D119; Arents (Add.) 75. CSt, CtY, DLC, ICJ, MH-A, MiU, NN-A, PU-B, RPB; BL, BN.   616/36

Drayton, Michael. Poems . . . Newly corrected by the authour. *London: W. Stansby, for J. Smethwick* [ca. 1616]. 3 pts; 8vo. 1st publ., London, 1605. STC 7219; Grolier Club (Langland to Wither) 88; Pforzheimer 306. CSmH, CtY, DFo, IU, MH, NN-RB, PPRF; BL.   616/37

Du Bartas, Guillaume de Salluste, seigneur. Les oeuvres poetiques et chrestiennes. *Geneva: P. & J. Chouët,* 1616. 3 v.; 12mo. In verse. Included are the author's *La sepmaine,* 1st publ., Paris, 1578, & his *La seconde sepmaine,* 1st publ., Paris, 1584; cf. 1601 edn. Holmes (DuBartas) I:77 no. 37n & I:91 no. 25abcd(n). Grenoble:BM.   616/38

—[Anr edn]. *Rouen: L. Loudet,* 1616. Holmes (DuBartas) I:77 no. 40n & I:91 no. 23abc(n).   616/39

——. Premiere sepmaine ou Creation du monde . . . En cette derniere edition on esté adjoustez la premiere & seconde partie de la suite . . . & explications des principales difficultez du texte, par S[imon]. G[oulart]. *Rouen: R. Du Petit Val, for D. Du Petit Val,* 1616. 2 pts; 12mo. In verse. Included are the author's *La sepmaine,* 1st publ. with Goulart's annotations, Geneva, 1581, & also *La seconde sepmaine,* 1st publ., Paris, 1584. Holmes (DuBartas) I:77 no. 39; Jones (Goulart) 20aa. BN.   616/40

——. La seconde sepmaine. *Paris: R. Du Petit Val, for D. Du Petit Val,* 1616. 12mo. In verse. 1st publ., Paris, 1584; cf. 1601 edn. Included are commentaries by Simon Goulart of 1589. Holmes (DuBartas) I:90 no. 21a(n). Toulouse: BM.   616/41

Dunbar, John. Epigrammaton . . . centuriae sex. *London: T. Purfoot,* 1616. 200 p.; 8vo. Tobacco is mentioned or the subject in, cent.v, epigrams xlv & lxxvii, and, cent. vi, nos vi, ix & xcviii. STC 7346; Arents (Add.) 174. CSmH, CtY, DFo, MH, NN-A; BL. 616/42

Dunoyer de Saint-Martin, François. Articles, moyens et raisons approuvez par les Estats Generaux . . . afin d'establir à Paris . . . la Royale compagnie françoise pour faire le commerce general. *Paris: Widow of J. Regnoul,* 1616. 73 p.; 8vo. Pages 33–36 describe proposed trade with New France; ref. is made to other European colonies in New World. JCB (3) II:111–12. RPJCB. 616/43

—[Anr edn]. *Paris: Widow of J. Regnoul,* 1616. 114 p.; 8vo. Unquestionably a reissue of the preceding item with the addition of p. 75 ff. MH-BA (microfilm); BN. 616/44

Durante, Castore. Il tesoro della sanità. *Venice: M. A. Zaltieri,* 1616. 334 p.; 16mo. 1st publ., [Rome?], 1586; cf. 1601 edn. Michel (Répertoire) II:191. DNLM; Paris:Arsenal. 616/45

Estienne, Charles. Maison rustique, or, The countrey farme . . . translated . . . by Richard Surflet. *London: A. Islip for J. Bill,* 1616. 732 p.; illus.; fol. 1st publ. as transl. from Estienne's *L'agriculture* (itself 1st publ., Paris, 1567); cf. 1606 edn above. Here added by Gervase Markham is further discussion of therapeutic uses of tobacco. STC 10549; Arents 123. CSmH, CtY, DLC, ICN, MH, NN-RB; BL. 616/46

Gallucci, Giovanni Paolo. Theatro, y descripcion del mundo, y del tiempo . . . Traducido de latin . . . por Miguel Perez. *Granada: S. Múñoz, for J. Castello,* 1616. 369 numb. lvs; illus., map; fol. 1st publ. in Spanish, Granada, 1606. MiU. 616/47

Garcilaso de la Vega, el Inca. Historia general del Peru, trata el descubrimiento del; y como lo ganaron los Españoles. *Córdova: Widow of A. de Barrera,* 1616. 300 numb. lvs; fol. Continues the author's *Commentarios,* Lisbon, 1609. Sabin 98754. BN. 616/48

Garzoni, Tommaso. La piazza universale di tutte le professioni del mondo . . . In questa ultima impressione corretta, e ristampata con quella, che l'istesso autore fece ristampare, e porre in luce. *Venice: O. Alberti,* 1616. 403 numb. lvs; 4to. 1st publ., Venice, 1585; cf. 1601 edn. Michel (Répertoire) IV:25. DLC, MH, PU; BN. 616/49

Gaultier, Jacques. Tabula chronographica status ecclesiae catolicae . . . ad annum MDCXIV. *Lyons: H. Cardon,* 1616. 838 p.; fol. Transl. by the author from his *Table chronologique de l'estat du christianisme,* 1st publ., Lyons, 1609. Backer III:1276; Cioranescu (XVII) 32621. BL, BN. 616/50

—[Anr edn]. *Cologne: P. Henning,* 1616. 838 p.; fol. Backer III:1276. NNUT; BN. 616/51

Gesner, Konrad. Quatre livres des Secrets de medecine et de la philosophie chimique faicts françois par m. Jean Liebault. *Rouen: P. Calles,* 1616. 358 p.; illus.; 8vo. 1st publ., as transl. by Liébault, Paris, 1573, from Gesner's *Euonymus. De remediis secretis, pars secunda* (Zurich, 1569). Included are prescriptions for treating syphilis ('mal de Naples') employing guaiacum. BN. 616/52

—[Anr edn]. *Lyons: P. Rigaud,* 1616. 293 numb. lvs; illus.; 8vo. London: Wellcome. 616/53

Gracián, Jerónimo. Obras. *Madrid: Widow of A. Martín,* 1616. 436 numb. lvs; fol. Included is Gracián's *Zelo de la propagacion de la fee,* 1st publ., Lisbon, 1586, under title *Stimulo dela propagacion dela fee;* cf. Gracián's 1604 *Lampara encendida.* Streit I:358; Pérez Pastor (Madrid) 1399; Palau 106774. Madrid:BU (San Isidro), Salamanca:BU. 616/54

Great Britain. Council for Virginia. A briefe declaration of the present state of things in Virginia, and a division to be now made, of some part of those lands in our actuall posession. [*London: T. Snodham,* 1616]. 8 p.; 4to. Sabin 99873; Clayton-Torrens 35B (& 29); Vail (Frontier) 41; STC 24834; JCB (3) II:115. CSmH, RPJCB; BL. 616/55

Guicciardini, Francesco. La historia d'Italia . . . divisa in venti libri. *Venice: P. M. Bertano,* 1616. 2 pts; 4to. 1st publ., Florence, 1561; cf. 1604 edn. Michel (Répertoire) IV:101. MnU, NcU; Paris:Ste Geneviève. 616/56

Gysius, Johannes. Oorsprong en voortgang der neder-landtscber beroerten ende ellendicheden. [*Leyden?*] 1616. 411 p.; ports; 4to. Includes refs to Peru & to Spanish massacre of French in Florida. Cf. Sabin 11256n. DFo, ICU, MH; BL.   616/57

Jack Drum's entertainment. Jacke Drums entertainment; or, The comedie of Pasquill and Katherine. *London: W. Stansby, for P. Knight,* 1616. [72] p.; 4to. 1st publ., London, 1601. STC 7244; Greg 77(bI); Arents 126. CSmH, DFo, NN-A; BL.   616/58

James I, King of Great Britain. Workes. *London: R. Barker & J. Bill,* 1616. 569 p.; illus., ports; fol. Includes James's *A counterblaste to tobacco,* 1st publ., London, 1604. STC 14344; Arents 124. CSmH, CtY, DLC, ICN, MH, MiU, MnU, NN-RB, PPL; BL.
616/59

Joel, Franciscus (1508–1579). Operum medicorum . . . tomus primus[-sextus]. *Hamburg: H. Carstens; Lüneburg: A. Michelson; Rostock: M. Sachs, for J. Hallervord,* 1616–31. 6 v.; illus.; 4to. Source of syphilis ascribed to New World, with guaiacum & sarsaparilla prescribed for its treatment; for asthma, use of tobacco is recommended. Wellcome I:3462. DNLM; BL.   616/60

Jonson, Ben. Workes. *London: W. Stansby,* 1616. 1015 p.; fol. Included are Jonson's *Every man in his humour* (1st publ., London, 1601); *Every man out of his humour* (1st publ., London, 1600) with its ref. to tobacco & its Cuban source; *Cynthias revels* (1st publ., London, 1601, as *The fountaine of selfe-love*); and *The alchemist* (1st publ., London, 1612). For variant issues, etc., see the STC & the Pforzheimer catalog. STC 14751–52; Arents 125; Pforzheimer 556. CSmH, CtY, DLC, ICN, InU-L, MH, MiU, MnU, NN-RB, PU, RPB; BL.   616/61

Liceti, Fortunio. De monstrorum caussis, natura et differentiis libri duo. *Padua: G. Crivellari,* 1616. 143 p.; 4to. Denies that giants described by Hondius, Hulsius, & Walter Raleigh in the Indies qualify as monsters. DNLM, NNNAM, PPC; BL, BN.
616/62

Linschoten, Jan Huygen van. Dritter Theil Indiae Orientalis. *Oppenheim: H. Galler, for J. T. de Bry,* 1616. 219 p.; illus., maps; fol.
(J. T. de Bry's *India Orientalis.* Pt 3. German). 1st publ. in this version, Frankfurt, 1599. Itself without Americana, includes also 1st pt of W. Lodewijcksz's *Der Holländer Schiffahrt in die Orientalische Insulen,* transl. from *D'eerste boeck; Historie van Indien,* 1st publ., Amsterdam, 1598. Church 231; JCB (3) I:428. CSmH, CtY, IU, MBAt, NN-RB, RPJCB; BL.   616/63

Lithgow, William. A most delectable, and true discourse, of an admirable . . . peregrination . . . Second impression. *London: N. Okes, for T. Archer,* 1616. [136] p.; 4to. 1st publ., London, 1614. STC 15711. CSmH, DFo; BL.   616/64

Locre, Ferry de. Chronicon Belgicum. Ab anno CCLVIII, ad annum usque M.D.C. . . . perductum. *Arras: G. Rivière,* 1616, '14. 3 v. (696 p.); 4to. Under year 1492 Columbus is noted as discovering the Canary Islands; under 1496 syphilis is described as brought from Indies by Spanish; under 1497 Vespucci is credited with discovery of America; etc. Wellcome I:3839. CtY, MiU, NNC; BL, BN.   616/65

Magati, Cesare. De rara medicatione vulnerum, seu De vulneribus raro tractandis. *Venice: A. & B. Dei,* 1616. 2 pts; fol. In bk 1, chapt. lxi describes oils employing Peruvian opobalsam. Wellcome I:3942. DNLM; London:Wellcome, BN.   616/66

Markham, Gervase. Cheape and good husbandry. *London: T. S[nodham]., for R. Jackson,* 1616. 182 p.; 4to. 1st publ., London, 1614. Poynter (Markham) 22.2; STC 17337. DFo, NN-RB; BL.   616/67

Marlowe, Christopher. The tragicall historie of the life and death of Doctor Faustus. *London: J. Wright,* 1616. [62] p.; 4to. Drama. 1st publ., London, 1604; here rev. & enl. STC 17432; Greg 205(d). BL.   616/68

Mercator, Gerardus. Atlas sive Cosmographicae meditationes de fabrica mundi et fabricati figura. Denuò auctus. Editio quarta. *Amsterdam: J. Hondius,* 1616. 365 p.; maps; fol. 1st publ., Amsterdam, 1606. Cf. Sabin 47882; Koeman (Me) 24. NN-RB; Paris: Inst. de France.   616/69

Mexía, Pedro. Les diverses leçons . . . Mises en françois par Claude Gruget . . . Plus la suite de celles d'Antoine du Verdier.

Tournon: C. Michel, 1616. 1032 p.; 8vo. 1st publ. in this version with American refs in Du Verdier's continuation, Lyons, 1577; cf. 1604 edn. Sabin 48245n; Palau 167325. DLC, NjP; BL, BN. 616/70

——. Selva rinovata di varia lettione di Pietro Messia . . . di Mambrino Roseo, divisa in cinque parti. *Venice: A. & B. Dei, bros,* 1616, '15. 3 pts; 4to. 1st publ. with addition of Francesco Sansovino's 'Della grandezza dell'Indie, & chi le trovò, & perche furono chiamate Indie', Venice, 1559–60, under title *Della selva di varia lettione;* cf. 1611 edn. Michel (Répertoire) V:161; Palau 167302. IU, NcD, MiU; Paris:Arsenal, Barcelona: BU. 616/71

Mey, Aurelio. Norte de la poesia española. Illustrado del sol de doze comedias . . . de laureados poetas valencianos. *Valencia: F. Mey, for J. Ferrer,* 1616. 105 numb. lvs; 4to. Included is Ricardo de Turia's 'La gran comedia de la Belligera española', inspired by the wars of the Araucanian Indians in Chile. Medina (BHA) 7758. BL. 616/72

—[Anr issue]. *Valencia: F. Mey, for F. Pincinali,* 1616. Medina (BHA) 7758n; Palau 167625. Madrid:BN. 616/73

Mocquet, Jean. Voyages en Afrique, Asie, Indes Orientales et Occidentales. *Paris: J. de Heuqueville,* 1616. 442 p.; illus.; 8vo. Sabin 49790; Brunet III:1782 (19994). 616/74

Montaigne, Michel Eyquem de. Les essais . . . Edition nouvelle enrichie d'annotations en marge. *Cologny: P. Aubert,* 1616. 1129 p.; port.; 8vo. 1st publ., Bordeaux, 1580; cf. 1602 edn. Tchémerzine VIII:417–18. BN. 616/75

—[Anr issue?]. Edition nouvelle prise sur l'exemplaire trouvé après le deces de l'autheur. *Cologny: P. Aubert,* 1616. Tchémerzine VIII:417–18. BN. 616/76

—[Anr issue?]. *Geneva: P. Aubert,* 1616. Imprint has reading 'De l'imprimerie de Philippe Albert'. Tchémerzine VIII:418. BN. 616/77

—[Anr issue?]. *Geneva: P. Aubert,* 1616. Imprint has reading 'Par Philippe Albert'. Tchémerzine VIII:418. BN. 616/78

—[Anr issue?]. *[Geneva:] P. Aubert,* 1616. Tchémerzine VIII:418. BN. 616/79

—[Anr edn]. *Geneva & Cologny: [P. Aubert],* 1616. 1031 p.; 8vo. A reissue with cancel t.p. of Doreau's 1602 edn. BN. 616/80

Müller, Philipp (1585–1659). Miracula & mysteria chymico-medica . . . Editio tertia. *[Wittenberg:] C. Berger,* 1616. 493 p.; illus.; 12mo. 1st publ., [Wittenberg], 1611. DNLM, WU. 616/81

Nieuwe ende warachtighe tijdinghe ghekomen van Sint Lucas de Barrameda . . . aengaende de heerlycke victorie . . . in de Zuytzee . . . door 't beleyt van . . . Joris van Speilbergen. *Amsterdam: B. Janszoon,* 1616. 4 p.; 4to. An early progress report on Spilbergen's voyage around the world. Cf. *Een waerachtige beschryvinghe* of this year below. Sabin 89441; Tiele 1024n. 616/82

Novus orbis regionum. Novus orbis, id est, Navigationes primae in Americam: quibus adjunximus Gasparis Varrerii Discursum super Ophyra regione. *Rotterdam: J. L. Berewout,* 1616. 2 pts; 8vo. Extracted from *Novus Orbis regionum,* 1st publ., Basel, 1532. The supplementary 'Discursus' of Barreiros, with title *Commentarius de Ophyra regione,* 1st publ., Coimbra, 1561, as part of his *Chorographia,* argues that the legendary land of 'Ophir' was in Asia, not America. Sabin 34105 & 3597; Streit I:360; JCB (3) II:111. Cu-A, CtY, DLC, MH, MiU-C, NN-RB, RPJCB (imp., wanting Barreiros's Discursus); BL (America), BN (Barreiros). 616/83

Orta, Garcia da. Dell'historia de i semplici, et altre cose che vengono portate dall'Indie Orientali pertinenti all'uso della medicina . . . Et due altri libri parimente di quelle cose che si portano dall' Indie Occidentali . . . Di Nicolò Monardes . . . Hora tradotti . . . da m. Annibale Briganti. *Venice: G. Salis,* 1616. 525 p.; illus.; 8vo. 1st publ. in Italian, Venice, 1576. Sabin 57670n; Guerra (Monardes) 38; Michel (Répertoire) VI:42; Palau 99522. DNLM, MH-A, MnU-B, NN-A, RPJCB; BL, BN. 616/84

Overbury, Sir Thomas. Sir Thomas Overburie his wife . . . Editio septima. *London: E. Griffin, for L. Lisle,* 1616. [250] p.; 8vo. 1st publ. with character of tobacco seller, London, 1615, under title *New and choise characters.* STC 18909; Murphy (Engl. char.-bks) 19. DFo, IU, MH; BL. 616/85

—[Anr edn]. The eight [*sic*] impression. *London: E. Griffin,* 1616. [271] p.; 8vo. STC 18910; Murphy (Engl. char.-bks) 20. CtY, DFo, IU, MB (imp.); Oxford:Bodl. (imp.).
616/86

—[Anr edn]. The ninth impression augmented. *London: E. Griffin, for L. Lisle,* 1616. [315] p.; 8vo. STC 18911; Murphy (Engl. char.-bks) 20. CSmH, DFo, IU, NN-RB; BL.
616/87

Paracelsus. Opera. Bücher und Schrifften. *Strassburg: Heirs of L. Zetzner,* 1616. 2 v.; fol. 1st publ. as here constituted, [Basel], 1589–90; cf. 1603 edn. Sudhoff (Paracelsus) 300–301; Wellcome I:4809. CSt, CtY, DLC, KU-M, PPPM; London:Wellcome, Munich:StB.
616/88

Pascal, Jacques. Discours contenant la conference de la pharmacie. *Béziers: J. Martel,* 1616. 333 p.; 8vo. Among substances enumerated are guaiacum, mechoacan, & sassafras. Wellcome I:4837. BL, BN.
616/89

—[Anr edn]. *Lyons: L. Vivian,* 1616. 333 p.; 8vo. Wellcome I:4838. London:Wellcome.
616/90

—[Anr edn]. *Toulouse: D. Bosc,* 1616. 333 p.; 8vo. WU; BL, BN.
616/91

Penot, Bernard Georges. Tractatus varii de vera praeparatione et usu medicamentorum chymicorum . . . Editio quarta. *Basel: L. König,* 1616. 246 p.; illus.; 12mo. 1st publ., Frankfurt a. M., 1594; cf. 1602 edn. BN.
616/92

Pigray, Pierre. Epitome des preceptes de medecine et chirurgie . . . Troisiesme edition. *Lyons: S. Rigaud,* 1616. 666 p.; 8vo. 1st publ., Paris, 1600, under title *La chirurgie;* cf. 1604 edn. BN.
616/93

Pindarus. Greek and Latin. Περίοδος, hoc est, Pindari . . . Ὀλυμπιονίκαι, Πυθιονίκαι . . . cum . . . discursu duplici, uno de dithrambis, altero de Insula atlantica . . . quae America hodie dicitur, opera Erasmi Schmidii. [*Wittenberg:*] *Z. Schürer,* 1616. 4 pts; 4to. Sabin 62917; Jantz (German Baroque) 193. CtY, DLC, NNH; BL, BN.
616/94

Potier, Pierre. Insignes curationes et singulares observationes centum. *Cologne: M. Schmitz,* 1616. 158 p.; 12mo. 1st publ., Venice, 1615. CtY-M, DNLM; BN.
616/95

Preguntas que se propusieron al maese de campo Don Diego Florez de Leon . . . acerca de la defensa y fortificacion del Perù, y sus costas. [*Madrid?* 1616?]. [13] p.; fol. Palau 236262 ('ca. 1650'); Maggs Cat. 496 (Americana VI):124. BL (Florez de Leon, Diego).
616/96

Rich, Barnabe. The honestie of this age. *London:* [*J. Legat,*] *for T. Adams,* 1616. 4to. 1st publ., London, 1614. STC 20988. CSmH, DFo, PPL; BL.
616/97

——. My ladies looking glasse. *London:* [*J. Legat,*] *for T. Adams,* 1616. 40 lvs; 4to. Continues author's earlier diatribes against tobacco in his *Honestie of this age* of 1614. STC 20991.7 (formerly 20984); Arents 127. CSmH, IU, MH, NN-A; BL.
616/98

A rich storehouse or treasurie for the diseased. Now sixtly augmented . . . by A. T. *London: R. Blower,* 1616. 176 (i.e., 146) numb. lvs; 4to. 1st publ., London, 1596; cf. 1601 edn. STC 23609. CSmH, DNLM, WU; London:UL.
616/99

Rivadeneira, Pedro de, S.J. The life of b. Father Ignatius of Loyola . . . translated out of Spanish, by W.M. [i.e., Michael Walpole]. [*St Omer: English College Press*] 1616. 358 p.; 8vo. 1st publ. in Spanish, Madrid, 1592; includes refs to Jesuits in Brazil. Allison & Rogers 712; STC 20967; Palau 266263. DFo; BL.
616/100

——. Vita b. Ignatii . . . quam r.p. Gaspar Quartemont . . . latine reddidit. *Augsburg: C. Mang,* 1616. 324 p.; port.; 12mo. 1st publ. in this version, Ypres, Belgium, 1612. Palau 266267. DGU; BL, BN.
616/101

——. Vita del p. Francesco Borgia . . . Tradotta dalla lingua spagnuola de f. Giulio da Zanchini. *Rome: B. Zannetti,* 1616. 289 p.; 4to. Transl. from author's *Vida del padre Francisco de Borja,* 1st publ. in Spanish, Madrid, 1592. Includes refs to Jesuits in Florida, Peru, & Mexico. Backer VI:1734; Palau 266318. RPJCB.
616/102

Rowlands, Samuel. Doctor Merry-man: or, Nothing but mirth. *London:* [*W. White,*] *for S. Rand,* 1616. [24] p.; 4to. In verse. 1st publ., London, 1607, under title *Democritus, or Doctor Merry-man his medicines.* STC 21373. BL.
616/103

Scot, Thomas. Philomythie or philomythologie. Wherein outlandish birds, beasts, and fishes, are taught to speake true English plainely. *London: [J. Legat,] for F. Constable,* 1616. 2 pts; 8vo. In verse. Includes section on 'Pandorus Waldolynnatus, the merrie American philosopher, or wise man of the New World' & also a diatribe against tobacco, 'the Indian divel'. Sabin 78188 & 78191; STC 21869; Arents 121. CSmH, DFo, ICN, MH, NN-A; BL.   616/104

—[Anr edn]. Second edition, much inlarged. *London: [E. Griffin,] for F. Constable,* 1616. Sabin 78189; STC 21870. CSmH, CtY, DFo, MH, NN-RB; BL.   616/105

Sharpham, Edward. Cupids whirligig. *London: T. Creede & B. Alsop; sold by A. Johnson,* 1616. 40 lvs; 4to. Comedy. 1st publ., London, 1607. STC 22382; Greg 247(c). DFo, IU, MB; BL.   616/106

Smith, Capt. John. A description of New England. *London: H. Lownes, for R. Clarke,* 1616. 61 p.; map; 4to. For variant states of the map, etc., see Sabin; of the t.p., the STC. Sabin 82819; Vail (Frontier) 40; STC 22788, 22788.3, 22788.5; Church 369; JCB (3) II:113. CSmH, DLC, ICN, MH, MiU-C, NN-RB, PPL, RPJCB; BL.   616/107

Sosa, Pedro de, O.F.M. Memorial del peligroso estado espiritual, y temporal del reyno de Chile. *[Madrid? 1616?].* 21 numb. lvs; fol. Sabin 87184; Medina (Chile) 214; Streit II:1456. BL.   616/108

——. Señor. Fray Pedro de Sosa de la Orden de san Francisco. Dize, que ha hecho quanto ha sido de su parte, porque V. M. sea satisfecho. *[Madrid? 1616?].* 4 (i.e., 10) numb. lvs; fol. Memorial to king of Spain on affairs of Chile. Sabin 87185; Medina (BHA) 215; Streit II:1457. NN-RB; BL.   616/109

Spain. Laws, statutes, etc., 1598–1621 (Philip III). El Rey. Por quanto por cedula mia fecha a dos de Otubre del año passado de 608. *[Madrid: 1616].* 5 numb. lvs; fol. Decree on commerce of foreigners with Spanish America. Subscribed at end: Fecha en Madrid, a veynte y cinco de Deziembre de mil y seyscientos y diez y seys. BL.   616/110

Suárez de Figueroa, Cristóbal. Hechos de Don Garcia Hurtado de Mendoça, marques de Cañete. *Madrid: Imprenta Real,* 1616. 324 p.; 4to. 1st publ., Madrid, 1613; here a reissue of that edn with cancel t.p. Sabin 93312; Medina (Chile) 41; Pérez Pastor (Madrid) 1433; JCB (3) II:115. RPJCB; Madrid:BU.   616/111

Tabourot, Estienne. Les bigarrures, et touches. *Rouen: D. Geuffroy,* 1616. 2 pts; illus., ports; 12mo. In verse. Includes only the 1st two pts as 1st publ. collectively, Paris, 1603, q.v. DLC, ICN, OCU; BL.   616/112

Tanner, Robert. A brief treatise of the use of the globe celestiall and terrestriall. *London: F. Kingston, for T. Man,* 1616. 8vo. Includes description of America as one of the four parts of the earth, enumerating its component areas. STC 23672. BL, Oxford: Bodl.   616/113

El venturoso descubrimiento de las insulas de la nueva y fertil tierra de Xauxa, por otro numbre llamada Mandrona. Descubierta por el . . . capitan llamado Longares de Sentlom y de Gorgans. En este año de 1616. *Barcelona: E. Liberós,* 1616. [4] p.; illus.; 4to. In verse. Palau 358785. Madrid:BN.   616/114

Villagrá, Gaspar Pérez de. El capitan Gaspar de Villagra, para que su Magestad le haga merced del govierno de Campeche, Nueva Vizcaya, ò corregimiento de Tabusco, ò Iztlavaca, suplica a V. merced passe los ojos por este memorial. *[Madrid? ca. 1616?].* 4 lvs; fol. Sabin 99640; Medina (BHA) 6981; Wagner (SW) 21. Seville:Archivo de Indias.   616/115

Een waerachtige beschryvinghe van de schoone victorie . . . door . . . Joris van Speelberghen in de Strate Magelanus enz. *Amsterdam: B. Janszoon,* 1616. 4 p.; 4to. Cf. the *Nieuwe ende warachtige tijdinghe* of this year above. Sabin 89442; Tiele 1024n.   616/116

Wecker, Johann Jakob. Le grand dispensaire. *Cologny: E. Gamonet,* 1616. 2 pts; illus.; 4to. Transl. from Wecker's *Antidotarium generale, et speciale,* 1st publ., Basel, 1574 & 1576; cf. 1601 edn. DNLM; BN.   616/117

——. Kunstbuch. Ein nutzliches Büchlein. *Basel: L. König,* 1616. 86 p.; 8vo. Transl. from Wecker's *Antidotarium generale,* 1st publ., Basel, 1576; cf. 1601 edn. Here a reissue of C. Waldkirch's 1605 edn. Well-

come I:6707. MoSW; London:Wellcome.
616/118

Wirsung, Christoph. Medecyn boec . . . nu
uyt de vijfde editie . . . overgheset door
d. Carolum Battum . . . De vijfde verbeterde druck. *Dordrecht: I. J. Canin,* 1616.
676 p.; fol. Transl. from Wirsung's *New
Artzney Buch,* 1st publ., Heidelberg, 1568;
cf. 1605 edn. DNLM. 616/119

1617

Abbot, George, Abp of Canterbury. A
briefe description of the whole worlde . . .
The fourth edition. *London: [T. Snodham,]
for J. Browne,* 1617. [170] p.; 4to. 1st publ.,
London, 1599. Sabin 21n; STC 28; Church
369A. CSmH, CtY, DLC, MBAt, MiU-C;
BL. 617/1

Acosta, José de, S.J. Histoire naturelle et
morale des Indes, tant Orientalles qu'Occidentalles . . . Composée en castillan . . .
& traduite . . . par Robert Regnault. *Paris:
A. Tiffaine,* 1617. 375 numb. lvs; 8vo. 1st
publ. in French, Paris, 1598; cf. year 1606.
A reissue, with cancel t.p., of printer's 1616
edn. Sabin 125n; Streit II:1464; Palau 1990;
JCB (3) II:116. DLC, MiU-C, RPJCB.
617/2

Agustí, Miguel. Llibre dels secrets de agricultura. *Barcelona: E. Liberós,* 1617. 194
numb. lvs; illus.; fol. Includes chapt. on tobacco, derived from Jean Liébault, found
in Charles Estienne's *L'agriculture.* Palau
4122. Barcelona:B. Central. 617/3

Airolo Calar, Gabriel de. Pensil de principes, y varones ilustres. *Seville: F. Rey,*
1617. 52 numb. lvs; 4to. In verse. Included
are refs to Mexico, where the author prac-
ticed law. Medina (BHA) 646; Escudero
(Seville) 1.111. BL, Madrid:BN. 617/4

Alemán, Mateo. Der Landtstörtzer. *Munich:
[N. Heinrich?]* 1617. 1st publ. in German,
Munich, 1615. Laurenti (Nov. pic. esp.)
605; Goedeke II:577. 617/5

Amati, Scipione. Histori dess haydnischen
Königreichs Voxu in Japonia . . . An jetzo
. . . von dem geistlichen Joanne Bürcken
auss der italienischen . . . ubergetragen.

Rottweil: J. M. Helmlin, 1617. 4to. Transl.
from the author's *Historia del regno di Voxu,*
1st publ., Rome 1615. For anr German
translation see Amati's *Relation* below.
Streit V:1157n. MH. 617/6

——. Relation und gründtlicher Bericht von
dess Königreichs Voxu im Japonischen
Keyserthumb gottseliger Bekehrung. An-
fangs in italienischer Sprach verfasset . . .
anjetzo aber zu Teutsch verwendet durch
R. P. F. Thobiam Hendschelium. *Ingolstadt:
Eder Press, by Elisabeth Angermaier,* 1617. 292
p.; 4to. Transl. from author's *Historia del
regno di Voxu del Giapone,* 1st publ., Rome,
1615. Includes refs to missions in Peru,
Guatemala, Nicaragua, etc. For anr German
translation see Amati's *Histori* above. Sabin
31333; cf. Streit V:1157; JCB (3) II:116.
DLC, RPJCB; BL. 617/7

—[Anr edn]. *Ingolstadt: Eder Press, by Elisabeth
Angermaier,* 1617. 359 p.; 4to. Streit V:1157.
Göttingen:UB. 617/8

Avity, Pierre d', sieur de Montmartin. Les
estats, empires et principautez du monde.
Paris: P. Chevalier, 1617. 1467 p.; 4to. 1st
publ., Paris, 1613. Cf. Sabin 2498. BL,
Munich:StB. 617/9

—[Anr issue]. *Paris: O. de Varennes,* 1617. Mu-
nich:StB. 617/10

Bacon, Francis, viscount St Albans. Saggi
morali. *London: J. Bill,* 1617. 2 pts; 8vo.
Transl., perhaps by Sir Tobie Mathews,
from Bacon's *Essays* as publ., London, 1612.
Gibson (Bacon) 33; STC 1153. MH; Lon-
don:Lambeth. 617/11

Banchieri, Adriano. Von dess Esels Adel
und der Saw Triumph. Ein sehr artige lustige und liebliche beschreibung Attabalippa dess peruanischen Esels Adel [pseud.]
. . . an tag gegeben durch Griphangno
Fabro-Miranda [i.e., G. F. Messerschmid].
[Strassburg: J. Carolus] 1617. 183 p.; illus.,
8vo. Transl. from the author's *La nobiltà
dell'asino,* 1st publ., Venice, 1592. American
only in choice of pseudonym. Goedeke
II:586; Holzmann-Bohatta IV:10882. IU;
Wolfenbüttel:HB. 617/12

Barclay, John. Euphormionis Lusinini Satyricon. *Leyden: J. Marci,* 1617. 4 pts; 8vo. Includes pt 2, 1st publ., Paris, 1607, & the

Icon animorum, 1st publ., London, 1614. Shaaber (Brit. auth.) B185. IU; Bonn:UB, Hamburg:StUB. 617/13

——. Icon animorum. *Paris:* 1617. 273 p.; 12mo. 1st publ., London, 1614; here printed 'juxta exemplar impressum Londini'. Shaaber (Brit. auth.) B166; Tchémerzine I:447. ICN; London:Lambeth, BN. 617/14

Baricelli, Giulio Cesare. Hortulus genialis: sive, Rerum jucundarum, medicarum, & memorabilium compendium. *Naples: S. Bonino,* 1617. 418 p.; 12mo. Includes discussion of tobacco, 'Daemonis astutia apud Indos', citing Monardes. DNLM. 617/15

Barrough, Philip. The method of phisick . . . The fifth edition. *London: R. Field,* 1617. 477 p.; 4to. 1st publ., London, 1583; cf. 1601 edn. STC 1513. CtY, DNLM, ICU, MiU, NNNAM; BL. 617/16

Benzoni, Girolamo. Americae pars quinta . . . secundae sectionis hīā: Hispanorum, tùm in nigrittas servos suos, tùm in Indos crudelitatem . . . Addita ad singula fere capita scholia, in quibus res Indiae luculenter exponuntur. [*Frankfurt a. M.: T. de Bry*] 1595 [i.e., *Oppenheim? H. Galler?* ca. 1617]. 72 p.; illus., map; fol. (Theodor de Bry's *America.* Pt 5. Latin). 1st publ. in this version, Frankfurt a. M., 1595; cf. earlier pt. (bk 1) of 1594. Cf. Sabin 8784; Church 157; JCB (3) I:395. CSmH, ICN, NN-RB, RPJCB; BL, BN. 617/17

——. Americae pars sexta, sive Historiae . . . sectio tertia. *Oppenheim: H. Galler, for J. T. de Bry,* 1617. 78 p.; illus., map; fol. (Theodor de Bry's *America.* Pt 6. Latin). 1st publ. in this version, Frankfurt a. M., 1596. Has engr. title of 1596, Frankfurt, edn, cut & remounted; imprint from t.p. to plates. Cf. Sabin 8784; Church 159 & 160; JCB (3) I:397. CSmH, ICN, NN-RB, RPJCB; BL, BN. 617/18

Berettari, Sebastiano, S.J. Josephi Anchietae soc. Jesu sacerdotis in Brasilia defuncti vita. *Lyons: H. Cardon,* 1617. 277 p.; 8vo. Sabin 4826; Medina (BHA) 651; Borba de Moraes I:85–86; Streit II: 2380; Backer I:1326. NN-RB; BL, BN. 617/19

—[Anr edn]. Vita r. p. Josephi Anchietae. Cologne: *J. Kinckius,* 1617. 427 p.; 12mo. Sabin 4827; Medina (BHA) 652; Borba de Moraes I:86; Streit II:2380; Backer I:1326; JCB (3) II:117. DLC, MH, NN-RB, RPJCB; BL, BN. 617/20

Besard, Jean Baptiste. Antrum philosophicum, in quo pleraque arcana physica . . . revelantur. *Augsburg: D. Franck, for the Author,* 1617. 248 p.; 4to. For syphilis, remedies employing guaiacum, sarsaparilla, & sassafras are described. DNLM, MnU, PPC, TxU, WU; BL, BN. 617/21

Blaeu, Willem Janszoon. Het licht der zeevaert. *Amsterdam: W. J. Blaeu,* 1617. 2 v.; illus., maps; obl. fol. 1st publ., Amsterdam, 1608. Koeman (M.B1) 4. London:Admiralty. 617/22

Boccalini, Traiano. De' ragguagli di Parnaso . . . Centuria prima . . . seconda [*sic*] impressione. *Venice: G. Guerigli,* 1617. 478 p.; 8vo. 1st publ., Venice, 1612. Firpo (Ragguagli) 13; Michel (Répertoire) I:176. CtY, DLC, MH, MnU, NNC, PPL; Paris:Ste Geneviève. 617/23

——. De' ragguagli di Parnaso . . . Centuria seconda . . . terza impressione. *Venice: G. Guerigli,* 1617. 453 p.; 4to. 1st publ., Venice, 1613; issued with Guerigli's Centuria prima of this year above. Firpo (Ragguagli) 13; Michel (Répertoire) I:176. MnU, N; Paris:Ste Geneviève. 617/24

——. Politischen Probiersteins ander Theil. Relation aus Parnasso. [*Tübingen?*] 1617. 4to. Transl. by Christoph Besold from Boccalini's *De' ragguagli di Parnaso . . . Centuria seconda,* 1st publ., Venice, 1613. CtY. 617/25

——. Politischen Probiersteins auss Parnasso. Erster Theil . . . Erstlich italianisch beschrieben. [*Tübingen? 1617?*]. 4to. Transl. by Christoph Besold from Boccalini's *De' ragguagli di Parnaso . . . Centuria prima,* 1st publ., Venice, 1612. CtY. 617/26

Boitel, Pierre, sieur de Gaubertin. Le tableau des merveilles du monde. *Paris: T. Du Bray,* 1617. 627 p.; 8vo. 'Invention d'Americ Vespuce gentilhomme florentin': p. 241–43; 'Invention d'Atapaliba roy du Peru': p. 420–22. Sabin 6164. CtY, MH; BL. 617/27

149

—[Anr issue]. *Paris: T. de La Ruelle*, 1617. BN.
617/28

Boulenger, Jules César. Historiarum sui temporis libri tredecim, quibus res toto orbe gestae ab anno 1560 ad annum usque 1612 continentur. *Lyons: Heirs of G. Rouillé*, 1617. 409 p.; fol. Included are refs to Columbus, Villegagnon, Florida, etc. Cioranescu (XVI) 4570. BN.
617/29

Bourne, William. [A regiment for the sea. *London: E. Weaver*, 1617?]. An edition the existence of which is conjectured from tables found in 1620 edn. Taylor (Regiment) 455.
617/30

Brathwait, Richard. A solemne joviall disputation . . . briefely shadowing the law of drinking. [*London: E. Griffin*] 1617. 194 p.; illus.; 8vo. Includes the author's *The smoaking age . . . with The life and death of tobacco* with numerous American refs, esp. to 'Burmuda'. STC 3585; Arents 129. CSmH, CtY, DFo, ICN, MH, NN-RB; BL.
617/31

Brunner, Balthasar. Consilia medica summo studio collecta & revisa Laurentio Hofmano. *Halle: P. Schmidt, for J. Krusecke*, 1617. 421 p.; illus.; 4to. Prescribed for a wide variety of ailments are guaiacum, sarsaparilla, & sassafras. DNLM, PPC; BL, BN.
617/32

Bry, Johann Theodor de, ed. America, das ist, Erfindung und Offenbahrung der newen Welt . . . zusammengefasset . . . durch M. Philippum Ziglerum. *Frankfurt a. M.: N. Hoffmann, for J. T. de Bry, at Oppenheim*, 1617. 433 p.; illus., maps; fol. Contains abridgment of the first 9 parts of de Bry's *America*, with addition of N. Herborn's 'Epitome, wie man die Indianer bekehren sol' (p. 423–33), 1st publ. in Latin, Cologne, 1532, in H. Cortés's *De Insulis nuper inventis*. Sabin 8784 (III:59); Baginsky (German Americana) 138; Streit I:366; JCB (3) II:123. DLC, MiU-C, NN-RB, RPJCB; BL, Breslau:BU.
617/33

Capivaccio, Girolamo. Opera omnia . . . *Venice: The Sessas*, 1617. 910 p.; fol. Includes the author's *De lue venerea acroaseis*, 1st publ., Speyer, 1590; cf. 1603 edn. DNLM; BN.
617/34

Catholic Church. Liturgy and ritual. Ritual. Brevis forma administrandi apud Indos sacramenta . . . per fratrem Michaelem à Za-

rate . . . denuó autem per . . . Joannem de la Roca in Limensi cathedrali ecclesia rectorem . . . limata. *Madrid: Imprenta Real*, 1617. 108 numb. lvs; 8vo. 1st publ., Mexico, 1583. Medina (BHA) 8471; Streit I:364; Pérez Pastor (Madrid) 1516; Palau 379716. Madrid:BN.
617/35

Cervantes Saavedra, Miguel de. Novelas exemplares. *Madrid: J. de la Cuesta, for F. de Robles*, 1617. 399 numb. lvs; 8vo. 1st publ., Madrid, 1613. Rius (Cervantes) 226; Palau 53405.
617/36

—[Anr edn]. *Pamplona: N. de Assiayn*, 1617. 391 numb. lvs; 8vo. Rius (Cervantes) 227; Palau 53406. NNH; BL.
617/37

—[Anr edn]. *Lisbon: A. Alvarez*, 1617. 236 p.; 8vo. Rius (Cervantes) 228; Palau 53407. NNH; BL.
617/38

——. Segunda parte del ingenioso cavallero Don Quixote de la Mancha. *Lisbon: J. Rodriguez*, 1617. 306 (i.e., 292) numb. lvs; 4to. 1st publ., Madrid, 1615. Rius (Cervantes) 15; Palau 51987n. NNH; BL.
617/39

—[Anr edn]. *Barcelona: S. Matevad, for R. Vives*, 1617. 357 p.; 8vo. Edition shared with other booksellers: M. Gracián and J. Simón. Rius (Cervantes) 16; Palau 51989. MB, NNH (Gracián); BL (Gracián).
617/40

Chronicon Hollandiae. De Hollandorum repub. & rebus gestis commentarii Hugonis Grotii. *Leyden: J. Maire*, 1617. 501 p.; 4to. Includes Grotius's *De antiquitate reipublicae Batavicae*, 1st publ., Leyden, 1610. Meulen/Diermanse 693; Bibl. Belg. G343. ICN, MiU-C, NNC; BL (Holland), The Hague: PP.
617/41

Clercq, Nikolaas de. Tooneel der beroemder hertogen, princen, graven ende krygshelden. *Delft: N. de Clercq*, 1617. 637 p.; illus.; fol. Includes biographies & ports of Cortés, Magellan, Montezuma, Atabalipa, Columbus, and Francisco Pizarro. Continues Clercq's *Tooneel der keyseren*, 1st publ., Delft, 1615. Cf. Sabin 13637; Muller (1872) 363. DFo, PBL.
617/42

—[Anr edn]. *Amsterdam:* 1617. illus.; fol. Sabin 13637 (a possible ghost).
617/43

Collibus, Hippolytus à. Fürstliche Tischreden . . . durch J. W. Gebharten [pseud.] . . . angefangen und . . . nochmals vermehret und . . . continuirt werden durch . . . G. Draudium. *Frankfurt a. M.: [N. Hoff-*

mann? for] *J. Bassé*, 1617. 2 pts; 8vo. 1st publ., Frankfurt a. M., 1597; cf. 1614 edn. Cf. Jantz (German Baroque) 838; cf. Goedeke II:473. BL (Gerhard). 617/44

Cotta, John. A true discovery of the empericke, with the fugitive, physition and quacksalver. *London: W. Jones, sold by E. Weaver,* 1617. 135 p.; 4to. 1st publ., London, 1612, under title *A short discoverie of the unobserved dangers of severall sorts of ignorant . . . practisers of physicke.* STC 5834. BL. 617/45

Crespin, Jean. Gross Martyrbuch und Kirchen-Historien . . . Ubergesetzt . . . durch D. Paulum Crocium. *Hanau: P. Antonius,* 1617. 1606 p.; fol. 1st publ. in German, Hanau, 1606; transl. from Crespin's *Histoire des martyrs,* Geneva, 1564. Includes (p. 819–29) 'Zustand der Kirchen in Bresilia'. Jones (Goulart) 23(f); cf. Borba de Moraes I:199; JCB (3) II:117. RPJCB; Basel:UB. 617/46

Del Rio, Martin Anton, S.J. Disquisitionum magicarum libri sex. *Mainz: J. Albin, for P. Henning, at Cologne,* 1617. 1070 p.; 4to. 1st publ., Louvain, 1599–1600; cf. 1603 edn. Backer II:1899. DLC, OCl, PU-S, WU; BN. 617/47

Durante, Castore. Herbario novo . . . con figure, che rappresentano le vive piante, che nascono in tutta Europa, & nell'Indie Orientali, & Occidentali. *Treviso: A. Reghettini, for the Sessas, at Venice,* 1617. 492 p.; illus., port.; fol. 1st publ., Rome, 1585; cf. 1602 edn. Pritzel 2552n; cf. Nissen (Bot.) 569. DNLM, MoSB, OCl; BL, BN. 617/48

Fennor, William. The compters commonwealth. *London: E. Griffin, for G. Gibbs,* 1617. 85 p.; 4to. Describing experiences as prisoner for debt, refers in chapt. ii to other prisoners' use of tobacco. Reprinted, 1619, under title *The miseries of a jaile,* and, 1629, as *A true description of the lawes . . . of a compter.* STC 10781; Arents (Add.) 177. CSmH, DLC, NN-A; BL. 617/49

Figueroa, Francisco de, S.J. Memorial presentado a Su Magestad por el p. Francisco de Figueroa, procurador de las provincias de las Indias de la Compañia. Y de otros dos religiosos. *Barcelona: L. Déu,* 1617. 11 numb. lvs; 4to. Anr edn of following item but including also at end 'Suma de los muertos y martyrizados que se referien en el presente memorial'. Sabin 24319 (dated

1616); Wagner (SW) 22a; Palau 91413. CSmH, MH, RPJCB. 617/50

——. Señor. Francisco de Figueroa de la Compañia de Jesus, procurador de las provincias de las Indias, dize: Que por quanto acerca del alçamiento, y rebelion de los Indios Tepehuanes, Zinaloas, y otras naciones, que sucedio por fin del año de mil y seiscientos y deziseis, se han esparcido varias relaciones, mezclandose . . . algunas cosas que causan confusion. [*Madrid?* 1617?]. 12 lvs; 4to. Medina (BHA) 6465; Wagner (SW) 22; Streit II:1469; Palau 19414. MH (imp.), NNH, RPJCB; Granada:BU. 617/51

——. Señor. El padre Francisco de Figueroa de la Compañia de Jesus, procurador de las Indias dize: Que fray Pedro de Sosa . . . llegó al reyno de Chile con otros frayles de su religion. [*Madrid?* 1617?]. 2 lvs; 8vo. Streit II:1470; Pérez Pastor (Madrid) 1463. 617/52

Fioravanti, Leonardo. De' capricci medicinali . . . libri quattro. *Venice: C. Gallina,* 1617. 230 numb. lvs; illus.; 8vo. 1st publ., Venice, 1561, under title *Capricci medicinali;* cf. 1602 edn. Michel (Répertoire) III:47. DNLM, WU; Paris:Sorbonne. 617/53

Gallucci, Giovanni Paolo. Theatro, y descripcion universal del mundo . . . Traduzido de latin . . . por Miguel Perez. *Granada: S. Múñoz,* 1617. 369 numb. lvs; illus., map; fol. 1st publ. in Spanish, Granada, 1606. ICN; BN. 617/54

Garcilaso de la Vega, el Inca. Historia general del Peru, trata el descubrimiento del, y come lo ganaron los Españoles. *Córdoba: Widow of A. de Barrera,* 1617. 300 numb. lvs; 4to. 1st publ., Córdoba, 1616; here a reissue of that edn with altered title page. Sabin 98755; Medina (BHA) 658; Palau 354789; JCB (3) II:118. CtY, DLC, InU-L, MH, MiU-C, NN-RB, PPRF, RPJCB; BL, BN. 617/55

Garimberto, Girolamo, Bp of Gallese. Problemi naturali e morali. *Vicenza: F. Bolzetta,* 1617. 239 p.; 8vo. 1st publ., Venice, 1549. Includes discussion of lost Atlantis, mentioning Columbus. CU; BN. 617/56

Garzoni, Tommaso. La piazza universale di tutte le professioni del mondo. *Venice: G. Valentini, & A. Giuliani,* 1617. 403 numb. lvs; 4to. 1st publ., Venice, 1586; cf. 1601

edn. Comprises v. 1 of Garzoni's *Opere* of this year. CU, NN, RPJCB; BL, BN.

617/57

Gerhard, Johann. Locorum theologicorum . . . tomus quintus. *Jena: T. Steinmann,* 1617. 4to. Includes chapt. 25, 'De ecclesia', with section on Spanish cruelties in America, Cuba, Peru, etc., citing Acosta, Las Casas, Benzoni, et al. For Gerhard's 6th volume, see the year 1619; the remaining volumes are without American interest. NNUT.

617/58

Gesner, Konrad. Historia animalium liber iii. qui est de avium nunc natura . . . nunc denuo recognita. *Frankfurt a. M.: E. Emmel, for H. Laurenszoon [at Amsterdam],* 1617. 732 p.; illus.; fol. 1st publ., Zurich, 1555; cf. 1604 edn. DLC, MH, MnU, NN, PU-F; BL, BN.

617/59

Great Britain. Council for Virginia. Whereas upon the returne of sir Thomas Dale. *[London: T. Snodham,* 1617?]. bds.; fol. Includes appeal for emigrants; identifies governor as Samuel Argall. Sabin 99874; Vail (Frontier) 42; Clayton-Torrence 29; STC 24839. CSmH.

617/60

Great Britain. Sovereigns, etc., 1603–1625 (James I). A proclamation for the better and more peaceable government of the middle shires. *London: B. Norton & J. Bill,* 1617. 4 lvs; fol. Notorious offenders are to be sent to Virginia or the wars. Crawford (Roy. procl.) 1202; Brigham (Roy. procl.) 7–8; STC 8557. CSmH; London:Soc. Ant.

617/61

Greene, Robert. Theeves falling out. *London: H. Bell,* 1617. 4to. 1st publ., London, 1592; cf. 1615 edn. STC 12236. BL, Oxford:Bodl.

617/62

Habicot, Nicolas. Problesmes medicinaux et chirurgicaux. *Paris: J. Corrozet,* 1617. 110 p.; 8vo. Problem x, on syphilis, describes it as unknown to the ancients, mentioning guaiacum & sarsaparilla. Wellcome 3038. DNLM; London:Wellcome.

617/63

Hamor, Ralph, the Younger. Dreyzehente Schiffahrt, darinnen ein warhafftiger und gründtlicher Bericht von . . . Virginien . . . Erstlichen in engelischer Sprach . . . beschrieben. *Hanau: The Hulsiuses,* 1617. 76 p.; illus., map; 4to. (Levinus Hulsius's *Sammlung von . . . Schiffahrten.* Pt 13.)

Transl. from Hamor's *True discourse of the present state of Virginia,* 1st publ., London, 1615. Sabin 30122 (& 33666b); Baginsky (German Americana) 140; Shaaber (Brit. auth.) H79; Church 303; JCB (3) I:463. CSmH, CtY, NN-RB, PU, RPJCB, ViU; BL, BN.

617/64

—[Anr issue]. Dreyzehende Schiffahrt. *Hanau: The Hulsiuses,* 1617. Sabin 33666b; Baginsky (German Americana) 141; Church 303a; JCB (3) I:463–64. NN-RB (imp.), RPJCB; BL.

617/65

Hendschel, Tobias, O.P. Englischen Liebbrinnendten S. Francisci Ordens Relations Continuation, oder Volführung angedeuter Excellentz und Fürtrafligkeit . . . Colligiert auss dem grossen Chronica . . . Herrn Francisci Gonzage . . . und p.f. Francisco de S. Columbano . . . Auss Latein . . . verwendet durch p.f. Thobiam Hendschelium. *Ingolstadt: Eder Press, by Elisabeth Angermaier,* 1617. 109 p.; 4to. Prob. drawn in part from Francisco Gonzaga's *De origine seraphicae religionis franciscanae,* 1st publ., Rome, 1587. Includes refs to Franciscan martyrdoms in West Indies, p. 63–64. Streit V:1159; JCB (3) II:116. DLC, DHN, RPJCB; BL, Göttingen:UB.

617/66

Hues, Robert. Tractatus de globis coelesti et terrestri . . . à J. Hondio excusa. *Amsterdam: J. Hondius,* 1617. 130 p.; illus.; 4to. 1st publ., London, 1594; cf. 1611 edn. Shaaber (Brit. auth.) H480. DLC, ICN, NN-RB, RPJCB; BL, BN.

617/67

Ibarra Gueztaraen, Juan de. Por la villa imperial de Potossi. En razon de que conviene alcançar de su Santidad que los Indios dedicados a la mita . . . de la labor . . . trabajen. *[Madrid:* 1617]. 9 lvs; fol. Subscribed at end at Madrid, 14 Aug. 1617. Medina (BHA) 660. BL.

617/68

—[Anr edn]. *[Madrid:* 1617?]. 6 lvs; fol. Medina (BHA) 660n. BL.

617/69

——. Señor. Cinco cosas son las que . . . Potosi à V.M. en este memorial, por . . . Iuan de Yvarra . . . se sirva de conceder. *[Madrid:* 1617?]. 8 numb. lvs; fol. On the administration of mines at Potosí and the treatment of Indians there. Medina (BHA) 6549. BL.

617/70

——. Señor. De parte de la villa imperial de Potosi, suplique a V. Magestad en otro memorial cinco cosas . . . necessarias para su conservacion. [*Madrid:* 1617?]. [4] p.; fol. Medina (BHA) 6547. BL.   617/71

——. Señor. El licenciado Juan de Ybarra, procurador general de la villa imperial de Potosi, dize, que entre otras cosas . . . una es, que se haga reducion general de los Indios [etc.]. [*Madrid:* 1617]. bds.; fol. Memorial to king of Spain. Medina (BHA) 6550. BL.   617/72

——. Suma de lo que el licenciado Juan de Ybarra, como procurador . . . de Potosi pide. [*Madrid:* 1617]. bds.; fol. Memorial to king of Spain dated 14 Aug. 1617. BL.   617/73

Keckermann, Bartholomaeus. Systema compendiosum totius mathematices. *Hanau: P. Antonius,* 1617. 607 p.; illus., map; 8vo. Includes the author's *Systema astronomiae compendiosum,* 1st publ. separately, Hanau, 1611, & his *Systema geographicum,* 1st publ., Hanau, 1611. MH, PPL, RPB; London:Wellcome, BN.   617/74

Lescarbot, Marc. Histoire de la Nouvelle-France. Contenant les navigations, découvertes, & habitations faites par les François és Indes Occidentales & Nouvelle-France . . . Troisiesme edition enrichie de plusieurs choses singulieres. *Paris: A. Périer,* 1617. 970 p.; maps; 8vo. 1st publ., Paris, 1609. Cf. Sabin 40173; Church 370; Rothschild 1965. CSmH, ICN; BN.   617/75

——. Les muses da la Nouvelle France. *Paris: A. Périer,* 1617. 76 p.; 8vo. 1st publ., Paris, 1609. Normally bound with, as issued, the author's *Histoire de la Nouvelle France* of 1618. DLC, MiU-C.   617/76

Liddel, Duncan. Ars medica, succincte . . . explicata. *Hamburg: Froben Bookshop (P. Lang),* 1617. 868 p.; 8vo. 1st publ., Hamburg, 1608. Wellcome I:3796. DNLM; London:Wellcome, BN.   617/77

Lodewijcksz, Willem. 'T eerste boeck; Historie van Indien. *Amsterdam: M. Colijn,* 1617. 83 numb. lvs; illus., maps; obl. 4to. 1st publ., Amsterdam, 1598; cf. year 1609. Ostensibly published separately in this form, this work also figures as pt 2 of Michiel Colijn's *Oost-Indische ende West-Indische voyagien,* Amsterdam, 1619, q.v. Tiele-Muller 117; JCB (3) II:118. RPJCB.   617/78

Loubayssin de Lamarca, Francisco. Histo-

ria tragicomica de Don Henrique de Castro. *Paris: A. Tiffaine, for the Widow of M. Guillemot,* 1617. 879 p.; 8vo. 1st publ., Paris, 1612. Medina (Chile) 42. BL, BN.   617/79

Loyseau, Guillaume. De internorum externorumque ferme omnium curatione libellus. *Bordeaux: G. Vernoy,* 1617. 246 p.; 12mo. Chapt. xxxv, 'De lue venerea' calls for treatment using guaiacum, sarsaparilla, & sassafras. CtY-M, DNLM; BL, BN.   617/80

——. Observations médicinales et chirurgicales, avec histoires, noms, pays, saisons et tesmoinages. *Bordeaux: G. Vernoy,* 1617. 130 p.; 12mo. Case history of 'Crane carié par verole', i.e., syphilis, cites use of guaiacum. Wellcome I:3880. NNNAM; London:Wellcome, BN.   617/81

Marees, Pieter de. Beschrijvinghe ende Historische verhael vant Gout Koninckrijck van Guinea. *Amsterdam: M. Colijn,* 1617. 104 numb. lvs; illus.; obl. 4to. 1st publ., Amsterdam, 1602. Ostensibly published separately in this form, this work also figures as pt 5 of Michiel Colijn's *Oost-Indische ende West-Indische voyagien,* Amsterdam, 1619, q.v. Tiele 716; Tiele-Muller 136; JCB (3) II:119. RPJCB.   617/82

Mariana, Juan de, S.J. Historia general de España. *Madrid: Widow of A. Martín* (v. 1) *& J. de la Cuesta* (v. 2) *for A. Pérez,* 1617, '16. 2 v.; fol. Transl., rev. & augm. by the author from his *Historiae de rebus Hispaniae,* 1st publ., Toledo, 1592; cf. 1601 edn. Sabin 44546n; Backer V:549; Pérez Pastor (Madrid) 1472; Palau 151668. RP; BL, BN.   617/83

Marinelli, Curzio. Pharmacopaea, sive De vera pharmaca conficiendi . . . a medicorum venetorum collegio comprobata. *Hanau: C. Schleich,* 1617. 599 p.; 8vo. On p. 482 an oil employing guaiacum is described. Wellcome I:4057. WU; London:Wellcome.   617/84

—[Anr edn]. *Venice:* 1617. 8vo. BL.   617/85

Markham, Gervase. Cavelarice, or The English horseman . . . Newly imprinted. *London: E. Allde, for E. White,* 1617, '16. 8 pts; 4to. 1st publ., London, 1607. Poynter (Markham) 19.2; STC 17335. CSmH, CtU, DFo, NjP, WU; BL.   617/86

Matthieu, Pierre. Histoire de France et des

chose memorables advenues aux provinces estrangeres durant sept années de paix du regne du roy Henry IIII. *Cologny: P. Aubert,* 1617. 2 v.; 8vo. 1st publ., Paris, 1605. MH.
617/87

Mercuriale, Girolamo. Medicina practica . . . libri v. *Lyons: C. Cayne, for A. Pillehotte,* 1617. 809 p.; 4to. 1st publ., Frankfurt a. M., 1601. DNLM (imp.); BL.
617/88

——. Praelectiones Patavinae. *Venice: The Giuntas,* 1617. 644 p.; fol. 1st publ., Frankfurt a. M., 1601, under title *Medica practica.* Wellcome I:4253. DNLM, MnU; London: Wellcome.
617/89

Mexía, Pedro. De verscheyden lessen . . . Hier zÿn noch by gevoecht seven verscheyden tsamensprekinghen, overgheset uyt den Fransoysche . . . tale. *Amsterdam: P. Ravesteyn, for P. J. Paets,* 1617. 2 pts; 8vo. 1st publ. in this version, Leyden, 1595. The 2nd pt, with title *De seven verscheyden tsamensprekinghe,* contains refs to syphilis & the Magellan circumnavigation. As indicated, transl. from the French version, 1st publ., Lyons, 1577, under title *Les diverses leçons . . . augmentées de trois dialogues.* The 'dialogues' were 1st publ., Seville, 1547, under title *Colóquios o dialogos.* Palau 167339. DNLM, RPJCB; Madrid:BN.
617/90

Middleton, Thomas. A faire quarrell . . . By Thomas Middleton and William Rowley. *London: [G. Eld,] for J. T[rundle]., sold [by E. Wright],* 1617. [61] p.; 4to. Drama. In act 4, scene 1, a character named 'Vapor', a tobacco seller, appears, occasioning discussion of evils of the weed. STC 17911; Greg 352 (aI); Arents 130. CSmH, CtY, DLC, MH, NN-A; BL.
617/91

—[Anr issue]. With new additions. *London: [G. Eld,] for J. T[rundle].; sold [by E. Wright]* 1617. [77] p.; 4to. STC 17911a; Greg 352 (aII). MH; London:V. & A.
617/92

Minsheu, John. Ἡγεμὼν εἰς τὰς γλῶσσας, id est, Ductor in linguas, the guide into tongues. *London: [W. Stansby & M. Bradwood]; sold by J. Browne,* 1617. 2 pts; fol. An etymological dictionary, with definitions & sources for numerous words relating to the Americas, e.g. 'Tabaco', 'Maize', 'Pockes', &c. For variant states see STC 17944a. Pt 2 comprises the author's *Vocabularium hispanicolatinum . . . A most copious Spanish dic-*tionarie, which includes entries anent the Americas, e.g., 'Mexico', 'Tuna', & 'Yuca'. STC 17944; Arents 131. CSmH, CtY, DFo, ICN, MH, MiU, MnU, NN-RB, PU-F, RPB; BL, BN.
617/93

Mocquet, Jean. Voyages en Afrique, Asie, Indes Orientales et Occidentales. *Paris: J. de Heuqueville,* 1617. 442 p.; illus.; 8vo. 1st publ., Paris, 1616; here a reissue with altered imprint date. Sabin 49790n; Borba de Moraes II:65. CSmH, CtY, MnU-B, NN-RB.
617/94

Montaigne, Michel Eyquem de. Les essais . . . Edition nouvelle enrichie d'annotations en marge. *Paris: F. Gueffier,* 1617. 1089 p.; port.; 4to. 1st publ., Bordeaux, 1580; cf. 1602 edn. Tchémerzine VIII:420. MiU, NjP; BN.
617/95

—[Anr issue]. *Paris: M. Nivelle,* 1617. Tchémerzine VIII:420. MH; BN.
617/96

—[Anr issue]. *Paris: J. Petit-Pas,* 1617. Tchémerzine VIII:420. BL, BN.
617/97

—[Anr issue]. *Paris: C. Rigaud,* 1617. Tchémerzine VIII:420. BN.
617/98

—[Anr issue]. *Paris: Widow D. Salis,* 1617. Tchémerzine VIII:420. CtY; BN.
617/99

—[Anr issue]. *Paris: C. Sevestre,* 1617. Tchémerzine VIII:420.
617/100

—[Anr edn]. *Rouen: N. Angot,* 1617. 1129 p.; port.; 8vo. Tchémerzine VIII:421.
617/101

—[Anr issue]. *Rouen: J. Berthelin,* 1617. Tchémerzine VIII:420.
617/102

—[Anr issue]. *Rouen: J. Besongne,* 1617. Tchémerzine VIII:420.
617/103

—[Anr issue]. *Rouen: T. Daré,* 1617. Tchémerzine VIII:420.
617/104

—[Anr issue]. *Rouen: J. Durand,* 1617. Tchémerzine VIII:420.
617/105

—[Anr issue]. *Rouen: J. Osmont,* 1617. Tchémerzine VIII:420. BN.
617/106

—[Anr issue]. *Rouen: M. de Preaulx,* 1617. Tchémerzine VIII:420. DFo, MH, MiU.
617/107

—[Anr issue]. *Rouen: R. Valentin,* 1617. Tchémerzine VIII:420. BN.
617/108

Moryson, Fynes. An itinerary. *London: J. Beale,* 1617. 3 pts; illus., maps; fol. In Pt iii, bk i, chapt. 1, a Spaniard is mentioned who, having contracted syphilis, went to America to learn its cure 'from those who first infected the Spaniards therewith'; tobacco is also mentioned. STC 18205; Arents (Add.) 180. CSmH, CtY, DLC, ICN, MH, NN-A, PU-F; BL. 617/109

Ortiz de Cervantes, Juan. Memorial que trata de la perpetuydad de los encomenderos de Indios del Peru. *Madrid: J. Sánchez,* 1617. 6 numb. lvs; fol. Medina (BHA) 661; Pérez Pastor (Madrid) 1485; Palau 205770. BL. 617/110

Ottsen, Hendrick. Journael oft Daghelijcx-register van de voyagie na Rio de Plata. *Amsterdam: M. Colijn,* 1617. 54 p.; illus.; obl. 4to. 1st publ., Amsterdam, 1603. Ostensibly published separately in this form, this work also figures as pt 8 of Michiel Colijn's *Oost-Indische ende West-Indische voyagien,* Amsterdam, 1619, q.v. Sabin 57901 (& 31228); Tiele-Muller 207; Tiele 836; JCB (3) II:120. DLC, InU-L, MnU-B, NNH, RPJCB. 617/111

Panciroli, Guido. Livre premier des antiquitez perdues . . . accompagné d'un second des choses nouvellement inventées . . . Traduits tant de l'italien que du latin en françois par Pierre de la Noue. *Lyons: P. Roussin,* 1617. 261 p.; 12mo. 1st publ. in Latin, Amberg, 1599–1602, & in Italian, Venice, 1612; cf. year 1602. Sabin 58414. ICN; BL, BN. 617/112

—[Anr issue]. *Lyons: J. Gaudion,* 1617. BN. 617/113

Pasquier, Etienne. Les recherches de la France. *Paris: L. Sonnius,* 1617. 694 p.; port.; 4to. 1st publ. with American content, Paris, 1596; cf. 1607 edn. Thickett (Pasquier) 14; Tchémerzine IX:84. CU, CtY, DLC, ICN, NjP; Strasbourg:BN, Vienna:NB. 617/114

Pisa, Francisco de. Descripcion de la imperial ciudad de Toledo . . . Primera parte . . . Publicada de nuevo despues de su muerte por el doctor don Thomas Tamaio de Vargas. *Toledo: D. Rodríguez,* 1617. 277 p.; fol. 1st publ., Toledo, 1605; here a reissue of sheets of that edn with differing preliminary pages & t.p. No more published. Pérez Pastor (Toledo) 456n; Palau 227400. ICU, NNH, RPB; BL, BN. 617/115

Popp, Johann. Chymische Medicin. *Frankfurt a. M.: E. Emmel, for S. Schamberger,* 1617. 523 p.; 8vo. Describes extracts, salts, etc., of guaiacum & sarsaparilla. Ferguson (Bibl.

chem.) II:213; Wellcome I:5170. BL, London:Wellcome. 617/116

Potgieter, Barent Janszoon. Historisch ende wijdtloopigh verhael van 'tghene de vijf schepen (die . . . door de Straet Magellana haren handel te dryven) wedervaren is. *Amsterdam: M. Colijn,* 1617. 73 p.; illus., obl. 4to. 1st publ., Amsterdam, 1600, under title *Wijdtloopigh verhael van tgene de vijf schepen.* Ostensibly published separately in this form, this work also figures as pt 9 of Michiel Colijn's *Oost-Indische ende West-Indische voyagien,* Amsterdam, 1619, q.v. Sabin 64582; Tiele-Muller 12; JCB (3) II:120. NNH, RPJCB. 617/117

Pretty, Francis. Beschryvinge vande overtreffelijcke ende wydtvermaerde zee-vaerdt vanden . . . Meester Thomas Candish . . . Hier noch by ghevoecht de voyagie van Siere François Draeck, en Siere Ian Haukens . . . Van nieus gecorrigeert ende verbeetert. *Amsterdam: M. Colijn,* 1617. 39 numb. lvs; obl. 4to. 1st publ., Amsterdam, 1598. Ostensibly published separately in this form, this work also figures as pt 6 of Michiel Colijn's *Oost-Indische ende West-Indische voyagien,* Amsterdam, 1619, q.v. Sabin 11606; Tiele 882n; Tiele-Muller 281; JCB (3) II:121. DLC, NNH, RPJCB. 617/118

Ptolemaeus, Claudius. Geographiae universae tum veteris tum novae. *Arnhem: J. Janszoon,* 1617. 2 pts; maps; 4to. 1st publ. as here ed. by G. A. Magini, Venice, 1596; cf. 1608 edn. Sabin 66496 (& 43822n); Stevens (Ptolemy) 60; Phillips (Atlases) 432; JCB (3) III:119. CtY, DLC, ICN, NN-RB, RPJCB; BL, BN. 617/119

Purchas, Samuel. Purchase his Pilgrimage . . . The third edition, much enlarged. *London: W. Stansby, for H. Fetherstone,* 1617. 1102 p.; fol. 1st publ., London, 1613. Sabin 66681; Streit I:365; STC 20507; JCB (3) II:120. CSmH, CtY, DLC, ICN, MH, MiU, NN-RB, PPL, RPJCB; BL. 617/120

Queiros, Pedro Fernandes de. Copie de la requeste presentee au Roy d'Espagne . . . sur la cinquiesme partie du monde, appelée la terre australe. *Paris:* 1617. 16 p.; 4to. Transl. from Spanish text, 1st publ., [Madrid? 1610]. Sabin 67356; Medina (BHA) 6456n (VI:82), Palau 89608; Kelly (Calendar of Docs) 593; JCB (3) II:117. InU-L, MnU-B, NcD, RPJCB; BL.   617/121

——. Terra Australis incognita, or A new southerne discoverie . . . Translated by W. B. *London: J. Hodgetts,* 1617. 27 p.; 4to. Transl. from the *Copie de la requeste presentee au Roy,* the preceding item. Sabin 67357; Medina (BHA) 558n (II:104); Palau 89609; STC 10822. CSmH, DLC, MH; BL.
    617/122

—[Anr issue]. *London: J. Hodgetts,* 1617. Title page lacks phrase 'translated by W. B.'. Kelly (Calendar of Docs.) 583; JCB (3) II:117–18. RPJCB.   617/123

Raleigh, Sir Walter. The history of the world. *London: W. Stansby, for W. Burre,* 1617. 2 v.; port., maps; fol. 1st publ., London, 1614. See also the year 1621. Sabin 67560n; Brushfield (Raleigh) 223(B); STC 20638. CtY, DFo, MiU-C, NN-RB, PU; BL.
    617/124

——. Warachtighe ende grondige beschryvinghe van . . . Guiana . . . ende den vermaerden zeevaerder Capiteyn Laurens Keymis. *Amsterdam: M. Colijn,* 1617. 49 numb. lvs; obl. 4to. 1st publ. in Dutch, Amsterdam, 1598; cf. year 1605. Ostensibly published separately in this form, this work also figures as pt 7 of Michiel Colijn's *Oost-Indische ende West-Indische voyagien,* Amsterdam, 1619, q.v. Includes, with special t.p., Lawrence Kemys's *Waerachtighe ende grondighe beschryvinghe vande tweede zeevaert . . . nae Guiana* (lvs [32]–49). Sabin 67597 & 37690; Tiele-Muller 287; Arents (Add.) 179; JCB (3) II:121–22. DLC, InU-L, NN-A, RPJCB.   617/125

Remón, Alonso, O. Merced. La vida del siervo de Dios Gregorio Lopez. *Madrid: Widow of A. Martín,* 1617. 140 numb. lvs; 8vo. Lopez was for 30 years a missionary to the Indians in Mexico. Medina (BHA) 664 (VII:318–21); Streit II:1475; Pérez Pastor (Madrid) 1501; Palau 260834. Madrid: BU (San Isidro).   617/126

——. Vida y muerte del siervo de Dios Don Fernando de Cordova y Bocanegra. *Madrid: L. Sánchez,* 1617 [colophon: 1616]. 130 numb. lvs; illus.; 4to. Cordova y Bocanegra (1565–89) was a Mexican-born priest who lived and died there. Cf. Sabin 16773; Me-

dina (BHA) 663; Pérez Pastor (Madrid) 1498; Palau 260831. RPJCB.   617/127

Rich, Barnabe. The Irish hubbub, or The English hue and crie. *London: [G. Purslowe,] for J. Marriott,* 1617. 56 p.; 4to. A further diatribe against tobacco, citing its West Indian source. On t.p. line 8 is in roman type. STC 20989. CSmH, CtY, MH; BL.
    617/128

—[Anr edn, rev.]. *London: [G. Purslowe,] for J. Marriott,* 1617. 56 p.; 4to. On t.p. line 8 is in italic. STC 20989; Arents 132. NN-A.
    617/129

Rubio, Antonio. Logica mexicana . . . Hoc est, Commentarii breviores . . . in universam Aristotelis Dialecticam . . . *Lyons: J. Pillehotte,* 1617. 683 p.; 8vo. 1st publ., Cologne, 1605. Cf. Sabin 73860; cf. Medina (BHA) 575; Palau 280356n. InU-L.
    617/130

Sacro Bosco, Joannes de. Sphaera . . . emendata. Eliae Vineti . . . Scholia . . . ab ipso autore restituta. *Lyons: A. Pillehotte,* 1617. 192 p.; illus.; 8vo. 1st publ. with Vinet's *Scholia,* Paris, 1551; cf. 1601 edn above. London:Wellcome, BN.   617/131

Schaller, Georg. Thierbuch, sehr künstliche und wolgerissene Figuren von allerley Thieren . . . menniglich . . . in Reimen gestellt durch Georg Schallern. *Frankfurt a. M.: A. Humm, for F. N. Roth,* 1617. 64 lvs; illus.; 4to. 1st publ., Frankfurt a. M., 1569. Included are illus. of turkey cock and hen by Jost Amman with descriptive verses by Schaller. Though Becker describes several edns of this work, we have confined ourselves to those of which we are able to locate copies, that of 1592 & the present. Becker (Amman) 15e; Nissen (Zool.) 431n; Dt. Ges. Kat. 4:293. BL, Munich:StB, Vienna:NB.
    617/132

Schmidel, Ulrich. Warhafftige und liebliche Beschreibung etlicher fürnemmen Indianischen Landschafften und Insulen . . . Zum dritten mal auffgelegt und gebessert durch Johan-Theodor de Bry. *Oppenheim: H. Galler,* 1617. 51 p.; illus.; fol. (Theodor de Bry's *America.* Pt 7. German). 1st publ. in this version, Frankfurt a. M., 1597. At head of title: Das VII. Theil America. For variant issue see Church. Cf. Sabin 8784; Baginsky (German Americana) 139; Church 192 & 193; JCB (3) I:400. CSmH, NN-RB, RPJCB; BL, BN. 617/133

Scortia, Joannes Baptista. De natura et incremento Nili libri duo. *Lyons: H. Cardon,* 1617. 148 p.; illus.; 8vo. In bk 1, chapt. v, the Nile is described as smaller than the New World's Oreanus (i.e., Orinoco), as reported by José de Acosta, and the Argentine (i.e., the River Plate), citing G. P. Maffei. Wellcome I:5878. NN, OkU; BL, BN. 617/134

Serres, Olivier de, seigneur du Pradel. Le theatre d'agriculture. *Paris: A. Saugrain,* 1617. 907 p.; illus.; 4to. 1st publ., Paris, 1600; cf. 1603 edn. DLC, MH; BL. 617/135

Seville. Casa de la Moneda. El Fiscal de su Magestad. Con Francisco Baptista Beintin ensayador de la Casa de la Moneda de Sevilla, y consortes. Sobre la falta de ley que se ha hallado en la moneda de oro y plata de 13. 14. y 15. [*Seville?* 1617?]. 11 numb. lvs; fol. Ref. is made to the mint at Mexico City. BL. 617/136

Smith, Capt. John. Viertzehende Schiffart oder . . . Beschreibung dess Neuwen Engellandts . . . Auss dem Englischen . . . versetzt. *Frankfurt a. M.: H. Palthenius, for the Hulsiuses,* 1617. 62 p.; illus., map.; 4to. (Levinus Hulsius's *Sammlung von . . . Schifffahrten.* Pt 14). Transl. from Smith's *Description of New England,* 1st publ., London, 1616. Sabin 33667 (& 82819n); Baginsky (German Americana) 142; Shaaber (Brit. auth.) S250; Church 304; JCB (3) I:464. CSmH, CtY, ICN, MH, MnU, NN-RB, RPJCB, ViU; BL, BN. 617/137

Sosa, Pedro de, O. F. M. Señor. Fray Pedro de Sosa . . . dize . . . de quan nocivos han side los medios que se han executado en el reyno de Chile. [*Madrid?* 1617?]. 10 lvs; fol. Supplements Sosa's *Memorial* of 1616. Sabin 87185; Medina (Chile) 215; Streit II:1457. NN-RB. 617/138

Spenser, Edmund. The faerie queen . . . Together with the other workes of England's arch-poët. *London: H. L[ownes]., for M. Lownes,* 1617. 4 pts; illus.; fol. 1st publ., London, 1590; here another issue, in part reset, of 1609 edn, q.v. Johnson (Spenser)

19; STC 23085; Arents (Add.) 144; Pforzheimer 1007–8. CSmH, CtY, DLC, ICN, InU-L, MH, NN-A, PPT; BL. 617/139

Spilbergen, Joris van. Copie van een brief . . . inhoudende de voyagie by hem gedaen door de Strate Magelanica, tot in de Zuydt-Zee. *Delft: J. A. Cloeting,* 1617. [8] p.; 4to. Sabin 89443; Palau 321546; Tiele 1024n; Knuttel 2320; JCB (3) II:122. NN-RB, RPJCB; The Hague:KB. 617/140

——. t'Historiael journael van tghene ghepasseert is van weghen drie schepen. *Amsterdam: M. Colijn,* 1617. 41 numb. lvs; illus., maps; obl. 4to. 1st publ., Delft, 1601. Ostensibly published separately in this form, this work also figures as pt 4 of Michiel Colijn's *Oost-Indische ende West-Indische voyagien,* Amsterdam, 1619, q.v. Tiele-Muller 142; Tiele 1021; JCB (3) II:122. RPJCB; Amsterdam:NHSM. 617/141

Stigliani, Tomaso. Del mondo nuovo . . . Venti primi canti. *Piacenza: A. Bazacchi,* 1617. 700 p.; 12mo. Sabin 91728. CSmH, NN-RB, RPJCB; BL, BN. 617/142

Sylvester, Joshua. Tobacco battered; & the pipes shattered. [*London: H. Lownes,* 1617?]. [81]–116 p.; 8vo. In verse. For printing variants, see the STC. Also found issued with the author's *The second session,* [1615], & his *Sacred works* of 1620. Sabin 96042; STC 23582a; Arents 128. CSmH, DLC, MH, NN-A; BL. 617/143

Tapp, John. The seamans kalendar . . . Sixth edition. *London: E. Allde, for J. Tapp,* 1617. 4to. 1st publ., London, 1602. STC 23680.3. Edinburgh:UL. 617/144

Tarcagnota, Giovanni. Delle historie del mondo . . . Aggiuntovi la quinta parte di B. D. da Fano; laquale, ripigliando dall' anno sudetto 1513 contiene quanto è successo sino all'anno 1606. *Venice: G. & V. Varischi,* 1617. 4 pts; 4to. 1st publ., Venice, 1562. Includes accounts of Columbus & New World. Cf. 1580 edn. ICU; BL. 617/145

Taylor, John, the Water-poet. Jack a Lent. His beginning and entertainment. [*London: G. Eld, for J. Trundele?* 1617?]. 4to. A voyage to the West Indies is mentioned, as are the turkey, America, & its mines. STC 23765. Oxford:Bodl. (imp.). 617/146

——. Three weekes, three daies, and three houres observations and travel, from London to Hamburgh. *London: E. Griffin; & sold by G. Gibbs*, 1617. 21 lvs; 4to. Speaks of fame of Jacomo Campostella in Europe, Asia, Africa, & America. STC 23807. CSmH, DFo, MH, PU; BL. 617/147

Tomkis, Thomas. Lingua, or The combat of the tongue. *London: N. Okes, for S. Waterson*, 1617. 4to. Drama. 1st publ., London, 1607. STC 24106; Greg 239(c); Arents 133. CSmH, DLC, ICU, MH, NN-A, PU; BL. 617/148

Vaughan, William. Directions for health . . . Newly enriched with large additions . . . The fift edition. *London: T. S[nodham]., for Roger Jackson*, 1617. 8vo. 1st publ., London, 1600, under title *Naturall and artificial directions for health;* cf. 1602 edn. STC 24616; Arents (Add.) 154. CSmH, NN-A; BL. 617/149

Vega Carpio, Lope Félix de. Arcadia, prosas y versos. *Antwerp: P. & J. Bellère*, 1617. 471 p.; 12mo. 1st publ., Madrid, 1598; cf. 1602 edns. Peeters-Fontainas (Impr. esp.) 1343; Palau 356301. NNH, NjP; BL, BN. 617/150

Warachtich verhael vanden slach oft scheeps-strijt inde Zuydt Zee, ontrent de vermaerde . . . zee-haven Caljolo de Lima, tusschen . . . capiteyn generael . . . don Rodrigo de Mendosa, ende . . . commandeur generael . . . Joris van Speelberghen . . . 1615. *Middelburg: R. Schilders*, 1617. [16] p.; 4to. Knuttel 2321. The Hague:KB. 617/151

Wecker, Johann Jakob. Antidotarium generale et speciale. *Basel: J. J. Genath, for L. König*, 1617. 2 pts; illus.; 4to. 1st publ., Basel, 1574 & 1576; cf. 1601 edn. CaBVaU; DNLM. 617/152

Wirsung, Christoph. Praxis medicinae universalis; or A generall practise of physicke. *London: [J. Legat,] for T. Adams*, 1617. 790 p.; fol. 1st publ. as here transl., London, 1598; cf. 1605 edn. STC 25865; Wellcome I:6760. DFo, MBCo, NNNAM; BL. 617/153

Wither, George. Abuses stript and whipt . . . Reviewed and enlarged. *London: H. Lownes, for F. Burton*, 1617. 387 p.; 8vo. In verse. 1st publ., London, 1613. STC 25897. CSmH, CtY, DFo, ICU, MH; BL. 617/154

Woodall, John. The surgions mate, or A treatise discovering . . . the due contents of the surgions chest. *London: E. Griffin, for L. Lisle*, 1617. 348 p.; 4to. Describes a 'sassafras water' derived from Monardes; uses of guaiacum & sarsaparilla are discussed. STC 25962; Wellcome I:6774. CSmH, CtY, DLC, MBCo, MiU; BL. 617/155

Young, Thomas. Englands bane: or, The description of drunkennesse. *London: W. Jones; sold by T. Bailey*, 1617. 24 lvs; 4to. The nakedness of Virginians & Indians and the use of tobacco are mentioned. For variant states of imprint, see the STC. STC 26116; Arents (Add.) 181. CSmH, MH, NN-A; BL. 617/156

Zecchi, Giovanni. Consultationes medicinales. *Venice: G. & V. Varisco & Bros*, 1617. 432 p.; 4to. 1st publ., Rome, 1599, under title *Liber primus Consultationum medicinalium;* cf. 1601 edn. Wellcome I:6803. DNLM, NNNAM; London:Wellcome. 617/157

1618

Alemán, Mateo. Der Landtstörtzer: Gusman von Alfarche . . . Durch Aegidium Albertinum . . . verteutscht. *Munich: N. Heinrich*, 1618. 541 p.; 8vo. 1st publ. in German, Munich, 1615. Dt. Ges. Kat. 3:871; Goedeke II:577. Berlin:StB. 618/1

Araujo, Antonio de, S. J. Catecismo na lingoa brasilica. *Lisbon: P. Craesbeeck, for the Jesuits of Brazil*, 1618. 179 numb. lvs; 8vo. Sabin 1889; Borba de Moraes I:39, Viñaza 149. Lisbon:BN. 618/2

Bacon, Francis, viscount St Albans. Saggi morali. *London: J. Bill*, 1618. 2 pts; 8vo. 1st publ. as here transl., London, 1617, of which this is anr issue with altered imprint date. Gibson (Bacon) 34; STC 1153a. DFo. 618/3

—[Anr edn]. *London: J. Bill*, 1618. 2 pts; 8vo. Gibson (Bacon) 35; STC 1154. CSmH, DLC, IU, MH, NNPM; BL, BN. 618/4

Bainbridge, John. An astronomicall description of the late comet. *London: E. Griffin, for H. Fetherstone,* 1618. 42 p.; 4to. In description of course of comet, Brazil & Peru are mentioned. STC 1207. CSmH, WU; Cambridge: Emmanuel. 618/5

Barlow, William (d. 1625). Magneticall advertisements . . . The second edition. *London: E. Griffin, for T. Barlow,* 1618. 2 pts; illus.; 4to. 1st publ., London, 1618; here a reissue of that edn with cancel t.p. and addition of Barlow's *A briefe discovery of the idle animadversions of M. Ridley* of this year. STC 1444. CSmH (pt 2 wanting); BL, Cambridge: UL. 618/6

Bauderon, Brice. Paraphrase sur la Pharmacopee. *Lyons: P. Rigaud,* 1618. 2 pts; 8vo. 1st publ., Lyons, 1588; cf. 1607 edn.ViU. 618/7

Béguin, Jean. Secreta spagyrica revelata, sive Tyrocinium chymicum. [*Frankfurt a.d.O.:*] *J. Eichorn* [1618]. 382 p.; 8vo. 1st publ., Paris, 1612, under title *Tyrocinium chymicum.* BL, BN 618/8

—[Anr edn]. Tyrocinium chymicum. *Königsberg: J. Fabricius,* 1618. 537 p.; 8vo. BL, BN. 618/9

—[Anr edn]. *Königsberg: C. Berger,* 1618. 480 p.; 8vo. Wellcome I:751. London.Wellcome 618/10

Belchier, Dabridgcourt. Hans Beer-pot his invisible comedie of See me, and see me not. [*London:*] *B. Alsop,* 1618. 32 lvs; 4to. Included are refs to turkey, tobacco, & English explorers, e.g., Drake & Cavendish. STC 1803; Greg 354; Arents 134. CSmH, CtY, DFo, IU, MH, NN-A; BL. 618/11

Benzi, Ugo. Regole della sanità et della natura de cibi . . . Opera utile, ornata di varie storie, et arricchita d'un trattato nuovo della ebbrietà, & dell'abuse del tabaco. *Turin: Heirs of G. D. Tarino,* 1618. 850 (i.e., 800) p.; 8vo. DLC, NN. 618/12.

Berettari, Sebastiano, S. J. Vida del padre Joseph de Ancheta de la Compañia de Jesus, y provincial del Brasil. Traduzida de latin . . . por el padre Estevan de Paternina. *Salamanca: Antonia Ramírez,* 1618. 430 p.; 8vo. Transl. from the author's *Josephi Anchietae . . . vita,* 1st publ., Lyons, 1617. Sabin 4828 (& 1373); Medina (BHA) 676; Borba

de Moraes I:86 & II:135; Streit II:2383; Backer I:1326; JCB (3) II:123–24.RPJCB. 618/13

Bertius, Petrus. La geographie racourcie . . . comprise en sept livres. *Amsterdam: J. Hondius,* 1618. 829 p.; maps; obl. 8vo. Transl. from author's *Tabularum geographicarum . . . libri septem,* 1st publ., Amsterdam, 1600. Koeman (Lan) 13B; Phillips (Atlases) 5925. CSmH, DLC, NNC; BL, BN. 618/14

—[Anr issue.] Tabularum geographicarum contractarum libri septem. *Amsterdam: J. Hondius,* 1618. With text in French, differs only in its Latin t.p. Cf. following item. Sabin 5014; Koeman (Lan) 13A. InU-L; BN. 618/15

——. Tabularum geographicarum contractarum libri septem. *Amsterdam: J. Hondius,* 1618. 829 p.; maps; 4to. 1st publ., Amsterdam, 1600; here a reissue of 1616 edn with altered imprint date on t.p. Sabin 5014n; Koeman (Lan) 11B; JCB (3) II:124. MiU-C, RPJCB; BN. 618/16

Blaeu, Willem Janszoon. Het licht der zeevaert. *Amsterdam: W. J. Blaeu,* 1618. 2 v.; illus., maps; obl. fol. 1st publ., Amsterdam, 1608. Koeman (M.Bl) 5. Lund: UB, Copenhagen: KB. 618/17

Boccalini, Traiano. De' ragguagli di Parnaso . . . Centuria prima . . . quarta impressione. *Venice: G. Guerigli,* 1618. 332 p.; 8vo. 1st publ., Venice, 1612. Firpo (Ragguagli) 15; Michel (Répertoire) I:176. CtY, MH, MiU; Paris:Mazarine. 618/18

——. De' ragguagli di Parnaso . . . Centuria seconda . . . quarta impressione. *Venice: G. Guerigli,* 1618. 292 p.; 8vo. 1st publ., Venice, 1613; issued with Guerigli's Centuria prima of this year above. Firpo (Ragguagli) 15; Michel (Répertoire) I:176. 618/19

Botero, Giovanni. Le relazioni universali . . . Nuovamente ristampate, & ricorrette. *Venice: A. Vecchi,* 1618 [colophon: 1617]. 8 pts; illus., maps; 4to. 1st publ., Rome, 1591–96; cf. 1602 edn. Sabin 6806; Streit I:368; Michel (Répertoire) I:202. DLC, ICN, MBAt; BL, BN. 618/20

Breton, Nicholas. Conceyted letters, newly layde open. *London: B. Alsop, for S. Rand,* 1618. 23 lvs; 4to. Includes ref. to 'the turkie

cocke beating his henne when hee hath trod her'. STC 3637. CSmH, MH; BL.
618/21

——. The court and country, or A briefe discourse . . . by N. B. *London: G. Eld, for J. Wright,* 1618. 20 lvs; 4to. Includes refs to tobacco. STC 3641. CSmH, MH; Oxford: Bodl. (imp.).
618/22

—[Anr issue]. *London: G. Eld, for J. Wright,* 1618. T.p. has two woodcuts. STC 3642. DFo.
618/23

Camerarius, Philipp. Operae horarum subcisivarum . . . Centuria tertia. *Frankfurt a.M.: N. Hoffmann, for P. Kopff,* 1618. 4to. 1st publ., Frankfurt a.M., 1609. DLC, MnU-B; BN.
618/24

Capitulo de una de las cartas que diversas personas embiaron desde Cartagena de las Indias a algunos amigos suyos a las ciudades de Sevilla y Cadiz. En que dan cuenta como una monja en habito de hombre anduvo gran parte de España y de Indias . . . Y assi mismo come fue soldado en Chile y Tipoan. *Seville: J. Serrano de Vargas y Ureña,* 1618. 2 lvs; fol. Medina (Chile) 43; Escudero (Seville) 1.168; Palau 43287.
618/25

Cardona, Tomás de. Señor. El capitan Tomas de Cardona, por si, y en nombre de los demas participes en el assiento que con V. magestad se hizo el año de 1612, de nuevos descubrimientos de perlas. [*Madrid?* 1618?]. 5 numb. 1vs; fol. 'Relacion que haze el capitan Tomas de Cardona, y compañia, de lo sucedico en el descubrimiento de las perlas, y el estado que oy tiene', mentioning not only island of Margarita but also Carib Indians, Mexico, California, etc. According to Wagner, prob. written by Nicolás de Cardona. Medina (BHA) 6316; Wagner (SW) 23. CU-B, ICN, NN-RB; BL.
618/26

Cats, Jacob. Maechden-plicht, ofte Ampt der jonck-vrouwen. *Middelburg: J. van der Hellen,* 1618. 92 p.; illus.; 4to. Description of whaling includes ref. to Greenland; on p. 86 appears a ref. to the pineapple. Text in Latin & Dutch, with some French. Collation of preliminary matter in this edn: ❧, ❧2, *2–**2. Vries 100; Mus. Cats. 54. Leyden: UB.
618/27

—[Anr edn]. *Middelburg: J. van der Hellen,* 1618.

92 p.; illus.; 4to. Collation of preliminary matter in this edn: *2–❧2. For other variations in this edn, cf. Vries. Vries 101; Mus. Cats. 55. MH; Leyden:UB. [Editions not differentiated:] CSmH, CtY, DLC, ICN, NjP.
618/28

—[Anr edn]. Monita amoris virginei, sive Officium puellarum . . . Maechden-plicht. *Amsterdam: W. J. Blaeu* [1618?]. 123 p.; illus.; 4to. Vries 108; Mus. Cats. 63. NcD; BL, BN.
618/29

——. Silenus Alcibiadis, sive Proteus. *Middelburg: J. van der Hellen,* 1618. 3 pts; illus.; 4to. Includes refs to tobacco smoking & related customs; text of various portions in Dutch, Latin, & French. Vries 78; cf. Arents 163n. [Locations may include both edns:] CSmH, CtY, DFo, ICN, NjP; BL, BN.
618/30

—[Anr edn]. *Middelburg: J. van der Hellen,* 1618. 3 pts; illus.; 4to. Pt 1 is identical to that of the preceding edn. On the verso of the engraved t.p. of pt 2, under the phrase 'Ad lectorem', is an explanation of the differences exhibited by pts 2 & 3. Here the emblemata are omitted, being replaced by further explanatory text in Latin & Dutch, in 2 columns—Vries. Vries 79; Mus. Cats. 27. Leyden:UB.
618/31

Cervantes Saavedra, Miguel de. Les nouvelles . . . Seconde edition. *Paris: J. Richer,* 1618. 2 v.; 8vo. 1st publ. as here transl. from the Madrid, 1613, Spanish text, Paris, 1615. Palau 53521.
618/32

——. Seconde partie de l'Histoire de . . . Don Quichot de la Manche . . . traduicte . . . par F. de Rosset. *Paris: Widow of J. Du Clou, & D. Moreau,* 1618. 878 p.; 8vo. Transl. from the Brussels, 1616, Spanish edn; 1st publ., Madrid, 1615. Ríus (Cervantes) 463; Rothschild 3070; Palau 52695. MH; BN.
618/33

Clavius, Christoph. In Sphaeram Joannis de Sacro Bosco. *Lyons: P. Rigaud,* 1618. 639 p.; illus.; 4to. 1st publ., Rome, 1570; cf. 1601 edn. DLC; BN.
618/34

Cole, Nathanael. Preservatives against sinne. *London: T. S[nodham]., for N. Bourne,* 1618. 556 p.; 4to. The discussion of the sin of drunkenness includes (p. 406–10) section 'Concerning drinking of Tobacco.'

STC 5538; Arents (Add.) 182. DFo, MH, NN-A; BL.   618/35

Cordus, Valerius. Dispensatorium, sive Pharmacorum conficiendorum ratio. *Leyden: J. Maire,* 1618. 547 p.; illus.; 16mo. 1st publ., Nuremberg, 1546; cf. 1606 edn. PPC; London:Wellcome.   618/36

A declaration of the demeanor and carriage of Sir Walter Raleigh . . . as well in his voyage, as in, and sithence his returne. *London: B. Norton & J. Bill,* 1618. 63 p.; 4to. Published in justification of Raleigh's execution; authorship has been ascribed to Francis Bacon. Discusses in part Raleigh's Guiana voyages. For a Dutch translation, see the year 1619, the *Verclaringe ende verhael . . . Wouter Raleigh.* Sabin 67550; Gibson (Bacon) 369c; STC 20652.5 (formerly 20654); Church 374; JCB (3) II:123. CSmH, DFo, ICN, MH, MiU-C, NN-RB, RPJCB; BL.   618/37

—[Anr edn]. *London: B. Norton & J. Bill,* 1618. 68 p.; 4to. A partially reset & reimposed version of the above. For variant phrasings of the imprint, see the STC. Sabin 67548–49; Gibson (Bacon) 369a–b; STC 20653. CSmH, CtY, DLC, ICN, MH, MiU, NN-RB, PBL; BL.   618/38

Dodoens, Rembert. Cruydt-boeck . . . volgens sijne laetste verbeteringe . . . met bii voegsels achter elck capittel, uut verscheyden cruydtbeschrijvers: item in 't laetste een beschrijvinge vande Indiaensche gewassen, meest getrocken uut de schriften van Carolus Clusius. *Leyden: Plantin Press,* 1618. 1495 p.; illus.; fol. 1st publ., Antwerp, 1583; cf. 1608 edn above. Pritzel 2345n; Nissen (Bot.) 518; Bibl. belg., 1st ser., IX, D120; Arents (Add.) 76. DNLM, ICJ, MH-A, NN-A; BL, BN.   618/39

Ens, Gaspar. West- unnd Ost Indischer Lustgart: Das ist, eygentliche erzehlung wann und von wem die Newe Welt erfunden . . . worden. *Cologne: W. Lützenkirchen,* 1618. 2 pts; maps; 4to. Sabin 22657 (& 42742); Baginsky (German Americana) 144; Palau 79882; JCB (3) II:126. CU, DLC, MH, MnU-B, NN-RB, PBL, RPJCB; BL.   618/40

Espinel, Vicente. Relaciones de la vida del escudero Marcos de Obregon. *Madrid: J. de*

la Cuesta, for M. Martínez, 1618. 187 numb. lvs; 4to. Picaresque novel which, in 3rd pt, descansos xix ff., presents fictional attempt to colonize the Strait of Magellan, with account of Patagonian 'giants'. Laurenti (Nov. pic. esp.) 853; Pérez Pastor (Madrid) 1538; Palau 82586. CU, NNH, PU; BL, BN.   618/41

—[Anr edn]. *Barcelona: S. de Cormellas,* 1618. 232 numb. lvs; 8vo. Laurenti (Nov. pic. esp.) 854; Palau 82587. NNH; BL.   618/42

—[Anr edn]. *Barcelona: J. Margarit,* 1618. 281 numb. lvs; 8vo. Laurenti (Nov. pic. esp.) 855; Palau 82588.   618/43

Estienne, Charles. Dictionarium historicum, geographicum, poeticum. *Cologny: S. Crispin,* 1618. 2032 cols; 4to. 1st publ. in this enl. edn, Lyons, 1595; cf. 1601 edn. NcU; BN.   618/44

Fernández, Alonso, O. P. Concertatio praedicatoria, pro eclesia [*sic*] catholica. *Salamanca: D. Cosío,* 1618. 498 p.; fol. Included are accounts of Dominican missions in Spanish America. Streit I:369. Rome: BN.   618/45

Field, Nathan. Amends for ladies. A comedie. *London: G. Eld, for M. Walbanke,* 1618. [62] p.; 4to. In acts 2 & 3 tobacco is mentioned. For a variant t.p. of dubious authenticity, see Greg 356aII & the Pforzheimer catalog. STC 10851; Greg 356aI; Arents 136; Pforzheimer 364. CSmH, CtY, DFo, NN-A; BL.   618/46

Fioravanti, Leonardo. Corona oder Kron der Artzney . . . in unsere hochteutsche Sprach . . . versetzt. *Frankfurt a. M.: A. Humm, for J. Berner,* 1618. 512 p.; illus.; 8vo. 1st publ. in German, Frankfurt a.M., 1604. DNLM, MiU.   618/47

Gabelkover, Oswald. Artzneybuch. *Tübingen: J. J. Porsch & J. Berner,* 1618. 3 pts; 4to. 1st publ., Tübingen, 1589, under title *Nützlich Artzneybuch;* cf. 1603 edn. DNLM; London:Wellcome.   618/48

Goulart, Simon. Histoires admirables et memorables. *Paris: J. Houzé,* 1618. 6 v.; 12mo. 1st publ., Paris, 1600–1601; cf. 1603 edn. Jones (Goulart) 54n. BN.   618/49

Le grand dictionnaire françois-latin, augmenté [par Guillaume Poille] . . . recueilli

des observations de plusieurs hommes doctes, entre autres de m. Nicot. *Paris: S. Chapellet,* 1618. [1164] p.; 4to. 1st publ., Paris, 1573, under title *Dictionaire françois-latin;* cf. year 1603. BN.   618/50
—[Anr edn]. *Rouen: R. L'Allemant,* 1618. 284 lvs; 4to. [1164] p.; 4to. BN.   618/51
—[Anr issue]. *Rouen: J. Osmont* 1618. MA, OClW.   618/52

Great Britain. Sovereigns, etc., 1603–1625 (James I). A proclamation declaring His Majesties pleasure concerning Sir Walter Rawleigh, and those who adventured with him. *London: B. Norton & J. Bill,* 1618. bds.; fol. On Raleigh's Guiana voyage. Sabin 67547; Crawford (Roy. procl.) 1213; Brigham (Roy. procl.) 8–9; STC 8569. CSmH; BL.   618/53
——. A proclamation, with articles . . . concerning ale-houses. *London:* 1618. *See the year* 1619.

Grotius, Hugo. Mare liberum, sive De jure quod Batavis competit ad Indicana commercia dissertatio. Ultima editio. *Leyden: Elsevier Office,* 1618. 108 p.; 8vo. 1st publ., Leyden, 1609. Meulen/Diermanse 543; Willems (Les Elzevier) 140; Bibl. Belg. G333. CtY, DLC, MH, NN-RB; BL, BN.
                                                 618/54

Guicciardini, Francesco. The historie of Guicciardin: Containing the warres of Italie . . . Reduced into English by Geffray Fenton. The third edition. *London: R. Field; sold by A. Johnson,* 1618. 821 p.; fol. Transl. from the author's *La historia di Italia,* 1st publ., Florence, 1561; 1st publ. in English, London, 1579. In book 6, discoveries of Columbus, Vespucci, & others are discussed. STC 12460. CSmH, CtY, DLC, IU, MH, MnU, NN, PBL; BL, BN.   618/55

Harington, Sir John. The most elegant and wittie epigrams. *London: G. P[urslowe]., for J. Budge,* 1618. 92 lvs; 8vo. In verse. In bk 2, Epigram 38 has title 'Why Paulus takes so much tobacco'; bk 3, no. 38, 'Of a sicknesse grew with a tobacco pipe; bk 4, no. 34, 'Of a drunken tobacconist', while in bk 3 no. 33 mentions 'potato rootes'. STC 12776. CSmH, DFo, MH; BL.   618/56

Heurne, Justus van. De legatione evangelica ad Indos capessanda admonitio. *Leyden: I.*

Elsevier, 1618. 300 p.; 8vo. Though written with the East rather than the West Indies in view, the New World is incidentally mentioned. Sabin 31623; Muller (1872) 996; JCB (3) II:126. DLC, MH, NNUT, PU, RPJCB; BL, BN.   618/57

Holyday, Barten. Τεχνογαμια: or, The marriages of the arts. A comedy. *London: W. Stansby, for J. Parker,* 1618. 56 lvs; 4to. In act 2, scene 2, a song of 7 stanzas on 'Indian tobacco' appears. STC 13617; Greg 353(a); Arents 137. CSmH, CtY, DFo, ICN, MH, NN-A; BL.   618/58

Hues, Robert. Traicté des globes, et de leur usage. Traduict du latin . . . Par D. Henrion. *Paris: F. Bourriquant, for A. Pacard,* 1618. 184 p.; 8vo. Transl. from Hues's *Tractatus de globis,* 1st publ., London, 1594; cf. 1611 edn. Sabin 33563; Shaaber (Brit. auth.) H482. MB, MH, MnU-B; BN.
                                                 618/59

Hulsius, Levinus, ed. Sechster Theil; Kurtze, warhafftige Relation und Beschreibung der wunderbarsten vier Schifffahrten . . . nemlich: Ferdinandi Magellani . . . Francisci Draconis . . . Thomae Candisch . . . Olivarii von Noort. *Frankfurt a.M.: Hulsius,* 1618. 53 p.; illus., maps; 4to. (Levinus Hulsius's *Sammlung von . . . Schiffahrten.* Pt. 6). 1st publ., Nuremberg, 1603. Sabin 33660; Baginsky (German Americana) 145; Church 283; JCB (3) I:458. CSmH, NN-RB, RPJCB; BN.   618/60

Ibarra Gueztaraen, Juan de. Señor. A nueve cosas que supliquè, en nombre de la villa imperial de Potosi. [*Madrid:* 1618?]. 4 numb. lvs; fol. Memorial to king of Spain on affairs of Potosí. Medina (BHA) 6545. BL.   618/61
——. Señor. De parte de la villa imperial de Potosi, se suplica a V. Magestad lo siguiente. [*Madrid:* 1618?]. [3] p.; fol. Memorial to king of Spain on affairs of Potosí. Medina (BHA) 6546. BL.   618/62
——. Señor. En el memorial que presento en este Real Consejo, en razon de los negocios de . . . Potosi. [*Madrid:* 1618?]. [3] p.; fol. Memorial to the king of Spain on working of mines. Medina (BHA) 6548. BL.
                                                 618/63

Jack Drum's entertainment. Jacke Drums entertainment; or, The comedie of Pasquill and Katherine. *London:* [*W. Stansby,*] *for N. Fosbrooke,* 1618. [72] p.; 4to. 1st publ., London, 1601; here a reissue with cancel t.p. of 1616 edn. STC 7245; Greg 177 (bII). MWiW-C; BL. 618/64

Jesuits. Letters from missions. Annuae litterae (1602) 1618. Litterae annuae . . . anni M.DC.II. *Antwerp: Heirs of M. Nuyts,* 1618. 775 p.; 8vo. Included is a report on the Mexican province. Streit I:375; JCB (3) II:127. ICN, RPJCB; BL, Rome: BN. 618/65

Jesuits. Letters from missions. Annuae litterae (1603) 1618. Annuae litterae . . . Anni M.DC.III. *Douai: Widow of L. Kellam & son Thomas,* 1618. 706 p.; 8vo. Included is a report on the province of Peru. Streit I:376. BL, Rome:BN. 618/66

Jesuits. Letters from missions. Annuae litterae (1604) 1618. Annuae litterae . . . Anni M.DC.IV. *Douai: Widow of L. Kellam & son Thomas,* 1618. 758 p.; 8vo. Included are reports on the provinces of Mexico & Peru. Streit I:377. RPJCB; BL, Rome:BN. 618/67

Jesuits. Letters from missions. Annuae litterae (1605) 1618. Annuae litterae . . . Anni M.DC.V. *Douai: Widow of L. Kellam & son Thomas,* 1618. 978 p.; 8vo. Included is a report on Peru. Streit I:378. NNH; BL, Fulda:B. Sem. 618/68

Jesuits. Letters from missions. Annuae litterae (1606, 1607 & 1608) 1618. Literae annuae . . . Anni 1606. 1607 & 1608. *Mainz: J. Albin,* 1618. 3 v.; 8vo. Included are reports on the provinces of Mexico & Peru. On variants in v. 3, see the JCB Catalogue as cited. Streit I:379–81; JCB (3) II:127. RPJCB; BL, Rome:BN. 618/69

Jesuits. Letters from missions. Annuae litterae (1609) 1618. Annuae litterae . . . anni M.DC.IX. *Dillingen: Widow of J. Mayer,* [1618?]. 667 p.; 8vo. Included are reports on the provinces of Peru & Mexico. Streit I:382; JCB (3) II:85. RPJCB; BL, Rome:BN. 618/70

Jesuits. Letters from missions. Annuae litterae (1610) 1618. Annuae litterae . . . anni M.DC.X. *Dillingen: Widow of J. Mayer,* [1618?]. 545 p.; 8vo. Included are reports on the provinces of Peru & Mexico. Sabin 1607n; Streit I:383; Palau 12796; JCB (3) II:85. DLC, InU-L, RPJCB; BL, Rome:BN. 618/71

Jesuits. Letters from missions. Annuae litterae (1611) 1618. Annuae litterae . . . anni M.DC.XI. *Dillingen: Mayer Press, by M. Algeyer* [1618]. 869 p.; 8vo. Included are reports on the provinces of Peru & Mexico. Streit I:384. NNH; BL, Rome:BN. 618/72

Jesuits. Letters from missions. Annuae litterae (1612) 1618. Annuae litterae . . . anni M.DC.XII. *Lyons: C. Cayne,* 1618. 757 p.; 8vo. Included are reports on Mexico & Peru. Ed. by Philibert Monet. Streit I:385; Backer V:1209. ICN, RPJCB; BL, Rome:BN. 618/73

Lescarbot, Marc. Histoire de la Nouvelle-France. Contenant les navigations, découvertes, & habitations faites par les François és Indes Occidentales & Nouvelle-France . . . Troisiesme edition enrichie de plusieurs choses singulieres. *Paris: A. Périer,* 1618. 970 p.; maps; 8vo. 1st publ., Paris, 1609; here anr issue of printer's 1617 edn, with altered imprint date. Sabin 40173; Harrisse (NF) 31; Streit II:2481; Church 372; JCB (3) II:127. CSmH, CtY, DLC, InU-L, MH, MiU-C, MnU-B, NN-RB, RPJCB; BL, Göttingen:UB. 618/74

——. Les muses de la Nouvelle France. *Paris: A. Périer,* 1618. 76 p.; 8vo. 1st publ., Paris, 1609; here another issue of Périer's 1617 edn with altered imprint date. Sabin 40174n; Harrisse (NF) 31n; Borba de Moraes I:407; Streit II:2481; Church 371; Rothschild 1965n; JCB (3) II:128. CSmH, CtY, InU-L, MH, MnU-B, RPJCB; BN. 618/75

——. Le tableau de la Suisse et autres alliez de la France és hautes Allemagnes. *Paris: A. Périer,* 1618. 79 p.; illus.; 4to. In the preface is a ref. to 'Nouvelle France'. Cioranescu (XVII) 43001; Maggs Cat. 502 (Americana VII):5032. MH, NjP, RPB; BL, BN. 618/76

L'Obel, Matthias de. Pharmacopoeia Rondeletii: cum Matthiae Lobelii & Lyd. Myrei animadversionibus. Item Stirpium adversaria, auctiora. *Leyden: J. Maire,* 1618. 2 pts. illus.; fol. A reissue with cancel t.p. of L'Obel's *In G. Rondelletii Pharmaceuticam*

. . . *animadversiones*, London, 1605. STC 19595.7. RPB.   618/77

Lundorp, Michael Caspar. Politische SchatzCammer oder Form zu regieren, ander Theil . . . in Truck gegeben durch Nicolaum Bellum. *Frankfurt a.M.: J. G. Schönwetter,* 1618. 254 p.; 4to. Includes refs (p. 10–11) to Columbus, Magellan, Peru, Florida, and Panama; cf. the author's *Politische SchatzCammer* of 1624. RPJCB.   618/78

Magnus, Olaus, Abp of Upsala. Historia . . . de gentibus septentrionalibus . . . In epitomen redacta. *Frankfurt a. M.: C. Vetter,* 1618. 461 p.; 8vo. 1st publ., Rome, 1555. Includes sections on Greenland, referring also to New World voyages by Portuguese, Spanish, & French. CtY, MH, PU.   618/79

Marradon, Bartolomeo. Dialogo del uso del tabaco . . . y del chocolate y otros bebidas. *Seville: G. Ramos Bejarano,* 1618. 8vo. A possible ghost. Muller:139; Escudero (Seville) 1.143.   618/80

Massaria, Alessandro. Practica medica. *Venice: T. Bertolotti,* 1618. 3 pts; fol. 1st publ., Frankfurt a.M., 1601. DNLM.   618/81

Matthieu, Pierre. Histoire de sainct Louys. *Paris: B. Martin,* 1618. 512 p.; 8vo. Includes mention of Columbus. Cioranescu (XVI) 14819. MH; BN.   618/82

Mattioli, Pietro Andrea. I discorsi . . . nelli sei libri di Pedacio Dioscoride . . . della materia medicinale. *Venice:* 1618. 1527 p.; illus., port.; fol. 1st publ. as here transl. from Latin, Venice, 1555; cf. 1604 edn above. Cf. Pritzel 5988n; cf. Nissen (Bot.) 1304. MnU-B.   618/83

Mazza, Marc' Antonio. Tesoro de secreti medicinali. *Macerata: P. Salvioni,* 1618. [16] p.; 8vo. Secret 10, 'Per le scrofole', employs tobacco. London:Wellcome.   618/84

Medina, Pedro de. L'art de naviguer . . . traduit . . . par Nicolas de Nicolai . . . nouvellement reveu . . . par Jean de Séville, dit Le Souci. *La Rochelle: J. Haultin,* 1618. 382 p.; illus.; 4to. 1st publ. as here transl., Lyons, 1553; cf. 1607, Rouen, edn. Palau 159676n. BN.   618/85

Mercuriale, Girolamo. Medicina practica . . . libri v. *Lyons: [C. Cayne,] for A. Pillehotte,* 1618. 809 p.; 4to. 1st publ., Frankfurt a.

M., 1601; here a reissue of Pillehotte's 1617 edn with altered imprint date? DNLM; BN.   618/86

Meteren, Emanuel van. Descriptio bellorum inferioris Germaniae ab anno 1597 ad annum usque 1610. *Amsterdam: J. Janszoon, the Younger,* 1618. 502 p.; ports; fol. 1st publ. in Latin, 1598, under title *Historia belgica;* cf. year 1610. BN.   618/87

——. L'histoire des Pays-Bas . . . ou Recueil des guerres et choses memorables advenues tant és dits pays, qu'és pays voysins, depuis l'an 1315 jusques à l'an 1612. Corrigé et augmenté. Traduit de flamend en francoys par J. D. L. Haye [Jean de La Haye]. *The Hague: H. Jacobszoon van Wouw,* 1618. 720 numb. lvs; illus., ports, map; fol. Prob. transl. from *Historie der Nederlandscher . . . oorloghen,* The Hague, 1614; 1st publ. in Dutch, Delft, 1599. Palau 166959; Brunet 24986. CSmH, MH, MdBP; BL, BN.   618/88

Middelgeest, Simon van, supposed author. Discurs und Muthmassung, oder New Mandat ausz Holland . . . Auss dem Niderländischen . . . gebracht. *Amsterdam: J. Mucken,* 1618. [16]p.; 4to. Transl. from the author's *Raedtsel,* 1st publ., [Amsterdam? 1608?]. Signed 'Yemant Adams'. Knuttel 2501. The Hague:KB.   618/89

Murner, Thomas. Der Schelmen Zunfft. *Frankfurt a. M.: L. Jennis* (pt 1) *& J. de Zetter* (pt 2), 1618–25. 2 pts; 8vo. Though Murner's work is itself without Americana, this edn includes as pt 2 Sebastian Brant's *Der Narren Zunfft,* 1st publ., Basel, 1494, under title *Das Narren Schyff.* Includes ref. to New World. Goedeke I:385 & II:216. BL, Göttingen:UB.   618/90

Murtola, Gasparo. Della creatione del mundo. *Macerata: P. Salvioni,* 1618. 646 p.; 12mo. 1st publ., Venice, 1608. CU, DFo.   618/91

Newes of Sr. Walter Rauleigh. With the true description of Guiana. *London: [G. Eld,] for H. G[osson].; sold by J. Wright,* 1618. 45 p.; 4to. In this issue a list of ships appears on p. [46]. Sabin 54971 & 67574 (& 67576?); Brushfield (Raleigh) 136; STC 17148; JCB (3) II:128. CSmH, DFo, NN-RB, RPJCB; BL.   618/92

—[Anr issue]. *London:* [*G. Eld,*] *for H. G*[*osson*].*; sold by J. Wright,* 1618. The final page is without list of ships; sheets B–D are reset. STC 17148.3. CSmH, MH, NN-RB.   618/93

Noort, Olivier van. Beschrijvinge van de voyagie om den geheelen werelt-kloot. *Amsterdam: M. Colijn,* 1618. 131 p.; illus., maps; obl. 4to. 1st publ., Rotterdam & Amsterdam, 1601. Ostensibly published separately in this form, this work also figures at pt 10 of Michiel Colijn's *Oost-Indische ende West-Indische voyagien,* Amsterdam, 1619, q.v. Sabin 55439; Tiele 808; Tiele-Muller 20; JCB (3) II:128–29. NNH, RPJCB.   618/94

Overbury, Sir Thomas. Sir Thomas Overbury his wife . . . The tenth impression augmented. *London: E. Griffin, for L. Lisle,* 1618. [292] p.; 8vo. 1st publ., London, 1615. STC 18912; Murphy (Engl. char.-bks) 21. CSmH, DFo (imp.), MH; BL.   618/95

Owen, John. Epigrammatum . . . libri tres. Editio secunda. *London: N. Okes, for S. Waterson,* 1618. 3 pts; 12mo. 1st publ., London, 1606. STC 18989. CSmH, IU, MH; BL.   618/96

Panciroli, Guido. Brief recueil des choses plus signalees qu'ont eu les anciens, et autres qu'ont trouvé les modernes . . . Traduit d'italien . . . par Pierre de La Noue. *Lyons: J. Gaudion,* 1618. 261 p.; 12mo. A reissue of Gaudion's 1617 edn with title *Livre premier* [*-second*] *des antiquitez perdues.* BL, BN.   618/97

Paracelsus. Chirurgische Bücher und Schrifften . . . an tag geben . . . Durch Johannem Huserum. *Strassburg: Heirs of L. Zetzner,* 1618. 795 p.; fol. 1st publ. as here constituted, [Basel], 1589–90; cf. 1603 edn. Sudhoff (Paracelsus) 302; Wellcome I:4812. CSt, DNLM, MiU, PPHa:BL, Munich:StB.   618/98

Piò, Giovanni Michele. Allegatione per confirmare quanto si scrive nell'annotationi all'Aviso di Parnaso [da G. Castellani]. al numero 57. Cavata dalla vita di f. Bartolomeo dalla Casa, vescovo di Chiapa. *Antipoli: Stamperia Regia* [i.e., *Venice?*], 1618. 22 p.; 4to. Extracted from Piò's *Delle vite de gli huomini illustri di S. Domenico,* Pavia, 1613. The 'Antibes' imprint is fictitious. Streit

I:371; Palau 227134; Church 385; JCB (3) II:129. CSmH, NN-RB, RPJCB; BL, BN.   618/99

Rich, Barnabe. The Irish hubbub, or The English hue and crie. *London:* [*G. Purslowe,*] *for J. Marriott,* 1618. 56 p.; 4to. 1st publ., London, 1617. STC 20989.7. Robt Taylor; Cambridge: Magdalene.   618/100

Riolan, Jean, the Younger. Gigantologie. Histoire de la grandeur des geants. *Paris: A. Périer,* 1618. 128 p.; 8vo. Mentioned is Vespucci's purported account of giants in Peru near the Strait of Magellan; elsewhere are refs to American giants, drawn in part from José de Acosta. BL, BN.   618/101

Ripa, Cesare. Nova iconologia. *Padua: P. P. Tozzi,* 1618. 648 p.; illus., port.; 4to. 1st publ. with American content, Rome, 1603, under title *Iconologia.* CU, DFo, ICN, MnU, NN, PU.   618/102

Rosaccio, Giuseppe. Le sei eta del mondo . . . Di nuovo corrette ed ampliate. *Rome: B. Cochi, & in Bologna,* 1618. 55 p.; 8vo. 1st publ., Brescia, 1593; cf. 1602 edn. Sabin 73197n. BL.   618/103

Rowlands, Samuel. Doctor Merry-man: or, Nothing but mirth. *London:* [*J. White,*] *for S. Rand,* 1618. 4to. In verse. 1st publ., London, 1607, under title *Democritus, or, Doctor Merry-man his medicines.* STC 21374. BL.   618/104

Royal College of Physicians of London. Pharmacopoea Londinensis, in qua medicamenta antiqua et nova usitatissima . . . describuntur. *London: E. Griffin, for J. Marriott,* 1618. 184 p.; fol. Amongst the ingredients called for are guaiacum & mechoacan. STC 16772. CtY-M, MBCo; BL.   618/105

—[Anr edn]. Diligenter revisa. *London:* [*E. Griffin,*] *for J. Marriott,* 1618. STC 16773. TxU; BL, Oxford:Bodl.   618/106

Sadeler, Raphael. Zodiacus christianus, seu signa 12. divinae praedestinationis. *Munich: Anna Berg, for R. Sadeler,* 1618. 126 p.; illus.; 8vo. Included is an emblematic rendering of tobacco plant in flower, symbolizing charity. Arents (Add.) 184. CtY, IU, NN-A.   618/107

Sala, Angelo. Ternarius bezoardicorum & hemetologia. *Erfurt: Heirs of E. Mechler,* 1618. 2 pts; illus.; 8vo. Formula for an 'unguentum bezoarticum' employs tobacco; another incorporates Peruvian opobalsam. DNLM, InU, MnU; BL, BN.   618/108

Sánchez, Francisco. De multum nobili & prima universali scientia quod nihil scitur, deque literarum pereuntium agone . . . libelli singulares duo. *Frankfurt a. M.: J. Berner,* 1618. 190 p.; 8vo. Includes Sánchez's *Quod nihil scitur,* 1st publ., Lyons, 1581, with refs to New World, Mexico, & West Indies, discussing character of life there. Palau 294104. BL, BN.   618/109

Sandoval, Prudencio de, Bp of Pamplona. Historia de la vida y hechos del Emperador Carlos V . . . Primer parte. *Barcelona: S. de Cormellas,* 1618. fol. 1st publ., Valladolid, 1604; ostensibly a reprinting to replace stock to be issued with the 1614 edn of v. 2. Cf. Sabin 76424; Palau 297147n. DLC, NN-RB, TxU; BL, BN.   618/110

Saulnier, Jean. Cosmologie du monde, tant celeste que terrestre. *Paris: M. Daniel,* 1618. 236 p.; 8vo. Includes, p. 174–75, brief section on American geography. Cioranescu (XVII) 61562. BL, BN.   618/111

Schouten, Willem Corneliszoon. Journal ofte Beschryvinghe van de wonderlicke reyse, ghedaen door . . . Schouten . . . bezuyden de Strate van Magellanes. *Amsterdam: W. J. Blaeu,* 1618. 92 p.; illus., ports, maps; 4to. Sabin 77920; Tiele-Muller 33; Tiele 981; Muller (1872) 1955; Knuttel 2494; JCB (3) II:129. DLC, NNH, RPJCB (imp.); The Hague:KB (imp.).   618/112

—[Anr issue]. Journael ofte Beschryvinghe. *Amsterdam: W. J. Blaeu,* 1618. Sabin 77921. NN-RB.   618/113

—[Anr edn]. Journael ofte Beschrijvinghe. *Arnhem: J. Janszoon,* 1618. 92 p.; illus., maps; 4to. A reprint of the preceding. Sabin 77922; Tiele-Muller 34; Tiele 982. NN-RB.   618/114

—[Anr issue]. [*Arnhem: J. Janszoon,*] *for J. Janszoon, the Younger, at Amsterdam,* 1618. Sabin 77923; Tiele-Muller 35; Tiele 982n. NN-RB.   618/115

—[Anr issue]. [*Arnhem: J. Janszoon,*] *for P. van der Keere, at Amsterdam,* 1618. Tiele 982n.   618/116

——. Journal ou Description de l'admirable voyage de Guillaume Schouten Hollandois. *Amsterdam: W. J. Blaeu* [1618?]. 88 p.; illus.,

maps; 4to. Transl. from Schouten's *Journal ofte Beschryvinghe* above. Sabin 77947; Palau 305108, Tiele-Muller 36; Tiele 983; JCB (3) II:141. NN-RB, RPJCB; BL, BN.   618/117

—[Anr edn]. Journal ou Description du merveilleux voyage. *Amsterdam: W. J. Blaeu,* 1618. 88 p.; illus., maps; 4to. Sabin 77948; Palau 305104; Tiele-Muller 37; Tiele 984; JCB (3) II:130. CSmH, MH, NN-RB, RPJCB.   618/118

—[Anr edn]. Journal ou Relation exacte du voyage . . . dans les Indes. *Paris: M. Gobert* (text) *& M. Tavernier* (maps), 1618. 232 p.; illus., maps; 8vo. Sabin 77952; cf. Tiele-Muller 42n. CtY, InU-L, MH, NN-RB; BL.   618/119

——. Warhaffte Beschreibung der wunderbarlichen Räyse und Schiffart. *Arnhem: J. Janszoon,* 1618. 34 p.; illus., maps; 4to. Transl. & abridged from Schouten's *Journal ofte Beschryvinghe* above. Sabin 77955; Palmer 386; Tiele-Muller 38. NN-RB; Munich:StB.   618/120

Sennert, Daniel. Epitome naturalis scientiae. *Wittenberg:* [*H. W. Fincelius? for*] *C. Heiden,* 1618. 643 p.; 8vo. Discussed are the Peruvian bezoar stone, mechoacan, & tobacco ('Hyoscyamus'). ICU; BN.   618/121

Seville. Consulado. Sepan quantos esta carta vieran como nos Crhistoval [*sic*] de Barnuevo Bonifaz, y Juan de Vergara Gaviria. [*Seville?* 1618]. [51] p.; fol. On duties imposed on commerce with the New World. Sabin 2234; Medina (BHA) 668; Palau 18673. BL.   618/122

Sir Walter Rauleigh his lamentation: who was beheaded the 29. of October. 1618. *London:* [*R. Blower,*] *for P. Birch* [1618]. bds.; fol. Ballad. Sabin 67599n (XVI:281); STC 20655. Cambridge: Magdalene (Pepys).   618/123

Spain. Consejo de las Indias. Assiento, y capitulacion que por mandado de su Magestad se ha tomado con diversas personas interesadas en el comercio de Indias, sobre la cobrança, y administracio del derecho de averia por tres años. [*Madrid?* 1618?]. 30 lvs; fol. Sabin 2230; Medina (BHA) 667; Pérez Pastor (Madrid) 1521; Palau 18673.   618/124

Spain. Laws, statutes, etc., 1598–1621 (Philip III). El Rey. Por quanto la experiencia y execucion de las ultimas ordenanças firmadas de mi mano a treze de Julio de mil y seiscientos y treze, sobre la forma de bagricar navios. [*Madrid:* 1618]. 24 numb. lvs; fol. Instructions relating both to building of ships & to naval operations, with refs to those of Spanish America. BL.
618/125

Stafford, Robert. A geographicall and anthologicall description of all the empires . . . in this . . . globe. *London: N. O[kes]., for S. W[aterson].,* 1618. 1st publ., London, 1607. STC 23136; JCB (3) II:131. CSmH, ICN, NN-RB, RPJCB; BL.
618/126
—[Anr issue, with cancel t.p.]. *London: N. O[kes]., for J. Parker,* 1618. STC 23136a; JCB (3) II:130. CSmH, DLC, NN-RB, RPJCB; BL.
618/127

Stow, John. The abridgement of the English chronicle . . . Continued . . . unto the beginning of the yeare, 1618. *London: [E. Allde & N. Okes,] for the Co. of Stationers,* 1618. 568 p.; 8vo. 1st publ. in abridged form London, 1566; cf. 1604 & subsequent edns of 1607 & 1611. Here, as of April 1618, is recorded Lord De La Warr's second going to Virginia. STC 23332 (& formerly also 23339). CSmH, CtY, DFo, ICU, MH, MiU, NNC, PU; BL.
618/128

Stucley, Sir Lewis. To the Kings most excellent majestie. The humble petition . . . for the bringing up of Sir Walter Raleigh. *London: B. Norton & J. Bill,* 1618. 17 p.; 4to. Includes refs to Raleigh's Guiana venture. For a Dutch translation, see the year 1619, the *Verclaringe ende verhael . . . Wouter Raleigh.* Sabin 67550 & 93235; Brushfield (Raleigh) 186; STC 23401; Church 374A; JCB (3) II:131. CSmH, CtY, DFo, ICN, MH, NN-RB, RPJCB; BL.
618/129

Taylor, John, the Water-poet. Master Thomas Coriat to his friends in England . . . from Agra. *London: J. B[eale].,* 1618. [52] p.; illus.; 4to. In prose & verse. Included is poem 'A short description of the longing desire that America hath to entertain this unmatchable perambulator', i.e., Coryate. STC 5809. DFo, MH; BL.
618/130

Thou, Jacques Auguste de. Historiarum sui temporis libri lxxx de cxxxxiii. Editio quarta. *Paris: R. Estienne,* 1618. 2 pts; fol. The title statement notwithstanding, includes 1st 26 bks only, 1st publ. (as 18 bks), Paris, 1604. For complete work, see the year 1620. Brunet V:840–41. BN.
618/131

Torquemada, Antonio de. The Spanish Mandeville of miracles. *London: B. Alsop,* 1618. 325 p.; 4to. Transl. from the author's *Jardin de flores curiosas,* 1st publ., Salamanca, 1570; 1st publ. as here transl. by Lewes Lewkenor, London, 1600. Includes numerous scattered refs to Spanish America. STC 24136; Palau 334927n. CSmH, CtY, DLC, ICU, MH, NNH, PU-F; BL.
618/132

Vespucci, Amerigo. Zehender Theil Americae; darinnen zubefinden: erstlich zwo Schiffahrten . . . Zum andern: ein gründlicher Bericht von dem jetzigen Zustand der Landschafft Virginien . . . durch Raphe Homar . . . beschrieben . . . Zum dritten: ein warhafftige Beschreibung dess Newen Engellands . . . von Capitein Johann Schmiden . . . beschrieben. *Oppenheim: H. Galler, for J. T. de Bry,* 1618. 73 p.; illus.; fol. (Theodor de Bry's *America.* Pt 10. German). Vespucci's two letters, possibly taken from the 1616, Rotterdam, collection *Novus Orbis,* concern his American voyages of 1497 & 1499; Ralph Hamor's work transl. from his *A true discourse* of Virginia, 1st publ., London, 1615; Smith's work transl. from his *A Description of New England,* 1st publ., London, 1616. Cf. Sabin 8784; Baginsky (German Americana) 143; Church 197; JCB (3) I:412–13. CSmH, DLC, ICN, IU, NN-RB, RPJCB; BL, BN.
618/133

Weckherlin, Georg Rodolph. Kurtze Beschreibung dess zu Stutgarten . . . jüngstgehaltenen Frewden-Fests. *Tübingen: D. Werlin,* 1618. 71 p.; obl. fol. Includes in 'Der Sibende Tag Hewmonats' (p. 63) an account of Spaniards on Haiti being entertained with a ballet of 300 naked dancing girls. Jantz (German Baroque) 2632; Faber du Faur 163; Goedeke III:31. CtY, NcD; BN.
618/134

Willis, John. Mnemonica, sive Reminiscendi ars. *London: H. Lownes, for N. Browne,* 1618. 177 p.; illus.; 12mo. Use of tobacco ('ab insula Tobacque tobacco dicitur'), is recommended (p. 168) for improving memory.

STC 25748; Arents (Add.) 185. DFo, IU, MH, NN-A; BL.   618/135

1619

Alemán, Mateo. Le gueux, ou La vie de Guzman d'Alfarache . . . Version nouvelle e fidelle d'espagnol [par Jean Chapelain]. Premiere partie. *Paris: P. Bilaine,* 1619. 2 pts; 8vo. Transl. from Alemán's *Primera parte de Guzman de Alfarache,* 1st publ., Madrid, 1599; cf. 1601 edn. Laurenti (Nov. pic. esp.) 615; cf. Cioranescu (XVII) 18474.   619/1

——. Der Landtstörtzer: oder Gusman von Alfarche . . . Zum vierten mal widerumb in Truck geben durch Aegidium Albertinum. *Augsburg: A. Aperger,* 1619. 723 p.; 8vo. 1st publ. in German, Munich, 1615. Laurenti (Nov. pic. esp.) 607; Dt. Ges. Kat. 3:872. BL, Vienna:NB.   619/2

——. Primera y segunda parte de Guzman de Alfarache. *Burgos: J. B. Varesio, for P. Gómez de Valdivielso,* 1619. 2 v.; 4to. Pt 1, 1st publ., Madrid, 1599; pt 2, 1st publ., Lisbon, 1604; cf. year 1601. Laurenti (Nov. pic. esp.) 562; Palau 6699. DFo, NNH, OU, PU; BL, BN.   619/3

Amphitheatrum sapientiae Socraticae jocoseriae. *Hanau: Wechel Press, for D. & D. Aubry & C. Schleich,* 1619. In v. 1, p. 822–54 contain Sir Thomas More's *Utopia,* 1st publ., Louvain, 1516; cf. 1601 edn. Gibson (More) 10.   619/4

Antidotario romano latino, tradotto da Ippolito Ceccarelli con l'aggiunta dell'elettione de' semplici. *Rome:* 1619. 4to. 1st publ. as here constituted, Rome, 1612. BL.   619/5

Αρχαιο-πλουτος. Containing, ten following bookes to the former Treasurie of auncient and moderne times . . . Translated out of . . . Pedro Mexia, and m. Francisco Sansovino . . . as also, of . . . Anthony du Verdier . . . Loys Guyon . . . Claudius Gruget &c. *London: W. Jaggard,* 1619. 977 p.; illus.; fol. Compiled & transl. by Thomas Milles. 'Chap. ii. A brief discourse, how those parts, and countries, commonly called, The New World, were first found. Also, by whom, and what things were there found, and

seene, and brought away thence': p. 916–24. The compiler's *Treasurie* was publ., London, 1613. Sabin 48248; STC 17936.5. CSmH, CtY, DLC, ICN, InU-L, MH, MiU, NN-RB, PP, RPJCB; BL.   619/6

Aventrote, Juan. Epistola . . . ad . . . regem Hispaniae. [*Amsterdam:* 1619?]. *See the year* 1615.

Avity, Pierre d', sieur de Montmartin. Les estats, empires et principautez du monde. *Geneva: P. Aubert,* 1619. 1464 p.; 4to. 1st publ., Paris, 1613. Cf. Sabin 2498. NN-RB; Berlin:StB.   619/7

—[Anr edn]. *Paris: P. Chevalier,* 1619. 1467 p.; 4to. Sabin 2498. BN.   619/8

—[Anr issue]. *Paris: N. Du Fossé,* 1619. Borba de Moraes I:52. BL.   619/9

—[Anr issue]. *Paris: O. de Varennes,* 1619. NNC; Königsberg:StB.   619/10

Bacon, Francis, viscount St Albans. Les essays politiques et moraux . . . Mis en nostre langue par J. Baudouin. *Paris: F. Julliot,* 1619. 162 numb. lvs; 8vo. Transl. from English text 1st publ. with 'Of atheisme', London, 1612. Gibson (Bacon) 44; Shaaber (Brit. auth.) B27. CtY, DFo; BL, BN.   619/11

—[Anr edn]. Essays moraux . . . traduits . . . par . . . Arthur Gorges. *London: J. Bill,* 1619. 139 p.; 12mo. Gibson (Bacon) 45; STC 1152. DLC, NNPM; BL, BN.   619/12

——. Saggi morali . . . data in luce dal sig. cavalier Andrea Cioli. *Florence: P. Cecconcelli,* 1619. 2 pts; 12mo. Transl. from Bacon's *Essaies* as publ., London, 1612. Gibson (Bacon) 36; Shaaber (Brit. auth.) B28; CCB, MH, NjP; BL.   619/13

—[Anr edn]. *Venice: P. Dusinelli,* 1619. 2 pts; 12mo. Gibson (Bacon) 37; Shaaber (Brit. auth.) B29. DFo, IU, NNC; Berlin:StB.   619/14

Bainbridge, John. An astronomicall description of the late comet. *London: E. Griffin, for J. Parker,* 1619. 42 p.; 4to. 1st publ., London, 1618; here a reissue with altered imprint. STC 1208. CSmH, CtY, DFo, MH, NN-RB; BL.   619/15

Barclay, John. Euphormionis Lusinini Satyricon. *Leyden: J. Marcus,* 1619. 478 p.; 12mo. Includes pt 2, 1st publ., Paris, 1607, & pt 4, Barclay's *Icon animorum,* 1st publ., London, 1614. Shaaber (Brit. auth.) B186. Cologne:StUB, Hannover:NLB, Wiesbaden: NLB. 619/16

Bauhin, Johann. Historiae plantarum generalis . . . prodromus. *Yverdon: P. de Candolle,* 1619. 124 p.; 4to. Included are numerous American plants, e.g., 'Choyne Americana', 'Papaiae Peruvianis', 'Cacao Americana, seu Avellaria Mexicana'. Written jointly with J. H. Cherler. Pritzel 503. MB, NNBG: BL, BN. 619/17

Béguin, Jean. Tyrocinium chymicum . . . Editio quinta. *Königsberg: A. Boreck, for C. Berger,* 1619. 480 p.; 8vo. 1st publ., Paris, 1612. Göttingen:UB. 619/18

Bembo, Pietro, Cardinal. Omnia opera, in unum corpus collecta. *Strassburg: L. Zetzner,* 1619. 3 v.; 8vo. 1st publ. as here collected, Basel 1556; Cf. 1609 edn. PU. 619/19

Benzoni, Girolamo. Das sechste Theil Americae oder der Historien . . . das dritte Buch. *Oppenheim: H. Galler, for J. T. de Bry, at Frankfurt a. M.,* 1619. 121 p.; illus., map; fol. (Theodor de Bry's *America.* Pt 6. German). 1st publ. in this version, Frankfurt a. M., 1597. Cf. earlier pts 1–2, publ. in 1594 & 1595. Cf. Sabin 8784; Baginsky (German Americana) 147; Church 189 & 190; JCB (3) I:398. CSmH, IU, NN-RB, RPJCB; BL, BN. 619/20

Berettari, Sebastiano, S. J. La vie miraculeuse du p. Joseph Anchieta . . . traduite du latin. *Douai: M. Wyon,* 1619. 462 p.; 12mo. Transl. by Pierre Outremann from the author's *Josephi Anchietae . . . vita,* 1st publ., Lyons, 1617. Sabin 4829; Medina (BHA) 652n (II:160); Borba de Moraes I:86 & II:125; Streit II:2384; Backer I:1326. RPJCB; BN. 619/21

Besold, Christoph. De Novo Orbe conjectanea. *Tübingen: J. A. Cellius* [1619?]. 25 p.; 4to. Discusses questions whether New World was known to the ancient world (citing Seneca's *Medea*), or was peopled by the lost tribes of Israel, or constitutes Ophir, etc. JCB (3) II:131. RPJCB; BN. 619/22

——. Dissertationes singulares. *Tübingen: J. A. Cellius,* 1619. 6 pts.; 4to. Includes as pt 2 Besold's *De Novo Orbe conjectanea*, with special t.p. & separate paging, also described separately above. ICN. 619/23

Blaeu, Willem Janszoon. Le flambeau de la navigation. *Amsterdam: W. J. Blaeu,* 1619. 2 v.; illus., maps; obl. fol. Transl. from Blaeu's *Het licht der zee-vaert,* 1st publ., Amsterdam, 1608. Title printed on slip pasted on engraved Dutch t.p. For variant, see Koeman. Koeman (M.Bl) 13; Tiele 122. BL, Amsterdam:NHSM. 619/24

Boccalini, Traiano. Pietra del paragone politico. *'Cosmopoli'* [i.e., *Venice*]: Z. Teler, 1619. 133 p.; 8vo. 1st publ., 'Cormopoli' (i.e., Venice), 1615. Michel (Répertoire) I:174. Lyons:BM. 619/25

—[Anr edn]. *Sabioneta: A. Visdomini,* 1619. 127 p.; 8vo. Michel (Répertoire) I:174. BN. 619/26

Botero, Giovanni. Della ragion di stato libri dieci . . . Una relatione del mare. *Venice: N. Misserini,* 1619. 2 pts; 8vo. 1st publ., Venice, 1589; cf. 1601 edn above. The 2nd pt comprises Botero's *Aggiunte . . . alla sua Ragion di stato,* 1st publ., Rome 1598; cf. 1606 edn. Michel (Répertoire) I:201. ICN, MH-BA, NjP, RPB; BN. 619/27

—[Anr issue?]. *Venice: A. Muschio,* 1619. Michel (Répertoire) I:201. BN. 619/28

Boulenger, Jules César. Historiarum sui temporis libri tredecim. *Lyons: The author,* 1619. 409 p.; fol. 1st publ., Lyons, 1617; here a reissue of that edn? DFo, MdBP; BL, BN. 619/29

Bry, Johann Theodor de, ed. Indiae Orientalis pars undecima. *Oppenheim: H. Galler,* 1619. 2 pts; illus.; fol. (J. T. de Bry's *India Orientalis.* Pt 11. Latin). Included are accounts of 3rd & 4th voyages of Vespucci as well as R. Coverte's journey through Persia and Barendsz's voyage to the north drawn from H. Gerritsz's *Histoire du pays nommé Spitsberghe,* Amsterdam, 1613. Church 223; JCB (3) I:442–43. CSmH, DLC, RPJCB; BL, BN. 619/30

Cabrera de Córdoba, Luis. Filipe Segundo rey de España. *Madrid: L. Sánchez,* 1619. 1176 p.; fol. 'La navegacion i robos que hizo Frãcisco Draque en las Indias': bk 12, chapt. 23; 'Descubrimiento del nuevo Mexico en la Nueva España, i lo acaecido en el': bk 13, chapt. 11. Wagner (SW) 25; Pérez Pastor (Madrid) 1586; Palau 38917. CtY, ICN, MH, PU, RPJCB; BL, BN. 619/31

Campion, Thomas. Epigrammatum libri ii.

London: E. Griffin, 1619. [72] p.; 12mo. In bk 1 the 4th & 51st epigrams are devoted to tobacco, as is no. 183 in bk 2. STC 4541; Arents (Add.) 187. CSmH, CtY, DFo, ICN, MH, NN-A; BL.   619/32

Cats, Jacob. Monita amoris virginei, sive Officium puellarum . . . Maechden-plicht. *Amsterdam: W. J. Blaeu,* 1619. 92 p.; illus.; 4to. 1st publ., Middelburg, 1618, under title Maechden-plicht. IU, OU.   619/33

——. Silenus Alcibiadis, sive Proteus. *Amsterdam: W. J. Blaeu* (Pt 1) & *J. van der Hellen, at Middelburg* (Pts 2 & 3), 1619. 3 pts; illus.; 4to. 1st publ., Middelburg, 1618. The copy described in Mus. Cats. omits the end of pt 1, containing the tobacco refs. Vries 80; Mus. Cats. 28. NjP; Leyden:UB.   619/34

Champlain, Samuel de. Voyages et descouvertes faites en la Nouvelle-France, depuis l'année 1615 jusques à la fin di l'année 1618. *Paris: C. Collet,* 1619. 158 numb. lvs; illus.; 8vo. Sabin 11836; Harrisse (NF) 32; Church 375; JCB (3) II:132. CSmH, DLC, InU-L, MnU-B, NN-RB, RPJCB; BN.
619/35

Colijn, Michiel, comp. Oost-Indische ende West-Indische voyagien. *Amsterdam: M. Colijn,* 1619. 10 pts; illus., maps; obl. 4to. Here brought together under this collective title is a group of pamphlets each of which, except for the 1st, has its own special t.p., separate paging & signatures, & ostensibly was also issued separately between the years 1617 & 1619. According to Tiele (as cited), most were printed for Colijn at Enkhuizen by J. L. Meyn, as indicated by his colophon dated 1617 at end of pt 1. In some copies the prelim. matter of pt 1 is signed by Marten Heubeldinck, to whom the compilation has been attributed. For fuller descriptions of the individual items, see, under the years indicated, the following: (1) G. de Veer, *De waerachtighe beschrijvinge, vande drie seylagien* (1619); (2) W. Lodewijcksz, *'T eerste boeck; Historie van Indien* (1617); (3) J. C. van Neck, *Historiale beschrijvinghe* (1619); (4) J. van Spilbergen, *t'Historiael journael* (1617); (5) P. de Marees, *Beschrijvinghe . . . van Guinea* (1617); (6) F. Pretty, *Beschryvinge vande overtreffelijcke . . . zee-vaerdt* (1617); (7) W. Raleigh, *Warachtighe . . . be-* schryvinghe van . . . Guiana (1617); (8) H. Ottsen, *Journael . . . van de voyagie na Rio de Plata* (1617); (9) B. J. Potgieter, *Historisch ende wijdtloopigh verhael* (1617); (10) O. van Noort, *Beschrijvinge van de voyagie* (1618). Sabin 14349; Tiele-Muller 1; Tiele 1178; cf. Shaaber (Brit. auth.) H15 & R20; cf. JCB (3) II:133–34. MiU-C (Heubeldinck), NN-RB; BL, Amsterdam:NHSM.   619/36

Collège des Maîtres chirurgiens de Paris. Traicté de la peste. *Paris: F. Jacquin,* 1619. 58 p.; 8vo. Amongst precautions against pestilence offered is use of a 'sudorifique medicament' containing guaiacum. BL.
619/37

Cotta, John. A short discoverie of the unobserved dangers of severall sorts of ignorant . . . practisers of physicke in England. *London: W. J[ones]., sold by J. Barnes,* 1619. 135 p.; 4to. 1st publ., London, 1612. STC 5835. CSmH; Oxford:Bodl.   619/38

Crato von Krafftheim, Johannes. Consiliorum et epistolarum medicinalium . . . liber quintus; nunc secondo labore & studio Laurentii Scholzii . . . in lucem editus. *Hanau: D. & D. Aubry & C. Schleich, for the Heirs of A. Wechel,* 1619. 643 p.; 8vo. 1st publ., Frankfurt a. M., 1595. In 'De morbo gallico commentarius' (p. [609]–43), syphilis is described as 'primum ab Indis Anno 1492. ortus'. Guaiacum is described as deriving from islands of Santo Domingo, Saint Croix, & St John (i.e., Puerto Rico). Sarsaparilla is named as a possible substitute for guaiacum. DNLM; BL, BN.   619/39

Crespin, Jean. Histoire des martyres, persécutez et mis a mour pour la vérité de l'evangile . . . Nouvelle & dernière édition, revue & augmentée. *Geneva: P. Aubert,* 1619. 778 numb. lvs; fol. 1st publ. as enl. by Simon Goulart, [Geneva?], 1582; cf. 1608 edn above. Borba de Moraes I:199; Jones (Goulart) 23(g). DLC; BN.   619/40

Dodoens, Rembert. A newe herbal . . . now first translated out of French . . . by Henry Lyte. *London: E. Griffin,* 1619. 564 p.; illus.; fol. 1st publ. in English, London, 1578; transl. from the author's *Cruydeboeck,* 1st publ., Antwerp, 1554. Includes numerous American plants. Pritzel 2345n; Nissen (Bot.) 516n; Henrey (Brit. bot.) 113; STC

6987; Arents (Add.) 188. CSmH, CtY, DLC, ICJ, MH, NN-A, PPL, RPB; BL. 619/41

Dominicans. Acta capituli generalis Ulyssiponae in conventu S. Dominici ordinis Praedicatorum celebrati . . . M.DC.XVIII. *Seville: F. de Lyra,* 1619. 22 numb. lvs; 4to. Included is a section 'Hae sunt provisiones pro bono regimine provinciarum Indiarum Occidentalium'. Sabin 20581n (& 29497n); Medina (BHA) 691; Escudero (Seville) 1.155; Palau 2127. BL, Seville:BM. 619/42

Du Bartas, Guillaume de Salluste, seigneur. Hebdomas II, a Samuel Benedicto . . . latinitate donata. *Leipzig:* 1619. In verse. Transl. from the author's *La seconde sepmaine,* 1st publ., Paris, 1584; cf. 1609 edn. Holmes (Du Bartas) I:107 no. 8. Copenhagen:KB. 619/43

Duchesne, Joseph. Le ricchezze della riformata farmacopoea . . . Nuovamente . . . traportata . . . dal sig. G. Ferrara. *Venice: G. Guerigli,* 1619. 256 p.; 4to. Transl. from Duchesne's *Pharmacopoea dogmaticorum restituta,* 1st publ., Paris, 1607. Michel (Répertoire) II:187. DNLM, MnU, NIC; London:Wellcome, Roanne:BM. 619/44

Duret, Claude. Thresor de l'histoire des langues de cest univers . . . Seconde edition. *Yverdon: Société Caldoresque (P. de Candolle),* 1619. 1030 p.; 4to. 1st publ., Cologny, 1613. Sabin 21420. DLC, MB, MnU-B, NN-RB; BL, BN. 619/45

Ercilla y Zúñiga, Alonso de. Historiale beschrijvinghe der goudtrijcke landen in Chili ende Arauco, ende andere provincien in Chili gheleghen . . . Overgheset uut de Spaensche . . . tale door Isaac Jansz. Byl. *Rotterdam: J. van Waesberghe,* 1619. 59 p.; 4to. Extracted & transl. from the author's *Araucana,* 1st publ. in all 3 pts, Madrid, 1590. Sabin 22728; Knuttel 2831; Palau 80447; JCB (3) II:132–33. NNH, RPJCB; BL, The Hague:KB. 619/46

Esternod, Claude d'. L'espadon satyrique. *Lyons: J. Lautret,* 1619. 129 p.; 12mo. In verse. In the 1st & 5th satires, the turkey (coq d'Inde) is mentioned. The 5th satire also includes refs to Magellan, Colum-

bus, & Francis Drake. In the 6th, Indians prostrating themselves before Pizarro are cited. Cioranescu (XVII) 28485. Aix-en-Provence:B. Méjanes. 619/47

—[Anr edn]. *Rouen: J. Besongne, N. LePrevost & J. Boulley,* 1619. 122 p.; 12mo. Cioranescu (XVII) 28486. 619/48

Fennor, William. The miseries of a jaile. *London: R. R.,* 1619. 85 p.; 4to. 1st publ., London, 1617, under title *The compters common-wealth.* STC 10782. Oxford:Bodl. 619/49

Fernel, Jean. Universa medicina. *Geneva: S. Gamonet, in shop of P. & J. Chouët,* 1619. 1172 p.; 4to. 1st publ. as here constituted, Paris, 1567; cf. 1601–2 edn. Sherrington (Fernel) 79.J23. CtY, DNLM, MH, RPB (imp.):Edinburgh:UL, Paris:Faculté de Médecine. 619/50

Fonseca, Rodrigo. Consultationum medicinalium singularibus remediis refertae. *Venice: G. Guerigli,* 1619–22. 2 v.; fol. Described are decoctions using guaiacum & sarsaparilla. BN. 619/51

Garzoni, Tommaso. Piazza universale, das ist: Allgemeiner Schauwplatz, oder Marckt, und Zusammenkunfft aller Professionen. *Frankfurt a.M.: N. Hoffmann,* 1619. 731 p.; fol. Transl. from the author's Italian text with title *La piazza universale,* 1st publ., Venice, 1585. Includes brief description of America. MH, WU. 619/52

Gemma, Reinerus, Frisius. Les principes d'astronomie et cosmographie. *Paris: J. Quesnel,* 1619. 120 p.; 8vo. 1st publ., Paris, 1556; transl. from the author's *De principiis astronomiae,* 1st publ., Antwerp, 1530. Includes minor American refs. MH. 619/53

Gerhard, Johann. Locorum theologicorum . . . tomus sextus. *Jena: T. Steinmann,* 1619. 4to. Includes chapt. 27, 'De magistratu politico', with refs to Spanish cruelties in New World. NNUT 619/54

Goes, Damião de. Chronica do felicissimo rey Dom Emanuel. *Lisbon: A. Alvarez,* 1619. 347 numb. lvs; fol. 1st publ., Lisbon, 1566–67. Includes account of Cabral's discovery of Brazil. Sabin 27687; Borba de Moraes I:303. DLC, MH, NN; BL, BN. 619/55

Great Britain. Sovereigns, etc., 1603–1625

(**James I**). An abstract of some branches of his Majesties late charter, granted to the tobacco-pipe makers of Westminster. [*London: B. Norton & J. Bill?* 1619]. bds.; fol. Crawford (Roy. procl.) 1257; Brigham (Roy. procl.) 12–14; STC 8611. London: Soc. of Antiquaries.   619/56

——. A proclamation concerning the viewing . . . of tobacco. *London: B. Norton & J. Bill*, 1619. 2 lvs; fol. Crawford (Roy. procl.) 1263; Brigham (Roy. procl.) 15–18; STC 8617. London:Soc. of Antiquaries.   619/57

—[Anr edn]. *London: B. Norton & J. Bill*, 1619. 2 lvs; fol. Crawford (Roy. procl.) 1264; STC 8618; Arents 139. CSmH, NN-A; Cambridge:UL.   619/58

——. A proclamation to restraine the planting of tobacco in England and Wales. [*London:*] *B. Norton & J. Bill*, 1619. 2 lvs; fol. Sabin 99841; Crawford (Roy. procl.) 1268; Brigham (Roy. procl.) 18–21; STC 8622; Arents 140. CSmH, NN-A; London: Soc. of Antiquaries.   619/59

——. A proclamation, with articles of directions thereunto annexed, concerning alehouses. *London: B. Norton, & J. Bill*, 1618 [i.e., 1619]. 3 lvs; fol. Forbids, *inter alia*, use of tobacco in alehouses. STC 8588; Crawford (Roy. procl.) 1233. CSmH; London: PRO.   619/60

—[Anr edn]. *London: B. Norton & J. Bill*, 1618 [i.e., 1619]. 17 p.; 4to. STC 8589; Crawford (Roy. procl.) 1234; Arents (Add.) 189. DLC, MH, NN-A; BL.   619/61

Grick, Friedrich. Regula vitae: das ist, Eine heylsame . . . Erinnerung an die Jenige, welche nach der . . . Fraternitet dess Rosencreutzes ein . . . verlangen tragen . . . Verfertiget durch . . . I. Agnostum [pseud.]. [*Nuremberg: S. Halbmeyer*] 1619. [38] p.; 8vo. Includes, in jest, a list of Rosicrucians to be sent to America to replace Jesuits. Jantz (German Baroque) 1216. NcD; BL (Agnostus, I.).   619/62

Gysius, Johannes. Origo et historia Belgicorum tumultuum. *Leyden: B. van der Bilt*, 1619. 288 p.; 8vo. Transl. from Gysius's *Oorsprong en voortgang der neder-landtscher beroerten*, 1st publ., [Leyden?], 1616. CSt, CtY, DFo, ICN, MnU-B; BL.   619/63

Harris, Robert. The drunkards cup. *London:*

F. Kingston, for T. Man, 1619. 4to. Sermon. Includes phrase 'the whole Land stinkes . . . unlesse it be where the brightnesse of his Maiestie dispels the smoke, and that is Tobacco'. STC 12827. MBrZ, NNUT; Oxford:Bodl., Cambridge:UL.   619/64

Hevia Bolaños, Juan de. Laberinto do comercio terrestre y naval. *Madrid: L. Sánchez, for G. de Courbes*, 1619. 664 p.; 4to. 1st publ., Lima, 1617. Included are numerous refs to the commerce of the Indies, esp. in the 3rd bk on 'Comercio naval'. Medina (BHA) 685; Pérez Pastor (Madrid) 1603; Palau 114532. InU-L, MnU-B, RPB; BL, BN.   619/65

—[Anr edn]. *Madrid: Widow of A. Martín*, 1619. 253 numb. lvs; 4to. Palau 114531.   619/66

Hospinianus, Rudolphus. Historia Jesuitica. *Zurich: J. R. Wolf*, 1619. 257 numb. lvs; fol. In bk 2, 'De propagatione Jesuitarum', the 'catalogus provinciarum' includes those of Brazil, Peru, Paraguay, & Mexico. Succeeding edns entered under L. Lucius, who contined & enl. the work. MH-AH, NNH, PPL; BL, BN.   619/67

al-Idrisi. Geographia Nubiensis. *Paris:* 1619. *See the year 1620.*

James I, King of Great Britain. Opera. *London: B. Norton & J. Bill*, 1619. 609 p.; fol. Transl. by Thomas Reid from James's *Workes*, 1st publ., London, 1616. For variant issues see the STC. STC 14346; Arents 143. CSmH, CtY, DFo, IU, MH, NN-A; BL, BN.   619/68

Jesuits. Letters from missions. Litterae Societatis Jesu . . . M DC XIII, et M DC XIV. *Lyons: C. Cayne*, 1619. 789 p.; 8vo. 'Provincia Peruana': p. 675–700; 'Provincia Mexicana': p. 701–13. Streit I:389; JCB (3) II:134. RPJCB; BL.   619/69

Junius, Hadrianus. Nomenclator octilinguis, omnium rerum propria nomina continens. *Geneva: J. Stoer*, 1619. 736 p.; 8vo. 1st publ., Antwerp, 1577; cf. 1602 edn. Wellcome I:3522. London:Wellcome, BN.   619/70

—[Anr issue]. [*Geneva:*] *J. Stoer*, 1619. ICU; BL.   619/71

Le Mire, Aubert. De statu religionis christianae per Europam, Asiam, Africam et Orbem novum, libri iv. *Cologne: B. Wolter*, 1619. 222 p.; 8vo. Rev. from the author's *Notitia episco-*

patuum orbis christiani, Antwerp, 1513. Sabin 49403; Streit I:388; Palau 171569. ICN, InU-L, MH, NN-RB, RPJCB; BL, BN.
619/72

Levantamiento, y principios de Yangua rey de los negros Cimarrones de la nueva España. Dase cuenta de como despuso y destribuyò los oficios de su republica . . . y assi mismo se dizen las muertes, robos, y crueldades que hizo en los caminos reales de la Veracruz y Mexico. *Málaga: J. René,* 1619. 2 lvs; fol. Medina (BHA) 686.
619/73

Linschoten, Jan Huygen van. Histoire de la navigation de Hugues de Linschot . . . aux Indes Orientales . . . Avec annotations de B. Paludanus . . . Deuxiesme edition augmentee. *Amsterdam: J. E. Cloppenburg,* 1619. 3 pts; illus., maps, port.; fol. Pts 2 & 3 transl. from the printer's 1614 edn of the author's *Itinerarium . . . naer Oost ofte Portugaels Indien,* the 1st pt (without American refs) having been 1st publ. in French, Amsterdam, 1610. Pt 2 has title *Le grand routier de mer . . . contenant une instruction des routes . . . en la navigation des Indes Orientales, & au voyage de la coste du Bresil, des Antilles, & du Cap de Lopo Gonsalves;* pt 3 has title *Description de l'Amerique.* Sabin 41370, 41371 & 41372 (& 19701); Borba de Moraes I:419; Tiele-Muller 87; JCB (3) II:134–35. ICN, InU-L, MH, MdBP, NN-RB, RPJCB; BN.
619/74

Lugo, Bernardo de, O.P. Gramatica en la lengua general del nuevo reyno, llamada Mosca. *Madrid: B. de Guzman,* 1619. 158 numb. lvs; 8vo. On the Chibcha language of Indians of Colombia, etc. Sabin 42667; Medina (BHA) 682; Viñaza 150; Pérez Pastor (Madrid) 1607; JCB (3) II:135. CU-B, DLC (imp.), InU-L, NN-RB, RPJCB; BL, Madrid:BN.
619/75

Mariana, Juan de, S.J. Historiae de rebus Hispaniae libri xxx. Editio nova, ab auctore recensita. *Mainz: D. & D. Aubry, & C. Schleich,* 1619. 2 pts; fol. 1st publ., Toledo, 1592; cf. 1605 edn. CtY, ICN, NcD.
619/76

———. Summarium ad Historiam Hispaniae quae acciderunt annis sequentibus. *Mainz: D. & D. Aubry & C. Schleich,* 1619. 41 p.; 4to. Supplements the author's *Historiae de rebus Hispaniae libri xxx* of this year above.

Under year 1596 Francis Drake's attack on Panama is mentioned. Backer V:548; Palau 151664. CtY, DLC, OU, RPJCB, WU; BN.
619/77

Marino, Giovanni Battista. La Murtoleide, fischiate. *'Nuremberg: J. Stamphier'* [i.e., *Venice?*], 1619. 142 p.; 12mo. In verse. The 1st 'fischiata' mentions Columbus. In this as in other edns, the imprint is fictitious. Michel (Répertoire) V:125. Paris:Arsenal.
619/78

Marlowe, Christopher. The tragicall historie of the life and death of Doctor Faustus. *London: J. Wright,* 1619. [62]p.; 4to. Drama. 1st publ., London, 1604; here a reprinting of Wright's rev. & enl. 1616 edn. STC 17433; Greg 605(e). NjP.
619/79

Mattioli, Pietro Andrea. Les commentaires . . . sur les six livres de Pedacius Dioscoride . . . de la matiere medecinale, traduits de latin . . . par m. Antoine du Pinet. *Lyons: P. Rigaud,* 1619. 606p.; illus., port.; fol. 1st publ. as here transl., Lyons, 1561; cf. 1605 edn above. Cf. Pritzel 5991n; cf. Nissen (Bot.) 1312n. DNLM.
619/80

Mercado, Luis. Opera omnia. *Frankfurt a. M.: H. Palthenius, for Heirs of Z. Palthenius,* 1619–29. 5 v.; fol. Included is the 2nd vol. 1st publ. as here constituted, Valladolid, 1605. Palau 164995. CtY-M, ICJ.
619/81

Mercator, Gerardus. Atlas sive Cosmographicae meditationes . . . Denuò auctus . . . Editio quarta. *Amsterdam: J. Hondius,* 1619. 378 p.; maps, ports; fol. 1st publ., Amsterdam, 1606. The text is in Latin. Sabin 47882n; Koeman (Me 25); Phillips (Atlases) 434. DLC.
619/82

—[Anr edn]. *Amsterdam: J. Hondius,* 1619. fol. The text is in French. For variants, see Koeman. Koeman (Me 26A & B). MiU-C; Fribourg:BC.
619/83

Moncada, Sancho de. Restauracion politica de España, primera parte, deseos publicos . . . Ocho discursos. *Madrid: L. Sánchez,* 1619. 2 pts; 4to. Ref. is made to Spanish America, its trade, & the effects of its conquest. NNC, RPJCB, WU; BL.
619/84

Montaigne, Michel Eyquem de. Les essais. *Rouen: Widow T. Daré,* 1619. 1129 p.; port.; 8vo. 1st publ., Bordeaux, 1580; cf. 1602 edn. According to Tchémerzine, the pres-

ent edn was prob., like earlier Rouen edns, shared between a variety of booksellers. We list here only those of which copies are known to us. Tchémerzine VIII:421. BN.
619/85

—[Anr issue]. *Rouen: J. Osmont,* 1619. Tchémerzine VIII:421. CLU-C, NjP; BN.
619/86

—[Anr issue]. *Rouen: A. Ouyn,* 1619. MH.
619/87

—[Anr issue]. *Rouen: R. Valentin,* 1619. DFo; BN.
619/88

—[Anr edn]. *Rouen: J. Durand, for N. Angot* [1619]. 1129 p.; port.; 8vo. Differs from preceding in that the front. contains port. & that the colophon identifies printer & year. Tchémerzine VIII:422. BN.
619/89

—[Anr issue]. *Rouen: J. Durand, for J. Berthelin* [1619]. Tchémerzine VIII:422. MWiW-C; BN.
619/90

—[Anr issue]. *Rouen: J. Durand, for J. Besongne* [1619]. Tchémerzine VIII:422. BL, BN.
619/91

Morejon, Pedro, S.J. A briefe relation of the persecution lately made against the Catholike Christians, in . . . Japonia . . . Written in Spanish, and printed first at Mexico in the West Indies . . . M.DC.XVI. and newly translated into English by W[illiam]. W[right]. . . . The first part. [*St Omer: English College Press*] 1619. 350 p.; 8vo. Transl. from Morejon's *Breve relacion de la persecucion . . . contra la iglesia de Japon,* Mexico, 1616. Sabin 7926; Streit V:1214; Allison & Rogers 550; STC 14527. DFo, InU-L, TxU; BL.
619/92

Neck, Jacob Corneliszoon van. Historiale beschrijvinghe, inhoudende een waerachtich verhael vande reyse ghedaen met acht schepen van Amsterdam. *Amsterdam: M. Colijn,* 1619. 64 numb. lvs; illus., maps; obl. 4to. 1st publ., Amsterdam, [1600], under title *Journael ofte Dagh-register;* cf. edn of 1601. Ostensibly published separately in this form, this work also figures as pt 3 of Michiel Colijn's *Oost-Indische ende West-Indische voyagien* of this year, q.v. Tiele-Muller 130; Tiele 784; JCB (3) II:137. DLC, MnU-B, RPJCB; Amsterdam:NHSM.
619/93

Nicolai, Eliud, comp. Newe und warhaffte

relation von deme was sich in beederley, dass ist, in den West- und Ost-Indien . . . zugetragen . . . Aus gewissen Castiglianischen und Portugesischen relationen colligiert. *Munich: N. Heinrich,* 1619. 158 p.; map; 4to. Sabin 55242; Baginsky (German Americana) 148; Palau 190345; JCB (3) II:137–38. CSmH, DLC, InU-L, MH, MiU-C, NN-RB, RPJCB; BL.
619/94

Orlers, Jan Jansz. De oorlochs-daden van Maurits, off den nieuwen vermeerderden Nassauschen Laurencrans. *Leyden:* 1619. 1st publ., Leyden, 1610, under title *Beschrijvinghe . . . van alle de victorien.* Molhuysen I:1392.
619/95

Orta, Garcia da. Histoire des drogues espiceries, et de certains medicamens simples, qui naissent és Indes & en l'Amérique . . . comprise en six livres . . . Seconde edition reveuë & augmentée. *Lyons: J. Pillehotte,* 1619. 4 pts; illus.; 8vo. 1st publ. in this version, Lyons, 1602. Sabin 14355 (& 115n); Pritzel 4316n & 6366; Guerra (Monardes) 39. CtY-M, DLC, MH, NN-RB, RPB; BL, BN.
619/96

—[Anr issue]. Divisé en deux parties . . . Seconde edition. . . . *Lyons: J. Pillehotte,* 1619. Sabin 13801; Nissen (Bot.) Suppl. 1397nd; Guerra (Monardes) 40. CtY-M, DNLM, ICN, MH, NN-A, PPC, RPJCB; BL (Colin, A.), BN.
619/97

Ortiz de Cervantes, Juan. Informacion en favor del derecho que tienen los nacidos en las Indias á ser preferidos en las prelacias. *Madrid: Widow of A. Martín,* 1619. 12 numb. lvs; fol. The author was resident in Peru. Medina (BHA) 8472; Pérez Pastor (Madrid) 1621; Palau 205771. BL, Madrid:BN.
619/98

——. Memoriál . . . a Su Magestad . . . Sobre pedir remedio del daño, y dimunicion de los Indios: y propone ser remedio eficaz la perpetuydad de encomiendas. [*Madrid?*] 1619. 18 numb. lvs; fol. Sabin 57718; Medina (BHA) 690; Pérez Pastor (Madrid) 1622; Palau 205769. DLC, WU: BL.
619/99

Owen, John. Epigrams . . . Translated by John Vicars. *London: W. S[tansby]., for J. Smethwick* [1619]. [111] p.; 8vo. In bk 2 as no. 148, is the translation of the epitaph on Sir Francis Drake 1st publ. in Latin, Lon-

don, 1606, in Owen's *Epigrammatum libri tres.*
STC 18993. CSmH, MH; Oxford:Bodl.
619/100

Pasquier, Etienne. Les lettres. *Paris: L. Sonnius,* 1619. 2 v.; port.; 8vo. 1st publ., Paris, 1586; cf. year 1607. Thickett (Pasquier) 24.
CtY, DLC, ICN; BL, BN. 619/101

—[Anr issue of v. 1]. *Paris: J. Petit-Pas,* 1619.
Thickett (Pasquier) 24n. 619/102

Purchas, Samuel. Purchas his pilgrim. Microcosmus, or The historie of man. *London: W. S[tansby]., for H. Fetherstone,* 1619. 818 p.; 8vo. A different work from the author's *Purchas his pilgrimage.* Chapt. vi cites Acosta on Indian (Aztec) sacrifices; chapt. xxxiii has ref. to cannibalism in America; in chapt. lxviii 'the chaunted conversions of the Americans and Indians' are mentioned; etc.
Sabin 66677; STC 20503; JCB (3) II:139.
CSmH, CtY, DLC, ICN, InU-L, MH, MiU-C, NN-RB, PPC, RPJCB; BL.
619/103

Pyrard, François. Voyage de François Pyrard, de Laval. Contenant sa navigation aux Indes Occidentales, Maldives, Moluques, Bresil . . . Troisiesme et derniere edition, reveue, corrigèe & augmentèe. *Paris: S. Thiboust, & Widow of R. Dallin,* 1619. 2 v.; 8vo. 1st publ., Paris, 1611, under title *Discours du voyage.* Sabin 66881; Borba de Moraes II:169. CtY, ICN, MH-BA, NN-RB, RPJCB; BL, BN. 619/104

Remesal, Antonio de. Historia de la provincia de S. Vicente de Chýapa ý Guatemala de la orden de . . . Sancto Domingo. *Madrid: F. Abarca de Angulo,* 1619. 784 p.; fol.
Sabin 69550; Medina (BHA) VII:330 (cf. 704); Streit II:1505; Pérez Pastor (Madrid) 1633. CU, CtY, DLC, ICU, InU-L, MH, MiU-C, NNH, PPL; BN. 619/105

Rich, Barnabe. The Irish hubbub, or, The English hue and crie. *London: [G. Purslowe,] for J. Marriott,* 1619. 56 p.; 4to. 1st publ., London, 1617; here a reissue with altered imprint date of 1618 edn. STC 20990; Arents 132-a. DFo, NN-A; Oxford:Bodl.
619/106

Ritter, Stephan. Cosmographia prosometrica: hoc est, Universi terrarum orbis regionum . . . tum ex variis variarum poetarum monumentis oratione ligata descriptio. *Marburg: P. Egenolff,* 1619. 1253 p.; 4to. 'Or-

bis terrarum partes', mentioning America: p. 42–45; 'America, novus orbis': p. 88–89.
Sabin 71596; JCB (3) II:140–41. ICN, MnU-B, PPL, RPJCB; BL, BN. 619/107

Rondelet, Guillaume. Opera omnia medica . . . studio & opera J. Croqueri . . . repurgata. *Geneva: S. Gamonet,* 1619. 1277 p.; 8vo. 1st publ., [Paris? 1563?], under title *Methodus curandorum omnium morborum corporis humani;* cf. 1601 edn. DNLM. 619/108

Rowlands, Samuel. Doctor Merry-man; or, Nothing but mirth. *London: A. M[athewes]., for S. Rand,* 1619. 12 lvs; 4to. In verse. 1st publ., London, 1607, under title *Democritus, or, Doctor Merry-man his medicines.* STC 21375. MH. 619/109

——. Well met gossip. *London: W. W[hite]., for J. Deane,* 1619. 4to. In verse. 1st publ., London, 1602, under title *Tis merrie when gossips meete.* STC 21411. BL, Oxford:Bodl.
619/110

Schouten, Willem Corneliszoon. Americae pars undecima; seu Descriptio admirandi itineris . . . qua ratione in Meridionali plaga freti Magellanici novum hactenusque incognitum in mare Australe transitum patefecerit. *Oppenheim: H. Galler, for J. T. de Bry,* 1619. 49 p.; illus., ports, maps; fol. (Theodor de Bry's *America.* Pt 11. Latin). 1st publ. in Dutch, Amsterdam, 1618; here a new Latin translation of author's *Journal ofte beschryvinghe van de wonderlicke reyse.* Cf. Joris van Spilbergen's *Appendix* of 1620. Cf. Sabin 8784; cf. Tiele-Muller, p. 40; Church 172; JCB (3) I:413. CSmH, DLC, ICN, NN-RB, RPJCB; BL, BN. 619/111

——. Historische Beschreibung der wunderbarlichen Reyse. *Frankfurt a. M.: P. Jacobi,* 1619. 35 p.; illus., ports, maps; fol. (Theodor de Bry's *America.* Pt 11. German). Prob. transl. from Schouten's *Journael ofte Beschrijvinghe* below; cf. Arnhem, 1618, German translation *(Warhaffte Beschreibung)* & anr translation in the Hulsius series below. Cf. also de Bry's Appendix of 1620. Cf. Sabin 8784; Baginsky (German Americana) 146; Tiele-Muller p. 40; Church 198; JCB (3) I:414–15. CSmH, DLC, ICN, NN-RB, RPJCB; BL, BN. 619/112

—[Anr edn]. Die sechtzehende Schifffahrt. Journal oder Beschreibung der wunderbaren Reise. *Frankfurt a. M.: N. Hoffmann, for the Hulsiuses,* 1619. 90 p.; illus., maps; 4to. (Levinus Hulsius's *Sammlung von . . . Schiffahrten.* Pt 16). A differing translation of Schouten's *Journael ofte Beschrijvinghe* below. Sabin 77956 & 33669; Church 308; JCB (3) I:465. CSmH, ICN, MnU-B, NN-RB, RPJCB; BL, BN. 619/113

——. Journael ofte Beschrijvinghe van de wonderlijcke reyse. *Amsterdam: H. Janszoon,* 1619. 92 p.; illus., maps; 4to. 1st publ., Amsterdam, 1618. Sabin 77924; Palau 305085; Tiele-Muller 39; Tiele 982n. 619/114

——. Journal ou Description du merveilleux voyage. *Amsterdam: J. Janszoon, the Younger,* 1619. 88 p.; illus., maps; 4to. 1st publ. in French, Amsterdam, 1618. Sabin 77949; Palau 305106; Tiele-Muller 40; Tiele 985. [Locations may be for one of the other issues:] CtY, NcU, NN-RB; London:Wellcome. 619/115

—[Anr issue]. *Amsterdam:* [*J. Janszoon, the Younger, for*] *P. van der Keere,* 1619. Sabin 77951; Palau 305107; Tiele-Muller 41; Tiele 985n. ICN; BL, Amsterdam:NHSM. 619/116

—[Anr issue]. *Amsterdam:* [*J. Janszoon, the Younger, for*] *H. Janszoon,* 1619. Sabin 77950; Palau 305105; Tiele-Muller 42; cf. Tiele 985n; Muller (1872) 1956; JCB (3) II:141. NN-RB, RPJCB; BL. 619/117

—[Anr edn]. Journal ou Relation exacte du voyage . . . dans les Indes. *Paris: M. Gobert* (text) *& M. Tavernier* (maps), 1619. 323 p.; illus., maps; 8vo. Perhaps a reissue with altered imprint date of booksellers' 1618 edn. Sabin 77953; Palau 305109; Tiele-Muller 42n; cf. Tiele 985n; JCB (3) II:141–42. DLC, MWA, MiU-C, NN-RB, PBL, RPJCB; BN. 619/118

——. Novi freti a parte meridionali freti Magellanici, in Magnum Mare Australe detectio. *Amsterdam: W. J. Blaeu,* 1619. 93 p.; illus., maps; 4to. Prob. transl. by Nicolaas van Wassenaer from Schouten's *Journal ofte Beschryvinghe,* 1st publ., Amsterdam, 1618. Sabin 77957; Palau 305115; Tiele-Muller 43; Tiele 987; Muller (1872) 1957; JCB (3) II:142. DLC, MiU-C, NN-RB, RPJCB; BL, BN. 619/119

—[Anr edn]. Diarium vel Descriptio laboriosissimi & molestissimi itineris. *Amsterdam: P. van der Keere,* 1619. 71 p.; illus., maps; 4to. A differing translation of unknown origin.

Sabin 77958; Palau 305113; Tiele-Muller 44; Tiele 988; Muller (1872) 1958; JCB (3) II:142. CtY, DLC, MoSW, NN-RB, RPJCB; BL, BN. 619/120

——. Relacion diaria del viage de Jacobo de Mayre y Guillelmo Cornelio Schouten. *Madrid: B. de Guzmán,* 1619. 26 numb. lvs; maps; 4to. Transl. from a Latin or French edn. of Schouten's *Journael ofte Beschrijvinghe* above. Sabin 77963 & 44058; Medina (Chile) 46; Palau 305111 & 134740; JCB (3) II:135. NN-RB, RPJCB; BL, Madrid:BN. 619/121

——. The relation of a wonderfull voiage. *London: T. D*[*awson*]*., for N. Newbery,* 1619. 82 p.; illus., port., maps; 4to. Transl. by William Phillip from Schouten's *Journael ofte Beschrijvinghe,* above, or perhaps from Gobert's French version of this year from which the maps and plates were taken. Sabin 77962; STC 21828; Palau 305124; Church 377; JCB (3) II:142. CSmH, MH, MiU-C, NN-RB, PP, RPJCB; BL, BN. 619/122

Scotland. Privy Council. [Forsamekle as the Kingis . . . *Edinburgh: T. Finlason,* 1619]. Forbids importation, sale, & use of tobacco in Scotland. Crawford (Roy. procl.) Scotland:1249. No copy known. 619/123

Serres, Jean de. Inventaire general de l'histoire de France. *Paris: S. Thiboust,* 1619. 2 v.; port.; 8vo. 1st publ. with American refs, Paris, 1600; cf. 1606 edn. BN. 619/124

—[Anr edn]. *Geneva: P. Aubert,* 1619. 2 v. NNU. 619/125

Serres, Olivier de, seigneur du Pradel. Le theatre d'agriculture. [*Geneva:*] *P. & J. Chouët,* 1619. 878 p.; illus.; 4to. 1st publ., Paris, 1600; cf. 1603 edn. BL. 619/126

Sesse, Josepe de. Libro de la cosmographia universal del mundo. *Saragossa: J. de Larumbe,* 1619. 111 numb. lvs; 4to. Sabin 79328; Jiménez Catalán (Saragossa) 189; Palau 11108. MH, NN-RB; BN. 619/127

Shakespeare, William. A most pleasaunt and excellent comedie, of syr John Falstaffe, and the merrie wives of Windsor. *London:* [*W. Jaggard,*] *for A. Johnson* [i.e., *T. Pavier*] 1619. 4to. 1st publ., London, 1602. STC 22300; Greg 187(b). CSmH, DFo, IU, MH, NN-RB. 619/128

Spain. Laws, statutes, etc., 1556–1598 (Philip II). Ordenanças para remedio de los daños, e inconvenientes, que se siguen de los descaminos, y arribadas . . . de los navios que navegan a las Indias Occidentales. *Madrid: Widow of A. Martín,* 1619. 24 numb. lvs; fol. 1st publ., Madrid, 1591. Sabin 57482; Medina (BHA) 689 & VII 321; Pérez Pastor (Madrid) 1619; Palau 202638. CSmH, InU-L; BL, Madrid:BN.

619/129

Spanisch Post und Wächterhörnlein an die teutsche Nation, das ist, Ein . . . Vermanungsschrifft. [*Heidelberg?*] 1619. 48 p.; 4to. Included is a ref. to the Spanish Indies as America. BL (Spanish Posthorn).

619/130

Spilbergen, Joris van. Oost ende West-Indische spiegel der nieuwe navigatien, daer in vertoont werdt de leste reysen ghedaen door Joris van Speilbergen. *Leyden: N. van Geelkercken,* 1619. 192 p.; illus., maps; obl. 4to. Includes extensive refs to Indians, Rio de la Plata, Strait of Magellan, Peru, Chile, etc. Includes also, p. 143–92, an abridged version of Schouten's voyage with Le Maire through the Strait of Magellan, 1st publ., Amsterdam, 1618, under title *Journal ofte Beschryvinghe.* Sabin 89444; Borba de Moraes II:276; Palau 321548; Tiele-Muller 64; Tiele 1024; JCB (3) II:143. RPJCB.

619/131

——[Anr issue]. Oost ende West-Indische spiegel der 2. leste navigatien . . . Met de Australische navigatien, van Jacob le Maire. *Leyden: N. van Geelkercken,* 1619. 192 p.; illus., maps; obl. 4to. Sabin 89445; Borba de Moraes II:275–76; Tiele-Muller 65; Tiele 1025; Muller (1872) 1968; JCB (3) II:143. MnU-B, NN-RB, RPJCB (imp.); BL.

619/132

——. Speculum Orientalis Occidentalisque Indiae navigationum . . . altera Jacobi le Maire auspiciis imperioque directa. *Leyden: N. van Geelkercken,* 1619. 175 p.; illus., maps; obl. 4to. Transl. from Spilbergen's *Oost en West-Indische spiegel* of this year above. Cf. Sabin 89450; Borba de Moraes II:276; Tiele-Muller 66; Tiele 1029. [Locations may include the following issue:] CtY, DLC, InU-L, MB, MiU-C, MnU-B, NN-RB, PBL; BL, BN.

619/133

——[Anr issue]. *Leyden: N. van Geelkercken, for J. Hondius* [*at Amsterdam*], 1619. Sabin 89450; Borba de Moraes II:276; Tiele-Muller 67; Tiele 1029n; JCB (3) II:143. RPJCB.

619/134

Taylor, John, the Water-poet. A kicksey winsey: or A lerry come-twang. *London: N. Okes, for M. Walbanck,* 1619. 8vo. In verse. Includes ref. to 'Indian vapour', i.e., tobacco. STC 23767. BL, Oxford:Bodl.

619/135

Thou, Jacques Auguste de. Historiarum sui temporis [. . . libri]. *Paris: A. & H. Drouart,* 1619. 10 v.; 12mo. Contains 80 bks, as 1st publ., Paris, 1606–9; cf. the 1609–14 Drouart edn also in 12mo format. Brunet V:840.

619/136

Twisck, Pieter Janszoon. Chronijck van den onderganc der tijrannen. *Hoorn: Z. Cornelis-zoon* (v. 1) & *I. Willemszoon* (v. 2), 1619–20. 1853 p.; 4to. Includes scattered refs to American places & events, citing explorers of various nations. MH-AH, ViHarEM (v. 1).

619/137

Valderrama, Pedro de. Histoire generale du monde, et de la nature . . . Composé en espagnol . . . et traduit sur le manuscrit espagnol . . . par le sr. de la Richardier . . . Seconde édition. *Paris: I. Mesnier,* 1619,'17. 2 pts; 8vo. Transl. from the author's *Teatro de las religiones,* 1st publ., Seville, 1612, the ref. to the Brazilian monster here appearing in pt 2, p. 35. NIC, PU; BL, BN.

619/138

Vargas Machuca, Bernardo de. Teorica y exercicios de la gineta. *Madrid: D. Flamenco,* 1619. 200 numb. lvs; illus.; 8vo. An expanded version of the author's *Libro de exercicios de la gineta,* 1st publ., Madrid, 1600. On the use of the lance as developed in the New World. Medina (BHA) 695 & VII:1322–30; Pérez Pastor (Madrid) 1637. NNH; BL (destroyed), Madrid:BN.

619/139

Veer, Gerrit de. De waerachtighe beschrijvinge vande drie seylagien. *Enkhuizen: J. L. Meyn, for M. Colijn, at Amsterdam,* 1619 [colophon:1617]. 80 numb. lvs; illus., maps; obl. 4to. 1st publ., Amsterdam, 1598; cf. 1605 edn. The present edn constitutes the 1st pt of Michiel Colijn's *Oost-Indische ende West-Indische voyagien,* described more fully above. Unlike the other pts, this does not have its own special t.p., the above title appearing solely in the list of contents in the collective title. In view of the colophon, dated 1617, it appears likely that this pt, like the others thus collected, may have been earlier issued separately with its own t.p., but no other evidence for this has been encountered. Sabin 14349; Muller (1872) 2077; Tiele-Muller 100 (& 1); Tiele 1129n; JCB (3) II:133–34. DLC, RPJCB.

619/140

Verclaringe ende verhael hoe de Heere Wouter Raleigh Ridder, hem ghedreghen heeft, soo wel in signe voyaghe, als in ende sedert sijne wedercomste . . . Naer de copye tot London, by Bonham Norton. *The Hague: A. Meuris,* 1619. 40 p.; 4to. Transl. from the *Declaration of the demeanor and cariage of Sir Walter Raleigh,* 1st publ., London, 1618; 'Oprecht ende waerachtich verhael': p. 26–31; 'Aende Coninncklicke Majesteyt', p. 32–40, transl. from Sir Lewis Stucley's *To the Kings most excellent majesties,* 1st publ., London, 1618. Sabin 67592 Knuttel 2811; JCB (3) II:139–40. NNH, NN-RB, RPJCB; BL, Amsterdam:NHSM.

619/141

Vespucci, Amerigo. Americae pars decima: qua continentur, I. Duae navigationes Dn. Americi Vesputii . . . II. Solida narratio de moderno provinciae Virginiae statu . . . authore Raphe Hamor . . . III. Vera descriptio Novae Angliae . . . à Capitaneo Johanne Schmidt. *Oppenheim: H. Galler, for J. T. de Bry,* 1619. 72 p.; illus., map; fol. (Theodor de Bry's *America.* Pt 10. Latin). Prob. transl. from de Bry's German version of previous year. Ralph Hamor's work 1st publ. in English, London, 1615; Smith's work 1st publ. in English, London, 1616. For variant issue see Church. Cf. Sabin 8784; Church 170 & 171; JCB (3) I:411–12. CSmH, DLC, ICN, NN-RB, RPJCB; BL, BN.   619/142

Vitorias felicissimas, que el Gran Turco se han tenido al presente; y otra vitoria que se alcanço en Indias contra Olandeses. *Seville: J. Serrano de Vargas y Ureña,* 1619. 2 lvs; fol. Medina (BHA) 688.

619/143

Welper, Eberhard. Observationes astronomicae & praedictiones astrologicae genommen auss dem Stand . . . des im . . . 1618. Jahrs im novembri erschinenen grossen Cometens. *Strassburg: C. von der Heyden,* 1619. 22 p.; 4to. Includes ref. to America (p. 16), referring to passage of comet. NNC; BL, BN.   619/144

Wirsung, Christoph. Ein newes Artzney Buch . . . *Frankfurt a. M.: H. Palthenius, for Heirs of Z. Palthenius,* 1619. 2 pts; fol. 1st publ., Heidelberg, 1568; cf. 1605 edn. DNLM.   619/145

162–?

Drayton, Michael. The owle. *London: E. A[llde]., for E. Whit [i.e., White],* 1604 [i.e., 162–?]. 4to. In verse. 1st publ., London, 1604. For reasons for the dating here assigned, see the Pforzheimer catalogue. STC 7213; Pforzheimer 304C. DFo, NN-RB; Oxford:Bodl.   62–/1

Flores de León, Diego. Señor. El maestre de campo don Diego Florez de Leon, cavallero de la Orden de Santiago. *[Madrid? 162–?].* 12 numb. lvs; fol. Memorial to king of Spain on affairs & administration of Peru, Chile, etc. Medina (Chile) 225. BL.   62–/2

Garavito, Gerónimo. Señor. Geronimo Garavito, procurador general del gremio de los azogueros de . . . Potosi del Pirù. Dize, que tiene suplicado a V.M. mande que se prosiga en la junta que se sirvio de formar del marques de Mansera, virrey que va al Pirù, y del principe de Esquilache, que lo avia sido, y de don Sebastian Zambrana de Villalobos. *[Madrid: 162–?].* 6 numb. lvs; fol. Memorial to king of Spain. Included are financial statistics on mines of Potosí. BL.   62–/3

Gaytán de Torres, Manuel. Que se dé diferente modo al govierno de las Indias, que se van perdiendo muy apriessa con el que sí tienen y modo para su práctica. *[Madrid? 162–?].* 21 numb. lvs; 4to. Palau 100943.   62–/4

1620

Abbot, George, Abp of Canterbury. A briefe description of the whole worlde . . . The fift edition. *London: J. Marriott,* 1602. 88 lvs; 4to. 1st publ., London, 1599. Sabin 21n; STC 29. CSmH, DFo, MH, NN-RB; BL.   620/1

Alemán, Mateo. Le voleur, ou La vie de Guzman d'Alfarache . . . Seconde partie. *Paris: T. DuBray,* 1620. 1209 p.; 8vo. Transl. by Jean Chapelain from Alemán's *Segunda parte de la vida de Guzman d'Alfarache.* 1st publ., Lisbon, 1604. For the 1st pt in French translation, see Alemán's *Le gueux,* 1st publ., Paris, 1619. Subsequent edns of this work are entered as v. 2 of Alemán's *Le gueux.* Laurenti (Nov. pic. esp.) 616. Paris:Arsenal.   620/2

Amatus Lusitanus. Curationum medicinalium centuriae septem. *Bordeaux: G. Vernoy,* 1620. 800 p.; fol. 1st publ., Venice, 1551–60. For treatment of syphilis, discusses use of sarsaparilla, described as derived from Peru & elsewhere in New World. Guaiacum, 'ex insulis noviter repertis', is also mentioned. CtY-M, NNC; BL, BN.   620/3

Aparisi, Francesco. Consilia medicinalia, de conservanda sanitate. *Edinburgh: T. Finlason,* 1620. 24 lvs; 4to. Describes therapeutic uses of tobacco, said to have been brought from the Indies by Columbus. STC 698a; Arents (Add.) 190. NN-A; BL, Aberdeen: UL.   620/4

Aramburu, Gerónimo. Memorial que presenta a su Magestad Geronimo de Aramburu gentilhombre de la Compañia de lanzas de la guarda del reyno del Piru. *Madrid: F. Correa de Montenegro,* 1620. 8 lvs; fol. Reproduced in facsim., Almeria, 1968.   620/5

Avisos de Roma, venidos en este ultimo ordinario que llego a los primeros deste mes de março 1620. *Valencia: F. Mey,* 1620. 8 p.; 4to. Mentioned is acquisition by Spanish of island in West Indies rich in gold, silver, & gems. Palau 20645; Maggs Cat. 479 (Americana V):4150a.   620/6

Bacon, Francis, viscount St Albans. Saggi morali . . . data in luce dal s. cavalier A. Cioli. *Milan: G. B. Bidelli,* 1620. 2 pts; 12mo. 1st publ. as here transl., Florence, 1619. Gibson (Bacon) 38; Shaaber (Brit. auth.) B30. CCB; BL, Munich:StB.   620/7

Baricelli, Giulio Cesare. Hortulus genialis, sive Rerum jucundarum, medicarum et memorabilium compendium. *Cologne: M. Smitz,* 1620. 353 p.; 12mo. 1st publ., Naples, 1617. DFo, NIC, PPC; BL, BN.   620/8

—[Anr edn]. *Geneva: P. Aubert,* 1620. 2 pts; 8vo. The 2nd pt, with title 'Liber de esculentorum facultatibus', is a translation by Arnald Freitag of Baldassare Pisanelli's *Trattato della natura de' cibi,* 1st publ., Venice, 1586, including discussion of turkey. BL, BN.   620/9

Baudart, Willem. Memorien, ofte korte verhael der ghedenckwerdighste gheschiedenisen van Nederlandt . . . van den jare 1612 . . . tot . . . 1620. *Arnhem: J. Janszoon,* 1620. 478 p.; 4to. Includes refs to the West Indies. MnU-B.   620/10

——. De Spaensche tiranije, dienende tot een morghen-wecker. . . . Nae de copye tot Danswijck, by Crijn Vermeulen de Jonghe. [*Amsterdam?* ca. 1620?]. [72] p.; 4to. 1st publ., [The Hague?], 1610, under title *Morghen-wecker.* Knuttel 1732; Meulman 1211; cf. Muller (1872) 2730n. BL, The Hague:KB.   620/11

Bauhin, Kaspar. Προδρομος. Theatri botanici. *Frankfurt a. M.: P. Jacobi, for J. Treudel,* 1620. 160 p.; illus.; 4to. Included are descriptions of numerous American plants identified as such, amongst them the potato (*Solanum*). Pritzel 507; Nissen (Bot.) 104. DLC, MH-A, MoSB, NIC; BL, BN.   620/12

Béguin, Jean. Les elemens de chymie. *Paris: M. Le Maître,* 1620. 398 p.; illus.; 8vo. 1st publ. as transl. from Béguin's *Tyrocinium chymicum* (Paris, 1612), Paris, 1615. CtY, DNLM, PP; Glasgow:UL.   620/13

Bennett, Edward. A treatise devided into three parts, touching the inconveniences, that the importation of tobacco out of Spaine hath brought into this land. [*London?* 1620?]. [7] p.; 4to. Recommends Virginia

& Bermuda tobaccos in preference to those of Spain. STC 1883. Cambridge:UL.
620/14

Benzi, Ugo. Regole della sanita et natura de' cibi . . . Et nuovamente in questa seconda impressione aggiontovi . . . i trattati di B Pisanelli, e sue Historie naturali; et annotationi del medico galina. *Turin: Heirs of G. D. Tarino,* 1620. 898 (i.e., 798) p.; 8vo. Pages 683–99 comprise an 'Altra gionta, dove tratta de molti cibi usati, in molte altre parti, e specialmente nell'Indie Orientali, & Occidentali', describing American foodstuffs, e.g., the potato & the passionflower. Cf. 1610 edn. Wellcome I:3355. DLC, DNLM; BL, BN.
620/15

Biancani, Giuseppe. Sphaera mundi, seu Cosmographia, demonstrativa . . . in qua totius mundi fabrica, una cum novis, Tychonis, Kepleri, Galiliae, aliorumque astronomorum inventis continetur. *Bologna: S. Buonuomo, for H. Tamburini,* 1620. 455 p.; illus., 4to. Sabin 5132. MnS, NN-RB.
620/16

Blaeu, Willem Janszoon. Le flambeau de la navigation. *Amsterdam: J. Janszoon, the Younger,* 1620. 2 v.; illus., maps; obl. fol. 1st publ. in French, Amsterdam, 1619; here an apparent piracy. French title on slip pasted on t.p. of Janszoon's 1620 Dutch edn. Koeman (M.Bl) 23 (J); Phillips (Atlases) 2829; Tiele 122n. CtY, DLC, ICN, MH; BL, BN.
620/17

—[Anr issue?]. Le phalot de la mer. *Amsterdam: J. Janszoon, the Younger,* 1620. Koeman (M.Bl) 24 (J).
620/18

——. Het licht der zee-vaert . . . Ook van . . . Guinea, Brasilien, Oost- ende West-Indien . . . enz. *Amsterdam: W. J. Blaeu,* 1620. 2 v.; illus., maps; obl. fol. Books i & ii dated 1619; for variant see Koeman. Sabin 35775; Koeman (M.Bl) 6; Tiele 121. Oxford:Bodl., BN, Amsterdam:NHSM.
620/19

—[Anr edn]. *Amsterdam: J. Janszoon, the Younger,* 1620. 2 pts; illus., maps; obl. fol. An apparent piracy. Koeman (M.Bl) 15 (J). Amsterdam:NHSM.
620/20

——. The light of navigation. *Amsterdam: J. Janszoon, the Younger,* 1620. 2 v.; illus., maps; obl. fol. 1st publ. in English, Amsterdam,

1612; here an apparent piracy. Koeman (M.Bl) 21 (J); STC 3111. Cambridge:St John's, Cambridge:Trinity.
620/21

Boemus, Johann. Mores, leges et ritus omnium gentium . . . Itidem et ex Brasiliana J. Lery historia. Fides, religio et mores Aethiopum . . . Damiano a Goes auctore. *Geneva: J. de Tournes,* 1620. 504 p.; 16mo. A reissue of de Tournes's 1604 edn? Sabin 6118; Borba de Moraes I:96. CtY, NN-RB; BL (imprint misdated 1600), BN.
620/22

Bogotá, Colombia. Por parte de las ciudades Santa Fé, y Cartagena, se suplica a V. vea los apuntamientos del hecho del pleito, que siguen con el capitan Alonso Turrillo, tesorero de la Casa de moneda, que se ha de hazer en . . . Santa Fè. [*Madrid?* ca. 1620?]. 12 numb. lvs; fol. Medina (BHA) 6332. BL, Seville:Archivo de Indias.
620/23

Bonoeil, John. Observations to be followed, for the making of fit roomes, to keepe silkwormes in . . . Published by authority for the benefit of the noble plantation in Virginia. *London: F. Kingston,* 1620. 28 p.; 4to. 'A valuation of the commodoties growing and to be had in Virginia': p. 25n–28. Sabin 99883; Clayton-Torrence 32; Vail (Frontier) 43; STC 18761; Church 382A; JCB (3) II:151. CSmH, CtY, MH, RPJCB; Oxford:Bodl.
620/24

A booke of cookerie, and the order of meates to be served to the table. *London: E. Allde,* 1620. 102 p.; 8vo. Included are instructions on how 'To bake a Turkie, and take out his bones'. STC 3300. BL.
620/25

Botero, Giovanni. Politia regia: in qua totus imperiorum mundus . . . accuratius edisseruntur . . . Justus Reifenberg emaculavit . . . denique illustravit. *Marburg: P. Egenolff,* 1620. 253 p.; 4to. Based on Botero's *Relationi universali,* 1st publ., Rome, 1591–96. RPJCB, NN-RB; BL, BN.
620/26

Bourne, William. A regiment for the sea . . . Newly corrected. *London: W. Jones, for E. Weaver,* 1620. 96 numb. lvs; 8vo. 1st publ., London, [1574], but cf. 1601 edn above. Taylor (Regiment) 455–56; STC 3430. BL.
620/27

Breton, Nicholas. A poste with a packet of

mad letters. *London: W. Stansby, for J. Smethwicke & J. Marriott,* 1620. 32 lvs; 4to. 1st publ., London, 1602. STC 3689. DFo.
620/28

Calvisius, Seth. Opus chronologicum . . . Editio altera & auctior & correctior. [*Leipzig: F. Lanckish, the Elder ? for*] *J. Thymiss, at Frankfurt a. d. O.,* 1620. 2 pts; fol. 1st publ., Leipzig, 1605, under title *Chronologia.* MB, NNC, NjP.
620/29

Camerarius, Philipp. Operae horarum subcisivarum . . . Centuria . . . altera. *Frankfurt a. M.: E. Emmel, for P. Kopff,* 1620. 391 p.; 4to. 1st publ., Frankfurt a. M., 1601. CtY, DLC, NN-RB.
620/30

Campanella, Tommaso. Von der Spanischen Monarchy. [*Tübingen? J. A. Cellius?*] 1620. 166 p.; 4to. Transl., possibly by Christophor Besold, from an Italian ms. 'Von der andern Hemispherio, und von der newen Welt': chapt. xxxi; 'Von der Schiffahrt' with refs to the Spanish Indies: chapt. xxxii. Cf. Sabin 10197; Firpo (Campanella) p. 63. MH, RPJCB; BL.
620/31

Canale, Floriano. De' secreti universali raccolti et esperimentati. *Venice: G. Imberti,* 1620. 304 p.; 8vo. 1st publ., Brescia (?), 1613. Michel (Répertoire) I:29. BN.
620/32

Cardona, Tomás de. Señor. Tomas de Cardona desseoso del servicio de V[uestra]. M[agestad]. y del bien publico . . . presento ante V. M. el año . . . 1615 la proposicion siguiente. [*Madrid? 1620?*]. 48 numb. lvs; fol. Memorial to king of Spain recommending means to increase royal revenues from New World. BL.
620/33

Caro de Torres, Francisco. Relacion de los servicios que hizo a Su Magestad . . . Felipe segundo y tercero, Don Alonso de Sotomayor . . . en los estados de Flandes, y en los provincios de Chile, y Tierrafirme, donde fue capitan general. *Madrid: Widow of C. Delgado,* 1620. 88 numb. lvs; 4to. Sabin 10952; Medina (Chile) 48; Pérez Pastor (Madrid) 1651; JCB (3) II:145. MH, MiU-C, NN-RB, RPJCB; BN, Madrid:Arch. Hist.
620/34

Cartagena, Colombia. Por parte de las ciudades de Cartagena, y santa Fé. Sobre el assiento y monedas, que conforme a el pre-

tende labrar el capitan Alonso Turrillo de Yebra, se advierte lo siguiente. [*Madrid? 1620?*]. 6 numb. lvs; fol. In this work, the first line of the title ends 'Civda-'. Medina (BHA) 6330. Seville:Archivo de Indias.
620/35

—[Anr edn?]. [*Madrid? 1620?*]. 6 numb. lvs; fol. In this edn, the first line of the title ends 'Civ-'. Medina (BHA) 6331. Seville:Archivo de Indias.
620/36

Casas, Bartolomé de las, O.P., Bp of Chiapa. Le miroir de la tyrannie espagnole perpetree aux Indes Occidentales . . . Nouvellement refaicte, avec les figurs en cuyvre. *Amsterdam: J. E. Cloppenburg,* 1620. 68 numb. lvs; illus.; 4to. Comprises pt 2 of Johannes Gysius's *Miroir de la cruelle & horrible tyrannie espagnole,* q.v.
620/37

——. Den spiegel der Spaensche tijrannije-geschiet in West-Indien. *Amsterdam: J. E. Cloppenburg,* 1620. 2 pts; illus.; 4to. The above work (pt 1) 1st publ. in Dutch, [Antwerp?], 1578, under title *Seer cort verhael vande destructie van d'Indien;* cf. 1607 edn above. Pt 2, with title *Tweede deel van de Spieghel der Spaensche tyrannye,* is an abridged version of Johannes Gysius's *Oorsprong en voortgang der Nederlandtschen bercerten,* 1st publ., [Leyden?], 1616; included is mention of Spanish massacre of French in Florida. In this edn the 1st title leaf is engraved. For edns with t.p. dated 1620 but with title printed rather than engraved, see the author's *Eerste deel* below and the year 1622. Sabin 11256; Medina (BHA) 1085n (II:477); Hanke/Giménez 515; Tiele-Muller 309; cf. Streit I:393. CSmH, DLC, ICN, NN-RB; BN.
620/37

—[Anr edn]. Eerste deel van den Spiegel der Spaensche tyrannye, gheschiet in West-Indien. *Amsterdam: J. E. Cloppenburg,* 1620. 104 p.; illus.; 4to. This edn has printed t.p. Sabin 11257; Tiele-Muller 310. NN-RB.
620/38

—[Anr edn]. Den spiegel der Spaensche tierannije geschiet in Westindien. *Amsterdam: C. L. van der Plasse,* 1620. [104] p.; illus.; 4to. Reprinted from the 1610 edn publ. by the Widow of C. Claeszoon. Sabin 11259; Medina (BHA) 1085n (II:477); Tiele-Muller 313; Streit I:394. NN-RB; BL.
620/39

Castro, Juan de. Historia de las virtudes y propriedades del tabaco. *Córdoba: S. de Cea Tesa,* 1620. 72 numb. lvs; 8vo. Sabin 11463; Medina (BHA) 701; Valdenebro (Córdoba) 102; Palau 48750. NNH; Madrid:BN.
620/40

Catholic Church. Commisarius Generalis Cruciatae. Instrucion y forma que se ha de tener y guardar en la publicacion, predicacion, administracion y cobrança de la Bula de la Santa Cruzada . . . la qual se ha de hazer en los arçobispados de los Reyes, Charcas, y obispados del Cuzco, la Barranca, Truxillo, Guamanga, Ariquipa, la Paz, Quito, Tucuman, y Santiago de Chile, y la Assuncion, y provincias del rio de la Plata, Panama, Cartagena, Santa Marta, y assimismo en el arçobispado del nuevo reyno de Granada, y obispados de Popayan, y Veneçuela. [*Madrid?* 1620?]. [16] p.; fol. Issued by Diego de Guzmán as Commissario Apostolico General de la Santa Cruzada; at end: Dada en Madrid a primero de Otubre de mil y seicientos y veinte años. Palau 111762; JCB (3) II:147–48. RPJCB.
620/41

Cats, Jacob. Silenus Alcibiadis, sive Proteus. *Amsterdam: W. J. Blaeu,* 1620, '19. 3 pts; illus.; 4to. 1st publ., Middelburg, 1618; pts 2 & 3 have imprints dated 1619, apparently reissues of Amsterdam & Middelburg, 1619, edns. Vries 81; Mus. Cats. 29. ICN, IU (imp.), PPL; BN, Leyden:UB.
620/42

Cervantes Saavedra, Miguel de. Les nouvelles. *Paris: J. Richer,* 1620–21. 2 v.; 8vo. 1st publ. as here transl. from the Madrid, 1613, Spanish text, Paris, 1615. Ríus (Cervantes) 886; Palau 53522. DLC, NNH, OU; BL, BN.
620/43

——. The second part of the history of Don Quixote. *London: [G. Purslow,] for E. Blount,* 1620. 504 p.; 8vo. Transl. by Thomas Shelton (?) from Cervantes's *Segunda parte,* 1st publ., Madrid, 1615. Ríus (Cervantes) 607; STC 4917. CSmH, CtY, DLC, MH, MiU, NN-RB, PPRF; BL.
620/44

Champlain, Samuel de. Voyages et descouvertes faites en la Nouvelle-France, depuis l'année 1615 jusques à la fin de l'année 1618. *Paris: C. Collet,* 1620. 158 numb. lvs; illus.; 8vo. 1st publ., Paris, 1619; here a reissue of that edn with altered imprint date.

Sabin 11837; Harrisse (NF) 33; Church 378; JCB (3) II:146. CSmH, NN-RB, RPJCB; BL, BN.
620/45

Codogno, Ottavio. Nuovo itinerario delle poste per tutto il mondo. *Venice: L. Spineda,* 1620. 446 p.; obl. 8vo. 1st publ., Venice, 1611. Michel (Répertoire) II:112. MnU-B; Paris:Mazarine.
620/46

Collibus, Hippolytus à. Fürstliche Tischreden . . . durch Johann Werner Gebharten [pseud.] . . . angefangen und kurtz verfasset . . . und nachmals vermehret und continuirt werden durch . . . Georgium Draudium. *Frankfurt a. M.: E. Emmel,* 1620. 2 pts; 8vo. 1st publ., Frankfurt a. M., 1597; cf. 1614 edn. CtY (pt 1), ICU; BN.
620/47

Compagnie de Montmorency pour la Nouvelle France. Articles accordez par monseigneur le duc de Montmorency . . . lieutenant general pour sa Majesté au pays de la nouvelle France appellé Canada . . . pour les voyages, commerces, traictes, & traffics audit pays de la nouvelle France. [*Paris?* 1620]. 8 p.; 4to. BN.
620/48

Córdoba, Antonio Laso de la Vega de. Por Don Antonio de Cordova de la Vega, capitan de las guardas de el Governador, y teniente general de la cavalleria del reyno de Chile. Con el Señor Fiscal del Consejo de Indias. [*Madrid?* 1620?]. 4 lvs; fol. Sabin 39132; Medina (Chile) 231.
620/49

Croll, Oswald. Basilica chymica . . . Additus est . . . Tractatus novus de signaturis rerum internis. *Frankfurt a. M.: J. F. Weiss, for G. Tampach,* 1620. 2 pts; illus.; 8vo. 1st publ., Frankfurt a. M., 1609. CU, CtY-M; London:Wellcome.
620/50

Dekker, Thomas. Villanies discovered . . . newly corrected and enlarged. *London: A. Mathewes,* 1620. [117] p.; illus.; 4to. 1st publ., London, 1608, under title *Lanthorne and candle-light.* STC 6489; Arents (Add.) 193. CSmH, DFo, MB, NN-A; BL.
620/51

Les delices satyriques, ou Suite du Cabinet des vers satyriques de ce temps. *Paris: A. de Sommaville,* 1620. 472 p.; 12mo. Included are the 1st & 5th satires from Claude d'Esternod's *L'espadon satyrique,* 1st publ., Lyons, 1619. Versailles:BM.
620/52

Desprez, Philippe. Le theatre des animaux, auquel sous . . . fables & histoires, est representé la plupart des actions de la vie humaine. *Paris: J. LeClerc,* 1620. 103 p.; illus.; 4to. In verse. Includes poem 'Le coq de Flandres, & le coq d'Inde' to exemplify moral 'Ne fouler l'estranger'. Cioranescu (XVII) 25737. MH; BL, BN. 620/53

Draud, Georg. Bibliotheca historica. *Leipzig:* 1620. 4to. Includes chapt. 'De scriptoribus rerum Americanarum'. Sabin 20908.
620/54

——. Fürstliche Tischreden. *Frankfurt a. M.:* 1620. *See* Collibus, Hippolytus à, *above.*

Drayton, Michael. Poems . . . collected into one volume. *London: W. Stansby, for J. Smethwick,* 1620. 492 p.; port.; fol. 1st publ., London, 1605. STC 7223. ICN, MH, ViU; BL.
620/55

Duchesne, Joseph. Pharmacopoea dogmaticorum restituta. *Geneva: P. Aubert,* 1620. 591 p.; 8vo. 1st publ., Paris, 1607. BN.
620/56

Dupleix, Scipion. La curiosité naturelle. *Lyons: S. Rigaud,* 1620. 269 p.; 8vo. 1st publ., Paris, 1606. CtY, DNLM. 620/57

Estienne, Charles. Lexicon historicum, geographicum, poeticum . . . Hanc postremam editionem Fed. Morellus . . . recensuit. *Paris: N. Buon,* 1620. 2038 cols; 4to. 1st publ. with American geographic refs, Lyons, 1595; cf. 1601 edn with title *Dictionarium historicum, geographicum, poeticum.* BN.
620/58

Fioravanti, Leonardo. Del compendio de' secreti rationali . . . libri cinque. *Venice: P. Miloco,* 1620. 8vo. 1st publ., Venice, 1564. Discussion of syphilis includes its treatment with guaiacum & sarsaparilla. Michel (Répertoire) III:47. DNLM (imp.); Paris: Mazarine. 620/59

Flóres de León, Diego. Informe a S.M. Don Felipe III y al Consejo de Indias sobre el viaje que ha de hacer la Armada al reino de Chile e instrucciones para occupar el puerto de Valdivia . . . y viaje que en 1615 hizo el holandés Jorge Esperuet. [*Madrid?* ca. 1620?]. 8 lvs; fol. Palau 92685.
620/60

Fonseca, Rodrigo. Consultationum medicinalium singularibus remediis refertae. *Venice: G. Guerigli,* 1620–22. 2 v.; fol. Vol. 1

1st publ., Venice, 1619. Wellcome I:2344. London:Wellcome, BN. 620/61

Gerhard, Johann. Locorum theologicorum . . . tomus quintus. *Jena: T. Steinmann,* 1620. 1327 p.; 4to. 1st publ., Jena, 1617. MH-AH. 620/62

Gonsalvius, Reginaldus, Montanus. Der heyliger Hispanischer inquisitie etliche listighe secrete consten ende practijcken ontdeckt . . . Eerst in Latyn beschreven. *The Hague: A. Meuris,* 1620. 156 p.; 4to. 1st publ. in Dutch, London, 1569; transl. from author's *Sanctae Inquisitionis Hispanicae artes,* 1st publ., Heidelberg, 1567. Cf. 1625 English edn. Petit 1281. Leyden: B. Thysiana.
620/63

Goulart, Simon. Thresor d'histoires admirables et memorables. *Geneva: S. Crespin,* 1620. 2 v.; 8vo. 1st publ., Paris, 1600–1601, under title *Histoires admirables et memorables;* cf. 1603 edn. Jones (Goulart) 54o. BL, BN.
620/64

Gracián, Jerónimo. Zelo della propagatione della fede. *Rome:* 1620. 18mo. 1st publ. in Italian, Rome, 1610. Streit I:391.
620/65

Great Britain. Council for Virginia. A declaration of the state of the colonie and affaires in Virginia . . . 22 Junii. 1620. *London: T. S[nodham & F. Kingston].,* 1620. 2 pts; 4to. For the distinguishing features of this edn, & other issues and edns of this year, see the STC Sabin 99877; Vail (Frontier) 45; STC 24841.2; JCB (3) II:151. MiD, RPJCB. 620/66

—[Anr issue]. *London: T. S[nodham & F. Kingston].,* 1620. 3 pts; 4to. Here added are 'Orders and constitutions collected by the . . . Companie of Virginia'. Sabin 99878; Vail (Frontier) 46; STC 24841.3 (formerly 24840); Church 381; JCB (3) II:151. CSmH, ICN, MHi, RPJCB; Oxford:Queen's.
620/67

—[Anr issue]. *London: T. S[nodham & F. Kingston].,* 1620. 3 pts; 4to. Here added on lf C4 is 'A declaration of the supplies'. Sabin 99879; Vail (Frontier) 47; STC 24821.4 (formerly 24835); JCB (3) II:150. CSmH, DFo, MH, NN-RB, RPJCB; BL.
620/68

—[Anr edn]. *London: T. Snodham [& F. Kingston].,* 1620. 92 p.; 4to. Sabin 99880; Vail

(Frontier) 48; STC 24821.6 (formerly 24836); JCB (3) II:151. CtY, DLC, NN-RB, RPJCB; BL.   620/69

—[Anr issue]. *London: T. Snodham* [*& F. Kingston*]., 1620. 97 p.; 4to. Here added as p. 93–97 are 'Proposals and inducements for settlers'. Sabin 99881; Vail (Frontier) 49; STC 24841.8; Church 382. CSmH, DFo, MiU-C, MnU-B, NN-RB.   620/70

Great Britain. Sovereigns, etc., 1603–1625 (James I). James, by the grace of God . . . [19 Jan. 1620]. *London:* [1620]. *See the year* 1621.

——. A proclamation commanding conformity to his Majesties pleasure, expressed in his late charter to the tobacco-pipe-makers. *London: R. Barker & J. Bill*, 1620. 2 lvs; fol. Crawford (Roy. procl.) 1282; Brigham (Roy. procl.) 24–26; STC 8636; Arents 141. CSmH, NN-A; London:Soc. of Antiquaries.
620/71

——. A proclamation declaring his Majesties pleasure concerning Captaine Roger North, and those who are gone foorth as adventurers with him. *London: R. Barker & J. Bill*, 1620. 2 lvs; fol. Ordering arrest of North, who has undertaken an expedition to Brazil. Crawford (Roy. procl.) 1280; Brigham (Roy. procl.) 21–23; STC 8634. CSmH; London:Soc. of Antiquaries.
620/72

——. A proclamation for restraint of the disordered trading for tobacco. *London: R. Barker & J. Bill,* 1620. 2 lvs; fol. Sabin 99842; Crawford (Roy. procl.) 1283; Brigham (Roy. procl.) 27–31; STC 8637; Arents 142. CSmH, NN-A; London:Soc. of Antiquaries.
620/73

——. Whereas, at the humble suit and request. *London:* 1620. *See the year* 1621.

Gysius, Johannes. Le miroir de la cruelle & horrible tyrannie espagnole perpetree au Pays-Bas . . . On a adjoinct la deuxiesme partie de les tyrannies commises aux Indes Occidentales par les Espagnoles. *Amsterdam: J. E. Cloppenburg,* 1620. 2 pts; illus.; 4to. Transl. from the Dutch edn of this year entered under Casas above, the two pts being here transposed. Pt 2, by Las Casas, has special t.p. with title *Le miroir de la tyrannie espagnole perpetree aux Indes Occidentales.* Gysius's work includes ref. to massacre of

French in Florida by Spanish; that of Las Casas, Spanish treatment of Indians. Sabin 11270; Medina (BHA) 1085n (II:472); Streit I:392; Tiele-Muller 312; JCB (3) II:145 & 146. CSmH, DLC, ICN, MH, MiU-C, NN-RB, RPJCB; BL, BN.
620/74

——. Tweede deel van de spieghel der Spaensche tyrannye. *Amsterdam: J. E. Cloppenburg,* 1620. 126 p.; illus.; 4to. Comprises pt 2 of las Casas's *Den spiegel der Spaensche tijrannije-geschiet* of this year above, q.v.

Hamcomius, Martinus. Frisia, seu De viris rebusque Frisiae illustribus libri duo. *Franeker: J. Lamrinck,* 1620. 131 p.; illus.; 4to. In verse. Included is a tale of a voyage by Frisians to America & Chile long before Columbus. Sabin 29937. DLC, MB, MiU, MnU-B, NN-RB, PU; BL.   620/75

Hariot, Thomas. Wunderbarliche, doch warhafftige Erklärung von der Gelegenheit und Sitten der Wilden in Virginia . . . Erstlich in engelländischer Spraach beschrieben . . . und newlich durch Christ. P. in Teutsch gebracht . . . zum drittenmal in Truck gegeben. *Oppenheim: H. Galler, for J. T. de Bry,* [*at Frankfurt a. M.*], 1620. 31 p.; illus.; maps; fol. (Theodor de Bry's *America.* Pt 1. German). 1st publ. in this version, Frankfurt a. M., 1590; transl. from Hariot's *A brief and true report of . . . Virginia,* 1st publ., London, 1588. Cf. Sabin 8784; Baginsky (German Americana) 149; Shaaber (Brit. auth.) H92; Church 178; JCB (3) I:387. CSmH, NN-RB, RPJCB; BL, BN.
620/76

Hernández, Melchor. Memorial de Chiriqui del padre Presentado fr. Melchor Hernandez. [*Madrid?* 1620]. 4 lvs; fol. Asks superior to retain priests in small Indian villages to protect latter from abuses. Subscribed in Panama, 12 June 1620. Medina (BHA) 702; Palau 113598. BL.   620/77

Herrera, Gabriel Alonzo de. Agricultura general . . . *Madrid: Widow of A. Martín, for D. González,* 1620. 270 numb. lvs; fol. Also included is Gonzalo de las Casas's *Arte nuevo para criar seda,* on the growing of silkworms in Yucatan, 1st publ. separately, Granada, 1581. Pérez Pastor (Madrid) 1660; Palau 114100n & 47016n. BL, BN.
620/78

Hieron, Samuel. The workes. *London: W. Stansby; sold by J. Parker* [1620?]. 2 v.; fol. Included in v. 1 is Hieron's *An answer to a popish rime*, 1st publ., London, 1604. STC 13380. CU-A, CtY, DLC; Cambridge:UL.
620/79

—[Anr issue?]. *London: W. Stansby & J. Beale* [1620?]. STC 13380a. NIC, NNUT, PPiPT; Cambridge:UL. 620/80

Holland, Henry. Herωlogia anglica, hoc est, Clarissimorum et doctissimorum aliqout [*sic*] Anglorum . . . vitae effigiae, vitae et elogia. [*Utrecht:*] *C. van de Passe & J. Janszoon, at Arnhem* [1620]. 240 p.; ports; fol. Includes accounts of early English navigators, with their portraits. Sabin 32505; STC 13582. CSmH, CtY, DLC, ICN, InU-L, MH, MiU-C, MnU-B, NN-RB, PPL; BL, BN.
620/81

al-Idrisi. Geographia Nubiensis, id est Accuratissima totius orbis . . . descriptio . . . ex arabico . . . versa a Gabriel Sionita . . . & Joanne Hesronita. *Paris: J. Blageart,* 1619 [i.e., 1620]. 2 pts; 4to. The translators' dedication mentions America. The privilege, on final page, is dated 1620. DLC, IU, NN-RB, PBL, RPJCB; BL, BN.
620/82

James I, King of Great Britain. Workes. *London: R. Barker & J. Bill,* 1616 [i.e., 1620]. 621 p.; illus., ports; fol. A reissue of 1st, 1616, edn, with supplementary text dated 1620. STC 14345. CSmH, DLC, ICN, MH, MnU, NN-RB, PU; BL. 620/83

Jamet, Denis, O.F.M. Rec. Coppie de la lettre escripte par le r.p. Denys Jamet, commissaire des pp. Recollestz de Canada, a monsieur de Rancé. [*Paris?* 1620?]. 8 p.; 8vo. At end: De Quebec . . . 15 Aoust 1620. Harrisse (NF) 39; Streit II:2488; JCB (3) II:200. RPJCB; BN. 620/84

Jesuits. Historiae Societatis Jesu pars prima . . . auctore Nicolao Orlandini. *Antwerp: Sons of M. Nuyts,* 1620. 426 p.; fol. 1st publ., Rome, 1615. Borba de Moraes I:119; Streit I:399; Backer V:1935. DLC, MnU-B, NNH, RPJCB; BL, BN. 620/85

——. Historiae Societatis Jesu pars secunda . . . auctore r.p. Francisco Sacchino. *Antwerp: Sons of M. Nuyts,* 1620. 340 p.; fol. Continues 1st pt above; for the subsequent 3rd pt, see the year 1649. Borba de Moraes

II:225; Streit I:400; Backer VII:366. DLC, MnU-B, NNH, RPJCB; BL, BN.
620/86

Jesuits. Letters from missions. Auss America, das ist, Auss der Newen Welt. Underschidlicher Schreiben Extract, von den Jaren 1616, 1617, 1618. Was gestalt acht Patres Societatis . . . ihr blut vergossen. Auss frantzösischer Sprach . . . ubergesetzt. *Augsburg: Sarah Mangin,* 1620. 91 p.; 4to. Transl. from the *Histoire du massacre de plusieurs religieux,* 1st publ. at Valenciennes, the following item. Sabin 1019; Baginsky (German Americana) 151; Wagner (SW) 22c; Streit II:1519; JCB (2) II:234. CU-B, DLC, MB, NN-RB, PPL, RPJCB, BL, Munich:StB. 620/87

——. Histoire du massacre de plusieurs religieux de S. Dominique, de S. François, et de la Compagnie de Jesus . . . advenu en la rebellion de quelques Indois de l'Occident contre les Espagnols. *Valenciennes: J. Vervliet,* 1620. 3 pts; 8vo. The 1st pt, p. 5–31, the *Memorial presenté a Sa Majeste catholique touchant de massacre,* transl. from Francisco de Figueroa's *Memorial* as publ., Barcelona, 1617. Sabin 32027; Wagner (SW) 22b; Streit II:1517–18; Backer VIII:241. DLC, RPJCB; BL (Dominicans). 620/88

King, John, Bp of London. Sermon at Paules Crosse, on behalfe of Paules Churche. *London: E. Griffin, for E. Adams,* 1620. 51 p.; 4to. Mentions funds raised in London for support of church in Virginia. Sabin 37811; STC 14982. CSmH, CtY, DFo, IU, NNUT; BL. 620/89

Knobloch, Tobias. De lue venerea, von Frantzosen kurtzer Bericht. *Giessen: N. Hampel,* 1620. 191 p.; 8vo. Drawing upon Jean Fernel's *De luis venereae curatione* (1st publ., Antwerp, 1579) ascribes American source to syphilis & prescribes use of guaiacum for its treatment. Wellcome I:3570. OClW-H; London:Wellcome. 620/90

Leech, John, poet. Musae priores, sive Poematum pars prior. *London:* [*J. Beale*] 1620. 3 pts; 8vo. In pt 2, in the 2nd of the 'Eclogae nauticae', Columbus & Magellan are mentioned; in the 4th, Columbus, Vespucci & Sir Francis Drake. In this issue, in the 3rd pt 1f Blr has caption 'Ad Musas' in roman type. STC 15365.7. CSmH, MH; London: UC.   620/91

—[Anr issue]. *London:* [*J. Beale*] 1620. In this issue, in the expanded & reset 3rd pt, lf Blr has caption 'Ad Musas' in italic type. STC 15366. CSmH, CtY, DLC, ICN, MH, NNC; BL.   620/92

Le Mire, Aubert. Geographia ecclesiastica, in qua provinciae metropoles, episcopatus, sive urbis titulo episcopali illustres . . . leguntur. *Lyons: C. Cayne, for A. Pillehotte,* 1620. 359 p.; 12mo. Extracted from the author's *Notitia episcopatuum orbis christiani,* Antwerp, 1613. Streit I:397. DFo, MH, MnU-B, NNH, PPL, RPJCB; BL, BN.   620/93

——. Politiae ecclesiasticae, sive Status religionis christianae per Europam, Asiam, Africam et Orbem novum, libri iv. *Lyons: A. Pillehotte,* 1620. 348 p.; 12mo. 1st publ., Cologne, 1619, under title *De statu religionis christianae.* Sabin 49405; Streit I:396. CtY-D, DFo, IU, MH, RPJCB; BN.
620/94

Liebfriedt, Christian, von Gross Seufftzen, pseud. An gantz Teutschlandt, von dess Spanniers Tyranney, welche er ohn unterscheidt der Religion auch an den aller Unschuldigsten verübt. [*Frankfurt a. M.?*] *F. Snuhcam',* 1620. [21] p.; 4to. Includes extensive account of Spanish atrocities against American Indians. Jantz (German Baroque) 2909. ICN, InU-L, NcD; BL.   620/95

Liñán y Verdugo, Antonio. Guia y avisos de forasteros, adonde se les enseña a huir de los peligros que ay en la vida de corte. *Madrid: Widow of A. Martín, for M. de Silis,* 1620. 148 numb. lvs; 8vo. The 7th tale describes career of a Peruvian-born adventuress. Pérez Pastor (Madrid) 1668; Palau 138643. NNH; Madrid:BN.   620/96

Linocier, Geoffroy. L'histoire des plantes, traduicte du latin en françois . . . Seconde edition. *Paris: G. Macé,* 1620, '19. 3 pts; illus.; 12mo. Based upon Antoine DuPinet's *Historia plantarum,* the French translation (with supplementary material by Linocier) was 1st publ., Paris, 1584, & has been entered previously as DuPinet's work. Divided into 7 sections, with special title pages, the 1st describes numerous American plants, & is followed by an *Histoire des plantes nouvellement trouvee en l'isle Virginie.* The *Histoire*

des animaux à quatre pieds describes the 'Su', said to live in giant-inhabited Patagonia, & also the armadillo. The *Histoire des oiseaux* mentions the parrots of Hispaniola, & describes the turkey. Sabin 72042 (& 32024); Pritzel 2539n (& 7672); cf. JCB (3) II:149. MH, RPJCB (*Histoire des plantes . . . en l'isle Virgine* only); BL, BN.   620/97

Loyseau, Guillaume. De internorum externorumque morborum ferme omnium curatione libellus. *Bordeaux: G. Vernoy,* 1620. 246 p.; 12mo. 1st publ., Bordeaux, 1617; here a reissue of that edn with altered imprint date? Wellcome I:3872. London:Wellcome.
620/98

Marcos da Lisboa, O.F.M., Bp. Erster[-dritter] Thail der Cronicken der eingesetzten orden dess heiligen Vatters Francisci . . . Erstlich in portugalischer Sprach zusammen getragen . . . und hernach in die castiglianische verendert . . . volgents in die italienische transferiert . . . und . . . in unser teutsche Sprach gebracht durch . . . Carl Kurtzen von Senfftenau. *Munich: Anna Berg, for J. Hertsroy,* 1620. 3 pts; 4to. Pt 3, with its refs to Franciscans in Mexico, 1st publ., Salamanca, 1570, under title *Tercera parte de las Chronicas.* Cf. Streit I:274 & 108. MdSsW, RPJCB (Pts 1 & 2); BL.
620/99

Marlowe, Christopher. The tragicall historie of the life and death of Doctor Faustus. *London: J. Wright,* 1620. [62] p.; 4to. Drama. 1st publ., London, 1604. STC 17434; Greg 205(f). NN-RB, Robt Taylor; BL.
620/100

Marquardus, Joannes. Practica medicinalis theorica empirica morborum internorum . . . Huic in fine accesserunt Institutionum chirurgicarum libri quinque cum practica chirurgica. Authore Sebastiano Castalione [i.e., Cortilio]. *Cologne: P. Henning,* 1620. 705 p.; 8vo. 1st publ., Speyer, 1589; cf. 1610 edn. PPC.   620/101

Mason, John. A briefe discourse of the New-found-land. *Edinburgh: A. Hart,* 1620. [14] p.; 4to. Sabin 45453; STC 17616; Church 379; JCB (3) II:148. CSmH, PP, RPJCB; BL.
620/102

Mattioli, Pietro Andrea. Les commentaires . . . sur les six livres de Pedacius Dioscoride . . . de la matiere medicinale, traduits de latin . . . par m. Antoine du Pinet. *Lyons: P. Rigaud,* 1620. 606 p.; illus., port.; fol. 1st publ. as here transl., Lyons, 1561; cf. 1605 edn above. Cf. Pritzel 5991n; Nissen (Bot.) 1312n. BL, BN.   620/103

Medina, Bartolomé de. Las poblaciones, assientos y reales de minas, que mediante Bartolome de Medina, y su invencion de sacar la plata de los metales . . . se han poblado en la Nueva España. [*Madrid?* 1620?]. bds.; fol. Medina (BHA) 6618. BL.   620/104

Mercado, Luis. Operum tomus primus[-III]. *Frankfurt a. M.: Heirs of Z. Palthenius,* 1620, '19. 3 v.; fol. Included is Mercado's Tomus secundus Operum, 1st publ., Valladolid, 1605. Palau 164995. CtY-M, DNLM, ICJ; BN.   620/105

Mercator, Gerardus. Atlas minor . . . à J. Hondius. . . illustratus. *Arnhem: J. Janszoon,* 1620. 683 p.; maps; obl. 12mo. 1st publ., Amsterdam, 1607. Cf. Sabin 47887; Koeman (Me) 192. CtY (imp.).   620/106

Merida, Yucatan. La ciudad de Merida, cabeça de la provincia de Yucatan . . . en las Indias, y los hijos, nietos . . . de los conquistadores. [*Madrid?* 1620?]. 3 numb. lvs; fol. Defense of encomiendas granted the conquistadors. BL.   620/107

Meteren, Emanuel van. Niderländischer histori . . . Supplementum. *Arnhem:* 1620. *See under title below.*

Montaigne, Michel Eyquem de. Les essais. *Rouen: M. de Préaulx,* 1620. 1129 p.; port.; 8vo. 1st publ., Bordeaux, 1580; cf. 1602 edn. According to Tchémerzine, this edn was shared with other Rouen booksellers, as with edns of 1617 & 1619. Tchémerzine VIII: 421. BN.   620/108

More, Sir Thomas, Saint. De optime reipublicae statu, de que nova insula Utopia. *Milan: G. B. Bidelli,* 1620. 228 p.; 12mo. 1st publ., Louvain, 1516; cf. 1601 edn. Gibson (More) 11. CSfU; London:Guildhall.   620/109

Mutoni, Niccolò. Μιϑριδατειοτεχνία: hoc est; De Mithridatii legitima constructione N. Mutoni collectanea . . . quorum prius exhibet ᾿Ακρόαμα medico-philosophicum . . . posterius Διατριβήν de opobalsamo Syriaco, Judaico, Aegyptio, Peruviano, Tolutano, et Europaeo, per M. Döringium.

Jena: J. Beithmann, for Heirs of J. Eyering & J. Perfert, 1620. 3 pts; 8vo. Wellcome I:4495. DNLM; BL, BN.   620/110

Mylius, Johann Daniel. Antidotarium medico-chymicum reformatum. *Frankfurt a. M.: L. Jennis,* 1620. 1044 p.; port.; 4to. In bk 2, chapt. iii discourses 'De chyna, sassafras, sarsaparilla, behen secachul, cubebis, & carpo balsamo', referring to the West Indies, Honduras, & Peru. Elsewhere mechoacan & guaiacum are mentioned. Ferguson (Bibl. chem.) II:121; Wellcome I:4501. DNLM, MBCo; BL, BN.   620/111

Niderländischer histori . . . Supplementum . . . vom Jahr 1613 biss auff . . . 1620. *Arnhem: J. Janszoon,* 1620. 684 p.; illus.; fol. Continues E. van Meteren's *Eigentlich und vollkomene historische Beschreibung des niderlendischen Kriegs,* Arnhem, 1614. Bruckner 12. Leyden:UB (imp.).   620/112

Oogh-teecken der inlantsche twisten ende beroerten . . . over-geset uyt het Latijnsche exemplaer. *The Hague: A. Meuris,* 1620. 38 p.; 4to. In discussing truce, ref. is made to gold & silver of West Indies & commercial possibilities there. In this edn, line 1 of p. 38 begins 'Laet ons'. Locations listed may include the following edn. Cf. Knuttel 3122. MnU-B, InU-L, NN; The Hague:KB.   620/113

—[Anr edn]. *The Hague: A. Meuris,* 1620. [38] p.; 4to. Line 1 of p. [38] begins 'daente'. Cf. Knuttel 3122. NN.   620/114

—[Anr edn]. *The Hague: A. Meuris,* 1620. [32] p.; 4to. Knuttel 3123. The Hague:KB.   620/115

Orlandini, Nicolò. Historiae Societatis Jesu pars prima. *Antwerp:* 1620. *See* Jesuits *above.*

Orlers, Jan Janszn. The triumphs of Nassau . . . translated out of the French by W. Shute. *London: A. Islip; sold by R. More,* 1620. 392 p.; fol. 1st publ. in English, London, 1613; here a reissue of that edn with cancel t.p. STC 17677. CaOHM, MH; BL, Glasgow:UL.   620/116

Ortiz de Cervantes, Juan. Informacion en favor del derecho que tienen los nacidos en las Indias à ser perferidos [*sic*] en la prelacias, dignidades, canongias, y otros beneficios eclesiasticos. *Madrid: Widow of A. Martín,* 1620. 12 numb. lvs; fol. 1st publ., Madrid, 1619. Medina (BHA) 703; Pérez

Pastor (Madrid) 1675; JCB (3) II:148. RPJCB.   620/117

——. Señor. El licenciado Juan Ortiz de Cervantes, abogado . . . del Pirú . . . Dize; que catorze leguas de la dicha ciudad [Cuzco] está el rio grande de Aporimac. [*Madrid?* ca. 1620?]. 2 lvs; fol. Memorial to king of Spain, requesting bridge over river. Medina (BHA) 6702. BL.   620/118

——. Señor. El licenciado Juan Ortiz de Cervantes, abogado . . . del Pirù . . . Dize; que como en este reyno estan eoncedidos . . . ferias libres [etc.]. [*Madrid?* ca. 1620?]. bds.; fol. Memorial to king of Spain, requesting that Cuzco be permitted public holidays. Medina (BHA) 6700. BL.   620/119

——. Señor. El licenciado Juan Ortiz de Cervantes, abogado . . . del Pirù . . . Dize: que en . . . Cuzco, donde ay el mas concurio de Indios [etc.]. [*Madrid?* ca. 1620]. bds.; fol. Memorial to king on protection of Indians. Medina (BHA) 6698. BL.   620/120

——. Señor. El licenciado Juan Ortiz de Cervantes, abogado . . . del Pirù . . . Dize; que en el reyno del Pirù solo ay universidad y estudio general . . . en Lima. [*Madrid?* ca. 1620?]. bds.; fol. Memorial to king of Spain, seeking establishment of a university at Cuzco. Medina (BHA) 6704. BL.
620/121

——. Señor. El licenciado Juan Ortiz de Cervantes, abogado . . . del Pirù . . . Dize; que en los pueblos de las diez leguas de [Cuzco, etc.]. [*Madrid?* ca. 1620]. bds.; fol. Memorial to king of Spain, requesting that one out of five Indians be released to maintain villages. Medina (BHA) 6699. BL.
620/122

——. Señor. El licenciado Juan Ortiz de Cervantes, abogado . . . del Pirù . . . Dize; que una de las mayores causas de la destruycion de aquel reyno, es, encomendar los Indios a los de acà. [*Madrid?* ca. 1620]. 2 lvs; fol. Medina (BHA) 6701. BL.   620/123

——. Señor. El licenciado Juan Ortiz de Cervantes, abogado . . . del Pirù . . . Dize; que V. Magestad tiene hecha merced a los decendientes de conquistadores y pobladores del Pirù . . . que en los cargos y oficios sean preferidos. [*Madrid?* ca. 1620?]. 2 lvs; fol. Memorial to king of Spain. Medina (BHA) 6703. BL.   620/124

Parisi, Antonio. Señor. Don Antonio Parisi, procurador del reyno de Chile, digo, que aviendo llegado à mis manos este memorial del padre Luis de Valdivia . . . por cumplir con mi oficio para servir à V.M. respondo en breve. [*Madrid?* ca. 1620?]. 12 numb. lvs; fol. For the memorial to which Parisi here replies, see entry for Valdivia below. Medina (Chile) 218; Streit II:1474.
620/125

Pérez de Nueros, Jacinto, S.J. Señor. Jacinto Perez de Nueros, religioso . . . residente en España con poderes de la provincia del Piru. [*Madrid:* ca. 1620?]. [15] p.; fol. Memorial to king of Spain urging merits of native-born clergy for Peru; cf. Ortiz de Cervantes *Informacion* of 1619. Medina (BHA) 6752. BL, Seville:B. Colombina.   620/126

Piò, Giovanni Michele. Delle vite de gli huomini illustri di S. Domenico. *Bologna: S. Bonomi,* 1620. 697 cols; fol. 1st publ., Bologna, 1607. Streit I:398; Palau 227138. ICN; BL, BN.   620/127

Plainte de la Nouvelle France dicte Canada, a la France sa germaine, pour servir de factum en une cause pandente [*sic*] au Conseil. [*Paris?* 1620?]. 15 p.; 8vo. Sabin 10543; Harrisse (NF) 42; JCB (3) II:98. RPJCB; BN (Lk12.774).   620/128

Porcacchi, Tommaso. L'isole più famose del mondo descritte da Thomaso Porcacchi . . . e intagliate da Girolamo Porro. *Padua: P. & F. Galignani,* 1620. 211 p.; illus., maps; fol. 1st publ., Venice, 1572; here anr impression of the 1604 edn above. Sabin 64152; Michel (Répertoire) VI:141: Palau 232896; JCB (3) II:148–49. CtY, DLC, IU, InU-L, MH, NN-RB, RPJCB; BL, BN.
620/129

Potosí, Bolivia. Gremio de Azogueros. Señor. Los azogueros dueños de minas, e ingenios de Potosi [etc.]. [*Madrid?* 1620?]. [10] p.; fol. Memorial to king of Spain on working of mines of Potosí. Medina (BHA) 6246. BL.   620/130

Remesal, Antonio de. Historia general de las Indias Ocidentales, y particular de la governacion de Chiapa, y Guatemala. *Madrid: F. Abarca de Angulo,* 1620. 784 p.; fol. A reissue of 1st, 1619, edn with title *Historia de la provincia de S. Vicente,* the above printed title leaf being here added. Sabin 69551; Medina (BHA) 704 (cf. VII:330); Streit II:1515; Pérez Pastor (Madrid) 1687. DLC, IMunS, MH, NN-RB, RPJCB; BL, BN.

620/131

Ríos Coronel, Hernando de los. Señor. Hernando de los Rios Coronel, procurador general de las islas Filipinas. [*Madrid?* ca. 1620?]. [4] p.; fol. Memorial to king of Spain, requesting that a fleet be sent for defense of Philippines from Dutch by way of the Cape of Good Hope because of delays inherent to route by way of Brazil, Chile, etc. InU-L; BL. 620/132

Rodríguez Bustamante, Sebastián. Señor. Sebastian Rodriguez Bustamante, vezino de Santa Marta de las Indias. [*Madrid?* 1620?]. 4 numb. lvs; fol. Memorial to king of Spain on problems of coinage. MH-BA.

620/133

Rondelet, Guillaume. Opera omnia medica. Nunc . . . opera J. Croqueri . . . repurgata. *Montpellier: P. & J. Chouët*, 1620. 1277 p.; 8vo. 1st publ., [Paris? 1563?], under title *Methodus curandorum omnium morborum corporis humani;* cf. 1601 edn. DNLM, NjP, PPC; BL. 620/134

Rosaccio, Giuseppe. Universale discrittione del teatro del cielo, et della terra. *Venice: G. B. Ciotti*, 1620. 141 p.; illus., maps; 8vo. 1st publ., Brescia, 1592, under title *Teatro del cielo e della terra.* Included are a map & description of America. IU. 620/135

Rowlands, Samuel. The night raven. *London: G. Eld, for J. Deane & T. Bailey*, 1620. 18 lvs; 4to. In verse. The poem 'The gull, and the domineering constable' mentions tobacco, as do those on 'An English cannibal' & 'Mistris Newfangle'. STC 21402. CSmH, DFo, NN-RB; Oxford:Bodl.

620/136

——. A paire of spy-knaves. [*London: G. Purslowe*, 1620?]. 4to. In verse. Includes poem 'Instructions given to a countrey clowne, to take tobacco, when he comes to towne'. STC 21404. BL (imp.). 620/137

Rubio, Antonio. Logica mexicana . . . Hoc est, Commentarii breviores . . . in universam Aristoteles Dialecticam. *Lyons: A. Pillehotte*, 1620. 683 p.; 8vo. 1st publ., Cologne, 1605. In this edn the index comprises 10 pages. Cf. Sabin 73860; Medina (BHA) 706;

Backer VII:281; Palau 280356. Seville:BU.

620/138

—[Anr edn]. *Lyons: A. Pillehotte*, 1620. 683 p. In this edn the index comprises 9 pages. Medina (BHA) 707. Seville:BU.

620/139

Sacchini, Francesco. Historiae Societatis Jesu pars secunda. *Antwerp:* 1620. *See* Jesuits *above.*

Sacro Bosco, Joannes de. Sphaera . . . emendata. Eliae Vineti . . . scholia. *Venice: Heirs of G. Scoto*, 1620. 168 p.; illus.; 8vo. 1st publ. with Vinet's *Scholia,* Paris, 1551; cf. 1601 edn above. Sabin 74807. CU, InU-L, MiU, NN-RB. 620/140

Santo Tomé, Venezuela. Señor. La ciudad de Santo Tome, e isla Trinidad de la . . . Guayana. [*Madrid?* ca. 1620?]. [4] p.; fol. Memorial to king of Spain seeking compensation for depredations of English corsairs in 1618. BL (Saint Thomas, City of).

620/141

Sardinha Mimoso, João, S.J. Relacion de la real tragicomedia con que los padres de la Compañia de Jesus, en su Collegio de S. Anton de Lisboa recibieron, a . . . Felipe II. de Portugal. *Lisbon: J. Rodríguez*, [1] 620. 163 numb. lvs; 4to. The play was written by Antonio de Sousa. Included is a section in which a ship captain 'announces the news of the discovery of Brazil. He has with him Tapuia and Aimore Indians, parrots and monkeys. They all sing a *Chorus brasilicus,* in Portuguese and Tupi. Next there is a dialogue between the King [D.Manoel], who speaks Portuguese, and a monkey who speaks alternately in Portuguese and Tupi'—Borba de Moraes. Sabin 69184; Borba de Moraes II:62–63; Backer IV: 1862–63; Palau 302072 (cf. 320757). ICN, InU-L, MH, RPJCB; BL, BN.

620/142

Sassonia, Ercole. De melancholia tractatus . . . Cui etiam adjectus est tractatus alius de lue venerea. *Venice: A. Polo [& F. Bolzetta]*, 1620. 30 p.; fol. The 'Tractatus . . . de lue venerea' 1st publ., Padua, 1597. Introduction of syphilis attributed to 'Indicarum congressus mulierum'; for it, treatment includes use of guaiacum, sarsaparilla, & sassafras. Wellcome:I:5801. DNLM, ICU; London:Wellcome. 620/143

Scaliger, Julius Caesar. Exotericarum exercitationum liber quintus decimus. *Hanau: Wechel Office, for D. & D. Aubry & C. Schleich,* 1620. 1074 p.; illus.; 8vo. 1st publ., Paris, 1557; cf. 1601 edn. DFo, ICN, MH; BN. 620/144

Scott, Thomas. Vox populi. Or Newes from Spain, translated according to the Spanish coppie. Which may serve to forewarn both England and the United Provinces how farre to trust to Spanish pretences. [*London?*] 1620. [25] p.; 4to. Included are refs to Spanish colonies in America and to Virginia & Bermuda. For the distinguishing features of this & the following edns, see the STC. See also W. W. Greg *Companion to Arber* (Oxford, 1967) p. 176–78. Sabin 78376; STC 22098; cf. Knuttel 3056. DFo, ICN, MH, MiU, NNH; BL. 620/145

—[Anr edn]. [*London?*] 1620. [25] p.; 4to. Sabin 78376n; STC 22098.5; Church 381; JCB (3) II:149. CSmH, DFo, IU, MH, NN-RB, RPJCB; Oxford:Exeter. 620/146

—[Anr edn]. [*London?*] 1620. [25] p.; 4to. Sabin 78376n; STC 22099. TxU; BL. 620/147

—[Anr edn]. [*London:*] 1620. [25] p.; 4to. STC 22100. DFo, MH, TxU; Oxford:Bodl. 620/148

—[Anr edn]. [*London:*] 1620. [25] p.; 4to. STC 22100.2. DFo, MH; BL. 620/149

—[Anr edn]. [*London:*] 1620. [25] p.; 4to. STC 22100.4. DFo, ICU, MH, TxU; Cambridge: UL. 620/150

—[Anr edn]. [*London:*] 1620. [25] p.; 4to. STC 22100.6; Church 380. CSmH, DFo, IU, MH, NN-RB; London:Lambeth. 620/151

—[Anr issue of preceding]. [*London:*] 1620. STC 22100.8. DFo, NNUT, RPJCB; Cambridge:King's. 620/152

Scotto, Benedetto. Deux cartes maritimes septentrionales ou sont figurez les trois voyages que les Holandois & Zellandois firent ez années 1594. 95. & 96. *Paris: N. Rousset,* 1620. 2 pts; maps; fol. In advancing merits of a northeast passage to Asia, adverts to Mexico & Panama. Also issued as pt of the author's *Globe maritime* of 1622. 620/153

Sennert, Daniel. Institutionum medicinae libri v . . . Editio secunda auctior. *Wittenberg: Heirs of J. Richter, for Z. Schürer, the Elder,* 1620. 1324 p.; illus., port.; 4to. 1st publ., Wittenberg, 1611. NNC. 620/154

Serrano, Martín. Copia de un memorial que se dio a su Magestad, y despues se remitio a las Cortes passadas el año de 619. [*Madrid?* 1620?]. [4] p.; fol. Included are refs to the resources of the New World and individuals who have served in Mexico & Peru. MH. 620/155

Smith, Capt. John. New Englands trials. Declaring the successe of 26. ships employed thither. *London: W. Jones,* 1620. [20] p.; 4to. On variant dedications, see the STC. Sabin 82833; Vail (Frontier) 44; STC 22792. CSmH, ICN; BL, Oxford:Bodl. 620/156

Sotomayor, Alonso de. Señor. Don Alonso de Sotomayor, dize, que las tierras . . . referidas en su relacion, se han visto por algunas partes, y por todas ellas se han reconocido estar muy pobladas de Indios. [*Madrid?* 1620?]. [4] p.; fol. Although Medina dated this [1606?], the British Library's later date is perhaps more likely. Cf. the following item. Sabin 87237; Medina (Chile) 200; Palau 320473. BL. 620/157

——. Señor. Don Alonso de Sotomayor, dize que son tan fuertes . . . las razones y causas que ay, para que se vean y abran las tierras que estan cerradas è incultas, convezinas al Pirù . . . se conocerà . . . ser una de las cosas mas importantes que . . . puede tener España. [*Madrid?* 1620?]. 3 lvs; fol. Cf. the preceding item. Sabin 87238; Medina (Chile) 199; Palau 320474. BL. 620/158

Spain. Consejo de las Indias. Assiento, y capitulacion que las señores Presidente y del Consejo real de las Indias, tomaron con los vezinos de . . . Cádiz, y Universidad de los mareantes de Sevilla sobre la cobrança y administracion del derecho de la averia, y despacho de las armadas, y flotas de las Indias, por tiempo de seys años. *Madrid: F. Correa de Montenegro,* 1620. 41 numb. lvs; fol. Cf. similar *assiento* of 1618. Sabin 2231; Pérez Pastor (Madrid) 1646; Palau 18675; JCB (3) II:144. RPJCB. 620/159

Spain. Laws, statutes, etc., 1598–1621 (Philip III). El Rey. Por quanto de ordinario se han ofrecido y ofrecen dudas en mi Consejo Real de las Indias. [*Madrid:*

1620]. bds.; fol. Decree concerning administration of justice in Spanish America. BL.					620/160

——. El Rey. Por quanto por cedula mia de dos de Otubre del año passado de seyscientos y ocho [etc.]. [*Madrid:* 1620?]. [2] p.; fol. Decree dated 28 Mar. 1620 on government of Spanish America. BL.					620/161

——. El Rey. Por quanto por cedula mia fecha en Madrid a catorze de Diziembre del año passado. [*Madrid:* 1620]. [4] p.; fol. Decree of 28 March 1620 concerning salable offices in Spanish Indies. BL.					620/162

——. El Rey. Por quanto por diferentes cedulas, leyes y ordenanças hechas para la buena governacion de mis Indias Occidentales [etc.]. [*Madrid?* 1620]. [6] p.; fol. Dated 12 Dec. 1619. BL.					620/163

Spain. Sovereigns, etc., 1598–1621 (Philip III). Instrucción y memoria de las relaciones que se han de hazer para la descripcion de las Indias. [*Madrid:* ca. 1620]. 3 p.; fol. Cf. similar instructions of 1577. Palau 120141.					620/164

Spain. Sovereigns, 1598–1621 (Philip III), addressee. Señor. El agravio que el principe de Esquilache, y el Arçobispo de Lima han intentado contra las religiones de santo Domingo, san Francisco, san Augustin [etc.]. [*Madrid?* 1620?]. 7 numb. lvs; fol. Includes 'Razones por las quales no conviene que se nombre jues Apostolico en las Indias, superior a todas las religiones'. BL.					620/165

Spanisch Mucken Pulver . . . Ein aussführlicher schöner Discurs; was gestalt sich Spanien . . . durch Mithülff der Jesuiten . . . unterstanden. [*Hannover?*] 1620. 108 p.; 4to. Excoriation of Spanish & Jesuit practices, including discussion of cruelty to Indians, citing Las Casas. Meulman 1700. NIC, PU; Ghent:BU.					620/166

Spilbergen, Joris van. Americae tomi undecimi appendix. Seu admirandae navigationis . . . per fretum Magellanicum & Mare meridionale . . . descriptio. *Frankfurt a. M.: J. Hofer, for J. T. de Bry,* 1620. 34 p.; illus., maps; fol. (Theodor de Bry's *America.* Pt 11. Appendix. Latin). Extracted & transl. from author's *Oost ende West-Indische Spiegel,* 1st publ., Leyden, 1619. Cf. Sabin 8784; Tiele-Muller p. 63; Church 172; JCB

(3) I:413–14. CSmH, DLC, ICN, NN-RB, RPJCB; BL, BN.					620/167

——. Appendix dess eilfften Theils Americae, das ist: Warhafftige Beschreibung der wunderbahren Schifffahrt . . . durch die Magellanische Strasse. . . . beschrieben durch M. Gotthard Arthus. *Oppenheim: H. Galler, for J. T. de Bry, at Frankfurt, a. M.,* 1620. 38 p.; illus., maps; fol. (Theodor de Bry's *America.* Pt 11. Appendix. German.) 1st publ. in Dutch, Leyden, 1619, under title *Oost ende West-Indische Spiegel.* Cf. Sabin 8784; Baginsky (German Americana) 150; Tiele-Muller p. 63; Church 198; JCB (3) I:415. CSmH, DLC, ICN, NN-RB, RPJCB; BL. BN.					620/168

——. Die siebenzehende Schiffart. Das ist: Eigentliche unnd warhaftige beschreibung der wunderbahren Reiss und Schiffart. *Frankfurt a. M.: J. Hofer, for Hulsius,* 1620. 93 p.; illus.; 4to. (Levinus Hulsius's *Sammlung von . . . Schiffahrten,* Pt 17). Transl. from J. van Spilbergen's *Oost ende West-Indische spiegel,* 1st publ., Leyden, 1619. Sabin 33670; Church 309; Tiele 1030n; JCB (3) I:466. CSmH, ICN, MH, MnU-B, NN-RB, RPJCB; BL, BN.					620/169

Strobelberger, Johann Stephan. Tractatus novus in quo de cocco baphica, et quae inde paratur confectionis alchermes recto usu disseritur. *Jena: J. Beithmann,* 1620. 54 numb. lvs; 4to. The French edn of which this is a translation has not been identified. Includes ref. to pearls found in West Indies citing José de Acosta, & to 'Moschus' (musk?) 'ex America Portugaliam [i.e., Brazil], & Inde ad nos affertur'. Wellcome I:6116. DNLM; BL, BN.					620/170

Sweerts, Emanuel. Florilegium amplissimum et selectissimum. *Amsterdam: J. Janszoon, the Younger,* 1620,'14. 2 v.; illus.; fol. 1st publ., Frankfurt a. M., 1612–14. Pritzel 9073n; Nissen (Bot.) 1921. MH, MH-A, RPB; BN.					620/171

Tabourot, Estienne. Les bigarrures et touches. *Rouen: J. Berthelin,* 1620. 5 pts; illus., ports; 12mo. In verse. 1st publ. in this collective edn, Paris, 1603, q.v. BN.					620/172

Tanner, Robert. A brief treatise of the use of the globe celestiall and terrestriall. *London: R. Field, for T. Man,* 1620. 54 p.; 8vo.

1st publ., London, 1616. STC 23673. DFo; BL.   620/173

Tapp, John. The seamans kalendar . . . Seventh edition. *London: E. Allde, for J. Tapp,* 1620. 48 lvs; illus.; 4to. 1st publ., London, 1602. STC 23680.5. BN.   620/174

Tassoni, Alessandro. Dieci libri di pensieri diversi . . . Aggiuntovi nuovamente il decimo libro . . . E corretti . . . in questa terza impressione. *Carpi: G. Vaschieri,* 1620. 584 p.; 4to. 1st publ., Modena, 1612, under title *Varieta di pensieri diversi.* In the 10th bk here added, chapt. xvi, on 'Agricoltura antica e moderna', corn (maize), 'sorte de grano portato dall'India Occidentali', is mentioned, while in chapt. xxv, on 'Geometri e cosmografi antichi e moderni', Columbus, Vespucci, Magellan, etc., are named. Puliatti (Tassoni) 4. CtY, ICN, MH; BL, BN.
620/175

Taylor, John, the Water-poet. Jack a Lent. *London: [G. Purslowe,] for J. T[rundle].,* 1620. 4to. 1st publ., [London, 1617?]. STC 23765.5. BL, London:Guildhall.
620/176

——. The praise of hemp-seed. *London: [E. Allde,] for H. Gosson; sold [by E. Wright?]* 1620. 24 lvs; 4to. In verse. Mentioned are the West Indies & Newfoundland, as well as tobacco, Columbus, Cortés, Magellan, Sir Francis Drake, etc. STC 23788; Arents (Add.) 194. CSmH, DFo, NN-A; BL.
620/177

Thou, Jacques Auguste de. Historiarum sui temporis ab anno Domini 1543. usque ad annum Domini 1607. Libri cxxxviii, quorum lxxx priores, multo quam antehac auctiores, reliqui lviii nunc primum prodeunt. *Geneva: P. de LaRovière,* 1620–21. 5 v.; fol. Includes earlier bks 1st publ., Paris, 1604 & 1606–9, here completed by bks lxxi–cxxxviii, containing extended accounts of the French, Dutch, & English (incl. Sir Francis Drake) in the New World. Brunet V:841. DLC, MH, NjP; BL, BN.   620/178

Torquemada, Antonio de. Giardino di fiori curiosi. *Venice: G. Alberti,* 1620. 402 p.; 8vo. 1st publ. in Spanish, Salamanca, 1570; as here transl. by Celio Malespina, Venice, 1604, q.v. Palau 334926. CtY.   620/179

Torsellino, Orazio, S.J. Epitomae historiarum libri x. *Lyons: J. Cardon & P. Cavellat,*

1620. 640 p.; 12mo. 1st publ., Rome, 1598. In bk 10, chapt. 4 mentions discovery of America as well as Vespucci, Mexico, & Brazil. Backer VIII:151. DLC; BN.
620/180

Turrillo, Alonso. El pleito que se ha començado a ver, que es entre el Capitan, y su Magestad, y las ciudades de Santa Fè y Cartagena, es sobre tres puntos, ò articulos. *[Madrid? ca. 1620?].* [4] p.; fol. On coinage of money in New World. Cf. entry under Bogotá above. Medina (BHA) 6333. BL.
620/181

Twisck, Pieter Janszoon. Chroniick van den Ondergangh der tyrannen . . . II. deel. *Hoorn:* 1620. *See the year* 1619.

Valdivia, Luis de, S.J. Señor. El padre Luys de Valdivia vice provincial de la Compañia de Jesus en . . . Chile. Digo, que la mayor parte de mi vida, he gastado en la conversion . . . del dicho reyno. *[Madrid? ca. 1620?].* 15 numb. lvs; 8vo. Memorial to king of Spain on conditions in Chile & treatment of Indians there. Sabin 98333; Medina (Chile) 219; Streit II:1529; JCB AR45:26–30. RPJCB; BL.   620/182

Vázquez de Serna, Juan. Libro intitulado Reduciones de oro, y señorage de plata, con las reglas, y tablas . . . de lo uno y de lo otro. *Cadiz: J. de Borja, for the Author,* 1620. 285 numb. lvs; 8vo. 'Declaracion del marco castellano, con que se pesa el oro, y la plata, y la diferencia que ay de la division de las pesas del oro a las pesas de la Plata', etc.: lvs 280–81. Palau 354285. ICN, NNH, NSyU; BL, BN.   620/183

Vega Carpio, Lope Félix de. Arcadia, prosas y versos. *Madrid: F. Correa de Montenegro, for A. Pérez,* 1620. 250 numb. lvs; 8vo. 1st publ., Madrid, 1598; cf. 1602 edns. Palau 356302. NNH; Madrid:BN.   620/184

Vege, Petrus de. Pax methodicorum . . . Accessit Conr. Gesneri Thesaurus Euonymi de remediis secretis. *Lyons: B. Vincent,* 1620. 2 pts; illus.; 16mo. Gesner's *Thesaurus,* 1st publ., Zurich, 1552, includes formulas employing guaiacum. Wellcome I:6522. DNLM, MnU; London:Wellcome.
620/185

Velasco, Diego de. Señor. Advertencias que . . . Diego de Velasco, provincial de la provincia del Cuzco . . . tiene hechas sobre los excessos que se cometen por el puerto de Buenos ayres, y los inconvencientes . . . que se siguen de no tomar medio eficaz en ceralle como V[uestra]. M[agestad]. siempre ha procurado. [*Madrid?* 1620?]. 4 lvs; fol. Sabin 98789; Medina (BHA) 6955; Palau 357082. BL. 620/186

——. Señor. Descubrimiento del camino que la ciudad de Quito, y su reyno, ha pretentido abrir para el puerto, y baya de Caracas. [*Madrid?* 1620?]. 2 lvs; fol. Sabin 98790; Medina (BHA) 6953; Palau 357082II. MnU-B; BL, Santiago, Chile:BN. 620/187

Venner, Tobias. Via recta ad vitam longam, or A plaine philosophical discourse of such things, as make for health. *London: E. Griffin, for R. More,* 1620. 4to. Includes mention of potato. STC 24643. DFo, IEN-M, MH, NNNAM; BL. 620/188

Virginia Company of London. By the Treasuror, Councell and Company for Virginia. [*London: F. Kingston,* 1620]. bds.; fol. Orders erection of guest house & provision of clergyman in every borough; dated 17 May 1620. Sabin 99876; Clayton-Torrence 36; STC 24841. NN-RB; Cambridge:Magdalene. 620/189

——. A note of the shipping, men, and provisions, sent to Virginia . . . 1619. [*London: F. Kingston,* 1620]. [4] p.; fol. Includes information to April 1620. Sabin 99882; Clayton-Torrence 31; Vail (Frontier) 50; STC 24842. NN-RB. 620/190

Visscher, Roemer. Sinnepoppen. *Amsterdam: W. J. Blaeu* [ca. 1620]. [367] p.; illus.; 12mo. 1st publ., Amsterdam, 1614. Vries 54; Arents (Add.) 196. ICN, NN-A; Leyden: MNL. 620/191

Wecker, Johann Jakob. Practica medicinae generalis. *Basel:* 1620. 1st publ., Basel, 1585; cf. 1602 edn. BL. 620/192

Whitbourne, Sir Richard. A discourse and discovery of New-found-land, with many reasons to proove how worthy and beneficiall a plantation may there be made. *London: F. Kingston, for W. Barret,* 1620. 69 p.; 4to. Sabin 103330; STC 25372; Church 383; JCB (3) II:151. CSmH, CtY, DLC, ICN, MH, MiU-C, NN-RB, RPJCB; BL. 620/193

Wright, Thomas. The passions of the minde. *London: A. M[athewes].,* *for Anne Helme,* 1620. 350 p.; 4to. 1st publ., London, 1601. STC 26041. DFo, IU, KU; Oxford: Bodl. 620/194

1621

Acosta, José de, S.J. Histoire naturelle et morale des Indes, tant Orientales, qu'Occidentales . . . Composee en castillan . . . & traduicte . . . par Robert Regnauld . . . Derniere edition, reveue, et corrigee de nouveau. *Paris: A. Tiffaine,* 1621. 375 numb. lvs; 8vo. 1st publ. in French, Paris, 1598; cf. 1606 edn above. Sabin 125n; Streit II:1521. NN-RB. 621/1

Aldrovandi, Ulisse. Quadrupedum omnium bisulcorum historia. *Bologna: S. Bonamo,* 1621. 1040 p. ; illus.; fol. In chapt. xxvii, 'De cervo', P. M. Anghiera on deer noted at 'Xapita, novi orbis regionem' is mentioned. Nissen (Zool.) 76. CLU-C, ICJ, MB, NN, PPC, RPB; BL, BN. 621/2

Alemán, Mateo. Le gúeux, ou La vie de Guzman d'Alfarache . . . Version nouvelle & fidelle d'espagnol en françois. Premiere partie. *Paris: G. Alliot,* 1621. 2 pts; 8vo. 1st publ. as here transl. by Jean Chapelain, Paris, 1619. Laurenti (Nov. pic. esp.) 617. BL. 621/3

——. Vita del picaro Gusmano d'Alfarace . . . tradotta . . . da Barezze. *Milan: G. B. Bidelli,* 1621. 2 v.; 8vo. Includes both 1st & 2nd pts, the former 1st publ., Madrid, 1599 (cf. 1601 edn above), the 2nd, Lisbon, 1604. Laurenti (Nov. pic. esp.) 713; Palau 6778. NNH, NjP; BN. 621/4

Avity, Pierre d', sieur de Montmartin. Wereld spiegel waer in vertoont word de beschrijvinge der rijken, staten ende vorstendommen. *Amsterdam: J. E. Cloppenburgh,* 1621. 695 p.; ports, maps; fol. Transl. from the author's *Les estats, empires et principautez de monde,* 1st publ., St. Omer, 1614. The American refs appear here on p. 150. Cf. Sabin 2498 & 18911. RPJCB (imp.). 621/5

Bacon, Francis, viscount St Albans. Essays politiques et moraux . . . Mis en nostre langue par J. Baudouin. *Paris: F. Julliot,* 1621. 162 numb. lvs; 12mo. 1st publ. as here

transl., Paris, 1619. Gibson (Bacon) 46; Shaaber (Brit. auth.) B31. MH: BL, BN.
621/6

——. Saggi morali . . . data in luce da sig. cavalier Andrea Cioli. *Bracciano: A. Fei, for P. Totti,* 1621. 475 p.; 12mo. 1st publ. as here transl., Florence, 1619. Gibson (Bacon) 39; Shaaber (Brit. auth.) B33. DFo; Munich:StB.
621/7

—[Anr edn]. *Venice: P. Dusinelli,* 1621. 259 p.; 12mo. Gibson (Bacon) 40; Shaaber (Brit. auth.) B32. BL, Munich:StB.
621/8

Bartholin, Caspar. Epigrammata extemporanea quae juvenis inter peregrinandum fudit . . . Ex autoris dispersis chartis collecta à M. Christ. Pet. *Copenhagen: H. Waldkirch,* 1621. 12mo. Poem on verso of lf D5 refers to America. CtY; BL.
621/9

Berettari, Sebastiano, S.J. Vita del p. Gioseppo Anchietto, religioso della Compagnia di Gesù apostolo del Brasile. *Turin: Heirs of G. D. Tarino,* 1621. 205 p.; 12mo. Transl. from the author's *Josephi Anchietae . . . vita,* 1st publ., Lyons, 1617. Sabin 4830; Medina (BHA) 652n (II:161); Borba de Moraes I:86; Streit II:2386; Backer I:1326. MBAt, NN-RB; BN.
621/10

Blasco de Lanuza, Vincenzio. Historias ecclesiasticas y seculares de Aragon, en que se continuan los annales de Çurita, y tiempos de Carlos V. *Saragossa: J. de Lanaja y Quartanet,* 1621, '19. 2 v.; fol. Included are accounts of Columbus, Magellan's circumnavigation, etc. Cf. Sabin 38949. CaBVaU, DLC; BN.
621/11

Brandon, Lorenço. Excelmo señor. Siendo la materia del valor de la plata tan importante [etc.]. *Madrid:* 1621. 59 p.; 4to. Memorial to king of Spain; drugs & silver from the New World are mentioned. Palau 34462. MH-BA; BL.
621/12

Brief gheschreven uyt Vranckryck . . . nopende eenighe handelinghe van Francoys Aerssens. [*The Hague?*] 1621. 8 p.; 4to. Expresses wish not to harm Spanish subjects in Europe, East or West Indies, but merely to negotiate for place in free commerce. The initial 'S' on p. 1 is unadorned in this edn. NN.
621/13

—[Anr edn]. Brief gescheven. [*The Hague?*] 1621. 8 p.; 4to. The initial 'S' on p. 1 is

enclosed within factotum block. Knuttel 3222. NN; The Hague:KB.
621/14

Buchanan, George. Poemata quae supersunt omnia. *Saumur: J. Burel, for C. Girard & D. Lerpinière,* 1621,'20. 3 pts; 12mo. 1st publ. as here constituted, Edinburgh, 1615. Shaaber (Brit. auth.) B703; Rahir (Les Elzevier) 3361. BN.
621/15

—[Anr issue]. [*Saumur: J. Burel, for*] *A. Elsevier, at Amsterdam,* 1621. Shaaber (Brit. auth.) B704; Rahir (Les Elzevier) 154; Willems (Les Elzevier) 182. CU, MH, PU; BN.
621/16

Burton, Robert. The anatomy of melancholy. *Oxford: J. Lichfield & J. Short, for H. Cripps,* 1621. 783 p.; 4to. Included are numerous scattered refs to the Americas; see the index provided by Floyd Dell & Paul Jordan Smith in their edn of the *Anatomy,* New York, 1927. Madan (Oxford) 1621:2; STC 4159. CSmH, CtY, DLC, IU, InU-L, MH, MiD, NN-RB, PBL, RPB; BL.
621/17

Camerarius, Philipp. The walking librarie, or Meditations and observations historical . . . Written in Latin . . . and done into English by John Molle. *London: A. Islip; sold by J. Partridge,* 1621. 403 p.; fol. Transl. from pt 1 of Camerarius's *Meditations historiques,* 1st publ., Paris, 1603, itself transl. by Simon Goulart from pts 1 & 2 of Camerarius's *Operae horarum subcisivarum,* 1st publ., Altdorf, 1591, & Frankfurt a. M., 1601. Cf. STC 4528. BL.
621/18

—[Anr issue]. *London: A. Islip,* 1621. STC 4528; Arents 145-A. CSmH, DFo, IU, MiU-C, NN-A; Oxford:Bodl.
621/19

—[Anr issue]. The living librarie. *London: A. Islip,* 1621. STC 4529; Arents (Add.) 197. CSmH, CtY, DFo, ICU, MH, MnU-B, NN-RB; BL.
621/20

Caron, Noel de. Nieus uyt Engelandt gheschreven door den heer ambassadeur . . . aende . . . Staten Generael der Vereenichde Nederlanden. [*The Hague?*] 1621. [6] p.; 4to. While primarily on East Indian commerce, relates also to the West-Indische Compagnie. Knuttel 3236. MnU-B; BL (Caron), The Hague:KB.
621/21

Carranza, Alonso. Por D. Luis Colon de Toledo, con D. Alvaro Colon de Portugal, conde de Gelbes . . . y don Diego Colon de Portugal . . . Sobre la propriedad del estado de Veragua que fundò don Christoval Colon primer descubridor, conquistador i almirante de las Indias. [*Madrid:* 1621]. 31 numb. lvs; fol. Palau 44940; JCB (3) II:152. NN-RB, RPJCB.				621/22

Casas, Bartolomé de las, O.P. Bp of Chiapa. Den vermeerderden spieghel de Spaensche tierannije-geschiet in Westindien. *Amsterdam: C. L. van der Plasse,* 1621. [104] p.; illus.; 4to. 1st publ. in Dutch, [Antwerp?], 1578; cf. 1607 edn above & present printer's 1620 edn with title *Den spiegel der Spaensche tierannije.* Here added are a 'Cort sommarisch verhael vande ontdeckinge vande Nieuwe-Wereldt ende Wereldt ende West-Indien, deur Christoffel Columbus' & a 'Corte Beschrijvinge der lande ende Provintien van America'. Sabin 11260; Medina (BHA) 1085n (II:477); Hanke/Giménez 517; Tiele-Muller 314; Streit I:403. DLC, NN-RB; BL.				621/23

—[Anr state?]. *Amsterdam: C. L. van der Plasse,* 1621. This issue differs from the above by its disfigured imprint date, which some bibliographers have interpreted as a scribal correction to 1623. It more likely represents a defect in the plate used for the engraved t.p. As with the above, the present issue has a 4-line title to the 'Prologhe', and the work ends with 'Finis' in uppercase gothic type. Cf. Sabin 11260; cf. Medina (BHA) 1085n (II:477); Hanke/Giménez 519; cf. Tiele-Muller 314 & 315; JCB (3) II:177. RPJCB.				621/24

—[Anr edn]. *Amsterdam: C. L. van der Plasse,* 1621. [104] p.; illus.; 4to. Imprint date disfigured as in the above. Here the 'Prologe' has a 6-line title; the work ends with 'Finis' in uppercase roman type. Sabin 11260n; Medina (BHA) 1085n (II:477); Tiele-Muller 315; JCB (3) II:177. DLC, NN-RB, RPJCB.				621/25

Catholic Church. Commisarius Generalis Cruciatae. Instrucción y forma que se ha de tener y guardar la publicación de la Bula de la Santa Cruzada en el arzobispado de México y obispados de Mechoacan, Gauxaca, Taxcala, Nueva Galicia, Yucatán Guatemala, Cuba, Jamayca y Filipinas. *Madrid:*

1621. 7 numb. lvs; fol. 1st (?) publ., [Barcelona? 1537?]; cf. 1608 edn. Palau 120142.				621/26

Cervantes Saavedra, Miguel de. Les nouvelles. *Paris: J. Richer,* 1621. 2 v.; 8vo. A reissue of the printer's 1620 edn with imprint date in v. 1 altered. BL.				621/27

Charron, Jacques de. Histoire universelle de toutes nations, et specialement des Gaulois ou François. *Paris: T. Blaise,* 1621. 1378 p.; fol. Included are numerous refs to the Americas. DLC (imp.); BL, BN.				621/28

Colle, Giovanni. Elucidarium anatomicum et chirurgicum ex Graecis, Arabibus et Latinis selectum. *Venice: E. Deuchino,* 1621,'20. 2 pts; fol. In pt 2, chapt. 'De Lue gallica brevis elucidatio' discusses American source, prescribing guaiacum & sarsaparilla for its treatment. CtY-M, ICJ; BL.				621/29

Discours. Daer in kortelijck ende grondigh wert verthoont, hoeveel de Vereenighde Nederlanden gheleghen is aen de Oost ende West-Indische navigatie. *Arnhem: J. Janszoon,* 1621. See the *Missive. Daer in kortelijck . . . wert verthoont* below.

Donne, John. The first anniversarie. *London: A. Mathewes, for T. Dewe,* 1621. 2 pts; 8vo. In verse. 1st publ., London, 1611, under title *An anatomy of the world.* STC 7024; Keynes (Donne) 76. MH; BL.				621/30

Du Bartas, Guillaume Salluste, seigneur. Bartas his devine weekes and workes . . . with a compleat collection of all the other workes translated and written by Josuah Sylvester. *London: H. Lownes,* 1621,'20. 1215 p.; illus., port.; fol. In verse. 1st publ. as thus transl. by Josuah Sylvester, London, 1605, here with additional text, including Sylvester's own poem 'Tobacco battered'. For variants, see the STC. STC 21653. CSmH, CtY, DFo, ICU, InU-L, MH, MiU, NN-RB, PPL, RPB; BL.				621/31

——. Wercken. [*Zwolle:* 1621]. 2 v.; illus., port.; 4to. Transl. by Zacharias Heyns from Du Bartas's *La sepmaine,* 1st publ., Paris, 1578, and his *Seconde sepmaine,* 1st publ., Paris, 1584; cf. year 1601. Holmes (DuBartas) I:108 no. 12. MH; BN.				621/32

——. A learned summary upon the famous poem of William of Saluste, lord of Bartas

. . . Translated out of French, by T[homas]. L[odge]. *London: [G. Purslowe,] for J. Grismand,* 1621. 2 pts; fol. Transl. from the illicit edn 1st publ., Paris, 1582, under title *Commentaires et annotations sur La sepmaine,* with notes, etc., by Simon Goulart, derived from the latter's Geneva, 1581, edn published under title *La sepmaine.* Included are numerous refs to New World in both text & commentary. STC 21666. CSmH, CtY, DFo, ICN, MH; BL. 621/33

Enchiridion practicum medico-chirurgicum, sive De internorum externorumque morborum curatione . . . tractatus duo. *Geneva: P. de LaRovière,* 1621. 495 p.; 8vo. Included is Antoine Chaumette's *Enchiridion chirurgicum,* 1st publ., Paris, 1560, with discussion of use of guaiacum for treatment of syphilis. CtHT, DNLM, NIC. 621/34

Esternod, Claude d'. L'espadon satyrique . . . Seconde edition. *Lyons: J. Lautret,* 1621. 143 p.; 8vo. In verse. 1st publ., Lyons, 1619. Cioranescu (XVII) 28487. Versailles:BM. 621/35

Estienne, Charles. Dictionarium historicum, geographicum, poeticum. [*Cologny:*] *S. Crispin,* 1621. 1132 cols; 4to. 1st publ. in this enl. edn, Lyons, 1595; cf. 1601 edn. MH, OU. 621/36
—[Anr edn]. *Yverdun: Société Caldoresque (P. de Candolle),* 1621. 2042 cols; 4to. BN. 621/37

Ferdinandi, Epifanio. Centum historiae, seu Observationes, et casus medici. *Venice: T. Baglioni,* 1621. 352 p.; fol. Hist. 17, 'casus decimus septimus, morbi gallici' discusses American origins of syphilis at length, advancing thesis 'ubi Deus opt. Max. permisit fieri morbos, statim eorum creavit remedia, s[cilicet]. lignum sanctum [guaiacum], salsam [sarsaparilla], Chinamque [& ginseng],' Discussed is use of guaiacum, sarsaparilla, & sassafras for treating syphilis. Other 'historiae' call for similar uses of guaiacum, sassafras, sarsaparilla, & tobacco. Wellcome I:2190. CtY-M, DNLM, ICJ, NNNAM, PPC; BL, BN. 621/38

Fernández Navarrete, Pedro. Discursos politicos. *Barcelona: S. de Cormellas,* 1621. 80 numb. lvs; 4to. Includes refs to 'carrera de Indias' (lf 13v), rewards given Hernando Cortés by Ferdinand & Isabella (lf 77r) and to the Consejo de las Indias (lf 79v). Reprinted, Madrid, 1626, under title *Conservacion de monarquias.* Palau 89491. CU, MH, MoSM, NNH, PU; BL. 621/39

Figueira, Luiz. Arte da lingua brasilica. *Lisbon: M. da Silva* [1621]. 91 numb. lvs; 12 mo. Borba de Moraes I:263; Streit II:2394n. Lisbon:BN, Rio de Janeiro:BN. 621/40

Fracastoro, Girolamo. Operum pars prior -[posterior]. *Geneva: S. Crespin,* 1621. 3 pts; diagrs; 8vo. 1st publ. as here collected, Venice, 1555. Includes the author's 'De contagione', 1st publ., Venice, 1546, in his *De sympathia . . . rerum,* with discussion of American origin of syphilis. Baumgartner (Fracastoro) 37. CtY-M, DNLM, IU, NNNAM, PSC; London: Wellcome, BN. 621/41

Fragoso, Juan. Cirugia universal, aora nuevamendada, y añadida en esta sexta impression. *Alcalá de Henares: Heirs of J. Gracián,* 1621. 685 p.; fol. 1st publ., Madrid, 1581; cf. 1607 edn. DNLM; BN. 621/42

France. Conseil d'état. Arrests, commissions et privileges du Conseil du Roy, pour l'establissement de la Royale & general compagnie du commerce. *Paris: B. Martin,* 1621. 16 p.; illus.; 8vo. Maggs:French ser., Cat. 8, no. 3; JCB AR38:28. RPJCB. 621/43

Gaultier, Jacques. Table chronologique de l'estat du christianisme . . . jusques à l'année MDXX . . . reveue pour la troisiesme fois . . . par l'autheur. *Lyons: Amy de Polier, for P. Rigaud,* 1621. 881 p.; fol. 1st publ., Lyons, 1609. Backer III:1275; Cioranescu (XVII) 32622. BN. 621/44

Gaytán de Torres, Manuel. Relacion, y vista de ojos que Don Manuel Gaytan de Torres Ventiquatro de la ciudad de Xerez, haze a su Magestad en el Real Consejo de las Indias, por comission que para ello tuvo de las minas de cobre que ay en las serranias de Cocorote, provincia de Veneçuela. [*Madrid:*] 1621. 22 numb. lvs; fol. Medina (BHA) 714. BL. 621/45

Goulart, Simon. The wise vieillard, or old man. Translated out of French . . . by . . . T. W[illiamson?]. *London: J. Dawson,* 1621. 205 p.; illus.; 4to. Transl. from Goulart's *Le sage vieillard,* 1st publ., Lyons, 1605. Jones (Goulart) 60(c); STC 12136. CLU-C,

CtY, DFo, ICN, IU, RPB (imp.): BL, Geneva:Bibl. Mus. de la Reformation.
621/46

—[Anr issue]. The wise old man. *London: N. Bourne,* 1621. A reissue, with cancel t.p., of the preceding. STC 12137. DFo; Dublin: Marsh's. 621/47

Great Britain. Sovereigns, etc., 1603–1625 (James I). James, by the grace of God . . . Whereas wee are credibly [etc., 19 Jan. 1620, i.e., 1621]. *London:* [*E. Allde, for*] *R. Wood & T. Symcock* [1621]. bds.; fol. Brief for collections on behalf of Anne Challons, whose husband, Capt. Henry Challons, on a Virginia voyage had been captured by Spaniards, losing his ship. STC 8652; Crawford (Roy. procl.) 8652. London:Soc. of Antiquaries. 621/48

——. Whereas at the humble suit and request of sundry. *London: R. Barker & J. Bill,* 1620 [i.e., 1621]. bds.; fol. Suspends permission granted for lotteries to benefit Virginia Company. Sabin 99843; Crawford (Roy. procl.) 1307; Brigham (Roy. procl.) 31–32; STC 8660. CSmH, RPJCB: London:Soc. of Antiquaries. 621/49

Greene, Robert. Theeves falling out. *London: B. Alsop, for H. Bell,* 1621. 4to. 1st publ., London, 1592; cf. 1615 edn. STC 12237. London:Guildhall, Oxford:Bodl. 621/50

Greevous grones for the poore. *London:* [*W. Jaggard,*] *for M. Sparke,* 1621. 22 p.; 4to. Dedicated to the Virginia Company, praised for its charitable intent and for offering opportunities for the poor as colonists. Authorship has been attributed to Thomas Dekker & to Michael Sparke. In some copies lf D2 is missigned C2. Sabin 88961; Vail (Frontier) 51; STC 12391; Church 387. CSmH, CtY, DLC, ICN, MiU-C, BL. 621/51

Guicciardini, Francesco. La historia d'Italia . . . di nuovo riveduta et corretta per Francesco Sansovino. *Geneva: J. Stoer,* 1621. 2 v.; 8vo. 1st publ., Florence, 1561; cf. 1604 edn. Michel (Répertoire) IV:101. BN.
621/52

—[Anr issue]. [*Geneva?*] *J. Stoer,* 1621. Michel (Répertoire) IV:101. MH; BN. 621/53

Gysius, Johannes. De spaensche tiranije gheschiet in Neder-Lant. *Amsterdam: C. L. van der Plasse,* 1621. 113 p.; illus.; 4to. 1st publ. as here abridged from the author's

Oorsprong en voortgang der Nederlandtscher beroerten, Amsterdam, 1620. Normally bound with, as issued, Las Casas's *Den vermeerderden Spieghel der Spaensche tierannije in Westindien* of this year. Authorship erroneously attributed to C. L. van der Plasse. Cf. Meulman 1728. CSmH, NN-RB. 621/54

Heylyn, Peter. Microcosmus, or A little description of the great world. A treatise historicall, geographicall, politicall, theologicall. *Oxford: J. Lichfield & J. Short,* 1621. 317 (i.e., 417) p.; 4to. 'Of America': p. 400–417. Sabin 31656; Madan (Oxford) 1621:4; STC 13276; JCB (3) II:153. CSmH, CtY, DFo, NN-RB, RPJCB; BL. 621/55

Hughes, Lewis. A plaine and true relation of the goodnes of God towards the Sommer Ilands. *London: E. Allde,* 1621. 24 lvs; 4to. STC 13920; Arents (Add.) 199; Church 383. CSmH, NN-A; BL. 621/56

Illescas, Gonzalo de. Segunda parte de la Historia pontifical y catolica. *Barcelona: S. de Cormellas,* 1621. 364 numb. lvs; fol. 1st publ. with American materials, Barcelona, 1596; cf. 1602 edn. MnU. 621/57

Jesuits. Historiae Societatis Jesu pars prima . . . Auctore Nicolao Orlandino. *Cologne: A. Hierat,* 1621. 578 p.; fol. 1st publ., Rome, 1615. Borba de Moraes I:119; Streit I:405.
621/58

Jesuits. Historiae Societatis Jesu pars secunda . . . auctore r. p. Francisco Sachino. *Cologne: A. Hierat,* 1621. 578 p.; fol. 1st publ., Antwerp, 1620. Borba de Moraes II:225; Streit I:406. 621/59

Keckermann, Bartholomaeus. Systema compendiosum totius mathematices. *Hanau: P. Antonius,* 1621. 607 p.; illus., map; 8vo. 1st publ. as here collected, Hanau, 1617. JCB (3) II:153–54. CU, ICU, MiU, NN-RB, RPJCB; London:Wellcome. 621/60

Liñán y Verdugo, Antonio. Aviso de los peligros que hay en la vida de corte: novelas morales y ejemplares. *Madrid: Widow of A. Martín,* 1621. 148 numb. lvs; 4to. 1st publ., Madrid, 1620, under title *Guia y avisos de forasteros;* here a reissue with cancel t.p.? Palau 138644. 621/61

—[Anr issue]. Guia y aviso de forasteros, a donde debaxo de novelas morales se le avisa y advierte. *Madrid: Widow of A. Martín, for M. de Silis,* 1621. Like the preceding, a

reissue of the 1621 edn with cancel t.p.?
Palau 138645. 621/62

López, Juan, O.P., Bp. Quinta parte de la
Historia de Santo Domingo, y de su Orden
de Predicatores. *Valladolid: J. de Rueda, 1621.*
451 numb. lvs; fol. Continues 4th pt, Valladolid, 1615. Includes accounts of Dominican missions in Spanish America. Streit
I:404; Alcocer (Valladolid) 663; Palau
140141. Granada:BU, Rome:Bibl. Casanatense. 621/63

Markham, Gervase. Hungers prevention:
or, The whole arte of fowling. *London: A.
Math[ewes]., for Anne Helme & T. Langley,*
1621. 285 p.; 8vo. Includes ref. to Virginia
plantation, 'the glorious star of example in
the South'. Poynter (Markham) 25.1; STC
17362. CSmH, CtY, DFo, ICN, MH; BL. 621/64

Marquardus, Joannes. Practica medicinalis
theorica empirica morborum internorum
. . . Huic accesserunt Institutionum chirurgicarum libri quinque cum practica chirurgica. Authore Sebastiano Castalione
[i.e., Cortilio]. *Cologne: P. Henning, 1621.*
705 p.; 8vo. 1st publ., Speyer, 1589; cf.
1610 edn. Wellcome I:4082a. London:
Wellcome. 621/65

Martyn, Joseph. New epigrams, and a satyre.
London: G. Eld, 1621. [66] p.; 4to. In verse.
Epigram 40 is 'To Verinus a Tobacco taker';
epigram 49 mentions tobacco. STC 17525;
Arents (Add.) 200. CSmH, DFo, NN-A; BL. 621/66

Mattioli, Pietro Andrea. I discorsi . . . nelli
sei libri di Pedacio Dioscoride . . . della
materia medicinale. *Venice: A. Muschio, for
M. Ginammi, 1621.* 843 p.; illus.; fol. 1st
publ., as here transl. from Latin; Venice,
1555; cf. 1604 edn above. Cf. Pritzel 5988n;
Nissen (Bot.) 1304n; Michel (Répertoire)
V:152. DNLM, NNBG; BL, Ajaccio:BM. 621/67

Mercator, Gerardus. Atlas minor . . . à J.
Hondius . . . illustratus. *Arnhem: J. Janszoon,*
1621. 684 p.; maps; obl. 12mo. 1st publ.,
Amsterdam, 1607. Sabin 47887n; Koeman
(Me) 193; Phillips (Atlases) 435. DLC, ICU,
MH, MiU-C, NNH; Marburg:StB. 621/68

Merula, Paulus. Cosmographiae generalis libri tres. *Amsterdam: H. Hondius, 1621 [colo-
phon: Leyden: I. Elsevier, for J. Hondius*

[*at Amsterdam*] 1620]. 1075 p.; illus., maps;
fol. 1st publ., Leyden, 1605. Willems (Les
Elzevier) 188; Rahir (Les Elzevier) 160;
Tiele 751n. CtY, DLC, ICN, InU, MiU-C,
NN-RB; BL, BN. 621/69

Missive. Daer in kortelijck ende grondigh
wert verthoont, hoeveel de Vereenighde
Nederlanden gheleghen is aen de Oost
ende West-Indische navigatie. *Arnhem: J.
Janszoon, 1621.* [36] p.; 4to. For a continuation of these arguments, cf. the *Anderde discours,* [Amsterdam?], 1622, & the *Derde discours. By forma van missive,* [Amsterdam],
1622. Sabin 49557; Asher 93; cf. Jameson
(Usselinx) p. 74n; Knuttel 3237. CSmH,
DLC, NN-RB, The Hague:KB. 621/70

—[Anr edn]. . . . eerst tot Arnhem by Jan
Jansz. *Amsterdam: B. Janszoon, 1621.* [28] p.;
illus.; 4to. Sabin 49558; Borba de Moraes
II:65; Asher 92; Knuttel 3238; JCB (3)
II:154. RPJCB; The Hague:KB. 621/71

—[Anr edn]. Discours. Daer in kortelijck ende
grondigh wert verthoont, hoeveel de Vereenighde Nederlanden gheleghen is aen de
Oost ende West-Indische navigatie. *Arnhem:
J. Janszoon, 1621.* [36] p.; 4to. Sabin 20233
(& 102890); Asher 94. DLC, MnU-B, NN-
RB, ViU; Leyden:B. Thysiana. 621/72

Missive van twee Indiaensche coninghen
aen den Vorst Mauritius van Oranje, by
dwelcke sy versoecken dat haere soonen
. . . in de Christl. religie mochten opge-
trocken worden. *The Hague: A. Meuris, 1621.*
4 p.; 4to. Sabin 49569; Petit 1320. Ley-
den:B. Thysiana. 621/73

Nederlandsche West-Indische Compagnie.
De ghemeene directeurs, ghestelt tottet formeren vande capitalen vande West-Indische Compagnie. [*Amsterdam? 1621*]. bds.;
fol. Sabin 102925. NN-RB. 621/74

—[Anr edn]. De gemeene directeurs. [*Amsterdam: 1621*]. bds.; fol. Knuttel 3234. The
Hague:KB. 621/75

——. Orders and articles granted by the . . .
States General . . . concerning the erecting
of a West India Companie. [*London:*] 1621.
[18] p.; 4to. Transl. from the *Ordonnantien
ende articulen* below. Sabin 57498 (&
102903); Borba de Moraes II:118; STC
18460; Church 118. CSmH, CtY, DFo, NN-
RB; BL. 621/76

——. Ordonnantien ende articulen beraemt

by de . . . Staten Generael . . . op het toe rusten ende toestellen, van eene West-Indische Compagnie. [*Amsterdam:*] 1621. [16] p.; 4to. This edn has woodcut of ship with sea monster on t.p. Cf. Sabin 57532–33 & 102905–5A; Borba de Moraes II:119; Knuttel 3229; Meulman 8955. [Edn uncertain:] CSmH, CtY, DLC; BL, The Hague:KB.

621/77

—[Anr edn]. [*Amsterdam?*] 1621. [16] p.; 4to. Has reading 'toe-rusten ende toe-stellen'; type-ornament appears on t.p. Meulman 1784; cf. Tiele (Pamfletten) 1863. Ghent:BU.

621/78

—[Anr edn]. [*Amsterdam?*] 1621. [16] p.; 4to. Vignette on t.p. of woman's head with cornucopia at both sides. Sabin 102905n. NN.

621/79

—[Anr edn]. [*Amsterdam?*] 1621. [16] p.; 4to. This edn has engraving on t.p. showing ships entering port of Hoorn. Sabin 102905n. Knuttel 3230; Tiele (Pamfletten) 1864; Petit 1318. The Hague:KB, Leyden:B. Thysiana.

621/80

—[Anr edn]. Octroy by de . . . Staten Generael, verleent aende West-Indische Compagnie. *The Hague: H. Jacobszoon van Wouw,* 1621. [20] p.; 4to. Sabin 56665; Stokes (Manhattan) VI:258; Knuttel 3232; JCB (3) II:154; JCB AR20:3. DLC, NN, RPJCB; The Hague:KB.

621/81

——. West Indianische compagnia: das ist: Artickel und Satzungen der . . . : General Staden in den Unirten Niderländischen Provintzen wegen Anstellung und Ausrüstung einer West Indianischen Compagni oder Gesellschaft . . . Auss niederländischer Sprache . . . ubersetzet. *Frankfurt a. M.: J. Schmidlin,* 1621. [20] p.; 4to. Transl. from the *Ordonnantien ende articulen . . . op het toe rusten ende toestellen,* 1st publ., [Amsterdam], 1621, and the *West-Indische Compaignie; de gemeene directeurs,* 1st publ., [Amsterdam: 1621]. Sabin 102923; Knuttel 3231. The Hague:KB

621/82

——. West-Indische Compagnie. [*Amsterdam?* 1621]. bds.; fol. Report, with blank spaces, of the administrators undertaking various posts. Not to be confused with a similar title described under year 1634. Knuttel 3235. The Hague:KB.

621/83

Nederlandsche West-Indische Compagnie.

Kamer Zealand. Ordre ende Reglement op de Comptoiren. *Middelburg: Widow & Heirs of S. Moulert* [1621?]. bds.; fol. Meulman 1786. Ghent:BU.

621/84

Netherlands (United Provinces, 1581–1795). Staten Generaal. Ordre by de . . . Staten Generael . . . ghemaeckt op het bevaren vande Middellantsche Zee ende het sout halen in West-Indien. *Amsterdam: M. Colijn,* 1621. [20] p.; 4to. Sabin 57535 (& 102905A); Petit 1319. CSmH, NN-RB; Leyden:B. Thysiana.

621/85

——. Placcaet . . . ghemaeckt op' t besluyt vande West-Indissche Compaignie. *The Hague: H. Jacobszoon van Wouw,* 1621. [5] p.; 4to. Sabin 63192; Knuttel 3233; JCB (3) II:154–55. NN-RB, RPJCB; BL, The Hague:KB.

621/86

——. Placcaet inhoudende verbodt dat niemandt varen en mach door de Strate van Gibraltar . . . anders als in admiraelschap. *The Hague: H. Jacobszoon van Wouw,* 1621. [5] p.; 4to. Includes mention of West Indies on 1f A2. JCB (3) II:155. NNH, RPJCB.

621/87

——. Placcaet . . . op 'tstuck vant verkoopen ende transporteren van actien inde Oost ende West Indische Compaignien. *The Hague: H. Jacobszoon van Wouw,* 1621. [6] p.; 4to. On sale and transfer of stock shares. Sabin 63198; Tiele (Pamfletten) 1868; JCB (3) II:155. NN-RB, RPJCB; BL.

621/88

—[Anr edn]. Placaet [etc.]. *The Hague: H. Jacobszoon van Wouw,* 1621. [6] p.; 4to. Meulman 1785. Ghent:BU.

621/89

Nodal, Bartolomé García de. Relacion del viaje que por orden de Su Mag[esta]d. y acuerdo del Real Consejo de Indias. hizieron los capitanes Bartolome Garcia de Nodal, y Gonzalo de Nodal hermanos . . . al descubrimiento del Estrecho nuebo de S. Vicente y reconosimi[ent]o. del de Magallanes. *Madrid: F. Correa de Montenegro,* 1621. 2 pts; illus., map; 4to. In some copies in pt 1 lvs 1, 7, 54 & 65 are cancels. Sabin 55394; Medina (Chile) 50; Pérez Pastor (Madrid) 1760; Church 386; JCB (3) II:156. CSmH, CtY, DLC (with & without cancel lvs), InU-L, MH, MiU-C, MnU-B, PPL, RPJCB; BL, BN.

621/90

A notable and wonderfull sea-fight. be-

tweene two great and wel-mounted Spanish shipps, and a small . . . English shipp. *Amsterdam: J. Veseler,* 1621. 4to. Abridged from the *True relation of of* [*sic*] *a wonderfull sea fight* of this year below. STC 22131. CSmH; BL.
621/91

Ochoa, Cristóbal de, O.F.M. Señor. Fray Cristoval de Ochoa de la orden de . . . san Francisco. [*Madrid?* 1621?]. [7] p.; fol. Memorial to king of Spain on distinction drawn between native & Spanish Franciscans in the New world. BL.
621/92

Ordóñez de Ceballos, Pedro. Eyghentlijcke beschryvinghe van West-Indien. *Amsterdam: M. Colijn,* 1621. 29 p.; fol. Transl. from that section relating to Spanish America in the author's *Viage del mundo,* 1st publ., Madrid, 1614. Issued as pt 2 of Antonio de Herrera y Tordesilla's *Nieuwe werelt,* Amsterdam, 1622. Sabin 14352; cf. Streit II:1533; Palau 203656n; JCB (3) II:156. CU-B, DLC, MWiW-C, MiU-C, MnU-B, NN-RB, RPJCB; BL.
621/93

Orlandini, Nicolò. Historiae Societatis Jesu, pars prima. *Cologne:* 1621. *See* Jesuits *above.*

Ortiz de Cervantes, Juan. Parabien al Rey D. Felip IIII. N.S. que da la cabeça del . . . Piru. [*Madrid?* 1621?]. 5 numb. lvs; fol. Seeks protection of Indians, the rewarding of merit & appointment of residents. Sabin 11716; Medina (BHA) 6697; Palau 205774. RPJCB; BL.
621/94

———. Patrocinium pro eo titulo toto terrarum orbe celebratissimo, magnae civitatis del Cuzco Peruani . . . a regibus Hispaniarum, & Indiarum concesso. [*Madrid?*] 1621. 8 numb. lvs; fol. Medina (BHA) 718; Palau 205773.
621/95

Pasquier, Etienne. Les recherches de la France. *Paris: J. Petit-Pas,* 1621. 1019 p.; port.; 4to. 1st publ. with American content, Paris, 1596; cf. 1607 edn. In this edn the American ref. appears in chapt. xxviii of bk 4. Thickett (Pasquier) 15; Tchémerzine IX:84. Oxford:Bodl., Heidelberg:UB.
621/96

—[Anr issue]. *Paris: L. Sonnius,* 1621. Thickett (Pasquier) 15; Tchémerzine IX:84. ICN, MH, NcD; BL, BN.
621/97

Piò, Giovanni Michele. Allegatione per confirmare quanto si scrive nell'annotationi all'Aviso de Parnaso [da G. Castellani]. al numero 57, cavata dalla vita di f. Bartolomeo dalla Casa. '*Antipoli: Stamperia Regia*' [i.e., *Venice?*], 1621. 22 p.; 4to. 1st publ. as here extracted, 'Antipoli', 1618, q.v. Here a reissue with altered imprint date of that edn? Hanke/Giménez 518; cf. Streit I:371; Palau 227135. DLC; BN.
621/98

Planis Campy, David de. La petite chirurgie chimique medicale, ou est traicté . . . de l'origine des maladies & curation. *Paris: J. Périer & A. Buissart,* 1621. 333 p.; 8vo. In chapt. xv, 'Curation de la maladie venerienne', use of the bark 'du bois d'Inde' (guaiacum) & of sarsaparilla is recommended. Wellcome I:5075. CtY, DNLM, MH; BL.
621/99

Plautius, Caspar, O.S.B., Abbot of Seitenstetten. Nova typis transacta navigatio. Novi orbis India Occidentalis . . . Nunc primum e varijs scriptoribus . . . Authore . . . Honorio Philopono [pseud.]. [*Linz:*] 1621. 101 p.; illus., ports; 4to. With accounts of the Benedictine monks who accompanied Columbus, includes also refs to Indian customs, agricultural products, etc. Exists in two issues, one with 5, the other with 3, prelim. lvs & differing supplementary matter. Sabin 63367 (& 82979n); Palau 224762; Arents (Add.) 201; Wolfenbüttel 32; JCB (3) II:157. Issues not differentiated: CU-B, CtY, DLC (both issues), InU-L, MH, MiU-C, MnU-B, NN-RB, PP, RPJCB (both issues); BL, BN.
621/100

Porreño, Baltasar. Dichos y hechos del Rey Phelipe II. *Cuenca: S. de Viader,* 1621. 8vo. In chapt. vi, on Philip's religion & faith, his support of the Jesuits, and their mission to Florida in 1566, is cited; in chapt. xiii, on his 'liberalidad y magnificiencia', military installations in the New World ordered by him are enumerated. Other refs to Spanish America occur. Palau 233064. 621/101

Ptolemaeus, Claudius. Geografia, cioè Descrittione universale della terra, partita in due volumi . . . Nuovamente . . . rincontrati, & corretti dall' eccell.mo sig. Gio. Antonio Magini . . . Dal latino . . . tradotta dal r. d. Leonardo Cernoti. *Padua: P. & F. Galignani,* 1621,'20. 2 pts; maps; fol. 1st publ. as here transl., Venice, 1598,'97. Sabin 66508; Stevens (Ptolemy) 61; Phillips (Atlases) 436; Michel (Répertoire) VI:151;

JCB (3) II:157. CU, CtW, DLC, ICN, InU-L, MiU, NN-RB, PP, RPJCB; BL, BN.
621/102

Raleigh, Sir Walter. The history of the world. *London: W. Jaggard, [W. Stansby & N. Okes] for W. Burre,* 1617 [i.e., 1621]. 2 v.; maps, port.; fol. 1st publ., London, 1614. Sabin 67560n; Brushfield (Raleigh) 223 (C); STC 20638a. CtY, NNC, MWiW-C; BL.
621/103

—[Anr state]. *London: W. Jaggard, for W. Burre,* 1621. Sabin 67560n; Brushfield (Raleigh) 223 (D); STC 20639. CSmH, CtY, DFo, ICU, MH; BL.
621/104

Entry Canceled.   621/105

Rosaccio, Giuseppe. Il medico . . . Aggiuntavi la distillatione di estrare e olii. *Venice: P. Farri,* 1621. 356 p.; 4to. Therapeutic formulas using guaiacum & sarsaparilla are provided. Wellcome I:5565. DNLM, ICU, MH, NNNAM; BL, BN (imp.).   621/106

Sacchini, Francesco. Historiae Societatis Jesu pars secunda. *Antwerp:* 1621. *See* Jesuits *above.*

Sandys, George. A relation of a journey . . . containing a description of the Turkish empire . . . Second edition. *London: [R. Field,] for W. Barrett,* 1621. 310 p.; illus., maps; fol. 1st publ., London, 1615. STC 21727. CSmH, CtY, DLC, ICN, MH, NN-RB; BL, BN.   621/107

Schouten, Willem Corneliszoon. Giornale overo Descrittione del faticossimo & travagliosissimo viaggio . . . Tradotto di Latino. *Venice: Santo Grillo & Bros,* 1621. [120] p.; 8vo. Transl. from Schouten's *Diarium vel Descriptio,* Amsterdam, 1619, itself transl. from his *Journal ofte Beschryvinghe,* 1st publ., Amsterdam, 1618. Sabin 77964. NN-RB; Amsterdam:NHSM.   621/108

Scott, Thomas, supposed author. Den compaignon vanden verre-sienden waerschouwer, thoonende met veele redenen. *The Hague: A. Meuris,* 1621. [12] p.; 4to. In arguing for war with Spain, discusses its benefits for the West-Indische Compagnie's ventures. Cf. *Den getrouwen . . . waerschouwer,* to which this refers, below. In this edn, the title & imprint comprise 12 lines, along with a vignette. The attribution of authorship to Scott is dubious. Knuttel 3204. [Locations may include the following edn:]

InU-L, MnU-B, NN, RPJCB; BL, The Hague:KB.   621/109

—[Anr edn]. *The Hague: A. Meuris,* 1621. [12] p.; 4to. Here the title and imprint comprise 13 lines, along with a portrait. Knuttel 3205. NN; The Hague:KB.   621/110

——. Nieuwe tydingen wt den Conseio, ofte Secreten raedt van Spangien. *Amsterdam: J. P. Wachter,* 1621. [50] p.; 4to. Transl. from *Vox populi, or Newes from Spayne,* 1st publ., [London?], 1620. Cf. Sabin 78376; Shaaber (Brit. auth.) S172; Knuttel 3207. MnU-B, NNH, NN; The Hague:KB.
621/111

—[Anr edn]. Consejo Españolesco, dat is, Den secreten raet van Spaengien. *Leyden: Z. de Smit,* 1621. [30] p.; 4to. Cf. Sabin 78376; Shaaber (Brit. auth.) S171; Knuttel 3208. MnU-B, NN, RPJCB; The Hague:KB.
621/112

——, **supposed author.** A relation of some speciall points concerning the state of Holland. Or The provident counsellours companion . . . shewing why for the good and security of the Netherland United Provinces warre is much better than peace. *'The Hague: A. Meuris'* [i.e., London: E. Allde] 1621. 19 p.; 4to. Transl. from *Den compaignon vanden . . . waerschouwer,* attrib. to Scott, above. STC 22083. CSmH, DFo, MH; BL; Oxford: Bodl.   621/113

Silva, Juan de, O.F.M. Advertencias importantes, acerca del buen govierno, y administracion de las Indias, assi en lo espiritual, como en lo temporal. *Madrid: Widow of F. Correa Montenegro,* 1621. 110 numb. lvs; fol. Sabin 81095; Medina (BHA) 719; Streit I:402; Pérez Pastor (Madrid) 1786; JCB (3) II:157–58. CU-B, NN-RB, RPJCB; BL, BN.
621/114

Spain. Consejo de las Indias. Assiento y capitulacion que los señores Presidente y del Consejo real de las Indias tomaron con los vezinos Sierralta, consul de la Universidad de los mercaderes de . . . Sevilla . . . sobre la prorrogacion y nueva concesion del derecho de la averia, por seys años. *Madrid: M. Clavijo,* 1621. 28 numb. lvs; fol. Cf. similar *assiento* of 1620. Palau 18676. BL.
621/115

Spilbergen, Joris van. Miroir Oost & West-Indical, auquel sont descripes les deux dernieres navigations . . . L'autre faicte par Jacob le Maire, lequel au costé du zud du Destroict de Magellan, a descouvert un nouveau destroict. *Amsterdam: J. Janszoon, the Younger,* 1621. 172 p.; illus., maps; obl. 4to. Transl. from Spilbergen's *Oost ende West-Indische spieghel* of this year below. Sabin 89451; Borba de Moraes II:276; Tiele-Muller 70; Tiele 1030; JCB (3) II:158. DLC, InU-L, MB, MnU-B, NN-RB, RPJCB; BL, BN.   621/116

——. Oost ende West-Indische spieghel, waer in beschreven werden de twee laetste navigatien . . . De andere ghedaen bij Jacob le Maire . . . in 't zuyden de Straet Magellanes. *Amsterdam: J. Janszoon, the Younger,* 1621. 192 p.; illus., maps; obl. 4to. 1st publ., Leyden, 1619. Sabin 89446; Borba de Moraes II:276; Tiele-Muller 68; Tiele 1026; JCB (3) II:158. RPJCB; BL.   621/117

—[Anr issue]. *Zutphen: A. J. van Aelst,* 1621. Sabin 89446; Borba de Moraes II:276; Tiele-Muller 69; Tiele 1026n. CSmH, NN-RB.   621/118

Suárez de Gamboa, Juan. Illustrissimo señor. Advertencias de daños que se siguen, assi para el real interesse de su Magestad, como en daño general del comun de la Nueva España, y su ruina. [*Madrid?* 1621]. 7 numb. lvs; fol. Memorial to king of Spain on affairs of Mexico. Subscribed at end, Madrid, Dec., 1621. Sabin 93320; Medina (BHA) 721. BL.   621/119

——. Señor. Tres cosas son las que obligan a credito, de los avisos que piden remedio de daños grandes. [*Madrid?* 1621]. 6 numb. lvs; fol. Anr memorial to king of Spain on affairs of Mexico, also subscribed at end, Madrid, Dec., 1621. Sabin 93321; Medina (BHA) 720. BL.   621/120

Tabourot, Estienne. Les bigarrures et touches. *Rouen: D. Geuffroy,* 1621. 5 pts; illus., ports; 12mo. In verse.1st publ. in this collective edn, Paris, 1603, q.v. Here perhaps a reissue of the Rouen, 1620, edn above. BN.   621/121

Taylor, John, the Water-poet. The praise, antiquity, and commodity, of beggery, beggers, and begging. *London: E. A[llde]., for H. Gosson; sold by E. Wright,* 1621. 12 lvs; 4to. In verse. Tobacco is mentioned. STC 23786; Arents (Add.) 203. CSmH, MH, NN-A; BL.   621/122

——. A shilling, or, The travailes of twelve-pence. [*London: E. Allde, for H. Gosson,* 1621]. [46] p.; 8vo. In verse. Preface (in prose) mentions Columbus; in text tobacco sellers are mentioned, as are America & the mines of 'Pottozzy' (Potosí). STC 23793; Arents (Add.) 204. CSmH, CtY, DFo, IU, MH, NN-A; BL.   621/123

——. Superbiae flagellum, or, The whip of pride. *London: G. Eld,* 1621. 31 lvs; 8vo. In verse. Mention of 'Indian mines and gems' patently refers to those of New World. For variant dedications, see the STC. STC 23796; Arents (Add.) 205. CSmH, DFo, ICN, MH, NN-A; BL.   621/124

——. Taylors goose. *London: E. Allde, for H. Gosson; sold by E. Wright,* 1621. 4to. In verse. The turkey and 'Spanish potatoes' are mentioned. STC 23799. London: Guildhall, Oxford:Bodl. (imp.).   621/125

——. Taylor's motto. *London: [E. Allde,] for J. T[rundle]. & H. G[osson].,* 1621. 36 lvs; 8vo. In verse. Tobacconists are mentioned. On lf B4r, line 1 has reading 'Libles.' STC 23800; Arents (Add.) 206. CSmH, DFo, MH, NN-A; BL.   621/126

—[Anr edn]. *London: [E. Allde] for J. T[rundle]. & H. G[osson].,* 1621. 36 lvs; 8vo. On lf B4r, line 1 has reading 'Libels', etc. STC 23800.5. BL (imp.), London:Guildhall, Cambridge:Trinity.   621/127

Thou, Jacques Auguste de. Historische Beschreibung deren namhafftigsten, geistlichen und weltlichen Geschichten . . . nun uber die 100. Jahr hero, denckwürdig zugetragen. *Frankfurt a. M.: E. Emmel, for P. Kopff,* 1621. 818 + p.; fol. Transl. from de Thou's *Historiarum sui temporis pars prima,* etc., 1st publ., Paris, 1604–6. NNH, PHi; BL (imp.).   621/128

Torquemada, Antonio de. Jardin de flores curiosas. *Barcelona: J. Margarit,* 1621. 258 numb. lvs; 8vo. 1st publ., Salamanca, 1570. Includes numerous scattered refs to Spanish America. Palau 334914.   621/129

Torsellino, Orazio, S.J. Epitomae historiarum libri x . . . Editio secunda. *Lyons: J. Cardon & P. Cavellat,* 1621. 12mo. 1st publ., Rome, 1598; cf. 1620 edn. Backer VIII:151. BL.   621/130

—[Anr edn]. *Cologne: B. Wolter,* 1621. 503 p.; 12mo. Backer VIII:151. 621/131

—[Anr edn]. *Milan: G. B. Bidelli,* 1621. 557 p.; 12mo. Backer VIII:151. ICN. 621/132

A true relation of of [*sic*] a wonderfull sea fight betweene two great and well appointed Spanish ships . . . And a small . . . English ship, who was constrained to enter into this conflict at the iland of Dominico in her passage to Virginia. *London: [E. Allde,] for N. B[utter].,* 1621. [21] p.; 8vo. For an abridgment, also of this year, see *A notable and wonderfull sea-fight* above. Sabin 97140; STC 22130. CSmH; BL, Oxford:Bodl. 621/133

Valdivia, Luis de. Sermon en lengua de Chile, de los mysterios de nuestra santa fe catholica, para predicarla a los Indios infieles del reyno de Chile. [*Valladolid:* 1621]. 76 p.; 4to. Text in Araucanian language, with marginal translation in Castilian. Reprinted as ed. by J. T. Medina, Santiago de Chile, 1897, under title *Nueve sermones en lengua de Chile.* Sabin 98334; Medina (Chile) 52; Streit II:1381n. 621/134

Vargas Machuca, Bernardo de. Compendio y doctrina nueva de la gineta. *Madrid: F. Correa de Montenegro,* 1621. 26 numb. lvs; 8vo. Cf. the author's *Teorica y exercicios de la gineta,* Madrid, 1619, & his *Libro de exercicios de la gineta,* Madrid, 1600. Medina (BHA) 723; Pérez Pastor (Madrid) 1795. BL, Madrid:BU (S. Isidro). 621/135

Venner, Tobias. A briefe and accurate treatise, concerning, the taking of the fume of tobacco. *London: W. J[ones]., for R. More,* 1621. [21] p.; 4to. Sabin 98890; STC 24642; Arents 146. CSmH, DFo, MH, NN-A; BL. 621/136

Verdadera relacion del viage y sucesso de los caravelones y galeoncetes de la guarda de Cartagena de las Indias y su costa. Y la grandiosa victoria que han tenido contra los corsarios paratas en aquel mar. *Seville: B. Gómez de Pastrana,* 1621. 2 lvs; fol. Also publ. this year at Madrid, under title *Viage, y suceso,* etc. Sabin 98945; Escudero (Seville) 1.233. RPJCB. 621/137

Viage, y sucesso de los caravelones, galeoncetes de la guarda de Cartagena . . . y su costa. Y la . . . victoria . . . contra los cor-

sarios piratas en . . . 1621. *Madrid: Widow of C. Delgado,* 1621. [4] p.; fol. Also publ. this year at Seville under title *Verdadera relacion del viage.* Sabin 11137; Medina (BHA) 724; Pérez Pastor (Madrid) 1805. RPJCB; BL. 621/138

Virginia Company of London. A note of the shipping, men, and provisions, sent and provided for Virginia . . . this yeare 1620 [i.e., 1621]. [*London: T. Snodham,* 1621]. bds.; fol. Cf. edn of 1620 above. Included here is information to Febr. 1621. Sabin 55947; Clayton-Torrence 34; Vail(Frontier) 52; STC 24842a. NN-RB; BL. 621/139

Winne, Edward. A letetr [*sic*] written . . . to Sir G. Calvert his Majesties principall secretary: from Feryland in Newfoundland [containing an account of the country]. [*London: B. Alsop*] 1621. 8vo. Sabin 104786; STC 25854. NIC; BL. 621/140

Wright, Thomas. The passions of the minde. *London: A. M[athewes]., for Anne Helme,* 1621. 350 p.; 4to. 1st publ., London, 1601; here anr issue of publisher's 1620 edn with altered imprint date. STC 26042. CSmH, DLC, NNNAM; BL. 621/141

Zacchia, Paolo. Quaestiones medico-legales. *Rome: A. Brugiotti* (v. 1) *& G. Facciotti* (v. 2-5), 1621-30. 5 v.; 4to. Includes *Liber quartus,* with passage on tobacco, referring to Monardes. For a sixth book, see the year 1634. ICU, MiEM. 621/142

Zambrana de Villalobos, Sebastián. Allegatio juris. Por licenciado Don Sebastian Zambrana de Villalobos, oydor de la real audiencia de las Charcas. Con el señor Fiscal del Consejo de Indias. Sobre la culpa que se le opone de averse casado don Christoval de Villalobos y Lara su hijo, con doña Ana Calderon de Robles. [*Madrid?* 1621]. 44 numb. lvs; fol. At end: Accepit finem hic labor Matriti 23. die mensis Junii . . . anno millesimo sexcentesimo vigesimo primo. Medina (BHA) 6433; Palau 378977; JCB (3) II:159. InU-L, RPJCB. 621/143

Zwey unterschiedliche nohtwendige Bedencken; und ausführliche Resolution deren Frage: ob die Herren General-Staaden . . . sich mit dem König zu Hispanien, etc. in . . . Friedens- und Anstandshandlung einlassen. . . . Auss niderländischer unnd . . . engeländischer . . . Sprach transferirt. [*The Hague?*] 1621. [48] p.; 4to. Pt 1, p. 1–18, transl. from *Den compaignon vanden verre-sienden waerschouwer,* attributed to Thomas Scott, above. Knuttel 3206. The Hague:KB.   621/144

1622

Alemán, Mateo. Der Landstörtzer: oder Gusman von Alfarche . . . zum 4. mal widerumb in Truck geben durch Aegidium Albertinum. *Munich: N. Heinrich,* 1622. 652 p. 1st publ. in German, Munich, 1615. Dt. Ges. Kat.3.873. Munich:StB.   622/1

——. The rogue: or, The life of Guzman de Alfarache. *London: G. E[ld].,* for E. Blount, 1622–23. 2 pts; fol. Transl. by James Mabbe from Aleman's *Primera parte de Guzman de Alfarache,* 1st publ., Madrid, 1599 (cf. the 1601 edn) & the *Segunda parte,* Lisbon, 1604. Laurenti (Nov. pic. esp.) 691; STC 288; Palau 6781. CSmH, CtY, DLC, ICU, MH, NN-RB, PU; BL.   622/2

——. Vita del picaro Gusmano d'Alfarace . . . tradotta da Barezzo Barezzi. *Venice: B. Barezzi,* 1622. 2 v.; 8vo. 1st publ. as here transl. in both pts, Venice, 1615. Laurenti (Nov. pic. esp.) 714; Palau 6779.

622/3

Anderde discours, by forma van messieve. Daer in kortelijck ende grondich verthoondt wort, de nootwendicheyt der Oost ende West Indische navigatie . . . Worden daerom alle getrouwe patriotten . . . vermaendt, om tot dese . . . West-Indiaensche Compagnie mildelijck te contribueren. [*Amsterdam?*] 1622. [23] p.; 4to. Continues the arguments of the *Missive. Daer in kortelijck . . . wert verthoont,* Arnhem, 1621; cf. also *Derde discours. By forma van missive* of this year below. Sometimes attrib. to W. Usselinx, but see Jameson (Usselinx), p. 74–75. In some copies a postscript is pasted on the blank verso of lf 12 (Knuttel). Sabin 102879; Asher 95; Knuttel 3360. MBAt, NN-RB; BL. With postscript:CSmH, DLC.

622/4

Apologus vanden krijch der gansen, met de vossen, gepractiseert door Philonem Patri-

cium, tot welstant . . . ende bevorderinghe vande aen-staende vloot op West-Indien. [*Amsterdam:*] 1622. [16] p.; 4to. Sabin 59074; Asher 90; Knuttel 3357; JCB (3) II:172. NN-RB, RPJCB; BL, The Hague:KB.

622/5

Ayalá y Rojas, Iñigo de. Don Iñigo de Ayala y Rojas, maestre de campo general del reyno de Chile, pide, que su Magestad le hago merced del govierno del dicho reyno. [*Madrid?* 1622?]. 2 lvs; fol. Medina (Chile) 53. Seville:Archivo de Indias.   622/6

Bacci, Andrea. De thermis . . . libri septem. *Rome: G. Mascardi,* 1622. 425 p.; fol. 1st publ., Venice, 1571. Includes discussions of volcanoes of America (p. 163), natural features of Peru (p. 222–23), & legend of Peruvian giants (p. 273). DNLM, MnU, PU, RPJCB; BL, BN.   622/7

Bacon, Francis, viscount St. Albans. Essays politiques et moraux . . . Mis en nostre langue par J. Baudouin. *Paris: F. Julliot,* 1622. 162 numb. lvs; 8vo. 1st publ. as here transl., Paris, 1619; here a reissue of the printer's 1621 edn with altered imprint date. Gibson (Bacon) 47; Shaaber (Brit. auth.) B34. BN.

622/8

——. Historia naturalis et experimentalis ad condendam philosophiam. *London: J. Haviland,* for M. Lownes & G. Barret, 1622. 285 p.; 8vo. Includes refs to Columbus & Peru, derived from or citing Acosta. Later edns have title *Historia naturalis . . . de ventis.* Gibson (Bacon) 108; STC 1155. CSmH, CtY, DLC, ICN, MH, MnU, NNPM, PPL; BL, BN.

622/9

——. The historie of the raigne of King Henry the seventh. *London: W. Stansby, for M. Lownes, & W. Barrett,* 1622. 248 p.; port.; fol. The voyages of Columbus & Sebastian Cabot are described, p. 187–89. For variants, see Gibson. Gibson (Bacon) 116a–b; STC 1159–60; Pforzheimer 32. CSmH, CtY-M, DLC, ICN, InU-L, MH, MiU-C, NN-RB, PU-F; BL, BN.   622/10

Belmonte y Bermúdez, Luis de. Algunas hazañas de las muchas de Don García Hurtado de Mendoça, marqués de Cañete. *Madrid: D. Flamenco,* 1622. 69 numb. lvs; 4to. Comedy. On author's collaborators, see Medina. Based upon the Araucanian Indian wars in

Chile. Sabin 4587; Medina (Chile) 54; Pérez Pastor (Madrid) 1809; Palau 26633; JCB (3) II:160. MB, RPJCB. 622/11

Benamati, Guido Ubaldo. Delle due trombe i primi fiati: cioè, Trè libri della vittoria navale, e trè libri del Mondo Nuovo; poemi eroici. *Parma: A. Viotti*, 1622. 228 p.; 12mo. Sabin 4632. CU, NN-RB. 622/12

Berettari, Sebastiano, S.J. Vida del padre Joseph de Ancheta de la Compania de Jesus, y provincial del Brasil. *Barcelona: E. Liberós*, 1622. 394 p.; 8vo. 1st publ. as here transl. by Esteban de Paternina from the author's *Josephi Anchietae . . . vita* (Lyons, 1617), Salamanca, 1618. Cf. Sabin 4828; Medina (BHA) 735; Borba de Moraes I:86; Streit II:2387; cf. Backer I:1326. ICN, MH. 622/13

Bermuda Islands. Laws, statutes, etc. Orders and constitutions, partly collected out of His Majesties letters patents; and partly by authority. *London: F. Kingston*, 1622. 83 p.; 4to. Sabin 57499; STC 1905; JCB (3) II:173. DLC, ICN, MH-L, MiU, NN-RB, RPJCB; BL. 622/14

Besler, Basilius. Continuatio rariorum et aspectu dignorum varii generis quae collegit . . . curavit . . . Basilius Besler. [*Nuremberg: The author*] 1622. 32 lvs; illus.; obl. 4to. An expanded version of the author's *Fasciculus*, [Nuremberg], 1616. Here added are illus. of an iguana, armadillo, & pineapple. Pritzel 746; Nissen (Zool.) 345. PPAN; BL, BN. 622/15

Blaeu, Willem Janszoon. The light of navigation. *Amsterdam: W. J. Blaeu*, 1622. 2 v.; illus., maps; fol. 1st publ. in English, Amsterdam, 1612. English title pasted on t.p. of 1620 Dutch edn; each 'book' has special t.p. Books 1 & 2 are dated '1621'. Koeman (M.Bl) 12; STC 3112. CtY, DFo, DLC; BL, Rome:BN. 622/16

Blasco de Lanuza, Vincenzio. Historias ecclesiasticas, y seculares de Aragon en que se continuan los annales de Çurita, y tiempos de Carlos V. *Saragossa: J. de Lanaja y Quartanet*, 1622. 2 v.; fol. 1st publ., Saragossa, 1621,'19; here a reissue of that edn with altered imprint dates? AzU, ICN, MH, NN-RB, NcU, PU; BL. 622/17

Blundeville, Thomas. M. Blundevile his Ex-

ercises . . . The sixth edition corrected and augmented. *London: W. Stansby; sold by R. Meighen*, 1622,'21. 799 p.; 4to. 1st publ., London, 1594; cf. 1606 edn. No edn designated the 5th has been traced. Also included is John Blagrave's *A very brief . . . description of Master Blagrave his Astrolabe*, 1st publ., London, 1585. Sabin 6024; STC 3150; JCB (3) II:160. CtY, DLC, MH, MiU, NNE, RPJCB, WU; BL. 622/18

Bodin, Jean. De republica libri sex. *Frankfurt, a. M.: H. Palthenius, for Widow of J. Rose*, 1622. 1121 (i.e., 1221) p.; illus.; 8vo. 1st publ. as transl. from Bodin's French text of 1576, Paris, 1586; cf. 1601 edn above. CU, MH-L, NIC; BN. 622/19

Bonoeil, John. His Majesties gracious letter to the Earle of South-hampton, treasurer, and to the Councell and Company of Virginia heere: commanding the present setting up of silke works, and planting of vines in Virginia. *London: F. Kingston*, 1622. 88 p.; illus.; 4to. Sabin 99886 (& 31998 & 35676); Clayton-Torrence 40; Vail (Frontier) 53; STC 14378; Arents (Add.) 207; Church 389; JCB (3) 160–61. CSmH, ICN, MH, NN-RB, PHi, RPJCB; BL. 622/20

Botero, Giovanni. Descripcion de todas las provincias y reynos del mundo, sacada de las Relaciones toscanas de Juan Botero . . . por fr. Jayme Rebullosa. *Gerona: G. Garrich*, 1622. 360 numb. lvs; 8vo. 1st publ. as here extracted & transl. by Rebullosa, Barcelona, 1603. Cf. Sabin 68338 (& 6810); Medina (BHA) 739; Streit I:411; Palau 33705n. Santiago, Chile:BN. 622/21

———. Le relationi universali . . . Alli quali vi sono aggiunte nuovamente i Capitani. *Venice: A. Vecchi*, 1622–23. 9 pts; illus., maps; 4to. 1st publ., Rome, 1591–96; here supplemented by the *Capitani*, 1st publ., Turin, 1607. Cf. 1601 edn. Sabin 6807; Michel (Répertoire) I:202; JCB (3) II:161, MH, NN-RB, PU, RPJCB; BN. 622/22

Brandon, Lorenzo. Señor. Medios para V. Magestad ahorrar lo mucho que gasta cada año en las Armadas del reyno de Portugal, y estado de la India, con mas fruto y comodidad, para poder venir la plata del Pirù con menos costa y riesgo. [*Madrid: 1622?*]. 7 numb. lvs; fol. Memorial to king of Spain, subscribed: Madrid 23. de Diziembre 1622. Sabin 7401; Medina (BHA) 727; Palau 34464.   622/23

Brerewood, Edward. Enquiries touching the diversity of languages and religions. *London: J. Bill,* 1622. 203 p.; 4to. 1st publ., London, 1614. Sabin 7732; STC 3619; JCB (3) II:162. CSmH, CtY, DFo, ICN, MH, MiU-C, NN-RB, RPJCB; BL.   622/24

Brinsley, John. Consolation for our grammar schooles, or Comfortable encouragement, for laying of a sure foundation of all good learning in our schooles; more especially for all those of an inferiour sort . . . namely for Ireland, Wales, Virginia, with the Sommer Islands. *London: R. Field,* 1622. 84 p.; 4to. Contains introduction addressed to Council and Company of Virginia and Sommer Islands, i.e., Bermuda. Sabin 7996 (& 16037); STC 3767; JCB (3) II:162. CSmH, CtY, DLC, MH, NN-RB, PHi, RPJCB; BL.   622/25

Brooke, Christopher. A poem on the late massacre in Virginia. With particular mention of those men of note that suffered in that disaster. *London: G. Eld, for R. Milbourne,* 1622. [23] p.; 4to. Sabin 100510; Vail (Frontier) 54. OkTG; London:PRO.
                                                  622/26

Camões, Luiz de. Lusiadum libri decem. Authore . . . Thoma de Faria. *Lisbon: G. da Vinha,* 1622. 179 numb. lvs; 4to. Transl. from Camões's *Os Lusiadas,* 1st publ. Lisbon, 1572. Silva (Camões) 142. DLC, MH, MnU-B, NNH, RPJCB; BN, Lisbon:BN.
                                                  622/27

Carrillo, Martín. Annales y memorias cronologica. Contienen las cossas mas notables . . . succedidas en el mundo . . . en España, desde su principio . . . hasta . . . 1620. *Huesca: P. Bluson, for the Widow of J. Pérez Valdivielso,* 1622. 452 p.; illus.; fol. Bk 5 contains chapt. 'Descubrimiento de las Indias Occidentales.' Medina (BHA) 728; Palau 45513. MH, NNH, OU, WU; BL, BN.
                                                  622/28

Casas, Bartolomé de las, O.P., Bp of Chiapa. Den spiegel der Spaensche tyranny gheschiet in West-Indien. *Amsterdam: J. E. Cloppenburg,* 1620 [i.e., ca. 1622?]. 1st publ. in Dutch, [Antwerp?], 1578; cf. 1607 edn

above & present printer's 1620 edn with engr. t.p.; the present edn. has a printed t.p. Sabin 11258; Medina (BHA) 1085n (II:479); Tiele-Muller 311; JCB (3) II:145. NN-RB, RPJCB.   622/29

Castillo, Juan del. Pharmacopoea, universa medicamenta in officinis pharmaceuticis usitata complectens, et explicans. *Cadiz: J. de Borja,* 1622. 335 numb. lvs; 4to. In bk 2, sect. 1, chapt. vii, describing 'Oleum Laurinum Mesuae', guaiacum is mentioned. Palau 48131. DNLM; BL, London:Wellcome.
                                                  622/30

Cats, Jacob. Emblemata, ofte Minnelycke, zedelycke ende stichtelycke sinnebeelden. [*Amsterdam?* 1622?]. 2 pts; illus.; obl. 24mo. 1st publ., Middelburg, 1618, under title *Silenus Alcibiadis;* Latin portions and notes omitted from this edition. Includes illus. of tobacco smoker. Title from engraved t.p.; printed half-title, generally used in describing subsequent edns, begins 'Minnelijcke, zedelijcke . . .'. Cf. Vries 91n–93; cf. Mus. Cats. 44n–46. ICN, MH.   622/31

——. Minnelijcke, zedelijcke en stichtelijcke sinne-beelden en ghedichten. [*Amsterdam?* 1622?]. See Cats's *Emblemata,* above.

——. Monita amoris virginei, sive Officium puellarum in castis amoribus, emblemate expressum. Maechden-plicht, ofte Ampt der jonckvrouwen. *Amsterdam: W. J. Blaeu,* 1622. 124 p.; illus.; 4to. 1st publ., Middelburg, 1618, under title *Maechden-plicht.* Vries 102; Mus.Cats. 56; cf. Arents (Add.) 208n. CtY, DFo, NN-A; BL, Leyden:UB.
                                                  622/32

——. Silenus Alcibiadis, sive Proteus. *Amsterdam: W. J. Blaeu,* 1622. 3 pts; illus.; 4to. 1st publ., Middelburg, 1618. Vries 82; Mus. Cats. 30; Arents (Add.) 208. DFo, NN-A; Leyden:UB.   622/33

Ceruto, Benedetto. Musaeum Franc. Calceolarii. *Verona: A. Tami,* 1622. 746 p.; illus.; fol. Described are numerous American plants, identified as such. Nissen (Zool.) 857. CU, CtY-M, DNLM, MH, WU; BL, BN.
                                                  622/34

Cervantes Saavedra, Miguel de. L'histoire de l'ingenieux . . . Dom Quichot . . . traduicte par F. de Rosset . . . Seconde edition. *Paris: D. Moreau,* 1622. 877 (i.e., 839) p.; 8vo. 1st publ. as here transl., Paris, 1618. Ríus (Cervantes) 464; Palau 52696n. DLC, MH, RPB; Barcelona:B. Central.   622/35

——. Novelas exemplares. *Madrid: Widow of A. Martín, for D. González,* 1622. 366 numb. lvs; 8vo. 1st publ., Madrid, 1613. Ríus (Cervantes) 229; Palau 53408. NNH; BL.
622/36

—[Anr edn]. *Pamplona: J. de Oteyza,* 1622. 391 numb. lvs; 8vo. Ríus (Cervantes) 230; Palau 53409. DLC, NNH; BL.   622/37

Collio, Francesco. De animabus paganorum libri quinque. *Milan: Ambrosian College,* 1622–23. 2 v.; 4to. Included is a plea for conversion of natives of New World. Streit I:408. MH, NNUT, OC; BL, BN.
622/38

Cooke, Jo. Greene's Tu quoque. *London: T. Dewe,* 1622. [87] p.; 4to. Drama. 1st publ., London, 1614. STC 5674; Greg 323(b). CSmH, DFo, ICU, MH; BL.   622/39

Copland, Patrick. A declaration how the monies . . . were disposed, which was gathered . . . at the Cape of good hope (towards the building of a free schoole in Virginia). *London: F. Kingston,* 1622. 7 p.; 4to. Sabin 99884; Vail (Frontier) 55; STC 5726; Church 392. CSmH; London:PRO.
622/40

——. Virginia's God be thanked, or A sermon of thanksgiving for the happie successe of the affaires in Virginia this yeare. *London: J. D[awson]., for W. Sheffard & J. Bellamy,* 1622. 36 p.; 4to. Includes the earliest account of present-day North Carolina. Sabin 16691; Clayton-Torrence 43; Vail (Frontier) 56; STC 5727; Church 390; JCB (3) II:163. CSmH, DFo, ICN, MH, NN-RB, RPJCB; BL.   622/41

Copye van eenen brieff van eenen vrient aen den anderen geschreven nopende het redres van de Oost-Indische Compaignie. *[Amsterdam? 1622].* 8 p.; 4to. Includes refs to the West-Indische Compagnie. Sabin 16737 (& 57378); Asher 89; Knuttel 3346. NN-RB; The Hague:KB.   622/42

Cordus, Valerius. Dispensatorium, cum Petri Coudebergi et Matthiae Lobelii scholiis. *Naples: G. Gaffaro,* 1622. 548 p.; 12mo. 1st publ., Nuremberg, 1546; cf. 1606 edn. BN.   622/43

Council for New England. A brief relation of the discovery and plantation of New England: and of sundry accidents therein occurring, from . . . M.DC.VII. to . . . M.DC.XXII. *London: J. Haviland, for W. Bladen,* 1622. [36] p.; 4to. Sabin 52619; Vail (Frontier) 57; STC 18483; Church 394; JCB (3) II:171. CSmH, DFo, ICN, MiU-C, NN-RB, PPL, RPJCB; BL.   622/44

Cushman, Robert. A sermon preached at Plimmoth in New England December 9. 1621. *London: J. D[awson]., for J. Bellamy,* 1622. 19 p.; 4to. Sabin 18132; Vail (Frontier) 58; STC 6149; Church 391; JCB (3) II:163–164. CSmH, CtY, ICN, MHi, RPJCB; Oxford: Bodl.   622/45

Deductie waer by onpartijdelijck overwogen . . . wort. *The Hague: [1622].* See the year 1638.

Derde discours. By forma van missive, daer in kortelijck ende grondich vertoont wort de nootwendicheyt des Oost ende West-Indische navigatie . . . in druck ghebracht by de liefhebbers der Nederlandtsche vryheyt. *[Amsterdam:]* 1622 [8] p.; 4to. Sometimes attrib. to W. Usselinx; see Jameson (Usselinx). Cf. the *Missive Daer in kortelijck . . . wert verthoont,* Arnhem, 1621, & the *Anderde discours* of this year above. The present work appears to be the 3rd in this series; it is not to be confused with the *Derde discours. Waer in by forme van missive . . .* below. Sabin 19670; Asher 96; Knuttel 3361; JCB (3) II:169. MWA, NN-RB, RPJCB; BL, The Hague:KB.   622/46

Derde discours. Waer in by forme van missive den geheelen staet van de Vereenichde Oost Indische compagnie wort ten vollen geremonstreert . . . Ende . . . bewesen . . . dat by soo verre dese geoctroyeerde West-Indische navigatie van Godt met gelijcken succes sal gesegent worden. *[Amsterdam?]* 1622. [24] p.; 4to. Not to be confused with the *Derde discours. By forma van missive* above. Sabin 19671; Asher 97; Knuttel 3351. NN-RB; The Hague:KB.   622/47

Doglioni, Giovanni Nicolò. Compendio historico universale di tutte le cose notabili historico sucesse nel mondo . . . la quarta volta riveduta, corretto & ampliato con nuova aggiunta fino all'anno 1618. *Venice:*

N. Misserini, 1622. 2 pts; port.; 4to. 1st publ., Venice 1594; here a probable reissue of Venice, 1605, edn with new t.p. & addition of the *Nuova aggiunta,* with special t.p. & separate paging & signatures. Added material includes sections on Virginia and Hudson's voyages, as well as refs to tobacco, the Spanish fleet of the Indies, and English voyages. Cf. 1601 edn. Michel (Répertoire) II:177. CU, CtY; Paris: Arsenal.   622/48

Donne, John. A sermon upon the viii. verse of the I. chapter of the Actes of the Apostles. Preached to the Honourable Company of the Virginian Plantation. 13°. Novemb. 1622. *London: A. Mat[hewes]., for T. Jones,* 1622. 49 p.; 4to. Sabin 20601; Clayton-Torrence 44; Vail (Frontier) 59; Keynes (Donne) 15; STC 7051; JCB (3) II:164. CSmH, CtY, DLC, ICN, MH, NN-RB, RPJCB; BL.   622/49

Drayton, Michael. A chorographicall description of . . . Great Britain . . . Digested into a poem. *London: J. Marriott, J. Grismond, & T. Dewe,* 1622. 303 p.; maps, port.; fol. 1st publ., London, [1612], under title *Poly-Olbion.* STC 7228; Grolier Club (Langland to Wither) 84; Pforzheimer 308. CSmH, CtY, DLC, ICN, InU-L, MH; BL.   622/50

Du Bartas, Guillaume de Salluste, seigneur. La seconde sepmaine . . . Die andere Woche . . . Aus dem Frantzösischen gegen übergesatzten in teutsche Reime . . . gegeben [von Tobias Hübner]. *Köthen:* 1622,'19. 4 pts; 4to. Transl. from author's *La seconde sepmaine,* 1st publ., Paris, 1584. Includes numerous refs to New World. Holmes (Du-Bartas) I:109 no. 21. CtY, ICU, MH; BL.   622/51

Duchesne, Joseph. Pharmacopoea dogmaticorum restituta . . . Editio tertia. *Marburg: P. Egenolff,* 1622. 448 p.; 8vo. 1st publ., Paris, 1607. DNLM, PPC.   622/52

Esternod, Claude d'. L'espadon satyrique . . . Reveu et augmentee de nouveau. *Lyons: J. Lautret,* 1622. 157 p.; 12mo. In verse. 1st publ., Lyons, 1619. Cioranescu (XVII) 28488.   622/53

Estienne, Charles. De veltbouw; ofte Lantwinninghe . . . Alles beschreven van M. Kaerle Stevens ende Jan Libaut . . . ende

nu vermeerdert door . . . Mechior Sebizius. *Amsterdam: M. Colijn,* 1622. 259 p.; fol. 1st publ. in this Dutch version, Amsterdam, 1588; transl. from Liébault's enl. version of Estienne's *L'agriculture,* 1st publ., Paris, 1567. CtY, MH, NNBG.   622/54

Foreest, Jan van. Hispanus redux. Sive exitus induciarum Belgicarum, ad Foederatos Belgas. *Hoorn: J. Claeszoon,* 1622. 88 p.; 4to. Includes, under title 'Expeditio in Americam facienda', 3 poems, followed by 'Aliud super immani crudelitate Hispani in Americanos' & similar verses. Knuttel 3328. BL, The Hague:KB.   622/55

Fotherby, Martin, Bp of Salisbury. Atheomastix clearing foure truthes against atheists. *London: N. Okes,* 1622. 362 p.; fol. Cited are Samuel Purchas's *Pilgrimage* & Grimstone's translation from Pierre d'Avity, *Estates, empires, and principalities of the world* (London, 1615) in support of thesis that 'all nations have . . . gods,' even 'Idolaters in America'. Also mentioned is Hakluyt in ref. to Drake's voyage to 'New Albion', i.e., California. STC 11205. CSmH, CtY, DLC, MBAt, NNUT; BL.   622/56

Fracastoro, Girolamo. Operum pars prior -[posterior]. *Geneva: P. & J. Chouët,* 1622. 3 pts; 8vo. 1st publ. as here collected, Venice, 1555; cf. 1621 edn. Baumgartner (Fracastoro) 38. CtY-M, DNLM, KU-M, NNC-M; Edinburgh:NL, Leipzig:UB.   622/57

Gaetani, Costantino, O.S.B. Ad universos ordinis . . . S. Benedicti abbates & praepositos, de erectione ipsius collegii, epistola encyclica. *Rome: Apostolic Camera,* 1622. 6 lvs; 4to. Plea for founding of Benedictine college to train missionaries to pagans, incl. those of America. Streit I:407. BN.

622/58

Gómez Solis, Duarte. Carta que Duarte Gomez escrivio al duque de Lerma en 20. de Noviembre de 612. [*Madrid:* 1622]. Bound with, as issued, the following item. CtY, ICN, MH, MnU-B, RPJCB; BL.   622/59

——. Discursos sobre los comercios de las dos Indias. [*Madrid:*] *P. Taso,* 1622. 256 numb. lvs; 4to. With this was issued the author's *Carta* above. Sabin 27759; Medina (BHA) 731; Pérez Pastor (Madrid) 1840; JCB (3) II:164. CtY, ICN, MH, MnU-B, RPJCB; BL.   622/60

Great Britain. Sovereigns, etc., 1603–1625 (James I). A proclamation prohibiting interloping and disorderly trading to New England. *London: B. Norton & J. Bill, 1622.* bds.; fol. Crawford (Roy. procl.) 1339; Brigham (Roy. procl.) 33–35; STC 8692; JCB (3) II:164. CSmH, RPJCB; BL.   622/61

Grotius, Hugo. Bewys van den waren godsdienst in ses boecken gestelt. [*Leyden?*] 1622. 111 p.; 4to. In verse. Includes scattered American refs, e.g. to Peru, Chile, & Brazil. This edn includes foreword by Rosaeus. Knuttel 3368; Meulen/Diermanse 143. BN, The Hague:PP.   622/62

—[Anr edn]. . . . in ses boecken ghestelt. [*Leyden?*] 1622. 111 p.; 4to. The foreword by Rosaeus here omitted. Knuttel 3369; Meulen/Diermanse 144. [Locations may include the preceding edn:] MH, NNC, NNUT; BL, The Hague:PP.   622/63

Gysius, Johannes. De Spaensche tiranije gheschiet in Neder-Lant. *Amsterdam: J. P. Wachter* [1622]. 112 p.; illus.; 4to. 1st publ. as here abridged from the author's *Oorsprong en voortgang der nederlandtscher beroerten,* Amsterdam, 1620. Erroneously attrib. to C. L. van der Plasse. Palau 111889; JCB (3) II:165. RPJCB; BL.   622/64

Harris, Robert. The drunkards cup. *London: B. Alsop, for T. Man, 1622.* 4to. Sermon. 1st publ., London, 1619. STC 12828. CtY, DFo; Oxford:Bodl.   622/65

Hawkins, Sir Richard. The observations of Sir Richard Hawkins . . . in his voiage into the South Sea . . . 1593. *London: J. D[awson].*, *for J. Jaggard, 1622.* 169 p.; fol. Includes descriptions of South America. Sabin 30957; STC 12962; Arents 147. CSmH, CtY, DLC, ICN, InU-L, MH, MiU-C, MnU-B, NN-RB, RPJCB; BL.   622/66

Herrera y Tordesillas, Antonio de. Description des Indes Occidentales . . . translatée d'espagnol . . . A laquelle sont adjoustées quelques autres descriptions des mesmes pays, avec la navigation du vaillant capitaine de mer Jacques Le Maire et de plusieurs autres [Pedro Ordóñez de Cevallos et P.Bertius]. *Amsterdam: M. Colijn, 1622.* 254 p.; illus., port., maps; fol. Transl. from the author's *Descripcion de las Indias Occidentales,* 1st publ., Madrid, 1601. Sabin 14351 & 31543; Medina (BHA) 455n; Wagner (SW)

12a; Tiele-Muller 295; Streit II:1532; JCB (3) II:166. [Locations may include the following issue:] ICN, MiU-C, MnU-B, NN-RB, PPL, RPJCB; BL, Göttingen:BU.   622/67

—[Anr issue]. *Amsterdam:* [*M. Colijn? for*] *E. Colijn & M. Soly, at Paris, 1622.* 254 p.; illus., port., maps; fol. Sabin 31543 (& 14351n); Medina (BHA) 455n; Wagner (SW) 12b; Tiele-Muller 296; JCB (3) II:166. RPJCB; BN.   622/68

——. Nieuwe werelt, anders ghenaemt West-Indien. *Amsterdam: M. Colijn, 1622.* 111 p.; illus., maps; fol. 1st publ. in Spanish, Madrid, 1601, under title *Descripcion de las Indias Occidentales;* cf. the author's Latin edn of this year below. Issued with P. Ordóñez de Ceballos's *Eyghentlijcke Beschryvinghe van West Indien,* Amsterdam, 1621, & J. LeMaire's *Spieghel der Australische navigatie* of this year below. Sabin 14348 & 31542; Wagner (SW) 12d; Streit II:1533; Palau 114296; Tiele-Muller 297; JCB (3) II:166. CU-B, DLC, MWiW-C, MiU-C, MnU-B, NN-RB, RPJCB; BL (West Indies).   622/69

——. Novus orbis, sive Descriptio Indiae Occidentalis . . . Accesserunt & aliorum Indiae Occidentalis descriptiones. *Amsterdam: M. Colijn, 1622.* 2 pts; illus., port., maps; fol. Included are Petrus Bertius's *Brevis ac succincta Americae . . . descriptio* and Jacob Le Maire's *Ephemerides sive Descriptio navigationis australis.* Sabin 31540; Medina (BHA) 455n; Wagner (SW) 12c; Streit II:1531; JCB (3) II:165. CtY, DLC, MH, MiU-C, MnU-B, NN-RB, PBL, RPJCB; BL, BN.   622/70

Hoorn, Netherlands. Ordinances, etc. Provisionele ordre ende reglement. Waer nae de schippers die met hunne schepen van dese stadt Hoorn, naer West-Indien . . . om sout te laden, sullen willen varen . . . hen sullen hebben te reguleren. *Hoorn: J. C. Coster, 1622.* 10 p.; 4to. Sabin 66395. NN-RB; BL.   622/71

Hues, Robert. Tractaet ofte Handelinge van het gebruyck der hemelscher ende aertscher globe . . . Van nieus oversien ende verbetert. *Amsterdam: M. Colijn, 1622.* 67 p.; illus.; 4to. 1st publ. in Dutch, Amsterdam, 1597; cf. year 1612. American refs here appear on p. 26–28. JCB (STL) 26. RPJCB.   622/72

Illescas, Gonzalo de. Segunda parte de la Historia pontifical y catolica. *Barcelona: S. de Cormellas,* 1622. 364 numb. lvs; fol. 1st publ. with American materials, Barcelona, 1596; cf. 1602 edn. Streit I:409. BL.

622/73

—[Anr edn]. *Madrid: J. de la Cuesta, for J. Hasrey,* 1622. Palau 118424n.   622/74

The inconveniencies that have happened to some persons which have transported themselves from England to Virginia, without provisions necessary to sustaine themselves. *London: F. Kingston,* 1622. bds.; fol. Includes list of clothing, utensils, &c. needed by prospective settlers. Also issued as part of Edward Waterhouse's *Declaration of the state of . . . Virginia* of this year below. Sabin 99887; Clayton-Torrence 47; Vail (Frontier) 62; STC 24844; JCB (3) II:174. CSmH, NN-RB, RPJCB; BL.

622/75

Jesuits. Letters from missions (South America). [Lettres des Indes Occidentales écrites par les pp. Jesuites partis de Flandre en 1615. *Mechlin: H. Jaey,* 1622.] The above title is that given by Sabin (under 'Zoes, ——') for a work described by Backer as in Flemish but recorded as 'Variae litterae missae a religiosis Societatis Jesu e Belgio ad vineam Indiae Occidentalis excolendam abierunt'. Sabin 106367; Backer VIII:1517.

622/76

Korte aenwysinghe der bewinthebbers regieringe. [*Amsterdam:* 1622]. [7] p.; 4to. Included are refs to both the 'West-Indische Compagnie' and the 'Oost-Indische Compagnie'. Sabin 38255; Asher 87. BL (Nederlandsche Oost-Indische Compagnie).

622/77

LeMaire, Jacob. Spieghel der australische navigatie, door den wijt vermaerden ende cloekmoedighen zee-heldt. *Amsterdam: M. Colijn,* 1622. 72 p.; illus., port., maps; fol. Issued as pt 3 of Antonio de Herrera y Tordesillas's *Nieuwe Werelt* of this year above. An account of voyage with Schouten through the Strait of Magellan, etc. Sabin 14353 & 44059; Tiele-Muller, p. 56–57; JCB (3) II:166. CU-B, DLC, MWiW-C, MiU-C, NNH, RPJCB.   622/78

Levendich discours vant ghemeyne lants welvaert voor desen de Oost ende nu oock de West-Indische generale Compaignie aenghevanghen seer notabel om lesen. [*Amsterdam:*] *B. Janszoon,* 1622. [24] p.; 4to. Woodcut on t.p. portrays city of Potosí. Sabin 40745; Knuttel 3362. DLC, NN-RB; BL, The Hague:KB.   622/79

Magnus, Olaus, Abp of Upsala. Historia . . . de gentibus septentrionalibus . . . In epitomen redacta. *Frankfurt a. M.: J. Schmidlin,* 1622. 468 p.; 8vo. 1st publ., Rome, 1555; cf. 1618 edn. BL.   622/80

Malynes, Gerard. The maintenance of free trade. *London: J. L[egat]., for W. Sheffard,* 1622. 105 p.; 8vo. Describes monetary effects of purchase of Spanish tobacco. STC 17226; Arents (Add.) 209; Kress 391. CtY, DLC, InU-L, MH-BA, NN-A; BL.

622/81

Massaria, Alessandro. Liber responsorum et consultationum medicinalium. Nunc primúm collectus, & in lucem editus. *Lyons: L. Durand,* 1622. 100 p.; 4to. 1st publ., Frankfurt a. M., 1601, in the author's *Practica medica.* DNLM; BL.   622/82

——. Practica medica, seu Praelectiones academicae. *Lyons: L. Durand,* 1622. 968 p.; 4to. 1st publ., Frankfurt a. M., 1601. BL.

622/83

—[Anr edn]. *Venice: G. A. Guliano,* 1622. 3 pts; fol. DNLM, NIC, PPC, WU.

622/84

Middelgeest, Simon van, supposed author. Den langh-verwachten donder-slach. [*Amsterdam?* 1622?]. *See the year* 1625.

——. Nootwendich discours oft Vertooch aan de . . . Staten Generaal van de participanten der Oost-Indische Compagnie tegens bewinthebbers. [*Amsterdam:*] 1622. [40] p.; 4to. Relates to the West-Indische Compagnie. Signed 'Ymant van Waar-mond'. Sometimes attrib. to Usselinx (cf. Sabin 99316). Cf. the Netherlands Staten Generaal's *Placcaet jeghens seecker fameus libel,* & their *Placcaet tegen het Nootwendich discours,* below, comprising edicts against this publication. Sabin 55449; Asher 77; Knuttel 3348. DLC, MnU-B; The Hague:KB.

622/85

—[Anr edn]. Ootmoedighe beklagh-redenen aen de . . . Staten Generael . . . gedaen door d'onderdanige deel-hebbers in de schadelijcke disordren. [*Amsterdam?*] 1622.

[33] p.; 4to. Sabin 57379; cf. Knuttel 3348n; Meulman 1838. Ghent:BU. 622/86

——. Tweede noot-wendiger discours ofte Vertooch aan alle lant-lievende, van de participanten der Oost-Indische Compagnie, tegens bewinthebbers. [*Amsterdam?* 1622]. [96] p.; 4to. Relates to the West-Indische Compagnie. Signed 'Yemant Adams'. Cf. the author's *Nootwendich discours* of this year above. Sabin 97530; Asher 78; Knuttel 3350. DLC, ICU, MnU-B, NN-RB; BL, The Hague:KB. 622/87

Middleton, Thomas. A faire quarrell. *London: A. M[athewes]., for T. Dewe,* 1622. 40 lvs; 4to. Drama. 1st publ., London, 1617. STC 17912; Greg 352 (b). CSmH, DLC, MH; BL. 622/88

Misselden, Edward. Free trade. or, The means to make trade flourish. *London: J. Legat, for S. Waterson,* 1622. 8vo. 'Sugars & Tobacco of the West Indies' & tobacco of 'Virginia and Barmuda's' are mentioned. STC 17986. MH (imp.); Cambridge:UL, Oxford:Christ Church. 622/89

—[Anr edn]. The second edition with some additions. *London: J. Legat, for S. Waterson,* 1622. 134 p.; 8vo. STC 17987. CtY, DFo, ICU, MH, NNC; BL. 622/90

More excellent observations of the estate and affaires of Holland. In a discourse, shewing how necessarie and convenient it is for their neighbouring countries, as well as the Netherland provinces, to trade into the West Indies. *London: E. A[llde]., for N. Bourne & T. Archer,* 1622. 37 p.; 4to. Transl. from the *Missive. Daer in kortelijcke ende grondigh wert verthoont,* 1st publ., Arnhem, 1621. Sabin 102898; STC 13573; JCB (3) II:171. CSmH, RPJCB; BL. 622/91

[**Mourning Virginia.** *London: H. Gosson,* 1622]. Known only from entry in Stationers' Register of 10 July 1622. Commemorates massacre in Virginia, April, 1622. Sabin 100489; Vail (Frontier) 64. 622/92

Mourt's relation. A relation or journall of the beginning of the English plantation at Plimoth. *London: [J. Dawson], for J. Bellamy,* 1622. 72 p.; 4to. Prob. written by William Bradford & Edward Winslow, giving an account of the voyage of the *Mayflower* & the settling of Plymouth. Sabin 51198; Vail (Frontier) 60; STC 20074; Church 393; JCB

(3) II:168. CSmH, CtY, DLC, MH, MiU-C, NN-RB, PPL, RPJCB; BL. 622/93

Murcía de la Llana, Francisco. Canciones lugubres, y tristes a la muerte de Don Christoval de Oñate, teniente de governador y capitan general de las conquistas del nuevo Mexico. *Madrid: Widow of F. Correa,* 1622. 54 numb. lvs; 4to. Cf. Sabin 51429; Medina (BHA) 734; Wagner (SW) 27; JCB AR40:17–18. RPJCB. 622/94

Naerder aenwysinghe der bewinthebbers regieringe. [*Amsterdam:* 1622]. [12] p.; 4to. Includes ref. to the West-Indische Compagnie, though chiefly concerned with East Indies. Cf. the *Korte aenwysinghe* of this year above. Sabin 51711; Knuttel 3354. MnU-B; BL, The Hague:KB. 622/95

Neander, Johann. Tabacologia: hoc est, Tabaci, seu nicotianae descriptio medico-cheirurgico-pharmaceutica. *Leyden: I. Elsevier,* 1622. 256 p.; illus., port.; 4to. Cf. Sabin 52173; Pritzel 6624; Rahir (Les Elzevier) 172; Willems (Les Elzevier) 257; cf. Arents 148. CU, DNLM, MH, MnU-B, NN-RB, RPJCB; BL. 622/96

Netherlands (United Provinces, 1581–1795). Staten Generaal. Ordonnantie, dienende tot versekeringe vande schepen uyt dese landen naer oosten. *The Hague: Widow & Heirs of H. Jacobszoon van Wouw,* 1622. [5] p.; 4to. On verso of 3rd leaf is mention of ships traveling toward the West [i.e., toward the Americas]. JCB (3) II:169. RPJCB. 622/97

——. Placaet [Nov. 26, 1622]. [*The Hague?* 1622?]. bds.; fol. Prohibits trade within the limits of the Dutch West India company. Sabin 63202. 622/98

——. Placcaet [June 10, 1622]. *The Hague: Widow & Heirs of H. Jacobszoon van Wouw,* 1622. bds.; fol. Refers to trade with Punta de Araya. This edn contains 47 lines. Sabin 63202; cf. Petit 1381. [Edn uncertain:] Leyden: B. Thysiana (imp.). 622/99

—[Anr edn]. *The Hague: Widow & Heirs of H. Jacobszoon van Wouw,* 1622. bds.; fol. This edn contains 51 lines. Sabin 63202. 622/100

——. Placcaet . . . daer by den koopluyden ende ingesetenen deser landen verboden werdt. *The Hague: Widow & Heirs of H. Jacobszoon van Wouw,* 1622. [5] p.; 4to. Includes ref. to 'Goederen, koopmanschappen, cargasoenen ende schepen toebehoorende de subjecten ende onderdanen van den voorsz Koning van Spaengien ende andere vyanden deser landen'. Meulman 1820; JCB (3) II:170. RPJCB; Ghent:BU.   622/101

——. Placcaet jeghens seecker fameus libel geintituleert, Nootwendigh discours, ofte Vertoogh. *The Hague: Widow & Heirs of H. Jacobszoon van Wouw,* 1622. [6] p.; 4to. Edict of July 22, 1622, against Middelgeest's *Nootwendich discours* of this year, above. Cf. Sabin 63197; Knuttel 3349. BL, The Hague:KB.   622/102

—[Anr edn]. Placcaet teghens seecker fameus libel. *The Hague: Widow & Heirs of H. Jacobszoon van Wouw,* 1622. 4 lvs.; 4to. Sabin 63197; Asher 80.   622/103

——. Placcaet tegen het: Nootwendich discours oft Vertooch. *Middelburg:* 1622. bds.; fol. Edict of July 17, 1622 against Middelgeest's *Nootwendich* discours of this year above. Sabin 63196; Asher 79.   622/104

Overbury, Sir Thomas. Sir Thomas Overbury his wife . . . The eleventh impression. *London:* [A. Griffin,] *for L. Lisle & sold by H. Seile,* 1622. [320] p.; 8vo. 1st publ., London, 1615. STC 18913; Murphy (Engl. char.-bks) 21. CSmH, DFo, MH, PBL; BL.   622/105

Oviedo, Luís de. Methodo de la coleccion y reposicion de las medicinas simples. *Madrid: L. Sánchez,* 1622. 524 p.; fol. 1st publ. in this enl. edn, Madrid, 1595; cf. 1609 edn. Pérez Pastor (Madrid) 1872; Palau 207731. DNLM; BL, BN.   622/106

Owen, John. Epigrammatum . . . libri tres . . . Editio quinta. *London: N. Okes, for S. Waterson,* 1622. 12mo. 1st publ., London, 1606. STC 18990. CSmH, DFo, IU, PBL; BL.   622/107

—[Anr edn]. Epigrammatum . . . libri decem. *Leipzig: Heirs of T. Schürer,* 1622. 5 pts; 8vo. Cf. 1612 edn. Shaaber (Brit. auth.) O88. CtY, BN.   622/108

Panciroli, Guido. Rerum memorabilium jam olim deperditam . . . Nunc vero latinitate . . . per Henricum Salmuth . . . Editio quarta. *Frankfurt a. M.: J. Schmidel,* 1622. 2 v.; 8vo. Includes, as v. 2, the author's *Nova reperta,* 1st publ., Amberg, 1602. Cf. Sabin 58413n. BL (v. 1), BN.   622/109

Pereira Corte Real, João. Discursos sobre

la navegacion de las naos de la India de Portugal. [*Madrid?* 1622?]. 16 numb. lvs; 4to. Memorial to king of Spain on ships and commerce of Brazil. Subscribed at end: Madrid a primero de enero de 622. Borba de Moraes I:185.   622/110

Petit recueil d'aucuns hommes illustres, & des plus signalés martyres de la Compagnie de Jesus. *Douai: L. Kellam, the Younger,* 1622. 103 p.; 12mo. Borba de Moraes II:142.   622/111

Pharmacopoeia Augustana. Jussu et auctoritate . . . Senatus a Collegio Medico rursus recognita . . . nunc septimum in lucem emissa. *Augsburg: A. Aperger, for J. Kruger,* 1622. 2 pts; fol. 1st publ., as prep. by Adolph Otto, Augsburg, [1564]; cf. 1613 edn ed. by R. Minderer. Wellcome I:4979. DNLM; London:Wellcome.   622/112

Potier, Pierre. Insignium curationum, & singularium observationum centuria prima. *Bologna: N. Tebaldini, for M. A. Bernia,* 1622. 8vo. 1st publ., Venice, 1615. Continued by the following. DNLM.   622/113

——. Insignium curationum, et singularium observationum centuria secunda. *Bologna: N. Tebaldini, for M. A. Bernia,* 1622. 8vo. Curatio xxvi utilizes sassafras; for treatment of epilepsy, tobacco smoke is recommended. Continues the preceding. DNLM; BL.   622/114

——. Pharmacopoea spagirica. *Bologna:* [*N. Tebaldini?*], 1622. 280 p.; 8vo. Included are formulas employing guaiacum, sarsaparilla, & sassafras. DNLM, InU.   622/115

Relacion de la plata y frutos que se embarcaron en la Armada de Nueva España. [*Madrid:*] 1622. Medina (BHA) 741n; Pérez Pastor (Madrid) 1890; Palau 257665.   622/116

Relacion de lo sucedido en los galeones y flota de Tierrafirme. [*Madrid?* 1622]. 5 numb. lvs; fol. Sabin 69204; Medina (BHA) 741; Pérez Pastor (Madrid) 1889; Palau 257664. DLC, FU.   622/117

Resende, Garcia de. Chronica dos valerosos e insignes feitos del rey Dom Joao II. *Lisbon: A. Alvarez,* 1622,'21. 174 numb. lvs; fol. 1st publ., Lisbon, 1545, under title *Lyvro . . . que trata da vida . . . do . . . rey don João o segundo;* cf. 1607 edn. Sabin 70063; cf. Borba de Moraes II:200; Palau 262163;

Maggs Cat. 502 (Americana VII) 5043. ICN, MH, MiU-C, NN-RB, RPJCB; BL.
          622/118

Ribera y Colindres, Luis de. Memorial que se dio por parte de Don Luys de Ribera a su Magestad . . . sobre quitar las dotrinas y curatos, que administran frayles en el . . . Pirù, y darlas à clerigos aprovados. [*Madrid? 1622?*]. 4 numb. lvs; fol. Subscribed at end: De Potosi, y Março 13. 1621. años. Palau 266953-II; JCB (3) II:157. RPJCB; BL.
          622/119

——. Señor. Don Luys de Ribera y Colindres, vezino de Sevilla, y residente en la Plata del Pirù. [*Madrid? 1622?*]. [3] p.; fol. Memorial to king of Spain on administration of Peru. Cf. Sabin 70805. BL.
          622/120

Rich, Barnabe. The Irish hubbub, or The English hue and crie. *London: A. Mathewes, for J. Marriott*, 1622. 56 p.; 4to. 1st publ., London, 1617. STC 20991. DFo; BL.
          622/121

Rivadeneira, Pedro de, S. J. Della religione del prencipe christiano contra li Machiavellisti. *Bologna: P. P. Tozzi*, 1622. 624 p.; port.; 8vo. 1st publ. in Italian, Genoa, 1598; cf. year 1601. Backer VI:1736; Palau 266345. ICN, OClJC.
          622/122

——. The life of the holy patriarch. [*St. Omer: English College Press*] 1622. 358 p.; 8vo. A reissue, with cancel t.p., of the *Life of . . . Ignatius of Loyola* as publ., St Omer, 1616, q.v. Allison & Rogers 712; STC 20968. CSmH; BL.
          622/123

——. Vida di San Ignacio patriarca y fundador de la Compañia de Jesus. *Madrid: L. Sánchez*, 1622. 126 lvs; 8vo. 1st publ. in Spanish, Madrid, 1583; includes refs to Jesuits in Brazil. Backer VI:1728; Palau 266228.
          622/124

——. Vita del p.s. Ignatio Loiola . . . hora di nuovo transportata nella nostra italiana. *Milan: G. B. Bidelli*, 1622. 113 p.; 8vo. Cf. year 1606 above. Palau 266243. IU; Rome:BN.
          622/125

Roca, Juan Antonio Vera Zúñiga y Figueroa, conde de la. Epitome de la vida i hechos del invicto emperador Carlos V. *Madrid: Widow of A. Martín*, 1622. 114 numb. lvs; 4to. Included are mentions of Magellan & of Pizarro's conquest of Peru. Pérez Pastor

(Madrid) 1906. ICU, NNH, TxHU; BL, Madrid:BU (San Isidro).
          622/126

Rowlands, Samuel. Good newes and bad newes. *London: [G. Purslowe,] for H. Bell*, 1622. 4to. In verse. Of the poems, three mention tobacco. STC 21382. CSmH; Oxford:Bodl.
          622/127

Sandys, Sir Edwin. A relation of the state of religion. *London: 'S. Waterson, 1605'* [i.e., *W. Stansby? 1622?*]. 179 p.; 4to. 1st publ., London, 1605; here a forgery of that edn, distinguished from it in having line 1 on 1f H3r end 'haue'. STC 21717.5 (formerly 21715). CSmH, DFo, ICN, MH, NNUT; BL.
          622/128

Scot, Thomas. Phylomythie or phylomythologie . . . Second edition, much inlarged. *London: [J. Legat,] for F. Constable*, 1622,'16. 2 pts; 8vo. In verse. 1st publ., London, 1616. Line 1 on verso of 1f A8 has reading 'sodain'd'. STC 21871. CSmH, DFo, ICU, MH; BL.
          622/129

—[Anr edn]. Second edition, much enlarged. *London: [J. Legat] for F. Constable*, 1622. Line 1 on verso 1f A8 has reading 'sodaind'. STC 21871a. CtY, DFo; BL.
          622/130

Scotland. Privy Council. [Forsamekle as it is weill knowin that his Majestie hes not onlie . . . *Edinburgh:* 1622]. Conditions whereby tobacco may be sold. Crawford (Roy. procl.) Scotland:1379. No copy known.
          622/131

——. [Forsamekle as the Kingis Majestie oute of his princelie and tender . . . *Edinburgh:* 1622]. Forbids import & sale of tobacco. Crawford (Roy. procl.) Scotland:1376. No copy known.
          622/132

Scott, Thomas. The Belgicke pismire: stinging the slothfull sleeper. *'London'* [i.e., *Utrecht?*]: 1622. 99 p.; 4to. Describes Columbus's discovery of New World as saving of the Old; predicts spreading of war in Europe to America. For distinguishing features of edns here listed, see the STC. Sabin 78357; STC 22069. CSmH, DFo, ICN, MH, NN-RB; BL.
          622/133

—[Anr edn]. *'London'* [i.e., *Utrecht?*]: 1622. 4to. STC 22069a. CSmH, DFo, IU, MH, NN-RB; BL.
          622/134

—[Anr edn]. *'London'* [i.e., *Utrecht?*]: 1622. 4to. STC 22069a.5. Cambridge:UL.
          622/135

Scotto, Benedetto. Globe maritime avec la cognoissance et pratique des longitudes proposée en une navigation qui est de passer par la mer septentrionale. *Paris: J. Bessin,* 1622. 6 pts; maps; fol. Included is Scotto's *Deux cartes maritimes septentrionales,* 1st publ. separately, Paris, 1620. BL, BN.
622/136

Shakespeare, William. The history of King Henrie the fourth [Pt 1]. *London: T. P[urfoot].; sold by M. Law,* 1622. 4to. 1st publ., London, 1598; cf. 1604 edn. CSmH, DFo, MB; BL.
622/137

Smith, Capt. John. New Englands trials. Declaring the successe of 80 ships employed thither within these eight yeares . . . The second edition. *London: W. Jones,* 1622. [32] p.; 4to. 1st publ., London, 1620. Sabin 82835; Vail (Frontier) 61; STC 22793; JCB (3) II:172–73. CSmH, ICN, NN-RB, PPL, RPJCB; BL.
622/138

Spain. Sovereigns, etc., 1621–1665 (Philip IV). El Rey. Concejo, justicia, veyntiquatros, cavalleros. [*Madrid?* 1622]. 14 numb. lvs; fol. Includes mention of depopulation of Spain by migration to Indies, which is therefore forbidden. MH.
622/139

Stolcius de Stolcenberg, Daniel. Trias hexastichorum, sive Tres centuriae Epigrammatum. *Frankfurt a. M.: L. Jennis,* 1622. [96] p.; 12mo. In verse. Includes epigram on America. Jantz (German Baroque) 2429. NcD.
622/140

Tapp, John. The seamans kalendar . . . Eighth edition. *London: E. Allde, for J. Tapp,* 1622. 4to. 1st publ., London, 1602. STC 23680.7. Horblit.
622/141

Tassoni, Alessandro. La secchia, poema eroicomico d'Androvinci Melisone [pseud.] . . . Aggiuntovi . . . il primo canto de l'Oceano. *Paris: T. DuBray,* 1622. 166 p.; 12mo. Includes a 'Lettera ad un amico sopra la materia del mondo nuovo' & in 'L'Oceano' refs to Columbus & the New World. In this edn the preface 'A chi legge' occupies prelim. lvs [2r]–[4r]. Sabin 94402; Puliatti (Tassoni) 97. MH, NN-RB, OU; Bologna: BN.
622/142

—[Anr edn]. *Paris: T. DuBray,* 1622. 166 p.; 12mo. In this edn the preface 'A chi legge' occupies prelim.lvs [4]r–[6]r. Puliatti (Tassoni) 98. BN, Rome:BN.
622/143

—[Anr edn]. *Paris: T. DuBray,* 1622. 166 p.; 12mo. Puliatti (Tassoni) 99. BL.
622/144

—[Anr edn]. '*Paris: T. DuBray*' [i.e., *Venice*], 1622. 166 p.; 12mo. A piracy of the preceding. Puliatti (Tassoni) 100. Florence:BN.
622/145

Taylor, John, the Water-poet. An arrant thiefe, whom every man may trust. *London: E. Allde, for H. Gosson,* 1622. [44] p.; 8vo. In verse. Tobacco is described as a thief. STC 23728; Arents (Add.) 210. CSmH, DFo, IU, MH, NN-A; BL.
622/146

——. A common whore with all these graces grac'd. *London: [E. Allde,] for H. Gosson,* 1622. 16 lvs; 8vo. In verse. Tobacco is described as 'Englands bainefull Diety'. In this edn the imprint has reading 'Pannier-Alley'. STC 23742; Arents (Add.) 211. CSmH, IU, MH, NN-A; BL.
622/147

—[Anr edn]. *London: [E. Allde,] for H. Gosson,* 1622. 16 lvs; 8vo. In this edn the imprint has reading 'Panier-Alley'. STC 23742.5.
622/148

——. The great O Toole. *London: [E. Allde,] for H. Gosson,* 1622. [21] p.; port.; 8vo. In verse. Tobacco is mentioned. Also issued as pt 2 of Taylor's *A verry merry wherry-ferry voyage* of 1623. STC 23762; Arents (Add.) 212. CSmH, CtY, MH, NN-A; BL.
622/149

——. Sir Gregory Nonsence his newes from no place. *London: N. O[kes].,* 1700 [i.e., 1622]. 14 lvs; 8vo. In verse. Tobacco is mentioned. STC 23795; Arents (Add.) 213. DFo, NN-A, TxU; BL.
622/150

——. A verry merry wherry-ferry voyage: or Yorke for my money. *London: E. Allde,* 1622. 8vo. Tobacco pipes are mentioned. STC 23812. CSmH; BL.
622/151

——. The water-comorant his complaint. *London: G. Eld,* 1622. 24 lvs; 4to. In verse. Section 'A drunkard' mentions 'th' Indian drug', i.e., tobacco, as does 'A prodigall country gallant' while 'A basket justice' mentions the turkey. STC 23813; Arents (Add.) 213. DFo, MH, NN-A; Oxford:Bodl.
622/152

Theatrum florae, in quo ex toto orbe selecti mirabiles . . . flores . . . proferuntur. *Paris: N. de Mathonière,* 1622. 69 numb. pls; illus.; fol. Included are illus. of American plants

yucca & prickly pear, drawn by Daniel Rabel. Pritzel 10855; Nissen (Bot.) 1575.
622/153

Tomkis, Thomas. Lingua, or The combat of the tongue. *London: N. Okes, for S. Waterson*, 1622. 4to. Drama. 1st publ., London, 1607. STC 24107; Greg 239(d); Arents (Add.) 215. CSmH, CtY, DFo, MH, NN-A; BL.
622/154

Torsellino, Orazio, S.J. Epitome historiarum libri x. *Cologne: Birckmann Office, for H. Mylius*, 1622. 326 p.; 12mo. 1st publ., Rome, 1598; cf. 1620 edn. MiU.
622/155

——. Histoire générale depuis la création du monde jusques a l'annee 1598. *Paris: R. Chaudière*, 1622. 806 p.; 8vo. Transl. from Rome, 1598, Latin text; cf. 1620 edn. Backer VIII:155. BN.
622/156

Usselinx, Willem. Korte onderrichtinghe ende vermaeninge aen alle liefhebbers des vaderlandts, om liberalijcken te teecken inde West-Indische Compagnie. *Leyden: I. Elsevier*, 1622. [20] p.; 4to. Sabin 98197; Jameson (Usselinx) 8; JCB (3) II:173. RPJCB.
622/157

—[Anr issue]. *Leyden: I. Elsevier, for J. van Waesberghe, at Rotterdam*, 1622. Sabin 38260; Jameson (Usselinx) 9; Knuttel 3363. BN, The Hague:KB.
622/158

—[Anr issue]. *Leyden: I. Elsevier, for D. Pieterszoon, at Amsterdam*, 1622. Sabin 102894. CSmH.
622/159

——. Politiicq discours, over den wel-standt van dese vereenichde Provincien. [*Netherlands:*] 1622. [27] p.; 4to. The Nederlandsche West-Indische compagnie is described as a defense against Spain. Sabin 98207; Borba de Moraes II:158; Jameson (Usselinx) 10; Knuttel 3358; JCB (3) II:170. MnU-B, RPJCB; The Hague:KB, Ghent:UB.
622/160

—[Anr edn]. Politiicq discours . . . Provintien. [*Netherlands:*] 1622. [20] p.; 4to. Sabin 63830; Asher 91; Jameson (Usselinx) 11; Knuttel 3359. NN-RB; The Hague:KB, Leyden:UB.
622/161

Vega Carpio, Lope Félix de. Les delices de la vie pastorale de l'Arcadie . . . Mis en françois par L.S.N. [N. Lancelot]. *Lyons: P. Rigaud*, 1622. 454 p.; illus.; 8vo. Transl. from the author's *Arcadia*, 1st publ., Madrid,

1598; cf. 1602 edns. Cf. Palau 356312. BN.
622/162

Venner, Tobias. Via recta ad vitam longam, or A plaine philosophical discourse of such things, as make health . . . The second edition, corrected, and enlarged. Whereunto is also annexed a Treatise of tobacco. *London: T. S[nodham]., for R. More*, 1622. 4to. The *Via recta*, 1st publ., London, 1620; the *Treatise of tobacco*, London, 1621. Of the copies today known, that at MH alone contains the latter. For variant title pages, see the STC. Sabin 98890n; STC 24643.5 & 24644; Arents (Add.) 216. CU, CtY, DNLM, MH, NN-A: Oxford:Bodl.
622/163

Vertooch aen de Ed. Ho. Mo. Heeren Staten Generael, aengaende de tegenwoordige regeringe van de . . . Oost-Indische Compangie [*sic*]. [*The Hague?* 1622]. [11] p.; 4to. Ref. is made also to the West Indies. Sabin 99306; Asher 76; Knuttel 3345. DLC, MnU-B; BL, The Hague:KB.
622/164

Victoria, Pedro Gobeo de, S.J. Wunderbarliche und seltzame Raiss dess jungen und edlen Herrn Petri de Victoria auss Hispanien in das Königreich Peru . . . auss dem lateinischen Exemplar . . . versetzt. *Ingolstadt: G. Hänlin*, 1622. 109 p.; 8vo. Transl. from the author's own published Latin version of his *Naufragio y peregrinacio*, 1st publ., Seville, 1610; described in Backer as 'inexacte et souvent inintelligible'. Sabin 99446; Backer I:1515; Palmer 405; JCB (3) II:172. InU-L, NN-RB, RPJCB; Munich:StB.
622/165

Virginia Company of London. A note of the shipping, men, and provisions, sent and provided for Virginia . . . in the yeere 1621. [*London: F. Kingston*, 1622]. 4 p.; fol. Cf. edns of 1620 & 1621 above. Included here is information to May, 1622. Sabin 99888; Clayton-Torrence 39; Vail (Frontier) 63; STC 24843. CSmH, NN-RB, PPRF; BL.
622/166

Waerschouwinghe op de West-Indissche Compagnie. [*The Hague?* 1622]. bds.; fol. Concerns salt trade with Punta de Araya. Sabin 100939; Asher 67; Petit 1382. Leyden:B. Thysiana.
622/167

Wassenaer, Nicolaes van. Historisch verhael alder ghedenck-weerdichste geschiedenissen, die hier en daer in Europa . . . van den beginne des jaers 1621, tot den herfst toe, voorgevallen syn. *Amsterdam: J. E. Cloppenburg*, 1622. 76 numb. lvs.; illus.; 4to. (N. van Wassenaer's *Historisch verhael*. Pt 1). This volume includes the articles of the Nederlandsche West-Indische Compagnie. Wassenaer's chronicle was continued in 20 additional volumes (1622–1635), each of which is described under the year of its publication. Pts 18–21 were written by Barent Lampe. Bibliographers and cataloguers have regrettably neglected, up till now, to describe individual volumes, limiting themselves to discussion of the collected 21-volume series. It is known that at least some of the volumes were reprinted, so that the sets in different libraries do not necessarily correspond. For this reason, it has not been possible to assign locations to each entry. Locations listed below are for libraries known to have all 21 pts. Sabin 102039; Vail (Frontier) 65; Borba de Moraes II:371–72; Muller (1872) 1745; Stokes (Manhattan) VI:264; JCB (3) II:174. CSmH, CtY, DLC, MH, MiU-C, MnU-B, NN-RB, RPJCB; BL, BN.   622/168

——. Tweede-deel ofte Vervolgh van het Historisch verhael aller gedencweerdigher geschiedenissen . . . *Amsterdam: J. E. Cloppenburg*, 1622. 92 numb. lvs; illus.; 4to. (N. van Wassenaer's *Historisch verhael*. Pt 2). Includes materials concerning formation of the West-Indische Compagnie. Cf. Sabin 102039; Borba de Moraes II:371–72; Muller (1872) 1745; cf. JCB (3) II:174. RPJCB.   622/169

Waterhouse, Edward. A declaration of the state of the colony and affaires in Virginia. With a relation of the barbarous massacre . . . executed by the native infidels . . . And A treatise annexed, written by . . . Henry Briggs, of the Northwest passage to the South Sea through the continent of Virginia, and by Fretum Hudson . . . And a note of the charges of necessary provisions fit for every man that intends to goe to Virginia. *London: G. Eld, for R. Milbourne*, 1622. 54 p.; 4to. The annexed note, a broadside with title *The inconveniencies that have happened*

. . . was also issued separately. Sabin 99885; Vail (Frontier) 66; STC 25104; JCB (3) II:174. CSmH, DLC, ICN, MH (lacks 'Note'), NN-RB, PPL, RPJCB; BL.   622/170

Whitbourne, Sir Richard. A discourse and discovery of New-found-land. *London: F. Kingston*, 1622. 107 p.; 4to. 1st publ., London, 1620; here added are letters of Capt. Edward Wynne relating to Maryland. Sabin 103331; Baer (Md) 2; STC 25373; Church 397; JCB (3) II:175. CSmH, CtY, DLC, ICN, InU-L, MH, MWA, MnU-B, PPL, RPJCB; BL.   622/171

——. A discourse containing a loving invitation . . . to all such as shall be adventurers . . . for the advancement of . . . New-found-land. *London: F. Kingston*, 1622. 46 p.; 4to. An expanded version of the appendix to Whitbourne's *Discourse and discovery* above. Sabin 103333; Harrisse (NF) 35; Baer (Md) 3; STC 25375; Church 398; JCB (3) II:175. CSmH, DLC, ICN, MH, MiU-C, NN-RB, RPJCB; Dublin:Trinity.   622/172

—[Anr edn]. *London: F. Kingston*, 1622. 2 pts; 4to. Here added as pt 2 are letters of Capt. Edward Wynne of July, 1622, etc., relating to Maryland. Sabin 103333n; Baer (Md) 3; STC 25375a. CSmH, DFo, ICN, MH, NN-RB; BL.   622/173

Wither, George. Juvenilia. A collection of those poemes heretofore imprinted. *London: T. S[nodham]., for J. Budge*, 1622. 8vo. Includes Wither's *Abuses stript, and whipt*, 1st publ., London, 1613. STC 25911 (& 25898). CSmH, CtY, DFo, ICN, MH, NN-RB; BL.   622/174

Zoes, Gerardus, S.J. [Relation de la mort de quelques religieux et autres chretiens dans une émeute excites contres les Espagnols dans les Indes Occidentales. *Mechlin: H. Jaey*, 1622.] The above title is that given by Sabin for a work described by Backer as in Flemish but recorded as 'Narratio mortis quorundam religiosorum, et aliorum christianorum in quadam seditione Indorum Occidentalium adversus Hispanos'. Sabin 106367; Backer VIII:1516.   622/175

1623

Aguilar del Rio, Juan. Memorial que ofrece el licenciado Don Juan de Aguilar del Rio, arcediano de la santa iglesia catedral de la ciudad de Arequipa . . . del Peru. [*Madrid:* 1623?]. 20 numb. lvs; fol. Memorial to king of Spain, seeking funds for repair of cathedral & for missionary efforts with Indians. Subscribed: En Los Reyes 20. de Junio de 1623. Sabin 71453; Medina (BHA) 6177; Streit II:1538; JCB (3) II:176. NNH, RPJCB; Santiago, Chile:BN. 623/1

Aldrovandi, Ulisse. De piscibus libri v. et de cetis liber i. *Frankfurt a. M.: J. N. Stoltzenberger, for J. Treudel,* 1623. 280 p.; illus.; fol. 1st publ., Bologna, 1612. Nissen (Zool.) 71. MH-Z; RPB; Munich:StB. 623/2

Alemán, Mateo. The rogue: or, The life of Guzman de Alfarache. *London: G. E[ld]., for E. Blount,* 1623. 2 pts; fol. 1st publ. as here transl. by James Mabbe, London, 1622; here a reissue with altered imprint date. Laurenti (Nov. pic. esp.) 692; STC 289; Palau 6782. CSmH, CtY, DLC, IU, MH, MiU, NjP; BL. 623/3

——. Vitae humanae proscenium: in quo sub persona Gusmani Alfaracii virtutes et vitia . . . graphice et ad vivum repraesantantur . . . Caspare Ens editore. *Cologne: P. von Brachel,* 1623–26. 3 v.; 12mo. Founded on Alemán's *Guzman de Alfarache,* of which pt 1 was 1st publ., Madrid, 1599 (cf. 1601 edn) & pt 2 1st publ., Lisbon, 1604. Vols 2–3 have title *Proscenii vitae humanae.* Laurenti (Nov. pic. esp.) 718–20; cf. Palau 6796. CtY, ICU; BN (v. 1). 623/4

Aviñón, Bartolomé, O.P. Vita, virtù e miracoli del beato Luigi Bertrandi del Ordine de' Predicatori . . . composta in lingua spagnola . . . Tradotta . . . dal sig. Giulio Caesare Cavalia Bottifango. *Rome: A. Ciaccone,* 1623. 522 p.; 8vo. Bertran's career included missions in Colombia. The Spanish text is unknown. Streit I:1539; Palau 20554. Rome:BN. 623/5

Bacon, Francis, viscount St. Albans. Opera: Tomus primus: qui continet De dignitate et augmentis scientiarum. *London: J. Haviland,* 1623. 494 p.; fol. In bk 1 Bacon cites legend of Columbus's use of an egg to demonstrate roundness of earth (promulgated by Benzoni & embellished by de Bry). In bk 5, chapt. 2, Bacon states that the West Indies would not have been discovered except for compass. In some copies the imprint date 'MDCXXIII' has an 'I' added by handstamp or in ink. Gibson (Bacon) 129 a–b; STC 1108. CtY, DNLM; BL, BN. 623/6

——. Historia vitae & mortis. *London: J. Haviland, for M. Lownes,* 1623. 454 p.; 8vo. In section 'Desiccatio' guaiacum is mentioned; under 'Longaevitas', the turkey; under 'Operatio super spiritus', tobacco. Scattered refs to Brazil, Peru, & Virginia also appear. Gibson (Bacon) 147; STC 1156; Arents 150. CSmH, CtY, DLC, ICN, MH, MnU, NN-RB; BL, BN. 623/7

Barclay, John. Euphormionis Lusinini Satyricon. *Leyden: J. Marcus,* 1623. 488 p.; 12mo. Includes pt 2, 1st publ., Paris, 1607, & pt 4, the *Icon animorum,* 1st publ., London, 1614. Shaaber (Brit. auth.) B187. BL, Wolfenbüttel:HB. 623/8

—[Anr edn]. *Frankfurt a. M.: J. Schmidlin,* 1623,'22. 4 pts; 8vo. Shaaber (Brit. auth.) B188. CtY; Oxford:Bodl., Munich:StB. 623/9

—[Anr edn]. *Amsterdam: W. J. Blaeu,* 1623. 8vo. Shaaber (Brit. auth.) B189. York:Minster. 623/10

—[Anr edn]. *Amsterdam: J. Hessius,* 1623–24. 635 p.; 8vo. Shaaber (Brit. auth.) B190. CU, DFo, ICN; Munich:StB, Vienna:NB. 623/11

Bauderon, Brice. Paraphrase sur la Pharmacopoee. *Lyons: P. Rigaud,* 1623. 496 p.; 8vo. 1st publ., Lyons, 1588; cf. 1607 edn. BN. 623/12

—[Anr edn]. *Paris: G. Clopejau,* 1623. 524 p.; 8vo. ViU. 623/13

—[Anr issue]. *Paris: M. Henault,* 1623. BN. 623/14

—[Anr issue]. *Paris: J. Villéry,* 1623. BN. 623/15

Bauhin, Kaspar. Πιναξ theatri botanici . . . opera. *Basel: L. König,* 1623. 522 p.; 4to. Includes descriptions of American plants. Müller 15; Pritzel 509. CU, CtY, DLC, MH,

NNNAM, OU, PPL; London:Wellcome, BN.
623/16

Besold, Christoph. Discursus politicus de incrementis imperiorum . . . Cui inserta est dissertatio singularis De novo orbe. *Strassburg: Heirs of L. Zetzner,* 1623. 65 p.; 4to. The author's *De novo orbe* 1st publ., Tübingen, 1619. Sabin 5048. DLC, NNC; BL, BN. 623/17

Blaeu, Willem Janszoon. Het licht der zeevaert. *Amsterdam: J. Janszoon, the Younger,* 1623-26. 2 v.; illus., maps; obl. fol. 1st publ., Amsterdam, 1608. Koeman (M.B1) 16 (J); Kebabian 296. CtY. 623/18

———. Het licht der zee-vaert [i.e., The light of navigation]. *Amsterdam:* 1623-25. Koeman (M.B1) 22 (J). *See* Blaeu's *The light of navigation* under year 1625.

———. Zeespiegel, inhoudende een korte onderwysinghe in de konst der zeevaert. *Amsterdam: W. J. Blaeu,* 1623. 3 pts; illus., maps; fol. In the 'Erste deel', chapt. xxv includes navigational refs to Peru. This edn includes an 'Almanak' for 1623-34; following the 'Voorreden', the caption title begins 'Cort onderwys'. Koeman (M.B1) 28; Tiele 124; Kebabian 295. CtY; BL (imp.), Zutphen:Librye. 623/19

—[Anr edn]. *Amsterdam: W. J. Blaeu,* 1623. 1 v.; illus.; fol. Of this edn, only pt 1 is known. Following the 'Voorreden', the caption title begins 'Kort onderwys'; the text has been reset. Koeman (M.B1) 29. Rotterdam:ML (imp.). 623/20

—[Anr edn]. *Amsterdam: W. J. Blaeu,* 1623 [i.e., 1627]. *See the year* 1627.

Braun, Georg. Civitates orbis terrarum [Liber primus]. *Cologne: P. von Brachel,* 1523 [i.e., 1623]. 59 double pls; fol. 1st publ., Cologne, 1572; cf. 1612 edn. Koeman II:12. BL (as [1577]), BN. 623/21

Breton, Nicholas. Cornu-copiae. Pasquil's night-cap: or, Antidot for the head-ache. The second impression corrected and amended. *London: T. Thorp,* 1623. 8vo. 1st publ., London, 1612. STC 3640. CSmH; London:V. & A. 623/22

———. A poste with a packet of madde letters. *London: J. Marriott* [1623?]. 4to. 1st publ., London, 1602. STC 3690. Oxford:Bodl.
623/23

Cabeças, Luis. Primera parte da Historia de

S. Domingos particular do reyno, e conquistas de Portugal. [*Lisbon:*] G. da Vinha, 1623. 369 numb. lvs; fol. Streit I:413.
623/24

Calestani, Girolamo. Delle osservationi . . . nella quale . . . s'insegna tutto cio, che fa di bisogno ad ogni diligente speciale. *Venice: P. Miloco,* 1623. 2 v.; 4to. 1st publ., Venice, 1564; cf. 1606 edn. London:Wellcome.
623/25

Campanella, Tommaso. Realis philosophiae epilogisticae partes quatuor . . . (cui Civitas solis juncta est) . . . A Thobia Adami nunc primum editae. *Frankfurt a. M.:* [*E. Emmel?*] *for W. Tampach,* 1623. 508 p.; illus.; 4to. In the *Civitas solis* are scattered refs to the New World. CLSU, MH, NN-RB, PU; BN. 623/26

———. Von der Spannischen Monarchy. [*Tübingen? J. A. Cellius?*] 1623. 166 p.; 4to. 1st publ. as here transl., [Tübingen?], 1620. Sabin 10200-201; Firpo (Campanella) p. 64. NN-RB; BN. 623/27

Casas, Bartolomé de las, O.P., Bp of Chiapa. Den vermeerderden spieghel der Spaensche tierrannije-geschiet in Westindien. *Amsterdam: C. L. van der Plasse,* 1621 [i.e., 1623?]. *See the year* 1621.

Chute, Anthony. Een korte beschrijvinge van het wonderlijcke kruyt tobacco, komende uyt verre ende vreemde landen . . . Overgeset uyt 'tEngels. *Rotterdam: J. Pauwelszoon,* 1623. [48] p.; 16mo. Transl. from Chute's *Tabaco,* 1st publ., London, 1595. Sabin 94165n; Arents 151; Maggs Cat. 502 (Americana VII):5044. DNLM, NN-A, OCl.
623/28

Claude d'Abbeville, O.F.M.Cap. L'arrivee des peres Capucins en l'Inde Nouvelle, appellée Maragnan. *Paris: J. Nigaut,* 1623. 20 p.; 8vo. 1st publ., Paris, 1612. Perhaps a ghost, derived from one of Nigaut's 1613 edns. Streit II:2388. 623/29

Codogno, Ottavio. Compendio delle poste. *Milan: G. B. Bidelli,* 1623. 509 p.; 16mo. 1st publ., Venice, 1611, under title *Nuovo itinerario delle poste.* 'Viaggio per andare da Sevilla alle Indie Occidentali, cioè a Cuba': p. 289-91; 'Relatione delle distanze d'alcuni luoghi, isole, & regni del Mondo nuovo, Nuova Spagna, & Indie Occidentali, per li mari del nort, & sur': p. 304-10. Cf.

Sabin 14142; Michel (Répertoire) II:112. IU; BL, BN. 623/30

Craig, Alexander. The poetical recreations. *Aberdeen: E. Raban, for D. Melvill*, 1623. 4to. 1st publ., Edinburgh, 1609. STC 5960; Arents (Add.) 217. CSmH, NN-A; Aberdeen:UL. 623/31

Crespo, Francisco, S.J. Señor. El padre Francisco Crespo de la Compañia de Jesus, procurador general de las Indias Occidentales en esta corte. Dice, que por los despachos que V[uestra]. M[agestad]. embió con el padre Luys de Valdivia . . . ad marques de Montesclaros virrey del Piru. [*Madrid:* 1623]. 4 numb. lvs; fol. Memorial to king of Spain on Jesuit missions in Chile, etc. Medina (Chile) 241; Streit II:1540; Backer IX:149. Santiago, Chile:BN. 623/32

——. Señor. Francisco Crespo de la Compañia de Jesus, procurador general de las provincias de Indias, dize: Que a sus manos ha llegado un memorial que fray Geronimo Maymon, religioso de la . . . Orden de Predicadores ha hecho imprimir, publicado, y dado por su mano, en defensa de don Melchor de Aguilera, governador de Cartagena. [*Madrid:* 1623?]. Memorial to king of Spain. 6 numb. lvs; fol. Streit II:1541. 623/33

Croll, Oswald. Basilica chymica: oder Alchÿmistisch königlich Kleÿnod . . . Deneben angehengtem seinem newen Tractat von den innerlichen Signaturn. *Frankfurt a. M.: J. F. Weiss, for G. Tampach* [1623]. 3 pts; illus.; 4to. Transl. from Croll's Latin text, *Basilica chymica,* 1st publ., Frankfurt a. M., 1609. CtY, NNE, WU; London:Wellcome. 623/34

Crusenius, Nicolaus, O.E.S.A. Monasticon Augustinianum: in quo omnium ordinum sub regula S. Augustini militantium . . . explicantur. *Munich: J. Hertsroy*, 1623. 262 p.; fol. Includes lists of Augustinian foundations in New World. Streit I:415. DLC, MH, NN-RB, PV; Rome: B. Casanatense. 623/35

Daniel, Samuel. The whole workes. *London: N. Okes, for S. Waterson*, 1623. 2 pts; 4to. Includes both Daniel's 'Musophilus', 1st publ., London, 1599 in his *Poeticall essayes* (cf. his 1602 *Works*), and his *Panegyrike congratulatorie*, 1st publ., London, 1603, as well

as his *The queenes arcadia*, 1st publ., London, 1606. STC 6238; Grolier Club (Langland to Wither) 64. CSmH, CtY, DLC, ICN, MH, NN-RB; BL. 623/36

Du Bartas, Guillaume de Salluste, seigneur. Les oeuvres poetiques. *Rouen: J. B. Behourt*, 1623. In verse. Included are the author's *La sepmaine,* 1st publ., Paris, 1578, & his *La seconde sepmaine,* 1st publ., Paris, 1584; cf. 1603 edn. Holmes (DuBartas) I:77 no. 41n; Jones (Goulart) 20bb; Tchémerzine X:197. Toulouse:BM. 623/37

—[Anr issue]. *Rouen: J. Cailloué*, 1623. Holmes (DuBartas) I:77 no. 41n. 623/38

—[Anr issue]. *Rouen: D. Cousturier*, 1623. Holmes (DuBartas) I:77 no. 41n. 623/39

—[Anr issue]. *Rouen: L. Loudet*, 1623. Holmes (DuBartas) I:77 no. 41. BL. 623/40

Du Chevreul, Jacques. Sphaera. *Paris: J. Moreau*, 1623. 256 p.; illus.; 8vo. Florida & the Strait of Magellan are given passing mention. BN. 623/41

Dupleix, Scipion. La curiosite naturelle. [*Rouen?*] 1623. 269 p.; 8vo. 1st publ., Paris, 1606. NjP; BN. 623/42

Durante, Castore. Il tesoro della sanità. *Venice: A. de' Vecchi*, 1623. 334 p.; 16mo. 1st publ., [Rome?], 1586; cf. 1601 edn. NN-RB, NNNAM. 623/43

Enríquez, Juan, O.P. Relacion de las exequias y honras funerales que por orden del maestro fr. Martin de Requena, provincial de la provincia de S. Hipolyto martyr de Oaxaca de la Orden de Predicadores, en la Nuevaespaña se hizieron a . . . Felipe Terzo . . . en el convento de . . . Santo Domingo de . . . Antequera a los 19. y 20. dias de Diziembre de 1621. *Madrid: Widow of C. Delgado*, 1623. 48 numb. lvs; 4to. Medina (BHA) 747; Pérez Pastor (Madrid) 1936. 623/44

Esternod, Claude d'. L'espadon satyrique. *Lyons: J. Lautret*, 1623. 157 p.; 12mo. In verse. 1st publ., Lyons, 1619. BL. 623/45

Estienne, Charles. L'agricoltura, e casa de villa. *Venice: G. A. Giuliani*, 1623. Cf. 1606 edn. MH; BL. 623/46

Eugalenus, Severinus. De scorbuto morbo liber. *Jena:* 1623. *See the year* 1624.

Fin de la guerre. Dialogus, of t'Samen-spre-

kinge P. Scipio Africanus raedt den Romey-
nen datmen naer Africam most trecken . . .
Dienende tot een exemplar . . . om te be-
wysẽ dat de West-Indische interprinse
d'eenige, ende beste middele is, . . . om
de Spaniaerden uyt den Nederlanden te
jagen. *Amsterdam: P. A. van Ravesteyn* [1623].
43 p.; 4to. Sabin 24340; Knuttel 3428. DLC,
MnU-B, NN-RB, RPJCB; BL (Scipio).

623/47

**Fortgang der West Indianischen Compa-
gnia** . . . In Deutsch gebracht und gedruckt nach der copey Marten Hans Bran-
den . . . zu Amsterdam, 1623. [*Amsterdam?*
1623?]. 19 p.; 4to. Transl. from the *Voortganck vande West-Indische Compaignie,* of this
year below. Sabin 102893; LeClerc (1878)
610n. 623/48

Grégoire, Pierre. Syntagma juris universi.
Geneva: M. Berjon, for Societas Typographica,
1623. 2 pts; fol. 1st publ., Lyons, 1582; cf.
1609 edn. CtY, MH-L. 623/49

—[Anr edn?]. *Geneva: P. Aubert,* 1623. 2 pts;
fol. NBuU-L. 623/50

—[Anr edn?]. *Geneva: S. Gamonet,* 1623. 2 pts;
fol. BN. 623/51

Guicciardini, Francesco. La historia d'Italia
. . . divisa in venti libri. *Venice: A. Pasini,*
1623. 2 pts; 4to. 1st publ., Florence, 1561;
cf. 1604 edn. Michel (Répertoire) IV:101.
MH; BL, Paris:Mazarine. 623/52

Gysius, Johannes. De Spaensche tiranije
gheschiet in Neder-lant. [*Amsterdam:* 1623?].
4to. 1st publ. in this version, Amsterdam,
1620; cf. 1621 edn. BL (Plasse).

623/53

Herrera y Tordesillas, Antonio de. Achtzehender Theil der Newen Welt, das ist:
Gründliche volkommene Entdeckung aller
der West Indianischen Landschafften . . .
Auss der hispanischen Sprach . . . ubergе-
setzet. Item, Gewisse Anzeig der jenigen
so durch die . . . Magellanischen Strassen
. . . passirt und den Erdtkreiss rings umb-
fahren haben. *Frankfurt a. M.: J. F. Weiss,
for the Hulsiuses,* 1623. 256 p.; maps; 4to.
(Levinus Hulsius's *Sammlung von . . . Schiffahrten.* Pt 18). Transl. from the author's
Descripcion de las Indias Occidentales, 1st publ.,
Madrid, 1601. For anr German edn of this
year, see the author's *Zwölffter Theil* below.

Sabin 33671; Baginsky (German Americana) 153; Streit II:1542; Church 310; JCB
(3) I:466. CSmH, CtY, ICN, NN-RB,
RPJCB; BL, BN. 623/54

——. Zwölffter Theil der Newen Welt, das
ist: Gründliche volkommene Entdeckung
aller der West Indianischen Landschafften
. . . auss der hispanischen Sprach . . .
ubergesetzet. Item, Gewisse Anzeigung der
jenigen, so durch die . . . Magellanischen
Strassen . . . passirt . . . haben. Item, Petti
Ordonnez de Cevallos Beschreibung der
West Indianischen Landschafften. *Frankfurt
a. M.: J. T. de Bry,* 1623. 131 p.; illus., maps;
fol. (Theodor de Bry's *America.* Pt 12. German). Herrera y Tordesillas's work transl.
from his *Descripcion de las Indias Occidentales,*
1st publ., Madrid, 1601; for anr German
edn of this year see the author's *Achtzehender
Theil* above. For de Bry's Latin version, see
the year 1624. P. Ordóñez de Ceballos's
work transl. from American section of his
Viage del mundo, 1st publ., Madrid, 1614. Cf.
Sabin 8784; Baginsky (German Americana)
152; Streit II:1543; Church 199; JCB (3)
I:416–17. CSmH, ICN, DLC, NN-RB,
RPJCB; BL, BN. 623/55

Hevia Bolaños, Juan de. Segunda parte de
la Curia philippica. *Valladolid: J. Morillo, for
A. López,* 1623. 664 p.; 8vo. 1st publ., Lima,
1617, under title *Laberinto de comercio terrestre
y naval;* cf. 1619 edn above. The present
edn constitutes the 2nd pt of the 1605 Valladolid edn of the *Curia philippica.* Alcocer
(Valladolid) 693; Palau 114534. BL.

623/56

Hexham, Henry. A tongue-combat lately
happening betweene two English souldiers
in the tilt-boat of Gravesend, the one going
to serve the King of Spaine, the other to
serve the States Generall of the United
Provinces. *London:* [*W. Jaggard?*] 1623. 104
p.; 4to. Mentions Drake's adventures in
West Indies, Sir Walter Raleigh, tobacco,
etc. Erroneously attributed to Thomas
Scott. Sabin 78371; STC 13264.8 (formerly
22090); Arents 154; Knuttel 3486. CSmH,
CtY, DLC, ICN, MH, MnU-B, NN-RB,
RPJCB; BL, The Hague:KB. 623/57

Hues, Robert. Tractaet; ofte Handelinge
van het gebruyck der hemelscher ende

aertscher globe . . . nu in Nederduytsch overgheset ende met vele annotationen vermeerdert door Judocum Hondium. *Amsterdam: J. Hondius,* 1623. 136 p.; illus.; 4to. Transl. from Hues's *Tractatus de globis,* 1st publ., London, 1594; 1st publ. in Dutch, Amsterdam, 1597; cf. Amsterdam, 1611, Latin edn. DLC. 623/58

Jobson, Richard. The golden trade: or, A discovery of the river Gambra, and the golden trade of the Aethiopians. *London: N. Okes; sold by N. Bourne,* 1623. 166 p.; 4to. Describes use in The Gambia of tobacco, introduced from New World. STC 14623; Arents 152. CSmH, CtY, DLC, IU, MH, MiU-C, MnU-B, NN-RB; BL. 623/59

Khunrath, Conrad. Medulla destillatoria et medica quintum aucta & renovata; das ist, Gründliches und vielbewertes Destillier und Artzney Buch. *Hamburg: Froben Office,* 1623,'21. 2 pts; 4to. 1st publ., Schleswig, [1594]; cf. 1601 edn. No 4th edn has been noted; cf. 3rd edn of 1605. Wellcome I:3553. DNLM (imp.); London: Wellcome. 623/60

León Pinelo, Antonio Rodríguez de. Discurso sobre la importancia, forma y disposicion de la recopilacion de las leyes de Indias Occidentales. [*Madrid:* 1623]. 28 numb. lvs; 4to. Sabin 40051; Medina (BHA) 7705; Palau 135734. Santiago, Chile:BN. 623/61

——. Memorial al Rey nuestro señor don Felipe Quarto. En favor . . . de Potosi, de . . . la Serena, en . . . Chile, del monasterio . . . de Santa Catalina . . . de Cordova de Tucuma, y de . . . la Trinidad, puerto de Santa Maria de Buenos Ayres, y governacion del Rio de la Plata. Sobre la licencia . . . que han suplicado para que entren por aquel puerto esclavos de Guinea. *Madrid: J. González,* 1623. 8 numb. lvs; fol. Medina (Chile) 55; Pérez Pastor (Madrid) 1956; Palau 135732. Seville:Archivo de Indias. 623/62

——. Señor. La ciudad de la Trinidad, puerto de Santa Maria de Buenos-Ayres, governacion del Rio de la Plata, suplica a V[uestra]. M[agestad]. se sirva de concederle permission para navegar por aquel puerto los frutos de su cosecha a Sevilla,

Brasil y Angola. [*Madrid:* 1623?]. 14 numb. 1vs; fol. Addressed to king of Spain. Medina (BHA) 7703; Palau 135733. Santiago, Chile:BN. 623/63

A letter from W. A., a minister in Virginia, to his friend T. B., merchant, of Gracious street, London, declaring the advantages to those minded to transport themselves thither. *London:* 1623. 8 p.; 4to. Sabin 40349. 623/64

Linschoten, Jan Huygen van. Beschrijvinge van de gantsche custe van Guinea . . . en tegen over de Cabo de S. Augustijn in Brasilien. *Amsterdam: J. E. Cloppenburg,* 1623. [82] p.; fol. 1st publ., Amsterdam, 1896; cf. 1605 edn. Ostensibly issued as a part of the author's *Itinerarium, ofte Schip-vaert* of this year, q.v. Sabin 41362n; Borba de Moraes I:420; Tiele-Muller 88. 623/65

——. Itinerarium, ofte Schip-vaert naer Oost ofte Portugaels Indien . . . Van nieus ghecorrigeert ende verbetert. *Amsterdam: J. E. Cloppenburg,* 1623. 3 pts; illus., port., maps; fol. 1st publ., Amsterdam, 1596 (cf. 1605 edn); here ostensibly issued with Linschoten's *Reys-gheschrift* & his *Beschrijvinge van . . . Guinea* of this year, the latter including an index for all three pts. Sabin 41362; Borba de Moraes I:419–20; Tiele-Muller 88; Tiele 681; JCB (3) II:178. DLC, NN-RB, RPJCB; BL, BN. 623/66

——. Reys-gheschrift van de navigatien der Portugaloysers in Orienten . . . Als oock van de gantsche kusten van Brasilien . . . Item 't vaste lant eñ die voor-eylanden Las Antilas ghenaemt van Spaensch Indien. *Amsterdam: J. E. Cloppenburg,* 1623. 147 p.; fol. 1st publ., Amsterdam, 1595 [i.e., 1596]; cf. 1604 edn. Ostensibly issued as a pt of Linschoten's *Itinerarium, ofte Schip-vaert* of this year, q.v. Sabin 41362n; Borba de Moraes I:420; Tiele 88. 623/67

Lithgow, William. A most delectable, and true discourse, of an admirable . . . peregrination . . . Newly imprinted, and inlarged. *London: N. Okes,* 1623. 205 p.; port.; 4to. 1st publ., London, 1614. STC 15712; Arents (Add.) 218. CSmH, CtY, NN-A; BL. 623/68

Malynes, Gerard de. The center of the circle of commerce. *London: W. Jones; sold by N.*

Bourne, 1623. 139 p.; 4to. Mentions effects of tobacco. STC 17221. CSmH, DLC, ICU, MnU-B; BL.　　　　　　　　　623/69

Marcos da Lisboa, O.F.M., Bp. La troisiesme partie des Chroniques des freres mineurs . . . Reduicte de castillan en italien par . . . Horace Diola . . . Et nouvellement traduicte par . . . Jean Blancone. *Paris: R. Foüet*, 1623. 774 p.; 4to. 1st publ. in Spanish, Salamanca, 1570; as transl. into Italian, Venice, 1591. Included are accounts of Franciscan missionaries in Mexico. MB; BN.　　　　　　　　　623/70

Mariana, Juan de, S.J. Historia general de España. *Madrid: L. Sánchez*, 1623. 2 v.; fol. Transl., rev. & augm. by the author from his *Historiae de rebus Hispaniae*, 1st publ., Toledo, 1592; cf. 1601 edn. Sabin 44546n; Backer V:549; Pérez Pastor (Madrid) 1965; Palau 151669. RPB; BN (v. 1).　　623/71

—[Anr edn?]. *Toledo: D. Rodríguez*, 1623. 2 v.; fol. Backer V:549–50; Pérez Pastor (Toledo) 512; Palau 151669. CU-A, IaU, NjP; BN (v. 2).　　　　　　　　　623/72

Marino, Giovanni Battista. L'Adone, poema. *Venice: G. Sarzina*, 1623. 577 p.; 4to. In canto 5, stanza 8, Columbus is mentioned as 'il domator de l'Oceano'; in canto 7, stanza 187, by name; in canto 10, stanza 45, as 'il Ligure Argonauta'. Michel (Répertoire) V:120. CU, CtY, DFo, ICN, MH, PU; BL, Paris:Sorbonne.　　623/73

—[Anr edn]. *Paris: O. de Varennes*, 1623. 575 p.; fol. Michel (Répertoire) V:120. MH, MnU, NNC, NcD, OCl; BL, BN.　　623/74

—[Anr edn]. *Turin: Compagnia della Concordia* [1623?]. 583 p.; 12mo. ICN; BN.
　　　　　　　　　623/75

Markham, Gervase. Cheape and good husbandry . . . The third edition. *London: T. S[nodham]., for R. Jackson*, 1623. 179 p.; 4to. (*In* Markham's *A way to get wealth*). 1st publ., London, 1614. Poynter (Markham) 34.1; STC 17338. CSmH, CtY, DFo, ICN, PU; BL.　　　　　　　　　623/76

——. Country contentments, or the English huswife. *London: J. B[eale]., for R. Jackson*, 1623. 133 (i.e., 233) p.; 4to. (In Markham's *A way to get wealth*). 1st publ., London, 1615, under title *The English huswife* as pt 2 of Markham's *Countrey contentments, in two bookes*. Reissued, 1625, as pt 3 of Markham's

A way to get wealth—cf. Poynter (Markham) 34.2. Poynter (Markham) 34.1; STC 17343; Hunt (Bot.) 207. CSmH, DFo, MiU, NN-RB; BL.　　　　　　　　　623/77

Matthieu, Pierre. Historia di Francia et delle cose memorabili occorse nelle provincie stranieri negl'anni di pace del regno del Re . . . Henrico IIII. . . . tradotta di francese . . . dal sig. conte Alessandro Senesio. *Venice: B. Fontana*, 1623. 3 pts; 4to. Transl. from Matthieu's *Histoire de France et des choses memorables advenues aux provinces estrangeres durant sept annees de paix du regne de Henry IV*, 1st publ., Paris, 1605. Michel (Répertoire) V:150. ICN; Nice:BM.　　623/78

Mercator, Gerardus. Atlas sive Cosmographicae meditationes . . . Denuò auctus. Editio quinta. *Amsterdam: H. Hondius*, 1623. fol. 1st publ., Amsterdam, 1606. For variants, see Koeman. Sabin 47882n; Koeman (Me 27A & B); JCB (3) II:179. CSmH, DLC, NN-RB, RPJCB; Paris: Inst. de France.
　　　　　　　　　623/79

Mercuriale, Girolamo. Medicina practica . . . libri v. *Lyons: A. Phillehotte*, 1623. 809 p.; 4to. 1st publ., Frankfurt a. M., 1601. CtY, DNLM; BL.　　　623/80

Meteren, Emanuel van. Historie der Nederlandscher ende haerder na-buren oorlogen ende geschiedenissen, tot dem jare M.VI.ᶜ XII . . . verbetert en in xxxii boecken voltrocken. Gedruckt . . . 1614. *The Hague: Widow & Heirs of J. Jacobszoon van Wouw*, 1623. 671 numb. lvs; illus., ports, map; fol. 1st publ. in Dutch, Delft, 1599; here a reissue of publisher's 1614 edn. ICN (imp.), MiU-C, PLatS; BL, BN.　　　623/81

Mexía, Pedro. The imperiall historie. *London: H. L[ownes]., for M. Lownes*, 1623. 867 p.; fol. 1st publ. in English as transl. by W. Traheron, London, 1604, under title *The historie of all the Romane emperors*. STC 17852. CSmH, CtY, DLC, ICN, InU-L, MH, MiU, NN-RB, PU; BL.　　　623/82

Müller, Philipp (1585–1659). Miracula & mysteria chymico-medica . . . Editio quatuor. *Wittenberg: J. Hake, for C. Berger*, 1623. 493 p.; illus.; 12mo. 1st publ., Wittenberg, 1611. Also included is Jean Béguin's *Tyrocinium chymicum*, 1st publ. with American material, Königsberg, 1618? CLU-C, CtY, DNLM, ICU, MnU; BL, BN.　　　623/83

Neck, Jacob Corneliszoon van. Fünffter Theil der Orientalischen Indien; Eygentlicher Bericht . . . der gantzen volkommenen Reyse oder Schiffahrt. *Frankfurt a. M.: J. F. Weiss,* 1623. 58 p.; illus., maps; fol. (J. T. de Bry's *India Orientalis.* Pt 5. German). 1st publ. in this version, Frankfurt a. M., 1601. Church 235; JCB (3) I:432–33. CSmH, CtY, IU, NN-RB, RPJCB; BL.
623/84

Nederlandsche Oost-Indische Compagnie. Het geamplieerde Octroy van de Oost-Indische Compagnie, by de . . . Staten Generael . . . Midtsgaders: eene corte verthooninge vande nootsakelickheyt vande geoctroyeerde West Indische navigatie. [*Amsterdam?*] 1623. 12 lvs; 4to. Sabin 26815; Asher 82. MiU-C, MnU-B, NN-RB; BL.
623/85

Nederlandsche West-Indische Compagnie. Bewilligungen bey den Staden General damit man die West Indianische Compagnia belehnet . . . Nach dem Original so ins Graven Hage . . . 1623. [*The Hague?* 1623?]. 13 lvs; 4to. Transl. from the Company's *Octroy* of this year below. Sabin 102884; LeClerc (1878) 610n.
623/86

——. Copye. Van seker articulen beraemt inde vergaderinghe vande bewindthebberen ende gecommitteerde der hooft-participanten vande West-Indische Compagnie, binnen Amsterdam. Streckende tot goede verseeckeringe der participanten. [*Amsterdam?*] 1623. 8 p.; 4to. Sabin 16731; Knuttel 3427. NN-RB; The Hague:KB.
623/87

——. Octroy by de Hooghe Mogende Heeren Staten Generael, verleent aende West-Indische Compagnie . . . Meete ampliatien van dien, ende het accoort. *The Hague: Widow & Heirs of H. Jacobszoon van Wouw,* 1623. [30] p.; 4to. The *Octroy* itself 1st publ., The Hague, 1621; here enlarged by addition of related material dated 1622 & 1623. Sabin 56666; Borba de Moraes II:110–11; Asher 55; Knuttel 3424; JCB (3) II:179. MnU-B, NN-RB, PHi, RPJCB; BL, The Hague:KB.
623/88

—[Anr edn]. . . . Mette . . . het accord. *The Hague: Widow & Heirs of H. Jacobszoon van Wouw,* 1623. [30] p.; 4to. Sabin 56667; Knuttel 3425. The Hague:KB.
623/89

—[Anr edn]. . . . Mette . . . het accourt. *The Hague: Widow & Heirs of H. Jacobszoon van Wouw,* 1623. [30] p.; 4to. Sabin 56668.
623/90

—[Anr edn]. Octroy, by de Hooghe Mogende Heeren Staten Generael . . . Na de copije ghedruckt in 'sGraven-Haghe. *Middelburg: Widow & Heirs of S. Moulert* [1623]. [32] p.; 4to. Sabin 102901. MnU-B.
623/91

——. Octroy concédé—par les . . . Estats Generaulx, de la Compagnie des Indes Occidentales . . . Ensemble la première et la seconde ampliation. *Amsterdam: J. P. Wachter,* 1623. 12 lvs; 4to. Transl. from the Dutch *Octroy* above. Sabin 56675; Borba de Moraes II:111; Asher 62; Petit 1405. Leyden: B. Thysiana.
623/92

——. Ordonnances, privileges, franchises, et assistances octroyez & concedez, par les . . . Estats Generaux . . . a la Compagnie des Indes Occidentales . . . Traduit du flaman. *Paris: J. A. Joallin,* 1623. 36 p.; 8vo. Transl. from the *Ordonnantien ende articulen* below. Sabin 102904. BN.
623/93

——. Ordonnantien ende articulen voor desen beraemt by de . . . Staten Generael . . . op het toerusten van eene West-Indische Compagnie. Midtsgaders de laeste ampliatie van de selve ghearresteert op den 21 Julij laestleden. *Arnhem: J. Janszoon,* 1623. [21] p.; 4to. 1st publ., [Amsterdam], 1621; here enl. Sabin 57534 (& 102905A); Asher 53; Meulman 1884. NN-RB; Ghent:BU.
623/94

Netherlands (United Provinces, 1581–1795). Staten Generaal. Placcaet ende ordonnantie . . . waer naer de ingesetenen vande selve landen varende naer westen door de Strate . . . van Gibraltar . . . hen sullen hebben te reguleren. *The Hague: Widow & Heirs of H. Jacobszoon van Wouw,* 1623. [6] p.; 4to. Includes refs to travel toward west (i.e. America), Spanish ships, etc.; cf. enlarged edn of 1625. JCB (3) II:179. RPJCB.
623/95

Novus orbis regionum. Novus orbis. Hoc est, Navigationes illustriores . . . Christophori Columbi, Vincentii Pinzoni, Americi Vesputii, Petri Martyris, Ferdinandi Cortesii, Nicolai Herbornii, quibus novi orbis Americae regnorum . . . situs . . . explicatio & historia continetur. Accessit Casparis Varrerii De Ophyra regione. *Amsterdam: J. Janszoon, the Younger,* 1623. 2 pts; 8vo. 1st publ. in this form, Rotterdam, 1616; here a reissue of that edn with cancel t.p. JCB (3) II:176–77. DLC, RPJCB.

623/96

Outreman, Pierre d', S.J. Tableaux des personnages signalés de la Comp[agn]. ie de Jesus. *Douai: B. Bellère,* 1623. 511 p.; 12mo. Included are accounts of Jesuit missions in the New World. Borba de Moraes II:125; Streit I:416; Backer VI:37. DGU, MoSU-D; BL, BN.

623/97

Pattenson, Matthew. The image of bothe churches, Hierusalem and Babel. *Tournai: A. Quinqué,* 1623. 461 p.; 8vo. Pages 3–4 contain a brief discussion of Virginia. In this issue, on p. 81, line 2 has reading 'mere'. STC 19480; Allison & Rogers 599. CtY, DFo, MBAt; Cambridge:UL.

623/98

—[Anr issue]. *Tournai: A. Quinqué,* 1623. In this issue the reading is 'more'. STC 19481; Allison & Rogers 600. CSmH, DFo, ICN, MH, NN-RB; BL.

623/99

Peraza de Ayala y Rojas, Antonio, conde de la Gomera. Señor. Don Antonio Peraça de Ayala y Rojas . . . presidente de la Real Audiencia . . . de Santiago de Guatemala . . . dize. [*Madrid?* 1623?]. 8 numb. lvs; fol. Memorial to king of Spain protesting actions of Juan de Ibarra & others. BL.

623/100

Perceval, Richard. A dictionary in Spanish and English . . . Now enlarged and amplified . . . by John Minsheu. *London: J. Haviland, for W. Aspley,* 1623. 391 p.; fol. 1st publ., London, 1599. Includes vocabulary relating to American topics. STC 19621. CSmH, CtY, DLC, ICN, MH, MiU, NN-RB, PU-F; BL.

623/101

—[Anr issue]. *London: J. Haviland, for E. Blount,* 1623. STC 19621a. IU, NN-RB, NNH; London:Dr. Williams's Library.

623/102

—[Anr issue]. *London: J. Haviland, for G. Latham,* 1623. STC 19621b. CU, DFo, ICN, MH; Oxford:Queen's College.

623/103

—[Anr issue]. *London: J. Haviland, for M.*

Lownes, 1623. STC 19621.5. CLSU, CtY, DFo, MH, NNH; Oxford:Oriel.

623/104

Pharmacopoeia Augustana. Jussu et auctoritati . . . Senatus a Collegio Medico rursus recognita, nunc septimum in lucem emissa. *Augsburg: A. Aperger, for J. Kruger,* 1623. 2 pts; 8vo. 1st publ., Augsburg, [1564]; cf. 1613 edn. T. Husemann, *A facsimile of the first edition of the Pharmacopoeia Augustana* (Madison, Wisc., 1927) xlii.

623/105

Planis Campy, David de. La verolle recogneue, combatue et abbatue . . . sans tenir chambre . . . Où est adjousté l'antidotaire venerien. *Paris: N. Bourdin,* 1623. 189 p.; 8vo. The introduction of syphilis to Europe is said to have been due to the Indian women who 'avoient esté menées & conduites là des Indes par des soldats Espagnols'. Also given is an extended description of Columbus & his 1st & 2nd voyages. 'Huile de Gaiac': p. 116. Wellcome I:5077. DNLM; BL, BN.

623/106

Plautius, Caspar, O.S.B., Abbot of Seitenstetten. Extract und Ausszug der grossen and wunderbarlichen Schiff-farth Buelij Cataloni . . . welcher anno 1423. mit Almirante Christoforo Columbo in Indiam americam oder Newe Welt . . . geschiffet. [*Linz:*] *J. Planck,* 1623. 37 lvs; illus.; fol. Extracted & transl. from the author's *Nova typis transacta navigatio,* 1st publ., [Linz], 1621. Cf. Sabin 23512. InU-L.

623/107

Pona, Giovanni. Del vero balsamo de gli antichi. *Venice: [B. Barezzi, for] R. Miglietti,* 1623. 54 p.; illus.; 4to. Denies efficacy of Peruvian opobalsam, as opposed to that described by Dioscorides. Wellcome I:5157. CtY, DNLM, MH-A; BL, BN.

623/108

Potier, Pierre. Insignium curationum . . . centuria secunda. *Cologne: M. Schmitz,* 1623. 235 p.; 12mo. 1st publ., Bologna, 1622. NPV.

623/109

Powell, Thomas (1572?–1635?). Wheresoever you see mee, trust unto your selfe. Or, The mysterie of lending and borrowing. *London: [Eliot's Court Press,] for B. Fisher,* 1623. 4to. Includes refs to tobacco. STC 20171; Arents 153. CSmH (imp.), NN-A; BL.

623/110

Recio de León, Juan. Breve relacion de la descripcion y calidad de las tierras, y rios de las provincias de Tipuane, Chunchos, y otras . . . del grande reyno del Paytite. [*Madrid?* 1623?]. 6 numb. lvs; fol. The area in question forms part of present-day Bolivia. Sabin 68358 (& 40075); Medina (Chile) 56; Palau 252304. BL.   623/111

Relacion de la gente de mar, y guerra, y passageros que se ahogaron en los dos galeones de plata, nombradas Nuestra Señora de Atocha, almirante de la flota de Tierrafirme, y Santa Margarita, que se perdieron en la boca de la canal de Bahamas. [*Madrid?* 1623?]. [12] p.; fol. Dated at end: En la Habana, a doze de diziembre de 1622 años. Palau 257649. CSmH, NN-RB.   623/112

—[Anr edn?]. [*Seville?* 1623?]. 5 numb. lvs; fol. DLC, FU.   623/113

Relacion de las vitorias que Don Diego de Arroyo y Daça, governador . . . de la provincia de Cumana, tuvo en la gran salina de Arraya a 30 de Noviembre, del año passado de Cumana. *Madrid: Widow of A. Martín* [1623]. [4] p.; fol. Sabin 69197; Medina (BHA) 752; Pérez Pastor (Madrid) 2000. NN-RB; BL, Madrid:BN.   623/114

—[Anr edn]. *Madrid: Widow of A. Martín* [1623]. [4] p.; fol. Title has reading 'Daza' for 'Daça.' Medina (BHA) 751; cf. Pérez Pastor (Madrid) 2001; Palau 257672. DLC, InU-L.   623/115

Renou, Jean de. Dispensatorium medicum. *Geneva: J. Stoer,* 1623. 1115 p.; 8vo. 1st publ., Paris, 1608, under title *Institutionum pharmaceuticarum libri quinque.* Wellcome I:5430. DNLM; London:Wellcome.   623/116

Ricettario Fiorentino di nuovo illustrato. *Florence: P. Cecconcelli,* 1623. 296 numb. lvs; illus.; fol. 1st publ., Florence, 1597. Described are formulas employing guaiacum & sarsaparilla. DLC, NIC, TxU, WU; BL.   623/117

Robin, Jean. Enchiridion isagogicum ad facilem notitiam stirpium, tam indigenarum, quàm exoticarum. Hae coluntur in horto Joannis & Vespasiani Robin. *Paris: P. de Bresche,* 1623. 71 p.; 8vo. Included are plants identified or identifiable as American. Pritzel 7673. BL.   623/118

Rowlands, Samuel. Doctor Merry-man: or, Nothing but mirth. *London: A. M[athewes]., for S. Rand,* 1623. 4to. In verse. 1st publ., London, 1607, under title *Democritus, or, Doctor Merry-man his medicines.* STC 21376. BL.   623/119

Ruyters, Dierick. Toortse der zee-vaert, om te beseylen de custen gheleghen bezuyden den Tropicus Cancri als Brasylien, West-Indien . . . &c. *Flushing: M. A. vander Nolck, for the Author,* 1623. 462 p.; 4to. Sabin 74515. BN.   623/120

Schyron, Jean. Methodi medendi, seu Institutionis medicinae faciendae . . . libri quatuor . . . Editio nova correcta. *Geneva: P. & J. Chouët,* 1623. 542 p.; 16mo. 1st publ., Montpellier, 1609. In the imprint 'St Gervais' has been overprinted with type ornaments & the Geneva location added. Wellcome I:6946. CtY-M, DNLM; London: Wellcome.   623/121

Scott, Thomas. The Belgicke pismire. [*London: J. Dawson*] 1623. 4to. 1st published, [*Utrecht?*], 1622. For variant states, see the STC. Sabin 78358; STC 22070. CSmH, DFo, TxU; BL.   623/122

——. An experimentall discoverie of Spanish practises. [*London:*] 1623. 54 p.; 4to. Includes copious refs to Spanish America, as well as to Sebastian Cabot & to Sir Francis Drake. The STC suggests that this work may actually have been written by Henry Hexham. For the distinguishing features of the edns listed below, see the STC. Sabin 78363; STC 22077. CSmH, DFo, ICN, MH; BL.   623/123

—[Anr edn]. [*London:*] 1623. 4to. STC 22077.3. ICN, OCl, RPJCB, ViU; BL.   623/124

—[Anr edn]. [*London:*] 1623. 4to. STC 22077.5. CSmH, InU-L, RPJCB; BL.   623/125

—[Anr edn]. [*London:*] 1623. 4to. STC 22077.7. CSmH, DFo, IU, NjP; Cambridge:UL.   623/126

——. The high-waies of God and the King . . . Two sermons. 'London' [i.e., *Utrecht?*]: 1623. 88 p.; 4to. Mentions the use of tobacco as thought necessary by some. Sabin 78365; STC 22079. CSmH, CtY, DLC, ICN, MH; BL.   623/127

——. A tongue-combat. *London:* 1623. *See* Hexham, Henry, *above.*

——. Vox Dei. [*Utrecht?* 1623?] 86 p.; 4to. Includes refs to Spanish West Indies. Also issued as pt of Scott's *Vox populi Vox Dei. Vox regis* of 1624. STC 22097a. CSmH, DFo, MH, NN-RB, RPJCB; Oxford:Bodl.
623/128

Serres, Olivier de, seigneur du Pradel. Le theatre d'agriculture. *Rouen: J. Osmont,* 1623. 908 p.; 4to. 1st publ., Paris, 1600; cf. 1603 edn. ICN; BL.   623/129

Shakespeare, William. Comedies, histories, & tragedies. *London: I. Jaggard & E. Blount, for W. Jaggard, E. Blount, J. Smethwick & W. Aspley,* 1623. 3 pts; fol. Here 1st publ. is *The tempest* with its Bermuda setting, inspired in part by Silvester Jourdan's *A discovery of the Barmudas* of 1610. Also here 1st publ. are *The comedy of errors* with, act 3, scene 3, mention of 'metal of Indies', i.e., gold; and *Twelfth night,* in which, act 2, scene 5, the turkey is mentioned, &, act 3, scene 2, a 'new map, with the augmentation of the Indies'. Also included are other works with American refs earlier published, e.g., *The merry wives of Windsor* (London, 1602). STC 22273. CSmH, CtY, DLC, ICN, InU-L, MH, MiU, NN-RB, PU-F, RPJCB; BL, BN.   623/130

A short discourse of the New-found-land: containing diverse reasons and inducements, for the planting of that countrey. *Dublin: Society of Stationers,* 1623. [27] p.; 4to. Dedication signed: T. C. Sabin 80620; Baer (Md) 4; STC 4311; JCB (3) II:177. MB, NN-RB, PPRF, RPJCB; BL.   623/131

Silva, Juan de, O.F.M. Santissimo padre. Fray Juan de Silva. [*Madrid:* 1623]. bds.; fol. Memorial, dated at Madrid, 1623, to the pope on spiritual & temporal conditions in Spanish America. Medina (BHA) 754. BL.
623/132

Smith, Capt. John. The generall history of Virginia, the Somer Iles, and New England. [*London: J. Dawson,* 1623]. [4] p.; fol. Prospectus for Smith's *Generall historie* of 1624. Sabin 82823; STC 22789. London: Soc. of Antiquaries.   623/133

Somma, Agacio di. Dell'America, canti cinque. *Rome: B. Zannetti,* 1623. 12mo. Sabin 86842.   623/134

Spain. Casa de Contratación de las Indias. Relacion de las cargas y obligaciones que tengo en el oficio de Contador desta Casa de la Contratacion de las Indias. *Seville: J. Serrano de Vargas y Ureña,* 1623. 12 numb. lvs; fol. Issued by Antonio López de Calatayd. NN-RB; BL.   623/135

Spain. Consejo de las Indias. Assiento y capitulacion que se tomo con Manuel Rodriguez Lamego, sobre la renta provision de esclavos negros que se navegan a las Indias por tiempos de ocho años. [*Madrid?* 1623]. 17 numb. lvs; 4to. Relates to trade in slaves from Cape Verde destined for Colombia & Mexico. Sabin 72556; Medina (BHA) 746; Palau 18677. BL.
623/136

Spain. Laws, statutes, etc., 1598–1621 (Philip III). Titulo de gran chanciller y registrador de las Indias, para el conde de Olivares. [*Madrid?* 1623]. 5 numb. lvs; fol. Dated 16 Oct. 1623. BL.
623/137

Taylor, John, the Water-poet. The praise and vertue of a jayle. *London: J. H[aviland]., for R. B[adger].,* 1623. 8vo. Tobacco is mentioned. STC 23785. CSmH (imp.); BL.
623/138

——. The praise of hemp-seed. *London: [E. Allde,] for H. Gosson; sold [by E. Wright?* 1623]. 24 lvs; 4to. In verse. 1st publ., London, 1620. STC 23789; Arents (Add.) 195. MH (imp.), NN-A.   623/139

—[Anr state]. *London: [E. Allde,] for H. Gosson; sold [by E. Wright?]* 1623. 4to. STC 23789.3. Oxford:Bodl.   623/140

——. A verry merry wherry-ferry voyage. *London: E. Allde,* 1623,'22. 2 pts; 8vo. 1st publ., London, 1622. The 2nd pt is a reissue of Taylor's 1622 *The great O Toole.* STC 23812.3. MH.   623/141

——. The world runnes on wheeles. *London: E. A[llde]., for H. Gosson,* 1623. 19 lvs; 8vo. In verse. Tobacco is mentioned. STC 23816; Arents (Add.) 220. NN-A (imp.); BL.
623/142

Torsellino, Orazio, S.J. Historiarum ab origine mundi usque ad annum 1598 epitome libri x. *Douai: B. Bellère,* 1623. 2 pts; 12mo. 1st publ., Rome, 1598; cf. 1620 edn. Backer VIII:151. BN.   623/143

——. Ristretto delle historie dalla creatione

del mondo . . . dalla latina . . . voltato do Lodovico Aurelii. *Perugia: P. G. Billi,* 1623. 507 p.; 12mo. Transl. from Latin text, 1st publ., Rome, 1598; cf. 1620 edn. Backer VIII:156.　　　　　　　　　　623/144

A true relation of that which lately hapned to the great Spanish fleet, and galeons of Terra Firma in America. *London: [G. Eld,] for N. Butter, N. Bourne & W. Sheffard,* 1623. 28 numb. lvs; 4to. Transl. from the 1622 *Relacion de lo sucedido en los galeones y flota de Tierrafirme.* Sabin 97141; STC 23009. CSmH, DFo; BL.　　　　　　623/145

Vallet, Pierre. Le jardin du roy très chrestien Loys XIII. *[Paris:]* 1623. 90 pls; illus.; fol. An enlarged version of edn publ., [Paris], 1608, under title *Le jardin du roy très chrestien Henry IV,* q.v. Pritzel 9672; Nissen (Bot.) 2039n. DDO, DeU, MH-A; BL.
　　　　　　　　　　　　　　　　623/146

Vázquez de Espinosa, Antonio. Confessario general, luz y guia del cielo . . . con los tratos y contratos de las Indias del Piru, y Nueva España. *Madrid: J. González,* 1623. 107 numb. lvs; 8vo. Sabin 98724 (& 22889); Medina (BHA) 777; Pérez Pastor (Madrid) 2029. NN-RB.　　　　　　　623/147

——. Tratado verdadero del viage y navegacion deste año de seiscientos y veinte y dos, que hizo la flota de Nueva España, y Honduras. *Málaga: J. René,* 1623. 80 numb. lvs; 8vo. Sabin 98726; cf. Medina (BHA) 755; JCB (3) II:181. RPJCB (imp.); BL, BN.
　　　　　　　　　　　　　　　　623/148

Voortganck vande West-Indische Compaignie. *Amsterdam: M. J. Brandt,* 1623. 19 p.; 4to. Sometimes attrib. to Usselinx, but see Jameson (Usselinx), p. 74–75. Sabin 100773; Asher 100; Knuttel 3426; Kress 408. CSmH, MH-BA, MnU-B, NN-RB, RPB; BL, The Hague:KB.　　623/149

Wassenaer, Nicolaes van. [T'derde-deel of t'vervolgh van het Historischer verhael aller ghedenckwaerdigher gheschiedenissen. *Amsterdam: J. E. Cloppenburg,* 1623]. 97 numb. lvs; illus.; 4to. (N. van Wassenaer's *Historisch verhael.* Pt 3). Includes refs to the West-Indische Compagnie, & to the Netherlands Staten Generaal's prohibition of trafficking with Punta de Araya. The existence of this edn is inferred from the t.p. of the Hoorn edn under year 1626. Sabin

102039; Borba de Moraes II:371–72; Muller (1872) 1745.　　　　　　　　623/150

——. T'vierde deel of t'vervolgh van het Historisch verhael aller ghedenckwaerdigher gheschiedenissen. *Amsterdam: J. E. Cloppenburg,* 1623. 148 numb. lvs; illus.; 4to. (N. van Wassenaer's *Historisch verhael.* Pt 4). Includes ref. to the Spanish loss of its silver fleet & to Spanish fortification of Punta de Araya. Cf. Sabin 102039; Borba de Moraes II:371–72; Muller (1872) 1745. RPJCB.
　　　　　　　　　　　　　　　　623/151

Whitbourne, Sir Richard. A discourse and discovery of New-found-land. *London: F. Kingston,* 1623. 97 p.; 4to. 1st publ., London, 1620. Some copies have reading 'Discoerus' in title; for 2 settings of sheet D, see Sabin. Sabin 103332; STC 25374. CSmH, ICN, MB, NN-RB; BL.　　623/152

Zárate, Agustín de. Conqueste van Indien. De wonderlijcke ende warachtighe historie vant coninckrijck van Peru . . . inde welcke verhaelt wort de gelegentheyt costuymen, manieren van leven, overvloedicheyt des goudts ende silvers . . . *Amsterdam: J. P. Wachter,* 1623. 154 numb. lvs; 8vo. 1st publ. in Dutch, Antwerp, 1563, under title *De wonderlijcke . . . historie . . . van Peru;* transl. from Zárate's *Historia,* 1st publ. in Spanish, Antwerp, 1555. Sabin 106258; Medina (BHA) 249 (I:414–15). DLC.　　623/153

1624

Abbot, George, Abp of Canterbury. A briefe description of the whole worlde . . . The sixt edition. *London: J. Marriott,* 1624. [174] p.; 4to. 1st publ., London, 1599. Cf. Sabin 21; STC 30. DLC, MBAt, NN-RB; BL.　　　　　　　　　　　　624/1

Acosta, José de, S.J. Historie naturael en morael van de Westersche Indien . . . Uyt den Spaenschen . . . tale overgheset door Jan Huyghen van Linschoten. De tweede editie. *Amsterdam: B. Janszoon,* 1624. 177 numb. lvs; 4to. 1st publ. in Dutch, Enkhuizen, 1598; transl. from Acosta's *Historia natural y moral delas Indias,* 1st publ., Seville, 1590. Sabin 127; Medina (BHA) 330n (I:502); Palau 1993; Tiele-Muller 290; Streit

II:1549; JCB (3) II:182. DLC, ICN, MH, MiU-C, RPJCB; BL, Göttingen:UB. 624/2

—[Anr issue]. *Amsterdam: B. Janszoon, for J. E. Cloppenburg,* 1624. Palau 1993n; Tiele-Muller 291. NN-RB. 624/3

—[Anr issue]. *Amsterdam: [B. Janszoon, for] H. Laurenszoon,* 1624. Medina (BHA) 330n (I:502); Palau 1993n; Tiele-Muller 292. MnU-B. 624/4

Alcalá Yáñez y Rivera, Jerónimo. Alonso, mozo de muchos amos. *Madrid: B. de Guzmán, for J. de Vicuña Carrasquilla,* 1624. 167 lvs; 8vo. Chapt. viii comprises a fictional account of Alonso's 'jornada que hizo á las Indias y los grandes trabajos que padeció'. Pérez Pastor (Madrid) 2038; Palau 5818. NNH. 624/5

Alsted, Johann Heinrich. Thesaurus chronologiae. *Herborn: [G. Rab]* 1624. 340 p.; 8vo. Under the year 1492 Columbus & Vespucci are discussed. LNHT, MBAt, NcD; Munich:StB. 624/6

Antidotario romano latino e volgare. Tradotto da Ippolito Ceccarelli . . . Con l'aggiunta dell'elettione de' semplici. *Rome: A. Fei, for G. A. Ruffinelli,* 1624. 232 p.; 4to. 1st publ. as here constituted, Rome, 1612. DNLM. 624/7

Bacon, Francis, viscount St Albans. De dignitate et augmentis scientiarum libri ix. *Paris: P. Mettayer,* 1624. 540 p.; fol. 1st publ., London, 1623, as *Opera: Tomus primus.* Gibson (Bacon) 130; Shaaber (Brit. auth.) B20. CSmH, CtY, DFo, ICN, MH, MnU, NjP; BL, BN. 624/8

——. The essaies. *London: J. D[awson]., for Elizabeth Jaggard,* 1624. 114 lvs; 8vo. 1st publ. with 'Of atheisme', London, 1612. Gibson (Bacon) 12; STC 1146. CtY, DLC, ICN, MH, NNPM; BL. 624/9

——. Le progrez et avancement aux sciences divines & humaines . . . Traduict . . . par A. Maugars. *Paris: P. Bilaine,* 1624. 636 p.; 8vo. Transl. from Bacon's *Twoo bookes . . . of the proficience and advancement of learning,* 1st publ., London, 1605. Gibson (Bacon) 84; Shaaber (Brit. auth.) B41. CU, DFo, MH, MiU; BL, BN. 624/10

Barclay, John. Euphormionis Lusinini . . . Satyricon. *Frankfurt a. M.: J. Schmidlin,* 1624–25. 4 pts; 8vo. Includes pt 2, 1st publ.,

Paris, 1607, & pt 4, the *Icon animorum,* 1st publ., London, 1614. Shaaber (Brit. auth.) B191. TNJ; Wolfenbüttel:HB, Vienna:NB. 624/11

Barrough, Philip. The method of phisick . . . The sixth edition. *London: R. Field,* 1624. 477 p.; 4to. 1st publ., London, 1583; cf. 1601 edn. STC 1514. CSmH, DNLM, MBCo, MnU, PU, WU; BL. 624/12

Baudart, Willem. Memoryen ofte Cort verhael der gedenck-weerdichste . . . gheschiedenisse . . . van den jaere 1603. tot . . . 1624. Tweede editie . . . vermeerdert. *Arnhem: J. Janszoon,* 1624 (pt 1); *Zutphen: A. Janssen,* 1625 (pt 2). 2 pts; port.; fol. 1st publ., Arnhem, 1620, but here including treatment of Dutch exploits in Brazil, New Netherland, & the West-Indische Compagnie's *Octroy.* Muller (1872) 2385; Rodrigues (Dom. Hol.) 106; Stokes (Manhattan) VI:258. CtY, DLC, MiU, NIC, WU; BL. 624/13

Béguin, Jean. Les elemens de chymie. *Geneva: J. Celerier,* 1624. 465 p.; 8vo. 1st publ. as here transl. from Béguin's *Tyrocinium chymicum* (Paris, 1612), Paris, 1615. CtY-M, DLC. 624/14

—[Anr edn]. Troisiesme edition. *Paris: M. Le Maître,* 1624. Glasgow:UL, BN. 624/15

Bertius, Petrus. Abrégé ou Sommaire description du globe de la terre . . . traduict en françois par N. Hallay. *Paris: J. Villéry* 1624. 92 p.; 8vo. Transl. from the author's *Breviarium totius orbis terrarum* of this year. Cf. Sabin 5013. BN. 624/16

——. Breviarium totius orbis terrarum. *Paris: M. Hénault,* 1624. 17 p.; map; 4to. Cf. Sabin 5013. BN. 624/17

Beschryvinge van 't in-nemen van de stadt Salvador inde Baya de todos os Sanctos in Brasil door den e. Admiral Jacob Willekes. *Amsterdam: C. J. Visscher,* 1624. bds.; illus.; fol. Sabin 76212. DLC. 624/18

Besold, Christoph. Juridico-politicae dissertationes. *Strassburg: Heirs of L. Zetzner,* 1624. 283 p.; 4to. Includes ref. to Spanish colonies in Indies, citing Botero. DLC; BN. 624/19

Boanerges. or The humble supplication of the ministers of Scotland. *'Edenburgh'* [i.e., *London*]: 1624. 34 p.; 4to. Deplores impact upon Virginia of surreptitious sale of Spanish tobacco. Authorship attrib. to Thomas Scott. STC 3171. CSmH, CtY, DFo, ICN, MH, NN-RB; BL. 624/20

—[Anr edn]. *'Edinburgh'* [i.e., *London*]: 1624. 34 p.; 4to. STC 3171.3; Arents (Add.) 221. CtY, DFo, InU-L, MH, NN-A; BL. 624/21

Boccalini, Traiano. De' ragguagli di Parnaso . . . Centuria prima . . . quinta impressione. *Venice: G. Guerigli*, 1624. 478 p.; 4to. 1st publ., Venice, 1612. Firpo (Ragguagli) 16; Michel (Répertoire) I:176. CU, InU, MH, MiU, NN; BN. 624/22

—[Anr edn]. *Venice: G. Guerigli*, 1624. 332 p.; 8vo. Firpo (Ragguagli) 17; Michel (Répertoire) I:176. Paris:Mazarine. 624/23

——. De' ragguagli di Parnaso . . . Centuria seconda . . . quarta impressione. *Venice: G. Guerigli*, 1624. 453 p.; 4to. 1st publ., Venice, 1613; issued with Guerigli's Centuria prima of this year above. Firpo (Ragguagli) 16; Michel (Répertoire) I:176. InU, MiU, NN; BN. 624/24

—[Anr edn]. Quinta impressione. *Venice: G. Guerigli*, 1624. 292 p.; 8vo. Firpo (Ragguagli) 17: Michel (Répertoire) I:176. BL, Paris:Mazarine. 624/25

Bozio, Tommaso. De signis ecclesiae Dei libri xxiiii. *Lyons*: 1624. 3 v.; 8vo. 1st publ., Rome, 1591; cf. 1602 edn. Streit I:418. 624/26

Brassillische Relation. inn America gelegen. Was gstaldt [*sic*] die Baija und Möhr buesen de Todos os Sanctos unnd Statt S. Salvator von den Hollendern eingenommen worden, geschehen diss 1624 Jahr. *Augsburg: D. Franck, in shop of W. P. Zimmermann*, 1624. [2] p.; illus., map; fol. BL. 624/27

Braun, Georg. Civitates orbis terrarum [Liber primus]. *Cologne: P. von Brachel*, 1624. 59 double pls; fol. 1st publ., Cologne, 1572; cf. 1612 edn. Koeman lists this edn but provides no specific location for it. Koeman II:12. 624/28

Braun, Samuel. Samuel Brun . . . Schiffarten, welche er in etliche newe Länder . . . gethan. *Basel: J. J. Genath*, 1624. 132 p.; 8vo. Includes refs to West Indies. BL. 624/29

Bry, Theodor de, comp. Novi Orbis pars

duodecima. *Frankfurt a. M.:* 1624. *See* Herrera y Tordesillas, Antonio de, *below*.

Burton, Robert. The anatomy of melancholy . . . The second edition, corrected and augmented by the author. *Oxford: J. Lichfield & J. Short, for H. Cripps*, 1624. 557 p.; fol. 1st publ., Oxford, 1621. Madan (Oxford) 1624:3; STC 4160; Arents (Add.) 222. CSmH, CtY, DLC, ICN, IU, InU-L, MH, MiU, NN-RB, PU, RPJCB; BL. 624/30

Camden, William. Annales des choses qui se sont passées en Angleterre . . . traduites par Paul de Bellegent. *London: R. Field*, 1624. 521 p.; 4to. Transl. from the author's Latin text, 1st publ., London, 1615. Sabin 10159; STC 4502. CSmH, DFo, MH; BL, BN. 624/31

Camerarius, Philipp. Operae horarum subcisivarum . . . Centuria prima. *Frankfurt a. M.: E. Emmel, for P. Kopff*, 1624. 474 p.; 4to. 1st publ., Altdorf, 1591; cf. 1602 edn. CtY, DLC. 624/32

Carrillo Altamirano, Fernando Alfonso. Señor. El doctor Hernan Carrillo Altamirano, vezino y natural de la ciudad de Mexico. [*Madrid?* 1624?]. 12 numb. lvs; fol. Memorial to king of Spain in reply to that of Cristóbal de Molina on services of Mexican Indians. Medina (BHA) 6319. BL, Seville: Archivo de Indias. 624/33

Carrillo de Mendoza y Pimentel, Diego, marqués de Gelves. Relacion del estado en que el marques de Gelves hallo los reynos de la Nueva España, de lo sucedido en el tiempo que la govierno, y del tumulto y lo demas, hasta que volvio a España. [*Madrid*: 1624]. 32 numb. lvs; fol. Cf. the *Relacion Sumaria* below. Sabin 69212. Medina (BHA) 6604; Palau 45598; Maggs Cat. 496 (Americana VI):134. CU-B, ICN. 624/34

Catholic Church in the West Indies. Los arçobispos y obispos de las Indias Occidentales, pretenden V[uestra]. Magestad les ampare en lo que por derecho comun Concilio Tridentino . . . està determinado . . . para que los religiosos de las tres ordenes mendicantes . . . en dichas Indias, esten subordinados immediatamente a los Ordinarios en la visita. [*Madrid*: 1624]. fol. Memorial to king of Spain. Sabin 102866. BL. 624/35

Cats, Jacob. Silenus Alcibiadis. [*Amsterdam?*] 1624. obl. 12mo. 1st publ., Middelburg, 1618; here abridged. Mus. Cats. 31.
624/36

Cervantes Saavedra, Miguel. Novelas exemplares. *Seville: F. de Lyra,* 1624. 371 numb. lvs; 8vo. 1st publ., Madrid, 1613. Ríus (Cervantes) 231; Palau 53410. BL.
624/37

Céspedes y Velasco, Francisco de. Memoria de diferentes piensons . . . para tener medrados, y luzidos los cavallos. Por don Francisco de Cespedes . . . Governador, y capitan general del puerto de Buenosayres, y provincia del Rio de la Plata. *Seville: F. de Lyra,* 1624. 8 numb. lvs; 4to. Medina (BHA) 764; Escudero (Seville) 1298; Palau 54217. Madrid:BN.
624/38

Een clare ende waerachtighe beschrijvinghe vande victorie, die de West-Indische Compagnie . . . gehad heeft in de Baye de Todos los Sanctos. *Utrecht: A. van Herwijck,* 1624. 4 p.; 4to. Amsterdam:NHSM.
624/39

Clüver, Philipp. Introductionis in universam geographiam, tam veterem quàm novam, libri vi. *Leyden: Elsevier Office,* 1624. 245 p.; illus.; 4to. Edited by Joseph Vorstius. Sabin 13805; Willems (Les Elzevier) 220; Rahir (Les Elzevier) 187. NN-RB, PU, ViU; BL, BN.
624/40

Coelho de Barbuda, Luiz. Empresas militares de Lusitanos. *Lisbon: P. Craesbeeck,* 1624. 334 numb. lvs; 4to. 'Descubrieron la tierra de Sanct Cruz llamada agora Brasil': lf 116; an account of Magellan appears on lvs 260v–262r. Borba de Moraes I:63; Maggs Cat. 502 (Americana VII):5047. ICN, MH, NN-RB, RPJCB; BL.
624/41

—[Anr issue]. Reyes de Portugal y empresas militares de Lusitanos. *Lisbon: P. Craesbeeck,* 1624. Palau 56169. BN.
624/42

Cortés, Jerónimo. Phisonomia. *Barcelona: S. de Cormellas,* 1624. 8vo. 1st publ., Valencia, 1597; cf. 1601 edn. Palau 63308.
624/43

Croll, Oswald. Basilica chymica . . . Additus est . . . Tractatus novus de signaturis rerum internis. *Geneva: J. Celerier,* 1624. 2 pts; 8vo. 1st publ., Frankfurt a. M., 1609. BN.
624/44

——. La royalle chymie. Traduitte . . . par J. Marcel de Boulenc. *Lyons: P. Drouet,* 1624. 3 pts; illus.; 8vo. Transl. from Croll's Latin *Basilica chymica,* 1st publ., Frankfurt a. M., 1609. MH; London:Wellcome, BN.
624/45

Del Rio, Martin Anton, S.J. Disquisitionum magicarum libri sex. *Mainz: [A. Strohecker?] for P. Henning, at Cologne,* 1624. 1070 p.; 4to. 1st publ., Louvain, 1599–1600; cf. 1603 edn. Backer II:1899. MH, MiU, NIC; London:Wellcome, BN.
624/46

Dessein perpetuel des Espagnols a la monarchie universelle . . . Reveu, corrigé, augmenté, & translaté . . . avec les extraicts des lettres du Roy d'Espagne. [*The Hague?*] 1624. 71 p.; 8vo. Beginning with p. 15, consists of citations from various official documents & statesmen's letters. On p. 53–55 is an account of the duke of Alba's counselling the king of Spain either to make peace with England or invade her, since war by itself would only teach her to be mischievous & to trouble the Indies. Knuttel 3512. DFo, MH, MnU-B; BL (Spaniards), The Hague:KB.
624/47

Donne, John. A sermon upon the eighth verse of the first chapter of the Actes of the Apostles. *London: [A. Mathewes,] for T. Jones,* 1624. 49 p.; 4to. 1st publ., London, 1622. Cf. Sabin 20601; cf. Clayton-Torrence 44; cf. Vail (Frontier) 59; Keynes (Donne) 18; STC 7052; Church 401; JCB (3) II:184. DFo, DLC, MH, RPJCB; Cambridge: Pembroke.
624/48

——. Three sermons upon speciall occasions. *London: [A. Mathewes?] for T. Jones,* 1624. 3 pts; 4to. Made up of works first publ. separately, the 2nd being the original 1622 edn of Donne's *A sermon upon the viii verse of the I. chapter of . . . Actes.* In this issue the imprint has reading 'are to sold' [*sic*]. Cf. Sabin 20601; Keynes (Donne) 17; STC 7057.
624/49

—[Anr issue]. *London: [A. Mathewes?] for T. Jones,* 1624. In this issue the imprint has reading 'are to be sold'. Keynes (Donne) 17a. R. S. Pirie.
624/50

Duchesne, Joseph. La pharmacopee des dogmatiques reformee. *Paris: C. Morel,* 1624. 2 pts. 8vo. Transl. from Duchesne's

Pharmacopoea dogmaticorum restituta, 1st publ., Paris, 1607. London:Wellcome.
624/51

Duport, François. Medica decas. Niort: J. Moussat, 1624. 306 p.; 8vo. In verse. 1st publ., Paris, 1584, under title *De signis morborum libri quatuor;* cf. 1613 edn. DNLM; BN.
624/52

Eburne, Richard. A plaine path-way to plantations. *London: G. P[urslowe]., for J. Marriott,* 1624. Includes discussion of Newfoundland & other regions of North America. Sabin 21752; Baer (Md) 6; STC 7471; JCB (3) II:184. CsmH, DFo, MH, NN-RB, RPJCB.
624/53

Estaço da Silveira, Simão. Relação summaria das cousas do Maranhão. *Lisbon: G. da Vinha,* 1624. [23] p.; fol. Sabin 81120; Borba de Moraes II:263–64; Palau 313855. DCU, MnU-B; Seville:Archivo de Indias.
624/54

Esternod, Claude d'. L'espadon satyrique. *Rouen: D. Ferrand,* 1624. 154 p.; 12mo. In verse. 1st publ., Lyons, 1619. Cioranescu (XVII) 28492.
624/55

Eugalenus, Severinus. De scorbuto morbo liber. *Jena: J. Beithmann, for B. Voigt,* 1623 [i.e., 1624?]. 453 p.; 8vo. 1st publ., Leipzig, 1604. DNLM, NNNAM; BN.
624/56

Fioravanti, Leonardo. Compendium oder Ausszug der Secreten, Gehaymnissen und verborgenen Künsten . . . Jetzund auss dem Italienischen . . . versetzet. *Darmstadt: J. Leinhose, for J. Berner [at Frankfurt a. M.?]* 1624. 399 p.; 8vo. Transl. from Fioravanti's *Del compendio de i secreti rationali,* 1st publ., Venice, 1564; cf. 1620 edn. Ferguson (Bibl. chem.) I:277. DNLM; London:Wellcome.
624/57

——. Dello specchio di scientia universale. *Venice: The Valentini,* 1624. 347 lvs; 8vo. 1st publ., Venice, 1564; cf. 1603 edn. Michel (Répertoire) III:48. Paris:Arsenal, Grenoble:BM.
624/58

Gardiner, Edmund. Physicall and approved medicines. *London: [H. Lownes,] for M. Lownes,* 1624. 58 numb. lvs; 4to. 1st publ., London, 1610, under title *The triall of tobacco;* here reissued with cancel t.p. Arents 155. NN-A.
624/59

Garzoni, Tommaso. Emporii emporiorum, sive Theatri vitae humanae . . . Interprete N. Bello [i.e., M. C. Lundorp]. *Frankfurt a. M.: J. T. Schönwetter,* 1624,'23. 3 pts; 4to. Transl. from Garzoni's *La piazza universale,* 1st publ., Venice, 1586; cf. 1601 edn. BL.
624/60

Gheluck-wenschinghe aan de West-Indische vlote. Afghevaren uyt Nederland in de maand Januario, des jaars 1624. *Amsterdam: B. Janszoon,* 1624. 8 p.; 4to. In verse. Signed 'A.H.' Sabin 27259; Borba de Moraes I:298; Knuttel 3538; Asher 103. The Hague:KB.
624/61

——[Anr edn?] Geluckwenschinghe. *Amsterdam:* 1624. 4to. Sabin 26847 (a possible ghost).
624/62

Good newes from Virginia, sent from James his towne this present moneth of March, 1623 [i.e., 1624], by a gentleman in that country. *London: J. Trundle* [1624?]. bds.; illus.; fol. Ballad concerning Indian massacre. Sabin 100478; Clayton-Torrence 49A. ViU; London:PRO.
624/63

Great Britain. Council for Virginia. By His Majesties Commissioners for Virginia. *London: F. Kingston,* 1624. bds.; fol. To further 'the present ordering of the affaires of the Colony and Plantation of Virginia' states that the Commissioners will be available weekly at the house of Sir Thomas Smith to give counsel to those seeking to emigrate or engage in commerce in the colony. STC 24844.3 (formerly 24837). BL.
624/64

Great Britain. Sovereigns, etc., 1603–1625 (James I). A proclamation concerning tobacco. *London: B. Norton & J. Bill,* 1624. 4 lvs; fol. Prohibits importation of tobacco not grown in Virginia or Bermuda. Sabin 99844; Crawford (Roy. procl.) 1385; STC 8738; Arents 154-A. CSmH, NN-A, RPJCB; BL.
624/65

——[Anr edn]. *London: B. Norton & J. Bill,* 1624. 4 lvs; fol. Crawford (Roy. procl.) 1386; Brigham (Roy. procl.) 35–42; STC 8739. London: Soc. of Antiquaries.
624/66

Guerreiro, Bartolomeu, S.J. Sermão que fez o padre Bartolameu Guerreiro . . . na cidade de Lisboa na Capella real, dia de São Thome, anno de 1623, cuja festa como de padroeiro da India celebra . . . com offertas publicas das drogas delle. *Lisbon: P.*

Craesbeeck, 1624. 14 numb. lvs; 4to. On verso of 3rd lf Brazil is mentioned. Innocencio I:332; Backer III:1912. MH.   624/67

Gunter, Edmund. The description and use of his Majesties dials in White-Hall Garden. *London: B. Norton & J. Bill*, 1624. 59 p.; 4to. Difference in time between London & Virginia is mentioned on p.59. STC 12524. CSmH, DFo, RPJCB; BL.   624/68

Herrera y Tordesillas, Antonio de. Comentarios de los hechos de los Españoles, Franceses, y Venecianos en Italia. *Madrid: J. Delgado*, 1624. 467 p.; fol. Includes ref. to Columbus's discovery of West Indies in 1492. Palau 114321. CU, InU-L; BL, BN.   624/69

——. Novi Orbis pars duodecima, sive Descriptio Indiae Occidentalis . . . Accesserunt et aliorum Indiae Occidentalis descriptiones . . . Quibus cohaerent Paralipomena Americae. *Frankfurt a. M.: E. K[empfer?]. for Heirs of J. T. de Bry*, 1624. 154 numb. lvs; illus., maps; fol. (Theodor de Bry's *America*. Pt 12. Latin). Herrera y Tordesillas's work 1st publ. in Latin, Amsterdam, 1622, under title *Novus Orbis*. Cf. de Bry's German version of 1623. The *Paralipomena Americae* extracted from J. de Acosta's *Historia natural*. Cf. Sabin 8784; Tiele-Muller, p. 312; Streit II:1553; Church 173; JCB (3) I:416. CSmH, DLC, ICN, NN-RB, RPJCB; BL, BN.   624/70

Hieron, Samuel. The sermons [The workes]. *London: J. Legat* (v. 1) *& W. Stansby* (v. 2), 1624–25. 2 v.; fol. Included in v. 1 is Hieron's *An answer to a popish rime*, 1st publ., London, 1604. STC 13381. CSmH, DFo, MH, NN-RB; BL.   624/71

Hoffer, Adriaan. Elegia . . . in expeditionem navalem potentissimorum ordd. foederati Belgii auspiciis anno 1624 in Indiam occidentalem susceptam. *Harderwijck: Widow of T. Henrickz*, 1624. 4 lvs; 4to. BN.   624/72

Hues, Robert. Tractatus de globis, coelesti et terrestri . . . à Judoco Hondio excusus. *Amsterdam: H. Hondius*, 1624. 130 p.; illus.; 4to. 1st publ., London, 1594; cf. 1611 edn. Shaaber (Brit. auth.) H483. CtY-M, DLC, NN-RB; BL, BN.   624/73

Inga, Athanasius, pseud.? West-Indische Spieghel. *Amsterdam: B. Janszoon & J. P.*

Wachter, 1624. 435 p.; illus., maps; 4to. Includes refs to Mexico, Peru, etc. Sabin 34722; Palau 119668; Tiele 520; Stokes (Manhattan) VI:264; JCB (3) II:186. CU-B, CtY, DLC, MB, MnU-B, NN-RB, RPJCB; BL, BN.   624/74

Juan de Jesús María, O.C.D. Epistolario espiritual . . . Compuesto por el p.f. Juan de Jesus Maria, prior del sagrado yermo de Nuestra Señora del Carmen de Descalços de la Nueva España. *Uclés: D. de la Iglesia*, 1624. 810 p.; fol. Included are refs to Mexico. Medina (BHA) 771; Palau 123846. NNH; Seville:BU.   624/75

Juncker, Johann. Compendiosa methodus therapeutica . . . et ligni guaiaci diversimode praeparati administratione. *[Erfurt:] H. Steinmann*, 1624. 72 lvs; 4to. BL, BN.   624/76

Levett, Christopher. A voyage into New England begun in 1623. and ended in 1624. *London: W. Jones*, 1624. 4to. On Maine & the Indians there. Cf. Sabin 40751; cf. Vail (Frontier) 71; STC 15553.5. BL.   624/77

Lima. Universidad de San Marcos. Constituciones añadidas por los virreyes, marques de Montesclaros, y principes de Esquilache, a los que hizo el virrey don Francisco de Toledo para la Real Universidad . . . de San Marcos . . . de Los Reyes del Piru. Confirmadas . . . por el Rey . . . don Felipe Quarto, en su Consejo Real de las Indias. *Madrid: Imprenta Real*, 1624. 11 numb lvs; fol. Sabin 41092; Medina (BHA) 765; Pérez Pastor (Madrid) 2054. Santiago, Chile:BN.   624/78

——. Prologo de las constituciones, que hizo y recopilò el virrey marques de Montesclaros. *[Madrid? 1624?]*. fol. Subscribed at Madrid, 3 Sept. 1624. BL.   624/79

Linschoten, Jan Huygen van. Voyasie, ofte Schip-vaert . . . van by noorden om langes Noorwegen. *Amsterdam: J. E. Cloppenburg*, 1624. 38 numb. lvs; illus., maps; fol. 1st publ., Franeker, 1601. Tiele 692; Tiele-Muller 156. DLC, MWA, MB, NN; BL.   624/80

Lopes, Duarte. Regnum Congo, hoc est Vera descriptio regni Africani . . . Latio sermone donata ab August. Cassiod. Reino. *Frankfurt a. M.: E. Kempfer, for Heirs of J. T.*

de Bry, 1624. 60 p.; illus., maps; fol. (J. T. de Bry's *India Orientalis*. Pt 1. Latin). 1st publ. in this version, Frankfurt a. M., 1598; transl. from *Relatione del reame di Congo*, 1st publ., Rome, 1591; cf. de Bry's German version of 1609. Church 206; JCB (3) I:420. CSmH, ICN, NN-RB, RPJCB; BL, BN.

624/81

López Madera, Gregorio. Excelencias de la monarquia y reyno de España. *Madrid: L. Sánchez*, 1624. 109 numb. lvs; fol. 1st publ., Valladolid, 1597. Chapt. 9 comprises accounts of Spanish discoveries in New World. BL, BN.

624/82

Lundorp, Michael Caspar. Politische Schatz Cammer oder Form zu regieren . . . in Truck gegeben durch Nicolaum Bellum [pseud.]. *Frankfurt a. M.: J. G. Schönwetter*, 1624. 223 p.; 4to. Includes scattered refs to Peru, Mexico, Columbus, Brazil, etc. Cf. *Politische SchatzCammer . . . ander Theil* of 1618. RPJCB.

624/83

Malingre, Claude. Troisiesme tome de l'Histoire de nostre temps. *Paris: J. Petit-Pas*, 1624. 803 p.; 8vo. Pages 159–61 describe the founding of the Nederlandsche West-Indische Compagnie. Prior volumes are without American refs. Cioranescu (XVII) 45425; JCB (3) II:167 & 178. RPJCB; BN.

624/84

Marees, Pieter de. Siebende Schiffahrt in das goldreiche Königreich Guineam. *Frankfurt a. M.: E. Emmel, for Heirs of L. Hulsius*, 1624. 232 p.; illus., map; 4to. (Levinus Hulsius's *Sammlung von . . . Schiffahrten*. Pt 7). 1st publ. in this version, Frankfurt a. M., 1603. Sabin 33661; Church 287; JCB (3) I:459. CSmH, ICN, NN-RB, RPJCB; BL.

624/85

Marino, Giovanni Battista. L'Adone, poema. *Turin: Concordia*, 1624. 583 p.; 12mo. 1st publ., Paris, 1623. Michel (Répertoire) V:121. Paris:Arsenal.

624/86

Marlowe, Christopher. The tragicall historie of the life and death of Doctor Faustus, with new additions. *London: J. Wright*, 1624. [62] p.; 4to. Drama. 1st publ., London, 1604. STC 17435; Greg 205(g). BL.

624/87

Matthieu, Pierre. Della perfetta historia di Francia, e delle cose piu memorabili occorse nelle provincie straniere ne gli anni di pace regnante . . . Henrico IV . . . Tradotta di francese . . . dal signor conte Alessandro Senesio. *Venice: B. Barezzi*, 1624. 5 pts; 4to. Transl. from Matthieu's *Histoire de France et des choses memorables advenues aux provinces estrangeres durant sept annes de paix, du regne de Henry IV*, 1st publ., Paris, 1605; cf. 1623 edn with title *Historia di Francia*. NIC, OC.

624/88

———. Historia di Francia e delle cose, memorabili occorse nelle provincie stranieri negl'anni di pace del regno del Re . . . Henrico IIII . . . tradotta di francese . . . dal sig. conte Alessando Senesio. *Venice: B. Fontana*, 1624. 4 pts; 4to. Transl. from Matthieu's *Histoire de France et des choses memorables advenues aux provinces estrangeres durant sept annees de paix du regne de Henry IV*, 1st publ., Paris, 1605. Michel (Répertoire) V:150. ICU; Montpellier:BM.

624/89

Melich, Georg. Dispensatorium medicum, sive De recta medicamentorum . . . parandorum ratione, commentarii . . . in latinum sermonem conversi a Sam. Keller. *Frankfurt a. M.: H. Palthenius, for Heirs of Z. Palthenius*, 1624. 2 pts; 8vo. 1st publ. as here transl., Frankfurt a. M., 1601. BL, BN.

624/90

Memorabilia, das ist . . . Beschreibung aller vornembsten . . . Eygenschaften . . . der himmlischen Cörpern, deren Influentz . . . in . . . Europa . . . und . . . America zu sehen sindt. [*Frankfurt a. M.?*] 1624. fol. Palmer 358. BL.

624/91

Moerbeeck, Jan Andries. Redenen waeromme de west-Indische Compagnie dient te trachten het landt van Brasilia den Coninck van Spangien te ontmachtigen. *Amsterdam: C. L. van der Plasse*, 1624. 15 p.; 4to. Sabin 49828 (& 68495); Borba de Moraes II:67; Knuttel 3541. NN-RB; The Hague: KB.

624/92

More, Sir Thomas, Saint. Utopia: containing, an excellent, learned, wittie, and pleasant discourse . . . translated . . . by Raphe Robinson . . . newly corrected. *London: B. Alsop*, 1624. 138 p.; 4to. 1st publ. as here transl., London, 1551. Set in New World, with ref. to Vespucci's voyages. Gibson (More) 28; STC 18097. CSmH, CtY, DFo, ICN, NNC, RPJCB; BL.

624/93

Munk, Jens. Navigatio septentrionalis. Det er: Relation eller bescriffuelse om seiglads

oc reyse paa denne Nordvestiske Passagie, som nu kaldis Nova Dania. *Copenhagen: H. Waldkirch,* 1624. [60] p.; illus., map; 4to. Sabin 51335; Pettersen (Before 1814) 2513; JCB (3) II:187–88. CSmH, MnU-B, RPJCB.
624/94

Nederlandsche Oost-Indische Compagnie. Het out Oost-Indische octroy, by de . . . Staten Generael . . . inden jare 1602. verleent ende wtgegeven . . . Int jaer dryentwintich der lang-geweygerde . . . reeckeninge. [*The Hague?* 1624?]. 20 p.; 4to. 1st publ., [The Hague? 1602?]. This edn includes list of new directors on p. 20. Tiele (Pamfletten) 490 (& 2061); Knuttel 3536. RPJCB; The Hague:KB.
624/95

—[Anr edn]. [*The Hague?* 1624?]. 44 p.; 4to. Differs from the preceding only by addition of an appendix 'Extracten tot wederlegginghe . . .', p. 21–44. Meulman 1907. Ghent:BU.
624/96

Nederlandsche West-Indische Compagnie. Octroy by de . . . Staten Generael, verleent aende West-Indische Compagnie . . . Ende: het accoordt. *The Hague: Widow & Heirs of H. Jacobszoon van Wouw,* 1624. [28] p.; 4to. 1st publ., The Hague, 1621; here enl. Sabin 56669; Knuttel 3542. BL, The Hague:KB.
624/97

——. De Staten Generael der Vereenichde Nederlanden . . . [*The Hague?* 1624]. bds.; fol. Ratification by the Staten Generaal of the 19 directors' resolution to raise capital, dated 16 Oct. 1624. Includes notice to stockholders dated 10 Nov. 1624. Meulman 1919. Ghent:BU.
624/98

Netherlands (United Provinces, 1581–1795). Staten Generaal. Placaet . . . op't stuck van 't verkoopen ende transporteren van actien inde West Indische Compagnie. *The Hague: Widow & Heirs of H. Jacobszoon van Wouw,* 1624. [7] p.; 4to. Cf. the Netherlands Staten Generaal's *Placcaet . . . op 'tstuck vant verkoopen . . . van actien inde Oost ende West Indische Compaignien,* 1st publ., The Hague, 1621. Petit 1445. MnU-B; Leyden:B. Thysiana.
624/99

——. Placcaet. De Staten Generael tot verbod den handel op West-Indien. [Dated May 24]. *The Hague: Widow & Heirs of H. Jacobszoon van Wouw,* 1624. bds.; fol. Refers to hiring of sailors by the West India Com-

pany. Sabin 63193 (& 102908n); Meulman 1918. NN-RB; Ghent:BU.
624/100

Ofwod, Stephen. A relation of sundry particular wicked plots . . . of the Spaniards. [*London?*] 1624. 14 p.; 4to. 1st publ., [Amsterdam], 1624, in Verheiden's *Oration* of this year below. STC 18756. BL (O., S.), Cambridge:St John's.
624/101

Orlers, Jan Janszn. La genealogie des illustres comtes de Nassau, nouvellement imprimée, avec la description de toutes les victoires. Deuxiesme edition. *Amsterdam: J. Janszoon, the Younger,* 1624. 305 p.; illus., ports, maps; fol. 1st publ. in this version, Leyden, 1615. DLC, NN-RB, OCl; BL.
624/102

Pick, Jan Cornelisz. Copie eens briefs geschreven uyt West-Indien inde hooft-stadt van Bresilien ghenaemt de Totus le Sanctus, den 23. Mey . . . 1624. *Delft: C. J. Timmer,* 1624. 4 p.; 4to. Sabin 62613; Borba de Moraes II:144; Knuttel 3539. The Hague:KB.
624/103

Plautius, Caspar, O.S.B., Abbot of Seitenstetten. Extract und Augsszug [!] der grossen und wunderbarlichen Schifffarth Buelij Cataloni . . . welcher anno 1423 [*sic*]. mit Almirante Christoforo Columbo in Indiam Americam . . . geschiffet. *Linz: J. Planck,* 1624. 19 lvs; illus.; fol. 1st publ. in German, [Linz], 1623. Sabin 23512; Palmer 319. NN-RB; Munich:StB.
624/104

Plinius Secundus, Caius. Historia natural . . . Traducida por . . . Geronimo de Huerta . . . y ampliado por el mismo. *Madrid: L. Sánchez & J. González,* 1624–29. 2 v.; fol. Included in v. 1 are sections on America (p. 233–37) & Peru (p. 237–48). Sabin 63421; Medina (BHA) 769; Pérez Pastor (Madrid) 2099. CU, DNLM, ICN, MH-A, MnU; BL.
624/105

Potier, Pierre. Pharmacopoea spagirica. *Cologne: M. Schmitz,* 1624. 3 pts; 12mo. Included is Potier's *Insignium curationum . . . centuria secunda,* 1st publ., Bologna, 1622. Ferguson (Bibl. chem.) II:219; Wellcome I:5234. NNNAM; London:Wellcome.
624/106

Raleigh, Sir Walter. Achter Theil Americae, darinnen erstlich beschrieben wird das . . . Königreich Guiana . . . Eine Reyse Herrn Thomas Candisch . . . Und dann drey son-

derbare Reysen Herrn Frantzen Drakens . . . Auss dem Hölländischen . . . ubersetzt . . . Von Neuem ubersehen in ein richtigere Ordnung gebracht. *Frankfurt a. M.: K. Rötel, for Heirs of J. T. de Bry,* 1624. 130 p.; illus., map; fol. (Theodor de Bry's *America.* Pt 8. German). 1st publ. in this version, Frankfurt a. M., 1599–1600. Cf. Sabin 8784; Baginsky (German Americana) 154; Shaaber (Brit. auth.) R22; Church 194n; JCB (3) I:405. NN-RB, RPJCB; BL, BN.
624/107

Relacion del alzamiento de los Indios de los pueblos de los Yungas, de la provincia de Larecaxa y su castigo, por . . . Diego de Lodeña. [*Seville?* 1624]. [3] p.; fol. The area concerned is in Bolivia. Medina (BHA) 774. Seville:Archivo de Indias.
624/108

Relacion sumaria y puntual del tumulto y sedicion que huvo en Mexico a los 15. de enero de 624. y de las cosas mas notables que le precedieron, y despues se han seguido. [*Madrid?* 1624]. 18 numb. lvs; fol. On the conflict between the marquis of Silva (viceroy of Mexico) and archbishop de la Serna. Sabin 69233; Medina (BHA) 773; Pérez Pastor (Madrid) 2113; Palau 257722. CU-B, InU-L, NN-RB.
624/109

Relation de la prinse de la ville de Sainct Salvador, scituee dans la baya de Todos los Santos au Bresil. *Paris: M. Tavernier,* 1624. bds.; illus.; fol. Borba de Moraes II:193.
624/110

Relation veritable de la prinse de la Baya de Todos los Santos & de la ville de S. Sauveur au Brasil, par la flotte Hollandoise. [*Paris?*] 1624. 12 p.; 8vo. Sabin 69294; Borba de Moraes II:193–94; JCB (3) II:188. MiU-C, NN-RB, RPJCB.
624/111

Renou, Jean de. Le grand dispensaire medicinal . . . Traduict par mr. Louys de Serres. *Lyons: P. Rigaud & Associates,* 1624. 982 p.; 4to. Transl. from Renou's *Institutionum pharmaceuticarum libri quinque,* 1st publ., Paris, 1608. DNLM, PPL.
624/112

Restauracion de la Bahia. [*Lisbon?* 1624?]. [34] p.; 8vo. In verse. On the recapture by the Portuguese of Bahia from the Dutch. Borba de Moraes II:201; Rodrigues (Dom. Hol.) 886.
624/113

Reynolds, John. Vox coeli, or Newes from heaven . . . wherein Spaines ambition and trecheries are unmasked. *'Elisium'* [i.e., *London: W. Jones*] 1624. 92 p.; 4to. Includes description of 'The West Indies, or new Spaine'. Hitherto attributed to Thomas Scott, but now assigned to Reynolds by the STC; see J. H. Bryant, 'John Reynolds . . . a footnote', *The Library,* 5th ser., XVIII (1963) 299–303. Sabin 78375; STC 20946.4 (formerly 22094). DFo, MH; Cambridge: Trinity.
624/114

—[Anr edn]. *'Elisium'* [i.e., *London*]: 1624. 92 p.; 4to. Title has reading 'treacheries'. STC 29046.5. CSmH, DFo, IU, NN-RB; BL.
624/115

—[Anr edn]. *'Elisium'* [i.e., *London*]: 1624. 70 (i.e., 60) p.; 4to. Sabin 100799; STC 20946.6 (formerly 22095). CU, DLC, ICN, MH, NNUT; BL.
624/116

—[Anr edn]. *'Elisium'* [i.e., *London*]: 1624. 60 p.; 4to. On lf Blr last line reads 'Palatinate'. STC 20946.7 (formerly 22096). CU, CtY, DFo, ICN, MH.
624/117

—[Anr edn]. *'Elesium'* [i.e., *London*]: 1624. 60 p.; 4to. On lf Blr last line reads 'his Palatinate'. Sabin 78374; STC 20946.8 (formerly 22096a). CSmH, DFo, MH; Oxford:Bodl.
624/118

Reys-boeck van het rijcke Brasilien, Rio de la Plata ende Magallanes . . . Als ooch De leste reyse van den Heer van Dort . . . tsamen ghestelt door N. G. [i.e., Nicolas van Geelkercken?]. [*Dordrecht?*] *J. Canin,* 1624. [67] p.; illus., maps; 4to. Sabin 7633; Borba de Moraes II:203; Asher 106; Knuttel 3540; JCB (3) II:183. DLC, MH, RPJCB; BL.
624/119

Robin, Jean. Enchiridion isagogicum ad facilem notitiam stirpium, tam indigenarum quam exoticarum. Hae coluntur in horto Joannis et Vespasiani Robin. *Paris: P. de Bresche,* 1624. 71 p.; 8vo. 1st publ., Paris, 1623. Cf. Pritzel 7673. BN.
624/120

Roca, Juan Antonio Vera Zúñiga y Figueroa, conde de la. Epitome de la vida, y hechos del invicto emperador Carlos V. *Madrid: Widow of A. Martín, for A. Pérez,* 1624. 118 numb. lvs; 4to. 1st publ., Madrid, 1622. Pérez Pastor (Madrid) 2138; Palau 358988. Madrid: BN.
624/121

Schouten, Willem Corneliszoon. Journael ofte Beschrijvinghe van de wonderlicke

reyse. *Amsterdam: J. Janszoon, the Younger,* 1624. 56 p.; illus., maps; 4to. 1st publ., Amsterdam, 1618; here a reprint of Janszoon's edn of that year. Sabin 77925; Palau 305086; Tiele-Muller 45. NN-RB; BL.
624/122

Scotland. Privy Council. [Our Soverane Lord being formarlie gratiouslie . . . *Edinburgh:* 1624]. On institution of Nova Scotian baronets. Crawford (Roy. procl.) Scotland:1413. No copy known. 624/123

Scott, Thomas. Workes. *Utrecht:* 1624. 4to. Comprises individual items 1st publ. separately and here brought together with a general t.p., a particular copy varying in contents, as recorded in the STC. Those works containing American items, for present purposes, have alone been described elsewhere. Sabin 78379; STC 22064. MH (24 items); Aberdeen:UL (9 items), Oxford: Bodl. (25 items). 624/124

——. The Belgick souldier: warre was a blessing. [*London:*] 1624. [42] p.; 4to. Spanish exploration & fishing off American coast are mentioned. Sabin 78360; STC 22071; Knuttel 3527. CSmH, DFo, MH, NNUT; BL, The Hague:KB. 624/125

—[Anr edn]. *'Dort'* [i.e., *London:*] 1624. 47 p.; 4to. Sabin 78359; STC 22072; Knuttel 3528. CSmH, CtY, DLC, ICN, MH, MiU, MnU-B; BL, The Hague:KB. 624/126

——. Certaine reasons and arguments of policie, why the King of England should hereafter give over all further treatie, and enter into warre with the Spaniard. [*London:*] 1624. 8 lvs; 4to. On lf A3r line 14 ends 'Spani-'; line 2, 'al mẽ'. STC 22073 (formerly also 9982). IU; Cambridge:UL (imp.), Lamport. 624/127

—[Anr edn]. [*London:*] 1624. 8 lvs; 4to. On lf A3r line 14 ends 'Spani-'; line 2, 'all men'. Sabin 78361; STC 22073.2. DFo, MH, MnU, NNH, BL. 624/128

—[Anr edn]. [*London:*] 1624. 8 lvs; 4to. On lf A3r line 14 ends 'Spani=' (double hyphen). STC 22073.4. CU, DLC, ICN, InU-L, NNPM; Oxford:Bodl. 624/129

—[Anr edn]. [*London:*] 1624. 8 lvs; 4to. On lf A3r line 14 ends 'Spaniard is'; line 9 begins 'Spaniards' (no comma). STC 22073.6. CSmH, DFo; Oxford:Bodl. 624/130

—[Anr edn]. [*London:*] 1624. 8 lvs; 4to. On

lf A3r line 14 ends 'Spaniard is'; line 9 begins 'Spaniards,'. STC 22073.8. CtY, DFo; Oxford:Bodl. 624/131

——. An experimentall discoverie of Spanish practises. [*London: N. Okes?* 1624]. 4to. 1st publ., London, 1623. Caption on lf A1r reads 'A true souldiers councel. Anno 1624.' STC 22078. NNH; Oxford:Bodl.
624/132

——. Politijcke redenen, waerom dat de Koning van Engelandt alle handelinge soude nalaten, maer oorloch aenvaerden tegen den Spangiart. *The Hague: A. Meuris,* 1624. [8] p.; 4to. Transl. from Scott's *Certaine reasons and arguments* of this year above. Shaaber (Brit. auth.) S173; Knuttel 3524. The Hague:KB, Leyden:UB.
624/133

—[Anr edn]. Politique redenen. *Utrecht: J. Amelisszoon,* 1624. [8] p.; 4to. Shaaber (Brit. auth.) S174; Knuttel 3525. The Hague:KB.
624/134

——. Robert earle of Essex his ghost, sent from Elizian: to the nobility, gentry, and communaltie of England. *'Paradise'* [i.e., *London: J. Beale?*] 1624. 2 pts; 4to. Included in the 2nd pt are refs to Spanish cruelty to Indians, derived from Las Casas. In this edn, on lf A2r, line 10 ends 'parti-'. Sabin 78369; STC 22084. CU, CtY, DFo, MH, NNC; BL. 624/135

—[Anr edn]. *'Paradise'* [i.e., *London: J. Beale?*] 1624. 2 pts; 4to. On lf A2r line 10 ends 'partici-'. STC 22084a. CSmH, CtY, DFo, ICN; BL. 624/136

——. The second part of Vox populi, or Gondomar appearing in the likeness of Matchiavell in a Spanish Parliament. *'Gorkum: A. Janss'* [i.e., *London: N. Okes & J. Dawson*] 1624. 60 p.; 4to. Continues Scott's *Vox populi* of 1620. Mentions Spanish evangelization in both Indies, as well as Sir Walter Raleigh's Guiana venture & the Dutch in Peru. For the distinguishing features of the edns described below, see the STC. Sabin 78377; STC 22103. CU, DFo, MH, NN-RB (imp.); Cambridge:UL. 624/137

—[Anr issue]. 'The second edition'. *'Gorkum: A. Janss'* [i.e., *London: N. Okes*] 1624. 60 p.; 4to. Sabin 78377n; STC 22103.7. MnU-B; BL. 624/138

—[Anr edn]. *'Gorkum: A. Janss'* [i.e., *London:*

N. Okes] 1624. 60 p.; 4to. STC 22103.3. DFo, MBAt, NN-RB, RPJCB; BL.

624/139

——[Anr edn]. 'The second edition'. *'Gorkum: A. Janss'* [i.e., London: W. Jones] 1624. 4to. A forgery of Okes's 2nd edn described above. STC 22104. CSmH, ICN, MH; BL.

624/140

——. Symmachia: or, A true-loves knot. Tyed, betwixt Great Britaine and the United Provinces. [*Utrecht?* 1624]. 34 p.; 4to. Includes ref. to footing recently secured by British in West Indies. Sabin 78370; STC 22089. CSmH, CtY, DFo, ICN, MH, NN-RB; BL. 624/141

——. Vox coeli. *Elisium:* 1624. *See* Reynolds, John, *above.*

——. Vox populi. Or News from Spaine. [*Utrecht?*] 1620 [i.e., 1624]. [25] p.; 4to. Preface signed: Thom: Scott. 1st publ., [London?], 1620. STC 22101. DFo, NN-RB; BL.

624/142

——. Vox populi, Vox Dei. Vox regis. Digitus Dei. The Belgick pismire. The tongue-combat. Symmachia. The high-wayes of God and the king. The projector. [*The Netherlands:* 1624]. 9 pts; 4to. Comprises, with general t.p., sheets of the works in question previously issued individually, identified by the STC. Those items alone containing American refs have, for present purposes, been described as separately published. Sabin 78378; STC 22102. CSmH, CtY, DFo, MH, MiU, NN-RB; BL. 624/143

——. Vox regis. [*Utrecht: A. van Herwijck,* 1624]. 74 p.; illus.; 4to. Mentioning Sir Walter Raleigh, states that 'the East and West Indies are not sufficient, nor all Europe' to satisfy Spanish ambitions. STC 22105. CSmH, DFo, ICN, MH (imp.), NNG; BL. 624/144

——[Anr issue]. [*Utrecht: A. van Herwijck,* 1624]. Here added are 5 p. (unpaged) of text. STC 22105.5; McAlpin I:364. CSmH, IU (imp.), MH, NN-RB, RPJCB; BL. 624/145

——. Vox regis, of De stemme des Conincks van Enghelant. *Utrecht: A. van Herwijck,* 1624. 86 p.; 4to. Transl. from the preceding item. Cf. Sabin 78378–79; Shaaber (Brit. auth.) S176; Knuttel 3530. The Hague:KB.

624/146

Scribanius, Carolus. Veridicus Belgicus . . .

Item reformata apocalypsis Batavica, aucta et recensita. [*Antwerp: M. Nuyts,* 1624]. This edn, described by Backer and cited by Knuttel, is, lacking other evidence, perhaps only a conjecture. Kleerkooper and others suggest that Scribanius's *Den Hollantschen apocalypsis,* 'Nieustadt' [i.e., Leyden?], 1625 (with its ref. to Peru & Mexico), was 1st publ. in the *Veridicus Belgicus.* Knuttel supports the belief that the work was 1st publ. in Latin in that year. The main body of the work consists of a dialogue between 2 Spanish cavaliers, & refers to America & Brazil. Cf. Knuttel 3609n; Backer VII:988; Briels 110; Kleerkooper 878. 624/147

Sennert, Daniel. Epitome naturalis scientiae. *Wittenberg: H. W. Fincelius, for C. Heiden,* 1624. 674 p.; 8vo. 1st publ., Wittenberg, 1618. CLU. 624/148

Serres, Jean de. A generall historie of France . . . Contynued by P. Mathew to . . . 1610. And . . . unto . . . 1622. By Edward Grimston. *London: G. Eld & M. Fletcher,* 1624. 2 pts; fol. 1st publ., in English, London, 1607; cf. 1611 edn. STC 22246. CSmH, DFo, ICN, MH, NNUT; BL. 624/149

——[Anr issue]. *London: G. Eld & M. Fletcher,* 1624. STC 22246.5. ICN, NN-RB.

624/150

Sgambata, Scipio, S.J. supposed author. Eloge du p. Joseph Anquieta, de la Compagnie de Jesus; lequel mourut au Brasil le 9. de juin 1597. *Paris: S. Cramoisy,* 1624. 8vo. Conjecturally attributed to Sgambata on basis of Naples, 1631, text, of which this is perhaps a translation, here from an earlier unrecorded edn. Maggs Cat. 412 (1921):60; cf. Backer VII:1174. 624/151

Smith, Capt. John. The generall historie of Virginia, New-England, and the Summer Isles. *London: J. D[awson]. & J. H[aviland].,* for M. Sparke, 1624. 248 p.; illus., ports, maps; fol. For fuller discussion of this work, largely made up of items previously issued separately, and of the states of the maps, see the refs cited. Sabin 82823; Vail (Frontier) 68; Clayton-Torrence 51 (1); Baer (Md) 7; STC 22790; Church 402; JCB (3) II:188. CSmH, CtY, DLC, ICN, InU-L, MH, MiU-C, NN-RB, PPL, RPJCB; BL.

624/152

Entry canceled. 624/153

Stevin, Simon. Le trouve-port, traduit d'alleman en françois. *Leyden: J. Maire,* 1624. 30 p.; illus.; 4to. Transl. from Stevin's *De havenfinding,* 1st publ., Leyden, 1599; here a reissue of the 1599 Leyden French edn, the earlier imprint being here covered by a paste-on cancel. Includes incidental mentions of America. BN.   624/154

Steyger-praetjen tusschen Jan Batavier en Maetroos over het apprehenderen van den Gouverneur ende Provinciael van gantsch Brasilien, met haer geselschap. *Amsterdam: C. J. Visscher,* 1624. bds.; ports; fol. In verse. Sabin 91715; Rodrigues (Dom. Hol.) 332; cf. Muller (1872) III:1538. RPJCB; Amsterdam:NHSM.   624/155

Stirling, William Alexander, 1st earl of. An encouragement to colonies. *London: W. Stansby,* 1624. 47 p.; map; 4to. Sabin 91853 (& 739); STC 341; Church 400; JCB (3) II:183–84. CSmH, NN-RB, RPJCB; BL.   624/156

Struzzi, Alberto. Dialogo sobre el commercio . . . de Castilla. *Madrid: L. Sánchez,* 1624. 15 numb. lvs; fol. Included are refs to West Indies. Sabin 93114n; Medina (BHA) 776; Pérez Pastor (Madrid) 2126; Palau 323007. MH; BL, Madrid:BN.   624/157

Tassoni, Alessandro. La secchia rapita, poema eroicomico, e 'l primo canto dell' Oceano. *'Ronciglione'* [i.e., *Rome*]: *'G. B. Brogiotti'* [pseud.], 1624. 166 p.; 12mo. 1st publ., Paris, 1622. Cf. Sabin 94402; Puliatti (Tassoni) 101. ICN, MH, NNC, ViU; BL, Munich:UB.   624/158

Taylor, John, the Water-poet. The scourge of baseness. Or the old Lerry with a new Kicksey. *London: N. O[kes]., for M. Walbanke,* 1624. 8vo. In verse. 1st publ., London, 1619, under title *A kicksey winsey.* STC 23768. CSmH; BL.   624/159

Teellinck, Willem. Davids danckbaerheyt voor Gods weldadicheyt voor gestelt, wt. Psalm. 116. . . . (Welcke text te St. Salvador in Brasilien oock alder eerst ghepredickt is gheweest). *Middelburg: J. van der Hellen, for M. J. Brandt, at Amsterdam,* 1624. 59 p.; 12mo. Sabin 94580; Borba de Moraes II:295.   624/160

Torsellino, Orazio, S.J. Historiarum ab origine mundi usque ad annum 1598 epitome libri x. *Cologne: B. Wolter,* 1624. 12mo. 1st

publ., Rome, 1598; cf. 1620 edn. Backer VIII:151.   624/161

Usselinx, Willem. Manifest und Vertragbrieff der Australischen Companey im Königreich Schweden auffgerichtet. [*Gothenburg:*] 1624. 12 p.; 4to. Prospectus of the Swedish Söder Compagniet. Sabin 98199; Jameson (Usselinx) 12 (& p. 101). MnU-B, PHi.   624/162

Valbuena, Bernardo de. El Bernardo, o Victoria de Roncesvalles, poema heroyco. *Madrid: D. Flamenco,* 1624. 290 (i.e., 270) p.; 4to. The author was 'abad major' in Jamaica. Included are refs to Columbus & the New World (see Pérez Pastor). Sabin 2864; Medina (BHA) 761; Pérez Pastor (Madrid) 2049; Palau 22340. DFo, IU, MH, NN-RB, PU; BL, Madrid:BN.   624/163

Valverde Turices, Santiago de. Al excelentissimo . . . Fernando Afan de Ribera . . . Un discurso del chocolate. *Seville: J. de Cabrera,* 1624. 16 numb. lvs; 4to. Palau 349421. Madrid:BN.   624/164

Vega Carpio, Lope Félix de. Les delices de la vie pastorale de l'Arcadie . . . Mis en françois par L. S. L. [N. Lancelot]. *Lyons: P. Rigaud & Associates,* 1624. 454 p.; 8vo. 1st publ. in French, Lyons, 1622, as transl. from the author's *Arcadia,* 1st publ., Madrid, 1598; cf. 1602 edns. Palau 356312. ICN.   624/165

——. Doze comedias . . . Quarta parte. *Pamplona: J. de Oteyza,* 1624. 296 numb. lvs; 4to. 1st publ., Madrid, 1614. Sabin 98767n; Palau 355280. BN.   624/166

Verheiden, Willem. An oration or speech appropriated unto the princes of Christendom. [*Amsterdam: Successors of G. Thorp*] 1624. 2 pts; 4to. Also included is Stephen Ofwod's 'An adjoynder of sundry other particular wicked plots and . . . unnaturall practises of the Spaniards' which cites an Indian chief's preference not to go to heaven if Spaniards are to be there. On authorship, see the STC. STC 18837 (& pt 2, formerly also 18757). CSmH, DFo, MH; BL.   624/167

——. A second part of Spanish practises . . . Whereunto is adjoyned a worthy oration. [*London: N. Okes*] 1624. [45] p.; 4to. Being found bound among other tracts by Thomas Scott in his *Workes* of this year, usually attributed to him; the item is however essentially a reprinting of Verheiden's *An oration or speech* publ. at Amsterdam in 1624, and includes as well Stephen Ofwod's 'An adjoynder of sundry other particular wicked plots' there included. The 1st pt referred to in the title is *An experimentall discoverie of Spanish practises*, assigned generally to Thomas Scott, but possibly by Henry Hexham, of 1623. Sabin 78364; STC 22078.5. CSmH, DFo, ICN, MH, NN-RB, RPJCB; BL.   624/168

Warhafft, Umbständ und gründlicher Bericht . . . wie es eigendlich mit Einnehmung der vortrefflichen Region Bahia im Königreich Brasilien gelegen. [*The Hague?*] 1624. 4 lvs; 4to. Sabin 7649; Borba de Moraes II:370; Rodrigues (Dom. Hol.) 333. NN-RB.   624/169

Wassenaer, Nicolaes van. T'seste deel of 't vervolgh van het Historisch verhael aller gedencwaerdiger geschiedenissen, die in Europa . . . in America, als West-Indien, d'eylanden, en Brasil . . . voorgevallen syn. *Amsterdam: J. Janszoon, the Younger* [1624]. 156 numb. lvs; illus.; 4to. (N. van Wassenaer's *Historisch verhael*. Pt 6.) Includes refs to undertakings of the Nederlandsche West-Indische Compagnie, as well as a descr. of New-Netherland. Cf. Sabin 102039; Borba de Moraes II:371; Muller (1872) 1745. MH, RPJCB.   624/170

——. T'vyfde-deel of t'vervolgh van het Historisch verhael aller gedencwaerdiger gheschiedenissen, die in Europa . . . in America, als West-Indien en d'eijlanden . . . voorgevallen sijn. *Amsterdam: J. Hondius,* 1624. 152 numb. lvs; illus.; 4to. (N. van Wassenaer's *Historisch verhael*. Pt 5). Includes accounts of Jacques L'Hermite's naval adventures & amplification of the West-Indische Compagnie's charter. Cf. Sabin 102039; Borba de Moraes II:371–72; Muller (1872) 1745. MH, RPJCB.   624/171

Wieroock-vath, of triumph-liedt over 't in-nemen vande Bai Todos los Sanctos ende de stadt Salvador in Brasiliën. *Utrecht: J. J. Amelisszoon,* 1624. bds. Amsterdam:NHSM.   624/172

Willekens, Jacob. Goede nieuwe tijdinghe ghecomen met het jacht de vos ghenaemt afghesonden von den generael Jacob Wilc-

kens uyt Bresilien aen de heeren bewinthebbers vande . . . West Indische Compagnie. [*Amsterdam?*] B. Janszoon, 1624. bds.; 4to. Sabin 27680; Borba de Moraes I:302; Asher 104; Petit 1443. Leyden: B. Thysiana.   624/173

Winslow, Edward. Good newes from New-England: or A true relation of things very remarkable at . . . Plimoth. *London: J. D*[*aw-son*]*., for W. Bladen & J. Bellamy,* 1624. 59 (i.e., 67) p.; 4to. Sabin 104795; Vail (Frontier) 69; STC 25855; Church 403; JCB (3) II:189–90. CSmH, CtY, ICN, MB, NN-RB, PPL, RPJCB; BL.   624/174

——[Anr issue]. *London: J. D*[*awson*]*., For W. Bladen,* 1624. Vail (Frontier) 69A; STC 25856; Church 404. CSmH, CtY, MHi, MiU-C; BL.   624/175

Wirsung, Christoph. Een medecyn-boeck . . . nu uyt de seste editie . . . overgheset door Carolum Battum. *Amsterdam: J. E. Cloppenburg,* 1624. 676 p.; illus.; fol. Transl. from Wirsung's *New Artzney Buch*, 1st publ., Heidelberg, 1568; cf. 1605 edn. BL.   624/176

Wonderlicke avontuer van twee goelieven . . . die . . . in vreughden zijn te samen ghekomen, mede brengende eenen uytnemenden schat van gout ende perlen uyt West-Indien. *Leyden: N. Geelkercken,* 1624. 36 p.; 4to. Sabin 105014. N.   624/177

1625

Aguilera, Cristóbal de, O.P. El presentado fray Christoval de Aguilera de la orden de Santo Domingo, procurador general de la provincia de Mexico. [*Madrid?* 1625?] [4] p.; fol. Memorial to king of Spain on ecclesiastical affairs of province. Medina (BHA) 6179; Streit II:2353. BL.   625/1

Agustí, Miguel. Libro de los secretos de agricultura. *Saragossa: P. Bueno* [1625?]. 512 p.; illus.; 4to. Transl. from the author's Catalan text, 1st publ., Barcelona, 1617. Includes chapt. on tobacco, derived from Jean Liébault. Palau 4123. NNC.   625/2

Alcalá Yáñez y Rivera, Jerónimo. Alonso moço de muchos amos. *Barcelona: E. Liberos, for M. Menescal,* 1625. 160 lvs; 8vo. 1st publ.,

Madrid, 1624. Palau 5818n. MB, NNH; BL, BN.   625/3

Aldini, Tobia. Exactissima descriptio rariorum plantarum . . . in Horto Farnesiano. *Rome:* 1625. *See* Castelli, Pietro, *below.*

Anghiera, Pietro Martire d'. The historie of the West-Indies, containing the actes and adventures of the Spaniards . . . Published in Latin by Mr. Hakluyt, and translated into English by M. Lok. *London: A. Hebb* [after 1625?]. 318 numb. lvs; 4to. 1st publ. as here transl., 1612; here a reissue of that edn with cancel t.p. Sabin 45011; STC 651; Arents 6; cf. Church 358; JCB (3) II:194. CSmH, DLC, ICN, MH, MWA, MiU-C, NN-A, PPL, RPJCB; BL.   625/4

Avendaño y Vilela, Francisco de. Relacino [*sic*] del viaje, y sucesso de la armada que por mandado de su Magestad partiò al Brasil. *Seville: F. de Lyra,* 1625. [7] p.; 4to. May have served as the basis for other accounts of the seizure of Bahia—Borba de Moraes. Cf. Toledo Osorio's *Relacion de la carta* of this year below. Sabin 69222; Medina (BHA) 778; Borba de Moraes I:48; Rodrigues (Dom. Hol.) 334; Palau 20165; JCB (3) II:190. RPJCB; BL.   625/5

——. Relacione del viaggio, e successo dell' armata, che per ordine de S.M. s'invió al Brasil . . . Stampata in Siviglia da Francesco de Lyra. *Milan: The Malatesti,* 1625. 4 lvs; 8vo. Transl. from the author's *Relacino del viaie* above. Borba de Moraes I:48; Rodrígues (Dom. Hol.) 335.
                                                    625/6

—[Anr edn]. *Rome: F. Pizzuto,* 1625. Borba de Moraes I:48n; Palau 20165n.   625/7

—[Anr edn]. *Naples: Roncagliolo,* 1625. A possible ghost. Borba de Moraes I:48n.
                                                    625/8

——, **supposed author.** Relation und eigentliche beschreibung. *Augsburg:* 1625. *See* Toledo Osorio y Mendoza, Fadrique, marqués de Villanueva de Valdueza, *below.*

Avity, Pierre d', sieur de Montmartin. Les estats, empires et principautez du monde. *Paris: P. Chevalier,* 1625. 1396 p.; fol. 1st publ., Paris, 1613. Cf. Sabin 2498. MB, MH (imp.), NcD; BN.   625/9

—[Anr issue]. *Paris: Widow of O. de Varennes,* 1625. Bonn:UB.   625/10

—[Anr edn]. *Rouen: A. Ouyn & J. Cailloué,* 1625.

Borba de Moraes I:52–53. DLC, NcD, PPL.
                                                    625/11

Bacon, Francis, viscount St Albans. The essayes or Counsels, civill and morall . . . Newly enlarged. *London: J. Haviland, for Hanah Barret & R. Whitaker,* 1625. 340 p.; 4to. A greatly enlarged edn beyond that of 1612. Included here are 'Of the true greatness of kingdomes & estates' mentioning 'wealth of both Indies'; 'Of plantations', citing American products, including 'tobacco in Virginia'; 'Of prophecies', quoting Seneca's *Medea* as a prophecy of the discovery of America; and 'Of vicissitude of things', mentioning the West Indies & the Andes. Gibson (Bacon) 13; STC 1147. CLU-C, DLC, ICN, MH, NN-RB, PBL; BL.
                                                    625/12

—[Anr edn]. *London: J. Haviland, for Hannah Barret,* 1625. 340 p.; 4to. Gibson (Bacon) 14; STC 1148; Pforzheimer 30. CSmH, CtY, DFo, MH, NNPM; BL.   625/13

Baerle, Kaspar van. Manes Auraici, sive In funus . . . Mauricii, principis ac domini Aurantiae, comitis Nassaviae . . . epicedium. *Leyden: G. Basson,* 1625. 16 p.; fol. Includes ref. to land discovered by Columbus. Dt. Ges. Kat. 11.6581. BL, Wolfenbüttel:HB.
                                                    625/14

Barclay, John. Icon animorum. *Frankfurt a. M.: D. & D. Aubry & C. Schleich,* 1625,'24. 187 p.; 8vo. 1st publ., London, 1614. Shaaber (Brit. auth.) B169. Göttingen:UB, Hamburg:StB, Vienna:NB.   625/15

——. Le pourtraict des esprits. *Paris: N. Buon,* 1625. 430 p.; 12mo. Transl. by Nanteuil de Bonham from Barclay's *Icon animorum,* 1st publ., London, 1614. Shaaber (Brit. auth.) B167. DFo; BN, Wolfenbüttel:HB.
                                                    625/16

—[Anr issue?]. *Paris: S. Thiboust,* 1625. Shaaber (Brit. auth.) B168. Edinburgh:NL, Greifswald:UB, Wolfenbüttel:HB.
                                                    625/17

——. Les satyres d'Euphormion de Lusine. *Paris: J. Petit-Pas,* 1625. 2 v.; 8vo. Transl. by 'I.T.P.A.E.P.'. Includes pt 2, 1st publ. in Latin, Paris, 1607 & pt 4, the *Icon animorum,* 1st publ., London, 1614. Shaaber (Brit. auth.) B182; Tchémerzine I:447. DFo,MH; BN, Berlin:StB.   625/18

——. Le tableau des esprits. *Paris: J. Petit-*

Pas, 1625. 443 p.; 8vo. Transl. from Barclay's *Icon animorum*, 1st publ., London, 1614; cf. translation of this year above with title *Le pourtraict des esprits*. Shaaber (Brit. auth.) B170. Edinburgh:NL, BN.
625/19

Bartholin, Caspar. Enchiridion physicum ex priscis et recentioribus philosophis accuratae concinnatum. *Strassburg: E. Zetzner*, 1625. 865 p.; 12mo. In bk 4, chapt. 8, on tides, Columbus & his voyage of discovery are mentioned. DLC, DNLM; BL, London: Wellcome.
625/20

Basuyne des oorloghs, ofte Waerschouwinghe aen de Vereenichde Nederlanden. [*Amsterdam:*] *P. Walschaert*, 1625. [23] p.; 4to. Includes refs to the West India Company, Brazil, & Spanish tyranny in West Indies. Sabin 3902; Borba de Moraes I:77; Knuttel 3608. InU, NN; The Hague:KB.
625/21

Bauhin, Kaspar. De lapidis bezaar Orientalis et Occidentalis cervini. *Basel: L. König*, 1625. 294 p.; illus.; 8vo. 1st publ., Basel, 1613. DNLM, MH, MiU, PPAN, TxLT; BL, BN.
625/22

Beaumont, Francis. The scorneful ladie. A comedie. *London: [A. Mathewes?] for M. P[artridge?]., & to be sold by T. Jones*, 1625. 36 lvs; 4to. 1st publ., London, 1616. STC 1687; Greg 334(b); Arents 156. CSmH, DFo, MH, NN-A; BL.
625/23

Béguin, Jean. Tyrocinium chymicum . . . Editio sexta. [*Königsberg: A. Boreck, for C. Berger*] 1625. 480 p.; 8vo. 1st publ., Paris, 1612. NjP.
625/24

Benítez Negrete, Sebastián. Señor. El aver entrado en estos reynos de España tan gran suma de moneda de bellon . . . que oy se hallan . . . despojadas de la plata y oro. [*Madrid:* 1625?]. 8 numb. lvs; fol. Memorial to the king of Spain; includes refs to gold & silver mines of the Indies, specifically mentioning Potosí, & citing use of tobacco as currency. BL.
625/25

Besold, Christoph. Dissertatio politico-juridica de majestate in genere. *Strassburg: Heirs of L. Zetzner*, 1625. 237 p.; 4to. Includes ref. to José de Acosta's history of the West Indies (*De natura Novi Orbis*, 1st publ., Salamanca, 1588). DLC; BN.
625/26

Blaeu, Willem Janszoon. Le flambeau de la navigation. *Amsterdam: W. J. Blaeu*, 1625. 2 v.; illus., maps; obl. fol. 1st publ. in French, Amsterdam, 1619. Title pasted on t.p. of 1620 Dutch edn. Bk 1 dated '1624'. Koeman (M.Bl) 14; Tiele 122n. ICN; BL.
625/27

——. The light of navigation. *Amsterdam: J. Janszoon, the Younger*, 1625. 2 v.; illus., maps; obl. fol. 1st publ. in English, Amsterdam, 1612. Title & imprint pasted on t.p. of Janszoon's 1623 Dutch edn. The Harvard copy lacks slips showing English title and 1625 imprint date on initial t.p. Koeman (M.Bl) 22 (J). MH (imp.); London:Admiralty, Amsterdam:UB.
625/28

——. The sea-mirrour, containing a brief instruction in the art of navigation . . . translated out of Dutch . . . by Richard Nynmers. *Amsterdam: W. J. Blaeu*, 1625. 3 pts; illus., maps; fol. Transl. from Blaeu's *Zeespiegel*, 1st publ., Amsterdam, 1623. Koeman (M.Bl) 48; STC 3113. CSmH; BL, Amsterdam:NHSM.
625/29

Blocius, Johannes. Historiae per Saturam ex Novi Orbis scriptoribus. Excerpta memorabilia. *Rostock: J. Fuess (Pedanus) for J. Hallervord*, 1625. 91 p.; 12mo. Contains refs to Columbus, to Vespucci, & to parts of North & South America. Sabin 5942. NN-RB; BL.
625/30

Bradwell, Stephen. A watch-man for the pest, teaching the true rules of preservation. *London: J. Dawson, for G. Vincent*, 1625. 57 p.; 4to. Approves of turkeys as food in avoidance of plague, but discourages use of tobacco. STC 3537; Arents (Add.) 232. NN-A; BL.
625/31

Brant, Sebastian. Der Narren Zunfft. *Frankfurt a. M.:* 1625. *See Thomas Murner's* Schelmen Zunfft *under the year* 1618.

Braun, Samuel. Anhang der Beschreibung dess Königreichs Congo. Innhaltend fünf Schiffarten Samuel Brauns. *Frankfurt a. M.: K. Rötel, for Heirs of J. T. de Bry*, 1625. 56 p.; illus.; fol. (J. T. de Bry's *India Orientalis*. Pt 1. Appendix. German). 1st publ., Basel, 1624, under title *Schiffarten*. Church 246; JCB (3) I:422. CSmH, DLC, NN-RB, RPJCB; BL, BN.
625/32

——. Appendix Regni Congo. Qua continentur navigationes quinque Samuelis Brunonis . . . Omnia ab ipso quidem authore

Germanico idiomate conscripta, nunc . . . translata. *Frankfurt a. M.: K. Rötel, for Heirs of J. T. de Bry,* 1625. 86 p.; illus.; fol. (J. T. de Bry's *India Orientalis.* Pt 1. Appendix. Latin). Transl. from Braun's *Schiffarten,* 1st publ., Basel, 1624; cf. de Bry's German version above. Church 225; JCB (3) I:420. CSmH, DLC, ICN, NN-RB, RPJCB; BL, BN.
625/33

Bry, Theodor de. Americae pars viii. Continens Primo, Descriptionem trium itinerum . . . Francisci Draken . . . Secundo, iter . . . Thomae Candisch . . . Tertio, duo itinera . . . Gualtheri Ralech [i.e., Raleigh]. *Frankfurt a. M.: E. Kempfer,* 1625. 160 p.; illus., maps; fol. (Theodor de Bry's *America.* Pt 8. Latin). 1st publ. in this version, Frankfurt a. M., 1599; transl. from a variety of English sources. Here added is the *Historiae antipodum . . . liber tertius,* an account of the Dutch expedition under Pieter van der Does against the Spaniards in 1599; for pts 1 & 2 of de Bry's *Historiae antipodum,* cf. B. J. Potgieter under year 1633. For variant issue see Church. Cf. Sabin 8784; Shaaber (Brit. auth.) R23; Church 166 & 167; JCB (3) I:402–3. CSmH, DLC, NN-RB, RPJCB: BL, BN.
625/34

Camden, William. Annales. The true and royall history of Elizabeth, queene of England. *London:* [*H. Lownes,*] *for B. Fisher,* 1625. 2 pts; port.; 4to. Transl. by Abraham Darcie from Paul de Bellegent's French translation (1st publ., London, 1624) of Camden's Latin text, 1st publ., London, 1615. Sabin 10158; STC 4497. CSmH, CtY, DLC, ICN, NN-RB, PPL; BL, BN.
625/35

——. Annales rerum Anglicarum, et Hibernicarum . . . Prima pars emendatior, altera pars nunc primum in lucem edita. *Leyden: Elsevier Office,* 1625. 855 p.; 8vo. Pt 1, 1st publ., London, 1615; v. 2, here 1st publ., includes numerous refs to exploits in New World of Sir Francis Drake & Sir Walter Raleigh. Sabin 10157n; Willems (Les Elzevier) 227; Rahir (Les Elzevier) 194; Shaaber (Brit. auth.) C18. CSmH, DFo, ICU, MH, NNUT, PPL, RP; BL, BN.
625/36

Camerarius, Philipp. The living librarie . . . Done into English by J. Molle . . . with some additions by H. Molle, his sonne. The second edition. *London: A. Islip; sold by J. Partridge,* 1625. 428 p.; fol. 1st publ., London, 1621. STC 4530; Arents (Add.) 198. CSt, CtY, DLC, ICN, MH, NN-A: BL, Oxford:Bodl.
625/37

—[Anr issue?]. The walking librarie. Second edition. *London:* 1625. DGU.
625/38

——. Operae horarum subcisivarum . . . Centuria tertia. *Frankfurt a. M.: W. Hoffmann, for P. Kopff,* 1625. 379 p.; 4to. 1st publ., Frankfurt a. M., 1609. CtY.
625/39

——. Operae horarum succisivarum . . . Das ist: Historischer Lustgarten. *Leipzig: M. Wachsman,* 1625. 702 p.; 4to. Transl. by Georg Maier from Camerarius's *Operae horarum subcisivarum . . . Centuria prima,* 1st publ., Altdorf, 1591; cf. 1602 edn. For the continuation of this translation, see the years 1628 (*Secunda centuria*) & 1630 (*Tertia Centuria*). Jantz (German Baroque) 47. Wroclaw:BU.
625/40

Carpenter, Nathaniel. Geography delineated forth in two bookes. *Oxford: J. Lichfield & W. Turner, for H. Cripps,* 1625. 2 v.; illus.; 4to. On the theory & principles of geography, but included are scattered refs to the Americas. Sabin 10999; Madan (Oxford) 1625:3; STC 4676; JCB (3) II:191. CSmH, CtY, DLC, ICN, MiU, MnU-B, NjP, RPJCB; BL.
625/41

Carta cierta y verdadera que vino a un cavallero desta ciudad, desde la ciudad de San Lucar, haziendole relacion de la conficion que hizo un maestre de una nao que cogio el armada del almirantazgo, en que declaro, que el Brasil estava ya por el Rey. *Seville: J. de Cabrera,* 1625. [4] p.; fol. Subscribed at San Lucar de Barrameda, 10 May 1625. Medina (BHA) 780; Escudero (Seville) 1.339; Palau 45722. RPJCB; Madrid:Acad. de la Hist.
625/42

Carta segunda: que vino a un cavallero desta ciudad, avisandole come el armada del almirãtaggo cogio una nao, la qual declaró, que el Brasil está por el Rey nuestro señor, y como le quemaron sus naos. *Valladolid: Widow of F. Fernández de Córdoba* [1625]. 4 p.; 4to. Borba de Moraes I:137.
625/43

Cartagena, Colombia (Province). A dos cosas se reduze la pretension de Cartagena y su provincia. [*Madrid?* ca. 1625?]. 13 numb. lvs; fol. Includes extended discussion of monetary problems of Spanish America in general. BL. 625/44

Casas, Bartolomé de las, O.P., Bp of Chiapa. Erudita & elegans explicatio quaestionis: Utrum reges vel principes, jure aliquo vel titulo . . . cives ac subditos . . . subjicere possint? . . . Accessit Guilielmi de Montserrat, De successione regum. *Tübingen: E. Wild,* 1625. 2 pts; 4to. 1st publ., Frankfurt a. M., 1571. Americana only as inferential of Las Casas's views. Sabin 11238; Hanke/ Giménez 521; Palau 46981. NN-RB (pt 1 only). 625/45

Casos notables, sucedidos en las costas de la ciudad de Lima, en las Indias, y como el armada Olandesa procurava coger el armadilla nuestra, que baxa con la plata de ordinario à Cartagena. *Seville: J. de Cabrera* [1625]. [4] p.; fol. Cf. the *Relacion de las cosas notables* of this year below. Sabin 41082; Medina (BHA) 781. BL, Madrid: Acad. de la Hist. 625/46

—[Anr edn]. *Madrid: J. González; sold by A. de Paredes,* 1625. [4] p.; fol. Text begins: 'Aviendo hecho el señor Inquisidor . . .'. Sabin 11342 (& 16989); Medina (BHA) 782; Palau 47347; Pérez Pastor (Madrid) 2146; JCB (3) II:191. DLC, RPJCB; Madrid:BN. 625/47

—[Anr edn]. *Madrid: B. de Guzman,* 1625. [4] p.; fol. Text begins: 'El Señor Inquisidor Juan de Mañeca, aviendo . . .'. Sabin 11342n; Palau 47347n; Pérez Pastor (Madrid) 2147; JCB (3) II:191. NN-RB, RPJCB; Madrid:BN. 625/48

Castelli, Pietro. Exactissima descriptio rariorum plantarum, quae continentur Romae in Horto Farnesiano. *Rome: G. Mascardi,* 1625. 109 p.; illus.; fol. Describes & illustrates several American plants, notably the yucca (agave). Though authorship is attributed on the t.p. to Tobia Aldini, it is recognized as Castelli's work. Pritzel 1590; Nissen (Bot.) 13; Hunt (Bot.) 208. CtY-M, DFo, MH-A, MiU, MnU, NN-RB, RPB; BL, BN. 625/49

Cervantes Saavedra, Miguel de. Dell'ingenoso cittadino Don Chisciotte della Mancia tradotta . . . da Lorenzo Franciosini fiorentino. *Venice: A. Baba,* 1625. 2 v.; 8vo. Includes the 2nd pt, 1st publ. in Spanish, Madrid, 1615. Ríus (Cervantes) 781; Palau 53136. DLC, MH. 625/50

——. L'histoire de . . . Dom Quichot . . . traduicte . . . par F. de Rosset . . . Troisiesme edition. *Paris: J. Mestais,* 1625. 877 p.; 8vo. 1st publ. as here transl. from the *Segunda parte,* Paris, 1618. Ríus (Cervantes) 462; Palau 52697. 625/51

——. Les nouvelles. *Paris: E. Saucié,* 1625. 2 v.; 8vo. 1st publ. as here transl. from the Madrid, 1613, Spanish text, Paris, 1615. Ríus (Cervantes) 887; Palau 53522n. 625/52

——. Novelas exemplares. *Brussels: H. Anthoine,* 1625. 608 p.; 8vo. 1st publ., Madrid, 1613. Ríus (Cervantes) 233; Palau 53412. DLC, ICU, NNH, PU; BL. 625/53

Clercq, Nikolaas de. Princelyck cabinet, verthoonende 't leven, afcomste ende afbeeldingen der voornaemste vorsten, graven ende heeren van Europa. *Delft: Heirs of N. de Clercq,* 1625. 140 p.; ports; fol. Section on king of Spain's properties details American possessions, e.g. California, Florida, Peru. MH; BL. 625/54

Correa, João de Medeiros. Relacam verdadeira de tudo o succedido na restauraçaõ da Bahia. *Lisbon: Pedro Craesbeeck; sold by Paulo Craesbeeck,* 1625. 8 lvs; 8vo. Sabin 16835 (& 69166); Borba de Moraes I:182–83; Rodrigues (Dom. Hol.) 344; Maggs Cat. 479 (Americana V):4175. DLC,RPJCB. 625/55

—[Anr edn]. *Oporto: J. Rodriguez,* 1625. 16 p.; 8vo. Contains additional text. Borba de Moraes I:183; Maggs Cat. 412 (1921):61. MnU-B. 625/56

—[Anr edn]. *Evora: M. Carvalho,* 1625. 16 p.; 4to. Contains additional text. Borba de Moraes I:183; Rodrigues (Dom. Hol.) 345. 625/57

Correa, Simão. Sermão no procissão de graças que a muito nobre villa de Villo-real, fez pela restauração da cidade da Bahia: pregado em 15 de Agosto de 1625. *Lisbon: G. da Vinha,* 1625. [22] p.; 4to. Sabin 16837; Borba de Moraes I:184. 625/58

Cortés de Monroy, Juan. Señor. Aviendo visto, y considerado las tres dudas que se han ofrecido en el discurso que hize . . . a V.M. sobre . . . la conquista de Chile . . . dire . . . lo que . . . se me ofrese. [*Madrid?* 1625]. [4] p.; fol. Memorial to the king of Spain; subscribed at Madrid, 30 Aug. 1625. Medina (Chile) 57. BL.   625/59

Crosse, William. Belgiaes troubles, and triumphs. Wherein are truly and historically related all the most famous occurrences, which have happened between the Spaniards, and Hollanders in these last foure yeares . . . with other accidents . . . as . . . the conquest of St. Salvador in Brasilia. *London: A. Mathewes & J. Norton*, 1625. 74 p.; 4to. In verse. STC 6072. CSmH, TxU; BL.   625/60

——, **supposed author.** The Dutch survay. Wherein are related . . . the chiefest losses and acquirements, which have past betweene the Dutch and Spaniards, in these last foure yeares warres of the Netherlands, with a comparative balancing of that which the Spaniards . . . have lost unto the Dutch and Persians in Brasilia, Lima, and Ormus. *London: E. Allde, for N. Butter*, 1625. 36 p.; 4to. Sabin 9758; Borba de Moraes I:238; STC 4318; Knuttel 3611. CSmH, RPJCB; BL, The Hague:KB.   625/61

Dávila Padilla, Augustín, O.P., Abp of Santo Domingo. Historia de la fundacion y discurso de la provincia, de Santiago de Mexico, de la orden de Predicadores . . . Edicion segunda. *Brussels: J. van Meerbeeck*, 1625. 654 p.; fol. 1st publ., Madrid, 1569. Sabin 18780; Medina (BHA) 784; Streit II:1555; Peeters-Fontainas (Impr. esp.) 286; JCB (3) II:191. CU-B, CtY, DLC, MH, NN-RB, OCU, PPL, RPJCB; BL, BN.   625/62

La defaite navale de trois mil, tant Espagnols que Portugais, mis & taillez en pièces par les Hollandois, à la Baya de Todos los Sanctos. Traduite de flamand en françois. *Paris: J. Martin*, 1625. 14 p.; 12mo. Presumably transl. from the *Waerachtigh verhael* of this year below. Borba de Moraes I:215; Rodrigues (Dom. Hol.) 342. NN-RB.   625/63

Descripcion de la Baia de Todos los Santos y ciudad de Sansalvador en la costa del Brasil en que se fortificaron los Olandeses: aora restaurado por don Fradique de Toledo.

Madrid: A. de Popma, 1625. bds.; illus.; fol. Borba de Moraes I:223. NN-RB.   625/64

Description de la Brasil & de la ville de Pernambuco; aussi de tout le païs, & des moulins de sucre . . . Et comment les Olandois pensoyent prendre possession de tout le pais & traficq. *Antwerp: A. Verhoeven* [1625?]. bds.; illus.; 4to. Sabin 60988. DLC.   625/65

Description de la reprise de la ville de S. Salvador, située en la Baye de Todos os sanctos en Brasil. *Antwerp: A. Verhoeven*, 1625. 4 lvs.; illus.; 4to. Includes view of San Salvador. Sabin 76213. DLC.   625/66

Discours sur l'affaire de la Valteline, et des Grisons. Dedié au . . . Roy d'Espagne. Traduit de l'italien. *Paris: J. Bouillerot*, 1625. 183 p.; 8vo. On p. 7–15 Atabalipa ('roy du Peru') & Pizarro are mentioned, and Las Casas is quoted in discussion of Spanish cruelty to Indians. The Italian text of which this purports to be a translation has not been identified if it in fact existed. Perhaps written by Jérémie Du Ferrier; cf. publications by him of this year. WU; BL.   625/67

Ditchfield, ——. Considerations touching the new contract for tobacco. [*London?*] 1625. 11 p.; 4to. Sabin 20328; Clayton-Torrence 52; STC 6918; Church 406. CSmH; BL, Cambridge:UL.   625/68

Donne, John. An anatomie of the world. *London: W. Stansby, for T. Dewe*, 1625. 2 pts; 8vo. In verse. 1st publ., London, 1611. STC 7025; Keynes (Donne) 77. CSmH, CtY, MH; BL.   625/69

——. Foure sermons upon speciall occasions. *London: [A. Mathewes?] for T. Jones*, 1625. 4pts; 4to. Made up of works 1st publ. separately, the 2nd being the 1624 edn of Donne's *A sermon upon the eighth verse of the first chapter of . . . Actes.* Cf. Sabin 20601; Keynes (Donne) 20. DFo, MiU, NN-RB; G. L. Keynes.   625/70

Draud, Georg. Bibliotheca classica, sive Catalogus officinalis. *Frankfurt a.M: B. Ostern*, 1625. 1654 p.; 4to. 1st publ., Frankfurt, 1611. Jantz (German Baroque) 836. DLC, ICU, MH, NN-RB, PPRF; BL, BN.   625/71

——. Bibliotheca librorum Germanicorum

classica, das ist, Verzeichnuss aller und jeder Bücher . . . bis auffs Jahr . . . 1625, in teutscher Spraach. *Frankfurt a. M.: E. Emmel, for B. Ostern,* 1625. 759 p.; 4to. 1st publ., Frankfurt a. M., 1611; here enlarged. This edn includes, p. 524–25, section of German books on America. Jantz (German Americana) 20; Jantz (German Baroque) 837. MnU-B, NNUT, NcD; BL. 625/72

Du Bartas, Guillaume de Salluste, seigneur. Part of Du Bartas, English and French . . . Englished, as may teach an English-man French, or a French-man English . . . With the commentary of S[imon]. G[oulart]. [de] S[enlis]. By William L'isle. *London: J. Haviland,* 1625. 186 (i.e., 273) p.; 4to. In verse. Comprises the four sections of the second day of Du Bartas's *La seconde sepmaine,* 1st publ., Paris, 1584, supplemented by Goulart's commentaries in English only, 1st publ., in the Geneva, 1589, edn. Reissued, 1637, under title *Foure bookes of Du Bartas.* The 3rd section, on 'The colonies' includes numerous refs to the New World. Cf. Sylvester's 1605 translation of Du Bartas's *Devine weekes,* etc. STC 21663. CSmH, CtY, DFo, IU; BL. 625/73

Duchesne, Joseph. Pharmacopoea restituta. Das ist Verbesserte apotecker-Kunst oder Zubereittung . . . in das teutsch versetzet. Durch Johann Adolph Ringelstein. *Strassburg: E. Zetzner,* 1625. 368 p.; port.; 4to. Transl. from Duchesne's *Pharmacopoea dogmaticorum restituta,* 1st publ., Paris, 1607. MiU. 625/74

———. Traicté de la cure generale et particuliere des arcbusades. *Paris: C. Morel,* 1625. 248 p.; 8vo. 1st publ. as transl. from Duchesne's *Sclopetarius* of the same year, [Geneva?], 1576. Included are directions for therapeutic use of tobacco. DNLM; London:Wellcome, BN. 625/75

Du Ferrier, Jérémie. Advertissement à tous les estats de l'Europe, touchant les maximes fondamentales du gouvernement et des desseins des Espagnols. *Paris:* 1625. 16 p.; 8vo. Included are refs to Spanish domination in both Indies. ICN; BN. 625/76

———. Le Catholique d'estat, ou Discours politique des alliances du Roy tres-chrestien. *Paris: J. Bouillerot,* 1625. 227 p.; 8vo. In commenting on cruelty of Spanish rule in the West Indies the author states that the Italian Benzo (i.e., Benzoni), Las Casas, & others have already said all that is necessary. BN. 625/77

—[Anr edn]. *Paris: J. Bouillerot,* 1625. 215 p.; 8vo. CtY, ICN, MH; BN. 625/78

—[Anr edn]. *Rouen: D. Du Petit-Val,* 1625. 227 p.; 8vo. BN. 625/79

Dupleix, Scipion. La curiosité naturelle. *Rouen: C. Loudet,* 1625. 12mo. 1st publ., Paris, 1606. CU; BL. 625/80

Durante, Castore. Il tesoro della sanità. *Venice: G. & I. Imberti,* 1625. 334 p.; 16mo. 1st publ., [Rome?], 1586; cf. 1601 edn. Here a reissue of M. A. Zaltieri's 1616, Venice, edn. DNLM; BL. 625/81

Esternod, Claude d'. L'espadon satyrique. *Rouen: D. Ferrand* [1625?]. 142 p.; 12mo. In verse. 1st publ., Lyons, 1619. Esternod, *L'espadon satyrique,* ed. Fleuret & Perceau (Paris, 1922) xliv–xlv. 625/82

Estienne, Charles. L'agriculture et maison rustique. *Rouen: L. Costé,* 1625,'24. 2 pts; 4to. 1st publ. as enl. by Liébault, Paris, 1567; cf. 1601 edn. Goldsmith (France) E329. BL. 625/83

Fernández Pereira, Ruy. Daños certissimos, y evidentes de la subida de la plata, que se à propuesto a su Magestad. [*Madrid?* 1625?]. [8] p.; fol. Memorial to king of Spain on royal revenues received from New World. BL. 625/84

Figueiredo, Manuel de. Hidrographia, exame de pilotos. *Lisbon: V. Alvarez,* 1625. 3 pts; illus.; 4to. 1st publ., Lisbon, 1608. Cf. Sabin 24316; Borba de Moraes I:265–66; Palau 91333; JCB (3) II:192. CtY, RPJCB; BL, BN. 625/85

Fonseca, Rodrigo. Consultationum medicinalium singularibus remediis refertae. *Frankfurt a. M.: Heirs of A. Wechel, for D. & D. Aubry & C. Schleich,* 1625. 2 v.; 8vo. 1st publ., Venice, 1619–22. Wellcome I:2345. London:Wellcome, BN. 625/86

France. Laws, statutes, etc., 1610–1643 (Louis XIII). Declaration du Roy, portant defenses a tous ses subjects de faire aucun traficq ny commerce au royaume d'Espagne. *Paris: P. Mettayer,* 1625. 13 p.; 8vo. Forbids seizure of Spanish ships en route to or from the Americas. MH-BA. 625/87

Freitas, Seraphim de. De justo imperio Lusitanorum asiatico. *Valladolid: J. Morillo,* 1625. 190 numb. lvs; 4to. A reply to Grotius's *Mare liberum,* 1st publ., Leyden, 1609. Includes refs to West Indies & America. Meulen/Diermanse, p. 212. CtY, DLC, InU-L, MH, MnU-B, NN-RB; BL, BN.   625/88

Frías, Manuel de. El capitan Manuel de Frias, Procurador general . . . del Rio de la Plata y Paraguay. [*Madrid?* 1625?]. 4 numb. lvs; fol. Memorial to king of Spain on commerce of provinces under procurator's control. Medina (BHA) 6472; Palau 95007. BL.   625/89

——. Señor. El capitan Manuel de Frias vezino del Rio de la Plata. Dize: que el viene por procurador de ocho ciudades . . . en aquellas provincias. [*Madrid?* 1625?]. [4] p.; fol. BL.   625/90

La furieuse défaite des Espagnols et la sanglante bataille donnee au Perou . . . entre les dits Espagnols et les Hollandois, conduits par leur admiral Jacques l'Hermite . . . jouxte la copie Flamande imprimée à Anvers. *Paris: J. Martin,* 1625. 16 p.; 8vo. Presumably transl. from the *Waerachtigh verhael van het succes* of this year below, itself transl. from the *Casos notables* of this year above. Sabin 31508; Palau 95907; Maggs Cat. 479 (Americana V):4173. CU-B, NN-RB, RPJCB.   625/91

—[Anr edn]. *Toulouse: J. Boude,* 1625. 15 p.; 8vo. Reprinted from the above. Sabin 31509; Palau 95908; Tiele 663n.   625/92

Gaitan de Torres, Manuel. Reglas par el govierno destos reynos y de los Indias. [*Jerez de la Frontera:*] 1625. 161 p.; 4to. Concerns administration & trade of Spanish America. MnU-B.   625/93

Garcés, García, S.J. Relacion de la persecucion que huvo en la iglesia de Japon. *Madrid: L. Sánchez,* 1625. 33 numb. lvs; 4to. 1st publ., Mexico, 1624. Medina (BHA) 786; Streit V:1345; Pérez Pastor (Madrid) 2165; Palau 98886n. MH; BN, Madrid:BU (San Isidro).   625/94

—[Anr edn]. *Valencia: J. C. Gárriz,* 1625. 140 p.; 12mo. Streit V:1346. Palma:BP.   625/95

García, Gregorio, O.P. Predicacion del Evangelio en el Nuevo Mundo, viviendo los Apostoles. *Baeza: P. de la Cuesta,* 1625. 250 numb. lvs; 8vo. Sabin 26588; Medina (BHA) 787; Streit II:1556; Palau 98008. NN-RB, RPJCB.   625/96

Gaspar d'Asençao, O.P. Sermam que prego o padre frey Gaspar d'Ascenção . . . na se da Bahia de todos os Santos na cidade de Salvador. Na primeira missa que disse, quando se derão as primeiras graças publicas, entrada a cidade pela vitoria alcançada dos Olandeses a 5. de mayo de 1625. [*Lisbon:*] G. da Vinha [1625?]. [15] p.; 4to. Borba de Moraes I:43; Rodrigues (Dom. Hol.) 885; Innocencio III:123. MH.   625/97

Gonsalvius, Reginaldus, Montanus. A discovery and plaine declaration of sundry subtill practices of the Holy Inquisition of Spaine. *London: J. Bellamy,* 1625. 198 p.; 4to. 1st publ. in English, London, 1568; transl. by Vincent Skinner from author's *Sanctae Inquisitiones Hispanicae artes,* 1st publ., Heidelberg, 1567. Includes account of Juan de Leon, formerly a 'taylor' in Mexico. STC 11998; McAlpin I:375. CSmH, CtY, NN; BL.   625/98

—[Anr issue]. A full, ample and punctuall discovery of the barbarous, bloudy, and inhumane practices of the Spanish Inquisition. *London: J. Bellamy,* 1625. STC 11999. CSmH, CtY, DFo, InNd; BL.   625/99

Gordon, Sir Robert, of Lochinvar. Encouragements. For such as shall have intention to bee under-takers in the new plantations of Cape Breton, now New Galloway in America. *Edinburgh: J. Wreittoun,* 1625. [34] p.; illus.; 4to. Sabin 27967 (misdated 1620) & 41715 (erroneously citing 1620 & 1624 edns); STC 12069; JCB AR27:14. CSmH, NN-RB, RPJCB; BL.   625/100

Le grand dictionaire françois-latin . . . recueilli des observations de plusieurs hommes doctes, entre autres de m. Nicod . . . et de nouveau reveu et augmenté par m. de Brosses . . . plus un recueil des noms modernes des peuples, régions, villes, montaignes, rivières et autres lieux. *Lyons: C. Larjot,* 1625. 1620 p.; 8vo. 1st publ., Paris, 1573, under title *Dictionaire françois-latin;* cf. year 1614. Includes, as 'Nicotiane', description of tobacco. BN.   625/101

—[Anr edn]. *Geneva: J. Stoer,* 1625. 1620 p.; 8vo. TxU; BL.   625/102

—[Anr edn]. . . . augmenté [par Guillaume Poille] . . . recueilli des observations de plusieurs hommes doctes, entre autres de m. Nicod [i.e., Nicot]. *Rouen: R. L'Allemant,* 1625. 284 lvs; 4to. BN. 625/103

Gravina, Domenico, O.P. Vox turturis, seu De florenti usque ad nostra tempora SS. Benedicti, Dominici, Francisci et aliarum sacrarum religionum statu. *Naples: S. Roncalioli,* 1625. 365 p.; 8vo. Contains discussion of missionary activity in New World. Streit I:422. BN. 625/104

Great Britain. Sovereigns, etc., 1603–1625 (James I). A proclamation for setling the plantation of Virginia. *London: B. Norton & J. Bill,* 1625. 2 lvs; fol. Sabin 99848; Crawford (Roy. procl.) 1423; Brigham (Roy. procl.) 52–55; STC 8774. CSmH, DFo; BL. 625/105

—[Anr edn]. *London: B. Norton & J. Bill,* 1625. 2 lvs; fol. Crawford (Roy. procl.) 1424; STC 8775. London:Soc. of Antiquaries. 625/106

——. A proclamation for the utter prohibiting the importation and use of all tobacco, which is not of the proper growth of . . . Virginia and the Summer Islands. *London: B. Norton & J. Bill,* 1624 [i.e., 1625]. 4 lvs; fol. Sabin 99845; Crawford (Roy. procl.) 1398; Brigham (Roy. procl.) 42–50; STC 8751. CSmH; BL. 625/107

Great Britain. Sovereigns, etc., 1625–1649 (Charles I). A proclamation touching tobacco. *London: B. Norton & J. Bill,* 1625. 2 lvs; fol. Reiterates prohibition of importation of tobacco not grown in Virginia or Bermuda, etc. Sabin 99846; Crawford (Roy. procl.) 1415; Brigham (Roy. procl.) 50–52; STC 8767. DFo; BL. 625/108

Grotius, Hugo. De jure belli ac pacis libri tres. *Paris: N. Buon,* 1625. 785 (i.e., 739) p.; 4to. The simple life of American natives is said to exemplify the communal state existing before the development of property. For variant edns, see Meulen/Diermanse as cited. Meulen/Diermanse 565(I)–565(III). CLSU, CtY, DLC, MH, MiU-C, MnU-B, NN-RB, PU-L, RPB; BL, BN. 625/109

Guerreiro, Bartolomeu, S.J. Jornada dos vassalos da coroa de Portugal, pera se recuperar a cidade do Salvador, na Bahya de Todos os Santos, tomada pollos Olandezes, a oito de Mayo de 1624. & recuperada ao primeiro de Mayo de 1625. *Lisbon: M. Pinheiro, for F. Alvarez,* 1625. 74 numb. lvs; map; 8vo. Sabin 29126; Borba de Moraes I:320; Rodrigues (Dom. Hol.) 341; Backer III:1912; JCB (3) II:192. DLC, MH, RPJCB; BL, BN. 625/110

Guibert, Philbert. Le prix et valeur des medicamens, tant simples que composes, desquels on se sert a la medecine. *Paris: D. Langlois,* 1625. 71 p.; 8vo. Listed, with prices, are guaiacum, mechoacan, sarsaparilla, sassafras, & tobacco ('Folium Indicum'). DNLM; BN. 625/111

Guyon, Louis, sieur de la Nauche. Les diverses leçons . . . Troisiesme edition. *Lyons: A. Chard,* 1625. 3 v.; 8vo. 1st publ., Lyons, 1604. BN. 625/112

Hagthorpe, John. England's-exchequer. or A discourse of the sea and navigation, with some things thereto coincident concerning plantations . . . Wherein . . . is likewise set downe the great commodoties and victories the Portingalls, Spaniards, Dutch, and others have gotten by navigation and plantations, in the West-Indies, and elsewhere. *London: N. Butter & N. Bourne,* 1625. 49 p.; 4to. Sabin 29522; STC 12603; JCB (3) II:192. CSmH, DLC, RPJCB; BL. 625/113

Harington, Sir John. The most elegant and wittie epigrams. *London: T. S[nodham]., for J. Budge,* 1625. 92 lvs; 8vo. In verse. 1st publ., London, 1618. STC 12777. CSmH, MH. 625/114

Heinsius, Daniel. Harangue funebre faite a la memoire du tres-illustre et invincible Prince Maurice de Nassau . . . Prince d'Orange . . . en l'Université de Leiden en Hollande, le xix jour de septembre 1625. Du latin [traduit par André Rivet]. *Leyden: I. Elsevier,* 1625. 85 p.; illus.; 4to. Transl. from the following item. Willems (Les Elzevier) 236; Rahir (Les Elzevier) 199; Knuttel 3597. BN, The Hague:KB. 625/115

——. Laudatio funebris invicto et excelsae memoriae principi Mauritio . . . principi Auriaco, Lugd. Bat. xix. septemb. publice dicta. *Leyden: Elsevier Office,* 1625. 76 p.; port.; fol. Heinsius describes Dutch overseas enterprises, first in the East Indies & soon after in the West Indies, whence were gained not only incredible wealth, but also an infinite number of plants, strange animals, drugs & spices, and roots hitherto unknown. Willem (Les Elzevier) 235; Rahir (Les Elzevier) 198. BL, BN. 625/116

Heylyn, Peter. Μικροκοσμος. A little description of the great world. Augmented and revised. *Oxford: J. Lichfield & W. Turner; sold by W. Turner & T. Huggins,* 1625. 812 p.; 8vo. 1st publ., Oxford, 1621. Sabin 31656n; Madan (Oxford) 1625:6; STC 13277. CSmH, CtY, DFo, NHi; BL. 625/117

Heyns, Zacharias. Emblemata. Emblemes chrestiennes et morales. Sinnebeelden. *Rotterdam: P. van Waesberghe,* 1625. 4 pts; illus.; 4to. Includes Heyns's *Emblemata moralia;* here lvs 38v–40r treat the 'kukuye', a small bird with luminescent eyes described in chapt. 8 of Oviedo's 'Indische historie'. 'De Indianen haer de oogen ende de borste strijckende met . . . dese vogelkens blinckens by nachte in hare dansen . . . als oft sy vierige vlammende geesten waren.' Also cited are Ortelius's *Caertboeck* & a lengthy passage from the '5th day' of Du Bartas. The creatures in question are more likely tropical American fireflies. Vries (Emblemata) 118. CSmH, CtY-M, DFo, IU (imp.), MH, MiU; BL, BN. 625/118

——. Emblemata moralia. Les emblemes morales. De sinne-beelden. *Rotterdam:* 1625. 50 numb. lvs; illus.; 4to. Issued as pt of Heyns's *Emblemata* above, q.v.

Hofmann, Lorenz. Θαυματαφυλακιον, sive Thesaurus variarum rerum antiquarum et exoticarum . . . Allerley Antiquiteten und seltsame sachen, auss Ost- unn West-Indien . . . und vielen andern frembden Landen. *Halle: C. Bismarck,* 1625. 120 lvs; 8vo. Arents (Add.) 234. NN-A. 625/119

Horst, Gregor. Observationum medicinalium singularium libri quatuor. *Ulm: J. Saur,* 1625. 584 p.; illus., port.; 4to. In pt 1 mechoacan is discussed, in pt 2 an unguent based on tobacco. DNLM. 625/120

Houtman, Cornelis de. Erste Schiffart in die Orientalische Indien, so die holländische Schiff . . . verricht . . . Editio quinta. *Frankfurt a. M.: H. Palthenius, for the Hulsiuses,* 1625. 67 p.; illus., maps; 4to. (Levinus Hulsius's *Sammlung von . . . Schiffahrten.* Pt 1).

1st publ. in this version, Nuremberg, 1598; cf. year 1602. Sabin 33653; Church 260; JCB (3) I:451. CSmH, ICN, NN-RB, RPJCB; BL, BN. 625/121

Hughes, Lewis. To the Right Honourable, the Lords and others of his Majesties most honourable privie Council. [*London?* 1625]. [27] p.; 8vo. Plea for redress of sufferings during service as clergyman in Bermuda. Sabin 96027; STC 13915; Arents (Add.) 233. NN-A; BL. 625/122

Insigne victoria que el senor marques de Guadalcazar, virrey en el reyno del Pirú ha alcançado en los puertos de Lima, y Callao, contra una armada poderosa de Olanda. [*Seville:*] *S. Fajardo* [1625]. [4] p.; fol. Cf. Sabin 34812; Medina (BHA) 788; Escudero (Seville) 1.332. RPJCB; BL, Madrid:Acad. de la Hist. 625/123

——[Anr edn]. *Lisbon: G. da Vinha* [1625]. [4] p.; fol. Sabin 34812; Medina (BHA) 789; Palau 11910. DLC, ICN. 625/124

Laet, Joannes de. Nieuwe Wereldt ofte Beschrijvinghe van West-Indien. *Leyden: I. Elsevier,* 1625. 510 p.; maps; fol. Sabin 38554; Vail (Frontier) 70; Rodrigues (Dom. Hol.) 82; Streit II:1557; JCB (3) II:193. CtY, DLC, MH, MiU-C, MnU-B, NN-RB, PU, RPJCB; BL, BN. 625/125

León Pinelo, Antonio Rodríguez de. Libros reales de govierno y gracia de la Secretaria del Perù, que por mandado del Real Consejo de las Indias, y orden del . . . Rodrigo de Aguiar y Acuña . . . ha leydo y passado . . . Antonio de Leon. [*Madrid?* ca. 1625?]. 11 numb. lvs; fol. Medina (BHA) 7704. BL, Santiago, Chile:BN. 625/126

——. Por Diego de Vega, vezino del puerto de Buenos-Ayres, governacion del Rio de la Plata, en . . . Perù. Con el señor fiscal del Consejo Real de las Indias. Sobre la causa de la pesquias, que por comission del presidente de los Charcas . . . hizo Hernando Arias de Saavedra. [*Madrid:* ca. 1625?]. 42 numb. lvs; fol. CU-B. 625/127

Lescarbot, Marc. Nova Francia, or the Description of that part of New France, which is one continent with Virginia . . . Translated out of French . . . by P[ierre]. E[rondelle]. *London: A. Hebb* [after 1625]. 307 p.; map; 4to. 1st publ. as here transl., London, 1609; here a reissue of that edn with dedication & preface canceled, and cancel t.p. Sabin 40176; cf. Harrisse (NF) 19; cf. Borba de Moraes I:407; STC 15492; Church 342; JCB (3) II:62. CSmH, CtY, DLC, ICN, MH, MiU-C, NN-RB, PPL, RPJCB; BL. 625/128

Lima. Universidad de San Marcos. Prologo de las constituciones, que hizo y recopilò el virrey marques de Montesclaros. *Seville: J. de Cabrera* [1625]. fol. 1st publ., [Madrid? 1624?]. BL. 625/129

Lo que sacara de frutos del Rio de la Plata un navio de setenta toneladas. [*Madrid?* 1625?] [2] p.; fol. BL. 625/130

López Madera, Gregorio. Excelencias de la monarquia y reyno de España. *Madrid: L. Sánchez, for M. Gil de Córdova,* 1625 (Colophon: 1624). 109 numb. lvs.; fol. 1st publ., Valladolid, 1597; here a reissue of 1624 edn. CaBVaU, DLC, ICU, NN, NNH; BL. 625/131

Lyste van 't ghene de Brasil jaerlijcks can opbrenghen. [*Amsterdam:* ca. 1625?]. bds.; 4to. Sabin 7600; Rodrigues (Dom. Hol.) 720; Petit 2028. Leyden:B. Thysiana. 625/132

Malingre, Claude. Quatriesme tome de l'Histoire de nostre temps. Ez années M.DC.XXIII. XXIV. & XXV. *Paris: J. Petit-Pas,* 1625. 689 p.; 8vo. Described are the recapture of Bahia, Brazil, from the Dutch (p. 125–30); & events in Mexico (p. 376–86). For prior vols, see the year 1624. Cioranescu (XVII) 45425; JCB (3) II:167. RPJCB; BN. 625/133

Marguérite d'Angoulême, Queen of Navarre. L'Heptameron. *Rouen: D. Du Petit-Val,* 1625. 12mo. 1st publ., Paris, 1558, under title *Histoire des amans fortunez;* cf. 1615 edn. Tchémerzine VII:395. 625/134

Marianus de Orscelar, O.F.M. Gloriosus Franciscus redivivus, sive Chronica observantiae strictioris . . . eiusdemque per Christianos orbes, non solùm, sed & Americam, Peru, Chinas . . . Indos Orientis, & occidui solis. *Ingolstadt: W. Eder,* 1625. 852 p.; 4to. Sabin 44556; Streit I:426; Palau 151767; JCB (3) II:194. CU, NN-RB, RPJCB; BL, BN. 625/135

Martini, Matthäus. De morbis mesenterii abstrusioribus. *Halle: M. Oelschlegel,* 1625. 486 p.; 8vo. Included are a discussion of Peru-

vian opobalsam & a formula for an infusion of tobacco. DNLM, PPC. 625/136

Mascarenhas, Antonio. Relação dos procedimentos que teve sendo o Commissario Geral da bulla da Sancta Cruzada, na declaraçao e decisão de algumas duvidas que moveu . . . João Baptista Pallota. [*Lisbon:* 1625?]. 60 lvs; 4to. On the functioning of the Catholic Church's Commisarius Generalis Cruciatae, with its American participation. Sabin 45403. 625/137

Matthieu, Pierre. Della perfetta historia di Francia, e delle cose piu memorabili occorse nelle provincie straniere ne gli anni di pace regnante . . . Henrico Quarto . . . libri sette; tradotti di francese . . . dal conte Alessandro Senesio. *Venice: B. Barezzi,* 1625. 717 p.; 4to. Transl. from Matthieu's *Histoire de France et des choses memorables advenues aux provinces estrangeres durant sept annees de paix, du regne de Henry IV,* 1st publ., Paris, 1605; cf. 1623 edn with title *Historia di Francia.* ICU. 625/138

Mexía, Pedro. Les diverses leçons . . . Mises de castillan en françois par Cl. Gruget . . . Plus la suite de celles d'Antoine du Verdier. *Geneva: P. Aubert,* 1625. 1032 p.; 8vo. 1st publ. in this version with American refs in Du Verdier's continuation, Lyons, 1577. Cf. Sabin 48245; Palau 167326. DFo, InNd. 625/139

Middelgeest, Simon van, supposed author. Den langh-verwachten dondersclach. Voorsien ende voorseyt in den Oost-Indischen Eclipsis . . . Uut ghegheven . . . door den gheest van . . . Ymant Adamsen. Tot Eenstadt in de Landts-trouwe, naest de welbekende waerheydt. [*Amsterdam?* ca. 1625?]. [44] p.; 4to. 1st publ., [Amsterdam? 1622], under title *Tweede noot-wendiger discours ofte Vertooch.* Sabin 39241 (& 97530); Knuttel 3585b; Petit 1379. The Hague:KB. 625/140

——. Den vervaerlijcken Oost-Indischen eclipsis vertoont aende Vereenichde Provincien door de participanten van d' Oost-Indische Compagnie. [*Amsterdam:*]1625. [20] p.; 4to. 1st publ., [Amsterdam], 1622, under title *Nootwendich discours oft Vertooch.* Sabin 99316; Knuttel 3585a; Petit 1377. RPJCB; The Hague:KB. 625/141

Minsheu, John. Minshaei emendatio, vel a

mendis expurgatio, seu augmentatio sui 'Ductoris in linguas, the guide into tongues' . . . The second edition. *London: J. Haviland,* 1625. 760 cols; fol. A new edn of pt 1 of the author's 1617 *Ductor in linguas.* STC 17945. CSmH, IU, MH; BL.   625/142

—[Anr issue]. *London: [J. Haviland;] sold by J. Browne,* 1625. STC 17945.5. DFo, MdBP, MH; Edinburgh:NL.   625/143

Montaigne, Michel Eyquem de. Essais. *Paris: F. Angat,* 1625. 1039 p.; 4to. 1st publ., Bordeaux; cf. 1602 edn. ICU, NjP.
                                        625/144

—[Anr issue]. *Paris: R. Bertault,* 1625. Tchémerzine VIII:424. BL, BN.
                                        625/145

—[Anr issue]. *Paris: R. Boutonné,* 1625. Tchémerzine VIII:424. BN.   625/146

—[Anr issue]. *Paris: M. Collet,* 1625. Tchémerzine VIII:424.   625/147

—[Anr issue]. *Paris: Widow R. Dallin,* 1625. Tchémerzine VIII:424. CLSU, MH; BN.
                                        625/148

—[Anr issue]. *Paris: C. Hulpeau,* 1625. Tchémerzine VIII:424. BN.   625/149

—[Anr issue]. *Paris: T. de LaRuelle,* 1625. OU.
                                        625/150

—[Anr issue]. *Paris: G. Loyson,* 1625. Tchémerzine VIII:424. BN.   625/151

—[Anr issue]. *Paris: G. & A. Robinot,* 1625. Tchémerzine VIII:424. CtY, MH; BN.
                                        625/152

—[Anr issue]. *Paris: P. Rocolet,* 1625. Tchémerzine VIII:424. BN.   625/153

—[Anr issue]. *Paris: E. Saucié,* 1625. Tchémerzine VIII:424. BN.   625/154

Morrell, William. New-England. or A briefe enarration of the ayre, earth, water, fish, and fowles of that country. With a description of . . . the natives; in Latine and English verse. *London: J. D[awson].,* 1625. 24 p.; 4to. Sabin 50786; STC 18169. CSmH, MHi (imp.); BL.   625/155

Moscoso y de Córdoba, Cristóbal de. Discurso juridico y politico en la sedicion que huvo en Mexico el año passado de 1624. [*Madrid?* 1625?]. 21 numb. lvs; fol. Medina (BHA) 6669. InU-L; Santiago, Chile:BN.
                                        625/156

Neander, Johann. Traicté du tabac, ou Nicotiane, panacee . . . mis . . . en françois par J[acques]. V[eyras]. *Lyons: B. Vincent,* 1625.

342 p.; illus.; 8vo. Transl. from the author's *Tabacologia,* 1st publ., Leyden, 1622. KyLoS, MH; BL, BN.   625/157

Netherlands (United Provinces, 1581–1795). Staten Generaal. Ampliatie op 'tvierde artijckel van de Ordonnantie vande verpachtinge van een vierde-part vande opheve vende convoye ende licente. *The Hague: Widow & Heirs of H. Jacobszoon von Wouw,* 1625. [2] p.; 4to. Apparently relates to the 4th article of the *Placcaet ordonnantie ende conditien* of this year, below. JCB (3) II:194–95. RPJCB.   625/158

——. Placcaet. De Staten Generael der Vereenichde Nederlanden . . . octroy tot het oprechten van een West-Indische compagnie . . . ghegheven in 's Graven-Haghe opten acht-en-twintichsten Octobris 1625, was gheparapheert G. Schaffer. *The Hague: Widow & Heirs of H. Jacobszoon van Wouw,* 1625. 4 lvs; 4to. Sabin 63194. DLC, ICN.
                                        625/159

——. Placcaet ende ordonnantie opte wapeninge ende manninge vande schepen. *The Hague: Widow & Heirs of H. Jacboszoon van Wouw,* 1625. [20] p.; 4to. 1st publ., The Hague, 1607; here enlarged. Petit 1480; JCB (3) II:195. RPJCB; Leyden:UB.
                                        625/160

——. Placcaet ende ordonnantie . . . tegens wechloopers die hun indienst vande West-Indische Compaignie begeven hebbende verloppen. *The Hague: Widow & Heirs of H. Jacobszoon van Wouw,* 1625. [4] p.; 4to. Lf 3v dated '. . . den twee-en-twintichsten Marty 1625, was geparapheert Anthonis de Rode v[t]'. Sabin 63195; Asher 110; JCB (3) II:195. RPJCB; BL.   625/161

—[Anr edn]. . . . in dienst vande Oost ofte West-Indische Compaignien . . . *The Hague: Widow & Heirs of H. Jacobszoon van Wouw,* 1625. [4] p.; 4to. Lf 3v dated '. . . den dertichsten May 1625, was geparapheert F. Graeff van Culenborgh v[t]'. Sabin 102908; Petit 1477; JCB (3) II:196. RPJCB; Leyden:B. Thysiana.   625/162

——. Placcaet ende ordonnantie . . . waer naer de inghesetenen vande selve landen varende naer westen . . . hen sullen hebben te reguleren. *The Hague: Widow & Heirs of H. Jacobszoon van Wouw,* 1625. [6] p.; 4to. 1st publ., The Hague, 1623; here enlarged.

Includes ref. in article XI to 'Terreneufve en elders aenloopen'. Petit 1479; JCB (3) II:195. RPJCB; Leyden:UB.   625/163

——. Placcaet ordonnantie ende conditien: waer op van weghens de . . . Heeren Staten Generael . . . sal werdē verpacht den meest ofte hoochst-mijnende een vierde-part vanden opheve der convoyen ende licenten. *The Hague: Widow & Heirs of H. Jacobszoon van Wouw,* 1625. [9] p.; 4to. Includes ref. to the West-Indische Compagnie. JCB (3) II:196. RPJCB.   625/164

Opmeer, Pieter van (1525–1595). Chronographia mundi. *Cologne: B. Wolter & P. Henning,* 1625. 2 pts; 4to. 1st publ., Antwerp, 1611, under title *Opus chronographicum.* ICN; BL, BN.   625/165

Pérez de Porres, Diego. A Melchor de Castro Macedo, secretario del Rey . . . y de su consejo. [*Madrid?* 1625]. [7] p.; fol. Memorial on armaments & equipment for a frigate for defense of Peru. BL.   625/166

Pigray, Pierre. Epitome des preceptes de medecine et chirurgie. *Rouen: J. Berthelin,* 1625. 764 p.; 8vo. 1st publ., Paris, 1600, under title *La chirurgie;* cf. 1604 edn. DNLM.   625/167

Platter, Felix. Praxeos medicae tomi tres. *Basel: J. Schroeter, for L. König,* 1625. 4 v.; 4to. Expanded version of the author's *Praxeos,* 1st publ., Basel, 1602–3. Wellcome I:5088. ICJ, NIC; London:Wellcome, BN.   625/168

Polo, Gaspar Gil. Casp. Barthi Erotodidascalus, sive Memorialium libri v. *Hanau: D. & D. Aubry & C. Schleich,* 1625. 315 p.; illus.; 8vo. Transl. from the author's *Diana enamorada;* cf. Brussels, 1613, edn above. Palau 102088. CtY, DLC, ICN, MH, NjP; BN.   625/169

Popp, Johann. Chymische Medicin. *Frankfurt a. M.: D. & D. Aubry & C. Schleich,* 1625. 523 p.; 8vo. 1st publ., Frankfurt a. M., 1617. DNLM.   625/170

Potier, Pierre. Insignes curationes et singulares observationes centum. *Cologne: M. Schmitz,* 1625. 2 pts; 12 mo. 1st publ., Venice, 1615. Also included is Potier's *Curationum . . . centuria secunda,* 1st publ., Bologna, 1622. DNLM; BL.   625/171

La prise de la ville d'Ordinguen par l'Evesque d'Halberstat, sur les Espagnols.

Paris: 1625. 14 p.; 8vo. Purported to have been printed 'jouxte la copie imprimée à Amsterdam', the latter has not been traced. Mention is made of 70 Dutch ships destined for West Indies & Brazil. MH.   625/172

Purchas, Samuel. Purchas his pilgrimes. *London: W. Stansby, for H. Fetherstone,* 1625. 4 v.; illus., maps; fol. In the tradition of Hakluyt, contains accounts of travel and exploration in various parts of the world. Added engraved t.p. in v. l, dated 1624 or 1625, has title *Hakluytus posthumus, or Purchas his pilgrimes.* For printing variants & description of contents, see Sabin. Sabin 66683 & 66686; Baer (Md) 8: Streit I:423; STC 20509; Arents 158; Church 401A; JCB (3) II:196–97. CSmH, CtY, DLC, ICN, MH, MWA, MiU-C, MnU-B, NN-RB, PPL, RPJCB; BL, BN.   625/173

La quarta carta, y verdadera relacion de todas las cosas que han sucedido hasta aora sobra la toma dela ciudad de San Salvador del Brasil. *Valladolid: Widow of F. Fernández de Córdoba,* 1625. 4 p.; fol. Borba de Moraes I:137 ('Carta, La quarta') & II:191; Rodrigues (Dom. Hol.) 338. NN-RB.   625/174

Quervau, Vincent, sieur du Sollier. Le tableau historiale du monde, depuis sa creation jusques à l'an present . . . mil six cens vingt-cinq. *Rennes: P. L'Oyselet,* 1625. 1161 p.; 8vo. CU.   625/175

Recio de León, Juan. Relation de los servicios que Juan Recio de Leon maese de campo general . . . de las provincias de Tipuane, Chunchos, Paytitis y Dorado, de los reynos del Perù, ha hecho a su Magestad de mas de veinte años. [*Madrid:* 1625]. [7] p.; fol. Subscribed at Madrid, 23 June 1625. On services in Bolivia. Medina (Chile) 63. Santiago, Chile:BN.   625/176

——. Señor. El maesse de campo Juan Recio de Leon. Dize, que el principio efecto que se sigue . . . del descubrimiento que ha hecho, no es el traer por el la plata . . . del Peru a España . . . que el menor dellos es de mas importancia que el traerla. [*Madrid?* 1625?]. [4] p.; fol. Sabin 68360 (BA=BL); Medina (Chile) 236. BL, Santiago, Chile:BN.   625/177

——. Señor. Juan Recio de Leon . . . hace

relacion a V[uestra]. M[agestad]. del nuevo camino y navegacion para traer la plata de Potosí y reyno del Perú en España. [*Madrid?* 1625?]. 5 lvs; fol. Memorial addressed to king of Spain. Sabin 68362 (BA=BL); Palau 252306. BL.   625/178

Relaçam do dia em que as armadas de sua Magestade chegarão á Baya, & do que se fez até vinte dous de abril, em que mandou a Pernambuco. [*Lisbon:*] *P. Craesbeeck,* 1625. 3 p.; fol. Describes attacks of Pieter Hein upon Espirito Santo, etc. Borba de Moraes II:182; Rodrigues (Dom. Hol.) 343.
625/179

Relacion de las cosas notables succedidas en la ciudad de Lima y como dexo burlados a los navios Olandeses, la armada de España. [*Seville? J. de Cabrera?*] 1625. Cf. the *Casos notables sucedidos en las costas* of this year above. Sabin 41126; Escudero (Seville) 1.338?; Ternaux-Compans (B. Amer.) 478; Tiele 663n.   625/180

Entry canceled.   625/181

Relacion du grand voyageur, de ce qu'il a veü de plus remarquable dans les principales parties de l'Amerique; avec les portraits des roys, & des sujets de diverses contrées. [*n.p.:* 1625?]. 16 lvs; illus.; 8vo. That its sheets are signed 'C–D' suggests that this item was part of a larger work; if so, the latter has escaped identification. NN-RB.   625/182

Relacion. verdadera, de la grandiosa vitoria que las armadas de España an tenido en la entrada del Brasil. *Cadiz:* 1625. 4 p.; 4to. A possible ghost. Cf. the *Verdadera relacion* below. Rodrigues (Dom. Hol.) 347.
625/183

[Relacion verdadera de las grandes hazañas . . . que una mujer hizo en veynte y quatro años que sirvio en . . . Chile y otras partes . . . de soldado. *Madrid: B. de Guzmán,* 1625?]. Known only from Seville edn below. The woman is identified as Doña Catalina de Erauso. For a continuation, see the *Segunda relacion* below. Medina (Chile) 58; Pérez Pastor (Madrid) 2214.   625/184

——. *Seville: S. Fajardo,* 1625. [4] p.; fol. Medina (Chile) 59. BL, Santiago, Chile:BN.
625/185

Relacion y copia de una carta, de las companias de infanteria, y de acavallo, que su Ma-

gestad tiene en el puerto de Callao, para defensa del dicho puerto, y de la isla del Brasil. *Madrid: B. de Guzman,* 1625. [4] p.; fol. Sabin 69238; Medina (BHA) 791; Borba de Moraes II:192; Pérez Pastor (Madrid) 2213.   625/186

Remón, Alonso, O. Merc. Relacion de como martirizaron los hereges Olandeses, Gelandeses, y Pechilingues . . . al . . . fray Alonso Gomez de Enzinas . . . en la entrada que hizieron este mes passado de Junio de 1624, en la ciudad de Guayaquil, en la provincia de Quito . . . y reynos del Peru. *Madrid: J. Delgado,* 1625. [4] p.; fol. Sabin 69570; cf. Medina (BHA) 792; cf. Streit II:1559; Pérez Pastor (Madrid) 2205. InU-L, NN-RB, RPJCB; BL.   625/187

Ripa, Cesare. Della novissima iconologia. *Padua: P. P. Tozzi,* 1625,'24. 734 p.; illus.; 4to. 1st publ. with American content, Rome, 1603, under title *Iconologia.* CtY, DFo, ICN, NcD, NNUT; BN.   625/188

Rivadeneira, Pedro de, S.J. Della religione del prencipe christiano contra li Machiavellisti. *Bologna: P. P. Tozzi,* 1625. 624 p.; 8vo. 1st publ. in Italian, Genoa, 1598; cf. 1601 edn. Here a reissue of printer's 1622 edn? Palau 266346.   625/189

Roca, Juan Antonio Vera Zúñiga y Figueroa, conde de la. Epitome de la vida y hechos del invicto emperador Carlos V. *Valencia: J. B. Marzal,* 1625. 330 p.; 8vo. 1st publ., Madrid, 1622. Palau 358989. BN.
625/190

Rodríguez Bustamante, Sebastián. Sebastian Rodriguez Bustamante, contador de la real hazienda de . . . Guayaquil en el Piru, al Reyno junto en Cortes. [*Madrid:* 1625]. [2] p.; fol. Memorial to king of Spain on sovereignty of the sea. BL.   625/191

Rodríguez de Burgos, Bartolomé. Relacion de la jornada del Brasil. *Cadiz: J. de Borja,* 1625. [4] p.; fol. On Fadrique de Toledo's victories. Medina (BHA) 796; Borba de Moraes II:212; Rodrigues (Dom. Hol.) 349. DLC, RPJCB.   625/192

Romero, Gonzalo. Señor. Gonzalo Remero [*sic*], en conformidad de lo que tiene ofrecido cerca de su adbitrio. [*Madrid?* 1625?]. 4 numb. lvs; fol. Memorial to king of Spain on registration of precious metals arriving from Indies. BL.   625/193

Rubio, Antonio. Logica mexicana . . . Hoc est, Commentarii breviores . . . in universam Aristotelis Dialecticam. *Lyons: J. Pillehotte*, 1625. 683 p.; 8vo. 1st publ., Cologne, 1625. Cf. Sabin 73860; Medina (BHA) 797; cf. Backer VII:281; Palau 280357. BL, Santiago, Chile:BN.   625/194

Sandoval, Prudencio de, Bp of Pamplona. Historia de la vida y hechos del Emperador Carlos V. *Barcelona: S. de Cormellas*, 1625. 2 v.; port.; fol. 1st publ., Valladolid, 1604–6. Sabin 76425; Palau 297148. DFo; BN.   625/195

Sandys, Sir Edwin. Relatione dello stato della religione. [*Mirandola?*] 1625. 192 p.; 4to. Transl. and annotated by Paolo Sarpi from the author's *A relation of the state of religion*, 1st publ., London, 1605. NcU, NjP; BL, BN.   625/196

Santander, Juan de, O.F.M. Señor. Fray Juan de Santander de la Orden de san Francisco, comissario general de las Indias, dize: que por cedula de 22. de junio . . . de 1624. fue V[uestra]. M[agestad]. servido de mandar, que los religiosos de . . . Neuva-España tengan las dotrinas, come hasta aqui las han tenido. [*Madrid? 1625?*]. [12] p.; fol. Memorial to king of Spain on regular clergy in Spanish America. Medina (BHA) 6880. Santiago, Chile:BN.   625/197

Schmidel, Ulrich. Vera et jucunda descriptio praecipuarum quarundam Indiae Occidentalis regionum & insularum . . . Correctius et tersius quam antehac edita. [*Frankfurt a. M.:*] *Widow & Heirs of J. T. de Bry*, 1625. 35 p.; illus.; fol. (Theodor de Bry's *America*. Pt 7. Latin). At head of title: Americae pars vii. 1st publ. in this version, [Frankfurt a. M.], 1599; transl. from Schmidel's *Neuwe Welt*, 1st publ., Frankfurt a. M., 1567; etc. Cf. Sabin 8784; Church 162; JCB (3) I:399. CSmH, DLC, NN-RB, RPJCB; BL, BN.   625/198

Scotland. Privy Council. [Forsamekle as our soveraine Lordis . . . *Edinburgh:* 1625]. For completing number of Nova Scotian baronets. Crawford (Roy. procl.) Scotland:1432. No copy known.   625/199

Scott, Thomas. Vox Dei. Of De stemme des Heeren . . . overgeset door Jacobum Hughes. *Utrecht: A. van Herwijck*, 1625. 84 p.; 4to. Transl. from English text 1st publ.,

[1623?]. Cf. Sabin 78378–79; Shaaber (Brit. auth.) S175; Knuttel 3627. The Hague:KB.   625/200

Scribanius, Carolus. Holländisch apocalypsis: oder Offenbarung . . . aussgelegt . . . durch Pambonem Verimundima [pseud.] *Augsburg: A. Aperger* [1625]. 23 p.; 4to. Transl. from the author's *Den Hollantschen apocalypsis*, below. Knuttel 3610. BL, The Hague:KB.   625/201

——. Den Hollantschen apocalypsis, vrijmoedelijck uytghellet door Pambonem Vreimundima [pseud.]. *Nieustadt: H. Waerseggher*, 1625. 23 p.; 4to. Perhaps 1st publ. in Latin, [Antwerp, 1624], as pt of Scribanius's *Veridicus Belgicus*. Includes refs to Dutch military & naval power in Peru, Brazil, Mexico, etc. For variant see Backer. Backer VII:988; Kleerkooper 878–79. NN-RB.   625/202

——. Den oor-sprongh, voort-gangh ende gewenscht eynde van den Nederlantschen krygh . . . door Veridicum Belgicum. *Amsterdam: J. Veselaer & B. Janszoon* [1625]. 208 p.; 8vo. Perhaps transl. from an Antwerp, 1624, Latin edn with title *Veridicus Belgicus*. Includes 'Den Hollantschen gereformeerden Apocalypsis', p. 158–208. Backer VII:988; Kleerkooper 878. CtY (as [1626]).   625/203

—[Anr edn]. Den Neder-landtschen waersegger . . . overgheset door B. B. B. B. . . . Nae de kopye ghedruckt t'Amsterdam by Joris Veseler ende Broer Jansz. [*The Netherlands:* 1625]. 144 p.; 8vo. Includes, p. 99–143, *Den ghereformeerden Hollandtschen apocalypsis*. Knuttel 3609; Backer VII:988. BL (as [1627?]), The Hague:KB.   625/204

—[Anr edn]. Den Nederlandschen waerzegger . . . uyt het fransch nae de copye ghedruckt t'Amsterdam. [*The Netherlands:* 1625?]. 8vo. Includes 'Le remonstrant hollandois ou le Brabançon vray disant par B. B. B. B.' Backer VII:988.   625/205

[Segunda relacion . . . Dizense en ella cosas admirables, y fidedignas de los valerosos hechos desta muger; de lo bien que empleó el tiempo en servicio de nuetro Rey y señor. *Madrid: B. de Guzmán*, 1625?]. Continues the conjectured *Relacion verdadera de las grandes hazañas* of this year above, dealing with Doña Catalina de Erausa, & like it known only in the Seville reprints below. Medina (Chile) 60. 625/206

—[Anr edn]. Segunda relacion la mas copiosa, y verdadera que ha salida, impressa por Simon Faxardo . . . Dizense en ellas cosas admirables. *Seville: S. Fajardo,* 1615 [i.e., 1625]. [4] p.; fol. Medina (Chile) 61; Pérez Pastor (Madrid) 61. Santiago, Chile:BN. 625/207

—[Anr edn]. Segunda relacion de los famosos hechos que en el reyno de Chile hizo una varonil muger sirviendo . . . de soldado. *Seville: J. de Cabrera,* 1625. [4] p.; fol. Medina (Chile) 62; Escudero (Seville) 1346. 625/208

Settala, Lodovico. Animadversionum et cautionum medicarum libri septem. *Strassburg: E. Zetzner,* 1625. 330 p.; 8vo. 1st publ., Milan, 1614. DNLM. 625/209

Smith, Capt. John. The generall historie of Virginia, New-England, and the Summer Isles. *London: J. D[awson]. & J. H[aviland].,* *for M. Sparke,* 1625. 248 p.; illus., ports, maps; fol. 1st publ., London, 1624; here a reissue with letterpress t.p. of that edn. Sabin 82825; Clayton-Torrence 51 (2); STC 22790a; Church 407. CSmH, CtY. 625/210

Spain. Laws, statutes, etc., 1556–1598 (Philip II). Nuevas leyes y ordenanzas, hechas por su Magestad . . . cerca de la forma que se ha de tener . . . en el descubrimiento, labor, y beneficio de las minas de oro . . . y otros metales. *Madrid: L. Sánchez,* 1625. 22 numb. lvs; fol. Laws promulgated in August 1584; body of text 1st publ., Madrid, 1585. Includes covering letter of Andres de Carrasquilla, 'secretario de don Juan de Oñate, adelantado del Nuevo Mexico, visitador general de las minas de España'. BL. 625/211

Spain. Sovereigns, etc., 1621–1665 (Philip IV), addressee. Señor. Un vasallo de V. Magestad . . . que ha estado en las Indias . . . representa a V. Magestad la inconveniencias que ay, para que en las plaças del Consejo de Indias sean proveydos de oydores. [*Madrid?* 1625?]. [3] p.; fol. Medina (BHA) 6211. BL. 625/212

Spain. Treaties, etc., 1621–1665 (Philip IV). Copia de las cartas y respuestas que huvo de parte de los olandeses, y don Fadrique de Toledo Ossorio, desde 28. de abril hasta 30. que se vindio la plaça. *Barcelona: S. & J. Matevad,* 1625. 4 lvs; 4to. Contains correspondence between the Dutch commandant & Don F. de Toledo Osório y Mendoza on terms of São Salvador's surrender—Borba de Moraes. Borba de Moraes I:174–75. NN-RB. 625/213

Spilbergen, Joris van. Dreyjährige Reise Georg von Spielbergen nach den orientalischen und occidentalischen Indien. *Frankfurt a. M.:* 1625. fol. 1st publ. in German, Frankfurt a. M., 1620, under title *Die siebenzehende Schiffart.* Sabin 89452. 625/214

Spinola, Ambrogio, marchese del Sesto e di Venafro. La sommation faite par le marquis de Spinola au gouverneur de la ville de Breda . . . Ensemble plusieurs particularitez de tout ce qui s'est passé, tant en Amerique, qu'en plusieurs endroicts de l'Europe. *Paris: J. Martin,* 1625. 16 p.; 8vo. Said by Martin to have been printed 'jouxte la copie imprimée à Amsterdam'. The latter edn has not been traced. Sabin 89456; Palau 321601; Knuttel 3603. The Hague:KB. 625/215

—[Anr edn]. *Toulouse: J. Boudé* [1625]. 12 p.; 8vo. Reprinted from the above. Sabin 89457; Palau 321602. NNH. 625/216

Staden, Hans. Beschrijvinghe van America . . . how hy selve onder de Brasilianen langhe ghevanghen gheseten heeft. *Amsterdam: B. Janszoon,* 1625. 72 p.; illus.; 4to. 1st publ. in Dutch, Antwerp, 1558, under title *Warachtige historie;* transl. from Staden's *Warhaftige Historia,* 1st publ., Marburg, 1557. Sabin 90043; Borba de Moraes II:284. NN-RB. 625/217

Stirling, William Alexander, 1st earl of. An encouragement to colonies. *London: W. Stansby,* 1625. 47 p.; map; 4to. 1st publ., London, 1624; here a reissue with altered imprint date. STC 341a; Arents (Add.) 231; Church 400n. DLC, MH, NN-A; BL. 625/218

Struzzi, Alberto. Dialogo sobre el comercio destos reynos de Castilla. [*Madrid? L. Sánchez?* 1625?]. 16 lvs; fol. 1st publ., Madrid, 1624. Sabin 93114n. NNC, NcD; BL. 625/219

Le succes de la nouvelle entreprise de la grande flotte des Anglois contre les Espagnols. *Paris: I. Mesnier,* 1625. 16 p.; 8vo. Ref. is made to Spanish subjugation of East & West Indies. MH.   625/220

Tabourot, Estienne. Les bigarrures et touches. *Rouen: D. Geuffroy,* 1625. 5 pts; illus., ports; 12mo. In verse. 1st publ. in this collective edn, Paris, 1603. CtY, NcD; BL.   625/221

Tapp, John. The seamans kalendar . . . Ninth edition. *London: E. Allde, for J. Tapp,* 1625. 4to. 1st publ., London, 1602. STC 23681. CSmH.   625/222

Tassoni, Alessandro. La secchia rapita, poema eroicomico, e 'l primo canto dell' Oceano. *Milan: G. B. Bidelli,* 1625. 249 p.; 12mo. 1st publ., Paris, 1622. Cf. Sabin 94402; Puliatti (Tassoni) 102. Madrid:BN.   625/223

—[Anr edn]. *Venice: G. Sarzina,* 1625. 333 p.; 12mo. Puliatti (Tassoni) 103. FU; Basel:UB.   625/224

Taylor, John, the Water-poet. An arrant thiefe. *London: [M. Fletcher,] for H. Gosson; sold [by E. Wright]* 1625. 8vo. In verse. 1st publ., London, 1622. STC 23729. BL, Oxford:Bodl.   625/225

——. The common whore. *London: [M. Fletcher,] for H. Gosson; sold [by E. Wright?]* 1625. 8vo. In verse. 1st publ., London, 1622. STC 23743. BL.   625/226

Teeling, Ewoud. De derde wachter. *The Hague: A. Meuris,* 1625. 32 p.; 4to. Cf. Teeling's *De tweede wachter* below. Includes ref. to Dutch expectations of Bahia. Knuttel 3607a. NN-RB; The Hague:KB.   625/227

——. De tweede wachter, brenghende tydinghe vande nacht, dat is, van het overgaen vande Bahia. *The Hague: A. Meuris,* 1625. 52 p.; 4to. Preface is signed 'Ireneus Philalethius', a pseud. of the author; sometimes attrib. to his brother, Willem Teelinck. Sabin 94579; Borba de Moraes I:214; Asher 109; Knuttel 3607. BL, The Hague: KB.   625/228

Teixeira, José, supposed author. The Spanish pilgrime; or, An admirable discovery of a Romish Catholike. *London: B. A[lsop]., for T. Archer,* 1625. 134 p.; 4to. Long & generally attributed to Teixeira, or to Antonio Pérez, the ascription is now held erroneous. 1st publ., London, 1598, under title *A trea-*

tise paraenetical, as transl. from the Paris, 1598, *Traicté paranaetique.* Included are numerous refs to the New World. STC 19838.5 (formerly 23863). CSmH, CtY, DLC, ICN, InU-L, MH, NN-RB, RPJCB; BL.   625/229

Theodorus, Jacobus. Neuw vollkommentlich Kreuterbuch . . . so in teutschen . . . Landen, auch in . . . West-Indien . . . gemehret durch Casparum Bauhinum. *Frankfurt a. M.: P. Jacobi, for J. Dreutel,* 1625. 3 pts; illus.; fol. 1st publ., Frankfurt a. M., 1588; cf. 1613 edn. Pritzel 9093; Nissen (Bot.) 1931n. CU, DNLM, ICJ, MH-A, NNBG, PPC; BL, BN.   625/230

Thorius, Raphael. Hymnus tabaci. *Leyden: I. Elsevier,* 1625. 55 p.; illus.; 4to. Sabin 95619; Arents 157. CU, DNLM, MH, NN-RB, OCl, PU; BN.   625/231

Thou, Jacques Auguste de. Historiarum sui temporis . . . libri cxxxviii. *Frankfurt a. M.: E. Emmel, for P. Kopff & B. Ostern,* 1625–28. 4 v.; fol. 1st publ. as here constituted, Geneva, 1620–21. NcD, PPLT; BN (imp.).   625/232

Toledo Osorio y Mendoza, Fadrique de, marqués de Villanueva de Valdueza. Relacion de la carta que embio a su Magestad el Señor Don Fadrique de Toledo, General de las Armadas, y poderoso exercito, que fue al Brasil, y del felicissimo sucesso. *Seville: S. Fajardo,* 1625. [4] p.; fol. Cf. Avendaño y Vilela's *Relacino del viaje* of this year. Sabin 96110; Medina (BHA) 799; Borba de Moraes II:187–88; Rodrigues (Dom. Hol.) 351. NN-RB, RPJCB; BL.   625/233

—[Anr edn]. Relacion del sucesso del armada, y exercito que fue al socorro del Brazil. *Cadiz: G. Vezino,* 1625. [3] p.; 4to. Sabin 96111; Medina (BHA) 800; Rodrigues (Dom. Hol.) 346. Amsterdam:NHSM; Madrid:Acad de la Hist.   625/234

—[Anr edn]. *[Madrid? 1625].* [4] p.; fol. Sabin 69217 & 96112; Medina (BHA) 801; Borba de Moraes II:190; Palau 257843; Pérez Pastor (Madrid) 2203. RPJCB.   625/235

—[Anr edn]. *Naples: Roncallolo,* 1625. 2 lvs; 4to. Rodrigues (Dom. Hol.) 352; Palau 257844.   625/236

——. Relation und Eigentliche beschreibung dess jenigen was sich mit der Schiff Armada und Kriegshör so nach Prasil [*sic*] abgefertigt worden . . . In spannischer Sprach in den Truck verferttigt und hernach verteutscht worden. *Augsburg: M. Langenwalter, for J. Keyltz,* 1625. 12 p.; 4to. Transl. from the author's *Relacion del sucesso del Armada* of this year above. Cf. Avendaño y Vilela's *Relacino del viaje* of this year. Sabin 69263 & 96114; Borba de Moraes II:194; Muller (1872) 2430; Rodrigues (Dom. Hol.) 336; JCB (3) II:190. RPJCB; BL.   625/237

Torquemada, Antonio de. Histoires en forme de dialogues serieux de trois philosophes . . . traduictes d'espagnol par G[abriel]. C[happuys]. *Rouen: J. Roger,* 1625. 546 p.; 12mo. Transl. from the author's *Jardin de flores curiosas,* 1st publ., Salamanca, 1570; 1st publ. as here transl., Lyons, 1579, under title *Hexameron;* cf. 1610 edn. Palau 334921. CtY; BN.   625/238

Torsellino, Orazio, S.J. Epitome historiarum libri x . . . Editio quarta. *Rome: G. Facciotti, for G. B. Brugiotti,* 1625. 416 p.; 12mo. 1st publ., Rome, 1598; cf. 1620 edn. Backer VIII:151.   625/239

A true relation of the fleet which went under the Admirall Jaquis le Hermite through the Straights of Magellane towards the coasts of Peru and the town of Lima. *London: Mercurius Britannicus,* 1625. 33 p.; 4to. Pages 1–6 transl. from part of the *Casos notables, sucedidos en las costas de la ciudad de Lima,* 1st publ., [Seville & Madrid], 1625; sometimes attrib. to Jacques L'Hermite. Also includes, p. 9–33, *An excellent discours,* transl. from the *Voortganck vande West-Indische compaignie,* 1st publ., Amsterdam, 1623. Sabin 31510 (& 31502); Palau 134561; STC 15571; Church 405; JCB (3) II:193; CSmH, NN-RB, PP, RPJCB; BL.   625/240

Usselinx, Willem. Der reiche Schweden General Compagnies handlungs contract, dirigiret naher Asiam, Africam, Americam und Magellanicam. *Stockholm:* 1625. [16] p.; 4to. Based on the author's *Manifest und Vertragbrieff,* 1st publ., [Gothenburg], 1624. Sabin 68983; Jameson (Usselinx) 13; JCB (3) II:197. CtY, DLC, NN-RB, RPJCB.   625/241

——. Sweriges Rijkes General Handels Compagnies contract, dirigerat til Asiam, Africam, Americam och Magellanicam. *Stock-*

holm: 1625. [15] p.; 4to. Prob. transl. from the author's *Der reiche Schweden General Compagnies handlungs contract* of this year, itself based on the *Manifest und Vertragbrieff,* 1st publ., [Gothenburg], 1624. Sabin 98210; Jameson (Usselinx) 14; JCB AR28:24. CtY, DLC, NN-RB, RPJCB; Stockholm:KB.   625/242

Valverde Turices, Santiago de. Al excelmo. S[eñ]or Don Gaspar de Guzman, conde de Olivares. *Seville: J. de Cabrera,* 1625. 8 lvs; 4to. 'Tratado de las propiedades medicinales de la Aloxa y el chocolate'. Palau 349422; Maggs Cat.479 (Americana V): 4179A. London:Wellcome, Madrid:BN.   625/243

Vander Hammen y León, Lorenzo. Don Filipe el Prudente, segundo deste nombre, Rey de las Españas y Nuevo-Mundo. *Madrid: Widow of A. Martín, for A. Pérez,* 1625. 192 numb. lvs; 4to. Described are the evacuation of the French from Florida & Francis Drake's raids in Caribbean. Sabin 30079; Pérez Pastor (Madrid) 2231; Maggs Cat. 479 (Americana V):4179. DLC, MH, NN-RB; BL.   625/244

Varaona, Sancho de. Carta . . . que se fulminò contra don M. Perez de Varaiz . . . a fray Nicolas de Origuen, maestro de dotrina de los Indios del pueblo . . . de Metepeque . . . en la Nueva España; y declaraciones de los Indios de Istlaguaca, Iocotitlan [etc.]. [*Madrid?* 1625?]. fol. Sabin 98593; Palau 351911. MB, NN; BL.   625/245

Vaughan, William. Cambrensium Caroleia. Quibus nuptiae regales celebrantur . . . reportata a Colchide Cambriola ex australissima nova terrae plaga. *London: W. Stansby,* 1625. [112] p.; map; 8vo. In verse. Some of the poems are dedicated to Lord Baltimore; others relate to Newfoundland. Sabin 98691; Baer (Md) 10; STC 24604; Arents (Add.) 235. CSmH, DFo, NN-A; BL.   625/246

Vázquez de Cisneros, Alonso. El doctor Alonso Vazquez de Cisneros oydor de la Real audiencia de México, suplica á V. Señoria que para mejor intelligencia de su justicia, è inocencia, se sirva de mandar advertir estos breves apuntamientos. [*Madrid?* ca. 1625?]. 4 numb. lvs; fol. Memorial to king of Spain on revolt in Mexico of 1624 against the marqués de Gelves. DLC.

625/247

Vázquez de Espinosa, Antonio. Señor. El maestro Fr. Antonio Basquez Despinosa. [*Madrid?* 1625?]. [4] p.; fol. Memorial to king of Spain on defense of province of Peru. Sabin 98725. MH; BL.   625/248

Vega Carpio, Lope Félix de. Parte veinte de las Comedias. *Madrid: Widow of A. Martín, for A. Pérez,* 1625. 298 numb. lvs; 4to. Included is 'Arauca domado', based on Pedro de Oña's poem of that title, 1st publ., Madrid, 1605. Sabin 98772; Medina (Chile) 64; Pérez Pastor (Madrid) 2233; Palau 355310. MB; BL, BN.   625/249

Verdadera relacion de la grandiosa vitoria que las armadas de España an tenido en la entrada del Brasil . . . Dasse tambien aviso de la refriega de los navios sobre la Baía, y los dias que duraron las batallas. [*Madrid?* 1625?]. [3] p.; fol. Cf. the *Relacion. verdadera* above. Borba de Moraes II:192.

625/250

Vergara Gaviria, Diego de. Nulidades expresas, y notorias. Que contiene la causa del alboreto sucedido en la ciudad de Mexico, a 15 de enero de 1624. assi en general, como particular. [*Madrid?* ca. 1625]. 3 lvs; fol. Palau 360150.   625/251

Verhael van 't ghene den Admirael l'Hermite in zyne reyse naer de custen van Peru verricht, ende och wat schepen hy ghenomen ende verbrandt heeft, inde haven van Callao . . . Ghetranslateert uyt het Spaensch. *Amsterdam: C. Meulemans,* 1625. [8] p.; 4to. Cf. the *Waerachtigh verhael van het succes* of this year below, describing the same events, but differing in wording & details. Sometimes ascribed to Jacques L'Hermite. Sabin 31501; Tiele-Muller 73; Knuttel 3586. The Hague:KB.   625/252

Vigna, Domenico. Animadversiones, sive Observationes in libros de historia, et de causis plantarum Theophrasti. *Pisa: S. Marchetti, & C. Massino,* 1625. 117 p.; 4to. Included are entries for guaiacum, tobacco ('Tornabona'), & sarsaparilla ('Zarzaparilla'). Pritzel 9203; Arents (Add.) 236; Wellcome I:6608. BL, BN.   625/253

Waerachtigh verhael van het succes van de vlote onder den Admirael Jaques l'Hermite,

in de Zuyt-Zee, op de custen van Peru, en de staet Lima. [*Amsterdam?*] 1625. [14] p.; 4to. Transl. from the *Casos notables, sucedidos en las costas de la ciudad de Lima,* 1st publ., [Seville & Madrid], 1625. Sometimes attrib. to Jacques L'Hermite. Cf. the *Verhael van 't ghene den Admirael l'Hermite . . . verricht,* of this year above, describing the same events, but differing in wording & details. Sabin 31502 & 100932; Tiele-Muller 74; Knuttel 3587; JCB AR49:50–51. DLC, NN-RB, RPJCB; The Hague:KB.

625/254

Warhaffte gründliche Relation was gestalt durch dero königl: Mayest: in Hispanien Obristen Don Friderico de Toleto mit beystand des Allmächtigen Brasilia den Holländern widerumb abtrungen und erobert worden. *Augsburg: A. Aperger,* 1625. 2 lvs; 4to. Cf. Toledo Osorio y Mendoza's *Relation und Eigentliche beschreibung* of this year below. Borba de Moraes II:370.   625/255

Wassenaer, Nicolaes van. T'achste deel of t'vervolch van het Historisch verhael aller gedenckwaerdiger geschiedenissen, die in Europa . . . in America, als West-Indien, Brasil en d'eylanden . . . voorgevallen syn. *Amsterdam: J. Janszoon, the Younger* [1625]. 156 numb. lvs; illus.; 4to. (N. van Wassenaer's *Historisch verhael.* Pt 8). Includes accounts of Dutch naval & commercial adventures, esp. the exploitation of Bahia, Brazil, as well as of English & Swedish undertakings. Cf. Sabin 102039; Borba de Moraes II:371; Muller (1872) 1745. RPJCB.

625/256

——. T'sevende-deel of t'vervolgh van het Historisch verhael aller gedencwaerdiger geschiedenissen, die in Europa . . . in America, als Brasilien, en Nová Espagná . . . voorgevallen syn. *Amsterdam: J. Janszoon, the Younger,* 1625. 155 numb. lvs; illus.; 4to. (N. van Wassenaer's *Historisch verhael.* Pt 7). Includes accounts of Dutch & Spanish colonies, and of activities of the West-Indische Compagnie. Cf. Sabin 102039; Borba de Moraes II:371–72; Muller (1872) 1745. RPJCB.   625/257

Zimara, Marco Antonio. Antrum magico-medicum. *Frankfurt a. M.: J. F. Weiss,* 1625–26. 2 v.; 8vo. In v. 1, remedies for syphilis employing guaiacum, sarsaparilla, & sassafras are provided. Wellcome I:6811. CU, DNLM, NNNAM, WU; BL.   625/258

1626

Advis au Roy, sur les affaires de la Nouvelle France. [*Paris?* 1626]. 23 p.; 8vo. Sabin 56081 & 56082; Harrisse (NF) 34 & 38; JCB (3) II:116. MH, MnU-B, RPJCB.   626/1

Agustí, Miguel. Libro de los secretos de agricultura. *Perpignan: L. Roure,* 1626. 654 p.; illus.; 4to. 1st publ. in Castilian, Saragossa [1625?]. Palau 4124; Arents (Add.) 41. NN-A.   626/2

—[Anr edn]. *Saragossa: P. Bueno,* 1626. 512 p.; 4to. Reissue of printer's 1625 edn with altered imprint date. Palau 4123n.
            626/3

Alcalá Yáñez y Rivera, Jerónimo. Segunda parte de Alonso mozo de muchos amos. *Valladolid: J. Morillo,* 1626. 322 p.; 8vo. Continues 1st pt, 1st publ., Madrid, 1624. In chapt. xiv the indifference of monkeys on the Rio de la Plata to death by drowning of fellows is cited. Later edns bear title *El donoso hablador.* Alcocer (Valladolid) 714; Palau 5818n. NNH; BL.   626/4

Aubigné, Théodore Agrippa d'. L'histoire universelle . . . Seconde édition. *Amsterdam: Heirs of H. Commelin,* 1626. 3 v.; fol. 1st publ., Maillé, 1616–20. CtY, DFo, ICN, MH; BN.   626/5

—[Anr edn]. [*n.p.: n.pr.*] 1626. 3 v.; fol. BL, BN.   626/6

Bachot, Gaspard. Erreurs populaires touchant la medicine et regime de santé. *Lyons: B. Vincent,* 1626. 509 p.; 8vo. In bk 2, chapt. 1, 'De l'air & vestements', Patagonia & Florida are mentioned, citing Thevet; chapt. 2 speaks of nudity of American Indians. CLU-C, CtY-M, DNLM, KU-M, MH, NIC; BL, BN.   626/7

—[Anr issue?]. Partie troisieme des Erreurs populaires . . . en suite de celles de feu m. Laurens Joubert. *Lyons: [B. Vincent?] for the Widow of T. Soubron,* 1626. 509 p.; 8vo. BN.   626/8

Bacon, Francis, viscount St Albans. Les oeuvres morales et politiques . . . de la version de J. Baudoin. *Paris: P. Rocolet & F. Targa,* 1626. 848 p.; port.; 8vo. Includes the *Essays politiques et moraux* as publ. Paris, 1619, in translation by Baudoin from the London, 1612, *Essaies.* Gibson (Bacon) 164; Shaaber (Brit. auth.) B12. CCB, DFo; BL, BN.   626/9

——. Saggi morali . . . data in luce dal sig. cavalier Andrea Cioli. *Bracciano: A. Fei, for P. Totti,* 1626. 475 p.; 12mo. 1st publ. as here transl., Florence, 1619. Gibson (Bacon) 42; Shaaber (Brit. auth.) B35. Rome: Vatican.   626/10

——. Sylva sylvarum. *London:* 1626. *See the year* 1627.

Barclay, John. Icon animorum. Editio postrema. *Milan: G. B. Bidelli,* 1626. 419 p.; 8vo. 1st publ., London, 1614. Shaaber (Brit. auth.) B173. MiU.   626/11

——. L'oeil clair-voyant d'Euphormion dans les actions des hommes. *Paris: A. Estoct,* 1626. 277 p.; 8vo. Transl. by Jean Nau from Barclay's *Icon animorum,* 1st publ., London, 1614; cf. French translation of 1625. Tchémerzine I:448; Shaaber (Brit. auth.) B172. BN, Berlin:StB, Wolfenbüttel:HB.
            626/12

Béguin, Jean. Les elemens de chymie . . . Troisiesme edition. *Paris: M. Le Maître,* 1626. 1st publ. as here transl. from Béguin's *Tyrocinium chymicum* (Paris, 1612), Paris, 1615. BN.   626/13

—[Anr edn]. Quatriesme edition. *Rouen: J. Boulley,* 1626. 432 p.; illus.; 8vo. BN.
            626/14

Bertius, Petrus. Breviarium totius orbis terrarum. *Paris: M. Hénault,* 1626. 63 p.; 8vo. 1st publ., Paris, 1624. Cf. Sabin 5013. BN.   626/15

Boccalini, Traiano. The new-found politicke. *London: [Eliot's Court Press,] for F. Williams,* 1626. 242 p.; 4to. Transl. by John Florio, Thomas Scott, & William Vaughan from Boccalini's *De' ragguagli di Parnaso,* pt 1, 1st publ., Venice, 1612, pt 2, Venice, 1613; & from his *Pietra del paragone politico,* 1st publ. [Venice], 1615. STC 3185. CSmH, DLC, ICU, MH, NN-RB; BL.   626/16

——. Pierre de touche politique . . . Traduicte . . . de l'italien [par Louis Giry]. *Paris: J. Villery,* 1626. 318 p.; 8vo. Transl. from Boccalini's *Pietra del paragone politico,* 1st publ., 'Cormopoli' (i.e., Venice), 1615. MdBJ, RPB; BN.   626/17

Bozio, Tommaso. De signis ecclesiae Dei, libri xxiii. *Cologne: J. Gymnicus,* 1626. 2 v.; 4to. 1st publ., Rome, 1591; cf. 1602 edn. BN. 626/18

Braun, Samuel. Die neuntzehende Schiffarth, inhaltendt fünff Schiffarthen. *Frankfurt a. M.: H. Palthenius, for the Hulsiuses,* 1626. 105 p.; illus.; 4to. (Levinus Hulsius's *Sammlung von . . . Schiffahrten.* Pt 19). 1st publ., Basel, 1624. Sabin 33672; Church 311; JCB (3) I:467. CSmH, ICN, MnU-B, NN-RB, RPJCB; BL, BN. 626/19

Breton, Nicholas. Fantasticks. *London: [M. Fletcher,] for F. Williams,* 1626. 23 lvs; illus.; 4to. Section for October notes that 'Tobacco is held very precious for the Rhewme'; that for December refers to turkeys for the feast. STC 3650. CSmH, DFo, MH, WU; BL, Oxford:Bodl. 626/20

Brochero, Luis de. Discurso breve del uso de exponer los ninos. En que se propone lo que observo la antiguedad, dispone el derecho, y importa a las republicas. *Seville: S. Fajardo,* 1626. 56 numb. lvs; 4to. On verso of lf 27 Brochero describes himself as a native of today's Colombia, mentioning a form of ferret found there. Though Brochero was the author of other works described by Medina, they appear to be without American relevance. Medina (BHA) 806; Escudero (Seville) 1.350; Palau 36098. NNH, NcD; Madrid:BN. 626/21

Bry, Johann Theodor de. Anthologia magna, sive Florilegium novum & absolutum. *Frankfurt a. M.: J. T. de Bry,* 1626. 142 pls; illus.; fol. 1st publ., [Oppenheim], 1612[-14], under title *Florilegium novum,* but here containing additional plates. Pritzel 1299n; Nissen (Bot.) 273. MH-A. 626/22

Calvo, Juan. Primera y segunda parte de la Cirugia universal. *Madrid: D. Flamenco, for D. Logroño,* 1626. 620 p.; fol. 1st publ., Seville, 1580. Includes statement that syphilis was introduced from New World. Cf. Medina (BHA) 1095; Palau 40552. 626/23

Camões, Luiz de. Os Lusiadas. *Lisbon: P. Craesbeeck,* 1626. 141 numb. lvs; 24mo. 1st publ., Lisbon, 1572; cf. 1609 edn above. In verse. Silva (Camões) 25. MH, NNH; BL. 626/24

Canale, Floriano. De' secreti universali raccolti et sperimentati. *Venice: G. & G. Imberti,* 1626. 304 p.; 8vo. 1st publ., Brescia (?), 1613. London:Wellcome. 626/25

Cartari, Vincenzo. Seconda novissima editione delle Imagini de gli dei delli antichi. *Padua: P. P. Tozzi,* 1626. 589 p.; illus.; 4to. 1st publ. with continuation by Lorenzo Pignoria, 'Imagine de gli Indiani Orientali et Occidentali', Padua, 1615. Cf. Sabin 11104; Michel (Répertoire) II:52; JCB (3) II:198. CU, IaU, MdBJ, RPJCB; BL, BN. 626/26

Casas, Bartolomé de las, O.P. Bp of Chiapa. Istoria, ò brevissima relatione della distruttione dell'Indie Occidentali . . . Con la traduttione . . . di Francesco Bersabito [i.e., Giacomo Castellani]. *Venice: M. Ginammi,* 1626. 154 p.; 4to. Transl. from author's *Brevissima relación,* 1st publ., Seville, 1552. Spanish & Italian texts in parallel columns. Sabin 11242; Medina (BHA) 1085n (II:473); Hanke/Giménez 522–23; Streit I:431; Palau 46955; JCB (3) II:199. CtY, DLC, MBAt, NN-RB, PPRF, RPJCB; BL, BN. 626/27

Catholic Church. Commisarius Generalis Cruciatae. Instrucción sobre la predicación y cobranza de la Bula de Cruzada en los arzobispados de Los Reyes, Charcas y obispados de Cuzco, Barranca, Truxillo, Guamanga, Arequipa, La Paz, Quito, Tucumán, Santiago de Chile, Assumpcion, Buenos Ayres, etc. *[Madrid:]* 1626. 8 numb. lvs; fol. 1st (?) publ., [Barcelona? 1537?]; cf. 1602 edn. Palau 120145. 626/28

Cervantes Saavedra, Miguel de. Il novelliere castigliano . . . Tradotta dalla lingua spagnuola . . . dal sig. Guglielmo Alessandro de Novilieri Clavelli. *Venice: The Barezzi,* 1626. 720 p.; 8vo. Transl. from text 1st publ., Madrid, 1613. Rius (Cervantes) 969; Palau 53548; Michel (Répertoire) II:84. CU, DLC, MH, PU; BL, Aix-en-Provence: Bibl. Méjanes. 626/29

Copye van een brief die een burgher van Sevilien geschreven heeft aen zijn vrient. *Amsterdam: C. Menlemand,* 1626. 7 p.; 4to. Announces a flood which destroyed goods recently received from the West Indies. Signed 'N.N.'. MnU-B, NN. 626/30

Cortés, Jerónimo. Phisonomia. *Saragossa: D. de la Torre,* 1626. 246 p.; 8vo. 1st publ., Valencia, 1597; cf. 1601 edn. MiU. 626/31

Cyriaque de Mongin, Clément. Cosmographie, ou Traicté general des choses tant celestes qu'elementaires . . . Seconde edition, reveuë, corrigée, & augmentée. *Paris: [S. Thiboust]* 1626. 113–934 p.; illus.; 8vo. The 1st, Paris, 1620, edn is without American content. Here included are mention of 'Apalchen', Virginia, & 'Norumbega'. Paging continues that of author's *Logocanon* of this year. DLC, MiU, NN-RB, RPJCB; BL, BN.   626/32

Davys, John. The seamans secrets . . . wherein is taught the three kindes of sayling . . . Fourth time imprinted. *London: J. Dawson; sold by J. Bellamy,* 1626. 2 pts; illus.; 4to. 1st publ., London, [1594?]; cf. 1607 edn. STC 6370. DFo, NHi; BL.   626/33

Discurso de lo sucedido en este año 1626 en galeones y flota de Nueva España, así desde que se juntaron en la ciudad de la Avana, come desde que salieron de ella . . . Dase cuenta de las facciones, que tuvieron con el enemigo, que descubrieron antes de entrar en la canal de Bahama, y de las rigurosas tormentas que se vieron sobre la Bermuda. *Seville: S. Fajardo,* 1626. 4 lvs; 4to. Medina (BHA) 810; Escudero (Seville) 1.379; Palau 74247.   626/34

Dispensatorium chymicum, hoc est, Nova et hactenus incognita rariora . . . remedia conficiendi ratio. *Frankfurt a. M.: P. Jacobi, for T. Schönwetter,* 1626. 3 pts; 8vo. Included are prescriptions employing guaiacum, sarsaparilla, & sassafras. DNLM; BL, London: Wellcome.   626/35

Les diversitez naturelles de l'univers, de la creation et origine de toutes choses. *Paris: G. Loyson,* 1626. 507 p.; 8vo. On p. 359 the author states that in the West Indies one finds no tree not always green; on p. 449 the bear is described as being numerous in the New World. NNC; BL.   626/36

Donne, John. Five sermons upon speciall occasions. *London: [A. Mathewes?] for T. Jones,* 1626. 5 pts; 4to. Made up of works 1st publ. separately, the 2nd being the 1624 edn of Donne's *A sermon upon the eighth verse of the first chapter of . . . Actes.* Included also is Donne's sermon preached before the Virginia Company of London 13 Nov. 1622, 1st publ., London, 1622. Cf. Sabin 20601; Keynes (Donne) 22; STC 7041. CSmH,

CtY, DLC, MH, NN-RB; Oxford:Merton.   626/37

——. Ignatius his conclave. *London: M. F[letcher]., for R. More,* 1626. 143 p.; 12mo. 1st publ. as transl. from Donne's *Conclave Ignatii* of the same year, London, 1611. Keynes (Donne) 7; STC 7028. BL, Cambridge:UL.   626/38

Duchesne, Joseph. Conseils de medecine. *Paris: C. Morel,* 1626. 316 p.; 8vo. Chapter 'De la grosse verole' calls for its treatment with sarsaparilla & sassafras as well as guaiacum, described at length as brought from the Indies by the Spanish, who had also introduced syphilis to Europe. Ferguson (Bibl. chem.) II:237. BL.   626/39

——. Traicté de la matiere, preparation et excellente vertu de la medecine balsamique. *Paris: C. Morel,* 1626. 215 p.; 8vo. Transl. from Duchesne's *Liber de priscorum philosophorum verae medicinae materia,* 1st publ., St Gervais, 1603. Wellcome I:1883. DNLM; BL, BN.   626/40

Du Ferrier, Jérémie. Advertissement à tous les estats de l'Europe, touchant les maximes . . . du gouvernement . . . des Espagnols. *Paris: J. Bouillerot,* 1626. 16 p.; 8vo. 1st publ., Paris, 1625; here a reissue of that edn. BL, BN.   626/41

——. Le Catholique d'estat, ou Discours politique des alliances du Roy tres-chrestien . . . Troisiesme edition. *Paris: J. Bouillerot,* 1626. 161 p.; 8vo. 1st publ., Paris, 1625. BL, BN.   626/42

Dupleix, Scipion. La curiosité naturelle. *Paris: C. Sonnius,* 1626. 296 p.; 8vo. 1st publ., Paris, 1606. DNLM, IU.   626/43

—[Anr edn]. *Rouen: M. de Préaulx,* 1626. 269 p.; 8vo. DNLM; London:Wellcome, BN.   626/44

Ercilla y Zúñiga, Alonso de. Primera, segunda, y tercera partes de la Araucana. *Cadiz: G. Vezino,* 1626. 398 numb. lvs; 8vo. In verse. 1st publ. in all 3 pts, Madrid, 1590; cf. 1610 edn. Cf. Sabin 22724; Medina (Arau.) 19; Medina (Chile) 65. MH, NNH; Santiago, Chile:BN.   626/45

Estaço da Silveira, Simão. El capitan Symon Estacio da Silveyra, procurador general de la conquista del Marañon. Dize, que la plata y riquezas del Piru vienen a España conduzidas por tierra a Arica. [*Madrid:* 1626]. [3]

p.; fol. Memorial to king of Spain; subscribed at Madrid, 15 June 1626. Medina (BHA) 811; Palau 313856. Madrid:BN, Seville:Archivo de Indias. 626/46

Esternod, Claude d'. L'espadon satyrique . . . Reveu et augmenté de nouveau. *Lyons: J. Lautret,* 1626. 144 p.; 12mo. In verse. 1st publ., Lyons, 1619. Paris:Arsenal. 626/47

Fernández Navarrete, Pedro. Conservacion de monarquias. *Madrid: Imprenta Real,* 1626. 344 p.; fol. 1st publ., Barcelona, 1621, under title *Discursos politicos.* 'De la despoblacion de Castilla, por los nuevos descubrimientos y colonias': chapt. ix. Palau 89491. CtY, ICN, MH, PU, WU; BL, BN. 626/48

—[Anr edn]. *Madrid:* 1626. 312 p.; fol. InU-L; BL. 626/49

Ferrer Maldonado, Lorenzo. Imagen del mundo, sobre la esfera, cosmografia, y geografia, teorica de planetas, y arte de navegar. *Alcalá de Henares: J. García & A. Duplastre,* 1626. 276 p.; illus.; 4to. Sabin 44108; Medina (BHA) 812; Palau 90524; JCB (3) II:199–200. DLC, IU, MB, MnU-B, NNH, RPJCB. 626/50

Fioravanti, Leonardo. A discourse upon chyrurgery . . . Translated out of Italian by John Hester, and now newly published and augmented . . . by Richard Booth. *London: E. Allde,* 1626. 118 p.; 8vo. 1st publ. as here transl. from Fioravanti's *Tesoro della vita humana* (Venice, 1570), London, 1580. Included are prescriptions employing guaiacum. STC 10882. DNLM; BL, Oxford: Bodl. 626/51

Francisco de Vitoria, O.P. Relectiones theologicae. *Venice: A. Pinelli,* 1626. 531 p.; 8vo. 1st publ., Lyons, 1557; cf. 1604 edn. Sabin 100620n; Palau 371072. BN. 626/52

Freudenhold, Martin. Der Landtstörtzer Gusman, von Alfarche . . . Dritter Theil . . . verteutscht durch Martinum Frewdenhold. *Frankfurt a. M.:* 1626. 494 p.; 8vo. Though ostensibly transl. from the Spanish, an independent German continuation. Deals initially with trip to Jerusalem & Turkey, but then later to West Indies. 'Caput xvi. Gusman wirdt auff fleissige Bitte dess Zuchthaus loss, begibt sich auff ein Schiff und kompt in die neuw erfundene Indien':

p. 251–70, with specific mention of Rio de Janeiro & Brazil. Faber du Faur 906. CtY, WaU; BL. 626/53

García, Gregorio, O.P. Historia ecclesiastica y seglar de la Yndia Oriental y Occidental, y predicacion del sancto evangelio en ella por los apostolos. *Baeza: P. de la Cuesta,* 1626. 250 numb. lvs; 8vo. Medina (BHA) 813; Streit II:1564; Palau 98009. DLC; BL, Granada:BU. 626/54

Garzoni, Tommaso. Piazza universale, das ist, Allgemeiner Schawplatz oder Marckt und Zusammenkunfft aller Professionen. *Frankfurt a. M.: L. Jennis,* 1626. 731 p.; fol. Transl. from Garzoni's *La piazza universale;* cf. 1619 German edn above. CtY, NNC; BL. 626/55

——. La piazza universale di tutte le professioni del mondo. *Venice: P. M. Bertano,* 1626. 403 numb. lvs; 4to. 1st publ., Venice, 1585; cf. 1601 edn. Michel (Répertoire) IV:25. MnU-B, NNC; BN. 626/56

Gaultier, Jacques, S.J. Table chronologique de l'estat du christianisme . . . jusques à l'année 1625 . . . Reveue pour la quatriesme fois . . . par l'autheur. *Lyons: P. Rigaud,* 1626. 886 p.; fol. 1st publ., Lyons, 1609. Backer III:1274; Cioranescu (XVII) 32623. InU-L, MiU; BN. 626/57

Gerhard, Johann. Locorum theologicorum . . . tomus sextus. *Jena: T. Steinmann,* 1626. 1316 p.; 4to. 1st publ., Jena, 1619. MH-AH. 626/58

Great Britain. Sovereigns, etc., 1625–1649 (Charles I). A proclamation touching tobacco. *London:* 1626. *See the year* 1627.

Grotius, Hugo. De jure belli ac pacis libri tres. *Frankfurt a. M.: The Wechels, Daniel & David Aubry, & C. Schleich [at Hanau]* 1626. 682 p.; 8vo. 1st publ., Paris, 1625. Meulen/Diermanse 566. CtY, MH, MnU-B, NN-RB, The Hague:PP. 626/59

Guibert, Philibert. Le prix et valeur des medicamens . . . desquels on se sert a la medecine . . . III. edition, reveuë & corrigee. *Paris: D. Langlois,* 1626. 71 p.; 8vo. 1st publ., Paris, 1625. The intervening 2nd edn has not been found. BL. 626/60

Guidi, Guido (d. 1569). Opera omnia, sive Ars medicinalis. *Frankfurt a. M.: Wechel Office, for D. & D. Aubry & C. Schleich,* 1626. 3 v.; illus.; fol. 1st publ., Frankfurt a. M., 1596, under title *Universae artis medicinalis;* cf. 1611 edn with title *Ars medicinalis.* Wellcome I:6602. CtY, DNLM, NNNAM; BL, BN.

626/61

Harcourt, Robert. The relation of a voyage to Guiana . . . performed . . . 1619 [i.e., 1609]. Now newly reviewed, & enlarged, by addition of some necessary notes. *London: E. Allde,* 1626. 84 p.; 4to. 1st publ., London, 1613. Sabin 30297; STC 12755; JCB (3) II:200. CSmH, DLC, MH, MnU-B, NN-RB, RPJCB; BL.

626/62

Harris, Robert. The drunkards cup. *London: G. Purslowe, for J. Bartlet,* 1626. 29 p.; 4to. Sermon. 1st publ., London, 1619. STC 12829; Arents (Add.) 237. CSmH, CtY, DFo, MH, MnU, NN-A; BL.

626/63

Heinsius, Daniel. Histoire de la vie et de la mort, du tres-illustre, Maurice de Nassau, prince d'Orange. Representee en l'oraison funebre, faicte en latin par Daniel Heinsius. Traduite de latin en françois, par André Rivet. *Leyden:* 1626. 110 p.; 8vo. 1st publ. as here transl., Leyden, 1625, under title *Harangue funebre,* etc. BL, BN.

626/64

Hondius, Jodocus. Nova et accurata Italiae hodiernae descriptio. *Amsterdam: J. Hondius,* 1626. 406 p.; illus., maps; obl. 4to. Includes refs to America. Cf. Sabin 32751. ICU, NcU; BL, BN.

626/65

Hornung, Johannes. Cista medica, qua in epistolae clarissimorum Germaniae medicorum, familiares, et in re medica . . . asservantur. *Nuremberg: S. Halbmeyer* [1626]. 516 p.; illus.; 4to. Letter 59 mentions mechoacan; 114, sarsaparilla; & 185, guaiacum. Wellcome I:3306. DNLM, ICJ; BL, BN.

626/66

Hulsius, Levinus, ed. Sechster Theil. Kurtze, warhafftige Relation und Beschreibung der wunderbarsten vier Schiffahrten. *Frankfurt a. M.: H. Palthenius, for the Hulsiuses,* 1626. 53 p.; illus., maps; 4to. (Levinus Hulsius's *Sammlung von . . . Schiffahrten.* Pt 6). 1st publ., Nuremberg, 1603. Sabin 33660; Baginsky (German Americana) 155; Church 284; JCB (3) I:458. CSmH, ICN, NN-RB, RPJCB, ViU; BL, BN.

626/67

Ibarra Gueztaraen, Juan de. Señor. El licenciado Juan de Ybarra, por lo que toca a . . . Potosi, dize, que por causa de la mucha necessidad que aquella villa y provincia de los Charcos tienen de esclavos negros años a esta parte, ha suplicado a V. Magestad en su nombre provea del remedio necessario. [*Madrid:* 1626]. [4] p.; fol. Medina (BHA) 6543. BL, Seville:Archivo de Indias.

626/68

Jenner, Thomas. The soules solace, or Thirtie and one spirituall emblems. [*London: J. Dawson,*] *sold by T. Jenner,* 1626. 52 lvs; illus.; obl. 8vo. The 31st emblem & poem are on tobacco. STC 14494 (formerly also 22940); Arents 160. BL.

626/69

Journael vande Nassausche vloot, ofte beschryvingh vande voyagie om den gantschen aerdt-kloot . . . Onder 't beleyd vanden Admirael Jacques l'Hermite ende Vice-Admirael Geen Huygen Schapenham. *Amsterdam: H. Gerritsz & J. P. Wachter,* 1626. 99 p.; illus., maps; 4to. Includes refs to Peru, Mexico, Tierra del Fuego, etc. Attrib. by Tiele to Johannes van Walbeeck. Sabin 31503; Tiele-Muller 75; Tiele 664; Muller (1872) 1932; Church 408; JCB (3) II:201. CSmH, MnU-B, NN-RB, RPJCB; BL, Amsterdam:NHSM.

626/70

Larrinaga Salazar, Juan de. Memorial discursivo sobre el oficio de protector general de los Indios del Piru. *Madrid: Imprenta Real,* 1626. 34 numb. lvs; 4to. Sabin 74599; Medina (BHA) 814; Palau 132212; JCB (3) II:201. MH, RPJCB.

626/71

Leake, Stephen Martin. Nummi Britannici historia. *London: W. Meadows,* 1626. *See the year* 1726.

Lucius, Ludwig, S.J. Jesuiter-Historii von des Jesuiter-Ordens Ursprung. *Basel: J. J. Genath,* 1626. 878 p.; illus.; 4to. Based on R. Hospinianus's Latin *Historia Jesuitica,* 1st publ., Zurich, 1619, but here enl., including (p. 530–34) account of American missions. Backer XI:62; Jöcher (Suppl.) IV:42; cf. Jöcher II:2569. ICU, MH-AH, NNH, RPJCB.

626/72

Malingre, Claude. Suite de l'Histoire de nostre temps. Ez années M.DC.XXIV. XXV. & XXVI. [*Paris: J. Petit-Pas,* 1626]. 988 p.; 8vo. The recapture of Bahia, Brazil, by the Portuguese from the Dutch is mentioned on p. 941–42. For prior vols, see the years 1624 & 1625. Cioranescu (XVII) 45424; JCB (3) II:137. RPJCB; BL, BN.

626/73

Marino, Giovanni Battista. L'Adone,

poema. *Venice: G. Sarzina, 1626.* 577 p.; 4to. 1st publ., Venice, 1523. Michel (Répertoire) V:121. FU, NNC, OCl; BL, Paris:Arsenal. 626/74

—[Anr edn]. *Venice: G. Sarzina* [1626?]. 577 p.; 4to. Michel (Répertoire) V:121. BL, BN. 626/75

——. La Murtoleide, fischiate. *'Frankfurt a. M.: G. Beyer'* [i.e., *Venice?*] 1626. 138 p.; 4to. In verse. 1st publ., [Venice?] 1619. In this as in other edns of this work, the imprint is fictitious. Michel (Répertoire) V:126. ICU, InU-L, MH, MdBJ, MiU; BL, BN. 626/76

—[Anr edn]. *'Frankfurt a. M.: G. Beyer'* [i.e., *Venice?*] 1626. 161 p.; 8vo. BL, BN. 626/77

Mascarenhas, Antonio. Relacam dos procedimentos que teve Dom Antonio Mascarenhas, Commissario geral da S. Cruzada . . . na decisaõ & declaraçaõ de algunas duvidas . . . acerca da dita Bulla. [*Lisbon?* 1626]. 59 lvs; 4to. 1st publ., [Lisbon, 1625]. Cf. Sabin 45403. ICN. 626/78

Mattioli, Pietro Andrea. Kreutterbuch. *Frankfurt a. M.: Heirs of J. Fischer, 1626.* 460 numb. lvs; illus.; fol. 1st publ. as here ed. by Joachim Camerarius, Frankfurt a. M., 1586; cf. 1611 edn above. Pritzel 5990n; Hunt (Bot.) 210. DNLM, MnU, NNBG; BN. 626/79

Mexía, Pedro. Les diverses leçons . . . mises de castillan en françois, par Claude Gruget . . . avec sept dialogues. *Rouen: J. Roger* [1626]. 1032 p.; 8vo. 1st publ. in this version with American refs, Paris, 1556; cf. 1604 edn. Sabin 48243 (misdated '1526'); Palau 167327. MiU, PU, WU; BN. 626/80

—[Anr issue]. [*Rouen: J. Roger*] *for C. Michel, at Lyons* [1626]. Sabin 48243 (misdated '1526'); Palau 167327n. BN. 626/81

——. Ragionamenti dottissimi et curiosi. *Venice: G. Imberti, 1626.* 90 p.; 4to. 1st publ. as here transl. from Mexía's *Colóquios* (Seville, 1547), Venice, 1557, under title *Dialoghi;* cf. 1615 edn. Palau 167382ii. 626/82

——. Selva rinovata di varia lettione di Pietro Messia . . . di Mambrin Roseo [e] Francesco Sansovino. *Venice: G. Imberti, 1626.* 5 pts; 4to. 1st publ. with addition of Sansovi-

no's pt, Venice, 1559–60; cf. 1616 edn. Palau 167303. IU. 626/83

Minsheu, John. Minshaei emendatio . . . The second edition. *London: J. Haviland, 1626.* 760 cols; fol. 1st publ., London, 1617; here a reissue of 1625 edn with altered imprint date. STC 17946. CU, IU, NNH, PPL; BL, BN. 626/84

Moerbeeck, Jan Andries. Spaenschen raedt. Om die geunieerde provincien te water ende te lande te benauwen. . . . Nae't Brabandsche exemplaer. *The Hague: A. Meuris, 1626.* [61] p.; 4to. A dialogue between 2 Spanish cavaliers, attrib. to Moerbeeck, or to C. Scribanius. Cf. the latter's *Veridicus belgicus,* 1st publ., [Antwerp, 1624], of which this is perhaps anr edn. Noted are potential dangers to Netherlands & West-Indische Compagnie in making peace with Spain. No Brabant edn with the present title has been traced. T.p. of this edn includes reading 'de selvige'. Knuttel 3681; cf. Kleerkooper 878. MnU-B; The Hague:KB. 626/85

—[Anr edn]. *The Hague: A. Meuris, 1626.* [61] p.; 4to. Here, the t.p. includes reading 'de selvevige'. Knuttel 3682; Meulman 1983. The Hague:KB, Ghent:BU. 626/86

Montaigne, Michel Eyquem de. Essais. *Paris: F. Targa, 1626.* 1039 p.; 8vo. 1st publ., Bordeaux, 1580; cf. 1602 edn. MH. 626/87

Neander, Johann. Tabacologia: hoc est, Tabaci, seu nicotianae descriptio medico-cheirurgico-pharmaceutica. *Leyden: I. Elsevier, 1626.* 256 p.; illus., port.; 4to. 1st publ., Leyden, 1622; a reissue of that edn with 1st 4 prelim. lvs here cancels. Sabin 52173; Willems (Les Elzevier) 257; Rahir (Les Elzevier) 219; Arents 148-a. CtY-M, DLC, InU-L, MH, MnU-B, NN-A, PU; BL, BN. 626/88

——. Traicté du tabac, ou Nicotiane, panacee . . . mis . . . en françois par J[acques]. V[eyras]. *Lyons: B. Vincent, 1626.* 343 p.; illus.; 8vo. 1st publ. as transl. from author's *Tabacologia* (Leyden, 1622), Lyons, 1625; here a reissue with altered imprint date of that edn? Arents 148-b. CtY-M, DNLM, InU-L, MH, NN-A; London:Wellcome. 626/89

—[Anr edn]. *Lyons: B. Vincent, 1626.* 2 pts; illus.; 8vo. Includes as pt 2 Laurent Catelan's *Traicté de la thériaque* 1st publ. separately Lyons, 1614. CtY-M, DNLM, InU-L, MH; London:Wellcome, BN. 626/90

Nichols, Philip. Sir Francis Drake revived: calling upon this dull or effeminate age to folowe his noble steps for golde & silver, by this memorable relation, of the rare occurrances . . . in a third voyage made by him into the West-Indies, in the years 72. & 73. *London: E. A[llde]., for N. Bourne,* 1626. 94 p.; port.; 4to. Sabin 20838; STC 18544; Church 407a; JCB (3) II:199. CSmH, CtY, DLC, MB, MiU-C, NN-RB; RPJCB; BL. 626/91

Ortiz de Salcedo, Francisco. Curia eclesiastica, para secretarios de prelados, juezes eclesiasticos, notarios apostolicos . . . Con una relacion de los arzobisbados, y obispados de España, y las Indias. *Madrid: Widow of A. Martín, for D. González,* 1626. 270 numb. lvs; 4to. Although the author's work appears to have been 1st publ. at Madrid in 1610, the present edn is the earliest noted to contain section relating to the Indies. Palau 205989. NNH; Madrid:BN. 626/92

Overbury, Sir Thomas. Sir Thomas Overbury his Observations in his travailes upon the state of the Xvii. provinces [of the Netherlands] . . . 1609. [*London: B. Alsop, for J. Parker*] 1626. 28 p.; 4to. Mentioned are the 'mynes of Peru'. STC 18903. CSmH, CtY, DLC, ICN, MH; BL. 626/93

——. Sir Thomas Overbury his wife . . . The twelfth impression. *Dublin: [A. Johnson, for the] Company of Stationers,* 1626. [255] p.; 8vo. 1st publ., London, 1615. STC 18914; Murphy (Engl. char.-bks) 22. DFo; BL, Cambridge:UL. · 626/94

Ovidius Naso, Publius. Metamorphoses. English. Ovid's Metamorphosis Englished by G[eorge]. S[andys]. *London: W. Stansby,* 1626. 326 p.; port.; fol. Bks 6–15 transl. by Sandys while resident in Virginia, supplementing the 1st five publ., 1621, prior to his departure from England (Sabin 76454). Sabin 76456; Grolier Club (Wither to Prior) 781; STC 18964. CSmH, CtY, DLC, ICN, InU-L, MH, MWA, MiU-C, NN-RB, RPJCB; BL. 626/95

Pazes entre España, Francia, y otros potentados, y mercedes que hizo su Magestad en las Cortes, en Balvastro . . . Y otras cosas dignas de saberse. *Seville: J. de Cabrera* [1626]. [4] p.; fol. Mentioned is the Dutch seizure of Puerto Rico. BL (Spain. Treaties). 626/96

Pérez de Montalván, Juan. [La monja alferez, comedia famosa. *Madrid?* 1626? 4to?]. On the adventures in Chile of Catalina de Erauso. Description & existence of such an edn conjectured. Sabin 50073; Medina (Chile) 67; Palau 221569. 626/97

Pérez de Navarrete, Francisco. Arte de enfrenar. Del capitan Don Francisco Perez de Navarrete, . . . corregidor . . . de los puertos . . . en el Pirù. *Madrid: J. González,* 1626. 2 pts; illus.; 4to. Medina (BHA) 816; Palau 221778. CU, CtY; BL. 626/98

A plaine and true relation, of the going forth of a Holland fleete the eleventh of November 1623, to the coast of Brasile . . . By I. B. *Rotterdam: M[athias?]. S[ebastiani?].,* 1626. 26 p.; 4to. 'I.B.' has been tentatively identified as Johannes Baers. Sabin 2553; Borba de Moraes I:352; STC 1042; JCB (3) II:197–98. CSmH, CtY, InU-L, RPJCB; BL. 626/99

Purchas, Samuel. Purchase his Pilgrimage . . . The fourth edition, much enlarged. *London: W. Stansby, for H. Fetherstone,* 1626. 1047 p.; illus., maps; fol. 1st publ., London, 1613. Cf. Sabin 66682; STC 20508. MWiW-C, MiU-C. 626/100

——[Anr issue]. Purchas his pilgrimage. *London: W. Stansby, for H. Fetherstone,* 1626. Sabin 66682; Streit I:433; STC 20508.5; Arents 158; JCB (3) II:196–97. CSmH, CtY, DLC, ICN, MH, MnU-B, NN-RB, PPL, RPJCB; BL. 626/101

Pyne, John. Epigrammata religiosa, officiosa, jocosa. Anglo-latina, latina, anglica. [*London: W. Stansby,* 1626]. 42 lvs; 4to. Prob. issued with the author's *Anagrammata regia* of this year. Includes 'The epitaph of a certaine tobacchonist'. STC 20521.4 (formerly 10428); Arents 162. CSmH, NN-A; BL, Oxford:Bodl.. 626/102

Recio de León, Juan. Peligros del dilitado camino, desde el reyno del Perú a España por Tierra firme. [*Madrid?* 1626?]. 10 lvs; fol. Sabin 68355; Medina (Chile) 68; Huth IV:1231; Palau 252308. 626/103

——. Señor. El maesse de campo Juan Recio

de Leon, dize, Que la riqueza que se ha sacado dello cerro de Potosi . . . no ha sido por causa de la mucha que los metales tienen. [*Madrid?* 1626?]. 3 lvs; fol. Sabin 68357 (BA = BL); Medina (Chile) 239. BL, Seville:Archivo de Indias.   626/104

——. Señor. El maesse de campo Juan Recio de Leon . . . propone a V[uestra]. M[agestad]. las cosas que . . . convienen para la execucion del nuevo camino y navegacion desde Perú a España, y otras de mucha importancia para remedio de aquel reyno. [*Madrid:* 1626]. 6 lvs; fol. Sabin 68359 (BA = BL). BL.   626/105

——. Señor. Juan Recio de Leon, masse [*sic*] de campo . . . de las provincias de Tipuane, Chunchos, y Paytitis . . . Advierte a V[uestra]. M[agestad]. de la de mas, consideracioñ e importancia dellos en el grado que parece. [*Madrid:* 1626?]. 3 numb. lvs; fol. Memorial to king of Spain on Bolivian provinces. Medina (Chile) 238. Seville:Archivo de Indias.   626/106

——. Señor. Quando el nuevo camino no fuera tan rico provechoso, y de tan grande remedio para tantas cosas come tiene dicho [etc.]. [*Madrid:* 1626?]. bds.; fol. Sabin 68363 (BA = BL). BL.   626/107

——. Señor. Relacion que Juan Recio de Leon . . . poblador de las provincias de Tipuane, Chunchos, y Paytitis . . . presento a V. magestad. [*Madrid?* 1626?]. 9 numb. lvs; fol. Memorial to king of Spain on administration of areas in present-day Bolivia. Sabin 68364 (BA = BL); Medina (Chile) 235. BL, Seville:Archivo de Indias.   626/108

——. Los servicios que refiero a V[uestra]. M[agestad]. en el memorial de la jornada y pacificacion que tengo hechos a V.M. antes della. [*Madrid?* 1626?]. 4 numb. lvs; fol. A further memorial to king of Spain reciting services in Bolivia; cf. that of 1625. Sabin 68365; Medina (Chile) 234; Maggs Cat. 479 (Americana V):4182. BL, Seville:Archivo de Indias.   626/109

Renou, Jean de. Les oeuvres pharmaceutiques . . . augmentées . . . en cette second edition par l'auteur; puis traduittes . . . par m. Louys de Serres. *Lyons: A. Chard,* 1626. 762 p.; illus.; fol. Transl. from Renou's *Institutionum pharmaceuticarum,* 1st publ., Paris,

1608. Wellcome I:5432. DNLM, MoSB, MnU, WU.   626/110

Reyd, Everhard van. Voornaemste gheschiedenissen inde Nederlanden. *Arnhem: J. Janszoon,* 1626. 734 p.; ports; 4to. In treating Dutch history, 1566–1601, includes passing refs to America, e.g. to Magellan's circumnavigation & Spanish silver fleet. Subsequently issued under titles *Oorspronck ende voortganck* (1633, 1644) & *Historie* (1650). Palau 265366. CtY, MH, NN.   626/111

——[Anr edn]. Historie der Nederlantscher oorlogen begin ende voortganck tot den jare 1601. *Arnhem:* 1626. 4to. A possible ghost. Catalogus van boeken VI:50; Buck (Geschiedenis) 2299; Aa X:56.   626/112

Rocaberti, Diego de. Epitome historico compendiosissimo, en diez romances. Contiene los casos mas notables acaecidos en el mundo desde su principio hasta . . . 1625. *Majorca: G. Guasp,* 1626. 98 p.; 8vo. In verse. Under years 1492 & 1519 Columbus & Cortés are mentioned. Palau 271630.   626/113

Rubio, Antonio, S.J. Logica mexicana . . . Hoc est, Commentarii breviores . . . in universam Aristotelis Dialecticam. *Brescia: L. Britannico,* 1626. 424 p.; 4to. 1st publ., Cologne, 1605. Cf. Sabin 73860; Backer VII:281–82; Palau 280358. MH.   626/114

Sandys, Sir Edwin. Relation de l'estat de la religion. *Geneva: P. Aubert,* 1626. 323 p.; 8vo. Transl. by Jean Diodati from Paolo Sarpi's Italian translation, with annotations, of Sandys's English text 1st publ. [Mirandola?], 1625 under title *Relatione dello stato della religione.* Of the present text as here recorded there may exist two or more editions or issues. CU, DLC, ICN; BL, BN.   626/115

Scott, Thomas. Sir Walter Rawleighs ghost, or Englands forewarner. '*Utrecht: J. Schellem*' [i.e., *London?*] 1626. 41 p.; 4to. Sabin 67586; Brushfield (Raleigh) 317; STC 22085; JCB (3) II:202. CSmH, CtY, DFo, ICN, MH, NN-RB, RPJCB; BL.   626/116

Scribanius, Carolus. L'Apocalipse hollandoise clairement expliquée, par Pambon Vreimundima [pseud.]. '*Villeneuve: J. LeVray*' [i.e., *The Netherlands?*] 1626. 51 p.; 8vo.

Transl. from the author's *Den Hollantschen apocalypsis* below. BN. 626/117

——. Apocalypsis Holandica: oder Eröffnung der geheimen und verborgenen Anschläge des . . . holländischen Löwens . . . in castilianischer Sprach . . . jetzo aber ubergesetzt durch Fagabundum Persuasorem: ill: Dn. Pamboni Veremontani sec. [*Strassburg?*] 'Parnassus Office', 1626. 23 p.; 4to. 1st publ. in German, Augsburg, [1625], under title *Der holländisch Apocalypsis*, despite statement on t.p., transl. from Scribanius's *Den Hollantschen apocalypsis*, 'Nieustadt' [i.e., Leyden?], 1625. For anr edn of this translation, see below. Concerning imprint, see Weller. Cf. Backer VII:989; cf. Weller (Falsch. & fing. Druckorte) I:23. RPJCB. 626/118

——. Copia de un papel impresso en Olanda con titulo de Apocalipsi de los Olandeses, que traducido en castellano contiene los miserables que han padecido . . . su grande empeño. *Seville: S. Fajardo*, 1626. [4] p.; fol. Presumably transl. from the *Hollantschen apocalypsis* of this year below. BL (Dutch). 626/119

——. Der holländisch Apocalypsis . . . ausgelegt und verfertiget durch Pambonem Verimundima [pseud.]. 'New Newenstatt' [i.e., *Augsburg?*]: 'Vielhüppens Warsagern', 1626. 23 p.; 4to. 1st publ. in this version, Augsburg, 1625. Backer VII:989; Weller (Falsch. & fing. Druckorte) I:23 (& III:24); JCB (3) II:202–3. CtY, RPJCB; Leyden:B. Thysiana. 626/120

——. Den Hollantschen apocalypsis . . . uytgheleet door Pambonen Vreimundima [pseud.]. [*Netherlands:*] 1626. 23 p.; 4to. 1st publ., 'Nieustadt' [i.e., Leyden?], 1625. For variant see Backer as cited. Knuttel 3676; Backer VII:988. NN-RB; The Hague:KB. 626/121

—[Anr edn]. . . . uytgheleet ende vermeerdert door Pambonem Vreimundima. 'Nieustadt: H. Waersegghe' [i.e., *Leyden?*] 1626. 28 p.; 4to. Knuttel 3677; Backer VII:988. The Hague:KB. 626/122

——. Den oor-sprongh, voort-gangh ende gewenscht eynde. *Amsterdam:* [1626]. *See the year* 1625.

——. Spaenschen raedt. *The Hague:* 1626. *See under* Moerbeeck, Jan Andries, *above.*

——. Veridicus Belgicus, quem auctor auxit, recensuit; e belgico latinum reddidit An. Dr. Accessit Apocalypsis Batavica, item auctior, emendatior. [*Antwerp: M. Nuyts*] 1626. 202 p.; 8vo. Though ostensibly 1st publ., [Antwerp, 1624], this edn is thought to have been transl. from the enl. Dutch edn; cf. *Den vernieuden waer-segger*, below, and Scribanius's Amsterdam, 1625, *Oorsprongh*. Knuttel 3678; Backer VII:988. MH, PCarlD; BL, BN. 626/123

——. Den vernieuden waer-segger, streckende tot een . . . eynde van d'inlandtsche oorloge . . . midtsgaders de macht vande Spaensche, West-Indische ende Nederlantsche provincien . . . [uyt het latyn van Car. Scribanus vertaelt]. *Amsterdam: J. Veselaer & B. Janszoon* [1626?]. 114 p.; 8vo. 1st publ. in Dutch, Amsterdam, 1625, under title *Oorsprongh*. Included, p. 97–144, is 'Den ghereformeerden Hollandschen apocalypsis'. Enlarged edn. Sabin 78474; Knuttel 3679; Backer VII:988. The Hague:KB, Ghent:BU. 626/124

Settala, Lodovico. Animadversionum, et cautionum medicarum libri septem. *Milan: G. B. Bidelli*, 1626. 2 pts; 8vo. 1st publ., Milan, 1614. Wellcome I:5948. CtY-M, DNLM, NNNAM, OU; London:Wellcome, BN. 626/125

Severim de Faria, Manuel. Relaçam universal do que succedeo em Portugal, & mais provincias do Occidente & Oriente, de março de 625. atè todo setembro de 626. *Lisbon: G. da Vinha*, 1626. [32] p.; 4to. Borba de Moraes I:259. MH, RPJCB. 626/126

Smith, Capt. John. An accidence or The path-way to experience. Necessary for all young sea-men. *London:* [*N. Okes,*] *for J. Man & B. Fisher*, 1626. 42 p.; 4to. America is mentioned only incidentally. Sabin 82812; STC 22784; JCB (3) II:203. CSmH, DN, RPJCB; BL. 626/127

——. The generall historie of Virginia, New-England, and the Summer Isles. *London: J. D[awson]. & J. H[aviland]., for M. Sparke*, 1626. 248 p.; illus., ports, maps; fol. 1st publ. London, 1624; here a reissue of that edn with altered imprint date. Sabin 82826; Clayton-Torrence 51 (3); Baer (Md) 11; STC 22790b; Church 408a; JCB (3) II:203.

CSmH, CtY, DLC, ICN, MH, NN-RB, PPRF, RPJCB; BL. 626/128

Söder Compagniet. Octroy eller privilegium. *Stockholm:* 1626. *See* Sweden. Sovereigns, etc., 1611–1632 (Gustaf II Adolf) *below.*

Spain. Laws, statutes, etc., 1598–1621 (Philip III). Instrucción de lo que han de observar los governadores, y corregidores de las provincias, y ciudades de la Nueva España en el uso de sus empleos. [*Madrid:* 1626]. 4 numb. lvs; fol. Palau 120146. Madrid:BN. 626/129

Sweden. Sovereigns, etc., 1611–1632 (Gustaf II Adolf). Octroy eller privilegium som . . . Gustaff Adolph, Sweriges . . . Konung . . . thet Swenska nyys uprättadhe Söder Compagniet . . . hafwer . . . bebrefwat. *Stockholm: I. Meurer,* 1626. [16] p.; 4to. Charter of the Swedish Söder Compagniet, drafted by Willem Usselinx, granting it commercial and navigational rights in 'Africa, Asia, America och Magellanica'. Sabin 98202; Jameson (Usselinx) 17 (& p. 114); JCB AR28:24–25. CtY, DLC, ICN, MnU-B, RPJCB; Stockholm:KB. 626/130

——. Octroy und privilegium, so . . . Herr Gustavus Adolphus, der Schweden . . . König . . . der . . . Süder Company . . . verliehen. *Stockholm: I. Meurer,* 1626. [13] p.; 4to. Prob. transl. from the *Octroy eller Privilegium* above. Sabin 98205; Jameson (Usselinx) 18. Stockholm:KB. 626/131

—[Anr edn]. Octroy oder Privilegium. '*Stockholm: I. Meurer*' [i.e., *Germany?*] 1626. [14] p.; 4to. Sabin 98203; James (Usselinx) 19. Stockholm:KB. 626/132

Tabourot, Estienne. Les bigarrures et touches. *Rouen: D. Geuffroy,* 1626. 5 pts; 24mo. 1st publ. in this collective edn, Paris, 1603. MH. 626/133

Taylor, John, the Water-poet. Wit and mirth. Chargeably collected out of tavernes, ordinaries, innes. *London:* [*M. Fletcher,*] for *H. Gosson; sold* [*by E. Wright*] 1626. 40 lvs; 8vo. A jest book. The 61st & 107th items mention tobacco. STC 23813.5; Arents (Add.) 238. NN-A. 626/134

Thorius, Raphael. Hymnus tabaci. *London:* [*J. Haviland,*] for *J. Waterson,* 1626. 48 p.; 12mo. 1st publ., Leyden, 1625. Sabin

95620; STC 24033; Arents 157-b. CSmH, DFo, MH, NN-A, PPL; BL, BN. 626/135

Thou, Jacques Auguste de. Historiarum sui temporis ab anno . . . 1543 usque ad annum . . . 1607. Libri CXXXVIII. *Geneva: P. de LaRovière,* 1626–30. 5 v.; fol. 1st publ. as here constituted, Geneva, 1620–21. CSt, CtY, ICN, MH, PPL; BN. 626/136

Torres, Pedro de. Libro que trata de la enfermedad de las bubas. *Alcalá de Henares: Widow of J. Gracián,* 1626. 59 p.; 4to. 1st publ., Madrid, 1600. Includes remedies for syphilis using American plants. Palau 336655n. London:Wellcome. 626/137

Usselinx, Willem. Aussführlicher Bericht über den Manifest: oder Vertrag Brieff der Australischen oder Süder Compagney . . . Auss dem Niederländischen . . . ubergesetzt. *Stockholm: C. Reusner,* 1626. [135] p.; 4to. For a full list of contents, including works previously publ., see Jameson. Sabin 98189; Jameson (Usselinx) 16; Palmer 401. CtY, DLC, PHi; BN. 626/138

—[Anr edn?]. Ausfuhrlicher Bericht. *Stockholm: C. Reusner,* 1626. [135] p.; 4to. Sabin 98188. NN-RB. 626/139

——. Uthförligh förklaring öfwer handels contractet angäendes thet Södre Compagniet . . . aff thet Nederländske Spräket uthsatl . . . aff Erico Schrodero. *Stockholm: I. Meurer,* 1626. [99] p.; 4to. Transl. in part from the author's *Naerder bericht,* itself 1st publ. as part of the *Octroy ofte Privilegie,* The Hague, 1627; cf. heading 'Sweden. Sovereigns, etc.' for that year. Includes extensive American refs. Sabin 98211; Muller (1872) 1143; Jameson (Usselinx) 15 (& p. 106–18); JCB (3) II:203–4. DLC, MiU-C, NN-RB, RPJCB; BL. 626/140

Valerius, Adrianus. Neder-landtsche gedenck-clanck. *Haarlem: Heirs of the author, at Veere,* 1626. 250 p.; illus.; obl. 4to. Includes account of the founding of the Dutch West India Company and its operations in Brazil under Pieter Hein, Pieter Schoutens, & Hillebrant Janssen; also includes mention of Spanish silver fleet and Virginia, 'nu 't Nieu-Nederlant genaemt'. Hertzberger Cat. 262, 140. CSmH, DFo, ICN, NN-RB; BL, BN. 626/141

Vaughan, William. Directions for health

. . . The sixth edition reviewed. *London: J. Beale, for F. Williams*, 1626. 4to. 1st publ., London, 1600, under title *Naturall and artificial directions for health*; cf. 1602 edn. STC 24617; Arents 161. CtY, DNLM, ICU, MH, NN-A; BL. 626/142

——. The golden fleece. *London: [W. Stansby, M. Fletcher & ?] For F. Williams*, 1626. 3 pts; map; 4to. The 'golden fleece' represents Newfoundland; Maryland is mentioned. Sabin 98693; STC 24609; Baer (Md) 12; Arents 161-A; Church 409; JCB (3) II:204. CSmH, CtY, DLC, ICN, MH, MWA, NN-RB, PHi, RPJCB; BL. 626/143

Vega Carpio, Lope Félix de. Arcadia, prosas y versos. *Cádiz: J. de Borja*, 1626. 250 numb. lvs; 8vo. 1st publ., Madrid, 1598; cf. 1602 edns. Palau 356303. Madrid:BN. 626/144

——. Parte veinte de las Comedias. *Madrid: Widow of A. Martín [colophon: J. González]*, 1626. 298 lvs; 4to. 1st publ., Madrid, 1625. Sabin 98772n; Palau 355311. BN. 626/145

Velázquez, Baltasar Mateo. El filosofo del aldea. *Pamplona: P. Dullort*, 1626. 88 numb. lvs; 8vo. The dedicatory epistle cites an unidentified history of the Indies; in the 'Relacion del caso de Agueda la mal casada', a character mentions voyage to Cartagena & Lima. Palau 357344. FU, NNH; Madrid:BN. 626/146

Vergilius, Polydorus. De rerum inventoribus libri octo . . . Accessit pars altera auctorum qui a Polydoro relicta per tractant. *Cologne: B. Wolter*, 1626. 790 p.; 8vo. 1st publ. as here constituted, Geneva, 1604. OCl, OkU, PPLT; BN. 626/147

Vicary, Thomas. The English-mans treasure . . . and now seventhly augmented. *London: B. Alsop & T. Fawcet*, 1626. 4to. 1st publ., London, 1548, but cf. 1613 edn. STC 24711. DFo (imp.), IU; BL. 626/148

Vondel, Joost van den. Begroetenis aen den doorluchtighsten en hoogh-geboren vorst Frederick Hendrick. *Amsterdam: W. J. Blaeu*, 1626. [16] p.; 4to. In verse. Includes ref. to mines of Peru & to the 'bragging' of silver fleets. Unger (Vondel) 115 (p. 35); Knuttel 3666. NN; The Hague:KB. 626/149

—[Anr edn]. *Amsterdam: W. J. Blaeu*, 1626. [16] p.; 4to. Includes a 'Klinckdicht' on p. ii.

Unger (Vondel) 111 (p.36). J. H. W. Unger. 626/150

Waerachtich verhael van de gantsche reyse ghedaen by . . . Jan Dircksz Lam, als admirael van een vloot schepen. *Amsterdam: J. van Hilten*, 1626. [15] p.; 4to. Includes refs to Brazilian naval operations. Sabin 38699; Asher 108; Knuttel 3665. DLC, NN-RB; The Hague:KB. 626/151

Wassenaer, Nicolaes van. T'derde-deel of t'vervolgh van het Historischer verhael aller ghedenckwaerdigher gheschiedenissen. *Amsterdam: J. E. Cloppenburg; Hoorn: I. Willemszoon*, 1626. 97 numb. lvs; illus.; 4to. (N. van Wassenaer's *Historisch verhael*. Pt 3). 1st publ., Amsterdam, 1623; here a reissue of Cloppenburg's sheets of that year, with addition of Willemszoon's appendix on astronomy mentioning the West Indies. Cf. Sabin 102039; Borba de Moraes II:371–72; Muller (1872) 1745. NN-RB, RPJCB. 626/152

——. T'neghenste deel of t'vervolgh van het Historisch verhael aller gedenckwaardighe geschiedenissen, die in Europa . . . in America, als West-Indien, Brasil en Peru . . . voorgevallen syn. *Amsterdam: J. Janszoon, the Younger [1626?]*. 154 numb. lvs; illus.; 4to. (N. van Wassenaer's *Historisch verhael*. Pt 9). Includes accounts of New Netherland, Jacques L'Hermite, the Spanish silver fleet, & the taking of San Salvador by Don Fadrique de Toledo Osorio y Mendoza. Cf. Sabin 102039; Borba de Moraes II:371; Muller (1872) 1745. RPJCB. 626/153

——. 'Thiende deel of t vervolgh van het Historisch verhael aller gedenck-waerdiger geschiedenissen, die in Europâ . . . in America, als West-Indien, Brasyl en Peru . . . voor-ghevallen syn. *Amsterdam: J. Janszoon, the Younger*, 1626. 150 numb. lvs; illus.; 4to. (N. van Wassenaer's *Historisch verhael*. Pt 10). Includes mention of arrival of ships from New Netherland. Cf. Sabin 102039; Borba de Moraes II:371; Muller (1872) 1745. RPJCB. 626/154

Weickard, Arnold. Thesaurus pharmaceuticus, sive Tractatus practicus . . . in sex peculiares libros digestus. *Frankfurt a. M.: J. T. Schönwetter & J. F. Weiss*, 1626. 2 v.;

fol. Formulas given call for use of guaiacum, sarsaparilla, sassafras, & mechoacan. Wellcome I:6727. PPC; BL.   626/155

1627

Advys op de presentatie van Portugael. Het eerste deel. [*Amsterdam? 1627?*]. *See the year* 1648.

Aldenburgk, Johannes Gregorius. West-Indianische Reisse und Beschreibung der . . . Eroberung der Statt S. Salvador . . . inn dem Lande von Brasilia. *Coburg: C. Bertsch, for F. Grüners,* 1627. [92] p.; 4to. Sabin 710; Borba de Moraes I:16–17; Rodrigues (Dom. Hol.) 354; JCB (3) II:204–5. MH, NN-RB, RPJCB; Amsterdam:NHSM; Munich:StB.   627/1

Alpini, Prosper. De plantis exoticis libri duo. *Venice: G. Guerigli,* 1627. 344 p.; illus.; 4to. Described (p. 325) is 'Hyosciamus virginianus', i.e., an American Oenothera. Pritzel 112; Nissen (Bot.) 21; Hunt (Bot.) 211. DFo, MoSB, MH-A, NIC, RPB; BL, BN.   627/2

Antwerp. Collegium Societatis Jesu. Typus mundi in quo calamitates et pericula . . . emblematicè proponuntur. *Antwerp: J. Cnobbaert,* 1627. 240 (i.e., 140) p.; illus.; 12mo. Includes, with emblematic illus., poem, in Latin, French & Dutch versions, by Gilles Tellier, on the slavery of the tobacco habit. Backer I:448; cf. Arents (Add.) 253. DFo; BL.   627/3

Araujo, Leonardo de, O.S.A. Relacion de las cosas que sucidieron en la ciudad de Quito, reyno del Pirù, con las Ordenes de Santo Domingo y san Agustin, por mano del licencido Juan de Mañosca. [*Madrid? 1627?*]. 7 numb. lvs; fol. For Mañosca's reply, see the year 1630. Medina (BHA) 6801. Seville:Archivo de Indias.   627/4

Aventrote, Juan. Epistola á los Peruleras en la qual está comprehendido el cathechismo de la verdadera religion Christiana, y una aliança de los muy poderosos señores estados de las Provincias Unidas del Pais Baxo. *Amsterdam:* 1627. For a Dutch transl. of the *Epistola* excluding the Heidelberg Cate-

chism, see the year 1630. Elst (Avontroot) 171–72; cf. Molhuysen I:200–201.   627/5

Avity, Pierre d', sieur de Montmartin. Les estats, empires et principautez du monde . . . Nouvelle edition. *Paris: G. Alliot,* 1627. 2 pts; fol. 1st publ., Paris, 1613. Cf. Sabin 2498. Greifswald:UB.   627/6

Bacon, Francis, viscount St Albans. Histoire du regne de Henry VII roy d'Angleterre. Traduicte de l'anglois [par La Tour Hotman]. *Paris: P. Rocolet & F. Targa,* 1627. 552 p.; port.; 8vo. Transl. from Bacon's *History of the raigne of King Henry the seventh,* 1st publ., London, 1622. Gibson (Bacon) 122; Shaaber (Brit. auth.) B36. DLC, MH, MiAC; BL, BN.   627/7

——. Sylva sylvarum: or, A naturall historie . . . Published after the authors death, by William Rawley. *London: J. H[aviland]., for W. Lee,* 1626 [i.e., 1627]. 2 pts; port.; fol. The added engr. t.p. is dated 1627. In discussion of syphilis, the disease is attributed to cannibalism, citing that in the West Indies. Also included is Bacon's *New Atlantis* with incidental refs to America & the West Indies. Gibson (Bacon) 170; STC 1168; Arents 159. CSmH, CtY, DFo, MH, NN-A; Oxford: Bodl.   627/8

——[Anr edn]. *London: J. H[aviland]., for W. Lee,* 1627. 2 pts; port.; fol. Cf. preceding item, of which this is a reissue with altered imprint date. Includes also Bacon's *New Atlantis.* Gibson (Bacon) 171; STC 1169. CSmH, CtY, DLC, MH, PPL, RPB; BL.   627/9

Barclay, John. Euphormionis Lusinini . . . Satyricon. *Amsterdam: J. Janszoon, the Younger,* 1627. 694 p.; 12mo. Includes pt 2, 1st publ., Paris, 1607, & pt 4, the *Icon animorum,* 1st publ., London, 1614. Shaaber (Brit. auth.) B192. DFo, NBu, PU; BL, Kiel:UB.   627/10

Bauderon, Brice. Paraphrase sur la Pharmacopoee. *Rouen: M. de LaMotte,* 1627. 2 pts; 8vo. 1st publ., Lyons, 1588; cf. 1607 edn. DNLM; London:Wellcome, BN.   627/11

Béguin, Jean. Les elemens de chymie. *Rouen: J. Boulley,* 1627. 432 p.; illus.; 8vo. 1st publ. as here transl. from Béguin's *Tyrocinium chymicum* (Paris, 1612), Paris, 1615. DNLM, MBCo, MiU; BN.   627/12

Bertius, Petrus. Breviarium totius orbis terrarum. *Frankfurt a. M.: K. Rötel, in de Bry Office*, 1627. 72 p.; 12mo. 1st publ., Paris, 1624. Sabin 5013. BL. 627/13

Blaeu, Willem Janszoon. Het licht der zeevaert. *Amsterdam: J. Janszoon, the Younger*, 1627. 2 v.; illus., maps; obl. fol. 1st publ., Amsterdam, 1608. Bk i dated '1626'; bk ii '1625'. Koeman (M.Bl) 17 (J). Leyden:UB, Amsterdam:UB. 627/14

——. Zeespiegel. *Amsterdam: W. J. Blaeu*, 1627. 3 pts; illus., maps; fol. 1st publ., Amsterdam, 1623. This edn includes an 'Almanak' for 1627–34; the 'Voorreden' here consist of a single page. Koeman (M.Bl) 32; Tiele 124n. BL(imp.), Amsterdam:KAW, Marburg:UB. 627/15

—[Anr issue]. *Amsterdam: W. J. Blaeu*, 1623 [i.e., 1627]. Koeman (M.Bl) 30. Amsterdam:UB. 627/16

Blocius, Johannes. Historiae per Saturam ex Novis Orbis scriptoribus. Excerpta memorabilia. *Rostock: J. Fuess (Pedanus), for J. Hallervord*, 1627. 117 p.; 12mo. 1st publ., Rostock, 1626. Sabin 5942. NN-RB. 627/17

Bry, Theodor de, ed. Continuatio Americae, das ist, Fortesetzung der Historien von der Newen Welt . . . Darinnen . . . ein . . . Beschreibung dess Newen Engellandts . . . Erzehlung von . . . Virginia, Brasilia, Guiana, und Insul Bermuda . . . Discurs wie die Statt S. Salvador und Baia in Brasilien . . . gewunnen worden. *Frankfurt a. M.: K. Rötel, for M. Merian*, 1627. 90 p.; illus., maps; fol. (Theodor de Bry's *America*. Pt 13. German). For a description of the 7 pts & their antecedents, see Church 174n (I:401–2) & 201. Cf. Sabin 8784; Shaaber (Brit. auth.) H83 & W66; Church 201; JCB (3) II:417–18. CSmH, RPJCB; BL. 627/18

Camden, William. Histoire d'Elizabeth, royne d'Angleterre . . . Traduit du latin . . . par Paul de Bellegent. *Paris: S. Thiboust*, 1627. 2 pts; port.; 4to. 1st pt 1st publ. as here transl., London, 1624; the 2nd pt transl. from text 1st publ., Leyden, 1625. Sabin 10159; Shaaber (Brit. auth.) C19. MiD-B; BL, BN. 627/19

——. Tomus alter Annalium rerum Anglicarum . . . sive Pars quarta. *London: W. Stansby, for S. Waterson*, 1627. 286 p.; fol. 1st publ., Leyden, 1625, as v. 2 of Camden's *Annales*. Sabin 10157; STC 4496 v. 2. CSmH, MH, NN-RB, PPL, RPJCB; BL. 627/20

Campo, Gonzalo de, Abp of Lima. Copia de un capitulo de una carta escrita de Llamellin en el Perù. *Seville: F. de Lyra*, 1627. [4] p.; fol. Medina (BHA) 821; Streit II:1568; cf. Palau 41323. RPJCB. 627/21

Canoniero, Pietro Andrea. Flores illustrium epitaphiorum. *Antwerp: H. Verdussen*, 1627. 544 p.; 8vo. 1st publ., Antwerp, 1613. Cf. Sabin 24830. ICN, OU; BL. 627/22

Casas, Bartolomé de las, O.P., Bp of Chiapa. Den spieghel der Spaensche tierannije geschiet in West-indien. *Amsterdam*: 1627. 1st publ. in Dutch, [Antwerp?], 1578; cf. 1607 edn above. Cf. Sabin 11258n; Tiele-Muller 316. 627/23

Cats, Jacob. Proteus ofte Minne-beelden. *Rotterdam: P. van Waesberghe*, 1627. 5 pts; illus.; 4to. 1st publ., Middelburg, 1618, under title *Silenus Alcibiadis*. Vries 89; Mus. Cats. 41; Arents 163. CtY, DLC, ICN, MH, NN-A; BN, Leyden:UB. 627/24

Cervantes Saavedra, Miguel de. Novelas exemplares. *Seville: F. de Lyra*, 1627. 338 numb. lvs; 8vo. 1st publ., Madrid, 1613. Rius (Cervantes) 234; Palau 53413. Barcelona:B. Central. 627/25

——. Novelle . . . Nuovamente transportate dalla lingua castigliana . . . da Donato Fontana milanese. *Milan: B. Vallo & A. Besozzo*, 1627. 591 p.; 8vo. Transl. from text 1st publ., Madrid, 1613; cf. other Venice, 1626, translation. Rius (Cervantes) 970; Palau 53549; Michel (Répertoire) II:84. DLC; BL, Paris:Arsenal. 627/26

Champlain, Samuel de. Voyages et descouvertures faites en la Nouvelle France, depuis l'année 1615. jusques à la fin de l'année 1618 . . . Seconde edition. *Paris: C. Collet*, 1627. 158 numb. lvs; illus.; 8vo. 1st publ., Paris, 1619; here a reissue of that edn with t.p. & prelim. matter reprinted. Sabin 11838; Harrisse (NF) 40; Lande 117; JCB (3) II:205. DLC, MH, MiU-C, MnU-B, NN-RB, RPJCB; BL, BN. 627/27

Clüver, Philipp. Introductionis in universam geographiam tam veterem quam novam libri vi . . . Editio ultima prioribus emenda-

tior. *Leyden: Elsevier Office,* 1627. 373 p.; illus.; 16mo. 1st publ., Leyden, 1624. Cf. Sabin 13805; Willems (Les Elzevier) 274; Rahir (Les Elzevier) 235. CtY, MH; BL, BN.
627/28

Compagnie de la Nouvelle France. Le Roy continuant le mesme desir que le defunct Roy Henry le Grand son pere, de glorieuse memoire, avait de faire rechercher & descouvrir és païs, terres & contrées de la nouvelle France, dite Canada. [*Paris?* 1627]. 27 p.; 8vo. Charter of the company. Sabin 10361; cf. Harrisse (NF) 43n; JCB (3) II:205. RPJCB.
627/29

Cordus, Valerius. Dispensatorium, sive Pharmacorum conficiendorum ratio. *Leyden: J. Maire,* 1627. 661 p.; illus.; 12mo. 1st publ., Nuremberg, 1546; cf. 1606 edn. DNLM; London:Wellcome, BN.
627/30

Cotta, John. Conatus sine exemplo: or The first and needfullest discoverie to the attainment of health. *London: L. Becket,* 1627. 135 p.; 4to. 1st publ., London, 1612, under title *A short discoverie of the . . . dangers of . . . ignorant practisers of physicke in England;* here a reissue of that edn with t.p. & 4th leaf reset. Arents (Add.) 156-A. NN-A.
627/31

Council for New England. An historicall discoverie and relation of the English plantations, in New England. *London: J. Bellamy,* 1627. [36] p.; 4to. 1st publ., London, 1622, under title *A brief relation of the discovery* [etc.]; here a reissue with cancel t.p. of that edn. Cf. Sabin 52619; STC 18484. BL.
627/32

Croll, Oswald. La royalle chymie . . . traduitte . . . par J. Marcel de Boulenc. *Lyons: P. Drouet,* 1627. 3 pts; illus.; 8vo. 1st publ. as here transl., Lyons, 1624. CtY-M, DNLM, MH; BN.
627/33

Delle rime piacevoli del Berni, Casa, Mauro, Varchi, Dolce, et d'altri auttori. *Venice:* 1627. 4 pts; 12mo. 1st publ. as here constituted, Venice, 1552–55; cf. 1603 edn. NcD, PU; BL (Berni, F.).
627/34

Drayton, Michael. The battaile of Agincourt. *London: [A. Mathewes,] for W. Lee,* 1627. 218 p.; port.; fol. In verse. Includes epistle addressed to George Sandys on latter's departure for Virginia. STC 7190; Grolier Club (Langland to Wither) 85;

Pforzheimer 301. CSmH, CtY, DLC, ICN, MH, MiU, NN-RB; BL.
627/35

Enchiridion practicum medico-chirurgicum. *Geneva: M. Berjon,* 1627. 2 pts; 8vo. The 2nd pt comprises Antoine Chaumette's *Enchiridion chirurgicum,* 1st publ., Paris, 1560; cf. French edn, Lyons, 1609. DNLM; BN.
627/36

Estienne, Charles. Dictionarium historicum, geographicum, poeticum. *Geneva: J. Crispin,* 1627. 1132 cols; 4to. 1st publ. in this enl. edn, Lyons, 1595; cf. 1601 edn. MB, MnU, TxU.
627/37

——. De velt-bow, ofte Landt-winninghe. *Amsterdam: H. Laurenszoon,* 1627. 259 p.; fol. 1st publ. in this Dutch version, Amsterdam, 1588; cf. 1622 edn. BN.
627/38

Fabronius, Hermann. Geographica historica: Newe summarische Welt-Historia, oder Beschreibunger aller Keyserthumb, Königreiche, Fürstenthumb und Völcker heutiges Tages auff Erden . . . Die fünfte Edition. *Schmalkalden: W. Ketzel,* 1627. 2 v.; illus., maps; 4to. 1st publ., Schmalkalden, 1612. Vol. 2 has subtitle *Von der Newen Welt.* The presumptive 3rd & 4th edns have not been traced. Sabin 23605. DLC.
627/39

Fernández Manjón, Lucas. Señor. Lucas Fernandez Manjon vezino del pueblo y minas de san Luis Potosi en la Nueva España. Dize, que ha mas de veinte y seis anos que reside y vive en ellas [etc.]. [*Madrid?* 1627]. 5 numb. lvs; fol. Memorial to king of Spain, offering historical account of mines at Potosí. Subscribed: Madrid 29. de Abril 1627. Medina (BHA) 823. BL, Seville:Archivo de Indias.
627/40

Fernel, Jean. De abditis rerum causis libri duo. *Geneva:* 1627. 8vo. 1st publ., Paris, 1548; cf. 1601–2 edn of Fernel's *Universa medicina.* Sherrington (Fernel) 41.F25. DNLM; Paris:Faculté de Médecine.
627/41

Fragoso, Juan. Cirugia universal aora nuevamente añadida . . . Nuevamente emendada en esta septima impression. Iten un tratado de todas las enfermedades de los riñones . . . par Francisco Diaz. *Madrid: Widow of A. Martín, for D. González,* 1627. 2 pts; fol. 1st publ., Madrid, 1581; cf. 1607 edn. BL.
627/42

Gabelkover, Wolfgang. Curationum et observationum, centuria V. *Tübingen: P. Brunn,* 1627. 226 p.; 8vo. Described are various decoctions using guaiacum; mentioned is the Peruvian bezoar stone. Wellcome I:2493. CtY-M, DNLM; BL, BN.

627/43

Gerritsz, Hessel, ed. Zwölffte Schiffahrt, oder Kurtze Beschreibung der newen Schiffahrt gegen Nord Osten uber die Amerische Inseln in Chinam und Japponiam, von . . . Heinrich Hudson newlich erfunden. *Oppenheim: H. Galler, for Widow of L. Hulsius,* 1627. 67 p.; illus., maps; 4to. (Levinus Hulsius's *Sammlung von . . . Schiffahrten.* Pt 12). 1st publ. in this version, Oppenheim, 1614; 1st publ. in this translation, Frankfurt a. M., 1613. Sabin 33666; Baginsky (German Americana) 156; Church 302; JCB (3) I:463. CSmH, MnU-B, NN-RB, RPJCB; ViU; BL, BN.

627/44

Góngora y Argote, Luis de. Obras en verso del Homero español. *Madrid: Widow of L. Sánchez, for A. Pérez,* 1627. 160 numb. lvs; 4to. An unauthorized publication including 'romances' earlier published in editions of the *Romancero general.* Here 1st publ. are the *Solidades* with numerous scattered refs to the New World, e.g., the Caribs, Magellan's ship *Vitoria,* the Isthmus of Panama, etc. Palau 104626. DLC, IU, MH, NNH; BL, BN.

627/45

Governor and Company of Noblemen and Gentlemen of England for the Plantation of Guiana. Breefe notes of the River Amazones, and of the coaste of Guiana. [*London?* 1627]. bds.; fol. London:PRO.

627/46

——. A breefe relation of the present state of the business of Guiana. [*London?* 1627]. bds.; fol. MnU-B; London:PRO.

627/47

——. The coppie of the preamble, for the subscriptions, intimating the conditions of adventure. [*London?* 1627]. bds.; fol. London:PRO.

627/48

Gravina, Domenico, O.P. Vox turturis, seu De florenti usque ad nostra tempora SS. Benedicti, Dominici, Francisci et aliarum sacrarum religionum statu. *Cologne: M. Demen,* 1627. 586 p.; 12mo. 1st publ., Naples, 1625. Cf. Streit I:422. BL, BN.

627/49

Great Britain. Sovereigns, etc., 1625–1649 (Charles I). A proclamation for the ordering of tobacco. *London: B. Norton & J. Bill,* 1627. 2 lvs; fol. Sabin 99850; Crawford (Roy. procl.) 1516; Brigham (Roy. procl.) 62–65; STC 8864; Arents (Add.) 240. CSmH, DFo, NN-A; BL.

627/50

——. A proclamation touching the sealing of tobacco. *London: B. Norton & J. Bill,* 1627. bds.; fol. Sabin 65936 & 99849; Crawford (Roy. procl.) 1509; Brigham (Roy. procl.) 61–62; STC 8857. CSmH; BL.

627/51

——. A proclamation touching tobacco. *London: B. Norton & J. Bill,* 1626 [i.e., 1627]. 3 lvs; fol. On importation & sale of tobacco. Sabin 99848; Crawford (Roy. procl.) 1505; Brigham (Roy. procl.) 55–61; STC 8853; Arents (Add.) 239. CSmH, DFo, NN-A; BL.

627/52

Grimestone, Edward. A generall historie of the Netherlands. Newly renewed, corrected . . . Continued from the yeare 1608 till the yeare . . . 1627 by William Crosse . . . The second impression. *London: A. Islip,* 1627. 1588 p.; ports; fol. 1st publ., London, 1608; here enl. Section for 1617 includes account of Spilbergen's passage through the Strait of Magellan; that for 1623 includes account of wreck of Spain's West India fleet in heavy storm. STC 12376. CSmH, CtY, DLC, IEN, PU, WU; BL, BN.

627/53

Grotius, Hugo. Sensus librorum sex, quos pro veritate religionis christianae Batavice. *Leyden: J. Maire,* 1627. 202 p.; 12mo. Prose adaptation of Grotius's *Bewys van den waren godsdienst,* 1st publ., [Leyden?], 1622; subsequently publ. under title *De veritate religionis christianae.* Includes refs to religious practices of American natives; to Indians of Cuba, Michoacana; & to Nicaragua, said to have had knowledge of the Flood & saving of animals. Meulen/Diermanse 944. MiU; BN, The Hague:KB.

627/54

—[Anr edn]. *Paris: J. Ruart,* 1627. 202 p.; 12mo. Meulen/Diermanse 945. BL, The Hague:PP.

627/55

Guibert, Philbert. Les oeuvres charitables. *Paris: D. Langlois,* 1627. 4 v.; 12mo. Included as v. 2 is Guibert's *Le prix et valeur des medicamens* of this year below, also issued separately. DNLM.

627/56

——. Le prix et valeur des medicamens . . .

Quatriesme edition. *Paris: D. Langlois,* 1627. 71 p.; 12mo. 1st publ., Paris, 1625. Wellcome I:2979. London:Wellcome, BN.

627/57

Hakewill, George. An apologie of the power and providence of God in the government of the world. *Oxford: J. Lichfield & W. Turner,* 1627. 473 p.; fol. In bk 3, chapt. 9, sect. 4, 'Of the art of navigation' refs to the New World, incl. Sir Francis Drake, occur; other American refs are found elsewhere. STC 12611; Madan (Oxford) I:1627:3. CSmH, CtY, DFo, IU, MH, MiU, NN-RB; BL.

627/58

Hein, Pieter Pieterszoon. Copia van het schryven ende bericht, geschreven ende gesonden aen de heeren bewindthebberen van de West-Indische compagnie . . . verkondigende de heerlicke victorie . . . inde Bahia, de Todos los Sanctos, onder de stadt . . . S. Salvador in West-Indien . . . den 16. Martii, 1627. [*The Hague?* 1627]. 4 lvs; 4to. NN-RB.

627/59

Heylyn, Peter. Μικροκοσμος. A little description of the great world. The third edition. *Oxford: J. L[ichfield]. & W. T[urner].,* for W. Turner & T. Huggins, 1627. 807 p.; 4to. 1st publ., Oxford, 1621. Sabin 31656; Madan (Oxford) 1627:4; STC 13278; JCB (3) II:206. CSmH, CtY, DLC, ICN, NN-RB, PBL, RPJCB; BL.

627/60

Hondius, Jodocus. Nova et accurata Italiae hodiernae descriptio. *Leyden: B. & A. Elsevier,* 1627. 406 p.; illus., maps; obl. 4to. 1st publ., Amsterdam, 1626. Sabin 32751; Willems (Les Elzevier) 279. DLC, NN-RB; BL, BN.

627/61

Hues, Robert. Tractatus de globis, coelesti et terrestri. *Frankfurt a. M.: D. & D. Aubry, for the House of Wechel,* 1627. 258 p.; 12mo. 1st publ., London, 1594; cf. 1611 edn. Shaaber (Brit. auth.) H484. MiU, NN-RB; BN.

627/62

——. Tractatus duo mathematici. Quorum primus De globis coelesti et terrestri . . . Alter Breviarium totius orbis terrarum, Petri Bertii. *Frankfurt a. M.: K. Rötel,* 1627. 2 pts; 12mo. 1st publ., London, 1594; cf. 1611 edn. Shaaber (Brit. auth.) H485. RPB; BN.

627/63

Hurtado de Mendoza, Diego. Guerra de Granada . . . contra los Moriscos. *Lisbon:*

G. de la Vinha, 1627. 127 numb. lvs; map; 4to. Includes mention of 'esmeraldas de América'. Palau 117245. CU-A, CtY, ICU, MH, MnU-B, NNH, PU; BL, BN.

627/64

Ibarra Gueztaraen, Juan de. Señor. El licenciado Iuan de Ybarra. [*Madrid?* 1627?]. bds.; fol. Memorial to king of Spain seeking reduction in number of Indians leaving their villages in Potosí province. Medina (BHA) 6550. BL.

627/65

Jesuits. Letters from missions. Lettere annue d'Etiopia, Malabar, Brasil, e Goa. Dall'anno 1620, fin' al 1624. *Rome: F. Corbelletti,* 1627. 343 p.; 8vo. Sabin 40561; Borba de Moraes I:408; Streit II:2392; JCB (3) II:206. CU, ICN, NN-RB, OCl, RPJCB; Munich:BU, Rome:BN.

627/66

Kepler, Johann. Tabulae Rudolphinae. *Ulm:* 1627. *See the year* 1629.

Lallemant, Charles, S.J. Lettre du pere Charles L'Allemant, superieur de la mission de Canadas; de la Compagnie de Jesus. *Paris: J. Boucher,* 1627. 16 p.; 8vo. Sabin 38680; Harrisse (NF) 41; Streit II:2490; Backer IV:1385; Church 410; JCB AR41: 25–30; cf. JCB (3) II:206–7. CSmH, NN-RB, RPJCB; BN.

627/67

Lucius, Ludwig, S.J. Historia Jesuitica; de Jesuitarum ordinis origine . . . nunc etiam latine edita per m. Ludovicum Lucium. *Basel: J. J. Genath,* 1627. 686 p.; illus.; 4to. Based on R. Hospinianus's *Historia Jesuitica,* 1st publ., Zurich, 1619; here enl. Cf. author's Basel, 1626, German edn. Backer XI:62; Jöcher II:2569. DFo, NN-RB; BL (Hospinianus), BN.

627/68

Marino, Giovanni Battista. L'Adone; poema. *Paris: M. Sonnius,* 1627. 16mo. 1st publ., Venice, 1623. Michel (Répertoire) V:121. MH; Paris:Mazarine.

627/69

—[Anr edn]. *Turin: Heirs of G. D. Tarino,* 1627. 583 p.; 12mo. Michel (Répertoire) V:121. Paris:Mazarine.

627/70

——. La Murtoleide, fischiate. *Paris: Heirs of A. Pacard,* 1627. 78 p.; 12mo. 1st publ., [Venice?], 1626. ICN; BN.

627/71

Mattioli, Pietro Andrea. Les commentaires . . . sur les six livres de Pedacius Dioscoride . . . de la matiere medicinale, traduits de latin . . . par m. Antoine du Pinet. *Lyons: C. Rigaud & C. Obert,* 1627. 603 p.; illus.;

fol. 1st publ. as here transl., Lyons, 1561; cf. 1605 edn above. Cf. Pritzel 5991n; Nissen (Bot.) 1312n. DNLM, MB, NN-RB; BL, BN.   627/72

Melich, Georg. Avertimenti nelle composizioni de' medicamenti. *Venice: G. Guerigli,* 1627. 522 p.; 4to. 1st publ., Venice, 1575; cf. [1605] edn. Wellcome I:4193. London: Wellcome.   627/73

Mercuriale, Girolamo. Praelectiones Patavinae. *Venice: The Giuntas,* 1627. 644 p.; fol. 1st publ., Frankfurt a. M., 1601, under title *Medica practica.* Wellcome I:4254. DNLM.
627/74

Meteren, Emanuel van. Eygentliche und vollkommene historische Beschreibung dess niderländischen Kriegs . . . vom Jahr 1560 biss auff 1620 . . . in Hochteutsch ubersetzt . . . und biss auff obgemelte Zeit continuirt. *Amsterdam: J. Janszoon, the Younger,* 1627. 2 pts; ports, map; fol. 1st publ. in German, Hamburg, 1596; cf. 1601 edn. Pt II has title: *Ander Theil der niderländischen Historien.* In 1630 the publisher issued a continuation, *Der niderländischen Historien dritter Theil.* Bruckner 34. ICN, ICU, NN-RB; Cambridge:UL, BN.   627/75

Minsheu, John. Minshaei emendatio . . . The second edition. *London: J. Haviland,* 1627. 760 cols; fol. 1st publ., London, 1617; here a reissue with altered imprint date of 1625 edn. STC 17947. CSmH, CtY, DFo, ICN, MH, NjP; BL, BN.   627/76

Montaigne, Michel Eyquem de. Essais. [*Rouen:*] *J. Besongne,* 1627. 1129 p.; 8vo. 1st publ., Bordeaux, 1580; cf. 1602 edn. Tchémerzine VIII:425. BN.   627/77

—[Anr issue]. *Rouen: J. Berthelin,* 1627. NjP, PPL.   627/78

—[Anr issue]. *Rouen: J. Caillouë,* 1627. Tchémerzine VIII:425. ICU; BN.   627/79

—[Anr issue]. *Rouen: L. DuMesnil,* 1627. Tchémerzine VIII:425. BN.   627/80

—[Anr issue]. *Rouen: R. Feron,* 1627. Tchémerzine VIII:425. BN.   627/81

—[Anr issue]. *Rouen: P. de LaMotte,* 1627. Tchémerzine VIII:425. MH; BN.
627/82

—[Anr issue]. *Rouen: R. Valentin,* 1627. Tchémerzine VIII:425. CtY; BN.
627/83

Nederlandschen verre-kijcker, om wt Hol-

land te konnen sien tot in de cancellerije van Spaignien. *The Hague: A. Meuris,* 1627. 23 p.; 4to. Includes discussions of Spanish brutality in Cuba, Jamaica, Hispaniola, and mainland of America, citing Las Casas. Not to be confused with similar title publ. 1626. Knuttel 3743. NN; The Hague:KB.
627/84

Netherlands (United Provinces, 1581–1795). Staten Generaal. Copia. De Staten Generael der Vereenichde Nederlanden: allen den genen, die desen sullen sien oft hooren lesen, saluyt. [*The Hague? 1627?*]. [8] p.; 4to. Resolutions concerning the West-Indische Compagnie's salt trade with Punta de Araya, 1626–27. Sabin 102889 (& 16664). DLC; BL.   627/85

——. Placcaet ende ordonnantie opte wapeninghe ende manninge vande schepen. *The Hague: Widow & Heirs of H. Jacobszoon van Wouw,* 1627. [20] p.; 4to. 1st publ., The Hague, 1607. Meulman 2006. Ghent:BU.
627/86

——. Placcaet opte grootte, equippagie, monture, manninghe ende admiraelschappen der schepen. *The Hague: Widow & Heirs of H. Jacobszoon van Wouw,* 1627. [7] p.; 4to. Includes ref. to shipping of goods from Mediterranean to New World. Meulman 2016; JCB (3) II:207. RPJCB; Ghent:BU.
627/87

Nonnius, Ludovicus. Diaeticon, sive De re cibaria. *Antwerp: P. & J. Bellère,* 1627. 638 p.; 8vo. In bk 2, chapt. xxv, the identity of the turkey is discussed. Cf. Palau 196869. CtY, DNLM, KMK, MeB; BL, BN.

627/88

Outreman, Pierre d', S.J. Tableaux des personnages signalez de la Compagnie de Jesus. *Lyons: C. Rigaud & C. Obert,* 1627. 511 p.; 8vo. 1st publ., Douai, 1623. Borba de Moraes II:126n; Streit I:436; Backer VI:37. BL, BN.   627/89

Overbury, Sir Thomas. Sir Thomas Overbury his wife . . . The twelfth [*sic*] impression. *London: I. J[aggard].*, *for R. Swain, Sr,* 1627. [320] p.; 8vo. 1st publ., London, 1615. STC 18915; Murphy (Engl. char.-bks) 22–23. CSmH, CtY, DFo, ICU, MH, PU; BL.   627/90

Paré, Ambroise. De chirurgie, ende alle de opera, ofte wercken . . . Nu eerst uyt de

françoysche . . . overgheset: door d. Carolum Battum. *Haarlem: H. Kranepoel, for H.
Laurenszoon, at Amsterdam, 1627.* 940 p.; illus.; fol. 1st publ. as here transl. from the
Paris, 1585, 4th edn, Dordrecht, 1592; cf.
the 1601 German edn. Doe (Paré) 61. Am-
sterdam:UB, Brussels:BR.   627/91

Pretty, Francis. Le voyage de l'illustre seigneur . . . François Drach. *Paris: 1627. See
under title below.*

Purchas, Samuel. Purchas his pilgrim. Microcosmus, or The historie of man. *London:
[B. Alsop & T. Fawcet,] for T. Alchorn, 1627.*
818 p.; 8vo. 1st publ., London, 1619; here
a reissue of that edn with cancel t.p. as here
given. Sabin 66677n; STC 20504; JCB (3)
II:209. CtY, IU, MiU, RPJCB; BL.
                                      627/92

Pyne, John. Epigrammata religiosa, officiosa, jocosa. Anglo-latina, latina, anglica.
[London: 1627?]. See the year 1626.

Recio de León, Juan. Señor. El maestro de
campo Juan Recio de Leon, dize: Que los
Indios que de ordinario estan obligadas
[*sic*] a entregar a los mineros del assiento
de minas de Potosi por ordenanças y repartimiento del Virrey. *[Madrid: 1627].* 10
numb. lvs; fol. Memorial to king of Spain
on decline of Indian population in Potosí,
subscribed at Madrid, 8 March 1627. Sabin
68361 (BA = BL), Medina (Chile) 237. BL,
Seville:Archivo de Indias.   627/93

**Roca, Juan Antonio Vera Zúñiga y Figueroa,
conde de la.** Epítome de la vida, y hechos
del invicto emperador Carlos V. *Madrid: L.
Sánchez, 1627.* 118 numb. lvs; 4to. 1st publ.,
Madrid, 1622. Palau 358990. ICN, NN-RB;
BN.   627/94

Rowlands, Samuel. Doctor Merry-man: or,
Nothing but mirth. *London: A. M[athewes].,
for S. Rand, 1627.* 4to. In verse. 1st publ.,
London, 1607, under title *Democritus, or,
Doctor Merry-man his medicines.* STC 21377.
Oxford: Bodl. (imp.).   627/95

——. Tis merrie when gossips meete. *London:
A. Mathewes; sold by M. Sparke, 1627.* 4to.
1st publ., London, 1602. In verse. STC
21412. NN-RB.   627/96

Royal College of Physicians of London.
Pharmacopoea Londinensis . . . Tertia editio. *London: [Eliot's Court Press,] for J. Marriott,
1627.* fol. 1st publ., London, 1618. STC

16774. WU; BL, Cambridge:UL, Oxford:
Bodl.   627/97

Sandys, George. A relation of a journey . . .
containing a description of the Turkish empire . . . Third edition. *London: [T. Cotes,]
for R. Allot, 1627.* 309 p.; illus., maps; fol.
1st publ., London, 1615. STC 21728.
CSmH, CtY, DFo, IU, InU-L, MH, NN-RB;
BL.   627/98

Scribanius, Carolus. Civilium apud Belgas
bellorum initia, progressus, finis optatus.
[Antwerp: M. Nuyts] 1627. 286 p.; 8vo. 1st
publ., [Antwerp, 1624], under title *Veridicus
Belgicus.* Includes, p. [213]–86, the author's
'Reformata apocalypsis Batavica'. Knuttel
3743a; Backer VII:988. ICN, MH, MnU; BL,
BN.   627/99

——. Le manifeste hollandoise . . . expliqué
par Pambon Nreimundima [*sic; pseud.*].
[Amsterdam? 1627?]. [31] p.; 8vo. 1st publ.
in French, 'Villeneuve' [i.e., The Netherlands?], 1626, under title *L'Apocalipse hollandoise;* transl. from the author's *Den Hollantschen apocalypsis,* 1st publ., 'Nieustadt'
[i.e., Leyden?], 1625. NN-RB; BL (as
[1626?]), BN.   627/100

Serres, Jean de. Inventaire general de l'histoire de France. *Paris: P. Mettayer, 1627.*
2077 p.; fol. 1st publ. with American refs,
Paris, 1600; cf. 1606 edn. BN.
                                  627/101

Settala, Lodovico. Animadversionum, et
cautionum medicarum libri septem. *Naples:
L. Scorigio, 1627.* 260 p.; 8vo. 1st publ., Milan, 1626. London:Wellcome.   627/102

Le siege de la ville de Groll . . . Ensemble
la defaitte de la flotte espagnolle; dans la
baye de Todos los Sanctos, au Bresil, par
les Hollandois. *Paris: P. Auvray, 1627.* Palau
312370. NNH.   627/103

—[Anr edn]. *[Paris?]* 1627. 7 p.; 8vo. MH.
                                  627/104

Simón, Pedro. Primera parte de las Noticias
historiales de las conquistas de tierra firme
en las Indias Occidentales. *Cuenca: D. de la
Iglesia* [1627]. 671 p.; fol. Sabin 81286; Medina (BHA) 818; Streit II:1565; Palau
314220; JCB (3) II:209. CU-B, CtY, DLC,
InU-L, MH, NNH, PPL, RPJCB; BL, Ma-
drid:BN.   627/105

Smith, Capt. John. An accidence or The
path-way to experience. Necessary for all

young sea-men. *London:* [*N. Okes,*] *for J. Man & B. Fisher,* 1627. 42 p.; 4to. 1st publ., London, 1626; here anr issue with altered imprint date. Sabin 82813; STC 22785. CSmH, NN-RB; Cambridge: Christ's (imp.).
627/106

——. The generall historie of Virginia, New-England, and the Summer Isles. *London: J. D*[*awson*]. *& J. H*[*aviland*]., *for M. Sparke,* 1627. 248 p.; illus., ports, maps; fol. 1st publ., London, 1624; here a reissue of that edn with altered imprint date. Sabin 82827; Clayton-Torrence 51 (4); Baer (Md) 13; STC 22790c; Arents 164; Church 411; JCB (3) II:209. CSmH, ICN, InU-L, MB, MWA, MnU-B, NN-RB, PPL, RPJCB; BL, BN.
627/107

——. A sea grammar, with the plaine exposition of Smith's Accidence for young seamen enlarged. *London: J. Haviland,* 1627. 86 p.; 8vo. Smith's *Accidence* had been publ. in 1626. Ref. is made to the West Indian 'hericana', while the prelim. matter includes a poem by Edw. Jorden mentioning praise of Smith by Indians in America. Sabin 82839; STC 22794; Church 412; JCB (3) II:209. CSmH, NN-RB, RPJCB; Oxford: Bodl.
627/108

Spain. Consejo de las Indias. Assiento y capitulacion, que los señores Presidente, y del Consejo real de las Indias tomaron con Adriano de Legafo, por si y en nombre del Prior y consules de la Universidad de los cargadores a las Indias de . . . Seville, y demas personas interessadas en el commercio dellas. *Madrid: J. González,* 1627. 44 1vs; fol. Sabin 2232; Medina (BHA) 820; Palau 18678. BL.
627/109

Speed, John. A prospect of the most famous parts of the world. Together with that large Theater of Great Brittaines empire. *London: J. Dawson, for G. Humble,* 1627. 44 (i.e., 86) p.; maps. fol. Sabin 89228n; STC 23039g.7; Phillips (Atlases) 5928. DLC, MH; BL, Cambridge:UL.
627/110

Staden, Hans. Beschrijvinghe van America. *Amsterdam: B. Janszoon,* 1627. 72 p.; illus.; 4to. 1st publ. in Dutch, Antwerp, 1558; cf. edn. of 1625. Sabin 90044; Borba de Moraes II:284; Palau 321858; JCB (3) II:210. NN-RB, RPJCB.
627/111

Stephens, John. The errors of men person-

ated in sundry essaies. *London:* [*E. Allde,*] *for W. Barrenger,* 1627. 434 p.; 8vo. 1st publ., London, 1615, under title *Satyrical essayes;* here a reissue with cancel t.p. of the 1615 'second impression with title *Essayes and characters*'. STC 23250.5 (formerly 10527 & 21502). DFo.
627/112

Sweden. Sovereigns, etc., 1611–1632 (Gustaf II Adolf). Octroy ofte Privilegie, soo by . . . Herr Gustaeff Adolph, der Sweden . . . Koningh . . . aen de . . . Zuyder Compagnie . . . Mitsgaders een naerder bericht over 'tselve Octroy . . . door Willem Usselinx. *The Hague: A. Meuris,* 1627. [98] p.; 4to. The *Octroy* itself 1st publ. in Swedish, Stockholm, 1626; here added are related materials, including works by Willem Usselinx. For a full list of contents, see Jameson. Sabin 98204; Knuttel 3735; Muller (1872) 1142; Jameson (Usselinx) 20. PHi; BL, The Hague:KB.
627/113

Tassoni, Alessandro. Dieci libri di pensieri diversi . . . Corretti . . . in questa quarta impressione. *Venice: M. A. Brogiollo,* 1627. 679 p.; 4to. 1st publ., Modena, 1612, under title *Varieta di pensieri diversi,* but see also enl. 1620 edn. Puliatti (Tassoni) 5. DFo, ICN, MH, NNC, PPL; BL, BN.
627/114

Taylor, John, the Water-poet. An armado, or navye, of 103. ships & other vessels; who have the art to sayle by land, as well as by sea. *London: E. A*[*llde*]., *for H. Gosson,* 1627. [54] p.; 8vo. Includes a ref. to Francis Drake's circumnavigation, as well as to tobacco. STC 23726; Arents (Add.) 241. CSmH, NN-A; BL.
627/115

Téllez, Gabriel. Doze comedias nuevas del maestro Tirso de Molina [pseud.] . . . la parte. *Seville: F. de Lyra, for M. de Sande,* 1627. 300 numb. 1vs; 4to. In the 'La villana de Vallescas' a principal character is one Don Pedro, born in Mexico, who has come to Spain to marry. Refs to American places and to tobacco & other American products occur. Palau 329475. BN.
627/116

Theatrum florae, in quo ex toto orbe selecti mirabiles . . . flores . . . proferuntur. *Paris: P. Firens,* 1627. 69 numb. pls; illus.; fol. 1st publ., Paris, 1622. Cf. Pritzel 10855; Nissen (Bot.) 1575n; Hunt (Bot.) 212. PPiHB; London:Wellcome.
627/117

Torsellino, Orazio, S.J. Historiarum ab origine mundi usque ad annum 1598 epitome libri x. *Douai: B. Billère,*1627. 416 p.; 12mo. 1st publ., Rome, 1598; cf. 1620 edn. Backer VIII:151.   627/118

Vega Carpio, Lope Félix de. Parte veinte de las Comedias. *Madrid: J. González, for A. Pérez,* 1627. 4to. 1st publ., Madrid, 1625. Sabin 98772n; cf. Palau 355311. BL.
                                          627/119

Vesga, Mateo de. Señor. El capitan y almirante Mateo de Vesga governador . . . que ha sido de las provincias de la Nueva Vizcaya en Nuevaespaña, dize, que aviendo servido à V. Magestad en diversos cargos [etc.]. [*Madrid?* 1627?]. 4 numb. 1vs; fol. Memorial to king of Spain written from Mexico seeking further advancement. Sabin 99326; Medina (BHA) 6966; Wagner (SW) 30; Palau 361065. Seville:Archivo de Indias.
                                          627/120

Le voyage de l'illustre seigneur et chevalier François Drach . . . à l'entour du monde. Augmentée de la seconde partie. *Paris: J. Gesselin,* 1627. 230 p.; 8vo. The 1st pt had been 1st publ. in French, Paris, 1613. Sabin 20845; Wagner (SW) 9c; Shaaber (Brit. auth.) H11. DLC, MH, MiU-C, NN-RB, PPRF, RPJCB; BL, BN.   627/121

Wake, Sir Isaac. Rex platonicus, sive De . . . Jacobi . . . Regis, ad . . . Academiam Oxoniensem adventu . . . 1605. narratio . . . Editio quarta. *Oxford: J. Lichfield,* 1627. 238 p.; 12mo. 1st publ., Oxford, 1607. STC 24941; Madan (Oxford) 1627:13. CSmH, CtY, DFo, IU, MH, NNUT; BL.
                                          627/122

Wassenaer, Nicolaes van. Het elfde deel of 't vervolgh van het Historisch verhael aller ghedencwaerdiger geschiedenissen, die in Europa . . . in America, als West-Indien, Brasil en d'eylanden . . . voorgevallen syn. *Amsterdam: J. Janszoon, the Younger* [1627?]. 138 numb. 1vs.; illus.; 4to. (N. van Wassenaer's *Historisch verhael.* Pt 11). Includes account of Bahia, Brazil, and of Admiral Boudewyn Hendrickszoon's West Indian voyage. Cf. Sabin 102039; Borba de Moraes II:371; Muller (1872) 1745. RPJCB.
                                          627/123

——. 'Twaelfde deel of 't vervolgh van het Historisch verhael aller gedenckwaerdiger geschiedeniss. die in Europa . . . in Amer-

ica, als West-Indien, d'eijlanden en Brasil . . . voorgevallen zijn. *Amsterdam: J. Janszoon, the Younger* [1627]. 118 numb. 1vs; illus.; 4to. (N. van Wassenaer's *Historisch verhael.* Pt 12). Includes discussion of New Netherland & arrival of silver fleet in Spain. Cf. Sabin 102039; Borba de Moraes II:371; Muller (1872) 1745. RPJCB.   627/124

Wirsung, Christoph. Medicyn-boeck . . . overgeset door d. Carolum Battum . . . 7. ed. *Amsterdam: J. E. Cloppenburg,* 1627. 676 p.; illus.; fol. Transl. from Wirsung's *New Artzney Buch,* 1st publ., Heidelberg, 1568; cf. 1605 edn. DNLM; BN.   627/125

1628

Alpherio, Hyacinthus de. De peste, et vera distinctione inter febrem pestilentem, et malignam, non hactenus perspecta. *Naples: A. Longhi,* 1628. 2 pts; 4to. In bk 4, 'De variolis, & morbillis' syphilis is discussed, in reference to Galen & Hippocrates, as a new disease introduced from the Indies, citing Oviedo y Valdés & Hernando Cortés. London:Wellcome.   628/1

Alsted, Johann Heinrich. Thesaurus chronologiae . . . Editio secunda. *Herborn:* [*G. Rab*] 1628. 592 p.; 8vo. 1st publ., Herborn, 1624. CtY, MH, MWA; BN.   628/2

Amatus Lusitanus. Curationum medicinalium centuriae septem. *Barcelona: S. & J. Matevad,* 1628. 1408 cols; fol. 1st publ., Venice, 1551–66; cf. 1620 edn. Palau 10867. CtY-M, MH-A; London:Wellcome.   628/3

Amsterdam. Citizens. Copie van requesten van de goede gehoorsame burgeren ende gemeente deser stede Amstelredamme . . . Requeste van de West Indische Compaignie. [*Amsterdam:*] 1628. 14 p.; 4to. Sabin 16680 (& 102889); Knuttel 3813. DLC, NN-RB, RPJCB; BL, The Hague:KB.   628/4

Anghiera, Pietro Martire d'. The famous historie of the Indies . . . Set forth first by Mr Hakluyt, and now published by L. M. gent. The second edition. *London: M. Sparke,* 1628. 318 numb. 1vs; 8vo. 1st publ. as here edited, London, 1612; here a reissue with cancel t.p. & dedication of that edn. Sabin 1564; STC 652; Palau 12609; Arents (Add.) 7; JCB (3) II:217. CSmH, ICN, MH, NN-A, RPJCB.   628/5

Augustinians. Bullarum Ordinis Eremitarum S. Augustini . . . A rev. p. magistro fr. Laurentio Empoli. *Rome: Apostolic Camera,* 1628. 406 p.; fol. Includes papal bulls of Clement VIII & Urban VIII relating to New World. Streit I:440. Rome:BN.   628/6

Avity, Pierre d', sieur de Montmartin. Archontologia cosmica; sive Imperiorum, regnorum, principatuum, rerumque publicarum per totum terrarum orbem commentarii. *Frankfurt a. M.: L. Jennisius,* 1628. 3 pts; illus., maps; fol. Transl. by J. L. Gottfried from the author's *Les estats, empires et principautez du monde,* 1st publ., Paris, 1613. Sabin 28070. DLC, RPJCB: Munich:StB.
628/7

Bacon, Francis, viscount St Albans. The history of the reigne of King Henry the seventh. *London: H. L[ownes]. & R. Y[oung].; sold by P. Stephens & C. Meredith,* 1628. 248 p.; fol. 1st publ., London, 1622. Gibson (Bacon) 117.   628/8

——. Sylva sylvarum. *London:* 1628. *See the year* 1629.

Baerle, Kaspar van. Poemata. *Leyden: G. Basson,* 1628. 2 pts; 8vo. In verse. Includes scattered American refs. Enl. in succeeding edns by added Americana. Cf. Sabin 3407; Dt. Ges. Kat. 11.6596; cf. Arents 172n. ICN, MNS, NcD, PP; BL, BN.   628/9

—[Anr edn]. *Amsterdam: Elsevier,* 1628. Sabin 3407n, but very possibly a ghost.
628/10

Barbón y Castañeda, Guillén. Provechosos adbitrios al consumo del vellon, conservacion de plata, poblacion de España, y relacion de avisos importantes. *Madrid: A. de Parra, for the Confraternity of Souls in Purgatory of the Parish of Santiago in Madrid,* 1628. 29 numb. 1vs; 4to. Refers in passing to 'las Indianas riquezas'. Colmeiro 106; Palau 23803; JCB (3) II:212. RPJCB; BL.
628/11

Barclay, John. Euphormionis Lusinini . . . Satyricon. *Amsterdam: J. Janszoon, the Younger,* 1628. 508 p.; 12mo. Includes pt 2, 1st publ., Paris, 1607, & pt 4, the *Icon animorum,* 1st publ., London, 1614. Shaaber (Brit. auth.) B196; Tchémerzine I:449–51. CtY, DFo, ICN, MiU, MnU; Oxford:Bodl., BN.
628/12

—[Anr edn]. *Leyden: J. Marcus,* 1628, '27. 252

p.; 8vo. Shaaber (Brit. auth.) B194. CU-S, IU, OU; BL, Munich:StB.   628/13
—[Anr edn]. *Rouen: J. de La Mare,* 1628. 8vo. Shaaber (Brit. auth.) B195. BL, Lübeck:StB, Santiago de Compostela:BU.   628/14

Barros, João de. Decada primeira[-terceira] da Asia. *Lisbon: J. Rodriguez, for A. Gonzalvez,* 1628. 3 v.; maps; fol. 1st publ., Lisbon, 1552–63. Included are accounts of the Portuguese discovery of Brazil, & of the Magellan circumnavigation. Cf. Sabin 3646; Borba de Moraes I:71; JCB (3) II:213. DLC, MH, NN-RB, RPJCB: BL, BN.   628/15

Bertius, Petrus. [Geographia vetus ex antiquis, et melioris notae scriptoribus nuper collecta. *Paris: M. Tavernier,* 1628]. 41 1vs; maps; obl. 4to. Hemispheric map shows New World. BN (imp.).   628/16

Boissard, Jean Jacques. Bibliotheca sive Thesaurus virtutis et gloriae in quo continentur illustrium eruditione et doctrina virorum effigies et vitae. *Frankfurt a. M.: W. Fitzer,* 1628–32. 5 pts; illus., ports; 4to. 1st publ., Frankfurt a. M., 1597–99, under title *Icones virorum illustrium doctrina et eruditione.* In pt 1 is a port. of Columbus. Graesse I:474. CSmH, CtY, DLC, MH, NN-RB; BL, BN.   628/17

Bruele, Gualtherus. Praxis medicinae theorica et empirica familiarissima. *Geneva: J. Chouët,* 1628. 476 p.; 8vo. 1st publ., Antwerp, 1579; cf. 1602 edn. CtY-M, DNLM, NNNAM; BN.   628/18
—[Anr issue]. *Geneva: P. Aubert,* 1628. BL.
628/19
—[Anr edn]. *Leyden: J. Maire,* 1628. 428 p.; 8vo. BN.   628/20

Bry, Johann Theodor de. Der dreyzehende Theil der Orientalischen Indien. *Frankfurt a. M.: K. Rötel, for W. Fitzer,* 1628. 184 p.; illus., map.; fol. (J. T. de Bry's *India Orientalis.* Pt 13. German). Ed. by William Fitzer. Includes, p. 147–49, description of Greenland. Tiele-Muller p. 198–202; Church 245; JCB (3) I:445–46. CSmH, CtY, DLC, NN-RB, RPJCB; BL, BN.   628/21

——. Historiarum Orientalis Indiae tomus XII. In tres libros . . . distributus . . . I. Ludovicus Gotofridus ex Anglico et Belgico sermone in Latinum transtulit. *Frankfurt a. M.: W. Fitzer,* 1628. 208 p.; illus., maps; fol. (J. T. de Bry's *India Orientalis.* Pt 12. Latin).

Text as here collected & ed. By William Fitzer, 1st publ. in de Bry's *Der zwölffte Theil der Orientalischen Indien* below and *Der drey-zehende Theil der Orientalischen Indien* above. Includes account of L'Hermite's circumnavigation and a description of Greenland. Cf. Tiele-Muller p. 198–202; Church 224; JCB (3) I:444–45. CSmH, NN-RB, RPJCB; ViU; BL, BN. 628/22

———. Der zwölffte Theil der Orientalischen Indien. Darinnen etliche newe gedenckwürdige Schifffarthen . . . Dessgleichen Die Reyss . . . der Nassawischen Floth, so unter dem Admiral Jacob l'Eremit . . . umb den gantzen Erdkreyss verrichtet worden. *Frankfurt a. M.: K. Rötel, for W. Fitzer,* 1628. 77 p.; illus., map; fol. (J. T. de Bry's *India Orientalis.* Pt 12 German). Ed. by William Fitzer. Includes, p. 36–66, account of L'Hermite's circumnavigation. Tiele-Muller p. 198–201; Church 244; JCB (3) I:445. CSmH, CtY, DLC, NN-RB, RPJCB; BL, BN. 628/23

Bry, Theodor de. Dreyzehender Theil Americae, das ist, Fortsetzung der Historien von der Newen Welt. *Frankfurt a. M.: K. Rötel, for M. Merian,* 1628. 90 p.; illus., maps; fol. (Theodor de Bry's *America.* Pt 13. German). 1st publ. in this version, Frankfurt a. M., 1627, under title *Continuatio Americae.* Cf. Sabin 8784; Baginsky (German Americana) 158; Shaaber (Brit. auth.) H82 & W66; Church 200 (cf. 174n). CSmH, DLC, ICN, NN-RB; BL, BN. 628/24

Buchanan, George. Poemata quae extant. Editio postrema. *Leyden: Elsevier Office,* 1628. 561 p.; 12mo. 1st publ. as here constituted, Edinburgh, 1615. Shaaber (Brit. auth.) B705; Willems (Les Elzevier) 292; Arents 165. CU, DLC, IEN, InU-L, MH, MiD, NN-A, PU, RPB; BL, BN. 628/25

Burton, Robert. The anatomy of melancholy . . . The thirde edition, corrected and augmented by the author. *Oxford: J. Lichfield & J. Short, for H. Cripps,* 1628. 646 p.; fol. 1st publ., Oxford, 1621. Madan (Oxford) 1628:4; STC 4161; Arents (Add.) 223. CSmH, CtY, DLC, ICN, MH, NN-RB; BL. 628/26

Camerarius, Philipp. Secunda centuria historica, das ist, Ander Theil des historischen Lustgartens. *Leipzig: M. Wachsman,* 1628.

624 p.; 4to. Transl. by Georg Maier from Camerarius's *Operae horarum subcisivarum . . . Centuria . . . altera,* 1st publ., Frankfurt a. M., 1601. Continues Maier's translation of pt 1, 1st publ. Leipzig, 1625; for pt 3, see the year 1630. Jantz (German Baroque) 47. NcD. 628/27

Cats, Jacob. Proteus, ofte Minne-beelden. [*The Hague:*] 1628. 2 pts; 8vo. 1st publ., Middelburg, 1618, under title *Silenus Alcibiadis.* BL.. 628/28

Cevicos, Juan. Discurso . . . Sobre una carta para Su Santidad. [*Madrid?* 1628]. 19 numb. 1vs; fol. Cevicos mentions having spent the years 1604–8 in Mexico before going on to Japan. Medina (BHA) 835. Granada:BU 628/29

Chaumette, Antoine. Le parfaict chirurgien, ou Recueil general de ce qu'il doit scavoir. *Paris: C. Besongne,* 1628. 4 pts; 8vo. Transl. from Chaumette's *Enchiridion chirurgicum,* 1st publ., Paris, 1560, and publ. in French, Lyons, 1571, under title *Enchiridion ou Livret portatif.* In section on syphilis ('mal de Naples'), use of 'lignum sanctum' (guaiacum) is discussed. DNLM; BL. 628/30

Clüver, Philipp. Introductionis in universam geographiam, tam veterem quàm novam, libri vi. *Leyden: J. Marcus,* 1628. 450 p.; illus.; 16mo. 1st publ., Leyden, 1624. Cf. Sabin 13805. MnU-B. 628/31

Codogno, Ottavio. Nuovo itinerario delle poste per tutto il mondo. *Venice: The Imberti,* 1628. 446 p.; obl. 16mo. 1st publ., Venice, 1611. Cf. Sabin 14142; Michel (Répertoire) II:112. BN. 628/32

Compagnie de la Nouvelle France. Articles accordés par le roi à la Compagnie de la Nouvelle-France. [*Paris?* 1628?]. 23 p.; 4to. Dated 6 Aug. 1628. Sabin 10360 (& 56079); Harrisse (NF) 43; JCB AR52:32–36. RPJCB; BN (Lk12.776). 628/33

———. Les noms, surnoms et qualitez des associez en la Compagnie de la Nouvelle France, suyvant les jours & dates de leurs signatures. [*Paris?* 1628?]. 8 p.; 4to. Harrisse (NF) 44. BN (Lk. 12.779). 628/34

Contant, Jacques. Les oeuvres de Jacques et Paul Contant, père et fils. *Poitiers: J. Thoreau & the Widow of A. Mesnier,* 1628. 4 pts; illus.; fol. In the 2nd pt, the son's 'Eden', in verse, numerous American plants are mentioned. The final pt, his 'Le jardin et cabinet poëtique' was 1st publ. Poitiers, 1609. Pritzel 1850; Arents (Add.) 242. DNLM, MH-A, NN-A; BL, BN.   628/35

Cooke, Jo. Greene's Tu quoque. *London: M. Fletcher* [1628?]. [80] p.; 4to. Drama. 1st publ., London, 1614. STC 5675; Greg 323(c). CSmH, CtY, DLC, ICN, MH; BL.   628/36

Drake, Sir Francis. The world encompassed by Sir Francis Drake, being his next voyage to that to Nombre de Dios . . . carefully collected out of the notes of Master Francis Fletcher. *London: [G. Miller?] for N. Bourne,* 1628. 108 p.; port., map; 4to. For discussion of the probable sources of this 'most untrustworthy' account, see H. R. Wagner, *Sir Francis Drake's voyage around the world* (San Francisco: 1926), p. 286–302. Sabin 20853; Wagner (SW) 31; STC 7161; Church 413; JCB (3) II:214. CSmH, DFo, MH, MiU-C, MnU-B, NN-RB, RPJCB; BL, BN.   628/37

Drayton, Michael. Poems . . . Collected into one volume. *London: W. Stansby, for J. Smethwick* [ca. 1628?]. 487 p.; fol. 1st publ., London, 1605. On date & variant title pages, see Pforzheimer. Sabin 20916; STC 7222; Pforzheimer 307. CSmH, CtY, DFo, ICN, MH, MiU, NN-RB, PU; BL.   628/38

Duchesne, Joseph de. Pharmacopoea dogmaticorum restituta. *Geneva: P. & J. Chouët,* 1628. 591 p.; 8vo. 1st publ., Paris, 1607. DNLM, NNC; London:Wellcome.   628/39

Du Jarric, Pierre, S.J. Nouvelle histoire des choses plus memorables advenuës tant ès Indes Orientales, qu'autres pays de la decouverte des Portugais. *Arras: G. Baudin,* 1628. 977 p.; 8vo. 1st publ., Bordeaux, 1610, as the *Seconde partie de l'Histoire des choses plus memorables;* cf. 1611 edn above. Cf. Sabin 35790; cf. Borba de Moraes I:359–60; Streit IV 155; Backer IV:751. BL, Lyons:BM.   628/40

Earle, John, Bp of Salisbury. Micro-cosmographie. or, A peece of the world discovered; in essayes and characters. *London: W. S[tansby]., for E. Blount,* 1628. [214] p.; 12mo. Includes a character of 'A Tobacco-

seller'. STC 7439; Murphy (Engl. char.-bks) 35–36. CSmH, DFo; BL.   628/41

—[Anr edn]. *London: W. Stansby, for E. Blount,* 1628. [213] p.; 12mo. STC 7440; Murphy (Engl. char.-bks) 36. CSmH, MH; BL.   628/42

—[Anr edn]. *London: W. Stansby, for R. Allott,* 1628. [213] p.; 12mo. STC 7441; Murphy (Engl. char.-bks) 36; Arents 166. DFo, MH, NN-A; BL.   628/43

Faber, Johannes. Animalia mexicana descriptionibus, scholiisq. exposita. *Rome: G. Mascardi,* 1628. 90 p.; fol. Bd with, as issued, Francisco Hernández, *Rerum medicarum Novae Hispaniae thesaurus* of this year, q.v.

Fabre, Pierre Jean. Myrothecium spagyricum; sive Pharmacopoea chymica, occultis naturae arcanis . . . illustrata. *Toulouse: N. d'Estey, for P. Bosc,* 1628. 448 p.; 8vo. For cure of syphilis, guaiacum & sarsaparilla are recommended; mechoacan is also discussed. DNLM, ICU, MH, NNNAM.   628/44

Faria e Sousa, Manuel de. Epitome de las historias portuguesas. *Madrid: F. Martínez, for P. Coello,* 1628. 2 v. (696 p.); illus.; 4to. Under year 1625, Brazil is mentioned. Sabin 23803; Palau 86682; Maggs Cat. 479 (Americana V):4192. DLC, MH; MnU-B, BL, BN.   628/45

Fitzer, William, ed. Orientalische Indien. Das ist Aussführliche und volkommene historische und geographische Beschreibung aller . . . Schifffarten. *Frankfurt a. M.: K. Rötel, for W. Fitzer,* 1628. 566 p.; illus.; fol. (J. T. de Bry's *India Orientalis.* Abridgment). Extracted from J. T. de Bry's *India Orientalis,* pts 1–11, Frankfurt a. M., 1590–1620. Includes account of Hudson's voyages & a description of Greenland. Palmer 368; Brunet I:1362; JCB (3) II:214. RPJCB; BL (Bry).   628/46

Fonseca, Rodrigo. Consultationum medicinalium singularibus remediis refertae. *Venice: G. Guerigli,* 1628. 2 v.; fol. 1st publ., Venice, 1619–22. Wellcome I:2346. DNLM; BL.   628/47

Garibáy y Zamálloa, Esteban de. Los quarenta libros del Compendio historial de las chronicas y universal historia de todos los reynos de España. *Barcelona: S. de Cormellas,* 1628. 4 v.; fol. 1st publ., Brussels, 1571.

Included are substantial accounts of Columbus & the New World. Sabin 26667; Palau 100102. CtY, IU, InU-L, MH, MiU, NNH, PU; BL, BN.   628/48

Gesner, Konrad. Quatre livres des secrets de medecine . . . faicts françois par m. Jean Liebault. *Rouen: J. B. Behourt,* 1628. 298 numb. lvs; illus.; 8vo. 1st publ., as transl. by Liébault, Paris, 1573; cf. 1616 edn. London:Wellcome, BN.   628/49

Gilbert, William. Tractatus, sive Physiologia nova de magnete . . . Omnia . . . recognita . . . operâ . . . Wolfgangi Lochmans. *Stettin: Götz Press, for J. Hallervord,* 1628. 232 p.; illus.; 4to. 1st publ., London, 1600, with refs in preface by Edward Wright to English explorers, e.g., Sir Francis Drake & Thomas Cavendish, here also reprinted. Shaaber (Brit. auth). G312. ICJ, MH, NN-RB, PPAmP; BL.   628/50

Goulart, Simon. Thresor d'histoires admirables et memorables. *Geneva: S. Crespin,* 1628. 2 v.; 8vo. 1st publ., Paris, 1600–1601, under title *Histoires admirables et memorables;* cf. 1603 edn. Jones (Goulart) 54p. BN, Berne:StB.   628/51

Le grand dictionnaire françois-latin, augmenté [par Guillaume Poille] . . . Recueilly des observations de plusieurs hommes doctes: entre autres de m. Nicod [i.e., Nicot]. *Rouen: J. Osmont,* 1628. [1164] p.; 4to. 1st publ. with section on tobacco by Nicot, Paris, 1573, under title *Dictionaire françois-latin;* cf. year 1603. DLC.   628/52

Gysius, Johannes. Tweede deel van de Spieghel der Spaense tyrannye, gheschiet in Nederlant. *Leyden: A. C. Hoogenacker & D. van Vreeswijck, for J. E. Cloppenburg, at Amsterdam,* 1628. 126 p.; illus.; 4to. 1st publ. in this version as issued with Las Casas's Amsterdam, 1620, *Den spiegel der Spaensche tijrannije-geschiet in West-Indien.* Issued with Cloppenburg edns of Las Casas's *Den spieghel der Spaensche tijrannije.* NN-RB.   628/53

Habrecht, Isaac. Planiglobium coeleste et terrestre, sive Globus coelestis atque terrestris nova forma ac norma in planum projectus. *Strassburg: M. von der Heyden,* 1628–29. 206 p.; map; 4to. Areas discussed include the Americas. Cf. Sabin 29470. CtY (p. 103–206 only); BN (p. 1–102 only).   628/54

Hayman, Robert. Quodlibets, lately come over from New Britaniola, old Newfoundland. Epigrams and other small parcels . . . The first foure bookes being the authors owne: the rest translated out of . . . John Owen and other rare authors . . . All of them composed and done at Harbor-Grace in Britaniola, anciently called Newfoundland. *London: Elizabeth Allde, for R. Michell,* 1628. 4 pts; 4to. Sabin 31036–37; Baer (Md) 14; Wegelin (Poetry) 198; Arents 167; JCB (3) II:335. CSmH, DLC, InU-L, MH, MiU-C, NN-RB, RPJCB; BL.   628/55

Hein, Pieter Pieterszoon. Beschreibung von Eroberung der spañischen Silber Flotta, wie solche von dem General Peter Peters Heyn. In Nova Hispania in der Insel Cuba im Baia Matanckha ist erobert worden. *Amsterdam: N. J. Fischer,* 1628. bds; illus.; fol. Perhaps transl. from Hein's *Extract* below. For variants see Muller. Palau 114574; Muller (1872) III:1543–45; Bruckner 36; JCB (3) II:216. RPJCB.   628/56

—[Anr edn]. Aussführlicher Bericht, wie es mit der Silber Flotta hergangen, wann . . . solche inn diesem 1628. Jahr erobert, fort und eingebracht. Nebenst Specificierung aller Gütter, auch wie sie unter die West-Indische Compagni aussgetheilt worden. Erstlich gedruckt zu Ambsterdam bey Heinrich Mellort Jano. [Germany? 1628?]. 6 lvs; 4to. Baginsky (German Americana) 157. NN-RB.   628/57

——. Extract uyt den Brief . . . aen de Geoctroyeerde West-Indische Compagnie, gheschreven in 't schip Amsterdam . . . bywesten't eylandt Bermuda. [The Hague? 1628?]. [4] p.; 4to. Cf. Hein's *Copia van het schryven,* 1st publ., [The Hague? 1627]. Sabin 31658; Borba de Moraes I:340; Palau 114575; Petit 1538; JCB (3) II:216. RPJCB; Leyden:B. Thysiana.   628/58

Hernández, Francisco. Rerum medicarum Novae Hispaniae thesaurus, seu Plantarum, animalium, mineralium Mexicanorum historia, ex . . . relationibus . . . conscriptis à Nardo Antonio Reccho. *Rome: G. Mascardi,* 1628. 950 p.; illus.; fol. Sabin 31515; cf. Pritzel 4000; Nissen (Bot.) 861; Nissen (Zool.) 1908; Palau 113534. DNLM; BL, Rome:Accad. Lincei.   628/59

Heurne, Justus van. De vocatione ethnicorum et Judaeorum ultima ad fidem christianam: admonitio. *Leyden: B. & A. Elsevier,* 1628. 300 p.; 8vo. 1st publ., Leyden, 1618, under title *De legatione evangelica,* etc.; here a reissue with cancel t.p. Cf. Sabin 31623; Willems (Les Elzevier) 296; Rahir (Les Elzevier) 115. NjP, PU.   628/60

Hieron, Samuel. Workes. *London: W. Stansby,* 1628–35. 2 v.; fol. Included in v. 1 is Hieron's *An answer to a popish rime,* 1st publ., London, 1604. STC 13382. ICU; Oxford: Bodl.   628/61

Horst, Gregor. Observationum medicinalium libri iv. priores . . . Editio nova. Cui auctuarium pharmaceuticar. recens additum. *Ulm: J. Saur,* 1628. 2 pts; 4to. 1st publ., Ulm, 1625. Wellcome I:3312. DNLM, MBCo, NIC; BL.   628/62

Jesuits. Letters from missions. Histoire de ce qui s'est passé en Ethiopie, Malabar, Brazil, et es Indes Orientales . . . Traduit de l'italien. *Paris: S. Cramoisy,* 1628. 451 p.; 8vo. Transl. by Jean Darde from the Rome, 1627, *Lettere annue d'Etiopia, Malabar, Brasil, e Goa.* Sabin 32008 (& 18538 & 40562); Borba de Moraes I:340; Streit II:2393; Backer II:1824; JCB (3) II:216. CU, DLC, ICN, NN-RB, RPJCB; BL.   628/63

Kort verhael van de exploicten door den manhaften held Pieter Pietersz Heyn als admirael . . . van de . . . West Indische Compagnie . . . in Brasil, in de baey, ende ontrent de stadt S. Salvador, geluckigh uytgevoert. *Amsterdam: H. Gerritsz.,* 1628. 2 lvs; illus.; fol. Sabin 76214.   628/64

La Brosse, Guy de. De la nature, vertu, et utilité des plantes. *Paris: R. Baragnes,* 1628. 849 p.; 8vo. In bk 5, chapt. i comprises a discussion of West Indian plants unknown to early physicians. Pritzel 1184. DNAL, MiU, MnU-B, NNNAM; BL, BN.
                                                      628/65

Levett, Christopher. A voyage into New England begun in 1623 and ended in 1624. *London: W. Jones; sold by E. Brewster,* 1628. 38 p.; 4to. 1st publ., London, 1624. Sabin 40751; Vail (Frontier) 71; STC 15554; JCB (3) II:216–17. CSmH, NHi, PP, RPJCB; BL.
                                                      628/66

Liddel, Duncan. Ars medica. *Hamburg: Froben Bookshop (P. Lang),* 1628. 2 pts; 8vo. 1st

publ., Hamburg, 1608. Wellcome I:3797. DNLM, NNNAM; BL, BN.   628/67

López de León, Pedro. Practica y teorica de las apostemas . . . Primera parte. *Seville: L. Estupiñán,* 1628. 372 numb. lvs; 4to. The author was a surgeon at Cartagena in New Granada, i.e., Colombia. Medina (BHA) 840; Escudero (Seville) 1.395; Palau 141306. DNLM, InU-L; BL, Madrid:Fac. de Med.   628/68

Marlowe, Christopher. The tragicall historie of the life and death of Doctor Faustus. *London: J. Wright,* 1628. [62] p.; 4to. Drama. 1st publ., London, 1604. STC 17435.5; Greg 205 (h). Oxford:Lincoln, Stockholm:KB   628/69

Matthieu, Pierre. Dell'historia di S. Luigi IX re di Francia . . . Tradotta di francese . . . dal signor Gio: Battista Parchi. *Venice: F. Baba,* 1628. 308 p.; 4to. Transl. from Matthieu's *Histoire de sainct Louys,* 1st publ., Paris, 1618. Michel (Répertoire) V:151. NNC; Montpellier:BM.   628/70

Medina, Pedro de. L'art de naviguer . . . traduit . . . par Nicolas de Nicolai . . . nouvellement reveu . . . par Jean de Séville, dit Le Souci. *Rouen: M. de Préaulx,* 1628. 227 (i.e., 263) p.; illus.; 4to. 1st publ. as here transl., Lyons, 1553; cf. 1607, Rouen, edn. Palau 159677. ICJ, ICN, InU-L; BL, BN.   628/71

Mercator, Gerardus. Atlas minor . . . à J. Hondio . . . illustratus: denuo recognit, additisque novis delineationibus emendatus. *Amsterdam: J. Janszoon, the Younger,* 1628. 655 p.; maps; obl. 12mo. A new rev. edn; cf. Amsterdam, 1607 edn. Sabin 47887n; Koeman (Me) 194; Phillips (Atlases) 437. DLC, IU, MiU-C, NjP; BL, BN.   628/72

——. Atlas minor, ofte Een korte doch grondige beschrijvinge der geheeler werelt. *Amsterdam: 1628. See the year 1630.*

——. Atlas sive Cosmographicae meditationes de fabrica mundi et fabricati figura . . . Editio decima. *Amsterdam: H. Hondius,* 1628. 712 p.; maps; fol. Though with Latin t.p., the text is in French; cf. years 1607 & 1609. Sabin 47882; Koeman (Me) 28A(cf. 28B); Phillips (Atlases) 438; CtY, DLC, MnU-B, NN-RB; BL, Zurich:ZB.   628/73

Moerbeeck, Jan Andries. Vereenighde Nederlandschen raedt, het eerste deel. *The*

Hague: A. Meuris, 1628. 40 p.; 4to. Relates to West Indian & Brazilian commerce. Cf. the 'tweede deel' below. Sabin 98961; Rodrigues (Dom. Hol.) 314; Knuttel 3797. DLC, MnU-B, NN-RB; BL, BN.

628/74

—[Anr edn]. Den tweeden druck gecorrigeert ende vermeerdert. *The Hague: A. Meuris*, 1628. 40 p.; 4to. Sabin 98961; Knuttel 3798. The Hague:KB.   628/75

—[Anr edn]. Den derden druck. *The Hague: A. Meuris*, 1628. 40 p.; 4to. Sabin 98961; Knuttel 3799. The Hague:KB   628/76

—[Anr edn]. Den vierden druck. *The Hague: A. Meuris*, 1628. 40 p.; 4to. Sabin 98961; Asher 127.   628/77

——. Vereenighde Nederlandschen raedt, het tweede deel. *The Hague: A. Meuris,* 1628. 60 p.; 4to. In opposing truce with Spain, refers to commerce with West Indies & Brazil. Cf. the 'eerste deel' above. Sabin 98962; Knuttel 3801. NN-RB; BN, The Hague:KB.

628/78

Molina, Cristóbal de. Señor. Christoval de Molina, regidor de la ciudad de Mexico . . . Dize, que como es notorio quedaron en aquellas provincias . . . muchos millones de Indios, de los quales de treinta partes faltan aora mas de veinte y nueve. [*Madrid:* 1628]. 9 numb. lvs; fol. Memorial to king of Spain, subscribed at Madrid, 4 April 1628. Medina (BHA) 841. Seville:Archivo de Indias.   628/79

——. Señor. Cristoval de Molina regidor de la ciudad . . . de Mexico. [*Madrid:* 1628]. [8] p.; fol. Memorial to king of Spain regarding treatment of native Indians; subscribed at Madrid, 28 June 1628. Medina (BHA) 842; Maggs Cat. 496 (Americana VI):218c. BL, Seville:Archivo de Indias.

628/80

Monet, Philibert, S.J. Nouveau et dernier dictionaire des langues françoise et latine. *Paris:* 1628. 4to. Presumably includes, as do later edns, entries for 'Amerique, Brasil, Bresil, terre decouverte par Americ Vespuce', 'Americain', 'Peru', 'Perüans', 'Tabac . . . herbe medicinale', etc. Also publ. under title *Invantaire des deus langues*, q.v. under the year 1635. Goujet (Bibl. franç.) II:434; Brunet III:1824; Graesse IV:575

628/81

Morel, Pierre. Systema parascevasticum ad praxin, materiae medicae sylvam complectans. *Geneva: J. Chouët,* 1628. 323 p.; 12mo. Included as therapeutic agents are guaiacum, mechoacan, & tobacco (*Nicotiana*). Subsequent edns appear in Morel's *Formulae remediorum*. DNLM; BL.   628/82

Morovelli de la Puebla, Francisco. Don Francisco Morovelli de Puebla defiende el patronato de Santa Teresa de Jesús. *Malagá: J. René,* 1628. 34 numb. lvs; 4to. Ascribes to Saint Teresa Spanish success over Dutch in seizing Bahia, Brazil. Palau 183226.

628/83

Münster, Sebastian. Cosmographia. das ist: Beschreibung der gantzen Welt. *Basel: Henricpetri Office,* 1628. 1752 p.; port., maps; fol. 1st publ., Basel 1544. Sabin 51396; Burmeister (Münster) 86. CtY, DLC, ICN, MB, NN-RB, PPLT; BL, BN.   628/84

Nájera, Antonio de. Navegacion especulativa, y pratica, reformadas sus reglas, y tablas por las observaciones de Ticho Brahe. *Lisbon: P. Craesbeeck,* 1628. 149 numb. lvs; illus.; 4to. Medina (BHA) 843; Palau 187291; Maggs Cat. 479 (Americana V):4189. BL, BN.   628/85

Netherlands (United Provinces, 1581–1795). Staten Generaal. Placcaet ende ordonnantie op de wapeninge ende manninghe vande schepen. *The Hague: Widow & Heirs of H. Jacobszoon van Wouw,* 1628. [20] p.; 4to. 1st publ., The Hague, 1607. JCB (3) II:217. RPJCB.   628/86

Nichols, Philip. Sir Francis Drake revived: calling upon this dull or effeminate age to folowe his noble steps. *London: [W. Stansby,] for N. Bourne,* 1628. 80 p.; 4to. 1st publ., London, 1626. Sabin 20838; STC 18545; JCB (3) II:213. CSmH, CtY, DLC, MH, NN-RB, RPJCB; BL.   628/87

Olmo, ——. Por el licenciado Don Sebastian Zambrana de Villalobos, oydor de la real audiencia de las Charcas. Con el señor fiscal. Sobre el atentado, y restitucion de la plaça de oydor de la dicha audiencia. [*Madrid?* 1628?]. 5 numb. lvs; fol. Medina (BHA) 8280; JCB (3) II:219. RPJCB.

628/88

Opitz, Martin. Deutscher Poematum erster [-anderer] Theil. *Breslau: D. Müller,* 1628–29. 2 v.; 8vo. 1st publ., Strassburg, 1624, under title *Teutsche Poemata*, but here including in pt 2 (1629) Opitz's 'Lob des Krieges Gottes', 1st publ. separately below. Cf. 1629 edn. Cf. Goedeke III:45; cf. Faber du Faur 213; Jantz (German Baroque) 1912. NcD; BL.   628/89

——. Laudes Martis . . . Poema Germanicum. *Brieg: A. Gründer, for D. Müller, at Breslau*, 1628. 48 p.; 4to. In verse. Includes 25-line section referring to Columbus, Cuba, Guiana, Mexico, the Orinoco, etc. Reprinted in succeeding edns of Opitz's collected poems under title 'Lob des Krieges Gottes'. Goedeke III:44; Jantz (German Baroque) 1917; Faber du Faur 212. CU, CtY, NcD; BL, Göttingen:StUB.   628/90

Ordóñez de Ceballos, Pedro. Tratado de los relaciones verdaderas de los reynos de la China, Cochinchina, y Champa, y otras cosas notables, y varios sucessos. *Jaen: P. de la Cuesta*, 1628. 52 numb. 1vs; port.; 4to. The author was 'chantre de la santa iglesia de la ciudad de Guamanga en el Piru'; describes voyage from Acapulco, Mexico, to the Orient. Sabin 57523; Medina (BHA) 844; Streit V:1624. MB, NIC, NN-RB; BL, BN.   628/91

Overbury, Sir Thomas. Sir Thomas Overburie his wife . . . The thirteen impression. *London: J. L[egat]., for R. Allott*, 1628. [320] p.; 8vo. 1st publ., London, 1615. STC 18916; Murphy (Engl. char.-bks) 23. CSmH, CtY, DFo, ICU, MH, PPL; BL.   628/92

Ovidius Naso, Publius. Metamorphoses. English. Ovid's Metamorphosis Englished by G[eorge]. S[andys]. *London: R. Young; sold by J. Grismond*, 1628. 445 p.; 12mo. 1st publ., London, 1626; here an unauthorized reprint. Sabin 76457; STC 18965. CSmH, DFo, ICU, MH, NN-RB; BL.   628/93

Owen, John. Certaine epigrams. *London:* 1628. *In* Hayman, Robert, *Quodlibets*, q.v. *above.*

——. Epigrammatum . . . editio postrema. *Leyden: Elsevier Office*, 1628. 280 p.; 24mo. 1st publ., London, 1606. According to Rahir there exist separate edns of this work, not differentiated by Willems. In what Rahir believed the earlier, 'Ad lectorem' on p. 3 is in roman rather than italic type. Shaaber

(Brit. auth.) O89–90; Willems (Les Elzevier) 299; Rahir (Les Elzevier) 267–69. DFo, ICU, MH, PU; BL, Stockholm:KB.   628/94

Paré, Ambroise. Les oeuvres . . . Reveuës . . . en ceste huictiesme edition. *Paris: N. Buon*, 1628. 1320 p.; illus., ports; fol. 1st publ., Paris, 1575; cf. the 1601 German edn. Doe (Paré) 37. CtY-M, DNLM, MiU; Cambridge:UL, BN.   628/95

Pharmacopoea sive Dispensatorium Coloniense. *Cologne: Birckmann Office, for H. Mylius* [1628]. 103 p.; illus.; fol. The catalogue of useful ingredients includes mechoacan, sarsaparilla, tobacco (*Nicotiana*), guaiacum, & the Peruvian (occidental) bezoar stone. Wellcome I:4982. DNLM, IU; BL.   628/96

Pigray, Pierre. Epitome des preceptes de medecine et chirurgie. *Lyons: J. A. Candy*, 1628. 764 p.; port.; 8vo. 1st publ., Paris, 1600, under title *La chirurgie*; cf. 1604 edn. CtY-M, DNLM.   628/97

Porreño, Baltasar. Dichos y hechos del señor Rey Don Felipe Segundo. *Cuenca: S. de Viader*, 1628. 192 numb. 1vs; 8vo. 1st publ., Cuenca, 1621. Sabin 64171; Palau 233065. BL.   628/98

Puteo, Zacharias. Historia de gumma indica, anteasthmatica, antehydropica, et antepodagrica. *Venice: G. de Imbertis*, 1628. [40] p.; 4to. The gum in question is described as being Peruvian in origin; also mentioned is mechoacan. MH-A; BL, BN.   628/99

Raleigh, Sir Walter. The historie of the world. *London: [H. Lownes,] for H. Lownes, G. Latham & R. Young*, 1628. 2 v.; maps, port.; fol. 1st publ., London, 1614. Sabin 67560n; Brushfield (Raleigh) 223 (E); STC 20640. CSmH, DFo, ICN, MH, NjP; BL.   628/100

——. The prerogative of parlaments [*sic*]. *'Hamburgh'* [i.e., *London: T. Cotes*] 1628. 65 p.; 4to. Includes statement that potential revenues from monasteries suppressed by Henry VIII would have exceeded those of Spain from both Indies. Line 17 on 1f D3v ends 'is'. Sabin 67599n; STC 20649. CSmH, CtY, DFo, IU, MH; BL.   628/101

—[Anr issue]. The prerogative of parliaments. *'Midelburge'* [i.e., *London: T. Cotes*]

1628. The t.p. of the preceding is here re-set. Sabin 67599n; STC 20649.1. CLL, DFo, MH; Oxford:Bodl.   628/102

—[Anr edn]. *'Midelburge''* [i.e., *London: T. Cotes*] 1628. 65 p.; 4to. Line 17 on 1f D3v ends *'more';* on D1r line 6 from bottom has reading 'seized'. STC 20649.3. CU, DLC, IU, NN-RB; BL.   268/103

—[Anr edn]. *'Midelburge'* [i.e., *London: T. Cotes*] 1628. 65 p.; 4to. The preceding, but with p. 9–48 reset. On D1r line 6 from bottom has reading 'seised'. STC 20649.5. CSmH, ICN, MH, MdBP, NNC; BL.   628/104

—[Anr edn]. *'Midelburge'* [i.e., *London: T. Cotes?*] 1628. 65 p.; 4to. Line 17 on 1f D3v ends 'more'. STC 20649.7 (formerly 20648). CSmH, CtY, DLC, ICN, MH, NN-RB, RPJCB; BL.   628/105

Relation véritable de huict navires venus des Indes Orientales & Occidentales. *Paris: J. Martin,* 1628. 14 p.; 8vo. Describes cargoes brought from the East & West Indies. CSmH, NN.   628/106

—[Anr edn]. *Lyons: C. Armand,* 1628. MnU-B.
628/107

Richeome, Louis, S. J. Les oeuvres . . . Re-veuës par l'autheur avant sa mort. *Paris: S. Cramoisy,* 1628. 2 v.; fol. In v. 1, p. 1–140 contain Richeome's *Trois discours pour la religion catholique,* 1st publ., Bordeaux, 1597; cf. 1601 edn above. Backer VI:1818 & 1830–31; Cioranescu (XVII) 59486.
628/108

Rivadeneira, Pedro de, S. J. Vies des saints Ignace Xavier et autres bienheureux pères de la Compagnie de Jesus. *Rouen:* 1628. 8vo. Cf. 1615 edn. Backer VI:1756; Palau 266255.   628/109

Roca, Balthasar Juan. Histoire veritable de la vie & miracles du b.p. S. Luis Bertran. *Tournai: A. Quinqué,* 1628. 536 p.; 8vo. Transl. by Jean d'Oye from the author's *Historia verdadera . . . del . . . padre S. Luys Bertran,* Valencia, 1608. Streit II:1573; Palau 271342.   628/110

Rocaberti, Diego de. Epitome historico en diez romances. Contiene las cosas mas notables acaecidas en el mundo . . . hasta . . . 1625. *Barcelona: S. de Cormellas,* 1628. 111 p.; 8vo. In verse. 1st publ., Majorca, 1626. Palau 271631. BL.   628/111

Rondelet, Guillaume. Opera omnia medica. [*Montpellier:*] *P. & J. Chouët,* 1628. 1359 p.; 8vo. 1st publ., [Paris? 1563?], under title *Methodus curandorum omnium morborum corporis humani;* cf. 1601 edn. DNLM, PPL, WU (imp.); BL.   628/112

Rosenberg, Johann Karl. Rhodologia, seu Philosophico-medica generosae rosae descriptio. *Strassburg: M. von der Heyden,* 1628. 316 p.; 8vo. In pt 2, chapt. vi, identification of marigold as form of rose is refuted; American roses are mentioned. Pritzel 7768. MH, MoSB, WU; BN.   628/113

Ruiz de Alarcón y Mendoza, Juan. Parte primera de las comedias. *Madrid: J. González,* 1628. 179 numb. lvs; 4to. Included is 'El semejante a si mismo' in which figure characters about to depart for Peru. Also mentioned is Luis de Velasco, marqués de Salinas, who had returned to Spain 'despues de tres virreinatos' in Mexico. Palau 281540. Madrid:BN.   628/114

Ruland, Martin (1532–1602). Curationum empiricarum et historicarum . . . centuriae decem. *Lyons: P. Ravaud,* 1628. 2 pts; 8vo. Here brought together are 'centuries' earlier publ. individually, Basel, 1580, *et seq.,* of which some appear to have been re-printed ca. 1610, but are not here entered in the absence of precise information. Included are numerous formulas employing guaiacum & sarsaparilla. DNLM; BL, BN.
628/115

—[Anr edn]. Thesaurus Rulandinus . . . Curationes empiricae. *Basel: Henricpetri Office,* 1628, '27. 2 pts; 8vo. Wellcome I:5639. CtY-M; BL.   628/116

Schrijver, Pieter. Saturnalia, seu De usu et abusu tabaci. *Haarlem:* 1628. 8vo. In verse. Waring II:709; cf. Arents 172.   628/117

Scribanius, Carolus. Discours d'estat: auquel sont proposez plusieurs maximes pour mettre fin aux guerres du Pays bas. *Brussels: J. Bernard & J. Pierre,* 1628. 86 p.; 8vo. Transl. from the author's *Veridicus Belgicus,* 1st publ., [Antwerp, 1624]. BL.
628/118

——. Weit und tieffsinnig Bedencken, auff das nach jetz wehrende Kriegswesen in Niderland . . . in latinischer Sprach erstlich eingestellt. Jetzo . . . ubergesetz. [*Augs-*

burg?] 1628. [84] p.; 4to. Transl. from the author's *Veridicus Belgicus*, 1st publ., [Antwerp, 1624]. Knuttel 3807; Meulman 2039; cf. Kleerkooper 878. The Hague:KB (imp.), Ghent:BU.   628/119

Sennert, Daniel. Institutionum medicinae . . . tertia editio. Libri v. *Wittenberg: [Heirs of S. Auerbach, for] Heirs of Z. Schürer, the Elder,* [1628]. 1518 p.; illus., port.; 4to. 1st publ, Wittenberg, 1611. Wellcome I:5923. DNLM, NNNAM; London:Wellcome.
                    628/120

Settala, Lodovico. Animadversionum et cautionum medicarum libri septem. *Padua: G. Tuilio, for P. Frambotti,* 1628. 2 pts; 8vo. 1st publ., Milan, 1622. Wellcome I:5949. DNLM, MnU, PCarlD; BL, BN.
                    628/121

Smith, Capt. John. Vierzehende Schiffart, oder Gründliche und warhaffte Beschreibung dess Newen Engellands. *Frankfurt a. M.: Heirs of L. Hulsius,* 1628. 62 p.; illus., map; 4to. (Levinus Hulsius's *Sammlung von . . . Schiffahrten.* Pt 14). 1st publ. in this version, Frankfurt a. M., 1617; transl. from Smith's *Description of New England,* 1st publ., London, 1616. Sabin 33667; Baginsky (German Americana) 159; Church 305; JCB (3) I:464. MH, NN-RB, RPJCB; BL.
                    628/122

Spain. Laws, statutes, etc. Sumarios de la recopilacion general de las leyes, ordenanças, provisiones, cedulas, instrucciones, y cartas accordadas, que por los Reyes catolicos de Castilla se han promulgado . . . para las Indias Occidentales, islas, y tierra firme del mar Occeano: desde el año, de mil y quatrocientos y noventa y dos . . . hasta . . . mil y seiscientos y veinto y ocho. *Madrid: J. González,* 1628. 385 numb. 1vs; fol. Sabin 525; Medina (BHA) 832; Streit I:439; JCB (3) II:212. RPJCB.   628/123

Spinola, Fabio Ambrosio, S.J. Vita del p. Carlo Spinola della Compagnia di Giesu, morto per la santa fede nel Giappone. *Rome: F. Corbelletti,* 1628. 223 p.; 8vo. Includes account of Spinola's missionary work in Brazil & Spanish America. Sabin 89458; Streit V:1407; Backer VII:1448. MH; BL.
                    628/124

Stigliani, Tomaso. Il mondo nuovo. *Rome:*

G. Mascardi, 1628. 1011 p.; 12mo. 1st publ., Piacenza, 1617. Sabin 91729; Arents (Add.) 243; JCB (3) II:218. CSmH, MH, NN-A, RPJCB; BL.   628/125

Tamayo de Vargas, Tomás. Restauracion de la ciudad del Salvador, y baìa de Todos-Sanctos, en la provincia del Brasil. *Madrid: Widow of A. Martín,* 1628. 178 numb. 1vs; 4to. Sabin 94280; Medina (BHA) 850; Borba de Moraes II:291–92; Palau 327113; JCB (3) II:218. DLC, ICN, InU-L, MH, NN-RB, RPJCB; BL, Amsterdam:NHSM, Madrid:BN.   628/126

Tassoni, Alessandro. Dieci libri di pensieri diversi. *Milan: G. B. Bidelli,* 1628. 630 p.; 8vo. 1st publ., Modena, 1612, under title *Varieta di pensieri diversi,* but see also enl. 1620 edn. Puliatti (Tassoni) 6. CU, NcU, PP; Madrid:BN, Zurich:ZB.   628/127

Taylor, John, the Water-poet. Wit and mirth. *London: [A. Mathewes,] for H. Gosson; sold by [E. Wright]* 1628. [80] p.; 8vo. 1st publ., London, 1626. STC 23813.5. MH.
                    628/128

Theatrum florae, in quo ex toto orbe selecti mirabiles . . . flores . . . proferuntur. *Paris: P. Firens,* 1628. 69 pls; illus.; fol. 1st publ., Paris, 1622. Cf. Pritzel 10855; cf. Nissen (Bot.) 1575. DNAL.   628/129

Tijdinge hoe dat den . . . Generael Pieter Pietersz. Heyn, ende den Vice-Admirael Loncq, de vlote van Nova-Spaengien inde Bahia Matanse hebben aenghetast, verovert ende verdestrueert, den 8. Septemb. 1628. *Amsterdam: J. F. Stam, for J. van Hilten,* 1628. bds.; fol. Knuttel 3796. The Hague:KB.
                    628/130

Tijdinghe hoe dat den heer commandeur Pieter Adriaensz. van Vlissinghen in't ghesichte van d'Havana de Hondurische vlote heeft verovert, aen strandt ghejaeght ende verbrandt, den eersten Augusti lestleden. *Amsterdam: Widow of J. Veselaer, for J. van Hilten,* 1628. bds.; 4to. Sabin 95815. NN-RB.
                    628/131

Torsellino, Orazio, S.J. Epitomae historiarum libri x . . . Editio tertia. *Lyons: J. Cardon,* 1628. 606 p.; 12mo. 1st publ., Rome, 1598; cf. 1620 edn. BN.   628/132

Velázquez Minaya, Francisco. Esfera, forma del mundo, con una breve descripcion del mapa. *Madrid: Widow of L. Sánchez,* 1628. 260 numb. 1vs; illus.; 8vo. Chapt. 8 (1vs 159–260) comprises a gazetteer of the Americas. Sabin 49191; Medina (BHA) 851; JCB (3) II:218. ICN, MH, NN-RB, RPJCB; BN. 628/133

Venner, Tobias. Via recta ad vitam longam, or A plaine philosophical discourse of such things as make for health. *London: F. Kingston, for R. More,* 1628. 2 pts; 4to. 1st publ., London, 1620. STC 24645. CSmH, CtY, DFo, ICN, MH; Oxford:Bodl. 628/134

Vera, e nuova relatione. d'un grandissimo mostro apparso nella città di Quito in India . . . 1628. Tradotta dalla lingua spaguola in italiana. *Florence: S. Fantucci* [1628?]. [8] p.; illus.; 8vo. The original Spanish text has not been identified. RPJCB. 628/135

Victoria, Pedro Gobeo de. Wunderbarliche und seltzame Raiss . . . in das Königreich Peru. *Ingolstadt: G. Hänlin,* 1628. 8vo. 1st publ. in German, Ingolstadt, 1622. Sabin 99446; Navarrete II:561; Palmer 405. 628/136

Wassenaer, Nicolaes van. Het dertiende ghedeelt of 't vervolch van het Historisch verhael aller gedenckwaerdiger geschiedeniss., die in Europa . . . in America, als West-Indien, Brasil en Peru . . . voorgevallen syn. *Amsterdam: J. Janszoon, the Younger,* 1628. 110 numb. 1vs; illus.; 4to. (N. van Wassenaer's *Historisch verhael.* Pt 13). Includes refs to Pieter Hein & Brazil. Cf. Sabin 102039; Borba de Moraes II:371; Muller (1872) 1745. RPJCB. 628/137

————. Het veertiende deel of 't vervolgh van het Historisch verhael aller gedenckwaerdiger geschiedeniss. die in Europa . . . In America, als West-Indien, d'eijlanden en Brasil . . . voorgevallen zijn. *Amsterdam: J. Janszoon, the Younger,* [1628]. 106 numb. 1vs; illus.; 4to. (N. van Wassenaer's *Historisch verhael.* Pt 14). Includes refs to Pieter Hein, Bahia, Brazil, & the Spanish silver fleet. Cf. Sabin 102039; Borba de Moraes II:371; Muller (1872) 1745. RPJCB. 628/138

Weickard, Arnold. Pharmacia domestica, dass ist: Hauss Apoteck. *Frankfurt a. M.: E. Kempfer, for J. T. Schönwetter,* 1628. 904 p.; 4to. Included is a formula for 'Tabac pulver'. Wellcome I:6728. BL. 628/139

Willemssz, Salomon. Rapport gedaen aen hare Ho. Mo. ende Sijn Excell. . . . over 't ver-overen vande silver-vlote, komende van nova Hispania, door 't beleyt van den Heer General Pieter Pieterssz Heyn. *The Hague: Widow & Heirs of H. Jacobszoon van Wouw,* 1628. [2] p.; 4to. Sabin 104134; Muller (1872) 955; Petit 1541; JCB (3) II:219. DLC, NN-RB, RPJCB; Amsterdam:NHSM, Leyden:UB. 628/140

————[Anr edn]. Rapport aen hare Ho. Mo. *The Hague: Widow & Heirs of H. Jacobszoon van Wouw,* 1628. [2] p.; 4to. Petit 1540. Leyden:B. Thysiana. 628/141

Wtenbogaert, Johannes. Ondersoeck der Amsterdamsche requesten tot verdedigingh der onschuldighe. [*Amsterdam? Rotterdam?*] 1628. 36 p.; 4to. A reply to the Amsterdam citizens' *Copie van requesten* of this year above. Provides insight into leading parties of Amsterdam, who played an important part in the development of the West-Indische Compagnie—Sabin. Sabin 57320 (& 102889); Asher 112. DLC; BL (Amsterdam). 628/142

1629

Aldrovandi, Ulisse. De piscibus libri v. et de cetis liber i. *Frankfurt a. M.: M. Kempffer, for J. Treudel,* 1629. 280 p.; illus.; fol. 1st publ., Bologna, 1612; cf. 1623 edn of which this is prob. a reissue. Nissen (Zool.) 71n. OC1W, RPB; BL, Berlin:StB. 629/1

Alemán, Mateo. Vita del picaro Gusmano d'Alfarache . . . tradotta . . . da Barezzo Barezzi. *Venice: The Barezzi,* 1629. 2 v.; 8vo. 1st publ. in translation of both pts, Venice, 1615. Laurenti (Nov. pic. esp.) 715; Palau 6780. Naples:BN, Vienna:NB. 629/2

Alpini, Prosper. De plantis exoticis libri duo. *Venice: G. Guerigli,* 1629. 344 p.; illus.; 4to. 1st publ., Venice, 1627; here a reissue of that edn with altered imprint date. Nissen (Bot.) 21n; Hunt (Bot.) 213. DNLM, MH-A, MoSB, PPL; BL. 629/3

Ampzing, Samuel. West-Indische triumph-basuyne, tot Godes ere, ende roem der Batavieren gesteken, van wegen de veroveringe der Spaensche silver-vlote van Nova

Hispania, inde Baij van Matanca . . . onder het beleyd van . . . Pieter Pieterszoon Heyn . . . ende . . . Lonck. *Haarlem: A. Roman,* 1629. 44 p.; ports; 4to. For a reply, see the *Reed-geld over betalinghe* under the year 1630. Sabin 1350; Knuttel 3859. DLC, LNHT, NN-RB; BL, BN. 629/4

Antwoordt, op sekeren brief Evlaly, vervatende de redenen waerom datmen met den vyandt in geen conferentie behoort te treden. [*Amsterdam?*] 1629. [16] p.; 4to. Includes refs to West Indian commerce and to Hein's capture of the Spanish silver fleet. Sabin 23103; Asher 126; Muller (1872) 413; Knuttel 3915. DLC, RPJCB; BL, The Hague:KB. 629/5

—[Anr edn]. Antwoordt . . . in gheen conferentie. [*Amsterdam?*] 1629. [16] p.; 4to. Sabin 23104; Knuttel 3916. DLC, ICU, MnU-B, NN-RB, PHi: The Hague:KB. 629/6

—[Anr edn]. Antwoordt op sekeren brieff Evlalii . . . [*Amsterdam?*] 1629. [16] p.; 4to. Sabin 23105. 629/7

Avellaneda Manrique, Juan de. Memorial de la culpa que resulta de la pesquisa hecha con comission de su Magestad, por el señor licenciado Don Geronimo de Avellaneda Manrique . . . contra el Don Juan de Benavides Baçan, y su Almirante don Juan de Leon [i.e., Leoz], otros consortes. Sobre la perdida de la flota, que el año passado de 1628 venia á estos reynos de la provincia de Nueva España, á cargo del dicho General, y la robó el enemigo Olandes en el puerto y baía de Matánças, apoderandose de su tesoro. [*Madrid?* 1629?]. 336 numb. 1vs; fol. Medina (BHA) 8070. Puebla: B. Palafoxiana. 629/8

Bacon, Francis, viscount St Albans. Certaine miscellany works . . . published by William Rawley. *London: J. Haviland, for H. Robinson,* 1629. 166 p.; 4to. Incudes Bacon's *Considerations touchinge a warre with Spaine* also published separately this year in a surreptitious edn, q.v. Gibson (Bacon) 191; STC 1124. CSmH, CtY, DLC, ICN, MH, NNPM; BL, BN. 629/9

——. Considerations touching a warre with Spaine. [*London:*] 1629. 46 p.; 4to. Includes descriptions of exploits of Sir Francis Drake & others against Spanish in Caribbean. A surreptitious edn; also publ. this year in Bacon's *Certaine miscellany works.* Gibson (Bacon) 187; STC 1126. CSmH, CtY, DLC, ICN, MH, NN-RB, RPJCB; BL. 629/10

——. The essayes or Counsels civill and morall. *London: J. Haviland; sold by R. Allott,* 1629. 340 p.; 4to. 1st publ. as here enl., London, 1625. Gibson (Bacon) 15; STC 1149; Pforzheimer 31. CSmH, CtY, DFo, ICN, MH, MiU, NNPM, PBm; BL, BN. 629/11

——. The historie of the raigne of King Henry the seventh. *London: J. H[aviland]. & R. Y[oung].; sold by P. Stephens & C. Meredith,* 1629. 248 p.; fol. 1st publ., London, 1622; here a reissue, with cancel t.p., of bookseller's 1628 edn. Gibson (Bacon) 118; STC 1161. CSmH, CtY, DLC, IU, MH, MnU-B, NjP; BL, BN. 629/12

——. Sylva sylvarum: or, A naturall historie . . . The second edition. *London: J. H[aviland], for W. Lee,* 1628 [i.e., 1629]. 2 pts; port.; fol. 1st publ., London, 1627. The added engr. t.p. is here dated 1629. Includes also Bacon's *New Atlantis,* 1st publ., London, 1627. Gibson (Bacon) 172; STC 1170. CSmH, CtY, DLC, ICN, MH, NjP, PU; BL. 629/13

——. The two bookes . . . of the proficience and advancement of learning. *London: [N. Okes,] for W. Washington,* 1629. 335 p.; 4to. 1st publ., London, 1605. Gibson (Bacon) 82; STC 1165. CSmH, CtY, DLC, ICU, MH, NN; BL, BN. 629/14

Baerle, Kaspar van. Argo Batava, inscripta virtuti ac fortunae fortissimi . . . herois Petri Heinii, classis quae, sub ductu et moderamine Societatis Indicae . . . ad Occidentem militat, praefecti. *Leyden: G. Basson,* 1629. 16 p.; 4to. In verse. Cf. Sabin 3407n; Dt. Ges. Kat. 11.6546. BN, Frankfurt a. M.:StUB. 629/15

Barclay, John. Satyricon. *Amsterdam: W. J. Blaeu,* 1629. 580 p.; 12mo. Includes pt 2, 1st publ., Paris, 1507, & the *Icon animorum,* 1st publ., London, 1614. Shaaber (Brit. auth.) B197; Tchémerzine I:452. DFo, MH, PBL, RPB; BL, BN. 629/16

Baudous, Wilhelmus de. Lof-dicht van alle de voornaemste exployten, ghedaen onder het bewint van de Gheoctroyeerde Westindische Compagnie, door het cloek beleyt van den . . . Generael Pieter Pietersz Heyn, beginnende vanden Jar 1624. 1625. 1626. ende 1628. *Dordrecht: F. Bosselaer,* 1629. 16 p.; 4to. Sabin 31659 (& 3978a); Muller (1872) 943; Asher 120. BL. 629/17

Baumann, Johann Nicolaus. Dissertatio inauguralis de tabaci virtutibus, usu et abusu. *Basel: J. J. Genath,* 1629. 31 p.; 4to. Includes description of American sources. DNLM, MH; BL. 629/18

Beaumont, Simon van (1574–1654). Rapport ghedaen by d'heer van Beaumont, ghedeputeerde der vergaderinghe vande . . . Staten van Zeelandt op den 17. October 1629. [*Middelburg? 1629?*]. [4] p.; fol. Relates to the West-Indische Compagnie. Knuttel 3913. The Hague:KB. 629/19

Bergeron, Pierre de. Traicté de la navigation et des voyages de descouverte & conqueste modernes, & principalement des François. *Paris: J. de Heuqueville & M. Soly,* 1629. 303 p.; 8vo. Issued as pt 2 of Pierre Bontier's *Histoire . . . des Canaries,* Paris, 1630, q.v.

Bertius, Petrus. Breviarium totius orbis terrarum. *Hanau: C. Schleich & P. de Zetter,* 1629. 76 p.; 12mo. 1st publ., Paris, 1624. Cf. Sabin 5013. DFo, NN-RB, RPJCB; BN. 629/20

Blaeu, Willem Janszoon. Het licht der zeevaert. *Amsterdam: J. Janszoon, the Younger,* 1629. 2 v.; illus., maps; obl. fol. 1st publ., Amsterdam, 1608. Koeman (M.Bl) 19 (J). Amsterdam:VBBB, Paris:Loeb-Laroque. 629/21

Boccalini, Traiano. De' ragguagli di Parnaso . . . Centuria prima . . . sesta impressione. *Venice: Heirs of G. Guerigli,* 1629. 332 p.; 8vo. 1st publ., Venice, 1612. Firpo (Ragguagli) 18; Michel (Répertoire) I:176. NIC, PPL; BN. 629/22

——. De' ragguagli di Parnaso . . . Centuria seconda . . . sesta impressione. *Venice: Heirs of G. Guerigli,* 1629. 292 p.; 8vo. 1st publ., Venice, 1613; issued with Guerigli's Centuria prima of this year above. Firpo (Ragguagli) 18; Michel (Répertoire) I:176. NIC, PPL; BN. 629/23

Bodin, Jean. Les six livres de la Republique. *Geneva: E. Gamonet,* 1629. 1060 p.; illus.; 8vo. 1st publ., Paris, 1576; cf. 1601 edn. CCC, ICJ, MH-L, NjP; BN. 629/24

A booke of cookerie, and the order of meates to be served to the table. *London: E. A[llde].; sold by F. Grove,* 1629. 102 p.; 8vo. 1st publ., London, 1620. CSmH. 629/25

Bonnart, Jean. La semaine des medicaments. *Paris: R. Baraignes,* 1629. 446 p.; 8vo. Amongst medicinal plants named are guaiacum & sarsaparilla. DNLM, MH, NNNAM; BL, BN. 629/26

Breton, Nicholas. Wits private wealth. *London: E. Allde, for F. Grove,* 1629. 4to. 1st publ., London, 1612. STC 3711. CSmH; Oxford:Bodl. 629/27

Calvisius, Seth. Opus chronologicum . . . Editio tertia. *Leipzig: F. Lanckisch, the Elder, for J. Thymiss, at Frankfurt a. d. O.,* 1629. 2 pts; 4to. 1st publ., Leipzig, 1605, under title *Chronologia.* CtY, IEN, MH, MnU, NNC. 629/28

Camden, William. Tomus alter et idem: or The historie of . . . Princesse Elizabeth. *London: T. Harper, & sold by W. Webb, at Oxford,* 1629. 384 p.; port.; 4to. Transl. by Thomas Browne from Latin text 1st publ., Leyden, 1625. Sabin 10158n; STC 4498. CSmH, CtY, DLC, ICU, MH, NN-RB; BL, BN. 629/29

Cargo de la culpa que resulta contra Juan de Reyna, alferez de la infanteria de la nao capitana, preso en la carcel real de . . . Cadiz. Sobre que aviendole dado orden el General don Juan de Benavides, el dia ocho de Setiembre . . . estando varadas en el puerto de Matanças la dicha capitama y demas naos de la flota, y el enemigo Olandes que las venia siguiendo . . . para que con la vandera real de su compañia, y otros soldados saltasse á tierra [etc.]. [*Madrid? 1629?*]. 18 lvs; fol. Medina (BHA) 8066. Puebla: B. Palafoxiana. 629/30

Caro de Torres, Francisco. Historia de las ordenes militares de Santiago, Calatrava, y Alcantara, desde su fundacion hasta el Rey Don Felipe Segundo. *Madrid: J. González,* 1629. 252 numb. lvs; fol. Includes numerous refs to Spanish America & Cortés. Sabin 10951; Palau 44869. CtY, DLC, NN-RB, OU, WU; BL, BN. 629/31

Carranza, Alonso. El ajustamiento i proporcion de las monedas de oro, plata, i cobre, i la reduccion destos metales a su debida estimacion. *Madrid: F. Martínez,* 1629. 387

p.; fol. Colmeiro 139; Kress 462; Palau 44950. CU, CtY, ICN, MH-BA, MnU-B, NN-RB, RPJCB; BL, BN.   629/32

Cats, Jacob. Proteus ofte Minne-beelden verandert in sinne-beelden. *The Hague: A. van der Venne & J. Ockerszoon,* 1629. 4 pts; illus.; 8vo. 1st publ., Middelburg, 1618, under title *Silenus Alcibiadis.* Vries 90; Mus. Cats. 43. Leyden:UB.   629/33

——. Silenus Alcibiadis, sive Proteus. [*Antwerp?*] 1629. [217] p.; illus.; obl. 12mo. 1st publ., Middelburg, 1618. Text in Dutch & French, the Latin parts being here omitted. Vries 83; Mus. Cats. 31. Leyden:UB.   629/34

Cervantes Saavedra, Miguel de. Novelle . . . Nuovamente transportate dalla lingua castigliana . . . da Donato Fontana milanese. *Milan: G. B. Canevese,* 1629. 591 p.; 8vo. A reissue of the Milan, 1627, edn as here transl. Palau 53549n. BL.   629/35

——. Il novelliere castigliano . . . Tradotto . . . dal sig. Guglielmo Alessandro de Novillieri, Clavelli. *Venice: The Barezzi,* 1629. 720 p.; 8vo. 1st publ. as here transl., Venice, 1626. Rius (Cervantes) 974; Palau 53548n; Michel (Répertoire) II:84. CU, DLC, ICN, MH, PU; Besançon:BM.   629/36

Clüver, Philipp. Introductionis in universam geographiam, tam veterem quàm novam, libri vi. *Leyden: Elsevier Office,* 1629. 252 (i.e., 352) p.; illus.; 16mo. 1st publ., Leyden, 1624. Cf. Sabin 13805; Willems (Les Elzevier) 309; Rahir (Les Elzevier) 278. CSmH, CtY, IaU, MH, PU, RPJCB; BL.   629/37

—[Anr edn]. *Amsterdam: J. Hondius,* 1629. 328 p.; illus.; 16mo. DLC, PU; BN.   629/38

Colonius, Daniel (1608–1672). Oratio panegyrica, de illustri victoria, quam amplissimi rerum Indiae Occidentalis administratores ductu . . . Petri Henrici . . . capta Hispanorum classe, retulerunt. *Leyden: A. Elsevier,* 1629. [23] p.; 4to. Willems (Les Elzevier) 310; Knuttel 3864. BL, The Hague:KB.   629/39

Cort verhael, hoe den edel. heer admirael Dirck Symonsz. voor de West-Indische compagnie den 30. October 1628. ontrent Farnabocque vijf schepen . . . heeft verovert ende verdestrueert. *Amsterdam: J. van Hilten,* 1629. bds.; fol. Muller (1872) 277. DLC.   629/40

Cortés, Jerónimo. Phisonomia. *Barcelona: L. Déu,* 1629. 107 numb. lvs; 8vo. 1st publ., Valencia, 1597; cf. 1601 edn. DNLM.   629/41

Cortesi, Giovanni Battista. Pharmacopoeia, seu Antidotarium messanense. *Messina: P. Brea,* 1629. 361 p.; ports; fol. Prescriptions described include use of guaiacum (cited as American), sarsaparilla, & sassafras. London:Wellcome, BN.   629/42

Discours, aengaende treves of vrede, met de infante ofte koning van Hispanien, ende dese Vereenighde Nederlanden. *Haarlem: A. Roman,* 1629. 40 p.; 4to. Includes refs to the West-Indische Compagnie. Knuttel 3919. CtY, MnU-B, NN-RB; BL (Spain), The Hague:KB.   629/43

Discours over den Nederlandtschen vredehandel. *Leeuwarden: D. Albertszoon,* 1629. 16 lvs; 4to. Relates to West Indian trade. Sabin 20236; Asher 129; Knuttel 3917. MnU-B, NN-RB; BL (Netherlands), The Hague:KB.   629/44

Diurnal der nassawischen Flotta, oder Tag-register . . . einer . . . Schiffahrt umb die gantze Erdkugel . . . Welcher auch . . . beygewohnet Adolph Decker . . . Vor niemalen vollkömlich in Truck gegeben aber nun alles aus flammischer Spraach . . . ubersetzet. *Strassburg: E. Zetzner,* 1629. 68 p.; illus., maps; 4to. Transl., with additional details, by Adolf Decker from the *Journael vande Nassausche vloot,* 1st publ., Amsterdam, 1626; authorship sometimes ascribed to Decker. The engraved t.p. begins 'Diurnal und historische Beschreibung'. Sabin 19152; Tiele-Muller, p. 80–81; Tiele 669n; JCB (3) II:221. CtY, DLC, NN-RB, RPJCB; BL, BN.   629/45

Du Chevreul, Jacques. Sphaera. *Paris: H. Du Mesnil,* 1629. 255 p.; illus.; 8vo. 1st publ., Paris, 1623. BL, BN.   629/46

Duircant, Andries, supposed author. Practiicke van den Spaenschen aes-sack. *The Hague:* 1629. *See under title below.*

——. Rym-vieren op de jeghen-woordige victorie, bekomen door den manhaften generael Pieter Pietersz. Heyn . . . in de veroveringe van de Spaensche silvere-vlote, onder 'teylandt Cubae, anno 1628. [*The Hague:* 1629]. [15] p.; 4to. Issued as part of the *Practiicke van den Spaenschen aes-sack* of this year. q.v. below. MiU-C. 629/47

Earle, John, Bp of Salisbury. Micro-cosmographie. or, A peece of the world discovered . . . The fift edn. *London: R. Allott,* 1629. [299] p.; 12mo. 1st publ., London, 1628. No 4th edn is known. STC 7442; Murphy (Engl. char. -bks) 38; Arents (Add.) 244. CSmH, DFo, IU (imp.), NN-A; BL.
629/48

Eibergen, Rutgerus. Swymel-klacht des Spaenschen conincks Philippi Quarti over het eerste verlies van sijn silver-vlote. *Amsterdam: J. F. Stam, for W. J. Stam,* 1629. 16 p.; 4to. Concerns Hein's capture of the silver fleet. Sabin 22075 (& 94086); Palau 78728; Muller (1872) 939; Asher 120; JCB (3) II:220. DLC, RPJCB. 629/49

Ens, Gaspar. Newer unpartheyischer teutscher Mercurius. *Cologne: P. von Brachel,* 1629. 98 p.; map; 4to. Refers to the West-Indische Compagnie's 1628 capture of the silver fleet. MnU-B. 629/50

Epicedium cum epitaphio appositum monumento . . . Petri Heinii . . . [Door N. R.]. *The Hague: A. Meuris,* 1629. [8] p.; 4to. Alludes to capture of Spanish silver fleet. Knuttel 3868. The Hague:KB. 629/51

Eroberung der reiche silber-vloot inde bay oder haven Matancae. An 1628. den 8. Sept. [*Amsterdam?* ca. 1629]. bds.; illus., map; fol. RPJCB. 629/52

Featley, John. A sermon preached to . . . Sir Thomas Warner: and the rest of his compagnie: bound to the West-Indies . . . at St. Buttolphs, Aldersgate, London. Septemb. 6. 1629. *London: N. Bourne,* 1629. 34 p.; 4to. Sabin 23965; STC 10743. DFo, MH, NNUT; BL. 629/53

Fennor, William. A true description of the lawes, justice, and equity of a compter. *London:* 1629, 85 p.; 4to. 1st publ., London, 1617, under title *The compters common-wealth.* STC 10786. BL, Oxford:Bodl. 629/54

Ferrufiño, Juan Bautista, S.J. Relacion del martirio de los padres Roque Gonçalez de Santacruz, Alonso Rodriguez, Juan del Castillo, de la Compañia de Jesus. Padecido en el Paraguay, a 16. de Noviembre de 1628. [*Madrid?* 1629?]. [59] p.; 4to. Sabin 24195; Medina (BHA) 6461 & VI:529n; Streit II:1616; cf. Backer III:699. RPJCB. 629/55

Fioravanti, Leonardo. De' capricci medicinali . . . libri quattro. *Venice: L. Spineda,* 1629. 251 numb. lvs; illus.; 8vo. 1st publ., Venice, 1561, under title *Capricci medicinali;* cf. 1602 edn. Michel (Répertoire) III:47. MiU; BN. 629/56

——. Della fisica . . . divisa in libri quattro . . . di nuovo ristampata. *Venice: L. Spineda,* 1629. 391 p.; 8vo. 1st publ., Venice, 1582; cf. 1603 edn. Michel (Répertoire) III:48. WU; Paris:Arsenal. 629/57

——. Il tesoro della vita humana . . . Di nuovo ristampato. *Venice: L. Spineda,* 1629. 327 numb. lvs; 8vo. 1st publ., Venice, 1570; cf. 1603 edn. Michel (Répertoire) III:48. DNLM; London:Wellcome, Paris:Ste Geneviève. 629/58

Fitzer, William, ed. Extract der Orientalischen Indien . . . Alles . . . beschrieben durch Caesarem Longinum. *Frankfurt a. M.: K. Rötel, for W. Fitzer,* 1629. illus., maps; fol. (J. T. de Bry's *India Orientalis.* Abridgment). 1st publ., Frankfurt a. M., 1628, under title *Orientalische Indien.* Brunet I:1362–63; Graesse I:560. BL (Bry). 629/59

Focanus, Jacobus. Adoni-beseck, of Lex talionis, dat is Rechtveerdighe straffe Godes over den tyrannen. Een meditatie, off discours. *Delft: J. A. Cloeting,* 1629. 232 p.; 4to. Though the work was apparently 1st publ. in 1622 (see Knuttel 3922n), information available on that edn has been insufficient to reconstruct it. The present edn includes sections on Spanish tyranny in West Indies, referring to Columbus, Las Casas, Benzoni, Pizarro, & various Indian kings. Further American refs occur in section on freedom of the seas. Knuttel 3922. The Hague:KB, Ghent:BU. 629/60

Ford, John. The lovers melancholy. *London: [F. Kingston,] for H. Seile,* 1629. 86 p.; 4to. Drama. In act I, scene 1, tobacco is mentioned. In some copies Seile's name appears simply as 'H.S.'. STC 11163; Greg 420; Arents 168; Pforzheimer 382. CSmH, CtY, DLC, MH, NN-A; BL. 629/61

Gallobelgicus, pseud. Wine, beere, and ale, together by the eares. *London: A. M[athewes]., for J. Grove,* 1629. [22] p.; 4to. Dramatic dialogue. Included is a discussion of tobacco (lf Blr-v). STC 11541; Greg 426(a). CSmH, MH; BL. 629/62

Geslin, Paul. La saincte chorographie, ou Description des lieux ou reside l'eglise chrestienne par tout l'univers. *Saumur: J. Lesnier & I. Desbordes, for C. Girard,* 1629. 109 p.; 8vo. In chapt. vii, section 1 describes the Church in the New World. Cioranescu (XVII) 32957. RPJCB. 629/63

Ghespreck van Langhe Piet met Keesje Maet, belanghende den treves met den Spaigniaert. [*The Hague?* 1629]. [14] p.; 4to. Relates to the West-Indische Compagnie. Knuttel 3924. The Hague:KB. 629/64

Gilbert, William. Tractatus, sive Physiologia nova de magnete . . . Omnia . . . recognita . . . opera . . . D. Wolfgang Lochmans. *Frankfurt a. M.:* 1629. 4to. 1st publ. as here ed., Stettin, 1628. Shaaber (Brit. auth.) G315. WU. 629/65

Gomberville, Marin Le Roy, sieur du Parc et de. L'exil de Polexandre. Première partie. *Paris: T. Du Bray,* 1629. 926 p.; 8vo. Novel with as a central figure a Peruvian prince enamored of a Mexican princess, reflecting author's awareness of writings on Spanish America. MdBP, NNU; BN. 629/66

—[Anr edn]. *Paris: T. Du Bray,* 1629. 638 p.; 8vo. NNC. 629/67

Grotius, Hugo. De veritate religionis christianae. Editio secunda, priore auctior & emendatior. *Leyden: J. Maire,* 1629. 233 p.; 12mo. 1st publ., Leyden, 1627, under title *Sensus librorum sex.* Meulen/Diermanse 946. BN, The Hague:PP. 629/68

Guibert, Philbert. Les oeuvres charitables. *Paris: J. Jost,* 1629. 686 p.; port.; 12mo. Included is Guibert's *Le prix et valeur des medicamens,* 1st publ., Paris, 1625. BN. 629/69

Haselbeeck, Johannes. Triumph-dicht over de gheluckighe ver-overinghe van de Spaensche silver-vlote, geschiet den 8. Septemb. anno 1628. Item, over de rasse veroveringhe van de Bahia de Todos os Sanctos, den 10 Maij, anno 1624. *Leeuwarden: C. Fonteyne,* 1629. [28] p.; 4to. In verse. Meulman 2051. Ghent:BU. 629/70

Helwig, Christoph. Theatrum historicum, sive Chronologiae systema novum. *Marburg: N. Hampel,* 1629. 169 p.; tables; fol. 1st (?) publ., Giessen, 1609, but here in-cluding for 1st time ref. to 'tumultus Mexici in nova Hispania' under years 1624–26. Edited by Johannes Steuberus. Cf. Jantz (German Baroque) 2293. ICN, PPPrHi, RPB; BL. 629/71

Hevia Bolaños, Juan de. Segunda parte de la Curia filipica. *Valladolid: J. Lasso de las Peñas,* 1629. 664 p.; 8vo. 1st publ., Lima, 1617, under title *Laberinto de comercio terrestre y moral;* cf. 1619 edn above. Alcocer (Valladolid) 753; Palau 114534n. RPJCB; Santiago de Compostela:Colegio de Misiones. 629/72

—[Anr edn]. *Madrid:* 1629. 4to. Palau 114534n. 629/73

Heylyn, Peter. Μικροκοσμος. A little description of the great world. The fourth edition. *Oxford: W. T[urner.] for W. Turner & T. Huggins,* 1629. 807 p.; 4to. 1st publ., Oxford, 1621. Sabin 31656n; Madan (Oxford) 1629:8; STC 13279. CSmH, CtY, DFo, ICN, MH, MiU-C, NN-RB, PU; BL. 629/74

Hulsius, Levinus. Die ein und zwanzigste Schifffahrt oder Gründliche und umbständliche fernere Beschreibung der . . . Landtschafft Brasilien Americae, und deroselben Innwohner und Sitten mit sampt einem angehenckten Verlauff, wie ein engellendischer Capiteyn Parcket genant S. Vincentem und den Portum Bellum erobert. Item: Was Gestalt der schöne Portus . . . Totos los Sanctos sampt der Statt Salvator in Anno 1624. von den Holländern gewunnen . . . worden. Item: Ein vollkömlicher Discurs, wie die spanische Silberflotta in der Insul Cuba . . . von . . . Heyn . . . erobert . . . worden. *Frankfurt a. M.: W. Hoffmann, for Heirs of Hulsius,* 1629. 131 p.; illus., port., map; 4to. (Levinus Hulsius's *Sammlung von . . . Schiffahrten.* Pt 21). Sabin 33674 (& 7567 & 7585); Church 313; JCB (3) I:467–68. CSmH, ICN, NN-RB, RPJCB; BL, BN. 629/75

Kannenburch, Hendrik van. Protest ofte Scherp dreyghement, 't welck den Coninck van Spagnen is doende . . . d'heeren bewint-hebbers vande Oost ende West-Indische Compagnien . . . ter occasie van't veroveren vande silver-vlote. *Middelburg: J. van de Vivere,* 1629. [15] p.; 4to. In verse. On Pieter Hein's victory in Matanzas Bay.

Sabin 66102; Asher 121; Knuttel 3861. DLC, NN-RB, NNH; The Hague:KB.
629/76

Kepler, Johann. Tabulae Rudolphinae, quibus astronomicae scientiae, temporum longinquitate collapsae restauratio continetur; a . . . Tychone . . . Braheorum . . . concepta. *Ulm: J. Saur,* 1627 [i.e., 1629]. 2 pts; illus., map; fol. In pt 1, America is mentioned on p. 42; world map includes America. Caspar (Kepler) 79. CU, CtY-M, DLC, ICJ, InU-L, MH, MiU, MnU, NN-RB, RPJCB; BL, BN.   629/77

Laet, Joannes de. Hispania, sive De regis Hispaniae regnis et opibus commentarium. *Leyden: Elsevier Office,* 1629. 498 p.; 16mo. Includes sections on Brazil (p. 185–88) & America (p. 189–242). Sabin 38560; Willems (Les Elzevier) 313; Rahir (Les Elzevier) 283; Palau 129562n; JCB (3) II:220. CSmH, IU, MH, MiU, MnU-B, NNH, PU, RPJCB; BL, BN.   629/78

—[Anr edn]. *Leyden: Elsevier Office,* 1629. 520 p.; 16mo. Cf. Sabin 38560; Borba de Moraes I:383; Willems (Les Elzevier) 313n; Rahir (Les Elzevier) 284; Palau 129562. CSmH, CtY, DCU, ICN, MH, NN-RB, PU; BL, BN.   629/79

Lalli, Giovanni Battista. Franceide, overo Del mal francese. Poemo giocoso. *Foligno: A. Alterio,* 1629. 235 p.; 12mo. The title poem discusses origin of syphilis & adventures in New World of one Gonzalvo, in his search for guaiacum, warring with Indians, etc. Brunet III:778 (14573n); Michel (Répertoire) V:11. DNLM, NSchU, OU; Paris:Arsenal.   629/80

—[Anr edn]. *Venice: G. Sarzina,* 1629. 177 p.; 12mo. Michel (Répertoire) V:11. Paris:Arsenal.   629/81

Leather: a discourse, tendered to the high court of Parliament. *London: T. C[otes]., for M. Sparke,* 1629. 27 p.; 4to. Ref. is made to the gold of Peru, tobacco of Virginia, & whales of Newfoundland. STC 15344; Arents (Add.) 245. CSmH, CtY, DFo, MH-BA, MiU-L, MnU-B, NN-A, PU; BL.   629/82

Lenton, Francis. The young gallants whirligigg; or Youths reakes. *London: M. F[letcher]., for R. Bostocke,* 1629. 22 p.; 4to. In verse. 'Potatoe pies' are mentioned on p. 19. STC 15467. CSmH, DFo, MH; BL.
629/83

León Pinelo, Antonio Rodríguez de. Epitome de la Biblioteca Oriental i Occidental, nautica i geografica. *Madrid: J. González,* 1629. 186 p.; 4to. Sabin 40052; Borba de Moraes II:150; Palau 135737; JCB (3) II:221. CtY, DLC, InU-L, MH, MiU-C, MnU-B, NN-RB, PBL, RPJCB; BL, BN.
629/84

Liefs, Jacob. Lof-dicht over de wijt-vermaerde . . . victorie, by het veroveren vande . . . silver-vloot des konings van Spangien door . . . Pieter Pietersz Heyn . . . ende Henderick Cornelisz Lonq, admirael over de . . . vloot der West-Indische compagnie. [*The Hague?*] 1629. [8] p.; 4to. Petit 1562. MiU-C; Leyden:B. Thysiana.
629/85

Linschoten, Jan Huygen van. Tertia pars Indiae Orientalis. *Frankfurt a. M.: K. Rötel, for W. Fitzer* (text); *E. Kempfer* (plates), 1629. 131 p.; illus., maps; fol. (J. T. de Bry's *India Orientalis.* Pt 3. Latin). 1st publ. in this version, Frankfurt a. M., 1601. Church 210n; JCB (3) I:426–27. CSmH, NN-RB, RPJCB; BL.   629/86

—[Anr edn]. *Frankfurt a. M.: K. Rötel, for W. Fitzer,* 1629. 170 p.; illus., maps; fol. (J. T. de Bry's *India Orientalis.* Pt 3. Latin). Reissue of sheets of 1601 edn with cancel t.p. and plates of this year. NN-RB; BN.
629/87

Lof des vrye vaerts, ende berisp tegen het misbruyck der selver, gecomponeert door J. M. Flissingano-Zelandum. [*Amsterdam?*] 1629. [12] p.; port.; 4to. Two poems in defense of privateering, referring to the West Indische Compagnie. Knuttel 3925. The Hague:KB.   629/88

Lommelin, D. Lof-dicht, ter eeren ende tot weerde fame vanden . . . Generael . . . Heyn . . . inghekomen met de silver-vlote. [*Amsterdam?*] 1629. 8 p.; 4to. Petit 1563. Leyden:B. Thysiana.   629/89

Maluenda, Jacinto Alonso. Cozquilla del gusto. *Valencia: S. Esparsa,* 1629. 8vo. In verse. Included are two poems disparaging tobacco. Palau 147975 (misdated 1619); Arents (Add.) 246. NN-A, NcU.
629/90

Marino, Giovanni Battista. La Murtoleide. *'Speyer'* [i.e., *Naples?*]: 1629. 284 p.; 12mo. In verse. 1st publ., [Venice?], 1619. Also included, *inter alia,* are 'Le strigliate a Tomaso Stigliani' of 'Robusto Pogommega', i.e., Andrea Barbazza, satirizing Stigliani's *Del mondo novo* of 1617. Cf. Sabin 51557; Michel (Répertoire) V:126. CU, DFo, ICN, MH, MiU, NIC; BL, BN.   629/91

Márquez de Cisneros, ——. Por Don Juan de Leoz, cavallero de la Orden de Santiago, almirante que fue de la flota de Nueva-España del año passado. Con el señor fiscal . . . Juan de Solorçano Pereira, del Consejo Real de las Indias, pue por mandado de su Magestad lo es en este pleito, sobre los cargos que al dicho almirante se le hacen en razon de la perdida de la dicha flota. [*Madrid:*] *F. Martínez* [1629]. 20 numb. lvs; fol. Medina (BHA) 7766. Puebla:B. Palafoxiana.   629/92

Martinius, Franciscus. Argo-nauta Batavus, sive expeditionis navalis, quam alter noster Jason, & heros fortissimus, Petrus Heinius . . . Societatis Indiae Occidentalis ductu nuper suscepit . . . historia carmine heroico discripta. *Kampen: P. H. Wyringanus,* 1629. 28 p.; 4to. In verse. On Hein's victory over Spanish silver fleet. Sabin 44968; Rodrigues (Dom. Hol.) 887; Muller (1872) 944; JCB (3) II:222. MHi, NN-RB, RPJCB.   629/93

Matthieu, Pierre. Dell'historia di S. Luigi IX, re di Francia . . . Tradotta di francese . . . dal signor Gio. Battista Parchi. *Venice: F. Baba,* 1629. 308 p.; 4to. Transl. from Matthieu's *Histoire de sainct Louys,* 1st publ., Paris, 1618; here anr issue of Baba's 1628 edn with altered imprint date? MH.   629/94

Mexía, Pedro. Verscheyden lessen, waarin beschreven worden de weerdichste gheschiedenissen. *Amsterdam:* 1629. 2 pts; 8vo. 1st publ. in this version, Leyden, 1595; cf. 1617 edn. Sabin 48152 (& 48248n); cf. Palau 167339.   629/95

Micrologia. Characters, or essayes, of persons, trades, and places . . . By R. M. *London: T. C[otes]., for M. Sparke,* 1629. [53] p.; 8vo. Character 6 describes 'A tobacconist'; in character 5, 'A smith', Peru is mentioned.

STC 17146; Murphy (Engl. char.-bks) 46–47. Oxford:Bodl.   629/96

Moerbeeck, Jan Andries. Vereenighde Nederlandschen raedt, het eerste deel . . . Den vierden druck. *The Hague: A. Meuris,* 1629. 40 p.; 4to. 1st publ., The Hague, 1628. Sabin 98961; Knuttel 3800; Meulman 2086. The Hague:KB, Ghent:BU.   629/97

——. Vereenighde Nederlandschen raedt, het tweede deel . . . den tweeden druck. *The Hague: A. Meuris,* 1629. 60 p.; 4to. 1st publ., The Hague, 1628. Sabin 98962; Asher 128; Knuttel 3802. DLC; The Hague:KB.   629/98

Molina, Cristóbal de. Señor. Cristoval de Molina, regidor perpetuo de la ciudad de Mexico en la Nuevaespaña, en continuacion de los discursos y memoriales que ha dada paraque el repartimiento, y servicio personal que los Indios de aquellas provincias . . . como en las del Piru. Suplica a V. Magestad mande se consideren los fundamentos siguentes. [*Madrid:* 1629]. 7 numb. lvs; fol. Memorial to king of Spain; subscribed at Madrid, 18 Aug. 1629. Medina (BHA) 855; Maggs Cat. 496 (Americana VI). Seville:Archivo de Indias.   629/99

More, Sir Thomas, Saint. De Utopia. *Hoorn:* 1629. *See the year* 1630.

——. Utopia à mendis vindicata. *Cologne: C. ab Egmondt & Co.,* 1629. 266 p.; 16mo. 1st publ., Louvain, 1516; cf. 1601 edn. Gibson (More) 12; Shaaber (Brit. auth.) M242. CSmH, CtY, MH, NjP; BL, BN.   629/100

Nederlandsche West-Indische Compagnie. Consideratien ende redenen der e. heeren bewind-hebberen vande geoctrojeerde West-Indische Compagnie. *Haarlem: A. Roman,* 1629. 32 p.; 4to. Concerns navigation & commerce. Sabin 15930; Asher 130; Knuttel 3909. DLC, MH-BA, NN, RPJCB; BL, The Hague:KB.   629/101

—[Anr edn]. *Haarlem: A. Roman,* 1629. 32 p.; 4to. In this & succeeding edns by Roman, the 'Remonstrantie . . . van Bohemen' is mentioned on t.p. Here line 1 of p. 32 begins 'Treves' & ends 'aenghebo-'. Cf. Sabin 15931–32; cf. Asher 132–33; Knuttel 3910. The Hague:KB.   629/102

—[Anr edn]. *Haarlem: A. Roman*, 1629. 32 p.; 4to. Here line 1 on p. 32 ends 'aen-'. Cf. Sabin 15931–32; Knuttel 3911. The Hague:KB. 629/103

—[Anr edn]. *Haarlem: A. Roman*, 1629. 32 p.; 4to. Here line 1 on p. 32 begins 'daen' & ends 'in-'. Cf. Sabin 15931–32; Knuttel 3912. The Hague:KB. 629/104

—[Anr edn]. . . . Na de copie gedruckt te Haerlem by Adriaen Rooman . . . 1629 [*Amsterdam?* 1629?]. [16] p.; 4to. Sabin 102888. NN. 629/105

——. Octroy by de . . . Staten Generael, verleent aende West-Indische Compagnie. *The Hague: Widow & Heirs of H. Jacobszoon van Wouw*, 1629. 18 lvs; 4to. 1st publ. in this enl. version, The Hague, 1623. Sabin 56670. 629/106

—[Anr edn]. *The Hague: Widow & Heirs of H. Jacobszoon van Wouw*, 1629. 16 lvs; 4to. Sabin 56671. 629/107

——. Verhooginge der capitalen vande West-Indische Compagnie voor een derde part. [*The Hague?* 1629]. bds.; fol. This edn has 56 lines of text. Sabin 102914; Knuttel 3869. [Locations cited may include the following edn.] DLC, NN-RB; The Hague:KB. 629/108

—[Anr edn]. [*The Hague?* 1629]. bds.; fol. This edn has 42 lines of text. Sabin 102914; Asher 71. 629/109

Netherlands (United Provinces, 1581–1795). Staten Generaal. Artickels-brief ende Instructie roerende den oorloghe ter zee. [*The Hague:* 1629]. [19] p.; 4to. Includes refs to tobacco. JCB (3) II:222–23. RPJCB. 629/110

—[Anr edn]. *The Hague: Widow & Heirs of H. Jacobszoon van Wouw*, 1629. [34] p.; 4to. Tiele (Pamfletten) 2262. 629/111

—[Anr edn]. Artijckel-brief . . . roerende den oorloge. *Middelburg: Widow & Heirs of S. Moulert*, 1629. [40] p.; 4to. Meulman 2054. Ghent:BU. 629/112

——. Placcaet ende ordonnantie op de wapeninge ende manninge vande schepen. *The Hague: Widow & Heirs of H. Jacobszoon van Wouw*, 1629. [20] p.; 4to. 1st publ., The Hague, 1607. JCB (3) II:223. RPJCB. 629/113

Neuhaus, Edo. Triumphalia Leowardiana, in victoriis Belgicis de Antichristo Antiochizante. Cum Corollario de negotio Hispanicae pacis ad Belgicos ordines. *Groningen: N. Roman*, 1629. 94 p.; 4to. Relates to the West-Indische Compagnie. Knuttel 3923. The Hague:KB. 629/114

Nierop, Adriaan van. Loff-dicht, ter eeren . . . Pieter Pietersz. Heyn, over het veroveren vande rijcke silver-vloot. *Delft: J. A. Cloeting*, 1629. [8] p.; 4to. Knuttel 3860. The Hague:KB. 629/115

Niess, Johann, S.J. Adolescens Europaeus ab Indo moribus christianis informatus. *Dillingen: C. Sutor*, 1629. 450 p.; 12mo. Though the 'Indian' in question, brought to Europe for education, was a Philippine, included is a discussion, with long poem, of the passionflower ('granadilla'), identified as Peruvian. Sabin 55273; Backer V:1768. DLC, NN-RB, RPJCB; BL, BN. 629/116

Nuevas ciertas y fidedignas de la vitoria que ha alcançado Don Fadrique de Toledo general de la armada . . . de ochenta y siete vaxeles de Olandeses en la isla de San Christoval cerca de la Avana [i.e., Habana] . . . Su fecha de 2. de diziembre 1629. *Barcelona: E. Liberós*, 1629. 2 lvs; illus.; 4to. Sabin 96109; Medina (BHA) 864; Rodrigues (Dom. Hol.) 376; Palau 196324. 629/117

Ontwerp, raeckende het op-rechten van een Camer van Asseurantie, ofte versekeringe vande zee-vaert, ende tot beschorminge vande navogatie. *Leeuwarden: D. Albertszoon*, 1629. 28 p.; 4to. Project for a chamber of maritime-assurance in cooperation with the East and West India companies, together with the letter-patent granted by the Staten Generaal. Knuttel 3865. RPJCB; The Hague:KB. 629/118

Opitz, Martin. Deutscher Poematum Erster[-Anderer] Theil. *Breslau: D. Müller*, 1629. 2 v.; 8vo. 1st publ. in this version, Breslau, 1628–29, with vol. 2 including the author's 'Lob des Krieges Gottes'. Goedeke III:45; Faber du Faur 213; Jördens IV:114. CU, CtY, MShM, PU; Göttingen:StUB. 629/119

Panciroli, Guido. Rerum memorabilium . . . pars prior [et posterior] . . . commentariis illustrata ab Henrico Salmuth. *Frank-*

furt a. M.: G. Tampach [1629]–31. 2 v.; 4to. 1st publ., Amberg, 1599–1602; cf. 1602 edn. Sabin 58411n; Jantz (German Baroque) 186. CSt, DLC, InU-L, MiDW, NNE, PP; BL, BN. 629/120

Parkinson, John. Paradisi in sole paradisus terrestris. Or a garden of . . . flowers with a kitchen garden and an orchard. *London: H. Lownes & R. Young,* 1629. 612 p.; illus.; fol. Included are numerous American plants. For printing variants see the STC & Henrey. Pritzel 6933; Nissen (Bot.) 1489; Henrey (Brit. bot.) 282–83; STC 19300; Arents 169. CSmH, CtY, DLC, MH-A, MoSB, NN-RB, PPL, RPJCB; BL, BN. 629/121

Pels, E. Lof-dicht des vermaerde, wyt-beroemde, manhaftige zee-heldt Pieter Pietersen Heyn . . . Waer in . . . verhaelt wordt . . . het veroveren vande silvere-vloot aen t eylant Cuba inde haven van Matanca. *Amsterdam: W. J. Wyngaert,* 1629. 6 lvs; 4to. Sabin 59591; Borba de Moraes I:425; Muller (1872) 945; Asher 119. NN-RB, NNH; Ghent:BU. 629/122

Peñalosa y Mondragón, Benito de. Libro de las cinco excellencias del Español que despueblan a España para su mayor potencia y dilatacion. *Pamplona: C. de Labàyen,* 1629. 178 numb. lvs; 4to. Sabin 59635; Medina (BHA) 857; Streit II:1581; Palau 217642; JCB (3) II:224. CtY, DLC, MH-BA, PU, RPJCB, TxU; BN. 629/123

Pharmacopoeia Augustana. Jussu et auctoritati . . . Senatus a Collegio Medico rursus recognita, nunc septimum in lucem emissa. *Augsburg: A. Aperger, for J. Kruger,* 1629. 2 pts; 8vo. 1st publ., Augsburg, [1564]; cf. 1613 edn. Here a reissue of 1623 edn with cancel t.p. Darmstadt:UB, Würzburg:UB. 629/124

Planis Campy, David de. Bouquet composé des plus belles fleurs chimiques. *Paris: P. Billaine,* 1629. 1005 p.; port.; 8vo. Includes formulas employing guaiacum, mechoacan, & tobacco. Wellcome I:5080. CtY, DNLM, MH, MnU, NNNAM; London:Wellcome, BN. 629/125

Plumptre, Huntingdon. Epigrammatων opusculum duobus distinctum. *London: T. Harper, for R. Allot,* 1629. 73 p.; 8vo. In verse. 'Tabaco tabes corporis': bk i, epigram lvi; 'In Christophorum Columbum

Americani orbis inventorum': bk ii, epigram xxxvii. STC 20051; Arents (Add.) 247. CSmH, CtY, DFo, ICN, MH, NN-A; Oxford:Bodl. 629/126

Practiicke van den Spaenschen aes-sack: aengewesen op de veroveringe en victorie van . . . Pieter Pietersz. Heyn. *The Hague:* 1629. [31] p.; illus.; 4to. In verse. Includes, p. [17–31], *Rym-vieren op de jeghenwoordige victorie, bekomen door . . . Pieter Pietersz. Heyn,* attributed to Andries Duircant, whose name appears at the end of the 'Treur-versen' in the *Rym-vieren;* sometimes attrib. to A. van de Venne. Sabin 31660; Asher 123; Muller (1872) 946; Knuttel 3862; JCB (STL) 28. RPJCB (imp.); BL, The Hague:KB. 629/127

—[Anr issue]. *The Hague: A. J. Tongerloo,* 1629. Sabin 31661; Palau 234701; JCB (3) II:224. NN-RB, RPJCB. 629/128

Recherches curieuses des mesures du monde. P. le S. C. de V. *Paris: M. Collet,* 1629. 48 p.; 8vo. America's size is discussed. RPJCB. 629/129

Rosaccio, Giuseppe. Universale discrittione del teatro del cielo, e della terra. *Venice: The Ciottis,* 1629. 141 p.; illus., maps; 8vo. 1st publ., Brescia, 1592, under title *Teatro del cielo e della terra;* cf. 1620 edn. CtY. 629/130

Saint-Amant, Marc Antoine de Gérard, sieur de. Les oeuvres. *Paris: R. Estienne, for F. Pomeray & T. Quinet,* 1629. 255 p.; 4to. In verse. Page 245 contains sonnet in praise of tobacco, beginning 'Assis sur un fagot, une pipe à la main'; the poem 'La chambre du desbauché' (p. 189–201) mentions it, as do the 'Cassation de sondrilles' (p. 230–33), & 'L'enamouré' (p. 236–37). In 'La gazette du Pont-Neuf' (p. 213–19) Peru is mentioned. In this edn, the 'achevé d'imprimer' is correctly dated '29 février 1629'. Cioranescu (XVII) 60671; Tchémerzine X:81. DLC, MH, OrU, TNJ; BN. 629/131

—[Anr edn]. 'Paris: R. Estienne, for F. Pomeray & T. Quinet, 1629.' 255 p.; 4to. A counterfeit of the above; the 'achevé d'imprimer' is misdated '29 février 1627'. Tchémerzine X:81. Caen:BU. 629/132

Sandys, Sir Edwin. Europae speculum; or, A view or survey of the state of religion.

The Hague: [*for M. Sparke, at London*] 1629. 248 p.; 4to. 1st publ., London, 1605, under title *A relation of the state of religion.* STC 21718. CSmH, CtY, DFo, ICN, MH, MiU-C, NNUT; BL. 629/133

Scribanius, Carolus. Ausführliches, wolgegründtes, politisches Bedencken auff das nach jetzwehrende Kriegswesen im Niderlandt . . . in lateinischer Sprach erstlich beschriben, jetzo . . . ubergesetzt. [*Augsburg?*] 1629. 76 p.; 4to. Transl. from the author's *Veridicus Belgicus,* 1st publ., [Antwerp, 1624]. BL. 629/134

—[Anr edn?]. Ausführliches wolgegründetes . . . Bedencken. [*Augsburg?*] 1629. 4to. BL. 629/135

Solórzano Pereira, Juan de. Disputationem de Indiarum jure, sive De justa Indiarum Occidentalium, inquisitione, acquisitione, et retentione. Tomus primus. *Madrid: F. Martínez,* 1629. 751 p.; fol. A second vol. was publ. in 1639. Sabin 86525; Medina (BHA) 863; Hanke/Giménez 525; Streit I:443; Palau 318974; JCB (3) II:224. CSmH, CtY, DLC, InU-L, MH, MiU-C, NN-RB, PU, RPJCB; BL, BN. 629/136

——. El doctor Juan de Solorzano Pereira, fiscal del Real Consejo de las Indias. Con los bienes i herederos del governador don Francisco Vanegas, cabo que fue de las galeras de Cartagena. Sobre si se pueden seguir, y sentenciar contra ellos que quedaron hechos al dicho don Francisco. *Madrid: F. Martínez,* 1629. 44 numb. lvs; fol. Sabin 86523; Medina (BHA) 7767. Puebla: B. Palafoxiana. 629/137

——. Memorial i discurso de las razones que se ofrecen para que el Real . . . Consejo de las Indias debe preceder en todos los actos publicos al que llaman de Flandres. *Madrid: F. Martínez,* 1629. 33 numb. lvs. fol. Sabin 86530; Medina (BHA) 862; Palau 318992. NN-RB; Oxford:Bodl., Santiago, Chile:BN (imp). 629/138

Spinola, Fabio Ambrosio, S.J. Vita del p. Carlo Spinola della Compagnia di Giesu, morto per la santa fede nel Giappone. *Bologna: C. Ferroni,* 1629. 235 p.; 4to. 1st publ., Rome, 1628. Sabin 89459. NNH. 629/139

Spranckhuysen, Dionysius. Tranen over den doodt van den grooten Admirael van Hollandt . . . Pieter Pietersz. Heyn. . . . Midtsgaders syn testament aen de . . . West Indische Compagnie. *Delft: A. J. Cloeting,* 1629. 20 p.; 4to. Sabin 89746; Asher 124; Muller (1872) 949; Knuttel 3867; JCB (STL) 28. MiU-C, NN-RB, RPJCB; BL, The Hague:KB. 629/140

——. Triumphe van weghen de . . . victorie, welcke de heere . . . verleent heeft aen de vlote van de West-Indische Compagnie onder . . . Pieter Pietersz. Heyn. . . . Teghen de silver-vlote onser vyanden komende van Nova Hispania. *Delft: J. A. Cloeting,* 1629. 80 p.; 4to. Some copies include port. of Hein with paean to him on verso. Sabin 89747; Knuttel 3858; Meulman 2050; Cf. Petit 1561; JCB (3) II:225. NN-RB, RPJCB; Amsterdam:NHSM, The Hague:KB. 629/141

Suárez de Figueroa, Cristóbal. Plaza universal de todas ciencias y artes. Parte traducida de toscana, y parte compuesta por el doctor Christoval Suarez de Figueroa. *Perpignan: L. Roure,* 1629. 379 numb. lvs; 4to. Transl. in part from Tommaso Garzoni's *La piazza universale,* 1st publ., Venice, 1587; cf. 1615, Madrid, Spanish edn. Palau 323909. CU-S, DNLM, NNU. 629/142

Taylor, John, the Water-poet. Wit and mirth, chargeably collected out of tavernes, ordinaries . . . tobacco shops, highwayes, and water-passages. *London: T. C*[*otes*]*., for J. Boler,* 1629. [80] p.; 8vo. 1st publ., London, 1626. STC 23814. CSmH, MH. 629/143

Tekel ofte Weech-schale vande groote monarchie van Spaingien . . . ter occasie vande silver vlote by den Generael Pieter Pieterssen Heyn verowert, neder-ghestelt. *Middelburg: J. van der Hellen, for J. vande Vivere,* 1629. 48 p.; 4to. Sabin 94599 & 31633; Asher 122. 629/144

Tractaet tegens pays, treves, en onderhandelinge met den Koningh van Spaignien. *The Hague: A. Meuris,* 1629. [32] p.; 4to. Includes refs to West Indian commerce & navigation. Continued in pt 2, *Redenen* (The Hague, 1630), & pt 3, *Klare aenwysinge* (The Hague, 1630), q.v. Cf. Sabin 38034; Asher 133; Muller (1872) 461; Knuttel 3918; JCB (STL) 28. CtY, DLC, MnU-B, NN-RB, RPJCB; The Hague:KB. 629/145

Vairo, Leonardo. De fascino libri tres. *Venice:* 1629. 375 p.; 12mo. 1st publ., Paris, 1583. In describing superstitions of West Indian natives, quotes Monardes on use of tobacco. Cf. Arents (Add.) 78. MWA.
629/146

Vargas, Manuel Antonio de, S.J. Relacion de los milagros que Dios . . . ha obrado por una imagen del glorioso p. S. Francisco de Borja en el nuevo reyno de Granada. *Madrid: A. de Parra,* 1629. [4] p.; fol. Said also to have been published in Italian translation this year at Naples by V. Franchi. Sabin 98602; Medina (BHA) 865; Palau 352366. BL, Madrid:Acad. de la Hist.
629/147

Veen, Jan van der. Siet den getaanden speck, Jan Dwars-voet den seinjoor, don Pock Mock, den Maraan . . . Pie'r Heyn verkrijght zijn schatten [*Haarlem?* 1629]. bds.; fol. In verse. Satirical poem alluding to Pieter Hein's capture of Spanish silver fleet. Knuttel 3863. The Hague:KB, Amsterdam: NHSM.
629/148

Vega Carpio, Lope Félix de. Arcadia, prosas y versos. *Cádiz: J. de Borja:* 1629. 250 numb. lvs; 8vo. 1st publ., Madrid, 1598; cf. 1602 edns. A reissue of the printer's 1626 edn? Palau 356304. Madrid:BN.
629/149

—[Anr edn]. *Segovia: D. Flamenco, for A. Pérez* [*at Madrid*], 1629. 250 numb. lvs; 8vo. Palau 356305. NNH; Madrid:BN.
629/150

——. Parte veinte de las Comedias. *Madrid: J. González,* 1629. 289 numb. lvs; 4to. 1st publ., Madrid, 1625. Sabin 98772n; Palau 355312.
629/151

Verovering vande silver-vloot inde Bay Matanca. *Amsterdam: C. J. Visscher* [1629]. bds.; illus.; fol. MnU-B.
629/152

Victorij sang en lof dicht ofer de heerlijcke veroveringe vande Spaensche silver-vloot uyt Nova Spanje door den generael Pieter Pietersz Heyn. *Haarlem:* 1629. bds.; fol. Sabin 31664.
629/153

Vondel, Joost van den. Op het ontset van Piet Heyns buyt, het West-Injes-huys spreeckt. [*Amsterdam? W. J. Blaeu?* 1629?]. bds.; 4to. A 24-line poem concerning troubles caused in Amsterdam by the return of Hein with the captured Spanish silver fleet—Muller. Cf. Vondel's *Op het tweede ontset* below. In this edition, line 11 reads 'Giert

wtebruyt die stong'. Sabin 100761; Muller (1872) 954; Unger (Vondel 169; Knuttel 3863a; JCB (3) II:218. RPJCB; The Hague:KB.
629/154

—[Anr edn]. [*Amsterdam?* 1629?]. bds.; 4to. Line 11 reads 'Giert Almans Hoer, die stong'. Unger (Vondel) 170. Amsterdam: UB.
629/155

—[Anr edn]. [*Amsterdam?* 1629?] bds.; 4to. Line 11 reads 'Giert Allemans-Hoer, die stong'. Unger (Vondel) 171. Amsterdam: UB.
629/156

——. Op het tweede ontset van Piet Heyns buyt. [*The Hague?* 1629]. bds.; 4to. A 34-line poem concerning Hein's arrival in Amsterdam with the Spanish silver fleet; cf. Vondel's *Op het ontset* above. Sabin 100762; Muller (1872) II:2765.
629/157

Wassenaer, Nicolaes van. Het ses'thiende deel of t vervolgh van het Historisch verhael aller gedenck-waerdiger geschiedenissen, die in Europa . . . in America, als West-Indien, Brasyl en Peru . . . voorghevallen syn. *Amsterdam: J. Janszoon, the Younger,* 1629. (N. van Wassenaer's *Historisch verhael.* Pt 16). Includes an account of Pieter Hein's capture of the Spanish silver fleet, and materials concerning the Nederlandsche West-Indische Compagnie. Cf. Sabin 102039; Borba de Moraes II:371; Muller (1872) 1745. RPJCB.
629/158

——. 'T vyfthiende deel of 't vervolgh van het Historisch verhael aller gedenckwaerdiger geschiedeniss. die in Europa . . . in America, als West-Indien, d'eijlanden en Brasil . . . voorgevallen zijn. *Amsterdam: J. Janszoon, the Younger,* 1629. 108 numb. lvs; illus.; 4to. (N. van Wassenaer's *Historisch verhael.* Pt 15). Under April, includes brief account of Dirk Symonszoon's capture of ships on Brazilian coast. Under August, describes a sea battle at Havana, in which 2 ships from Honduras are captured by the Dutch. Cf. Sabin 102039; Borba de Moraes II:371; Muller (1872) 1745. RPJCB.
629/159

Whitbourne, Sir Richard. Zwantzigste Schifffahrt, oder Gründliche . . . Beschreibung dess Newen Engellands, wie auch Aussführliche Erzehlung von . . . Virginia, und der Insel Barmuda. *Frankfurt a. M.: W. Hoffmann, for Heirs of Hulsius,* 1629. 116 p.;

illus., map; 4to. (Levinus Hulsius's *Sammlung von . . . Schiffahrten*. Pt 20). Transl. from Whitbourne's *Discourse and discovery of Newfound-land*, 1st publ., London, 1620; here added is an account of Virginia & the Bermuda Islands, prob. extracted & transl. from Smith's *Generall history of Virginia*, 1st publ., [London, 1623]. Sabin 33673; Baginsky (German Americana) 160 (& 161); Shaaber (Brit. auth.) W68; Church 312; JCB (3) I:467. CSmH, CtY, ICN, MH, MnU-B, NN-RB, RPJCB, ViU; BL, BN.

629/160

Wijnandts, Willem. Lobspruch uber die heerliche Victori. In Eroberung der Silberflotta in dem Bay Matanca. [*Netherlands:*] 1629. [10] p.; 4to. Transl. from the author's *Lof-dicht* of this year below. Sabin 41714 (& 103943); Palmer 353; JCB (3)II:222. NN-RB, RPJCB: Wolfenbüttel:HB.   629/161

——. Lof-dicht over de heerlijcke victorie, in het veroveren van de silver vlote in de Baey van Matanca onder het beleyt van . . . Heer Generael Pieter Pietersz Heyn. *Middelburg: Z. Roman*, 1629. [9] p.; 4to. Sabin 41779 (& 103943); Muller (1872) 942; Asher 118; JCB (3) II:225. DLC, NN-RB, RPJCB.   629/162

——. Spaensche tryumphe over de begintselen haerder victory. *Middelburg: Z. Roman*, 1629. [12] p.; 4to. In beginning of poem 'Den tweeden Heems-kerck heeft Nederland verloren', Spaniards portrayed as rejoicing over death of Pieter Hein, who was infamous for his 1628 capture of Spanish silver fleet. Meulman 2074. Ghent:BU.

629/163

Wilkins, George. The miseries of inforst marriage. *London: A. Mathewes, for R. Thrale & G. Vincent, the Younger*, 1629. [79] p.; 4to. Drama. 1st publ., London, 1607. STC 25637; Greg 249 (c). CSmH, CtY, DLC, ICN, MH; BL.   629/164

Zacutus, Abraham, Lusitanus. De medicorum principum historia libri sex. *Cologne: J. F. Stam*, 1629. 624 p.; 8vo. In bk 1, as hist. 73ff., whether or not syphilis was known to Galen is discussed, with refs to Monardes, Oviedo, & Cortés; but its American origin is denied. Waller 10451; Palau 378670. DNLM, MBCo, NNJ; Uppsala:UB.

629/165

——[Anr issue?]. *Leyden: J. Maire*, 1629. Palau 378670n.   629/166

163–?

Garavito, Gerónimo. Cuenta que Geronimo Garavito procurador general del gremio de los azugeros de . . . Potosi del Perù ha hecho de la mucha plata que pierde el Rey . . . y los particulares que la traen de las Indias, por no se la dexar labrar à ellos en moneda. [*Madrid?* 163–?]. 7 numb. lvs; fol. Memorial to king of Spain. BL.

63–/1

——. Señor. Aviendo los Españoles descubierto los dilatados reynos de las Indias Occidentales, y en particular los del Pirù tan ricos, y abundantes en oro, y plata [etc.]. [*Madrid?* 163–?]. 4 numb. lvs; fol. Memorial to king of Spain. BL.   63–/2

——. Señor. Geronimo Garavito en nombre de don Juan de Lizaraçu . . . presidente de la real audiencia de S. Francisco de Quito, dize, que aviendo despachado V. Magestad cedula para que se pregonasse la empressa, entrada poblacion, y fortificacion del gran rio de las Amaçonas [etc.]. [*Madrid:* 163–?]. [3] p.; fol. Memorial to the king of Spain. BL.   63–/3

——. Señor. Geronimo Garavito en nombre de don Juan de Lizaraçu . . . presidente de la real audiencia de S. Francisco de Quito, dize, que reconociendo el dicho presidente las cosas de aquella provincia, le ha parecido . . . consultar a V. Mag. la necessidad que ay, se haga casa de moneda en aquella ciudad. [*Madrid:* 163–?]. bds.; fol. Memorial to king of Spain. BL.

63–/4

——. Señor. Geronimo Garavito en nombre del presidente don Juan de Lizaraçu . . . dize: Que el presentò en el Real Consejo de las Indias doz memoriales, en siete de noviembre del año passado [etc.]. [*Madrid:* 163–?]. [2] p.; fol. Memorial to king of Spain. BL.   63–/5

——. Señor. Geronimo Garavito, procurador general del gremio de los azugueros de . . . Potosi del Pirù . . . Digo, que tengo presentados muchos memoriales, en que . . . manifestè lo que pierde la hazienda de V.

Magestad . . . en la dicha villa y provincia . . . por la mala administracion de algunos ministros de aquel reino. [*Madrid:* 163–?]. [4] p.; fol. Memorial to king of Spain. BL.
63–/6

——. Señor. Geronimo Garavito, procurador general del gremio de los azogueros de . . . Potosi del Pirù, dize: que aviendo presentado muchos memoriales a V.M. y al Consejo de las Indias . . . no ha tenido modo de saber lo decretado. [*Madrid?* 163–?]. [4] p.; fol. Memorial to king of Spain. BL.
63–/7

——. Señor. Geronimo Garavito, procurador general del gremio de los azogueros de . . . Potosi del Pirù, dize: Que ha mas de 5. años que vino a esta corte desde la dicha villa de Potosi por los dichos azogueros y mineros, para que representasse a V.M. y al Consejo de las Indias el infeliz estado en que se hallava aquella republica. [*Madrid:* 163–?]. 8 numb. lvs; fol. Memorial to king of Spain. BL.
63–/8

——. Señor. Geronimo Garabito, procurador general del gremio de los azogueros, y mineros de . . . Potosi del Perù . . . dize, que ha tenido noticia que el Arçobispo de Santa Cruz de la Sierra ha dada un memorial en forma de arbitrio, diziendo, que conviene que el Arçobispo de los Charcas . . . sea una persona sola que ocupe todas tres plaças [etc.]. [*Madrid:* 163–?]. [3] p.; fol. Memorial to king of Spain. BL.
63–/9

——. Señor. Geronymo Garavito en nombre de Don Juan de Lizarazu . . . presidente de la real chancilleria de . . . San Francisco de Quito . . . dize: que a los siete deste mes de noviembre entregò al secretario Don Gabriel de Ocaña y Alarcon, para que leyesse en el Consejo de las Indias un memorial impresso en tres pliegos . . . en que se dio noticia . . . del grandioso descubrimiento de los tres cerros de plata de la jurisdicion de los Indios Yumbos. [*Madrid:* 163–?]. 4 numb. lvs; fol. Memorial to king of Spain. BL.
63–/10

Moscoso y de Córdoba, Cristóbal de. El licenciado Don Christoval de Moscoso y Cordova . . . fiscal en el Real de las Indias. Con el duque del Infantado. Sobre la encomienda de Indias, que tuvo en segunda vida la duquesa del Infantado, marquesa

de Montesclaros. [*Madrid?* 163–?]. 22 lvs; fol. Medina (BHA) 8263.
63–/11

Relacion del nuevo descubrimiento de las minas ricas del assiento de san Miguel de Oruro de la provincia de Paria, juridicion de la real audiencia de la Plata, y villa de san Felipe de Austria, que en ella fundò el licenciado don Manuel de Castro y Padilla. [*Madrid:* 163–?]. 8 numb. lvs; fol. BL (Castro y Padilla, M. de).
63–/12

1630

Aldrovandi, Ulisse. Ornithologiae . . . libri xii. *Frankfurt a. M.: W. Richter, for Heirs of N. Basse,* 1630. 2 v.; illus.; fol. 1st publ., Bologna, 1599–1603; here a reissue of vols. 1 & 2 of 1610 edn with altered imprint date. Dt. Ges. Kat. 3.499. BL, Breslau:StB.
630/1

Alemán, Mateo. Le gueux, ou La vie de Guzman d'Alfarache. *Lyons: S. Rigaud,* 1630. 2 v.; 8vo. 1st publ. as here transl. by Jean Chapelain, Paris, 1619, & Paris, 1620. Vol. 2 has title *Le voleur, ou La vie de Guzman d'Alfarache.* Laurenti (Nov. pic. esp.) 620; Cioranescu (XVII) 18475. BL.
630/2

——. The rogue: or, The life of Guzman de Alfarache. *Oxford: W. Turner, & R. Allott, at London,* 1630. 2 pts; fol. 1st publ. as here transl. by James Mabbe, London, 1622. Laurenti (Nov. pic. esp.) 693; STC 290; Madan (Oxford) 1630:1; Palau 6783. CSmH, CtY, DLC, ICN, InU-L, MH, MiU, MnU, NNPM; BL, BN.
630/3

Almansa, Bernardino de. Por parte del Dean y cabildo de la santa iglesia de la ciudad de la Plata . . . en el . . . Pirù, en razon de las prebendas . . . se suplica a V.M. se sirva de considerar lo siguiente. [*Madrid?* 1630?]. 3 numb. lvs; fol. Medina (BHA) 6188; Palau 7875; JCB (3) II:176. RPJCB; BL.
630/4

Alsted, Johann Heinrich. Encyclopaedia, septem tomis distincta. *Herborn:* [*G. Rab*] 1630. 2404 p.; illus., maps; fol. The 'Geographiae pars iii, caput iv' concerns America, discussing its discovery & exploration, ancient foreknowledge of its existence, and the meaning of specific place names, e.g. New France, Canada, Nicaragua, & Brazil.

Scattered refs to the Americas occur in other chapters. Cf. Jantz (German Baroque) 361. CtY, IU, MH, NN, PPL, RPB (imp.); BL, BN. 630/5

Ampzing, Samuel. Fasciculus epigrammatum super expugnatâ & devictâ Olinda, ditionis Fernambuci, in Brasilia, a classe et milite Societatis Indiae Occidentalis, ductu . . . Henrici Lonquii . . . & Diderici à Waerdenburg . . . Een bondelken sindichten van wegen de veroveringe van Olinda. *Haarlem: A. Roman*, 1630. 16 p.; 4to. Rodrigues (Dom. Hol.) 888; Meulman 2114. Ghent:BU. 630/6

Antwerp. Collegium Societatis Jesu. Typus mundi in quo calamitates et pericula . . . emblematicè proponuntur . . . Editio altera. *Antwerp: J. Cnobbaert*, 1630. 144 p.; illus.; 12mo. 1st publ., Antwerp, 1627. Arents (Add.) 252. NN-A; Antwerp:Plantin Mus. 630/7

The armes of the tobachonists. *London: R. Shorleyker*, 1630. bds.; illus.; fol. STC 776; Arents 169-A. BL. 630/8

Arnauld, Antoine (1560–1619). La premiere et seconde Savoisienne. *Grenoble: P. Marnioles*, 1630. 2 pts; 8vo. Pt 1 by Arnauld; pt 2 (La seconde Savoisienne) attrib. variously to Bernard de Rechignevoisin, seigneur de Guron, Paul Hay, sieur de Chastelet, & Matthieu de Morgues, sieur de Saint Germain. The latter includes (p. 238) refs to Brazil, Pernambuco, & the Spanish fleet of the Indies. ICN, NIC; BL, BN. 630/9

—[Anr edn]. [*Grenoble?*] 1630. 2 pts; 8vo. [Locations may refer to the preceding edn:] CtY, NjPT, WU; BN. 630/10

Aventrote, Juan. Sendt-brief aen die van Peru, met een Aliance van de . . . heeren Staten der Vereenigder Provintien des Nederlands. Getranslateert uyt de Spaensche tale. *Amsterdam: P. A. van Ravesteyn*, 1630. [29] p.; 4to. Transl. from Aventrote's *Epistola á los Peruleras*, 1st publ., Amsterdam, 1627. Millares Carlo (Aventroot) 14; Knuttel 4001; Molhuysen I:200–201. The Hague:KB, Madrid:BN. 630/11

Avity, Pierre d', sieur de Montmartin. Les estats, empires et principautez du monde. *Paris: M. Henault*, 1630. 1048 p.; fol. 1st publ., Paris, 1613. Cf. Sabin 2498. Berlin:StB. 630/12

—[Anr edn]. *Rouen: J. Cailloué & A. Ouyn*, 1630. 1396 p.; fol. ICU, MB; Munich:StB. 630/13

Baardt, Pieter. Friesche Triton. Over t'geluckich veroveren van de stercke stadt Olinda met alle de forten in Fernambucq. *Leeuwarden: C. Fonteyne*, 1630. [16] p.; port.; fol. In verse. Borba de Moraes I:55; Rodrigues (Dom. Hol.) 399; Muller (1872) 220; JCB (3) II:226. DCU, RPJCB. 630/14

Baerle, Kaspar van. Poemata, tum quae antehac ed. fuerunt, tum quae iam singulari libro nova in lucem prodierunt. *Leyden: [G. Basson &] A. Cloucq*, 1630. 3 pts; 8vo. Here issued under collective t.p. are G. Basson's Leyden, 1628, edn of Baerle's *Poemata*, along with the author's *Poematum liber novus* of this year, below. Each has special t.p. Dt. Ges. Kat. 11.6598. Rostock:UB. 630/15

——. Poematum liber novus. *Leyden: A. Cloucq*, 1630. 183 p.; 8vo. In verse. 1st publ., Leyden, 1628, but here including for 1st time, 'Triumphus supra capta Olinda, Pernambuci urbe, Brasiliae metropoli', also issued separately as described below. Sabin 3407n; cf. Borba de Moraes I:65; Dt. Ges. Kat. 11.6597. IU, RPJCB; Munich:StB, Cologne:StUB. 630/16

——. Triumphus super captâ Olinda, Pernambuci urbe, Brasiliae metropoli. *Leyden: G. Basson*, 1630. 8 p.; fol. In verse. Sabin 3407n; Borba de Moraes I:65; Rodrigues (Dom. Hol.) 891. CtY, RPJCB; BL, BN. 630/17

Baers, Johannes. Olinda, ghelegen int landt van Brasil, inde capitania van Phernambuco . . . inghenomen ende . . . verovert . . . onder het beleydt vanden . . . zee-helt, den Heere Henrick Lonck, Generael weghen de Geoctroyeerde West-Indische Compagnie . . . door den . . . Heere Diederich van Weerdenburg. *Amsterdam: H. Laurenszoon*, 1630. 38 p.; 4to. Sabin 2712; Borba de Moraes I:56; Rodrigues (Dom. Hol.) 390; Knuttel 3997; JCB (3) II:226. DLC, KMK, NN-RB, RPJCB; BL, The Hague:KB. 630/18

Batavier gaet hem verblije. Singioor kryght de popelcye, over het innemen der . . . stadt Farnambucque [door S. B.]. [*Amsterdam?*] 1630. bds.; fol. In verse. Rodrigues

(Dom. Hol.) 392; Petit 1626b. Leyden: B. Thysiana. 630/19

Beaumont, Francis. The scornefull ladie. A comedie . . . The third edition. *London: B. A[lsop]. & T. F[awcet].*, *for T. Jones*, 1630. 36 lvs; 4to. 1st publ., London, 1616. STC 1688; Greg 334(c). DLC, ICU, MH; BL. 630/20

Benavides, Alonso de, O.F.M. Memorial que fray Juan de Santander . . . Comissario General de Indias, presenta a la majestad catolica del Rey Don Felipe quarto . . . Hecho por el padre fray Alonso de Benavides . . . custodio que ha sido de las provincias y conversiones del Nuevo-Mexico. *Madrid: Imprenta Real*, 1630. 109 p.; 4to. For anr state see Wagner. Sabin 4636 & 76810; Medina (BHA) 868; Streit II:1583; Wagner (SW) 33; JCB (3) II:226. CSmH, CtY, DLC, ICN, MH, NHi, RPJCB; BL, Madrid:BN. 630/21

Bertius, Petrus. Geographia vetus ex antiquis, et melioris notae scriptoribus nuper collecta. *Paris: M. Tavernier*, 1630. 41 lvs; maps; obl. 4to. 1st publ., Paris, 1628. BN. 630/22

Beschreibung, welcher Gestalt die Hauptstatt des Königreichs Brasilien, Phernambuco, in America gelegen, von Heinrich Cornelio Lonch . . . und Dieterich Wardenburg belägert, auch . . . erobert worden. Auss dem Niederländischen . . . ubergesetzt. Erstlich gedruckt zu Ambsderdamm bey Hessel Getritsz [sic], 1630. [*The Hague? 1630?*]. 8 p.; 4to. Transl. from the *Veroveringh van de stadt Olinda* of this year below. For a similar but differing translation of this year see entry under title *Warhaffter Bricht* [sic] . . . below. Sabin 41850; Borba de Moraes I:90. DLC, NN-RB; BL (Loncq), Amsterdam: NHSM. 630/23

Biancani, Giuseppe. Sphaera mundi, seu Cosmographia demonstrativa. *Modena: G. Cassiano*, 1630. fol. 1st publ., Bologna, 1620. Cf. 1635 edn of same printer. Sabin 5132n. 630/24

Blaeu, Willem Janszoon. Atlantis appendix, sive Pars altera continens tab. geographicas diversarum orbis regionum, nunc primum editas. *Amsterdam: W. J. Blaeu*, 1630. 60 maps; fol. Includes several American maps. Subsequently publ. under title *Appendix* *Theatri A. Ortelii*. For variants see Koeman. Koeman (Bl) 1. BL, Amsterdam:UB. 630/25

——. Het licht der zee-vaert. *Amsterdam: W. J. Blaeu*, 1630. 2 v.; illus., maps; obl. fol. 1st publ., Amsterdam, 1608. Books I & II dated '1629'. Koeman (M.Bl) 7. Paris: Loeb-Larocque, Stockholm:KB. 630/26

Boccalini, Traiano. De' ragguagli di Parnaso . . . Centuria prima . . . quinta impressione. *Venice: Heirs of G. Guerigli*, 1630. 478 p.; 4to. 1st publ., Venice, 1612. Firpo (Ragguagli) 19; Michel (Répertoire) I:176. IU, NNC, OU; BL, Paris:Mazarine. 630/27

——. De' ragguagli di Parnaso . . . Centuria seconda . . . quinta [sic] impressione. *Venice: Heirs of G. Guerigli*, 1630. 453 p.; 8vo. 1st publ., Venice, 1613; issued with the Guerigli Centuria prima of this year above. Firpo (Ragguagli) 19; Michel (Répertoire) I:176. IU, NNC, OU; BL, Paris:Mazarine. 630/28

Bock, Hieronymus. Kraütterbuch . . . Ubersehen . . . durch M. Sebizium. *Strassburg: W. C. Glaser*, 1630. 892 p.; illus.; fol. 1st publ., Strassburg, 1539. Included are descriptions of numerous American plants. Pritzel 866; cf. Nissen (Bot.) 182. MH, NNBG, NNU-H; BL. 630/29

Bompart, Marcellin. Nouveau chasse peste. *Paris: P. Gaultier*, 1630. 178 p.; 8vo. A formula (p. 108) calls for use of 'Balsamus Peruviani'; another (p. 112), for 'Lignum Guaiaci'. DNLM, MnU; BL, BN. 630/30

Bonham, Thomas. The chyrurgeons closet: or An antidotarie chyrurgicall . . . now drawne into forme, by Edward Poeton. *London: G. Miller*, *for E. Brewster*, 1630. 359 p.; 4to. Described are formulas for treatment of syphilis (*lues venerea*) employing guaiacum, & sarsaparilla; elsewhere tobacco is also called for. STC 3279; Arents (Add.) 248. CSmH, DFo, MBCo, MiU, MnU, NN-A, PPC; BL. 630/31

Bontier, Pierre. Histoire de la premiere descouverte et conqueste des Canaries. Faite dés l'an 1402. par messire Jean de Bethencourt . . . Plus un Traicté de la navigation et des voyages de descouverte & conqueste modernes, & principalement des François.

Paris: J. de Heuqueville, 1630. 2 pts; port.; 8vo. The 2nd pt, the *Traicté de la navigation,* etc., has special t.p. with joint imprint of Heuqueville & Soly, dated 1629, and includes accounts of Columbus's & Vespucci's voyages, as well as those of English, Dutch, & French navigators. Sabin 32016 (& 4850 & 5073); Cioranescu (XVII) 11470–71; Palau 32885; JCB (3) II:219–20 & 227. CtY, DLC, MWiW, MiU-C, MnU-B, NN-RB, PBL, RPJCB; BN.   630/32
—[Anr issue]. *Paris: M. Soly,* 1630. BN.
                                                           630/33

Botero, Giovanni. Relations of the most famous kingdomes. *London: J. Haviland, sold by J. Partridge,* 1630. 644 p.; map; 4to. 1st publ. in English, London, 1601, under title *The travellers breviat & The worlde;* also publ., London, 1603, under title *An historical description.* Sabin 6812 (& 36283n); Borba de Moraes I:101; STC 3404; JCB (3) II:227. DLC, ICN, MBAt, MnU, NN-RB, RPJCB; BL.   630/34

Bottifango, Giulio Cesare. Lettera dell'elefante. *Rome: F. Corbelletti,* 1630. 16 p.; illus., 8vo. The elephant in question is described as able to smoke tobacco. Arents (Add.) 249. CtY, NN-A.   630/35

Breton, Nicholas. A poste with a packet of madde letters. Newly imprinted. *London: J. Marriott,* 1630. 4to. 1st publ., London, 1602. STC 3691. London:Guildhall.
                                                           630/36

Bry, Theodor de. Vierzehender Theil Amerikanischer Historien, inhaltend, erstlich, Warhafftige Beschreibung etlicher West-Indianischer Landen. *Hanau: D. Aubry, for M. Merian, at Frankfurt a. M.,* 1630. 72 p.; illus., maps; fol. (Theodor de Bry's *America.* Pt 14. German). Includes accounts of New Mexico, Jacques L'Hermite, Pieter Hein, etc. For a description of the 8 pts, see Church 174n (I:401–2) & 202. Cf. Sabin 8784; Baginsky (German Americana) 162; Church 202; JCB (3) I:418–19. CSmH, DLC, ICN, NN-RB, RPJCB; BL, BN.   630/37

Camden, William. The historie of the most renowned . . . Princesse Elizabeth. *London: [N. Okes?,] for B. Fisher,* 1630. 4 pts; port.; fol. Transl. by R. N., i.e., Robert Norton, from Latin texts 1st publ. London, 1615 & Leyden, 1625. Sabin 10158n; STC 4500;

Arents 170. CSmH, CtY, DLC, InU-L, MH, NN-A; BL, BN.   630/38

Camerarius, Philipp. Tertia centuria historica, das ist, Dritter Theil des historischen Lustgartens. *Leipzig: Heirs of M. Wachsman,* 1630. 519 p.; 4to. Transl. by Georg Maier from Camerarius's *Operae horarum subcisivarum . . . Centuria tertia,* 1st publ., Frankfurt a. M., 1609. Continues Maier's German translation of pt 1 (Leipzig, 1625) & pt 2 (Leipzig, 1628). Jantz (German Baroque) 47. NcD; Wolfenbüttel:HB.   630/39

Cargo que resulta contra don Feliciano Navarro, gentilhombre de la dicha flota. Sobre que aviendole nombrado el Almirante don Juan de Leoz el dia ocho de setiembre . . . estando varados las naos de la dicha flota en el puerto de Matanças . . . saliessen á tierra [etc.]. *[Madrid? 1630?].* 14 numb. lvs; fol. Medina (BHA) 8067. Puebla: B. Palafoxiana.   630/40

Casas, Bartolomé de las, O.P., Bp of Chiapa. Istoria ò brevissima relatione della distruttione dell'Indie Occidentali . . . Tradotta . . . dall'eccell. sig. Giacomo Castellani già sotto nome di Francesco Bersabita. *Venice: M. Ginammi,* 1630. 150 p.; 4to. 1st publ. as here transl., Venice, 1626. Text in Spanish & Italian in parallel columns. Sabin 11243; Medina (BHA) 1085n (II:473); Hanke/Giménez 527; Streit I:446; JCB (3) II:228. CtY, DLC, MH, NN-RB, OU, PBL, RPJCB; Rouen:BM.   630/41

——. Tyrannies et cruautez des Espanols, commises es Indes Occidentales, qu'on dit le Nouveau Monde . . . Traduitte . . . par Jacques de Miggrode. *Rouen: J. Cailloué,* 1630. 214 p.; 4to. 1st publ. as here transl. from the work known as the *Brevíssima relación,* Antwerp, 1579; here reprinted 'jouxte la coppie imprimée à Paris par Guillaume Julien', in 1582. Sabin 11271; Medina (BHA) 1085n (II:472); Hanke/Giménez 529; Streit I:445; Palau 46963; JCB (3) II:228. CtHT, DLC, MWA, NN-RB, RPJCB; BL, BN.   630/42

Cats, Jacob. Silenus Alcibiadis, sive Proteus. *Amsterdam: W. J. Blaeu* [1630?]. 244 p.; illus.; 4to. 1st publ., Middelburg, 1618. Vries 84; Mus. Cats. 32. BL, Leyden:UB.   630/43

——[Anr edn]. . . . dit zijn zedelycke verclaeringen over syne siñe beelden. *[Amsterdam?*

1630?]. [176] p.; illus.; 8vo. The similarity of this edn to later edns cited in Mus. Cats. suggests that a later imprint date, e.g. [1680?], may be likelier. Cf. Vries 88; cf. Mus. Cats. 37. ICU.   630/44
—[Anr edn]. *Dordrecht: M. de Bot* [n.d.]. Arents 163-A. *See the year* 1645.

Champlain, Samuel de. Au Roy. Sire, Le sieur de Champlain remontre tres-humblement à Vostre Majesté, que les travaux par luy soufferts aux descouvertes de plusieurs terres . . . du pays de . . . Nouvelle France. [*Paris?* 1630?]. 25 p.; 4to. Cioranescu (XVII) 18331; JCB AR53:3–9. RPJCB; BN.
                                                                630/45

Clüver, Philipp. Introductionis in universam geographiam, tam veterem quàm novam libri vi. Editio ultima priorib. emendatior. *Amsterdam: Hondius Office* [1630?]. 2 pts; illus.; 16mo. 1st publ., Leyden, 1624. Includes also Petrus Bertius's *Breviarium totius orbis terrarum*, 1st publ., Paris, 1624. Cf. Sabin 13805. CtY, ICN, OU; BL.   630/46
—[Anr edn]. *Paris: M. Soly*, 1630. 506 p.; illus.; 16mo. BN.   630/47

Cortés, Martín. The arte of navigation. *London: B. A. & T. Fawcet, for J. Tapp*, 1630. 4to. Transl. by Richard Eden from Cortés's *Breve compendio de la sphera*, 1st publ., Seville, 1551; cf. English edn, London, 1609, above. STC 5805.5; A. F. Allison, *English translations from the Spanish* (Folkestone, 1974) 47.8.   630/48

Cotton, John. Gods promise to His plantation . . . a sermon. *London: W. Jones for J. Bellamy*, 1630. 20 p.; 4to. Delivered in Boston, Lincolnshire, on occasion of John Winthrop's departure for New England; preface refers directly to Virginia, Bermuda, etc., while the sermon provides biblical support for the undertaking. Sabin 17065; Tuttle (Cotton) 1; STC 5854; JCB (3) II:228. CtY, DLC, ICN, MH, NN-RB, RPJCB; BL, Cambridge:UL.   630/49

Crexel de San Martín, Juan. Señor. El capitan Juan Crexel de San Martin procurador general del govierno del Espiritu Santo de la Grita, jurisdicion del nuevo reyno de Granada de las Indias. [*Madrid?* ca. 1630]. 4 numb. lvs; fol. Memorial addressed to king of Spain. Medina (BHA) 8144. RPJCB.
                                                                630/50

Daniel, Charles. La prise d'un seigneur escossois et de ses gens qui pilloient les navires pescheurs de France. Ensemble le razement de leur fort, & l'establissement d'un autre pour le service du Roy, & l'assurance des pescheurs françois en la Nouvelle France par monsieur Daniel de Dieppe . . . general de la flotte en la Nouvelle France. *Rouen: J. LeBoullenger*, 1630. 24 p.; 12mo. Sabin 44089; Harrisse (NF) 45. BL.
                                                                630/51

Dekker, Thomas. The second part of the Honest whore. *London: Elizabeth Allde, for N. Butter*, 1630. [85] p.; 4to. Drama. The 1st pt, without American content, had appeared in 1604. Tobacco is mentioned. STC 6506; Greg 435; Arents 171; Pforzheimer 278. CSmH, CtY, DLC, ICN, MH, NN-A; BL.   630/52
——. Villanies discovered. *London: A. Mathewes*, 1630. 4to. 1st publ., London, 1608, under title *Lanthorne and candle-light*. STC 6490. Oxford:Bodl.   630/53

Dialogus ofte t'Samenspreekinge tusschen Jan Andersorgh ende Govert Eygensin. [*Amsterdam?*] 1630. [32] p.; 4to. Argues for war with Spain in interest of Dutch commerce with West Indies. Knuttel 4020. MnU-B, NN; The Hague:KB.
                                                                630/54

Discours, aengaende treves of vrede, met de infante ofte koning van Hispanien, ende dese Vereenighde Nederlanden. *Haarlem: A. Roman*, 1630. [39] p.; 4to. 1st publ., Haarlem, 1629. Knuttel 4024. The Hague:KB.
                                                                630/55

Drayton, Michael. Poems . . . Newly corrected & augmented. *London: W. Stansby, for J. Smethwick*, 1630. 3 pts; 8vo. 1st publ., London, 1605. STC 7224; Grolier Club (Langland to Wither) 91. CSmH, CtY, DFo, ICN, MH, NN-RB; BL.   630/56

Duchesne, Joseph. La pharmacopee des dogmatiques reformee . . . Seconde edition, revue & augmentée. *Paris: C. Morel*, 1630. 2 pts; port.; 8vo. 1st publ. Paris, 1624, as here transl. from Duchesne's *Pharmacopoea dogmaticorum restituta*, 1st publ., Paris, 1607. DNLM; London:Wellcome.
                                                                630/57

Earle, John, Bp of Salisbury. Micro-cosmographie. or, A peece of the world discovered . . . The sixth edition, augmented. *London: R. B[adger]., for R. Allott,* 1630. [299] p.; 12mo. 1st publ., London, 1628. STC 7443; Murphy (Engl. char.-bks) 39–40. DFo; BL. 630/58

Entwerffung von Eroberung der Stadt Olinda, so in der Hauptmanschafft Pharnambuco gelegen, und durch den . . . Herrn Heinrich Cornelis Lonck . . . und Herrn Colonell Wartenburg . . . eingenommen. [*Frankfurt a. M.? Amsterdam?* 1630]. bds.; illus.; fol. Extracted & transl. from the *Veroveringh van de stadt Olinda* of this year below. Sabin 41848; Borba de Moraes I:246; JCB (3) II:231. DLC, RPJCB. 630/59

—[Anr edn]. Von Eroberung der Stadt Olinda, so in der Hauptmanschafft Pharnembuco gelegen. [*Frankfurt a. M.?*] 1630. 3 lvs; illus.; 4to. Borba de Moraes I:247. Vienna:NB. 630/60

Erschröckliche Zeittung wie inn die neun Tausent Häuser in der Stadt-Mexico . . . worbey viel tausent seelen durch ein erschröckliches Wetter, sturmwind und Wasserflut vor 6. Wochen dieses 1630 Jars ertruncken und untergangen. *Frankfurt a. M.:* [1630]. 4to. Palmer 319. BL (Mexico, City of). 630/61

Este es la verdaderissima relacion de la feliz vitoria que ha tenido Don Fadrique de Toledo, general de la Real Armada de su Magestad, de quarenta naos Olandesas, las seys que encontro en . . . las Canarias, y las quatro que estavan en la isla de San Lorenço, dando careno. *Granada: M. Fernández Zambrano,* 1630. [4] p.; fol. The 2nd encounter took place off the coast of Peru. See also entries of this year under *Feliz. vitoria.* Medina (BHA) 875. Seville:BU. 630/62

Feliz. vitoria. que ha tenido Don Fadrique de Toledo, general de la Real Armada de su Magestad, de quarenta naos Olandesas, las seis . . . en la altura . . . de las Canarias, y las trienta y quatro que estavan en la isla de S. Lorenço, en las Indias, dando carena. *Seville: F. de Lyra,* 1630. [4] p.; fol. The 2nd encounter took place off the coast of Peru. See also entry of this year under title *Este es la verdaderissima relacion,* &, as transl. into Dutch, the *Translaet uyt den Spaenschen.* Me-

dina (BHA) 877; Escudero (Seville) 1.430; Palau 87530 (& 257989?). RPJCB. 630/63

—[Anr edn]. *Valladolid: J. Lasso,* 1630. 2 lvs; fol. Alcocer (Valladolid) 761; Palau 87529. 630/64

Fernández de Santiestevan, Blas. Relacion verdadera y cierta de la desseada y felice venida de la flota de Nueva España, y galeones de Tierra Firme, y de la armada real del Mar Oceano. Da se quenta de las mercaderias, plata, oro, y perlas que truxo registrada y valor dellas. *Granada: M. Fernández,* 1630. [3] p.; fol. Medina (BHA) 870. Granada:BU. 630/65

Fernández Manjón, Lucas. Por Lucas Fernandez Manjon, procurador general del pueblo, y mineros de san Luis, Potosi de Nueva España. En el pleyto de capitulos con don Pedro de Salazar, alcalde mayor que fue de las dichas minas. [*Madrid?* ca. 1630?]. 13 numb. lvs; fol. Medina (BHA) 6451. Santiago, Chile:BN. 630/66

Ferrufiño, Juan Bautista, S.J. Señor. Juan Bautista Ferrufino procurador general de la provincia del Paraguay . . . dize: Que como constanta de las informaciones . . . los venerables padres Roque Gonzales de Santa-Cruz, Juan de Castillo, y Alonson Rodriguez . . . padieceron martirio en la provincia de Uruguay, muriendo a manos de los Indios. [*Madrid:* ca. 1630]. [4] p.; fol. Memorial to king of Spain. Cf. Sabin 24195; Medina (BHA) 6462; Streit II:1617; Backer III:699 & IX:333–34. BL. 630/67

Fioravanti, Leonardo. La cirugia . . . Con una gionta de secreti nuovi. *Venice: L. Spineda,* 1630. 182 numb. lvs; 8vo. 1st publ., Venice, 1570; cf. 1610 edn. Michel (Répertoire) III:47; Wellcome I:2303. DNLM, NNH; BL, Avignon:BM. 630/68

——. Del compendio de' secreti rationali. *Venice: L. Spineda,* 1630. 190 numb. lvs; 8vo. 1st publ., Venice, 1564; cf. 1620 edn. Michel (Répertoire) III:47. Montpellier:Ecole de Médecine. 630/69

Freitag, Johann. Aurora medicorum Galeno-chymicorum . . . libri iv. *Frankfurt a. M.: J. T. Schönwetter,* 1630. 642 p.; 4to. In bk 2, chapt. xxix, mechoacan is discussed; in bk 3, chapt. xxix, Peruvian opobalsam.

Wellcome I:2415. DNLM, MH, WU; BL, BN.   630/70

Gallobelgicus, pseud. Wine, beere, ale and tobacco contending for superiority . . . The second edition, much enlarged. *London: T. C[oles]., for J. Grove,* 1630. [26] p.; 4to. Dramatic dialogue. 1st publ., London, 1629; here tobacco is given a separate identity. STC 11542; Greg 426 (b); Arents 174. CSmH, DLC, MH, NN-A; BL.   630/71

García de Avila, Francisco. Para que se devan preferir todos los que huvieran servido en las Indias a su Magestad. [*Madrid?* 1630?]. 9 numb. lvs; 4to. Medina (BHA) 6489. BL.   630/72

General opinion es en la Nuevaespaña . . . que los repartimientos delos Indios, para las minas y labores, es la causa mas eficaz para consumirlos. [*Madrid?* 1630?]. [4] p.; fol. BL.   630/73

Ghedenck-weerdich verhael van t'ghene datter ghepasseert is tusschen de ghecommitteerden vande . . . Staten ter eener zijde ende van weghen de Hertoginne en de Koninck van Hispanien ter ander zijde . . . Midtsgaders een naerder advijs vande treffelijcke vlooten vande . . . West Indische Compaignye wat by deselve ghepasseert is. *Rotterdam: J. Janszoon,* 1630. [8] p.; 8vo. Asher 144.   630/74

Goodall, Baptist. The tryall of travell. *London: J. Norton; sold by J. Upton,* 1630. [80] p.; 4to. In verse. Included are refs to Columbus & other explorers of America. Sabin 27842; STC 12007; Church 415. CSmH, DFo, MH; BL.   630/75

Great Britain. Sovereigns, etc., 1625–1649 (Charles I). A proclamation concerning tobacco. *London:* 1630. *See the year* 1631.

———. A proclamation forbidding the disorderly trading with the salvages in New England . . . especially the furnishing of the natives . . . by the English with weapons, and habilments of warre. *London: R. Barker & assigns of J. Bill,* 1630. 2 lvs; fol. Sabin 65938?; Crawford (Roy. procl.) 1627; Brigham (Roy. procl.) 66–68; STC 8969. CSmH, MH; London:Soc. of Antiquaries.   630/76

Guibert, Philbert. Les oeuvres charitables. *Paris: J. Jost,* 1630, '29. 2 pts; 12mo. Included

in pt 1 is Guibert's *Le prix et valeur des medicamens,* 1st publ., Paris, 1625. WU.   630/77

Hakewill, George. An apologie or declaration of the power and providence of God in the government of the world . . . The second edition revised. *Oxford: W. Turner, for R. Allot, at London,* 1630. 523 p.; fol. 1st publ., Oxford, 1627. STC 12612; Madan (Oxford) I:1630:6. CSmH, CtY, DLC, ICU, MBC, MWA, MiD, MnU, NN-RB, PPL; BL, BN.   630/78

Harris, Robert. Six sermons of conscience. *London: H. L[ownes]., for J. Bartlet,* 1630. 5 pts; 4to. Includes Harris's *The drunkards cup,* 1st publ., London, 1619. STC 12852 (& 12830). CSmH, CtY, DFo, ICU, MH, NN-RB; BL.   630/79

Higginson, Francis. New-Englands plantation. Or, A short and true description of that countrey. *London: T. C[otes]. & R. C[otes]., for M. Sparke,* 1630. [22] p.; 4to. Description of Plymouth Colony, July–Sept. 1629. Sabin 31739; Vail (Frontier) 72; STC 13449; Church 416; JCB (3) II:229. CSmH, DLC, ICN, InU-L, MH, NN-RB, RPJCB; Oxford:Bodl.   630/80

——[Anr edn]. The second edition. *London: T. & R. Cotes, for M. Sparke,* 1630. [28] p.; 4to Vail (Frontier) 73; STC 13450. CSmH, CtY, MB, NN-RB; Dublin:Marsh's.   630/81

——[Anr edn]. The third edition. *London: T. & R. Cotes, for M. Sparke,* 1630. [26] p.; 4to. Sabin 31740; Vail (Frontier) 74; STC 13451; JCB (3) II:229. CSmH, CtY, DLC, ICN, MB, NN-RB, RPJCB; BL.   630/82

Holyday, Barten. Τεχνογαμια: or, The marriages of the arts. A comedy. *London: J. Haviland, for R. Meighen,* 1630. 56 lvs; 4to. 1st publ., London, 1618. STC 13618; Greg 353 (b); Arents (Add.) 250. CSmH, CtY, DLC, ICU, MH, NN-RB; BL.   630/83

Horst, Jakob. Herbarium Horstianum. *Marburg: C. Chemlin,* 1630. 414 p.; 8vo. In the appendix several American plants are mentioned. Pritzel 4275. DNLM, MH-A, MnU, NNBG, RPB; BL, BN.   630/84

Hulsius, Levinus. Die zwey und zwäntzigste Schiffart, das ist, Historische eygentliche Beschreibung der . . . Schiffahrt, so under dem Admiral Jacob l'Hermite . . . umb die gantzen Welt beschehen . . . von Adolph Deckern . . . erzehlt. . . . *Frankfurt a. M.: Heirs of Hulsius,* 1630. 114 p.; illus., map; 4to. (Levinus Hulsius's *Sammlung von . . . Schiffahrten.* Pt 22). 1st publ. in German, Strassburg, 1629, under title *Diurnal der nassawischen Flotta.* Sabin 33675; Church 314; JCB (3) I:468. CSmH, CtY, ICN, NN-RB, RPJCB; WiU; BL, BN. 630/85

Klare aenwijsinge. Dat de Vereenighde Nederlanden, gheen treves met den vyandt dienen te maecken. Sijnde net Derden deel van't Tractaet tegens pays, treves ende Onderhandelinghe . . . *The Hague: A. Meuris,* 1630. [72] p.; 4to. Pt 3 of the *Tractaet tegens pays,* 1st publ., The Hague, 1629. For pt 2, see the *Redenen* of this year below. For a reply to this pt, see Wtenbogaert's *Wtwissinge der schandelicker blamen* of this year below. Sabin 38034; Asher 136; Muller (1872) 461; Knuttel 4014. RPJCB; The Hague:KB. 630/86

Kurtze Erzehlung: was massen vom Herrn General Long nebenst dem Colonel, Dietrich von Wartenburg, die Hauptstadt Fernambuco in Brassilien, so ein Theil der Landschafft Americae, wie auch die beyde dabey liegende . . . castel . . . eingenommen worden. [*Hamburg?*] 1630. 4 lvs; illus.; 4to. Narrative on the taking of Olinda extracted from the *Entwerffung von Eroberung der Stadt Olinda* of this year above. Borba de Moraes I:375–76. Vienna:NB. 630/87

Laet, Joannes de. Beschrijvinghe van West-Indien . . . Tweede druck . . . verbetert, vermeerdert. *Leyden: The Elseviers,* 1630. 622 p.; maps; fol. 1st publ., Leyden, 1625, under title *Nieuwe Wereldt.* Sabin 38555; Borba de Moraes I:384; Vail (Frontier) 75; Streit II:1587; Willems (Les Elzevier) 327; JCB (3) II:229. CtY, DLC, InU, MH, NN-RB, PU, RPJCB; BL, BN. 630/88

Lalli, Giovanni Battista. Opere poetiche. *Milan: D. Fontana & G. Scaccabarozzo,* 1630. 2 pts; 12mo. Includes the author's *La franceide,* 1st publ., Foligno, 1629. Brunet III:778 (14573). CU, CtY, ICN; BL, BN. 630/89

Lampe, Barent. Het achtiende deel of 't vervolgh van het Historisch verhael aller ge-denckwaerdiger geschiedeniss. die in Europa . . . in America, als in West-Indien, d'eijlanden en Brasil . . . voorgevallen zijn. *Amsterdam: J. Janszoon, the Younger* [1630?]. 108 numb. lvs; illus., 4to. (N. van Wassenaer's *Historisch verhael.* Pt 18). Includes, under segment for February, account of the conquest of Olinda. Under March is included the Nederlandsche West-Indische Compagnie's *Vryheden ende exemptien voor de patronen,* 1st publ. this year, described below under a slightly differing title. Cf. Sabin 102039 (& 102920n); Borba de Moraes II:371; Muller (1872) 1745. RPJCB. 630/90

Ledesma, Diego de, S.J. Doctrine chrestienne . . . Traduite en langage Canadois, pour la conversion des habitants dudit pays. *Rouen: R. Lallemant,* 1630. 26 p.; 12mo. Transl. by Jean de Brébeuf from the Spanish. Sabin 39682; Harrisse (NF) 46; Backer IV:1650; Palau 134152; JCB (3) II:230. RPJCB; BN. 630/91

León Pinelo, Antonio Rodríguez. Tratado de confirmaciones reales de encomiendas, oficios i casos, en que se requieren para las Indias Occidentales. *Madrid: J. González,* 1630. 173 numb. lvs; 4to. Sabin 40057; Palau 135740; JCB (3) II:230. CU-B, CtY, DLC, InU-L, MH, MnU-B, NN-RB, PBL, RPJCB; BL, BN. 630/92

Leonardo y Argensola, Bartolomé Juan. Primera parte de los Anales de Aragon. *Saragossa: P. Bueno, for J. de Lanaja,* 1630. 1128 p.; fol. Includes refs to Cortés, Magellan, & Las Casas. Sabin 1950; Hanke/Giménez 526; Palau 16096; JCB (3) II:230. CU-A, CtY, DLC, MiU, NNH, PU, RPJCB. 630/93

Liefs, Jacob. Den lof vande geoctroyeerde Oost ende West-Indische Compagnye ende lofrijcke zee-vaert. *Delft: J. P. Waalpots,* 1630. 16 p.; 4to. Petit 1625. Leyden:B. Thysiana. 630/94

Loarte Dávila, ——. Informacion en derecho del que tiene su Magestad para proveer el oficio de Colector general de Lima. [*Madrid?* 1630?]. [4] p.; fol. BL. 630/95

Loncq, Hendrik Cornelis. Copia wt de missiven oft briefen van . . . Lonck . . . ende . . . Diedrich Waerbenburgh [*sic*]. *Amster-

dam: G. van Breughel [1630?]. bds.; fol. Dated at Pernambuco, March 1630. Cf. Waerdenburgh's *Copie vande missive* of this year below. Petit 1626c. Leyden:UB.   630/96

——, **supposed author.** Vera relatione della presa della città d'Olinda di Fernambuco, città capitale del gran regno di Brasil. *Venice: The Reghettini*, 1630. [8] p.; 8vo. ICN.
630/97

López Solis, Francisco. Por los religiosos de la provincia de san Hipolyto Martyr de Guaxaca . . . en defensa de la jurisdiccion del . . . padre . . . Diego Ibañez . . . guardian del convento de Mexico. [*Madrid?* 1630?]. fol. Signed in ms. at end: Don Lopes de Solis. BL.   630/98

Mañozca, Juan de. Señor. El licencido Juan de Mañozca, inquisidor apostolico de la ciudad de Lima, en . . . Pirù, y vuestro visitador, que fue de la Real Audiencia de S. Francisco del Quito. Dize [etc.]. [*Madrid?* ca. 1630?]. [52?] p.; fol. Reply to Leonardo de Araujo's *Relacion de las cosas que sucidieron en la ciudad de Quito*, [Madrid? 1627?]. Sabin 44359; Medina (BHA) 6602. RPJCB (imp.).
630/99

Martini, Matthäus. De morbis mesenterii abstrusioribus. *Leipzig: K. Klosemann*, 1630. 365 p.; 8vo. 1st publ., Halle, 1625. Wellcome I:4091. CtY-M, DNLM; BL, BN.
630/100

Massachusetts (Colony). The humble request of his Majesties loyall subjects . . . late gone for New-England. *London:* [*M. Fletcher,*] *for J. Bellamy*, 1630. 10 p.; 4to. Authorship ascribed to the Rev. George Phillips; explains motives for settling the colony. Sabin 104846; Vail (Frontier) 76; STC 18485 (& formerly also 25858); JCB (3) II:231–32. CSmH, MB, MiU-C, RPJCB; Oxford:Bodl.   630/101

Memoria de lo que an de advertir los pilotos de la Carrera de las Indias, a cerca de la reformacion del padron delas cartas de marear. [*Madrid?* 1630?]. bds.; fol. BL.
630/102

Mendoça, Lourenço de, Bp of Rio de Janeiro. El doctor Lorenço de Mendoça prelado, con jurisdicion y oficio episcopal, de la diocesi del Rio de Janeiro. [*Madrid?* 1630?]. 6 numb. lvs; fol. Memorial to king of Spain on dangers to Spanish colonies

from frequent appearance there of heretics; &, in general, on the state of Brazil. Medina (BHA) 6629. BL.   630/103

——. Suplicacion a Su Magestad . . . Antes sus Reales Consejos de Portugal y de las Indias, en defensa de los Portugueses. *Madrid:* 1630. 58 numb. lvs; 4to. Seeks equal treatment with Spanish of Portuguese in America, also subjects of the king of Spain. Sabin 47830; Medina (BHA) 872. ICN, MnU-B, NN-RB; BL.   630/104

Mercator, Gerardus. Atlantis majoris appendix, sive Pars altera, continens geographicas tabulas diversarum orbis regionum & provinciarum octoginta, nunc primum editas. *Amsterdam: J. Janszoon, the Younger*, 1630. 80 maps; fol. Includes various American maps. For variants see Koeman as cited. Koeman (Me) 31A, B, C. Paris: Ste Geneviève, Erlangen:UB.   630/105

——. Atlas minor, ofte Een korte doch grondige beschrijvinge der geheeler werelt . . . eerstlije . . . in't latijn beschreven ende vervolghens door Judocum Hondium met vele caerten verbetert ende vermeerdert ende . . . overgeset door Ernestus Brinck. *Amsterdam: J. Janszoon, the Younger*, 1628 [i.e., 1630]. 763 p.; maps; obl. 12mo. Transl. from Amsterdam, 1628, edn. The preface is dated 29 Dec. 1629. The Dutch title is on a paste-on slip over 1628 Latin title. Koeman (Me) 197; Phillips (Atlases) 439, 5929, & 5930. DLC, NjP, Wa; Geneva:BP.
630/106

——. Atlas minor, ou Brièfve, & vive description de tout le monde . . . composée premièrement en latin . . . & depuis reveu, corrigé & augmenté de plusieurs tables nouvelles, par Judocus Hondius: & traduict . . . par le sieur de la Popelinière. *Amsterdam: J. Janszoon, the Younger*, 1630. 643 p.; maps; obl. 12mo. 1st publ. in French, Amsterdam, 1608. Title & imprint are paste-on slips on 1628 Latin t.p. Sabin 47888; Koeman (Me) 196; Phillips (Atlases) 3419. CtY (paste-on slips wanting), DLC, MiU-C; BL, BN.   630/107

——. Atlas, or A geographicke description . . . of the world. *Amsterdam:* 1630. *See the year* 1636.

——. Atlas, sive Cosmographicae meditationes . . . Editio decima. *Amsterdam: H.*

Hondius, 1630. 391 lvs; maps; ports; fol. 1st publ., Amsterdam, 1606. Text in Latin. For variants, see Koeman. Koeman (Me 29A & B); Phillips (Atlases) 441. CtY, DLC, InU-L, NNH, PPL; BN. 630/108

—[Anr edn]. *Amsterdam: J. E. Cloppenburg,* 1630. 676 p.; maps; obl. 8vo. Text in French. Phillips (Atlases) 440. DLC.
630/109

Meteren, Emanuel van. Der niderländischen Historien dritter Theil. *Amsterdam:* 1630. *See under title below.*

Middleton, Thomas. The phoenix. *London: T. H[arper]., for R. Meighen,* 1630. [69] p.; 4to. Drama. 1st publ., London, 1607. STC 17893; Greg 243 (b). CSmH, CtY, DLC, MH, NNPM; BL. 630/110

Missive, inhoudende den aerdt vanden treves tusschen den Koninck van Spaengien ende de Gheunieerde Provincien. [*The Hague?*] 1630. [39] p.; 4to. Mentions West Indies, Spanish Silver fleet, & West-Indische Compagnie. Knuttel 4023. CtY, MnU-B, NN-RB; The Hague:KB. 630/111

More, Sir Thomas, Saint. De Utopia . . . Over-geset in't Nederduytsch. *Hoorn: I. Willemszoon, for M. Gerbrantszoon,* 1629 [colophon: 1630]. 236 p.; 8vo. Transl. from Latin text 1st publ., Louvain, 1516; cf. 1601 edn. Gibson (More) 40; Shaaber (Brit. auth.) M243. Amsterdam:UB. 630/112

—[Anr issue]. *Hoorn: I. Willemszoon, for M. Gerbrantszoon,* 1630. A reissue of the above with cancel t.p. Gibson (More) 41; Shaaber (Brit. auth.) M244. CtY, ICJ; London:UL, Groningen:UB. 630/113

Neander, Johann. Traicté du tabac, ou Nicotiane, panacee . . . mis . . . en françois, par J[acques]. V[eyras]. *Lyons:* 1630. 8vo. 1st publ. as transl. from author's *Tabacologia* (Leyden, 1622), Lyons, 1625. Arents 148-c. NN-A. 630/114

Nederlandsche West-Indische Compagnie. Articulen, met approbatie vande . . . Staten Generael . . . provisioneelijck beraemt by bewinthebberen . . . over het open ende vry stellen vanden handel ende negotie opde stadt Olinda de Parnambuco, ende custen van Brasil. *Amsterdam: P. A. van Ravesteyn,* 1630. [8] p.; 4to. Sabin 102924; Asher 160; Knuttel 3998. NN-RB; The Hague:KB. 630/115

—[Anr edn]. *Middelburg: Widow & Heirs of S. Moulert* [1630?]. 4 lvs; 4to. Sabin 102924; Le Clerc (1878) 1675; Knuttel 3999. The Hague:KB. 630/116

——. Three severall treatises concerning the truce . . . The first, laying open divers considerations and reasons why a truce ought not to be contracted, propounded . . . by the . . . commissioners and deputies of the . . . Company of West India . . . Translated out of the Low-Dutch copie. *London: [B. Alsop & T. Fawcet,] for N. Butter & N. Bourne,* 1630. 28 p.; 4to. Transl. from Nederlandsche West-Indische Compagnie's *Consideratien ende redenen,* 1st publ., Haarlem, 1629. Sabin 95749; STC 24258; JCB (3) II:234. CSmH, DFo, MBAt, RPJCB; BL. 630/117

——. Vryheden by de vergaderinghe van de negenthiene vande Geoctroyeerde West-Indische Compagnie vergunt aen allen den ghenen, die eenighe colonien in Nieu-Nederlandt sullen planten. *Amsterdam: M. J. Brandt,* 1630. [15] p.; illus.; 4to. For variant states see Sabin. Sabin 102920; Vail (Frontier) 79; Knuttel 4000; JCB (3) II:232. CSmH, DLC, MB, MiU-C, NN-RB, RPJCB; BL, The Hague:KB. 630/118

Netherlands (United Provinces, 1581–1795). Staten Generaal. Placcaet . . . op't stuck van't verkoopen ende transporteren van actien inde West-Indische Compaignie. *The Hague: Widow & Heirs of H. Jacobszoon van Wouw,* 1630. [5] p.; 4to. 1st publ., The Hague, 1621. Sabin 63200; Asher 72; Petit 1628. DLC; BL, Leyden:B. Thysiana. 630/119

—[Anr edn]. Placaet . . . op 't stuck van 't verkoopen . . . van actien inde Oost ende West-Indische Compagnien. *The Hague: Widow & Heirs of H. Jacobszoon van Wouw,* 1630. 8 p.; 4to. Sabin 63201; Asher 73. 630/120

——. De Staten Generael . . . *The Hague: Widow & Heirs of H. Jacobszoon van Wouw,* 1630. bds.; fol. Orders protection for holdings of Portuguese inhabitants of Brazil. Asher 143; Petit 1630. Leyden:B. Thysiana. 630/121

Der niderländischen Historien dritter Theil . . . vom jahr 1620 biss auff 1630. *Amsterdam: J. Janszoon, the Younger,* 1630. 686 p.;

illus.; fol. Continues E. van Meteren's *Eygentliche und vollkommene historische Beschreibung dess niderländischen Kriegs*, Amsterdam, 1627. Cambridge:UL, BN, Uppsala:UB.
630/122

Nieremberg, Juan Eusebio, S.J. Curiosa filosofia, y tesoro de maravillas de la naturaleza. *Madrid: Imprenta Real,* 1630. 264 numb. lvs; 8vo. Included are numerous scattered refs to the New World, e.g., to the passionflower, Sir Francis Drake, and Magellan. Cf. the author's *Historia naturae . . . libris xvi* of 1635. Backer V:1730; Palau 190662. BN.
630/123

Nijkerke, Joost Willemszoon. Klaer-bericht ofte Aenwysinghe. Hoe ende op wat wijse, de tegenwoordige dierte der granen sal konnen geremedieert werden, ende de schipvaert deser landen vergroot. *The Hague: A. Meuris,* 1630. [23] p.; 4to. The West-Indische Compagnie & West Indian trade are mentioned, as well as Greenland. Knuttel 4004. ICJ; BL (Netherlands), The Hague:KB.
630/124

—[Anr edn]. *Hoorn: M. Gerbrantszoon,* 1630. [24] p.; 4to. Knuttel 4005. The Hague:KB.
630/125

Norton, Samuel. Metamorphosis lapidum ignobilium in gemmas quasdam pretiosas. *Frankfurt a. M.: K. Rötel, for W. Fitzer,* 1630. 12p.; illus.; 4to. Described (p. 8–12) is a certain mineral called 'Electrum', 'inventum in India occidentali', which served as an 'antidotum contra omnia venena', perhaps referring to the bezoar stone of Peru. Shaaber (Brit. auth.) N38; Ferguson (Bibl. chem.) II:142; Wellcome I:4573. CtY, DNLM, MH, WU; BL, BN.
630/126

Osorio de Erasso, Diego. Señor. Celebre fue la vitoria. [*Madrid?* 1630?]. 10 numb. lvs; 4to. Memorial to king of Spain on conversion of Indians. BL.
630/127

Overbury, Sir Thomas. Sir Thomas Overbury his wife . . . The fourteenth impression. *London: [B. Alsop & T. Fawcet,] for R. Allott,* 1630. [320] p.; 8vo. 1st publ., London, 1615. STC 18917; Murphy (Engl. char.-bks) 23. CSmH, DFo, NIC; BL.
630/128

Ovidius Naso, Publius. Amores. English. All Ovids elegies. '*Middlebourgh*' [i.e., *London:* ca. 1630]. [96] p.; 8vo. For earlier edns see

the year 1602. Title page has ornament of 3 leaves & 2 hands. STC 18932. CSmH, CtY, DFo, NNPM; BL.
630/129

Palafox y Mendoza, Juan de, Bp of Puebla de los Angeles. Por Don Juan de Palafox, y Mendoza, fiscal del Consejo de Indias. Con Don Geronimo de Sandoval, general que fue de la flota de Nueva-España el año de 628. [*Madrid?* ca. 1630?]. 7 numb. lvs; fol. Medina (BHA) 6719. Seville:Archivo de Indias.
630/130

Pardoux, Barthélemy. Universa medicina ex medicorum principium sententiis consiliisque collecta. *Paris: M. Henault,* 1630. 943 p.; 4to. In bk 4, sect. 2, chapt. x, the food values of the turkey are described; in bk 8, chapt. xxi, 'De oleis chimisticis', guaiacum is discussed; in bk 12, chapt. ix, 'De lue venerea', syphilis is described as American in origin, & guaiacum is prescribed. Wellcome I:4898. DNLM, PPC; London: Wellcome, BN.
630/131

Pigray, Pierre. Epitome des preceptes de medecine et chirurgie. *Rouen: L. Loudet,* 1630. 8vo. 1st publ., Paris, 1600, under title *La chirurgie;* cf. 1604 edn. NNNAM.
630/132

Pinon, Jacques. De anno romano carmen . . . Seconda editio. *Paris: S. Cramoisy,* 1630. 2 pts; 8vo. 1st publ., Paris, 1615. ICU; BL, BN.
630/133

A proposition of provisions needfull for such as intend to plant themselves in New England. *London: F. Clifton,* 1630. bds.; fol. Sabin 66013; STC 18486. BL, Lincoln:Cathedral.
630/134

Randolph, Thomas. Aristippus, or The jovial philosopher . . . To which is added, The conceited pedlar. *London: T. Harper, for J. Marriott, & sold by R. Myn,* 1630. 44 p.; 4to. Drama. In *Aristippus*, tobacco is mentioned; in *The conceited pedlar*, America. On 1f A2r, line 2 of speech has reading 'steep'd'. STC 20686; Greg 431/432(a); Arents (Add.) 251. CSmH, DLC, NN-RB, PU; BL.
630/135

—[Anr edn]. *London: T. Harper, for J. Marriott, & sold by R. Myn,* 1630. 44 p.; 4to. On 1f A2r, line 2 has reading 'steept'. STC 20686.5. CSmH, DFo, ICN, MH, NN-RB; Oxford:Bodl.
630/136

—[Anr edn]. *London: [J. Beale?] for R. Allott,*

1630. 44 p.; 4to. STC 20687; Greg 431/432(d). CSmH, DFo; BL. 630/137

Rapine, Charles, O.F.M. Histoire generale de l'origine et progrez des freres mineurs de S. François . . . appellés . . . Recollects . . . ou Deschaux, tant en toutes les provinces & royaumes catholiques, comme dans les Indes Orientales & Occidentales, & autres parties des nouveaux mondes. *Paris:* 1630. 2 pts; 4to. Cf. Sabin 67915; Streit I:448. Romc:OFM. 630/138

Redenen, waeromme dat de Vereenighde Nederlanden geensints eenighe vrede met den Koningh van Spaignien konnen mogen, noch behooren te maecken. Zijnde het Tweede deel van't Tractaet tegens pays, treves en onderhandelinge . . . *The Hague:* A. Meuris, 1630. [66] p.; 4to. Pt 2 of the *Tractaet tegens pays,* 1st publ., The Hague, 1629. For a 3rd pt, see the *Klare aenwysinge* of this year above. Cf. Sabin 38034; Muller (1872) 461; Asher 135; Knuttel 4013. RPJCB; The Hague:KB. 630/139

Reed-geld over betalinghe der ongefondeerde lasteringen . . . teghens de Roomsche kercke . . . door Samuel Ampsing . . . so in syn West-Indische triumph-basuyne. [*Haarlem?*] 1630. 12 p.; 4to. A reply to Ampzing's *West-Indische triumph-basuyne,* Haarlem, 1629, and other works. Knuttel 4115. The Hague:KB. 630/140

Relaçam verdadeira, e breve da tomada da villa de Olinda, e lugar do Recife na costa do Brazil pellos rebeldes de Olanda, tirada de huma carta que escreveo hum religioso. *Lisbon: M. Rodriguez,* 1630. [6] p.; fol. Sabin 69167; Borba de Moraes II:183–84. NN-RB. 630/141

Relacion verdadera, de la grandiosa vitoria que dios . . . fue servido de darle a don Fadrique de Toledo, general de la armada real de su Magestad . . . contra ochenta naves que yvan en la carrera de Indias. *Granada: B. de Lorenzana,* 1630. [4] p.; fol. Medina (BHA) 876. Granada:BU. 630/142

Relatione venuta de Madrid a Roma con lettere de 20 di gennaro 1630. de progressi fatti sin hora nel mare Oceano dal sig. Don Fradique de Toledo Ossorio . . . Tradotta da Gio. Francesco Pizzuto. *Rome: L. Grignani,* 1630. 4 lvs; 12mo. Borba de Moraes II:195–96; Rodrigues (Dom. Hol.) 361. BL. 630/143

Remón, Alonso de. Vida i muerte misteriosas del . . . siervo de Dios Gregorio Lopez . . . Ultima impression. *Madrid: F. Martínez, for P. Coello,* 1630. 150 numb. lvs; 8vo. 1st publ., Madrid, 1617. Medina (BHA) 878; Streit II:1591. NN-RB, PCarlD; BL, BN. 630/144

Respublica Hollandiae, et urbes. *Leyden: J. Maire,* 1630. 434 p.; 8vo. Includes Grotius's *De antiquitate reipublicae Batavicae,* 1st publ., Leyden, 1610. Meulen/Diermanse 694; Bibl. Belg. G345. CU-B, DLC, IU, MH, MiU-C, NN-RB, PPL, RPB; BN, The Hague:PP. 630/145

—[Anr edn]. *Leyden: J. Maire,* 1630. 514 p.; 8vo. Meulen/Diermanse 695. NN-RB, NNC, PPiPT; BN (imp.), The Hague:PP. 630/146

—[Anr edn]. *Leyden: J. Maire,* 1630. 526 p.; 8vo. Meulen/Diermanse 696. BN, The Hague:PP. 630/147

Reves, Jacques de. Biechte des Conincx van Spanien . . . over het verlies van Pernambuco. [*Amsterdam?* 1630]. bds.; fol. In verse. Sabin 70323; Rodrigues (Dom. Hol.) 889. 630/148

A rich storehouse, or treasurie for the diseased . . . Now seventhly augmented . . . by A. T. *London: R. Badger, for P. Stephens & C. Meredith,* 1630. 317 p.; 4to. 1st publ., London, 1596; cf. 1601 edn. STC 23610. CLU-C, DNLM, MH (wants t.p.), MnU-B, NIC; London:Wellcome. 630/149

Ripa, Cesare. Della piu che novissima iconologia . . . Ampliata dal sig. cav. Zaratino Castellini. *Padua: D. Pasquardo,* 1630. 3 pts; illus.; 4to. 1st publ. with American content, Rome, 1603, under title *Iconologia.* ICN, MH, MiU, NcU; BL, BN. 630/150

Sala, Angelo. Ternarius ternariorum hermeticorum bezoardicorum laudanorum. *Erfurt: Heirs of E. Mechler, for J. Birckner,* 1630. 684 p.; illus.; 8vo. 1st publ., Erfurt, 1618. Wellcome I:5712. DNLM, ICU, MnU, NNNAM, PPC; BL, BN. 630/151

San Felipe de Austria, Venezuela. Señor. El cabildo, justicia, y regimiento, y vezinos mineros de la villa de San Felipe de Austria, dizen: Que desde que la dicha villa se fundò, el dicho cabildo, y vezinos han hecho

. . . muchas labores de minas, con que el sitio, y fundacion de la dicha villa, es de los mas ricos . . . en todas las Indias. [*Madrid?* 1630?]. 8 numb. lvs; fol. Memorial to king of Spain, seeking additional Indians to work local mines & comparing production with that of Potosí. BL.   630/152

Santorio, Santorio. Methodi vitandorum errorum omnium, qui in arte medica contingunt libri quindecim . . . Nova editio. *Venice: M. A. Brogiollo,* 1630. 972 cols; 4to. 1st publ., Venice, 1603. Wellcome I:5758. DNLM, OkU; BL.   630/153

—[Anr edn]. *Geneva: P. Aubert,* 1630. 2 pts; illus.; 4to. DNLM, KU-M, NNNAM, PPC; BN.   630/154

Schouten, Willem Corneliszoon. Journal ou Relation exacte du voyage . . . dans les Indes. *Paris: J. Guignard & H. LeGras,* 1630. 232 p.; illus., maps; 8vo. 1st publ. in French, Amsterdam, 1618; here a reissue of Gobert's 1619 Paris edn. Sabin 77954; Palau 305110. MiU-C, NN-RB; BN, Amsterdam:NHSM.   630/155

Schrijver, Pieter. Saturnalia, ofte Poëtisch Vasten-avond-spel, vervatende het gebruyk ende misbruyk van den taback, onlangs . . . in 't Latijn beschreven . . . Nu verrijkt ende herdrukt . . . in Neder-Duytsch vertaeld door Samuel Ampzing. *Haarlem: A. Roman,* 1630. 47 p.; 4to. Transl. from Haarlem, 1628, Latin text. Includes verse in Latin & Dutch. Arents 172. MH, NN-A; BL.   630/156

Seeckere tijdinghe vande vlote vande gheoctroyeerde West-Indische Compagnie, onder den Generael Hendrick Cornelisz. Loncq, over 't innemen van Fernambucque. *Amsterdam: F. Lieshout,* 1630. bds.; fol. Rodrigues (Dom. Hol.) 394; Meulman 2113. Ghent:BU.   630/157

Seville. Señor. La ciudad de Sevilla, dize que el daño que causa sacar la plata y oro de España es . . . conocido . . . Y assi . . . se he de servir V. Magestad de mandar que . . no . . . se de licencia. [*Seville?* 1630?]. fol. Memorial to king of Spain, on monetary problems, referring in passing to Spanish silver fleet. BL.   630/158

Shakespeare, William. The merry wives of Windsor . . . Newly corrected. *London: T. H[arper]., for R. Meighen,* 1630. [78] p.; 4to.

1st publ., London, 1602. STC 22301; Greg 187(d). CSmH, DFo, MH, NN-RB; BL.   630/159

Sharpe, Edward. England's royall fishing revived. *London: [W. Jaggard,] for N. Bourne,* 1630. [47] p.; 4to. 1st publ., London, 1615, under title *Britaines busse;* here a reissue with cancel t.p. STC 21487; Kress 470. CSmH, DLC, MH, NNC, PU; London:UL.   630/160

Sharpham, Edward. Cupids whirligig. *London: T. H[arper]., for R. Meighen,* 1630. 40 lvs; 4to. Comedy. 1st publ., London, 1607. STC 22383; Greg 247(d). CSmH, CtY, DLC, ICU, MH, MiU, PU; BL.   630/161

Smith, Capt. John. The true travels, adventures, and observations of Captaine John Smith, in Europe, Asia, Affrika, and America . . . 1593. to 1629. *London: J. H[aviland]., for T. Slater; sold [by M. Sparke],* 1630. 60 p.; illus.; fol. For variants, see Sabin. Sabin 82851–52; Vail (Frontier) 77; Arents 173; STC 22796; JCB (3) II:233. CSmH, DLC, ICN, MH, MiU-C, NN-RB, RPJCB; BL.   630/162

Souter, Daniel. Eben-ezer, tot hier toe heeft ons de Heere gheholpen. *Haarlem: H. P. van Wesbusch,* 1630. 184 p.; illus.; 4to. Also issued as pt of his *Seer uytmuntende . . . victorien* of this year below, q.v. Includes refs to Olinda, Brazil, & Pieter Hein's capture of Spanish silver fleet. Cf. JCB (3) II:233–34.   630/163

——. Seer uytmuntende Nederlandtsche victorien. *Haarlem: H. P. van Wesbusch,* 1630. 2 pts; illus.; 4to. Includes, under collective added t.p., the author's *Eben-ezer* and *Sené-boher,* each with special t.p. & separate paging & signatures. JCB (3) II:233. RPJCB.   630/164

——. Sené-boher. Brandende-Bosch uyt welckers voncken, d'over-groote victorie vande stercke stadt s'Hertoghen-bosch. *Haarlem: H. P. van Wesbusch,* 1630. 356 p.; illus.; 4to. Also issued as pt of the author's *Seer uytmuntende . . . victorien* of this year above, q.v. Includes refs to Salvador, Olinda, Matanzas Bay, & Spanish silver fleet. Cf. JCB (3) II:234.   630/165

Spaensche vosse-vel, ofte Copye van een Missive die ghehouden mach werden seer avontuyrlick inde handen van een oprecht patriot . . . gekomen. *Leeuwarden: C. Fonteyne,* 1630. 32 p.; 4to. Refers to capture of Spanish silver fleet by Hein & to dangers inherent in power of the West-Indische Compagnie & its sister company. Knuttel 4022. The Hague:KB.   630/166

—[Anr edn]. Copie van een missive. . . . [*Amsterdam?*] 1630. 22 p.; 4to. Knuttel 4021. The Hague:KB.   630/167

Spain. Laws, statutes, etc., 1621–65 (Philip IV). Ordenes, y providencias, que Su Magestad . . . se ha servido expedir, y se han de executar en el recibo de la capitane de Barlovento. *Madrid: A. Bizarron* [ca. 1630]. 8 p.; 4to. On handling of Spanish cargo from West Indies. MnU-B.   630/168

Spain. Sovereigns, etc., 1621–1665 (Philip IV), addressee. Señor. Los cargadores interessados en la plata y mercadarias. [*Madrid?* 1630?] [4] p.; fol. Memorial relating to commerce of Indies. BL.

630/169

Spinola, Fabio Ambrosio, S.J. Vita del p. Carlo Spinola, della Compagnia di Giesù, morto per la santa fede nel Giappone. *Rome: F. Corbelletti,* 1630. 223 p.; plan; 8vo. 1st publ., Rome, 1628. Cf. Sabin 89458; Streit V:1448; Backer VII:1448.   630/170

——. Vita p. Caroli Spinolae Societatis Jesu, pro christiano religione in Japonia mortui. Italice scripta . . . latine reddita a p. Hermann Hugone. *Antwerp: Plantin Press (B. Moretus),* 1630. 186 p.; port., plan; 8vo. Transl. from author's *Vita del p. Carlo Spinola,* 1st publ., Rome, 1628. Sabin 89460; Streit V:1449; cf. Backer VII:1448; JCB (3) II:234. CtY, DGU, NN-RB, RPJCB; BL, BN.

630/171

Staden, Hans. Beschrijvinghe van America. *Amsterdam: B. Janszoon,* 1630. 72 p.; illus.; 4to. 1st publ. in Dutch, Antwerp, 1558; cf. 1625 edn. Sabin 90045. BL.   630/172

——. Historiae Antipodum, sive Novi Orbis qui vulgo Americae & Indiae Occidentalis nomine usurpatur, pars tertia, . . . Quorum I. Primo continetur narratio profectionis Joannis Stadii Hessi in Brasiliam . . . II. Diegesis historica naturam coeli solique Brasiliensis . . . III. Luculentissima descriptio itineris Johannis Lerij . . . quod in easdem terras suscepit. *Frankfurt a. M.: M. Merian,*

1630. 294 p.; illus., map; fol. (Theodor de Bry's *America.* Pt 3. Latin). 1st publ. in this version, Frankfurt a. M., 1592, under title *Americae tertia pars;* cf. 1605 edn. Cf. Sabin 8784; Church 152; JCB (3) I:391–92. CSmH, NN-RB, RPJCB; BL, BN.

630/173

Stirling, William Alexander, 1st earl of. The mapp and description of New-England; together with a discourse of plantation, and collonies. *London: N. Butter,* 1630. 47 p.; map; 4to. 1st publ., London, 1624, under title *Encouragement to colonies;* here a reissue of that edn with t.p. & dedication canceled by new t.p. Sabin 740; STC 342; Church 414; JCB (3) II:225–26. CSmH, DFo, ICN, MH, MiU-C, NN-RB, RPJCB; BL.   630/174

Strobelberger, Johann Stephan. De dentium podagra. *Leipzig: J. Gross,* 1630. 238 p.; 8vo. Tobacco is recommended for relief of toothache. Arents (Add.) 252. DNLM, NN-A, PU-D; BL, BN.   630/175

Suárez de Figueroa, Cristóbal. Plaza universal de todas sciencias y artes, parte traduzida de toscano y parte compuesta por el doctor Christoval Suarez de Figueroa. *Perpignan: L. Roure,* 1630. 379 numb. lvs; 4to. Transl. in part from Tommaso Garzoni's *La piazza universale,* 1st publ., Venice, 1585; cf. Madrid, 1615, Spanish edn. Here a reissue of the printer's 1529 edn? Palau 323910. MiU, NNH, PU; BN.   630/176

Tassoni, Alessandro. La secchia rapita, poema eroicomico . . . e 'l primo canto dell'Oceano. *Venice: G. Scaglia,* 1630. 384 p.; 12mo. 1st publ., Paris, 1622. Cf. Sabin 94402; Puliatti (Tassoni) 104. ICN, MH; Rome:BN.   630/177

Taylor, John, the Water-poet. All the workes of John Taylor the Water-poet. Beeing sixty and three in number . . . with sundry new additions, corrected, revised, and newly imprinted. *London: J. B[eale, Elizabeth Allde, B. Alsop & T. Fawcet]., for J. Boler,* 1630. 2 pts; illus.; fol. Here included are numerous poems on a wide variety of American topics earlier publ. separately. Apparently now 1st publ. is 'Honour conceal'd; strangely reveal'd', with mention, in 'The peace of France', of Virginia & Powhatan the Indian sachem. STC 23725; Arents

3277; Pforzheimer 1006. CSmH, CtY, DLC, ICN, MH, MnU, NN-RB, PBL; BL.
                                                                    630/178

———. The great eater, of Kent. *London: Elizabeth Allde, for H. Gosson,* 1630. 20 p.; 4to. Includes ref. to tobacco. STC 23761. CSmH, NcU; BL.   630/179

———. Jacke a Lent. *London: J. B., for J. Boler,* 1630. 26 p.; 4to. 1st publ., [London, 1617?]. KMK.   630/180

Toledo Osorio y Mendoza, Fadrique de, marqués de Villanueva de Valdueza. Relacion embiado . . . al . . . marques de Cerralvo, virrey de la nueva España, avisando de lo sucedido a la armada desde que salío de España hasta que entró en Cartagena. *Seville: F. de Lyra,* 1630. [8] p.; 4to. 1st publ., Mexico, 1629. Sabin 96113; Medina (BHA) 882; Escudero (Seville) 96113; Palau 333045. Seville:B. Colombina.   630/181

—[Anr edn]. *Granada: B. de Lorenzana,* 1630. [4] p.; fol. Sabin 96113; Medina (BHA) 883; Palau 333046. Granada:BU.   630/182

———. Relatione venuta de Madrid a Roma . . . de progressi fatti fin hora nel mare Oceano dal sig. Don Fadrique di Toledo Ossorio . . . Tradotta da Giovanni Francesco Pizzuto. *Rome:* 1630. Sabin 96115. BL.   630/183

———. Warhaffte Relation, von dem grossen herrlichen Sig welchen dess Herrn Don Federico de Toledo Osorio . . . erhalten . . . wider die Holländer . . . Aus einer . . . italianischen Beschreibung . . . ubergesetzt. *Passau: T. Nenninger & C. Frosch,* 1630. [7] p.; 4to. 1st publ., Mexico, 1629, under title *Relacion embiada por Don Fadrique;* here transl. from the *Relatione venuta de Madrid* above. Cf. Sabin 96113; cf. Palau 333045. NN-RB, RPJCB.   630/184

Tomasini, Jacopo Philippo, Bp of Città Nuova. Illustrium virorum elogio, inconibus exornata. *Padua: D. Pasquardo & Associates,* 1630. 374 p.; illus., ports; 4to. Columbus is mentioned as 'ulterius navigationis occasio', while one 'Jacobus Thienaeus' is named as discoverer of the island of Florida. CU, DLC, ICU, MH, MiU, MnU, NN, PU; BL, BN.   630/185

Torsellino, Orazio, S.J. Historiarum ab origine mundi usque ad annum 1598 epitome libri x. *Douai: B. Bellère,* 1630. 416 p.; 12mo.

1st publ., Rome, 1598; cf. 1620 edn. Backer VIII:151.   630/186

—[Anr edn]. *Rome: G. Facciotti,* 1630. 8vo. Backer VIII:151.   630/187

Translaet uyt den Spaenschen. Vande geluckige victorie verkregen bij don Fredrico de Toledo . . . Nae de copie . . . ghedruckt tot Sevillien. *Amsterdam: F. Lieshout,* 1630. [8] p.; 4to. Transl. from the *Feliz vitoria que ha tenido* of this year above, the text of which is here included. Rodrigues (Dom. Hol.) 362; Meulman 2116. Ghent:BU.
                                                                    630/188

A true relation of the vanquishing of the town Olinda, cituated in the capitania of Phernambuco. Through . . . Lonck . . . and . . . Wardenburgh . . . Hereto is also annexed a letter of the Coronell Wardenburgh to the States Generall. *Amsterdam: J. F. Stam,* 1630. 15 p.; map; 4to. Transl. from the *Veroveringh van de stadt Olinda* of this year below. Here included in waerdenburgh's letter, transl. from his *Copie vande missive* of this year below. Sabin 97144; Borba de Moraes II:194–95; STC 16699; JCB (3) II:231. RPJCB; BL (Loncq).   630/189

Usselinx, Willem. Waerschouwinghe over den treves met den Coninck van Spaengien. *Flushing: S. C. Versterre,* 1630. [48] p.; 4to. Includes refs to the Nederlandsche West-Indische Compagnie & to Spanish governance of Chilean natives. Sabin 98214; Asher 49; Jameson (Usselinx) 21; Knuttel 4016. NN-RB; BL, The Hague:KB.
                                                                    630/190

—[Anr edn]. Waerschouwinge over den treves . . . *Flushing: S. C. Versterre,* 1630. [34] p.; 4to. Sabin 98215; Jameson (Usselinx) 22; Knuttel 4017; JCB (3) II:235. DLC, NN-RB, RPJCB; BN, The Hague:KB.
                                                                    630/191

Vande geluckige victorie. *Amsterdam:* 1630. See entry under *Translaet uyt den Spaenschen* above.

Vaughan, William. The arraignment of slander, perjury, blasphemy, and other malicious sinnes. *London: F. Constable,* 1630. 351 p.; 4to. In preface 'To the Reader' tobacco is discussed, with statement 'It is no shame to be drunke with Tobacco', while West Indian 'furicanoes' are also mentioned. STC 24623. BL.   630/192

——. Cambrensium Caroleja. *London:* [*N. Okes,*] *for F. Constable,* 1630. [112] p.; 8vo. In verse. 1st publ., London, 1625; here a reissue of that edn with cancel t.p. Sabin 98692; Baer (Md) 15; STC 24605. CSmH.
630/193

——. The Newlanders cure. Aswell of those violent sicknesses which distemper most minds in these latter dayes; as also by a cheape and newfound dyet. *London: N. O[kes]., for F. Constable,* 1630. 143 p.; 8vo. The earliest medical work written in America; includes section on scurvy in Maryland. Sabin 98694; Vail (Frontier) 78; Baer (Md) 16; STC 24619; Arents (Add.) 255; JCB (3) II:235. CSmH, DFo (imp.), MH, NN-A, RPJCB; BL.
630/194

Veen, Jan van der. Schimp-ghedicht. Van Fernabuco. [*Haarlem?* 1630?]. bds.; fol. In verse. Meulman 2115. Ghent:BU.
630/195

Vega Carpio, Lope Félix de. Arcadia, prosas y versos. *Barcelona: J. Margarit,* 1630. 285 numb. lvs; 8vo. 1st publ., Madrid, 1598; cf. 1602 edns. Palau 356306. MH, MiU (imp.), NNH; BN.
630/196

——. Laurel de Apolo, con otra rimas. *Madrid: J. González,* 1630. 129 numb. lvs; port.; 4to. The title poem includes numerous refs to the New World & to its writers, esp. in the 2nd 'Silva'. Sabin 98770; Palau 356475. ICU, MH, MnU, NN-RB, PU, RPB; BL, BN.
630/197

——. Parte veinte de las Comedias. *Barcelona: E. Liberós, for R. Vives,* 1630. 298 numb. lvs; 4to. 1st publ., Madrid, 1625. Sabin 98772n; Palau 355313. BL, BN.
630/198

——. Parte veynte y dos de las Comedias. *Saragossa: P.Verges, for J.de Ginobart,* 1630. 235 numb. lvs; 4to. Despite attribution to Lope de Vega, includes Juan Rúiz de Alarcón's *La verdad sospechosa*, in which the principal character, Don García, pretends to have been born in the Indies, and to be endowed with wealth therefrom. Rúiz de Alarcón was himself born in Mexico, but migrated to Spain, where in 1626 he was named 'relator' of the Council of the Indies. Palau 355318.
630/199

Veroveringh van de stadt Olinda, gelegen in de capitania van Phernambuco, door . . . Heyndrick C. Lonck . . . Mitsgaders: Dide-

rick van Waerdenburgh. *Amsterdam: H. Gerritsz* [1630]. [12] p.; 4to. For an English translation of this year, see *A true relation of the vanquishing of . . . Olinda* above. Sabin 41849; Borba de Moraes II:344; Rodrigues (Dom. Hol.) 388; Knuttel 3996; JCB (3) II:230–31. DLC, NN-RB, RPJCB; BL (Loncq), The Hague:KB.
630/200

Von Eroberung der Stadt Olinda. [n.p.] 1630. See the *Entwerffung von Eroberung der Stadt Olinda* of this year above.

De vruchten van't monster van den treves, toe-ghevoeght aen . . . allen patriotten van ons lieve vader-landt, ende Oost ende West-Indische compagnie. [*Amsterdam?*] 1630. [8] p.; 4to. Sabin 100858; Asher 138; Knuttel 4019. MnU-B, NN-RB; The Hague:KB.
630/201

——[Anr edn]. [*Amsterdam?*] 1630. [12] p.; 4to. Meulman 2128. Ghent:BU.
630/202

Wadsworth, James. The present estate of Spayne, or A true relation of some remarkable things touching the court, and government of Spayne. *London: A M[athewes]., for R. Thrale & A. Ritherdon,* 1630. 84 p.; 4to. Included are mentions of offices in Spanish America & those who hold them. STC 24929. CSmH, DFo, ICN, InU-L, MH; BL.
630/203

——[Anr issue]. *London: A M[athewes]., for A. Ritherdon,* 1630. STC 24929a. CSmH, DLC, InU-L, NNH, RPJCB; Oxford:Bodl.
630/204

Waerdenburgh, Dirk van. Copia wt de missiven. *Amsterdam:* [1630?]. *See* Loncq, Hendrik Cornelis, *above.*

——. Copie de la lettre escrite a Messieurs les Estats Generaux des Provinces Unies des Pays-bas . . . touchant la prise de la ville de Olinda de Fernabouc sur l'Espagnol. *Paris: J. Bessin,* 1630. 15 p.; 8vo. Transl. from Waerdenburgh's *Copie vande missive* of this year below. Sabin 100933; Borba de Moraes II:363; Rodrígues (Dom. Hol.) 397. MnU-B, NN-RB, RPJCB; BN.
630/205

——[Anr edn]. *Paris: J. Bessin,* 1630. 16 p.; 8vo. Text printed in 8 pages, followed by, p. 9–16, *La seconde lettre du roy de Suède aux Electeurs,* dated 13 Sept. 1630 and signed Goustave Adolphe. BN.
630/206

——[Anr issue]. *Paris: J. Bessin,* 1630. Title lacks

phrase 'sur l'espagnol'. BN.   630/207

—[Anr edn]. La prise de la ville de Olinda de Fernabouc . . . Suyvant la coppie imprimée a Paris, chez Jean Bassin. [*Antwerp?*] 1630. 15 p.; 12mo. Borba de Moraes II:364. ICN.   630/208

——. Copie eines Schreibens an die hochmögende Herrn Staden General . . . Betreffend die Eroberung der Statt Olinda de Fernabuco . . . Auss dem niederländischen . . . ubergesetzet. [*Frankfurt a. M.?*] 1630. [8] p.; 12mo. Transl. from Waerdenburgh's *Copie vande missive* of this year below. Sabin 100934; Borba de Moraes II:363–64; Rodrigues (Dom. Hol.) 398. DLC.   630/209

——. Copie vande missive, gheschreven . . . aende Ho.Mo. Heeren Staten Generael, noopende de veroveringhe vande stadt Olinda de Fernabuco. *The Hague: Widow & Heirs of H. Jacobszoon van Wouw,* 1630. [8] p.; 4to. Sabin 100935 & 16678; Borba de Moraes II:363; Rodrigues (Dom. Hol.) 396; Knuttel 3995. DLC, NN-RB; BL, The Hague:KB.   630/210

—[Anr edn]. . . . Na de copye in 's Gravenhage. *Utrecht: L. S. de Vries,* 1630. [4] p.; 4to. Sabin 102497; Borba de Moraes II:363; Asher 140.   630/211

——. Two memorable relations. The one a letter written . . . out of the West-India, from Farnabuck . . . touching the surprisall of the towne of Olinda in Farnabuck . . . Translated out of the Dutch . . . Printed at Roane by Tho. Mallard. *London: N. Bourne,* 1630. 12 p.; 4to. Transl. from Waerdenburgh's *Copye vande missive* of this year above; the Rouen French edn cited in the title has not been traced. Sabin 102498; STC 25219. CSmH.   630/212

Warhaffter Bricht [*sic*], welcher Massen die Statt Olinda in Brasillia . . . durch . . . Loncq . . . unnd . . . Wardenburg . . . ist eroberet unnd eingenommen worden . . . Nach den Exemplaren die zu Ambsterdam getruckt. [*The Hague?* 1630]. [11] p.; 8vo. Transl. from the *Veroveringh van de stadt Olinda* of this year above. For a similar but differing translation of this year, see entry under title *Beschreibung, welcher Gestalt . . .* above. Sabin 101421; Borba de Moraes II:370. DLC, NN-RB   630/213

Wassenaer, Nicolaes van. Het seventiende

ghedeelt of 't vervolch van het Historisch verhael aller gedenckwaerdiger geschiedeniss., die in Europa . . . in America, als West-Indien, Brasil en Peru . . . voorghevallen syn. *Amsterdam: J. Janszoon, the Younger,* 1630. 126 numb. lvs; illus.; 4to. (N. van Wassenaer's *Historisch verhael.* Pt 17). Includes refs to the West-Indische Compagnie, Pieter Hein & Dirk Symonszoon. Cf. Sabin 102039; Borba de Moraes II:371; Muller (1872) 1745. RPJCB.   630/214

Wecker, Johann Jakob. Practica medicinae generalis. *Venice: D. Pasquardo & Associates,* 1630. 542 p.; 16mo. 1st publ., Basel, 1585; cf. 1602 edn. Wellcome I:6721. DNLM.   630/215

White, John. The planters plea. Or the grounds of plantations examined, and usual objections answered. Together with a manifestation of the causes mooving such as have lately undertaken a plantation in New-England. *London: W. Jones,* 1630. 84 p.; 4to. Sabin 103396; Vail (Frontier) 80; STC 25399; Church 418; JCB (3) II:235. CSmH, CtY, DLC, ICN, MH, MiU, MWA, NN-RB, PHi, RPJCB; BL.   630/216

Wijnbergen, J. Vol-maeckte lauwer-crans . . . Waer in verhaelt worden . . . het inbrenghen van de Silvervloot. *Harderwyck: N. van Wieringen,* 1630. 70 p.; 4to. Includes account of Hein's capture of Spanish silver fleet. Sabin 100684; Asher 117; Knuttel 3992. MiU; The Hague:KB.   630/217

Wright, Thomas. The passions of the minde. *London: M. Fletcher; sold by R. Dawlman,* 1630. 352 p.; 4to. 1st publ., London, 1601. STC 26043. CSmH, CtY, DFo, ICN, MH, MiU; BL.   630/218

Wtenbogaert, Johannes. Tsamen-spraeck over de twee slechte gesellen van Treveskrack. [*The Hague?*] 1630. [16] p.; 4to. A reply to those advocating continued war with Spain on behalf of the West-Indische Compagnie. Knuttel 4028. MnU-B; The Hague:KB.   630/219

——, **supposed author.** Wtwissinge der schandelicker blamen, daer mede de schryver vande Tractaten tegen pays, treves etc. de remonstranten t'onrecht bewerpt in sijn Derde deel, ghedruckt in 's Graven-Haghe by Aert Meuris, anno 1630. [*The Hague?*] 1630. [19] p.; 4to. A reply to the *Klare aen-*

wysinge of this year above. Sabin 98247; Asher 137; Knuttel 4015. CtY, MnU, NN; The Hague:KB.   630/220

Zacchia, Paolo. Quaestiones medico-legales, liber quartus. *Leipzig:* [*F. Lanckisch?* *for*] *E. Rehefeld,* 1630. 224 p.; 8vo. 1st publ. as book 4 of the author's *Quaestiones,* Rome, 1621–30. Cf. Wellcome I:6787. NNNAM; London:Wellcome.   630/221

1631

Alemán, Mateo. Der Landstörtzer: Gusman von Alfarche . . . Durch Aegidium Albertinum . . . verteutscht. [*Munich: N. Heinrich*] 1631. 454 p.; 8vo. 1st publ. in German, Munich, 1615. Dt. Ges. Kat. 3:874; Goedeke II:577. Berlin:StB, Breslau:BU, Munich: StB.   631/1

Bacon, Francis, viscount St Albans. Histoire naturelle. *Paris: A. de Sommaville & A. Soubron,* 1631. 567 p.; 8vo. Transl. by Pierre d'Amboise, sieur de La Magdelaine, from Bacon's *Sylva sylvarum: or A naturall historie* (incl. also his *New Atlantis*), 1st publ., London, 1627. Gibson (Bacon) 184; Shaaber (Brit. auth.) B38; Cioranescu (XVII) 7088. CLU-C, CtY-M, DFo; BN.   631/2

——. Sylva sylvarum: or, A naturall historie . . . The third edition. *London: J. H[avi-land].*, *for W. Lee,* 1631. 2 pts; port.; fol. 1st publ., London, 1627. Includes, as pt 2, Bacon's *New Atlantis,* 1st publ., London, 1627. Gibson (Bacon) 173; STC 1171. CSmH, CtY, DFo, IEN, MH, MiU, MnU-B, NNBG; BL.   631/3

Baerle, Kaspar van. Poematum editio nova, priore castigatior et altera parte auctior. *Leyden: Elsevier Office,* 1631. 511 p.; 12mo. In verse. 1st publ., Leyden, 1628; cf. 1630 edn. Sabin 3407n; cf. Borba de Moraes I:65; Willems (Les Elzevier) 344. ICU, MH, MnU-B, PPL, RPJCB; BL, BN.   631/4

——. Trophaeum Arausionense, sive In interceptam ad scaldis ostia. *Amsterdam: W. J. Blaeu,* 1631. 12 p.; fol. Includes mention of Matanzas & Olinda. Knuttel 4151. CtY; BN, The Hague:KB.   631/5

Barclay, John. The mirrour of mindes, or, Barclay's Icon animorum. Englished by T[homas]. M[ay]. *London: J. Norton, for T. Walkley,* 1631. 2 pts; 12mo. Transl. from Barclay's Latin *Icon animorum,* 1st publ., London, 1614. STC 1399. CSmH, CtY, DFo, ICN, MH, MiU, MnU, NNUT; BL.   631/6

Benavides, Alonso de, S.J. Requeste oft Verhael d'welck den . . . Pater . . . J. de Santander Commissarius Generael der Minder-broeders Orden van Indien presenteert aen . . . Philippus den iv., door . . . A.de Benavides . . . custos der provincie ende bekeeringhen van Nieuw-Mexico. *Antwerp: W. Lesteens,* 1631. 86 p.; 8vo. Transl. from Benavides's *Memorial,* 1st publ., Madrid, 1630. Sabin 76812; Medina (BHA) 868n; Streit II:1594; Wagner (SW) 33b. BL.   631/7

——. Requeste remonsrative [!] au Roy d'Espagne sur la conversion de Nouveau-Mexico, traduit de l'Espagnol. *Brussels: F. Vivien,* 1631. 120 p.; 8vo. Transl. by François Paludanus from Benavides's *Memorial,* 1st publ., Madrid, 1630. Sabin 4637 & 76811; Medina (BHA) 868n; Streit II:1593; Wagner (SW) 33a; JCB (3) II:238. DGU, ICN, NHi, RPJCB; BL, BN.   631/8

Blaeu, Willem Janszoon. Appendix Theatri A. Ortelii et Atlantis G. Mercatoris, continens tabulas geographicas diversarum orbis regionum. *Amsterdam: W. J. Blaeu,* 1631. 98 maps; fol. 1st publ., Amsterdam, 1630, under title *Atlantis appendix;* here enl. introduction by Philip Cluverius includes refs to Brazil, Peru, Paraguay, etc. 'Insulae Barmudas' is signed 'Mmmm'; '104' added at head of page in manuscript. Koeman (M.Bl) 2. [Edition uncertain: CtY, DFo; BN], Amsterdam:UB.   631/9

—[Anr edn]. *Amsterdam: W. J. Blaeu,* 1631. 99 maps; fol. 'Insulae Barmudas' is signed 'AAAAAAA'. Koeman (M.Bl) 3. BL, Paris: Arsenal.   631/10

——. Zeespiegel. *Amsterdam: W. J. Blaeu,* 1631. 3 pts; illus., maps.; fol. 1st publ., Amsterdam, 1623. Koeman (M.Bl) 33; cf. Tiele 124. NN-RB (imp.); Amsterdam:UB, BN.   631/11

Bourne, William. A regiment for the sea . . . Newly corrected. *London: W. Jones, for T. Weaver,* 1631. 96 numb. lvs; 8vo. 1st publ., London, [1574], but cf. 1601 edn above. Taylor (Regiment) 456; STC 3431. MH; Oxford:Bodl. 631/12

Brathwaite, Richard. Whimzies: or, A new cast of characters. *London: F. K[ingston].*, *sold by A. Ritherdon*, 1631. 2 pts; 12mo. The 'character' of a ballad-monger includes description of 'two naked Virginians [who in an ale-house] will call for a great potte, a toast, and a pipe [of tobacco].' Also issued with Ritherdon's name given as 'A.R'. STC 3591; Arents (Add.) 256. CSmH, CtY, DFo, MH, NN-A; BL. 631/13

—[Anr issue]. *London: F. K[ingston].*, *sold by R. B[ostock].*, 1631. 631/14

Bredan, Daniel. Desengano a los pueblos del Brasil, y demas partes en los Indias Occidentales, para quitarles las dudas y falsas imaginaciones que podrian tener acerca de las declaraciones de los . . . Estados Generales, y los administradores de la Compania. *Amsterdam: P. A. van Ravesteyn*, 1631. 14 p.; 4to. Defense of the Dutch West India Company's occupation of Brazil. Sabin 7696; Medina (BHA) 888; Borba de Moraes I:109; Rodrigues (Dom. Hol.) 400. 631/15

Breton, Nicholas. Crossing of proverbs. *London: J. Wright*, 1631–32. 22 lvs; 8vo. 1st publ., London, 1616. STC 3645.5. ICN. 631/16

Brito Lemos, João de. Abecedario militar do que o soldado deve fazer até chegar a ser capitão, & sargento-mór. *Lisbon: P. Craesbeeck*, 1631. 2 pts; 4to. Includes lists of participants, ships, supplies, etc., engaged in 1624 recapture of Bahia from Dutch. Innocencio III:331; Rodrigues (Dom. Hol.) 363. 631/17

Camões, Luiz de. Os Lusiadas. *Lisbon: P. Craesbeeck*, 1631. 140 numb. lvs; 24mo. In verse. 1st publ., Lisbon, 1572; cf. 1609 edn above. Silva (Camões) 27. DLC, MH; BL, Lisbon:BN. 631/18

Cats, Jacob. Maegden-plicht, ofte Ampt der jonghvrouwen. *[Antwerp:] J. Cnobbaert*, 1631. [176] p.; illus.; obl. 8vo. 1st publ., Middelburg, 1618. At end: 'Finis'; caption on lf *8 reads 'Aende . . . Jonck-vrou'. Name of printer appears in colophon. Perhaps a pirated edn. For a critical discussion of this and similar edns, see P. Minderaa, ed., *Aandacht voor Cats bij zijn 300-ste sterfdag* (Zwolle,

1962), p. 45–47. Vries 103; Mus. Cats. 57. Leyden:UB. 631/19

—[Anr edn]. *[Antwerp? 1631?]*. [178] p.; illus.; obl. 8vo. At end: 'Eynde'; lacks colophon. Caption on lf *8 reads 'Aende . . . Jongvrou'; that on *2 reads 'Maeghden Toe-ge-eyghent'. Vries 104; Mus. Cats. 58. Leyden:UB. 631/20

—[Anr edn]. *[Antwerp? 1631?]*. [178] p.; illus.; obl. 8vo. At end: 'Finis'; caption on *2 reads 'Maechden Toe-ghe-eyghent'. Vries 105; Mus. Cats. 59. Leyden:UB. 631/21

—[Anr edn]. Maeghden-plicht. *[Antwerp? 1631?]* [176] p.; illus.; obl. 8vo. At end: 'Eynde'; caption on *2 reads 'Maeghden Toe-ge-eyghent'. Vries 106; Mus. Cats. 60. Leyden:UB. 631/22

—[Anr edn]. *[Antwerp? 1631?]*. [176] p.; illus.; obl. 8vo. The emblemata here are smaller and reversed, or otherwise altered. The engraved t.p. has heading 'E.Pels, Amsterdams Fluytertie', anr published work. Vries 107; Mus. Cats. 61. Leyden:UB. 631/23

—[Anr edn?]. Maegden-plicht. *[Antwerp? 1631?]*. 4 pts; illus. ICU, MnU-B. 631/24

——. Minnelijcke, zedelijcke en stichtelijcke sinne-beelden en ghedichten. *[Amsterdam? 1631?]*. 2 pts; illus.; obl. 16mo. 1st publ. in this abridged version, *[Amsterdam? 1622?]*. Engraved t.p. begins 'Emblemata, ofte Minnelycke . . .'. Cf. Vries 91–93; cf. Mus. Cats. 44–46. BN. 631/25

—[Anr edn?]. *[Amsterdam? 1631?]*. 4 pts; illus. Cf. Vries 91–93; cf. Mus. Cats. 44–46. ICN (imp). 631/26

Cervantes Saavedra, Miguel de. Novelas exemplares. *Barcelona: E. Liberós*, 1631. 360 numb. lvs; 8vo. 1st publ., Madrid, 1613. Rius (Cervantes) 235; Palau 53414. MB, NNH; BL, Barcelona:B. Central. 631/27

Céspedes y Meneses, Gonzalo de. Primera parte de la Historia de D. Felippe el IIII. rey de las Españas. *Lisbon: P. Craesbeeck*, 1631. 607 p.; fol. Included are numerous chapts relating to Spanish America, Brazil, & Dutch activity there. Palau 54200. MH, RPJCB; BL, BN. 631/28

Clüver, Philipp. Introduction a la geographie universelle, tant nouvelle qu'ancienne. Traduitte du latin. *Paris: P. Billaine*, 1631.

318

496 p.; illus.; 16mo. Transl. from the author's *Introductionis in universam geographiam,* 1st publ., Leyden, 1624. Cf. Sabin 13805. MH. 631/29

——. Introductionis in universam geographiam, tam veterem quàm novam libri vi. *Paris: G. Pelé,* 1631. 506 p.; illus.; 16mo. 1st publ., Leyden, 1624. Cf. Sabin 13805. BN. 631/30

Colmenero de Ledesma, Antonio. Curioso tratado de la naturaleza y calidad del chocolate. *Madrid: F. Martínez,* 1631. 11 numb. lvs; 4to. Sabin 14542; Medina (BHA) 889; Müller 51; Palau 56904. MH; BL, BN. 631/31

Een cort ende warachtich verhael van de . . . victorie die Godt . . . verleent heeft de generale West-Indische compagnie onder 't beleyt vanden . . . Generael Adrien Janssen Pater ende . . . Maerten Tyssen teghen de Spaensche armade . . . geschiet op de cust van Brasil. *Middelburg: Z. Roman,* 1631. 8 p.; 4to. Sabin 7573 (& 16926); Borba de Moraes I:242; Asher 146; Knuttel 4153. The Hague:KB, Amsterdam:NHSM. 631/32

Croll, Oswald. Basilica chymica . . . Additus . . . est Tractatus novus de signaturis rerum internis. *Geneva: P. Aubert,* 1631. 3 pts; illus.; 8vo. 1st publ., Frankfurt a. M., 1609. DNLM, InU, MH, NIC, PPHa. 631/33

Dekker, Thomas. Penny-wise, pound foolish, or, A Bristol diamond. *London: A M[athewes]., for E. Blackmore,* 1631. 4to. Keeping a tobacco shop is depicted as sign of degradation. STC 6516. CSmH; Oxford: Bodl. 631/34

Drayton, Michael. The battaile of Agincourt. *London: A. M[athewes]., for W. Lee,* 1631. 8vo. 1st publ., London, 1627. STC 7191. CSmH, CtY, DFo, ICU, MH, NjP, PBL; BL. 631/35

Du Bartas, Guillaume de Salluste, seigneur. Erste Woche, von Erschaffung der Welt . . . auss den frantzösischen . . . Versen . . . übersetzet. *Köthen: J. Röhner, for M. Götze, at Leipzig,* 1631. 351 p.; 8vo. In verse. Transl. from the author's *La Sepmaine,* 1st publ., Paris, 1578. Includes numerous refs to New World, with French & German text on facing pages. Goedeke III:33; Holmes (DuBartas) I:109: no. 23. CtY, IU, MH; BL, Göttingen:UB. 631/36

Duchesne, Joseph. Drey medicinische Tractätlein . . . in die teutsche Sprach ubergesetzet. Durch m. Thomam Keszlern. *Strassburg: E. Zetzner,* 1631. 2 pts; port.; 4to. Transl. from Duchesne's *Ad Jacobi Auberti . . . explicationem,* 1st publ., Lyons, 1575, & his *Sclopetarius,* 1st publ., Lyons, 1576. The latter text describes salves employing tobacco for treatment of wounds. Wellcome I:1906. DNLM; London:Wellcome. 631/37

Du Gardin, Louis. Medicamenta purgantia, simplicia & composita. *Douai: P. Auroy,* 1631,'30. 2 pts; 12mo. Amongst the ingredients cited is mechoacan (cf. 'Pilulae mechoacanae', p. 66–67). DNLM; BL, BN. 631/38

Dupleix, Scipion. La curiosité naturelle. *Paris: J. Bessin,* 1631. 269 p.; 8vo. 1st publ., Paris, 1606. ICN; BN. 631/39

Epithalamium symbolicum conjugibus porphyrogenitis . . . Ferdinando III, Hungarorum, Boemorumque Regi. *Graz: E. Widmanstätter,* 1631. [200] p.; illus.; fol. Emblem book including some American allusions. Jantz (German Baroque) 3064. NcD. 631/40

Estado en que se hallan las Indias Occidentales. [*Madrid?* 1631?]. [4] p.; fol. CSmH. 631/41

Figueira, Luiz, S.J. Relaçam de varios successos acontecidos no Maranham e Gram Para assim de paz como de guerra, contra o rebelde Olandes, Ingleses & Franceses, & autras nações. *Lisbon: M. Rodriguez,* 1631. [4] p.; fol. Borba de Moraes I:264; Streit II:2394. Madrid:Acad. de la Hist. 631/42

Geraldini, Alessandro, O.S.B. Itinerarium ad regiones sub aequinoctiali plaga constitutas Alexandri Geraldini . . . episcopi civitatis S. Dominici apud Indos Occidentales. *Rome: G. Facciotti,* 1631. 284 p.; 8vo. Written in 1524 by a friend of Columbus; describes discovery of West Indies. Sabin 27116; Medina (BHA) 890; Streit II:1600; JCB (3) II:236–37. CSmH, CtY, DLC, ICN, MH, MiU-C, MnU-B, NN-RB, PBL, RPJCB; BL, BN. 631/43

Gottfried, Johann Ludwig, ed. Newe Welt

und Amerikanische Historien, inhaltende Warhafftige und vollkommene Beschreibungen aller West-Indianischen Landschafften . . . Alles auss verscheidenen . . . Historien-Schreibern unnd mancherley Sprachen . . . zusammen getragen/extrahirt. *Frankfurt a. M.: M. Merian,* 1631. 2 pts; illus., maps; fol. (Theodor de Bry's *American.* Abridgment). Extracted from pts 1–12 of de Bry's *America;* issued with an appendix, itself a reissue of de Bry's *Vierzehender Theil,* 1st publ., Hanau, 1630. Authorship erroneously attrib. to J. P. Abelin. Engraved t.p. begins 'Historia antipodum oder Newe Welt'. Sabin 50n; cf. Borba de Moraes I:311–13; Palau 106386; Baginsky (German Americana) 163; Streit II:1601; JCB (3) II:237. CtY, DLC, InU, MiU-C, MnU-B, NN-RB, RPJCB; BL, BN.   631/44

Great Britain. Sovereigns, etc., 1625–1649 (Charles I). A proclamation concerning tobacco. *London: R. Barker & assigns of J. Bill,* 1630 [i.e., 1631]. 2 lvs; fol. Sabin 99851; Crawford (Roy. procl.) 1629; Brigham (Roy. procl.) 68–71; STC 8971; Arents (Add.) 237. CSmH, NN-A; BL.   631/45

Greene, Robert. Philomela, the Lady Fitzwaters nightingale. *London: G. Purslowe,* 1631. [76] p.; 4to. 1st publ., London, 1592; cf. 1615 edn. STC 12298; Pforzheimer 433. CSmH, DFo; BL.   631/46

Grotius, Hugo. De jure belli ac pacis libri tres . . . Editio secunda emendatior. *Amsterdam: W. J. Blaeu,* 1631. 554 p.; fol. 1st publ., Paris, 1625. Meulen/Diermanse 567. CLL, CtY, DLC, IU, MH-BA, MiU-C, MnU-B, NjP; BL, BN.   631/47

——. Die Meinung der Bücher . . . Von der Warheit der christlichen Religion . . . Auss dem Holländischen inn Latein, und aus diesem inn das Deutsche gezogen, durch Christoph Colerum. [*Breslau:*] *D. Müller,* 1631. 290 p.; 12mo. Transl. from Grotius's *Sensus librorum sex,* 1st publ., Leyden, 1627, itself a prose adaptation of Grotius's *Bewys van den waren godsdienst,* 1st publ., [Leyden?], 1622. Cf. the verse translation of that work by Opitz below. Meulen/Diermanse 1008. Amsterdam:UB.   631/48

——. Von der Warheit der christlichen Religion, auss holländischer Sprache hochdeutsch gegeben, durch Martin Optizen.

Brieg: A. Gründer, for D. Müller, at Breslau, 1631. 159 p.; 4to. In verse. Transl. from Grotius's *Bewys van den waren godsdienst,* 1st publ., [Leyden?], 1622. Added American refs occur in Opitz's introduction. Cf. above the German translation of Grotius's prose adaptation. Jantz (German Baroque) 1931; Faber du Faur 220; Meulen/Diermanse 152; Goedeke III:46. CU, CtY, MH; BL, The Hague:PP.   631/49

Grüling, Philipp Gerhard. Florilegium chymicum, hoc est, Libellus insignis de quorundam medicamentorum chymicorum . . . vera praeparatione, recto usu et certa dosi. *Leipzig: G. Gross,* 1631. 476 p.; 12mo. Described are extracts of guaiacum & mechoacan. Wellcome I:2949. DNLM, NNNAM; London:Wellcome.   631/50

Harris, Robert. The arraignment of the whole creature, at the barre of religion, reason, and experience. *London: B. Alsop & T. Fawcet,* 1631. 335 p.; 4to. Includes refs to tobacco (p. 27), gold of Peru (p. 62), & 'American Palmitos and Potatos' (p. 120). STC 13069. CSmH, CtY, DFo, ICN, MH, MiU, NNUT, PPPrHi; BL.   631/51

Heinsius, Daniel. Histoire du siége de Bolduc, et de ce qui s'est passé es Paisbas Unis l'an M DC XXIX. faicte françoise du latin. *Leyden: Elsevier Office,* 1631. 212 p.; maps; fol. Transl. by André Rivet from the following item. Willems (Les Elzevier) 352. IEN, MH, PU; BN.   631/52

——. Rerum ad Sylvam-Ducis atque alibi in Belgio aut a Belgis anno M DC XXIX gestarum historia. *Leyden: Elsevier,* 1631. 141 p.; maps; fol. Includes account of capture of Spanish silver fleet by Piet Hein. Willems (Les Elzevier) 351. CtY, ICN, MH, MnU, NN, PU; BL, BN.   631/53

Heresbach, Conrad. The whole art and trade of husbandry . . . translated by Barnaby Googe . . . now renewed, corrected, enlarged, and adorned . . . By Captaine Gervase Markham. *London: T. C[otes].,* for *R. More,* 1631. 385 p.; 4to. Transl. from author's *Rei rusticae,* 1st publ., Cologne, 1570; cf. 1601 English edn with title *Foure books of husbandry.* STC 13202; Poynter (Markham) 33. CSmH, CtY, DFo, MH, NNC, PPAmP.   631/54

Heylyn, Peter. Μικροκοσμος, A little description of the great world. The fifth edition. *Oxford: W. Turner & R. Allott,* [at London,] 1631. 807 p.; 4to. 1st publ., Oxford, 1621. Sabin 31656n (misdated 1632); Madan (Oxford) 1631:15; STC 13280. CtY, DLC, ICN, MH, MiU, NNC; BL.   631/55

Horst, Gregor. Observationum medicinalium singularium. Libri quatuor posteriores. *Heilbronn: C. Krause,* 1631. 652 p.; 4to. 1st publ., Ulm, 1628. DNLM.   631/56

Jenner, Thomas. The soules solace, or Thirtie and one spiritual emblems. [*London: J. Dawson,*] sold by *T. Jenner,* 1631. illus., 8vo. 1st publ., London, 1626. STC 14495 (formerly also 22941). CSmH; BL, Oxford: Bodl.   631/57

Jonson, Ben. Bartholmew fayre: a comedie. *London: J. B[eale]., for R. Allott,* 1631. 88 p.; fol. Also included are Jonson's *The divell is an asse* & his *The staple of newes. Bartholmew fayre* contains an extended dialog on tobacco; the other two plays mention it. The present work was apparently intended & distributed as a continuation of Jonson's *Workes* of 1616; it was also reissued, 1640, as pt of his *Workes . . . The second volume.* STC 14753.5; cf. Arents 211. CSmH, MH, TxU.   631/58

Journael van de Nassausche vloot . . . Den derden druck oversien ende doorgaens vermeerdert. *Amsterdam: H. Gerritsz & J. P. Wachter,* 1631. 110 p.; illus., maps; 4to. 1st publ., Amsterdam, 1626. No further evidence of a 2nd edn. has been discovered. Tiele 665.   631/59

Lenton, Francis. Characterismi; or, Lentons leasures. *London: J. B[eale]., for R. Michell,* 1631. [173] p.; 12mo. In characters 11, 'A pander', & 29, 'A yong Innes a Court Gentleman', tobacco is mentioned. Reissued, 1632, under title *Spare time;* 1636, as *Lentons leisures described;* 1640, as *A piece of the world.* STC 15463; Murphy (Engl. char.-bks) 48–49. CSmH, IU; BL.   631/60

León, Luis Ponce de. Obras proprias . . . Con la parafrasi de algunos psalmos y capitulos de Job. *Madrid: Imprenta Real (Widow of L. Sánchez), for D. González,* 1631. 203 numb. lvs; 8vo. In his commentary on the Book of Job the author sees in chapt. 28 a prediction of the discovery of the New World & its riches, mentioning specifically

the mines of Potosí. Palau 135199. NNH.   631/61

—[Anr edn]. *Milan: P. Guisolfi,* 1631. 312 p.; 12mo. Palau 135199n. NNH.   631/62

León Pinelo, Antonio Rodríguez de. Por la Real Universidad y escuelas generales de S. Marcos de . . . Lima, en . . . Peru. Con el Arzobispo, dean y cabildo de la santa iglesia de la ciudad de La Plata, y cabildos seculares . . . de Potosi, en . . . los Charcas. [*Madrid?* 1631?]. 10 numb. lvs; fol. Medina (BHA) 7710. Santiago, Chile:BN.   631/63

Lloyd, David. The legend of captaine Jones. [*London: R. Young,*] for *J. M[arriott].,* 1631. 4to. In verse. Satire on Capt. John Smith, mentioning Florida & America. Cf. Sabin 41683; STC 16614. MH; BL, London:Sion College.   631/64

Markham, Gervase. Cheape and good husbandry . . . Fift edition. *London: N. Okes, for J. Harrison,* 1631. 188 p.; 4to. (*In* Markham's *A way to get wealth*). 1st publ., London, 1614. Poynter (Markham) 34.5; STC 17339. CSmH, CtY, DFo, IU, MH; BL.   631/65

—[Anr edn]. The sixt edition. *London: Anne Griffin, for J. Harrison,* 1631. [216] p.; 8vo. (*In* Markham's *A way to get wealth*). Poynter (Markham) 34.6; STC 17340. CSmH, DFo, MH, MiU, NIC; BL.   631/66

——. The English house-wife. *London: N. Okes, for J. Harrison,* 1631. 252 p.; 4to. (*In* Markham's *A way to get wealth*). 1st publ., London, 1615, as pt 2 of Markham's *Countrey contentments.* Poynter (Markham) 34.5; STC 17353. CSmH, CtY, DLC; BL.   631/67

Marlowe, Christopher. The tragicall historie of the life and death of Doctor Faustus. *London: J. Wright,* 1631. [62] p.; 4to. Drama. 1st publ., London, 1604. STC 17436; Greg 205(i). CSmH, CtY, DFo, ICN, MH; BL.   631/68

Matthieu, Pierre. Histoire de France soubs les regnes de François I, Henry II, François II, Charles IX, Henry III, Henry IV, Louys XIII, et des choses plus memorables advenues aux autres estats de la chrestienté depuis cent ans. *Paris: Widow of N. Buon,* 1631. 3 pts; fol. Pt 2 contains a ref. to the riches afforded Philip II by the New World. BN.   631/69

—[Anr issue?]. *Paris: C. Sonnius*, 1631. 3 pts;
fol. BL, BN.   631/70.

Mendoça, Francisco de, S.J. Viridarium sacrae ac profanae eruditionis. *Lyons: J. Cardon*, 1631. 350 p.; port.; fol. In bk 4, Probl. xxxvii, 'De hemisphaerio', mentions New World in general; bk 4, Probl. xliv, mentions Brazil, citing Osorio; bk 4, Probl. xxxviii, mentions Columbus. Backer V:900–901; Palau 163629.   631/71

Mercator, Gerardus. Atlantis majoris appendix, sive Pars altera. *Amsterdam: H. Hondius*, 1631. 83 maps; fol. 1st publ., Amsterdam, 1630. Koeman (Me) 33. Freiburg:UB.
                                                631/72

——. Atlas minor, das ist: Ein kurtze jedoch gründliche Beschreibung der gantzen Welt . . . Erstlich . . . in Latein beschrieben: folgends durch Jodocum Hondium mit vielen Kupffern gebessert und vermehret: und endlich in unsere hochteutsche Sprach versetzt. *Amsterdam: J. Janszoon, the Younger*, 1631. 600 p.; maps; obl. 12mo. Transl. from 1628 Latin text. Sabin 47889; Koeman (Me) 199; Phillips (Atlases) 5932. DLC, LNHT; BL, Amsterdam:UB.   631/73

More, Sir Thomas, Saint. Utopia a mendis vindicata. *Amsterdam: J. Janszoon, the Younger*, 1631. 263 p.; 16mo. 1st publ., Louvain, 1516; cf. 1601 edn. Gibson (More) 14; Shaaber (Brit. auth.) M245. CSmH, CtY, DFo, ICN, MH, RPJCB; BL, Vienna:BN.
                                                631/74

Nederlandsche West-Indische Compagnie. Articulen, met approbatie vande . . . Staten Generael . . . over het open ende vry stellen vanden handel ende negotie opde stadt Olinda . . . Brasil. Hier zijn achter by ghedruckt De vryheden van Nieu-Nederlant. *Amsterdam: T. Jacobszoon, for M. J. Brandt*, 1631. [23] p.; 4to. 1st publ., Amsterdam, 1630; here enl. by the company's *Vryheden ende exemptien voor de patroonen . . . op Nieu-Nederlandt*, 1st publ., Amsterdam, 1630, under title *Vryheden by de vergaderinghe.* Sabin 102924 & 102921; Borba de Moraes II:374–75; Vail (Frontier) 83; Knuttel 4152; JCB (3) II:239. MiU-C, RPJCB; BL, The Hague:KB.   631/75

——. Extract uyt de Notulen der vergaderinge der XIX, in dato den 17. October 1631. [*Amsterdam*: 1631?] bds.; 4to. Con-

cerns commerce with Brazil, touching relations with Portuguese & Spanish. Berès (Pays-Bas anciens) 107.   631/76

——. Octroy by de . . . Staten generael, verleent aende West-Indische compaignie . . . Mette ampliatien van dien, ende het accoord. *The Hague: Widow & Heirs of H. Jacobszoon van Wouw*, 1631. 16 lvs; 4to. 1st publ. in this enl. version, The Hague, 1623. Cf. Sabin 56666. NN-RB.
                                                631/77

——. Vryheden ende exemptien voor de patroonen, meesters ofte particulieren die op Nieu-Nederlandt eenighe colonien ende vee sullen planten geconsidereert ten dienst van de Generale West-Indische Compagnie in Nieu-Nederlandt. *Amsterdam: T. Jacobszoon*, 1631. [11] p.; 4to. 1st publ., Amsterdam, 1630, under title *Vryheden by de vergaderinghe*. While this reprinting may have been issued separately, it is more likely a fragment of the company's *Articulen* of this year above, q.v. Sabin 102921; Vail (Frontier) 82.   631/78

Nieremberg, Juan Eusebio, S.J. De arte voluntatis libri sex . . . Accedit . . . Historia panegyrica de tribus martyribus . . . in Urugai pro fide occisis. *Lyons: J. Cardon*, 1631. 543 p.; 8vo. Sabin 55267; cf. Medina (BHA) 717; Backer V:1731; Palau 190701 (cf. 190602 & 190603). MoU, WU.
                                                631/79

Ossorio y Guadalfaxara, Juan. Por Lelio Imbrea cavallero de la Orden de Santiago . . . con Bernal Perez. [*Seville*: 1631?]. 14 numb. lvs; fol. On failure of Pérez to ship tobacco pipes to Mexico. Arents (Add.) 258. NN-A.   631/80

Pedro de Santiago, O.S.A.D. Relacion del transito que hizieron à las Indias los padres Agustinos descalços de España el año de 1605. y progressos . . . el año de 1630 [*Madrid*: 1631]. 75 numb. lvs; 4to. Sabin 69219; Medina (BHA) 880; Streit II:1590 & V:797; Palau 299884; JCB(3) II:232. RPJCB.
                                                631/81

Peleus, Julien. Les oeuvres . . . contenant plusieurs questions illustres. *Paris: M. Guillemot*, 1631. 2 pts; fol. The author's *Questions illustres*, with ref. to the Sieur de Monts's trading company in Acadia, 1st publ., Paris, 1608. BL.   631/82

—[Anr issue]. *Paris: N. Rousset,* 1631. DLC.
631/83

Pellham, Edward. Gods power and providence: shewed in the miraculous preservation . . . of eight Englishmen, left by mischance in Green-land anno 1630 . . . With a description of the chiefe places . . . of that . . . countrey. *London: R. Y[oung]., for J. Partridge,* 1631. 35 p.; map; 4to. Sabin 59586; STC 19566; JCB (3) II:237. CSmH, DLC, ICN, MH, MnU-B, NN-RB, RPJCB; BL.
631/84

La prise de l'isle de Santo Paulo, et seize navires espagnolles, par les Hollandois . . . *Lyons, suivant les copies envoyees d'Hollande,* 1631. 8vo. The original Dutch text has not been identified. Sabin 65702.
631/85

Randolph, Thomas. Aristippus, or The joviall philosopher . . . To which is added, The conceited pedlar. *London: [Elizabeth Allde,] for R. Allot,* 1631. 44 p.; 4to. Drama. 1st publ., London, 1630. STC 20688; Greg 431/432(d). CSmH, CtY, DFo, MB, MiU; BL.
631/86

Rapine, Charles, O.F.M. Histoire generale de l'origine et progrez des freres mineurs de S. François . . . appellés . . . Recollects . . . ou Deschaux tant en toutes les provinces & royaumes catholiques, comme dans les Indes Orientales & Occidentales, & autres parties des nouveaux mondes depuis . . . 1486 . . . à . . .1606. *Paris: C. Sonnius,* 1631. 775 p.; ports; 4to. 1st publ., Paris, 1630. Sabin 67915; Streit I:451. BL, BN.
631/87

Relacion de la jornada que la armada de Su Magestad à hecho al socorro del Brasil, y batalla que entre ella, y la de los estados de Olanda se dieron en doze de septiembre deste año de 1631. *Seville: F. de Lyra,* 1631. 2 lvs; fol. Sabin 69178; Medina (BHA) 802; Rodrigues (Dom. Hol.) 421; Escudero (Seville) 1.631; Palau 258004. NN-RB; Madrid:Acad. de la Hist., Seville:BM. 631/88

Relacion del lastisomo incendio que el 6 de julio de 1631 . . . y las alegres nuevas de las pazes de Italia, y llegada de nuestra armada à Pernambuco. *Granda: M. Fernández Zambrano,* 1631. 4 p.; fol. Rodrigues (Dom. Hol.) 401; Palau 258003.
631/89

Renou, Jean de. Dispensatorium Galeno chymicum continens primo Joannis Reno-daei Institutionum pharmoceuticarum [*sic*] lib. v; De materia medica lib. iii., et antidotarium varium et absolutissima. Secudo Josephi Quercetani Pharmacopoeam dogmaticorum restitutam. Per Petrum Uffenbachium . . . revisum. *Hanau: D.Aubry,* 1631. 869 p.; 4to. Renou's *Institutionum* 1st publ., Paris, 1608; Duchesne's *Pharmacopoeam . . . restitutam,* Paris, 1607. Wellcome I:5431. WU; London:Wellcome.
631/90

Rezende, Luis Vaz de. Contrato do pao Brasil, que o Capitam Luis Vaz de Rezende . . . fez con a fazenda de sua Magestad, por tempo de dez annos. *Lisbon: P. Craesbeeck,* 1631. 6 lvs; 4to. Borba de Moraes I:172.
631/91

A rich storehouse or treasury for the diseased. *London: R. Badger, for P. Stephens & C. Meredith,* 1631. 317 p.; 4to. 1st publ., London, 1596; cf. 1601 edn; here a reissue of 1630 edn with altered imprint date. STC 23611. CSmH, DFo, MH(imp.), PPC; BL.
631/92

Río de Janeiro (Diocese). Por la administracion y prelacia eclesiastica del Rio de Janeiro, en . . . Brasil, y de lo que en ella tiene gran necessidad de remedio. *Madrid:* 1631. 4 numb. lvs; fol. BL.
631/93

Rosenberg, Johann Karl. Rhodologia, seu Philosophico-medica generosae descriptio . . . Editio novissima aucta. *Frankfurt a. M.: H. Palthenius,* 1631. 403 p.; 8vo. 1st publ., Frankfurt a. M., 1628. Pritzel 7768n. DNLM, MH-A, MoSB; BL, BN. 631/94

Santorio, Santorio. Methodi vitandorum errorum omnium, qui in arte medica contingunt libri quindecim. *Geneva: P. Aubert,* 1631. 2 pts; illus., 4to. 1st publ., Venice, 1603; here a reissue of Aubert's 1630 edn with altered imprint date? Wellcome I:5759. CtY-M, DNLM; London:Wellcome.
631/95

Schemering, Daniel. Nova Zemla, sive descriptio contracta navigationum trium admirandarum. *Flushing: S. Versterre,* 1631. 22 lvs; 4to. In verse. Includes refs to Greenland. Sabin 77559. DLC, MH. 631/96

Schrijver, Pieter. Vasten-avond-spel, den tweeden druck vervatende 't ghebruyk en 't misbruyk van den taback uyt het Latijn in 't Neder-duytsch vertaelt. *Leyden: W.*

Christiaens, 1631. 96 p.; obl. 16mo. 1st publ.
in Dutch, Haarlem, 1630, under title *Saturnalia* Bragge 34. BL.   631/97

Sennert, Daniel. Institutionum medicinae,
libri v. *Paris:* 1631. 1363 p.; illus.; 4to. 1st
publ., Wittenberg, 1611. CaBVaU, DNLM.
631/98

Sgambata, Scipio, S.J. Elogio del p. Giuseppe Anchieta della Compagnia di Gesù
il quale . . . morí nel Brasile il giorno 9
giugno dell'anno 1622. *Naples: Il Scoriggio*,
1631. fol. Borba de Moraes II:252; Streit
I:2395; Backer VII:1174.   631/99

Sharpham, Edward. The fleire. *London: B.
A[lsop]. & T. Fawcet, for N. Butter*, 1631. 30
lvs; 4to. Drama. 1st publ., London, 1607.
STC 22387; Arents (Add.) 259. CSmH,
CtY, DFo, ICN, MH, MiU, NN-A; BL.
631/100

Smith, Capt. John. Advertisements for the
unexperienced planters of New England, or
any where. *London: J. Haviland; sold by R.
Milbourne*, 1631. 40 p.; map; 4to. For discussion of 9 states of map, etc., see Sabin. Sabin 82815; Vail (Frontier) 81; STC 22787;
Church 419; JCB (3) II:238. CSmH, CtY,
DLC, ICN, MH, MiU-C, PP, RPJCB; BL.
631/101

——. The generall historie of Virginia, New-
England, and the Summer Isles. *London: J.
D[awson]. & J. H[aviland]., for M. Sparke*,
1631. 248 p.; illus., ports, maps; fol. 1st
publ., London, 1624; here a reissue with
altered imprint date. Sabin 82828; Clayton-
Torrence 51 (5); Baer (Md) 17; STC
22790c.5; JCB AR19:4–5. DFo, RPJCB.
631/102

Solórzano Pereira, Juan de. Discurso i alegacion en derecho sobre la culpa que resulta contra el general don Juan de Benavides Baçan i Almirante don Juan de Leoz
. . . i otros consortes, en razon de aver desamparado la flota de su cargo, que el año
passado de 1628. venía à estos reinos de
la provincia de Nueva España, dexandola
. . . en manos del cossario Olandes, en el
puerto . . . de Matanças. *Madrid: F. Martinez*, 1631. 98 numb. lvs; fol. Sabin 86531;
Medina (BHA) 894; Palau 318993. InU-L,
RPJCB; Seville:BU.   631/103

Sousa de Macedo, Antonio de. Flores de
España excelencias de Portugal. En que
. . . se trata los mejor de sus historias, y
de todos las del mundo . . . primera parte.
Lisbon: J. Rodriguez, 1631. 252 numb. lvs;
fol. DLC, InU-L, KU; BL.   631/104

Spaensche vosse-vel, ofte Copye van een
missive, die gehouden mach werden seer
avontuyrlijck in de handen van een oprecht
patriot . . . ghekomen. *Leeuwarden: C. Fonteyne*, 1631. [21] p.; 4to. 1st publ., Leeuwarden, 1630. MnU-B.   631/105

Spain. Consejo de las Indias. Memorial de
lo que contienen los papeles presentados
por . . . Juan de Mañozca, inquisidor apostolico del Peru, visitador que fue de la Audiencia real de Quito. [*Madrid:* 1631]. 10
numb. lvs; fol. Sabin 98809; Medina (BHA)
895. NN-RB.   631/106

Speed, John. A prospect of the most famous
parts of the world. *London: J. Dawson, for
G. Humble*, 1631. 44 p.; illus., maps; fol. 1st
publ., London, 1627. Cf. Sabin 89228; Phillips (Atlases) 442; STC 23040. CSmH,
DLC, MH(imp.), MiU-C, NNC; BL.
631/107

Stephens, John. New essayes and characters.
London: [Elizabeth Allde,] for L. Fawne, 1631.
434 p.; 8vo. 1st publ., London, 1615 under
title *Satyrical essayes;* here a reissue with
cancel t.p. of 1615 'second impression'
with title *Essayes and characters.* STC 23251;
Murphy (Engl. char-bks) 31. DFo; BL,
Cambridge: UL, Oxford:Bodl.
631/108

Stow, John. The annales . . . of England
. . . Continued unto 1631. By Edmund
Howes. *London: [J. Beale, B. Alsop, T. Fawcet
&] A. Mathewes, for R. Meighen*, 1631. 1087
p.; fol. 1st publ. with American refs; London, 1592. To those found in 1601 & 1615
edns are added, under year 1618, account
of Virginia & mention of tobacco. STC
23340; Arents 176. CSmH, CtY, DLC, ICN,
MH, MiU, MnU, NN-A, PU, RPB; BL, BN.
631/109

Sweerts, Emanuel. Florilegium amplissimum et selectissimum. *Amsterdam: J. Janszoon, the Younger*, 1631,'14. 2 v.; illus.; fol.
1st publ., Frankfurt a. M., 1612–14. MBH,
MiU-C, NIC; BN.   631/110

Tapp, John. The seamans kalendar . . .

Twelfth impression. *London: B. Alsop & T. Fawcet, for J. Tapp,* 1631. 4to. 1st publ., London, 1602; no 10th & 11th edn or impression has been traced. STC 23682. Oxford: Bodl. 631/111

Taylor, John, the Water-poet. The needles excellency. *London: [T. Harper,] for J. Boler,* 1631. illus.; obl. 4to. In verse. 'Great Mexico' & the 'Indies West' are mentioned. STC 23775.5. Cambridge: Magdalene (Pepys). 631/112

Téllez, Gabriel. Doze comedias nuevas del maestro Tirso de Molina. *Valencia: P. P. Mey,* 1631. 300 numb. lvs; 4to. 1st publ., Seville, 1627; here a reissue of that edn with cancel t.p. Palau 329475. 631/113

Torsellino, Orazio, S.J. Chronicon ab orbe condito ad haec tempora brevi compendio digestum. *Cologne: Birckmann Office, for H. Mylius,* 1631. 524 p.; 8vo. 1st publ., Rome, 1598; cf. 1620 edn with title, like those below, *Historiarum . . . epitome.* Backer VIII:152. 631/114

——. Historiarum ab origine mundi usque ad annum 1630 epitome libri x. *Paris: M. Henault,* 1631. 3 pts; 12mo. 1st publ., Rome, 1598; cf. 1620 edn. Backer VIII:152. BN. 631/115

—[Anr edn]. *Paris: J. Branchu,* 1631. 3 pts; 12mo. BN. 631/116

—[Anr issue of preceding]. *Paris: M. Soly,* 1631. BN. 631/117

Trebiño, Antonio, S.J. Señor. El maestro fray Francisco de Herrera, definidor y procurador general de la provincia de San Agustin de Quito, en . . . Pirù, dize: Que estando la dicha su provincia preseguida y oprimada de algunos de los juezues [sic] de aquella audiencia, viene con muchas dificultades y peligros a buscar el remedio. [*Madrid:* 1631]. 12 numb. lvs; fol. Memorial to king of Spain. Sabin 96757; Medina (BHA) 7768; Palau 339980. 631/118

Walkington, Thomas. The optick glasse of humors. *Oxford: W. T[urner].; sold by M. S[parke, at London,* 1631]. 168 p.; 8vo. 1st publ., London, 1607. STC 24968; Madan (Oxford) 1631:30; Arents 175. CSmH, CtY, DFo, MH, NN-A, WU; BL. 631/119

1632

Acarete du Biscay. Relation des voyages dans la riviere de la Plata et au-de-la aux terres du Pérou. *Paris:* 1632. fol. Very possibly a ghost. Sabin 88; Palau 1688. 632/1

Alemán, Mateo. Le gueux, ou La vie de Guzman d'Alfarache. *Paris: H. LeGras* (v. 1) & *N. Gasse* (v. 2), 1632. 2 v.; 8vo. 1st publ. as here transl. by Jean Chapelain, Paris, 1619 & 1620. Vol. 2 has title *Le voleur, ou La vie de Guzman d'Alfarache.* Laurenti (Nov. pic. esp.) 621. Paris:Arsenal. 632/2

—[Anr edn]. *Rouen: J. de LaMare,* 1632–33. 2 v.; 8vo. Cf. Laurenti (Nov. pic. esp.) 622. IU; BN. 632/3

——. Der Landstörtzer. *Munich:* [*N. Heinrich?*] 1632. 8vo. 1st publ. in German, Munich, 1615. Goedeke II:577. 632/4

Altamirano, Diego. Por Don Juan de Benavides Baçan . . . general de la flota de Nueva-España, con el señor fiscal. [*Madrid:*] *F. Martínez,* [1632?]. 35 numb. lvs; fol. Memorial to king of Spain. Medina (BHA) 8058; Palau 8863; cf. JCB AR44:18–23. RPJCB. 632/5

——. Por la Real audiencia de Mexico. Con el marques de Gelves. Prespuesto el tumulto y alteracion popular que huvo en la ciudad de Mexico, lunes 15. de enero de 1624. en descontento y odio de la persona del virrey marques de Gelves. [*Madrid?* 1632?]. 22 numb. lvs; fol. NN-RB. 632/6

Avendaño, Francisco de. Señor: El general don Francisco de Avendaño. [*Madrid?* 1632?]. 8 numb. lvs; fol. Memorial to king of Spain on affairs & administration of Chile. Medina (Chile) 246. BL. 632/7

Bacon, Francis, viscount St Albans. The essayes or Counsels, civill and morall. *London: J. Haviland,* 1632. 340 p.; 4to. 1st publ. as here enl., London, 1625. Gibson (Bacon) 16; STC 1150. CSmH, CtY, DLC, ICN, MH, NN-RB, PPL, RPB; BL. 632/8

——. Neuf livres de la dignité et l'accroissement des sciences . . . traduits . . . par le sieur de Golefer. *Paris: J. Dugast,* 1632. 717 numb. lvs; 4to. 1st publ., London, 1623. as *Opera: Tomus primus* but here prob. transl.

from Paris, 1624, edn with title *De dignitate . . . scientiarum libri ix.* Gibson (Bacon) 137; Shaaber (Brit. auth.) B21–B22. CtY, DLC, ICU, MH; BL, BN.　　　　　632/9

Baerle, Kaspar van. Athenaeum, sive In illustris Amstelodamensium scholae inaugurationem poemation. *Amsterdam: W. J. Blaeu,* 1632. 15 p.; fol. In verse. Includes ref. to Olinda. CtY; BL, BN.　　　　632/10

——. Mercator sapiens, sive Oratio. *Amsterdam: W. J. Blaeu,* 1632. 37 p.; fol. Includes refs to American gold & silver, Columbus, Vespucci, & Mexico. CtY, DLC; BL, BN.　　　　　632/11

Basso, Gerardo. Discurso sobre la proposicion de labrar buenas monedas de valor intrinseco. [*Madrid?*] 1632. 36 numb. lvs; fol. Memorial to king of Spain, mentioning Mexico & Peru, & the export thither of mercury. BL.　　　　632/12

Béguin, Jean. Les elemens de chymie . . . Quatriesme edition. *Paris: J. B. Behourt,* 1632. 432 p.; illus.; 8vo. 1st publ. as here transl. from Béguin's *Tyrocinium chymicum* (Paris, 1612), Paris, 1615. PU-S; Glasgow: UL.　　　　632/13

Benavides, Alonso de, O.F.M. Carta de fr. Alonso de Benavides a los religiosos de la custodia de San Pueblo del Nuevo Mexico. *Madrid:* 1632. Being unknown to H. R. Wagner & others, this may well be a ghost. Medina (BHA) 897.　　　　632/14

Bethune, Philippe de, comte de Selles et de Charost. Le conseiller d'estat, ou Recueil des plus grandes considerations servans au maniment des affaires publique. [*Paris?*] 1632. 496 p.; 4to. Chapt. xv describes Christianization of peoples of Brazil, Peru, Mexico, etc.; scattered American refs occur elsewhere. Cioranescu (XVII) 11974. BL.　　　　632/15

Breton, Nicholas. Conceited letters, newly laid open. *London: A. Mathewes, for S. Rand,* 1632. 4to. 1st publ., London, 1618. STC 3638. CSmH; BL.　　　　632/16

Bruele, Gualtherus. Praxis medicinae, or, The physicians practise. *London: J. Norton, for W. Sheares,* 1632. 407 p.; 4to. Transl. from the author's *Praxis medicinae,* 1st publ., Antwerp, 1579; cf. 1602 edn. STC 3929. CSmH, NNNAM, WU; BL.　　　　632/17

Burton, Robert. The anatomy of melancholy . . . The fourth edition, corrected and augmented by the author. *Oxford: J. Lichfield & J. Short, for H. Cripps,* 1632. 722 p.; fol. 1st publ., Oxford, 1621. Madan (Oxford) 1632:3; STC 4162; Arents (Add.) 224. CSmH, CtY, DLC, ICN, InU-L, MH, NN-RB, PPL; BL.　　　　632/18

Castillo Solórzano, Alonso de. La niña de los embustes. *Barcelona: J. Margarit, for J. Sepera,* 1632. 118 numb. lvs; 8vo. Novel, containing, in chapt. xviii, as character one Jorge de Miranda, former resident in Peru, who describes his life there. Palau 48395. MB; Paris:Arsenal.　　　　632/19

Champlain, Samuel de. Les voyages de la Nouvelle France, dicte Canada, faits par le sr de Champlain . . . & toutes les descouvertes qu'il a faites en ce pais depuis l'an 1603. jusques en l'an 1629. *Paris: C. Collet,* 1632. 5 pts; map; 4to. Pages 27–30 (1st count) occur in two settings, the 1st having the 1st paragraph on p. 27 end 'telles descouvertes . . . pour ne l'avoir jamais practique', the 2nd ending with 'telles descouvertes'. In this issue the map bears the legend 'faict par le sieur de Champlain suivant les memoires de P. du Val—en l'isle du Palais'. Sabin 11839; Streit II:2493n; Church 420; Lande 118; JCB (3) II:239. CSmH, MH, RPJCB; BL, BN.　632/20

—[Anr issue]. *Paris: P. LeMur,* 1632. The map differs in being larger & bearing legend 'Faict l'an 1632 par le sieur du Champlain'. Sabin 11839n; Harrisse (NF) 51; Bell (Jes. rel.) 239–47; Wolfenbüttel 96. MWiW-C, MnU-B; Wolfenbüttel:HB.　　632/21

—[Anr issue]. *Paris: L. Sevestre,* 1632. Map as in LeMur issue. Sabin 11839n; Harrisse (NF) 50; Streit II:2493. BN.　　　632/22

Copye van 't proces ende sententie teghens Joan Avontroot, die gekomen is in Spangien . . . om te spreken met den koningh van liberteyt van conscientie . . . overgeset in onse tale. *Amsterdam: G. J. Arensteyn* [1632?]. [8] p.; 4to. Mentions Aventrote's visit to Peru. No Spanish or Latin edn has been traced. Knuttel 4204. The Hague:KB, Ghent:BU.　　　　632/23

Cotgrave, Randle. A dictionarie of the English & French tongues. *London: A. Islip,* 1632. 2 pts; fol. 1st publ., London, 1611.

STC 5831. CSmH, CtY, DFo, ICN, MH, MnU, NN-RB, PU-F; BL, BN.   632/24

Dalechamp, Caleb. Christian hospitalitie, handled common-place-wise. *Cambridge: T. Buck,* 1632. 2 pts; 4to. Includes condemnation of tobacco, citing views of James I, and Burton's *Anatomy of melancholy.* STC 6192; Arents (Add.) 260. CSmH, CtY, DFo, ICN, MH, MnU, NN-RB; BL.   632/25

Dekker, Thomas. English villanies six severall times prest to death. *London: A. Mathewes; sold by J. Grismond,* 1632. 56 lvs; 4to. 1st publ., London, 1608, under title *Lanthorne and candle-light.* STC 6491. CLU, DFo, MH; London:V. & A.   632/26

Díaz del Castillo, Bernal, O. Merced. Historia verdadera de la conquista de la Nueva-España . . . Sacada a luz por el p. fr. Alonso Remon. *Madrid: Imprenta Real,* 1632. 254 numb. lvs; fol. Sabin 19978; Medina (BHA) 898; Streit II:1609; Palau 72354; Arents 177. CU, CtY, DLC, InU-L, MH, MiU-C, NN-RB, PPL; BL.   632/27

—[Anr edn]. *Madrid: Imprenta Real* [1632?]. 256 numb. lvs; fol. Sabin 19979; Medina (BHA) 899; Streit II:1609n; Palau 72354n. CtY, DLC, InU-L, MH, NN-RB, PPL, RPJCB; BL, BN.   632/28

Díaz Taño, Francisco, S.J. Señor. El padre Francisco Diaz Taño de la Compañia de Jesus, y procurador general della, de las provincias del Paraguay, Tucumán, y Rio de la Plata, dize. [*Madrid?* 1632?]. [4] p.; fol. Memorial to king of Spain seeking services of 60 Jesuits. Sabin 19989; Streit II:1610; Backer III:48. InU-L.   632/29

Du Bartas, Guillaume de Salluste, seigneur. Les oeuvres poetiques et chrestiennes. *Geneva: P. & J. Chouët,* 1632. 701 p.; 12mo. In verse. Included are the author's *La sepmaine,* 1st publ., Paris, 1578, & his *La seconde sepmaine,* 1st publ., Paris, 1584; cf. 1603 edn. Holmes (DuBartas) I:77 no.38. ICN, NcU, WU; Paris:Ste Geneviève.   632/30

Dupleix, Scipion. La curiosité naturelle. *Paris: C. Sonnius,* 1632. 296 p.; 8vo. 1st publ., Paris, 1606. BN.   632/31

Durante, Castore. Il tesoro della sanità. *Rome: G. Facciotto,* 1632. 334 p.; 8vo. 1st publ., [Rome?], 1586; cf. 1601 edn. Michel (Répertoire) II:191. BL, BN.   632/32

Ercilla y Zúñiga, Alonso de. Araucana . . .

Divida en tres partes. *Madrid: Imprenta Real,* 1632. 453 numb. lvs; 8vo. In verse. 1st publ. in all 3 pts, Madrid, 1590; cf. 1610 edn. above. Medina (Chile) 82; Medina (Arau.) 20; Palau 80423n. InU-L, MiU, NN-RB, RPJCB; BL.   632/33

Estienne, Charles. L'argiculture et maison rustique. *Rouen: J. Berthelin,* 1632. 2 pts; 4to. 1st publ. as enl. by Liébault, Paris, 1567; cf. 1601 edn. Goldsmith (France) E330. BL.   632/34

Fabre, Pierre Jean. Myrothecium spagyricum; sive, Pharmacopoea chymica. *Strassburg: Heirs of L. Zetzner,* 1632. 2 pts; 8vo. 1st publ., Toulouse, 1628. DNLM, WU; London:Wellcome.   632/35

Figueiredo, Manuel de. Hidrographia, exame de pilotos. *Lisbon: J. Rodríguez,* 1632. 3 pts; illus.; 4to. 1st publ., Lisbon, 1608. Cf. Sabin 24316; Borba de Moraes I:266; cf. Palau 91333.   632/36

France. Treaties, etc., 1610–1643 (Louis XIII). Traicté entre le Roy Louis XIII. et Charles roy de la Grand' Bretagne, pour la restitution de la Nouvelle France, la Cadie, & Canada . . . 1632. le 29. mars. [*Paris?* 1632?]. 11 p.; 4to. Sabin 96516; Harrisse (NF) 47; JCB AR52:37–38. CSmH, RPJCB; BL, BN (Lk 12.1057).   632/37

Freylin, Juan Maria, S.J. Catalogo de algunos varones insignes en santidad, de la provincia del Perú de la Compañia de Jesus. Hecho por orden de la congregacion provincial, que se celebro en el Colegio de S. Pablo de Lima. *Seville: F. de Lyra,* 1632. 26 p.; 4to. Streit II:1614; Backer III:973–74.   632/38

Gomberville, Marin Le Roy, sieur du Parc et de. La premiere [-seconde] partie de Polexandre . . . revue, changée et augmentee en cette nouvelle edition. *Paris: T. Du Bray,* 1632. 2 v.; 4to. A reworking of author's *Exil de Polexandre,* Paris, 1629, retaining Peruvian prince, but with less New World background. BN.   632/39

Greiff, Friedrich. Consignatio medicamentorum omnium tam simplicium quam compositorum tam Galenice quam chymice praeparatorem quae pro tempore in officina m. Friderici Greiffii . . . prostant. *Tübingen: P. Brunn,* 1632. [32] p.; 4to. Offered for sale for medicinal uses are guaiacum, mechoacan, sassafras, & tobacco. Wellcome I:6900. London:Wellcome. 632/40

Grotius, Hugo. De jure belli ac pacis libri tres . . . Editio tertia emendatior. *Amsterdam: J. Janszoon, the Younger,* 1632. 548 p.; 8vo. 1st publ., Paris, 1625. This edn not authorized by Grotius. Meulen/Diermansc 568. DLC, OC1W; The Hague:PP. 632/41

—[Anr edn]. Editio nova ab auctore ipso recognita & correcta. *Amsterdam: W. J. Blaeu,* 1632. 421 p.; 8vo. Meulen/Diermanse 569. CtY, DLC, MH, MiU-C, NN-RB, PPL; BN, The Hague:PP. 632/42

—[Anr edn]. Editio ultima, post editionem G. Blaeu, in 8°. Tractatu de mari libero adaucta. *Amsterdam: J. Janszoon, the Younger,* 1632. 2 pts; 8vo. A reissue of Janszoon's unauthorized edition of this year, with new t.p. and the addition at end of Grotius's *Mare liberum,* 1st publ., Leyden, 1609, with special t.p. & separate paging & signatures. Meulen/Diermanse 570 (& 544). The Hague:PP. 632/43

——. Mare liberum, sive De jure quod Batavis competit ad Indicana commercia dissertatio. Ultima editio. *Amsterdam: J. Janszoon, the Younger,* 1632. 39 p.; 8vo. Issued as part of J. Janszoon's 2nd edn of Grotius's *De jure belli ac pacis* of this year above, q.v. Meulen/Diermanse 544; Bibl. Belg. G334. 632/44

——. True religion explained . . . in six bookes. Written in Latine . . . and now done in English. *London: J. H[aviland]., for R. Royston,* 1632. 350 p.; 12mo. Prob. transl. from Maire's Leyden, 1629, edn of Grotius's *De veritate religionis Christianae.* STC 12400; Meulen/Diermanse 1015. CSmH, CtY, DFo, ICU; BL, BN. 632/45

Guibert, Philbert. Les oeuvres charitables. *Paris: J. Jost,* 1632. 602 p.; 12mo. Included is Guibert's *Le prix et valeur des medicamens,* 1st publ., Paris, 1625. DNLM, WU; BN. 632/46

Hoyarsabal, Martin de. Les voyages avantureux du Capitaine Martin de Hoyarsabal. *Rouen: D. Du Petit Val,* 1632. 114 p.; 4to. Includes sailing directions to Newfoundland. ICN, MnU-B. 632/47

Jonstonus, Joannes. Thaumatographia naturalis. *Amsterdam: W. J. Blaeu,* 1632. 501

p.; 12mo. Includes refs to American flora & fauna. Jantz (German Baroque) 1452; Arents (Add.) 261. DLC, ICU, MH, MiU-C, MnU-B, NN-A, PPL; BL, BN. 632/48

Lampe, Barent. Het negentiende deel of 't vervolgh van het Historisch verhael aller gedencwaerdiger gheschiedenissen, die in Europa . . . in America als West-Indien en d'eijlanden . . . voorgevallen zijn. *Amsterdam: J. Janszoon, the Younger,* 1632. 118 numb. lvs; illus., 4to. (N. van Wassenaer's *Historisch verhael.* Pt 19). Includes refs to Pernambuco & the Spanish silver fleet. Cf. Sabin 102039; Borba de Moraes II:371; Muller (1872) 1745. RPJCB; Amsterdam:NHSM. 632/49

Lauremberg, Peter. Apparatus plantarius primus. *Frankfurt a. M.: M. Merian* [1632]. 168 p.; illus.; 4to. In bk 2, chapts iii–iv discuss 'adenes Canadensis' & 'Virginiani', i.e., potatoes & yams. Pritzel 5089; Nissen (Bot.) 1146; Hunt (Bot.) 221. CU, DNAL, ICJ, MH-A, NNBG, RPB; BL. 632/50

Ledesma, Diego de, S.J. Doctrine chrestienne . . . Traduicte en langage canadois . . . par le r.p. Breboeuf. [*Paris:* 1632]. *In* Champlain's *Les voyages de la Nouvelle France* of this year above.

Le Jeune, Paul, S.J. Brieve relation du voyage de la Nouvelle France, fait au mois d'Avril dernier par le p. Paul le Jeune de la Compagnie de Jesus. *Paris: S. Cramoisy,* 1632. 68 p.; 8vo. For variant states, see McCoy. Sabin 39946; Harrisse (NF) 49; Streit II:2494; Backer IV:795; McCoy 1–2; JCB (3) II:242. ICN, NN-RB, RPJCB; BN. 632/51

Lenton, Francis. Spare time. Expressed in essayes and characters. *London: [J. Beale,] for J. Boler,* 1632. [173] p.; 12mo. 1st publ., London, 1631, under title *Characterismi;* here a reissue with cancel t.p. STC 15463.5; Arents (Add.) 263. NN-A. 632/52

Lima. Consulado de mercaderes. Relacion de las fiestas que el comercio, y consulado de los mercaderes de Lima, celebrò al nacimiento del principe nuestro señor don Baltasar Carlos de Austria. 1630. *Seville:* 1632. 7 p.; fol. Medina (BHA) 904. MB. 632/53

Lithgow, William. The totall discourse, of

the rare adventures, of long nineteene yeares travayles. *London: N. Okes,* 1632. 507 p.; illus., port.; 4to. 1st publ., London, 1614, under title *A most delectable and true discourse;* here revised and enlarged. STC 15712.5; Arents 179. IU, NN-A, WU; Cambridge:Christ's. 632/54

—[Anr issue]. *London: N. Okes, sold by N. Fussell & H. Moseley,* 1632. STC 15713. CSmH, CtY, DLC, ICN, MH, NN-RB; BL. 632/55

Lucius, Ludwig, S.J. Historia Jesuitica. *Basel:* 1632. 4to. 1st publ. in this version, Basel, 1627. Jöcher II:1725–26. BL (Hospinianus). 632/56

Lugo y Dávila, Francisco de. Desenganos y replicas a las proposiciones de Gerardo Basso, en razon de las monedas ligadas de nueve y tres dineros de ley. *Madrid: Imprenta Real,* 1632. 36 numb. lvs; 4to. A reply to Gerardo Basso's *Arbitrios y discursos politicos,* Madrid, 1627. Included are numerous refs to precious metals of Spanish America. Medina (Lima) 156; Palau 14767; JCB (3) II:240. RPJCB; BL, BN. 632/57

Malingre, Claude. Remarques d'histoire, ou Description chronologique des choses . . . passées, tant en France, qu'és pays estrangers, depuis . . . 1600. *Paris: C. Collet,* 1632. 984 p.; 8vo. Included are scattered refs to events in the New World. BL, BN. 632/58

Marmion, Shackerley. Hollands leaguer. An excellent comedy. *London: J. B[eale]., for J. Grove,* 1632. [86] p.; 4to. In act 1, scene 5, & act 5, scene 2, tobacco is mentioned. Imprint has reading 'Swan-Alley'. STC 17443. CSmH. 632/59

—[Anr issue]. *London: J. B[eale]., for J. Grove,* 1632. Imprint has reading 'Swan-Yard'. STC 17443.5; Greg 461; Arents 180. CSmH, CtY, DLC, ICN, MH, NN-RB, PU; BL. 632/60

Mendoça, Francisco de, S.J. Viridarium sacrae profanae eruditionis. *Lyons: J. Cardon,* 1632. 350 p.; fol. 1st publ., Lyons, 1631; here anr issue of that edn with altered imprint date. Backer V:901; Palau 163629n. CoU. 632/61

Mercator, Gerardus. Atlas, sive Cosmographicae meditationes de fabrica mundi et fabricati figura. De novo . . . emendatus . . .

studio Judoci Hondii. *Amsterdam: J. E. Cloppenburg,* 1632. 749 p.; maps; obl. 4to. 1st publ. in this version, Amsterdam, 1630. Sabin 47882n; Koeman (Me) 200; Phillips (Atlases) 443. DLC, IU, PBL; BL, Madrid:BN. 632/62

Micalori, Jacomo. Crisis . . . de Erycii Puteani circulo urbiniano. *Urbino: M. & A. Ghisoni,* 1632. 20 p.; 4to. A reply to Puteanus's *Circulus Puteanus,* the text of which occupies p. 15–20. Both Micalori & Puteanus, discussing time measurement, refer to the New World, citing Columbus, Pope Alexander's demarcation line, etc. RPJCB; BN. 632/63

Montaigne, Michel Eyquem de. Essais. *Paris: P. Chevalier,* 1632. 1129 p.; 8vo. 1st publ., Bordeaux, 1580; cf. 1602 edn. Tchémerzine VIII:426. BN. 632/64

——. The essayes . . . Third edition. *London: M. Fletcher, for R. Royston,* 1632. 631 p.; fol. 1st publ. as here transl. by John Florio, London, 1603. STC 18043. CSmH, CtY, MH, MiU, MnU, NNC, PPL; BN. 632/65

Netherlands (United Provinces, 1581–1795). Staten Generaal. Placaet ende Ordonnantie op de wapeninge ende manninghe vande schepen. *The Hague: Widow & Heirs of H. Jacobszoon van Wouw,* 1632. 24 p.; 4to. 1st publ., The Hague, 1607; here rev. Meulman 2192. Ghent:BU. 632/66

——. Placcaet. De Staten Generael tot verbod van den handel op West-Indien. *The Hague:* 1632. bds.; fol. Dated June 14, 1632. 1st publ., The Hague, 1624. Sabin 63193n; Petit 1765. Leyden:B. Thysiana (imp.). 632/67

Nieremberg, Juan Eusebio, S.J. Curiosa filosofia, y tesoro de maravillas de la naturaleza. *Madrid: Imprenta Real,* 1632. 214 numb. lvs; 8vo. 1st publ., Madrid, 1630. Palau 190662-II. 632/68

Oliva, Anelio, S.J. Catalogo de algunos varones illustres in santidad de la Compañia de Jesus de la provincia del Piru. *Seville: F. de Lyra,* 1632. 327 p.; 4to. Sabin 57186n; Backer V:1883; Escudero (Seville) 1460. 632/69

Overbury, Sir Thomas. Sir Thomas Overbury his wife . . . The fifteenth impression. *London: R. B[adger]., for R. Allott,* 1632. [320] p.; 8vo. STC 18918; Murphy (Engl. char.-

bks) 23–24. CSmH, CtY, DFo, ICN, MH, MiU, NIC; BL. 632/70

Ovidius Naso, Publius. Metamorphoses. English. Ovid's Metamorphosis. Englished . . . by G[eorge]. S[andys]. *Oxford: J. Lichfield,* 1632. 549 p.; illus.; fol. 1st publ., London, 1626; here a rev. edn. Sabin 76458 (& 57984); Grolier Club (Wither to Prior) 782; Madan (Oxford) 1632:7; STC 18966. CSmH, CtY, DLC, ICN, InU-L, MH, MiU-C, NN-RB, PPL, RPB; BL. 632/71

Owen, John. Epigrammatum . . . editio postrema. *Amsterdam: J. Janszoon, the Younger,* 1632. 280 p.; 8vo. 1st publ., London, 1606. Shaaber (Brit. auth.) O91. IaU; BN.

632/72

Paulo do Rosario, O.S.B. Relacam breve, e verdadeira de memoravel victoria, que ovve o capitão môr da capitania da Paraiva Antonio de Albuquerque, dos rebeldes de Olanda. *Lisbon: J. Rodriguez,* 1632. 16 numb. lvs; 8vo. Sabin 73207 (& 677 & 59227); Borba de Moraes II:219; Rodrigues (Dom. Hol.) 191; JCB (3) II:243. RPJCB.

632/73

Perea, Estevan de, O.F.M. Verdadera relacion, de la grandiosa conversion que ha avido en el Nuevo Mexico. *Seville: L. Estupiñán,* 1632. [4] p.; fol. For a 2nd *relacion* by Perea, see the year 1633. Sabin 76810n; Medina (BHA) 901; Wagner (SW) 35. Madrid:Acad. de la Hist. 632/74

Pinto Ribeiro, João. Discurso sobre os fidalgos, e soldados portugueses não militarem em conquistas alheas desta coroa. *Lisbon: P. Craesbeeck,* 1632. 15 numb. lvs; 4to. Complains of reluctance of Portuguese nobles to serve in Indies, thus abandoning Brazil to Dutch. Borba de Moraes II:204; Rodrigues (Dom. Hol.) 403. DLC, MH.

632/75

Ponce de Léon, Francisco, O.Merced. Relacion de los servicios que ha hecho a su Magestad en . . . Peru . . . fray Ponce de Leon, del orden . . . de la Merced. [*Madrid?* 1632?]. [4] p.; fol. BL. 632/76

A publication of Guiana's plantation, newly undertaken by . . . the Earl of Barkshire . . . and Company, for that most famous river of the Amazones in America. *London: W. Jones, for T. Paine,* 1632. 24 p.; 4to. Sabin 29190; STC 12456; JCB (3) II:241. DLC,

MB, MiU-C, MnU-B, NN-RB, PPL, RPJCB; BL. 632/77

Pulgar, Hernando de. Los claros varones de España. *Antwerp: J. de Meurs,* 1632. 91 numb. lvs; 8vo. 1st publ. with ref. to discovery of New World, Saragossa, 1561. Peeters-Fontainas (Impr. esp.) 1084; Palau 242120. NNH; BL, Brussels:BR.

632/78

Relacion de la jornada que la armada de su Magestad, cuyo capitan general es don Antonio de Oquendo, hizo al Brazil para correr las plaças de aquella provincia. *Barcelona: E. Liberós,* 1632. [4] p.; fol. 1st publ., Seville, 1631. Cf. Medina (BHA) 903; cf. Borba de Moraes II:188; Palau 258005. RPJCB. 632/79

—[Anr edn]. *Madrid: F. de Ocampo,* 1632. [4] p.; fol. Medina (BHA) 903; cf. Borba de Moraes II:188; Palau 258006. RPJCB.

632/80

Relaes ende 't cargo van't silver ende coopmanschappen diegheregistreert quamen inde vlote van Nova Hispania . . . vertrocken den 14. Octob. 1631 uyt Nova Vera Croce. *Amsterdam: J. F. Stam, for J. van Hilten* [1632?]. bds.; fol. Sabin 69241; Muller (1872) 1281. NNH. 632/81

Reves, Jacques de. Historia pontificorum romanorum. *Amsterdam: J. Janszoon, the Younger,* 1632. 322 p.; 8vo. Section on Pope Alexander VI includes ref. to papal division of lands discovered by Columbus. Jöcher (Suppl.) VI:1903. CtY, IEG, NcD; BL, BN.

632/82

Richelieu, Armand Jean du Plessis, Cardinal, duc de. Furent presens en leurs personnes par devant le notaire . . . A Sanjon ce 2 jour de décembre, 1632 . . . Signé le Cardinal de Richelieu. [*Paris?* 1632?]. 7 p.; fol. On rival aspirations of de Caen and Champlain respecting Canada. Sabin 71103; Harrisse (NF) 48. MnU-B.

632/83

Rowley, William. A new wonder, a woman never vext. A . . . comedy. *London: G. P[urslowe]., for F. Constable,* 1632. 81 p.; 4to. In act 3, cochineal, the dye produced by West Indian insects, is mentioned; in act 4, the phrase 'this new-found land' presumably refers to Newfoundland; tobacco is also cited. STC 21423; Greg 460; Arents (Add.)

264. CSmH, CtY, DLC, ICN, MH, NN-RB; BL. 632/84

Royal College of Physicians of London. Pharmacopoea Londinensis. . . Quarta editio. *London: J. Marriott,* 1632. 217 p.; fol. 1st publ., London, 1618. STC 16775. CSmH, DLC, MBCo, PPC; Oxford:Bodl. 632/85

Sagard, Gabriel, O.F.M. Dictionaire de la langue Huronne. *Paris:* 1632. *See the following item.*

———. Le grand voyage du pays des Hurons, situé en Amérique . . . és derniers confins de la nouvelle France, dite Canada . . . Avec un Dictionaire de la langue Huronne. *Paris: D. Moreau,* 1632. 2 pts; 8vo. The 2nd pt, the *Dictionaire de la langue Huronne,* has special t.p. Sabin 74883 (& 74881); Harrisse (NF) 52 (& 53); Streit II:2495; Arents 181; Church 421; JCB (3) II:243–44. CSmH, CtY, DLC, IHi, InU-L, MH, MiU-C, MnU-B, NN-A, RPJCB; BL, BN. 632/86

Saint-Amant, Marc Antoine de Gérard, sieur de. Les oeuvres. *Paris: R. Estienne, for F. Pomeray & T. Quinet,* 1632. 2 pts; 4to. In verse. 1st publ., Paris, 1629. Cioranescu (XVII) 60673; Tchémerzine X:83. BN. 632/87

Sandys, Sir Edwin. Europae speculum; or, A view or survey of the state of religion. *London: T. Cotes, for M. Sparke,* 1632. 4to. 1st publ., London, 1605, under title *A relation of the state of religion.* STC 21719. CtY, DFo, ICN, MH, MiU; BL. 632/88

—[Anr issue]. . . . Whereunto is added an Appendix. *London: T. Cotes, for M. Sparke,* 1632. 2 pts; 4to. STC 21720. CSmH, DFo, NNG; BL. 632/89

———. A relation of a journey . . . containing a description of the Turkish empire . . . Third edition. *London: [G. Miller] for R. Allot,* 1632. 309 p.; illus., maps; fol. 1st publ., London, 1615. STC 21729. CSmH, CtY, DFo, ICU, MH, MiU, NN-RB, PPL; BL, BN. 632/90

Satyre Ménippée. Satyre Menippée . . . augmenté . . . de l'interpretation du mot de Higueiro d'inferno. *[Paris?]* 1632. [559] p.; illus.; 12mo. 1st publ. in this version, Paris, 1594; cf. 1612 edn. MH; BL. 632/91

Schouten, Willem Corneliszoon. Journael

ofte Beschryvinghe van de wonderlijcke reyse. *Amsterdam: J. Janszoon, the Younger,* 1632. 56 p.; illus., maps; 4to. 1st publ., Amsterdam, 1618. Sabin 77926; Palau 305087; Tiele-Muller 46; Tiele 982n; JCB (3) II:244. NN-RB, RPJCB. 632/92

Sennert, Daniel. Epitome naturalis scientiae. Editio tertia, auctior & correctior. *Oxford: J. Lichfield, for H. Cripps,* 1632. 632 p.; 8vo. 1st publ., Wittenberg, 1618. STC 22231; Madan (Oxford) 1632:9. CSmH, DLC, MoSW; BL. 632/93

———. Institutionum medicinae libri v. *Paris:* 1632. 1363 p.; illus.; 4to. 1st publ., Wittenberg, 1611. MnU-B. 632/94

Severino, Marco Aurelio. De recondita abscessum natura libri vii. *Naples: O. Baltrano,* 1632. [548] p.; illus.; 8vo. Use of sarsaparilla is recommended for treatment of 'fluxions'. CtY-M, InU-L, NIC. 632/95

Shakespeare, William. Comedies, histories, and tragedies . . . The second impression. *London: T. Cotes, for R. Allott,* 1632. 3 pts; port.; fol. 1st publ. as here collected, 1623. For the numerous bibliographical variants in all their complexity, see the STC. STC 22274 ff.; Church 614; JCB (3) II:245. CSmH, CtY, DLC, ICN, MH, MiU, MnU, NN-RB, PU, RPJCB; BL, BN. 632/96

———. The historie of Henrie the fourth [Pt 1]. *London: J. Norton, sold by W. Sheares,* 1632. 4to. 1st publ., London, 1598; cf. 1604 edn. STC 22286. DFo, MH; London:Sir J. Soane's Mus. 632/97

Shirley, James. Changes: or, Love in a maze. A comedie. *London: G. P[urslowe]., for W. Cooke,* 1632. 69 p.; 4to. In act 3 the West Indies are mentioned. STC 22437; Greg 462. CSmH, CtY, DLC, ICN, MH, PU; BL. 632/98

Smith, Capt. John. The generall historie of Virginia, New-England, and the Summer Isles. *London: J. D[awson]. & J. H[aviland]., for E. Blackmore,* 1632. 248 p.; illus., ports, maps; fol. 1st publ., London, 1624; here a reissue with altered imprint. Sabin 82829; Clayton-Torrence 51 (6); Baer (Md) 19; STC 22790d; Church 422; JCB (3) II:245. CSmH, CtY, DLC, ICN, MH, MWA, MiU-C, NN-RB, PPRF, RPJCB; London:UL, BN. 632/99

Tapp, John. The seamans kalendar . . .

Thirteenth impression. *London: B. A[lsop]. & T. F[awcet]., for J. Hurlock,* 1632. 4to. 1st publ., London, 1602. STC 23682.7. Aberdeen:UL, London:Trinity House (imp.).
632/100

Tomkis, Thomas. Lingua, or The combat of the tongue. *London: A. Mathewes, for S. Waterson,* 1632. [83] p.; 4to. Drama. 1st publ., London, 1607. STC 24108; Greg 239(e); Arents 133a. CSmH, CtY, DLC, ICN, MH, MnU-B, NN-A, PU; BL.
632/101

Valcarcel, Francisco de. Por Don Carlos Vazquez Coronado, vezino de Guatimala. Con el Señor Fiscal. Sobre los treynta y un mil tostones, en que se le remato el officio de alguazil mayor de la Audiencia de Guatimala, para don Antonio Vazquez Coronado su hijo. [*Madrid?* 1632]. 5 numb. lvs; fol. Sabin 98301 (& 16825); Medina (BHA) 6942. BL.
632/102

Vander Hammen y León, Lorenzo. Don Filipe el Prudente, segundo deste nombre. *Madrid: Widow of A. Martín, for D. González,* 1632. 137 numb. lvs; 8vo. 1st publ., Madrid, 1625. Palau 351488. CLU, InU-L, MH, NNH; BL, BN.
632/103

Velázquez, Juan. Relacion que el licenciado Don Juan Velazquez hizo en el Consejo Real de las Indias . . . Señor, Las religiones de las ordenes mendicantes de santo Domingo, san Francisco, san Agustin, la Merced, y los padres de la Compañia de Jesus . . . del Peru, y Nueva España . . . sobre las dotrinas que poseen oy los religiosos destas ordenes. [*Madrid?* 1632?]. 27 numb. lvs; fol. Memorial addressed to the king of Spain. Sabin 98811; Medina (BHA) 907; Streit II:1613; Palau 357429. InU-L, RPJCB; BL.
632/104

Vera relacion de la famosa vitoria y buen sucesso que tuvo el capitan Benito Arias Montano con el enemigo Olandes en la isla de la Tortuga . . . treynta y seis leguas de el puerto de la Guayra, y ciudad de Santiago de Leon de Caracas . . . el año de mil y seiscientos y treynta y uno. *Jérez de la Frontera: F. Rey,* 1632. [4] p.; fol. Sabin 98942; Medina (BHA) 908.
632/105

Zacutus, Abraham, Lusitanus. De medicorum principum historia. *Amsterdam: H. Lau-*

renszoon, 1632–42. 11 v.; 8vo. 1st publ., Cologne, 1629. KU-M, PPC.
632/106

Zambrana de Villalobos, Sebastián. Por el licenciado Don Sebastian Zambrana de Villalobos, fiscal de su Magestad en su Consejo supremo de Castilla. Contra el General don Juan de Benavides Baçan, y Almirante don Juan de Leoz, y demas complices. Sobre aver perdido la flota de Nueva-España. [*Madrid?* 1632?]. 43 numb. lvs; fol. Subscribed at end, Madrid, 15 December 1632. Medina (BHA) 896 & 7770; Palau 378978. Lisbon:BN.
632/107

1633

Avity, Pierre d', sieur de Montmartin. Les estats, empires et principautez du monde. *Rouen: J. Cailloué,* 1633. 1396 p.; fol. 1st publ., Paris, 1613. Cf. Sabin 2498. Munich:StB.
633/1

Baardt, Pieter. Loff-en-lijck-gedicht over het onduldich afflijven van . . . Ernest Casimyr. *Leeuwarden: C. Fonteyne,* 1633. [11] p.; port.; fol. Includes ref. to Peruvian gold & to Spanish silver fleet. JCB (3) II:245. RPJCB.
633/2

Bacon, Francis, viscount St Albans. Les oeuvres morales et politiques . . . de la version de J. Baudoin. *Paris: P. Rocolet & F. Targa,* 1633. 848p.; 8vo. 1st publ. in this form, Paris, 1626. Gibson (Bacon) 165; Shaaber (Brit. auth.) B13. CCB, DLC, MH, NNC; BL, BN.
633/3

——. The two bookes . . . of the proficience and advancement of learning. *Oxford: J. L[ichfield]., for T. Huggins,* 1633. 335 p.; 4to. 1st publ., London, 1605. Gibson (Bacon) 83; STC 1166; Madan (Oxford) 1633:3. CSmH, CtY, DLC, ICN, MH, MiU, NNPM; BL.
633/4

Baerle, Kaspar van. Amor sapiens, sive Epithalamium in nuptias . . . d. Cornelii Graef. *Amsterdam: W. J. Blaeu,* 1633. 8 p.; fol. Includes refs to Chile, Potosí, Peru, Olinda. CtY; BN.
633/5

Banister, John. The workes . . . digested into five bookes. *London: T. Harper,* 1633. 4 pts; 4to. Included are the author's *Antidotary,* 1st publ., London, 1589, describing medicinal uses of tobacco, & his *Needeful . . . treatise of chyrurgerie,* 1st publ., London, 1575, describing use of guaiacum for treatment of syphilis. STC 1357. CSmH, CtY-M, DNLM, ICU, NN-RB; BL.

633/6

Barclay, John. The mirror of minds, or, Barclays Icon animorum. Englished, by Tho. May. *London: J. B[eale]., for T. Walkley,* 1633. 380 p.; 12mo. 1st publ. as here transl., London, 1631. STC 1400. CtY, DLC, MiU, NjP; BL.

633/7

Bethune, Philippe de, comte de Selles et de Charost. Le conseiller d'estat, ou Recueil des plus generales considerations servant au maniment des affaires publiques. *Paris: E. Richer,* 1633. 503 p.; 4to. 1st publ., [Paris?], 1632. CtY, ICN, MiU; BN.

633/8

—[Anr edn]. *Paris: E. Richer,* 1633. 496 p.; 4to. BN.

633/9

Beverwijck, Jan van. Medicinae encomium. Eiusdem Montanus ἐλεγχομενος: sive Refutatio argumentorum, quibus necessitatem medicinae impugnat Mich. seigneur de Montaigne. *Dordrecht: H. van Esch,* 1633. 8vo. The latter work includes scattered refs to Indies and Indians in Beverwijck's replies to assertions by Montaigne. Also noted is the Spaniards' transmission of 'Spanish pox', i.e. syphilis, from the West Indies and infection of Indians with smallpox in turn. In discussing logic of name 'Spanish pox', Beverwijck draws analogy with use of Nicot's name for tobacco, stating that it was he who first introduced the plant in Europe. Van de Velde 75. BL.

633/10

Bradwell, Stephen. Helps for suddain accidents endangering life. *London: T. Purfoot, for T. S[later].; sold by H. Overton,* 1633. 127 p.; 16mo. Describes therapeutic uses for tobacco. STC 3535; Arents 182. CSmH, DFo, NN-A; BL.

633/11

Breton, Nicholas. A poste with a packet of madde letters. *London: J. Marriott,* 1633. 2 pts; 4to. 1st publ., London, 1602–5. STC 3692. BL, Oxford:Bodl.

633/12

Bry, Theodor de. Historiae antipodum, sive Novi Orbis . . . pars nona. Frankfurt a. M.: 1633. *See* Potgieter, Barent Janszoon, *below.*

633/13

Butron, Juan Alonso de. Por Simon Ribero ausente, passagero que fue en la nao S. Pedro, y dueño de algunos esclavos que ivan en ella, maestre Jacinto de Silva, que arribò a la Habana. Con el señor fiscal del Real Consejo de las Indias. [*Madrid?* 1633]. 18 numb. lvs; fol. Medina (BHA) 7771. Puebla:B. Palafoxiana.

633/14

Camões, Luiz de. Os Luciadas. *Lisbon: L. Craesbeeck,* 1633. 140 numb. lvs; 24mo. In verse. 1st publ., Lisbon, 1572; cf. 1609 edn above. Silva (Camões) 30. MH, NNH; Lisbon:BN.

633/15

Cats, Jacob. Mägden-plicht. [*Amsterdam?* 1633?]. 48 lvs; illus.; 8vo. 1st publ., Middelburg, 1618. Latin text probably omitted from this edn. Mus. Cats. 62. DFo; BL.

633/16

——. Minnelijcke, zedelijcke en stichtelijcke sinne-beelden met der selve ghedichten. [*Amsterdam?* ca. 1633]. 4 pts; illus.; 8vo. 1st publ. in this abridged version, [Amsterdam? 1622?]. Vries 91; Mus. Cats. 44. BL, Leyden:UB.

633/17

——. Silenus Alcibiadis. [*Amsterdam?* ca. 1633]. 8vo. 1st publ., Middelburg, 1618; emblemata omitted from this edn. Mus. Cats. 33. Leyden:UB.

633/18

Cervantes Saavedra, Miguel de. Les nouvelles . . . Reveuë & corrigée. *Paris: N. & J. de La Coste,* 1633. 695 p.; 8vo. 1st publ. as transl. from Madrid, 1613, Spanish text, Paris, 1615. Ríus (Cervantes) 888; Palau 53523. BN.

633/19

Compagnie de la Nouvelle France. Edict du roy pour l'establissement de la Compagnie de la Nouvelle France. *Paris: S. Cramoisy,* 1633. 26 p.; illus.; 8vo. Sabin 56086; Harrisse (NF) 54; Wroth & Annan 16. BN.

633/20

——. Sommaire de l'instance pendante au Conseil privé du roy. Entre les associez en la Compagnie de la Nouvelle France, defendeurs. Et le sieur Guillaume de Caën. [*Paris:* 1633]. 8 p.; 4to. Sabin 86843. BN.

633/21

Croll, Oswald. La royalle chymie . . . traduitte . . . par J. Marcel de Boulenc. *Paris: M. Henault,* 1633. 3 pts; illus.; 8vo. 1st publ. as here transl., Lyons, 1624. MH, NIC, PU-S, WU; BN.

633/22

Davys, John. The seamans secrets . . . wherein is taught the three kindes of sayling. *London: J. Dawson, 1633.* 2 pts; illus.; 4to. 1st publ., London, [1594?]; cf. 1607 edn. Cf. Sabin 18842; STC 6371; JCB (3) II:245–46. RPJCB; BL.   633/23

Del Rio, Martin Anton, S.J. Disquisitionum magicarum libri sex. *Cologne: P. Henning,* 1633. 1070 p.; 4to. 1st publ., Louvain, 1599–1600; cf. 1603 edn. Backer II:1899. CLU, InU, MH, NN, PPL; BN.   633/24

Diez de Auxarmendáriz, Lope, marqués de Caderayta. Relacion de la famosa vitoria. *Seville:* 1633. *See under title* below.

Discours sur la bataille de Lutzen. Du 6./ 16. novembre 1632. [*Paris?* 1633?]. 26 p.; 8vo. 'Discours sur la proposition de trefve au Pays-bas' (p. 15–26) mentions desire of Spanish to regain prestige in New World & elsewhere. MH.   633/25

Donne, John. Poems. *London: M. F[letcher].,* for J. Marriott, 1633. 406 p.; 4to. Includes Donne's *An anatomie of the world,* 1st publ., London, 1611. STC 7045; Keynes (Donne) 78; Arents (Add.) 192; Pforzheimer 296. CSmH, CtY, DFo, ICN, InU-L, MH, MiU, NN-A, PPL; BL.   633/26

Du Bartas, Guillaume Salluste, seigneur. Bartas his devine weekes and workes. *London: R. Young,* 1633,'32. 657 p.; port.; fol. In verse. 1st publ. as here transl. by Josuah Sylvester, London, 1605, supplemented by additional text including Sylvester's *Tobacco battered* (London, [1616–17]); cf. 1620–21 edn. STC 21654; Arents 128-b. CSmH, CtY, DFo, ICN, MH, MiU, MnU, NN-RB, PU-F, RPB; BL.   633/27

Earle, John, Bp of Salisbury. Micro-cosmographie. or, A piece of the world discovered . . . The sixth [*sic*] edition augmented. *London: Elizabeth A[llde].,* for R. Allott, 1633. [300] p.; 12mo. 1st publ., London, 1628. STC 7444; Murphy (Engl. char.-bks) 40. CSmH, DFo, ICN, MH; BL.   633/28

Estienne, Charles. Dictionarium historicum, geographicum, poeticum. *Geneva: J. Crispin,* 1633. 1132 cols; 4to. 1st publ. in this enl. edn, Lyons, 1595; cf. 1601 edn. DFo, IU, MH, NNUT, TxU; BN.   633/29

Fernández de Bivero, Juan. Señor. Juan Fernandez de Bivero, natural . . . de Tlax-

cala de la Nueva-España . . . de donde actualmente vengo sola a informar a V. Magestad, del remedio que puede tener la inundacion de la ciudad de Mexico. *Madrid: Imprenta Real,* 1633. 10 numb. lvs; fol. Medina (BHA) 910. DLC; Seville:Archivo de Indias.   633/30

Fernel, Jean. Traité de . . . la parfaite cure de la maladie venerienne . . . Traduit par m. le Long. *Paris: N. & J. de La Coste,* 1633. 230 p.; 12mo. Transl. from Fernel's *De luis venereae curatio,* 1st publ., Antwerp, 1579. Chapt. ii asserts syphilis to be American in origin; chapt. x describes guaiacum at length, identifying it as American. Sherrington (Fernel) 100N3; Wellcome I:2214. London:Wellcome, BN.   633/31

Ferrari, Giovanni Battista. De florum cultura libri iv. *Rome: S. Paolini,* 1633. 522 p.; illus.; 4to. Among the American plants described & their culture discussed are the yucca ('fiore dell'India occidentale') and the passionflower ('Granadiglia'), identified as deriving from Mexico & Peru. Pritzel 2877; Nissen (Bot.) 620; Hunt (Bot.) 222. CU, DNAL, ICN, MH, MiU, PPAN; BL (Ferrarius, Joannes Baptista), BN.   633/32

Fioravanti, Leonardo. Dello specchio di scientia universale . . . libri tre. *Venice: Heirs of M. Sessa,* 1633. 360 numb. lvs; 8vo. 1st publ., Venice, 1564; cf. 1603 edn. MiU.   633/33

Freylin, Juan Maria, S.J. Catalogo de algunos varones insignes en santidad, de la provincia del Peru de la Compañia de Jesus. *Seville: F. de Lyra,* 1633. 26 p.; 4to. 1st publ., Seville, 1632; here a reissue with altered t.p.? Medina (BHA) 917; Streit II:1621; Escudero (Seville) 1.460. Madrid: Acad. de la Hist.   633/34

Frias, Pedro de, O.F.M. Relacion del martirio de treinta y un martires, religiosos, y terceros, hijos de . . . San Francisco . . . en al Japon, y los dos en las Indias de Nuevo-Mexico. *Madrid: Imprenta Real,* 1633. [3] p.; fol. Medina (BHA) 912; Wagner (SW) 36; Streit II:1618; Palau 95014; Maggs Cat. 502 (Americana VII):5058. CtY, RPJCB.   633/35

Fuente, Gaspar de la, O.F.M. Historia del capitulo general, que celebrò la religion serafica en la imperial Toledo este año de 1633. *Madrid: Imprenta Real*, 1633. 2 pts; 4to. Included are accounts of missionary martyrs of Spanish America. Medina (BHA) 913; Streit I:453; Palau 95271. Valencia: BU. 633/36

Garcilaso de la Vega, el Inca. Le commentaire royal, ou L'histoire des Incas, roys du Peru . . . traduitte . . . par J. Baudoin. *Paris: A. Courbé*, 1633. 1319 p.; 4to. Transl. from the author's *Primera parte de los Commentarios reales*, 1st publ., Lisbon, 1609. Sabin 98743; Medina (BHA) 658; Palau 354820; Arents (Add.) 269; JCB (3) II:247. CtY, DLC, MB, NN-RB, RPJCB; BL (Lasso de la Vega, G.), BN. 633/37

Gaultier, Jacques. Table chronologique de l'estat du christianisme . . . jusques à l'année 1631 . . . Reveue pour la cinquiesme fois . . . par l'autheur. *Lyons: C. Cayne, for the Widow of C. Rigaud & C. Obert*, 1633. 899 p.; fol. 1st publ., Lyons, 1609. Backer III:1275; Cioranescu (XVII) 32624. BN. 633/38

Gerard, John. The herball or Generall historie of plantes . . . very much enlarged and amended by Thomas Johnson. *London: A. Islip, J. Norton & R. Whitaker*, 1633. 1630 p.; illus.; fol. 1st publ., London, 1597. Virtually a translation, by Robert Priest, of Rembert Dodoens's *Stirpium historiae*, 1st publ., Antwerp, 1583. Included are numerous descriptions & illus. of American plants. Pritzel 3282n; Nissen (Bot.) 698n; Henrey (Brit. bot.) 155; STC 11751; Arents 184. CSmH, CtY, DLC, ICN, MH, MiU, NN-A, PU, RPB; BL. 633/39

Gerritsz, Hessel, ed. Indiae Orientalis pars X. Qua continetur, Historica relatio sive Descriptio novi ad aquilonem transitus, supra terras americanas in Chinam. *Frankfurt a. M.: W. Fitzer*, 1633. 26 p.; illus., maps; fol. (J. T. de Bry's *India Orientalis*. Pt 10. Latin). 1st publ. in this version, Frankfurt a. M., 1613. Brunet I:1341; Church 222n. NN-RB; BL. 633/40

Gilbert, William. Tractatus, sive Physiologia nova de magnete . . . Omnia . . . recognita . . . opera . . . Wolfgangi Lochmans. *Stettin: Götz Press*, 1633. 232 p.; illus.; 4to. 1st publ. as here ed., Stettin, 1628; here a reissue of that edn? Shaaber (Brit. auth.) G314. CtY, DFo, MH, NNNAM, PPL, WU; BL, BN. 633/41

Góngora y Argote, Luis de. Todas las obras. *Madrid: Imprenta Real, for A. Pérez*, 1633. 234 numb. lvs; port.; 4to. In verse. Included is Góngora's *Las soledades*, 1st publ., Madrid, 1627, in his *Obras en verso*. Palau 104627. MH, NNH, NcD; BL, BN. 633/42

Great Britain. Laws, statutes, etc., 1625–1649 (Charles I). A commission for the well governing of our people . . . in New-found-land. *London:* 1633. *See the year 1634.*

Great Britain. Sovereigns, etc., 1625–1649 (Charles I). A proclamation for preventing of the abuses growing by the unordered retailing of tobacco. *London: R. Barker & assigns of J. Bill*, 1633. 2 lvs; fol. Crawford (Roy. procl.) 1661; Brigham (Roy. procl.) 71–74; STC 9003. BL. 633/43

—[Anr edn]. *London: R. Barker & assigns of J. Bill*, 1633. 2 lvs; fol. Crawford (Roy. procl.) 1662; STC 9004. London:Privy Council. 633/44

Grotius, Hugo. Liber de antiquitate et statu reipublicae Batavicae . . . Editio nova. *Amsterdam: J. Charpantier*, 1633. 84 p.; 8vo. 1st publ., Leyden, 1610. Meulen/Diermanse 697. PBL; The Hague:PP. 633/45

——. Mare liberum; sive De jure quod Batavis competit ad indicana commercia dissertatio. Editio nova, prioribus longe emendatior. *Amsterdam: W. J. Blaeu*, 1633. 26 p.; 8vo. 1st publ., Leyden, 1609. Meulen/Diermanse 547. CtY, DLC, MH-L, NN-RB; The Hague:PP. 633/46

—[Anr edn]. De mari libero et P. Merula De maribus. *Leyden: Elsevier Office*, 1633. 308 p.; 24mo. Here added is Merula's *De maribus*, with refs to Columbus's discoveries, & to Vespucci, Magellan, Drake, Cavendish, Sebastian Cabot, Verrazano, etc. Meulen/Diermanse 545; Willems (Les Elzevier) 385; Bibl. Belg. G335. CSmH, CtY, MH-BA, NNG, ViW; BL, BN, The Hague:PP. 633/47

—[Anr edn]. *Leyden: Elsevier Office*, 1633. 267 p.; 24mo. Meulen/Diermanse 546; cf. Willems (Les Elzevier) 385; Bibl. Belg. G336. CSmH, DLC, MiU-C, NN-RB, PU-L; BN, The Hague:PP. 633/48

Guibert, Philbert. Toutes les oeuvres charitables. *Paris: J. Jost,* 1633. 1046 p.; 8vo. Included is Guibert's *Le prix & valeur des medicamens,* 1st publ., Paris, 1625. DNLM.
633/49

Gysius, Johannes. De Spaensche tirannij in Neder-Lant. *Amsterdam: J. P. Wachter,* 1633. 122 p.; illus.; 4to. 1st publ. as here abridged from the author's *Oorsprong en voortgang der Nederlandtscher beroerten,* Amsterdam, 1620. Issued with Las Casas's *Den vermeerderden Spieghel der Spaensche tierrannije in Westindien.* Authorship erroneously attributed to C. L. van der Plasse. DLC.
633/50

Harington, Sir John. The most elegant and wittie epigrams. *London: G. Miller,* 1633. 8vo. In verse. 1st publ. with refs to tobacco & potatoes, London, 1618. Also issued as pt of Lodovico Ariosto's *Orlando furioso* as transl. by Harington, London, 1634 (STC 748). STC 12778; Arents 188. CtY, ICU, MiU, PU; BL.
633/51

Hart, James. Κλινική, or The diet of the diseased. *London: J. Beale, for R. Allott,* 1633. 411 p.; fol. American foodstuffs mentioned include maize, 'cassani' (i.e., manioc), potatoes, & the turkey, as is also tobacco. STC 12888; Arents 185. CSmH, CtY, DFo, MBCo, MiU, MnU, NN-RB, PPC, RB; BL.
633/52

Hartmann, Johann (1568–1631). Praxis chymiatrica. *Leipzig: J. A. Minzel, for G. Gross,* 1633. 238 p.; 4to. For tertian fever an 'aqua tabaci' is described; for syphilis, guaiacum, sarsaparilla, & sassafras are named; an extract of mechoacan is mentioned. Wellcome I:3064. DNLM; BL, BN.
633/53

Hernodius, Jacob Olaf. De praeclaris herbae nicotianae, sive Tabaci virtutibus disputatio. *Upsala: E. Matthiae,* 1633. [16] p.; 4to. Cf. Arents 186. Stockholm:KB.
633/54

Hester, John. The secrets of physick and philosophy . . . now published in the English tongue, by John Hester. *London: A. M[athewes]., for W. Lugger,* 1633. 196 p.; 12mo. Transl. in part from Paracelsus's *Secreet der Philosophijen,* 1st publ., Antwerp, 1553. Includes directions 'To make oyle of Lignum Vitae or Guaiacum'. Sudhoff (Paracelsus) 356; STC 19182; Wellcome I:4813. CSmH, DNLM, MBCo, WU; London:Wellcome.
633/55

—[Anr edn]. A storehouse of physicall and philosophicall secrets. *London: T. Harper,* 1633. 57 p.; 4to. STC 19182.5 (formerly 23293). CtY, DFo, WU; BL.
633/56

—[Anr issue of preceding]. *In* Banister, John. Workes. *London: T. Harper,* 1633. STC 1357. CSmH, CtY-M, DNLM, ICU, NN-RB, PU; BL.
633/57

Heylyn, Peter. Μικροκοσμος, A little description of the great world. The sixth edition. *Oxford: W. Turner, & R. Allott, at London,* 1633. 807 p.; 4to. 1st publ., Oxford, 1621. Sabin 31656n; Madan (Oxford) 1633:22; STC 13281. CSmH, CtY, DLC, IU, InU-L, MH, MiU-C, NN-RB; BL, BN.
633/58

Histoire de ce qui s'est passé au royaume du Japon, es annees 1625. 1626. & 1627 . . . Traduite d'italien [par Jean Vireau]. *Paris: S. Cramoisy,* 1633. 485 p.; 8vo. Transl. from earlier *Lettere annue* but with here added (p. 474–85) a 'Relation de la mort des pères Roch Gonzales, A. Rodriguez et J. de Castillio, S.J., occis par les Indiens en Paraguay'. Sabin 32007; Streit II:1625 & V:1488; Backer VIII:834. DLC.
633/59

Hoyarsabal, Martin de. Les voyages avantureux du Capitaine Martin de Hoyarsabal . . . Seconde édition, reveuë et corrigée. *Bordeaux: G. Millanges,* 1633. 122 p.; 8vo. 1st publ., Bordeaux, 1579; cf. 1632 edn. DLC; BL, BN.
633/60

Isaacson, Henry. Saturni ephemerides; sive Tabula historico-chronologica, containing a chronological series . . . of the foure monarchyes. *London: B. A[lsop]., & T. F[awcet]., for H. Seile & H. Robinson,* 1633. ccclxxxiii p.; fol. Under appropriate years American figures & events are mentioned, e.g., 1492, Columbus, & 1580, Sir Francis Drake. STC 14269. CSmH, CtY, DLC, ICU, InU, MH, MiU, MnU, NNC, PPAmP; BL.
633/61

James, Thomas. The strange and dangerous voyage of Captaine Thomas James, in his intended discovery of the Northwest Passage into the South Sea. *London: J. Legat, for J. Partridge,* 1633. 120 p.; map; 4to. Sabin 35711; STC 14444; Church 423; JCB (3) II:246. CSmH, CtY, DLC, ICN, MH, MiU-C, NN-RB, RPJCB; BL, BN.
633/62

Jonckheer, M. Teghen-worp op het onwa-rachtich schrijven van eenen verwaenden Papist op de handelinghe van den treves. *Flushing: J. Janszoon de Jonghe,* 1633. [8] p.; 4to. In verse. Notes danger to the Spanish fleet of falling into the hands of a Pieter Hein. NN. 633/63

Jonstonus, Joannes. Thaumatographia na-turalis. *Amsterdam: J. Janszoon, the Younger,* 1633. 578 p.; 12mo. 1st publ., Amsterdam, 1632. CU, MiU-C, NNBG; London:Well-come. 633/64

Laet, Joannes de. Novus Orbis, seu, De-scriptionis Indiae Occidentalis. Libri xviii. *Leyden: The Elseviers,* 1633. 104, 205–690 p.; illus., maps; fol. Transl. from the author's *Beschrijvinghe van West-Indien,* Leyden, 1630, itself an enlargement of his Nieuwe We-reldt, 1st publ., Leyden, 1625. Sabin 38557; Borba de Moraes I:384; Vail (Frontier) 84; Streit II:1619; Rodrigues (Dom. Hol.) 84 Rahir (Les Elzevier) 367; Willems (Les El-zevier) 382; JCB (3) II:246. CU-B, CtY, DLC, InU, MH, MnU-B, NN-RB, PU, RPJCB; BL, BN. 633/65

Lampe, Barent. Het twintigste deel of t'ver-volgh van het Historisch verhael aller ge-dencwaerdiger gheschiedenissen, die in Eu-ropa . . . in America, als West-Indien en d'eijlanden . . . voorgevallen syn. *Amster-dam: J. Janszoon, the Younger,* 1633. 182 numb. lvs; illus.; 4to. (N. van Wassenaer's *Historisch verhael.* Pt 20). Includes refs to Pernambuco, Brazil. Cf. Sabin 102039; Borba de Moraes II:371; Muller (1872) 1745. RPJCB. 633/66

Langham, William. The garden of health . . . Second edition corrected. *London: T. Harper,* 1633. 702 p.; 4to. 1st publ., Lon-don, 1597. Included are chapts on guaia-cum & sarsaparilla. STC 15196. CSmH, CtY, DLC, ICJ, MH, MiU, NN-RB, PPC; BL. 633/67

Lizana, Bernardo de. Historia de Yucatan; devocionario de nuestra Señora de Izmal, y conquista espiritual. *Valladolid: G. Morillo,* 1633. 204 numb. lvs; 8vo. Medina (BHA) 915; Streit II:1620; Palau 159153. BL. 633/68

Marmion, Shackerley. A fine companion. Acted before the King and Queene at White-hall. *London: A. Mathewes, for R.*

Meighen, 1633. [77] p.; 4to. In act 2, scene 3, 'the rich Indian vapour' of tobacco is mentioned. STC 17442; Greg 481; Arents (Add.) 265; Pforzheimer 646. CSmH, CtY, DLC, ICN, MH, PU; BL. 633/69

Marston, John. The workes . . . being tra-gedies and comedies. *London: [A. Mathewes,] for W. Sheares,* 1633. [416] p.; 8vo. Included is Marston's *What you will,* 1st publ., Lon-don, 1607. STC 17471; Greg 252 (bI); Pforzheimer 667. CSmH, CtY, DLC, ICU, MH, MiU; BL. 633/70

—[Anr issue]. Tragedies and comedies. *Lon-don: [A. Mathewes,] for W. Sheares,* 1633. [412] p.; 8vo. A reissue of the above with cancel t.p., etc. STC 17472; Greg 252 (bII); Arents 187. CSmH, CtY, DLC, ICU, MH, NN-A; BL. 633/71

Massinger, Philip. A new way to pay old debts. A comoedie. *London: E. P[urslowe]., for H. Seile,* 1633. [92] p.; 4to. In act 2, scene 3, 'Potato rootes' are mentioned, as else-where is tobacco. STC 17639; Greg 474; Arents (Add.) 266. CSmH, CtY, DLC, ICN, InU-L, MH, MiU, NN-RB, PU; BL. 633/72

Medina, Pedro de. L'art de naviguer . . . traduit . . . par Nicolas de Nicolai. *Rouen: D. Ferrand,* 1633. 227 p.; illus.; 4to. 1st publ. as here transl., Lyons, 1553; cf. 1607 edn. Sabin 47345n; Palau 159678. Paris:Arsenal. 633/73

Memorial del processo causado en el Santo Oficio de las Inquisiciones de Cartagena de las Indias, y Sevilla, a instancia de los fis-cales, contra el capitan Juan de Urbina, vezino de la dicha ciudad de Cartagena, por casado segunda vez, viviendo la primera mujer. [*Seville?* 1633?]. 29 numb. lvs; fol. Medina (BHA) 916. Santiago, Chile:BN. 633/74

Mendoça, Francisco de, S.J. Viridarium sa-crae profanae eruditionis. *Cologne: P. Hen-ning,* 1633. 948 p.; 8vo. 1st publ., Lyons, 1631. Backer V:901; Palau 163630; Well-come I:4200. CoU, NNH. 633/75

Mercator, Gerardus. L'appendice de l'atlas de Gerard Mercator et Judocus Hondius: contenant diverses nouvelles tables et de-scriptions . . . de l'Allemaigne . . . et de l'on et l'autre Inde . . . Traduit du Latin. *Amsterdam: H. Hondius,* 1633. 104 maps; fol.

Transl. from Mercator's *Atlantis majoris appendix*, 1st publ., Amsterdam, 1630, but here enl. Also issued as pt of Mercator's *Atlas ou Representation* below. Koeman (Me) 35. BL, Amsterdam:NHSM.   633/76

——. Atlas, das ist, Abbildung der gantzen Welt . . . Sonderlich von Teutschland . . . Ost und West Indien. *Amsterdam: H. Hondius & J. Janszoon, the Younger,* 1633. 680 p.; illus., maps; fol. Perhaps transl. from Mercator's Latin version, the *Atlas sive Cosmographicae meditationes,* 1st publ., Amsterdam, 1606. Here the title & imprint appear on slips pasted on the t.p. of the French edn below. For Mercator's *Appendix Atlantis oder des Weltbuchs,* see the year 1636. Koeman (Me) 37; Phillips (Atlases) 444; Tiele 743n. CSmH, CtY, DLC, ICN, NNH; BL (imp.), Marburg:StB.   633/77

—[Anr issue]. *Amsterdam: H. Hondius,* 1633. Koeman (Me) 38. Copenhagen:KB.
                                             633/78

——. Atlas, or A geographicke description . . . of the world. *Amsterdam: 1633. See the year* 1638.

——. Atlas, ou Representation du monde universel . . . devisé en deux tomes. Edition nouvelle Augmenté d'un appendice . . . et descriptions de . . . l'une et l'autre Inde. *Amsterdam: H. Hondius,* 1633. 2 v.; maps; fol. 1st publ. in French, Amsterdam, 1609; here added is Mercator's *Appendice,* also issued separately, q.v. above. For variants see Koeman as cited. Sabin 47884; Koeman (Me) 36A,B,C; Phillips (Atlases) 445; Tiele 743n; Muller (III) 1879; JCB (3) II:248. CtY, DLC, IU, MiU-C, NPV, RPJCB; London:RGS, Paris:Arsenal.   633/79

Merindol, Antoine. Ars medica. *Aix-en-Provence: J. Roize,* 1633. 2 pts; port.; fol. On p. 417 is cited on an 'ex nova Hispania lapidem advehi nigrum, lenem, gravem, & figurae ovalis, qui sub umbilico alligatus suffocationes ab utero reprimat.' Also discussed is mechoacan. DNLM; BL, BN.   633/80

Meteren, Emanuel van. Meteranus novus, das ist: Warhafftige Beschreibung aller denckwürdigsten Geschichten, so sonderlich in den Nederlanden . . . sich zugetragen . . . Von neuen ins Hochteutsche ubersetzet und biss auff das Jahr 1633 auffs fleisigste continuiert. *Amsterdam: W. J. Blaeu,* 1633. 726 p.; illus., ports; fol. 1st publ. in German, Hamburg, 1596; cf. year 1601. Continued in pt 2, *Meterani novi continuatio,* Amsterdam, 1635. Bruckner 62. Amsterdam:UB (imp.), Stockholm:KB.   633/81

Montaigne, Michel Eyquem de. Saggi . . . overo Discorsi naturali, politici e morali. *Venice: M. Ginammi,* 1633. 782 p.; 4to. Transl. by Girolamo Canini d'Anghieri from Montaigne's *Essais,* 1st publ., Bordeaux, 1580; cf. Paris, 1602, edn. CU, ICN, MH, MiU (imp.), RPB; BN.   633/82

Nash, Thomas (1588–1648). Quaternio, or A fourefold way to a happie life. *London: J. Dawson,* 1633. 280 p.; 4to. On p. 41 the gains of a tobacco-seller from 'Indian weedes' is mentioned; elsewhere numerous scattered refs to America occur, e.g., to the Northwest Passage and Columbus. STC 18382; Arents (Add.) 267; Pforzheimer 766. CSmH, CtY, DLC (imp.), ICN, MH, NN-A; BL.   633/83

Netherlands (United Provinces, 1581–1795). Staten Generaal. Ordre ende reglement . . . waer op, ende waer naer alle gemonteerde schepen uyt dese respective provincien, sullen vermogen te varen in seecker gedeelte vande limiten van't Octroy vande West-Indische Compaignie, hier nae gheexprimeert. *The Hague: Widow & Heirs of H. Jacobszoon van Wouw,* 1633. 4 lvs; 4to. Sabin 57536; Borba de Moraes II:119; Asher 161. BL.   633/84

Neuhaus, Edo. Theatrum ingenii humani. *Amsterdam: J. Janszoon, the Younger,* 1633–34. 2 v.; 8vo. Includes refs to Canada, Cuba, Florida, etc. Jöcher (Suppl.) V:555. CtY, ICN, NjP; BL, BN.   633/85

Owen, John. Epigrammatum . . . libri decem . . . Editio sexta. *London: A. Math[ewes], for S. Waterson,* 1633. 12mo. 1st publ., London, 1606. STC 18991. CSmH, CtY, MH, NN-A; BL.   633/86

—[Anr edn]. Editio postrema. *Amsterdam: J. Janszoon, the Younger, for W. J. Blaeu,* 1633. 12mo. Shaaber (Brit. auth.) O92. ICU, MH, MnU; BL.   633/87

Oxenstierna, Axel Gustafsson, grefve. Wir Burgermeister und Rhat desz heiligen Reichs Stadt Nürnberg. [*Nuremberg:* 1633].

bds; fol. Invites German investment in the Swedish Söder Compagniet. MnU-B.

633/88

Paré, Ambroise. Les oeuvres . . . Neufiesme edition. *Lyons: Widow of C. Rigaud, & C. Obert,* 1633. 986 p.; illus., port.; fol. 1st publ., Paris, 1575; cf. 1601 German edn. Doe (Paré) 38. CtY-M, DLC, ICJ, MBCo, MiU; London: Roy. Soc. of Med., BN.

633/89

Pascal, Jacques. Traicté contenant la pharmacie chymique. *Lyons: L. Vivian,* 1633. 330 p.; 8vo. 1st publ., Lyons, etc., 1616, under title *Discours contenant la conference de la pharmacie.* DNLM.

633/90

Pasquier, Etienne. Les recherches de la France. *Paris: M. Colet,* 1633. 1019 p.; port.; 4to. 1st publ. with American content, Paris, 1596; cf. the 1607 edn, the American ref. here appearing in chapt. xxviii of bk 4. Thickett (Pasquier) 16; Tchémerzine IX:84. The following American locations may represent any one of the issues here described: CU, MWalB, NN; Avignon:Mus. Calvet, Amsterdam: UB.

633/91

—[Anr issue]. *Paris: P. Ménard,* 1633. Thickett (Pasquier) 16; Tchémerzine IX:84. Cambridge:Trinity, Lyons:BM.

633/92

—[Anr issue]. *Paris: T. Quinet,* 1633. Thickett (Pasquier) 16; Tchémerzine IX:84. FTaSU, MH; Frieburg i. Br.:UB, Nantes:BM.

633/93

—[Anr issue]. *Paris: O. de Varennes,* 1633. Thickett (Pasquier) 16; Tchémerzine IX:84. Cambridge:UL, BN.

633/94

Perea, Estevan de. Segunda relacion, de la grandiosa conversion que ha avido en el Nuevo Mexico. *Seville: L. Estupiñán,* 1633. [4] p.; fol. Continues Perea's *Verdadera relacion,* Seville, 1632. Wagner (SW) 37; Palau 218275. ICN, NN-RB, RPJCB.

633/95

Por los interesados en los quatro generos de mercaderias, grana, añil, açucar, y palo, qui vinieron de Indias el año passado de 1632. Con los interesados en plata, y oro del mismo año. [*Seville?* 1633?]. 20 numb. lvs; fol. Medina (BHA) 6208. Seville:BU.

633/96

Potgieter, Barent Janszoon. Historiae antipodum sive Novi Orbis, qui vulgo Americae et Indiae Occidentalis nomine usurpatur, pars nona: continens veram descriptionem duarum navigationum Hollandicarum. *Frankfurt a. M.: M. Merian* (Pt 1) *& W. Hoffmann* (Pt 2), 1633. 102p.; illus.; fol. (Theodor de Bry's *America,* Pt 9. Latin). Potgieter's work 1st publ. in this version, Frankfurt a. M., 1602, as pt 2 of Acosta's *Americae nona & postrema pars.* Here included is O. van Noort's *Vera et accurata descriptio . . . navigationis,* 1st publ. in this version, Frankfurt a. M., 1602, under title *Additamentum nonae partis Americae.* Cf. *Historiae Antipodum . . . liber tertius* in de Bry's *Americae pars viii,* Frankfurt a. M., 1625, above. Cf. Sabin 8784; Church 169; JCB (3) I:408. CSmH, NN-RB, RPJCB; BL, BN.

633/97

Prado Beltran, Bernardino de. Razonamiento panegyrico . . . en favor del Colegio Real y mayor de S. Felipe, y S. Marcos de la ciudad de los Reyes. *Madrid: Imprenta Real,* 1633. 46 numb. lvs; 4to. Medina (BHA) 919; Palau 234915. Madrid:Acad. de la Hist.

633/98

Prynne, William. Histrio-mastix. The players scourge. *London: E. A[llde, A. Mathewes, T. Cotes]. & W. J[ones]., for M. Sparke,* 1633. 1006 p.; 4to. Included are scattered refs to the New World, and its inhabitants, e.g., to Brazil, Florida, & Peru, citing P. M. d'Anghiera's *De orbe novo* & Samuel Purchas's *Purchas his pilgrimage.* In this issue the verso of lf ✱*✱ is blank. STC 20464. CSmH, ICU, MB, MiU, MnU, NNCC, PU-F; London:UL.

633/99

—[Anr issue]. *London: E. A[llde, A. Mathewes, T. Cotes]. & W. J[ones]., for M. Sparke,* 1633. In this issue the verso of lf ✱*✱ contains a list of 'Errataes'. STC 20464a; Arents (Add.) 268; Pforzheimer 809. CSmH, CtY, DLC, ICN, MH, MWA, NN-RB, PU, RPB; BL.

633/100

Quesada, Ginés de, O.F.M. Relacion verdadera del martirio que dieron en el Japon a veynte y nueve martyres . . . Avisase tambien de la embaxada que embió el Emperador de Japon al Virey de Mexico. *Seville: S. Fajardo,* 1633. [4] p.; fol. Medina (BHA) 920; Streit V:1485; Palau 243308. Seville: Seminario.

633/101

Relacion de la famosa vitoria, que la armada

que fue a las Indias este año de 1633. de que fue general el marquès de Cadereyta, alcançò del enemigo Olandes, echandole . . . de S. Martin. *Seville: P. Gómez de Pastrana*, 1633. [4] p.; fol. Medina (BHA) 922 (& 924); Palau 258035; Maggs Cat. 479 (Americana V):4208. InU-L, RPJCB; BL, (imp.), Madrid:Acad. de la Hist.

633/102

Relacion del sucesso que ha tenido el marques de Cadreyta en desalojar el enemigo Olandes de un fuerte que tenia en la isla de San Martin. *Barcelona: E. Liberòs*, 1633. [8] p.; 4to. Palau 258016. RPJCB.

633/103

Relacion verdadera de la famosa victoria que ha tenido el marques de Cadereita . . . contra el enemigo Olandes, *Seville: J. Gómez de Blas* [1633]. [4] p.; fol. Medina (BHA) 923; Palau 258037; Maggs Cat. 479 (Americana V):4209. BL.

633/104

Remón, Alonso, O. Merced. Historia general de la Orden de Nra S[eñor]a. de la Merced, redencion de cautivos. Tomo II. *Madrid: Imprenta Real*, 1633. 290 numb. lvs; fol. Continues 1st vol. publ., Madrid, 1618, without American refs. In this vol. are included accounts of Mercedarian missions in Spanish America. Medina (BHA) 925; Streit I:372; Perez Pastor (Madrid) 1906; Palau 260838. MH; BN, Rome:Bibl. Casanatense.

633/105

Reyd, Everhard van. Belgarum, aliarumque gentium, annales . . . Dionysio Vossio interprete. *Leyden: J. Maire*, 1633. 561 p.; fol. Transl. from Reyd's *Historie der Nederlantscher oorlogen*, 1st publ., Arnhem, 1626. Includes minor refs to America, e.g., the Strait of Magellan. CLU, CtY, DLC, ICU, MH, MnU-B, PPL; BL, BN.

633/106

——. Oorspronck ende voortganck vande Nederlantsche oorloghen . . . tot het jaer 1601 . . . tweede editie. *Arnhem: J. van Biesen*, 1633. 791 p.; illus.; fol. 1st publ., Arnhem, 1626. Aa X:56. BN, Amsterdam:NHSM.

633/107

Roca, Juan Antonio Vera Zúñiga y Figueroa, conde de la. Histoire de l'empereur Charles V. . . . traduite par le sieur Du Perron Le Hayer. *Paris:* 1633. 4to. Transl.

from the author's *Epitome de la vida . . . del . . . imperador Carlos V*, 1st publ., Madrid, 1622. Palau 358996.

633/108

Saint-Amant, Marc Antoine de Gérard, sieur de. Les oeuvres . . . Seconde edition. *Paris: N. Traboulliet*, 1633. 2 pts; 8vo. In verse. 1st publ., Paris, 1629. Cioranescu (XVII) 60674; Tchémerzine X:83. BN.

633/109

Scotland. Laws, statutes, etc. The acts made in the first parliament of our . . . soveraigne Charles . . . at Edinburgh, twentie eight day of June . . . 1633. *Edinburgh: R. Young*, 1633. 66 p.; fol. Act xxviii consists of the 'Ratification in favour of the Viscount of Sterling, of the infestments and signature granted to him of the dominions of new Scotland [i.e., Nova Scotia] and Canada in America . . .'. For an edn publ. by E. Tyler, dated 1633, see item entered under [164–]. STC 21902. CSmH, CtY-L, DLC, ICN, MH, MiU, MnU-L, NN-RB; BL.

633/110

Sennert, Daniel. Epitome naturalis scientiae. *Paris:* 1633. 297 p.; 4to. 1st publ., Wittenberg, 1618. MH, NIC; BN.

633/111

——[Anr edn]. *Wittenberg: J. Helwig*, 1633. 706 p.; 8vo. BN.

633/112

——. Institutionum medicinae libri v. *Wittenberg: Heirs of Z. Schürer, the Elder*, 1633. 2 v.; illus.; 8vo. 1st publ., Wittenberg, 1611. CtY-M, NcD.

633/113

Spiegel, Adriaan van de. Isagoges in rem herbariam. *Leyden: Elsevier Office*, 1633. 272 p.; 8vo. 1st publ., Padua, 1606: here appended is a catalog, compiled by A. Vorstius, of plants grown at the Leyden Botanic Garden, including numerous items designated as American Brazilian, Canadian, or Virginian. Pritzel 8827; Willems (Les Elzevier) 391; Wellcome I:6041. CU-S, DNLM, MH-A, MiU, NNNAM, PU; BL, BN.

633/114

Spinelli, Giovanni Paolo. Lectiones aureae in omni quod pertinet ad artem pharmacopoeam lucubratae . . . secunda impressione. *Bari: G. Gudoni, for G. Montini*, 1633. 2 pts; illus.; 4to. 1st publ., Bari, 1605. WU; Wellcome I:6044.

633/115

Sweden. Sovereigns, etc., 1611–1632 (Gustaf II Adolf). Ampliatio oder Erweiterung dess Privilegii so . . . Gustavus Adolphus

. . . der newen Australischen oder Süder-Compagnie . . . verliehen. *Heilbronn: C. Krause*, 1633. [7] p.; 4to. Presumably drafted by W. Usselinx. Clarifies *Octroy* of 1626. Sabin 98186; Jameson (Usselinx) 23; Palmer 401. MnU-B; Stockholm:KB (imp.).
633/116

Theatrum florae, in quo ex toto orbe selecti mirabiles . . . flores . . . proferuntur. *Paris: P. Firens*, 1633. 69 numb. pls; illus.; fol. 1st publ., Paris, 1622. Pritzel 10855n. DDO, MH-A; BL (imp.). 633/117

—[Anr issue?]. *Paris: P. Mariette*, 1633. Nissen (Bot.) 1575n. 633/118

Torsellino, Orazio, S.J. Histoire universelle depuis la création du monde. *Paris: T. de LaRuelle*, 1633. 888 p.; 8vo. 1st publ. as here transl., Paris, 1622. Backer VIII:155. BN.
633/119

Usselinx, Willem. Ampliatio. *Heilbronn:* 1633. *See* Sweden. Sovereigns, etc., *above.*

——. Argonautica Gustaviana, das ist: Nothwendige Nachricht von der newen Seefahrt und Kauffhandlung . . . durch anrichtung einer general handel-compagnie. *Frankfurt a. M.: K. Rötel*, 1633. 2 pts.; fol. Issued with the *Mercurius Germaniae*, with caption title & separate paging & signatures. For a detailed descr. of these documents concerning the Söder Compagniet, see Jameson. Sabin 98187; Vail (Frontier) 85; Asher 43; Jameson (Usselinx) 26; Kress S.635; JCB (3) II:248. CSmH, CtY, DLC, MH, MnU-B, NN-RB, PHi, RPJCB; BN.
633/120

——. Instruction oder Anleitung: welcher gestalt die Einzeichnung zu der newen Süder Compagnie durch Schweden und nunmehr auch Teutschland zubefördern. *Heilbronn: C. Krause*, 1633. [7] p.; 4to. Sabin 98196; Jameson (Usselinx) 25; Palmer 401. Stockholm:KB. 633/121

——. Kurtzer Extract der vornemsten Hauptpuncten . . . in Sachen der newen Süder Compagnie. *Heilbronn: C. Krause*, 1633. [5] p.; 4to. Sabin 98198; Jameson (Usselinx) 24; Palmer 401. Stockholm:KB.
633/122

Vaughan, William. Directions for health . . . The seventh edition. *London: T. Harper, for J. Harison the 4th*, 1633. 4to. 1st publ.,

London, 1600, under title *Naturall and artificial directions for health;* cf. 1602 edn. For variant states of imprint see the STC. STC 24618. CSmH, DFo, MBCo, NN; BL.
633/123

Vicary, Thomas. The English-mans treasure . . . And now eighthly augmented. *London: B. Alsop & T. Fawcet*, 1633. 264 p.; 4to. 1st publ., London, 1548, but cf. 1613 edn. STC 24712; Wellcome I:6582. CSmH, DNLM, IEN-M, MBCo, MiU, NNNAM; BL.
633/124

Victoria, Francisco de. Por los regidores de la ciudad de la Habana. Con el señor fiscal. Sobre las sentencias que contra ellos dio y pronunciò . . . don Francisco de Prada, fiscal de la audiencia de Santo Domingo, y juez de residencia y visita de don Lorenço de Cabrera, governador de la dicha ciudad. *Madrid: Widow of J. González*, 1633. 4 numb. lvs; fol. Sabin 99437; Medina (BHA) 7778; Palau 362300. 633/125

——. Por los regidores de la ciudad de la Havana en las Indias, que admetieron al oficio de governador della a don Lorenço de Cabrera. *Madrid: Widow of A. Martín*, 1633. 2 lvs; fol. Sabin 99438; Medina (BHA) 7777; Palau 362301. 633/126

Welper, Eberhard. Compendium geographicum, das ist Kurtze und eigentliche Beschreibung der gantzen Erdkugel. *Strassburg: The author*, 1633. 128 p.; 4to. Baginsky (German Americana) 166. CtY. NN-RB.
633/127

White, Andrew, S. J. A declaration of the Lord Baltemore's plantation in Mary-land, nigh upon Virginia: manifesting the nature, quality, condition, and rich utilities it contayneth. [*London: B. Alsop & T. Fawcet*, 1633]. 8 p.; 4to. Sabin 103351; cf. Baer (Md) 20; Vail (Frontier) 85A; STC 25375a.10. Ware, Herts.:St Edmund's College. 633/128

Yañez Fajardo, Diego Antonio. Memorial en nombre de fr. Juan Mendez, del Orden de San Juan de Dios, sobre reformacion del real decreto de 30. de enero de 1632. en quanto à la forma que havian de observar los religiosos de ella, en las Indias, con una relacion de la religion en ellas, i en España. [*Madrid?*] 1633. fol. Medina (BHA) 926.
633/129

1634

Abbot, George, Abp of Canterbury. A briefe description of the whole worlde . . . *London: [T. Harper?] for W. Sheares,* 1634. 329 p.; port.; 12mo. 1st publ., London, 1599. Sabin 21; STC 31; JCB (3) II:248. CSmH, CtY, DLC, MB, MnU-B, NN-RB, RPJCB; London: Wellcome, Oxford: Bodl.
634/1

Aldrovandi, Ulisse. De piscibus libri v. et de cetis liber i. *Frankfurt a. M.: K. Rötel, for J. Treudel,* 1634. 280 p.; illus.; fol. 1st publ., Bologna, 1612. Breslau:StB.
634/2

Alemán, Mateo. The rogue . . . Third edition. *London: R. B[adger]., for R. Allott,* 1634, '33. 2 pts; fol. 1st publ. as here transl. by James Mabbe, London, 1622. Laurenti (Nov. pic. esp.) 694; STC 291; Palau 6784. CSmH, CtY, DLC, ICN, MH, NN-RB, PPRF; BL.
634/3

Altamirano, Diego. Por el duque del infantado. Con el señor fiscal. Sobre la encomienda de Indios. *[Madrid: 1634?].* 8 numb. lvs; fol. Medina (BHA) 8057. BL, Puebla: B. Palafoxiana.
634/4

Ariosto, Lodovico. Orlando furioso, in English heroical verse. By Sr John Harington . . . Now thirdly revised and amended with the addition of the authors Epigrams. *London: G. Miller, for J. Parker,* 1634, '33. 2 pts. illus.; fol. Pt 2 comprises Harington's *Most elegant and wittie epigrams,* 1st publ. separately, London, 1633. STC 748; Arents 188. CSmH, CtY, DLC, ICN, MH, MnU, NN-RB, PU-F; BL, BN.
634/5

Avity, Pierre d', sieur de Montmartin. Les estats, empires et principautez du monde. *Geneva: P. Aubert,* 1634. 1869 p.; 8vo. 1st publ., Paris, 1613. Cf. Sabin 2498. NNH; Königsberg:StB.
634/6

Bacon, Francis, viscount St Albans. Considerations politiques pour entreprendre la guerre contre l'Espagne . . . traduites . . . par le sieur Maugars. *Paris: S. Cramoisy,* 1634. 74 p.; 4to. Transl. from Bacon's *Considerations touching a warre with Spaine,* 1st publ., [London], 1629. Gibson (Bacon) 188; Shaaber (Brit. auth.) B19. CtY; BL, BN.
634/7

——. Neuf livres de la dignité et l'accroissement des sciences. *Paris: J. Dugast,* 1634.

717 numb. lvs; 4to. 1st publ. as here transl. from Bacon's *Opera: Tomus primus* (London, 1623), Paris, 1632; here a reissue of that edn with cancel t.p. Gibson (Bacon) 138; Shaaber (Brit. auth.) B23. CCB.
634/8

Barclay, John. Euphormionis Lusinini . . . Satyricon. *Amsterdam: J. Hessius,* 1634. 8vo. Includes pt 2, 1st publ., Paris, 1607, & the *Icon animorum,* 1st publ, London, 1614. Shaaber (Brit. auth.) B193. York: Minster.
634/9

—[Anr edn]. Satyricon. *Amsterdam: W. J. Blaeu,* 1634. 580 p.; 12mo. In this edn the imprint date is in arabic numerals. Shaaber (Brit. auth.) B198. CtY, DFo; BN, Bonn:UB.
634/10

—[Anr edn]. Satyricon. *Amsterdam: W. J. Blaeu,* 1634. 16mo. In this edn the imprint date is in roman numerals. Shaaber (Brit. auth.) B199; Tchémerzine I:452. CtY, ICU, InU, PU, ViU; BL, Munich: StB.
634/11

—[Anr edn]. *Oxford: J. L[ichfield]., for H. Cripps,* 1634. 782 p.; 12mo. STC 1397; Madan (Oxford) 1634:2; Arents (Add.) 270. CSmH, CtY, ICU, MB, MnU, NN-A; BL.
634/12

Barriasa, Mateo de. Por Fernando de Almonte Veinticuatro de Sevilla, y consortes, interessados en la plata y oro que se traxo de las Indias el año passado de 632. en la armada de los galeones, General Tomas de Arraspurù, que son, añir, cochinilla, azucar y palo, que vinieron en la dicha armada. *Madrid: Widow of J. González,* 1634. 23 numb. lvs; fol. Medina (BHA) 7780. Puebla: B. Palafoxiana.
634/13

Barrough, Philip. The method of phisick . . . The seventh edition. *London: G. Miller,* 1634. 477 p.; 4to. 1st publ., London, 1583; cf. 1601 edn. STC 1515. CSmH, DFo, NNNAM; BL.
634/14

Bate, John. The mysteryes of nature and art. *London: T. Harper, for R. Mabb.* 1634. 192 p.; illus.; 4to. Includes section on 'How to take the Smoake of Tobacco through a glasse of water'. STC 1577. CSmH (imp.), DLC, MH; BL.
634/15

—[Anr issue]. *[London: T. Harper,] for R. Mabb, & sold by J. Jackson & F. Church,* 1634. STC 1577.2; Arents (Add.) 272. CoDU, DFo, NN-A; BL.
634/16

Béguin, Jean. Tyrocinium chymicum. *Whit-*

tenberg: *Widow of G. Müller, for Heirs of C. Berger*, 1634. 480 p.; 8vo. 1st publ., Paris, 1612. Ferguson I:93; Wellcome I:752. MeB, NIC; Glasgow:UL. 634/17

Benavides, Alonso de, O.F.M. Relatio quam Philippo iv . . . exhibuit reverendiss. p.f. Joannes de Santander . . . per manus adm. r.p.f. Alphonsi de Benavides. *Salzburg: C. Katzenberger*, 1634. 158 p.; 8vo. Transl. by Jean Gravendonc (or Cranendonc) from Benavides's *Memorial*, 1st publ., Madrid, 1630. Sabin 76813 (& 4638 & 43826); Medina (BHA) 928; Wagner (SW) 33c; Streit II:1626; JCB (3) II:249. DGU, NN-RB, RPJCB; Munich:StB. 634/18

——. Relatio, welche Philippo iv. . . . & r.p.f. Joannes de Santander . . . uber Indien General Commissarius, durch r.p.f. . . . Benavides . . . uber die Provintz dess newbekerten Mexico custoden . . . ubergeben lassen . . . Erstlich zu Madril . . . in Hispanisch volgents in Lateinisch an jetzo in hochteutscher sprach nachgetruckt. *Salzburg: C. Katzenberger* [1634?]. 130 p.; 12mo. Transl. from Benavides's *Memorial*, 1st publ., Madrid, 1630. Sabin 76814; Streit II:1627; Wagner (SW) 33d; JCB (3) II:249. RPJCB. 634/19

Bertius, Petrus. Abrégé ou Sommaire description du globe de la terre . . . traduict en françois par N. Hallay. *Paris: J. Villery*, 1634. 188 p.; 8vo. 1st publ., as here transl., Paris, 1624. Cf. Sabin 5013. BN. 634/20

Betancurt, Luis de. Memorial i informacion por las iglesias metropolitanas, i catedrales de las Indias. *Madrid: F. Martínez*, 1634. 24 numb. lvs; fol. Sabin 47635 (cf. 5064); Medina (BHA) 934; Palau 28775. BL, Palma: BP. 634/21

Bethune, Philippe de, comte de Selles et de Charost. Counsellor of estate . . . Written in French . . . Translated by E[dward]. G[rimestone]. *London: N. Okes*, 1634. 336p.; port.; 4to. Transl. from Bethune's *Le conseiller d'estat*, 1st publ., [Paris?], 1632. STC 1977. CtY, DLC, ICN, MH-BA, MnU-L, NN-RB; BL. 634/22

Blaeu, Willem Janszoon. Institutio astronomica de usu globorum & sphaerarum caelestium ac terrestrium . . . Latinè reddita à M. Hortensio. *Amsterdam: W. J. Blaeu*,

1634. 246 p.; illus.; 8vo. Transl. from Blaeu's *Tweevoudigh onderwijs* below. Keuning (Blaeu) 62–63; Houzeau/Lancaster I:9714. NN, NjP; BN. 634/23

——. Het nieuwe licht der zeevaert ofte havenwyser van de Oostersche, Noordsche en Westersche zeen. *Amsterdam: W. J. Blaeu*, 1634. 2 v.; illus., map; obl. fol. 1st publ., Amsterdam, 1608, under title *Het licht der zeevaert*. Imprint on slip pasted over original imprint, dated '1635'. Tiele 125. NN-RB. 634/24

—[Anr edn]. Het nieuw vermeerde licht. *Amsterdam: J. Janszoon, the Younger*, 1634. 2 v.; illus., maps; obl. fol. This edn rev. & enl. by Joris Carolus. Koeman (M.Bl) 20 (J). The Hague:AR, Copenhagen:KB. 634/25

——. Novus atlas, das ist, Abbildung und Beschreibung von allen Ländern des Erdreichs, gantz vernewt und verbessert. *Amsterdam: W. J. Blaeu*, 1634. 159 maps; fol. Includes several American maps; the introduction is translated from that by Philipp Clüver to Blaeu's *Appendix Theatri A. Ortelii*, Amsterdam, 1631, including refs to Brazil, Peru, Paraguay, etc. Koeman (Bl) 4; Wieder (Mon. Cart.) 84–85. 634/26

——. Tweevoudigh onderwijs van de hemelsche en aerdsche globen. *Amsterdam: W. J. Blaeu*, 1634. illus.; 4to. Though a 1st edn of 1620 is generally referred to, the work was not listed in a Blaeu catalogue until 1633; a privilege was granted by the States General in 1634. In pt 1, chapt. iv includes refs to Brazil, Peru, Paraguay, Chile, Magellanica; scattered refs to Lima occur elsewhere. Keuning (Blaeu) 62–63; Houzeau/Lancaster I:9714. 634/27

A booke of cookerie, and the order of meates to be served to the table. *London: Elizabeth Allde*, 1634. 102 p.; 8vo. 1st publ., London, 1620. BL. 634/28

Braun, Georg. Civitates orbis terrarum [Liber primus]. [*Cologne?* 1634?]. 58 double pls; fol. 1st publ., Cologne, 1572; cf. 1612 edn. ICJ. 634/29

Breton, Nicholas. A poste with a packet of madde letters. *London: [M. Fletcher,] for J. Marriott*, 1634. 2 pts; 4to. 1st publ., London, 1602–5. STC 3693. CSmH, DFo (imp.). 634/30

——. Wits private wealth. *London: B. Alsop & T. Fawcet, for G. Hurlock*, 1634. 4to. 1st publ., London, 1612. STC 3712. CSmH; BL.   634/31

Broeck, Pieter van den. Korte historiael ende journaelsche aenteyckeninghe, van al 't gheen merck-waerdich voorgevallen is. *Haarlem: H. P. van Wesbusch*, 1634. 163 p.; illus., port.; obl. 4to. Includes minor refs to Brazil. Tiele-Muller 209. NN-RB; BL.   634/32

—[Anr edn]. *Amsterdam: J. Broerszoon, for H. J. Brouwer*, 1634. 130 p.; illus., port.; obl. 4to. Tiele-Muller 210. MnU-B; BL.   634/33

Brugge, Jacob Segersz. van der. Journael, of Dagh-register, gehouden . . . op Spitsbergen. *Amsterdam:* [1634?]. *See the year* 1663.

Bry, Theodor de. Decima tertia pars Historiae Americanae, quae continet exactam et accuratum descriptionem I. Novae Angliae, Virginiae, Brasiliae, Guianae, & insulae Bermudae . . . II. Terrae australis incognitae . . . III. Expugnationis urbis S. Salvatoris . . . ab Hollandis factae . . . IV. Novi Mexici, Cibolae, Quivirae, rerumque memorabilium, quae in Iucatan, Guatimala, Fonduris & Panama observatae sunt . . . V. Navigationis Hollandorum per universum orbem . . . VI. Classis Hispanicae praedivitis ab Hollandis . . . in portu insulae qui Matanza dicitur, interceptae. VII. Urbis Olindae de Fernambucco in Brasilia ab Hollandis . . . occupatae. *Frankfurt a. M.:* [*K. Rötel?*] *for M. Merian*, 1634. 149 p.; illus.; maps; fol. Transl. from the de Bry, Frankfurt a. M., 1628, *Continuatio Americae* & the Hanau, 1630, *Vierzehender Theil Americanischer Historien.* Shaaber (Brit. auth.) W69; Church 174; JCB (3) I:417. CSmH, DLC, ICN, NN-RB, RPJCB; BL, BN.   634/34

——. Historia Americae, sive Novi Orbis. *Frankfurt a. M.: M. Merian*, 1634. [20] p.; fol. (Theodor de Bry's America. General title and preface. Latin). Intended as a collective t.p., preface & table of contents for de Bry's *America.* For a description of the two later reprintings, see JCB (3). Cf. Church 175; JCB (3) I:382. RPJCB; BL, BN.   634/35

Bucholtzer, Abraham. Index chronologicus

monstrans annorum seriem a mundo condito usque ad 1634. *Frankfurt A. M.: W. Hoffmann, for the Widow of J. Rose*, 1634. 1st publ., Görlitz, 1584; cf. 1612 edn. NNH (imp.).   634/36

Camden, William. Tomus alter et idem: or The historie of . . . Princesse Elizabeth. *London* [*T. Harper,*] *for W. Webb,* [*at Oxford,*] 1634. 384 p.; port.; 4to. 1st publ. as trans. by Thomas Browne for Latin text (1st publ., Leyden, 1625, & London, 1629); here a reissue of that edn. STC 4499. BL.   634/37

Cárdenas, Bernardino de, Bp of Paraguay. Memorial, y relacion verdadera para el Rei . . . y su Real Consejo de las Indias, de cosas del reino del Peru. *Madrid: F. Martínez*, 1634. 64 numb. lvs; 4to. Sabin 10807; Medina (BHA) 929; Streit II:1628; Palau 43890; JCB (3) II:250. NN-RB, RPJCB; BL.   634/38

Cardona, Nicolás de. Señor. El capitan Nicolas de Cardona, dize: que sirve a V[uestra]. M[agestad]. desde el año de 610. en la carrera de las Indias. [*Madrid?* 1634]. 8 numb. lvs; fol. On voyage to California. Medina (BHA) 6315; Wagner (SW) 38. BL, Seville:Archivo de Indias.   634/39

Carrillo, Martín. Anales cronologicos del mundo . . . Añadese en este segunda impression en diversas partes adiciones . . . Mas se añaden los años 1621. hasta 1630. *Saragossa: Hospital Real de Nuestra Señora de Gracia, for P. Escuer*, 1634. 525 numb. lvs; fol. 1st publ., Huesca, 1622. In added section, under year 1624, ref. is made to Dutch in Brazil. For a variant title leaf, see Medina. Medina (BHA) 930; Jiménez Catalan (Saragossa) 332; Palau 45513n. IU, NNH, RPJCB; BL, BN.   634/40

Casas, Bartolomé de las, O.P., Bp of Chiapa. Den vermeerderden spiegel der Spaensche tierannije geschiet in Westindien. *Amsterdam: C. L. van der Plasse*, 1634. [104]p.; illus.; 4to. 1st publ. in Dutch, [Antwerp?], 1578; cf. 1607 edn above & Plasse's 1621 edn, of which this is a reprint. Sabin 11261; Medina (BHA) 1085n (II:477); Hanke/ Giménez 530; Tiele-Muller 317; Streit I:456; Meulman 1729; JCB (3) II:250. DLC, NN-RB, RPJCB; Ghent:BU.   634/41

Céspedes y Meneses, Gonzalo de. Historia

de Don Felipe IIII, rey de las Españas. *Barcelona: S. de Cormellas, 1634.* 281 numb. lvs; fol. 1st publ., Lisbon, 1631. Rodrigues (Dom. Hol.) 88; Palau 54200n. ICU, NNH, PU, RPB; BL, BN. 634/42

Copye van twee geintercipieerde brieven komende wt Westindien. [*Amsterdam?* 1634]. bds.; fol. Letters dated 15 & 18 Feb. 1634. Meulman 2282. Ghent: BU.
634/43

Cotton, John. Gods promise to His plantations . . . a sermon. *London: W. Jones, for J. Bellamy, 1634.* 20 p.; 4to. 1st publ., London, 1630. Cf. Sabin 17065; Tuttle (Cotton) 2; STC 5855. CtY, ICN, MH; BL, Oxford: Bodl. 634/44

Crisci, Giovanni Battista. Lucerna de corteggiani. *Naples: G. D. Roncaglioli, 1634.* 348 p.; port.; 4to. In section suggesting menus for a full year turkeys ('gallotti d'India') figure frequently in varying forms. DLC; London: Wellcome. 634/45

Croll, Oswald. Basilica chymica . . . Additus est . . . Tractatus novus de signaturis rerum internis. *Leipzig: G. Gross, 1634.* 3 pts; 8vo. 1st publ., Frankfurt a. M., 1609. PBa; BN. 634/46

——. La royale chymie. Traduitte . . . par J. Marcel de Boulenc. *Rouen: J. Berthelin, 1634.* 3 pts; illus.; 8vo. 1st publ. as here transl., Lyons, 1624. BN. 634/47

—[Anr issue?]. *Rouen: J. Osmont, 1634.* CtY-M, DLC, WU; BN. 634/48

Dávila Padilla, Augustín, Abp of Santo Domingo. Varia historia de Nueva España y Florida . . . Edicion segunda. *Valladolid: J. B. Varesio, 1634.* 654 p.; fol. 1st publ., Madrid, 1590; here a reissue with cancel t.p. of sheets of the Brussels, 1625, edn, with title *Historia de la fundacion,* etc. Sabin 18781; Medina (BHA) 931; Streit II:1629; JCB (3) II:251. NcD, RPJCB (imp.); BL. 634/49

Donne, John. Ignatius his conclave. *London: J. Marriott; sold by W. Sheares, 1634.* 135 p.; 12mo. 1st publ. as transl. from Donne's *Conclave Ignatii* of same year, London, 1611. Keynes (Donne) 8; STC 7029; Grolier Club (Wither to Prior) 278. CSmH, CtY, DFo, MH; BL. 634/50

Fabricius, Hieronymus, ab Aquapendente. Medecina practica. *Paris: C. Cottard, 1634.*

799 p.; 4to. Use of guaiacum is described at length, as well as of sarsaparilla. PPL; BL, BN. 634/51

Faye, Charles, sieur d'Espesses. Memoires de plusieurs choses considerables avenües en France . . . depuis le commencement de l'année 1607. *Paris: T. Blaise, 1634.* 147 p.; 8vo. Includes account of voyage to New France by the sieur de Poutrincourt. MnU-B, RPJCB; BL. 634/52

France. Conseil d'Etat. Extraict des registres du Conseil d'Estat. Entre m[ait]re Jean Jacques Dolu, Arnoul de Nouveau, Guillaume de Caën, Mathieu d'Eustrelot, & consors, cy devant Associez pour les voyages de la Nouvelle France de la Compagnie dicte de Montmorency . . . et Claude Roquemont, Louys Houel, Gabriel Lattaignant, David du Chesne & Jacques Castillon, tant pour eux que pour les autres nouveaux Associez de la Compagnie de la dite Nouvelle France. [*Paris?* 1634]. 14 p.; 4to. BN. 634/53

France. Sovereigns, etc., 1610–1643 (Louis XIII). Declaration du Roy, portant defenses a ses sujets d'entreprendre sur les Espagnols & Portugais au deça du premier meridien. Verifiée en Parlemont le 27 juillet 1634. *Paris: S. Cramoisy, 1634.* 16 p.; 8vo. On seizure of ships trading to America; cf. 1625 edn. Wroth/Annan 20; JCB (3) II:251. RPJCB. 634/54

Gallego Benítez de la Serna, Juan. Opera physica, medica, ethica, quinque tractatibus comprehensa. *Lyons: J. & P. Prost, 1634.* 2 pts; fol. In pt 1, bk 1, chapt. xxii, chocolate, 'ex Indiis exportatis', is mentioned. Palau 97157. DNLM; BL. 634/55

Góngora y Argote, Luis de. Todas las obras. *Madrid: Imprenta Real, for A. Pérez, 1634.* 232 numb. lvs; 4to. In verse. Included is Góngora's *Soledades,* 1st publ., Madrid, 1627, in his *Obras en verso.* Palau 104627n. DPU, MH, NNH; BN. 634/56

Le grande deffaite des Espagnols tant par mer que par terre, avec la prise du fort de la Christine, et de dix vaisseaux de guerre, par les Hollandois. *Paris: M. Colombel, 1634.* 16 p.; 8vo. Borba de Moraes I: 315.
634/57

Graswinckel, Dirk. Libertas Veneta. *Leyden: A. Commelin, 1634.* 510 p.; 4to. On p. 121

is a ref. to Pope Alexander VI's arbitration of dispute between Spain & Portugal 'super navigatione maris Indici'. CtU, ICN, MH; BL, BN.   634/58

Great Britain. Laws, statutes, etc., 1625–1649 (Charles I). A commission for the well governing of our people, inhabiting in New-found-land; or, Traffiquing in bayes, creekes, or fresh rivers there. *London: R. Barker, & assigns of J. Bill*, 1633 [i.e., 1634]. 22 (i.e., 18) p.; 4to. STC 9255; JCB AR41:9–14 & AR43:18–23. CSmH, DFo, MH, RPJCB; BL.   634/59

Great Britain. Sovereigns, etc., 1625–1649 (Charles I). A proclamation concerning tobacco. *London: R. Barker & assigns of J. Bill*, 1634. 2 lvs; fol. Crawford (Roy. procl.) 1677; Brigham (Roy. procl.) 75–78; STC 9016. BL.   634/60

——. A proclamation restraining the abusive venting of tobacco. *London: R. Barker & assigns of J. Bill*, 1633 [i.e., 1634]. bds.; fol. Crawford (Roy. procl.) 1671; Brigham (Roy. procl.) 74–75; STC 9011; Arents 190. NN-A; BL.   634/61

—[Anr edn]. *London: R. Barker & assigns of J. Bill*, 1633 [i.e., 1634]. bds.; fol. Crawford (Roy. procl.) 1672; STC 9012. London: PRO.   634/62

Guibert, Philbert. Les oeuvres du medecin charitable. *Lyons: J. Huguetan*, 1634. 684 p.; 12mo. Included is Guibert's *Le prix et valeur des medicaments*, 1st publ., Paris, 1625. BN.
                                                634/63

—[Anr edn]. *Paris: C. Griset*, 1634. 718 p.; 8vo. BN.   634/64

—[Anr issue]. *Paris: C. Collet*, 1634. MnU.
                                                634/65

Hartmann, Johann (1568–1631). Praxis chymiatrica. *Frankfurt a. M.: K. Rötel*, 1634, 652 p.; 8vo. 1st publ., Leipzig, 1633. Wellcome I:3065. DNLM; London:Wellcome.
                                                634/66

Hay, Paul, sieur du Chastelet (1592–1636), ed. Le mercure d'estat. *Geneva: P. Aubert*, 1634. 484 p.; 8vo. Includes refs to America, West Indies, Atabalipa, Pizarro, etc. BL (Mercury), BN.   634/67

Herbert, Sir Thomas. A relation of some yeares travaile, begunne anno 1626. into Afrique and the greater Asia. *London: W. Stansby & J. Bloome*, 1634. 225 p.; illus.,

maps; fol. 'A discourse and proofe that Madoc ap Owen Gwynedd first found out that continent now call'd America': p. 217–224. Sabin 31471; STC 13190; Arents 191; JCB (3) II:413. CSmH, CtY, DLC, ICN, MH, MnU-B, NN-RB, PPL, RPJCB; BL.
                                                634/68

Herckmans, Elias. Der zee-vaert lof handelende vande gedenckwaerdighste zee-vaerden. . . . *Amsterdam: J. F. Stam, for J. P. Wachter*, 1634. 235 p.; illus.; fol. In verse. Includes accounts of voyages to America & Dutch conquest of Brazil. Sabin 31476; Borba de Moraes I:335; JCB (3) II:251–52. CtY, DLC, InU-L, MiU-C, MnU-B, PP, RPJCB; BL.   634/69

Héry, Thierry de. La methode curatoire de la maladie venerienne. *Paris: E. d'Aubin*, 1634. 208 p.; 8vo. 1st publ., Paris, 1552. Offers as possible source of syphilis 'une isle incogneue aux anciens, & n'a pas long temps descouverte par les Espaignols navigans, environs le temps qu'elle nous est apparue'. 'La description du bois de gaiac': p. 56–72. BL.   634/70

—[Anr issue]. *Paris: J. Gesselin*, 1634. Wellcome I:3145. London:Wellcome.
                                                634/71

Joernael. ofte. Voyagie vande Groenlantsvaerders, namelijck vande seven matrosz. die ghebleven waren op het eylant genaemt Mauritius. *Rotterdam: A. Nering*, 1634. [45] p.; 4to. Sometimes attrib. to Outgert Jacobszoon, commander of the marooned sailors. Sabin 34968; Tiele-Muller 249; Tiele 565; Knuttel 4346; JCB (3) II:252. NN-RB, RPJCB; The Hague:KB.
                                                634/72

—[Anr edn]. Journael ofte waerachtige beschrijvinge van al het gene datter voorghevallen is op het eylandt Mauritius in Groenlandt. *Leiden: W. Christiaens., for J. Roels*, 1634. 20 p.; 4to. Knuttel 4345. CSmH, DLC; BL (Jacobsz, Outgert), The Hague:KB.
                                                634/73

Keulen, Mathias van. Extract wtten brief van mijn Herr Keulen, bewint hebber van de West-Indische Compagnie, residerende . . . tot Fernambuco in Brasilien. *The Hague: L. Breeckevelt*, 1634. bds.; 4to. Borba de Moraes I:257; Rodrigues (Dom. Hol.) 192; Meulman 2280. Ghent:BU.   634/74

La Serre, Jean Puget de. Balet des princes indiens. *Brussels: F. Vivien,* 1634. 30 p.; 4to. Of the dancers represented, two are Tupinambi (Brazilian) Indians. MH; BL, BN.
634/75

Leiva y Aguilar, Francisco de. Desengaño contra el mal uso del tabaco. *Córdoba: S. de Cea Tesa,* 1634. 278 numb. lvs; 4to. Medina (BHA) 982; Valdenebro (Córdoba) 155; Palau 134674; Arents 192. DLC, NN-A, OCl, PPB; BL, Madrid:BN.
634/76

Le Jeune, Paul, S.J. Relation de ce qui s'est passé en la Nouvelle France en l'annee 1633. *Paris: S. Cramoisy,* 1634. 216 p.; 8vo. The headpiece on p. 3 depicts a cupid. For variants, see McCoy. Sabin 39947; Harrisse (NF) 55; Church 424; McCoy 3–6. CSmH, CtY, MiU-C, RPJCB; BL, BN.
634/77

—[Anr edn]. *Paris: S. Cramoisy,* 1634. 216 p.; 8vo. The headpiece on p. 3 depicts a ram's head. For variants, see McCoy. Sabin 39948; Harrisse (NF) 56; Bell (Jes. rel.) 1; McCoy 7–9. ICN, MH, MnU-B, NN-RB, RPJCB; BN.
634/78

Leonardo y Argensola, Lupercio. Rimas de Lupercio i del dotor Bartolome Leonardo de Argensola. *Saragossa: Hospital Real de Nuestra Señora de Gracia,* 1634. 501 p.; 4to. Poems by Bartolomé include one 'A Don Fernando de Borja' mentioning Potosí & another 'A Nuño de Mendoza' citing the evil effects of gold from the Indies. Jiménez Catalan (Saragossa) 328; Palau 16101. Those copies listed below may include the present edn. Saragossa:BU.
634/79

—[Anr edn]. *Saragossa: Hospital Real de Nuestra Señora de Gracia,* 1634. 502 p.; 4to. Jiménez Catalan (Saragossa) 329; Palau 16102. CU, DLC, ICN, MH, MiU, MnU, NN, PU, RPB; BL, BN.
634/80

Liceti, Fortunio. De monstrorum caussis, natura, et differentiis libri duo. *Padua: P. Frambotti,* 1634. 262 p.; illus.; 4to. 1st publ., Padua, 1616. Wellcome I:3768. CLSU, DNLM, ICJ, MBCo, MiU, NNAM, PPC; BL, BN.
634/81

Lowe, Peter. A discourse of the whole art of chyrurgerie . . . Third edition. *London: T. Purfoot,* 1634. 2 pts; illus.; 4to. 1st publ., London, 1597; cf. 1612 edn. STC 16871.

CSmH, CtY-M, DFo, IU, MH MiU, NN; BL, Oxford:Bodl.
634/82

Markham, Gervase. The art of archerie. *London: B. A[lsop]. & T. F[awcet]., for B. Fisher,* 1634. 172 p.; 8vo. On p. 50–51 bows used by Indians of Brazil are described. STC 17333; Poynter (Markham) 185–87. CSmH, CtY (imp.), DFo, ICN (imp.), WU; BL.
634/83

Márquez de Cisneros, ——. Por el Consulado de Sevilla, è interessados en la plata y oro, que el año passado de 31. se salvò en la provincia de Tabasco en la nao San Antonio, que llego a ella derrotada de la flota de aquel año . . . Con el señor Fiscal. *Madrid: Widow of J. González,* 1634. 16 numb. lvs; fol. Medina (BHA) 7783. Puebla:B. Palafoxiana.
634/84

——. Por el señor D. Carlos de Ibarra . . . almirante general de la armada de la Guarda de las Indias . . . Sobre los cargos de su residencia del dicho oficio de almirante de la armada ultima de los galeones que vino a estos reynos, General marques de Cadereyta. *Madrid: Widow of J. González,* 1634. 19 numb. lvs; fol. Medina (BHA) 7784. BL, Puebla:B. Palafoxiana. 634/85

Massaria, Alessandro. Opera medica. *Lyons: J. A. Candy,* 1634. 865 p.; fol. 1st publ., Frankfurt a.M., 1601, under title *Practica medica.* CtY-M, DNLM, NIC, WU. 634/86

Mercator, Gerardus. Atlas minor . . . à J. Hondius . . . illustratus. *Amsterdam: J. Janszoon, the Younger,* 1634. 651 p.; maps; obl. 12mo. 1st publ. in this version, Amsterdam, 1628. Cf. Sabin 47887; Koeman (Me) 201A; Phillips (Atlases) 446. DLC, ICN, MiU-C, NNUT; BL, Vienna:NB. 634/87

——. Atlas ofte Afbeeldinghe vande gantsche weerldt . . . uyt het Latyn . . . getranslateert. [*Amsterdam: J. Janszoon, the Younger,* 1634]. 400 lvs; maps; fol. Transl. by Ernest Brinck from Mercator's *Atlas sive Cosmographicae meditationes,* 1st publ., Amsterdam, 1606. Title & imprint appear on slips pasted on t.p. of 1633 French edn. For variant see Koeman. Koeman (Me) 39A–39B; Phillips (Atlases) 447; Tiele 744. DLC; Amsterdam:UB, Leyden:UB.
634/88

Moffett, Thomas. Insectorum, sive minimorum animalium theatrum. *London: T. Cotes,*

& sold by B. Allen, 1634. 326 p.; fol. Includes scattered refs to insects of America, Virginia, Peru, Hispaniola, etc. STC 17993. CU, DCU, MH, MiU, NNNAM; BL, Oxford: Christ Church.   634/89

—[Anr issue]. *London: T. Cotes, & sold by W. Hope*, 1634. STC 17993a. CSmH, DFo, MH, NN-RB; BL, Oxford:Bodl.   634/90

—[Anr issue]. *London: T. Cotes*, 1634. STC 17993b; Wellcome I:4380. CU, DFo, IU, MnU, NN-RB; London:Wellcome, Oxford: Bodl.   634/91

Moscoso y de Córdoba, Cristóbal de. El licenciado D. Christoval de Moscoso y Cordova, fiscal del Real Consejo de Indias. Con Don Juan de Amassa . . . Sobre que sea condenado en quarenta mil ducados, por los dos navios que no ha entregado. *Madrid: Widow of J. González*, 1634. 18 numb. lvs; fol. Sabin 51043n. BL.   634/92

——. El licenciado D. Christoval de Moscoso y Cordova, fiscal del Real Consejo de Indias. Con el Consulado de Sevilla, e interessados en la plata y oro . . . que el año passado de treinta y uno se salvó en la provincia de Tabasco en la nao San Antonio, que llegó a ella derrotada de la flota de aquel año. *Madrid: Widow of J. González*, 1634. 22 numb. lvs; fol. Sabin 51043n; Medina (BHA) 7788; Palau 183358. TxU-L; BL.   634/93

——. El licenciado Don Christoval de Moscoso y Cordova, fiscal del Consejo Real de Indias, con Don Juan de Meneses, governador que fue de la provincia de Veneçuela. Sobre la inteligencia de la sentencia de revista, y pretension de que està condenado en cincuenta y quatro esclavos. *Madrid: Widow of J. González*, 1634. 13 numb. lvs; fol. Sabin 51043; Medina (BHA) 7789. BL, Puebla:B. Palafoxiana.   634/94

——. El licenciado Don Christoval de Moscoso y Cordova, fiscal del Real Consejo de las Indias. Con el duque del Infantado. Sobre la encomienda de Indios, que tuvo . . . la duquesa del Infantado. [*Madrid? 1634?*]. 22 numb. lvs; fol. Sabin 51043n. BL.   634/95

——. El licenciado Don Christoval de Moscoso y Cordova . . . fiscal en el Real [Consejo] de las Indias. Con Alonso de Carrion,

escrivano publico, y del cabildo de . . . Lima. *Madrid: Widow of J. González*, 1634. 13 numb. lvs; fol. Sabin 51043n. BL.
                                            634/96

Nederlandsche West-Indische Compagnie. West-Indische Compagnie. [*Amsterdam? 1634?*]. bds.; fol. Forbids hoarding of certain goods without foreknowledge of the directors. Dated 9 Dec. 1634. Petit 1872. Leyden:B. Thysiana.   634/97

Netherlands (United Provinces, 1581–1795). Staten Generaal. Nader ordre ende reglement vande . . . Staten Generael . . . over het open ende vry stellen vanden handel ende negotie op de stadt Olinda de Pernambuco ende custen van Brasil [9 Jan. 1634]. *The Hague: Widow & Heirs of H. Jacobszoon van Wouw*, 1634. 8 p.; 4to. Tiele (Pamfletten) 2529.   634/98

——. Ordre ende reglement . . . gearresteert by advijs ende deliberatie vande bewint-hebberen vande . . . West-Indische Compagnie ter vergaderinge vande negenthiene over het bewoonen ende cultiveren der landen . . . in Brasil. *The Hague: Widow & Heirs of H. Jacobszoon van Wouw*, 1634. [11] p.; 4to. Sabin 57537 (& 102905); Borba de Moraes II: 119. DLC.   634/99

——. Placaet, alle realen van Spaignen, Mexico ende Peru vande meeste totte minste toe . . . *The Hague: Widow & Heirs of H. Jacobszoon van Wouw*, 1634. bds.; illus.; fol. On coinage. Cf. the following item. Meulman 2294. Ghent:BU.   634/100

——. Placaet ende ordonnantie . . . tegens wechloopers die hun in dienst vande Oostofte West-Indische Compaignien begeven hebbende, verloopen. *The Hague: Widow & Heirs of H. Jacobszoon van Wouw*, 1634. [4] p.; 4to. 1st publ., The Hague, 1625. Petit 1478. Leyden: B. Thysiana.   634/101

——. Placaet ende ordonnantie . . . teghens alle realen van Spaignen, Mexico ende Peru. *The Hague: Widow & Heirs of H. Jacobszoon van Wouw*, 1634. [8] p.; illus.; 4to. Cf. the preceding item. Petit 1869. Leyden:B. Thysiana.   634/102

Nieremberg, Juan Eusebio, S.J. Curiosa filosofia y tesoro de las maravillas de la naturaleza . . . De nuevo impressa, y añadida por el mismo autor. *Madrid: Imprenta Real,*

1634. 248 p.; 8vo. 1st publ., Madrid, 1630. Backer V:1730; Palau 190663. 634/103

Ortiz de Salcedo, Francisco. Curia eclesiastica, para secretarios . . . Con una relacion de los arzobispados, y obispados de España, y las Indias. *Madrid: F. Martínez,* 1634. 278 numb. lvs; 4to. 1st publ. with section on West Indian prelates, Madrid, 1626. Palau 205989n. DLC (imp.). 634/104

Owen, John. Epigrammatum . . . libri decem . . . Editio sexta. *London: A. Mathewes, for S. Waterson,* 1634. 12mo. 1st publ., London, 1606; here a reissue of 1633 edn with engr. t.p. with altered imprint date. STC 18992. ICU, MH, PPL; Oxford:Bodl. 634/105

Palafox y Mendoza, Juan de, Bp of Puebla de los Angeles. Por el licenciado don Iuan de Palafox y Mendoza, fiscal de su Magestad en su Consejo Real de las Indias. Con Doña Francisca Arze de Otalora . . . Sobre que los [31550] . . . pesos que estan en el depositorio . . . de Lima . . . se traygan al Recetor del Consejo. [*Madrid:* 1634]. 14 numb. lvs; fol. Cf. Medina (BHA) 7790. BL. 634/106

Paré, Ambroise. The workes of . . . Ambrose Parey translated out of Latine and compared with the French by Th: Johnson. *London: T. Cotes & R. Young,* 1634. 1173 p.; illus., port.; fol. Transl. from 1582 Latin text; cf. 1601 German edn. For variant dedications, see the STC. Doe (Paré) 51; STC 19189; Wellcome I:4825. CSmH, CtY-M, DNLM, ICJ, MBCo, MiU, NNNAM, PPC; BL. 634/107

Pertinent bericht. Van alle de particulariteyten soo sich hebben toeghedragen in West-Indien, 't welck geadviseert wert vande gedeligeerde heeren, van weghen de gheoctroyeerde West-Indische Compagnie tot Farnumbuco van date den 18. April 1634. *The Hague: L. Breeckevelt,* 1634. 3 p.; 4to. Borba de Moraes II:141; Asher 147; Knuttel 4347. DLC; The Hague:KB. 634/108

Pharmacopoea Blaesensis. *Blois: J. & M. Cottereau,* 1634. 36 p.; 16mo. Amongst the ingredients cited is 'Tabaci Indici', p. 7. BL. 634/109

Por Alonso de Carrion escrivano publico, y del cabildo, justicia y regimiento de la ciu-

dad de los Reyes. *Madrid: Widow of J. González,* 1634. 10 lvs; fol. Memorial on produce of Peru. Medina (BHA) 927. BL. 634/110

Potosí, Bolivia. Por la villa imperial de Potosi. En el pleyto con el señor fiscal. Sobre la visita de las pulperias. [*Madrid:* 1634?]. [8] p.; fol. Medina (BHA) 8095; JCB (3) II:253–54. RPJCB. 634/111

Raleigh, Sir Walter. The historie of the world. *London: [R. Young,] for G. Latham & R. Young,* 1634. 2 v.; port., maps; fol. 1st publ., London, 1614. Sabin 67560n; Brushfield (Raleigh) 223(F); STC 20641. CSmH, CtY, DLC, ICN, MH, NN-RB, RPB; BL. 634/112

Relacion cierta y verdadera, del famoso sucesso y vitoria que tuvo el capitan Benito Arias . . . contra los . . . Olandeses, que estavan fortificados en una salina . . . del rio Unare. *Seville: F. de Lyra,* 1634. [4] p.; fol. On events in Venezuela. Sabin 50084 & 69173; Medina (BHA) 936. NN-RB; BL. 634/113

A relation of the successefull beginnings of the Lord Baltemore's plantation in Maryland. Being an extract of certain letters written from thence. [*London?* 1634]. 14 p.; 4to. A later, 1635, edn has title *A relation of Maryland.* Sabin 45316; Baer (Md) 21; Vail (Frontier) 86; STC 4371; JCB (3) II:250. RPJCB; BL. 634/114

Rocquigny, Adrian de. La muse chrestienne . . . revuë, embellie & augmentee d'une seconde partie par l'autheur. [*London: G. Miller*] 1634. 262 p.; port.; 4to. Amongst prefatory verses, those of P. Béraud mention 'Petun', i.e., tobacco; in 2nd pt a poem (p. 139–49) 'Du petun' appears. STC 21139; Arents (Add.) 274. NN-A; BL, BN. 634/115

Rowlands, Samuel. The night raven. *London: W. J[ones]., for T. Bailey,* 1634. 4to. 1st publ., London, 1620. In verse. STC 21403; Arents (Add.) 275. ICN, NN-RB; BL. 634/116

Rowley, Samuel. The noble souldier. or A contract broken justly reveng'd. *London: [J. Beale,] for N. Vavasour,* 1634. [62] p.; 4to. Drama. In act 2, scene 1, English use of tobacco as snuff is mentioned; in act 3, Spain's 'Indian Treasury'; in act 5, the West

Indies. STC 21416; Greg 490; Arents
(Add.) 276. CSmH, CtY, DLC, ICN, MH,
NN-A; BL.   634/117

Rúa, Fernando de. Por Don Juan Meneses,
castellano de Perpiñan, governador que fue
. . . de Veneçuela . . . Con el señor fiscal,
sobre de declaracion de un capitulo de la
sentencia de su residencia. *Madrid: A. de
Parra,* 1934 [i.e., 1634]. 15 numb. lvs; fol.
Mentions the growing of cacao. Cf. Medina
(BHA) 8064. BL.   634/118

Ruiz de Alarcón y Mendoza, Juan. Parte
segunda de las Comedias. *Barcelona: S. de
Cormellas,* 1634. 269 numb. lvs; 4to. Continues the 1st pt publ. at Madrid, 1628. Included is the author's *La verdad sospechosa*
1st publ. as attrib. to Lope de Vega in the
latter's *Comedias,* pte 22, at Saragossa, 1630.
Palau 281540. BN.   634/119

Sánchez, Alfonso. De rebus Hispaniae anacephalaeosis libri septem. A condita Hispania ad annum 1633. *Alcalá de Henares: A.
Duplastre,* 1634. 401 p.; 4to. 'Indicae navigationes': p. 355; 'De Ferdinando Cortesio':
p. 355–61; 'Cortesius Mexicanum regnum
invadit': p. 361–68. Sabin 76316; Medina
(BHA) 939; García López (Alcalá de Henares) 950; Palau 294034. MdAN, PU, WU;
BL, BN.   634/120

Sandoval, Prudencio de, Bp of Pamplona.
Historia de la vida y hechos del Emperador
Carlos V. *Pamplona: B. Paris, for P. Escuer,
at Saragossa,* 1634. 2 v.; port.; fol. 1st publ.,
Valladolid, 1604–6; here a reissue with cancel title pages of Paris's edns of 1614 (v.
2) & 1618 (v. 1). Sabin 76426; Palau
297147n. CU-B, CtY, DLC, MH, NNH; BL,
BN.   634/121

Sandoval y Guzmán, Sebastián de. El doctor don Sebastian de Sandoval y Guzman,
procurador general de . . . Potosi . . .
digo, que las barras que vinieron del Perù
en los galeones . . . se bolvieron a ensenyar
[etc]. [*Madrid:* 1634]. [4] p.; fol. Medina
(BHA) 8342; JCB (3) II:253–54. RPJCB.
                                       634/122

——. Epilogo de las Pretensiones de la villa
imperial de Potosi, y lo que han acordado
. . . don Garcia de Haro y Avellaneda. [*Madrid:* 1634?]. 6 numb. lvs; fol. Medina (BHA)
8344; Palau 297176; JCB (3) II:253–54.
RPJCB.   634/123

——. Pretensiones de la villa imperial de Potosi, propuestas en el Real Consejo de las
Indias. *Madrid: Widow of J. González,* 1634.
157 numb. lvs; fol. Sabin 76431; Medina
(BHA) 7791; Palau 297175; JCB (3) II:253–
54. MH, RPJCB; Puebla:B. Palafoxiana.
                                       634/124

Scaliger, Julius Caesar. Exotericarum exercitationum liber quintus decimus. *Hanau:
Wechel Office, for C. Schleich,* 1634. 1076 p.;
illus.; 8vo. 1st publ., Paris, 1557; cf. 1601
edn. CU-M, ICU, MH, NNG; BL.
                                       634/125

Seville. Consulado. Por el consulado de Sevilla, è interessados en la plata y oro, que
el año . . . de 31. Se salvo en . . . Tabasco
. . . Con el . . . fiscal [C. de Moscoso y
Cordova]. *Madrid: Widow of J. González,*
1634. 16 numb. lvs; fol. BL.   634/126

Spain. Junta de Guerra de Indias. Ordenanzas de la Junta de Guerra de Indias. *Madrid:* 1634. fol. Perhaps a ghost; cf. 1636
edn. Sabin 57474; Palau 202985n.
                                       634/127

**Spain. Sovereigns, etc., 1598–1621 (Philip
III).** El Rey [27 Sept. 1634]. [*Madrid:*
1634]. 10 numb. lvs; fol. On the pacification
and conversion of the Indians of New Granada (Colombia) & the working of mines.
Sabin 98825. BL.   634/128

Staden, Hans. Beschrijvinghe van America.
Amsterdam: B. Janszoon, 1634. 72 p.; illus.;
4to. 1st publ. in Dutch, Antwerp, 1558; cf.
1625 edn. For variant see Borba de Moraes.
Sabin 90046; Borba de Moraes II:285; Palau 32185; JCB (3) II:254. RPJCB.
                                       634/129

Stafford, Robert. A geographicall and anthologicall description of all the empires
. . . in this . . . globe. *London: N. Okes, for
S. Waterson,* 1634. 55 p.; 4to. 1st publ., London, 1607. STC 23137; Arents (Add.) 277;
JCB (3) II:254. CSmH, DFo, IU, MB, NN-
RB, RPJCB; BL.   634/130

A strange metamorphosis of man . . . Deci-
phered in characters. *London: T. Harper; sold
by L. Chapman,* 1634. [212] p.; 12mo. In
character 12, 'The coalepit', Peru & Havana
are mentioned; the 36th discusses tobacco.
STC 3587; Murphy (Engl. char.-bks) p. 52;
Arents 189. CSmH, CtY, DLC, IU, MH,
NN-RB; BL.   634/131

Tapp, John. The seamans kalendar . . . [Fourteenth? impression. *London: B. Alsop & T. Fawcet, for J. Hurlock, 1634?*]. 4to. 1st publ., London, 1602. STC 23682.7. Horblit (lacks t.p.). 634/132

Taylor, John, the Water-poet. The needles excellency . . . The 10th edition inlarged. *London: J. Boler, 1634.* illus.; obl. 4to. In verse. 1st publ., London, 1631. STC 23776. CSmH. 634/133

Tomkis, Thomas. Albumazar. A comedy . . . Newly revised and corrected by a speciall hand. *London: N. Okes, 1634.* [82] p.; 4to. 1st publ., London, 1615. The catchword on lf D1r is 'O'. For anr edn dated 1634 see the year 1640. STC 24102; Greg 330 (c). CSmH, DLC, IU, MH, NNS, PU; BL. 634/134

Torsellino, Orazio, S.J. Ristretto dell'historie del mondo . . . volgarizzate dal sig. Lodovico Aurelii. *Rome: G. Mascardi, for P. Totti, 1634.* 575 p.; illus., port.; 12mo. Transl. from Latin text 1st publ., Rome, 1598; cf. 1620 edn. BL, BN. 634/135

Trophaeum hermetico-Hippocraticum post feliciter restauratus Thuringorum Hierosolymas . . . Homiliâ ecclesiasticâ, orationibus, quaestionibus & responsis chymiatricis . . . ornatum. *Erfurt: 1634.* 4to. Includes section on tobacco provided by Querinus Schmaltz describing its nature & therapeutic uses, based in part on Monardes. Arents 193. NN-A. 634/136

Untzer, Matthias. Tractatus medico-chymici septem. *Halle: M. Oelschlegel, 1634.* 2511 cols; 4to. On the bezoar stone Monardes is quoted; elsewhere formulas employing guaiacum, sarsaparilla, & sassafras are given. Wellcome I:6408. London: Wellcome, BN. 634/137

Venne, Adriaen van de. Sinne-vonck op den Hollandtschen turf . . . Hier noch by-gevoegt een vermakelijcken Hollandtschen sinne droom op het Nieuw wys-mal . . . mitsgaders de vindinge der tabacks wondersmoock. *The Hague: I. Burchoorn; sold by A. van de Venne & Heirs, 1634.* 2 pts; illus., port.; 16mo. In verse. In the author's *Sinne-vonck*, a farmer on a ship, having lighted his pipe, is thought by onlookers to be on fire. The *Nieuw wys-mal* is a fable on the propagation & beneficial uses of tobacco. Abkoude

525; Arents 194. MH, NN-A, NcD; BL, BN. 634/138

Vitoria Baraona, Francisco de. Señor, el capitan Francisco de Vitoria Baraona dize. [*Madrid: 1634?*]. fol. Memorial to king of Spain on management of Peruvian mines, etc. Sabin 100624. BL. 634/139

——. Señor. El capitan Francisco de Vitoria Baraona dize. [*Madrid? 1634?*] 6 numb. lvs; fol. Memorial addressed to king of Spain. Includes also 'Proposicion tocante a las dos naos que van todos los años del puerto de Acapulco . . . con el socorro a las islas Filippinas y las que baxan del Piru, y puerto del Callao de Lima, al dicho puerto de Acapulco.' Sabin 100625. BL. 634/140

White, Andrew. A relation of the successefull beginning of the Lord Baltemore's plantation. [*London?*] 1634. *See under title above.*

Wood, William. New Englands prospect. A true, lively, and experimentall description . . . discovering the state of that countrie, both as it stands to our new-come English planters; and to the old native inhabitants. *London: T. Cotes, for J. Bellamy, 1634.* 98 p.; map; 4to. Sabin 105074; Vail (Frontier) 87; STC 25957; Church 427; JCB (3) II:254. CSmH, CtY, DLC, MH, MiU-C, NN-RB, PHi, RPJCB; BL. 634/141

Young, Thomas. Englands bane: or, The description of drunkennesse. *London: W. J[ones]., for T. Bailey, 1634.* 8vo. 1st publ., London, 1617. STC 26117. DFo (imp.); BL. 634/142

Zacchia, Paulo. Quaestiones medico-legales, liber VI. *Rome: Heirs of G. Facciotti, 1634.* 256 p.; 4to. Includes passage on tobacco, noting American origin, & referring to Monardes. Continues Zacchia's bks 1–5, 1st publ., Rome, 1621–30. NNNAM. 634/143

Zacutus, Abraham, Lusitanus. De praxi medica admiranda. Libri tres. *Amsterdam: C. van Breughel, for H. Laurenszoon, 1634.* 492 p.; 8vo. In bk 1, Observatio xx treats 'Epileptici, syrupo Nicotianae curati'; in bk 3, Observatio xciv, 'De morbis novis. Morbus Brasiliensis, vermis dictus', also mentioning tobacco. DNLM, ICJ, PPPH. 634/144

1635

Abbot, George, Abp of Canterbury. A briefe description of the whole world. *London: [T. Harper?] for W. Sheares,* 1635. 350 p.; port.; 12mo. 1st publ., London, 1599. Sabin 21n; cf. STC 31. CtY, DLC, MH, NjP.
635/1

Advertencias para el papel de crecimiento de la plata. *[Madrid? ca. 1635?].* 17 numb. lvs; fol. Commentary on the *Medio* of this year below, with refs to silver received from New World. MH-BA; BL (Spain).
635/2

Antidotario romano latino, et volgare. Tradotto da Hippolito Cesarelli [i.e., Ceccarelli] . . . Con l'aggionta dell'electione de semplici. *Milan: G. B. Bidelli,* 1635. 2 pts; 4to. 1st publ. in this expanded version, Rome, 1612. DNLM.
635/3

Aviendo el marques de Cadereyta desalojado al enemigo Olandes desta isla de san Martin en primero de Julio de mil y seiscientos y treinta y tres años, venia en el armada don Cebrían de Lizaraçu [etc.]. *[Madrid? 1635?].* 14 numb. lvs; fol. Medina (BHA) 7792. Puebla: B. Palafoxiana.
635/4

Avity, Pierre d', sieur de Montmartin. Les estats, empires et principautez du monde. *Paris: A. Courbé,* 1635. 3 pts; port.; fol. 1st publ., Paris, 1613. Cf. Sabin 2498. CU; BL.
635/5

—[Anr issue]. *Paris: J. Jost,* 1635. Rome:BN.
635/6

Bacon, Francis, viscount St Albans. De dignitate et augmentis scientiarum . . . libri ix. *Strassburg: Heirs of L. Zetzner,* 1635. 500 p.; 8vo. 1st publ., London, 1623, under title *Opera: Tomus primus.* Gibson (Bacon) 131; Shaaber (Brit. auth.) B25. DFo, ICN, MH; BL, Vienna:NB.
635/7

——. Sylva sylvarum: or, A naturall historie. *London: J. Haviland for W. Lee, & sold by J. Williams,* 1635. 2 pts; port.; fol. 1st publ., 1627; includes also Bacon's *New Atlantis.* Gibson (Bacon) 174; STC 1172. CSmH, CtY, MH, NN-RB, PPAN, RPB; BL, BN.
635/8

Baillou, Guillaume de. Consiliorum medicinalium libri ii. a Jacobo Thevart . . . editi. *Paris: J. Quesnel,* 1635. 572 p.; 4to. Included are prescriptions employing guaiacum for

ailments other than syphilis; for syphilis itself both guaiacum & sarsaparilla are cited. Subsequent vols, not publ. till 1649, are without American refs. CLU-M, DNLM, PPL, WU; BL, BN.
635/9

Bate, John. The mysteries of nature and art . . . The second edition. *London: [T. Harper,] for R. Mabb,* 1635. 288 p.; illus.; 4to. 1st publ., London, 1634. STC 1578; Arents 195. CSmH, CtY, DLC, ICN, MH, MWA, MiU (imp.), NN-RB, PPL; BL.
635/10

Beaumont, Francis. The knight of the burning pestle. *London: N. O[kes]., for J. S[penser?].,* 1635. [77] p.; 4to. Comedy, written jointly with John Fletcher; 1st publ., London, 1613. STC 1675; Greg 316(b); Arents (Add.) 278. CSmH, CtY, DLC, ICN, MH, NN-RB, PU; BL.
635/11

—[Anr edn]. *London: N. [Okes]., for J. S[penser?].,* 1635. 4to. STC 1675a; Greg 316(c); Arents 196; Pforzheimer 49. CSmH, CtY, DFo, InU-L, MH, NN-A; BL.
635/12

——. The scornfull ladie. A comedy . . . The fourth edition. *London: A. M[athewes].,* 1635. 36 lvs; 4to. 1st publ., London, 1616. STC 1689; Greg 334(d). CSmH, CtY, DFo, ICN, MH; BL.
635/13

Betancurt, Luis de. Derecho de las iglesias metropolitanas i catedrales de las Indias, sobre que sus prelacias sean proveidas en los capitulares dellas, i naturales de sus provincias. *Madrid: F. Martínez,* 1635. 55 numb. lvs; 4to. 1st publ., Madrid, 1634, under title *Memorial y informacion por las iglesias metropolitanas.* Sabin 5063; Streit I:454. Palma:BP.
635/14

Beverwijck, Jan van. Lof der medicine. *Dordrecht: H. van Esch,* 1635. fol. Transl. from the author's *Medicinae encomium,* 1st publ., Dordrecht, 1633. Presumably includes the author's 'Bergh-val, ofte Wederlegginge van Michiel de Montaigne', which normally appeared as part of this work, with refs to Indians, tobacco, disease in West Indies, etc. Van de Velde 75; Catalogus van boeken VII:10.
635/15

Biancani, Giuseppe. Sphaera mundi, seu Cosmographia demonstrativa. *Modena: G. Cassiano,* 1635. 232 p.; illus.; fol. 1st publ., Bologna, 1620. Sabin 5132n. CtY, MH, MiU, NN-RB, PU.
635/16

Biondi, Sir Giovanni Francesco. Donzella

desterrada, or, The banish'd virgin. Written originally in Italian . . . and Englished by J. H. *London: T. Cotes, for H. Moseley,* 1635. 235 p.; fol. Translator's preface mentions 'the savage American'. STC 3074. CSmH, CtY, DLC, ICN, MH, MnU, PU; BL.

                635/17

Blaeu, Willem Janszoon. Ander Theil Novi atlantis. *Amsterdam:* 1635. See Blaeu's *Novus atlas* below.

——. Le nouveau phalot de la mer. *Amsterdam: J. Janszoon, the Younger,* 1635. 2 v.; illus., maps; obl. fol. Transl. from Blaeu's *Het nieuw vermeerde licht,* as revised by Joris Carolus, Amsterdam, 1634; cf. Blaeu's *Le flambeau de la navigation,* 1st publ., Amsterdam, 1619. Koeman (M.Bl) 25A (J); Kebabian 323. CtY.   635/18

——. Novus atlas, das ist, Abbildung und Beschreibung van allen Ländern des Erdreichs. *Amsterdam: W. J. [& J.] Blaeu,* 1635. 2 v.; maps; fol. 1st publ., Amsterdam, 1634; here added is the *Ander Theil,* with map of 'Nova Belgica et Anglia Nova' & supporting text. In this edn, v. 1 has 155 maps. Koeman (Bl) 5–6. CCC (v. 1); Amsterdam:UB, Munich:StB.   635/19

—[Anr edn]. *Amsterdam: W. J. [& J.] Blaeu,* 1635. 2 v.; maps; fol. The maps of the preceding edn are here differently arranged in both volumes, with some additional maps. Here, v. 1 has 109 maps; the American maps are largely allocated to the 2nd volume in this edn. Koeman (Bl) 7A–8A; Phillips (Atlases) 5933. DLC; Vienna:NB, Stuttgart:LB.   635/20

——. The sea-mirror. *Amsterdam: W. J. Blaeu,* 1635. 3 pts; illus., maps; fol. 1st publ. in this English translation, Amsterdam, 1625. Koeman (M.Bl) 49. Oxford:Bodl., The Hague:KB.   635/21

——. Le theatre du monde, ou Nouvel atlas. *Amsterdam: W. J. & J. Blaeu,* 1635. 105 maps; fol. Cf. pt 1 of Blaeu's German version of this year, the *Novus atlas, das ist Abbildung* above. Includes map of America, with accompanying text. Issued with Blaeu's *Le theatre . . . seconde partie* below. Koeman (Bl) 11. DLC, MiU-C; BL, BN.   635/22

——. Le theatre du monde, ou Nouvel atlas . . . Seconde partie. *Amsterdam: W. J. & J. Blaeu,* 1635. 103 maps; fol. Cf. pt 2 of

Blaeu's German version of this year, the *Novus atlas, das ist Abbildung* above. Includes various American maps. Issued with Blaeu's *Le theatre* above. Koeman (Bl) 12. DLC, MiU-C; BL, BN.   635/23

——. Theatrum orbis terrarum, sive Atlas novus. *Amsterdam: W. J. & J. Blaeu,* 1635. 105 maps; fol. Cf. pt 1 of Blaeu's German version of this year, the *Novus atlas, das ist Abbildung* above. Includes map of America, with accompanying text. Issued with Blaeu's *Theatrum . . . pars secunda* below. Koeman (Bl) 13. CLU (imp.), DLC, ICJ, MiU-C; Amsterdam:UB, Milan:BN.   635/24

——. Theatrum orbis terrarum, sive Atlas novus, pars secunda. *Amsterdam: W. J. & J. Blaeu,* 1635. 102 maps; fol. Cf. pt 2 of Blaeu's German version of this year, the *Novus atlas, das ist Abbildung* above. Includes various American maps. Issued with Blaeu's *Theatrum* above. Koeman (Bl) 14. CLU (imp.), DLC, ICJ, MiU-C; Amsterdam:UB, Milan:BN.   635/25

——. Toonneel des aerdriicx; ofte Nieuwe atlas. *Amsterdam: W. J. & J. Blaeu,* 1635. 104 maps; fol. Cf. pt 1 of Blaeu's German version of this year, the *Novus atlas, das ist Abbildung* above. Here included is a world map showing America; the introduction includes refs to Brazil, Peru, Paraguay, etc. Issued with Blaeu's *Tweede deel van't toonneel* below. Sabin 5721; Koeman (Bl) 9; Phillips (Atlases) 448; Tiele 130. DLC, MH; Amsterdam: UB, Louvain:UB.   635/26

——. Tweede deel van't toonneel des aerdriicx, ofte Nieuwe atlas. *Amsterdam: W. J. & J. Blaeu,* 1635. 103 maps; fol. Cf. pt 2 of Blaeu's German version of this year, the *Novus atlas, das ist Abbildung* above. Includes a variety of American maps. Issued with Blaeu's *Toonneel des aerdriicx* above. Sabin 5721; Koeman (Bl) 10; Phillips (Atlases) 448; cf. Tiele 130. DLC, MH, RPJCB; BN, Amsterdam:UB, Louvain:UB.   635/27

Boccalini, Traiano. Pierre de touched [*sic*] ou Satyres du temp. *Paris: J. Villery & J. Guignard,* 1635. 250 p.; 8vo. 1st publ. as here transl., Paris, 1626. ICN, MH; BN.

                635/28

Botero, Giovanni. The cause of the greatnesse of cities. Three bookes. With certaine observations concerning the sea. Written in Italian . . . and translated . . . by Sir T[homas]. H[awkins]. *London: E[lizabeth]. P[urslowe]., for H. Seile,* 1635. 236 p.; 12mo. The 'Observations concerning the sea,' with geographic refs to New World, were transl. from Botero's *Aggiunte fatte . . . alla sua Ragion di stato,* 1st publ., Rome, 1598; cf. 1606 edn above. STC 3396; JCB (3) II:255. CSmH, CtY, DFo, ICN, MH-BA, NNC, RPJCB; Oxford:Bodl. 635/29

Brerewood, Edward. Enquiries touching the diversity of languages and religions. *London: J. Norton, for Joyce Norton & R. Whitaker,* 1635. 203 p.; 4to. 1st publ., London, 1614. Sabin 7732; STC 3621. CSmH, CtY, DFo, ICN, MH, MnU-B, NN-RB, PU, RPJCB; BL. 635/30

Buck, George. The great Plantagenet, or, A continued succession of the royal name. *London: N. & J. Okes,* 1635. [54] p.; 4to. Preface mentions Madoc's purported discovery of West Indies; cf. Caradog of Llancarvan's *Historie of Cambria,* London, 1584. STC 3997. CSmH, CtY, DFo, ICN, MH, NjP; BL. 635/31

Camden, William. Annals, or The historie of . . . Princesse Elizabeth. *London: T. Harper, for B. Fisher,* 1635. 586 p.; port.; fol. 1st publ. as here transl. by Robert Norton, London, 1630. Sabin 10158; STC 4501. CSmH, DFo, ICU, MH, NN-RB, PU, RPB: BL. 635/32

Carpenter, Nathaniel. Geographie delineated forth in two bookes . . . The second edition corrected. *Oxford: J. Lichfield, for H. Cripps,* 1635. 2 v.; illus.; 4to. 1st publ., Oxford, 1625. Cf. Sabin 10999; Madan (Oxford) 1635:2; STC 4677; JCB (3) II:255. CSmH, CtY, DFo, ICU, MH, NN-RB, RPJCB; BL. 635/33

Cats, Jacob. Monita amoris virginei. *Amsterdam: W. J. Blaeu* [ca. 1635]. 4to. 1st publ., Middelburg, 1618, under title *Maechdenplicht.* Mus. Cats. 63. 635/34

Clüver, Philipp. Introductionis in universam geographiam, tam veterem quàm novam, libri vi. *Paris: M. Soly,* 1635. 360 p.; illus.; 16mo. 1st publ., Leyden, 1624. Cf. Sabin 13805. BN. 635/35

—[Anr issue]. *Paris: J. Libert,* 1635. BN. 635/36

Cornut, Jacques Philippe. Canadensium plantarum, aliarumque nondum editarum historia. *Paris: S. LeMoine,* 1635. 238 p.; illus.; 4to. Sabin 16809; Harrisse (NF) 59; Pritzel 1894; Nissen (Bot.) 406; JCB (3) II:255. CU, CtY, DLC, MH, MiU, MnU-B, NN-RB, PPAmP, RPJCB; BL, BN. 635/37

Croll, Oswald. Basilica chymica . . . Additus est . . . Tractatus novus de signaturis rerum internis. *Geneva: P. Chouët,* 1635. 3 pts; illus.; 8vo. 1st publ., Frankfurt a. M., 1609. CtY-M, DNLM, MH, WU; BL, BN. 635/38

Davenant, Sir William. The triumphs of the Prince d'Amour. A masque. *London: [M. Parsons,] for R. Meighen,* 1635. 16 p.; 4to. The opening episode has for setting a village of alehouses and tobacco shops, with 'black Indian Boyes . . . bestriding roles [*sic*] of tobacco'. STC 6308; Greg 502; Arents (Add.) 279. CSmH, CtY, DFo, MB, MiU; BL. 635/39

Díez de Auxarmendáriz, Lope, marqués de Cadereyta. Por Don Lope Diez de Aux Armendariz marques de Cadereita . . . capitan general de la Real Armada de la guarda de la Carrera de las Indias. Con el . . . fiscal del Real Consejo de las Indias. [i.e., C. de Moscoso y Cordova]. [*Madrid?* 1635?]. 56 numb. lvs; fol. BL. 635/40

——. Por Don Lope Diez de Auxarmendariz marques de Cadereita . . . capitan general de la Real Armada de la guarda de la carrera de las Indias. Sobre los cargos de la residencia del dicho oficio. [*Madrid?* 1635?]. 51 numb. lvs; fol. BL. 635/41

Donne, John. Ignatius his conclave. *London: J. Marriott; sold by W. Sheares,* 1635. 135 p.; 12mo. 1st publ. as transl. from Donne's *Conclave Ignatii* of same year, London, 1611; here anr issue of 1634 edn with in-press alteration of imprint date. Keynes (Donne) 9; STC 7030. CSmH, CtY, DLC, ICN, MH, MnU, NjPT; BL. 635/42

——. Poems. *London: M. F[letcher]., for J. Marriott,* 1635. 388 p.; port.; 8vo. Includes Donne's *An anatomie of the world,* 1st publ., London, 1611. STC 7046; Keynes (Donne) 79. CSmH, CtY, DFo, ICN, MH, NNC, PU; BL. 635/43

Drake, Sir Francis. The world encompassed

by Sir Francis Drake being his next voyage to that to Nombre de Dios . . . carefully collected out of the notes of Master Francis Fletcher. *London: E[lizabeth]. P[urslowe]., for N. Bourne,* 1635. 90 p.; 4to. 1st publ., London, 1628. Sabin 20854; Wagner (SW) 31a; STC 7132; Church 428; JCB (3) II:256. DLC, MH, RPJCB; BL.   635/44

Dupleix, Scipion. La curiosité naturelle. *Rouen: C. Malassis,* 1635. 474 p.; 12mo. 1st publ., Paris, 1606. BN.   635/45

Du Rocher, R.M. L'Indienne amoureuse, ou L'heureux naufrage Tragi-comedie. *Paris: J. Corrozet,* 1635. 133 p.; 8vo. In verse. The characters are designated as Peruvian, Mexican, & Florida royalty, etc. Cioranescu (XVII) 27903. MnU-B, OCU; BN.
635/46

Fox, Luke. North-West Fox, or Fox from the North-west passage . . . Following with briefe abstracts of the voyages of Cabot, Frobisher . . . Mr. James Hall's three voyages to Groynland. *London: B. Alsop & T. Fawcet,* 1635. 269 p.; illus., map; 4to. Sabin 25410; STC 11221; Church 429; JCB (3) II:256. CSmH, CtY, DLC, ICN, InU-L, MH, MWA, MiU-C, MnU-B, NN-RB, PPL, RPJCB; BL.   635/47

Gellibrand, Henry. A discourse mathematical of the variation of the magneticall needle. *London: W. Jones,* 1635. 22 p.; 4to. Mentioned are the 'streights of Magellan' & 'the backe parts of America in the South Sea', etc. STC 11712. DFo, ICJ, MH, NNE; BL, Oxford:Bodl.   635/48

Góngora y Argote, Luis de. Todas las obras. *Madrid: Maria de Quiñones,* 1635. 438 p.; 4to. In verse. 1st publ., Madrid, 1627. Palau 104627n.   635/49

Great Britain. Laws, statutes, etc., 1625–1649 (Charles I). The rates of marchandizes: as they are set downe in the Booke of rates. *London: R. Barker & assigns of J. Bill,* 1635. [110] p.; 8vo. 1st publ., London [1611?]. STC 7695; Kress 510. CSmH, MH-BA.   635/50

Grotius, Hugo. Drie boecken . . . nopende het recht des oorloghs ende des vredes . . . Eerst in 't Latijn uyt-gegeven, ende nu . . . vertaelt, door H.V. *Haarlem: A. Roman,* 1635. 401 [i.e., 421] p.; port.; 4to. Transl. from Grotius's *De jure belli ac pacis,* 1st

publ., Paris, 1625. Meulen/Diermanse 620. DLC, NN-RB, NNC; The Hague:PP.
635/51

Hakewill, George. An apologie or declaration of the power and providence of God in the government of the world . . . The third edition revised. *Oxford: W. Turner, for R. Allott, at London,* 1635. 2 pts; fol. 1st publ., Oxford, 1627. STC 12613; Madan (Oxford) I:1635:9. CSmH, CtY, DFo, ICN, MH, MiU, NNC, PU; BL.   635/52

Hartmann, Johann (1568–1631). Praxis chymiatrica. *Geneva: J. de Tournes & J. de La Pierre,* 1635. 2 pts; 8vo. 1st publ., Leipzig, 1633. NN; BN.   635/53

—[Anr issue]. *Geneva: P. Chouët,* 1635. Wellcome I:3066. London: Wellcome.
635/54

Hay, Paul, sieur du Chastelet (1592–1636), ed. Le mercure d'estat. *Geneva: P. Aubert,* 1635. 484 p.; 8vo. 1st publ., Geneva, 1634; here a reissue? BN.   635/55

—[Anr issue?]. [*Paris:*] 1635. ICN, NNC; BL (Mercury).   635/56

——. Recueil de diverses pieces pour servir a l'histoire. [*Paris:*] 1635. 922 p.; fol. Includes J. Du Ferrier's *Le Catholique d'estat, ou Discours politique* (1st publ., Paris, 1625), with refs to Spanish cruelties in Indies, citing example of Atabalipa. Minor refs to Spanish West Indies occur in other pts of the collection. Cioranescu (XVII) 35054. CtY, ICU, MiU, RPB; BL, BN.   635/57

Heywood, Thomas. Philocothonista, or The drunkard. *London: R. Raworth,* 1635. 91 p.; 4to. In chapt. xii tobacco is mentioned. STC 13356. CSmH, DFo, MH, TxU; BL.
635/58

Hieron, Samuel. The workes. *London: W. Stansby & J. Beale* [1635,'34]. 2 v.; fol. Included in v. 1 is Hieron's *An answer to a popish rime,* 1st publ., London, 1604. STC 13384. CtY, DFo, ICU, MH; BL.
635/59

Hoffer, Adriaan. Nederduytsche poemata. *Amsterdam: B. Janszoon,* 1635. 400 p.; illus.; 4to. Includes poems on Pieter Hein & capture of the Spanish silver fleet. Sabin 32382; Rodrigues (Dom. Hol.) 893; cf. Molhuysen VI:790. DLC, ICN, NNC; BL, BN.
635/60

Jones, John (fl. 1635). Adrasta: or, The

womans spleene . . . A tragi-comedie. *London:* [*M. Fletcher?*] *for R. Royston,* 1635. [88] p.; 4to. In act 2, scene 1, is described 'a swaggering wench that will take Tobacco eight and forty times in four and twenty houres'; in act 4, scene 1, potatoes are mentioned. STC 14721; Greg 501; Arents (Add.) 280. CSmH, CtY, DLC, ICN, MH, NN-A, PU; BL. 635/61

Lampe, Barent. Het eenentwintichste deel of 't vervolgh van het Historisch verhael aller gedencwaerdiger gheschiedenissen, die in Europa . . . in America als West-Indien en d'eijlanden . . . voorgevallen zijn. *Amsterdam: J. Janszoon, the Younger,* 1635. 174 numb. lvs; illus.; 4to. (N. van Wassenaer's *Historisch verhael.* Pt 21). Includes refs to ships of the West-Indische Compagnie, Mexico, Pernambuco, and a naval battle off the Brazilian coast. Cf. Sabin 102039; Borba de Moraes II:371–72; Muller (1872) 1745. RPJCB. 635/62

Le Jeune, Paul, S.J. Relation de ce qui s'est passé en la Nouvelle France, en l'annee 1634. *Paris: S. Cramoisy,* 1635. 342 p.; 8vo. In this edn blank lvs follow p. 342. For variant states, see McCoy as cited. Sabin 39949; Harrisse (NF) 60; Streit II:2501; Backer IV:795; Church 430; Bell (Jes. rel) 2; McCoy 10–13; JCB (3) II:257. CSmH, CtY, DLC, InU-L, MH, MiU-C, MnU-B, NN-RB, RPJCB; BL, Paris:Mazarine. 635/63

—[Anr edn]. *Paris: S. Cramoisy,* 1635. 342 p.; 8vo. In this edn a 'Privilege' appears on lf following p. 342. Sabin 39949; Harrisse (NF) 61; Bell (Jes. rel.) 3; McCoy 14; Streit II:2501; Church 431. CSmH, MnU-B, NN-RB, MiU-C, MnU-B. 635/64

Lenton, Francis. The puisne gallants progresse. *London:* 1635. 22 p.; 4to. In verse. 1st publ., London, 1629, under title *The young gallants whirligigg;* here a reissue of that edn with cancel t.p. & dedication. STC 15467.5. Robert Taylor, Princeton, N.J. 635/65

León Garavito, Andrés de. Memorial discursivo, en que se muestra la obligacion que V. Magestad tiene en justicia, conciencia, y razon politica de reformar el govierno de la provincia del Rio de la Plata, y otros de las Indias. *Madrid: Widow of J. González,*

1635. 72 numb. lvs; fol. Medina (BHA) 944; Palau 135591. Santiago, Chile:BN. 635/66

Liñán y Verdugo, Antonio. Guia y avisos de forasteros, adonde se les enseña a huir de los peligros que ay en la vida de corte. *Valencia: S. Esparsa, for J. Sonzonio,* 1635. 148 numb. lvs; 8vo. 1st publ., Madrid, 1620. Palau 138647. NNH; BL. 635/67

Malpaeus, Petrus, O.P. Palma fidei s. Ordinis praedicatorum. *Antwerp: J. Cnobbaert,* 1635. 314 p.; 8vo. Included are accounts of Dominicans who found martyrdom in America & elsewhere. Streit I:461. BN. 635/68

Mariana, Juan de, S.J. Historia general de España. *Madrid: F. Martínez,* 1635. 2 v.; fol. Transl., rev. & augm. by the author from his *Historiae de rebus Hispaniae,* 1st publ., Toledo, 1592; cf. 1601 edn. Cf. Sabin 44546; Backer V:550; Palau 151670. RPJCB, WU; BN. 635/69

Márquez de Cisneros, ——. Por Don Lope de Hozes y Cordova, del Consejo de Guerra de su Magestad . . . Capitan general de la armada real que partio la buelta del Brasil . . . Sobre los quatro cargos remitidos en discordia, de la residencia que se le tomò de la flota de la Nueva España, del año passado de 634. *Madrid: Widow of J. González,* 1635. 28 numb. lvs; fol. Medina (BHA) 7794. Puebla: B. Palafoxiana. 635/70

Márquez de Torres, Francisco. Medio suave y facil para impossibilitar a los estrangeros la introduccion de moneda de vellon falsa. [*Madrid?* ca. 1635?]. 10 numb. lvs; fol. Mentioned are the Indians of Mexico & Peru, & also cacao, citing José de Acosta. BL. 635/71

Mayerne, Louis Turquet de. Histoire generale d'Espagne. *Paris: S. Thiboust,* 1635. 3 v.; fol. 1st publ., Geneva, 1587; cf. 1608 edn. Cf. Sabin 47117. ICN, ICU, NNH; BL, BN. 635/72

Medio que el reyno propone para el consumo del vellon, y las razones que le mueven a ello. [*Madrid?* ca. 1635?]. 11 numb. lvs; fol. A discussion of Spain's monetary problems involving Spanish America. Kress 222. MH-BA; BL (Spain. Cortes). 635/73

Memorial de advertencias convenientes

para esta monarquia. [*Madrid?* ca. 1635?].
18 numb. lvs; fol. On Spanish monetary
problems, discussing gold & silver of New
World. BL. 635/74

Mendoça, Francisco de, S.J. Viridarium sacrae profanae eruditionis. *Lyons: G. Boissat,*
1635. 350 p.; fol. 1st publ., Lyons, 1631.
Backer V:901; Palau 163630n. 635/75

Mendoça, Lourenço de. Memorial a Su Magestad . . . en razon de la seguridad de
su plata, y armada del Piru, y de los galeones de Tierrafirme. [*Madrid?* 1635?]. 10
numb. lvs; fol. BL. 635/76

Mercator, Gerardus. Atlas, ou Representation du monde universel . . . divisé en deux
tomes. Edition nouvelle. Augmenté d'un
appendice de plusieurs nouvelles tables
. . . de diverses regions d'Allemaigne . . .
et de l'une et l'autre Indie. *Amsterdam: H.
Hondius,* 1635. 1 v.; maps; fol. 1st publ. in
this enlarged version, Amsterdam, 1633. Of
this edn., only v. 1 is known. Koeman (Me)
40. BN (v. 1). 635/77

——. Historia mundi, or Mercator's atlas
. . . enlarged by Judocus Hondy . . . Englished by W[ye]. S[altonstall]. *London: T.
Cotes, for M. Sparke & S. Cartwright,* 1635.
930 p.; illus., maps; fol. Transl. from Mercator's *Atlas minor,* 1st publ., Amsterdam,
1607. Cf. Sabin 47885; Koeman II:549 &
(Me) 41A(n); cf. Phillips (Atlases) 4255 &
451; STC 17824; JCB (3) II: 257–58. CtY,
DFo, ICN, InU, MH (imp.), NN-RB, RPJCB;
BL, Oxford:Bodl. 635/78

—[Anr issue]. *London: T. Cotes, for M. Sparke,*
1635. STC 17824.5. CSmH, DFo; BL.
635/79

—[Anr issue?]. *London: M. Sparke,* 1635. Sabin
32750; Koeman II:549n. 635/80

Meteren, Emanuel van. Historie der Nederlandscher ende haerder na-buren oorlogen
ende geschiedenissen . . . verbetert en in
xxxii boecken voltrocken. *The Hague: Widow
& Heirs of H. Jacobszoon van Wouw,* 1635.
[1368] p.; map; fol. 1st publ. in Dutch,
Delft, 1599; cf. years 1605 & 1610. BL,
Amsterdam:NHSM. 635/81

——. Meterani novi continuatio, das ist:
Warhafftige Beschreibung aller denckwürdigsten Geschichten. *Amsterdam: W.
Blaeu,* 1635. 713 p.; illus., ports; fol. Continues the author's *Meteranus novus, das ist: War-*

hafftige Beschreibung, Amsterdam, 1633.
Bruckner 62. Amsterdam: UB (imp.), Stockholm:KB. 635/82

Monet, Philibert, S.J. Invantaire des deus
langues, françoise et latine. *Lyons: Widow of
C. Rigaud & P. Borde,* 1635. 990 p.; fol. 1st
publ., Paris, 1628, under title *Nouveau et dernier dictionaire.* Backer V:1211. BL, BN.
635/83

Montaigne, Michel Eyquem de. Essais.
Paris: J. Camusat, 1635. 871 p.; fol. 1st publ.,
Bordeaux, 1580; cf. 1602 edn. Tchémerzine
VIII:428. DFo, ICN, MH, MiU, MnU, NjP;
BL, BN. 635/84

—[Anr issue]. *Paris: T. DuBray & P. Rocolet,*
1635. CLU, CtY, MH; BN. 635/85

—[Anr issue]. *Paris: P. Rocolet,* 1635.
Tchémerzine VIII:428. MWiW-C; BN.
635/86

Moscoso y de Córdoba, Cristóbal de. Alegacion en derecho en competencia de jurisdicion, entre el Consejo Real y de las Ordenes. *Madrid: Widow of J. González,* 1635.
7 numb. lvs; fol. Sabin 51041. BL.
635/87

——. Discurso legal militar . . . contra Francisco Diez Pimienta, almirante de la Flota
de Nueva España. Sobre aver desamparado
las naos saltando à la obligacion de su oficio, y causando cogiera una los enemigos,
y otros graves daños. [*Madrid:* 1635?]. [35]
p.; fol. Sabin 51042; Medina (BHA) 8265.
RPJCB. 635/88

——. El l[icendia]do Don Christoval de Moscoso y Cordova . . . fiscal en Real de las
Indias, en defensa de su jurisdiccion, con
Don Martin Carrillo de Aldrete del Consejo
de la . . . Inquisicion, visitador de la Nueva
España, y obispo de Oviedo . . . sobre el
pleyto con don Juan Blazquez Mayoralgo,
y Diego de Valle Alvarado, contador y tesorero, juezes, oficiales reales de la Veracruz. [*Madrid:* 1635?]. 6 numb. lvs; fol.
Sabin 51043n; Medina (BHA) 8264. BL.
635/89

——. Señor. La resolucion de V. Magestad.
[*Madrid: Widow of J. González?* 1635?]. 16
numb. lvs; fol. Memorial to king of Spain
on ecclesiastical affairs of Curaçao. Sabin
51044. BL. 635/90

Nederlandsche West Indische Compagnie.
Extract uyt den brief vande politijcque rae-

den in Brasil aen de . . . West-Indische Compagnie, over de veroveringe vande stadt Philippia nu Frederickstadt . . . inde capitania van Paraiba. *The Hague: Widow & Heirs of H. Jacobszoon van Wouw,* 1635. [4] p.; 4to. Sabin 7579; Borba de Moraes I:257; Rodrigues (Dom. Hol.) 193; Knuttel 4384. DLC; The Hague:KB. 635/91

Netherlands (United Provinces, 1581–1795). Staten Generaal. Nader ordre ende Reglement vande . . . Staten Generael . . . gearresteert by advijs ende deliberatie vande bewint-hebberen vande . . . West-Indische Compagnie. *The Hague: Widow & Heirs of H. Jacobszoon van Wouw,* 1635. [5] p.; 4to. Concerns trade in tobacco & other wares. Cf. Sabin 51705. OCl. 635/92

—[Anr edn]. [*Amsterdam?* 1635]. bds.; fol. Sabin 51705 (& 102899). 635/93

Nieremberg, Juan Eusebio, S.J. Historia naturae, maximae peregrinae, libris xvi. distincta. *Antwerp: Plantin Office (B. Moretus),* 1635. 502 p.; illus.; fol. Deals largely with the natural history of Mexico, with discussion of passionflower, p. 299ff. Sabin 55268; Pritzel 6701; Nissen (Zool.) 2974; Backer V:1736; Arents 3278 (IV:416); JCB (3) II:258. CLU-C, CtY, DLC, InU-L, MH-A, MiU, MnU, NN-A, PU-Mus, RPJCB; BL, BN. 635/94

Olearius, Adam. Lustige Historie, woher das Toback-Trincken kommt, etwas nach dem Niederländischen beschrieben durch Ascanium de Oliva. *Leipzig:* 1635. Said to be a loose translation of Rowlands's poem 'To smokey noses, and stinking nostrils', 1st publ., London, [1613], in that author's *More knaves yet?*—Arents. Lohmeier (Olearius) 8; cf. Arents 224. 635/95

Pagitt, Ephraim. Christianographie. or The description of the multitude and sundry sorts of Christians in the world not subject to the Pope. *London: T. P[aine]. & W. J[ones]., for M. Costerden,* 1635. 2 pts; maps; 4to. 'America and the Christians therein': p. 53–54. STC 19110; McAlpin I:481. CSmH, CtY, DLC, InU-L, MH, NNUT (imp.), PPL, RPJCB; BL, BN. 635/96

Paré, Ambroise. Wund Artzney oder Artzney spiegell . . . Von Petro Uffenbach . . . auss der lateinischen edition Jacobi Guillemeau . . . transferirt und gesetzt. Und nun zum andernmal in Truck verfertiget. *Frankfurt a. M.: K Rötel, for Heirs of J. Fischer,* 1635. 984 p.; illus., ports; fol. 1st publ. as here transl., Frankfurt a. M., 1601. Doe (Paré) 57. DNLM; Wolfenbüttel:HB. 635/97

Parkinson, John. Paradisi in sole paradisus terrestris. Or a garden of . . . flowers. *London: T. Cotes; sold by R. Royston,* 1635. 612 p.; illus.; fol. 1st publ., London, 1629; here reissued with letterpress t.p. added. STC 19301; Henrey (Brit. bot.) 284; Arents 197. NN-A. 635/98

Pedrera, Andrés. Andres Pedrera, ensayador mayor, y visitador del oro, y plata destos reynos. [*Madrid?* ca. 1635?]. [8] p.; fol. In discussion of Spain's monetary problems, copper coming from Havana is mentioned. BL. 635/99

Person, David. Varieties: or, A surveigh of rare and excellent matters. *London: R. Badger [& T. Cotes], for T. Alchorn,* 1635. 2 pts; 4to. In bk 4, sect. 11, to Columbus's 'practicall-curiosity' is attributed his discovery 'of the new World of America'. STC 19781; Wellcome I:4918. CSmH, CtY, DLC, ICN, MH, MiU, MnU, NN-RB, PU; BL. 635/100

Postel, Guillaume. De universitate libri duo: in quibus astronomiae, doctrinaeve coelistis compendium . . . Editio tertia. *Leyden: J. Maire,* 1635. 261 p.; port.; 12mo. 1st publ., Paris, 1552. Includes section 'Devisio terrae', referring to New World; 'De regionibus extra Priscorum cognitionem' includes American refs. CSmH, CtY, DLC, MH, MiU, NN; BN. 635/101

Potier, Pierre. Pharmacopoea spagirica . . . Tertia editio. *Bologna: G. Monti & C. Zenaro,* 1635. 387 (i.e., 427) p.; illus., port.; 4to. Included is Potier's *Insignium curationum . . . centuria secunda,* 1st publ., Bologna, 1622. Cf. 1624 Cologne work with above title; a presumptive 2nd edn has not been located. DNLM; BN. 635/102

Powell, Thomas (1572?–1635?). The art of thriving. *London:* 1635. *See the year* 1636.

Quarles, Francis. Emblemes. *London: G. M[iller]., sold by J. Marriott,* 1635. 307 p.; illus.; 8vo. In verse. Included is an emblem depicting a cupid smoking a pipe, with verses derived from poem by Gilles Pellier in *Typus mundi* produced by the Jesuits at

Antwerp. In this edn p. 46, 92, 200, 268, & 280 are misnumbered. Normally issued with this was E. Benlowe's *Quarleis.* STC 20540; Horden (Quarles) X, 1. CSmH, CtY, ICN, MH, NN-RB; BL. 635/103

—[Anr edn]. *London: G. M[iller]., sold by J. Marriott,* 1635. 307 p.; illus.; 8vo. Without the errors in paging of the foregoing. STC 20540.5; Horden (Quarles) X, 2; Arents (Add.) 281; Pforzheimer 811. CSmH, DFo, MB; BL. 635/104

Ramón, Tómas. Nueva prematica de reformacion, contra los abusos de los afeytes, calçado . . . y excesso en el uso del tabaco. *Saragossa: D. Dormer,* 1635. 390 p.; 8vo. Theological reasons for avoiding excesses, directed against clergy. Jiménez Catalan (Saragossa) 341; Palau 247399; Arents 198. NN-A, OCl, WU; BL, BN. 635/105

Randolph, Thomas. Aristippus, or The joviall philosopher . . . To which is added, The conceited pedlar. *London: [Elizabeth Purslowe,] for R. Allot,* 1635. 44 p.; 4to. Drama. 1st publ., London, 1630. STC 20689; Greg 431/432(f); Pforzheimer 826. CSmH, DFo, MWiW-C, TxU; BL. 635/106

—[Anr edn]. *Dublin: Society of Stationers* [1635?]. 37 p.; 4to. STC 20690; Greg 431/432(c). BL (imp.). 635/107

A relation of Maryland; together with a map of that countrey, the conditions of plantation, His Magesties charter to the Lord Baltemore. *[London:] W. Peasley & J. Morgan,* 1635. 2 pts; map; 4to. 1st publ., [London? 1634], under title *A relation of the successefull beginnings of the Lord Baltemore's plantation in Maryland.* Sabin 45314; STC 17571; Baer (Md) 22; Church 432; JCB (3) II:257. CSmH, DLC, ICN, MH, MiU-C, MnU-L, NN-RB, RPJCB (imp.); BL. 635/108

Rijpen raedt ende Salighe resolutie. 'The Hague' [i.e., *Antwerp]:* 1635. 16 p.; 4to. Includes refs to the West Indies, characterizing commerce there as piracy. Knuttel 4394; Meulman 2335. InU-L, NN; The Hague:KB, Ghent:BU. 635/109

—[Anr edn]. 'The Hague' [i.e., *Antwerp]:* 1635. 15 p.; 4to. This edn has reading 'Salige resolutie' on t.p. Meulman 2336; Petit 1916. Ghent:BU, Leyden:B. Thysiana. 635/110

Ritratti et elogii di capitani illustri che ne' secoli moderni hanno gloriosamente guerreggiato. *Rome: A Fei, for P. Totti,* 1635. 295 p.; 4to. Based on A. Capriolo's *Ritratti di cento capitani illustri,* Rome, 1596 & 1600. Included is a port. & account of Columbus. Cf. Sabin 71587. CtY, ICN, NN-RB; BL. 635/111

Saint-Amant, Marc Antoine de Gérard, sieur de. Les oeuvres. *Paris: N. Trabouillet,* 1635. 2 pts; 8vo. In verse. 1st publ., Paris, 1629. Tchémerzine X:83. 635/112

Sandoval y Guzman, Sebastian de. El doctor don Sebastian de Sandoval y Guzman, procurador general de . . . Potosi, digo, que de pedimiento mio embio V. A. orden por el mes de Junio deste presente año de 635. a los juezes de la Casa de Contratacion de Sevilla, para hacer ciertas diligencias en razon de la ley con que vienen ensayadas las barras del Perù [etc.]. *[Madrid?* 1635]. 7 numb. lvs; fol. Medina (BHA) 7797. RPJCB; Puebla:B. Palafoxiana. 635/113

Selden, John. Mare clausum, seu De dominio maris libri duo. *London: W. Stansby, for R. Meighen,* 1635. 304 p.; illus., map; fol. A reply to Hugo Grotius's *Mare liberum,* Leyden, 1609. Includes refs to America, Greenland, etc. Sabin 78971; Meulen/Diermanse, p. 212; STC 22175. CSmH, DFo, ICN, MH, NNC, RPJCB; BL, BN. 635/114

Serres, Olivier de, seigneur du Pradel. Le theatre d'agriculture. *Rouen: R. Valentin,* 1635. 908 p.; illus.; 8vo. 1st publ., Paris, 1600; cf. 1603 edn. MH. 635/115

Swan, John. Speculum mundi. or A glasse representing the face of the world. *Cambridge: T. Buck & R. Daniel,* 1635. 504 p.; 4to. In 'The third dayes work', chapt. 3, sect. 3, the origin of the New World is discussed; in chapt. 6, sect. 4, tobacco & its American sources, etc. STC 23516; Arents 199; McAlpin I:484. CSmH, CtY, DLC, ICN, MH, MiU, NN-RB; BL. 635/116

Taylor, John, the Water-poet. An armado, or navy, of 103. ships & other vessels. *London: E. A[llde]., for H. Gosson,* 1635. [54] p.; 8vo. 1st publ., London, 1627; in part reprinted from same setting of type. STC 23726a. MH; Oxford:Bodl. 635/117

——. An arrant thiefe. *London: [A. Mathewes,] for H. Gosson,* 1635. 8vo. In verse. 1st publ.,

London, 1621. STC 23730. CSmH, MH; Oxford:Bodl. 635/118

——. A bawd. A vertuous bawd, a modest bawd. *London: [A. Mathewes?] for H. Gosson,* 1635. [45] p.; 8vo. Describes syphilis as brought to France from Naples where it had been introduced from America by the Spanish. STC 23731. CSmH; Oxford:Bodl. 635/119

——. A common whore. *London: [A. Mathewes,] for H. Gosson,* 1635. 8vo. In verse. 1st publ., London, 1622. STC 23744. CSmH; Oxford:Bodl. 635/120

——. The olde, old, very olde man. *London: [A. Mathewes,] for H. Gosson,* 1635. 15 lvs; port.; 4to. In verse. Tobacco is mentioned. STC 23781; Arents 200. CtY, MH, NN-A; BL. 635/121

—[Anr edn]. *London: [A. Mathewes,] for H. Gosson,* 1635. 16 lvs; 4to. Includes postscript stating that tobacco was 1st brought to England in 1565 by Sir John Hawkins, but was not brought into general use till much later when introduced by Sir Walter Raleigh. STC 23781. CSmH, DFo, MH, NNPM; BL. 635/122

—[Anr issue]. *London: [A. Mathewes,] for H. Gosson,* 1635. Title includes added text with phrase '15 of Novem. 1635'. STC 23782.5; Arents (Add.) 283. CSmH, MH, NN-A; Oxford:Bodl. 635/123

——. The travels of twelve-pence. *London: [A. Mathewes,] for H. Gosson,* 1635. [46] p.; 8vo. 1st publ., [London, 1621], under title *A shilling.* STC 23794. MH (imp.); Oxford: Bodl. (imp.). 635/124

——. Wit and mirth. *London: [T. Cotes,] for J. Boler,* 1635. [80] p.; 8vo. 1st publ., London, 1626. STC 23815. CSmH. 635/125

——. The world runnes on wheeles. *London: [A. Mathewes,] for H. Gosson,* 1635. 8vo. In verse. 1st publ., London, 1623. STC 23817. Oxford:Bodl. 635/126

Téllez, Gabriel. Deleytar aprovechando. *Madrid: Imprenta Real, for D. González,* 1635. 334 numb. lvs; 4to. Dramas. Includes 'Los hermanos parecidos' in which a character designated 'America' speaks of the New World's riches. Palau 329483. MH, MNS, PU; BL. 635/127

——. Quarta parte de las Comedias del maestro Tirso de Molina. *Madrid: María de Quiñones, for P. Coello & M. López,* 1635. 308 numb. lvs; 4to. Includes Téllez's trilogy known as the 'Hazañas de los Pizarros' comprising 'Todo es dar en una cosa', 'Amazonas en las Indias' & 'La lealtad contra la enviada', based on the life of Francisco Pizarro. Elsewhere in Téllez's writings will be found scattered refs to the New World, where he himself spent some two years, ca. 1615–1618. On such refs see Angela B. Dellepiane, *Presencia de America en la obra de Tirso de Molina.* Madrid, 1968. Cf. Medina (BHA) 945; Palau 329478. BL. 635/128

Vega Carpio, Lope Félix. Veinte y una parte verdadera de las comedias del Fénix de España. *Madrid: Widow of A. Martín, for D. Logroño,* 1635. 260 lvs; 4to. Included is 'El premio del bien hablar' set in Seville, with numerous refs to Spanish Indies. Also included is 'La noche de San Juan' with mention of New World. Palau 355314. CU, MB, PU; BL, BN. 635/129

Venne, Adriaen van de. Tafereel van de belacchende werelt. *The Hague: The author,* 1635. 280 p.; illus.; 4to. In verse. A dialogue includes exchange on tobacco as vice & benefit. Gathering A, p. 1–8, has catchwords as follows: 'Op', 'Boer-', 'Daer', 'Be-', 'Fijt-', 'Fijt-', 'En', 'Of'. Arents (Add.) 284. NN-A, NN-RB; BL (edn uncertain), BN. 635/130

—[Anr edn]. *The Hague: The author,* 1635. 280 p.; illus.; 4to. Signature marks & catchwords of gathering A are said to exhibit differences from the preceding. BN. 635/131

Vernulz, Nicolás de, C. Or. Apologia pro augustissima . . . gente austriaca, in qua illius magnitudo, imperium, virtus adversus ejus hoc tempore aemulos asseritur. *Louvain: F. Simon & J. Zeger,* 1635. 310 p.; 4to. Section 'De provinciis . . . in Indis' (p. 90–107) mentions Columbus, Magellan, & Vespucci. Palau 360819. ICN, MH; BL, BN. 635/132

Wake, Sir Isaac. Rex platonicus, sive De . . . Jacobi . . . Regis, ad . . . Academiam Oxoniensem adventu . . . 1605. narratio . . . Editio quinta. *Oxford: L. Lichfield,* 1635. 239 p.; 12mo. 1st publ., Oxford, 1607. STC 24942; Madan (Oxford) 1635:18. CU, CtY, DFo, IU; BL. 635/133

Wood, William. New Englands prospect. A true, lively, and experimentall description of that part of America, commonly called New England. *London: T. Cotes, for J. Bellamy,* 1635. 83 p.; map; 4to. 1st publ., London, 1634. Sabin 105075; Vail (Frontier) 89; STC 25958; Church 433; JCB (3) II:258. CSmH, CtY, DLC, ICN, MH, NN-RB; BL.
635/134

Zeitungen wie die Keyserlichen Herszprug belägert . . . Item particularia, wie die Holländer in Brassilien, die Stadt Pariba beneben dreyen Forten eingenommen. [*Cologne?*] 1635. 8 p.; 4to. Meulman 2302. Ghent:BU.
635/135

1636

Abbot, George, Abp of Canterbury. A briefe description of the whole worlde. *London: T. H[arper]., for W. Sheares,* 1636. 350 p.; 12mo. 1st publ., London, 1599. Sabin 21n; STC 32. CLU-C, DFo, IU, MnU-B, NNC; BL.
636/1

Agustí, Miguel. Libro de los secretos de agricoltura. *Saragossa:* 1636. 4to. 1st publ. in Castilian, Saragossa, [1625?]. Palau 4125.
636/2

Bacon, Francis, viscount St Albans. Historia vitae et mortis. *Leyden: J. Maire,* 1636. 476 p.; 12mo. 1st publ., London, 1623. Gibson (Bacon) 148; Shaaber (Brit. auth.) B39. CU-I, DLC, IU, MH, PHC; BL, Berlin:StB.
636/3

——. Les oeuvres morales et politiques . . . de la version de J. Baudoin. *Paris: P. Rocolet & F. Targa,* 1636. 639 p.; 8vo. 1st publ. in this version, Paris, 1626. Gibson (Bacon) 166; Shaaber (Brit. auth.) B14. CLU-C, CtY, MH, NjP; BL, BN.
636/4

Baerle, Kaspar van. Oratio de coeli admirandis habita in illustri Amstelodamensium schola. *Amsterdam: J. Blaeu,* 1636. 28 p.; fol. Includes ref. to America on p. 18. CtY; BL, BN.
636/5

Bauderon, Brice. Pharmacopee. *Paris: J. Laquehay,* 1636. 2 pts; 8vo. 1st publ., Lyons, 1588, under title *Paraphrase sur la Pharmacopoee;* cf. 1607 edn. WU.
636/6

Beverwijck, Jan van. De excellentia foeminei sexus. *Dordrecht:* 1636. 12mo. Cites Isabella of Castile as the power behind Columbus's discovery of the New World. Grässe I:357–58.
636/7

——. Schat der gesontheyt. Met verssen verçiert door Heer Jacob Cats. [*Dordrecht?* 1636?] 2 pts; illus.; 8vo. Existence of this edn deduced from description of Dordrecht, 1637, edn in Arents. Though that edn is there cited as '1st edn', the t.p. of pt 1 includes the phrase 'Na de copye', indicating an earlier 1637 or 1636 edn. Pt 2 of the 1637 edn has a 1636 imprint, suggesting a reissue. American refs encountered in later edns are as follows: Pt 1 includes section on tobacco, preceded by a 16-line poem by Cats, 'De taback-blaser spreeckt'; another poem in section on sugar includes a ref. to Brazil. Pt 2 includes mention of 'brown balsam' from the West Indies. Cf. Arents (Add.) 287; cf. Grässe I:357; cf. Molhuysen I:331.
636/8

Blundeville, Thomas. Mr. Blundevil his exercises . . . The seventh edition corrected and somewhat enlarged by Ro. Hartwell. *London: R. Bishop; sold by B. Allen,* 1636. 799 p.; illus.; 4to. 1st publ., London, 1594; cf. 1606 edn. Also included is John Blagrave's *A very brief . . . description of Master Blagrave his Astrolabe,* 1st publ., London, 1585. Sabin 6024; STC 3151; JCB (3) II:259. CSmH, DLC, ICN, MB, MiU, NHi, RPJCB; BL.
636/9

Bradwell, Stephen. Physick for the sicknesse, commonly called the plague. *London: B. Fisher,* 1636. 53 p.; 4to. In avoidance of plague, eating of turkey is approved; cf. author's 1625 *A watch-man for the pest.* STC 3536. CSmH, DFo, MBCo, NNNAM; BL.
636/10

Brathwaite, Richard. Barnabae itinerarium, Mirtili & Faustuli nominibus insignitum. [*London: J. Haviland,* 1636?]. 2 pts; 16mo. Latin verse. In penultimate stanza couplet 'Officina juncta Baccho / Juvenilem fert Tobacco' appears. STC 3555.7. MH.
636/11

Calvo, Juan. Primera y segunda parte de la Cirugia universal. *Perpignan: L. Roure,* 1636. 620 p.; fol. 1st publ., Seville, 1580; cf. 1626 edn. Cf. Medina (BHA) 1095; Palau 40553. London:Wellcome.
636/12

Canoniero, Pietro Andrea. Illustrium epitaphiorum . . . flores. *Douai: B. Bellère, 1636.* 544 p.; 8vo. 1st publ., Antwerp, 1613, under title *Flores illustrium epitaphiorum.* Cf. Sabin 24830. BL.   636/13

Casas, Bartolomé de las, O.P., Bp of Chiapa. Il supplice schiavo indiano . . . conforme al suo vero originale spagnuolo già stampato in Siviglia. Tradotto . . . per opera di Marco Ginammi. *Venice: M. Ginammi,* 1636. 118 p.; 4to. Spanish & Italian texts in parallel cols. Spanish text 1st publ., Seville, 1552, as *Tratado . . . sobre la materia de los Yndios* (No. 552/10). Sabin 11246; Medina (BHA) 1085n (II:474); Streit I:464; Palau 46956. CtY, DLC, ICU, MH, MiU-C, NN-RB, PBL, RPJCB; BL, BN.   636/14

Chinchón, Luis Gerónimo Fernández de Cabrera y Bobadilla, conde de. Carta del conde de Chinchon virrey del Peru, à Su Magestad del rey nuestro . . . sobre la canoniçacion del siervo de Dios fray Francisco Solano patron del Peru. [*Madrid?* 1636]. 2 p.; fol. Medina (BHA) 951. Santiago, Chile:BN.   636/15

Clüver, Philipp. Introduction a la geographie universelle, tant nouvelle, qu'ancienne. Traduitte du latin de Philippe de Cluvier Seconde edition reveuë, corrigée & augmentée de figures. *Paris: P. Bilaine,* 1636. 496 p.; illus.; 8vo. 1st publ. as here transl., Paris, 1631. Cf. Sabin 13805. ViU.   636/16

Corte, Corneille de, O.S.A. Virorum illustrium ex ordine Eremitarum d. Augustini elogia. *Antwerp: J. Cnobbaert,* 1636. 288 p.; 4to. Includes account of Cornelius de Bye, missionary in Mexico. Streit I:463. ICN, MiU, NNUT; BN.   636/17

Dekker, Thomas. The wonder of a kingdome. *London: R. Raworth, for N. Vavasour,* 1636. [56] p.; 4to. Drama. In act 1, scene 1, tobacco is described as 'that chopping herbe of hell'; elsewhere it is mentioned. STC 6533; Greg 508; Arents 201. CSmH, CtY, DLC, MH, NN-A; BL.   636/18

Dioscorides, Pedanius. Acerca de la materia medicinal, y de los venenos mortiferos. Traducido de lengua griega . . . con anotaciones . . . por el Doctor Andres de Laguna . . . y aora en esta ultima impression corregido. *Valencia: M. Sorolla,* 1636. 616 p.; illus.; fol. Laguna's annotations, with numerous

refs to American plants, 1st publ. separately Lyons, 1554, & in the present form, Antwerp, 1555. Pritzel 2313n; Palau 74025. BL, London:Wellcome.   636/19

Du Bartas, Guillaume de Salluste, seigneur. A learned summary upon the famous poem of William of Saluste, lord of Bartas . . . Translated out of French, by T[homas]. L[odge]. *London: [G. Purslowe,] for R. M[ilbourne?].,* 1636. 2 pts; fol. 1st publ. as here transl., London, 1621; a reissue with cancel t.p. of that edn. STC 21666.5. CU; Cambridge:UL.   636/20

Durante, Castore. Herbario nuovo . . . ove son figure che rappresentano le vive piante, che nascono in tutta Europa, & nell'Indie Orientali, & Occidentali. *Venice: The Giuntas,* 1636. 515 p.; illus.; 4to. 1st publ., Rome, 1585; cf. year 1602. Pritzel 2552n; Nissen (Bot.) 569n; Arents (Add.) 83; Hunt (Bot.) 229. DNAL, MH-A, NN-A, PPAmP; London:Wellcome, BN.   636/21

Du Rocher, R.M. L'Indienne amoureuse, ou L'heureux naufrage. Tragi-comedie. *Paris: J. Corrozet,* 1636. 133 p.; 8vo. In verse. 1st publ., Paris, 1635; here a reissue of that edn with altered imprint date? RPJCB; BL.   636/22

García de Zurita, Andrés. Discurso de las missas conventuales que Su Magestad manda se digan en las iglesias de las Indias. *Madrid: F. Martínez,* 1636. 22 numb. lvs; 4to. IU, NcD.   636/23

Gaultier, Jacques, S.J. Tabula chronologica status ecclesiae catolicae . . . ad annum 1631. *Lyons: H. Cardon,* 1636. 838 p.; fol. 1st publ. as transl. by the author into Latin from his *Table chronologique de l'estat du christianisme* (Lyons, 1609), Lyons, 1616. Backer III:1276. MiD.   636/24

Gerard, John. The herball or Generall historie of plantes. *London: A. Islip, J. Norton & R. Whitaker,* 1636. 1630 p.; illus.; fol. 1st publ., London, 1597; cf. 1633 edn, of which this is a reissue with altered imprint date. Pritzel 3282n; Nissen (Bot.) 698n; Henrey (Brit. bot) 156; STC 11752. CSmH, DLC, IU, MH-A, MnU, NN-RB, PPL, RPB; BL.   636/25

Góngora y Argote, Luis de. Las obras. *Madrid: Imprenta Real, & D. Díaz de la Carrera* (v. 2), 1636–48. 2 v.; 4to. In verse. Vol. 1

contains Góngora's *Soledades,* 1st publ., Madrid, 1627, in his *Obras en verso.* Palau 104628. CU, MoU, NIC, PU; Madrid:BN.
636/26

———. Soledades . . . Comentadas por d. Garcia de Salcedo Coronel. *Madrid: Imprenta Real, for D. González,* 1636. 312 numb. lvs; 4to. In verse. 1st publ., Madrid, 1627, in Góngora's *Obras en verso.* Palau 104671. ICU, MH, NN-RB; BL, BN.
636/27

Grotius, Hugo. Inleydinghe tot de Hollandsche rechts-gheleerdheydt . . . Hier is noch by ghevoeght . . . Van de oudheydt der Batavische, nu Hollandsche republijcke. Ende de Vrije zee-vaert. [*Haarlem: A. Roman,* 1636]. 3 pts; port.; 4to. Here brought together under this collective half title are the three works described. Of these the *Inleydinghe* was 1st publ. at the Hague, 1631, the *Van de oudheydt,* 1st publ. there in Dutch in 1610, and the last, in Dutch, at Leyden, 1614. Each of the three, with its special t.p., separate paging & signatures, was also issued separately in this year. Meulen/Diermanse 762. CU, CtY-L; The Hague:PP.
636/28

———. Traicté de la verité de la religion chrestienne . . . Traduit du latin de l'aucteur. *Amsterdam: J. Blaeu,* 1636. 191 p.; 12mo. Transl. from Grotius's *Sensus librorum sex,* 1st publ., Leyden, 1627. Meulen/Diermanse 1060. BN, The Hague:PP.
636/29

———. Van de oudheydt der Batavische, nu Hollandsche republique. *Haarlem: A. Roman,* 1636. 44 p.; port.; 4to. 1st publ. in Dutch, The Hague, 1610, under title *Tractaet vande oudtheyt.* Also issued as part of Grotius's *Inleydinghe tot de Hollandsche rechtsgheleerdheydt* of this year, q.v. above. Meulen/Diermanse 699; Bibl. Belg. G346. The Hague:PP.
636/30

———. Vrye zeevaert, ofte Bewys van het recht dat de inghesetenen deser gheunieerde landen toekomt over de Oost ende West-Indische koophandel. *Haarlem: A. Roman,* 1636. 42 p.; 4to. 1st publ. in Dutch, Leyden, 1614. Also issued as part of Grotius's *Inleydinghe tot de Hollandsche rechts-gheleerdheydt* of this year, q.v. above. Meulen/Diermanse 555 (& 762); Bibl. Belg. G337. MH, NNC; BL, The Hague:PP.
636/31

Guicciardini, Francesco. La historia d'Italia . . . Di nuovo riveduta et corretta per Francesco Sansovino. *Geneva: J. Stoer,* 1636. 2 v.; 4to. 1st publ., Florence, 1561; cf. 1604 edn. Michel (Répertoire) IV:101. The present issue may be represented by copies recorded below.
636/32

—[Anr issue]. [*Geneva:*] *J. Stoer,* 1636. Michel (Répertoire) IV:101. CSmH, CtY, ICU, MH, NjP, PBm; BL, BN.
636/33

—[Anr edn]. *Venice: A. Baba,* 1636. 2 pts; 4to. Michel (Répertoire) IV:101. Versailles:BM.
636/34

Heylyn, Peter. Μικροκοσμος: A little description of the great world. The seventh edition. *Oxford: W. Turner,* 1636. 808 p.; 4to. 1st publ., Oxford, 1621. Sabin 31656; Madan (Oxford) 1636:10; STC 13282; JCB (3) II:260. CSmH, CtY, DLC, MH, MnU-B, NN-RB, RPJCB; BL.
636/35

Horst, Gregor. Centuria problematum medicorum. *Nuremberg: W. Endter,* 1636. 240 (i.e., 430) p.; 4to. 1st publ., Wittenberg, 1610. DNLM, MBCo, MnU.
636/36

Jesuits. Letters from missions (South America). Litterae annuae provinciae Paraquariae Societatis Jesu. *Antwerp: J. de Meurs,* 1636. 168 p.; 18mo. Sabin 21407; Medina (BHA) 953; Streit II:1641; Backer VI:1438. CtY, DLC, MH, NN-RB, RPJCB; Göttingen:UB.
636/37

La Brosse, Guy de. Description du jardin royal des plantes medicinales estably par le roy Louis le Juste, avec le catalogue des plantes. *Paris:* 1636. 107 p.; 4to. In the catalogue numerous plants of American origin are listed & described as such. Pritzel 1187. BL, BN.
636/38

Le Jeune, Paul, S.J. Relation de ce qui s'est passé en la Nouvelle France en l'annee 1634. *Avignon: J. Bramereau,* 1636. 416 p.; 8vo. 1st publ., Paris, 1635, but includes also the 1635 *Relation* publ. at Paris in this year. Sabin 39951; Harrisse (NF) 64; Bell (Jes. rel.) 7; McCoy 15; Streit II:2507. CSmH, MiD, MnU-B, NN-RB (imp.); Avignon:Mus. Calvet.
636/39

———. Relation de ce qui s'est passé en la Nouvelle France en l'annee 1635. *Paris: S. Cramoisy,* 1636. 246 p.; 8vo. For variant states, see McCoy as cited. Sabin 39950;

Harrisse (NF) 63; Bell (Jes. rel.) 5–6; McCoy 18; Streit II:2506; Church 434; JCB (3) II:260. CSmH, CtY, DLC, InU-L, MH, MiU-C, MnU-B, NN-RB, RPJCB; BL, BN.
636/40

Lenton, Francis. Lentons leisures described, in divers moderne characters. *London:* [*J. Beale*] 1636. [173] p.; 12mo. 1st publ., London, 1631, under title *Characterismi;* here reissued with cancel t.p. & prelim. lvs. STC 15464; Murphy (Engl. char.-bks) 49. CSmH.
636/41

León Pinelo, Antonio Rodríguez de. Question moral si el chocolate quebranta el ayuno eclesiastico. *Madrid: Widow of J. González,* 1636. 122 numb. lvs; 4to. Sabin 62932; Medina (BHA) 950; Müller 168; Arents 202; Kress 5657; JCB (3) II:260–61. CU-B, DNLM, ICN, InU-L, MH, NN-A, RPJCB; BL, BN.
636/42

Lloyd, David. The legend of captaine Jones. *London:* [*M. Fletcher,*] *for J. M*[*arriott*]., 1636. [22] p.; illus.; 4to. In verse. 1st publ., London, 1631. Sabin 41683n; Grolier (Wither to Prior) 524; STC 16615. CtY, DFo; BL.
636/43

Lupton, Donald. Emblems of rarities: or Choice observations out of worthy histories of many remarkable histories of many remarkable passages, and renowned actions of divers princes and severall nations. *London: N. Okes,* 1636. 478 p.; 12mo. Includes (p. 372) brief description of America. STC 16942; Wellcome I:3913. CSmH, DLC, ICN, MHi, MiU; BL.
636/44

Maffei, Giovanni Pietro, S.J. Historiarum Indicarum libri xvi. *Lyons: J. Champion,* 1636. 718 p.; 8vo. 1st publ., Florence, 1588; cf. 1605 edn. Cf. Sabin 43774; Borba de Moraes II:10; Backer V:298.
636/45

Malynes, Gerard de. Consuetudo, vel, Lex mercatoria, or, The antient law-merchant. *London: A. Islip,* 1636. 333 p.; fol. Mentioned are tobacco trade & monopolies, & the Bermuda & Virginia companies, while chapt. xlvi treats 'Of plantations of people, and new Discoveries'. STC 17222. CSmH, CtY, DFo, IU, MH, NNC-L; Oxford:Bodl.
636/46

—[Anr issue, with cancel t.p.]. *London: A. Islip; sold by N. Bourne,* 1636. STC 17223. CLU-C, CtY, DLC, ICN, MH; BL.
636/47

—[Anr edn]. *London: A. Islip & R. Young; sold by N. Bourne,* 1636. 2 pts; fol. Pt 2 comprises R. Dafforne's *Merchants mirror.* For complex variants, see STC 17224 & 17224.5. CSmH (pt 1 only), CtY, DLC (pt 1 only), IU, MBAt, MH (pt 1 only), N; BL.
636/48

Mariana, ——, licenciado. Carta que escrivio el licenciado Mariana al doctor don Juan Sanchez Duque . . . obispo . . . de Guadalaxara en Indias. [*Madrid?* 1636]. fol. Includes also the bishop's reply. Medina (BHA) 959. BL.
636/49

Mercator, Gerardus. Appendix Atlantis oder dess WeltBuchs, darinnen . . . Tabellen von Teutschland . . . auch einer und der andern Indien begrieffen. *Amsterdam: J. Janszoon, the Younger,* 1636. 128 maps; fol. Perhaps transl. from Mercator's Latin version, the *Atlantis majoris appendix,* 1st publ., Amsterdam, 1630; sometimes issued with Mercator's 1633 *Atlas, das ist Abbildung,* q.v. Koeman (Me) 44. CtY; Marburg:StB, Copenhagen:KB.
636/50

——. Atlantis novi pars tertia, Italiam . . . nec non . . . Americam continens, Editio ultima. *Amsterdam: H. Hondius,* 1636. 1 v.; 98 maps; fol. Based on Mercator's *Atlantis majoris appendix,* 1st publ., Amsterdam, 1630; here enl. Cf. the author's similar *Appendix novi atlantis* as publ. by Janszoon, Amsterdam, 1637. Includes new maps of North & South America. Koeman (Me) 50A. Antwerp:Mus. Plantin.
636/51

——. Atlas, das ist, Abbildung der gantzen Welt. *Amsterdam: H. Hondius,* 1636. 1 v.; illus., maps; fol. 1st publ. in German, Amsterdam, 1633; cf. Mercator's *Appendix Atlantis* above. Koeman (Me) 42. Greenwich:NMM.
636/52

——. Atlas oder Ander Theil des grossen Welt-Buchs. *Amsterdam:* 1636. See Mercator's *Newer Atlas* below.

——. Atlas, or A geographicke description of the . . . world, through Europe, Asia, Africa, and America . . . Translated by Henry Hexham. *Amsterdam: H. Hondius & J. Janszoon, the Younger,* 1636. 2 v.; illus., maps; fol. Prob. transl. from Mercator's *Atlas sive Cosmographicae meditationes,* 1st publ., Amsterdam, 1606. Title & imprint appear on slips pasted on 1633 French t.p.; some copies lack one or both imprint slips. Sabin

47886; Koeman (Me) 41A; Phillips (Atlases) 449; STC 17827; JCB (3) II:271. CSmH, DLC, ICN (imp., with Latin t.p. dated 1630), IU, MH, MiU-C (v. 1), NN (imp.), RPJCB (v. 1), ViU; BL, Amsterdam:NHSM.
636/53

———. Atlas, sive Cosmographicae meditationes de fabrica mundi . . . emendatus . . . studio Judoci Hondii. *Amsterdam: J. E. Cloppenburg,* 1636. 2 pts; maps; obl. 8vo. A reissue of publisher's 1630 edn with altered imprint date. Cf. Sabin 47887; Koeman (Me) 202; Phillips (Atlases) 450. DLC.
636/54

———. Newer Atlas, oder Grosses Weltbuch . . . auch von . . . West Indien . . . in zwei Theille. *Amsterdam: J. Janszoon, the Younger [& H. Hondius],* 1636. 2 v.; maps; fol. 1st publ. in German, Amsterdam, 1633, under title *Atlas, das ist Abbildung der gantzen Welt;* here added, as pt of the *Atlas oder Ander Theil* are 73 maps from Mercator's *Appendix Atlantis oder des Weltbuchs* above. Koeman (Me) 45–46. Zurich:ZB.
636/55

Merula, Paulus. Cosmographiae generalis libri tres. *Amsterdam: W. J. Blaeu,* 1636. 372 p.; 12mo. 1st publ., Leyden, 1605. Tiele 751n. CtY, MH; BL, BN.
636/56

Monet, Philibert, S.J. Invantaire des deus langues françoise et latine. *Lyons: Widow of C. Rigaud, & P. Borde,* 1636 (Colophon: 1635). 990 p.; fol. 1st publ., Paris, 1628, under title *Nouveau . . . dictionaire;* here a reissue of Lyons, 1635, edn under present title. MH.
636/57

—[Anr issue?]. *Lyons: C. Obert,* 1636. Backer V:1211–12. BN.
636/58

—[Anr issue?]. *Lyons: A. Pillehotte,* 1636. Backer V:1211–12.
636/59

Montaigne, Michel Eyquem de. Essais. *Paris: P. Billaine,* 1636. 1129 p.; 8vo. 1st publ., Bordeaux, 1580; cf. 1602 edn. Tchémerzine VIII:429. ViU, NjP; BN.
636/60

—[Anr issue]. *Paris: M. Blageart,* 1636. Tchémerzine VIII:429. BN.
636/61

—[Anr issue]. *Paris: L. Boulanger,* 1636. Tchémerzine VIII:429. MH; BN.
636/62

—[Anr issue]. *Paris: M. Collet,* 1636. Tchémerzine VIII:429. BN.
636/63

—[Anr issue]. *Paris: J. Germont,* 1636. Tchémerzine VIII:429. BN.
636/64

—[Anr issue]. *Paris: S. de La Fosse,* 1636. Tchémerzine VIII:429. BN.
636/65

—[Anr issue]. *Paris: P. L'Amy,* 1636. Tchémerzine VIII:429. BL, BN.
636/66

—[Anr issue]. *Paris: G. Loyson,* 1636. Tchémerzine VIII:429.
636/67

—[Anr issue]. *Paris: J. Villery & J. Guignard,* 1636. Tchémerzine VIII:429. MiU; BN.
636/68

Nash, Thomas (1588–1648). Quaternio, or A fourefold way to a happy life. *London: N. Okes, sold by J. Benson,* 1636. 280 p.; 4to. 1st publ., London, 1633; here a reissue with cancel t.p. STC 18383. CtY, DFo, IU, MH, NNC; BL.
636/69

Nederlandsche West Indische Compagnie. Nieuwe in-teyckeninge ende verhooginge der capitalen van de . . . West-Indische Compagnie. *[The Hague? 1636].* bds.; fol. Extracted from the resolutions of the Staten Generaal, June 15, 1636. Sabin 55286 & 102900; Knuttel 4513. NN-RB; The Hague:KB.
636/70

Olearius, Adam. Lustige historia, woher das Toback-Trincken kommt. *Hamburg:* 1636. 1st publ., Leipzig, 1635. Lohmeier (Olearius) 8a.
636/71

Oviedo Pedrosa, Francisco de, O. Merced. Epitome de las razones que alega en los memoriales y informes, que diò . . . Francisco de Oviedo . . . Procurador . . . de Lima y Chile, del orden . . . de la Merced . . . al Rey. *Madrid: Widow of J. González,* 1636. 12 lvs; fol. Memorial to king of Spain requesting that a chapter general of the order of Our Lady of Mercy not be held without representation from Spanish America. Medina (BHA) 962; Palau 207766; Maggs Cat. 496 (Americana VI): 249. BL, Seville:BU.
636/72

Pagitt, Ephraim. Christianographie. or The description of the multitude and sundry sorts of Christians in the world not subject to the Pope . . . The second edition, inlarged. *London: W. J[ones]. & N. O[kes]., for M. Costerden,* 1636. 2 pts; 4to. 1st publ., London, 1635. STC 19111. CSmH, CtY, DLC, ICN, MH, MWA, NN-RB, PPFr, RPJCB; BL.
636/73

Paré, Ambroise. De chirurgie, ende alle de opera, ofte wercken . . . Nu eerst uyt de françoysche . . . overgeset: door d. Carolum Battum. *Amsterdam: C. van Breughel, for H. Laurenszoon,* 1636. 940 p.; illus.; fol. 1st publ. as here transl. from the Paris, 1585, 4th edn, Dordrecht, 1592; cf. the 1601 German edn. Doe (Paré) 62. NNC; Cambridge: St John's.   636/74

—[Anr edn]. *Rotterdam: Widow of M. Bastiaenszoon,* 1636. 940 p.; illus.; fol. Doe (Paré) 63. CtY-M, DNLM; London:Med. Soc., Amsterdam:UB.   636/75

—[Anr issue]. *Rotterdam: J. van Waesberghe,* 1636. Doe (Paré) 64. MiU; Amsterdam:UB.
636/76

Peacham, Henry (1576?–1643?). Coach and sedan, pleasantly disputing for place and precedence. *London: R. Raworth, for J. Crouch,* 1636. [55] p.; illus.; 4to. On p. [15] 'Rattle-Snakes in New-England' are discussed; on p. [50], tobacco. STC 19501.5. MH.   636/77

—[Anr issue]. *London: R. Raworth, for J. Crouch; sold by E. Paxton,* 1636. STC 19501; Arents (Add.) 285. CSmH, DFo, NN-A; BL.
636/78

Pharmacopoea Amstelredamensis, Senatus auctoritata munita. *Amsterdam: W. & J. Blaeu,* 1636. 126 p.; 4to. Among the ingredients called for are mechoacan, sarsaparilla, & Guaiacum. DNLM, NjP; BL.   636/79

—[Anr edn]. Editio altera. *Amsterdam: A. Jacobus,* 1636. 126 p.; 12mo. London:Wellcome.
636/80

—[Anr edn]. Editio secunda. *Amsterdam: W. & J. Blaeu,* 1636. 134 p.; 8vo. London:Wellcome.   636/81

—[Anr edn]. *Franeker: B. Barentsma,* 1636. 12mo.   636/82

Postel, Guillaume. De cosmographica disciplina . . . libri ii. *Leyden: J. Maire,* 1636. 2 pts; illus.; 16mo. 1st publ., Basel, 1561. Included are refs to New World. Sabin 64523; Wellcome I:5230. CtY, DLC, MiU, NN-RB; BL.   636/83

Potosí, Bolivia. Gremio de los azogueros. El gremio de los azogueros de . . . Potosi . . . suplica a V[uestra]. M[agestad]. . . . se sirva de passar los ojos por este papel, y mandar lo vea el Real Consejo de las Indias. [*Madrid?* 1636?]. 20 numb. lvs; fol. In caption title line 5 ends 'mandar lo'. Sabin 64595. BL.   636/84

—[Anr edn]. [*Madrid?* 1636?]. 20 numb. lvs;

fol. In caption title line 5 ends 'mādar lo'. Sabin 64595. BL.   636/85

Powell, Thomas (1572?–1635?). The art of thriving . . . Together with The mysterie and miserie of lending and borrowing. *London: T. H[arper]., for B. Fisher,* 1635 [i.e., 1636]. 8vo. *The mysterie,* etc., with its refs to tobacco, 1st publ., London, 1623, under title *Wheresoever you see me.* STC 20162. CSmH, CtY, DFo, MnU-B, NNC; BL.
636/86

Proeve, over eenen Rypen-raet ende zalige resolutie . . . ingestelt by . . . J. G. B. S. G. M. *Tholen: C. Speckaert,* 1636. 45 p.; 4to. Calls on East & West India Companies to discontinue piracy; cf. the *Rijpen raedt,* [Antwerp], 1635. Knuttel 4436. MnU-B; The Hague:KB.   636/87

Reden van dat die West-Indische Compagnie oft handelinge, niet alleen profijtelijck, maer oock noodtsaeckelijck is. [*The Hague?*] 1636. 14 p.; 4to. Sabin 68493 (& 102910 ff.); Borba de Moraes II:175–76; Knuttel 4425. DLC, MnU-B, NN-RB; BL, The Hague:KB.   636/88

Relacion de la toma de Parayba por los Olandeses el año de 1628 y de la aliança de los Indios con ellos. [*Seville?*] 1636. fol. Sabin 58555; Borba de Moraes II:188–89.
636/89

Relacion del felice sucesso que ha tenido el Armada que llevò el socorro al Brasil el año passado de 1635. *Seville: A. Grande,* 1636. [4] p.; 4to. Borba de Moraes II:189. BL (Spain. Appendix).   636/90

Relacion del pleyto, i cause que en govierno i justicia se sigue por los interesados, i dueños de barras del Perù, i en particular por Gregorio de Ibarra. i don Juan Fermin de Izu . . . con los compradores de oro i plata de Sevilla . . . Sobre la apelacion i revocacion de tres autos proveidos por el presidente y juezes letrados de la Casa de Contratacion, en que mandaron ensayar, i labrar en moneda cierto numero de barras. i otros articulos deducidos en razon de la ley de las del Perù, y su baxa, i restitucion, costas i gastos de su labor, i modo de su fundirlas, i pedimentos hechos sobre todo por el señor fiscal. [*Madrid?* 1636]. 33 p.; fol. Medina (BHA) 7802. Puebla:B. Palafoxiana.   636/91

Ritter, Stephan. Theatrum cosmographicum, hoc est Totius terrarum orbis regionum . . . tum ex variis variorum poetarum monumentis oratione ligata descriptio . . . nova editione adornata. *Marburg: N. Hampel,* 1636. 1253 p.; 4to. 1st publ., Marburg, 1619, under title *Cosmographica prosometrica.* Cf. Sabin 71596. BN.   636/92

Roco de Córdoba, Francisco. Por Don Martin y Aldrete, obispo de Oviedo . . . en el pleyto con Don Juan Blazquez Mayoralgo, y Diego del Valle Alvarado, oficiales reales de la . . . Nueva Vera Cruz. Sobre los diez mil pesos, daños, e interesses que el dicho obispo pretende le satisfagan por el embargo, y registro que dellos hizieron, y perdida que se ocasiò de averlos embiado á España contra la voluntad del dicho don Martin, en la flota que se llevò el Olandes el año de 628. del cargo de don Juan de Benavides. *Madrid: Widow of J. González,* 1636. 31 numb. lvs; fol. Medina (BHA) 7801. Puebla:B. Palafoxiana.   636/93

Ruland, Joannes David. Inauguralis de lue sive lepra venerea disputatio. [*Frankfurt a. M.:*] *M. Koch* [1636]. 8 lvs; 4to. Describes syphilis as brought from America by Columbus & Vespucci; mentions Santo Domingo, Florida, guaiacum, sarsaparilla, sassafras, & mechoacan. Wellcome I:5627. London:Wellcome.   636/94

Sagard, Gabriel, O.F.M. Histoire du Canada et voyages que les freres mineurs Recollects y ont faicts pour la conversion des infidelles. *Paris: C. Sonnius,* 1636. 1005 p.; 8vo. 'D'une lecture aussi difficile qu'ingrate'— Harrisse. Bks ii–iii are an enlargement of Sagard's *Le grand voyage du pays des Hurons,* Paris, 1632. Sabin 74885; Harrisse (NF) 62; Streit II:2508; Church 435; JCB (3) II:261. CSmH, DLC, ICN, MH, MiU-C, MnU-B, PHi, RPJCB; BL, BN.   636/95

Saltonstall, Charles. The navigator, shewing and explaining all the chiefe principles and parts . . . in the famous art of navigation. *London: [B. Alsop & T. Fawcet] for G. Hurlock,* 1636. 124 p.; illus., port.; 4to. In section 'Of the distance of places' ref. is made to the Lucayan (i.e., Turks & Caicos) Islands & to the Bahamas. Sabin 75851; STC 21640. CSmH (imp.), CtY (imp.), DLC (imp.), PPAmP; BL (imp.), BN.   636/96

Sánchez, Francisco. Opera medica. His juncti sunt tractatus quidam philosophici non insubtiles. *Toulouse: P. Bosc,* 1636. 2 pts; 4to. Includes as pt 2 the author's *Tractatus philosophici,* with (p. 81–134) *Quod nihil scitur,* 1st publ., Lyons, 1581; cf. 1618 edn. Palau 294100. CLSU, CtY-M, DNLM, NNNAM; BL.   636/97

Sandys, George. A paraphrase upon the Psalmes of David. *London: [A. Hebb,]* 1636. 271 p.; 8vo. In verse. Includes, p. 242–43, poem 'Deo Opt. Max.' mentioning 'New-found-world' & Indian massacres. Sabin 76464; STC 21724. CSmH, CtY, DLC, ICU, MH, NN-RB; BL.   636/98

Selden, John. Mare clausum, seu De dominio maris libri duo . . . juxta exemplar Londinense, W. Stanesbeii pro Richard Meighen. [*Leyden: B. & A. Elsevier*] 1636. 567 p.; 12mo. 1st publ., London, 1635. Sabin 78971n; STC 22175.3; Willems (Les Elzevier) 449. CSmH, DLC, NIC, NjP, RPB; BL, BN.   636/99

—[Anr edn]. *Leyden: J. & T. Maire,* 1636. 244 p.; 4to. Sabin 78971n; STC 22175.7. MH, NN-RB, NjP; BL, BN.   636/100

—[Anr edn]. 'London' [i.e., *Amsterdam?*]: 1636. 504 p.; 8vo. Sabin 78972; STC 22175.3. DLC, MH, NN-RB, RPB; BL, BN.
636/101

Serres, Jean de. Inventaire general de l'histoire de France . . . jusques en l'an 1636. *Paris: G. Pelé,* 1636. 1526 p.; fol. 1st publ. with American refs, Paris, 1600; cf. 1606 edn. IaU; BN.   636/102

—[Anr edn]. *Paris: C. Morlot, J. Petrinae, & I. Dedin,* 1636. 4 v.; 8vo. 'Finissant à Louys XIII'. TxDaM-P; BN.   636/103

Smith, Capt. John. An accidence for the sea. Very necessary for all young seamen. *London: T. H[arper]., for B. Fisher,* 1636. 62 p.; 8vo. 1st publ., London, 1626. Sabin 82814; STC 22786. CtY; BL.
636/104

Spain. Consejo de las Indias. Ordenanzas del Consejo Real de las Indias . . . recopiladas, y por el Rey . . . para su govierno, establecidas. Año de M.DC.XXXVI. *Madrid: Widow of J. González,* 1636. 112 p.; fol. A revision of the *Ordenanças,* 1st publ., Seville, 1571. Medina (BHA) 960. DLC; BL, Seville:BM.   636/105

Spain. Junta de Guerra de Indias. Ordenanzas de la Junta de guerra de Indias, nuevamente recopiladas. *Madrid: Widow of J. González, 1636.* 7 p.; fol. Medina (BHA) 961. ICN. 636/106

Tassoni, Alessandro. Dieci libri di pensieri diversi . . . Corretti in questa ottava impressione. *Venice: M. A. Brogiollo, 1636.* 551 p.; 4to. Despite edn statement on t.p., constitutes sixth edn. 1st publ., Modena, 1612, under title *Varieta di pensieri diversi,* but see also enl. 1620 edn. Puliatti (Tassoni) 7; Wellcome I:6229. DLC, MH, NNC, WU; BL, BN. 636/107

Taylor, John, the Water-poet. Beschrijvinge van den ouden, ouden, heel ouden man . . . Overgeset upt' t' Engelsch . . . door H. H. *Delft: J. P. Waalpot, 1636.* 8 p.; 4to. Transl. from Taylor's *The olde, old, very olde man,* 1st publ., London, 1635. BL, BN. 636/108

——. The needles excellency . . . The 10th edition inlarged. *London: J. Boler, 1636.* illus.; obl. 4to. In verse. 1st publ., London, 1631. STC 23776.5. 636/109

Vitoria Baraona, Francisco de. Señor. El capitan Francisco de Vitoria Baraona, representa a V.M. los servicios que ha hecho . . . para que en justicia . . . le haga merced. [*Madrid:* 1636]. 16 numb. lvs; fol. Memorial to king of Spain discussing possible means of increasing revenues from Spanish America; included is section on cochineal. BL. 636/110

Vives, Juan Luis. De disciplinis libri xii. *Leyden: J. Maire, 1636.* 693 p.; 12mo. 1st publ., Antwerp, 1531; cf. 1612 edn. DFo, MH, MWA; BL, BN. 636/111

Wake, Sir Isaac. Rex platonicus sive De . . . Jacobi . . . Regis, ad . . . Academiam Oxoniensem adventu . . . 1605. narratio . . . Editio quinta. *Oxford: L. Lichfield, 1636.* 239 p.; 12mo. 1st publ., Oxford, 1607; here a reissue with altered imprint date of printer's 1635 edn. STC 24942.5. MH. 636/112

Wurfbain, Leonhart. Relatio historica Habspurgico-Austriaca, durch was mittel das . . . Hauss der Ertz-Hertzogen zu Oesterreich in Europa, Africa, Asia und America zu denen . . . Königreichen kommen und gelanget. *Nuremberg:* 1636. fol. Cf. Wurf-

bain's *Vier unterschiedliche Relationes historicae* of this year below. Sabin 105640. 636/113

——. Vier unterschiedliche Relationes historicae. *Nuremberg: W. Endter, 1636.* 4 pts; fol. Pts ii & iii concern territorial acquisitions of the Hapsburgs, including America. Cf. Sabin 105640; Jantz (German Baroque) 2758. NcD; BL. 636/114

Zacutus, Abraham, Lusitanus. Historiarum medicarum libri sex. *Arnhem: J. Jacobszoon, for H. Laurenszoon at Amsterdam, 1636–39.* 6 v.; 8vo. 1st publ., Cologne, 1629, under title *De medicorum principium historia libri sex.* Wellcome I:6790. DN-MS, MBCo; London: Wellcome. 636/115

Zucchi, Francesco. Poesie, divise in scherzi, aborti, & ombra. *Ascoli: M. Salvioni, 1636.* 2 pts; 8vo. Includes, with special t.p., Zucchi's 'La tabbaccheide, scherzo estivo sopra il tabacco'. Arents 203. ICN, MH, NN-A; BL. 636/116

1637

Aldrovandi, Ulisse. De quadrupedibus digitatis viviparis libri tres et de quadrupedibus digitatis oviparis libri duo. *Bologna: N. Tebaldini, for M. A. Bernia, 1637.* 718 p.; illus.; fol. In bk 2, chapt. xxx of the 'De quadrupedibus digitatis viviparis' the armadillo is mentioned; in bk 1, chapt. xiii of the 'De quadrupedibus digitatis oviparis' discusses the alligator, mentioning the iguana. Nissen (Zool.) 77. ICJ, MB, NN-RB, PPAN, RPB; BL, BN. 637/1

——. Ornithologiae tomus alter. *Bologna:* 1637. *See the year* 1640.

Alsted, Johann Heinrich. Thesaurus chronologiae . . . Editio tertia. *Herborn: [G. Rab]* 1637. 610 p.; 8vo. 1st publ., Herborn, 1624. CU, IU; BN. 637/2

Aprosio, Angelico. Il vaglio critico di Masoto Galistoni [pseud.] . . . sopra il Mondo nuovo del cavalier Tomaso Stigliani. '*Rostock: I. Steinman, for W. Wallop*' [i.e., *Treviso: G. Righettini*], 1637. 86 p.; 12mo. For Stigliani's *Mondo nuovo,* of which this is a critique, see the year 1617. Michel (Répertoire) I:61. DLC; BL, Paris:Mazarine. 637/3

Avity, Pierre d', sieur de Montmartin. Le monde, ou La description generale de ses quatre parties. *Paris: C. Sonnius, 1637.* 7 v. in 5; maps; fol. 1st publ., Paris, 1613, under title *Les estats, empires, et principautez du monde.* Vol. IV contains a 'Description de l'Amerique'. Sabin 18912; Cioranescu (XVII) 23603. RPJCB; BN. 637/4

—[Anr issue]. *Paris: P. Bilaine, 1637.* CU-B. 637/5

Bacon, Francis, viscount St Albans. Historia vitae et mortis. *Leyden: J. Maire, 1637.* 476 p.; 12mo. 1st publ., London, 1623; here a reissue of printer's 1636 edn with altered imprint date? Gibson (Bacon) 149; Shaaber (Brit. auth.) B40. CU, DLC, ICU, MH, NNNAM, PU; BL, BN. 637/6

——. The historie of the reigne of King Henrie the seaventh. *London: [W. Stansby,] for G. Latham, 1637.* 248 p.; fol. 1st publ., London, 1622; here a reissue with cancel t.p. of Gibson 116b. Gibson (Bacon) 119. MH. 637/7

——. Neuf livres de la dignité et l'accroissent des sciences. *Paris: J. Dugast, 1637.* 717 numb. lvs; 4to. 1st publ. as here transl. from Bacon's *Opera: Tomus primus* (London, 1623), Paris, 1632; here a reissue of that edn with cancel t.p. Gibson (Bacon) 139; Shaaber (Brit. auth.) B24. CCB. 637/8

——. Les oeuvres morales et politiques . . . de la version de J. Baudoin. *Paris: J. Guierche, 1637.* 639 p.; 8vo. 1st publ. in this form, Paris, 1626. Gibson (Bacon) 167a; Shaaber (Brit. auth.) B15. CCB, MH; BN. 637/9

—[Anr issue]. *Paris: H. LeGras, 1637.* Gibson (Bacon) 167b; Shaaber (Brit. auth.) B16. CCB; BN. 637/10

—[Anr issue]. *Paris: N. Bourdin & L. Périer, 1637.* Gibson (Bacon) 167c; Shaaber (Brit. auth.) B17. CCB; BL, BN. 637/11

—[Anr issue]. *Paris: J. Promé, 1637.* MH, MnU. 637/12

Barclay, John. Euphormionis Lusinini . . . Satyricon. *Leyden: Elsevier Office, 1637.* 717 p.; 12mo. Includes pt 2, 1st publ., Paris, 1607, & pt 4, the *Icon animorum,* 1st publ., London, 1614. Of this there are two separate edns, in one of which p. 207 & 209 are misnumbered 107 & 109. Shaaber (Brit. auth.) B200; Willems (Les Elzevier) 452;

Tchémerzine I:453. CU, DLC, ICN, MH, MiU, NNC, PPL, RPB; BL, Munich:StB. 637/13

Basset, Robert. Curiosities: or The cabinet of nature. *London: N. & J. Okes, 1637.* 287 p.; 12mo. In section 'Of smelling' tobacco is mentioned. STC 1557; Arents (Add.) 286. CSmH, DFo, ICU, MH, NN-A; BL. 637/14

Béguin, Jean. Les elemens de chymie . . . Quatriesme edition. *Rouen: M. de La Motte, 1637.* 432 p.; illus.; 8vo. 1st publ. as here transl. from Béguin's *Tyrocinium chymicum* (Paris, 1612), Paris, 1615. MH; Glasgow:UL, BN. 637/15

Betancurt, Luis de. Derecho de las iglesias metropolitanas, i catedrales de las Indias. *Madrid: F. Martínez, 1637.* 51 numb. lvs; 4to. 1st publ., Madrid, 1634, under title *Memorial i informacion por las iglesias metropolitanas;* cf. 1635 edn. Medina (BHA) 964; Streit I:465; Palau 28774; JCB (3) II:262. CU, CtY, MH, RPJCB; BL. 637/16

Beverwijck, Jan van. Idea medicinae veterum. *Leyden: Elsevier Office, 1637.* 390 p.; 8vo. Section on syphilis includes ref. to Columbus's voyages. Van de Velde 75; Molhuysen I:331; Willems (Les Elzevier) 453. CtY-M, DNLM, ICU, MH, MiU-C, NNC, PU; BL, BN. 637/17

——. Schat der gesontheyt. Met versssen verçiert door Heer Jacob Cats. Gedruckt na de copye. *Dordrecht: H. van Esch, for M. Havius, 1637,'36.* 2 pts; illus.; 8vo. 1st publ., [Dordrecht? 1636?]; pt 2 has colophon: Dordrecht, 1636, an apparent reissue. Arents (Add.) 287. NN-A; London: Wellcome. 637/18

—[Anr edn]. *[Dordrecht: H. van Esch, 1637].* 2 pts; illus.; 8vo. Existence of this edn inferred from pt 2 of the 1638 edn in National Library of Medicine. 637/19

Blaeu, Joan. Atlas minor, sive Tabulae geographicae orbis terrarum. *Amsterdam: J. Blaeu, 1637.* 224 maps; obl. 8vo. Maps, including several of America, are reissues of those from Hondius plates used for Bertius's *Tabularum geographicarum,* 1st publ., Amsterdam, 1600. Cf. Koeman (Lan) 14 (& v. I:71). RPJCB; Louvain:UB. 637/20

—[Anr issue?]. *Amsterdam: J. Blaeu, 1737 [i.e., 1637].* 226 maps; obl. 8vo. 637/21

——. Le nouveau phalot de la mer. *Amsterdam: J. Janszoon, the Younger*, 1637. 2 v.; illus., maps; obl. fol. 1st publ. in this revised French version, Amsterdam, 1635. Koeman (M. Bl) 25B (J). Amsterdam:UB.　637/22

Boccalini, Traiano. De' ragguagli di Parnaso . . . Centuria prima . . . settima impressione. *Venice: Heirs of G. Guerigli*, 1637. 8vo. 1st publ., Venice, 1612. Firpo (Ragguagli) 20. DLC, MiU.　637/23

——. De' ragguagli di Parnaso Centuria seconda . . . settima impressione. *Venice: Heirs of G. Guerigli*, 1637. 292 p.; 8vo. 1st publ., Venice, 1613; issued with the Guerigli Centuria prima of this year above. Firpo (Ragguagli) 20. DLC, MiU, RPB.　637/24

Boey, Cornelis. Illustrissimo heroi Mauritio, Comitii Nassovio . . . Rerum Indicarum ad Occidentem duci terra marique generalissimo, cum post expugnatam in Batavis Schenckianam Arcem, in Brasilia Portumcalvum hostile armamentarium subegisset, acto in fugam Hispanorum exercito. *The Hague: A. Tongerloo*, 1637. bds.; fol. Basis for Borba de Moraes's attribution of this work to Boey is unknown. Borba de Moraes I:96; Knuttel 4493. The Hague:KB.　637/25

Brébeuf, Jean de, S.J. Relation. *Paris*: 1637. See Paul LeJeune's *Relation* of this year below.

Breton, Nicholas. A poste with a packet of mad letters. Newly imprinted. *London: [M. Fletcher,] for J. Marriott*, 1637. 2 pts; 4to. 1st publ., London, 1602–5. STC 3694. DFo; BL.　637/26

Cats, Jacob. 's Werelts begin, midden, eynde, besloten in den trou-ringh, met den proef-steen van den selven. *Dordrecht: H. van Esch, for M. Havius*, 1637. 3 pts; illus.; 4to. In verse. Includes a fable, 'Roosen-krygh, ofte Herders trou-bedrogh', in imitation of Greek mythology, but with characters' names apparently drawn from American Indian culture, e.g. 'Chile', 'Mechoakanou', 'Xajonca', 'Ungas', 'Xancho', 'Napulka', 'Zumpogande', 'Taponga', 'Zeibo'. For variants see Mus. Cats. as cited. Mus. Cats. 171–73; Hoe (Foreign, 1909) I:223. ICN, NN-RB, NNC; BL, BN.　637/27

Cervantes Saavedra, Miguel de. Primera y Segunda parte del ingenioso hidalgo Don Quixote de la Mancha. *Madrid: F. Martínez, for D. González*, 1637,'36. 2 v.; 4to. Pt 2, with American refs, 1st publ., Madrid, 1615. Ríus (Cervantes) 17; Palau 51990. DLC, MH, NNH.　637/28

Clowes, William. A profitable and necessarie booke of observations . . . Last of all is adjoyned a short treatise, for the cure of Lues venerea . . . The third edition. *London: M. Dawson; sold by B. Allen & P. Cole*, 1637. 229 p.; 4to. 1st publ., London, 1596. For treatment of syphilis, use of *lignum sanctum* (guaiacum) or sarsaparilla is recommended. STC 5443. CSmH, CtY, DLC, IEN-M, NNNAM, PPC; BL.　637/29

Clüver, Johannes. Historiarum totius mundi epitome a prima rerum origine usque ad annum Christi MDCXXX. *Leyden: J. Marcus*, 1637. 816 p.; 4to. Included are refs to Columbus, Vespucci, and Magellan, and to syphilis as brought from New World, etc. ICU, OU, WU; BN.　637/30

Clüver, Philipp. Introductionis in universam geographiam, tam veterem quàm novam, libri vi. Editio ultima priorib. emendatior. *Amsterdam: Hondius Office*, 1637. 352 p.; illus.; 16mo. 1st publ., Leyden, 1624. Cf. Sabin 13805. ICN, N.　637/31

Coppie de la fleur de la passion qui croist dans les Indes Occidentales [Faict . . . par I. V. E.]. *Paris*: 1637. bds.; illus.; fol. BL (E., I.V.).　637/32

Drayton, Michael. Poems . . . Newly corrected & augmented. *London: J. Smethwick*, 1637. 487 p.; 12mo. 1st publ., London, 1605. STC 7225. CSmH, CtY, DFo, ICN, MH, MiU, MnU, NNPM, PU; BL.　637/33

Du Bartas, Guillaume de Salluste, seigneur. Foure bookes of Du Bartas. *London: T. Paine, for F. Eglesfield*, 1637. 186 (i.e., 273) p.; 4to. 1st publ. as transl. by William L'Isle from the 2nd day of Du Bartas's *La seconde sepmaine*, London, 1625, under title *Part of Du Bartas;* here a reissue of that edn with the 1st sheet reset. STC 21663a.5. CSmH, DFo (imp.), MH, ViU.　637/34

——. A learned summary upon the famous poem of William of Saluste, lord of Bartas . . . Translated out of French, by T[homas]. L[odge]. *London: [A. Mathewes,] for A. Crooke*, 1637. 2 pts; fol. 1st publ. as here transl., London, 1621; a reissue with cancel t.p. of that edn. STC 21667. CtY, DFo, DLC; Cambridge:UL. 637/35

—[Anr issue]. *London: [A. Mathewes,] for A. C[rooke].,* 1637. 'Part of the impression to be vented for the benefit of E. Minsheu'. STC 21667.5. DFo, IU, MH; BL. 637/36

Estienne, Charles. L'agriculture et maison rustique. *Lyons: C. Rigaud & P. Borde,* 1637. 709 p.; illus.; 4to. 1st publ. as here enl. by Liébault, Paris, 1567; cf. 1601 edn. BN. 637/37

Examen over het Vertoogh tegen het ongefondeerde ende schadelijck sluyten der vryen handel in Brasil. Door een onder soecker der waerheyt. [*The Hague?*] 1637. 16 p.; 4to. A reply to the *Vertoogh by een lief-hebber* of this year below. Sabin 7575; Asher 165; Petit 1990. DLC; Leyden:B. Thysiana. 637/38

—[Anr edn]. [*The Hague?*] 1637. 15 p.; 4to. This edn has reading 'onghefondeerde' on t.p. Sabin 7576; Borba de Moraes I:253; Rodrigues (Dom. Hol.) 728; Knuttel 4515; Kress 526. MH-BA; The Hague: KB. 637/39

—[Anr edn]. [*The Hague?*] 1637. 16 p.; 4to. This edn has reading 'ongefondeerde' & 'waerheydt' on t.p. Tiele (Pamfletten) 2607. 637/40

—[Anr edn]. [*The Hague?*] 1637. 16 p.; 4to. This edn has reading 'ongefondeerde' & 'schadelijcke' on t.p. Tiele (Pamfletten) 2608. 637/41

Fernel, Jean. Universa medicina. *Geneva: J. Stoer,* 1637. 1172 p.; 4to. 1st publ. as here constituted, Paris, 1567; cf. 1601–2 edns. Sherrington (Fernel) 81.J25. CtY-M, DNLM; London:Wellcome, Paris:Faculté de Médecine. 637/42

Fracastoro, Girolamo. Opera pars prior. Philosophica et medica continens. *Geneva: J. Stoer,* 1637. 3 pts; 8vo. 1st publ. as here collected, Venice, 1555; cf. 1621 edn. Baumgartner (Fracastoro) 41; Waller 3170. CtY-M, DNLM, MH, WU-M; Oxford:Bodl., BN. 637/43

France. Amirauté. Reglement donné par monseigneur le Cardinal de Richelieu . . . sur le faict des congez donnez aux m[aitr]es de navires. *Rouen: D. Du Petit Val & J. Viret,* 1637. 8 p.; 8vo. 'Extrait du Registre des expeditions du greffe de l'Amirauté de France pour le siege de Grandcamp . . . '—caption title, p. [3]; 'Faict à Paris le deuxiesme jour de Janvier mil six cens vingt-sept'—p. [7]. Mentions 'les navires qui feront voyage en la Terre-neufve, Canadas', etc. RPJCB. 637/44

Garavito, Gerónimo. Señor. Geronimo Garavito procurador general del gremio de los açogueros dela villa . . . de Potosi del Pirú, digo, que a los doze . . . de noviembre del año passado de 1636. puse en las reales manos . . . tres memoriales, en que ponia el lamentable estado que tenia los cosas del Cerro rico. [*Madrid:* 1637]. [4] p.; fol. Memorial to king of Spain. BL. 637/45

——. Señor. Geronimo Garavito, procurador general del gremio de los azogueros de . . . Potosi del Piro. Digo, que tengo presentados a V.M. muchos memoriales, suplicando . . . quel el Consejo de las Indias resolviesse los catorze puntos del primero que puse en los reales manos . . . a los doze de noviembre del año passado de mil y seiscientos y treinta y seis. [*Madrid:* 1637]. [4] p.; fol. Memorial to king of Spain in behalf of Indians of Potosí. BL. 637/46

——. Señor. Geronimo Garavito, procurador general del gremio de los azogueros, y mineros de . . . Potosi del Piru, dize: Que es notorio, y en el Real Consejo de Indias paracen los muchos memoriales que ha presentado desde los doze de noviembre del año passado de mil y seiscientos y treinta y seis hasta oy, pues los mas dellos han sidos dirigidos a manifestar el gran tesoro que ha perdido . . . en aquella villa, y provincia de los Charcas V. Mag. [*Madrid?* 1637]. [3] p.; fol. BL. 637/47

Gomberville, Marin Le Roy, sieur du Parc et de. La première [-quatriesme] partie de Polexandre. *Paris: A. Courbé,* 1637. 5 v.; 8vo. A further reworking & expansion of author's *Exil de Polexandre,* Paris, 1629; cf.1632 edn. American materials are retained from the latter. 637/48

Grau y Monfalcón, Juan. Memorial informativo al Rey . . . en su Real . . . Consejo de las Indias. Por la . . . ciudad de Manila . . . sobre las pretensiones de aquella ciudad y islas . . . y moradores, y comercio con la Nueva España. *Madrid: Imprenta Real,* 1637. 21 numb. lvs; fol. Medina (BHA) 967; Palau 108813. CSmH; Madrid:Acad. de la Hist. 637/49

Great Britain. Sovereigns, etc., 1625–1649 (Charles I). A proclamation against the disorderly transporting His Majesties subjects to . . . America. *London: R. Barker & assigns of J. Bill,* 1637. bds.; fol. Sabin 65939; Crawford (Roy. procl.) 1745; Brigham (Roy. procl.) 80–82; STC 9086. MB, MH; BL. 637/50

——. A proclamation concerning tobacco. *London: R. Barker & assigns of J. Bill,* 1637 [i.e., 1638]. *See the year* 1638.

Greene, Robert. Theeves falling out. *London: H. & M. Bell,* 1637. 4to. 1st publ., London, 1592; cf. 1615 edn. STC 12238. CSmH, DFo; BL. 637/51

Guibert, Philbert. Les oeuvres du medecin charitable. *Paris: J. Gesselin,* 1637. 735 p.; 8vo. Included is Guibert's *Le prix et valeur des medicaments,* 1st publ., Paris, 1625. BN. 637/52

——. Toutes les oeuvres charitables. *Paris: J. Jost,* 1637. 874 p.; 8vo. Included is Guibert's *Le prix & valeur des medicamens,* 1st publ., Paris, 1625. BN. 637/53

Guillén y Colón, Francisco, O. Merced. Vita, muerte y milagros del prodigioso varon . . . fray Gonçalo Diaz, religioso lego del Orden de N. Señora de la Merced . . . hijo professo de la casa de Lima. *Seville: S. Fajardo,* 1637. 27 numb. lvs; 4to. Medina (BHA) 968; Palau 110863. 637/54

Den handel ende wandel van den stichtsen joncker. [*Amsterdam?* 1637?]. [8] p.; 4to. Charges Ernst van Rede, Heer van der Vuyrst, director of the West-Indische Compagnie, & other directors with intrigues with that company's suppliers. Knuttel 4519. The Hague: KB. 637/55

Horst, Gregor. Observationum medicinalium singularium libri quatuor posteriores . . . Editio nova completa. *Nuremberg: W. Endter,* 1637. 652 p.; 4to. 1st publ., Ulm, 1628. Wellcome I:3313. DNLM; London: Wellcome. 637/56

Inquisition. Spain. Copia de la consulta que el Consejo supremo de la general Inquisicion hizo a Su Magestad en 2. de abril deste año de 637. sobre la persona del . . . d.

Domingo Velez de Assas y Argos inquisidor . . . de la Inquisicion de Cartagena de las Indias. [*Madrid?* 1637?]. [3] p.; fol. Medina (BHA) 966. Santiago, Chile:BN. 637/57

Le Jeune, Paul, S.J. Relation de ce qui s'est passé en la Nouvelle France en l'année 1636. *Paris: S. Cramoisy,* 1637. 2 pts (272 & 223 p.); 8vo. The 2nd pt comprises Jean de Brébeuf's *Relation de ce qui s'est passé dans le pays des Hurons en l'année 1636.* For variants, see McCoy. Sabin 39952; Harrisse (NF) 65; Bell (Jes. rel.) 8; McCoy 21–22; Streit II:2510; Church 436; JCB (3) II:264. CSmH, CtY, DLC, MH, MiU-C, MnU-B, NN-RB, RPJCB; Göttingen:UB. 637/58

——[Anr edn]. *Paris: S. Cramoisy,* 1637. 2 pts (199 & 163 p.); 8vo. Sabin 39952; Harrisse (NF) 66; McCoy 23; Streit II:2510. CSmH, InU-L; BL, BN. 637/59

Linden, Johannes Antonides van der. De scriptis medicis, libri duo. *Amsterdam: J. Blaeu,* 1637. 559 p.; 8vo. Includes categories for mechoacan, tobacco, guaiacum (as both *lignum sanctum* & *Guaiacum*), sarsaparilla, & sassafras. Wellcome I:3807. CU-M; BL, BN. 637/60

López de Altuna, Pedro, O.SS.Tr. Primera parte de la Coronica general del Orden de la Santissima Trinidad. *Segovia: D. Díaz de la Carrera,* 1637. 637 p.; fol. The 3rd bk discusses the order's missions in America. Streit I:466. BL, Rome:B. Casanatense. 637/61

Maffei, Giovanni Pietro, S.J. Historiarum Indicarum libri xvi. *Lyons: J. Champion,* 1637. 718 p.; 8vo. 1st publ., Florence, 1588; cf. 1605 edn. Here a reissue of printer's 1636 edn with altered imprint date? Sabin 43774; cf. Borba de Moraes II:10; Streit V:336; Backer V:299; Palau 146985. RPJCB; BL, BN. 637/62

Markham, Gervase. The English housewife. *London: Anne Griffin, for J. Harrison,* 1637. 252 p.; 4to. (*In* Markham's *A way to get wealth,* London, 1638). 1st publ., London, 1615, as pt 2 of Markham's *Countrey contentments.* Poynter (Markham) 34.6; STC 17397. CSmH, CtY, MH, NNNAM, PPL; BL. 637/63

Menéndez Silva, Rodrigo. Catalogo real de España. *Madrid: Imprenta Real,* 1637. 135 numb. lvs; 8vo. Account of Ferdinand &

Isabella mentions Columbus & his discoveries; the account of Charles V, the further discoveries in the West Indies, Mexico, & Peru of Cortés, Magellan, & Pizarro. BL.
637/64

Mercator, Gerardus. Appendix Atlantis, ofte Vervolgh van de gantsche Werelt-beschrijvinghe. *Amsterdam: J. Janszoon, the Younger, & H. Hondius,* 1637. 1 v.; 106 maps; fol. Prob. transl. from Mercator's *Appendix novi Atlantis* below. Koeman (Me) 48; Tiele 744. Leeuwarden:PB. 637/65

——. Appendix novi atlantis, continens regiones . . . Galliae . . . Americae, &c. *Amsterdam: J. Janszoon, the Younger,* 1637. 108 maps; fol. 1st publ., Amsterdam, 1630, under title *Atlantis majoris appendix,* but here enl. by addition of maps introduced in intervening French and German edns. Koeman (Me) 47. Leeuwarden: Buma, Vienna:NB. 637/66

——. Historia mundi, or Mercator's atlas . . . Englished by W[ye]. S[altonstall]. . . . Second edytion. *London: M. Sparke,* 1637. 930 p.; illus., maps; fol. 1st publ. in this version, London, 1635; here a reissue with added engr. t.p., the original printed t.p. with 1635 imprint date being retained. Also added is Ralph Hall's 1636 map of Virginia & an expanded introduction. Sabin 47785; Koeman II:549; Phillips (Atlases) 451 & 4255; STC 17825; JCB (3) II:265. CSmH, CtY, DLC, ICN, InU, MH, MiU-C, NN-RB, RPJCB; BL, Oxford:Bodl. 637/67

More, Sir Thomas, Saint. Utopia . . . traducida de latin . . . por Don Gregorio Antonio de Medinilla i Porres. *Córdoba: S. de Cea Tesa,* 1637. 51 numb. lvs; 8vo. 1st publ. in Latin, Louvain, 1516; cf. Valdenebro (Córdoba) 166; Palau 300427. NNH; Madrid:BN. 637/68

Morton, Thomas. New English Canaan or new Canaan. Containing an abstract of New England. *Amsterdam: J. F. Stam,* 1637. 188 p.; 4to. Describes both Plymouth & Massachusetts Bay settlements, as well as natural history & Indians, in a satirical vein that caused Morton's banishment. Sabin 51028; Vail (Frontier) 90; STC 18202; Church 437; JCB (3) II:265-66. CSmH, CtY, DLC, ICN, MH, MiU-C, MWA, NN-RB, PPL, RPJCB; BL. 637/69

—[Anr issue]. [*Amsterdam: J. F. Stam,*] *for C. Greene, at London* [1637?]. Sabin 51028n; Vail (Frontier) 90n; STC 18203. BL, Chatsworth. 637/70

Murga, Francisco de. Señor. El maestro de campo Francisco de Murga . . . governador . . . de Cartagena, y su provincia. [*Madrid?* 1637]. 20 numb. lvs; fol. Memorial to king of Spain on affairs of Colombia. BL. 637/71

Nederlandsche West-Indische Compagnie. Octroy by de . . . Staten Generael, verleent aende West-Indische Compagnie. *The Hague: Widow & Heirs of H. Jacobszoon van Wouw,* 1637. [32] p.; 4to. 1st publ. in this enl. version, The Hague, 1623. Sabin 56672 (& 102901). DLC, NN-RB. 637/72

Netherlands (United Provinces, 1581–1795). Staten Generaal. Nader ordre ende reglement vande . . . Staten Generael . . . ghearresteert by advijs . . . vande bewindthebberen vande . . . West-Indische Compagnie. *The Hague: Widow & Heirs of H. Jacobszoon van Wouw,* 1637. [6] p.; 4to. 1st publ., The Hague, 1635. Sabin 51706; Borba de Moraes II:94; Asher 163. BL. 637/73

—[Anr edn]. *The Hague: Widow & Heirs of H. Jacobszoon van Wouw,* 1637. [6] p.; 4to. This edn has reading 'bewint-hebberen' on t.p. Meulman 2406. DLC, NN-RB; Ghent:BU. 637/74

Norwood, Richard. The sea-mans practice, contayning a fundamentall probleme in navigation, experimentally verified. *London: [B. Alsop & T. Fawcet, for] G. Hurlock,* 1637. 88 lvs; illus.; 4to. Dedication refers to conversion of 'silly catives of Sathan in America' by settlements there; in text, Virginia, New England, Sir Francis Drake, the West Indies, etc., are mentioned. STC 18691. CtY, DFo; BL. 637/75

Opitz, Martin. Deutscher Poematum. Erster[-Anderer] Theil. Zum drittenmal . . . herausgegeben. [*Breslau? Lübeck?*] 1637. 697 p.; 8vo. 1st publ. in this version, Breslau, 1628–29; imprint date from pt 2. Goedeke III:48. InU-L, MB, MdBJ; Göttingen: StUB. 637/76

Pardoux, Barthélemy. Ars sanitatis tuendae. *Paris: L. Boullenger & J. Laquehay,* 1637. 239

p.; 12mo. 1st publ., Paris, 1630, as bk 4 of the author's *Universa medicina*. In discussion of food values of fowl, the turkey, 'gallo indico', is mentioned. BL, BN.   637/77

Perea, Pedro de. Señor. Don Pedro de Perea, governador y capitan de la provincia de Sinaloa, y la Nueva Andaluzia. Dice [etc.]. [*Madrid?* 1637?]. 6 numb. 1vs; fol. A detailed account, addressed to the king of Spain, of Perea's services as governor of the province. CtY.   637/78

Pigray, Pierre. Epitome des preceptes de medecine et chirurgiae. *Lyons: P. Bailly,* 1637. 764 p.; port.; 8vo. 1st publ., Paris, 1600, under title *La chirurgie;* cf. 1604 edn. London:Wellcome.   637/79

—[Anr issue?]. *Lyons: L. Odain,* 1637. MH.   637/80

—[Anr issue?]. *Lyons: Widow of C. Rigaud, & P. Borde,* 1637. DNLM.   637/81

Pinto de Moraes, Jorge. Maravillas del Parnaso y flor de los mejores romances. *Lisbon: L. Craesbeeck,* 1637. 96 numb. 1vs; 4to. Includes the 'Jugete satirico' of Quevedo y Villegas beginning 'Poderoso cavallero es don Dinero' found earlier in Pedro de Espinosa's *Flores de poetas ilustres,* Valladolid, 1605. Other poems also include refs to the Indies. Palau 226691. NNH.   637/82

Pontanus, Johannes Isaacus. Discussionum historicarum libri duo. Quibus praecipuè quatenus & quodnam mare liberum vel non liberum clausumque accipiendum dispicitur expenditurque. *Harderwijk: N. van Wieringen,* 1637. 431 p.; 8vo. In bk 1, chapt. xiv, Camden on Drake's exploits of 1580 in New World is quoted; chapt. xxiii discusses Greenland. Sabin 64001. CLL, DLC, MH, MiU-C, NN-RB, RPJCB; BL, BN.   637/83

Remonstrance tres-humble en forme d'advertissement, qui font au Roy & a nosseigneurs de son Conseil, les capitaines de la marine de France. [*Paris?* 1637?]. 16 p.; 8vo. Petition seeking permission for arming of French vessels for protection from Spanish & Portuguese, citing past attacks by them. Borba de Moraes II:198. BN.   637/84

Renou, Jean de. Les oeuvres pharmaceutiques . . . Augmentées . . . en cette seconde edition par l'auteur; puis traduittes . . . par m. Louys de Serres. *Lyons: N. Gay,*

1637. 762 p.; illus.; fol. 1st publ., Paris, 1608, under title *Institutionum pharmaceuticarum.* DNLM.   637/85

Saint-Amant, Marc Antoine de Gérard, sieur de. Les oeuvres. *Lyons: J. Jacquemetton,* 1637. 408 p.; 8vo. In verse. 1st publ., Paris, 1629. Tchémerzine X:83.   637/86

Saldías, Pedro de. Tabla para la reducion de barras de plata de todas leyes a maravedis. *Seville: F. de Lyra,* 1637. 4 pts; obl. 4to. Medina (BHA) 972. CtY; Santiago, Chile:BN (missing, 1942).   637/87

Sánchez, Antonio. Todo el pleyto que siguen los dueños de barras del Pirù, con los compradores de plata de la ciudad de Sevilla, se reduce . . . en una demonstracion mathematica innegable. [*Madrid?* 1637]. 7 numb. 1vs; fol. Subscribed: Madrid, á 12 de Octubre de 1637. Medina (BHA) 974; Palau 294050. BL.   637/88

Sandys, Sir Edwin. Europae speculum; or, A view or survey of the state of religion. *London: T. Cotes, for M. Sparke; sold by G. Hutton,* 1637. 248 p.; 4to. 1st publ., London, 1605, under title *A relation of the state of religion.* STC 21721. CSmH, CtY, DFo, ICN, MH, NHi; BL, BN.   637/89

Sandys, George. A relation of a journey . . . containing a description of the Turkish empire . . . Fourth edition. *London: [T. Cotes,] for A. Crooke,* 1637. 309 p.; illus., maps; fol. 1st publ., London, 1615. STC 21730. CSmH, DFo, IU, MH, PPL; Oxford:Bodl.   637/90

Schouten, Willem Corneliszoon. Journael ofte Beschryvinghe vande wonderlijcke reyse. *Rotterdam: I. van Waesberghen,* 1637. 53 p.; illus., maps; 4to. 1st publ., Amsterdam 1618. Sabin 77927; Palau 305088; Tiele-Muller 47; JCB (3) II:266. NN-RB, RPJCB; BL.   637/91

Simón, Pedro. Noticias historiales de las conquistas de Tierra Firme, en las Indias Occidentales. *Cuenca: D. de la Iglesia,* 1637. 671 p.; fol. 1st publ., Cuenca, 1627; here a reissue of that edn with cancel t.p. Cf. Sabin 81286; cf. Medina (BHA) 818; Streit II:1649; JCB (3) II:266. ICN, RPJCB.   637/92

Speagle, Huldricke van, pseud. Drinke and welcome. *London:* 1637. *See* Taylor, John, the Water-poet, *below.*

Tassoni, Alessandro. La secchia rapita, poema eroicomico . . . e 'l primo canto dell'Oceano. *Venice: G. Scaglia,* 1637. 388 p.; 12mo. 1st publ., Paris, 1622. Cf. Sabin 94402; Puliatti (Tassoni) 105. BN.
637/93

Taylor, John, the Water-poet. Drinke and welcome: or the Historie of the most part of drinks in use now in Great Brittaine and Ireland . . . Compiled first in the high Dutch tongue, by Huldricke van Speagle [pseud.] . . . and translated into English prose and verse. By John Taylor. *London: Anne Griffin,* 1637. [25] p.; 4to. In discussing perry (derived from pears), records theory that it derives from 'Perrue in America'. STC 23749. CSmH, MH, PBL; BL.
637/94

Torsellino, Orazio, S.J. Historiarum ab origine mundi ad annum 1630 epitome libri x. *Paris:* 1637. 12mo. 1st publ., Rome, 1598; cf. 1620 edn. Backer VIII:152. 637/95

——. Ristretto delle historie del mondo . . . volgarizzato dal sig. Lodovico Aurelii. *Rome: G. Mascardi, for P. Totti,* 1637. 720 p.; port.; 12mo. 1st publ. as here transl. from Latin text (1st publ., Rome, 1598), Rome, 1634. Backer VIII:156. BL, BN. 637/96

Udemans, Godefridus Corneliszoon. Geestelick compas, dat is Nut en nootwendigh bericht voor alle zee-varende . . . Den derden druck verbetert ende seer verm. . . . met een nieu tractaet van den coophandel, ende de coop-vaert. Item De vaert op Oost ende West-Indien. *Dordrecht: H. van Esch, for F. Boels,* 1637. 396 p.; 8vo. Though no earlier edn has been found, the work was perhaps 1st publ., Zierikzee, 1617, as dated at end of preface. Though no special section on commerce or Indian navigation is present, the work does include minor American refs. Cf. Muller (1872) 1536. MH-BA. 637/97

Venner, Tobias. Via recta ad vitam longam . . . As also an accurate treatise concerning tobacco. *London: R. Bishop, for H. Hood,* 1637. 364 p.; 4to. The treatise of tobacco 1st publ., London, 1621. Sabin 98890n; STC 24646; Arents 146-a. CSmH, DFo, ICU, MiU, NN-A; BL. 637/98

Vertoogh by een lief-hebber des vaderlants vertoont. Teghen het ongefondeerde ende

schadelijck sluyten vryen handel in Brazil. [*The Hague:*] 1637. [6] p.; 4to. For a reply, see the *Examen over het Vertoogh* of this year above. Sabin 99308; Borba de Moraes II:345; Rodrigues (Dom. Hol.) 727; Knuttel 4514; JCB (3) II:266. DLC, NN-RB, RPJCB; BL (Brazil), The Hague:KB. 637/99

Villa, Esteban de. Ramillete de plantas. *Burgos: P. Gómez de Valdivielso,* 1637. 148 numb. 1vs; 4to. On 1f 7v Monardes's work on plants of New Spain is mentioned; on 1f 23r medical use of mechoacan & sarsaparilla is cited; elsewhere further refs to the New World occur. Pritzel 9770; Palau 366188. DNLM, MH-A; BL. 637/100

Vincent, Philip. A true relation of the late battell fought in New England, between the English, and the salvages: with the present state of things there. *London: M. P[arsons]., for N. Butter & J. Bellamy,* 1637. 23 p.; 4to. For variant states, see Sabin. Sabin 99760–62; Vail (Frontier) 91; STC 24758; JCB (3) II:267. CSmH, MHi, MiU (imp.), NN-RB, RPJCB; BL. 637/101

Wilkins, George. The miseries of inforst mariage. *London: J. N[orton]., for R. Thrale,* 1637. 38 1vs; 4to. Drama. 1st publ., London, 1607. STC 25638; Greg 249 (d). CSmH, CtY, DLC, ICN, MH, MiU, NN-RB; BL. 637/102

Zacutus, Abraham, Lusitanus. De medicorum principum historia. *Amsterdam: H. Laurenszoon,* 1637. 2 v.; fol. 1st publ., Cologne, 1629. OCH. 637/103

——. Praxis medica admiranda. *Lyons: J. A. Huguetan,* 1637. 634 p.; 8vo. 1st publ., Amsterdam, 1634. Wellcome I:6791. CtY, DNLM, MBCo, NNJ; London:Wellcome. 637/104

1638

Aldrovandi, Ulisse. De piscibus libri v. et de cetis lib. unus. *Bologna: N. Tebaldini,* 1638. 732 p.; illus.; fol. 1st publ., Bologna, 1612. Nissen (Zool.) 70n. CU, DNLM, ICJ, MH, MiU, MnU, PPL; BL, BN. 638/1

Alemán, Mateo. Le gueux, ou La vie de Guzman d'Alfarache. *Paris: A. Cotinet,* 1638–39. 2 v.; 8vo. 1st publ. as here transl. by Jean Chapelain, Paris, 1619 & 1620. Vol. 2 has

title *Le voleur, ou La vie de Guzman d'Alfarache.*
Laurenti (Nov. pic. esp.) 624? DLC.
                                                    638/2

—[Anr issue?]. *Paris: D. Houssaye,* 1638–39.
2 v.; 8vo. Laurenti (Nov. pic. esp.) 623.
                                                    638/3

Avila y Lugo, Francisco de. Memorial al
Rey. [*Madrid:* 1638]. [4] p.; fol. Relates ser-
vices of ancestors in Spanish America &
own as governor of Honduras, capture by
Dutch, and adventures with Indians. Maggs
Cat. 496 (Americana VI):90.   638/4

Avity, Pierre d', sieur de Montmartin. Archontologia cosmica, sive Imperiorum, regnorum principatuum, rerumque publicarum omnium per totum terrarum orbem
commentarii. *Frankfurt a.M.: W. Hoffmann,
for M. Merian,* 1638. 1154 p.; illus., maps;
4to. Transl. by J. L. Gottfried from the author's *Les estats, empires et principautez du
monde,* 1st publ., Paris, 1613.; cf. 1628 Latin
edn. NNH; BN, Munich:StB.   638/5

——. Les estats, empires et principautez du
monde. *Rouen: J. Berthelin,* 1638. 1396 p.;
fol. 1st publ., Paris, 1613. Cf. Sabin 2498.
Vienna:BN.   638/6

——. Neuwe Archontologia cosmica, das ist,
Beschreibung aller Käyserthumben, König-
reichen und Republicken der gantzen
Welt. *Frankfurt a. M.: W. Hoffman, for M.
Merian,* 1638. 760 p.; illus., maps; fol.
Transl. by J. L. Gottfried from the author's
Les estats, empires et principautez du monde, 1st
publ., Paris, 1613. Jantz (German Baroque)
1135. DLC, IU, NcU; BL, BN.   638/7

Bacon, Francis, viscount St Albans. Historia naturalis et experimentalis de ventis etc.
Leyden: F. Heger & F. Haack, 1638. 340 p.;
12mo. 1st publ., London, 1622, under title
*Historia naturalis . . . ad condendam philoso-
phiam.* Gibson (Bacon) 109; Shaaber (Brit.
auth.) B37. CU, CtY, DLC, MH, PPL, WU;
BL, BN.   638/8

——. The historie of life and death. *London:
J. Okes, for H. Moseley,* 1638. 323 p.; 12mo.
Transl. from Bacon's *Historia vitae & mortis*
of 1623; an unauthorized version, by an unknown hand, differing from that entered below. Gibson (Bacon) 153; STC 1157; Arents
204. CSmH, CtY, DLC, IU, MH, NN-RB,
PPC; BL.   638/9

——. History naturall and experimentall, of

life and death. *London: J. Haviland; for W.
Lee & H. Moseley,* 1638. 434 p.; 12mo. Translation prepared by William Rawley from
Bacon's *Historia vitae & mortis* of 1623; a
differing version from that entered
above. Gibson (More) 154; STC 1158.
CSmH, CtY, DLC, ICN, MH, NNC; BL.
                                                    638/10

——. Opera moralium et civilium tomus ab
ipso . . . auctore . . . latinite donatus. *London: E. Griffin, for R. Whitaker,* 1638. 2 pts;
port.; fol. Included in translation are Bacon's *Historie of the raigne of King Henry the
Seventh,* 1st publ., London, 1622; and his
New Atlantis, London, 1626; as well as the
*Historia naturalis . . . ad condendam philoso-
phiam* (here designated *Historia ventorum*),
London, 1622, & the *Historia vitae et mortis,*
London, 1623. For variant issues, see Gibson. Gibson (Bacon) 196–97; STC 1109–
10. CSmH, CtY, DLC, InU-L, MH, MiU,
PU; BL, BN.   638/11

Barnuevo, Rodrigo, S.J. Muy poderoso
señor. El padre Rodrigo de Barrionuevo,
de la Compañia de Jesus. [*Madrid?* 1638?].
[4] p.; fol. Memorial to king of Spain on
Jesuits in Peru. Medina (BHA) 6254. BL.
                                                    638/12

Beverwijck, Jan van. Schat der gesontheyt.
Tweede druck; met veersen verçiert door
. . . Jacob Cats. Merckelick vermeedert.
Dordrecht: H. van Esch, for M. Havius,
1638,'37. 778 p.; illus.; 8vo. 1st publ., [Dor-
drecht? 1636?]. Pt 2, an apparent reissue,
has imprint: Dordrecht: H. van Esch, 1637.
Cf. Molhuysen I:331. DNLM, IaU, NN-RB.
                                                    638/13

Blaeu, Willem Janszoon. Appendice dela i
& ii parties du Théatre du monde, ou nouvel atlas. [*Amsterdam: W. J. & J. Blaeu,* ca.
1638]. 24 maps; fol. Cf. Blaeu's *Theatre du
monde . . . 3me partie,* Amsterdam, 1640,
with which this was sometimes issued. Includes map of Florida, & another of arctic
regions, showing part of North America.
Koeman (Bl) 15.   638/14

——. Novus atlas, das ist Weltbeschreibung
. . . erster Theil. *Amsterdam: J. & C. Blaeu,*
1638. 1st publ., Amsterdam, 1634; cf. 1635
edn. Koeman (Bl) 7B. Wertheim:RL.
                                                    638/15

——. Le theatre du monde, ou Nouvel atlas.

Amsterdam: W. J. & J. Blaeu, 1638. 2 pts; 120 maps; fol. 1st publ. in French, Amsterdam, 1635; here added are 20 maps from Blaeu's *Appendice* above, including 'Pays sous le Pole Arctique', showing part of North America. Issued with Blaeu's *Theatre . . . seconde partie*, Amsterdam, 1640. Koeman (Bl) 16A. DLC, MiU-C; BL, Amsterdam:UB.
638/16

——. Tweevoudigh onderwijs. *Amsterdam:* 1638. 4to. 1st publ., Amsterdam, 1634. Keuning (Blaeu) 62–63; Houzeau/Lancaster I:9714.
638/17

——. Zeespiegel. *Amsterdam: W. J. & J. Blaeu*, 1638. 3 pts; illus., maps; fol. 1st publ., Amsterdam, 1623. Koeman (M.Bl) 34; Tiele 124n.
638/18

Bloys, William. Adam in his innocence. *London: R. Young, for G. Latham*, 1638. 279 p.; 12mo. On p. 26 the failures of those seeking a Northwest Passage are mentioned. STC 3139. DFo, MH; BL.
638/19

Blundeville, Thomas. Mr. Blundevil his exercises . . . The seventh edition corrected and somewhat enlarged by Ro. Hartwell. *London: R. Bishop; sold by W. Hope*, 1638,'36. 799 p.; illus., map; 4to. 1st publ., London, 1594; cf. 1606 edn; here a reissue of the printer's 1636 edn. Also included is John Blagrave's *A very brief . . . description of Master Blagrave his Astrolabe*, 1st publ., London, 1585. STC 2151a. CSmH, MeB, NN-RB; Dublin:Marsh's Libr.
638/20

Brathwaite, Richard. Barnabae itinerarium, Mirtili & Faustuli nominibus insignitum. [*London: J. Haviland*, 1638?]. [448] p.; 16mo. In verse. In 4 bks, the 1st two of which had been publ., [London: ca. 1636] in Latin alone. Here Latin & English texts appear on facing pages. STC 3556; Arents 205. CSmH, CtY, DFo, IU, NN-A; BL.
638/21

Breton, Nicholas. Conceited leters, newly layd open. *London: M. Parsons, for S. Rand*, 1638. [45] p.; 4to. 1st publ., London, 1618. ICN.
638/22

Bril-gesicht voor de verblinde eyghen baetsuchtige handelaers op Brasil. By forme van adviis door enn lief-hebber van 't vaderlant geschreven aen synen vriendt. [*Amsterdam?*] 1638. 7 p.; 4to. Sabin 7345 (& 7981); Borba de Moraes I:110; Rodrigues (Dom. Hol.)

432 & 733; JCB (3) II:267. DLC, RPJCB.
638/23

Burton, Robert. The anatomy of melancholy . . . The fift edition, corrected and augmented by the author. *Oxford: [R. Young, at Edinburgh, J. Lichfield & W. Turner] for H. Cripps*, 1638. 723 p.; fol. 1st publ., Oxford, 1621. Madan (Oxford) 1638:3; STC 4163; Arents (Add.) 225. CSmH, CtY, DFo, ICN, InU-L, MH, NN-A, PPL; BL.
638/24

Calancha, Antonio de la, O.S.A. Coronica moralizada del orden de San Augustin en el Peru . . . Primer tomo. *Barcelona: P. Lacavallería*, 1638. 922 p.; illus.; 8vo. The earliest work to mention use by Indians of cinchona, 'Peruvian' or 'Fever' bark, for treatment of fever. A 2nd vol. was printed at Lima in 1653. Sabin 9870; Medina (BHA) 977; cf. Streit II:1663; Palau 39450; cf. JCB (3) II:267. CtY, ICN, MH, NN-RB; BL.
638/25

Casas, Bartolomé de las, O.P., Bp of Chiapa. Den spiegel der Spaense tyrannye geschiet in West-Indien. [*Amsterdam: E. Cloppenburg*, 1638]. [104] p.; illus.; 4to. 1st publ. in this version, Amsterdam, 1620. Sometimes bound with Gysius's continuation *Tweede deel van de Spiegel der Spaense tyrannye*, q.v. below. Sabin 11262; Medina (BHA) 1085n (II:477); Tiele-Muller 318; Meulman 1730; cf. Streit I:472. CtY, NN-RB; Ghent:BU.
638/26

—[Anr edn]. Den spieghel der Spaensche tyrannye. *Amsterdam: E. Cloppenburg*, 1638. [104] p.; illus.; 4to. This edn has imprint on t.p. and slight variations in title. Hanke/Giménez 532; Meulman 1731; JCB (3) II:268. CtY, DLC, RPJCB; Ghent:BU.
638/27

Cats, Jacob. 's Werelts begin, midden, eynde. *Dordrecht: H. van Esch, for M. Havius*, 1638. 639 p.; illus., port.; 8vo. 1st publ., Dordrecht, 1637. Mus. Cats. 174. BL, Leyden:UB.
638/28

Consideratien als dat de negotie op Brasil behoort open gestelt te worden . . . door Jor. H. Gr. Gron[ingen]. [*Amsterdam?*] 1638. 9 p.; 4to. Relates to the West-Indische Compagnie. Borba de Moraes I:170; Asher 167; Knuttel 4580. BL (Gron, H. Gr.), The Hague:KB.
638/29

Contreras y Valverde, Blasco de. Discurso, que propone en justicia el derecho que tienen los cabildos, y capitulares del Perù a la reformacion de la cédula, que les prohibe las visitas. *Madrid: F. Martínez,* 1638. 33 numb. lvs; fol. Medina (BHA) 978; Palau 60828. Seville:BU.   638/30

Deductie waer by onpartijdelijck over-wogen ende bewesen wort, wat het beste voor de Compagnie van West-Indien zy. *The Hague: I. Burchoorn* [1638?]. 32 p.; 4to. Relates to commerce with Brazil. Sabin 19227 (& 102890); Rodrigues (Dom. Hol.) 739; Knuttel 4581. DLC, ICU, NN-RB; BL (as [1622]), The Hague:KB.   638/31

Dekker, Thomas. English villanies seven severall times prest to death. *London: M. Parsons, sold by J. Becket,* 1638. [111] p.; illus.; 4to. 1st publ., London, 1608, under title *Lanthorne and candle-light.* STC 6492. CSmH, CtY, DLC, NNPM; BL.   638/32

Du Bartas, Guillaume de Salluste, seigneur. A learned summary upon the famous poem of William of Saluste, lord of Bartas . . . Translated out of French, by T[homas]. L[odge]. *London:* [*R. Young,*] *for P. Nevill,* 1638. 2 pts; fol. 1st publ. as here transl., London, 1621; a reissue with cancel t.p. of that edn. STC 21668. CSmH, IU, MdBP; Oxford:Queen's.   638/33

Duchesne, Joseph. Le ricchezze della riformata farmacopoea . . . Nuovamente . . . traportata . . . dal sig. Giacomo Ferrara. *Venice: The Guerigli,* 1638. 256 p.; 4to. 1st publ. as here transl., Venice, 1619, from Duchesne's *Pharmacopoea dogmaticorum restituta,* Paris, 1607. DNLM, NNBG; London: Wellcome.   638/34

Du Monstier, Arthur, O.F.M. Martyrologium Franciscanum. *Paris: D. Moreau,* 1638. 657 p.; fol. Included are numerous accounts of Franciscans who were born in the New World or found martyrdom there. ICU, NNH; BL, BN.   638/35

Dupleix, Scipion. La curiosité naturelle. *Rouen: D. Loudet,* 1638. 269 p.; 8vo. 1st publ., Paris, 1606. BN.   638/36

Earle, John, Bp of Salisbury. Micro-cosmographie. or, A piece of the world discovered . . . The seventh edition augmented. *London: J. L[egat].,, for A. Crooke,* 1638. [288] p.; 12mo. 1st publ., London, 1628. STC

7445; Murphy (Engl. char.-bks) 40–41. DFo, ICU, MH; BL.   638/37

Estienne, Charles. Dictionarium historicum, geographicum, poeticum. *Geneva: J. Crispin,* 1638. 2110 cols; 4to. 1st publ. in this enl. edn, Lyons, 1595; cf. 1601 edn. MiU, NBu.   638/38

Fernel, Jean. Universa medicina. *Geneva: P. Chouët,* 1638. 3 pts; 8vo. 1st publ. as here constituted, Paris, 1567; cf. 1601–2 edn. Sherrington (Fernel) 82.J26. DNLM; London:Wellcome, BN.   638/39

Ferrari, Giovanni Battista. Flora, overo Cultura di fiori . . . trasportata dalla lingua latina . . . da Lodovico Aureli. *Rome: P. A. Facciotti,* 1638. 520 p.; illus.; 4to. Transl. from the author's *De florum cultura,* 1st publ., Rome, 1633, with its descriptions of American plants, amongst them the yucca & passionflower. Pritzel 2877n; Nissen (Bot.) 620n. CU, DNLM, MH-A, MiU, RPB; BL, BN.   638/40

Franck, Johann. Speculum botanicum. In quo praecipuarum herbarum, arborum, fruticum et suffruticum nomenclaturae . . . tam in suetica quam latina lingua, ad lustrandum proponuntur. *Uppsala: A. Matthias,* 1638. 24 lvs; 4to. Listed are the marigold ('Cariophyllus Indicus'), mechoacan, 'Nicotiana; Tabacum', & sarsaparilla. Pritzel 3020; Wellcome I:2405. DLC; BL.
                      638/41

García de Zurita, Andrés. Por la iglesia metropolitana de Los Reyes en el Peru. [*Madrid?*] 1638. [62] p.; fol. Medina (BHA) 979; JCB (3) II:269. RPJCB.   638/42

Garzoni, Tommaso. La piazza universale di tutte le professioni del mondo. *Venice: P. M. Bertano,* 1638. 402 numb. lvs; 4to. 1st publ., Venice, 1585; cf. 1601 edn. Michel (Répertoire) IV:25. MH, OCl; BL, BN.
                      638/43

De ghepretendeerden overlast van eenighe ingebooRenen ende inghesetenen voor de Zeeuwen ende uytheemsche Rameren haer in Brasil aengedaen. [*Middelburg?*] 1638. [4] p.; 4to. Sabin 7584; Rodrigues (Dom. Hol.) 734; Knuttel 4584. The Hague:KB.
                      638/44

Gomberville, Marin Le Roy, sieur du Parc et de. La premiere [-cinquiesme et dernière] partie de Polexandre. *Paris: A. Courbé,*

1638,'37. 5 v.; 8vo. A revision of author's 1637 edn, with added passage (v. 1, p. 210–14) on merits of New World civilization; cf. original 1629 version. BL, BN.

638/45

Gottfried, Johann Ludwig. Neuwe Archontologia cosmica. *Frankfurt a.M.:* 1638. *See* Avity, Pierre d', sieur de Montmartin, *above.*

Gravina, Domenico, O.P. Vox turturis, seu De florenti usque ad nostra tempora SS. Benedicti, Dominici, Francisci et aliarum sacrarum religionum statu. *Cologne: H. Krafft,* 1638. 140 p.; 4to. 1st publ., Naples, 1625. Cf. Streit I:422. BN. 638/46

Great Britain. Sovereigns, etc., 1625–1649 (Charles I). A proclamation concerning tobacco. *London: R. Barker & assigns of J. Bill,* 1637. [i.e., 1638]. 4 lvs; fol. Sabin 99852; Crawford (Roy. procl.) 1769; Brigham (Roy. procl.) 82–87; STC 9109. BL.

638/47

——. A proclamation to restraine the transporting of passengers and provisions to New England, without licence. *London: R. Barker & assigns of J. Bill,* 1638. Sabin 65939n; Crawford (Roy. procl.) 1778; Brigham (Roy. procl.) 87–88; STC 9113. DFo; London:PRO. 638/48

Gysius, Johannes. Tweede deel van de Spiegel der spaense tyrannye geschiet in Nederlant. *Amsterdam: J. E. Cloppenburg, for E. Cloppenburg,* 1638. 126 p.; illus.; 4to. 1st publ. as here abridged from the author's *Oorsprong en voortgang der Nederlandtscher beroorten,* Amsterdam, 1620. The present edn is a reissue of the sheets of J. E. Cloppenburg's 1620 edn. As indicated by title, issued as continuation of Las Casas's *Den spiegel der Spaense tyrannye geschiet in West-Indien* with which it is found bound; cf. entry under Casas of this year above. Meulman 1732. CtY, NN-RB, RPJCB; Ghent:BU.

638/49

Hay, Paul, sieur du Chastelet (1592–1636), ed. Recueil de diverses pieces pour servir a l'histoire. [*Paris:*] 1638. 908 p.; 4to. 1st publ., [Paris], 1635. MnU. 638/50

Helwig, Christoph. Theatrum historicum et chronologicum . . . Nunc continuatum et revisum à Johan. Balthasar Schuppio. *Marburg: N. Hampel,* 1638. 169 p.; fol. 1st publ. with American refs, Marburg, 1629. Jantz

(German Baroque) 2293. MiU-C, PPLT; BL. 638/51

Herbert, Sir Thomas. Some yeares travels into divers parts of Asia and Afrique. *London: R. Bishop, for J. Bloome & R. Bishop,* 1638. 364 p.; illus., maps; fol. 1st publ., London, 1634, under title *A relation of some yeares travaile.* Sabin 31471n; STC 13191; Maggs Cat. 502 (Americana VII):5061. CSmH, CtY, DLC, ICN, MH, MiU, NN-RB, PPL; BL, BN. 638/52

Hernando de Talavera, Abp of Granada. Reforma de trages . . . ilustrado por . . . Bartolome Ximenez Paton . . . Enseñase el buen uso del tabaco. *Baeza: J. de la Cuesta,* 1638. 2 pts; 4to. The section on tobacco is by Ximénez Patón. Sabin 105734; Palau 326755 & 377224; Arents 206. NN-A, NNH. 638/53

Hues, Robert. A learned treatise of globes, both coelestiall and terrestriall . . . Written first in Latine . . . And now lastly made English . . . by John Chilmead. *London: The assigne of T. P[urfoote]., for P. Stephens & C. Meredith,* 1638. 186 (i.e., 286) p.; diagrs; 8vo. 1st publ. in Latin, London, 1594 under title *Tractatus de globis;* cf. 1611 edn. STC 13907. BL. 638/54

Ireland. Lord Deputy, 1633–41 (Thomas Wentworth, 1st earl of Strafford). A proclamation concerning the importation of tobaccoe. *Dublin: Society of Stationers,* 1637 [i.e., 1638]. bds.; fol. Crawford (Roy. procl.) Ireland:324; STC 14255. Dublin:PRO (destroyed). 638/55

——. A proclamation concerning the sealing of tobaccoe. *Dublin: Society of Stationers,* 1637, [i.e., 1638]. Crawford (Roy. procl.) Ireland:326; STC 14247. Dublin:PRO (destroyed). 638/56

Jansson, Jan. Newer Atlas oder Weltbeschreibung . . . Sampt Ost- und West-Indien. *Amsterdam: J. Janszoon, the Younger,* 1638. 2 v.; illus., maps; fol. Based on Mercator's *Newer Atlas,* as publ. by Janszoon, Amsterdam, 1636, but here omitting for 1st time Mercator's name. Cf. Mercator's *Atlas novus* of this year below. Koeman (Me) 120–21; cf. Tiele 533. Zurich:ZB, Wolfenbüttel:HB. 638/57

——. Nieuwen atlas, ofte Werelt Beschryvinge ende volkomene afbeeldinge van alle coninckrycken . . . als meede Oost en West Indien, alles in twee deelen begrepen. *Amsterdam: J. Janszoon, the Younger,* 1638. 2 v.; illus., maps; fol. Based on Mercator's *Atlas ofte Afbeeldinghe* & incorporating maps appearing in Mercator's Dutch Appendix of 1637, but here omitting Mercator's name. For variants of v. 2 see Koeman. Cf. Mercator's *Atlas novus* of this year below. Koeman (Me) 69, 70A & 70B; Tiele 533. Utrecht: Geog. Inst., Marburg:StB. 638/58

Jesuits. Letters from missions (South America). Relation des insignes progrez de la religion chrestiene, faits au Paraquai . . . & dans les vastes regions de Guair & d'Uraig. Nouvellement decouvertes . . . és annees 1626 & 1627 . . . Traduite de latin [par Jacques Machault]. *Paris: S. Cramoisy,* 1638. 162 p.; 8vo. Transl. from the Paris, 1636, Latin edn. Sabin 21408 (& 43302, misdated '1636'); Medina (BHA) 953n; Streit II:1654; Backer V:254; JCB (3) II:269. CtY, DLC, MH, NN-RB, RPJCB.
638/59

Khunrath, Conrad. Medulla destillatoria et medica sextum aucta & renovata; das ist, Gründliches und vielbewehrtes Destillier und Artzney Buch. *Hamburg: Froben Office,* 1638. 2 pts; 4to. 1st publ., Schleswig, [1594]; cf. 1601 edn. DNLM, ICJ.
638/60

Kirke, John. The seven champions of Christendome. *London: J. Okes; sold by J. Becket,* 1638. [81] p.; 4to. Drama. Act 1 includes ref. to 'India's precious weede', i.e., tobacco. STC 15014; Greg 545; Arents (Add.) 289; Pforzheimer 574. CSmH, CtY, DLC, ICN, MH, NN-A, PU; BL. 638/61

Le Jeune, Paul, S.J. Relation de ce qui s'est passé en la Nouvelle France en l'annee 1637. *Rouen: J. Le Boullenger,* 1638. 2 pts; 8vo. Pt 2 comprises François Joseph Le Mercier's *Relation de ce qui s'est passé en la mission . . . au pays des Hurons.* For variant states, see Bell & McCoy. Sabin 39953; Harrisse (NF) 67; Bell (Jes. rel.) 9–10; McCoy 24–25. CSmH, CtY, DLC, InU-L, MH, MiU-C, MnU-B, NN-RB; BL, BN.
638/62

—[Anr issue]. *Rouen: J. Le Boullenger, & P. de Bresche, at Paris,* 1638. A reissue with cancel t.p. of the above; for variants, see Bell &

McCoy. Sabin 39953; Harrisse (NF) 68; Bell (Jes. rel.) 11–12; McCoy 26–27; Church 438; JCB (3) II:270. CSmH, MnU-B, RPJCB. 638/63

——. Relation de ce qui s'est passé en la Nouvelle France en l'année 1638. *Paris: S. Cramoisy,* 1638. 2 pts; 8vo. Pt 2 comprises François Joseph Le Mercier's *Relation de ce qui s'est passé en la mission des Hurons.* Sabin 39954; Harrisse (NF) 69; Bell (Jes. rel.) 13; McCoy 28; Church 439; JCB (3) II:271. CSmH, CtY, DLC, InU-L, MH, NN-RB, RPJCB; BL, BN. 638/64

—[Anr edn]. *Paris: S. Cramoisy,* 1638. 2 pts; 8vo. For distinguishing elements of this edition, see Bell. Sabin 39955; Harrisse (NF) 70; Bell (Jes. rel.) 14; McCoy 29; Church 440. CSmH, CtY, MiU-C, MnU-B, NN-RB; BN. 638/65

Le Mercier, François Joseph, S.J. Relation . . . 1637. *Rouen:* 1638. See Paul Le Jeune's *Relation* above.

——. Relation . . . 1637 & 1638. *Paris:* 1638. See Paul Le Jeune's *Relation* above.

León Pinelo, Antonio Rodríguez de. Relacion que en el Consejo real de las Indias hizo el licenciado Antonio de Leon Pinelo . . . sobre la pacificacion y poblacion de las provincias del Manché, i Lacandon. [*Madrid:* ca. 1638]. 8 numb. lvs; fol. Sabin 62933 (& 40056). RPJCB. 638/66

Linschoten, Jan Huygen van. Histoire de la navigation . . . Troisieme edition augmentée. *Amsterdam: E. Cloppenburg,* 1638. 3 pts; illus., maps; fol. 1st publ. as here translated, Amsterdam, 1619, including also the author's *Description de l'Amerique* & his *Grand routier de mer.* Sabin 41373 (& 28266); Tiele 686–88; Palau 138584; JCB (3) II:271. CU-B, DLC, InU-L, MB, MiU-C, NN-RB, RPJCB; BN. 638/67

Losa, Francisco de. The life of Gregorie Lopes . . . written in Spanish by father Losa . . . and set out by father Alonza Remon . . . with some additions of his owne. *Paris: [Widow of J. Blagaert]* 1638. 24mo. Transl. from the author's *Vida que el siervo de Dios Gregorio Lopez hizo en algunos lugares de la Nueva España,* 1st publ., Mexico City, 1613. Cf. Sabin 42584; cf. Medina (BHA) 624; Allison & Rogers 471; STC 16828; Palau 142535. DFo; BL. 638/68

Malingre, Claude. Remarques d'histoire, ou Description chronologique des choses . . . passées, tant en France, qu'és pays estrangers, depuis 1600. *Paris: C. Collet*, 1638. 960 p.; 8vo. 1st publ., Paris, 1632. BN.
638/69

Malvezzi, Virgilio, marchese. La libra de Grivilio Vezzalmi [pseud.]. Traducida de italiano . . . Pesanse las ganancias y las perdidas de la monarquia de España en el . . . reynado de Felipe IV el Grande. [*Pamplona?* 1638?]. Description conjectured on basis of [1639?] edn containing ref. to earlier edn. Mentioned are Brazil, Peru & Mexico. The Italian text is not known in printed form prior to 1651; it is possible that the present work was transl. from the author's manuscript, Malvezzi being in Spain at this time. Palau 148060.
638/70

Martyn, William. The historie and lives of the kings of England. *London: R. Young*, 1638. 843 p.; ports; fol. In this enl. edn are numerous refs to Drake, Hawkins, & Raleigh. STC 17529. CSmH, CtY, DFo, ICN, InU-L, MH, NNUT, PP; BL, BN.
638/71

Matthieu, Pierre. Dell'historia de S. Luigi IX . . . Tradotta di francese . . . dal signor Gio. Battista Parchi. *Venice: The Giuntas*, 1638. 142 p.; 4to. (His *Opere*, v. 1). Transl. from Matthieu's *Histoire de sainct Louys*, 1st publ., Paris, 1618. Michel (Répertoire) V:151. NIC; BL, Aix-en-Provence:Bibl. Méjanes.
638/72

——. Della perfetta historia di Francia e delle cose piu memorabili occorse nelle provincie straniere ne gli anni di pace regnante . . . Henrico quarto . . . libri sette . . . tradotti di francese . . . dal signor conte Alessandro Senesio. *Venice: B. Barezzi*, 1638. 717 p.; 4to. (His *Opere*, v. 3). Transl. from Matthieu's *Histoire de France et des choses memorables advenues aux provinces estrangeres durant sept annees de paix, du regne de Henry IV*, 1st publ., Paris, 1605; cf. 1623 edn with title *Historia di Francia*. Michel (Répertoire) V:150. ICN; BL, Aix-en-Provence:Bibl. Méjanes.
638/73

Medina de las Torres, Gaspar de Guzmán y Acevedo, duque de. Relacion. Muerte de Pie de Palo. Segunda relacion, y muy copiosa de una carta que embio el señor Duque de Medina a la contratacion de Se-villa. Dase cuenta de la batalla que han tenido los galeones con 40 navios de Olandeses, siendo general de ellos Pie de Palo. Assi mismo se da cuenta de su muerte, con perdida de siete navios, en cabo de S. Anton. *Madrid: A. Duplastre*, 1638. [4] p.; 4to. Cf. the *Relacion verdadera* of this year below. Sabin 51243; Medina (BHA) 990; Palau 258135.
638/74

Mendoça, Lourenço de, Bp of Rio de Janeiro. Señor. El prelado del Rio de Janeiro, digo, que en otro memorial doi cuenta . . . di mi venida a esta corte [etc.]. [*Madrid?* 1638?]. 3 numb. lvs; fol. Continues memorial to king of Spain of 1630. Sabin 47844? BL.
638/75

Mercator, Gerardus. Atlantis novi pars tertia . . . Americam continens. *Amsterdam:* 1638. See Mercator's *Atlas novus* of this year below.

——. Atlas novus, sive Descriptio geographica totius orbis terrarum . . . tribus tomis distinctus. *Amsterdam: J. Janszoon, the Younger & H. Hondius*, 1638. 3 v.; illus., maps; fol. Based on Mercator's *Atlas*, 1st publ., Amsterdam, 1606, as modified by Hondius & Jansson. Vol. 3, the *Atlantis novi pars tertia*, represents a reissue of 1636 edn with altered imprint date (q.v.). For variant see Koeman. Vols. 1 & 3 include Americana. Subsequent edns entered under Jansson. Sabin 47883; Koeman (Me) 51A–51B, 52A–52B, 50B; Tiele 745; JCB (3) II:271. MH, RPJCB; BN (v. 3), Utrecht:UB, Warsaw:BU.
638/76

——. Atlas, or A geographicke description . . . of the world . . . Translated by Henry Hexham. *Amsterdam: H. Hondius*, 1638. 2 v.; illus., maps; fol. 1st publ. in English, Amsterdam, 1636; here a reissue of that edn. Koeman (Me) 41B; STC 17828. PU (v. 2), RPJCB (v. 2); Oxford:Bodl.
638/77

Mexía, Pedro. Selva rinovata di varia lettione di Pietro Messia . . . di Mambrin Roseo [e] Francesco Sansovino. *Venice: G. Imberti*, 1638. 5 pts; 4to. 1st publ. with addition of Sansovino's pt, Venice, 1559–60; cf. 1611 edn. Michel (Répertoire) V:161. CU; BL, BN.
638/78

Nederlandsche West-Indische Compagnie. Reglement byde West-Indische Compagnie ter vergaderinge vande negentiene, met approbatie vande . . . Staten Generael, over het openstellen vanden handel op Brasil provisioneel ghearresteert. *The Hague: Widow & Heirs of H. Jacobszoon van Wouw,* 1638. [6] p.; 4to. Borba de Moraes states that there is anr edn comprising 1 lf. Sabin 68899 (& 102926); Borba de Moraes II:375; Asher 168; JCB (3) II:274. DLC, MnU-B, RPJCB; BL.   638/79

—[Anr edn]. *Amsterdam: J. Broerszoon,* 1638. 8 p.; 4to. Cf. Borba de Moraes II:375; Meulman 2439. BL, Ghent:BU.   638/80

Netherlands (United Provinces, 1581–1795). Staten Generaal. Naerder ordre ende reglement vande . . . Staten Generael . . . gearresteert by adviis ende deliberatie van de bewindthebberen van de . . . West-Indische Compagnie . . . over het open ende vry stellen van den handel . . . op de stadt Olinda de Parnambuco, ende custen van Brasil [9 Jan. 1634]. *Amsterdam: J. F. Stam,* 1638. 8 p.; 4to. 1st publ., The Hague, 1634. Meulman 2281. Ghent:BU.

638/81

Onbedriegh'lijcke leyd-sterre, tot geluckige voyage vande machtige scheeps-vloten der generale gheoctroyeerde West-Indische Compagnie. [*Amsterdam?* 1638?]. 20 p.; 4to. Meulman 2433. Ghent:BU.   638/82

Opitz, Martin. Weltliche Poemata das erste Theil. Zum vierdten mal . . . herausgegeben. *Breslau: Heirs of D. Müller,* 1638. 573 p.; 8vo. 1st publ. with American refs, Breslau, 1628–29, under title *Deutscher Poematum.* Goedeke III:49; cf. Faber du Faur 228; cf. Jördens IV:116. Berlin:StB.   638/83

Overbury, Sir Thomas. Sir Thomas Overbury his wife . . . The sixteenth impression. *London: J. Haviland, for A. Crooke,* 1638. [320] p.; 8vo. 1st publ., London, 1615. STC 18919; Murphy (Engl. char.-bks) 24. CSmH, CtY, DFo, IU, MH, NjP; BL.

638/84

Ovidius Naso, Publius. Metamorphoses. English. Ovid's Metamorphosis Englished by Geo: Sandys. The third edition. *London: R. B[adger]., for A. Hebb,* 1638. 316 p.; 12mo. 1st publ., London, 1626. Sabin 57984 & 76459; STC 18967. CSmH, DFo, InU-L, MH, NN-RB; BL.   638/85

Owen, John. Rosarium, dat is, Rosen-Garden . . . overgesettet . . . dorch Bernhar-

dum Nicoeum Ancumanum. *Emden: H. Kallenbach,* 1638. 8vo. Transl. from Owen's *Epigrammatum libri tres,* 1st publ., London, 1606. Shaaber (Brit. auth.) O93. Kassel:LB.

638/86

Oxford. University. Statuta selecta è corpore statutorum. [*Oxford:*] *W. Turner, for W. Webb,* 1638. 213 p.; 8vo. Includes regulation against smoking tobacco & frequenting places where it is sold. STC 19007; Madan (Oxford) 1638:17; Arents (Add.) 290. CSmH, CtY, DFo, IU, MH, NN-A; BL.

638/87

Pax Christi. En esta referire a V. R. las nuevas que tenemos por aca despues de la ultima que en la armada que fue a cargo del marques de Cadereyta escrivi a V. R. [*Madrid:* ca. 1638]. [8] p.; fol. Cf. entry under Pedro Porter y Casanate below. RPJCB.

638/88

Philopatroös, Erasmus. Nieuw-keulsch of Spaensch bedrogh. [*Amsterdam?*] 1638. 43 p.; 4to. Includes refs to West Indies, Peruvian gold, & the West-Indische Compagnie. Knuttel 4575. InU-L, NN; The Hague:KB.

638/89

Pigray, Pierre. Epitome des preceptes de medecine et chirurgiae. *Rouen: D. Ferrand,* 1638. 764 p.; 8vo. 1st publ., Paris, 1600, under title *La chirurgie;* cf. 1604 edn. London:Wellcome.   638/90

—[Anr issue?]. *Rouen: L. DuMesnil,* 1638. DNLM.   638/91

Porter y Casanate, Pedro. Señor. El capitan Don Pedro Porter y Cassanate, dize: Que el año de mil y seiscientos y treinta y seis, por servir a V. Magestad, ofreciò al Virrey marques de Cadereyta hazer viage a la California, saber si era isla, ò tierrafirme, y descubrir lo occidental, y septentrional de la Nueva-España. [*Madrid?* 1638?]. [8] p.; fol. Memorial to king of Spain. Medina (Chile) 255; Wagner (SW) 39. InU-L, RPJCB; Madrid:BN.   638/92

Primerose, James. De vulgi in medicina erroribus libri quatuor. *London: B. A[lsop]. & T. F[awcet]., for H. Robinson,* 1638. 431 p.; 12mo. In bk 4 chapts 31–34 discuss the medicinal use of tobacco, & chapt. 35 the bezoar stone produced by Peruvian llamas. STC 20384. CSmH, CtY, DFo, TxU; BL.

638/93

Randolph, Thomas. Poems; with The muses looking-glasse. *Oxford: L. Lichfield, for F. Bowman,* 1638. 3 pts; 4to. In addition to using the phrase 'both the Indies', Randolph in 'An epithalamium to Mr. F. H.' mentions 'the metals in Guiana', & in 'The muses looking-glasse', in act 3, scene 1, tobacco. STC 20694; Greg 547 (a); Madan (Oxford) 1638:19; Pforzheimer 828. CSmH, CtY, DFo, ICN, InU-L, MH, NN-RB, PPL; BL.
638/94

Relacion de la vitoria que alcanzaron las armas catolicas en la baía de Todos Santos, contra Olandeses, que fueron a sitiar aquella plaça, en 14. de Junio de 1638. *Madrid: F. Martínez,* 1638. 6 numb. lvs; fol. Sabin 69187; Medina (BHA) 983; Borba de Moraes II:189; Palau 258124; JCB (3) II:272. DLC, InU-L, NN-RB, RPJCB; Amsterdam:NHSM.
638/95

Relacion de lo sucedido a la Armada Real de la guarda de la carrera de las Indias, desde el dia que se hizo a la vela en la vaia de Cadiz, hasta el en que dio fondo en el puerto de la Vera Cruz en la Nueva España. [*Seville?* 1638]. 8 numb. lvs; 4to. Sabin 69202; Medina (BHA) 989.
638/96

Relacion de los muertos, y heridos que huvo en la Real Armada de la guardia de las Indias, las dos vezes que peleó con el enemigo, sobre Pan de Cavañas. [*Madrid?* 1638?]. [4] p.; 4to. Sabin 69206; Medina (BHA) 988.
638/97

Relacion verdadera, de la gran vitoria que han alcançado en el Brasil la gente de la baia de Todos Santos, contra los Olandeses. *Seville: N. Rodríguez,* 1638. [4] p.; 4to. Sabin 7622; Medina (BHA) 985; Borba de Moraes II:191; Rodriguez (Dom. Hol.) 466. NN-RB.
638/98

Relacion verdadera de la refriega que tuvieron nuestros galeones de la plata en el cabo de San Anton con catorze navios de Olanda. *Seville: F. de Lyra,* 1638. [4] p.; 4to. Sabin 69235; Medina (BHA) 986; JCB (3) II:272. RPJCB.
638/99

—[Anr edn]. *Madrid: D. Díaz de la Carrera,* 1638. Palau 258134. NN-RB; BL.
638/100

Relacion verdadera del viaje de los galeones, y de las dos batallas que tuvieron sobre Pan de Cavañas, con los Olandeses, en este año de 1638. *Seville: N. Rodríguez,* 1638. [4] p.; 4to. Sabin 69237.
638/101

Roberts, Lewes. The merchants mappe of commerce: wherein, the universall manner and matter of trade, is compendiously handled. *London: R. O[ulton, Eliot's Court Press?, T. Harper & F. Kingston]., for R. Mabb,* 1638. 3 pts; port., maps; fol. 'America and the provinces thereof': pt 2, p. 51–64. On division of printing, see the STC. Sabin 71906; STC 21094; Arents (Add.) 292; Kress 535. CSmH, CtY, DLC, ICU, InU-L, MH-BA, MWA, MiU-C, MnU-B, NN-RB, PPL, RPJCB; BL.
638/102

Rodríguez de León, Juan. El predicador delas gentes. *Madrid: María de Quiñones,* 1638. 256 numb. lvs; 4to. In bk 3, chapt. 10 discusses the 'Modo de predicar a los gentiles de las Indias'. Streit I:473. InU-L; Valencia:BU.
638/103

Saint-Amant, Marc Antoine de Gérard, sieur de. Les oeuvres. *Paris: N. Traboulliet,* 1638. 2 pts; 8vo. In verse. 1st publ., Paris, 1629. Tchémerzine X:83. BN.
638/104

—[Anr edn]. *Rouen: J. Osmont, the Younger,* 1638. 8vo. BL (Gérard, M. A. de).
638/105

Sandys, Sir Edwin. Europae speculum; or A view or survey of the state of religion. *London: T. Cotes, for M. Sparke, the Elder,* 1638. 358 p.; illus.; 12mo. 1st publ., London, 1605, under title *A relation of the state of religion.* STC 21722. CSmH, CtY, DFo, IU, MiU; BL, BN.
638/106

Sandys, George. A paraphrase upon the divine poems. [*London: J. Legat, for A. Hebb*] 1638. 3 pts; fol. In verse. 1st publ., London, 1636, under title *A paraphrase upon the Psalmes of David.* For printing variants, see the STC. Sabin 76465; STC 21725; Pforzheimer 825. CSmH, CtY, DLC, ICN, InU-L, MB, MiU-C, NN-RB, PPL; BL, BN.
638/107

Sibbes, Richard. Light from heaven, discovering the fountaine opened. *London: Elizabeth Purslowe & R. Badger, for N. Bourne & R. Harford,* 1638. 4 pts; 4to. The preface mentions 'great discoverers in the Newfound Lands in America'. In this edn t.p. includes reading 'Copies'. STC 22498. CtY,

DFo, ICN, MH, MiU, MnU, NN-RB, PU
(imp.); Oxford:Bodl.   638/108
—[Anr edn]. *London: Elizabeth Purslowe & R.
Badger, for N. Bourne & R. Harford, 1638.* 4
pts; 4to. In this edn t.p. includes reading
'Coppies'. STC 22498a. CSmH, NN-RB;
BL.   638/109
Entry canceled.   638/110
Het spel van Brasilien, vergheleken by een
goedt verkeer-spel. [*Amsterdam?*] 1638. 7 p.;
4to. Sabin 7638; Borba de Moraes I:339;
Rodrigues (Dom. Hol.) 736; Knuttel 4582;
JCB (3) II:269. NN-RB, RPJCB; BL (Brazil),
The Hague:KB.   638/111
—[Anr edn]. . . . vergeleecken by een goet
verkeer-spel. [*Amsterdam?*] 1638. bds.; fol.
Knuttel 4583; Asher 150. DLC; The
Hague:KB.   638/112
Spinola, Fabio Ambrosio, S.J. Vita del p.
Carlo Spinola della Compagnia di Giesu,
morto per la santa fede nel Giappone. *Rome:
F. Corbelletti, 1638.* 223 p.; port., plan; 8vo.
1st publ., Rome, 1628. Cf. Sabin 89458;
Streit V:1524; Backer VII:1448.
                                    638/113
Spranckhuysen, Dionysius. Tranen over
den doodt van den grooten Admirael van
Hollandt . . . Pieter Pietersz. Heyn. *Delft:
A. J. Cloeting, 1638.* 4to. 1st publ., Delft,
1629. Sabin 89746; Muller (1872) 950.
                                    638/114
Staden, Hans. Beschrijvinghe van America.
Amsterdam: B. Janszoon, 1638. 72 p.; illus.;
4to. 1st publ. in Dutch, Antwerp, 1558; cf.
1625 edn. Sabin 90046. NN-RB.
                                    638/115
—[Anr edn]. *Amsterdam: B. Janszoon* [1638?].
72 p.; illus.; 4to. Sabin 90047. MH, NN-
RB.   638/116
Sumario, y compendio de lo sucedido en España, Italia, Flandes, Francia, y otras partes.
Desde Febrero de 637. hasta el de 638. [*Madrid:* 1638]. [12] p.; fol. 'Toma de las provincias de la Cumanogotos, e islas de Barlovento': 1f 6. Palau 325173; Maggs Cat. 502
(Americana VII):5062. RPJCB.
                                    638/117
Taylor, John, the Water-poet. Newes and
strange newes from St. Christophers of a
hurry-cane. In August last, about the 5. day
of 1638. *London: J. O[kes]., for F. Coules,
1638.* 8vo. Sabin 54942 & 75017; STC

23778.5 (formerly 21558). CSmH; Oxford:
Worcester.   638/118
——. Taylors feast: containing twenty-
seaven dishes of meate. *London: J. Okes,
1638.* 8vo. Under 'Strong beere', 'petars
of tobacco' are mentioned; elsewhere, in
'A bill of fare', 'West-India cheese' and pine-
apples. STC 23798. CSmH.   638/119
Theatrum florae, in quo ex toto orbe selecti
mirabiles . . . flores . . . proferuntur. *Paris:*
1638. 69 numb. pls; illus.; fol. 1st publ.,
Paris, 1622. Cf. Pritzel 10855; cf. Nissen
(Bot.) 1575. MoSB.   638/120
Udemans, Godefridus Corneliszoon. 't
Geestelyck roer van 't coopmans schip, dat
is: Trouw bericht, hoe dat een coopman,
en coopvaerder, hemselven dragen moet in
syne handelinge . . . insonderheyt onder
de heydenen in Oost ende West-Indien.
*Gouda: W. vander Hoeve, for F. Boels, at Dor-
drecht,* 1638. 360 numb. lvs; 4to. Sabin 97664;
Tiele 1119; Asher 23. DLC, MnU-B, NN-
RB; BL, Amsterdam:NHSM.   638/121
Underhill, John. Newes from America; or
A new and experimentall discoverie of New
England; containing, a true relation of their
war-like proceedings these two yeares last
past. *London: J. D. [awson]., for P. Cole, 1638.*
44 p.; map; 4to. Sabin 97733; Vail (Fron-
tier) 92; STC 24518; Church 441; JCB (3)
II:273. CSmH, DLC, ICN, MH, NN-RB,
PPL, RPJCB; BL.   638/122
Venner, Tobias. Via recta ad vitam longam
. . . As also an accurate treatise concerning
tobacco. *London: R. Bishop, for H. Hood,
1638.* 364 p.; 4to. The treatise of tobacco
1st publ., London, 1621. The present edn
is a reissue of that of 1637 with altered imprint date. Sabin 98890n; STC 24647;
Arents 146-b. CSmH, DLC, MBCo, NN-A,
OCl; BL.   638/123
Vincent, Philip. A true relation of the late
battell fought in New England, between the
English, and the Pequet [*sic*] salvages. *London: M. P[arsons]., for N. Butter & J. Bellamy,
1638.* 23 p.; 4to. 1st publ., London, 1637;
here a reissue with new t.p. Sabin 99763–
65; Vail (Frontier) 93; STC 24759; Church
442; JCB (3) II:273–74. CSmH, DFo, ICN,
MB, NN-RB, PPL, RPJCB; Oxford:Lincoln.
                                    638/124
—[Anr edn]. *London: T. Harper, for N. Butter*

& J. Bellamy, 1638. [22] p.; 4to. Sabin 99766; Vail (Frontier) 94; STC 24760; Church 443; JCB (3) II:273–74. CSmH, MH(imp.), NN-RB, PPAmP, RPJCB; BL.   638/125

1639

Alemán, Mateo. Le gueux, ou La vie de Guzman d'Alfarache. *Lyons: S. Rigaud*, 1639. 2 v.; 8vo. 1st publ. as here transl. by Jean Chapelain, Paris, 1619, & Paris, 1620. Vol. 2 has title *Le voleur, ou La vie de Guzman d'Alfarache*. Laurenti (Nov. pic. esp.) 625. BN.   639/1

—[Anr edn]. *Dijon*: 1639. Laurenti (Nov. pic. esp.) 626.   639/2

——. Primera parte de la vida del picaro Gusman de Alfarache. *Brussels: J. Mommaert*, 1639. 215 (i.e., 198) numb. lvs; 8vo. 1st publ., Madrid, 1599; cf. 1601 edn. A reissue of the printer's 1604 edn, with the first gathering a cancel. Laurenti (Nov. pic. esp.) 563; Peeters-Fontainas (Impr. esp.) 34; Palau 6700. Brussels:BR.   639/3

Alfaro, Francisco de. Tractatus de officio fiscalis. *Madrid: F. Martínez.* 1639. 352 p.; fol. 1st publ., Valladolid, 1606. Medina (BHA) 992; Palau 6984; JCB (3) II:274. ICN, MH-L, RPJCB; BN.   639/4

Antidotario romano latino, e vulgare. Tradotto da Ippolito Ceccarelli. *Rome: P. Totti, for P. A. Facciotti*, 1639. 359 p.; 4to. 1st publ. as here constituted, Rome, 1612. DNLM.   639/5

Bacon, Francis, viscount St Albans. The essayes or, Counsels, civill and morall. *London: J. Beale*, 1639. 340 p.; 4to. 1st publ. as here enl., London, 1625. Gibson (Bacon) 17; STC 1151. CSmH, CtY, DLC, ICN, MH, MiD, NN-RB, RPB; BL.   639/6

——. Les oeuvres morales et politiques . . . de la version de J. Baudoin. *Paris: M. Henault*, 1639. 639 p.; 8vo. 1st publ. in this form, Paris, 1626. Gibson (Bacon) 168b. DFo, MdE.   639/7

—[Anr issue]. *Paris: J. Roger*, 1639. Gibson (Bacon) 168a; Shaaber (Brit. auth.) B18. CCB; BL.   639/8

——. Opere morali. *Venice: A. Bariletti*, 1639. 327 p.; 12mo. Ostensibly transl. from Jean Baudoin's French version as publ., Paris,

1626, under title *Les oeuvres morales et politiques.* Gibson (Bacon) 169. Rome:BN.   639/9

——. Sylva sylvarum: or, A naturall historie . . . The fifth edition. *London: J. Haviland, for W. Lee*, 1639. 2 pts; port.; fol. 1st publ., London, 1627. Includes also Bacon's *New Atlantis*. Gibson (Bacon) 175; STC 1173. CSmH, CtY, DLC, IEN, MH, MnU-B, NjP, RPB; BL, BN.   639/10

Bancroft, Thomas. Two bookes of epigrammes and epitaphs. *London: J. Okes, for M. Walbanke*, 1639. [87] p.; 4to. 'To Captaine James, after his intended discovery of the North-west passage': no. 159; 'On the searchers of the North-west passage': no. 160; 'On Tobacco taking': no. 183; 'To his Brother John Bancroft deceased', mentioning brother's plans to go to New England prior to his death: no. 193. STC 1354; Arents (Add.) 294. CSmH, CtY, DLC, NN-A; BL.   639/11

Barnuevo, Rodrigo, S.J. Señor. Rodrigo Barnueuo de la Compañia de Jesus. [*Madrid?* 1639?]. [3] p.; fol. Memorial to king of Spain on services in Peru. Medina (BHA) 6253; Streit II:1660; Backer I:606. BL, Seville:Archivo de Indias.   639/12

Barrough, Philip. The method of phisick . . . The eighth edition. *London: G. Miller*, 1639. 477 p.; 4to. 1st publ., London, 1583; cf. 1601 edn. STC 1516. CSmH, CtY-M, DNLM, MBCo, NNNAM; London:Wellcome.   639/13

Bauderon, Brice. Pharmacopoea, cui adjecta sunt paraphrasis et miscendorum medicamentorum modus. Primum gallice scripta . . . Nunc vero a Philemone Hollando . . . in latinum sermonem conversa. *London: E. Griffin, for R. Whitaker*, 1639. 2 pts; fol. Transl. from Bauderon's *Paraphrase sur la Pharmacopoee*, 1st publ., Lyons, 1588; cf. 1607 edn. STC 1592. London:Wellcome, BN.   639/14

Beaumont, Francis. The scornfull lady. A comedy . . . The fift edition. *London: M. P[arsons]., for R. Wilson*, 1639. 35 lvs; 4to. 1st publ., London, 1616. STC 1690; Greg 334(e). CSmH, CtY, DFo, MH, NjP; BL.   639/15

——. Wit without money. London: 1639. *See* Fletcher, John, *below*.

Berettari, Sebastiano, S.J. Vita del padre Giuseppe Anchieta . . . apostolo del Brasile. *Messina: P. Brea,* 1639. 8vo. 1st publ. as here transl. from the author's *Josephi Anchietae . . . vita* (Lyons, 1617), Turin, 1621. Cf. Sabin 4830; Medina (BHA) 676n (II:175); Streit II:2396; Backer III:806. 639/16

Beverwijck, Jan van. Spaensche Xerxes, ofte Beschrijvinge ende vergelijckinge van den scheep-strijdt tusschen de groote koningen van Persen ende Spaengjen, tegen de verbonde Griecken ende Nederlanders. *Dordrecht: H. van Esch, for J. Gorisszoon,* 1639. 96 p.; 4to. Includes refs to West Indies, Pieter Hein (battle of Matanzas Bay; capture of Spanish silver fleet), & a ship from Seville to America. Palau 28844; Catalogus van boeken VI:51; Knuttel 4631. BL, The Hague:KB. 639/17

——. Van de uitnementheyt des vrouwelicken geslachts. Verçiert met verssen van Mr. Corn. Boy. *Dordrecht: [H. van Esch,] for J. Gorisszoon,* 1639. 679 p.; illus., ports; 8vo. Transl. from Beverwijck's *De excellentia foeminei sexus,* 1st publ., Dordrecht, 1636. Grässe I:357–58. NN-RB; BL. 639/18

Blaeu, Willem Janszoon. Zeespiegel. *Amsterdam: W. J. Blaeu,* 1639. 3 pts; illus., maps; fol. 1st publ., Amsterdam, 1623. Koeman (M.Bl) 35. CtY. 639/19

Bodecherus Banninghius, Janus. Epigrammata americana. *Leyden: W. Christiaens, for D. Lopez de Haro,* 1639. 15 p.; 12mo. Describes the author's voyage to Brazil, where he served as political counselor to the West-Indische Compagnie. Borba de Moraes I:60; Rodrigues (Dom. Hol.) 895. 639/20

Breton, Nicholas. Wits private wealth. *London: B. Alsop & T. Fawcet, for G. Hurlock,* 1639. 12 lvs; 4to. 1st publ., London, 1612. CSmH; BL. 639/21

Breve, y ajustada relacion de lo sucedido en España, Flandes, Alemania, Italia, Francia, y otras partes de Europa, desde fin de febrero de mil seyscientos y treynta y siete, hosta todo el mes de deziembre de mil y seyscientos treynta y ocho. *Barcelona: J. Romeu,* 1639. [20] p.; 4to. Section on Spain mentions arrival at Lisbon of ships with sugar & fruit from Brazil, reporting defeat of Dutch there. Section on Flanders reports death of Pie de Palo in attack by Dutch on Spanish silver fleet. Ref. is made to the defense of Pernambuco, and a special section describes events in Brazil. Rodrigues (Dom. Hol.) 467. RPJCB. 639/22

Een brief, gheschreven van een goet patriot woonachtich tot 's Hartogenbosch . . . Nae de copye. *'s Hertogenbosch: J. van Dockum,* 1639. [16] p.; 4to. The final page contains an extract from a letter written at Bahia by António d'Igal Castillo dealing with Brazil & speaking of the attack on Pernambuco. Borba de Moraes I:241–42; Rodrigues (Dom. Hol.) 408; Tiele (Pamfletten) 2668; Knuttel 4626. MnU; The Hague:KB 639/23

Bruele, Gualtherus. Praxis medicinae, or, The physicians practise . . . The second edition, newly corrected and amended. *London: J. Norton, for W. Sheares,* 1639. 407 p.; 4to. 1st publ. as here transl., London, 1632. STC 3930. CLU-M, CtY-M, DFo; BL. 639/24

Bustamante y Loyola, Sebastián de. Señor. El licenciado Don Sebastian de Bustamente [*sic*] y Loyola. [*Madrid?* 1639]. bds.; fol. Memorial to king of Spain reciting services of ancestors in Peru & New Granada (i.e., Colombia). BL. 639/25

Calancha, Antonio de la, O.S.A. Coronica moralizada del orden de San Augustin en el Peru . . . Primer tomo. *Barcelona: P. Lacavallería,* 1639. 922 p.; illus.; fol. 1st publ., Barcelona, 1638; here a reissue with altered date on t.p. A 2nd vol. was publ. at Lima in 1653. Cf. Sabin 9870; cf. Medina (BHA) 977; Streit II:1663; cf. Palau 39450; JCB (3) II:267. CU, DLC, RPJCB (with substitution of 1638 date on t.p.). 639/26

Calestani, Girolamo. Delle osservationi . . . parte prima[-seconda]. *Venice: G. Imberti,* 1639. 2 v.; 4to. 1st publ., Venice, 1564; cf. 1606 edn. DNLM. 639/27

Camden, William. Rerum Anglicarum . . . annales . . . Ultima editio. *Leyden: Elsevier Office,* 1639. 856 p.; port.; 8vo. 1st publ. as here issued with both pts, Leyden, 1625, with title *Annales rerum Anglicanarum.* Sabin 10157n; Willems (Les Elzevier) 475; Rahir (Les Elzevier) 472; Shaaber (Brit. auth.) C20. CU, DFo, IU, MiU, NPV, PU, RPB; BL, BN. 639/28

Camões, Luiz de. Lusiadas . . . comentadas por Manuel de Faria i Sousa. *Madrid: J. Sánchez, for P. Coello,* 1639. 4 v. in 2; illus., ports, maps; fol. 1st publ., Lisbon, 1572. Here given is the Portuguese text with prose commentary in Spanish. Sabin 28002n; Silva (Camões) 31; Palau 41053. CU, CtY, DLC, MH, NN-RB, PU, RPJCB; BN, Lisbon:BN. 639/29

Caramuel Lobkowitz, Juan, Bp of Campagna. Philippus prudens. Caroli V. imp. filius Lusitaniae, Algarbiae, Indiae, Brasiliae, legitimus rex demonstratus. *Antwerp: Plantin Press (B. Moretus),* 1639. 430 p.; illus., ports; fol. Asserts legitimacy of Spanish claims to Portuguese throne & hence to Brazil. Maggs Cat. 479 (Americana V):4227. DLC, InU-L, NN, PP, RPJCB; BL, BN. 639/30

Cepeda, Fernando de. Señor. Con orden que he tenido del marquès de Cadereyte, virrey desta Nueva España. *Madrid: D. Díaz de la Carrera,* 1639. 6 lvs; fol. 1st publ., Mexico, 1638. 'Relacion que embiò à su Magestad el marquès del Cadereyta, Virrey de la Nueva España, en que dà cuenta del feliz sucesso que ha tenido esta monarquia en la detencion de la flota, por el gran peligro que tenia de los enemigos en el camino. . . '. Medina (BHA) 994; Palau 51559; Maggs Cat. 479 (Americana V):4223. BL, Seville:B. Colombina. 639/31

Cervantes Saavedra, Miguel de. Le valeureux Dom Quixote. *Paris: A. Cotinet* (v. 1) *& A. Coulon* (v. 2), 1639. 2 v.; 8vo. Includes the 2nd pt, 1st publ. as here transl., Paris, 1618. Ríus (Cervantes) 466; Palau 52699. 639/32

Chamberlain, Robert. Conceits, clinches, flashes, and whimsies. *London: R. Hodgkinson, for D. Frere,* 1639. [132] p.; 12mo. Conceits 59 & 207 discuss tobacco. Reprinted, 1640, under title *Jocabella, or A cabinet of conceits.* STC 4942. MH; BL. 639/33

Chapman, George. The ball. A comedy . . . Written by George Chapman, and James Shirly. *London: T. Cotes & W. Cooke,* 1639. [72] p.; 4to. In act 4 'tobacco merchants' are mentioned. STC 4995; Greg 549; Arents (Add.) 295; Pforzheimer 144. CSmH, CtY, DLC, ICN, MH, NN-RB, PU; BL. 639/34

Clüver, Johannes. Historiarum mundi epitome. *Leyden:* 1639. *See the year* 1641.

Díaz Taño, Francisco, S.J. La mort glorieuse du pere Christophe de Mendoza, de la Compagnie de Jesus, cruellement massacré pour la foy, au Paraguay, province du Peru l'an 1636. Ainsi le rapporte le père François Drezzanio [i.e., Francisco Díaz Taño]. *Lille: P. de Rache,* 1639. 8 p.; 8vo. Sabin 20945; Streit II:1666; Backer III:206; Palau 72907. 639/35

Donne, John. Poems. *London: M. F[letcher]., for J. Marriott,* 1639. 388 p.; port.; 8vo. Includes Donne's *An anatomie of the world,* 1st publ., London, 1611. STC 7047; Keynes (Donne) 80; Pforzheimer 297. CSmH, CtY, ICN, MH, MiU, PU; BL. 639/36

Drezzanio, François, S.J. La mort glorieuse du pere Christophe de Mendoza. *Lille:* 1639. *See* Diaz Taño, Francisco, *below.*

Duchesne, Joseph. La pharmacopee des dogmatiques reformée. *Rouen: O. Seigneurée & L. Oursel, for C. Pitreson,* 1639. 2 pts; port.; 8vo. 1st publ., Paris, 1624, as here transl. from Duchesne's *Pharmacopoea dogmaticorum restituta,* 1st publ., Paris, 1609. DNLM, WU; London:Welcome. 639/37

Dugres, Gabriel. Dialogi gallico-anglico-latini. *Oxford: L. Lichfield,* 1639. 195 p.; 8vo. The 6th dialogue mentions turkeys, the 8th, tobacco. STC 7295; Madan (Oxford) 1639:5; Arents (Add.) 296. NN-RB; BL, Oxford:Bodl. 639/38

Field, Nathan. Amends for ladies . . . A comedy. *London: J. Okes, for M. Walbanke,* 1639. [62] p.; 4to. 1st publ., London, 1618. STC 10853; Greg 356 (b); Arents (Add.) 297. CSmH, CtY, DLC, ICN, MH, NN-A; BL. 639/39

Fletcher, John. Wit without money. A comedie . . . Written by Francis Beaumont, and John Flecher. *London: T. Cotes, for A. Crooke, & W. Cooke,* 1639. [64] p.; 4to. 'English tobacco' is mentioned on lf Hlr. Despite author statement on t.p., prob. the work of Fletcher alone. STC 1691; Greg 563; Arents 207; Pforzheimer 374. CSmH, CtY, DLC, ICN, MH, NN-RB, PU; BL. 639/40

Fonteyn, Nicolaus. Responsionum et curationum medicinalium liber unus. *Amsterdam: J. Janszoon, the Younger,* 1639. 179 p.; 12mo.

In discussing case of inherited syphilis, calls for use of guaiacum & sarsaparilla. Wellcome I:2354. DLC, NN, PPL; BL, BN.

639/41

Fragoso, Juan. Della cirugia . . . parti due . . . Tradotte dalla lingua spagnola . . . da Baldassar Grasso. *Palermo: A. Martarello,* 1639. 424 p.; fol. Transl. from the author's *Cirugia universal,* 1st publ., Madrid, 1581; cf. 1607 edn. DNLM, NcD-MC. 639/42

Gerhard, Johann. Locorum theologicorum . . . tomus primus [-nonus]. *Geneva: P. Gamonet,* 1639. 9 v.; fol. Includes Gerhard's *Tomus quintus* (1st publ., Jena, 1617) & *Tomus sextus* (1st publ., Jena, 1619). Jantz (German Baroque) 1077. NcD, PPiPT (vols 1–6); BL, BN. 639/43

González de Mendoza, Pedro. El licenciado Don Pedro Gonçalez de Mendoça, del Consejo de su Magestad, fiscal en el Real de las Indias. Con Diego de Vergara Gaviria . . . Sobre que pretende que la baxa de la moneda de vellon . . . que el dicho Diego de Vergara Gaviria dize estava extante de la hazienda del Opispo de Chile. [*Madrid:* 1639?]. 8 numb. lvs; fol. BL. 639/44

Goodall, Baptist. The tryall of travell. *London: J. Norton,* 1639. 4to. In verse. 1st publ., London, 1630. STC 12008. BL.

639/45

Great Britain. Sovereigns, etc., 1625–1649 (Charles I). A proclamation concerning tobacco. *London: R. Barker & assigns of J. Bill,* 1638 [i.e., 1639]. 3 lvs; fol. Crawford (Roy. procl.) 1798; Brigham (Roy. procl.) 88–92; STC 9138. London: Soc. of Antiquaries.

639/46

—[Anr edn]. *London: R. Barker & assigns of J. Bill,* 1638 [i.e., 1639]. 3 lvs; fol. Crawford (Roy. procl.) 1799; STC 9139. Oxford: Bodl. 639/47

——. A proclamation declaring His Majesties gratious pleasure touching sundry grants, licences, and commissions, obtained under untrue surmises. *London: R. Barker & assigns of J. Bill,* 1639. 2 lvs; fol. Amongst those affected are tobacco sellers & tobacco-pipe makers. Crawford (Roy. procl.) 1800; STC 9140. MH; BL. 639/48

—[Anr edn]. *London: R. Barker & assigns of J. Bill,* 1639. 2 lvs; fol. Crawford (Roy.procl.) 1801; STC 9141. Oxford:Bodl. 639/49

——. A proclamation declaring His Majesties pleasure . . . for licensing retailors of tobacco. *London: R. Barker & assigns of J. Bill,* 1639. bds.; fol. Crawford (Roy. procl.) 1808; Brigham (Roy. procl.) 92–93; STC 9147. Oxford:Bodl. 639/50

Grégoire, Pierre. Syntagma juris universi. *Geneva: J. Stoer,* 1639. 5021 p.; fol. 1st publ., Lyons, 1582; cf. 1609 edn. MH-L; BN.

639/51

Grotius, Hugo. De veritate religionis christianae. Editio quinta. *Oxford: L. L[ichfield].,* *for W. Webb,* 1639. 180 p.; 8vo. 1st publ., Leyden, 1627, under title *Sensus librorum sex.* STC 12399; Madan (Oxford) II:918; Meulen/Diermanse 948. Cambridge:UL, The Hague:PP. 639/52

—[Anr edn]. *Leyden: J. Maire,* 1639. 180 p.; 8vo. Meulen/Diermanse 949. Oxford: Bodl.

639/53

——. Inleydinghe tot de Hollandsche rechts-gheleerdheydt. [*Haarlem: A. Roman,* 1639]. 3 pts; port.; 4to. 1st publ. in this version including also Grotius's *Van de oudheydt* & his *Vrye zeevaert,* each with special t.p., & separate paging & signatures, Haarlem, 1636; the latter works were also issued separately in this year as described below. Meulen/Diermanse 763. BL, BN, The Hague:KB. 639/54

——. Van de oudheydt der Batavische, nu Hollandsche republique. *Haarlem: A. Roman,* 1639. 44 p.; port.; 4to. 1st publ. in Dutch, The Hague, 1610, under title *Tractaet vande oudtheyt.* Also issued as part of Grotius's *Inleydinghe tot de Hollandsche rechts-gheleerdheydt* of this year, q.v. above. Meulen/Diermanse 700; Bibl. Belg. G347. CSmH, MH, MiU-C; The Hague:PP.

639/55

——. Vrye zeevaert . . . Nu uyt den Latijne op een nieuw vertaeld door A. Iekerman. *Haarlem: A. Roman,* 1639. 40 p.; 4to. 1st publ. in Dutch, Leyden, 1614; here newly transl. from Grotius's *Mare liberum,* 1st publ., Leyden, 1609. Also issued as part of Grotius's *Inleydinghe tot de Hollandsche rechts-gheleerdheydt* of this year, q.v. above. Meulen/Diermanse 556; Bibl. Belg. G338; Meulman 2494. DLC; The Hague:KB, Ghent:BU. 639/56

Guibert, Philbert. Toutes les oeuvres charitables. *Paris: J. Jost,* 1639. 880 p.; port.; 8vo. Included is Guibert's *Le prix & valeur des medicamens,* 1st publ., Paris, 1625. DNLM, PPC. 639/57

Hartmann, Johann (1568–1631). Praxis chymiatrica. *Geneva: P. Chouët,* 1639. 2 pts; 8vo. 1st publ., Leipzig, 1633. CtY, DNLM; BN. 639/58

—[Anr issue]. [*Geneva:*] *J. de La Planche,* 1639. Wellcome I:3067. London:Wellcome. 639/59

Hay, Paul, sieur du Chastelet (1592–1636), ed. Recueil de diverses pieces pour servir a l'histoire. [*Paris:*] 1639. 908 p.; 4to. 1st publ., [Paris], 1635. CtY, UU; BL, BN. 639/60

Herbert, Sir Thomas. Travels in Africa and Asia. *London: W. Stansby,* 1639. fol. 1st publ., London, 1634, under title *A relation of some yeares travaile.* Cf. Sabin 31471; STC 13192. Winchester:Cathedral. 639/61

Heylyn, Peter. Μικροκοσμος, A little description of the great world. *Oxford: W. Turner,* 1639. 808 p.; 4to. 1st publ., Oxford, 1621. Cf. Sabin 31656n; Madan (Oxford) 1639:11; STC 13283. DLC, IU, MH, MnU, NHi; BL, BN. 639/62

—[Anr state]. *Oxford: W. Turner,* 1939 [i.e., 1639]. Sabin 31656n; Madan (Oxford) 1639:11n; STC 13284. CSmH, CtY, DLC, ICU, MH, NN-RB; Oxford:Bodl. 639/63

Hondius, Hendrik. Nouveau theatre du monde, ou Nouvel atlas . . . divise en deux tomes. *Amsterdam: H. Hondius,* 1639. 2 v.; maps; fol. Vol. 1 based on Mercator's *Atlas ou Representation* as publ., Amsterdam, 1633. Here pt 2 lacks American material; for a 3rd vol. including American maps, see below. Cf. Mercator's *Atlas novus,* Amsterdam, 1638. Koeman (Me) 91, 92A; cf. Tiele 533n. NNH; London:RGS, BN (v. 1; Mercator). 639/64

—[Anr edn]. Nouveau théâtre du monde . . . devisé en trois tomes. *Amsterdam: J. Janszoon, the Younger,* 1639. 3 v.; maps; fol. Includes a 3rd vol. also issued separately, q.v. below. Phillips (Atlases) 452 (cf. 3422); Tiele 533n; cf. Koeman 92B. DLC; BL (v. 2). 639/65

——. Le nouveau theatre du monde, ou Nouvel atlas, tome troisiesme. *Amsterdam: H.*

Hondius, 1639. 1 v.; maps; fol. Based in pt on Mercator's *L'appendice de l'atlas,* 1st publ., Amsterdam, 1633. Issued as a supplementary volume to Hondius's *Nouveau theatre* above. Includes various American maps. Koeman (Me) 93A. NNH; London:RGS, Paris:Arsenal. 639/66

—[Anr edn]. Editio ultima. *Amsterdam: J. Janszoon, the Younger,* 1639. 1 v., maps; fol. Koeman (Me) 93B. CtY; Wroclaw:BU. 639/67

Hues, Robert. A learned treatise of globes, both coelestiall and terrestriall . . . Written first in Latine . . . An now lastly made English . . . by John Chilmead. *London: The assigne of T. P[urfoote]., for P. Stephens & C. Meredith,* 1639. 186 (i.e., 286) p.; diagrs; 8vo. 1st publ. in Latin, London, 1594, under title *Tractatus de globis;* cf. 1611 edn. 1st publ. in English, London, 1638; here a reissue of that edn with altered imprint date? STC 13908. CSmH, DLC, IU, MH, MiU-C, NN-RB, RPJCB; Oxford:Bodl. 639/68

Jansson, Jan. Nouveau theatre du monde. *Amsterdam:* 1639. *See* Hondius, Hendrik, above.

Jenner, Thomas. The soules solace, or Thirtie and one spiritual emblems. *London: E[lizabeth]. Purslowe., for H. Overton,* 1639. 27 lvs; illus.; 8vo. 1st publ., London, 1626. STC 14496. CSmH. 639/69

Khunrath, Conrad. Medulla destillatoria et medica. Zum sechsten Mahl . . . revidirt . . . und gebessert. *Hamburg: Froben Office,* 1639,'38. 2 pts; 4to. 1st publ., Schleswig, [1594]; cf. 1601 edn. BL. 639/70

The ladies cabinet opened: wherein is found hidden severall experiments in preserving and conserving, physicke, . . . cookery and huswifery. *London: M. P[arsons]., for R. Meighen,* 1639. 32 lvs; 4to. Includes recipe for 'Oyle of tobacco'. STC 15119; Arents (Add.) 298. NN-A; BL, Oxford:Bodl. 639/71

Laynez, Juan, S.J. Copia de una carta . . . a el . . . fr. Joseph de Sisneros . . . En que le da cuenta del viage de los galeones, batalla con Pie de palo, y otros sucessos hasta que llegaron a España. *Malaga: J. Serrano de Vargas y Ureña,* 1639. 32 p.; 4to. Medina (BHA) 997; Maggs Cat. 479 (Americana V): 4225. Seville: Residencia de Jesuitas.   639/72

Le Brun, Laurent, S.J. Nova Gallia delphino. *Paris: J. Camusat,* 1639. 63 p.; 4to. In verse. A sequence of elegies relating to Canada & Indians there. Reprinted, 1649, in Le Brun's *Ecclesiastes . . . Salomonis . . . paraphrasi poetica.* The 1649 edn described in Backer (IV:1629) perhaps represents a typographic error. NN-RB; BN.
                                             639/73

Malvezzi, Virgilio, marchese. La libra de Grivilio Vezzalmi [pseud.]. *Pamplona:* [1639?]. 188 p.; 4to. 1st publ., [Pamplona? 1638?]. As with the 1640 edn, the Pamplona imprint may be fictitious. Toda y Güell (Bibl. esp. d'Italia) 3032n; Palau 148060. NNH, WU.   639/74

—[Anr edn]. *Naples: G. Gafaro,* 1639. 233 p.; 12mo. Toda y Güell (Bibl. esp. d'Italia) 3032. MH, NNH; BL (Vezzalmi, G.).
                                             639/75

Mascardi, Agostino. Ethicae prolusiones. *Paris: S. Cramoisy,* 1639. 232 p.; 4to. Describes introduction in Europe of tobacco from West Indies where it had been used by native priests; deplores its social use. Arents 3279. NN-A, NNC; BL, BN.
                                             639/76

Mayne, Jasper. The cityе match. A comoedye. *Oxford: L. Lichfield,* 1639. 64 p.; fol. In act 1, scene 3, the 'wealthier mines in the Indies' are cited; in act 3, scene 1, a 'man fish [i.e., manatee]' taken 'strangely in the Indies, neere the mouth of Rio de la plata' & Sir Francis Drake are mentioned; in act 4, scene 3, 'Ladies of New England' are described as marrying in haste. STC 17750; Madan (Oxford) 1639:16; Greg 568. CSmH, CtY, DLC, ICN, MH, NNC, PBL; BL.   · 639/77

Mercator, Gerardus. Historia mundi, or Mercator's atlas . . . Englished by W[ye]. S[altonstall]. . . . Second edytion. *London: M. Sparke,* 1639. 930 p.; illus., maps; fol. 1st publ. in this version with enl. introduction & map of Virginia, London, 1637; the original printed t.p. with 1635 imprint date is retained in this reissue. Cf. Sabin 47885; Koeman II:549; cf. Phillips (Atlases) 4255 & 451; STC 17826. IU, MiU-C, NN-RB.
                                             639/78

——. Nouveau theatre du monde. *Amsterdam:* 1639. *See* Hondius, Hendrik, *above.*

More, Sir Thomas, Saint. The commonwealth of Utopia. *London: B. Alsop & T. Fawcet; sold by W. Sheares,* 1639. 315 p.; 12mo. 1st publ. as here transl. by R. Robinson, London, 1551; cf. 1624 edn. Gibson (More) 29; STC 18098; JCB (3) II:275. CSmH, CtY, DFo, ICN, MH, RPJCB; BL.   639/79

Morel, Pierre. Methodus praescribendi formulas remediorum elegantissima, cum annexo Systemate materiae medicae. [*Geneva:*] *J. Chouët,* 1639. 2 pts; 8vo. The *Systemate materiae medicae* 1st publ., Geneva, 1628. DNLM; BN.   639/80

Múñoz, Bernardo. Relacion verdadera, y carta nueva de un traslado embiado del Brasil, por . . . Bernardo Muñoz, a un hijo suyo: dandole cuenta de una grande victoria . . . 29. de noviembre . . . 1638. *Madrid: A. Duplastre,* 1639. [4] p.; 4to. Sabin 51341; Medina (BHA) 1000; Borba de Moraes II:90; Rodrigues (Dom. Hol.) 464. DLC, NN-RB; BL, BN.   639/81

Nash, Thomas (1588–1648). Miscelanea, or, A fourefold way to a happie life. *London: J. Dawson, sold by T. Slater,* 1639. 280 p.; 4to. 1st publ., London, 1633, under title *Quaternio, or A fourefold way;* here a reissue with cancel t.p. STC 18384. CSmH, ICN; BL.   639/82

Nederlandsche West-Indische Compagnie. Also tot welstant vande generale West-Indische Compagnie . . . [*Amsterdam?* 1639?]. Meulman 2477. *See* the company's Verhooginghe vande capitalen *below.*

——. Verhooginghe vande capitalen inde West-Indische Compagnie, ghearresteert byde vergaderinghe vande negentiene van de selve compagnie. *The Hague: Widow & Heirs of H. Jacobszoon van Wouw,* 1639. [4] p.; 4to. For variant, see Sabin. The item described under Meulmann 2477 ('Also tot welstant') apparently represents a copy of the present work lacking t.p. Sabin 102915–16; Asher 75; Knuttel 4633. DLC, NN-RB; BL, The Hague:KB.   639/83

—[Anr edn]. [*The Hague?* 1639]. bds.; fol. Sabin 102917; Asher 74; Rodrigues (Dom. Hol.) 39n.   639/84

Nieremberg, Juan Eusebio, S.J. De arte voluntatis libri sex . . . Accedit . . . Historia panegyrica de tribus martyribus . . . in Urugai pro fide occisis. *Paris: N. Charles,* 1639. 543 p.; 8vo. 1st publ., Lyons, 1631; here, as suggested by Backer, a reissue of that edn with cancel t.p. Sabin 55267; Backer V:1731; Palau 190702. BL, BN. 639/85

Ontdeckinghe van rijcke mijnen in Brasil. *Amsterdam: J. van Hilten,* 1639. [8] p.; 4to. Concerns navigation & commerce. Sabin 7612; Borba de Moraes II:115; Rodrigues (Dom. Hol.) 740; Asher 172; Knuttel 4634. DLC, NN-RB; BL (Brazil), The Hague:KB. 639/86

Pagitt, Ephraim. A relation of the Christians in the world. *London: J. Okes,* 1639. 79 p.; 4to. 'In America': p. 42–43. STC 19113. NN-RB, NNUT; BL. 639/87

Pardoux, Barthélemy. Universa medicina. Editio secunda studio et opera G. Sauvageon. *Paris: L. Boullenger, for J. Bessin,* 1639. 943 p.; 4to. 1st publ., Paris, 1630. DNLM, PPL; BN. 639/88

—[Anr issue]. *Paris: L. Boullenger, for J. Jost,* 1639. BN. 639/89

Paredes, Antonio de. Señor. Entre diversos memoriales que truxo el pliego de Castilla por otubre de 38. he visto dos, que se dieron a V.Magestad. [*Madrid:* 1639?]. [58] p.; fol. Memorial to king of Spain on the mines of Potosí. Dated Potosí, 24 Jan. 1639. Maggs Cat. 496 (Americana VI):261. ICN. 639/90

Perucci, Francesco. Pompe funebri. Di tutte le nationi del mondo. *Verona: F. di Rossi,* 1639. 97 numb. lvs; illus.; fol. The illus. are engravings 1st used in Tommaso Porcacchi's Venice, 1591, *Funerali antichi.* In the 7th bk, 'Del' essequie dell' Indiani', the author speaks of 'Bramani del regno del Perù' with depiction of a Hindu funeral pyre. Michel (Répertoire) VI:102. CU, CtY, ICN, MH, MdBJ, NNC; BL, BN. 639/91

Pharmacopoea Amstelredamensis . . . Editio tertia. *Amsterdam: W. & C. Blaeu,* 1639. 12mo. 1st publ., Amsterdam, 1636. 639/92

Pizarro y Orellana, Fernando. Varones ilustres del Nuevo mundo . . . sus vidas, virtud . . . y claros blasones. Ilustrados . . . con . . . observaciones politicas y morales. *Madrid: D. Díaz de la Carrera,* 1639. 427 p.; fol.

Sabin 63189; Medina (BHA) 999; Palau 227687; JCB (3) II:276. CU, CtY, DLC, InU-L, MH-P, MiU-C, MnU-B, NN-RB, PPL, RPJCB; BL, BN. 639/93

Plattes, Gabriel. A discovery of subterraneall treasure, viz. Of all manner of mines and mineralls from the gold to the coal. *London: J. Okes, for J. Emery,* 1639. 60 p.; 4to. Mentions gold & silver mines in Peru, New England, Virginia, Bermuda, & elsewhere in the New World. Sabin 63360; STC 20000; Kress S.676; Maggs Cat. 502 (Americana VII):5063. CSmH, CtY, DFo, IU, MH-BA, NN-RB; BL. 639/94

Porreño, Baltasar. Dichos y hechos del señor Rey D. Felipe. *Madrid: Widow of J. Sánchez, for L. Sánchez,* 1639. 156 numb. lvs; 8vo. 1st publ., Cuenca, 1621. Palau 233066. NNH; BL. 639/95

—[Anr edn]. *Seville: P. Gómez de Pastrana,* 1639. 140 numb. lvs; 8vo. CU, CtY, DLC, NNH; BN. 639/96

Primerose, James. De vulgi erroribus in medicina libri quatuor. *Amsterdam: J. Janszoon, the Younger,* 1639. 237 p.; 12mo. 1st publ., London, 1638. Arents (Add.) 299. DNLM, NN-A; BL, BN. 639/97

Quarles, Francis. Emblemes. *London: J. Dawson, for F. Eglesfield,* 1639. 381 p.; illus.; 8vo. In verse. 1st publ., London, 1635; here enlarged. STC 20542. CSmH, DFo, MH; BL. 639/98

Raven, Dirck Albertsz. Journael van de ongeluckighe voyagie . . . naer Groenlandt. *Amsterdam: G. J. Saeghman* [1639?]. *See the year* 1663.

Royal College of Physicians of London. Pharmacopoea Londinensis . . . Quinta editio. *London: J. Marriott,* 1639 [at end: 1638]. 212 p.; fol. 1st publ., London, 1618. STC 16776. DFo, DNLM, TxU; BL. 639/99

Ruiz de Montoya, Antonio, S.J. Conquista espiritual hecha por los religiosos de la Compañia de Jesus, en . . . Paraguay, Parana, Uruguay, y Tape. *Madrid: Imprenta Real,* 1639. 103 numb. lvs; 4to. Sabin 74029; Medina (BHA) 1001; Borba de Moraes II:78; Streit II:1670; JCB (3) II:277. DLC, ICN, InU-L, MnU-B, NN-RB, PU, RPJCB; BL, BN. 639/100

——. Haseme mandado, que assi como representè a su Magestad, y señores del

Real Consejo, en un memorial impresso los agravios enormes, que los vezinos de la villa de S. Pablo, y demas villas de la costa del Brasil han hecho, y al presente hazen a los Indios christianos, è infideles de las provincias del Paraguay, y Rio de la Plata. [*Madrid?* 1639]. 7 numb. lvs; fol. Sabin 74031; Medina (BHA) 6844; Backer VII:720; Palau 282111; JCB (3) II:87. RPJCB.   639/101

——. Señor. Antonio Ruiz de Montoya de la Compañia de Jesus, y su procurador general de la provincia del Paraguay, dize: Que estando prohibido por cedulas, y ordenes reales, so graves penas que los Portugueses del Brasil no puedan entrar en la dicha provincia [etc.]. [*Madrid:* 1639]. [4] p.; fol. Memorial to king of Spain accusing one Antonio Raposo de Tavares of having led force from Buenos Aires in attack on Jesuit mission in Paraguay. Sabin 74030; Medina (BHA) 6843; Streit II:1671; Borba de Moraes II:79–81; Backer V:320; Palau 282111; JCB (3) II:88. RPJCB; BL, BN.   639/102

——. Tesoro de la lengua guarani. *Madrid: J. Sánchez*, 1639. 2 pts; 4to. Sabin 74027; Medina (BHA) 1002; Borba de Moraes II:78; Streit II:1670n; Viñaza 175; Backer VII:321; JCB (3) II:277. NNH, RPJCB, ViU; BL.   639/103

Salinas y Córdova, Buenaventura de O.F.M. Memorial del padre fray Buenaventura de Salinas y Cordova . . . procurador general de . . . Lima . . . Cuya grandeza . . . representa a la magestad del Rey . . . Felipe IIII . . . Para que pida a Su Santidad la canonizacion de . . . el venerable padre fray Francisco Solano. *Madrid:* 1639. 26 numb. lvs; fol. Solano had served as a Franciscan missionary in Peru; he was canonized in 1725. Medina (BHA) 1003; Streit II:1674; Palau 287612. NN-RB; Seville:BU.   639/104

Sánchez de Aguilar, Pedro. Informe contra idolorum cultores del obispado de Yucatán. Dirigido al Rey . . . en su real Consejo de las Indias. *Madrid: Widow of J. González*, 1639. 124 numb. lvs; 4to. Sabin 76295 (& 527); Medina (BHA) 1004 (VII:335); Streit II:1675; JCB (3) II:277. CtY, RPJCB, TxU.   639/105

Sassonia, Ercole. Opera practica. *Padua: F.*

Bolzetta, 1639. 5 pts; fol. Includes the author's *De lue venerea*, 1st publ., Padua, 1597; & his *De melancholia tractatus* of 1620. CtY-M, DNLM.   639/106

Serres, Olivier de, seigneur du Pradel. Le theatre d'agriculture. *Geneva: P. & J. Chouët*, 1639. 878 p.; 4to. 1st publ., Paris, 1600; cf. 1603 edn. DNAL.   639/107

Shakespeare, William. The history of Henrie the fourth [Pt 1]. *London: J. Norton, sold by H. Perry*, 1639. 4to. 1st publ., London, 1598; cf. 1604 edn. STC 22287. CSmH, DFo, IU, MH, NN-RB, PU-F; BL.   639/108

Slichtenhorst, Arend van. Oratio de navigationibus ac commerciis Foederatum Belgarum. *Leyden: W. Christiaens, for D. Lopez de Haro*, 1639. 26 p.; 4to. Includes refs to Columbus & Magellan, to tobacco, & to Spanish America & Brazil. Sabin 82133. BL.   639/109

Soler, Vincent Joachim. Brief, & singulier relation d'un lettre de monsieur Soler, ministre du S. Evangile és Eglises reformees du Bresil: où il entretient quelques uns de ses amis à qui il escrit, de plusieurs singularitez du pays. *Amsterdam: B. de Preys*, 1639. 10 p.; 4to. Describes plants & natural history of Brazil. RPJCB.   639/110

——. Cort ende sonderlingh verhael van eenen brief van Monsieur Soler, bedienaer des H. Evangelij inde Ghereformeerde Kercke van Brasilien . . . Uyt de Francoysche . . . tale overgeset. *Amsterdam: B. de Preys*, 1639. 12 p.; 4to. Transl. from preceding. Sabin 86375; Borba de Moraes II:267; Rodrigues (Dom. Hol.) 436; JCB (3) II:278. InU-L, NN-RB, RPJCB; The Hague:KB.   639/111

Solórzano Pereira, Juan de. Disputationum de Indiarum jure, sive De justa Indiarum Occidentalium gubernatione, tomus alter. *Madrid: F. Martínez*, 1639. 1076 p.; illus., port.; fol. Continues 1st vol. publ. at Madrid, 1629. Sabin 86526; Medina (BHA) 1006; Palau 318975; JCB (3) II:278. CSmH, CtY, DLC, InU-L, MH, MiU-C, NN-RB, PU, RPJCB; BL, BN.   639/112

——. Traduccion de la dedicatoria real, i epistolas proemio del segundo tomo del Derecho, i govierno de las Indias Occidentales . . . Hecha, i illustrada con notas marge-

nales . . . por Don Gabriel de Solorzano Paniagua. [*Madrid:*] *F. Martínez*, 1639. 62 numb. lvs; fol. Extracted & transl. from the author's *Disputationum* of this year described above. Sabin 86532; Medina (BHA) 1005; Palau 318979. CtY, ICN, RPJCB (imp.); BN.
639/113

Spain. Consejo de las Indias. Culpa que resulta contra el licenciado Pedro de Vergara Gaviria, oydor que fue de la audiencia de Mexico, en la perdida de la flota de Nueva-España, del cargo del General don Juan de Benavides, donde venia el susodicho á estos reynos por passagero. [*Madrid? 1639?*]. 34 numb. lvs; fol. Medina (BHA) 8083. Puebla: B. Palafoxiana.
639/114

——. Memorial del pleyto que el señor fiscal del Consejo de Indias trata. Contra Diego de Vergara Gaviria . . . Sobre la baxa de la moneda de vellon . . . procedido de los bienes de don fray Juan Perez de Espinosa obispo que fue de . . . Santiago . . . de Chile. [*Madrid? 1639?*]. 7 numb. lvs; fol. Cf. Vergara Gaviria's own memorial of this year below. Medina (Chile) 250. BL, Seville: Archivo de Indias.
639/115

Spain. Laws, statutes, etc., 1621–1665 (Philip IV). Capitulaciones de el assiento que con . . . el Rey Don Felipe . . . hizo don Diego de Vera con el Real Consejo de las Indias . . . para la conquista . . . y poblacion de el Prospero, (aliàs el Lacandon y dè los demas Indios . . .) . . . en la Nueva España. [*Madrid:*] 1639. 8 numb. lvs; fol. Dated 29 Mar. 1639. Sabin 10759; Medina (BHA) 996. BL (lacks lvs 4–5).
639/116

——. Prematica en que Su Magestad manda, que desde primero de enero del año de 1640. en adelante, no se puede hazer ni escrivir ninguna escritura . . . en todos los reynos . . . de las Indias. [*Madrid:*] *J. Sánchez, at Imprenta Real*, 1639. 6 numb. lvs; fol. Medina (BHA) 7805. CU, RPJCB.
639/117

Translaet uyt den Spaenschen, weghens 't gevecht tusschen des conincx silvervloot, en den Admirael Houte-been in West-Indien op den 31 Augustus 1638. 12 mylen van de Havana. . . . Eerst gedruckt in Spaensch tot Calis [i.e., Cadiz] door Fernando Rey. Anno 1639. *Amsterdam: F. Lies-*

hout, 1639. [10] p.; 4to. A 3rd-person account based on Carlos de Ibarra's report to the Marqués de Cadereyta. The Spanish text of which this is a translation has not been identified. Sabin 96455; Palau 265096 & 258138; Muller (1872) 273; Asher 154; Knuttel 4620; JCB (3) II:278. RPJCB; BL (Ibarra), The Hague:KB.
639/118

Two famous sea-fights. Lately made, betwixt the fleetes of the king of Spaine, and the fleetes of the Hollanders. The one, in the West-Indyes: the other . . . betwixt Callis and Gravelin. *London:* [*B. Alsop & T. Fawcet,*] *for N. Butter & N. Bourne*, 1639. [16] p.; 4to. The 1st account was transl. from the *Relacion verdadera, de la gran vitoria . . . en el Brasil*, Seville, 1638. Sabin 97556; STC 22132; JCB (3) II:278–79. CSmH, DFo, NN-RB, RPJCB; BL.
639/119

Vasconcellos, Agostinho Manuel de. Vida y acciones del Rey Don Juan el Segundo, decimotercio de Portugal. *Madrid: Maria de Quiñones*, 1639. 348 p.; 4to. Includes description (p. 293–300) of meeting of King João with Columbus, of the latter's discoveries, & of the demarcation line of Pope Alexander VI. Borba de Moraes II:332; Palau 150185. CtY, ICN, MH, MdBP, MiU, MnU-B, RPJCB.
639/120

Vergara Gaviria, Diego de. Adicion a la informacion de Diego de Vergara . . . receptor del Consejo Real de las Indias. En el pleyto con el señor Fiscal, sobre la baxa de la moneda. [*Madrid? 1639?*]. [4] p.; fol. BL.
639/121

——. Por Diego de Vergara Gaviria . . . recetor del Consejo Real de las Indias. Con el señor fiscal. Sobre la baxa de la moneda de vellon, que procedio de la hazienda del Obispo de Chile. [*Madrid? 1639?*]. 7 numb. lvs; fol. Cf. the *Memorial del pleyto* of this year entered under 'Spain. Consejo de las Indias' above. BL.
639/122

Vitoria Baraona, Francisco de. El capitan Francisco de Vitoria, vezino de la puebla de los Angeles de la nueva España . . . suplica humildissimamente . . . a V.S. y demas señores de el Consejo Real de Indias, le haga merced de passar los ojos por este breve discurso . . . [tocante a] los dos naos que todos los años se despachan del puerto de Acapulcro [*sic*] en la Mar del Sur, para las islas Filipinas. [*Madrid:* 1639]. 5 (i.e., 6) numb. lvs; fol. Signed by Vitoria Baraona & Marcos de Theca & dated at Madrid, 6 Jan. 1639. Sabin 100623; Medina (BHA) 1008 & 8389 (VII:266). BL.

639/123

Walkington, Thomas. The optick glasse of humors. *London: For [& by] J. D[awson].; sold by L. B[lacklock].,* 1639. 168 p.; 8vo. 1st publ., London, 1607. STC 24969. CSmH, CtY, DLC, ICN, MH, NjP; BL.   639/124

Wood, Owen. An alphabeticall book of physicall secrets. *London: J. Norton, for W. Edmonds,* 1639. 238 p.; 8vo. Included are various medicinal formulas employing mechoacan, sassafras, sarsaparilla, guaiacum, & tobacco. STC 25955; Arents (Add.) 303; Wellcome I:6773. DNLM, NN-A; BL, London:Wellcome.

639/125

Wood, William. New Englands prospect. A true, lively, and experimentall description of that part of America, commonly called New England. *London: J. Dawson; sold by J. Bellamy,* 1639. 83 p.; map; 4to. 1st publ., London, 1634. Sabin 105076; Vail (Frontier) 95; STC 25959; Church 444; JCB (3) II:279. CSmH, ICN, MH, MiU-C, NN-RB, PPL, RPJCB; BL.   639/126

Zacchia, Paolo. De' mali hipochondriaci libri due. *Rome: P. A. Facciotti, for F. Corbo,* 1639. 413 p.; 8vo. Includes ref. to chocolate. Müller 223. DNLM; London:Wellcome.

639/127

164–?

Allo, Pedro de. Señor. El desseo del servicio de V. magestad. [*Madrid?* 164–?]. 6 numb. lvs; fol. Memorial to king of Spain 'de la necessidad que ay de remedio en los aprestos de la armada de la guarda de las Indias, flotas de Nuevaespaña y Tierrafirme'. Medina (BHA) 6203. BL.   64–/1

Apuntamientos para mejor inteligencia de la duda que se ofrece, sobre si se podrà continuar el repartimiento de Indios . . . para la labor de las minas de azogue de Guancabelica. [*Madrid?* 164–?]. 6 numb. lvs; fol. CtY; BL.   64–/2

Espinosa Montero, Agustín de. Señor. El

doctor Agustin de Espinosa Montero. [*Madrid?* 164–?]. 4 lvs; 4to. Memorial to king on working of Peruvian mines. Medina (BHA) 6436. BL, Seville:Archivo de Indias.

64–/3

El estado en que oy se halla el comercio de Sevilla, y de todo el reyno, con la detencion de los galeones de la plata. [*Seville?* 164–?]. [3] p.; fol. Relates to Spanish silver fleet. BL.   64–/4

Garavito, Gerónimo. Señor. Geronimo Garavito . . . en nombre de los curas, beneficiados, y sacristanes . . . de la . . . iglesia parroquil [de Potosí]. [*Madrid?* 164–?]. [4] p.; fol. Memorial to king of Spain on behalf of clergy, etc., of parish. Medina (BHA) 6485. BL.   64–/5

——. Señor. Gerónimo Garavito, procurador general del gremio de los azogueros de . . . Potosi del Pirù, dize: Que a los 17. de mayo deste presente año presentò . . . un memorial impresso en 4. fojas, y en el refirió los 91. que avia puesto en las reales manos de V. M. y en el Consejo de las Indias. [*Madrid?* 164–?]. 6 numb. lvs; fol. Memorial to king of Spain. Cf. Medina (BHA) 8168. BL.

64–/6

——. Señor. Geronimo Garavito, procurador general del gremio delos azogueros delle villa . . . de Potosi del Pirù, dize: Que de nuevo represento a V. M. los dos capitulos delos catorze que puso en las reales manos . . . a los 12. de noviembre del año passado de 1636. sobre que se embian a sus partes los 6 [mil] quintales de hierro, y los 10 [mil] quintales de azogue, que tienen pedido en cada un año, porque dello pende el venir plata del Pirù. [*Madrid:* 164–?]. 8 numb. lvs; fol. Memorial to the king of Spain. BL.

64–/7

González de Najera, Alonso. El quinto, y sexto punto de la Relacion del desengaño de la guerra de Chile. [*Madrid?* 164–?]. 16 numb. lvs; 4to. Relates to the author's larger work, the *Relacion,* not publ. till 1866. Sabin 27785; Medina (Chile) II:201; Palau 105577. BL.   64–/8

Grau y Monfalcón, Juan. Señor. Don Juan Grau y Monfalcon, procurador general de . . . Manila cabeça de las Islas Filipinas. [*Madrid?* 164–?]. 42 numb. lvs; fol. Me-

morial to king of Spain, chiefly on the affairs of the Philippines but stressing the importance of maintaining regular communication with Mexico & Peru. BL.
64–/9

Pérez Manrique de Lara, Dionisio, marqués de Santiago. Señor. Don Dionisio Perez Manrique . . . presidente en la audiencia real de los Charcas en . . . Pirù, dize: Que estando occupado en este ministerio [etc.]. [*Madrid?* 164–?]. 6 numb. lvs; fol. Memorial to king of Spain on administration of area in question. Medina (BHA) 6751. BL.
64–/10

Scotland. Laws, statutes, etc. The acts made in the first parliament of our . . . soveraigne Charles . . . 1633. *Edinburgh: E. Tyler,* 1633 [i.e., 164–?]. 66 p.; fol. 1st publ., Edinburgh, 1633. STC 21902.5. CSmH, CtY, DLC, MH, MnU-L, NN-RB: St Andrews:UL.
64–/11

Seville. Junta del Almirantazgo. Por la Junta del Real Almirantazgo de la ciudad de Sevilla, en el pleyto que de oficio se sigue por el señor Don Juan de la Calle . . . juez del Real Almirantazgo, sobre el tabaco que aprendio de contra bando. [*Seville?* 164–?]. [9] p.; fol. On illegal trade with the Dutch & Virginia, Barbados, etc., & traffic in tobacco thence by Luis Méndez Enríquez. BL.
64–/12

Tapia de Vargas, Juan. Por D. Juan Tapia de Vargas, fiador de Andres de Aranburo . . . juez oficial por su Magestad de la ciudad de la Veracruz, en las Indias. En la escriptura con Jaques Bules sobre la nulidad de la dicha fianza. [*Madrid?* 164–?]. 13 numb. lvs; fol. Sabin 94351; Medina (BHA) 6906. Seville:BU.
64–/13

Vaz, Cristóbal, O.F.M. Fray Cristobal Vaz, del orden de San Francisco, provincial que fue de la dicha orden en la provincia de Mechoacan. [*Madrid?* 164–?]. [3] p.; fol. Medina (BHA) 7614.
64–/14

Vizcaya, Spain. Señorío. Proposiciones que haze el Señorío de Vizcaya a los cavalleros vizcaynos sus hijos, que residen en las partes de las Indias, Flandes, Italia, y otras provincias. *Valladolid: A. Vázquez de Velasco y Esparza* [164–?]. 4 numb. lvs; fol. RPJCB.
64–/15

1640

Abreu y Figueroa, Fernando de, O.S.A. Adiciones al memorial que pretende los aumentos de la real hazienda en el tesoro que su Magestad tiene en el Perú, y en todas las Indias. [*Madrid?* 1640?]. 3 lvs; fol. Medina (BHA) 6168; cf. Palau 1013. BL.
640/1

——. Excmo Señor. El maestro fray Fernando de Abreu y Figueroa . . . representa . . . que aun medianamente sepa, y entienda el manejo de las minas. [*Madrid?* 1640?]. 7 lvs; fol. On mines of Peru. Medina (BHA) 6167. BL.
640/2

——. El maestro fray Fernando de Abreu y Figueroa . . . dize: Que depues de aver . . . representado en otro memorial a V. Magestad, el notorio derecho que tiene a los sinodos que le reparten a los dotrineros de Indias [etc.]. [*Madrid?* 1640]. 8 numb. lvs; fol. Medina (BHA) 6154. BL.
640/3

——. Señor. El maestro fray Fernando de Abreu y Figueroa . . . natural de . . . Lima . . . del Peru, dize: Que aviendosele intimado de orden de V. Magestad que proponga de nuevo los fundamentos . . . en razon de reformados sinodos que gozan . . . los ministros eclasiasticos en . . . las Indias Occidentales. [*Madrid?* 1640?]. 20 numb. lvs; fol. Medina (BHA) 6153. BL, Seville: Archivo de Indias.
640/4

Acuña, Cristóbal de, S.J. Señor. Christoval de Acuña, religioso de la Compañia de Jesus, que vino por orden de V. Magestad, al descubrimiento del gran rio de las Amazonas. [*Madrid?* 1640?]. 4 p.; fol. Memorial to king of Spain. Medina (BHA) 6174; Borba de Moraes I:12; Streit II:1691; Backer I:39; JCB (3) II:280. NN-RB, RPJCB.
640/5

Af-beeldinghe van d'eerste eeuwe der Societeyt Jesu. *Antwerp: Plantin Press,* 1640. 712 p.; illus.; 4to. Translated by p. Laurentius Uwens from the *Imago primi saeculi Societatis Jesu* below. Backer I:1626; JCB (3) II:283. MH-AH, MiU-C, NN-RB, RPJCB; BL, BN.
640/6

Aldrovandi, Ulisse. De piscibus libri v. et de cetis liber i. *Frankfurt a. M.: K. Rötel, for J. Treudel,* 1640. 280 p.; illus.; fol. 1st publ.,

Bologna, 1612. Nissen (Zool.) 71n. MH.
640/7

———. Ornithologiae . . . libri xii[–xx]. *Frankfurt a. M.: W. Richter, for Heirs of N. Basse,* 1640, '35. 3 v.; illus,; fol. 1st publ., Bologna, 1599–1603; cf. Frankfurt, 1610 edn. Vol. 3 has 1635 imprint date. Dt. Ges. Kat. 3.502. DNAL (v. 3), NcD (v. 1); Berlin:StB, Marburg: UB (v. 1, 2), Munich:StB (v. 3).
640/8

———. Ornithologiae tomus alter[–tertius]. *Bologna: N. Tebaldini, for M. A. Bernia,* 1637 [colophon: 1640]. 2 v.; illus.; fol. 1st publ. as vols 2–3 of the author's 3 v. work, Bologna, 1599–1603; cf. 1610 edn. For v. 1, see the year 1646. Cf. Nissen (Birds) 82; Mengel (Ellis) 44–45; Dt. Ges. Kat. 3.503. CU, DNLM (v. 3), NN (v. 3), WU; BL, BN.
640/9

Articul-brief. Beraemt over het scheeps ende crijgs-volck ten dienste van de geoctroyeerde West-Indische Compagnie in Brasyl, Guinea ende vonders de limiten van den Octroye. *Groningen: H. Sas,* 1640. 64 p.; 4to. Sabin 7519; Borba de Moraes I:42; Asher 159; Rodrigues (Dom. Hol.) 769, Leyden: B. Thysiana.
640/10

Au Roi. Raisons qui font voir combien il est important au Roy & à son estat, de deffendre ses sujets de la nouvelle France, dite Canada, contre les invasions des Iroquois & d'estrendre sa protection sur ce nouveau monde. [*Paris?* 1640]. 3 p.; fol. Sabin 56080.
640/11

Auctentijck verhael van 't remarcquabelste is voorgevallen in Brasil, tusschen den Hollandtschen Admirael Willem Cornelisz. ende de Spaensche vloot. *Amsterdam: J. van Hilten,* 1640. [12] p.; 4to. For variant collations see Knuttel. Sabin 7522 (& 2443); Borba de Moraes I:46; Asher 157; Palau 265097; Knuttel 4685; JCB (3) II:281. DLC, NN-RB, RPJCB; BL (Cornelisz.; imp.), The Hague:KB.
640/12

Bacon, Francis, viscount St Albans. Of the advancement and proficiencie of learning . . . Interpreted by Gilbert Wats. *Oxford: L. Lichfield, for R. Young & E. Forrest,* 1640. 477 p.; port.; 4to. Transl. from Bacon's *Opera: Tomus primus: qui continet De dignitate et augmentis scientiarum,* 1st publ., London, 1623. For printing variants, see Gibson.

Gibson (Bacon) 141a–c; Madan (Oxford) 1640:1. CSmH, CtY, DLC, ICN, MH, MiU, MnU, NN-RB, PU; BL, BN.
640/13

———. Le progrez et avancement aux sciences divines & humaines . . . Traduict . . . par A. Maugars. *Paris: A. Soubron,* 1640. 636 p.; 8vo. 1st publ. as here transl., Paris, 1624; here a reissue of that edn? Shaaber (Brit. auth.) B42. CCB.
640/14

Ballet du Bureau d'adresse. *Dijon:* 1640. *See the year* 1641.

Barba, Alvaro Alonso. Arte de los metales en que se ensaña el verdadero beneficio de los de oro, y plata por açoque. El modo de fundirlos todos. *Madrid: Imprenta Real,* 1640. 120 numb. lvs; illus.; 4to. 'One of the few significant works on metallurgy in colonial Spanish America'—Lewis Hanke. Based on Barba's residence at Potosí. Sabin's 1630 edn is a ghost. Sabin 3253; Medina (BHA) 1010; Palau 23622; JCB AR40:34–36. CtY, NNE, PU-S, RPJCB; BL, BN.
640/15

Barclay, John. L'oeil clair-voyant d'Euphormion. *Paris: T. Quinet* [ca. 1640]. 277 numb. lvs. 8vo. 1st publ. under the above title, Paris, 1626, as transl. from Barclay's *Icon animorum,* 1st publ., London, 1614. Shaaber (Brit. auth.) B175. BN, Kassel:LB, Schwerin:MLB.
640/16

———. La satyre d'Euphormion . . . mise nouvellement en françois. *Paris: J. Guignard,* 1640. 648 p.; 8vo. Transl. from Barclay's *Satyricon,* of which pt 2 had been 1st publ., Paris, 1607, and, pt 4, the *Icon animorum,* London, 1614. Shaaber (Brit. auth.) B178; Tchémerzine I:453. DFo, ICN, PU; Karlsruhe:BLB.
640/17

Bauderon, Brice. Pharmacopee. *Lyons: Widow of C. Rigaud & P. Borde,* 1640. 2 pts; 8vo. 1st publ., Lyons, 1588, under title *Paraphrase sur la Pharmacopoee;* cf. 1607 edn. DNLM, NNNAM.
640/18

Béguin, Jean. Tyrocinium chymicum. *Wittenberg: [J. Röhner, for] Heirs of C. Berger,* 1640. 480 p.; 8vo. 1st publ., Paris, 1612. BN.
640/19

Bertius, Petrus. Breviarium totius orbis terrarum. *Frankfurt a. M.: C. Schleich & Co.,* 1640. 76 p.; 12mo. 1st publ., Paris, 1614. Sabin 5013n. BL.
640/20

Besold, Christoph. Discursus politicus de

incrementis imperiorum . . . Cui inserta est dissertatio singularis, De novo orbe. *Strassburg: Heirs of L. Zetzner,* 1640. 55 p.; 4to. 1st publ. in this version with the *De novo orbe,* Strassburg, 1623. Cf. Sabin 5048. DLC, NIC; BN. 640/21

Beverwijck, Jan van. Schat der gesontheydt. *Dordrecht:* 1640. 8vo. 1st publ., [Dordrecht? 1636?]. Catalogus van boeken VII:40. 640/22

——. Spaensche Xerxes, ofte Beschrijvinge ende vergelijckinge van den scheepstrijdt . . . Den tweeden druck. *The Hague: I. Burchoorn,* 1640. 64 p.; 4to. 1st publ., Dordrecht, 1639. Cf. Palau 28844; Van de Velde 75; Knuttel 4683. MnU-B; The Hague:KB. 640/23

Blaeu, Willem Janszoon. [Appendice I & II partium. *Amsterdam:* 1640]. *See* Blaeu's *Theatrum orbis terrarum . . . Tertia pars* below.

——. Institutio astronomica. *Amsterdam: J. & C. Blaeu,* 1640. 246 p.; illus.; 8vo. 1st publ., Amsterdam, 1634. CtY, DLC, MiU; BN. 640/24

——. The sea-mirrour. *Amsterdam: W. J. Blaeu, for W. Lugger* [*at London,*] 1640. 3 pts; illus., maps; fol. 1st publ. in English, Amsterdam, 1625; here a reissue of 1635 edn with new, collective t.p. added. Koeman (M.Bl) 50B (& 49); Kebabian 330. CtY. 640/25

—[Anr issue?]. *Amsterdam: W. J. Blaeu,* 1640. Koeman (M.Bl) 50A. Edwards. 640/26

——. Theatre du monde, ou Nouvel atlas . . . seconde partie. *Amsterdam: J. & C. Blaeu,* 1640. 2 pts; 93 maps; fol. 1st publ. in French, Amsterdam, 1635; here added are 4 maps from Blaeu's French *Appendice,* 1st publ., [Amsterdam, ca. 1638], including map of Florida. Issued with Blaeu's *Theatre,* Amsterdam, 1638. Koeman (Bl) 17. ICN; BL, Amsterdam:UB. 640/27

—[Anr edn]. *Amsterdam: J. & C. Blaeu,* 1640. 2 pts; 93 maps; fol. Text pages are numbered. Koeman (Bl) 18A. [Edn uncertain: DLC, MiU-C]; BN. 640/28

——. Theatre du monde . . . Troisiesme partie, avec L'appendice des deux precedentes parties. *Amsterdam: J. & C. Blaeu,* 1640. 2 pts; 86 maps; fol. This edn differs from others of this year by the inclusion of Blaeu's *Appendice dela i & ii parties du Theatre,* 1st publ., [Amsterdam, ca. 1638], with

maps including Florida & pt of North America. Koeman (Bl) 35B (& 15); Phillips (Atlases) 3421. DLC; BN, Amsterdam:UB. 640/29

——. Theatrum orbis terrarum, sive Atlas novus. *Amsterdam: J. & C. Blaeu,* 1640. 2 pts; 120 maps; fol. 1st publ., Amsterdam, 1635; among added maps is 'Regiones sub Polo Arctico' from Blaeu's Latin 'Appendice' of this year, showing pts of North America. Issued with Blaeu's *Theatrum . . . pars secunda* below. Sabin 5720n; Koeman (Bl) 21A. Rotterdam:MA, Rome:Vatican. 640/30

——. Theatrum orbis terrarum, sive Atlas novus pars secunda. *Amsterdam: J. & C. Blaeu,* 1640. 2 pts; 91 maps; fol. 1st publ., Amsterdam, 1635; among the maps added to this edn from Blaeu's Latin 'Appendice' of this year is one of Florida, 'Virginiae partis australis.' Issued with Blaeu's *Theatrum* above. Sabin 5720n; Koeman (Bl) 22. Rotterdam:MA, Rome:Vatican. 640/31

——. Theatrum orbis terrarum, sive Atlas novus. Tertia pars cum Appendice I & II partium antehac editarum. *Amsterdam: J. & C. Blaeu,* 1640. 2 pts; 87 maps; fol. This edn of pt 3 differs from the other of this year by the inclusion of Blaeu's Latin 'Appendice', with 2 maps relating to America. Cf. Blaeu's French edn, the *Appendice . . . du Theatre,* [Amsterdam, ca. 1638]. Koeman (Bl) 36A & 20. Milan:BN 640/32

——. Zeespiegel. *Amsterdam: W. J. Blaeu,* 1640. 3 pts; illus., maps; fol. 1st publ., Amsterdam, 1623. Koeman (M.Bl) 36. Amsterdam:NHSM. 640/33

Boccalini, Traiano. Lapis lydius politicus. Latinitate donavit Ern. Joan. Creutz. *Amsterdam: L. Elsevier,* 1640. 196 p.; 12mo. Transl. from Boccalini's *Pietra del paragone politico,* 1st publ., 'Cormopoli' (i.e., Venice), 1615. Willems (Les Elzevier) 966. ICU, PU; BL, BN. 640/34

——. Pietra del paragone politico. '*Cosmopoli: G. Teler*' [i.e., *Leyden: B. & A. Elsevier, for L. Elsevier, at Amsterdam*], 1640. 268 p.; 12mo. 1st publ. 'Cormopoli' (i.e., Venice), 1615. Willems (Les Elzevier) 965; Michel (Répertoire) I:174. PU, WU; BL, Paris: Arsenal. 640/35

Boodt, Anselm Boëce de. Florum, herba-

rum, ac fructuum selectiorum icones. *Bruges: J. B. & L. Kerchovius,* 1640. 119 p.; illus.; obl. 4to. 1st publ., Frankfurt a. M., 1609. Pritzel 989; Nissen (Bot.) 208n. DNAL, ICJ, MH-A; BL, BN.
                                    640/36

Botero, Giovanni. Della ragion di stato libri dieci, con tre libri Delle cause della grandezza delle città. *Venice: The Giuntas,* 1640. 264 p.; 4to. 1st publ., Venice, 1589; cf. 1601 edn. The *Delle cause della grandezza delle città,* 1st publ., Rome, 1588, with refs to riches of New World, mentioning Canada, Brazil, & Peru. Michel (Répertoire) I:201. NN; Orléans:BM.   640/37

Botero, Giovanni. Relationi universali. *Venice: The Giuntas,* 1640. 800 p., maps; 4to. 1st publ., Rome, 1591–96; cf. 1601 edn. Sabin 6807n; Streit I:479. RPJCB; Strasbourg:BN.   640/38

—[Anr edn]. Aggiuntovi di nuovo la Ragione di stato. *Venice: The Giuntas,* 1640. 2 pts; maps; 4to. Maggs Cat. 465 (Americana IV):2745; Michel (Répertoire) I:202. CU, CtY, DLC, NN-RB; BN.   640/39

Bouton, Jacques, S.J. Relation de l'establissement des François depuis . . . 1635 . . . en Martinique . . . Des moeurs des sauvages. *Paris: S. Cramoisy,* 1640. 141 p.; 8vo. Sabin 6948; Streit II:1680; Backer II:53; Maggs Cat. 479 (Americana V):4234. CtY, DLC, InU-L, MiU-C, MnU-B, NN-RB, RPJCB; BN.   640/40

Brerewood, Edward. Recherches curieuses sur la diversité des langues et religions par toutes les principales parties du monde . . . mises en français par J. de La Montagne. *Paris: O. de Varennes,* 1640. 338 p.; 8vo. Transl. from author's *Enquiries touching the diversity of languages and religions,* 1st publ., London, 1614. Sabin 7733; Shaaber (Brit. auth.) B651; JCB (3) II:281. CSmH, ICU, NN-RB, RPJCB; BL, BN.   640/41

Campanella, Tommaso. De monarchia Hispanica discursus. [*Leyden: Elsevier Press, for*] *L. Elsevier, at Amsterdam,* 1640. 560 p.; 12mo. Ostensibly transl. from German text, 1st publ., [Frankfurt a. M.?], 1620. Sabin 10197; Willems (Les Elzevier) 967. CSmH, ICN, MH, NNC, PU; BN.   640/42

—[Anr issue]. [*Leyden: Elsevier Press, for L. Elsevier, at*] *Amsterdam,* 1640. Firpo (Campa-

nella) p. 64; Willems (Les Elzevier) 967n. BN.   640/43

—[Anr edn]. *Harderwijk:* 1640. 415 p.; 12mo. Sabin 10197n; Firpo (Campanella) p. 64; Willems (Les Elzevier) 967n. CSmH, CtY, PU; BL, BN.   640/44

Canale, Floriano. De' secreti universali raccolti, et esperimentati. *Venice: G. Imberti,* 1640. 304 p.; 8vo. 1st publ., Brescia (?), 1613. Michel (Répertoire) I:29. DNLM; BL, BN.   640/45

Casas, Bartolomé de las, O.P., Bp of Chiapa. La libertà pretesa dal supplice schiavo indiano . . . Tradotto . . . per . . . Marco Ginammi. *Venice: M. Ginammi,* 1640. 155 p.; 4to. Transl. from the author's *Entre los remedios que don fray Bartolomé delas Casas . . . refirio,* 1st publ., Seville, 1552. Text in Spanish & Italian in parallel columns. Sabin 11245; Medina (BHA) 1085n (II:474); Hanke/Giménez 534; Streit I:480; Palau 46957; JCB (3) II:281. CU, DLC, MH, NN-RB, PU, RPJCB; BL, BN.   640/46

——. Den vermeerderden spieghel der Spaensche tierannije-geschiet in Westindien. *Amsterdam: C. L. van der Plasse,* 1640. [104] p.; illus.; 4to. 1st publ. in Dutch, [Antwerp?], 1578; cf. 1607 edn above. Hanke/Giménez 533. CtY; Haarlem:StB.

                                    640/47

Castelli, Pietro. Balsamum examinatum. *Messina: G. F. Bianco,* 1640. 63 (i.e., 163) p.; port.; 4to. Describes American opobalsam as adequate substitute for Arabian type. DNLM; BL, BN.   640/48

—[Anr edn]. Opobalsamum triumphans. *Basel: F. Perna,* 1640. 51 p.; 4to. BN.

                                    640/49

—[Anr edn]. Opobalsamum triumphans. [*Rome:* 1640]. 44 (i.e., 54) p.; 4to. DNLM.
                                    640/50

—[Anr edn]. Opobalsamum. *Venice: P. Tomasini,* 1640. 163 p.; 4to. Michel (Répertoire) II:64; Wellcome I:1352. BL, BN.

                                    640/51

——. Hortus Messanensis. *Messina: Widow of G. F. Bianco,* 1640. 51 p.; illus.; 4to. Described as growing in the garden are several American plants, identified as such, among them the prickly pear. Pritzel 1591; Nissen (Bot.) 335; Michel (Répertoire) II:63. MH-A, NNBG; BL, BN.   640/52

Castro de Torres, El capitán. Panegirico del chocolate. *Segovia: D. Díaz de la Carrera,* 1640. 10 lvs; 4to. Medina (BHA) 1011; Müller 42; Palau 49050. 640/53

Cats, Jacob. Maechden-plicht. *Gouda: P. Rammazeyn* [ca. 1640]. 8vo. 1st publ., Middelburg, 1618. For variant edn, see Mus. Cats. as cited. Mus. Cats. 64 & 65. 640/54

——. Minnelijcke, zedelijcke en stichtelijcke sinne-beelden en ghedichten. [*Amsterdam?* ca. 1640]. [217] p.; illus.; obl. 12mo. 1st publ. in this abridged version, [Amsterdam? 1622?]. Engraved t.p. begins 'Emblemata, ofte Minnelycke . . .'; vignette portrays two couples; in center is Cupid carrying globe, on which 'Europa' can be read. Vries 92; Mus. Cats. 45. Leyden:UB. 640/55

—[Anr edn?]. . . . zinnebeelden . . . [*Amsterdam?* ca. 1640]. [217] p.; illus. DLC, ICU. 640/56

——. Silenus Alcibiadis, sive Proteus, voorghestelt in minn'-en-sinne-beelden. *Gouda: P. Rammazeyn* [ca. 1640]. 4 pts; illus.; 8vo. 1st publ., Middelburg, 1618. Vries 85; Mus. Cats. 34. Leyden:UB. 640/57

Cervantes Saavedra, Miguel de. Exemplarie novells . . . Turned into English by Don Diego Puede-Ser [i.e., James Mabbe]. *London: J. Dawson, for R. M[abb]. & L. Blacklock,* 1640. 323 p.; 8vo. Transl. from Spanish text 1st publ., Madrid, 1613. Ríus (Cervantes) 925; STC 4914; Palau 53553. DFo, PPL. 640/58

——. Les nouvelles. *Paris: J. Bouillerot,* 1640. 695 p.; 8vo. 1st publ. as transl. from Madrid, 1613, Spanish text, Paris, 1615. Ríus (Cervantes) 889; Palau 53524. DLC, MB; BL, BN. 640/59

Céspedes y Meneses, Gonzalo de. Historia del Rey Don Felipe Quarto. *Lisbon: P. Craesbeeck,* 1640. 607 p.; fol. 1st publ., Lisbon, 1631. Palau 54201. 640/60

Chamberlain, Robert. Jocabella, or A cabinet of conceits. *London: R. Hodgkinson, for D. Frere,* 1640. 106 lvs; 12mo. 1st publ., London, 1639, under title *Conceits, clinches, flashes, and whimsies;* here enl. with additional refs to tobacco. STC 4943; Arents 208. DFo, MH, NN-A; BL. 640/61

Champlain, Samuel de. Les voyages de la Nouvelle France Occidentale, dite Canada. *Paris: C. Collet,* 1640. 4 pts; illus., map; 4to. 1st publ., Paris, 1632; here a reissue of that edn with cancel t.p. Sabin 11840; Harrisse (NF) 72; Streit II:2522; Church 446; JCB (3) II:280. CSmH, DLC, MnU-B, NN-RB, RPJCB. 640/62

Chaumette, Antoine. Handt-boeck der chirurgie . . . Waer by gekomen is een wel besochte maniere om de Spaensche pocken te ghenesen . . . In onse Nederlandtsche tale over-gheset door Gysbert Coets. *Arnhem: J. Jacobszoon,* 1640. 488 p.; 12mo. Transl. from Chaumette's *Enchiridion chirurgicum,* 1st publ., Paris, 1560, with discussion of use of guaiacum for treating syphilis. DNLM. 640/63

Cianca, Alonso de. Discourso breve hecho por . . . Alonso de Cianca, juez que ha side de su Magestad, en que se muestra . . . la causa que [a] enflaquecido el comercio de las flotas de Nueva España. [*Madrid:* 1640?]. 6 numb. lvs; fol. Medina (BHA) 6365; BL. 640/64

Clüver, Johannes. Historiarium totius mundi epitome . . . Editio tertia correctior. *Leyden: J. Marcus,* 1640. 852 p.; 4to. 1st publ., Leyden, 1637. ICN. 640/65

Collart, P., S.J., pseud. Het hoogh-loffelijcke jubel-jaer van de . . . Societeyt Jesu. *Antwerp: H. Pers,* 1640. [26] p.; 4to. Includes ref. to conversion of Indians. Backer II:1291; Knuttel 4710. NN-RB; The Hague:KB. 640/66

—[Anr edn]. *Antwerp: H. Pers,* 1640. [19] p.; 4to. Backer II:1291; Meulman 2525. Ghent:BU. 640/67

Colmenero de Ledesma, Antonio. A curious treatise of the nature and quality of chocolate . . . put into English by Don Diego de Vadesforte [i.e., James Wadsworth]. *London: J. Okes,* 1640. 21 p.; 4to. Transl. from author's *Curioso tratado . . . de chocolate,* 1st publ., Madrid, 1631. Müller 52; STC 5570. CSmH, DFo; BL. 640/68

Copye ofte Cort ende waerachtigh verhael van 't gene ghepasseert is soo te water als te lande, sint de komste ende vertreck van de Spaensche vloot in Brasil, overgesonden door . . . Mauritz van Nassau. *Amsterdam: P. Matthijszoon, for F. Lieshout,* 1640. [14] p.; 4to. Sabin 7561 & 16739; Borba de Moraes I:178; Rodrigues (Dom. Hol.) 476. DLC,

NN-RB; Ghent:BU, Rio de Janeiro:BN.
640/69

Cort verhael vande ordre die sijne Conincklicke Majesteyt van Spagnien aen sijn Generalissimo den Graef de la Torre inde Bay de todos los Sanctos gegeven heeft, om int werck te stellen al 'tghene hy tot recuparatie van Brasil noodigh achten soude . . . Beschreven door den eern. N. N. *Amsterdam: J. van Hilten* [1640]. [12] p.; 4to. Sabin 51680 [& 45404]; Borba de Moraes I:185; Rodrigues (Dom. Hol.) 475; Knuttel 4688; JCB (3) II:282. DLC, NN-RB, RPJCB; The Hague:KB (imp.). 640/70

Declaracion del valor justo, dela plata que viene de las Indias, en barras quintadas. [*Madrid?* 1640?]. 4 numb. lvs; fol. BL (Indies). 640/71

Del Rio, Martin Antón, S.J. Disquisitionum magicarum libri sex. *Venice: The Guerigli,* 1640. 768 p.; 4to. 1st publ., Louvain, 1599–1600; cf. 1603 edn. Backer II:1899. NNH; London:Wellcome. 640/72

Discurso de los sucessos de España, prevenciones de guerra, y muestros que han dado todos los reynos, con la salida de la cavalleriza. *Madrid: J. Sánchez,* 1640. [4] p.; 4to. In verse. 'Has los Indios agora quisieron mostrar su afecto para que aun del nuevo mundo muestren lo que al Rey devieron.' BL. 640/73

Donne, John. LXXX sermons. *London:* [*M. Fletcher*] *for R. Royston & R. Marriott,* 1640. 826 p.; port.; fol. In sermon xxiv, for Easter day 1629, the Strait of Magellan & the search for a Northwest passage are mentioned. Keynes (Donne) 29; STC 7038. CSmH, CtY, DLC, ICN, MH, MiU, MnU, NN-RB, PPL; BL, BN. 640/74

Du Bartas, Guillaume de Salluste, seigneur. Die erste und andere Woche . . . Aus dem Frantzösischen . . . ausgegangen. *Köthen:* 1640. 668 p.; illus.; 4to. In verse. 1st publ. in German, Köthen, 1622,'19 (*La seconde sepmaine . . . Die andere Woche*) and 1631 (*Erste Woche*); transl. by Tobias Hübner. Includes French and German text on facing pages. Goedeke III:34; Holmes (DuBartas) I:109:no. 24. MH; Göttingen:UB. 640/75

Durante, Castore. Il tesoro della sanità. *Venice: G. Imberti,* 1640. 324 p.; 8vo. 1st publ.,

[Rome?], 1586; cf. 1601 edn. Michel (Répertoire) II:191. Versailles:BM. 640/76

Elías, Juan, fray. Señor. Un libelo infamatorio se ha impresso, y publicado en 29. hojas . . . su fecha en Potosí, en 24. de enero del año passado de 1639. firmado de Antonio de Paredes. [*Madrid?* 1640]. 16 numb. lvs; fol. Memorial to king of Spain on mines of Potosí. For the 'libelo' of Antonio de Paredes see the year 1639. Medina (BHA) 1012. BL. 640/77

Estienne, Charles. L'agriculture et maison rustique. *Paris: N. de La Vigne,* 1640. 2 pts; illus.; 4to. 1st publ. as enl. by Liébault, Paris, 1567; cf. 1601 edn. BN. 640/78

Figueroa, Antonio de. Don Antonio de Figueroa, procurador general de los mineros de la Nueva España. [*Madrid?* 1640?]. 5 numb. lvs; fol. Memorial to the Consejo de las Indias on means of attracting Indians to work in Mexican mines. Medina (BHA) 6463. BL. 640/79

Fioravanti, Leonardo. De' secreti rationali . . . libri cinque. *Venice: G. Imberti,* 1640. 190 numb. lvs; 8vo. 1st publ., Venice, 1564, under title *Del compendio de i secreti rationali;* cf. 1620 edn. Michel (Répertoire) III:47. London:Wellcome, BN. 640/80

Gad ben-Arod ben Balaam, pseud. The wandering Jew, telling fortunes to Englishmen. *London: J. Raworth, for N. Butter,* 1640. 67 p.; 4to. Includes character of 'A tobacconist, or A gallant smelling strong of tobacco'. STC 11512; Arents 213. DFo, NN-A; BL. 640/81

Garavito, Gerónimo. Geronimo Garavito procurador general del gremio de los azogueros y mineros dela villa imperial de Potosi del Perù, dize, que teniendo noticia que don Juan de Carvajal y Sande . . . queria entrar por Consejero de Indias. [*Madrid?* 1640]. [8] p.; fol. Memorial to king of Spain, opposing naming of Carvajal y Sande to Consejo de las Indias. RPJCB; BL. 640/82

——. Señor. Geronimo Garavito, procurador general del gremio de los azogueros de . . . Potosi del Pirù, dize: Que alos 3. de enero del año passado de 1639. teniendo noticia, que por parte de don Pablo Vazquez, Indio Atunruna y Chontal, y de los del servicio del Cerro de la dicha villa se avian presentado ciertos recaudos en el Consejo de las Indias [etc.]. [*Madrid?* 1640]. 3 numb. lvs; fol. Denies merits of the Indian Pablo's petition. BL. 640/83

Glapthorne, Henry. Wit in a constable. A comedy. *London: J. Okes, for F. C[onstable].*, 1640. [64] p.; 4to. In act 1, scene 1, & act 3, scene 1, tobacco is mentioned; in act 5, scene 1, the 'Brethren at Amsterdam, And in new England' are cited. STC 11914; Greg 591; Arents 209. CSmH, CtY, DLC, ICN, MH, NN-RB; BL. 640/84

González de Ribero, Blas. Por Andres de Zavala, contador . . . mayor del Tribunal de la Santa Cruzada de . . . Lima . . . y don Tomas de Vibanco, notario . . . Con el fiscal del Consejo Real de las Indias. Sobre que el conocimiento destas causas toca al Consejo de la santa Cruzada. [*Madrid?* 1640?]. 13 numb. lvs; fol. Relates to the Catholic Church's Commisarius generalis cruciatae in Peru. Medina (BHA) 7004. BL, Seville:BM. 640/85

Gough, John. The strange discovery: a tragicomedy. *London: E. G[riffin], for W. Leake*, 1640. [86] p.; 4to. The prologue mentions Columbus & Peru. On t.p. author statement reads 'J. G. Gent.'. STC 12133; Greg 584; Pforzheimer 418. CSmH, DFo, MH, MiU, PU; BL. 640/86

—[Anr issue]. *London: E. G[riffin]., for W. Leake*, 1640. On t.p. author statement reads 'J. Gough. Gent.'. STC 12135; Greg 584. CSmH, CtY, DFo, ICN; BL. 640/87

Grau y Monfalcón, Juan. Justificacion de la conservacion, y comercio de las islas Filipinas. [*Madrid:* 1640]. 2 pts; 4to. Pt 2 comprises a *Cedula de informe, sobre en que cantidad, y en que forma ha de correr . . . el comercio de las islas con Nueva-España.* Medina (Phil.) 148; Palau 108816; Maggs Cat. 479 (Americana V):4231; JCB (3) II:282. DLC, ICN, RPJCB; BL. 640/88

Grotius, Hugo. De veritate religionis christianae. Editio nova additis annotationibus in quibus testimonia. *Paris: S. Cramoisy*, 1640. 581 p.; 12mo. 1st publ., Leyden, 1627, under title *Sensus librorum sex.* This issue has vignette on t.p. of Jesus & instruments of Passion. Meulen/Diermanse 950. BL, BN, Leyden:UB. 640/89

—[Anr issue?]. *Paris: S. Cramoisy*, 1640. This issue has royal French coat of arms on t.p. Meulen/Diermanse 950n. BN. 640/90

—[Anr edn]. Iuxta exemplar Parisiense, sumptibus Seb. Cramoisy . . . MDCXL. [*Amsterdam? J. Janszoon, the Younger?* 1640?]. 274 [i.e., 374] p.; 12mo. Meulen/Diermanse 951. The Hague:PP. 640/91

—[Anr edn]. *Leyden: J. Maire*, 1640. 2 pts; 12mo. For variants cf. Meulen/Diermanse as cited. Meulen/Diermanse 952–53. CSmH, CtY-D, DLC, ICN, NNC, PPL; BL, BN, The Hague:PP. 640/92

——. La verité de la religion chrestienne. *Paris:* [1640?]. 541 p.; 8vo. *See the year* 1644.

Guelen, August de. Brieve relation de l'estat de Phernambucq. *Amsterdam: L. Elsevier*, 1640. [43] p.; 4to. Sabin 29100; Borba de Moraes II:170; Rodrigues (Dom. Hol.) 439; Willems (Les Elzevier) 970; JCB (3) II:283. RPJCB; BL, Ghent:BU. 640/93

——. Kort verhael vanden staet van Fernanbuc [*sic*] . . . Wt het Francois . . . vertaelt. *Amsterdam:* 1640. [30] p.; 4to. Transl. from Guelen's *Brieve relation* of this year above. Sabin 29101; Borba de Moraes I:170; Rodrigues (Dom. Hol.) 440; Knuttel 4689; JCB (3) II:283. DLC, MnU-B, NN-RB, RPJCB; Amsterdam:NHSM, The Hague:KB. 640/94

Guibert, Philbert. Toutes les oeuvres charitables. *Lyons: Widow of C. Rigaud & P. Borde*, 1640. 766 p.; 8vo. Included is Guibert's *Le prix & valeur des medicamens*, 1st publ., Paris, 1625. DNLM. 640/95

—[Anr issue]. *Lyons: N. Gay*, 1640. DNLM. 640/96

Guicciardini, Francesco. La historia d'Italia . . . divisa in venti libri. *Venice: E. Baba*, 1640. 2 pts; 4to. 1st publ., Florence, 1561; cf. 1604 edn. Michel (Répertoire) IV:101. CtY, DLC, NN, WU; Lyons:BM. 640/97

Hay, Paul, sieur du Chastelet (1592–1636), ed. Recueil de diverses pieces pour servir à l'histoire. [*Paris:*] 1640. 921 p.; 4to. 1st publ., [Paris], 1635. DFo; BL, BN. 640/98

Hodson, William. The divine cosmographer, or A brief survey of the whole world delineated. *Cambridge: R. Daniel*, 1640. 154 p.; 12mo. In sect. 9, phrase 'gold from India' presumably refers to that from Amer-ica. Sabin 32367; STC 13554. CSmH, CtY, DLC; BL. 640/99

Hondius, Hendrik. Nouveau theatre du monde, ou Nouvel atlas . . . divise en trois tomes. *Amsterdam: J. Janszoon, the Younger,* 1640. 3v.; maps; fol. 1st publ. in this enl. version, Amsterdam, 1639. Koeman (Me) 94–96; cf. Phillips (Atlases) 3422. DLC (v. 2, 3); BN (v. 2–3; Jansson), Louvain:BU. 640/100

Horatius Flaccus, Quintus. Q. Horatius Flaccus: his Art of poetry. Englished by Ben: Jonson. With other works . . . never printed before. *London: J. Okes, for J. Benson,* 1640. 138 p.; port.; 12mo. Included are Jon-son's 'Execration against Vulcan', also publ. separately in this year, and his 'Masque of the gypsies', mentioning both tobacco & the turkey. An added engraved t.p. exists in two states, one with imprint reading 'Printed for John Benson', the other, 'Printed for J. Benson and are sold by W. Ley at Paules-Chayne'. STC 13798; Grolier Club (Lang-land to Wither) 151; Arents 210; Pforz-heimer 548. CSmH, CtY, DFo, IU, MH, MiU, NN-RB, PU; BL. 640/101

Howell, James. Δενδρολογια. Dodona's grove, or The vocall forest. [*London:*] T. B[adger]., for H. Moseley, 1640. 219 p.; illus.; fol. STC 13872; Arents (Add.) 308; Hunt (Bot.) 234; Pforzheimer 512. CSmH, CtY, DLC, ICN, InU-L, MH, MnU, NN-RB, PU; BL, BN. 640/102

Hulsius, Levinus, comp. Achte Schiffahrt, oder Kurtze Beschreibung etlicher Reysen. *Frankfurt a. M.: C. LeBlon,* 1640. 56 p.; illus., maps; 4to. (Levinus Hulsius's *Sammlung von . . . Schiffahrten.* Pt 8). 1st publ., Frankfurt a. M., 1605. Sabin 33662; Church 290; JCB (3) I:460. CSmH, NN-RB, RPJCB, ViU; BL. 640/103

Imago primi saeculi Societatis Jesu. *Antwerp: Plantin Office (B. Moretus)* 1640. 952 p.; fol. Includes accounts of Jesuits in Brazil, Mex-ico, Canada, etc. Sometimes ascribed to Jean de Tollenaer, but chiefly the work of Joannes Bollandus & Godefridus Hen-schenius. For a Dutch translation, see the *Af-beeldinghe,* &c., above. Streit I:481; Backer I:1625. CLU, DLC, NN-RB, OCl; BL, BN. 640/104

Inquisition. Peru. Auto de la fe celebrado en Lima a 23. de enero de 1639 al tribunal del Santo Officio de la Inquisicion, de los reynos del Perù, Chile, Paraguay, y Tucu-man, por . . . Fernando de Montesinos. *Madrid: Imprenta Real,* 1640. 28 numb. lvs; 4to. 1st publ., Lima 1639. Cf. Sabin 50124; Medina (BHA) 1017; Palau 178980n; JCB (3) II:284. CtY, MH, RPJCB; BL, Madrid:BN. 640/105

Jansson, Jan. Nouveau theatre. *Amsterdam:* 1640. *See* Hondius, Hendrik, *above.*

Jesuits. Servicios de la Compañia de Jesus hizieron a V. Mag[estad]. en el Brasil. [*Madrid? ca. 1640?*]. 8 numb. lvs; fol. Borba de Moraes II:252; Maggs Cat. 496 (Ameri-cana VI):367 640/106

Jonson, Ben. The workes [Vol. I]. *London: R. Bishop; sold by A. Crooke,* 1640. fol. 1st publ., London, 1616. STC 14753. CSmH, CtY, DLC, ICN, MH, MiU, NN-RB, PU, RPB; BL. 640/107

——. The workes . . . The second[-third] volume. *London: [B. Alsop & T. Fawcet; & J. Dawson,] for R. Meighen & T. Walkley,* 1640–41. [835] p.; fol. In pt a reissue of sheets of the 1631 edn of Jonson's *Bartholo-mew fayre,* etc. Here 1st publ., in v. 3, is *The magnetick lady* with, in act 3, scene vi (i.e., vii), mention of tobacco. For the com-plex printing history & variant issue of this work, see the STC. STC 14754 & 14754a; Arents 211; Pforzheimer 560. CSmH, CtY, DLC, ICN, MH, MiU, NN-RB, PU, RPB; BL. 640/108

——. Ben: Jonson's Execration against Vul-can. With divers epigrams. *London: J. O[kes]., for J. Benson [& A. Crooke],* 1640. [57] p.; port.; 4to. Includes mention of tobacco. For variant states, see the STC. STC 14771; Grolier Club (Langland to Wither) 152; Pforzheimer 546. CSmH, CtY, DLC (imp.), ICN, MH, MiU, NN-RB; BL. 640/109

Journalier verhael ofte copie van sekeren brief geschreven uit Brasijl, nopende de vic-torie van januarij 1640, aan de bewintheb-beren ter Kamer van de Mase. [*Rotterdam?*] 1640. 4to. Cf. the *Naderste ende sekerste journa-lier verhael* of this year below, of which this presumably represents anr edn. Sabin 7592. 640/110

Laet, Joannes de. L'histoire du Nouveau

Monde, ou Description des Indes Occidentales. *Leyden: B. & A. Elsevier,* 1640. 632 p.; illus., maps; fol. Transl. from the author's *Beschrijvinghe van West-Indien,* Leyden, 1630, itself an enlargement of his *Nieuwe Wereldt,* 1st publ., Leyden, 1625. Here added are vocabularies of Indian languages & other material—Sabin. Some copies include a 2-page dedication to Richelieu—Willems. For another variant see Rahir. Sabin 38558; Borba de Moraes I:384; Vail (Frontier) 96; Streit II;1682; Rahir (Les Elzevier) 492–494; Willems (Les Elzevier) 497; JCB (3) II:283. CSt, CtY, DLC, ICJ, MH, MiU-C, MnU-B, NN-RB, RPJCB; BL, BN.
640/111

Lallemant, Jérôme, S.J. Relation de ce qui s'est passé dans le pays des Hurons. [*Paris:* 1640]. See Paul Le Jeune's *Relation* of this year below.

Le Jeune, Paul, S.J. Relation de ce qui s'est passé en la Nouvelle France en l'année 1639. *Paris: S. Cramoisy,* 1640. 2 pts; 8vo. Pt 2 comprises Jérôme Lallemant's *Relation de ce qui s'est passé dans les pays des Hurons.* Sabin 39956; Harrisse (NF) 74; Bell (Jes. rel.) 15; McCoy 36; Church 447; JCB (3) II:184. CSmH, CtY, DLC, MH, MiU-C, MnU-B, NN-RB, RPJCB; BL, BN.
640/112

—[Anr edn]. *Paris: S. Cramoisy,* 1640. 2 pts; 8vo. For distinguishing elements of this edn, see Bell. Sabin 39956; Harrisse (NF) 75; Bell (Jes. rel.) 16; McCoy 35; Church 448; JCB (3) II:284. CSmH, InU-L, MnU-B, NN-RB, RPJCB; BN.
640/113

Le Mire, Aubert. Politiae ecclesiasticae, sive Status religionis christianae per Europam, Asiam, Africam et Orbem novum, libri iv. *Lyons: J. Huguetan,* 1640. 348 p.; 12mo. 1st publ., Cologne, 1619, under title *De statu religionis christianae.* BN.
640/114

Lenton, Francis. A piece of the world, painted in proper colours. *London: J. Raworth,* 1640. [173] p.; 12mo. 1st publ., London, 1631, under title *Characterismi;* here reissued with cancel t.p. & prelim. lvs; with sheets D & E prob. reset. STC 15464.5. DFo, ICN.
640/115

Lithgow, William. The totall discourse, of the rare adventures, of long nineteene yeares travayles. *London: J. Okes,* 1640. 514;

p.; illus., port.; 4to. 1st publ., London, 1614, under title *A most delectable and true discourse.* STC 15714; Arents (Add.) 219. CSmH, CtY, DFo, ICN, MH, NN-RB, RPB; BL.
640/116

López de Guitian Sotomayor, Diego. Señor. El capitan Diego Lopez de Guitian Sotomayor. [*Madrid?* 1640?]. 6 numb. lvs; fol. A memorial to the king of Spain on the building & equipping of the Spanish silver fleet. Cf. Medina (BHA) 8209 & 8210. BL.
640/117

Malvezzi, Virgilio, marchese. La libra de Grivilio Vezzalmi [pseud.]. *Pamplona* [i.e., *Madrid: Imprenta Real*]: 1640. 4to. 1st publ., [*Pamplona?* 1638?]. BL (Vezzalmi, G.).
640/118

——. Successi principali della monarchia di Spagna nell'anno M.DC.XXXIX. [*Madrid?* 1640?]. 296 p.; 12mo. Bk 2 includes discussion of economic effects of truce between Spain & the Netherlands permitting trade by the latter with the New World. Michel (Répertoire) V:90. BN.
640/119

—[Anr issue?]. [*Madrid?* 1640?]. 269 (i.e., 296) p.; 12mo. Michel (Répertoire) V:90. DFo, MH.
640/120

——. Sucesos principales de la monarquía de España en el año de mil i seiscientos i treinta i nueva. *Madrid: Imprenta Real.* 1640. 131 numb. lvs; 4to. Transl. from Malvezzi's *Successi* of this year above. Palau 148063. DLC, NNH; BL, BN.
640/121

Mañozca y Zamora, Juan de. Memorial al Rey y satisfaccion a los 56 cargos sobre la visita de la Audiencia de Quito. *Madrid:* 1640. fol. Medina (BHA) 1015.
640/122

Meteren, Emanuel van. Meteranus novus, das ist: Warhafftige Beschreibung des niederländischen Krieges . . . in das Hochteutsch getrewlich ubergesetzt . . . und biss auff das Jahr 1638 continuirt. *Amsterdam: J. Janszoon, the Younger,* 1640. 4 pts; ports, plans; fol. 1st publ. in German, Hamburg, 1596. Reissue of publisher's 1627–30 edn with a 4th pt added. For variant issues of pt 4, see Bruckner, Pts 2, 3, & 4 have special title pages and were evidently also issued separately: *Meterani novi, oder Niederländischer Historien ander[–dritter, vierdter] Theil.* Sabin 48177; Palmer 358; Bruckner 34. MH (pts 2-4); Oxford:Bodl., BN.
640/123

Mexico (City). Consulado. Señor. El Prior y consules de la Universidad de los Mercaderes de la Nueva España. [*Madrid?* 1640?]. 4 numb. lvs; fol. Memorial to king of Spain on commerce of Mexico. Sabin 98020. InU-L; BL. 640/124

Middleton, Thomas. A mad world, my masters. *London: [J. Okes,] for J. S[penser].; sold by J. Becket,* 1640. 40 lvs; 4to. Comedy. 1st publ., London, 1608. STC 17889; Greg 276(b); Pforzheimer 696. CSmH, CtY, DFo, ICN, MH, MiU, NNPM, PU; BL. 640/125

Montaigne, Michel Eyquem de. Essais. *Paris: M. Blageart,* 1640. 750 p.; port.; fol. 1st publ., Bordeaux, 1580; cf. 1602 edn. Tchémerzine VIII:430. ICN, MH, MiU; BL, BN. 640/126

—[Anr issue]. *Paris: A. Courbé,* 1640. Courbé's name is stamped by hand over that of Blageart. BN. 640/127

—[Anr issue]. *Paris: A. Courbé,* 1640. Tchémerzine VIII:430. NcGuG; BN. 640/128

Moris, Gedeon. Copye. Van 't Journael gehouden by Gedeon Moris, koopman op het schip . . . uytgevaren naer Bresilien van Zeelandt den 27 Februarij 1640. *Amsterdam: F. Lieshout,* 1640. [5] p.; 4to. Moris's journal also publ. as pt of *Het naderste ende sekerste journalier verhael* of this year below. Sabin 50709; Rodrigues (Dom. Hol.) 477; Asher 152; Knuttel 4687; Meulman 2514; JCB (3) II:285. RPJCB; BL, BN. 640/129

—[Anr edn?]. *Amsterdam: F. Lieshout,* 1640. 4 lvs; 4to. This edn has reading 'uytghevaren' on t.p. Borba de Moraes II:87; Tiele (Pamfletten) 2705. 640/130

Moscherosch, Johann Michael. Les Visiones de don Francesco de Quevedo Villegas, oder Wunderbare satyrische Gesichte verteutscht durch Philander von Sittewalt [pseud.]. *Strassburg: J. P. Mülbe* [1640]. 681 p.; 8vo. Transl. by Moscherosch from the Caen, 1633, French translation, by the Sieur de la Geneste, of Francisco de Quevedo y Villegas's *Sueños,* 1st publ., Barcelona, 1627, but with additions & alterations. Among Moscherosch's additions are refs to American straits & treasures, in a satirical vein, in 'Welt-Wesen,' the 2nd of the 'Gesichte.' Bechtold 'A'; Faber du Faur 423;

cf. Goedeke III:233. CU, CtY, MdBJ; Berlin:StB, Frankfurt a. M.:StB. 640/131

Het naderste ende sekerste journalier verhael, ofte copye van sekeren brieff, gheschreven uyt Brasyl, aen de . . . bewinthebberen der . . . West-Indische Compagnye. *The Hague: I. Burchoorn,* 1640. 24 p.; 4to. Included is G. Moris's 'Journael gehouden op het schip de Princesse Aemilia', also publ. separately this year under slightly differing title. Knuttel 4686. NN-RB; The Hague:KB. 640/132

—[Anr edn]. *The Hague: I. Burchoorn,* 1640. 16 p.; 4to. This edn lacks Moris's journal. Sabin 7608; Rodrigues (Dom. Hol.) 478; Asher 151. DLC; Amsterdam:NHSM. 640/133

Entry canceled. 640/134

Nueva relacion y curioso romance, en que se declara, y dà cuenta de lo que passa en las visitas con las señoras mugeres. [*Madrid?* ca. 1640?]. [4] p.; 4to. In verse. The serving of chocolate is mentioned. BL. 640/135

Ocampo, Martín de. Señor. El capitan Martin de Ocampo, corregidor que fue de . . . Cuenca del Piru. [*Madrid?* 1640?]. 4 numb. lvs; fol. Memorial to king of Spain on mercury mines of Almaden. Medina (BHA) 6686. BL. 640/136

Opitz, Martin. Deutsche Poemata. [*Danzig:* 1640]. 697 p.; 8vo. 1st publ. in this version, Breslau, 1628–29. Goedeke III:49; Faber du Faur 226. CtY, ICU, PU; Göttingen:StUB, Berlin:StB. 640/137

Ovidius Naso, Publius. Amores. English. All Ovids elegies. '*Middlebourgh*' [i.e., *London: T. Cotes?* ca. 1640]. [96]p.; 8vo. For earlier edns see the year 1602. Title page has square of 4 type ornaments. STC 18933; Arents 144; Pforzheimer 641. CSmH, CtY, DFo, ICN, MH, NN-A; BL. 640/138

——. **Metamorphoses. English.** Ovids Metamorphosis Englished . . . by G[eorge]. S[andys]. *London: J. L[egat].,* for *A. Hebb,* 1640. 363 p.; illus., port.; fol. 1st publ., London, 1626. Sabin 76460; STC 18968. CSmH, DLC, IU, MH, MiU-C, NN-RB; BL, BN. 640/139

Owen, John. Epigrammatum editio postrema. *Amsterdam: J. Janszoon, the Younger,* 1640. 249 p.; 8vo. 1st publ., London, 1606.

Shaaber (Brit. auth.) O94. IU, NN; BL.
640/140

Pagitt, Ephraim. Christianographie. or The description of the multitude and sundry sorts of Christians in the world not subject to the Pope . . . The third edition inlarged. *London: J. Okes, for M. Costerden, 1640.* 3 pts; fol. 1st publ., London, 1635. STC 19112; McAlpin I:552–53. CSmH, CtY, DFo, ICN, MH, MWA, MiU, MnU-B, NNUT, RPB; BL.
640/141

Pardoux, Barthélemy. Universa medicina. Editio secunda, studio & opera G. Sauvageon. *Paris: O. de Varennes, 1640.* 2 pts; 8vo. 1st publ., Paris, 1630. DNLM.
640/142

Parkinson, John. Theatrum botanicum: The theater of plants. Or, An herball of a large extent. *London: T. Cotes, 1640.* 1755 p.; illus.; fol. Müller 163; Pritzel 6934; Nissen (Bot.) 1490; STC 19302; Arents 212; Hunt (Bot.) 235. CSmH, CtY, DLC, ICN, InU-L, MH, MiU, MnU-B, NN-A, PU, RPB; BL.
640/143

Pharmacopoeia Augustana, auspicio . . . Senatus cura octava Collegii Medici . . . locupletata. *Augsburg: A. Aperger, 1640.* 2 pts; fol. 1st publ., Augsburg, [1564]; cf. 1613 edn. Arents (Add.) 304. NN-A.
640/144

Pharmacopoeia Lillensis . . . optima quaeque pharmaca a medicis ejusdem urbis selecta & usitata continens. *Lille: S. Le Francq, 1640.* 241 p.; 4to. Amongst the ingredients cited are mechoacan, 'Bryoniae peruvianae', 'Sarzeparigliae' (sarsaparilla), 'Lignum guaiaci, Santi, Indici'. BL.
640/145

Pinto de Moraes, Jorge. Maravillas del Parnaso y flor de los mejores romances. *Barcelona: S. & J. Matevad, for J. Prats, 1640.* 99 numb. lvs; 8vo. 1st publ., Lisbon, 1637. Palau 226691n. NNH.
640/146

Pizarro y Orellana, Fernando. Discurso . . . en que se muestra la obligacion que Su Magestad tiene en justicia, conciencia, y razon politica à cumplir, y mandar executar la merced, que la magestad imperial hizo à Don Francisco Pizarro del titulo de marquès, con veinte mil vassallos en la parte donde mas bien le estuviesse, como à descubridor, conquistador, y pacificador de los opulentissimos reynos del Perù, en favor, y gracia de los sucessores de su casa. [*Madrid?* ca. 1640?]. 36 numb. lvs; fol. Sabin 63188 (& 20250); Medina (BHA) 6758; Palau 227687–II. BL, Santiago, Chile:BN.
640/147

Porreño, Baltasar. Dichos i hechos del señor Rei D. Phelipe II. *Seville: Press of the Siete Revueltas* [ca. 1640?]. 149 numb. lvs; 8vo. 1st publ., Cuenca, 1621. Palau 233067.
640/148

Porter y Casanate, Pedro de. Relacion de los servicios del capitan Don Pedro Porter y Casanate. Por fees de oficios de la Armada del mar Occeano, y guardia de las Indias. [*Madrid:* ca. 1640?]. [4] p.; fol. Memorial to king of Spain seeking naval appointment. Sabin 64325; cf. Medina (Chile) 257; Wagner (SW) 39A. RPJCB; BL.
640/149

Prado, Esteban de. Por Francisco Nuñez Melian, governador . . . que fue . . . de Veneçuela . . . Con Bartolome de Monesterio, vezino . . . de Caracas, en la causa de querella y capitulos. [*Madrid?* 1640?] 49 numb. lvs; fol. BL.
640/150

Quadro, Diego Felipe de. Todo el pleyto que siguen los dueños de Barras del Pirù, con los compradores de plata de la ciudad de Sevilla. [*Seville?* 1640?]. 7 numb. lvs; fol. BL.
640/151

Raleigh, Sir Walter. The prerogative of parliaments in England. [*London: T. Cotes?*] 1640. 65 p.; 4to. 1st publ., London, 1628; here a reissue of that 1628 edn (STC 20649.7) in which on lf D3v line 17 ends 'none'. Sabin 67599n; STC 20649.9. DLC. MH, NN-RB; BL.
640/152

—[Anr edn]. The perogative [*sic*] of parliaments. [*London: T. Cotes*] 1640. 65 p.; 4to. On lf D3v line 17 ends *'none'*. Sabin 67599n; STC 20650. CSmH, CtY, DFo, ICN, InU-L, MH, NN-RB; BL.
640/153

Ranchin, François. Opuscules, ou Traictés divers et curieux. *Lyons: P. Ravaud, 1640.* 824 p.; 8vo. A 'Traictté de l'origine, nature, causes, curation & preservation de la verolle' (p. 513–647) discusses the American origins of syphilis & its transmission by the Spanish. For its treatment both guaiacum & sarsaparilla are recommended. Wellcome I:5331. DNLM, NNNAM, OClW; BL, BN.
640/154

Randolph, Thomas. Poems, with the Muses looking-glasse, and Amyntas . . . The second edition. *Oxford: L. Lichfield, for F. Bowman,* 1640. 3 pts; 8vo. 1st publ., Oxford, 1638. STC 20695; Greg 547 (b); Madan (Oxford) 1640:16. CSmH, CtY, DFo. ICN, MH, MiU, NNC, PU, RPB; BL.
640/155

—[Anr issue.]. *Oxford: [L. Lichfield,] for F. B[owman].; sold by L. Chapman [at London,]* 1640. STC 20695.5. Manchester:UL. 640/156

Relacion muy verdadera de los felices sucessos que ha tenido el señor don Fernando Mascareñas general de la armada de Portugal. Dase cuente de la batalla que tuvieron contra treynta y seys navios de Olanda, que ivan a socorrer la plaça de Pernambuc, a donde murio en ella el general de Olanda. *Barcelona: S. & J. Matevad,* 1640. 2 lvs; 4to. In verse. Reprinted from the Madrid *Relacion nueva y verdadeira* of this year below. Borba de Moraes II:190; Rodrigues (Dom. Hol.) 479; Palau 258209. 640/157

Relacion nueva y verdadera, de los felizes sucessos que ha tenido el señor Don Fernando Mascareñas, general de la armada de Portugal. Dase cuenta de la batalla que tuvieron contra treinta y seis navios de Olanda, que iban a socorrer la plaça de Pernambuc, adonde murio en ella el general de Olanda. *Madrid: A. Duplastre,* 1640. 4 p.; 4to. In verse. Sabin 45405; Borba de Moraes II:190; Rodrigues (Dom. Hol.) 897. NN-RB. 640/158

Relation du combat donné par l'armée navale du roy aux mers de ponant . . . contre l'armée navale du roy d'Espagne s'en allant aux Indes Occidentales pres Calis. *[Paris:] Bureau d'Adresse,* 1640. 8 p.; 4to. Sabin 69280. NNH. 640/159

—[Anr edn]. *[Amsterdam?]* 1640. 8vo. Reprinted 'sur l'imprimé à Paris, en l'île du Palais'. BN (Lb36.3211). 640/160

Rivière, Lazare. Methodus curandorum febrium. *Paris: O. de Varennes,* 1640. 247 p.; 8vo. In chapt. 'De variolis & morbilis' ref. is made to the West Indies & the arrival of the Spanish there; in that 'De febre pestilenti' to a plant 'quae nostro saeculo ab Hispanis ex India allata est, quam *contrayervam* nominant, quod vocabulum herbam alxipharmacam significat, quonium illius

pulvis adversus venena praesentissimum est remedium, eaque per sudores, aut insensibilem transpirationem evacuat . . .', conceivably a ref. to cinchona or opobalsam. DNLM; BL. 640/161

—. Praxis medica. *Paris: O. de Varennes,* 1640. 568 p.; 8vo. Prescribed for a wide variety of ailments (as well as for syphilis) are guaiacum, sassafras, Peruvian opobalsam, sassafras, & tobacco *(Nicotiana)*. Wellcome I:5500. London:Wellcome, BN. 640/162

Romances varios. De diversos autores. *Saragossa: P. Lanaja,* 1640. 323 p.; 12mo. In verse. Includes 'baile' of Quevedo y Villegas mentioning Puerto Rico, Havana, Buenos Aires, etc. Jiménez Catalán (Saragossa) 414; Palau 277065. Madrid:BN. 640/163

Ruiz de Montoya, Antonio, S.J. Arte y bocabulario de la lengua Guarani. *Madrid: J. Sánchez,* 1640. 2 pts; 4to. Sabin 74026; Medina (BHA) 1019; Borba de Moraes II:78; Streit II:1670n; Backer VII:321; Palau 282097; JCB AR40:25–29. NN-RB, RPJCB, ViU (imp.). 640/164

—. Catecismo de la lengua guarani. *Madrid: D. Díaz de la Carrera,* 1640. 336 p.; 12mo. Sabin 74028; Medina (BHA) 1020; Borba de Moraes II:78; Viñaza 178; Streit II:1670n; Backer VII:322; JCB AR40:25–29. NN-RB, NNH, RPJCB; BL. 640/165

Saavedra Fajardo, Diego de. Idea de un principe christiano. *Munich: N. Heinrich,* 1640. 710 p.; illus.; 4to. Empresa xvii mentions Columbus & Cortés as lawgivers; in Empresa xxvi Cortés's valor is cited; he is again mentioned in Empresa lii. Empresa lxix discusses the riches of the New World. Scattered American refs appear elsewhere. Palau 283442. CtY, DFo, MH, NN-RB, OU; BL, BN. 640/166

Scot, Thomas. Philomythie or philomythologie. *London: F. Constable,* 1640. 2 pts; 8vo. 1st publ., London, 1616; here a reissue of a 1622 edn. STC 2187la.3. MH. 640/167

Shepard, Thomas. The sincere convert, discovering the paucity of true believers. *London: T. Paine, for M. Simmons,* 1640. 267 p.; 8vo. In chap. v America is mentioned as

one of the 4 parts of the world, of which Europe is the best. Cf. Sabin 80218; STC 22404.7; JCB (3) II:285–86. RPJCB; BL.
640/168

—[Anr issue]. *London: T. P[aine]., for M. S[immons].; sold by H. Blunden,* 1640. STC 22404.8. NjPT, ViU. 640/169

—[Anr issue]. *London: T. Paine, for H. Blunden,* 1640. STC 22404.9. London:Dulwich.
640/170

Shirley, James. The constant maid. A comedy. *London: J. Raworth, for R. Whitaker,* 1640. [71] p.; 4to. Act 2 mentions Virginia tobacco. STC 22438; Greg 592; Arents (Add.) 307. CSmH, CtY, DLC, ICN, MH, NN-A, PU; BL. 640/171

Spain. Consejo de las Indias. Assiento y capitulacion, que los señores presidente, y del Consejo Real de las Indias tomaron con el prior, y consules y comercio de Sevilla, sobra la cobrança, y administracion del derecho de la averia, y despacho de las armadas, y flotas de las Indias, por tiempo de tres años. *Madrid: A. de Parra,* 1640. 50 lvs; fol. Cf. earlier edn of 1620. Sabin 2233; Medina (BHA) 1009. NcD; BL.
640/172

Spain. Laws, statutes, etc., 1621–1665 (Philip IV). Cedula de informe. [*Madrid:* 1640]. *See* Grau y Monfalcón, Juan, *above.*

Spain. Sovereigns, etc., 1621–1665 (Philip IV), addressee. Señor. Muy notorio es à V. Magestad, y sus Reales Consejos de quan grande importancia sea . . . la navegacion, y commercio de los mareantes . . . que navegan la carrera de las Indias. [*Madrid?* 1640?]. 10 numb. lvs; fol. BL.
640/173

Strafford, Thomas Wentworth, 1st earl of, defendant. Depositions and articles against Thomas earle of Strafford. [*London:*] 1640. *See the year* 1641.

Sucessos de la armada que fue al Brasil, y el largo viaje que tuvieron por tierra. Dase cuenta de los encuentros que tuvieron con el Olandés. *Seville: N. Rodríguez,* 1640. 2 lvs; 4to. Sabin 93392; Borba de Moraes II:290–91; Rodrigues (Dom. Hol.) 480; Maggs Cat. 479 (Americana V):4235. São Paulo:BM.
640/174

Tabourot, Estienne. Les bigarrures et touches. *Rouen: L. DuMesnil,* 1640. 5 pts;

illus., ports; 8vo. In verse. 1st publ. in this collective edn, Paris, 1603, q.v. CtY, ICU; BL, BN. 640/175

Tatham, John. The fancies theater. *London: J. Norton, for R. Best,* 1640. [162] p.; 8vo. In verse. Poem 'Meeting a peece of mortality val'd' mentions tobacco. Reissued, 1657, under title *The mirrour of fancies.* STC 23704; Arents (Add.) 308. CSmH, CtY, DFo, ICN, MH, NN-A; BL. 640/176

Taylor, John, the Water-poet. The needles excellency . . . The 12th edition inlarged. *London: [J. Dawson?] for J. Boler,* 1640. [9] p.; illus.; obl. 4to. 1st publ., London, 1631. STC 23777. MH, NjP; BL. 640/177

——. A valorous and perillous sea-fight. Fought with three Turkish ships . . . on the coast of Cornewall . . . by the good ship . . . Elizabeth, of Plimmouth. *London: E. P[urslowe]., for E. Wright,* 1640. 4to. The *Elizabeth* is described as returning from Virginia & New England. STC 23809. BL.
640/178

—[Anr issue]. A brave and valiant sea-fight, upon the coast of Cornewall. *London: [B. Alsop & T. Fawcet] for N. Butter,* 1640. A reissue of the above with cancel t.p. & additional text. STC 23809.5 (formerly 23734). CSmH; Oxford:Bodl. 640/179

Tijdinghe van Bresiel door den super cargo vant schip den Saeyer van Farnabock gesonden. *Delft: Widow of J. A. Cloeting,* 1640. bds.; fol. On operations of Dutch, Portuguese, & Spanish fleets off coast of Brazil. Sabin 95816. NN-RB. 640/180

—[Anr edn]. *Amsterdam: F. Lieshout,* 1640. bds. This edn in title has reading 'supper cargo'. NNH. 640/181

Tomkis, Thomas. Albumazar. A comedy . . . Newly revised and corrected by a speciall hand. *London: N. Okes,* 1634 [i.e., 1640]. [82] p.; 4to. 1st publ., London, 1615. In this edn the catchword on lf D1r is 'drops'. STC 24103; Greg 330 (d); Arents (Add.) 172. CSmH, CtY, DFo, ICN, InU-L, MH, NN-A; BL. 640/182

Torriano, Giovanni. The Italian tutor, or A new . . . Italian grammar. *London: T. Paine; sold by H. Robinson,* 1640. 2 pts; 4to. In 2nd pt, in 8th dialogue, tobacco is mentioned. STC 24137; Arents (Add.) 309. CSmH, MH, MiU, NN-A; BL. 640/183

—[Anr issue]. *London: T. Paine; sold by H. Robinson . . . for the author,* 1640. STC 24137.5. CtY, DFo; Oxford:Bodl. 640/184

Torsellino, Orazio, S.J. Historiarum ab origine mundi ad annum 1630 epitome libri x. *Paris:* 1640. 12mo. 1st publ., Rome, 1598; cf. 1620 edn. Backer VIII:152.

640/185

Traslado de una carta, embiada del Brasil à un cavallero desta corte, dandole cuenta de las grandes vitorias que han tenido las armas catolicas de . . . Felipe IIII. *Madrid: Catalina de Barrio y Angulo* [1640]. [4] p.; fol. On forts and ships seized from the Dutch by Spanish forces. Sabin 7640; cf. Medina (BHA) 6238; Borba de Moraes II:312–13; Palau 339133. NN-RB, RPJCB; São Paulo: BM. 640/186

A true relation of a late very famous sea-fight, made betwixt the Spaniard and the Hollander in Brasil, for many dayes together . . . but at last the Hollander got the victory . . . Truely translated out of the low Dutch originall copie first printed at Amsterdam. *London:* [*T. Harper?*] *for N. Butter,* 1640. 8 lvs; 4to. The work of which this is a translation has not been identified. Sabin 97139; Rodrigues (Dom. Hol.) 474; STC 18507.339; Maggs Cat. 479 (Americana V):4232. NIC; BL, Oxford:Bodl.

640/187

Udemans, Godefridus Corneliszoon. 't Geestelyck roer van 't coopmans schip. *Dordrecht:* 1640. *See the year* 1641.

Vaughan, William. The church militant, historically continued. *London: T. Paine, for H. Blunden,* 1640. 345 p.; 12mo. In verse. Included are numerous refs to the Americas. STC 24606; Maggs Cat. 465 (Americana IV):2744. CSmH, CtY, DLC, ICN, MH, NN-RB; BL. 640/188

Vernulz, Nicolás de, C. Or. Virtutum augustissimae gentis Austriacae libri tres. *Louvain: J. Seger,* 1640. 254 p.; 4to. In bk 2, chapt. iii, 'De prudentia', the exploits of Hernando Cortés in the New World under Charles V are mentioned, as is Spanish overseas expansion under Philip II; in bk 3, chapt.ii, 'De majestate & auctoritate', America is cited in section on Philip II; in bk 3, chapt iv, 'De contemptu regnorum & divitiarum', America is again mentioned in relation to

Philip II. Palau 360820. CtY; BL (Vernulaeus, N.), BN. 640/189

Entry canceled. 640/190

Wit's recreations. Wits recreations. Selected from the finest fancies of moderne muses. *London: R. H*[*odgkinson*]*., for H. Blunden,* 1640. 3 pts; 8vo. Compilation attributed to Sir John Mennes. Comprises epigrams & epitaphs of which eight relate in some way to tobacco. STC 25870; Arents 214. CSmH, CtY, DFo, MH, NN-A; BL. 640/191

Zavala, Andrés de. Por Andres de Zavala, contador . . . [*Madrid?* 1640?]. *See under* González de Ribero, Blas. 640/192

Zeiller, Martin. Ein Hundert Episteln oder Sendschreiben von underschidlichen politischen, historischen und andern Materien. *Heilbronn: C. Krause, for J. Görlin, at Ulm,* 1640. 614 p.; 8 vo. Includes refs to discovery of America, American gold, etc. Continued by Zeiller's *Das andere Hundert Episteln* (Ulm, 1641), *Das dritte Hundert* (Ulm, 1643), *Das vierdte Hundert* (Ulm, 1644), *Das sechste und letzte Hundert* (Ulm, 1651), q.v. The six-volume collection is in the British Library. Cf. Sabin 106295; cf. Palmer 411; Jantz (German Baroque) 2771; Jördens V:600. NcD; BL. 640/193.

1641

Abreu y Figueroa, Fernando de, O.S.A. El maestro fray Fernando de Abreu y Figueroa . . . dize: Que en el año passado de 1640, puso en la Real mano de V. Magestad dos memoriales impressos . . . en razon de poderse reformar los sinodos de los dotrinantes de Indias [etc.]. [*Madrid?* 1641]. 12 numb. lvs; fol. Medina (BHA) 6155.

641/1

Acuña, Cristóbal de, S.J. Nuevo descubrimiento del gran rio de las Amazonas . . . el año de 1639. *Madrid: Imprenta Real,* 1641. 46 numb. lvs; 4to. On expedition of Pedro Teixeira. Sabin 150; Medina (BHA) 1022; Borba de Moraes I:10; Streit II:1692; Backer I:39; JCB (3) II:287. CtY, DLC, MH, MiU-C, MnU-B, PBL, RPJCB; BL, BN.

641/2

Aldrovandi, Ulisse. Quadrupedum omnium bisulcorum historia . . . Marcus Antonius

Bernia denuò in lucem edidit. *Bologna: G. B. Ferroni, for M. A. Bernia,* 1641. 1040 p.; illus.; fol. 1st publ., Bologna, 1621. Cf. Nissen (Zool.) 76. Naples:BN. 641/3

Alemán, Mateo. Primera y segunda parte de Guzman de Alfarache. *Madrid: P. de Val, for P. García Sodruz,* 1641. 475 p.; 4to. Pt 1, 1st publ., Madrid, 1599 (cf. 1601 edn); pt 2, 1st publ., Lisbon, 1604. Laurenti (Nov. pic. esp.) 564; Palau 6701. NNH; BL. 641/4

—[Anr edn]. *Madrid: Imprenta Real, for the Brotherhood of Booksellers (Hermandad de los Mercaderes de libros),* 1641. 229 numb. lvs; 4to. Palau 6702. MH. 641/5

Bacon, Francis, viscount St Albans. Considerationi politiche . . . per movere la guerra contra la Spagna, tradotte dal inglese in francese dal sig^r Mangars [i.e., A. Maugars] e dal francese in italiano da Antonello Tutuccio. *Turin:* 1641. 49 p.; 4to. 1st publ. in English, London, 1629, under title *Considerations touching a warre with Spaine.* Copies are found with imprint date altered by hand to read 'MDCXXXXV'. Gibson (Bacon) 189–90. MH; BL, Rome:BN. 641/6

——. The historie of the reigne of King Henrie the seaventh. *London: R. Y[oung]. & R. H.; sold by R. Meighen,* 1641. 248 p.; port.; fol. 1st publ., London, 1622. Gibson (Bacon) 120; Wing (2) B299; Pforzheimer 33. CSmH, CtY, DLC, ICN, InU-L, MH, NN-RB, PU, RPB; BL, BN. 641/7

——. Sermones fideles, ethici, politici. *Leyden: F. Haack,* 1641. 439 p.; port.; 12mo. Transl. from Bacon's *Essayes,* as 1st publ. in enl. form, London, 1625. Gibson (Bacon) 51. CSmH, DLC, ICN, MH, NN; BL, BN. 641/8

——. Three speeches. *London: R. Badger, for S. Browne,* 1641. 88 p.; 4to. In speech 'Concerning the post-nati' ref. is made to Columbus's offer of the Indies to Henry VII of England. Gibson (Bacon) 206; Wing (2) B337. CSmH, CtY, DLC, NNUT; BL. 641/9

Baerle, Kaspar van. Verstandighe coopman of Oratie, handelende van de t'samen-voeginghe des koop-handels, ende der philosophie . . . Wt de Latijnsche . . . sprake . . . vertaelt door W. A. Buijserius. *Enkhuizen:*

The author, 1641. 16 lvs; 4to. Transl. from Baerle's *Mercator sapiens,* 1st publ., Amsterdam, 1632. Petit 1810. NN; Leyden:B. Thysiana. 641/10

Ballet du Bureau d'adresse, dansé devant Monseigneur le Prince par Monseigneur le duc d'Enguien le trentiesme décembre 1640. *Dijon:* 1640 [i.e., 1641?]. 17 p.; 8vo. Includes text for section assigned to 'un Américain et un More'—cf. Paul Lacroix, *Ballets et mascarades* (Geneva, 1868–70) VI:19. 641/11

Besold, Christoph. Juridico-politicae dissertationes. *Strassburg: Heirs of L. Zetzner,* 1641. 234 p.; 4to. 1st publ., Strassburg, 1624. DLC; BN. 641/12

Bethune, Philippe de, comte de Selles et de Charost. Le conseiller d'estat. . . . Jouxte la copie imprimee à Paris. *[Leyden? F. Heger?]* 1641. 501 p.; 12mo. 1st publ., [Paris?], 1632. Willems disputes belief that this or the 1645 edn without imprint originated at the Elsevier press. Willems (Les Elzevier) 973; Rahir (Les Elzevier) 968. ICN, PU, WU; BN. 641/13

Beverwijck, Jan van. Lof der medicine, ofte Genees-konste. *[Dordrecht:* 1641]. 152 p.; 8vo. 1st publ. in Dutch, Dordrecht, 1635; transl. from the author's *Medicinae encomium,* 1st publ., Dordrecht, 1633. Includes his 'Bergh-val, ofte Wederlegginge van Michiel de Montaigne, Tegens de notsakelickheyt der genees-konste'. Catalogus van boeken VII:10. CtY-M, DNLM. 641/14

——. Schat der ongesontheit. *Dordrecht:* 1641. Catalogus van boeken VII:39. *See the year* 1642.

——. Wonderbaerlijcken strydt tusschen de kickvorschen ende de muysen, toegepast op de Nederlandtsche oorloghe. *Dordrecht: H. van Esch, for J. Gorisszoon,* 1641. 50 p.; 4to. In verse. An adaptation of the *Batrachomyomachia.* 'Gelyckheyt der vrije Vereenighde Nederlanden' (p. 38–60) comments substantially on Spanish in West Indies, citing Las Casas, while elsewhere an account of Dutch exploits in Brazil & West Indies appears. Sabin 104998; Knuttel 4781a. BL (Homer. Batrachomyomachia), The Hague:KB. 641/15

The Bishops potion. or, A dialogue betweene the Bishop of Canterbury, and his phisitian. [*London:*] 1641. [6] p.; illus.; 4to. Satire on Abp Laud, mentioning his involvement in tobacco patent & adverting to therapeutic uses of tobacco. Wing B3032; Arents (Add.) 311. DFo, MH, MnU, NN-A, PHi; BL.   641/16

Blaeu, Willem Janszoon. Novus atlas, das ist Weltbeschreibung . . . erster Theil. *Amsterdam: J. & C. Blaeu,* 1641–42. 2 pts; 120 maps; fol. 1st publ., Amsterdam, 1634; cf. 1635 edn. In this edn, 2 maps relate to America. Issued with Blaeu's *Novus atlas . . . ander Theil,* Amsterdam, 1642. Koeman (B1) 31A; Phillips (Atlases) 5936. DLC, IU, PPL; BL, Cologne:UB.   641/17

——. Novus atlas, das ist Welt-beschreibung . . . ander Theil. *Amsterdam: J. & C. Blaeu,* 1641. 1st publ., Amsterdam, 1635. Koeman (B1) 8B. Cologne:UB, Zurich:ZB.

641/18

——. Theatrum orbis terrarum, sive Atlas novus. *Amsterdam: J. & C. Blaeu,* 1641. 2 pts; 120 maps; fol. 1st publ., Amsterdam, 1635. Koeman (B1) 21B. BL (imp.).   641/19

Boccalini, Traiano. Hundert ein und dreissig Relationes, oder Newe Zeitungen aus Parnasso. *Leyden: J. Marcus,* 1641. 2 pts; 4to. Transl. from Boccalini's *De' ragguagli di Parnaso . . . Centuria prima,* 1st publ., Venice, 1612, & his *Pietra del paragone politico,* 1st publ., [Venice], 1615. BL.   641/20

Bologna. Università. Collegio di Medicina. Antidotarium Bononien. *Bologna: Heirs of V. Benacci,* 1641. 506 p.; 4to. Included is a formula for an 'Oleum Guaiaci'. CtY-M, DNLM; London:Wellcome.   641/21

Bry, Johann Theodor de. Florilegium renovatum et auctum, das ist, Vernewertes und vermehrtes Blumenbuch. *Frankfurt a. M.: Merian,* 1641. 178 pls; illus.; fol. 1st publ., [Oppenheim], 1612[–14], but here enl.; cf. 1626 edn. Also included are 32 plates copied from G. B. Ferrari's *De flora cultura,* 1st publ. Rome, 1633. Nissen (Bot.) 274; Hunt (Bot.) 237. DNAL, MH-A, OU, RPB; BL.

641/22

Buchanan, George. Poemata quae extant. *Amsterdam: J. Janszoon, the Younger,* 1641. 561 p.; port.; 12mo. 1st publ. as here constituted, Edinburgh, 1615. CtY, NNC, PPL; BL, BN.   641/23

Campanella, Tommaso. De monarchia His-

panica . . . Editio novissima, aucta et emendata. [*Leyden: B. & A. Elsevier, for*] *L. Elsevier, at Amsterdam,* 1641. 379 p.; 12mo. 1st publ. as here transl., Amsterdam, 1640. Sabin 10197; Willems (Les Elzevier) 971; Rahir (Les Elzevier) 964. CU-S, DFo, ICN, MH, NN-RB, PU; BL, BN.   641/24

Castell, William. A petition of W.C. exhibited to the high court of Parliament now assembled, for the propagating of the gospel in America, and the West Indies. [*London:*] 1641. 19 p.; 4to. Sabin 11397; Wing C1230; Church 449; JCB (3) II:28. CSmH, CtY, DLC, ICN, InU-L, MH, MiU-C, NN-RB, PHi, RPJCB.   641/25

Cervantes Saavedra, Miguel de. Novelas ejemplares. *Seville: F. de Lyra,* 1641. 332 numb. lvs; 8vo. 1st publ., Madrid, 1613. Rius (Cervantes) 236; Palau 53414n. BL, BN.   641/26

Clüver, Johannes. Historiarum mundi epitome . . . Editio tertia correctior. *Leyden: J. Marcus; sold also by L. Elsevier at Amsterdam,* 1639 [i.e., 1641]. 852 p.; 4to. 1st publ., Leyden, 1637. Notwithstanding the t.p. date of 1639, the colophon, with ref. to Elsevier, is dated 1641. Willems (Les Elzevier) 964. MH, MeB; BN.   641/27

—[Anr state?]. *Leyden: J. Marcus,* 1641. Rahir (Les Elzevier) 967. MnU.   641/28

Clüver, Philipp. Introductionis in universam geographiam, tam veterem quam novam, libri vi. *Braunschweig: B. Gruber, for G. Müller,* 1641. 214 p.; illus., maps; 4to. 1st publ., Leyden, 1624. Cf. Sabin 13805; JCB (3) II:288. CSmH, CtY, DLC, RPJCB.

641/29

—[Anr edn]. *Leyden: Elsevier Office,* 1641. 2 pts; illus.; 16mo. Includes also Petrus Bertius's *Breviarium totius orbis terrarum.* Sabin 5013n; Willems (Les Elzevier) 513; Rahir (Les Elzevier) 514. CSmH, IU, MB, NN-RB, PU, ViU; BL, BN.   641/30

Cotton, John. An abstract or [*sic*] the lawes of New England as they are now established. *London: F. Coules & W. Lee,* 1641. 15 p.; 4to. Sabin 17042 & 52595; Tuttle (Cotton) 14; Wing C6408; Church 450; JCB (3) II:286–87. CtY, DLC, ICN, MH, MiU-C, MnU-L, NN-RB, PU, RPJCB; BL, Oxford: Bodl.   641/31

——. A coppy of a letter of Mr. Cotton of

Boston, in New England, sent in answer of certaine objections. [*London:*] 1641. 6 p.; 4to. Refers to Roger Williams and others banished from Boston. Sabin 17057; Tuttle (Cotton) 16; Wing C6422; JCB (3) II:288. CtY, DLC, MH, MiU-C, NN-RB, RPJCB; BL, Oxford:Bodl. 641/32

Damiens, Jacques, S.J. Synopsis primi saeculi Societatis Jesu. *Tournay: A. Quinqué,* 1641. 365 p.; fol. Included are accounts of Jesuit missions in Brazil, Mexico, & elsewhere in the Americas. Backer I:288. DLC, MiU-C, N; BN. 641/33

Du Bartas, Guillaume de Salluste, seigneur. Du Bartas his divine weekes, and workes . . . translated and written by . . . Josuah Sylvester. *London: R. Young,* 1641. 670 p.; ports; fol. In verse. 1st publ. as here transl., London, 1605. Also included is Sylvester's *Tobacco battered,* 1st publ., London, [1616–17]. Wing D2405; Arents 128-c. CSmH, CtY, DLC, ICN, InU-L, MH, MiU, NN-RB, PBm, RPB; BL. 641/34

—[Anr issue]. *London: R. Young; sold by W. Hope,* 1641. Wing D2405A. Oxford:Christ Church. 641/35

Enrique, Pedro. Relacion verdadera, y copia sacada, y embiada por un capitan de los galeones de España . . . de los sucessos, victoria, y batalla que han tenido los galeones, de nueva España, contra veinte y seis vaxeles de Olanda. *Madrid: A. Duplastre,* 1641. [4] p.; fol. Cf. Sabin 22654; cf. Medina (BHA) 1029n; Palau 79776. NN-RB, RPJCB. 641/36

Espinel, Vicente. Relaciones de la vida del escudero Marcos de Obregon. *Seville: P. Gómez de Pastrana,* 1641. 148 numb. lvs; 4to. 1st publ., Madrid, 1618. Escudero (Seville) 1558; Palau 82589. NNH. 641/37

Estienne, Charles. L'agriculture et maison rustique. *Rouen: J. Berthelin,* 1641. 2 pts; illus.; 4to. 1st publ. as enl. by Liébault, Paris, 1567; cf. 1601 edn. BN. 641/38

Evelyn, Robert. A direction for adventurers . . . with small stock to get two for one . . . And a true description of the healthiest, pleasantest, and richest plantation of new Albion, in North Virginia. [*London?*] 1641. [8] p.; 4to. Sabin 63312; Vail (Frontier) 97; Baer (Md) 23; Wing E3524; Church 451. CSmH. 641/39

Fruchtbringende Gesellschaft. Kurtzer Bericht von der Fruchtbringenden Geselschaft Vorhaben, auch dero Namen, Gemählde und Wörter in achtzeilige Reimgesetze verfasset. *Köthen:* 1641. [131] p.; 4to. Includes sections on sunflower, tobacco, Brazilian pineapple, peanuts, and 'Indian' plants of uncertain origin. Goedeke III:6; Faber du Faur 165. CtY; Göttingen:UB. 641/40

Gabelkover, Oswald. Artzneybuch. [*Frankfurt a.M.:*] *J. J. Porsch & Widow & Heirs of J. Berner,* 1641. 2 pts; 4to. 1st publ., Tübingen, 1589, under title *Nützlich Artzneybuch;* cf. 1603 edn. DNLM. 641/41

Garavito, Gerónimo. Señor. Geronimo Garavito, procurador general del gremio de los azogueros de . . . Potosi del Pirù: Dize, que desde los 12. . . . de noviembre del año passado de 1636. hasta los de 16. de enero deste año de 1641. ha presentado a V. M. y en el Real Consejo de las Indias 91. memoriales, y ocho peticiones: y en los 17. dellos ha significado, y mostrado muy en particular el lamentable estado de aquella villa y provincia. [*Madrid:* 1641]. 4 numb. lvs; fol. Memorial to king of Spain. BL. 641/42

Garzoni, Tommaso. Piazza universale, das ist Allgemeiner Schawplatz, Marckt und Zusammenkunfft aller Professionen. *Frankfurt a. M.: W. Hoffmann,* 1641. 1084 p.; illus.; 4to. Transl. from the author's *La piazza universale,* 1st publ., Venice, 1587; cf. 1619 German edn. BL, BN. 641/43

Geslin, Paul. La sainte chorographie, ou Description des lieux ou reside l'eglise chrestienne par tout l'univers. *Amsterdam: L. Elsevier,* 1641. 101 p.; 12mo. 1st publ., Saumur, 1629. Issued with Elsevier's edn of Edwin Sandys's *Relation de l'estat de la religion* of this year. Willems (Les Elzevier) 978. MH, PU; BN. 641/44

Gomberville, Marin Le Roy, sieur du Parc et de. La premiere [-cinquiesme et dernière] partie de Polexandre. *Paris: A. Courbé,* 1641. 5 v.; 8vo. 1st publ. in this version, Paris, 1638; cf. Paris, 1629, version. MdBP; BL. 641/45

Grau y Monfalcón, Juan. Memorial . . . en defensa de Don Antonio Urrutia de Vergara, apoderado en México del ex-virey

marquís de Cerralvo. [*Madrid?* 1641?]. 16
numb. lvs; 4to. Subscribed: Madrid à 2. de
agosto de 1641 años. DLC.　　　641/46

Greiff, Friedrich. Decas nobilissimorum
medicamentorum Galeno-chymico modo
compositorum et praeparatorum . . .
Accessit Consignatio medicamentorum,
quae in officina . . . reperiuntur. *Tübingen:
P. Brunn,* 1641. 2 pts; 4to. The *Consignatio
medicamentorum* had 1st been publ. separately, Tübingen, 1632. BL, BN.
　　　　　　　　　　　　　　　641/47

Grimston, Sir Harbottle, bart. Mr Grymstons speech in Parliament upon the accusation and impeachment of William Laud,
Arch-bishop of Canterbury. [*London:*] 1641.
5 p.; 4to. Includes accusation that Laud has
impoverished tradesmen by requiring licensing of tobacco sellers. Wing G2037;
Arents 215. DFo, ICN, InU-L, MB, NN-A,
PU; BL.　　　　　　　　　　　641/48

Groote schrijf-almanach . . . op het jaer
1641 . . . door D. Origanus. *Amsterdam: C.
L. van der Plasse,* 1641. 8vo. Includes account
of Columbus's discovery of New World. Sabin 28931; Muller (1872) 404.　　641/49

Grotius, Hugo. Inleydinghe tot de Hollandsche rechts-gheleerdheydt. [*Haarlem:
A. Roman,* 1641]. 3 pts; 4to. 1st publ. in
this version, including also Grotius's *Van
de oudheydt* & his *Vrye zeevaert*, each with special t.p. & separate paging & signatures,
Haarlem, 1636; the latter works were also
issued separately in this year as described
below. Meulen/Diermanse 764. IaU (imp.),
ViU (imp.); The Hague:PP.　　　641/50

———. Van de oudheydt der Batavische, nu
Hollandsche republique. *Haarlem: A. Roman,* 1641. 44 p.; port.; 4to. 1st publ., The
Hague, 1610, under title *Tractaet vande
oudtheyt*. Also issued as part of Grotius's *Inleydinghe tot de Hollandsche rechts-gheleerdheydt*
of this year above. Meulen/Diermanse 701;
Bibl. Belg. G348. DS, NcD; BL, The
Hague:PP.　　　　　　　　　　641/51

———. Vrye zeevaert . . . Nu uyt den Latijne
op een nieuw vertaeld door A. Iekerman.
Haarlem: A. Roman, 1641. 40 p.; port.; 4to.
1st publ. in this translation, Haarlem, 1639.
Also issued as a part of Grotius's *Inleydinghe
tot de Hollandsche rechts-gheleerdheydt* of this
year. Meulen/Diermanse 557; Bibl. Belg.

G339; Meulman 2495. MiU, NcD; The
Hague:PP, Ghent:BU.　　　　　641/52

Guibert, Philbert. Toutes les oeuvres charitables. *Rouen: O. Seigneuré, for C. Pitreson,*
1641. 880 p.; 8vo. Included is Guibert's *Le
prix & valeur des medicamens*, 1st publ., Paris,
1625. DNLM, MH; BN.　　　　641/53

Gysius, Johannes. Origo et historia Belgicorum tumultuum. *Amsterdam: J. Janszoon, the
Younger,* 1641. 449 p.; 12mo. 1st publ.
in Latin, Leyden, 1619. CU, ICN, MH,
MiU-C; BL.　　　　　　　　　641/54

———. De Spaensche tirannye gheschiet in
Nederlant. *Amsterdam: Widow of C. L. van der
Plasse,* 1641. 112 p.; illus.; 4to. 1st publ.
in this version, Amsterdam, 1620; cf. 1621
edn. Meulman 1733. CtY; Ghent:BU.
　　　　　　　　　　　　　　　641/55

Hall, Joseph, Bp of Norwich. A survay of
that foolish, seditious, scandalous, pro-
phane libell, The protestation protested.
London: 1641. 40 p.; 4to. A reply to Henry
Burton's *The protestation protested* ([London?]
1641), attacking views of Puritans & mentioning New England & Virginia. Wing
H418; McAlpin II:43. CSmH, CtY, MH,
MiU-C, MnU-B, NNUT, RPJCB; BL.
　　　　　　　　　　　　　　　641/56

Harsdörffer, Georg Philipp. Frauenzimmer
Gesprechspiele. *Nuremberg:* 1641–49. 8 pts.
For pts of this work containing Americana
see the years 1643, 1644, 1645, 1646, 1647,
& 1649.

Herckmans, Elias. Theatrum victoriae, ofte
het thoneel der zeeslagen, uytbeeldende
alle de treffelijcke overwinningen . . . over
de vyanden van onses vryheyds. *The Hague:
I. Burchoorn,* 1641. [32] p.; 4to. Extracted
by the publisher from Canto V of Herckmans's *Der zee-vaert lof*, 1st publ., Amsterdam, 1634. Includes refs to Pieter Hein's
naval victories. Sabin 31477; cf. Borba de
Moraes I:335; Knuttel 4781. DLC, NN-RB;
BL(H., E.), The Hague:KB.　　　641/57

Heywood, Thomas. Machiavel. as he has
lately appeared to his deare sons. *London:
J. O[kes].,* for F. Constable, 1641. [30] p.;
4to. Includes attack on tobacco monopolies, mentioning the 'Summer Islands', i.e.,
the Bermudas. Wing H1787; Arents 3280.
CSmH, DFo, MH, MnU, NN-A; BL.
　　　　　　　　　　　　　　　641/58

—[Anr edn]. Machiavels ghost. *London: J. O[kes]., for F. Constable,* 1641. [30] p.; 4to. Wing H1788. CSmH; Oxford:Bodl.
641/59

Hondius, Hendrik. Nouveau theatre du monde ou Nouvel atlas . . . divise en trois tomes. *Amsterdam: H. Hondius,* 1641. 3 v.; maps; fol. 1st publ. in this version, Amsterdam, 1639. For a description of differences exhibited by the following edn see Koeman. Koeman 97A, 98A, 99A. CU; BN.
641/60

—[Anr edn]. *Amsterdam: J. Janszoon, the Younger,* 1641. 3 v.; maps; fol. For variants of v. 2–3, see Koeman. Koeman 97B, 98B (cf. 98C), 99B, 99C, 99D. MdBP; BL (v. 3), BN (v. 1), Basel:UB (v. 3).
641/61

Hooke, William. New Englands teares, for old Englands feares. Preached in a sermon on July 23, 1640. *London: E. G[riffin]., for J. Rothwell & H. Overton,* 1641. 23 p.; 4to. Sabin 32810; Wing H2624; McAlpin II:46–47; JCB (3) II:289. CtY, DLC, MH, MiU-C, NNUT, RPJCB; BL, Edinburgh:NL.
641/62

—[Anr edn]. *London: T. P[ayne]., for J. Rothwell & H. Overton,* 1641. 23 p.; 4to. Sabin 32811; Wing H2625; JCB (3) II:289. MWiW-C, MiU-C, RPJCB; BL.
641/63

—[Anr edn]. *London: J. D[awson]., for J. Rothwell & H. Overton,* 1641. 23 p.; 4to. Wing H2626; Church 452. CSmH, MBAt, NN-RB; BL.
641/64

Hooker, Thomas. The danger of desertion: or a Farwell sermon of Mr. Thomas Hooker . . . now of New England. Preached immediately before his departure out of old England. *London: G. M[iller]., for G. Edwards,* 1641. 29 p.; 4to. The gold of the New World is mentioned. Sabin 32834; Wing H2645; McAlpin II:47; JCB (3) II:290. CSS, CtY, DLC, InU-L, MH, MWA, NN-RB, RPJCB; BL.
641/65

—[Anr edn]. The second edition. *London: G. M[iller]., for G. Edwards,* 1641. 28 p.; 4to. Sabin 32834; Wing H2646. BL.
641/66

Howell, James. Dendrologie, ou La forest de Dodonne. *Paris: A. Courbé,* 1641. 322 p.; illus.; 4to. Transl. (by Jean Baudouin?) from Howell's Δενδρολογια; *Dodona's grove,* 1st publ., London, 1640. Arents (Add.) 306. CSmH, CtY, MH, NN-A; BL.
641/67

—[Anr issue]. *Paris: [A. Courbé, for the] Widow of J. Camusat,* 1641. BN.
641/68

Ireland. Parliament. The humble and just remonstrance, of the knights, citizens, and burgesses. *[London:] H. Perry,* 1641. 11 p.; 4to. Includes passage on the injustices inherent to tobacco monopoly in Ireland. At head of title: To the Right Honourable, the Lord Deputie. Wing I414; Arents (Add.) 312. ICN, InU-L, MH, NN-A; BL.
641/69

—[Anr edn]. *[London:] H. Perry,* 1641. 11 p.; 4to. At head of title: To the Right Honorable, the Lord Deputie. CU-A, CtY, MH.
641/70

Jansson, Jan. Atlas novus, sive Theatrum orbis terrarum . . . in tres tomos distinctus. *[Amsterdam:] J. Janszoon, the Younger,* 1641. 3 v.; maps; fol. 1st publ. in this version, Amsterdam, 1638, as Mercator's *Atlas novus,* Mercator's name being here omitted. Cf. Sabin 35773; Koeman (Me) 53. Leningrad: Saltykov PL.
641/71

——. Nieuwen atlas, ofte Werelt Beschryvinge . . . als mede Oost en West Indien . . . in twee deelen begrepen. *Amsterdam: J. Janszoon, the Younger,* 1641. 2 v.; illus., maps; fol. 1st publ. in this version, Amsterdam, 1638. Koeman (Me) 71 & 72. Breda: MA (v. 1).
641/72

——. Nouveau theatre. *Amsterdam:* 1641. See Hondius, Hendrik, *above.*

——. Novi Atlantis Anhang, oder Neuer Weltbeschreibung dritter Theil. *Amsterdam: J. Janszoon, the Younger,* 1641. 1 v.; maps; fol. Issued as a supplement to Jansson's *Newer Atlas,* Amsterdam, 1638. Includes several American maps. Koeman (Me) 122. Berne:ML.
641/73

Kircher, Athanasius. Magnes, sive De arte magnetica opus tripartitum. *Rome: L. Grignani, for H. Scheus,* 1641. 916 p.; illus.; 4to. In bk 3, chapt. ii, tides as related to navigation in the New World are discussed, naming Mexico, Acapulco, California, Virginia, Florida, etc. Elsewhere scattered refs to America occur. CtY-M, DNLM, MH, PPAmP; BL, BN.
641/74

Kort en grondigh verhael van alle 't gene sich heeft toe-ghedragen in Portugael, tot op den 23 Maert 1641 . . . uyt den Portugeesch. *Amsterdam: C. van de Pas,* 1641. [24]

p.; illus.; 4to. The Portuguese text of which this is a translation has not been identified. On p. [6] America is named, solely amongst continents. BL (John IV., King of Portugal). 641/75

La Brosse, Guy de. Catalogue des plantes cultivées . . . au jardin . . . des plantes medicinales . . . à Paris. *Paris: J. Dugast,* 1641. 101 p.; 4to. Amongst the plants named are numerous specimens of American origin, e.g., 'Aconitum Americanum', 'Aloë Americana', 'Calceolus Mariae Americanus', 'Nardus Americana', & 'Polygonatum Virginianum'. Pritzel 1189. BL, BN. 641/76

Laet, Joannes de. Portugallia, sive De regis Portugalliae regnis et opibus commentarius. *Leyden: Elsevier Office,* 1641. 460 p.; 16mo. 1st publ., Leyden, 1629, as section of De Laet's *Hispania,* with description of Brazil. Borba de Moraes I:383; Willems (Les Elzevier) 525; Rahir (Les Elzevier) 523. CU-S, CtY, ICN, MnU-B, NN-RB, RPJCB; BN. 641/77

The lamentable complaints of Hop the brewer. [*London:*] 1641. [8] p.; illus.; 4to. Includes mention of 'Indian smoake', i.e., tobacco. Wing L267; Arents (Add.) 313. CtY, NN-A. 641/78

The lamentable complaints of Nick Froth. [*London:*] 1641. 7 p.; illus.; 4to. Tobacco is mentioned. Wing L268; Arents (Add.) 314. CtY, MH, NN-A; BL. 641/79

León Pinelo, Antonio Rodríguez de. Velos antiguos i modernos en los rostros de las mugeres sus con veniençias [*sic*] i daños. Ilustracion de la real prematica de las tapadas. *Madrid: J. Sánchez,* 1641. 137 numb. lvs; 4to. Includes (lvs 106–8) discussion of the use of veils in Peru & Mexico. Medina (BHA) 7717 (VIII:lxxxi); Palau 135751. RPJCB; BL, BN. 641/80

A little true forraine newes: better than a greate deale of domestick spurious false newes. *London: N. Butter,* 1641. 11 p.; 4to. 'An extract out of divers letters written in Brazeil': p. 1–8; 'A copy of John Coulombeil's letter sent from Pernambuck': p. 9–11. Borba de Moraes I:423; Wing L2553; JCB (3) II:290. NNUT, RPJCB; BL. 641/81

Malvezzi, Virgilio, marchese. Successi prin-

cipali della monarchia di Spagna nell'anno M.DC.XXXIX. *Antwerp: Plantin Press,* 1641. 270 p.; 12mo. 1st publ., [Madrid? 1640?]. Palau 148061; Michel (Répertoire) V:90. ICN, OC1, PU, RPB; BL, BN. 641/82

—[Anr edn]. *Geneva: P. Aubert* [1641?]. 296 p.; 12mo. Michel (Répertoire) V:90. Lyons:BM. 641/83

Manasseh ben Joseph ben Israel. Segunda parte del Conciliador o De la conviniencia de los lugares de la S. Escripura, que repugnantes entre si parecen. *Amsterdam: N. de Ravesteyn,* 5401 [i.e., 1641]. 195 p.; 4to. Dedicatory letter to Nederlandsche West-Indische Compagnie discusses Jews in Brazil as does also the preface to the reader. Continues 1st vol., of 1632, with title *Conciliator* & Frankfurt imprint, though actually printed at Amsterdam. Borba de Moraes II:54. MH, NN-RB, PU; BL. 641/84

Méndez, Juan Francisco. Panegyrico funeral a D. Tomas Tamaio de Vargas, chronista mayor de las Indias. [*Madrid?*] 1641. 4to. Sabin 47806. 641/85

Mercator, Gerardus. Atlas novus, sive Theatrum. [*Amsterdam:*] 1641. *See* Jansson, Jan, *above.*

——. Atlas, or A geographicke description . . . of the world. *Amsterdam: H. Hondius,* 1641. 2 v.; illus., maps; fol. 1st publ. in English, Amsterdam, 1636. Koeman (Me) 49; JCB (3) II:291. RPJCB (imp.). 641/86

Mervyn, Sir Audley. A speech made before the Lords in . . . Parliament in Ireland . . . March the 4th. 1640 [i.e., 1641]. [*London?*] 1641. 27 p.; 4to. Includes attack on tobacco monopoly established in Ireland by Thomas Wentworth. Wing M1888A; Arents 216. CSmH, DFo, MH, NN-A; BL. 641/87

—[Anr edn]. [*London:*] *H. Perry,* 1641. 14 p.; 4to. Wing M1889. CtY, DFo, ICN, InU-L, MH, MdBP, MiU; BL, BN. 641/88

Miguel de la Purificación, O.F.M. Vida evangelica y apostolica de los frayles menores. *Barcelona: G. Nogues,* 1641. 572 p.; fol. In pt 2, trat. 3, Franciscan missions in America are described. Streit I:483; Palau 242333. 641/89

Montaigne, Michel Eyquem de. Essais. *Rouen: J. Berthelin,* 1641. 1129 p.; 8vo. 1st

publ., Bordeaux, 1580; cf. 1602 edn. Tchémerzine VIII:431. NjP; BL, BN.
641/90

—[Anr issue?]. *Rouen: J. Berthelin* [1641?]. BL, BN.
641/91

—[Anr issue?]. *Rouen: J. Besongne, the Younger,* 1641. Tchémerzine VIII:431.
641/92

Montalvão, Jorge Mascarenhas, marquez de. Carta, que o Visorrey do Brasil Dom Jorge Mascarenhas marquez de Montalvão escreveo ao . . . conde de Nassau. *Lisbon: J. Rodriguez, for L. de Queiros,* 1641. [3] p.; 4to. On accession of João IV to the throne of Portugal. Sabin 45409; Borba de Moraes II:75–76; JCB (3) II:290. InU-L, RPJCB; BN.
641/93

——. Cartas que escreveo o marquez de Montalvam sendo visorey do estado do Brasil, ao conde de Nassau, que governava as armas em Pernambuco. *Lisbon: D. Lopes Rosa, for D. Alvarez,* 1641. [8] p.; 4to. Borba de Moraes II:76; Rodrigues (Dom. Hol.) 607. NN-RB (imp.); Evora:BP.
641/94

——. Copyen van drie missiven, Een door den marquis du Montuval . . . gheschreven . . . aen . . . Mauritius van Nassau, tot Fernambock . . . Noch een missive gheschreven van Fernanbock, dat van daer gheordineert ende vertrocken waren gecommitteerden aen den voorsz. Marquis, om met den selven te handelen. *Amsterdam: J. van Hilten,* 1641. [7] p.; 4to. Montalvão's letter transl. from his *Carta* of this year above. Sabin 50231; Asher 174; Borba de Moraes II:76; Rodrigues (Dom. Hol.) 610; Knuttel 4774. DLC, ICJ; The Hague:KB; Leyden:B. Thysiana.
641/95

——. Segunda carta. Da un cortezano de Madrid. *Lisbon: J. Rodriguez,* 1641. [7] p.; 4to. Continues the *Carta que o . . . marquez de Montalvão escreveo ao . . . conde de Nassau* above. Rodrigues (Dom. Hol.) DLC.
641/96

Nederlandsche West-Indische Compagnie. Voorslack by eenige hooftparticipanten, uyt Hollandt ghesonden rakende de West-Indische Compagnie. [*Amsterdam?* 1641]. bds.; fol. Sabin 102918. DLC.
641/97

Opitz, Martin. Deutsche Poëmata. *Danzig: A. Hünefeld,* 1641. 952 (i.e., 752) p.; 8vo. 1st publ. in this version, Breslau, 1628–29;

pt 2 includes the 'Lob des Krieges Gottes'. Goedeke III:49; Faber du Faur 227; Jantz (German Baroque) 1911; Jördens IV:115. CU, CtY, NcD, WU; BL, Göttingen:StUB.
641/98

A pack of patentees. opened. shuffled. cut. dealt. and played. *London:* 1641. 15 p.; 4to. In verse. Includes passage on tobacco, mentioning St Kitts & Virginia. Wing P156; Arents 217. CSmH, MH, NN-A; BL.
641/99

Paes Viegas, Antonio. Manifest van 't Koninghrijck van Portugael, in d'welcke verklaert wort de gerechte oorsake ende reden waerom de inwoonders sich hebben getrocken uyt de gehoorsaemheyt des Konings van Castilien . . . Gedruckt naer de coppe tot Lisbona, by Paulus van Craesbeecke, ende nu . . . overgheset . . . door C. F. *Amsterdam: P. Matthijszoon, for B. Janszoon, J. van Hilten, & C. de Pas,* 1641. 23 p.; 4to. Transl. from the author's *Manifesto do reino de Portugal* below. Sabin 44268; Borba de Moraes II:15; Asher 173; Knuttel 4767. RPJCB; BL, The Hague:KB.
641/100

——. Manifesto do Reino de Portugal. No qual se declara o direyto as causas, e o modo qu teve para exemirse da obediencia del rey de Castella. *Lisbon: P. Craesbeeck,* 1641. 42 numb. lvs; 4to. Includes refs to Brazil & West Indies. MH; BN.
641/101

Palafox y Mendoza, Juan de, Bp of Puebla de los Angeles. Discursos espirituales. *Madrid: F. Martínez,* 1641. 126 numb. lvs; port.; 4to. Includes, lvs 119–26, the bishop's 'Carta pastoral á la venerable congregacion de San Pedro, de la ciudad de los Angeles,' 1st publ., Mexico, 1640. Sabin 58290; Medina (BHA) 1026; Streit II:1697; Backer VIII:544. PBL.
641/102

Paré, Ambroise. Les oeuvres . . . Dixiesme edition. *Lyons: P. Borde,* 1641. 840 p.; illus., port; fol. 1st publ., Paris, 1575; cf. the 1601 German edn. Doe (Paré) 39. BL, Louvain:BU.
641/103

—[Anr issue]. *Lyons: C. Prost,* 1641. Doe (Paré) 40. CtY-M, ICJ, MiU, Oxford:Bodl., Paris: Arsenal.
641/104

—[Anr issue]. *Lyons: Widow of C. Rigaud, & P. Rigaud, the Younger,* 1641. Doe (Paré) 41.

DNLM, PPC, Aberdeen:Marischal, Rennes:BU. 641/105

Pharmacopoeia Bruxellensis: jussu amplissimi Senatus edita. *Brussels: J. Mommaert,* 1641. 224 p.; 4to. Amongst the ingredients specified are mechoacan, sarsaparilla, guaiacum, sassafras, Peruvian opobalsam, tacamahac, & the marigold ('Garyophylli seu Tunicis officinarum'). In section 'De cognitione & delectu medicamentorum simplicium' further descriptions are provided for the bezoar stone, guaiacum, mechoacan, sarsaparilla, sassafras, & tacamahac. BL, London:Wellcome. 641/106

Platter, Felix. Observationum, in hominis affectibus . . . libri tres . . . Secunda nunc vice typis mandati. *Basel: L. König,* 1641. 912 p.; 8vo. 1st publ., Basel, 1614. DNLM, KU-M, MnU; BL. 641/107

Den Portugaelsen donder-slagh, tot ontwakinge van alle trouhertighe Neder-landtsche regenten ende ondersaten . . . Door Theophilus Anti-Pater. *Groningen: Heirs of N. Roman,* 1641. 36 p.; 4to. Relates to Brazil. Sabin 1708; Borba de Moraes I:217; Asher 175; Knuttel 4773. RPJCB; BL (Anti-Pater), The Hague:KB. 641/108

Portugal. Sovereigns, etc., 1640–1656 (John IV). Andere declaratie von Jean de Vierde, Koninck van Portugael. Aen alle koninghen, potentaten en natien . . . Nae de . . . originale copye, uyt den Portugeesch. *Amsterdam: C. van de Pas; sold by J. van Hilten & B. Janszoon,* 1641. [17] p.; 4to. The Portuguese original of this work, stated to have been 1st printed at Lisbon by Manuel da Sylva in 1641, has not been identified. The present edn includes a ref. to America. Sabin 36131; Knuttel 4770. RPJCB; BL (John IV), The Hague:KB. 641/109

——. Manifest van 't Koninghrijck van Portugael. *Amsterdam:* 1641. *See* Paes Viegas, Antonio, *above.*

——. Manifesto do Reino de Portugal. *Lisbon:* 1641. *See* Paes Viegas, Antonio, *above.*

Portugal. Treaties, etc., 1640–1656 (John IV). Accoort ende articulen tusschen de croone van Portugael ende de . . . Staten Generael der vrye Vereenichde Nederlanden weghens de West Indische Compagnie deser landen. *Amsterdam: F. Lieshout,* 1641.

[6] p.; 4to. Sabin 102875; Borba de Moraes I:9–10; Asher 181. DLC, MnU-B; BL. 641/110

—[Anr edn]. Accoort ende artijckelen . . . *Middelburg: Widow & Heirs of S. Moulert* [1641]. [8] p.; 4to. Sabin 102875; Borba de Moraes I:9–10(n); Asher 182. DLC. 641/111

——. Extract uyt d'Articulen van het tractaet van bestant ende ophoudinge van alle acten van vyantschap, als oock van traffijcq ende commercie. *The Hague: Widow & Heirs of H. Jacobszoon van Wouw,* 1641. [5] p.; 4to. Includes articles 1, 23 & 25–34 of the treaty; cf. the *Tractaet van bestant* itself under year 1642. Line 1 on p. [3] ends 'isser'. Sabin 23509; Knuttel 4775; Tiele (Pamfletten) 2750. DLC, NN-RB; The Hague:KB. 641/112

—[Anr edn]. *The Hague: Widow & Heirs of H. Jacobszoon van Wouw,* 1641. [5] p.; 4to. T.p. includes reading 'vyandtschap'; line 1 on p. [3] ends 'een goet'. Meulman 2556. Ghent:BU. 641/113

—[Anr edn]. . . . na de copie van de weduwe van Wouw, gedruckt in 's Graven-hage. . . . *Amsterdam: F. Lieshout,* 1641. [5] p.; 4to. Sabin 102891; Borba de Moraes I:256; JCB (3) II:291. RPJCB; BL. 641/114

——. Verkondinghe van het bestant ende ophoudinghe van alle acten van vyandtschap . . . *The Hague: Widow & Heirs of H. Jacobszoon van Wouw,* 1641. [8] p.; 4to. Relates to the West-Indische Compagnie & Brazil. Sabin 98988; Borba de Moraes II:344; Asher 179. 641/115

—[Anr edn]. *The Hague: Widow & Heirs of H. Jacobszoon van Wouw,* 1641. bds.; fol. Sabin 98988; Knuttel 4776. The Hague:KB; Leyden:B. Thysiana. 641/116

Prevost, Jean. Medicina pauperum. *Frankfurt a. M.: [K. Rötel, for] J. Beyer,* 1641. 377 p.; 12mo. In addition to formulas employing the Peruvian bezoar stone, guaiacum, Peruvian opobalsam, & sarsaparilla, an unguent based on the yucca ('Americanae succus') is described as an antidote to poisons. DNLM, NN, ViRA. 641/117

Pym, John. A speech delivered in Parliament, by a worthy member thereof . . . concerning the grievances of the kingdome. *London: R. Lowndes,* 1641. 40 p.; 4to. Criticizes, *inter alia,* effect on English colonies in America of taxes levied, mentioning tobacco. Wing P4284. CSmH, MH, RPJCB; BL. 641/118

—[Anr edn]. *London: R. L[owndes].,* 1641. 40 p.; 4to. CtY, MH, MiU; BL. 641/119

Relaçam da aclamação que se fez na capitania do Rio de Janeiro do estado do Brasil, & nas mais do Sul, ao Senhor Rey Dom João o IV. por verdadeiro rey. *Lisbon: J. Rodriguez, for D. Alvarez,* 1641. 8 lvs; 4to. Sabin 7620 & 69163; Borba de Moraes II:181. InU-L. 641/120

Relacion verdadera de todos los sucessos y encuentros que ha tenido la Real armada de la Flota, en la carrera de las Indias, con los Olandeses . . . Viniendo por Generales don Geronimo de Sandoval, y don Juan de Vega Baçan. *Madrid: J. Sánchez,* 1641. [4] p.; fol. Sabin 76421; Medina (BHA) 1028; Palau 258221; Maggs Cat. 479 (Americana V):4240. RPJCB; Santiago, Chile:BN. 641/121

Relacion verdadera, del felice sucesso, con que la Real Armada de Barlovento ha empeçado, cumpliendo con las esperanças, que en ella tienen todas estas Indias Occidentales . . . en este año de 1641. [*Madrid?* 1641]. fol. Medina (BHA) 1029. 641/122

Rivière, Lazare. Methodus curandorum febrium. *Paris: O. de Varennes,* 1641. 247 p.; 8vo. lst publ., Paris, 1640; here a reissue with altered imprint date of that edn? BN. 641/123

Roberts, Lewes. The treasure of traffike. or A discourse of forraigne trade. *London: E[lizabeth]. P[urslowe]. for N. Bourne,* 1641. 95 p.; 4to. Included are numerous refs to the New World, its wealth & commerce, Spanish as well as English, with mention of both Columbus & Sebastian Cabot. Sabin 71910; Wing R1602; Kress 595; Arents (Add.) 315. CtY, DLC, MH-BA, MnU-B, NN-RB, PU, RPJCB; BL. 641/124

Robinson, Henry. England's safety, in trades encrease. *London: E[lizabeth]. P[urslowe]., for N. Bourne,* 1641. 62 p.; 4to. English plantations in Virginia, Bermuda, St Kitts, etc., are mentioned. Sabin 72083; Wing R1671. CSmH, CtY, ICN, MH-BA, MdBJ, NN-RB, PU; BL. 641/125

Roche, John. Moravian heresy. *Dublin:* 1641. *See the year* 1741.

Rudyerd, Sir Benjamin. A speech concerning a West Indie association, at a committee of the whole house in the Parliament. *London:* 1641. 7 p.; 4to. Urges the establishment of a company for West Indian settlement & commerce to counter Spain's presence there. Wing R2191; JCB (3) II:293. CSmH, CtY, MH, MnU-B, NN-RB, PPRF, RPJCB. 641/126

Sad news from the seas. Being a true relation of the losse of that good ship called the Merchant Royall, which was cast away ten leagues from the Lands end . . . 23. of Septemb. last, 1641. [*London:*] 1641. [6] p.; 4to. Describes seizure by Spanish of British vessel for West Indian voyage & its subsequent loss. Wing S258; Thomason I:29; JCB (3) II:293. RPJCB; BL. 641/127

Sala, Gaspar, O.S.A. Secretos publicos, piedra de toque, de las intenciones del enemigo, y luz de la verdad . . . Traduzidos fielmente de catalan. [*Barcelona?* 1641?]. [92] p.; 4to. Transl. from the following item. Palau 285721. MiU, WU. 641/128

——. Secrets publichs, pedra de toch, de les intencions del enemich, y llum de la veritat. [*Barcelona:* 1641]. [48] p.; 4to. Includes (p. [15–24]) description of Spanish cruelties in West Indies, quoted from Las Casas; on p. [11], tobacco is mentioned. Palau 285720. RPJCB. 641/129

—[Anr edn]. [*Barcelona:* 1641?]. 100 p.; 4to. 'Va en esta ultima impressio sinch cartas.' MH. 641/130

——. Segredos publicos. Pedra de toque, dos intentos do inimigo . . . Traducido de catalão. *Lisbon: L. de Anveres, for L. de Queiros,* 1641. 35 numb. lvs; 4to. Transl. from Sala's *Secrets publichs* of this year above. Palau 285721. 641/131

Sandys, Sir Edwin. Relation de l'estat de la religion. *Amsterdam: L. Elsevier,* 1641. 416 p.; 12mo. lst publ. as here transl. by Jean Diodati from Paolo Sarpi's Italian translation, with additions, Geneva, 1626. CtY, NNUT, PU; BL, BN. 641/132

Scarioni, Francesco. Centuria seconda de' secreti mirabili, medicinali, & curiosi. *Viterbo, Bologna, Verona, Brescia, & Piacenza: G. A. Ardizzoni,* 1641. [16] p.; 8vo. The 22nd 'secret', to promote digestion, employs sassafras. London:Wellcome. 641/133

Schröder, Johann (1600–1664). Pharmacopeia medico-chymica, sive Thesaurus pharmacologicus. *Ulm: J. Görlin,* 1641. 1 v.; illus.; 4to. Invoked for therapeutic use are Peruvian opobalsam, the Peruvian bezoar stone, mechoacan (& its related jalapa), guaiacum, sarsaparilla, sassafras, & tobacco. DNLM. 641/134

Sennert, Daniel. Epitome naturalis scientiae. *Venice: F. Baba,* 1641. 118 p.; fol. 1st publ., Wittenberg, 1618. MiU, PBa. 641/135

Shepard, Thomas. The sincere convert. *London: T. P[aine]. & M. S[immons].,* for H. Blunden, 1641. 266 p.; 8vo. 1st publ., London, 1640. Sabin 80218; Wing S3118. InU-L, MH; BL. 641/136

Strafford, Thomas Wentworth, 1st earl of, defendant. Depositions and articles against Thomas earle of Strafford. [*London:*] 1640 [i.e., 1641]. 45 p.; 4to. The 12th article accuses Strafford of having, while lieutenant governor of Ireland, monopolized to his own profit the tobacco trade there. Of this work related to the earl's subsequent execution there are at least four edns, with further variants, on which the STC should be consulted. STC 25247–25248.7; Wing E2572; Arents (Add.) 310. The locations here given represent one or more edns, etc.: CSmH, CtY, DLC, ICU, InU-L, MH, MiU, MnU, NN; BL. 641/137

—[Anr edn]. *London:* 1641. 4to. Wing E2572A. MnU, NPV. 641/138

Sweden. Sovereigns, etc., 1632–1654 (Christina). Förordning huru medh tobaks handelen skal blifwa hällit [8. Febr. anno 1641]. [*Stockholm:* 1641]. [3] p.; 4to. MnU-B. 641/139

Sweerts, Emanuel. Florilegium amplissimum et selectissimum. *Amsterdam: J. Janszoon, the Younger,* 1641. 2 v.; illus.; fol. 1st publ., Frankfurt a. M., 1612–14. MH, NNBG; BL, BN. 641/140

Taylor, John, the Water-poet. The complaint of M. Tenter-hooke the projector, and Sir Thomas Dodger the patentee. *London: E. P[urslowe].,* for F. Coules, 1641. bds.; illus.; fol. In verse. Mentioned is tobacco & various areas in America where grown. Wing T443. BL. 641/141

Teixeira, José, supposed author. Seigneur ofte den groten meester van Castilien, dat is, Levende afbeeldinge van die . . . tyrannye . . . Philippi des II. conincks van Hispanien . . . Uyt den Castiliaenschen in de Fransche tale overgeset door J.d. Dralymont . . . [i.e., Jean de Montlyard] . . . ende naederhandt int Nederduytsche door C. P. Boeyt. [*Amsterdam?*] 1641. 39 numb. lvs; 4to. 1st publ. in Dutch, [Amsterdam?], 1598, under title *Tractaet paraeneticq,* as transl. from [Paris?], 1597, text. On disputed authorship see STC 19837.5. Includes numerous refs to New World. NN-RB. 641/142

Torsellino, Orazio, S.J. Historiarum ab origine mundi ad annum 1630 epitome libri x. *Munich:* 1641. 1st publ., Rome, 1598; cf. 1620 edn. Backer VIII:152. 641/143

Udemans, Godefridus Corneliszoon. 't Geestelyck roer van 't coopmans schip . . . Den tweeden druck. *Dordrecht: F. Boels,* 1640 [colophon: *Dordrecht: H. van Esch,* 1641]. 721 p.; 4to. 1st publ., Gouda & Dordrecht, 1638. Sabin 97664; Tiele 1119n; Asher 24; Muller (1872) 1534; JCB (3) II:286. MnU-B. N, RPJCB; BL. 641/144

Veen, Jan van der. Over-zeesche zege, en Bruylofts-zangen . . . De derde druk, oversien ende vermeerdert. *Haarlem: H. P. van Wesbusch,* 1641. 476 p.; obl. 16mo. In verse. No earlier edn has been traced. The 'Feestdicht tot . . . Walewyn van der Veen' (p. 247–51) mentions America. Aa XI:V15. BL. 641/145

Velasco, Pedro de, S.J. Señor. Pedro de Velasco . . . procurador general de la provincia de Nueva España dize, Que los religiosos de la Compañia de Jesus se emplean en la predicacion del santo evangelio, conversion de los Indios gentiles, y dotrina de los nuevamente convertidos, en las missiones de la Nueva Vizcaya. [*Madrid:* 1641?]. 2 lvs; fol. Memorial to king of Spain. Sabin 98805; Medina (BHA) 6956; Wagner (SW) 41; Palau 357198. Seville:Archivo de Indias (missing). 641/146

Venero, Alonso. Enchiridion, o Manual de los tiempos . . . Continuando las cosas mas dignas de memoria, que han sucedido desde el año de 1582 hasta el de 1640. *Alcalá de Henares: A. Vázquez, for M. López,* 1641. 353 p.; 8vo. 1st publ. with American refs, Saragossa, 1548. Sabin 98865n; Palau 358458. DLC, PU.   641/147

Vicary, Thomas. The English-mans treasure . . . ninthly augmented. *London: B. Alsop & T. Fawcet,* 1641. 292 p.; illus.; 4to. 1st publ., London, 1548, but cf. 1613 edn. Wing V334. CtY, DLC, MBCo, MnU-B, PPC; BL.   641/148

Vimont, Barthélemy, S.J. Relation de ce qui s'est passé en la Nouvelle France en l'anne M. DC. XL. *Paris: S. Cramoisy,* 1641. 2 pts; 8vo. Pt 2 comprises J. Lallemant's *Relation de ce qui s'est passé dans le pays des Hurons.* For variant states, see Bell as cited. Sabin 99748; Harrisse (NF) 76; Bell (Jes. rel.) 17–18; McCoy 38–39; Streit II:2531; JCB (3) II:293–94. CSmH, CtY, ICN, InU-L, MH, MiU-C, MnU-B, NN-RB, RPJCB; BL, BN.   641/149

Vox borealis. or The northern discoverie: by way of dialogue. [*London:*] 'Margery Mar-Prelat', 1641. 14 numb. lvs; 4to. Includes mention of tobacco. Wing V712; Arents 219. CSmH, CtY, DFo, ICU, MH, NN-RB; BL.   641/150

Le voyage curieux, faict autour du monde, par François Drach . . . Augmenté de la seconde partie. *Paris: A. Robinot,* 1641. 230 p.; map; 8vo. 1st publ. with 2nd pt, Paris, 1627, as here transl. by François de Louvencourt, under title *Le voyage de l'illustre . . . François Drach.* On disputed authorship, see the 1613 edn. Sabin 20846; Wagner (SW) 9d; Maggs Cat. 479 (Americana V): 4237; JCB (3) II:292. CU, DLC, MiU-C, NNH, RPJCB; BL, BN.   641/151

Watts, Richard. The young mans looking-glass. or, A summary discourse between the ant and the grashopper. *London: E. Blackmore,* 1641. 2 pts; 8vo. Prose and verse. Included are disparaging refs to tobacco. Wing W1155; Arents (Add.) 316. CtY, NN-A, BL.   641/152

Wit's recreations. Wit's recreations. *London: T. Cotes, for H. Blunden,* 1641. [347] p.; 8vo. 1st publ., London, 1640. Wing M1720. CSmH, CtY, DFo, MH; BL.   641/153

Zeiller, Martin. Das andere Hundert Episteln, oder Sendschreiben. *Ulm: J. Görlin,* 1641. 537 p.; 8vo. Includes refs to American discovery & exploration, to Peruvian natives' acceptance of Christian beliefs, etc. Cf. Zeiller's *Hundert Episteln,* 1st publ., Heilbronn & Ulm, 1640. Jantz (German Baroque) 2771; Jördens V:600. NcD, RPJCB.   641/154

1642

Abbot, George, Abp of Canterbury. A briefe description of the whole world. *London: B. Alsop, for J. M., & W. Sheares* [1642]. 329 p.; port.; 12mo. 1st publ., London, 1599. Sabin 21n; Wing A60. CtY, DFo, IU; Cambridge:Trinity.   642/1

Aldrovandi, Ulisse. Monstrorum historia, cum Paralipomenis historiae omnium animalium. *Bologna: N. Tebaldini, for M. A. Bernia,* 1642. 2 pts; illus.; fol. Described are numerous American birds & beasts, with native names cited, including an 'Elaphocamelus', i.e., a llama. Nissen (Zool.) 74. CU, DNLM, ICJ, MB, MiU, NN-RB, PPC, RPB; BL, Rome:BN.   642/2

——. Quadrupedum omnium bisulcorum historia . . . Marcus Antonius Bernia denuò in lucem edidit. *Bologna: G. B. Ferroni,* 1642 [colophon: 1641]. 1040 p.; illus.; fol. 1st publ., Bologna, 1621; here a reissue of printer's 1641 edn with altered imprint date? Nissen (Zool.) 74n. CU, CtY, DNLM, ICJ, MiU, NN-RB, PPC; BN.   642/3

Andrade Leitão, Francisco de. Copia das proposições, e secunda allegaçam . . . em 14 de Junho de 1642. *Lisbon: L. de Anveres,* 1642. [30] p.; 4to. Transl. from author's *Copia propositionum* of this year below. Cf. Sabin 39940; Borba de Moraes I:396; Rodrigues (Dom. Hol.) 620; Innocencio II:344. MH.   642/4

——. Copia primae allegationis . . . legatus ad . . . ordines generales Foederati Belgij; eisdem obtulit, pro restitutione civitatis Sancti Pauli de Loanda in Angola, insularumque Sancti Thomae, necnon etiam de Maranham, 18. die May anno 1642. [*The Hague:* 1642]. 5 lvs; 4to. Protest against

Dutch seizure of Portuguese colonies. Cf. Sabin 39940; Borba de Moraes I:395–96; Rodrigues (Dom. Hol.) 617. MH.
642/5

——. Copia propositionum, & secundae allegationis . . . renovatae die 14. Junii anno 1641 [i.e., 1642]. [*The Hague?* 1642]. 13 lvs; 4to. Continues author's *Copia primae allegationis* of this year above. Cf. Sabin 39940; Borba de Moraes I:396; Rodrigues (Dom Hol.) 619.
642/6

——. Discurso politico sobre o se aver de largar a coroa de Portugal, Angola, S. Thome, e Maranhão, exclamado aos . . . estados de Olanda. *Lisbon: A. Alvarez, for A. Godinho,* 1642. [12] p.; 4to. Transl. from author's *Copia primae allegationis* of this year above. Sabin 39940; Borba de Moraes I:396; Innocencio II:450. MH, RPJCB; BL.
642/7

Bacon, Francis, viscount St Albans. The essayes or, Counsels, civill and morall. *London: J. Beale, for R. Royston,* 1642. 340 p.; port.; 4to. 1st publ. as here enl., London, 1625; here a reissue of 1639 edn with cancel t.p. & port. added. Gibson (Bacon) 18; Wing (2) B283. CSmH, DFo, MH.
642/8

——. Historia regni Henrici septimi. *Leyden: F. Haack,* 1642. 406 p.; 12mo. Transl. from Bacon's *History of the raigne of King Henry the seventh,* 1st publ., London, 1622. Gibson (Bacon) 125. DLC, ICU, MH, PMA; BL, BN.
642/9

Baltimore, George Calvert, 1st baron. The answer to Tom-Tell-Troth. The practise of princes and the lamentations of the kirke. *London:* 1642. 30 p.; 4to. Included are minor refs to Spanish Indies & to Greenland. Wing (2) B611; JCB AR50:26–30. CtY, ICN, MH, MnU, NjP, RPJCB; BL.
642/10

Barba, Pedro. Vera praxis ad curatione tertianae. *Seville:* 1642. 'The first publication on cinchona bark and its use in the treatment of malaria'—Morton & Garrison, *Medical bibliography* (New York, 1961) 5230. The fact remains that the text as presumably reprinted below contains no such ref, & this edn remains unlocated.
642/11

—[Anr edn]. [*Louvain?* 1642?]. [26] p.; 4to. Palau 23647. DNLM.
642/12

Beroa, Diego de, S.J. Litterae annuae provinciae Paraquariae Societatis Jesu . . . Ex hispanico autographo latinè redditae à p. Francisco de Hamal. *Lille: T. LeClercq,* 1642. 347 p.; 8vo. Covers years from 1635 to July, 1637. Sabin 4956; Medina (BHA) 1034; Streit II:1700; Backer I:1355; Palau 33170; JCB (3) II:295. CtY, DLC, RPJCB; BL, BN.
642/13

Besler, Michael Rupert. Gazophylacium rerum naturalium e regno vegetabili, animali et minerali depromptarum. *Leipzig: J. Wittigau,* 1642. 36 lvs; illus.; fol. Included are illus. & notes on an 'Amaranthus mexicanus' & tobacco pipes. Pritzel 747; Nissen (Zool.) 346. MiU (imp.), NNBG; BL, BN.
642/14

Besold, Christoph. Dissertatio politico-juridica de majestate in genere. *Strassburg: Heirs of L. Zetzner,* 1642. 197 p.; 4to. 1st publ., Strassburg, 1625. DLC; BN.
642/15

Beverwijck, Jan van. Inleydinge tot de Hollandsche geneesmiddelen. *Dordrecht: J. Gorisszoon,* 1642. 8vo. Includes discussion of pox (syphilis), native to West Indies. In the course of defending the import of sugar, herbs, & medicine from foreign lands, Beverwijck notes that the West Indian peoples' riches in gold & silver have regrettably led to the destruction of those peoples. Van de Velde 76; Catalogus van boeken VII:94.
642/16

——. Schat der gesontheydt ofte Geneeskonste van de sieck. Het tweede deel. *Dordrecht:* 1642. 12mo. 1st publ., [Dordrecht? 1636?]. Graesse I:357; cf. Molhuysen I:331
642/17

——. Schat der ongesontheit, ofte Geneeskonste van de siecken . . . met verssen van . . . Jacob Cats. *Dordrecht: H. van Esch, for J. Gorisszoon,* 1642. 632 p.; illus.; 8vo. Included are refs to bezoar stone in West Indies (i.e., Peru), mechoacan of Mexico, tacamahac, caranna, sassafras, Florida, etc. A special t.p. is dated 1641. For a differing and supplementary pt 2, see the year 1644. Cf. Beverwijck's *Schat der gesontheyt . . . tweede deel* of this year, above. Van de Velde 76; cf. Catalogus van boeken VII:39. CtY-M, DNLM.
642/18

Blaeu, Willem Janszoon. Aenhangsel van 't i & ii deel van 't Toonneel des aerdryks.

[*Amsterdam: J. Blaeu*, ca. 1642?]. 24 maps; fol. Cf. Blaeu's French version, the *Appendice*, 1st publ., [Amsterdam, ca. 1638]. Includes maps showing Florida & pt of North America. Sometimes issued as pt of Blaeu's *Toonneel . . . derde deel* below. Koeman (Bl) 25. 642/19

——. Institution astronomique de l'usage des globes et spheres. *Amsterdam: J. & C. Blaeu*, 1642. 277 p.; illus.; 4to. Transl. from Blaeu's *Tweevoudigh onderwijs*, 1st publ., Amsterdam, 1634. Keuning (Blaeu) 63; Houzeau/Lancaster I:9714. CtY, DLC, NN-RB; BN. 642/20

——. Novus atlas, das ist Welt-beschreibung . . . ander Theil. *Amsterdam: J. & C. Blaeu*, 1642. 2 pts; 92 maps; fol. 1st publ., Amsterdam, 1635. Issued with Blaeu's *Novus atlas*, Amsterdam, 1641–42. Koeman (Bl) 32A; Phillips (Atlases) 5936. DLC; BL. 642/21

——. Le theatre du monde, ou Nouvel atlas. *Amsterdam: J. & C. Blaeu*, 1642. 2 pts; 120 maps; fol. 1st publ. in French, Amsterdam, 1635. Koeman (Bl) 16B. BN. 642/22

——. Toonneel des aerdriicx, ofte Nieuwe atlas, dat is beschryving van alle landen. *Amsterdam: J. & C. Blaeu*, 1642. 2 pts; 120 maps; fol. 1st publ., Amsterdam, 1635. This edn includes 3 p. section, 'Oude ende nieuwe schipvaert', with refs to American voyages. In this edn, several maps from Blaeu's *Aenhangsel* of this year have been added without alteration of their signatures. For variant see Koeman. Koeman (Bl) 26A; Tiele 130. DeU (state uncertain); Deventer:Athenaeum. 642/23

—[Anr state]. *Amsterdam: J. & C. Blaeu*, 1642. 2 pts; 120 maps; fol. Here the maps inserted from the *Aenhangsel* have had their signatures adapted to the numbering of the pages. Koeman (Bl) 26B. Amsterdam: NHSM. 642/24

——. Toonneel des aerdrycx, oft Nieuwe atlas . . . Tweede deel. *Amsterdam: J. Blaeu*, 1642. 2 pts; 92 maps; fol. 1st publ., Amsterdam, 1635, under title *Tweede deel*. Title printed on slips pasted on engr. t.p. Some maps from Blaeu's *Aenhangsel* are inserted with their original signatures. Koeman (Bl) 27A. DeU (edn uncertain), RPB; Deventer: Athenaeum. 642/25

—[Anr state]. *Amsterdam: J. Blaeu*, 1642. Here the signatures of maps added are adapted to the numbering of the pages. Koeman (Bl) 27B. Amsterdam:NHSM. 642/26

—[Anr edn]. *Amsterdam: J. Blaeu*, 1642. 2 pts; 92 maps.; fol. Here the text has been reset & a new map of 'Brasilia' added. Koeman (Bl) 28. Utrecht:UB. 642/27

——. Toonneel des aerdrycx, oft Nieuwe atlas . . . Derde deel, met een Aenhangsel tot de twee voorgaende deelen. *Amsterdam: J. Blaeu*, 1642. 86 maps; fol. The present edn differs from others of this year in having an additional 24 maps from Blaeu's *Aenhangsel* of this year above. Map no. 63, 'Regiones sub polo arctico' shows pt of North America, while no. 86 portrays Florida. Koeman (Bl) 39A; Phillips (Atlases) 454. DLC; Middelburg:PL. 642/28

Boccalini, Traiano. Pietra del paragone politico. *'Cosmopoli: G. Teler'* [i.e., *Amsterdam?*] 1642. 287 p.; 8vo. 1st publ., 'Cormopoli' (i.e., Venice), 1615. Willems (Les Elzevier) 965n; Michel (Répertoire) I:175. DLC; Paris:Ste Geneviève. 642/29

Breton, Nicholas. Wits private wealth. *London: T. Fawcet, for G. Hurlock*, 1642. 4to. 1st publ., London, 1612. Wing B4393. BL. 642/30

Camerarius, Philipp. Operae horarum subcisivarum . . . Centuria . . . altera. *Frankfurt a. M.: W. Hoffmann*, 1642. 4to. 1st publ., Frankfurt a. M., 1601. CU. 642/31

Caramuel Lobkowitz, Juan, Bp. Joannes Bargantinus Lusitaniae illegitimus rex demonstratus . . . translatus in idioma latinum a d. Leandro van der Brandt. *Louvain: E. de Witte*, 1642. 221 p.; 4to. Transl. from the author's *Respuesta* below; includes text of A. Paes Viegas's *Manifesto del Reino*, 1st publ., Lisbon, 1641. BL (Portugal), BN. 642/32

——. Respuesta al Manifesto del reyno de Portugal. *Antwerp: Plantin Office (B. Moretus)*, 1642. 198 p.; 4to. A reply to Antonio Paes Viegas's *Manifesto do Reino de Portugal*, Lisbon, 1641, the text of which is here included. The present work includes a few additional American refs. ICN, MH; BL, BN. 642/33

Carvalho, Jorge de. Relação verdadeira dos sucessos do conde de Castel Melhor, preso na cidade de Cartagena de Indias, & hoje livre, por particular merce do Ceo, & favor del Rey Dom João IV. *Lisbon: D. Lopes Rosa,* 1642. Sabin 69171; Innocencio IV:164–65; Palha 2952. MH, NN-RB, OCl, RPJCB.

642/34

Casas, Bartolomé de las, O.P., Bp of Chiapa. Histoire des Indes Occidentales. Ou l'on reconnoit la bonté de ces pais, & de leurs peuples; et les cruautez tyrraniques des Espagnols . . . fidellement traduite en françois. *Lyons: J. Caffin & F. Plaignard,* 1642. 299 p.; 8vo. 1st publ. in French, Antwerp, 1579, under title *Tyrannies et cruautez des Espagnols.* Sabin 11272; Medina (BHA) 1085n (II:472); Hanke/Giménez 535; Streit I:486; Palau 46964; JCB (3) II:295. DLC, MH, NN-RB, RPJCB; BL, BN. 642/35

Catholic Church. Pope, 1623–1644 (Urban VIII). Nuestro mui santo p. Urbano . . . à mandado por su breve apostolico . . . a 30. de enero de 1642 [etc.] . . . Sevilla . . . 27. de julio de 1642. [*Seville:* 1642]. bds.; fol. Bull forbidding use of tobacco in any form in churches of Seville. Arents (Add.) 322. NN-A. 642/36

Clément, Claude, S.J. Tabla chronologica de los descubrimientos, conquistas, fundaciones, poblaciones . . . de las Indias Orientales, islas y tierra firme del Mar Oceano, desde 1492, hasta el presente de 1642. *Madrid: D. Díaz de la Carrera,* 1642. bds.; fol. Cf. Medina (BHA) 1047; Palau 190947. NNH. 642/37

——. Tabla cronologica del govierno secular y eclesiastico de las Indias Occidentales. *Madrid: D. Díaz de la Carrera,* 1642. bds.; fol. Palau 190948. 642/38

Clüver, Johannes. Historiarum totius mundi epitome . . . Editio quinta correctior. *Leyden: F. Moyaert,* 1642. 658 (i.e., 850) p.; 4to. 1st publ., Leyden, 1637. CtY. 642/39

Clüver, Philipp. Introduction à la geographie universelle tant nouvelle que ancienne. Traduitte du latin de Philippe de Cluvier. . . . Seconde édition. *Paris: M. Henault,* 1642. 496 p.; illus.; 8vo. 1st publ. as here transl., Paris, 1631. Cf. Sabin 13805. CtY; BN. 642/40

——. Introductionis in universam geographiam tam veterem quàm novam, libri vi. Editio ultima prioribus multò emendatior.

Caen: A. Cavelier, 1642. 496 p.; 16mo. 1st publ., Leyden, 1624. Cf. Sabin 13805. ICN (imp.); BN. 642/41

Collibus, Hippolytus à. Fürstliche Tischreden . . . continuirt . . . durch . . . G. Draudium. *Basel: J. J. Genath, for Heirs of L. König,* 1642–45. 2 pts; 8vo. 1st publ., Frankfurt a. M., 1597; cf. 1614 edn. Jantz (German Baroque) 838; Goedeke II:473. NNC (pt 1), NcD; BL (Gebhard). 642/42

Compagnie de la Nouvelle France. Estat general des debts passives de la Compagnie generale de la Nouvelle France. [*Paris:* 1642]. 32 numb. lvs; fol. Sabin 56087; Harrisse (NF) 78. 642/43

Conestaggio, Girolamo Franchi di. Dell' unione del regno di Portugallo alla corona di Castiglia. *Florence: A. Massi & L. Landi,* 1642. 373 p.; 4to. 1st publ., Genoa, 1585; cf. 1616 edn. Michel (Répertoire) 123; Palau 313375n. DLC, NIC; BN. 642/44

——[Anr edn]. Terza impressione. *Venice & Verona: F. di Rossi,* 1642. 295 p.; 8vo. Michel (Répertoire) 123; Palau 313375. CU, DLC, MH, PU; BL, BN. 642/45

Cotton, John. The churches resurrection . . . by . . . John Cotton, teacher to the church of Boston in New England. *London: R. O[ulton]. & G. D[exter]., for H. Overton,* 1642. 30 p.; 4to. In part a comparison of New England religious life with that of Europe. Sabin 17054; Tuttle (Cotton) 22; Wing C6419; JCB (3) II:296. CSmH, CtY, DLC, ICN, MH, MiU-C, NNUT, RPJCB; BL, Oxford:Bodl. 642/46

——. The powring out of the seven vials . . . Preached . . . at Boston in New-England. *London: R. S[mith?].; sold by H. Overton,* 1642. [175] p.; 4to. Includes ref. to seasonal croaking of American frogs. Sabin 17074; Tuttle (Cotton) 25; Wing C6449; JCB (3) II:296–97. CSmH, CtY, DLC, MH, RPJCB; BL, Oxford:Bodl. 642/47

——[Anr edn]. *London: H. Overton,* 1642. 4to. Cf. Sabin 17074; Wing C6449A. CtY. 642/48

Damiens, Jacques, S.J. Tableau racourci de ci qui s'est fait par la Compagnie de Jesus durant son premier siecle . . . Traduit . . . par le r.p. François Lahier. *Tournay: A. Quinqué,* 1642. 511 p.; 4to. Transl. from

the author's *Synopsis primi saeculi Societatis Jesu.* Backer I:288. MB, MiU; BL.
642/49

Davenport, John. The profession of faith of . . . Mr. J. D., sometime preacher of Stevens Coleman-street. London. Made publiquely before the congregation at his admission into one of the churches of God in New-England. *London: J. Hancock,* 1642. 8 p.; 4to. Sabin 18709; Wing (2) D364; JCB (3) II:297. CSmH, CtY, DLC, ICN, MH, RPJCB; BL.
642/50

Draud, Georg. Fürstliche Tischreden. *Basel:* 1642–45. *See* Collibus, Hippolytus à, *above.*

Eras Pantoja, Nicolás. Señor. Don Nicolas Eras Pantoja, vezino y regidor de . . . Cartagena de las Indias. [*Madrid?* 1642?]. 18 numb. lvs; fol. Memorial on government and affairs of city & province of Cartagena. Medina (BHA) 6428. BL.
642/51

Extract uyt verscheyden brieven gheschreven in Brasil. [*Middelburg:* 1642]. 4 lvs.; 4to. Rodrigues (Dom. Hol.) 486. DLC.
642/52

France. Sovereigns, etc., 1610–1643 (Louis XIII). Lettres de ratification du Roi des contrats du 12. fev. 1635. & 29 janv. 1642. faits par le Cardinal de Richelieu avec le sieur Berruyer pour les associez en la Compagnie des isles de l'Amerique. Données à Narbonne au mois de mars . . . mil six cens quarante deux. [*Paris?* 1642?]. [9] p.; 4to. Printed on vellum, perhaps in a single copy. Sabin 75014 & 75016; cf. Wroth & Annan 25 & 26; Maggs: French ser. Cat. 8 (1936) 6.
642/53

Friesland, Netherlands. Provinciale Staten. Copye van het Octroy, by de Staten van Frieslandt. *Leeuwarden: J. & P. van den Rade,* 1642. [16] p.; 4to. While concerned primarily with East Indian trade, relates also to the West-Indische Compagnie. Knuttel 4888. MnU-B; The Hague:KB.
642/54

Fuller, Thomas. The holy state. *Cambridge: R. Daniel, for J. Williams* [*at London*], 1642. 441 p.; illus., ports; fol. Includes life of Sir Francis Drake, mentioning American voyages. Sabin 26181; Murphy (Eng. charbks)55; Wing F2443; McAlpin II:130; JCB AR44:28. CSmH, CtY, DLC, ICN, MH, MiU, MnU, NN-RB, PU, RPJCB; BL, BN.
642/55

González de Legaria, Juan. Aqui se contiene una obra graciosa . . . para reir . . . y es un cuento que le passò a un soldado, con un gato . . . Juntamente con la respuesta que dio el gato al autor. *Madrid: C. Sánchez, for L. Sánchez,* 1642. [8] p.; illus.; 4to. In verse. 1st publ., Lisbon, 1608. Palau 105415n; Salvá 50. BL.
642/56

Great Britain. Treaties, etc., 1625–1649 (Charles I). Articles of peace and commerce, between . . . Charles . . . And John the 4th King of Portugal . . . Concluded at London the nine and twentieth day of January . . . 1642. stilo novo. Translated out of Latin into English. *London: R. Barker, & assigns of J. Bill,* 1642. [22] p.; 4to. Article xvi relates to commerce with Brazil. Wing (2) C2147. CSmH, DFo, ICN, RPJCB; BL.
642/57

—[Anr edn]. *London: J. Harrison,* 1642. 4to. Wing C2147A. MH.
642/58

—[Anr edn]. *London: H. Seile,* 1642. 55 p.; 4to. Issued with phrase 'Published by authority . . .' or 'Allowed and published for . . . Scotland' on t.p. Wing C2147C. CtY, MH, NNUT; Cambridge:UL.
642/59

Grégoire, Pierre. De republica, libri sex et viginti . . . Editio germaniae tertia. *Frankfurt a. M.: M. Kempfer, for P. J. Fischer,* 1642. 908 p.; 4to. 1st publ., Pont-à-Mousson, 1596; cf. 1609 edns above. MiU; BN.
642/60

Grotius, Hugo. De jure belli ac pacis libri tres . . . Editio nova cum annotatis auctoris. *Amsterdam: J. & C. Blaeu,* 1642. 601 p.; 8vo. 1st publ., Paris, 1625. Meulen/Diermanse 571. CU-S, CtY, DLC, MiU-C, NNC; BN, The Hague:PP.
642/61

——. De origine gentium Americanarum dissertatio. [*Paris?*] 1642. 15 p.; 4to. For a refutation of this work, see J. de Laet's *Notae ad dissertationem,* 1st publ., Amsterdam, 1643; cf. also Georg Horn's *De originibus Americanis libri quatuor,* 1st publ., Leyden & The Hague, 1652. Sabin 28957; Borba de Moraes I:317; Meulen/Diermanse 725. CtY, DLC, MH, RPJCB; BN, The Hague:PP.
642/62

—[Anr edn]. *Amsterdam:* 1642. 8vo. Sabin 28957.
642/63

—[Anr edn]. Dissertatio de origine gentium Americanarum. [*Paris?*] 1642. 13 p.; 8vo.

Meulen/Diermanse 726. DFo, ICJ, NN-RB;
The Hague:PP.   642/64

Guerreiro, Bartholomeu, S.J. Gloriosa coroa d'esforçados religiosos da Companhia
de Jesu nas conquistas dos reynos . . . de
Portugal. Mortos polla fe catholica. *Lisbon:
A. Alvarez,* 1642. 736 p.; fol. The 3rd pt
(p. 300–387) describes Jesuit missionaries
of Brazil. Sabin 29127 (&27587); Borba de
Moraes I:320; Streit I:485; Backer III:1913.
DLC, ICN, MH; BL, BN.   642/65

Homburg, Ernst Christoph. Schimpff- und
ernsthaffte Clio, erster[-ander] Theil. Zum
andern mal umb die Helffte vermehret.
Jena: B. Lobenstein, for Z. Hertel, at Hamburg,
1642. 2 pts; 8vo. 1st publ., [Hamburg],
1638; here enlarged. This edn includes refs
to tobacco & to trade with Brazil & Peru.
Jantz (German Baroque) 1395; Faber du
Faur 257; Goedeke III:78. CtY, NcD; BL,
Göttingen:UB.   642/66

Hondius, Hendrik. Nouveau theatre du
monde, ofte Nouvel atlas . . . divise en
trois tomes. *Amsterdam: J. Janszoon, the Younger,* 1642. 3 v.; maps; fol. 1st publ. in this
version, Amsterdam, 1639. Of this edn,
only vols 1 & 3 are known. Subsequent edns
entered under Jansson. Koeman 100A,
100B, 101. ICN (v. 3); BL (v. 1).
                                    642/67

Jansson, Jan. Nieuwen atlas, ofte Werelt
beschryvinge . . . als meede Oost en West
Indien . . . in twee deelen. *Amsterdam: J.
Janszoon, the Younger,* 1642. 2 v.; illus., maps;
fol. 1st publ. in this version, Amsterdam,
1638. Koeman (Me) 73 & 74; Phillips (Atlases) 5937. DLC; Brussels:BR, Leeuwarden (v. 2).   642/68

——. Nouveau theatre. *Amsterdam:* 1642. *See*
Hondius, Hendrik, *above.*

——. Novi Atlantis Anhang, oder Neuer
Weltbeschreibung dritter Theil. *Amsterdam:
J. Janszoon, the Younger,* 1642. 1 v.; maps;
fol. 1st publ., Amsterdam, 1641. Koeman
(Me) 123 (cf. 126). Wolfenbüttel:KB, Co-
penhagen:KB.   642/69

——. [Novus Atlas, das ist Weltbeschreibung. *Amsterdam: J. Janszoon, the Younger,*
1642]. 3 v.; illus., maps; fol. 1st publ., Amsterdam, 1638; here enl. by Jansson's appendix. Koeman (Me) 124–126. Wolfen-
büttel:HB, Warsaw:BN (pt 3).   642/70

Lechford, Thomas. Plain dealing: or, Newes
from New-England. *London: W. E[llis?]. &
J. G[rismond?]. for N. Butter,* 1642. 80 p.; 4to.
Reissued, 1644, under title *New-Englands advice to Old-England.* Sabin 39640; Baer (Md)
24; Wing L810; Arents (Add.) 317; Church
454; JCB (3) II:298. CSmH, CtY, DLC, ICN,
MH, MiU-C, NN-RB, PPL, RPJCB; BL, BN.
                                    642/71

Léry, Jean de. Histoire d'un voyage fait en
la terre de Bresil. *Geneva:* 1642. 8vo. 1st
publ., La Rochelle, 1578; cf. 1604 edn. Sabin 40152; cf. Borba de Moraes I:400–404.
                                    642/72

Losa, Francisco de. Vida que el siervo de
Dios Gregorio Lopez hizo en algunos lugares de la Nueva España, y principalmente
en el pueblo de Santa Fé. *Madrid: Imprenta
Real, for A. del Ribero Rodríguez,* 1642. 114
numb. lvs; port.; 4to. 1st publ., Mexico City,
1613; cf. 1615 edn. Sabin 42576; Medina
(BHA) 1037; Streit II:1703; Palau 142525.
DLC, InU-L, NN-RB, RPJCB; BL, BN.
                                    642/73

Madeira Arraes, Duarte. Methodo de conhecer e curar o morbo gallico. Primeira
parte. . . . E largamente se trata do
azougue, salsa parrilha, guiacão, pau
sancto, raiz de China, e de todos os mais
remedios d'esta enfermidade. *Lisbon: L. de
Anveres,* 1642. 523 p.; 4to. Innocencio II:209
(380).   642/74

Maiolo, Simeone, Bp of Volturara. Dierum
canicularum tomi septem. *Frankfurt a. M.:
J. G. Schönwetter,* 1642. 2 pts; fol. 1st publ.,
Rome, 1597; cf. 1607 edn. Sabin 44056n.
BN.   642/75

Maldonado, José. Relacion del primer descubrimiento del rio de las Amazonas, por
otro nombre, del Marañon . . . Para informe . . . del Rey . . . y su Real Consejo
de las Indias. [*Madrid?* 1642?]. 15 numb.
lvs; 4to. Borba de Moraes II:12. NN-RB;
BL.   642/76

Manasseh ben Joseph ben Israel. Gratulaçao de Menasseh ben Israel, em nome de
sua nacão, ao celsissimo Principe de Orange
Frederique Henrique, na sua vinda a nossa
synagoga de T[almud]. T[ora]. *Amsterdam:*
5402 [i.e., 1642]. 8 p.; 4to. Includes refs
to Dutch colony in Brazil. Maggs Cat. 502
(Americana VII):5066. OCH.   642/77

Marín de Armendariz, Pedro. Condiciones que el veedor Pedro Marin de Amendariz, por si, y en nombre del capitan D. Pedro de Lugo Albarracin, administrator de las minas del cobre del lugar del Prado de la isla de Santiago de Cuba por su Magestad . . . en razon del assiento que tratan de efectuar . . . en cada uno dellos mil y quinientos quintales de artilleria de broçe fundida a toda satisfacion. [*Madrid?* 1642]. 5 numb. lvs; fol. BL.   642/78

Marino, Giovanni Battista. La Murtoleide . . . '*Nuremberg: J. Stamphier*' [i.e., *Venice?*] 1642. 144 p.; 12mo. In verse. 1st publ., [Venice?], 1619, but also containing Andrea Barbazza's 'Le stigliate a Tomaso Stigliani' 1st publ. in 1629 edn, possibly at Venice. Sabin 51557; Michel (Répertoire) V:126. CtY, MH; BL, BN.   642/79

Mariz Carneiro, Antonio de. Regimento de pilotos, e roteiro da navegaçam, e conquistas do Brasil, Angola . . . Maranhaõ, ilhas e Indias, agora novamente emendado & acresentado. *Lisbon: L. de Anveres*, 1642. 2 pts; maps; 4to. 1st publ., 1625. Sabin 44607; Borba de Moraes I:132; Innocencio I:1106. DLC, MB; BL, BN.   642/80

Massaria, Alessandro. Practica medica. *Venice: B. Barezzi*, 1642. 499 p.; fol. 1st publ., Frankfurt a. M., 1601. DNLM; London: Wellcome.   642/81

Mattioli, Pietro Andrea. Les commentaires . . . sur les six livres de Pedacius Dioscoride . . . de la matiere medecinale, traduits de latin . . . par m. Antoine du Pinet. *Lyons: Widow of C. Rigaud & sons P. & C. Rigaud*, 1642. 605 p.; illus.; fol. 1st publ. as here transl., Lyons, 1561; cf. 1605 edn above. Cf. Pritzel 5991n; Nissen (Bot.) 1312n. DNLM, MH-A, NNC.   642/82

Mela, Pomponius. La geographia . . . que traduxo de Latin . . . Luis Tribaldos de Toledo, chronista mayor de las Indias. *Madrid: D. Díaz de la Carrera, for P. Lasso*, 1642. 88 numb. lvs; 8vo. 1st publ. with American refs, Salamanca, 1498, as Mela's *Cosmographia*. In the present edn, P. Lasso's preface refers to translator's service for Consejo de las Indias, & to 'heroicos versos procuró celebrar los doctos y nunca bastantemente alabados libros de V.S. *de Indiarum jure & gubernatione*'. Book 3, chapt. vii ('La India')

includes gloss 'Piraguas se llaman en las Indias Occidentales.' MH, NNH.   642/83

Merlo de la Fuente, Alonso. Señor. Por dos informaciones de oficio, recebidas ambas por la real audiencia de Lima, los años de 638. y 40. [*Madrid?* 1642?] [3] p.; fol. Memorial to king of Spain reciting own services & those of father in Spanish Indies. BL.   642/84

Messina. Ospedale di Santa Maria della Pietà. Antidotarium speciale sacrae domus magni hospitalis . . . Messanae sub titulo Sanctae Mariae Pietatis. *Venice: Giunta Office*, 1642. 336 p.; 4to. Various remedies call for use of guaiacum, sarsaparilla, & sassafras. London:Wellcome.   642/85

Montalvão, Jorge Mascarenhas, marquez de. Copyen van drie missiven . . . Tweede druck. *Amsterdam:* 1642. 4to. 1st publ., Amsterdam, 1641. Sabin 50231; cf. Borba de Moraes II:76.   642/86

Moscherosch, Johann Michael. Visiones de don Quevedo; Wunderliche und warhafftige Gesichte Philanders von Sittewalt [pseud.] . . . Zum andern mahl auffgelegt . . . übersehen, vermehret und gebessert. *Strassburg: J. P. Mülbe*, 1642–43. 2 pts; 8vo. 1st publ., Strassburg, [1640]; here expanded by Moscherosch's *Ander Theil*, Strassburg, 1643. Bechtold 'B'; Faber du Faur 424; Goedeke III:233. CtY, NIC (pt. 1); BL (pt. 1), Munich:StB.   642/87

Nederlandsche West-Indische Compagnie. Octroy by de . . . Staten Generael, verleent aende West-Indische Compaignie. *The Hague: Widow & Heirs of H. Jacobszoon van Wouw*, 1642. [32] p.; 4to. 1st publ. in this enl. version, The Hague, 1623. This edn has reading 'Moghende' in title; 1st line of text reads 'DE Staten gene-'. Sabin 56673; Knuttel 4880. DLC; The Hague:KB.   642/88

—[Anr edn?]. *The Hague: Widow & Heirs of H. Jacobszoon van Wouw*, 1642. [30] p.; 4to. This edn has reading 'Mog:' in title. Sabin 56674 (& 102901). DLC, N, NN-RB.   642/89

—[Anr edn]. *The Hague: Widow & Heirs of H. Jacobszoon van Wouw*, 1642. [24] p.; 4to. Here the 1st line of text reads 'DE Staten Generael der ver-'. Knuttel 4881. The Hague:KB.   642/90

Newes from New-England: of a most strange

and prodigious birth, brought to Boston in New-England, October the 17. being a true and exact relation, brought over April 19. 1642. by a gentleman of good worth, now resident in London. *London: J. G. Smith*, 1642. [8] p.; illus.; 4to. Sabin 54970; Wing N984; Thomason I:105. BL, Oxford:Bodl.
642/91

Observations upon Prince Rupert's white dogge. [*London:*] 1642. *See the year* 1643.

Ofwod, Stephen. The wicked plots and perfidious practices of Spaniards against the seventeen provinces of the Netherlands. [*London:* 1642]. 8 p.; 4to. Authorship mistakenly attributed to Thomas Scott; a reprinting of Ofwod's 'An adjoynder of sundry other particular wicked plots', 1st publ. at Amsterdam, 1624, in Willem Verheiden's *An oration or speech* and also in its London, 1624, reprinting with title *A second part of Spanish practises.* Wing S2087 (formerly STC 22105a); Thomason I:183; Knuttel 4676a. BL, Oxford:Bodl, The Hague: KB.
642/92

Olearius, Adam. Lustige Historia woher das Tabacktrincken kömpt. [*Hamburg:*] 1642, [7] p.; 8vo. 1st publ., Leipzig, 1635. Lohmeier (Olearius) 8b; Faber du Faur 322. CtY.
642/93

Ortiz de Salcedo, Francisco. Curia eclesiastica, para secretarios de prelados . . . Con una relacion de los arzobispados, y obispados España, y los Indios. *Madrid:* 1642. 4to. 1st publ. with section on West Indian prelates, Madrid, 1626. Palau 205989n.
642/94

Ovalle, Alonso de, S.J. Memorial y carta en que el padre Alonso del Valle procurador general de la provincia de Chile, representa . . . la necessidad que sus missiones tienen de sugetos para los gloriosos empleos de sus apostolicos ministerios. [*Seville?* 1642]. 14 lvs; fol. Subscribed: Sevilla y Março 12 de 1642. Streit II:1705.
642/95

——. Relacion verdadera de las pazes que capituló con el Araucano rebelado, el marques de Baides . . . governador . . . de Chile . . . Sacada de sus informes, y cartas, y de los padres de la Compañia de Jesus, que acompañaron el real exercito . . . el año passado de 1641. *Madrid: F. Maroto*, 1642. [8] p.; fol. Sabin 12802; Medina

(Chile) 108; Streit II:1709; Backer VI:40; JCB (3) II:299. NN-RB, RPJCB; BL.
642/96

Owen, John. Epigrammatum . . . libri decem. *Leyden: F. Heger*, 1642. 268 p.; 12mo. 1st publ., London, 1606. BN.
642/97

Pacheco Ossorio, Rodrigo, marqués de Cerralvo. Por el marques de Zerralvo, difunto, virrey . . . de la Nueva España. Con . . . Francisco de la Torre . . . y . . . Fiscal del Consejo real de las Indias. Sobre la enmienda, ò reformacion de una sentencia pronunciada por algunas señores del dicho Consejo, contra el dicho marques. [*Madrid:* 1642]. 9 numb. lvs; fol. Dated at Madrid 18 Jan. 1642. BL.
642/98

Palafox y Mendoza, Juan de, Bp of Puebla de los Angeles. Señor. Aviendo informado a V. Mag. desde que he llegado a esta provincia de todo lo q[ue] toca a su govierno . . . he dilatado el escrivir sobre los diezmos, pleytos, y diferencias entre el clero, y las religiones. [*Madrid?* 1642?]. 31 numb. lvs; fol. Report to king of Spain on diocese of Puebla de los Angelos in Mexico. NN-RB.
642/99

Pigray, Pierre. Epitome des preceptes de medecine et chirurgie. *Rouen: J. Berthelin*, 1642. 764 p.; 8vo. 1st publ., Paris, 1600, under title *La chirurgie;* cf. 1604 edn. BN.
642/100

——[Anr issue]. *Rouen: D. Ferrand*, 1642. London:Wellcome.
642/101

——[Anr issue]. *Rouen: D. Loudet*, 1642. DNLM.
642/102

Planis Campy, David de. La chirurgie chimique medicale. *Rouen: J. Cailloüe*, 1642. 2 pts; 8vo. 1st publ., Paris, 1621, under title *La petite chirurgie chimique medicale.* DNLM; London:Wellcome.
642/103

Portugal. Treaties, etc., 1640–1656 (John IV). Tractaet van bestant ende ophoudinge van alle Acten van vyandtschap, als oock van traffijcq, commercien ende secours, gemaeckt . . . den twaelfden Junii 1641. *The Hague: Widow & Heirs of H. Jacobszoon van Wouw*, 1642. [16] p.; 4to. Transl. from the *Tractatus induciarum* of this year below. Sabin 96517; Borba de Moraes II:313; Rodrigues (Dom. Hol.) 624; Asher 178; Knuttel 4875. CtY, DLC, MH, NN-RB, RPJCB; The Hague:KB.
642/104

——. Tractatus induciarum & cessationus omnis hostilitatis actus, ut & navigationis ac commercij, pariterque succurssus factus, initus & conclusus Hagae Comitis die duodecimâ Junii 1641. *The Hague: Widow & Heirs of H. Jacobszoon van Wouw,* 1642. [15] p.; 4to. Includes refs to Brazilian & West Indian claims of Portuguese & Dutch. Sabin 96518; Borba de Moraes II:311; Asher 176; Knuttel 4874. ICN; BL, The Hague:KB.
642/105

——. Trattado das tregoas e suspensãó de todo o acto de hostilidade ebem assi de navegação, comercio ejuntamente soccorro . . . *The Hague: Widow & Heirs of H. Jacobszoon van Wouw,* 1642. [14] p.; 4to. Transl. from the *Tractatus induciarum* of this year above. Sabin 96519; Borba de Moraes II:315; Rodrigues (Dom. Hol.) 622; Maggs Cat. 479 (Americana V):4246; Knuttel 4876. CtY, DLC, MnU-B, RPJCB; The Hague:KB.
642/106

—[Anr edn]. Tregoas entre o prudentissimo Rey Dom Joam o IV. de Portugal & os poderosos estados das Provincias Unidas. *Lisbon: A. Alvarez,* 1642. [16] p.; 4to. Sabin 96520; Borba de Moraes II:314–15; Rodrigues (Dom. Hol.) 623; Maggs Cat. 479 (Americana V):4244. BL.
642/107

Pym, John. A speech delivered in Parliament by a worthy member thereof. *London: R. Lowndes,* 1642. 40 p.; 4to. 1st publ., London, 1641. Cf. Wing P4285. CSmH, DLC, ICN, MH, NNC; BL.
642/108

Quintanadueñas, Antonio de, S. J. Explicacion de la Bula de Urbano VIII. que prohibe en Sevilla y su arzobispado el uso de tabaco en las iglesias, sus patios y ambitos. *Seville: S. Fajardo,* 1642. 40 p.; 4to. Medina (BHA) 1040; Escudero (Seville) 1.573; Palau 244918. Seville:BM.
642/109

Relación de algunas perdidas, que tuvo Filippe IV. rey de Castilla, para siempre jámás. *Lisbon: D. Lopez Rosa,* 1642. [7] p.; 4to. Amongst the losses enumerated are those in Brazil. Palau 258254; Maggs Cat. 502 (Americana VII):5071. MH.
642/110

Relacion del sucesso que tuvo Francisco Diaz Pimienta, general de la Real Armada de las Indias, en la isla de santa Catalina. Dase cuenta como la tomò a los enemigos que la posseìan, enchandolos della. *Madrid: J. Sánchez,* 1642. [6] p.; fol. The island of Santa Catalina, 'noventa leguas distante de Cartagena de las Indias' had been occupied by English settlers who grew tobacco & engaged in piracy. Sabin 62885; Medina (BHA) 1041; Palau 258262; Maggs Cat. 479 (Americana V):4248; JCB (3) II:297. RPJCB.
642/111

—[Anr edn.] *Seville: F. de Lyra,* 1642. [12] p.; 4to. Sabin 62886; Medina (BHA) 1042; Palau 258263; JCB (3) II:297–98. RPJCB.
642/112

Rosaccio, Giuseppe. Teatro del cielo e della terra. *Treviso: G. Righettini,* 1642. 141 p.; illus., maps; 8vo. 1st publ., Brescia, 1592. Includes a description & map of America. Cf. Sabin 73198. CtY, DLC, NNH; BL.
642/113

Rowlands, Samuel. Doctor Merrie-man: or, Nothing but mirth. *London: J. D[awson]., for S. Rand,* 1642. 4to. In verse. 1st publ., London, 1607, under title *Democritus, or, Doctor Merry-man his medicines.* Wing R2080A. DFo.
642/114

Rudyerd, Sir Benjamin. Two speeches in Parliament: The one concerning religion . . . The other concerning a West Indie Association at a committee of the whole House . . . 21. Jacobi. *London: B. A[lsop]., for H. Seile,* 1642. Wing R2203; McAlpin II:164. CLU-C, CtY, ICU, MH, NN-RB, RPJCB; BL.
642/115

Ruiz de Montoya, Antonio, S.J. Señor: Antonio Ruiz de Montoya . . . procurador de la provincia del Paraguay y Rio de la Plata, dize: Que Don Pedro de Lugo . . . fué proveido por governador del Paraguay [etc.]. [*Madrid:* 1642?]. [3] p.; fol. Memorial to king of Spain defending Jesuits from charges against them, esp. in relations with Indians. Medina (BHA) 6845; Streit II:1723.
642/116

Saavedra Fajardo, Diego de. Idea de un principe christiano. *Milan:* 1642. *See the year* 1643.

Saint-Amant, Marc Antoine de Gérard, sieur de. Les oeuvres. *Rouen: J. Boulley,* 1642. 276 p.; 12mo. In verse. 1st publ., Paris, 1629. Tchémerzine X:83. BN
642/117

—[Anr issue]. *Rouen: D. Ferrand,* 1642. 12mo.

Tchémerzine X:83. BL (Gérard, M. A. de).
642/118

—[Anr edn]. *Paris: T. Quinet*, 1642–43. 3 pts; 4to. Cioranescu (XVII) 60675; Arents (Add.) 318. DLC, MH, NN-A, PU; BN.
642/119

Sala, Gaspar de, O.S.A. Secrets publiques de la Catalogne, ou La pierre de touche des intentions de l'enemy . . . Traduit fidelement de catalan. *Rouen: J. Berthelin*, 1642. 44 p.; 4to. Transl. from Sala's *Secrets publichs*, [Barcelona, 1641]. Palau 285723.
642/120

Saltonstall, Charles. The navigator . . . Second edition. *London: [B. Alsop & T. Fawcet?] for G. Hurlock*, 1642. 124 p.; illus., port.; 4to. 1st publ., London, 1636. Sabin 75852; Wing S508. RPJCB (imp.); Oxford: Bodl.
642/121

Scott, Thomas. The wicked plots and practises of the Spaniards against the seventeen provinces of the Netherlands. [*London:* 1642]. *See* Ofwod, Stephen, *above*.

Shepard, Thomas. The sincere convert. *London: T. P[aine] & M. S[immons].*, *for H. Blunden*, 1642. 266 p.; 8vo. 1st publ., London, 1640. Sabin 80219; Wing S3118A. ICN.
642/122

Solorzano Pereira, Juan de. Memorial, o discurso informativo . . . de los derechos, honores . . . i otras cosas, que se debendar . . . a los consejeros. *Madrid: F. Martínez*, 1642. 272 p.; 4to. Sabin 86533; Medina (BHA) 1044; Palau 318994. InU-L, RPJCB, UU; BL.
642/123

The speech of a cavaleere to his comrades. *London:* 1642. 4 lvs; 4to. A satire with several refs to tobacco. Wing S4858; Arents (Add.) 320. CtY, NN-A; BL, Dublin:Trinity.
642/124

Stratenus, Gulielmus, praeses. Disputationum medicarum de erroribus popularis, secunda de abusu tabaci. *Utrecht: A. Roman*, 1542 [i.e., 1642?]. [8] p.; 4to. Henricus Wils, respondent. MH.
642/125

Tassoni, Alessandro. La secchia rapita, poema eroicomico . . . e 'l primo canto dell'Oceano. *Venice:* 1642. 388 p.; 12mo. 1st publ., Paris, 1622. Cf. Sabin 94402; Puliatti (Tassoni) 106. MH, NcD; BN.
642/126

Taylor, John, the Water-poet. The devil turn'd Round-head: or, Pluto become a Brownist. [*London:* 1642]. [8] p.; 4to. The Puritans of New England are mentioned. Sabin 94477; Wing T449. CSmH, CtY, InU-L, MH; BL.
642/127

——. St. Hillaries teares. Shed upon all professions. *London: N. V[avasour]. & J. B[eckett?].*, 1642. 4 lvs; 4to. Tobacco shops are mentioned. Wing T507. MH, NNUT; BL.
642/128

—[Anr edn]. *London:* 1642. 4to. Wing T508; Arents (Add.) 321. CSmH, NN-A, TxU; BL.
642/129

Torsellino, Orazio, S.J. Ristretto delle historie del mondo . . . volgarizate dal sig. Lodovico Aurelii. *Venice: C. Tomasini*, 1642. 703 p.; 12mo. 1st publ. as here transl. from Latin text (1st publ., Rome, 1598), Rome, 1634. BN.
642/130

Veen, Jan van der. Over-zeesche zege, en Bruylofts-zangen . . . De derde druk. *Haarlem:* 1642. 476 p.; obl. 16mo. 1st publ., Haarlem, 1641 (?); here a reissue of the 'derde druk' of that year? BL.
642/131

——. Zinne-beelden, oft Adams appel. *Amsterdam: E. Cloppenburg*, 1642. 523 p.; illus.; 4to. Includes author's poem 'Siet den getaanden speck', 1st publ., [Haarlem? 1629]. CLU, DFo, ICN, NNC; BL.
642/132

Vimont, Barthélemy, S.J. Relation de ce qui s'est passé en la Nouvelle France, es années 1640 et 1641. *Paris: S. Cramoisy*, 1642. 2 pts; 8vo. Pt 2 comprises Jérôme Lallemant's *Relation de ce qui s'est passé . . . en la mission . . . Aux Hurons*. For variant states see McCoy. Sabin 99749; Harrisse (NF) 77; Bell (Jes. rel.) 19; McCoy 40-43; Streit II:2535; Church 455; JCB (3) II:299–300. CSmH, CtY, DLC, ICN, InU-L, MH, MiU-C, MnU-B, NN-RB, RPJCB; BL, BN.
642/133

Wecker, Johann Jakob. Antidotarium generale et speciale. *Basel: J. J. Genath, for Heirs of L. König*, 1642. 2 pts; illus.; 4to. 1st publ., Basel, 1574 & 1576; cf. 1601 edn. CaBVaU, DNLM.
642/134

Zeiller, Martin. Ein hundert Episteln, oder Sendschreiben . . . Jetzt zum andernmal fleissig durchsehen und . . . vermehrt. *Ulm: J. Görlin*, 1642. 614 p.; 8vo. 1st publ., Heilbronn & Ulm, 1640. Cf. Sabin 106295; cf. Jördens V:600. RPJCB.
642/135

1643

Abreu y Figueroa, Fernando de, O.S.A.
Señor. El maestro fr. Fernando de Abreu
y Figueroa . . . Dize, que el año de 36. que
vino . . . a ruego del maestro de campo
don Pedro Estevan Davila governador de
Buenos Ayres, para tratar negocios importantes de aquella tierra, y en especial, que
aquel puerto se fortificasse [etc.]. [*Madrid?*
1643?]. [3] p.; fol. Memorial to king of
Spain. Medina (BHA) 6157. BL. 643/1

——. Sumario en hecho, y derecho de lo que
resulta de los memoriales, y decretos que
ha avido en la propuesta que el padre . . .
Fernando de Abreu y Figueroa hizo a su
Magestad . . . el año 1634. sobre retener
los sinodos, ò estipendios que paga en la
Indias a los curas dotrineros [etc.]. [*Madrid?*
1643]. [45] p.; fol. Medina (BHA) 6156.
643/2

Ashe, Simeon. A letter of many ministers.
London: 1643. *See* Ball, John, *below.*

Avity, Pierre d', sieur de Montmartin. Le
monde, ou La description générale de ses
quatre parties . . . Deuxième édition revue,
corrigée et augmentée. *Paris: C. Sonnius &*
D. Bechet, 1643. 7 v. in 5; illus., maps; fol.
1st publ., Paris, 1613, under title *Les estats,*
empires et principautez du monde; cf. 1637 edn
with this title. The 4th vol. has title 'Description de l'Amérique'. NNH; BL, BN.
643/3

—[Anr issue]. *Paris: L. Cottereau,* 1643. Cf.
Borba de Moraes I:53. RPJCB (v. 4 only);
Berlin:StB, Milan:BN. 643/4

Bacon, Francis, viscount St Albans. Nova
Atlantis. *Utrecht: J. van Waesbergen,* 1643. 96
p.; 16mo. 1st publ. in Latin, as transl. by
Bacon from his *New Atlantis* (1st publ., London, 1626) in his *Operum moralium,* London,
1638. Included are incidental refs to America & the West Indies. *In* Joseph Hall, Bp
of Norwich, *Mundus alter, below,* q.v.

Baerle, Kaspar van. Orationum liber, accesserunt alia nonnulla varii et amoenioris
argumenti. *Amsterdam: J. Blaeu,* 1643. 514
p.; 12mo. Includes refs to Brazil. Borba de
Moraes I:65. ICU, IaU, MNS; BN, Stutt-
gart:LB. 643/5

Baker, Sir Richard. A chronicle of the kings
of England. *London: D. Frere,* 1643. 4 pts;

fol. Included are accounts of Drake,
Frobisher, & Raleigh. Wing B501; Arents
220. CSmH, CtY, DFo, ICU, MH, NN-RB;
BL, BN. 643/6

—[Anr issue?]. *London: R. C[otes]. & R. H[odg-*
kinson?]., for D. Frere, 1643. Wing B502.
DFo. 643/7

Balde, Jakob. Lyricorum lib. iv. Epodon lib.
unus. *Munich: Heirs of C. Leysser,* 1643. 318
p.; illus.; 12mo. Includes 2 odes to Sabinus
Fuscus on his departure for Mexico. Backer
I:820, cf. Jantz (German Baroque) 433. CtY,
NjP, OCl; BL, BN. 643/8

Ball, John. A letter of many ministers in Old
England, requesting the judgement of their
reverend brethren in New England. *London:*
T. Underhill, 1643. 90 p.; 4to. Sabin 40355
(& 2171); Wing B583A (& L1573A); McAl-
pin II:219; Church 456; JCB (3) II:300. CtY,
DLC, MH, MWA, MiU-C, NN-RB, RPJCB;
BL. 643/9

Bauderon, Brice. Pharmacopee. *Paris: J. Bes-*
sin, 1643. 2 pts; 8vo. 1st publ., Lyons, 1588,
under title *Paraphrase sur la Pharmacopoee;* cf.
1607 edn. BN. 643/10

Bedenckingen over het thien-hoornigh en
seven-hoofdigh treves ofte pays Munsters-
Monster, by den Paus Urbanum ontfangen
. . . door E. P. [*The Hague?*] 1643. [32] p.;
4to. Includes mention of West Indies. Knuttel 5015. NN; The Hague:KB. 643/11

—[Anr edn]. Bedenckingen over het thien
hoornig en seven-hoofdigh trefves. [*The*
Hague?] 1643. [32] p.; 4to. NN.
643/12

Béguin, Jean. Tyrocinium chymicum. *Venice:*
P. Baleoni, 1643. 480 p.; 8vo. 1st publ., Paris,
1612. In this edn, in bk 2 chapt. ix calls
for use of guaiacum *(lignum sanctum)* in an
'Essentia Chynae'. CtY, DLC, ICU, MBCo,
PU-S; Glasgow:UL. 643/13

Benavides y de la Cueva, Diego, conde de
Santistevan del Puerto, Viceroy of Peru.
Señor. El conde de Santistevan, marques
de Moya, dize: que por cartas del marques
de Villena [etc.]. [*Madrid? 1643?*]. 8 numb.
lvs; fol. Memorial to king of Spain defending writer's father from charges made by
Juan de Palafox y Mendoza. Medina (BHA)
6374. Santiago, Chile:BN. 643/14

Berettari, Sebastiano, S.J. Vita del padre
Gioseffo Anchieta. *Bologna: Heir of Benacci,*

1643. 227 p.; 12mo. 1st publ. in Italian, Turin, 1621. Cf. Sabin 4830; cf. Medina (BHA) 652; cf. Borba de Moraes I:86; Streit II:2397.　643/15

Beverwijck, Jan van. Schat der gesontheyt; verciert met historyen; als oock met verssen van Heer Jacob Cats . . . In desen sesten druck van nieuws oversien. *Amsterdam: Widow of E. Cloppenburg,* 1643. 736 p.; illus.; 8vo. 1st publ., [Dordrecht? 1636?]. Van de Velde 95. DFo; Ghent:BU.　643/16

――. Van de uitnementheyt des vrouwelicken geslachts. Verçiert met historyen . . . als oock latijnsche ende nederlantsche verssen van Corn. Boy. In desen tweeden druck op verscheyde plaetschen vermeerdert. *Dordrecht: H. van Esch, for J. Gorisszoon,* 1643. 3 pts; illus., ports; 8vo. 1st publ. in Dutch, Dordrecht, 1639. Grässe I:357–58. ICU, MH, NNC, PPeSchw; BL.　643/17

—[Anr edn]. *Leyden: H. van der Deyster,* 1643. 8vo. A possible ghost. Abkoude 61.
　643/18

Blaeu, Willem Janszoon. Novus atlas, das ist Welt-beschreibung . . . ander Theil. *Amsterdam: J. & C. Blaeu,* 1643. 1st publ., Amsterdam, 1635. Koeman (Bl) 32B. Tübingen:UB.　643/19

――. The sea-beacon . . . translated out of Dutch . . . by Richard Hynmers. *Amsterdam: J. Blaeu,* 1643–44. 3 pts; illus., maps; fol. 1st publ. in English, Amsterdam, 1625, under title *Sea-mirrour;* here revised and publ. in larger format. Koeman (M.Bl) 51; Wing B3108B. BL, Amsterdam:VBBB.
　643/20

――. Le theatre du monde, ou Nouvel atlas. *Amsterdam: J. Blaeu,* 1643–44. 2 pts; 120 maps; fol. 1st publ. in French, Amsterdam, 1635. Koeman (Bl) 19A. ICN, MiU-C, PPL; BN, Florence:BN.　643/21

――. Theatrum orbis terrarum, sive Atlas novus. *Amsterdam: J. & C. Blaeu,* 1643, '40. 2 pts; 120 maps; fol. 1st publ., Amsterdam, 1635. Koeman (Bl) 21C. MBAt; Rome:Vatican.　643/22

――. Zeespiegel. *Amsterdam: J. Blaeu,* 164[3?]. 3 pts; illus., maps; fol. 1st publ., Amsterdam, 1623. Here pt 3, dated 164[3?], is printed by *J. Blaeu.* Koeman (M.Bl) 37 (I), 37 (III). Rome:Bibl. Palatinum (imp.).　643/23

—[Anr issue?]. *Amsterdam: J. [& C.] Blaeu,* 1643. Here pt 3, dated 164[3], is printed by J. & C. Blaeu. In pts 2 & 3 a '3' has been added in manuscript to the incomplete imprint date. For other differences from the preceding, see Koeman (M.Bl) 37 (I–III). Koeman (M.Bl) 38 (I), 37 (II), 37 (III). Leyden:UB.　643/24

—[Anr edn]. *Amsterdam: J. Blaeu,* 1643–44. 3 pts; illus., maps; fol. Here, pt 3 has 1644 imprint date. Koeman (M.Bl) 38 (n). DLC.
　643/25

Campanella, Tommaso. Civitas solis poetica. Idea reipublicae philosophicae. *Utrecht: J. van Waesbergen,* 1643. 106 p.; 16mo. 1st publ., Frankfurt a. M., 1623, in the author's *Realis philosophiae epilogisticae partes quatuor;* here issued as pt of Joseph Hall, Bp of Norwich, *Mundus alter,* q.v. below.

Cañizares, Martín de, O.S.A. El maestro fr. Martin de Cañizares de la orden de S. Agustin, difinidor, y procurador general de la provincia del nuevo reyno en Indias, con fr. Franc. de la Resurreccion, Descalzo . . . Excepciones . . . en el pleito . . . ante su M. en su Real consejo de Indias, contra la provincia . . . de Granada [i.e., Colombia]. [*Madrid?* ca. 1643?]. 4 lvs; fol. Sabin 56282; Medina (BHA) 6306.　643/26

Canne, Abednego, pseud. A new wind-mil, a new. *'Oxford: L. Lichfield'* [i.e., *London*]: 1643. 6 p.; 4to. Contains purported letter from Boston, satirizing Puritan objection to display of cross. Sabin 10688; Madan (Oxford) II:1389; Wing N797. CtY; BL, Oxford:Bodl.　643/27

Cárdenas, Alonso de. A speech, or complaint, lately made by the Spanish embassadour to his Majestie at Oxford, upon occasion of the taking of a ship called Sancta Clara in the port of Sancto Domingo, richly laden with plate, cocheneal, and other commodoties of great value . . . Translated out of the Spanish, in Oxford, by S[igno]r Torriano, an Italian. *London: N. Butter,* 1643. 8 p.; 4to. Madan (Oxford) II:1191; Wing C496; Thomason I:213. DLC, MH, MiU-C, MnU-B, RPJCB; BL.
　643/28

Casas, Bartolomé de las, O.P., Bp of Chiapa. Istoria, ò Brevissima relatione della distruttione dell'Indie Occidentali . . . Conforme al suo vero originale spagnnuolo già stampato in Siviglia. Tradotta . . . dell'eccell. sig. Giacomo Castellani, già sotto nome di Francesco Bersabita [pseud.]. *Venice: M. Ginammi,* 1643. 150 p.; 4to. 1st publ. in this translation, Venice, 1626. Text in both Spanish & Italian in parallel columns. Sabin 11244; Medina (BHA) 1085n (II:473); Hanke/Giménez 536; Streit II:446; JCB (3) II:228. CtY, DLC, MH, MiU-C, NN-RB, PU, RPJCB; BL, BN. 643/29

Cats, Jacob. 's Werelts begin, midden, eynde. *Amsterdam: N. van Ravesteyn, for E. Cloppenburg,* 1643. 1 v.; illus., port.; 4to. 1st publ., Dordrecht, 1637. Mus. Cats. 175. Leyden:UB. 643/30

Certain inducements to well minded people, who are here straitned in their estates . . . to transport themselves, or some servants, or agents for them into the West-Indies, for the propagating of the Gospel and increase of trade. [*London:* 1643?]. 16 p.; 4to. Provides glowing account of foodstuffs & other products readily available in the Caribbean. Sabin 11709; Wing C1701; JCB (3) II:314. ICU, RPJCB; BL. 643/31

Clément, Claude, S.J. Tabla chronologica de los descubrimientos, conquistas, fundaciones, poblaciones, y otras cosas ilustres. *Madrid: D. Dìaz de la Carrera,* 1643. bds.; fol. 1st publ., Madrid, 1642. NNH. 643/32

——. Tablas chronologicas, en que se contienen los sucesos eclesiásticos y seculares de España, Africa, Indias Orientales y Occidentales desde su principio hasta el año 1642. *Madrid: D. Díaz de la Carrera,* 1643. fol. Medina (BHA) 1047; Streit I:489; Backer II:1227; Palau 190949. 643/33

Colmenero de Ledesma, Antonio. Du chocolate, discours curieux . . . traduit de l'espagnol . . . et eclaircy de quelques annotations par René Moreau . . . Plus est adjousté un dialogue touchent le meme chocolate par Marradon. *Paris: S. Cramoisy,* 1643. 59 p.; 4to. Transl. from the author's *Curioso tratado,* 1st publ., Madrid, 1631; Marradon's dialogue here extracted from his *Dialogo . . . de tabaco,* 1st publ., Seville, 1618. Sabin 14544; Müller 51; Palau 56905; Arents (Add.) 324. DNLM, MH-A, NN-A; BL, BN. 643/34

Compagnie de la Nouvelle France. Extraict des registres du Conseil d'estat. Entre les directeurs de la Compagnie generale de la Nouvelle France . . . en execution de l'arrest . . . du 5. fevrier 1642 . . . et messire Jacques Bordier [etc.]. [*Paris:* 1643]. 26 p.; fol. MnU-B. 643/35

Córdoba y Salinas, Diego de, O.F.M. Vida, virtudes, y milagros del apostol del Peru el venerable p[adr],e fray Francisco Solano . . . En . . . segunda edicion añadida por . . . fray Alonso de Mendieta. *Madrid: Imprenta Real,* 1643. 686 p.; 4to. 1st publ., Lima, 1630. Sabin 86228; Medina (BHA) 1048; Streit II:1716; Palau 61941n. BL, Santiago, Chile:BN. 643/36

Cotton, John. A letter of Mr. John Cottons, teacher of the church in Boston in New England, to Mr. [Roger] Williams a preacher there. *London: B. Allen,* 1643. 13 p.; 4to. Sabin 17069; Tuttle (Cotton) 27; Wing C6441; JCB (3) II:303. CtY, DLC, MH, RPJCB; BL, Oxford:Balliol. 643/37

Croll, Oswald. Basilica chymica . . . Additus est . . . Tractatus novus de signaturis rerum internis. *Geneva: P. Chouët,* 1643. 2 pts; illus.; 8vo. 1st publ., Frankfurt a. M., 1609. CtY, DNLM, ICU, MH, MiU, NNNAM, PPL; BL. 643/38

——[Anr edn]. *Venice: Combi,* 1643. 469 p.; 8vo. CSt, PU-S; BN. 643/39

Digby, Sir Kenelm. Observations upon Religio medici. *London: R. C[otes]., for D. Frere,* 1643. 124 p.; 8vo. Includes ref. to addictive properties of tobacco. Keynes (Browne) 218; Wing D1442; Arents 221. CSmH, CtY-M, MH, NN-A; BL. 643/40

——[Anr issue]. *London: R. C[otes]., for L. Chapman & D. Frere,* 1643. Keynes (Browne) 219; Wing D1441; Arents 221n. CtY-M, MH; Cambridge:UL. 643/41

Directeurs compagnie binnen Middelburgh in Zeelant, bestaende in acht schepen ghedestineert tot veylinghe vande zee . . . mitsgaders de voordeelen ende premien daer op ghestelt, door ordre vande . . . Staten Generael. *Middelburg: Z. Roman,* 1643. [12] p.; 4to. Relates to the West-Indische Compagnie. Knuttel 5020. The Hague:KB. 643/42

Durante, Castore. Il tesoro della sanità. *Venice: D. Imberti,* 1643. 324 p.; 8vo. 1st publ.,

[Rome?], 1586; cf. 1601 edn. Michel (Répertoire) II:191. Aix-en-Province:Bibl. Méjanes.   643/43

Entremeses nuevos. De diversos autores. Para honesta recreacion. *Alcalá de Henares: F. Ropero,* 1643. 119 numb. lvs; 8vo. Includes dialogue *Las sombras,* containing mention of defense of Brazil & Puerto Rico, & another dialogue on tobacco. Palau 80102.   643/44

Fernel, Jean. Universa medicina. *Geneva: P. Chouët,* 1643. 3 pts; 8vo. 1st publ. as here constituted, Paris, 1567; cf. 1601–2 edn. Sherrington (Fernel) 83.J27. London:Wellcome, Paris:Faculté de Médecine.
    643/45

Focanus, Jacobus. Adoni-Beseck, of Lex talionis, dat is, Rechtveerdighe straffe Godts over den tyrannen . . . De derde editie. *Leeuwarden: G. Sybes,* 1643. 238 p.; 4to. Prob. 1st publ. in 1622; cf. 1629 edn. NNC.
    643/46

Fournier, Georges, S.J. Hydrographie, contenant la theorie et la practique de toutes les parties de la navigation. *Paris: M. Soly,* 1643. 922 p.; fol. Included are refs to the Americas, e.g., in bk iv, chapt. xxi, 'Des navigations angloises' & in bk xviii, possibility of a canal across the isthmus of Panama. Backer III:909. BL, BN.   643/47

Fragoso, Juan. Cirugia universal aora nuevamente añadida . . . Nuevamente enmendada en esta octava impression. *Madrid: C. Sánchez, for D. de Palacio y Villegas,* 1643. 2 pts; fol. 1st publ., Madrid, 1581; cf. 1607 edn. Palau 94187. London:Wellcome.
    643/48

Geslin, Paul. Die heilige Weltsbeschreibung . . . Verfertigt in frantzösischer Sprache . . . und . . . übergesetzt. *Köthen:* 1643. 58 p.; 4to. Transl. by Ludwig, prince of Anhalt-Köthen, from Geslin's *La saincte chorographie,* 1st publ., Saumur, 1629, but more prob. from the Amsterdam, 1641 edn. Cf. Jöcher (Suppl.) II:1433. CtY; BL.   643/49

Gesner, Konrad. Secrets de medecine, et la philosophie chimique, par m. Jean Liebault. *Rouen: N. L'Oyselet,* 1643. 297 p.; illus.; 8vo. 1st publ. as transl. by Liébault, Paris, 1573; cf. 1616 edn. Ferguson (Bibl. chem.) II:36. BN.   643/50

Gölnitz, Abraham. Compendium geographicum succinctá methodo adornatum. *Amsterdam: L. Elsevier,* 1643. 278 p.; 12mo. Chapts xviii–xx concern America. For variants, see Rahir as cited. Willems (Les Elzevier) 1000; Rahir (Les Elzevier) 994–996. CtY, IEN, MiU-C, NjP; BL, BN.
    643/51

Góngora y Argote, Luis de. Todas las obras. *Saragossa: P. Verges, for P. Escuer,* 1643. 120 numb. lvs; 12mo. In verse. Included is Góngora's *Soledades,* 1st publ., Madrid, 1627, in his *Obras en verso.* Palau 104629. NNH.   643/52

González de Mendoza, Juan, Bp. Histoire du grand royaume de la Chine situé aux Indes Orientales . . . nouvellement traduite de Latin. *Rouen: N. Angot,* 1643. 388 p.; 8vo. 1st publ. in French, Paris, 1588; cf. 1606 edn. InU-L.   643/53

Goulart, Simon. Der weise Alte . . . Aus dem frantzösischen . . . versetzet. *Köthen:* 1643. 187 p.; 4to. Transl. by Ludwig, prince of Anhalt-Köthen from Goulart's *Le sage vieillard,* 1st publ., Lyons, 1605. Jones (Goulart) 60(d). CtY; BL.   643/54

Great Britain. Laws, statutes, etc., 1625–1649 (Charles I). An order of Parliament for the putting in due execution . . . the statutes made for the observation of the Sabath day. *[London:] R. Cotes,* 1643. 4 lvs; 4to. Forbids, *inter alia,* use of tobacco in taverns, etc., on Sunday. Wing E1692; Arents (Add.) 325. DFo, MH, NN-A; BL.
    643/55

——. An ordinance of the Lords and Commons . . . concerning the excise of tobacco. *London: R. Cotes & J. Raworth,* 1643. 6 p.; 4to. Wing E1821. DFo, DLC, MH; London: Wellcome.   643/56

—[Anr edn]. *London: R. Cotes & J. Raworth* [1643]. 8 p.; 4to. Wing E1822; Arents 222; JCB (3) II:316. DLC, MH, NN-A, RPJCB; BL.   643/57

——. An ordinance of the Lords and Commons . . . whereby Robert earle of Warwicke is made governour in chiefe . . . of all those islands and other plantations . . . belonging to . . . the King of Englands subjects, within the bounds, and upon the coasts of America. *London: J. Wright,* 1643.

6 p.; 4to. Sabin 57510; Wing (2) E2104; JCB (3) 2104. CSmH, DFo, ICN, NN-RB, RPJCB; BL. 643/58

Great Britain. Sovereigns, etc., 1625–1649 (Charles I). A proclamation prohibiting the buying or disposing of any the lading of the ship . . . Sancta Clara. [*Oxford: L. Lichfield*, 1643]. bds.; fol. The ship, carrying silver, cochineal, etc., had been seized from Spanish owners at Santo Domingo; cf. entry under Cardenas, Alonso de, above. Cf. Crawford (Roy. procl.) 2338; Madan (Oxford) 1158; Wing C2691. Oxford:Bodl. 643/59

—[Anr edn]. [*London: A. Norton?* 1643]. bds.; fol. Crawford (Roy. procl.) 2338. CtY, MH; BL. 643/60

——. A proclamation to give assurance unto all His Majesties subjects in the islands and continent of America, of His Majesties royall care over them, and to preserve them in their due obedience. [*Oxford: L. Lichfield*, 1643]. bds.; fol. Crawford (Roy. procl.) 2512; Brigham (Roy. procl.) 94–96; Madan (Oxford) 1643: 1493; Wing C2701. Oxford:Bodl. 643/61

Grenaille, François de, sieur de Chatounières. Le mercure Portugais, ou Relations politiques de la . . . révolution d'Estat arrivée en Portugal depuis la mort de D. Sebastien jusques au couronnement de D. Jean IV. *Paris: A. de Sommaville & A. Courbé*, 1643. 483 (i.e., 683) p.; 8vo. The final chapter contains a brief description of Brazil. ICN; BL, BN. 643/62

Grotius, Hugo. De jure belli ac pacis libri tres. *Amsterdam:* 1643. 1st publ., Paris, 1625. WU. 643/63

——. De origine gentium Americanarum dissertatio. *Paris: G. Pelé*, 1643. 1st publ., [Paris?], 1642. Sabin 28957. 643/64

——. De origine gentium Americanarum dissertatio altera, adversus obtrectatorem. *Paris: S. Cramoisy*, 1643. 35 p.; 8vo. A reply to Laet's *Notae* of this year below; cf. Grotius's *De origine gentium Americanarum*, 1st publ., [Paris?], 1642. Cf. Sabin 28957n; Meulen/Diermanse 731; JCB (3) II:304. ICN, NN-RB, RPJCB; BN, Leyden:UB. 643/65

—[Anr edn]. Dissertatio altera de origine gen-

tium Americanarum, adversus obtrectatorem. [*Paris? S. Cramoisy?*] 1643. 30 p.; 8vo. Sabin 28957n; Meulen/Diermanse 732. MiU-L; BL, Amsterdam:UB. 643/66

Hall, Joseph, Bp of Norwich. Mundus alter et idem . . . Accessit . . . Thomae Campanellae, Civitas solis. Et Nova Atlantis. Franc. Baconis. *Utrecht: J. van Waesbergen*, 1643. 3 pts; illus., maps; 12mo. Hall's *Mundus alter* 1st publ., [London, 1605?]; Campanella's *Civitas solis*, Frankfurt a. M., 1623, in his *Reales philosophiae epilogisticae partes quatuor;* and Bacon's *Nova Atlantis*, transl. from his *New Atlantis* (1st publ., London, 1626), 1st publ. in Latin in his *Operum moralium*, London, 1638. Sabin 29819n; Gibson (Bacon) 213; Arents (Add.) 326; JCB (3) II:301. CLU-C, CtY, DLC, MiU, NN-RB, RPJCB; BL, BN. 643/67

Harsdörffer, Georg Philipp. Gesprachspiele . . . Dritter Theil . . . verfasset durch einen Mitgenossen der . . . Fruchtbringenden Geselschaft. *Nuremberg: W. Endter*, 1643. 472 p.; illus., music.; obl. 8vo. In chapt. cxxxii, sect.15 includes poem on smoking of tobacco. Forms pt 3 of the author's *Frauenzimmer Gesprechspiele*, Nuremberg, 1641–49. Goedeke III:108; Faber du Faur 502. CU, CtY, DLC; BL. 643/68

Hay, Paul, sieur du Chastelet (1592–1636), ed. Recueil de diverses pieces pour servir a l'histoire. [*Paris:*] 1643. 1025 p.; 4to. 1st publ., [Paris], 1635. DLC, IU, MH, MnU, NIC. 643/69

Heyden, Hermann van der. Discours et advis sur les flus du ventre douloureux. *Ghent: S. Manilius*, 1643. 120 p.; 4to. Reports use of cinchona for treatment of fever. CtY-M, DNLM; BN. 643/70

Ireland. Lords Justices and Council. We haveing taken into our . . . *Dublin: W. Bladen*, 1643. bds.; fol. For laying an impost on tobacco. Crawford (Roy. procl.) Ireland:387; Wing I 686. Dublin:PRO (destroyed). 643/71

James I, King of Great Britain. King James his Apopthegmes; or, Table-talke. *London: B. W.*, 1643. 14 p.; 4to. Includes attack on tobacco. Wing J127; Arents (Add.) 323. MH, NN-A; BL, BN. 643/72

Journael vande Nassausche vloot . . . Wy

hebben hier noch achter by gevoeght een Beschryvinghe vande regeringe van Peru door Pedro de Madriga . . . Als mede een verhael van Pedro Fernandez de Quir, aengaende de ontdeckinge van 't onbekent Austrialia. *Amsterdam: J. P. Wachter,* 1643. 122 p.; illus., maps; 4to. 1st publ., Amsterdam, 1626. Also issued as pt. 2 of the *Journalen van drie voyagien* of this year below, q.v. Sabin 31504 & 11607; Muller (1872) 1933; Tiele-Muller 76; Tiele 666; JCB (3) II:306. RPJCB. 643/73

Journalen van drie voyagien, te weten: 1. Van Mr. Thomas Candish . . . 2. Vande Heer Fransoys Draeck . . . Nassausche vloot, 3. ofte Beschryvinge vande voyagie . . . vanden Admirael Jaques L'Heremite . . . by ghevoeght een Beschrijvinghe vande regeringhe van Peru, door Pedro de Madriga. *Amsterdam: J. P. Wachter,* 1643. 2 pts; illus., maps; 4to. Includes Pretty's *Beschryvinge vande overtreffelijcke . . . zee-vaerdt,* 1st publ., Amsterdam, 1598; cf. 1617 edn. The *Journael vande Nassausche vloot,* 1st publ., Amsterdam, 1626, has special t.p. & separate paging & signatures. Sabin 11607; Borba de Moraes I:149; Tiele-Muller 282; Tiele 569; JCB (3) II:305. ICN, NN-RB, RPJCB; BL (imp.). 643/74

Kircher, Athanasius. Magnes, sive De arte magnetica opus tripartitum . . . Editio secunda post romanum multò emendatior. *Cologne: J. Kalckhoven,* 1643. 797 p.; illus.; 4to. 1st publ., Rome, 1641. CSt, CtY, DLC, ICJ, MH, MnU, NN, PPF; BL, BN. 643/75

Laet, Joannes de. Notae ad dissertationem Hugonis Grotii De origine gentium Americanarum. *Amsterdam: L. Elsevier,* 1643. 223 p.; 8vo. Refutes Grotius's *De origine gentium Americanarum,* 1st publ., [Paris?], 1642, the text of which is here reprinted. Included, p. 140–51, are comparative vocabularies of some European & American Indian languages. In this issue, printer's name appears as 'Elzevirium'; title of Grotius's work in italics. Sabin 38561n; Borba de Moraes I:385; Meulen/Diermanse 727; Willems (Les Elzevier) 997; JCB (3) II:305–6. DLC, IEN, MH, MiU-C, NN-RB, PPL, RPJCB; BL, BN. 643/76

—[Anr issue]. *Amsterdam: L. Elsevier,* 1643. In this issue, printer's name appears as 'Elzevi-

rivm'; title of Grotius's work is in roman. Meulen/Diermanse 727.3. CtY, DLC, IU, InU-L, MB, MiU-C, NN-RB, PU, RPJCB; The Hague:KB. 643/77

—[Anr edn]. *Paris: Widow of G. Pelé,* 1643. 223 p.; 8vo. Sabin 38561; Borba de Moraes I:385; Meulen/Diermanse 728; JCB (3) II:306. DLC, MH, NN-RB, PPM, RPJCB, WU; BL, BN. 643/78

Lallemant, Jérôme, S.J. Relation de ce qui s'est passé en la mission des Hurons. *Paris:* 1643. *See* Barthélemy Vimont's *Relation* below.

Liébault, Jean. Warhaffte Beschreibung dess edelen Krauts Nicotianae . . . von uns Teutschen Taback genennet . . . wie es auss Florida in Portugal . . . kommen . . . Erstlichen von Carolo Stephano und Johanne Libaldo in frantzösischer, hernacher aber von Melchiore Sebitio . . . und Joanne Fischardo . . . in unsere teutsche Sprach an Tag gegeben. Jetzunder aber . . . vermehret und verbessert. [*Frankfurt a. M.?*] 1643. 10 lvs; illus.; 4to. Extracted from Charles Estienne's *Siben Bücher von dem Feldbau,* 1st publ., Strassburg, 1579, itself transl. from the Paris, 1578, edn of Estienne's *L'agriculture,* as expanded by Liébault. Probably a pirated edn. Ferguson (Bibl. chem.) II:36; Arents 223. NN-A. 643/79

Liebergen, Arnout van. Apologiae, ofte Waerachtighe verantwoordinghe . . . over de enorme . . . proceduren tegens zijnen persoon gebruyckt by de gewesene Hooge Raden van Brasil, wegen eenige gedeclareerde verraders, als Gabriel Soaris ende Franciscus Vas, cum Socis [!]. *Amsterdam: The author,* 1643. 182 p.; 4to. Sabin 40988; Borba de Moraes I:412; Asher 183; Knuttel 5022. BL, The Hague:KB. 643/80

Lopes, Francisco. Milagroso successo do Conde de Castel Milhor . . . Em verso. *Lisbon: M. da Silva,* 1643. 15 numb. lvs; 8vo. Innocencio II:421; Maggs Cat. 502 (Americana VII):5072. CtY, MH. 643/81

Massachusetts (Colony). Laws, statutes, etc. The capitall lawes of New-England, as they stand now in force in the common-wealth. By the Court, in the years 1641. 1642. *London: B. Allen,* 1643. bds.; fol. Reprinted from Cambridge, Mass., test of 1642 of which no copy is today known. Wing C479; Thomason I:229. BL. 643/82

Mexía, Pedro. Les diverses leçons . . . Mises de castillan en françois par Claude Gruget . . . Avec sept dialogues de l'autheur . . . quartriesme edition. *Rouen: J. Berthelin,* 1643. 1032 p.; 8vo. Cioranescu (Bibl. francoespañola) 2053; Palau 167328. BN, Madrid: BN. 643/83

More, Sir Thomas, Saint. L'Utopie . . . traduicte par Samuel Sorbiere. *Amsterdam: J. Blaeu,* 1643. 210 p.; 12mo. Transl. from Latin text, 1st publ., Louvain, 1516. Set in New World, with ref. to Vespucci's voyages. Gibson (More) 21; Willems (Les Elzevier) 1628. CtY, MH, MiU, NjP; BL, BN. 643/84

Morisot, Claude Barthélemy. Orbis maritimi, sive Rerum in mari et littoribus gestarum generalis historia. *Dijon: P. Palliot,* 1643. 725 p.; illus., maps; fol. In bk 2, chapt. xvii, 'Anglorum res mari gestae', chapt. xx, 'Imperiorum Hispanorum maritinum', & chapts xxxiv–xxxvii deal with American matters. Sabin 50723; Borba de Moraes II:87–88; JCB (3) II:307–8. CtY, DFo, ICN, MH, MiU-C, MnU-B, NNH, PPL, RPJCB; BL, BN. 643/85

Moscherosch, Johann Michael. Visiones de don Quevedo; Wunderliche und warhaffte Gesichte Philanders von Sittewalt [pseud.]. *Strassburg: J. P. Mülbe,* 1643. 2 pts; 8vo. 1st publ., Strassburg, [1640]. Bechtold 'C'; cf. Goedeke III:233–34. Berlin:StB; Nuremberg:Germ. Mus. 643/86

New Englands first fruits; in respect. First of the conversion . . . of the Indians. 2. Of the progresse of learning, in the Colledge at Cambridge in Massacusets Bay. *London: R. O[ulton]. & G. D[exter]., for H. Overton,* 1643. 26 p.; 4to. The 1st of the 11 pamphlets known as the Eliot Indian tracts. Sabin 52758; Vail (Frontier) 98; Wing E519; Church 458; JCB (3) II:308. CSmH, CtY, DLC, ICN, MH, NN-RB, PPL, RPJCB; BL. 643/87

Nieremberg, Juan Eusebio, S.J. Curiosa y occulta filosofia. Primera y segunda parte de las maravillas de la naturaleza . . . Tercera impression añadida por el mismo autor. *Madrid: Imprenta Real, for J. A. Bonet,* 1643. 438 p.; 4to. 1st publ., Madrid, 1630,

with here added the *Oculta filosofia* of 1638. Backer V:1730; Palau 190667. NNNAM, WU; BL. 643/88

——. Ideas de virtud en algunos claros varones de la Compañia de Jesus. *Madrid: María de Quiñones,* 1643. 804 p.; fol. Includes accounts of Jesuits who served in New World. Sabin 55269; Medina (BHA) 1053; Streit I:491; Backer V:1746; JCB (3) II:308. DLC, RPJCB; BN. 643/89

Noodige bedenckingen der troughertighe Nederlanders over de aen-staende Munstersche handelinghe van vrede. [*The Hague?*] 1643. [32] p.; 4to. Includes mentions of Dutch conquests in West Indies & Brazil. For variant see Knuttel. Knuttel 5014. The Hague:KB. 643/90

Observations upon Prince Rupert's white dogge, called Boye: carefully taken by T. B. [*London:*] 1642 [i.e., 1643]. 10 p.; 4to. Satire upon Puritans with ref. to the 'Colonies of new England' as perhaps coming to the aid of King Charles's opponents. Sabin 2558; Wing B194; Thomason I:229 (2 Feb. 1643). CtY, ICN, MH, MnU, TxU; BL. 643/91

Olearius, Adam. Lustige Historia, woher das Taback-trincken kompt. [*Hamburg?*] 1643. [8] p.; 4to. Lohmeier (Olearius) 8c; Arents 224. MH, MH-BA, NN-A; Göttingen:StUB. 643/92

Pasquier, Etienne. Les recherches de la France. *Paris: P. Ménard,* 1643. 1019 p.; port.; 4to. 1st publ. with American content, Paris, 1596; cf. the 1607 edn, the American ref. here appearing in chapt. xxviii of bk 4. Thickett (Pasquier) 17. CtY-M, DLC, ICN, InU, MH, NjP; London:Wellcome, BN. 643/93

Pharmacopoea Amstelredamensis . . . Editio quarta. *Amsterdam: J. Blaeu,* 1643. 12mo. 1st publ., Amsterdam, 1636. 643/94

Pharmacopoea Burdigalensis, seu Descriptio medicamentorum. *Bordeaux: G. Millanges,* 1643. 75 p.; 4to. Amongst the ingredients listed is guaiacum. BL. 643/95

Pharmacopoeia Augustana, auspicio . . . Senatus cure octava Collegii Medici recognita. *Augsburg:* 1643. 2 pts; 8vo. 1st publ., Augsburg, [1564]; cf. 1613 edn. DNLM. 643/96

Pigray, Pierre. Epitome des preceptes de

medecine et chirurgie. *Lyons: J. Huguetan,* 1643. 1st publ., Paris, 1600, under title *La chirurgie;* cf. 1604 edn. DNLM.   643/97

Pona, Francesco. Trattato de' veleni, e lor cura. *Verona: B. Merlo,* 1643. 96 p.; 4to. Distinguishes, as antidote to poisons, between Occidental (i.e., Peruvian) & Oriental bezoar stones. DNLM, ICU, MnU; BL, BN.
                                              643/98

Potier, Pierre. Libri duo de febribus . . . Centuriae tres, & Pharmacopoea spagirica. *Bologna: G. Monti,* 1643. 5 pts; port.; 4to. Included are Potier's *Insignes curationes,* 1st publ., Venice, 1615, & Bologna, 1622, as well as the *Pharmacopoea spagirica,* 1st publ., Bologna, 1624. DNLM; BL, BN.
                                              643/99

Prevost, Jean. Medicina pauperum. *Lyons: P. Ravaud,* 1643. 718 p.; 12mo. 1st publ., Frankfurt a. M.?, 1641? DNLM, WU.
                                              643/100

Randolph, Thomas. Poems, with the Muses looking-glasse, and Amyntas . . . the third edition. *London:* 1643. 3 pts; 8vo. 1st publ., Oxford, 1638. Wing R241; Greg 547(c). CSmH, CtY, DFo, ICN, MH, NjP; BL.
                                              643/101

Rensselaer, Kiliaen van. Insinuatie, protestatie, ende presentatie van weghen den patroon van de colonie van Rensselaerswijck. *[Amsterdam:* 1643]. bds.; fol. Sabin 98544; Van Rensselaer Bowier 697; Vail (Frontier) 99.   643/102

———. Redres van de abuysen ende faulten in de colonie van Rensselaers-wijck. *Amsterdam: T. Jacobszoon,* 1643. [15] p.; 4to. Sabin 98545; Van Rensselaer Bowier 686; Vail (Frontier) 100.   643/103

———. Waerschouwinge, verboth, ende toelatinghe, weghens de colonie van Renselaers-wyck. *Amsterdam: T. Jacobszoon* [1643]. bds.; fol. Sabin 98546; Van Rensselaer Bowier 682; Vail (Frontier) 100.
                                              643/104

Rivadeneira, Pedro de, S.J. Bibliotheca scriptorum Societatis Jesu, post excusum anno M.DC.VIII. catalogum r.p. Petri Ribadeneira, nunc hoc novo apparatu librorum ad annum . . . M.DC.XLII . . . a Philippo Allegambe . . . Accedit Catalogus religiosum Societatis Jesu, qui . . . interempti sunt. *Antwerp: J. Meurs,* 1643. 568 p.; fol.

1st publ., Antwerp, 1608, under title *Illustrium scriptorum religionis Societatis Jesu catalogus;* republished, Antwerp, 1613, as *Catalogus scriptorum religionis Societatis Jesu;* here substantially expanded. Sabin 70776 (& 712); Backer I:151; Palau 266561. CLgA, CtY, DLC, InU-L, MH, N, PU, RPJCB; BL, BN.   643/105

Robinson, Henry. Liberty of conscience: or The sole means to obtaine peace and truth. *[London:]* 1643. 62 p.; 4to. Includes mention (p. 8) of massacre by Spaniards of 'many millions of West-Indians'. Authorship has been mistakenly ascribed to Roger Williams. Wing R1675; McAlpin II:246; Thomason I:316. CSmH, CtY, DFo, ICN, MH, MWA, MiU-C, NNUT, PPPrHi, RPJCB; BL.   643/106

Romances varios. De diversos autores. Añadidos y enmendados en esta tercera [*sic*] impression. *Saragossa: P. Lanaja,* 1643. 432 p.; 12mo. Collection 1st publ., Saragossa, 1640. No copy of the 2nd impression has been traced. Jiménez Catalan (Saragossa) 447; Palau 277065-II. BL.   643/107

Saavedra Fajardo, Diego de. Idea de un principe christiano. *Milan:* 1642 [i.e., 1643]. 753 p.; illus.; fol. 1st publ., Munich, 1640. Prelim. matter is dated 1643. Palau 283442. DFo, MB, NcD, PU; BL.   643/108

Saint-Amant, Marc Antoine de Gérard, sieur de. Les oeuvres. *Lyons: J. Huguetan,* 1643. 2 pts; 8vo. In verse. 1st publ., Paris, 1629. Also issued with imprints of N. Gay, Philippe Borde, the Widow Jean Jacquemetton, and F. La Bottière & N. Arnon. Tchémerzine X:83. MH; BN (Widow Jacquemetton).   643/109

Scarron, Paul. Recueil de quelques vers burlesques. *Paris: T. Quinet,* 1643. 2 pts; 4to. 'Epistre' to Sarrazin mentions Peru, Canada, & Mexico; 'Remerciment a monsieur le Cardinal' mentions Atabalipa, the Peruvian chief. Magne (Scarron) 8; Cioranescu (XVII) 61733. CtY, MH, NNC; BN.
                                              643/110

Schenck von Grafenberg, Johann. Observationum medicarum rariorum, libri vii. *Lyons: J. A. Huguetan,* 1643. 892 p.; illus., port.; fol. 1st publ., Frankfurt a. M., 1600; cf. 1609 edn with title Παρατηρησεων. DNLM, NNNAM, PPL; BN.   643/111

Schouten, Willem Corneliszoon. Journael ofte Beschryvinge vande wonderlijcke reyse. *Rotterdam: I. van Waesberghen, 1643.* 53 p.; illus., maps; 4to. 1st publ., Amsterdam, 1618. Sabin 77928. NN-RB.
643/112

Serres, Jean de. Inventaire general de l'histoire de France. Depuis Pharamond jusques à present . . . Augmenté en cette derniere edition, de ce qui s'est passé durant ces dernieres années jusques à present. *Paris: A. Alazart, J. Villery, C. Besongne, & J. Promé,* 1643. 1306 p.; ports; fol. 1st publ., Paris, 1597–1600, but here lacking the ref. to Villegagnon's Brazilian venture. As here expanded, however, under the year 1598 are refs to Dutch expeditions to both Indies in defiance of the Spanish & Portuguese. Described here from the JCB copy, this work, patently issued jointly by the booksellers named in the above imprint, may exist with variant title pages carrying the name of a single bookseller, as in the case of the BL copy with that of Villery alone. CLSU (Besongne), RPJCB; BL(Villery).
643/113

Severino, Marco Aurelio. De recondita abscessum natura libri viii . . . [Editio secunda]. *Frankfurt a. M.: J. Beyer,* 1643. 168 (i.e., 468) p.; illus.; 4to. 1st publ., Naples, 1632. CLU-M, CtY-M, DNLM, ICJ, MiU, NNNAM; BL, BN.
643/114

Shepard, Thomas. The sincere convert. *London: T. P[aine]. & M. S[immons]., for H. Blunden,* 1643. 266 p.; 8vo. 1st publ., London, 1640. Sabin 80220; Wing S3119. IU; BL, Oxford:Bodl.
643/115

Steuart, Adam. Some observations. *London:* 1643. *See the year* 1644.

Swan, John. Speculum mundi. or A glasse representing the face of the world . . . The second edition enlarged. *Cambridge: R. Daniel,* 1643. 504 p.; 4to. 1st publ., Cambridge, 1635. Wing S6238. CSmH, CtY, DFo, IU, NNUT; BL.
643/116

Taylor, John, the Water-poet. A letter sent to London from a spie at Oxford. *[Oxford: H. Hall]* 1643. 14p.; 4to. Includes ref. to 'New-England spirituall fathers'. Madan (Oxford) 1447; Wing T474. CSmH; Cambridge:UL, Oxford:Bodl.
643/117

——. The noble cavalier caracterised. *[Ox-*

ford? 1643]. 8 p.; 4to. Mentions one Francis Beale, a sometime 'tobacco-man'. Madan (Oxford) 1584**; Wing T490. CSmH; Oxford:Bodl.
643/118

Torsellino, Orazio, S.J. Historiarum ab origine mundi usque ad annum 1630 epitome libri x. *Lyons: A. Rigaud,* 1643. 2 pts; 12mo. 1st publ., Rome, 1598; Cf. 1620 edn. Backer VIII:152.
643/119

Trou-hertighe onderrichtinge, aen alle hooft participanten en lief-hebbers vande . . . West-Indische Compagnie, nopende het open stellen vanden handel op de cust van Africa . . . mitsgaders . . . Nieu Nederlant ende West-Indien, door . . . V. W. C. *[Amsterdam?]* 1643. 10 lvs; 4to. Includes (lf 10) 'Extract wt de missive van sijn excellentie en Hooghe raden in Brasil.' Sabin 9757; Asher 333; Knuttel 5021. CLU, MnU-B, NN-RB; BL, The Hague:KB.
643/120

Vasconcellos, João de, S.J. Restauração de Portugal prodigiosa . . . Por Gregoria de Almarez [pseud]. *Lisbon: A. Alvarez,* 1643. 399 p.; 4to. Authorship also attrib. to Manuel de Escobar. Includes refs to Portuguese possessions in America. Sabin 22835; Innocencio IV:1349; Backer VIII:484. ICN, MH.
643/121

Les veritables motifs de messieurs et dames de la Societé de Nostre Dame de Montreal, pour la conversion des sauvages de la nouvelle France. *[Paris:]* 1643. 127 p.; 4to. Sabin 50292; Harrisse (NF) 79; Streit II:2546. CSmH, MH, MnU-B, NN-RB; BN.
643/122

Vimont, Barthélemy, S.J. Relation de ce qui s'est passé en la Nouvelle France en l'anne 1642. *Paris: S. Cramoisy,* 1643. 2 pts; 8vo. Pt 2 comprises Jérôme Lallemant's 'Relation de ce qui s'est passé en la mission des Hurons'. For variants, see Bell McCoy as cited. Sabin 99750; Harrisse (NF) 80; Bell (Jes. rel.) 20–22; McCoy 44–48; Streit II:2544; Church 459–459A; JCB (3) II: 311–312. CSmH, CtY, DLC, ICN, InU-L, MH, MiU-C, MnU-B, NN-RB, RPJCB; BL, BN.
643/123

Weidner, Johann Leonhard. Hispanicae dominationis arcana. *Leyden: A. Commelin D. López de Haro,* 1643. 224 p.; 12mo. Chapt. xxvii describes 'Hispanorum in America & India crudelitates barbaries'. Sabin 102504;

Palau 374466. DFo, ICN, MH, NNC, PU, RPJCB; BL (W., J. L.).   643/124

Williams, Roger. A key into the language of America: or, An help to the language of the natives in that part of America, called New-England. *London: G. Dexter,* 1643. 197 p.; 8vo. Sabin 104339; Vail (Frontier) 102; Wing W2766; Arents 3281; Church 460; JCB (3) II:312. CSmH, ICN, MH, MWA, MiU-C, NN-RB, PHi, RPJCB; BL.
                                       643/125

Zeiller, Martin. Das dritte Hundert Episteln. *Ulm: J. Görlin,* 1643. 724 p.; 8vo. Continues Zeiller's *Ein Hundert Episteln,* 1st publ., Heilbronn & Ulm, 1640. Stated by Jantz to be rich in Americana. Jantz (German Baroque) 2771; Jördens V:600. NcD.   643/126

1644

Abreu y Figueroa, Fernando de, O.S.A. Señor. Index, y sumario de lo que contiene el memorial. que en la real mano de V. M. . . . fray Fernando de Abreu y Figueroa . . pone. [*Madrid?* 1644]. 5 lvs; fol. On customs duties relating to Peru; addressed to king of Spain. Medina (BHA) 6162. BL.   644/1

Aenwysinge: datmen vande Oost en West-Indische Compagnien een compagie [sic] dient te maken. *The Hague: J. Veely,* 1644. [36] p.; 4to. For variant see Sabin. Sabin 102878; Borba de Moraes I:14; Rodrigues (Dom. Hol.) 49; Asher 187; Knuttel 5117; JCB (3) II:319. DLC, ICU, MH-BA, MiU-C, NN-RB, RPJCB; BL, The Hague:KB.
                                       644/2

—[Anr edn]. . . . vermeerderd en verbetert. *The Hague:* 2644 [i.e., 1644]. Sabin 102878; Muller (1872) 412. NNH; Leyden:B. Thysiana.   644/3

—[Anr edn]. *Amsterdam: F. Pels,* 1644. [36] p.; 4to. Sabin 102878; Knuttel 5118. NN-RB; The Hague:KB.   644/4

Aldrovandi, Ulisse. De piscibus libri v. et de cetis lib, unus. *Bologna: N. Tebaldini, for M. A. Bernia,* 1644. 732 p.; illus.; fol. 1st publ., Bologna, 1612. Nissen (Zool.) 70n.
                                       644/5

Antworp, en voor-stel. [*The Hague?*] 1644. *See entry under title* Ontworp *below.*

Augspurger, Johann Paul. Kurtze und warhaffte Beschreibung der See-Reisen von Amsterdam in Holland nacher Brasilien in America . . . *Schleusingen: J. M. Schall,* 1644. 79 p.; 8vo. Sabin 2379; Borba de Moraes I:46–47; Rodrigues (Dom. Hol.) 488; JCB (3) II:312–313. RPJCB.
                                       644/6

Avity, Pierre d', sieur de Montmartin. Les estats, empires et principautez du monde. *Rouen: A Ouyn,* 1644. 1469 p.; 4to. 1st publ., Paris, 1613. Sabin 18913. DLC, NN-RB; BL.
                                       644/7

—[Anr issue]. *Rouen: J. Cailloué,* 1644. RPJCB.
                                       644/8

——. Nouveau théatre du monde, contenant les estats, empires, royaumes et principautez. *Paris: P. Rocolet,* 1644. 1414 p.; fol. 1st publ., Paris, 1613, under title *Les estats, empires et principautez du monde.* ICN.
                                       644/9

—[Anr edn]. *Rouen: D. Du Petit Val,* 1644. 1469 p.; fol. Berlin:StB.   644/10

Bacon, Francis, viscount St Albans. Sermones fideles, ethici, politici. *Leyden: F. Haack,* 1644. 404 p.; port.; 12mo. 1st publ. as here transl., Leyden, 1641. Gibson (Bacon) 52. Copies of this edn will prob. be found amongst those entered for the following item. BL.   644/11

—[Anr edn]. *Leyden: F. Haack,* 1644. 416 p.; port.; 12mo. Gibson (Bacon) 53. CU, DLC, ICJ, MH, NN, PSC; BN.   644/12

Baerle, Kasper van. Laurus Flandrica, sive In expugnationem validissimi Flandriae propugnaculi . . . ductu armisque . . . Frederici Henrici, Arausionensium principis comitis Nassaviae, &c. *Amsterdam: J. Blaeu,*1644. 12 p.; fol. Includes ref. to Matanzas Bay, Cuba. Dt. Ges. Kat. 11.6580. BL, Leipzig:StB.   644/13

——. Mauritius redux, sive, Gratulatio ad excellentissimum & illustrissimum comitem, J. Mauritium comitem Nassaviae . . . cum ex orbe Americano in European sospes appulisset. *Amsterdam: J. Blaeu,* 1644. 12 p.; fol. In verse. On Johan Maurits van Nassau, governor in Brazil for the Nederlandsche West-Indische Compagnie. Cf. Sabin 3407n; Dt. Ges. Kat. 11.6583. DLC; BL, Leipzig:StB.   644/14

—[Anr edn]. [*Amsterdam?* 1644]. 4 lvs; 8vo.

Has reading 'Nassoviae' in title. Dt. Ges. Kat. 11.6582. Marburg:UB, Halle:UB.
644/15

Ball, John. A tryall of the new-church way in New-England and in Old. *London: T. Paine & M. Simmons, for T. Underhill,* 1644. 90 p.; 4to. 1st publ., London, 1643, under title *A letter of many ministers in Old England;* here reissued with cancel t.p. Sabin 2939; Wing T2229; JCB (3) II:313. CtY, DLC, MH, RPJCB; BL.
644/16

Barnstein, Heinrich. Taback das Wunder: Künst undt Artzney mittel. *Erfurt: T. Fritsche,* 1644. 18 lvs; 8vo. Dt. Ges. Kat. 11.7680; Arents 229n. Munich:StB.
644/17

Basilius Valentinus, O.S.B. Haliographia. De praeparatione, usu, ac virtutibus omnium salium. *Bologna: N. Tebaldini, for A. Salmincio,* 1644. 102 p.; 8vo. On p. 78 a salt of guaiacum is described, on p. 88 a salt of tobacco. CtY-M, PPC, WU; BL, BN. 644/18

Bauderon, Brice. Pharmacopee. *Rouen: C. Malassis,* 1644. 2 pts; 8vo. 1st publ., Lyons, 1588, under title *Paraphrase sur la Pharmacopoee;* cf. 1607 edn. DNLM, MH; BL.
644/19

Bedenckinge over d'Antwoordt der heeren bewint-hebbers vande Oost-Indische Compagnie: aen d'edele . . . Staten van Hollandt en West Vrieslant, in twee schriften, overgelevert, belanghende de combinatie der twee compagnien. *The Hague: J. Veely,* 1644. 2 pts; 4to. Concerns union with the West-Indische Compagnie. Vignette of ship appears on t.p. Sabin 4275 & 102883; JCB (3) II: 319. NN-RB. [Issues not differentiated: DLC, MnU-B, RPJCB (imp.); BL].
644/20

—[Anr issue]. *The Hague: J. Veely,* 1644. Coat of arms of the province of Holland on t.p. Sabin 102883n; Knuttel 5116. NN-RB; The Hague:KB.
644/21

Benzoni, Girolamo. Historia antipodum, sive Novi Orbis, qui vulgo Americae et Indicae Occidentalis nomine usurpatur, Liber quartus. *Frankfurt a. M.: M. Merian,* 1644. 74 p.; illus.; fol. 1st publ. as transl. by Urbain Chauveton from Benzoni's *Historia del Mondo Nuovo* (1st publ., Venice, 1565) under title *Americae pars quarta,* Frankfurt a. M., 1594. Cf. Sabin 8784; Church 155n. NN-RB (imp.); BN.
644/22

Beschrijvinghe vande landen van Brasilien ende het veroveren. van Bahia de todos los Santos. *Amsterdam: Widow of C. L. van der Plasse,* 1644. 8 lvs; 4to. Extracted from the *Reys boeck van het rijcke Brasilien,* [Dordrecht?] 1624. Borba de Moraes I:90; Rodrigues (Dom. Hol.) 366.
644/23

Beverwijck, Jan van. Αὐτάρχεια Bataviae, sive Introductio ad medicinam indigenam. *Leyden: J. Maire,* 1644. 162 p.; 12mo. Transl. from the author's *Inleydinge tot de Hollandsche geneesmiddelen,* 1st publ., Dordrecht, 1642. Van de Velde 76; Catalogus van boeken VII:10 (& VII:94). NNNAM; BL, BN.
644/24

——. Schat der gesontheyt. *Amsterdam:* 1644. 4to. 1st publ., [Dordrecht? 1636?]. Graesse I:357.
644/25

——. Schat der ongesontheyt ofte Geneeskonste . . . Der tweeden druck. *Dordrecht: J. Gorisszoon,* 1644. 632 p.; illus.; 8vo. 1st publ., Dordrecht, 1642. For a second pt, see below. Van de Velde 96–98. Ghent:BU.
644/26

—— Schat der ongesontheyt, ofte Geneeskonste . . . Het tweede deel. *Dordrecht: J. Gorisszoon,* 1644. 593 p.; illus.; 8vo. Intended for issue with the preceding; not to be confused with a previous 'tweede deel'. The present volume includes refs to American origin of 'pox' (syphilis), noting its various names & stating that Spaniards, as discoverers of the New World, brought the disease back to their country & Naples in the years 1492–96. The author cites Guicciardini, Fioravanti, & others in advancing idea that syphilis developed because of cannibalism by Indians, & by Neapolitans under seige in West Indies. Also present is poem transl. by J. Cats from Du Bartas, referring to West Indian pox. Waller 1016; Cushing B362. CtY-M, DFo; London:Wellcome, Amsterdam:MBG.
644/27

Birago, Giovanni Battista. Historia del regno di Portogallo. *Lyons:* 1644. 2 pts; 4to. Included is material on Brazil. Cf. Borba de Moraes I:93. ICN, NN; BL, BN.
644/28

Blaeu, Willem Janszoon. Le theatre du monde, ou Nouvel atlas . . . Seconde partie. *Amsterdam: J. Blaeu,* 1644. 2 pts; 93 maps;

fol. 1st publ., Amsterdam, 1635; here a reissue, with minor changes, of the 2nd Amsterdam edn of 1640. Printer's address and date appear as paste-on slips on t.p. Koeman (B1) 18B (cf. 18A). DLC; BN, Florence:BN.
644/29

——. Theatrum orbis terrarum, sive Atlas novus. *Amsterdam: J. Blaeu,* 1644. 2 pts, 120 maps; fol. 1st publ., Amsterdam, 1635. Issued with Blaeu's *Theatrum . . . pars secunda,* Amsterdam, 1645. Cf. Sabin 5720n; Koeman (B1) 23A. Leeuwarden: PLF, Florence:B Marucel. 644/30

Boccalini, Traiano. De' ragguagli di Parnaso . . . Centuria prima . . . ottava impressione. *Venice: Heirs of G. Guerigli,* 1644. 8vo. 1st publ., Venice, 1612. Firpo (Ragguagli) 21; Michel (Répertoire) I:176. MH, MnU, PPL; BN. 644/31

——. De' ragguagli di Parnaso . . . Centuria seconda . . . ottava impressione. *Venice: Heirs of G. Guerigli,* 1644. 292 p.; 8vo. 1st publ., Venice, 1613; issued with Guerigli Centuria prima of this year above. Firpo (Ragguagli) 21; Michel (Répertoire) I:176. MH, MnU, PPL; BN. 644/32

——. Relation aus Parnasso, erster, zweyter und dritter Theil . . . Erstlich . . . in italianischer Sprach beschrieben. *Frankfurt a. M.: J. Beyer,* 1644. 702 p.; 4to. 1st publ. in German, [Tübingen? 1617] as transl. from Boccalini's *De' ragguagli di Parnaso,* the 1st pt 1st publ., Venice, 1612, the 2nd, Venice, 1613. DLC; BL. 644/33

Brevis assertio et apologia acclamationis et justitiae . . . Portugalliae regis Joannis inter veros, & legitimos Lusitaniae reges nomine Quarti. [*Amsterdam?* 1644?]. [20] p.; 4to. Defending João IV's legitimacy as king of Portugal following the country's regained independence from Spain, the writer comments on Dutch intrusions in Brazil. Knuttel 5092. RPJCB; The Hague: KB. 644/34

—[Anr edn]. [*The Hague?* 1644?]. [11] p.; fol. NjP. 644/35

Camerarius, Philipp. Operae horarum subcisivarum, sive Meditationes historicae . . . Centuria prima. *Frankfurt a.M.: K. Rötel, for J. Hallerford & J. Wild,* 1644. 4to. 1st publ., Altdorf, 1591; cf. 1602 edn. CU, MnU-B, NjP, OC1W; BL, BN. 644/36

Camões, Luiz de. Os Lusiadas. *Lisbon: P. Craesbeeck,* 1644. 204 numb. lvs; 24mo. In verse. 1st publ., Lisbon, 1572; cf. 1609 edn above. Silva (Camões) 32. MH, NNH; Lisbon:BN. 644/37

Casas, Bartolomé de las, O.P., Bp of Chiapa. Conquista dell'Indie Occidentali . . . Tradotta . . . per opera di Marco Ginammi. *Venice: M. Ginammi,* 1644. 184 p.; 4to. Transl. from author's *Aqui se contiene una disputa . . . entre el Obispo . . . Bartholomé de las Casas . . . y el Doctor Gines de Sepulveda,* Seville, 1552. Text in Spanish & Italian in parallel columns. Cf. Sabin 11248; cf. Medina (BHA) 1085n (II:472); Hanke/Giménez 536; cf. Streit I:499. DLC, MB; BL. 644/38

Castell, William. A short discoverie of the coasts and continent of America. *London:* 1644. 2 pts; 4to. Sabin 11398; Baer (Md) 25; Wing C1231; Church 461; JCB (3) II:313. CSmH, CtY, DLC, ICN, MH, MiU-C, NN-RB, PBL, RPJCB; BL. 644/39

Cats, Jacob. Maechden-plicht. *Amsterdam: T. Jacobszoon,* 1644. [104] p.; illus.; 8vo. 1st publ., Middelburg, 1618. Vries 109; Mus. Cats. 66. 644/40

——. Proef-steen van den trou-ring. [*Amsterdam?*] 1644. 1 v.; illus.; port.; 8vo. 1st publ., Dordrecht, 1637, under title '*s Werelts begin.* Mus. Cats. 176. Leyden:UB (imp.). 644/41

Claer licht. [*Amsterdam?* 1644?]. See **Klaer licht** *below.*

Clément, Claude, S.J. Tablas chronologicas, en que se contienen los sucesos eclesiásticos y seculares de España, Africa, Indias Orientales y Occidentales . . . hasta el año 1642. *Madrid: D. Díaz de la Carrera,* 1644. 13 lvs; fol. 1st publ., Madrid, 1643. Cf. Medina (BHA) 1047; Palau 190949. 644/42

Colmenero de Ledesma, Antonio. Chocolata Inda, opusculum de qualitate & naturâ chocolatae . . . hispanico antehac idiomate editum, nunc vero curante Marco Aurelio Severino [a Joanne Georgio Volmanero] in latinum translatum. *Nuremberg: W. Endter,* 1644. 73 p.; 24mo. Transl. from the author's *Curioso tratado . . . de chocolate,* 1st publ., Madrid, 1631. Sabin 14543 (& 12861n); Medina (BHA) 1056; Müller 52;

Palau 56906. CtY, DNLM, ICJ, MH-A, PPL, RPJCB; BL, BN. 644/43

Commelin, Izaäk, ed. Begin ende voortgang vande Vereenigde Neederlandtsche Geoctroyeerde Oost-Indische Compagnie, 't eerste[–tweede] deel. [*Amsterdam: J. Janszoon, the Younger* 1644?]. 2 v.; obl. 4to. A collection of voyages in 22 pts, each pt being separately paged. For a complete list of included items, many of which include American refs, see Tiele-Muller as cited. Sabin 14957 (& 11608, 37691, 67558, & 89447); Tiele-Muller 2 (cf. 6); cf. Muller (1872) 1871. 644/44

Comtaeus, Robertus. De origine gentium Americanarum dissertatio. *Amsterdam: N. van Ravesteyn*, 1644. 41 p.; 8vo. Sabin 15079; JCB (3) II:314. DLC, NN-RB, RPJCB; BL 644/45

Consideratie over de tegenwoordige ghelegentheydt van Brasil. In twee deelen ghestelt. *Amsterdam: J. Jaquet, for J. van Hilten*, 1644. 34 p.; 4to. Concerns commerce. For variant see Knuttel. Sabin 7553; Borba de Moraes I:170; Asher 184; Knuttel 5124. NN-RB, NNH, RPB; BL (Brazil), The Hague:KB. 644/46

Consideratie, overgelevert by de heeren bewinthebberen van de Oost-Indische Compagnie aen de . . . Staten van Hollant ende West-Vrieslant, waeromme het voor de selve. Compagnie onmogelick . . . is, om met de West-Indische Compagnie te treden in handelinge. *The Hague: J. Fransen*, 1644. [7] p.; 4to. Also publ., as part of the Nederlandsche West-Indische Compagnie's *Remonstrantie ende Consideratie* of this year below. Sabin 15929 (& 102887); Knuttel 5115. DLC, NN-RB; BL, The Hague:KB. 644/47

A coole conference between the cleared reformation and the apologeticall narration. [*London:* 1644?]. 18 p.; 4to. A reply to Thomas Goodwin's *An apologeticall narrative* of 1643. Included is mention of 'our brethren in New England & of 'Colonies of Saints' in Frankfurt, Holland, & New England. Wing C6044A. CSmH, CtY, DFo, MH, MiU-C, NN-RB. 644/48

Cotton John. The keyes of the kingdom of heaven . . . by . . . John Cotton . . . at Boston in New England. *London: M. Sim-*

mons, for H. Overton, 1644. 59 p.; 4to. Includes ref. to requirements of Indians wishing to enter the church. For variant states see Tuttle and Wing as cited. Sabin 17067; Tuttle (Cotton) 28–31; Wing C6437–C6438; JCB (3) II:314–315. CSmH, CtY, DLC, ICN, MH, NNUT, RPJCB; BL, Oxford:Bodl. 644/49

—[Anr edn]. The second time imprinted. *London: M. Simmons, for H. Overton*, 1644. 59 p.; 4to. Imprint contains reading 'at his shop in Popes-head-Alley'. Sabin 17067; Tuttle (Cotton) 33; Wing C6439. CSmH, CtY, DLC, MH; BL, Cambridge:UL. 644/50

—[Anr issue?]. *London: M. Simmons, for H. Overton*, 1644. 59 p.; 4to. Imprint contains reading 'at his shop entring into Popes-head Alley'. Sabin 17067; Tuttle (Cotton) 34; Wing C6440. MHi; Maldon:Plume, Dublin:Trinity. 644/51

——. Sixteene questions of serious and necessary consequence, propounded unto Mr. John Cotton of Boston in New-England. *London: E[lizabeth?]. P[urslowe?].*, *for E. Blackmore*, 1644. 14 p.; 4to. Sabin 81490; Tuttle (Cotton) 35; Wing C6458; JCB (3) II:315. CtY, DFo, MH, NN-RB, RPJCB; BL, Wolfenbüttel:HB. 644/52

Dialogus oft T'samensprekinge, ghemaeckt op den vrede-handel. *Antwerp:* 1644. [14] p.; 4to. 1st publ., [Amsterdam?] 1608. Knuttel 5102; Meulman 2696. InU-L; The Hague:KB, Ghent:BU. 644/53

Digby, Sir Kenelm. Observations upon Religio medici. *London: F. L[each].*, *for L. Chapman & D. Frere*, 1644. 124 p.; 8vo. 1st publ., London, 1643. Keynes (Browne) 220. MH; Keynes. 644/54

—[Anr state]. The second edition corrected and amended. *London: F. L[each].*, *for L. Chapman & D. Frere*, 1644. The t.p. has been partly reset to include edn statement. Keynes (Browne) 221; Wing D1443. CtY-M, MH; BL. 644/55

Dodoens, Rembert. Cruydt-boeck . . . volghens sijne laetste verberinghe . . . met biivoeghsels achter elck capitel, uyt verscheyden cruydt-beschrijvers: item, in 't laetste een beschrijvinghe vande Indiaensche ghewassen, meest ghetrocken uyt de schriften van Carolus Clusius. Nu wederom van nieuws oversien ende verbetert.

Antwerp: Plantin Press, 1644. 1492 p.; illus.; fol. 1st publ., Antwerp, 1583; cf. 1608 edn above. Pritzel 2345n; Nissen (Bot.) 518n; Bibl. belg., 1st ser., IX:D121. CU, DNLM, IU, MH-A, MnU, NNBG, PPAmP, RPB; BL, BN.   644/56

Dominicans. [Acta capituli generalissimum Romae . . . Ordinis Predicatorum celebrati . . . xiv. Maij anno Domini M. DC. XLIV. *Rome:* 1644]. 112 + p.; 4to. Included are reports on Dominican provinces in Spanish America. RPJCB (lacks prelim. matter & all after p. 112).   644/57

Edwards, Thomas. Antapologia; or, A full answer to the Apologeticall narration of Mr Goodwin, Mr Nye, Mr Sympson [etc.]. *London: G. M[iller]., for J. Bellamy,* 1644. 307 p.; 4to. Included are numerous refs to New England & to Roger Williams. Sabin 21991; Wing E222; JCB (3) II:315. CLU-C, DLC, MH, MiU, NN-RB, RPJCB; BL.   644/58

—[Anr issue]. *London: G. M[iller]., for R. Smith,* 1644. Wing E223. CSmH, DFo, MWiW-C, MnU, NN-RB, PPPrHi, ViU; BL, BN.   644/59

Enchiridion practicum medico-chirurgicum. [*Geneva:*] *P. & J. Chouët,* 1644. 2 pts; 8vo. 1st publ., Geneva, 1621, including Antoine Chaumette's *Enchiridion chirurgicum,* itself 1st publ., Paris, 1560. Here a reissue of Berjon's Geneva, 1627, edn? DNLM, MnU; London: Wellcome.   644/60

Estienne, Charles. Lexicon historicum, geographicum, poeticum. *Paris: J. Libert,* 1644. 2058 cols; 4to. 1st publ. in this enl. edn, Lyons, 1595, under title *Dictionarium historicum, geographicum, poeticum;* cf. 1601 edn; cf. also the 1620, Paris, edn with the above title. BN.   644/61

Everard, Giles. De herba panacea, quam alii tabacum, alii petum aut nicotianum vocant, brevis commentariolo . . . auctore Aegidio Everario . . . Johannis Neandri . . . Tabacologia . . . Misocapnus, sive De abuso tobacci lusus regius. Hymnus tabaci, autore Raphaele Thorio. *Utrecht: D. van Hoogenhuysen,* 1644. 305 p.; 8vo. Everand's *De herba panacea* 1st publ., Antwerp, 1587; Neander's *Tabacologia,* Leyden, 1622; James I's 'Misocapnus', as here transl. from his 1604 *Counter-blaste to tobacco,* in his *Opera,* London,

1619; Thorius's *Hymnus tabaci,* Leyden, 1625. Sabin 23218n; Pritzel 2767; Arents 226. CU, DNLM, MH, NN-RB, OCl, RPJCB; BL, BN.   644/62

Fernel, Jean. Universa medicina. *Geneva: J. Chouët,* 1644. 3 pts; 8vo. 1st publ. as here constituted, Paris, 1567; cf. 1601–2 edn. Sherrington (Fernel) 84.J28. DNLM, PPC; Paris:Faculté de Médecine.   644/63

Forbes, Alexander. An anatomy of independency. *London: R. Bostock,* 1644. 52 p.; 4to. Includes (p. 9 & 11) refs to Nonconformists in New England. Sabin 27953; Wing F1439. CSmH, CtY, ICU, InU-L, MH, MnU, NN-RB; BL.   644/64

Friesland, Netherlands. Provinciale Staten. Copye van het Octroy, by de Staten van Frieslandt. *The Hague: A. J. Tongerloo,* 1644. [16] p.; 4to. 1st publ., Leeuwarden, 1642. Knuttel 5111. BL, The Hague:KB.
                                                644/65

Goodwin, John. M. S. to A. S. with a plea for libertie of conscience, against the cavils of A. S[teuart]. *London: F. N[eile]., for H. Overton,* 1644. 110 p.; 4 to. Included are numerous refs to New England. Sabin 74624; Wing G1180; McAlpin II:289; JCB (3) II:323. CSmH, CtY, DLC, ICN, MWiW-C, NN-RB, PPL, RPJCB; BL.   644/66

——, **supposed author.** A reply of two of the brethren to A[dam]. S[teuart]. *London: M. Simmons, for H. Overton,* 1644. 112 p.; 4to. Numerous refs are made to churches of New England. Sabin 69679; Wing G1198. CtY, MWA.   644/67

—[Anr edn]. The second edition, corrected, and enlarged. *London: M. Simmons, for H. Overton,* 1644. 112 p.; 4to. Sabin 69679n; McAlpin II:289; Thomason I:322. MH, MiU-C, NN-RB; BL.   644/68

Great Britain. Laws, statutes, etc., 1625–1649 (Charles I). An ordinance . . . for the regulating of the rates on the customes and excise of tobacco. *London: R. Cotes & J. Raworth,* 1644. bds.; fol. At head of title: Die lunae 4 martii 1643. Crawford (Roy. procl.) 2538; Thomason I:313; cf. Wing E2025.   644/69

—[Anr edn]. *London: R. Cotes & J. Raworth,* 1644. [59]–66 p.; 4to. Cf. Wing E2025; Arents 225. CSmH, DLC, MH, NN-A, RPJCB.   644/70

Grotius, Hugo. De veritate religionis christianae. Editio tertia. *Leyden: J. Maire, 1644.* 327 p.; 12mo. 1st publ., Leyden, 1627, under title *Sensus librorum sex.* Meulen/Diermanse 947. ICU, InU, NNC; BN, The Hague:PP. 644/71

——. La verité de la religion chrestienne. Ouvrage traduit du Latin. *Paris: 'Printshop of the New Type invented by P. Moreau'; sold by F. Rouvelin* [1644]. 541 p.; 8vo. Transl. from Grotius's *Sensus librorum sex,* 1st publ., Leyden, 1627; cf. Amsterdam, 1636, French edn. Meulen/Diermanse 1061. BL (as 1640?), BN, The Hague:PP. 644/72

Grüling, Philipp Gerhard. Florilegium Hippocrateo-Galeno-chymicorum novum longe pluris priore auctum et quasi prodromis practici operis. *Leipzig: T. Ritzsch, for Heirs of G. Gross,* 1644. 479 p.; 4to. 1st publ., Leipzig, 1631, but here substantially rev. & enl. In pt 1, chapt. 14 describes an extract of mechoacan, identified as Mexican, mentioning Cortés; chapt. xv describes a second type of mechoacan; chapt. xvi, 'De extracto seu magisterio gummi laxativi, aliàs gummi de Peru, vel de Goa', i.e., of opobalsam, descr. as coming from 'provincia Carthaginae vel Carthagenâ in Americâ (aliàs Nova Hispania, dicta).' In pt 25, chapt. iii, 'Essentia ligni sassafras' is recommended for treatment of arthritis. CtY-M, DNLM; London:Wellcome. 644/73

Guidi, Ippolito Camillo. Caduta del conte d'Olivares . . . M.DC.XXXXIII. *Ivrea:* 1644. 56 p.; 4to. Ref. is made to loss to king of Spain brought on by Olivares, through Portugal's regaining its sovereignty, of 'Fernambouc' & Brazil. Also mentioned is Olivares's personal trade with the Indies, patently West as well as East. MnU-B; BL. 644/74

Harsdörffer, Georg Philipp. Gesprachspiele . . . vierter Theil. *Nuremberg: W. Endter,* 1644. 622 p.; illus., music; obl. 8vo. Chapt. CLXVIII (sects 20–23) advises against use of symbols based on unfamiliar animals & plants of the Indies. Chapt. CLXXXVIII, sect. 3, notes Indians' attitude toward Spaniards' recreational walking. Chapt. CXCVIII, sect. 31, notes that Christians have planted religion in Indians, but extirpated their virtue & piety through trad-ing ventures. Forms pt 4 of the author's *Frauenzimmer Gesprechspiele,* 1641–49. Goedeke III:108; Faber du Faur 502. CU, CtY, DLC; BL. 644/75

Heilsame en onpartijdige raat aan alle d' inwoonders van Nederlandt, die onder . . . den Koning van Spanien zijn, gestelt . . . in de Franse sprake en nu . . . overgeset. [*The Hague?*] 1544 [i.e., 1644]. [24] p.; 4to. Capture of fleet from West Indies is discussed on lf B3. Knuttel. 5096. NN; The Hague:KB. 644/76

Herrera, Tomás de, O.S.A. Alphabetum Augustinianum . . . Tomus I. *Madrid: G. Rodríguez,* 1644. 2 v.; fol. Includes biographical & bibliographical notices of Augustinians who served in the New World. Medina (BHA) 1059; Streit I:496; Palau 114184. NNAHi; Rome:BN. 644/77

Hevia Bolaños, Juan de. Curia filipica. *Madrid: C. Sánchez, for D. de Palacio y Villegas,* 1644. 2 pts; fol. The 2nd pt was 1st publ., Lima, 1617, under title *Laberinto de comercio terrestre y naval;* cf. 1619 edn above. Medina (BHA) 1060; Palau 114535. InU-L, MH, RPB; BN. 644/78

Holmes, Nathaniel. Gospel musick. or, The singing of David's Psalms, &c., in the publick congregation . . . Unto which is added, The judgment of our worthy brethren of New-England touching singing of psalms, as it is learnedly and gravely set forth in their preface to the singing psalms, by them translated into metre. *London: H. Overton,* 1644. 30 p.; 4to. Reprints most of the preface to the Bay Psalm Book, publ. at Cambridge, Mass., 1640. Sabin 28050; Wing H2567. CSmH, CtY, MH, MiU-C, NN-RB; BL. 644/79

Howell, James. Δενδρολογια. Dodona's grove, or The vocall forrest. The second edition. [*Oxford: H. Hall*] 1644. 172 p.; 4to. 1st publ., [London,] 1640. Wing H3059; Madan (Oxford) 1692; Arents 226-A. CSmH, CtY, ICU, MH, NN-A, RPB; BL. 644/80

James I, King of Great Britain. De abusu tobacci discursus. *Rostock: J. Hallervord,* 1644. 34 p.; 12 mo. Extracted from Thomas Reid's Latin translation of King James's works, publ., London, 1619; English text 1st publ., London, 1604, under title *A coun-*

terblaste to tobacco. Arents 227. CSmH, NN-A, PPC. 644/81

Jansson, Jan. [Atlas novus . . . tribus tomis distinctus. *Amsterdam: J. Janszoon, the Younger,* 1644]. 3 v.; illus., maps; fol. 1st publ. in this version, Amsterdam, 1638, as Mercator's *Atlas novus.* Koeman (Me) 54, 55, 56. CtY (imp.); Cracow:PAN. 644/82

——. Des nieuwen atlantis aenhang; ofte des Nieuwen wereld-beschrijvinghe . . . derde deel. *Amsterdam: J. Janszoon, the Younger,* 1644. 1 v.; maps; fol. Includes maps of Florida & North & South America. Intended as a supplement to Jansson's Nieuwen atlas, Amsterdam, 1642. For variant see Koeman. Koeman (Me) 75A & 75B; Phillips (Atlases) 4258 & 5937. DLC; Leeuwarden:PL, Haarlem:MA. 644/83

——. Nouveau theatre du monde, ou Nouvel atlas . . . divise en trois tomes. *Amsterdam: J. Janszoon, the Younger,* 1644. 3 v.; maps; fol. 1st publ. in this version, Amsterdam, 1639, as H. Hondius's *Nouveau theatre.* Of this edn, only v. 1 & 2 are known. Koeman (Me) 102, 103. BN (v. 2), Marburg:StB (v. 1). 644/84

——. [Novus Atlas, das ist Weltbeschreibung. *Amsterdam: J. Janszoon, the Younger,* 1644]. 3 v.; maps; fol. 1st publ., Amsterdam, 1638. Koeman (Me) 127–129. Leningrad:Saltykov PL. 644/85

Jonstonus, Joannes. Idea universae medicinae practicae libris viii absoluta. *Amsterdam: L. Elsevier,* 1644. 759 p.; 12mo. For treatment of syphilis & gonorrhea, guaiacum is specified. Willems (Les Elzevier) 1012. CLU-M, CtY-M, DNLM, MiU, NNNAM, PU; London:Wellcome, BN. 644/86

Klaer licht, ofte Vertoogh van 's lants welvaeren, aengaende de combinatie van de Oost en West-Indische Compagnien. [*Amsterdam?* 1644]. 12 p.; 4to. Sabin 38029 (& 102886); Knuttel 5120. DLC; BL, The Hague:KB. 644/87

—[Anr edn]. Claer licht, ofte Vertooch van 's lants wervaeren. [*Amsterdam?* 1644?]. [18] p.; 4to. Sabin 102886; Knuttel 5121. NNH; The Hague:KB. 644/88

Kort discours, ofte naardere verklaringe van de onderstaende v. poincten, 1. Aengaende de verlichtinghe die desen staat heeft ghenooten, door de oprechtinghe en oorlo-

ghen van de West-Indische Compagnie. [*The Hague?*] 1644. [35] p.; 4to. Sabin 38245; Asher 194; Knuttel 5122. DLC, NN-RB; BL, The Hague:KB. 644/89

La Barre, Antoine de. Les leçons publiques du sieur de La Barre, prises sur les questions curieuses et problematiques des plus beaux esprits de ce temps. *Leyden: Heirs of J. N. van Dorp,* 1644. 188 p.; 8vo. Included is a chapter on tobacco. Arents 228. ICN, NN-A; BL. 644/90

Laet, Joannes de. Historie ofte Jaerlijck verhael van de verrichtinghen der Geoctroyeerde West-Indische Compagnie. *Leyden: B. & A. Elsevier,* 1644. 544 p.; illus., maps; fol. 1st publ., Leyden, 1625, under title *Nieuwe Wereldt;* cf. enlarged edn. of 1630. Sabin 38556; Borba de Moraes I:383; Vail (Frontier); 103; Asher 22; Willems (Les Elzevier) 571; JCB (3) II:316. CtY, DLC, InU, MH-A, MiU-C, MnU-B, NN-RB, PU, RPJCB; BL, BN. 644/91

——. Responsio ad dissertationem secundam Hugonis Grotii, de Origine gentium Americanarum. *Amsterdam: L. Elsevier,*1644. 116 p.; map; 8vo. A response to Grotius's *De origine gentium Americanarum dissertatio altera,* 1st publ., Paris, 1642, the text of which is here included. Sabin 38562; Meulen/Diermanse 733; Willems (Les Elzevier) 1007. CtY, DLC, InU-L, MB, MiU-C, NN-RB, PU, RPJCB, WU; BL, BN. 644/92

Lechford, Thomas. New-Englands advice to Old-England. [*London:*] 1644. 80 p.; 4to. 1st publ., London, 1642, under title *Plain dealing;* here a reissue of that edn with cancel t.p. Sabin 39641; Baer (Md) 26; Wing L809; JCB (3) II:317. CSmH, MdBJ-G, NN-RB, RPJCB; BL. 644/93

Le Moyne, Pierre, S.J. Manifeste apologetique pour la doctrine des religeux de la Compagnie de Jesus. *Paris:* 1644. 150 p.; 4to. Defends motives of Jesuit missions in Canada, Brazil, & elsewhere. Backer V:1361; Lande (Canadiana) 522; Cioranescu (XVII) 42352. CaQMM; BL, BN. 644/94

—[Anr edn]. *Paris:* 1644. 174 p.; 8vo. Backer V:1361. BN. 644/95

—[Anr edn]. *Rouen: J. Le Boullenger & J. de Manneville,* 1644. 271 p.; 8vo. Backer V:1361. ICN. 644/96

Linschoten, Jan Huygen van. Beschrijvinge vande gantsche custe van Guinea . . . eñ tegen over de Cabo de S. Augustijn in Brasilien . . . *Amsterdam: E. Cloppenburg, 1644.* [86] p.; fol. 1st publ., Amsterdam, 1596; cf. 1605 edn. Ostensibly issued as a part of the author's *Itinerarium ofte schip-vaert* of this year below, q.v., since the present item includes an index for all 3 pts. Sabin 41363n; Tiele-Muller 90. MH. 644/97

——. Itinerarium, ofte Schip-vaert naer Oost ofte Portugaels Indien. *Amsterdam: E. Cloppenburg, 1644.* 3 pts; port., maps; fol. 1st publ., Amsterdam, 1596 (cf. 1605 edn); here ostensibly issued with Linschoten's *Reys-gheschrift* & his *Beschrijvinghe van . . . Guinea* of this year, the latter including an index for all three pts. Each pt has a special t.p. as well as separate paging & signatures. Sabin 41363; cf. Borba de Moraes I:419–20; Tiele-Muller 90; Tiele 682; JCB (3) II:317. DLC, MnU-B, NN-RB, RPJCB; BL. 644/98

——. Reys-gheschrift van de Navigatien der Portugaloysers in Orienten . . . Als oock van de gantsche custen van Brasilien . . . Item van 't vaste land enn die voor eylanden Las Antilas ghenaemt, van Spaensch Indien. *Amsterdam: E. Cloppenburg, 1644.* 147 p.; maps; fol. 1st publ., Amsterdam, 1595 [i.e., 1596]; cf. 1604 edn. Ostensibly issued as a part of the author's *Itinerarium ofte Schip-vaert* of this year above, q.v. Sabin 41363n; Tiele-Muller 90. MH. 644/99

Losa, Francisco de, S.J. La vie de Gregoire Lopez dans la Nouvelle Espagne. Composée en espagnol . . . et traduite nouvellement en françois, par un pere de la Compagnie de Jesus [Louis Conart]. *Paris: M. & J. Henault, 1644.* 264 p.; 12 mo. Transl. from Losa's *Vida que el siervo de Dios Gregorio Lopez hizo,* 1st publ., Mexico City, 1613; cf. 1615, Lisbon, edn. Sabin 42580; Medina (BHA) 624n (II:141); Streit II:1728; JCB (3) II:318. InU-L, RPJCB; BN. 644/100

Maldonado, José, O.F.M. Memorial y discurso que se dió al . . . señor don García de Haro y Avellaneda conde de Castrillo . . . por p. fr. Joseph Maldonado . . . commissario general del nuevo mundo de las Indias; cerca de la autoridad, y preeminencias de su oficio. [*Saragossa:* 1644?]. 32 lvs;

fol. On Franciscan missions in the Indies. Palau 147690. InU-L. 644/101

Megapolensis, Johannes. Een kort ontwerp vande Mahakuase Indianen, haer landt, tale, statuere, dracht, godes-dienst ende magistrature . . . opgesonden uit Nieuwe Neder-lant . . . Mitsgaders een Kort verhael van het leven . . . der Staponjers in Brasiel. *Alkmaar: Y. J. van Houten,* [1644]. [32] p.; illus.; 8vo. Includes, with special t.p., Gerrit Gerbrantszoon Hulck's 'Een korte beschrijvinge vande Staponjers in Brasiel'. Vail (Frontier) 104; Muller (1872) 1089; Stokes (Manhattan) VI:259; Meulman 2702. Ghent:BU. 644/102

Mercator, Gerardus. Atlas novus, sive Theatrum. *Amsterdam:* 1644. *See* Jansson, Jan, *above.*

Merinero, Juan, O.F.M. Fray Juan Merinero . . . A todos los religiosos de nuestras provincias de las Indias Occidentales . . . Salud y paz. [*Madrid:* 1644]. [17] p.; fol. Subscribed at Madrid, 16 March 1644. On conflict between native-born & Spanish-born Franciscans in Mexico. Medina (BHA) 1064. BL. 644/103

Moscherosch, Johann Michael. Visiones de don Quevedo, das ist, Wunderliche satyrische und war-hafftige Gesichte Philanders von Sittewald [pseud.]. *Frankfurt a. M.: A. Humme, 1644.* 985 p.; 8vo. 1st publ., Strassburg, [1640]; here an unauthorized reprint of the Strassburg, 1642, edn. Bechtold 'b'; Faber du Faur 427. CU, CtY, MH, MdBJ (imp.), PSt; Berlin:StB; Würzburg:UB. 644/104

Müller, Philipp (1585–1659). Miracula chymica, et mystica medica. *Paris: M. Mondière, 1644.* 191 p.; illus.; 12 mo. 1st publ., [Wittenberg], 1611. DNLM, MBCo. 644/105

Nederlandsche West-Indische Compagnie. Remonstrantie ende consideratien aengaende de vereeninghe vande Oost ende West-Indische Compagnien . . . Midtsgaders de Consideratien ende andtwoorden by de . . . bewinthebberen. *The Hague: L. de Langhe, 1644.* 40 p.; 4to. Includes the Nederlandsche West-Indische Compagnie's *Twee deductien* of this year below. Sabin 69586 (& 102911); Knuttel 5114. DLC; The Hague:KB. 644/106

—[Anr edn?] *The Hague:* [1644]. 4to. BL.
644/107

——. Twee deductien, aen-gaende de ver-eeninge van d'Oost ende West-Indische Compagnien. *The Hague: J. Veely,* 1644. 21 p.; 4to. This issue has vignette of ship on t.p. under phrase 'Concordia res parvae crescunt'. Sabin 97527 (& 102913); Asher 198; Knuttel 5112; JCB (3) II:319. DLC, NN-RB, RPJCB; The Hague:KB.
644/108

—[Anr issue]. *The Hague: J. Veely,* 1644. Coat of arms of province of Holland appears on t.p. under Latin motto. Knuttel 5113. The Hague:KB. 644/109

—[Anr state of preceding]. *The Hague: J. Veely,* 1644. Lacks Latin motto above vignette. Cf. Sabin 97527n; Asher 197; cf. Knuttel 5113n. BL. 644/110

Netherlands (United Provinces, 1581–1795). Laws, statutes, etc. Nederlandtsche placcaet-boeck: waerinne alle voornaemste placcaten, ordonnantien, accorden ende andere acten ende munimenten . . . begrepen worden. *Amsterdam: J. Janszoon, the Younger,* 1644. 2 pts; fol. Includes numerous items relating to Brazil, West Indies, trade, etc. JCB (3) II:319. CtY, DLC, NN-RB, RPJCB. 644/111

Nieremberg, Juan Eusebio, S.J. Curiosa filosofia y tesoro de las maravillas de la naturaleza. *Barcelona: P. Lacavallería,* 1644. 214 numb. lvs; 8vo. 1st publ., Madrid, 1630. Backer V:1731; Palau 190664. MH-A; BN.
644/112

——. Firmamento religioso de luzidos astros, en algunos claros varones de la Compañia de Jesus. *Madrid: María de Quiñones,* 1644. 798 p.; fol. Continues the author's *Ideas de virtud* of 1643, as v. 4 of his *Varones de la Compañia de Jesus.* Sabin 55270; Medina (BHA) 1066; Streit I:495; Backer V:1746; JCB (3) II:320. ICN, InU-L, RPJCB; BL.
644/113

——. Vida del santo padre . . . el b. Francisco de Borja, tercero general de la Compañia de Jesus. *Madrid: Maria de Quiñones,* 1644. 515 p.; port.; fol. In bk 3, chapts 8–9 & 11 describe beginnings of Jesuit missions in New World. Text extracted from the author's *Ideas de virtud,* Madrid, 1643.

Backer V:1747; Palau 191036. RPJCB; BN.
644/114

Noodige bedenckingen der trouhertighe Nederlanders over de aen-staende Munstersche handelinge van vrede ofte treves. . . . den tweeden druck, oversien en verbetert. [*The Hague?*] 1644. [22] p.; 4to. 1st publ., [The Hague?], 1643. Knuttel 5103. InU-L, NN; The Hague:KB.
644/115

Norwood, Richard. The sea-mans practice. *London: T. Fawcet, for G. Hurlock,* 1644. 142 p.; illus.; 4to. 1st publ., London, 1637. Wing N1354. CSmH, NN-RB; Cambridge: Emmanuel, BN. 644/116

Ontworp, en voor-stel tot remedie van twee swarigheden inde West-Indische Compagnie. [*The Hague?*] 1644. 8 p.; 4to. Sabin 57373; Asher 190; Meulman 2704. Ghent:BU. 644/117

—[Anr edn?]. Antworp [etc.]. [*The Hague?*] 1644. 4to. BL (Ned. West-Ind. Comp).
644/118

Ooghen-salve tot verlichtinghe, van alle participanten, so vande Oost, ende West-Indische Compaignien. *The Hague: L. de Langhe,* 1644. 35 p.; 4to. Sabin 57376 (& 102903); Asher 193; Knuttel 5123; JCB (3) II:319. DLC, MH-BA, MiU-C, MnU-B, NN-RB, RPJCB; BL, The Hague:KB.
644/119

Opitz, Martin. Weltliche Poemata. *Frankfurt a. M.: T. M. Götz,* 1644. 2 pts; 8vo. 1st publ. with American refs, Breslau, 1628–29, under title *Deutscher Poematum.* Opitz's 'Lob des Krieges Gottes' appears here in pt 1. Goedeke III:49; Faber du Faur 228; Jantz (German Baroque) 1932; Jördens IV:116. CU, CtY, DLC, MH, NNC, PU; BL, Göttingen: StUB. 644/120

Owen, John. Epigrammatum editio postrema. *Amsterdam: J. Janszoon, the Younger,* 1644. 215 p.; port.; 8vo. 1st publ., London, 1606. NNC, ViU. 644/121

Palma y Freitas, Luis de la. Por las religiones de Santo Domingo, Santo Francisco, y . . . San Agustin . . . de Nueva-España. En defensa de las doctrina de que fueron removidos de hecho sus religiosos por . . . Don Juan de Palafox y Mendoza, obispo de Tlaxcala. *Madrid: Imprenta Real,* 1644. 34

numb. lvs; fol. Medina (BHA) 1067; Streit II:1731. RPJCB; BL. 644/122

Paris, Université. III. [i.e., Troisième] requeste de l'Université de Paris, presentée a la cour de Parlement. Le 7 decembre 1644, contre les libelles que les Jesuites ont publiez. *Paris: The University,* 1644. 2 pts; 8vo. Includes refs to Jesuits' relations with natives of New France. MnU-B, N; BL. 644/123

Parker, Thomas. The true copy of a letter: written by Mr. Thomas Parker, a learned . . . minister, in New-England . . . Declaring his judgement touching the government practised in the churches of New-England. *London: R. Cotes, for R. Smith,* 1644. 4 p.; 4to. Sabin 58770; Wing P482; JCB (3) II:320. CtY, MiU-C, NN-RB, RPJCB; BL. 644/124

Peralta, Pedro de. Señor. El capitan Don Pedro de Peralta contador, oficio real . . . de Veneçuela, y Caracas . . . . dize. [*Madrid:* 1644?]. 4 numb. lvs; fol. Memorial to king of Spain describing conditions in Venezuela & conflict with bishop there. BL. 644/125

Poisson, Jean Baptiste. Animadversio . . . ad ea quae . . . Hugo Grotius & Joannes Lahetius de origine gentium Peruvianarum et Mexicanarum scripserunt. *Paris:* 1644. 23 p.; 12 mo. Sabin 63711. NN-RB; BN. 644/126

Ponce de León, Francisco. Descripcion del reyno de Chile, de sus puertos, caletas, y sitio de Valdivia. [*Madrid:* 1644?]. 15 numb. lvs; 4to. Preface dated Madrid, 1 Oct. 1644. Sabin 63969; Medina (Chile) 111; Streit II:1733; JCB (3) II:321. OCl, RPJCB; BL. 644/127

Pretty, Francis. Beschrijvinge vande overtreffelijcke ende wydtvermaerde see-vaert van . . . Thomas Candish. [*Amsterdam:*] 1644. 78 p.; obl. 4to. Sabin 11608. *See* Commelin, Izaäk, *above.*

Prevost, Jean. Medicina pauperum. *Lyons: P. Ravaud,* 1644. 718 p.; 12mo. 1st publ., Frankfurt a. M.?, 1641? Here a reissue of Ravaud's 1643 edn, with altered imprint date? BL, BN. 644/128

Primerose, James. De vulgi erroribus in medicina libri quatuor. *Amsterdam: J. Jans-*zoon, the Younger, 1644. 237 p.; 12mo. 1st publ., London, 1638. CtHT, DNLM, MH. 644/129

Raleigh, Sir Walter. Grondige ende waerachtige beschrijvinge van . . . Guiana. [*Amsterdam:*] 1644. [98] p.; obl. 4to. Sabin 67558 (& 37691). *See* Commelin, Izaäk, *above.*

Rathband, William. A briefe narration of some courses held in opinion and practise in the churches lately erected in New England. *London: G. M[iller]., for E. Brewster,* 1644. Sabin 67947; Wing R298; McAlpin II:312, JCB (3) II:322. CSmH, CtY, ICN, MH, MWA, NNUT, RPJCB; BL. 644/130

Reyd, Everhard van. Oorspronck ende voortganck vande Nederlantsche oorloghen . . . derde editie. Naer des autheurs originael oversien, ende . . . vermeerdert . . . Ende hier is nu nieulijcks by gevoeght 't vervolgh van 1601 tot . . . 1644. *Amsterdam: Widow of E. Cloppenburg,* 1644. 2 v.; illus.; fol. 1st publ., Arnhem, 1626; the continuator is unknown. For a differing continuation, see the year 1650. DLC, ICU; BL. 644/131

Rimphoff, Heinrich. Aurea pacis corona, & catena, das ist Güldene Friedens Frewden Bundes-Cron und Kette. *Rinteln a. d. Weser: P. Lucius,* 1644. [8] p.; 4to. Discusses riches brought by Spaniards from Indies, as reported by Surius, asserting that Germans would prefer peace to Indian treasures. Cf. Jöcher (Suppl.) VI:2172. NN (imp.). 644/132

Ripa, Cesare. Iconologia, of Uytbeeldingen des verstands . . . Uyt het italiaans vertaelt door D. P. Pers. *Amsterdam: J. Lescaille, for D. P. Pers,* 1644. 638 p.; illus.; 4to. Transl. from Ripa's *Iconologia,* 1st publ. with American content, Rome, 1603. CtY, MoSU, PP; BL. 644/133

——. Iconologie, ou Explication nouvelle de plusieurs images . . . Moralisées par J[ean]. Baudoin. *Paris: M. Guillemot,* 1644, '43. 2 pts; illus.; 4to. The earliest edn of this French version of the Italian text (1st publ. with American content, Rome, 1603) containing pt 2 and the emblematic representation of America. In the prose commentary the discovery of the continent is attrib. to Vespucci. CLU-C, DLC, MH, NN, MoSW; BL, BN.   644/134

Rivière, Lazare. Praxis medica. Editio secunda. *Paris: O. de Varennes, 1644–45.* 2 v.; 8vo. 1st publ., Paris, 1640. DNLM.

644/135

Romance en alabansa del tabaco, y de sus virtudes, sacadas del libro Historia plantarum, y de otros muchos, y graves autores. *Barcelona: G. Nogues, 1644.* [4] p.; 4to. In verse. BL.   644/136

Rutherford, Samuel. The due right of presbyteries or, A peaceable plea for the government of the Church of Scotland, wherein is examined 1. The way of the church of Christ in New England . . . 2. Their apology for the said government [etc.]. *London: E. Griffin, for R. Whitaker & A. Crooke, 1644.* 468 p.; 4to. Sabin 74456; Wing R2378; McAlpin II:314; JCB (3) II:322–323. CSmH, CtY, DLC, ICN, InU-L, MH, MiU-C, MnU, NN-RB, PPT, RPJCB; BL.

644/137

Scarron, Paul. Typhon, ou La gigantomachie. Poëme burlesque. *Paris: T. Quinet, 1644.* 4 pts; 4to. Tobacco ('Petun') is mentioned. Magne (Scarron) 17; Cioranescu (XVII) 61809. CtY, MH; BN.   644/138

Schaede die den staet der Vereenichde Nederlanden, en d' inghesetenen van dien, is aenstaende, by de versuymenisse van d' Oost en West-Indische negotie onder een octroy en societeyt te begrijpen. *The Hague: J. Veely, 1644.* 51 p.; 4to. Sabin 77475; Asher 191; Knuttel 5119. DLC, MnU-B, NN-RB; BL, The Hague:KB.   644/139

—[Anr edn]. *The Hague: J. Veely, 1644.* [54] p.; 4to. This edn has reading 'die den staat' in title. Asher 192.   644/140

Schenck von Grafenberg, Johann. Observationum medicarum rariorum libri vii. *Lyons: J. A. Huguetan, 1644.* 892 p.; port.; fol. 1st publ., Frankfurt a. M., 1600; cf. 1609 edn with title Παρατηρησεων; here anr edn of Huguetan's 1643 edn with altered imprint date? DNLM, ICJ, NIC, PPGenH; BL, BN.

644/141

Schouten, Willem Corneliszoon. Journael ofte Beschryvinghe vande wonderlijcke Reyse. *Amsterdam: J. Janszoon, the Younger, 1644.* 56 p.; illus., maps; 4to. 1st publ., Amsterdam, 1618. Sabin 77929; Palau 305089; Tiele-Muller 48; cf. Tiele 982n; Muller (1872) 1959; JCB (3) II:323. NN-RB, RPJCB; BL.   644/142

Schröder, Johann (1600–1664). Pharmacopoeia medico-chymica, sive Thesaurus pharmacologicus . . . editione secundà correctius & auctius. *Ulm: J. Görlin, 1644.* 3 pts; 4to. 1st publ., Ulm, 1641. InU.

644/143

Sennert, Daniel. Institutionum medicinae libri v. *Wittenberg: M. Wendt, for Heirs of T. Mevius, 1644.* 1523 p.; illus., port; 4to. DNLM, OClStM, WU.   644/144

Siri, Vittorio. Il mercurio, overo Historia de correnti tempi. *Casale: C. della Casa, 1644.* 853 p.; 4to. Account of treaty between Portugal & the Netherlands (p. 827–841) refers to Nederlandsche West-Indische Compagnie. For a 2nd vol., see the year 1647. Sabin 81447; Brunet V:402; Graesse VI: 417. CU, CtY, ICN, MH, MdBP, NN-RB, RPJCB; BL, BN.   644/145

Spilbergen, Joris van. Historisch journael van der voyagie . . . door de straete Magallanes. [*Amsterdam:* 1644?]. 118 p.; illus.; obl. 4to. Sabin 89447. *See* Commelin, Izaäk, *above.*

Steuart, Adam. An answer to a libell intituled, A coole conference. *London:* 1644. 62 p.; 4to. Ref. is made, p. 51, to separatism of New England churches. Sabin 91381; Wing S5489; McAlpin II:319. CtY, DFo, MWiW-C, NN-RB, RPJCB; BL.

644/146

——. The second part of the duply to M.S. alias Two brethren . . . With a brief epitome and refutation of all the whole independent-government. *London: J. Field, 1644.* 194 p.; 4to. A reply to John Goodwin, *A reply of two of the brethren to A. S.* Included are numerous disparaging comments on the Puritan establishment in New England. Sabin 91382; Wing S5491; McAlpin II:319; JCB (3) II:323. CSmH, CtY, DLC, ICU, MH, MnU, NN-RB, RPJCB; BL.

644/147

——. Some observations and annotations upon the Apologeticall narration. *London: C. Meredith, 1643* [i.e., 1644]. 71 p.; 4to. Included are numerous derogatory refs to clergy of New England. Entered in Stationers' Register 21 Febr. 1644. Sabin 91383; Wing S5492; McAlpin II:252; JCB (3) II:311. CSmH, DLC, MH, NN-RB, RPJCB; BL. 644/148

—[Anr issue]. *London: C. Meredith,* 1644. Sabin 91383 (& 56461); Wing S5493; McAlpin II:319; JCB (3) II:323. CU-B, CtY, DLC, IU, MB, MnU, NNUT, RPJCB; BL. 644/149

Swan, John. Speculum mundi. or A glasse representing the face of the world . . . The second edition enlarged. *Cambridge: R. Daniel [for T. Atkinson],* 1643 [i.e., 1644]. 504 p.; 4to. 1st publ., Cambridge, 1636; here a reissue of 1643 edn with added engr. t.p. dated 1644 with bookseller's name in imprint. Wing S6238A. DFo, MH. 644/150

—[Anr issue]. *Cambridge: R. Daniel, [for J. Williams, at London],* 1643 [i.e., 1644]. As above, with added engraved t.p. RPJCB. 644/151

Syms, Christopher. The swords apology, and necessity in the act of reformation. *London: T. Warren,* 1644. 15 p.; illus.; 4to. Mentions trade in West Indian tobacco. Wing S6364; Arents (Add.) 327. CtY, NN-A; BL, Cambridge:UL. 644/152

Tanara, Vincenzo. L'economia del cittadino in villa. *Bologna: G. Monti,* 1644. 594 p.; illus.; 4to. Mentioned are not only the turkey but also various American plants, amongst them the 'Granatilia' (passionflower), 'portata dall'Indiche piaggie'. CU, MH-A, MiU, NNNAM. 644/153

Taylor, John, the Water-poet. Crop-eare curried. [*Oxford;*] 1644. *See the year* 1645.

——. John Taylor being yet unhanged, sends greeting to John Booker. [*Oxford: L. Lichfield*] 1644. 4to. Rivalry between Columbus & Vespucci is described. Madan (Oxford) 1695; Wing T434. BL. 644/154

Theophrastus. De historia plantarum libri x, graece et latine . . . cum notis tum commentariis, item rariorum plantarum iconibus illustravit Joannes Bodaeus a Stapel. *Amsterdam: H. Laurenszoon,* 1644. 1187 p.; illus.; fol. The editor's commentary contains refs to numerous American plants. Nissen (Bot.) 1947nc; Hunt (Bot.) 240. CtY, DLC, IU, InU-L, MH-A, MiU, NNC, PU, RPB; BL. BN. 644/155

Tomasini, Jacopo Philippo, Bp of Città Nuova. Elogia virorum literis & sapientia illustrium. *Padua: S. Sardi,* 1644. 411 p.; illus., ports; 4to. 1st publ., Padua, 1630, under title *Illustrium virorum elogia.* CtY, DFo, ICN, MH, MiU, PPT; BL, BN. 644/156

A true state of the case between the heires and assignes of Sir William Courteen, knight . . . and the late Earl of Carlisle, and planters in the island of Barbadoes . . . exhibited in Parliament. [*London:* ca. 1644]. bds.; fol. Handler (Barbados) 1–2. BL. 644/157

Tydingh uyt Brasil aende heeren bewinthebberen van de West-Indische Compagnie, van wegen den tocht by den Generael Brouwer nae de Zuyd-Zee gedaen. *Amsterdam: F. Lieshout,* 1644. bds.; fol. Sabin 7641; Borba de Moraes II:317–18; Asher 185. 644/158

Vargas Carvajal, Francisco. Peticion de Don Francisco de Vargas Carvajal correo mayor del Peru. [*Madrid?* 1644.]. [8] p.; fol. Protests against changes in postal administration instituted by the viceroy, the marqués de Mancera. Medina (BHA) 1071. Santiago, Chile:BN. 644/159

Vesling, Johann. Opobalsami veteribus cogniti vindiciae. *Padua: P. Frambotti,* 1644. 108 p.; 4to. Opobalsam as produced in Peru & Tolu is cited. DNLM, NNBG; London:Wellcome, BN. 644/160

Vimont, Barthélemy, S.J. Relation de ce qui s'est passé en la Nouvelle France en l'annee 1642. & 1643. *Paris: S. Cramoisy, & G. Cramoisy,* 1644. 309 p.; 8vo. For variants, see Bell & McCoy as cited. Sabin 99751; Harrisse (NF) 81; Streit II:2553; Bell (Jes. rel.) 25–26; McCoy 49–52; Church 472; JCB (3) II:324. CSmH, CtY, DLC, ICN, InU-L, MH, MiU-C, MnU-B, NN-RB, RPJCB; BL, BN. 644/161

Volkamer, Johann Georg, ed. Opobalsami orientalis in theriaces confectionem Romae revocati examen. *Nuremberg: W. Endter,* 1644. 224 p.; 24 mo. Includes comparisons of therapeutic value of oriental opobalsam with that found 'in nova Hispaniâ' (Mexico) & in Peru. Normally bound with, as issued, A. Colmenero de Ledesma's *Chocolata Inda* of this year. CtY, DNLM, ICJ, NjP, RPJCB; BL, BN. 644/162

Vondel, Joost van den. Verscheide gedichten . . . Verzamelt door D. B. D. L. B. [i.e., Gerrit Brandt]. *Amsterdam: J. Lescaille for J. Hartgers*, 1644. 406 p.; 8vo. Includes, p. 133, the author's 'Op Pieter Pietersz Heyn', referring to naval activity in West Indies. Unger (Vondel) 1. MH; BL, Amsterdam: UB.   644/163

Warwick, Robert Rich, 2d earl of. A declaration of the Right Honourable Robert, earle of Warwick, Lord High Admirall of England, and of all the plantations . . . upon the coasts of America, Governour of the Company . . . of the Summer Islands . . . To the colony and plantation there. [*London:* 1644]. 12 p.; 4to. Dated (p. 4): 23 October, 1644. Sabin 101508; Wing W995; JCB (3) II:335. MH, NHi, RPJCB; BL.
644/164

Wecker, Johann Jakob. Practica Weckeri. *Venice: G. B. Combi*, 1644. 489 p.; 16mo. 1st publ., Basel, 1585; cf. 1602 edn. DNLM, ICU, NIC.   644/165

Weld, Thomas. An answer to W. R. his Narration of the opinions and practises of the churches lately erected in New-England . . . By Thomas Welde, pastour of the church of Roxborough in New-England. *London: T. Paine, for H. Overton*, 1644. 68 p.; 4to. A reply to William Rathband's *Briefe narration* of this year. Sabin 102551; Wing W1262; JCB (3) II:324. CSmH, CtY, DLC, ICN, MH, MWA, MiU-C, RPJCB: BL.
644/166

——. A short story. *London:* 1644. *See* Winthrop, John, *below.*

Williams, Roger. The bloudy tenent of persecution. [*London:*] 1644. 247 p.; 4to. For a reply, see John Cotton's *The bloody tenent, washed*, London, 1647. This edn includes errata, p. 247. Sabin 104332; Wing W2758; Church 467; JCB (3) II:325. CSmH, CtY, DLC, MH, MiU, NN-RB, RPJCB; BL, Oxford:Bodl.   644/167

—[Anr edn]. The bloudy tenet. [*London:*] 1644. 247 p.; 4to. This edn lacks errata at end, the text being corrected. Sabin 104331; Wing 2759; JCB (3) II:326. RPJCB; Dublin:Trinity.   644/168

——. Mr. Cottons letter lately printed, examined and answered. *London:* 1644. 47 p.; 4to. A reply to John Cotton's *Letter . . . to Mr.*

Williams, London, 1643. Sabin 104341 (& 17082); Wing W2767; Church 468; JCB (3) II:326. CSmH, CtY, MH, NN-RB, RPJCB; BL.   644/169

Winthrop, John, supposed author. Antinomians and Familists condemned by the synods of elders in New-England: with the proceedings of the magistrates against them. *London: R. Smith*, 1644. 66 p.; 4to. On Anne Hutchinson & the Antinomian controversy. Attrib. to Winthrop by C. F. Adams in his *Antinomianism in the colony of Massachusetts Bay* (Boston, 1894). Sabin 104843; Wing W3094; McAlpin II:265; Church 465; JCB (3) II:325. CSmH, CtY, DLC, ICN, InU-L, MH, MWA, MiU-C, NN-RB, PHC, RPJCB; BL.   644/170

—[Anr edn]. A short story of the rise, reign, and ruine of the Antinomians, Familists & libertines, that infected the churches of New-England. *London: R. Smith*, 1644. 66 p.; 4to. Here added is a preface signed 'T. Welde' to whom the work has sometimes been ascribed. In this edn p. 56 is misnumbered 57. Sabin 104848; JCB (3) II:325. MH, MiU-C, NN-RB, RPJCB.   644/171

—[Anr edn]. *London: R. Smith*, 1644. 66 p.; 4to. Differs from preceding in having p. 56 correctly numbered, etc. Sabin 104848; Church 466; JCB (3) II:325. CSmH, CtY, ICN, MH, RPJCB; BL.   644/172

Zacchia, Paolo. De' mali hipochondriaci libri tre. *Rome: V. Mascardi, for E. Ghezzi*, 1644. 527 p.; 4to. 1st publ., Rome, 1639. CLU-M, DNLM, ICU, NNNAM. 644/173

Zacutus, Abraham, Lusitanus. Praxis historiarum . . . Accessit Praxis medica admiranda. *Lyons: J. A. Huguetan*, 1644. 2 pts; fol. (His Opera omnia. Lyons, 1643–44, v. 2). The *Praxis medica admiranda* 1st publ., Amsterdam, 1634. DCU-IA, MBCo, MnU-B.   644/174

Zeiller, Martin. Das vierdte Hundert Episteln. *Ulm: J. Görlin*, 1644. 716 p.; 8vo. Continues Zeiller's *Ein Hundert Episteln*, 1st publ., Heilbronn & Ulm, 1640. On p. 623 ff. is a discussion of whether the ancients knew of America, & by whom it was populated, mentioning Asians crossing the 'Anian Strait' & Scandinavians settling in Iceland & Greenland. Jantz (German Baroque) 2771; Jördens V:600. CtY, NcD.   644/175

1645

Aldrovandi, Ulisse. De quadrupedibus digitatis viviparis libri tres et de quadrupedibus digitatis oviparis libri duo. *Bologna: N. Tebaldini, for M. A. Bernia*, 1645. 718 p.; illus.; fol. 1st publ., Bologna, 1637. Nissen (Zool.) 77n. CU, CtY, DNLM, ICJ, MB, MiU, MnU, NN-RB, PPC; BL, BN. 645/1

——. Ornithologiae [. . . libri]. *Bologna:* 1645. *See the years* 1646 & 1652.

Alegambe, Philippe, S.J. De vita, & morib. p. Joannis Cardim lusitani è Societate Jesu liber. *Rome: F. Cavalli*, 1645. 135 p.; port.; 8vo. Includes account of Jesuit missions in Brazil. Borba de Moraes I:17; Backer I:152. BN, Munich:StB, Rome:BN. 645/2

Alemán, Mateo. Le gueux, ou La vie de Guzman d'Alfarache. *Rouen: D. Ferrand*, 1645–46. 2 v.; 8vo. 1st publ. as here transl. by Jean Chapelain, Paris, 1619, & Paris, 1620. Vol. 2 has title *Le voleur, ou La vie de Guzman d'Alfarache.* Laurenti (Nov. pic. esp.) 627. BN. 645/3

Antwoort vanden ghetrouwen Hollander. Op den Aenspraeck van den heetgebaeckerden Hollander. [*The Hague?*] 1645. [16] p.; 4to. A reply to D. Graswinckel's *Aenspraek aen den getrouwen Hollander* of this year below. Sabin 7515; Borba de Moraes I:35; Asher 207; Knuttel 5229. DLC; The Hague:KB. 645/4

Autentyck verhael van 't gene in Brasiel tot den 15 September is voorgevallen, geschreven uyt 't Resif. *Amsterdam: J. van Hilten*, 1645. bds.; fol. Sabin 7521; Borba de Moraes I:47; Asher 205; Knuttel 5556. The Hague:KB. 645/5

Ayo, Cristóbal de. Tratado de las excelencias y virtudes del tabaco. *Salamanca:* 1645. 32 p.; 4to. Medina (BHA) 1073; Palau 20892. Seville:B. Colombina. 645/6

Baardt, Pieter. Deughden-spoor; in de ondeughden des werelts aff-gebeeldt. *Leeuwarden: S. Geerts*, 1645. 326 p.; illus.; 8vo. In verse. Poem 'Medicus' includes ref. to Indians; 'Apothecarius' has ref. to mechoacan; further ref. to America on p. 178. ICN, MH. 645/7

—[Anr edn]. *Leeuwarden: H. W. Coopman*, 1645. 394 p.; illus.; 8vo. DFo; BL. 645/8

Bacon, Francis, viscount St Albans. De aug-

mentis scientiarum. Libri ix . . . Editio nova. *Leyden: F. Moyaert & A. Wijngaerden*, 1645. 749 p.; 12mo. 1st publ., London, 1623, under title *Opera: Tomus primus.* Gibson (Bacon) 132. CU, DFo, IU, MH, NjPT; BL, BN. 645/9

——. Historia vitae et mortis. *Dillingen:* 1645. 526 p.; 18mo. 1st publ., London, 1623. Gibson (Bacon) 150. DFo, DLC, MiU; BL. 645/10

Baerle, Kaspar van. Poemata. Editio iv. Altera plus parte auctior. Pars i[–ii]. *Amsterdam: J. Blaeu*, 1645–46. 2 pts; 12mo. 1st publ., Leyden, 1628. Sabin 3407; Borba de Moraes I:65; Willems (Les Elzevier) 344n; Rahir (Les Elzevier) 1955. CtY, ICN, MH, MiU-C, NNU, NcD, PU, RPJCB; BL, BN. 645/11

Baillie, Robert. A dissuasive from the errours of the time: wherein the tenets of the principall sects, especially of the Independents, are drawn together in one map. *London: S. Gellibrand*, 1645. 252 p.; 4to. Chapt. 3 comprises 'The origins and progress of the Independents, and of their carriage in New-England'. Sabin 4059; Wing B456; McAlpin II:330; JCB (3) II:327. CSmH, CtY, ICN, InU-L, MH, MiU-C, MnU, NN-RB, RPJCB; BL. 645/12

Baldani, Fulgenzio, O.S.A. Vita del . . . fra Diego Ortiz, protomartire nel regno del Peru, martizzato l'ano 1571. *Genoa: Pavonum*, 1645. 4to. Based upon Antonio de la Calancha's *Coronica moralizada* of 1638. Sabin 57715; Streit II:1738; Palau 22371. 645/13

Balde, Jakob, S.J. Lyricorum libri iv & Epodon lib. unus. Editio secunda, auctior & emendatior. *Cologne: J. Kalckhoven*, 1645. 329 p.; illus.; 12mo. 1st publ., Munich, 1643. Some copies have added engraved t.p. dated 1646. Backer I:820. MH, MiDU, NNUT, OCl, PU; BL. 645/14

Barnstein, Heinrich. Tabacologia, das ist: Beschreibung des Tabacks . . . was er vor Tugenden und Eygenschafften an sich habe . . . *Erfurt: T. Fritsche*, 1645. 12 lvs; 4to. 1st publ., Erfurt, 1644, under title *Taback das Wunder.* Dt. Ges. Kat. 11.7681; Arents 229. NN-A; Gotha:HB. 645/15

—[Anr edn]. Kurtze Beschreibung dess Tabacks. *Erfurt: T. Fritsche*, 1645. 18 lvs; 8vo.

Dt. Ges. Kat. 11.7682; Arents 229n. BL,
Erlangen:UB. 645/16

Béguin, Jean. Les elemens de chymie. *Lyons:
C. Chancey,* 1645. 384 p.; illus.; 8vo. 1st publ.
as here transl. from Béguin's *Tyrocinium chymicum* (Paris, 1612), Paris, 1615. BN.
645/17

Bertius, Petrus. Geographia vetus ex antiquis, et melioris notae scriptoribus nuper
collecta. *Paris: J. Boisseau,* 1645. 20 lvs;
maps; obl. 4to. 1st publ., Paris, 1628. BL,
BN. 645/18

**Bethune, Philippe de, comte de Selles et de
Charost.** Le conseiller d'estat. *Paris: M. Bobin,* 1645. 496 p.; 4to. 1st publ., [Paris?],
1632. InU-L, MH-BA. 645/19

——[Anr edn]. 'Suivent la copie imprimee à
Paris.' [*Leyden? F. Heger?*] 1645. 539 p.;
12mo. Willems (Les Elzevier) 973n. MnU,
RPB; BL, BN. 645/20

Beverwijck, Jan van. Heel-konste, ofte
Derde deel van de geneeskonste om de
uytwendige gebreken te heelen. *Dordrecht:
H. van Esch, for P. Looymans & M. de Bot,*
1645. 487 p.; illus.; 8vo. Chapt. vi includes
discussion of West Indian medicines tacamahac & caranna, & their use by Indians.
Van de Velde 76. CtY-M, DNLM; BL, BN.
645/21

Blaeu, Willem Janszoon. Le theatre du
monde, ou Nouvel atlas. *Amsterdam: J. Blaeu,*
1645. 2 pts; 120 maps; fol. 1st publ., Amsterdam, 1635. Issued with Blaeu's *Le theatre
. . . seconde partie* below. Here, a dedication
has been added to 'Regiones sub polo arctico'. The copy described by Phillips represents anr edn of pt 1, lacking text and excluding Americana. Koeman (Bl) 19B; cf.
Phillips (Atlases) 5938. NNE, NNH.
645/22

——. Le theatre du monde, ou Nouvel atlas
. . . Seconde partie. *Amsterdam: J. Blaeu,*
1645. 2 pts; 93 maps; fol. 1st publ., Amsterdam, 1635; here a reissue of the Amsterdam, 1644, edn with date altered by paste-
on slip. Issued with Blaeu's *Le theatre* above.
Koeman (Bl) 18C. NNH. 645/23

——[Anr edn]. *Amsterdam: J. Blaeu,* 1645. Lacks
the text normally accompanying maps. Phillips (Atlases) 5938. DLC. 645/24

——. Theatrum orbis terrarum, sive Atlas
novus, pars secunda. *Amsterdam: J. Blaeu,*

1645. 2 pts; 92 maps; fol. 1st publ., Amsterdam, 1635. Issued with Blaeu's *Theatrum,*
Amsterdam, 1644. Sabin 5720n; Koeman
(Bl) 24A. MB, MnHi, NPV; Leeuwarden:PFL, Florence:B. Marucel. 645/25

Boissard, Jean Jacques. Icones et effigies
virorum doctorum . . . artificiosissime in
aes incisae a Joh. Theodoro de Brÿ. *Frankfurt a. M.: J. Ammon,* 1645. 2 v.; ports; 4to.
1st publ., Frankfurt a. M., 1597–99, under
title *Icones quinquaginta virorum illustrium,*
etc., but here without Boissard's text; cf.
1628–31 edn. Cf. Sabin 6162. ICN; London: Wellcome, BN. 645/26

Canale, Floriano. De' secreti universali raccolti, et esperimentati. *Venice: Heirs of G. Imberti,* 1645. 304 p.; 8vo. 1st publ., Brescia
(?), 1613. BL. 645/27

Casas, Bartolomé de las, O.P., Bp of Chiapa.
Conquista dell'Indie Occidentali . . . Tradotta . . . per opera di Marco Ginammi.
Venice: M. Ginammi, 1645. 184; p.; 4to. 1st
publ. in this translation, Venice, 1644; here
a reissue with altered imprint date. Text
in Spanish & Italian in parallel columns.
Sabin 11248; Medina (BHA) 1085n
(II:472); Hanke/Giménez 538; Streit I:499;
Palau 46958; JCB (3) II:327–328. CtY,
DLC, KU, MH, NN-RB, PU, RPJCB; BL.
645/28

Cats, Jacob. Minnelijcke, zedelijcke en
stichtelijcke zinnebeelden en ghedichten.
[*Amsterdam?* ca. 1645.] [217] p.; illus.; obl.
12mo. 1st publ. in this abridged version,
[Amsterdam? 1622?]. Engraved t.p. begins
'Emblemata ofte Minnelijcke . . .'; vignette
portrays various persons; on globe carried
by Cupid, 'Europa' & 'America' can be read.
Vries 93; Mus. Cats 46. Leyden:UB.
645/29

——. Poëtische wercken . . . namentlijck
Emblemata, Maegden-plicht . . . [*Antwerp?*
ca. 1645]. [394] p.; illus.; 8vo. Cats's *Emblemata* 1st publ., Middelburg, 1618, here
abridged; his *Maegden-plicht* 1st publ., Middelburg, 1618. Vries 94; Mus. Cats. 47.
645/30

——. Silenus Alcibiadis, sive Proteus. *Dordrecht: M. de Bot* [ca. 1645]. 4 pts; illus.; 8vo.
1st publ., Middelburg, 1618; here an apparent reissue of Rammazeyn's Gouda, [ca.
1640], edn, with cancel t.p. Vries 86; Mus.

Cats. 35; Arents 163-a. NN-A; Leyden:UB.
645/31

—[Anr edn]. [*Rotterdam?* ca. 1645]. 4 pts; illus.; 8vo. Vries 87; Mus. Cats. 36. Leyden: UB. 645/32

Cawdry, Daniel. Vindiciae clavium, or, A vindication of the keyes of the kingdome of heaven . . . being some animadversions upon a tract of Mr. J. C[otton]. . . . as also upon . . . his . . . The way of the churches of New-England. *London: T. H[arper?]., for P. Whaley,* 1645. 90 p.; 4to. A reply to John Cotton's *Keyes of the kingdom of heaven,* 1st publ., London, 1644, & his *The way of the churches* of this year below. Sabin 17091n & 11616 (& 99832); Wing C1640; JCB (3) II:328. CSmH, CtY, DLC, InU, MH, MiU-C, NN-RB, PPL, RPJCB; BL, Oxford:Bodl.
645/33

Clüver, Johannes. Historiarum mundi epitome . . . Editio quarta correctior. *Leyden: D. López de Haro,* 1645. 850 p.; 4to. 1st publ., Leyden, 1637. BL. 645/34

—[Anr issue?]. *Leyden: H. de Vogel,* 1645. IU.
645/35

Commelin, Izaäk, ed. Begin ende voortgangh van de Vereenighde Nederlantsche Geoctroyeerde Oost-Indische Compagnie. [*Amsterdam: J. Janszoon, the Younger*] 1645. 2 v.; illus., maps; obl. 4to. 1st publ., [Amsterdam, 1644?]. Sabin 14958; Tiele-Muller 4; Tiele ̓81; Muller (1872) 3286; JCB (3) II:328. DLC, NN-RB, RPJCB. 645/36

Compagnie de la Nouvelle France. Articles accordez entre les directeurs et associez en la Compagnie de la Nouvelle France; et les députez des habitans dudit pays: agrees et confirmez par le roi. *Paris: S. Cramoisy,* 1645. 14 p.; fol. Sabin 10359; Harrisse (NF) 82. MnU-B; BN (Lk12.778). 645/37

Coppier, Guillaume. Histoire et voyage des Indes Occidentales, et de plusieurs autres regions maritimes, & esloignées. *Lyons: J. Huguetan,* 1645. 182 p.; 8vo. Sabin 16710; Cioranescu (XVII) 20388; JCB (3) II:328. DLC, MH, MiU-C, MnU-B, NN-RB, RPJCB; BL, BN. 645/38

Cortés de Mesa, Diego. Señor. Don Diego Cortes de Mesa, regidor de la ciudad de Cartaxena de las Indias, sindico procurador general della, en virtud de los poderes è instruciones que tiene para pedir y repre-

sentar a V. Mag. el estado en que se halla dicha ciudad, y su provincia, y suplicar todo lo que mas convenga a su real servicio [etc.]. [*Madrid?* 1645?]. 11 numb. lvs; fol. Memorial to king of Spain. Medina (BHA) 7813. Seville:Archivo de Indias. 645/39

Cotton, John. The covenant of Gods free grace . . . Whereunto is added A profession of faith . . . by John Davenport, in New-England. *London: M. Simmons,* 1645. 40 p.; 4to. Cf. Sabin 17058; Wing C6423. DFo, MBAt, NN-RB, PPL; BL, Oxford:Bodl.
645/40

—[Anr issue]. *London: M. S[immons]., for J. Hancock,* 1645. Sabin 17058; Tuttle (Cotton) 37; Wing C6424; JCB (3) II:329. CSmH, CtY, ICN, MH, NN-RB, PPL, RPJCB; BL, Cambridge:St John's.
645/41

——. The powring out of the seven vials. *London: R. S[mith?]., sold by H. Overton,* 1645. 156 p.; 4to. 1st publ., London, 1642. Sabin 17074; Tuttle (Cotton) 26; Wing C6450; JCB (3) II:329. CtY, DLC, MH, RPJCB; BL, Cambridge:UL. 645/42

——. The way of the churches of Christ in New-England. *London: M. Simmons,* 1645. 116 p.; 4to. In this 1st printing, the 7th line of t.p. ends 'or'. Sabin 17090; Tuttle (Cotton) 38; Wing C6471; JCB (3) II:329. CSmH, DFo, ICN, MH, NNUT, RPJCB; BL, Oxford:Bodl. 645/43

—[Anr edn]. *London: M. Simmons,* 1645. 116 p.; 4to. In this 2nd printing, the 7th line of t.p. ends 'co-'. Sabin 17090; Tuttle (Cotton) 39; Wing C6471; JCB (3) II:329–330. CtY, MH, RPJCB. 645/44

Díez de la Calle, Juan. Memorial informativo al Rey . . . en su Real y Supremo Consejo de las Indias . . . Contiene lo que su Magestad provee en su Consejo . . . y por las dos secretarias de la Nueva España, y Pirù, eclesiastico, secular, salarios, estipiendios, y presidios, su gente, y costa, y de que cajas, y hacienda real se paga: valor de las encomiendas de Indios, y otras cosas curiosas y necessarias. [*Madrid?*] 1645. 32 numb. lvs; 4to. Sabin 20133 (& 10057); Medina (BHA) 1076; Maggs Cat. 479 (Americana V):4258; JCB (3) II:330. NN-RB, RPJCB, TxU. 645/45

Discours op verscheyde voorslaghen rakende d'Oost en West-Indische trafyken. Het eerste deel. [*The Hague?*] 1645. 39 p.; 4to. For variant see Asher & Knuttel. Sabin 20235; Asher 199 & 200; Knuttel 5224; JCB (3) II:330. DLC, MiU-C, MnU-B, NN-RB, RPJCB; BL, The Hague:KB.   645/46

Du Mas de Flores, Israel. La clef de la geographie generale, ou Sommaire discours pour l'intelligence de la mappemonde droicte du sieur Boisseau. *Paris: J. Boisseau & L. Vendosme,* 1645. 76 p.; map; 8vo. 'Le continant [*sic*] de l'Amerique': p. 57–59. Other refs to the Americas occur. MiU-C, MnU-B; BL.   645/47

Dupleix, Scipion. La curiosité naturelle. *Rouen: R. L'Allemant,* 1645. 269 p.; 8vo. 1st publ., Paris, 1606. BN.   645/48

Eaton, Samuel. A defense of sundry positions & scriptures alledged to justifie the Congregationall-way . . . By Samuel Eaton . . . and Timothy Taylor. *London: M. Simmons, for H. Overton,* 1645. 130 p.; 4to. A reply to Richard Hollingworth's *Examination of sundry scriptures* of this year below, including refs to New England. Sabin 29402; Wing E118; Thomason I:405. CtY, DLC, MBAt, MWA, NN-RB; BL.   645/49

Espinosa Centeno, Alonso de. Señor. El doctor don Alonso de Espinosa Centeno. [*Madrid?* 1645?]. 4 lvs; fol. Memorial to king of Spain on government of Jamaica, of which the writer was a native. BL.
645/50

Fernel, Jean. Universa medicina. *Leyden: F. Haack,* 1645. 2 v.; port.; 8vo. 1st publ. as here constituted, Paris, 1567; cf. 1601–2 edn. Cf. Sherrington (Fernel) 85.J29. CtY-M, DNLM, NNNAM, PPL; BL, BN.
645/51

Ferriol, José. Señor. Joseph Ferriol, en nombre del prior, y consules, consulado y comercio . . . de Mexico, y de toda la Nueva España. [*Madrid?* 1645?]. 9 numb. lvs; fol. Memorial to king of Spain on commerce of Mexico. Medina (BHA) 6460. BL.
645/52

Franciscans. Provincia de los Angeles (Mexico). Breve resumen, que se haze, para la mejor inteligencia del pleyto que litiga la religion de San Francisco . . . de la Nueva España, con el clero . . . del obispado de la Puebla de los Angeles. [*Madrid?* 1645?].

22 p.; fol. BL (Mexico, Province of).
645/53

Fueldez, Antoine. Observations curieuses, touchant la petite verole . . . et le Bezahar son antidote. *Lyons: J. A. Huguetan,* 1645. 157 p.; 8vo. In chapt. vi, 'Du Bezaar' there is quoted at length a letter to Monardes from one Pierre de Osma describing a hunting expedition in Peru to secure bezoar stones produced by llamas. OClW-H; London:Wellcome, BN.   645/54

Gillespie, George. Wholsome severity reconciled with Christian liberty. or, The true resolution of a present controversie concerning liberty of conscience. *London: C. Meredith,* 1645. 40 p.; 4to. Included are refs to Roger Williams's *The bloudy tenent* of 1644 & to the clergy of New England. Sabin 17046 (& 103852); Wing G765; McAlpin II:348; JCB (3) II:331. CU-A, CtY, DLC, MH, MiU-C, NN-RB, PPPrHi, RPJCB; BL, Oxford:Bodl.   645/55

Gomberville, Marin Le Roy, sieur du Parc et de. La première [–cinquiesme et dernière] partie de Polexandre. *Paris: A. Courbé,* 1645. 5 v.; 8vo. 1st publ. in this version, Paris, 1638; cf. Paris, 1629, version. CU, ICU, MiU-C, NjP; BL.   645/56

Góngora y Argote, Luis de. Obras. *Madrid: D. Díaz de la Carrera, for P. Laso,* 1645–48. 3 pts; 4to. In verse. 1st publ., Madrid, 1627. BL.   645/57

Graswinckel, Dirk. Aen-spraek aen den getrouwen Hollander, nopende de proceduren der Portugesen in Brasill. *The Hague: I. Burchoorn,* 1645. 24 p.; 8vo. This edn has vignette of stork on t.p. Sabin 7504; Borba de Moraes I:14; Asher 206; Knuttel 5227; JCB (3) II:326–27. NN-RB, RPJCB; BL (Portuguese), The Hague:KB.   645/58

—[Anr edn]. Nae de copye in 's Graven-Hage, gedruckt by Isaac Burghoorn. [*Amsterdam?*] 1645. 15 p.; 4to. This edn has vignette of dog on t.p. Cf. Borba de Moraes I:14n; Knuttel 5228. DLC, NN-RB; The Hague:KB. [Edition uncertain: MnU-B, PHi.]   645/59

Great Britain. Laws, statutes, etc., 1625–1649 (Charles I). Two ordinances. *London:* 1645. *See the year* 1646.

Grüling, Philipp Gerhard. Florilegium Hippocrateo-Galeno-chymicorum. *Leipzig: T.*

Ritzsch, for Heirs of G. Gross, 1645. 479 p.;
4to. 1st publ. in this version, Leipzig, 1644;
here a reissue of that edn with altered imprint date? PPC; BL. 645/60

Guibert, Philbert. Toutes les oeuvres charitables. *Rouen: N. Loyselet,* 1645. 880 p.; 8vo.
Included is Guibert's *Le prix & valeur des
medicamens,* 1st publ., Paris, 1625. DNLM,
MiU. 645/61

Guicciardini, Francesco. La historia d'Italia
. . . di nuovo riveduta et corretta per Francesco Sansovino. [*Geneva:*] *J. Stoer,* 1645. 3
pts; 4to. 1st publ., Florence, 1561; cf. 1604
edn. Michel (Répertoire) IV:101. IU, MBAt,
NPV, PPL; BN. 645/62

Harduin, Philippe. Codex medicamentarius, seu Pharmacopoea Parisiensis. *Paris: O.
de Varennes,* 1645. 122 p.; 4to. Section on
oils mentions Peruvian opobalsam as possible substitute for oriental variety; the unguents described include one based on tobacco (*Nicotianum*). London:Wellcome.
645/63

Harsdörffer, Georg Philipp. Gesprechspiele fünfter Theil. *Nuremberg: W. Endter,*
1645. 499 p.; illus.; obl. 8vo. Poem
'Erklärung des Sinnbildes' describes ship
bound for Peru, Mexico, & elsewhere,
mentioning gold-rich gorge of Potosí. The
present vol. forms pt 5 of the author's
Frauenzimmer Gesprechspiele, Nuremberg,
1641. Goedeke III:108; cf. Faber du Faur
502. CtY, DLC, MdBJ, NN; BL.
645/64

Herrera, Gabriel Alonzo de. Agricultura
general . . . *Madaid* [i.e., *Madrid*]: *C.
Sánchez, for A. de Ribero,* 1645. 243 numb.
lvs; fol. 1st publ. with inclusion of Gonzalo
de las Casas's *Arte nuevo para criar seda,* Madrid, 1620. Palau 114100n & 47016n. DLC,
ICJ, MiU; BN. 645/65

Heyden, Hermann van der. Discours et advis sur les flus du ventre douloureux. *Ghent:
S. Manilius,* 1645. 182 p.; 4to. 1st publ.,
Ghent, 1643; here a reissue of that edn with
cancel t.p. & addition of p. 121–82. DNLM;
BL (imp.); London:Wellcome. 645/66

Hollingworth, Richard. An examination of
sundry scriptures, alleadged by our brethren [of New England] in defence of some
particulars of their church-way. *London: J.
R[aworth]. for L. Fawne,* 1645. 30 p.; 4to.

A reply to John Cotton's *The way of the
churches of Christ in New-England* of this year
above. Sabin 29401; Wing H2491; McAlpin
II:353–354. CSmH, MHi, MWA, NNUT;
BL. 645/67

—[Anr issue]. *London: J. R[aworth]., for T.
Smith,* 1645. Wing H2492. BL, Dublin:Trinity. 645/68

Hooke, William. New-Englands sence, of
old-England and Ireland sorrowes. A sermon preached upon a day of generall humiliation in the churches of New-England.
London: J. Rothwell, 1645. 34 p.; 4to. Sabin
32809; Wing H2623; Church 470; JCB (3)
II:331. CSmH, DLC, MH, NN-RB, RPJCB;
BL, Dublin:Trinity. 645/69

Howell, James. Δενδρολογια. Dodona's
grove, or the vocall forrest. The third edition. *Cambridge: R. D[aniel]., for H. Moseley,
at London,* 1645. 191 p.; illus.; 12mo. 1st
publ., [London,] 1640. Wing H3060.
CSmH, CtY, DFo, ICN, InU-L, MH, MnU,
NN-RB; BL, BN. 645/70

——. Epistolae Ho-elianae. Familiar letters,
domestic and forren . . . partly historicall,
politicall, philosophicall. *London: H. Moseley,*
1645. 5 pts; 4to. In pt 1, letter iv, dated
28 March 1618, reports at length on Sir
Walter Raleigh's return from his 2nd voyage to Guiana; in pt 3, letter xxi, dated 16
Aug. 1623, describes fire caused by tobacco
ashes; elsewhere refs to Spanish America,
the Dutch in Brazil, etc., occur. Wing
H3071; Grolier Club (Wither to Prior) 482;
Arents (Add.) 330; Pforzheimer 513.
CSmH, CtY, DLC, ICN, MH, NN-A, RPB;
BL. 645/71

Hudson, Samuel. The essence and unitie of
the church catholike visible. *London: G.
Miller, for C. Meredith,* 1645. 52 p.; 4to. A
reply to John Cotton & the New England
clergy. Sabin 33495; Wing H3265; McAlpin
II:354. CSmH, CtY, ICN, MH, NN-RB; BL.
645/72

Hurtado, Tomás. Chocolate y tabaco, ayuno
eclesiastico y natural. *Madrid: F. García, for
M. López* [1645]. 144 numb. lvs; 8vo. The
1642 edn cited at Medina (BHA) 1036 may
be a ghost. Medina (BHA) 1077; Arents
(Add.) 331. CtY, NN-A, NNH; BL, BN.
645/73

Illustrissimo heroi, Joanni Mauritio, comiti

Nassaviae, &c. cum post supremam terra marique Brasiliae in Occidentali India praefacturam, foederatorum Belgarum nomine gestam, desideratissimus patriae redderetur. *Leyden: W. C. van der Boxe,* 1645. [12] p.; fol. A collection of poems by D. Heinsius & others honoring John Maurice, prince of Nassau, on his return from Brazil, where he had been commander general. Borba de Moraes II:95; Rodrigues (Dom. Hol.) 898; Van Alphen 179. BL (John Maurice), Groningen:UB.   645/74

Independency accused by nine severall arguments: written by a godly learned minister. *London: H. Overton,* 1645. 34 p.; 4to. Dedication signed: J. P. The 'Argum. iii' discusses the power of the civil magistrate in New England to question theological doctrine. Wing P71; McAlpin II:367; JCB (3) II:332. CU, CtY, DFo, MH, MWA, NNUT, RPJCB; BL, Dublin:Trinity.
                    645/75

Jansson, Jan. Nieuwen atlas, ofte Whereltbeschrijvinge. Vermeerdert . . . in drie deelen. *Amsterdam: J. Janszoon, the Younger,* 1645. 3 v.; illus., maps; fol. 1st publ., Amsterdam, 1638, but here appearing in 3 v., incorporating maps introduced in Jansson's *Des nieuwen atlantis aenhang,* 1st publ., Amsterdam, 1644. For variant of v. 1, see Koeman. Koeman (Me) 76–78; Tiele 533n. Leyden:UB.   645/76

——. Novus Atlas, das ist Weltbeschreibung . . . Abgetheilt in drey theile. *Amsterdam: J. Janszoon, the Younger,* 1645. 3 v.; illus., maps; fol. 1st publ., Amsterdam, 1638. Koeman (Me) 130. NNC (imp.); Leningrad: Saltykov PL.   645/77

Jesuits. Letters from missions (South America). Letras anuas dela Compañia de Jesus dela provincia del nuevo reyno de Granada. Desde el año de mil y seyscientos y treinta y ocho, hasta el año de mil y seys cientos y quarenta y tres. *Saragossa:* 1645. 239 p.; 4to. Signed at end: Sebastian Hazañero. Sabin 40251; Medina (BHA) 1078; Streit II:1747; Backer IV:181. CtY; BL, BN.
                    645/78

Lallemant, Jérôme, S.J. Relation de ce qui s'est passé dans le pays des Hurons. *Paris:* 1645. *See* Barthélemy Vimont's *Relation* of this year below.

Magnus, Olaus, Abp of Upsala. Historiae septentrionalium gentium breviarium. Libri xxii. *Leyden: A. Wijngaerden & F. Moyaert,* 1645. 589 p.; 12mo. Extracted from the author's *Historia,* 1st publ., Rome, 1555; cf. 1618 edn of that work. The present volume includes briefer treatment of Greenland, omitting refs to other nations' voyages. CtY, NjR, OCl; BL, BN.   645/79

Maldonado, José, O.F.M. Señor. Fray Joseph Maldonado . . . comissario general de las Indias, dize. Que entre las constituciones que se han hecho este año de 1645, en este Capitulo general de su orden, para las provincias de las Indias Occidentales, las tres primeras son del tenor siguiente. [*Madrid?* 1645]. 9 numb. lvs; fol. Memorial to king of Spain. Medina (BHA) 7814. Puebla, Mexico:B. Palafoxiana.   645/80

Mattioli, Pietro Andrea. I discorsi . . . ne i sei libri di Pedacio Dioscoride . . . ricorretti, e . . . aumentati. *Venice: M. Ginammi,* 1645. 842 p.; illus.; fol. 1st publ. as here transl. from Latin, Venice, 1555; cf. 1604 edn above. Cf. Pritzel 5988n; cf. Nissen (Bot.) 1304n. DNLM, MH-A, NNBG; BL.
                    645/81

Mello, Francisco Manuel de. Ecco polytico. Responde en Portugal a la voz de Castilla: y satisface a un papel . . . sobre los intereses de la corona Lusitana, y del Occeanico, Indico, Brasilico, Ethiopico. *Lisbon: P. Craesbeeck,* 1645. 100 numb. lvs; 4to. Medina (BHA) 1079; Rodrigues (Dom. Hol.) 90; Palau 160449. DCU, MH, NN-RB, RPJCB; BN.   645/82

Mocquet, Jean. Voyages en Afrique, Asie, Indes Orientales, & Occidentales. *Rouen: J. Cailloué,* 1645. 442 p.; illus.; 8vo. 1st publ., Paris, 1616. Sabin 49790n; Borba de Moraes II:65; Maggs Cat. 479 (Americana V):4259; JCB (3) II:332–333. DLC, NN-RB, RPJCB; BL, BN.   645/83

Monet, Philibert, S.J. Nouveau et dernier dictionaire des langues françoise et latine . . . nouvelle ed. *Paris: C. Le Beau,* 1645. 2 pts; 4to. 1st publ., Paris, 1628; cf. Lyons, 1635 edn, under title *Invantaire.* Backer V:1210. CtY.   645/84

Montesinos, Fernando de. Señor. El licenciado D. Fernando de Montesinos . . . dize; Que el consumo, ò perdida de cinco a seis mil quintales de açogue, que todos los años se pierden en las Indias beneficiando la plata, consiste, en que como padece obrundo con tan violentos repassos [etc.]. [*Madrid?* 1645]. [4] p.; fol. Memorial to king of Spain. Medina (BHA) 6656. BL, Seville:BU. 645/85

Morisot, Claude Barthélemy. Orbis maritimi sive Rerum in mari et littoribus gestarum generalis historia. *Dijon: P. Palliot,* 1645. 725 p.; fol. 1st publ., Dijon, 1643. NcD. 645/86

——. Peruviana. *Dijon: G. A. Guyot,* 1645–46. 2 pts; 4to. A political allegory depicting under 'Peruvian' names Richelieu & other French figures. Sabin 50722; Borba de Moraes II:88n. CtY, DFo, ICN, MH, NN-RB, PBL; BL, BN. 645/87

Moscherosch, Johann Michael. Visiones de don de Quevedo, das ist, Wunderliche satyrische und warhafftige Gesichte Philanders von Sittewalt [pseud.] . . . In zwei Theile abgetheilet. [*Frankfurt a. M.: J. G. Schönwetter*] 1645. 10068 (i.e., 1068) p.; 12mo. 1st publ., Strassburg, [1640]; succeeding volumes of this unauthorized edn include some material in imitation of Moscherosch. The added engraved t.p. to this 1st volume is dated 1644. Bechtold 'c'; Goedeke III:233. BN, Göttingen:UB. 645/88

—[Anr edn]. [*Frankfurt a. M.: J. G. Schönwetter*] 1645. 706 p.; 12mo. *See the year* 1647.

——. Les visiones de don de Quevedo; Satyrische Gesichte Philanders von Sittewalt [pseud.] iiii. [*sic*] theil. *Leyden: F. Heger,* 1645–46. 4 pts; 12mo. 1st publ., Strassburg, [1640]; an unauthorized edition. Bechtold 'e'; Goedeke III:233. ICU (imp.); Würzburg:UB, Breslau:UB. 645/89

Nápoles, Juan de, O.F.M. Señor. El general de toda la Orden de s. Francisco, dize. [*Madrid?* 1645?]. 24 p.; fol. Memorial to king of Spain on Franciscan order in Mexico & Peru. BL. 645/90

Nederlandsche West-Indische Compagnie. Vryheden ende exemptien t'accorderen ende toe te staen, weghen de . . . West-Indische Compagnie, uyt krachte van den Octroye by . . . de . . . Staten Generael . . . de selve verleent, aen alle de gene die hun met hare woonstede naer Brasil sullen

willen begeven, ofte jegenwoordig daer woonen. [*Amsterdam:* 1645]. bds.; fol. Sabin 7648; Borba de Moraes II:363; Knuttel 5230. The Hague:KB. 645/91

Nieremberg, Juan Eusebio, S.J. Honor del gran patriarca San Ignacio de Loyola, fundador de la Compañia de Jesus . . . y las noticias de . . . multitud e hijos del mismo. *Madrid: Maria de Quiñones,* 1645. 784 p.; fol. Included are accounts of numerous Jesuits who had served in Spanish America, in continuation of the author's *Ideas de virtud* of 1643. Sabin 55271; Medina (BHA) 1080; Streit I:502; Backer V:1746–1747; JCB (3) II:333. CSmH, DLC, MH, PU, RPJCB; BL, BN. 645/92

Nonnius, Lodovicus. Diaeticon, sive De re cibaria . . . Secunda editio et auctior. *Antwerp: P. Bellère,* 1645. 526 p.; 4to. 1st publ., Antwerp, 1627. Palau 196869. CtY, DLC, ICJ, NN, PPL; BL, BN. 645/93

Opitz, Martin. Weltliche Poemata. Der ander Theil. *Amsterdam:* 1645. *See* Opitz's *Opera poetica,* Amsterdam, 1646.

Pagitt, Ephraim. Heresiography: or, A description of the heretickes and sectaries of these latter times. *London: Marie Okes; sold by R. Trot,* 1645. 131 p.; 4to. Among the heretics discussed are those of New England. Wing P174; McAlpin II:367. CSmH, CtY, ICU, MH, NNUT; BL. 645/94

—[Anr edn]. The second edition. *London: W. Wilson, for J. Marshall & R. Trot,* 1645. 4to. Wing P175. BL, Dublin:Trinity. 645/95

Pérez de Ribas, Andrés, S.J. Historia de los triumphos de nuestra santa fee entre gentes los mas barbaros y fieras del nuevo orbe: conseguidos por los soldados . . . de la Compañia de Jesus en las missiones de la provincia de Nueva España. *Madrid: A. de Paredes,* 1645. 763 p.; fol. Sabin 60895 & 70789; Medina (BHA) 1083; Wagner (SW) 43; Streit II:1745; JCB (3) II:333. CU-B, CtY-D, DLC, MH, MiU-C, NN-RB, PU-Mus, RPJCB; BN. 645/96

Pérez Rocha, Antonio. Al Rey nuestro señor. Discurso politico. [*Madrid?* ca. 1645?]. 20 numb. lvs; fol. Includes ref. to commerce with Indies. MH; BL. 645/97

Potier, Pierre. Opera omnia medica et chy-

mica. *Lyons: J. A. Huguetan,* 1645. 792 p.;
8vo. Included is Potier's *Insignium curationum . . . centuria secunda,* 1st publ., Bologna,
1622. DNLM, ICJ, NjP; BL, BN.

645/98

Primerose, James. De vulgi erroribus in
medicina libri quatuor. *Amsterdam: J. Janszoon, the Younger,* 1645. 237 p.; 12mo. 1st
publ., London, 1638; here anr issue of the
printer's 1644 edn with altered imprint
date? CtY-M.   645/99

Prynne, William A fresh discovery of some
prodigious new-wandring-blasing-stars, &
firebrands, stiling themselves New-Lights.
London: J. Macock, for M. Sparke, 1645. 2pts;
4to. The 2nd pt comprises *A transcript of a
letter lately written from the Sommer Islands,* consisting of letters of Richard Beake & Richard Norwood. Sabin 66417; Wing P3963;
McAlpin II:370; JCB (3) II:333–334.
CSmH, CtY, DLC, InU-L, MH, MnU-B,
NN-RB, PHi, RPJCB; BL, Dublin:Trinity.

645/100

Quiñones, Diego de. Oracion funebre en
las honras que celebro el convento de Nuestra Señora de la Merced de la ciudad de
Toro. A la muerte de . . . D. fr. Geronimo
Manrique de Lara, obispo de Santiago de
Cuba. *Valladolid: A. de Rueda,* 1645. 12
numb. lvs; 4to. RPJCB.   645/101

Relation d'un voyage aux Indes Orientales,
par un gentil-homme françois arrivé depuis
trois ans. *Paris: P. Villéry & J. Guignard,* 1645.
190 p.; 8vo. Includes (p. 179–90) section
on 'Les isles de l'Amerique'. Sabin 69248.
NN-RB.   645/102

Ripa, Cesare. Iconologia . . . Ampliata dal
sig. cav. Gio. Zaratino Castellini. *Venice: C.
Tomasini,* 1645. 685 p.; illus.; 4to. 1st publ.
with American content, Rome, 1603. DLC,
NIC, PBm; BN.   645/103

**Roca, Juan Antonio Vera Zúñiga y Figueroa,
conde de la.** Epitome de la vida, y hechos
del invicto emperador Carlos V. *Milan: F.
Ghisolfi, for G. B. Bidelli,* 1645. 444 p.; 12mo.
1st publ., Madrid, 1622. Palau 358991.
DFo; BL, BN.   645/104

Romances varios de diversos autores.
Corregido y enmendado en esta tercera [*sic*]
impression. *Madrid: Imprenta Real,* 1645.
309 p.; 12mo. Collection 1st publ., Saragossa, 1640. CU.   645/105

Scarron, Paul. Recueil de quelques vers burlesques. *Paris: T. Quinet,* 1645. 164 p.; 4to.
1st publ., Paris, 1643. Magne (Scarron) 9.
DLC, MH; BN.   645/106

Serres, Jean de. Inventaire general de l'histoire de France . . . jusques a la majorite
de Louys XIII. *Geneva: J. Stoer,* 1645. 8vo.
1st publ. with American refs, Paris, 1600;
cf. 1606 edn. BN.   645/107

Shepard, Thomas. New Englands lamenta-
tion for old Englands present errours and
divisions. *London: G. Miller,* 1645. 6 p.; 4to.
Sabin 80211; Wing S3113; JCB (3) II:335.
DLC, InU-L, MH, MiU-C, NN-RB, RPJCB;
BL.   645/108

Spiegel, Adriaan van de. Opera quae extant
omnia. *Amsterdam: J. Blaeu,* 1645. 2 v.; illus.,
port.; fol. Included is the author's *Isagoges
in rem herbariam,* 1st publ., Padua, 1606.
DNLM, ICU, MiU, MnU, NNNAM, PPL;
BL, BN.   645/109

Taylor, John, the Water-poet. Crop-eare
curried, or, Tom Nash his ghost. [*Oxford:
L. Lichfield*] 1644 [i.e., 1645]. 40 p.; 4to. Tobacco & tobacco pipes are mentioned. Madan (Oxford) 1725; Wing M446. CSmH,
MH; BL.   645/110

Torsellino, Orazio, S.J. Historiarum ab origine mundi ad annum 1630 epitome libri
x. *Paris: J. Libert,* 1645. 12mo. 1st publ.,
Rome, 1598; cf. 1620 edn. Backer VIII:152.

645/111

Tuscany. Laws, statutes, etc. Bando, et ordine da osservarsi per l'appalto, e vendita
del tabacco. Rinovato, & ampliato sotto li
ii. maggio 1645. *Florence: Ducal Press* [1645].
[7] p.; 4to. Arents 230. CtY, NN-A.

645/112

Uyt-vaert vande West-Indische Compagnie,
met een propositie ende vertooninghe, ghedaen door een seker heere aenden Coninck
van Castilien. [*Amsterdam?*] *The author,* 1645.
[20] p.; 4to. The fourth line of title here
ends 'ghedaen door een'. Sabin 98248 (&
102913); Borba de Moraes II:318; Asher
204; Knuttel 5225; JCB (3) II:336. [Loca-
tions may include the following edn:] DLC,
MnU-B, NN-RB, RPJCB; BL, The
Hague:KB.   645/113

—[Anr edn]. [*The Hague?*] *The author,* 1645.
[20] p.; 4to. The fourth line of title
here ends 'ghedaen door'. Sabin 98248;

458

Knuttel 5226. NN-RB; The Hague:KB.
645/114

Vega Carpio, Lope Félix de. Arcadia, prosas y versas. *Madrid: G. Rodríguez, for R. Lorenzo,* 1645. 281 numb. lvs; 8vo. 1st publ., Madrid, 1598; cf. 1602 edns. Palau 356307. IU, NNH; Madrid:BN. 645/115

Vimont, Barthélemy, S.J. Relation de ce qui s'est passé en la Nouvelle France és années 1643. & 1644. *Paris: S. Cramoisy & G. Cramoisy,* 1645. 2 pts; 8vo. Pt 2 comprises Jérôme Lallemant's *Relation de ce qui s'est passé dans le pays des Hurons.* For variants, see Bell & McCoy as cited. Sabin 99752; Harrisse (NF) 83; Streit II:2555; Bell (Jes. rel.) 25–26; McCoy 53–56; Church 472; JCB (3) II:336. CSmH, CtY, DLC, ICN, InU-L, MH, MiU-C, MnU-B, NN-RB, RPJCB; BL, BN. 645/116

Waller, Edmund. The workes of Edmond Waller. *London: [T. Warren?] for T. Walkley,* 1645. 111 p.; 8vo. In verse. Included is Waller's 'The battle of the Summer [i.e., Bermuda] Islands', in 3 cantos. Wing W495; Grolier Club (Wither to Prior) 917. CSmH, DLC, IU, MWiW-C; BL. 645/117

—[Anr edn]. *London: T. W[arren]., for H. Moseley,* 1645. 111 p.; 8vo. Wing W496. MH; BL. 645/118

—[Anr edn]. Poems, &c. *London: T. W[arren]., for H. Moseley,* 1645. 96 p.; 8vo. In this edn the imprint has reading 'Princes armes'. Wing W511; Grolier Club (Wither to Prior) 918. CsmH, CtY, DFo, MWiW-C, NN-RB; BL. 645/119

—[Anr edn]. Poems, &c. *London: T. W[arren]., for H. Moseley,* 1645. 107 p.; 8vo. In this edn the imprint has reading 'Princes arms'. Wing W512; Grolier Club (Wither to Prior) 919. CSmH, CtY, MH; BL. 645/120

—[Anr edn]. Poems, &c. *London: J. N[orton]., for H. Moseley,* 1645. 212 p.; 8vo. Wing W513; Grolier Club (Wither to Prior) 920. CSmH, CtY, IU, MH; BL. 645/121

Weld, Thomas. A brief narration of the practices of the churches in New-England. *London: M. Simmons, for J. Rothwell,* 1645. 18 p.; 4to. Sabin 52617 (& 51775 & 102552); Wing W1263; JCB (3) II:334–35. CSmH, CtY, DLC, MH, RPJCB; BL. 645/122

Wheelwright, John. Mercurius Americanus, Mr. Welds his Antitype, or, Massachusetts great apologie examined, being observations upon a paper styled, A short story of the . . . Familists, libertines, etc. *London:* 1645. 24 p.; 4to. A reply to John Winthrop's *Short story* of 1644, discussing Anne Hutchinson & participants in the antinomian controversy. Sabin 103223; Wing W1605; JCB (3) II:336. CSmH, DLC, MH, NN-RB, RPJCB; BL. 645/123

White, Nathaniel. Truth gloriously appearing . . . Or, A vindication of the practice of the church of Christ in the Summer-Islands. *London: G. Calvert* [1645]. 168 p.; 4to. A reply to William Prynne's *A fresh discovery* of this year. Sabin 103440; Wing W1799; McAlpin II: 385; Thomason I:401; JCB (3) II:337. CSmH, CtY, MB, NNUT, RPJCB, ViU; BL. 645/124

Williams, Roger. Christenings make not Christians. *London:*1645. See the year 1646.

Wit's recreations. Recreation for ingenious head-pieces. or, A pleasant grove for their wits to walke in . . . Third edition. *London: R. Cotes, for H. B[lunden].,* 1645. 3 pts; illus.; 8vo. 1st publ., London, 1640, under title *Wits recreation.* Wing M1712. DFo; BL (Wit). 645/125

1646

Agustí, Miguel. Libro de los secretos de agricoltura. *Saragossa: Widow of P. Verges,* 1646. 592 p.; 8vo. 1st publ. in Castilian, Saragossa [1625?]. Jiménez Catalán (Saragossa) 488; Palau 4126. CU; BN, Saragossa:BU. 646/1

Alcázar y Zúñiga, Jacinto de, conde de la Marquina. Medios politicos para el remedio . . . de España. *Madrid: D. Díaz de la Carrera,* 1646. 18 numb. lvs; fol. Mentioned is the impact on Castile of gold & silver from the Indies. Palau 6008n. MH; BL. 646/2

—[Anr edn]. *Madrid: F. García de Arroyo,* 1646. fol. BL. 646/3

—[Anr edn]. *Córdova: S. de Cea Tesa,* 1646. 18 numb. lvs; fol. Palau 6008. 646/4

—[Anr edn]. *Seville: J. Gómez de Blas,* 1646. fol. BL. 646/5

Aldrovandi, Ulisse. Ornithologiae . . . libri xii. *Bologna: N. Tebaldini, for M. A. Bernia,*

1646 [colophon: 1645]. 893 p.; illus., fol.
1st publ. as v. 1 of the author's 3 v. work,
Bologna, 1599; cf. 1610 edn. For vols 2
& 3 see the year 1640. Cf. Nissen (Birds)
82; Mengel (Ellis) 43; Dt. Ges. Kat. 3.503.
CtY, DNLM, ICJ, MiU, NN-RB; BL, BN.
                                        646/6

Alegambe, Philippe, S.J. De vita & moribus
p. Joannis Cardim lusitani . . . liber. *Antwerp: H. Aertssens,* 1646. 114 p.; 12 mo. 1st
publ., Rome, 1645. Backer I:152. Mu-
nich:StB, Rome:BN.   646/7

—[Anr edn]. *Munich: L. Straub, for J. Wagner,*
1646. 91 p.; 12mo. Backer I:152. BL, Ber-
lin:StB.   646/8

Antwooordt [sic] op 't Munsters praetie.
Dordrecht: C. Claeszoon, 1646. [44] p.; 4to.
Includes refs to Brazil, Peru, Mexico, the
West-Indische Compagnie & Spanish silver
fleet. A reply to *Munsters praetie* of this year
below. In some copies the last e of 'Praetie'
is inverted, but no other variation is present. Knuttel 5296. NN; The Hague:KB.
                                        646/9

Antwoordt op seeckere missive van een Ve-
netiaens edelman aen sijn vriendt tot Tui-
rin, uyttet Italiaens ende Frans over gheset.
[*Amsterdam?* 1646?]. [16] p.; 4to. Neither an
Italian nor a French edn has been traced.
Includes ref. to Brazil. Knuttel 5301 (cf.
5300). The Hague:KB.   646/10

—[Anr edn?]. [*Amsterdam?* 1646?]. [16] p.; 4to.
This edn has reading 'aen sijn vrient' on
t.p. NN (dated [1636?] & [1639?]).
                                        646/11

—[Anr edn]. Antwoort op een seker brief geschreven aen sijn vrient, dienende tot vervolgh van 't Fransch en Munsters praetje.
[*Amsterdam?* 1646?]. Knuttel 5302. NN; The
Hague:KB.   646/12

Avila y Sotomayor, Fernando de. El arbitro
entre el Marte francés y las Vindicias galli-
cas. *Pamplona: C. Juan,* 1646. 111 numb. lvs;
4to. A reply to the *Vindiciae Gallicae* of Daniel
de Priezac and to Las Casas, including
chapt. 'De la conquista de las Indias — su
grandeza, su utilidad'. Hanke/Giménez
539; Palau 20901. NNH.   646/13

Avity, Pierre d', sieur de Montmartin. Newe
archontologia cosmica; das ist, Beschreibung aller Kaÿserthumben, Königreichen
und Republicken der gantzen Welt. *Frank-*

furt a. M.: W. Hoffmann, for M. Merian, 1646.
760 p.; illus., maps; fol. 1st publ., as here
transl. by J. L. Gottfried, Frankfurt a. M.,
1638. Cf. Phillips (Atlases) 456. DLC, MH,
NN-RB; Munich:StB.   646/14

Bacon, Francis, viscount St Albans. De
proef-stucken (beschreven in 't Engelsch)
. . . in 't Latijn . . . Nu . . . overgeset . . .
door Peter Böener. *Leyden: W. C. vander Boxe,*
1646. Transl. from the 1641, Leyden, Latin
text, itself transl. from the London, 1625,
English original. Gibson (Bacon) 57.
                                        646/15

Baerle, Kaspar van. Poematum pars ii, Ele-
giarum et miscellaneorum carminum. *Amsterdam:* 1646. *See* Baerle's *Poemata,* Amsterdam, 1645.

Baillie, Robert. A dissuasive from the errours of the time. *London: S. Gellibrand,*
1646. 252 p.; 4to. 1st publ., London, 1645;
seemingly here printed from same setting
of type, possibly reimposed. Cf. Sabin 4059;
Wing B457; McAlpin II:389; JCB (3) II:337.
DLC, MH, MiU-C, NNUT, RPJCB; BL.
                                        646/16

Balde, Jakob. Lyricorum libri iv, & Epodon
lib. unus. *Cologne: J. Kalckhoven,* 1646. 329
p.; 12mo. 1st publ., Munich, 1643. Backer
I:820; Jantz (German Americana) 19; Jantz
(German Baroque) 433. NcD; BN.
                                        646/17

—[Anr edn]. *Cologne: J. Busäus & J. Blaeu, at
Amsterdam,* 1646. 12mo. Backer I:820.
                                        646/18

——. Sylvae lyricae. Editio secunda. *Cologne:
J. Kalckhoven,* 1646. 390 p.; 12 mo. In verse.
1st publ., Munich, 1643; here enl. This edn
includes an 8th book with ode 'De herba
tabaco', mentioning Virginia & Brazil. Ode
iii refers to Kaspar van Baerle & Dutch involvement in Brazil, mentioning gold & silver. CtY, ICN, MH, MiU, NNUT, PU: BL,
BN.   646/19

Barnstein, Heinrich. Kurtze Beschreibung
dess Tabacks. *Erfurt: T. Fritsche,* 1646. 18
lvs; 8vo. 1st publ. in this version, Erfurt,
1645. Dt. Ges. Kat. 11.7683. Freiburg:UB.
                                        646/20

Birago, Giovanni Battista. Historia del
regno di Portogallo. *Lyons:* 1646. 681 p.;
4to. 1st publ., Lyons, 1644. Borba de Moraes I:93. CU, IU.   646/21

——. Historia delle rivolutioni del regno di Portogallo. *Geneva: S. Gamonet,* 1646. 681 p.; 8vo. 1st publ., Lyons, 1644, under title *Historia del regno di Portogallo.* Cf. Borba de Moraes I:93; Palau 29948. DLC, NN, TxU; BL, BN. 646/22

Le bon voisin; c'est a dire le Portugais. [*Amsterdam?*] 1646. [19] p.; 4to. On Portuguese uprising in Brazil. Borba de Moraes I:97; Rodrigues (Dom. Hol.) 518; Maggs Cat. 479 (Americana V):4267; Knuttel 5356. MH; The Hague:KB, Leyden:B. Thysiana. 646/23

Bontekoe, Willem Ysbrandsz. Journael ofte Gedenckwaerdige beschrijvinghe vande Oost-Indische reyse. *Hoorn: I. Willemszoon, for J. J. Deutel,* 1646 [colophon: *Haarlem: T. Fonteyn,* 1646]. 72 p.; illus., port.; 4to. Issued with Dirk Albertsz. Raven's *Journael ofte Beschrijvinge vande reyse,* with special t.p. & separate signatures & paging. Bontekoe's work includes a ref. to Brazil; Raven's work describes an attempted voyage to Greenland. Both works also issued separately. Cf. Sabin 6337 & 67980; Tiele-Muller 168; JCB (3) II:338 & 347. CU, DLC, MnU-B, NN-RB, RPJCB; BL, BN. 646/24

Boothby, Richard. A briefe discovery or description of the most famous island of Madagascar. *London: E. G[riffin]., for J. Hardesty,* 1646. 72 p.; 4to. Chapt. xv discusses 'The valour of the English nation against the salvages in Virginia and New-England, also of the Spaniards against a civill nation in America, or in the west Indies, also of the Spaniards and Portugals against the Brasilians, and against the Indians a mighty warlike nation', etc. Wing B3743; Thomason I:449; JCB (3) II:338. CSmH, CtY, DFo, MH, RPJCB; BL. 646/25

Bos, Lambert van den. Essays ofte Poëtische betrachtungen. *Amsterdam: J. Lescaille, for the Author,* 1646. 360 p.; 12mo. In verse. The 'Belgiados', bk 1, includes ref. to 'naackten Indiaan'. MH. 646/26

Brouwer, Hendrick. Journael ende Historis verhael van de reyse gedaen by oosten de Straet le Maire, naer de custen van Chili . . . door het schip Castricum. *Amsterdam: B. Janszoon,* 1646. 104 p.; illus., maps; 4to. Sabin 8427; Palau 36206; Tiele-Muller 204. NN-RB. 646/27

—[Anr issue]. . . . schip Castricom. *Amsterdam: B. Janszoon,* 1646. JCB (3) II:338. NN-RB, RPJCB. [Issues not differentiated: DLC, MH, MnU-B; BL (imp.)]. 646/28

Browne, Sir Thomas. Pseudodoxia epidemica: or, Enquiries into very many received tenents and commonly presumed truths. *London: T. Harper, for E. Dod,* 1646. 386 p.; 4to. Bk ii, chapt. 2, 'Concerning the loadstone', discusses variations of the compass in the New World, mentioning Columbus & Sebastian Cabot. In bk vi, chapt. 8, 'On the River Nilus', the Nile is compared with the rivers Plate & Amazon ('Oregliana'), with refs to writings of J. B. Scortia, G. P. Maffei, G. A. Magini, J. de Acosta & G. Cardano. Elsewhere minor refs to America occur. Keynes (Browne) 73 (a); Wing B5159A. Oxford:Worcester. 646/29

—[Anr state]. *London: T. H[arper]., for E. Dod,* 1646. Keynes (Browne) 73 (b); Wing B5159. CSmH, CtY, DLC, IU, MH, MiU, MnU, NNNAM, PU; BL, BN. 646/30

Bulkeley, Peter. The gospel-covenant; or The covenant of grace opened . . . Preached in Concord in New-England. *London: M. S[immons]., for B. Allen,* 1646. 383 p.; 4to. In pt 1, chapt. i, Bulkeley addresses those of New England for whom it offers spiritual hope; in pt 4, chapt. ii, Anne Hutchinson is mentioned as 'that wretched Jezebel'. Sabin 9096; Wing B5403; Thomason I:431. CLU-C, CtY, DLC, ICN, MHi, MiU-C, NNUT; BL. 646/31

Camargo, Gerónimo de. Por el real fisco, y . . . Geronimo de Camargo . . . fiscal en el Real [Consejo] de las Indias. Con don Alvaro de Quiñones y Neira, nieto de don Alvaro de Quiñones marques de Lorençana, presidente que fue . . . de Guatemala. [*Madrid?* ca. 1646?]. 16 numb. lvs; fol. NN-RB. 646/32

Campuzano, Baltasar, O.S.A. Planeta catholico sobre el Psalmo. 18. *Madrid: D. Díaz de la Carrera* [1646]. 267 p.; 4to. On missionary efforts in Peru, exhorting Philip IV to further them. Privilege & approbations, etc., dated 1646. Medina (BHA) 1084; Streit I:497; Palau 45255. OU; Seville:BU. 646/33

Casas, Bartolomé de las, O.P., Bp of Chiapa. Obras. *Barcelona: A. Lacavalleria,* 1646. 214

numb. lvs; 4to. 1st publ., Seville, 1552, as work known collectively as the author's *Brevíssima relación,* relating to treatment of Indians in New World. Sabin 11239; Medina (BHA) 1085; Hanke/Giménez 540; Streit I:504; JCB (3) II:339. MH, NN-RB, RPJCB; BL, BN.   646/34

The case of Mainwaring, Hawes, Payne, and others, concerning a depredation made by the Spanish West India fleete upon the ship Elizabeth. [*London:*] 1646. 17 p.; 4to. The ship was en route to Virginia. Sabin 44055; Wing M296; Thomason I:466; McAlpin II:399; JCB (3) II:344. CSmH, DFo, ICN, MH, MnU-B, NN-RB, RPJCB; BL.
646/35

Catholic Church. Liturgy and ritual. Ritual. Brevis forma administrandi apud Indos sacramenta . . . per fratrem Michaelem à Zarate . . . denuo autem per doctorem Joannem de la Roca in Limensi Cathedrali ecclesia rectorem studio, ac diligentia limata . . . aucta. *Madrid: Imprenta Real,* 1646. 80 numb. lvs; 8vo. 1st publ., Mexico, 1583; cf. 1617 edn. Medina (BHA) 7821; Streit I:508; Palau 379716n. Lima, Peru:BN.
646/36

Cervantes Saavedra, Miguel de. Le valeureux Dom Quixote. *Rouen: D. Ferrand* (v. 1) *& J. Cailloué* (v. 2), 1646. 2 v.; 8vo. Includes the 2nd pt, 1st publ. as here transl. by F. de Rosset, Paris, 1618. Ríus (Cervantes) 467; Palau 52701. MH; BL.
646/37

—[Anr issue?]. *Rouen: J. Berthelin,* 1646. Ríus (Cervantes) 467n. BN.   646/38

Clarke, Samuel (1599–1683). A mirrour or looking-glasse both for saints and sinners. *London: R. Cotes, for J. Bellamy,* 1646. 227 p.; 8vo. Includes mention of Patagonian giants, while amongst heretics & schismatics described are the wife of William Dyer & Anne Hutchinson of Boston, citing John Winthrop's *A short story* of 1644. Sabin 13447; Wing C4548; Thomason I:424. MB, MnU-B; BL.   646/39

Clüver, Philipp. Introductionis in universam geographiam, tam veterem quàm novam, libri vi. Accessit P. Bertii Breviarium orbis terrarum. *Venice: Turrino Press,* 1646. 2 pts; illus.; 16mo. 1st publ., Leyden, 1624. Sabin 13805n. ICN, NN-RB.   646/40

Commelin, Izaäk, ed. Begin ende voortgangh van de Vereenighde Nederlantsche Geoctroyeerde Oost-Indische Compagnie . . . in twee deelen verdeelt. [*Amsterdam: J. Janszoon, the Younger*] 1646. 2 v.; illus., maps; obl. 4to. 1st publ., [Amsterdam, 1644?]. For variant, see Tiele-Muller as cited. Sabin 14959–60; Tiele-Muller 5–6; Tiele 82; Muller (1872) 1871; JCB (3) II:339. CtY, DLC, ICJ, MH-A, MnU-B, NIC, RPJCB; BL, BN.
646/41

Copie van een Missive, gheschreven by een vry man in Brasil . . . gevonden onder de verdroncken brieven uyt het schip Zeelandia . . . ende de West-Indische Compagnie ter hand gekomen. [*Amsterdam:*] F. Lieshout, 1646. bds.; fol. Signed 'A. T. secretaris van de gewesene Raet der Justitien', & dated at Recife, Dec. 11, 1645. Relates to Portuguese uprising. Sabin 7562 & 16679; Borba de Moraes I:177; Knuttel 5352. The Hague:KB, Leyden:B. Thysiana.   646/42

Cort ende waerachtich verhael van . . . Brasil. [n. p., 1646]. *See the year* 1647.

Cotton, John. A conference Mr. John Cotton held at Boston with the elders of New England. *London: J. Dawson; sold by F. Eglesfield,* 1646. 2 pts; 8vo. Sabin 17055; Tuttle (Cotton) 41; Wing C6335. DLC, MH, NjPT, ViU; BL, Oxford:Bodl.   646/43

—[Anr issue?]. Gospel conversion. *London: J. Dawson,* 1646. 2 pts; 8vo. Tuttle (Cotton) 42; Wing C6435 & C6336; JCB (3) II:339–40. CSmH, DLC, MH, NN-RB, RPJCB; BL.
646/44

Diemerbroeck, Isbrandus de. De peste libri quatuor. *Arnhem: J. Jacobszoon,* 1646. 337 p.; 4to. Includes discussion of therapeutic uses of tobacco during plagues. Arents 231. CtY-M, DLC, NN-A, PPL; London:Wellcome.   646/45

Díez de la Calle, Juan. Memorial, y noticias sacras, y reales del imperio de las Indias Occidentales . . . Comprehende lo eclesiastico, secular, politico, y militar. [*Madrid:*] 1646. 172 (i.e., 164) numb. lvs; 4to. Sabin 20134; Medina (BHA) 1086n; cf. Wagner (SW) 44. CU, CtY, DLC, MH, NNH; BN.   646/46

—[Anr edn]. [*Madrid: 1646?*]. 183 (i.e., 175) numb. lvs; 4to. Differs from the above, apparently earlier, printing in having lvs 10,

11, 22, 23, & 38 reset with additional text, & with errata preceding text. Sabin 10058; Medina (BHA) 1086; Streit II:1751; Wagner (SW) 44; Palau 73743. CtY, DLC, MnU-B, NN-RB, RPJCB; BL. 646/47

Duchesne, Joseph. Le richezze della riformata farmacopoea . . . traportata . . . dal signor Giacomo Ferrari. *Venice: The Guerigli,* 1646. 264 p.; 4to. 1st publ. as here transl., Venice, 1619, from Duchesne's *Pharmacopoea dogmaticorum restituta,* Paris, 1607. DNLM. 646/48

Dudley, Sir Robert, styled duke of Northumberland and earl of Warwick. Dell'arcano del mare . . . libri sei. *Florence: F. Onofri,* 1646–47. 3 v.; maps; fol. In v. 3, bk 6, pt 4 includes maps, etc., of America. Phillips (Atlases) 457; Michel (Répertoire) II:187–188. CSmH, DLC, InU-L, MH; BL, BN. 646/49

Durante, Castore. Il tesoro della sanità. *Venice: G. B. Cestaro,* 1646. 320 p.; 8vo. 1st publ., [Rome?], 1586; cf. 1601 edn. DNLM. 646/50

Eaton, Samuel. The defence of sundry positions & scriptures for the Congregationalway justified . . . By Sam: Eaton [&] Tim: Taylor. *London: M. Simmons, for H. Overton,* 1646. 46 p.; 4to. Mentioned are the 'Elders of New England' & John Cotton. Cf. Wing E120; McAlpin II:408; Thomason I:453. MH, MWA, NN-RB, RPJCB; BL. 646/51

Edwards, Thomas. Antapologia: or, A full answer to the Apologeticall narration. *London: T. R[atcliffe]. & E. M[ottershead]., for J. Bellamy,* 1646. 159 (i.e., 253) p.; 4to. 1st publ., London, 1644. CtY, MH, NNUT; Oxford:Corpus. 646/52

—[Anr issue]. *London: T. R[atcliffe]. & E. M[ottershead]., for R. Smith,* 1646. MH, NNUT, RPJCB; BL. 646/53

——. The first and second part of Gangraena: or A catalogue and discovery of many of the errors . . . of the sectaries of this time . . . Third edition corrected and much enlarged. *London: T. R[atcliffe]. & E. M[ottershead]., for R. Smith,* 1646. 2 pts; 4to. Here issued together are items issued separately in this year. Wing E227; McAlpin II:409. CLU-C, CtY, ICN, MH, MiU, NNUT; Cambridge:UL. 646/54

——. Gangraena; or A catalogue and discovery of many of the errours, heresies, blasphemies and pernicious practices of the sectaries of this time. *London: [T. Ratcliffe & E. Mottershead?] for R. Smith,* 1646. 184 p.; 4to. Included are numerous critical comments on the clergy of New England, esp. Hugh Peters. Wing E228; McAlpin II:409; Thomason I:413; JCB (3) II:342. CLU-C, CtY, DLC, ICN, MH, MnU, NN-RB, PPT, RPJCB; BL. 646/55

—[Anr edn]. Second edition enlarged. *London: [T. Ratcliffe & E. Mottershead?] for R. Smith,* 1646. 124 (i.e., 224) p.; 4to. Wing E229. CSmH, CtY, ICN, MH, PHC; BL. 646/56

—[Anr edn]. Third edition corrected and much enlarged. *London: [T. Ratcliffe & E. Mottershead?] for R. Smith,* 1646. 178 p.; 4to. Wing E230. CtY, ICN, MBAt, NHC; BL. 646/57

——. The second part of Gangraena. *London: T. R[atcliffe]. & E. M[ottershead]., for R. Smith,* 1646. 182 p.; 4to. Continues the 1st pt of this year above. Included are further refs to events & individuals in New England, e.g., Roger Williams & Samuel Gorton. Wing E234; McAlpin II:409; Thomason I:441. NNUT; BL. 646/58

—[Anr edn]. *London T. R[atcliffe]. & E. M[ottershead]., for R. Smith,* 1646. 178 p.; 4to. McAlpin II:409. NNUT. 646/59

—[Anr edn]. Third edition. *London: T. R[atcliffe]. & E. M[ottershead]., for R. Smith,* 1646. 212 p.; 4to. Wing E235; McAlpin II:409. ICN, NNUT; Cambridge:UL. 646/60

——. The third part of Gangraena. *London: [T. Ratcliffe & E. Mottershead?] for R. Smith,* 1646. 295 p.; 4to. As in prior two parts of this year includes refs to New England, amongst them, to Anne Hutchinson. Wing E237; McAlpin II:409; Thomason I:483. CSmH, CtY, DFo, MH; BL. 646/61

Entremeses nuevos. De diversos autores. Para honesta recreacion. *Alcalá de Henares: F. Ropero,* 1646. 119 numb. lvs; 8vo. 1st publ., Alcalá de Henares, 1643. Arents (Add.) 329. NN-A. 646/62

Extract ende copye van verscheyde brieven en schriften, belangende de rebellie der Paepsche Portugesen van desen staet in Brasilien. *[Amsterdam?]* 1646. 31 p.; 4to. Sabin 7577; Borba de Moraes I:256; Knuttel 5353. DLC, NN-RB, NNH; Amsterdam:NHSM; The Hague:KB.   646/63

Fabre, Pierre Jean. Myrothecium spagyricum; sive Pharmacopoea chymica. *Toulouse: P. Bosc,* 1646. 448 p.; 8vo. 1st publ., Toulouse, 1623. DNLM.   646/64

Ferrari, Giovanni Battista. Flora, seu De flora cultura lib. iv. Editio nova. *Amsterdam: J. Janszoon, the Younger,* 1646. 522 p.; illus.; 4to. 1st publ., Rome, 1633. Pritzel 2877n; Nissen (Bot.) 620n. MH-A, NNBG; BL, BN.   646/65

Fontana, Francesco. Novae coelestium terrestriumque rerum observationes. *Naples: Il Gaffaro,* 1646. 152 p.; illus., port., 4to. Dedicatory epistle names Columbus as discoverer of America. DLC, MH, MiU, NN, PPAmP; BL, BN.   646/66

Franciscans. Renuncia que hizo la religion de S. Francisco de todas las doctrinas, y conversiones que tiene en la Nueva-España, è islas Filipinas, año de 1645. [*Madrid?* 1646?]. [4] p.; fol. Sabin 69643; Medina (BHA) 6807; Palau 313245; Maggs Cat. 479 (Americana V):4261. CSmH.   646/67

Fransch praetie. Münster: N. Staets, 1646. [22] p.; 4to. A continuation of *Munsters praetie* of this year below. Mentions Spanish 'extremes' in Brazil [*sic*] & elsewhere. Knuttel 5297. InU-L, MnU-B, NN-RB; The Hague:KB.   646/68

—[Anr edn]. Fransch praetje. *Münster: N. Staets,* 1646. [12] p.; 4to. Knuttel 5298. BL(?), The Hague:KB.   646/69

—[Anr edn]. Fransch praetje. *Münster: N. Staets,* 1646. [16] p.; 4to. This edn has vignette of bear with greenery on t.p. Knuttel 5299. NN; The Hague:KB.   646/70

Fruchtbringende Gesellschaft. Der Fruchtbringenden Geselschaft Nahmen, Vorhaben, Gemählde und Wörter. *Frankfurt a. M.: M. Merian,* 1646. 4 pts; illus.; 4to. Includes emblems portraying more than a dozen native American plants. Authorship attrib. to Ludwig von Anhalt-Köthen. Jantz (German Baroque) 1673; Faber du Faur 166–166a; Nissen (Bot.) 1343. CSmH, CtY, DLC, MH, NNC, OCU; BL, Wolfenbüttel:HB.   646/71

Het ghelichte Munstersche mom-aensicht,

ofte de Spaensche eclipse. [*Vlissingen?*] 1646. [23] p.; 4to. Discusses Spanish & Dutch interests in West Indies, & problems of the West-Indische Compagnie. Knuttel 5326. MnU-B, NN; The Hague:KB.   646/72

Góngora y Argote, Luis de. Obras. *Lisbon: P. Craesbeeck,* 1646–47. 2 v.; 12mo. In verse. Included is Góngora's *Soledades,* 1st publ., Madrid, 1627, in his *Obras en verso.* Palau 104630. CLU, NNH.   646/73

Gorton, Samuel. Simplicities defence against seven-headed policy. or Innocency vindicated, being unjustly accused . . . by that seven-headed church-government united in New-England. *London: J. Macock, for L. Fawne,* 1646. 111 p.; 4to. The contentious author, in attacking his opponents at Boston, Plymouth, & Providence, provides an account of his settlement at Warwick (Rhode Island) & treaties with the Narragansets; cf. Edward Winslow's *Hypocrosie unmasked* of this year below. Sabin 28044; Wing G1308; Thomason I:473; Church 475; JCB (3) II:343. CSmH, DLC, ICN, MH, MWA, MiU-C, NN-RB, PPL, RPJCB; BL.   646/74

Great Britain. Laws, statutes, etc., 1625–1649 (Charles I). Two ordinances of the Lords and Commons . . . the one dated November 2. 1643. the other March 21. 1645. Whereby Robert earle of Warwick is made Governor in chief . . . of all those islands and other plantations, inhabited, planted, or belonging to any . . . the King of Englands subjects, within the bounds, and upon the coasts of America. And a committee appointed to be assisting unto him for the better governing . . . of the said plantations; but chiefly for the advancement of the true Protestant religion. *London: J. Wright,* 1645 [i.e., 1646]. 6 p.; 4to. Wing E2418; Thomason I:427. InU-L, MH, MiU-C, RPJCB; BL.   646/75

——. Whereas the severall plantations in Virginia. *London:* 1646. *See the year* 1647.

Grenaille, François de, sieur de Chatounières. Le théatre de l'univers, ou L'abbregé du monde. *Paris: A. Robinot,* 1646. 470 numb. lvs; ports; 8vo. 'Description du Nouveau Monde, où il est discouru de sa découverte, de l'Amerique, du Mexico, du Perou, des Terres-Neuves, & de leurs proprietez': lvs 57v–64r. Cioranescu (XVII) 34060. RPJCB; BN.   646/76

Grotius, Hugo. De jure belli ac pacis libri tres . . . Editio nova. *Amsterdam: J. Blaeu,* 1646. 618 p.; 8vo. 1st publ., Paris, 1625. Meulen/Diermanse 572. CtY, DLC, MH, NNUT, MiU-C, PPL; The Hague:PP.
646/77

Harsdörffer, Georg Philipp. Gesprech-spiele sechster Theil. *Nuremberg: W. End-ler,* 1646. 345 p.; obl. 8vo. Includes ref. to Dutch ambitions & treasures brought home from East & West Indies. Forms pt 6 of the author's *Frauenzimmer Gesprechspiele,* Nuremberg, 1641–49. Goedeke III:108; Faber du Faur 502. CU, CtY, DLC; BL.
646/78

Hollandsche Sybille. *Amsterdam: R. Heyn-drickz,* 1646. 31 p.; 4to. Includes ref. to the West-Indische Compagnie. Knuttel 5304. DLC, MnU-B, NN; The Hague:KB.
646/79

—[Anr edn]. *Amsterdam: R. Heyndrickz,* 1646. 32 p.; 4to. Fully reset. Meulman 2782. Ghent:BU.   646/80

—[Anr edn]. [*The Hague?*] 1646. 22 p.; 4to. Knuttel 5305. The Hague:KB.   646/81

—[Anr edn]. Hollandtsche Sybille. [*The Hague?*] 1646. 22 p.; 4to. Knuttel 5306. The Hague:KB.   646/82

Hollants praetie. [*Amsterdam?*] 1646. 28 p.; 4to. Mentions hindrances to the West-Indische Compagnie brought about by earlier truce. Knuttel 5317. NN; The Hague:KB.
646/83

—[Anr edn]. Munsters discours, ofte 'tSamen-sprekinge over de laetste tijdinghe van Munster. [*The Hague?*] 1646. 28 p.; 4to. This edn has vignette of bear with leaves on t.p. Knuttel 5318. MnU-B, NN; The Hague:KB.   646/84

—[Anr edn]. Munsters discours, ofte t'Samen-sprekinghe. [*The Hague?*] 1646. 22 p.; 4to. This edn has title vignette of dragon with gunpowder & weapons. Knuttel 5319. NN; The Hague:KB.   646/85

Jansson, Jan. Novus atlas, sive Theatrum orbis terrarum . . . in quatuor tomos distinctus. *Amsterdam: J. Janszoon, the Younger,* 1646–47. 4 v.; illus., maps; fol. 1st publ. in this version, Amsterdam, 1638, as Mercator's

Atlas novus; here enl. by a 4th vol. Pts 2–4 issued 1647. As with earlier edns, vols 1 & 3 include Americana. Cf. Sabin 35773; Koeman (Me) 57, 58, 59 (cf. 152–153). Amsterdam:UB (v. 1–3), Madrid:BN (v. 1–3).   646/86

Kircher, Athanasius, S.J. Ars magna lucis et umbrae in decem libros digesta. *Rome: L. Grignani, for H. Scheus,* 1646. 935 p.; illus., maps; fol. Quotes Charles L'Ecluse on 'mira proprietas Laricis Americanae', i.e., the American larch. Map facing p. 460 showing northern hemisphere includes America. CSmH, CtY, DNLM, ICJ, InU, MnU, NNC, PPL; BL, BN.   646/87

Labbe, Philippe, S.J. La geographie royale. *Paris: M. Henault & J. Henault,* 1646. 589 p.; maps; 8vo. Includes sections on New World. Backer IV:1301; Cioranescu XVII:37320. MiU-C.   646/88

—[Anr issue?]. *Paris: M. Henault,* 1646. PBL; BL, BN.   646/89

—[Anr issue?]. *Paris: J. Henault,* 1646. CtY.
646/90

——. Les tableaux methodiques de la geographie royale. *Paris: M. Henault & J. Henault,* 1646. 3 pts; fol. 'De l'Amerique et Magellanique': pt 1, p. 24–25. Pt 2, 'Geographiae ecclesiastica delineatio', includes accounts of sees of Mexico, Santo Domingo & Lima. Backer IV:1301; Cioranescu (XVII) 37322. BL, BN.   646/91

Le Candele, P. Wel-vaert vande West-Indische Compagnie. [*Middelburg:* 1646]. [34] p.; 4to. Concerns commerce with Brazil. Sabin 102922; Borba de Moraes II:374; Asher 211; Knuttel 5357. MH, NN-RB, RPJCB; BL, The Hague:KB.   646/92

Lof der Oost-Indise [!] **Compagnie.** *Amsterdam: H. J. Visscher,* 1646. 18 p.; 4to. Relates to question of union with the West-Indische Compagnie. Sabin 41778; Asher 203; Knuttel 5358. DLC, NN; The Hague:KB, Ghent:BU.   646/93

Manifest door d'inwoonders van Parnambuco uytgegeven tot hun verantwoordinge op 't aennemen der wapenen tegens de West-Indische Compagnie . . . uyt het Portugies overgeset. *Antwerp: P. van den Cruyssen,* 1646. 12 p.; 4to. The Portuguese text of which this purports to be a translation has not been identified. For a reply to this,

see the *Korte antwoort,* [The Hague?], 1647.
Sabin 44263; Asher 214; Knuttel 5354.
DLC, MnU-B, NN-RB; The Hague:KB,
Ghent:BU. 646/94

—[Anr edn]. [*The Hague?*] 1646. 12 p.; 4to.
In this edn the title has reading 'uytghege-
ven'. Sabin 102895; Borba de Moraes II:14;
Asher 215; Knuttel 5355; JCB (3) II:344.
NN-RB, RPJCB; The Hague:KB.

646/95

A moderate and safe expedient to remove
jealouses and feares, of any danger . . . by
the Roman Catholickes of this kingdome.
[*London?*] 1646. 16 p.; 4to. Promotional
tract in behalf of colonization of Maryland.
Sabin 49802; Baer (Md) 27; Vail (Frontier)
106; Wing M2322; JCB (3) II:344. MdBJ-G,
NNUT, RPJCB; London:Law Soc.

646/96

Moscherosch, Johann Michael. Les visions
de don de Quevedo, das ist, Wunderliche
satyrische unnd warhaftige Gesichte Philanders von Sittewaldt [pseud.] . . . in fünff
[i.e., sieben] Theilen begriffen. *Leyden: A.
Wijngaerden,* 1646[–47]. 7 pts; 12mo. 1st
publ., Strassburg, [1640]; pts 1–4 represent
a reissue of the unauthorized 1645 Leyden
edn with cancel t.p., while pts 5–7 include
material 1st publ. in corresponding pts of
the [Frankfurt], 1645–47, edn. Bechtold 'f';
Faber du Faur 429; Goedeke III:233. CU,
CtY, IU, MH, MdBJ; Berlin:StB, Mu-
nich:StB. 646/97

Munsters discours, ofte 'tSamen-sprekinge.
[*The Hague?*] 1646. *See* Hollants praetie *of
this year above.*

Munsters praetie. Deliberant dum fingere
nesciunt. [*Amsterdam?*] 1646. [22] p.; 4to.
Signed 'Vaertwel. Deventer'. Includes refs
to Brazil & the West-Indische Compagnie.
In this edn, the 10th line of text ends
'Duyn–'. Knuttel 5291; JCB (STL) 34. [Edi-
tion uncertain: MnU-B], NN, RPJCB; The
Hague:KB. 646/98

—[Anr edn]. [*Amsterdam?*] 1646. [22] p.; 4to.
The 10th line of text ends 'Duvn'. Knuttel
5290. The Hague:KB. 646/99

—[Anr edn]. [*Amsterdam?*] 1646. [22] p.; 4to.
The 1st line of text ends 'soo'; in the preceding 2 edns, it ends 'so schrij–'. Knuttel
5292. The Hague:KB. 646/100

—[Anr edn]. Munsters praetje. [*Amsterdam?*]

1646. [16] p.; 4to. Vignette on t.p. Knuttel
5293. The Hague:KB. 646/101

—[Anr edn]. [*Amsterdam?*] 1646. [12] p.; 4to.
Printed in 2 columns; the catchword on p.
10 is 'Medecide'. Knuttel 5294. InU-L; The
Hague:KB. 646/102

—[Anr edn?]. [*Amsterdam?*] 1646. [11] p.; 4to.
Printed in two columns; the catchword on
p. 10 is 'Medecine'. This edn has vignette
at end. Van Alphen 186. Groningen:UB.

646/103

—[Anr edn]. [*Amsterdam?*] 1646. [12] p.; 4to.
Not printed in columns; the 1st line of text
ends 'ick'. NN. 646/104

—[Anr edn]. Munsters praetie . . . Na de
oprechte origenale copije. [*Amsterdam?*]
1646. [24] p.; 4to. Knuttel 5295; Meulman
2779. The Hague:KB; Ghent:BU.

646/105

—[Anr edn]. Munsters praetien. [*Amsterdam?*]
1646. [24] p.; 4to. Meulman 2778. Ghent:
BU. 646/106

—[Anr edn]. [*Amsterdam?*] 1646. [16] p.; 4to.
NN. 646/107

—[Anr edn]. Munsters vrede-praetje. Vol alderhande opinien. [*Amsterdam?*] 1646. [24]
p.; 4to. Van Alphen 185. Groningen:UB.

646/108

Nonnius, Lodovicus. Diaeticon, sive De re
cibaria . . . Secunda editio et auctior. *Antwerp: P. Bellère,* 1646. 526 p.; 4to. 1st publ.,
Antwerp, 1627; here anr issue of Bellère's
1645 edn with altered imprint date. Palau
196870. BL. 646/109

Den ongeveynsden Nederlandschen patriot.
Tweede deel van den Ongeveynsden patriot. *Middelburg: S. Verhoeven,* 1646. [40] p.;
4to. Includes mention of French engage-
ment in Dutch affairs in both Indies. The
earlier pt, also published this year (Knuttel
5321), is without American matter. Knuttel
5323. The Hague:KB. 646/110

Opitz, Martin. Opera poetica, das ist Geistliche und weltliche Poemata. *Amsterdam: J.
Janszoon, the Younger,* 1646,'45. 3 v.; 12mo.
1st publ. with American refs, Breslau,
1628–29, under title *Deutscher Poematum.*
The 'Lob des Krieges Gottes' appears here
in pt 1. Pt 2 has title *Weltliche Gedichte
. . . ander Theil.* Goedeke III:49; Faber du
Faur 229–230; Jantz (German Baroque)
1920; Jördens IV:116–117. CU, CtY, ICN,

InU, MH, NNC, PU; BL, BN (pts 1 & 2), Göttingen:StUB.   646/111

Ovalle, Alonso de, S.J. Historica relacion del reyno de Chile, y delas missiones, y ministerios que exercita en el la Compañia de Jesus. *Rome: F. Cavalli,* 1646. 455 p.; illus., ports, maps; fol. Sabin 57972; Medina (Chile) 118; Streit II:1752; Backer VI:40; Palau 207397; JCB (3) II:345. CU, CtY, DLC, InU-L, MnU-B, NN-RB, PPL, RPJCB; BL, BN.   646/112

———. Historica relatione del regno di Cile, e delle missioni, e ministerii che esercita in quelle la Compagnia di Giesu. *Rome: F. Cavalli,* 1646. 378 p.; illus., ports, maps; 4to. Transl. from the preceding item. Sabin 57971; Streit II:1753; Backer VI:60; Michel (Répertoire) VI:48; Palau 207399; JCB (3) II:346. CtY, DLC, ICN, InU-L, MH, MiU, MnU-B, NN-RB, PPL, RPJCB; BL, BN.   646/113

Pacifique de Provins, O.F.M. Cap. Brieve relation du voyage des isles de l'Amerique. *Paris: N. & J. de LaCoste,* 1646. 30 p.; 8vo. Sabin 58095 & 66393; Streit II:2398; Maggs Cat. 479 (Americana V):4265; JCB (3) II:346. MnU-B, RPJCB.   646/114

Palafox y Mendoza, Juan de, Bp of Puebla de los Angeles. Carta que . . . Don Juan de Palafox y Mendoza . . . escribio al padre Oratio Carocchi . . . de la sagrada Compañia de Jesus. Sacada de su original, que se halla en el noviciado de Carmelitas descalzes de la Puebla de los Angeles en la Nueva España. '*Madrid: G. Rodriguez, for F. Serrano,* 1646'. 248 (i.e., 284) p.; 16mo. An attack on the Jesuit order in Mexico. Though hitherto accepted at face value, that the work here described is as represented is beyond question false. Not only does the text contain a letter dated 1647, but Palafox is described on the t.p. as bishop of Osma, to which see he was not translated till 1653. The present item constitutes the first of three in a volume typographically consistent throughout, being followed by a *Carta segunda* with Seville imprint of 'Francisco Lira' dated 1650 & a *Carta tercera,* likewise attributed to 'Lira', but dated 1750. All three bear on the t.p. an identical ornament. It is perhaps significant, moreover, that on the title pages of all three

Palafox is designated as 'venerable', a designation canonically correct following the introduction, in 1694, of his cause for the process of canonization. Preliminary investigations by Danial Elliott point to the real possibility that these items were in fact printed at Puebla around the middle of the 18th century, and hence, technically speaking, are outside the scope of the present undertaking. Palau 209675. ICN, InU-L, RPJCB.   646/115

Panciroli, Guido. Rerum memorabilium . . . pars prior[–posterior]. *Frankfurt a. M.: J. G. Schönwetter,* 1646. 2 pts; 4to. 1st publ., Amberg, 1599–1602; cf. 1602 edn. Sabin 58412. DNLM, MiU, NNC, PPL; BN.   646/116

Pastor, Juan, S.J. Señor. Juan Pastor . . . procurador general . . . por la provincia del Paraguay, dize: que de seis en seis años viene de su provincia un procurador della sacerdote, y otro compañero. [*Madrid:* 1646?], bds.; fol. Memorial to king of Spain. Medina (BHA) 6732; Streit II:1754; Backer VI:339. Seville:Archivo de Indias.   646/117

———. Señor. Juan Pastor . . . procurador general . . . por la provincia del Paraguay. Dize, que los Indios [etc.]. [*Madrid:* 1646?]. [1] p.; fol. Memorial to king of Spain seeking continuance of prohibition of forcing Indians to work for Spanish against their will in Paraguay. Medina (BHA) 6734; Streit II:1756. Seville:Archivo de Indias.   646/118

———. Señor. Juan Pastor . . . procurador . . . por la provincia del Paraguay dize, que los Indios del Uruay, y del Parana. [*Madrid:* 1646?]. [1] p.; fol. Memorial to king of Spain praising Indians for support in struggle against Portuguese in Brazil. Medina (BHA) 6733; Streit II:1755. Seville:Archivo de Indias.   646/119

Pérez, Jacinto, S.J. Razon que da de si el padre Jacinto Perez . . . En los cargos que le haze don Juan de Medina Avila, en el libelo infamatorio que ha sacado contra el. *Madrid:* 1646. 46 numb. lvs; fol. The writer defends his conduct in Lima, where he was the Jesuit provincial. Medina (BHA) 1090. BL.   646/120

Perucci, Francesco. Pompe funebri di tutte

le nationi del mondo . . . Seconda impressione. *Verona: F. Rossi* [1646]. 146 p.; illus.; obl. fol. 1st publ., Verona, 1639. Michel (Répertoire) VI:102. DNLM, ICU, MH; BL, BN.   646/121

Pharmacopoeia Augustana, auspicio . . . Senatus, cura octava Collegii Medici. *Augsburg: A. Aperger,* 1646. 2 pts; fol. 1st publ., Augsburg, [1564]; cf. 1613 edn. CaBVaU; BL.   646/122

Planis Campy, David de. Les oeuvres . . . contenant les plus beaux traicté de la medecine chymique. *Paris: D. Moreau,* 1646. 752 p.; port.; fol. Included are the author's *Bouquet,* 1st publ., Paris, 1629, & his *Chirurgie chimique medicale,* 1st publ., Paris, 1621. DLC, MH, WU; BN.   646/123
—[Anr issue]. *Paris: E. Danguy,* 1646. ICU, DNLM.   646/124

Porter y Casanate, Pedro. Relacion en que se ciñen los servicios del almirante Don Pedro Casanate, cavallero de la orden de Santiago. [*Madrid:* 1646]. 2 lvs; fol. Cf. entries for writer under years 1638 & 1640. Cf. Sabin 64325; Wagner (SW) 45. CSmH.
                                              646/125

Poty, Pieter. Copye van een Brasiliaenschen brieff gheschreven van Pieter Potty Brasiliaen en commanderende over 't regiment Brasilianen van Paraiba, aen Camaron mede Brasiliaen en overste vande Brasilianen van die van de Bahia dato 31 October 1645. Geschreven in de Brasiliaensche tale en daer uyt getranslateert. [*Amsterdam:*] *F. Lieshout,* 1646. bds.; fol. Transl. from ms. letter of the author's in Tupi—see C. R. Boxer, *The Dutch in Brazil* (Oxford, 1957), p. 185. Borba de Moraes I:178; Asher 209; Petit 2298. Leyden:UB.   646/126

Prevost, Jean. La medecine des pauvres. *Paris: G. Clousier,* 1646. 259 p.; 8vo. Transl. from the author's *Medicina pauperum,* 1st publ., Frankfurt a. M.?, 1641? DNLM; BN.
                                              646/127

Prynne, William. A fresh discovery of some prodigious new wandring-blasing-stars, & firebrands, stiling themselves New Lights . . . The second edition. *London: J. Macock, for M. Sparke,* 1646. 88 p.; 4to. 1st publ., London, 1645. Sabin 66417; Wing P3964; Thomason I:410; JCB (3) II:346. CtY, ICN, MdBP, RPJCB; BL.   646/128

Raven, Dirck Albertsz. Journael ofte Beschrijvinge vande reyse ghedaen by den Commandeur Dirck Albertsz. Raven . . . ten dienste vande . . . bewindthebbers vande Groenlandtsche Compagnie tot Hoorn. *Hoorn: I. Willemszoon, for J. J. Deutel,* 1646. 16 p.; illus.; 4to. Issued as pt of W. Y. Bontekoe's *Journael . . . vande Oost-Indische reyse* above, q.v.

Ritratti et elogii di capitani illustri che ne' secoli moderni hanno gloriosamente guerregiato. Descritti da Giulio Roscio, Monsig. Agostino, Mascardi, Fabio Leonida, Ottavio Tronsarelli, & altri. *Rome: G. Mascardi, for F. de' Rossi,* 1646. 404 p.; ports; 4to. 1st publ., Rome, 1635. Cf. Sabin 71587. ICN, MH, MiU; BN.   646/129

Rivière, Lazare. Observationes medicae et curationes insignae. *Paris: S. Piquet,* 1646. 2 pts; 4to. In Centuria ii, Observatio lxxxi, on syphilis, prescribes use of guaiacum & sarsaparilla. DNLM, MiU, NNNAM; London:Wellcome.   646/130
—[Anr edn]. *London: M. Fletcher,* 1646. 451 p.; 8vo. Wing R1557. DNLM, NIC, PPC; BL.   646/131
—[Anr edn?]. [*London?*] 1646. 8vo. Wing R1558. Cambridge:Trinity.   646/132

Rutherford, Samuel. The divine right of church-government and excommunication. *London: J. Field, for C. Meredith,* 1646. 2 pts; 4to. Includes (pt 1, p. 625–28) discussion of 'Indian and American governments', citing Roger William's *Bloudy Tenent* of 1644. Sabin 74455; Wing R2377; McAlpin II:446–447. CLU-C, CtY, ICU, InU-L, NNUT, PPPrHi; BL.   646/133

Salinas y Córdova, Buenaventura de, O.F.M. Memorial, informe, y manifiesto del p.f. Buenaventura de Salinas y Cordova . . . commissario general de las provincias de la Nueva-España. Al Rey nuestro señor, en su . . . Consejo de las Indias. Representa las acciones proprias . . . Informa, la buena dicha, y meritos de los que nacen en las Indias, de padres Españoles . . . Manifesta, la piedad y zelo con que su Magestad govierno toda la America. [*Madrid:* ca. 1646]. 2 pts; fol. Sabin 75785 (& 75782?); Medina (BHA) 6858; Streit II:1758; Palau 287614; JCB (3) II:454–55. NNH, RPJCB; Seville:B. Colombina.   646/134

Salmerón, Marcos, O. Merced. Recuerdos historicos y politicos de los servicios que los generales, y varones ilustres de la religion de Nuestra Señora de la Merced, Redencion de Cautivos han hecho a los reyes de España en los dos mundos, desde . . . 1218, hasta . . . 1640. *Valencia: Heirs of C. Gárriz, for B. Nogues, 1646.* 550 p.; fol. Relates in part to Order's missions in Mexico. Sabin 75813; Medina (BHA) 1091; Streit I:507; Palau 287722; JCB (3) II:347. CtY, ICN, InU-L, MH, NN-RB, RPJCB; BL, BN.
646/135

Saltmarsh, John. The smoke in the temple. Wherein is a designe for peace and reconciliation. *London: Ruth Raworth, for G. Calvert, 1646.* 2 pts; 4to. On p. 38 is a ref. to Roger Williams's *The bloudy tenet* of 1644. Wing S498; McAlpin II:449. CSmH, CtY, DLC, ICN, MH, NNUT, RPJCB; BL.
646/136

Sánchez de Espejo, Andrés. Discurso político del estado de las cosas de España; sobre carta para Indias. Granada primero de Julio de 1646. *[Granada:] V. Alvarez [1646].* 6 numb. lvs; fol. Includes refs to uncertain departure of Spanish fleet for Mexico. Palau 295355; Maggs Cat. 496 (Americana VI):359. ICN, NN-RB, RPJCB.
646/137

Sennert, Daniel. Institutionum medicinae. Libri v. *Geneva: P. Gamonet, 1646.* 2 v.; 8vo. 1st publ., Wittenberg, 1611. ICJ.
646/138

Serres, Olivier de, seigneur du Pradel. Le theatre d'agriculture. *Rouen: J. Berthelin, 1646.* 908 p.; illus.; 4to. 1st publ., Paris, 1600; cf. 1603 edn, BN.
646/139

Shepard, Thomas. The sincere convert . . . The fourth edition, corrected and much amended. *London: M. Simmons, for J. Sweeting, 1646.* 270 p.; 8vo. 1st publ., London, 1640. Sabin 80221; Wing S3120. CtY, MH.
646/140

Siri, Vittorio. Il mercurio, overo Historia de' correnti tempi. *Casale: C. della Casa, 1646.* 853 p.; 4to. 1st publ., Casale, 1644. Cf. Sabin 81447; Brunet V:402; Grasse VI:417. BN.
646/141

Speed, John. A prospect of the most famous parts of the world. *London: M. F[letcher]., for W. Humble, 1646.* 206 p.; maps; 8vo. 1st

publ., London, 1627. Sabin 89228n; Wing S4882. CtY, DLC, ICN, MH, MiU-C; BL.
646/142

—[Anr edn]. *London: J. Legatt, for W. Humble, 1646.* 5 pts; ports, maps; fol. ICN.
646/143

Suchtich en trouwhertich discours over dese . . . gestalte des lants . . . door E. P. *[Amsterdam?] 1646.* [23] p.; 4to. Includes ref. to role of East & West Indies in truce negotiations. 'Discours' appears in roman type. Knuttel 5312. NN; BL, The Hague:KB.
646/144

—[Anr edn]. Suchtigh en trouwhertigh discours. *[Amsterdam?] 1646.* [23] p.; 4to. 'Discours' is in black letter. Knuttel 5313. InU, MnU, NN; BL, The Hague:KB.   646/145

Tassoni, Alessandro. De' pensieri diversi . . . libri dieci. *Venice: B. Barezzi, 1646.* 445 p.; 4to. 1st publ., Modena, 1612, under title *Varieta di diversi pensieri,* but see also enl. 1620 edn. Puliatti (Tassoni) 8. CU, ICN, InU, MH, MiDW; BL, BN.   646/146

Tweede deel van den Ongeveynsden patriot. *Middelburg: 1646.* See Den ongeveynsden Nederlandschen patriot *above.*

Twisse, William. A treatise of Mr. Cottons . . . concerning predestination. *London: J. D[awson?]., for A. Crooke, 1646.* 288 p.; 4to. A reply to John Cotton, mentioning New England; it does not contain Cotton's treatise. Sabin 17088 & 97545; Wing C6464 & T3425; McAlpin II:458; JCB (3) II:340. CSmH, CtY, DLC, MH, MnU, NNUT, PPL, RPJCB; BL, Oxford:Bodl.   646/147

Vaughan, Henry. Poems. *London: G. Badger, 1646.* 8vo. On p. 27 tobacco is mentioned. Wing V124 (STC 24914). CSmH, CtY, IU, MH; BL.   646/148

Vieira, Antonio, S.J. Sermam, que pregou o p. Antonio Vieira da Companhia de Jesus na Misericordia da Bahia de todos os Santos, em dia da Visitação de Nossa Senhora, Orago da Casa assistindo o marquez de Montalvão visorrey daquelle estado do Brasil. *[Lisbon? 1646?].* [16] p.; 4to. Cf. Backer VIII:655; Leite IX:202–203. RPJCB.
646/149

—[Anr edn]. *Lisbon: D. Lopes Rosa, 1646.* [25] p.; 4to. Backer VIII:655; Leite IX:203.
646/150

Villa, Esteban de. Ramillete de plantas. *Bur-*

gos: *P. Gómez de Valdivielso,* 1646. 148 numb. lvs; 4to. 1st publ., Burgos, 1637. Cf. Pritzel 9770; Palau 366189. MH-A, NNH; León: BP.　　　　　　　　　　　　　　646/151

Vimont, Barthélemy, S.J. Relation de ce qui s'est passé en la Nouvelle France, és années 1644. & 1645. *Paris: S. Cramoisy & G. Cramoisy,* 1646. 183 p.; 8vo. 'Lettre du p. Hierosme Lalemant, escrite des Hurons': p. 136–83. For variants, see Bell & McCoy as cited. Sabin 99753; Streit II:2560; Bell (Jes. rel.) 27–29; McCoy 57–60; Church 476; JCB (3) II:348. CSmH, CtY, DLC, ICN, InU-L, MH, MiU-C, MnU-B, NN-RB, RPJCB; BL, BN.　　　　　　　　　　　　　　646/152

A vindication of learning from unjust aspersions. Wherein is set forth, the learning of the ancient fathers, and patriarches, prophets, and apostles of Jesus Christ. *London: J. Hardesty,* 1646. 30 p.; 4to. On p. 21–22 is a paragraph on America, referring to Anghiera, Oviedo, & de Laet. Wing V480; Thomason I:467. CSmH, IEN, MH, RPJCB; BL.　　　　　　　　　　　　　　646/153

Voor-looper, brenghende oprecht bescheyt uyt Amsterdam, aen een . . . heer in 's Gravenhaghe, weghens de verraderije in Brasil, met het schip Zeelandia, afgevaerdicht den twaelfden December 1645. van Pharnambuco. [*The Hague?*] 1646. [4] p.; 4to. Relates to Portuguese uprising. Signed by the 'Bewinthebberen vande West-Indische Compagnie'. Sabin 7647; Borba de Moraes II:362; Knuttel 5351. The Hague: KB.　　　　　　　　　　　　　　646/154

Weerts, Paul, O.F.M. Histoire admirable de la vie du père . . . S. François. *Antwerp: M. vanden Enden & A. van Brakel* [1646]. 136 p.; illus. Chapt. 6 describes Franciscan missions in New World. DHN.　　　646/155

Williams, Roger. Christenings make not Christians, or A briefe discourse concerning that name heathen, commonly given to the Indians. *London: Jane Coe, for J. H[ancock?].,* 1645 [i.e., 1646]. 21 p.; 8vo. Recorded by Thomason as publ. 23 Jan. 1646. Sabin 104334; Wing W2761; Thomason I:416. BL.　　　　　　　　　　646/156

Winslow, Edward. Hypocrisie unmasked: by a true relation of the proceedings of the Governour and Company of the Massachusets against Samuel Gorton (and his accom-

plices) a notorious disturber of the peace. *London: R. Cotes, for J. Bellamy,* 1646. 103 p.; 4to. A reply to Gorton's *Simplicities defence* of this year. Sabin 104796; Vail (Frontier) 107; Wing W3037; Church 477; JCB (3) II:349. CSmH, CtY, DLC, ICN, MB, MiU-C, NN-RB, RPJCB; BL.　　　646/157

Workman, Giles. Private-men no pulpitmen: or, A modest examination of lay-mens preaching. Discovering it to be neither warranted by the word of God; nor allowed by the judgement, or practise, of the churches of Christ in New England. *London: F. Neile, for T. Underhill,* 1646. 28 p.; 4to. Included are refs to John Cotton's writings. Sabin 105475; Wing W3583; McAlpin II:465; JCB (3) II:349. CSmH, MH, MiU-C, NNUT, RPJCB; BL.　　　646/158

—[Anr issue]. *London: F. N[eile]., for T. Langford, at Gloucester,* 1646. Wing W3584. CtY.　　　　　　　　　　　　　　646/159

Wurffbain, Johann Sigmund. Reiss-Beschreibung . . . Gestelt durch seinen Vattern Leonhardi Wurffbain . . . und auff desselben Verlag und Unkosten. *Nuremberg: M. Endter,* 1646. 65 p.; 4to. Includes, p. 37–65, section on East & West Indies & the Netherlands. An inaccurate account based on Wurffbain's letters and later suppressed; cf. Wurffbain's own *Reise nach den Molukken,* Nuremberg, 1686. Cf. Sabin 105639. CtY, MnU-B, NN-RB.　　　　　　646/160

Ximénez de Torres, Jacinto. Medica resolucion, en que se prueba ser el otoño, tiempo conveniente para dar las unciones a los enfermos galicos. *Seville:* 1646. 11 numb. lvs; 4to. Medina (BHA) 1092; Palau 377302. Granada:BU.　　　　　　　　　　646/161

1647

Aldrovandi, Ulisse. De piscibus libri v. et de cetis liber i. *Frankfurt a. M.: K. Rötel, for J. D. Zunner & P. Haubold,* 1647. 280 p.; illus.; fol. 1st publ., Bologna, 1612. Nissen (Zool.) 71n. MH; Munich:StB.　　647/1

——. Quadrupedum omnium bisulcorum historia . . . Marcus Antonius Bernia denuò in lucem edidit. *Frankfurt a. M.: K. Rötel, for J. D. Zunner & P. Haubold,* 1647. 425 p.;

illus.; fol. 1st publ., Bologna, 1621. Nissen (Zool.) 74n. KU, MiU, NjP, RPB; BL. 647/2

Authenthijcque copye van het Recif van den 12 December 1647, vervattende 't gheene aldaer van de Portuguisen is voorghevallen. [*Amsterdam?* 1647?]. bds.; fol. Knuttel 5563a. The Hague:KB 647/3

Avila y Lugo, Francisco de. El governador Don Francisco Davila y Lugo: Dize, que necessitado de sus obligaciones, informò por carta, que remitio al Consejo real de las Indias, la demarcacion, importancia, y peligroso estado que tiene el reyno de Guatemala . . . causado . . . por el modo de govierno del licenciado Don Diego de Avendaño, presidente de aquella audiencia. [*Madrid:* 1647?]. [4] p.; fol. Medina (BHA) 6406. Seville:Archivo de Indias. 647/4

Bacon, Francis, viscount St Albans. Histoire de la vie, et de la mort . . . fidelement traduite par J[ean]. Baudoin. *Paris: G. Loyson & J.-B. Loyson,* 1647. 508 p.; 8vo. Transl. from Bacon's *Historia vitae & mortis,* 1st publ., London, 1623. Reissued, 1653, under title *Le medecin françois.* Gibson (Bacon) 155. DFo, MH; BL, BN. 647/5

——. Historia regni Henrici septimi. *Leyden: F. Haack,* 1647. 403 p.; 12mo. 1st publ. in Latin, Leyden, 1642. In this edition p. 159 is correctly numbered. Gibson (Bacon) 126a. The locations here given may include the following item. CU, IU, InU-L, MH, NN-RB, PPL, RPJCB; BL. 647/6

—[Anr edn]. *Leyden: F. Haack,* 1647. 403 p.; 12mo. In this edn p. 159 is misnumbered 195. Gibson (Bacon) 126b. 647/7

——. De proef-stucken (beschreven in 't Engelsch) . . . in 't Latijn . . . beschreven . . . overgeset . . . door Peter Böener. *Leyden: W. C. vander Boxe,* 1647. 194 p.; port.; 4to. 1st publ. in Dutch, Leyden, 1646; here a reissue with cancel t.p. of that edn. Gibson (Bacon) 58. DFo. 647/8

Baerle, Kaspar van. Rerum per octennium in Brasilia et alibi nuper gestarum, sub praefectura . . . J. Mauritii, Nassoviae, &c., comitis . . . historia. *Amsterdam: J. Blaeu,* 1647. 340 p.; illus., port., maps; fol. Includes also section on language of Araucanian Indians. Sabin 3408; Borba de Moraes I:65–66; Rodrigues (Dom. Hol.) 449; JCB (3) II:350. DLC, InU-L, MH, MiU-C, MnU-B, NNC, RPJCB; BL, BN. 647/9

——. Uytvaert der Vereenichde Nederlanden, gehouden over . . . Frederic Henric . . . nu in nederduyts naegevolgt door J. Westerbaen. *The Hague: A. J. Tongerloo,* 1647. 36 p.; 4to. The complete Latin text from which this was translated has not been traced. Includes (p. 16–18) refs to Peru, Cuba, Potosí, to Atabalipa, Pizarro, & Brazil. Cf. Baerle's *Argo Batava,* 1st publ., Leyden, 1629. Knuttel 5576. BL, The Hague:KB, Ghent:BU. 647/10

Baillie, Robert. Anabaptism, the true fountaine of independency, antinomy, Brownisme, familisme . . . unsealed. *London: M. F[letcher]., for S. Gellibrand,* 1647. 179 p.; 4to. Included are refs to Anabaptists in New England, to Roger Williams & his *Bloudy tenent,* & to Anne Hutchinson. Sabin 2762; Wing B452; McAlpin II:469; JCB (3) II: 351. CLU-C, CtY, DFo, ICN, MH, MiU-C, MnU-B, NNUT, PPPrHi, RPJCB; BL. 647/11

Barnstein, Heinrich. Kurtze Beschreibung dess Tabacks. *Erfurt: T. Fritsche,* 1647. 16 lvs; 8vo. 1st publ. in this version, Erfurt, 1645. Dt. Ges. Kat. 11.7684. Munich:UB. 647/12

Bartholin, Thomas. De luce animalium libri iii. Admirandis historiis rationibusque novis refertis. *Leyden: F. Haack,* 1647. 396 p.; 8vo. In bk 1, chapt. vi 'Ab affectionibus seu passionibus agrorum, in homine lucem inferimus', it is stated that 'In America aegri ex calore comburi videntur.' CtY-M, DNLM, MWA, MiU, NjP; BL, BN. 647/13

Beaumont, Francis. Comedies and tragedies written by Francis Beaumont and John Fletcher never printed before. *London: H. Robinson & H. Moseley,* 1647. 9 pts; port.; fol. Includes, with anachronistic refs to tobacco, *The mad lover, The queene of Corinth,* and *The honest mans fortune.* Wing B1581; Greg 637(a), 662(a), & 663(a); Arents 232. CSmH, CtY, DLC, ICN, MH, MiU, MnU, NN-RB, PU; BL. 647/14

Béguin, Jean. Les elemens de chymie . . . Quatriesme edition. *Rouen: J. Behourt,* 1647. 432 p.; illus.; 8vo. 1st publ. as here transl. from Béguin's *Tyrocinium chymicum*

(Paris, 1612), Paris, 1615. MH; Glasgow: UL. 647/15

Beneficien voor de soldaten gaende naer Brasil. *The Hague: Widow & Heirs of H. Jacobszoon van Wouw,* 1647. 4 p.; 4to. Sabin 7525. 647/16

—[Anr edn]. *The Hague: Widow & Heirs of H. Jacobszoon van Wouw,* 1647. bds.; fol. Van Alphen 195. Groningen:UB. 647/17

—[Anr edn]. Beneficien voor soldaten [etc.]. *The Hague: Widow & Heirs of H. Jacobszoon van Wouw,* 1647. 3 p.; fol. Petit 2372. Leyden:B. Thysiana. 647/18

Besoignes en communicatien over de ligue garentie van de . . . Staten Generael. Den 2. 4. en 5. Julij 1647. *The Hague: Widow of H. Jacobszoon van Wouw,* 1647. [8] p.; 4to. Relates in part to the West-Indische Compagnie. Sabin 52225; Asher 268; Knuttel 5484. The Hague:KB. 647/19

—[Anr edn]. *The Hague: J. J. Verhuel,* 1647. [8] p.; 4to. Petit 2355. Leyden:B. Thysiana, BL. 647/20

—[Anr edn]. *The Hague: Widow of H. Jacobszoon van Wouw,* 1647. [8] p.; 4to. This edn has reading 'de ligve' on t.p.; the last page begins 'voorts geresolveert'. Knuttel 5485. The Hague:KB. 647/21

—[Anr edn]. *The Hague: Widow of H. Jacobszoon van Wouw,* 1647. [4] p.; 4to. This edn has reading 'garantie' on t.p. Knuttel 5486; Meulman 2848. MnU-B, NN; Ghent:BU, The Hague:KB. 647/22

Beverwijck, Jan van. Heel-konste. *Dordrecht: J. Gorisszoon,* 1647. 12mo. 1st publ., Dordrecht, 1645. Catalogus van boeken VII:71. 647/23

——. Lof der genees-konste, Weder-legginge van Montaigne over de nootsakelickheydt van de selve. *Dordrecht: J. Braat,* 1647. 155 p.; 8vo. 1st publ. in Dutch, Dordrecht, 1635; transl. from 1633 Latin text. Van de Velde 75–76. DFo, DNLM. 647/24

——. Schat der ongesontheyt; ofte Geneeskonste . . . mitsgaders met verssen door . . . Jacob Cats. *Dordrecht: J. Braat,* 1647. 693 p.; illus., port.; 8vo. 1st publ., Dordrecht, 1642. Van de Velde 76. DFo, DNLM. 647/25

Bible. O.T. English. Paraphrases. 1647. Bay Psalm Book. The whole book of psalmes, faithfully translated into English metre.

[*London?*] 1647. 274 p.; 12mo. 1st publ., Cambridge, Mass., 1640. Sabin 66430; Evans 20; Holmes (MM) 53AA; Wing B2427; JCB (3) II:351. RPJCB; BL. 647/26

Birago, Giovanni Battista. Historia della disunione del regno di Portugallo dalla corona di Castiglia . . . Novamente corretta, emendata & illustrata. *Amsterdam: N. van Ravesteyn,* 1647. 796 p.; 8vo. 1st publ., Lyons, 1644, under title *Historia del regno di Portogallo.* Cf. Borba de Moraes I:93; Palau 29947; JCB (3) II:351. CtY, DLC, MH, MnU-B, NN, RPJCB; BL. 647/27

Bissel, Johannes, S.J. Argonauticon Americanorum, sive, Historiae periculorum Petri de Victoria, ac sociorum eius, libri vi. *Munich: L. Straub, for J. Wagner,* 1647. 480 p.; map; 12mo. Though conventionally described as a Latin version of the Ingolstadt, 1622, German translation of Pedro Gobeo de Victoria's *Naufragio y peregrinatio,* 1st publ., Seville, 1610, Harold Jantz points out that this is in fact a novel for which Gobeo's account was 'merely . . . raw material'. Sabin 99443; Medina (BHA) 1094; Borba de Moraes I:93; Backer I:1514–1515; Jantz (German Baroque) 513; JCB (3) II:360. CtY, DLC, ICN, MH, MnU-B, NN-RB, PPL, RPJCB; BL, Wolfenbüttel:HB. 647/28

Blaeu, Willem Janszoon. Novus atlas, das ist Weltbeschreibung. *Amsterdam: J. Blaeu,* 1647. 1st publ., Amsterdam, 1634, cf. 1635 edn. Koeman (Bl) 31B. Berlin:StB, Innsbruck:UB. 647/29

——. Novus atlas, das ist Welt-beschreibung . . . ander Theil. *Amsterdam: J. Blaeu,* 1647. 2 pts; 92 maps; fol. 1st publ., Amsterdam, 1635. Issued with Blaeu's *Novus atlas,* Amsterdam, 1649, '47. Sabin 5719; Koeman (Bl) 34. MH; Leeds:UL, Amsterdam: NHSM. 647/30

——. Le theatre du monde ou Nouvel atlas. *Amsterdam: J. Blaeu,* 1647. 2 pts; 120 maps; fol. 1st publ. in French, Amsterdam, 1635; here largely a reissue of the Amsterdam, 1645, edn. Issued with Blaeu's *Le theatre . . . seconde partie* of this year, below. For variant see Koeman. Koeman (Bl) 19C. ICN; Paris:Ste Geneviève, Cracow:BCzart. 647/31

—[Anr edn]. *Amsterdam: J. Blaeu,* 1647–50. 2 pts; 120 maps; fol. 1st publ. in French, Amsterdam, 1635. Issued with Blaeu's *Le theatre . . . seconde partie*, Amsterdam, 1650. Koeman (Bl) 19D. ICN; Paris:Loeb-Larocque. 647/32

——. Le theatre du monde, ou Nouvel atlas . . . Seconde partie. *Amsterdam: J. Blaeu,* 1647. 2 pts; 93 maps; fol. 1st publ., Amsterdam, 1635; here a reissue of 1645 edn. Issued with Blaeu's *Le theatre* of this year above. Koeman (Bl) 18D. Paris:Ste Geneviève, Cracow:BCzart. 647/33

——. Toonneel des aerdrycx, ofte Nieuwe atlas. *Amsterdam: J. Blaeu,* 1647. 2 pts; 120 maps.; fol. 1st publ., Amsterdam, 1635; cf. 1642 edn. Koeman (Bl) 29A. RPB; Utrecht:UB. 647/34

——. Tweevoudigh onderwijs van de hemelsche en aerdsche globen. *Amsterdam: J. Blaeu,* 1647. 2pts; illus.; 4to. 1st publ., Amsterdam, 1634. Keuning (Blaeu) 62–63. DLC. 647/35

Bontekoe, Willem Ysbrandsz. Journael ofte Gedenckwaerdige beschryvinghe van de Oost-Indische reyse. *Utrecht: G. Bilsteyn, for E. W. Snellaert,* 1647. 72 p.; illus.; 4to. 1st publ., Haarlem & Hoorn, 1646. Issued with D. A. Raven's *Journael ofte Beschryvinge vande reyse,* with special t.p. & separate signatures & paging. Sabin 67980n; Tiele-Muller 169; Tiele 158n; cf. JCB (3) II:359 (Raven). NN-RB; BL. [Raven only: DLC, MiHM, RPJCB]. 647/36

—[Anr edn]. *Rotterdam: I. van Waesberghe,* 1647. 2 pts; illus.; 4to. Sabin 67980n; Tiele-Muller 170 647/37

Boodt, Anselm Boèce de. Gemmarum et lapidum historia . . . Cui accedunt Joannis de Laet . . . De gemmis et lapidibus libri ii. *Leyden: J. Maire,* 1647. 2 pts; illus.; 8vo. Laet's *De gemmis* includes discussion of American fossils. CtY, DLC, MCM, MnU-B, NNE, PU-S; BL, BN. 647/38

Boothby, Richard. A briefe discovery or description of the most famous island of Madagascar . . . The second edition corrected and amended. *London: [E. Griffin?] for J. Hardesty,* 1647. 72 p.; 4to. 1st publ., London, 1646. Wing B3744. CSmH, DLC, MH; Glasgow:Hunterian Mus. 647/39

De Brasilsche Breede-byl; ofte T'samenspraek, tusschen Kees Jansz. Schott komende uyt Brasil, en Jan Maet, koopmans-knecht, hebbende voor desen ook in Brasil geweest, over den verloop in Brasil. [*Amsterdam?*] 1647. 36 p.; 4to. Sabin 7534; Borba de Moraes I:107; Asher 230; Knuttel 5546; JCB (3) II:606. DLC, MnU-B, NN-RB, RPJCB; BL (Schott, K.), The Hague:KB. 647/40

Brasilsche gelt-sack, waer in dat klaerlijck vertoont wort, waer dat de participanten van de West-Indische Compagnie haer geldt ghebleven is. *'Recife, Brazil'* [i.e., *Amsterdam?*]: 1647. [28] p.; 4to. Sabin 7535; Borba de Moraes I:108; Asher 231; Muller (1872) 226; Knuttel 5547; JCB (3) II:351. MnU-B, RPJCB; BL (Brazilian Money-bag), The Hague:KB. 647/41

—[Anr edn]. . . . claerlijck vertoont wordt . . . *'Recife, Brazil'* [i.e., *Amsterdam?*]: 1647. [28] p.; 4to. Sabin 102885; Knuttel 5548; JCB (3) II:352. DLC, NN-RB, RPJCB; BL, The Hague:KB. 647/42

Brilleman, Jan. Collyrium, ofte Costelijcke ooghen-salve. *Leeuwarden: H. de Bock,* 1647. 30 p.; 4to. Includes ref. to a Heer Gijselingh & ships from Brazil, affording a taste of sugar. Knuttel 5591; Petit 2384. MnU-B, NN; The Hague:KB, Leyden:B. Thysiana. 647/43

Bruele, Gualtherus. Praxis medicinae theorica et empirica familiarissima. *Leyden: J. Maire,* 1647. 2 pts; 8vo. 1st publ., Antwerp, 1579; cf. 1602 edn. DNLM; London: Wellcome, BN. 647/44

Calvo, Juan. Primera y segunda parte de la Cirugia universal. *Valencia: Heirs of C. Gárriz, for B. Nogués,* 1647. 618 p.; fol. 1st publ., Seville, 1580; cf. 1626 edn. Medina (BHA) 1095; Palau 40554. DNLM; León:BP. 647/45

Cartari, Vincenzo. Imagini delli dei de gl'antichi. *Venice: The Tomasini,* 1647. 400 p.; illus.; 4to. 1st publ., Padua, 1615, with Lorenzo Pignoria's pt 2, his 'Imagine de gli Indiani Orientali et Occidentali'. Sabin 11104n. CtY, ICN, NN-RB, PPL, RPJCB. 647/46

Cervantes Saavedra, Miguel de. Primera y segunda parte del incenioso [*sic*] hidalgo Don Quixote de la Mancha. *Madrid: Imprenta Real, for J. A. Bonet, & F. Serrano,* 1647. 481 numb. lvs; 4to. Pt 2, with American refs, 1st publ., Madrid, 1615. Ríus (Cervantes)

18; Palau 51991. DLC, MB, MiU, NNH; BL.
647/47

Child, John. New-Englands Jonas cast up in London: or, A relation of the proceedings of the court at Boston against divers honest and godly persons. *London: T. R[atcliffe]. & E. M[ottershead].*, 1647. Sabin 12705; Wing C3851; Church 578; JCB (3) II:353. CSmH, DLC, MBAt, MiU-C, NN-RB, PPL, RPJCB; BL.
647/48

Claar vertooch van de verradersche en vyant-lijcke acten en proceduren van Poortugaal, in't verwecken ende stijven van de rebellie ende oorloghe in Brasil. *Amsterdam: Widow of J. Broerszoon*, 1647. [39] p.; 4to. Sabin 7547; Borba de Moraes I:161; Asher 228; Knuttel 5544; JCB (3) II:352. DLC, NN-RB, RPJCB; BL (Portugal), The Hague:KB.
647/49

Company of Adventurers for the Plantation of the Islands of Eleutheria, formerly called Buhama. Articles and orders, made and agreed upon the 9th day of July, 1647. [*London:* 1647]. bds.; fol. Wing C5583. BL.
647/50

Consideratien op de Cautie van Portugael. [*Amsterdam?*] 1647. 15 p.; 4to. Supports Portuguese interests in opposition to the West-Indische Compagnie's undertakings in Brazil. Cf. a related work of this year, the *Vertooch aen de . . . Staten Generael* below. Sabin 15933; Borba de Moraes I:171; Asher 225; Knuttel 5554. DLC, MnU-B, NN-RB, RPJCB; BL (Portugal), The Hague:KB.
647/51

Contreras, Francisco de, S.J. Informacion sobre que los electos para obispos no pueden consagrarse, ni tomar la possession de sus obispados sin que primero reciban las letras apostolicas de su Santidad: hecho en abono de el que hizieron los padres de la Compania de Jesus de la provincia del Paraguay. [*Madrid?*] 1647. 44 lvs; 4to. Medina (BHA) 1097; Palau 60775. Santiago, Chile:BN.
647/52

Corbeius, Theodorus. Pathologia. *Nuremberg: W. Endter*, 1647. 564 p.; 8vo. 1st publ., Frankfurt a. M., 1615. PPC; BL, BN.
647/53

Corbet, Miles. A most learned and eloquent speech . . . at Westminster . . . on the 31th day of July, 1647. [*London:* 1647]. 8 p.; fol.

Defends Puritans from charge of desecrating communion tables by smoke of a cheap tobacco, 'Mundungo'. Wing C6268; Arents (Add.) 333. CSmH, CtY, ICN, MH, NN-A; BL.
647/54

Cort ende waerachtich verhael van der Portugysen in Brasil revolte. [*Amsterdam?* 1647]. 8 p.; 4to. Sabin 7565; Borba de Moraes I:184; Petit 2328. Leyden:B. Thysiana.
647/55

Cotton, John. The bloudy tenent, washed, and made white . . . Whereunto is added a Reply to Mr. Williams answer to Mr. Cottons letter. *London: M. Simmons, for Hannah Allen*, 1647. 2 pts; 4to. Includes refs to relations with Indians. 'A reply to Mr. Williams', pt 2, is answer to Roger Williams's *Bloudy tenent of persecution*, 1st publ., [London], 1644. For a further reply see Williams's *The bloody tenent yet more bloody*, London, 1652. Sabin 17045 (& 17077); Tuttle (Cotton) 55; Wing C6409; Church 479; JCB (3) II:353. CSmH, CtY, DLC, ICN, MH, MiU-C, NN-RB, RPJCB; BL, Oxford: Bodl.
647/56

——. Severall questions of serious and necessary consequence, propounded by the teaching elders, unto M. John Cotton . . . with his . . . answer. *London: T. Banks*, 1647. 10 p.; 4to. 1st publ., London, 1644, under title *Sixteene questions*. Sabin 17080; Tuttle (Cotton) 36; Wing C6455; JCB (3) II:354. CSmH, MB, RPJCB; BL, Oxford:Bodl.
647/57

Croll, Oswald. Hermetischer probier stein . . . Neben angehengten Crollischen Tractätlein von den innerlichen Signaturen. *Frankfurt a. M.: J. G. Schönwetter*, 1647. 3 pts; illus.; 4to. 1st publ. as here transl., Frankfurt a. M., [1623], under title *Basilica chymica, oder, Alchÿmistisch königlich Kleynod*. DLC, PU-S, WU.
647/58

Declaratie, ofte precijse Verklaringe van de plenipotentiarisen ende ambassadeurs van . . . den . . . Coningh van Spangien, nopende de versochte treves voor Portugael . . . Declaration des ambassadeurs d'Espaigne, touchant une trefve pour Portugal. *Münster:* 1647. [8] p.; 4to. Relates to 1647 uprising in Brazil. Text in Dutch & French. Sabin 19154; Knuttel 5549. NN; The Hague:KB.
647/59

—[Anr edn]. Declaratie, ofte precijse Verklaringhe. *Münster:* 1647. [4] p.; 4to. French text omitted in this edn. Knuttel 5550. The Hague:KB. 647/60

Discours de la paix, contre le Portugais. [*Amsterdam?*] 1647. [15] p.; 4to. Sabin 20234; Borba de Moraes I:226; Rodrigues (Dom. Hol.) 631; Knuttel 5555. DLC; The Hague:KB. 647/61

Donne, John. Βιαϑανατος. A declaration of that paradoxe . . . that selfe-homicide is not so naturally sinne, that it may never be otherwise. *London: J. Dawson* [1647]. 218 p.; 4to. Includes, pt 1, dist. 1, sect. 9, mention of religious sacrifice of children in Hispaniola, derived from Jean Matal's preface to Jerónimo Osorio's *De rebus Emmanuelis . . . gestis,* as 1st publ., Cologne, 1574. Prob. printed in 1644, but not publ. till 1647. Keynes (Donne) 47; Wing D1858. CSmH, CtY, ICN, MH, MWA, MiU, NN-RB, PU; BL. 647/62

Duliris, Leonard, O.R.S.A. La theorie des longitudes, reduite en pratique sur le globe celeste. *Paris: J. Guillemot,* 1647. 268 p.; illus.; 4to. Includes observations from voyages between La Rochelle & Canada, & also an 'Abregé du journal fait en la navigation de Canada'. Houzeau & Lancaster 10338. NN, RPJCB; BL, BN. 647/63

Du Val, Guillaume. Phytologia, sive Philosophia plantarum. *Paris: G. Meturas,* 1647. 472 p.; 8vo. Includes chapt. on mechoacan, identified as Mexican, derived from Monardes. Pritzel 2572. DNAL, MH-A, NNBG; BL, BN. 647/64

Escalona y Agüero, Gaspar de. Arcae Limensis gazophilatium regium, Perubicum. *Madrid: Imprenta Real,* 1647. 2 pts; fol. Sabin 22820 (& 521); Medina (Chile) 120; Palau 80775. CtY, MH, NN-RB, NcD; Santiago, Chile:BN. 647/65

Examen over seker boecxken, genaemt Nederlants beroerde inghewanden: over . . . de Munstersche vredehandelinghe. [*The Hague?*] 1647. [10] p.; 4to. Refers to *Nederlants beroerde ingewanden* of this year below. Includes refs to the West-Indische Compagnie. Knuttel 5520. NN; The Hague:KB. 647/66

Fioravanti, Leonardo. De' capricci medicinali . . . libri quattro. *Venice: Cestaro,* 1647.

267 numb. lvs; illus.; 8vo. 1st publ., Venice, 1561, under title *Capricci medicinali;* cf. 1602 edn. Michel (Répertoire) III:47. DNLM, NNC, WU; Paris:Arsenal. 647/67

France. Sovereigns, etc., 1643–1715 (Louis XIV). Le Roy estant en son Conseil, la Reyne [etc.] . . . Paris, 27 mars 1647. [*Paris:* 1647]. [4] p.; 4to. 'Reglement pour établir un bon ordre de police au Canada'—Harrisse. Sabin 73741; Harrisse (NF) 85. 647/68

Gomberville, Marin Le Roy, sieur du Parc et de. The history of Polexander . . . Done into English by William Browne. *London: T. Harper, for T. Walkley,* 1647. 2 pts; fol. Transl. from the author's *Polexandre* as publ., Paris, 1638, '37. Wing G1025. CSmH, CtY, ICN, MH, NjP, ViU; BL. 647/69

——. Il Polessandro . . . diviso in cinque libri, trasportato dal francese da Paris Cerchieri. *Venice: The Guerigli,* 1647. 636 p.; 12mo. Transl. from Paris, 1638, '37, version; cf. 1629 version. Michel (Répertoire) IV:68. Grenoble:BM. 647/70

Gorton, Samuel. Simplicities defence against seven-headed policy, or A true complaint of a peaceable people, being part of the English in New England, made . . . against cruell persecutors. *London: J. Macock, for G. Wittington,* 1647. 4to. 1st publ., London, 1646. Sabin 28045. 647/71

Great Britain, Laws, statutes, etc., 1625–1649 (Charles I). Whereas the severall plantations in Virginia, Bermudas, Barbados, and other places of America have been much beneficiall to this kingdome by the increase of navigation . . . be it ordained . . . that all merchandize, goods, and necessaries, shall, or may be exported thither . . . without paying or yeelding any custom. *London: J. Wright,* 1646 [i.e., 1647]. bds.; fol. At head of title: Die sabbathi 23 januarii 1646 [i.e., 1647]. Wing E2186 & E2496; Crawford (Roy. procl.) 2677. CSmH, RPJCB; BL. 647/72

Grotius, Hugo. De jure belli ac pacis libri tres . . . Editio nova. *Amsterdam: H. Laurenszoon,* 1647. 554 p.; fol. 1st publ., Paris, 1625. Meulen/Diermanse 573. The Hague:PP. 647/73

Guibert, Philbert. Toutes les oeuvres charitables. *Paris: J. Jacquin,* 1647. 880 p.; port.; 8vo. Included is Guibert's *Le prix & valeur des medicamens,* 1st publ., Paris, 1625. CtY-M, DNLM. 647/74

Harsdörffer, Georg Philipp. Gesprächspiele, siebender Theil. *Nuremberg: W. Endter,* 1647. 440 p.; obl. 8vo. Includes ref. to 'Indianische Leinwa[n]d' as symbol on p. 100; on p. 282 is a ref. to relative merits of making long voyage to New World in order to flee poverty or to convert Indians, with apparently fictional account of French voyage toward Strait of Magellan presented on following pages. Forms pt 7 of the author's *Frauenzimmer Gesprechspiele,* 1641–49. Goedeke III:108; Faber du Faur 502. CU, CtY, DLC; BL. 647/75

Hartmann, Johann (1568–1631). Praxis chymiatrica. *Geneva: P. Chouët,* 1647. 2 pts; 8vo. 1st publ., Leipzig, 1633. Copies may occur without place in imprint. Ferguson (Bibl. chem.) I:365. CtY, WU; BL, London:Wellcome. 647/76

—[Anr edn]. *Mainz: N. Heill, for J. G. Schönwetter [at Frankfurt a. M.?],* 1647. 246 p.; 4to. London:Wellcome. 647/77

Hemmersam, Michael. Guineische und West-Indianische Reissbeschreibung de an. 1639. biss 1645. Von Ambsterdam nach . . . Brasilien. *Nuremberg: P. Fürst* [1647]. 109 p.; 8vo. The similarity of this to the edns of 1663 & 1669 suggests that such an edn may be a ghost. Sabin 31289 (& 37685); cf. Borba de Moraes I:334 & 276; Palmer 335. 647/78

Hille, Carl Gustav von. Der teutsche Palmenbaum; das ist, Lobschrift von der . . . Fruchtbringenden Gesellschaft . . . Tugendruhm. *Nuremberg: W. Endter,* 1647. 231 p.; illus., port.; obl. 8vo. Dedicatory verses by Johann Rist praise the Fruchtbringende Gesellschaft for its symbolic German palm, now exalted above the American original. Goedeke III:6; Faber du Faur 167; Wolfenbüttel 122. CtY, MH, NN-RB; BL, Wolfenbüttel:HB. 647/79

Hofmann, Caspar. De medicamentis officinalibus . . . libri duo. *Paris: G. Meturas,* 1647. 707 p.; 4to. Included is a comprehensive survey of American plants used as materia medica. DNLM; London:Wellcome, BN. 647/80

Holland (Province). Hof. Copie vande twee sententien uytgesproocken vanden Hove Provinciael van Hollandt . . . ende . . . de sententie van appel vanden Hoghen Rade van Hollandt . . . tegens Gaspar Dias de Fereira. [*The Hague?*] 1647. 8 p.; 4to. Dias Fereira, having been in Brazil, used his knowledge of Brazilian affairs to damage the West-Indische Compagnie. Sabin 24085 (& 16681); Knuttel 5548a; Tiele (Pamfletten) 3200. The Hague:KB. 647/81

Hollandt gedoodt-verwet. 't Samenspraeck, tusschen Teeuwes ende Keesie Maet. Verhalende de groote goodtloose gelt-giericheydt. [*The Hague?*] 1647. 8 p.; 4to. In verse. Includes ref. to the Dutch traveling to Brazil to fight Portuguese, mentioning an army of over 9,000 men. Sabin 99317n; Knuttel 5599. BL (Teeuwis; imp.), The Hague:KB. 647/82

Howell, James. A new volume of letters partly philosophicall, politicall, historicall. *London: T. W[arren?], for H. Moseley,* 1647. [271] p.; 8vo. Continues Howell's *Epistolae Ho-elianae,* London, 1645. Letter lxi, addressed to Sir Walter Raleigh's son Carew, recounts in detail circumstances and incidents of former's 2nd voyage to Guiana. The purported discovery of America by the Welshman Madog ab Owain Gwynedd is mentioned in letter lvi. Wing H3096; Grolier Club (Wither to Prior) 483. CLU-C, CtY, ICN, MH, MnU-B; BL. 647/83

Jansson, Jan. Atlas novus . . . in quo Hispaniae . . . nec-non Americae tabulae . . . tomus tertius. *Amsterdam.* 1647. *See* Jansson's *Novus atlas,* Amsterdam, 1646.

——. Nieuwen atlas, ofte Whereltbeschrijvinge . . . In drie deelen. *Amsterdam: J. Janszoon, the Younger,* 1647. 3 v.; illus., maps; fol. 1st publ. in this enl. version, Amsterdam, 1645. Koeman (Me) 79–81; Tiele 533n. Rotterdam:ML. 647/84

——. Nouvel atlas, ou Theatre du monde . . . divisé en quatre tomes. *Amsterdam: J. Janszoon, the Younger,* 1647. 4 v.; maps; fol. 1st publ. in this version, Amsterdam, 1639, as H. Hondius's *Nouveau theatre;* cf. Jansson's 1644 edn. Here added is a 4th vol. lacking Americana. Koeman (Me) 104–106, 160. Paris:CD, Basel:UB (v. 2, 3). 647/85

———. Novus Atlas, das ist Abbildung und Beschreibung von allen Ländern dess Erdreichs. *Amsterdam: J. Janszoon, the Younger,* 1647. 3 v.; illus., maps; fol. 1st publ., Amsterdam, 1638. Koeman (Me) 131–133. CtY (v. 1); Marburg:StB. 647/86

Jonstonus, Joannes. Idea universae medicinae practicae, libris xii absoluta. *Venice: 'Sub signo Minervae',* 1647. 580 p.; 8vo. 1st publ., Amsterdam, 1644. DNLM; London:Wellcome. 647/87

Journael ofte Kort discours, nopende de rebellye ende verradelijcke desseynen der Portugesen, alhier in Brasil voorgenomen, 't welck in Junio 1645. is ontdeckt. *Arnhem: J. Jacobszoon,* 1647. [80] p.; 4to. Sabin 7593; Borba de Moraes I:364; Asher 229; Knuttel 5545; JCB (3) II:352. DLC, InU-L, NN-RB, RPJCB; BL (Portuguese), Amsterdam: NHSM. 647/88

Korte antwoort, tegens't Manifest ende remonstrantie, overgelevert door d'Portugesche natie, en inwoonderen van Pharnambuco, wegens 't aen-nemen der wapenen tegens de West-Indische Compagnie. [*The Hague?*] 1647. 10 p.; 4to. A reply to the *Manifest door d'inwoonders van Parnambuco,* 1st publ., Antwerp, 1646. Sabin 38256; Borba de Moraes I:369; Asher 216; Knuttel 5563. BL, The Hague:KB, Leyden:B. Thysiana. 647/89

Korte observatien op het Vertoogh . . . nopende de voor-gaende ende tegenwoordige proceduren van Brasil. *Amsterdam: P. van Marel,* 1647. [8] p.; 4to. A reply to the *Vertooch aen de . . . Staten Generael* of this year below. Sabin 7595; Borba de Moraes I:370; Asher 218; Knuttel 5559. DLC, InU-L, NN-RB; BL, The Hague:KB. 647/90

Labbe, Philippe, S.J. Les tableaux méthodiques de la géographie royalle . . . Seconde edition. *Paris: M. Henault & J. Henault,* 1647. 350 p.; 12mo. 1st publ., Paris, 1646. MiU-C; BN. 647/91

Laet, Joannes de. De gemmis et lapidibus libri ii. *Leyden:* 1647. *See* Boodt, Anselm Boèce de, *of this year above.*

Lallemant, Jérôme, S.J. Relation de ce qui s'est passé de plus remarquable ès missions des peres de la Compagnie de Jesus, en la Nouvelle France, ès années 1645. & 1646. *Paris: S. Cramoisy,* 1647. 2 pts; 8vo. The 2nd pt comprises Paul Ragueneau's *Relation de ce qui s'est passé . . . aux Hurons.* For variants, see Bell & McCoy as cited. Sabin 38684; Harrisse (NF) 86; Streit II:2563; Bell (Jes. rel.) 30–32; McCoy 61–63; Church 481; JCB (3) II:357. CSmH, CtY, DLC, MH, MiU-C, MnU-B, NN-RB, RPJCB; BL, BN. 647/92

La Peyrère, Isaac de. Relation du Groenland. *Paris: A. Courbé,* 1647. 278 p.; illus., map; 8vo. Includes accounts of the Norse in North America and the search for a Northwest passage, including Jens Munk's voyage of 1619–20. Sabin 38970; JCB (3) II:357. CtY, DLC, ICJ, MH, MiU, MnU, NN-RB, PPL, RPJCB; BL (Greenland), BN. 647/93

Le Moyne, Pierre, S.J. La gallerie des femmes fortes. *Paris: A. de Sommaville,* 1647. 378 p.; illus.; fol. Account of Queen Isabella of Spain mentions Columbus. Backer V:1362; Cioranescu (XVII) 42356. CtY, ICU; BL, BN. 647/94

Lydius, Jacobus. Historie der beroerten van Engelandt, aengaende de veelderley secten. *Dordrecht: H. van Esch,* 1647. 224 p.; 8vo. Includes material on Protestant sects in America, e.g., in Boston. Sabin 42757; McAlpin II:508. CtY, DLC, NNUT, PCC. 647/95

Malvenda, Tommaso. De antichristo tomus primus [-secundus]. *Lyons: Societas Bibliopolarum,* 1647. 2 v.; illus.; fol. 1st publ., Rome, 1604. Cf. Sabin 44176. NN-RB, OU; BL, BN. 647/96

Malvezzi, Virgilio, marchese. The chiefe events of the monarchie of Spaine, in the yeare 1639 . . . Translated out of th' Italian copy, by Robert Gentilis. *London: T. W[arren?]., for H. Moseley,* 1647. 208 p.; 12mo. Transl. from Malvezzi's *Successi,* 1st publ., [Madrid? 1640?]. Wing M355; Palau 148064; Thomason I:581. CSmH, CtY, DFo, ICN, MH, MnU, PU; BL. 647/97

Mather, Richard. A reply to Mr. Rutherford. *London: J. Rothwell & H. Allen,* 1647. 109 p.; 4to. 'Of Mr Rutherfords report of synodicall propositions in new-England': chapt. xviii. Sabin 46782; Holmes (MM) 54; Wing M1275; McAlpin II:510. CtY, DLC, MH, MiU-C, NN-RB; BL. 647/98

Meteren, Emanuel van. Historien der Nederlanden, en haar naburen oorlogen tot het jaar 1612. *Amsterdam: J. J. Schipper,* 1647. 673 numb. lvs; ports; fol. 1st publ. in Dutch, Delft, 1599; cf. years 1605 & 1610. RPJCB; BN.   647/99

—[Anr edn]. *Dordrecht: M. de Bot,* 1647. PU.
647/100

—[Anr edn]. *Leyden:* 1647. fol. BL.
647/101

Missive uyt Middelburg aen syn vrient in Hollandt. *Middelburg: G. Verdussen,* 1647. [19] p.; 4to. In supporting peace with Spain, mentions Brazil. In this edn, p. [19] begins 'Charron . . .'. Knuttel 5496. . MnU-B, NN; BL (Middelburg), The Hague:KB.
647/102

—[Anr edn]. *Middelburg: G. Verdussen,* 1647. [19] p.; 4to. Here, p. [19] begins 'gaet anders'. Knuttel 5497. NN; BL (Middelburg), The Hague:KB.   647/103

—[Anr edn]. *Middelburg: G. Verdussen,* 1647. [16] p.; 4to. Here, p. [9], line 1 reads 'dat de Koninck . . . aen de Koninck van Spangien'. Knuttel 5498. NN; The Hague:KB.
647/104

—[Anr edn]. *Middelburg: G. Verdussen,* 1647. [16] p.; 4to. Here, p. [9], line 1 reads 'Dat de Coningh . . . aende Coningh van Span-'. Knuttel 5499. The Hague:KB (imp).
647/105

Montstopping aende vrede-haters. *Leiden: C. M. van Schie,* 1647. [20] p.; 4to. Mentions commerce of Spanish in West Indies & Portuguese in Brazil. Knuttel 5514. MnU, NN; BL (Mondstopping), The Hague:KB.
647/106

Morel, Pierre. Formulae remediorum . . . cujus accedit Systema materiae medicae. *Padua: P. Frambotti,* 1647, '46. 2 pts; 8vo. The *Systema materiae medicae* 1st publ., Geneva, 1628. CtY-M, DNLM; BN.
647/107

Moro-mastix: Mr John Goodwin whipt with his own rod. *London: T. Underhill,* 1647. 15 p.; 4to. Included are critical comments on the New England clergy. Sabin 50773; Wing M2807; McAlpin II:512; Thomason I:498. CSmH, CtY, MH; BL.   647/108

Morone, Mattia. Directorium medico-practicum. *Lyons: J. A. Huguetan,* 1647. 400 p.; 8vo. Index to selected medical literature, containing entries for syphilis ('Gallicus

morbus'), guaiacum, sarsaparilla, & sassafras. CtY-M, DNLM; London:Wellcome.
647/109

Moscherosch, Johann Michael. Visiones de don de Quevedo, das ist, Wunderliche satirische und warhafftige Gesichte Philander von Sittewalt [pseud.] . . . in zwei Theil abgetheilet. [*Frankfurt a. M.: J. G. Schönwetter*] 1645 [i.e., 1647]. 706 (i.e., 1006) p.; 12mo. 1st publ., Strassburg, [1640]; 1st publ. in Schönwetter's unauthorized version, [Frankfurt a. M.], 1645. Succeeding volumes include some material in imitation of Moscherosch. Bechtold states that the work was entirely reset; the added engraved t.p. to this volume is dated 1647. Bechtold 'd'; Faber du Faur 428; cf. Goedeke III:233–234. CtY; BN, Berlin:StB.   647/110

Den naeckten Spangjaert. Vertoonende sijn listige gheveynstheden. [*Amsterdam?*] 1647. [8] p.; 4to. In verse. In opposing truce with Spain, includes mention of Peru. Signed 'P. E. N.' Knuttel 5528; Meulman 2862. NN; The Hague:KB, Ghent:BU.   647/111

—[Anr edn]. Den naeckten Spagniaerdt. [*Amsterdam?*] 1647. [8] p.; 4to. Meulman 2861. Ghent:BU.   647/112

Nederlandsche West-Indische Compagnie. Antwoorde vande gedeputeerde der Westindische Companie op de propositien van den Portugaelschen ambassadeur. [*Amsterdam?*] 1647. 8 p.; 4to. A reply to the *Vertooch* of this year below. Meulman 2870. Ghent: BU.   647/113

Nederlants beroerde ingewanden, over de laetste tijdinge van de Munstersche vrede handelinge. [*The Hague?*] 1647. [16] p.; 4to. Includes refs to Brazil & the West-Indische Compagnie. Knuttel 5519. MnU-B, NN; BL (Netherlands), The Hague:KB.   647/114

Netherlands (United Provinces, 1581–1795). Staten Generaal. Extract auss dem Buch der Friedenshandlungen . . . den 15 Novemb. 1647. [*Brussels:* 1647]. 4to. *See* Spain. Treaties, etc. . . . *Articulen dess Friedens* of this year below.

——. Extract uyt het Boeck vande vrede-handelingh. [*Dordrecht?*] 1647. [8] p.; 4to. Includes mention of an expedition to Brazil & of the West-Indische Compagnie. For variant see Tiele. Knuttel 5492; Meulman 2850 (& 2851); cf. Tiele (Pamfletten) 3165–

3166. InU-L, MnU-B, NN-RB; The Hague:KB, Ghent:BU.   647/115

—[Anr edn]. *Dordrecht: S. Moulaert*, 1647. [8] p.; 4to. Knuttel 5493. BL, The Hague:KB.   647/116

—[Anr edn?]. . . . vreed-handeling. *Dordrecht: S. Moulaert*, 1647. [6] p.; 4to. JCB (STL) 35. RPJCB.   647/117

——. Extract uyttet register der resolutien vande . . . Staten Generael. *Alkmaar: J. Claeszoon*, 1647. 8 p.; 4to. Sabin 23513; Borba de Moraes I:257; Asher 234; Meulman 2840. Ghent:BU.   647/118

—[Anr edn]. *Amsterdam: S. van der Made*, 1647. 8 p.; 4to. Meulman 2839. Ghent:BU.   647/119

——. Extract uyttet rigister der resolutien van der . . . Staten der Vereenighde Nederlanden van datum 6, ende 19 Februarii 1647, waer door de vermelte heeren ratificieren den vrede gheteeckent van hunne Plenipotentiarissen tot Munster. *Amsterdam:* 1647. 45 p.; 4to. Includes refs to sections in 1647 Treaty of Munster relating to Brazil & the West-Indische Compagnie. Cf. Spain. Treaties, etc. . . . *Articulen dess Friedens* below, the earliest edn traced of that special peace treaty. BL.   647/120

——. Poincten der artijckulen ter vergaderinghe van de Staten Generael . . . gearresteert, waer na de . . . plenipotentiarisen . . . in het tractaet van vreden tot Munster . . . hebben te verhandelen. *Dordrecht: Moulaert*, 1647. [18] p.; 4to. 'Point' 5 concerns commerce with West Indies & Brazil; points 6 & 7 refer to the West-Indische Compagnie. Knuttel 5430; Tiele (Pamfletten) 3129. InU-L, MnU-B, NN; The Hague:KB.   647/121

—[Anr edn]. Poincten der artijckulen, gearresteert. [*Dordrecht: S. Moulaert &*] *J. van Benden* [*at Amsterdam*], 1647. [18] p.; 4to. Sheet A is here reset, sheets B & C being reissued from the preceding. Page 1 has heading 'Artijculen van de vrede'. Knuttel 5432; Tiele (Pamfletten) 3130. The Hague:KB.   647/122

—[Anr edn]. Poincten der artyculen ter vergaderinge. *Dordrecht: S. Moulaert*, 1647. 8 lvs; 4to. Knuttel 5431; Meulman 2828. The Hague:KB, Ghent:BU.   647/123

—[Anr edn]. Poincten der artijckelen, ter ver-

gaderinghe. *Dordrecht: S. Moulaert*, 1647. 7 lvs.; 4to. Meulman 2829. BL, Ghent:BU.   647/124

Netherlands (United Provinces, 1581–1795). Treaties, etc. Articulen, nopende de conditien des pays aenghetroffen tot Munster. *Middelburg: A. P. van Hagedoorn*, 1647. [7] p.; 4to. Includes ref. to the West Indies. Knuttel 5434; Meulman 2831. NN; The Hague:KB, Ghent:BU.   647/125

—[Anr edn]. *Middelburg: A. P. van Hagedoorn*, 1647. bds.; fol. Knuttel 5435. The Hague:KB.   647/126

Neville, Henry. The parliament of ladies. or Divers remarkable passages. [*London:*] 1647. [16] p.; 4to. Mentioned is 'a Seafaring man' who may 'goe a long voyage to Sea, as to the East or West Indies, or to the straights of Magellan'. Wing N511. Thomason I:504. CSmH, MH; BL.   647/127

—[Anr edn]. The second edition. [*London:*] 1647. 15 p.; 4to. Here added is a ref. to tobacco. Wing N512; Arents (Add.) 334. CtY, ICJ, MnU, NN-A.   647/128

—[Anr edn]. The ladies parliament. [*London:* 1647]. 4to. Wing N508; Thomason I:532. BL.   647/129

Nieremberg, Juan Eusebio, S.J. Vidas exemplares y venerables memorias de la Compañia de Jesus, de los quales es este tomo quarto. *Madrid: A. de Paredes*, 1647. 748 p.; fol. Included are accounts of Jesuits who had served in Spanish America, in continuation of the author's *Honor del gran patriarca San Ignacio de Loyola* of 1645. Sabin 55272; Medina (BHA) 1101; Streit I:510; Backer V:1747; JCB (3) II:357. CSmH, ICN, InU-L, RPJCB; BL, BN.   647/130

Nieuwenborgh, Johann. Het nederlantsche lust-hofken. *Amsterdam: G. Joosten*, 1647. 160 p.; illus.; 12mo. Included are numerous scattered refs to New World phenomena, with illustration & description, p. 17, of passionflower, 'dien Granadil-Struyck, ofte Passie-bloem' from 'de geberghten van Peru'. MH-A.   647/131

Olearius, Adam. Offt begehrte Beschreibung der newen orientalischen Reise. *Schleswig: J. Zur Glocken*, 1647. 2 pts; illus., port., maps; fol. Includes accounts of punishment for tobacco use in Russia, as well as Persian tobacco customs. Lohmeier (Olearius) 14; Arents 233. CLSU, ICU, NN-A; BN, Göttingen:StUB.   647/132

Den ongeveynsden Nederlandschen patriot. Den ongeveynsden Nederlantschen patriot, voorstaende de intressen van sijn vaderlandt . . . Tweede deel. *Middelburg: S. Verhoeven* [1647]. [40] p.; 4to. 1st publ., Middelburg, 1646. The work of which this is a continuation (Knuttel 5321) is not to be confused with *Den ongeveynsden . . . patriot* (Alkmaar, 1647), q.v. below. MnU-B.
                                                    647/133

—[Anr edn?]. Tweede deel van den Ongeveynsden Nederlantschen patriot. *Middelburg: S. Verhoeven* [1647]. [40] p.; 4to. MnU-B.   647/134

—[Anr issue?]. Tweede deel van den Ongeveynsden patriot. *Middelburg: G. Vermeyde, for S. Verhoeven,* 1647. Knuttel 5324. NN; The Hague:KB.   647/135

Den ongeveynsden Nederlantschen patriot. *Alkmaar: J. Claeszoon,* 1647. [31] p.; 4to. Includes the 'Extract uyttet register der resolutien vande . . . Staten Generael' of 6 & 19 Feb. 1647, with refs to the West-Indische Compagnie. This should not be confused with a work with similar title described under Knuttel 5321. Knuttel 5507 (cf. 5506). [Edition uncertain:] MnU-B, NN, WU; BL (Dutch patriot), The Hague:KB.
                                                    647/136

—[Anr edn]. Den ongeveynsden Nederlandtschen patriot. *Alkmaar: J. Claeszoon,* 1647. 24 p.; 4to. Knuttel 5508. The Hague:KB.   647/137

Owen, John. Epigrammatum . . . editio postrema. *Amsterdam: L. Elsevier,* 1647. 212 p.; port.; 8vo. 1st publ., London, 1606. In this edn the headpiece on p. 1 consists of type ornaments. Willems (Les Elzevier) 1051. MH; BN.   647/138

—[Anr edn]. *Amsterdam: L. Elsevier,* 1647. 212 p.; port.; 8vo. In this edn the headpiece on p. 1 contains an X within a triangle; there is a tailpiece on p. 204. Willems (Les Elzevier) 1051. DLC, MH.   647/139

—[Anr edn]. *Amsterdam: L. Elsevier,* 1647. 212 p.; port.; 8vo. In this edn the headpiece on p. 1 contains an X within a triangle; there is no tailpiece on p. 204. Willems (Les Elzevier) 1051.   647/140

Pagitt, Ephraim. Heresiography . . . Third [*sic*] edition. *London: W. L[ee].,* 1647. 4to. 1st publ., London, 1645. Cf. Sabin 31483; Wing P177. BL, BN.   647/141

—[Anr edn]. The fourth edition. *London: W. W[ilson]., for W. Lee,* 1647. 164 p.; 4to. Cf. Sabin 31483; Wing P178; McAlpin II:515. CLU-C, CtY, DLC, ICN, MH, MdBP, MnU-B, NN-RB; BL.   647/142

Plante, Franciscus. Mauritiados libri xii. Hoc est: Rerum ab . . . Joanne Mauritio, comite Nassauiae &c. in Occidentali Indiâ gestarum descriptio poetica. *Leyden: J. Maire; sold by J. Blaeu, at Amsterdam,* 1647. 196 p.; illus., port., maps; fol. Sabin 63319; Borba de Moraes II:156; Rodrigues (Dom. Hol.) 900; Tiele 868; JCB (3) II:358–359. RPJCB; BL, BN.   647/143

Portugal. Sovereigns, etc., 1640–1656 (John IV). Copye vande volmacht van don Juan . . . coninck van Portugael . . . Ghesonden . . . aen Francisco de Sousa Coutinho sijnen raet . . . om met . . . de bewintheberen vande Oost- ende West-Indische Compagnie te handelen. [*The Hague?* 1647]. bds.; fol. Sabin 16735; Borba de Moraes I:179; Asher 219; Knuttel 5557. RPJCB; The Hague:KB.   647/144

Ragueneau, Paul, S.J. Relation de ce qui s'est passé . . . aux Hurons. [*Paris:* 1647]. *See* Lallemant, Jérôme, *above.*

Raven, Dirck Albertsz. Journael ofte Beschryvinge vande reyse gedaen . . . nae Spitsbergen. *Utrecht: E. W. Snellaert,* 1647. 16 p.; illus.; 4to. Issued as a part of W. Y. Bontekoe's *Journael . . . van de Oost-Indische reyse* of this year above, q.v.

Remonstrantie aen alle de steden ende vroetschappen der vrye vereenighde Nederlanden . . . door A.P. '*Dordrecht: Philips van Macedonien*' [i.e., *The Hague? L. Breeckevelt?*] 1647. 24 p.; 4to. Dialogue includes 2 p. section on possibility of military service in West Indies, with speculation on age & condition of officers employed by the West-Indische Compagnie. Knuttel 5589. MnU-B, NN; The Hague:KB.   647/145

—[Anr edn]. '*Dordrecht: Philips van Mascedonien*' [i.e., *The Hague? L. Breeckevelt?*] 1647. [12] p.; 4to. Knuttel 5590. The Hague:KB, Ghent:BU.   647/146

Ritratti et elogii di capitani illustri che

ne' secoli moderni hanno gloriosamente guerregiato. *Rome: G. Mascardi, for F. de' Rossi,* 1647. 404 p.; ports; 4to. 1st publ., Rome, 1635. Sabin 71587. NNC.
647/147

Rivière, Lazare. Praxis medica . . . Editio tertia. *Paris: O. de Varennes,* 1647–48. 3 pts; 8vo. 1st publ., Paris, 1640. NIC; London: Wellcome, BN. 647/148

Saint-Amant, Marc Antoine de Gérard, sieur de. Les oeuvres. *Paris: N. Bessin,* 1647. 274 p.; 8vo. In verse. 1st publ., Paris, 1629. Tchémerzine X:83. BN. 647/149

Sala, Angelo. Opera medico-chymica quae extant omnia. *Frankfurt a. M.: J. Beyer,* 1647. 856 p.; illus.; 4to. Oils employing Peruvian opobalsam, guaiacum, sassafras, & tobacco are described. DNLM, MnU, NNC; BL, BN.
647/150

San Juan, Puerto Rico (Diocese). Synod, 1645. Constituciones synodales, hechas por . . . Damian Lopez de Haro, obispo de la ciudad de San Juan. *Madrid: Catalina de Barrio y Angulo,* 1647. 128 numb. lvs; fol. Sabin 30410; Medina (BHA) 1100; Palau 141244. BL (López de Haro, D.).
647/151

Scarron, Paul. La suite des oeuvres burlesques . . . Seconde partie. *Paris: T. Quinet,* 1647. 2 pts; 4to. In verse. 'A monseigneur le Prince' predicts that Louis II de Bourbon 'portera le beau nom de Bourbon de la Mexique aux isles de Jappon'; 'Estocade a monseigneur le Cardinal Mazarin' mentions the Strait of Magellan; 'Revelations' refers to 'renifleurs de Petun', i.e., of tobacco. Magne (Scarron) 13; cf. Cioranescu (XVII) 61735. Grenoble:BM. 647/152

Serres, Jean de. Inventaire general de l'histoire de France . . . Augmentée . . . jusques à present [2 novembre 1646]. *Paris: C. Marette,* 1647. 1451 p.; ports; fol. 1st publ. with American refs, Paris, 1600; cf. 1606 edn. BN. 647/153

—[Anr edn]. . . . Augmenté . . . jusques à present [5 août 1647]. *Rouen: L. DuMesnil,* 1647. 1354 p.; ports; fol. BN. 647/154

—[Anr issue]. *Rouen: C. Malassis,* 1647. CU-A.
647/155

Shepard, Thomas. The day-breaking, if not the sun-rising of the Gospell with the Indians in New-England. *London: R. Cotes, for F. Clifton,* 1647. 25 p.; 4to. The 2nd of the Eliot Indian tracts. *See under* Wilson, John, *below.*

——. The sincere convert. *Edinburgh: G. Lithgow,* 1647. 8vo. 1st publ., London, 1640. Sabin 80222; Wing S3121. Edinburgh:NL, Innerpeffray Libr. 647/156

Entry canceled. 647/157

Sheppard, Samuel. The committee-man curried. A comedy. [*London?*] 1647. 13 p.; 4to. Includes two refs to tobacco. Wing S3160; Greg 630; Arents (Add.) 335. CSmH, DLC, ICN, MB, NjP; BL.
647/158

Shinkin ap Shone, pseud. The honest Welch-cobler, for her do scorne to call her selfe the simple Welch-cobler: although her thinkes . . . that her have not so much wit as her prother cobler of America. [*London:*] '*M. Shinkin, printer to S. Taffie*', 1647. 8 p.; 4to. A satire on Nathaniel Ward's *Simple cobler of Aggawam in America* of this year below. Sabin 32778; Wing W780; Thomason I:499. CtY, NN-RB; BL. 647/159

Silva, Antonio Telles da. Successo della guerra de portugueses levantados em Pernambuco contra Olandeses, como por carta del maestro a campo Martino Soarez, et Andrea Vidal de Negreiros, por Antonio Telles de Silva. [*Lisbon? 1647?*]. [20] p.; 4to. Borba de Moraes II:290; Rodrigues (Dom. Hol.) 520; Maggs Cat. 479 (Americana V):4269. 647/160

——. Sucesso della guerra de' Portoghesi solevati in Pernambuco contra Olandesi, come appare per lettera del maestro di campo Martins Soares, & d' Andrea Vidal de Negreiros, indrizzata à Antonio Telles da Silva l'anno 1646. [*Rome? 1647?*]. 16 p.; 4to. Translated from the preceding item. Sabin 81078; Borba de Moraes II:290; Rodrigues (Dom. Hol.) 520n. 647/161

Siri, Vittorio. Del mercurio, overo Historia de' correnti tempi . . . Tomo secondo. *Casale: C. della Casa,* 1647. 1724 p.; 4to. Continues 1st vol., publ., Casale, 1644. In section on 'Affari di Portugallo' a summary of Portugal's oversea enterprises is given (p. 1129–37), mentioning Columbus & Brazil. Sabin 81447; Graesse VI:417. CU, CtY, ICN, MH, MdBP, NN-RB, RPJCB; BL, BN.
647/162

—[Anr edn]. *Geneva: P. Aubert,* 1647. 4to. NjP; BN. 647/163

Sousa Coutinho, Francisco de. Brevis repetitio omnium quae . . . legatus Portugalliae ad componendas res Brasilicanas proposuit vel egit a die 23. Maij. usque ad. 1. Novembris hujus anni 1647. *The Hague: L. Breeckevelt,* 1647. [14] p.; 4to. Abridged Latin version of Sousa Coutinho's *Propositio facta* & his *Naerdere propositie* of this year below. Sabin 7543 & 88754; Borba de Moraes I:110; Asher 224; Knuttel 5562. BL (Portugal), The Hague:KB. 647/164

——. Naerdere propositie ghedaen door de heer ambassadeur van den coningh van Portugael. *The Hague:* 1647. [4] p.; 4to. Includes refs to Brazil. Sabin 88755; Borba de Moraes I:191; Asher 222. NN-RB; BL (Portugal). 647/165

—[Anr edn]. *The Hague:* [1647]. [6] p.; 4to. In this edn the title contains reading 'koningh van Portugael'. Sabin 88756; cf. Borba de Moraes I:191; Asher 223. RPJCB. 647/166

—[Anr edn]. [*The Hague?* 1647]. [6] p.; 4to. Knuttel 5560; Meulman 2871. InU-L; The Hague:KB, Ghent:BU. 647/167

—[Anr edn]. [*Amsterdam?*] 1647. [4] p.; 4to. In this edn the title contains reading 'coningh van Portugael'. Sabin 88756n; Knuttel 5561. BL (Portugal), The Hague:KB. 647/168

——. Propositie ghedaen ter vergaderinghe van . . . d'heeren Staten Generael der Vereenichde Nederlanden. [*The Hague?*] 1647. 16 p.; 4to. Transl. from Sousa's Latin *Propositio* or French *Proposition* of this year below. Sabin 17198; cf. Borba de Moraes I:191; Asher 221; Knuttel 5552; JCB (3) II:357. DLC, MnU-B, NN-RB, RPJCB; BL (Portugal), The Hague:KB. 647/169

—[Anr edn]. [*The Hague?*] 1647. [14] p.; 4to. Borba de Moraes I:191. 647/170

—[Anr edn]. [*The Hague?*] 1647. [7] p.; 4to. Cf. Borba de Moraes I:191; Knuttel 5553. The Hague:KB. 647/171

——. Propositio facta . . . dominis ordinibus generalibus Confoederatarum Provinciarum Belgii in concessu publico 16. Augusti 1647. *The Hague: J. Breeckevelt,* 1647. 12 p.; 4to. Perhaps transl. from Sousa's French version of this year, the following item. Sa-

bin 88757; Borba de Moraes I:191; Asher 220; Knuttel 5551. DLC; BL (Portugal), The Hague:KB. 647/172

——. La proposition faicte à l'assemblée publie des . . . Estats Generaux des Provinces Unies des Païs-Bas, le 16 d'Aougst 1647. *The Hague: J. Breeckevelt,* 1647. 16 lvs. Includes refs to Brazil. Cf. Latin & Dutch edns of this year above. Sabin 17197; cf. Borba de Moraes I:191; Rodrigues (Dom. Hol.) 643; cf. Knuttel 5551. 647/173

Spaensche triumphe over haer onlanghs bekomen victorien in de Gheunieerde Nederlanden . . . Ghestelt door . . . L. G. J. M. [*Amsterdam?*] 1647. [8] p.; 4to. Includes refs to Brazil & the West-Indische Compagnie. Knuttel 5522. The Hague:KB, Ghent:BU. 647/174

—[Anr edn]. Spaensche triumphe . . . inde Geunieerde Nederlandtsche Provintien. [*Amsterdam?*] 1647. [8] p.; 4to. Knuttel 5523. The Hague:KB, Ghent:BU. 647/175

—[Anr edn]. Spaensche thriomphe . . . inde Gheunieerde Nederlanden. [*Amsterdam?*] 1647. [8] p.; 4to. Knuttel 5524. NN; The Hague:KB, Ghent:BU. 647/176

Spain. Casa de Contratación de las Indias. Ordenanzas reales, para la Casa de la Contratacion de Sevilla, y para otras cosas de las Indias, y de la navegacion y contratacion de ellas. *Seville: F. de Lyra,* 1647. 2 pts; fol. 1st publ., Seville, 1553; cf. 1604 edn. Sabin 57485n; Medina (BHA) 1102; Escudero (Seville) 1.623; Palau 203204. ICN, InU-L, RPJCB; BL. 647/177

Spain. Treaties, etc., 1621–1665 (Philip IV). Articulen dess Friedens so zwischen ihrer königlichen majestät in Hispanien und den HH. General Staden der vereinigten Niederlanden geschlossen und ratificiert [8. Jan. 1647.] Aus der Niederländischen copey . . . ubergesetzt. [*Brussels: H. A. Velpius*] 1647. 2 pts; 4to. Apparently transl. from the *Poincten der Artijckelen,* entered under Netherlands . . . Staten Generaal above. Cf. Spain. Treaties, etc. . . . *Articulen en conditien,* Ghent, 1648. Article 5 mentions West Indies, America, and the Dutch East & West India companies, while Article 6 relates to the West India Company. Coat of arms on t.p. is that of Spain also found on 1648 *Traicté de paix.* With this was issued the Netherlands Staten Generaal's *Extract auss dem Buch der Friedenshandlungen*, [Brussels, 1647], transl. from the *Extract uyt het boeck* of this year above. Knuttel 5433; Meulman 2830. BL, The Hague:KB. 647/178

Spinola, Fabio Ambrosio, S.J. Vita del p. Carlo Spinola della Compagnia di Giesu, morto per la santa fede nel Giappone. *Bologna: Heir of Benacci*, 1647. 205 p.; 8vo. 1st publ., Rome, 1628. Cf. Sabin 89458; Streit V:1565; Backer VII:1448–1449.
647/179

Stengel, Karl. Hortensius et dea flora cum pomona historice . . . descripti. *Augsburg: A. Aperger*, 1647. 2 v.; 12mo. Included are descriptions of American plants. Pritzel 8932. CU, NNBG; BN. 647/180

Sweerts, Emanuel. Florilegium amplissimum et selectissimum. *Amsterdam: J. Janszoon, the Younger*, 1647–54. 2 v.; illus.; fol. 1st publ., Frankfurt a. M., 1612–14. BL, BN.
647/181

Tanner, Robert. A brief treatise of the use of the globe celestial and terrestrial. *London: T. Fawcet, for W. Lugger*, 1647. 35 p.; 8vo. 1st publ., London, 1616. MB. 647/182

Taxa medicamentorum, tam simplicium, quam compositorum, in officiniis Argentinensibus prostantium. Tax und Preiss aller unnd jeder Artzneyen. [*Strassburg:*] *Heirs of J. Carolus*, 1647. 36 lvs; 4to. Included in listing are mechoacan, sarsaparilla, sassafras, guaiacum, tacamahac, & the bezoar stone ('Lapis bezoar Occidentalis, Bezoar auss Peru'). London:Wellcome. 647/183

Taylor, John, the Water-poet. The Kings most excellent majesties wellcome to his owne house . . . Hampton Court. [*London:*] 1647. 6 p.; 4to. In verse. Mentioned are New England, Virginia, Bermuda, & British Caribbean islands. CSmH, KMK, MH, PU; BL. 647/184

Tesillo, Santiago de. Guerra de Chile, causas de su duracion, medios para su fin, exemplificado en el govierno de Don Francisco Lasso de la Vega. *Madrid: Imprenta Real*, 1647. 100 numb. lvs.; 4to. Sabin 94898; Medina (Chile) 121; Palau 330851; JCB (3) II:359. CU, NN-RB, RPJCB; BN.
647/185.

Torsellino, Orazio, S.J. Histoire universelle depuis la creation du monde jusques a l'an 1598 . . . traduite de nouveau . . . et continuee jusques a present par le sieur Coulon. *Paris:* 1647. 1st publ. in Latin, Rome, 1598; cf. 1622 French translation. Cioranescu (XVII) 22250. 647/186

——. Historiarum ab origine mundi usque ad annum 1640 epitome libri x. *Lyons: S. Rigaud*, 1647. 2 pts; 12mo. 1st publ., Rome, 1598; cf. 1620 edn. Backer VIII:152.
647/187

Traslados de algunas cartas sacadas de sus proprios originales, para prueba de la inocencia del p. Jacinto Perez de la Compañia de Jesus, en el testimonio que han levantado en el Peru de aver alcançado algunos decretos de su Magestad, contra los Españoles criollos de aquel reyno. [*Madrid?* 1647]. 5 numb. lvs; fol. Memorial to king of Spain; subscribed: Madrid y mayo 30 de 1647. Medina (BHA) 1110; Streit II:1771; Palau 339135. Madrid: Acad. de la Hist.
647/188

Tweede deel van den Ongeveynsden patriot. *Middleburg:* 1647. *See* Den ongeveynsden Nederlandschen patriot *above.*

Udemans, Godefridus Corneliszoon. Geestelick compas, dat is Nut ende nootwendigh bericht voor alle zee-varende . . . Den vierden druck verbetert ende seer vermeerdert . . . met een nieuw tractaet van den coophandel ende de coopvaert. Item De vaert op Oost- ende West-Indiën. *Dordrecht:* [*H. van Esch,*] *for F. Boels*, 1647. 393 p.; 8vo. Cf. Dordrecht, 1637, edn. Though no earlier edn has been found, the work was perhaps 1st publ, Zierikzee, 1617. Issued with the author's *Koopmans jacht* below. Muller (1872) 1536. MnU-B, NN-RB.
647/189

——. Koopmans jacht, brenghende goede tijdinghe. *Dordrecht: H. van Esch, for F. Boels*, 1647. 183 p.; 8vo. Includes refs to West Indies & Mexico. Issued with the author's *Geestelijck compas* of this year above. Muller (1872) 1537. MnU-B, NN-RB. 647/190

Valle, Francisco. Methodus medendi. *Louvain: J. Nempe*, 1647. 296 p.; 8vo. In bk 4, chapt. ii, the bezoar stone as found in America is mentioned. London:Wellcome.
647/191

Vasselli, Giovanni Francesco. L'apicio, overo Il maestro de'conviti. *Bologna: Heirs*

of E. Dozza, 1647. 117 p.; 4to. Describes banquet tendered Alexander, duke of Mirandola, including turkeys; numerous other menus call for 'pollastri d'India'—i.e., young turkeys. London:Wellcome.
647/192

Velle, Nicasius Martens van. De oprechte waeghschaele der Vereenighde Neder-landen. *Arnhem: J. T. van Westerloo,* 1647. 21 p.; 4to. Page 21 mentions incidentally East & West Indies. Meulman 2854. MnU-B; BL, Ghent:BU.
647/193

—[Anr edn]. De oprechte waeg-schaele. *Antwerp: P. de Hollander,* 1647. [10] p.; 4to. Knuttel 5505. MnU-B; BN, The Hague:KB.
647/194

Vertooch aen de . . . Staten Generael der Vereenichde Nederlanden, nopende de voorgaende ende tegenwoordighe proceduren van Brasil. *Amsterdam: J. van Marel,* 1647. [32] p.; 4to. Concerns the West-Indische Compagnie & Brazil; includes, at end, Francisco de Sousa Coutinho's *Propositien* & his *Naerder propositie*, also publ. separately this year. See also the *Korte observatien* of this year above. Sabin 7643 (& 99306); Borba de Moraes II:345; Asher 217; Knuttel 5558; JCB (3) II:352. DLC, MnU-B, NN-RB, RPJCB; BL (Netherlands), The Hague:KB.
647/195

't Vervolgh op de t' samen-spraeck, tusschen Teeuwes ende Keesje Maet. Verhalende hoe dat sommige persoonen haer begeven hebben inden dienst vande West-Indische Compagnie na Brasil, ende daer na haer selven met groot geldt af-gekocht hebben. [*The Hague?* 1647]. [8] p.; 4to. In verse. Sabin 99317; Borba de Moraes II:345; Knuttel 5600; Petit 2386. DLC, MnU-B; The Hague:KB, Leyden:B. Thysiana.
647/196

Victoria, Pedro Gobeo de. Joannis Bisselii . . . Argonauticon Americanorum. *Munich:* 1647. *See* Bissel, Johannes, *above*.

Vondel, Joost van den. Poesy, ofte Verscheide gedichten. Het tweede deel. *Schiedam: The author* [i.e., *Rotterdam? J. Naeranus?*] 1647. 159 p.; 12mo. Includes Vondel's *Op het ontset van Piet Heyns buyt*, 1st publ., [Amsterdam? 1629?]. Unger (Vondel) 2 (cf. 169n). Amsterdam:UB.
647/197

—[Anr edn]. Den tweeden druck. *Schiedam:*

The author [i.e., *Rotterdam? J. Naeranus?*] 1647. 214 p.; 12mo. Unger (Vondel) 3. Amsterdam:UB.
647/198

Vrymoedigh discours tusschen twee Paepsche Hollanders, over de tegenwoordighe Munstersche vrede-handelinge. [*The Hague?*] 1647. [14] p.; 4to. Includes ref. to the West-Indische Compagnie. Knuttel 5510. MnU-B, NN; The Hague:KB.
647/199

Ward, Nathaniel. The simple cobler of Aggawam in America. Willing to help 'mend his native country . . . By Theodore de la Guard [pseud.]. *London: J. Dever & R. Ibbitson, for S. Bowtell,* 1647. 80 p.; 4to. Sabin 101323; Wing W786; Church 484; JCB (3) II:360. CSmH, CtY, MH, NN-RB, RPJCB; BL.
647/200

—[Anr edn]. *London: J. D[ever]. & R. I[bbitson]., for S. Bowtell,* 1647. 80 p.; 4to. Sabin 101324; Wing W787; Church 483; JCB (3) II:360. CSmH, CtY, DLC, ICN, InU-L, MH, MiU-C, NN-RB, PPL, RPJCB; BL.
647/201

—[Anr edn]. The third edition, with some additions. *London: J. D[ever]. & R.I[bbitson]., for S. Bowtell,* 1647. 80 p.; 4to. Sabin 101325; Wing W788; JCB (3) II:361. CSmH, CtY, MH, MWA, NN-RB, RPJCB.
647/202

—[Anr edn]. The fourth edition, with some amendments. *London: J. D[ever]. & R. I[bbitson]., for S. Bowtell,* 1647. 89 p.; 4to. Sabin 101326; Wing W789; Church 485; JCB (3) II:361. CSmH, CtY, MH, MiU-C, MnHi, NN-RB, PPL, RPJCB.
647/203

—[Anr edn]. '*London: J. Dever & R. Ibbitson, for S. Bowtell,* 1647'. [47] p.; 4to. Prob. a piracy of the 1st edn. Sabin 101327; Wing W790?; JCB (3) II:361. CtY, NjP, RPJCB; BL.
647/204

Weerts, Paul, O. F. M. Cort begryp van 't wonderlyck leven des . . . Vader Franciscus . . . Met een cort begryp vande vruchten ende zilwinninghe die de . . . Ordre inde vier deelen der werelts ghedaen heeft. *Antwerp: A. van Brakel,* 1647. 167 p.; 12mo. Prob. transl. from the author's *Histoire admirable*, 1st publ., Antwerp, [1646]. Streit I:512. Ghent:O.F.M.
647/205

Weld, Thomas. A brief narration of the practices of the churches in New-England. *London: M. Simmons, for J. Pouncet,* 1647. 18 p.;

4to. 1st publ., London, 1645; here a reissue of that edn with cancel t.p. & errata leaf added. Sabin 52618; Wing W1264. MH, MiU-C, NN-RB; BL. 647/206

Wilson, John (1588–1667), supposed author. The day-breaking, if not the sun-rising of the gospell with the Indians in New-England. *London: R. Cotes, for F. Clifton,* 1647. 25 p.; 4to. The 2nd of the Eliot Indian tracts. Sabin 80207 (& 22146); Wing S3110; Church 482; JCB (3) II:359. CSmH, CtY, DLC, InU-L, MH, MWA, MiU-C, NN-RB, PPRF, RPJCB; BL. 647/207

Winslow, Edward. New-Englands salamander, discovered by an irreligious and scornefull pamphlet, called New-Englands Jonas cast up at London, &c. Owned by Major John Childe, but not probably written by him. Or, A satisfactory answer to many aspersions cast upon New-England therein. *London: R. Cotes, for J. Bellamy,* 1647. 29 p.; 4to. Sabin 104797; Wing W3038; JCB (3) II:362. CSmH, CtY, InU-L, MH, MiU-C, NN-RB, NcU, RPJCB; BL. 647/208

Wortley, Sir Francis. Mercurius Britannicus, his welcome to hell. [*London?*] 1647. 8 p.; 4to. In verse. Mentions social use of tobacco. Wing W3641; Arents (Add.) 336. CSmH, MH, MnU-B, NN-RB; BL. 647/209

Zeiller, Martin. [Das sechste und letzte Hundert Episteln.] *Ulm: J. Görlin,* 1647. 8vo. Continues Zeiller's *Ein Hundert Episteln,* 1st publ., Heilbronn & Ulm, 1640. Cf. Jantz (German Baroque) 2771; Jördens V:600. 647/210

Ziegler, Jakob. Fermentatio, generationis et corruptionis causa. Ein kurtzer Bericht. *Basel: J. J. Genath,* 1647. 64 p.; illus.; 4to. Includes passage on therapeutic use of tobacco in time of plague. Ferguson (Bibl. chem.) II:565–566; Arents 3282. MnU, NN-A; BL. 647/211

1648

Advys op de presentatie van Portugal. Het eerste deel. [*Amsterdam?* 1648]. 21 p.; 4to. Concerns the West-Indische Compagnie & Brazil. The author promises & outlines a 'Tweede deel' (q.v. below) & a 'Derde deel' (unknown). Cf. the *Tegen-advys* of this year

below. Sabin 7503 (& 60987n); Borba de Moraes I:14; Knuttel 5784; JCB (3) II:364. MnU-B, RPJCB; BL, The Hague:KB. 648/1

Advys op de presentatie van Portugael. Het tweede deel. Met een remonstrantie aen sijn konincklijcke majesteyt van Portugael by de inwoonders . . . van Parnambocq overgelevert. [*Amsterdam?*] 1648. 37 p.; 4to. Cf. pt 1 of the *Advys* above. Cf. Sabin 60987; Borba de Moraes I:14; Knuttel 5785. BL (Portugal; edn uncertain), The Hague:KB. 648/2

—[Anr state?]. . . . Met een remonstranci. [*Amsterdam?*] 1648. 37 p.; 4to. Cf. Knuttel 5785n; JCB (3) II:364. RPJCB. 648/3

—[Anr state?]. . . . Met een remonstrancie. [*Amsterdam?*] 1648. 37 p.; 4to. Sabin 60987. DLC. 648/4

Aldrovandi, Ulisse. Musaeum metallicum in libros iiii distributum. *Bologna: G. B. Ferroni, for M. A. Bernia,* 1648. 979 p.; illus.; fol. An Aztec ceremonial knife is described & illustrated (p. 156–57); abundance of lead in New World is mentioned (p. 166). Nissen (Zool.) 75; Brunet I:156; Graesse I:65. CU, CtY, DNLM, InU-L, MB, MiU, MnU, NN, PPAN, RPJCB; BL, BN. 648/5

Allin, John. A defence of the answer made unto the nine questions or positions sent from New-England, against the reply thereunto by . . . John Ball; entituled, A tryall of the new church-way in New-England and in old . . . By John Allin, pastor of Dedham [&] Tho. Shepard of Cambridge in New-England. *London: R. Cotes, for A. Crooke,* 1648. 211 p.; 4to. Sabin 921; Wing A1036; JCB (3) II:362. CtY, DLC, MH, MWA, NN-RB, PPPrHi, RPJCB; BL. 648/6

Amatus Lusitanus. Curationum medicinalium centuriae septem. *Barcelona: S. & J. Matevad,* 1648. 1408 cols; fol. 1st publ., Venice, 1551–60; cf. Bordeaux, 1620, edn above. MH-A. 648/7

Avity, Pierre d', sieur de Montmartin. Les estats, empires et principautez du monde. *Geneva: J. Stoer,* 1648. 4to. 1st publ., Paris, 1613. Cf. Sabin 2498. BN. 648/8

Bacon, Francis, viscount St. Albans. Historia naturalis & experimentalis de ventis &c. *Leyden: F. Haack,* 1648. 232 p.; 12mo. 1st publ., London, 1622, under title *Historia* *naturalis . . . ad condendam philosophiam.* In this edn p. 150 is correctly numbered, etc. Gibson (Bacon) 110a. For locations see following item.   648/9

—[Anr edn]. *Leyden: F. Haack,* 1648. 232 p.; 12mo. In this edn p. 150 is misnumbered 105, etc. Gibson (Bacon) 110b. Editions undifferentiated: CU, CtY-M, DLC, ICJ, MH, MnU, NN, PPJ, RPB; BL.   648/10

——. Sylva sylvarum, sive Hist. naturalis. [*Leyden: F. Haack, for*] *L. Elsevier, at Amsterdam,* 1648. 2 pts; 12mo. Transl. by Jacob Gruter from Bacon's *Sylva sylvarum: or A naturall historie,* 1st publ., London, 1627. Gibson (Bacon) 185a; Willems (Les Elzevier) 1058. DLC, NNUT, PU, TxU; BL.
                                                    648/11

—[Anr issue]. *Leyden: F. Haack,* 1648. Gibson (Bacon) 185b; Willems (Les Elzevier) 1058n. CtY, ICN, MH, NN-RB, PPL; BL.
                                                    648/12

Barnstein, Heinrich. Kurtze Beschreibung dess Tabacks. *Erfurt: T. Fritsche,* 1648. 16 lvs; 8vo. 1st publ. in this version, Erfurt, 1645. Dt. Ges. Kat. 11.7685. Bonn:UB.
                                                    648/13

Bellinzani, Lodovico. Il mercurio estinto resuscitato. *Rome: F. Cavalli,* 1648. 24 p.; 4to. In advocating use of mercury for treatment of syphilis, adverts to sarsaparilla & guaiacum. DNLM; London:Wellcome.
                                                    648/14

Benzoni, Girolamo. Novae Novi Orbis historiae, das ist Aller Geschichten, so in der newen Welt, welche Occidentalis India . . . genent wird . . . Dessgleichen von der Frantzosen Meerfahrt . . . in das Land Floridam . . . auss dem Latein gebracht. *Hamburg: B. Arens,* 1648. 537 p.; 4to. Transl. from Benzoni's [Geneva], 1578, Latin text, itself a translation of his *Historia del Mondo Nuovo,* 1st publ., Venice, 1565; the present edn is an apparent reissue of sheets of the 1590, Helmstedt, edn, only the preface being reset. Sabin 4796; Streit II:1794; Palau 27639; JCB (3) II:364. RPJCB.   648/15

Bible. O. T. Psalms. English. Paraphrases. 1648. Bay Psalm Book. The psalms, hymns, and spiritual songs of the Old and New Testament . . . For the use, edification and comfort of the saints . . . especially in New-England. *Cambridge:* [*R. Daniel,*] *for*

H. Usher, of Boston [1648]. 96 + p.; 18mo. 1st publ., Cambridge, Mass. 1640. JCB AR42:45–47. RPJCB (imp.).   648/16

Blaeu, Willem Janszoon. Novus atlas, das ist Weltbeschreibung. *Amsterdam: J. Blaeu,* 1648. 120 maps; fol. 1st publ., Amsterdam, 1634; cf. 1635 edn. Koeman (Bl) 31C. Marburg:StB.   648/17

——. Toonneel des aerdriicx. *Amsterdam:* 1648. *See the years* 1650 & 1658.

Bobart, Jacob. Catalogus plantarum Horti medici Oxoniensis. [*Oxford:*] *H. Hall,* 1648. 2 pts; 8vo. Describes numerous American plants identified as such, some of them specifically as Virginian. Pt 2, with English text, has title *An English catalogue,* etc. In some copies 'Catalogus' in title is misspelled 'Catologus'. Madan (Oxford) 2003; Henrey (Brit. bot.) 279–280; Wing B3376. CLU-C, CtY, MH-A, PPL; BL, BN.   648/18

Bontekoe, Willem Ysbrandsz. Journael ofte Gedenckwaerdighe beschrijvinghe vande Oost-Indische reyse . . . Waer by ghevoeght is het Journael van Dirck Albertsz. Raven. *Hoorn: I. Willemszoon, for J. J. Deutel,* 1648 [colophon: *Haarlem: T. Fonteyn,* 1646]. 2 pts; illus., port.; 4to. 1st publ., Haarlem & Hoorn, 1646; here an apparent reissue of that edn. Sabin 67980n; Tiele-Muller 172.   648/19

—[Anr edn]. *Hoorn: I. Willemszoon, for J. J. Deutel,* 1648. 80 p.; illus., port.; 4to. Lacks colophon; paged continuously. Sabin 67980n; Tiele-Muller 171; JCB (3) II:364. RPJCB; BL.   648/20

—[Anr edn]. *Amsterdam: J. Hartgers,* 1648. 56 (i.e., 76) p.; illus.; 4to. Sabin 6337 & 67980n; Tiele-Muller 173. DLC, NN-RB; BL.   648/21

—[Anr issue of the preceeding]. *Zaandam: W. Willemszoon,* 1648. Sabin 67980n; Tiele-Muller 176. NN-RB.   648/22

—[Anr edn]. *Amsterdam: J. Hartgers,* 1648. 76 p.; illus.; 4to. (Joost Hartgers's *Oost en West-Indische voyagien.* Pt 10). Sabin 6337 & 67980n; Tiele-Muller 174. NN-RB.
                                                    648/23

—[Anr edn]. Die vier und zwanzigste Schiffahrt. . . . Demnach, eine andere Reyse, durch . . . Raven. *Frankfurt a. M.: P. Fievet, for C. LeBlon,* 1648. 81 p.; illus., port.; 4to. (Levinus Hulsius's *Sammlung von . . . Schif-*

fahrten. Pt 24). Sabin 33677 (& 6340); Church 317; JCB (3) I:469. CSmH, ICN, NN-RB, RPJCB; BL, BN.   648/24

Brandt in Brasilien. [*Amsterdam?*] 1648. 9 p.; 4to. Includes, p. 3–5, 'Copie translaet van Joan Fernandus Vieras brieff aende Koopluyden van 't Reciff, den 11. en 12. September 1646'. Cf. the *Advys op de presentatie* above & the *Tegen-advys* below. Sabin 7528; Borba de Moraes I:106; Asher 235; Knuttel 5786; JCB (3) II:364. NN-RB, RPJCB; BL, The Hague:KB.   648/25

Brasilsche oorloghs overwegingh. [*Delft:*] 1648. 4 lvs; 4to. Sabin 7536; Borba de Moraes I:108; Asher 246. BL.   648/26

Briet, Philippe, S.J. Parallela geographiae veteris et novae. *Paris: S. Cramoisy & G. Cramoisy,* 1648–49. 3 v.; maps; 4to. In v. 1 is a brief description of the New World, incl. America. Backer II:156–157. DNLM, MnU-B, NNH, PPL; BL, BN.   648/27

The British bell-man. [*London:*] 1648. 20 p.; 4to. The Royalist author urges (p. 3) the 'Caterpillers of our Common-wealth', i.e., the Puritan faction, to seek gold sent away to New England & elsewhere. Wing B4823; Thomason I:620. CSmH, CtY, DFo, MH, MnU, RPJCB; BL.   648/28

Broeck, Pieter van den. Wonderlijcke historische ende Journaelsche aenteyckeningh. *Amsterdam: J. Hartgers,* 1648. 112 p.; illus.; 4to. (Joost Hartgers's *Oost en Westindische voyagien* . . . [Pt 7]). 1st publ., Haarlem, 1634; enlarged as pt of Commelin's *Begin ende voortgang,* 1st publ., [Amsterdam, 1644?]. Tiele-Muller 211; Tiele 195; Muller (1872) 2117; JCB (3) II:365. CtY, InU, MiU-C, NHi; BL.   648/29

Bruele, Gualtherus. Praxis medicinae; or, The physitians practice . . . The third edition newly corrected and amended. *London: R. Cotes, for W. Sheares,* 1648. 407 p.; 4to. 1st publ. as here transl., London, 1632. Wing B5221A. DFo, ICJ, MBCo, MnU, PPC; BL.   648/30

Caballero de Cabrera, Juan. Obra postuma. Sermones a diversos intentos . . . Diolos a la estampa . . . Blas Cavallero de Cabrera. *Madrid: D. García Morrás,* 1648. 306 numb. lvs; 4to. In his preface the editor pleads on behalf of the native-born American clergy for recognition. The author had been

a canon of the cathedral at Lima. Medina (BHA) 1131; Palau 38459; JCB (3) II:384. RPJCB; Santiago, Chile:BN.   648/31

Calado, Manuel, O.E.S.P. O valeroso Lucideno. E triumpho da liberdade. Primeira parte. *Lisbon: P. Craesbeeck,* 1648. 356 p.; fol. No more publ. The author, resident in Brazil, describes the expulsion by the Portuguese of the Dutch. Sabin 9865; Borba de Moraes I:123; Rodrigues (Dom. Hol.) 540; Innocencio V:385; JCB (3) II:365. InU-L, MH, NN-RB, RPJCB; BL.   648/32

Carlyle, James Hay, 2nd earl of. A declaration of James earl of Carlile, lord of the Caribee Islands . . . manifesting his care of, and affection to, the good and welfare of the inhabitants of . . . Barbadoes, and of all other people under his government . . . 22 day of November . . . 1647. [*London:* 1648?]. bds.; fol. Handler (Barbados) 2; Crawford (Roy. procl.) 2735; Wing C594. BL.   648/33

Carta de aviso de la muerte y virtudes del padre Alonso de Medrano, de la Compañia de Jesus. [*Granada?* 1648]. 8 lvs; fol. Subscribed: Granada, á 6 de octubre de 1648. Medrano had been a missionary in Mexico. Medina (BHA) 1117; Streit II:1813. Granada:BU.   648/34

Catholic Church. Commisarius Generalis Cruciatae. Instruccion, y forma que se ha de tener y guardar en la publicacion . . . i cobrança de la Bula dela santa Cruzada . . . concedido por . . . Paulo V . . . i mandada publicar por . . . Innocencio X . . . la qual se ha de hazer en el arçobispado de Mexico, i obispado de Mechoacan, Guatimala, Honduras, Chiapa, Verapaz, i Nicaragua, i en el arçobispado de Santo Domingo, i obispado de Puertorico, i de Cuba, i abadia de Jamaica. Y assimismo en las islas Filipinas. [*Madrid?* 1648]. 8 numb. lvs; fol. 1st (?) publ., [Barcelona? 1537?]; cf. 1608 edn. Medina (BHA) 1128; Palau 120170.   648/35

Catholic Church. Pope, 1644–1655 (Innocentius X). [Breve Sanctissimi Domini Nostri Innocentii X. in causa Angelopolitana jurisdictionis in Indiis Occidentalis Novae Hispaniae. *Rome: Apostolic Camera,* 1648]. On controversy between the Jesuits in Mexico & Bp Juan de Palafox y Mendoza.

Existence inferred from refs to it in later edns, etc. Cf. Sabin 7704; Palau 119833n.
648/36

—[Anr edn]. *Saragossa: D. Dormer*, 1648. 11 p.; 4to. Medina (BHA) 1115; Streit II:1803; Palau 119833. Granada:BU. 648/37

——. Breve Sanctissimi Domini Nostri Innocentii X. in cause Angelopolitana jurisdictionis in Indiis Occidentalis Novae Hispaniae. Bref de Nostre Saint Pere le Pape Innocent X, sur le differend d'entre l'Evesque d'Angelopolis . . . & les pp. Jesuites. *Paris: A. Vitré*, 1648. 19 p.; fol. Cf. the preceding item. Text in both Latin & French. Cf. Sabin 7704; cf. Streit II:1804; Palau 119833n. MiU-C. 648/38

Cervantes Saavedra, Miguel de. Novelas ejemplares. *Seville: P. Gómez de Pastrana*, 1648. 333 numb. lvs; 8vo. 1st publ., Madrid, 1613. Ríus (Cervantes) 237; Palau 53415. NNH. 648/39

Clüver, Philipp. Introduction à la geographie universelle tant nouvelle que ancienne, traduitte du latin de Philippe de Cluvier . . . Deuxième [*sic*] édition. *Paris: Widow Saussier & D. David*, 1648. 496 p.; illus.; 8vo. 1st publ. as here transl., Paris, 1631. Cf. Sabin 13805. BN. 648/40

——. Introductionis in universam geographiam, tam veterem quam novam, libri vi. Editio ultima, prioribus emendator [*sic*]. *Paris: Widow of J. Libert*, 1648. 2 pts; illus.; 16mo. 1st publ., Leyden, 1624. Includes also Petrus Bertius's *Breviarium totius orbis terrarum*, 1st publ., Paris, 1624. Cf. Sabin 13805. DLC. 648/41

Cobbet, Thomas. A just vindication of the covenant and church-estate of children of church members. *London: R. Cotes, for A. Crooke*, 1648. 296 p.; 4to. Includes (p. 186) mention of 'Indian papouses'. Cobbet was pastor of the church at Lynn in the Massachusetts Bay. Sabin 13867; Wing C4778; McAlpin II:551; JCB (3) II:366. CtY, DFo, MB, NN-RB, NcD, RPJCB; Cambridge:UL. 648/42

Coignet de la Thuillerie, Gaspard. Twee propositien gedaen door den Heer de La Thullerie . . . ter vergaderinge van . . . Staten Generael . . . Mitsgaders eenige consideratien. [*The Hague: J. Veely*] for *F. Levyn, at Utrecht*, 1648. [38] p.; 4to. The 1st

anonymous 'Consideratie' includes a ref. to Brazil. Authorship of the pamphlet attrib. by Knuttel to Adriaan Pauw. In this issue, the device of J. Veely appears on t.p. Knuttel 5696. Locations may include the following issue. MnU, NN; BN, The Hague:KB.
648/43

—[Anr issue?]. [*The Hague? J. Veely?*] for *F. Levyn, at Utrecht*, 1648. [38] p.; 4to. Here a vignette replaces the printer's device used above. Knuttel 5697. The Hague:KB.
648/44

—[Anr edn]. *Utrecht: F. Levyn*, 1648. [20] p.; 4to. T.p. includes reading 'vergaderinghe'. Knuttel 5698. The Hague:KB, Ghent:BU.
648/45

—[Anr edn]. Aaloude heersch-en-oorlogssught van Louis de XIV tot nadeel en verderf . . . ofte Twee propositien gedaen door den heer de la Thullerie . . . nae de copy. *Utrecht: F. Levyn* [1648?]. [20] p.; 4to. Knuttel 5699. NN; The Hague:KB.
648/46

—[Anr edn]. Propositien gedaen door den Heere de la Thuillerye. [*Amsterdam?* 1648]. [20] p.; 4to. Knuttel 5700. BL, The Hague:KB. 648/47

Colom, Jacob Aertszoon. Toortse der Zeevaerdt, verlichtende West Indien, Brasilien . . . en Angola. *Amsterdam: J. A. Colom*, 1648. 183 p.; maps; 4to. Cf. Sabin 14550. BL.
648/48

La confession de l'imprimeur, traduitte du flamend en françois. [*Antwerp?*] 1648. 62 p.; 4to. Transl. from *Des druckers belydenisse* of this year below. Knuttel 5766. The Hague:KB. 648/49

Cooke, James. Mellificium chirurgiae. or, The marrow of many good authours, wherein is . . . handled the art of chyrurgery. *London: S. Cartwright*, 1648. 478 p.; 12mo. Cures for syphilis include use of guaiacum & sarsaparilla. Wing C6012. CU-M, CtY-M, DNLM, MnU, NNNAM, PPC; London:Wellcome. 648/50

Cotton, John. The way of congregational churches cleared. *London: M. Simmons, for J. Bellamy*, 1648. 2 pts; 4to. Included is a substantial discussion of the church of New England. Also issued as pt of Thomas Hooker's *A survey of the summe of church discipline* of this year, q.v. below. In part a reply to Daniel Cawdry's *Vindiciae clavium* (London, 1645). In this state, the last line on verso of lf A3 has reading 'Godly Elder'; recto of lf A4 (lines 27–28) has reading 'to throw the scum upon one another'. Sabin 17091; Tuttle (Cotton) 59; Wing C6469; JCB (3) II:367. CSmH, CtY, DFo, MH, MiU-C, NNUT, RPJCB; BL, BN. 648/51

—[Anr state]. *London: M. Simmons, for J. Bellamy,* 1648. The last line on verso of lf A3 has reading 'Godly Elders'; recto of lf A4 (lines 27–28) has reading 'to throw the steem upon one another'. The locations given above may include this state. Tuttle (Cotton) 59; JCB (3) II:367. RPJCB.
648/52

Des druckers belydenisse. [*Amsterdam?*] 1648. [56] p.; 4to. Prob. 1st publ. in French, according to Knuttel, but see the French version, with title *La confession de l'imprimeur,* of this year above. Includes refs to the West-Indische Compagnie & war with Portuguese in Brazil. Knuttel 5765. NN; BL, The Hague:KB. 648/53

Díez de la Calle, Juan. Memorial y compendio breve del libro intitulado Noticias sacras y reales de los dos imperios de la Nueva España, el Perù y sus islas de las Indias Occidentales. [*Madrid:* 1648]. 16 numb. lvs; fol. Cf. the author's larger *Memorial* of 1646 to which this is a supplement. Medina (BHA) 1119; Wagner (SW) 46; Streit II:1801; Palau 73744. CtY, NN-RB, RPJCB; BL. 648/54

Donne, John. Βιαθανατος. A declaration . . . that selfe-homicide is not so naturally sinne. *London:* [*J. Dawson,*] *for H. Moseley,* 1648. 218 p.; 4to. 1st publ., London, [1647]; here a reissue of that edn with cancel t.p. Keynes (Donne) 48; Wing D1859; Grolier Club (Wither to Prior) 294. CSmH, CtY, DLC, IU, MH, MnU, NN-RB; BL, BN.
648/55

Duchesne, Joseph. La pharmacopee des dogmatiques reformée. *Lyons: J. de LaGarde,* 1648. 3 pts; 8vo. 1st publ., as here transl. from Duchesne's *Pharmacopoea dogmaticorum restituta* (Paris, 1607), Paris, 1624. BL.
648/56

——. Quercetanus redivivus, hoc est Ars medica dogmatica hermetica . . . tomis tribus digesta. *Frankfurt a. M.: J. Beyer,* 1648. 3 v.;

4to. Digested from Duchesne's works by J. Schröder. Vol. 2 includes refs to guaiacum, sarsaparilla, & peoples of the Indies. DNLM, ICU, NNC, PPL; BN. 648/57

Duliris, Leonard, O.R.S.A. Apologie; ou Juste deffence du secret des longitudes pratiqué en mer. *Paris: A. Bertier,* 1648. 2 pts; 4to. Included is the author's *La théorie des longitudes,* 1st publ., Paris, 1647. Houzeau & Lancaster 10341. NN. 648/58

Eenige advijsen ende verklaringhen uyt Brasilien. In dato den 19. Mey 1648. '*Amsterdam: Philips van Macedonien, printer, in the press of J. R. Toorn*' [i.e., *The Hague: L. Breeckevelt*] 1648. [8] p.; 4to. Includes report sent out by Dirck van Hoorn. Sabin 7573 (& 7502); Borba de Moraes I:242; Rodrigues (Dom. Hol.) 541; Knuttel 5782; JCB (3) II:365. NN-RB, RPJCB; BL (Brazil), The Hague:KB. 648/59

—[Anr edn]. Eenighe advijsen . . . In dato den 29 May, 1648. '*Amsterdam: Phlips* [*sic*] *van Macedonien, printer, in the press of J. R. Toorn*' [i.e., *The Hague? L. Breeckevelt?*] 1648. [8] p.; 4to. Borba de Moraes I:242; Knuttel 5783. The Hague:KB. 648/60

Eerste schip-vaert der Hollanders naer Oost-Indien . . . onder 't beleydt van Cornelis Houtman. *Amsterdam: J. Hartgers,* 1648. 102 p.; illus.; 4to. (Joost Hartgers's *Oost en Westindische voyagien* . . . [Pt 2]). 1st publ. as a pt of Commelin's *Begin ende voortgang,* [Amsterdam, 1644?]; based largely on W. Lodewijcksz's *D'eerste boeck,* 1st publ., Amsterdam, 1598 (cf. 1609 edn), but includes material from Houtman's *Verhael vande reyse,* 1st publ., Middelburg, 1597. Includes mention of Brazil & West Indies. Tiele-Muller 120; Tiele 512; Muller (1872) 2171. NIC. 648/61

Estienne, Charles. L'agricoltura, e casa di villa. *Venice: M. Ginammi,* 1648. Cf. 1606 edn. MH. 648/62

Extract van seeckeren brief, gheschreven uyt Loando St. Paulo, in Angola, van weghen de groote victorie die de onse verkregen hebben. *The Hague: L. Breeckevelt,* 1648. [8] p.; 4to. On battle between forces of the West-Indische Compagnie & Portugal. Rodrigues (Dom. Hol.) 490; Asher 238; Knuttel 5780. RPJCB; The Hague:KB; Amsterdam:NHSM. 648/63

Fernel, Jean. La therapeutique, ou La methode universelle de guerir les maladies . . . mis en françois par le sieur Du Teil. *Paris: J. Guignard, father & son,* 1648. 648 p.; 8vo. Transl. from Fernel's *Therapeutices universalis,* 1st publ., Paris, 1567, as part of his *Universa medicina,* and separately, Lyons, 1571. Includes refs to Brazil & to tacamahac, citing Monardes. Sherrington (Fernel) 91.K3. DNLM; Paris:Faculté de Médecine. 648/64

—[Anr issue]. *Paris: Widow of J. LeBouc,* 1648. BN. 648/65

Fournier, Georges. Geographica orbis notitia. Per litora maris & ripas fluviorum. *Paris: J. Henault,* 1648. 651 p.; 12mo. In bk 1, chapt. v mentions Vespucci & Magellan in passing. A 2nd pt was publ. in 1651. Backer III:910. BL, BN. 648/66

Fuller, Thomas. The holy state . . . The second edition enlarged. *Cambridge: R. D[aniel]., for J. Williams [at London],* 1648. 510 p.; illus., ports; fol. 1st publ., London, 1642. Cf. Sabin 26181; Murphy (Engl. char.-bks) 57; Wing F2444; McAlpin II:565. CSmH, CtY, ICN, MH, MWA, NNUT, PHi; BL. 648/67

Gage, Thomas. The English-American his travail by sea and land: or, A new survey of the West-India's, containing a journall of three thousand and three hundred miles within the main land of America. *London: R. Cotes, to be sold by H. Blunden & by T. Williams,* 1648. 220 p.; fol. Sabin 26298; Streit II:505; Wing G109; McAlpin II:565; JCB (3) II:369. CSmH, CtY, DLC, ICN, InU-L, MH, MWA, MiU-C, NN-RB, PP, RPJCB; BL. 648/68

Golding, William. Servants on horse-back . . . Being a representation of the dejected state of the inhabitants of Summer Islands. *[London:]* 1648. 24 p.; 4to. Sabin 27713; Wing G1020; Arents (Add.) 337; JCB (3) II:369. MiU-C, NN-A, RPJCB; BL. 648/69

Gomberville, Marin Le Roy, sieur du Parc et de. The history of Polexander . . . Done into English by William Browne. *London: T. Harper, for T. Walkley,* 1648. 2 pts; fol. 1st publ. in English, London, 1647; here a reissue with altered imprint date? Wing G1026. ICN, PPL, ViU; Cambridge:UL. 648/70

Góngora y Argote, Luis de. Todas las obras. *Seville: N. Rodríguez,* 1648. 234 numb. lvs; 4to. In verse. Included is Góngora's *Soledades.* 1st publ., Madrid, 1627, in his *Obras en verso.* Escudero (Seville) 1624; Palau 104630. NNH, PU; BL, Madrid:BN. 648/71

González Chaparro, Juan, S.J. Carta del p. Juan Gonzalez Chaparro . . . para el p. Alonso de Ovalle y del Manzano . . . en que le dà cuento del lastimoso sucesso del terremoto que huvo en la ciudad de Santiago de Chile en Indias. *Madrid: D. Díaz de la Carrera,* 1648. [4] p.; fol. Sabin 11937; Medina (Chile) 123; Streit II:1796; Backer III:1588; Palau 105269. BL, Santiago, Chile:BN. 648/72

—[Anr edn]. *[Madrid? 1648?].* 3 numb. lvs; fol. Medina (Chile) 124; Streit II:1797; Palau 105269n. Madrid:Acad. de la Hist., Seville: Seminario. 648/73

—[Anr edn]. Relacion del gran terremoto, o temblor de tierra que assolò toda la ciudad de Chile en el nuevo mundo. *Seville: F. de Lyra,* 1648. [4] p.; 4to. Medina (Chile) 125; Streit II:1798; Palau 105270. Seville:B. Colombina. 648/74

——. Lettera . . . ove s'intendono casi stravagantissimi del terremoto ivi seguito alli 13 di maggio 1647. *Rome: L. Grignani,* 1648. 4 lvs; 4to. Transl. from the preceding. Sabin 13038; Backer III:1587; Palau 105272. 648/75

——. Relation dell'horrible tremblement. qui a ruyné de fons en comble la florissante cité de S. Jaques de Chile aux Indes Occidentales. *Brussels: J. Mommaert,* 1648. 18 p.; 4to. Transl. from the Spanish text above. Sabin 69262; Medina (Chile) 125n; Streit II:1799; Backer III:1587; Palau 105272. BL. 648/76

Grotius, Hugo. Bewijs van de ware godtsdienst, gestelt in ses boecken. *Amsterdam: Widow of R. D. van Baardt,* 1648. 143 p.; 8vo. 1st publ., [Leyden?], 1622. Meulen/ Diermanse 145. NNC; BL, The Hague:PP. 648/77

Guibert, Philbert. Toutes les oeuvres charitables. *Paris: C. Marette,* 1648. 799 p.; port.; 8vo. Included is the author's *Le prix & valeur des medicamens,* 1st publ., Paris, 1625. BN. 648/78

Hall, Joseph, Bp of Norwich. Mundus alter et idem . . . Authore Mercurio Britannico. *Frankfurt a. M.: Heirs of Ascanius de Rinialme,* 1648. 224 p.; illus., maps; 8vo. 1st publ., Frankfurt a. M. [i.e., London, 1605?]. As with the 1st edn, the above imprint is no doubt fictitious. Sabin 29819n; Brunet III:20.   648/79

Hartgers, Joost, comp. Oost-Indische voyagien, door dien Begin en voortgangh van de Vereenighde Nederlandtsche Geoctroyeerde Oost-Indische Compagnie . . . 1. deel. Daer in begrepen zijn 16 voyagien. *Amsterdam: J. Hartgers,* 1648. 13 pts in 1 v.; illus.; 4to. Here brought together under this collective title, with introduction & binding instructions, is a group of 13 pamphlets, each of which has its own special t.p., & separate paging & signatures. Each was also issued separately this year and several were reissued 1648–1652; some copies of the collection include individual pts with the later imprint date. All but pts 10 (Bontekoe) & 11 (Pelsaert) are reprinted from Commelin's *Begin ende voortgang,* 1st publ., [Amsterdam, 1644?]. Commelin's introduction includes scattered American refs. For fuller descriptions of those items including Americana, see the following under the present year: (1) G. de Veer, *Verhael van de eerste schip-vaert;* (2) the *Eerste schip-vaert der Hollanders;* (3) J. van Neck, *Waerachtigh verhael;* (4) O. van Noort, *Wonderlijcke voyagie;* (5) J. van Spilbergen, *Historis journael;* (6) C. Matelief, *Journael;* (7) P. van den Broecke, *Wonderlijcke historische . . . aenteyckeningh;* (8) J. van Spilbergen, *Oost- en West-Indische voyagie;* (9) the *Journael vande Nassausche vloot;* (10) W. Y. Bontekoe, *Journael.* In some copies, the order of pts 10 & 11 is reversed. For a variant edn omitting Matelief's voyage, see Tiele-Muller. A planned 2nd volume of the work was not published. Sabin 30680; Tiele-Muller 7–8; Tiele 1179; Muller (1872) 3288; JCB (3) II:370. CSt, DLC, NN-RB, RPJCB; BL, BN.   648/80

Hernández, Francisco. Rerum medicarum Novae Hispaniae thesaurus, seu Plantarium, animalium, mineralium Mexicanorum. *Rome: V. Mascardi,* 1648. 950 p.; illus.; fol. 1st publ., Rome, 1628. Cf. Sabin 31515;

cf. Pritzel 4000; Nissen (Zool.) 1908a; Palau 113537. Vienna:NB.   648/81

Hinc illae lachrymae. or The impietie of impunitie. Containig [*sic*] a short, serious and most serious . . . demonstration of . . . all the grand grievances . . . over the whole kingdome. *London:* 1648. 29 p.; 4to. On p. 4, Samuel Gorton, an 'audicious Malefactor in New-England', is mentioned. The title leaf is a cancel. Dubiously attrib. to John Gauden, bp of Worcester. Wing G358; McAlpin II:572; Thomason I:579 (23 Dec. 1647) & I:720 (30 Jan. 1649). ICU, MB, NNUT, RPJCB; BL.   648/82

Hooker, Thomas. A survey of the summe of church-discipline, wherein the way of the churches of New-England is warranted. *London: A M[iller]., for J. Bellamy,* 1648. 4 pts; 4to. Also issued with John Cotton's *The way of congregational churches* under collective t.p., as described below. Sabin 32860; Wing H2658; JCB (3) II:371. CSmH, CtY, DLC, ICN, MH, MiU-C, NNUT, RPJCB; BL, BN.   648/83

——. A survey of the summe of church-discipline, wherein the way of the congregationall churches of Christ in New-England is warranted . . . in two books, the first, by Mr. Thomas Hooker . . . at Hartford . . . the second, by Mr. John Cotton . . . at Boston. *London: A. M[iller]., for J. Bellamy,* 1648. 6 pts; 4to. Here issued under collective t.p. are Hooker's *Survey* & Cotton's *The way of congregational churches,* also described separately above. Sabin 32861; JCB (3) II:371. RPJCB.   648/84

Johnson, Edward. Good news from New England: with an exact relation of the first planting that countrey. *London: M. Simmons,* 1648. 25 p.; 4to. In verse. Authorship attrib. to Johnson by H. S. Jantz in his *The first century of New England verse* (Worcester, 1944). Sabin 27832; Vail (Frontier) 109; Wing G1062; JCB (3) II:369–370. CSmH, ICN, RPJCB.   648/85

Jonstonus, Joannes. Idea universae medicinae practicae, libris xii absoluta. *Amsterdam: L. Elsevier,* 1648. 756 p.; 12mo. 1st publ., Amsterdam 1644. Willems (Les Elzevier) 1069. CtW, DNLM, IU, NNNAM, PPL; BN.   648/86

Journael, van de reyse van de vlote uyt de

Vereenighde Nederlanden na Brasilien . . . mitsgaders de batalie tusschen den . . . Ghenerael Sigismundus Schoppe ende . . . de Portugiesen. *Amsterdam: J. van Hilten,* 1648. [7] p.; 4to. Sabin 77898; Borba de Moraes I:364; Rodrigues (Dom. Hol.) 544; Knuttel 5781a. DLC, NN; The Hague:KB, Leyden:UB. 648/87

Journael vande Nassausche vloot. *Amsterdam: J. Hartgers,* 1648. 76 p.; illus., maps; 4to. (Joost Hartgers's *Oost en Westindische voyagien* . . . [Pt 9]). 1st publ., Amsterdam, 1626. Here included is Madriga's narrative of Peru and an extract from Lawrence Kemys's 2nd voyage, the *Kort journael gedaen naer Guiana,* as taken from C. Claeszoon's 1598, Amsterdam, Dutch translation of Raleigh's *Waerachtighe . . . beschryvinge.* Sabin 31505; Muller (1872) 1935; Tiele-Muller 77; Tiele 667; JCB (3) II:372. RPJCB; BL, Ghent:BU. 648/88

Lallemant, Jérôme, S.J. Relation de ce qui s'est passé de plus remarquable és missions des pères de la Compagnie de Jesus, en la Nouvelle France, sur le grand fleuve de S. Laurens en l'année 1647. *Paris: S. Cramoisy,* 1648. 276 p.; 8vo. For variants, see Bell & McCoy as cited. Sabin 38685; Harrisse (NF) 87; Streit II:2566; Bell (Jes. rel.) 33–34; McCoy 63–68; Church 487; JCB (3) II:372. CSmH, DLC, ICN, MH, MnU-B, NN-RB, RPJCB; BL, BN. 648/89

Le Blanc, Vincent. Les voyages fameux du sieur Vincent Le Blanc marseillois, qu'il a faits depuis l'âge de douze ans jusques à soixante, aux quatres parties du monde . . . le tout recueilly . . . par le sieur Coulon. *Paris: G. Clousier,* 1648. 3 pts; 4to. Whether this work is authentic or a work of Coulon's imagination is uncertain. Sabin 39590n; Borba de Moraes I:392n; Cioranescu (XVII) 41090. DLC, MiU, MnU-B, NN-RB; BL, BN. 648/90

Lloyd, David. The legend of captaine Jones. *London: M. F[letcher]., for R. Marriott,* 1648. 2 pts; 4to. In verse. Pt 1 1st publ., London, 1631; pt 2, here 1st publ., includes refs to Drake, Cavendish & 'Cortes's Montezuma'. Sabin 41683; Wing L2630; Thomason I:633. CSmH, CtY, ICN, MH; BL. 648/91

Losa, Francisco de. Vida que el siervo de

Dios Gregorio Lopez hizo. *Madrid:* 1648. *See the year 1658.*

Magnen, Jean Chrysostôme. Exercitationes de tabaco. *Pavia: G. A. Magri,* 1648. 192 p.; 4to. Cf. Sabin 43825; Pritzel 6410; Waring II:710; Arents 234. CtY, DNLM, InU, MH, NN-RB, PPC, RPJCB; BL, BN. 648/92

Markham, Gervase. Cheape and good husbandry . . . Seventh edition. *London: B. Alsop, for J. Harrison,* 1648. 188 p.; 4to. (In Markham's *A way to get wealth*). 1st publ., London, 1614. Poynter (Markham) 34.7; Wing M611. CSmH, CtY, IU, MH, NN-RB; BL. 648/93

Matelief, Cornelis. Journael ende Historische verhael van de treffelijcke reyse gedaen naer Oost-Indien. *Amsterdam: A. H. Roest, for J. Hartgers,* 1648. 142 p.; illus.; 4to. (Joost Hartgers's *Oost en Westindische voyagien* . . . [Pt 6]). 1st publ. as pt of Commelin's *Begin ende voortgang,* [Amsterdam, 1644?]. Includes minor refs to resources of Peru & Mexico, & to maize eaten by Indians there. Tiele-Muller 167; Tiele 723; Muller (1872) 2208; JCB (3) II:373. CU, InU-L, MSaE, NN-RB, RPJCB. 648/94

Mayerne, Louis Turquet de, fl. 1648. Discours sur la carte universelle, en laquelle le globe terrestre est entierement reduit et represente dans un seul cercle. *Paris:* 1648. 78 p.; 12mo. DLC; BN. 648/95

Melich, Georg. Avvertimenti nelle compositioni de' medicamenti. *Venice: The Guerigli,* 1648. 344 p.; 4to. 1st publ., Venice, 1575; cf. [1605] edn. DNLM. 648/96

Mercator, Gerardus. Atlas minor, das ist: Eine kurtze jedoch gründliche Beschreibung der gantzen Welt. *Amsterdam: J. Janszoon, the Younger,* 1648. 2 pts; maps; obl. 8vo. 1st publ. in this German translation, Amsterdam, 1631. Cf. Sabin 47889; Koeman (Me) 203; Phillips (Atlases) 5940. DLC, InU-L, NN-RB; Wolfenbüttel:HB. 648/97

Morisot, Claude Barthélemy. Orbis maritimi, sive Rerum in mari et littoribus gestarum generalis historia. *Dijon: P. Palliot,* 1648. 725 p.; fol. 1st publ., Dijon, 1643. NcD. 648/98

Morone, Mattia. Directorium medico-practicum. *Lyons: J. A. Huguetan,* 1648. 400 p.;

8vo. 1st publ., Lyons, 1647; here a reissue of that edn with altered imprint date? PPL.
648/99

Neck, Jacob Corneliszoon van. Waerachtigh verhael van de schip-vaert op Oost-Indien . . . Hier achter is aen-ghevoeght De voyagie van Sebald de Weert, naer de Strate Magalanes. *Amsterdam: J. Hartgers, 1648.* 92 p.; illus.; 4to. (Joost Hartgers's *Oost en Westindische voyagien . . .* [Pt 3]). Neck's voyage 1st publ., Amsterdam [1600], under title *Journael ofte Dagh-register;* cf. 1601 edn (*Het tweede* boeck). The present version is abridged as 1st publ. in Commelin's *Begin ende voortgang,* [Amsterdam, 1644?]. De Weert's voyage, also reprinted from *Begin ende voortgang,* had been extracted from B. J. Potgieter's *Wijdtloopigh verhael,* 1st publ., Amsterdam, [1600]; cf. 1617 edn. Sabin 52214; cf. Tiele-Muller 131; Tiele 787; Muller (1872) 2213; JCB (3) II:373. MB, RPJCB; BL. 648/100

—[Anr edn]. *Amsterdam: J. Hartgers, 1648* [colophon: *Amsterdam: C. Cunradus, 1650*]. *See the year 1650.*

Nederlandsche West-Indische Compagnie. Reglement by de West-Indische Compagnie, ter vergaderinge vande negentiene, met approbatie vande . . . Staten Generael over het open-stellen vanden handel op Brazil, provisioneel ghearresteert. *The Hague: Widow & Heirs of H. Jacobszoon van Wouw, 1648.* [7] p.; 4to. 1st publ., The Hague, 1638. Cf. the Netherlands Staten Generaal's *Concept* of this year below, the text of which is here included. Sabin 102927; Borba de Moraes II:375; Asher 242; Knuttel 5790. NN-RB; BL, The Hague:KB. 648/101

——. Reglement by de West-Indische Compagnie, ter vergaderinge vande negentiene, met approbatie vande . . . Staten Generael, over het open-stellen vanden handel op S. Paulo de Loanda, provisioneel gearresteêrt. *The Hague: Widow & Heirs of H. Jacobszoon van Wouw, 1648.* [5] p.; 4to. Sabin 102928; Borba de Moraes II:375; Asher 241; Knuttel 5790a. BL, The Hague:KB. 648/102

Nederlandsche West-Indische Compagnie. Hooghe en Secrete Raad. Extract uyt de Missive vanden president ende raden aende . . . Staten Generael. Op 't Recif den 22.

April 1648. *The Hague: L. Breeckevelt, 1648.* [8] p.; 4to. Report on Dutch wounded & dead in Brazil. Sabin 7578; Borba de Moraes I:256; Asher 247; Knuttel 5781; JCB (3) II:374. MnU-B, NN-RB, RPJCB; BL, The Hague:KB. 648/103

Nederlantsche absolutie op de Fransche belydenis. '*Amsterdam: J. Nes*' [i.e., *The Hague? J. Veely?*], 1684 [i.e., 1648]. [29] p.; 4to. Concerns peace negotiations with Spain; includes refs to war in Brazil. Knuttel 5770. MnU-B, NN-RB, RPJCB; The Hague:KB. 648/104

Netherlands (United Provinces, 1581–1795). Staten Generaal. Concept van Reglement op Brasil ghenomen by . . . de Heeren Staten Generael der Vereenighde Nederlanden ende de bewindt-hebberen der Geoctroyeerde West-Indische Compaignie. [*The Hague: L. Breeckevelt*] 1648. [8] p.; 4to. Cf. the Nederlandsche West-Indische Compagnie's *Reglement . . . op Brazil* of this year above. Sabin 7552 (& 102886); Borba de Moraes I:170; Asher 240. DLC, NN-RB; Amsterdam:NHSM. 648/105

——. Vercondinge van de vrede den dertichsten Januarij deses loopende jaers . . . geslooten binnen Munster. *The Hague: Widow & Heirs of H. Jacobszoon van Wouw, 1648.* bds.; fol. Includes ref. to West Indies & the West-Indische Compagnie. Also appears in Spain. Treaties, etc. *Tractaet van vrede* of this year below. Knuttel 5730. InU-L, MnU-B; BL, The Hague:KB. 648/106

—[Anr edn]. . . . gesloten . . . Nae de copye. *The Hague: Widow & Heirs of H. Jacobszoon van Wouw, 1648.* bds.; fol. Knuttel 5731. The Hague:KB. 648/107

Neuhaus, Edo. Theatrum ingenii humani . . . Editio novissima. *Amsterdam: 1648.* 12mo. 1st publ., Amsterdam, 1633. BL. 648/108

Noort, Olivier van. Wonderlijcke voyagie, by de Hollanders gedaen, door de Strate Magalanes . . . onder . . . van Noort, uytgevaren anno 1598. Hier achter is by-gevoeght De tweede voyagie van Jacob van Neck, naar Oost-Indien. *Amsterdam: J. Hartgers, 1648.* 88 p.; illus.; 4to. (Joost Hartgers's *Oost en Westindische voyagien.* [Pt 4]). Noort's voyage 1st publ., Rotterdam & Am-

sterdam, 1601, under title *Beschryvinghe van de voyagie;* this abridged version 1st publ., as part of Commelin's *Begin ende voortgangh,* [Amsterdam, 1644]. Roelof Roelofsz's account of the Neck voyage, *Korte ende waerachtig verhael van de tweede schipvaert by de Hollanders,* with refs to potatoes, Brazil, & the Strait of Magellan, was 1st publ. in *Begin ende voortgangh,* but bears some similarity to the Roelofsz account in pt 8 of J. T. de Bry's *India Orientalis* (Frankfurt a. M., 1606); for a discussion of the 2 versions see Tiele-Muller, p. 162–66. Sabin 55440; Tiele-Muller 21 (& p. 163); Tiele 809; JCB (3) II:374.
648/109

Norton, John. Responsio ad totam quaestionum syllogen à . . . Guilielmo Apollonio, ecclesiae Middleburgensis pastore, propositam. Ad componendas controversias quasdam circa politiam ecclesiasticam in Anglia nunc temporis agitatas spectantem. *London: R. B[ishop]., for A. Crooke,* 1648. 170 p.; 8vo. Included are numerous refs to the clergy of New England. Sabin 55888; Wing N1322; JCB (3) II:374. CSmH, CtY, DLC, InU-L, MWA, NN-RB, RPJCB; Oxford: Bodl.
648/110

Ocampo y Velasco, Juana. A Doña Juana de Ocampo y Velasco se sirvio su Magestad hazerla merced. [*Madrid?* 1648?]. [3] p.; fol. Petition regarding grant of monopoly for growing tobacco in Oran. BL.   648/111

Ondermarck, Nataneel. Copye van seeckeren send-brieff geschreven . . . aen sijnen goeden vriend Joris Pietersz. [*Middelburg?*] 1648. [8] p.; 4to. Includes ref. to the West-Indische Compagnie. Knuttel 5719. MnU-B, NN; BN, The Hague:KB.
648/112

Ontdeckinghe van een wonderlick Monster onlanghs in Hollandt geopenbaert door een ghemeynden brief. [*Amsterdam?*] 1648. [13] p.; 4to. A reply to N. Ondermarck's *Copye* of this year above. Includes ref. to the West-Indische Compagnie. Knuttel 5720. NN; The Hague:KB.   648/113

Openhertige en trouhertige requeste . . . aen de . . . Staten van Zeelant. [*Middelburg?*] 1648. [8] p.; 4to. Includes ref. to the West-Indische Compagnie. Printed in black letter. Knuttel 5712. MnU, NN; The Hague:KB.   648/114

—[Anr edn]. [*Middelburg?*] 1648. [8] p.; 4to. Printed in roman type. Knuttel 5713; Meulman 2949. The Hague:KB, Ghent:BU.
648/115

—[Anr edn]. Open-hertige en trou-hertige requeste. [*Middelburg?*] 1648. [8] p.; 4to. Knuttel 5714. NN; The Hague:KB.
648/116

—[Anr edn]. Openhertige ende trouhertige requeste. [*Middelburg?*] 1648. [7] p.; 4to. Knuttel 5715. MnU, NN; The Hague:KB.
648/117

Opitz, Martin. Weltliche Poemata. *Frankfurt a. M.:* 1648. 2 pts; 8vo. 1st publ. with American refs, Breslau, 1628–29, under title *Deutscher Poematum.* Optiz's 'Lob des Kriegesgottes' appears here in pt 2. Goedeke III:50; Jördens IV:117.   648/118

Ortiz de Valdes, Fernando. Defensa canonica por la dignidad del Obispo de la Puebla de los Angeles [i.e., Juan de Palafox y Mendoza], por su jurisdiccion ordinaria, i por la auctoridad de sus puestos. En el pleito que han movido los padres de la Compañia de Jesus de la dicha ciudad. [*Madrid:* 1648]. 240 numb. lvs; 4to. Dated at end, Madrid, 16 June 1648. Medina (BHA) 6722; Palau 209720; JCB (3) II:375. RPJCB, WU.
648/119

Ovalle, Alonso de, S.J. Historica relacion del reyno de Chile, y delas missiones. *Rome: F. Cavalli,* 1648. 455 p.; illus., ports, maps; fol. 1st publ., Rome, 1646. The MH copy dated as above & described by Sabin proves on examination to be another copy of the 1646 edn with imprint date altered by hand in ink. It also contains, however, preceding the t.p., a printed leaf beginning 'Varias y curiosas noticias del reino de Chile' containing an extended description of the contents, emphasizing that these also treat other areas of Spanish America. One infers a conscious effort, presumably by Cavalli, to stimulate lagging sales. Sabin 57973. MH.   648/120

Pace di Olanda. *Florence: Ducal Press,* 1648. [8] p.; 4to. Includes statement that Treaty of Munster is to come into effect in Spanish America 16 months after 15 May 1648. BL (Netherlands).   648/121

Pagitt, Ephraim. Heresiography . . . The fourth [*sic*] edition. *London: W. W[ilson]., for*

W. Lee, 1648. 4to. 1st publ., London, 1645. Wing P179. ICN; Oxford:Bodl.

648/122

Palma, Luis de la, S.J. Informe juridico a favor de los religiosos doctrineros de la Nueva España. [*Madrid?*] 1648. fol. Medina (BHA) 1123; Palau 210298. 648/123

Palma Fajardo, Francisco de, O.F.M. Sermon predicado . . . a las obsequias de . . . Pedro de Irramain, calificador del Consejo supremo de la Santa Inquisicion, perpetuo de . . . los doze Apostolos de Lima, visitador general de todos los reynos, y provincias del Pirù y tierra firme, custodio, y guardian dignissimo del convento grande de Jesus de Lima, y provincial actual meritismo della. *Cadiz: F. J. de Velazco,* 1648. 12 lvs; 4to. Medina (BHA) 1124; Streit II:1809.

648/124

Paulli, Simon. Flora Danica, det er: Dansk urtebog. *Copenhagen: M. Martzen, for J. Molikens & J. Holstis* (pt 1); *Antwerp: Plantin Office* (pt 2), 1648,'47. 2 pts; illus.; 4to. Included are illus. & descriptions of the marigold ('Flos Africanus'), of 'Nicotiana foemina', & also of tobacco, with an extended discussion of its American origins. Pritzel 6993; Nissen (Bot.) 1497. CtY, DNLM, MoSB, NNBG; BL, BN. 648/125

De penitentie gegeven aen den Franschen drucker op syn paes-biecht. *Amsterdam: J. Nes* [i.e., *The Hague? J. Veely?*], 1648. 72 p.; 4to. Includes sections on confrontation with Portuguese in Brazil. A rebuttal of *Des druckers belydenisse* of this year above. Knuttel 5769. DLC, MnU-B, NN; The Hague:KB.

648/126

Pigray, Pierre. Epitome des preceptes de medecine et chirurgie. *Lyons: C. Prost,* 1648. 764 p.; 8vo. 1st publ., Paris, 1600, under title *La chirurgie;* cf. 1604 edn. BN.

648/127

Piso, Willem. Historia naturalis Brasiliae . . . in qua non tantum plantae et animalia, sed et indigenarum morbi, ingenia et mores describuntur et iconibus . . . illustrantur. *Leyden: F. Haack & L. Elsevier, at Amsterdam,* 1648. 2 pts; illus.; fol. Pt 1 has special t.p., with title *Guilielmi Pisonis . . . Medicina Brasiliensis libri quatuor;* pt 2, *Georgi Marcgravi . . . Historiae rerum naturalium Brasiliae libri octo.* Sabin 63028 (& 7588); Borba de Moraes

II:152; Nissen (Bot.) 1533; Willems (Les Elzevier) 1068; JCB (3) II:375. CtY, DLC, ICJ, InU-L, MB, MiU, NN-RB, PPL, RPJCB; BL, BN. 648/128

Plantagenet, Beauchamp. A description of the province of New Albion. And a direction for adventurers with small stock to get two for one, and good land freely . . . Together with a letter from master Robert Evelin. [*London:*] 1648. 32 p.; illus.; 4to. Perhaps written by Sir Edmond Plowden. Evelyn's 'letter' 1st publ. separately, London, 1641, under title *A direction for adventurers.* Sabin 63310 (& 19724); Vail (Frontier) 110; Baer (Md) 28; Wing P2378; Church 488; JCB (3) II:376. CSmH, ICN, MH, MiU-C, NN-RB, PPL, RPJCB; BL. 648/129

Poincten van consideratie, raeckende de vrede met Portugal. *Amsterdam:* 1648. 8 p.; 4to. Includes refs to Brazil & the West-Indische Compagnie. Sabin 63682; Borba de Moraes II:158; Asher 245; Knuttel 5788; JCB (3) II:365. DLC, MnU-B, RPJCB; BL (Portugal). 648/130

Poirier, Hélie. Deus harangues panégyriques, l'une de la pais, l'autre de la concorde . . . Ensemble un traité de Monsieur Grotius: De l'antiquité de la république des Hollandois. *Amsterdam: J. Blaeu,* 1648. 191 p.; 12mo. Grotius's work transl. by Poirier from the *Liber de antiquitate,* 1st publ., Leyden, 1610. Meulen/Diermanse 709; Willems (Les Elzevier) 1651. PPRF; BN, The Hague: PP. 648/131

Quevedo y Villegas, Francisco Gómez de. Enseñança entretenida, y donairosa moralidad. *Madrid: D. Díaz de la Carrera, for P. Coello,* 1648. 396 p.; 4to. Included is 'El entremetido, la dueña y el soplón', in which are refs to the devils of tobacco & of chocolate, introduced from the Indies. Palau 243569. 648/132

———. El parnasso español . . . donde se contienen poesias. *Madrid: D. Díaz de Carrera, for P. Coello,* 1648. 666 p.; illus.; 4to. Includes sonnet 'Tumulo a Colón: Habla un pedazo de la nave en que describío el Nuevo Mundo'; elsewhere incidental refs to the New World occur. Palau 244329. CU; BN, Madrid:BN. 648/133

Raleigh, Sir Walter, defendant. The arraignment and conviction of Sr Walter

Rawleigh, at the Kings Bench-barre at Winchester. on the 17. of November. 1603. *London: W. Wilson, for A. Roper,* 1648. 38 p.; 4to. Includes refs to Raleigh's voyage to Guiana. Sabin 67545; Brushfield (Raleigh) 164; Wing A3744; JCB (3) II:376. CSmH, CtY, DLC, ICN, MH, MnU-B, NN-RB, RPJCB; BL.   648/134

Reina Maldonado, Pedro de. Apologia por la santa iglesia de Trujillo pidiendo que fuese a gobernarla su obispo D. Pedro de Ortega Sotomayor. *Madrid:* 1648. Medina (BHA) 1126.   648/135

Remonstrance on behalf of the merchants trading to Spain, East Indies, and New-foundland. *London:* 1648. fol. Sabin 69584.
648/136

Rivière, Lazare. Methodus curandorum fe-brium. *Paris: O. de Varennes,* 1648. 247 p.; 8vo. 1st publ., Paris, 1640. DNLM; London: Wellcome.   648/137

Rochas, Henry de. La physique reformée, contenant la refutation des erreurs popu-laires, et le triomphe des veritez philosophi-ques. *Paris: The author,* 1648. 567 p.; 4to. Includes accounts of Columbus's discovery of New World, Spanish conquests there, etc. DNLM, ICU, MH; BL, BN.
648/138

Romances varios. De diversos autores, cor-regido y enmendado en esta tercera [*sic*] impression. *Madrid: Imprenta Real,* 1648. 309 p.; 12mo. Collection 1st publ., Sara-gossa, 1640. Palau 277066.   648/139

Rutherford, Samuel. A survey of the spiri-tuall antichrist. *London: J. D[awson].& R. I[bbitson].,* for A. Crooke, 1648. 2 pts; 4to. Chapt. xv discusses Familists & Antinomi-ans of New England. Sabin 74459; Wing R2394; McAlpin II:599; JCB (3) II:377. CSmH, CtY, DCU, ICN, MH, MiU-C, NN-RB, PPPrHi, RPJCB; BL.   648/140

Saavedra Fajardo, Diego de. L'idea di un prencipe politico christiano . . . traspor-tata dalla lingua spagnuola, dal . . . dottor Paris Cerchieri. *Venice: M. Garzoni,* 1648. 388 p.; illus.; 4to. Transl. from the author's *Idea de un principe christiano,* Munich, 1640. Palau 283473. DFo, ICN, PU; BN.
648/141

Sandys, George. A paraphrase upon the di-

vine poems. [*London:*] 1648. 5 pts; 8vo. In verse. 1st publ., London, 1636, under title *A paraphrase upon the Psalmes of David.* Sabin 76466; Wing S673. CtY, DLC, ICN, InU-L, MH, NNUT, PBL, RPB; BL.
648/142

—[Anr edn]. *London: O. D.,* 1648. 8vo. Wing S674. CtY; Cambridge: UL, Oxford:Bodl.
648/143

Scarron, Paul. Recueil des oeuvres bur-lesques . . . Première partie. *Paris: T. Qui-net,* 1648. 2 pts; 4to. In verse. 1st publ., Paris, 1643, under title *Recueil de quelques vers burlesques.* Magne (Scarron) 10. MH; Paris:Mazarine.   648/144

——. La relation veritable, de tout ce qui s'est passé . . . au combat des parques & des poëtes, sur la mort de Voitture. *Paris: T. Quinet,* 1648. 55 p.; 4to. In verse. In 'Ro-gatum', 'Sauvages Occidentaux' are men-tioned, citing 'les Ameriquains'. Magne (Scarron) 75; Cioranescu (XVII) 61763. ICN, MH; BN.   648/145

——. La suite des oeuvres burlesques . . . Seconde partie. *Paris: T. Quinet,* 1648. 2 pts; 4to. In verse. 1st publ., Paris, 1647. Magne (Scarron) 14; Cioranescu (XVII) 61735. BL, BN.   648/146

——. Typhon, ou La gigantomachie. Poëme burlesque. *Paris: T. Quinet,* 1648. 87 p.; 4to. 1st publ., Paris, 1644. Magne (Scarron) 18; cf. Cioranescu (XVII) 61809. MH; BN.
648/147

——. Le Virgile travesty en vers burlesque. *Paris: T. Quinet,* 1648–53. 7 pts; illus.; 4to. In bk 1 (p. 117), Dido is described as de-manding tobacco to smoke. Magne (Scar-ron) 19, 22, 25, 27, 29, 31, & 33. DLC, MH, NjP, PU; BL, BN.   648/148

Schouten, Willem Corneliszoon van. Dia-rium vel descriptio laboriosissimi & molestissimi itineris. *Amsterdam: [J. Janszoon, the Younger?]* for L. Vlasbloem, at Dokkum, 1648. 71 p.; illus., maps; 4to. 1st publ. in this Latin version, Amsterdam, 1619. Sabin 77959; Palau 305118; Tiele-Muller 49; Tiele 988n. MH; BN.   648/149

—[Anr edn?] *Dokkum: L. Vlasbloem,* 1648. 71 p.; illus., maps; 4to. Sabin 77960. BL.
648/150

——. Journael ofte Beschrijvinghe vande

wonderlijcke reyse . . . Desen laetsten druck verbetert en uyt eenige geschreven journalen van Aris Claessz. en andere . . . vermeerdert. *Hoorn: I. Willemszoon, for M. Gerbrantszoon,* 1648. 56 p.; illus., maps; 4to. 1st publ., Amsterdam, 1618; here added are extracts from three other journals of the same voyage—Sabin. Sabin 77930; Muller (1872) 1960. DLC, MH, NN-RB.

648/151

—[Anr issue]. *Hoorn: I. Willemszoon, for M. J. Appel,* 1648. Sabin 77931; Palau 305091; Tiele-Muller 51; Tiele 989; Muller (1872) 1961; JCB (3) II:378. NN-RB, RPJCB.

648/152

—[Anr issue]. *Hoorn: I. Willemszoon, for J. J. Deutel,* 1648. Sabin 77932; Palau 305092; Tiele-Muller 52; Tiele 989n; Muller (1872) 1960n; JCB (3) II:378. DLC, NN-RB, RPJCB. Issue not differentiated:BL.

648/153

Schultze, Gottfried. Kurtze Welt-Beschreibung. *Lübeck: G. Jäger, for H. Schernwebel,* 1648. 522 p.; 12mo. Includes (p. 212–24) section on New World, discussing places, natural history, & Indian folkways. Scattered American refs occur elsewhere. NNH.

648/154

Seeckere naedere missive, geschreven uyt Brasilien . . . waer in klaerlijck verhaelt wordt het ghevecht het welcke tusschen de onse ende de Portugijsen op den 19 April is geschiedt. *The Hague: L. Breeckevelt,* 1648. 8 p.; 4to. Sabin 7634; Borba de Moraes II:245; Asher 244.

648/155

Serres, Jean de. Le veritable inventaire de l'histoire de France. *Paris: A. Cotinet, J. Roger, & F. Preuveray,* 1648. 2 v.; fol. 1st publ. with American refs, Paris, 1600, under title *Inventaire general de l'histoire de France;* cf. 1606 edn. MH; BL.

648/156

Shepard, Thomas. The clear sun-shine of the Gospel breaking forth upon the Indians in New England. *London: R. Cotes, for J. Bellamy,* 1648. 38 p.; 4to. The 3rd of the Eliot Indian tracts. Sabin 80205; Vail (Frontier) 111; Wing S3109; Church 489; JCB (3) II:378–379. CSmH, CtY, DLC, InU-L, MH, MWA, MiU-C, NN-RB, PHi, RPJCB; BL.

648/157

——. The sincere convert . . . The fifth edi-

tion. *London: R. Cotes, for J. Sweeting,* 1648. 270 p.; 8vo. 1st publ., London, 1640. Sabin 80223; Wing S3122; McAlpin II:602; JCB (3) II:379. MH, MiU, NNUT, RPJCB.

648/158

Solórzano Pereira, Juan de. Politica indiana. Sacada en lengua castellana de los dos tomos del derecho, i govierno . . . de las Indias Occidentales. *Madrid: D. Díaz de la Carrera,* 1648. 1040 p.; fol. Transl. from the author's *Disputationem de Indiarum jure,* Madrid, 1629–39. Sabin 86534; Medina (BHA) 1130; Streit I:513; Palau 318981; JCB (3) II:379. CLL, CtY, DLC, InU-L, MH, NHi, PPL, RPJCB; BL, BN.

648/159

Spain. Treaties, etc., 1621–1665 (Philip IV). The articles and conditions of the perpetuall peace, concluded between the . . . king of Spaine . . . and . . . the States Generall . . . the 13th [i.e., the 30th] of January 1648, at Munster. Printed at Rotterdam by Haest van Voortganck . . . 1648. *London: R. White,* 1648. 28 p.; 4to. Transl. from the *Articulen en conditien* of this year below. For a similar translation, see the *Treatie of peace* of this year below. Wing A3810; Maggs Cat. 502 (Americana VII):5085. CtY, DFo, MH; BL, Oxford:Bodl.

648/160

——. Articulen en conditien van den eeuwigen vrede gesloten den dertichsten Januarii . . . Naer de coppe ghedruckt tot s'Gravenhaghe by de Weduwe . . . van . . . Wouw. *Ghent: S. Manilius,* 1648. 23 p.; 4to. Includes articles of the Treaty of Münster, also publ. under title *Tractaet van vrede,* q.v. below. Present are refs to West Indies & the West-Indische Compagnie. Cf. Knuttel 5733–5736 & 5674–5675. MnU-B.

648/161

—[Anr edn]. *Ghent: S. Manilius,* 1648. 34 p.; 4to. This edn has reading 'eeuwighen vrede, besloten' & 'Naer de copye' on t.p. For contents see Meulman. Meulman 2937. Ghent: BU.

648/162

—[Anr edn]. . . . geslooten tusschen den koninck van Hispaignen . . . ende de . . . Staten Generael. *Rotterdam: 'Haest van Voortganck',* 1648. 30 p.; 4to. Knuttel 5674; cf. Meulman 2935. BL, The Hague:KB.

648/163

—[Anr edn]. . . . geslooten tusschen den

koning. *Rotterdam: 'Haest van Voortgangk',* 1648. 26 p.; 4to. Knuttel 5675; Meulman 2936. CSmH, NN-RB; BL, The Hague:KB.
648/164

—[Anr edn]. . . . gesloten tusschen den . . . koninck. *Rotterdam: 'Haest van Voortgangk',* 1648. 16 p.; 4to. Sabin 52223; Asher 269.
648/165

—[Anr edn]. *Dordrecht: S. Moulaert,* 1648. 24 p.; 4to. NN-RB.   648/166

——. Capitulaciones de la paz hecha entre el Rey nuestro señor, y los Estados Unidos de las provincias de Olanda. *Madrid: D. García Morrás,* 1648. 55 p.; fol. Cf. other versions of this year herewith. Palau 43268. ICN.   648/167

—[Anr edn]. *Madrid: D. García Morrás,* 1648. 32 numb. lvs; 8vo. Rodrigues (Dom. Hol.) 649; Palau 43269. Madrid:BN.
648/168

—[Anr edn]. *Saragossa: P. Lanaja y Lamarca,* 1648. 36 p. Palau 43271.   648/169

——. Tractaet van vrede, beslooten den dertichsten Januarij deses jegenwoordigen jaers . . . binnen de stadt van Munster in Westphalen . . . *The Hague: Widow & Heirs of H. Jacobszoon van Wouw,* 1648. [27] p.; 4to. This edn has the 'Privilegie' on verso of t.p.; the Dutch lion appears below the title. Includes refs to the West Indies & the West-Indische Compagnie. Cf. the *Articulen en conditien,* with similar contents, above. Palau 338556; Knuttel 5733. RPJCB; The Hague:KB.   648/170

—[Anr edn]. *The Hague: Widow & Heirs of H. Jacobszoon van Wouw,* 1648. [26] p.; 4to. This edn does not have the 'Privilegie'. [Locations may include the preceding edn:] DLC, InU-L, MnU-B, N, RPJCB; BL, The Hague:KB.   648/171

—[Anr edn]. . . . besloten . . . *The Hague: Widow & Heirs of H. Jacobszoon van Wouw,* 1648. [28] p., 4to. The 'Privilegie' omitted. Knuttel 5735. The Hague: KB.
648/172

—[Anr edn]. . . . besloten . . . Nae de copye. *The Hague: Widow & Heirs of H. Jacobszoon van Wouw,* 1648. [26] p.; 4to. Vignette of Dutch lion appearing on the t.p. of other edns is here omitted; probably a pirated edn. Knuttel 5726. The Hague:KB (imp.).
648/173

—[Anr edn]. Tractaet van peys. *Brussels: H. A. Velpius,* 1648. 42 p.; 4to. Includes the 'Prokuratien' but lacks the 'Ratificatien' & 'Verkondinge' included in preceding edns. Meulman 2964. Ghent:BU.   648/174

——. Tractatus pacis inter Catholicam suam majestatem et dominos Ordines Generales Provinciarum Unitarum Inferioris Germaniae signatus . . . 30. Januarij . . . anno 1648, e Gallico et Belgico sermonibus, . . . aliisque nuspiam antehac editis . . . translatus a Johanne Cools. *Münster: B. Raesfeldt,* 1648. [64] p.; 4to. Translated in part from the *Tractaet van vrede* of this year above. Knuttel 5738. BL, The Hague:KB.
648/175

——. Traicté de la paix, conclu le trentiesme Janvier . . . 1648. en la ville de Munster. *The Hague: Widow & Heirs of H. Jacobszoon van Wouw,* 1648. [30] p.; 4to. Transl. in part from the *Tractaet van vrede* of this year above, with 2 pts remaining in Dutch. Knuttel 5737. InU-L; The Hague:KB.   648/176

—[Anr edn]. Traicte de paix entre sa majesté catholique et les srs. Estats General des Provinces Unies du Pais-bas. *Brussels: H. A. Velpius,* 1648. [16] p.; 4to. This edn lacks the 'Ratificatien' & 'Verkondinge'. Meulman 2964. ICN; BL, Ghent:BU.
648/177

——. A treatie of peace, concluded the thirteth [*sic*] of Januarie . . . within the city of Munster . . . Translated out of Netherdutch . . . by H. H. according to the original . . . printed by . . . Wauw . . . Anno. 1648. *The Hague: S. Browne* [1648]. 31 p.; 4to. Transl. from the *Tractaet van vrede* of this year above; for a similar translation cf. the *Articles and conditions* of this year above. Wing P1987A. CSmH; BL, Oxford:Bodl.
648/178

Speculatien op't concept van reglement op Brasil. *Amsterdam: S. Vermeer,* 1648. 22 p.; 4to. Includes the articles of the Netherlands Staten Generaal *Concept van reglement* of this year above. Sabin 7636; Borba de Moraes II:275; Rodrigues (Dom. Hol.) 753; Knuttel 5789; JCB (3) II:365. DLC, NN-RB, RPJCB.
648/179

—[Anr edn?]. *Amsterdam: S. Vermeer,* 1648. 14 p.; 4to. Sabin 7637.   648/180

Spilbergen, Joris van. Historis journael van

de voyage gedaen met 3 schepen . . . naer d'Oost-Indien. *Amsterdam: J. Hartgers,* 1648. 96 p.; illus.; 4to. (Joost Hartgers's *Oost en Westindische voyagien* [Pt 5]). 1st publ., Delft, 1601. Tiele-Muller 143; Tiele 1022; Muller (1872) 2255; JCB (3) II:380. DLC, NN-RB, RPJCB; BL, BN.   648/181

——. Oost- en West-Indische voyagie, door de Strate Magallanes . . . onder . . . Spilbergen. Als mede de . . . reyse . . . door Willem Cornelisz Schouten . . . en Jacob le Maire . . . Hoe sy bezuyden de Straet van Magallanes een nieuwe passagie . . . ontdeckt. *Amsterdam: J. Hartgers,* 1648. 120 p.; illus.; 4to. (Joost Hartger's *Oost en Westindische voyagien.* [Pt 8]). 1st publ., Leyden, 1619; here reprinted in a shortened version as 1st publ. in Commelin's *Begin ende voortgang,* [Amsterdam, 1644?]. Here added is Schouten's *Journael,* 1st publ., Amsterdam, 1618. Sabin 89448 (& 77933); Borba de Moraes II:277; Tiele-Muller 71 (& 50); Tiele 1027; Muller (1872) 1972; JCB (3) II:380. NNH, NjP, RPJCB.   648/182

Tabourot, Estienne. Les bigarrures et touches. *Rouen: L. DuMesnil,* 1648. 5 pts; illus., ports; 8vo. 1st publ. in this collective edn, Paris, 1603, q.v. CtY, MH, NNH; BN.   648/183

Tanara, Vincenzo. L'economia del cittadino in villa. *Bologna: Heirs of Dozza,* 1648. 594 p.; illus.; 4to. 1st publ., Bologna, 1644. DLC, MH-A, MiU.   648/184

Taylor, John, the Water-poet. Ἱππάνθρωπος: or, An ironical expostulation with death and fate, for the losse of the late mayor of London. [*London:*] 1648. 4to. In verse. Mentioned are 'potato-pies'. Wing T466. ICN, TxU; BL.   648/185

Tegen-advys, op de presentatie van Portugal . . . 't Eenemael oock dienende om den brant in Brasilien . . . uyt te blusschen. [*The Hague?*] 1648. 7 p.; 4to. Concerns Portugal's treatment of the West-Indische Compagnie, etc. Signed 'P.T.'. Cf. the *Advys op de presentatie* & the *Brandt in Brasilien* of this year above. Sabin 94591; Borba de Moraes II:295; Asher 236; Knuttel 5787. BL (T., P.), The Hague:KB.   648/186

Tomkis, Thomas. Lingua; ofte Strijd tusschen de tong, en de vyf zinnen. *Amsterdam: G. van Goedesberg,* 1648. [64] p.; 4to. Transl.

by Lambert van der Bos from the English text, 1st publ., London, 1607. IU; BL.   648/187

Torsellino, Orazio, S. J. Histoire universelle depuis la creation du monde jusques à l'an 1598 . . . Traduitte de nouveau en nostre langue, et continuée jusques à present par le sieur Coulon. *Paris: G. Clouzier,* 1648,'47. 2 pts; 8vo. 1st publ. as here transl. from 1620 Latin text, Paris, 1622. BL.   648/188

——. Historiarum ab origine mundi usque ad annum 1641 libri x. *Lyons: J. A. Candy,* 1648. 12mo. 1st publ., Rome, 1598; cf. 1620 edn. Backer VIII:152.   648/189

Urrutia de Vergara, Antonio. El maesse de campo Don Urrutia de Vergara, dize: Que aviendo acabado su oficio de Virrey de la Nueva España el marques de Cerralvo, teniendo licencia de bolver à Castilla, le dexò sus poderes [etc.]. [*Madrid:* 1648]. 15 numb. lvs; fol. Memorial to king of Spain. Sabin 98161; Medina (BHA) 6926; Palau 346069. Seville:Archivo de Indias.   648/190

Veer, Gerrit de. Verhael van de eerste schipvaert der Hollandische ende Zeeusche schepen door't Way-Gat. *Amsterdam: J. Hartgers,* 1648. 57 p., illus., 4to. (Joost Hartgers's *Oost en Westindische voyagien.* [Pt 1]). 1st publ., Amsterdam, 1598, under title *Waerachtighe beschryvinghe.* The present abridged version, with added accounts, was 1st publ. as pt of Commelin's *Begin ende voortgang,* [Amsterdam, 1644?]. Added narratives include an account of Hudson's 1609 voyage in search of a Northwest passage, taken from van Meteren. This is a pirated edn; cf. J. Janszoon's edn below. Sabin 98739; Tiele-Muller 101; Tiele 1132; Muller (1872) 2079. NIC, RPJCB.   648/191

—[Anr edn]. Eerste schip-vaert der Hollanderen nae de Oost-Indien door de Waygats. *Amsterdam: J. Janszoon, the Younger,* 1648. 92 p.; illus.; 4to. Includes preface decrying the preceding pirated edn. Tiele-Muller 103; Tiele 1134; Muller (1872) 2080. CLU, NN-RB.   648/192

Les visions de don Queveto Philandri von Sittewaldt [pseud.] Complementum; das ist, Discursus historico politici don Experti Ruperti, von Wunder-Geschichten der Welt. *Frankfurt a. M.: J. G. Schönwetter,* 1648. 776

p.; 12mo. A sequel of unknown authorship to J. M. Moscherosch's *Visiones de don Quevedo*, 1st publ., Strassburg, [1640], though frequently ascribed to him. Includes some American material. Cf. Schönwetter's unauthorized edn, [Frankfurt a. M., 1647], of Moscherosch's work. Jantz (German Baroque) 1822; Bechtold, p. 36–37; Goedeke III:233–34. ICU, NcD; Munich:StB.

648/193

Vondel, Joost van den. De getemde Mars. *Amsterdam: A. de Wees,* 1648. [12] p.; 4to. Poem 'Aen onze vredevaders' includes ref. to 'vier deelen des aertkloots'; the 'Vredezang', p. [9–12], includes refs to Dutch exploration of new worlds & a new ocean. Unger (Vondel) 442. RPB; Amsterdam:UB.

648/194

—[Anr edn]. *Amsterdam: A. de Wees,* 1648, 8 p.; fol. Apparently lacks the 'Vredezang'. Unger (Vondel) 441. Amsterdam:UB.

648/195

Walker, Clement. Anarchia anglicana . . . The first part. [*London?*] 1648. *See the year* 1649.

——. The history of Independency. [*London?*] 1648. 174 p.; 4to. A substantially enl. edn of work of above title in 72 p. publ. earlier in this year. Here are now appended 'Prolegomena' in which Walker states that 'The Independents [in Parliament are] provided by places of retreat to flie to', naming New England, the Bermudas, 'Barbadas, the Carybi Isles, the Isle of Providence, Eleutheria, Lygonia', etc. Also publ. in this year under title *Relations and observations, historical and politick, upon the Parliament begun anno Dom. 1640.* Copies of the two titles are dated by Thomason as of 14 Sept. Also issued, presumably in 1649, under title *Anarchia anglicana . . . The first part.* That the publishing history of this & its related works is more complex than has been previously recognized seems likely, but resolution of the problems is disproportionate to our present purpose. For a continuation of the above work, with title *Anarchia anglicana . . . The second* part, see the year 1649. Wing W329; Thomason I:673. CSmH, DFo, IEN, MH, MnU, NIC; BL. 648/196

——. Relations and observations, historical and politick, upon the Parliament begun

anno Dom. 1640. [*London?*] 1648. 2 pts; 4to. Also issued under title *The history of Independency,* q.v. above. Of this title the British Library records three edns dated as above, of which one has bound with it *The High Court of Justice* dated on p. [72] 28 March 1660 & hence was presumably not printed till that year. Wing W334; McAlpin II:611; Thomason I:673. The locations here given may represent one or more editions: CSmH, CtY, DLC, ICN, MH, NN, PPAmP, RPB; BL, BN. 648/197

With, Witte Corneliszoon de. Copie de trois lettres escrittes du Bresil, par l'Admiral Wit Witsen. *Amsterdam:* [1648]. 4to. Catalogus van boeken VI:214. 648/198

1649

Agustí, Miguel. Libro de los secretos de agricoltura. *Barcelona:* 1649. 4to. 1st publ. in Castilian, Saragossa [1625?]. Palau 4127.

649/1

Alegambe, Philippe, S.J. De vita et moribus p. Joannis Cardim lusitani . . . liber. *Rome: F. Cavalli,* 1649. 12mo. 1st publ., Rome, 1645. Backer I:152. 649/2

Alsted, Johann Heinrich. Scientiarum omnium encyclopaediae, tomus primus[-quartus]. *Lyons: J. A. Huguetan, the Younger, & M. A. Ravaud,* 1649. 4 v.; port.; fol. 1st publ., Herborn, 1630, under title *Encyclopaedia.* KU, MH, MdBJ, NNC; BL, BN.

649/3

Amsterdam. Burgemeester. Copye van de resolutie van de heeren burgemeesters ende raden tot Amsterdam. Op 't stuck vande West-Indische Compagnie. [*Amsterdam?* 1649]. [16] p.; 4to. Third line of title ends 'burgemee-'. For a reply, see the *Examen vande falsche resolutie* of this year below. Sabin 16732 (& 102889); cf. Borba de Moraes I:178–179; Asher 250; Knuttel 6469. DLC, NN-RB, RPJCB; Amsterdam:NHSM, The Hague:KB. 649/4

—[Anr edn]. [*Amsterdam?* 1649?]. [16] p.; 4to. Third line of title ends 'burgemeesters'; title comprises 8 lines. Cf. Sabin 16733; Knuttel 6470. The Hague:KB, Ghent:BU.

649/5

—[Anr edn]. [*Amsterdam?* 1649]. [16] p.; 4to.

Title as in the preceding edn, but comprises 9 lines. Sabin 16733; Asher 251; Knuttel 6471. MWA; The Hague:KB. 649/6

—[Anr edn]. *Utrecht: J. Havick*, 1649. [18] p.; 4to. This edn has reading 'burghemeesters' on t.p. Sabin 16734; Borba de Moraes I:178–179; Asher 252; Knuttel 6472; JCB (3) II:383. DLC, MnU-B, NN-RB, RPJCB; BL, The Hague:KB. 649/7

Amsterdams dam-praetje. *Amsterdam: J. van Soest* [i.e., *J. van Hilten?*], 1649. [39] p.; 4to. Dialogue concerning Portuguese interests versus those of the West-Indische Compagnie in Brazil. Cf. the *Amsterdams vuur-praetje & Amsterdams tafel-praetje* below, as well as the *Amsterdamsche veerman*, 1st publ., Flushing, 1650. Sabin 1351; Borba de Moraes I:27; Asher 263; Knuttel 6477. DLC, MnU-B, NN-RB; BL, The Hague:KB. 649/8

Amsterdams tafel-praetje. *Gouda: J. Corneliszoon* [i.e., *Amsterdam? J. van Hilten?*], 1649. [31] p.; 4to. Dialogue advancing Portuguese cause against the West-Indische Compagnie in Brazil. Sabin 1352; Borba de Moraes I:27; Rodrigues (Dom. Hol.) 69; Knuttel 6479. DLC, LNHT, NN-RB; BL, The Hague:KB. 649/9

Amsterdams vuur-praetje. *Amsterdam: C. Pieterszoon* [i.e., *J. van Hilten?*], 1649. [36] p.; 4to. On F. de Sousa Coutinho's negotiations over Dutch interests in Brazil. Sabin 1353; Borba de Moraes I:27; Rodrigues (Dom. Hol.) 70; Knuttel 6478; JCB (3) II:388. MnU-B, NN-RB, RPJCB; BL, The Hague:KB. 649/10

L'arrivee des ambassadeurs du royaume de Patagoce et de la Nouvelle France . . . Traduit par le sieur I. R. *Paris: Widow of J. Remy*, 1649. 8 p.; 4to. A political allegory attacking Cardinal Mazarin, without American substance. Sabin 10358; Harrisse (NF) 483; Moreau (Mazarinades) 390; JCB (3) II:381–382. DFo, MH, MnU-B, NN-RB, RPJCB; BN (Lb 37.642). 649/11

Avity, Pierre d', sieur de Montmartin. Archontologia cosmica; sive Imperiorum, regnorum, principatuum, rerumque omnium per totum terrarum orbem commentarii . . . Editio secunda. *Frankfurt a. M.: M. Merian*, 1649. 3 pts; illus., maps; fol. 1st publ. as here transl. & ed. by J. L. Gottfried,

Frankfurt a. M., 1628. Sabin 28070. ICN, NNH, WU; Berlin:StB. 649/12

——. Les estats, empires et principautez du monde. *Rouen: J. Cailloué*, 1649. 1466 p.; 4to. 1st publ., Paris, 1613. Sabin 18913n. PPL; BL. 649/13

Bacon, Francis, viscount St Albans. Histoire des vents . . . traduitee par J. Baudoin. *Paris: C. Besongne*, 1649. 222 p.; 8vo. Transl. from Bacon's *Historia naturalis . . . ad condendam philosophiam*, 1st publ., London, 1622. Gibson (Bacon) 113. DFo; BN. 649/14

Barclay, John. Icon animorum oder Gründtliche Beschreibung menschlicher Gemüths Verwirrungen und Endrungen . . . Ins Teutsche auffgesetzet, durch Johann Seyferten. [*Frankfurt a. M.?, for*] E. Berger, at Bremen, 1649. 284 p.; 8vo. Transl. from Barclay's London, 1614, Latin text. Berlin:StB, Danzig:StB, Göttingen:UB. 649/15

Beverwijck, Jan van. Schat der gesontheydt. *Amsterdam: J. J. Schipper*, 1649. 8vo. 1st publ., [Dordrecht? 1636?]. Catalogus van boeken VII:108. 649/16

——. Schat der ongesontheyt; ofte Geneeskonste . . . Neerstelijck op nieuws by den autheur oversien en gecorrigeert . . . het tweede deel. *Dordrecht: J. Braat*, 1649. 553 p.; illus., 8vo. 1st publ., Dordrecht 1644. DNLM, IU; BL. 649/17

Blaeu, Willem Janszoon. Novus atlas, das ist Weltbeschreibung. *Amsterdam: J. Blaeu*, 1649,'47. 2 pts; 120 maps; fol. 1st publ., Amsterdam, 1634; cf. 1635 edn. Issued with Blaeu's *Novus atlas . . . ander Theil*, Amsterdam, 1647. Sabin 5719; Koeman (Bl) 33. MH; Leeds:UL, Amsterdam:NHSM. 649/18

——. Le theatre du monde, ou Nouvel atlas. *Amsterdam: J. Blaeu*, 1649–50. 2 pts; 120 maps; fol. 1st publ., Amsterdam, 1635. The introduction to this edn includes various American refs; America appears in 2 maps. Cf. Blaeu's *Le theatre . . . Seconde partie*, Amsterdam, 1650. Koeman (Bl) 19E. CaOOA (imp.), MHi; Wroclaw:BU. 649/19

——. Theatrum orbis terrarum, sive Atlas novus. *Amsterdam: J. Blaeu*, 1649. 2 pts; 120 maps; fol. 1st publ., Amsterdam, 1635. Issued with Blaeu's *Theatrum . . . pars secunda,*

Amsterdam, 1650. Sabin 5720; Koeman (Bl) 23B. Leyden:UB, Madrid:BN. 649/20

—[Anr edn]. *Amsterdam: J. Blaeu*, 1649–50. 2 pts; 120 maps; fol. Cf. Koeman (Bl) 23B; Phillips (Atlases) 5941. DLC.   649/21

—[Anr edn]. *Amsterdam: J. Blaeu*, 1649–55. 2 pts; 120 maps; fol. Koeman (Bl) 23C. TxU.
649/22

Le bon advis, mesprisé ou la lettre de Mons. Tristan de Mendosse jadis, ambassadeur pour le nouveau eletto don Joan el Quarto . . . Roy de Portugael. Escrite à son successeur l'ambassadeur de Portugal, Francisco de Sousa Coutinho, presente a la Haye. [*The Hague?*] 1649. [8] p.; 4to. A diatribe against the Portuguese ambassador & government at Amsterdam, which opposed the West-Indische Compagnie. Sabin 47832; Borba de Moraes I:96–97; Rodrigues (Dom. Hol.) 653; Knuttel 6476. The Hague:KB, Ghent:BU.   649/23

Bontekoe, Willem Ysbrandsz. Journael, ofte Gedenckwaerdige beschrijvinge van de Oost-Indische reyse . . . Waer by gevoeght is het Journael van Dirck Albertsz Raven. *Utrecht: L. de Vries*, 1649. 78 p.; illus.; 4to. 1st publ., Haarlem & Hoorn, 1646. Sabin 6337 & 67980n; Tiele-Muller 176; Tiele 159n. NN-RB (imp.); BL.   649/24

—[Anr edn]. *Utrecht: Widow of E. W. Snellaert*, 1649. 2 pts; illus.; 4to. Sabin 67980n; cf. Tiele-Muller 178. BL (lacks Raven).
649/25

Bovionier, François. Quaestio medica . . . in Scholis Medicorum, die Jovis ix Decembris, M. Francisco Bovionier . . . moderatore. Estne certa & optima luis venereae per solam hydrargyrosim curatio. [*Paris:* 1649]. 4 p.; 4to. 'Proponebat Lutetiae Robertus Patin . . . M.DC.XLIX'. Disparages use of guaiacum & sarsaparilla for treatment of syphilis. BL (Patin, Robert).
649/26

Boxhorn, Marcus Zuerius. Commentariolus de statu Confoederatarum provinciarum Belgii. *Leyden: P. de Croy, for J. Verhoeve, at The Hague*, 1649. 194 p.; 12mo. Chapt. viii, 'De Collegiis Societatum utriusque Indiae quibus in Orientem aut Occidentem navigatur', includes refs to Brazil & West Indies. IU; BL, BN.   649/27

——. De majestate regum principumque.

Leyden: Boxe Press, for P. Leffen, 1649. 100 p.; 4to. In discussion of King Philip on p. 95, mention is made of ownership of the Indies. IU, MH; BL.   649/28

Braga, Bernardo de, O.S.B. Sermão . . . na festa que fez o mestre de campo André Vidal de Negreiros. *Lisbon: P. Craesbeeck*, 1649. 28 p.; 4to. Includes expression of hope for downfall of Dutch at Pernambuco. Borba de Moraes I:104; Innocencio I:371. DCU, RPJCB.   649/29

——. Sermão que prègou na sé da [Bahia] . . . a 18 de junho de 1644 em a nova publicação da bulla da Sancta Cruzada. *Lisbon: P. Craesbeeck*, 1649. 26 p.; 4to. Borba de Moraes I:104; Innocencio I:371.   649/30

Brasyls schuyt-praetjen ghehouden tusschen een officier, een domine, en een coopman, noopende den staet van Brasyl. '*West-Indische Kamer: Maerten*' [i.e., *The Hague? F. Breeckevelt?*] 1649. [23] p.; 4to. Sabin 7537; Borba de Moraes I:108; Asher 265; Knuttel 6482; JCB (3) II:282. DLC, MnU-B, NN-RB, RPJCB; BL, The Hague:KB.   649/31

Breeden-raedt aende Vereenichde Nederlandsche Provintien . . . Door I. A., G. W. C. *Antwerp: F. van Duynen*, 1649. 45 p.; 4to. Contains refs to Peter Stuyvesant, New Netherland, Brazil, & the West-Indische Compagnie. Sometimes attrib. to Cornelis Melyn. Sabin 26272 (cf. 23521); Vail (Frontier) 112; Knuttel 6481; JCB (3) II:382. CSmH, CtY, DLC, MWiW-C, MiU-C, MnU-B, NN-RB, PHi, RPJCB; The Hague:KB.   649/32

Een brief uyt den Haegh over 't redres vande militie [30 Oct. 1649]. *Utrecht: S. de Roover*, 1649. [8] p.; 4to. In discussing induction, mentions Frisians' refusal to provide subsidy for the West-Indische Compagnie. Knuttel 6492. MnU, NN; The Hague:KB.   649/33

Brouwer, Hendrick. Die fünff und zweyntzigste Schifffahrt, nach dem Königreich Chili in West-Indien. *Frankfurt a. M.: C. Le-Blon*, 1649. 62 p.; illus.; 4to. (Levinus Hulsius's *Sammlung von . . . Schiffahrten*. Pt 25). 1st publ., Amsterdam, 1646, under title *Journael ende Historis verhael*. Sabin 33678 (& 7465); Church 318; JCB (3) I:469. CSmH, ICN, NN-RB, RPJCB; BL, BN.   649/34

Bullock, William. Virginia impartially examined . . . Under which title, is comprehended the degrees from 34 to 39, wherein lyes the rich and healthfull countries of Roanock, the now plantations of Virginia and Mary-land. *London: J. Hammond,* 1649. 66 p.; 4to. Sabin 9145; Vail (Frontier) 113; Baer (Md) 29; Clayton-Torrence 57; Wing B5428; Arents 235; Church 490; JCB (3) II:383. CSmH, CtY, DLC, ICN, MH, MiU-C, NN-RB, RPJCB; BL, BN. 649/35

Cambridge. University. To our reverend and deare brethren the ministers of England and Wales. [*Cambridge?* 1649]. bds.; fol. Dated 24 October 1649; signed by 'Ant: Tuckney, *procan.*' & 11 others. Exhorts clergy to undertake collections on behalf of the Society for Propagation of the Gospel in New-England. Cf. Sabin 34590; William Kellaway, *The New England Company, 1649–1776* (London, 1961), p. 26. Oxford:Worcester. 649/36

Cats, Jacob. 's Werelts begin, midden, eynde. *Leyden: P. de Croy,* 1649. 1 v.; illus.; 12mo. 1st publ., Dordrecht, 1637. Engraved t.p. dated 1645. Mus. Cats. 177. Leyden:UB. 649/37

—[Anr edn]. *Amsterdam: J. J. Bouman,* 1649. 1 v.; illus., ports; 8vo. Mus. Cats. 178. Leyden:UB. 649/38

Clüver, Johannes. Historiarum mundi epitome . . . Editio quinta correctior. *Leyden: F. Moyaert,* 1649. 650 (i.e., 850) p.; 4to. 1st publ., Leyden, 1637. BN. 649/39

—[Anr issue?]. *Leyden: D. López de Haro,* 1649. NNUT. 649/40

Clüver, Philipp. Introduction a la geographie universelle, tant nouvelle, qu'ancienne. Traduitte du latin de Philippe de Cluvier. Dernière édition, reveuë, corrigée & augmentée de figures. *Rouen: J. Berthelin,* 1649. 496 p.; illus.; 8vo. 1st publ., as here transl., Paris, 1631. Cf. Sabin 13805. CU. 649/41

Companhia geral para o estado do Brazil. Articles accordées par le Roy de Portugal, à la compagnie qui s'établit dans son royaume, pour l'estat general du Brazil. Traduit de portugais en françois. *Rouen: J. Besongne, the Younger,* 1649. 26 p.; 4to. Presumably transl. from the *Instituiçam* described below. Borba de Moraes I:42;

Maggs Cat. 479 (Americana V):4281. 649/42

—. De instellinge van de Generale Compagnie ghemaeckt in Portugael, na Brasil, toelatinge met de acte van Sijn Maiesteyt, gepasseert den 10 Meert, 1649. *Amsterdam: Widow of F. Lieshout* [1649?]. [22] p.; 4to. Translated from the following item. Borba de Moraes I:213; Asher 257; Knuttel 6466; JCB (3) II:383. RPJCB; BL (Portugal), The Hague:KB. 649/43

—. Instituiçam da Companhia geral para o estado do Brazil. *Lisbon: A. Alvarez,* 1649. [22] p.; fol. Borba de Moraes I:353. MnU-B, NNH. 649/44

Copie. Gheschreven uyt den Haeghe, den 25 September 1649 . . . uit het Reciffo de Pernambuco in Brasilien, den xxiii Julius, 1649. [*The Hague?* 1649]. bds.; fol. Concerns relief ships equipped by the States General for the West-Indische Compagnie. Borba de Moraes I:177; Rodrigues (Dom. Hol.) 551; Knuttel 6474. The Hague:KB. 649/45

Copie translaet uit het Portogijs, waer in verhaelt wort de vreede . . . tusschen de onderdanen vanden Koningh van Hispanien ende den Koningh van Portugael, by die van Rio Plato. *The Hague: J. Breeckevelt & M. Stael,* 1649. bds.; fol. The original Portuguese text has not been traced. Sabin 16677; Borba de Moraes I:177; Rodrigues (Dom. Hol.) 652; Knuttel 6475. The Hague:KB. 649/46

Culpeper, Nicholas. A physicall directory or A translation of the London dispensatory made by the Colledge of Physicians in London . . . By Nich. Culpeper. *London: P. Cole,* 1649. 345 (i.e., 315) p.; port.; 4to. Transl. & adapted from the 1638 edn of the *Pharmacopoeia Londinensis,* 1st publ., London, 1618, by the Royal College of Physicians of London. Among pharmaceutical ingredients cited are mechoacan, sarsaparilla, & tobacco. Wing C7540; Arents (Add.) 338. CtY-M, DLC, MBCo, NN-A, PPC; BL. 649/47

Dias Ferreira, Gaspar. Epistola Gasparis Dias Fereira in carcere, unde erupit scripta die 17 August. 1649. [*The Hague?* 1649]. 8 p.; 4to. The Portuguese author, long resident in Brazil & made prisoner in the Neth-

erlands, here discusses Portuguese & Dutch policy in Brazil. Sabin 24085; Borba de Moraes I:262; Rodrigues (Dom. Hol.) 454; Knuttel 6467a. The Hague:KB, Ghent:BU.
649/48

——. Een zent-brief . . . den 17. Augustus 1649. Uyt 't Latin overgheset. [*Amsterdam:*] *J. Colom,* 1649. [4] p.; 4to. Transl. from the preceding item. Rodrigues (Dom. Hol.) 454n. Ghent:BU.
649/49

Les divers entretiens de la fontaine de Vaucluse; balet dansé a la Grande Salle du Roure l'année 1649. *Avignon: J. Bramereau,* 1649. 31 p.; 4to. The descriptive text refers to the Americas' doing homage to Europe—cf. P. LaCroix, *Ballets et mascarades* (Geneva: 1868) I:193ff.
649/50

Donne, John. Poems. *London: M. F[letcher].,* *for J. Marriott,* 1649. 388 p.; port.; 8vo. Includes Donne's *An anatomie of the world,* 1st publ., London, 1611. Wing D1868; Keynes (Donne) 81. CSmH, CtY, IU, MH; G. L. Keynes.
649/51

Examen vande valsche resolutie vande heeren burgemeesters ende raden tot Amsterdam. Op 't stuck vande West-Indische Compagnie. *Amsterdam: A. de Bruyn,* 1649. 36 p.; 4to. A reply to the Amsterdam Burgermeester's *Copye van de resolutie* of this year above. Sabin 23344 (& 102890); cf. Borba de Moraes I:253; Rodrigues (Dom. Hol.) 75; Knuttel 6473; JCB (3) II:383. DLC, NHi, RPJCB; The Hague:KB.
649/52

—[Anr edn?]. *Amsterdam: A. de Bruyn,* 1649. 36 p.; 4to. In this printing, the title contains reading 'op't stuck'. Borba de Moraes I:253. DLC, MnU-B, NN-RB; BL (Amsterdam).
649/53

Extract uyt een brief gheschreven in Maurits-Stadt de Pernambuco in Brasil. [*Amsterdam?*] 1649. 8 p.; 4to. Sabin 23511; Borba de Moraes I:257; Rodrigues (Dom. Hol.) 552; Meulman 3078. Ghent:BU.
649/54

Fournier, Georges. Geographica orbis notitia. *Paris: J. Henault,* 1649. 651 p.; 12mo. 1st publ., Paris, 1648; here a reissue of that edn with altered imprint date? Cf. Backer III:910. ICU.
649/55

Franck, Sebastian. Werelt-spiegel, oft Beschryvinge des gehelen aert-bodems, met sijn vier gedeelten, Europa, Asia, Africa, America, &c. Verbetert, vermeerdert . . .

door d. Joh. Phocylides Holwarda. *Bolsward: S. van Haringhouck,* 1649. 652 p.; 4to. 1st publ. in Dutch, [Antwerp? 1550?]; transl. from Franck's *Weltbüch,* 1st publ., Tübingen, 1534. Includes additional 4 pages on America by Holwarda. Sabin 25473; JCB (3) II:386. DLC, NNH, RPJCB.
649/56

Godefroy, Théodore. Le ceremonial français. *Paris: S. Cramoisy & G. Cramoisy,* 1649. 2 v.; fol. Includes mentions of participation of American & Brazilian Indians in royal ceremonies. Copies exist on fine paper. Borba de Moraes I:300–301. CtY, DLC, NjP, RPB; BL, BN.
649/57

Gölnitz, Abraham. Compendium geographicum succinctá methodo adornatum. *Amsterdam: [J. Blaeu? for] L. Elsevier,* 1649. 278 p.; 12mo. 1st publ., Amsterdam, 1643. Willems (Les Elzevier) 1086; Rahir (Les Elzevier) 1098. CSmH, CtY, MiU-C, NN, PU; BL, BN.
649/58

González Dávila, Gil. Teatro eclesiastico de la primitiva iglesia de las Indias Occidentales, vidas de sus arzobispos, obispos, y cosas . . . de sus sedes. *Madrid: D. Díaz de la Carrera,* 1649–55. 2 v.; illus., map; fol. Sabin 18777; Medina (BHA) 1133 & 1235; Streit II:1815; Palau 105289; JCB (3) II:386 & 449. CU-B, CtY, DLC, ICN, MH, MiU-C, NN-RB, RPJCB; BL, BN.
649/59

Grotius, Hugo. A treatise of the antiquity of the commonwealth of the Battavers, which is now the Hollanders . . . translated out of both the Latin and Dutch . . . by Tho. Woods. *London: J. Walker,* 1649. 149 p.; 8vo. Transl. from Grotius's *Liber de antiquitate,* 1st publ., Leyden, 1610; cf. also his *Tractaet vande oudheyt,* 1st publ., The Hague, 1610. Meulen/Diermanse 710; Bibl. Belg. G349. CtY, NIC; BL, The Hague:PP.
649/60

Haerlems schuyt-praetjen op't redres vande West-Indische Compagnie. [*Amsterdam?*] 1649. [23] p.; 4to. Sometimes attrib. to Cornelis Melin. Sabin 7586 & 29505; Borba de Moraes I:327; Rodrigues (Dom. Hol.) 68; Knuttel 6480. DLC, MnU-B, NN-RB, RPJCB (imp.); BL, The Hague:KB.
649/61

Harsdörffer, Georg Philipp. Gesprächspiele achter und letzter Theil. *Nuremberg:*

W. Endter, 1649. 600 p.; illus.; obl. 8vo. Poem on Adam Olearius at end, citing journey to Moscow, judges him 'equal to Columbus & better in skill'. This vol. forms pt 8 of the author's *Frauenzimmer Gesprechspiele*, Nuremberg, 1641. Goedeke III:108; cf. Faber du Faur 502. CtY, DLC, MdBJ, NN; BL. 649/62

Hernández, Francisco. Rerum medicarum Novae Hispaniae thesaurus, seu Plantarum, animalium, mineralium Mexicanorum historia. *Rome: V. Mascardi*, 1649. 950 p.; illus.; fol. 1st publ., Rome, 1628; here a reissue of Mascardi's 1648 edn with altered imprint date? Cf. Sabin 31515; Nissen (Zool.) 1908a; Palau 113537n; Hunt (Bot.) 200. PPiHB. 649/63

Howell, James. Δενδρολογια. Dodona's grove, or The vocall forrest. *London: T. W[arren?] for H. Moseley* [1649]. 2 pts; 12mo. 1st publ., London, 1640. Wing H3061. CSmH, CtY, IU, MH, MiU; BL. 649/64

Ibarra, Alvaro de. Informe en derecho por el illmo. s[eñ]or. dom. fray Christoval de Mancha, obispo de la provincia de Buenos Aires, en defensa de la libertad ecclesiastica, contra los estatutos, que promulgo Don Jacinto de Laris . . . governador del puerto de Buenos Aires. [*Madrid?* 1649]. 7 lvs; fol. Medina (BHA) 6541; Palau 117587; Maggs Cat. 479 (Americana V):4285. Madrid:Ministerio del Ultramar. 649/65

Jansson, Jan. Nouvel atlas ou Theatre du monde . . . divisé en quatre tomes. *Amsterdam: J. Janszoon, the Younger*, 1649. 4 v.; maps; fol. 1st publ. in 4 vols., Amsterdam, 1647. For a 5th vol., see the year 1650. Koeman (Me) 107, 108, 109, 161. BN (v. 1), Paris: DM (v. 2–4), Madrid:BN. 649/66

——. Novus Atlas, das ist Welt-beschreibung . . . abgetheilt in vier Theile. *Amsterdam: J. Janszoon, the Younger*, 1649. 4 v.; maps; fol. 1st publ., Amsterdam, 1638. For variants of v. 2 & 3, see Koeman as cited. The 4th vol. added in this edn lacks Americana. Koeman (Me) 134, 135A, 136A, 135B, 136B (cf. 162–163). CSmH, CtY (v. 2, 3); BL, Marburg:StB. 649/67

——. Novus atlas, sive Theatrum orbis terrarum . . . in quinque tomos distinctus. *Amsterdam: J. Janszoon, the Younger*, 1649–50. 5 v.; illus., maps; fol. 1st publ., in this version,

Amsterdam, 1638, as Mercator's *Atlas novus;* cf. Jansson's 1641 & succeeding edns. Here added is Jansson's *Atlantis majoris quinta pars*, Amsterdam, 1650, also described separately, q.v. Cf. Sabin 35773; Koeman (Me) 60–62, 164; Phillips (Atlases) 459. DLC (v. 1–3); Rotterdam (v. 1–3, 5), Copenhagen:KB (v. 1, 2, 5). 649/68

Jesuits. Historiae Societatis Jesu, pars tertia, sive Borgia. *Rome: M. Manelfi*, 1649. 432 p.; fol. Continues the work 1st publ., Antwerp, 1620. Borba de Moraes II:225; Streit I:516; Backer VII:366. DLC, MnU-B, NNH; BL, BN. 649/69

Joosten, Jacob. De kleyne wonderlycke wereldt, bestaende in deze keyzerrycken . . . het nieuwe Jerusalem en Bresilien, beschreven en door reyst van Jacus Joostz. en Tylg. *Amsterdam: The author*, 1649. 86 lvs.; 8vo. Cf. Sabin 36640; Arents (Add.) 340. NN-A. 649/70

——[Anr edn]. De kleyne wonderlijke werelt . . . *Amsterdam: D. Uittenbroek, for the author* [1649]. 80 p.; port., maps; 4to. Sabin 36640; Borba de Moraes I:363; Rodrigues (Dom. Hol.) 456; Tiele 561; Arents (Add.) 340n; JCB (3) II:387. DLC, NN-RB, RPJCB (imp.); BL. 649/71

Lallemant, Jérôme, S.J. Relation de ce qui s'est passé de plus remarquable ès missions des pères de la Compagnie de Jesus, en la Nouvelle France, ès années 1647. & 1648. *Paris: S. Cramoisy*, 1649. 2 pts; 8vo. The 2nd pt comprises Paul Ragueneau's *Relation de ce qui s'est passé dans le pays des Hurons*. For variants, see McCoy as cited. Sabin 38686; Harrisse (NF) 89; Streit II:2575; Bell (Jes. rel.) 35; McCoy 69–70; Church 493; JCB (3) II:387–388. CSmH, CtY, ICN, InU-L, MH, MWiW-C, MiU-C, MnU-B, NN-RB, RPJCB, ViU; BL, BN. 649/72

Le Blanc, Vincent. Les voyages fameux du sieur Vincent Le Blanc marseillois . . . aux quatre parties du monde . . . rédigez . . . par Pierre Bergeron. *Paris: G. Clousier*, 1649. 3 pts; 4to. 1st publ., Paris, 1648; here a reissue of that edn with cancel t.p. Sabin 39590; Borba de Moraes I:392; Cioranescu (XVII) 41091 (& 11475); JCB (3) II:388. CtY, DLC, IEN, InU-L, NN-RB, RPJCB; BL. 649/73

Le Brun, Laurent, S.J. Ecclesiastes qui ab

Hebraeis Coheleth appellatur, sive Salomonis de contemptu rerum humanarum concio, paraphrasi poetica explicata. *Rouen: J. LeBoullenger,* 1649. 4to. In verse. Presumably includes, under title 'Franciados', Le Brun's *Nova Gallia delphino* on Canada, 1st publ., Paris, 1639. Backer IV:1630. No copy known; cf. 1650 edn.   649/74

Lisle, Francis. The kingdoms divisions anatomized, together with a vindication of the armies proceedings . . . By Franciscus Leinsula [pseud.]. *London: J. Clowes, for Hannah Allen,* 1649. 13 p.; 4to. On p. 1 & 9 John Cotton of New England is cited; on p. 12, John Wheelwright's banishment to colony. Sabin 39934; Wing L2369; McAlpin II:646; Thomason I:727. CLU-C, MH, MiU, NNUT; BL.   649/75

Lyste vande hoge ende lage officieren, mitsgaders de gemeene soldaten, dewelcke in batalie teghens de Portugiesen aen den Bergh van de Guararapes (3 mijl van 't Recif) doot zijn gebleven op den 19 Februarius 1649. [*The Hague? 1649?*]. bds.; fol. Borba de Moraes I:427; Rodrigues (Dom. Hol.) 548; Knuttel 6465. The Hague:KB.
649/76

Maldonado, José, O.F.M. De la autoridad que tiene el Comisario general de enviar comisarios a las Indias Occidentales. *Madrid:* 1649. fol. Medina (BHA) 1138; Streit II:1817; Palau 147694.   649/77

Mendes Silva, Rodrigo. Epitome de la admirable y exemplar vida de D. Fernando de Cordoba Bocanegra. *Madrid: P. Coello,* 1649. 74 numb. lvs; 8vo. Includes refs to Mexico & Central America. Palau 163275. ICN.
649/78

Mendoça, Francisco de, S.J. Viridarium sacrae profanae eruditionis. *Lyons: L. Anisson,* 1649. 360 p.; fol. 1st publ., Lyons, 1631. Backer V:901, Palau 163630n. DCU.
649/79

Montaigne, Michel Eyquem de. Essais. *Paris: M. Blageart,* 1649. 1129 p.; 8vo. 1st publ., Bordeaux, 1580; cf. 1602 edn. Tchémerzine VIII:432. MdBJ, MiU, MnU; BN.   649/80

Nederlandsche West-Indische Compagnie. Aen de . . . Staten Generael. [*Amsterdam?* 1649]. 20 p.; 4to. Request of the company's

participants, with the States General's resolutions of 19 Jan.—26 March 1649. Petit 2533. Leyden:UB.   649/81

Netherlands (United Provinces, 1581–1795). Staten Generaal. Ses poincten. [n.p., 1649]. *See under title below.*

Nieremberg, Juan Eusebio, S.J. Curiosa y oculta filosofia. Primera y segunda parte de las maravillas de la naturaleza . . . Tercera impression anadida por el mismo autor. *Alcalá de Henares: María Fernández, for J. A. Bonet, at Madrid,* 1649. 439 p.; fol. 1st publ., Madrid, 1630; cf. bookseller's 1643 edn. Backer V:1731; Palau 190668. InU-L, TxU; BN.   649/82

——. De arte voluntatis libri sex . . . Accedit . . . Historia panegyrica de tribus martyribus . . . in Urugai pro fide occisis. *Lyons: L. Anisson,* 1649. 2 pts; 8vo. 1st publ., Lyons, 1631. Cf. Medina (BHA) 717; Backer V:1731; Palau 190704. CU.   649/83

Noort, Olivier van. Wonderlijcke voyagie, by de Hollanders ghedaen door de Strate Magalanes. *Utrecht: L. de Vries,* 1649. 67 p.; illus., maps; 4to. 1st publ., Rotterdam & Amsterdam, 1601; cf. 1648 edn. This edn lacks the Roelofsz account of Neck's 2nd voyage. Sabin 55441; Tiele-Muller 22; Tiele 809n; JCB (3) II:389. MH, NN-RB, RPJCB; BL.   649/84

Owen, John. Epigrammatum . . . libri x. *Mainz: N. Heil, the Elder, for J. G. Schönwetter [at Frankfurt a. M.?]* 1649. 90 p.; 8vo. 1st publ., London, 1606. PV.   649/85

Oxford. University. To our reverend brethren the ministers of the Gospel in England and Wales. [*Oxford?* 1649]. bds.; fol. Dated 22 October 1649; signed 'in the name and by the authority of the delegates of the University of Oxford by Ed: Reynolds Vicecan: Oxon'. Exhorts clergy to undertake collections on behalf of the Society for Propagation of the Gospel in New-England. Cf. Sabin 34590; William Kellaway, *The New England Company, 1649–1776* (London, 1961), p. 26. Sabin 58037. Oxford: Worcester.   649/86

Pardoux, Barthélemy. Universa medicina. *Lyons: S. Rigaud,* 1649. 2 pts; 4to. 1st publ., Paris, 1630. BN.   649/87

—[Anr issue?] *Lyons: [S. Rigaud?] for J. Car-*

teron, 1649. DNLM, KyU.   649/88

Paré, Ambroise. De chirurgie, ende opera van alle de wercken. *Amsterdam: J. J. Schipper,* 1649. 940 p.; illus.; fol. 1st publ. as here transl., Dordrecht, 1592; here reprinted from 1604 edn; cf. the 1601 German edn. Doe (Paré) 65. CtY-M, DNLM; Dublin:Trinity, Amsterdam:UB.   649/89

——[Anr edn]. *Amsterdam: G. Willemszoon,* 1649. 940 p.; illus.; fol. A reissue of H. Laurenszoon's 1636 edn with cancel t.p. Doe (Paré) 66. Amsterdam:UB, Groningen-UB.
          649/90

——. The workes of . . . Ambrose Parey, translated out of Latine and compared with the French by Tho: Johnson. *London: R. Cotes & W. DuGard; sold by J. Clarke,* 1649. 781 p.; illus.; port.; fol. 1st publ. as here transl., London, 1634; cf. the 1601 German edn. Doe (Paré) 52; Wing P349. CtY-M, DLC, ICU, MBCo, NNNAM, PPC; BL.
          649/91

Pedraza, Julián de, S.J. Señor. Julian de Pedraza . . . procurador general de las Indias en esta corte . . . dize: Que avendose quexado la provincia de Mexico á V. Magestad, y su Real Consejo de las Indias, de que don Juan de Palafox, obispo de la Puebla de los Angeles despojó violentamente a las tres comunidades que dicha su religion tiene en la dicha ciudad [etc.]. [*Madrid:* 1649]. 4 lvs; fol. Medina (BHA) 6737; Streit II:1825. Seville: Archivo de Indias.
          649/92

Pérez de Ribas, Andrés, S.J. Señor. Andres Perez . . . procurador general a esta corte, y a la de Roma, por su provincia de la Nueva-España, parece, y se presenta con este memorial . . . en razon de dar satisfacion, y responder a ciertas propositiones, que el Obispo de la ciudad de los Angeles don Juan de Palafox y Mendoça, en memorial para V. M[agestad]. presentó primero aqui en Madrid, y despues impresso se ha publicado en la Nueva-España. [*Madrid:* ca. 1649]. 10 lvs; fol. Medina (BHA) 6742; Streit II:1827. Seville:BU.   649/93

Pérez de Rocha, Antonio. Al Rey nuestro señor. Compendio de medios politicas que afianzan todo lo que prometen los siente tratados siguientes. [*Madrid?* 1649?]. 30

numb. lvs; fol. Includes section on 'Crecimiento de la plata de Indias'. BL.
          649/94

A perfect description of Virginia: being, a full and true relation of the present state of the plantation, their health, peace, and plenty. *London: R. Wodenothe,* 1649. 19 p.; 4to. Sabin 60918; Vail (Frontier) 115; Clayton-Torrence 58; Baer (Md) 30; Wing P1486; Church 496; JCB (3) II:389. CSmH, CtY, DLC, ICN, MH, MiU-C, NN-RB, PPL, RPJCB; BL.   649/95

Pigray, Pierre. Epitome des preceptes de medecine et chirurgie. *Rouen: J. Hollant,* 1649. 764 p.; 8vo. 1st publ., Paris, 1600, under title *La chirurgie;* cf. 1604 edn. London:Wellcome.   649/96

De Portogysen goeden buyrman, ghetrocken uyt de registers van sijn goet gebuerschap . . . Dienende tot antwoort op het ongefondeerde Brasyls-schuyt-praetjen. *'Lisbon'* [i.e., The Hague?]: 1649. 15 p.; 4to. A reply to the *Brasyls schuyt-praetjen* of this year above. Sabin 7538; Rodrigues (Dom. Hol.) 492; Asher 266; Knuttel 6483. DLC, NN-RB; The Hague:KB.   649/97

Portugal. Sovereigns, etc., 1640–1656 (John IV). Articles accordées par le Roy de Portugal. *Rouen:* 1649. *See the* Companhia geral para o estado do Brazil *above.*

——. Copye, van een brief van den Koningh van Portugael, gheschreven aen Francisco de Souza Coutinho. *Amsterdam: N. van Ravesteyn,* 1649. 8 p.; 4to. Relates to Brazil. Sabin 16730; Borba de Moraes I:178; Rodrigues (Dom. Hol.) 651.   649/98

——. Declaratie van sijn Koninghlijcke Majesteyt van Portugael Don Juan . . . besloten tot Lisbona den 7 Februarius anno 1649. Gedruckt na de copye tot Lissebon. [*Amsterdam?*] 1649. 3 lvs; 4to. The Portuguese original has not been traced. Relates to Brazil. Sabin 19155; Borba de Moraes I:215; Rodrigues (Dom. Hol.) 797; Knuttel 6464. NN; The Hague:KB, Ghent:BU.
          649/99

Quevedo y Villegas, Francisco Gómez de. Parnasso español. *Saragossa: Hospital Real de Nuestra Señora de Gracia, for P. Escuer,* 1649. 506 p.; 4to. In verse. 1st publ., Madrid, 1649. Jiménez Catalán (Saragossa) 548; Palau 244330. NNH. 649/100

Ragueneau, Paul, S.J. Relation de ce qui s'est passé dans le pays des Hurons. [*Paris:* 1649]. *See* Jérôme Lallemant's *Relation* of this year above.

Relacion de la victoria que los portugueses de Pernambuco alcançaron de los de la Compañia del Brasil en los Garerapes a 19. de febrero de 1649. Traducido del aleman, publicada en Viena de Austria. [*Madrid?*] 1649. 6 lvs; 4to. The text of which this is a translation has not been identified. Medina (BHA) 1140; Rodrigues (Dom. Hol.) 554. MH, NN-RB; BL. 649/101

Remonstrantie van de hooft-partijcipanten ende geintresseerde vande West-Indische Compagnie aen alle de regenten des vaderlandts. [*The Hague?*] 1649. 16 p.; 4to. Sabin 69588 (& 102911); Borba de Moraes II:198; Rodrigues (Dom. Hol.) 76; Knuttel 6468. CSmH, DLC, NN-RB; BL, The Hague:KB. 649/102

Rivière, Lazare. Methodus curandarum febrium. *Gouda: W. van der Hoeve,* 1649. 166 p.; 8vo. 1st publ., Paris, 1640. DNLM. 649/103

——. Praxis medica. *Gouda: W. van der Hoeve,* 1649. 3 pts; 8vo. 1st publ., Paris, 1640. CtY, DNLM, NIC, RPB; BN. 649/104

Robinson, Henry. Briefe considerations. *London:* 1649. *See the year* 1650.

Roca, Juan Antonio Vera Zúñiga y Figueroa, conde de la. Epitome de la vida, y hechos del invicto emperador Carlos Quinto . . . sétima impression. *Madrid: J. Sánchez, for P. García,* 1649. 131 numb. lvs; 4to. 1st publ., Madrid, 1622. Palau 358992. CtY, TxU, WU. 649/105

Rutherford, Samuel. A free disputation against pretended liberty of conscience. *London: R. I[bbitson]., for A. Crooke,* 1649. 410 p.; 4to. Included are refs to the churches of New England & Roger Williams. Sabin 74457; Wing R2379; McAlpin II:666; Thomason I:761. CSmH, CtY, MH, NN-RB, PPPrHi, RPJCB; BL. 649/106

Saavedra Fajardo, Diego de. Idea principis christiano politici. *Brussels: J. Mommaert & F. Vivien,* 1649. 722 p.; illus.; fol. Transl. by the author from his *Idea de un principe*

christiano, 1st publ., in Spanish, Munich, 1640. Palau 283477. CtY, DLC, ICN, NN-RB, PPL; BN. 649/107

Sacchini, Francesco, S. J. Historiae Societatis Jesu, pars tertia. *Rome:* 1649. *See entry under* Jesuits *above.*

Saint-Amant, Marc Antoine de Gérard, sieur de. Les oeuvres. *Rouen: R. Daré,* 1649. 277 p.; 8vo. In verse. 1st publ., Paris, 1629. Tchémerzine X:83. BN. 649/108

——. La Rome ridicule. Caprice. [*Leyden: P. de Croy?*] 1649. 46 p.; 12mo. In verse. For the 1st edn, [Paris,] 1643, see the Addenda (A643/1 & 2). Tchémerzine X:74; Willems (Les Elzevier) 1658. ICU, MH. 649/109

Sánchez, Francisco. Tractatus philosophici: Quod nihil scitur. *Rotterdam: A. Leers,* 1649. 420 p.; 12mo. Includes the author's *Quod nihil scitur,* 1st publ., Lyons, 1581, with refs to New World; cf. 1618 edn. Palau 294101. CLSU, CtY, DNLM, ICN, NjNbS; BL, BN. 649/110

Satyre Ménippée. Satyre Menippée de la vertu du Catholicon d'Espagne. [*Leyden?*] 1649. 206 p.; 12mo. 1st publ. in this version, Paris, 1594; cf. 1612 edn. Willems (Les Elzevier) 1659. NcU; BL. 649/111

Schirmbeck, Adam, S.J. Messis Paraquariensis a patribis Societatis Jesu per sexenium in Paraquaria collecta, annis videlicet M.DC.XXXVIII. XXXIX. XL. XLI. XLII. XLIII. *Munich: L. Straub, for J. Wagner,* 1649. 365 p.; 12mo. Sabin 77636 (& 48157); Streit II:1830; Backer VII:788; Palau 33171; JCB (3) II:390. DLC, InU-L, MH, NN-RB, RPJCB; BL, BN. 649/112

Schouten, Willem Corneliszoon. Journael ofte Beschryving [*sic*] vande wonderlijcke voyagie. *Dokkum: L. Vlasbloem,* 1649. 56 p.; illus., maps; 4to. 1st publ., Amsterdam, 1618. For variant issue see Sabin. Sabin 77934 & 77935; Palau 305093; Tiele-Muller 53; cf. Tiele 989n; JCB (3) II:390. NN-RB, RPJCB. 649/113

Schröder, Johann (1600–1664). Pharmacopeia medico-chymica, sive Thesaurus pharmacologicus. *Lyons: P. & C. Rigaud,* 1649. 3 pts; 4to. 1st publ., Ulm, 1641. NNBG, ViN; London:Wellcome, BN. 649/114

——[Anr edn]. Editio tertia. *Ulm: J. Görlin,* 1649.

2 pts; illus.; 4to. CtY-M, DNLM.

649/115

Ses poincten welcke by de . . . Staten ende alle de steden zijn vast gestelt den 14 Januarij 1649. [*The Hague? 1649?*]. bds.; fol. Relates to the Nederlandsche West-Indische Compagnie. Borba de Moraes II:252; Knuttel 6467; Petit 2532. The Hague:KB, Leyden:UB.

649/116

Siri, Vittorio. Del mercurio, overo Historia de' correnti tempi . . . Tomo secondo. *Geneva: P. Aubert,* 1649. 4to 1st publ., Casale, 1647. Cf. Sabin 81447; Brunet V:402; Graesse VI:417. BL.

649/117

——. Il mercurio, overo Historia de' correnti tempi. *Geneva: P. Aubert,* 1649. 4to. 1st publ., Casale, 1644. Cf. Sabin 81447; Brunet V:402; Graesse VI:417. BL, BN.

649/118

Society for Propagation of the Gospel in New-England. An act for the promoting and propagating the gospel of Jesus Christ in New England. *London: E. Husband,* 1649. [405]–412 p.; fol. The pagination is that of the collection of the several acts of Parliament from 16 January 1649 to 8 April 1653, Thomason II:10. Sabin 52600; McAlpin II:551–552 & 616; JCB (3) II:386. CtY, DLC, ICN, InU-L, MH, MiU-C, NN-RB, PPRF, RPJCB; BL.

649/119

Spain. Treaties, etc., 1621–1665 (Philip IV). Traicté de paix entre sa majesté catholique et les srs Estats Generaux de Provinces Unies du Païs-bas jouxte la copie imprimée a Bruxelles. *Paris: J. Du Crocq,* 1649. 32 p.; 4to. 1st publ. in French, The Hague, 1648. Moreau 3798. MH, NNC.

649/120

Steendam, Jacob. Den Distelvink. Eerste deel, Minne-sang. *Amsterdam: P. D. Boeteman, for G. van Goedesberg,* 1649. 101 p.; 4to. Collection of poems by the 1st poet of New Netherlands, published before his arrival. Continued in Steendam's pt 2 of this year below; for a 3rd pt, see the year 1650. Sabin 91166; Muller (1872) 1092; JCB (3) II:391. DLC, IaU, MWiW-C, NN-RB, RPJCB.

649/121

——. Den Distelvink. Twede deel, Zegenzang. *Amsterdam: P. D. Boeteman, for the author,* 1649. 207 p.; 4to. Continues Steendam's *Den Distelvink. Eerste deel* of this year above.

Includes mention of Piet Hein, Brazil, the Nederlandsche West-Indische Compagnie, & Pernambuco. For a 3rd pt, see the year 1650. Sabin 91166; Muller (1872) 1092; JCB (3) II:391. DLC, IaU, MWiW-C, NN-RB, RPJCB; BL.

649/122

Taylor, John, the Water-poet. John Taylors wandering, to see the wonders of the West. [*London:*] 1649. 21 p.; 4to. Tobacco is mentioned. Wing T528. CSmH, CtY, IU, MH, MnU-B, NNC; BL.

649/123

Thoner, Augustinus. Observationum medicinalium, haud triialium, libri quatuor. *Ulm: J. Görlin,* 1649. 368 p.; 4to. Remedies prescribed employ guaiacum, opobalsam, sarsaparilla, sassafras, & tobacco. CtY-M, DNLM; London:Wellcome, BN.

649/124

Toledo y Leiva, Pedro de, marqués de Mancera. Relacion del estado del gobierno del Peru, que haze el marques de Mancera al señor Virrey Conde de Salvatierra. [*Madrid? 1649*]. 18 lvs; fol. Dated at Lima, 8 Oct. 1648. Maggs Cat. 479 (Americana V):4283.

649/125

Torsellino, Orazio, S.J. Epitome historiarum ab orbe condito usque ad annum 1595. *Cologne: J. A. Kinckius,* 1649. 262 p.; 8vo. 1st publ., Rome, 1598; cf. 1620 edn. MiU-C.

649/126

Walker, Clement. Anarchia anglicana: or, The history of Independency . . . By Theodorus Verax [pseud.]. The first part. [*London?*] 1648 [i.e., 1649?]. 174 p.; 4to. Ostensibly 1st publ., [London?], 1648, under title *The history of Independency,* in its expanded text; apparently a reissue of that edn or that with title *Relations and Observations* here with cancel t.p. to conform with that of *Anarchia anglicana . . . The second part* of this year described below, with which this is normally bound. Wing W315. CU-A, ICN, MH, MiD, MnU, PPPrHi, RPJCB; Cambridge:UL.

649/127

——. Anarchia anglicana: or The history of Independency. The second part . . . By Theodorus Verax [pseud.]. [*London?*] 1649. 254 (i.e., 262) p.; 4to. Continues the author's *The history of Independency.* As with the latter the publishing history of this work is at best uncertain. Thus that edn contain-

ing 262 p. despite its imprint date of 1649 appears to have been printed in 1660. In section no. 24, an army officer is described as detaining members of the House of Commons in 'the Tobacco Roome'. Wing W316. CLU-C, DFo, InU, MH-AH; BL, BN.
649/128

—[Anr edn]. [*London?*] 1649. 256 p.; 4to. Wing W317. CSmH, CtY, DLC, MH, OU, PU, RPJCB.   649/129

Winslow, Edward. The dangers of tolerating levellers in a civill state: or, An historicall narration of the dangerous practices and opinions, wherewith Samuel Green and his levelling accomplices so much disturbed and molested the severall plantations in New England. *London: R. Cotes, for J. Bellamy,* 1649. 103 p.; 4to. 1st publ., London, 1646, under title *Hyprocrisie unmasked;* here a reissue of that edn with t.p. & dedication lf canceled. Sabin 104794; Vail (Frontier) 116; Wing W3035; JCB (3) II:392–393. MB, MH, NN-RB, RPJCB; BL.   649/130

——. The glorious progress of the Gospel, amongst the Indians in New England. Manifested by three letters, under the hand of . . . John Eliot, and another from Mr. Thomas Mayhew jun. . . . Published by Edward Winslow. *London: Hannah Allen,* 1649. 28 p.; 4to. The 4th of the Eliot Indian tracts. Sabin 22152; Vail (Frontier) 114; Wing W3936; Church 497; JCB (3) II:385–386. CSmH, CtY, DLC, ICN, MB, MiU-C, NN-RB, RPJCB; BL.   649/131

Zacutus, Abraham, Lusitanus. Opera omnia. *Lyons: J. A. Huguetan, the Younger & M. A. Ravaud,* 1649. 2 v.; port.; fol. Included are the author's *De medicorum principum historia,* 1st publ., Cologne, 1629, & his *De praxi medica admiranda,* 1st publ., Amsterdam, 1634. DNLM, ICJ, MiU, NIC; BL.
649/132

De Zeeusche verre-kyker. *Flushing:* 1649. [15] p.; 4to. Opposes Dutch policy in Brazil. Sabin 106293; Borba de Moraes I:214; Asher 264; Knuttel 6484; JCB (3) II:393. DLC, MnU-B, NN-RB, RPJCB; BL, The Hague:KB.   649/133

Zesen, Philipp von. Durch-aus vermehrter und zum dritt- und letzten mahl in dreien teilen aus gefartigter Hoch-deutscher Helikon. *Wittenberg: J. Röhner, for J. Seelfisch,*

1649. 3 pts; 8vo. 1st publ., Wittenberg, 1640, but here including (pt 2) a Latin poem dated 12 March 1648 by Johannes Casparus Clusius at Pernambuco, & (pt 3) letter of John Wilhelm Marschalk, Pernambuco, including Marschalk's German poem on Zesen, with refs to the West Indies. Marschalk's encounters with other admirers of Zesen in the Indies are discussed in the letter. Jantz (German Baroque) 2789; Otto 44; Goedeke III:21. CU; Leyden:UB, Göttingen:UB.   649/134

165–?

Clüver, Philipp. Introductionis in universam geographiam, tam veterem quám novam, libri vi. Editio ultima priorib. emendatior. *Amsterdam: Hondius Office* [165–?]. 2 pts; 12mo. 1st publ., Leyden, 1624. Includes also Petrus Bertius's *Breviarium totius orbis terrarum,* 1st publ., Paris, 1624. Cf. Sabin 13805. CSmH.   65–/1

Pedraza, Julian de, S.J. Señor. Julian de Pedraza, procurador general de la Compañia de Jesus de las Indias Occidentales por la provincia del Paraguay. [*Madrid?* 165–?]. 7 numb. lvs; fol. MH.   65–/2

Plaza, Juan de la. Por el maestro Juan Baptista del Campo Claro, canonigo de la iglesia metropolitana de . . . La Plata, en las provincias del Pirù. Sobre que se revoque un auto que proveyò la Real audiencia de aquella ciudad, condenandole en mil pesos ensayados, y se le manden bolver. [*Madrid?* 165–?]. 12 numb. lvs; fol. Medina (BHA) 6762. Santiago, Chile:BN.   65–/3

1650

Aitzema, Lieuwe van. Verhael van de Nederlantsche vreede-handeling. *The Hague: J. Veely,* 1650. 2 v.; 4to. Includes refs to West Indian navigation, & the West-Indische Compagnie. RPB; BN.   650/1

Alsted, Johann Heinrich. Thesaurus chronologiae . . . Editio quarta. *Herborn:* [*Heirs of G. Rab?*] 1650. 691 p.; 8vo. 1st publ., Herborn, 1624. DLC, NN, OU, PPL; BL, BN.   650/2

Amsterdam. Burgemeester. Extract uyttet

register der Resolutien van den heeren bur-germeesteren en de ses en dertigh raden der stadt Amsteldamme. [*Amsterdam:*] 1650. [16] p.; 4to. Includes ref. to the West-Indische Compagnie & Portuguese in Brazil. Cf. Knuttel 6662–6667. Knuttel 6668. NN; The Hague:KB. 650/3

Amsterdams buer-praetje. *Amsterdam:* 1650. [16] p.; 4to. Includes ref. to rebels in Brazil, charging complicity with the king of Portu-gal. Knuttel 6868. MnU-B, NN, WU; The Hague:KB. 650/4

Amsterdamsche veerman op Middelburgh. '*Flushing: J. J. Pieck*' [i.e., *Amsterdam? J. van Hilten?*] 1650. [11] p.; 4to. Defends Portu-guese interests against those of the West-Indische Compagnie in Brazil. Cf. the *Am-sterdams dam-praetje,* 1st publ., Amsterdam, 1649. Sabin 1354 (&102878); Borba de Moraes I:27; Rodrigues (Dom. Hol.) 78; Asher 267; Knuttel 6627. NN-RB, RPJCB; BL, The Hague:KB. 650/5

Angulo, Nicolas de, O. F. M. Señor. Fray Nicolas de Angulo. [*Madrid?* 1650?]. [4] p.; fol. Petition to king of Spain, seeking recog-nition for Franciscan convents in Mexico. BL. 650/6

Avila, Pedro Estevan de. Señor. Don Pedro Estevan de Avila. [*Madrid?* 1650?]. 8 numb. lvs; fol. Memorial to king of Spain, reciting services at Rio de la Plata, i.e., Buenos Aires. BL. 650/7

Bacon, Francis, viscount St Albans. His-toire des vents . . . traduitte par J. Baudoin. *Paris: C. Besongne,* 1650. 222 p.; 8vo. 1st publ. as here transl., Paris, 1649; here a reissue of that edn with altered imprint date. Gibson (Bacon) 114. BL, BN. 650/8

——. History naturall and experimentall, of life and death. *London:* 1650. *See* Bacon's *Sylva sylvarum,* London: 1651.

Bartolommei Smeducci, Girolamo. L'Amer-ica, poema eroico. *Rome: L. Grignani,* 1650. 564 p.; illus., port.; 4to. Celebrates voyages of Vespucci, in imitation of the Odyssey. Sabin 3797; Palau 25119; JCB (3) II:393. CtY, DLC, ICU, MH, NN-RB, RPJCB; BL, BN. 650/9

Bauderon, Brice. Pharmacopee. *Paris: J. Jost,* 1650. 3 pts; 8vo. 1st publ., Lyons, 1588, under title *Paraphrase sur la Pharmacopoee* cf. 1607 edn. DNLM; BN. 650/10

Bauhin, Johann. Historia plantarum univer-salis . . . quam recensuit et auxit Domini-cus Chabraeus. *Yverdon: Typographia Caldo-riana (P. de Candolle),* 1650–51. 3 v.; illus.; fol. Expanded version of Bauhin's *Historiae plantarum generalis novae . . . prodromus,* Yverdon, 1619. For variant issues, see the Hunt catalog. Pritzel 504; Nissen (Bot.) 103; Hunt (Bot.) 251. CU, DLC, ICJ, MH-A, MiU, MnU, NNNAM, PPL; BL, BN. 650/11

Bedenkingen en antwoord op de vrymoe-dige aenspraek aen zyn hoogheit, den heere Prince van Oranje . . . gestelt door den ge-leerden Maximiliaen Teelinck. *Flushing: G. de Laet,* 1650. 21 p.; 4to. A reply to Maximi-liaan Teellinck's *Vrymoedige aenspraeck,* 1st publ., at Middelburg, in this year. Includes section on the West-Indische Compagnie & Brazil. Signed 'O. M. P.'. Knuttel 6862; JCB (STL) 36. MH-AH, MnU-B, NN-RB, RPJCB; BL, The Hague:KB. 650/12

——[Anr edn]. *Flushing: G. de Laet,* 1650. [21] p.; 4to. Includes, at end, a 'Waarschou-winge des schrijvers', a reply to Teellinck's *Onderrichtinge,* stating that his *Vrymoedige aen-spraeck* below corresponds word for word with the dedication to Willem Teellinck's *Den politijcken Christen* of this year below. Knuttel 6863. NN; The Hague:KB. 650/13

Béguin, Jean. Tyrocinium chymicum. *Witten-berg: J. Röhner, for A. Hartmann,* 1650. 480 p.; 8vo. 1st publ., Paris, 1612. CtY-M, DNLM, ICJ, NNC; BL. 650/14

Benavides Bazán, Juan de. Demas de lo ale-gado y advertido por . . . don Juan de Be-navides Baçan en su causa sobre la perdida de la flota de nueva España. [*Madrid?* 1650?]. 6 lvs. fol. Continues the following item. Medina (BHA) 6265 & VII:366. BL. 650/15

——. Señor. Don Juan de Benavides Baçan, general que fue de la flota de Nueva-España que se perdio el año de 628 . . . se postra a los pies de V. Magestad. [*Madrid?* 1650?]. 10 numb. lvs; fol. Petition of king of Spain, defending writer for losses of the Spanish silver fleet in 1628. See also the preceding item. Palau 27182 (dated ca. 1632?). BL. 650/16

Bertius, Petrus. Beschreibung der gantzen

Welt, abgebildet mit sehr schoen cosmogra-
phischen Land-Tafeln. *Amsterdam: J. Janszoon, the Younger,* 1650. 830 p.; maps; obl.
8vo. Except for t.p., identical with 1612
German edn. Sabin 5012; Koeman (Lan)
16; Phillips (Atlases) 5942. DLC.
                                                    650/17

Bickerse beroerten, ofte Hollandtschen
eclypsis teghen den helderen dagheraedt
der provintie van Hollandt. [*Amsterdam?*]
1650. [25] p.; 4to. Topics discussed include
the beleaguered West-Indische Compagnie, which the author supports. This edn
has vignette of Dutch lion on t.p. Knuttel
6845. NN; The Hague:KB.   650/18

—[Anr edn]. [*Amsterdam?*] 1650. [23] p.; 4to.
This edn has type-ornament on t.p. Cf.
Knuttel 6846. NN; The Hague:KB.
                                                    650/19

—[Anr edn]. *Brussels: J. Verdussen,* 1650. [25]
p.; 4to. This edn has reading 'Hollantschen
eclipsis' & vignette of woman on t.p. Knuttel 6843. NN; The Hague:KB.   650/20

—[Anr edn]. *Brussels: J. Verdussen,* 1650. [25]
p.; 4to. This edn lacks vignette. For variant
see Knuttel. Knuttel 6844. The Hague:KB.
                                                    650/21

Blaeu, Willem Janszoon. Le theatre du
monde, ou Nouvel atlas . . . Seconde partie. *Amsterdam: J. Blaeu,* 1650. 2 pts; 92 maps;
fol. 1st publ. in French, Amsterdam, 1635.
Issued with Blaeu's *Le theatre,* Amsterdam,
1647–50. Koeman (Bl) 18E. CaOOA, ICN,
MB (imp.), MHi; Paris: Loeb-Larocque.
                                                    650/22

——. Theatrum orbis terrarum, sive Atlas
novus, pars secunda. *Amsterdam: J. Blaeu,*
1650. 2 pts; 92 maps; fol. 1st publ., Amsterdam, 1635. Issued with Blaeu's *Theatrum,*
Amsterdam 1649. Sabin 5720; Koeman (Bl)
24B; Phillips (Atlases) 5941. DLC; Lei-
den:UB, Madrid: BN.   650/23

——. Toonneel des aerdriicx, ofte Nieuwe
atlas. *Amsterdam: J. Blaeu,* 1649 [i.e., 1650].
2 pts; 120 maps; fol. 1st publ., Amsterdam,
1635. Imprint date inferred from preface
dated 1650. Issued with Blaeu's *Toonneel
. . . tweede deel* below. Cf. edn of [1658],
with initial t.p. dated 1649. Koeman (Bl)
29B. Amsterdam:UB, Leningrad:Saltykov
PL.   650/24

——. Toonneel des aerdrycx, oft Nieuwe at-

las . . . tweede deel. *Amsterdam: J. Blaeu,*
1650. 2 pts; 91 maps.; fol. 1st publ., Amsterdam, 1635. Issued with Blaeu's *Toonneel*
above. For variant American maps see Koeman. Sabin 5721; Koeman (Bl) 30A. NN
(imp.), NcU (imp.), PU (imp.); Amster-
dam:UB, Leningrad: Saltykov PL.
                                                    650/25

——. Zeespiegel . . . verbetert en vermeerdert. *Amsterdam: J. Blaeu,* 1650, '48. 3 v.; illus., maps; fol. 1st publ., Amsterdam, 1623.
Pt 2 has a 1648 imprint date. Koeman
(M.Bl) 44; Tiele 126. Oxford:Bodl., BN.
                                                    650/26

Boccalini, Traiano. De' ragguagli di Parnaso
. . . Centuria prima. *Venice: Heirs of G. Gue-
rigli,* 1650. 8vo. 1st publ., Venice, 1612.
Firpo (Ragguagli) 21; Michel (Répertoire)
I:176. KMK, MWA; Rouen:BM.
                                                    650/27

——. De' ragguagli di Parnaso . . . Centuria
seconda . . . ottava [*sic*] impressione. *Venice:
Heirs of G. Guerigli,* 1650. 292 p.; 8vo. 1st
publ., Venice, 1615; issued with the Guerigli Centuria prima of this year above.
Firpo (Ragguagli) 21; Michel (Répertoire)
I:176. KMK, MWA; Rouen:BM.   650/28

Bodin, Jean. Methodus ad facilem historiarum cognitionem. *Amsterdam: J. Ravestein,*
1650. 412 p.; 12mo. 1st publ., Paris, 1566;
cf. 1607 edn. CLSU, IU, N, NcD, PU; BL,
BN.   650/29

Boissard, Jean Jacques. Bibliotheca chalcographica, illustrium virtute atque eruditione
in tota Europa clarissimorum virorum.
Frankfurt a. M.: J. Ammon, 1650–54. 9 pts;
ports; 4to. 1st publ., Frankfurt a. M., 1597–
99, under title *Icones virorum illustrium doctrina et eruditione;* cf. 1628–31 edn. Graesse
I:475; JCB (3) II:394. CSmH, DCU, MH,
MnU-B, RPJCB; BL, BN.   650/30

Bontekoe, Willem Ysbrandsz. Journael ofte
Gedenckwaerdige beschrijvinge van de
Oost-Indische reyse . . . Waer by gevoeght
is het Journael van Dirck Albertsz Raven.
Amsterdam: C. Cunradus, for J. Hartgers, 1650.
76 p.; illus.; 4to. (Joost Hartgers's *Oost en
West-Indische voyagien.* [Pt 10]). 1st publ.,
Haarlem & Hoorn, 1646. Sabin 67980n;
Tiele-Muller 177. DLC, NN-RB; BL.
                                                    650/31

—[Anr edn?]. Verhael van de avontuerlijke

reyse . . . Journael van de reyse gedaen by
. . . Raven, naer Groen-landt. *Amsterdam:
J. Hartgers,* 1650. 76 p.; illus.; 4to. BN.
650/32

A booke of cookerie. *London: Jeane Bell,*
1650. 102 p.; 8vo. 1st publ., London, 1620.
Wing B3705. BL. 650/33

Botero, Giovanni. Relationi universali. *Ven-*
ice: The Giuntas, 1650. 800 p.; map; 4to. 1st
publ., Rome, 1591–96; cf. 1601 edn. Cf.
Sabin 6806n. RPJCB. 650/34

Boxhorn, Marcus Zuerius. Commentariolus
de statu Confoederatum provinciarum Belgii. Editio secunda. *Leyden: P. de Croy, for*
J. Verhoeve, at The Hague, 1650. 3 pts; 12mo.
1st publ., Leyden & The Hague, 1649.
CSmH, IU, MH; BL, BN. 650/35

—[Anr edn]. Editio tertia. *Leyden: P. de Croy,*
for J. Verhoeve, at The Hague, 1650. 3 pts;
12 mo. BN. 650/36

Bradstreet, Anne (Dudley). The tenth muse
lately sprung up in America . . . Also a dialogue between old England and new, concerning the late troubles. *London: S. Bowtell,*
1650. 207 p.; 8vo. In verse. Sabin 7296;
Wegelin (Poetry) 28; Grolier Club (Langland to Wither) 56; Wing B4167; Church
498; Thomason I:804; JCB (3) II:395.
CSmH, CtY, DLC, InU-L, MB, MiU-C, NN-
RB, RPJCB; BL. 650/37

Breton, Nicholas. A poste with a packet of
mad letters. *London: J. Marriott* [1650?]. 2
pts; 4to. 1st publ., London, 1602–5. Wing
B4387. BL, Oxford: Bodl. 650/38

Brouwer, Hendrick. Journael ende historis
verhael van de reyse gedaen . . . naer de
custen van Chili. *Amsterdam: J. Bouman*
[1650?]. 104 p.; illus.; 4to. 1st publ., Amsterdam, 1646. BL. 650/39

Browne, Sir Thomas. Pseudodoxia epidemica: or, Enquiries into very many received
tenents and commonly presumed truths.
The second edition, corrected and much
enlarged. *London: A. Miller, for E. Dod & N.*
Ekins, 1650. 329 p.; 4to. 1st publ., London,
1646. Keynes (Browne) 74; Wing B5160.
CSmH, CtY, DLC, IEN, InU-L, MWA,
MnU-B, NNNAM, PPL; BL. 650/40

Calderón, Juan Alonso. Memorial historico,
juridico, politico, de la s. iglesia catedral
de la Puebla de los Angeles, en la Nueva-
España. Sobre restituirla las armas reales

de Castilla, Leon, Aragon, y Navarra. [*Ma-*
drid? ca. 1650]. 89 numb. lvs; illus.; fol. The
royal arms had been placed at the altar by
Juan Palafox y Mendoza as bishop but were
removed by civil authorities. Medina (BHA)
6293; Palau 39726. MB, NN-RB, RPJCB;
BL, Seville:BU. 650/41

Calvisius, Seth. Opus chronologicum . . .
Editio quarta emendatior. *Frankfurt a. M.*
& Emden: C. Gerlach & S. Beckenstein, 1650.
1030 p.; fol. 1st publ., Leipzig, 1605, under
title *Chronologia.* CU, DLC, ICU, MnU, PPL,
RPB; BL. 650/42

Camerarius, Philipp. Operae horarum sub-
cisivarum, sive Meditationes historicae . . .
Centuria ii. *Frankfurt a.M.: J. F. Weiss, for*
J. Wild, 1650. 4to. 1st publ., Frankfurt a.
M., 1601. NjP. 650/43

——. Operae horarum subcisivarum, sive
Meditationes historicae . . . Centuria tertia.
Frankfurt a. M.: J. F. Weiss, for J. Wild, 1650.
379 p.; 4to. 1st publ., Frankfurt, a. M., 1609.
NjP, OClW. 650/44

Conveniencias en la institucion del comis-
sario general en esta corte, y de vicarios
generales en las provincias de Indias, del
Orden de San Agustin. [*Madrid?* ca. 1650?].
2 numb. lvs; fol. Relates specifically to
Spanish America. RPJCB. 650/45

Cotgrave, Randle. A French-English dic-
tionary . . . with another in English and
French, whereunto are newly added the ani-
madversions and supplements . . . of
James Howell. *London: W. H[unt]. for M. M.*
T. C. & G. Bedell, 1650. 2 pts; fol. 1st publ.,
London, 1611. Wing C6376. CSmH, CtY;
Cambridge:UL. 650/46

—[Anr issue]. *London: W. H[unt]., for L. Fawne,*
1650. Wing C6377D. ICN, IU. 650/47

—[Anr issue]. *London: W. H[unt]., for G. La-*
tham, 1650. Wing C6377A. DFo. 650/48

—[Anr issue]. *London: W. H[unt]., for O. Pul-*
leyn, 1650. Wing C6375. BL. 650/49

—[Anr issue]. *London: W. H[unt]., for H. Robin-*
son, 1650. Wing C6377C. Cambridge:
King's. 650/50

—[Anr issue]. *London: W. H[unt]., for A. Roper,*
1650. Wing C6377B. MBAt. 650/51

—[Anr issue]. *London: W. H[unt]., for R. Whit-*
aker, 1650. Wing C6374. ICN, NjP, OU.
650/52

—[Anr issue]. *London: W. H[unt]., for J. Wil-*

liams, 1650. Wing C6377. DFo, NNC, TxU; BL, Oxford:Chr. Ch.   650/53

Cotton, John. Of the holinesse of church-members. *London: F. N[eile?]., for Hannah Allen,* 1650. 95 p.; 4to. Includes refs to Boston, New England, & lower religious status of Indians. Sabin 17073; Tuttle (Cotton) 61; Wing C6448; JCB (3) II:396. CSmH, CtY, DLC, MH, NNUT, RPJCB; BL, Oxford:Bodl.   650/54

Cramer, Barent. Voor-looper van d'hr. Witte Cornelissz. de With, admirael van de West-Indische Compagnie, nopende den Brasijlschen handel. *[Amsterdam?]* 1650. [20] p.; 4to. Dated 30 May 1650. Sabin 100772 & 104925; Borba de Moraes II:362; Asher 270; Knuttel 6628. DLC; BL (With, Witte de), The Hague:KB.   650/55

Culpeper, Nicolas. A physical directory: or a translation of the dispensatory made by the Colledge of Physitians of London . . . The second edition, much enlarged. *London: P. Cole,* 1650. 242 (i.e., 212) p.; port.; fol. 1st publ. as here transl., London, 1649; for the Latin text, see the year 1618. Wing C7541. CSmH, CtY-M, MH, PPL; London: Wellcome.   650/56

Los daños que se seguirian que la plata corriente con que se ha comerciado en las provincias del nuevo reyno de Granada se consumiesse en su lugar moneda provincial. *[Seville? 1650?].* [4] p.; BL.   650/57

Donck, Adriaen van der. Vertoogh van Nieu-Neder-Land. Weghens de gheleghentheydt, vruchtbaerheydt, en soberen staet desselfs. *The Hague: M. Stael,* 1650. 49 p.; 4to. Sabin 20595; Vail (Frontier) 117; Church 499; Asher 5; JCB (3) II:396. CSmH, DLC, ICN, MWiW-C, MiU-C, NNRB, RPJCB; BL, Ghent:BU.   650/58

Donne, John. Poems. *London: J. Marriott; & sold by R. Marriott,* 1650. 392 p.; port.; 8vo. Includes Donne's *An anatomie of the world,* 1st publ., London, 1611. Wing D1869; Keynes (Donne) 82. CtY, DFo, ICN, MH, NNC; BL, BN.   650/59

Earle, John, Bp of Salisbury. Micro-cosmographie. or, A piece of the world characteri'd . . . *London: W. Bentley, for W. Sheares,* 1650. 105 p.; 12mo. 1st publ., London, 1628. Wing E88; Murphy (Engl. char.-bks) 41. ICN; BL.   650/60

—[Anr edn]. *London: W. Bentley, for W. Sheares,* 1650. 131 p.; 12mo. Wing E89; Murphy (Engl. char.-bks) 41–42. BL.   650/61

I. [i.e., Eerste] Conferentie van eenige Nederlandtsche heeren op den tegenwoordigen staet deser landen. *Middleburg: 'J. de Laet',* 1650. [33] p.; 4to. Includes ref. to Count Johan Maurits of Nassau's fame in Europe, Africa, & America, as soldier & governor, mentioning the West-Indische Compagnie. Knuttel 6899. MnU-B, NN, WU; The Hague:KB.   650/62

Eerste schip-vaert der Hollanders naer Oost-Indien. *Amsterdam: J. Hartgers,* 1650. 102 p.; illus.; 4to. (Joost Hartgers's *Oost en Westindische voyagien,* [Pt 2]). 1st publ. in this separate version, Amsterdam, 1648. Tiele-Muller 121; Tiele 512n; Muller (1872) 2172; JCB (3) II:397. DLC, NHi, RPJCB.   650/63

Estienne, Charles. Dictionarium historicum, geographicum, poeticum. *Geneva: J. Stoer,* 1650. 2110 cols; 4to. 1st publ. in this enl. edn, Lyons, 1595; cf. 1601 edn. CU, IaU, MH.   650/64

Extract eens briefs uyt Vlissingen; inhoudende een roef-praatje. *The Hague: D. H. van Waalsdorp [i.e., Antwerp: H. Verdussen]* 1650. 24 p.; 4to. Includes refs to the West-Indische Compagnie & Brazil. Knuttel 6855. MnU-B, NN, RPJCB, WU; The Hague:KB.   650/65

Extract uyt een brief gheschreven aen . . . de . . . Staten Generael der Vereenighde Nederlanden . . . verhalende den grooten rijckdom vande silver-mijne inde capitania van Siara gelegen. *Leyden: C. Banheyning,* 1650. bds.; fol. Borba de Moraes I:257; Knuttel 6629. The Hague:KB.   650/66

Fernández Rebolledo, Rodrigo. Contiene este papel la forma que parece se podra tomar, para que . . . se pueda reformar . . . la moneda labrada en Potosí. *[Seville? 1650].* 9 numb. lvs; fol. 'Fecho en Sevilla a doze de Octubre de 1650'. Medina (BHA) 1145. BL.   650/67

Figueroa, Juan de. Juan de Figueroa, regidor de la ciudad de los Reyes, en el Perù. *[Madrid? 1650?].* 3 numb. lvs; fol. Defense against charges brought against author. BL.   650/68

Forest du Chesne, Nicolas. Florilegium

universale liberalium artium et scientiarum. *Paris: A. Lesselin,* 1650. 576 p.; illus.; 4to. In tract 12, section xxv treats briefly 'De partibus novi orbis'. BL, BN. 650/69

Foster, Nicholas. A briefe relation of the late horrid rebellion acted in the island Barbadas, in the West Indias . . . Acted by the Waldronds and their abettors, anno 1650. *London: J. G[rismond]., for R. Lowndes & R. Boydell,* 1650. 112 p.; 8vo. Sabin 25260; Handler (Barbados) 2; Wing F1627; JCB (3) II:396. CSmH, CtY, DLC, MH, MWA, MiU-C, NN-RB, PPL, RPJCB; BL. 650/70

Garcilaso de la Vega, el Inca. Histoire des guerres civiles des Espagnols dans les Indes . . . Escrite en espagnol . . . et mise en françois, par J. Baudoin. *Paris: A. Courbé & E. Couterot,* 1650. 2 v.; 4to. Transl. from the author's *Historia general del Peru,* 1st publ., Córdova, 1617. Sabin 98750; Medina (BHA) 658n (II:165); Palau 354827; JCB (3) II:398. DLC, MB, NN-RB, RPJCB. 650/71

De gesteeurde Hollantsche leeuw, ofte het belegerde Amsterdam [*sic*]. [*The Hague?*] 1650. [28] p.; 4to. Includes ref. to military service in Brazil. Knuttel 6865. NN; The Hague:KB. 650/72

—[Anr edn]. De gesteeurde Hollantsche leeuw, ofte het belegerde Amsterdam . . . Gedruckt na de copye van den Haegh. [*Amsterdam?*] 1650. [28] p.; 4to. Knuttel 6866. NN; The Hague:KB. 650/73

—[Anr state of preceding]. [*Amsterdam?*] 1650. [28] p.; 4to. To the title has been added 'als mede de . . . geboorte van den . . . Prins van Orangien'. Knuttel 6867; Meulman 3170. The Hague:KB, Ghent:BU. 650/74

Gómez Tejada de los Reyes, Cosmé. El filosofo. Ocupacion de nobles, y discretos contra la cortesana ociosidad. *Madrid: D. García Morrás, for S. Martín Véllaz,* 1650. 140 numb. lvs; 4to. In bk 1 chapt. ix describes 'Como pasaron á las Indias Occidentales hombres y brutos'. Medina (BHA) 1146; Palau 104494. BL, Santiago, Chile:BN. 650/75

Great Britain. Laws, statutes, etc., 1649–1660 (Commonwealth). An act for charging of tobacco brought from New-England

with custome and excise. [*London:* 1650]. [2] p.; fol. At head of title: Die Iovis 20 Iunii 1650. Sabin 52599; Wing E1004A; Arents 237; JCB AR32:9–12. NN-A, RPJCB. 650/76

——. An act prohibiting trade with the Barbada's, Virginia, Bermuda's and Antego; die Jovis, 30 Octobr. 1650. *London: E. Husband & J. Field,* 1650. [1025]–1034 p.; fol. With paging of volume entered in Thomason (II:10) as *A collection of the several actes of Parliament from the 16 of January 1649 to the 8 of April 1653* this act was manifestly also issued separately. This item was unknown to Steele while he compiled the Crawford catalogue of Royal proclamations; Sabin's description of it as a folio broadside is probably in error. Sabin 145; Clayton-Torrence 59; McAlpin II:679. MnU-B, NNUT, RPJCB, ViU; BL. 650/77

——. Een acte van het Parlament van Engelandt, verbiedende den handel met die vande Barbades, Verginia, Bermudes ende Antigos, die Jovis 3. October, 1650 . . . Naer de copie tot London, gheprent by Edwaerd Hus-band aud [*sic*] Joan Field. [*Amsterdam?* 1650?]. 8 p.; 4to. Transl. from *An act prohibiting trade with the Barbada's* of this year above. Cf. Sabin 145. RPJCB. 650/78

—[Anr edn]. Een acte, verbiedende den handel met de Barbadas, Virginia, Bermudas ende Antego . . . Wt het Engels . . . overgheset door I[saac?]. B[urchoorn?]. *Rotterdam: M. Wagens* [1650?]. 8 p.; 4to. Petit 2545. Leyden:B. Thysiana. 650/79

Grotius, Hugo. Annotationum in Novum Testamentum pars tertia et ultima. Cui subiuncti sunt eiusdem auctoris libri pro veritate religionis Christianae. *Paris: Widow of T. Pepingué & S. Maucroy,* 1650. 2 pts; 4to. Includes Grotius's *De veritate religionis christianae,* with special t.p., separate signatures & paging, also issued separately below. Meulen/Diermanse 1141 (Cf. 954). ICU, NN-RB, Wa; BN, The Hague:PP. 650/80

——. De jure belli ac pacis libri tres . . . Editio nova. *Amsterdam: J. Blaeu,* 1650. 618 p.; 8vo. 1st publ., Paris, 1625. Meulen/Diermanse 574. CtY, DLC, OO; BL, The Hague:PP.   650/81

——. De veritate religionis christianae. . . . Editio novissima. *Paris:* [*Widow of T. Pepingué & S. Maucroy?*] 1650. 205 p.; 4to. 1st publ., Leyden, 1627, under title *Sensus librorum sex;* also issued as pt of Grotius's *Annotationum* of this year above. Meulen/Diermanse 954. BN, The Hague:PP.   650/82

—[Anr edn]. Editio decima additis annotationibus, in quibus testimonia. *Oxford: W. Webb,* 1650. 416 p.; 8vo. Wing G2100; Madan (Oxford) II:2032 & III, p. 465–466; Meulen/Diermanse 955. MB, NNUT; BL, Oxford:Corpus.   650/83

Guidi, Ippolito Camillo. Relation de ce qui s'est passé en Espagne, à la disgrace du comte-duc d'Olivares. Traduite d'italien. *Paris: A. Courbé,* 1650. 157 p.; 8vo. Transl. by A. Félibien des Avaux from Guidi's *Caduta del conte d'Olivares,* Ivrea, 1644. BL.   650/84

Harsdörffer, Georg Philipp. Nathan und Jotham: das ist Geistliche und weltliche Lehrgedichte . . . durch ein Mitglied der . . . Fruchtbringenden Gesellschaft. [Theil 1–2]. *Nuremberg: N. Endter,* 1650–51. 2 pts; 8vo. In verse. Pt 1 includes poems on turkeys ('Die Indianischen Haanen') & tobacco; section 'Die Faulheit' in pt 2 describes behavior of South American sloth, setting its 'song' to music. Goedeke III:109; Faber du Faur 506; Wolfenbüttel 126. CSt (pt 1), CtY, MH (pt 1); Wolfenbüttel:HB, Göttingen:UB.   650/85

Helwig, Johann. Die Nymphe Noris in zweyen Tagzeiten vorgestellet. *Nuremberg: J. Dümler,* 1650. 197 p.; illus.; 4to. Includes refs to America. Jantz (German Baroque) 1325; Faber du Faur 556; Goedeke III:112. CU, CtY, ICU, NcD, NjP, WU; BL (Noris), Göttingen:StUB.   650/86

Heurne, Johan van. Praxis medicinae nova ratio . . . Ex accurata recensione Zachariae Sylvii. *Rotterdam: A. Leers,* 1650. 721 p.; illus.; 8vo. 1st publ., Leyden, 1587; cf. 1609 edn. CtY, DNLM; London:Wellcome, BN.   650/87

Holland (Province). Staten. Brief vande groot-mog: heeren Staten van Hollandt ende West-Vrieslandt aen de respective provincien . . . nopende de cassatie van de militie. [*The Hague?*] 1650. [8] p.; 4to. Includes discussion of subsidy for the West-Indische Compagnie's defense of Brazilian conquests. Knuttel 6675. NN; The Hague:KB.   650/88

—[Anr edn]. Missive van . . . de . . . Staten van Hollandt . . . aen alle de andere . . . Provintie [*sic*]. *Rotterdam: J. Verburch,* 1650. 12 p.; 4to. Knuttel 6676. The Hague:KB.   650/89

—[Anr edn]. Missive aende Staten vande Provintien. [*Amsterdam?*] 1650. [8] p.; 4to. Knuttel 6677. MnU-B, NN; The Hague:KB.   650/90

—[Anr edn]. Copie van een missive, gesonden by de Staten van Hollandt, den 27. July 1650 aen de . . . Provintien. [*Amsterdam?*] 1650. [8] p.; 4to. Knuttel 6678. MnU-B, NN; The Hague:KB.   650/91

——. Extract uyt de resolutien vande ed. groot mo: heeren Staten van Hollant ende West-Frieslant, genomen den 10. ende 11. November 1650. Gedruckt nae 't extract. [*Amsterdam?*] 1650. [5] p.; 4to. Relates to maintenance of the West-Indische Compagnie. Knuttel 6731. MnU-B, NN; The Hague:KB.   650/92

——. Provintiael advijs van Hollant ende West-Frieslandt roerende de ratificatie van de tractaten, jongst met . . . Deenemarken aengegaen; mitsgaders het offensijf secours vande Compagnie van West-Indien. *Amsterdam: J. Pieterszoon,* 1650. 6 p.; 4to. Amsterdam:NHSM.   650/93

't Hollandts rommelzootje, vertoonende de gantsche ghelegentheyd van het benaudt, ontzet, en gewapent Amsterdam. [*Amsterdam?* 1650]. [8] p.; 4to. In verse. Refers to capture of two Spanish fleets, & to Brazilian sugar trade. Knuttel 6783. MnU-B, NN; The Hague:KB.   650/94

—[Anr edn]. [*Amsterdam?* 1650]. [8] p.; 4to. T.p. includes reading 'benaaudt'. Knuttel 6782. The Hague:KB.   650/95

Howell, James. Epistolae Ho-elianae. Familiar letters domestic and forren . . . The second edition, enlarged. *London: W. H[unt]., for H. Moseley,* 1650. 3 pts; 8vo. Comprises text 1st publ., London, 1645, & the *New Volume of letters,* London, 1647, with the addition here of a 3d pt, in which letter vii, accompanying a 'parcel of Indian perfume', i.e., tobacco, discusses its therapeutic uses, quoting Raphael Thorius's *Hymnus tabaci*. In turn, letter xxx mentions Madog's West Indian voyages. Wing H3072; Arents 238. CSmH, CtY, DFo, ICN, MH, MnU-B, NN-A; BL, BN. 650/96

Hudson, Samuel. A vindication of the essence and unity of the church catholike visible. *London: A. M[athewes]., for C. Meredith,* 1650. 265 p.; 4to. Included are refs to the churches & brethren of New England, as well as to the writings of clergy resident there. Sabin 33496; Wing H3266; McAlpin II:703–704. CtY, MH, MWA, NNUT, PPPrHi; BL. 650/97

Hunt, Robert, Lieut. Col. The island of Assada, near Madagascar impartially defined. *London: N. Bourne* [1650]. 8 p.; 4to. The author mentions having been governor in the Bahamas, and compares Madagascar with Barbados. Wing H3744; Thomason I:808; Maggs Cat. 502 (Americana VII):5093. CSmH, OCl; BL. 650/98

Jansson, Jan. Atlantis majoris quinta pars. *Amsterdam: J. Janszoon, the Younger,* 1650. 1 v.; maps; fol. Includes maps showing Hispaniola, Cuba, Puerto Rico, etc. Intended for sale as pt 5 of Jansson's *Novus atlas*, Amsterdam, 1649 (q.v.), and as a supplementary volume to Jansson's 1646–47 edn. Koeman (Me) 164. ICN; Madrid:BN. 650/99

——. Cinquiesme partie du Grand atlas contenant une parfaicte description du monde maritime. *Amsterdam: J. Janszoon, the Younger,* 1650. 1 v.; maps; fol. Transl. from Jansson's *Atlantis majoris quinta pars* of this year above. Intended as a supplement to Jansson's *Nouvel Atlas,* Amsterdam, 1649. Koeman (Me) 171. MnU-B; BN, Amsterdam:NHSM. 650/100

——. Das fünffte Theil des Grossen Atlantis, welches begreiffet die Wasser Welt, das ist: Eine sehr kunstreiche Abbildung . . . alles Wasser und Meeren. *Amsterdam: J. Janszoon, the Younger,* 1650. 1 v.; maps; fol. Transl. from Jansson's *Atlantis majoris quinta pars.* Intended as a supplement to Jansson's *Novus Atlas,* Amsterdam, 1649. Koeman (Me) 174. CtY. 650/101

——. Het vijfde deel des Grooten atlas, vervatende de water-weereld, ofte Een naarstige beschryving van alle zeen. *Amsterdam:*

J. Janszoon, the Younger, 1650. 1 v.; maps; fol. Transl. from Jansson's *Atlantis majoris quinta pars* above. Intended as a supplement to Jansson's *Nieuwen atlas,* Amsterdam, 1647. Koeman (Me) 168. Amsterdam: NHSM. 650/102

Jonstonus, Joannes. Historiae naturalis de avibus libri vi. *Frankfurt a. M.: M. Merian,* 1650. 227 p.; illus.; fol. Included are descriptions of American birds, with bk vi specifically 'De avibus exoticis, Americanis inprimis'. Nissen (Birds) 482; Nissen (Zool.) 2132. CtY, DFo, MH-Z, MiU, NN-RB; BL, BN. 650/103

——. Historiae naturalis de piscibus et cetis libri v. *Frankfurt a. M.: M. Merian* [1650?]. 228 p.; illus.; fol. Included are descriptions of American fishes, amongst them the manatee. Nissen (Zool.) 2133. CtY, DFo, MH, NN-RB, PPAN, RPB; BL, BN. 650/104

——. Historiae naturalis de quadrupetibus [*sic*] libri. *Frankfurt a. M.: M. Merian* [1650?]. 231 p.; illus., port.; fol. Described are numerous American quadrupeds, e.g., the alligator ('Senembi Brasiliensibus'), lizards, & the armadillo ('Tatu seu Armadillo'). Nissen (Zool.) 2131. CtY, DFo, MH, MiU, NN; BL, BN. 650/105

Journael, of Dagh-register gehouden by seven matroosen, in het over-winteren op 't eylandt Mauritius in Groenlandt, in 't jaer 1633. en 1634. *Amsterdam: G. J. Saeghman* [1650?]. 16 p.; illus.; 4to. 1st publ., Rotterdam, 1634, under title *Joernael, ofte Voyagie.* Sometimes attrib. to Outgert Jacobszoon, the commander. Not to be confused with Jacob Segersz. van der Brugge's *Journael of Daghregister* (Amsterdam, [1633?]), with similar title but concerning 7 sailors marooned contemporaneously on Spitsbergen. Cf. Sabin 78900; cf. Tiele-Muller 249; cf. Tiele 565. CtY. 650/106

—[Anr edn]. Journael of Dagh-register . . . Mitsgaders een kort verhael van 't vangen der walvissen en andere avontueren . . . in Groenlant. *Amsterdam:* [*G. J. Saeghman?* 1650?]. 24 p.; illus.; 4to. Includes account (p. 20–24) of D. A. Raven's voyage to Greenland. Sabin 78900. BL (Jacobsz, O.). 650/107

Kort verhael van 't gene onlangs in Hollandt en Amsterdam is voor-gevallen. [*The*

Hague?] 1650. [32] p.; 4to. Includes letter from states of Holland & West Friesland (also publ. separately this year), with section discussing subsidy for the West-Indische Compagnie's defense of Brazilian conquests. Knuttel 6708. NN; The Hague:KB.   650/108

—[Anr edn]. [*The Hague?*] 1650. [60] p.; 4to. Knuttel 6707. MnU-B; The Hague:KB.
650/109

La Peyrère, Isaac. Die xxvi. Schiff-Fahrt; Beschreibung einer höchst-mühseligen . . . Reyse durch . . . Johann Müncken inn Jahren 1619. und 1620. verricht . . . nach dem Freto oder der Enge Hudsons. *Frankfurt a. M.: C. Le Blon,* 1650. 63 p.; illus., map; 4to. (Levinus Hulsius's *Sammlung von . . . Schiffahrten.* Pt 26). Though generally ascribed to Jens Munk, actually a truncated translation of La Peyrère's *Relation du Groenland,* 1st publ., Paris, 1647. Here added is supplementary material ed. by Christoph Le Blon. Sabin 33679; Baginsky (German Americana) 170; Church 319; JCB (3) I:470. CSmH, CtY, ICN, MH, NN-RB, RPJCB; BL, BN.   650/110

Le Brun, Laurent, S.J. Ecclesiastes Salomonis paraphrasi poëticâ explicatus. Editio tertia. *Rouen: J. LeBoullenger,* 1650. 245 p.; 12mo. 1st (?) publ., Rouen, 1649. No edn designated as the 2nd has been traced. Backer IV:1630; JCB (3) II:398. DLC, RPJCB; BL, BN.   650/111

Le Moyne, Pierre, S.J. Les poesies. *Paris: A. Courbé,* 1650. 603 p.; 4to. 'Les Alpes humiliées' mentions Magellan; 'Elegie' (p. 576–579) mentions Peru. Backer V:1364–1365; Cioranescu 42379. DLC, MH; BN.
650/112

León Pinelo, Antonio Rodríguez de. Oracion panegirica a la presentacion de la Sacratissima Virgin . . . dirigese al Supremo i Real Consejo de las Indias. *Madrid: D. Díaz de la Carrera,* 1650. 120 p.; 4to. Palau 135756. InU-L.   650/113

Lopes, Duarte. Beschrijvinge van 't koningkrijck Congo. *Amsterdam: A. Roest, for J. Hartgers,* 1650. 96 p.; illus.; 4to. 1st publ. in this version, Amsterdam, 1596; transl. from Lopes's *Relatione del reame di Congo,* 1st publ., Rome, 1591; cf. de Bry's German version of 1609. Tiele-Muller 299. DLC.   650/114

Magano, Juan. Memorial a los eminentissimos . . . cardenales, y prelados de la Congregacion indiana . . . por . . . Juan Magano, agente en la Curia . . . por . . . Juan de Palafox y Mendoza, Obispo . . . en la controversia . . . con los religiosos de la Compañia de Jesus de la Nueva España . . . Traducido de italiano. [*Rome?* 1650?]. 126 p.; 4to. The Italian text, if published, has not been identified. Medina (BHA) 6595; Streit II:1834; Backer XI:1332; Palau 147040. MH, RPJCB; BL, BN.   650/115

Manasseh ben Joseph ben Israel. Esto es, Esperança de Israel. *Amsterdam: Semuel ben Israel Soreiro,* 5410 [i.e., 1650]. 126 p.; 8vo. Title in Hebrew at head of t.p. Develops theory that American Indians represent lost tribes of Israel, applying it to Indians of Brazil. Sabin 44191; Medina (BHA) 1148; Borba de Moraes II: 53; Palau 162816; JCB (3) II:398. CtY, NN-RB, OCH, RPJCB; BL, Madrid:BN.   650/116

——. Hoc est, Spes Israelis. *Amsterdam:* 1650. 111 p.; 8vo. Latin version of the preceding. Sabin 44192; Palau 162817n. CSmH, NN-RB, OCH; BL.   650/117

——. The hope of Israel. *London: R. I[bbitson]. for Hannah Allen,* 1650. 90 p.; 8vo. Transl. from the above by Moses Wall. Sabin 44193; Wing M375; Thomason I:804. CSmH, MH; BL.   650/118

Mariana, Juan de, S.J. Historia general de España . . . Ultima impression. *Madrid: C. Sánchez for G. de León,* 1650. 2 v.; fol. Transl., rev. & augm. by the author from his *Historiae de rebus Hispaniae,* 1st publ., Toledo, 1592; cf. 1601 edn. Sabin 44546n; Backer V:550; Palau 151671. DLC; BL, BN.   650/119

Martínez de Mata, Francisco. Memorial en razon de la despoblacion, pobreza de España, y su remedio. [*Madrid?* 1650?]. 24 numb. lvs; fol. Mentioned are Spanish America & artisan skills needed there. Palau 155312.   650/120

—[Anr edn]. [*Madrid?* 1650?]. 8 numb. lvs; fol. Includes text of covering letter dated 8 Nov. 1650. MH.   650/121

—[Anr edn]. [*Madrid?* 1650?]. 8 numb. lvs; fol. Lacks covering letter of preceding item. CtY, MH.   650/122

Mather, Richard. An heart-melting exhortation, together with a cordiall consolation,

presented in a letter from New-England. *London: A. M[athewes]., for J. Rothwell*, 1650. 84 p.; 12mo. Sabin 46780; Holmes (MM) 42; Wing M1273. CtY, ViU; Oxford:Bodl.
650/123

Mello, Francisco Manuel de. Relaçam dos successos da armada, que a Companhia geral de commercio expediu ao estado do Brasil o anno passado de 1649. [*Lisbon:*] *Craesbeeck Office*, 1650. [16] p.; 4to. Sabin 44425; Borba de Moraes II:50; Innocencio II:1264. BN, Lisbon:BN.
650/124

Mendoça, Francisco de, S.J. Viridarium sacrae ac profanae eruditionis. *Cologne: P. Henning*, 1650. 1012 p.; 8vo. 1st publ., Lyons, 1631. Cf. Backer V:900–901. MnCS.
650/125

Mendoça, Lourenço de, Bp of Rio de Janeiro. Señor. El doctor Lorenço de Mendoça. [*Madrid?* 1650?]. [4] p.; fol. Memorial to king of Spain reciting past services, in Peru, etc. BL.
650/126

Merlo de la Fuente, Alonso. Copia de un memorial, que en 7. de noviembre de 1650. diò al Rey . . . el Doctor Don Alonso Merlo de la Fuente . . . en razon de la moneda falsa que de algunos años a esta parte se ha labrado en la villa de Potosi. [*Madrid:* 1650]. 41 (i.e., 14) numb. lvs; fol. Subscribed: Madrid, y noviembre siete, de mil y seiscientos y cinquenta años. Palau 165841. BL.
650/127

Morales, Juan de. Señor. El capitan don Juan de Morales dize. [*Madrid?* ca. 1650?]. [4] p.; fol. Memorial to king of Spain on commerce between Mexico & Philippines. Medina (BHA) 6660. BL.
650/128

Morone, Mattia. Directorium medico-practicum. *Lyons: J. A. Huguetan & M. A. Ravaud*, 1650. 523 p.; 8vo. 1st publ., Lyons, 1647. DNLM, PPC.
650/129

Moscherosch, Johann Michael. Wunderliche und warhafftige Gesichte Philanders von Sittewald [pseud.] . . . Erster[-Ander] Theil. *Strassburg: J. P. Mülbe & J. Städel*, 1650. 2 pts; 8vo. 1st publ., Strassburg, [1640]. For variant see Bechtold. Bechtold (E1)–(E2); Faber du Faur 425; Goedeke III:234. CU, CtY, DLC, MnU-B; Göttingen:UB.
650/130

—[Anr edn?]. *Strassburg:* [1650]. 2 pts; 8vo. BL (pt 2 wanting).
650/131

Munk, Jens. Die xxvi. Schiff-Fahrt. *Frankfurt a. M.: C. Le Blon*, 1650. 63 p.; illus., map; 4to. See Isaac La Peyrère's *Die xxvi. Schiff-Fahrt* of this year above.

Naples (Kingdom). Laws, statutes, etc. Philippus Dei gratia rex. Pragmatica circa illius prohibendi del tabaco. *Naples: E. Longo*, [1650]. [3] p.; fol. MH.
650/132

De na-ween vande vrede, ofte Ontdeckinge vande kommerlijcke gheleghentheydt . . . Door Ιρενευμ φιλαλεθιυμ [*sic*] '*Poste*' [i.e., *Amsterdam?*]: 1650. [24] p.; 4to. Refs to Indies & Brazil include writer's question whether Dutch are aware their emissaries can lose Brazil, tying the state's hands, reducing its commerce, & ruining its best patriots. Knuttel 6756. The Hague:KB.
650/133

—[Anr edn]. '*Poste*' [i.e., *Amsterdam?*]: 1650. [20] p.; 4to. This edn has reading 'ontdeckinghe . . . ghelegentheyt' on t.p. Knuttel 6757. The Hague:KB.
650/134

—[Anr edn]. '*Poste*' [i.e., *Amsterdam?*]: 1650. [20] p.; 4to. This edn has reading 'ghelentheydt [*sic*] . . . Door en lief-hebber der waerheydt' on t.p. The last line begins 'soo sy het'. Knuttel 6758. BL (Netherlands), The Hague:KB.
650/135

—[Anr state of preceding]. '*Poste*' [i.e., *Amsterdam?*]: 1650. [20] p.; 4to. Here the reading on t.p. has been improved to 'ghelegentheydt'. Knuttel 6759. MnU-B, NN, WU; BL (Netherlands), The Hague:KB.
650/136

Neck, Jacob Corneliszoon van. Waerachtigh verhael van de schip-vaert op Oost-Indien . . . Hier achter is aen-ghevoeght De voyagie van Seebald de Weert, naer de Strate Magalanes. *Amsterdam: J. Hartgers, 1648* [colophon: *Amsterdam: C. Cunradus, 1650*]. 92 p.; illus.; 4to. (Joost Hartgers's *Oost en West-indische voyagien.* [Pt 3]. 1st publ. in this version, Amsterdam, 1648; here a reissue of that edn? Cf. Sabin 52214; Tiele-Muller 131; cf. Tiele 787.
650/137

—[Anr edn]. *Amsterdam: J. Hartgers*, 1650. 76 p.; illus.; 4to. Sabin 52215; Tiele-Muller 132; Tiele 787n. DLC, NN-RB; BL.
650/138

Netherlands (United Provinces, 1581–1795). Staatsraad. Adviis van den Raedt van staten, voort-ghebracht aen de . . . Staten

Generael der Vereenighde Nederlanden. *The Hague: G. Pieterszoon,* 1650. [4] p.; 4to. Relates to Brazil. Sabin 484; Borba de Moraes I:14; Rodrigues (Dom. Hol.) 77; Knuttel 6630. DLC, NNH; The Hague:KB.
650/139

—[Anr edn]. *The Hague: J. Stael,* 1650. [4] p.; 4to. In some copies the erroneous reading 'beblieven' appears in 1st line of p. [4]. Borba de Moraes I:14; Knuttel 6631–6632. NN-RB; The Hague: KB, Ghent:BU.
650/140

Neville, Henry. Newes from the New-exchange, or The commonwealth of ladies, drawn to the life. *London:* 1650. 22 p.; 4to. Speaks caustically of use of tobacco by women. In some copies errors in paging occur. Wing N510; Arents 240. CSmH, CtY, DFo, ICN, NN-A; BL.
650/141

Noodige aenmerckingen op seeckere propositie, in Junio 1650. gedaen inde Hollantsche steden. *Amsterdam: P. Rombouts,* 1650. [16] p.; 4to. Includes ref. to subsidies for the West-Indische Compagnie. This edn has reading 'Eynnde' at end. Knuttel 6767. MnU-B, NN; The Hague:KB.
650/142

—[Anr edn?]. *Amsterdam: P. Rombouts,* 1650. [16] p.; 4to. This edn has reading 'Eynde' at end. Knuttel 6768. The Hague:KB.
650/143

—[Anr edn]. *'The Hague'* [i.e., *Amsterdam]: P. Rombouts,* 1650. [8] p.; 4to. The verso of t.p. is blank. NN.
650/144

—[Anr edn]. Noodige aenmerckinge. *'The Hague'* [i.e., *Amsterdam:]* P. Rombouts, 1650. [8] p.; 4to. The verso of t.p. contains text. For variant, see Meulman. Meulman 3162–3163. MnU-B, NN; Ghent:Bu.
650/145

—[Anr edn]. [*Amsterdam?*] 1650. [8] p.; 4to. The verso of t.p. contains text while vignette of double cornucopia appears on t.p. Knuttel 6769. MnU-B, NN; The Hague:KB, Ghent:Bu.
650/146

Noort, Olivier van. Wonderlijcke voyagie, by de Hollanders ghedaen, door de Strate Magalanes . . . Hier achter is by-ghevoeght De tweede voyage van Jacob van Neck. *Amsterdam: J. Hartgers,* 1650. 88 p.; illus.; 4to. 1st publ., Rotterdam & Amsterdam, 1601; cf. 1648 edn, of which this is a reprint. Sabin 55442; Tiele-Muller 23 (& p. 163); Tiele 809n. DLC, MH, NN-RB.
650/147

Nootwendige aenmerkinge op een fameus libel, ghenaemt de Bickerse beroerte, ofte den Hollantsen eclipsis. *Antwerp: J. van Waesbergen,* 1650. [15] p.; 4to. Relates to the West-Indische Compagnie. Knuttel 6847. MnU-B, NN, WU; BL (Bicker), The Hague:KB.
650/148

Den ommeganck van Amsterdam. *Breda:* 1650. 11 p.; 4to. Refers to situation of the West-Indische Compagnie in Brazil. Knuttel 6773. The Hague:KB.
650/149

—[Anr edn]. Na de copye van Breda. *Rotterdam:* 1650. 12 p.; 4to. Knuttel 6774. NN; The Hague:KB.
650/150

—[Anr edn]. Den ommegank . . . Nae de copye gedruckt tot Breda. [*Breda?*] 1650. 8 p.; 4to. Knuttel 6775. MnU-B; The Hague:KB.
650/151

—[Anr edn]. Na de copye gedruckt tot Breda in Augustus. [*Amsterdam?*] 1650. 8 p.; 4to. Knuttel 6776. The Hague:KB.
650/152

—[Anr edn]. Den omme-ganck. *Leeuwarden: C. Martensz,* 1650. 12 p.; 4to. For anr state see Knuttel as cited. Knuttel 6777. The Hague:KB., Ghent:BU.
650/153

—[Anr edn]. Den ommeganck. [*Amsterdam?* 1650?]. 8 p.; 4to. Knuttel 6778 (cf. 6779). The Hague:KB.
650/154

d'Onstelde Amsterdammer met sijn trouwe waerschouwinghe, raed en antwoort op bickers beroerten. Eerste deel. *Brussels: 'S. Vermeer',* 1650. [22] p.; 4to. Includes ref. to the West-Indisch-Huys. Knuttel 6849. MnU-B, NN, WU; BL(?), The Hague:KB.
650/155

—[Anr edn]. *Brussels: 'S. Vermeer',* 1650. [24] p.; 4to. Knuttel 6850. The Hague:KB.
650/156

—[Anr edn]. *Brussels: 'S. Vermeer',* 1650. [32] p.; 4to. Knuttel 6848. The Hague:KB.
650/157

Owen, John. Epigrammatum . . . editio postrema. *Amsterdam: J. Janszoon, the Younger,* 1650. 212 p.; port.; 8vo. 1st publ., London, 1606. CLU-C, CtY, ICU.
650/158

Palafox y Mendoza, Juan de, Bp of Puebla de los Angeles. Carta segunda de tres, que el venerable señor Don Juan de Palafox escribio al sumo pontifice Inocencio X. sobre dos pleytos, que, litigaba con los padres Jesuitas; sobre diezmos, y jurisdicion. *'Se-*

ville: F. Lira, 1650'. 94 p.; 16mo. On the Jesuits in Mexico. That this was written by Palafox is questionable. Continues, & was undoubtedly issued with, Palafox's first letter entered under the year 1646, q.v., and like it of dubious authenticity. Palau 209689. IU, NN-RB, RPJCB. 650/159

——. Vida de S. Juan el Limosnero. *Madrid: D. García Morrás,* 1650. 150 numb. lvs; 4to. Includes a prefatory letter to the faithful of the author's see of Puebla de los Angeles, describing his return to Spain from Mexico. Medina (BHA) 1149; Palau 209709. IU, RPJCB. 650/160

——. [Virtudes del Indio.] Señor. Poco ministros han ido a la Nueva España, ni buelta della, mas obligados que yo al amparo de los Indios. [*Madrid?* ca. 1650?]. 93 p.; 8vo. Issued without t.p., but known as the *Virtudes* etc. Sabin 58307; Medina (BHA) 7680; Streit II:1837; Palau 209711; Maggs Cat. 502 (Americana VII):5091; JCB (3) II:399. DLC, InU-L, MH, MiU-C, NN-RB, RPJCB; BL. 650/161

Pardoux, Barthélemy. Universa medicina. *Lyons: S. Rigaud,* 1650. 2 pts; 4to. 1st publ., Paris, 1630; here a reissue with altered imprint date of Rigaud's 1649 edn? DNLM, NIC, NNNAM; BL. 650/162

Pemell, Robert. Πτωχοφαρμακον, seu Medicamen miseris, or . . . Help for the poor, collected for the benefit of such as are not able to make use of physitians and chirurgians. *London: F. L[each]., for P. Stephens,* 1650. 70 p.; 8vo. Includes formula for ointment employing tobacco. Cf. Wing P1133; Arents (Add.) 341. DNLM, NN-A. 650/163

Piccino, Giovanni. Il petopiccino, overo Eccellenza, e doti del tabacco. *Viterbo: The Diotallevi* [ca. 1650]. 83 lvs; 12mo. Arents (Add.) 342. NN-A; BL. 650/164

Plantagenet, Beauchamp. A description of the province of New Albion. *London: J. Moxon,* 1650. 32 (i.e., 24) p.; 4to. 1st publ., London, 1648. Sabin 63311; Vail (Frontier) 118; Baer (Md) 31; Wing P2379; Church 504. CSmH, DLC. 650/165

Porta, Giovanni Battista della. Phytognomonica . . . octo libris contenta. *Rouen: J. Berthelin,* 1650. 605 p.; illus.; 8vo. 1st publ., Naples, 1588; cf. 1608 edn. Pritzel 7273n;

Nissen (Bot.) 463n. DLC, MN, PU-S; BL, BN. 650/166

De Portogysen goeden buyrman . . . Dienende tot antwoort op het ongefondeerde Brasyls-schuyt-praetjen. *'Lisbon'* [i.e., *The Hague?*]: 1650. 15 p.; 4to. 1st publ., Lisbon [i.e., The Hague?], 1649; here a reissue of sheets of that edn with cancel t.p? Cf. Sabin 7538; Knuttel 6626; Meulman 3116. NN-RB; The Hague:KB, Ghent:BU. 650/167

Quevedo y Villegas, Francisco Gómez de. La fortuna con seso . . . autor Rifroscrancot Viveque Vasgel duacense [pseud.], tr. del latin en español por Don Estevan Pluvianes del Padron. *Saragossa: Heirs of P. Lanaja y Lamarca, for R. de Uport,* 1650. 220 p.; 8vo. Chapt. xxviii, on the Dutch, discusses their presence in Brazil; chapt. xxxvi discusses 'Los de Chile y los Holandeses'. Palau 244353. MH, NNH. 650/168

—[Anr edn]. *Saragossa: Heirs of P. Lanaja y Lamarca, for R. de Uport,* 1650. 220 p.; 8vo. In this edn the pseud. in title has reading 'Nifroscrancod'. Palau 244354. IU. 650/169

——. Parnasso español. *Madrid: D. Díaz de la Carrera,* 1650. 502 p.; illus.; 4to. In verse. 1st publ., Madrid, 1648. Palau 244331. MB, NjP; BL. 650/170

——. Todas las obras en prosa. *Madrid: D. Díaz de la Carrera,* 1650. 2 v.; 4to. Included in v. 2 is the 'El entremetido, la dueña y el soplón, 1st publ., Madrid, 1648, in Quevedo's *Enseñanzas.* Palau 243570. CLSU, MH. 650/171

Ragueneau, Paul, S.J. Narratio historica eorum, quae Societas Jesu in Nova Francia fortiter egit, & passa est, annis M.DC.XLIIX. & XLIX. è gallico . . . translata a p. Georgio Gobat. *Innsbruck: H. Agricola,* 1650. 232 p.; 12mo. Transl. from the following item. Sabin 67494; Harrisse (NF) 93; Streit II:2576; Bell (Jes. rel.) 38; McCoy 73; Church 507; JCB (3) II:400. CSmH, DLC, MH, MiU-C, MnU-B, NN-RB, RPJCB; BL. 650/172

——. Relation de ce qui s'est passé en la mission des peres de la Compagnie de Jesus aux Hurons, pays de la Nouvelle France, és années 1648. & 1649. *Paris: S. Cramoisy & G. Cramoisy,* 1650. 103 p.; 8vo. Sabin

67491; Harrisse (NF) 90; Streit II:2577; Bell (Jes. Rel.) 36; McCoy 71; Church 505; JCB (3) II:400. CSmH, DLC, MH, MiU-C, MnU-B, NN-RB, RPJCB; BL, BN.

650/173

—[Anr edn]. *Paris: S. Cramoisy & G. Cramoisy,* 1650. 116 p.; 8vo. Sabin 67491; Harrisse (NF) 91; Streit II:2577n; Bell (Jes. Rel.) 37; McCoy 72; Church 506; JCB (3) II:400. CSmH, CtY, DLC, ICN, InU-L, MiU-C, NN-RB, RPJCB; BL, BN.

650/174

—[Anr edn]. *Lille: Widow of P. de Rache,* 1650. 121 p.; 8vo. Sabin 67493; Harrisse (NF) 92; Streit II:2577n; McCoy 74. NN-RB.

650/175

Raleigh, Sir Walter. Judicious and select essayes. By . . . Sir Walter Raleigh . . . With his Apologie for his voyage to Guiana. *London: T. W[arren]., for H. Moseley,* 1650. 4 pts; port.; 8vo. In pt 1, 'A discourse of the invention of ships', American Indians, the Strait of Magellan, the West Indies, etc., are mentioned. In pt 2 'A discourse of . . . warre', 'Atatalipa King of Peru' is cited. In some copies the 2nd pt, 'A discourse' has reading 'misery' for 'mystery' in title. Sabin 67561; Brushfield (Raleigh) 218; Wing R170; JCB (3) II: 400–401. CSmH, CtY, DFo, ICN, InU-L, MH, MiU-C, MnU-B, RPJCB; BL, BN.

650/176

——. Sir Walter Rawleigh his Apologie for his voyage to Guiana. *London: T. W[arren]., for H. Moseley,* 1650. 69 p.; 8vo. Also issued as pt of Raleigh's *Judicious and select essayes* of this year. Cf. Sabin 67561; Brushfield (Raleigh) 135; Wing R154; JCB (3) II:401. CtY, NNC, NcU, PHi, RPJCB; Cambridge:UL.

650/177

Den rechten konink Midas ondekt in sijn lange Ezels-oren. *Delft: The author* [1650?]. [8] p.; 4to. Includes paragraph on the West-Indische Compagnie, mentioning Portuguese. Knuttel 6784. NN; The Hague:KB.

650/178

Reineccius, Felix, O.F.M. Solon franciscanus, sive Sapientiae franciscanae . . . Partis primae, liber tertius. *Innsbruck: M. Wagner,* 1650. 363 p.; 12mo. Describes Franciscan missions in Orient & America. For other vols in series see Streit. Streit I:515. Munich:StB.

650/179

Relaçam dos sucessos da armada. *Lisbon:* 1650. *See* Mello, Francisco Manuel de, *above.*

Relacion de la vitoria que la armada de Inglaterra que está sobre Cascaes, ha tenido con los navios de la flota de Portugal que venia del Brasil. *Seville: J. Gómez de Blas,* 1650. [4] p.; 4to. Medina (BHA) 1151; Palau 258369; Maggs Cat. 479 (Americana V): 4289. Seville: B. Colombina.

650/180

Reyd, Everhard van. Historie der Nederlantscher oorlogen begin ende voortganck tot den jaere 1601 . . . deer bÿ gevoegt de Nederlandsche geschiedenissen dienende voor continuatie tot . . . 1640. Beschreven door wijlen Johan van Sande. *Groningen: H. Mucerus, for G. Sybes, at Leeuwarden,* 1650. 2 pts; illus., ports; fol. Pt 1 1st publ., Arnhem, 1626. Pt 2, J. van Sande's *Nederlandtsche Historie,* gives details on Dutch in West Indies & Brazil, Pieter Hein, the West-Indische Compagnie, etc. ICU, MH, MiU, NN (pt 2), PU, RPJCB; BL, BN.

650/181

Ribera, Hernando Matias de. Por Hernando Matias de Ribera heredero de Juan Luys de Ribera, tesorero que fue de la Casa de la moneda de Mexico. Con el señor fiscal. Sobre que en cumplimento de las executorias del Consejo, se le buelvan y restituyan de la caxa real de la dicha ciudad . . . los . . . pesos. [*Madrid?* 1650?]. 13 numb. lvs; fol. BL.

650/182

A rich store-house, or Treasury for the diseased . . . By G[eorge]. W[ateson]. The eighth edition, augmented and enlarged, by D. B. *London: J. Clowes,* 1650. 4to. 1st publ., London, 1596; cf. 1601 edn. Wing W31. CSmH, CtY, DNLM; London:Royal College of Surgeons.

650/183

Robinson, Henry. Briefe considerations concerning the advancement of trade. *London: M. Simmons,* 1649 [i.e., 1650]. 10 p.; 4to. Sabin 72083n; Wing R1667; Kress 797; Thomason I:782 (8 Jan. 1650). CSmH, CtY, DFo, MH-BA, NNC; BL.

650/184

Rodríguez Pizarro, Juan. Señor. Ivan Rodriguez Pizarro, como procurador general del gremio de los azogueros . . . de Potosi. [*Madrid?* 1650?]. 8 lvs; fol. Memorial to king of Spain on working of mines of Potosí. Medina (BHA) 6824. BL, Seville:Archivo de Indias.

650/185

Royal College of Physicians of London.

Pharmacopoea Londinensis. *London: G. Du-Gard, for S. Bowtell,* 1650. 212 p.; fol. 1st publ., London, 1618. Wing R2111. CtY-M, DNLM; BL, Oxford:Bodl. 650/186

Ruland, Martin (1532–1602). Curationum empyricarum & historicarum . . . centuriae decem. *Rouen: J. Berthelin,* 1650. 2 pts; 8vo. 1st publ. as here brought together, Lyons, 1628. DNLM, MBCo, NNNAM; BN. 650/187

Saavedra Fajardo, Diego de. Idea principis christiano-politici. *Cologne: C. Münich,* 1650. 795 p.; illus., 12mo. 1st publ. in Latin as transl. by author, Brussels, 1649. Palau 283478. DLC, FU, MoSU. 650/188

Sala, Angelo. Opera medico-chymica quae extant omnia. *Rouen: J. Berthelin,* 1650. 449 (i.e., 749) p.; 4to. 1st publ., Frankfurt a.M., 1647. CLU-C, DNLM, ICU, MH, PPL; BN. 650/189

Sande, Johan van den. Kort begrijp der Nederlandtsche historien . . . tot in't jaer 1648. *Amsterdam: J. Hartgers,* 1650. 690 p.; ports; 12mo. Includes the author's continuation of Reyd's *Historie* of this year. ICN, ICU, WU. 650/190

——[Anr edn]. *Amsterdam: J. Hartgers,* 1650. 714 p.; 12mo. This edn has reading 'tot het jaer 1648 . . . den tweeden druck' on t.p. Amsterdam:NHSM. 650/191

——. Nederlandtsche historie . . . dienende voor continuatie vande Historie van . . . Everhard van Reyd. *Groningen: H. Mucerus, for G. Sybes, at Leeuwarden,* 1650. 217 p.; ports; fol. Issued as pt 2 of E. van Reyd's *Historie* of this year above, q.v.

Sanderson, Sir William. Aulus Coquinariae. *London:* 1650. *See the year* 1651.

Sennert, Daniel. Epitome naturalis scientiae. *Frankfurt a. M.: C. Wächter,* 1650. 706 p.; 8vo. 1st publ., Wittenberg, 1618. TxU; London:Wellcome. 650/192

Settala, Lodovico. Animadversionum, & cautionum medicarum libri novem. *Dordrecht: V. Caimax,* 1650. 3 pts; 8vo. 1st publ. as 7 bks, Milan, 1626. CtY-M, DNLM, NNNAM, PPL, WU; BL, BN. 650/193

Seville. Por el comercio de la ciudad de Sevilia [*sic*] . . . En el pleyto con el señor fiscal . . . Sobre los derechos de una partida de tabaco que vino de la Virginea. [*Seville?* 1650?]. 4 numb. lvs; fol. BL. 650/194

Shepard, Thomas. The sincere convert . . . the fifth [*sic*] edition. *London: M. Simmons, for J. Sweeting,* 1650. 270 p.; 8vo. 1st publ., London, 1640. Sabin 80224. CLU-C, InU-L, MH; BL. 650/195

——[Anr edn]. *London: M. S[immons]., for J. Sweeting,* 1650. 354 (i.e., 154) p.; 8vo. Sabin 80225; Wing S3123. CtY, DLC, ICN, MH; BL. 650/196

Sibelius, Caspar. Of the conversion of five thousand and nine hundred East Indians, in the isle Formose . . . With a post-script of the Gospel's good successe among the West-Indians, in New England. *London: J. Hammond., sold by Hannah Allen,* 1650. 38 p.; 4to. The postscript consists of extracts from the Eliot Indian tracts & from a letter of John Eliot to Hugh Peters. Sabin 80815 (& 56742); Wing J697 & S3748; Thomason I:804; JCB (3) II:402. CSmH, DLC, ICN, MH, NN-RB, PPL, RPJCB; BL. 650/197

Spain. Laws, statutes, etc., 1621–1665 (Philip IV). Pregon en que el Rey nuestro señor manda, que todos los reales de à ocho, y à quatro del Perù . . . valgan los de a ocho à seis reales de plata, y los d' à quatro à tres. *Madrid: D. García Morrás,* 1650. 2 lvs; fol. Dated Oct. 1650. Sabin 65039; Palau 235487n. BL. 650/198

——[Anr edn?]. Prematica [etc.]. *Madrid: D. García Morrás,* 1650. 2 lvs; fol. Palau 235487. 650/199

——. Prematica en que su Magestad manda, que toda la moneda de plata labrada en . . . Perù se reduzca, y ponga conforme a la ley. *Madrid: D. García Morrás,* 1650. 5 numb. lvs; fol. Dated 1 Oct. 1650. Sabin 65048; Palau 235484. BL. 650/200

——[Anr edn]. *Seville: J. Gómez de Blas,* 1650. Medina (BHA) 1150; Palau 235485. MH-L; Seville:Seminario. 650/201

Steendam, Jacob. Den Distelvink. Darde deel, Hemel-sang. *Amsterdam: P. D. Boeteman, for H. Doncker,* 1650. 199 p.; 4to. Continues Steendam's *Distelvink*, 1st publ., Amsterdam, 1649, q.v. One prayer, p. 104–108, includes invocation on behalf of Dutch countrymen in Brazil. Sabin 91166; Muller (1872) 1092; JCB (3) II:391. DLC, IaU, MWiW-C, NN-RB, RPJCB. 650/202

——. Den Distelvink in't geheel: singende

(in drie deelen . . .). *Amsterdam:* 1650, '49, '50. 3 pts; 4to. Pts 1 & 2 1st publ., Amsterdam, 1649; pt 3 1st publ. this year as above. Cf. Sabin 91166. BL. 650/203

Stengel, Karl. Hortorum, florum, et arborum historia . . . Editio altera auctior. *Augsburg: A. Aperger,* 1650. 2 v.; 12mo. 1st publ., Augsburg, 1647. Cf. Pritzel 8932. DNAL, MH-A, MoSB; BL, BN. 650/204

Teellinck, Maximiliaan. Vrymoedige aenspraeck aen syn hoogheyt de heere Prince van Oraengjen . . . Nae de copye. *Middelburg: A. de Later,* 1650. 16 p.; 4to. 1st publ. as dedication to Willem Teellinck's *Den politijcken Christen,* of this year below. Includes argument for trade & the West-Indische Compagnie, of which the author was a proprietor. In this edn., p. 16 begins '14.v.14'. For a reply, see the *Bedenckingen en antwoort* of this year above. Knuttel 6857; JCB (STL) 37. [Locations may include other edns:] InU, MnU-B, RPJCB; BL, BN, The Hague:KB. 650/205

—[Anr edn]. *Middelburg: A. de Later,* 1650. 16 p.; 4to. Page 16 begins 'volgens'. Knuttel 6858. NN; The Hague:KB. 650/206

—[Anr edn]. . . . Nae de copie. *Middelburg: A. de Later,* 1650. 16 p.; 4to. Page 16 begins '1 Tim. 4'. Knuttel 6859. The Hague:KB. 650/207

—[Anr edn]. . . . aen zijn hoogheyt . . . Na de copye. *Middelburg: A. de Later,* 1650. 16 p.; 4to. Page 16 begins 'Uwe Hoogheyt'. Knuttel 6860. NN; The Hague:KB. 650/208

Teellinck, Willem. Den politijcken Christen. *Middelburg: A. de Later,* 1650. 8vo. Includes dedication by the author's son Maximiliaan with refs to Brazil & the West-Indische Compagnie. The dedication was separately reprinted without knowledge of the author, under title *Vrymoedige aenspraeck,* q.v. above. Molhuysen V:899; cf. Knuttel 6857n. 650/209

Thorowgood, Thomas. Jews in America, or, Probabilities that the Americans are of that race. *London: W. H.[unt?]., for T. Slater,* 1650. 136 p.; 4to. Reissued, London, 1652, under title *Digitus Dei.* Of this work a continuation appeared in 1660. Sabin 95651; Baer (Md) 32; Wing T1067; JCB (3) II:403. CSmH,

CtY, DLC, ICN, MH, MiU-C, NN-RB, PPL, RPJCB; BL, BN. 650/210

To the supreme authority the Parliament. [*London:* 1650]. Sabin 101443. *See the year 1651.*

A treatise of New England published in anno Dom. 1637. and now reprinted. [*London?* 1650 *or earlier*]. 16 p.; 4to. The earlier 1637 edn is untraced, unless this be a summary of Thomas Morton's *New English Canaan* of that year. Sabin 96741; Vail (Frontier) 119. MH. 650/211

The troubles of Amsterdam, or the disturbed . . . Amsterdammer, with his . . . answer upon Bicker's commotions. The first part . . . Translated . . . by L. W. *London: W. DuGard,* 1650. 32 p.; 4to. Transl. from d'Onstelde Amsterdammer of this year above. Wing T2309; McAlpin II:722. CtY, NNUT-Mc; BL (Amsterdam), Dublin: Trinity. 650/212

Utrecht (Province). Laws, statutes, etc. Ordonnantie volgens dewelcke d'ed: mog: Heeren Staten 's landts van Utrecht sullen verpachten van nu voort-aen den impost van drie stuyvers op elck pont tabacco . . . *Utrecht: A. van Paddenburch,* 1650. 4 lvs; 4to. Arents 239. NN-A. 650/213

Valdés, Juan de. Por el licenciado Don Juan de Valdes . . . con el Comercio de la ciudad de Sevilla. [*Seville?* 1650?]. 14 numb. lvs; fol. States that the 'isla de la Virginea' forms part of the king of Spain's domains, & hence that tobacco from ship *Carlos,* Jorge Vrete master, out of Bristol, with cargo of tobacco, was contraband; trade in tobacco with British islands in West Indies, e.g., Barbados, is also discussed. BL. 650/214

Varen, Bernhard. Geographia generalis. *Amsterdam: L. Elsevier,* 1650. 786 p.; illus.; 12mo. Included are numerous refs to America. Willems (Les Elzevier) 1120. CU-S, CtY, DLC, ICJ, MiD, NN, PPL, RPJCB; BL. 650/215

Vargas, Luis de, O.P. Por fray Geronimo Alonso de la Torre y fray Miguel de Gauna, difinidores actuales de la provincia de los Doze apostoles de Lima. Con el padre Alonso Velazquez . . . electo vicario provincial . . . Sobre nulidad de la dicha eleccion. [*Madrid?* 1650?]. 29 numb. lvs; fol. Sabin 98600; Medina (BHA) 6938; Palau 352356. InU-L; BL. 650/216

Vaughan, Thomas. The man-mouse taken in a trap. *London:* 1650. 116 p.; 8vo. Ref. is made to the ashes of tobacco. Wing V153; Arents (Add.) 343. CSmH, CtY, DNLM, ICN, MH, MiU, MnU-B, NN-A; BL. 650/217

Veer, Gerrit de. Verhael van de eerste Schip-vaert der Hollandische ende Zeeusche schepen door 't Way-Gat . . .den tweeden druck. *Amsterdam: A. Roest, for J. Hartgers,* 1650. 63 p.; illus.; 4to. (Joost Hartger's *Oost en Westindische voyagien.* [Pt 1]. 1st publ., Amsterdam, 1598, under title *Waerachtighe beschryvinghe;* cf. 1648 edn. Sabin 98739; Tiele-Muller 102; Tiele 1133; Muller (1872) 2081; JCB (3) II:403. NN-RB, RPJCB; BL. 650/218

Velázquez, Baltasar Mateo. El filosofo del aldea. *Saragossa: D. Dormer* [ca. 1650]. 106 numb. lvs; 8vo. 1st publ., Pamplona, 1626. Palau 357345. NNH. 650/219

Venner, Tobias. Via recta ad vitam longam, or A plaine philosophical discourse of such things . . . As also an accurate treatise concerning tobacco. *London: J. Fletcher, for H. Hood,* 1650. 4to. The *Via recta* 1st publ., London, 1620; the *Treatise concerning tobacco,* London, 1621. Sabin 98890n; Wing V195; Arents 146-c. CLU-C, CtY-M, DNLM, ICJ, MBCo, NN-A; BL. 650/220

Villagómez, H. de. El Fiscal de Indias, con Francisco de Vides y su defensor y herederos. [*Madrid?* 1650?]. 4 numb. lvs; fol. Relates to the province of Cumana, in Venezuela. BL (Vides, Francisco de). 650/221

Villagómez, Pedro, Abp of Lima. D. Petri de Villiagomez . . . Por edicto suo contra laicos comis habitum clericalem deturpantes. *Madrid: D. García Morrás,* 1650. 72 numb. lvs; 4to. Subscribed at end: Lima, 17 Oct. 1648. Sabin 99634; Medina (BHA) 1153; Palau 366636; JCB (3) II:404. RPJCB; Madrid:BN. 650/222

The Virginia trade stated. [*London:* ca. 1650?]. bds.; fol. Remonstrance against levying further customs duty on tobacco. Sabin 100570; STC 24838. BL. 650/223

Vitoria, Paulo de. Por el ilustrissimo señor el maestro d.f. Diego de Hevia y Valdes, obispo de la Nueva Vizcaya, del Consejo de Su Magestad. Y por clero de su diocesi. Con las religiones de San Francisco y de la Compañia de Jesus. Sobre las dotrinas, que en execucion de las reales cedulas, les fuesen removidas, y proveidas en clerigos seculares en aquel obispado. [*Madrid?* 1650?]. 19 lvs; fol. Sabin 99442; Medina (BHA) 6986; Palau 371163. Seville:BU. 650/224

Vondel, Joost van den. Poëzy, of Verscheide gedichten . . . vermeert. *Amsterdam: J. Hartgers,* 1650. 610 p.; illus.; 8vo. Includes poem 'Op Pieter Pietersz Hein', referring to naval activity in West Indies; *De getemde Mars,* 1st publ., Amsterdam, 1648, is reprinted here in its entirety. The 'Lofzang van de zeevaert der Vereenichde Nederlanden' includes refs to Drake, Cavendish, Houtman, Noort, etc., referring also to Strait of Magellan, Chile, & Peru. Unger (Vondel) 4. CtY, ViHarEM, ViU; BL, Amsterdam:UB. 650/225

Voor-looper van d'hr. Witte Cornelissz. de With. [*Amsterdam?*] 1650. *See* Cramer, Barent, *above.*

Vox veritatis. [*The Hague?*] 1650. 34 p.; 4to. Mentioned is Sir Henry Vane's expulsion as governor in New England. Sabin 100802; Wing V741; Thomason I:817. CLU-C, ICN, RPJCB; BL. 650/226

Walker, Clement. Anarchia anglicana: or The history of Independency. The second part. [*London?*] 1650. 4to. 1st publ., [London?] 1649. WU. 650/227

———. Relations and observations, historicall and politick, upon the Parliament begun anno Dom. 1640. [*London?*] 1650. 161 p.; 4to 1st publ., [London?], 1648, under title *The history of Independency.* C, WU; BN. 650/228

Ward, Nathaniel. Discolliminium. or, A most obedient reply to a late book, called Bounds & Bonds . . . By B:. *London:* 1650. On p. 2 a 'Turky-cocks quill' is contrasted to the author's 'honest plain-hearted goose-quill'. In some copies 3 lines of errata appear at end. Wing W779; McAlpin II:725; Thomason I:793. CSmH, CtY, DFo, ICN,

MH, NN-RB, PPPrHi, RPJCB, ViU; BL.
650/229

Williams, Edward. Virginia's discovery of silke-wormes . . . Together with the making of the saw-mill, very useful in Virginia. *London: T. H[arper]., for J. Stephenson,* 1650. 75 p.; illus.; 4to. Also issued as pt 2 of the following item. Sabin 104192; Vail (Frontier) 122; Clayton-Torrence 62; Wing W2659; Church 509n; JCB (3) II:404. CSmH, CtY, DLC, ICN, MH, MiU-C, NN-RB, PHi, RPJCB; BL.
650/230

——. Virgo triumphans: or, Virginia richly and truly valued; more especially the south part thereof: viz the fertile Carolina, and no lesse excellent isle of Roanoak. *London: T. Harper, for J. Stephenson,* 1650. 47 p.; 4to. Sabin 104193; Vail (Frontier) 120; Clayton-Torrence 60; Wing W2661; Church 509; JCB (3) II:404–409. CSmH, DLC, ICN, MH, NN-RB, PPL, RPJCB; BL.
650/231

—[Anr edn]. Virginia: more especially the south part thereof . . . The second edition, with addition of the discovery of silkworms. *London: T. H[arper]., for J. Stephenson,* 1650. 2 pts; illus.; 4to. For the 2nd pt as separately issued, see Williams's *Virginia's discovery* above. Reissued, 1651, as pt of Sabin 100450. Sabin 104190; Vail (Frontier) 121; Clayton-Torrence 61; Wing W2658; Church 509n. CSmH, DLC, ICN, MH, MiU-C, NN-RB, PHi; BL.   650/232

With, Witte Corneliszoon de. Voor-looper. *[Amsterdam?]* 1650. *See* Cramer, Barent, *above.*

Wit's recreations. Recreation for ingenious head-peeces. *London: M. Simmons; sold by J. Hancock,* 1650. [400] p.; illus.; 8vo. 1st publ., London, 1640, under title *Wit's recreation.* Wing M1713; Arents 214-a(n). DFo, ICN; BL.   650/233

Zavona, Massimiano. Abuso del tabacco de' nostri tempi. *Bologna: G. B. Ferroni,* 1650. 55 p.; 4to. Arents 241. DNLM, MH, NN-A; BL.   650/234

Zecchi, Giovanni. Consultationes medicinales. *Frankfurt a. M.: J. Beyer,* 1650. 955 p.; 8vo. 1st publ., Rome, 1599, under title *Liber primus Consultationum me-* *dicinalium;* cf. 1601 edn. DNLM, PCarlD.
650/235

Addenda

Boemus, Johann. Historia moralis, das ist, warhafftige Erzelung aller vornemsten geistlichen unnd weltlichen Regimenten, mancherley Sitten und Gewonheiten, welche alle . . . Völker . . . in . . . Europa und America vorzeiten gehabt. *Frankfurt a. M.: L. Bitsch,* 1604. 2 pts; 8vo. Comp. & transl. from various sources by Johann Homberg, who perhaps contributed the section on America. Cf., however, Boemus's Latin edn of 1604. MnU-B.
A604/1

Netherlands (Southern Provinces, 1581–1793). Sovereigns, etc., 1596–1621 (Albert and Isabella). Copie de l'instruction donne par leur Altesses au Marquis Ambrosio Spinola. *[Brussels?]* 1608. [8] p.; 4to. Trade by Dutch to be permitted with Spain, but not with East & West Indies. This edn dated 'les xvi de Janvier'. Knuttel 1532. [Locations may include the following edn:] MH-L, MnU-B; The Hague:KB.
A608/1

—[Anr edn]. *[Brussels?]* 1608. [8] p.; 4to. This edn dated 'le xvi de Janvier'. Knuttel 1533. The Hague:KB.   A608/2

——. Copye van de instructie by hare hoocheden ghegheven aen den Marquis Ambrosio Spinola . . . Wt het Fransche vertaelt. *[Brussels:]* 1608. 4 lvs; 4to. Transl. from the preceding. Knuttel 1534. NN; BL, The Hague:KB.   A608/3

—[Anr edn]. Instructie ofte Register-brief. *[Brussels? 1608?].* 8 p.; 4to. A reprinting of the preceding translation. Knuttel 1535. The Hague:KB.   A608/4

—[Anr edn]. Instructie gegeven . . . aenden Marquiz . . . Spinola . . . Wt het Fransoys . . . overghezet. *[Antwerp?]* 1608. 8 p.; 4to. Here, a differing translation. Knuttel 1536. The Hague:KB.   A608/5

—[Anr edn]. Wt het Francoys . . . overghezet. *[Antwerp?]* 1608. 8 p.; 4to. A reprinting of the preceding translation. Knuttel 1537. BL, The Hague:KB.   A608/6

Netherlands (Southern Provinces, 1581–1793). Sovereigns, etc., 1596–1621 (Albert and Isabella). Copie de l'instruction donnee par leurs Altesses, au Marquis Ambrosio Spinola. [*Brussels?*] 1609. 23 p.; 12mo. 1st publ., [Brussels], 1608. Cf. Knuttel 1532. ICN.   A609/1

Teixeira, Pedro. Relaciones . . . del origen . . . de los reyes de Persia. *Antwerp: H. Verdussen,* 1610. 384 p.; 8vo. Includes refs to Mexico, Peru, tobacco, etc. Palau 328892; Peeters-Fontainas (Impr. esp.) 1255; JCB (STL) 22. CU, CtY, DLC, ICN, InU, MH, MnU-B, NN, PPL, RPJCB; BL, BN.

A610/1

Clemens, Venceslaus. Trinobantiados Augustae sive Londini libri VI. [*Leyden: J. Maire,* 1636]. 204 p.; 4to. Refers to properties & virtues of tobacco (p. 91); mentions America, Virginia, Brazil, etc. (p. 166). CSmH, CtY, ICU, MdBP, NN; BL, BN.

A636/1

Boxhorn, Marcus Zuerius. Historia obsidionis Bredae et rerum. anni MDCXXXVII. *Leyden: I. Commelin,* 1640. 176 p.; illus., maps; fol. Included are poems on Pieter

Hein and the Nederlandsche West-Indische Compagnie. Rodrigues (Dom. Hol.) 896. MH, MiU, WaU; BL, BN.   A640/1

Liceti, Fortunio. Litheosphorus, sive De lapide bononiensi lucem in se conceptam ab ambiente claro mox in tenebris mire conservante. *Udine: N. Schiratti,* 1640. 280 p.; port; 4to. Refers to stones of Paraguay. NN, RPJCB, WU; BL, BN.   A640/2

Nicolosi, Giovanni Battista. Teorica del globo terrestre et explicatione della carta da navigare. *Rome: M. Manelfi,* 1642. 235 p.; 12mo. Included are refs to the Americas and its component countries. Michel (Répertoire) VI:19. DFo, InU-L, MB, NN-RB; Paris:Sorbonne.   A642/1

Saint-Amant, Marc Antoine de Gérard, sieur de. La Rome ridicule. Caprice. [*Paris:* 1643]. 53 p.; 4to. In verse. In stanza xix the sun is described as 'ce Dieu du Perou'. For a later edn, see the year 1649. Cioranescu (XVII) 60694. ICU, MH, NjP; BL, BN.   A643/1

—[Anr edn]. [*Paris:*] 1643. 53 p.; 8vo. CtY, DLC, ICU; BL, BN, Wolfenbüttel:HB.

A643/2

A Geographical Index of Printers and Booksellers
& Their Publications

The asterisk before a name indicates that there were two printers or booksellers of the same name, and that, in some of the books listed, it is not certain to which of them the name in the imprint refers.

FICTITIOUS LOCATIONS

ANTIPOLI
Stamperia Regia, pseud.
For the following works *see* Italy—Venice—Printer unidentified
1618 Piò, G. M. Allegatione
1621 Piò, G. M. Allegatione

CORMOPOLI
1615 Boccalini, T. Pietra del paragone. *See* Italy—Venice—Teler, Ambros; Teler, Giorgio; Teler, Zorzi

COSMOPOLI
1619 Boccalini, T. Pietra. *See* Italy—Venice—Teler, Zorzi
Teler, Giorgio, pseud.
1640 Boccalini, T. Pietra. *See* The Netherlands—Leyden—Elsevier, Bonaventura & Abraham
1642 Boccalini, T. Pietra. *See* The Netherlands—Amsterdam—Printer unidentified

DANSWIJCK
See also Schotlandt, outside Danswijck, *below*.
Vermeulen de Jonge, Crijn, pseud.
1610 Baudart, W. Morghenwecker. *See* The Netherlands—The Hague—Printer unidentified

ELISIUM
1624 Reynolds, J. Vox coeli. *See* Great Britain—London—

Printer unidentified;
London—Jones, William

FRANC END AL
Vrije, Frederijck de, pseud.
1609 Middelgeest, S. van. Testament. *See* The Netherlands—Amsterdam—Printer unidentified

NEW NEWENSTATT
Warsagern, Vielhüppens, pseud.
1626 Scribanius, C. Der holländisch Apocalypsis. *See* Germany—Augsburg—Printer unidentified

NIEUSTADT
Waersegger, Hans, pseud.
For the following works *see* The Netherlands—Leyden—Printer unidentified
1625 Scribanius, C. Den Hollantschen apocalypsis
1626 Scribanius, C. Den Hollantschen apocalypsis

PARADISE
1624 Scott, T. Robert . . . of Essex. *See* Great Britain—London—Beale, John

POSTE
1650 De na-ween. *See* The Netherlands—Amsterdam—Printer unidentified

RONCIGLIONE
Brogiotti, G. B.
1624 Tassoni, Alessandro. La

Secchia. *See* Italy—Rome—Brugiotti, Giovanni Battista

SCHOTLAND, OUTSIDE DANSWIJCK
Loven, Hermes van.
For the following works *see* The Netherlands—The Hague—Loven, Hermes van
1609 Meteren, E. van. Belgische . . . oorlogen
1609 Meteren, E. van. Commentarien
1610 Meteren, E. van. Commentarien
1611 Meteren, E. van. Belgische . . . oorlogen

SPA, OUTSIDE ALTENA
1608 Hovt en beleght; een oud schipper

UTOPIA
1613 Taylor, J. Odcombs complaint. *See* Great Britain—London—Eld, George

VILLENEUVE
Le Vray, Jean, pseud.
1626 Scribanius, C. L'apocalipse. *See* The Netherlands—Printer unidentified

WEST INDISCHE KAMER
Maerten, pseud.
1649 Brasyls schuyt-praetjen. *See* The Netherlands—The

Hague—Breeckevelt,
Ferdinandus

AMERICA

BOSTON
Usher, Hezekiah.
1648 Bible. O. T. Psalms.
English, Paraphrases. 1648.
Bay Psalm Book. The psalms

BRAZIL
Jesuits of Brazil
1618 Araujo, A. de. Catecismo
na lingoa brasilica

RECIFE
1647 Brasilsche gelt-sack. *See
under* The Netherlands—
Amsterdam—Printer
unidentified

AUSTRIA

GRAZ
Widmanstätter, Ernst
1631 Epithalamium symbolicum
Widmanstetter, Georg
1609 Cabredo, L. de. Historia
insignis miraculi

INNSBRUCK
Agricola, Hieronymus
1650 Ragueneau, P. Narratio
historica
Wagner, Michael
1650 Reineccius, F. Solon
franciscanus

LINZ
Printer unidentified
1621 Plautius, C. Nova typis
transacta navigatio. Novi orbis
Planck, Johann
1623 Plautius, C. Extract und
Ausszug der grossen . . .
Schiff-farth
1624 Plautius, C. Extract und
Augsszug der grossen . . .
Schifffarth

SALZBURG
Katzenberger, Christoph
1634 Benavides, A. de. Relatio
1634? Benavides, A. de. Relatio

BELGIUM

ANTWERP
Printer unidentified
1603 Ortelius, A. Epitome
1604 Francisco de Vitoria.
Relectiones morales
1608A Netherlands (Southern,
Provinces, 1581–1793).
Sovereigns, etc., 1596–1621.
Instructie (2)
1608 Walerande, J. B. de. Le
plaidoyer (2)
1629 Cats, J. Silenus Alcibiadis
1630 Waerdenburgh, D. van. La
prise de la ville de Olinda
1631? Cats, J. Maegden-plicht
(5)
1635 Rijpen raedt (2)
1644 Dialogus oft T'samensprekinge
1645 Cats, J. Poëtische wercken
1648 La confession de l'imprimeur
Aertssens, Henri
1614 Aldrete, B. J. Varias
antiguedades de Espanã
1646 Alegambe, P. De vita et
moribus p. Joannis Cardim
Bellère, Pierre
1645 Nonnius, L. Diaeticon
1646 Nonnius, L. Diaeticon
Bellère, Pierre & Jean
1617 Vega Carpio, L. F. de.
Arcadia
1627 Nonnius, L. Diaeticon
Brakel, Arnout van
1646 Weerts, P. Histoire
admirable
1647 Weerts, P. Cort begryp
Cnobbaert, Jan
1627 Antwerp. Collegium
Societatis Jesu. Typus mundi
1630 Antwerp. Collegium
Societatis Jesu. Typus mundi
1631 Cats, J. Maegden-plicht
1635 Malpaeus, P. Palma
fidei s. Ordinis praedicatorum
1636 Corte, C. de. Virorum
illustrium . . . elogia
Cruyssen, Pieter van den
1646 Manifest door d'inwoonders van Parnambuco
Duynen, Françoys van
1649 Breeden-raedt

Enden, Martinus van den
1646 Weerts, P. Histoire
admirable
Fuet, Jean
1605 Rabelais, F. Oeuvres
Hasrey, Jean
1614 Aldrete, B. J. Varias
antiguedades de España
Hollander, Peter de
1647 Velle, N. M. van. De
oprechte waeg-schaele
Hubert, Adrien
1604 Verstegen, R. Theatrum
crudelitatum haereticorum
1607 Verstegen, R. Theatre des
cruautez des hereticques
Keerberghen, Jan van
1601 Ortelius, A. Epitome
theatri
1602 Ortelius, A. L'épitome du
théâtre
1604 Ortelius, A. Ausszug
1615 Molina, L. de. De justitia et
jure
Lesteens, Willem
1631 Benavides, A. de. Requeste
oft Verhael
Maire, Abraham
1608? Montaigne, M. E. de. Les
essais
Martin, David
1611 Le Mire, A. Notitia
patriarchatuum
1612 Le Mire, A. Notitia
episcopatuum
Meurs, Jean de
1632 Pulgar, H. de. Los claros
varones de España
1636 Jesuits. Letters from
missions (South America).
Litterae annuae provinciae
Paraquariae Societatis Jesu
1643 Rivadeneira, P. de.
Bibliotheca scriptorum
Societatis Jesu
Moretus, Jean
1610? Ortelius, A. Theatrum
orbis terrarum . . . Tonneel
des aert-bodems
*Nuyts, Marten
1604 Torres Bollo, D. de. De
rebus Peruanis . . . commentarius
1605 Hay, J. De rebus Japonicis
1605 Maffei, G. P. Historiarum
Indicarum libri xvi

1609 Gracián, J. Zelo de la
propagacion de la fee
1639 Alemán, M. Gusman de
Alfarache, la pte
1641 Pharmacopoeia
Bruxellensis
1648 González Chaparro, J.
Relation dell'horrible
tremblement
1649 Saavedra Fajardo, D. de.
Idea principis christiano-
politici
Pierre, Jean
1628 Scribanius, C. Discours
d'estat
**Velpius, Hubert Antoine (the
Younger)**
1647 Spain. Treaties, etc., 1621–
1665. Articulen dess Friedens
1648 Spain. Treaties, etc., 1621–
1665. Tractaet van peys
1648 Spain. Treaties, etc., 1621–
1665. Traicte de paix
Velpius, Rutger
1604 Martí, J. J. Guzman de
Alfarache, 2a pte
1609 Du Bartas, G. de S.,
seigneur. De eerste weke
1613 Polo, G. G. Diana
enamorada
1614 Cervantes Saavedra, M. de.
Novelas exemplares
Verdussen, Johan
1650 Bickerse beroerten (2)
Vermeer, Symon
1650 d'Onstelde Amster-
dammer . . . Eerste deel (3)
Vivien, François
1631 Benavides, A. de. Requeste
remonsrative au Roy
1634 La Serre, J. P. de. Balet des
princes indiens
1649 Saavedra Fajardo, D. de.
Idea principis christiano-
politici

GHENT
Manilius, Servais
1643 Heyden, H. van der.
Discours et advis sur les flus
1645 Heyden, H. van der.
Discours et advis sur les flus
1648 Spain. Treaties, etc., 1621–
1665. Articulen en conditien
(2)

LIÈGE
Glen, Jean de
1601 Glen, J. B. de. Des habits
. . . du monde

LOUVAIN
Printer unidentified
1642? Barba, P. Vera praxis
Nempe, Jérémie
1647 Valle, F. Methodus
medendi
Simon, F.
1635 Vernulz, N. de. Apologia
Witte, Everaerdt de
1642 Caramuel Lobkowitz, J.
Joannes Bargantinus
Lusitaniae
Zeger, Jacob
1635 Vernulz, N. de. Apologia
1640 Vernulz, N. de.
Virtutum . . . gentis Austriacae
libri tres

MECHLIN
Jaey, Henri
1622 Jesuits. Letters from
missions (South America).
[Lettres des Indes
Occidentales]
1622 Zoes, G. [Relation]

SPA
1608 Hovt en beleght. *See*
Fictitious Locations—Spa,
outside Altena

TOURNAI
Laurent, Nicolas
1610 Rivadeneira, P. de. La vie
du . . . pere Ignace de Loyola
Martin, Charles
1613 Maffei, G. P. La vie
du . . . p. Ignace de Loyola
Quinqué, Adrien
1623 Pattenson, M. The image
of bothe churches (2)
1628 Roca, B. J. Histoire . . . du
b.p. S. Luis Bertran
1641 Damiens, J. Synopsis primi
saeculi Societatis Jesu
1642 Damiens, J. Tableau
racourci

YPRES
Bellettus, Franciscus
1612 Rivadeneira, P. de. Vita
beati patris Ignatii

CZECHOSLOVAKIA

PRAGUE
Marino, Wenceslao
1602 Martini, L. Der christlichen
Jungkfrawen Ehrenkräntzlein

DENMARK

COPENHAGEN
Holstis, J.
1648 Paulli, S. Flora Danica
(pt 1)
Laurentz, Benedict
1608 Lyskander, C. C. Den
Grønlandske chronica
Martzen, Melchior
1648 Paulli, S. Flora Danica
(pt 1)
Molikens, J.
1648 Paulli, S. Flora Danica
(pt 1)
Waldkirch, Henricus
1614 Martini, L. Alle christelige
. . . jomfruers aerekrantz
1621 Bartholin, C. Epigrammata
extemporanea
1624 Munk, J. Navigatio
septentrionalis

FRANCE

AIX-EN-PROVINCE
Roize, Jean
1633 Mérindol, A. Ars medica

ARRAS
Bauduin, Gilles
1611 Du Jarric, P. L'histoire des
choses plus memorables
1613 Conestaggio, G. F. di.
L'union du royaume de
Portugal
1628 Du Jarric, P. Nouvelle
histoire des choses plus
memorables
La Rivière, Guillaume de
1604 Goulart, S. Histoires
admirables et memorables
1611 Du Jarric, P. L'histoire des
choses plus memorables (2)
1615 Rivadeneira, P. de. Les vies
des bien-heureux peres

1616 Locre, F. de. Chronicon Belgicum

AVIGNON
Bramereau, Jacques
1636 Le Jeune, P. Relation de ce qui s'est passé en la Nouvelle France en l'annee 1634
1649 Les divers entretiens

BESANÇON
Moingesse, Nicolas de
1601 Conestaggio, G. F. di. L'union du royaume de Portugal

BÉZIERS
Martel, Jean
1616 Pascal, J. Discours . . . de la pharmacie

BLOIS
Cottereau, Jacques & Michel
1634 Pharmacopoea Blaesensis

BORDEAUX
Millanges, Guillaume
1633 Hoyarsabal, M. de. Les voyages avantureux
1643 Pharmacopoea Burdigalensis
Millanges, Simon
1610 Du Jarric, P. Seconde partie de l'Histoire
Vernoy, Gilbert
1617 Loyseau, G. De internorum externorumque ferme omnium curatione libellus
1617 Loyseau, G. Observations medicinales
1620 Amatus Lusitanus. Curationum medicinalium centuriae septem
1620 Loyseau, G. De internorum externorumque morborum ferme omnium curatione libellus

CAEN
Cavelier, Adam
1614 Maffei, G. P. Historiarum Indicarum libri xvi
1642 Clüver, P. Introductionis in universam geographiam . . . libri vi
Mangeant, Jacques
1614 Maffei, G. P. Historiarum Indicarum libri xvi (2)

CALAIS
Dacivelle, Bonaventure
1601 Neck, J. C. van. Le second livre, Journal ou Comptoir

DIE
Fabri, Jean Rodolphe
1613 Owen, J. Epigrammatum libri tres
1614 Owen, J. Epigrammatum libri tres

DIJON
Printer unidentified
1639 Alemán, M. Le gueux
1641? Ballet du Bureau d'adresse
Guyot, Guy-Anne
1645 Morisot, C. B. Peruviana
Palliot, Pierre
1643 Morisot, C. B. Orbis maritimi
1645 Morisot, C. B. Orbis maritimi
1648 Morisot, C. B. Orbis maritimi

DOUAI
Auroy, Pierre
1607 Wytfliet, C. Histoire universelle des Indes
1631 Du Gardin, L. Medicamenta purgantia
Bellère, Baltazar
1603 Rivadeneira, P. de. La vie du pere François de Borja
1623 Outreman, P. de. Tableaux des personnages signales
1623 Torsellino, O. Historiarum . . . epitome libri x
1627 Torsellino, O. Historiarum . . . epitome libri x
1630 Torsellino, O. Historiarum . . . epitome libri x
1636 Canoniero, P. A. Illustrium epitaphiorum . . . flores
Bogard, Jean
1605 Wytfliet, C. Histoire universelle des Indes
1610 Rivadeneira, P. de. Traité de la religion
Boremann, Pierre
1613 Soto, D. de. De justitia et jure
Fabri, François
1603 Wytfliet, C. Descriptionis Ptolemaicae augmentum (2)

1605 Wytfliet, C. Histoire universelle des Indes
1607 Wytfliet, C. Histoire universelle des Indes
1611 Wytfliet, C. Histoire universelle des Indes
Kellam, Laurence, the Younger
1622 Petit recueil d'aucuns hommes illustres
Kellam, Laurence, Widow of
1618 Jesuits. Letters from missions, Annuae litterae (1603) 1618. Annuae litterae . . . Anni M.DC.III
1618 Jesuits. Letters from missions, Annuae litterae (1604) 1618. Annuae litterae . . . Anni M.DC.IV
1618 Jesuits. Letters from missions, Annuae litterae (1605) 1618. Annuae litterae . . . Anni M.DC.V
Kellam, Thomas
1618 Jesuits. Letters from missions, Annuae litterae (1603) 1618. Annuae litterae . . . Anni M.DC.III
1618 Jesuits. Letters from missions, Annuae litterae (1604) 1618. Annuae litterae . . . Anni M.DC.IV
1618 Jesuits. Letters from missions, Annuae litterae (1605) 1618. Annuae litterae . . . Anni M.DC.V
Wyon, Marc
1619 Berettari, S. La vie miraculeuse du p. Joseph Anchieta

GEX
L'Abbé, Balthazar
1610 Estienne, C. Dictionarium historicum, geographicum

GRENOBLE
Printer unidentified
1630 Arnauld, A. La premiere et seconde Savoisienne
Marnioles, Pierre
1630 Arnauld, A. La premiere et seconde Savoisienne

LA ROCHELLE
Printer unidentified
1606 Lescarbot, M. [Adieu a la France]

Brethommé, Jean
1615 Medina, P. de. L'art de naviguer
Haultin, Jérome
1618 Medina, P. de. L'art de naviguer
Haultin, Jérome, Heirs of
1605 Alfonce, J., i.e., Jean Fonteneau, known as. Les voyages avantureux
1606? Lescarbot, M. A Dieu aux François retournans de la Nouvelle France
1608 Usselinx, W. Sommaire recueil
La Forge, André de
1615 Medina, P. de. L'art de naviguer

LILLE
Beys, Christophe
1614 Claude d'Abbeville. Les fruicts de la mission
Le Clercq, Toussaint
1642 Beroa, D. de. Litterae annuae provinciae Paraquariae
Le Francq, Simon
1640 Pharmacopoeia Lillensis
Rache, Pierre de
1639 Díaz Taño, F. La mort glorieuse du pere Christophe de Mendoza
Rache, Pierre de, Widow of
1650 Ragueneau, P. Relation de ce qui s'est passé en la mission . . . aux Hurons

LYONS
Printer unidentified
1602 Arnauld, A. Ingenua et vera oratio
1602 Bozio, T. De signis ecclesiae Dei
1605 Goulart, S. Le sage vieillard
1607 Erastus, T. Examen de simplicibus
1622 Molina, L. de. De justitia et jure
1624 Bozio, T. De signis ecclesiae Dei
1630 Neander, J. Traicté du tabac
1631 La prise de l'isle de Santo Paulo
1644 Birago, G. B. Historia del regno di Portogallo

1646 Birago, G. B. Historia del regno di Portogallo
Ancelin, Thibaud
1606 Du Bartas, G. de S., seigneur. Les oeuvres poëtiques
1607 Du Bartas, G. de S., seigneur. Les oeuvres poëtiques
Anisson, Laurent
1649 Mendoça, F. de. Viridarium sacrae profanae eruditionis
1649 Nieremberg, J. E. De arte voluntatis libri sex
Armand, Claude
1628 Relation véritable de huict navires
Arnon, Nicolas
1643 Saint-Amant, M. A. de Gérard, sieur de. Les oeuvres
Arnoullet, François
1608 Du Bartas, G. de S., seigneur. Premiere sepmaine
1608 Du Bartas, G. de S., seigneur. La seconde sepmaine
1609 González de Mendoza, J. Histoire . . . de la Chine
Bailly, Pierre
1637 Pigray, P. Epitome des preceptes de medecine
Boissat, Gabriel
1635 Mendoça, F. de. Viridarium sacrae profanae eruditionis
Borde, Philippe
1635 Monet, P. Invantaire des deus langues
1636 Monet, P. Invantaire des deus langues
1637 Estienne, C. L'agriculture
1637 Pigray, P. Epitome des preceptes de medecine
1640 Bauderon, B. Pharmacopee
1640 Guibert, P. Toutes les oeuvres charitables
1641 Paré, A. Les oeuvres
1643 Saint-Amant, M. A. de Gérard, sieur de. Les oeuvres
Boulenger, Jules César
1619 Boulenger, J. C. Historiarum sui temporis libri tredecim
Caffin, Jean
1642 Casas, B. de las. Histoire des Indes Occidentales

Candy, Jean Aymé
1628 Pigray, P. Epitome des preceptes de medecine
1634 Massaria, A. Opera medica
1648 Torsellino, O. Historiarum . . . libri x
Cardon, Horace
1608 Del Rio, M. A. Disquisitionum magicarum libri sex
1612 Del Rio, M. A. Disquisitionum magicarum libri sex
1616 Gaultier, J. Tabula chronographica status ecclesiae catolice
1617 Berettari, S. Josephi Anchietae . . . vita
1617 Scortia, J. B. De natura et incremento Nili
1636 Gaultier, J. Tabula chronologica status ecclesiae catolicae
Cardon, Jacob
1620 Torsellino, O. Epitomae historiarum libri x
1621 Torsellino, O. Epitomae historiarum libri x
1628 Torsellino, O. Epitomae historiarum libri x
1631 Mendoça, F. de. Viridarium sacrae ac profanae eruditionis
1631 Nieremberg, J. E. De arte voluntatis libri sex
1632 Mendoça, F. de. Viridarium sacrae profanae eruditionis
Carteron, Jean
1649 Pardoux, B. Universa medicina
Cavellat, Pierre
1620 Torsellino, O. Epitomae historiarum libri x
1621 Torsellino, O. Epitomae historiarum libri x
Cayne, Claude
1617 Mercuriale, G. Medicina practica . . . libri
1618 Jesuits. Letters from missions, Annuae litterae (1612) 1618. Annuae litterae . . . anni M.DC.XII
1618 Mercuriale, G. Medicina practica . . . libri
1619 Jesuits. Letters from missions. Litterae Societatis Jesu . . . M DC XIII, et M DC XIV
1620 Le Mire, A. Geographia ecclesiastica

1633 Gaultier, J. Table chronologique
1633 Paré, A. Les oeuvres
1636 Monet, P. Invantaire des deus langues
Odain, Louis
1637 Pigray, P. Epitome des preceptes de medecine
Pailly, Guichard
1613 Claude d'Abbeville. L'arrivee des peres Capucins en l'Inde Nouvelle
Pillehotte, Antoine
1617 Mercuriale, G. Medicina practica . . . libri
1617 Sacro Bosco, J. de. Sphaera
1618 Mercuriale, G. Medicina practica . . . libri
1620 Le Mire, A. Geographia ecclesiastica
1620 Le Mire, A. Politiae ecclesiasticae
1620 Rubio, A. Logica mexicana (2)
1623 Mercuriale, G. Medicina practica . . . libri
1636 Monet, P. Invantaire des deus langues
Pillehotte, Jean
1602 Orta, G. da. Histoire des drogues espiceries
1603 Maffei, G. P. Histoire des Indes
1604 Del Rio, M. A. Disquisitionum magicarum libri sex
1604 Maffei, G. P. Histoire des Indes
1608 Del Rio, M. A. Disquisitionum magicarum libri sex
1609 Génebrard, G. Chronographiae libri quatuor
1609 Grégoire, P. De republica libri sex
1609 Grégoire, P. Syntagma juris universi
1609 Rivadeneira, P. de. Illustrium scriptorum religionis Societatis Jesu catalogus
1611 Rubio, A. Logica mexicana
1612 Del Rio, M. A. Disquisitionum magicarum libri sex
1617 Rubio, A. Logica mexicana
1619 Orta, G. da. Histoire des drogues espiceries (2)
1625 Rubio, A. Logica mexicana

Plaignard, François
1642 Casas, B. de las. Histoire des Indes Occidentales
Polier, Amy de
1621 Gaultier, J. Table chronologique
Poyet, Jean
1606 Goulart, S. Le sage vieillard
1613 Pezieu, L. de. Brief recueil . . . de l'isle de Marignan
Prost, Claude
1641 Paré, A. Les oeuvres
1648 Pigray, P. Epitome des preceptes de medecine
Prost, Jacob & Pierre
1634 Gallego Benítez de la Serna, J. Opera physica, medica, ethica
Ravaud, Marc Antoine
1649 Alsted, J. H. Scientiarum omnium encyclopaediae, t 1–4
1649 Zacutus, A. Opera omnia
1650 Morone, M. Directorium medico-practicum
Ravaud, Pierre
1628 Ruland, M. Curationum empiricarum . . . centuriae decem
1640 Ranchin, F. Opuscules
1643 Prevost, J. Medicina pauperum
1644 Prevost, J. Medicina pauperum
Rigaud, Antoine
1643 Torsellino, O. Historiarum . . . epitome libri x
*** Rigaud, Claude**
1627 Mattioli, P. A. Les commentaires
1627 Outreman, P. de. Tableaux des personnages signales
1637 Estienne, C. L'agriculture
Rigaud, Claude, Widow of
1633 Gaultier, J. Table chronologique
1633 Paré, A. Les oeuvres
1635 Monet, P. Invantaire des deus langues
1636 Monet, P. Invantaire des deus langues
1637 Pigray, P. Epitome des preceptes de medecine
1640 Bauderon, B. Pharmacopee
1640 Guibert, P. Toutes les oeuvres charitables

1641 Paré, A. Les oeuvres
1642 Mattioli, P. A. Les commentaires

Rigaud, Pierre
1601 Richeome, L. Trois discours
1603 Du Bartas, G. de S., seigneur. Les oeuvres poetiques
1605 Mattioli, P. A. Les commentaires
1607 Bauderon, B. Paraphrase sur la Pharmacopoee
1607 Richeome, L. Trois discours
1608 Du Bartas, G. de S., seigneur. Premiere sepmaine
1608 Du Bartas, G. de S., seigneur. La seconde sepmaine
1609 Rivadeneira, P. de. La vie du . . . père François de Borgia
1609 Rivadeneira, P. de. La vie du b.p. Ignace de Loyola
1610 Bauderon, B. Paraphrase sur la Pharmacopoee
1611 Guillaumet, T. Traicté
1614 Bauderon, B. Paraphrase sur la Pharmacopee
1616 Gesner, K. Quatre livres des Secrets de medecine
1618 Bauderon, B. Paraphrase sur la Pharmacopee
1618 Clavius, C. In Sphaeram Joannis de Sacro Bosco
1619 Mattioli, P. A. Les commentaires
1620 Mattioli, P. A. Les commentaires
1621 Gaultier, J. Table chronologique
1622 Vega Carpio. L. F. de. Les delices de la vie pastorale
1623 Bauderon, B. Paraphrase sur la Pharmacopoee
1626 Gaultier, J. Table chronologique
Rigaud, Pierre, & Associates
1624 Renou, J. de. Le grand dispensaire medicinal
1624 Vega Carpio, L. F. de. Les delices de la vie pastorale
Rigaud, Pierre & Claude
1649 Schröder, J. Pharmacopeia medico-chymica

1628? Compagnie de la Nouvelle France. Les noms, surnoms et qualitez

1628 Monet, P. Nouveau et dernier dictionaire

1630? Champlain, S. de. Au Roy sire, Le sieur de Champlain remontre

1630 Rapine, C. Histoire generale . . . des freres mineurs

1631 Sennert, D. Institutionum medicinae, libri v

1632 Acarete du Biscay. Relation des voyages

1632 Bethune, P. de. Le conseiller d'estat

1632? France. Treaties, etc., 1610–1643. Traicté

1632? Richelieu, A. J. du Plessis, Cardinal, duc de. Furent presens en leurs personnes par devant le notaire

1632 Satyre Ménippée

1632 Sennert, D. Institutionum medicinae libri v

1633 Compagnie de la Nouvelle France. Sommaire de l'instance

1633? Discours sur la bataille de Lutzen

1633 Roca, J. A. Vera Zúñiga y Figueroa, conde de la. Histoire de l'empereur Charles v

1633 Sennert, D. Epitome naturalis scientiae

1634 France. Conseil d'état. Extraict des registres

1635 Hay, P. Le mercure d'estat

1635 Hay, P. Recueil de diverses pieces

1636 La Brosse, G. de. Description du jardin royal des plantes medicinales

1637 Coppie de la fleur de la passion

1637? Remonstrance tres-humble

1637 Torsellino, O. Historiarum . . . epitome libri x

1638 Hay, P. Recueil de diverses pieces

1638 Theatrum florae

1639 Hay, P. Recueil de diverses pieces

1640 Au Roi. Raisons qui font voir combien il est important au Roy

1640 Hay, P. Recueil de diverses pieces

1640 Torsellino, O. Historiarum . . . epitome libri x

1642 Compagnie de la Nouvelle France. Estat general des debts passives

1642? France. Sovereigns, etc., 1610–1643. Lettres de ratification

1642 Grotius, H. De origine gentium Americanarum dissertatio (2)

1643 Compagnie de la Nouvelle France. Extraict des registres

1643 Hay, P. Recueil de diverses pieces

1643 Saint-Amant, M. A. de Gérard, sieur de. La Rome ridicule (2; see Addenda)

1643 Les veritables motifs

1644 Le Moyne, P. Manifeste apologetique (2)

1644 Poisson, J. B. Animadversio

1647 France. Sovereigns, etc., 1643–1715. Le Roy estant en son Conseil

1647 Torsellino, O. Histoire universelle

1648 Mayerne, L. T. de. Discours sur la carte universelle

1649 Bovionier, F. Quaestio medica . . . in Scholis Medicorum

Alazart, Anthoine
1643 Serres, J. de. Inventaire general

Alliot, Gervais
1621 Alemán, M. Le gueux
1627 Avity, P. d'. Les estats

Angat, F.
1625 Montaigne, M. E. de. Essais

Aubin, Eustache d'
1634 Héry, T. de. La methode curatoire

Auvray, Pierre
1627 Le siege de la ville de Groll

Baragnes (Baraignes), Rolin
1628 La Brosse, G. de. De la nature . . . des plantes
1629 Bonnart, J. La semaine des medicaments

Bechet, Denis
1643 Avity, P. d'. Le monde

Behourt, Jean Baptiste
1632 Béguin, J. Les elemens de chymie

Berjon, Jean
1608 Serres, O. de. Le theatre d'agriculture
1612 Lancre, P. de. Tableau de l'inconstance des mauvais anges
1613 Champlain, S. de. Les voyages
1613 Lancre, P. de. Tableau de l'inconstance des mauvais anges

Bertault, Pierre
1603 Du Bartas, G. de S., seigneur. La seconde sepmaine

Bertault, Robert
1625 Montaigne, M. E. de. Essais

Bertier, Antoine
1648 Duliris, L. Apologie

Besongne, Cardin
1628 Chaumette, A. Le parfaict chirurgien
1643 Serres, J. de. Inventaire general
1649 Bacon, F. Histoire des vents
1650 Bacon, F. Histoire des vents

Bessin, Jean
1615 Marguérite d'Angoulême. L'Heptameron
1615? Matthieu, P. Histoire de France (t 2me)
1622 Scotto, B. Globe maritime
1630 Waerdenburgh, D. van. Copie de la lettre (3)
1631 Dupleix, S. La curiosité naturelle
1639 Pardoux, B. Universa medicina
1643 Bauderon, B. Pharmacopee

Bessin, Nicolas
1647 Saint-Amant, M. A. de Gérard, sieur de. Les oeuvres

Beys, Adrian
1611 Fontaine, J. Practica curandorum morborum
1611 Reneaulme, P. de. Specimen historiae plantarum

Bilaine, Pierre
1619 Alemán, M. Le gueux

1627 Champlain, S. de. Voyages
1632 Champlain, S. de. Les voyages
1632 Malingre, C. Remarques d'histoire
1634 Guibert, P. Les oeuvres du medecin charitable
1638 Malingre, C. Remarques d'histoire
1640 Champlain, S. de. Les voyages

Collet, Martin
1625 Montaigne, M. E. de. Essais
1629 Recherches curieuses des mesures
1633 Pasquier, E. Les recherches de la France
1636 Montaigne, M. E. de. Essais

Colombel, Mathieu
1634 La grande deffaite

Corrozet, Jean
1617 Habicot, N. Problesmes medicinaux
1635 Du Rocher, R. M. L'Indienne amoureuse
1636 Du Rocher, R. M. L'Indienne amoureuse

Cotinet, Arnould
1638 Alemán, M. Le gueux
1639 Cervantes Saavedra, M. de. Le valeureux Dom Quixote
1648 Serres, J. de. Le veritable inventaire

Cottard, Clovis
1634 Fabricius, H. Medecina practica

Cottereau, Joseph
1608 Camerarius, P. Les meditations historiques, t 2me
1610 Camerarius, P. Les heures desrobees

Cottereau, Laurent
1643 Avity, P. d'. Le monde

Coulon, Antoine
1639 Cervantes Saavedra, M. de. Le valeureux Dom Quixote

Courbé, Augustine
1633 Garcilaso de la Vega. Le commentaire royal
1635 Avity, P. d'. Les estats
1637 Gomberville, M. Le Roy, sieur du Parc et de. Polexandre
1638 Gomberville, M. Le Roy, sieur du Parc et de. Polexandre
1640 Montaigne, M. E. de. Essais (2)

1641 Gomberville, M. Le Roy, sieur du Parc et de. Polexandre
1641 Howell, J. Dendrologie (2)
1643 Grenaille, F. de Le mercure Portugais
1645 Gomberville, M. Le Roy, sieur du Parc et de. Polexandre
1647 La Peyrère, I. de. Relation du Groenland
1650 Garcilaso de la Vega. Histoire des guerres civiles
1650 Guidi, I. C. Relation
1650 Le Moyne, P. Les poesies

Couterot, Edme
1650 Garcilaso de la Vega Histoire des guerres civiles

Cramoisy, Gabriel
1644 Vimont, B. Relation de ce qui s'est passé . . . en l'annee 1642. et 1643
1645 Vimont, B. Relation de ce qui s'est passé . . . és années 1643. et 1644
1646 Vimont, B. Relation de ce qui s'est passé . . . és années 1644. et 1645
1648 Briet, P. Parallela geographiae
1649 Godefroy, T. Le ceremonial françois
1650 Ragueneau, P. Relation de ce qui s'est passé en la mission . . . aux Hurons (2)

Cramoisy, Sebastien
1624 Sgambata, S. Eloge du p. Joseph Anquieta
1628 Jesuits. Letters from missions. Histoire de ce qui s'est passé
1628 Richeome, L. Les oeuvres
1630 Pinon, J. De anno romano carmen
1632 Le Jeune, P. Brieve relation
1633 Compagnie de la Nouvelle France. Edict du roy
1633 Histoire de ce qui s'est passé
1634 Bacon, F. Considerations politiques
1634 France. Sovereigns, etc., 1610–43. Declaration
1634 Le Jeune, P. Relation de ce qui s'est passé . . . en l'annee 1633 (2)
1635 Le Jeune, P. Relation de ce qui s'est passé . . . en l'annee 1634 (2)

1636 Le Jeune, P. Relation de ce qui s'est passé . . . en l'annee 1635
1637 Le Jeune, P. Relation de ce qui s'est passé . . . en l'année 1636 (2)
1638 Jesuits. Letters from missions (South America). Relation
1638 Le Jeune, P. Relation de ce qui s'est passé . . . en l'année 1638 (2)
1639 Mascardi, A. Ethicae prolusiones
1640 Bouton, J. Relation
1640 Grotius, H. De veritate religionis christianae (2)
1640 Le Jeune, P. Relation de ce qui s'est passé . . . en l'année 1639 (2)
1641 Vimont, B. Relation de ce qui s'est passé . . . en l'anne M.DC.XL
1642 Vimont, B. Relation de ce qui s'est passé . . . es années 1640 et 1641
1643 Colmenero de Ledesma, A. Du chocolate, discours curieux
1643 Grotius, H. De origine gentium Americanarum dissertatio altera (2)
1643 Vimont, B. Relation de ce qui s'est passé . . . en l'annee 1642
1644 Vimont, B. Relation de ce qui s'est passé . . . en l'annee 1642. et 1643
1645 Compagnie de la Nouvelle France. Articles
1645 Vimont, B. Relation de ce qui s'est passé . . . és années 1643. et 1644
1646 Vimont, B. Relation de ce qui s'est passé . . . és années 1644. et 1645
1647 Lallemant, J. Relation de ce qui s'est passé . . . ès années 1645. et 1646
1648 Briet, P. Parallela geographiae
1648 Lallemant, J. Relation de ce qui s'est passé . . . en l'année 1647
1649 Godefroy, T. Le ceremonial françois

1611 Montaigne, M. E. de. Essais
1613 Dupleix, S. La curiosite
    naturelle
1617 Montaigne, M. E. de. Les
    essais
Guierche, Jean
1637 Bacon, F. Les oeuvres
    morales et politiques
Guignard, Jean
1630 Schouten, W. C. Journal
1635 Boccalini, T. Pierre de
    touched
1636 Montaigne, M. E. de. Essais
1640 Barclay, J. La satyre
    d'Euphormion
1645 Relation d'un voyage
Guignard, Jean, father & son
1648 Fernel, J. La therapeutique
Guillemot, Jean
1647 Duliris, L. La theorie des
    longitudes
*Guillemot, Matthieu
1605 Matthieu, P. Histoire de
    France
1606 Matthieu, P. Histoire de
    France
1609 Matthieu, P. Histoire de
    France
1614 Matthieu, P. Histoire de
    France
1615 Matthieu, P. Histoire de
    France
1631 Peleus, J. Les oeuvres
1644 Ripa, C. Iconologie
Guillemot, Matthieu, Widow of
1612 Loubayssin de Lamarca, F.
    Historia tragicomica de Don
    Henrique de Castro
1617 Loubayssin de Lamarca, F.
    Historia tragicomica de Don
    Henrique de Castro
Henault, Jean
1646 Labbe, P. La geographie
    royalle (2)
1646 Labbe, P. Les tableaux
    méthodiques
1647 Labbe, P. Les tableaux
    méthodiques
1648 Fournier, G. Geographica
    orbis notitia
1649 Fournier, G. Geographica
    orbis notitia
Henault, Mathurin
1623 Bauderon, B. Paraphrase
    sur la Pharmacopoee
1624 Bertius, P. Breviarium
    totius orbis terrarum

1626 Bertius, P. Breviarium
    totius orbis terrarum
1630 Avity, P. d'. Les estats
1630 Pardoux, B. Universa
    medicina
1631 Torsellino, O. Historia-
    rum . . . epitome libri x
1633 Croll, O. La royalle chymie
1639 Bacon, F. Les oeuvres
    morales et politiques
1642 Clüver, P. Introduction à
    la geographie universelle
1646 Labbe, P. La geographie
    royalle (2)
1646 Labbe, P. Les tableaux
    methodiques
1647 Labbe, P. Les tableaux
    methodiques
Henault, Mathurin & Jean
1644 Losa, F. de. La vie de
    Gregoire Lopez
Heuqueville, Jean de
1616 Mocquet, J. Voyages en
    Afrique, Asie, Indes
1617 Mocquet, J. Voyages en
    Afrique, Asie, Indes
1629 Bergeron, P. de. Traicté de
    la navigation
1630 Bontier, P. Histoire . . . des
    Canaries
Houssaye, Denys
1638 Alemán, M. Le gueux
Houzé, Jean
1601 Goulart, S. Histoires de
    nostre temps, t 2–3
1603 Du Bartas, G. de S.,
    seigneur. Premiere
    sepmaine . . . La seconde
    sepmaine
1603 Goulart, S. Histoires
1606 Goulart, S. Histoires
1607 Goulart, S. Histoires
1618 Goulart, S. Histoires
Huby, François
1607 Barclay, J. Euphormionis
    Lusinini Satyricon pars
    secunda
1609 Barclay, J. Euphormionis
    Lusinini Satyricon. pars
    secunda (2)
1613 Barclay, J. Euphormionis
    Lusinini Satyricon: pars ii
1613 Doglioni, G. N. Le théâtre
    universel des princes
1613 Quervau, V. Epitome . . .
    de l'histoire

1614 Claude d'Abbeville.
    Histoire de la mission des
    peres Capucins (2)
1615 Yves d'Evreux. Suitte de
    l'Histoire
Hulpeau, Claude
1625 Montaigne, M. E. de. Essais
Jacquin, François
1608 Coquerel, N. de. Discours
    de la perte
1613 Duport, F. Medica decas (2)
1619 Collège des Maîtres
    chirurgiens de Paris. Traicté
    de la peste
Jacquin, Julien
1647 Guibert, P. Toutes les
    oeuvres
Joallin, Jean Anthoine
1623 Nederlandsche West-
    Indische Compagnie.
    Ordonnances
Jost, Jean
1629 Guibert, P. Les oeuvres
1630 Guibert, P. Les oeuvres
1632 Guibert, P. Les oeuvres
1633 Guibert, P. Toutes les
    oeuvres
1635 Avity, P. d'. Les estats
1637 Guibert, P. Toutes les
    oeuvres
1639 Guibert, P. Toutes les
    oeuvres
1639 Pardoux, B. Universa
    medicina
1650 Bauderon, B. Pharmacopee
Julliot, François
1619 Bacon, F. Les essays
    politiques
1621 Bacon, F. Essays politiques
1622 Bacon, F. Essays politiques
La Coste, Nicholas & Jean de
1633 Cervantes Saavedra, M. de.
    Les nouvelles
1633 Fernel, J. Traité de . . . la
    parfaite cure
1646 Pacifique de Provins.
    Brieve relation du voyage des
    isles de l'Amerique
La Fosse, Solomon de
1636 Montaigne, M. E. de. Essais
L'Amy, Pierre
1636 Montaigne, M. E. de. Essais
L'Angelier, Abel
1602 Montaigne, M. E. de. Les
    essais
1604 Montaigne, M. E. de. Essais

1608 Mayerne, L. T. de. Histoire generale d'Espagne

Langlois, Denis
1613 Claude d'Abbeville. Discours
1625 Guibert, P. Le prix et valeur des medicamens
1626 Guibert, P. Le prix et valeur des medicamens
1627 Guibert, P. Le prix et valeur des medicamens

La Nouë, Denis de
1608 Renou, J. de. Institutionum pharmaceuticarum libri quinque

La Nouë, Guillaume de, Widow of
1605 Ribera, J. de. Lettre annuelle de la province
1608 Renou, J. de. Institutionum pharmaceuticarum libri quinque

Laquehay, Jean
1636 Bauderon, B. Pharmacopee
1637 Pardoux, B. Ars sanitatis tuendae

La Ruelle, Thomas de
1601 Du Périer, A. Les amours de Pistion
1602 Du Périer, A. Les amours de Pistion
1603 Du Bartas, G. de S., seigneur. Premiere sepmaine . . . La seconde sepmaine
1606 Du Périer, A. Les amours de Pistion
1617 Boitel, P. Le tableau des merveilles
1625 Montaigne, M. E. de. Essais
1633 Torsellino, O. Histoire universelle

La Vigne, Nicolas de
1640 Estienne, C. L'agriculture

Le Beau, Claude
1645 Monet, P. Noveau et dernier dictionaire

Le Bouc, Jean, Widow of
1648 Fernel, J. La therapeutique

Le Clerc, David
1605 Laffémas, B. Instruction du plantage des meuriers
1611 Pyrard, F. Discours du voyage . . . aux Indes

Le Clerc, Jean
1620 Desprez, P. Le theatre des animaux

Le Fevre, Abraham
1612 Claude d'Abbeville. L'arrivee des peres Capucins en l'Inde Nouvelle

Le Gras, Henry
1630 Schouten, W. C. Journal
1632 Alemán, M. Le gueux
1637 Bacon, F. Les oeuvres morales et politiques

Le Maître, Mathieu
1612 Béguin, J. Tyrocinium chymicum
1615 Béguin, J. Les elemens de chymie
1620 Béguin, J. Les elemens de chymie
1624 Béguin, J. Les elemens de chymie
1626 Béguin, J. Les elemens de chymie

Le Moine, Simon
1635 Cornut, J. P. Canadensium plantarum . . . historia

Le Mur, Pierre
1612 Guicciardini, F. Histoire des guerres d'Italie
1632 Champlain, S. de. Les voyages de la Nouvelle France

Lesselin, Alexandre
1650 Forest du Chesne, N. Florilegium universale

Libert, Jean
1615 Pinon, J. De anno romano carmen
1635 Clüver, P. Introductionis in universam geographiam . . . libri vi
1644 Estienne, C. Lexicon historicum, geographicum
1645 Torsellino, O. Historiarum ab origine mundi . . . epitome libri x

Libert, Jean, Widow of
1648 Clüver, P. Introductionis in universam geographiam . . . libri vi

Loyson, Guillaume
1625 Montaigne, M. E. de. Essais
1626 Les diversitez naturelles de l'univers
1636 Montaigne, M. E. de. Essais
1647 Bacon, F. Histoire de la vie

Loyson, Jean Baptiste
1647 Bacon, F. Histoire de la vie

Macé, Barthélemy
1607 Paré, A. Les oeuvres
1614 Paré, A. Les oeuvres

Macé, Guillaume
1620 Linocier, G. L'histoire des plantes

Marceau, P.
1606 Serres, J. de. Inventaire general

Marette, Claude
1647 Serres, J. de. Inventaire general
1648 Guibert, P. Toutes les oeuvres

Mariette, Pierre
1633 Theatrum florae

Marnef, H. de
1608 Sacro Bosco, J. de. Sphaera

Martin, Bertrand
1618 Matthieu, P. Histoire de sainct Louys
1621 France. Conseil d'état. Arrests, commissions et privileges

Martin, Jean
1625 Le defaite navale
1625 La furieuse défaite des Espagnols
1625 Spinola, A. La sommation
1628 Relation véritable de huict navires

Mathonière, Nicolas de
1622 Theatrum florae

Maucroy, Stephan
1650 Grotius, H. Annotationum in Novum Testamentum pars tertia
1650 Grotius, H. De veritate religionis christianae

Ménard, Pierre
1633 Pasquier, E. Les recherches de la France
1643 Pasquier, E. Les recherches de la France

Mesnier, Isaac
1619 Valderrama, P. de. Histoire generale

Mestais, Jean
1625 Cervantes Saavedra, M. de. L'histoire de . . . Dom Quichot

Mettayer, Jamet
1603 Du Bartas, G. de S., seigneur. Premiere sepmaine . . . La seconde sepmaine
1605 Matthieu, P. Histoire de France
1606 Matthieu, P. Histoire de France

1609 Matthieu, P. Histoire de France

1614 Matthieu, P. Histoire de France

1615 Matthieu, P. Histoire de France

Mettayer, Jamet & Pierre

1602 Estienne, C. L'agriculture

Mettayer, Pierre

1614 Barclay, J. Icon animorum

1624 Bacon, F. De dignitate . . . scientiarum

1625 France. Laws, statutes, etc., 1610–43. Declaration

1627 Serres, J. de. Inventaire general

Meturas, Gaspar

1647 Du Val, G. Phytologia

1647 Hofmann, C. De medicamentis officinalibus

Millot, Jean

1609 Lescarbot, M. Histoire de la Nouvelle France

1609 Lescarbot, M. Les muses de la Nouvelle France

1610 Lescarbot, M. La conversion des sauvages (2)

1610 Lescarbot, M. Les muses de la Nouvelle France

1610 Sonnet, T. Satyre

1611 Lescarbot, M. Histoire de la Nouvelle-France

1612 Lescarbot, M. Histoire de la Nouvelle-France

1612 Lescarbot, M. Les muses de la Nouvelle France

1612 Lescarbot, M. Relation derniere

Mondière, Melchior

1613 Duport, F. Medica decas

1644 Müller, P. Miracula chymica, et mystica medica

Monstr'oeil, Claude de

1603? Champlain, S. de. Des sauvages

1604 Champlain, S. de. Des sauvages

Moreau, Denys

1618 Cervantes Saavedra, M. de. Histoire de . . . Don Quichot

1622 Cervantes Saavedra, M. de. L'histoire de . . . Dom Quichot

1632 Sagard, G. Le grand voyage du pays des Hurons

1638 Du Monstier, A. Martyrologium Franciscanum

1646 Planis Campy, D. de. Les oeuvres

Moreau, Jean

1623 Du Chevreul, J. Sphaera

Moreau, Pierre, Printshop of the New Type invented by

1644 Grotius, H. La verité de la religion chrestienne

Morel, Charles

1607 Duchesne, J. Pharmaco-poea dogmaticorum restituta (2)

1624 Duchesne, J. La pharma-copee

1625 Duchesne, J. Traicté de la cure generale

1626 Duchesne, J. Conseils de medecine

1626 Duchesne, J. Traicté . . . de la medecine balsamique

1630 Duchesne, J. La pharma-copee

Morlot, Claude

1636 Serres, J. de. Inventaire general

Nigaut, Jean

1613 Arsène de Paris. Derniere lettre

1613 Claude d'Abbeville. L'arrivee des peres Capucins (2)

1623 Claude d'Abbeville. L'arrivee des peres Capucins

Nivelle, Michel

1608 Montaigne, M. E. de. Les essais

1611 Montaigne, M. E. de. Essais

1617 Montaigne, M. E. de. Les essais

Niverd, Catherine (Widow of Monstr'oeil)

1604 Torres Bollo, D. de. La nouvelle histoire du Perou

Orry, Jeanne

1612 Guicciardini, F. Histoire des guerres d'Italie

Orry, Marc

1604 Pigray, P. La chirurgie

1606 Acosta, J. de. Histoire naturelle

1609 Pigray, P. Chirurgia.

1609 Pigray, P. Epitome des preceptes de medecine

Orry, Marc, Widow of

1612 Pigray, P. Epitome Praeceptorum medicinae

Pacard, Abraham

1618 Hues, R. Traicté des globes

Paris, University of

1644 Paris. Université. III. [i.e., Troisiesme] requeste

Patisson, Mamert, Widow of

1604 Thou, J. A. de. Historarium sui temporis, t 1(2)

Patisson, Philippe

1605 France. Sovereigns, etc., 1589–1610. Commissions du Roy . . . pour l'habitation és terres de Lacadie

Pelé, Guillaume

1631 Clüver, P. Introductionis in universam geographiam . . . libri vi

1636 Serres, J. de. Inventaire general

1643 Grotius, H. De origine gentium Americanarum dissertatio

Pelé, Guillaume, Widow of

1643 Laet, J. de. Notae ad dissertationem Hugonis Grotii

Pépingué, Théodore, Widow of

1650 Grotius, H. Annotationum in Novum Testamentum pars tertia

1650 Grotius, H. De veritate religionis christianae

Périer, Adrien

1603 Du Bartas, G. de S. seigneur. Premiere sepmaine . . . La seconde sepmaine

1603 Du Bartas, G. de S., seigneur. La seconde sepmaine

1612 Fontaine, J. Opera . . . artis medicae

1615 Boccalini, T. Les cent premieres nouvelles

1617 Lescarbot, M. Histoire de la Nouvelle-France

1617 Lescarbot, M. Les muses de la Nouvelle France

1618 Lescarbot, M. Histoire de la Nouvelle-France

1618 Lescarbot, M. Les muses de la Nouvelle France

1618 Lescarbot, M. Le tableau de la Suisse

1618 Riolan, J. Gigantologie

Périer, Jeremie

1608 Lescarbot, M. La defaite des sauvages

1633 Bacon, F. Les oeuvres morales et politiques
1635 Montaigne, M. E. de. Essais (2)
1636 Bacon, F. Les oeuvres morales et politiques
1644 Avity, P. d'. Noveau théatre du monde

Roger, Jean
1639 Bacon, F. Les oeuvres morales et politiques
1648 Serres, J. de. Le veritable inventaire

Rousset, Nicolas
1615 Histoire veritable
1620 Scotto, B. Deux cartes maritimes septentrionales
1631 Peleus, J. Les oeuvres

Rouvelin, F.
1644 Grotius, H. La verite de la religion chrestienne

Ruart, Jacques
1627 Grotius, H. Sensus librorum sex

Salis, Dominique (Widow)
1608 Montaigne, M. E. de. Les essais
1617 Montaigne, M. E. de. Les essais

Saucié, Estienne
1625 Cervantes Saavedra, M. de Les nouvelles
1625 Montaigne, M. E. de. Essais

Saugrain, Abraham
1603 Serres, O. de. Le théatre d'agriculture
1604 Duchesne, J. Ad veritatem hermeticae medicinae
1605 Serres, O. de. Le theatre de'agriculture
1608 Serres, O. de. Le theatre d'agriculture
1613 Duport, F. Medica decas
1615 Serres, O. de. Le theatre d'agriculture
1617 Serres, O. de. Le theatre d'agriculture

Saussier, Widow
1648 Clüver, P. Introduction à la geographie universelle

Sevestre, Charles
1608 Montaigne, M. E. de. Les essais
1611 Montaigne, M. E. de. Essais
1617 Montaigne, M. E. de. Les essais

Sevestre, Louis
1632 Champlain, S. de. Les voyages de la Nouvelle France

Soly, Michel
1622 Herrera y Tordesillas, A. de. Description des Indes Occidentales
1629 Bergeron, P. de. Traicté de la navigation
1630 Bontier, P. Histoire de la premiere descouverte . . . des Canaries
1630 Clüver, P. Introductionis in universam geographiam . . . libri vi
1631 Torsellino, O. Historiarum . . . epitome libri x
1635 Clüver, P. Introductionis in universam geographiam . . . libri vi
1643 Fournier, G. Hydrographie

Sommaville, Antoine de
1620 Les delices satyriques
1631 Bacon, F. Histoire naturelle
1643 Grenaille, F. de. Le mercure Portugais
1647 Le Moyne, P. La gallerie

Sonnius, Claude
1626 Dupleix, S. La curiosité naturelle
1631 Matthieu, P. Histoire de France
1631 Rapine, C. Histoire . . . des freres mineurs
1632 Dupleix, S. La curiosité naturelle
1636 Sagard, G. Histoire du Canada
1637 Avity, P. d'. Le monde
1643 Avity, P. d'. Le monde

Sonnius, Laurent
1601 Gómara, F. L. de. Histoire . . . des Indes Occidentales
1606 Dupleix, S. La curiosite
1607 Pasquier, E. Les recherches
1610 Pasquier, E. Les recherches
1611 Pasquier, E. Les recherches
1617 Pasquier, E. Les recherches
1619 Pasquier, E. Les lettres
1621 Pasquier, E. Les recherches

Sonnius, Michel
1605 Gómara, F. L. de. Histoire . . . des Indes Occidentales

1606 Gómara, F. L. de. Histoire . . . des Indes Occidentales (2)
1627 Marino, G. B. L'Adone

Soubron, André
1631 Bacon, F. Histoire naturelle
1640 Bacon, F. Le progrez

Targa, François
1626 Bacon, F. Les oeuvres morales et politiques
1626 Montaigne, M. E. de. Essais
1627 Bacon, F. Histoire du regne de Henry VII
1633 Bacon, F. Les oeuvres morales et politiques
1636 Bacon, F. Les oeuvres morales et politiques

Tavernier, Melchior
1618 Schouten, W. C. Journal
1619 Schouten, W. C. Journal
1624 Relation de la prinse
1628 Bertius, P. [Geographia]
1630 Bertius, P. Geographia

Thiboust, Samuel
1615 Pyrard, F. Voyage . . . aux Indes
1619 Pyrard, F. Voyage . . . aux Indes
1619 Serres, J. de. Inventaire general
1625 Barclay, J. Le pourtraict des esprits
1626 Cyriaque de Mangin, C. Cosmographie
1627 Camden, W. Histoire d'Elizabeth
1635 Mayerne, L. T. de. Histoire generale d'Espagne

Tiffaine, Adrien
1616 Acosta, J. de. Histoire naturelle
1617 Acosta, J. de. Histoire naturelle
1617 Loubayssin de Lamarca, F. Historia tragicomica
1621 Acosta, J. de. Histoire naturelle

Traboulliet, Nicolas
1633 Saint-Amant, M. A. de Gérard, sieur de. Les oeuvres
1635 Saint-Amant, M. A. de Gérard, sieur de. Les oeuvres
1638 Saint-Amant, M. A. de Gérard, sieur de. Les oeuvres

University of Paris. *See* Paris, University of

*Varennes, Olivier de
1613 Avity, P. d'. Les estats
1614 Avity, P. d'. Les estats
1617 Avity, P. d'. Les estats
1619 Avity, P. d'. Les estats
1623 Marino, G. B. L'Adone
1633 Pasquier, E. Les recherches
1640 Brerewood, E. Recherches
. . . sur la diversité des langues
1640 Pardoux, B. Universa
medicina
1640 Rivière, L. Methodus
curandorum febrium
1640 Rivière, L. Praxis medica
1641 Rivière, L. Methodus
curandorum febrium
1644 Rivière, L. Praxis medica
1645 Harduin, P. Codex
medicamentarius
1647 Rivière, L. Praxis medica
1648 Rivière, L. Methodus
curandorum febrium
Varennes, Olivier de, Widow of
1625 Avity, P. d'. Les estats
Vendosme, Louis
1645 Du Mas de Flores, I. La clef
de la geographie generale
Verard, Martin
1602 Richeome, L. Trois
discours
Villéry, Jacques
1623 Bauderon, B. Paraphrase
sur la Pharmacopoee
1624 Bertius, P. Abrégé ou
Sommaire description du
globe
1626 Boccalini, T. Pierre de
touche politique
1634 Bertius, P. Abrégé ou
Sommaire description du
globe
1635 Boccalini, T. Pierre de
touched
1636 Montaigne, M. E. de. Essais
1643 Serres, J. de. Inventaire
general
Villéry, Pierre
1645 Relation d'un voyage
Vitre, Antoine
1648 Catholic church. Pope,
1644–1655. Breve

PERPIGNAN
Roure, Louis
1626 Agustí, M. Libro de los
secretos de agricultura

1629 Suárez de Figueroa, C.
Plaza universal
1630 Suárez de Figueroa, C.
Plaza universal
1636 Calvo, J. Cirugia universal,
1a–2a pte

POITIERS
Mesnier, Antoine
1609 Contant, P. Le jardin et
cabinet poétique
Mesnier, Antoine, Widow of
1628 Contant, J. Les oeuvres
Thoreau, Julien
1628 Contant, P. Les oeuvres

PONT-À-MOUSSON
Bernard, Melchior
1608 Rivadeneira, P. de. La vie
du b.p. Ignace de Loyola

RENNES
Glamet, Noël
1603 Du Fail, N. Les contes et
discours d'Eutrapel
L'Oyselet, Pierre
1625 Quervau, V. Le tableau
historiale du monde

ROUEN
Printer unidentified
1623 Dupleix, S. La curiosite
naturelle
1628 Rivadeneira, P. de. Vies des
saints
Angot, Nicolas
1614 González de Mendoza, J.
Histoire . . . de la Chine.
1617 Montaigne, M. E. de. Les
essais
1619 Montaigne, M. E. de. Les
essais
1643 González de Mendoza, J.
Histoire . . . de la Chine
Beauvais, Romain de
1610 Torquemada, A. de.
Hexameron
Behourt, Jean
1647 Béguin, J. Les elemens de
chymie
Behourt, Jean Baptiste
1623 Du Bartas, G. de S.,
seigneur. Les oeuvres
poetiques
1628 Gesner, K. Quatre livres
des secrets de medecine

Berthelin, Jean
1617 Montaigne, M. E. de. Les
essais
1619 Montaigne, M. E. de. Les
essais
1620 Tabourot, E. Les
bigarrures
1625 Pigray, P. Epitome des
preceptes de medecine
1627 Montaigne, M. E. de. Essais
1632 Estienne, C. L'agriculture
1634 Croll, O. La royale chymie
1638 Avity, P. d'. Les estats
1641 Estienne, C. L'agriculture
1641? Montaigne, M. E. de.
Essais
1641 Montaigne, M. E. de. Essais
1642 Pigray, P. Epitome des
preceptes de medecine
1642 Sala, G. Secrets publiques
1643 Mexía, P. Les diverses
leçons
1646 Cervantes Saavedra, M. de.
Le valeureux Dom Quixote
1646 Serres, O. de. Le theatre
d'agriculture
1649 Clüver, P. Introduction a
la geographie
1650 Porta, G. B. della. Phytognomonica
1650 Ruland, M. Curationum
empyricarum . . . centuriae
decem
1650 Sala, A. Opera medico-
chymica
Besongne, Jacques
1617 Montaigne, M. E. de. Les
essais
1619 Esternod, C. d'. L'espadon
satyrique
1619 Montaigne, M. E. de. Les
essais
1627 Montaigne, M. E. de. Essais
1649 Companhia geral para o
estado do Brazil. Articles
**Besongne, Jacques, the
Younger**
1641 Montaigne, M. E. de. Essais
Boulley, Jean
1619 Esternod, C. d'. L'espadon
satyrique
1626 Béguin, J. Les elemens de
chymie
1627 Béguin, J. Les elemens de
chymie
1642 Saint-Amant, M. A. de
Gérard, sieur de. Les oeuvres

Cailloué, Jacques
1623 Du Bartas, G. de S., seigneur. Les oeuvres poetiques
1625 Avity, P. d'. Les estats
1627 Montaigne, M. E. de. Essais
1630 Avity, P. d'. Les estats
1630 Casas, B. de las. Tyrannies . . . des Espanols
1633 Avity, P. d'. Les estats
1642 Planis Campy, D. de. La chirurgie
1644 Avity, P. d'. Les estats
1645 Mocquet, J. Voyages en Afrique, Asie, Indes
1646 Cervantes Saavedra, M. de. Le valeureux Dom Quixote
1649 Avity, P. d'. Les estats

Calles, Pierre
1610 Du Bartas, G. de S., seigneur. Les oeuvres poetiques
1616 Gesner, K. Quatre livres des Secrets de medecine

Costé, Louys
1625 Estienne, C. L'agriculture

Cousturier, Daniel
1623 Du Bartas, G. de S., seigneur. Les oeuvres poetiques

Daré, Robert
1649 Saint-Amant, M. A. de Gérard, sieur de. Les oeuvres

Daré, Thomas
1606 Goulart, S. Histoires admirables et memorables
1615 Matthieu, P. Histoire de France (t 1)
1617 Montaigne, M. E. de. Les essais

Daré, Thomas, Widow of
1619 Montaigne, M. E. de. Les essais

Du Mesnil, Louis
1627 Montaigne, M. E. de. Essais
1638 Pigray, P. Epitome des preceptes de medecine
1640 Tabourot, E. Les bigarrures
1647 Serres, J. de. Inventaire general
1648 Tabourot, E. Les bigarrures

Du Petit Val, David
1616 Du Bartas, G. de S., seigneur. Premiere sepmaine

1625 Du Ferrier, J. Le Catholique d'estat
1625 Marguérite d'Angoulême. L'Heptameron
1632 Hoyarsabal, M. de. Les voyages
1637 France. Amirauté. Reglement
1644 Avity, P. d'. Noveau théatre du monde

Du Petit Val, Raphael
1602 Du Bartas, G. de S., seigneur. Premiere sepmaine . . . La seconde sepmaine (2)
1602 Du Bartas, G. de S., seigneur. La seconde sepmaine
1603 Du Hamel, J. Acoubar
1608 Du Bartas, G. de S., seigneur. Premiere sepmaine
1608 Du Bartas, G. de S., seigneur. La seconde sepmaine
1611 Du Hamel, J. Acoubar
1616 Du Bartas, G. de S., seigneur. Premiere sepmaine

Durand, Jean
1617 Montaigne, M. E. de. Les essais
1619 Montaigne, M. E. de. Les essais (3)

Feron, Robert
1627 Montaigne, M. E. de. Essais

Ferrand, David
1624 Esternod, C. d'. L'espadon satyrique
1625? Esternod, C. d'. L'espadon satyrique
1633 Medina, P. de. L'art de naviguer
1638 Pigray, P. Epitome des preceptes de medecine
1642 Pigray, P. Epitome des preceptes de medecine
1642 Saint-Amant, M. A. de Gérard, sieur de. Les oeuvres
1645 Alemán, M. Le gueux
1646 Cervantes Saavedra, M. de. Le valeureux Dom Quixote

Geuffroy, David
1616 Tabourot, E. Les bigarrures
1621 Tabourot, E. Les bigarrures
1625 Tabourot, E. Les bigarrures

1626 Tabourot, E. Les bigarrures

Hollant, J.
1649 Pigray, P. Epitome des preceptes de medecine

L'Allemant, Richard
1618 Le grand dictionnaire françois-latin
1625 Le grand dictionare françois-latin
1630 Ledesma, D . de. Doctrine chrestienne
1645 Dupleix, S. La curiosité naturelle

La Mare, Jean de
1628 Barclay, J. Euphormionis Lusinini . . . Satyricon
1632 Alemán, M. Le gueux

La Motte, Martin de
1627 Bauderon, B. Paraphrase sur la Pharmacopoee
1637 Béguin, J. Les elemens de chymie

La Motte, Pierre de
1627 Montaigne, M. E. de. Essais

Le Boullenger, Jacques
1630 Daniel, C. La prise d'un seigneur escossois
1638 Le Jeune, P. Relation de ce qui s'est passé . . . en l'année 1637 (2)
1644 Le Moyne, P. Manifeste apologetique
1649 Le Brun, L. Ecclesiastes
1650 Le Brun, L. Ecclesiastes

Le Prevost, Nicolas
1619 Esternod, C. d'. L'espadon satyrique

Loudet, Clovys (Louis)
1625 Dupleix, S. La curiosité naturelle

Loudet, Daniel
1638 Dupleix, S. La curiosité naturelle
1642 Pigray, P. Epitome des preceptes de medecine

Loudet, Louis
1616 Du Bartas, G. de S., seigneur. Les oeuvres poetiques
1623 Du Bartas, G. de S., seigneur. Les oeuvres poetiques
1630 Pigray, P. Epitome des preceptes de medecine

L'Oyselet, Nicolas
1643 Gesner, K. Secrets de medecine
1645 Guibert, P. Toutes les oeuvres
Malassis, Clément
1635 Dupleix, S. La curiosité naturelle
1644 Bauderon, B. Pharmacopee
1647 Serres, J. de. Inventaire general
Manneville, Jean de
1644 Le Moyne, P. Manifeste apologetique
Osmont, Jean
1602 Richeome, L. Trois discours
1604 Richeome, L. Trois discours
1613 Estienne, C. L'agriculture
1615 Matthieu, P. Histoire de France (t 1)
1617 Montaigne, M. E. de. Les essais
1618 Le grand dictionnaire françois-latin
1619 Montaigne, M. E. de. Les essais
1623 Serres, O. de. Le theatre d'agriculture
1628 Le grand dictionnaire françois-latin
1634 Croll, O. La royale chymie
Osmont, Jean, the Younger
1638 Saint-Amant, M. A. de Gérard, sieur de. Les oeuvres
Oursel, Louis
1639 Duchesne, J. La pharmacopee
Ouyn, Adrian
1610 Du Bartas, G. de S., seigneur. Les oeuvres poetiques
1612 Bauderon, B. Paraphrase sur la Pharmacopoee
1615 Pigray, P. Epitome des preceptes de medecine
1619 Montaigne, M. E. de. Les essais
1625 Avity, P. d'. Les estats
1630 Avity, P. d'. Les estats
1644 Avity, P. d'. Les estats
Petit, Jean
1606 Lescarbot, M. Adieu a la France
1608 Usselinx, W. Sommaire recueil

Pitreson, Corneille
1639 Duchesne, J. La pharmacopee
1641 Guibert, P. Toutes les oeuvres charitables
Préaulx, Manasses de
1617 Montaigne, M. E. de. Les essais
1620 Montaigne, M. E. de. Les essais
1626 Dupleix, S. La curiosité naturelle
1628 Medina, P. de. L'art de naviguer
Reinsart, Théodore
1602 Alfonce, J., i.e., Jean Fonteneau, known as. Les voyages avantureux
1602 Du Bartas, G. de S., seigneur. Premiere sepmaine . . . La seconde sepmaine
1602 Du Bartas, G. de S., seigneur. La seconde sepmaine
1602 Medina, P. de. L'art de naviguer
1607 Medina, P. de. L'art de naviguer
Roger, Jean
1625 Torquemada, A. de. Histoires en forme de dialogues
1626 Mexía, P. Les diverses leçons (2)
Seigneuré, Ozée
1639 Duchesne, J. La pharmacopee
1641 Guibert, P. Toutes les oeuvres
Valentin, Robert
1617 Montaigne, M. E. de. Les essais
1619 Montaigne, M. E. de. Les essais
1627 Montaigne, M. E. de. Essais
1635 Serres, O. de. Le theatre d'agriculture
Viret, Jean
1637 France. Amirauté. Reglement

ST GERVAIS
Crespin, Samuel
1602 Clavius, C. In Sphaeram Joannis de Sacro Bosco commentarius

1607 Clavius, C. In Sphaeram Joannis de Sacro Bosco commentarius
1608 Clavius, C. In Sphaeram Joannis de Sacro Bosco commentarius
Vignon, Eustache, Heirs of
1603 Duchesne, J. Liber de priscorum philosphorum verae medicinae materia

ST OMER
Boscard, Charles
1614 Avity, P. d'. Les empires
1614 Avity, P. d'. Les estats
English College Press
1612 Floyd, J. The overthrow of the Protestants pulpitbabels
1616 Rivadeneira, P. de. The life of . . . Ignatius of Loyola
1619 Morejon, P. A briefe relation of the persecution
1622 Rivadeneira, P. de. The life of the holy patriarch

SAUMUR
Burel, Jean
1621 Buchanan, G. Poemata (2)
Desbordes, Isaac
1629 Geslin, P. La saincte chorographie
Girard, Claude
1621 Buchanan, G. Poemata
1629 Geslin, P. La saincte chorographie
Lerpinière, Daniel
1621 Buchanan, G. Poemata
Lesnier, Jean
1629 Geslin, P. La saincte chorographie
Portau, Thomas
1607 Buchanan, G. Franciscanus et fratres

STRASBOURG. *See* Germany—Strassburg

TOUL
Philippe, Sébastien
1614 Guibert, N. De interitu alchymiae

TOULOUSE
Bosc, Dominique
1616 Pascal, J. Discours . . . de la pharmacie

Bosc, Pierre
1628 Fabre, P. J. Myrothecium
   spagyricum
1636 Sánchez, F. Opera medica
1646 Fabre, P. J. Myrothecium
   spagyricum
Boudé, Jean
1625 La furieuse défaite des
   Espagnols
1625 Spinola, A. La sommation
Estey, Nicolas d'
1628 Fabre, P. J. Myrothecium
   spagyricum

TOURNON
Michel, Claude
1604 Mexía, P. Les diverses
   leçons
1609 Mexía, P. Les diverses
   leçons
1610 Mexía, P. Les diverses
   leçons
1613 Claude d'Abbeville.
   Discours
1616 Mexía, P. Les diverses
   leçons
Soubron, Thomas
1604 Mexía, P. Les diverses
   leçons

VALENCIENNES
Vervliet, Jean
1611 Du Jarric, P. L'histoire des
   choses plus memorables
1620 Jesuits. Letters from
   missions. Histoire du massacre

VILLENEUVE
1626 Scribanius, C. *See* The
   Netherlands—Printer
   unidentified

GERMANY

Printer unidentified
1608 Ein Dialogus oder
   Gespräch
1608 Usselinx, W. Aussführung
   allerhand wolbedencklicher
   Argumenten
1626 Sweden. Sovereigns, etc.,
   1611–1632. Octroy oder Privilegium
1628? Hein, P. P. Aussführlicher
   Bericht

ALTENA
1608 Hovt en beleght. *See* Fictitious Locations—Spa, outside
   Altena

AMBERG
Forster, Michael
1602 Panciroli, G. Nova reperta
   sive Rerum memorabilium recens inventarum . . . Liber secundus
1607 Panciroli, G. Rerum memorabilium libri duo
1612 Panciroli, G. Rerum memorabilium libri duo
Schönfeld, Johann
1608 Owen, J. Epigrammatum libri tres
1611 Beringer, J. Hispanicae Inquisitionis . . . secretiora
1611 Owen, J. Epigrammatum libri tres
1612 Beringer, J. Der tyrannischen hispanischen Inquisition
   Heimligkeiten . . . offenbaret

ARNSTADT
Vögelin Press
1601 Wittich, J. Bericht
1603 Wittich, J. Von dem Ligno
   Guayaco

AUGSBURG
Printer unidentified
1626 Scribanius, C. Der
   holländisch Apocalypsis
1628 Scribanius, C. Weit und
   tieffsinnig Bedencken
1629 Scribanius, C. Aussführliches . . . politisches Bedencken (2)
1643 Pharmacopoeia Augustana
Aperger, Andreas
1619 Alemán, M. Der Landtstörtzer
1622 Pharmacopoeia Augustana
1623 Pharmacopoeia Augustana
1625 Scribanius, C. Holländisch
   apocalypsis
1625 Warhaffte gründliche Relation
1629 Pharmacopoeia Augustana
1640 Pharmacopoeia Augustana
1646 Pharmacopoeia Augustana
1647 Stengel, K. Hortensius et
   dea flora cum pomona historice . . . descripti

1650 Stengel, K. Hortorum . . .
   historia
Besard, Jean Baptiste
1617 Besard, J. B. Antrum philosophicum
Custos, Dominicus
1615? Abriss der Blümen
Dabertzhofer, Chrysostomus
1611 Jesuits. Letters from missions. Drey newe Relationes
1611 Queiros, P. F. de. Relation
1613 Claude d'Abbeville. Die
   Ankunfft
1613 Lescarbot, Marc. Nova
   Francia. Gründliche History
Franck, David
1617 Besard, J. B. Antrum philosophicum
1624 Brassillische Relation
Keyltz, Johann
1625 Toledo Osorio y Mendoza,
   F. de. Relation
Kruger, Johann
1613 Pharmacopoeia Augustana
1622 Pharmacopoeia Augustana
1623 Pharmacopoeia Augustana
1629 Pharmacopoeia Augustana
Langenwalter, Matthäus
1625 Toledo Osorio y Mendoza,
   F. de. Relation
Mang, Christoph
1613 Pharmacopoeia Augustana
1615? Abriss der Blümen
1616 Rivadeneira, P. de. Vita b.
   Ignatii
Mangin, Sarah
1620 Jesuits. Letters from missions. Auss America
Zimmermann, W. P.
1624 Brassillische Relation

BRAUNSCHWEIG
Gruber, Balthasar
1641 Clüver, P. Introductionis in
   universam geographiam . . .
   libri vi
Müller, Gottfried
1641 Clüver, P. Introductionis in
   universam geographiam . . .
   libri vi

BREMEN
Berger, Erhard
1649 Barclay, J. Icon animorum
   oder Gründtliche Beschreibung

BRESLAU

Printer unidentified

1637 Opitz, M. Deutscher Poematum. Erster[-Anderer] Theil

Müller, David

1628 Opitz, M. Deutscher Poematum Erster[-Anderer] Theil

1628 Opitz, M. Laudes Martis . . . Poema Germanicum

1629 Opitz, M. Deutscher Poematum Erster[-Anderer] Theil

1631 Grotius, H. Die Meinung der Bücher . . . Von der Warheit

1631 Grotius, H. Von der Warheit

Müller, David, Heirs of

1638 Opitz, M. Weltliche Poemata

BRIEG

Gründer, Augustin

1628 Opitz, M. Laudes Martis . . . Poema Germanicum

1631 Grotius, H. Von der Warheit

COBURG

Bertsch, Caspar

1627 Aldenburgk, J. G. West-Indianische Reisse

Grüner, Friedrich

1627 Aldenburgk, J. G. West-Indianische Reisse

COLOGNE

Printer unidentified

1634? Braun, G. Civitates orbis terrarum

1635 Zeitungen . . . wie die Holländer in Brassilien . . . Forten eingenommen

Birckmann, House of

1602 Mylius, A. De rebus hispanicis

1602 Rivadeneira, P. de. Vita p. Ignatii Loiolae

1602 Sepúlveda, J. G. de. Opera

Birckmann Office

1622 Torsellino, O. Epitome historiarum libri x

1628 Pharmacopoea sive Dispensatorium Coloniense

1631 Torsellino, O. Chronicon ab orbe condito

Boetzer, Anton

1612 Béguin, J. Tyrocinium chymicum

1614 Béguin, J. Tyrocinium chymicum

1615 Béguin, J. Tyrocinium chymicum

Brachel, Peter von

1612 Braun, G. Civitates orbis terrarum

1623 Alemán, M. Vitae humanae proscenium

1623 Braun, G. Civitates orbis terrarum

1624 Braun, G. Civitates orbis terrarum

1629 Ens, G. Newer . . . teutscher Mercurius

Braun, Georg

1612 Braun, G. Civitates orbis terrarum

Busäus, Johann

1646 Balde, J. Lyricorum libri iv

Bussemacher, Johann

1608 Quad, M. Fasciculus geographicus

Cholinus, Goswin

1601 Sacro Bosco, J. de. Sphaera

1610 Sacro Bosco, J. de. Sphaera

Christoffel, Johann

1610 Jesuits. Verzeichnuss alle Provintzen

Demen, Michael

1627 Gravina, D. Vox turturis

Egmondt, Cornelis ab, & Co.

1629 More, Sir T. Utopia à mendis vindicata

Greuenbruch, Gerhard

1613 Deliciae lusitano-hispanicae

Gymnicus, Johannes

1607 Possevino, A. Bibliotheca selecta

1610 Possevino, A. Cultura ingeniorum

1626 Bozio, T. De signis ecclesiae Dei

Henning, Peter

1615 Du Jarric, P. Thesaurus rerum indicarum

1616 Gaultier, J. Tabula chronographica

1617 Del Rio, M. A. Disquisitionum magicarum libri sex

1620 Marquardus, J. Practica medicinalis

1621 Marquardus, J. Practica medicinalis

1624 Del Rio, M. A. Disquisitionum magicarum libri sex

1625 Opmeer, P. van. Chronographia mundi

1633 Del Rio, M. A. Disquisitionum magicarum libri sex

1633 Mendoça, F. de. Viridarium sacrae profanae eruditionis

1650 Mendoça, F. de. Viridarium sacrae ac profanae eruditionis

Hierat, Anton

1611 Botero, G. Allgemeine historische Weltbeschreibung

1612 Botero, G. Allgemeine historische Weltbeschreibung

1615 Jesuits. Historiae Societatis Jesu prima pars

1621 Jesuits. Historiae Societatis Jesu pars prima

1621 Jesuits. Historiae Societatis Jesu pars secunda

Kalckhoven, Jost

1643 Kircher, A. Magnes

1645 Balde, J. Lyricorum libri iv

1646 Balde, J. Lyricorum libri iv

1646 Balde, J. Sylvae lyricae

Kempen, Arnold

1609 Morellas, C. G. Compendiosa relatio

Keschedt, Peter

1608 Ptolemaeus, C. Geographiae universae . . . opus

Kinckius, Johann

1617 Berettari, S. Vita r.p. Josephi Anchietae

Kinckius, Johann Anton

1649 Torsellino, O. Epitome historiarum

Krafft, Heinrich

1638 Gravina, D. Vox turturis

Lützenkirchen, Wilhelm

1604 Quad, M. Enchiridion cosmographicum

1606 Botero, G. Macht, Reichthum und Einkommen

1608 Arthus, G. Historia Indiae Orientalis

1612 Ens, G. Indiae Occidentalis historia

1612 Ens, G. Mauritiados libri vi

1618 Ens, G. West- unnd Ost Indischer Lustgart

Münich, Constantin
1650 Saavedra Fajardo, D. de.
Idea principis christiano-politici
Mylius, Arnold
1602 Rivadeneira, P. de. Vita p.
Ignatii Loiolae
1602 Sepúlveda, J. G. de. Opera
**Mylius, Arnold (House of
Birckmann)**
1605 Rubio, A. Logica mexicana
Mylius, Hermann
1614 Molina, L. de. De justitia et
jure
1622 Torsellino, O. Epitome
historiarum libri x
1628 Pharmacopoea sive Dispensatorium Coloniense
1631 Torsellino, O. Chronicon
ab orbe condito
**Mylius, J. (House of Birck-
mann)**
1604 Fregoso, B. Factorum et
dictorum memorabilium lib. ix
Schmitz (Smitz), Matthäus
1616 Potier, P. Insignes curationes
1620 Baricelli, G. C. Hortulus
genialis
1623 Potier, P. Insignium curationum . . . centuria secunda
1624 Potier, P. Pharmacopoea
spagirica
1625 Potier, P. Insignes curationes
Stam, Jan Frederickszoon
1629 Zacutus, A. De medicorum
principum historia
Wolter, Bernhard
1604 Rivadeneira, P. de. Princeps christianus
1619 Le Mire, A. De statu religionis christianae
1621 Torsellino, O. Epitomae
historiarum libri x
1624 Torsellino, O. Historiarum . . . epitome libri x
1625 Opmeer, P. van. Chronographia mundi
1626 Vergilius, P. De rerum inventoribus libri octo

DANZIG. *See* Poland—Danzig

DARMSTADT
Leinhose, Johannes
1624 Fioravanti, L. Compendium . . . der Secreten

Porsch, Johann Jakob
1611 Kornmann, H. Templum
naturae historicum

DILLINGEN
Printer unidentified
1645 Bacon, F. Historia vitae
Algeyer, Melchior
1618 Jesuits. Letters from missions. Annuae litterae (1611)
1618. Annuae litterae-
. . . anni M.DC.XI
Mayer, Johann, Widow of
1618? Jesuits. Letters from missions. Annuae litterae (1609)
1618. Annuae litterae . . . anni
M.DC.IX
1618? Jesuits. Letters from missions. Annuae litterae (1610)
1618. Annuae litterae . . . anni
M.DC.X
Mayer Press
1618 Jesuits. Letters from missions. Annuae litterae (1611)
1618. Annuae litterae . . . anni
M.DC.XI
Sutor, Caspar
1629 Niess, J. Adolescens Europaeus ab Indo moribus christianis informatus

EISLEBEN
Apel, Jakob
1603 Thoelde, J. Haliographia
Gaubisch, Jakob
1603 Thoelde, J. Haliographia

EMDEN
Gerlach, Christian
1650 Calvisius, S. Opus chronologicum
Kallenbach, Helwig
1638 Owen, J. Rosarium

ERFURT
Printer unidentified
1634 Trophaeum hermetico-
Hippocraticum
Birckner, Johann
1630 Sala, A. Ternarius ternariorum
Fritsche, Tobias
1644 Barnstein, H. Taback das
Wunder
1645 Barnstein, H. Kurtze Beschreibung dess Tabacks
1645 Barnstein, H. Tabacologia

1646 Barnstein, H. Kurtze Beschreibung dess Tabacks
1647 Barnstein, H. Kurtze Beschreibung dess Tabacks
1648 Barnstein, H. Kurtze Beschreibung dess Tabacks
Mechler, Esaias, Heirs of
1618 Sala, A. Ternarius bezoardicorum
1630 Sala, A. Ternarius ternariorum
Steinmann, Hieronymus
1624 Juncker, J. Compendiosa
methodus therapeutica

FRANKFURT AM MAIN
Printer unidentified
1612 Rauw, J. Weltbeschreibung
1613 Barclay, J. Euphormionis
Lusinini Satyricon
1616 Barclay, J. Euphormionis
Lusinini Satyricon
1624 Memorabilia, das ist
. . . Beschreibung
1625 Spilbergen, J. van.
Dreyjährige Reise
1626 Freudenhold, M. Der
Landtstörtzer, 3. Theil
1629 Gilbert, W. Tractatus
. . . de magnete
1630 Entwerffung von Eroberung der Stadt Olinda (2)
1630 Erschröckliche Zeitung
1630 Waerdenburgh, D. van.
Copie eines Schreibens
1643 Liébault, J. Warhaffte Beschreibung
1648 Opitz, M. Weltliche Poemata
1649 Barclay, J. Icon animorum
oder Gründliche Beschrei-
bung
Albert, L.
1602 Duchesne, J. Opera medica
Ammon, Johann
1645 Boissard, J. J. Icones
1650 Boissard, J. J. Bibliotheca
chalcographica
Aubry, Daniel & David
1625 Barclay, J. Icon animorum
1625 Fonseca, R. Consultationum medicinalium singularibus remediis refertae
1625 Popp, J. Chymische Medicin
1626 Guidi, G. Opera

1627 Hues, R. Tractatus de globis

Aubry, Johann, Heirs of

1601 Le Paulmier de Grentemesnil, J. De morbis contagiosis libri septem

1601 Scaliger, J. C. Exotericarum exercitationum liber xv

1601 Silvaticus, J. B. Controversiae numero centum

1602 Conestaggio, G. F. di. De Portugalliae conjunctione

1603 Maffei, R. Commentariorum urbanorum libri

1603 Schottus, A. Hispaniae illustratae

1606 Mariana, J. de. Historiae hispanicae appendix

1606 Steeghius, G. Ars medica

1607 Fernel, J. De abditis rerum causis

1607 Fernel, J. Universa medicina

1607 Peucer, K. Commentarius

1607 Scaliger, J. C. Exotericarum exercitationum liber xv

1608 Schottus, A. Hispaniae bibliotheca

1609 Croll, O. Basilicus chymica

Aubry Office

1614 Gruterus, J. Chronicon

Basse, Johann

1613 Theodorus, J. Neuw . . . Kreuterbuch

1614 Collibus, H. à. Fürstliche Tischreden

1617 Collibus, H. à. Fürstliche Tischreden

Basse, Nikolaus

1601 Massaria, A. Practica medica

Basse, Nikolaus, Heirs of

1608 Romanus, A. Parvum theatrum urbium

1610 Aldrovandi, U. Ornithologiae . . . libri xii

1610 Bauhin, K. De compositione medicamentorum

1630 Aldrovandi, U. Ornithologiae . . . libri xii

1640 Aldrovandi, U. Ornithologiae . . . libri xii

Beatus, Georg

1601 Columba, G. Disputationum medicarum . . . libri duo

Beatus, Romanus, Heirs of

1601 Columba, G. Disputationum medicarum . . . libri duo

Beckenstein, Simon

1650 Calvisius, S. Opus chronologicum

Becker, Matthäus

1601 Acosta, J. de. Neundter . . . Theil Americae, pt 2

1601 Linschoten, J. H. van. Tertia pars Indiae Orientalis

1601 Neck, J. C. van. Fünffter Theil der Orientalischen Indien

1601 Neck, J. C. van. Quinta pars Indiae Orientalis

1601 Potgieter, B. J. Historische Relation

1602 Acosta, J. de. Americae nona et postrema pars

1602 Noort, O. van. Additamentum . . . dess neundten Theils Americae

1602 Noort, O. van. Additamentum nonae partis Americae

1602 Noort, O. van. Neue Schiffart

1602 Potgieter, B. J. Relatio historica

1605 Cesalpino, A. Katoptron

1605 Spilbergen, J. van. Newe Schifffahrt

1605 Spilbergen, J. van. Siebender Theil der Orientalischen Indien (2)

1605 Staden, H. Americae tertia pars

1608 Hulsius, L. Achte Schiffart

1609 Lopes, D. Regnum Congo

1610 Boutrays, R. Historiopolitographia

1610? Langenes, B. Thrésor de chartes

1612 Bertius, P. Geographischer . . . Tabeln fünff . . . Bücher

Becker, Mätthäus, Widow of

1613 Benzoni, G. Das vierdte Buch von der neuwen Welt (2)

1613 Gerritsz, H. Indiae Orientalis Pars X

1613 Gerritsz, H. Zehender Theil der Orientalischen Indien

1613 Verken, J. Continuatio . . . dess neundten Theils (2)

Berner, Johann

1604 Fioravanti, L. Corona; oder, Kron der Artzney

1604 Fioravanti, L. Physica

1610 Gabelkover, O. Artzneybuch

1618 Fioravanti, L. Corona . . . der Artzney

1618 Sánchez, F. De multum nobili et prima universali scientia

1624 Fioravanti, L. Compendium oder Ausszug

Berner, Johann, Widow & Heirs of

1641 Gabelkover, O. Artzneybuch

Beyer, Johann

1626 Marino, G. B. La Murtoleide. *See under* Italy—Venice—Printer unidentified

1641 Prevost, J. Medicina pauperum

1643 Severino, M. A. De recondita abscessum natura

1644 Boccalini, T. Relation aus Parnasso

1647 Sala, A. Opera medicochymica

1648 Duchesne, J. Quercetanus redivivus

1650 Zecchi, G. Consultationes medicinales

Bitsch, Johann Ludwig

1601 Columba, G. Disputationum medicarum . . . libri duo

Bitsch, Ludwig

1604A Boemus, J. Historia moralis

Bringer, Johann

1611 Porta, G. B. della. Ars destillatoria

1614 Collibus, H. à. Fürstliche Tischreden

1614 Owen, J. Epigrammatum libri tres

1616 Camden, W. Annales

Bry, Johann Theodor de

1613 Benzoni, G. Das vierdte Buch von der neuwen Welt (2)

1613 Verken, J. Continuatio oder Ergäntzung dess neundten Theils (2)

1619 Benzoni, G. Das sechste Theil Americae

1620 Hariot, T. Wunderbarliche . . . Erklärung von . . . Virginia

1620 Spilbergen, J. van. Americae tomi undecimi appendix

1620 Spilbergen, J. van. Appendix dess eilfften Theils Americae

1623 Herrera y Tordesillas, A. de. Zwölffter Theil der Newen Welt

1626 Bry, J. T. de. Anthologia magna

Bry, Johann Theodor de, Heirs of

1624 Herrera y Tordesillas, A. de. Novi Orbis pars duodecima

1624 Lopes, D. Regnum Congo

1624 Raleigh, Sir W. Achter Theil Americae

1625 Braun, S. Anhang der Beschreibung dess Königreichs Congo

1625 Braun, S. Appendix Regni Congo

Bry, Johann Theodor de, Widow & Heirs of

1608 Schenck, J. G. Hortus Patavinus

1625 Schmidel, U. Americae pars vii

1625 Schmidel, U. Vera . . . descriptio . . . Indiae Occidentalis

Bry, Johann Theodor & Johann Israel de

1601 Linschoten, J. H. van. Tertia pars Indiae Orientalis

1604 Marees, P. de. Indiae Orientalis, pars vi

1609 Lopes, D. Regnum Congo

Bry, Theodor de

1605 Staden, H. Americae tertia pars

1606 Staden, H. Dritte Buch Americae

1608 Hariot, T. Admiranda narratio . . . Virginiae

1609 Laudonnière, R. G. de. Brevis narratio

Bry, Theodor de, Widow & Sons of

1603 Laudonnière, R. G. de. Der ander Theil der . . . Landtschafft Americae

Bry Office

1627 Bertius, P. Breviarium totius orbis terrarum

Cambier, Andreas

1604 Gesner, K. Historia animalium

Dreutel, Johann

1613 Theodorus, J. Neuw vollkommentlich Kreuterbuch

1625 Theodorus, J. New vollkommentlich Kreuterbuch

Emmel, Egenolff

1615 Camerarius, P. Operae horarum subcisivarum . . . Centuria prima

1617 Gesner, K. Historia animalium

1617 Popp, J. Chymische Medicin

1620 Camerarius, P. Operae horarum subcisivarum . . . Centuria . . . altera

1620 Collibus, H. à. Fürstliche Tischreden

1621 Thou, J. A. de. Historische Beschreibung

1623 Campanella, T. Realis philosophiae epilogisticae partes quatuor

1624 Camerarius, P. Operae horarum subcisivarum . . . Centuria prima

1624 Marees, P. de. Siebende Schiffahrt

1625 Draud, G. Bibliotheca librorum Germanicorum classica

1625 Thou, J. A. de. Historiarum sui temporis . . . libri

Feyerabend, Sigmund

1608 Hariot, T. Admiranda narratio . . . Virginiae

1609 Laudonnière, R. G. de. Brevis narratio

Fievet, Philipp

1648 Bontekoe, W. Y. Die vier und zwantzigste Schiffahrt

Fischer, Jakob

1610 Uffenbach, P. Thesaurus chirurgiae

1611 Mattioli, P. A. Kreutterbuch

1612 Paré, A. Opera chirurgica

Fischer, Jakob, Heirs of

1626 Mattioli, P. A. Kreutterbuch

1635 Paré, A. Wund Artzney

Fischer, Peter

1601 Paré, A. Wundt Artzney

Fischer, Peter Jacob

1642 Grégoire, P. De republica, libri sex

Fitzer, Wilhelm

1628 Boissard, J. J. Bibliotheca sive Thesaurus virtutis

1628 Bry, J. T. de. Der dreyzehende Theil der Orientalischen Indien

1628 Bry, J. T. de. Historiarum Orientalis Indiae tomus XII

1628 Bry, J. T. de. Der zwölffte Theil der Orientalischen Indien

1628 Fitzer, W. Orientalische Indien

1629 Fitzer, W. Extract der Orientalischen Indien

1629 Linschoten, J. H. van. Tertia pars Indiae Orientalis (2)

1630 Norton, S. Metamorphosis lapidum ignobilium

1633 Gerritsz, H. Indiae Orientalis Pars X

Götz, Thomas Matthias

1644 Opitz, M. Weltliche Poemata

Hallervord, Johann

1644 Camerarius, P. Operae horarum subcisivarum . . . Centuria prima

Hartmann, Melchior

1601 Massaria, A. Practica medica

Haubold, Peter

1647 Aldrovandi, U. De piscibus libri v

1647 Aldrovandi, U. Quadrupedum omnium bisulcorum historia

Hofer, Johann

1620 Spilbergen, J. van. Americae tomi undecimi appendix

1620 Spilbergen, J. van. Die siebenzehende Schiffart

Hoffmann, Nikolaus, the Elder

1604 Fioravanti, L. Corona; oder, Kron der Artzney

1604 Fioravanti, L. Physica

1608 Macchelli, N. Tractatus methodicus

1608 Porta, G. B. della. Phytognomonica

1609 Bodin, J. De republica libri sex

Kempfer, Matthäus
1629 Aldrovandi, U. De piscibus libri v
1642 Grégoire, P. De republica, libri sex

Kempner, Anton
1612 Sweerts, E. Florilegium

Koch, Michael
1636 Ruland, J. D. Inauguralis de lue . . . venerea disputatio

Kopff, Peter
1601 Camerarius, P. Operae horarum subcisivarum . . . Centuria altera
1601 More, Sir T. De optimo reipublicae statu
1602 Camerarius, P. Operae horarum subcisivarum . . . Centuria prima
1603 Libavius, A. Alchymistische Practic
1604 Libavius, A. Praxis alchymiae
1606 Camerarius, P. Operae horarum subcisivarum . . . Centuria . . . altera
1606 Libavius, A. Alchymia
1607 Libavius, A. Alchymia triumphans
1609 Camerarius, P. Operae horarum subcisivarum . . . Centuria tertia
1609 Thou, J. A. de. Historiarum sui temporis. Opera
1611 Draud, G. Bibliotheca classica
1611 Libavius, A. Syntagma selectorum
1614 Thou, J. A. de. Historiarum sui temporis . . . libri
1615 Camerarius, P. Operae horarum subcisivarum . . . Centuria prima
1615 Libavius, A. Sintagmatis selectorum
1618 Camerarius, P. Operae horarum subcisivarum . . . Centuria tertia
1620 Camerarius, P. Operae horarum subcisivarum . . . Centuria . . . altera
1621 Thou, J. A. de. Historische Beschreibung
1624 Camerarius, P. Operae horarum subcisivarum . . . Centuria prima

1625 Camerarius, P. Operae horarum subcisivarum . . . Centuria tertia
1625 Thou, J. A. de. Historiarum sui temporis . . . libri cxxxviii

Le Blon, Christoph
1640 Hulsius, L. Achte Schiffahrt
1648 Bontekoe, W. Y. Die vier und zwanzigste Schiffahrt
1649 Brouwer, H. Die fünff und zweyntzigste Schifffahrt
1650 La Peyrère, I. de. Die xxvi. Schiff-Fahrt

Marne, Claude de
1601 Le Paulmier de Grentemesnil, J. De morbis contagiosis libri septem
1601 Scaliger, J. C. Exotericarum exercitationum liber xv
1601 Silvaticus, J. B. Controversiae numero centum
1602 Conestaggio, G. F. di. De Portugalliae conjunctione
1603 Maffei, R. Commentariorum urbanorum libri
1603 Schottus, A. Hispaniae illustratae
1606 Mariana, J. de. Historiae hispanicae appendix
1606 Steeghius, G. Ars medica
1607 Fernel, J. De abditis rerum causis
1607 Fernel, J. Universa medicina
1607 Peucer, K. Commentarius
1607 Scaliger, J. C. Exotericarum exercitationum liber xv
1608 Schottus, A. Hispaniae bibliotheca
1609 Boodt, A. B. de. Florum . . . icones
1609 Croll, O. Basilicus chymica

Marne, Claude de, Heirs of (Johannes & Andreas Marne)
1612 Scaliger, J. C. Exotericarum exercitationum liber quintus decimus

Megiser, Hieronymus
1603 Megiser, H. Thesaurus polyglottus

Merian, Matthäus
1627 Bry, T. de. Continuatio Americae, das ist, Fortsetzung
1628 Bry, T. de. Dreyzehender Theil Americae

1630 Bry, T. de. Vierzehender Theil Amerikanischer Historien
1630 Staden, H. Historiae Antipodum . . . pars tertia
1631 Gottfried, J. L. Newe Welt
1632 Lauremberg, P. Apparatus plantarius primus
1633 Potgieter, B. J. Historiae antipodum
1634 Bry, T. de. Decima tertia pars Historiae Americanae
1634 Bry, T. de. Historia Americae
1638 Avity, P. d'. Archontologia cosmica
1638 Avity, P. d'. Neuwe Archontologia cosmica
1641 Bry, J. T. de. Florilegium renovatum
1644 Benzoni, G. Historia antipodum . . . Liber quartus
1646 Avity, P. d'. Newe archontologia cosmica
1646 Fruchtbringende Gesellschaft. Der Fruchtbringenden Geselschaft Nahmen
1649 Avity, P. d'. Archontologia cosmica
1650 Jonstonus, J. Historiae naturalis de avibus
1650? Jonstonus, J. Historiae naturalis de piscibus
1650? Jonstonus, J. Historiae naturalis de quadrupetibus libri

Musculus, Petrus
1610 Marquardus, J. Practica medicinalis

Neben, Conrad
1605 Duchesne, J. Ad veritatem hermeticae medicinae

Ostern, Balthasar
1625 Draud, G. Bibliotheca classica,
1625 Draud, G. Bibliotheca . . . das ist, Verzeichnuss
1625 Thou, J. A. de. Historiarum sui temporis . . . libri cxxxviii

Palthenius, Hartmann
1615 Corbeius, T. Pathologia
1616 Corbeius, T. Pathologia
1617 Smith, Capt. J. Viertzehende Schiffart
1619 Wirsung, C. Ein newes Artzney Buch
1622 Bodin, J. De republica libri sex

556

1624 Melich, G. Dispensatorium medicum

1625 Houtman, C. de. Erste Schiffart

1626 Braun, S. Die neuntzehende Schiffarth

1626 Hulsius, L. Sechster Theil. Kurtze, warhafftige Relation

1631 Rosenberg, J. K. Rhodologia

Palthenius, Zacharias

1601 Paré, A. Wundt Artzney

1608 Mercado, L. Opera

Palthenius, Zacharias, Heirs of

1619 Wirsung, C. Ein newes Artzney Buch

1620 Mercado, L. Operum tomus primus[-III]

1624 Melich, G. Dispensatorium medicum

Palthenius Office

1601 Melich, G. Dispensatorium medicum

1603 Capivaccio, G. Opera omnia

1603? Sassonia, E. Pantheum medicinae selectum

1609 Foreest, P. van. Observationum . . . medicinalium . . . libri

Pistorius, Rupert

1610 Marquardus, J. Practica medicinalis

Porsch, Johann Jakob

1610 Gabelkover, O. Artzneybuch

1613 Donati, M. De historia medica mirabili libri sex

1641 Gabelkover, O. Artzneybuch

Richter, Wolfgang

1601 Acosta, J. de. Neundter . . . Theil Americae, pt 1

1602 Noort, O. van. Additamentum . . . dess neundten Theils Americae

1603 Laudonnière, R. G. de. Der ander Theil . . . Americae

1603 Marees, P. de. Sechster Theil der Orientalischen Indien

1603 Marees, P. de. Siebende Schiffahrt in . . . Guineam

1604 Marees, P. de. Indiae Orientalis, pars vi

1604 Ottsen, H. Warhafftige Beschreibung der Schiffarht

1605 Duchesne, J. Ad veritatem hermeticae medicinae

1605 Hulsius, L. Achte Schiffart

1605 Roelofsz, R. Zwo underschiedliche newe Schiffarten

1606 Bry, J. T. de. Achter Theil der Orientalischen Indien

1606 Houtman, C. de. Erste Schiffahrt

1606 Marees, P. de. Siebende Schiffart

1606 Spilbergen, J. van. Indiae Orientalis pars septima

1607 Bry, J. T. de. Indiae Orientalis, pars octava

1608 Romanus, A. Parvum theatrum urbium

1610 Aldrovandi, U. Ornithologiae . . . libri xii

1630 Aldrovandi, U. Ornithologiae . . . libri xii

1640 Aldrovandi, U. Ornithologiae . . . libri xii

Rinialme, Ascanius de, Heirs of

1605 Hall, J. Mundus alter. *See under* Great Britain—London —Lownes, Humphrey

1606 Hall, J. Mundus alter. *See under* Hanau—Antonius, Wilhelm

1648 Hall, J. Mundus alter

Rötel, Kaspar

1624 Raleigh, Sir W. Achter Theil Americae

1625 Braun, S. Anhang

1625 Braun, S. Appendix

1627 Bertius, P. Breviarium totius orbis terrarum

1627 Bry, T. de. Continuatio Americae

1627 Hues, R. Tractatus duo mathematici

1628 Bry, J. T. de. Der dreyzehende Theil

1628 Bry, J. T. de. Der zwölffte Theil

1628 Bry, T. de. Dreyzehende Theil Americae

1628 Fitzer, W. Orientalische Indien

1629 Fitzer, W. Extract der Orientalischen Indien

1629 Linschoten, J. H. van. Tertia pars Indiae Orientalis (2)

1630 Norton, S. Metamorphosis lapidum ignobilium

1633 Usselinx, W. Argonautica Gustaviana

1634 Aldrovandi, U. De piscibus libri v

1634 Hartmann, J. Praxis chymiatrica

1635 Paré, A. Wund Artzney

1640 Aldrovandi, U. De piscibus libri v

1641 Prevost, J. Medicina pauperum

1644 Camerarius, P. Operae horarum subcisivarum . . . Centuria prima

1647 Aldrovandi, U. De piscibus libri v

1647 Aldrovandi, U. Quadrupedum omnium bisulcorum historia

Roht, Nikolaus

1610 Meteren, E. van. Historia . . . aller . . . Kriegshändel

Rose, Jonas

1603 Capivaccio, G. Opera omnia

1607 Croce, G. A. della. Officina aurea

1609 Durante, C. Hortulus sanitatis

1609 Schenck von Grafenberg, J. Paratēreseōn

1612 Bucholtzer, A. Index chronologicus

1616 Bucholtzer, A. Index chronologicus

Rose, Jonas, Widow of

1622 Bodin, J. De republica libri sex

1634 Bucholtzer, A. Index chronologicus

Roth, F. N.

1617 Schaller, G. Thierbuch

Rulands, The

1616 Camden, W. Annales

Sauer, Johannes

1601 Camerarius, P. Operae horarum subcisivarum . . . Centuria altera

1601 More, Sir T. De optimo reipublicae statu

1602 Camerarius, P. Operae horarum subcisivarum . . . Centuria prima

1603 Libavius, A. Alchymistische Practic

1603 Solinus, C. Julius. Memorabilia mundi

1604 Libavius, A. Praxis alchymiae

1606 Camerarius, P. Operae horarum subcisivarum . . . Centuria altera

1606 Libavius, A. Alchymia

1607 Croce, G. A. della. Officina aurea

1607 Libavius, A. Alchymia triumphans

1609 Thou, J. A. de. Historiarum sui temporis. Opera

Schamberger, Simon

1617 Popp, J. Chymische Medicin

Schleich, Clemens

1625 Barclay, J. Icon animorum

1625 Fonseca, R. Consultationum medicinalium singularibus remediis refertae

1625 Popp, J. Chymische Medicin

1626 Guidi, G. Opera omnia

Schleich, Clemens, & Co.

1640 Bertius, P. Breviarium totius orbis terrarum

Schmidlin, Johann

1621 Nederlandsche West-Indische Compagnie. Artickel

1622 Magnus, O. Historia . . . de gentibus septentrionalibus

1622 Panciroli, G. Rerum memorabilium . . . libri duo

1623 Barclay, J. Euphormionis Lusinini Satyricon

1624 Barclay, J. Euphormionis Lusinini . . . Satyricon

Schönwetter, Johann Gottfried

1618 Lundorp, M. C. Politische SchatzCammer . . . ander Theil

1624 Lundorp, M. C. Politische SchatzCammer

1642 Maiolo, S. Dierum canicularum tomi septem

1645 Moscherosch, J. M. Visiones de don de Quevedo

1646 Panciroli, G. Rerum memorabilium . . . pars prior[-posterior]

1647 Croll, O. Hermetischer probier stein

1647 Hartmann, J. Praxis chymiatrica

1647 Moscherosch, J. M. Visiones de don de Quevedo

1648 Les visions de don Queveto . . . Complementum

1649 Owen, J. Epigrammatum . . . libri x

Schönwetter, Johann Theobald

1601 Mercuriale, G. Medicina practica . . . libri

1602 Mercuriale, G. Medicina practica . . . libri

1609 Renou, J. de. Dispensatorium medicum

1610 Boutrays, R. Historiopolitographia

1615 Renou, J. de. Dispensatorium medicum

1624 Garzoni, T. Emporii emporiorum

1626 Weickard, A. Thesaurus pharmaceuticus

1628 Weickard, A. Pharmacia domestica

1630 Freitag, J. Aurora medicorum

Schönwetter, Theobald

1603 Solinus, C. Julius. Memorabilia mundi

1626 Dispensatorium chymicum

Snuhcam, Friedenreich, pseud.

1620 Liebfriedt, C., pseud. An gantz Teutschlandt

Stoltzenberger, Johann Nikolaus

1623 Aldrovandi, U. De piscibus libri v

Tampach, Gottfried

1611 Croll, O. Basilica chymica

1620 Croll, O. Basilica chymica

1623 Croll, O. Basilica chymica: oder . . . Kleÿnod

1629 Panciroli, G. Rerum memorabilium . . . pars prior [-posterior]

Tampach, Wilhelm

1623 Campanella, T. Realis philosophiae epilogisticae partes quatuor

Treudel, Johann

1620 Bauhin, K. Prodromos Theatri botanici

1623 Aldrovandi, U. De piscibus libri v

1629 Aldrovandi, U. De piscibus libri v

1634 Aldrovandi, U. De piscibus libri v

1640 Aldrovandi, U. De piscibus libri v

Vetter, Christoph

1618 Magnus, O. Historia . . . de gentibus septentrionalibus

Wächter, C.

1650 Sennert, D. epitome naturalis scientiae

Wechel, Andreas, Heirs of

1601 Silvaticus, J. B. Controversiae numero centum

1625 Fonseca, R. Consultationum medicinalium singularibus remediis refertae

Wechel, Johann [i.e., Heirs]

1608 Hariot, T. Admiranda narratio . . . Virginiae

1609 Laudonnière, R. G. de. Brevis narratio

Wechel, Johann, Heirs of

1603 Paracelsus. Bücher und Schrifften

Wechel Office

1601 Scaliger, J. C. Exotericarum exercitationum liber xv

1607 Scaliger, J. C. Exotericarum exercitationum liber xv

1612 Scaliger, J. C. Exotericarum exercitationum liber quintus decimus

1626 Grotius, H. De jure belli ac pacis

1626 Guidi, G. Opera omnia

1627 Hues, R. Tractatus de globis

Weiss, Johann Friedrich

1611 Croll, O. Basilica chymica

1620 Croll, O. Basilica chymica

1623 Croll, O. Basilica chymica: oder Alchÿmistisch . . . Kleÿnod

1623 Herrera y Tordesillas, A. de. Achtzehender Theil der Newen Welt

1623 Neck, J. C. van. Fünffter Theil der Orientalischen Indien

1625 Zimara, M. A. Antrum magico-medicum

1626 Weickard, A. Thesaurus pharmaceuticus

1650 Camerarius, P. Operae horarum subcisivarum . . . Centuria ii

1650 Camerarius, P. Operae horarum subcisivarum . . . Centuria tertia

Wild, Joachim
1644 Camerarius, P. Operae horarum subcisivarum . . . Centuria prima
1650 Camerarius, P. Operae horarum subcisivarum . . . Centuria ii
1650 Camerarius, P. Operae horarum subcisivarum . . . Centuria tertia
Zetter, Jacob de
1618 Murner, T. Der Schelmen Zunfft
Zetzner, Lazarus
1605 Cesalpino, A. Katoptron
Zunner, Johann David
1647 Aldrovandi, U. De piscibus libri v
1647 Aldrovandi, U. Quadrupedum omnium bisulcorum historia

FRANKFURT AN DER ODER
Eichorn, Johann
1618 Béguin, J. Secreta spagyrica
Thymiss, Johann
1620 Calvisius, S. Opus chronologicum
1629 Calvisius, S. Opus chronologicum

GERA
Apel, Jakob
1613 Suchten, A. von. Antinomii mysteria gemina

GIESSEN
Chemlin, Caspar
1612 Bickerus, J. Hermes redivivus
Hampel, Nikolaus
1620 Knobloch, T. De lue venerea
Humm, Anton
1612 Bickerus, J. Hermes redivivus

HALLE
Bismarck, Christoph
1625 Hofmann, L. Thaumatophylakion
Krusecke, Joachim
1617 Brunner, B. Consilia medica
Oelschlegel, Melchior
1625 Martini, M. De morbis mesenterii abstrusioribus

1634 Untzer, M. Tractatus medico-chymici septem
Schmidt, Peter
1617 Brunner, B. Consilia medica

HAMBURG
Printer unidentified
1601 Meteren, E. van. Historia
1628 Raleigh, Sir W. The perogative. See Great Britain—London—Cotes, Thomas
1630 Kurtze Erzehlung . . . vom Herrn General Long
1636 Olearius, A. Lustige historia
1642 Olearius, A. Lustige Historia
1643 Olearius, A. Lustige Historia
Arens, Bernd
1648 Benzoni, G. Novae Novi Orbis historiae
Carstens, Heinrich
1616 Joel, F. Operum medicorum . . . tomus
Froben Bookshop (P. Lang)
1608 Liddel, D. Ars medica
1617 Liddel, D. Ars medica
1628 Liddel, D. Ars medica
Froben Office
1601 Khunrath, C. Medulla destillatoria et medica
1605 Khunrath, C. Medulla destillatoria et medica
1623 Khunrath, C. Medulla destillatoria et medica
1638 Khunrath, C. Medulla destillatoria et medica
1639 Khunrath, C. Medulla destillatoria et medica
Hertel, Zacharias
1642 Homburg, E. C. Schimpff- und ernsthaffte Clio

HANAU
Printer unidentified
1603 Arnauld, A. Ingenua et vera oratio
1611 Donne, J. Conclave Ignatii
Antonius, Peter
1617 Crespin, J. Gross Martyrbuch
1617 Keckermann, B. Systema compendiosum totius mathematices

1621 Keckermann, B. Systema compendiosum totius mathematices
Antonius, Wilhelm
1606 Crespin, J. Gross Martyrbuch
1606? Hall, J. Mundus alter
1607 Hall, J. Mundus alter
1607 Peucer, K. Commentarius
1610 Keckermann, B. De natura et proprietatibus historiae
Antonius, Wilhelm, Heirs of
1611 Keckermann, B. Systema astronomiae compendiosum
1611 Keckermann, B. Systema geographicum
1611 Ortelius, A. Thesaurus geographicus
1612 Keckermann, B. Systema geographicum
1613 Keckermann, B. Systema astronomiae compendiosum
Aubry, David
1630 Bry, T. de. Vierzehender Theil Amerikanischer Historien
1631 Renou, J. de. Dispensatorium Galeno chymicum
Aubry, Daniel & David
1619 Amphitheatrum sapientiae Socraticae
1619 Crato von Krafftheim, J. Consiliorum . . . medicinalium . . . liber quintus
1620 Scaliger, J. C. Exotericarum exercitationum liber quintus decimus
1625 Polo, G. G. Casp. Barthi Erotodidascalus
1626 Grotius, H. De jure belli ac pacis
Aubry, Johann, Heirs of
1605 Fernel, J. Pharmacia
1605 Lange, J. Epistolarum medicinalium
1610 Scholtz, L. Consiliorum medicinalium
1610 Scholtz, L. Epistolarum philosophicarum . . . volumen
1611 Manardo, G. Iatrologia epistolikē
1613 Perlinus, H. Binae historiae
Henne, Hans Jakob
1613 More, Sir T. De optimo rei publicae statu

Hulsiuses, The
1617 Hamor, R. Dreyzehente Schiffahrt (2)
Kopff, Peter
1613 More, Sir T. De optimo rei-publicae statu
Marne, Claude de
1605 Bodin, J. Universae naturae theatrum
1605 Fernel, J. Pharmacia
1605 Lange, J. Epistolarum medicinalium
Marne, Claude de, Heirs of
1610 Fernel, J. Universa medicina
Schleich, Clemens
1617 Marinelli, C. Pharmacopaea
1619 Amphitheatrum sapientiae Socraticae
1619 Crato von Krafftheim, J. Consiliorum . . . medicinalium . . . liber quintus
1620 Scaliger, J. C. Exotericarum exercitationum liber quintus decimus
1625 Polo, G. G. Casp. Barthi Erotodidascalus
1626 Grotius, H. De jure belli ac pacis
1629 Bertius, P. Breviarium totius orbis terrarum
1634 Scaliger, J. C. Exotericarum exercitationum liber quintus decimus
Wechel, Andreas, Heirs of
1605 Lange, J. Epistolarum medicinalium
1610 Scholtz, L. Consiliorum medicinalium
1610 Scholtz, L. Epistolarum philosophicarum . . . volumen
1611 Manardo, G. Iatrologia epistolikē
1613 Perlinus, H. Binae historiae
1619 Crato von Krafftheim, J. Consiliorum . . . medicinalium . . . liber quintus
Wechel Office
1605 Bodin, J. Universae naturae theatrum
1605 Fernel, J. Pharmacia
1619 Ampitheatrum sapientiae Socraticae
1620 Scaliger, J. C. Exotericarum exercitationum liber quintus decimus

1634 Scaliger, J. C. Exotericarum exercitationum liber quintus decimus
Zetter, Petrus de
1629 Bertius, P. Breviarium totius orbis terrarum

HANNOVER
Printer unidentified
1620 Spanisch Mucken Pulver

HEIDELBERG
Printer unidentified
1602 Arnauld, A. Bedencken
1603 Arnauld, A. Bedencken
1619 Spanisch Post
Cambier, Andreas
1606 Gesner, K. Icones avium omnium
1606 Gesner, K. Nomenclator aquatilium
1606 Gesner, K. Thierbuch
Commelin Office
1603 Heresbach, C. Rei rusticae
1609 Buchanan, G. Franciscanus et fratres
Lancellot, Johann
1606 Gesner, K. Icones avium omnium
1606 Gesner, K. Nomenclator aquatilium
1606 Gesner, K. Thierbuch
Vögelin, Gotthard
1602 Keckermann, B. Meditatio
1613? Hues, R. Tractatus de globis
1615? Hues, R. Tractatus de globis

HEILBRONN
Krause, Christoff
1631 Horst, G. Observationum medicinalium . . . Libri quatuor
1633 Sweden. Sovereigns, etc., 1611–1632. Ampliatio . . . dess Privilegii
1633 Usselinx, W. Instruction . . . der newen Süder Compagnie
1633 Usselinx, W. Kurtzer Extract der . . . Hauptpuncten
1640 Zeiller, M. Ein Hundert Episteln

HERBORN
Corvinus (Rab), Christoph
1606 Chytraeus, N. Variorum in Europa itinerum deliciae
Rab, Georg
1624 Alsted, J. H. Thesaurus chronologiae
1628 Alsted, J. H. Thesaurus chronologiae
1630 Alsted, J. H. Encyclopaedia
1637 Alsted, J. H. Thesaurus chronologiae
Rab, Georg, Heirs of
1650 Alsted, J. H. Thesaurus chronologiae

INGOLSTADT
Angermaier, Andreas
1610 Hollings, E. Medicamentorum oeconomia nova
1613 Rivadeneira, P. de. Leben Francisci Borgiae

Angermaier, Elisabeth
1614 Riyadeneira, P. de. Leben dess seligen p. Ignatii
1615 Hollings, E. Medicamentorum oeconomia nova
1617 Amati, S. Relation . . . dess Königreichs Voxu (2)
1617 Hendschel, T. Englischen Liebbrinnendten . . . Relations Continuation
Eder, Wilhelm
1625 Marianus de Orscelar. Gloriosus Franciscus redivivus
Eder Press
1610 Hollings, E. Medicamentorum oeconomia nova
1615 Hollings, E. Medicamentorum oeconomia nova
1617 Amati, S. Relation . . . dess Königreichs Voxu (2)
1617 Hendschel, T. Englischen Liebbrinnendten . . . Relations Continuation
Hänlin, Gregor
1622 Victoria, P. G. de. Wunderbarliche und seltzame Raiss
1628 Victoria, P. G. de. Wunderbarliche und seltzame Raiss

JENA
Beithmann, Johann
1620 Mutoni, N. Mithridateiotechnia

Schürer, Thomas, Heirs of
1622 Owen, J. Epigrammatum
. . . libri decem
Valentin Heirs
1615 Owen, J. Epigrammatum
. . . libri decem
Vögelin Press
1605 Camerarius, J. Symbolorum . . . centuriae tres
Voigt, Bartholomaeus
1604 Eugalenus, S. De scorbuto
morbo liber
1613 Duchesne, J. Liber de priscorum philosophorum verae
medicinae materia
1613 Duchesne, J. Pharmacopoea dogmaticorum restituta
1614 Duchesne, J. Opera medica
Wachsman, Michael
1625 Camerarius, P. Operae horarum succisivarum
1628 Camerarius, P. Secunda
centuria historica
Wachsman, Michael, Heirs of
1630 Camerarius, P. Tertia centuria historica
Wittigau, Johann
1642 Besler, M. R. Gazophylacium rerum naturalium

LÜBECK
Printer unidentified
1637 Opitz, M. Deutscher Poe-
matum. Erster theil
Jäger, Gottfried
1648 Schultze, G. Kurtze Welt-
Beschreibung
Schernwebel, Heinrich
1648 Schultze, G. Kurtze Welt-
Beschreibung

LÜNEBURG
Michelson, Andreas
1616 Joel, F. Operum medicorum . . . tomus

MAGDEBURG
Franck, Johann
1607 Penot, B. G. Theophrastisch Vade mecum
1608 Penot, B. G. Theophrastisch Vade mecum

MAINZ
Albin, Johann
1603 Del Rio, M. A. Disquisitionum magicarum libri sex

1607 Maiolo, S. Dies caniculares
1612 Del Rio, M. A. Disquisitionum magicarum libri sex
1617 Del Rio, M. A. Disquisitionum magicarum libri sex
1618 Jesuits. Letters from missions. Annuae litterae (1606,
1607 et 1608) 1618. Literae
annuae
Aubry, Daniel & David
1619 Mariana, J. de. Historiae de
rebus Hispaniae
1619 Mariana, J. de. Summarium
ad Historiam Hispaniae
Butgen, Conrad
1603 Rivadeneira, P. de. Princeps christianus
1604 Rivadeneira, P. de. Princeps christianus
*Heil, Nikolaus
1647 Hartmann, J. Praxis
chymiatrica
1649 Owen, J. Epigrammatum
. . . libri x
König, Jakob
1606 Del Rio, M. A. Disquisitionum magicarum libri sex
Lipp, Balthasar
1602 Molina, L. de. De justitia et
jure tomi duo
1603 Rivadeneira, P. de. Vita
Francisci Borgiae
1604 Torres Bollo, D. de. Brevis
relatio historica
1605 Mariana, J. de. Historiae de
rebus Hispaniae
1611 Castile. Laws, statutes, etc.,
1252–1284. Las siete partidas
1614 Molina, L. de. De justitia et
jure
Mylius, Arnold
1602 Molina, L. de. De justitia et
jure
Schleich, Clemens
1619 Mariana, J. de. Historiae de
rebus Hispaniae
1619 Mariana, J. de. Summarium
ad Historiam Hispaniae
Schönwetter, Johann Theobald
1610 Maiolo, S. Dies caniculares
1614 Maiolo, S. Dies caniculares
1615 Maiolo, S. Dies caniculares
Strohecker, Anton
1624 Del Rio, M. A. Disquisitionum magicarum libri sex

Wechel, Andreas, Heirs of
1605 Mariana, J. de. Historiae de
rebus Hispaniae

MARBURG
Chemlin, Caspar
1630 Horst, J. Herbarium
Horstianum
Egenolff, Paul
1615 Petraeus, H. Nosologia
harmonica
1615 Petraeus, H. Nosologia
harmonica
1619 Ritter, S. Cosmographia
prosometrica
1620 Botero, G. Politia regia
1622 Duchesne, J. Pharmacopoea dogmaticorum restituta
Hampel, Nikolaus
1629 Helwig, C. Theatrum historicum
1636 Ritter, S. Theatrum cosmographicum
1638 Helwig, C. Theatrum historicum

MÜNSTER
Printer unidentified
1647 Declaratie, ofte precijse
Verklaringe (2)
Raesfeldt, Bernhard
1648 Spain. Treaties, etc., 1621–
1665. Tractatus pacis
Staets, Niclaes
1646 Fransch praetie (3)

MUNICH
Printer unidentified
1641 Torsellino, O. Historiarum . . . epitome libri x
Berg, Anna
1618 Sadeler, R. Zodiacus christianus
1620 Marcos da Lisboa. Cronicken
Heinrich, Nikolaus
1604 Mayr, J. Epitome cronicorum seculi moderni
1611 Botero, G. Allgemeine historische Weltbeschreibung
1612 Botero, G. Allgemeine historische Weltbeschreibung
1615 Alemán, M. Der Landtstörtzer
1616 Alemán, M. Der Landtstörtzer (2)

1617 Alemán, M. Der Landtstörtzer

1618 Alemán, M. Der Landtstörtzer

1619 Nicolai, E. Newe und warhaffte relation

1622 Alemán, M. Der Landtstörtzer

1631 Alemán, M. Der Landtstörtzer

1632 Alemán, M. Der Landtstörtzer

1640 Saavedra Fajardo, D. de.
Idea de un principe christiano

Herstroy, Johann

1620 Marcos da Lisboa. Cronicken

1623 Crusenius, N. Monasticon
Augustinianum

Leysser, Cornelius, Heirs of

1643 Balde, J. Lyricorum lib. iv

Sadeler, Raphael

1618 Sadeler, R. Zodiacus christianus

Straub, Lucas

1646 Alegambe, P. De vita . . . p.
Joannis Cardim

1647 Bissel, J. Argonauticon
Americanorum

1649 Schirmbeck, A. Messis Paraquariensis

Wagner, Johannes

1646 Alegambe, P. De vita . . . p.
Joannis Cardim

1647 Bissel, J. Argonauticon
Americanorum

1649 Schirmbeck, A. Messis Paraquariensis

NUREMBERG

Printer unidentified

1613 Besler, B. Hortus eystettensis

1633 Oxenstierna, A. G., grefve.
Wir Burgermeister

1636 Wurfbain, L. Relatio historica

1641 Harsdörffer, G. P. Frauenzimmer Gesprechspiele

Besler, Basilius

1616 Besler, B. Fasciculus rariorum

1622 Besler, B. Continuatio rariorum

Dümler, Jeremias

1650 Helwig, J. Die Nymphe
Noris

Endter, Michael

1646 Wurffbain, J. S. Reiss-Beschreibung

1650 Harsdörffer, G. P. Nathan
und Jotham

Endter, Wolfgang

1636 Horst, G. Centuria problematum medicorum

1636 Wurfbain, L. Vier unterschiedliche Relationes

1637 Horst, G. Observationum
medicinalium . . . libri quator

1643 Harsdörffer, G. P. Gesprachspiele . . . Dritter Theil

1644 Colmenero de Ledesma, A.
Chocolata Inda

1644 Harsdörffer, G. P. Gesprachspiele . . . vierter Theil

1644 Volkamer, J. G. Opobalsami orientalis . . . examen

1645 Harsdörffer, G. P. Gesprechspiele fünfter Theil

1646 Harsdörffer, G. P. Gesprechspiele sechster Theil

1647 Corbeius, T. Pathologia

1647 Harsdörffer, G. P. Gesprächspiele, siebender Theil

1647 Hille, C. G. von. Der
teutsche Palmenbaum

1649 Harsdörffer, G. P. Gesprächspiele achter . . . Theil

Fürst, Paul

1647 Hemmersam, M. Gui-
neische und West-Indianische
Reissbeschreibung

Halbmeyer, Simon

1619 Grick, F. Regula vitae

1626 Hornung, J. Cista medica

Hentzner, Paul

1612 Hentzner, P. Itinerarium
Germaniae

Hulsius, Levinus

1601 Raleigh, Sir W. Kurtze
wunderbare Beschreibung
. . . Guianae (2)

1602 Houtman, C. de. Erste
Schiffart

1602 Neck, J. C. van. Ander
Schiffart

1602 Schmidel, U. Vierte Schiffart

1602 Veer, G. de. Dritte Theil,
warhafftige Relation (2)

1603 Hulsius, L. Sechste Theil,
Kurtze, warhafftige Relation

1603 Raleigh, Sir W. Die fünffte
kurtze . . . Beschreibung

Kaufmann, Paul

1604 Camerarius, J. Symbolorum et emblematum . . . centuria quarta

Lochner, Christoph

1601 Raleigh, Sir W. Kurtze
wunderbare Beschreibung
. . . Guianae (2)

1602 Neck, J. C. van. Ander
Schiffart

1603 Hulsius, L. Sechste Theil,
Kurtze . . . Relation

1603 Raleigh, Sir W. Die
fünffte kurtze wunderbare
Beschreibung

Stamphier, Joseph, pseud.

For the following works *see*
Italy—Venice—Printer uni-
dentified

1619 Marino, G. B. La Murtoleide

1642 Marino, G. B. La Murtoleide

Wagenmann, Abraham

1612 Hentzner, P. Itinerarium
Germaniae

OBERURSEL

Rose, Jonas

1601 Bodin, J. De republica libri
sex

1602 Penot, B. G. Tractatus
varii

Sutor, Cornelius

1601 Bodin, J. De republica libri
sex

1601 Estienne, C. Dictionarium
historicum geographicum

1602 Botero, G. Mundus imperiorum . . . das ist Beschreibung

1602 Botero, G. Tractatus duo

1602 Penot, B. G. Tractatus
varii

1603 Botero, G. Mundus imperiorum

1605 Acosta, J. de. America

1605 Wirsung, C. Ein new Artzney Buch

OFFENBACH

Neben, Conrad

1609 Thou, J. A. de. Historiarum
sui temporis. Opera

1610 Bauhin, K. De compositione medicamentorum

OPPENHEIM
Bry, Johann Theodor de
1611 Röslin, E. Mitternächtige Schiffarth
1612 Bry, J. T. de. Florilegium novum
1613 Casas, B. de las. Warhafftiger und gründlicher Bericht
1614 Casas, B. de las. Narratio regionum Indicarum
1616 Linschoten, J. H. van. Dritter Theil Indiae Orientalis
1617 Benzoni, G. Americae pars sexta
1617 Bry, J. T. de. America, das ist, Erfindung
1618 Vespucci, A. Zehender Theil Americae
1619 Schouten, W. C. Americae pars undecima
1619 Vespucci, A. Americae pars decima
Galler, Hieronymus
1611 Röslin, E. Mitternächtige Schiffarth
1614 Casas, B. de las. Narratio regionum Indicarum
1614 Gerritsz, H. Zwölffte Schiffahrt (2)
1616 Linschoten, J. H. van. Dritter Theil Indiae Orientalis
1617 Benzoni, G. Americae pars sexta
1617 Benzoni, G. Americae pars quinta
1617 Schmidel, U. Warhafftige und liebliche Beschreibung
1618 Vespucci, A. Zehender Theil Americae
1619 Benzoni, G. Das sechste Theil Americae
1619 Bry, J .T. de. Indiae Orientalis pars undecima
1619 Schouten, W. C. Americae pars undecima
1619 Vespucci, A. Americae pars decima
1620 Hariot, T. Wunderbarliche . . . Erklärung von . . . Virginia
1620 Spilbergen, J. van. Appendix dess eilfften Theils Americae
1627 Gerritsz, H. Zwölffte Schiffahrt

Hulsius, Levinus, Widow of
1614 Gerritsz, H. Zwölffte Schiffahrt (2)
1627 Gerritsz, H. Zwölffte Schiffahrt

PADERBORN
Brückner, Matthäus
1601 Sostmann, J. Indianische Reise

PASSAU
Nenninger, Tobias, & Conrad Frosch
1630 Toledo Osorio y Mendoza, F. de. Warhaffte Relation

RINTELN AN DER WESER
Lucius, Petrus
1644 Rimphoff, H. Aurea pacis corona

ROSTOCK
Fuess (Pedanus), Joachim
1625 Blocius, J. Historiae per Saturam . . . memorabilia
1627 Blocius, J. Historiae per Saturam . . . memorabilia
Hallervord, Johann
1616 Joel, F. Operum medicorum . . . tomus
1625 Blocius, J. Historiae per Saturam . . . memorabilia
1627 Blocius, J. Historiae per Saturam . . . memorabilia
1644 James I, King. De abusu tobacci discursus
Mölemann, Staffan
1608 Martini, L. Christeliga jungfrwrs ärakrantz
Sachs, Moritz
1616 Joel, F. Operum medicorum . . . tomus
Steinmann, I., & W. Wallop, pseud.
1637 Aprosio, A. Il vaglio. *See under* Italy—Treviso—Righettini, Girolamo
Wallop, W. *See* Steinmann, I., *above*

ROTTWEIL
Helmlin, Johann Maximilian
1617 Amati, S. Histori dess . . . Königreichs Voxu

SCHLESWIG
Zur Glocken, Jakob
1647 Olearius, A. Offt begehrte Beschreibung

SCHLEUSINGEN
Schall, Johann Michael
1644 Augspurger, J. P. Kurtze . . . Beschreibung der See-Reisen

SCHMALKALDEN
Ketzel, Wolfgang
1612 Fabronius, H. Newe summarische Welt-Historia
1614 Fabronius, H. Newe summarische Welt-Historia
1627 Fabronius, H. Geographica historica: Newe . . . Welt-Historia

SPEYER
1629 Marino, G. B. La Murtoleide. *See under* Italy—Naples—Printer Unidentified

STETTIN
Götz Press
1628 Gilbert, W. Tractatus . . . de magnete
1633 Gilbert, W. Tractatus . . . de magnete
Hallervord, Johann
1628 Gilbert, W. Tractatus . . . de magnete

STRASSBURG
Printer unidentified
1650 Moscherosch, J. M. Wunderliche und warhafftige Gesichte
Carolus, Johann
1617 Banchieri, A. Von dess Esels Adel
Carolus, Johann, Heirs of
1647 Taxa medicamentorum
Glaser, Théodore
1615 Fuchs, S. Metoposcopia
Glaser, Wilhelm Christian
1630 Bock, H. Kraütterbuch
Heyden, Christoph von der
1619 Welper, E. Observationes astronomicae
Heyden, Marx von der
1628 Habrecht, I. Planiglobium coeleste et terrestre

WITTENBERG

Auerbach, Salomon, Heirs of
1628 Sennert, D. Institutionum medicinae . . . libri

Berger, Clemens
1606 Benzoni, G. Chronicon, das ist: Beschreibung
1610 Horst, G. Centuria problematum medicorum
1611 Müller, P. Miracula chymica et misteria medica
1614 Müller, P. Miracula . . . chymico-medica
1616 Müller, P. Miracula . . . chymico-medica
1623 Müller, P. Miracula . . . chymico-medica

Berger, Clemens, Heirs of
1634 Béguin, J. Tyrocinium chymicum
1640 Béguin, J. Tyrocinium chymicum

Crato Press
1608 Horst, G. Problematum medicorum decades

Fincelius, Hiob Wilhelm
1618 Sennert, D. Epitome naturalis scientiae
1624 Sennert, D. Epitome naturalis scientiae

Gormann, Johann
1608 Horst, G. Problematum medicorum decades

Hake, Johann
1623 Müller, P. Miracula . . . chymico-medica

Hartmann, Andreas
1650 Béguin, J. Tyrocinium chymicum

Heiden, C.
1618 Sennert, D. Epitome naturalis scientiae
1624 Sennert, D. Epitome naturalis scientiae

Helwig, J.
1633 Sennert, D. Epitome naturalis scientiae

Lehmann, Zacharias, Widow of
1606 Benzoni, G. Chronicon, das ist: Beschreibung

Meisner, Wolfgang
1611 Sennert, D. Institutionum medicinae libri v

Mevius, Tobias, Heirs of
1644 Sennert, D. Institutionum medicinae libri v

Müller, Georg, Widow of
1634 Béguin, J. Tyrocinium chymicum

Richter, Johann
1615 Praetorius, M. Syntagma musicum

Richter, Johann, Heirs of
1620 Sennert, D. Institutionum medicinae libri v

Röhner, Johann
1640 Béguin, J. Tyrocinium chymicum
1649 Zesen, P. von. Durch-aus vermehrter . . . Helikon
1650 Béguin, J. Tyrocinium chymicum

Schmidt, Johann
1610 Horst, G. Centuria problematum medicorum

Schürer, Zacharias, the Elder
1611 Sennert, D. Institutionum medicinae libri v
1616 Pindarus. Greek and Latin. Periodos
1620 Sennert, D. Institutionum medicinae libri v

Schürer, Zacharias, the Elder, Heirs of
1628 Sennert, D. Institutionum medicinae . . . libri
1633 Sennert, D. Institutionum medicinae libri v

Seelfisch, Johann
1649 Zesen, P. von. Durch-aus vermehrter . . . Helikon

Seuberlich, Lorenz
1611 Müller, P. Miracula chymica et . . . medica

Wendt, Michael
1644 Sennert, D. Institutionum medicinae libri v

WOLFENBÜTTEL
Holwein, Elias
1615 Praetorius, M. Syntagma musicum

WÜRZBURG
Fleischmann, Georg
1604 Torres Bollo, D. de. Kurtzer Bericht

GREAT BRITAIN

ABERDEEN
Melvill, David
1623 Craig, A. The poetical recreations

Raban, Edward
1623 Craig, A. The poetical recreations

CAMBRIDGE
Printer unidentified
1608 Cambridge. University. Act verses. Anima unita corpori est perfectior
1649 Cambridge. University. To our reverend . . . brethren

Atkinson, Troylus
1644 Swan, J. Speculum mundi

Buck, Thomas
1632 Dalechamp, C. Christian hospitalitie
1635 Swan, J. Speculum mundi

Daniel, Roger
1635 Swan, J. Speculum mundi
1640 Hodson, W. The divine cosmographer
1642 Fuller, T. The holy state
1643 Swan, J. Speculum mundi
1644 Swan, J. Speculum mundi (2)
1645 Howell, J. Dendrologia
1648 Bible. O.T. Psalms. English. Paraphrases. 1648. Bay Psalm Book. The psalms
1648 Fuller, Thomas. The holy state

EDINBURGH
Printer unidentified
1622 Scotland. Privy Council. [Forsamekle as it is weill knowin]
1622 Scotland. Privy Council. [Forsamekle as the Kingis Majestie]
1624 Boanerges. *See under* London—Printer unidentified
1624 Scotland. Privy Council. [Our Soverane Lord]
1625 Scotland. Privy Council. [Forsamekle as our soveraine Lordis]

Finlason, Thomas
1609 Craig, A. The poetical recreations
1609 Grahame, S. The anatomie of humors
1619 Scotland. Privy Council. [Forsamekle as the Kingis]
1620 Aparisi, F. Consilia medicinalia

Hart, Andreas
1614 Bacon, F. The essaies
1614 Barclay, W. Nepenthes
1615 Buchanan, G. Poemata omnia
1620 Mason, J. A briefe discourse
Lithgow, Gideon
1647 Shepard, T. The sincere convert
Tyler, Evan
164– Scotland. laws, statutes, etc. The acts
Wreittoun, John
1625 Gordon, Sir R. Encouragements
Young, Robert
1633 Scotland. Laws, statutes, etc. The acts

GLOUCESTER
Langford, Toby
1646 Workman, G. private-men

LONDON
Printer unidentified
1602 Copley, A. Another letter
1602 Ovidius Naso, P. Amores. English. All Ovids elegies
1602 Ovidius Naso, P. Amores. English. Ovids elegies
1608 Virginia Company of London. Whereas [blank] hath paid in readie monie
1609? Great Britain. Council for Virginia. Considering there is no publicke action
1620? Bennett, E. A treatise
1620 Scott, T. Vox populi. Or Newes from Spain (8)
1621 Nederlandsche West-Indische Compagnie. Orders and articles
1622 Scott, T. The Belgick pismire. *See under* The Netherlands—Utrecht—Printer unidentified
1623 A letter from W. A.
1623 Scott, T. An experimentall discoverie of Spanish practises (4)
1623 Scott, T. The high-waies. *See under* The Netherlands—Utrecht—Printer unidentified
1624 Boanerges. or The humble supplication (2)

1624 Ofwod, S. A relation
1624 Reynolds, J. Vox coeli (4)
1624 Scott, T. The Belgick souldier (2)
1624 Scott, T. Certaine reasons (5)
1625 Camerarius, P. The walking librarie
1625 Ditchfield,——. Considerations
1625 Hughes, L. To the Right Honourable
1626 Scott, T. Sir Walter Rawleighs ghost
1627 Governor & Company . . . of Guiana. Breefe notes
1627 Governor & Company . . . of Guiana. A breefe relation of . . . Guiana
1627 Governor & Company . . . of Guiana. The coppie of the preamble
1629 Bacon, F. Considerations
1629 Fennor, W. A true description of the lawes
1630 Ovidius Naso, P. Amores. English. All Ovids elegies
1634 A relation of . . . Lord Baltemore's plantation
1635 Lenton, F. The puisne gallants progresse
1636 Selden, J. Mare clausum. *See under* The Netherlands—Amsterdam—printer unidentified
1641 The Bishops potion
1641 Castell, W. A petition
1641 Cotton, J. A coppy of a letter
1641 Evelyn, R. A direction for adventurers
1641 Grimston, Sir H. Mr Grymstons speech in Parliament
1641 Hall, J. A survay
1641 The lamentable complaints of Hop the brewer
1641 The lamentable complaints of Nick Froth
1641 Mervyn, Sir A. A speech
1641 A pack of patentees. opened
1641 Rudyerd, Sir B. A speech
1641 Sad news from the seas
1641 Strafford, T. Wentworth, 1st earl of, defendant. Depositions and articles (2)

1642 Baltimore, G. Calvert, 1st baron. The answer to Tom-Tell-Troth
1642 Ofwod, S. The wicked plots
1642 The speech of a cavaleere
1642 Taylor, J. The devil turn'd Round-head
1642 Taylor, J. St. Hillaries teares
1643 Canne, Abednego, pseud. A new wind-mil
1643? Certain inducements
1643 Observations
1643 Randolph, T. Poems
1643 Robinson, H. Liberty of conscience
1644 Castell, W. A short discoverie
1644? A coole conference
1644 Lechford, T. New-Englands advice
1644 Steuart, A. An answer to a libell
1644 A true state of the case
1644 Warwick, R. Rich, 2d earl of. A declaration
1644 Williams, R. The bloudy tenent
1644 Williams, R. The bloudy tenet
1644 Williams, R. Mr. Cottons letter . . . examined
1645 Wheelwright, J. Mercurius Americanus
1646 The case of Mainwaring
1646 A moderate and safe expedient
1646 Rivière, L. Observationes medicae
1647 Bible. O.T. Psalms. English. Paraphrases. 1647. Bay Psalm Book. The whole book of psalmes
1647 Company of Adventurers for . . . Eleutheria. Articles and orders
1647 Corbet, M. A most learned . . . speech
1647 Neville, H. The ladies parliament
1647 Neville, H. The parliament of ladies (2)
1647 Sheppard, S. The committee-man curried
1647 Taylor, J. The Kings most excellent majesties wellcome

1647 Wortley, Sir F. Mercurius Britannicus
1648 The British bell-man
1648? Carlyle, J. Hay, 2nd earl of. A declaration
1648 Golding, W. Servants on horse-back
1648 Hinc illae lachrymae
1648 Plantagenet, B. A description . . . of New Albion
1648 Remonstrance
1648 Sandys, G. A paraphrase upon the divine poems
1648 Taylor, J. Hipp-anthrōpos
1648 Walker, C. The history of Independency
1648 Walker, C. Relations and observations
1649 Taylor, J. John Taylors wandering
1649? Walker, C. Anarchia anglicana, pt 1
1649 Walker, C. Anarchia anglicana, pt 2 (2)
1650 Great Britain. laws, statutes, etc., 1649–1660. An act for charging of tobacco
1650 Neville, H. Newes from the New-exchange
1650 A treatise of New England
1650 Vaughan, T. The man-mouse
1650? The Virginia trade stated
1650 Walker, C. Anarchia anglicana, pt 2
1650 Walker, C. Relations and observations
1650 Ward, N. Discolliminium

A., B.
1630 Cortés, M. The arte of navigation

Adams, Elizabeth
1620 King, J. Sermon at Paules Crosse

Adams, Thomas
1605 Stow, J. The annals of England
1609 Crakanthorpe, R. A sermon
1612 Anghiera, P. M. d'. De novo orbe
1612 Rich, B. A true and a kinde excuse
1613 Rich, B. Opinion diefied
1614 Ravenscroft, T. A briefe discourse
1614 Rich, B. The honestie of this age

1615 Rich, B. The honestie of this age (2)
1615 Stow, J. The annales . . . of England
1616 Rich, B. The honestie of this age
1616 Rich, B. My ladies looking glasse
1617 Wirsung, C. Praxis medicinae universalis

Alchorn, Thomas
1627 Purchas, S. Purchas his pilgrim. Microcosmus
1635 Person, D. Varieties: or, A surveigh

Allde, Edward
1602 Dekker, T. Satiro-mastix (2)
1602 Tapp, J. The seamans kalendar
1603 Dekker, T. The pleasant comodie
1604 Drayton, M. The owle (2)
1604 Rowlands, S. Looke to it
1605 Breton, N. An olde mans lesson
1605 Rowlands, S. Humors antique faces
1607 Markham, G. Cavelarice
1607 Middleton, T. The phoenix
1607 Nicholl, J. An houre glasse
1607 Rowlands, S. Humors ordinarie
1607 Sharpham, E. Cupids whirligig
1607 Sharpham, E. The fleire
1608 Day, J. Law-trickes
1608 Rowlands, S. Humors looking glasse
1608 Smith, Capt. J. A true relation of . . . Virginia (4)
1608 Tapp, J. The seamans kalendar
1609 Everie woman in her humor
1609 Melton, Sir J. A sixe-folde politician
1609 Rowlands, S. The knave of clubbes
1610 Dawson, T. The good huswifes jewell
1610 Rich, R. Newes from Virginia
1610 Rowlands, S. Humors ordinarie
1611 Davies, J. The scourge of folly

1611 Rowlands, S. The knave of clubbes
1612 Breton, N. Wits private wealth
1612? Rowlands, S. The knave of clubbes
1612 Taylor, J. The sculler
1613 Breton, N. Wits private wealth
1613 Rowlands, S. More knaves yet?
1613? Rowlands, S. More knaves yet?
1614 Ravenscroft, T. A briefe discourse
1614 Rowlands, S. A fooles bolt is soon shot
1615 Stephens, J. Essayes and characters
1615 Tapp, J. The seamans kalendar
1617 Markham, G. Cavelarice
1617 Tapp, J. The seamans kalendar
1618 Stow, J. The abridgment of the English chronicle
162–? Drayton, M. The owle
1620 A booke of cookerie
1620 Tapp, J. The seamans kalendar
1620 Taylor, J. The praise of hemp-seed
1621 Great Britain. Sovereigns, etc., 1603–1625. James, by the grace of God.
1621 Hughes, L. A plaine and true relation
1621 Scott, T. A relation of some speciall points
1621 Taylor, J. The praise . . . of beggery
1621 Taylor, J. A shilling
1621 Taylor, J. Taylor's motto (2)
1621 Taylor, J. Taylors goose
1621 A true relation
1622 More excellent observations
1622 Tapp, J. The seamans kalendar
1622 Taylor, J. An arrant thiefe
1622 Taylor, J. A common whore (2)
1622 Taylor, J. The great O Toole
1622 Taylor, J. A verry merry wherry-ferry voyage

1641 Vicary, T. The English-
   mans treasure
1642 Abbott, G. A briefe description
1642 Rudyerd, Sir B. Two
   speeches
1642 Saltonstall, C. The navigator
1648 Markham, G. Cheape and
   good husbandry
Archer, Thomas
1604 Dekker, T. Newes from
   Graves-end
1609 Everie woman in her humor
1610 Rowlands, S. Humors ordinarie
1611 Middleton, T. The roaring
   girle
1614 Lithgow, W. A most delectable . . . discourse
1616 Lithgow, W. A most delectable . . . discourse
1622 More excellent observations
1625 Teixeira, J. The Spanish
   pilgrime
Aspley, William
1603 A letter written to the
   governours
1604 Acosta, J. de. The naturall
   and morall historie
1604 Marston, J. The malcontent
1605 Chapman, G. Eastward
   Hoe (4)
1623 Perceval, R. A dictionary
1623 Shakespeare, W. Comedies, histories, & tragedies
B., J.
1630 Taylor, J. Jacke a Lent
Bache, John
1612 Rowlands, S. The knave of
   harts
1613 Rowlands, S. The knave of
   harts
Badger, George
1646 Vaughan, H. Poems
Badger, Richard
1623 Taylor, J. The praise and
   vertue of a jayle
1630 Earle, J. Micro-
   cosmographie
1630 A rich storehouse
1631 A rich storehouse
1632 Overbury, Sir T. Sir
   Thomas Overbury his wife
1634 Alemán, M. The rogue

1635 Person, D. Varieties: or, A
   surveigh
1638 Ovidius Naso, P.
   Metamorphoses. English.
   Metamorphosis
1638 Sibbes, R. Light from
   heaven (2)
1641 Bacon, F. Three speeches
Badger, Thomas
1640 Howell, J. Dendrologia
Bailey, Thomas
1617 Young, T. Englands bane
1620 Rowlands, S. The night
   raven
1634 Rowlands, S. The night
   raven
1634 Young, T. Englands bane
Ballard, Henry
1608 Middleton, T. A mad world
Banks, Thomas
1647 Cotton, J. Severall
   questions
Bankworth, Richard
1612 Thompson, T. A diet for
   a drunkard
Barker, Robert
1603 Great Britain. Sovereigns,
   etc., 1603–1625. A proclamation . . . against rogues
1604 James I, King of Great
   Britain. A counterblaste
1605 Great Britain. Treaties,
   etc., 1603–1625. Articles of
   peace
1605 Great Britain. Treaties,
   etc., 1603–1625. Articulen. *See
   under* The Netherlands—
   Middelburg—Printer
   unidentified
1616 James I, King of Great
   Britain. Workes
1620 Great Britain. Sovereigns,
   etc., 1603–1625. A proclamation commanding conformity
1620 Great Britain. Sovereigns,
   etc., 1603–1625. A proclamation . . . concerning Captaine
   Roger North
1620 Great Britain. Sovereigns,
   etc., 1603–1625. A proclamation for restraint
1620 James I, King of Great
   Britain. Workes
1621 Great Britain. Sovereigns,
   etc., 1603–1625. Whereas at
   the humble suit

1630 Great Britain. Sovereigns,
   etc., 1625–1649. A proclamation forbidding the disorderly
   trading
1631 Great Britain. Sovereigns,
   etc., 1625–1649. A proclamation concerning tobacco.
1633 Great Britain. Sovereigns,
   etc., 1625–1649. A proclamation for preventing of the abuses . . . of tobacco (2)
1634 Great Britain. Laws,
   statutes, etc., 1625–1649. A
   commission for the well
   governing of . . . Newfoundland
1634 Great Britain. Sovereigns,
   etc., 1625–1649. A proclamation concerning tobacco.
1634 Great Britain. Sovereigns,
   etc., 1625–1649. A proclamation restraining the abusive
   venting of tobacco (2)
1635 Great Britain. Laws,
   statues, etc., 1625–1649. The
   rates of marchandizes
1637 Great Britain. Sovereigns,
   etc., 1625–1649. A proclamation against the disorderly
   transporting
1638 Great Britain. Sovereigns,
   etc., 1625–1649. A proclamation concerning tobacco
1638 Great Britain. Sovereigns,
   etc., 1625–1649. A proclamation to restraine the transporting of passengers
1639 Great Britain. Sovereigns,
   etc., 1625–1649. A proclamation concerning tobacco (2)
1639 Great Britain. Sovereigns,
   etc., 1625–1649. A proclamation . . . touching sundry
   grants (2)
1639 Great Britain. Sovereigns,
   etc., 1625–1649. A proclamation . . . for licensing retailors
   of tobacco
1642 Great Britain. Treaties,
   etc., 1625–1649. Articles of
   peace and commerce
Barley, William
1601 A rich storehouse
1607 Dekker, T. A knights
   conjuring
1608 Weelkes, T. Cantus. Ayeres
   or phantasticke spirites

1637 Venner, T. Via recta
1638 Blundeville, T. Mr. Blundevil his exercises
1638 Herbert, Sir T. Some yeares travels
1638 Venner, T. Via recta
1640 Jonson, B. Workes
1648 Norton, J. Responsio
Blacklock, Lawrence
1639 Walkington, T. The optick glasse of humors
1640 Cervantes Saavedra, M. de. Exemplarie novells
Blackmore, Edward
1631 Dekker, T. Penny-wise
1632 Smith, Capt. J. The generall historie
1641 Watts, R. The young mans looking-glass
1644 Cotton, J. Sixteene questions
Bladen, William
1622 Council for New England. A brief relation . . . of New England
1624 Winslow, E. Good newes from New-England (2)
Bloome, Jacob
1634 Herbert, Sir T. A relation
1638 Herbert, Sir T. Some yeares travels
Blount, Edward
1603 Daniel, S. A panegyricke congratularie (3)
1603 Montaigne, M. E. de. The essayes
1604 Acosta, J. de. The naturall and morall historie
1609? Hall, J. The discovery of a new world
1611 Florio, J. Queen Anna's new world of words
1613 King, H. An halfe-penny-worth of wit
1613 Montaigne, M. E. de. Essayes
1620 Cervantes Saavedra, M. de. History of . . . Don Quixote, Pt 2
1622 Alemán, M. The rogue
1623 Alemán, M. The rogue
1623 Perceval, R. A dictionary
1623 Shakespeare, W. Comedies, histories, and tragedies
1628 Earle, J. Micro-cosmographie (2)

Blower, Ralph
1601 A rich storehouse
1606 Breton, N. A poste, pt 2
1607 A rich storehouse
1612 A rich storehouse
1615 Rowlands, S. The melancholie knight
1615 Taylor, J. Faire and fowle weather
1616 A rich storehouse
1618 Sir Walter Rauleigh his lamentation
Blunden, Humphrey
1640 Shepard, T. The sincere convert (2)
1640 Vaughan, W. The church militant
1640 Wit's recreations
1641 Shepard, T. The sincere convert
1641 Wit's recreations
1642 Shepard, T. The sincere convert
1643 Shepard, T. The sincere convert
1645 Wit's recreations. Recreation for ingenious head-pieces
1648 Gage, T. The English-American
Boler, James
1629 Taylor, J. Wit and mirth
1630 Taylor, J. All the works
1630 Taylor, J. Jacke a Lent
1631 Taylor, J. The needles excellency
1632 Lenton, F. Spare time
1634 Taylor, J. The needles excellency
1635 Taylor, J. Wit and mirth
1636 Taylor, J. The needles excellency
1640 Taylor, J. The needles excellency
Bollifant, Edmund
1601 Botero, G. The travellers breviat
1601 Botero, G. The worlde
Bonion, Richard
1610 Hobbes, S. Margarita chyrurgica
Bostock, Robert
1629 Lenton, F. The young gallants whirligigg
1631 Brathwaite, R. Whimzies
1644 Forbes, A. An anatomy of independency

Bourne, Nicholas
1614 Davies, W. A true relation
1618 Cole, N. Preservatives against sinne
1621 Goulart, S. The wise old man
1622 More excellent observations
1623 Jobson, R. The golden trade
1623 Malynes, G. de. The center of the circle of commerce
1623 A true relation of . . . the . . . Spanish fleet
1625 Hagthorpe, J. England's-exchequer
1626 Nichols, P. Sir Francis Drake revived
1628 Drake, Sir F. The world encompassed
1628 Nichols, P. Sir Francis Drake revived
1629 Featley, J. A sermon
1630 Sharpe, E. England's royall fishing revived
1630 Three severall treatises
1630 Waerdenburgh, D. van. Two memorable relations
1635 Drake, Sir F. The world encompassed
1636 Malynes, G. de. Consuetudo, vel, Lex mercatoria (2)
1638 Sibbes, R. Light from heaven (2)
1639 Two famous sea-fights
1641 Roberts, L. The treasure of traffike
1641 Robinson, H. England's safety
1650 Hunt, R. The island of Assada
Bowtell, Stephen
1647 Ward, N. The simple cobler of Aggawam (5)
1650 Bradstreet, A. The tenth muse
1650 Royal College of Physicians of London. Pharmacopoea Londinensis
Boydell, Robert
1650 Foster, N. A briefe relation of the . . . rebellion
Boyle, Richard
1612 Cotta, J. A short discoverie

Bradock, Richard
1602 Vaughan, W. Naturall and artificial directions for health (2)
1606 Dekker, T. Newes from hell
1606? Drayton, M. Poemes lyrick and pastorall
1607 Vaughan, W. Naturall and artificial directions for health
1616 Beaumont, F. The scornful ladie

Bradwood, Melchisidec
1606 The copy of a letter ... written by E. D.
1607 Daniel, S. A panegyrike congratulatorie
1611 Florio, J. Queen Anna's new world of words
1612 Donne, J. The first anniversarie
1613 Montaigne, M. E. de. Essayes
1617 Minsheu, J. Ductor in linguas

Brewster, Edward
1628 Levitt, C. A voyage into New England
1630 Bonham, T. The chyrurgeons closet
1644 Rathband, W. A briefe narration

Browne, John
1605 Abbot, G. A briefe description
1605 Breton, N. A poste, pt 2
1606 Breton, N. A poste, pt 2
1607 Breton, N. A poste
1608 Abbot, G. A brief description
1608 Vaughan, W. The golden-grove
1609 Breton, N. A poste
1612 Drayton, M. Poly-Olbion
1613 Drayton, M. A choro-graphicall description
1613 Drayton, M. Poly-Olbion
1617 Abbot, G. A briefe description
1617 Minsheu, J. Ductor in linguas
1625 Minsheu, J. Minshaei emendatio

Browne, Nathaniel
1618 Willis, J. Mnemonica

Browne, Samuel
1641 Bacon, F. Three speeches

Budge, John
1612 Chapman, G. An epicede
1615 Harington, Sir J. Epigrams
1616 Breton, N. The good and the badde
1618 Harington, Sir J. The most elegant and wittie epigrams
1622 Wither, G. Juvenilia
1625 Harington, Sir J. The most elegant and wittie epigrams

Burby, Cuthbert
1601 Neck, J. C. van. The journall

Burre, Walter
1601 Jonson, B. Every man in his humor
1601 Jonson, B. The fountaine of selfe-love
1601 Wright, T. The passions of the minde
1604 Wright, T. The passions of the minde
1608 Middleton, T. A mad world
1610 Donne, J. Pseudo-martyr
1611 Donne, J. Conclave Ignatii
1612 Jonson, B. The alchemist
1612 Strachey, W. For the colony in Virginea
1613 Beaumont, F. The knight of the burning pestle
1613 Taylor, J. Odcombs complaint
1614 Raleigh, Sir W. The history of the world
1615 An advice how to plant tobacco
1615 Kayll, R. The trades increase
1615 Tomkis, T. Albumazar. A comedy (2)
1617 Raleigh, Sir W. The history of the world
1621 Raleigh, Sir W. The history of the world (2)

Burton, Francis
1607 Sharpham, E. The fleire
1613 Wither, G. Abuses stript, and whipt (4)
1614 Wither, G. Abuses stript, and whipt
1615 Wither, G. Abuses stript and whipt
1617 Wither, G. Abuses stript and whipt

Busby, John
1608 Dekker, T. Lanthorne and candle-light

1609 Dekker, T. Lanthorne and candle-light
1609 Melton, Sir J. A six-folde politician
1612 Dekker, T. O per se O, or A new cryer
1612 Drayton, M. Poly-Olbion
1613 Drayton, M. A choro-graphicall description
1613 Drayton, M. Poly-Olbion
1616 Dekker, T. Villanies discovered

Bushell, Thomas
1602 Work for chimney-sweepers
1604 Marlowe, C. Doctor Faustus

Butler, William
1615 Taylor, J. Faire and fowle weather

Butter, Nathaniel
1605 Crosse, H. The schoole of pollicie
1607 Dekker, T. Jests to make you merie
1607 Dekker, T. The whore of Babylon
1607 Nicholl, J. An houre glasse
1609 Dekker, T. Worke for armourours
1609 The man in the moone
1610 Sharpham, E. The fleire
1612 Taylor, J. The sculler
1613 Hoby, Sir E. A counter-snarle (2)
1614 Gentleman, T. Englands way to win wealth
1614 Taylor, J. The nipping ... of abuses
1614 Taylor, J. Taylors water-worke
1615 Hoby, Sir E. A curry-combe for a coxe-combe
1615 Sharpham, E. The fleire
1621 A true relation of of a wonderfull sea fight
1623 A true relation of ... the ... Spanish fleet
1625 Crosse, W. The Dutch survay
1625 Hagthorpe, J. England's-exchequer
1630 Dekker, T. The honest whore, pt 2
1630 Nederlandsche West-Indische Compagnie. Three severall treatises

1632 Sandys, Sir E. Europae speculum (2)

1632 Shakespeare, W. Comedies, histories, and tragedies

1633 Prynne, W. Histrio-mastix (2)

1634 Moffett, T. Insectorum . . . theatrum (3)

1634 Paré, A. The workes

1634 Wood, W. New Englands prospect

1635 Biondi, Sir G. F. Donzella desterrada

1635 Mercator, G. Historia mundi, or . . . atlas (2)

1635 Parkinson, J. Paradisi in sole paradisus terrestris

1635 Person, D. Varieties

1635 Taylor, J. Wit and mirth

1635 Wood, W. New Englands prospect

1637 Sandys, G. A relation of a journey

1637 Sandys, Sir E. Europae speculum

1638 Sandys, Sir E. Europae speculum

1639 Chapman, G. The ball

1639 Fletcher, J. Wit without money

1640 Ovidius Naso, P. Amores. English. All Ovids elegies

1640 Parkinson, J. Theatrum botanicum

1640 Raleigh, Sir W. The prerogative of parliaments (2)

1641 Wit's recreations

Cotton, William

1604 Cooke, J. Epigrames

Coules, Francis

1638 Taylor, J. Newes

1641 Cotton, J. An abstract or the lawes

1641 Taylor, J. The complaint of M. Tenter-hooke

Creede, Thomas

1601 Jack Drum's entertainment

1602 Breton, N. A poste

1602 Shakespeare, W. A most pleasaunt . . . comedie, of syr John Falstaffe

1603 Breton, N. A poste

1603 Dekker, T. The wonderfull yeare

1603 Lodge, T. A treatise of the plague

1604 Dekker, T. Newes from Graves-end

1604? Dekker, T. The wonderfull year

1604 Middleton, T. The blacke booke

1605? Breton, N. [A poste]

1605 Breton, N. A poste, pt 2

1605? Dekker, T. The wonderfull year

1605 Duchesne, J. The practise of chymicall . . . physicke

1606 Chapman, G. Monsieur d'Olive. A comedie (2)

1607 Dekker, T. A knights conjuring

1607 Stafford, R. A geographi-call and anthologicall description

1610 Hobbes, S. Margarita chyrurgica

1611 Sharpham, E. Cupids whirligig

1612 Dekker, T. If it be not good

1613 Vicary, T. The English-mans treasure

1613 Wither, G. Abuses stript, and whipt

1614 Borough, W. A discours

1614 Norman, R. The new attractive

1615 Breton, N. Wits private wealth

1615 Overbury, Sir T. New and choise characters

1615 Parrot, H. The mastive

1616 Sharpham, E. Cupids whirligig

Crooke, Andrew

1637 Du Bartas, G. de S., seigneur. A learned summary (2)

1637 Sandys, G. A relation of a journey

1638 Earle, J. Micro-cosmographie

1638 Overbury, Sir T. Sir Thomas Overbury his wife

1639 Fletcher, J. Wit without money

1640 Jonson, B. Execration

1640 Jonson, B. Workes

1644 Rutherford, S. The due right

1646 Twisse, W. A treatise of Mr. Cottons

1648 Allin, J. A defence of the answer

1648 Cobbet, T. A just vindication

1648 Norton, J. Responsio

1648 Rutherford, S. A survey

1649 Rutherford, S. A free disputation

Crouch, John

1636 Peacham, H. Coach and sedan (2)

D., O.

1648 Sandys, G. A paraphrase

Dawlman, Robert

1630 Wright, T. The passions of the minde

Dawson, John

1621 Goulart, S. The wise vieillard

1622 Copland, P. Virginia's God be thanked

1622 Cushman, R. A sermon

1622 Hawkins, Sir R. The observations

1622 Mourt's relation. A relation . . . of . . . Plimoth

1623 Scott, T. The Belgicke pismire

1623 Smith, Capt. J. The generall history

1624 Bacon, F. The essaies

1624 Scott, T. Vox populi, pt 2

1624 Smith, Capt. J. The generall historie

1624 Winslow, E. Good newes from New-England (2)

1625 Bradwell, S. A watch-man for the pest

1625 Morrell, W. New-England

1625 Smith, Capt. J. The generall historie

1626 Davys, J. The seamans secrets

1626 Jenner, T. The soules solace

1626 Smith, Capt. J. The generall historie

1627 Smith, Capt. J. The generall historie

1627 Speed, J. A prospect

1631 Jenner, T. The soules solace

1631 Smith, Capt. J. The generall historie

1631 Speed, J. A prospect

1632 Smith, Capt. J. The generall historie

1618 Newes of Sr. Walter Rauleigh (2)
1620 Rowlands, S. The night raven
1621 Martyn, J. New epigrams
1621 Taylor, J. Superbiae flagellum
1622 Alemán, M. The rogue
1622 Brooke, C. A poem on the late massacre
1622 Taylor, J. The water-comorant
1622 Waterhouse, E. A declaration of the state of . . . Virginia
1623 Alemán, M. The rogue
1623 A true relation of . . . the . . . Spanish fleet
1624 Serres, J. de. A generall historie (2)

Eliot's Court Press
1601 Stow, J. The annales
1605 Rosier, J. A true relation
1605 Stow, J. The annales
1607 Stradling, Sir J. Epigrammatum libri quatuor
1608? Ortelius, A. Theatrum orbis terrarum . . . The theatre of the whole world
1609 Lescarbot, M. Nova Francia, or the description of . . . New France
1610 Virginia Company of London. A true declaration
1623 Powell, T. Wheresoever you see mee
1625 Lescarbot, M. Nova Francia
1626 Boccalini, T. The new-found politicke
1627 Royal College of Physicians of London. Pharmacopoea Londinensis
1638 Roberts, L. The merchants mappe of commerce

Ellis, William
1642 Lechford, T. Plain dealing

Emery, Jaspar
1639 Plattes, G. A discovery

Fawcet, Thomas
1626 Vicary, T. The English-mans treasure
1627 Purchas, S. Purchas his pilgrim. Microcosmus
1630 Beaumont, F. The scornefull ladie
1630 Cortés, M. The arte of navigation

1630 Nederlandsche West-Indische Compagnie. Three severall treatises
1630 Overbury, Sir T. Sir Thomas Overbury his wife
1630 Taylor, J. All the workes
1631 Harris, R. The arraignment
1631 Sharpham, E. The fleire
1631 Stow, J. The annales
1631 Tapp, J. The seamans kalendar
1632 Tapp, J. The seamans kalendar
1633 Isaacson, H. Saturni ephemerides
1633 Vicary, T. The English-mans treasure
1633 White, A. A declaration
1634 Breton, N. Wits private wealth
1634 Markham, G. The art of archerie
1634? Tapp, J. The seamans kalendar
1635 Fox, L. North-West Fox
1636 Saltonstall, C. The navigator
1637 Norwood, R. The sea-mans practice
1638 Primerose, J. De vulgi in medicina erroribus
1639 Breton, N. Wits private wealth
1639 More, Sir T. The common-wealth of Utopia
1639 Two famous sea-fights
1640 Jonson, B. The workes, v. 2–3
1640 Taylor, J. A brave and valiant sea-fight
1641 Vicary, T. The English-mans treasure
1642 Breton, N. Wits private wealth
1642 Saltonstall, C. The navigator
1644 Norwood, R. The sea-mans practice
1647 Tanner, R. A brief treatise

Fawne, Luke
1631 Stephens, J. New essayes
1645 Hollingworth, R. An examination
1646 Gorton, S. Simplicities defence
1650 Cotgrave, R. A French-English dictionary

Ferbrand, William
1604 Rowlands, S. Looke to it (2)
1605? Rowlands, S. Humors ordinarie
1606 Dekker, T. Newes from hell
1607 Rowlands, S. Humors ordinarie
1608 Rowlands, S. Humors looking glasse
1609 Rowlands, S. The knave of clubbes

Featherstone, Henry
1609 Wybarne, J. The new age
1613 Purchas, S. Purchas his Pilgrimage
1614 Purchas, S. Purchas his Pilgrimage
1617 Purchas, S. Purchase his Pilgrimage
1618 Bainbridge, J. An astronomicall description
1619 Purchas, S. Purchas his prilgrim. Microcosmus
1625 Purchas, S. Purchas his pilgrimes
1626 Purchas, S. Purchas his pilgrimage
1626 Purchas, S. Purchase his Pilgrimage

Field, John
1644 Steuart, A. The second part of the duply
1646 Rutherford, S. The divine right
1650 Great Britain. Laws, statutes, etc., 1649–1660. An act prohibiting trade

Field, Richard
1601 Barrough, P. The method of phisick
1602 Marbecke, R. A defence of tabacco
1603 Du Bartas, G. de S., seigneur. The second day
1604 Du Bartas, G. de S., seigneur. The third dayes creation
1605 Wirsung, C. Praxis medicinae
1610 Barrough, P. The method of phisick
1612 Cotta, J. A short discoverie
1615 Sandys, G. A relation of a journey
1616 Deacon, J. Tobacco tortured

1617 Barrough, P. The method
of phisick
1618 Guicciardini, F. The
historie
1620 Tanner, R. A brief treatise
1621 Sandys, G. A relation of a
journey
1622 Brinsley, J. Consolation
1624 Barrough, P. The method
of phisick
1624 Camden, W. Annales
Fisher, Benjamin
1623 Powell, T. Wheresoever
you see mee
1625 Camden, W. Annales
1626 Smith, Capt. J. An
accidence
1627 Smith, Capt. J. An
accidence
1630 Camden, W. The historie
of . . . Princesse Elizabeth
1634 Markham, G. The art of
archerie
1635 Camden, W. Annals
1636 Bradwell, S. Physick
1636 Powell, T. The art of
thriving
1636 Smith, Capt. J. An
accidence
Flasket, John
1601 Neck, J. C. van. Journall
1602 Beaumont, Sir J. The
metamorphosis of tabacco
1606? Drayton, M. Poemes lyrick
and pastorall
Fletcher, James
1650 Venner, T. Via recta
Fletcher, Miles
1624 Serres, J. de. A generall
historie of France (2)
1625 Taylor, J. An arrant thiefe
1625 Taylor, J. The common
whore
1626 Breton, N. Fantasticks
1626 Donne, J. Ignatius his
conclave
1626 Taylor, J. Wit and mirth
1626 Vaughan, W. The golden
fleece
1628? Cooke, J. Greene's Tu
quoque
1629 Lenton, F. The young
gallants whirligigg
1630 Massachusetts (Colony).
The humble request
1630 Wright, T. The passions of
the minde

1632 Montaigne, M. E. de. The
essayes
1633 Donne, J. Poems
1634 Breton, N. A poste
1635 Donne, J. Poems
1635 Jones, J. Adrasta
1636 Lloyd, D. The legend of
captaine Jones
1637 Breton, N. A poste
1639 Donne, J. Poems
1640 Donne, J. LXXX sermons
1646 Rivière, L. Observationes
medicae
1646 Speed, J. A prospect
1647 Baillie, R. Anabaptism
1648 Lloyd, D. The legend of
captaine Jones
1649 Donne, J. Poems
Fosbrooke, Nathaniel
1618 Jack Drum's entertainment
Frere, Daniel
1639 Chamberlain, R. Conceits,
clinches, flashes
1640 Chamberlain, R. Jocabella
1643 Baker, Sir R. A chronicle
of the kings (2)
1643 Digby, Sir K. Observations
(2)
1644 Digby, Sir K. Observations
(2)
Fussell, Nicholas
1632 Lithgow, W. The totall
discourse
Gellibrand, Samuel
1645 Baillie, R. A dissuasive
from the errours
1646 Baillie, R. A dissuasive
from the errours
1647 Baillie, R. Anabaptism
Gibbs, George
1617 Fennor, W. The compters
common-wealth
1617 Taylor, J. Three weekes
Gosson, Henry
1612 Taylor, J. Laugh, and be
fat
1618 Newes of Sr. Walter
Rauleigh (2)
1620 Taylor, J. The praise of
hemp-seed
1621 Taylor, J. The praise . . . of
beggery
1621 Taylor, J. A shilling
1621 Taylor, J. Taylor's motto
(2)
1621 Taylor, J. Taylors goose
1622 [Mourning Virginia]

1622 Taylor, J. An arrant thiefe
1622 Taylor, J. A common
whore (2)
1622 Taylor, J. The great
O Toole
1623 Taylor, J. The praise of
hemp-seed (2)
1623 Taylor, J. The world
runnes on wheeles
1625 Taylor, J. An arrant thiefe
1625 Taylor, J. The common
whore
1626 Taylor, J. Wit and mirth
1627 Taylor, J. An armado
1628 Taylor, J. Wit and mirth
1630 Taylor, J. The great eater
1635 Taylor, J. An armado
1635 Taylor, J. An arrant thiefe
1635 Taylor, J. A bawd
1635 Taylor, J. A common
whore
1635 Taylor, J. The olde,
old . . . man (3)
1635 Taylor, J. The travels of
twelve-pence
1635 Taylor, J. The world
runnes on wheeles
Greene, Charles
1637? Morton, T. New English
Canaan
Griffin, Anne
1622 Overbury, Sir T. Sir
Thomas Overbury his wife
1631 Markham, G. Cheape and
good husbandry
1637 Markham, G. The English
housewife
1637 Taylor, J. Drinke and
welcome
Griffin, Edward, the Elder
1614 Taylor, J. The nipping
. . . of abuses
1616 Barlow, W. Magneticall
advertisements
1616 Overbury, Sir T. Sir
Thomas Overburie his wife (3)
1616 Scot, T. Philomythie
1617 Brathwaite, R. A solemne
joviall disputation
1617 Fennor, W. The compters
common-wealth
1617 Taylor, J. Three weekes
1617 Woodall, J. The surgions
mate
1618 Bainbridge, J. An
astronomicall description (2)

1618 Barlow, W. Magneticall advertisements
1618 Overbury, Sir T. Sir Thomas Overbury his wife
1618 Royal College of Physicians of London. Pharmacopoea Londinensis (2)
1619 Campion, T. Epigrammatum libri ii
1619 Dodoens, R. A newe herbal
1620 King, J. Sermon at Paules Crosse
1620 Venner, T. Via recta

Griffin, Edward, the Younger
1638 Bacon, F. Opera moralium et civilium
1639 Bauderon, B. Pharmacopoea
1640 Gough, J. The strange discovery (2)
1641 Hooke, W. New Englands teares
1644 Rutherford, S. The due right
1646 Boothby, R. A briefe discovery
1647 Boothby, R. A briefe discovery

Grismond, John
1621 Du Bartas, G. de S., seigneur. A learned summary
1622 Drayton, M. A chorographicall description
1628 Ovidius Naso, P. Metamorphoses. English. Metamorphosis
1632 Dekker, T. English villanies
1642 Lechford, T. Plain dealing
1650 Foster, N. A briefe relation

Grove, Francis
1629 A booke of cookerie
1629 Breton, N. Wits private wealth

Grove, John
1629 Gallobelgicus, pseud. Wine, beere, and ale
1630 Gallobelgicus, pseud. Wine, beere, ale and tobacco
1632 Marmion, S. Hollands leaguer (2)

Gubbin, Thomas
1615 Greene, R. Theeves falling out

H., R.
1641 Bacon, F. The historie of . . . King Henrie

Hall, William
1611 De La Warr, T. West, 3rd baron. Relation
1612 Taylor, J. Laugh, and be fat

Hammond, John
1649 Bullock, W. Virginia impartially examined
1650 Sibelius, C. Of the conversion

Hancock, John
1642 Davenport, J. The profession of faith
1645 Cotton, J. The covenant
1646 Williams, R. Christenings
1650 Wit's recreations. Recreation for ingenious head-peeces

Hardesty, John
1646 Boothby, R. A briefe discovery
1646 A vindication of learning
1647 Boothby, R. A briefe discovery

Harford, Raphael
1638 Sibbes, R. Light from heaven (2)

Harper, Thomas
1629 Camden, W. The historie of . . . Princess Elizabeth
1629 Plumptre, H. Epigrammatōn opusculum duobus distinctum
1630 Middleton, T. The phoenix
1630 Randolph, T. Aristippus (2)
1630 Shakespeare, W. The merry wives of Windsor
1630 Sharpham, E. Cupids whirligig
1631 Taylor, J. The needles excellency
1633 Banister, J. The workes
1633 Hester, J. A storehouse
1633 Langham, W. The garden of health
1633 Vaughan, W. Directions for health
1634 Abbot, G. A briefe description
1634 Bate, J. The mysteryes of nature and art (2)
1634 Camden, W. The historie of . . . Princesse Elizabeth
1634 A strange metamorphosis
1635 Abbot, G. A briefe description

1635 Bate, J. The mysteries of nature and art
1635 Camden, W. Annals
1636 Abbot, G. A briefe description
1636 Powell, T. The art of thriving
1636 Smith, Capt. J. An accidence
1638 Roberts, L. The merchants mappe of commerce
1638 Vincent, P. A true relation
1640 A true relation of a . . . sea-fight
1645 Cawdry, D. Vindiciae clavium
1646 Browne, Sir T. Pseudodoxia epidemica (2)
1647 Gomberville, M. Le Roy, sieur du Parc et de. The history of Polexander
1648 Gomberville, M. Le Roy, sieur du Parc et de. The history of Polexander
1650 Williams, E. Virginia
1650 Williams, E. Virginia's discovery of silke-wormes
1650 Williams, E. Virgo triumphans

*Harrison, John
1608 Middleton, R. Epigrams
1631 Markham, G. Cheape and good husbandry (2)
1631 Markham, G. The English house-wife
1633 Vaughan, W. Directions for health
1637 Markham, G. The English housewife
1642 Great Britain. Treaties, etc., 1625–1649. Articles of peace
1648 Markham, G. Cheape and good husbandry

Hatfield, Arnold
1604 Herring, F. A modest defence
1606 Estienne, C. Maison rustique

Haveland, Thomas
1610 Great Britain. Council for Virginia. By the Counsell of Virginia. Whereas the good shippe
1610 Great Britain. Council for Virginia. A publication

1648 Rutherford, S. A survey

1649 Rutherford, S. A free disputation

1650 Manasseh ben Joseph ben Israel. The hope of Israel

Islip, Adam

1604 Wright, T. The passions of the minde

1606 Bodin, J. Of the lawes and customes

1608 Grimestone, E. A generall historie

1609 Grimestone, E. A generall historie

1611 Cotgrave, R. A dictionarie

1612 Mayerne, L. T. de. The generall historie

1613 Orlers, J. J. The triumphs of Nassau

1615 Avity, P. d'. The estates

1616 Estienne, C. Maison rustique

1620 Orlers, J. J. The triumphs of Nassau

1621 Camerarius, P. The living librarie

1621 Camerarius, P. The walking librarie (2)

1625 Camerarius, P. The living librarie

1627 Grimestone, E. A generall historie

1632 Cotgrave, R. A dictionarie

1633 Gerard, J. The herball

1636 Gerard, J. The herball

1636 Malynes, G. de. Consuetudo, vel, Lex mercatoria (3)

Jackson, John

1634 Bate, J. The mysteryes of nature and art

Jackson, Roger

1607 Vaughan, W. Naturall and artificial directions for health

1611 Vaughan, W. Approved directions for health

1612 Vaughan, W. Approved directions for health

1614 Markham, G. Cheape and good husbandry

1615 Markham, G. Countrey contentments

1616 Markham, G. Cheape and good husbandry

1617 Vaughan, W. Directions for health

1623 Markham, G. Cheape and good husbandry

1623 Markham, G. Country contentments

Jaggard, Elizabeth

1624 Bacon, F. The essaies

Jaggard, Isaac

1623 Shakespeare, W. Comedies, histories, and tragedies

1627 Overbury, Sir T. Sir Thomas Overbury his wife

Jaggard, John

1601 Botero, G. The travellers breviat

1601 Botero, G. The worlde

1603 Botero, G. An historicall description

1608 Botero, G. Relations

1611 Botero, G. Relations

1612 Bacon, F. The essaies

1613 Bacon, F. The essaies (3)

1616 Botero, G. Relations

1622 Hawkins, Sir R. The observations

Jaggard, William

1602 Arnauld, A. Le franc discours. A discourse

1606? Rowlands, S. A terrible battell

1607 Dekker, T. West-ward hoe

1607 Markham, G. Cavelarice

1607 Rowlands, S. Democritus

1607 Topsell, E. The historie of foure-footed beastes

1607 Wilkins, G. The miseries of inforst mariage

1608 Botero, G. Relations

1608 Topsell, E. The historie of serpents

1609 Crakanthorpe, R. A sermon

1609 Rowlands, S. A whole crew of kind gossips

1612 Bacon, F. The essaies

1613 Bacon, F. The essaies (3)

1613 The treasurie of auncient and moderne times

1615 Sharpe, E. Britaines busse

1616 Botero, G. Relations

1619 Archaio-ploutos

1619 Shakespeare, W. A most pleasaunt . . . comedie, of syr John Falstaffe

1621 Greevous grones

1621 Raleigh, Sir W. The history of the world (2)

1623 Hexham, H. A tongue-combat

1623 Shakespeare, W. Comedies, histories, and tragedies

1630 Sharpe, E. England's royall fishing revived

Jenner, Thomas

1626 Jenner, T. The soules solace

1631 Jenner, T. The soules solace

Johnson, Arthur

1602 Shakespeare, W. A most pleasaunt . . . comedie, of syr John Falstaffe

1607 Middleton, T. The phoenix

1607 Sharpham, E. Cupids whirligig

1611 Du Bartas, G. de S., seigneur. Du Bartas his devine weekes

1611 Sharpham, E. Cupids whirligig

1614 Rowlands, S. A fooles bolt

1616 Sharpham, E. Cupids whirligig

1618 Guicciardini, F. The historie

1619 Shakespeare, W. See London—Pavier, Thomas

Jones, Thomas

1615 Parrot, H. The mastive

1622 Donne, J. A sermon

1624 Donne, J. A sermon

1624 Donne, J. Three sermons (2)

1625 Beaumont, F. The scorneful ladie

1625 Donne, J. Foure sermons

1626 Donne, J. Five sermons

1630 Beaumont, F. The scornefull ladie

Jones, William

1604 Herring, F. A modest defence

1612 Cotta, J. A short discoverie

1617 Cotta, J. A true discovery of the empericke

1617 Young, T. Englands bane

1619 Cotta, J. A short discoverie

1620 Bourne, W. A regiment for the sea

1620 Smith, Capt. J. New Englands trials

1621 Venner, T. A briefe and accurate treatise

1622 Smith, Capt. J. New Englands trials

Lee, William
1627 Bacon, F. Sylva sylvarum (2)
1627 Drayton, M. The battaile of Agincourt
1629 Bacon, F. Sylva sylvarum
1631 Bacon, F. Sylva sylvarum
1631 Drayton, M. The battaile of Agincourt
1635 Bacon, F. Sylva sylvarum
1638 Bacon, F. History naturall
1639 Bacon, F. Sylva sylvarum
1641 Cotton, J. An abstract or the lawes of New England
1646 Pagitt, E. Heresiography
1647 Pagitt, E. Heresiography (2)
1648 Pagitt, E. Heresiography
Legat, John
1611 Daniel, S. Certain small works
1612 Owen, J. Epigrammatum . . . libri tres
1615 Rich, B. The honestie of this age (2)
1616 Rich, B. The honestie of this age
1616 Rich, B. My ladies looking glasse
1616 Scot, T. Philomythie
1617 Wirsung, C. Praxis medicinae
1622 Malynes, G. The maintenance of free trade
1622 Misselden, E. Free trade (2)
1622 Scot, T. Phylomythie (2)
1624 Hieron, S. The sermons
1628 Overbury, Sir T. Sir Thomas Overburie his wife
1633 James, T. The strange and dangerous voyage
1638 Earle, J. Micro-cosmographie
1638 Sandys, G. A paraphrase
1640 Ovidius Naso, P. Metamorphoses. English. Metamorphosis
1640 Scot, T. Phylomathie
1646 Speed, J. A prospect
Ling, Nicholas
1603 Lodge, T. Treatise of the plague
1604 Drayton, M. The owle (2)
1605 Drayton, M. Poems
1606? Drayton, M. Poems lyrick and pastorall

Lisle, Laurence
1615 Overbury, Sir T. New and choise characters
1616 Overbury, Sir T. Sir Thomas Overburie his wife (2)
1617 Woodall, J. The surgions mate
1618 Overbury, Sir T. Sir Thomas Overbury his wife
1622 Overbury, Sir T. Sir Thomas Overbury his wife
Loftus, George
1602 Rowlands, S. Tis merrie
1604 Rowlands, S. Looke to it (2)
1612 Rowlands, S. The knave of harts
1614 Rowlands, S. A fooles bolt
1615 Rowlands, S. The melancholie knight (2)
Lowndes, Richard
1641 Pym, J. A speech (2)
1642 Pym, J. A speech
1650 Foster, N. A briefe relation of the . . . rebellion
Lownes, Humphrey
1605 Du Bartas, G. de S., seigneur. Bartas: his divine weekes
1605? Hall, J. Mundus alter
1606 Du Bartas, G. de S., seigneur. Bartas his devine weekes
1606 Palmer, Sir T. An essay
1607 Owen, J. Epigrammatum . . . libri tres
1608 Du Bartas, G. de S., seigneur. Bartas his devine weekes
1608 Greene, R. Greenes carde of fancie
1608 Hieron, S. An answere to a popish ryme
1609 Spenser, E. The faerie queene
1610 Gardiner, E. The triall of tabacco
1611 Donne, J. An anatomy of the world
1611 Du Bartas, G. de S., seigneur. Du Bartas his devine weekes
1611 Gardiner, E. Phisicall and approved medicines
1611 Spenser, E. The faerie queene
1612 Drayton, M. Poly-Olbion

1612 Spenser, E. The faerie queene
1613 Drayton, M. A choro-graphicall description
1613 Drayton, M. Poly-Olbion
1613 Du Bartas, G. de S., seigneur. Du Bartas his devine weekes
1613 Spenser, E. The faerie queene
1615? Spenser, E. The faerie queene
1615 Wither, G. Abuses stript and whipt
1616 Smith, Capt. J. A description of New England
1617 Spenser, E. The faerie queen
1617? Sylvester, J. Tobacco battered
1617 Wither, G. Abuses stript and whipt
1618 Willis, J. Mnemonica
1621 Du Bartas, G. de S., seigneur. Bartas his devine weekes
1623 Mexía, P. The imperiall historie
1624 Gardiner, E. Physicall and approved medicines
1625 Camden, W. Annales
1628 Bacon, F. The history of . . . King Henry
1628 Raleigh, Sir W. The historie of the world
1629 Parkinson, J. Paradisi in sole paradisus terrestris
1630 Harris, R. Six sermons
Lownes, Matthew
1602 Meteren, E. van. A true discourse historicall
1604 Mexía, P. The historie of all the Romane emperors
1606 Palmer, Sir T. An essay
1608 Greene, R. Greenes carde of fancie
1609 Spenser, E. The faerie queene
1609 Virginia richly valued
1610 Gardiner, E. The triall of tabacco
1611 Gardiner, E. Phisicall and approved medicines
1611 Spenser, E. The faerie queene
1611 The worthye . . . history of . . . Terra Florida

1630 Wadsworth, J. The present estate of Spayne (2)
1631 Dekker, T. Penny-wise
1631 Drayton, M. The battaile of Agincourt
1631 Stow, J. The annales . . . of England
1632 Breton, N. Conceited letters
1632 Dekker, T. English villanies
1632 Tomkis, T. Lingua
1633 Hester, J. The secrets of physick
1633 Marmion. S. A fine companion
1633 Marston, J. Tragedies and comedies
1633 Marston, J. The workes
1633 Owen, J. Epigrammatum . . . libri decem
1633 Prynne, W. Histrio-mastix (2)
1634 Owen, J. Epigrammatum . . . libri decem
1635 Beaumont, F. The scornfull ladie
1635 Taylor, J. An arrant thiefe
1635 Taylor, J. A bawd
1635 Taylor, J. A common whore
1635 Taylor, J. The olde, old . . . man (3)
1635 Taylor, J. The travels of twelve-pence
1635 Taylor, J. The world runnes on wheeles
1637 Du Bartas, G. de S., seigneur. A learned summary (2)
1650 Hudson, S. A vindication
1650 Mather, R. An heart-melting exhortation
Meighen, Richard
1615 Parrot, H. The mastive
1622 Blundevile, T. M.Blundevile his Exercises
1630 Holyday, B. Technogamia
1630 Middleton, T. The phoenix
1630 Shakespeare, W. The merry wives of Windsor
1630 Sharpham, E. Cupids whirligig
1631 Stow, J. The annales . . . of England
1633 Marmion, S. A fine companion
1635 Davenant, Sir. W. The triumphs

1635 Selden, J. Mare clausum
1639 The ladies cabinet opened
1640 Jonson, B. The workes, v. 2–3
1641 Bacon, F. The historie of . . . King Henrie
Mercurius Britannicus
1625 A true relation of the fleet
Meredith, Christopher
1628 Bacon, F. History of . . . King Henry
1629 Bacon, F. Historie of . . . King Henry
1630 A rich storehouse
1631 A rich storehouse
1638 Hues, R. A learned treatise
1639 Hues, R. A learned treatise
1643 Steuart, A. Some observations
1644 Steuart, A. Some observations
1645 Gillespie, G. Wholsome severity
1645 Hudson, S. The essence and unitie
1646 Rutherford, S. The divine right
1650 Hudson, S. A vindication
Meteren, Emanuel van
1609 Meteren, E. van. Commentarien ofte Memorien
1610 Meteren, E. van. Commentarien ofte Memoiren
1611 Meteren, E. van. Belgische ofte Nederlantsche oorlogen
Michell, Roger
1628 Hayman, R. Quodlibets
1631 Lenton, F. Characterismi
Milbourne, Robert
1622 Brooke, C. A poem on the late massacre
1622 Waterhouse, E. A declaration of . . . Virginia
1631 Smith, Capt. J. Advertisements for the unexperienced planters
1636 Du Bartas, G. de S., seigneur. A learned summary
Miller, Abraham
1648 Hooker, T. A survey of the summe of church-discipline (2)
1650 Browne, Sir T. Pseudodoxia epidemica
Miller, George
1628 Drake, Sir F. The world encompassed

1630 Bonham, T. The chyrurgeons closet
1632 Sandys, G. A relation of a journey
1633 Harrington, Sir J. The most elegant and wittie epigrams
1634 Ariosto, L. Orlando furioso, in English
1634 Barrough, P. The method of phisick
1634 Rocquigny, A. de. La muse chrestienne
1635 Quarles, F. Emblemes (2)
1639 Barrough, P. The method of phisick
1641 Hooker, T. The danger of desertion (2)
1644 Edwards, T. Antapologia; or, A full answer (2)
1644 Rathband, W. A briefe narration
1645 Hudson, S. The essence and unitie
1645 Shepard, T. New Englands lamentation
More, Richard
1608 Day, J. Law-trickes
1610 Folkingham, W. Feudigraphia
1611 Donne, J. Ignatius his conclave
1614 Heresbach, C. The whole art and trade of husbandry
1620 Orlers, J. J. The triumphs of Nassau
1620 Venner, T. Via recta
1621 Venner, T. A briefe and accurate treatise
1622 Venner, T. Via recta
1626 Donne, J. Ignatius his conclave
1628 Venner, T. Via recta
1631 Heresbach, C. The whole art . . . of husbandry
Morgan, John
1635 A relation of Maryland
Moseley, Humphrey
1632 Lithgow, W. The totall discourse
1635 Biondi, Sir G. F. Donzella desterrada
1638 Bacon, F. The historie of life
1638 Bacon, F. History naturall
1640 Howell, J. Dendrologia
1645 Howell, J. Dendrologia

Norton Office
1611 Hues, R. Tractatus de globis
Ockould, Richard
1606 Botero, G. A treatise
Okes, John
1638 Bacon, F. The historie of life
1638 Kirke, J. The seven champions of Christendome
1638 Taylor, J. Newes and strange newes
1638 Taylor, J. Taylors feast
1639 Bancroft, T. Two bookes of epigrammes
1639 Field, N. Amends for ladies
1639 Pagitt, E. A relation of the Christians
1639 Plattes, G. A discovery
1640 Colmenero de Ledesma, A. A curious treatise
1640 Glapthorne, H. Wit in a constable
1640 Horatius Flaccus, Q. Art of poetry
1640 Jonson, B. Execration against Vulcan
1640 Lithgow, W. The totall discourse
1640 Middleton, T. A mad world
1640 Pagitt, E. Christianographie
1641 Heywood, T. Machiavel
1641 Heywood, T. Machiavels ghost
Okes, Marie
1645 Pagitt, E. Heresiography
Okes, Nicholas
1607 Dekker, T. Jests to make you merie
1608 Middleton, R. Epigrams
1609 Blagrave, J. The art of dyalling
1609 Dekker, T. The guls hornebooke
1611 Donne, J. Ignatius his conclave
1611 Middleton, T. The roaring girle
1612 Owen, J. Epigrammatum libri decem
1613 Ridley, M. A short treatise of magneticall bodies (2)
1614 Lithgow, W. A most delectable . . . discourse
1614 The maske of flowers

1615 An advice how to plant tobacco
1615 Kayll, R. The trades increase
1615 Stephens, J. Satyrical essayes
1615 Tomkis, T. Albumazar. A comedy (2)
1615 Tomkis, T. Lingua
1616 Lithgow, W. A most delectable . . . discourse
1617 Tomkis, T. Lingua
1618 Owen, J. Epigrammatum . . . libri tres
1618 Stafford, R. A geographicall and anthologicall description (2)
1618 Stow, J. The abridgment of the English chronicle
1619 Taylor, J. A kicksey winsey
1621 Raleigh, Sir W. The history of the world
1622 Fotherby, M. Atheomastix clearing foure truthes
1622 Owen, J. Epigrammatum . . . libri tres
1622 Taylor, J. Sir Gregory Nonsence
1622 Tomkis, T. Lingua
1623 Daniel, S. The whole workes
1623 Jobson, R. The golden trade
1623 Lithgow, W. A most delectable . . . discourse
1624 Scott, T. An experimentall discoverie
1624 Scott, T. Vox populi, pt 2 (3)
1624 Taylor, J. The scourge of baseness
1624 Verheiden, W. A second part of Spanish practises
1626 Smith, Capt. J. An accidence
1627 Smith, Capt. J. An accidence
1629 Bacon, F. The two bookes . . . of the proficience . . . of learning
1630 Camden, W. The historie of . . . Princesse Elizabeth
1630 Vaughan, W. Cambrensium Caroleja
1630 Vaughan, W. The Newlanders cure

1631 Markham, G. Cheape and good husbandry
1631 Markham, G. The English house-wife
1632 Lithgow, W. The totall discourse (2)
1634 Bethune, P. de. Counsellor of estate
1634 Stafford, R. A geographicall and anthologicall description
1634 Tomkis, T. Albumazar. A comedy
1635 Beaumont, F. The knight of the burning pestle (2)
1636 Lupton, D. Emblems of rarities
1636 Nash, T. Quaternio
1636 Pagitt, E. Christianographie
1640 Tomkis, T. Albumazar. A comedy.
Okes, Nicholas & John
1635 Buck, G. The great Plantagenet
1637 Basset, R. Curiosities
Olive, Richard
1601 Jack Drum's entertainment
Oulton, Richard
1638 Roberts, L. The merchants mappe of commerce
1642 Cotton, J. The churches resurrection
1643 New Englands first fruits
Overton, Henry
1633 Bradwell, S. Helps for suddain accidents
1639 Jenner, T. The soules solace
1641 Hooke, W. New Englands teares (3)
1642 Cotton, J. The churches resurrection
1642 Cotton, J. The powring out of the seven vials (2)
1643 New Englands first fruits
1644 Cotton, J. The keyes of the kingdom of heaven (3)
1644 Goodwin, J. M.S. to A.S.
1644 Goodwin, J. A reply of two of the brethren (2)
1644 Holmes, N. Gospel musick
1644 Weld, T. An answer to W.R.
1645 Cotton, J. The powring out of the seven vials

1632 Rowley, W. A new wonder
1632 Shirley, J. Changes
1636 Du Bartas, G. de S.,
seigneur. A learned summary

R., R.
1619 Fennor, W. The miseries
of a jaile

Rand, Samuel
1614 Rowlands, S. Doctor
Merrie-man
1616 Rowlands, S. Doctor
Merry-man
1618 Breton, N. Conceyted
letters
1618 Rowlands, S. Doctor
Merry-man
1619 Rowlands, S. Doctor
Merry-man
1623 Rowlands, S. Doctor
Merry-man
1627 Rowlands, S. Doctor
Merry-man
1632 Breton, N. Conceited
letters
1638 Breton, N. Conceited
letters
1642 Rowlands, S. Doctor
Merrie-man

Ratcliffe, Thomas
1646 Edwards, T. Antapologia;
or, A full answer (2)
1646 Edwards, T. Gangraena (3)
1646 Edwards, T. Gangraena, pt
1–2
1646 Edwards, T. Gangraena, pt
2 (3)
1646 Edwards, T. Gangraena,
pt 3
1647 Child, J. New Englands
Jonas

Raworth, John
1640 Gad ben-Arod ben Balaam,
pseud. The wandering Jew
1640 Lenton, F. A piece of the
world
1640 Shirley, J. The constant
maid
1643 Great Britain. Laws,
Statutes, etc., 1625–1649. An
ordinance . . . concerning . . .
tobacco (2)
1644 Great Britain. Laws,
statutes, etc., 1625–1649. An
ordinance . . . for the
regulating of the rates (2)
1645 Hollingworth, R. An
examination (2)

Raworth, Robert
1635 Heywood, T. Philo-
cothonista
1636 Dekker, T. The wonder of
a kingdome
1636 Peacham, H. Coach and
sedan (2)

Raworth, Ruth
1646 Saltmarsh, J. The smoke in
the temple

Read, Richard
1601 Jonson, B. The fountaine
of selfe-love
1607 Daniel, S. A panegyrike
congratulatorie

Redmer, Richard
1611 Davies, J. The scourge of
folly
1614 Tailor, R. The hogge hath
lost his pearle
1615 Brathwaite, R. A strappado
1615 Johnson, J. Epigrammatum
libellus

Ritherdon, Ambrose
1630 Wadsworth, J. The present
estate of Spayne (2)
1631 Brathwaite, R. Whimzies

Robinson, Humphrey
1629 Bacon, F. Certaine
miscellany works
1633 Isaacson, H. Saturni
ephemerides
1638 Primerose, J. De vulgi in
medicina erroribus
1640 Torriano, G. The Italian
tutor (2)
1647 Beaumont, F. Comedies
and tragedies
1650 Cotgrave, R. A French-
English dictionary

Rocket, Henry
1603 Dekker, T. The pleasant
comodie
1605 Rowlands, S. Humors
antique faces

Roper, Abel
1648 Raleigh, Sir W., defendant.
The arraignment and
conviction
1650 Cotgrave, R. A French-
English dictionary

Rothwell, John
1641 Hooke, W. New Englands
teares (3)
1645 Hooke, W. New-Englands
sence
1645 Weld, T. A brief narration

Rutherford
1647 Mather, R. A reply to Mr.
Rutherford
1650 Mather, R. An heart-
melting exhortation

Royston, Richard
1632 Grotius, H. True religion
explained
1632 Montaigne, M. E. de. The
essayes
1635 Jones, J. Adrasta
1635 Parkinson, J. Paradisi in
sole paradisus terrestris
1640 Donne, J. LXXX sermons
1642 Bacon, F. The essayes

Seile, Henry
1622 Overbury, Sir T. Sir
Thomas Overbury his wife
1629 Ford, J. The lovers
melancholy
1633 Isaacson, H. Saturni
ephemerides
1633 Massinger, P. A new way
to pay old debts
1635 Botero, G. The cause of the
greatnesse
1642 Great Britain. Treaties,
etc., 1625–1649. Articles of
peace and commerce
1642 Rudyerd, Sir B. Two
speeches

Sergier, Richard
1607 Serres, O. de. The perfect
use of silk-wormes
1608 Vaughan, W. The golden-
grove
1609 Dekker, T. The guls horne-
booke

Shaw, James
1602 Teixeira, J. The true
historie of . . . Don Sebastian
1603 Du Bartas, G. de S.,
seigneur. The second day
1603 Ortelius, A. Epitome

Sheares, William
1632 Bruele, G. Praxis
medicinae
1632 Shakespeare, W. The
historie of Henrie the fourth
[Pt 1]
1633 Marston, J. Tragedies and
comedies
1633 Marston, J. The workes
1634 Abbot, G. A briefe
description
1634 Donne, J. Ignatius his
conclave

1635 Abbot, G. A briefe
description
1635 Donne, J. Ignatius his
conclave
1636 Abbot, G. A briefe
description
1639 Bruele, G. Praxis
medicinae
1639 More, Sir T. The common-
wealth of Utopia
1642 Abbot, G. A briefe
description
1648 Bruele, G. Praxis
medicinae
1650 Earle, J. Micro-
cosmographie (2)
Sheffard, William
1622 Copland, P. Virginia's God
be thanked
1622 Malynes, G. The
maintenance of free trade
1623 A true relation
Shinkin, M., pseud.
1647 Shinkin ap Shone, pseud.
The honest Welch-cobler
Shorleyker, Richard
1630 The armes of the
tobachonists
Simmes, Valentine
1601 Daniel, S. The works
1601 Wright, T. The passions of
the minde
1602 Daniel, S. The works
1603 Daniel, S. A panegyricke
congratularie (3)
1603 A letter written to the
governours
1603 Lodge, T. A treatise of the
plague
1603 Montaigne, M. E. de. The
essayes
1604 Acosta, J. de. The naturall
and morall historie
1604 Marlowe, C. Doctor
Faustus
1604 Marston, J. The malcontent
1604 Shakespeare, W. The
history of Henrie the fourth
[Pt 1]
1604 Wright, T. The passions of
the minde
1605 Crosse, H. The schoole of
pollicie
1605 Drayton, M. Poems
1605 Sandys, Sir E. A relation
1606 Rich, B. Faultes faults

Simmons, Matthew
1640 Shepard, T. The sincere
convert (2)
1641 Shepard, T. The sincere
convert
1642 Shepard, T. The sincere
convert
1643 Shepard, T. The sincere
convert
1644 Ball, J. A tryall of the new-
church way
1644 Cotton, J. The keyes of the
kingdom of heaven (3)
1644 Goodwin, J. A reply of two
of the brethren (2)
1645 Cotton, J. The way of the
churches of Christ in New-
England (2)
1645 Cotton, J. The covenant of
Gods free grace (2)
1645 Eaton, S. A defence of
sundry positions
1645 Weld, T. A brief narration
1646 Bulkeley, P. The gospel-
covenant
1646 Eaton, S. The defence of
sundry positions
1646 Shepard, T. The sincere
convert
1647 Cotton, J. The bloudy
tenant, washed
1647 Weld, T. A brief narration
1648 Cotton, J. The way of
congregational churches
cleared (2)
1648 Johnson, E. Good news
from New England
1650 Robinson, H. Briefe
considerations
1650 Shepard, T. The sincere
convert (2)
1650 Wit's recreations.
Recreation for ingenious
head-peeces
Slater, Thomas
1630 Smith, Capt. J. The true
travels
1633 Bradwell, S. Helps for
suddain accidents
1639 Nash, T. Miscelanea
1650 Thorowgood, T. Jewes in
America
Smethwick, John
1602 Breton, N. A poste
1603 Breton, N. A poste
1605? Breton, N. [A poste]
1605 Breton, N. A poste, pt 2

1606 Breton, N. A poste, pt 2
1607 Breton, N. A poste
1608 Drayton, M. Poems
1609 Breton, N. A poste
1610 Drayton, M. Poems
1613 Drayton, M. Poems
1616 Drayton, M. Poems
1619 Owen, J. Epigrams
1620 Breton, N. A poste
1620 Drayton, M. Poems
1623 Shakespeare, W.
Comedies, histories, &
tragedies
1628? Drayton, M. Poems
1630 Drayton, M. Poems
1637 Drayton, M. Poems
Smith, John G.
1642 Newes from New-England
Smith, Ralph
1642 Cotton, J. The powring out
of the seven vials
1644 Edwards, T. Antapologia;
or, a full answer
1644 Parker, T. The true copy
of a letter
1644 Winthrop, J. Antinomians
and Familists
1644 Winthrop, J. A short story
(2)
1645 Cotton, J. The powring out
of the seven vials
1646 Edwards, T. Antapologia;
or, A full answer
1646 Edwards, T. Gangraena (3)
1646 Edwards, T. Gangraena, pt
1–2
1646 Edwards, T. Gangraena, pt
2 (3)
1646 Edwards, T. Gangraena,
pt 3
Smith, Thomas
1645 Hollingworth, R. An
examination of sundry
scriptures
Snodham, Thomas
1611 Bourne, W. A regiment for
the sea
1611 Vaughan, W. Approved
directions for health
1611 Vaughan, W. The spirit of
detraction conjured and
convicted (2)
1612 Chapman, G. An epicede
or funerall song
1612 Jonson, B. The alchemist
1612 Rowlands, S. The knave of
harts (2)

1612 Vaughan, W. Approved directions for health
1613 Hoby, Sir E. A counter-snarle (2)
1613 Rowlands, S. The knave of harts
1613 Zouch, R. The dove
1614 Heresbach, C. The whole art and trade of husbandry
1614 Markham, G. Cheape and good husbandry
1614 Taylor, J. Taylors water-worke
1614 Wither, G. Abuses stript, and whipt
1615 Sharpham, E. The fleire
1616 Canterbury, Eng. (Province). Commissary General. To the minister and church-wardens
1616 Great Britain. Council for Virginia. A briefe declaration
1616 Markham, G. Cheape and good husbandry
1617 Abbot, G. A briefe description
1617? Great Britain. Council for Virginia. Whereas upon the returne of sir Thomas Dale
1617 Vaughan, W. Directions for health
1618 Cole, N. Preservatives against sinne
1620 Great Britain. Council for Virginia. A declaration of the state of . . . Virginia (5)
1621 Virginia Company of London. A note of the shipping
1622 Venner, T. Via recta
1622 Wither, G. Juvenilia. A collection of those poemes
1623 Markham, G. Cheape and good husbandry
1625 Harington, Sir J. The most elegant and wittie epigrams
Snowdon, George & Lionel
1605 Sandys, Sir E. A relation
*Sparke, Michael
1621 Greevous grones
1624 Smith, Capt. J. The generall historie
1625 Smith, Capt. J. The generall historie
1626 Smith, Capt. J. The generall historie

1627 Rowlands, S. Tis merrie when gossips meete
1627 Smith, Capt. J. The generall historie
1628 Anghiera, P. M. d'. The famous historie of the Indies
1629 Leather: a discourse
1629 Micrologia. Characters, or essayes
1629 Sandys, Sir E. Europae speculum
1630 Higginson, F. New-Englands plantation (3)
1630 Smith, Capt. J. The true travels
1631 Smith, Capt. J. The generall historie
1631 Walkington, T. The optick glasse of humors
1632 Sandys, Sir E. Europae speculum (2)
1633 Prynne, W. Histrio-mastix
1635 Mercator, G. Historia mundi, or . . . atlas (3)
1637 Mercator, G. Historia mundi, or . . . atlas
1637 Sandys, Sir E. Europae speculum
1638 Sandys, Sir E. Europae speculum
1639 Mercator, G. Historia mundi, or . . . atlas
1645 Prynne, W. A fresh discovery
1646 Prynne, W. A fresh discovery
Spenser, John
1635 Beaumont, F. The knight of the burning pestle (2)
1640 Middleton, T. A mad world
Stafford, Simon
1601 Jonson, B. Every man in his humor
1601 Neck, J. C. van. The journall
1602 Teixeira, J. The true historie of . . . Don Sebastian
1604 Hieron, S. An answer to a popish ryme
1608 Vaughan, W. The golden-grove
Stansby, William
1608 Drayton, M. Poems
1610 Donne, J. Pseudo-martyr
1610 Drayton, M. Poems
1610 Virginia Company of London. A true declaration

1611 Coryat, T. Coryats crudities
1611 L'Obel, M. de. Perfuming of tabacco
1611 Vaughan, W. The spirit of detraction (2)
1612 Strachey, W. For the colony in Virginea
1612 Thompson, T. A diet for a drunkard
1612 Vives, J. L. Libri xii de disciplinis (2)
1613 Blundeville, T. M.Blundeville his Exercises
1613 Drayton, M. Poems
1613 Jourdain, S. A plaine description
1613 Purchas, S. Purchas his Pilgrimage
1614 Brerewood, E. Enquiries
1614 Purchas, S. Purchas his Pilgrimage
1614 Raleigh, Sir W. The history of the world
1615 Camden, W. Annales rerum Anglicarum
1615 Cortés, M. the arte of navigation
1615 Digges, Sir D. The defence of trade.
1615 Hoby, Sir E. A curry-combe
1616 Drayton, M. Poems
1616 Jack Drum's entertainment
1616 Jonson, B. Workes
1617 Minsheu, J. Ductor in linguas
1617 Purchas, S. Purchase his Pilgrimage
1617 Raleigh, Sir W. The history of the world
1618 Holyday, B. Technogamia
1618 Jack Drum's entertainment
1619 Owen, J. Epigrams
1619 Purchas, S. Purchas his pilgrim. Microcosmus
1620 Breton, N. A poste
1620 Drayton, M. Poems
1620? Hieron, S. The workes (2)
1621 Raleigh, Sir W. The history of the world
1622 Bacon, F. The historie of . . . King Henry
1622 Blundeville, T. M. Blundevile his Exercises
1622? Sandys, Sir E. A relation
1624 Hieron, S. The sermons

Upton, James
1630 Goodall, B. The tryall of travell

Vavasour, Nicholas
1634 Rowley, S. The noble souldier
1636 Dekker, T. The wonder of a kingdome
1642 Taylor, J. St. Hillaries teares

Vincent, George
1607 Wilkins, G. The miseries of inforst mariage
1611 Wilkins, G. The miseries of inforst marriage
1625 Bradwell, S. A watch-man for the pest
1629 Wilkins, G. The miseries of inforst marriage

W., B.
1643 James I, King of Great Britain. King James his Apopthegmes

Walbanke, Matthew
1618 Field, N. Amends for ladies
1619 Taylor, J. A kicksey winsey
1624 Taylor, J. The scourge of baseness
1639 Bancroft, T. Two bookes of epigrammes
1639 Field, N. Amends for ladies

Walker, John
1649 Grotius, H. A treatise

Walkley, Thomas
1631 Barclay, J. The mirrour of mindes
1633 Barclay, J. The mirror of minds
1640 Jonson, B. The workes, v. 2–3
1645 Waller, E. The workes
1647 Gomberville, M. Le Roy, sieur du Parc et de. The history of Polexander
1648 Gomberville, M. Le Roy, sieur du Parc et de. The history of Polexander

Walley, Henry
1610 Hobbes, S. Margarita chyrurgica

Warren, Thomas
1644 Syms, C. The swords apology
1645 Waller, E. Poems (2)
1645 Waller, E. The workes (2)
1647 Howell, J. A new volume of letters

1647 Malvezzi, V. The chiefe events
1649 Howell, J. Dendrologia
1650 Raleigh, Sir W. Apologie for his voyage to Guiana
1650 Raleigh, Sir W. Judicious and select essayes

Washington, William
1629 Bacon, F. The two bookes . . . of the proficience . . . of learning

Waterson, John
1626 Thorius, R. Hymnus tabaci

Waterson, Simon
1601 Daniel, S. The works
1602 Daniel, S. The works
1605 Sandys, Sir E. A relation (2). For a piracy, see London—Stansby, William, under 1622?
1606 Daniel, S. The queenes arcadia
1606 Owen, J. Epigrammatum libri tres (2)
1607 Daniel, S. Certain small works
1607 Owen, J. Epigrammatum . . . libri tres
1607 Stafford, R. A geographicall and anthologicall description
1607 Tomkis, T. Lingua
1609 Blagrave, J. The art of dyalling
1611 Daniel, S. Certain small works
1612 Owen, J. Epigrammatum . . . libri tres
1612 Owen, J. Epigrammatum libri decem
1613 Hieron, S. An answere to a popish ryme
1615 Camden, W. Annales rerum Anglicarum
1615 Tomkis, T. Lingua
1617 Tomkis, T. Lingua
1618 Owen, J. Epigrammatum . . . libri tres
1618 Stafford, R. A geographicall and anthologicall description
1622 Misselden, E. Free trade (2)
1622 Owen, J. Epigrammatum . . . libri tres
1622 Tomkis, T. Lingua
1623 Daniel, S. The whole workes

1627 Camden, W. Annalium rerum Anglicarum, t. 2
1632 Tomkis, T. Lingua
1633 Owen, J. Epigrammatum . . . libri decem
1634 Owen, J. Epigrammatum . . . libri decem
1634 Stafford, R. A geographicall and anthologicall description

Weaver, Edmund
1606? Bourne, W. [A regiment for the sea]
1611 Bourne, W. A regiment for the sea
1617? Bourne, W. [A regiment for the sea]
1617 Cotta, J. A true discovery of the empericke
1620 Bourne, W. A regiment for the sea

Weaver, Thomas
1631 Bourne, W. A regiment for the sea

Welby, William
1608 Smith, Capt. J. A true relation of . . . Virginia (4)
1609 Gray, R. A good speed to Virginia
1609 Symonds, W. Virginia. A sermon
1610 Crashaw, W. A sermon
1610 Great Britain. Council for Virginia. A publication
1611 De La Warr, T. West, 3rd baron. The relation
1611 Great Britain. Council for Virginia. By the Counsell of Virginia. Seeing it hath pleased God
1611? Virginia Company of London. Whereas [blank] hath paid in ready mony
1612 Great Britain. Council for Virginia. [The articles sett down for the second lottery]
1612 Great Britain. Council for Virginia. By his Majesties Counsell for Virginea . . . for the advancement of . . . Virginea
1612 Great Britain. Council for Virginia. [The lottery for Virginea]
1612 Johnson, R. The new life of Virginea

1613 Great Britain. Council for Virginia. By his Majesties Councell for Virginia . . . a little standing lotterie

1613 Harcourt, R. A relation of a voyage to Guiana

1613 Jourdain, S. A plaine description

1613 Whitaker, A. Good newes from Virginia

1615 Hamor, R. A true discourse

1615 Hughes, L. A letter

1615 Virginia Company of London. A declaration

Whaley, Peter

1645 Cawdry, D. Vindiciae clavium

Whitaker, Richard

1625 Bacon, F. The essayes

1633 Gerard, J. The herball

1635 Brerewood, E. Enquiries

1636 Gerard, J. The herball

1638 Bacon, F. Opera moralium

1639 Bauderon, B. Pharmacopoea

1640 Shirley, J. The constant maid

1644 Rutherford, S. The due right

1650 Cotgrave, R. A French-English dictionary

White, Edward

1602 Dekker, T. Satiro-mastix (2)

1603 Lodge, T. A treatise

1604 Drayton, M. The owle (2)

1605 Breton, N. An olde mans lesson

1607 Markham, G. Cavelarice

1610 Dawson, T. The good huswifes jewell

1617 Markham, G. Cavelarice

162–? Drayton, M. The owle

White, John

1618 Rowlands, S. Doctor Merry-man

White, Robert

1648 Spain. Treaties, etc., 1621–1665. The articles and conditions

White, William

1602 Rowlands, S. Tis merrie

1604 Rowlands, S. Looke to it

1609 Rowlands, S. Doctor Merrie-man

1609 Veer, G. de. The true and perfect description

1611 Digges, Sir D. Fata mihi totum mea sunt agitanda per orbem

1611 Rowlands, S. The letting of humours blood

1611 Wilkins, G. The miseries of inforst marriage

1612 Digges, Sir D. Of the circumference

1613 Rowlands, S. The letting of humours blood

1613? Rowlands, S. Tis merrie

1613 Shakespeare, W. The history of Henrie the fourth [Pt 1]

1614 Rowlands, S. Doctor Merrie-man

1616 Rowlands, S. Doctor Merry-man

1619 Rowlands, S. Well met gossip

Wight, Thomas

1601 Bourne, W. A regiment for the sea

1601 Heresbach, C. Foure bookes of husbandry

Williams, Francis

1626 Boccalini, T. The new-found politicke

1626 Breton, N. Fantasticks

1626 Vaughan, W. Directions for health

1626 Vaughan, W. The golden fleece

Williams, John

1635 Bacon, F. Sylva sylvarum

1642 Fuller, T. The holy state

1644 Swan, J. Speculum mundi

1648 Fuller, T. The holy state

1650 Cotgrave, R. A French-English dictionary

Williams, Thomas

1648 Gage, T. The English-American

Wilson, Robert

1614 The maske of flowers

1639 Beaumont, F. The scornfull lady

Wilson, William

1645 Pagitt, E. Heresiography

1647 Pagitt, E. Heresiography

1648 Pagitt, E. Heresiography

1648 Raleigh, Sir W., defendant. The arraignment and conviction

Windet, John

1605 Hume, T. Ayres

1606 The araignement and execution

1606 Blundeville, T. M. Blundeville his Exercises

1606 Owen, J. Epigrammatum libri tres (2)

1606 A true report of the imprisonment

1607 Breton, N. A poste

1607 Daniel, S. Certain small works

1607 Walkington, T. The optick glasse of humors

1608 Shakespeare, W. The historie of Henrie the fourth [Pt 1]

1608 Weelkes, T. Cantus. Ayres

1609 Breton, N. A poste

1609 Johnson, R. Nova Britannia

1609 The man in the moone

1609 Price, D. Sauls prohibition staide

1609 Symonds, W. Virginia. A sermon

1609 Virginia Company of London. For the plantation in Virginia

1609 Wybarne, J. The new age of old names

1610 Heath, J. Two centuries of epigrammes

1610 Jourdain, S. A discovery of the Barmudas

Wittington, George

1647 Gorton, S. Simplicities defence

Wodenothe, Richard

1649 A perfect description of Virginia

Wood, Roger

1621 Great Britain. Sovereigns, etc., 1603–1625. James, by the grace of God

Wright, Edward

1615 Taylor, J. Faire and fowle weather

1617 Middleton, T. A faire quarrell (2)

1620 Taylor, J. The praise of hemp-seed

1621 Taylor, J. The praise . . . of beggery

1621 Taylor, J. Taylors goose

1623 Taylor, J. The praise of hemp-seed (2)

1625 Taylor, J. An arrant thiefe

1625 Taylor, J. The common
  whore
1626 Taylor, J. Wit and mirth
1628 Taylor, J. Wit and mirth
1640 Taylor, J. A valorous and
  perillous sea-fight
Wright, John
1606 Return from Parnassus.
  The returne from Pernassus
  (2)
1609 Marlowe, C. Doctor
  Faustus
1610 Rich, R. Newes from
  Virginia
1611 Marlowe, C. Doctor
  Faustus
1611 Rich, R. The last news from
  Virginia
1616 Breton, N. Crossing of
  proverbs
1616 Marlowe, C. Doctor
  Faustus
1618 Breton, N. The court and
  country (2)
1618 Newes of Sr. Walter
  Rauleigh (2)
1619 Marlowe, C. Doctor
  Faustus
1620 Marlowe, C. Doctor
  Faustus
1624 Marlowe, C. Doctor
  Faustus
1628 Marlowe, C. Doctor
  Faustus
1631 Breton, N. Crossing of
  proverbs
1631 Marlowe, C. Doctor
  Faustus
1643 Great Britain. Laws,
  statutes, etc., 1625–1649. An
  ordinance
1646 Great Britain. Laws,
  statutes, etc., 1625–1649. Two
  ordinances
1647 Great Britain. Laws,
  statutes, etc., 1625–1649.
  Whereas the severall
  plantations
Young, Robert
1628 Bacon, F. The history of
  . . . King Henry
1628 Ovidius Naso, P.
  Metamorphoses. English.
  Metamorphosis
1628 Raleigh, Sir W. The history
  of the world

1629 Bacon, F. The historie
  of . . . King Henry
1629 Parkinson, J. Paradisi in
  sole paradisus terrestris
1631 Lloyd, D. The legend of
  captaine Jones
1631 Pellham, E. Gods power
1633 Du Bartas, G. de S.,
  seigneur. Bartas his devine
  weekes
1634 Paré, A. The workes
1634 Raleigh, Sir W. The
  historie of the world (2)
1636 Malynes, G. de.
  Consuetudo, vel, Lex
  mercatoria
1638 Bloys, W. Adam in his
  innocence
1638 Burton, R. The anatomy of
  melancholy
1638 Du Bartas, G. de S.,
  seigneur. A learned summary
1638 Martyn, W. The historie
  and lives
1641 Bacon, F. The historie
  of . . . King Henrie
1641 Du Bartas, G. de S.,
  seigneur. Du Bartas his devine
  weekes (2)

OXFORD
Printer unidentified
1643 Taylor, J. The noble
  cavalier
1649 Oxford. University. To our
  reverend brethren
Barnes, Joseph
1607 Wake, Sir I. Rex platonicus
  (2)
1612 Smith, Capt. J. A map of
  Virginia
1615 Wake, Sir I. Rex platonicus
Bowman, Francis
1638 Randolph, T. Poems
1640 Randolph, T. Poems (2)
Cripps, Henry
1621 Burton, R. The anatomy of
  melancholy
1624 Burton, R. The anatomy of
  melancholy
1625 Carpenter, N. Geography
  delineated
1628 Burton, R. The anatomy of
  melancholy
1632 Burton, R. The anatomy of
  melancholy

1632 Sennert, D. Epitome
  naturalis scientiae
1634 Barclay, J. Euphormionis
  Lusinini . . . Satyricon
1635 Carpenter, N. Geographie
  delineated
1638 Burton, R. The anatomy of
  melancholy
Forrest, Edward
1640 Bacon, F. Of the advancement . . . of learning
Hall, Henry
1643 Taylor, J. A letter
1644 Howell, J. Dendrologia
1648 Bobart, J. Catalogus
  plantarum Horti medici
Huggins, Thomas
1625 Heylyn, P. Mikrokosmos
1627 Heylyn, P. Mikrokosmos
1629 Heylyn, P. Mikrokosmos
1633 Bacon, F. The two
  bookes . . . of the proficience . . . of learning
Lichfield, John
1621 Burton, R. The anatomy of
  melancholy
1621 Heylyn, P. Microcosmus
1624 Burton, R. The anatomy of
  melancholy
1625 Carpenter, N. Geography
  delineated
1625 Heylyn, P. Mikrokosmos
1627 Hakewill, G. An apologie
1627 Heylyn, P. Mikrokosmos
1627 Wake, Sir I. Rex platonicus
1628 Burton, R. The anatomy of
  melancholy
1632 Burton, R. The anatomy of
  melancholy
1632 Ovidius Naso, P.
  Metamorphoses. English.
  Metamorphosis
1632 Sennert, D. Epitome
  naturalis scientiae
1633 Bacon, F. The two
  bookes . . . of the proficience . . . of learning
1634 Barclay, J. Euphormionis
  Lusinini . . . Satyricon
1635 Carpenter, N. Geographie
  delineated
1638 Burton, R. The anatomy of
  melancholy
Lichfield, Leonard
1635 Wake, Sir I. Rex platonicus
1636 Wake, Sir I. Rex platonicus
1638 Randolph, T. Poems

Cocchi, Bartolomeo
1609 Donato d'Eremita. Il fiore della granadiglia
1618 Rosaccio, G. Le sei eta del mondo
Dozza, Evangelista, Heirs of
1647 Vasselli, G. F. L'apicio
Dozza, Heirs of
1648 Tanara, V. L'economia
Ferroni, Clemente
1629 Spinola, F. A. Vita del p. Carlo Spinola
Ferroni, Giovanni Battista
1641 Aldrovandi, U. Quadrupedum omnium bisulcorum historia
1642 Aldrovandi, U. Quadrupedum omnium bisulcorum historia
1648 Aldrovandi, U. Musaeum metallicum
1650 Zavona, M. Abuso del tabacco
Monti, Giacomo
1635 Potier, P. Pharmacopoea spagirica
1643 Potier, P. Libri duo de febribus
1644 Tanara, V. L'economia del cittadino
Pariasca, Simone
1609 Donato d'Eremita. Il fiore della granadiglia
Salmincio, Andrea
1644 Basilius Valentinus. Haliographia
Tamburini, Geronimo
1612 Aldrovandi, U. De piscibus libri v
1613 Aldrovandi, U. De piscibus libri v
1620 Biancani, G. Sphaera mundi
Tebaldini, Nicolo
1622 Potier, P. Insignium curationum . . . centuria prima
1622 Potier, P. Insignium curationum . . . centuria secunda
1637 Aldrovandi, U. De quadrupedibus
1638 Aldrovandi, U. De piscibus libri v
1640 Aldrovandi, U. Ornithologiae tomus alter
1642 Aldrovandi, U. Monstrorum historia

1644 Aldrovandi, U. De piscibus libri v
1644 Basilius Valentinus. Haliographia
1645 Aldrovandi, U. De quadrupedibus
1646 Aldrovandi, U. Ornithologiae . . . libri xii
Tozzi, Pietro Paolo
1622 Rivadeneira, P. de. Della religione del prencipe christiano
1625 Rivadeneira, P. de. Della religione del prencipe christiano
Zenaro, Carlo
1635 Potier, P. Pharmacopoea spagirica

BRACCIANO
Fei, Andrea
1621 Bacon, F. Saggi morali
1626 Bacon, F. Saggi morali
Totti, Pompilio
1621 Bacon, F. Saggi morali
1626 Bacon, F. Saggi morali

BRESCIA
Ardizzoni, Giovanni Antonio
1641 Scarioni, F. Centuria seconda de' secreti mirabili
Britannico, Ludovico
1626 Rubio, A. Logica mexicana
Compagnia Bresciana
1609 Rivadeneira, P. de. Trattato della religione
Fontana, Bartolomeo
1613 Canale, F. De' secreti universali raccolti

CARPI
Vaschieri, Girolamo
1620 Tassoni, A. Dieci libri di pensieri diversi

CASALE
Casa, Christoforo della
1644 Siri, V. Il mercurio
1646 Siri, V. Il mercurio
1647 Siri, V. Del mercurio . . . Tomo secondo

FLORENCE
Cecconcelli, Pietro
1619 Bacon, F. Saggi morali
1623 Ricettario Fiorentino

Ducal Press
1645 Tuscany. Laws, statutes, etc. Bando, et ordine
1648 Pace di Olanda
Fantucci, Stefano
1628? Vera, e nuova relatione
Giunta, Cosmo
1602 Villifranchi, G. Copia del . . . canto
1611 Gualterotti, R. L'America
Giunta, Filippo
1601 Jesuits. Letters from missions. Annuae litterae (1593) 1601. Annuae litterae . . . anni MDXCII
Giuntas, The
1609 Bocchi, F. Elogiorum . . . liber
Landi, Lorenzo
1642 Conestaggio, G. F. di. Dell'unione del regno di Portugallo
Marescotti, Christofano
1604 Valori, F. Termini di mezzo rilievo
Massi, Amadore
1642 Conestaggio, G. F. di. Dell'unione del regno di Portugallo
Onofri, Francesco
1646 Dudley, Sir R. Dell'arcano del mare
Ruoti, Bartolomeo
1613 Ripa, C. Iconologia
Sermatelli Press
1609 Bocchi, F. Elogiorum . . . liber
Sermatellis, The
1602 Villifranchi, G. Copia del . . . canto
Tedesco, Volkmar
1615? Rosaccio, G. Discorso

FOLIGNO
Alterio, Agostino
1629 Lalli, G. B. Franceide

GENOA
Pavoni, Giuseppe
1602 Paschetti, B. Del conservare la sanità
1606 Chiabrera, G. Delle poesie . . . Parte seconda
Pavonum
1645 Baldani, F. Vita del . . . fra Diego Ortiz

IVREA
Printer unidentified
1644 Guidi, I. C. Caduta del
conte d'Olivares

MACERATA
Salvioni, Pietro
1618 Mazza, M. A. Tesoro
1618 Murtola, G. Della creazione

MESSINA
Bianco, Giovanni Francesco
1640 Castelli, P. Balsamum examinatum
**Bianco, Giovanni Francesco,
Widow of**
1640 Castelli, P. Hortus Messanensis
Brea, Pietro
1629 Cortesi, G. B. Pharmacopoeia
1639 Berettari, S. Vita del padre
Giuseppe Anchieta

MILAN
Printer unidentified
1643 Saavedra Fajardo, D. de.
Idea
Ambrosian College
1622 Collio, F. De animabus paganorum
Besozzo, Alberto
1627 Cervantes Saavedra, M. de.
Novelle
Bidelli, Giovanni Battista
1613 Boccalini, T. De' ragguagli
di Parnaso . . . Centuria prima
1614 Boccalini, T. De' ragguagli
di Parnaso . . . Centuria seconda
1614 Settala, L. Animadversionum . . . libri septem
1615 Alemán, M. De la vida del
picaro Guzman de Alfarache
1615 Boccalini, T. De' ragguagli
di Parnaso . . . Centuria prima
1615 Boccalini, T. De' ragguagli
di Parnaso . . . Centuria seconda
1615 Cervantes Saavedra, M. de.
Novelas exemplares
1616 Conestaggio, G. F. di.
Dell'unione del regno di Portugallo
1620 Bacon, F. Saggi morali
1620 More, Sir T. De optimo reipublicae statu

1621 Alemán, M. Vita del picaro
Gusmano d'Alfarace
1621 Torsellino, O. Epitomae
historiarum libri x
1622 Rivadeneira, P. de. Vita del
p.s. Ignatio Loiola
1623 Codogno, O. Compendio
delle poste
1625 Tassoni, A. La secchia
1626 Barclay, J. Icon animorum
1626 Settala, L. Animadversionum . . . libri septem
1628 Tassoni, A. Dieci libri di
pensieri diversi
1635 Antidotario romano
1645 Roca, J. A. Vera Zúñiga y
Figueroa, conde de la. Epitome
Bordone, Girolamo
1603 Alemán, M. De la vida del
picaro Guzman de Alfarache,
la pte
1603 Martí, J. J. De la vida del
picaro Guzman de Alfarache,
2a pte
1605 Marcos da Lisboa, Bp.
Delle croniche de gli ordini
instituti dal p.s. Francisco,
parte terza
1614 Colón, F. Historie . . . della
vita . . . dell'ammariglio Don
Christoforo Colombo
1616 Codogno, O. Nuovo itinerario delle poste
Canevese, Giovanni Battista
1629 Cervantes Saavedra, M. de.
Novelle
Fontana, D.
1630 Lalli, G. B. Opere poetiche
Ghisolfi (Guisolfi), Filippo
1631 León, L. Ponce de. Obras
proprias
1645 Roca, J. A. Vera Zúñiga y
Figueroa, conde de la. Epitome
Guisolfi, P. *See* Ghisolfi, Filippo
Locarno, Pietro Martire
1603 Alemán, M. De la vida del
picaro Guzman de Alfarache,
la pte
1603 Martí, J. J. De la vida del
picaro Guzman de Alfarache,
2a pte
1605 Marcos da Lisboa, Bp.
Delle croniche de gli ordini
instituti dal p.s. Francisco,
parte terza

1613 Boccalini, T. De' ragguagli
. . . Centuria prima
Malatesti, The
1612 Coppino, A. De Hispanicae
monarchiae amplitudine . . .
oratio
1625 Avendaño y Vilela, F. de.
Relacione
Piccaglia, Giovanni Battista
1603 Torres Bollo, D. de. Relatione breve
Ponte, Paolo da, Heirs of
1603 Torres Bollo, D. de. Relatione breve
Scaccabarozzo, G.
1630 Lalli, G. B. Opere poetiche
Vallo, Bartolomeo
1627 Cervantes Saavedra, M. de.
Novelle

MIRANDOLA
Printer unidentified
1625 Sandys, Sir E. Relatione

MODENA
Cassiano, Giuliano
1630 Biancani, G. Sphaera
mundi
1635 Biancani, G. Sphaera
mundi
Verdi, Giovanni Maria, Heirs of
1612 Tassoni, A. Varietà di pensieri
1613 Tassoni, A. Varietà di pensieri

NAPLES
Printer unidentified
1629 Marino, G. B. La Murtoleide
Baltrano, Ottavio
1632 Severino, M. A. De recondita abscessum natura
Bonino, Scipione
1607 Rivadeneira, P. de. Vita del
b.p. Ignatio Loiola
1617 Baricelli, G. C. Hortulus
genialis
Carlino, Giovanni Giacomo
1607 Catholic Church. Liturgy
and ritual. Peru. Rituale
1609 Zappullo, M. Sommario istorico
Gafaro, Giacomo
1639 Malvezzi, V. La libra

Gaffaro, G.
1622 Cordus, V. Dispensatorium
Gaffaro, Il
1646 Fontana, F. Novae coelestium terrestriumque rerum observationes
Longo, Egidio
1628 Alpherio, H. de. De peste
1650 Naples (Kingdom). Laws, statutes, etc. Pragmatica
Longo, Tarquinio
1604 Jesuits. Letters from missions. Annuae litterae (1594–1595) 1604. Litterae . . . annorum M.D.XCIIII. et M.D.XCV
1605 Jesuits. Letters from missions. Annuae litterae (1596) 1605. Annuae litterae . . . anni M.D.XCVI
1606 Rivadeneira, P. de. Catalogus
1607 Jesuits. Letters from missions. Annuae litterae (1597) 1607. Annuae litterae . . . anni M.D.XCVII
Roncaglioli, Giovanni Domenico
1634 Crisci, G. B. Lucerna de corteggiani
Roncagliolo
1625 Avendaño y Vilela, F. de. Relacione del viaggio
1625 Toledo Osorio y Mendoza, F. de. Relacion del sucesso
Roncalioli, Secondino
1625 Gravina, D. Vox turturis
Roncallolo. *See* Roncagliolo
Scoriggio, Il
1631 Sgambata, S. Elogio
Scorigio, Lazaro
1627 Settala, L. Animadversionum . . . libri septem
Sottile, Giovanni Battista
1607 Rivadeneira, P. de. Vita del b.p. Ignatio Loiola
Vitale, Costantino
1607 Catholic Church. Liturgy and ritual. Ritual. Peru. Rituale
1609 Zappullo, M. Sommario istorico

PADUA
Bolzetta, Francesco
1611 Alpini, P. De medicina methodica
1639 Sassonia, E. Opera practica

Crivellari, Gasparo
1616 Liceti, F. De monstrorum caussis
Frambotti, Paolo
1628 Settala, L. Animadversionum . . . libri septem
1634 Liceti, F. De monstrorum caussis
1644 Vesling, J. Opabalsami veteribus cogniti vindiciae
1647 Morel, P. Formulae remediorum
Galignani, Paolo & Francesco
1620 Porcacchi, T. L'isole più famose del mondo
1621 Ptolemaeus, C. Geografia
Meietti, Paolo
1606 Spiegel, A. van de. Isagoges
Pasquardo, Donato
1630 Ripa, C. Della piu che novissima iconologia
Pasquardo, Donato, & Associates
1630 Tomasini, J. P. Illustrium virorum elogio
Pasquato, Lorenzo
1606 Spiegel, A. van de. Isagoges
1611 Alpini, P. De medicina methodica
Pasquato Office
1611 Ripa, C. Iconologia
Sardi, Sebastiano
1644 Tomasini, J. P. Elogia
Tozzi, Pietro Paolo
1611 Ripa, C. Iconologia
1615 Cartari, V. Le vere e nove imagini
1618 Ripa, C. Nova iconologia
1625 Ripa, C. Della novissima iconologia
1626 Cartari, V. Imagini de gli dei delli antichi
Tuilio, Giovanni
1628 Settala, L. Animadversionum . . . libri septem

PALERMO
Francisci, Giovanni Antonio de
1609 Cabredo, R. de. Copia d'una lettera
Martarello, Antonio
1639 Fragoso, J. Della cirugia

PARMA
Viotti, Anteo
1622 Benamati, G. U. Delle due trombe i primi fiati

PAVIA
Ardizzoni, Giacomo
1613 Piò, G. M. Delle vite de gli huomini illustri di S. Domenico. Seconda parte
Magri, Giovanni Andrea
1648 Magnen, J. C. Exercitationes de tabaco
Rossi, Giovanni Battista de
1613 Piò, G. M. Delle vite de gli huomini illustri di S. Domenico. Seconda parte

PERUGIA
Billi, P. Giacomo
1623 Torsellino, O. Ristretto delle historie

PIACENZA
Ardizzoni, Giovanni Antonio
1641 Scarioni, F. Centuria seconda de' secreti mirabili
Bazacchi, Alessandro
1617 Stigliani, T. Del mondo nuovo

PISA
Marchetti, Salvestro
1625 Vigna, D. Animadversiones
Massino, Carlo
1625 Vigna, D. Animadversiones

ROME
Printer unidentified
1610 Perlinus, H. De alexiteriis
1619 Antidotario romano
1620 Gracián, J. Zelo della propagatione della fede
1630 Toledo Osorio y Mendoza, F. de. Relatione
1640 Castelli, P. Opobalsamum triumphans
1644 Dominicans. [Acta capituli generalissimum Romae]
1647? Silva, A. T. da. Sucesso
1650? Magano, J. Memorial
Apostolic Camera
1608 Porta, G. B. della. De distillatione (4)
1622 Gaetani, C. Ad universos ordinis . . . S. Benedicti abbates

1628 Augustinians. Bullarum
   Ordinis Eremitarum S. Augustini
1648 Catholic Church. Pope,
   1644–1655. [Breve . . . in
   causa Angelopolitana jurisdic-
   tionis]
Bonfadino, Bartolomeo
1602 Montoya, J. de. Relacion
Brogiotti, G. B.
See Brugiotti, Giovanni Battista
Brugiotti, Andrea
1621 Zacchia, P. Quaestiones
   medico-legales
Brugiotti, Giovanni Battista
1624 Tassoni, A. La secchia
1625 Torsellino, O. Epitome historiarum libri x
Cavalli, Francesco
1645 Alegambe, P. De vita, et
   morib. p. Joannis Cardim
1646 Ovalle, A. de. Historica relacion
1646 Ovalle, A. de. Historica relatione
1648 Bellinzani, L. Il mercurio
   estinto resuscitato
1648 Ovalle, A. de. Historica relacion
1649 Alegambe, P. De vita et
   moribus p. Joannis Cardim
Ciaccone, Alfonse
1623 Aviñón, B. Vita . . . del
   beato Luigi Bertrandi
Cocchi, Bartolomeo
1618 Rosaccio, G. Le sei eta del
   ·mondo
Corbelletti, Francesco
1627 Jesuits. Letters from missions. Lettere annue d'Etiopia,
   Malabar, Brasil
1628 Spinola, F. A. Vita del p.
   Carlo Spinola
1630 Bottifango, G. C. Lettera
   dell'elefante
1630 Spinola, F. A. Vita del p.
   Carlo Spinola
1638 Spinola, F. A. Vita del p.
   Carlo Spinola
Corbo, Francesco
1639 Zacchia, P. De' mali hipochondriaci libri due
Facciotti, Guglielmo
1601 Zecchi, G. Liber primus
   Consultationum medicinalium
1602 Canevari, D. De ligno
   sancto commentarium

1606 Colonna, F. Minus cognitarum stirpium aliquot
1610 Colonna, F. Minus cognitarum stirpium aliquot
1621 Zacchia, P. Quaestiones
   medico-legales
1625 Torsellino, O. Epitome historiarum libri x
1630 Torsellino, O. Historiarum
   ab origine mundi . . . epitome
   libri x
1631 Geraldini, A. Itinerarium
1632 Durante, C. Il tesoro della
   sanitá
Facciotti, Guglielmo, Heirs of
1634 Zacchia, P. Quaestiones
   medico-legales, liber VI
Facciotti, Pietro Antonio
1638 Ferrari, G. B. Flora, overo
   Cultura di fiori
1639 Antidotario romano
1639 Zacchia, P. De' mali hipochondriaci libri due
Facio, Lepido
1603 Ripa, C. Iconologia
Fei, Andrea
1624 Antidotario romano
1635 Ritratti et elogii di capitani
Gelli, Giovanni Paolo
1606 Clavius, C. In Sphaeram
   Joannis de Sacro Bosco commentarius
1607 Clavius, C. In Sphaeram
   Joannis de Sacro Bosco commentarius
Ghezzi, Egidio
1644 Zacchia, P. De' mali hipochondriaci libri tre
Grignani, Ludovico
1630 Relatione venuta de Madrid
1641 Kircher, A. Magnes
1646 Kircher, A. Ars magna lucis
1648 González Chaparro, J. Lettera
1650 Bartolommei Smeducci, G.
   L'America
Jesuit College
1606 Jesuits. Compendium, privilegiorum. Compendium facultatum
1606 Jesuits. Compendium, privilegiorum. Literae apostolicae
1615 Jesuits. Compendium, privilegiorum. Compendium fa-
   cultatem

Manelfi, Manelfo
1642A Nicolosi, G. B. Teorica
   del globo terrestre
1649 Jesuits. Historiae Societatis
   Jesu, pars tertia
Martinelli, Giovanni
1601 Zecchi, G. Liber primus
   Consultationum medicinalium
Mascardi, Giacomo
1615 Amati, S. Historia del
   regno di Voxu
1616 Colonna, F. Minus cognitarum rariorumque . . . stirpium
1622 Bacci, A. De thermis
1625 Castelli, P. Exactissima descriptio rariorum plantarum
1628 Faber, J. Animalia mexicana
1628 Hernández, F. Rerum medicarum Novae Hispaniae thesaurus
1628 Stigliani, T. Il mondo
   nuovo (2)
1634 Torsellino, O. Ristretto
   dell' historie
1637 Torsellino, O. Ristretto
   delle historie
1646 Ritratti et elogii
1647 Ritratti et elogii
Mascardi, Vitale
1644 Zacchia, P. De' mali hipochondriaci libri tre
1648 Hernández, F. Rerum medicarum Novae Hispaniae thesaurus
1649 Hernández, F. Rerum medicarum Novae Hispaniae thesaurus
Paolini, Stefano
1610 Gracián, J. Zelo della propagazione della fede
1633 Ferrari, G. B. De florum
   cultura
Pizzuto, Francisco
1625 Avendaño y Vilela, F. de.
   Relazione del viaggio
Rossi, Francesco de'
1646 Ritratti et elogii
1647 Ritratti et elogii
Ruffinelli, Giovanni Angelo
1601 Tasso, T. Il Goffredo
1624 Antidotario romano
Scheus, Hermannus
1641 Kircher, A. Magnes
1646 Kircher, A. Ars magna
   lucis

Totti, Pompilio
1634 Torsellino, O. Ristretto dell'historie
1635 Ritratti et elogii
1637 Torsellino, O. Ristretto delle historie
1639 Antidotario romano
Vullietti, Carlo
1604 Malvenda, T. De antichristo libri undecim
1608 Dominicans. Acta capituli generalis Romae
Zannetti, Antonio
1602 Cesalpino, A. Artis medicae pars prima
1603 Bertonio, L. Arte breve dela lengua aymara
1603 Bertonio, L. Arte y grammatica . . . de la lengua aymara
1603 Lima (Ecclesiastical Province). Council, 1583. Catecismo en la lengua española. y quichua
1603 Torres Bollo, D. de. Relatione breve
1605 Bertonio, L. Arte y grammatica . . . de la lengua aymara
1606 Clavius, C. In Sphaeram Joannis de Sacro Bosco commentarius
1607 Clavius, C. In Sphaeram Joannis de Sacro Bosco commentarius
1608 Bertonio, L. Arte y grammatica . . . de la lengua aymara
Zannetti, Bartolomeo
1611 Cebà, A. Rime
1612 Antidotario romano
1615 Jesuits. Historiae Societatis Jesu prima pars
1616 Rivadeneira, P. de. Vita del p. Francesco Borgia
1623 Somma, A. di. Dell'America, canti cinque
Zannetti, Luigi
1601 Tasso, T. Il Goffredo
1605 Ribera, J. de. Lettera annua della v. provincia

SABBIONETA
Visdomini, Alessandro
1619 Boccalini, T. Pietra del paragone politico

SIENA
Florimi, Mattheo, Heirs of
1613 Ripa, C. Iconologia

Marchetti, Salvestro
1604 Sacro Bosco, J. de. Sfera

TREVISO
Deuchino, Evangelista
1604 Rosaccio, G. Mondo elementare, et celeste
1606 Cesalpino, A. Praxis universae artis medicae
1607 Massaria, A. Practica medica
Meietti, Roberto
1606 Cesalpino, A. Praxis universae artis medicae
Pulciano, Giovanni Battista
1607 Massaria, A. Practica medica
Reghettini, Angelo
1613 Claude d'Abbeville, Father. Relatione del viaggio
1617 Durante, C. Herbario novo
Righettini, Girolamo
1637 Aprosio, A. Il vaglio critico
1642 Rosaccio, G. Teatro del cielo
Zanetti, Fabritio
1602 Wecker, J. J. Practica medicina generalis
1604 Guicciardini, F. La historia d'Italia

TURIN
Printer unidentified
1641 Bacon, F. Considerationi politiche
Cavaleri Brothers
1612 Bertaldi, G. L. Medicamentorum apparatus
Concordia, Compagnia della
1623? Marino, G. B. L'Adone
1624 Marino, G. B. L'Adone
Tarino, Giovanni Domenico
1601 Botero, G. Relationi universali
1607 Botero, G. I capitani
1608 Botero, G. I capitani
1609 Estienne, C. L'agricoltura
1612 Durante, C. Il tesoro della sanità
Tarino, Giovanni Domenico, Heirs of
1618 Benzi, U. Regole della sanità
1620 Benzi, U. Regole della sanita

1621 Berettari, S. Vita del p. Gioseppo Anchietto
1627 Marino, G. B. L'Adone

UDINE
Schiratti, Nicolò
1640A Liceti, F. Litheosphorus

URBINO
Ghisoni, Mazantinus & Aloysius
1632 Micalori, J. Crisis

VENICE
Printer unidentified
1602 Rosaccio, G. Le sei eta del mondo
1611 Codogno, O. Nuovo itinerario delle poste
1617 Marinelli, C. Pharmacopaea
1618 Mattioli, P. A. I discorsi . . . nelli sei libri di Pedacio Dioscoride
1618 Piò, G. M. Allegatione per confirmare quanto si scrive
1619 Marino, G. B. La Murtoleide, fischiate
1621 Piò, G. M. Allegatione
1622 Tassoni, A. La secchia
1626 Marino, G. B. La Murtoleide, fischiate (2)
1627 Delle rime piacevoli
1629 Vairo, L. De fascino
1642 Marino, G. B. La Murtoleide
1642 Tassoni, A. La secchia
Alberti, Bartholomeo degli
1604 Mattioli, P. A. De i discorsi . . . nelli sei libri di Pedacio Dioscoride
Alberti, Giovanni
1610 Caro, A. De le lettere familiari
1620 Torquemada, A. de. Giardino di fiori curiosi
Alberti, Olivier
1616 Garzoni, T. La piazza universale
Angelieri, Agostino
1606 Calestani, G. Delle osservationi
1608 Botero, G. Relationi universali
Aureati, Leo
1612 Puteo, Z. Clavis medica rationalis

Combi, Giovanni Battista
1644 Wecker, J. J. Practica Weckeri
Combi, Sebastiano
1605 Chiabrera, G. Rime
1610 Chiabrera, G. Rime
Concordia, Sign of
1608 Giovio, P. Delle istorie del suo tempo
Dei, Ambrosio & Bartholomeo
1613 Guarguante, O. Responsa varia
1615 Mexía, P. Ragionamenti dottissimi
1616 Magati, C. De rara medicatione vulnerum
1616 Mexía, P. Selva rinovata di varia lettione
Deuchino, Evangelista
1608 Murtola, G. Della creatione del mundo
1621 Colle, G. Elucidarium anatomicum
Dusinelli, Pietro
1619 Bacon, F. Saggi morali
1621 Bacon, F. Saggi morali
Farri, Domenico
1603 Durante, C. Il tesoro della sanità
Farri, Domenico, Heirs of
1606 Durante, C. Il tesoro della sanità
Farri, Pietro
1612 Boccalini, T. De' ragguagli di Parnaso . . . Centuria prima (2)
1621 Rosaccio, G. Il medico
Fiorini, Vincento
1616 Del Rio, M. A. Disquisitionum magicarum libri sex
Fontana, Bartolomeo
1623 Matthieu, P. Historia di Francia
1624 Matthieu, P. Historia di Francia
Francisci, Giovanni Antonio & Jacopo de
1606 Del Rio, M. A. Disquisitionum magicarum libri sex
1608 Duchesne, J. Pharmacopoea dogmaticorum restituta
Francisci, Jacopo de
1614 Duchesne, J. Pharmacopoea dogmaticorum restituta
Galignani, Simon, Heirs of
1603 Porcacchi, T. L'isole piu famose del mondo

1604 Porcacchi, T. L'isole piu famose del mondo
1605 Porcacchi, T. L'isole piu famose del mondo
Gallina, Comino
1617 Fioravanti, L. De' capricci medicinali . . . libri quattro
Garzoni, M.
1648 Saavedra Fajardo, D. de. L'idea di un prencipe politico christiano
Ginammi, Marco
1621 Mattioli, P. A. I discorsi . . . nelli sei libri di Pedacio Dioscoride
1626 Casas, B. de las. Istoria ò brevissima relatione
1630 Casas, B. de las. Istoria ò brevissima relatione
1633 Montaigne, M. E. de. Saggi
1636 Casas, B. de las. Il supplice schiavo indiano
1640 Casas, B. de las. La liberta pretesa dal supplice schiavo indiano
1643 Casas, B. de las. Istoria ò brevissima relatione
1644 Casas, B. de las. Conquista dell'Indie Occidentali
1645 Casas, B. de las. Conquista dell'Indie Occidentali
1645 Mattioli, P. A. I discorsi . . . ne i sei libri di Pedacio Dioscoride
1648 Estienne, C. L'agricoltura
Giolitis, The
1601 Botero, G. Della ragion di stato
Giuliani, Antonio
1617 Garzoni, T. La piazza universale
Giuliani, Giovanni Antonio
1616 Calestani, G. Delle osservationi
1622 Massaria, A. Practica medica
1623 Estienne, C. L'agricoltura
Giunta, Bernardo
1608 Lorenzini, N. Le lagrime del peccatore
1608 Mercado, L. Praxis medica
1609 Mercado, L. Opera omnia
1610 Mercado, L. Praxis medica
1611 Mercado, L. Praxis medica
1611 Mercado, L. Tomus secundus Operum

1612 Panciroli, G. Raccolta breve
Giunta Office
1611 Guidi, G. Ars medicinalis
1642 Messina. Ospedale di Santa Maria della Pietà. Antidotarium speciale
Giuntas, The
1603 Mercuriale, G. Praelectiones Patavinae
1606 Mercuriale, G. Praelectiones Patavinae
1606 Ramusio, G. B. Delle navigationi et viaggi . . . Volume primo
1606 Ramusio, G. B. Delle navigationi et viaggi . . . Volume secondo
1606 Ramusio, G. B. Delle navigationi et viaggi . . . Volume terzo
1613 Ramusio, G. B. Delle navigationi et viaggi . . . Volume primo
1617 Mercuriale, G. Praelectiones Patavinae
1627 Mercuriale, G. Praelectiones Patavinae
1636 Durante, C. Herbario nuovo
1638 Matthieu, P. Dell'historia di S. Luigi
1640 Botero, G. Della ragion di stato
1640 Botero, G. Relationi universali (2)
1650 Botero, G. Relationi universali
Guerigli, Giovanni
1614 Boccalini, T. De' ragguagli di Parnaso . . . Centuria prima (2)
1614 Boccalini, T. De' ragguagli . . . Centuria seconda
1616 Boccalini, T. De' ragguagli . . . Centuria prima
1616 Boccalini, T. De' ragguagli . . . Centuria seconda
1617 Boccalini, T. De' ragguagli . . . Centuria prima
1617 Boccalini, T. De' ragguagli . . . Centuria seconda
1618 Boccalini, T. De' ragguagli . . . Centuria prima
1618 Boccalini, T. De' ragguagli . . . Centuria seconda

Salicato, Altobello
1603 Possevino, A. Biblioteca selecta
Salis, Giovanni
1616 Orta, G. da. Dell'historia de i semplici
Santo Grillo & Bros
1621 Schouten, W. C. Giornale overo Descrittione
Sarzina, Giacomo
1611 Durante, C. Il tesoro della sanita
1623 Marino, G. B. L'Adone, poema
1625 Tassoni, A. La secchia
1626? Marino, G. B. L'Adone, poema
1626 Marino, G. B. L'Adone, poema
1629 Lalli, G. B. Franceide
Scaglia, Giacomo
1630 Tassoni, A. La secchia
1637 Tassoni, A. La secchia
Scoto, Girolamo, Heirs of
1605 Orta, G. da. Dell'historia de i semplici
1620 Sacro Bosco, J. de. Sphaera
Sessa, Marchio, Heirs of
1633 Fioravanti, L. Dello specchio di scientia universale
Sessas, The
1602 Durante, C. Herbario novo
1606 Capivaccio, G. Opera omnia
1611 Molina, L. de. De justitia et jure
1614 Molina, L. de. De justitia et jure opera omnia
1617 Capivaccio, G. Opera omnia
1617 Durante, C. Herbario novo
Societas Venetas
1602 Bruele, G. Praxis medicinae
Somasco, Giacomo Antonio
1605 Gallucci, G. P. Coelestium corporum et rerum . . . accurata explicatio
Spineda, Lucio
1601 Durante, C. Il tesoro della sanità
1602 Fioravanti, L. De' capricci medicinali . . . libri quattro
1603 Fioravanti, L. Della fisica
1603 Fioravanti, L. Dello specchio di scientia universale

1603 Fioravanti, L. Il tesoro della vita humana
1607 Tagault, J. Institutione di cirugia
1610 Fioravanti, L. La cirugia
1614 Durante, C. Il tesoro della sanità
1620 Codogno, O. Nuovo itinerario delle poste
1629 Fioravanti, L. De' capricci medicinali . . . libri quattro
1629 Fioravanti, L. Della fisica
1629 Fioravanti, L. Il tesoro della vita humana
1630 Fioravanti, L. La cirugia
1630 Fioravanti, L. Del compendio de' secreti rationali
Sub signo Minervae
1647 Jonstonus, J. Idea universae medicinae
Teler, Ambros
1615 Boccalini, T. Pietra del paragone politico
Teler, Giorgio
1615 Boccalini, T. Pietra del paragone politico (4)
Teler, Zorzi
1615 Boccalini, T. Pietra del paragone politico (4)
1619 Boccalini, T. Pietra del paragone politico
Tomasini, Cristoforo
1642 Torsellino, O. Ristretto delle historie del mondo
1645 Ripa, C. Iconologia
Tomasini, Pietro
1640 Castelli, P. Opobalsamum
Tomasini, The
1647 Cartari, V. Imagini delli dei de gl'antichi
Turino, Antonio
1611 Bonardo, G. M. La minera del mondo
Turrino Press
1646 Clüver, P. Introductionis in universam geographiam . . . libri vi
Ugolino, Paolo
1603 Caro, A. De le lettere familiari
Valentin, Mattio
1606 Estienne, C. Agricoltura
Valentini, Giorgio
1617 Garzoni, T. La piazza universale

Valentini, The
1624 Fioravanti, L. Dello specchio di scientia universale
Varisco (Varischi), Giorgio
1608 Wecker, J. J. Antidotarium generale
Varisco, Giorgio & Varisco
1617 Tarcagnota, G. Delle historie del mondo
1617 Zecchi, G. Consultationes medicinales
Vecchi, Alessandro de'
1606 Ulloa, A. de. Vita, et fatti dell'invitissimo imperatore Carlo Quinto
1612 Botero, G. Le relazioni universali
1618 Botero, G. Le relazioni universali
1622 Botero, G. Le relazioni universali
1623 Durante, C. Il tesoro della sanita
Vincenti, Giacomo
1605 Melich, G. Avertimenti nelle compositioni de' medicamenti
Viotti, Erasmo
1606 Marcos da Lisboa. Delle croniche . . . parte terza
Zaltieri, Marc Antonio
1616 Durante, C. Il tesoro della sanita
Zenaro, Damiano
1601 Doglioni, G. N. Compendio historico
1602 Augenio, O. Epistolarum . . . libri xii

VERONA
Ardizzoni, Giovanni Antonio
1641 Scarioni, F. Centuria seconda de' secreti mirabili
Merlo, Bartolomeo
1643 Pona, F. Trattato de' veleni
Rossi, Francesco di
1639 Perucci, F. Pompe funebri
1642 Conestaggio, G. F. di. Dell'unione del regno di Portugallo
1646 Perucci, F. Pompe funebri
Tami, Angelo
1622 Ceruto, B. Musaeum Franc. Calceolarii

VICENZA
Bertelli, Pietro
1603 Delle rime piacevoli
Bolzetta, Francesco
1617 Garimberto, G. Problemi naturali e morali
Greco, Giorgio
1603 Zappullo, M. Historie di quattro principali città del mondo
Grossi, Francesco
1609 Delle rime piacevoli

VITERBO
Ardizzoni, Giovanni Antonio
1641 Scarioni, F. Centuria seconda de' secreti mirabili
Diotallevi, The
1650 Piccino, G. Il petopiccino

THE NETHERLANDS

Printer unidentified
1607? Migoen, J. W. Eene treffelijcke tzamensprekinghe (4)
1608 Consideratien vande vrede (2)
1608 Discours by forme van remonstrantie (3)
1608 Usselinx, W. Naerder bedenckingen over de zee-vaerdt (2)
1608 Usselinx, W. Vertoogh, hoe nootwendich (2)
1608 Usselinx, W. Waerschouwinghe van de ghewichtighe redenen
1622 Usselinx, W. Politiicq discours (2)
1623? Scott, T. Vox Dei
1624 Scott, T. Vox populi, Vox Dei. Vox regis
1625 Scribanius, C. Den Nederlandtschen waer-segger
1625? Scribanius, C. Den Nederlandschen waerzegger
1626 Scribanius, C. L'Apocalipse hollandoise
1626 Scribanius, C. Den Hollantschen apocalypsis
1629 Wijnandts, W. Lobspruch

ALKMAAR
Claeszoon, Jan
1647 Netherlands (United Provinces, 1581–1795). Staten Generaal. Extract uyttet register
1647 Den ongeveynsden Nederlantschen patriot (2)
Houten, Ysbrant Janszoon van
1644 Megapolensis, J. Een kort ontwerp vande Mahakuase Indianen

AMSTERDAM
Printer unidentified
160–? Vertooninghe aen de Vereenichde Provintien
1603 Meteren, E. van. Historia oder eigentliche . . . Beschreibung
1605 Sande, J. van den. Trouhertighe vermaninghe (2)
1607 Nierop, A. van. Echo ofte galm
1607? Nieuwen, klaren astrologen-bril
1608? Antwoordt op het tweede refereyn
1608? Bulle oft Mandaet
1608 Bulle oft Mandaet (2)
1608 Buyr-praetjen: ofte Tsamensprekinge (2)
1608 Catechismus ofte Tsamen-spreeckinghe
1608? Dees wonder-maer
1608 Dialogus oft Tsamensprekinge (3)
1608? Discours van Pieter en Pauwels (2)
1608 Ghetrouwen raedt
1608? Middelgeest, S. van. Discours of t'samensprekinghe
1608 Middelgeest, S. van. Droom oft t'samensprekinge
1608? Middelgeest, S. van. Raedtsel (2)
1608 Middelgeest, S. van. Raedtsel
1608? Middelgeest, S. van. Raedtslagh
1608 Migoen, J. W. Proeve des nu onlangs uyt-ghegheven drooms
1608 Den Nederlandtschen byecorf (3)
1608 Nierop, A. van. Echo ofte galm (2)
1608? Een oud schipper
1608 Schuyt-praetgens
1608? Schuyt-praetgens (2)

1608 Het secreet des Conings van Spangien
1608 Usselinx, W. Bedenckinghen
1608 Usselinx, W. Grondich discours (2)
1608 Usselinx, W. Memorie vande gewichtige redenen (3)
1608? Usselinx, W. Onpartydich discours (2)
1608 Verheiden, W. Nootelijcke consideratien
1609 Middelgeest, S. van. Testament (3)
1614? Krachteloose donder (3)
1617 Clercq, N. de. Tooneel der beroemder hertogen
1620? Baudart, W. De Spaensche tiranije
1621 Nederlandsche West-Indische Compagnie. De ghemeene directeurs (2)
1621 Nederlandsche West-Indische Compagnie. Ordonnantien ende articulen (4)
1621 Nederlandsche West-Indische Compagnie. West-Indische Compagnie
1622 Anderde discours
1622 Apologus vanden krijch
1622? Cats, J. Emblemata
1622 Copye van eenen brieff
1622 Derde discours. By forma van missive
1622 Derde discours. Waer in by forme van missive . . .
1622 Korte aenwysinghe
1622 Middelgeest, S. van. Nootwendich discours
1622 Middelgeest, S. van. Ootmoedighe beklagh-redenen
1622 Middelgeest, S. van. Tweede noot-wendiger discours
1622 Naerder aenwysinghe
1623? Fortgang der West Indianischen Compagnia
1623? Gysius, J. De Spaensche tiranije
1623 Nederlandsche Oost-Indische Compagnie. Het geamplieerde Octroy
1623 Nederlandsche West-Indische Compagnie. Copye. Van seker articulen
1624 Cats, J. Silenus Alcibiadis

1624 Geluckwenschinghe aan de West-Indische vlote
1624 Nederlandsche West-Indische Compagnie. Acte, waer by een yeder gheaccordeert werdt
1625? Lyste van 't ghene de Brasil jaerlijcks can opbrenghen
1625? Middelgeest, S. van. Den langh-verwachten donder-slach
1625 Middelgeest, S. van. Den vervaerlijcken Oost-Indischen eclipsis
1625 Waerachtigh verhael van het succes
1627 Aventrote, J. Epistola á los Peruleras
1627 Casas, B. de las, Bp. Den spieghel der Spaensche tierannije
1627? Scribanius, C. Le manifeste hollandoise
1628 Amsterdam. Citizens. Copie van requesten
1628 Wtenbogaert, J. Ondersoeck der Amsterdamsche requesten
1629 Antwoordt, op sekeren brief Evlaly (3)
1629 Eroberung der reiche silber-vloot
1629 Lof des vrye vaerts
1629 Lommelin, D. Lof-dicht
1629 Mexía, P. Verscheyden lessen
1629? Nederlandsche West-Indische Compagnie. Consideratien ende redenen
1629? Vondel, J. van den. Op het ontset van Piet Heyns buyt (2)
1630 Batavier gaet hem verblije
1630? Cats, J. Silenus Alcibiadis
1630 Copie van een missive
1630 Dialogus ofte t'Samenspreekinge tusschen Jan . . . ende Govert
1630 Entwerffung von Eroberung der Stadt Olinda
1630 Reves, J. de. Biechte des Conincx van Spanien
1630 De vruchten van't monster van den treves (2)
1631? Cats, J. Minnelijcke . . . sinne-beelden (2)

1631? Nederlandsche West-Indische Compagnie. Extract uyt de Notulen
1633? Cats, J. Mägden-plicht
1633 Cats, J. Minnelijcke . . . sinne-beelden
1633 Cats, J. Silenus Alcibiadis
1634 Copye van twee . . . brieven
1634? Nederlandsche West-Indische Compagnie. West-Indische Compagnie
1635 Netherlands (United Provinces, 1581–1795). Staten Generaal. Nader ordre ende Reglement
1636 Selden, J. Mare clausum
1637? Den handel ende wandel
1638 Blaeu, W. J. Tweevoudigh onderwijs
1638 Bril-gesicht
1638 Consideratien als dat de negotie op Brasil . . . .
1638? Onbedriegh'lijcke leyd-sterre
1638 Philopatroös, E. Nieuwkeulsch of Spaensch bedrogh
1638 Het spel van Brasilien (2)
1640 Cats, J. Minnelijcke . . . sinne-beelden (2)
1640 Guelen, A. de. Kort verhael . . . van Fernanbuc
1640 Relation du combat
1640? Staden, H. Beschrijvinghe van America
1641 Nederlandsche West-Indische Compagnie. Voorslack
1641 Teixeira, J. Seigneur ofte den groten meester
1642 Boccalini, T. Pietra del paragone politico
1642 Grotius, H. De origine gentium Americanarum dissertatio
1642 Manasseh ben Joseph ben Israel. Gratulaçao
1642 Montalvão, J. Mascarenhas, marquez de. Copyen van drie missiven
1643 Grotius, H. De jure belli ac pacis
1643 Rensselaer, K. van. Insinuatie
1643 Trou-hertighe onderrichtinge
1644 Baerle, K. van. Mauritius redux

1644 Beverwijck, J. van. Schat der gesontheyt
1644? Brevis assertio et apologia
1644 Cats, J. Proef-steen van den trou-ringh
1644? Claer licht, ofte Vertooch
1644 Klaer licht, ofte Vertoogh
1645 Cats, J. Minnelijcke . . . zinnebeelden
1645 Graswinckel, D. Aenspraek aen den getrouwen Hollander
1645 Nederlandsche West-Indische Compagnie. Vryheden ende exemptien
1645 Uyt-vaert vande West-Indische Compagnie
1646? Antwoordt op seeckere missive (2)
1646? Antwoort op een seker brief
1646 Le bon voisin
1646 Extract ende copye van verscheyde brieven
1646 Hollants praetie
1646 Munsters praetie (10)
1646 Munsters vrede-praetje
1646 Suchtich en trouwhertich discours (2)
1647? Authenthijcque copye van het Recif
1647 Brasilsche gelt-sack (2)
1647 De Brasilsche Breede-byl
1647 Consideratien op de Cautie
1647 Cort ende waerachtich verhael van der Portugysen in Brasil revolte
1647 Discours de la paix
1647 Den naeckten Spangjaert (2)
1647 Nederlandsche West-Indische Compagnie. Antwoorde vande gedeputeerde
1647 Netherlands (United Provinces, 1581–1795). Staten Generaal. Extract uyttet register
1647 Sousa Coutinho, F. de. Naerdere propositie
1647 Spaensche triumphe (3)
1648 Advys op de presentatie van Portugael . . . 2. dl. (3)
1648 Advys op de presentatie van Portugal . . . 1. dl.
1648 Brandt in Brasilien
1648 Coignet de la Thuillerie, Gaspard. Propositien

1642 Blaeu, W. J. Institution astronomique
1642 Blaeu, W. J. Novus atlas, das ist Welt-beschreibung . . . ander Theil
1642 Blaeu, W. J. Le theatre du monde
1642 Blaeu, W. J. Toonneel des aerdriicx (2)
1642 Grotius, H. De jure belli ac pacis
1643 Blaeu, W. J. Novus atlas, das ist Welt-beschreibung . . . ander Theil
1643 Blaeu, W. J. Theatrum orbis terrarum
1643 Blaeu, W. J. Zeespiegel

Blaeu, Willem Janszoon
1608 Blaeu, W. J. Het licht der zee-vaert
1610 Blaeu, W. J. Het licht der zee-vaert
1612 Blaeu, W. J. The light of navigation
1613 Blaeu, W. J. Het licht der zee-vaert
1614 Grotius, H. Vrye zeevaert
1614 Visscher, R. Sinne-poppen
1617 Blaeu, W. J. Het licht der zee-vaert
1618 Blaeu, W. J. Het licht der zee-vaert
1618? Cats, J. Monita amoris virginei
1618 Schouten, W. C. Journael ofte Beschryvinghe
1618 Schouten, W. C. Journal ofte Beschryvinghe
1618? Schouten, W. C. Journal ou Description
1618 Schouten, W. C. Journal ou Description
1619 Blaeu, W. J. Le flambeau de la navigation
1619 Cats, J. Monita amoris virginei
1619 Cats, J. Silenus Alcibiadis
1619 Schouten, W. C. Novi Freti . . . detectio
1620 Blaeu, W. J. Het licht der zee-vaert
1620 Cats, J. Silenus Alcibiadis (2)
1620 Visscher, R. Sinnepoppen
1622 Blaeu, W. J. The light of navigation

1622 Cats, J. Monita amoris virginei
1622 Cats, J. Silenus Alcibiadis
1623 Barclay, J. Euphormionis Lusinini Satyricon
1623 Blaeu, W. J. Zeespiegel (2)
1625 Blaeu, W. J. Le flambeau de la navigation
1625 Blaeu, W. J. The sea-mirrour
1626 Vondel, J. van den. Begroetenis aen den . . . vorst (2)
1627 Blaeu, W. J. Zeespiegel (2)
1629 Barclay, J. Satyricon
1629? Vondel, J. van den. Op het ontset van Piet Heyns buyt
1630 Blaeu, W. J. Atlantis appendix
1630 Blaeu, W. J. Het licht der zee-vaert
1630? Cats, J. Silenus Alcibiadis
1631 Baerle, K. van. Trophaeum Arausionense
1631 Blaeu, W. J. Appendix Theatri A. Ortelii (2)
1631 Blaeu, W. J. Zeespiegel
1631 Grotius, H. De jure belli ac pacis
1632 Baerle, K. van. Athenaeum
1632 Baerle, K. van. Mercator sapiens
1632 Grotius, H. De jure belli ac pacis
1632 Jonstonus, J. Thaumatographia naturalis
1633 Baerle, K. van. Amor sapiens
1633 Grotius, H. Mare liberum
1633 Meteren, E. van. Meteranus novus, das ist: Warhafftige Beschreibung
1633 Owen, J. Epigrammatum . . . editio postrema
1634 Barclay, J. Satyricon (2)
1634 Blaeu, W. J. Institutio astronomica
1634 Blaeu, W. J. Het nieuwe licht der zeevaert
1634 Blaeu, W. J. Novus atlas, das ist, Abbildung . . . von allen Ländern
1634 Blaeu, W. J. Tweevoudigh onderwijs
1635 Blaeu, W. J. The sea-mirror
1635 Cats, J. Monita amoris virginei

1635 Meteren, E. van. Meterani novi continuatio, das ist: Warhafftige Beschreibung
1636 Merula, P. Cosmographiae generalis libri tres
1639 Blaeu, W. J. Zeespiegel
1640 Blaeu, W. J. The sea-mirrour (2)
1640 Blaeu, W. J. Zeespiegel

Blaeu, Willem Janszoon & Cornelis
1639 Pharmacopoea Amstelredamensis

Blaeu, Willem Janszoon & Joan
1635 Blaeu, W. J. Novus atlas, das ist, Abbildung . . . von allen Ländern (2)
1635 Blaeu, W. J. Le theatre du monde
1635 Blaeu, W. J. Le theatre du monde . . . Seconde partie
1635 Blaeu, W. J. Theatrum orbis terrarum
1635 Blaeu, W. J. Theatrum orbis terrarum . . . pars secunda
1635 Blaeu, W. J. Toonneel des aerdriicx
1635 Blaeu, W. J. Toonneel des aerdriicx. 2. dl
1636 Pharmacopoea Amstelredamensis (2)
1638 Blaeu, W. J. Appendice . . . du Théatre du monde
1638 Blaeu, W. J. Le theatre du monde
1638 Blaeu, W. J. Zeespiegel

Boeteman, Pieter Dirckszoon
1649 Steendam, J. Den Distelvink. Eerste deel
1649 Steendam, J. Den Distelvink. Twede deel
1650 Steendam, J. Den Distelvink. Darde deel

Bos, Lambert van den
1646 Bos, L. van den. Essays

Bouman, J.
1650? Brouwer, H. Journael . . . van Chili

Bouman, Jan Jacobszoon
1649 Cats, J. 's Werelts begin

Brandt, Marten Janszoon
1623 Voortganck vande West-Indische Compaignie
1624 Teellinck, W. Davids danckbaerheyt
1630 Nederlandsche West-Indische Compagnie. Vryheden

1621 Avity, P. d', sieur de Montmartin. Wereld spiegel

1622 Casas, B. de las. Den spiegel der Spaensche tyranny

1622 Wassenaer, N. van. Historisch verhael

1622 Wassenaer, N. van.
Tweede-deel . . . van het Historisch verhael

1623 Linschoten, J. H. van.
Beschrijvinge . . . van
Guinea

1623 Linschoten, J. H. van. Itinerarium, ofte Schip-vaert

1623 Linschoten, J. H. van.
Reys-gheschrift

1623 Wassenaer, N. van.
T'derde-deel . . . van het Historischer verhael

1623 Wassenaer, N. van.
T'vierde deel . . . van het Historisch verhael

1624 Acosta, J. de. Historie naturael en morael

1624 Linschoten, J. H. van. Voyasie, ofte Schip-vaert

1624 Wirsung, C. Een medecyn-
boeck

1626 Wassenaer, N. van.
T'derde-deel . . . van het Historischer verhael

1627 Wirsung, C. Medicyn-
boeck

1628 Gysius, J. De spieghel der
Spaense tyrannye, 2de dl

1630 Mercator, G. Atlas sive
Cosmographicae meditationes

1632 Mercator, G. Atlas, sive
Cosmographicae meditationes

1636 Mercator, G. Atlas, sive
Cosmographicae meditationes

1638 Gysius, J. De spiegel der
spaense tyrannye, 2de dl

Colijn, Michiel

1612 Hues, R. Tractaet . . . van
het gebruijck der . . . globe

1617 Lodewijcksz, W. 'T eerste
boeck; Historie van Indien

1617 Marees, P. de. Beschrijvinghe . . . van Guinea

1617 Ottsen, H. Journael oft
Daghelijcx-register

1617 Potgieter, B. J. Historisch
ende wijdtloopigh verhael

1617 Pretty, F. Beschryvinge
vande . . . zee-vaerdt

1617 Raleigh, Sir W. Warachtighe ende grondige beschryvinghe van . . . Guiana

1617 Spilbergen, J. van. t'Historiael journael

1618 Noort, O. van. Beschrijvinge van de voyagie

1619 Colijn, M. Oost-Indische
ende West-Indische voyagien

1619 Neck, J. C. van. Historiale
beschrijvinghe

1619 Veer, G. de. De waerachtighe beschrijvinge vande drie
seylagien

1621 Netherlands (United Provinces, 1581–1795). Staten
Generaal. Ordre . . . ghemaeckt op . . . het sout halen in
West-Indien

1621 Ordóñez de Ceballos, P.
Eyghentlijcke beschryvinghe
van West-Indien

1622 Estienne, C. De veltbouw

1622 Herrera y Tordesillas, A.
de. Description des Indes Occidentales (2)

1622 Herrera y Tordesillas, A.
de. Nieuwe werelt

1622 Herrera y Tordesillas, A.
de. Novus orbis

1622 Hues, R. Tractaet . . . van
het gebruyck der . . . globe

1622 Le Maire, J. Spieghel der
australische navigatie

Colom, Jacob Aertszoon

1648 Colom, J. A. Toortse der
zeevaerdt

Colom, Johannes

1649 Dias Ferreira, G. Zent-brief

**Commelin, Hieronymus, Heirs
of**

1626 Aubigné, T. A. d'. L' histoire universelle

Cunradus, Christoffel

1650 Bontekoe, W. Y. Journael
. . . vande Oost-Indische reyse

1650 Neck, J. C. van. Waerachtigh verhael van de schip-
vaert

Doncker, Hendrick

1650 Steendam, J. Den Distelvink. Darde deel

Elsevier

1628 Baerle, K. van. Poemata

Elsevier, Abraham

1621 Buchanan, G. Poemata

Elsevier, Louis

1640 Boccalini, T. Lapis lydius
politicus

1640 Boccalini, T. Pietra del paragone politico

1640 Campanella, T. De monarchia Hispanica discursus
(2)

1640 Guelen, A. de. Brieve relation de . . . Phernambucq

1641 Campanella, T. De monarchia Hispanica

1641 Clüver, J. Historiarum
mundi epitome

1641 Geslin, P. La sainte chorographie

1641 Sandys, Sir E. Relation
. . . de la religion

1643 Gölnitz, A. Compendium
geographicum

1643 Laet, J. de. Notae ad dissertationem Hugonis Grotii De
origine gentium Americanarum (2)

1644 Jonstonus, J. Idea universae medicinae

1644 Laet, J. de. Responsio ad
dissertationem secundam Hugonis Grotii, de Origine gentium Americanarum

1647 Owen, J. Epigramma-
tum . . . editio postrema (2)

1648 Bacon, F. Sylva sylvarum

1648 Jonstonus, J. Idea universae medicinae

1648 Piso, W. Historia naturalis
Brasiliae

1649 Gölnitz, A. Compendium
geographicum

1650 Varen, B. Geographia generalis

Fischer, Nicolas Janszoon

1628 Hein, P. P. Beschreibung
von Eroberung der spanischen
Silber Flotta

Gerritsz, Hessel

1612 Gerritsz, H. Beschryvinghe
van der Samoyeden landt (2)

1612 Gerritsz, H. Descriptio ac
delineatio geographica detectionis freti

1612 Gerritsz, H. Exemplar libelli supplicis potentissimo
Hispaniarum Regi

1613 Gerritsz, H. Descriptio ac
delineatio geographica detectionis freti (2)

1609 Mercator, G. L'atlas ou Méditations cosmographiques

1610 Mercator, G. Atlas minor (2)

1611 Hues, R. Tractatus. de globis

1611 Mercator, G. Atlas sive Cosmographicae meditationes

1611 Pontanus, J. I. Rerum et urbis Amstelodamensium historia

1612 Mercator, G. Atlas, sive Cosmographicae meditationes

1613 Mercator, G. Atlas minor . . . Traduict

1613 Mercator, G. L'atlas ou Méditations cosmographiques

1613 Mercator, G. Atlas, sive Cosmographicae meditationes

1614 Mercator, G. Atlas minor . . . Traduict

1614 Pontanus, J. I. Historische beschrijvinghe

1616 Bertius, P. Tabularum geographicarum contractarum libri septem

1616 Mercator, G. Atlas sive Cosmographicae meditationes

1617 Hues, R. Tractatus de globis

1618 Bertius, P. La geographie racourcie

1618 Bertius, P. Tabularum geographicarum contractarum libri septem (2)

1619 Mercator, G. Atlas sive Cosmographicae meditationes (2)

1619 Spilbergen, J. van. Speculum Orientalis Occidentalisque Indiae navigationum

1621 Merula, P. Cosmographiae generalis libri tres

1623 Hues, R. Tractaet . . . van het gebruyck der . . . globe

1624 Wassenaer, N. van. T'vyfde-deel . . . van het Historisch verhael

1626 Hondius, J. Nova et accurata Italiae hodiernae descriptio

1629 Clüver, P. Introductionis in universam geographiam . . . libri vi

Hondius Office

1630? Clüver, P. Introductionis in universam geographiam . . . libri vi

1637 Clüver, P. Introductionis in universam geographiam . . . libri vi

165–? Clüver, P. Introductionis in universam geographiam . . . libri vi

Jacobszoon, Theunis

1631 Nederlandsche West-Indische Compagnie. Articulen, met approbatie . . . vanden handel

1631 Nederlandsche West-Indische Compagnie. Vryheden ende exemptien

1636 Pharmacopoea Amstelredamensis

1643 Rensselaer, K. van. Redres van de abuysen

1643 Rensselaer, K. van. Waerschouwinge, verboth, ende toe-latinghe

1644 Cats, J. Maechden-plicht

Janszoon, Broer

1616 Nieuwe ende warachtighe tijdinghe

1616 Een waerachtige beschryvinghe van de schoone victorie

1621 Missive. Daer in kortelijck . . . wert verthoont . . .

1622 Levendich discours

1624 Acosta, J. de. Historie naturael en morael (3)

1624 Gheluck-wenschinghe aan de West-Indische vlote

1624 Inga, A., pseud.? West-Indische Spieghel

1624 Willekens, J. Goede nieuwe tijdinghe

1625 Scribanius, C. Den oor-sprongh, voort-gangh ende gewenscht eynde

1626? Scribanius, C. Den vernieuden waer-segger

1627 Staden, H. Beschrijvinghe van America

1630 Staden, H. Beschrijvinghe van America

1634 Staden, H. Beschrijvinghe van America

1635 Hoffer, A. Nederduytsche poemata

1638? Staden, H. Beschrijvinghe van America

1638 Staden, H. Beschrijvinghe van America

1641 Paes Viegas, A. Manifest . . . van Portugael

1641 Portugal. Sovereigns, etc., 1640–1656. Andere declaratie

1646 Brouwer, H. Journael ende Historis verhael van . . . Chili (2)

Janszoon, Harmen

1619 Schouten, W. C. Journael ofte Beschrijvinghe

1619 Schouten, W. C. Journal ou Description

*Janszoon, Jan (the Younger)

1618 Meteren, E. van. Descriptio bellorum

1618 Schouten, W. C. Journael ofte Beschrijvinghe

1619 Schouten, W. C. Journal ou Description (3)

1620 Blaeu, W. J. Le flambeau de la navigation

1620 Blaeu, W. J. Het licht der zee-vaert

1620 Blaeu, W. J. The light of navigation

1620 Blaeu, W. J. Le phalot de la mer

1620 Sweerts, E. Florilegium

1621 Spilbergen, J. van. Miroir Oost et West-Indical

1621 Spilbergen, J. van. Oost ende West-Indische spieghel

1623 Blaeu, W. J. Het licht der zee-vaert

1623 Novus orbis regionum. Novus orbis

1624 Orlers, J. J. La genealogie des illustres comtes de Nassau

1624 Schouten, W. C. Journael ofte Beschrijvinghe

1624 Wassenaer, N. van. T'seste deel . . . van het Historisch verhael

1625 Blaeu, W. J. The light of navigation

1625 Wassenaer, N. van. T'achste deel . . . van het Historisch verhael

1625 Wassenaer, N. van. T'sevende-deel . . . van het Historisch verhael

1647 Jansson, J. Novus Atlas, das ist Abbildung

1647 Sweerts, E. Florilegium

1648 Mercator, G. Atlas minor, das ist . . . Beschreibung

1648 Schouten, W. C. Diarium vel descriptio . . . itineris

1648 Veer, G. de. Eerste schipvaert

1649 Jansson, J. Nouvel atlas

1649 Jansson, J. Novus atlas

1649 Jansson, J. Novus Atlas, das ist Welt-beschreibung

1650 Bertius, P. Beschreibung der gantzen Welt

1650 Jansson, J. Atlantis majoris quinta pars

1650 Jansson, J. Cinquiesme partie du Grand atlas

1650 Jansson, J. Das fünffte Theil des Grossen Atlantis

1650 Jansson, J. Het vijfde deel des Grooten atlas

1650 Owen, J. Epigrammatum . . . editio postrema

Jaquet, Johannes

1644 Consideratie . . . van Brasil

Joosten, Gillis

1647 Nieuwenborgh, J. Het nederlantsche lust-hofken

Joosten, Jacob

1649 Joosten, J. De kleyne wonderlycke wereldt (2)

Keere, Pieter van der

1618 Schouten, W. C. Journael ofte Beschrijvinghe

1619 Schouten, W. C. Diarium vel Descriptio

1619 Schouten, W. C. Journal ou Description

Laurenszoon, Hendrick

1610? Langenes, B. Thrésor de chartes

1610 Linschoten, J. H. van. Histoire de la navigation

1612 Bertius, P. Geographischer . . . Tabeln fünff . . . Bücher

1615 Paré, A. De chirurgie

1617 Gesner, K. Historia animalium

1624 Acosta, J. de. Historie naturael en morael

1627 Estienne, C. De velt-bow

1627 Paré, A. De chirurgie

1630 Baers, J. Olinda

1632 Zacutus, A. De medicorum principum historia

1634 Zacutus, A. De praxi medica admiranda

1636 Paré, A. De chirurgie

1636 Zacutus, A. Historiarum medicarum libri sex

1637 Zacutus, A. De medicorum principum historia

1644 Theophrastus. De historia plantarum

1647 Grotius, H. De jure belli ac pacis

Lescaille, Jacob

1644 Ripa, C. Iconologia, of Uytbeeldingen

1644 Vondel, J. van den. Verscheide gedichten

1646 Bos, L. van den. Essays ofte Poëtische betrachtungen

Liebergen, Arnout van

1643 Liebergen, A. van. Apologiae, ofte Waerachtighe verantwoordinghe

Lieshout, François

1630 Seeckere tijdinghe vande vlote

1630 Translaet uyt den Spaenschen. Vande geluckige victorie

1639 Translaet uyt den Spaenschen, weghens 't gevecht

1640 Copye ofte Cort ende waerachtigh verhael

1640 Moris, G. Copye. Van 't Journael (2)

1640 Tijdinghe van Bresiel

1641 Portugal. Treaties, etc., 1640–1656. Accoort ende articulen

1641 Portugal. Treaties, etc., 1640–1656. Extract uyt d'Articulen

1644 Tydingh uyt Brasil

1646 Copie van een Missive

1646 Poty, P. Copye van een Brasiliaenschen brieff

Lieshout, François, Widow of

1649? Companhia geral para o estado do Brazil. De instellinge

Macedonien, Philips van, pseud.

1648 Eenige advijsen. See under The Hague—Breeckevelt, Ludolph

Made, Sybrandt van der

1647 Netherlands (United Provinces, 1581–1795). Staten Generaal. Extract uyttet register der resolutien

Marel, Johannes van

1647 Vertooch aen de . . . Staten Generael

Marel, Pieter van, pseud.

1647 Korte observatien op het Vertoogh

Matthijszoon, Paul

1640 Copye ofte Cort . . . verhael

1641 Paes Viegas, A. Manifest . . . van Portugael

Menlemand, C.

1626 Copye van een brief

Meulemans, Christiaan

1625 Verhael van 't ghene den Admirael l'Hermite in . . . Peru verricht

Meyne, David de

1612 Casas, B. de las. Den spiegel der Spaensche tierannyegeschiet

Mucken, Jans

1618 Middelgeest, S. van. Discurs und Muthmassung

Nes, Jacob, pseud.

1648 Nederlantsche absolutie. See under The Hague—Veely, Johan

1648 De penitentie. See under The Hague—Veely, Johan

Paets, Jacob Pieterszoon

1610 Ulloa, A. de. Historie ende het leven

Paets, Pieter Jacobszoon

1617 Mexía, P. De verscheyden lessen

Pas, Crispin van de

1641 Kort en grondigh verhael

1641 Paes Viegas, A. Manifest . . . van Portugael

1641 Portugal. Sovereigns, etc., 1640–1656. Andere declaratie

Pels, Frans

1644 Aenwysinge . . . vande Oost en West-Indische Compagnien

Pers, Dirck Pieterszoon

1610 Linschoten, J. H. van. Histoire de la navigation

1622 Usselinx, W. Korte onderrichtinghe

1622 Gysius, J. De Spaensche ti-
    ranije
1623 Nederlandsche West-In-
    dische Compagnie. Octroy
1623 Zárate, A. de. Conqueste
    van Indien
1624 Inga, A., pseud.? West-In-
    dische Spieghel
1626 Journael vande Nassausche
    vloot
1631 Journael van de Nas-
    sausche vloot
1633 Gysius, J. De Spaensche ti-
    rannij
1634 Herckmans, Elias. Der zee-
    vaert lof
1643 Journael vande Nassausche
    vloot
1643 Journalen van drie voya-
    gien
Walschaert, Johannes
1614 Linschoten, J. H. van. Navi-
    gatio ac itinerarium
1614 Lodewijcksz, W. Pirma pars
    Descriptionis itineris navalis
Walschaert, Pieter
1625 Basuyne des oorloghs
Wees, Abraham de
1648 Vondel, J. van den. De ge-
    temde Mars (2)
Willemszoon, Gerrit
1649 Paré, A. De chirurgie
Wyngaert, Willem Janszoon
1629 Pels, E. Lof-dicht

ARNHEM
Printer unidentified
1626 Reyd, E. van. Historie der
    Nederlantscher oorlogen
Biesen, Jacob van
1633 Reyd, E. van. Oorspronck
    ende voortganck van de . . .
    oorloghen
Jacobszoon, Jan
1636 Zacutus, A. Historiarum
    medicarum libri sex
1640 Chaumette, A. Handt-
    boeck der chirurgie
1646 Diemerbroeck, I. de. De
    peste libri quatuor
1647 Journael ofte Kort discours
Janszoon, Jan
1601 Neck, J. C. van. Journal
1602 Bertius, P. Tabularum geo-
    graphicarum contractarum
    libri quinque

1604 Meteren, E. van. Historia,
    oder Eigentliche . . . beschrei-
    bung
1605 Meteren, E. van. Historia,
    oder Eigentliche . . . Beschrei-
    bung
1607 Mercator, G. Atlas minor
1608 Mercator, G. Atlas minor
    . . . Traduict
1609 Mercator, G. Atlas minor
    . . . Traduict
1609 Mercator, G. Atlas minor,
    das ist . . . Beschreibung
1609 Meteren, E. van. Niederlen-
    discher Historien ander Theil
1610 Mercator, G. Atlas minor
1610 Meteren, E. van. Belli civilis
    in Belgio . . . historia
1612 Meteren, E. van. Nieder-
    ländische Historien
1613 Mercator, G. Atlas minor
    . . . Traduict
1614 Mercator, G. Atlas minor
    . . . Traduict
1614 Meteren, E. van. Eigentlich
    und volkomene historische
    beschreibung
1614 Passe, C. van de. Hortus
    floridus
1615? Passe, C. van de. Jardin
    de fleurs
1615 Wytfliet, C. Descriptionis
    Ptolemicae augmentum
1617 Ptolemaeus, C. Geogra-
    phiae universae
1618 Schouten, W. C. Journael
    ofte Beschrijvinghe (3)
1618 Schouten, W. C. Warhaffte
    Beschreibung der wunderbar-
    lichen Räyse
1620 Baudart, W. Memorien,
    ofte korte verhael
1620 Holland, H. Herōlogia an-
    glica
1620 Mercator, G. Atlas minor
1620 Niderländischer
    histori . . . Supplementum
1621 Discours. Daer in korte-
    lijck . . . wert verthoont
1621 Mercator, G. Atlas minor
1621 Missive. Daer in kortelijck
    . . . wert verthoont
1623 Nederlandsche West-In-
    dische Compagnie. Ordon-
    nantien ende articulen
1624 Baudart, W. Memoryen
    ofte Cort verhael. Pt 1

1626 Reyd, E. van. Voornaemste
    gheschiedenissen
Westerloo, Joost Thyssens van
1647 Velle, N. M. van. De
    oprechte waeghschaele

BOLSWARD
Haringhouck, Samuel van
1649 Franck, S. Werelt-spiegel

BREDA
Printer unidentified
1650 Den ommeganck (2)

DELFT
Printer unidentified
1648 Brasilsche oorloghs over-
    wegingh
1650? Den rechten konink Midas
Balthasar, Floris
1601 Spilbergen, J. van. t'Histo-
    riael journael
1605 Spilbergen, J. van. t Histo-
    riael journael
1605 Spilbergen, J. van. Het
    journael (2)
**Beyeren, Adriaen Gerritszoon
    van**
1610 Ulloa, A. de. Historie
    . . . van den . . . Keyser Caerle
Clercq, Nicolaes de
1615 Clercq, N. de. Tooneel der
    keyseren
1617 Clercq, N. de. Tooneel der
    beroemder hertogen
Clercq, Nicolaes de, Heirs of
1625 Clercq, N. de. Princelyck
    cabinet
Cloeting, Andriesz Janszoon
1629 Spranckhuysen, D. Tranen
    over den doodt van . . . Heyn
1638 Spranckhuysen, D. Tranen
    over den doodt van . . . Heyn
Cloeting, Jan Andrieszoon
1614 Goulart, S. Schat-camer
    der . . . historien
1617 Spilbergen, J. van. Copie
    van een brief
1629 Focanus, J. Adoni-beseck
1629 Nierop, A. van. Loff-dicht
1629 Spranckhuysen, D. Tri-
    umphe van weghen de . . . vic-
    torie
**Cloeting, Jan Andrieszoon,
    Widow of**
1640 Tijdinghe van Bresiel

1647 Remonstrantie. *See under* The Hague—Breeckevelt, Ludolph

Moulaert, Symon

1647 Netherlands (United Provinces, 1581–1795). Staten Generaal. Extract uyt het Boeck (2)

1647 Netherlands (United Provinces, 1581–1795). Staten Generaal. Poincten der artijckulen (4)

1648 Spain. Treaties, etc., 1621–1665. Articulen en conditien

Verhagen, Pieter

1605 Wirsung, C. Medecyn boec

ENKHUIZEN

Baerle, Kaspar van

1641 Baerle, K. van. Verstandighe coopman

Linschoten, Jan Huygen van

1601 Linschoten, J. H. van. Voyagie

Meyn, Jacob Lenaertszoon

1619 Veer, G. de. De waerachtighe beschrijvinge vande drie seylagien

FLUSHING

Printer unidentified

1646 Het ghelichte Munstersche mom-aensicht

1649 De Zeeusche verre-kyker

Janszoon de Jonghe, Jan

1633 Jonckheer, M. Teghenworp

Laet, Geraerdt de

1650 Bedenkingen en antwoort (2)

Langenes, Baernaerdt

1611 Clyte, N. van der. Cort verhael der destructie

Nolck, Maarten Abraham van der

1623 Ruyters, D. Toortse der zee-vaert

Pieck, Jacob Janszoon, pseud.

1650 Amsterdamsche veerman. *See under* Amsterdam—Hilten, Jan van

Ruyters, Dierick

1623 Ruyters, D. Toortse der zee-vaert

Versterre, Samuel Claeys

1630 Usselinx, W. Waerschouwinghe over den treves (2)

1631 Schemering, D. Nova zemla

FRANEKER

Barentsma, B.

1636 Pharmacopoea Amstelredamensis

Ketel, Gerhard

1601 Linschoten, J. H. van. Voyagie

Lamrinck, Jan

1620 Hamcomius, M. Frisia

GORINCHEM (GORKUM)

Helmichszoon, Adriaen

1608 Blefken, D. Een corte ende warachtige beschrijvinge

Janss, A., pseud.

1624 Scott, T. The second part of Vox populi. *See under* Great Britain—London—Okes, Nicholas; Dawson, John; Jones, William

GORKUM. *See* Gorinchem

GOUDA

Corneliszoon, Jasper, pseud.

1649 Amsterdams tafel-praetje. *See under* Amsterdam—Hilten, Jan van

Hoeve, Willem van der

1638 Udemans, G. C. Geestelyck roer

1649 Rivière, L. Methodus curandorum febrium

1649 Rivière, L. Praxis medica

Rammazeyn, Pieter

1640 Cats, J. Maechden-plicht

1640 Cats, J. Silenus Alcibiadis

GRONINGEN

Mucerus, Hendrick

1650 Reyd, E. van. Historie der Nederlantscher oorlogen

1650 Sande, J. van den. Nederlandtsche historie

Roman, Nathanael

1629 Neuhaus, E. Triumphalia Leowardiana

Roman, Nathanael, Heirs of

1641 Den Portugaelsen donderslagh

Sas, Hans

1640 Articul-brief. Beraemt over het scheeps ende crijgs-volck

HAARLEM

Printer unidentified

1626 Valerius, A. Nederlandtsche gedenck-clanck

1628 Schrijver, P. Saturnalia

1629 Veen, J. van der. Siet den getaanden speck

1629 Victorij sang

1630 Reed-geld over betalinghe

1630? Veen, J. van der. Schimpghedicht. Van Fernabuco

1642 Veen, J. van der. Overzeesche zege

Fonteyn, Thomas

1646 Bontekoe, W. Y. Journael

1648 Bontekoe, W. Y. Journael

Kranepoel, Harman

1627 Paré, A. De chirurgie

Roman, Adriaan

1629 Ampzing, S. West-Indische triumph-basuyne

1629 Discours, aengaende treves

1629 Nederlandsche West-Indische Compagnie. Consideratien ende redenen (4)

1630 Ampzing, S. Fasciculus epigrammatum

1630 Discours, aengaende treves

1630 Schrijver, P. Saturnalia

1635 Grotius, H. Drie boecken . . . nopende het recht des oorloghs

1636 Grotius, H. Inleydinghe tot de Hollandsche rechts-gheleerdheydt

1636 Grotius, H. Van de oudheydt der Batavische . . . republique

1636 Grotius, H. Vrye zeevaert

1639 Grotius, H. Inleydinghe tot de Hollandsche rechts-gheleerdheydt

1639 Grotius, H. Van de oudheydt der Batavische . . . republique

1639 Grotius, H. Vrye zeevaert

1641 Grotius, H. Inleydinghe tot de Hollandsche rechts-gheleerdheydt

1641 Grotius, H. Van de oudheydt der Batavische . . . republique

1641 Grotius, H. Vrye zeevaert

Wesbusch, Hans Passchiers van

1610 Benzoni, G. De historie van de nieuwe weerelt

1610 Benzoni, G. De historie vande nieuwe werelt

1630 Souter, D. Eben-ezer

1649? Ses poincten
1650 De gesteeerde Hollantsche leeuw
1650 Holland (Province). Staten. Brief
1650 Kort verhael (2)
1650 Vox veritatis
Breeckevelt, Ferdinandus
1649 Brasyls schuyt-praetjen
Breeckevelt, Johannes
1647 Sousa Coutinho, F. de. Propositio
1647 Sousa Coutinho, F. de. La proposition
1649 Copie translaet uit het Portogijs
Breeckevelt, Ludolph
1634 Keulen, M. van. Extract wtten brief
1634 Pertinent bericht
1647 Remonstrantie aen alle de steden (2)
1647 Sousa Coutinho, F. de. Brevis repetitio
1648 Eenige advijsen ende verklaringhen (2)
1648 Extract van seeckeren brief
1648 Nederlandsche West-Indische Compagnie. Hooghe en Secrete Raad. Extract uyt de Missive
1648 Netherlands (United Provinces, 1581–1795). Staten Generaal. Concept van Reglement op Brasil
1648 Seeckere naedere missive
Browne, Samuel
1648 Spain. Treaties, etc., 1621–1665. Treatie of peace
Burchoorn, Isaac
1634 Venne, A. van de. Sinnevonck
1638? Deductie
1640 Beverwijck, J. van. Spaensche Xerxes
1640 Het naderste . . . journalier verhael . . . uyt Brasyl (2)
1641 Herckmans, E. Theatrum victoriae
1645 Graswinckel, D. Aenspraek
Fransen, J.
1644 Consideratie, overgelevert
Langhe, Lieven de, pseud.?
1644 Nederlandsche West-Indische Compagnie. Remon-

strantie . . . aengaende de vereeninghe
1644 Ooghen-salve
Loven, Hermes van
1609 Meteren, E. van. Belgische ofte Nederlantsche oorlogen
1609 Meteren, E. van. Commentarien ofte Memorien
1610 Meteren, E. van. Commentarien ofte Memoiren
1611 Meteren, E. van. Belgische ofte Nederlantsche oorlogen
Meuris, Aert
1619 Verclaringe ende verhael hoe de Heere Wouter Raleigh . . . hem ghedreghen heeft
1620 Gonsalvius, R. Der heyliger Hispanischer inquisitie etliche . . . consten
1620 Oogh-teecken der inlantsche twisten (3)
1621 Missive van twee Indiaensche coninghen
1621 Scott, T. Den compaignon vanden verre-sienden waerschouwer (2)
1621 Scott, T. Relation. *See under* Great Britain—London—Allde, Edward
1624 Scott, T. Politijcke redenen
1625 Teeling, E. De derde wachter
1625 Teeling, E. De tweede wachter
1626 Moerbeeck, J. A. Spaenschen raedt (2)
1627 Nederlandschen verrekijcker
1627 Sweden. Sovereigns, etc., 1611–1632. Octroy ofte Privilegie
1628 Moerbeeck, J. A. Vereenighde Nederlandschen raedt, het eerste deel (4)
1628 Moerbeeck, J. A. Vereenighde Nederlandschen raedt, het tweede deel
1629 Epicedium cum epitaphio . . . Petri Heinii
1629 Moerbeeck, J. A. Vereenighde Nederlandschen raedt, het eerste deel
1629 Moerbeeck, J. A. Vereenighde Nederlandschen raedt, het tweede deel
1629 Tractaet tegens pays
1630 Klare aenwijsinge

1630 Nijkerke, J. W. Klaerbericht
1630 Redenen
Ockerszoon, Joost
1629 Cats, J. Proteus ofte Minnebeelden
Pieterszoon, Gillis
1650 Netherlands (United Provinces, 1581–1795). Staatsraad. Adviis
Rombouts, P., *See* Amsterdam—Rombouts, Pieter
Stael, Jacob
1650 Netherlands (United Provinces, 1581–1795). Staatsraad. Adviis
Stael, Michiel
1649 Copie translaet uit het Portogijs
1650 Donck, A. van der. Vertoogh van Nieu-Neder-Land
Tongerloo, Anthony Janszoon
1629 Practiicke van den Spaenschen aes-sack
1637 Boey, C. Illustrissimo heroi Mauritio
1644 Friesland, Netherlands. Provinciale Staten. Copye van het Octroy
1647 Baerle, K. van. Uytvaert der Vereenichde Nederlanden
Veely, Johan
1644 Aenwysinge . . . vande Oost en West-Indische Compagnien
1644 Bedenckinge over d'Antwoordt der heeren bewinthebbers (2)
1644 Nederlandsche West-Indische Compagnie. Twee deductien, aen-gaende de vereeninge (3)
1644 Schaede die den staet . . . is aenstaende (2)
1648 Coignet de la Thuillerie, G. Twee propositien (2)
1648 Nederlandtsche absolutie
1648 De penitentie gegeven aen den Franschen drucker
1650 Aitzema, L. van. Verhael van de Nederlantsche vreedehandeling
Venne, Adriaen van de
1629 Cats, J. Proteus ofte Minnebeelden
1635 Venne, A. van de. Tafereel van de belacchende werelt (2)

Generaal. Placaet ende Ordonnantie op de wapeninge
1633 Netherlands (United Provinces, 1581–1795). Staten
Generaal. Ordre ende reglement
1634 Netherlands (United Provinces, 1581–1795). Staten
Generaal. Nader ordre ende
reglement . . . vanden handel . . . op de stadt Olinda
1634 Netherlands (United Provinces, 1581–1795). Staten
Generaal. Ordre ende reglement
1634 Netherlands (United Provinces, 1581–1795). Staten
Generaal. Placaet, alle realen
1634 Netherlands (United Provinces, 1581–1795). Staten
Generaal. Placaet ende Ordonnantie . . . tegens wechloopers
1634 Netherlands (United Provinces, 1581–1795). Staten
Generaal. Placaet . . . teghens
alle realen
1635 Meteren, E. van. Historie
der Nederlandscher . . . oorlogen
1635 Nederlandsche West Indische Compagnie. Extract uyt
den brief vande politijcque
raeden in Brasil
1635 Netherlands (United Provinces, 1581–1795). Staten
Generaal. Nader ordre ende
Reglement
1637 Nederlandsche West-
Indische Compagnie.
Octroy
1637 Netherlands (United Provinces, 1581–1795). Staten
Generaal. Nader ordre ende
reglement (2)
1638 Nederlandsche West-Indische Compagnie. Regle-
ment . . . vanden handel op
Brasil
1639 Nederlandsche West-Indische Compagnie. Verhoo-
ginghe vande capitalen
1641 Portugal. Treaties, etc.,
1640–1656. Extract uyt d'Articulen van het tractaet van bestant (2)

1641 Portugal. Treaties, etc.,
1640–1656. Verkondinghe van
het bestant (2)
1642 Nederlandsche West-Indische Compagnie. Octroy (3)
1642 Portugal. Treaties, etc.,
1640–1656. Tractaet van bestant
1642 Portugal. Treaties, etc.,
1640–1656. Tractatus induciarum
1642 Portugal. Treaties, etc.,
1640–1656. Trattado das tregoas
1647 Beneficien voor de soldaten (3)
1648 Nederlandsche West-Indische Compagnie. Regle-
ment . . . vanden handel op
Brazil
1648 Nederlandsche West-Indische Compagnie. Regle-
ment . . . vanden handel op S.
Paulo de Loanda
1648 Netherlands (United Provinces, 1581–1795). Staten
Generaal. Vercondinge van de
vrede (2)
1648 Spain. Treaties, etc., 1621–
1665. Tractaet van vrede (4)
1648 Spain. Treaties, etc., 1621–
1665. Traicté de la paix
**Wouw, Hillebrant Jacobszoon
van, Widow of**
1647 Besoignes en communicatien (3)

HARDERWIJK
Printer unidentified
1640 Campanella, T. De monarchia Hispanica discursus
Henrickz, Thomas, Widow of
1624 Hoffer, A. Elegia
Wieringen, Nicolaes van
1630 Wijnbergen, J. Vol-
maeckte lauwer-crans
1637 Pontanus, J. I. Discussionum historicarum libri duo

'S HERTOGENBOSCH
Dockum, Jan van
1639 Een brief, gheschreven van
een goet patriot

HOORN
Appel, Mieus Janszoon
1648 Schouten, W. C. Journael

Claeszoon, Jelis
1622 Foreest, J. van. Hispanus
redux
Corneliszoon, Zacharias
1619 Twisck, P. J. Chronijck
Coster, Jelis Claeszoon
1622 Hoorn, Netherlands. Ordinances, etc. Provisionele ordre
Deutel, Jan Janszoon
1646 Bontekoe, W. Y. Journael
1648 Bontekoe, W. Y. Journael
(2)
1648 Schouten, W. C. Journael
Gerbrantszoon, Marten
1630 More, Sir T. De Utopia (2)
1630 Nijkerke, J. W. Klaer-
bericht
1648 Schouten, W. C. Journael
Willemszoon, Isaack
1619 Twisck, P. J. Chronijck
1626 Wassenaer, N. van.
T'derde-deel . . . van het Historischer verhael
1630 More, Sir T. De Utopia (2)
1646 Bontekoe, W. Y. Journael
1648 Bontekoe, W. Y. Journael
(2)
1648 Schouten, W. C. Journael
(3)

KAMPEN
Wyringanus, Petrus Henricus
1629 Martinius, F. Argo-nauta
Batavus

LEEUWARDEN
Albertszoon, Dirck
1629 Discours over den Nederlandtschen vrede-handel
1629 Ontwerp, raeckende het
op-rechten van een Camer
Bock, Harman de
1647 Brilleman, J. Collyrium,
ofte Costelijcke ooghen-salve
Coopman, Hans Willemszoon
1645 Baardt, P. Deughden-spoor
Fonteyne, Claude
1629 Haselbeeck, J. Triumph-
dicht
1630 Baardt, P. Friesche Triton
1630 Spaensche vosse-vel
1631 Spaensche vosse-vel
1633 Baardt, P. Loff-en-lijck-
gedicht
Geerts, Steffen
1645 Baardt, P. Deughden-spoor

Martensz, Cornelis
1650 Den omme-ganck
Rade, Jan & Pieter van den
1642 Friesland, Netherlands. Provinciale Staten. Copye van het Octroy
Sybes, Gijsbert
1643 Focanus, J. Adoni-Beseck
1650 Reyd, E. van. Historie der Nederlantscher oorlogen
1650 Sande, J. van den. Nederlandtsche historie

LEYDEN
Printer unidentified
1603 Arnauld, A. Ingenua et vera oratio
1615 Orlers, J. J. Généalogie des illustres comtes de Nassau
1616 Gysius, J. Oorsprong en voortgang
1619 Orlers, J. J. De oorlochsdaden
1622 Grotius, H. Bewys van den waren godsdienst (2)
1625 Scribanius, C. Den Hollantschen apocalypsis
1626 Heinsius, D. Historie de la vie
1626 Scribanius, C. Den Hollantschen apocalypsis
1647 Meteren, E. van. Historien der Nederlanden
1649 Satyre Ménippée
Banheyning, Cornelis
1650 Extract uyt een brief . . . vande silver-mijne
Basson, Godefrid
1625 Baerle, K. van. Manes Auraici
1628 Baerle, K. van. Poemata
1629 Baerle, K. van. Argo Batava
1630 Baerle, K. van. Poemata
1630 Baerle, K. van. Triumphus super captâ Olinda
Bilt, Bartholomeus van der
1619 Gysius, J. Origo et historia Belgicorum tumultuum
Bonaventure, Corneille
1608 Matthieu, P. Histoire de France
Bouwenszoon, Jan
1604 Paré, A. De chirurgie
Boxe, Willem Christiaens van der
1645 Illustrissimo heroi Joanni Mauritio

1646 Bacon, F. De proef-stucken
1647 Bacon, F. De proef-stucken
Boxe Press
1649 Boxhorn, M. Z. De majestate regum principumque
Christiaens, Willem
1631 Schrijver, P. Vasten-avondspel
1634 Journael ofte waerachtige beschrijvinge
1639 Bodecherus Banninghius, J. Epigrammata americana
1639 Slichtenhorst, A. van. Oratio de navigationibus
Cloucq, Andries
1630 Baerle, K. van. Poemata
1630 Baerle, K. van. Poematum
Commelin, Abraham
1634 Graswinckel, D. Libertas Veneta
1643 Weidner, J. L. Hispanicae dominationis arcana
Commelin, Isaac
1640A Boxhorn, M. Z. Historia obsidionis Bredae
Croy, Philips de
1649 Boxhorn, M. Z. Commentariolus de statu Confoederatarum provinciarum Belgii
1649 Cats, J. 's Werelts begin, midden, eynde
1649 Saint-Amant, M. A. de. Gérard, sieur de. La Rome ridicule
1650 Boxhorn, M. Z. Commentariolus de statu Confoederatarum provinciarum Belgii (2)
Deyster, H. van der
1643 Beverwijck, J. van. Van de uitnementheyt
Doreau, Jean
1602 Montaigne, M. E. de. Les essais (2)
1609 Montaigne, M. E. de. Essais
Dorp, Jan Niclas van, Heirs of
1644 La Barre, A. de. Les leçons publiques
Elsevier, Bonaventura & Abraham
1627 Hondius, J. Nova et accurata Italiae hodiernae descriptio
1628 Heurne, J. van. De vocatione ethnicorum
1629 Colonius, D. Oratio panegyrica
1636 Selden, J. Mare clausum

1640 Boccalini, T. Pietra del paragone politico
1640 Laet, J. de. L'histoire du Nouveau Monde
1641 Campanella, T. De monarchia Hispanica
1644 Laet, J. de. Historie ofte Iaerlijck verhael
Elsevier, Isaak
1618 Heurne, J. van. De legatione evangelica
1621 Merula, P. Cosmographiae generalis libri tres
1622 Neander, J. Tabacologia
1622 Usselinx, W. Korte onderrichtinghe (3)
1625 Heinsius, D. Harangue funebre
1625 Laet, J. de. Nieuwe Wereldt
1625 Thorius, R. Hymnus tabaci
1626 Neander, J. Tabacologia
Elsevier, Louis
1602 Dickenson, J. Speculum tragicum
1603 Dickenson, J. Speculum tragicum
1605 Dickenson, J. Speculum tragicum
1609 Grotius, H. Mare liberum (2)
1611 Dickenson, J. Speculum tragicum
Elsevier Office
1618 Grotius, H. Mare liberum
1624 Clüver, P. Introductionis in universam geographiam . . . libri vi
1625 Camden, W. Annales rerum Anglicarum
1625 Heinsius, D. Laudatio funebris
1627 Clüver, P. Introductionis in universam geographiam . . . libri vi
1628 Buchanan, G. Poemata
1628 Owen, J. Epigrammatum . . . editio postrema
1629 Clüver, P. Introductionis in universam geographiam . . . libri vi
1629 Laet, J. de. Hispania (2)
1630 Laet, J. de. Beschrijvinghe van West-Indien
1631 Baerle, K. van. Poematum
1631 Heinsius, D. Histoire du siége de Bolduc

1631 Heinsius, D. Rerum ad Sylvam-Ducis . . . historia
1633 Grotius, H. De mari libero (2)
1633 Laet, J. de. Novus Orbis
1633 Spiegel, A. van de. Isagoges in rem herbariam
1637 Barclay, J. Euphormionis Lusinini . . . Satyricon
1637 Beverwijck, J. van. Idea medicinae veterum
1639 Camden, W. Rerum Anglicarum . . . annales
1640 Campanella, T. De monarchia Hispanica discursus (2)
1641 Clüver, P. Introductionis in universam geographiam . . . libri vi
1641 Laet, J. de. Portugallia

Geelkercken, Nicolaes van
1619 Spilbergen, J. van. Oost ende West-Indische spiegel (2)
1619 Spilbergen, J. van. Speculum Orientalis Occidentalisque Indiae navigationum (2)
1624 Wonderlicke avontuer

Guyot, Christoffel
1602 Langenes, B. Thrésor de chartes

Haack, François
1638 Bacon, F. Historia naturalis . . . de ventis
1641 Bacon, F. Sermones fideles
1642 Bacon, F. Historia regni Henrici septimi
1644 Bacon, F. Sermones fideles (2)
1645 Fernel, J. Universa medicina
1647 Bacon, F. Historia regni Henrici septimi (2)
1647 Bartholin, T. De luce animalium libri iii
1648 Bacon, F. Historia naturalis . . . de ventis (2)
1648 Bacon, F. Sylva sylvarum (2)
1648 Piso, W. Historia naturalis Brasiliae

Haestens, Hendrick van
1607 Blefken, D. Islandia
1610 Orlers, J. J. Beschrijvinghe . . . van alle de victorien
1612 Orlers, J. J. Description . . . de toutes de victoires

Heger, Frans
1638 Bacon, F. Historia naturalis . . . de ventis
1641 Bethune, P. de. Le conseiller d'estat
1642 Owen, J. Epigrammatum . . . libri decem
1645 Bethune, P. de. Le conseiller d'estat
1645 Moscherosch, J. M. Les visiones de don de Quevedo

Hoogenacker, Arent Corsen
1628 Gysius, J. De spieghel der Spaense tyrannye, 2de dl

Huybertszoon, Jan
1614 Grotius, H. Vrye zeevaert (3)

Leffen, Pieter
1649 Boxhorn, M. Z. De majestate regum principumque

López de Haro, David
1639 Bodecherus Banninghius, J. Epigrammata americana
1639 Slichtenhorst, A. van. Oratio de navigationibus
1643 Weidner, J. L. Hispanicae dominationis arcana
1645 Clüver, J. Historiarum mundi epitome
1649 Clüver, J. Historiarum mundi epitome

Maire, Jean
1617 Chronicon Hollandiae
1618 Cordus, V. Dispensatorium
1618 L'Obel, M. de. Pharmacopoeia Rondeletii
1624 Stevin, S. Le trouve-port
1627 Cordus, V. Dispensatorium
1627 Grotius, H. Sensus librorum sex
1628 Bruele, G. Praxis medicinae
1629 Grotius, H. De veritate religionis christianae
1629 Zacutus, A. De medicorum principum historia
1630 Respublica Hollandiae (3)
1633 Grotius, H. De veritate religionis christianae
1633 Reyd, E. van. Belgarum . . . annales
1635 Postel, G. De universitate libri duo
1636 Bacon, F. Historia vitae
1636 Clemens, V. Trinobantiados Augustae

1636 Postel, G. De cosmographica disciplina
1636 Vives, J. L. De disciplinis libri xii
1637 Bacon, F. Historia vitae
1639 Grotius, H. De veritate religionis christianae
1640 Grotius, H. De veritate religionis christianae
1644 Beverwijck, J. van. Autarcheia Bataviae
1647 Boodt, A. B. de. Gemmarum et lapidum historia
1647 Bruele, G. Praxis medicinae
1647 Plante, F. Mauritiados libri xii

Maire, Jean & Théodore
1636 Selden, J. Mare clausum

Marcus, Jacobus
1617 Barclay, J. Euphormionis Lusinini Satyricon
1619 Barclay, J. Euphormionis Lusinini Satyricon
1623 Barclay, J. Euphormionis Lusinini Satyricon
1628 Barclay, J. Euphormionis Lusinini . . . Satyricon
1628 Clüver, P. Introductionis in universam geographiam . . . libri vi
1637 Clüver, J. Historiarum totius mundi epitome
1640 Clüver, J. Historiarum totius mundi epitome
1641 Boccalini, T. Hundert ein und dreissig Relationes
1641 Clüver, J. Historiarum mundi epitome (2)

Moyaert, Franciscus
1642 Clüver, J. Historiarum totius mundi epitome
1645 Bacon, F. De augmentis scientiarum
1645 Magnus, O. Historiae septentrionalium gentium breviarium. Libri xxii
1649 Clüver, J. Historiarum mundi epitome

Orlers, Jan Janszn
1610 Orlers, J. J. Beschrijvinghe . . . van alle de victorien
1612 Orlers, J. J. Description . . . de toutes de victoires
1615 Orlers, J. J. Généalogie des illustres comtes de Nassau

ROTTERDAM
Printer unidentified
1615 Aventrote, J. Epistola...
ad... regem Hispaniarum
1616 Aventrote, J. Epistola...
ad... regem hispaniarum
1628 Wtenbogaert, J. Ondersoeck der Amsterdamsche requesten
1640 Journalier verhael... uit
Brasijl
1645 Cats, J. Silenus Alcibiadis
1650 Den ommeganck
Bastiaenszoon, Mathys, Widow of
1636 Paré, A. De chirurgie
Berewout, Jan Leendertszoon
1616 Novus orbis regionum. Novus orbis
Janszoon, Jacob
1630 Ghedenck-weerdich verhael
Leers, Arnout
1649 Sánchez, F. Tractatus philosophici
1650 Heurne, J. van. Praxis medicinae
Naeranus, Joannes
1647 Vondel, J. van den. Poesy
... Het tweede deel (2)
Nering, Abraham
1634 Joernael. ofte. Voyagie
vande Groenlants-vaerders
Pauwelszoon, Joris
1623 Chute, A. Een korte beschrijvinge van... tobacco
Sebastiani, Mathias
1626 A plaine and true relation
Verburch, Jacob
1650 Holland (Province). Staten.
Missive
Voortganck, Haest van, pseud.
1648 Spain. Treaties, etc., 1621–
1665. Articulen en conditien
van den eeuwigen vrede (3)
Waesberghe, Isaac van
1637 Schouten, W. C. Journael
1643 Schouten, W. C. Journael
1647 Bontekoe, W. Y. Journael
*****Waesberghe, Jan van**
1601 Noort, O. van. Beschryvinghe van de voyage
1601 Noort, O. van. Extract oft
Kort verhael
1602 Noort, O. van. Beschryvinghe van de voyage

1619 Ercilla y Zúñiga, A. de.
Historiale beschrijvinghe
1622 Usselinx, W. Korte onderrichtinghe
1636 Paré, A. De chirurgie
Waesberghe, Pieter van
1625 Heyns, Z. Emblemata
1627 Cats, J. Proteus ofte Minne-
beelden
Waesberghen, I. van. *See*
Waesberghe, Isaac van
Wagens, Matthys
1650? Great Britain. Laws, statutes, etc., 1649–1660. Een
acte, verbiedende den handel

SCHIEDAM
1647 Vondel, J. van den. Poesy.
See under Rotterdam—Naeranus, Joannes

THOLEN
Speckaert, Christoffel
1636 Proeve, over eenen Rypen-
raet

UTRECHT
Printer unidentified
1622 Scott, T. The Belgicke pismire (3)
1623 Scott, T. The high-waies of
God
1624 Scott, T. Symmachia: or, A
true-loves knot
1624 Scott, T. Vox populi. Or
News from Spaine
1624 Scott, T. Workes
Amelisszoon, Jan
1624 Scott, T. Politique redenen
1624 Wieroock-vath, of triumph-
liedt
Bilsteyn, Gillis
1647 Bontekoe, W. Y. Journael
Havick, Jan
1649 Amsterdam. Burgemeester. Copye van de resolutie
Herwijck, Abraham van
1624 Een clare ende waerachtighe beschrijvinghe
1624 Scott, T. Vox regis (2)
1624 Scott, T. Vox regis, of De
stemme des Conincks
1625 Scott, T. Vox Dei. Of De
stemme des Heeren
Hoogenhuysen, Dirk van
1644 Everard, G. De herba panacea

Levyn, Frans
1648? Coignet de la Thuillerie,
G. Aaloude heersch-en-oorlogs-sught
1648 Coignet de la Thuillerie, G.
Twee propositien (3)
Paddenburch, Amelis van
1650 Utrecht (Province). Laws,
statutes, etc. Ordonnan-
tie... op... tabacco
Passe, Crispin van de
1614 Passe, C. van de. Den blomhof
1615 Passe, C. van de. A garden
of flowers
1615? Passe, C. van de. Jardin
de fleurs
1620 Holland, H. Herōologia anglica
Roman, Aegidius
1642? Stratenus, G., praeses.
Disputationum medicarum
... secunda
Roover, Symon de
1649 Een brief uyt den Haegh
Roy, Salomon de
1615 Passe, C. van de. A garden
of flowers
Schellem, John, pseud.
1626 Scott, T. Sir Walter Rawleighs ghost. *See under* Great
Britain—London—Printer unidentified
Snellaert, Esdras Willemsen
1647 Bontekoe, W. Y. Journael
Snellaert, Esdras Willemsen, Widow of
1649 Bontekoe, W. Y. Journael
Vries, Lucas de
1649 Bontekoe, W. Y. Journael
1649 Noort, O. van. Wonderlijcke voyagie
Vries, Lucas Symonszoon de
1630 Waerdenburgh, D. van.
Copie vande missive
Waesbergen, Johannes van
1643 Hall, J. Mundus alter

VEERE
Valerius, Adrianus, Heirs of
1626 Valerius, A. Neder-
landtsche gedenck-clanck

VLISSINGEN. *See* Flushing

ZAANDAM
Willemszoon, Willem
1648 Bontekoe, W. Y. Journael

ZUTPHEN
Aelst, Andries Janszoon van
1621 Spilbergen, J. van. Oost ende West-Indische spieghel
1625 Baudart, W. Memoryen ofte Cort verhael. Pt 2
Janssen, A. *See* Aelst, Andries Janszoon van

ZWOLLE
Printer unidentified
1621 Du Bartas, G. de S., seigneur. Wercken

POLAND

BRZEG. *See* Germany—Brieg

CRACOW
Lob, Nicolaus
1606 Rivadeneira, P. de. Catalogus quorundam e Societate Jesu qui . . . sunt interfecti
Piotrkowczyk, Andrzey
1603 Torres Bollo, D. de. O rozszerzeniu wiary . . . w Americe
Skalskus, Bazyl
1613 Syreniusz Syrénski, S. Zielnik

DANZIG
Printer unidentified
1640 Opitz, M. Deutsche Poemata
Hünefeld, Andreas
1641 Opitz, M. Deutsche Poëmata

SZCZECIN. *See* Germany—Stettin

WROCŁAW. *See* Germany—Breslau

PORTUGAL

EVORA
Carvalho, Manoel
1625 Correa, J. de M. Relacam verdadeira

LISBON
Printer unidentified
1624? Restauracion de la Bahia
1625? Mascarenhas, A. Relação dos procedimentos
1626 Mascarenhas, A. Relacam dos procedimentos
1646? Vieira, A. Sermam, que pregou . . . Antonio Vieira
1647? Silva, A. T. da. Successo della guerra
1649 De Portogysen . . . buyrman. *See under* The Netherlands—The Hague—Printer unidentified
Alvarez, Antonio
1601 Teixeira Pinto, B. Naufragio que passou Jorge Dalbuquerque Coelho
1603 Martí, J. J. De la vida del picaro Guzman de Alfarache, 2a pte
1604 Amaral, M. E. do. Das batalhas do galeaom Sanctiago
1604 Amaral, M. E. do. Tratado das batalhas . . . do galeão Sanctiago
1605 Alemán, M. La vida de Guzman de Alfarache, 2a pte
1617 Cervantes Saavedra, M. de. Novelas exemplares
1619 Goes, D. de. Chronica do felicissimo rey Dom Emanuel
1622 Resende, G. de. Chronica . . . del rey Dom Joao II
1642 Andrade Leitão, F. de. Discurso politico
1642 Guerreiro, B. Gloriosa coroa d'esforçados religiosos
1642 Portugal. Treaties, etc., 1640–1656. Tregoas
1643 Vasconcellos, J. de. Restauração de Portugal prodigiosa
1649 Companhia geral para o estado do Brazil. Instituiçam
Alvarez, Domingo
1641 Montalvão, J. M., marquez de. Cartas
1641 Relaçam da aclamação
Alvarez, Francisco
1625 Guerreiro, B. Jornado dos vassalos
Alvarez, Vicente
1608 Figueiredo, M. de. Hydrographia
1608 González de Legaria, J. Aqui se contiene una obra nueva, graciosa
1612 Camões, L. de. Os Lusiadas
1614 Figueiredo, M. de. Hydrographia
1625 Figueiredo, M. de. Hidrographia
Anveres, Lourenço de
1641 Cristovão de Lisboa. Sermão
1641 Sala, G. Segredos publicos
1642 Andrade Leitão, F. de. Copia das proposições
1642 Madeira Arraes, D. Methodo de conhecer e curar o morbo gallico
1642 Mariz Carneiro, A. de. Regimento de pilotos
Craesbeeck, Lourenço
1633 Camões, L. de. Os Lusiadas
1637 Pinto de Moraes, J. Maravillas del Parnaso
Craesbeeck, Paolo
1625 Correa, J. de M. Relacam verdadeira
1641 Cristovão de Lisboa. Sermão da quarta domingo da quaresma
1641 Paes Viegas, A. Manifesto do Reino de Portugal
1644 Camões, L. de. Os Lusiadas
1645 Mello, F. M. de. Ecco polytico
1646 Góngora y Argote, L. de. Obras
1648 Calado, M. O valeroso Lucideno
1649 Braga, B. de. Sermão . . . na festa
1649 Braga, B. de. Sermão que prègou na sé da [Bahia]

Craesbeeck, Pedro
1602 Barco Centenera, M. del. Argentina y conquista del río de La Plata
1602 Torres, J. de. Philosophia moral
1603 Brito, B. de. Elogios
1604 Alemán, M. La vida de Guzman de Alfarache, 2a pte
1605 Alemán, M. La vida de Guzman de Alfarache, 2a pte
1605 Garcilaso de la Vega. La Florida
1606 Oliveira, S. d'. Arte de navegar
1609 Camões, L. de. Os Lusiadas
1609 Camões, L. de. Os Lusiadas
1609 Figueiredo, M. de. Roteiro e navegação

629

1609 Garcilaso de la Vega. Commentarios reales, 1a pte

1609 Guerreiro, F. Relaçam anual das cousas que fezeram os padres da Companhia de Jesus

1613 Camões, L. de. Os Lusiados (2)

1615 Losa, F. de. La vida, que hizo el siervo de Dios Gregorio Lopez

1615 Marcos da Lisboa. Chronicas da ordem dos Frades menores, pte 1a–3a

1618 Araujo, A. de. Catecismo na lingoa brasilica

1624 Coelho de Barbuda, L. Empresas militares de Lusitanos

1624 Coelho de Barbuda, L. Reyes de Portugal y empresas militares

1624 Guerreiro, B. Sermão que fez o padre Bartolameu Guerreiro

1625 Correa, J. de M. Relacam verdadeira

1625 Relaçam do dia em que as armadas

1626 Camões, L. de. Os Lusiadas

1628 Nájera, A. de. Navegacion especulativa

1631 Brito Lemos, J. de. Abecedario militar

1631 Camões, L. de. Os Lusiadas

1631 Céspedes y Meneses, G. de. Historia de D. Felippe el IIII

1631 Rezende, L. V. de. Contrato do pao Brasil

1632 Pinto Ribeiro, J. Discurso sobre os fidalgos

1640 Céspedes y Meneses, G. de. Historia del Rey Don Felipe Quarto

Craesbeeck Office

1650 Mello, F. M. de. Relaçam dos successos da armada

Estupiñán, Luis

1608 Mendes de Vasconcelos, L. Do sitio de Lisboa

Fernandes, Domingo

1609 Camões, L. de. Os Lusiadas (2)

1612 Camões, L. de. Os Lusiados

1613 Camões, L. de. Os Lusiados (2)

Godinho, Andre

1642 Andrade Leitão, F. de. Discurso politico

Gonçalvez, Antonio

1628 Barros, J. de. Asia

Jesuits of Brazil

1618 Araujo, A. de. Catecismo na lingoa brasilica

Lopes Rosa, Domingos

1641 Montalvão, J. M., marquez de. Cartas

1642 Carvalho, J. de. Relação verdadeira dos sucessos

1642 Relación de algunas perdidas

1646 Vieira, A. Sermam, que pregou . . . Antonio Vieira

Lopez, Estavão

1602 Avelar, A. do. Chronographia

Pinheiro, Mattheus

1625 Guerreiro, B. Jornado dos vassalos

Queiros, Lourenzo de

1641 Montalvão, J. M., marquez de. Carta

1641 Sala, G. Segredos publicos

Ramires, Pero

1603 Figueiredo, M. de. Chronographia

Ribeiro, Antonio

1601 Teixeira Pinto, B. Naufragio que passou Jorge Dalbuquerque Coelho

Rodríguez, Jorge

1601 Cortés, J. El curioso de varios secretos de naturaleza

1602 Avelar, A. do. Chronographia

1603 Figueiredo, M. de. Chronographia

1603 Martí, J. J. De la vida del picaro Guzman de Alfarache, 2a pte

1605 Guerreiro, F. Relaçam anual

1607 Resende, G. de. Choronica . . . do christianissimo . . . Joao o segundo

1617 Cervantes Saavedra, M. de. Don Quixote, 2a pte

1620 Sardinha Mimoso, J. Relacion de la real tragicomedia

1628 Barros, J. de. Asia

1631 Sousa de Macedo, A. de. Flores de España

1632 Figueiredo, M. de. Hidrographia

1632 Paulo do Rosario. Relacam breve

1641 Montalvão, J. M., marquez de. Carta

1641 Montalvão, J. M., marquez de. Segunda carta

1641 Relaçam da aclamação

Rodríguez, Matías

1630 Relaçam verdadeira, e breve da tomada da villa de Olinda

1631 Figueira, L. Relaçam de varios successos acontecidos no Maranham

Silva, Manuel da

1621 Figueira, L. Arte da lingua brasilica

1643 Lopes, F. Milagroso successo do Conde de Castel Milhor

Valle, Tomás do

1615 Marcos da Lisboa. Chronicas da ordem dos Frades menores, pte 1a–3a

Vinha, Geraldo da

1622 Camões, L. de. Lusiadum libri decem

1623 Cabeças, L. Historia de S. Domingos 1a pte

1624 Estaço da Silveira, S. Relação summaria das cousas do Maranhão

1625 Correa, S. Sermão

1625? Gaspar d'Asenção. Sermam que prego o padre

1625 Insigne victoria que el señor marques de Guadalcazar . . . ha alcançado

1626 Severim de Faria, M. Relaçam universal do que succedeo em Portugal

1627 Hurtado de Mendoza, D. Guerra de Granada

OPORTO

Rodriguez, Juan

1625 Correa, J. de M. Relacam verdadeira

SPAIN

ALCALÁ DE HENARES

Printer unidentified

1616? Carmelites. Chapter General. Constituciones

1622 Berettari, S. Vida del padre Joseph de Ancheta

1625 Alcalá Yáñez y Rivera, J. Alonso moço de muchos amos

1629 Nuevas ciertas y fidedignas de la vitoria

1630 Vega Carpio, L. F. de. Comedias, pte 20

1631 Cervantes Saavedra, M. de. Novelas exemplares

1632 Relacion de la jornada

1633 Relacion del sucesso

Manescal, M. *See* Menescal, Miguel

Margarit, Jerónimo

1608 Botero, G. Historia

1610 Cortés, J. Phisonomia

1614 Cortés, J. Phisonomia

1618 Espinel, V. Relaciones de la vida del escudero Marcos de Obregon

1621 Torquemada, A. de. Jardin de flores curiosas

1630 Vega Carpio, L. F. de. Arcadia

1632 Castillo Solórzano, A. de. La niña de los embustes

Matevad, Sebastián

1604 Botero, G. Theatro . . . del mundo

1605 Botero, G. Theatro . . . del mundo

1609 Cabredo, R. de. Copia di una carta

1610 Dessi, J. La divina semana

1617 Cervantes Saavedra, M. de. Don Quixote, 2a pte

Matevad, Sebastián & Jaume

1625 Spain. Treaties, etc., 1621–1665. Copia de las cartas

1628 Amatus Lusitanus. Curationum medicinalium centuriae septem

1640 Pinto de Moraes, J. Maravillas del Parnaso

1640 Relacion muy verdadera

1648 Amatus Lusitanus. Curationum medicinalium centuriae septem

Menescal, Miguel

1604 Vega Carpio, L. F. de. La hermosura de Angelica

1605 Alemán, M. La vida de Guzman de Alfarache, 2a pte

1615 Valderrama, P. de. Teatro de las religiones

1625 Alcalá Yáñez y Rivera, J. Alonso moço de muchos amos

Nogués, Gabriel

1641 Miguel de la Purificación. Vida evangelica

1644 Romance en alabansa del tabaco

Prats, Jusepe

1640 Pinto de Moraes, J. Maravillas del Parnaso

Ribera, Antich

1602 Martí, J. J. Guzman de Alfarach, 2a pte

Romeu, Jaime

1639 Breve, y ajustada relacion

Sepera, Juan

1632 Castillo Solórzano, A. de. La niña de los embustes

Simón, Juan

1602 Martí, J. J. Guzman de Alfarach, 2a pte

Vives, Rafael

1617 Cervantes Saavedra, M. de. Don Quixote, 2a pte

1630 Vega Carpio, L. F. de. Comedias, pte 20

BURGOS

Cañas, Sebastián de

1603 Botero, G. Razon d'estado

Gómez de Valdivielso, Pedro

1619 Alemán, M. Guzman de Alfarache, 1a–2a pte

1637 Villa, E. de. Ramillete de plantas

1646 Villa, E. de. Ramillete de plantas

Pérez, Diego

1602 Torres, J. de. Philosophia moral

Varesio, Juan Baptista

1602 Torres, J. de. Philosophia moral

1619 Alemán, M. Guzman de Alfarache, 1a–2a pte

CADIZ

Printer unidentified

1625 Relacion. verdadera, de la grandiosa vitoria

Borja, Juan de

1620 Vázquez de Serna, J. Libro intitulado Reduciones de oro

1622 Castillo, J. del. Pharmacopoea, universa medicamenta

1625 Rodríguez de Burgos, B. Relacion de la jornada del Brasil

1626 Vega Carpio, L. F. de. Arcadia

1629 Vega Carpio, L. F. de. Arcadia

Hidalgo, Clemente

1610 Suárez de Salazar, J. B. Grandezas y antiguedades

Vázquez de Serna, Juan

1620 Vazquez de Serna, J. Libro intitulado Reduciones de oro

Velazco, Francisco Juan de

1648 Palma Fajardo, F. de. Sermon

Vezino, Gaspar

1625 Toledo Osorio y Mendoza, F. de. Relacion del sucesso del armada

1626 Ercilla y Zúñiga, A. de. La Araucana, Ptes 1a–3a

CÓRDOBA

Printer unidentified

1601 Cortés, J. Libro de phisonomia

Barrera, Andrés de, Widow of

1616 Garcilaso de la Vega. Historia general del Peru

1617 Garcilaso de la Vega. Historia general del Peru

Cea Tesa, Salvador de

1620 Castro, J. de. Historia de las virtudes . . . del tabaco

1634 Leiva y Aguilar, F. de. Desengaño contra el mal uso del tabaco

1646 Alcázar y Zúñiga, J. de. Medios politicos

CUENCA

Bodán, Cornelio

1602 Nueva instruction

Iglesia, Domingo de la

1627 Simón, P. Noticias historiales de las conquistas

1637 Simón, P. Noticias historiales de las conquistas

Viader, Salvador de

1621 Porreño, B. Dichos y hechos

1628 Porreño, B. Dichos y hechos

GERONA
Garrich, Gaspar
1622 Botero, G. Descripcion
. . . del mundo

GRANADA
Printer unidentified
1603? Baño, P. de. Yo . . . doy fé
y verdadero testimonio
1648 Carta de aviso de la
muerte . . . del padre Alonso
de Medrano
Alvarez, Vicente
1646 Sánchez de Espejo, A. Discurso político
Castello, Juan
1612 Gallucci, G. P. Theatro del
mundo
1616 Gallucci, G. P. Theatro
. . . del mundo
Fernández, Martin
1630 Fernández de Santiestevan,
B. Relacion verdadera . . . de
la flota
Fernández Zambrano, Martin
1630 Este es la verdaderissima relacion de la feliz
vitoria
1631 Relacion del lastisomo incendio
Lorenzana, Bartolomé de
1630 Relacion verdadera de la
grandiosa vitoria
1630 Toledo Osorio y Mendoza,
F. de. Relacion . . . de lo sucedido a la armada
Múñoz, Sebastian
1606 Gallucci, G. P. Theatro del
mundo
1611 Gallucci, G. P. Theatro del
mundo
1612 Gallucci, G. P. Theatro del
mundo
1614 Gallucci, G. P. Theatro
. . . del mundo
1616 Gallucci, G. P. Theatro
. . . del mundo
1617 Gallucci, G. P. Theatro
. . . del mundo

HUESCA
Blusson, Pedro
1622 Carrillo, M. Annales
Valdivielso, Juan, Widow of
1622 Carrillo, M. Annales

JAEN
Cuesta, Pedro de la
1628 Ordóñez de Ceballos, P.
Tratado de los relaciones

JEREZ DE LA FRONTERA
Printer unidentified
1625 Gaitan de Torres, M.
Reglas par el govierno
Rey, Fernando
1632 Vera relacion de la famosa
vitoria

LÉRIDA
Margarit, Jerónimo
1612 Vega Carpio, L. F. de. Arcadia
Menescal, Luis
1612 Vega Carpio, L. F. de. Arcadia
1614 Granado, D. Libro del arte
de cozina
Menescal, Miguel
1612 Vega Carpio, L. F. de. Arcadia

MADRID
Printer unidentified
1601? Spain. Sovereigns, etc.,
1598–1621. Lo que por mi
mandado del rey nuestro
señor se assienta
1603 Spain. Sovereigns, etc.,
1598–1621. Instrucion para el
virrey del Piru
1603 Spain. Sovereigns, etc.,
1598–1621. El Rey. Lo que por
mi mandado se assienta, y concierta con Juan Nuñez Correa
1604? Eliseo, Father. Aviendo
representado el conde de
Monterey . . . los agravios
1604 Monsalve, M. de. Reducion
universal de todo el Piru
1604 Spain. Consejo de las Indias. Interrogatorio para todas
la ciudades
1605? Spain. Sovereigns, etc.,
1598–1621. La orden e in-
struccion
1605? Torres, M. de. El licendiado . . . contra Doña Francisca Colon
1606 Relacion de los sucesos que
tuvo Don Luis Fajardo
1606? Rodríguez de Robles, A.
Señor. Antonio de Rodriguez

de Robles dize, que quando la
Nueva España se gano . . . .
1606? Rodríguez de Robles, A.
Señor. Antonio Rodriguez de
Robles dize, que ahora quar-
enta y cinquanta años . . . .
1606? Rodríguez de Robles, A.
Señor. Antonio Rodriguez de
Robles dize, que assi como los
mineros sacan la plata . . . .
1606? Rodríguez de Robles, A.
Señor. Antonio Rodriguez de
Robles dize, que aunque de algunos años a esta parte . . . .
1606? Rodríguez de Robles, A.
Señor. Antonio Rodriguez de
Robles dize, que como a V.
Magestad . . . es notorio
1606? Rodríguez de Robles, A.
Señor. Antonio Rodriguez de
Robles dize, que de 9. años
. . . han residido
1606? Spain. Sovereigns, etc.,
1598–1621. El Rey [14 Dec.
1606]
1607? Baeza, P. de. Este memorial es traslado
1607? Baeza, P. de. Traslado del
memorial
1607? González de Nájera. A. El
quinto, y sexto punto de la relacion
1607 Spain. Consejo de las Indias. Memorial del pleyto
1608? Avendaño y Villela, P.
Señor. Quien considerare la
opulencia
1608? Catholic Church. Commisarius Generalis Cruciatae. Instruccion y forma
1608? Colón y Pravia, F., plaintiff. Allegacion de derecho
1608? Esquibel, J. de. Copia de
una carta
1608 Lemos, P. F. de Castro,
conde de. Relacion de la provincia de los Quixos
1609? Spain. Laws, statutes, etc.,
1598–1621. Este en em traslado bien y fielmente sacado
1609 Spain. Laws, statutes, etc.,
1598–1621. Instrucion de la
forma
1609 Spain. Laws, statutes, etc.,
1598–1621. Lo que se ordena
de nuevo

1609 Spain. Laws, statutes, etc., 1598–1621. El Rey. Marques de Montes Claros

1609 Spain. Sovereigns, etc., 1598–1621. El Rey [26 May 1609] (2 differing memorials)

1609? Valdivia, L. de. Copia de una carta

1609? Valdivia, L. de. Señor. El Padre . . . dize: que el Virrey de Pirù ha escrito

1610? Queiros, P. F. de. Señor . . . con este son ocho los memoriales

1610? Sandoval, F. de. Advertencia en fabor . . . del arbitrio

1610? Sandoval, F. de. Señor. Por aver entendido quan del servicio

1610? Sandoval, F. de. Señor. Si conviniere al servicio de V.M.

1610? Spain. Consejo de las Indias. El fiscal con doña Francisca Colon de Toledo

1610? Spain. Consejo de las Indias. Memorial del pleyto que tratan . . . doña Francisca Colon de Toledo

1610? Spain. Laws, statutes, etc., 1598–1621. Este es un traslado bien y fielmente sacado

1610? Valdivia, L. de. Señor. El padre . . . digo, que siendo V.M. informado

1611? Duarte Navarro, ——. El almirante don Fernando Martinez de Leyva

1611? Spain. Consejo de las Indias. Sentencias de revista

1612? Núñez Correa, J. Resolucion y resumen del estado

1612? Sologuren, J. de. Señor. Diferentes ministros

1612? Sologuren, J. de. Señor. Los sueldos

1612? Urdiñola, F. de. Francisco de Urdinola, governador . . . de la Nueva Vizcaya

1612? Villagrá, G. P. de. El capitan . . . para justificacion de las muertes (2)

1613 Potosí, Bolivia. Señor. Cinco cosas

1613 Spain. Sovereigns, etc., 1598–1621. Cedula

1613 Villerias, M. de. El capitan Mateo de Villerias vezino de Mexico

1614 Oré, L. J. de. Relacion de la vida . . . del venerable padre f. Francisco Solano

1614 Por los hijos, y nietos de conquistadores

1614? Sosa, P. de. Señor. Fray Pedro de Sossa . . . dize, que el dicho reyno le embia a dar quenta

1615? Asiento que se tomò con Antonio Fernandez Delbas

1615? González de Azevedo, J. Señor. El capitan Iuan Goncalez de Azevedo

1615? González de Azevedo, J. Señor. El capitan Juan Gonçalez de Azevedo, por lo que toca al servicio de Dios

1615? Guerrero, M. Por los herederos

1615? Sobrino, G. Señor, El padre Gaspar Sobrino

1615? Spain. Sovereigns, etc., 1598–1621. Cedula

1615? Valdivia, L. de. Relacion de lo que sucedio en el reyno de Chile

1615? Vaz Coutinho, G. Copia de la carta

1615? Villagrá, G. P. de. Servicios

1616? Carrasco del Saz, F. Initium a Domino

1616? Preguntas que se propusieron al maese de campo

1616? Sosa, P. de. Memorial del peligroso estado . . . de Chile

1616? Sosa, P. de. Señor. Fray Pedro de Sosa . . . Dize, que ha hecho quanto ha sido de su parte

1616 Spain. Laws, statutes, etc., 1598–1621. El Rey. Por quanto por cedula mia fecha a dos de Otubre del año passado . . . .

1616? Villagrá, G. P. de. El capitan Gaspar de Villagra, para que su Magestad le haga merced

1617? Figueroa, F. de. Señor. El padre Francisco de Figueroa

1617? Figueroa, F. de. Señor. Francisco de Figueroa de la Compañia de Jesus

1617? Ibarra Gueztaraen, J. de. Por la villa imperial de Potossi

1617 Ibarra Gueztaraen, J. de. Por la villa imperial de Potossi

1617? Ibarra Gueztaraen, J. de. Señor. Cinco cosas

1617? Ibarra Gueztaraen, J. de. Señor. De parte de la villa imperial de Potosi

1617 Ibarra Gueztaraen, J. de. Señor. El licenciado Juan de Ybarra

1617 Ibarra Gueztaraen, J. de. Suma de lo que el licenciado . . . pide

1617? Sosa, P. de. Señor. Fray Pedro de Sosa . . . dize . . .

1618? Cardona, T. de. Señor. El capitan Tomas de Cardona

1618? Ibarra Gueztaraen, J. de. Señor. A nueve cosas que supliquè

1618? Ibarra Gueztaraen, J. de. Señor. De parte de la villa imperial de Potosi

1618? Ibarra Gueztaraen, J. de. Señor. En el memorial que presento en este Real Consejo

1618? Spain. Consejo de las Indias. Assientos, y capitulacion

1618 Spain. Laws, statutes, etc., 1598–1621. El Rey. Por quanto la experiencia . . . .

1619 Ortiz de Cervantes, J. Memorial

162–? Flores de León, D. Señor. El maestre de campo

162–? Garavito, G. Señor. Geronimo Garavito . . . Dize, que tiene suplicado a V.M. . . . .

162–? Gaytán de Torres, M. Que se dé diferente modo al govierno de la Indias

1620? Bogotá. Por parte de las ciudades Santa Fé, y Cartagena

1620? Cardona, T. de. Señor. Tomas de Cardona . . . presento . . . la proposicion siguente

1620? Cartagena, Colombia. Por parte de las ciudades de Cartagena, y santa Fé (2)

1624? Carrillo Altamirano, F. A. Señor. El doctor

1624 Carrillo de Mendoza y Pimentel, D. Relacion del estado

1624 Catholic Church in the West Indies. Los arçobispos y obispos

1624? Lima. Universidad de San Marcos. Prologo de las constituciones

1624 Relacion sumaria . . . del tumulto . . . en Mexico

1625? Aguilera, C. de. El presentado fray Christoval de Aguilera

1625? Benítez Negrete, S. Señor. El aver entrado en estos reynos de España

1625? Cartagena, Colombia (Province). A dos cosas se reduze la pretension de Cartagena

1625 Casos notables, sucedidos en las costas de la ciudad de Lima

1625 Cortes de Monroy, J. Señor. Aviendo visto, y considerado las tres dudas

1625? Fernández Pereira, R. Daños certissimos

1625? Frias, M. de. El capitan Manuel de Frias

1625? Frias, M. de. Señor. El capitan Manuel de Frias

1625? León Pinelo, A. R. de. Libros reales de govierno

1625? León Pinelo, A. R. de. Por Diego de Vega

1625? Lo que sacara de frutos del Rio de la Plata

1625? Moscoso y de Córdoba, C. de. Discurso juridico

1625 Pérez de Porres, D. A Melchor de Castro Macedo

1625 Recio de León, J. Relation de los servicios

1625? Recio de León, J. Señor. El maesse de campo

1625? Recio de León, J. Señor. Juan Recio de Leon

1625 Rodríguez Bustamante, S. Sebastian Rodriguez Bustamante

1625? Romero, G. Señor. Gonzalo Remero

1625? Santander, J. de. Señor. Fray Juan de Santander

1625? Spain. Sovereigns, etc., 1621–1665 . . . addressee. Señor. Un vasallo de V. Magestad

1625 Toledo Osorio y Mendoza, F. de. Relacion del sucesso

1625? Varaona, S. de. Carta

1625? Vázquez de Cisneros, A. El doctor

1625? Vázquez de Espinosa, A. Señor. El maestro Fr. Antonio Basquez Despinosa

1625? Verdadera relacion

1625 Vergara Gaviria, D. de. Nulidades expresas

1626 Catholic Church. Commisarius Generalis Cruciatae. Instrucción sobre la predicación

1626 Estaço da Silveira, S. El capitan

1626 Fernández Navarrete, P. Conservacion de monarquias

1626 Ibarra Gueztaraen, J. de. Señor. El licenciado Juan de Ybarra

1626? Pérez de Montalván, J. [La monja alferez]

1626? Recio de León, J. Peligros del dilitado camino

1626 Recio de León, J. Señor. El maesse de campo . . . dize, que la riqueza . . . .

1626? Recio de León, J. Señor. El maesse de campo . . . propone

1626? Recio de León, J. Señor. Juan Recio de Leon, masse de campo

1626? Recio de Léon, J. Señor. Quando el nuevo camino no fuera tan rico provechoso

1626? Recio de León, J. Señor. Relacion

1626? Recio de León, J. Los servicios

1626 Spain. Laws, statutes, etc., 1598–1621. Instrucción

1627? Araujo, L. de. Relacion de las cosas que sucidieron

1627 Fernández Manjon, L. Señor. Lucas Fernandez Manjon

1627 Recio de León, J. Señor. El maestro de campo Juan Recio de Leon

1627? Vesga, M. de. Señor. El capitan y almirante Mateo de Vesga

1628 Cevicos, J. Discurso . . . Sobre una carta

1628 Molina, C. de. Señor. Christoval de Molina

1628 Molina, C. de. Señor. Cristoval de Molina

1628? Olmo, ———. Por el licenciado Don Sebastian Zambrana de Villalobos

1629? Avellaneda Manrique, J. de. Memorial de la culpa

1629? Cargo de la culpa

1629? Ferrufiño, J. B. Relacion del martirio

1629 Hevia Bolaños, J. de. Curia filipica

1629 Molina, C. de. Señor. Cristoval de Molina

163–? Garavito, G. Cuenta que Geronimo Garavito . . . ha hecho de la mucha plata

163–? Garavito, G. Señor. Aviendo los Españoles descubierto los dilatados reynos

163–? Garavito, G. Señor. Geronimo Garabito . . . dize, que ha tenido noticia que el Arçobispo de Santa Cruz ha dada un memorial

163–? Garavito, G. Señor. Geronimo Garavito . . . Digo, que tengo presentados muchos memoriales

163–? Garavito, G. Señor. Gerónimo Garavito . . . dize: que aviendo presentado muchos memoriales . . . .

163–? Garavito, G. Señor. Geronimo Garavito . . . dize: Que ha mas de 5. años

163–? Garavito, G. Señor. Geronimo Garavito en nombre de don Juan de Lizaraçu (2 differing memorials)

163–? Garavito, G. Señor. Geronimo Garavito en nombre del presidente

163–? Garavito, G. Señor. Geronymo Garavito

163–? Moscoso y de Córdoba, C. de. El licenciado . . . Con el duque del Infantado

163–? Relacion del nuevo descubrimiento de las minas

1638 García de Zurita, A. Por la iglesia

1638 Hurtado de Mendoza, L. Memorial

1638 León Pinelo, A. R. de. Relacion . . . sobre la pacificacion

1638? Mendoça, L. de., Bp. Señor. El prelado del Rio de Janeiro

1638 Pax Christi. En esta referire a V.R. las nuevas

1638? Porter y Casanate, P. Señor. El capitan Don Pedro Porter y Cassanate

1638? Relacion de los muertos

1638 Sumario, y compendio de lo sucedido en España

1639? Barnuevo, R. Señor. Rodrigo Barnueuo de la compañia de Jesus

1639 Bustamante y Loyola, S. de. Señor. El licenciado

1639? González de Mendoza, P. El licenciado Don Pedro Gonçalez de Mendoça

1639? Paredes, A. de. Señor. Entre diversos memoriales

1639 Ruiz de Montoya, A. Haseme mandado, que assi como represente

1639 Ruiz de Montoya, A. Señor. Antonio Ruiz de Montoya

1639 Salinas y Córdova, B. de. Memorial

1639? Spain. Consejo de las Indias. Culpa que resulta

1639 Spain. Consejo de las Indias. Memorial del pleyto

1639 Spain. Laws, statutes, etc., 1621–1665. Capitulaciones

1639? Vergara Gaviria, D. de. Adicion a la informacion

1639? Vergara Gaviria, D. de. Por Diego de Vergara Gaviria

1639 Vitoria Baraona, F. de. El capitan

164–? Allo, P. de. Señor. El desseo del servicio

164–? Apuntamientos para mejor inteligencia

164–? Espinosa Montero, A. de. Señor. El doctor

164–? Garavito, G. Señor. Geronimo Garavito . . . dize: Que a los 17. de mayo . . . .

164–? Garavito, G. Señor. Geronimo Garavito . . . dize: Que

nuevo represento a V.M. los dos capitulos

164–? Garavito, G. Señor. Geronimo Garavito . . . en nombre de los curas

164–? Grau y Monfalcón, J. Señor. Don Juan Grau y Monfalcon

164–? Pérez Manrique de Lara, D. Señor. Don Dionisio Perez Manrique

164–? Tapia de Vargas, J. Por D. Juan Tapia de Vargas

164–? Vaz, C. Fray Cristobal Vaz

1640? Abreu y Figueroa, F. de. Adiciones

1640? Abreu y Figueroa, F. de. Excmo Señor. El maestro

1640? Abreu y Figueroa, F. de. Señor. El maestro . . . dize: Que despues de aver . . . representado el notorio

1640 Abreu y Figueroa, F. de. Señor. El maestro . . . sobre lo que tiene representado a V. Magestad

1640? Acuña, C. de. Señor. Christoval de Acuña

1640? Cianca, A. de. Discourso breve

1640? Declaracion del valor justo

1640 Elías, J. Señor. Un libelo infamatorio

1640? Figueroa, A. de. Don Antonio de Figueroa

1640 Garavito, G. Geronimo Garavito . . . dize, que teniendo noticia . . . .

1640 Garavito, G. Señor. Geronimo Garavito . . . dize: Que alos 3. de enero . . . .

1640? González de Ribero, B. Por Andres de Zavala

1640 Grau y Monfalcón, J. Justificacion

1640? Jesuits. Servicios

1640? López de Guitian Sotomayor, D. Señor. El capitan

1640? Malvezzi, V. Successi principali (2)

1640 Mañozca y Zamora, J. de. Memorial

1640? Mexico (City). Consulado. Señor. El Prior y consules de la Universidad

1640? Nueva relacion

1640? Ocampo, M. de. Señor. El capitan Martin de Ocampo

1640? Pizarro y Orellana, F. Discurso

1640? Porter y Casanate, P. de. Relacion

1640? Prado, E. de. Por Francisco Nuñez Melian

1640? Spain. Sovereigns, etc., 1621–1665 . . . addressee. Señor. Muy notorio es à V. Magestad

1641 Abreu y Figueroa, F. de. El maestro fray Fernando de Abreu y Figueroa

1641 Garavito, G. Señor. Geronimo Garavito . . . Dize, que desde los 12. . . . de noviembre . . . .

1641? Grau y Monfalcón, J. Memorial

1641 Méndez, J. F. Panegyrico funeral

1641 Relacion verdadera

1641? Velasco, P. de. Señor. Pedro de Valasco

1642? Eras Pantoja, N. Señor. Don Nicolas Eras Pantoja

1642? González, J. El licenciado

1642? Maldonado, J. Relacion del primer descubrimiento

1642 Marín de Armendariz, P. Condiciones

1642? Merlo de la Fuente, A. Señor. Por dos informaciones de oficio

1642 Ortiz de Salcedo, F. Curia eclesiastica

1642 Pacheco Ossorio, R. Por el marques de Zerralvo

1642? Palafox y Mendoza, J. de. Señor. Aviendo informado . . . .

1642? Ruiz de Montoya, A. Señor: Antonio Ruiz de Montoya

1643? Abreu y Figueroa, F. de. Señor. El maestro fr. Fernando de Abreu y Figueroa

1643 Abreu y Figueroa, F. de. Sumario

1643? Benavides y de la Cueva, D. Señor. El conde de Santistevan

1643? Cañizares, M. de. El maestro fr. Martin de Cañizares

1639 Camões, L. de. Lusiadas
1648 Quevedo y Villegas,
    F. G. de. Enseñança entrete-
    nida
1648 Quevedo y Villegas,
    F. G. de. El parnasso español
1649 Mendes Silva, R. Epitome
**Confraternity of Souls in Pur-
gatory of the Parish of Santiago in Madrid**
1628 Barbón y Castañeda, G.
    Provechosos adbitrios
**Correa de Montenegro, Fer-
nando**
1620 Aramburu, G. Memorial
1620 Spain. Consejo de las In-
    dias. Assiento, y capitulacion
1620 Vega Carpio, L. F. de. Ar-
    cadia
1621 Nodal, B. G. de. Relacion
    del viaje
1621 Vargas Machuca, B. de.
    Compendio y doctrina nueva
    de la gineta
**Correa de Montenegro, Fer-
nando, Widow of**
1621 Silva, J. de. Advertencias
    importantes
1622 Murcia de la Llana, F. Can-
    ciones lugubres
Courbes, Gieronymo de
1619 Hevia Bolanos, J. de. La-
    berinto de comercio
Cuesta, Juan de la
1604 Gracián, J. Lampara encen-
    dida
1604 Romancero general
1605 Oña, P. de. Arauco do-
    mado
1605 Vega Carpio, L. F. de. Ar-
    cadia
1605 Vega Carpio, L. F. de. La
    hermosura de Angelica
1606 García de Céspedes, A. Re-
    gimiento de navegacion
1608 Suárez de Argüelo, F.
    Ephemerides generales
1610 Ercilla y Zúñiga, A. de. La
    Araucana, Ptes 1a–3a
1613 Cervantes Saavedra, M. de.
    Novelas exemplares
1613 Illescas, G. de. Historia
    pontifical, 2a pte
1614 Cervantes Saavedra, M. de.
    Novelas exemplares
1614 Romancero general

1615 Cervantes Saavedra, M. de.
    Don Quixote, 2a pte
1617 Cervantes Saavedra, M. de.
    Novelas exemplares
1617 Mariana, J. de. Historia
    general
1618 Espinel, V. Relaciones de
    la vida del escudero Marcos de
    Obregon
1622 Illescas, G. de. Historia
    pontifical, 2a pte
Delgado, Cosme, Widow of
1620 Caro de Torres, F. Rela-
    cion
1621 Viage, y sucesso de los ca-
    ravelones
1623 Enríquez, J. Relacion de las
    exequias
Delgado, Juan
1624 Herrera y Tordesillas,
    A. de. Comentarios
1625 Remón, A. Relacion de
    como martirizaron
Díaz de la Carrera, Diego
1636 Góngora y Argote, Luis de.
    Las obras
1638 Relacion verdadera de la
    refriega
1639 Cepeda, F. de. Señor. Con
    orden que he tenido del mar-
    quès de Cadereyte
1639 Pizarro y Orellana, F. Va-
    rones ilustres del Nuevo
    mundo
1640 Ruiz de Montoya, A. Cate-
    cismo
1642 Clément, C. Tabla chro-
    nologica de los descubrimien-
    tos
1642 Clément, C. Tabla cronolo-
    gica del govierno
1642 Mela, P. La geographia
1643 Clément, C. Tabla chro-
    nologica de los descubrimien-
    tos
1643 Clément, C. Tablas chro-
    nologicas
1644 Clément, C. Tablas chro-
    nologicas
1645 Góngora y Argote, L. de.
    Obras
1646 Alcázar y Zúñiga, J. de.
    Medios politicos
1646 Campuzano, B. Planeta
    catholico
1648 González Chaparro, J.
    Carta

1648 Quevedo y Villegas,
    F. G. de. Enseñança entrete-
    nida
1648 Quevedo y Villegas,
    F. G. de. El parnasso español
1648 Solórzano Pereira, J. de.
    Politica indiana
1649 González Dávila, G. Teatro
    eclesiastico
1650 León Pinelo, A. R. de. Ora-
    cion panegirica
1650 Quevedo y Villegas,
    F. G. de. Parnasso español
1650 Quevedo y Villegas,
    F. G. de. Todas las obras
Duplastre, Antonio
1638 Medina de las Torres,
    G. de Guzman y Acevedo,
    duque de. Relacion
1639 Múñoz, B. Relacion ver-
    dadera, y carta nueva
1640 Relacion nueva y verdadera
1641 Enrique, P. Relacion ver-
    dadera . . . de los sucessos
Espino, Francisco de
1601 Alemán, M. Guzman de Al-
    farache, 1a pte
Falorsí, Aníbal
1615 Barros, J. de. Asia. 4a de-
    cada
Flamenco, Diego
1619 Vargas Machuca, B. de.
    Teorica y exercicios de la
    gineta
1622 Belmonte y Bermúdez,
    L. de. Algunas hazañas de las
    muchas
1624 Valbuena, B. de. El Ber-
    nardo, o Victoria de Ronces-
    valles
1626 Calvo, J. Cirugia universal,
    1a–2a pte
Flamenco, Juan
1601 Herrera y Tordesillas,
    A. de. Descripcion de las In-
    dias Occidentales
1601 Herrera y Tordesillas,
    A. de. Historia general
1603 Martí, J. J. Guzman de Al-
    farache, 2a pte
1605 José de Sigüenza. Historia
    de la orden de San Geronimo,
    pte 3a
1612 Salazar, P. de. Coronica
García, Francisco. *See* García de
    Arroyo, Francisco

1601 Herrera y Tordesillas, A. de. Historia general

1605 José de Sigüenza. Historia de la orden de San Geronimo, pte 3a

1610 Pérez de Lara, A. Compendio

1612 Herrera y Tordesillas, A. de. Tratado . . . de Aragón (2)

1612 Salazar, P. de. Coronica

1613 Illescas, G. de. Historia pontifical, 2a pte

1613 Suárez de Figueroa, C. Hechos de Don Garcia Hurtado de Mendoza

1615 Barros, J. de. Asia. 4a decada

1615 Juan de Santa María. Chronica de la provincia de San Joseph

1616 Suárez de Figueroa, C. Hechos de Don Garcia Hurtado de Mendoça

1617 Catholic church. Liturgy and ritual. Ritual. Brevis forma

1624 Lima. Universidad de San Marcos. Constituciones

1626 Fernández Navarrete, P. Conservacion de monarquias

1626 Larrinaga Salazar, J. de. Memorial discursivo

1630 Benavides, A. de. Memorial

1630 Nieremberg, J. E. Curiosa filosofia

1631 León, L. P. de. Obras proprias

1632 Díaz del Castillo, B. Historia verdadera . . . de la Nueva-España

1632? Díaz del Castillo, B. Historia verdadera . . . de la Nueva-España

1632 Ercilla y Zúñiga, A. de. Araucana

1632 Lugo y Dávila, F. de. Desenganos

1632 Nieremberg, J. E. Curiosa filosofia

1633 Fernández de Bivero, J. Señor. Juan Fernandez de Bivero

1633 Frias, P. de. Relacion del martirio

1633 Fuente, G. de la. Historia del capitulo general

1633 Góngora y Argote, L. de. Todas las obras

1633 Prado Beltran, B. de. Razonamiento panegyrico

1633 Remón, A. Historia general de la Orden

1634 Gongora y Argote, L. de. Todas las obras

1634 Nieremberg, J. E. Curiosa filosofia

1635 Téllez, G. Deleytar aprovechando

1636 Góngora y Argote, L. de. Las obras

1636 Góngora y Argote, L. de. Soledades

1637 Grau y Monfalcón, J. Memorial

1637 Menéndez Silva, R. Catalogo real

1639 Ruiz de Montoya, A. Conquista espiritual

1639 Spain. Laws, statutes, etc., 1621–1665. Prematica

1640 Barba, A. A. Arte de los metales

1640 Inquisition. Peru. Auto de la fe

1640 Malvezzi, V. La libra de Grivilio Vezzalmi

1640 Malvezzi, V. Sucesos principales . . . de España

1641 Acuña, C. de. Nuevo descubrimiento

1641 Alemán, M. Guzman de Alfarache, 1a–2a pte

1642 Losa, F. de. Vida que el siervo de Dios Gregorio Lopez hizo

1643 Córdoba y Salinas, D. de. Vida, virtudes, y milagros del apostal del Peru

1643 Nieremberg, J. E. Curiosa y occulta filosofia

1644 Palma y Freitas, L. de la. Por las religiones de Santo Domingo

1645 Romances varios

1646 Catholic church. Liturgy and ritual. Ritual. Brevis forma

1647 Cervantes Saavedra, M. de. Don Quixote

1647 Escalona y Agüero, G. de. Arcae Limensis gazophilatium regium, Perubicum

1647 Tesillo, S. de. Guerra de Chile

1648 Romances varios

Lasso, Pedro

1642 Mela, P. La geographia

1645 Góngora y Argote, L. de. Obras

León, Gabriel de

1650 Mariana, J. de. Historia general

Logroño, Diego

1626 Calvo, J. Cirugia universal, 1a–2a pte

1635 Vega Carpio, L. F. de. Comedias, pte 21

López, Baptista

1603 Boaistuau, P. Historias prodigiosas

López, Francisco

1603 Martí, J. J. Guzman de Alfarache, 2a pte

1604 Romancero general

1605 Oña, P. de. Arauco domado

López, Manuel

1635 Téllez, G. Comedias, 4a pte

1645 Hurtado, T. Chocolate y tabaco

Lorenzo, Roberto

1645 Vega Carpio, L. F. de. Arcadia

Madrigal, Pedro

1601 Cortés, J. Libro de phisonomia

1602 Vega Carpio, L. F. de. Arcadia

1602 Vega Carpio, L. F. de. La hermosura de Angelica

1603 Vega Carpio, L. F. de. Arcadia (2)

Maroto, Francisco

1642 Ovalle, A. de. Relacion verdadera de las pazes

Martín, Alonso

1608 Acosta, J. de. Historia natural

1608 Valbuena, B. de. Siglo de oro

1609 Granado, D. Libro del arte de cozina

1609 Leonardo y Argensola, B. J. Conquista de las islas Malucas

1610? Spain. Consejo de las Indias. [Traslado del despacho del servicio personal]

1611 Vega Carpio, L. F. de. Arcadia

1612 Herrera y Tordesillas, A. de. Historia general, pte 3a

1620 Vega Carpio, L. F. de. Arcadia

1624 Roca, J. A. Vera Zúñiga y Figueroa, conde de la. Epitome

1625 Vander Hammen y Léon, L. Don Filipe el Prudente

1625 Vega Carpio, L. F. de. Comedias, pte 20

1627 Góngora y Argote, L. de. Obras en verso

1627 Vega Carpio, L. F. de. Comedias, pte 20

1629 Vega Carpio, L. F. de. Arcadia

1633 Góngora y Argote, L. de. Todas las obras

1634 Góngora y Argote, L. de. Todas las obras

Popma, Alardo de
1625 Descripcion de la Baia de Todos los Santos

Quiñones, María de
1635 Góngora y Argote, L. de. Todas las obras

1635 Téllez, G. Comedias, 4a pte

1638 Rodríguez de León, J. El predicador delas gentes

1639 Vasconcellos, A. M. de. Vida y acciones del Rey Don Juan

1643 Nieremberg, J. E. Ideas de virtud

1644 Nieremberg, J. E. Firmamento religioso de luzidos astros

1644 Nieremberg, J. E. Vida del santo padre . . . el b. Francisco de Borja

1645 Nieremberg, J. E. Honor del gran patriarca San Ignacio de Loyola

Ribero, A. de
1645 Herrera, G. A. de. Agricultura general

Ribero Rodríguez, Antonio del
1642 Losa, F. de. Vida que el siervo de Dios Gregorio Lopez hizo

Robles, Francisco de
1613 Cervantes Saavedra, M. de. Novelas exemplares

1614 Cervantes Saavedra, M. de. Novelas exemplares

1615 Cervantes Saavedra, M. de. Don Quixote, 2a pte

1617 Cervantes Saavedra, M. de. Novelas exemplares

Rodríguez, Gregorio
1644 Herrera, T. de. Alphabetum Augustinianum . . . t 1

1645 Vega Carpio, L. F. de. Arcadia

1646 Palafox y Mendoza, J. de. Carta

Sánchez, Carlos
1642 González de Legaria, J. Aqui se contiene una obra graciosa

1643 Fragoso, J. Cirugia universal

1644 Hevia Bolaños, J. de. Curia filipica

1645 Herrera, G. A. de. Agricultura general

1650 Mariana, J. de. Historia general de España

Sánchez, Juan
1614 Lima (Ecclesiastical Province). Council, 1583. Concilium Limense

1617 Ortiz de Cervantes, J. Memorial

1639 Camões, L. de. Lusiadas

1639 Ruiz de Montoya, A. Tesoro de la lengua guarani

1639 Spain. Laws, statutes, etc., 1621–1665. Prematica

1640 Discurso de los sucessos de España

1640 Ruiz de Montoya, A. Arte, y bocabulario de la lengua Guarani

1641 León Pinelo, A. R. de. Velos antiguos i modernos

1641 Relacion verdadera de todos los sucessos

1642 Relacion del sucesso

1649 Roca, J. A. Vera Zúñiga y Figueroa, conde de la. Epitome

Sánchez, Juan, Widow of
1639 Porreño, B. Dichos y hechos

Sánchez, Lorenzo
1639 Porreño, B. Dichos y hechos

1642 González de Legaria, J. Aqui se contiene una obra graciosa

Sánchez, Luis
1601 Herrera y Tordesillas, A. de. Historia general, pte 1a

1601 Rivadeneira, P. de. Tratado de la religion

1602 Vega Carpio, L. F. de. Arcadia

1603 Boaistuau, P. Historias prodigiosas

1605 Rivadeneira, P. de. Las obras

1608 Colón y Pravia, F., plaintiff. Alegacion en derecho

1608 Mariana, J. de. Historia general de España

1609 Avila, E. de. Tratado de domicilio

1609 Oviedo, L. de. Methodo de la coleccion

1611 Covarrubias Horozco, S. de. Tesoro de la lengua castellana

1613 Matienzo, J. de. Commentaria

1614 Acosta, J. de. Historia natural y moral

1614 Ordóñez de Ceballos, P. Viage del mundo

1615 Suárez de Figueroa, C. Plaza universal

1617 Remón, A. Vida y muerte del siervo

1619 Cabrera de Córdoba, L. Filipe Segundo rey de España

1619 Hevia Bolaños, J. de. Laberinto de comercio

1619 Moncada, S. de. Restauracion politica

1622 Oviedo, L. de. Methodo de la coleccion

1622 Rivadeneira, P. de. Vida di San Ignacio

1623 Mariana, J. de. Historia general

1624 López Madera, G. Excelencias de la monarquia

1624 Plinius Secundus, C. Historia natural

1624 Struzzi, A. Dialogo sobre el commercio

1625 Garcés, G. Relacion de la persecucion

1625 López Madera, G. Excelencias de la monarquia

1625 Spain. Laws, statutes, etc., 1556–1598. Nuevas leyes

1625? Struzzi, A. Dialogo sobre el comercio

1648 Spain. Treaties, etc., 1621–
1665. Capitulaciones de la paz
**Lanaja y Lamarca, Pedro, Heirs
of**
1650 Quevedo y Villegas, F. G.
de. La fortuna (2)
Lanaja y Quartanet, Juan de
1610 Zurita y Castro, G. Anales
1621 Blasco de Lanuza, V. Historias . . . de Aragon
1622 Blasco de Lanuza, V. Historias . . . de Aragon
1630 Leonardo y Argensola, B. J.
Anales, pte 1a
Larumbe, Juan de
1619 Sesse, J. de. Libro de la cosmographia
Ormer, D. d'. *See* Dormer, Diego
Robles, Lorenço de
1610 Zurita y Castro, G. Anales
Rodríguez, Alfonso
1601 Lobo Lasso de la Vega, G.
Elogios
St. Vincent Ferrer, College of
1610 Zurita y Castro, G. Anales
Sanz, Francisco
1601 Lobo Lasso de la Vega, G.
Manojuelo de romances
Tavano, Angelo
1603 Alemán, M. Guzman de Alfarache, 1a pte
1603 Martí, J. J. Guzman de Alfarache, 2a pte
Torre, Diego de la
1626 Cortés, J. Phisonomia
Uport, Roberto de
1650 Quevedo y Villegas, F. G.
de. La fortuna (2)
Verges, Pedro
1630 Vega Carpio, L. F. de. Comedias, pte 22
1643 Góngora y Argote, L. de.
Todas las obras
Verges, Pedro, Widow of
1646 Agustí, M. Libro de los secretos de agricoltura

SEGOVIA
Díaz de la Carrera, Diego
1637 López de Altuna, P. Coronica general del Orden
1640 Castro de Torres. Panegirico del chocolate
Flamenco, Diego
1629 Vega Carpio, L. F. de. Arcadia

SEVILLE
Printer unidentified
1612? Spain. Casa de Contratación de las Indias. Relacion de
las obligaciones
1617? Seville. Casa de la Moneda. El Fiscal de su Magestad
1618 Seville. Consulado. Sepan
quantos esta carta vieran
1623 Relacion de la gente de mar
1624 Relacion del alzamiento de
los Indios
1630? Seville. Señor. La ciudad
1631? Ossorio y Guadalfaxara, J.
Por Lelio imbrea cavallero
1632 Lima. Consulado de mercaderes. Relacion de las fiestas
1633? Memorial del processo
causado en el Santo Oficio
1633? Por los interesados en los
quatro generos de mercaderias
1636 Relacion de la toma de Parayba
1638 Relacion de lo sucedido a
la Armada Real
164–? El estado en que oy se
halla el comercio
164–? Seville. Junta del Almirantazgo. Por la Junta del Real Almirantazgo
1640? Quadro, D. F. de. Todo el
pleyto
1642 Barba, P. Vera praxis
1642 Catholic Church. Pope,
1623–1644. Nuestro mui santo
p. Urbano
1642 Ovalle, A. de. Memorial
1646 Ximénez de Torres, J. Medica resolucion
1650? Los daños que se seguirian
1650 Fernández Rebolledo, R.
Contiene este papel la forma
1650? Seville. Por el comercio
1650? Valdés, J. de. Por el licenciado
Cabrera, Juan de
1624 Valverde Turices, S. de. Al
excelentissimo . . . Fernando
Afan de Ribera
1625 Carta cierta y verdadera
1625 Casos notables
1625 Lima. Universidad de San
Marcos. Prologo de las constituciones

1625 Relacion de las cosas notables
1625 Segunda relacion de los famosos hechos
1625 Valverde Turices, S. de. Al
excelmo. S[eñ]or Don Gaspar
de Guzman
1626 Pazes entre España, Francia, y otros potentados
Clavijo, Matias
1614 Lima (Ecclesiastical Province). Council, 1567. Sumario
1615 Torquemada, J. de. Veynte
y un libros rituales, pte 1a–3a
Estupiñán, Luis
1610 Queiros, P. F. de. Memorial
1610 Queiros, P. F. de. Relacion
1611 Cano, T. Arte para fabricar . . . naos
1612 Valderrama, P. de. Teatro
de las religiones
1628 López de León, P. Practica
y teorica de las apostemas
1632 Perea, E. de. Verdadera relacion
1633 Perea, E. de. Segunda relacion
Fajardo, Simón
1625 Insigne victoria
1625 Relacion verdadera de las
grandes hazañas
1625 Segunda relacion la mas
copiosa
1625 Toledo Osorio y Mendoza,
F. de. Relacion de la carta
1626 Brochero, L. de. Discurso
breve
1626 Discurso de lo sucedido en
este año 1626
1626 Scribanius, C. Copia de un
papel
1633 Quesada, G. de. Relacion
verdadera del martirio
1637 Guillén y Colón, F. Vita,
muerte y milagros del prodigioso varon
1642 Quintanadueñas, A. de. Explicacion de la Bula
Gómez, Bartolomé
1603 Spain. Audiencia territorial. Seville. Ordenanças
1604 Lima (Ecclesiastical Province). Council, 1583. Catecismo
Gómez de Blas, Juan
1633 Relacion verdadera de la
famosa victoria

1608 Roca, B. J. Historia verdadera

1625 Garcés, G. Relacion de la persecucion

Marzal, Juan Batista

1625 Roca, J. A. Vera Zúñiga y Figueroa, conde de la. Epitome

Mey, Felipe

1616 Mey, A. Norte de la poesia española (2)

1620 Avisos de Roma

Mey, Pedro Patricio

1602 Martí, J. J. Guzman de Alfarach, 2a pte

1604 Beuter, P. A. Coronica general, 1a pte

1605 Alemán, M. Guzman de Alfarache, 1a pte

1605 Alemán, M. Guzman de Alfarache, 2a pte

1607 García, G. Origen de los indios

1610 Aguilar, G. H. de. Expulsion de los Moros

1616 Cervantes Saavedra, M. de. Don Quixote, 2a pte

1631 Téllez, G. Doze comedias nuevas

Miguel, Francisco

1602 Martí, J. J. Guzman de Alfarach, 2a pte

1602 Syria, P. de. Arte de la verdadera navegacion

1602 Vega Carpio, L. F. de. Arcadia

Nogués, Bernardo

1646 Salmerón, M. Recuerdos historicos

1647 Calvo, J. Cirugia universal, 1a–2a pte

Pincinali, Filippo

1616 Mey, A. Norte de la poesia española

Sonzonio, Juan

1635 Liñán y Verdugo, A. Guia y avisos

Sonzonio, Roque

1602 Vega Carpio, L. F. de. Arcadia

1605 Alemán, M. Guzman de Alfarache, 1a pte

1605 Alemán, M. Guzman de Alfarache, 2a pte

1616 Cervantes Saavedra, M. de. Don Quixote, 2a pte

Sorolla, Miguel

1636 Dioscorides, P. Acerca de la materia medicinal

VALLADOLID

Printer unidentified

1601? Lerma, F. de Sandoval y Rojas, duque de. Señor. Por las razones

1602 Catholic Church. Commisarius Generalis Cruciatae. Instruction y forma

1603 Ayanz, G. de. Respuesta

1603 López de Castro, B. Baltasar Lopez de Castro, criado de su Magestad

1603 Spain. Sovereigns, etc., 1598–1621. Este es un traslado . . . de una cedula

1605 Núñez, P. Advertencias

1605 Núñez, P. Excellencias y calidades del arbitrio

1605 Núñez, P. Señor. Pedro Nuñez, vezino de la ciudad de Sevilla

1606 Núñez, P. Tassa y postura en el valor de las mercadurias

1609 Arias, J. L. Señor. El doctor

1621 Valdivia, L. de. Sermon

Cañas, Sebastian de

1604 Alfonso X, el Sabio. Coronica

1604 Sandoval, P. de. Vida y hechos del emperador Carlos Quinto, pte 1a–2a

1606 Sandoval, P. de. Vida y hechos del emperador Carlos Quinto, pte 1a–2a

Castro, Varez de

1603 Spain. Consejo de las Indias. Ordenanzas reales

1603 Spain. Laws, statutes, etc., 1516–1556. Leyes y ordenanças

Córdova, Diego de

1611 Daza, A. Chronica general, 4a pte

Córdova, Martin de

1603 Botero, G. Relaciones universales

Cuello, Antonio

1602 Romancero general

1603 Botero, G. Razon d'estado

1604 Alfonso X, el Sabio. Coronica

Fernández de Córdoba, Francisco

1615 López, J. Bp. Historia general de Santo Domingo, pte 4a

Fernández de Córdoba, Francisco, Widow of

1625 Carta segunda

1625 La quarta carta

Fernández de Córdova, Diego, Heirs of

1603 Botero, G. Relaciones universales

García, Anton

1605 Madrigal, M. de. Romancero general, 2a pte

Godínez de Millis, Juan

1606 Herrera y Tordesillas, A. de. Historia general, pte 1a

1606 Herrera y Tordesillas, A. de. Historia general, pte 2a

1611 Daza, A. Chronica general, 4a pte

Iñíguez de Lequérica, Juan, Heirs of

1604 Spain. Casa de Contratación de las Indias. Ordenanzas reales

Lasso, Juan

1630 Feliz. vitoria. que ha tenido Don Fadrique de Toledo

Lasso, Pedro

1604 San Antonio, G. Q. de. Breve y verdadera relacion

Lasso de las Penas, Juan

1629 Hevia Bolaños, J. de. Curia filipica

Lasso Vaca, Cristóbal

1609 Zapata y Sandoval, J. De justitia distributiva

López, Andrés

1623 Hevia Bolaños, J. de. Curia philippica

Morillo, Jerónimo

1623 Hevia Bolaños, J. de. Curia philippica

1625 Freitas, S. de. De justo imperio Lusitanorum asiatico

1626 Alcalá Yáñez y Rivera, J. Alonso mozo de muchos amos, 2a pte

1633 Lizana, B. de. Historia de Yucatan

Ossete, Pedro de

1602 Romancero general

1603 Botero, G. Razon d'estado

Pérez, Diego
1603 San Román de Ribade-
neyra, A. Historia general de
la Yndia Oriental
Rueda, Antonio de
1645 Quiñones, D. de. Oracion
funebre
Rueda, Juan de
1621 López, J. Historia de Santo
Domingo, pte 5a
Sánchez, Luis
1603 San Román de Ribade-
neyra, A. Historia general de
la Yndia Oriental
1605 Espinosa, P. Flores de poetas ilustres
1605 León, A. de. Practico de
morbo gallico
1605 Madrigal, M. de. Ro-
mancero general, 2a pte
1605 Mercado, L. Tomus secundus Operum
1606 Alfaro, F. de. Tractatus de
officio fiscalis
1606 Spain. Consejo de las Indias. Ordenanzas reales
Varesio, Juan Baptista
1634 Dávila Padilla, A. Varia historia de Nueva España
**Vázquez de Velasco y Esparza,
Antonio**
164–? Vizcaya, Spain. Señorío.
Proposiciones

SWEDEN

GOTHENBURG
Printer unidentified
1624 Usselinx, W. Manifest
. . . der Australischen Companey

STOCKHOLM
Printer unidentified
1625 Usselinx, W. Der reiche
Schweden General Com-
pagnies handlungs contract
1625 Usselinx, W. Sweriges
Rijkes General Handels Compagnies contract
1641 Sweden. Sovereigns, etc.,
1632–1654. Förordning huru
medh tobaks handelen skal
blifwa hällit

Meurer, Ignatius
1626 Sweden. Sovereigns, etc.,
1611–1632. Octroy eller privilegium
1626 Sweden. Sovereigns, etc.,
1611–1632. Octroy und Privilegium. *See also* Germany—
Printer unidentified
1626 Usselinx, W. Uthförligh
förklaring
Reusner, Christoffer
1626 Usselinx, W. Auss-
führlicher Bericht (2)

UPPSALA
Matthias, Aeschillus
1633 Hernodius, J. O. De praeclaris herbae nicotianae
1638 Franck, J. Speculum botanicum

SWITZERLAND

BASEL
Printer unidentified
1612 La Noue, F. de. Discours
politiques
1620 Wecker, J. J. Practica medicinae generalis
1632 Lucius, L. Historia Jesuitica
Episcopius Heirs
1601 Wecker, J. J. Antidotarium
generale
Genath, Johann Jakob
1617 Wecker, J. J. Antidotarium
generale
1624 Braun, S. Schiffarten
1626 Lucius, L. Jesuiter-Histori
1627 Lucius, L. Historia Jesuitica
1629 Baumann, J. N. Dissertatio
inauguralis
1642 Collibus, H. à. Fürstliche
Tischreden
1642 Wecker, J. J. Antidotarium
generale
1647 Ziegler, J. Fermentatio,
generationis . . . causa
Henricpetri, Sebastian
1601 Emili, P. De rebus gestis
Francorum
1614 Münster, S. Cosmaphey
1615 Münster, S. Cosmographia
Henricpetri Office
1628 Münster, S. Cosmographia
1628 Ruland, M. Thesaurus Rulandinus

König, Ludwig
1614 Platter, F. Observationum,
in hominis affectibus . . . libri
tres
1616 Penot, B. G. Tractatus varii
1616 Wecker, J. J. Kunstbuch
1617 Wecker, J. J. Antidotarium
generale
1623 Bauhin, K. Pinax
1625 Bauhin, K. De lapidis bezaar
1625 Platter, F. Praxeos
1641 Platter, F. Observationum,
in hominis affectibus . . . libri
tres
König, Ludwig, Heirs of
1642 Collibus, H. à. Fürstliche
Tischreden
1642 Wecker, J. J. Antidotarium
generale
Perna, F.
1640 Castelli, P. Opobalsamum
triumphans
Schroeter, Johann
1625 Platter, F. Praxeos
Waldkirch, Conrad
1601 Wecker, J. J. Antidotarium
generale
1602 Platter, F. Praxeos
1605 Wecker, J. J. Ein nutzliches
Büchlein
1609 Platter, F. Praxeos
1613 Bauhin, K. De lapidis bezaar
1614 Platter, F. Observationum,
in hominis affectibus . . . libri
tres

COLOGNY
Aubert, Philippe
1616 Avity, P. d'., sieur de Montmartin. Les estats
1616 Montaigne, Michel Eyquem
de. Les essais (3)
1617 Matthieu, P. Histoire de
France
Bérjon, Mathieu
1613 Duret, C. Thresor de l'histoire des langues
Chouët, Pierre & Jacques
1613 Fontaine, J. Opera in quibus universae artis medicae
. . . explicantur
Crespin (Crispin), Samuel
1618 Estienne, C. Dictionarium
historicum

1621 Estienne, C. Dictionarium historicum
Doreau, Jean
1602 Montaigne, M. E. de. Les essais
Gamonet, Estienne
1616 Wecker, J. J. Le grand dispensaire
Société Caldoresque
1613 Duret, C. Thresor de l'histoire des langues

GENEVA
See also Cologny
Printer unidentified
1602 Goulart, S. Les memoires de la Ligue . . . Premier volume
1602 Goulart, S. Le second recueil
1604 Goulart, S. Le quatriesme recueil
1612 La Noue, F. de. Discours politiques
1627 Fernel, J. De abditis rerum causis
1642 Léry, J. de. Histoire d'un voyage
Arnaud, Jean
1606 González de Mendoza, J. Histoire . . . de la Chine (2)
Aubert, Philippe
1614 Keckermann, B. Operum omnium quae extant tomus primus[-secundus]
1616 Montaigne, M. E. de. Les essais (4)
1619 Avity, P. d'. Les estats
1619 Crespin, J. Histoire des martyres
1619 Serres, J. de. Inventaire general
1620 Baricelli, G. C. Hortulus genialis
1620 Duchesne, J. Pharmacopoea dogmaticorum restituta
1623 Grégoire, P. Syntagma juris universi
1625 Mexía, P. Les diverses leçons
1626 Sandys, Sir E. Relation de l'estat de la religion
1628 Bruele, G. Praxis medicinae
1630 Santorio, S. Methodi vitandorum errorum omnium . . . libri quindecim

1631 Croll, O. Basilica chymica
1631 Santorio, S. Methodi vitandorum errorum omnium . . . libri quindecim
1634 Avity, P. d'. Les estats
1634 Hay, P. Le mercure d'estat
1635 Hay, P. Le mercure d'estat
1641? Malvezzi, V. Successi principali
1647 Siri, V. Del mercurio . . . Tomo secondo
1649 Siri, V. Del mercurio . . . Tomo secondo
1649 Siri, V. Il mercurio
Berjon, Mathieu
1611 Serres, O. de. Le théatre d'agriculture
1623 Grégoire, P. Syntagma juris universi
1627 Enchiridion practicum medico-chirurgicum
Can, Jean
1609 Montaigne, M. E. de. Essais
Cartier, Gabriel
1608 Bodin, J. Discours . . . sur le rehaussement
1608 Bodin, J. Les six livres de la Republique
1608 Du Bartas, G. de S., seigneur. Les oeuvres poétiques
Celerier, J.
1624 Béguin, J. Les elemens de chymie
1624 Croll, O. Basilica chymica
Chouët, Jacques
1601 Du Bartas, G. de S., seigneur. Les oeuvres poétiques
1601 Du Bartas, G. de S., seigneur. La sepmaine
1628 Bruele, G. Praxis medicinae
1628 Morel, P. Systema parascevasticum
1639 Morel, P. Methodus praescribendi formulas remediorum
1644 Fernel, J. Universa medicina
Chouët, Pierre
1635 Croll, O. Basilica chymica
1635 Hartmann, J. Praxis chymiatrica
1638 Fernel, J. Universa medicina
1639 Hartmann, J. Praxis chymiatrica
1643 Croll, O. Basilica chymica

1643 Fernel, J. Universa medicina
1647 Hartmann, J. Praxis chymiatrica
Chouët, Pierre & Jacques
1608 Du Bartas, G. de S., seigneur. Les oeuvres poétiques
1608 Du Bartas, G. de S., seigneur. La seconde sepmaine
1610 La Faye, A. de. Emblemata et epigrammata
1613 Fontaine, J. Opera in quibus universae artis medicae . . . explicantur
1614 La Noue, F. de. Discours politiques
1615 Du Bartas, G. de S., seigneur. Les oeuvres poétiques
1616 Du Bartas, G. de S., seigneur. Les oeuvres poétiques
1619 Fernel, J. Universa medicina
1619 Serres, O. de. Le theatre d'agriculture
1622 Fracastoro, G. Operum pars prior
1623 Schyron, J. Methodi medendi . . . libri quatuor
1628 Duchesne, J. Pharmacopoea dogmaticorum restituta
1632 Du Bartas, G. de S., seigneur. Les oeuvres poétiques
1639 Serres, O. de. Le theatre d'agriculture
1644 Enchiridion practicum medico-chirurgicum
Crespin, Samuel
1608 Clavius, C. In Sphaeram Joannis de Sacro Bosco commentarius
1608 Du Bartas, G. de S., seigneur. Les oeuvres poétiques
1615 Du Bartas, G. de S., seigneur. Les oeuvres poetiques
1620 Goulart, S. Thresor d'histoires admirables
1621 Fracastoro, G. Operum pars prior
1628 Goulart, S. Thresor d'histoires admirables
Crispin, Jacques
1627 Estienne, C. Dictionarium historicum
1633 Estienne, C. Dictionarium historicum

Appendix II

An Alphabetical Index of Printers and Booksellers
& Their Geographic Location

The asterisk before a name indicates that there were two printers or booksellers of the same name, and that, in some of the books listed, it is not certain to which of them the name in the imprint refers.

A., B. (1630): London
Abarca de Angulo, Francisco (1619–20): Madrid
Abbatus, B. *See* L'Abbé, Balthazar
Adams, Elizabeth (1620): London
Adams, Thomas (1605–17): London
Aelst, Andries Janszoon van (1621–25): Zutphen
Aertssens, Henri (1614–46): Antwerp
Agricola, Hieronymus (1650): Innsbruck
Alazart, Anthoine (1643): Paris
Albert, L. (1602): Frankfurt a. M.
Albert, Philippe. *See* Aubert, Philippe
Alberti, Bartholomeo degli (1604): Venice
Alberti, Giovanni (1610–20): Venice
Alberti, Olivier (1616): Venice
Alberto, Philipp. *See* Aubert, Philippe
Albertszoon, Dirck (1629): Leeuwarden
Albin, Johann (1603–18): Mainz
Alchorn, Thomas (1627–35): London
Aleu, Geronimo (1602–3): Barcelona
Algeyer, Melchior (1618): Dillingen
Allde, Edward (1602–35): London
Allde, Elizabeth (1628–34): London
Allen, Benjamin (1634–46): London
Allen, Hannah (1647–50): London .
Alliot, Gervais (1621–27): Paris
Allott, Robert (1627–35): London
Alsop, Bernard (1616–48): London
Alterio, Agostino (1629): Foligno
Alvarez, Antonio (1601–49): Lisbon
Alvarez, Domingo (1641): Lisbon
Alvarez, Francisco (1625): Lisbon
Alvarez, Vicente (1608–25): Lisbon
Alvarez, Vicente (1646): Granada
Ambrosian College (1622): Milan
Amelisszoon, Jan (1624): Utrecht
Amello, Juan (1602–4): Barcelona
Ammon, Johann (1645–50): Frankfurt a. M.
Ancelin, Thibaud (1606–7): Lyons
Angat, F. (1625): Paris
Angelieri, Agostino (1606–8): Venice
Angermaier, Andreas (1610–13): Ingolstadt

Angermaier, Elisabeth (1614–17): Ingolstadt
Anglada, Honofre (1604–8): Barcelona
Angot, Nicolas (1614–43): Rouen
Anisson, Laurent (1649): Lyons
Anthoine, Hubert (1613–25): Brussels
Antonius, Peter (1617–21): Hanau
Antonius, Wilhelm (1606–10): Hanau
Antonius, Wilhelm, Heirs of (1611–13): Hanau
Anveres, Lourenço de (1641–42): Lisbon
Apel, Jakob (1603): Eisleben; (1604–13): Leipzig; (1613): Gera
Aperger, Andreas (1619–50): Augsburg
Apostolic Camera (1608–48): Rome
Appel, Mieus Janszoon (1648): Hoorn
Archer, Thomas (1604–25): London
Ardizzoni, Giacomo (1613): Pavia
Ardizzoni, Giovanni Antonio (1641): Bologna, Brescia, Piacenza, Verona, Viterbo
Arens, Bernd (1648): Hamburg
Arensteyn, Gerrit Janszoon (1632): Amsterdam
Armand, Claude (1628): Lyons
Arnaud, Jean (1606): Geneva
Arnon, Nicolas (1643): Lyons
Arnoullet, François (1608–9): Lyons
Aspley, William (1603–23): London
Assiayn, Nicolás de (1614–17): Pamplona
Atkinson, Troylus (1644): Cambridge
Aubert, Philippe (1614–49): Geneva; (1616–17): Cologny
Aubin, Eustache d' (1634): Paris
Aubry, David (1630–31): Hanau
Aubry, Daniel & David (1619–26): Hanau; (1619): Mainz; (1625–27): Frankfurt a. M.
Aubry, Johann, Heirs of (1601–9): Frankfurt a. M.; (1605–13): Hanau
Aubry Office (1614): Frankfurt a. M.
Auerbach, Salomon, Heirs of (1628): Wittenberg
Aureati, Leo (1612): Venice
Auroy, Pierre (1607–31): Douai
Auvray, Pierre (1627): Paris

B., J. (1630): London
Baardt, Rieuwert Dirckszoon van, Widow of (1648): Amsterdam
Baba, Andrea (1625–36): Venice
Baba, Evangelista (1640): Venice
Baba, Francesco (1611–41): Venice
Bache, John (1612–13): London
Badger, George (1646): London
Badger, Richard (1623–41): London
Badger, Thomas (1640): London
Baerle, Kaspar van (1641): Enkhuizen
Baglioni, Tommaso (1609–21): Venice
Bailey, Thomas (1617–34): London
Bailly, Pierre (1637): Lyons
Baleoni, Paolo (1643): Venice
Ballard, Henry (1608): London
Balthasar, Floris (1601–5): Delft
Baltrano, Ottavio (1632): Naples
Banheyning, Cornelis (1650): Leyden
Banks, Thomas (1647): London
Bankworth, Richard (1612): London
Baragnes (Baraignes), Rolin (1628–29): Paris
Barentsma, B. (1636): Franeker
Barentszoon, Hendrick (1606): Amsterdam
Barezzi, Barezzo (1601–46): Venice
Barezzi, The (1626–29): Venice
Bariletti, Antonio (1639): Venice
Bariletti, Francesco (1603): Venice
Barker, Robert (1603–42): London
Barley, William (1601–8): London
Barlow, Timothy (1616–18): London
Barnes, John (1611–19): London
Barnes, Joseph (1607–15): Oxford
Barnes, Roger (1610–15): London
Barrenger, William (1627): London
Barrera, Andrés de, Widow of (1616–17): Cordoba
Barret, Hannah (1625): London
Barrett, William (1609–22): London
Barrio y Angulo, Catalina de (1640–47): Madrid
Bartlet, John (1626–30): London
Basse, Johann (1613–17): Frankfurt a. M.
Basse, Nikolaus (1601): Frankfurt a. M.
Basse, Nikolaus, Heirs of (1608–40): Frankfurt a. M.
Basson, Godefrid (1625–30): Leyden
Bastiaenszoon, Mathys, Widow of (1636): Rotterdam
Bauduin, Gilles (1611–28): Arras
Bazacchi, Alessandro (1617): Piacenza
Beale, John (1612–42): London
Beatus, Georg (1601): Frankfurt a. M.
Beatus, Romanus, Heirs of (1601): Frankfurt a. M.
Beauvais, Romain de (1610): Rouen
Bechet, Denis (1643): Paris
Beckenstein, Simon (1650): Frankfurt a. M .
Becker, Matthäus (1601–12): Frankfurt a. M.

Becker, Matthäus, Widow of (1613): Frankfurt a. M.
Becket, James (1638–42): London
Becket, Leonard (1627): London
Bedell, Gabriel (1650): London
Beeck, Isaack Willemszoon van der. *See* Willemszoon, Isaack
Behourt, Jean (1647): Rouen
Behourt, Jean Baptiste (1623–28): Rouen; (1632): Paris
Beithmann, Johann (1620–24): Jena
Bell, Henry (1617–22): London
Bell, Henry & Moses (1637): London
Bell, Jeane (1650): London
Bellagamba, Giovanni Battista (1601–13): Bologna
Bellamy, John (1622–49): London
Bellère, Balthazar (1603–36): Douai
Bellère, Pierre (1645–46): Antwerp
Bellère, Pierre & Jean (1617–27): Antwerp
Bellettus, Franciscus (1612): Ypres
Benacci, Heir of (1643–47): Bologna
Benacci, Vittorio, Heirs of (1641): Bologna
Benden, Jan van (1647): Amsterdam
Benson, John (1636–40): London
Bentley, William (1650): London
Berewout, Jan Leendertszoon (1616): Rotterdam
Berg, Anna (1618–20): Munich
Berger, Clemens (1606–23): Wittenberg; (1618–25): Königsberg
Berger, Clemens, Heirs of (1634–40): Wittenberg
Berger, Erhard (1649): Bremen
Berjon, Jean (1608–13): Paris
Berjon, Mathieu (1611–27): Geneva; (1613): Cologny
Bernard, Jean (1628): Brussels
Bernard, Melchior (1608): Pont-a-Mousson
Berner, Johann (1604–24): Frankfurt a. M.; (1618): Tübingen
Berner, Johann; Widow & Heirs of (1641): Frankfurt a. M.
Bernia, Marco Antonio (1622–48): Bologna
Berrillo, Juan (1608): Madrid
Bertano, Giovanni Antonio, Heirs of (1602): Venice
Bertano, Pietro (1612–13): Venice
Bertano, Pietro Maria (1608–38): Venice
Bertault, Pierre (1603): Paris
Bertault, Robert (1625): Paris
Bertelli, Pietro (1603): Vicenza
Berthelin, Jean (1617–50): Rouen
Bertier, Antoine (1648): Paris
Bertolotti, Trivisano (1613–18): Venice
Bertsch, Caspar (1627): Coburg
Besard, Jean Baptiste (1617): Augsburg
Besler, Basilius (1616–22): Nuremberg
Besongne, Cardin (1628–50): Paris
Besongne, Jacques (1617–49): Rouen

Besongne, Jacques, the Younger (1641): Rouen
Besozzo, Alberto (1627): Milan
Bessin, Jean (1615–43): Paris
Bessin, Nicolas (1647): Paris
Best, Richard (1640): London
Beyer, Giovanni [i.e., Johann], pseud. (1626): 'Frankfurt a. M.'
Beyer, Johann (1641–50): Frankfurt a. M.
Beyeren, Adriaen Gerritszoon van (1610): Delft
Beys, Adrian (1611): Paris
Beys, Christophe (1614): Lille
Beys, Hadrianus. See Beys, Adrian
Bianco, Giovanni Francesco (1640): Messina
Bianco, Giovanni Francesco, Widow of (1640): Messina
Bidelli, Giovanni Battista (1613–45): Milan
Biesen, Jacob van (1633): Arnhem
Bilaine, Pierre (1619–37): Paris
Bill, John (1606–27): London
Bill, John, Assigns of (1630–42): London
Billi, P. Giacomo (1623): Perugia
Bilsteyn, Gillis (1647): Utrecht
Bilt, Bartholomeus van der (1619): Leyden
Birch, Philip (1618): London
Birckmann, House of (1602): Cologne. See also Mylius
Birckmann Office (1622–31): Cologne
Birckner, Johann (1630): Erfurt
Bishop, George (1601–9): London
Bishop, Richard (1636–48): London
Bismarck, Christoph (1625): Halle
Bitsch, Johann Ludwig (1601): Frankfurt a. M.
Bitsch, Ludwig [i.e., Johann Ludwig?] (1604): Frankfurt a. M.
Bizarron, Antonio (1630): Madrid
Blacklock, Lawrence (1639–40): London
Blackmore, Edward (1631–44): London
Bladen, William (1622–24): London; (1643): Dublin
Blaeu, Joan (1636–50): Amsterdam
Blaeu, Joan & Cornelis (1638–43): Amsterdam
Blaeu, Willem Janszoon (1608–40): Amsterdam
Blaeu, Willem Janszoon & Cornelis (1639): Amsterdam
Blaeu, Willem Janszoon & Joan (1635–38): Amsterdam
Blageart, Jérôme (1620): Paris
Blageart, Jérôme, Widow of (1638): Paris
Blageart, Michel (1636–49): Paris
Blaickelocke, Lawrence. See Blacklock, Lawrence
Blaise, Thomas (1621–34): Paris
Blaizot, Gilles (1612): Paris
Bloome, Jacob (1634–38): London
Blount, Edward (1603–28): London
Blower, Ralph (1601–18): London
Blunden, Humphrey (1640–48): London
Blusson, Pedro (1622): Huesca

Bobin, Michel (1645): Paris
Bock, Harman de (1647): Leeuwarden
Bodán, Cornelio (1602): Cuenca
Boels, Françoys (1637–47): Dordrecht
Boeteman, Pieter Dirckszoon (1649–50): Amsterdam
Boetzer, Anton (1612–15): Cologne
Bogard, Jean (1605–10): Douai
Boissat, Gabriel (1635): Lyons
Boisseau, Jean (1645): Paris
Boler, James (1629–40): London
Bollifant, Edmund (1601): London
Bolzetta, Francesco (1608–20): Venice; (1611–39): Padua; (1617): Vicenza
Bonamo, S. See Bonomi, Sebastiano
Bonaventure, Corneille (1608): Leyden
Bonet, Juan Antonio (1643–49): Madrid
Bonfadino, Bartolomeo (1602): Rome
Bonilla, Juan de (1602–14): Barcelona
Bonino, Scipione (1607–17): Naples
Bonion, Richard (1610): London
Bonomi, Sebastiano (1620–21): Bologna
Borde, Philippe (1635–43): Lyons
Bordeaulx, Jean de (1611): Paris
Bordone, Girolamo (1603–16): Milan
Boreck, August (1619–25): Königsberg
Boremann, Pierre (1613): Douai
Borja, Juan de (1620–29): Cádiz
Bos, Lambert van den (1646): Amsterdam
Bosc, Dominique (1616): Toulouse
Bosc, Pierre (1628–46): Toulouse
Boscard, Charles (1614): St Omer
Bosselaer, Françoys (1629): Dordrecht
Bostock, Robert (1629–44): London
Bot, Adrian (1610): Dordrecht
Bot, Marten de (1645–47): Dordrecht
Boucher, Jean (1627): Paris
Boudé, Jean (1625): Toulouse
Bouillerot, Joseph (1625–40): Paris
Boulay, Jean. See Boulley, Jean
Boulenger, Jules César (1619): Lyons
Boullenger, Louis (1636–39): Paris
Boulley, Jean (1619–42): Rouen
Bouman, J. (1650): Amsterdam
Bouman, Jan Jacobszoon (1649): Amsterdam
Bourdin, Nicolas (1623–37): Paris
Bourne, Nicholas (1614–50): London
Bourriquant, Fleury (1607–18): Paris
Boutonné, Rolet (1625): Paris
Bouwenszoon, Jan (1604): Leyden
Bowman, Francis (1638–40): Oxford
Bowtell, Stephen (1647–50): London
Boxe, Willem Christiaens van der, (1645–47): Leyden
Boxe Press (1649): Leyden
Boydell, Robert (1650): London
Boyle, Richard (1612): London

Braat, Jacob (1647–49): Dordrecht
Brachel, Peter von (1612–29): Cologne
Bradock, Richard (1602–16): London
Bradwood, Melchisidec (1606–17): London
Brakel, Arnout van (1646–47): Antwerp
Bramereau, Jacques (1636–49): Avignon
Branchu, Jean (1631): Paris
Brandt, Marten Janszoon (1623–31): Amsterdam
Braun, Georg (1612): Cologne
Brea, Pietro (1629–39): Messina
Breeckevelt, Ferdinandus (1649): The Hague
Breeckevelt, Johannes (1647–49): The Hague
Breeckevelt, Ludolph (1634–48): The Hague
Bresche, Pierre de (1623–38): Paris
Bresciana, Compagnia (1609): Brescia
Brethommé, Jean (1615): La Rochelle
Breughel, Cornelis van (1634–36): Amsterdam
Breughel, Gherrit van (1630): Amsterdam
Brewster, Edward (1628–44): London
Bringer, Johann (1611–16): Frankfurt a. M.
Britannico, Ludovico (1626): Brescia
Broerszoon, Joost (1634–38): Amsterdam
Broerszoon, Joost, Widow of (1647): Amsterdam
Brogiollo, Marc Antonio (1627–36): Venice
Brogiotti, G. B. *See* Brugiotti, Giovanni Battista
Brotherhood of Booksellers (1641): Madrid
Brouwer, Herman Janszoon (1634): Amsterdam
Browne, John (1605–25): London
Browne, Nathaniel (1618): London
Browne, Samuel (1641): London; (1648): The Hague
Brückner, Matthäus (1601): Paderborn
Brugiotti, Andrea (1621): Rome
Brugiotti, Giovanni Battista (1624–25): Rome
Brunn, Philibert (1627–41): Tübingen
Bruyn, Abraham de (1649): Amsterdam
Bry, Johann Theodor de (1611–19): Oppenheim; (1613–26): Frankfurt a. M.
Bry, Johann Theodor de, Heirs of (1624–25): Frankfurt a. M.
Bry, Johann Theodor de, Widow & Heirs of (1608–25): Frankfurt a. M.
Bry, Johann Theodor & Johann Israel de (1601–9): Frankfurt a. M.
Bry, Theodor de (1605–9): Frankfurt a. M.
Bry, Theodor de, Widow & Sons of (1603): Frankfurt a. M.
Bry Office (1627): Frankfurt a. M.
Buck, Thomas (1632–35): Cambridge
Budge, John (1612–25): London
Bueno, Pascual (1625–30): Saragossa
Buissart, Abdias (1621): Paris
Buon, Nicolas (1605–28): Paris
Buon, Nicolas, Widow of (1631): Paris
Buonuomo, S. *See* Bonomi, Sebastiano
Burby, Cuthbert (1601): London
Burchoorn, Isaac (1634–45): The Hague

Bureau d'Adresse (1640): Paris
Burel, Jean (1621): Saumur
Burre, Walter (1601–21): London
Burton, Francis (1607–17): London
Busäus, Johann (1646): Cologne
Busby, John (1608–16): London
Bushell, Thomas (1602–4): London
Bussemacher, Johann (1608): Cologne
Butgen, Conrad (1603–4): Mainz
Butler, N. *See* Butter, Nathaniel
Butler, William (1615): London
Butter, Nathaniel (1605–43): London

C., M. M. T. (1650): London
Caballo, F. *See* Cavalli, Francesco
Cabrera, Juan de (1624–26): Seville
Caffin, Jean (1642): Lyons
Cailloué, Jacques (1623–49): Rouen
Caimax, Vincent (1650): Dordrecht
Calles, Pierre (1610–16): Rouen
Calvert, Giles (1645–46): London
Cambier, Andreas (1604): Frankfurt a. M.; (1606): Heidelberg
Camusat, Jean (1635–39): Paris
Camusat, Jean, Widow of (1641): Paris
Can, Jean (1609): Geneva
Cañas, Sebastián de (1603): Burgos; (1604–6): Valladolid
Candolle, P. de (1619): Yverdon. *See also* Société Caldoresque; Typographia Caldoriana
Candy, Jean Aymé (1628–48): Lyons
Canevese, Giovanni Battista (1629): Milan
Canin, Abraham (1605): Dordrecht
Canin, Isaac Janszoon (1601–16): Dordrecht
Canin, Jacob (1624): Dordrecht
Cardon, Horace (1608–36): Lyons
Cardon, Jacob (1620–32): Lyons
Carlino, Giovanni Giacomo (1607–9): Naples
Carolus, Johann (1617): Strassburg
Carolus, Johann, Heirs of (1647): Strassburg
Carstens, Heinrich (1616): Hamburg
Carteron, Jean (1649): Lyons
Cartier, Gabriel (1608): Geneva
Cartwright, Samuel (1635–48): London
Carvalho, Manoel (1625): Evora
Casa, Christoforo della (1644–47): Casale
Cassiano, Giuliano (1630–35): Modena
Castello, Juan (1612–16): Granada
Castro, Varez de (1603): Valladolid
Cavaleri Bros (1612): Turin
Cavalier, A. *See* Cavelier, Adam
Cavalli, Francesco (1645–49): Rome
Cavelier, Adam (1614–42): Caen
Cavellat, Denise (1608): Paris
Cavellat, Pierre (1620–21): Lyons
Cayne, Claude (1617–33): Lyons

Cea Tesa, Salvador de (1620–46): Córdoba
Cecconcelli, Pietro (1619–23): Florence
Celerier, J. (1624): Geneva
Cellier, J. *See* Celerier, J.
Cellius, Johann Alexander (1619–23): Tübingen
Cendrat, Jaime (1603–8): Barcelona
Cestaro (1647): Venice
Cestaro, Giovanni Battista (1646): Venice
Champion, Jean (1636–37): Lyons
Chancey, C. (1645): Lyons
Chapellet, Sébastien (1618): Paris
Chapman, Lawrence (1634–44): London
Chappelet, Claude (1608): Paris
Chard, Antoine (1625–26): Lyons
Charles, Noel (1639): Paris
Charpantier, Jacobus (1633): Amsterdam
Chaudière, Guillaume (1606): Paris
Chaudière, Guillaume, Widow of (1604): Paris
Chaudière, Regnaud (1611–22): Paris
Chaunod, Guillaume (1646): Lyons
Chemlin, Caspar (1612): Giessen; (1630): Marburg
Chevalier, Pierre (1610–32): Paris
Cholinus, Goswin (1601–10): Cologne
Chorlton, Jeffrey (1604–6): London
Chouët, François (1609): Montpellier
Chouët, Jacques (1601–44): Geneva
Chouët, Pierre (1635–47): Geneva
Chouët, Pierre & Jacques (1608–44): Geneva; (1613): Cologny; (1620–28): Montpellier
Christiäens, Willem (1631–39): Leyden
Christoffel, Johann (1610): Cologne
Church, Francis (1634): London
Ciaccone, Alfonse (1623): Rome
Ciera, B. (1604): Venice
Ciotti, Giovanni Battista (1601–20): Venice
Ciotti, Giovanni Battista, & Co. (1608–12): Venice
Ciottis, The (1629): Venice
Claeszoon, Claes (1646): Dordrecht
Claeszoon, Cornelis (1601–14): Amsterdam
Claeszoon, Cornelis, Widow of (1610): Amsterdam
Claeszoon, Jan (1647): Alkmaar
Claeszoon, Jelis (1622): Hoorn
Clarke, John (1649): London
Clarke, Martin (1607): London
Clarke, Robert (1616): London
Clarke, Thomas (1604): London
Claseri, Marco (1605): Venice
Clavijo, M. (1621): Madrid
Clavijo, Matias (1614–15): Seville
Clercq, Nicolaes de (1615–17): Delft
Clercq, Nicolaes de, Heirs of (1625): Delft
Clifton, Fulke (1630–47): London
Cloeting, Andriesz Janszoon (1629–38): Delft
Cloeting, Jan Andrieszoon (1614–29): Delft
Cloeting, Jan Andrieszoon, Widow of (1640): Delft
Clopejau, Gabriel (1623): Paris
Cloppenburg, Evert (1638–44): Amsterdam

Cloppenburg, Evert, Widow of (1643–44): Amsterdam
Cloppenburg, Jan Evertszoon (1610–38): Amsterdam
Closemann, Caspar. *See* Klosemann, Kaspar
Cloucq, Andries (1630): Leyden
Clousier, Gervais (1646–49): Paris
Clouzier, G. *See* Clousier, Gervais
Clowes, John (1649–50): London
Cnobbaert, Jan (1627–36): Antwerp
Cocchi, Bartolomeo (1609–18): Bologna; (1618): Rome
Coe, Jane (1646): London
Coello, Antonio. *See* Cuello, Antonio
Coello, Pedro (1628–49): Madrid
Cole, Peter (1637–50): London
Coles, T. (1630): London
Colet, M. *See* Collet, Martin
Colijn, Emanuel (1622): Paris
Colijn, Michiel (1612–22): Amsterdam
Collet, Claude (1619–40): Paris
Collet, Martin (1625–36): Paris
Collosini, Matteo (1601): Venice
Colom, Jacob Aertszoon (1648): Amsterdam
Colom, Johannes (1649): Amsterdam
Colombel, Mathieu (1634): Paris
Combi (1643): Venice
Combi, Giovanni Battista (1644): Venice
Combi, Sebastiano (1605–10): Venice
Commelin, Abraham (1634–43): Leyden
Commelin, Hieronymus, Heirs of (1626): Amsterdam
Commelin, Isaac (1640): Leyden
Commelin Office (1603–9): Heidelberg
Compagnia Bresciana (1609): Brescia
Concordia, Compagnia della (1623–24): Turin
Concordia, Sign of (1608): Venice
Confraternity of Souls in Purgatory of the Parish of Santiago in Madrid (1628): Madrid
Constable, Francis (1616–41): London
Cooke, William (1632–39): London
Coopman, Hans Willemszoon (1645): Leeuwarden
Corbelletti, Francesco (1627–38): Rome
Corbo, Francesco (1639): Rome
Córdova, Diego de (1611): Valladolid
Córdova, Martin de (1603): Valladolid
Cormellas, Sebastian de (1601–34): Barcelona
Corneliszoon, Jasper, pseud. (1649): Gouda
Corneliszoon, Zacharias (1619): Hoorn
Correa, F., Widow of. *See* Correa de Montenegro, Fernando, Widow of
Correa de Montenegro, Fernando (1620–21): Madrid
Correa de Montenegro, Fernando, Widow of (1621–22): Madrid
Corrozet, Jean (1617–36): Paris
Cortés, Jeronimo, Widow of (1613): Valencia

Corvinus (Rab), Christoph (1606): Herborn
Corvinus, Georg. *See* Rab, Georg
Cosío, Diego de (1618): Salamanca
Costé, Louys (1625): Rouen
Coster, Jelis Claeszoon (1622): Hoorn
Costerden, Matthew (1635–40): London
Cotes, Richard (1630–49): London
Cotes, Thomas (1627–41): London
Cotinet, Arnould (1638–48): Paris
Cottard, Clovis (1634): Paris
Cottereau, Jacques & Michel (1634): Blois
Cottereau, Joseph (1608–10): Paris
Cottereau, Laurent (1643): Paris
Cotton, William (1604): London
Coules, Francis (1638–41): London
Coulon, Antoine (1639): Paris
Courbé, Augustin (1633–50): Paris
Courbes, Gieronymo de (1619): Madrid
Cousturier, Daniel (1623): Rouen
Couterot, Edme (1650): Paris
Craesbeeck, Lourenço (1633–37): Lisbon
Craesbeeck, Paulo (1625–50): Lisbon
Craesbeeck, Pedro (1602–40): Lisbon
Craesbeeck Office (1650): Lisbon
Cramoisy, Gabriel (1644–50): Paris
Cramoisy, Sebastien (1624–50): Paris
Crato Press (1608): Wittenberg
Creede, Thomas (1601–16): London
Crespin, J. *See* Crispin, Jacques
Crespin, Samuel (1602–8): St. Gervais; (1608–28): Geneva; (1618–21): Cologny
Cripps, Henry (1621–38): Oxford
Crispin, Jacques (1627–38): Geneva
Crispin, S. *See* Crespin, Samuel
Crivellari, Gasparo (1616): Padua
Crooke, Andrew (1637–49): London
Crouch, John (1636): London
Croy, Philips de (1649–50): Leyden
Cruyssen, Pieter van den (1646): Antwerp
Cuello, Antonio (1602–4): Valladolid
Cuesta, Juan de la (1604–22): Madrid; (1638): Baeza
Cuesta, Pedro de la (1625–26): Baeza; (1628): Jaen
Cunradus, Christoffel (1650): Amsterdam
Custos, Dominicus (1615): Augsburg

D., O. (1648): London
Dabertzhofer, Chrysostomus (1611–13): Augsburg
Dacivelle, Bonaventure (1601): Calais
Dallin, Rémy (1615): Paris
Dallin, Rémy, Widow of (1619–25): Paris
Danguy, Estienne (1646): Paris
Daniel, Michel (1618): Paris
Daniel, Roger (1635–48): Cambridge
Daré, Robert (1649): Rouen
Daré, Thomas (1606–17): Rouen

Daré, Thomas, Widow of (1619): Rouen
David, D. (1648): Paris
Dawlman, Robert (1630): London
Dawson, John (1621–48): London
Dawson, Mary (1637): London
Dawson, Thomas (1607–19): London
Deane, John (1602–20): London
Dedin, Isaac (1636): Paris
Dei, Ambrosio & Bartholomeo (1613–16): Venice
Delgado, Cosme, Widow of (1620–23): Madrid
Delgado, Juan (1624–25): Madrid
Demen, Michael (1627): Cologne
Desbordes, Isaac (1629): Saumur
Déu, Lorenzo (1609–29): Barcelona
Deuchino, Evangelista (1604–7): Treviso; (1608–21): Venice
Deutel, Jan Janszoon (1646–48): Hoorn
Dever, John (1647): London
Dewe, Thomas (1621–25): London
Dexter, Gregory (1642–43): London
Deyster, H. van der (1643): Leyden
Díaz de la Carrera, Diego (1637–40): Segovia; (1636–50): Madrid
Diotallevi, The (1650): Viterbo
Dockum, Jan van (1639): 's Hertogenbosch
Dod, Edward (1646–50): London
Doncker, Hendrick (1650): Amsterdam
Doreau, Jean (1602): Cologny, Switzerland; (1602–9): Leyden
Dormer, Diego (1635–50): Saragossa
Dorp, Jan Nicolas van, Heirs of (1644): Leyden
Dotil, Giraldo (1603–9): Barcelona
Douceur, David (1602–6): Paris
Dozza, Evangelista, Heirs of (1647): Bologna
Dozza, Heirs of (1648): Bologna
Dreutel, Johann (1613–25): Frankfurt a. M.
Drouart, Ambroise & Hieronymus (1604–19): Paris
Drouet, Pierre (1624–27): Lyons
Du Bray, Toussainct (1611–35): Paris
Du Breuil, Anthoine (1612): Paris
Ducal Press (1645–48): Florence
Du Carroy, Jean (1603): Paris
Du Clou, Jacques, Widow of (1618): Paris
Du Crocq, Jean (1649): Paris
Dümler, Jeremias (1650): Nuremberg
Du Fossé, Nicolas (1619): Paris
DuGard, William (1649–50): London
Dugast, Jacques (1632–41): Paris
Du Guy, Y. (1615): Paris
Dullort, Pedro (1626): Pamplona
Du Mesnil, Hervet (1629): Paris
Du Mesnil, Louis (1627–48): Rouen
Du Petit Val, David (1616–25): Paris; (1616–44): Rouen
Du Petit Val, Raphael (1602–16): Rouen; (1616): Paris

Duplastre, Antonio (1626–34): Alcalá de Henares; (1638–41): Madrid
Durand, Jean (1617–19): Rouen
Durand, Laurent (1622): Lyons
Durand, Pierre (1614): Paris
Dusinelli, Pietro (1619–21): Venice
Duynen, Francoys van (1649): Antwerp

East, Thomas (1602): London
Eder, Wilhelm (1625): Ingolstadt
Eder Press (1610–17): Ingolstadt
Edgar, Eleazar (1609): London
Edmonds, Walter (1639): London
Edwards, George (1641): London
Egenolff, Paul (1615–22): Marburg
Eglesfield, Francis (1637–46): London
Egmondt, Cornelis ab, & Co. (1629): Cologne
Eichorn, Johann (1618): Frankfurt a. d. O.
Ekins, Nathaniel (1650): London
Eld, George (1604–24): London
Eliot's Court Press (1601–38): London
Ellis, William (1642): London
Elsevier (1628): Amsterdam
Elsevier, Abraham (1621): Amsterdam
Elsevier, Bonaventura & Abraham (1627–44): Leyden
Elsevier, Isaak (1618–26): Leyden
Elsevier, Louis (I) (1602–11): Leyden
Elsevier, Louis (III) (1640–50): Amsterdam
Elsevier Office (1618–41): Leyden
Elzevier. See Elsevier
Emery, Jaspar (1639): London
Emmel, Egenolff (1615–25): Frankfurt a. M.
Enden, Martinus van den (1646): Antwerp
Endter, Michael (1646–50): Nuremberg
Endter, Wolfgang (1636–49): Nuremberg
English College Press (1612–22): St Omer
Episcopius Heirs (1601): Basel
Esch, Hendrick van (1633–47): Dordrecht
Escuer, Pedro (1634–49): Saragossa
Esparsa, Silvestre (1629–35): Valencia
Espino, Francisco de (1601): Madrid
Estey, Nicolas d' (1628): Toulouse
Estienne, Robert (1611–32): Paris
Estoct, Anthoine (1626): Paris
Estupiñán, Luis (1608): Lisbon; (1610–33): Seville
Eyering, Johann, Heirs of (1620): Jena

Fabri, François (1603–11): Douai
Fabri, Jean Rodolphe (1613–14): Die
Fabri Office (1610): Geneva
Fabricius, J. (1618): Königsberg
Facciotti, Guglielmo (1601–32): Rome
Facciotti, Guglielmo, Heirs of (1634): Rome
Facciotti, Pietro Antonio (1638–39): Rome

Facciotto, G. See Facciotti, Guglielmo
Facio, Lepido (1603): Rome
Fajardo, Simón (1625–42): Seville
Falorsí, Aníbal (1615): Madrid
Fantucci, Stefano (1628): Florence
Farri, Domenico (1603): Venice
Farri, Domenico, Heirs of (1606): Venice
Farri, Pietro (1612–21): Venice
Fawcet, Thomas (1626–47): London
Fawne, Luke (1631–50): London
Fei, Andrea (1621–26): Bracciano; (1624–35): Rome
Ferbrand, William (1604–9): London
Fernandes, Domingo (1609–13): Lisbon
Fernández, María (1649): Alcalá de Henares
Fernández, Martin (1630): Granada
Fernández de Córdoba, Francisco (1615): Valladolid
Fernández de Córdoba, Francisco, Widow of (1625): Valladolid
Fernández de Córdova, Diego, Heirs of (1603): Valladolid
Fernandez Zambrano, Martin (1630–31): Granada
Feron, Robert (1627): Rouen
Ferrand, David (1624–46): Rouen
Ferrer, Jusepe (1610–16): Valencia
Ferroni, Clemente (1629): Bologna
Ferroni, Giovanni Battista (1641–50): Bologna
Fetherstone, Henry (1609–26): London
Feyerabend, Sigmund (1608–9): Frankfurt a. M.
Field, John (1644–50): London
Field, Richard (1601–24): London
Fievet, Philipp (1648): Frankfurt a. M.
Fincelius, Hiob Wilhelm (1618–24): Wittenberg
Finlason, Thomas (1609–20): Edinburgh
Fiorini, Vincento (1616): Venice
Firebrand. See Ferbrand
Firens, Pierre (1627–33): Paris
Fischer, Jakob (1610–12): Frankfurt a. M.
Fischer, Jakob, Heirs of (1626–35): Frankfurt a. M.
Fischer, Nicolas Janszoon (1628): Amsterdam
Fischer, Peter (1601): Frankfurt a. M.
Fischer, Peter Jacob (1642): Frankfurt a. M.
Fisher, Benjamin (1623–36): London
Fitzer, Wilhelm (1628–33): Frankfurt a. M.
Flamenco, Diego (1619–26): Madrid; (1629): Segovia
Flamenco, Juan (1601–12): Madrid
Flasket, John (1601–6): London
Fleischmann, Georg (1604): Würzburg
Fletcher, James (1650): London
Fletcher, Miles (1624–49): London
Florimi, Mattheo, Heirs of (1613): Siena
Foillet, Jacques (1608): Montbeliard
Fontana, Bartolomeo (1613): Brescia; (1623–24): Venice

Fontana, D. (1630): Milan
Fonteyn, Thomas (1646): Haarlem
Fonteyne, Claude (1629–33): Leeuwarden
Forrest, Edward (1640): Oxford
Forster, Michael (1602–12): Amberg
Fortuño Sánchez, Miguel (1601): Saragossa
Fosbrooke, Nathaniel (1618): London
Fouët, Robert (1608–23): Paris
Frambotti, Paolo (1628–47): Padua
Franceschi. *See* Francisci
Francisci, Giovanni Antonio de (1609): Palermo
Francisci, Giovanni Antonio & Jacopo de
     (1606–8): Venice
Francisci, Jacopo de (1614): Venice
Franck, David (1617–24): Augsburg
Franck, Johann (1607–8): Magdeburg
Fransen, J. (1644): The Hague
Frellon, Paul (1607): Lyons
Frere, Daniel (1639–44): London
Fritsche, Tobias (1644–48): Erfurt
Froben Bookshop (P. Lang). (1608–28): Hamburg
Froben Office (1601–39): Hamburg
Frosch, Conrad (1630): Passau
Fürst, Paul (1647): Nuremberg
Fuess, (Pedanus), Joachim (1625–27): Rostock
Fuet, Jean (1605): Antwerp
Fussell, Nicholas (1632): London

Gabiano, J. A. (1602): Lyons
Gabiano, Jean de (1602–7): Lyons
Gafaro, Giacomo (1639): Naples
Gaffaro, G. (1622): Naples
Gaffaro, Il (1646): Naples
Galignani, Paolo & Francesco (1620–21): Padua
Galignani, Simon, Heirs of (1603–5): Venice
Galler, Hieronymus (1611–27): Oppenheim
Gallina, Comino (1617): Venice
Gamonet, Estienne (1609–46): Geneva; (1616):
     Cologny
Gamonet, Philippe (1639–46): Geneva
Gamonet, Stephan. *See* Gamonet, Estienne
García, Anton (1605): Valladolid
García, Francisco. *See* García de Arroyo, Francisco
García, Juan (1626): Alcalá de Henares
García, Pedro (1649): Madrid
García de Arroyo, Francisco (1645–46): Madrid
García Morrás, Diego (1648–50): Madrid
García Sodruz, Pedro (1641): Madrid
Garrich, Gaspar (1622): Gerona
Garriz, Crisóstomo, Heirs of (1646–47): Valencia
Garriz, Juan Crisóstomo (1602–25): Valencia
Garzoni, M. (1648): Venice
Gasse, Nicolas (1632): Paris
Gaubisch, Jakob (1603): Eisleben
Gaudion, Jacob (1617–18): Lyons
Gaultier, Philippe (1630): Paris

Gay, Nicolas (1637–43): Lyons
Gazeau, Hugo (1606): Lyons
Geelkercken, Nicolaes van (1619–24): Leyden
Geerts, Steffen (1645): Leeuwarden
Gelli, Giovanni Paolo (1606–7): Rome
Gellibrand, Samuel (1645–47): London
Genath, Johann Jakob (1617–47): Basel
Gerbrantszoon, Marten (1630–48): Hoorn
Gerlach, Christian (1650): Emden
Germont, Jean (1636): Paris
Gerritsz, Adriaen. *See* Beyeren, A. G. van
Gerritsz, Hessel (1612–31): Amsterdam
Gesselin, Jean (1603–37): Paris
Geuffroy, David (1616–26): Rouen
Ghezzi, Egidio (1644): Rome
Ghisolfi, Filippo (1645): Milan
Ghisoni, Mazantinus & Aloysius (1632): Urbino
Gibbs, George (1617): London
Gil de Cordova, Martin (1625): Madrid
Ginammi, Marco (1621–48): Venice
Ginobart, José de (1630): Saragossa
Giolitis, The (1601): Venice
Girard, Claude (1621–29): Saumur
Girard, Samuel (1602): Lyons
Giuliani, Antonio (1617): Venice
Giuliani, Giovanni Antonio (1616–23): Venice
Giunta, Bernardo (1608–12): Venice
Giunta, Cosmo (1602–11): Florence
Giunta, Filippo (1601): Florence
Giunta Office (1611–42): Venice
Giuntas, The (1603–50): Venice; (1609): Florence
Glamet, Noël (1603): Rennes
Glaser, Théodore (1615): Strassburg
Glaser, Wilhelm Christian (1630): Strassburg
Glen, Jean de (1601): Liège
Gobert, Martin (1618–19): Paris
Godinez de Millis, Juan (1602): Medina del Campo;
     (1606–11): Valladolid
Godinho, Andre (1642): Lisbon
Goedesberg, Gerrit van (1648–49): Amsterdam
Görlin, Johann (1640–49): Ulm
Götz, Thomas Matthias (1644): Frankfurt a. M.
Götz Press (1628–33): Stettin
Götze, Matthäus (1631): Leipzig
Gómez, Bartolomé (1603–4): Seville
Gómez de Blas, Juan (1633–50): Seville
Gómez de Pastrana, Bartolomé (1621): Seville
Gómez de Pastrana, Pedro (1633–48): Seville
Gómez de Valdivielso, Pedro (1619–46): Burgos
Gonçalvez, Antonio (1628): Lisbon
González, Domingo (1620–37): Madrid
González, Juan (1623–30): Madrid
González, Juan, Widow of (1633–39): Madrid
Gorisszoon, Jasper (1639–47): Dordrecht
Gormann, Johann (1608): Wittenberg
Gosson, Henry (1612–35): London

Gracián, Juan, Heirs of (1603–21): Alcalá de Henares
Gracián, Juan, Widow of (1601–26): Alcalá de Henares
Graells, Gabriel (1603–9): Barcelona
Grande, Andrés (1636): Seville
Grande, Luís Martínez (1606): Alcalá de Henares
Greco, Giorgio (1603): Vicenza
Greene, Charles (1637): London
Grevenbruch, Gerhard (1613): Cologne
Griffin, Anne (1622–37): London
Griffin, Edward, the Elder (1614–20): London
Griffin, Edward, the Younger (1638–47): London
Grignani, Ludovico (1630–50): Rome
Griset, Claude (1634): Paris
Grismond, John (1621–50): London
Gross, Gottfried (1631–34): Leipzig
Gross, Gottfried, Heirs of (1644–45): Leipzig
Gross, Henning (1604): Leipzig
Gross, Henning, the Younger (1612–13): Leipzig
Gross, Johann (1630): Leipzig
Grossi, Francesco (1609): Vicenza
Grove, Francis (1629): London
Grove, John (1629–32): London
Gruber, Balthasar (1641): Braunschweig
Gründer, Augustin (1628–31): Brieg
Grüner, Friedrich (1627): Coburg
Gruppenbach, Georg (1603–6): Tübingen
Guasp, Gabriel (1626): Majorca
Gubbin, Thomas (1615): London
Gudoni, Giacomo (1633): Bari
Gueffier, François (1608–17): Paris
Guerigli, Giovanni (1614–29): Venice
Guerigli, Giovanni, Heirs of (1629–50): Venice
Guerigli, The (1638–48): Venice
Guierche, Jean (1637): Paris
Guignard, Jean (1630–45): Paris
Guignard, Jean, father and son (1648): Paris
Guillemot, Jean (1647): Paris
*Guillemot, Matthieu (1605–44): Paris
Guillemot, Matthieu, Widow of (1612–17): Paris
Guisolfi, Phelipe (1631): Milan
Guliano, G. A. See Giuliani, Giovanni Antonio
Guyot, Christoffel (1602): Leyden
Guyot, Guy-Anne (1645): Dijon
Guzmán, Bernardino de (1619–25): Madrid
Gymnicus, Johannes (1607–26): Cologne

H., R. (1641): London
Haack, François (1638–48): Leyden
Hänlin, Gregor (1622–28): Ingolstadt
Haestens, Hendrick van (1607–12): Leyden
Hagedoorn, Abraham Pieterszoon van (1647): Middelburg
Hake, Johann (1623): Wittenberg
Halbmeyer, Simon (1619–26): Nuremberg

Hall, Henry (1643–48): Oxford
Hall, William (1611–12): London
Hallervord, Johann (1616–44): Rostock; (1628): Stettin; (1644): Frankfurt a. M.
Hammond, John (1649–50): London
Hampel, Nikolaus (1620): Giessen; (1629–38): Marburg
Hancock, John (1642–50): London
Hardesty, John (1646–47): London
Harford, Raphael (1638): London
Haringhouck, Samuel van (1649): Bolsward
Harper, Thomas (1629–50): London
*Harrison, John (1608–48): London
Harsy, Antoine de (1603–6): Lyons
Harsy, Antoine de, Widow of (1610–15): Lyons
Hart, Andreas (1614–20): Edinburgh
Hartgers, Joost (1644–50): Amsterdam
Hartmann, Andreas (1650): Wittenberg
Hartmann, Melchior (1601): Frankfurt a. M.
Hasrey, Juan (1611–22): Madrid; (1614): Antwerp
Hatfield, Arnold (1604–6): London
Haubold, Peter (1647): Frankfurt a. M.
Haultin, Jérome (1618): La Rochelle
Haultin, Jérome, Heirs of (1605–8): La Rochelle
Haveland, Thomas (1610–11): London
Havick, Jan (1649): Utrecht
Haviland, John (1622–39): London
Havius, Matthias (1637–38): Dordrecht
Hebb, Andrew (1625–40): London
Heger, Frans (1638–45): Leyden
Heiden, C. (1618–24): Wittenberg
*Heil, Nikolaus (1647–49): Mainz
Heinrich, Nikolaus (1604–40): Munich
Hellen, Johannes van der (1618–29): Middelburg
Helme, Anne (1620–21): London
Helme, John (1612–13): London
Helmichszoon, Adriaen (1608): Gorinchem
Helmlin, Johann Maximilian (1617): Rottweil
Helwig, J. (1633): Wittenberg
Henault, Jean (1646–49): Paris
Henault, Mathurin (1623–47): Paris
Henault, Mathurin & Jean (1644): Paris
Henne, Hans Jakob (1613): Hanau
Henning, Peter (1615–50): Cologne
Henrickz, Thomas, Widow of (1624): Harderwijck
Henricpetri, Sebastian (1601–15): Basel
Henricpetri Office (1628): Basel
Hentzner, Paul (1612): Nuremberg
Hermann, Johann (1613): Leipzig
Hertel, Zacharias (1642): Hamburg
Hertsroy, Johann (1620–23): Munich
Herwijck, Abraham van (1624–25): Utrecht
Hessius, Joannes (1623–34): Amsterdam
Heuqueville, Jean de (1616–30): Paris
Heyden, Christoph von der (1619): Strassburg
Heyden, Marx von der (1628): Strassburg
Heyll, Nikolaus. See Heil, Nikolaus

Heyndrickz, Roelof (1646): Amsterdam
Heyns, Zacharias (1601): Amsterdam
Hidalgo, Clemente (1603–10): Seville; (1610): Cadiz
Hierat, Anton (1611–21): Cologne
Hilten, Jan van (1626–50): Amsterdam
Hodgets, John (1607–17): London
Hodgkinson, Richard (1639–43): London
Hoeve, Willem van der (1638–49): Gouda
Hofer, Johann (1620): Frankfurt a. M.
Hoffmann, Nikolaus, the Elder (1604–19): Frankfurt a. M.
Hoffmann, Wolfgang (1625–46): Frankfurt a. M.
Hollander, Peter de (1647): Antwerp
Hollant, J. (1649): Rouen
Holmes, William (1606): London
Holstis, J. (1648): Copenhagen
Holwein, Elias (1615): Wolfenbüttel
Hondius, Henricus (1621–41): Amsterdam
Hondius, Jodocus (1605–29): Amsterdam
Hondius Office (1630–5–): Amsterdam
Hood, Henry (1637–50): London
Hoogenacker, Arent Corsen (1628): Leyden
Hoogenhuysen, Dirk van (1644): Utrecht
Hope, William (1634–41): London
Hospital Real de Nuestra Señora de Gracia (1634–49): Saragossa
Houssaye, Denys (1638): Paris
Houten, Ysbrant Janszoon van (1644): Alkmaar
Houzé, Jean (1601–18): Paris
Hubert, Adrien (1604–7): Antwerp
Huby, François (1607–15): Paris
Hünefeld, Andreas (1641): Danzig
Huggins, Thomas (1625–33): Oxford
Huguetan, A. (1609): Lyons
Huguetan, Jean (1634–45): Lyons
Huguetan, Jean Antoine (1606–50): Lyons
Huguetan, Jean Antoine, the Younger (1649): Lyons
Hulpeau, Claude (1625): Paris
Hulsius (The Hulsiuses). (1617–36): Frankfurt a. M.; (1617): Hanau
Hulsius, Heirs of (1629–30): Frankfurt a. M.
Hulsius, Levinus (1601–3): Nuremberg; (1603–5): Frankfurt a. M.
Hulsius, Levinus, Heirs of (1606–28): Frankfurt a. M.
Hulsius, Levinus, Widow of (1608–15): Frankfurt a. M.; (1614–27): Oppenheim
Humble, George (1627–31): London
Humble, William (1646): London
Humm, Anton (1611–44): Frankfurt a. M.; (1612): Giessen
Hunt, Joseph (1613): London
Hunt, William (1650): London
Hurlock, George (1634–44): London
Hurlock, Joseph (1632–34): London

Husband, Edward (1649–50): London
Hutton, George (1637): London
Huybertszoon, Jan (1614): Leyden

Ibbitson, Robert (1647–50): London
Iglesia, Domingo de la (1624): Ucles; (1627–37): Cuenca
Imberti, Domenico (1603–43): Venice
Imberti, Ghirardo (1620–40): Venice
Imberti, Ghirardo & Gioseffo (1625–26): Venice
Imberti, Ghirardo, Heirs of (1645): Venice
Imberti, Gioseffo (1628): Venice
Imberti, Iseppo. See Imberti, Gioseffo
Imberti, The (1628): Venice
Imprenta Real (1601–48): Madrid
Iñíguez de Lequérica, Juan, Heirs of (1604): Valladolid
Islip, Adam (1604–36): London

Jackson, John (1634): London
Jackson, Roger (1607–23): London
Jacobi, Paul (1615–26): Frankfurt a. M.
Jacobszoon, Hillebrant. See Wouw, Hillebrant Jacobszoon van
Jacobszoon, Jan (1636–47): Arnhem
Jacobszoon, Theunis (1631–44): Amsterdam
Jacobus, Anthoni. See Jacobszoon, Theunis
Jacquemetton, Jean (1637): Lyons
Jacquemetton, Jean, Widow of (1643): Lyons
Jacquin, François (1608–19): Paris
Jacquin, Julien (1647): Paris
Jäger, Gottfried (1648): Lübeck
Jaey, Henri (1622): Mechlin
Jaggard, Elizabeth (1624): London
Jaggard, Isaac (1623–27): London
Jaggard, John (1601–22): London
Jaggard, William (1602–30): London
Janss, A., pseud. (1624): Gorkum
Janssen, Andries (1625): Zutphen
Jansson, Jan. See Janszoon, Jan (the Younger)
Janszoon, Broer (1616–46): Amsterdam
Janszoon, Harmen (1619): Amsterdam
Janszoon, Jacob (1630): Rotterdam
Janszoon, Jan (1601–26): Arnhem
*Janszoon, Jan (the Younger). (1618–50): Amsterdam
Janszoon, Symon (1608): Middelburg
Janszoon, Willem. See Blaeu, Willem Janszoon
Janszoon de Jonghe, Jan (1633): Flushing
Jaquet, Johannes (1644): Amsterdam
Jenner, Thomas (1626–31): London
Jennis, Lucas (1618–28): Frankfurt a. M.
Jesuit College (1606–15): Rome
Jesuits of Brazil (1618): Lisbon
Joallin, Jean Anthoine (1623): Paris

Johnson, Arthur (1602–19): London; (1626): Dublin
Jones, Thomas (1615–30): London
Jones, William (1604–36): London
Joosten, Gillis (1647): Amsterdam
Joosten, Jacob (1649): Amsterdam
Jost, Jean (1629–50): Paris
Juan, Carlos (1646): Pamplona
Juliano. *See* Giuliano
Julliot, François (1619–22): Paris

Kalckhoven, Jost (1643–46): Cologne
Kallenbach, Helwig (1638): Emden
Katzenberger, Christoph (1634): Salzburg
Kaufmann, Paul (1604): Nuremberg
Keerberghen, Jan van (1601–15): Antwerp
Keere, Pieter van der (1618–19): Amsterdam
Kellam, Laurence, the Younger (1622): Douai
Kellam, Laurence, Widow of (1618): Douai
Kellam, Thomas (1618): Douai
Kempen, Arnold (1609): Cologne
Kempfer, Erasmus (1612–29): Frankfurt a. M.
Kempfer, Matthäus (1629–42): Frankfurt a. M.
Kempner, Anton (1612): Frankfurt a. M.
Kerchovius, J. Baptiste & L. (1640): Bruges
Keschedt, Peter (1608): Cologne
Ketel, Gerhard (1601): Franeker
Ketzel, Wolfgang (1612–27): Schmalkalden
Keyltz, Johann (1625): Augsburg
Kieffer, Karl (1612): Strassburg
Kinckius, Johann (1617): Cologne
Kinckius, Johann Anton (1649): Cologne
Kingston, Felix (1601–38): London
Klosemann, Kaspar (1630): Leipzig
Knight, Philip (1615–16): London
Koch, Michael (1636): Frankfurt a. M.
König, Jakob (1606): Mainz
König, Ludwig (1614–41): Basel
König, Ludwig, Heirs of (1642): Basel
Kopff, Peter (1601–25): Frankfurt a. M.; (1613): Hanau
Krafft, Heinrich (1638): Cologne
Kranepoel, Harman (1627): Haarlem
Krause, Christoff (1631–40): Heilbronn
Kruger, Johann (1613–29): Augsburg
Krusecke, Joachim (1617): Halle

Labayen, Carlos de (1610–29): Pamplona
L'Abbé, Balthazar (1610): Gex
La Bottière, François de (1643): Lyons
Lacavallería, Antonio (1646): Barcelona
Lacavallería, Pedro (1638–44): Barcelona
La Coste, Nicolas & Jean de (1633–46): Paris
Lacquahay, J. *See* Laquehay, Jean
Laet, Geraerdt de (1650): Flushing

Laet, Jan de (1650): Middelburg
La Fontaine, Charles (1601): Geneva
La Forge, André de (1615): La Rochelle
La Fosse, Solomon de (1636): Paris
La Garde, Jérôme de (1648): Lyons
L'Allemant, Richard (1618–45): Rouen
La Mare, Jean de (1628–32): Rouen
Lamberg, Abraham (1608): Leipzig
La Motte, Martin (1627–37): Rouen
La Motte, Pierre (1627): Rouen
Lamrinck, Jan (1620): Franeker
L'Amy, Pierre (1636): Paris
Lanaja, Juan de. *See* Lanaja y Quartanet, Juan de
Lanaja, Pedro. *See* Lanaja y Lamarca, Pedro
Lanaja y Lamarca, Pedro (1640–48): Saragossa
Lanaja y Lamarca, Pedro, Heirs of (1650): Saragossa
Lanaja y Quartanet, Juan de (1610–30): Saragossa
Lancellot, Johann (1606): Heidelberg
Lanckisch, Friedrich, the Elder (1620–30): Leipzig
Landi, Lorenzo (1642): Florence
Lang, P. *See* Froben Bookshop
L'Angelier, Abel (1602–8): Paris
Langenes, Baernaerdt (1601): Middelburg; (1611): Flushing
Langenwalter, Matthäus (1625): Augsburg
Langford, Toby (1646): Gloucester
Langhe, Lieven de, pseud. (1644): The Hague
Langley, Thomas (1621): London
Langlois, Denis (1613–27): Paris
La Noüe, Denis de (1608): Paris
La Noüe, Guillaume de, Widow of (1605–8): Paris
Lantzenberger, Michael (1604–12): Leipzig
Lantzenberger, Michael, Heirs of (1613): Leipzig
La Pierre, Jacques de (1635): Geneva
La Planche, Johannes de (1639): Geneva
La Porte, Hugues de (1607): Lyons
Laquehay, Jean (1636–37): Paris
La Rivière, Guillaume de (1604–16): Arras
Larjot, Claude (1625): Lyons
La Rovière, Pierre de (1604): Orleans; (1612–26): Geneva
La Ruelle, Thomas de (1601–33): Paris
Larumbe, Juan de (1619): Saragossa
Lasso, Juan (1630): Valladolid
Lasso, Pedro (1604): Valladolid; (1642–45): Madrid
Lasso de las Peñas, Juan (1629): Valladolid
Lasso Vaca, Cristóbal (1602): Medina del Campo; (1609): Valladolid
Later, Anthony de (1650): Middelburg
Latham, George (1623–50): London
Laurenszoon, Hendrick (1610–46): Amsterdam
Laurent, Nicolas (1610): Tournai
Laurentz, Benedict (1608): Copenhagen
Lautret, Jean (1619–26): Lyons
La Vigne, Nicolas de (1640): Paris

Law, Matthew (1604–22): London
Leach, Francis (1644–50): London
Leake, William (1640): London
Le Beau, Claude (1645): Paris
Le Blon, Christoph (1640–50): Frankfurt a. M.
Le Bouc, Jean, Widow of (1648): Paris
Le Boullenger, Jacques (1630–50): Rouen
Le Clerc, David (1605–11): Paris
Le Clerc, Jean (1620): Paris
Le Clercq, Toussaint (1642): Lille
Ledertz, Paul (1612–15): Strassburg
Lee, William (1627–48): London
Leers, Arnout (1649–50): Rotterdam
Le Fevre, Abraham (1612): Paris
Leffen, Pieter (1649): Leyden
Le Francq, Simon (1640): Lille
Legat, John (1611–46): London
Le Gras, Henry (1630–37): Paris
Lehmann, Zacharias, Widow of (1606): Wittenberg
Leinhose, Johannes (1624): Darmstadt
Le Maître, Mathieu (1612–26): Paris
Le Moine, Simon (1635): Paris
Le Mur, Pierre (1612–32): Paris
Leon, Gabriel de (1650): Madrid
Leon, Juan de (1602): Seville
Le Prevost, Nicolas (1619): Rouen
Lerpinière, Daniel (1621): Saumur
Lertout, Jean (1601): Lyons
Lescaille, Jacob (1644–46): Amsterdam
Lesnier, Jean (1629): Saumur
Lesselin, Alexandre (1650): Paris
Lesteens, Willem (1631): Antwerp
Le Vray, Jean, pseud. (1626): 'Villeneuve'
Levyn, Frans (1648): Utrecht
Leysser, Cornelius, Heirs of (1643): Munich
Liberòs, Esteban (1616–33): Barcelona
Libert, Jean (1615–45): Paris
Libert, Jean, Widow of (1648): Paris
Lichfield, John (1621–38): Oxford
Lichfield, Leonard (1635–45): Oxford
Liebergen, Arnout van (1643): Amsterdam
Lieshout, François (1630–46): Amsterdam
Lieshout, François, Widow of (1649): Amsterdam
Ling, Nicholas (1603–6): London
Linschoten, Jan Huygen van (1601): Enkhuizen
Lipp, Balthasar (1602–14): Mainz
Lira, F., pseud. (1650): Seville. *See also* Lyra, Francisco de
Lisle, Laurence (1615–22): London
Lithgow, Gideon (1647): Edinburgh
Lob, Nicolaus (1606): Cracow
Lobenstein, Blasius (1642): Jena
Locarno, Pietro Martire (1603–5): Milan
Locarno, Pietro Martire, Heirs of (1613): Milan
Lochner, Christoph (1601–3): Nuremberg
Loftus, George (1602–15): London
Logroño, Diego (1626–35): Madrid

Longhi, Aegidius. *See* Longo, Egidio
Longo, Egidio (1628–50): Naples
Longo, Tarquinio (1604–7): Naples
Looymans, Pieter (1645): Dordrecht
Lopes Rosa, Domingos (1641–46): Lisbon
López, Andrés (1623): Valladolid
López, Baptista (1603): Madrid
López, Baptista (1610): Alcalá de Henares
López, Estavão (1602): Lisbon
López, Francisco (1603–5): Madrid
López, Manuel (1635–45): Madrid; (1641): Alcalá de Henares
López de Haro, David (1639–49): Leyden
Lopez Rosa, D. *See* Lopes Rosa, Domingos
Lorenzana, Bartolomé de (1630): Granada
Lorenzo, Roberto (1645): Madrid
Loudet, Clovys (Louis) (1625): Rouen
Loudet, Daniel (1638–42): Rouen
Loudet, Louis (1616–30): Rouen
Loven, Hermes van (1609–11): The Hague
Lowndes, Richard (1641–50): London
Lownes, Humphrey (1605–30): London
Lownes, Matthew (1602–24): London
L'Oyselet, Nicolas (1643–45): Rouen
L'Oyselet, Pierre (1625): Rennes
Loyson, Guillaume (1625–47): Paris
Loyson, Jean Baptiste (1647): Paris
Lucius, Petrus (1644): Rinteln a. d. Weser
Lützenkirchen, Wilhelm (1604–18): Cologne
Lugger, William (1633–47): London
Lyra, Francisco de (1616–48): Seville. *See also* Lira, F., pseud.

M., J. (1642): London
Mabb, Ralph (1634–40): London
Macé, Barthélemy (1607–14): Paris
Macé, Guillaume (1620): Paris
Macedonien, Philips van, pseud. (1647): Dordrecht; (1648): Amsterdam
Macham, Samuel (1608–12): London
Macock, John (1645–47): London
Made, Sybrandt van der (1647): Amsterdam
Madrigal, Pedro (1601–3): Madrid
Maerten, pseud. (1649): 'West Indische Kamer'
Magri, Giovanni Andrea (1648): Pavia
Maire, Abraham (1608): Antwerp
Maire, Jean (1617–47): Leyden
Maire, Jean & Théodore (1636): Leyden
Malassis, Clément (1635–47): Rouen
Malatesti, The (1612–25): Milan
Mallet, Jacques (1614): Lyons
Man, Jonas (1626–27): London
Man, Thomas (1602–22): London
Manelfi, Manelfo (1642–49): Rome
Manescal, M. *See* Menescal, Miguel
Mang, Christoph (1613–16): Augsburg

Mangeant, Jacques (1614): Caen
Mangin, Sarah (1620): Augsburg
Manilius, Servais (1643–48): Ghent
Manneville, Jean de (1644): Rouen
Marceau, P. (1606): Paris
Marceau, Paul (1610): Geneva
Marchant, Jean (1612): London
Marchetti, Salvestro (1604): Siena; (1625): Pisa
Marcus, Jacobus (1617–41): Leyden
Marel, Johannes van (1647): Amsterdam
Marel, Pieter van, pseud. (1647): Amsterdam
Marescotti, Christofano (1604): Florence
Marette, Claude (1647–48): Paris
Margarit, Jerónimo (1608–32): Barcelona; (1612): Lérida
Mariette, Pierre (1633): Paris
Marino, Wenceslao (1602): Prague
Marne, Claude de (1601–9): Frankfurt a. M.; (1605): Hanau
Marne, Claude de, Heirs of (1610): Hanau; (1612): Frankfurt a. M.
Marne, Johannes & Andreas (1612): Frankfurt a. M. See also Marne, Claude de, Heirs of
Marnef, H. de (1608): Paris
Marnioles, Pierre (1630): Grenoble
Maroto, Francisco (1642): Madrid
Mar-Prelate, Margery, pseud. (1641): London
Marriott, John (1617–50): London
Marriott, Richard (1640–50): London
Marshall, John (1645): London
Martarello, Antonio (1639): Palermo
Martel, Jean (1616): Beziers
Martensz, Cornelis (1650): Leeuwarden
Martín, Alonso (1608–12): Madrid
Martín, Alonso, Widow of (1616–35): Madrid
Martin, Bertrand (1618–21): Paris
Martin, Charles (1613): Tournai
Martin, David (1611–12): Antwerp
Martín, Hieronymo (1603): Tarragona
Martin, Jean (1625–28): Paris
Martin, Jost (1601): Strassburg
Martín Vellaz, Santiago (1650): Madrid
Martinelli, Giovanni (1601): Rome
Martínez, Francisco (1628–42): Madrid
Martínez, Juan (1601): Madrid
Martínez, Miguel (1601–18): Madrid
Martínez Grande, Luis (1610): Alcalá de Henares
Martzen, Melchior (1648): Copenhagen
Marzal, Juan Batista (1625): Valencia
Mascardi, Giacomo (1615–47): Rome
Mascardi, Jacobus. See Mascardi, Giacomo
Mascardi, Vitale (1644–49): Rome
Massi, Amadore (1642): Florence
Massino, Carlo (1625): Pisa
Matevad, Sebastián (1604–17): Barcelona
Matevad, Sebastián & Jaume (1625–48): Barcelona
Mathewes, Augustine (1619–50): London

Mathonière, Nicolas de (1622): Paris
Matthiae, E. See Matthias, A.
Matthias, Aeschillus (1633–38): Uppsala
Matthijszoon, Paul (1640–41): Amsterdam
Maucroy, Stephan (1650): Paris
Mayer, Johann, Widow of (1618): Dillingen
Mayer Press (1618): Dillingen
Mechler, Esaias, Heirs of (1618–30): Erfurt
Meder, Johann (1612): Ulm
Meerbeeck, Jan van (1625): Brussels
Megiser, Hieronymus (1603): Frankfurt a. M.
Meietti, Paolo (1606): Padua
Meietti, Roberto (1601–5): Venice; (1606): Treviso
Meighen, Richard (1615–41): London
Meisner, Wolfgang (1611): Wittenberg
Melvill, David (1623): Aberdeen
Ménard, Pierre (1633–43): Paris
Menescal, Luis (1612–14): Lérida
Menescal, Miguel (1604–25): Barcelona; (1612): Lérida
Menlemand, C. (1626): Amsterdam
Mercurius Britannicus (1625): London
Meredith, Christopher (1628–50): London
Merian, Matthäus (1627–50): Frankfurt a. M.
Merlo, Bartolomeo (1643): Verona
Mesnier, Antoine (1609): Poitiers
Mesnier, Antoine, Widow of (1628): Poitiers
Mesnier, Isaac (1619): Paris
Mestais, Jean (1625): Paris
Meteren, Emanuel van (1609–11): London
Mettayer, Jamet (1603–15): Paris
Mettayer, Jamet & Pierre (1602): Paris
Mettayer, Pierre (1614–27): Paris
Meturas, Gaspar (1647): Paris
Meulemans, Christiaan (1625): Amsterdam
Meurer, Ignatius (1626): Stockholm
Meuris, Aert (1619–30): The Hague
Meurs, Jean de (1632–43): Antwerp
Mevius, Tobias, Heirs of (1644): Wittenberg
Mey, Felipe (1616–20): Valencia
Mey, Pedro Patricio (1602–31): Valencia
Meyn, Jacob Lenaertszoon (1619): Enkhuizen
Meyne, David de (1612): Amsterdam
Michel, Claude (1604–16): Tournon; (1626): Lyons
Michell, Roger (1628–31): London
Michelson, Andreas (1616): Lüneburg
Miglietti, Roberto (1623): Venice
Miguel, Francisco (1602): Valencia
Milbourne, Robert (1622–36): London
Millanges, Guillaume (1633–43): Bordeaux
Millanges, Simon (1610): Bordeaux
Miller, Abraham (1648–50): London
Miller, George (1628–45): London
Millot, Jean (1609–12): Paris
Miloco, Pier (1620–23): Venice
Minervae, Sub signo (1647): Venice

Minims, Society of (1602): Venice
Minzel, Johann Albrecht (1633): Leipzig
Misserini, Nicolò (1605–22): Venice
Mölemann, Staffan (1608): Rostock
Moingesse, Nicolas de (1601): Besançon
Molikens, J. (1648): Copenhagen
Mommaert, Jean (1604–49): Brussels
Mondière, Melchior (1613–44): Paris
Monstr'oeil, Claude de (1603–4): Paris
Monstr'oeil, Widow of. *See* Niverd, Catherine
Monti, Giacomo (1635–44): Bologna
Montini, Giovanni (1633): Bari
Montoya, Joã de (1601–5): Madrid
More, Richard (1608–31): London
Moreau, Denys (1618–46): Paris
Moreau, Jean (1623): Paris
Moreau, Pierre, Printshop of the New Type
    invented by (1644): Paris
Morel, Charles (1607–30): Paris
Moretus, Balthazar. *See* Plantin Office (B. Moretus)
Moretus, Jean (1610): Antwerp. *See also* Plantin
    Office (J. Moretus)
Morgan, John (1635): London
Morillo, G. *See* Morillo, Jerónimo
Morillo, Jerónimo (1623–33): Valladolid
Morillon, Claude (1604–15): Lyons
Morlot, Claude (1636): Paris
Moseley, Humphrey (1632–50): London
Mottershead, Edward (1646–47): London
Moulaert, Symon (1647–48): Dordrecht
Moulert, Simon, Widow & Heirs of (1621–41):
    Middelburg
Mourentorff, Jan. *See* Moretus, Jean; *see also* Plantin
    Press (J. Moretus)
Moussat, Jean (1616): Maillé
Moussat, Jean (1624): Niort
Moxon, James (1650): London
Moyaert, Franciscus (1642–49): Leyden
Mucerus, Hendrick (1650): Groningen
Mucken, Jans (1618): Amsterdam
Mülbe, Johann Philipp (1640–50): Strassburg
Müller, David (1628–31): Breslau
Müller, David, Heirs of (1638): Breslau
Müller, Georg, Widow of (1634): Wittenberg
Müller, Gottfried (1641): Braunschweig
Münich, Constantin (1650): Cologne
Muguet, Louis (1616): Lyons
Muñoz, Sebastian (1606–17): Granada
Muschio, Andrea (1619–21): Venice
Musculus, Petrus (1610): Frankfurt a. M.
Mylius, Arnold (1602): Cologne; (1602): Mainz
Mylius, Arnold (House of Birckmann). (1605):
    Cologne
Mylius, Hermann (1614–31): Cologne
Mylius, J. (House of Birckmann). (1604): Cologne
Myn, Richard (1630): London

Naeranus, Joannes (1647): Rotterdam
Neben, Conrad (1605): Frankfurt a. M.; (1609–10):
    Offenbach
Neile, Francis (1644–50): London
Nempe, Jérémie (1647): Louvain
Nenninger, Tobias (1630): Passau
Nering, Abraham (1634): Rotterdam
Nerlich, Nikolaus, Heirs of (1613): Leipzig
Nes, Jacob, pseud. (1648): Amsterdam
Nevill, Philip (1638): London
Newbery, John (1602–3): London
Newbery, Nathaniel (1619): London
Newbery, Ralph (1601): London
Nicod, Michelle (1608): Geneva
Nicolai. *See* Claeszoon
Nicolino, Domenico (1604): Venice
Nigaut, Jean (1613–23): Paris
Nivelle, Michel (1608–17): Paris
Niverd, Catherine (Widow of Monstr'oeil). (1604):
    Paris
Nogués, Bernardo (1646–47): Valencia
Nogués, Gabriel (1641–44): Barcelona
Nolck, Maarten Abraham van der (1623): Flushing
Norton, Alice (1643): London
Norton, Bonham (1614–27): London
Norton, George (1611–13): London
*Norton, John (1601–45): London
Norton, Joyce (1635): London
Norton Office (1611): London
Nutius, Martinus. *See* Nuyts, Marten
*Nuyts, Marten (1604–27): Antwerp
Nuyts, Marten, Heirs of (1618): Antwerp
Nuyts, Marten, Sons of (1620): Antwerp

Obert, Claude (1627–36): Lyons
Ocampo, Francisco de (1632): Madrid
Ockerszoon, Joost (1629): The Hague
Ockould, Richard (1606): London
Odain, Louis (1637): Lyons
Oelschlegel, Melchior (1625–34): Halle
Okes, John (1611–41): London
Okes, Marie (1645): London
Okes, Nicholas (1607–40): London
Okes, Nicholas & John (1635–37): London
Olive, Richard (1601): London
Onofri, Francesco (1646): Florence
Orlers, Jan Janszn (1610–15): Leyden
Ormer, Diego de. *See* Dormer, Diego
Orry, Jeanne (1612): Paris
Orry, Marc (1604–9): Paris
Orry, Marc, Widow of (1612): Paris
Osmont, Jean (1602–34): Rouen
Osmont, Jean, the Younger (1638): Rouen
Ossete, Pedro de (1602–3): Valladolid
Ostern, Balthasar (1625): Frankfurt a. M.
Oteyza, Juan de (1622–24): Pamplona

Oulton, Richard (1638–43): London
Oursel, Louis (1639): Rouen
Ouyn, Adrian (1610–44): Rouen
Overton, Henry (1633–46): London

Pacard, Abraham (1618): Paris
Paddenburch, Amelis van (1650): Utrecht
Paets, Jacob Pieterszoon (1610): Amsterdam
Paets, Pieter Jacobszoon (1617): Amsterdam
Pailly, Guichard (1613): Lyons
Paine, Thomas (1632–44): London
Palacio y Villegas, Domingo de (1643–44): Madrid
Palliot, Pierre (1643–48): Dijon
Palthenius, Hartmann (1615–31): Frankfurt a. M.
Palthenius, Zacharias (1601–8): Frankfurt a. M.
Palthenius, Zacharias, Heirs of (1619–24): Frankfurt a. M.
Palthenius Office (1601–9): Frankfurt a. M.
Paolini, Stefano (1610–33): Rome
Paredes, Alonso de (1625–47): Madrid
Pariasca, Simone (1609): Bologna
París, Bartholomé (1614–34): Pamplona
Paris, University of (1644): Paris
Parker, John (1618–34): London
Parnassus Office (1626): Strassburg
Parra, Andres de (1628–40): Madrid
Parsons, Marmaduke (1635–39): London
Partridge, John (1621–33): London
Partridge, Miles (1616–25): London
Pas, Crispin van de (1641): Amsterdam
Pas, Crispin van de, the Elder. See Passe, Crispin van de
Pasini, Agostino (1623): Venice
Pasquardo, Donato (1630): Padua
Pasquardo, Donato, & Associates (1630): Padua; (1630): Venice
Pasquato, Lorenzo (1606–11): Padua
Pasquato Office (1611): Padua
Passe, Crispin van de (1614–20): Utrecht
Passe, Crispin van de, the Younger. See Pas, Crispin van de
Patisson, Mamert, Widow of (1604): Paris
Patisson, Philippe (1605): Paris
Pauwelszoon, Joris (1623): Rotterdam
Pavier, Thomas (1609–19): London
Pavoni, Giuseppe (1602–6): Genoa
Pavonum (1645): Genoa
Paxton, Edward (1636): London
Payne, Thomas. See Paine, Thomas
Peasley, William (1635): London
Pedanus. See Fuess
Pelé, Guillaume (1631–43): Paris
Pelé, Guillaume, Widow of (1643): Paris
Pels, Frans (1644): Amsterdam
Pépingué, Théodore, Widow of (1650): Paris
Pérez, Alonso (1608–34): Madrid

Pérez, Diego (1602): Burgos; (1603): Valladolid
Pérez, Francisco (1603): Seville
Perfert, Johann (1620): Jena
Périer, Adrien (1603–18): Paris
Périer, Jeremie (1608–21): Paris
Périer, Louis (1637): Paris
Perna, F. (1640): Basel
Perry, Hugh (1639–41): London
Pers, Dirck Pieterszoon (1610–44): Amsterdam
Pers, Hans (1640): Antwerp
Petit, Jean (1606–8): Rouen
Petit-Pas, Jean (1608–26): Paris
Petrinae, Jean (1636): Paris
Philippe, Sébastien (1614): Toul
Piccaglia, Giovanni Battista (1603): Milan
Pieck, Jacob Janszoon, pseud. (1650): Flushing
Pierre, Jean (1628): Brussels
Pierre, Theodore. See Pers, Dirck Pieterszoon
Pieterszoon, Claes, pseud. (1649): Amsterdam
Pieterszoon, D. See Pers, Dirck Pieterszoon
Pieterszoon, Gillis (1650): The Hague
Pieterszoon, J. (1650): Amsterdam
Pillehotte, Antoine (1617–36): Lyons
Pillehotte, Jean (1603–25): Lyons
Pincinali, Filippo (1616): Valencia
Pinelli, Antonio (1626): Venice
Pinheiro, Mattheus (1625): Lisbon
Piotrkowczyk, Andrzey (1603): Cracow
Piquet, Sebastien (1646): Paris
Pistorius, Rupert (1610): Frankfurt a. M.
Pitreson, Corneille (1639–41): Rouen
Pizzuto, Francisco (1625): Rome
Plaignard, François (1642): Lyons
Planck, Johann (1623–24): Linz
Plantin, Christophe, Widow of (1610): Antwerp
Plantin Office (1601–48): Antwerp
Plantin Office (1608–18): Leyden
Plantin Office (Balthazar Moretus) (1630–42): Antwerp
Plantin Office (Franciscus Raphelengius) (1605–12): Leyden
Plantin Office (Jean Moretus) (1608): Antwerp
Plantin Office (Widow & Sons of Jean Moretus) (1613): Antwerp
Plasse, Cornelis Lodewijckszoon van der (1620–41): Amsterdam
Plasse, Cornelis Lodewijckszoon van der, Widow of (1641–44): Amsterdam
Polier, Amy de (1621): Lyons
Polo, Alessandrus (1620): Venice
Polo, Nicolò (1610): Venice
Polo, Nicolò, & Co. (1602): Venice
Pomeray, François (1629–32): Paris
Ponte, Paolo da, Heirs of (1603): Milan
Popma, Alardo de (1625): Madrid
Porsch, Johann Jakob (1610–41): Frankfurt a. M.; (1611): Darmstadt; (1618): Tübingen

Portau, Thomas (1607): Saumur
Potter, George (1606): London
Pouncet, John (1647): London
Poyet, Jean (1606–13): Lyons
Prats, Jusepe (1640): Barcelona
Preaulx, Manasses de (1617–28): Rouen
Preuveray, François (1648): Paris
Preys, Boudewijn de (1639): Amsterdam
Promé, Jean (1637–43): Paris
Prost, Claude (1641–48): Lyons
Prost, Jacob & Pierre (1634): Lyons
Pulciano, Giovanni Battista (1607): Treviso;
   (1608): Venice
Pulleyn, Octavian (1650): London
Purfoot, Thomas (1605–34): London
Purfoot, Thomas, Assignee of (1638–39): London
Purset, Christopher (1607): London
Purslowe, Elizabeth (1633–44): London
Purslowe, George (1615–36): London

Queiros, Lourenzo de (1641): Lisbon
Quesnel, Jacques (1619–35): Paris
Quinet, Toussaint (1629–49): Paris
Quiñones, Maria de (1635–45): Madrid
Quinqué, Adrien (1623–42): Tournai

R., R. (1619): London
Rab, Christoph. See Corvinus, Christoph
Rab, Georg (1624–37): Herborn
Rab, Georg, Heirs of (1650): Herborn
Raban, Edward (1623): Aberdeen
Rache, Pierre de (1639): Lille
Rache, Pierre de, Widow of (1650): Lille
Rade, Jan & Pieter van den (1642): Leeuwarden
Raesfeldt, Bernard (1648): Münster
Ramires, Pero (1603): Lisbon
Ramirez, Antonia (1618): Salamanca
Rammazeyn, Pieter (1640): Gouda
Ramos Bejarano, Gabriel (1618): Seville
Rampazetto, Francesco (1610): Venice
Rand, Samuel (1614–42): London
Raphelengius, Franciscus. See Plantin Office
Ratcliffe, Thomas (1646–47): London
Ravaud, Marc Antoine (1649–50): Lyons
Ravaud, Pierre (1628–44): Lyons
Ravestein, Jan (1650): Amsterdam
Ravesteyn, Nicolaes van (1641–49): Amsterdam
Ravesteyn, Paulus Aertszoon van (1613–31):
   Amsterdam
Raworth, John (1640–45): London
Raworth, Robert (1635–36): London
Raworth, Ruth (1646): London
Read, Richard (1601–7): London
Redmer, Richard (1611–15): London
Reghettini, Angelo (1613–17): Treviso

Reghettini, The (1630): Venice
Reghettini. See also Righettini
Regnoul, Jean (1610): Paris
Regnoul, Jean, Widow of (1616): Paris
Rehefeld, Elias (1630): Leipzig
Reinsart, Théodore (1602–7): Rouen
Rémy, Jean, Widow of (1649): Paris
Renaut, Andres (1603): Salamanca
René, Juan (1619–28): Málaga
Reusner, Christoffer (1626): Stockholm
Rey, Fernando (1617): Seville; (1632): Jerez de la
   Frontera
Rezé, J. (1602): Paris
Rezé, Pierre (1608): Paris
Rhode, J. See Rose, Jonas
Ribeiro, Antonio (1601): Lisbon
Ribera, Antich (1602): Barcelona
Ribero, A. de (1645): Madrid
Ribero Rodríguez, Antonio del (1642): Madrid
Richer, Estienne (1633): Paris
Richer, Jean (1603–21): Paris
Richter, Johann (1615): Wittenberg
Richter, Johann, Heirs of (1620): Wittenberg
Richter, Wolfgang (1601–40): Frankfurt a. M.
Rigaud, Antoine (1643): Lyons
*Rigaud, Claude (1608–17): Paris; (1627–37):
   Lyons
Rigaud, Claude, Widow of (1633–42): Lyons
Rigaud, Pierre (1601–26): Lyons
Rigaud, Pierre, & Associates (1624): Lyons
Rigaud, Pierre & Claude (1649): Lyons
Rigaud, Pierre & Claude, Sons of (1642): Lyons
Rigaud, Pierre, the Younger (1641): Lyons
Rigaud, Simon (1616–50): Lyons
Righettini, Girolamo (1637–42): Treviso
Righettini. See also Reghettini
Rinialme, Ascanius de, Heirs of, pseud. (1605–48):
   Frankfurt a. M.
Ritherdon, Ambrose (1630–31): London
Ritzsch, Timotheus (1644–45): Leipzig
Rivière, Guillaume. See La Rivière, Guillaume de
Roberto, Felipe (1603–9): Tarragona
Robinot, Anthoine (1641–46): Paris
Robinot, Gilles & Anthoine (1625): Paris
Robinson, Humphrey (1629–50): London
Robles, Francisco de (1613–17): Madrid
Robles, Lorenço de (1610): Saragossa
Rochas, Henry de (1648): Paris
Rocket, Henry (1603–5): London
Rocolet, Pierre (1625–44): Paris
Rodríguez, Alfonso (1601): Saragossa
Rodríguez, Diego (1617–23): Toledo
Rodríguez, Gregorio (1644–46): Madrid
Rodríguez, Jorge (1601–41): Lisbon
Rodríguez, Juan (1625): Porto
Rodríguez, Matías (1630–31): Lisbon
Rodríguez, Nicolás (1638–48): Seville

Rodríguez, Pedro (1601–5): Toledo
Rodríguez, Pedro, Widow of (1611): Toledo
Rodríguez Gamarra, Alonso (1608): Seville
Röhner, Johann (1631): Köthen; (1640–50):
　Wittenberg
Roels, Jacob (1634): Leyden
Roest, Adriaan Harmenszoon (1648–50):
　Amsterdam
Rötel, Kaspar (1624–47): Frankfurt a. M.
Roger, Jean (1625–26): Rouen
Roger, Jean (1639–48): Paris
Roht, Nikolaus (1610): Frankfurt a. M.
Roize, Jean (1633): Aix-en-Province
Roman, Adriaan (1629–41): Haarlem
Roman, Aegidius (1642): Utrecht
Roman, Nathanael (1629): Groningen
Roman, Nathanael, Heirs of (1641): Groningen
Roman, Zacharias (1629–43): Middelburg
Rombouts, Pieter (1650): Amsterdam
Romeu, Jaime (1639): Barcelona
Roncaglioli, Giovanni Domenico (1634): Naples
Roncagliolo (1625): Naples
Roncalioli, Secondino (1625): Naples
Roncallolo. See Roncagliolo
Roover, Symon de (1649): Utrecht
Roper, Abel (1648–50): London
Ropero, Francisco (1643–46): Alcalá de Henares
Rose, Jonas (1601–2): Oberursel; (1603–16):
　Frankfurt a. M.
Rose, Jonas, Widow of (1622–34): Frankfurt a. M.
Rossi, Francesco de' (1646–47): Rome
Rossi, Francesco di (1639–46): Verona; (1642):
　Venice
Rossi, Giovanni Battista de (1613): Pavia
Roth, F. N. (1617): Frankfurt, a. M.
Rothwell, John (1641–50): London
Rouillé, Guillaume, Heirs of (1606–17): Lyons
Roure, Louis (1626–36): Perpignan
Rousset, Nicolas (1615–31): Paris
Roussin, Jacques (1607–13): Lyons
Roussin, Pierre (1617): Lyons
Rouvelin, F. (1644): Paris
Roy, Salomon de (1615): Utrecht
Royston, Richard (1632–42): London
Ruart, Jacques (1627): Paris
Rueda, Antonio de (1645): Valladolid
Rueda, Juan de (1621): Valladolid
Ruffinelli, Giovanni Angelo (1601–24): Rome
Rulands, The (1616): Frankfurt a. M.
Ruoti, Bartolomeo (1613): Florence
Ruyters, Dierick (1623): Flushing

Sachs, Moritz (1616): Rostock
Sadeler, Raphael (1618): Munich
Saeghman, Gilles Joosten (1650): Amsterdam
St. Vincent Ferrer, College of (1610): Saragossa

Salicato, Altobello (1603): Venice
Salis, Dominique (Widow). (1608–17): Paris
Salis, Giovanni (1616): Venice
Salmincio, Andrea (1644): Bologna
Salvioni, Maffeo (1636): Ascoli
Salvioni, Pietro (1618): Macerata
Sánchez, Carlos (1642–50): Madrid
Sánchez, Juan (1614–49): Madrid
Sánchez, Juan, Widow of (1639): Madrid
Sánchez, Lorenzo (1639–42): Madrid
Sánchez, Luis (1601–27): Madrid; (1603–6):
　Valladolid
Sánchez, Luis, Widow of (1627–31): Madrid
Sande, Manuel de (1627): Seville
Santo Grillo & Bros (1621): Venice
Sanz, Francisco (1601): Saragossa
Sardi, Sebastiano (1644): Padua
Sarzina, Giacomo (1611–29): Venice
Sas, Hans (1640): Groningen
Sassier, E. See Saucié, Estienne
Saucié, Estienne (1625): Paris
Sauer (Saur), Johannes (1601–9): Frankfurt a. M.
Saugrain, Abraham (1603–17): Paris
Saur, Johannes. See Sauer, Johannes
Saur, Jonas (1625–28): Ulm
Saussier, Widow (1648): Paris
Savine, Leon (1609): Lyons
Scaccabarozzo, G. (1630): Milan
Scaglia, Giacomo (1630–37): Venice
Schall, Johann Michael (1644): Schleusingen
Schamberger, Simon (1617): Frankfurt a. M.
Schellem, John, pseud. (1626): Utrecht
Schernwebel, Heinrich (1648): Lübeck
Scheus, Hermannus (1641–46): Rome
Schie, Cornelis Martenszoon van (1647): Leyden
Schilders, Richard (1610–17): Middelburg
Schipper, Jan Jacobszoon (1647–49): Amsterdam
Schiratti, Nicolò (1640): Udine
Schleich, Clemens (1617–34): Hanau; (1619):
　Mainz; (1625–26): Frankfurt a. M.
Schleich, Clemens, & Co. (1640): Frankfurt a. M.
Schmidlin, Johann (1621–24): Frankfurt a. M.
Schmidt, Johann (1610): Wittenberg
Schmidt, Peter (1617): Halle
Schmitz, Matthäus (1616–25): Cologne
Schönfeld, Johann (1608–12): Amberg
Schönwetter, Johann Gottfried (1618–49):
　Frankfurt a. M.
Schönwetter, Johann Theobald (1601–30):
　Frankfurt a. M.; (1610–15): Mainz
Schönwetter, Theobald [i.e., Johann Theobald?]
　(1603–26): Frankfurt a. M.
Schroeter, Johann (1625): Basel
Schürer, Thomas (1613–15): Leipzig
Schürer, Thomas, Heirs of (1622): Leipzig
Schürer, Zacharias, the Elder (1611–20):
　Wittenberg

Schürer, Zacharias, the Elder, Heirs of (1628–33): Wittenberg

Scoriggio, Il (1631): Naples

Scorigio, Lazaro (1627): Naples

Scoto, Girolamo, Heirs of (1605–20): Venice

Sebastiani, Mathias (1626): Rotterdam

Seelfisch, Johann (1649): Wittenberg

Seger, J. *See* Zeger, Jacob

Seigneuré, Ozée (1639–41): Rouen

Seile, Henry (1622–42): London

Semuel ben Israel Soreiro (1650): Amsterdam

Sepera, Juan (1632): Barcelona

Sergier, Richard (1607–9): London

Sermatelli Press (1609): Florence

Sermatellis, The (1602): Florence

Serrano, Francisco (1646–47): Madrid

Serrano de Vargas, Miguel (1614): Madrid

Serrano de Vargas y Ureña, Juan (1618–23): Seville; (1639): Málaga

Sessa, Marchio, Heirs of (1633): Venice

Sessas, The (1602–17): Venice

Seuberlich, Lorenz (1611): Wittenberg

Sevestre, Charles (1608–17): Paris

Sevestre, Louis (1632): Paris

Shaw, James (1602–3): London

Sheares, William (1632–50): London

Sheffard, William (1622–23): London

Shinkin, M., pseud. (1647): London

Shorleyker, Richard (1630): London

Short, James (1621–32): Oxford

Siete Revueltas, Press of the (1640): Seville

Siles, Miguel de (1614–21): Madrid

Silva, Manuel da (1621–43): Lisbon

Simmes, Valentine (1601–6): London

Simmons, Matthew (1640–50): London

Simon, F. (1635): Louvain

Simón, Juan (1602): Barcelona

Skalskus, Bazyl (1613): Cracow

Slater, Thomas (1630–50): London

Smethwick, John (1602–37): London

Smit, Zacharias de (1621): Leyden

Smith, John G. (1642): London

Smith, Ralph (1642–46): London

Smith, Thomas (1645): London

Smitz, Matthäus (1620): Cologne

Snellaert, Esdras Willemsen (1647): Utrecht

Snellaert, Esdras Willemsen, Widow of (1649): Utrecht

Snodham, Thomas (1611–25): London

Snowdon, George & Lionel (1605): London

Snuhcam, Friedenreich, pseud. (1620): Frankfurt a. M.

Societas Bibliopolarum (1647): Lyons

Societas Typographica (1623): Geneva

Societas Venetas (1602): Venice

Société Caldoresque (1613): Cologny

Société Caldoresque (P. de Candolle) (1619–21): Yverdon. *See also* Typographia Caldoriana

Soeira, Samuel ben Israel. *See* Semuel ben Israel Soreiro

Soest, Jan van, pseud. (1649): Amsterdam

Soly, Michel (1622–43): Paris

Somasco, Giacomo Antonio (1605): Venice

Sommaville, Antoine de (1620–47): Paris

Sonnius, Claude (1626–43): Paris

Sonnius, Laurent (1601–21): Paris

Sonnius, Michel (1605–27): Paris

Sonzonio, Juan (1635): Valencia

Sonzonio, Roque (1602–16): Valencia

Soreiro, Semuel ben Israel. *See* Semuel ben Israel Soreiro

Sorolla, Miguel (1636): Valencia

Sottile, Giovanni Battista (1607): Naples

Soubron, André (1631–40): Paris

Soubron, Thomas (1601–4): Lyons; (1604): Tournon

Soubron, Thomas, Widow of (1626): Lyons

*Sparke, Michael (1621–46): London

Speckaert, Christoffel (1636): Tholen

Spenser, John (1635–40): London

Spineda, Lucio (1601–30): Venice

Städel, Josias (1650): Strassburg

Stael, Jacob (1650): The Hague

Stael, Michiel (1649–50): The Hague

Staets, Niclaes (1646): Münster

Stafford, Simon (1601–8): London

Stam, Jan Frederickszoon (1628–38): Amsterdam; (1629): Cologne

Stam, Willem Janszoon (1629): Amsterdam

Stamperia Regia, pseud. (1618): 'Antipoli'

Stamphier, Joseph, pseud. (1619–42): Nuremberg

Stansby, William (1608–39): London

Stationers, Company of (1618): London; (1626): Dublin

Stationers, Society of (1623–38): Dublin

Steendam, Jacob (1649): Amsterdam

Steinmann, Hieronymus (1624): Erfurt

Steinmann, I. pseud. (1637): Rostock

Steinmann, Tobias (1617–26): Jena

Stephens, Philemon (1628–50): London

Stephenson, John (1650): London

Stepneth, John (1610–12): London

Stoer, Jacques (1602–50): Geneva

Stoltzenberger, Johann Nikolaus (1623): Frankfurt a. M.

Straub, Lucas (1646–49): Munich

Strohecker, Anton (1624): Mainz

Sub signo Minervae (1647): Venice

Sutor, Caspar (1629): Dillingen

Sutor, Cornelius (1601–5): Oberursel

Swain, Robert, Sr (1627): London

Sweeting, John (1646–50): London

Swingen, Henrick (1601): Antwerp

Sybes, Gijsbert (1643–50): Leeuwarden
Symcock, Thomas (1621): London

Taffie, S., pseud. (1647): London
Tamburini, Geronimo (1612–20): Bologna
Tamburini, H. *See* Tamburini, Geronimo
Tami, Angelo (1622): Verona
Tampach, Gottfried (1611–29): Frankfurt a. M.
Tampach, Wilhelm (1623): Frankfurt a. M.
Tapp, John (1602–31): London
Targa, François (1626–36): Paris
Tarino, Giovanni Domenico (1601–12): Turin
Tarino, Giovanni Domenico, Heirs of, (1618–27): Turin
Taso, Pedro (1622): Madrid
Tavano, Angelo (1603): Saragossa
Tavernier, Melchior (1618–30): Paris
Tebaldini, Nicolo (1622–46): Bologna
Tedesco, Volkmar (1615): Florence
Teler, Ambros (1615): 'Cormopoli' [i.e., Venice]
Teler, Giorgio (1615): 'Cormopoli' [i.e., Venice]
Teler, Giorgio, pseud. (1640–42): 'Cosmopoli'
Teler, Zorzi (1615–19): 'Cormopoli' [i.e., Venice]
Theuniszoon, Jan (1605): Amsterdam
Thiboust, Samuel (1615–35): Paris
Thoreau, Julien (1628): Poitiers
Thorp, Giles, Successors of (1624): Amsterdam
Thorpe, Thomas (1603–23): London
Thrale, Richard (1629–37): London
Thymiss, Johann (1620–29): Frankfurt a. d. O.
Tiffaine, Adrien (1616–21): Paris
Timmer, Cornelis Janszoon (1624): Delft
Tomasini, Cristoforo (1642–45): Venice
Tomasini, Pietro (1640): Venice
Tomasini, The (1647): Venice
Tomes, Henry (1605–6): London
Tongerloo, Anthony Janszoon (1629–47): The Hague
Toorn, Jan Roonpoorts, pseud. (1648): Amsterdam
Torre, Diego de la (1626): Saragossa
Torriano, Giovanni (1640): London
Totti, Pompilio (1621–26): Bracciano; (1634–39): Rome
Tournes, Jean de (1604–35): Geneva
Tozzi, Pietro Paolo (1611–26): Padua; (1622–25): Bologna
Traboulliet, Nicolas (1633–38): Paris
Treudel, Johann (1620–40): Frankfurt a. M.
Trognaesius, Johannes (1603–13): Antwerp
Troost, Dirck Corneliszoon (1605): Amsterdam
Trot, Robert (1645): London
Trundle, John (1612–24): London
Tuilio, Giovanni (1628): Padua
Turino, Antonio (1611): Venice
Turner, William (1625–39): Oxford

Turrino Press (1646): Venice
Tyler, Evan (1633): Edinburgh
Typographia Caldoriana (P. de Candolle) (1650): Yverdon. *See also* Société Caldoresque

Ugolino, Paulo (1603): Venice
Uittenbroek, Dirck (1649): Amsterdam
Underhill, Thomas (1643–47): London
University of Paris. *See* Paris
Uport, Roberto de (1650): Saragossa
Upton, James (1630): London
Usher, Hezekiah (1648): Boston (America)
Ustupiñan, Luis. *See* Estupiñan, Luis

Vaguenar, Jean (1614): Nimes
Val, Pablo de (1641): Madrid
Valdivielso, Juan, Widow of (1622): Huesca
Valentin, Mattio (1606): Venice
Valentin, Robert (1617–35): Rouen
Valentin Heirs (1615): Leipzig
Valentini, Giorgio (1617): Venice
Valentini, The (1624): Venice
Valerius, Adrianus, Heirs of (1626): Veere
Valle, Tomás do (1615): Lisbon
Vallo, Bartolomeo (1627): Milan
*Varennes, Olivier de (1613–48): Paris
Varennes, Olivier de, Widow of (1625): Paris
Varesio, Juan Baptista (1602–19): Burgos; (1634): Valladolid
Varischi. *See* Varisco
Varisco, Giorgio (1608): Venice
Varisco, Giovanni & Varisco (1617): Venice
Vaschieri, Girolamo (1620): Carpi
Vavasour, Nicholas (1634–42): London
Vázquez, Antonio (1641): Alcalá de Henares
Vázquez de Serna, Juan (1620): Cadiz
Vázquez de Velasco y Esparza, Antonio (164–): Valladolid
Vecchi, Alessandro de' (1606–23): Venice
Veely, Johan (1644–50): The Hague
Vejarano, Gabriel Ramos (1615): Seville
Velazco, Francisco Juan de (1648): Cadiz
Velpius, Hubert Antoine, the Elder. *See* Anthoine, Hubert
Velpius, Hubert Antoine, the Younger (1647–48): Brussels
Velpius, Rutger (1604–14): Brussels
Vendosme, Louis (1645): Paris
Venne, Adriaen van de (1629–35): The Hague
Venne, Adriaen van de, & Heirs (1634): The Hague
Vennecool, Jacob Corneliszoon (1601–5): Delft
Ventura, Cominus (1605–13): Bergamo
Ventura, Giulio Cesare (1605): Bari
Verard, Martin (1602): Paris
Verburch, Jacob (1650): Rotterdam

Verdi, Giovanni Maria, Heirs of (1612–13):
  Modena
Verdussen, Gijsbert (1647): Middelburg
Verdussen, Hieronymus (1608–50): Antwerp
Verdussen, Johan (1650): Brussels
Verges, Pedro (1630–43): Saragossa
Verges, Pedro, Widow of (1646): Saragossa
Verhagen, Pieter (1605): Dordrecht
Verhoeve, Johannes (1649–50): The Hague
Verhoeven, Abraham (1625): Antwerp
Verhoeven, Symon (1646–47): Middelburg
Verhuel, Joost Janszoon (1647): The Hague
Vermeer, Samuel (1648): Amsterdam
Vermeer, Symon, pseud. (1650): Brussels
Vermeulen de Jonge, Crijn, pseud. (1610):
  'Danswijck'
Vermeyde, Gijsbert (1647): Middelburg
Vernoy, Gilbert (1617–20): Bordeaux
Versterre, Samuel Claeys (1630–31): Flushing
Vervliet, Jean (1611–20): Valenciennes
Veselaer, Joris (1621–26): Amsterdam
Veselaer, Joris, Widow of (1628): Amsterdam
Veseler, George. See Veselaer, Joris
Vetter, Christoph (1618): Frankfurt a. M.
Veyrat, Jean (1601–4): Lyons
Vezino, Gaspar (1625–26): Cadiz
Viader, Salvador de (1621–28): Cuenca
Vicuña Carrasquilla, Juan de (1624): Madrid
Vignon, Eustache, Heirs of (1603): Saint Gervais
Vignon, Jean (1608–11): Geneva
Villéry, Jacques (1623–43): Paris
Villéry, Pierre (1645): Paris
Vincent, Barthélemy (1605–26): Lyons
Vincent, George (1607–29): London
Vincenti, Giacomo (1605): Venice
Vinha, Geraldo da (1622–27): Lisbon
Viotti, Anteo (1622): Parma
Viotti, Erasmo (1606): Venice
Viret, Jean (1637): Rouen
Visdomini, Alessandro (1619): Sabbioneta
Visscher, Claes Janszoon (1624–29): Amsterdam
Visscher, Hendrick Janszoon (1646): Amsterdam
Vitale, Costantino (1607–9): Naples
Vitre, Antoine (1648): Paris
Vivere, Jacob van de (1629): Middelburg
Vives, Rafael (1617–30): Barcelona
Vivian, Louis (1616–33): Lyons
Vivien, François (1631–49): Brussels
Vlasbloem, Louis (1648–49): Dokkum
Vögelin, Gotthard (1602–15): Heidelberg
Vögelin Press (1601–3): Arnstadt; (1605): Leipzig
Vogel, Hieronymus de (1645): Leyden
Voigt, Bartholomaeus (1604–14): Leipzig; (1624):
  Jena
Voortganck, Haest van, pseud. (1648): Rotterdam
Voskuyl, Dirck Pieterszoon (1612): Amsterdam
Vreeswijck, Dirck van (1628): Leyden

Vrients, Jean Baptiste (1601–10): Antwerp
Vries, Lucas de (1649): Utrecht
Vries, Lucas Symonszoon de (1630): Utrecht
Vrije, Frederijck de, pseud. (1609): 'Franc en dal'
Vullietti, Carlo (1604–8): Rome

W., B. (1643): London
Waalpots, Jan Pieterszoon (1630–36): Delft
Waalsdorp, D. H. van, pseud. (1650): The Hague
Wachsman, Michael (1625–28): Leipzig
Wachsman, Michael, Heirs of (1630): Leipzig
Wachter, Jacob Pieterszoon (1621–43):
  Amsterdam
Wächter, C. (1650): Frankfurt a. M.
Waersegger, Hans, pseud. (1625–26): 'Nieustadt'
Waesbergen, Jan van (1650): Antwerp
Waesbergen, Johannes van (1643): Utrecht
Waesberghe, Isaac van (1637–47): Rotterdam
*Waesberghe, Jan van (1601–36): Rotterdam
Waesberghe, Pieter van (1625–27): Rotterdam
Wagenmann, Abraham (1612): Nuremberg
Wagens, Matthys (1650): Rotterdam
Wagner, Johannes (1646–49): Munich
Wagner, Michael (1650): Innsbruck
Walbanke, Matthew (1618–39): London
Waldkirch, Conradus (1601–14): Basel
Waldkirch, Henricus (1614–24): Copenhagen
Walker, John (1649): London
Walkley, Thomas (1631–48): London
Walley, Henry (1610): London
Wallop, W., pseud. (1637): Rostock
Walschaert, Johannes (1614): Amsterdam
Walschaert, Pieter (1625): Amsterdam
Warren, Thomas (1644–50): London
Warsagern, Vielhüppens, pseud. (1626): 'New
  Newenstatt'
Washington, William (1629): London
Waterson, John (1626): London
Waterson, Simon (1601–34): London
Weaver, Edmund (1606–20): London
Weaver, Thomas (1631): London
Webb, William (1629–50): Oxford
Wechel, Andreas, Heirs of (1601–25): Frankfurt
  a. M.; (1605–19): Hanau; (1605): Mainz
Wechel, Johann [i.e., Heirs] (1608–9): Frankfurt
  a. M.
Wechel, Johann, Heirs of (1603): Frankfurt a. M.
Wechel Office (1601–27): Frankfurt a. M.; (1605–
  34): Hanau
Wees, Abraham de (1648): Amsterdam
Weiss, Johann Friedrich (1611–50): Frankfurt
  a. M.
Welby, William (1608–15): London

Welper, Eberhard (1633): Strassburg
Wendt, Michael (1644): Wittenberg
Werlin, Dietrich (1618): Tübingen
Wesbusch, Hans Passchiers van (1610–41):
  Haarlem
Wessel, Wilhelm (1601): Kassel
Westerloo, Joost Thyssens van (1647): Arnhem
Whaley, Peter (1645): London
Whitaker, Richard (1625–50): London
White, Edward (1602–2–): London
White, John (1618): London
White, Robert (1648): London
White, William (1602–19): London
Widmanstätter, Ernst (1631): Graz
Widmanstetter, Georg (1609): Graz
Wieringen, Nicolaes van (1630–37): Harderwijk
Wight, Thomas (1601): London
Wijngaerden, Adriaen (1645–46): Leyden
Wild, Eberhard (1625): Tübingen
Wild, Joachim (1644–50): Frankfurt a. M.
Willemszoon, Gerrit (1649): Amsterdam
Willemszoon, Isaack (1619–48): Hoorn
Willemszoon, Willem (1648): Zaandam
Williams, Francis (1626): London
Williams, John (1635–50): London
Williams, Thomas (1648): London
Wilson, Robert (1614–39): London
Wilson, William (1645–48): London
Windet, John (1605–10): London
Witte, Everaerdt de (1642): Louvain
Wittigau, Johann (1642): Leipzig
Wittington, George (1647): London
Wodenothe, Richard (1649): London
Wolf, Johannes (1602): Zurich
Wolf, Johannes Rudolf (1619): Zurich
Wolf Press (1610): Zurich
Wolsschaten, Geraert van (1614): Antwerp

Wolter, Bernhard (1604–26): Cologne
Wood, Roger (1621): London
Wouw, Hillebrant Jacobszoon van (1607–21): The
  Hague
Wouw, Hillebrant Jacobszoon van, Widow & Heirs
  of (1622–48): The Hague
Wouw, Hillebrant Jacobszoon van, Widow of
  (1647): The Hague
Wreittoun, John (1625): Edinburgh
Wright, Edward (1615–40): London
Wright, John (1606–47): London
Wyngaert, Willem Janszoon (1629): Amsterdam
Wyon, Marc (1619): Douai
Wyringanus, Petrus Henricus (1629): Kampen

Young, Robert (1628–41): London; (1633–38):
  Edinburgh; (1640): Oxford

Zaltieri, Marc Antonio (1616): Venice
Zanetti, Fabritio (1602–4): Treviso
Zannetti, Antonio (1602–8): Rome
Zannetti, Bartolomeo (1611–23): Rome
Zannetti, Luigi (1601–5): Rome
Zeger, Jacob (1635–40): Louvain
Zenaro, Carlo (1635): Bologna
Zenaro, Damiano (1601–2): Venice
Zetter, Jacob de (1625): Frankfurt a. M.
Zetter, Petrus de (1629): Hanau
Zetzner, Eberhard (1625–31): Strassburg
Zetzner, Lazarus (1602–19): Strassburg; (1605):
  Frankfurt a. M.
Zetzner, Lazarus, Heirs of (1616–42): Strassburg
Zimmerman, W. P. (1624): Augsburg
Zunner, Johann David (1647): Frankfurt a. M.
Zur Glocken, Jakob (1647): Schleswig

General Index

Authors, Titles, and Subjects

In the preparation of this index it was believed that the user would be better served, not by references to entry numbers in the text, but by the fuller forms adopted, incorporating the year where a work is described and by which it can be located. This should facilitate a visual grasp in quantitative terms of the dissemination of a given work. We trust that our practices in such matters will be self-evident, but when publication dates span more than a single year, the entry will be found under the first given. Where a date appearing on a title page has proven in some way erroneous, the correct year and actual location is indicated by bracketed information. Those items with the letter A appended to the date will be found in the Addenda, while multiple editions or issues of a given item are indicated by a figure within parentheses following the year.

For the purposes of this computer-generated index, the word 'for' in an imprint may represent either 'for' or 'sold by'; the precise relationship will be found in the actual entry. Variant spellings of a title are sometimes condensed and subordinated to that of the earliest edition; all Greek words are transliterated.

The high proportion of works which appeared in multiple editions has led us to adopt the expedient of simply providing references from titles to the main entry. Under subject entries (represented by use of full capitals) we have included only the earliest edition of a work and of its translations.

A., I. *See* Breeden-raedt. Antwerp: 1649

A., W. *See* A letter from W. A.

A Dieu aux Francois retournans de la Nouvelle France. *See* Lescarbot, Marc

A Doña Juana de Ocampo y Velasco se sirvio su Magestad hazerla merced. *See* Ocampo y Velasco, Juana

A dos cosas se reduze la pretension de Cartagena. *See* Cartagena, Colombia (Province)

A Melchor de Castro Macedo, secretario del Rey. *See* Pérez de Porres, Diego

A messieurs des estat. *See* Fresneau, Jacques

Aaloude heersch-en-oorlogs-sught. *See* Coignet de la Thuillerie, Gaspard

Abbeville, Claude d', Father. *See* Claude d'Abbeville, Father

Abbot, George, Abp of Canterbury. A briefe description of the whole worlde. London: J. Browne, 1605

——London: J. Browne, 1608

——London: [T. Snodham] for J. Browne, 1617

——London: J. Marriott, 1620

——London: J. Marriott, 1624

——London: [T. Harper?] for W. Sheares, 1634

——London: [T. Harper?] for W. Sheares, 1635

——London: [T. Harper] for W. Sheares, 1636

——London: B. Alsop, for J. M., & W. Sheares [1642]

Abecedario militar. *See* Brito Lemos, João de

Abelin, Johann Philipp, supposed author. Newe Welt. *See* Gottfried, Johann Ludwig. Newe Welt und Amerikanische Historien. Frankfurt a.M.: 1631

Abrégé du Théâtre. *See* Ortelius, Abraham

Abrégé ou Sommaire description du globe. *See* Bertius, Petrus

Abreu y Figueroa, Fernando de. Adiciones al memorial. [Madrid? 1640?]

—Excmo Señor. El maestro fray Fernando de Abreu y Figueroa. [Madrid? 1640?]

—El maestro fray Fernando de Abreu y Figueroa ... dize: Que en el año passado de 1640. [Madrid? 1641]

—Señor. El maestro fr. Fernando de Abreu y Figueroa. [Madrid? 1643?]

—Señor. El maestro fray Fernando de Abreu y Figueroa ... dize: Que despues de aver ... representado el notorio. [Madrid? 1640?]

—Señor. El maestro fray Fernando de Abreu y Figueroa ... sobre lo que tiene representado a V. Magestad. [Madrid? 1640]

—Señor. Index, y sumario de lo que contiene el memorial. [Madrid? 1644]

—Sumario en hecho . . . sobre retener los sinodos, ò estipendios que paga en la Indias. [Madrid? 1643]

The abridgment of the English chronicle. *See* Stow, John

Abriss der Blü[men]. Augsburg: C. Mang, for D. Custos [ca. 1615?]

An abstract of some branches of his Majesties late charter. *See* Great Britain. Sovereigns, etc., 1603–1625 (James I)

An abstract or the lawes of New England. *See* Cotton, John

Abuses stript and whipt. *See* Wither, George

Abuso del tabacco. *See* Zavona, Massimiano

ACAPULCO, MEXICO

—Baeza, P. de. Este memorial es traslado. [Madrid: 1607?]

Acarete du Biscay. Relation des voyages dans la riviere de la Plata. Paris: 1632

An accidence. *See* Smith, Capt. John

Accoort ende articulen. *See* Portugal. Treaties, etc., 1640–1656 (John IV)

Accoort ende artijckelen. *See* Portugal. Treaties, etc., 1640–1656 (John IV)

Acerca de la materia medicinal. *See* Dioscorides, Pedanius

T'achste deel . . . van het Historisch verhael. *See* Wassenaer, Nicolaes van

Achte Schiffahrt. *See* Hulsius, Levinus

Achte Schiffart. *See* Hulsius, Levinus

Achter Theil Americae. *See* Raleigh, Sir Walter

Achter Theil der Orientalischen Indien. *See* Bry, Johann Theodor de

Het achtiende deel . . . van het Historisch verhael. *See* Lampe, Barent

Achtzehender Theil der Newen Welt. *See* Herrera y Tordesillas, Antonio de

Acosta, José de. America, oder . . . die Neuwe Welt. Oberursel: C. Sutor, 1605

—Americae nona et postrema pars. Frankfurt a.M.: M. Becker, 1602

—Histoire naturelle et moralle des Indes. Paris: M. Orry, 1606

— —Paris: A. Tiffaine, 1616

— —Paris: A. Tiffaine, 1617

— —Paris: A. Tiffaine, 1621

—Historia natural y moral de las Indias. Madrid: A. Martín, for J. Berrillo, 1608

— —Madrid: L. Sánchez, 1614

—Historie naturael en morael van de Westersche Indien. Amsterdam: B. Janszoon, 1624

— —Amsterdam: B. Janszoon, for J. E. Cloppenburg, 1624

— —Amsterdam: [B. Janszoon, for] H. Laurenszoon, 1624

—The naturall and morall historie of the . . . Indies. London: V. Simmes, for E. Blount, & W. Aspley, 1604

—Neundter und letzter Theil Americae. Frankfurt a.M.: W. Richter & M. Becker, 1601

—Paralipomena Americae. *In* Herrera y Tordesillas, Antonio de. Novi Orbis pars duodecima. Frankfurt a.M.: 1624

—*See also* Lima (Ecclesiastical Province). Council, 1583. Concilium Limense. Celebratum anno 1583. Madrid: 1614

ACOSTA, JOSÉ DE

—Bacon, F. Historia naturalis . . . ad condendam philosophiam. London: 1622

—Besold, C. Dissertatio politico-juridica. Strassburg: 1625

—Cortés, J. Libro de phisonomia natural. Madrid: 1601

—Donne, J. Pseudo-martyr. London: 1610

—Márquez de Torres, F. Medio suave y facil. [Madrid? ca. 1635?]

—Rivadeneira, P. de. Tratado de la religion. Madrid: 1601

—Scortia, J. B. De natura et incremento Nili. Lyons: 1617

Acoubar. *See* Du Hamel, Jacques

An act for charging of tobacco. *See* Great Britain. Laws, statutes, etc., 1649–1660 (Commonwealth)

An act for the promoting . . . the gospel . . . in New England. *See* Society for Propagation of the Gospel in New-England

An act prohibiting trade with the Barbada's, Virginia, Bermuda's and Antego. *See* Great Britain. Laws, statutes, etc., 1649–1660 (Commonwealth)

Acta capituli generalis Romae. *See* Dominicans

Acta capituli generalis Ulyssiponae. *See* Dominicans

[Acta capituli generalissimum Romae.] *See* Dominicans

Een acte van het Parlament van Engelandt, verbiedende den handel. *See* Great Britain. Laws, statutes, etc., 1649–1660 (Commonwealth)

Een acte, verbiedende den handel met de Barbadas. *See* Great Britain. Laws, statutes, etc., 1649–1660 (Commonwealth)

Acte, waer by een yeder gheaccordeert werdt. *See* Nederlandsche West-Indische Compagnie

The acts made in the first parliament. *See* Scotland. Laws, statutes, etc.

Acuña, Cristóbal de. Neuva descubrimiento del gran rio de las Amazonas. Madrid: Imprenta Real, 1641

—Señor. Christoval de Acuña. [Madrid? 1640?]

Ad universos ordinis . . . S. Benedicti abbates. *See* Gaetani, Costantino

Ad veritatem hermeticae medicinae. *See* Duchesne, Joseph

Adam in his innocence. *See* Bloys, William

Adams, Yemant. *See* Middelgeest, Simon van

Additamentum . . . dess neundten Theils Americae. *See* Noort, Olivier van

—Alonso mozo de muchos amos,
2a pte. Valladolid: J. Morillo,
1626

**Alcázar y Zúñiga, Jacinto de,
conde de la Marquina.** Medios politicos. Córdova: S. de
Cea Tesa, 1646

— —Madrid: D. Díaz de la Carrera, 1646

— —Madrid: F. García de
Arroyo, 1646

— —Seville: J. Gómez de Blas,
1646

The alchemist. *See* Jonson, Ben

Alchymia. *See* Libavius, Andreas

Alchymistische Practic. *See* Libavius, Andreas

Aldenburgk, Johannes Gregorius. West-Indianische Reisse.
Coburg: C. Bertsch, for
F. Grüners, 1627

Aldini, Tobia. Exactissima descriptio. *See* Castelli, Pietro. Exactissima descriptio rariorum
plantarum. Rome: 1625

Aldrete, Bernardo José. Varias
antiguedades de España. Antwerp: G. van Wolsschaten, &
H. Aertssens, for J. Hasrey,
1614

Aldrovandi, Ulisse. De piscibus
libri v. Bologna: G. B. Bellagamba, for G. Tamburini,
1612

— —Bologna: G. B. Bellagamba,
for G. Tamburini, 1613

— —Frankfurt a.M.: J. N. Stoltzenberger, for J. Treudel,
1623

— —Frankfurt a.M.:
M. Kempffer, for J. Treudel,
1629

— —Frankfurt a.M.: K. Rötel, for
J. Treudel, 1634

— —Bologna: N. Tebaldini,
1638

— —Frankfurt a.M.: K. Rötel, for
J. Treudel, 1640

— —Bologna: N. Tebaldini, for
M. A. Bernia, 1644

— —Frankfurt a.M.: K. Rötel, for
J. D. Zunner, & P. Haubold,
1647

—De quadrupedibus. Bologna:
N. Tebaldini, for M. A. Bernia,
1637

— —Bologna: N. Tebaldini, for
M. A. Bernia, 1645

—Monstrorum historia. Bologna: N. Tebaldini, for M. A.
Bernia, 1642

—Musaeum metallicum. Bologna: G. B. Ferroni, for M. A.
Bernia, 1648

—Ornithologiae . . . libri xii.
Frankfurt a.M.: W. Richter, for
Heirs of N. Basse, 1610–13

— —Frankfurt a.M.: W. Richter,
for Heirs of N. Basse, 1630

— —Frankfurt a.M.: W. Richter,
for Heirs of N. Basse, 1640,'35

— —Bologna: N. Tebaldini, for
M. A. Bernia, 1646

—Ornithologiae tomus alter
[-tertius] Bologna: N. Tebaldini, for M. A. Bernia, 1637
[colophon: 1640]

—Quadrupedum omnium bisulcorum historia. Bologna:
S. Bonamo, 1621

— —Bologna: G. B. Ferroni, for
M. A. Bernia, 1641

— —Bologna: G. B. Ferroni,
1642

— —Frankfurt a.M.: K. Rötel, for
J. D. Zunner, & P. Haubold,
1647

Alegacion en derecho. *See* Colón
y Pravia, Francisca, plaintiff

Alegacion en derecho en competencia de jurisdicion. *See* Moscosa y de Córdoba, Cristóbal
de

Alegambe, Philippe. De vita et
moribus p. Joannis Cardim.
Rome: F. Cavalli, 1645

— —Antwerp: H. Aertssens,
1646

— —Munich: L. Straub, for
J. Wagner, 1646

— —Rome: F. Cavalli, 1649

Alemán, Mateo. De la vida del
picaro Guzman de Alfarache.
See his Guzman de Alfarache,
below

—Le gueux. Paris: P. Bilaine,
1619

— —Paris: G. Alliot, 1621

— —Lyons: S. Rigaud, 1630

— —Paris: H. LeGras, &
N. Gasse, 1632

— —Rouen: J. de LaMare, 1632–
33

— —Paris: A. Cotinet, 1638–39

— —Paris: D. Houssaye, 1638–
39

— —Dijon: 1639

— —Lyons: S. Rigaud, 1639

— —Rouen: D. Ferrand, 1645–
46

—Gusman de Alfarache, 1a pte.
Brussels: J. Mommaert, 1639

—Guzman de Alfarache. Milan:
G. B. Bidelli, 1615

—Guzman de Alfarache, 1a pte.
Madrid: F. de Espino, for
J. Martínez, 1601

— —Seville: J. de León, 1602

— —Milan: G. Bordone &
P. M. Locarno, 1603

— —Saragossa: A. Tavanno,
1603

— —Tarragona: F. Roberto, for
H. Martín, 1603

— —Brussels: J. Mommaert,
1604

— —Barcelona: S. de Cormellas,
1605

— —Valencia: P. P. Mey, for
R. Sonzonio, 1605

—Guzman de Alfarache, 1a–2a
pte. Burgos: J. B. Varesio, for
P. Gomez de Valdivielso, 1619

— —Madrid: Imprenta Real, for
Brotherhood of Booksellers,
1641

— —Madrid: P. de Val, for
P. García Sodruz, 1641

—Guzman de Alfarache, 2a pte.
Lisbon: P. Craesbeeck, 1604

— —Barcelona: H. Anglada, for
M. Manescal, 1605

— —Barcelona: S. Cormellas,
1605

— —Lisbon: A. Alvarez, 1605

— —Lisbon: P. Craesbeeck,
1605

— —Valencia: P. P. Mey, for
R. Sonzonio, 1605

—Der Landstörtzer. Munich:
N. Heinrich, 1622

— —[Munich: N. Heinrich,]
1631

— —Munich: [N. Heinrich?]
1632

—Der Landtstörtzer. Munich:
N. Heinrich, 1615

— —Munich: N. Heinrich, 1616
(2)

——Munich: [N. Heinrich?]
1617

——Munich: N. Heinrich, 1618

——Augsburg: A. Aperger,
1619

—The rogue. London: G. E[ld].,
for E. Blount, 1622–23

——London: G. E[ld]., for
E. Blount, 1623

——Oxford: W. Turner, &
R. Allott, at London, 1630

——London: R. B[adger]., for
R. Allott, 1634,'33

—La vida de Guzman de Alfarache. *See his* Guzman de Alfarache, *above*

—Vida del picaro Guzman de Alfarache. *See his* Guzman de Alfarache, *above*

—Vita del picaro Gusmano d'Alfarace. Venice: B. Barezzi,
1606

——Venice: B. Barezzi, 1612

——Venice: B. Barezzi, 1615

——Milan: G. B. Bidelli, 1621

——Venice: B. Barezzi, 1622

—Vita del picaro Gusmano d'Alfarache. Venice: The Barezzi,
1629

—Vitae humanae proscenium.
Cologne: P. von Brachel,
1623–26

—Le voleur. Paris: T. DuBray,
1620

——*See also his* Le gueux, *above*

—*See also* Freudenhold, Martin.
Der Landtstörtzer Gusman,
von Alfarche . . . Dritter Theil.
Frankfurt a.M.: 1626

—*See also* Martí, Juan José. De la
vida del picaro Guzman de Alfarach, 2a pte. Valencia: 1602

Alexander, William, earl of Stirling. *See* Stirling, William Alexander, 1st earl of

ALEXANDER VI, POPE. *See also*
DEMARCATION LINE OF
ALEXANDER VI

—Graswinckel, D. Libertas Veneta. Leyden: 1634

Alfaro, Francisco de. Tractatus
de officio fiscalis. Valladolid:
L. Sánchez, 1606

——Madrid: F. Martínez, 1639

**Alfonce, Jean, i.e., Jean Fonte-
neau, known as.** Les voyages

avantureux. Rouen: T. Reinsart, 1602

——LaRochelle: Heirs of
J. Haultin, 1605

**Alfonso X, el Sabio, King of
Castile and Leon.** Coronica de
España. Valladolid: S. de
Cañas, for A. Cuello, 1604

Algunas hazañas de las muchas.
See Belmonte y Bermúdez,
Luis de

All Ovids elegies. *See* Ovidius
Naso, Publius. Amores. English

Alle christelige . . . jomfruers
aerekrantz. *See* Martini, Lucas

Allegacion de derecho. *See* Colón
y Pravia, Francisca, plaintiff

Allegatio iuris. *See* Zambrana de
Villalobos, Sebastián

Allegatione per confirmare
quanto si scrive. *See* Pio, Giovanni Michele

Allgemeine historische Weltbeschreibung. *See* Botero, Giovanni

ALLIGATORS

—Aldrovandi, U. De quadrupedibus. Bologna: 1637

—Besler, B. Fasciculus rariorum.
[Nuremberg:] 1616

—Ripa, C. Della novissima iconologia. Padua: 1625

——Iconologia. Rome: 1603

——Iconologia, of Uytbeeldingen. Amsterdam: 1644

——Iconologie, ou Explication
nouvelle. Paris: 1644

——Nova iconologia. Padua:
1618

—Topsell, E. The historie of serpents. London: 1608

Allin, John. A defence of the answer made unto . . . questions
. . . sent from New-England.
London: R. Cotes, for
A. Crooke, 1648

Allo, Pedro de. Señor. El desseo
del servicio de V. magestad.
[Madrid? 164–?]

Almansa, Bernardino de. Por
parte del Dean y cabildo . . . de
la ciudad de la Plata. [Madrid?
1630?]

El almirante don Fernando Martinez de Leyva. *See* Duarte Navarro, ——

Almoneda general. *See* Salazar,
Ambrosio de

ALOE

—Colonna, F. Minus cognitarum stirpium aliquot. Rome:
1606

Alonso moço de muchos amos.
See Alcalá Yáñez y Rivera,
Jerónimo

Alonso mozo de muchos amos,
2a pte. *See* Alcalá Yáñez y Rivera, Jerónimo

**Alonso y de los Ruyses de
Fontecha, Juan.** Diez previ-
legios para mugeres preñadas.
Alcalá de Henares: L. M.
Grande, 1606

An alphabeticall book of physicall secrets. *See* Wood, Owen

Alphabetum Augustinianum
. . . Tomus I. *See* Herrera, Tomás de

Alpherio, Hyacinthus de. De
peste. Naples: A. Longhi, 1628

Alpini, Prosper. De medicina
methodica. Padua: L. Pas-
quato, for F. Bolzetta, 1611

—De plantis exoticis. Venice:
G. Guerigli, 1627

—De plantis exoticis libri duo.
Venice: G. Guerigli, 1629

Alsted, Johann Heinrich. Encyclopaedia. Herborn: [G. Rab]
1630

—Scientiarum omnium encyclopaediae, tomus primus-quar-
tus. Lyons: J. A. Huguetan, &
M. A. Ravaud, 1649

—Thesaurus chronologiae. Herborn: [G. Rab] 1624

——Herborn: [G. Rab] 1628

——Herborn: [G. Rab] 1637

——Herborn: [Heirs of
G. Rab?] 1650

Alstedius, Joannes Henricus. *See*
Alsted, Johann Heinrich

Altamirano, Diego. Por Don
Juan de Benavides Baçan. [Ma-
drid:] F. Martínez [1632?]

—Por el duque del Infantado.
[Madrid: 1634?]

—Por la Real audiencia de Mexico. [Madrid? 1632?]

Amaral, Melchior Estacio do.
Das batalhas do galeaom Sanctiago. Lisbon: A. Alvarez, 1604

—Tratado das batalhas . . . do galeão Sanctiago. Lisbon: A. Alvarez, 1604

AMARANTHUS—MEXICO
—Besler, M. R. Gazophylacium rerum naturalium. Leipzig: 1642

Amati, Scipione. Histori dess haydnischen Königreichs Voxu. Rottweil: J. M. Helmlin, 1617

—Historia del regno di Voxu. Rome: G. Mascardi, 1615

—Relation . . . dess Königreichs Voxu. Ingolstadt: Eder Press, by Elisabeth Angermaier, 1617 (2)

Amatus Lusitanus. Curationum medicinalium centuriae septem. Bordeaux: G. Vernoy, 1620

— —Barcelona: S. & J. Matevad, 1628

— —Barcelona: S. & J. Matevad, 1648

AMAZON RIVER
—Acuña, C. de. Nuevo descubrimiento del gran rio de las Amazonas. Madrid: 1641

— —Señor. Christoval de Acuña. [Madrid? 1640?]

—Governor and Company of Noblemen and Gentlemen of England for the Plantation of Guiana. Breefe notes of the River Amazones. [London? 1627]

—A publication of Guiana's plantation. London: 1632

AMAZON RIVER—DEFENSE
—Garavito, G. Señor. Geronimo Garavito en nombre de don Juan de Lizaraçu . . . dize, que aviendo despachado. . . . [Madrid: 163–?]

AMAZON RIVER—DESCRIPTION
—Davies, W. A true relation of the travailes. London: 1614

AMAZON RIVER—DISCOVERY & EXPLORATION
—Maldonado, J. Relacion del primer descubrimiento del rio de las Amazonas. [Madrid? 1642?]

Amelung, Peter. Tractatus nobilis secundus. Leipzig:

A. Lamberg, for J. Apel, 1608

Amends for ladies. See Field, Nathan

L'America. See Bartolommei Smeducci, Girolamo; and also Gualterotti, Raffaello

America, das ist, Erfindung . . . der Newen Welt. See Bry, Johann Theodor de

America, oder . . . die Neuwe Welt. See Acosta, José de

AMERICA IN ART
—Dilich, Wilhelm Schäffer, called. Beschreibung und Abriss dero Ritterspiel. Kassel: 1601

—Epithalamium symbolicum. Graz: 1631

—Ripa, C. Della novissima iconologia. Padua: 1625

— —Iconologia. Rome: 1603

— —Iconologia, of Uytbeeldingen. Amsterdam: 1644

— —Iconologie, ou Explication nouvelle. Paris: 1644

— —Nova iconologia. Padua: 1618

AMERICA IN DRAMA. See also subheading 'Drama' under specific names and topics
—Mayne, J. The cityc match. A comoedye. Oxford: 1639

—Shakespeare, W. Comedies, histories, and tragedies. London: 1623

—Tailor, R. The hogge hath lost his pearle. [London:] 1614

—Téllez, G. Deleytar aprovechando. Madrid: 1635

— —Doze comedias nuevas. Seville: 1627

—Vega Carpio, L. F. de. Doze comedias . . . Quarta parte. Madrid: 1614

AMERICA IN LITERATURE
—Alemán, M. De la vida del picaro Guzman de Alfarache. Milan: 1615

— —Le gueux. Paris: 1619

— —Guzman de Alfarache, 1a pte. Madrid: 1601

— —Der Landtstörtzer. Munich: 1615

— —The rogue. London: 1622–23

— —La vida de Guzman de Alfarache, 2a pte. Lisbon: 1604

— —Vita del picaro Gusmano d'Alfarace. Venice: 1606

— —Vitae humanae proscenium. Cologne: 1623–26

— —Le voleur. Paris: 1620

—Bissel, J. Argonauticon Americanorum. Munich: 1647

—Breton, N. Cornu-copiae. London: 1612

—Cats, J. Proef-steen van den trou-ringh. [Amsterdam?] 1644

— —'s Werelts begin, midden, eynde. Dordrecht: 1637

—Daniel, S. The whole workes. London: 1623

— —The works. London: 1601

—Dekker, T. If it be not good. London: 1612

—Dessi, J. La divina semana. Barcelona: 1610

—Esternod, C. d'. L'espadon satyrique. Lyons: 1619

—Freudenhold, M. Der Landtstörtzer Gusman, von Alfarche . . . Dritter Theil. Frankfurt a.M.: 1626

—Gomberville, M. Le Roy, sieur du Parc et de. Il Polessandro. Venice: 1647

— —Polexandre. Paris: 1638

—Harsdörffer, G. P. Frauenzimmer Gesprechspiele. Nuremberg: 1641–49

— —Gesprachspiele . . . vierter Theil. Nuremberg: 1644

—Helwig, J. Die Nymphe Noris. Nuremberg: 1650

—Heyns, Z. Emblemata. Rotterdam: 1625

—Jonson, B. Every man in his humor. London: 1601

—Lalli, G. B. Franceide, overo Del mal francese. Foligno: 1629

—Marlowe, C. Doctor Faustus. London: 1604

—Moscherosch, J. M. Les Visiones de don Francesco de Quevedo Villegas, oder Wunderbare satyrische Gesichte. Strassburg: [1640]

—Pinto de Moraes, J. Maravillas del Parnaso. Lisbon: 1637

—Polo, G. G. Casp. Barthi Erotodidascalus. Hanau: 1625

Amphitheatrum sapientiae Socraticae. Hanau: Wechel Press, for D. & D. Aubry, & C. Schleich, 1619

Ampliatie op 'tvierde artijckel. *See* Netherlands (United Provinces, 1581–1795). Staten Generaal

Ampliatio oder Erweiterung dess Privilegii. *See* Sweden. Sovereigns, etc., 1611–1632 (Gustaf II Adolf)

Ampsing, Samuel. *See* Ampzing, Samuel

Ampzing, Samuel. Fasciculus epigrammatum super expugnatâ et devictâ Olinda. Haarlem: A. Roman, 1630

—West-Indische triumph-basuyne. Haarlem: A. Roman, 1629

——*See also* Reed-geld over betalinghe. [Haarlem?] 1630

Amsterdam. Burgemeester. Copye van de resolutie . . . op 't stuck vande West-Indische Compagnie. [Amsterdam? 1649] (3)

——Utrecht: J. Havick, 1649

—Extract uyttet register der Resolutien. Amsterdam: 1650

Amsterdam. Citizens. Copie van requesten. [Amsterdam:] 1628

Amsterdams buer-praetje. Amsterdam: 1650

Amsterdams dam-praetje. Amsterdam: 'J. van Soest' [i.e., J. van Hilten?] 1649

Amsterdams tafel-praetje. 'Gouda: J. Corneliszoon' [i.e., Amsterdam? J. van Hilten?] 1649

Amsterdams vuur-praetje. Amsterdam: 'C. Pieterszoon' [i.e., J. van Hilten?] 1649

Amsterdamsche veerman. 'Flushing: J. J. Pieck' [i.e., Amsterdam? J. van Hilten?] 1650

An gantz Teutschlandt. *See* Liebfriedt, Christian, von Gross Seufftzen, pseud.

Anabaptism, the true fountaine. *See* Baillie, Robert.

ANABAPTISTS IN NEW ENGLAND
—Baillie, Robert. Anabaptism, the true fountaine. London: 1647

Anales cronologicos del mundo. *See* Carrillo, Martín.

Anales de Aragon, pte 1a. *See* Leonardo y Argensola, Bartolomé Juan

Anales de la corona de Aragon. *See* Zurita y Castro, Gerónimo

Anarchia anglicana. *See* Walker, Clement

The anatomie of humors. *See* Grahame, Simion

An anatomie of the world. *See* Donne, John

An anatomy of independency. *See* Forbes, Alexander

The anatomy of melancholy. *See* Burton, Robert

An anatomy of the world. *See* Donne, John

ANCHIETA, JOSÉ DE
—Sgambata, S. Eloge du p. Joseph Anquieta. Paris: 1624

——Elogio del p. Giuseppe Anchieta. Naples: 1631

Ander Schiffart in die Orientalische Indien. *See* Neck, Jacob Corneliszoon van

Der ander Theil der . . . Landtschafft Americae. *See* Laudonnière, René Goulaine de

Anderde discours, by forma van messieve. [Amsterdam?] 1622

Andere declaratie von Jean de Vierde. *See* Portugal. Sovereigns, etc., 1640–1656 (John IV)

Das andere Hundert Epistlen. *See* Zeiller, Martin

ANDES
—Bacon, F. The essayes. London: 1625

——De proef-stucken. Leyden: 1646

——Sermones fideles. Leyden: 1641

Andrade Leitão, Francisco de. Copia das proposições. Lisbon: L. de Anveres, 1642

—Copia primae allegationis. [The Hague: 1642]

—Copia propositionum. [The Hague? 1642]

—Discurso politico. Lisbon: A. Alvarez, for A. Godinho, 1642

Andres de Carrasquilla. *See* Carrasquilla, Andres de

Andres Pedrera, ensayador mayor, y visitador del oro. *See* Pedrera, Andrés

Anghiera, Pietro Martire d'. De novo orbe, or The Historie of the West Indies. London: T. Adams, 1612

—The famous historie of the Indies. London: M. Sparke, 1628

—The historie of the West-Indies. London: A. Hebb [after 1625?]

ANGHIERA, PIETRO MARTIRE D'
—Aldrovandi, U. Quadrupedum omnium bisulcorum historia. Bologna: 1621

—Camerarius, P. The living librarie. London: 1625

——Les meditations historiques. Lyons: 1603

——Operae horarum subcisivarum . . . Centuria prima. Frankfurt a.M.: 1602

——Operae horarum succisivarum . . . Das ist: Historischer Lustgarten. Leipzig: 1625

——The walking librarie. London: 1621

—Gesner, K. Mithridates Gesneri, Zurich: 1610

——Thierbuch, Heidelberg: 1606

—Prynne, W. Histrio-mastix. London: 1633

—A vindication of learning. London: 1646

—Vives, J. L. Libri xii de disciplinis. [London:] 1612

Angulo, Nicolas de. Señor. Fray Nicolas de Angulo. [Madrid? 1650?]

Anhalt-Köthen, Ludwig von. Kurtzer Bericht. *See* Fruchtbringende Gesellschaft. Kurtzer Bericht. Köthen: 1641

—*See also* Fruchtbringende Gesellschaft. Der Fruchtbringenden Geselschaft Nahmen. Frankfurt a.M.: 1646

—Ingenua et vera oratio. Lyons: 1602

— —Hanau: 1603

— —Leyden: 1603

—La premiere et seconde Savoisienne. [Grenoble?] 1630

— —Grenoble: P. Marnioles, 1630

Aromatum, fructuum et simplicium aliquot medicamentorum . . . opera. *See* Fragoso, Juan

The arraignment and conviction of Sr Walter Rawleigh. *See* Raleigh, Sir Walter, defendant

The arraignment of slander. *See* Vaughan, William

The arraignment of the whole creature. *See* Harris, Robert

An arrant thiefe. *See* Taylor, John, the Water-poet

Arrests, commissions et privileges du Conseil du Roy. *See* France. Conseil d'état

L'arrivee des ambassadeurs du royaume de Patagoce et de la Nouvelle France. Paris: Widow of J. Remy, 1649

L'arrivee des peres Capucins. *See* Claude d'Abbeville, Father

Ars destillatoria. *See* Porta, Giovanni Battista della

Ars magna lucis. *See* Kircher, Athanasius

Ars medica. *See* Liddel, Duncan; Mérindol, Antoine; Steeghius, Godefridius

Ars medicinalis. *See* Guidi, Guido

Ars sanitatis tuendae. *See* Pardoux, Barthélemy

Arsène de Paris. Derniere lettre du pere . . . au r.p. provincial. [Paris: 1613]

—Derniere lettre du reverend pere . . . estant de present en l'Inde Occidentale. Paris: J. Nigaut, 1613

L'art de naviguer. *See* Medina, Pedro de

The art of archerie. *See* Markham, Gervase

The art of dyalling. *See* Blagrave, John

Art of poetry. *See* Horatius Flaccus, Quintus

The art of thriving. *See* Powell, Thomas

Arte breve dela lengua aymara. *See* Bertonio, Ludovico

Arte da lingua brasilica. *See* Figueira, Luiz

Arte de enfrenar. *See* Pérez de Navarrete, Francisco

Arte de la verdadera navegacion. *See* Syria, Pedro de

Arte de los metales. *See* Barba, Alvaro Alonso

Arte de navegar. *See* Oliveira, Simão d'

Arte del navigare. *See* Medina, Pedro de

The arte of navigation. *See* Cortés, Martín

Arte para fabricar, fortificar, y apareiar naos. *See* Cano, Tomé

Arte y bocabulario de la lengua Guarani. *See* Ruiz de Montoya, Antonio

Arte y grammatica . . . de la lengua aymara. *See* Bertonio, Ludovico

Arthus, Gotthard. Historia Indiae Orientalis, Cologne: W. Lützenkirchen, 1608

Artickel und Satzungen der . . . General Staden. *See* Nederlandsche West-Indische Compagnie

Artickels-brief . . . roerende den oorloghe. *See* Netherlands (United Provinces, 1581–1795). Staten Generaal

Articles accordées par le Roy de Portugal. *See* Companhia geral para o estado do Brazil

Articles accordés par le roi. *See* Compagnie de la Nouvelle France

Articles accordez entre les directeurs et associez. *See* Compagnie de la Nouvelle France

Articles accordez par monseigneur le duc de Montmorency. *See* Compagnie de Montmorency pour la Nouvelle France

The articles and conditions of the perpetuall peace. *See* Spain, Treaties, etc., 1621–1665 (Philip IV)

Articles and orders, made and agreed upon. *See* Company of Adventurers for the Plantation of the Islands of Eleutheria

Articles, moyens et raisons. *See* Dunoyer de Saint-Martin, François

Articles of peace and commerce. *See* Great Britain. Treaties, etc., 1625–1649 (Charles I)

Articles of peace, entercourse, and commerce. *See* Great Britain. Treaties, etc., 1603–1625 (James I)

The articles sett down for the second lottery. *See* Great Britain. Council for Virginia

Articul-brief. Beraemt over het scheeps ende crijgs-volck. Groningen: H. Sas, 1640

Articulen dess Friedens. *See* Spain. Treaties, etc., 1621–1665 (Philip IV)

Articulen en conditien van den eeuwigen vrede. *See* Spain. Treaties, etc., 1621–1665 (Philip IV)

Articulen, met approbatie . . . over het open ende vry stellen vanden handel. *See* Nederlandsche West-Indische Compagnie

Articulen, nopende de conditien des pays. *See* Netherlands (United Provinces, 1581–1795). Treaties, etc.

Articulen van het contract ende accoort. *See* Great Britain. Treaties, etc., 1603–1625 (James I)

Artijckel-brief . . . roerende den oorloge. *See* Netherlands (United Provinces, 1581–1795). Staten Generaal

De artijckelen van den peys. *See* Great Britain. Treaties, etc., 1603–1625 (James I)

Artis medicae pars prima. *See* Cesalpino, Andrea

ARTISANS

—Martínez de Mata, F. Memorial en razon de la despoblacion. [Madrid? 1650]

Artzneybuch. *See* Gabelkover, Oswald

Ascenção, Gaspar d'. *See* Gaspar d'Asenção

Ashe, Simeon. *See* Ball, John

Asia. *See* Barros, João de

Asiento que se tomò con Antonio Fernandez Delbas. [Madrid? 1615?]

Assiento y capitulacion. *See titles under* Spain. Consejo de las Indias

An astronomicall description. *See* Bainbridge, John

ATABALIPA. *See* ATAHUALPA

ATAHUALPA

—Boitel, P. Le tableau des merveilles. Paris: 1617

—Clercq, N. de. Tooneel der beroemder hertogen. Delft: 1617

—Dickenson, J. Speculum tragicum. Delft: 1601

—Discours sur l'affaire de la Valteline. Paris: 1625

—Goulart, S. Le quatriesme recueil contenant l'histoire de la Ligue. [Geneva?] 1604

—Hay, P. Le mercure d'estat. Geneva: 1634

—Raleigh, Sir W. Judicious and select essayes. London: 1650

—Scarron, P. Recueil de quelques vers burlesques. Paris: 1643

Athenaeum. *See* Baerle, Kaspar van

Atheomastix clearing foure truthes. *See* Fotherby, Martin, Bp

Atlantis appendix. *See* Blaeu, Willem Janszoon

Atlantis maioris appendix. *See* Mercator, Gerardus

Atlantis majoris quinta pars. *See* Jansson, Jan

Atlantis novi pars tertia. *See* Mercator, Gerardus

Atlas, das ist, Abbildung der gantzen Welt. *See* Mercator, Gerardus

Atlas minor. *See titles under* Mercator, Gerardus; *and also* Blaeu, Joan

L'atlas nouveau. *See* Bacon, Francis. Histoire naturelle. Paris: 1631

Atlas novus. *See* Jansson, Jan; *and also* Mercator, Gerardus

Atlas, ofte Afbeeldinghe. *See* Mercator, Gerardus

Atlas, or A geographicke description. *See* Mercator, Gerardus

L'atlas, ou Meditations cosmographiques. *See* Mercator, Gerardus

Atlas, ou Representation du monde. *See* Mercator, Gerardus

Atlas, sive Cosmographicae meditationes. *See* Mercator, Gerardus

Attabalippa des peruanischen Esels Adel. *See* Banchieri, Adriano. Von dess Esels Adel. [Strassburg:] 1617

Au Roi. Raisons qui font voir combien il est important au Roy. [Paris? 1640]

Au Roy sire, Le sieur de Champlain remontre. *See* Champlain, Samuel de

Aubigné, Théodore Agrippa d'. L'histoire universelle. Maillé: J. Moussat, 1616–20

— —[n.p.:n.pr.] 1626

— —Amsterdam: Heirs of H. Commelin, 1626

Auctentijck verhael van 't remarcquabelste . . . in Brasil. Amsterdam: J. van Hilten, 1640

Augenio, Orazio. Epistolarum et consultationum medicinalium . . . libri xii. Venice: D. Zenari, 1602

Augspurger, Johann Paul. Kurtze und warhaffte Beschreibung der See-Reisen . . . nacher Brasilien. Schleusingen: J. M. Schall, 1644

Augustinians. Bullarum Ordinis Eremitarum S. Augustini. Rome: Apostolic Camara, 1628

AUGUSTINIANS IN AMERICA

—Cañizares, M. de. El maestro fr. Martin de Cañizares. [Madrid? ca. 1643?]

—Conveniencias en la institucion del comissario general. [Madrid? ca. 1650?]

—Crusenius, N. Monasticon Augustinianum. Munich: 1623

—Herrera, T. de. Alphabetum Augustinianum . . . Tomus I. Madrid: 1644

—Pedro de Santiago. Relacion del transito. [Madrid: 1631]

AUGUSTINIANS IN MEXICO

—Corte, C. de. Virorum illustrium . . . elogia. Antwerp: 1636

AUGUSTINIANS IN PERU

—Calancha, A. de la. Coronica moralizada del orden de San Augustin en el Peru. Barcelona: 1638

Aurea pacis corona. *See* Rimphoff, Heinrich

La aurora de Cristo. *See* Belmonte y Bermúdez, Luis de

Aurora medicorum. *See* Freitag, Johann

Ausfuhrlicher Bericht. *See* Usselinx, Willem

Auss America. *See* Jesuits. Letters from missions

Ausführlicher Bericht über den Manifest. *See* Usselinx, Willem

Ausführlicher Bericht, wie es mit der Silber Flotta hergangen. *See* Hein, Pieter Pieterszoon

Ausführliches wolgegründetes, politisches Bedencken. *See* Scribanius, Carolus

Ausführung allerhand wolbedencklicher Argumenten. *See* Usselinx, Willem

Ausszug auss des Abrahami Ortelÿ Theatro orbis. *See* Ortelius, Abraham

Autarcheia Bataviae. *See* Beverwijck, Jan van

Autentyck verhael van 't gene in Brasiel . . . is voorgevallen. Amsterdam: J. Van Hilten, 1645

Authenthijcque copye van het Recif. [Amsterdam? 1647?]

AUTHORS, LATIN AMERICAN

—Vega Carpio, L. F. de. Laurel de Apolo. Madrid: 1630

Auto de la fe celebrado en Lima. *See* Inquisition. Peru

Avelar, André do. Chronographia ou Reportorio dos tempos. Lisbon: J. Rodríguez, for E. López, 1602

Avellaneda Manrique, Juan de. Memorial de la culpa que resulta de la pesquisa. [Madrid? 1629?]

Avendaño, Francisco de. Señor: El general don Francisco de Avendaño. [Madrid? 1632?]

Avendaño y Vilela, Francisco de. Relacino del viaje, y sucesso . . . al Brasil. Seville: F. de Lyra, 1625

—Relacione del viaggio, e successo . . . al Brasil. Milan: The Malatesti, 1625

——Naples: Roncagliolo, 1625

——Rome: F. Pizzuto, 1625

—, **supposed author.** Relation und eigentliche Beschreibung. *See* Toledo Osorio y Mendoza, Fadrique de. Relation und Eigentliche beschreibung. Augsburg: 1625

Avendaño y Villela, Pedro. Señor. Quien considerare la opulencia. [Madrid? 1608?]

Aventroot, Johann. *See* Aventrote, Juan

Aventrootus, Johannes. *See* Aventrote, Juan

Aventrote, Juan. Epistola á los Peruleras. Amsterdam: 1627

—Epistola . . . ad . . . regem Hispaniarum. [Rotterdam?] 1615

——[Rotterdam?] 1616

—Sendbrief . . . tot den . . . Coninck van Spaengien. Amsterdam: P. A. van Ravesteyn, 1613

—Sendt-brief aen die van Peru. Amsterdam: P. A. van Ravesteyn, 1630

Avertimenti nelle compositioni de' medicamenti. *See* Melich, Georg

Aviendo el marques de Cadereyta desalojado al enemigo Olandes . . . [Madrid? 1635?]

Aviendo representado el conde de Monterey . . . los agravios . . . que los Indios de la Nueva España recibian. *See* Eliseo, Father

Avignone, Bartolomeus. *See* Aviñón, Bartolomé

Avila, Esteban de. Tratado de domicilio. Madrid: L. Sánchez, 1609

Avila, Pedro Estevan de. Señor. Don Pedro Estevan de Avila. [Madrid? 1650?]

Avila y Lugo, Francisco de. El governador Don Francisco Davila y Lugo. [Madrid: 1647?]

—Memorial al Rey. [Madrid: 1638]

Avila y Sotomayor, Fernando de. El arbitro. Pamplona: C. Juan, 1646

Aviñón, Bartolomé. Vita, virtù e miracoli del beato Luigi Bertrandi. Rome: A. Ciaccone, 1623

Aviso de los peligros. *See* Liñán y Verdugo, Antonio

Avisos de Roma. Valencia: F. Mey, 1620

Avity, Pierre d', sieur de Montmartin. Archontologia cosmica. Frankfurt a.M.: L. Jennis, 1628

——Frankfurt a.M.: [W. Hoffmann? for] M. Merian, 1638

——Frankfurt a.M.: M. Merian, 1649

—Les empires, royaumes, estats . . . et principautez du monde. St Omer: C. Boscard, 1614

—The estates, empires, and principallities of the world. London: A. Islip, for M. Lownes, & J. Bill, 1615

—Les estats, empires et principautez du monde. Paris: P. Chevalier, 1613

——Paris: O. de Varennes, 1613

——Paris: O. de Varennes, 1614

——St Omer: C. Boscard, 1614

——Paris: P. Chevalier, 1615

——Cologny: P. Aubert, 1616

——Paris: P. Chevalier, 1616

——Paris: P. Chevalier, 1617

——Paris: O. de Varennes, 1617

——Geneva: P. Aubert, 1619

——Paris: P. Chevalier, 1619

——Paris: N. Du Fossé, 1619

——Paris: O. de Varennes, 1619

——Paris: P. Chevalier, 1625

——Paris: Widow of O. de Varennes, 1625

——Rouen: A. Ouyn, & J. Cailloué, 1625

——Paris: G. Alliot, 1627

——Paris: M. Henault, 1630

——Rouen: J. Cailloué, & A. Ouyn, 1630

——Rouen: J. Cailloué, 1633

——Geneva: P. Aubert, 1634

——Paris: A. Courbé, 1635

——Paris: J. Jost, 1635

——Rouen: J. Berthelin, 1638

——Rouen: J. Cailloué, 1644

——Rouen: A. Ouyn, 1644

——Geneva: J. Stoer, 1648

——Rouen: J. Cailloué, 1649

—Le monde, ou La description générale. Paris: P. Bilaine, 1637

——Paris: C. Sonnius, 1637

——Paris: L. Cottereau, 1643

——Paris: C. Sonnius, & D. Bechet, 1643

—Neuwe Archontologia cosmica; das ist, Beschreibung aller Käyserthumben. Frankfurt a.M.: W. Hoffmann, for M. Merian, 1638

——Frankfurt a.M.: W. Hoffmann, for M. Merian, 1646

—Nouveau théatre du monde. Paris: P. Rocolet, 1644

——Rouen: D. Du Petit Val, 1644

—Wereld spiegel . . . der rijken. Amsterdam: J. E. Cloppenburgh, 1621

—*See also* Fotherby, Martin, Bp. Atheomastix clearing foure truthes. London: 1622

Avontroot, Joan Bartholomaeus. *See* Aventrote, Juan

Avvertimenti nelle compositioni de' medicamenti. *See* Melich, Georg

Ayala y Rojas, Iñigo de. Don Iñigo de Ayala y Rojas. [Madrid? 1622?]

Ayanz, Gerónimo de. Respuesta . . . a lo que el Reyno le preguntó acerca de las minas. Valladolid: 1603

AYMARA LANGUAGE

—Bertonio, L. Arte breve dela lengua aymara. Rome: 1603

——Arte y grammatica . . . de la lengua aymara. Rome: 1603

—Lima (Ecclesiastical Province). Council, 1583. Catecismo en la lengua española, y aymara. Seville: 1604

Barbados . . . . London: 1646
[i.e., 1647]

BARBADOS—DESCRIPTION
—Hunt, R. The island of Assada.
London: [1650]

BARBADOS—HISTORY
—Foster, N. A briefe relation of
the . . . rebellion . . . in . . . Barbadas. London: 1650
—A true state of the case between the heires . . . of Sir William Courteen. [London: ca.
1644]

BARBADOS—POLITICS &
GOVERNMENT
—Carlyle, J. Hay, 2nd earl of. A
declaration by James earl of
Carlile. [London: 1648?]

Barbazza, Andrea. See Barbazza,
Giovanni Andrea

Barbazza, Giovanni Andrea.
Strigliate. See Marino, Gio-
vanni Battista. La Murtoleide.
[Naples?] 1629
——See the same. [Venice?] 1642

Barbón y Castañeda, Guillén.
Provechosos adbitrios. Madrid: A. de Parra, for the Confraternity of Souls, 1628

Barclay, John. Euphormionis
Lusinini Satyricon. [Frankfurt
a.M.?] 1613–15
— —[Frankfurt a.M.?] 1616
— —Leyden: J. Marcus, 1617
— —Leyden: J. Marcus, 1619
— —Amsterdam: W. J. Blaeu,
1623
— —Amsterdam: J. Hessius,
1623–24
— —Frankfurt a.M.: J. Schmid-
lin, 1623, '22
— —Leyden: J. Marcus, 1623
— —Frankfurt a.M.: J. Schmid-
lin, 1624–25
— —Amsterdam: J. Janszoon the
Younger, 1627
— —Amsterdam: J. Janszoon the
Younger, 1628
— —Leyden: J. Marcus, 1628,
'27
— —Rouen: J. de La Mare, 1628
— —Amsterdam: J. Hessius,
1634
— —Oxford: J. L[ichfield]., for
H. Cripps. 1634
— —Leyden: Elsevier Office,
1637

—Euphormionis Lusinini Satyri-
con pars secunda. Paris:
F. Huby, 1607
— —Paris: F. Huby, 1609
— —[Paris? F. Huby?] 1609
— —[Paris? F. Huby?] 1613
—Icon animorum. In his Euphor-
mionis Lusinini Satyricon.
[Frankfurt a.M.?] 1613–15
— —London: B. Norton, for
J. Bill, 1614
— —Paris: P. Mettayer, 1614
— —Paris: 1617
— —Frankfurt a.M.: D. & D. Au-
bry, & C. Schleich, 1625, '24
— —Milan: G. B. Bidelli, 1626
—Icon animorum oder Gründt-
liche Beschreibung. [Frankfurt
a.M.? for] E. Berger at Bre-
men, 1649
—The mirror of minds. London:
J. B[eale]., for T. Walkley,
1633
—The mirrour of mindes. Lon-
don: J. Norton, for T. Walkley,
1631
—L'oeil clair-voyant. Paris: A.
Estoct, 1626
— —Paris: T. Quinet, [ca. 1640]
—Le pourtraict des esprits.
Paris: N. Buon, 1625
— —Paris: S. Thiboust, 1625
—La satyre d'Euphormion.
Paris: J. Guignard, 1640
—Les satyres d'Euphormion.
Paris: J. Petit-pas, 1625
—Satyricon. Amsterdam.
W. J. Blaeu, 1629
— —Amsterdam: W. J. Blaeu,
1634 (2)
—Le tableau des esprits. Paris:
J. Petit-pas, 1625

Barclay, William. Nepenthes, or
The vertues of tobacco. Edinburgh: A. Hart, 1614

Barco Centenera, Martín del.
Argentina y conquista del río
de La Plata. Lisbon: P. Craesbeeck, 1602

Baricelli, Giulio Cesare. Hortulus genialis. Naples: S. Bonino,
1617
— —Cologne: M. Smitz, 1620
— —Geneva: P. Aubert, 1620

Barlaeus, Caspar. See Baerle,
Kaspar van

Barlow, William. Magneticall
advertisements. London: E.
Griffin, for T. Barlow, 1616
— —London: E. Griffin, for
T. Barlow, 1618

Barnabae itinerarium. See Brathwaite, Richard

Barnstein, Heinrich. Kurtze
Beschreibung dess Tabacks.
Erfurt: T. Fritsche, 1645
— —Erfurt: T. Fritsche, 1646
— —Erfurt: T. Fritsche, 1647
— —Erfurt: T. Fritsche, 1648
—Taback das Wunder. Erfurt:
T. Fritsche, 1644
—Tabacologia, das ist: Beschrei-
bung des Tabacks. Erfurt:
T. Fritsche, 1645

Barnuevo, Rodrigo. Muy poderoso señor. [Madrid? 1638]
—Señor. Rodrigo Barnueuo de
la compañia de Jesus. [Ma-
drid? 1639?]

Barré, Nicolas. Colloquio. In
Staden, Hans. Dritte Buch
Americae. Frankfurt a.M.: [ca.
1606]
—Descriptio morum et ferocita-
tis incolarum illius regionis. In
Staden, Hans. Americae tertia
pars. Frankfurt a.M.: 1605
— —In Staden, Hans. Historiae
Antipodum . . . pars tertia.
Frankfurt a.M.: 1630

Barreiros, Gaspar. Commentarius de Ophyra regione. In Novus orbis regionum. Novus orbis. Rotterdam: 1616
— —In the same. Amsterdam:
1623

Barriasa, Mateo de. Por Fernando de Almonte Veinticuatro de Sevilla. Madrid: Widow
of J. González, 1634

Barrionuevo, Rodrigo de. See
Barnuevo, Rodrigo

Barros, João de. Asia. Lisbon:
J. Rodríguez, for A. Gonçal-
vez, 1628
—Asia. 4a decada. Madrid: A.
Falorsi, for Imprenta Real,
1615

Barrough, Philip. The method
of phisick. London: R. Field,
1601
— —London: R. Field, 1610
— —London: R. Field, 1617

——London: R. Field, 1624
——London: G. Miller, 1634
——London: G. Miller, 1639
Bartas, his devine weekes. *See* Du
  Bartas, Guillaume de Salluste,
  seigneur
Bartholin, Caspar. Enchiridion
  physicum. Strassburg: E. Zetz-
  ner, 1625
—Epigrammata extemporanea.
  Copenhagen: H. Waldkirch,
  1621
Bartholin, Thomas. De luce ani-
  malium libri iii. Leyden: F.
  Haack, 1647
Bartholmew fayre. *See* Jonson,
  Ben
Bartolinus, Casparus. *See* Bartho-
  lin, Caspar
**Bartolommei Smeducci, Giro-
  lamo.** L'America. Rome:
  L. Grignani, 1650
Basilica chymica. *See* Croll, Os-
  wald
Basilicus chymica. *See* Croll, Os-
  wald
Basilius Valentinus. Haliogra-
  phia. De praeparatione . . .
  omnium salium. Bologna:
  N. Tebaldini, for A. Salmincio,
  1644
Basque Despinosa, Antonio. *See*
  Vazquez de Espinosa, Antonio
Basset, Robert. Curiosities: or
  The cabinet of nature. Lon-
  don: N. & J. Okes, 1637
Basso, Gerardo. Discurso sobre
  la proposicion. [Madrid?]
  1632
Basuyne des oorloghs. [Amster-
  dam:] P. Walschaert, 1625
Batavier gaet hem verblije.
  [Amsterdam?] 1630
Bate, John. The mysteries of na-
  ture and art. London: T.
  Harper, for R. Mabb, 1635
—The mysteryes of nature and
  art. London: T. Harper, for R.
  Mabb, 1634
——London: [T. Harper,] for
  R. Mabb, J. Jackson, &
  F. Church, 1634
Batrachomyomachia. *See* Bever-
  wijck, Jan van. Wonderbaer-
  lijcken strydt. Dordrecht: 1641
The battaile of Agincourt. *See*
  Drayton, Michael

Baudart, Willem. Memorien,
  ofte korte verhael. Arnhem:
  J. Janszoon, 1620
—Memoryen ofte Cort verhael.
  Arnhem: J. Janszoon, &
  A. Janssen, at Zutphen, 1624–
  25
—Morghen-wecker. Amsterdam:
  J. E. Cloppenburg, 1610?
——'Danswick: C. Vermeulen
  de Jonge' [i.e., The Hague?]
  1610 (3)
—De Spaensche tiranije. [Am-
  sterdam? ca. 1620?]
Baudartius, Wilhelmus. *See* Bau-
  dart, Willem
Bauderon, Brice. Paraphrase sur
  la Pharmacopee. Lyons: P. Ri-
  gaud, 1614
——Lyons: P. Rigaud, 1618
—Paraphrase sur la Pharmaco-
  poee. Lyons: P. Rigaud, 1607
——Lyons: P. Rigaud, 1610
——Rouen: A. Ouyn, 1612
——Lyons: P. Rigaud, 1623
——Paris: G. Clopejau, 1623
——Paris: M. Henault, 1623
——Paris: J. Villéry, 1623
——Rouen: M. de La Motte,
  1627
—Pharmacopee. Paris: J. Laque-
  hay, 1636
——Lyons: Widow of C. Ri-
  gaud, & P. Borde, 1640
——Paris: J. Bessin, 1643
——Rouen: C. Malassis, 1644
——Paris: J. Jost, 1650
—Pharmacopoea. London: E.
  Griffin, for R. Whitaker, 1639
Baudous, Wilhelmus de. Lof-
  dicht van alle de . . . exployten.
  Dordrecht: F. Bosselaer, 1629
Bauhin, Johann. Historia plan-
  tarum universalis. Yverdon:
  Typographia Caldoriana,
  1650–51
—Historiae plantarum generalis
  . . . prodromus. Yverdon: P. de
  Candolle, 1619
Bauhin, Kaspar. De composi-
  tione medicamentorum. Of-
  fenbach: C. Neben, for Heirs
  of N. Basse, [at Frankfurt
  a.M.,] 1610
—De lapidis bezaar. Basel:
  C. Waldkirch, 1613
——Basel: L. König, 1625

—Pinax, theatri botanici . . .
  opera. Basel: L. König, 1623
—Prodromos Theatri botanici.
  Frankfurt a.M.: P. Jacobi, for
  J. Treudel, 1620
—*See also* Theodorus, Jacobus.
  Neuw vollkommentlich Kreu-
  terbuch. Frankfurt a.M.: 1613
Baumann, Johann Nicolaus.
  Dissertatio inauguralis de ta-
  baci virtutibus. Basel: J. J. Ge-
  nath, 1629
A bawd. *See* Taylor, John, the
  Water-poet
Beake, Richard. *See* Prynne, Wil-
  liam. A fresh discovery. Lon-
  don: 1645
BEARS
—Les diversitez naturelles de
  l'univers. Paris: 1626
Beaumont, Francis. Comedies
  and tragedies. London: H.
  Robinson, & H. Moseley, 1647
—The knight of the burning pes-
  tle. London: W. Burre, 1613
——London: N. O[kes]., for
  J. S[penser?], 1635 (2)
—The scornful ladie. London:
  [R. Bradock] for M. Partridge,
  1616
[And variant spellings]
——London: [A. Mathewes?]
  for M. P[artridge?]., &
  T. Jones, 1625
——London: B. A[lsop]., &
  T. F[awcet]., for T. Jones,
  1630
——London: A. M[athewes].,
  1635
——London: M. P[arsons]., for
  R. Wilson, 1639
—Wit without money. *See*
  Fletcher, John. Wit without
  money. London: 1639
Beaumont, Sir John. The meta-
  morphosis of tabacco. Lon-
  don: [F. Kingston] for
  J. Flasket, 1602
Beaumont, Simon van. Rapport
  ghedaen by d'heer van Beau-
  mont. [Middelburg? 1629?]
Bedencken an die königliche
  May[estät]. *See* Arnauld, An-
  toine
Bedenckinge over d'Antwoordt
  der heeren bewint-hebbers.
  The Hague: J. Veely, 1644 (2)

Oppenheim? H. Galler? ca. 1617]

—Americae pars sexta. Oppenheim: H. Galler, for J. T. de Bry, 1617

—Chronicon, das ist: Beschreibung der . . . indianischen Ländern. Wittenberg: Widow of Z. Lehmann, for C. Berger, 1606

—Historia antipodum . . . Liber quartus. Frankfurt a.M.: M. Merian, 1644

—De historie van de nieuwe weerelt. Haarlem: H. P. van Wesbusch, 1610 (2)

—Novae Novi Orbis historiae, das ist Aller Geschichten, so in der newen Welt. Hamburg: B. Arens, 1648

—Recentes Novi Orbis historiae. Geneva: 1612. *See under title*

—Das sechste Theil Americae. Oppenheim: H. Galler, for J. T. de Bry, at Frankfurt a.M., 1619

—Das vierdte Buch von der neuwen Welt. Frankfurt a.M.: Widow of M. Becker, for J. T. de Bry, 1613

— —Frankfurt a.M.: Widow of M. Becker, for J. T. de Bry, 1613

—*See also* Goulart, Simon. Histoires de nostre temps, t 2–3. Paris: 1601

Berettari, Sebastiano. Josephi Anchietae . . . vita. Lyons: H. Cardon, 1617

—Vida del padre Joseph de Ancheta. Salamanca: Antonia Ramírez, 1618

— —Barcelona: E. Liberòs, 1622

—La vie miraculeuse du p. Joseph Anchieta. Douai: M. Wyon, 1619

—Vita del p. Gioseppo Anchietto. Turin: Heirs of G. D. Tarino, 1621

—Vita del padre Gioseffo Anchieta. Bologna: Heirs of Benacci, 1643

—Vita del padre Giuseppe Anchieta. Messina: P. Brea, 1639

—Vita r.p. Josephi Anchietae. Cologne: J. Kinckius, 1617

Bergeron, Pierre de. Traicté de la navigation. Paris: J. de Heuqueville, & M. Soly, 1629

Bericht von den . . . Bezoardischen Steinen. *See* Wittich, Johann

Bering, Joachim. *See* Beringer, Joachim

Beringer, Joachim. Hispanicae Inquisitionis . . . secretiora. Amberg: J. Schönfeld, 1611

—Der tyrannischen hispanischen Inquisition Heimligkeiten . . . offenbaret. Amberg: J. Schönfeld, 1611 [i.e., 1612]

Bermuda Islands. Laws, Statutes, etc. Orders and constitutions. London: F. Kingston, 1622

BERMUDA ISLANDS

—Brathwaite, R. A solemne joviall disputation. [London:] 1617

—Brinsley, J. Consolation for our grammar schooles. London: 1622

—Dekker, T. A strange horserace. London: 1613

—Golding, W. Servants on horse-back. [London:] 1648

—Great Britain. Sovereigns, etc., 1603–1625 (James I). A proclamation for the utter prohibiting the importation and use of all tobacco. London: 1624 [i.e., 1625]

—Great Britain. Sovereigns, etc., 1625–1649 (Charles I). A proclamation touching tobacco. London: 1625

—Hein, P. P. Extract uyt den Brief . . . aen de Geoctroyeerde West-Indische Compagnie. [The Hague? 1628?]

—Heywood, T. Machiavel. as he has lately appeared. London: 1641

—Hughes, L. A letter, sent into England from the Summer Ilands. London: 1615

— —A plaine and true relation of the goodness of God. London: 1621

—Jourdain, S. A discovery of the Barmudas. London: 1610

— —A plaine description of the Barmudas. London: 1613

—Kayll, R. The trades increase. London: 1615

—Malynes, G. de. Consuetudo, vel, Lex mercatoria. London: 1636

—Prynne, W. A fresh discovery. London: 1645

—Scott, T. Nieuwe tydingen wt den Conseio. Amsterdam: 1621

— —Vox populi. Or Newes from Spain. [London?] 1620

—Shakespeare, W. Comedies, histories, and tragedies. London: 1623

—Sharpe, E. Britaines busse. London: 1615

— —England's royall fishing revived. London: 1630

—Smith, Capt. J. The generall history of Virginia. [London: 1623]

—Taylor, J. The watermens suit. [London: 1614?]

—Warwick, R. Rich, 2d earl of. A declaration . . . To the colony. [London: 1644]

—Whitbourne, Sir R. Zwantzigste Schifffahrt. Frankfurt a.M.: 1629

BERMUDA ISLANDS—
CHURCH HISTORY

—White, N. Truth gloriously appearing. London: [1645]

BERMUDA ISLANDS—
COMMERCE

—Great Britain. Laws, statutes, etc., 1625–1649 (Charles I). Whereas the severall plantations in Virginia, Bermudas, Barbados . . . . London: 1646 [i.e., 1647]

—Misselden, Edward. Free trade. London: 1622

BERMUDA ISLANDS—
HISTORY

—Discurso de lo sucedido en este año 1626. Seville: 1626

—Hughes, L. To the Right Honourable, the Lords and others. [London? 1625]

—Smith, Capt. J. The generall historie of Virginia. London: 1624

BERMUDA ISLANDS—
POETRY
—Chapman, G. An epicede or
funerall song. London: 1612
—Rich. R. Newes from Virginia.
London: 1610
—Waller, E. The workes. London: 1645
BERMUDA ISLANDS IN LITERATURE
—Taylor, J. Odcombs complaint.
[London]: 1613
El Bernardo, o Victoria de Roncesvalles. *See* Valbuena, Bernardo de
Beroa, Diego de. Litterae annuae provinciae Paraquariae.
Lille: T. Le Clercq, 1642
Bertaldi, Giovanni Lodovico.
Medicamentorum apparatus.
Turin: Cavaleri Bros, 1612
Bertius, Petrus. Abrégé ou Sommaire description du globe.
Paris: J. Villéry, 1624
——Paris: J. Villéry, 1634
—Beschreibung der gantzen
Welt. Amsterdam: J. Janszoon
the Younger, 1650
—Breviarium totius orbis terrarum. Paris: M. Hénault, 1624
——Paris: M. Hénault, 1626
——Frankfurt a.M.: K. Rötel, for
de Bry Office, 1627
——*In* Hues, Robert. Tractatus
duo mathematici. Frankfurt
a.M.: 1627
——Hanau: C. Schleich, & P. de
Zetter, 1629
——*In* Clüver, Philipp. Introductionis in universam geographiam . . . libri vi. Amsterdam: [1630?]
——Frankfurt a.M.: C. Schleich
and Co., 1640
——*In* Clüver, Philipp. Introductionis in universam geographiam . . . libri vi. Leyden:
1641
——*In the same.* Venice: 1646
——*In the same.* Paris: 1648
——*In the same.* Amsterdam:
[165–?]
—Brevis ac succincta Americae
. . . descriptio. *In* Herrera y
Tordesillas, Antonio de. Novus orbis, sive Descriptio In-

diae Occidentalis. Amsterdam:
1622
—[Geographia vetus ex antiquis.
Paris: M. Tavernier, 1628]
——Paris: M. Tavernier, 1630
——Paris: J. Boisseau, 1645
—La geographie racourcie. Amsterdam: J. Hondius, 1618
—Geographischer . . . Tabeln
fünff . . . Bücher. Frankfurt
a.M.: M. Becker, for H. Laurenszoon, at Amsterdam, 1612
—Tabularum geographicarum
contractarum libri quinque.
Amsterdam: C. Claeszoon, for
J. Janszoon, at Arnhem, 1602
——Amsterdam: C. Claeszoon,
1606
—Tabularum geographicarum
contractarum libri septem.
Amsterdam: J. Hondius, 1616
——Amsterdam: J. Hondius,
1618 (2)
—*See also* Herrera y Tordesillas,
Antonio de. Description des
Indes Occidentales. Amsterdam: 1622
Bertonio, Ludovico. Arte breve
dela lengua aymara. Rome:
A. Zannetti, 1603
—Arte y grammatica . . . de la
lengua aymara. Rome: A. Zannetti, 1603
——Rome: A. Zannetti, 1605
——Rome: A. Zannetti, 1608
Bertrán, Luis. *See* Luis Bertrán,
Saint.
Bertrand, ——. Lettre missive,
touchant la conversion. Paris:
J. Regnoul, 1610
Besard, Jean Baptiste. Antrum
philosophicum. Augsburg:
D. Franck, for J. B. Besard,
1617
Beschreibung der gantzen Welt.
See Bertius, Petrus
Beschreibung des Tabacks. *See*
Barnstein, Heinrich. Tabacologia, das ist: Beschreibung
des Tabacks. Erfurt: 1645
Beschreibung und Abriss dero
Ritterspiel. *See* Dilich, Wilhelm
Schäffer, called
Beschreibung von Eroberung
der spanischen Silber Flotta.
See Hein, Pieter Pieterszoon

Beschreibung, welcher Gestalt
die Hauptstatt des Königreichs Brasilien . . . erobert
worden. [The Hague? 1630?]
Beschrijvinge van de gantsche
custe van Guinea. *See* Linschoten, Jan Huygen van
Beschrijvinge van de voyagie om
den geheelen werelt-kloot. *See*
Noort, Olivier van
Beschrijvinge van den ouden,
ouden . . . man. *See* Taylor,
John, the Water-poet
Beschrijvinge van 't koningkrijck
Congo. *See* Lopes, Duarte
Beschrijvinge vande gantsche
custe van Guinea. *See* Linschoten, Jan Huygen van
Beschrijvinghe ende af-beelding van alle de victorien. *See*
Orlers, Jan Janszn
Beschrijvinghe ende Historische
verhael . . . van Guinea. *See*
Marees, Pieter de
Beschrijvinghe van America. *See*
Staden, Hans
Beschrijvinghe van de gantsche
custe van Guinea. *See* Linschoten, Jan Huygen van
Beschrijvinghe van West-Indien.
See Laet, Joannes de
**Beschrijvinghe vande landen
van Brasilien.** Amsterdam:
Widow of C. L. van der Plasse,
1644
Beschryvinge ende historische
verhael . . . van Gunea. *See*
Marees, Pieter de
Beschryvinge van 't in-nemen
van . . . Salvador. Amsterdam:
C. J. Visscher, 1624
Beschryvinge vande overtreffelijcke . . . zee-vaerdt. *See*
Pretty, Francis
Beschryvinge van de voyagie
om den geheelen werelt cloot.
See Noort, Olivier van
Beschryvinghe van der Samoyeden landt. *See* Gerritsz, Hessel
Besler, Basilius. Continuatio
rariorum. [Nuremberg:
B. Besler] 1622
—Fasciculus rariorum. [Nuremberg:] B. Besler, 1616
—Hortus eystettensis. [Nuremberg:] 1613

Besler, Michael Rupert. Gazophylacium rerum naturalium.
Leipzig: J. Wittigau, 1642

Besoignes en communicatien.
The Hague: [1647]

—The Hague: J. J. Verhuel, 1647

—The Hague: Widow of
H. J. van Wouw, 1647 (3)

Besold, Christoph. De Novo
Orbe conjectanea. Tübingen:
J. A. Cellius [1619?]

— —*In his* Discursus politicus.
Strassburg: 1623

— —*In the same.* Strassburg: 1640

—Discursus politicus de incrementis imperiorum. Strassburg: Heirs of L. Zetzner,
1623

— —Strassburg: Heirs of
L. Zetzner, 1640

—Dissertatio politico-juridica.
Strassburg: Heirs of L. Zetzner, 1625

— —Strassburg: Heirs of
L. Zetzner, 1642

—Dissertationes singulares.
Tübingen: J. A. Cellius, 1619

—Juridico-Politicae dissertationes. Strassburg: Heirs of
L. Zetzner, 1624

— —Strassburg: Heirs of
L. Zetzner, 1641

Besoldo, Christoforo. *See* Besold,
Christoph

Besoltus, Christophorus. *See* Besold, Christoph

Betancurt, Luis de. Derecho de
las iglesias . . . de las Indias.
Madrid: F. Martínez, 1635

— —Madrid: F. Martínez, 1637

—Memorial i informacion por las
iglesias . . . de las Indias. Madrid: F. Martínez, 1634

**Bethune, Philippe de, comte de
Selles et de Charost.** Le conseiller d'estat. [Paris?] 1632

— —Paris: E. Richer, 1633 (2)

— —[Leyden? F. Heger?] 1641

— —[Leyden? F. Heger?] 1645

—Paris: M. Bobin, 1645

—Counsellor of estate. London:
N. Okes, 1634

Beuter, Pedro Antonio. Coronica general de toda España.
1a pte. Valencia: P. P. Mey,
1604

BEVERAGES

—Taylor, John, the Water-poet.
Drinke and welcome. London:
1637

—Valverde Turices, Santiago
de. Al excelmo. S[eñ]or Don
Gaspar de Guzman. Seville:
1625

Beverwijck, Jan van. Autarcheia
Bataviae. Leyden: J. Maire,
1644

—De excellentia foeminei sexus.
Dordrecht: 1636

—Heel-konste. Dordrecht:
H. van Esch, for P. Looymans,
& M. de Bot, 1645

— —Dordrecht: J. Gorisszoon,
1647

—Idea medicinae veterum. Leyden: Elsevier Office, 1637

—Inleydinge tot de Hollandsche
geneesmiddelen. Dordrecht:
J. Gorisszoon, 1642

—Lof der genees-konste. Dordrecht: J. Braat, 1647

—Lof der medicine. Dordrecht:
H. van Esch, 1635

— —[Dordrecht: 1641]

—Medicinae encomium. Dor-
drecht: H. van Esch, 1633

—Schat der gesontheydt. Dordrecht: 1640

— —Dordrecht: 1642

— —Amsterdam: J. J. Schipper,
1649

—Schat der gesontheyt. [Dor-
drecht? 1636?]

— —[Dordrecht: H. van Esch,
1637]

— —Dordrecht: H. van Esch, for
M. Havius, 1637, '36

— —Dordrecht: H. van Esch, for
M. Havius, 1638, '37

— —Amsterdam: Widow of E.
Cloppenburg, 1643

— —Amsterdam: 1644

—Schat der ongesontheit. Dordrecht: H. van Esch, for J.
Gorisszoon, 1642

—Schat der ongesontheyt. Dordrecht: J. Gorisszoon, 1644

— —Dordrecht: J. Braat, 1647

—Schat der ongesontheyt
. . . Het tweede deel. Dordrecht: J. Gorisszoon, 1644

— —Dordrecht: J. Braat, 1649

—Spaensche Xerxes. Dordrecht:
H. van Esch, for J. Gorisszoon,
1639

— —The Hague: I. Burchoorn,
1640

—Van de uitnementheyt des
vrouwelicken geslachts. Dordrecht: [H. van Esch] for
J. Gorisszoon, 1639

— —Dordrecht: H. van Esch, for
J. Gorisszoon, 1643

— —Leyden: H. van der Deyster,
1643

—Wonderbaerlijcken strydt.
Dordrecht: H. van Esch, for
J. Gorisszoon, 1641

Bewijs van de ware godts-dienst.
See Grotius, Hugo

Bewilligungen bey den Staden
General. *See* Nederlandsche
West-Indische Compagnie

Bewys van den waren gods-
dienst. *See* Grotius, Hugo

BEZOAR

—Bauhin, K. De lapidis bezaar.
Basel: 1613

—Beverwijck, J. van. Schat der
ongesontheit. Dordrecht:
1642

—Fueldez, A. Observations curieuses, touchant la petite verole. Lyons: 1645

—Gabelkover, W. Curationum et
observationum, centuria V.
Tübingen: 1627

—Norton, S. Metamorphosis lapidum ignobilium. Frankfurt
a.M.: 1630

—Perlinus, H. De alexiteriis.
Rome: 1610

—Pona, F. Trattato de' veleni.
Verona: 1643

—Primerose, J. De vulgi in medicina erroribus. London: 1638

—Sala, A. Ternarius bezoardicorum. Erfurt: 1618

—Sennert, D. Epitome naturalis
scientiae. Wittenberg: 1618

—Untzer, M. Tractatus medico-
chymici septem. Halle: 1634

—Valle, F. Methodus medendi.
Louvain: 1647

Biancani, Giuseppe. Sphaera
mundi, seu Cosmographia.
Bologna: S. Bonomi, for
H. Tamburini, 1620

— —Modena: G. Cassiano, 1630

——Amsterdam: J. Janszoon the Younger, 1625

—Het nieuw vermeerde licht. Amsterdam: J. Janszoon the Younger, 1634

—Het nieuwe licht der zeevaert. Amsterdam: W. J. Blaeu, 1634

—Le nouveau phalot de la mer. Amsterdam: J. Janszoon the Younger, 1635

——Amsterdam: J. Janszoon the Younger, 1637

—Novus atlas, das ist, Abbildung . . . von allen Ländern. Amsterdam: W. J. Blaeu, 1634

——Amsterdam: W. J. [& J.] Blaeu, 1635 (2)

—Novus atlas, das ist Weltbeschreibung. Amsterdam: J. Blaeu, 1647

——Amsterdam: J. Blaeu, 1648

——Amsterdam: J. Blaeu, 1649, '47

—Novus atlas, das ist Welt-beschreibung . . . ander Theil. Amsterdam: J. & C. Blaeu, 1641

——Amsterdam: J. & C. Blaeu, 1642

——Amsterdam: J. & C. Blaeu, 1643

——Amsterdam: J. Blaeu, 1647

—Novus atlas, das ist Weltbeschreibung . . . erster Theil. Amsterdam: J. & C. Blaeu, 1638

——Amsterdam: J. & C. Blaeu, 1641–42

—Le phalot de la mer. Amsterdam: J. Janszoon the Younger, 1620

—The sea-beacon. Amsterdam: J. Blaeu, 1643–44

—The sea-mirror. Amsterdam: W. J. Blaeu, 1635

—The sea-mirrour. Amsterdam: W. J. Blaeu, 1625

——Amsterdam: W. J. Blaeu, 1640

——Amsterdam: W. J. Blaeu, for W. Lugger [at London] 1640

—Le theatre du monde. Amsterdam: W. J. & J. Blaeu, 1635

——Amsterdam: W. J. & J. Blaeu, 1638

——Amsterdam: J. & C. Blaeu, 1642

——Amsterdam: J. Blaeu, 1643–44

——Amsterdam: J. Blaeu, 1645

——Amsterdam: J. Blaeu, 1647

——Amsterdam: J. Blaeu, 1647–50

——Amsterdam: J. Blaeu, 1649–50

—Le theatre du monde . . . Seconde partie. Amsterdam: W. J. & J. Blaeu, 1635

——Amsterdam: J. & C. Blaeu, 1640 (2)

——Amsterdam: J. Blaeu, 1644

——Amsterdam: J. Blaeu, 1645 (2)

——Amsterdam: J. Blaeu, 1647

——Amsterdam: J. Blaeu, 1650

—Theatre du monde . . . Troisiesme partie. Amsterdam: J. & C. Blaeu, 1640

—Theatrum orbis terrarum. Amsterdam: W. J. & J. Blaeu, 1635

——Amsterdam: J. & C. Blaeu, 1640

——Amsterdam: J. & C. Blaeu, 1641

——Amsterdam: J. & C. Blaeu, 1643, '40

——Amsterdam: J. Blaeu, 1644

——Amsterdam: J. Blaeu, 1649

——Amsterdam: J. Blaeu, 1649–50

——Amsterdam: J. Blaeu, 1649–55

—Theatrum orbis terrarum . . . pars secunda. Amsterdam: W. J. & J. Blaeu, 1635

——Amsterdam: J. & C. Blaeu, 1640

——Amsterdam: J. Blaeu, 1645

——Amsterdam: J. Blaeu, 1650

—Theatrum orbis terrarum . . . Tertia pars. Amsterdam: J. & C. Blaeu, 1640

—Toonneel des aerdriicx. Amsterdam: W. J. & J. Blaeu, 1635

——Amsterdam: J. & C. Blaeu, 1642

——Amsterdam: J. & C. Blaeu, 1642

——Amsterdam: J. Blaeu, 1647

——Amsterdam: J. Blaeu, 1649 [i.e., 1650]

—Toonneel des aerdriicx. 2de dl. Amsterdam: W. J. & J. Blaeu, 1635

——Amsterdam: J. Blaeu, 1642 (3)

——Amsterdam: J. Blaeu, 1650

—Toonneel des aerdrycx . . . derde deel. Amsterdam: J. Blaeu, 1642

—Tweevoudigh onderwijs. Amsterdam: W. J. Blaeu, 1634

——Amsterdam: 1638

——Amsterdam: J. Blaeu, 1647

—Zeespiegel. Amsterdam: W. J. Blaeu, 1623

——Amsterdam: W. J. Blaeu, 1623

——Amsterdam: W. J. Blaeu, 1627

——Amsterdam: W. J. Blaeu, 1623 [i.e., 1627]

——Amsterdam: W. J. Blaeu, 1631

——Amsterdam: W. J. & J. Blaeu, 1638

——Amsterdam: W. J. Blaeu, 1639

——Amsterdam: W. J. Blaeu, 1640

——Amsterdam: J. Blaeu, 164[3?]

——Amsterdam: J. Blaeu, 1643–44

——Amsterdam: J. [& C.] Blaeu, 1643

——Amsterdam: J. Blaeu, 1650, '48

Blagrave, John. The art of dyalling. London: N. O[kes]., for S. Waterson, 1609

—A very brief . . . description. *In* Blundeville, Thomas. M. Blundeville his Exercises. London: 1606

——*In the same.* London: 1613

——*In the same.* London: 1622

——*In the same.* London: 1636

——*In the same.* London: 1638

Blasco de Lanuza, Vincenzio. Historias ecclesiasticas y seculares de Aragon. Saragossa: J. de Lanaja y Quartanet, 1621, '19

——Saragossa: J. de Lanaja y Quartanet, 1622

Blefken, Dithmar. Een corte ende warachtige beschrijvinge

Boemus, Johann. Historia moralis. Frankfurt a.M.: L. Bitsch, 1604A
—The manners, lawes and customs of all nations. London: G. Eld, 1611
—Mores, leges, et ritus omnium gentium. [Geneva:] J. de Tournes, 1604
— —Geneva: J. de Tournes, 1620
Boey, Cornelis. Illustrissimo heroi Mauritio. The Hague: A. Tongerloo, 1637
—*See also* Beverwijck, Jan van. Van de uitnementheyt des vrouwelicken geslachts. Dordrecht: 1639
Bogotá. Por parte de las ciudades Santa Fé, y Cartagena. [Madrid? 1620?]
Boissard, Jean Jacques. Bibliotheca chalcographica. Frankfurt a.M.: J. Ammon, 1650–54
—Bibliotheca sive Thesaurus virtutis. Frankfurt a.M.: W. Fitzer, 1628
—Icones et effigies virorum doctorum. Frankfurt a.M.: J. Ammon, 1645
Boitel, Pierre, sieur de Gaubertin. Le tableau des merveilles. Paris: T. Du Bray, 1617
— —Paris: T. de La Ruelle, 1617
BOLIVIA
—Recio de León, J. Peligros del dilitado camino. [Madrid? 1626?]
— —Señor. El maesse de campo Juan Recio de Leon. [Madrid? 1625?]
— —Los servicios que refiero a V[uestra]. M[agestad]. en el memorial. [Madrid? 1626?]
BOLIVIA—ADMINISTRATION
—Pérez Manrique de Lara, D. Señor. Don Dionisio Perez Manrique. [Madrid? 164–?]
—Recio de León, J. Señor. Relacion que Juan Recio de Leon . . . presento a V. magestad. [Madrid? 1626?]

BOLIVA—DESCRIPTION
—Recio de León, J. Breve relacion de la descripcion . . . de las tierras. [Madrid? 1623?]
BOLIVIA—HISTORY
—Garavito, G. Señor. Geronimo Garavito . . . digo, que . . . puse en las reales manos . . . tres memoriales. [Madrid: 1637]
— —Señor. Geronimo Garavito . . . dize: Que es notorio. [Madrid? 1637]
— —Señor. Geronimo Garavito en nombre del presidente. [Madrid: 163–?]
—Olmo, ——. Por el licenciado Don Sebastian Zambrana de Villalobos. [Madrid? 1628?]
—Recio de León, J. Relation de los servicios . . . de las provincias de Tipuane. [Madrid: 1625]
— —Señor. Juan Recio de Leon, masse de campo . . . de las provincias de Tipuane. [Madrid? 1626?]
—Relacion del alzamiento de los Indios. [Seville? 1624]
—Zambrana de Villalobos, Sebastian. Allegatio iuris. [Madrid? 1621]
Bollandus, Joannes, ed. *See* Afbeeldinghe van d'eerste eeuwe. Antwerp: 1640
—*See also* Imago primi saeculi Societatis Jesu. Antwerp: 1640
Bologna. Università. Collegio di Medicina. Antidotarium Bononien. Bologna: Heirs of V. Benacci, 1641
Bompart, Marcellin. Nouveau chasse peste. Paris: P. Gaultier, 1630
Le bon advis. [The Hague?] 1649
Le bon voisin. [Amsterdam?] 1646
Bonardo, Giovanni Maria, conte. La minera del mondo. Venice: A. Turino, 1611
Bonham, Thomas. The chyrurgeons closet. London: G. Miller, for E. Brewster, 1630
Bonnart, Jean. La semaine des medicaments. Paris: R. Baraignes, 1629

Bonoeil, John. His Majesties gracious letter. London: F. Kingston, 1622
—Observations to be followed. London: F. Kingston, 1620
Bontekoe, Willem Ysbrandsz. Journael ofte Gedenckwaerdige beschrijvinghe vande Oost-Indische reyse. Hoorn: I. Willemszoon, for J. J. Deutel, 1646 [colophon: Haarlem: T. Fonteyn, 1646]
— —Rotterdam: I. van Waesberghe, 1647
— —Utrecht: G. Bilsteyn, for E. W. Snellaert, 1647
— —Amsterdam: J. Hartgers, 1648 (2)
— —Hoorn: I. Willemszoon, for J. J. Deutel, 1648 (2)
— —Zaandam: W. Willemszoon, 1648
— —Utrecht: Widow of E. W. Snellaert, 1649
— —Utrecht: L. de Vries, 1649
— —Amsterdam: C. Cunradus, for J. Hartgers, 1650
—Verhael van de avontuerlijke reyse. Amsterdam: J. Hartgers, 1650
—Die vier und zwantzigste Schiffahrt. Frankfurt a.M.: P. Fievet, for C. LeBlon, 1648
Bontier, Pierre. Histoire de la premiere descouverte . . . des Canaries. Paris: J. de Heuqueville, 1630
— —Paris: M. Soly, 1630
Boodt, Anselm Boèce de. Florum, herbarum, ac fructuum selectiorum icones. Frankfurt a.M.: C. Marne, 1609
— —Bruges: J. B. & L. Kerchovius, 1640
—Gemmarum et lapidum historia. Leyden: J. Maire, 1647
A booke of cookerie. London: E. Allde, 1620
—London: E. A[llde]., for F. Grove, 1629
—London: Elizabeth Allde, 1634
—London: Jeane Bell, 1650
Boothby, Richard. A briefe discovery . . . of Madagascar. London: E. G[riffin]., for J. Hardesty, 1646

——London: [E. Griffin?] for J. Hardesty, 1647

Borough, William. A discours of the variation of the cumpas. London: T. C[reede]., for J. Tapp, 1614

Bos, Lambert van den. Essays ofte Poëtische betrachtungen. Amsterdam: J. Lescaille, for L. van den Bos, 1646

BOSTON

—Canne, Abednego, pseud. A new wind-mil. [London]: 1643

BOTANY. *See also* BOTANY, MEDICAL *below, & names of plants*

—Abriss der Blü[men]. Augsburg: [ca. 1615?]

—Bauhin, J. Historiae plantarum generalis . . . prodromus. Yverdon: 1619

—Bauhin, K. Pinax, theatri botanici . . . opera. Basel: 1623

——Prodromos Theatri botanici. Frankfurt a.M.: 1620

—Besler, B. Hortus eystettensis. [Nuremberg:] 1613

—Bobart, J. Catalogus plantarum Horti medici. [Oxford:] 1648

—Bock, H. Kraütterbuch. Strassburg: 1630

—Bonardo, G. M., conte. La minera del mondo. Venice: 1611

—Bry, J. T. de. Anthologia magna, sive Florilegium novum. Frankfurt a.M.:1626

——Florilegium novum . . . New Blumenbuch. [Oppenheim:] 1612[–14]

——Florilegium renovatum . . . das ist, Vernewertes . . . Blumenbuch. Frankfurt a.M.: 1641

—Camerarius, P. Les heures desrobees, ou Meditations historiques. Paris: 1610

——Operae horarum subcisivarum . . . Centuria tertia. Frankfurt a.M.: 1609

——Tertia centuria historica, das ist, Dritter Theil des historischen Lustgartens. Leipzig: 1630

—Castelli, P. Exactissima descriptio rariorum plantarum. Rome: 1625

——Hortus Messanensis. Messina: 1640

—Ceruto, B. Musaeum Franc. Calceolarii. Verona: 1622

—Contant, J. Les oeuvres de Jacques et Paul Contant. Poitiers: 1628

—Cotgrave. R. A dictionarie of the French and English tongues. London: 1611

—Dalechamps, J. Histoire generale des plantes. Lyons: 1615

—Dioscorides, P. Acerca de la materia medicinal. Valencia: 1636

—Dodoens, R. A newe herbal. London: 1619

——Stirpium historiae pemptades sex. Antwerp: 1616

—Durante, C. Herbario novo. Venice: 1602

——Hortulus sanitatis. Das ist Ein heylsam . . . Gährtlin der Gesundtheit. Frankfurt a.M.: 1609

—Duret, C. Histoire admirable des plantes. Paris: 1605

—Ferrari, G. B. De florum cultura. Rome: 1633

——Flora, overo Cultura di fiori. Rome: 1638

—Fruchtbringende Gesellschaft. Der Fruchtbringenden Geselschaft Nahmen. Frankfurt a.M.: 1646

——Kurtzer Bericht von der Fruchtbringenden Geselschaft Vorhaben. Köthen: 1641

—Gerard, J. The herball or Generall historie of plantes. London: 1633

—Harris. R. The arraignment of the whole creature. London: 1631

—Hart, J. Klinikē, or The diet of the diseased. London: 1633

—Heinsius, D. Laudatio funebris . . . principi Mauritio. Leyden: 1625

—Horst, J. Herbarium Horstianum. Marburg: 1630

—Jonstonus, J. Thaumatographia naturalis. Amsterdam: 1632

—L'Ecluse, C. de. Curae posteriores. [Leyden:] 1611

——Exotericorum libri decem. [Leyden:] 1605

——Rariorum plantarum historia. Antwerp: 1601

—Parkinson, J. Paradisi in sole paradisus terrestris. London: 1629

——Theatrum botanicum: The theater of plants. London: 1640

—Passe, C. van de. Den blomhof. Utrecht: 1614

——A garden of flowers. Utrecht: 1615

——Hortus floridus. Arnhem: 1614

——Jardin de fleurs. Utrecht: [1615?]

—Pilletier, C. Plantarum tum patriarum . . . synonymia. Middelburg: 1610

—Por los interesados en los quatro generos de mercaderias. [Seville? 1633?]

—Possevino, A. Cultura ingeniorum. Cologne: 1610

—Reneaulme, P. de. Specimen historiae plantarum. Paris: 1611

—Robin, J. Enchiridion isagogicum. Paris: 1623

—Scaliger, J. C. Exotericarum exercitationum liber xv. Frankfurt a.M.: 1601

—Schenck, J. G. Hortus Patavinus. Frankfurt a.M.: 1608

—Spiegel, A. van de. Isagoges in rem herbariam. Leyden: 1633

—Stengel, K. Hortensius et dea flora cum pomona historice . . . descripti. Augsburg: 1647

—Sweerts, E. Florilegium. Frankfurt a.M.: 1612

—Theodorus, J. Neuw vollkommentlich Kreuterbuch. Frankfurt a.M.: 1613

—Theophrastus. De historia plantarum. Amsterdam: 1644

—Vallet, P. Le jardin du roy très chrestien Henry IV. [Paris:] 1608

—Villa, E. de. Ramillete de plantas. Burgos: 1637

BOTANY—CANADA
—Cornut, J. P. Canadensium plantarum . . . historia. Paris: 1635

BOTANY, MEDICAL. *See also* GUAIACUM, SARSAPARILLA, TOBACCO, etc.

—Antidotario romano. Rome: 1612
—Beverwijck, J van. Schat der ongesontheit. Dordrecht: 1642
—Crato von Krafftheim, J. Consiliorum et epistolarum medicinalium . . . liber quintus. Hanau: 1619
—Dodoens, R. Cruydt-boeck. Leyden: 1608
—Duchesne, J. Conseils de medecine. Paris: 1626
——La pharmacopee des dogmatiques reformee. Paris: 1624
——Pharmacopoea dogmaticorum restituta. Paris: 1607
——Pharmacopoea restituta. Das ist Verbesserte apotecker Kunst. Strassburg: 1625
——Le ricchezze della riformata farmacopoea. Venice: 1619
—Ferdinandi, E. Centum historiae. Venice: 1621
—Fioravanti, L. Della fisica. Venice: 1603
——Physica, das ist: Experientz. Frankfurt a.M.: 1604
—Fragoso, J. Aromatum, fructuum et simplicium aliquot medicamentorum . . . opera. Strassburg: 1601
—Greiff, F. Consignatio medicamentorum. Tübingen: 1632
—Grüling, P. G. Florilegium Hippocrateo-Galeno-chymicorum. Leipzig: 1644
—Hartmann, J. Praxis chymiatrica. Leipzig: 1633
—Hofmann, C. De medicamentis officinalibus. Paris: 1647
—Joel, F. Operum medicorum . . . tomus primus[-sextus]. Hamburg: 1616
—La Brosse, G. de. Catalogue des plantes cultivées. Paris: 1641
——De la nature, vertu, et utilité des plantes. Paris: 1628

——Description du jardin royal des plantes medicinales. Paris: 1636
—Le Paulmier de Grentemesnil, J. De morbis contagiosis libri septem. Frankfurt a.M.: 1601
—Linden, J. A. van der. De scriptis medicis. Amsterdam: 1637
—L'Obel, M. de. In G. Rondelletii . . . Pharmaceuticam . . . animadversiones. London: 1605
——Pharmacopoeia Rondeletii. Leyden: 1618
—Mattioli, P. A. Les commentaires . . . sur les six livres de Pedacius Dioscoride. Lyons: 1605
——De i discorsi . . . nelli sei libri di Pedacio Dioscoride. Venice: 1604
——Kreutterbuch. Frankfurt a.M.: 1611
—Mercado, L. Opera omnia. Frankfurt a.M.: 1608
——Praxis medica. Venice: 1608
——Tomus secundus Operum. Valladolid: 1605
—Morone, M. Directorium medico-practicum. Lyons: 1647
—Mylius. J. D. Antidotarium medico-chymicum reformatum. Frankfurt a.M.: 1620
—Orta, G. da. Dell'historia de i semplici. Venice: 1605
——Histoire des drogues espiceries. Lyons: 1619
—Planis Campy, D. de. Les oeuvres. Paris: 1646
—Rivière, L. Methodus curandorum febrium. Paris: 1640
—Ruland, J. D. Inauguralis de lue . . . venerea disputatio. [Frankfurt a.M.: 1636]
—Ruland, M. Propugnaculum chymiatriae. Leipzig: 1608
—Sala, A. Opera medico-chymica. Frankfurt a.M.: 1647
—Sassonia, E. De melancholia tractatus. Venice: 1620
—Scholtz, L. Epistolarum philosophicarum . . . volumen. Hanau: 1610
—Sennert, D. Institutionum medicinae libri v. Wittenberg: 1611

—Settala, L. Animadversionum . . . libri septem. Milan: 1614
—Steeghius, G. Ars medica. Frankfurt a.M.: 1606
—Torres, P. de. Libro que trata de la enfermedad. Alcalá de Henares: 1626
—Untzer, M. Tractatus medicochymici septem. Halle: 1634
—Wecker, J. J. Antidotarium generale. Basel: 1601
——Le grand dispensaire. Geneva: 1609
——Kunstbuch. Basel: 1616
——Ein nutzliches Büchlein. Basel: 1605
—Weickard, A. Thesaurus pharmaceuticus. Frankfurt a.M.: 1626
—Wood, O. An alphabeticall book of physicall secrets. London: 1639

Botero, Giovanni. Aggiunte alla Ragion di stato. *In his* I prencipi. Venice: 1601
——*In his* Della ragion di stato. Venice: 1606
——*In the same.* Venice: 1619
—Allgemeine historische Weltbeschreibung. Munich: N. Heinrich, for A. Hierat, at Cologne, 1611
——Munich: N. Heinrich, for A. Hierat, at Cologne, 1612
—I capitani. Turin: G. D. Tarino, 1607
——Turin: G. D. Tarino, 1608
—The cause of the greatnesse of cities. London: E[lizabeth]. P[urslowe]., for H. Seile, 1635
—Della ragion di stato. Venice: The Giolitis, 1601
——Venice: N. Misserini, 1606
——Venice: N. Misserini, 1619
——Venice: A. Muschio, 1619
——Venice: The Giuntas, 1640
—Descripcion de todas las provincias . . . del mundo. Barcelona: G. Graells, & G. Dotil, 1603
——Gerona: G. Garrich, 1622
—Historia ecclesiástica y estado. Barcelona: J. Cendrat, for J. Margarit, 1608
—An historicall description of the most famous kingdomes. London: J. Jaggard, 1603

702

—Macht, Reichthum und Einkommen aller Keyser. Cologne: W. Lützenkirchen, 1606

—Mundus imperiorum . . . das ist Beschreibung aller Keyserthumb. Oberursel: C. Sutor, 1602

—Mundus imperiorum, sive De mundis imperiis. Oberursel: C. Sutor, 1603

—Politia regia. Marburg: P. Egenolff, 1620

—I prencipi . . . con le Aggiunte alla Ragion di stato. Venice: G. B. Ciotti, 1601

—Razon d'estado. Burgos: S. de Cañas, for P. de Ossete, & A. Cuello, at Valladolid, 1603

—Relaciones universales del mundo. Valladolid: Heirs of D. Fernández de Córdova, for M. de Córdova, 1603

—Relationi universali. Turin: G. D. Tarino, 1601

— —Venice: N. Polo and Co., 1602

— —Venice: A. Angelieri, 1608, '07

— —Venice: A. Vecchi, 1612

— —Venice: A. Vecchi, 1618

— —Venice: A. Vecchi, 1622–23

— —Venice: The Giuntas, 1640(2)

— —Venice: The Giuntas, 1650

—Relations of the most famous kingdomes. London: [W. Jaggard] for J. Jaggard, 1608

— —London: J. Jaggard, 1611

— —London: [W. Jaggard] for J. Jaggard, 1616

— —London: J. Haviland, for J. Partridge, 1630

—Theatro de los mayores principes del mundo. Barcelona: S. Matevad, & H. Anglada, 1604

— —Barcelona: S. Matevad, & H. Anglada, 1605

—Tractatus duo. Oberursel: C. Sutor, for L. Zetzner, at Strassburg, 1602

—The travellers breviat. London: E. Bollifant, for J. Jaggard, 1601

—A treatise, concerning the . . . greatness of cities. London: T. P[urfoot]., for R. Ockould, & H. Tomes, 1606

—The worlde. London: E. Bollifant, for J. Jaggard, 1601

Boterus, Rodolphus. *See* Boutrays, Raoul

Bottifango, Giulio Cesare. Lettera dell'elefante. Rome: F. Corbelletti, 1630

Boulenger, Jules César. Historiarum sui temporis libri tredecim. Lyons: Heirs of G. Rouillé, 1617

— —Lyons: J. C. Boulenger, 1619

Bouquet composé des plus belles fleurs chimiques. *See* Planis Campy, David de

Bourne, William. De conste der zee-vaert. Amsterdam: C. Claeszoon, 1609

—A regiment for the sea. London: T. Wight, 1601

— —[London: E. Weaver, 1606?]

— —London: T. Snodham, for E. Weaver, 1611

— —[London: E. Weaver, 1617?]

— —London: W. Jones, for E. Weaver, 1620

— —London: W. Jones, for T. Weaver, 1631

Bouton, Jacques. Relation de l'establissement des François . . . en Martinique. Paris: S. Cramoisy, 1640

Boutrays, Raoul. De rebus in Gallia . . . commentariorum lib. xvi. Paris: P. Chevalier, 1610

—Historiopolitographia. Frankfurt a.M.: M. Becker, for J. T. Schönwetter, 1610

Bovionier, François. Quaestio medica . . . in Scholis Medicorum. [Paris: 1649]

BOW AND ARROW

—Guyon, L. Les diverses leçons. Lyons: 1604

—Markham, G. The art of archerie. London: 1634

—The maske of flowers. London: 1614

Boxhorn, Marcus Zuerius. Commentariolus de statu Confoederatarum provinciarum Belgii. Leyden: P. de Croy, for

J. Verhoeve, at The Hague, 1649

— —Leyden: P. de Croy, for J. Verhoeve, at The Hague, 1650(2)

—De majestate regum principumque. Leyden: Boxe Press, for P. Leffen, 1649

—Historia obsidionis Bredae. Leyden: I. Commelin, 1640A

Bozio, Tommaso. De signis ecclesiae Dei. Lyons: 1602

— —Lyons: 1624

— —Cologne: J. Gymnicus, 1626

Bradford, William. *See* Mourt's relation. A relation or journall of the beginning of the English plantation at Plimoth. London: 1622

Bradstreet, Anne (Dudley). The tenth muse. London: S. Bowtell, 1650

Bradwell, Stephen. Helps for suddain accidents. London: T. Purfoot, for T. S[later]., & H. Overton, 1633

—Physick for the sicknesse. London: B. Fisher, 1636

—A watch-man for the pest. London: J. Dawson, for G. Vincent, 1625

Braga, Bernardo de. Sermão . . . na festa. Lisbon: P. Craesbeeck, 1649

—Sermão que prègou . . . . Lisbon: P. Craesbeeck, 1649

Brandon, Lorenço. Excelmo señor. Siendo la materia del valor de la plata. Madrid: 1621

—Señor. Medios para V. Magestad ahorrar lo mucho. [Madrid: 1622?]

Brandt, Geeraert, supposed author. *See* Bedenkingen en antwoort op de vrymoedige aenspraek. Flushing: 1650

Brandt in Brasilien. [Amsterdam?] 1648

Brant, Sebastian. Narren Zunfft. *In* Murner, Thomas. Der Schelmen Zunfft. Frankfurt a.M.: 1618–25

De Brasilsche Breede-byl. [Amsterdam?] 1647

Brasilsche gelt-sack. 'Recife, Brazil' [i.e., Amsterdam?]: 1647(2)

—Portugal. Sovereigns, etc., 1640–1656 (John IV). Copye vande volmacht. [The Hague? 1647]

— —Copye, van een brief van den Koningh. Amsterdam: 1649

— —Declaratie van sijn Koninghlijcke Majesteyt. [Amsterdam?] 1649

—Portugal. Treaties, etc., 1640–1656 (John IV). Extract uyt d'Articulen van het tractaet van bestant. The Hague: 1641

— —Tractaet van bestant. The Hague: 1642

— —Tractatus induciarum. The Hague: 1642

— —Trattado das tregoas. The Hague: 1642

— —Verkondinghe van het bestant. The Hague: 1641

—Poty, P. Copye van een Brasiliaenschen brieff. [Amsterdam:] 1646

—Relaçam da aclamação. Lisbon: 1641

—Relacion de la vitoria que alcanzaron las armas catolicas. Madrid: 1638

—Relacion verdadera de la refriega. Madrid: 1638

— —Seville: 1638

—Relacion y copia de una carta. Madrid: 1625

—Relation de la prinse. Paris: 1624

—Rodríguez de Burgos, B. Relacion de la jornada del Brasil. Cadiz: 1625

—Ruiz de Montoya, A. Haseme mandado, que assi como representè. [Madrid? 1639]

—San Román de Ribadeneyra, A. Historia general de la Yndia Oriental. Valladolid: 1603

—Silva, A. T. da. Successo della guerra de portugueses. [Lisbon? 1647?]

— —Sucesso della guerra de' Portoghesi. [Rome? 1647?]

—Souter, D. Sené-boher. Haarlem: 1630

—Tegen-advys, op de presentatie van Portugal. [The Hague?] 1648

—Traslado de una carta, embiada del Brasil. Madrid: [1640]

—Tydingh uyt Brasil. Amsterdam: 1644

—Vertooch aen de . . . Staten Generael . . . nopende de . . . proceduren van Brasil. Amsterdam: 1647

—Voor-looper, brenghende oprecht bescheyt. [The Hague?] 1646

—De Zeeusche verre-kyker. Flushing: 1649

—Zeitungen . . . wie die Holländer in Brassilien . . . Forten eingenommen. [Cologne?] 1635

BRAZIL—HISTORY—DUTCH CONQUEST. *See also* DUTCH IN BRAZIL

—Aldenburgk, J. G. West-Indianische Reisse. Coburg: 1627

—Amsterdams buer-praetje. Amsterdam: 1650

—Amsterdams dam-praetje. Amsterdam: 1649

—Amsterdams tafel-praetje. [Amsterdam?] 1649

—Amsterdams vuur-praetje. Amsterdam: 1649

—Andrade Leitão, F. de. Copia das proposições. Lisbon: 1642

— —Copia primae allegationis. [The Hague: 1642]

— —Copia propositionum. [The Hague? 1642]

— —Discurso politico. Lisbon: 1642

—Antwoort vanden ghetrouwen Hollander. [The Hague? 1645]

—Auctentijck verhael van 't remarcquabelste . . . in Brasil. Amsterdam: 1640

—Autentyck verhael van 't gene in Brasiel . . . is voorgevallen. Amsterdam: 1645

—Authenthijcque copye van het Recif. [Amsterdam? 1647?]

—Avendaño y Vilela, F. de. Relacino del viaje, y sucesso . . . al Brasil. Seville: 1625

— —Relacione del viaggio, e successo . . . al Brasil. Milan: 1625

—Baardt, P. Friesche Triton. Leeuwarden: 1630

—Baerle, K. van. Poematum. Leyden: 1630

— —Rerum per octennium in Brasilia . . . nuper gestarum . . . historia. Amsterdam: 1647

—Batavier gaet hem verblije. [Amsterdam?] 1630

—Beneficien voor de soldaten. The Hague: 1647

—Beschreibung, welcher Gestalt die Hauptstatt des Königreichs Brasilien . . . erobert worden. [The Hague? 1630?]

—Beschryvinge van 't in-nemen van . . . Salvador. Amsterdam: 1624

—Le bon voisin. [Amsterdam?] 1646

—Brandt in Brasilien. [Amsterdam?] 1648

—De Brasilsche Breede-byl. [Amsterdam?] 1647

—Brasilsche gelt-sack. [Amsterdam?] 1647

—Brasilsche oorloghs overwegingh. [Delft:] 1648

—Brasyls schuyt-praetjen. [The Hague?] 1649

—Een brief, gheschreven van een goet patriot. 's Hertogenbosch: 1639

—Brito Lemos, J. de. Abecedario militar. Lisbon: 1631

—Claar vertooch van de verradersche . . . acten. Amsterdam: 1647

—Een clare ende waerachtighe beschrijvinghe. Utrecht: 1624

—La confession de l'imprimeur. [Antwerp?] 1648

—Consideratien als dat de negotie op Brasil behoort open gestelt te worden. [Amsterdam?] 1638

—Consideratien op de Cautie. [Amsterdam?] 1647

—Copye ofte Cort ende waerachtigh verhael van 't gene ghepasseert is. Amsterdam: 1640

—Correa, J. de Medeiros. Relacam verdadeira de tudo o succedido na restauração da Bahia. Lisbon: 1625

——Two memorable relations. London: 1630

—Warhafft, Umbständ und gründlicher Bericht. [The Hague?] 1624

—Warhaffte gründliche Relation. Augsburg: 1625

—Warhaffter Bricht welcher Massen die Statt Olinda . . . ist eroberet . . . worden. [The Hague? 1630]

—Wieroock-vath, of triumphliedt. Utrecht: 1624

—Willekens, J. Goede nieuwe tijdinghe. [Amsterdam?] 1624

—With, W. C. de. Copie de trois lettres. Amsterdam: [1648]

BRAZIL—HISTORY—
FRENCH COLONY

—Gaultier, J. Table chronologique de l'estat du christianisme. Lyons: 1609

——Tabula chronographica status ecclesiae catolicae. Lyons: 1616

—Léry, J. de. Histoire d'un voyage fait en la terre de Bresil. Geneva: 1611

BRAZIL—HISTORY, NAVAL

—Amaral, M. E. do. Tratado das batalhas . . . do galeão Sanctiago. Lisbon: 1604

—Carta segunda: que vino a un cavallero desta ciudad. Valladolid: [1625]

—Relacion de la jornada. Seville: 1631

—Relacion de la vitoria que la armada de Inglaterra . . . ha tenido. Seville: 1650

—Relacion del felice sucesso. Seville: 1636

—Relacion del lastisomo incendio. Granada: 1631

—Relacion muy verdadera. Barcelona: 1640

—Relacion nueva y verdadera. Madrid: 1640

—Relacion verdadera, de la gran vitoria. Seville: 1638

—Relacion. verdadera, de la grandiosa vitoria. Cadiz: 1625

—Relatione venuta de Madrid. Rome: 1630

—Le siege de la ville de Groll. Paris: 1627

—Sucessos de la armada que fue al Brasil. Seville: 1640

—Tijdinghe van Bresiel door den super cargo . . . gesonden. Delft: 1640

—A true relation of a late very famous sea-fight. London: 1640

BRAZIL—POETRY

—Baardt, P. Friesche Triton. Leeuwarden: 1630

—Buchanan, G. Franciscanus et fratres. Saumur: 1607

——Poemata omnia. Edinburgh: 1615

—Homburg, E. C. Schimpff- und ernsthaffte Clio. Jena: 1642

—Saint-Amant, M. A. de Gérard, sieur de. Les oeuvres . . . Seconde partie. Paris: 1643

—Steendam, J. Den Distelvink. Darde deel. Amsterdam: 1650

——Den Distelvink. Twede deel. Amsterdam: 1649

BRAZIL—POLITICS & GOVERNMENT

—Caramuel Lobkowitz, J. Philippus prudens. Antwerp: 1639

—Liebergen, A. van. Apologiae, ofte Waerachtighe verantwoordinghe. Amsterdam: 1643

—Nederlandsche West-Indische Compagnie. Vryheden ende exemptien t'accorderen. [Amsterdam: 1645]

—Steyger-praetjen. Amsterdam: 1624

BRAZIL NUT

—Besler, B. Fasciculus rariorum. [Nuremberg:] 1616

Brébeuf, Jean de. Relation de ce qui s'est passé dans le pays des Hurons en l'année 1636. *In* Le Jeune, Paul. Relation de ce qui s'est passé en la Nouvelle France en l'année 1636. Paris: 1637

Bredan, Daniel. Desengano a los pueblos del Brasil. Amsterdam: P. A. van Ravesteyn, 1631

Breeden-raedt. Antwerp: F. van Duynen, 1649

Breefe notes of the River Amazones. *See* Governor and Company of Noblemen and Gentle-

men of England for the Plantation of Guiana

A breefe relation of . . . Guiana. *See* Governor and Company of Noblemen and Gentlemen of England for the Plantation of Guiana

Brereton, John. A brief and true relation of . . . Virginia. London: G. Bishop, 1602(2)

Brerewood, Edward. Enquiries touching the diversity of languages. London: [W. Stansby] for J. Bill, 1614

——London: J. Bill, 1622

——London: J. Bill, 1624

——London: J. Norton, for Joyce Norton, & R. Whitaker, 1635

—Recherches curieuses sur la diversité des langues. Paris: O. de Varennes, 1640

Breton, Nicholas. Conceited letters. London: M. Parsons, for S. Rand, 1638

—Conceited letters. London: A. Mathewes, for S. Rand, 1632

—Conceyted letters. London: B. Alsop, for S. Rand, 1618

—Cornu-copiae. London: T. Thorp, 1612

——London: T. Thorp, 1623

—The court and country. London: G. Eld, for J. Wright, 1618(2)

—Crossing of proverbs. London: J. Wright, 1616

——London: J. Wright, 1631–32

—Fantasticks. London: [M. Fletcher] for F. Williams, 1626

—The good and the badde. London: G. Purslowe, for J. Budge, 1616

—An olde mans lesson. London: [E. Allde] for E. White, 1605

—A poste with a madde packet of letters. London: [T. Creede] for J. Smethwicke, 1602

—A poste with a packet of mad letters. London: J. W[indet]., for J. Smethwicke, & J. Browne, 1607

——London: W. Stansby, for J. Smethwicke, & J. Marriott, 1620

——London: [M. Fletcher] for J. Marriott, 1637

——London: J. Marriott [1650?]

—A poste with a packet of madde letters. London: [T. Creede?] for J. Smethwicke, 1603

——[London? T. Creede? for J. Smethwicke? 1605]

——London: J. W[indet]., for J. Smethwicke, & J. Browne, 1609

——London: J. Marriott [1623?]

——London: J. Marriott, 1630

——London: J. Marriott, 1633

——London: [M. Fletcher] for J. Marriott, 1634

—A poste with a packet of madde letters. The second part. London: T. Creede, for J. Browne, & J. Smethwicke, 1605

——London: R. B[lower?]., for J. Browne, & J. Smethwicke, 1606

—Wits private wealth. London: E. Allde, for J. Tapp, 1612

——London: E. Allde, for J. Tapp, 1613

——London: T. Creede, for J. Tapp, 1615

——London: E. Allde, for F. Grove, 1629

——London: B. Alsop, & T. Fawcet, for G. Hurlock, 1634

——London: B. Alsop, & T. Fawcet, for G. Hurlock, 1639

——London: T. Fawcet, for G. Hurlock, 1642

—Wonders worth the hearing. London: J. Tapp, 1602

Breve . . . in causa Angelopolitana jurisdictionis. *See* Catholic Church. Pope, 1644–1655 (Innocentius X)

Breve compendio dal Theatro. *See* Ortelius, Abraham

Breve relacion de la descripcion . . . de las tierras. *See* Recio de León, Juan

Breve relatione. *See* Torres Bollo, Diego de

Breve resumen, que se haze, para la mejor inteligencia del pleyto. *See* Franciscans. Provincia de los Angeles (Mexico)

Breve, y ajustada relacion de lo sucedido. Barcelona: J. Romeu, 1639

Breve y verdadera relacion. *See* San Antonio, Gabriel Quiroga de

Breviarium totius orbis terrarum. *See* Bertius, Petrus

Brevis assertio et apologia acclamationis et justitiae. [Amsterdam? 1644?]

—[The Hague? 1644?]

Brevis forma administrandi apud Indos sacramenta. *See* Catholic church. Liturgy and ritual. Ritual

Brevis narratio eorum quae in Florida . . . Gallis acciderunt. *See* Laudonnière, René Goulaine de

Brevis relatio historica in provincia Peruana. *See* Torres Bollo, Diego de

Brevis repetitio omnium quae . . . legatus Portugalliae . . . proposuit. *See* Sousa Coutinho, Francisco de

BRIDGES—LATIN AMERICA

—Ortiz de Cervantes, J. Señor. El licenciado Juan Ortiz de Cervantes . . . Dize; que catorze leguas . . . . [Madrid? ca. 1620?]

A brief and true relation of . . . Virginia. *See* Brereton, John

Brief, et singulier relation d'un lettre. *See* Soler, Vincent Joachim

Brief geschreven uyt Vranckryck. [The Hague?] 1621

Brief ghescreven uyt Vranckryck. [The Hague?] 1621

Een brief, ghescreven van een goet patriot. 's Hertogenbosch: J. van Dockum, 1639

A brief narration . . . of the churches in New-England. *See* Weld, Thomas

Brief recueil des choses plus signalees. *See* Panciroli, Guido

Brief recueil des particularitez . . . de l'isle de Marignan. *See* Pezieu, Louis de

A brief relation of the discovery . . . of New England. *See* Council for New England

A brief treatise of . . . the globe. *See* Tanner, Robert

Een brief uyt den Haegh. Utrecht: S. de Roover, 1649

Brief vande . . . Staten van Hollandt. *See* Holland (Province). Staten

A briefe and accurate treatise, concerning . . . tobacco. *See* Venner, Tobias

Briefe considerations concerning . . . trade. *See* Robinson, Henry

A briefe declaration of the present state of things in Virginia. *See* Great Britain. Council for Virginia

A briefe description of the whole worlde. *See* Abbot, George, Abp of Canterbury

A briefe discourse of the Newfound-land. *See* Mason, John

A briefe discourse of the true . . . use of charact'ring the degrees. *See* Ravenscroft, Thomas

A briefe discovery . . . of Madagascar. *See* Boothby, Richard

A briefe narration of some courses. *See* Rathband, William

A briefe relation of the late . . . rebellion . . . in . . . Barbadas. *See* Foster, Nicholas

A briefe relation of the persecution . . . in . . . Japonia. *See* Morejon, Pedro

Briet, Philippe. Parallela geographiae veteris et novae. Paris: S. Cramoisy, & G. Cramoisy, 1648–49

Brieve relation de l'estat de Phernambucq. *See* Guelen, August de

Brieve relation du voyage de la Nouvelle France. *See* Le Jeune, Paul

Brieve relation du voyage des isles de l'Amerique. *See* Pacifique de Provins, O. F. M. Cap

Bril-gesicht. [Amsterdam?] 1638

Brilleman, Jan. Collyrium, ofte Costelijcke ooghen-salve. Leeuwarden: H. de Bock, 1647

Brinsley, John. Consolation for our grammar schooles. London: R. Field, 1622

Britaines busse. *See* Sharpe, Edward

The British bell-man. [London:] 1648

BRITISH IN AMERICA

—Norwood, R. The sea-mans practice. London: 1637

—Rudyerd, Sir B. A speech concerning a West Indie association. London: 1641

——Two speeches in Parliament. London: 1642

—Sibbes, R. Light from heaven. London: 1638

—Stow, J. The annales . . . of England. London: 1615

—Thou, J. A. de. Historiarum sui temporis . . . Libri cxxxviii. Geneva: 1620

—Wassenaer, N. van. T'achste deel . . . van het Historisch verhael. Amsterdam: [1625]

BRITISH IN GUIANA

—A publication of Guiana's plantation. London: 1632

BRITISH IN THE WEST INDIES

—Sad news from the seas. [London:] 1641

—Santo Tomé, Venezuela. Señor. La ciudad de Santo Tome. [Madrid? ca. 1620?]

—Scott, T. Symmachia: or, A true-loves knot. [Utrecht? 1624]

Brito, Bernardo de. Elogios dos reis de Portugal. Lisbon: P. Craesbeeck, 1603

Brito Lemos, João de. Abecedario militar. Lisbon: P. Craesbeeck, 1631

Brochero, Luis de. Discurso breve del uso de exponer los ninos. Seville: S. Fajardo, 1626

Broeck, Pieter van den. Korte historiael ende journaelsche aenteyckeninghe. Amsterdam: J. Broerszoon, for H. J. Brouwer, 1634

——Haarlem: H. P. van Wesbusch, 1634

—Wonderlijcke historische ende Journaelsche aenteyckeningh. Amsterdam: J. Hartgers, 1648

Broecke, Pieter van den. See Broeck, Pieter van den

Brooke, Christopher. A poem on the late massacre in Vir-

ginia. London: G. Eld, for R. Milbourne, 1622

Brouwer, Hendrick. Die fünff und zweyntzigste Schifffahrt. Frankfurt a.M.: C. LeBlon, 1649

—Journael ende historis verhael van de reyse . . . naer de custen van Chili. Amsterdam: B. Janszoon, 1646 (2)

——Amsterdam: J. Bouman [1650?]

Browne, Sir Thomas. Pseudodoxia epidemica: or, Enquiries. London: T. Harper, for E. Dod, 1646

——London: T. H[arper]., for E. Dod, 1646

——London: A. Miller, for E. Dod, & N. Ekins, 1650

Bruele, Gualtherus. Praxis medicinae. Venice: Societas Venetas, 1602

——Leyden: Plantin Press (Raphelengius), 1612

——Geneva: P. Aubert, 1628

——Geneva: J. Chouët, 1628

——Leyden: J. Maire, 1628

——Leyden: J. Maire, 1647

—Praxis medicinae, or, The physicians practise. London: J. Norton, for W. Sheares, 1632

——London: J. Norton, for W. Sheares, 1639

——London: R. Cotes, for W. Sheares, 1648

Brun, Samuel. See Braun, Samuel

Brunner, Balthasar. Consilia medica. Halle: P. Schmidt, for J. Krusecke, 1617

Bry, Johann Theodor de, comp. India Orientalis. Abridgment. See Fitzer, William. Orientalischè Indien. Frankfurt a.M.: 1628

——See also Fitzer, William. Extract der Orientalischen Indien. Frankfurt a.M.: 1629

—India Orientalis, pt 1. German. See Lopes, Duarte. Regnum Congo, hoc est Warhaffte . . . Beschreibung. Frankfurt a.M.: 1609

——, pt 1. Latin. See Lopes, Duarte. Regnum Congo, hoc est Vera descriptio. Frankfurt a.M.: 1624

——, pt 1. Appendix. German. See Braun, Samuel. Anhang der Beschreibung dess Königreichs Congo. Frankfurt a.M.: 1625

——, pt 1. Appendix. Latin. See Braun, Samuel. Appendix Regni Congo. Frankfurt a.M.: 1625

——, pt 3. German. See Linschoten, Jan Huygen van. Dritter Theil Indiae Orientalis. Oppenheim: 1616

——, pt 3. Latin. See Linschoten, Jan Huygen van. Tertia pars Indiae Orientalis. Frankfurt a.M.: 1601

———See the same. Frankfurt a.M.: 1629

——, pt 5. German. See Neck, Jacob Corneliszoon van. Fünffter Theil der Orientalischen Indien. Frankfurt a.M.: 1601

———See the same. Frankfurt a.M.: 1623

——, pt 5. Latin. See Neck, Jacob Corneliszoon van. Quinta pars Indiae Orientalis. Frankfurt a.M.: 1601

——, pt 6. German. See Marees, Pieter de. Sechster Theil der Orientalischen Indien. Frankfurt a.M.: 1603

——, pt 6. Latin. See Marees, Pieter de. Indiae Orientalis, pars vi. Frankfurt a.M.: 1604

——, pt. 7. German. See Spilbergen, Joris van. Siebender Theil der Orientalischen Indien. Frankfurt a.M.: 1605

——, pt 7. Latin. See Spilbergen, Joris van. Indiae Orientalis pars septima. Frankfurt a.M.: 1606

——, pt 8. German. See Bry, Johann Theodor de. Achter Theil der Orientalischen Indien. Frankfurt a.M.: 1606

——, pt 8. Latin. See Bry, Johann Theodor de. Indiae Orientalis, pars octava. Frankfurt a.M.: 1607

——, pt 9. Appendix. German. See Verken, Johann. Continuatio oder Ergäntzung dess neundten Theils. Frankfurt a.M.: 1613

By his Majesties Commissioners for Virginia. *See* Great Britain. Council for Virginia

By his Majesties Councell for Virginia . . . a little standing lotterie. *See* Great Britain, Council for Virginia

By his Majesties Counsell for Virginea . . . for the advancement of . . . Virginea. *See* Great Britain. Council for Virginia

By the Counsell of Virginia. *See titles under* Great Britian. Council for Virginia

By the Treasuror, Councell and Company for Virginia. *See* Virginia Company of London

BYE, CORNELIUS DE

—Corte, C. de. Virorum illustrium . . . elogia. Antwerp: 1636

C., G. W. *See* Breeden-raedt. Antwerp: 1649

C., T. *See* A short discourse of the New-found-land. Dublin: 1623

C., V. W. *See* Trou-hertighe onderrichtinge. [Amsterdam?] 1643

Caballero de Cabrera, Juan. Obra postuma. Madrid: D. García Morrás, 1648

Cabeças, Luis. Historia de S. Domingos, la pte. [Lisbon:] G. da Vinha, 1623

Cabot, Sebastian. *See* Chytraeus, Nathan. Variorum in Europa itinerum deliciae. [Herborn:] 1606

CABOT, SEBASTIAN

—Bacon, F. Histoire du regne de Henry VII. Paris: 1627

— —Historia regni Henrici septimi. Leyden: 1642

— —The historie of . . . King Henry. London: 1622

—Gentleman, T. Englands way to win wealth. London: 1614

—Ramusio, G. B. Delle navigationi et viaggi . . . Volume secondo. Venice: 1606

—Roberts, L. The treasure of traffike. London: 1641

—Scott, T. An experimentall discoverie of Spanish practises. [London:] 1623

CABRAL, PEDRO ALVARES

—Goes, D. de. Chronica do felicissimo rey Dom Emanuel. Lisbon: 1619

—Wytfliet, C. Histoire universelle des Indes. Douai: 1605

Cabredo, Luis de. Historia insignis miraculi. Graz: G. Widmanstetter, 1609

Cabredo, Rodrigo de. Copia d'una lettera. Palermo: G. A. di Franceschi, 1609

—Copia di una carta. Barcelona: S. Matevad, & L. Déu, 1609

Cabrera de Córdoba, Luis. Filipe Segundo rey de España. Madrid: L. Sánchez, 1619

CACAO

—Márquez de Torres, F. Medio suave y facil. [Madrid? ca. 1635?]

—Rúa, F. de. Por Don Juan Meneses. Madrid: [1634]

CACTUS. *See* PRICKLY-PEAR

Cadereyta, Lope Díez de Auxarmendáriz, marqués de. *See* Díez de Auxarmendáriz, Lope, marqués de Cadereyta

Cadogno, Ottavio. *See* Codogno, Ottavio

Caduta del conte d'Olivares. *See* Guidi, Ippolito Camillo

Caesalpinus, Andreas. *See* Cesalpino, Andrea

Caietanus, Constantinus. *See* Gaetani, Costantino

Calado, Manuel. O valeroso Lucideno. Lisbon: P. Craesbeeck, 1648

Calancha, Antonio de la. Coronica moralizada del orden de San Augustin en el Peru. Barcelona: P. Lacavallería, 1638

— —Barcelona: P. Lacavallería, 1639

— —*See also* Baldani, Fulgenzio. Vita del . . . fra Diego Ortiz. Genoa: 1645

Calderón, Juan Alonso. Memorial historico, juridico, politico. [Madrid? ca. 1650]

Calestani, Girolamo. Delle osservationi. Venice: A. Angelieri, 1606

— —Venice: G. A. Giuliani, 1616

— —Venice: P. Miloco, 1623

— —Venice: G. Imberti, 1639

CALIFORNIA

—Fotherby, M. Atheomastix clearing foure truthes. London: 1622

—Villerias, M. de. El capitan Mateo de Villerias vezino de Mexico. [Madrid? 1613]

CALIFORNIA—DISCOVERY & EXPLORATION

—Cardona, N. de. Señor. El capitan Nicolas de Cardona, dize: que sirve a V[uestra]. M[agestad]. [Madrid? 1634]

—Porter y Casanate, P. Señor. El capitan Don Pedro Porter y Cassanate. [Madrid: 1638?]

CALLAO, PERU—HISTORY

—La furieuse défaite des Espagnols et la . . . bataille donnee au Perou. Paris: 1625

—Relacion y copia de una carta. Madrid: 1625

Calvisius, Seth. Chronologia. Leipzig: J. Apel, 1605

—Opus chronologicum. [Leipzig: F. Lanckisch the Elder? for] J. Thymiss, at Frankfurt a.d.O., 1620

— —Leipzig: F. Lanckisch the Elder, for J. Thymiss, at Frankfurt a.d.O., 1629

— —Frankfurt a.M.: S. Beckenstein, & C. Gerlach, at Emden, 1650

Calvo, Juan. Cirugia universal, la-2a pte. Madrid: D. Flamenco, for D. Logroño, 1626

— —Perpignan: L. Roure, 1636

— —Valencia: Heirs of C. Garriz, for B. Nogués, 1647

Camargo, Gerónimo de. Por el real fisco. [Madrid? ca. 1646?]

Cambrensium Caroleia. *See* Vaughan, William

Cambridge. University. To our reverend and deare brethren. [Cambridge? 1649]

Cambridge. University. Act verses. Anima unita corpori est perfectior. [Cambridge: ca. 1608]

Camden, William. Annales. London: [H. Lownes] for B. Fisher, 1625

—Annales des choses que se sont passées. London: R. Field, 1624

—Annales rerum Anglicarum. London: W. Stansby, for S. Waterson, 1615

——Frankfurt a.M.: J. Bringer, for The Rulands, 1616

——Leyden: Elsevier Office, 1625

—Annalium rerum Anglicarum, t.2. London: W. Stansby, for S. Waterson, 1627

—Annals. London: T. Harper, for B. Fisher, 1635

—Histoire d'Elizabeth. Paris: S. Thiboust, 1627

—The historie of . . . Princesse Elizabeth. London: T. Harper, for W. Webb, at Oxford, 1629

——London: [N. Okes?] for B. Fisher, 1630

——London: [T. Harper] for W. Webb [at Oxford] 1634

—Rerum Anglicarum . . . annales. Leyden: Elsevier Office, 1639

—Tomus alter et idem. *See his* The historie of . . . Princesse Elizabeth

Camerarius, Joachim, the Younger. Symbolorum et emblematum . . . centuria quarta. [Nuremberg? P. Kaufmann?] 1604

—Symbolorum et emblematum . . . centuriae tres. [Leipzig:] Vögelin Press, 1605

Camerarius, Philipp. Les heures desrobees, ou Meditations historiques. Paris: J. Cottereau, 1610

—The living librarie. London: A. Islip, 1621

——London: A. Islip, for J. Partridge, 1625

—Les meditations historiques. Lyons: A. de Harsy, 1603

——Paris: J. Gesselin, 1608

——Lyons: Widow of A. de Harsy, 1610

—Les meditations historiques, t 2me. Paris: J. Cottereau, 1608

—Operae horarum subcisivarum . . . Centuria altera. Frankfurt a.M.: J. Saur, for P. Kopff, 1601

——Frankfurt a.M.: J. Saur, for P. Kopff, 1506 [i.e., 1606]

——Frankfurt a.M.: E. Emmel, for P. Kopff, 1620

——Frankfurt a.M.: W. Hoffmann, 1642

——Frankfurt a.M.: J. F. Weiss, for J. Wild, 1650

—Operae horarum subcisivarum . . . Centuria prima. Frankfurt a.M.: J. Saur, for P. Kopff, 1602

——Frankfurt a.M.: E. Emmel, for P. Kopff, 1615

——Frankfurt a.M.: E. Emmel, for P. Kopff, 1624

——Frankfurt a.M.: K. Rötel, for J. Hallerford, & J. Wild, 1644

—Operae horarum subcisivarum . . . Centuria tertia. Frankfurt a.M.: N. Hoffmann, for P. Kopff, 1609

——Frankfurt a.M.: N. Hoffmann, for P. Kopff, 1618

——Frankfurt a.M.: W. Hoffmann, for P. Kopff, 1625

——Frankfurt a.M.: J. F. Weiss, for J. Wild, 1650

—Operae horarum succisivarum . . . Das ist: Historischer Lustgarten. Leipzig: M. Wachsman, 1625

—Secunda centuria historica, das ist, Ander Theil des historischen Lustgartens. Leipzig: M. Wachsman, 1628

—Tertia centuria historica, das ist, Dritter Theil des historischen Lustgartens. Leipzig: Heirs of M. Wachsman, 1630

—The walking librarie. London: A. Islip, 1621

——London: A. Islip, for J. Partridge, 1621

——London: 1625

Camões, Luiz de. Os Lusiadas. Lisbon: P. Craesbeeck, for D. Fernandes, 1609

——Lisbon: P. Craesbeeck, for D. Fernandes, 1609

——Lisbon: V. Alvares, for D. Fernandes, 1612

——Lisbon: P. Craesbeeck, for D. Fernandes, 1613 (2)

——Lisbon: P. Craesbeeck, 1626

——Lisbon: P. Craesbeeck, 1631

——Lisbon: L. Crasbeeck, 1633

——Madrid: J. Sánchez, for P. Coello, 1639

——Lisbon: P. Craesbeeck, 1644

—Lusiadum libri decem. Lisbon: G. da Vinha,1622

Campanella, Tommaso. Civitas solis poetica. *In* Hall, Joseph, Bp. Mundus alter. Utrecht: 1643

—De monarchia Hispanica. Harderwijk: 1640

——[Leyden: Elsevier Press, for] L. Elsevier, at Amsterdam, 1640

——[Leyden: Elsevier Press, for L. Elsevier, at] Amsterdam, 1640

——[Leyden: B. & A. Elsevier, for] L. Elsevier, at Amsterdam, 1641

—Realis philosophiae epilogisticae partes quatuor. Frankfurt a.M.: [E. Emmel?] for W. Tampach, 1623

—Von der Spanischen Monarchy. [Tübingen?: J. A. Cellius?] 1620

——[Tübingen?: J. A. Cellius?] 1623

Campion, Thomas. Epigrammatum libri ii. London: E. Griffin, 1619

Campo, Gonzalo de, Abp. Copia de un capitulo de una carta. Seville: F. de Lyra, 1627

Campuzano, Baltasar. Planeta catholico. Madrid: D. Díaz de la Carrera [1646]

CANADA. *See also* NEW FRANCE, FRENCH IN CANADA, *etc.*

—France. Sovereigns, etc., 1643–1715 (Louis XIV). Le Roy estant en son Conseil. [Paris: 1647]

—Neuhaus, E. Theatrum ingenii humani. Amsterdam: 1633

CANADA—COMMERCE

—Dunoyer de Saint-Martin, F. Articles, moyens et raisons. Paris: 1616

—France. Conseil d'état. Extraict des registres du Conseil d'Estat. [Paris? 1634]

paña conduzidas por tierra a Arica. *See* Estaço da Silveira, Simão

El capitan Francisco de Vitoria. *See* Vitoria Baraona, Francisco de

El capitan Gaspar de Villagra. *See titles under* Villagrá, Gaspar Pérez de

El capitan Manuel de Frias. *See* Frias, Manuel de

El capitan Mateo de Villerias. *See* Villerias, Mateo de

I capitani. *See* Botero, Giovanni

Capitulaciones de el assiento. *See* Spain. Laws, statutes, etc., 1621–1665 (Philip IV)

Capitulaciones de la paz. *See* Spain. Treaties, etc., 1621–1665 (Philip IV)

Capitulo de una de las cartas que diversas personas embiaron. Seville: J. Serrano de Vargas y Ureña, 1618

Capivaccio, Girolamo. Opera omnia. Frankfurt a.M.: Palthenius Office, for J. Rose, 1603

— —Venice: The Sessas, 1606

— —Venice: The Sessas, 1617

Capreolus, Jacobus. *See* Du Chevreul, Jacques

Caprioli, Aliprando. *See* Capriolo, Aliprando

Capriolo, Aliprando. Ritratti di cento capitani illustri. *See* Ritratti et elogii di capitani. Rome: 1635

CAPUCHINS IN BRAZIL

—Arsène de Paris. Derniere lettre du pere . . . au r.p. provincial. [Paris: 1613]

—Claude d'Abbeville, Father. Die Ankunfft der Vätter Capuciner Ordens. Augsburg: 1613

— —L'arrivee des peres Capucins en l'Inde Nouvelle. Paris: 1612

— —Les fruicts de la mission. Lille: 1614

— —Histoire de la mission des peres Capucins. Paris: 1614

— —[Relatione del viaggio . . . d'alcuni padri capuccini. Bergamo: 1613]

—Yves d'Evreux, Father. Suitte de l'Histoire des choses . . . advenues en Maragnan. Paris: 1615

Caramuel Lobkowitz, Juan, Bp. Joannes Bargantinus Lusitaniae. Louvain: E. de Witte, 1642

—Philippus prudens. Antwerp: Plantin Press (B. Moretus), 1639

—Respuesta al Manifesto. Antwerp: Plantin Office (B. Moretus), 1642

CARANNA

—Beverwijck, J. van. Heelkonste. Dordrecht: 1645

Cárdenas, Alonso de. A speech, or complaint. London: N. Butter, 1643

Cárdenas, Bernardino de, Bp. Memorial, y relacion verdadera para el rei. Madrid: F. Martínez, 1634

Cardona, Nicolás de. Señor. El capitan Nicolas de Cardona, dize: que sirve a V[uestra]. M[agestad]. [Madrid? 1634?]

—*See also* Cardona, Tomás de. Señor. El capitan Tomas de Cardona. [Madrid? 1618?]

Cardona, Tomás de. Señor. El capitan Tomas de Cardona, por si, y en nombre de los demas participes. [Madrid? 1618?]

—Señor. Tomas de Cardona . . . presento . . . la proposicion siguente. [Madrid? 1620?]

Cargo de la culpa que resulta contra Juan de Reyna. [Madrid? 1629?]

Cargo que resulta contra don Feliciano Navarro. [Madrid? 1630?]

CARIB INDIANS

—Cardona, T. de. Señor. El capitan Tomas de Cardona. [Madrid? 1618?]

CARIBBEAN SEA

—Boutrays, R. De rebus in Gallia . . . commentariorum lib. xvi. Paris: 1610

—Relacion de lo que le sucedio a Don Luis Fajardo. Malaga: 1606

Carlyle, James Hay, 2nd earl of. A declaration. [London: 1648?]

Carmelites. Chapter General. Constituciones pro regimine provinciae S. Alberti Novae Hispaniae. [Alcalá de Henares? 1616?]

CARMELITES IN MEXICO

—Carmelites. Chapter General. Constituciones. [Alcalá de Henares? 1616?]

Caro, Annibale. De le lettere familiari. Venice: P. Ugolino, 1603

— —Venice: G. Alberti, 1610

Caro de Torres, Francisco. Historia de las ordenes militares. Madrid: J. González, 1629

—Relacion de los servicios. Madrid: Widow of C. Delgado, 1620

CAROLINA—DESCRIPTION

—Williams, E. Virgo triumphans: or, Virginia richly . . . valued. London: 1650

Caron, Noel de. Nieus uyt Engelandt. [The Hague?] 1621

Carpenter, Nathaniel. Geographie delineated. Oxford: J. Lichfield, for H. Cripps, 1635

—Geography delineated. Oxford: J. Lichfield, & W. Turner, for H. Cripps, 1625

Carranza, Alonso. El ajustamiento i proporcion de las monedas de oro. Madrid: F. Martínez, 1629

—Por D. Luis Colon de Toledo. [Madrid: 1621]

Carrasco del Saz, Francisco. Initium a Domino. [Madrid? 1616?]

Carrasquilla, Andres de. *See* Spain. Laws, statutes, etc., 1556–1598 (Philip II). Nuevas leyes y ordenanzas, hechas por su Magestad. Madrid: 1625

Carrillo, Martín. Anales cronologicos del mundo. Saragossa: Hospital Real, for P. Escuer, 1634

—Annales y memorias cronologicas. Huesca: P. Blusson, for Widow of J. Valdivielso, 1622

Carrillo Altamirano, Fernando Alfonso. Señor. El doctor

Hernan Carrillo Altamirano. [Madrid? 1624?]

Carrillo de Mendoza y Pimentel, Diego, marqués de Gelves. Relacion del estado. [Madrid: 1624]

Carrión, Alonso de. *See* Por Alonso de Carrion escriuano publico. Madrid: 1634

Carta . . . a los religiosos. *See* Benavides, Alonso de, fray

Carta [. . . al padre Oratio Carocchi]. *See* Palafox y Mendoza, Juan de, Bp

Carta . . . que se fulminò contra don M. Perez de Varaiz. *See* Varaona, Sancho de

Carta cierta y verdadera que vino a un cavallero desta ciudad. Seville: J. de Cabrera, 1625

Carta de aviso de la muerte . . . del padre Alonso de Medrano. [Granada? 1648]

Carta del conde de Chinchon. *See* Chinchón, Luis Gerónimo Fernández de Cabrera y Bobadilla

Carta del p. Juan Gonzalez Chaparro. *See* González Chaparro, Juan

Carta que Duarte Gomez escrivio. *See* Gómez Solis, Duarte

Carta que escrivio el licenciado Mariana. *See* Mariana, ——, licenciado

Carta, que o Visorrey do Brasil . . . escreveo. *See* Montalvão, Jorge Mascarenhas, marquez de

Carta segunda. *See* Palafox y Mendoza, Juan de, Bp

Carta segunda: que vino a un cavallero desta ciudad. Valladolid: Widow of F. Fernández de Córdoba [1625]

Cartagena, Colombia. Por parte de las ciudades de Cartagena, y santa Fé. [Madrid? 1620?] (2)

Cartagena, Colombia (Province). A dos cosas se reduze la pretension de Cartagena. [Madrid? ca. 1625?]

CARTAGENA, COLOMBIA
—Capitulo de una de las cartas que diversas personas embiaron. Seville: 1618

—Carvalho, J. de. Relação verdadeira dos sucessos. Lisbon: 1642

—López de León, P. Practica y teorica de las apostemas. Seville: 1628

—Velázquez, B. M. El filosofo del aldea. Pamplona: 1626

CARTAGENA, COLOMBIA—HISTORY
—Cortés de Mesa, D. Señor. Don Diego Cortes de Mesa, regidor de la ciudad de Cartaxena. [Madrid? 1645?]

—Solórzano Pereira, J. de. El doctor Juan de Solorzano Pereira. Madrid: 1629

CARTAGENA, COLOMBIA—POLITICS & GOVERNMENT
—Eras Pantoja, N. Señor. Don Nicolas Eras Pantoja. [Madrid? 1642?]

Cartari, Vincenzo. Imagini de gli dei delli antichi. Padua: P. P. Tozzi, 1626

—Imagini delli dei de gl'antichi. Venice: The Tomasini, 1647

—Le vere e nove imagini. Padua: P. P. Tozzi, 1615

Cartas que escreveo o marquez de Montalvam. *See* Montalvão, Jorge Mascarenhas, marquez de

CARTIER, JACQUES
—Du Fail, N., seigneur de La Herissaye. Les contes et discours d'Eutrapel. Rennes: 1603

—Marguérite d'Angoulême, Queen of Navarre. L'Heptameron. Paris: 1615

—Rabelais, F. Oeuvres. Antwerp: 1605

CARTOGRAPHY
—Mayerne, L. T. de, fl. 1648. Discours sur la carte universelle. Paris: 1648

Carvalho, Jorge de. Relação verdadeira dos sucessos. Lisbon: D. Lopes Rosa, 1642

Casas, Bartolomé de las, Bp. Conquista dell'Indie Occidentali, Venice: M. Ginammi, 1644

——Venice: M. Ginammi, 1645

—Erudita et elegans explicatio quaestionis. Tübingen: E. Wild, 1625

—Histoire des Indes Occidentales. Lyons: J. Caffin, & F. Plaignard, 1642

—Istoria ò brevissima relatione. Venice: M. Ginammi, 1626

——Venice: M. Ginammi, 1630

——Venice: M. Ginammi, 1643

—La liberta pretesa dal supplice schiavo indiano. Venice: M. Ginammi, 1640

—Miroir de la tyrannie espagnole. *See* Gysius, Johannes. Le miroir de la cruelle . . . tyrannie. Amsterdam: 1620

—Narratio regionum Indicarum. Oppenheim: H. Galler, for J. T. de Bry, 1614

—Obras. Barcelona: A. Lacavalleria, 1646

—Den spiegel der Spaensche tierannye-geschiet in Westindien. Amsterdam: D. de Meyne, & D. P. Voskuyl, 1612 [And variant spellings]

——Amsterdam: D. P. Voskuyl, 1612

——Amsterdam: C. L. van der Plasse, 1620

——Amsterdam: J. E. Cloppenburg, 1620 (2)

——Amsterdam: J. E. Cloppenburg, 1620 [i.e., ca. 1622?]

——Amsterdam: 1627

——[Amsterdam: E. Cloppenburg, 1638]

——Amsterdam: E. Cloppenburg, 1638

—Spieghel der Spaenscher tyrannie, in West-Indien. Amsterdam: C. Claeszoon, 1607

——Amsterdam: Widow of C. Claeszoon, 1610

—Den spieghel vande Spaensche tyrannie beeldelijcken afgemaelt. Amsterdam: C. Claeszoon, 1609

—Il supplice schiavo indiano. Venice: M. Ginammi, 1636

—Tyrannies et cruautez des Espanols. Rouen: J. Cailloué, 1630

—Den vermeerderden spieghel der Spaensche tierannije-

geschiet. Amsterdam: C. L. van der Plasse, 1621 (3)
— —Amsterdam: C. L. van der Plasse, 1634
— —Amsterdam: C. L. van der Plasse, 1640
—Warhafftiger und gründlicher Bericht. Oppenheim: J. T. de Bry, 1613
See also the following:
—Clyte, Nicasius van der. Cort verhael der destructie van d'Indien. Flushing: [1611]
—Discours sur l'affaire de la Valteline. Paris: 1625
—Sala, Gaspar. Secrets publichs. [Barcelona: 1641]
CASAS, BARTOLOMÉ DE LAS, BP
—Avila y Sotomayor, F. de. El arbitro. Pamplona: 1646
—Leonardo y Argensola, B. J. Anales de Aragon, pte 1a. Saragossa: 1630
—Middelgeest, S. van. Het testament ofte wtersten wille. [Amsterdam?] 1609
—Nederlandschen verre-kijcker. The Hague: 1627
—Sepúlveda, J. G. de. Opera. Cologne: 1602
Casas, Gonzalo de las. Arte nuevo para criar seda. *In* Herrera, Gabriel Alonzo de. Agricultura general. [Madrid:] 1620
— —*In the same.* Madrid: 1645
The case of Mainwaring, Hawes, Payne, and others. [London:] 1646
Casos notables, sucedidos en las costas de la ciudad de Lima. Madrid: 1625
—Madrid: J. González, for A. de Paredes, 1625
—Madrid: B. de Guzman, 1625
—Seville: J. de Cabrera [1625]
Casp. Barthi Erotodidascalus. *See* Polo, Gaspar Gil
CASTEL MILHOR, ——, CONDE DE
—Lopes, F. Milagroso successo do Conde de Castel Milhor. Lisbon: 1643
Castell, William. A petition . . . exhibited to the high court of Parliament. [London:] 1641

—A short discoverie of the coasts . . . of America. London: 1644
Castelli, Pietro. Balsamum examinatum. Messina: G. F. Bianco, 1640
—Exactissima descriptio rariorum plantarum. Rome: G. Mascardi, 1625
—Hortus Messanensis. Messina: Widow of G. F. Bianco, 1640
—Opobalsamum. Venice: P. Tomasini, 1640
—Opobalsamum triumphans. Basel: F. Perna, 1640
— —[Rome: 1640]
Castile. Laws, statutes, etc., 1252–1284 (Alfonso X). Las siete partidas nuevamente glosadas. Mainz: B. Lipp, for J. Hasrey, at Madrid, 1611
Castilho, António d'Igual. *See* Een brief, gheschreven van een goet patriot. 's Hertogenbosch: 1639
Castillo, Juan del. Pharmacopoea, universa medicamenta. Cadiz: J. de Borja, 1622
Castillo Solórzano, Alonso de. La niña de los embustes. Barcelona: J. Margarit, for J. Sepera, 1632
Castro, Juan de. Historia de las virtudes . . . del tabaco. Córdoba: S. de Cea Tesa, 1620
Castro, Pedro de. *See* Lemos, Pedro Fernández de Castro, conde de
Castro de Torres, El capitán. Panegirico del chocolate. Segovia: D. Díaz de la Carrera, 1640
Catalogo de algunos varones illustres. *See* Oliva, Anelio
Catalogo de algunos varones insignes. *See* Freylin, Juan Maria
Catalogue des plantes cultivées. *See* La Brosse, Guy de
Catalogus plantarum Horti medici. *See* Bobart, Jacob
Catalogus quorundam e Societate Jesu qui . . . sunt interfecti. *See* Rivadeneira, Pedro de
Catalogus scriptorum religionis Societatis Jesu. *See* Rivadeneira, Pedro de

Catechismus ofte Tsamenspreeckinghe. [Amsterdam?] 1608
Catecismo de la lengua guarani. *See* Ruiz de Montoya, Antonio
Catecismo en la lengua española, y aymara. *See* Lima (Ecclesiastical Province). Council, 1583
Catecismo en la lengua española, y quichua. *See* Lima (Ecclesiastical Province). Council, 1583
Catecismo na lingoa brasilica. *See* Araujo, Antonio de
Catelan, Laurent. Discours et demonstration des ingrediens. Lyons: J. Mallet, 1614
Catholic Church. Commisarius Generalis Cruciatae. Instrucción sobre la predicación y cobranza de la Bula de Cruzada. [Madrid:] 1626
—Instruccion y forma que se ha de tener . . . en la publicacion . . . de la bula. [Madrid? 1608?]
— —Madrid: 1621
— —[Madrid? 1648]
—Instrucion y forma que se ha de tener . . . en la publicacion . . . de la Bula. [Madrid? 1620?]
—Instruction y forma que se ha de tener en la publicación . . . de la Bula. Valladolid: 1602
CATHOLIC CHURCH. COMMISARIUS GENERALIS CRUCIATAE
—Mascarenhas, A. Relação dos procedimentos. [Lisbon: 1625?]
—Pérez de Lara, A. Compendio de las tres gracias. Madrid: 1610
Catholic Church. Liturgy and ritual. Ritual. Brevis forma administrandi apud Indos sacramenta. Madrid: Imprenta Real, 1617
— —Madrid: Imprenta Real, 1646
Catholic Church. Liturgy and ritual. Ritual. Peru. Rituale, seu Manuale peruanum, et forma brevis. Naples: G. G. Carlino, & C. Vitale, 1607

Catholic Church. Pope, 1623–1644 (Urban VIII). Nuestro mui santo p. Urbano. [Seville: 1642]

Catholic Church. Pope, 1644–1655 (Innocentius X). Breve . . . in causa Angelopolitana jurisdictionis. Paris: A. Vitre, 1648

— —[Rome: Apostolic Camara, 1648]

— —Saragossa: D. Dormer, 1648

Catholic Church in the West Indies. Los arçobispos y obispos de las Indias Occidentales. [Madrid: 1624]

CATHOLIC CHURCH—MISSIONS. *See also* MISSIONS

—Bozio, T. De signis ecclesiae Dei. Lyons: 1602

—Catholic Church in the West Indies. Los arçobispos y obispos de las Indias Occidentales. [Madrid: 1624]

Le Catholique d'estat. *See* Du Ferrier, Jérémie

Cats, Jacob. Emblemata, ofte Minnelycke . . . sinnebeelden. [Amsterdam? 1622?]

— —*In his* Poëtische wercken. [Antwerp? ca. 1645]

—Maechden-plicht. Middelburg: J. van der Hellen, 1618 (2)

— —Gouda: P. Rammazeyn, [ca. 1640]

— —Amsterdam: T. Jacobszoon, 1644

—Maegden-plicht. [Antwerp? 1631?] (3)

— —[Antwerp:] J. Cnobbaert, 1631

— —[Amsterdam? 1633?]

— —*In his* Poëtische wercken. [Antwerp? ca. 1645]

—Maeghden-plicht. [Antwerp? 1631?] (2)

—Minnelijcke . . . sinne-beelden. [Amsterdam? 1631?] (2)

— —[Amsterdam? ca. 1633]

— —[Amsterdam? ca. 1640]

—Minnelijcke . . . zinnebeelden. [Amsterdam? ca. 1640]

— —[Amsterdam? ca. 1645]

—Monita amoris virginei. Amsterdam: W. J. Blaeu [1618?]

— —Amsterdam: W. J. Blaeu, 1619

— —Amsterdam: W. J. Blaeu, 1622

— —Amsterdam: W. J. Blaeu [ca. 1635]

—Poëtische wercken. [Antwerp? ca. 1645]

—Proef-steen van den trouringh. [Amsterdam?] 1644

—Proteus ofte Minne-beelden. Rotterdam: P. van Waesberghe, 1627

— —[The Hague:] 1628

— —The Hague: A. van der Venne, & J. Ockerszoon, 1629

—Silenus Alcibiadis. Middelburg: J. van der Hellen, 1618

— —Middelburg: J. van der Hellen, 1618

— —Amsterdam: W. J. Blaeu, & J. van der Hellen, at Middelburg, 1619

— —Amsterdam: W. J. Blaeu, 1620, '19

— —Amsterdam: W. J. Blaeu, 1622

— —[Amsterdam?] 1624

— —[Antwerp?] 1629

— —[Amsterdam? 1630?]

— —Amsterdam: W. J. Blaeu [1630?]

— —[Amsterdam? ca. 1633]

— —Gouda: P. Rammazeyn [ca. 1640]

— —Dordrecht: M. de Bot [ca. 1645]

— —[Rotterdam? ca. 1645]

—'s Werelts begin, midden, eynde. Dordrecht: H. van Esch, for M. Havius, 1637

— —Dordrecht: H. van Esch, for M. Havius, 1638

— —Amsterdam: N. van Ravesteyn, for E. Cloppenburg, 1643

— —Amsterdam: J. J. Bouman, 1649

— —Leyden: P. de Croy, 1649

Caudry, Daniel. *See* Cawdry, Daniel

The cause of the greatnesse of cities. *See* Botero, Giovanni

Cavelarice, or The English horseman. *See* Markham, Gervase

Cavendish, Thomas. Reyse. *In* Raleigh, Sir Walter. Achter

Theil Americae. Frankfurt a.M.: 1624

CAVENDISH, THOMAS

—Bry, T. de. Americae pars viii. Frankfurt a.M.: 1625

—Davys, J. The seamans secrets. London: 1607

—Dekker, T. Newes from Graves-end. London: 1604

—Gilbert, W. Tractatus . . . de magnete. Stettin: 1628

—Journalen van drie voyagien. Amsterdam: 1643

—Lloyd, D. The legend of captaine Jones: London: 1648

—Lopes, D. Beschrijvinge van 't koningkrijck Congo. Amsterdam: 1650

— —Regnum Congo, hoc est Vera descriptio. Frankfurt a.M.: 1624

— —Regnum Congo, hoc est Warhaffte . . . Beschreibung. Frankfurt a.M.: 1609

—Pretty, F. Beschryvinge vande overtreffelijcke . . . zee-vaerdt. Amsterdam: 1617

—Stow, J. The annales of England. London: [1601]

Cawdrey, Daniel. *See* Cawdry, Daniel

Cawdry, Daniel. Vindiciae clavium, or, A vindication. London: T. H[arper?]., for P. Whaley, 1645

Cayet, Pierre Victor Palma. Chronologie novenaire. Paris: J. Richer, 1608

—Chronologie septenaire. Paris: J. Richer, 1605 (3)

— —Paris: J. Richer, 1606

— —Paris: J. Richer, 1607

— —Paris: J. Richer, 1609

— —Paris: J. Richer, 1611

— —Paris: J. Richer, 1612 (2)

Cebà, Ansaldo. Rime. Rome: B. Zannetti, 1611

Cedula en que Su Magestad da licencia. *See* Spain. Sovereigns, etc., 1598–1621 (Philip III)

Cedula en que su Magestad reprehende gravemente. *See* Spain. Sovereigns, etc., 1598–1621 (Philip III)

CENSORSHIP—LATIN AMERICA

—Spain. Laws, statutes, etc.,

Champlain, Samuel de. Au Roy sire, Le sieur de Champlain remontre. [Paris? 1630?]
—Des sauvages. Paris: C. de Monstr'oeil [1603?]
— —Paris: C. de Monstr'oeil, 1604
—Les voyages de la Nouvelle France. Paris: C. Collet, 1632
— —Paris: P. LeMur, 1632
— —Paris: L. Sevestre, 1632
— —Paris: C. Collet, 1640
—Voyages et descouvertures faites en la Nouvelle-France. Paris: C. Collet, 1619
— —Paris: C. Collet, 1620
— —Paris: C. Collet, 1627
Changes. *See* Shirley, James
Chapman, George. Al fooles, a comedy. London: [G. Eld] for T. Thorpe, 1605
—The ball. A comedy. London: T. Cotes, & W. Cooke, 1639
—Eastward Hoe. London: [G. Eld] for W. Aspley, 1605 (4)
—An epicede or funerall song. London: T. S[nodham]., for J. Budge, 1612
—The memorable maske of the two honorable houses. London: G. Eld, for G. Norton [1613?]
— —London: F. K[ingston]., for G. Norton [1613?]
—Monsieur d'Olive. A comedie. London: T. C[reede]., for W. Holmes, 1606 (2)
Chappuys, Gabriel. Histoire de nostre temps. Paris: G. Chaudière, 1606
Characterismi; or, Lentons leasures. *See* Lenton, Francis
Charron, Jacques de. Histoire universelle de toutes nations. Paris: T. Blaise, 1621
Chatalogo real de España. *See* Menéndez Silva, Rodrigo
Chaumette, Antoine. Enchiridion chirurgicum. *In* Enchiridion practicum medico-chirurgicum. [Geneva:] 1621
— —*In the same.* Geneva: 1627
— —*In the same.* Geneva: 1644
—Enchiridion, ou Livret portatif pour les chirurgiens. Lyons: A. Huguetan, 1609

—Handt-boeck der chirurgie. Arnhem: J. Jacobszoon, 1640
—Le parfaict chirurgien. Paris: C. Besongne, 1628
Cheape and good husbandry. *See* Markham, Gervase
CHEESE—WEST INDIES
—Taylor, J. Taylors feast. London: 1638
Chiabrera, Gabriello. Belle poesie . . . Parte seconda. Genoa: G. Pavoni, 1606
—Rime. Venice: S. Combi, 1605
— —Venice: S. Combi, 1610
CHIAPAS, MEXICO—HISTORY
—Remesal, A. de. Historia de la provincia de S. Vicente. Madrid: 1619
— —Historia general de las Indias Ocidentales. Madrid: 1620
CHIBCHA LANGUAGE
—Lugo, B. de. Gramatica en la lengua general del nuevo reyno. Madrid: 1619
The chiefe events . . . of Spaine. *See* Malvezzi, Virgilio, marchese
Child, John. New Englands Jonas. London: T. R[atcliffe]., & E. M[ottershead]., 1647
— —*See also* Winslow, E. New-Englands salamander. London: 1647
CHILE. *See also* JESUITS IN CHILE, *etc.*
—Baerle, K.van. Amor sapiens. Amsterdam: 1633
—Capitulo de una de las cartas que diversas personas embiaron. Seville: 1618
—Caro de Torres, F. Relacion de los servicios. Madrid: 1620
—Grotius, H. Bewys van den waren godsdienst. [Leyden?] 1622
— —Von der Warheit der christlichen Religion. Brieg: 1631
—Quevedo y Villegas, F. G. de. La fortuna. Saragossa: 1650
—Recio de León, J. Señor. El maesse de campo Juan Recio de Leon. [Madrid? 1625?]
CHILE—DESCRIPTION
—Brouwer, H. Die fünff und

zweyntzigste Schifffahrt. Frankfurt a.M.: 1649
— —Journael ende Historis verhael van de reyse . . . naer de custen van Chili. Amsterdam: 1646
—Ponce de León, F. Descripcion del reyno de Chile. [Madrid: 1644?]
CHILE—DISCOVERY & EXPLORATION
—Hamcomius, M. Frisia. Franeker: 1620
—Nodal, B. G. de. Relacion del viaje. Madrid: 1621
—Porter y Casanate, P. Señor. El capitan Don Pedro Porter y Cassanate. [Madrid: 1638?]
CHILE—FICTION
—Loubayssin de Lamarca, F. Historia tragicomica de Don Henrique de Castro. Paris: 1612
CHILE—HISTORY
—Ayala y Rojas, I. de. Don Iñigo de Ayala y Rojas. [Madrid? 1622?]
—Baerle, K. van. Rerum per octennium in Brasilia . . . nuper gestarum . . . historia. Amsterdam: 1647
—Cortes de Monroy, J. Señor. Aviendo visto, y considerado las tres dudas. [Madrid? 1625]
—González de Nájera, A. El quinto, y sexto punto de la relacion. [Madrid? ca. 1607?]
—Oña, P. de. Arauco domado. Madrid: 1605
—Ovalle, A. de. Historica relacion del reyno de Chile. Rome: 1646
— —Historica relatione del regno di Cile. Rome: 1646
— —Relacion verdadera de las pazes. Madrid: 1642
—Parisi, A. Señor. Don Antonio Parisi, procurador del reyno de Chile. [Madrid? ca. 1620?]
—[Relacion verdadera de las grandes hazañas. Madrid: 1625?]
—[Segunda relacion . . . Dizense en ella cosas admirables. Madrid: 1625?]
—Sobrino, G. Señor, El padre

Coelho de Barbuda, Luiz.
Empresas militares de Lusitanos. Lisbon: P. Craesbeeck, 1624
—Reyes de Portugal y empresas militares. Lisbon: P. Craesbeeck, 1624
Coignet, Michel. Épitomé du théâtre. *See* Ortelius, Abraham. L'épitome du théâtre de l'univers
—Epitome of the theater. *See* Ortelius, Abraham. Epitome of the theater of the worlde
—Epitome theatri orbis. *See* Ortelius, Abraham. Epitome theatri orbis terrarum
—Epitome theatri Orteliani. *See* Ortelius, Abraham. Epitome theatri Orteliani
Coignet de la Thuillerie, Gaspard. Aaloude heersch-en-oorlogs-sught. Utrecht: F. Levyn [1648?]
—Propositien. [Amsterdam? 1648]
—Twee propositien. [The Hague: J. Veely] for F. Levyn, at Utrecht, 1648
— —[The Hague? J. Veely?] for F. Levyn, at Utrecht, 1648
— —Utrecht: F. Levyn, 1648
COINAGE. *See also* MINTS
—Bogotá. Por parte de las ciudades Santa Fé, y Cartagena. [Madrid? 1620?]
—Rodríguez Bustamante, S. Señor. Sebastian Rodriguez Bustamante, vezino de Santa Marta. [Madrid? 1620?]
—Spain. Consejo de las Indias. Memorial del pleyto que el señor fiscal . . . trata. [Madrid? 1639]
—Spain. Laws, statutes, etc., 1598–1621 (Philip III). Este es un traslado bien y fielmente sacado . . . Para que no se tomen ningun dineros. [Madrid: 1610?]
—Turrilo, A. El pleito que se ha començado a ver . . . es sobre tres puntos. [Madrid? ca. 1620?]
COINAGE—PERU
—Spain. Laws, statutes, etc., 1621–1665 (Philip IV). Pregon

en que el Rey nuestro señor manda. Madrid: 1650
— —Prematica en que su Magestad manda, que toda la moneda . . . labrada en . . . Perù se reduzca. Madrid: 1650
COINAGE—SPANISH AMERICA
—Netherlands (United Provinces, 1581–1795). Staten Generaal. Placaet, alle realen van Spaignen, Mexico ende Peru. The Hague: 1634
— —Placaet ende Ordonnantie . . . teghens alle realen van Spaignen, Mexico ende Peru. The Hague: 1634
Cole, Nathanael. Preservatives against sinne. London: T. S[nodham]., for N. Bourne, 1618
Colijn, Michiel. Oost-Indische ende West-Indische voyagien. Amsterdam: M. Colijn, 1619
— —[Pt 1]. Veer, Gerrit de. De waerachtighe beschrijvinge vande drie seylagien. Enkhuizen: 1619
— —[Pt 2]. Lodewijcksz, Willem. 'T eerste boeck; Historie van Indien. Amsterdam: 1617
— —[Pt 3]. Neck, Jacob Corneliszoon van. Historiale beschrijvinghe. Amsterdam: 1619
— —[Pt 4]. Spilbergen, Joris van. t'Historiael journael. Amsterdam: 1617
— —[Pt 5]. Marees, Pieter de. Beschrijvinghe ende Historische verhael . . . van Guinea. Amsterdam: 1617
— —[Pt 6]. Pretty, Francis. Beschryvinge vande overtreffelijcke . . . zee-vaerdt. Amsterdam: 1617
— —[Pt 7]. Raleigh, Sir Walter. Warachtighe ende grondige beschryvinghe van . . . Guiana. Amsterdam: 1617
— —[Pt 8]. Ottsen, Hendrick. Journael oft Daghelijcx-register van de voyagie. Amsterdam: 1617
— —[Pt 9]. Potgieter, Barent Janszoon. Historisch . . . verhael. Amsterdam: 1617

— —[Pt 10]. Noort, Olivier van. Beschrijvinge van de voyagie. Amsterdam: 1618
Collart, P. Het hoogh-loffelijcke jubel-jaer. Antwerp: H. Pers, 1640 (2)
Colle, Giovanni. Elucidarium anatomicum. Venice: E. Deuchino, 1621, '20
Collège des Maîtres chirurgiens de Paris. Traicté de la peste. Paris: F. Jacquin, 1619
Collibus, Hippolytus à.
Fürstliche Tischreden. Frankfurt a.M.: J. Bringer, for J. Basse, 1614
— —Frankfurt a.M.: [N. Hoffmann? for] J. Basse, 1617
— —Frankfurt a.M.: E. Emmel, 1620
— —Basel: J. J. Genath, for Heirs of L. König, 1642–45
Collio, Francesco. De animabus paganorum. Milan: Ambrosian College, 1622–23
Collius, Franciscus. *See* Collio, Francesco
Collyrium, ofte Costelijcke ooghen-salve. *See* Brilleman, Jan
Colmenero de Ledesma, Antonio. Chocolata Inda. Nuremberg: W. Endter, 1644
—Curioso tratado . . . del chocolate. Madrid: F. Martínez, 1631
—A curious treatise of . . . chocolate. London: J. Okes, 1640
—Du chocolate, discours curieux. Paris: S. Cramoisy, 1643
Colom, Jacob Aertszoon.
Toortse der zeevaerdt. Amsterdam: J. A. Colom, 1648
COLOMBIA
—Brochero, L. de. Discurso breve del uso de exponer los ninos. Seville: 1626
—Bustamante y Loyola, S. de. Señor. El licenciado Don Sebastian de Bustamente y Loyola. [Madrid? 1639]
COLOMBIA—CHURCH HISTORY
—Aviñón, B. Vita, virtù e miracoli del beato Luigi Bertrandi. Rome: 1623

—Roca, B. J. Histoire veritable . . . du b.p. S. Luis Bertran. Tournai: 1628

——Historia verdadera . . . del . . . padre S. Luys Bertran. Valencia: 1608

—Vargas, M. A. de. Relacion de los milagros. Madrid: 1629

COLOMBIA—ECONOMIC CONDITIONS

—Los daños que se seguirian. [Seville? 1650?]

COLOMBIA—HISTORY

—Crexel de San Martín, J. Señor. El capitan Juan Crexel de San Martin. [Madrid? ca. 1630]

—Murga, F. de. Señor. El maestro de campo Francisco de Murga. [Madrid? 1637]

COLOMBIA—HISTORY, NAVAL

—Verdadera relacion del viage y sucesso de los caravelones. Seville: 1621

—Viage, y sucesso de los caravelones. Madrid: 1621

COLOMBIA—POLITICS & GOVERNMENT

—Cañizares, M. de. El maestro fr. Martin de Cañizares. [Madrid? ca. 1643?]

—Cartagena, Colombia. Por parte de las ciudades de Cartagena, y santa Fé. [Madrid? 1620?]

Colombo, Cristoforo. De insulis . . . nuper inventis. *In* Schottus, Andreas. Hispaniae illustratae. Frankfurt a.M.: 1603–08

COLOMBO, CRISTOFORO. *See also* COLÓN FAMILY

—Aldrete, B. J. Varias antiguedades de España. Antwerp: 1614

—Alsted, J. H. Thesaurus chronologiae. Herborn: 1624

—Aparisi, F. Consilia medicinalia, de conservanda sanitate. Edinburgh: 1620

—Bacon, F. De dignitate . . . scientiarum. Paris: 1624

——Histoire des vents. Paris: 1649

——Histoire du regne de Henry VII. Paris: 1627

——Historia naturalis . . . ad condendam philosophiam. London: 1622

——Historia regni Henrici septimi. Leyden: 1642

——The historie of . . . King Henry. London: 1622

——Neuf livres de la dignité . . . des sciences. Paris: 1632

——Of the advancement . . . of learning. Oxford: 1640

——Opera: Tomus primus. London: 1623

——Three speeches. London: 1641

—Baerle, K. van. Manes Auraici. Leyden: 1625

——Mercator sapiens. Amsterdam: 1632

——Verstandighe coopman. Enkhuizen: 1641

—Barclay, J. Icon animorum. London: 1614

——The mirrour of mindes. London: 1631

——L'oeil clair-voyant. Paris: 1626

——Le pourtraict des esprits. Paris: 1625

——Les satyres d'Euphormion. Paris: 1625

——Satyricon. Amsterdam: 1629

——Le tableau des esprits. Paris: 1625

—Barrough, P. The method of phisick. London: 1601

—Bartholin, C. Enchiridion physicum. Strassburg: 1625

—Beverwijck, J. van. De excellentia foeminei sexus. Dordrecht: 1636

——Idea medicinae veterum. Leyden: 1637

——Van de uitnementheyt des vrouwelicken geslachts. Dordrecht: 1639

—Blocius, J. Historiae per Saturam . . . memorabilia. Rostock: 1625

—Boccalini, T. Les cent premieres nouvelles. Paris: 1615

——De' ragguagli di Parnaso . . . Centuria prima. Venice: 1612

——De' ragguagli di Parnaso . . . Centuria seconda. Venice: 1613

——The new-found politicke. London: 1626

——Politischen Probiersteins . . . Erster Theil. [Tübingen? 1617?]

——Politischen Probiersteins ander Theil. [Tübingen?] 1617

——Relation aus Parnasso. Frankfurt a.M.: 1644

—Boemus, J. Mores, leges, et ritus omnium gentium. [Geneva:] 1604

—Boissard, J. J. Bibliotheca chalcographica. Frankfurt a.M.: 1650

——Bibliotheca sive Thesaurus virtutis. Frankfurt a.M.: 1628

——Icones et effigies virorum doctorum. Frankfurt a.M.: 1645

—Boulenger, J. C. Historiarum sui temporis libri tredecim. Lyons: 1617

—Buonfiglio Costanzo, G. Prima parte dell'Historia siciliana. Venice: 1604

—Cano, T. Arte para fabricar, fortificar, y apareiar naos. Seville: 1611

—Cesalpino, A. Artis medicae pars prima. Rome: 1602

—Chiabrera, G. Rime. Venice: 1605

—Colón, F. Historie . . . della vita . . . dell'ammariglio Don Christoforo Colombo. Milan: [1614]

—Conestaggio, G. F. di. De Portugalliae conjunctione. Frankfurt a.M.: 1602

——Dell'unione del regno di Portugallo. Milan: 1616

——Historia de la union del reyno de Portugal. Barcelona: 1610

——L'union du royaume de Portugal. Besançon: 1601

—Croce, G. A. della. Cirugia universale. Venice: 1605

——Officina aurea; das ist, Guldene Werckstatt der Chirurgy. Frankfurt a.M.: 1607

—Doglioni, G. N. Compendio historico universale di tutte le cose notabili. Venice: 1601

—Drayton, M. A chorographicall description. London: 1613

— —Poly-Olbion. London: [1612]

—Emili, P. De rebus gestis Francorum. Basel: [1601]

—Fontana, F. Novae coelestium terrestriumque rerum observationes. Naples: 1646

—Fregoso, B. Factorum et dictorum memorabilium lib. ix. Cologne: 1604

—Fuchs, S. Metoposcopia et ophthalmoscopia. Strassburg: 1615

—Garibáy y Zamálloa, E. de. Los quarenta libros del Compendio historial. Barcelona: 1628

—Garimberto, G. Problemi naturali e morali. Vicenza: 1617

—Geraldini, A. Itinerarium ad regiones sub aequinoctiali plaga. Rome: 1631

—Glen, J. B. de Des habits, moeurs, ceremonies . . . du monde. Liège: 1601

—Gough, J. The strange discovery. London: 1640

—Groote schrijf-almanach. Amsterdam: 1641

—Guicciardini, F. La historia d'Italia. Treviso: 1604

— —The historie of Guicciardin. London: 1618

—Harsdörffer, G. P. Gesprächspiele achter . . . Theil. Nuremberg: 1649

—Herrera y Tordesillas, A. de. Comentarios de los hechos. Madrid: 1624

—Isaacson, H. Saturni ephemerides. London: 1633

—La Faye, A. de. Emblemata et epigrammata. Geneva: 1610

—Le Moyne, P. La gallerie des femmes fortes. Paris: 1647

—Léon, A. de. Practico de morbo gallico. Valladolid: 1605

—Maffei, R. Commentariorum urbanorum libri. Frankfurt a.M.: 1603

—Malvenda, T. De antichristo libri undecim. Rome: 1604

—Marino, G. B. La Murtoleide, fischiate. [Venice?] 1619

—Matthieu, P. Dell'historia di S. Luigi. Venice: 1628

— —Histoire de sainct Louys. Paris: 1618

—Mendoça, F. de. Viridarium sacrae ac profanae eruditionis. Lyons: 1631

—Micalori, J. Crisis . . . de Erycii Puteani circulo urbiniano. Urbino: 1632

—Murtola, G. Della creatione del mundo. Venice: 1608

—Nash, T. Quaternio, or A fourefold way. London: 1633

—Panciroli, G. Livre premier des antiquitez perdues. Lyons: 1617

— —Raccolta breve d'alcune cose piu segnalate. Venice: 1612

—Person, D. Varieties: or, A surveigh. London: 1635

—Petraeus, H. Nosologia harmonica. Marburg: 1615

—Peucer, K. Commentarius, de praecipuis divinationum generibus. Frankfurt a.M.: 1607

—Pinon, J. De anno romano carmen. Paris: 1615

—Planis Campy, D. de. La verolle recogneue. Paris: 1623

—Plautius, C. Extract und Ausszug der grossen . . . Schiff-farth Buelij Cataloni. [Linz:] 1623

— —Nova typis transacta navigatio. Novi orbis. [Linz:] 1621

—Resende, G. de. Choronica . . . do christianissimo . . . Joao o segundo. Lisbon: 1607

—Reves, J. de Historia pontificorum romanorum. Amsterdam: 1632

—Ritratti et elogii di capitani. Rome: 1635

—Roberts, L. The treasure of traffike. London: 1641

—Rocaberti, D. de. Epitome historico. Majorca: 1626

—Rochas, H. de. La physique reformée. Paris: 1648

—Rosaccio, G. Le sei eta del mondo. Venice: 1602

—Saavedra Fajardo, D. de. Idea de un principe christiano. Munich: 1640

— —Idea di un prencipe . . . christiano. Venice: 1648

— —Idea principis christiano-politici. Brussels: 1649

—Scott, T. The Belgicke pismire. [Utrecht?] 1622

—Siri, V. Del mercurio . . . Tomo secondo. Casale: 1647

—Tarcagnota, G. Delle historie del mondo. Venice: 1617

—Tassoni, A. La secchia. Paris: 1622

—Taylor, J. John Taylor being yet unhanged. [Oxford:] 1644

— —A shilling, or The travailes. [London: 1621]

—Tomasini. J. P. Illustrium virorum elogio. Padua: 1630

—Valbuena, B. de. El Bernardo, o Victoria de Roncesvalles. Madrid: 1624

—Valori, F. Termini di mezzo rilievo. Florence: 1604

—Vasconcellos, A. M. de. Vida y acciones del Rey Don Juan. Madrid: 1639

—Vega Carpio, L. F. de. Doze comedias . . . Quarta parte. Madrid: 1614

—Vernulz, N. de. Apologia pro augustissima . . . gente austriaca. Louvain: 1635

—Zurita y Castro, G. Anales de la corona de Aragon. Saragossa: 1610

COLOMBO, CRISTOFORO—POETRY

—Canoniero, P. A. Flores illustrium epitaphiorum. Antwerp: 1613

— —Illustrium epitaphiorum . . . flores. Douai: 1636

—Cebà, A. Rime. Rome: 1611

—Chiabrera, G. Delle poesie . . . Parte seconda. Genoa: 1606

—Marino, G. B. L'Adone, poema. Venice: 1623

—Plumptre, H. Epigrammatōn opusculum duobus distinctum. London: 1629

—Quevedo y Villegas, F. G. de. El parnasso español. Madrid: 1648

728

—Serres, O. de, seigneur du Pradal. The perfect use of silk-wormes. London: 1607

—Tasso, T. Il Goffredo. Rome: 1601

—Villifranchi, G. Copia del primo e del secondo canto del Colombo. Florence: 1602

Colombo, Fernando. *See* Colón, Fernando

Colón, Fernando. Historie . . . della vita . . . dell'ammariglio Don Christoforo Colombo. Milan: G. Bordone [1614]

COLÓN FAMILY

—Carranza, A. Por D. Luis Colon de Toledo. [Madrid: 1621]

—Colón y Pravia, F., plaintiff. Alegacion en derecho. Madrid: 1608

—Spain. Consejo de las Indias. El fiscal con doña Francisca Colon de Toledo. [Madrid? ca. 1610?]

——Memorial del pleyto sobre la sucession . . . del estado . . . de Veragua. [Madrid: 1607]

——Sentencias de revista . . . sobre la paga y consignacion. [Madrid? 1611?]

—Torres, M. de. El licenciado Marcos de Torres . . . contra Doña Francisca Colon. [Madrid? ca. 1605?]

Colón y Pravia, Francisca, plaintiff. Alegacion en derecho. Madrid: L. Sánchez, 1608

—Allegacion de derecho [Madrid? 1608?]

Colonius, Daniel. Oratio panegyrica, de illustri victoria. Leyden: B. & A. Elsevier, 1629

Colonna, Fabio. Minus cognitarum rariorumque . . . stirpium. Rome: J. Mascardi, 1616

—Minus cognitarum stirpium aliquot. Rome: G. Facciotti, 1606

——Rome: G. Facciotti, 1610

Columba, Gerardus. Disputationum medicarum . . . libri duo. Frankfurt a.M.: Heirs of R. Beatus, & G. Beatus, & J. L. Bitsch, 1601

Columbus, Christopher. *See* Colombo, Cristoforo

Comedias. *See* Ruiz de Alarcón y Mendoza, Juan; Téllez, Gabriel; Vega Carpio, Lope Félix de

Comedies and tragedies. *See* Beaumont, Francis

Comedies, histories, and tragedies. *See* Shakespeare, William

Comentarios de los hechos. *See* Herrera y Tordesillas, Antonio de

COMETS

—Welper, E. Observationes astronomicae. Strassburg: 1619

Commelin, Izaäk, ed. Begin ende voortgang. [Amsterdam: J. Janszoon the Younger, 1644?]

—Begin ende voortgangh. [Amsterdam: J. Janszoon the Younger] 1645

——[Amsterdam: J. Janszoon the Younger] 1646

Le commentaire royal. *See* Garcilaso de la Vega, el Inca

Les commentaires . . . sur les six livres de Pedacius Dioscoride. *See* Mattioli, Pietro Andrea

Commentaria. *See* Matienzo, Juan de

Commentarien ofte Memoiren van den Nederlandtschen staet. *See* Meteren, Emanuel van

Commentarii in universam Aristotelis Logicam. *See* Rubio, Antonio

Commentariolus de statu Confoederatarum provinciarum Belgii. *See* Boxhorn, Marcus Zuerius

Commentariorum urbanorum libri. *See* Maffei, Raffaele

Commentarios reales, la pte. *See* Garcilaso de la Vega, el Inca

Commentarius, de praecipuis divinationum generibus. *See* Peucer, Kaspar

COMMERCE. *See also names of companies, e.g.* Söder Compagniet, *& sub-heading* Commerce *under place names*

—Cristovão de Lisboa. Sermão da quarta domingo da quaresma. Lisbon: 1641

—Fioravanti, L. Dello specchio di scientia universale. Venice: 1603

——[Miroir universel des arts et des sciences.] Paris: 1602

—Gómez Solis, D. Discursos sobre los comercios. [Madrid:] 1622

—Great Britain. Laws, statutes, etc., 1625–1649 (Charles I). The rates of marchandizes. London: 1635

—Great Britain. Laws, statutes, etc., 1649–1660 (Commonwealth). An act prohibiting trade with the Barbada's, Virginia, Bermuda's and Antego. London: 1650

——Een acte ban het Parlament van Engelandt, verbiedende den handel. [Amsterdam? 1650?]

—Great Britain. Treaties, etc., 1603–1625 (James I). Articles of peace, entercourse, and commerce. London: 1605

——Articulen van het contract ende accoort. [Middelburg: 1605]

—Grotius, H. Mare liberum. Leyden: [1609]

——Vrye zeevaert. Leyden: 1614

—Hevia Bolaños, J. de. Curia philippica. Valladolid: 1623

——Laberinto de comercio terrestre y naval. Madrid: 1619

—Klare aenwijsinge. The Hague: 1630

—Malvezzi, V., marchese. The chiefe events . . . of Spaine. London: 1647

——Successi principali . . . di Spagna. [Madrid? 1640?]

——Sucesos principales . . . de España. Madrid: 1640

—Nederlandsche West-Indische Compagnie. Consideratien ende redenen der e. heeren bewind-hebberen. Haarlem: 1629

——Three severall treatises concerning the truce. London: 1630

—Netherlands (Southern Provinces, 1581–1793). Sovereigns, etc., 1596–1621. Copie

——L'idea di un prencipe . . . christiano. Venice: 1648

——Idea principis christiano-politici. Brussels: 1649

—Sánchez, A. De rebus Hispaniae anacephalaeosis. Alcalá de Henares: 1634

—Thou, J. A. de. Historiarum sui temporis, t 1. Paris: 1604

—Torres, J. de. Philosophia moral. Burgos: 1602

—Vega Carpio, L. F. de. Arcadia. Barcelona: 1602

——Les delices de la vie pastorale. Lyons: 1622

—Zacutus, A. De medicorum principum historia. Cologne: 1629

——Historiarum medicarum libri sex. Arnhem: 1636

CORTÉS, HERNANDO—POETRY

—Lobo Lasso de la Vega, G. Manojuelo de romances nuevas. Barcelona: 1601

Cortés, Jerónimo. El curioso de varios secretos de naturaleza. Lisbon: J. Rodríguez, 1601

—Libro de phisonomia natural. Cordova: 1601

——Madrid: P. Madrigal, for M. Martínez, 1601

——Alcalá de Henares: Heirs of J. Gracián, 1603

——Alcalá de Henares: Heirs of J. Gracián, 1607

——Tarragona: F. Roberto, 1609

—Phisonomia. Saragossa: 1601

——Barcelona: J. Margarit, 1610

——Pamplona: C. Labáyen, 1611

——Alcalá de Henares: Heirs of J. Gracián, 1612

——Valencia: Widow of J. Cortés, 1613

——Barcelona: J. Margarit, 1614

——Barcelona: S. de Cormellas, 1624

——Saragossa: D. de la Torre, 1626

——Barcelona: L. Déu, 1629

Cortes, Martin. The arte of navigation. London: [F. Kingston?] for J. Tapp, 1609

——London: W. Stansby, for J. Tapp, 1615

——London: B. A. & T. Fawcet, for J. Tapp, 1630

Cortés de Mesa, Diego. Señor. Don Diego Cortes de Mesa, regidor de la ciudad de Cartaxena. [Madrid? 1645?]

Cortes de Monroy, Juan. Señor. Aviendo visto, y considerado las tres dudas. [Madrid? 1625]

Cortesi, Giovanni Battista. Pharmacopoeia, seu Antidotarium messanense. Messina: P. Brea, 1629

Cortilio, Sebastiano. De chirurgica lib. v. *In* Marquardus, Joannes. Practica medicinalis. Frankfurt a.M.: 1610

——*In the same.* Cologne: 1620

——*In the same:* Cologne: 1621

Coryat, Thomas. Coryats crudities. London: W. S[tansby]., 1611

Coryats crudities. *See* Coryat, Thomas

Cosmographey: das ist Beschreibung aller Länder. *See* Münster, Sebastian

Cosmographia das ist, Aussführliche . . . beschreibung. *See* Münster, Sebastian

Cosmographia. das ist: beschreibung der gantzen Welt. *See* Münster, Sebastian

Cosmographia prosometrica. *See* Ritter, Stephan

Cosmographiae generalis libri tres. *See* Merula, Paulus

Cosmographie, ofte Beschrijvinge der geheelder werelt. *See* Apianus, Petrus

Cosmographie, ou Traicte general. *See* Cyriaque de Mangin, Clement

COSMOGRAPHY. *See also* GEOGRAPHY

—Memorabilia, das ist . . . Beschreibung aller vornembsten . . . Eygenschaften. [Frankfurt a.M.?] 1624

Cosmologie du monde. *See* Saulnier, Jean

Costa, Christovam da. *See* L'Ecluse, Charles. Exoticorum libri decem. [Leyden:] 1605

—*See also* Orta, Garcia da. Histoire des drogues espiceries. Lyons: 1619

COSTUME—BRAZIL

—Dracht-thoneel. Amsterdam: [1601]

Cotgrave, Randle. A dictionarie of the English and French tongues. London: A. Islip, 1632

—A dictionarie of the French and English tongues. London: A. Islip, 1611

—A French-English dictionary. London: W. H[unt]., for M. M. T. C., & G. Bedell, 1650

——London: W. H[unt]., for L. Fawne, 1650

——London: W. H[unt]., for G. Latham, 1650

——London: W. H[unt]., for O. Pulleyn, 1650

——London: W. H[unt]., for H. Robinson, 1650

——London: W. H[unt]., for A. Roper, 1650

——London: W. H[unt]., for R. Whitaker, 1650

——London: W. H[unt]., for J. Williams, 1650

Cotogno, Ottavio. *See* Codogno, Ottavio

Cotta, John. Conatus sine exemplo: or The first . . . discoverie . . . of health. London: L. Becket, 1627

—A short discoverie of the unobserved dangers . . . of physicke. London: [R. Field] for W. Jones, & R. Boyle, 1612

——London: W. J[ones]., for J. Barnes, 1619

—A true discovery of the empericke. London: W. Jones, for E. Weaver, 1617

Cottogno, Ottavio. *See* Codogno, Ottavio

Cotton, John. An abstract or the lawes of New England. London: F. Coules, & W. Lee, 1641

—The bloudy tenant, washed. London: M. Simmons, for Hannah Allen, 1647

—Officina aurea; das ist, Guldene Werckstatt der Chirurgy. Frankfurt a.M.: J. Sauer, for J. Rose, 1607

Crocius, Paulus. Gross Martyrbuch. *See* Crespin, Jean. Gross Martybuch

Croll, Oswald. Basilica chymica. Geneva: Fabri Office, 1610

— —Frankfurt a.M.: J. F. Weiss, for G. Tampach [1611]

— —Frankfurt a.M.: J. F. Weiss, for G. Tampach, 1620

— —Geneva: J. Celerier, 1624

— —Geneva: P. Aubert, 1631

— —Leipzig: G. Gross, 1634

— —Geneva: P. Chouët, 1635

— —Geneva: P. Chouët, 1643

— —Venice: Combi, 1643

—Basilica chymica: oder Alchÿmistisch . . . Kleÿnod. Frankfurt a.M.: J. F. Weiss, for G. Tampach [1623]

—Basilicus chymica. Frankfurt a.M.: C. Marne, & Heirs of J. Aubry, 1609

—Hermetischer probier stein. Frankfurt a.M.: J. G. Schönwetter, 1647

—La royale chymie. Rouen: J. Berthelin, 1634

— —Rouen: J. Osmont, 1634

—La royalle chymie. Lyons: P. Drouet, 1624

— —Lyons: P. Drouet, 1627

— —Paris: M. Henault, 1633

Cronicken der eingesetzten Orden dess heiligen Vatters Francisci. *See* Marcos da Lisboa, Bp

Crop-eare curried. *See* Taylor, John, the Water-poet

Crosse, Henry. The schoole of pollicie. London: V. Simmes, for N. Butter, 1605

—Vertues commonwealth. London: J. Newbery, 1603

Crosse, William. Belgiaes troubles. London: A. Mathewes, & J. Norton, 1625

—The Dutch survay. London: E. Allde, for N. Butter, 1625

—*See also* Grimestone, Edward. A generall historie of the Netherlands. London: 1627

Crossing of proverbs. *See* Breton, Nicholas

CRUSADE BULLS

—Pérez de Lara, A. Compendio de las tres gracias. Madrid: 1610

Crusenius, Nicolaus. Monasticon Augustinianum. Munich: J. Hertsroy, 1623

Cruydt-boeck. *See* Dodoens, Rembert

CUBA

—Gesner, K. Mithridates Gesneri. Zurich: 1610

—Jonson, B. Workes. London: 1616

—Neuhaus, E. Theatrum ingenii humani. Amsterdam: 1633

CUBA—HISTORY

—Marín de Armendariz, P. Condiciones que el veedor Pedro Marin de Armendariz . . . tratan de efectuar. [Madrid? 1642]

CUBA—HISTORY, NAVAL

—Duircant, A. Rym-vieren. [The Hague: 1629]

—Nuevas ciertas y fidedignas de la vitoria que ha alcançado Don Fadrique de Toledo. Barcelona: 1629

CUENCA, ECUADOR

—Ocampo, M. de. Señor. El capitan Martin de Ocampo, corregidor. [Madrid? 1640?]

Cuenta que Geronimo Garavito . . . ha hecho de la mucha plata. *See* Garavito, Gerónimo

Cueva, Juan de la. Conquista de la Betica. Seville: F. Pérez, 1603

Culpa que resulta contra el licenciado Pedro de Vergara Gaviria. *See* Spain. Consejo de las Indias

Culpeper, Nicholas. A physical directory. London: P. Cole, 1650

—A physicall directory. London: P. Cole, 1649

Cultura ingeniorum. *See* Possevino, Antonio

CUMANA, VENEZUELA—HISTORY

—Relacion cierta y verdadera, del famoso sucesso. Seville: 1634

—Relacion de las vitorias que Don Diego de Arroyo y Daça . . . tuvo. Madrid: [1623]

—Villagómez, H. de. El Fiscal de Indias. [Madrid? 1650?]

CUMANA INDIANS

—Sumario, y compendio de lo sucedido en España. [Madrid: 1638]

Cumanagoto Indians. *See* Cumana Indians

Cupids whirligig. *See* Sharpham, Edward

Curae posteriores. *See* L'Ecluse, Charles de

Curationum empiricarum . . . centuriae decem. *See* Ruland, Martin

Curationum et observationum, centuria V. *See* Gabelkover, Wolfgang

Curationum medicinalium centuriae septem. *See* Amatus Lusitanus

Curia eclesiastica. *See* Ortiz de Salcedo, Francisco

Curia filipica. *See* Hevia Bolaños, Juan de

Curia philippica. *See* Hevia Bolaños, Juan de

Curiosa filosofia. *See* Nieremberg, Juan Eusebio

Curiosa y oculta filosofia. *See* Nieremberg, Juan Eusebio

La curiosité naturelle. *See* Dupleix, Scipion

Curiosities: or The cabinet of nature. *See* Basset, Robert

El curioso de varios secretos de naturaleza. *See* Cortés, Jerónimo

Curioso tratado . . . del chocolate. *See* Colmenero de Ledesma, Antonio

A curious treatise of . . . chocolate. *See* Colmenero de Ledesma, Antonio

A curry-combe for a coxecombe. *See* Hoby, Sir Edward

Curtis, Martine. *See* Cortés, Martín

Cushman, Robert. A sermon preached at Plimmoth. London: J. D[awson]., for J. Bellamy, 1622

Derde discours. By forma van missive. [Amsterdam:] 1622

Derde discours. Waer in by forme missive den geheelen staet . . . wort . . . geremonstreert. [Amsterdam?] 1622

De derde wachter. *See* Teeling, Ewoud

T'derde-deel . . . van het Historischer verhael. *See* Wassenaer, Nicolaes van

Derecho de las iglesias . . . de las Indias. *See* Betancurt, Luis de

Derniere lettre du pere . . . au r.p. provincial. *See* Arsène de Paris

Derniere lettre du reverend pere . . . estant de present en l'Inde Occidentale. *See* Arsène de Paris

Het dertiende ghedeelt . . . van het Historisch verhael. *See* Wassenaer, Nicholaes van

Des Accord, Estienne Tabourot. *See* Tabourot, Estienne

Des Combes, ——, sieur. Coppie d'une lettre envoyee de Nouvelle France. Lyons: L. Savine, 1609

Des druckers belydenisse. [Amsterdam?] 1648

Des habits, moeurs, ceremonies . . . du monde. *See* Glen, Jean Baptiste de

Des sauvages. *See* Champlain, Samuel de

Descripcion de la Baia de Todos los Santos. Madrid: A. de Popma, 1625

Descripcion de la imperial ciudad de Toledo. *See* Pisa, Francisco de

Descripcion de las Indias Occidentales. *See* Herrea y Tordesillas, Antonio de

Descripcion de todas las provincias . . . del mundo. *See* Botero, Giovanni

Descripcion del reyno de Chile. *See* Ponce de León, Francisco

Descriptio ac delineatio geographica detectionis freti. *See* Gerritsz, Hessel

Descriptio bellorum inferioris Germaniae. *See* Meteren, Emanuel van

The description and use of his Majesties dials. *See* Gunter, Edmund

Description de la Brasil. Antwerp: A. Verhoeven [1625?]

Description de la reprise de la ville de S. Salvador. Antwerp: A. Verhoeven, 1625

Description des Indes Occidentales. *See* Herrera y Tordesillas, Antonio de

Description du jardin royal des plantes medicinales. *See* La Brosse, Guy de

Description du penible voyage. *See* Noort, Olivier van

Description et recit historial . . . de Gunea. *See* Marees, Pieter de

Description et representation de toutes de victoires. *See* Orlers, Jan Janszn

A description of New England. *See* Smith, Capt. John

A description of the province of New Albion. *See* Plantagenet, Beauchamp

Descriptionis Ptolemaicae augmentum. *See* Wytfliet, Corneille

Descubrimiento de los terros. Barcelona: H. Anglada, 1608

Desengano a los pueblos del Brasil. *See* Bredan, Daniel

Desengaño contra el mal uso del tabaco. *See* Leiva y Aguilar, Francisco de

Desenganos y replicas a las proposiciones de Gerardo Basso. *See* Lugo y Dávila, Francisco de

Les desirs amoureux de Dom Philippe. *See* Esternod, Claude d' ·

Desprez, Philippe. Le theatre des animaux. Paris: J. Le Clerc, 1620

Dessein perpetuel des Espagnols. [The Hague?] 1624

Dessi, Juan. La divina semana. Barcelona: S. Matevad, & L. Déu, 1610

Deughden-spoor. *See* Baardt, Pieter

Deus harangues panégyriques. *See* Poirier, Hélie

Deutsche Poemata. *See* Opitz, Martin

Deutscher Poematum Erster [-Anderer] Theil. *See* Opitz, Martin

Deux cartes maritimes septentrionales. *See* Scotto, Benedetto

The devil turn'd Round-head. *See* Taylor, John, the Waterpoet

Diaeticon, sive De re cibaria. *See* Nonnius, Ludovicus

Dialogi gallico-anglico-latini. *See* Dugres, Gabriel

Dialogo del uso del tabaco . . . y del chocolate. *See* Marradon, Bartolomeo

Dialogo sobre el comercio. *See* Struzzi, Alberto

Ein Dialogus oder Gespräch. [Germany?] 1608

Dialogus oft T'samensprekinge. Antwerp: 1644

Dialogus oft Tsamensprekinge. [Amsterdam?] 1608 (2)

Dialogus oft Tzamensprekinge. [Amsterdam?] 1608

Dialogus ofte t'Samensprekinge tusschen Jan . . . ende Govert. [Amsterdam?] 1630

Diana enamorada. *See* Polo, Gaspar Gil

Diarium vel Descriptio . . . itineris. *See* Schouten, Willem Corneliszoon

DIAS, GONZALO
—Guillén y Colón, F. Vita, muerte y milagros del prodigioso varon. Seville: 1637

Dias Ferreira, Gaspar. Epistola Gasparis Dias Fereira in carcere. [The Hague? 1649]
—Een zent-brief. [Amsterdam:] J. Colom, 1649

DIAS FERREIRA, GASPAR
—Holland (Province). Hof. Copie vande twee sententien. [The Hague?] 1647

Diaz de Armendaris, Lope. *See* Diez de Auxarmendariz, Lope

Díaz de Vivar Hurtado de Mendoza, Rodrigo, duque del Infantado. *See* Altamirano, Diego. Por el duque del Infantado. [Madrid: 1634?]

Díaz del Castillo, Bernal. Historia verdadera de la conquista de la Nueva-España. Madrid: Imprenta Real [1632?]

——Madrid: Imprenta Real, 1632

Díaz Taño, Francisco. La mort glorieuse du pere Christophe de Mendoza. Lille: P. de Rache, 1639

—Señor. El padre Francisco Diaz Taño. [Madrid? 1632?]

Dichos i hechos del señor Rei. *See* Porreño, Baltasar

Dichos y hechos del Rey. *See* Porreño, Baltasar

Dichos y hechos del señor Rey. *See* Porreño, Baltasar

Dickenson, John. Speculum tragicum. Delft: J. C. Vennecool, 1601

——Delft: J. C. Vennecool, 1602

——Delft: J. C. Vennecool, [for] L. Elsevier, [at Leyden,] 1602

——[Delft: J. C. Vennecool, for] L. Elsevier, at Leyden, 1603

——[Delft: J. C. Vennecool, for] L. Elsevier, at Leyden, 1605

——Leyden: L. Elsevier, 1611

Dickensonus, Joannes. *See* Dickenson, John

A dictionarie of the English and French tongues. *See* Cotgrave, Randle

A dictionarie of the French and English tongues. *See* Cotgrave, Randle

Dictionarium historicum, geographicum. *See* Estienne, Charles

A dictionary in Spanish and English. *See* Perceval, Richard

Die sabbathi 23 januarii. *See* Great Britain. Laws, statutes, etc., 1625–1649 (Charles I). Whereas the severall plantations in Virginia, Bermudas, Barbados . . . . London: [1647]

Dieci libri di pensieri diversi. *See* Tassoni, Alessandro

Diemerbroeck, Isbrandus de. De peste libri quatuor. Arnhem: J. Jacobszoon, 1646

Dierum canicularum tomi septem. *See* Maiolo, Simeone, Bp

Dies caniculares. *See* Maiolo, Simeone, Bp

A diet for a drunkard. *See* Thompson, Thomas

Díez de Auxarmendáriz, Lope, marqués de Cadereyta. Por

Don Lope Diez de Aux Armendariz . . . Con el . . . fiscal del Real Consejo. [Madrid? 1635?]

—Por Don Lope Diez de Auxarmendariz . . . Sobre los cargos de la residencia. [Madrid? 1635?]

DÍEZ DE AUXARMENDÁRIZ, LOPE, MARQUÉS DE CADEREYTA

—Pax Christi. En esta referire a V. R. las nuevas. [Madrid: ca.1638]

—Relacion de la famosa vitoria. Seville: 1633

—Relacion verdadera de la famosa vitoria. Seville: [1633]

Díez de la Calle, Juan. Memorial informativo al Rey. [Madrid?] 1645

—Memorial y compendio breve. [Madrid: 1648]

—Memorial, y noticias sacras. [Madrid:] 1646

——[Madrid: 1646?]

Diez previlegios para mugeres preñadas. *See* Alonso y de los Ruyses de Fontecha, Juan

Digby, Sir Kenelm. Observations upon Religio medici. London: R. C[otes]., for L. Chapman, & D. Frere, 1643 (2)

——London: F. L[each]., for L. Chapman, & D. Frere, 1644 (2)

Digges, Sir Dudley. The defence of trade. London: W. Stansby, for J. Barnes, 1615

—Fata mihi totum mea sunt agitanda per orbem. [London:] W. W[hite]., for J. Barnes, 1611

—Of the circumference of the earth. London: W. W[hite]., for J. Barnes, 1612

Dilich, Wilhelm Schäffer, called. Beschreibung und Abriss dero Ritterspiel. Kassel: W. Wessel, 1601

Dioscorides, Pedanius. Acerca de la materia medicinal. Valencia: M. Sorolla, 1636

Directeurs compagnie binnen Middelburgh. Middelburg: Z. Roman, 1643

A direction for adventurers . . . And a true description of

. . . new Albion, in North Virginia. *See* Evelyn, Robert

Directions for health. *See* Vaughan, William

Directorium medico-practicum. *See* Morone, Mattia

Discolliminium. *See* Ward, Nathaniel

I discorsi. *See* Mattioli, Pietro Andrea

Discorso della nobiltà. *See* Rosaccio, Giuseppe

Discours . . . sur le rehaussement. *See* Bodin, Jean

Discours, aengaende treves of vrede. Haarlem: A. Roman, 1629

—Haarlem: A. Roman, 1630

Discours au Roi Henri III. *See* Goulart, Simon. Les memoires de la Ligue . . . Premier volume. [Geneva?] 1602

Discours by forme van remonstrantie. [Netherlands:] 1608

—[Netherlands: 1608?]

Discours by forme van remonstrantye. [Netherlands:] 1608

Discours contenant la conference de la pharmacie. *See* Pascal, Jacques

Discours d'estat. *See* Scribanius, Carolus

Discours. Daer in kortelijck ende grondigh wert verthoont, hoeveel . . . gheleghen is. Arnhem: J. Janszoon, 1621

Discours de la paix, contre le Portugais. [Amsterdam?] 1647

Discours de la perte. *See* Coquerel, Nicolas de

Discours du voyage . . . aux Indes. *See* Pyrard, François

Discours et advis sur les flus. *See* Heyden, Hermann van der

Discours et congratulation a la France. *See* Claude d'Abbeville, Father

Discours et demonstration des ingrediens. *See* Catelan, Laurent

Discours, of t'samensprekinghe. *See* Middelgeest, Simon van

A discours of the variation of the cumpas. *See* Borough, William

Discours op verscheyde voorslaghen. [The Hague?] 1645

**Discours over den Neder-
landtschen vrede-handel.**
Leeuwarden: D. Albertszoon,
1629
Discours politiques et militaires.
See La Noue, François de
Discours sur l'affaire de la
Valteline. Paris: J. Bouillerot,
1625
Discours sur la bataille de Lut-
zen. [Paris? 1633?]
Discours sur la carte universelle.
See Mayerne, Louis Turquet
de, fl. 1648
Discours van Pieter en Pauwels.
[Amsterdam? 1608?] (2)
A discourse . . . for the advance-
ment of . . . New-found-land.
See Whitbourne, Sir Richard
A discourse and discovery of
New-found-land. *See* Whit-
bourne, Sir Richard
A discourse mathematical. *See*
Gellibrand, Henry
A discourse of . . . chyrurgerie.
See Lowe, Peter
A discourse upon chyrurgery. *See*
Fioravanti, Leonardo
Discourso breve. *See* Cianca,
Alonso de
The discoveries of the world. *See*
Galvão, António
DISCOVERIES
—Anghiera, P. M. d'. De novo
orbe, or The Historie of the
West Indies. London: 1612
— —The historie of the West-
Indies. London: [after
1625?]
—Archaio-ploutos. Containing,
ten following bookes. London:
1619
—Avelar, A. do. Chronographia
ou Reportorio dos tempos.
Lisbon: 1602
—Bacon, F. De dignitate . . .
scientiarum. Paris: 1624
— —Neuf livres de la dignité
. . . des sciences. Paris: 1632
— —Of the advancement . . . of
learning. Oxford: 1640
— —Opera: Tomus primus.
London: 1623
— —Le progrez et avancement
aux sciences. Paris: 1624

— —The twoo bookes . . . of the
proficience . . . of learning.
London: 1605
—Blagrave, J. The art of dyal-
ling. London: 1609
—Blasco de Lanuza, V. Historias
ecclesiasticas y seculares de
Aragon. Saragossa: 1621
—Boccalini, T. Hundert ein und
dreissig Relationes. Leyden:
1641
—Bontier, P. Histoire de la pre-
miere descouverte . . . des Ca-
naries. Paris: 1630
—Bry, J. T. de America, das ist,
Erfindung . . . der Newen
Welt. Frankfurt a.M.: 1617
—Buck, G. The great Planta-
genet. London: 1635
—Camerarius, P. The living li-
brarie. London: 1625
— —Les meditations histo-
riques. Lyons: 1603
— —Operae horarum subcisiva-
rum . . . Centuria prima.
Frankfurt a.M.: 1602
— —Operae horarum succisiva-
rum . . . Das ist: Historischer
Lustgarten. Leipzig: 1625
— —The walking librarie. Lon-
don: 1621
—Camões, L. de. Os Lusiados.
Lisbon: 1613
—Casas, B. de las, Bp. Den ver-
meerderden spieghel der
Spaensche tierannije-geschiet.
Amsterdam: 1621
—Cayet, P. V. P. Chronologie
septenaire. Paris: 1605
—Clément, C. Tabla chronolo-
gica de los descubrimientos.
Madrid: 1642
—Clercq, N. de. Tooneel der
keyseren. Delft: 1615
—Doglioni, G. N. Del theatro
universale de' prencipi. Ven-
ice: 1606
— —Le théâtre universel des
princes. Paris: 1613
—Ens, G. Indiae Occidentalis
historia. Cologne: 1612
— —West- unnd Ost Indischer
Lustgart. Cologne: 1618
—Fernel, J. De abditis rerum
causis. Lyons: 1604
— —Universa medicina. Lyons:
1601

—Galvão, A. The discoveries of
the world. London: 1601
—Gottfried, J. L. Newe Welt und
Amerikanische Historien.
Frankfurt a.M.: 1631
—Guicciardini, F. La historia
d'Italia. Treviso: 1604
— —The historie of Guicciardin.
London: 1618
—Lange, J. Epistolarum medici-
nalium. Hanau: 1605
—León, L. P. de. Obras proprias.
Madrid: 1631
—Linschoten, J. H. van. Voyagie,
ofte Schip-vaert. Franeker:
1601
—Locre, F. de. Chronicon Belgi-
cum. Arras: 1616
—Magnus, O. Historia . . . de
gentibus septentrionalibus.
Frankfurt a.M.: 1618
—Nieremberg, J. E. Curiosa filo-
sofia. Madrid: 1630
—Opmeer, P. van. Opus chrono-
graphicum orbis universi. Ant-
werp: 1611
—Orlers, J. J. Beschrijvinghe
ende af-beeldinge van alle de
victorien. Leyden: 1610
— —Description et representa-
tion de toutes de victoires.
Leyden: 1612
— —De oorlochs-daden van
Maurits. Leyden: 1619
— —The triumphs of Nassau.
London: 1613
—Panciroli, G. Livre premier des
antiquitez perdues. Lyons:
1617
— —Nova reperta sive Rerum
memorabilium recens inventa-
rum . . . Liber secundus. Am-
berg: 1602
— —Rerum memorabilium libri
duo. Amberg: 1607
—Pisa, F de. Descripcion de la
imperial ciudad de Toledo.
Toledo: 1605
—Pulgar, H. de. Los claros va-
rones de España. Antwerp:
1632
—Sacro Bosco, J. de. Sphaera.
Cologne: 1601
—Scott, T. The Belgicke pis-
mire. [Utrecht?] 1622
—Sibbes, R. Light from heaven.
London: 1638

—Solinus, C. Julius, Memorabilia mundi. Frankfurt a.M.: 1603

—Soto, D. de. De justitia et jure. Venice: 1602

—Tassoni, A. La secchia. Paris: 1622

—Thou, J. A. de. Historiarum sui temporis, t 1. Paris: 1604

—Torsellino, O. Chronicon ab orbe condito. Cologne: 1631

— —Epitomae historiarum libri x. Lyons: 1620

— —Histoire générale depuis la création. Paris: 1622

— —Historiarum ab origine mundi . . . epitome libri x. Paris: 1637

— —Ristretto dell'historie del mondo. Rome: 1634

—Twisck, P. J. Chronijck van den onderganc der tijrannen. Hoorn: 1619

—Zappullo, M. Historie di quattro principali città del mondo. Vicenza: 1603

— —Sommario istorico. Naples: 1609

—Zeiller, M. Das andere Hundert Episteln. Ulm: 1641

— —Ein Hundert Episteln. Heilbronn: 1640

DISCOVERIES—DANISH
—Munk, J. Navigatio septentrionalis. Copenhagen: 1624

DISCOVERIES—DUTCH
—Pontanus, J. I. Historische beschrijvinghe der . . . coopstadt Amsterdam. Amsterdam: 1614

— —Rerum et urbis Amstelodamensium historia. Amsterdam: 1611

DISCOVERIES—ENGLISH
—Belchier, D. Hans Beer-pot his invisible comedie. [London:] 1618

—Doglioni, G. N. Compendio historico universale di tutte le cose notabili. Venice: 1622

—Fournier, G. Hydrographie, contenant la theorie . . . de la navigation. Paris: 1643

—Norwood, R. The sea-mans practice. London: 1637

—Raleigh, Sir W. Judicious and select essayes. London: 1650

—Smith, Capt. J. The true travels, adventures, and observations. London: 1630

DISCOVERIES—NORSE
—La Peyrère, I. de. Relation du Groenland. Paris: 1647

DISCOVERIES—POETRY
—Benamati, G. U. Delle due trombe i primi fiati. Parma: 1622

DISCOVERIES—PORTUGUESE
—Bembo, P., Cardinal. Omnes . . . opera, in unum corpus. Strassburg: 1609

— —Venetae historiae . . . libri xii. Strassburg: 1611

DISCOVERIES—SPANISH
—Bembo, P., Cardinal. Omnes . . . opera, in unum corpus. Strassburg: 1609

— —Venetae historiae . . . libri xii. Strassburg: 1611

—Carrillo, M. Annales y memorias cronologicas. Huesca: 1622

—Catechismus ofte Tsamenspreeckinghe. Amsterdam?: 1608

—López Madera, G. Excelencias de la monarquia. Madrid: 1624

—Menéndez Silva, R. Catalogo real de España. Madrid: 1637

—Murtola, G. Della creatione del mundo. Venice: 1608

—Porter y Casanate, P. Señor. El capitan Don Pedro Porter y Cassanate. [Madrid: 1638?]

—Queiros, P. F. de. Copia de unos avisos muy notables. Barcelona: 1609

—Sánchez, A. De rebus Hispaniae anacephalaeosis. Alcalá de Henares: 1634

DISCOVERIES—WELSH. *See also* MADOG AB OWAIN GWYNEDD
—Herbert, Sir T. A relation of some yeares travaile. London: 1634

— —Some yeares travels. London: 1638

— —Travels in Africa and Asia. London: 1639

—Howell, J. Epistolae Ho-elianae. Familiar letters. London: 1650

— —A new volume of letters. London: 1647

A discovery and plaine declaration. *See* Gonsalvius, Reginaldus, Montanus

The discovery of a new world. *See* Hall, Joseph, Bp

A discovery of subterraneall treasure. *See* Plattes, Gabriel

A discovery of the Barmudas. *See* Jourdain, Silvester

Discurs und Muthmassung. *See* Middelgeest, Simon van

Discurso . . . Sobre una carta. *See* Cevicos, Juan

Discurso breve del uso de exponer los ninos. *See* Brochero, Luis de

Discurso de las missas conventuales. *See* García de Zurita, Andrés

Discurso de lo sucedido en este año 1626. Seville: S. Fajardo, 1626

Discurso de los sucessos de España. Madrid: J. Sánchez, 1640

Discurso en que se muestra la obligacion. *See* Pizarro y Orellana, Fernando

Discurso i alegacion en derecho. *See* Solórzano Pereira, Juan de

Discurso juridico y politico. *See* Moscoso y de Córdoba, Cristóbal de

Discurso legal militar. *See* Moscoso y de Córdoba, Cristóbal de

Discurso politico. *See* Andrade Leitão, Francisco de; *and also* Sánchez de Espejo, Andrés

Discurso, que propone . . . el derecho. *See* Contreras y Valverde, Blasco de

Discurso sobre la importancia . . . de la recopilacion de las leyes. *See* León Pinelo, Antonio Rodríguez de

Discurso sobre la proposicion. *See* Basso, Gerardo

Discurso sobre os fidalgos. *See* Pinto Ribeiro, João

Discursos espirituales. *See* Palafox y Mendoza, Juan de, Bp

Discursos politicos. *See* Fernández Navarrete, Pedro

Discursos sobre la navegacion. *See* Pereira Corte Real, João

—Dominicans. Acta capituli generalis Ulyssiponae. Seville: 1619

—Malpaeus, P. Palma fidei s. Ordinis praedicatorum. Antwerp: 1635

—Piò, G. M. Allegatione per confirmare quanto si scrive. [Venice?] 1618

— —Delle vite de gli huomini illustri di S. Domenico. Bologna: 1607

— —Delle vite de gli huomini illustri di S. Domenico. Seconda parte. Pavia: 1613

DOMINICANS IN MEXICO

—Dávila Padilla, A., Abp. Historia de la fundacion . . . de la provincia, de Santiago de Mexico. Brussels: 1625

— —Varia historia de Nueva España y Florida. Valladolid: 1634

—Ojea, H. La venida de Christo. Medina del Campo: 1602

DOMINICANS IN SPANISH AMERICA

—Remesal, A. de. Historia de la provincia de S. Vicente. Madrid: 1619

— —Historia general de las Indias Ocidentales. Madrid: 1620

Don Antonio de Figueroa, procurador general. See Figueroa, Antonio de

Don Filipe el Prudente, segundo deste nombre. See Vander Hammen y León, Lorenzo

Don Francisco Morovelli de Puebla defiende el patronato. See Morovelli de la Puebla, Francisco

Don Iñigo de Ayala y Rojas. See Ayala y Rojas, Iñigo de

Don Quixote. See Cervantes Saavedra, Miguel de

Donati, Marcello. De historia medica mirabili libri sex. Frankfurt a.M.: E. Kempfer, for J. J. Porsch, 1613

Donato d'Eremita. Il fiore della granadiglia. Bologna: B. Cocchi, for S. Pariasca, 1609

Donck, Adriaen van der. Vertoogh van Nieu-Neder-Land. The Hague: M. Stael, 1650

Donne, John. An anatomie of the world. London: W. Stansby, for T. Dewe, 1625

—An anatomy of the world. London: [H. Lownes] for S. Macham, 1611

— —In his Poems. London: 1633

—Biathanatos. A declaration. London: J. Dawson [1647]

— —London: [J. Dawson] for H. Moseley, 1648

—Conclave Ignatii. [Hanau? 1611]

— —[London: W. Burre, 1611]

—LXXX sermons. London: [M. Fletcher] for R. Royston, & R. Marriott, 1640

—The first anniversarie. London: M. Bradwood, for S. Macham, 1612

— —London: A. Mathewes, for T. Dewe, 1621

—Five sermons. London: [A. Mathewes?] for T. Jones, 1626

—Foure sermons. London: [A. Mathewes?] for T. Jones, 1625

—Ignatius his conclave. London: N. O[kes]., for R. More, 1611

— —London: M. F[letcher]., for R. More, 1626

— —London: J. Marriott, for W. Sheares, 1634

— —London: J. Marriott, for W. Sheares, 1635

—Poems. London: M. F[letcher]., for J. Marriott, 1633

— —London: M. F[letcher]., for J. Marriott, 1635

— —London: M. F[letcher]., for J. Marriott, 1639

— —London: M. F[letcher]., for J. Marriott, 1649

— —London: J. Marriott, & R. Marriott, 1650

—Pseudo-martyr. London: W. Stansby, for W. Burre, 1610

—A sermon upon the viii. verse. London: A. Mat[hewes]., for T. Jones, 1622

— —In his Three sermons. London: 1624

—A sermon upon the eighth verse. London: [A. Mathewes] for T. Jones, 1624

— —In his Foure sermons. London: 1625

— —In his Five sermons. London: 1626

—Three sermons. London: [A. Mathewes?] for T. Jones, 1624 (2)

Donzella desterrada, or, The banish'd virgin. See Biondi, Sir Giovanni Francesco

DORTH, JOHAN VAN, HEER VAN DER HORST

—Reys-boeck van . . . Brasilien. [Dordrecht?] 1624

The dove. See Zouch, Richard

Doze comedias nuevas. See Téllez, Gabriel

Doze comedias . . . Quarta parte. See Vega Carpio, Lope Félix de

Dracht-thoneel. Amsterdam: Z. Heyns [1601]

Drake, Sir Francis. Drey sonderbare Reysen. In Raleigh, Sir Walter. Achter Theil Americae. Frankfurt a.M.: 1624

—The world encompassed by Sir Francis Drake. London: [G. Miller?] for N. Bourne, 1628

— —London: E[lizabeth]. P[urslowe]., for N. Bourne, 1635

DRAKE, SIR FRANCIS

—Bacon, F. Considerationi politiche . . . per movere la guerra. Turin: 1641

— —Considerations. [London:] 1629

—Baker, Sir R. A Chronicle of the kings. London: 1643

—Boutrays, R. De rebus in Gallia . . . commentariorum lib. xvi. Paris: 1610

—Bry, T. de. Americae pars viii. Frankfurt a.M.: 1625

—Cabrera de Córdoba, L. Filipe Segundo rey de España. Madrid: 1619

—Camden, W. Annales. London: 1625

— —Annales des choses que se sont passées. London: 1624

— —Annales rerum Anglicarum. London: 1615

— —Histoire d'Elizabeth. Paris: 1627

— —The historie of . . . Princesse Elizabeth. London: 1630

— —Rerum Anglicarum . . . annales. Leyden: 1639

——Frankfurt a.M.: W. Richter, for C. Neben, 1605
—Conseils de medecine. Paris: C. Morel, 1626
—Drey medicinische Tractätlein. Strassburg: E. Zetzner, 1631
—Liber de priscorum philosophorum verae medicinae materia. Saint Gervais: Heirs of E. Vignon, 1603
——Geneva: J. Vignon, 1609
——Leipzig: T. Schürer, & B. Voigt, 1613
—Opera medica. Frankfurt a.M.: L. Albert, 1602
——Leipzig: T. Schürer, & B. Voigt, 1614
—La pharmacopee des dogmatiques reformée. Paris: C. Morel, 1624
——Paris: C. Morel, 1630
——Rouen: O. Seigneuré, & L. Oursel, for C. Pitreson, 1639
——Lyons: J. de La Garde, 1648
—Pharmacopoea dogmaticorum restituta. Paris: C. Morel, 1607
——Paris: C. Morel, 1607
——Venice: G. A. & J. de Francisci, 1608
——Leipzig: Heirs of M. Lantzenberger, for T. Schürer, & B. Voigt, 1613
——Venice: J. de Francisci, 1614
——*In* Renou, Jean de. Dispensatorium medicum. Frankfurt a.M.: 1615
——Geneva: P. Aubert, 1620
——Marburg: P. Egenolff, 1622
——Geneva: P. & J. Chouët, 1628
——*In* Renou, Jean de. Dispensatorium. Hanau: 1631
—Pharmacopoea restituta. Das ist Verbesserte apotecker Kunst. Strassburg: E. Zetzner, 1625
—The practise of chymicall . . . physicke. London: T. Creede, 1605
—Quercetanus redivivus. Frankfurt a.M.: J. Beyer, 1648
—Le ricchezze della riformata farmacopoea. Venice: G. Guerigli, 1619
——Venice: The Guerigli, 1638
——Venice: The Guerigli, 1646

—Sclopetarius, *In his* Opera medica. Frankfurt a.M.: 1602
—Traicté de la cure generale. Paris: C. Morel, 1625
—Traicté de la matiere . . . de la medecine balsamique. Paris: C. Morel, 1626
Du Chevreul, Jacques. Sphaera. Paris: J. Moreau, 1623
——Paris: H. Du Mesnil, 1629
Ductor in linguas, the guide into tongues. *See* Minsheu, John
Dudley, Sir Robert, styled duke of Northumberland. Dell'arcano del mare. Florence: F. Onofri, 1646–47
The due right of presbyteries. *See* Rutherford, Samuel
Du Fail, Noël, seigneur de La Herissaye. Les contes et discours d'Eutrapel. Rennes: N. Glamet, 1603
Du Ferrier, Jérémie. Advertissement à tous les estats. Paris: 1625
——Paris: J. Bouillerot, 1626
—Le Catholique d'estat. Paris: J. Bouillerot, 1625 (2)
——Rouen: D. Du Petit Val, 1625
——Paris: J. Bouillerot, 1626
——*In* Hay, Paul, sieur du Chastelet. Recueil de diverses pieces. [Paris:] 1635
—*See also* Discours sur l'affaire de la Valteline. Paris: 1625
Du Gardin, Louis. Medicamenta purgantia. Douai: P. Auroy, 1631, '30
Dugres, Gabriel. Dialogi gallicoanglico-latini. Oxford: L. Lichfield, 1639
Du Hamel, Jacques. Acoubar. Rouen: R. Du Petit Val, 1603
——Rouen: R. Du Petit Val, 1611
Duircant, Andries. Rym-vieren. [The Hague: 1629]
—, supposed author. *See* Practiicke van den Spaenschen aessack. The Hague: 1629
Duirkant, Andries. *See* Duircant, Andries
Du Jardin, Garcie. *See* Orta, Garcia da

Du Jarric, Pierre. L'histoire des choses plus memorables. Arras: G. Bauduin, 1611
——Arras: G. de La Rivière, 1611
——Arras: G. de La Rivière, for J. Vervliet, at Valenciennes, 1611
—Nouvelle histoire des choses plus memorables. Arras: G. Baudin, 1628
—Seconde partie de l'Histoire des choses plus memorables. Bordeaux: S. Millanges, 1610
—Thesaurus rerum indicarum. Cologne: P. Henning, 1615
Duliris, Leonard. Apologie; ou Juste deffence du secret des longitudes. Paris: A. Bertier, 1648
—La theorie des longitudes. Paris: J. Guillemot, 1647
Du Mas de Flores, Israel. La clef de la geographie generale. Paris: J. Boisseau, & L. Vendosme, 1645
Du Monstier, Arthur. Martyrologium Franciscanum. Paris: D. Moreau, 1638
Dunbar, John. Epigrammaton. London: T. Purfoot, 1616
Dunoyer de Saint-Martin, François. Articles, moyens et raisons. Paris: Widow of J. Regnoul, 1616 (2)
Du Périer, Anthoine, sieur de La Salargue. Les amours de Pistion. Paris: T. de La Ruelle, 1601
——Paris: T. de La Ruelle, 1602
——Paris: T. de La Ruelle, 1606
——*See also* Du Hamel, Jacques. Acoubar. Rouen: 1603
Dupleix, Scipion. La curiosité naturelle. Paris: L. Sonnius, 1606
——Paris: F. Gueffier, 1613
——Lyons: S. Rigaud, 1620
——[Rouen?] 1623
——Rouen: C. Loudet, 1625
——Paris: C. Sonnius, 1626
——Rouen: M. de Préaulx, 1626
——Paris: J. Bessin, 1631
——Paris: C. Sonnius, 1632
——Rouen: C. Malassis, 1635
——Rouen: D. Loudet, 1638
——Rouen: R. L'Allemant, 1645

Copie de l'instruction. [Brussels?] 1608A

——Copye van de instructie. [Brussels:] 1608A

—Netherlands (United Provinces, 1581–1795). Staten Generaal. Placcaet ende ordonnantie . . . tegens wechloopers. The Hague: 1625

—Nuevas ciertas y fidedignas de la vitoria que ha alcançado Don Fadrique de Toledo. Barcelona: 1629

—Den ongeveynsden Nederlandschen patriot. Tweede deel. Middelburg: 1646

—Reed-geld over betalinghe. [Haarlem?] 1630

—Remonstrantie aen alle de steden. [The Hague?] 1647

—Solórzano Pereira, J. de. Discurso i alegacion en derecho. Madrid: 1631

—Tijdinghe hoe dat . . . Pieter Adriaensz. van Vlissinghen . . . de Hondurische vlote heeft verovert. Amsterdam: 1628

DUTCH IN VENEZUELA

—Netherlands (United Provinces, 1581–1795). Staten Generaal. Placcaet. The Hague: 1622

—Wassenaer, N. van. T'derdedeel . . . van het Historischer verhael. Amsterdam: 1623

The Dutch survay. *See* Crosse, William

Du Val, Guillaume. Phytologia, sive Philosophia plantarum. Paris: G. Meturas, 1647

Du Verdier, Antoine. Diverses leçons. *In* Mexía, Pedro. Les diverses leçons. Tournon: 1604

——*In the same.* Tournon: 1609

——*In the same.* Tournon: 1610

——*In the same.* Tournon: 1616

——*In the same.* Tournon: 1625

—*See also* Archaio-ploutos. Containing, ten following bookes. London: 1619

Duyrcant, Andries. *See* Duircant, Andries

E., I. V. *See* Coppie de la fleur de la passion. Paris: 1637

Earle, John, Bp. Micro-cosmographie. London: W. Stansby, for R. Allot, 1628

——London: W. Stansby, for E. Blount, 1628

——London: W. S[tansby]., for E. Blount, 1628

——London: R. Allott, 1629

——London: R. B[adger]., for R. Allott, 1630

——London: E. A[llde]., for R. Allott, 1633

——London: J. L[egat]., for A. Crooke, 1638

——London: W. Bentley, for W. Sheares, 1650 (2)

EARTHQUAKES

—Keckermann, B. Meditatio de insolito et stupendo illo terraemotu. Heidelberg: 1602

EARTHQUAKES—CHILE

—González Chaparro, J. Carta del p. Juan Gonzalez Chaparro. Madrid: 1648

——Lettera . . . ove s'intendono casi . . . del terremoto. Rome: 1648

——Relation dell'horrible tremblement. Brussels: 1648

Eastward Hoe. *See* Chapman, George

Eaton, Samuel. A defence of sundry positions and scriptures alledged to justifie the Congregationall-way. London: M. Simmons, for H. Overton, 1645

—The defence of sundry positions and scriptures for the Congregational-way. London: M. Simmons, for H. Overton, 1646

Eben-ezer. *See* Souter, Daniel

Eburne, Richard. A plaine pathway to plantations. London: G. P[urslowe]., for J. Marriott, 1624

Ecclesiastes. *See* Le Brun, Laurent

Ecco polytico. *See* Mello, Francisco Manuel de

Echo ofte galm. *See* Nierop, Adriaan van

ECLIPSES

—Suárez de Argüelo, F. Ephemerides generales. Madrid: 1608

L' economia del cittadino. *See* Tanara, Vincenzo

ECONOMICS

—Malynes, G. The maintenance of free trade. London: 1622

—Medio que el reyno propone para el consumo del vellon. [Madrid? ca. 1635?]

—Memorial de advertencias convenientes para esta monarquia. [Madrid? ca. 1635?]

ECUADOR

—Lemos, P. F. de Castro, conde de. Relacion de la provincia de los Quixos. [Madrid: 1608]

ECUADOR–HISTORY

—Garavito, G. Señor. Geronimo Garavito en nombre de don Juan de Lizaraçu . . . dize, que reconociendo . . . [Madrid: 163–?]

—Spain. Consejo de las Indias. Memorial de lo que contienen los papeles. [Madrid: 1631]

—Trebiño, A., fray. Señor. El maestro fray Francisco de Herrera. [Madrid: 1631]

Edict du roy. *See* Compagnie de la Nouvelle France

EDUCATION

—Brinsley, J. Consolation for our grammar schooles. London: 1622

EDUCATION—MASSACHUSETTS

—New Englands first fruits. London: 1643

EDUCATION—PERU

—Ortiz de Cervantes, J. Señor. El licenciado Juan Ortiz de Cervantes . . . Dize; que en el reyno del Pirù . . . . [Madrid? ca. 1620?]

EDUCATION—VIRGINIA

—Copland, P. A declaration how the monies . . . were disposed. London: 1622

Edwards, Thomas. Antapologia; or, A full answer to the . . . narration. London: G. M[iller]., for J. Bellamy, 1644

——London: G. M[iller]., for R. Smith, 1644

——London: T. R[atcliffe]., & E. M[ottershead]., for J. Bellamy, 1646

— —London: T. R[atcliffe]., & E. M[ottershead]., for R. Smith, 1646

—Gangraena. London: [T. Ratcliffe, & E. Mottershead?] for R. Smith, 1646 (3)

—Gangraena, pt 1–2. London: T. R[atcliffe]., & E. M[ottershead]., for R. Smith, 1646

—Gangraena, pt 2. London: T. R[atcliffe]., & E. M[ottershead]., for R. Smith, 1646 (3)

—Gangraena, pt 3. London: [T. Ratcliffe, & E. Mottershead?] for R. Smith, 1646

Het eenentwintichste deel . . . van het Historisch verhael. *See* Lampe, Barent

Eenige advijsen ende verklaringhen. Amsterdam: P. van Macedonien, in press of J. R. Toorn [i.e., The Hague: L. Breeckevelt] 1648

Eenighe advijsen . . . [The Hague? L. Breeckevelt?] 1648

'T eerste boeck; Historie van Indien. *See* Lodewijcksz, Willem

I. [i.e., Eerste] conferentie van eenige Nederlandtsche heeren. Middelburg: J. de Laet, 1650

Eerste schip-vaert der Hollanderen. *See* Veer, Gerrit de

Eerste schip-vaert der Hollanders. Amsterdam: J. Hartgers, 1648

—Amsterdam: J. Hartgers, 1650

De eerste weke. *See* Du Bartas, Guillaume de Salluste, seigneur

Eibergen, Rutgerus. Swymelklacht des Spaenschen conincks. Amsterdam: J. F. Stam, for W. J. Stam, 1629

Eigentlich und volkomene historische beschreibung des niderlendischen Kriegs. *See* Meteren, Emanuel van

Eigentliche und warhafftige Beschreibung der wunderbärlichen Schiffarth. *See* Noort, Olivier van

LXXX [i.e., Eighty] sermons. *See* Donne, John

Die ein und zwanzigste Schifffahrt. *See* Hulsius, Levinus

Elegia . . . in expeditionem navalem . . . foederati Belgii. *See* Hoffer, Adriaan

Les elemens de chymie. *See* Béguin, Jean

Het elfde deel . . . van het Historisch verhael. *See* Wassenaer, Nicolaes van

Elías, Juan, fray. Señor. Un libelo infamatorio se ha impresso . . . su fecha en Potosí. [Madrid? 1640]

Eliot, John. *See* Winslow, Edward. The glorious progress of the Gospel, amongst the Indians. London: 1649

—*See also* Sibelius, Caspar. Of the conversion of five thousand. London: 1650

Eliseo, Father. Aviendo representado el conde de Monterey . . . los agravios . . . que los Indios de la Nueva España recibian. [Madrid? 1604?]

Eloge du p. Joseph Anquieta. *See* Sgambata, Scipio

Elogia virorum literis et sapientia illustrium. *See* Tomasini, Jacopo Philippo, Bp

Elogio del p. Giuseppe Anchieta. *See* Sgambata, Scipio

Elogiorum . . . liber primus [secundus]. *See* Bocchi, Francesco

Elogios dos reis de Portugal. *See* Brito, Bernardo de

Elogios en loor de los tres famosos varones. *See* Lobo Lasso de la Vega, Gabriel

Elsum, John. *See* Cooke, Jo. Epigrames. London: [1604]

Elucidarium anatomicum. *See* Colle, Giovanni

Emblemata. *See* Heyns, Zacharias

Emblemata et epigrammata. *See* La Faye, Antoine de

Emblemata, ofte Minnelycke . . . sinnebeelden. *See* Cats, Jacob

Emblemes. *See* Quarles, Francis

Emblems of rarities. *See* Lupton, Donald

EMERALDS

—Hurtado de Mendoza, D. Guerra de Granada. Lisbon: 1627

EMIGRATION AND IMMIGRATION

—Daniel, S. A panegyricke congratulatorie. London: 1603

—Great Britain. Sovereigns, etc., 1625–1649 (Charles I). A proclamation against the disorderly transporting. London: 1637

—Harsdörffer, G. P. Gesprächspiele, siebender Theil. Nuremberg: 1647

—Spain. Sovereigns, etc., 1621–1665 (Philip IV). El Rey. Conceio, justicia, veyntiquatros, cavalleros. [Madrid? 1622]

—Tassoni, A. Varietà di pensieri. Modena: 1612

Emili, Paolo. De rebus gestis Francorum. Basel: S. Henricpetri [1601]

Emilio, Paulo. *See* Emili, Paolo

Les empires, royaumes, estats . . . et principautez du monde. *See* Avity, Pierre d', sieur de Montmartin

Emporii emporiorum. *See* Garzoni, Tommaso

Empresas militares de Lusitanos. *See* Coelho de Barbuda, Luiz

Enchiridion cosmographiae. *See* Honter, Johannes

Enchiridion cosmographicum. *See* Quad, Matthias

Enchiridion isagogicum. *See* Robin, Jean

Enchiridion, o Manual de los tiempos. *See* Venero, Alonso

Enchiridion, ou Livret portatif pour les chirurgiens. *See* Chaumette, Antoine

Enchiridion physicum. *See* Bartholin, Caspar

Enchiridion practicum medicochirurgicum. Geneva: P. de La Rovière, 1621

—Geneva: M. Berjon, 1627

—[Geneva:] P. & J. Chouët, 1644

ENCOMIENDAS

—Altamirano, D. Por el duque del Infantado. [Madrid: 1634?]

—Merida, Yucatan. La ciudad de Merida. [Madrid? 1620?]

—Ortiz de Cervantes, J. Memorial . . . a Su Magestad. [Madrid?] 1619

An encouragement to colonies.

See Stirling, William Alexander, 1st earl of

Encouragements. *See* Gordon, Sir Robert, of Lochinvar

Encyclopaedia. *See* Alsted, Johann Heinrich

Englands bane. *See* Young, Thomas

Englands bright honour. *See* Satyre Menippee. English

England's-exchequer. *See* Hagthorpe, John

England's royall fishing revived. *See* Sharpe, Edward

England's safety. *See* Robinson, Henry

Englands way to win wealth. *See* Gentleman, Tobias

Englischen Liebbrinnendten S. Francisci Ordens Relations Continuation. *See* Hendschel, Tobias

ENGLISH. *See* BRITISH IN AMERICA

The English house-wife. *See* Markham, Gervase

English villanies. *See* Dekker, Thomas

The English-American. *See* Gage, Thomas

The English-mans treasure. *See* Vicary, Thomas

Enquiries touching the diversity of languages. *See* Brerewood, Edward

Enrique, Pedro. Relacion verdadera . . . de los sucessos, victoria, y batalla que han tenido los galeones de nueva España. Madrid: A. Duplastre, 1641

Enríquez, Juan. Relacion de las exequias y honras funerales . . . de la Orden de Predicadores, en la Nuevaespaña. Madrid: Widow of C. Delgado, 1623

Ens, Gaspar. Indiae Occidentalis historia. Cologne: G. Lützenkirchen, 1612

—Mauritiados libri vi. Cologne: W. Lützenkirchen, 1612

—Newer unpartheyischer teutscher Mercurius. Cologne: P. von Brachel, 1629

—West- unnd Ost Indischer Lustgart. Cologne: W. Lützenkirchen, 1618

Enseñança entretenida. *See* Quevedo y Villegas, Francisco Gómez de

ENTOMOLOGY
—Moffett, T. Insectorum . . . theatrum. London: 1634

Entremeses nuevos. De diversos autores. Alcalá de Henares: F. Ropero, 1643

—Alcalá de Henares: F. Ropero, 1646

Entwerffung von Eroberung der Stadt Olinda. [Frankfurt a.M.? Amsterdam? 1630]

Ephemerides generales. *See* Suárez de Argüelo, Francisco

An epicede or funerall song. *See* Chapman, George

Epicedium cum epitaphio . . . Petri Heinii. The Hague: A. Meuris, 1629

Epigrames. *See* Cooke, Jo.

Epigrammata americana. *See* Bodecherus Banninghius, Janus

Epigrammata extemporanea. *See* Bartholin, Caspar

Epigrammata religiosa. *See* Pyne, John

Epigrammaton. *See* Dunbar, John

Epigrammatōn opusculum duobus distinctum. *See* Plumptre, Huntingdon

Epigrammatum . . . libri. *See titles under* Owen, John

Epigrammatum editio postrema. *See* Owen, John

Epigrammatum libellus. *See* Johnson, Jacob

Epigrammatum libri decem. *See* Owen, John

Epigrammatum libri ii. *See* Campion, Thomas

Epigrammatum libri quatuor. *See* Stradling, Sir John

Epigrammatum libri tres. *See* Owen, John

Epigrams. *See* Owen, John

Epigrams and satyres. *See* Middleton, Richard

Epigrams both pleasant and serious. *See* Harington, Sir John

Epilogo de las pretensiones. *See* Sandoval y Guzmán, Sebastián de

Epistola . . . ad . . . regem Hispaniarum. *See* Aventrote, Juan

Epistola á los Peruleras. *See* Aventrote, Juan

Epistola Gasparis Dias Fereira in carcere. *See* Dias Ferreira, Gaspar

Epistolae Ho-elianae. Familiar letters. *See* Howell, James

Epistolario espiritual. *See* Juan de Jesús María, Father

Epistolarum et consultationum medicinalium . . . libri xii. *See* Augenio, Orazio

Epistolarum medicinalium. *See* Lange, Johannes

Epistolarum philosophicarum . . . volumen. *See* Scholtz, Lorenz, ed

Epithalamium symbolicum. Graz: E. Widmanstätter, 1631

Epitomae historiarum libri x. *See* Torsellino, Orazio

Epitome cronicorum seculi moderni . . . mit vilen Historien. *See* Mayr, Johann

Epitome de la admirable y exemplar vida. *See* Mendes Silva, Rodrigo

Epitome de la Biblioteca Oriental i Occidental. *See* León Pinelo, Antonio Rodríguez de

Epitome de la vida . . . del . . . emperador Carlos V. *See* Roca, Juan Antonio Vera Zúñiga y Figueroa, conde de la

Epitome de las historias portuguesas. *See* Faria e Sousa, Manuel de

Epitome de las razones. *See* Oviedo Pedrosa, Francisco de

Epitome des preceptes de medecine. *See* Pigray, Pierre

L'épitome du théâtre de l'univers. *See* Ortelius, Abraham

Epitome historiarum ab orbe condito. *See* Torsellino, Orazio

Epitome historiarum libri x. *See* Torsellino, Orazio

Epitome historico. *See* Rocaberti, Diego de

Epitome naturalis scientiae. *See* Sennert, Daniel

An epitome of Ortelius. *See* Ortelius, Abraham

Epitome of the theater of the worlde. *See* Ortelius, Abraham

Epitome ou brief recueil de l'histoire universelle. *See* Quervau, Vincent, sieur du Sollier

Epitome praeceptorum medicinae. *See* Pigray, Pierre

Epitome theatri orbis terrarum. *See* Ortelius, Abraham

Epitome theatri Orteliani. *See* Ortelius, Abraham

Eras Pantoja, Nicolás. Señor. Don Nicolas Eras Pantoja. [Madrid? 1642?]

Erastus, Thomas. Examen de simplicibus. Lyons: 1607

ERAUSO, CATALINA DE
—Pérez de Montalván, J. [La monja alferez, comedia famosa. Madrid? 1626?]
—Segunda relacion . . . Dizense en ella cosas admirables. Madrid: [1625?]

Ercilla y Zúñiga, Alonso de. Araucana. Madrid: Imprenta Real, 1632
— —, ptes 1a-3a. Madrid: J. de la Cuesta, for M. Martínez, 1610
— —Cadiz: G. Vezino, 1626
—Historiale beschrijvinghe der goudtrijcke landen in Chili ende Arauco. Rotterdam: J. van Waesberghe, 1619
—*See also* Oña, Pedro de. Arauco domado. Madrid: 1605

Eremita, Donato d'. *See* Donato d'Eremita

Eroberung der reiche silbervloot inde bay . . . Matancae. [Amsterdam? ca. 1629]

Erreurs populaires. *See* Bachot, Gaspard

The errors of men. *See* Stephens, John

Erschröckliche Zeitung wie . . . in der Stadt-Mexico . . . viel tausent seelen . . . ertruncken. Frankfurt a.M.: [1630]

Erste Schiffahrt. *See* Houtman, Cornelis de

Erste Schiffart. *See* Houtman, Cornelis de

Die erste und andere Woche. *See* Du Bartas, Guillaume de Salluste, seigneur

Erste Woche. *See* Du Bartas, Guillaume de Salluste, seigneur

Erudita et elegans explicatio quaestionis. *See* Casas, Bartolomé de las, Bp

Escalona y Agüero, Gaspar de. Arcae Limensis gazophilatium regium, Perubicum. Madrid: Imprenta Real, 1647

Escobar, Manuel de, supposed author. *See* Vasconcellos, João de. Restauração de Portugal prodigiosa. Lisbon: 1643

Esfera, forma del mundo. *See* Velázquez Minaya, Francisco

L'espadon satyrique. *See* Esternod, Claude d'

Esperança de Israel. *See* Manasseh ben Joseph ben Israel

ESPERUET, JORGE
—Flóres de León, D. Informe a S. M. Don Felipe III. [Madrid? ca. 1620?]

Espinel, Vicente. Relaciones de la vida del escudero Marcos de Obregon. Barcelona: S. de Cormellas, 1618
— —Barcelona: J. Margarit, 1618
— —Madrid: J. de la Cuesta, for M. Martínez, 1618
— —Seville: P. Gómez de Pastrana, 1641

Espinosa, Pedro, comp. Flores de poetas ilustres. Valladolid: L. Sánchez, 1605

Espinosa Centeno, Alonso de. Señor. El doctor don Alonso de Espinosa Centeno. [Madrid? 1645?]

Espinosa Montero, Agustín de. Señor. El doctor Agustin de Espinosa Montero. [Madrid? 164–?]

Esquibel, Juan de. Copia de una carta que el maese de campo . . . escrivio. [Madrid? 1608?]

The essaies. *See* Bacon, Francis

Essais. *See* Montaigne, Michel Eyquem de

An essay of the means. *See* Palmer, Sir Thomas

The essayes. *See* Bacon, Francis; *and also* Montaigne, Michel Eyquem de

Essayes and characters. *See* Stephens, John

Essays moraux. *See* Bacon, Francis

Essays ofte Poëtische betrachtungen. *See* Bos, Lambert van den

Essays politiques. *See* Bacon, Francis

The essence and unitie of the church. *See* Hudson, Samuel

Estaço da Silveira, Simão. El capitan . . . Dize, que la plata y riquezas del Piru vienen a España conduzidas por tierra a Arica. [Madrid? 1626]
—Relação summaria das cousas do Maranhão. Lisbon: G. da Vinha, 1624

El estado en que oy se halla el comercio. [Seville? 164–?]

Estado en que se hallan las Indias Occidentales. [Madrid? 1631?]

Estat general des debts passives. *See* Compagnie de la Nouvelle France

The estates, empires, and princepallities of the world. *See* Avity, Pierre d', sieur de Montmartin

Les estats, empires, et principautez du monde. *See* Avity, Pierre d', sieur de Montmartin

Este en em traslado bien y fielmente sacado . . . para que la plata . . . se labre. *See* Spain. Laws, statutes, etc., 1598–1621 (Philip III)

Este es la verdaderissima relacion de la feliz vitoria que ha tenido Don Fadrique de Toledo. Granada: M. Fernández Zambrano, 1630

Este es un traslado . . . de una cedula de su Magestad . . . para que los . . . maravedis . . . se muden. *See* Spain. Sovereigns, etc., 1598–1621 (Philip III)

Este es un traslado bien y fielmente sacado . . . Para que no se tomen ningun dineros. *See* Spain. Laws, statutes, etc., 1598–1621 (Philip III)

Este memorial es traslado. *See* Baeza, Pedro de

Esternod, Claude d'. Les desirs amoureux de Dom Philippe. Paris: P. Durand, 1614
—L'espadon satyrique. Lyons: J. Lautret, 1619

Exoticorum libri decem. *See*
L'Ecluse, Charles de

An experimentall discoverie of
Spanish practises. *See* Scott,
Thomas

Explicacion de la Bula. *See* Quintanadueñas, Antonio de

EXPLORERS. *See also* names of
explorers

—Bucholtzer, A. Index chronologicus. Frankfurt a.M.: 1612

—Calvisius, S. Chronologia.
Leipzig: 1605

—Clercq, N. de. Tooneel der
. . . hertogen. Delft: 1617

—Clüver, J. Historiarum totius
mundi epitome. Leyden: 1637

—Hall, J., Bp. The discovery of
a new world. London: [1609?]

——Mundus alter. [London:
1605?]

—Hulsius, L. Sechste Theil,
Kurtze, warhafftige Relation.
Nuremberg: 1603

—Lundorp, M. C. Politische
SchatzCammer . . . ander
Theil. Frankfurt a.M.: 1618

—Opmeer, P. van. Opus chronographicum orbis universi. Antwerp: 1611

—Slichtenhorst, A. van. Oratio
de navigationibus. Leyden:
1639

—Tassoni, A. Dieci libri di pensieri diversi. Carpi: 1620

EXPLORERS—POETRY

—Cooke, J. Epigrames. London:
[1604]

—Goodall, B. The tryall of travell. London: 1630

—Leech, J. Musae priores. London: 1620

—Taylor, J. The praise of hemp-
seed. London: 1620

—Vondel, J. van den. Poëzy. Amsterdam: 1650

EXPLORERS, ENGLISH

—Holland, H. Herōlogia anglica.
[Utrecht: 1620]

—Hues, R. A learned treatise of
globes. London: 1639

—Linton, A. Newes of the complement . . . of navigation.
London: 1609

Expulsion de los Moros. *See*
Aguilar, Gaspar Honorato de

Extract der Orientalischen Indien. *See* Fitzer, William

**Extract eens briefs uyt Vlissin-
gen.** 'The Hague: D. H. van
Waalsdorp' [i.e., Antwerp: H.
Verdussen] 1650

Extract ende copye van verscheyde brieven . . . belangende de rebellie . . . in Brasilien. [Amsterdam?] 1646

Extract oft Kort verhael uit het
groote journael. *See* Noort,
Olivier van

Extract und Ausszug der grossen . . . Schiff-farth Buelij Cataloni. *See* Plautius, Caspar,
Abbot

Extract uyt d'Articulen van het
tractaet van bestant. *See* Portugal. Treaties, etc., 1640–1656
(John IV)

Extract uyt de Missive vanden
president ende raden. *See* Nederlandsche West-Indische
Compagnie. Hooghe en Se-
crete Raad

Extract uyt de Notulen. *See* Nederlandsche West-Indische
Compagnie

Extract uyt de resolutien vande
. . . Staten van Hollant. *See*
Holland (Province). Staten

Extract uyt den Brief . . . aen de
Geoctroyeerde West-Indische
Compagnie. *See* Hein, Pieter
Pieterszoon

Extract uyt den brief vande poli-
tijcque raeden in Brasil. *See*
Nederlandsche West Indische
Compagnie

Extract uyt een brief gheschreven aen . . . de . . . Staten Generael . . . vande silver-mijne.
Leyden: C. Banheyning,
1650

Extract uyt een brief gheschreven in Maurits-Stadt de Pernambuco. [Amsterdam?] 1649

Extract uyt het Boeck vande
vrede-handelingh. *See* Netherlands (United Provinces,
1581–1795). Staten Generaal

Extract uyt het Boeck vande
vreed-handeling. *See* Netherlands (United Provinces,
1581–1795). Staten Generaal

**Extract uyt verscheyden
brieven** gheschreven in Brasil.
[Middelburg: 1642]

Extract uyttet register der resolutien. *See titles under* Netherlands (United Provinces,
1581–1795). Staten Generaal;
and also Amsterdam. Burgemeester

Extract van seeckeren brief,
gheschreven uyt Loando St.
Paulo. The Hague: L. Breeckevelt, 1648

Extract wtten brief van mijn Herr
Keulen . . . residerende . . . tot
Fernambuco. *See* Keulen, Ma-
thias van

Extraict des registres. *See* Compagnie de la Nouvelle France;
and also France. Conseil d'état

Eygentliche und vollkommene
historische Beschreibung dess
niderländischen Kriegs. *See*
Meteren, Emanuel van

Eyghentlijcke beschryvinghe van
West-Indien. *See* Ordóñez de
Ceballos, Pedro

Faber, Johannes. Animalia mexicana. Rome: G. Mascardi,
1628

Fabre, Pierre Jean. Myrothecium spagyricum. Toulouse:
N. d'Estey, for P. Bosc, 1628

——Strassburg: Heirs of L. Zetzner, 1632

——Toulouse: P. Bosc, 1646

**Fabricius, Hieronymus, ab
Aquapendente.** Medecina
practica. Paris: C. Cottard,
1634

Fabronius, Hermann. Geographica historica: Newe summarische Welt-Historia. Schmalkalden: W. Ketzel, 1627

—Newe summarische Welt-Historia. Schmalkalden: W. Ketzel, 1612

——Schmalkalden: W. Ketzel,
1614

Factorum et dictorum memorabilium lib. ix. *See* Fregoso, Battista

Factum du procez. *See* Poutrincourt, Jean de Biencourt, sieur
de

The faerie queene. *See* Spenser,
Edmund

Field, Nathan. Amends for ladies. London: G. Eld, for M. Walbanke, 1618
——London: J. Okes, for M. Walbanke, 1639
Figueira, Luiz. Arte da lingua brasilica. Lisbon: M.da Silva [1621]
—Relaçam de varios successos acontecidos no Maranham. Lisbon: M. Rodríguez, 1631
Figueiredo, Manuel de. Chronographia, reportorio dos tempos. Lisbon: J. Rodríguez, for P. Ramires, 1603
—Hidrographia. Lisbon: V. Alvarez, 1625
——Lisbon: J. Rodríguez, 1632
—Hydrographia. Lisbon: V. Alvarez, 1608
——Lisbon: V. Alvarez, 1614
—Roteiro e navegação das Indias Occidentais. Lisbon: P. Craesbeeck, 1609
Figueroa, Antonio de. Don Antonio de Figueroa, procurador general. [Madrid? 1640?]
Figueroa, Francisco de. Memorial presentado a Su Magestad . . . acerca del martyrio. Barcelona: L. Déu, 1617
——*In* Jesuits. Letters from missions. Histoire du massacre. Valenciennes: 1620
—Señor. El Padre Francisco de Figueroa. [Madrid? 1617?]
—Señor. Francisco de Figueroa de la Compañia de Jesus. [Madrid? 1617?]
Figueroa, Juan de. Juan de Figueroa, regidor de la cuidad de los Reyes. [Madrid? 1650?]
Filipe Segundo rey de España. *See* Cabrera de Córdoba, Luis
El filosofo. *See* Gómez Tejada de los Reyes, Cosmé
El filosofo del aldea. *See* Velázquez, Baltasar Mateo
Fin de la guerre. Dialogus, of t'Samen-sprekinge. Amsterdam: P. A. van Ravesteyn [1623]
A fine companion. *See* Marmion, Shackerley
Fioravanti, Leonardo. La cirugia. Venice: L. Spineda, 1610
——Venice: L. Spineda, 1630

—Compendium oder Ausszug der Secreten. Darmstadt: J. Leinhose, for J. Berner, [at Frankfurt a.M.?] 1624
—Corona, oder Kron der Artzney. Frankfurt a.M.: N. Hoffmann, for J. Berner, 1604
——Frankfurt a.M.: A. Humm, for J. Berner, 1618
—De' capricci medicinali . . . libri quattro. Venice: L. Spineda, 1602
——Venice: C. Gallina, 1617
——Venice: L. Spineda, 1629
——Venice: Cestaro, 1647
—De' secreti rationali . . . libri cinque. Venice: G. Imberti, 1640
—Del compendio de' secreti rationali. Venice: P. Miloco, 1620
——Venice: L. Spineda, 1630
—Della fisica. Venice: L. Spineda, 1603
——Venice: L. Spineda, 1629
—Dello specchio di scientia universale. Venice: L. Spineda, 1603
——Venice: The Valentini, 1624
——Venice: Heirs of M. Sessa, 1633
—A discourse upon chyrurgery. London: E. Allde, 1626
—[Miroir universel des arts et des sciences.] Paris: D. Douceur, 1602
—Physica, das ist: Experientz. Frankfurt a.M.: N. Hoffman, for J. Berner, 1604
—Il tesoro della vita humana. Venice: L. Spineda, 1603
——Venice: L. Spineda, 1629
Il fiore della granadiglia. *See* Donato d'Eremita
FIREFLIES
—Heyns, Z. Emblemata. Rotterdam: 1625
Firenzuola, Agnolo. *See* Delle rime piacevoli. Vicenza: 1603
Firmamento religioso de luzidos astros. *See* Nieremberg, Juan Eusebio
The first anniversarie. *See* Donne, John
First part of Ayres. *See* Hume, Tobias. Ayres, French, Pollish, and others. London: 1605

El fiscal con doña Francisca Colon de Toledo. *See* Spain. Consejo de las Indias
El Fiscal de Indias. *See* Villagómez, H. de
El Fiscal de su Magestad. *See* Seville. Casa de la Moneda
FISHERIES
—Gerritsz, H. Historie du pays nomme Spitsberghe. Amsterdam: 1613
—Kayll, R. The trades increase. London: 1615
—Scott, T. The Belgick souldier. [London]: 1624
FISHES. *See also* CODFISH
—Jonstonus, J. Historiae naturalis de piscibus. Frankfurt a.M.: [1650?]
Fitzer, William. Extract der Orientalischen Indien. Frankfurt a.M.: K. Rötel, for W. Fitzer, 1629
—Orientalische Indien. Frankfurt a.M.: K. Rötel, for W. Fitzer, 1628
See also the following:
—Bry, Johann Theodor de. Der dreyzehende Theil der Orientalischen Indien. Frankfurt a.M.: 1628
——Historiarum Orientalis Indiae tomus XII. Frankfurt a.M.: 1628
——Der zwölffte Theil der Orientalischen Indien. Frankfurt a.M.: 1628
Five sermons. *See* Donne, John
Le flambeau de la navigation. *See* Blaeu, Willem Janszoon
The fleire. *See* Sharpham, Edward
Fletcher, John. The knight of the burning pestle. *See under* Beaumont, Francis
—Wit without money. London: T. Cotes, for A. Crooke, & W. Cooke, 1639
—*See also* Beaumont, Francis. Comedies and tragedies. London: 1647
FLOODS—MEXICO
—Fernández de Bivero, J. Señor. Juan Fernandez de Bivero. Madrid: 1633
Flora Danica. *See* Paulli, Simon

Flora, overo Cultura di fiori. *See* Ferrari, Giovanni Battista

Flora, seu De flora cultura. *See* Ferrari, Giovanni Battista

Florence. Arte de' medici e degli speziali. *See* Ricettario Fiorentino. Florence: 1623

Flores de España. *See* Sousa de Macedo, Antonio de

Flores de León, Diego. Informe a S. M. Don Felipe III. [Madrid? ca. 1620?]

—Señor. El maestre de campo don Diego Florez de Leon, cavallero. [Madrid? 162–?]

—*See also* Preguntas que se propusieron al maese de campo. [Madrid? 1616?]

Flores de poetas ilustres. *See* Espinosa, Pedro, comp

Flores illustrium epitaphiorum. *See* Canoniero, Pietro Andrea

FLORIDA. *See also* FRENCH IN FLORIDA

—Bachot, G. Erreurs populaires. Lyons: 1626

—Beverwijck, J. van. Schat der ongesontheit. Dordrecht: 1642

—Boulenger, J. C. Historiarum sui temporis libri tredecim. Lyons: 1617

—Du Chevreul, J. Sphaera. Paris: 1623

—Le Paulmier de Grentemesnil, J. De morbis contagiosis libri septem. Frankfurt a.M.: 1601

—Lundorp, M. C. Politische SchatzCammer . . . ander Theil. Frankfurt a.M.: 1618

—Neuhaus, E. Theatrum ingenii humani. Amsterdam: 1633

—Prynne, W. Histrio-mastix. London: 1633

—Relacion de lo sucedido en los galeones. [Madrid? 1622]

—Renou, J. de. Le grand dispensaire medicinal. Lyons: 1624

——Institutionum pharmaceuticarum libri quinque. Paris: 1608

——Les oeuvres pharmaceutiques. Lyons: 1626

—Ruland, J. D. Inauguralis de lue . . . venerea disputatio. [Frankfurt a.M.: 1636]

—Sacro Bosco, J. de. Sfera. Siena: 1604

—A true relation of that which . . . hapned to the . . . Spanish fleet. London: 1623

—Villerias, M. de. El capitan Mateo de Villerias vezino de Mexico. [Madrid? 1613]

FLORIDA—DESCRIPTION & TRAVEL

—Virginia richly valued, by the description of . . . Florida. London: 1609

—The worthye and famous history of . . . Terra Florida. London: 1611

FLORIDA—DISCOVERY & EXPLORATION

—Laudonnière, R. G. de. Der ander Theil der . . . Landtschafft Americae. Frankfurt a.M.: 1603

——Brevis narratio eorum quae in Florida . . . Gallis acciderunt. Frankfurt a.M.: [1609]

—Tomasini, J. P., Bp. Illustrium virorum elogio. Padua: 1630

FLORIDA—HISTORY

—Aubigné, T. A. d'. L'histoire universelle. Maillé: 1616

—Gysius, J. Le miroir de la cruelle . . . tyrannie espagnole. Amsterdam: 1620

—Lescarbot, M. Histoire de la Nouvelle France. Paris: 1609

La Florida del Ynca. *See* Garcilaso de la Vega, el Inca

Florilegium. *See* Sweerts, Emanuel

Florilegium chymicum. *See* Grüling, Philipp Gerhard

Florilegium Hippocrateo-Galeno-chymicorum. *See* Grüling, Philipp Gerhard

Florilegium novum . . . New Blumenbuch. *See* Bry, Johann Theodor de

Florilegium renovatum . . . das ist, Vernewertes . . . Blumenbuch. *See* Bry, Johann Theodor de

Florilegium universale. *See* Forest du Chesne, Nicholas

Florio, John. Queen Anna's new world of words. London: M. Bradwood, for E. Blount, & W. Barret, 1611

Florum, herbarum, ac fructuum selectiorum icones. *See* Boodt, Anselm Boèce de

Floyd, John. The overthrow of the Protestants pulpitbabels. [St. Omer: English College Press] 1612

Focanus, Jacobus. Adoni-beseck. Delft: J. A. Cloeting, 1629

—Leeuwarden: G. Sybes, 1643

Fockens, Jacob. *See* Focanus, Jacobus

Förordning huru medh tobaks handelen skal blifwa hällit. *See* Sweden. Sovereigns, etc., 1632–1654 (Christina)

Folkingham, William. Feudigraphia. London: R. More, 1610

Fonseca, Rodrigo. Consultationum medicinalium singularibus remediis refertae. Venice: G. Guerigli, 1619–22

——Venice: G. Guerigli, 1620–22

——Frankfurt a.M.: Heirs of A. Wechel, for D. & D. Aubry, & C. Schleich, 1625

——Venice: G. Guerigli, 1628

Fontaine, Jacques. Opera in quibus universae artis medicae . . . explicantur. Paris: A. Périer, 1612

——Cologny: P. & J. Chouët, 1613

——Geneva: P. & J. Chouët, 1613

—Practica curandorum morborum. Paris: A. Beys, 1611

Fontana, Francesco. Novae coelestium terrestriumque rerum observationes. Naples: Il Gaffaro, 1646

Fontanus, Jacobus. *See* Fontaine, Jacques

Fontanus, Nicolaus. *See* Fonteyn, Nicolaus

Fonteyn, Nicolaus. Responsionum et curationum medicinalium liber unus. Amsterdam: J. Janszoon the Younger, 1639

FOOD. *See also* particular foods, e.g., MAIZE

—Benzi, U. Regole della sanita. Turin: 1620

—Hart, J. Klinikē, or The diet of the diseased. London: 1633

A fooles bolt is soon shot. *See* Rowlands, Samuel

For the colony in Virginea Britannia. Laws divine. *See* Strachey, William

For the plantation in Virginia. *See* Virginia Company of London

Forbes, Alexander. An anatomy of independency. London: R. Bostock, 1644

Ford, John. The lovers melancholy. London: [F. Kingston] for H. Seile, 1629

Foreest, Jan van. Hispanus redux. Hoorn: J. Claeszoon, 1622

—Idyllia sive Heroes. [Leyden:] Plantin Office (Raphelengius), 1605

Foreest, Pieter van. Observationum et curationum medicinalium . . . libri xxx. xxxi. et xxxii. Frankfurt a.M.: Palthenius Office, 1609

—Observationum et curationum medicinalium liber xxxii. Leyden: Plantin Press (Raphelengius), 1606

Forest du Chesne, Nicholas. Florilegium universale. Paris: A. Lesselin, 1650

Forestus, Joannes. *See* Foreest, Jan van

Forestus, Petrus. *See* Foreest, Pieter van

Formulae remediorum. *See* Morel, Pierre

[Forsamekle as it is weill knowin.] *See* Scotland. Privy Council

[Forsamekle as our soveraine Lordis . . . .] *See* Scotland. Privy Council

[Forsamekle as the Kingis . . . .] *See* Scotland. Privy Council

[Forsamekle as the Kingis Majestie oute of his princelie . . . .] *See* Scotland. Privy Council

FORT CHRISTINA

—La grande deffaite des Espagnols. Paris: 1634

Fortgang der West Indianischen Compagnia. [Amsterdam? 1623?]

La fortuna. *See* Quevedo y Villegas, Francisco Gómez de

Foster, Nicholas. A briefe relation of the late . . . rebellion . . . in . . . Barbadas. London: J. G[rismond]., for R. Lowndes, & R. Boydell, 1650

Fotherby, Martin, Bp. Atheomastix clearing foure truthes. London: N. Okes, 1622

The fountaine of selfe-love. *See* Jonson, Ben

Foure bookes of Du Bartas. *See* Du Bartas, Guillaume de Salluste, seigneur

Foure bookes of husbandry. *See* Heresbach, Conrad

Foure sermons. *See* Donne, John

Fournier, Georges. Geographica orbis notitia. Paris: J. Henault, 1648

——Paris: J. Henault, 1649

—Hydrographie, contenant la theorie . . . de la navigation. Paris: M. Soly, 1643

Fox, Luke. North-West Fox. London: B. Alsop, & T. Fawcet, 1635

Fracastoro, Girolamo. Opera pars prior. Geneva: J. Stoer, 1637

—Operum pars prior. Geneva: S. Crespin, 1621

——Geneva: P. & J. Chouët, 1622

Fragoso, Juan. Aromatum, fructuum et simplicium aliquot medicamentorum . . . opera. Strassburg: J. Martin, 1601

—Cirugia universal. Alcalá de Henares: Heirs of J. Gracián, 1607

——Alcalá de Henares: Heirs of J. Gracián, 1621

——Madrid: Widow of A. Martín, for D. González, 1627

——Madrid: C. Sánchez, for D. de Palacio y Villegas, 1643

—Della cirugia. Palermo: A. Martarello, 1639

Le franc discours. A discourse, presented . . . to the French king. *See* Arnauld, Antoine

Le franc et veritable discours. *See* Arnauld, Antoine

France. Amirauté. Reglement donné par monseigneur le

Cardinal de Richelieu. Rouen: D. Du Petit Val, & J. Viret, 1637

France. Conseil d'état. Arrests, commissions et privileges du Conseil du Roy. Paris: B. Martin, 1621

—Extraict des registres du Conseil d'Estat. [Paris? 1634]

France. Laws, statutes, etc., 1610–1643 (Louis XIII). Declaration du Roy, portant defenses a tous ses subjects. Paris: P. Mettayer, 1625

France. Sovereigns, etc., 1589–1610 (Henry IV). Commissions du Roy & de monseigneur l'Admiral . . . pour l'habitation és terres de Lacadie, Canada. Paris: P. Patisson, 1605

France. Sovereigns, etc., 1610–1643 (Louis XIII). Declaration du Roy, portant defenses a ses sujets. Paris: S. Cramoisy, 1634

—Lettres de ratification du Roi des contrats du 12. fev. 1635. [Paris? 1642?]

France. Sovereigns, etc., 1643–1715 (Louis XIV). Le Roy estant en son Conseil. [Paris: 1647]

France. Treaties, etc., 1610–1643 (Louix XIII). Traicté entre le Roy Louis XIII. et Charles roy de la Grand'Bretagne. [Paris? 1632?]

Franceide, overo Del mal francese. *See* Lalli, Giovanni Battista

Francis Solanus, Saint. *See* Solano, Francisco, Saint

Franciscans. Renuncia que hizo la religion de S. Francisco. [Madrid? 1646?]

Franciscans. Provincia de los Angeles (Mexico). Breve resumen, que se haze, para la mejor inteligencia del pleyto. [Madrid? 1645?]

FRANCISCANS

—Quesada, G. de. Relacion verdadera del martirio. Seville: 1633

—Relacion verdadera, y de mucho aprovachamiento para del

leges du Conseil du Roy. Paris: 1621

—France. Sovereigns, etc., 1610–1643 (Louis XIII). Declaration du Roy, portant defenses a ses sujets. Paris: 1634

——Lettres de ratificatéon du Roi des contrats du 12. fev. 1635. [Paris? 1642?]

—Relation d'un voyage aux Indes Orientales. Paris: 1645

—Thou, J. A. de. Historiarum sui temporis . . . Libri cxxxviii. Geneva: 1620

FRENCH IN BRAZIL

—Crespin, J. Gross Martyrbuch und Kirchen-Historien. Hanau: 1606

——Histoire des martyres. [Geneva:] 1608

FRENCH IN CANADA

—Jamet, D. Coppie de la lettre escripte par le r.p. Denys Jamet. [Paris? 1620?]

—Lescarbot, M. A Dieu aux Francois retournans de la Nouvelle France. [La Rochelle: 1606?]

——[Adieu a la France. La Rochelle: 1606]

—Quervau, V., sieur du Sollier. Epitome ou brief recueil de l'histoire universelle. Paris: 1613

—Richelieu, A. J. du Plessis, Cardinal, duc de. Furent presens en leurs personnes par devant le notaire. [Paris? 1632?]

FRENCH IN FLORIDA

—Gysius, J. Oorsprong en voortgang der neder-landtscher beroerten. [Leyden?] 1616

——Origo et historia Belgicorum tumultuum. Leyden: 1619

——De spaensche tiranije gheschiet in Neder-Lant. Amsterdam: 1621

—Thou, J. A. de. Historiarum sui temporis, t 1–3. Paris: 1606

—Vander Hammen y León, L. Don Filipe el Prudente, segundo deste nombre. Madrid: 1625

A fresh discovery. See Prynne, William

Fresneau, Jacques. A messieurs des estat. [Paris?] 1615

Freudenhold, Martin. Der Landtstörtzer Gusman, von Alfarche . . . Dritter Theil. Frankfurt a.M.: 1626

Freylin, Juan Maria. Catalogo de algunos varones insignes. Seville: F. de Lyra, 1632

——Seville: F. de Lyra, 1633

Frias, Manuel de. El capitan Manuel de Frias, Procurador general. [Madrid? 1625?]

—Señor. El capitan Manuel de Frias vezino del Rio de la Plata. [Madrid? 1625?]

Frias, Pedro de. Relacion del martirio de treinta y un martires. Madrid: Imprenta Real, 1633

Fricius, Valentinus. Indianischer Religionstandt. In Amati, Scipione. Relation . . . dess Königreichs Voxu. Ingolstadt: 1617

Friesche Triton. See Baardt, Pieter

FRIESIANS IN AMERICA

—Hamcomius, M. Frisia. Franeker: 1620

Friesland, Netherlands. Provinciale Staten. Copye van het Octroy by de Staten van Frieslandt. Leeuwarden: J. & P. van den Rade, 1642

——The Hague: A. J. Tongerloo, 1644

Frisia. See Hamcomius, Martinus

FROBISHER, MARTIN

—Baker, Sir R. A chronicle of the kings. London: 1643

—Stow, J. The annales of England. London: [1601]

FROGS

—Cotton, J. The powring out of the seven vials. London: 1642

Fruchtbringende Gesellschaft. Der Fruchtbringenden Gesellschaft Nahmen. Frankfurt a.M.: M. Merian, 1646

—Kurtzer Bericht von der Fruchtbringenden Gesellschaft Vorhaben. Köthen: 1641

Les fruicts de la mission. See Claude d'Abbeville, Father

Fuchs, Samuel. Metoposcopia et ophthalmoscopia. Strassburg: T. Glaser, for P. Ledertz, 1615

Fuchsius, S. See Fuchs, Samuel

Fueldez, Antoine. Observations curieuses, touchant la petite verole. Lyons: J. A. Huguetan, 1645

Die fünff und zweyntzigste Schifffahrt. See Brouwer, Hendrick

Die fünffte kurtze wunderbare Beschreibung. See Raleigh, Sir Walter

Das fünffte Theil des Grossen Atlantis. See Jansson, Jan

Fünffter Theil der Orientalischen Indien. See Neck, Jacob Corneliszoon van

[Fünfzehn] Bücher Von dem Feldbaw. See Estienne, Charles XV. Bücher Von dem Feldbaw

Fuente, Gaspar de la, fray. Historia del capitulo general. Madrid: Imprenta Real, 1633

Fürstliche Tischreden. See Collibus, Hippolytus à

Fulgosis, Baptista. See Fregoso, Battista

A full, ample and punctuall discovery. See Gonsalvius, Reginaldus, Montanus

Fuller, Thomas. The holy state. Cambridge: R. Daniel, for J. Williams, at London, 1642

——Cambridge: R. D[aniel]., for J. Williams, at London, 1648

FUNERAL RITES AND CEREMONIES—PERU

—Perucci, F. Pompe funebri. Verona: 1639

Furent presens en leurs personnes par devant le notaire. See Richelieu, Armand Jean du Plessis, Cardinal, duc de

La furieuse défaite des Espagnols et la . . . bataille donnee au Perou. Paris: J. Martin, 1625

—Toulouse: J. Boudé, 1625

G., N. See Reys-boeck van . . . Brasilien. [Dordrecht?] 1624

Gabelkover, Oswald. Artzneybuch. Tübingen: G. Gruppenbach, 1603

——Tübingen: G. Gruppenbach, 1606

——Frankfurt a.M.: J. J. Porsch, & J. Berner, 1610

——Tübingen: J. J. Porsch, & J. Berner, 1618

——[Frankfurt a.M.:] J. J. Porsch, & Widow & Heirs of J. Berner, 1641

Gabelkover, Wolfgang. Curationum et observationum, centuria V. Tübingen: P. Brunn, 1627

Gabriel Sionita, tr. *See* al-Idrisi. Geographia Nubiensis. Paris: [1620]

Gad ben-Arod ben Balaam, pseud. The wandering Jew. London: J. Raworth, for N. Butter, 1640

Gaebelchover, Wolfgang. *See* Gabelkover, Wolfgang

Gaetani, Costantino. Ad universos ordinis . . . S. Benedicti abbates. Rome: Apostolic Camara, 1622

Gage, Thomas. The English-American. London: R. Cotes, for H. Blunden, & T. Williams, 1648

Gaitan de Torres, Manuel. Reglas par el govierno destos reynos. [Jerez de la Frontera:] 1625

—*See also* Gaytan de Torres, Manuel, *below*

Galistoni, Masotto, pseud. *See* Aprosio, Angelico

Gallego Benítez de la Serna, Juan. Opera physica, medica, ethica. Lyons: J. & P. Prost, 1634

La gallerie des femmes fortes. *See* Le Moyne, Pierre

Gallobelgicus, pseud. Wine, beere, ale and tobacco. London: T. C[oles]., for J. Grove, 1630

—Wine, beere, and ale. London: A. M[athewes]., for J. Grove, 1629

Gallucci, Giovanni Paolo. Coelestium corporum et rerum . . . accurata explicatio. Venice: R. Meietti, 1603

——Venice: G. A. Somasco, 1605

—Theatro del mundo. Granada: S. Muñoz, 1606

——Granada: S. Muñoz, 1611

——Granada: [S. Muñoz] for J. Castello, 1612

—Theatro . . . del mundo. Granada: S. Muñoz, 1614

——Granada: S. Muñoz, for J. Castello, 1616

——Granada: S. Muñoz, 1617

Galvão, António. The discoveries of the world. London: G. Bishop, 1601

Gangraena. *See* Edwards, Thomas

Garavito, Gerónimo. Cuenta que Geronimo Garavito . . . ha hecho de la mucha plata. [Madrid? 163–?]

—Geronimo Garavito . . . dize, que teniendo noticia que don Juan de Carvajal y Sande . . . . [Madrid? 1640]

—Señor. Aviendo los Españoles descubierto los dilatados reynos. [Madrid? 163–?]

—Señor. Geronimo Garabito . . . dize, que ha tenido noticia que el Arçobispo de Santa Cruz ha dada un memorial. [Madrid: 163–?]

—Señor. Geronimo Garavito . . . digo, que . . . puse en las reales manos . . . tres memoriales. [Madrid: 1637]

—Señor. Geronimo Garavito . . . Digo, que tengo presentados a V. M. muchos memoriales. [Madrid: 1637]

—Señor. Geronimo Garavito . . . Digo, que tengo presentados muchos memoriales. [Madrid: 163–?]

—Señor. Gerónimo Garavito . . . dize: Que a los 17. de mayo . . . [Madrid? 164–?]

—Señor. Geronimo Garavito . . . dize: Que alos 3. de enero . . . . [Madrid? 1640]

—Señor. Geronimo Garavito . . . dize: que aviendo presentado muchos memoriales . . . .[Madrid? 163–?]

—Señor. Geronimo Garavito . . . dize: Que de nuevo represento a V. M. los dos capitulos. [Madrid? 164–?]

—Señor. Geronimo Garavito . . . Dize, que desde los 12. . . . de noviembre . . . . [Madrid: 1641]

—Señor. Geronimo Garavito . . .

dize: Que es notorio. [Madrid? 1637]

—Señor. Geronimo Garavito . . . dize: Que ha mas de 5. años. [Madrid: 163–?]

—Señor. Geronimo Garavito . . . Dize, que tiene suplicado a V. M. . . . . [Madrid: 162–?]

—Señor. Geronimo Garavito . . . en nombre de los curas. [Madrid? 164–?]

—Señor. Geronimo Garavito en nombre de don Juan de Lizaraçu . . . presidente de la real audiencia . . . dize, que aviendo despachado . . . . [Madrid: 163–?]

—Señor. Geronimo Garavito en nombre de don Juan de Lizaraçu . . . presidente de la real audiencia . . . dize, que reconociendo . . . . [Madrid: 163–?]

—Señor. Geronimo Garavito en nombre del presidente. [Madrid: 163–?]

—Señor. Geronymo Garavito en nombre de Don Juan de Lizarazu . . . presidente de la real chancilleria. [Madrid: 163–?]

Garcés, Garcia. Relacion de la persecucion. Madrid: L. Sánchez, 1625

——Valencia: J. C. Gárriz, 1625

García, Gregorio. Historia eclesiastica y seglar. Baeza: P. de la Cuesta, 1626

—Origen de los indios. Valencia: P. P. Mey, 1607

—Predicacion del Evangelio. Baeza: P. de la Cuesta, 1625

García de Avíla, Francisco. Para que se devan preferir todos. [Madrid? 1630?]

Garcia de Céspedes, Andrés. Regimiento de navegacion. Madrid: J. de la Cuesta, 1606

García de Zurita, Andrés. Discurso de las missas conventuales. Madrid: F. Martínez, 1636

—Por la iglesia metropolitana de Los Reyes. [Madrid?] 1638

Garcilaso de la Vega, el Inca. Le commentaire royal. Paris: A. Courbé, 1633

—Commentarios reales, la pte. Lisbon: P. Craesbeeck, 1609

—La Florida del Ynca. Lisbon: P. Craesbeeck, 1605

—Histoire des querres civiles des Espagnols. Paris: A. Courbé, & E. Couterot, 1650

—Historia general del Peru. Córdoba: Widow of A. de Barrera, 1616

——Córdoba: Widow of A. de Barrera, 1617

Garden of . . . flowers. *See* Parkinson, John. Paradisi in sole paradisus terrestris. London: 1629

A garden of flowers. *See* Passe, Crispijn van de

The garden of health. *See* Langham, William

Gardiner, Edmund. Phisicall and approved medicines. London: [H. Lownes] for M. Lownes, 1611

—Physicall and approved medicines. London: [H. Lownes] for M. Lownes, 1624

—The triall of tabacco. London: H. L[ownes]., for M. Lownes, 1610

Garibáy y Zamálloa, Esteban de. Los quarenta libros del Compendio historial. Barcelona: S. de Cormellas, 1628

Garimberto, Girolamo. Problemi naturali e morali. Vicenza: F. Bolzetta, 1617

Garzoni, Tommaso. Emporii emporiorum. Frankfurt a.M.: J. T. Schönwetter, 1624

—La piazza universale. Venice: R. Meietti, 1601

——Venice: M. Claseri, for R. Meietti, 1605

——Venice: T. Baglioni, 1610

——Venice: O. Alberti, 1616

——Venice: G. Valentini, & A. Giuliani, 1617

——Venice: P. M. Bertano, 1626

——Venice: P. M. Bertano, 1638

——*See also* Suárez de Figueroa, Cristóbal. Plaza universal. Madrid: 1615

—Piazza universale, das ist Allgemeiner Schauwplatz. Frankfurt a.M.: N. Hoffmann, 1619

——Frankfurt a.M.: L. Jennis, 1626

——Frankfurt a.M.: W. Hoffmann, 1641

Gaspar d'Asenção. Sermam que prego o padre frey Gaspar d'Ascenção. [Lisbon:] G. da Vinha [1625?]

Gauden, John, Bp, supposed author. *See* Hinc illae lachrymae. or The impietie of impunitie. London: 1648

Gaultier, Jacques. Table chronologique de l'estat du christianisme. Lyons: J. Roussin, 1609

——Lyons: J. Roussin, 1613

——Lyons: Amy de Polier, for P. Rigaud, 1621

——Lyons: P. Rigaud, 1626

——Lyons: C. Cayne, for Widow of C. Rigaud, & C. Obert, 1633

—Tabula chronographica status ecclesiae catolicae. Cologne: P. Henning, 1616

——Lyons: H. Cardon, 1616

—Tabula chronologica status ecclesiae catolicae. Lyons: H. Cardon, 1636

Gaytán de Torres, Manuel. Que se dé diferente modo al govierno de la Indias. [Madrid? 162–?]

—Relacion, y vista de ojos. [Madrid:] 1621

—*See also* Gaitan de Torres, Manuel, *above*

Gazophylacium rerum naturalium. *See* Besler, Michael Rupert

Het geamplieerde Octroy. *See* Nederlandsche Oost-Indische Compagnie

Gebhard, Johann Werner, pseud. *See* Collibus, Hippolytus à

Gebhart, Johann Werner, pseud. *See* Collibus, Hippolytus à

Geelkercken, Nicolas van, supposed author. Reys-boeck. *See* Reys-boeck van . . . Brasilien. [Dordrecht?] 1624

Geestelick compas. *See* Udemans, Godefridus Corneliszoon

Geestelyck roer. *See* Udemans, Godefridus Corneliszoon

Gellibrand, Henry. A discourse mathematical. London: W. Jones, 1635

Geluckwenschinghe aan de West-Indische vlote. Amsterdam: 1624

Gelves, Marqués de. *See* Carrillo de Mendoza y Pimentel, Diego, marqués de Gelves

De gemeene directeurs, ghestelt tottet formeren vande capitalen. *See* Nederlandsche West-Indische Compagnie

Gemma, Reinerus, Frisius. Les principes d'astronomie. Paris: J. Quesnel, 1619

Gemmarum et lapidum historia. *See* Boodt, Anselm Boèce de

Généalogie des illustres comtes de Nassau. *See* Orlers, Jan Janszn

Génebrard, Gilbert, Abp. Chronographiae libri quatuor. Lyons: J. Pillehotte, 1609, '08

A general inventorie of the history of France. *See* Serres, Jean de

General opinion es en la Nuevaespaña. [Madrid? 1630?]

A generall historie of France. *See* Serres, Jean de

The generall historie of Spaine. *See* Mayerne, Louis Turquet de

A generall historie of the Netherlands. *See* Grimestone, Edward

The generall historie of Virginia. *See* Smith, Capt. John

The generall history of Virginia. *See* Smith, Capt. John

Genesius de Sepulveda, Joannes. *See* Sepúlveda, Juan Ginés de

Gentleman, Tobias. Englands way to win wealth. London: N. Butler, 1614

Geografia. *See* Ptolemaeus, Claudius

La geographia. *See* Mela, Pomponius

Geographia ecclesiastica. *See* Le Mire, Aubert

Geographia generalis. *See* Varen, Bernhard

Geographia Nubiensis. *See* al-Idrisi

Geographia vetus ex antiquis. *See* Bertius, Petrus

GERMANS IN AMERICA
—Zesen, P. von. Durch-aus vermehrter . . . Helikon. Wittenberg: 1649
Geronimo Garavito . . . dize, que
teniendo noticia que don Juan
de Carvajal y Sande . . . . See
Garavito, Gerónimo
Gerritsz, Hessel. Beschryvinghe
van der Samoyeden landt. Amsterdam: H. Gerritsz, 1612 (2)
—Descriptio ac delineatio geographica detectionis freti. Amsterdam: H. Gerritsz, 1612
— —Amsterdam: H. Gerritsz,
1613 (2)
— —See also Recentes Novi Orbis
historiae. Geneva: 1612
—Exemplar libelli supplicis po-
tentissimo Hispaniarum Regi.
Amsterdam: H. Gerritsz, 1612
—Histoire du pays nomme Spits-
berghe. Amsterdam: [H. Ger-
ritsz] 1613
— —See also Bry, Johann Theo-
dor de. Indiae Orientalis pars
undecima. Oppenheim: 1619
—Indiae Orientalis Pars X.
Frankfurt a.M.: Widow of M.
Becker, 1613
— —Frankfurt a.M.: W. Fitzer,
1633
—Zehender Theil der Orientali-
schen Indien. Frankfurt a.M.:
Widow of M. Becker, 1613
—Zwölffte Schiffahrt. Oppen-
heim: H. Galler, for Widow of
L. Hulsius, 1614 (2)
— —Oppenheim: H. Galler, for
Widow of L. Hulsius, 1627
Geslin, Paul. Die heilige Welts-
beschreibung. Köthen: 1643
—La saincte chorographie. Sau-
mur: J. Lesnier, & I. Des-
bordes, for C. Girard, 1629
—La sainte chorographie. Am-
sterdam: L. Elsevier, 1641
Gesner, Konrad. Historia ani-
malium. Frankfurt a.M.: A.
Cambier, 1604
— —Frankfurt a.M.: E. Emmel,
for H. Laurenszoon [at Am-
sterdam], 1617
— —See also Topsell, Edward.
The historie of foure-footed
beastes. London: 1607
—Icones avium omnium. Heidel-

berg: J. Lancellot, for A. Cam-
bier, 1606
—Köstlicher Artzneyschatz. Zu-
rich: 1608
—Mithridates Gesneri. Zurich:
Wolf Press, 1610
—Nomenclator aquatilium. Hei-
delberg: J. Lancellot, for A.
Cambier, 1606
—Quatre livres des Secrets de
medecine. Lyons: P. Rigaud,
1616
— —Rouen: P. Calles, 1616
— —Rouen: J. B. Behourt, 1628
—Secrets de medecine. Rouen:
N. L'Oyselet, 1643
—Thesaurus Euonymi. In Vege,
Petrus de. Pax methodicorum.
Lyons: 1620
—Thierbuch. Heidelberg: J.
Lancellot, for A. Cambier,
1606
Gesprachspiele. See Harsdörffer,
Georg Philipp
Gesprächspiele. See Harsdörffer,
Georg Philipp
Gesprechspiele. See Harsdörffer,
Georg Philipp
**De gesteeurde Hollantsche
leeuw.** [Amsterdam?] 1650 (2)
—[The Hague?] 1650
De getemde Mars. See Vondel,
Joost van den
Ghedenck-weerdich verhael
van t'ghene datter ghepasseert
is. Rotterdam: J. Janszoon,
1630
**Het ghelichte Munstersche
mom-aensicht.** [Flushing?]
1646
Gheluck-wenschinghe aan de
West-Indische vlote. Amster-
dam: B. Janszoon, 1624
De ghemeene directeurs, ghe-
stelt tottet formeren vande ca-
pitalen. See Nederlandsche
West-Indische Compagnie
De ghepretendeerden overlast.
[Middelburg?] 1638
Ghespreck van Langhe Piet.
[The Hague? 1629]
Ghetrouwen raedt. [Amster-
dam? 1608] (See Een oud
schipper)
GIANTS
—Bacci, A. De thermis. Rome:
1622

—Clarke, S. A mirrour or look-
ing-glasse. London: 1646
—Espinel, V. Relaciones de la
vida del escudero Marcos de
Obregon. Madrid: 1618
—Leonardo y Argensola, B. J.
Conquista de las islas Malucas.
Madrid: 1609
—Liceti, F. De monstrorum caus-
sis. Padua: 1616
—Riolan, J., the Younger. Gigan-
tologie. Paris: 1618
—Topsell, E. The historie of
foure-footed beastes. London:
1607
Giardino di fiori curiosi. See Tor-
quemada, Antonio de
Gigantologie. See Riolan, Jean,
the Younger
Gil Polo, Gaspar. See Polo, Gas-
par Gil
Gilbert, William. Tractatus
. . . de magnete. Stettin: Götz
Press, for J. Hallervord, 1628
— —Frankfurt a.M.: 1629
— —Stettin: Götz Press, 1633
Gillespie, George. Wholsome
severity. London: C. Meredith,
1645
Giornale overo Descrittione. See
Schouten, Willem Cornelis-
zoon
Giovio, Paolo, Bp. Delle istorie
del suo tempo. Venice: Sign of
Concordia, 1608
Glapthorne, Henry. Wit in a
constable. London: J. Okes,
for F. C[onstable], 1640
Glen, Jean Baptiste de. Des ha-
bits, moeurs, ceremonies
. . . du monde. Liège: J. de
Glen, 1601
Globe maritime. See Scotto, Be-
nedetto
Gloriosa coroa d'esforçados reli-
giosos. See Guerreiro, Bartho-
lomeu
Gloriosus Franciscus redivivus.
See Marianus de Orscelar
The glorious progress of the
Gospel, amongst the Indians.
See Winslow, Edward
Gobeo de Victoria, Pedro. See
Victoria, Pedro Gobeo de
Goddard, William. A neaste of
waspes. Dort: 1615

Godefroy, Théodore. Le ceremonial françois. Paris: S. Cramoisy, for G. Cramoisy, 1649

Gods power and providence:
shewed . . . in Green-land. *See*
Pellham, Edward

Gods promise to His plantation.
See Cotton, John

Goede nieuwe tijdinghe. *See* Willekens, Jacob

Gölnitz, Abraham. Compendium geographicum. Amsterdam: L. Elsevier, 1643

——Amsterdam: [J. Blaeu? for]
L. Elsevier, 1649

Goes, Damião de. Chronica do
felicissimo rey Dom Emanuel.
Lisbon: A. Alvarez, 1619

—Fides, religio, et mores Aethiopum. *In* Boemus, Johann.
Mores, leges, et ritus omnium
gentium. [Geneva:] 1604

——*In the same.* Geneva: 1620

—*See also* Mylius, Arnold, comp.
De rebus hispanicis. Cologne:
1602

Il Goffredo. *See* Tasso, Torquato

GOLD

—Collibus, H. à. Fürstliche
Tischreden. Frankfurt a.M.:
1614

—Hieron, S. An answer to a popish ryme. London: 1604

—Hodson, W. The divine cosmographer. Cambridge: 1640

—Hooker, T. The danger of desertion. London: 1641

—Rowlands, S. A fooles bolt is
soon shot. London: 1614

—Vázquez de Serna, J. Libro intitulado Reduciones de oro.
Cadiz: 1620

—Vertooninghe aen de Vereen-
nichde Provintien. [Amster-
dam? 160–?]

—Wonderlicke avontuer van
twee goelieven. Leyden: 1624

—Wright, T. The passions of the
minde. London: 1601

—Zeiller, M. Ein Hundert Episteln. Heilbronn: 1640

GOLD—PERU

—Baardt, P. Loff-en-lijck-gedicht. Leeuwarden: 1633

—Bodin, J. Discours . . . sur le
rehaussement. [Geneva?]
1608

—Glen, J. B. de. Des habits,
moeurs, ceremonies . . . du
monde. Liège: 1601

—Harris, R. The arraignment of
the whole creature. London:
1631

—Leather: a discourse. London:
1629

—Philopatroös, E. Nieuw-
keulsch of Spaensch bedrogh.
[Amsterdam?] 1638

GOLD—POETRY

—Leonardo y Argensola, L. Rimas de Lupercio. Saragossa:
1634

GOLD MINES AND MINING

—Dekker, T. Worke for armorours. London: 1609

—Foreest, J. van. Idyllia sive Heroes. [Leyden:] 1605

—The treasurie of auncient and
moderne times. London: 1613

The golden fleece. *See* Vaughan,
William

The golden-grove. *See* Vaughan,
William

The golden trade. *See* Jobson,
Richard

Golding, William. Servants on
horse-back. [London:] 1648

Gómara, Francisco López de.
Histoire generalle des Indes
Occidentales. Paris: L. Son-
nius, 1601

——Paris: M. Sonnius, 1605

——Paris: M. Sonnius, 1606 (2)

GÓMARA, FRANCISCO LÓ-
PEZ DE

—Del Rio, M. A. Les controverses et recherches magiques.
Paris: 1611

——Disquisitionum magicarum
libri sex. Mainz: 1603

**Gomberville, Marin Le Roy,
sieur du Parc et de.** L'exil de
Polexandre. Paris: T. Du Bray,
1629 (2)

—The history of Polexander.
London: T. Harper, for
T. Walkley, 1647

——London: T. Harper, for
T. Walkley, 1648

—Il Polessandro. Venice: The
Guerigli, 1647

—Polexandre. Paris: T. Du Bray,
1632

——Paris: A. Courbé, 1637

——Paris: A. Courbé, 1638

——Paris: A. Courbé, 1641

——Paris: A. Courbé, 1645

Gómes Solis, Duarte. *See* Gómez
Solis, Duarte

Gómez Solis, Duarte. Carta que
Duarte Gomez escrivio. [Ma-
drid: 1622]

—Discursos sobre los comercios.
[Madrid:] P. Taso, 1622

**Gómez Tejada de los Reyes,
Cosmé.** El filosofo. Madrid: D.
García Morrás, for S. Martín
Velláz, 1650

Góngora y Argote, Luis de.
Obras. Madrid: Imprenta Real,
& D. Díaz de la Carrera, 1636–
48

——Madrid: D. Díaz de la Carrera, for P. Laso, 1645–48

——Lisbon: P. Craesbeeck,
1646–47

—Obras en verso del Homero
español. Madrid: Widow of L.
Sánchez, for A. Pérez, 1627

—Soledades. Madrid: Imprenta
Real, for D. González, 1636

——*In his* Obras en verso. Madrid: 1627

—Todas las obras. Madrid: Imprenta Real, for A. Pérez, 1633

——Madrid: Imprenta Real, for
A. Pérez, 1634

——Madrid: Maria de Qui-
ñones, 1635

——Saragossa: P. Verges, for P.
Escuer, 1643

——Seville: N. Rodríguez,
1648

**Gonsalvius, Reginaldus, Mon-
tanus.** A discovery and plaine
declaration. London: J. Bellamy, 1625

—A full, ample and punctuall
discovery. London: J. Bellamy,
1625

—Der heyliger Hispanischer inquisitie etliche . . . consten.
The Hague: A. Meuris, 1620

—Sanctae Inquisitionis Hispanicae. *See* Beringer, Joachim.
Hispanicae Inquisitionis . . .
secretiora. Amberg: 1611

Gonzaga, Francisco, Bp. De origine seraphicae religionis franciscanae. Venice: D. Imberti,
1603

—*See also* Hendschel, Tobias. Englischen Liebbrinnendten S. Francisci Ordens Relations Continuation. Ingolstadt: 1617

González, Juan. El licenciado don Iuan Gonçalez. [Madrid? 1642?]

González Chaparro, Juan. Carta del p. Juan Gonzalez Chaparro. [Madrid? 1648?]

——Madrid: D. Díaz de la Carrera, 1648

—Lettera . . . ove s'intendono casi . . . del terremoto. Rome: L. Grignani, 1648

—Relacion del gran terremoto. Seville: F. de Lyra, 1648

—Relation dell'horrible tremblement. Brussels: J. Mommaert, 1648

González Dávila, Gil. Teatro eclesiastico de la primitiva iglesia. Madrid: D. Díaz de la Carrera, 1649–55

González de Azevedo, Juan. Señor. El capitan Iuan Goncalez de Azevedo. [Madrid: 1615?]

—Señor. El capitan Juan Gonçalez de Azevado, por lo que toca al servicio de Dios. [Madrid? 1615?]

González de Legaria, Juan. Aqui se contiene una obra graciosa. Madrid: C. Sánchez, for L. Sánchez, 1642

—Aqui se contiene una obra nueva, graciosa. Lisbon: V. Alvarez, 1608

González de Mendoza, Juan, Bp. Histoire du grand royaume de la Chine. [Geneva:] J. Arnaud, 1606

——Geneva: J. Arnaud, 1606

——Lyons: F. Arnoullet, 1609

——Rouen: N. Angot, 1614

——Rouen: N. Angot, 1643

González de Mendoza, Pedro. El licenciado Don Pedro Gonçalez de Mendoça. [Madrid: 1639?]

González de Nájera, Alonso. El quinto, y sexto punto de la relacion. [Madrid? ca. 1607?]

González de Ribero, Blas. Por Andres de Zavala. [Madrid? 1640?]

The good and the badde. *See* Breton, Nicholas

The good huswifes jewell. *See* Dawson, Thomas

Good newes. *See* Rowlands, Samuel

Good newes from New-England. *See* Winslow, Edward

Good newes from Virginia. London: J. Trundle [1624?]

Good newes from Virginia. *See* Whitaker, Alexander

Good news from New England. *See* Johnson, Edward

A good speed to Virginia. *See* Gray, Robert

Goodall, Baptist. The tryall of travell. London: J. Norton, for J. Upton, 1630

——London: J. Norton, 1639

Goodwin, John. M. S. to A. S. London: F. N[eile]., for H. Overton, 1644

—A reply of two of the brethren. London: M. Simmons, for H. Overton, 1644 (2)

——*See also* Steuart, Adam. The second part of the duply. London: 1644

Gordon, Sir Robert, of Lochinvar. Encouragements. Edinburgh: J. Wreittoun, 1625

Gorton, Samuel. Simplicities defence. London: J. Macock, for L. Fawne, 1646

——London: J. Macock, for G. Wittington, 1647

GORTON, SAMUEL

—Edwards, T. Gangraena, pt 2. London: 1646

—Hinc illae lachrymae. or The impietie of impunitie. London: 1648

—Winslow, E. The dangers of tolerating levellers. London: 1649

——Hypocrisie unmasked. London: 1646

Gospel conversion. *See* Cotton, John

The gospel-covenant. *See* Bulkeley, Peter

Gospel musick. *See* Holmes, Nathaniel

Gottfried, Johann Ludwig. Newe Welt und Amerikanische Historien. Frankfurt a.M.: M. Merian, 1631

Gough, John. The strange discovery. London: E. G[riffin]., for W. Leake, 1640 (2)

Goulart, Simon. Admirable and memorable histories. London: G. Eld, 1607

—Histoires admirables et memorables. Paris: J. Houzé, 1603

——Arras: G. de La Rivière, 1604

——Paris: J. Houzé, 1606

——Rouen: T. Daré, 1606

——Paris: J. Houzé, 1607

——Paris: J. Houzé, 1618

—Histoires de nostre temps, t 2–3. Paris: J. Houzé, 1601

—Les memoires de la Ligue . . . Premier volume. [Geneva?] 1602

—Le quatriesme recueil contenant l'histoire de la Ligue [Geneva?] 1604

—Le sage vieillard. Lyons: 1605

——Lyons: [J. Poyet] for A. de Harsy, 1606

—[Schat-camer der wonderbare ende gedencweerdige historien.] Delft: J. A. Cloeting, 1614

—Schatzkammer uber naturlicher . . . Geschichten. Strassburg: P. Ledertz, 1613–14

—Le second recueil, contenant l'histoire des choses plus memorables advenues sous la Ligue. [Geneva?] 1602

—Thresor d'histoires admirables. [Geneva:] P. Marceau, 1610

——Geneva: S. Crespin, 1620

——Geneva: S. Crespin, 1628

—Der weise Alte. Köthen: 1643

—The wise old man. London: N. Bourne, 1621

—The wise vieillard. London: J. Dawson, 1621

See also the following:

—Du Bartas, Guillaume de Salluste, seigneur. A learned summary. London: 1621

——Les oeuvres poétiques. [Geneva:] 1601

— —Premiere sepmaine . . . La seconde sepmaine. Rouen: 1602

— —La seconde sepmaine. Rouen: 1602

— —La sepmaine. [Geneva:] 1601

Goveo de Victoria, Pedro. *See* Victoria, Pedro Gobeo de

El governador Don Francisco Davila y Lugo. *See* Avila y Lugo, Francisco de

Governor and Company of Noblemen and Gentlemen of England for the Plantation of Guiana. Breefe notes of the River Amazones. [London? 1627]

—A breefe relation of the present state of the business of Guiana. [London? 1627]

—The coppie of the preamble, for the subscriptions. [London? 1627]

Gracián, Jerónimo. Lampara encendida. Madrid: J.de la Cuesta, 1604

—Obras. Madrid: Widow of A. Martín, 1616

—Zelo de la propagacion de la fee. Brussels: J. Mommaert, 1609

— —*In his* Obras. Madrid: 1616

—Zelo della propagatione della fede. Rome: 1620

—Zelo della propagazione della fede. Rome: S. Paolini, 1610

Grahame, Simion. The anatomie of humors. Edinburgh: T. Finlason, 1609

Gramatica en la lengua general del nuevo reyno. *See* Lugo, Bernardo de

Granado, Diego. Libro del arte de cozina. Madrid: A. Martín, 1609

— —Lérida: L. Menescal, 1614

Le grand dictionaire françoislatin. [Geneva:] J. Stoer, 1603

—Geneva: J. Stoer, 1625

—Lyons: C. Larjot, 1625

—Rouen: R. L'Allemant, 1625

Le grand dictionnaire françoislatin. Paris: N. Buon, 1614

—Paris: S. Chapellet, 1618

—Rouen: R. L'Allemant, 1618

—Rouen: J. Osmont, 1618

—Rouen: J. Osmont, 1628

Le grand dispensaire. *See* Wecker, Johann Jakob

Le grand dispensaire medicinal. *See* Renou, Jean de

Le grand voyage du pays des Hurons. *See* Sagard, Gabriel

La grande chirurgie. *See* Paracelsus

La grande deffaite des Espagnols. Paris: M. Colombel, 1634

Grandezas y antiguedades. *See* Suárez de Salazar, Juan Bautista

Graswinckel, Dirk. Aen-spraek aen den getrouwen Hollander. [Amsterdam?] 1645

— —The Hague: I. Burchoorn, 1645

—Libertas Veneta. Leyden: A. Commelin, 1634

Gratulaçao de Menasseh ben Israel. *See* Manasseh ben Joseph ben Israel

Grau y Monfalcón, Juan. Justification de la conservacion. [Madrid: 1640]

—Memorial . . . en defensa de Don Antonio Urrutia de Vergara. [Madrid? 1641?]

—Memorial informativo al Rey. Madrid: Imprenta Real, 1637

—Señor. Don Juan Grau y Monfalcon, procurador general. [Madrid? 164–?]

Gravina, Domenico. Vox turturis. Naples: S. Roncalioli, 1625

— —Cologne: M. Demen, 1627

— —Cologne: H. Krafft, 1638

Gray, Robert. A good speed to Virginia. London: F. Kingston, for W. Welby, 1609

Great Britain. Council for Virginia. [The articles sett down for the second lottery. London: W. Welby, 1612]

—A briefe declaration of the present state of things in Virginia. [London: T. Snodham, 1616]

—By His Majesties Commissioners for Virginia. London: F. Kingston, 1624

—By his Majesties Councell for Virginia . . . a little standing lotterie. [London:] F. Kingston, for W. Welby, 1613

—By his Majesties Counsell for Virginea . . . for the advancement of . . . Virginia. London: F. Kingston, for W. Welby, 1612

—By the Counsell of Virginia. Seeing it hath pleased God. London: [T. Haveland] for W. Welby, 1611

—By the Counsell of Virginia. Whereas the good shippe . . . is now preparing. [London: T. Haveland, 1610]

—Considering there is no publicke action. [London: 1609?]

—A declaration of the state of the colonie . . . in Virginia. London: T. S[nodham, & F. Kingston]. 1620 (3)

— —London: T. Snodham [& F. Kingston], 1620 (2)

—[The lottery for Virginea. London: W. Welby, 1612]

—A publication by the Counsell of Virginea. London: T. Haveland, for W. Welby, 1610

—Whereas upon the returne of sir Thomas Dale. [London: T. Snodham, 1617?]

Great Britain. Laws, statutes, etc., 1625–1649 (Charles I). A commission for the well governing of our people . . . in New-foundland. London: R. Barker, & Assigns of J. Bill, 1633 [i.e., 1634]

—An order of Parliament for . . . the observation of the Sabath day. [London:] R. Cotes, 1643

—An ordinance . . . for the regulating of the rates. London: R. Cotes, & J. Raworth, 1644 (2)

—An ordinance of the Lords and Commons . . . concerning . . . tobacco. London: R. Cotes, & J. Raworth, 1643

— —London: R. Cotes, & J. Raworth [1643]

—An ordinance of the Lords and Commons . . . whereby Robert earle of Warwicke is made governour. London: J. Wright, 1643

—The rates of marchandizes.

—True religion explained. London: J. H[aviland]., for R. Royston, 1632

—Van de oudheydt der Batavische . . . republique. Haarlem: A. Roman, 1636

——Haarlem: A. Roman, 1639

——Haarlem: A. Roman, 1641

—La verité de la religion chrestienne. Paris: Printshop of the New Type invented by P. Moreau, for F. Rouvelin [1644]

—Von der Warheit der christlichen Religion. Brieg: A. Gründer, for D. Müller, at Breslau, 1631

——*See also his* Die Meinung der Bücher. [Breslau:] 1631

—Vrye zeevaert. Leyden: J. Huybertszoon, 1614 (2)

——Leyden: J. Huybertszoon, for W. J. Blaeu, at Amsterdam, 1614

——Haarlem: A. Roman, 1636

——Haarlem: A. Roman, 1639

——Haarlem: A. Roman, 1641

GROTIUS, HUGO

—Freitas, S. de. De justo imperio Lusitanorum asiatico. Valladolid: 1625

—Poisson, J. B. Animadversio. Paris: 1644

—Selden, J. Mare clausum. London: 1635

Grüling, Philipp Gerhard. Florilegium chymicum. Leipzig: G. Gross, 1631

—Florilegium Hippocrateo-Galeno-chymicorum. Leipzig: T. Ritzsch, for Heirs of G. Gross, 1644

——Leipzig: T. Ritzsch, for Heirs of G. Gross, 1645

Gruelingius, Philippus. *See* Grüling, Philipp Gerhard

Gründliches . . . Artzney Buch. *See* Khunrath, Conrad. Medulla destillatoria et medica. Hamburg: 1605

Gruterus, Janus. Chronicon chronicorum ecclesiastico-politicum. Frankfurt a.M.: Aubry Office, 1614

GUADALAJARA, MEXICO—HISTORY

—Mariana, ——, licenciado.

Carta que escrivio el licenciado Mariana. [Madrid? 1636]

GUAIACUM

—Alonso y de los Ruyses de Fontecha, J. Diez previlegios para mugeres preñadas. Alcalá de Henares: 1606

—Amatus Lusitanus. Curationum medicinalium centuriae septem. Bordeaux: 1620

—Augenio, O. Epistolarum et consultationum medicinalium . . . libri xii. Venice: 1602

—Bacon, F. Histoire de la vie. Paris: 1647

——Historia vitae. London: 1623

——The historie of life. London: 1638

——History naturall. London: 1638

—Baillou, G. de. Consiliorum medicinalium libri ii. Paris: 1635

—Banister, J. The workes. London: 1633

—Barrough, P. The method of phisick. London: 1601

—Basilius Valentinus. Haliographia. De praeparatione . . . omnium salium. Bologna: 1644

—Bauderon, B. Paraphrase sur la Pharmacopoee. Lyons: 1607

——Pharmacopee. Paris: 1636

——Pharmacopoea. London: 1639

—Bauhin, K. De compositione medicamentorum. Offenbach: 1610

—Béguin, J. Les elemens de chymie. Paris: 1615

——Tyrocinium chymicum. Paris: 1612

—Bellinzani, L. Il mercurio estinto resuscitato. Rome: 1648

—Bertaldi, G. L. Medicamentorum apparatus. Turin: 1612

—Besard, J. B. Antrum philosophicum. Augsburg: 1617

—Blundeville, T. M. Blundeville his Exercises. London: 1606

—Bologna. Università. Collegio di Medicina. Antidotarium Bononien. Bologna: 1641

—Bompart, M. Nouveau chasse peste. Paris: 1630

—Bonham, T. The chyrurgeons closet. London: 1630

—Bonnart, J. La semaine des medicaments. Paris: 1629

—Bovionier, F. Quaestio medica . . . in Scholis Medicorum. [Paris: 1649]

—Bruele, G. Praxis medicinae. Venice: 1602

——Praxis medicinae, or, The physicians practise. London: 1632

—Brunner, B. Consilia medica. Halle: 1617

—Calestani, G. Delle osservationi. Venice: 1606

—Canale, F. De' secreti universali raccolti. Brescia: 1613

—Canevari, D. De ligno sancto commentarium. Rome: 1602

—Capivaccio, G. Opera omnia. Frankfurt a.M.: 1603

—Caro, A. De le lettere familiari. Venice: 1603

—Castillo, Juan del. Pharmacopoea, universa medicamenta. Cadiz: 1622

—Cesalpino, A. Artis medicae pars prima. Rome: 1602

—Chaumette, A. Enchiridion, ou Livret portatif pour les chirurgiens. Lyons: 1609

——Handt-boeck der chirurgie. Arnhem: 1640

——Le parfaict chirurgien. Paris: 1628

—Clowes, W. A profitable and necessarie booke. London: 1637

—Colle, G. Elucidarium anatomicum. Venice: 1621

—Collège des Maîtres chirurgiens de Paris. Traicté de la peste. Paris: 1619

—Columba, G. Disputationum medicarum . . . libri duo. Frankfurt a.M.: 1601

—Cooke, J. Mellificium chirurgiae . . . the art of chyrurgery. London: 1648

—Cortesi, G. B. Pharmacopoeia, seu Antidotarium messanense. Messina: 1629

—Croce, G. A. della. Cirugia universale. Venice: 1605

——Officina aurea; das ist, Guldene Werckstatt der Chirurgy. Frankfurt a.M.: 1607

—Dispensatorium chymicum. Frankfurt a.M.: 1626

—Donati, M. De historia medica mirabili libri sex. Frankfurt a.M.: 1613

—Duchesne, J. Ad veritatem hermeticae medicinae. Paris: 1604

— —Liber de priscorum philosophorum verae medicinae materia. Saint Gervais: 1603

— —The practise of chymicall . . . physicke. London: 1605

— —Quercetanus redivivus. Frankfurt a.M.: 1648

— —Traicté de la matiere . . . de la medecine balsamique. Paris: 1626

—Du Fail, N., seigneur de La Herissaye. Les contes et discours d'Eutrapel. Rennes: 1603

—Duport, F. Medica decas. Paris: 1613

—Emili, P. De rebus gestis Francorum. Basel: [1601]

—Enchiridion practicum medico-chirurgicum. Geneva: 1621

—Erastus, T. Examen de simplicibus. Lyons: 1607

—Eugalenus, S. De scorbuto morbo liber. Leipzig: 1604

—Fabre, P. J. Myrothecium spagyricum. Toulouse: 1628

—Fabricius, H. Medecina practica. Paris: 1634

—Fernel, J. Traité de . . . la parfaite cure. Paris: 1633

— —Universa medicina. Lyons: 1601

—Fioravanti, L. La cirugia. Venice: 1610

— —Compendium oder Ausszug der Secreten. Darmstadt: 1624

— —Del compendio de' secreti rationali. Venice: 1620

— —A discourse upon chyrurgery. London: 1626

— —Il tesoro della vita humana. Venice: 1603

—Fonseca, R. Consultationum medicinalium singularibus remediis refertae. Venice: 1619

—Fonteyn, N. Responsionum et

curationum medicinalium liber unus. Amsterdam: 1639

—Foreest, P. van. Observationum et curationum medicinalium liber xxxii. Leyden: 1606

—Fragoso, J. Cirugia universal. Alcalá de Henares: 1607

— —Della cirugia. Palermo: 1639

—Gabelkover, W. Curationum et observationum, centuria V. Tübingen: 1627

—Gesner, K. Köstlicher Artzneyschatz. Zurich: 1608

— —Quatre livres des Secrets de medecine. Rouen: 1616

—Grüling, P. G. Florilegium chymicum. Leipzig: 1631

—Guarinoni, C. Consilia medicinalia. Venice: 1610

—Guibert, P. Le prix et valeur des medicamens. Paris: 1625

—Guidi, G. Ars medicinalis. Venice: 1611

—Guillaumet, T. Traicté de la maladie nouvellement appelee cristaline. Lyons: 1611

— —Traicté second de la maladie appelee cristaline. Nîmes: 1614

—Habicot, N. Problesmes medicinaux et chirurgicaux. Paris: 1617

—Héry, T. de. La methode curatoire de la maladie venerienne. Paris: 1634

—Hester, J. The secrets of physick. London: 1633

—Hobbes, S. Margarita chyrurgica. London: 1610

—Hollings, E. Medicamentorum oeconomia nova. Ingolstadt: 1610

—Hornung, J. Cista medica. Nuremberg: [1626]

—Jonstonus, J. Idea universae medicinae practicae. Amsterdam: 1644

—Juncker, J. Compendiosa methodus therapeutica. [Erfurt:] 1624

—Junius, H. Nomenclator octilinguis. Geneva: 1602

—Khunrath, C. Medulla destillatoria et medica. Hamburg: 1601

—Knobloch, T. De lue venerea,

von Frantzosen kurtzer Bericht. Giessen: 1620

—Lange, J. Epistolarum medicinalium. Hanau: 1605

—Langham, W. The garden of health. London: 1633

—León, A. de. Practico de morbo gallico. Valladolid: 1605

—Libavius, A. Alchymia. Frankfurt a.M.: 1606

— —Alchymia triumphans. Frankfurt a.M.: 1607

— —Alchymistische Practic. Frankfurt a.M.: 1603

— —Praxis alchymiae. Frankfurt a.M.: 1604

— —Syntagma selectorum. Frankfurt a.M.: 1611

—Lodge, T. A treatise of the plague. London: 1603

—Lowe, P. A discourse of . . . chyrurgerie. London: 1612

—Loyseau, G. De internorum externorumque ferme omnium curatione libellus. Bordeaux: 1617

— —Observations medicinales et chirurgicales. Bordeaux: 1617

—Macchelli, N. Tractatus methodicus . . . de lue venerea. Frankfurt a.M.: 1608

—Madeira Arraes, D. Methodo de conhecer e curar o morbo gallico. Lisbon: 1642

—Manardo, G. Iatrologia epistolikē, sive Curia medica. Hanau: 1611

—Marinelli, C. Pharmacopaea. Hanau: 1617

—Marquardus, J. Practica medicinalis. Frankfurt a.M.: 1610

—Massaria, A. Liber responsorum et consultationum medicinalium. Lyons: 1622

— —Opera medica. Lyons: 1634

— —Practica medica. Frankfurt a.M.: 1601

—Mercuriale, G. Medicina practica. Frankfurt a.M.: 1601

— —Praelectiones Patavinae. Venice: 1603

—Messina. Ospedale di Santa Maria della Pietà. Antidotarium speciale. Venice: 1642

778

bocabulario de la lengua Guarani. Madrid: 1640

——Catecismo de la lengua guarani. Madrid: 1640

——Tesoro de la lengua guarani. Madrid: 1639

GUARARAPES, BATTLE OF, 1649

—Relacion de la victoria que los portugueses . . . alcançaron. [Madrid?] 1649

Guarguante, Orazio. Responsa varia, ad varias aegritudines. Venice: A. & B. Dei, 1613

Guarinoni, Cristoforo. Consilia medicinalia. Venice: T. Baglioni, 1610

GUATEMALA—HISTORY

—Avila y Lugo, F. de. El governador Don Francisco Davila y Lugo [Madrid: 1647?]

—Peraza de Ayala y Rojas, A. Señor. Don Antonio Peraça de Ayala y Rojas. [Madrid? 1623?]

—Remesal, A. de. Historia de la provincia de S. Vincente. Madrid: 1619

——Historia general de las Indias Ocidentales. Madrid: 1620

—Valcarcel, F. de. Por Don Carlos Vazquez Coronado, vezino de Guatimala. [Madrid? 1632]

GUATEMALA—POLITICS & GOVERNMENT

—Camargo, G. de. Por el real fisco. [Madrid? ca. 1646?]

GUAYAQUIL

—Rodríguez Bustamante, S. Sebastian Rodriguez Bustamante, contador de la real hazienda. [Madrid: 1625]

Guelen, August de. Brieve relation de l'estat de Phernambucq. Amsterdam: L. Elsevier, 1640

—Kort verhael vanden staet van Fernanbuc. Amsterdam: 1640

Guerra de Chile. See Tesillo, Santiago de

Guerra de Granada. See Hurtado de Mendoza, Diego

Guerreiro, Bartholomeu. Gloriosa coroa d'esforçados religiosos. Lisbon: A. Alvarez, 1642

—Jornado dos vassalos da coroa

de Portugal. Lisbon: M. Pinheiro, for F. Alvarez, 1625

—Sermão que fez o padre Bartolameu Guerreiro. Lisbon: P. Craesbeeck, 1624

Guerreiro, Fernão. Relaçam anual das cousas que fezeram os padres de Companhia de Jesus. Lisbon: J. Rodriguez, 1605

——Lisbon: P. Craesbeeck, 1609

Guerrero, Marcos. Por los herederos del doctor don Marcos Guerrero. [Madrid: 1615?]

Le gueux. See Alemán, Mateo

Guia y avisos de forasteros. See Liñán y Verdugo, Antonio

GUIANA

—Governor and Company of Noblemen and Gentlemen of England for the Plantation of Guiana. Breefe notes of the River Amazones. [London? 1627]

—Raleigh, Sir W. Apologie for his voyage to Guiana. London: 1650

——, defendant. The arraignment and conviction of Sr Walter Rawleigh. London: 1648

—Stucley, Sir L. To the Kings most excellent majestie. London: 1618

GUIANA—COMMERCE

—Governor and Company of Nobleman and Gentlemen of England for the Plantation of Guiana. A breefe relation of the present state of the business of Guiana. [London? 1627]

——The coppie of the preamble, for the subscriptions. [London? 1627]

GUIANA—DESCRIPTION

—Harcourt, R. A relation of . . . Guiana. London: 1613

—Newes of Sr. Walter Rauleigh. London: 1618

—Raleigh, Sir W. Achter Theil Americae. Frankfurt a.M.: 1624

——Die fünffte kurtze wunderbare Beschreibung. Nuremberg: 1603

——Kurtze wunderbare Be-

schreibung dess . . . Königreichs Guianae. Nuremberg: 1601

——Warachtighe ende grondighe beschryvinghe van . . . Guiana. Amsterdam: 1605

GUIANA—DISCOVERY AND EXPLORATION

—A declaration of the demeanor . . . of Sir Walter Raleigh. London: 1618

—Great Britain. Sovereigns, etc., 1603–1625 (James I). A proclamation declaring His Majesties pleasure concerning Sir Walter Rawleigh. London: 1618

—Howell, J. Epistolae Ho-elianae. Familiar letters. London: 1645

——A new volume of letters. London: 1647

—Verclaringe ende verhael hoe de Heere Wouter Raleigh . . . hem ghedreghen heeft. The Hague: 1619

GUIANA—DRAMA

—Shakespeare, W. A most pleasaunt . . . comedie, of syr John Falstaffe, and the merrie wives of Windsor. London: 1602

Guibert, Nicolas. De interitu alchymiae. Toul: S. Philippe, 1614

Guibert, Philbert. Les oeuvres charitables. Paris: J. Jost, 1629

——Paris: J. Jost, 1630, '29

——Paris: J. Jost, 1632

—Les oeuvres du medecin charitable. Lyons: J. Huguetan, 1634

——Paris: C. Collet, 1634

——Paris: C. Griset, 1634

——Paris: J. Gesselin, 1637

—Le prix et valeur des medicamens. Paris: D. Langlois, 1625

——Paris: D. Langlois, 1626

——Paris: D. Langlois, 1627

——*In his* Les oeuvres charitables. Paris: 1629, *et seq.*

——*In his* Toutes les oeuvres, charitables. Paris: 1633, *et seq.*

——*In his* Les oeuvres du medecin charitable. Lyons: 1634, *et seq.*

——Lyons: G. Chaunod, 1646

—Toutes les oeuvres charitables. Paris: J. Jost, 1633
— —Paris: J. Jost, 1637
— —Paris: J. Jost, 1639
— —Lyons: N. Gay, 1640
— —Lyons: Widow of C. Rigaud, & P. Borde, 1640
— —Rouen: O. Seigneuré, for C. Pitreson, 1641
— —Rouen: N. Loyselet, 1645
— —Paris: J. Jacquin, 1647
— —Paris: C. Marette, 1648

Guicciardini, Francesco. Historie des guerres d'Italie. Paris: P. Le Mur, 1612
— —Paris: J. Orry, 1612
—La historia d'Italia. Treviso: F. Zanetti, 1604
— —Venice: N. Polo, & F. Rampazetto, 1610
— —Venice: P. M. Bertano, 1616
— —[Geneva?] J. Stoer, 1621
— —Geneva: J. Stoer, 1621
— —Venice: A. Pasini, 1623
— —Geneva: J. Stoer, 1636
— —[Geneva:] J. Stoer, 1636
— —Venice: A. Baba, 1636
— —Venice: E. Baba, 1640
— —[Geneva:] J. Stoer, 1645
—The historie of Guicciardin. London: R. Field, for A. Johnson, 1618

Guidi, Guido. Ars medicinalis. Venice: Giunta Office, 1611
—Opera omnia, sive Ars medicinalis. Frankfurt a.M.: Wechel Office, for D. & D. Aubry, & C. Schleich, 1626

Guidi, Ippolito Camillo. Caduta del conte d'Olivares. Ivrea: 1644
—Relation de ce qui s'est passé en Espagne. Paris: A. Courbé, 1650

Guilbert, Philibert. *See* Guibert, Philbert

Guillaumet, Tannequin. Traicté de la maladie nouvellement appelee cristaline. Lyons: P. Rigaud, 1611
—Traicté second de la maladie appelee cristaline. Nîmes: J. Vaguenar, 1614

Guillén y Colón, Francisco. Vita, muerte y milagros del prodigioso varon. Seville: S. Fajardo, 1637

Guineische und West-Indianische Reissbeschreibung. *See* Hemmersam, Michael

The guls horne-booke. *See* Dekker, Thomas

GUMS AND RESINS
—Puteo, Z. Historia de gumma indica. Venice: 1628

Gunter, Edmund. The description and use of his Majesties dials. London: B. Norton, & J. Bill, 1624

Guron, Bernard de Rechignevoisin, seigneur de. *See* Rechignevoisin, Bernard de, seigneur de Guron

Guyon, Louis, sieur de la Nauche. Les diverses leçons. Lyons: C. Morillon, 1604
— —Lyons: C. Morillon, 1605
— —Lyons: C. Morillon, 1610
— —Lyons: C. Morillon, 1613
— —Lyons: A. Chard, 1625

Guzman de Alfarache. *See* Alemán, Mateo

Guzman, Luis de. Historia de las missiones. Alcalá de Henares: Widow of J. Gracian, 1601

Gysius, Johannes. Le miroir de la cruelle . . . tyrannie espagnole. Amsterdam: J. E. Cloppenburg, 1620
—Oorsprong en voortgang der neder-landtscher beroerten. [Leyden?] 1616
—Origo et historia Belgicorum tumultuum. Leyden: B. van der Bilt, 1619
— —Amsterdam: J. Janszoon the Younger, 1641
—De Spaensche tiranije gheschiet in Neder-Lant. Amsterdam: C. L. van der Plasse, 1621
— —Amsterdam: J. P. Wachter [1622]
— —[Amsterdam: 1623?]
— —Amsterdam: Widow of C. L. van der Plasse, 1641
—De Spaensche tirannij in Neder-Lant. Amsterdam: J. P. Wachter, 1633
—De spiegel der spaense tyrannye, 2de dl. Amsterdam: J. E. Cloppenburg, for E. Cloppenburg, 1638
—De spieghel der Spaensche

tyrannye, 2de dl. *In* Casas, Bartolome de las, Bp. Den spiegel der Spaensche tijrannije-geschiet in West-Indien. Amsterdam: 1620
— —Leyden: A. C. Hoogenacker, & D. van Vreeswijck, for J. E. Cloppenburg, at Amsterdam, 1628

H., A. *See* Gheluck-wenschinghe aan de West-Indische vlote. Amsterdam: 1624

Habicot, Nicolas. Problesmes medicinaux et chirurgicaux. Paris: J. Corrozet, 1617

Habrecht, Isaac. Planiglobium coeleste et terrestre. Strassburg: M.von der Heyden, 1628–29

Haerlems schuyt-praetjen. [Amsterdam?] 1649

Haestens, Hendrick van, jt. auth. *See* Orlers, Jan Janszn. Beschrijvinghe ende af-beeldinge van alle de victorien. Leyden: 1610

Hagthorpe, John. England's-exchequer. London: N. Butter, & N. Bourne, 1625

Hakewill, George. An apologie of the power . . . of God. Oxford: J. Lichfield, & W. Turner, 1627
—An apologie or declaration of the power . . . of God. Oxford: W. Turner, for R. Allott, at London, 1630
— —Oxford: W. Turner, for R. Allott, at London, 1635

Hakluyt, Richard. *See* Virginia richly valued, by the description of . . . Florida. London: 1609
—*See also* Le voyage de l'illustre . . . François Drach. Paris: 1613

HAKLUYT, RICHARD
—Fotherby, M., Bp. Atheomastix clearing foure truthes. London: 1622

An halfe-penny-worth of wit. *See* King, Humphrey

Haliographia. *See* Basilius Valentinus; *and also* Thoelde, Johann

Hall, Joseph, Bp. The discovery of a new world. London: [G.

Eld] for E. Blount, & W. Barrett [1609?]

—Mundus alter. Frankfurt a.M.: Heirs of A. de Rinialme [i.e., London: H. Lownes, 1605?]

——Frankfurt a.M.: Heirs of Rinialme [i.e., Hanau: W. Antonius, 1606?]

——Hanau: W. Antonius, 1607

——Utrecht: J. van Waesbergen, 1643

——Frankfurt a.M.: Heirs of Ascanius de Rinialme, 1648

—Mundus alter . . . verteutscht. Leipzig: J. Hermann, for H. Gross the Younger, 1613

—A survay of that foolish . . . libell. London: 1641

Hamcomius, Martinus. Frisia. Franeker: J. Lamrinck, 1620

Hamor, Ralph, the Younger. Dreyzehende Schiffahrt. Hanau: The Hulsiuses, 1617

—Dreyzehente Schiffahrt . . . von . . . Virginien. Hanau: The Hulsiuses, 1617

—Gründlicher Bericht von . . . Virginien. *In* Vespucci, Amerigo. Zehender Theil Americae. Oppenheim: 1618

—Solida narratio de moderno provinciae Virginiae statu. *In* Vespucci, Amerigo pars decima. Oppenheim: 1619

—A true discourse of . . . Virginia. London: J. Beale, for W. Welby, 1615

Hand-boeck, of Cort begrijp der caerten. *See* Langenes, Barent

Den handel ende wandel. [Amsterdam? 1637?]

Handt-boeck der chirurgie. *See* Chaumette, Antoine

Hans Beer-pot his invisible comedie. *See* Belchier, Dabridgcourt

Harangue funebre . . . du tres-illustre . . . Maurice de Nassau. *See* Heinsius, Daniel

Harcourt, Robert. A relation of a voyage to Guiana. London: J. Beale, for W. Welby, 1613

——London: E. Allde, 1626

Harduin, Philippe. Codex medicamentarius. Paris: O. de Varennes, 1645

Harington, Sir John. Epigrams both pleasant and serious. London: J. Budge, 1615

—The most elegant and wittie epigrams. London: G. P[urslowe]., for J. Budge, 1618

——London: T. S[nodham]., for J. Budge, 1625

——London: G. Miller, 1633

——*In* Ariosto, Lodovico. Orlando furioso, in English. London: 1634

Hariot, Thomas. Admiranda narratio . . . Virginiae. Frankfurt a.M.: J. Wechel, for T. de Bry, S. Feyerabend, 1590 [i.e., ca. 1608]

—Wunderbarliche . . . Erklärung von . . . Virginia. Oppenheim: H. Galler, for J. T. de Bry [at Frankfurt a.M.], 1620

Harrington, Sir John. *See* Harington, Sir John

Harris, Robert. The arraignment of the whole creature. London: B. Alsop, & T. Fawcet, 1631

—The drunkards cup. London: F. Kingston, for T. Man, 1619

——London: B. Alsop, for T. Man, 1622

——London: G. Purslowe, for J. Bartlet, 1626

——*In his* Six sermons. London: 1630

—Six sermons of conscience. London: H. L[ownes]., for J. Bartlet, 1630

Harsdörffer, Georg Philipp. Frauenzimmer Gesprechspiele. Nuremberg: 1641–49

—Gesprachspiele . . . dritter Theil. Nuremberg: W. Endter, 1643

—Gesprachspiele . . . vierter Theil. Nuremberg: W. Endter, 1644

—Gesprächspiele achter . . . Theil. Nuremberg: W. Endter, 1649

—Gesprächspiele siebender Theil. Nuremberg: W. Endter, 1647

—Gesprechspiele fünfter Theil. Nuremberg: W. Endter, 1645

—Gesprechspiele sechster Theil. Nuremberg: W. Endter, 1646

—Nathan und Jotham. Nuremberg: M. Endter, 1650–51

Hart, James. Klinikē, or The diet of the diseased. London: J. Beale, for R. Allott, 1633

Hartgers, Joost. Oost-Indische voyagien. Amsterdam: J. Hartgers, 1648

—Oost en Westindische voyagien, pt 1. Veer, Gerrit de. Verhael van de eerste schipvaert der Hollandische . . . schepen. Amsterdam: 1648

————Amsterdam: 1650

——, pt 2. Eerste schip-vaert der Hollanders. Amsterdam: 1648

———Amsterdam: 1650

——, pt 3. Neck, Jacob Cornelis-zoon van. Waerachtigh verhael van de schip-vaert op Oost-Indien. Amsterdam: 1648

——, pt 4. Noort, Olivier van. Wonderlijcke voyagie, by de Hollanders gedaen. Amsterdam: 1648

——, pt 5. Spilbergen, Joris van. Historis journael. Amsterdam: 1648

——, pt 6. Matelief, Cornelis. Journael ende Historische verhael van de treffelijcke reyse. Amsterdam: 1648

——, pt 7. Broeck, Pieter van den. Wonderlijcke historische ende Journaelsche aenteyckeningh. Amsterdam: 1648

——, pt 8. Spilbergen, Joris van. Oost- en West-Indische voyagie. Amsterdam: 1648

——, pt 9. Journael vande Nassausche vloot. Amsterdam: 1648

——, pt 10. Bontekoe, Willem Ysbrandsz. Journael . . . vande Oost-Indische reyse. Amsterdam: 1648

————Amsterdam: 1650

Hartmann, Johann. Praxis chymiatrica. Leipzig: J. A. Minzel, for G. Gross, 1633

——Frankfurt a.M.: K. Rötel, 1634

——Geneva: P. Chouët, 1635

——Geneva: J. de Tournes, & J. de La Pierre, 1635

——Geneva: P. Chouët, 1639

— —Oxford: W. Turner, & R. Allott, at London, 1633

— —Oxford: W. Turner, 1636

— —Oxford: W. Turner, 1639

— —Oxford: W. Turner, 1939 [i.e., 1639]

Heyn, Pieter. *See* Hein, Pieter Pieterszoon

Heyns, Zacharias. Dracht-tho-neel. *See under title*

—Emblemata. Rotterdam: P. van Waesberghe, 1625

Heywood, Thomas. Machiavel. as he has lately appeared. London: J. O[kes]., for F. Constable, 1641

—Machiavels ghost. London: J. O[kes]., for F. Constable, 1641

—Philocothonista, or The drunkard. London: R. Raworth, 1635

Hidrographia. *See* Figueiredo, Manuel de

Hieron, Samuel. An answer to a popish ryme. London: S. Stafford, 1604

—An answere to a popish ryme. [London:] H. L[ownes]., for S. Macham, 1608

— —London: S. Waterson, 1613

— —*In his* Workes. London: [1620?] (2)

— —*In his* Sermons. London: 1624–25

— —*In his* Workes. London: 1628–35

— —*In the same.* London: [1635, '34]

—The sermons. London: J. Legat, & W. Stansby, 1624–25

—Workes. London: W. Stansby, & J. Beale [1620?]

— —London: W. Stansby, for J. Parker [1620?]

— —London: W. Stansby, 1628–35

— —London: W. Stansby, & J. Beale [1635, '34]

HIERONYMITES IN SPANISH AMERICA

—José de Sigüenza. Historia de la orden de San Geronimo, pte 3a. Madrid: 1605

Higginson, Francis. New-Englands plantation. London: T. C[otes]., & R. C[otes]., for M. Sparke, 1630

— —London: T. Cotes, & R. Cotes, for M. Sparke, 1630 (2)

The high-waies of God. *See* Scott, Thomas

Hille, Carl Gustav von. Der teutsche Palmenbaum. Nuremberg: W. Endter, 1647

Hinc illae lachrymae. or The impietie of impunitie. London: 1648

Hind, John, supposed author. *See* Work for chimney-sweepers. London: 1602

Hipp-anthrōpos: or, An ironical expostulation. *See* Taylor, John, the Water-poet

His Majesties gracious letter. *See* Bonoeil, John

Hispania, sive De regis Hispaniae regnis . . . commentarium. *See* Laet, Joannes de

Hispaniae bibliotheca. *See* Schottus, Andreas

Hispaniae illustratae. *See* Schottus, Andreas

Hispanicae dominationis arcana. *See* Weidner, Johann Leonhard

Hispanicae Inquisitionis . . . secretiora. *See* Beringer, Joachim

HISPANIOLA. *See also* SANTO DOMINGO

—Gesner, K. Mithridates Gesneri. Zurich: 1610

—Lodge, T. A treatise of the plague. London: 1603

—Raleigh, Sir W. The history of the world. London: 1614

HISPANIOLA—HISTORY

—López de Castro, B. Baltasar Lopez de Castro, criado de su Magestad. Valladolid: 1603

Hispanus redux. *See* Foreest, Jan van

Histoire admirable . . . du père . . . S. Francois. *See* Weerts, Paul

Histoire admirable des plantes. *See* Duret, Claude

Histoire d'Elizabeth. *See* Camden, William

Histoire d'un voyage fait en la terre de Bresil. *See* Léry, Jean de

Histoire de . . . Don Quichot. *See* Cervantes Saavedra, Miguel de

Histoire de ce qui s'est passé au royaume du Japon. Paris: S. Cramoisy, 1633

Histoire de ce qui s'est passé en Ethiopie, Malabar, Brasil. *See* Jesuits. Letters from missions

Histoire de France. *See* Matthieu, Pierre

Histoire de l'empereur Charles V. *See* Roca, Juan Antonio Vera Zúñiga y Figueroa, conde de la

Histoire de la mission des peres Capucins. *See* Claude d'Abbeville, Father

Histoire de la navigation. *See* Linschoten, Jan Huygen van

Histoire de la Nouvelle France. *See* Lescarbot, Marc

Histoire de la premiere descouverte . . . des Canaries. *See* Bontier, Pierre

Histoire de la vie. *See* Bacon, Francis

Histoire de la vie . . . du tres-illustre, Maurice de Nassau. *See* Heinsius, Daniel

Histoire de nostre temps. *See* Chappuys, Gabriel; *and also* Malingre, Claude

Histoire de sainct Louys. *See* Matthieu, Pierre

L'histoire des choses plus memorables. *See* Du Jarric, Pierre

Histoire des drogues espiceries. *See* Orta, Garcia da

Histoire des guerres civiles des Espagnols. *See* Garcilaso de la Vega, el Inca

Histoire des guerres d'Italie. *See* Guicciardini, Francesco

Histoire des Indes. *See* Maffei, Giovanni Pietro

Histoire des Indes Occidentales. *See* Casas, Bartolomé de las, Bp

Histoire des martyres. *See* Crespin, Jean

L'histoire des Pays-Bas. *See* Meteren, Emanuel van

L'histoire des plantes. *See* Linocier, Geoffroy

Histoire des vents. *See* Bacon, Francis

Histoire du Canada. *See* Sagard, Gabriel

Histoire du grand royaume de la

Historisch ende wijdtloopigh verhael. *See* Potgieter, Barent Janszoon

Historisch verhael. *See* Wassenaer, Nicolaes van

Historische Beschreibung der wunderbarlichen Reyse. *See* Schouten, Willem Corneliszoon

Historische Beschreibung deren . . . weltlichen Geschichten. *See* Thou, Jacques Auguste de

Historische beschrijvinghe der . . . coopstadt Amsterdam. *See* Pontanus, Johannes Isaacus

Historische Relation, oder Eygendtliche . . . Beschreibung. *See* Potgieter, Barent Janszoon

History naturall. *See* Bacon, Francis

History of . . . Don Quixote, Pt 2. *See* Cervantes Saavedra, Miguel de

The history of . . . King Henry. *See* Bacon, Francis

The history of Henrie the fourth [Pt 1]. *See* Shakespeare, William

The history of Independency. *See* Walker, Clement

The history of King Henrie the fourth [Pt 1]. *See* Shakespeare, William

The history of Polexander. *See* Gomberville, Marin Le Roy, sieur du Parc et de

The history of the world. *See* Raleigh, Sir Walter

Histrio-mastix. *See* Prynne, William

Hobbes, Stephen. Margarita chyrurgica. London: T. C[reede]., for R. Bonion, & H. Walley, 1610

Hoby, Sir Edward. A countersnarle. London: [T. Snodham] for N. Butter, 1613 (2)

—A curry-combe for a coxecombe. London: W. Stansby, for N. Butter, 1615

Hodson, William. The divine cosmographer. Cambridge: R. Daniel, 1640

Hoffer, Adriaan. Elegia . . . in expeditionem navalem . . . foederati Belgii. Harderwijck:

Widow of T. Henrickz, 1624

—Nederduytsche poemata. Amsterdam: B. Janszoon, 1635

Hoffmann, Caspar. *See* Hofmann, Caspar

Hofmann, Caspar. De medicamentis officinalibus. Paris: G. Meturas, 1647

Hofmann, Lorenz. Thaumatophylakion, sive Thesaurus . . . Allerley Antiquiteten. Halle: C. Bismarck, 1625

—*See also* Brunner, Balthasar. Consilia medica. Halle: 1617

Hogenberg, Franz, engr. *See* Braun, Georg. Civitates orbis terrarum Cologne: 1612, *et seq.*

The hogge hath lost his pearle. *See* Tailor, Robert

HOLIDAYS

—Ortiz de Cervantes, J. Señor. El licenciado Juan Ortiz de Cervantes . . . Dize; que como en este reyno. . . . [Madrid? ca. 1620?]

Holländisch apocalypsis. *See* Scribanius, Carolus

Holland, Henry. Herōlogia anglica. [Utrecht:] C. van de Passe, & J. Janszoon, at Arnhem [1620]

Holland, Hugh. *See* Coryat, Thomas. Coryats crudities. London: 1611

Holland (Province). Hof. Copie vande twee sententien. [The Hague?] 1647

Holland (Province). Staten. Brief vande . . . Staten van Hollandt. [The Hague?] 1650

——*In* Kort verhael. [The Hague?] 1650

—Copie van een missive, gesonden by de Staten. [Amsterdam?] 1650

—Extract uyt de resolutien vande . . . Staten van Hollant. [Amsterdam?] 1650

—Missive aende Staten vande Provintien. [Amsterdam?] 1650

—Missive van . . . de . . . Staten van Hollandt. Rotterdam: J. Verburch, 1650

—Provintiael advijs van Hollant. Amsterdam: J. Pieterszoon, 1650

Hollands leaguer. *See* Marmion, Shackerley

Hollandsche Sybille. Amsterdam: R. Heyndrickz, 1646 (2)

—[The Hague?] 1646

Hollandt gedoodt-verwet. [The Hague?] 1647

't Hollandts rommelzootje. [Amsterdam?] 1650 (2)

Hollandtsche Sybille. [The Hague?] 1646

Hollants praetie. [Amsterdam?] 1646

Den Hollantschen apocalypsis. *See* Scribanius, Carolus

Hollings, Edmund. Medicamentorum oeconomia nova. Ingolstadt: Eder Press, for A. Angermaier, 1610

——Ingolstadt: Eder Press, for Elizabeth Angermaier, 1615

Hollingworth, Richard. An examination of sundry scriptures. London: J. R[aworth]., for L. Fawne, 1645

——London: J. R[aworth]., for T. Smith, 1645

Holmes, Nathaniel. Gospel musick. London: H. Overton, 1644

Holwarda, Johannes Phocylides. *See* Franck, Sebastian. Wereltspiegel, oft Beschryvinge des gehelen aert-bodems. Bolsward: 1649

The holy state. *See* Fuller, Thomas

Holyday, Barten. Technogamia: or, The marriages of the arts. London: W. Stansby, for J. Parker, 1618

——London: J. Haviland, for R. Meighen, 1630

Homberg, Johann, ed. *See* Boemus, Johann. Historia moralis. Frankfurt a.M.: 1640A

Homburg, Ernst Christoph. Schimpff- und ernsthaffte Clio. Jena: B. Lobenstein, for Z. Hertel, at Hamburg, 1642

Hondius, Hendrik. Nouveau theatre du monde. Amsterdam: H. Hondius, 1639

——Amsterdam: J. Janszoon the Younger, 1639

——Amsterdam: J. Janszoon the Younger, 1640

——Amsterdam: H. Hondius, 1641

——Amsterdam: J. Janszoon the Younger, 1641

——Amsterdam: J. Janszoon the Younger, 1642

——1644. *See* Jansson, Jan. Nouveau theatre du monde. Amsterdam: 1644

—Le nouveau theatre du monde . . . tome troisiesme. Amsterdam: H. Hondius, 1639

——Amsterdam: J. Janszoon the Younger, 1639

Hondius, Jodocus. Atlas minor. *See* Mercator, Gerardus. Atlas minor. Amsterdam: 1607

—Nova et accurata Italiae hodiernae descriptio. Amsterdam: J. Hondius, 1626

——Leyden: B. & A. Elsevier, 1627

HONDURAS

—Avila y Lugo, F. de. Memorial al Rey. [Madrid: 1638]

HONDURAS—HISTORY, NAVAL

—Vázquez de Espinosa, A. Tratado verdadero del viage y navegacion deste año. Málaga: 1623

The honest Welch-cobler. *See* Shinkin ap Shone, pseud.

The honest whore, pt 2. *See* Dekker, Thomas

The honestie of this age. *See* Rich, Barnabe

Honor del gran patriarca San Ignacio de Loyola. *See* Nieremberg, Juan Eusebio

Honter, Johannes. Enchiridion cosmographiae. Zurich: J. Wolf, 1602

Het hoogh-loffelijcke jubel-jaer. *See* Collart, P

Hooke, William. New Englands teares. London: J. D[awson]., for J. Rothwell, & H. Overton, 1641

——London: E. G[riffin]., for J. Rothwell, & H. Overton, 1641

——London: T. P[ayne]., for J. Rothwell, & H. Overton, 1641

—New-Englands sence. London: J. Rothwell, 1645

Hooker, Thomas. The danger of desertion. London: G.

M[iller], for G. Edwards, 1641 (2)

—A survey of the summe of church-discipline. London: A. M[iller?]., for J. Bellamy, 1648 (2)

Hoorn, Dirck van. *See* Eenige advijsen ende verklaringhen. [The Hague]: 1648

Hoorn, Netherlands, Ordinances, etc. Provisionele ordre ende reglement. Hoorn: J. C. Coster, 1622

The hope of Israel. *See* Manasseh ben Joseph ben Israel

Horatius Flaccus, Quintus. Art of poetry. London: J. Okes, for J. Benson, 1640

Hornung, Johannes. Cista medica. Nuremberg: S. Halbmeyer [1626]

Horozco, Sebastian de Covarrubias. *See* Covarrubias Horozco, Sebastián de

HORSES

—Céspedes y Velasco. F. de. Memoria de diferentes piensons. Seville: 1624

Horst, Gregor. Centuria problematum medicorum. Wittenberg: J. Schmidt, for C. Berger, 1610

——Nuremberg: W. Endter, 1636

—Observationum medicinalium . . . libri quaturo. Ulm: J. Saur, 1625

——Ulm: J. Saur, 1628

——Heilbronn: C. Krause, 1631

——Nuremberg: W. Endter, 1637

—Problematum medicorum decades. Wittenberg: Crato Press, for J. Gormann, 1608

Horst, Jakob. Herbarium Horstianum. Marburg: C. Chemlin, 1630

Hortensius et dea flora cum pomona historice . . . descripti. *See* Stengel, Karl

Hortorum, florum, et arborum historia. *See* Stengel, Karl

Hortulus genialis. *See* Baricelli, Giulio Cesare

Hortulus sanitatis. Das ist Ein heylsam . . . Gährtlin der Ge-

sundtheit. *See* Durante, Castore

Hortus eystettensis. *See* Besler, Basilius

Hortus floridus. *See* Passe, Crispijn van de

Hortus Messanensis. *See* Castelli, Pietro

Hortus Patavinus. *See* Schenck, Johann Georg

Hospinianus, Rudolphus. Historia Jesuitica. Zurich: J. R. Wolf, 1619

——1627. *See* Lucius, Ludwig. Historia Jesuitica. Basel: 1627

——1632. *See* Lucius, Ludwig. Historia Jesuitica. Basel: 1632

—*See also* Lucius, Ludwig. Jesuiter-Histori. Basel: 1626

An houre glasse of Indian news. *See* Nicholl, John

Houtman, Cornelis de. Erste Schiffahrt. Frankfurt a.M.: W. Richter, for Heirs of L. Hulsius, 1606

—Erste Schiffart. Nuremberg: L. Hulsius, 1602

——Frankfurt a.M.: H. Palthenius, for The Hulsiuses, 1625

HOUTMAN, CORNELIS DE

—Eerste schip-vaert der Hollanders. Amsterdam: 1648

Hovt en beleght; een oud schipper. [Spa, outside Altena: 1608] (*See under* Een oud schipper)

Howell, James. Dendrologia. Dodona's grove. [London:] T. B[adger]., for H. Moseley, 1640

——[Oxford: H. Hall] 1644

——Cambridge: R. D[aniel]., for H. Moseley, at London, 1645

——London: T. W[arren?]., for H. Moseley [1649]

—Dendrologie, ou La forest de Dodonne. Paris: A. Courbé, 1641

——Paris: [A. Courbé, for] Widow of J. Camusat, 1641

—Epistolae Ho-elianae. Familiar letters. London: H. Moseley, 1645

——London: W. H[unt]., for H. Moseley, 1650

—A new volume of letters. Lon-

Zwölffte Schiffahrt. Oppenheim: 1614

— — — —Oppenheim: 1627

— —, pt 13. Hamor, Ralph, the
Younger. Dreyzehente Schiffahrt . . . von . . . Virginien.
Hanau: 1617

— —, pt 14. Smith, Capt. John.
Viertzehende Schiffart oder
. . . Beschreibung dess Neuwen Engellandts. Frankfurt
a.M.: 1617

— — — —Frankfurt a.M.: 1628

— —, pt 16. Schouten, Willem
Corneliszoon. Die sechtzehende Schifffahrt. Frankfurt
a.M.: 1619

— —, pt 17. Spilbergen, Joris
van. Die siebenzehende Schiffart. Frankfurt a.M.: 1620

— —, pt 18. Herrera y Tordesillas, Antonio de. Achtzehender Theil der Newen Welt.
Frankfurt a.M.: 1623

— —pt 19. Braun, Samuel. Die
neuntzehende Schiffarth.
Frankfurt a.M.: 1626

— —, pt 20. Whitbourne, Sir
Richard, Zwantzigste Schifffahrt. Frankfurt a.M.: 1629

— —, pt 21. Hulsius, Levinus.
Die ein und zwantzigste
Schifffahrt. Frankfurt a.M.:
1629

— —, pt 22. Hulsius, Levinus.
Die zwey und zwäntzigste
Schiffart. Frankfurt a.M.: 1630

— —, pt 24. Bontekoe, Willem
Ysbrandsz. Die vier und zwantzigste Schiffahrt. Frankfurt
a.M.: 1648

— —, pt 25. Brouwer, Hendrick.
Die fünff und zweyntzigste
Schifffahrt. Frankfurt a.M.:
1649

— —, pt 26. La Peyrère, Isaac de.
Die xxvi. Schiff-Fahrt. Frankfurt a.M.: 1650

The humble and just remonstrance. *See* Ireland. Parliament

The humble request of his Majesties loyall subjects. *See* Massachusetts (Colony)

Hume, Tobias. Ayres, French,
Pollish, and others. London: J.
Windet, 1605

Humors antique faces. *See* Rowlands, Samuel

Humors looking glasse. *See* Rowlands, Samuel

Humors ordinarie. *See* Rowlands,
Samuel

Hundert ein und dreissig Relationes. *See* Boccalini, Traiano

Ein Hundert Episteln. *See* Zeiller,
Martin

Hungers prevention. *See* Markham, Gervase

Hunt, Robert. The island of Assada. London: N. Bourne
[1650]

Hurault, Michel, sieur de Belesbat et du Fay. Le recueil des
excellens . . . discours. [Paris?]
1606

HURON INDIANS

—Le Jeune, P. Relation de ce qui
s'est passé en la Nouvelle
France en l'année 1636. Paris:
1637

— —Relation de ce qui s'est passé . . . en l'année 1637. Rouen:
1638

— —Relation de ce qui s'est passé . . . en l'année 1638. Paris:
1638

— —Relation de ce qui s'est passé . . . en l'année 1639. Paris:
1640

—Sagard, G. Le grand voyage du
pays des Hurons. Paris: 1632

— —Histoire du Canada. Paris:
1636

—*See also publications listed under*
Lallemant, Jérôme, *and* Vimont, Barthélemy

HURON LANGUAGE

—Sagard, G. Le grand voyage du
pays des Hurons. Paris: 1632

HURRICANES

—Smith, Capt. J. A sea grammar.
London: 1627

—Taylor, J. Newes and strange
newes. London: 1638

—Vaughan, W. The arraignment
of slander. London: 1630

— —The spirit of detraction
conjured and convicted. London: 1611

Hurtado, Tomás. Chocolate y
tabaco. Madrid: F. García, for
M. López [1645]

Hurtado de Mendoza, Diego.
Guerra de Granada. Lisbon: G.
de la Vinha, 1627

HURTADO DE MENDOZA,
GARCIA, MARQUÉS DE
CAÑETE

—Suárez de Figueroa, C. Hechos
de Don Garcia Hurtado de
Mendoza. Madrid: 1613

**Hurtado de Mendoza, Lorenzo,
Bp.** Memorial ad Rey pidiendo
remedio. [Madrid?] 1638

HUTCHINSON, ANNE

—Baillie, R. Anabaptism, the
true fountaine. London: 1647

—Bulkeley, P. The gospel-covenant. London: 1646

—Edwards, T. Gangraena, pt 3.
London: 1646

—Wheelwright, J. Mercurius
Americanus. London: 1645

—Winthrop, J. Antinomians and
Familists. London: 1644

Hydrographia. *See* Figueiredo,
Manuel de

Hydrographie, contenant la
theorie . . . de la navigation.
See Fournier, Georges

Hymnus tabaci. *See* Thorius, Raphael

Hypocrisie unmasked. *See* Winslow, Edward

I. Conferentie van eenige . . .
heeren. *See* I. [i.e., Eerste] conferentie

Iatrologia epistolikē, sive Curia
medica. *See* Manardo, Giovanni

Ibarra, Alvaro de. Informe en
derecho por el illmo. señor.
dom. fray Christoval de Mancha. [Madrid? 1649]

Ibarra, Carlos de, vizconde de
Centenera, supposed author.
See Marquez de Cisneros, ——.
Por el señor D. Carlos de
Ibarra. Madrid: 1634

—*See also* Translaet uyt den
Spaenschen. Amsterdam:
1639

IBARRA, JUAN DE

—Peraza de Ayala y Rojas,
A., conde de la Gomera.
Señor. Don Antonio Peraça
de Ayala y Rojas. [Madrid?
1623?]

regidor perpetuo. [Madrid: 1629]

—Nederlandschen verre-kijcker. The Hague: 1627

—Ofwod, S. A relation of sundry particular wicked plots. [London?] 1624

——The wicked plots . . . of Spaniards. [London: 1642]

—Ortiz de Cervantes, J. Parabien al Rey D. Felip IIII. [Madrid? 1621?]

——Señor. El licenciado Juan Ortiz de Cervantes . . . Dize: que en . . . Cuzco. . . . [Madrid? ca. 1620]

——Señor. El licenciado Juan Ortiz de Cervantes . . . Dize; que en los pueblos. . . . [Madrid? ca. 1620]

——Señor. El licenciado Juan Ortiz de Cervantes . . . Dize; que una de las mayores causas de la destruycion . . . . [Madrid? ca. 1620]

—Palafox y Mendoza, J. de, Bp. [Virtudes del Indio.] [Madrid? ca. 1650?]

—Robinson, H. Liberty of conscience. [London:] 1643

—Sala, G. Secretos publicos. [Barcelona? 1641?]

——Secrets publichs. [Barcelona: 1641]

——Secrets publiques. Rouen: 1642

——Segredos publicos. Lisbon: 1641

—Schuyt-praetgens. [Amsterdam? 1608?]

—Scott, T. Robert earle of Essex. [London]: 1624

—Sepúlveda, J. G. de. Opera. Cologne: 1602

—Silva, J. de. Advertencias importantes. Madrid: 1621

—Spain. Laws, statutes, etc., 1598–1621 (Philip III). El Rey. Marques de Montes Claros . . . gouernador . . . del Piru. [Madrid? 1609]

—Spain. Sovereigns, etc., 1598–1621 (Philip III). El Rey [26 May 1609]. [Madrid: 1609]

—Spanisch Mucken Pulver. [Hannover?] 1620

—The treasurie of auncient and

moderne times. London: 1613

—Usselinx, W. Onpartydich discours. [Amsterdam? 1608?]

—Valdivia, L. de. Señor. El padre Luys de Valdivia . . . Digo, que la mayor parte de mi vida, he gastado en la conversion. [Madrid? ca. 1620?]

—Vaughan, W. The goldengrove. London: 1608

—Verheiden, W. Nootelijcke consideratien. [Amsterdam?] 1608

——An oration or speech. [Amsterdam:] 1624

—t'Vertoig der Zeeuscher nymphen. [Middelburg? 1609?]

—Weidner, J. L. Hispanicae dominationis arcana. Leyden: 1643

INDIANS IN LITERATURE

—Lalli, G. B. Franceide, overo Del mal francese. Foligno: 1629

INDIANS OF CENTRAL AMERICA—PANAMA

—Hernández, M. Memorial de Chiriqui. [Madrid? 1620]

INDIANS OF MEXICO

—Carrillo Altamirano, F. A. Señor. El doctor Hernan Carrillo Altamirano. [Madrid? 1624?]

—Márquez de Torres, F. Medio suave y facil. [Madrid? ca. 1635?]

—Melich, G. Avertimenti nelle compositioni de' medicamenti. Venice: [1605]

——Dispensatorium medicum. Frankfurt a.M.: 1601

—Palafox y Mendoza, J. de, Bp. [Virtudes del Indio.] [Madrid? ca. 1650?]

—Pérez de Ribas, A. Historia de los triumphos de nuestra santa fee. Madrid: 1645

—Rodríguez de Robles, A. Señor. Antonio de Rodriguez de Robles dize, que quando la Nueva España se gano . . . . [Madrid? 1606?]

——Señor. Antonio Rodriguez de Robles dize, que ahora quarenta y cinquenta anos . . . . [Madrid? 1606?]

——Señor. Antonio Rodriguez de Robles dize, que como a V.

Magestad . . . es notorio. [Madrid? 1606?]

—Spain. Consejo de las Indias. [Traslado del despacho del servicio personal. Madrid: 1610?]

—Spain. Sovereigns, etc., 1598–1621 (Philip III). El Rey [26 May 1609]. [Madrid: 1609]

—Varaona, S. de. Carta . . . que se fulminò contra don M. Perez de Varaiz. [Madrid? 1625?]

INDIANS OF MEXICO—MISSIONS

—Gracián, J. Lampara encendida. Madrid: 1604

——Zelo de la propagacion de la fee. Brussels: 1609

——Zelo della propagazione della fede. Rome: 1610

—Velasco, P. de. Señor. Pedro de Velasco . . . procurador general. [Madrid? 1641?]

INDIANS OF MEXICO—RELIGION AND MYTHOLOGY

—Sánchez de Aguilar, P. Informe contra idolorum cultores del obispado de Yucatán. Madrid: 1639

—Torres, J. de. Philosophia moral. Burgos: 1602

INDIANS OF NORTH AMERICA

—Champlain, S. de. Des sauvages. Paris: [1603?]

—The maske of flowers. London: 1614

—Smith, Capt. J. A sea grammar. London: 1627

INDIANS OF NORTH AMERICA—CANADA

—Champlain, S. de. Voyages et descouvertures faites en la Nouvelle-France. Paris: 1619

—Ledesma, D. de. Doctrine chrestienne. Rouen: 1630

—Lescarbot, M. La defaite des sauvages armouchiquois. Paris: [1608]

—Paris. Université. III. [i.e., Troisième] requeste. Paris: 1644

—Les veritables motifs. [Paris:] 1643

liaenschen brieff. [Amsterdam:] 1646

—Pyrard, F. Discours du voyage . . . aux Indes. Paris: 1611

—Sardinha Mimoso, J. Relacion de la real tragicomedia. Lisbon: 1620

—Staden, H. Beschrijvinghe van America. Amsterdam: 1625

—Yves d'Evreux, father. Suitte de lHistoire des choses . . . advenues en Maragnan. Paris: 1615

INDIANS OF SOUTH AMERICA—BRAZIL—LANGUAGES

—Figueira, L. Arte da lingua brasilica. Lisbon: [1621]

INDIANS OF SOUTH AMERICA—BRAZIL—MISSIONS

—Claude d'Abbeville, Father. Die Ankunfft der Vätter Capuciner Ordens. Augsburg: 1613

——L'arrivee des peres Capucins en l'Inde Nouvelle. Paris: 1612

INDIANS OF SOUTH AMERICA—BRAZIL—SOCIAL LIFE AND CUSTOMS

—Pasquier, E. Les lettres. Lyons: 1607

INDIANS OF SOUTH AMERICA—CHILE

—Usselinx, W. Waerschouwinghe over den treves. Flushing: 1630

—Valdivia, L. de. Relacion de lo que sucedio en el reyno de Chile. [Madrid? 1615?]

——Señor. El padre Luys de Valdivia . . . Digo, que la mayor parte de mi vida, he gastado en la conversion. [Madrid? ca. 1620?]

INDIANS OF SOUTH AMERICA—COLOMBIA

—Spain. Sovereigns, etc., 1621–1655 (Philip IV). El rey. [Madrid: 1634]

INDIANS OF SOUTH AMERICA—LANGUAGES

—Catholic Church. Liturgy and ritual. Ritual. Peru. Rituale, seu Manuale peruanum, et forma brevis. Naples: 1607

INDIANS OF SOUTH AMERICA—MISSIONS

—Arias, J. L. Señor. El doctor Juan Luis Arias. [Valladolid: 1609]

INDIANS OF SOUTH AMERICA—PARAGUAY

—Histoire de ce qui s'est passé au royaume du Japon. Paris: 1633

—Pastor, J. Señor. Juan Pastor . . . procurador general . . . Dize, que los Indios [etc.]. [Madrid: 1646?]

—Ruiz de Montoya, A. Señor: Antonio Ruiz de Montoya . . . procurador de la provincia del Paraguay. [Madrid: 1642?]

INDIANS OF SOUTH AMERICA—PERU

—Cárdenas, B. de, Bp. Memorial, y relacion verdadera para el rei. Madrid: 1634

—Garcilaso de la Vega, el Inca. Le commentaire royal. Paris: 1633

——Commentarios reales, la pte. Lisbon: 1609

——Histoire des guerres civiles des Espagnols. Paris: 1650

——Historia general del Peru. Córdoba: 1616

—González de Azevedo, J. Señor. El capitan Iuan Goncalez de Azevedo. [Madrid: 1615?]

——Señor. El capitan Juan Gonçalez de Azevedo, por lo que toca al servicio de Dios. [Madrid? 1615?]

—Márquez de Torres, F. Medio suave y facil. [Madrid? ca. 1635?]

—Ortiz de Cervantes, J. Parabien al Rey D. Felip IIII. [Madrid? 1621?]

——Señor. El licenciado Juan Ortiz de Cervantes . . . Dize: que en . . . Cuzco . . . . [Madrid? ca. 1620]

——Señor. El licenciado Juan Ortiz de Cervantes . . . Dize: que en los pueblos . . . . [Madrid? ca. 1620]

—Pérez de Nueros, J. Señor. Jacinto Perez de Nueros, religioso. [Madrid: ca. 1620?]

—Spain. Consejo de las Indias.

[Traslado del despacho del servicio personal. Madrid: 1610?]

—Zárate, A. de. Conqueste van Indien. Amsterdam: 1623

—Zeiller, M. Das andere Hundert Episteln. Ulm: 1641

INDIANS OF SOUTH AMERICA—PERU—MISSIONS

—Aguilar del Rio, J. Memorial que ofrece el licenciado. [Madrid: 1623?]

INDIANS OF THE WEST INDIES

—León, A. de. Practico de morbo gallico. Valladolid: 1605

—Planis Campy, D. de. La verolle recogneue. Paris: 1623

—Plautius, C., Abbot. Extract und Ausszug der grossen . . . Schiff-farth Buelij Cataloni. [Linz:] 1623

——Nova typis transacta navigatio. Novi orbis. [Linz:]1621

—Weckherlin, G. R. Kurtze Beschreibung dess . . . Frewden-Fests. Tübingen: 1618

INDIANS OF THE WEST INDIES—HISPANIOLA

—Donne, J. Biathanatos. A declaration. London: [1647]

—Lancre, P. de. Tableau de l'inconstance des mauvais anges. Paris: 1612

INDIANS OF THE WEST INDIES—LANGUAGES

—Duret, C. Thresor de l'histoire des langues. Cologny: 1613

INDIANS OF THE WEST INDIES—POETRY

—Wither, G. Abuses stript, and whipt. London: 1613

L'Indienne amoureuse. *See* Du Rocher, R. M.

Informacion en derecho. *See* Loarte Davila, ——

Informacion en favor del derecho. *See* Ortiz de Cervantes, Juan

Informacion sobre que los electos para obispos no pueden consagrarse. *See* Contreras, Francisco de

Informe a S. M. Don Felipe III. *See* Flóres de León, Diego

Informe contra idolorum cul-

de la Compañia de Jesus. [Madrid? 165–?]

—Ruiz de Montoya, A. Conquista espiritual. Madrid: 1639

——Señor: Antonio Ruiz de Montoya . . . procurador de la provincia del Paraguay. [Madrid: 1642?]

——Señor. Antonio Ruiz de Montoya . . . procurador general . . . del Paraguay. [Madrid: 1639]

—Schirmbeck, A. Messis Paraquariensis. Munich: 1649

JESUITS IN PERU

—Barnuevo, R. Muy poderoso señor. [Madrid? 1638?]

——Señor. Rodrigo Barnueuo de la compañia de Jesus. [Madrid? 1639?]

—Figueroa, J. de. Juan de Figueroa, regidor de la ciudad de los Reyes. [Madrid? 1650?]

—Freylin, J. M. Catalogo de algunos varones insignes. Seville: 1632

—Jesuits. Letters from missions. Annuae litterae (1603) 1618. Annuae litterae . . . Anni M.DC.III. Douai: 1618

——Annuae litterae (1605) 1618. Annuae litterae . . . Anni M.DC.V. Douai: 1618

—Oliva, A. Catalogo de algunos varones illustres. Seville: 1632

—Pérez, J. Razon que da de si el padre Jacinto Perez . . . . Madrid: 1646

—Pérez de Nueros, J. Señor. Jacinto Perez de Nueros, religioso. [Madrid: ca. 1620?]

—Torres Bollo, D. de. Brevis relatio historica in provincia Peruana. Mainz: 1604

——De rebus Peruanis . . . commentarius. Antwerp: 1604

——Kurtzer Bericht was Gott . . . in den Peruanischen Ländern aussgericht. Würzburg: 1604

——La nouvelle histoire du Perou. Paris: 1604

——O rozszerzeniu wiary . . . w Americe. Cracow: 1603

——Relatione breve. Rome: 1603

—Traslados de algunas cartas sa-

cadas de sus proprios originales. [Madrid: 1647]

JESUITS IN SOUTH AMERICA

—Díaz Taño, F. Señor. El padre Francisco Diaz Taño. [Madrid? 1632?]

—Jesuits. Letters from missions. Auss America. Augsburg: 1620

——Histoire du massacre de plusieurs religieux. Valenciennes: 1620

—Jesuits. Letters from missions (South America). Relation des insignes progrez de la religion chrestienne. Paris: 1638

JESUITS IN SPANISH AMERICA

—Nieremberg, J. E. Honor del gran patriarca San Ignacio de Loyola. Madrid: 1645

——Vidas exemplares. Madrid: 1647

JESUITS IN URUGUAY

—Ferrufiño, J. B. Señor. Juan Bautista Ferrufino procurador general. [Madrid: ca. 1630]

—Nieremberg, J. E. De arte voluntatis libri sex. Lyons: 1631

—Ruiz de Montoya, A. Conquista espiritual. Madrid: 1639

Jesús María, Juan de. *See* Juan de Jesús María, Father

Jewes in America. *See* Thorowgood, Thomas

JEWS IN BRAZIL

—Manasseh ben Joseph ben Israel. Conciliador, pte 2a. Amsterdam: [1641]

Jiménez Paton, Bartolomé. *See* Hernando de Talavera, Abp. Reforma de trages. Baeza: 1638

Joannes Bargantinus Lusitaniae. *See* Caramuel Lobkowitz, Juan, Bp

Joannes Hesronita, tr. *See* al-Idrīsī. Geographia Nubiensis. Paris: [1620]

Jobson, Richard. The golden trade. London: N. Okes, for N. Bourne, 1623

Jocabella. *See* Chamberlain, Robert

Joel, Franciscus. Operum medicorum . . . tomus primus [-sextus]. Hamburg: H. Carstens;

Lüneburg: A. Michelson; Rostock: M. Sachs, for J. Hallervord, 1616–31

Joernael. ofte. Voyagie vande Groenlants-vaerders. Rotterdam: A. Nering, 1634

Johan Maurits, prince of Nassau-Siegen. *See* Copye ofte Cort ende waerachtigh verhael van 't gene ghepasseert is. Amsterdam: 1640

JOHAN MAURITS, PRINCE OF NASSAU-SIEGEN

—Baerle, K. van. Mauritius redux. Amsterdam: 1644

—I. [i.e., Eerste] conferentie van eenige . . . heeren. Middelburg: 1650

—Illustrissimo heroi Joanni Mauritio. Leyden: 1645

—Montalvão, J. Mascarenhas, marquez de. Copyen van drie missiven. Amsterdam: 1641

—Plante, F. Mauritiados libri xii. Leyden: 1647

John Taylor being yet unhanged. *See* Taylor, John, the Water-poet

John Taylors wandering. *See* Taylor, John, the Water-poet

Johnson, Edward. Good news from New England. London: M. Simmons, 1648

Johnson, Jacob. Epigrammatum libellus. London: J. Beale, for R. Redmer, 1115 [i.e., 1615]

—Schediasmata poetica. London: J. Beale, 1615

Johnson, Robert. The new life of Virginea. London: F. Kingston, for W. Welby, 1612

—Nova Britannia. London: [J. Windet] for S. Macham, 1609

Jonckheer, M. Teghen-worp op het onwarachtich schrijven. Flushing: J. Janszoon de Jonghe, 1633

Jones, John (fl. 1635). Adrasta: or, The womans spleene. London: [M. Fletcher?] for R. Royston, 1635

Jonson, Ben. The alchemist. London: T. Snodham, for W. Burre & J. Stepneth, 1612

——*In his* Workes. London: 1616

Juan de Jesús María, Father.
Epistolario espiritual. Uclés:
D. de la Iglesia, 1624

Juan de Leon. *See* Leon, Juan de

Juan de Santa María, fray.
Chronica de la provincia de
San Joseph. Madrid: Imprenta
Real, 1615–18

Juan de Urbina. *See* Urbina, Juan
de

Judicious and select essayes. *See*
Raleigh, Sir Walter

Juncker, Johann. Compendiosa
methodus therapeutica. [Erfurt:] H. Steinmann, 1624

Junius, Hadrianus. Nomenclator octilinguis. Geneva: J.
Stoer, 1602

——Lyons: J. A. Gabiano, & S.
Girard, 1602

——Paris: D. Douceur, 1606

——Frankfurt a.M.: N. Hoffmann, 1611

——Geneva: J. Stoer, 1619

——[Geneva:] J. Stoer, 1619

Juridico-politicae dissertationes.
See Besold, Christoph

A just vindication of the covenant. *See* Cobbet, Thomas

JUSTICE, ADMINISTRATION
OF—SPANISH AMERICA

—Spain. Laws, statutes, etc.,
1598–1621 (Philip III). El Rey.
Por quanto de ordinario se han
ofrecido y ofrecen dudas . . . .
[Madrid: 1620]

—Zapata y Sandoval, J. De justitia distributiva. Valladolid:
1609

Justificacion de la conservacion.
See Grau y Monfalcón, Juan

Justiniano, Vincente. *See* Antist,
Vincente Justiniano, fray

Juvenilia. A collection of those
poemes. *See* Wither, George

Kallwitz, Seth. *See* Calvisius, Seth

Kannenburch, Hendrik van.
Protest ofte Scherp dreyghement. Middelburg: J. van de
Vivere, 1629

Katoptron; sive, Speculum artis
medicae. *See* Cesalpino, Andrea

Kayll, Robert. The trades increase. London: N. Okes, for
W. Burre, 1615

KECHUA LANGUAGE

—Lima (Ecclesiastical Province).
Council, 1583. Catecismo en
la lengua española. y quichua.
Rome: 1603

——Confessario para los curas
de Indios. Seville: 1603

Keckermann, Bartholomaeus.
De natura et proprietatibus
historiae. Hanau: W. Antonius, 1610

—Meditatio de insolito et stupendo illo terrae-motu. Heidelberg: G. Vögelin, 1602

—Operum omnium quae extant
tomus primus [-secundus]. Geneva: P. Aubert, 1614

—Systema astronomiae compendiosum. Hanau: Heirs of W.
Antonius, 1611

——Hanau: Heirs of W. Antonius, 1613

——*In his* Operum omnium
quae extant tomus. Geneva:
1614

——*In his* Systema compendiosum totius mathematices. Hanau: 1617

—Systema compendiosum totius
mathematices. Hanau: P. Antonius, 1617

——Hanau: P. Antonius, 1621

—Systema geographicum. Hanau: Heirs of W. Antonius,
1611

——Hanau: Heirs of W. Antonius, 1612

——*In his* Operum omnium
quae extant tomus. Geneva:
1614

——*In his* Systema compendiosum totius mathematices. Hanau: 1617

Kemys, Lawrence. Kort journael, gedaen naer . . . Guiana.
1648. *In* Journael vande Nassausche vloot. Amsterdam:
1648

—Waerachtighe . . . beschryvinghe vande . . . zeevaert. *In*
Raleigh, Sir Walter. Warachtighe ende grondighe beschryvinghe van . . . Guiana. Amsterdam: 1605

——*In the same.* Amsterdam:
1617

Kepler, Johann. Tabulae Rudolphinae. Ulm: J. Saur, 1627
[i.e., 1629]

Kerkhove, Jan van. Nouvelles
des choses qui se passent.
Paris: F. Bourriquant, 1607

Keulen, Mathias van. Extract
wtten brief van mijn Herr Keulen . . . residerende . . . tot
Fernambuco. The Hague: L.
Breeckevelt, 1634

A key into the language of America. *See* Williams, Roger

The keyes of the kingdom of
heaven. *See* Cotton, John

Keymis, Lorenz. *See* Kemys, Lawrence

Khunrath, Conrad. Medulla
destillatoria et medica. Hamburg: Froben Office, 1601

——Hamburg: Froben Office,
1605

——Hamburg: Froben Office,
1623, ’21

——Hamburg: Froben Office,
1638

——Hamburg: Froben Office,
1639, ’38

A kicksey winsey. *See* Taylor,
John, the Water-poet

King, Humphrey. An halfepenny-worth of wit. London:
T. Thorp, for E. Blount, 1613

King, John, Bp. Sermon at
Paules Crosse. London: E.
Griffin, for E. Adams, 1620

King James his Apopthegmes.
See James I, King of Great Britain

The kingdoms divisions anatomized. *See* Lisle, Francis

The Kings most excellent majesties wellcome. *See* Taylor,
John, the Water-poet

Kircher, Athanasius. Ars magna
lucis. Rome: L. Grignani, for
H. Scheus, 1646

—Magnes, sive De arte magnetica opus. Rome: L. Grignani,
for H. Scheus, 1641

——Cologne: J. Kalckhoven,
1643

Kirke, John. The seven champions of Christendome. London:
J. Okes, for J. Becket, 1638

Klaer-bericht ofte Aenwysinghe.

See Nijkerke, Joost Willems-
zoon
Klaer licht, ofte Vertoogh. [Am-
sterdam? 1644]
Klare aenwijsinge. The Hague:
A. Meuris, 1630
—*See also* Wtenbogaert, Johan-
nes. Wtwissinge der schande-
licker blamen. [The Hague?]
1630
De kleyne wonderlijke werelt. *See*
Joosten, Jacob
De kleyne wonderlycke wereldt.
See Joosten, Jacob
Klinikē, or The diet of the dis-
eased. *See* Hart, James
The knave of clubbes. *See* Row-
lands, Samuel
The knave of harts. *See* Row-
lands, Samuel
The knight of the burning pestle.
See Beaumont, Francis
A knights conjuring. *See* Dekker,
Thomas
Knobloch, Tobias. De lue ve-
nerea, von Frantzosen kurtzer
Bericht. Giessen: N. Hampel,
1620
Köstlicher Artzneyschatz. *See*
Gesner, Konrad
Koopmans jacht. *See* Udemans,
Godefridus Corneliszoon
Kornmann, Heinrich. Tem-
plum naturae historicum.
Darmstadt: J. J. Porsch, 1611
Kort begrijp der Nederlandtsche
historien. *See* Sande, Johan van
den
Kort discours, ofte naardere
verklaringe. [The Hague?]
1644
Kort en grondigh verhael van
alle 't gene sich heeft toe-ghe-
dragen. Amsterdam: C. van de
Pas, 1641
Een kort ontwerp vande Maha-
kuase Indianen. *See* Megapo-
lensis, Johannes
**Kort verhael van de exploicten
door** . . . Pieter Pietersz Heyn.
Amsterdam: H. Gerritsz, 1628
Kort verhael van 't gene onlangs . . . is voor-gevallen.
[The Hague?] 1650 (2)
Kort verhael vanden staet van
Fernanbuc. *See* Guelen, August
de

Korte aenwysinghe der be-
winthebbers regieringe. [Am-
sterdam: 1622]
Korte antwoort, tegens 't Mani-
fest ende remonstrantie. [The
Hague?] 1647
Een korte beschrijvinge van het
. . . kruyt tobacco. *See* Chute,
Anthony
Korte historiael ende jour-
naelsche aenteyckeninghe. *See*
Broeck, Pieter van den
Korte observatien op het Ver-
toogh. Amsterdam: P. van
Marel, 1647
Korte onderrichtinghe ende Ver-
maeninge. *See* Usselinx, Wil-
lem
Krachteloose donder van den
Helschen hondt. [Amsterdam?
1614?] (3)
Kraütterbuch. *See* Bock, Hierony-
mus
Kreutterbuch. *See* Mattioli, Pietro
Andrea
Kunstbuch. *See* Wecker, Johann
Jakob
Kurtze Beschreibung dess
. . . Frewden-Fests. *See* Weck-
herlin, Georg Rodolph
Kurtze Beschreibung dess Ta-
backs. *See* Barnstein, Heinrich
Kurtze Erzehlung: was massen
vom Herrn General Long
. . . die Hauptstadt Fernam-
buco . . . eingenommen wor-
den. [Hamburg?] 1630
Kurtze und warhaffte Beschrei-
bung der See-Reisen . . .
nacher Brasilien. *See* Augspur-
ger, Johann Paul
Kurtze Welt-Beschreibung. *See*
Schultze, Gottfried
Kurtze wunderbare Beschreibung dess . . . Königreichs
Guianae. *See* Raleigh, Sir Walter
Kurtzer Bericht von der Fruchtbringenden Geselschaft Vorhaben. *See* Fruchtbringende
Gesellschaft
Kurtzer Bericht was Gott . . . in
den Peruanischen Ländern
aussgericht. *See* Torres Bollo,
Diego de
Kurtzer Extract der vornemsten

Hauptpuncten. *See* Usselinx,
Willem
L., G. M. A. W. *See* Lodewijcksz,
Willem
La Barre, Antoine de. Les le-
çons publiques. Leyden: Heirs
of J. N. van Dorp, 1644
Labbe, Philippe. La geographie
royale. Paris: J. Henault, 1646
——Paris: M. Henault, 1646
——Paris: M. Henault, & J. He-
nault, 1646
—Les tableaux méthodiques de
la géographie royale. Paris: M.
Henault, & J. Henault, 1646
——Paris: M. Henault, & J. He-
nault, 1647
Laberinto de comercio terrestre
y naval. *See* Hevia Bolaños,
Juan de
La Brosse, Guy de. Catalogue
des plantes cultivées. Paris: J.
Dugast, 1641
—De la nature, vertu, et utilité
des plantes. Paris: R. Ba-
ragnes, 1628
—Description du jardin royal des
plantes medicinales. Paris:
1636
LACANTÚN (PROVINCE)
—Spain. Laws, statutes, etc.,
1621–1665 (Philip IV). Capitu-
laciones de el assiento. [Ma-
drid:] 1639
La Coste, Christ. de. *See* Costa,
Christovam da
The ladies cabinet opened.
London: M. P[arsons]., for R.
Meighen, 1639
The ladies parliament. *See* Ne-
ville, Henry
Laet, Joannes de. Beschrij-
vinghe van West-Indien. Ley-
den: The Elseviers, 1630
—Hispania, sive De regis Hispa-
niae regnis . . . commenta-
rium. Leyden: Elsevier Office,
1629 (2)
—L'histoire du Nouveau Monde.
Leyden: B. & A. Elsevier, 1640
—Historie ofte Iaerlijck verhael.
Leyden: B. & A. Elsevier, 1644
—Nieuwe Wereldt. Leyden: I.
Elsevier, 1625
—Notae ad dissertationem Hu-
gonis Grotii De origine gen-
tium Americanarum. Amster-

dam: L. Elsevier, 1643 (2)

——Paris: Widow of G. Pelé, 1643

—Novus Orbis seu, Descriptionis Indiae Occidentalis. Leyden: The Elsevier, 1633

—Portugallia, sive De regis Portugalliae regnis . . . commentarius. Leyden: Elsevier Office, 1641

—Responsio ad dissertationem secundam Hugonis Grotii, de Origine gentium Americanarum. Amsterdam: L. Elsevier, 1644

LAET, JOANNES DE

—Poisson, J. B. Animadversio. Paris: 1644

—A vindication of learning. London: 1646

La Faye, Antoine de. Emblemata et epigrammata. Geneva: P. & J. Chouët, 1610

Laffémas, Barthélemy, sieur de Bauthor. Instruction du plantage des meuriers. Paris: D. Le Clerc, 1605

Le lagrime del peccatore. *See* Lorenzini, Niccolò

La Guard, Theodore, pseud. *See* Ward, Nathaniel

Laguna, Andrés de. *See* Dioscorides, Pedanius. Acerca de la materia medicinal. Valencia: 1636

Lallemant, Charles. Lettre du pere Charles L'Allemant. Paris: J. Boucher, 1627

Lallemant, Jérôme. Lettre . . . escrite des Hurons. *In* Vimont, Barthélemy. Relation de ce qui s'est passé en la Nouvelle France, és années 1644. et 1645. Paris: 1646

—Relation de ce qui s'est passé dans le pays des Hurons. *In* Le Jeune, Paul. Relation de ce qui s'est passé . . . en l'année 1539. Paris: 1640

——*In* Vimont, Barthélemy. Relation de ce qui s'est passé . . . en l'anne M. DC. XL. Paris: 1641

——*In* Vimont, Barthélemy. Relation de ce qui s'est passé . . . és annés 1643. et 1644. Paris: 1645

—Relation de ce qui s'est passé en la mission aux Hurons. *In* Vimont, Barthélemy. Relation de ce qui s'est passé . . . es années 1640 et 1641. Paris: 1642

—Relation de ce qui s'est passé en la mission des Hurons. *In* Vimont, Barthélemy. Relation de ce qui s'est passé . . . en l'annee 1642. Paris: 1643

—Relation de ce qui s'est passé . . . en la Nouvelle France . . . en l'année 1647. Paris: S. Cramoisy, 1648

—Relation de ce qui s'est passé . . . en la Nouvelle France, ès années 1645. et 1646. Paris: S. Cramoisy, 1647

—Relation de ce qui s'est passé . . . en la Nouvelle France, ès années 1647 et 1648. Paris: S. Cramoisy, 1649

Lalli, Giovanni Battista. Franceide, overo Del mal francese. Foligno: A. Alterio, 1629

——*In his* Opere poetiche. Milan: 1630

——Venice: G. Sarzina, 1629

—Opere poetiche. Milan: D. Fontana, & G. Scaccabarozzo, 1630

LAM, JAN DIRKSZOON

—Waerachtich verhael van de gantsche reyse. Amsterdam: 1626

The lamentable complaints of Hop the brewer. [London:] 1641

The lamentable complaints of Nick Froth. [London:] 1641

Lampara encendida. *See* Gracián, Jerónimo

Lampe, Barent. Het achtiende deel . . . van het Historisch verhael. Amsterdam: J. Janszoon the Younger [1630?]

—Het eenentwintichste deel . . . van het Historisch verhael. Amsterdam: J. Janszoon the Younger, 1635

—Het negentiende deel . . . van het Historisch verhael. Amsterdam: J. Janszoon the Younger, 1632

—Het twintigste deel . . . van het Historisch verhael. Amster-

dam: J. Janszoon the Younger, 1633

LANCES

—Vargas Machuca, B. de. Compendio y doctrina nueva de la gineta. Madrid: 1621

——Teorica y exercicios de la gineta. Madrid: 1619

Lancre, Pierre de. Tableau de l'inconstance des mauvais anges. Paris: J. Berjon, 1612

——Paris: J. Berjon, 1613

——Paris: N. Buon, 1613

LANDA, DIEGO DE

—Salazar, P. de. Coronica y historia de la fundacion. Madrid? [1612]

Der Landstörtzer. *See* Alemán, Mateo

Der Landtstörtzer. *See* Alemán, Mateo

Der Landtstörtzer . . . Dritter Theil. *See* Freudenhold, Martin

Lange, Johannes. Epistolarum medicinalium. Hanau: Heirs of A. Wechel, for C. Marne, & Heirs of J. Aubry, 1605

Langenes, Barent. Erste Schiffart. *See* Houtman, Cornelis de. Erste Schiffart. Inn die Orientalische Indien. Nuremberg: 1602

—Hand-boeck, of Cort begrijp der caerten. Amsterdam: C. Claeszoon, 1609

—Thrésor de chartes. Leyden: C. Guyot, for C. Claeszoon, at Amsterdam, 1602

——[Frankfurt a.M.:] M. Becker, for H. Laurenszoon, at Amsterdam [ca. 1610?]

Langham, William. The garden of health. London: T. Harper, 1633

Den langh-verwachten donderslach. *See* Middelgeest, Simon van

La Noue, François de. Discours politiques et militaires. [Basel? Geneva?] 1612

——Geneva: P. & J. Chouët, 1614

Lanthorne and candle-light. *See* Dekker, Thomas

La Peyrère, Isaac de. Relation du Groenland. Paris: A. Courbé, 1647

LAW—MASSACHUSETTS

—Cotton, J. An abstract or the lawes of New England. London: 1641

—Massachusetts (Colony). Laws, statutes, etc. The capitall lawes of New-England. London: 1643

LAW—SPANISH AMERICA

—León Pinelo, A. R. de. Discurso sobre la importancia . . . de la recopilacion de las leyes. [Madrid: 1623]

—Solórzano Pereira, J. de. Disputationem de Indiarum jure . . . Tomus primus. Madrid: 1629

— —Disputationum de Indiarum jure . . . tomus alter. Madrid: 1639

— —Politica indiana. Madrid: 1648

— —Traduccion de la dedicatoria real. [Madrid:] 1639

—Spain. Laws, statutes, etc. Sumarios de la recopilacion general de las leyes. Madrid: 1628

—Spain. Laws, statutes, etc., 1516–1556 (Charles I). Leyes y ordenanças nuevamente hechas por su Magestad. Valladolid: 1603

LAW—VIRGINIA

—Strachey, W. For the colony in Virginea Britannia. Laws divine. London: 1612

Law-trickes. *See* Day, John

Laynez, Juan. Copia de una carta . . . a el . . . fr. Joseph de Sisneros. Malaga: J. Serrano de Vargas y Ureña, 1639

A learned summary. *See* Du Bartas, Guillaume de Salluste, seigneur

A learned treatise of globes. *See* Hues, Robert

Leather: a discourse. London: T. C[otes]., for M. Sparke, 1629

Leben dess seligen p. Ignatii. *See* Rivadeneira, Pedro de

Leben Francisci Borgiae. *See* Rivadeneira, Pedro de

Le Blanc, Vincent. Les voyages fameux. Paris: G. Clousier, 1648

— —Paris: G. Clousier, 1649

Le Blon, Christoph, ed. *See* La Peyrère, Isaac de. Die xxvi. Schiff-Fahrt. Frankfurt a.M.: 1650

Le Brun, Laurent. Ecclesiastes. Rouen: J. Le Boullenger, 1649

— —Rouen: J. Le Boullenger, 1650

—Nova Gallia delphino. Paris: J. Camusat, 1639

— —In his Ecclesiastes. Rouen: 1649

Le Candele, P. Wel-vaert vande West-Indische Compagnie. [Middelburg: 1646]

Lechford, Thomas. New-Englands advice. [London:] 1644

—Plain dealing. London: W. E[llis?]., & J. G[rismond?]., for N. Butter, 1642

L'Ecluse, Charles de. Curae posteriores. [Leyden:] Plantin Press [Raphelengius], 1611 (2)

—Exoticorum libri decem. [Leyden:] Plantin Office (Raphelengius), 1605

—Rariorum plantarum historia. Antwerp: Plantin Press, 1601

—*See also* Kircher, Athanasius. Ars magna lucis. Rome: 1646

Les leçons publiques. *See* La Barre, Antoine de

Lectiones aureae. *See* Spinelli, Giovanni Paolo

Ledesma, Diego de. Doctrine chrestienne. Rouen: R. Lallemant, 1630

Leech, John, poet. Musae priores. London: [J. Beale] 1620 (2)

Le Ferron, Arnoul. De rebus gestis Gallorum. *In* Emili, Paolo. De rebus gestis Francorum. Basel: [1601]

The legend of captaine Jones. *See* Lloyd, David

Leinsula, Franciscus. *See* Lisle, Francis

Leitão, Francisco de Andrade. *See* Andrade Leitão, Francisco de

Leiva y Aguilar, Francisco de. Desengaño contra el mal uso del tabaco. Córdova: S. de Cea Tesa, 1634

Le Jeune, Paul. Brieve relation du voyage de la Nouvelle France. Paris: S. Cramoisy, 1632

—Relation de ce qui s'est passé en la Nouvelle France en l'année 1633. Paris: S. Cramoisy, 1634 (2)

—Relation de ce qui s'est passé . . . en l'année 1634. Paris: S. Cramoisy, 1635 (2)

— —Avignon: J. Bramereau, 1636

—Relation de ce qui s'est passé . . . en l'année 1635. Paris: S. Cramoisy, 1636

—Relation de ce qui s'est passé . . . en l'année 1636. Paris: S. Cramoisy, 1637 (2)

—Relation de ce qui s'est passé . . . en l'année 1637. Rouen: J. Le Boullenger, 1638

— —Rouen: J. Le Boullenger, & P. de Bresche, at Paris, 1638

—Relation de ce qui s'est passé . . . en l'année 1638. Paris: S. Cramoisy, 1638 (2)

—Relation de ce qui s'est passé . . . en l'année 1639. Paris: S. Cramoisy, 1640 (2)

Le Maire, Jacob. Ephemerides sive Descriptio navigationis australis. *In* Herrera y Tordesillas, Antonio de. Novus orbis, sive Descriptio Indiae Occidentalis. Amsterdam: 1622

—Spieghel der australische navigatie. Amsterdam: M. Colijn, 1622

—*See also* Herrera y Tordesillas, Antonio de. Description des Indes Occidentales. Amsterdam: 1622

LE MAIRE, JACOB

—Spilbergen, J. van. Oost ende West-Indische spiegel. Leyden: 1619

LE MAIRE STRAIT

—Nodal, B. G. de. Relacion del viaje. Madrid: 1621

Le Mercier, François Joseph. Relation de ce qui s'est passé . . . en la mission des Hurons. *In* Le Jeune, Paul. Relation de ce qui s'est passé . . . en l'année 1638. Paris: 1638

—Relation de ce qui s'est passé

LÉRY, JEAN DE
—Camerarius, P. Operae horarum subcisivarum . . . Centuria altera. Frankfurt a.M.: 1601
— —Secunda centuria historica, das ist, Ander Theil. Leipzig: 1628
Lescarbot, Marc. A Dieu aux Francois retournans de la Nouvelle France. [La Rochelle: Heirs of J. Haultin, 1606?]
—Adieu a la France. [La Rochelle: 1606]
— —Rouen: J. Petit, 1606
—La conversion des sauvages. Paris: J. Millot [1610] (2)
—La defaite des sauvages armouchiquois. Paris: J. Périer [1608]
—Histoire de la Nouvelle France. Paris: J. Millot, 1609
— —Paris: J. Millot, 1611
— —Paris: J. Millot, 1612
— —Paris: A. Périer, 1617
— —Paris: A. Périer, 1618
—Les muses de la Nouvelle France. Paris: J. Millot, 1609
— —Paris: J. Millot, 1610
— —Paris: J. Millot, 1612
— —Paris: A. Périer, 1617
— —Paris: A. Périer, 1618
—Nova Francia. Gründliche History von Erfündung der grossen Landschafft. Augsburg: C. Dabertzhofer, 1613
—Nova Francia, or The Description of . . . New France. London: [Eliot's Court Press] for G. Bishop, 1609
— —London: [Eliot's Court Press] for A. Hebb [after 1625]
—Relation derniere. Paris: J. Millot, 1612
—Le tableau de la Suisse. Paris: A. Périer, 1618
A letetr [sic] written . . . to Sir G. Calvert. *See* Winne, Edward
Letras anuas dela Compañia de Jesus dela provincia . . . de Granada. *See* Jesuits. Letters from missions (South America)
A letter from W. A. London: 1623
A letter of many ministers. *See* Ball, John
A letter of Mr. John Cottons . . .

to Mr. Williams. *See* Cotton, John
A letter, sent into England from the Summer Ilands. *See* Hughes, Lewis
A letter sent to London. *See* Taylor, John, the Water-poet
A letter written . . . to Sir G. Calvert. *See* Winne, Edward
A letter written to the governours. London: [V. Simmes?] for T. Thorpe, & W. Aspley, 1603
Lettera . . . ove s'intendono casi . . . del terremoto. *See* González Chaparro, Juan
Lettera annua della v. provincia. *See* Ribera, Juan de
Lettera dell'elefante. *See* Bottifango, Giulio Cesare
Lettere annue d'Ethiopia, Malabar, Brasil. *See* Jesuits. Letters from missions
The letting of humours blood. *See* Rowlands, Samuel
Lettre annuelle de la province. *See* Ribera, Juan de
Lettre d'un pere capucin. *See* Claude d'Abbeville, Father
Lettre du pere Charles L'Allemant. *See* Lallemant, Charles
Lettre missive, touchant la conversion. *See* Bertrand, ——
Les lettres. *See* Pasquier, Etienne
Lettres de ratification du Roi des contrats du 12. fev. 1635. *See* France. Sovereigns, etc., 1610–1643 (Louis XIII)
[Lettres des Indes Occidentales.] *See* Jesuits. Letters from missions (South America)
Leubelfing, Johann von. Ein schön lustig Reissbuch. Ulm: J. Meder, 1612
Leublfing, Johann von. *See* Leubelfing, Johann von
Leubling, Johann von. *See* Leubelfing, Johann von
Levantamiento, y principios de Yangua. Málaga: J. René, 1619
Levendich discours vant ghemeyne lants wel-vaert. [Amsterdam:] B. Janszoon, 1622
Levett, Christopher. A voyage into New England. London: W. Jones, 1624

— —London: W. Jones, for E. Brewster, 1628
Lexicon historicum, geographicum. *See* Estienne, Charles
Leyes y ordenanças nuevamente hechas por su Magestad. *See* Spain. Laws, statutes, etc., 1516–1556 (Charles I)
L'Hermite, Jacques, supposed author. *See the following:*
—Journael vande Nassausche vloot. Amsterdam: 1626
—A true relation of the fleet. London: 1625
—Verhael van 't ghene den Admirael l'Hermite in . . . Peru verricht. Amsterdam: 1625
—Waerachtigh verhael van het success van de vlote. [Amsterdam?] 1625
L'HERMITE, JACQUES
—Bry, J. T. de. Historiarum Orientalis Indiae tomus XII. Frankfurt a.M.: 1628
— —Der zwölffte Theil der Orientalischen Indien. Frankfurt a.M.: 1628
—Bry, T. de. Vierzehender Theil Amerikanischer Historien. Hanau: 1630
—Casos notables, sucedidos en las costas de la ciudad de Lima. Seville: [1625]
—Diurnal der nassawischen Flotta. Strassburg: 1629
—La furieuse défaite des Espagnols et la . . . bataille donnee au Perou. Paris: 1625
—Hulsius, L. Die zwey und zwäntzigste Schiffart. Frankfurt a.M.: 1630
—Journael vande Nassausche vloot. Amsterdam: 1626
—Wassenaer, N. van. T'vyfdedeel . . . van het Historisch verhael. Amsterdam: 1624
Libavius, Andreas. Alchymia. Frankfurt a.M.: J. Sauer, for P. Kopff, 1606
—Alchymia triumphans. Frankfurt a.M.: J. Sauer, for P. Kopff, 1607
—Alchymistische Practic. Frankfurt a.M.: J. Sauer, for P. Kopff, 1603
—Praxis alchymiae. Frankfurt

a.M.: J. Sauer, for P. Kopff, 1604

—Sintagmatis selectorum. Frankfurt a.M.: N. Hoffmann, for P. Kopff, 1615

—Syntagma selectorum. Frankfurt a.M.: N. Hoffmann, for P. Kopff, 1611–13

Liber de antiquitate reipublicae Batavicae. *See* Grotius, Hugo

Liber de priscorum philosophorum verae medicinae materia. *See* Duchesne, Joseph

Liber primus Consultationum medicinalium. *See* Zecchi, Giovanni

Liber responsorum et consultationum medicinalium. *See* Massaria, Alessandro

La liberta pretesa dal supplice schiavo indiano. *See* Casas, Bartolomé de las, Bp

Libertas Veneta. *See* Graswinckel, Dirk

Liberty of conscience. *See* Robinson, Henry

La libra de Grivilio Vezzalmi. *See* Malvezzi, Virgilio, marchese

Libri duo de febribus. *See* Potier, Pierre

Libri xii de disciplinis. *See* Vives, Juan Luis

Libro de la cosmographia universal. *See* Sesse, Josepe de

Libro de las cinco excellencias del Español. *See* Peñalosa y Mondragón, Benito de

Libro de los secretos de agricultura. *See* Agustí, Miguel

Libro de phisonomia natural. *See* Cortés, Jerónimo

Libro del arte de cozina. *See* Granado, Diego

Libro intitulado Reduciones de oro. *See* Vázquez de Serna, Juan

Libro que trata de la enfermedad. *See* Torres, Pedro de

Libros reales de govierno . . . de la Secretaria del Peru. *See* León Pinelo, Antonio Rodríguez de

El licenciado d. Christoval de Moscoso y Cordova. *See* titles *under* Moscoso y de Córdoba, Cristóbal de

El licenciado don Christoval de Moscoso y Cordova. *See* titles

under Moscoso y de Córdoba, Cristóbal de

El licenciado don Iuan Gonçalez. *See* González, Juan

El licenciado Don Pedro Gonçalez de Mendoça. *See* González de Mendoza, Pedro

El licendiado D. Christoval de Moscoso y Cordova. *See* titles *under* Moscoso y de Córdoba, Cristóbal de

El licenciado Don Christoval de Moscoso y Cordova. *See* titles *under* Moscoso y de Córdoba, Cristóbal de

El licenciado Marcos de Torres . . . contra Doña Francisca Colon. *See* Torres, Marcos de

Liceti, Fortunio. De monstrorum caussis. Padua: G. Crivellari, 1616

— —Padua: P. Frambotti, 1634

—Litheosphorus. Udine: N. Schiratti, 1640A

Het licht der zee-vaert. *See* Blaeu, Willem Janszoon

Liddel, Duncan. Ars medica. Hamburg: Froben Bookshop (P. Lang), 1608

— —Hamburg: Froben Bookshop (P. Lang), 1617

— —Hamburg: Froben Bookshop (P. Lang), 1628

Liébault, Jean. Warhaffte Beschreibung dess edelen Krauts Nicotianae. [Frankfurt a.M.?] 1643

See also the following:

—Agustí, Miguel. Libro de los secretos de agricultura. Saragossa: [1625]?

— —Llibre dels secrets de agricultura. Barcelona: 1617

—Estienne, Charles. L'agriculture et maison rustique. [Geneva:] 1601

— —XV. Bücher Von dem Feldbaw. Strassburg: 1607

— —De veltbouw. Amsterdam: 1622

Liebergen, Arnout van. Apologiae, ofte Waerachtighe verantwoordinghe. Amsterdam: A. van Liebergen, 1643

Liebfriedt, Christian, von Gross Seufftzen, pseud. An gantz

Teutschlandt. [Frankfurt a.M.?] F. Snuhcam, 1620

Liefs, Jacob. Den lof vande geoctroyeerde Oost ende West-Indische Compagnye. Delft: J. P. Waalpots, 1630

—Lof-dicht over de wijt-vermaerde . . . victorie. [The Hague?] 1629

The life of b. Father Ignatius of Loyola. *See* Rivadeneira, Pedro de

The life of Gregorie Lopes. *See* Losa, Francisco de

The life of the holy patriarch. *See* Rivadeneira, Pedro de

Light from heaven. *See* Sibbes, Richard

The light of navigation. *See* Blaeu, Willem Janszoon

Lima. Consulado de mercaderes. Relacion de las fiestas. Seville: 1632

Lima. Universidad de San Marcos. Constituciones añadidas por los virreyes. Madrid: Imprenta Real, 1624

—Prologo de las constituciones. [Madrid? 1624?]

— —Seville: J. de Cabrera [1625]

LIMA. UNIVERSIDAD DE SAN MARCOS

—León Pinelo, A. R. de. Por la Real Universidad . . . de . . . Lima. [Madrid? 1631]

—Prado Beltran, B. de. Razonamiento panegyrico. Madrid: 1633

Lima (Ecclesiastical Province). Council, 1567. Sumario del concilio provincial. Seville: M. Clavijo, 1583

Lima (Ecclesiastical Province). Council, 1583. Catecismo en la lengua española, y aymara. Seville: B. Gómez, 1604

—Catecismo en la lengua española, y quichua. Rome: A. Zannetti, 1603

—Concilium Limense. Celebratum anno 1583. Madrid: J. Sánchez, 1614

—Confessario para los curas de Indios. Seville: C. Hidalgo, 1603

LIMA—CHURCH HISTORY

—Guillén y Colón, F. Vita,

muerte y milagros del prodigioso varon. Seville: 1637

—Lima (Ecclesiastical Province). Council, 1583. Concilium Limense. Celebratum anno 1583. Madrid: 1614

— —Confessario para los curas de Indios. Seville: 1603

—Mañozca, J. de. Señor. El licenciado Juan de Mañozca, inquisidor apostolico. [Madrid? ca. 1630?]

—Oré, L. J. de. Relacion de la vida . . . del venerable padre f. Francisco Solano. [Madrid: 1614]

—Vargas, L. de. Por Fray Geronimo Alonso de la Torre. [Madrid? 1650?]

—Villagómez, P. Abp. D. Petri de Villiagomez . . . Por edicto suo contra laicos. Madrid: 1650

LIMA—COMMERCE

—Lima. Consulado de mercaderes. Relacion de las fiestas. Seville: 1632

LIMA—HISTORY

—Crosse, W. The Dutch survay. London: 1625

—Lima (Ecclesiastical Province). Council, 1567. Sumario del concilio provincial. Seville: 1614

—Moscoso y de Córdoba, C. de. El licenciado Don Christoval de Moscoso y Cordoba . . . con Alonso de Carrion. Madrid: 1634

—Palafox y Mendoza, J. de, Bp. Por el licenciado don Iuan de Palafox y Mendoza. [Madrid: 1634]

—Pérez, J. Razon que da de si el padre Jacinto Perez . . . . Madrid: 1646

LIMA IN LITERATURE

—Velázquez, B. M. El filosofo del aldea. Pamplona: 1626

Liñán y Verdugo, Antonio. Aviso de los peligros. Madrid: Widow of A. Martín, 1621

—Guia y avisos de forasteros. Madrid: Widow of A. Martín, for M. de Silis, 1620

— —Madrid: Widow of A. Martín, for M. de Silis, 1621

— —Valencia: S. Esparsa, for J. Sonzonio, 1635

Linden, Johannes Antonides van der. De scriptis medicis. Amsterdam: J. Blaeu, 1637

Lingua; ofte Strijd. *See* Tomkis, Thomas

Lingua, or The combat. *See* Tomkis, Thomas

Linocier, Geoffroy. L'histoire des plantes. Paris: G. Macé, 1620, '19

Linschoten, Jan Huygen van. Beschrijvinghe van de gantsche custe van Guinea. Amsterdam: C. Claeszoon, 1605

— —Amsterdam: J. E. Cloppenburg, 1614

— —Amsterdam: J. E. Cloppenburg, 1623

— —Amsterdam: E. Cloppenburg, 1644

—Descriptio totius Guineae. *In his* Navigatio ac itinerarium. Amsterdam: 1614

—Description de l'Amerique. *In his* Histoire de la navigation. Amsterdam: 1619

—Dritter Theil Indiae Orientalis. Oppenheim: H. Galler, for J. T. de Bry, 1616

—Grand routier de mer. *In his* Histoire de la navigation. Amsterdam: 1619

—Histoire de la navigation. Amsterdam: H. Laurenszoon, 1610

— —Amsterdam: T. Pierre [i.e., D. P. Pers?] 1610

— —Amsterdam: J. E. Cloppenburg, 1619

— —Amsterdam: E. Cloppenburg, 1638

—Itinerario, voyage ofte Schipvaert. Amsterdam: C. Claeszoon, 1605, '04

—Itinerarium, ofte Schipvaert. Amsterdam: J. F. Cloppenburg, 1614

— —Amsterdam: J. E. Cloppenburg, 1623

— —Amsterdam: E. Cloppenburg, 1644

—Navigatio ac itinerarium. Amsterdam: J. Walschaert, 1614

—Reys-gheschrift. Amsterdam: C. Claeszoon, 1604

— —Amsterdam: J. E. Cloppenburg, 1614

— —Amsterdam: J. E. Cloppenburg, 1623

— —Amsterdam: E. Cloppenburg, 1644

—Tertia pars Indiae Orientalis. Frankfurt a.M.: M. Becker, for J. T. & J. I. de Bry, 1601

— —Frankfurt a.M.: K. Rötel, for W. Fitzer, & E. Kempfer, 1629

— —Frankfurt a.M.: K. Rötel, for W. Fitzer, 1629

—Voyagie, ofte Schip-vaert. Franeker: G. Ketel, for J. H. van Linschoten, at Enkhuizen, 1601

—Voyasie, ofte Schip-vaert. Amsterdam: J. E. Cloppenburg, 1624

Linton, Anthony. Newes of the complement . . . of navigation. London: F. Kingston, 1609

Lisboa, Christoval de. *See* Cristovão de Lisboa

Lisle, Francis. The kingdoms divisions anatomized. London: J. Clowes, for Hannah Allen, 1649

Literae annuae . . . Anni 1606. 1607 et 1608. *See* Jesuits. Letters from missions. Annuae litterae (1606, 1607 et 1608) 1618

Literae apostolicae. *See* Jesuits. Compendium privilegiorum

Litheosphorus. *See* Liceti, Fortunio

Lithgow, William. A most delectable . . . discourse. London: N. Okes, for T. Archer, 1614

—London: N. Okes, for T. Archer, 1616

— —London: N. Okes, 1623

—The totall discourse. London: N. Okes, 1632

— —London: N. Okes, for N. Fussell, & H. Moseley, 1632

— —London: J. Okes, 1640

Litterae . . . annorum M.D.XC-III. et M.D.XCV. *See* Jesuits. Letters from missions. Annuae litterae (1594–95) 1604

Litterae annuae . . . anni M.DC.II. *See* Jesuits. Letters

Lopes, Duarte. Beschrijvinge van 't koningkrijck Congo. Amsterdam: A. Roest, for J. Hartgers, 1650

—Regnum Congo, hoc est Vera descriptio. Frankfurt a.M.: E. Kempfer, for Heirs of J. T. de Bry, 1624

—Regnum Congo, hoc est Warhaffte . . . Beschreibung. Frankfurt a.M.: M. Becker, for J. T. & J. I. de Bry, 1609

Lopes, Francisco. Milagroso successo do Conde de Castel Milhor. Lisbon: M. da Silva, 1643

Lopez, Eduart. *See* Lopes, Duarte

Lopez, Francisco. *See* Lopes, Francisco

López, Gregorio, ed. *See* Castile. Laws, statutes, etc., 1252–1284 (Alfonso X). Las siete partidas nuevamente glosadas. Mainz: 1611

LÓPEZ, GREGORIO

—Losa, F. de. The life of Gregorie Lopes. Paris: 1638

— —La vida, que hizo el siervo de Dios Gregorio Lopez. Lisbon: 1615

— —La vie de Gregoire Lopez. Paris: 1644

—Remón, A. Relacion de como martirizaron. Madrid: 1625

— —La vida del siervo de Dios Gregorio Lopez. Madrid: 1617

López, Juan, Bp. Historia de Santo Domingo, pte 5a. Valladolid: J. de Rueda, 1621

—Historia general de Santo Domingo, pte 4a. Valladolid: F. Fernández de Córdoba, 1615

López de Altuna, Pedro. Coronica general del Orden de la Santissima Trinidad, pte 1a. Segovia: D. Díaz de la Carrera, 1637

López de Calatyd, Antonio. *See* Spain. Casa de Contratación de las Indias. Relacion de las obligaciones. [Seville? 1612?]

—*See also* Spain. Casa de Contratación de las Indias. Relacion de las cargas y obligaciones. Seville: 1623

López de Castro, Baltasar. Baltasar Lopez de Castro, criado de su Magestad. Valladolid: 1603

López de Guitian Sotomayor, Diego. Sẽnor. El capitan Diego Lopez de Guitian Sotomayor. [Madrid? 1640?]

López de Haro, Damian. Constituciones. *See* San Juan, Puerto Rico (Diocese). Synod, 1645. Constituciones synodales. Madrid: 1647

López de León, Pedro. Practica y teorica de las apostemas. Seville: L. Estupiñán, 1628

López Madera, Gregorio. Excelencias de la monarquia. Madrid: L. Sanchez, 1624

— —Madrid: L. Sanchez, for M. Gil de Córdova, 1625

López Solis, Francisco. Por los religiosos de la provincia de san Hipolyto Martyr de Guaxaca. [Madrid? 1630?]

Lorenzini, Niccolò. Le lagrime del peccatore. Venice: B. Giunta, & G. B. Ciotti and Co., 1608

Losa, Francisco de. The life of Gregorie Lopes. Paris: [Widow of J. Blagaert] 1638

—Vida que el siervo de Dios Gregorio Lopez hizo. Madrid: Imprenta Real, for A.del Ribero Rodríguez, 1642

—La vida, que hizo el siervo de Dios Gregorio Lopez. Lisbon: P. Craesbeeck, 1615

—La vie de Gregoire Lopez. Paris: M. & J. Hénault, 1644

Lossa, Francisco. *See* Losa, Francisco de

LOTTERIES

—Great Britain. Sovereigns, etc., 1603–1625 (James I). Whereas at the humble suit and request of sundry. London: [1621]

—Great Britain. Council for Virginia. The articles sett down for the second lottery. London: 1612

— —By his Majesties Councell for Virginia . . . a little standing lotterie. [London:] 1613

— —By his Majesties Counsell for Virginea . . . for the advancement of . . . Virginea. London: 1612

— —The lottery for Virginea. London: 1612

—Virginia Company of London. A declaration for the certaine time. London: 1615

— —[A declaration of the presente estate. London: 1614]

The lottery for Virginea. *See* Great Britain. Council for Virginia

Loubayssin de Lamarca, Francisco. Historia tragicomica de Don Henrique de Castro. Paris: Widow of M. Guillemot, 1612

— —Paris: A. Tiffaine, for Widow of M. Guillemot, 1617

The lovers melancholy. *See* Ford, John

Lowe, Peter. A discourse of . . . chyrurgerie. London: T. Purfoot, 1612, '11

— —London: T. Purfoot, 1634

Loyseau, Guillaume. De internorum externorumque ferme omnium curatione libellus. Bordeaux: G. Vernoy, 1617

—De internorum externorumque morborum ferme omnium curatione libellus. Bordeaux: G. Vernoy, 1620

—Observations medicinales et chirurgicales. Bordeaux: G. Vernoy, 1617

Loza, Francisco. *See* Losa, Francisco de

Lucerna de corteggiani. *See* Crisci, Giovanni Battista

Lucius, Ludwig. Historia Jesuitica. Basel: J. J. Genath, 1627

— —Basel: 1632

—Jesuiter-Histori. Basel: J. J. Genath, 1626

Ludwig, prince of Anhalt-Köthen. *See* Anhalt-Köthen, Ludwig von

Lugo, Bernardo de. Gramatica en la lengua general del nuevo reyno. Madrid: B. de Guzman, 1619

Lugo y Dávila, Francisco de. Desenganos y replicas a las proposiciones de Gerardo Basso. Madrid: Imprenta Real, 1632

Anales de Aragon, pte 1a. Saragossa: 1630

—Mexía, P. Les diverses leçons. Tournon: 1604

— —Ragionamenti dottissimi et curiosi. Venice: 1615

— —De verscheyden lessen. Amsterdam: 1617

—Reyd, E. van. Voornaemste gheschiedenissen. Arnhem: 1626

—Roca, J. A. Vera Zúñiga y Figueroa, conde de la. Epitome de la vida . . . del . . . emperador Carlos V. Madrid: 1622

— —Histoire de l'empereur Charles V. Paris: 1633

—Veer, G. de. Dritte Theil, und warhafftige Relation der dreyen . . . Schiffart. Nuremberg: 1602

— —Le trois navigations. Paris: 1610

— —The true . . . description of three voyages. London: 1609

— —Vraye description de trois voyages. Amsterdam: 1604

— —Waerachtighe beschryvinghe van drie seylagien. Amsterdam: 1605

—Vernulz, N. de. Apologia pro augustissima . . . gente austriaca. Louvain: 1635

MAGALHÃES, FERNÃO DE— POETRY

—Le Moyne, P. Les poesies. Paris: 1650

Magano, Juan. Memorial a los eminentissimos . . . cardenales. [Rome? 1650?]

Magati, Cesare. De rara medicatione vulnerum. Venice: A. & B. Dei, 1616

Magellan, Ferdinand. *See* Magalhães, Fernão de

MAGELLAN, STRAIT OF

—Camerarius, J. Symbolorum et emblematum . . . centuria quarta. [Nuremberg?] 1604

—Discours by forme van remonstrantie. [Netherlands:] 1608

—Donne, J. LXXX sermons. London: 1640

—Du Chevreul, J. Sphaera. Paris: 1623

—Gellibrand, H. A discourse mathematical. London: 1635

—Grimestone, E. A generall historie of the Netherlands. London: 1627

—Houtman, C. de. Erste Schiffart. Inn die Orientalische Indien. Nuremberg: 1602

—Le Maire, J. Spieghel der australische navigatie. Amsterdam: 1622

—Merula, P. Cosmographiae generalis libri tres. [Leyden:] 1605

—Neck, J. C. van. Waerachtigh verhael van de schip-vaert op Oost-Indien. Amsterdam: 1648

—Nederlandsche Oost-Indische Compagnie. Het out Oost-Indische octroy. [The Hague? 1602?]

—Neville, H. The parliament of ladies. [London:] 1647

—Nodal, B. G. de. Relacion del viaje. Madrid: 1621

—Noort, O. van. Extract oft Kort verhael uit het groote journael. Rotterdam: 1601

— —Wonderlijcke voyagie, by de Hollanders gedaen. Amsterdam: 1648

—Potgieter, B. J. Historiae antipodum sive Novi Orbis. Frankfurt a.M.: 1633

— —Historisch ende wijdtloopigh verhael. Amsterdam: 1617

— —Historische Relation. Frankfurt a.M.: 1601

— —Relatio historica. Frankfurt a.M.: 1602

—Reyd, E. van. Belgarum . . . annales. Leyden: 1633

—Riolan, J. Gigantologie. Paris: 1618

—Schouten, W. C. Americae pars undecima. Oppenheim: 1619

— —Giornale overo Descrittione. Venice: 1621

— —Historische Beschreibung der . . . Reyse. Frankfurt a.M.: 1619

— —Journal . . . van de wonderlicke reyse. Amsterdam: 1618

— —Journal . . . de l'admirable voyage. Amsterdam: [1618?]

— —Novi Freti . . . detectio. Amsterdam: 1619

— —Relacion diaria del viage. Madrid: 1619

— —The relation of a wonderfull voiage. London: 1619

— —Die sechtzehende Schifffahrt. Frankfurt a.M.: 1619

— —Warhaffte Beschreibung der . . . Räyse. Arnhem: 1618

—Spilbergen, J. van. Copie van een brief. Delft: 1617

— —t'Historiael journael. Delft: 1601

— —Indiae Orientalis pars septima. Frankfurt a.M.: 1606

— —Het journael. Delft: 1605

— —Siebender Theil der Orientalischen Indien. Frankfurt a.M.: 1605

—Een waerachtige beschryvinghe van de schoone victorie. Amsterdam: 1616

—Zouch, R. The dove. London: 1613

MAGELLAN, STRAIT OF— FICTION

—Espinel, V. Relaciones de la vida del escudero Marcos de Obregon. Madrid: 1618

MAGELLAN, STRAIT OF— POETRY

—Scarron, P. La suite des oeuvres burlesques . . . Seconde partie. Paris: 1647

Magini, Giovanni Antonio. Histoire universelle des Indes Orientales. *In* Wytfliet, Corneille. Histoire universelle des Indes. Douai: 1607

See also the following:

—Ptolemaeus, Claudius. Geografia. Padua: 1621, '20

— —Geographiae libri octo. Amsterdam: 1605

—Wytfliet, Corneille. Histoire universelle des Indes. Douai: 1605

Magnen, Jean Chrysostôme. Exercitations de tabaco. Pavia: G. A. Magri, 1648

Magnes, sive De arte magnetica opus. *See* Kircher, Athanasius

Magneticall advertisements. *See* Barlow, William

Magnus, Olaus, Abp. Historia . . . de gentibus septen-

of all nations. *See* Boemus, Johann

Manojuelo de romances nuevas. *See* Lobo Lasso de la Vega, Gabriel

Mañozca, Juan de. Señor. El licenciado Juan de Mañozca, inquisidor apostolico. [Madrid? ca. 1630?]

Mañozca y Zamora, Juan de. Memorial al Rey y satisfaccion a los 56 cargos. Madrid: 1640

MANRIQUE DE LARA, GERÓNIMO, BP
—Quiñones, D. de. Oracion funebre. Valladolid: 1645

MANRIQUE DE LARA, JORGE
—Spain. Sovereigns, etc., 1598–1621 (Philip III). Cedula en que Su Magestad da licencia. [Madrid? 1615?]

Manuel de Mello, Francisco. *See* Mello, Francisco Manuel de

A map of Virginia. *See* Smith, Capt. John

The mapp and description of New-England. *See* Stirling, William Alexander, 1st earl of

MARANHÃO, BRAZIL
—Estaço da Silveira, S. Relação summaria das cousas do Maranhão. Lisbon: 1624
—Histoire veritable de ce qui c'est passé. Paris: 1615
—Histoire veritable du combat. Paris: 1615
—Pezieu, L. de. Brief recueil des particularitez . . . de l'isle de Marignan. Lyons: 1613

MARANHÃO, BRAZIL—DISCOVERY & EXPLORATION
—Maldonado, J. Relacion del primer descubrimiento del rio de las Amazonas. [Madrid? 1642?]

MARANHÃO, BRAZIL—HISTORY
—Yves d'Evreux. Suitte de lHistoire des choses . . . advenues en Maragnan. Paris: 1615

Maravillas del Parnaso. *See* Pinto de Moraes, Jorge

Marbecke, Roger. A defence of tabacco. London: R. Field, for T. Man, 1602

Marcgraf, Georg. Historiae rerum naturalium Brasiliae libri

octo. *See* Piso, Willem. Historia naturalis Brasiliae. Leyden: 1648

Marcos da Lisboa, Bp. Chronicas da ordem dos Frades menores, pte 1a–3a. Lisbon: P. Craesbeeck, for T. do Valle, 1615
—Chroniques des Frères mineurs, pte 3me. Paris: Widow of G. Chaudière, 1604
——Paris: R. Fouët, 1623
—Cronicken der eingesetzten Orden dess heiligen Vatters Francisci. Munich: Anna Berg, for J. Hertsroy, 1620
—Delle chroniche de' Frati minori . . . parte terza. Venice: B. Barezzi, 1612
—Delle chroniche dell'Ordine . . . parte quarta. *See* Daza, Antonio. Delle chroniche . . . parte quarta. Venice: 1608
—Delle croniche de gli ordini instituti dal p.s. Francisco, parte terza. Milan: G. Bordone, & P. M. Locarno, 1605
——Venice: E. Viotti, 1606

Mare clausum. *See* Selden, John
Mare liberum. *See* Grotius, Hugo

Marees, Pieter de. Beschrijvinghe ende Historische verhael . . . van Guinea. Amsterdam: M. Colijn, 1617
—Beschryvinge ende historische verhael . . . van Gunea. Amsterdam: C. Claeszoon, 1602
—Description et recit historial . . . de Gunea. Amsterdam: C. Claeszoon, 1605
—Indiae Orientalis, pars vi. Frankfurt a.M.: W. Richter, for J. T. & J. I. de Bry, 1604
—Sechster Theil der Orientalischen Indien. Frankfurt a.M.: W. Richter, 1603
—Siebende Schifffahrt in . . . Guineam. Frankfurt a.M.: W. Richter, for L. Hulsius, 1603
——Frankfurt a.M.: E. Emmel, for Heirs of L. Hulsius, 1624
—Siebende Schiffart. Frankfurt a.M.: W. Richter, for Heirs of L. Hulsius, 1606

Margarita chyrurgica. *See* Hobbes, Stephen

Marguérite d'Angoulême, Queen of Navarre. L'Heptameron. Paris: J. Bessin, 1615
——Rouen: D. Du Petit-Val, 1625

Mariana, ——, licenciado. Carta que escrivio el licenciado Mariana. [Madrid?: 1636]

Mariana, Juan de. Historia general de España. Toledo: P. Rodríguez, 1601
——Madrid: L. Sánchez, 1608
——Madrid: Widow of A. Martín, & J.de la Cuesta, for A. Pérez, 1617, '16
——Madrid: L. Sánchez, 1623
——Toledo: D. Rodríguez, 1623
——Madrid: F. Martínez, 1635
——Madrid: C. Sánchez, for G. de León, 1650
—Historiae de rebus Hispaniae. Mainz: B. Lipp, for Heirs of A. Wechel, 1605
——Mainz: D. & D. Aubry, & C. Schleich, 1619
—Historiae hispanicae appendix. Frankfurt a.M.: C.de Marne, & Heirs of J. Aubry, 1606
—Summarium ad Historiam Hispaniae. Mainz: D. & D. Aubry, & C. Schleich, 1619

Marianus de Orscelar. Gloriosus Franciscus redivivus. Ingolstadt: W. Eder, 1625

MARIGOLDS
—Boodt, A. B. de. Florum . . . icones. Frankfurt a.M.: 1609
—Duchesne, J. Ad veritatem hermeticae medicinae. Paris: 1604
——The practise of chymicall . . . physicke. London: 1605
—Franck, J. Speculum botanicum. Uppsala: 1638
—Martini, L. Alle christelige . . . jomfruers aerekrantz. Copenhagen: 1614
——Christeliga jungfrwrs ärakrantz. Rostock: 1608
—Der christlichen Jungkfrawen Ehrenkräntzlein. Prague: 1602
—Paulli, S. Flora Danica. Copenhagen & Antwerp: 1648, '47
—Rosenberg, J. K. Rhodologia. Strassburg: 1628

—Spiegel, A. van de. Isagoges in rem herbariam. Padua: 1606

—Syreniusz Syrénski, S. Zielnik. Cracow: 1613

Marín de Armendariz, Pedro. Condiciones que el veedor Pedro Marin de Armendariz . . . tratan de efectuar. [Madrid? 1642]

Marinelli, Curzio. Pharmacopaea. Hanau: C. Schleich, 1617

— —Venice: 1617

Marino, Giovanni Battista. L'Adone, poema. Paris: O. de Varennes, 1623

— —Turin: Compagnia della Concordia [1623?]

— —Venice: G. Sarzina, 1623

— —Turin: Concordia, 1624

— —Venice: G. Sarzina [1626?]

— —Venice: G. Sarzina, 1626

— —Paris: M. Sonnius, 1627

— —Turin: Heirs of G. D. Tarino, 1627

—La Murtoleide. 'Nuremberg: J. Stamphier' [i.e., Venice?] 1619

— —'Frankfurt a.M.: G. Beyer' [i.e., Venice?] 1626 (2)

— —'Speyer' [i.e., Naples?] 1629

— —'Nuremberg: J. Stamphier' [i.e., Venice?] 1642

MARITIME LAW. *See also* FREEDOM OF THE SEAS

—Great Britain. Sovereigns, etc., 1625–1649 (Charles I). A proclamation against the disorderly transporting. London: 1637

— —A proclamation to restraine the transporting of passengers. London: 1638

—Selden, J. Mare clausum. London: 1635

Mariz Carneiro, Antonio de. Regimento de pilotos. Lisbon: L. de Anveres, 1642

Markham, Gervase. The art of archerie. London: B. A[lsop]., & T. F[awcett]., for B. Fisher, 1634

—Cavelarice, or The English horseman. [London: E. Allde, & W. Jaggard] for E. White, 1607

— —London: E. Allde, for E. White, 1617, '16

—Cheape and good husbandry. London: T. S[nodham]., for R. Jackson, 1614

— —London: T. S[nodham]., for R. Jackson, 1616

— —London: T. S[nodham]., for R. Jackson, 1623

— —London: Anne Griffin, for J. Harrison, 1631

— —London: N. Okes, for J. Harrison, 1631

— —London: B. Alsop, for J. Harrison, 1648

—Countrey contentments. London: J. B[eale]., for R. Jackson, 1615

— —London: J. B[eale]., for R. Jackson, 1623

—The English house-wife. London: N. Okes, for J. Harrison, 1631

— —London: Anne Griffin, for J. Harrison, 1637

— —*See also his* Countrey contentments. London: 1615

—Hungers prevention. London: A. Math[ewes]., for Anne Helme, & T. Langley, 1621

—*See also* Estienne, Charles. Maison rustique, or, The countrey farme. London: 1616

Marlowe, Christopher. Doctor Faustus. London: V. S[immes]., for T. Bushell, 1604

— —London: G. E[ld]., for J. Wright, 1609

— —London: G. E[ld]., for J. Wright, 1611

— —London: J. Wright, 1616

— —London: J. Wright, 1619

— —London: J. Wright, 1620

— —London: J. Wright, 1624

— —London: J. Wright, 1628

— —London: J. Wright, 1631

Marmion, Shackerley. A fine companion. London: A. Mathewes, for R. Meighen, 1633

—Hollands leaguer. London: J. B[eale]., for J. Grove, 1632 (2)

Marquardus, Joannes. Practica medicinalis. Frankfurt a.M.: N. Hoffmann, for P. Musculus, & R. Pistorius, 1610

— —Cologne: P. Henning, 1620

— —Cologne: P. Henning, 1621

Márquez de Cisneros, ——. Por Don Juan de Leoz, cavallero. [Madrid:] F. Martínez [1629]

—Por Don Lope de Hozes y Cordova. Madrid: Widow of J. González, 1635

—Por el Consulado de Sevilla. Madrid: Widow of J. González, 1634

—Por el señor D. Carlos de Ibarra. Madrid: Widow of J. González, 1634

Márquez de Torres, Francisco. Medio suave y facil. [Madrid? ca. 1635?]

Marradon, Bartolomeo. Dialogo del uso del tabaco . . . y del chocolate. Seville: G. Ramos Bejarano, 1618

—*See also* Colmenero de Ledesma, Antonio. Du chocolate, discours curieux. Paris: 1643

Marschalk, Johan Wilhelm. *See* Zesen, Philipp von. Durch-aus vermehrter . . . Helikon. Wittenberg: 1649

Marston, John. The malcontent. London: V. S[immes]., for W. Aspley, 1604

—Tragedies and comedies. London: [A. Mathewes] for W. Sheares, 1633

—What you will. London: G. Eld, for T. Thorpe, 1607

— —*In his* Workes. London: 1633

—The workes . . . being tragedies and comedies. London: [A. Mathewes] for W. Sheares, 1633

See also the following:

—Chapman, George. Eastward Hoe. London: 1605

—Jack Drum's entertainment. Jacke Drums entertainment. London: 1601

Martens van Velle, Nicasius. *See* Velle, Nicasius Martens van

Martensz., Frans. *See* Martinius, Franciscus

Martí, Juan José. De la vida del picaro Guzman de Alfarach, 2a pte. Barcelona: J. Amello, for A. Ribera, 1602

— —Barcelona: J. Amello, for J. Simón, 1602

————Valencia: P. P. Mey, for F. Miguel, 1602

——Barcelona: J. Cendrat, 1603

——Barcelona: S. de Cormellas, for G. Aleu, 1603

——Lisbon: A. Alvarez, 1603

——Lisbon: J. Rodriguez, 1603

——Madrid: J. Flamenco, for F. López, 1603

——Milan: G. Bordone, & P. M. Locarno, 1603

——Salamanca: A. Renaut, 1603

——Saragossa: A. Tavano, 1603

——Brussels: R. Velpius, 1604

—*See also* Alemán, Mateo. Der Landtstörtzer. Munich: 1615

Martínez, Francisco. *See* Martinius, Franciscus

MARTÍNEZ DE LEYVA, FERNANDO

—Duarte Navarro, ——. El almirante don Fernando Martinez de Leyva. [Madrid? 1611?]

Martínez de Mata, Francisco. Memorial en razon de la despoblacion. [Madrid? 1650?] (3)

Martini, Franciscus. *See* Martinius, Franciscus

Martini, Lucas. Alle christelige . . . jomfruers aerekrantz. Copenhagen: H. Waldkirch, 1614

—Christeliga jungfrwrs ärakrantz. Rostock: S. Mölemann, 1608

—Der christlichen Jungkfrawen Ehrenkräntzlein. Prague: W. Marino, 1602

Martini, Matthäus. De morbis mesenterii abstrusioribus. Halle: M. Oelschlegel, 1625

——Leipzig: K. Klosemann, 1630

MARTINIQUE

—Bouton, J. Relation de l'establissement des François . . . en Martinique. Paris: 1640

Martinius, Franciscus. Argonauta Batavus. Kampen: P. H. Wyringanus, 1629

Martyn, Joseph. New epigrams. London: G. Eld, 1621

Martyn, William. The historie and lives of the kings of England. London: R. Young, 1638

Martyrologium Franciscanum. *See* Du Monstier, Arthur

MARYLAND

—Eburne, R. A plaine path-way to plantations. London: 1624

—Hayman, R. Quodlibets, lately come over from New Britaniola. London: 1628

—Plantagenet, B. A description of . . . New Albion. [London:] 1648

—Vaughan, W. The golden fleece. London: 1626

——The Newlanders cure. London: 1630

MARYLAND—COLONIZATION

—A moderate and safe expedient. [London?] 1646

MARYLAND—DESCRIPTION

—Bullock, W. Virginia impartially examined. London: 1649

—Evelyn, R. A direction for adventurers . . . And a true description of . . . new Albion. [London?] 1641

—White, A. A declaration of the Lord Baltimore's plantation. [London? 1633]

MARYLAND—HISTORY

—A relation of the . . . Lord Baltemore's plantation. [London? 1634]

—Whitbourne, Sir R. A discourse . . . for the advancement of . . . New-found-land. London: 1622

——A discourse and discovery of New-found-land. London: 1622

Mascardi, Agostino. Ethicae prolusiones. Paris: S. Cramoisy, 1639

Mascarenhas, Antonio. Relacam dos procedimentos. [Lisbon? 1626]

—Relação dos procedimentos. [Lisbon: 1625?]

Mascarenhas, Jorge. *See* Montalvão, Jorge Mascarenhas, marquez de

The maske of flowers. London: N. O[kes]., for R. Wilson, 1614

Mason, John. A briefe discourse of the New-found-land. Edinburgh: A. Hart, 1620

Massa, Isaac. Beschryvinghe van der Samoyeden landt. *See* Gerritsz, Hessel. Beschryvinghe

van der Samoyeden landt. Amsterdam: 1612

—Descriptio terrae Samojedarum. *In* Gerritsz, Hessel. Descriptio ac delineatio geographica detectionis freti. Amsterdam: 1612

Massachusetts (Colony). The humble request of his Majesties loyall subjects. London: [M. Fletcher] for J. Bellamy, 1630

Massachusetts (Colony). Laws, statutes, etc. The capitall lawes of New-England. London: B. Allen, 1643

MASSACHUSETTS

—Newes from New-England: of a most strange . . . birth. London: 1642

MASSACHUSETTS—CHURCH HISTORY

—Child, J. New Englands Jonas. London: 1647

—Cobbet, T. A just vindication of the covenant. London: 1648

—Cushman, R. A sermon preached at Plimmoth. London: 1622

—Lydius, J. Historie der beroerten van Engelandt. Dordrecht: 1647

MASSACHUSETTS—COLONIZATION

—Massachusetts (Colony). The humble request of his Majesties loyall subjects. London: 1630

MASSACRES

—[Mourning Virginia. London: 1622]

—Sandys, G. A paraphrase upon the Psalmes of David. London: 1636

Massaria, Alessandro. Liber responsorum et consultationum medicinalium. Lyons: L. Durand, 1622

—Opera medica. Lyons: J. A. Candy, 1634

—Practica medica. Frankfurt a.M.: M. Hartmann, for N. Basse, 1601

——Treviso: E. Deuchino, for G. B. Pulciano, 1607

——Venice: T. Bertolotti, 1613

——Venice: T. Bertolotti, 1618

— —Lyons: L. Durand, 1622
— —Venice: G. A. Guliano, 1622
— —Venice: B. Barezzi, 1642
Massinger, Philip. A new way to pay old debts. London: E. P[urslowe]., for H. Seile, 1633
The mastive. *See* Parrot, Henry
MATAL, JEAN
—Donne, J. Biathanatos. London: [1647]
— —Conclave Ignatii. [London: 1611]
— —Ignatius his conclave. London: 1611
MATANZAS BAY, CUBA
—Ampzing, S. West-Indische triumph-basuyne. Haarlem: 1629
—Avellaneda Manrique, J. de. Memorial de la culpa que resulta de la pesquisa. [Madrid? 1629?]
—Baerle, K. van. Laurus Flandrica. Amsterdam: 1644
— —Trophaeum Arausionense. Amsterdam: 1631
—Eibergen, R. Swymel-klacht des Spaenschen conincks. Amsterdam: 1629
—Eroberung der reiche silbervloot inde bay . . . Matancae. [Amsterdam? ca. 1629]
—Hein, P. P. Beschreibung von Eroberung der . . . Flotta. Amsterdam: 1628
—Kannenburch, H. van. Protest ofte Scherp dreyghement. Middelburg: 1629
—Pels, E. Lof-dicht des vermaerde . . . zee-heldt Pieter Pietersen Heyn. Amsterdam: 1629
—Solórzano Pereira, J. de. Discurso i alegacion en derecho. Madrid: 1631
—Souter, D. Sené-boher. Haarlem: 1630
—Tijdinge hoe dat . . . Pieter Pietersz. Heyn, ende . . . Loncq, de vlote . . . hebben aenghetast. Amsterdam: 1628
—Verovering vande silver-vloot. Amsterdam: [1629]
—Wijnandts, W. Lobspruch uber die herrliche Victori. [Netherlands:] 1629
— —Lof-dicht over de heerlijcke victorie. Middelburg: 1629

Matelief, Cornelis. Journael ende Historische verhael van de treffelijcke reyse. Amsterdam: A. H. Roest, for J. Hartgers, 1648
MATERIA MEDICA. *See also* BOTANY, MEDICAL *and* DRUGS *and* specific medicines
—Fernel, J. Pharmacia. Hanau: 1605
—Fioravanti, L. Dello specchio di scientia universale. Venice: 1603
— —[Miroir universel des arts et des sciences.] Paris: 1602
—Norton, S. Metamorphosis lapidum ignobilium. Frankfurt a.M.: 1630
—Pharmacopoea sive Dispensatorium Coloniense. Cologne: [1628]
—Pharmacopoeia Augustana. Augsburg: 1613
—Pharmacopoeia Bruxellensis. Brussels: 1641
—Piso, W. Historia naturalis Brasiliae. Leyden: 1648
—Prevost, J. La medicine des pauvres. Paris: 1646
— —Medicina pauperum. Frankfurt a.M.: 1641
—Renou, J. de. Dispensatorium Galeno chymicum. Hanau: 1631
— —Dispensatorium medicum. Frankfurt a.M.: 1609
— —Le grand dispensaire medicinal. Lyons: 1624
— —Institutionum pharmaceuticarum libri quinque. Paris: 1608
— —Les oeuvres pharmaceutiques. Lyons: 1626
—Rivière, L. Praxis medica. Paris: 1640
—Schröder, J. Pharmacopeia medico-chymica. Ulm: 1641
—Taxa medicamentorum. [Strassburg:] 1647
—Thoner, A. Observationum medicinalium . . . libri quatuor. Ulm: 1649
—Wittich, J. Bericht von den . . . Bezoardischen Steinen. [Arnstadt:] 1601
MATERIA MEDICA—MEXICO
—Hernández, F. Rerum medica-

rum Novae Hispaniae thesaurus. Rome: 1628
Mather, Richard. An heart-melting exhortation. London: A. M[athewes]., for J. Rothwell, 1650
—A reply to Mr. Rutherford. London: J. Rothwell, & H. Allen, 1647
Matienzo, Juan de. Commentaria. Madrid: L. Sánchez, for J. Hasrey, 1613
Matthieu, Pierre. Dell'historia di S. Luigi. Venice: F. Baba, 1628
— —Venice: F. Baba, 1629
— —Venice: The Giuntas, 1638
—Della perfetta historia di Francia. Venice: B. Barezzi, 1624
— —Venice: B. Barezzi, 1625
— —Venice: B. Barezzi, 1638
—Histoire de France. Paris: J. Mettayer, & M. Guillemot, 1605
— —Paris: J. Mettayer, & M. Guillemot, 1606
— —Leyden: C. Bonaventure, 1608–10
— —Paris: J. Mettayer, & M. Guillemot, 1609
— —Paris: J. Mettayer, & M. Guillemot, 1614
— —Paris: J. Mettayer, & M. Guillemot, 1615
— —Rouen: J. Osmont, & T. Daré, 1615 (v. 1); Paris: J. Bessin [1615?] (v. 2)
— —Cologny: P. Aubert, 1617
—Histoire de France soubs les regnes de Francois I . . . . Paris: Widow of N. Buon, 1631
— —Paris: C. Sonnius, 1631
—Histoire de sainct Louys. Paris: B. Martin, 1618
—Historia di Francia. Venice: B. Fontana, 1623
— —Venice: B. Fontana, 1624
—Historia Henrici IV. *See* Boutrays, Raoul. Historiopolitographia. Frankfurt a.M.: 1610
—Opere. t 1. *See his* Dell'historia di S. Luigi. Venice: 1638
—Opere. t 3. *See his* Della perfetta historia di Francia. Venice: 1638
Mattioli, Pietro Andrea. Les commentaires . . . sur les six

livres de Pedacius Dioscoride. Lyons: P. Rigaud, 1605

——Lyons: P. Rigaud, 1619

——Lyons: P. Rigaud, 1620

——Lyons: C. Rigaud, & C. Obert, 1627

——Lyons: Widow of C. Rigaud, & Sons of P. & C. Rigaud, 1642

—De i discorsi . . . nelli sei libri di Pedacio Dioscoride. Venice: B. degli Alberti, & D. Nicolino, 1604

—I discorsi. Venice: 1618

——Venice: A. Muschio, for M. Ginammi, 1621

——Venice: M. Ginammi, 1645

—Kreutterbuch. Frankfurt a.M.: N. Hoffmann, for J. Fischer, 1611

——Frankfurt a.M.: Heirs of J. Fischer, 1626

Mauritiados libri vi. *See* Ens, Gaspar

Mauritiados libri xii. *See* Plante, Franciscus

Mauritius redux. *See* Baerle, Kaspar van

Mayerne, Louis Turquet de (d. 1618). The generall historie of Spaine. London: A. Islip, & G. Eld, 1612

—Histoire generale d'Espagne. Paris: A. L'Angelier, 1608

——Paris: S. Thiboust, 1635

Mayerne, Louis Turquet de (fl. 1648). Discours sur la carte universelle. Paris: 1648

Mayhew, Thomas (1621–1657). *See* Winslow, Edward. The glorious progress of the Gospel, amongst the Indians. London: 1649

Mayne, Jasper. The citye match. A comoedye. Oxford: L. Lichfield, 1639

Mayr, Johann. Epitome cronicorum seculi moderni . . . mit vilen Historien. Munich: N. Heinrich, 1604

Mazza, Marc' Antonio. Tesoro de secreti medicinali. Macerata: P. Salvioni, 1618

MECHOACAN

—Alonso y de los Ruyses de Fontecha, J. Diez previlegios para mugeres preñadas. Alcalá de Henares: 1606

—Alpini, P. De medicina methodica. Padua: 1611

—Amelung, P. Tractatus nobilis secundus. Leipzig: 1608

—Baardt, P. Deughden-spoor. Leeuwarden: 1645

—Canale, F. De' secreti universali raccolti. Brescia: 1613

—Culpeper, N. A physicall directory. London: 1649

—Du Gardin, L. Medicamenta purgantia. Douai: 1631

—Du Val, G. Phytologia, sive Philosophia plantarum. Paris: 1647

—Fabre, P. J. Myrothecium spagyricum. Toulouse: 1628

—Fontaine, J. Opera in quibus universae artis medicae . . . explicantur. Paris: 1612

——Practica curandorum morborum. Paris: 1611

—Franck, J. Speculum botanicum. Uppsala: 1638

—Freitag, J. Aurora medicorum. Frankfurt a.M.: 1630

—Grüling, P. G. Florilegium chymicum. Leipzig: 1631

—Guibert, P. Le prix et valeur des medicamens. Paris: 1625

—Hornung, J. Cista medica. Nuremberg: [1626]

—Horst, G. Observationum medicinalium . . . libri quatuor. Ulm: 1625

—Jacobi, H. Den cleynen herbarius. Amsterdam: 1606

—Mérindol, A. Ars medica. Aix-en-Province: 1633

—Morel, P. Systema parascevasticum. Geneva: 1628

—Pascal, J. Discours contenant la conference de la pharmacie. Béziers: 1616

——Traicté contenant la pharmacie chymique. Lyons: 1633

—Pharmacopoea Amstelredamensis. Amsterdam: 1636

—Pharmacopoeia Lillensis. Lille: 1640

—Planis Campy, D. de. Bouquet composé des plus belles fleurs chimiques. Paris: 1629

—Puteo, Z. Clavis medica rationalis. Venice: 1612

——Historia de gumma indica. Venice: 1628

—Royal College of Physicians of London. Pharmacopoea Londinensis. London: 1618

—Scholtz, L., ed. Consiliorum medicinalium. Hanau: 1610

—Sennert, D. Epitome naturalis scientiae. Wittenberg: 1618

—Wecker, J. J. Practica medicinae generalis. Treviso: 1602

MECHOACAN—POETRY

—Tabourot, E. Les bigarrures. Paris: 1603

Medecina practica. *See* Fabricius, Hieronymus, ab Aquapendente

La medecine des pauvres. *See* Prevost, Jean

Medecyn boec. *See* Wirsung, Christoph

Medica decas. *See* Duport, François

Medica resolucion. *See* Ximénez de Torres, Jacinto

Medicamenta purgantia. *See* Du Gardin, Louis

Medicamentorum apparatus. *See* Bertaldi, Giovanni Lodovico

Medicamentorum oeconomia nova. *See* Hollings, Edmund

Medicina pauperum. *See* Prevost, Jean

Medicina practica. *See* Mercuriale, Girolamo

Medicinae encomium. *See* Beverwijck, Jan van

MEDICINE. *See also* MATERIA MEDICA

—Bickerus, J. Hermes redivivus. Giessen: 1612

—Vaughan, W. The Newlanders cure. London: 1630

Il medico. *See* Rosaccio, Giuseppe

Medicyn-boeck. *See* Wirsung, Christoph

Medina, Bartolomé de. Las poblaciones, assientos y reales de minas. [Madrid? 1620?]

Medina, Pedro de. L'art de naviguer. Rouen: T. Reinsart, 1602

——Rouen: T. Reinsart, 1607

——La Rochelle: J. Brethommé, for A. de La Forge, 1615

——La Rochelle: J. Haultin, 1618

——Rouen: M. de Préaulx, 1628

— —Rouen: D. Ferrand, 1633

—Arte del navigare. Venice: T. Baglioni, 1609

Medina de las Torres, Gaspar de Guzmán y Acevedo, duque de. Relacion. Muerte de Pie de Palo. Madrid: A. Duplastre, 1638

Medio que el reyno propone para el consumo del vellon. [Madrid? ca. 1635?]

Medio suave y facil. *See* Márquez de Torres, Francisco

Medios politicos. *See* Alcázar y Zúñiga, Jacinto de, conde de la Marquina

Meditatio de insolito et stupendo illo terrae-motu. *See* Keckermann, Bartholomaeus

Les meditations historiques. *See* Camerarius, Philipp

Medulla destillatoria et medica. *See* Khunrath, Conrad

Megapolensis, Johannes. Een kort ontwerp vande Mahakuase Indianen. Alkmaar: Y. J. van Houten [1644]

Megiser, Hieronymus. Septentrio novantiquus, oder Die newe nort Welt. Leipzig: Heirs of N. Nerlich, & J. Hermann, for H. Gross the Younger, 1613

—Thesaurus polyglottus. Frankfurt a.M.: H. Megiser, 1603

Die Meinung der Bücher. *See* Grotius, Hugo

Mejía, Diego de. *See* Mexía y Fernangil, Diego de, tr

Mejía, Pedro de. *See* Mexía, Pedro

Mela, Pomponius. La geographia. Madrid: D. Díaz de la Carrera, for P. Lasso, 1642

The melancholie knight. *See* Rowlands, Samuel

Melich, Georg. Avertimenti nelle compositioni de' medicamenti. Venice: C. Vincenti [1605]

— —Venice: G. Guerigli, 1627

— —Venice: The Guerigli, 1648

—Dispensatorium medicum. Frankfurt a.M.: Palthenius Office, 1601

— —Frankfurt a.M.: H. Palthe-

nius, for Heirs of Z. Palthenius, 1624

Melichius, Georg. *See* Melich, Georg

Melin, Cornelis. *See* Melyn, Cornelis

Mellificium chirurgiae . . . the art of chyrurgery. *See* Cooke, James

Mello, Francisco Manuel de. Ecco polyt ico. Lisbon: P. Craesbeeck, 1645

—Relaçam dos successos da armada. [Lisbon:] Craesbeeck Office, 1650

Melton, Sir John. A sixe-folde politician. London: E. A[llde]., for J. Busby, 1609

Melyn, Cornelis. *See* Breedenraedt. Antwerp: 1649

—*See also* Haerlems schuytpraetjen. [Amsterdam?] 1649

Les memoires de la Ligue . . . Premier volume. *See* Goulart, Simon

Memoires de plusieurs choses considerables. *See* Faye, Charles, sieur d'Espesses

Memorabilia, das ist . . . Beschreibung aller vornembsten . . . Eygenschaften. [Frankfurt a.M.?] 1624

Memorabilia mundi. *See* Solinus, C. Julius

The memorable maske. *See* Chapman, George

Memoria de diferentes piensons. *See* Céspedes y Velasco, Francisco de

Memoria de lo que an de advertir los pilotos de la Carrera de las Indias. [Madrid? 1630?]

Memòrial. *See* Queiros, Pedro Fernandes de

Memorial . . . a Su Magestad. *See* Ortiz de Cervantes, Juan

Memorial . . . en defensa de Don Antonio Urrutia de Vergara. *See* Grau y Monfalcón, Juan

Memorial a los eminentissimos . . . cardenales. *See* Magano, Juan

Memorial a Su Magestad . . . en razon de la seguridad de su plata. *See* Mendoça, Lourenço de

Memorial ad Rey pidiendo reme-

dio. *See* Hurtado de Mendoza, Lorenzo, Bp

Memorial al Rey. *See* Avila y Lugo, Francisco de

Memorial al Rey nuestro señor don Felipe Quarto. *See* León Pinelo, Antonio Rodríguez de

Memorial al Rey y satisfaccion a los 56 cargos. *See* Mañozca y Zamora, Juan de

Memorial de advertencias convenientes para esta monarquia. [Madrid? ca. 1635?]

Memorial de Chiriqui. *See* Hernández, Melchor

Memorial de la culpa que resulta de la pesquisa. *See* Avellaneda Manrique, Juan de

Memorial de lo que contienen los papeles. *See* Spain. Consejo de las Indias

Memorial del padre. *See* Salinas y Córdova, Buenaventura de

Memorial del peligroso estado . . . de Chile. *See* Sosa, Pedro de

Memorial del pleyto que el señor fiscal . . . trata. *See* Spain. Consejo de las Indias

Memorial del pleyto que tratan . . . doña Francisca Colon de Toledo. *See* Spain. Consejo de las Indias

Memorial del pleyto sobre la sucession . . . del estado . . . de Veragua. *See* Spain. Consejo de las Indias

Memorial del processo causado en el Santo Oficio . . . de Cartagena. [Seville? 1633?]

Memorial discursivo. *See* León Garavito, Andrés de

Memorial discursivo sobre el oficio de protector general. *See* Larrinaga Salazar, Juan de

Memorial en nombre de fr. Juan Mendez. *See* Yañez Fajardo, Diego Antonio

Memorial en razon de la despoblacion. *See* Martínez de Mata, Francisco

Memorial historico, juridico, politico. *See* Calderón, Juan Alonso

Memorial i discurso de las razones que se ofrecen. *See* Solórzano Pereira, Juan de

Memorial i informacion por las iglesias . . . de las Indias. *See* Betancurt, Luis de

Memorial informativo al Rey. *See* Díez de la Calle, Juan; *and also* Grau y Monfalcón, Juan

Memorial, informe, y manifiesto. *See* Salinas y Córdova, Buenaventura de

Memorial, o discurso informativo. *See* Solórzano Pereira, Juan de

Memorial presentado a Su Magestad . . . acerca del martyrio. *See* Figueroa, Francisco de

Memorial que fray Ivan de Santander . . . presenta. *See* Benavides, Alonso de

Memorial que ofrece el licenciado. *See* Aguilar del Rio, Juan

Memorial que presenta a su Magestad Geronimo de Aramburu. *See* Aramburu, Gerónimo

Memorial que se dio por parte de Don Luys de Ribera. *See* Ribera y Colindres, Luis de

Memorial que trata de la perpetuydad de los encomenderos. *See* Ortiz de Cervantes, Juan

Memorial y carta en que el padre . . . representa . . . la necessidad. *See* Ovalle, Alonso de

Memorial y compendio breve. *See* Díez de la Calle, Juan

Memorial y discurso. *See* Maldonado, José

Memorial, y noticias sacras. *See* Díez de la Calle, Juan

Memorial, y relacion verdadera para el rei. *See* Cárdenas, Bernardino de, Bp

Memorie vande gewichtige redenen. *See* Usselinx, Willem

Memorie vande ghewichtighe redenen. *See* Usselinx, Willem

Memorien, ofte korte verhael. *See* Baudart, Willem

Memoryen ofte Cort verhael. *See* Baudart, Willem

Menasseh ben Joseph ben Israel. *See* Manasseh ben Joseph ben Israel

Mendes de Vasconcelos, Luiz. Do sitio de Lisboa. Lisbon: L. Estupiñán, 1608

Mendes Silva, Rodrigo. Epitome de la admirable y exemplar vida. Madrid: P. Coello, 1649

Méndez, Juan Francisco. Panegyrico funeral a D. Tomas Tamaio de Vargas. [Madrid?] 1641

Mendez de Vasconcelos, Luys. *See* Mendes de Vasconcelos, Luiz

Mendoça, Francisco de. Viridarium sacrae ac profanae eruditionis. Lyons: J. Cardon, 1631

——Lyons: J. Cardon, 1632

——Cologne: P. Henning, 1633

——Lyons: G. Boissat, 1635

——Lyons: L. Anisson, 1649

——Cologne: P. Henning, 1650

Mendoça, Lourenço de. Memorial a Su Magestad . . . en razon de la seguridad de su plata. [Madrid? 1635?]

Mendoça, Lourenço de, Bp of Rio de Janeiro. El doctor Lorenço de Mendoça prelado. [Madrid? 1630?]

—Señor. El doctor Lorenço de Mendoça. [Madrid? 1650?]

—Señor. El prelado del Rio de Janeiro. [Madrid? 1638?]

—Suplicacion a Su Magestad. Madrid: 1630

Menéndez Silva, Rodrigo. Catalogo real de España. Madrid: Imprenta Real, 1637

Mennes, Sir John, comp. *See* Wit's recreations. Wits recreations. London: 1640

Mercado, Luis. Libri duo. De communi et peculiari praesidiorum artis medicae indicatione. *In his* Tomus secundus Operum. Valladolid: 1605

——*In his* Opera omnia. Frankfurt a.M.: 1608

—Opera omnia. Frankfurt a.M.: Z. Palthenius, 1608

——Venice: B. Giunta, & G. B. Ciotti and Co, 1609

—Operum tomus primus [–III]. Frankfurt a.M.: Heirs of Z. Palthenius, 1620, '19

—Praxis medica. Venice: B. Giunta, & G. B. Ciotti and Co., 1608

——Venice: B. Giunta, 1610

——Venice: B. Giunta, & G. B. Ciotti and Co., 1611

—Tomus secundus Operum. Valladolid: L. Sánchez, 1605

——Venice: B. Giunta, G. B. Ciotti and Co., 1611

Mercator, Gerardus. L'appendice de l'atlas. Amsterdam: H. Hondius, 1633

—Appendix Atlantis oder dess WeltBuchs. Amsterdam: J. Janszoon the Younger, 1636

—Appendix Atlantis, ofte Vervolgh. Amsterdam: J. Janszoon the Younger, & H. Hondius, 1637

—Appendix novi atlantis. Amsterdam: J. Janszoon the Younger, 1637

—Atlantis maioris appendix. Amsterdam: J. Janszoon the Younger, 1630

——Amsterdam: H. Hondius, 1631

—Atlantis novi pars tertia. Amsterdam: H. Hondius, 1636

—Atlas, das ist, Abbildung der gantzen Welt. Amsterdam: H. Hondius, 1633

——Amsterdam: H. Hondius, & J. Janszoon the Younger, 1633

——Amsterdam: H. Hondius, 1636

—Atlas minor. Amsterdam: J. Hondius, & C. Claeszoon, for J. Janszoon, at Arnhem, 1607

——Dordrecht: A. Bot, for J. Hondius, & C. Claeszoon, at Amsterdam, & J. Janszoon, at Arnhem, 1610 (2)

——Arnhem: J. Janszoon, 1620

——Arnhem: J. Janszoon, 1621

——Amsterdam: J. Janszoon, 1628

——Amsterdam: J. Janszoon the Younger, 1634

—Atlas minor . . . Traduict de latin. Amsterdam: J. Hondius, for J. Janszoon, at Arnhem, 1608

——Amsterdam: J. Hondius, for J. Janszoon, at Arnhem, 1609

——Amsterdam: J. Hondius, & C. Claeszoon, for J. Janszoon, at Arnhem, 1613

——Amsterdam: J. Hondius, &

C. Claeszoon, for J. Janszoon, at Arnhem, 1614

—Atlas minor, das ist, Ein kurtze . . . Beschreibung. [Amsterdam:] J. Hondius, & C. Claeszoon, for J. Janszoon, at Arnhem [1609]

— —Amsterdam: J. Janszoon the Younger, 1631

— —Amsterdam: J. Janszoon the Younger, 1648

—Atlas minor, ofte Een korte . . . beschrijvinge. Amsterdam: J. Janszoon the Younger, 1628 [i.e., 1630]

—Atlas minor, ou Brièfve- . . . description. Amsterdam: J. Janszoon the Younger, 1630

—Atlas novus. Amsterdam: J. Janszoon the Younger, & H. Hondius, 1638

— —1641. *See* Jansson, Jan. Atlas novus. [Amsterdam:] 1641

— —1644. *See* Jansson, Jan. [Atlas novus. Amsterdam: 1644]

—Atlas ofte Afbeeldinghe. [Amsterdam: J. Janszoon the Younger, 1634]

—Atlas, or A geographicke description. Amsterdam: H. Hondius, & J. Janszoon the Younger, 1636

— —Amsterdam: H. Hondius, 1638

— —Amsterdam: H. Hondius, 1641

—L'atlas ou Méditations cosmographiques. Amsterdam: J. Hondius, 1609

— —Amsterdam: J. Hondius, 1613

—Atlas, ou Representation du monde. Amsterdam: H. Hondius, 1633

— —Amsterdam: H. Hondius, 1635

—Atlas sive Cosmographicae meditationes. Amsterdam: J. Hondius, 1606

— —Amsterdam: C. Claeszoon, 1607

— —Amsterdam: C. Claeszoon, & J. Hondius, 1607

— —Amsterdam: J. Hondius, 1607

— —Amsterdam: C. Claeszoon, 1608

— —Amsterdam: J. Hondius, 1611

— —Amsterdam: J. Hondius, 1612

— —Amsterdam: J. Hondius, 1613

— —Amsterdam: J. Hondius, 1616

— —Amsterdam: J. Hondius, 1619 (2)

— —Amsterdam: H. Hondius, 1623

— —Amsterdam: H. Hondius, 1628

— —Amsterdam: J. E. Cloppenburg, 1630

— —Amsterdam: H. Hondius, 1630

— —Amsterdam: J. E. Cloppenburg, 1632

— —Amsterdam: J. E. Cloppenburg, 1636

—Historia mundi, or . . . atlas. London: T. Cotes, for M. Sparke, 1635

— —London: T. Cotes, for M. Sparke, & S. Cartwright, 1635

— —London: M. Sparke, 1635

— —London: M. Sparke, 1637

— —London: M. Sparke, 1639

—Newer Atlas. Amsterdam: J. Janszoon the Younger [& H. Hondius], 1636

—Nouveau theatre. *See* Hondius, Hendrik. Nouveau theatre du monde. Amsterdam: 1639, *et seq.*

—Novus atlas. *See* Jansson, Jan. Novus atlas, sive Theatrum orbis terrarum. Amsterdam: 1646–47, *et seq.*

Mercator sapiens. *See* Baerle, Kaspar van

MERCEDARIANS IN AMERICA

—Remón, A. Historia general de la Orden. Madrid: 1633

MERCEDARIANS IN MEXICO

—Salmerón, M. Recuerdos historicos y politicos. Valencia: 1646

MERCEDARIANS IN PERU

—Guillén y Colón, F. Vita, muerte y milagros del prodigioso varon. Seville: 1637

—Ponce de León, F. Relacion de los servicios. [Madrid? 1632?]

The merchants mappe of commerce. *See* Roberts, Lewes

Le mercure d'estat. *See* Hay, Paul, sieur du Chastelet

Le mercure Portugais. *See* Grenaille, François de, sieur de Chatounières

Mercuriale, Girolamo. Medicina practica. Frankfurt a.M.: J. T. Schönwetter, 1601

—Medicina practica . . . libri v. Frankfurt a.M.: J. T. Schönwetter, 1602

— —Lyons: C. Cayne, for A. Pillehotte, 1617

— —Lyons: [C. Cayne] for A. Pillehotte, 1618

— —Lyons: A. Pillehotte, 1623

—Praelectiones Patavinae. Venice: The Giuntas, 1603

— —Venice: The Giuntas, 1606

— —Venice: The Giuntas, 1617

— —Venice: The Giuntas, 1627

Il mercurio. *See* Siri, Vittorio

Il mercurio estinto resuscitato. *See* Bellinzani, Lodovico

Mercurius Americanus. *See* Wheelwright, John

Mercurius Britannicus. *See* Wortley, Sir Francis

Mercurius Germaniae. *See* Usselinx, Willem. Argonautica Gustaviana. Frankfurt a.M.: 1633

Merian, Matthaeus, ed. *See the following:*

—Bry, Theodor de. Continuatio Americae. Frankfurt a.M.: 1627

— —Decima tertia pars Historiae Americanae. Frankfurt a.M.: 1634

— —Dreyzehender Theil Americae. Frankfurt a.M.: 1628

Merida, Yucatan. La ciudad de Merida. [Madrid? 1620?]

Mérindol, Antoine. Ars medica. Aix-en-Province: J. Roize, 1633

Merinero, Juan. Fray Juan Merinero . . . A todos los religiosos de nuestras provincias. [Madrid: 1644]

Merlo de la Fuente, Alonso. Copia de un memorial. [Madrid: 1650]

—Señor. Por dos informaciones de oficio. [Madrid? 1642?]

The merry wives of Windsor. *See* Shakespeare, William

Merula, Paulus. Cosmographiae generalis libri tres. [Leyden:] Plantin Office (Raphelengius), for C. Claeszoon, at Amsterdam, 1605

— —[Leyden: I. Elsevier, for J. Hondius &] H. Hondius, at Amsterdam, 1621

— —Amsterdam: W. J. Blaeu, 1636

—De maribus. *In* Grotius, Hugo. De mari libero et P. Merula De maribus. Leyden: 1633

Mervyn, Sir Audley. A speech made before the Lords. [London?] 1641

— —[London:] H. Perry, 1641

Messia, Pietro. *See* Mexía, Pedro

Messina. Ospedale di Santa Maria della Pietà. Antidotarium speciale. Venice: Giunta Office, 1642

Messis Paraquariensis. *See* Schirmbeck, Adam

Metamorphosis. *See* Ovidius Naso, Publius. Metamorphoses. English

Metamorphosis lapidum ignobilium. *See* Norton, Samuel

The metamorphosis of tabacco. *See* Beaumont, Sir John

Meterani novi continuatio, das ist: Warhafftige Beschreibung. *See* Meteren, Emanuel van

Meteranus novus, das ist: Warhafftige Beschreibung. *See* Meteren, Emanuel van

Meteren, Emanuel van. Belgische ofte Nederlantsche historie. Delft: J. C. Vennecool, 1605

—Belgische ofte Nederlantsche oorlogen. 'Schotland outside Danswijck' [i.e., The Hague?]: H. van Loven, 1609

— —'Schotland outside Danswijck' [i.e., The Hague?]: H. van Loven, for E. van Meteren, [at London] 1611

—Belli civilis in Belgio . . . historia. [Arnhem? J. Janszoon?] 1610

—Commentarien ofte Memoiren

van den Nederlandtschen staet. 'Schotlandt outside Danswijck' [i.e., The Hague?]: H. van Loven, for E. van Meteren, at London, 1609

— —'Schotland outside Danswijck' [i.e., The Hague?]: H. van Loven, for E. van Meteren, at London, 1610

—Descriptio bellorum inferioris Germaniae. Amsterdam: J. Janszoon the Younger, 1618

—Eigentlich und volkomene historische beschreibung des niderlendischen Kriegs. Arnhem: J. Janszoon, 1614

— —, pt 3. *See* Niderländischer histori . . . Supplementum. Arnhem: 1620

—Eygentliche und vollkommene historische Beschreibung. Amsterdam: J. Janszoon the Younger, 1627

— —, pt 3. *See* Der niderländischen Historien dritter Theil. Amsterdam: 1630

—L'histoire des Pays-Bas. The Hague: H. J. van Wouw, 1618

—Historia, oder Eigentliche . . . Beschreibung aller Kriegshändel. [Hamburg?] 1601

— —[Amsterdam? Dordrecht?] 1603

— —Arnhem: J. Janszoon, 1604

— —Arnhem: J. Janszoon, 1605

— —Frankfurt a.M.: N. Roht, 1610

—Historie der Nederlandscher . . . oorlogen. The Hague: H. J. van Wouw, 1611

— —The Hague: H. J. van Wouw, 1614

— —The Hague: Widow & Heirs of H. J. van Wouw, 1623

— —The Hague: Widow & Heirs of H. J. van Wouw, 1635

—Historien der Nederlanden. Amsterdam: J. J. Schipper, 1647

— —Dordrecht: M. de Bot, 1647

— —Leyden: 1647

—Meterani novi continuatio, das ist: Warhafftige Beschreibung. Amsterdam: W. J. Blaeu, 1635

—Meteranus novus, das ist: Warhafftige Beschreibung. Amsterdam: W. J. Blaeu, 1633

— —Amsterdam: J. Janszoon the Younger, 1640

—Nederlantsche historien ofte geschiedenissen. [Dordrecht? 1612]

—Niderlendischer Historien ander Theil. [Arnhem? J. Janszoon?] 1609

—Niederländische Historien. [Arnhem: J. Janszoon] 1612, '09

—A true discourse historicall. London: [F. Kingston] for M. Lownes, 1602

The method of phisick. *See* Barrough, Philip

La methode curatoire de la maladie venerienne. *See* Héry, Thierry de

Methodi medendi . . . libri quatuor. *See* Schyron, Jean

Methodi vitandorum errorum omnium . . . libri quindecim. *See* Santorio, Santorio

Methodo de conhecer e curar o morbo gallico. *See* Madeira Arraes, Duarte

Methodo de la coleccion . . . de las medicinas simples. *See* Oviedo, Luís de

Methodus ad facilem historiarum cognitionem. *See* Bodin, Jean

Methodus curandorum febrium. *See* Rivière, Lazare

Methodus curandorum omnium morborum. *See* Rondelet, Guillaume

Methodus medendi. *See* Valle, Francisco

Methodus praescribendi formulas remediorum. *See* Morel, Pierre

Metoposcopia et ophthalmoscopia. *See* Fuchs, Samuel

Mexía, Pedro. Les diverses leçons. Tournon: C. Michel, & T. Soubron, 1604

— —Tournon: C. Michel, 1609

— —Tournon: C. Michel, 1610

— —Tournon: C. Michel, 1616

— —Geneva: P. Aubert, 1625

— —Rouen: J. Roger [1626]

— —[Rouen: J. Roger] for C. Michel, at Lyons [1626]

— —Rouen: J. Berthelin, 1643

—The historie of all the Romane

—Eliseo, Father. Aviendo representado el conde de Monterey . . . los agravios . . . que los Indios de la Nueva España recibian. [Madrid? 1604?]

—Enríquez, J. Relacion de las exequias y honras funerales . . . de la Orden de Predicadores, en la Nuevaespaña. Madrid: 1623

—León Pinelo, A. R. de. Question moral si el chocolate quebranta el ayuno eclesiastico. Madrid: 1636

—López Solis, F. Por Los religiosos de la provincia de san Hipolyto Martyr de Guaxaca. [Madrid? 1630?]

—Ortiz de Valdes, F. Defensa canonica por la dignidad del Obispo. [Madrid: 1648]

—Palafox y Mendoza, J. de, Bp. Carta. Madrid: 1646

— —Discursos espirituales. Madrid. 1641

— —Señor. Aviendo informado a V. Mag. desde que he llegado a esta provincia. [Madrid? 1642?]

—Palma, L. de la. Informe juridico a favor de los religiosos doctrineros. [Madrid?] 1648

—Palma y Freitas, L. de la. Por las religiones de Santo Domingo . . . de Nueva-España. Madrid: 1644

—Pedraza, J. de. Señor. Julian de Pedraza . . . procurador general de las Indias. [Madrid: 1649]

—Pérez de Ribas, A. Señor. Andres Perez . . . procurador general a esta corte. [Madrid: ca. 1649]

—Velázquez, J. Relacion que el licenciado Don Juan Velazquez hizo. [Madrid? 1632?]

MEXICO—COMMERCE

—Barriasa, M. de. Por Fernando de Almonte Veinticuatro de Sevilla. Madrid: 1634

—Esquibel, J. de. Copia de una carta que el maese de campo . . . escrivio. [Madrid? 1608?]

—Ferriol, J. Señor. Joseph Ferriol, en nombre del prior. [Madrid? 1645?]

—Grau y Monfalcón, J. Justificacion de la conservacion. [Madrid: 1640]

— —Memorial informativo al Rey. Madrid: 1637

—Mexico (City). Consulado. Señor. El Prior y consules de la Universidad. [Madrid? 1640?]

—Morales, J. de. Señor. El capitan don Juan de Morales dize. [Madrid? 1650?]

—Relacion de la plata y frutos. [Madrid:] 1622

—Vitoria Baraona, F. de. Señor. El capitan Francisco de Vitoria Baraona dize. [Madrid?: 1634?] (634/140)

MEXICO—DESCRIPTION

—Reynolds, J. Vox coeli. [London]: 1624

MEXICO—DISCOVERY & EXPLORATION

—Cabrera de Córdoba, L. Filipe Segundo rey de España. Madrid: 1619

MEXICO—DRAMA

—Ruiz de Alarcón y Mendoza, J. Comedias, pte 1a. Madrid: 1628

MEXICO—HISTORY

—Calderón, J. A. Memorial historico, juridico, politico. [Madrid? ca. 1650]

—Díaz del Castillo, B. Historia verdadera de la conquista de la Nueva-España. Madrid: 1632

—General opinion es en la Nuevaespaña. [Madrid? 1630?]

—Grau y Monfalcón, J. Memorial . . . en defensa de Don Antonio Urrutia de Vergara. [Madrid? 1641?]

—Guerrero, M. Por los herederos del doctor don Marcos Guerrero. [Madrid: 1615?]

—Helwig, C. Theatrum historicum, sive Chronologiae systema novum. Marburg: 1629

—Juan de Santa María, fray. Chronica de la provincia de San Joseph. Madrid: 1615

—Levantamiento, y principios de Yangua. Málaga: 1619

—Lizana, B. de. Historia de Yucatan. Valladolid: 1633

—Malingre, C. Histoire de nostre temps, t 4. Paris: 1625

—Molina, C. de. Señor. Christoval de Molina, regidor de la ciudad de Mexico . . . Dize. [Madrid: 1628]

— —Señor. Christoval de Molina, regidor perpetuo. [Madrid: 1629]

—Moscosa y de Córdoba, C. de. El l[icencia]do Don Christoval de Moscoso y Cordova . . . en defensa de su jurisdiccion. [Madrid: ca. 1635?]

—Pacheco Ossorio, R., marqués de Cerralvo. Por el marques de Zerralvo. [Madrid: 1642]

—Palafox y Mendoza, J. de, Bp. Por Don Juan de Palafox y Mendoza, fiscal del Consejo de Indias. [Madrid? ca. 1630?]

—Por los hijos, y nietos de conquistadores. [Madrid? 1614]

—Relacion sumaria . . . del tumulto . . . en Mexico. [Madrid? 1624]

—Rodríguez de Robles, A. Señor. Antonio Rodriguez de Robles dize, que como a V. Magestad . . . es notorio. [Madrid? 1606?]

— —Señor. Antonio Rodriguez de Robles dize, que de 9. años . . . han residido. [Madrid? 1606?]

—Salinas y Córdova, B. de. Memorial, informe, y manifiesto. [Madrid: ca. 1646]

—Sánchez, A. De rebus Hispaniae anacephalaeosis. Alcalá de Henares: 1634

—Sandoval, P. de, Bp. Historia de la vida . . . del Emperador Carlos V. Pamplona: 1614

— —Vida y hechos del emperador Carlos Quinto, pte 1a–2a. Valladolid: 1604

—Spain. Laws, statutes, etc., 1598–1621 (Philip III). Instrucción de lo que han de observar los governadores . . . de la Nueva España. [Madrid: 1626]

—Spain. Laws, statutes, etc., 1621–1665 (Philip IV). Capitulaciones de el assiento. [Madrid:] 1639

—Suárez de Gamboa, J. Illustrissimo señor. Advertencias de daños. [Madrid? 1621]

——Señor. Tres cosas son las que obligan a credito. [Madrid? 1621]

—Ulloa, A. de. Historie . . . van den . . . Keyser Caerle de vijfde. Dordrecht: [1610]

——Vita, et fatti dell'invitissimo imperatore Carlo Quinto. Venice: 1606

—Urrutia de Vergara, A. Señor. El maesse de campo don Antonio Urrutia de Vergara. [Madrid: 1648]

—Varaona, S. de. Carta . . . que se fulminò contra don M. Perez de Varaiz. [Madrid? 1625?]

—Vázquez de Cisneros, A. El doctor Alonso Vazquez de Cisneros. [Madrid? ca. 1625?]

—Vázquez de Espinosa, A. Confessario general. Madrid: 1623

—Vesga, M. de. Señor. El capitan y almirante Mateo de Vesga. [Madrid? 1627?]

—Villagrá, G. P. de. El capitan Gaspar de Villagra, para que su Magestad le haga merced. [Madrid? ca. 1616?]

—Vitoria Baraona, F. de. El capitan Francisco de Vitoria, vezino de la puebla de los Angeles. [Madrid: 1639]

MEXICO—HISTORY, NAVAL
—Altamirano, D. Por Don Juan de Benavides Baçan. [Madrid: 1632?]

—Cepeda, F. de. Señor. Con orden que he tenido del marqués de Cadereyte. Madrid: 1639

—Enrique, P. Relacion verdadera . . . de los sucessos. Madrid: 1641

—Moscoso y de Córdoba, C. de. Discurso legal militar. [Madrid: 1635?]

—Relacion de lo sucedido a la Armada Real. [Seville? 1638]

—Vázquez de Espinosa, A. Tratado verdadero del viage y navegacion deste año. Málaga: 1623

—Zambrana de Villalobos, S. Por el licenciado Don Sebas-

tian Zambrana de Villalobos. [Madrid? 1632?]

MEXICO—POETRY
—Balde, J. Lyricorum lib. iv. Munich: 1643

—Cueva, J. de la. Conquista de la Betica. Seville: 1603

—Romancero general. Romancero general, en que se contienen todos los romances. Madrid: 1604

—Scarron, P. La suite des oeuvres burlesques . . . Seconde partie. Paris: 1647

—Taylor, J. The needles excellency. London: 1631

—Valbuena, B. de. Siglo de oro. Madrid: 1608

MEXICO—POLITICS & GOVERNMENT
—Altamirano, D. Por la Real audiencia de Mexico. [Madrid? 1632?]

—Carrillo de Mendoza y Pimentel, D., marqués de Gelves. Relacion del estado. [Madrid: 1624]

—Moscoso y de Córdoba, C. de. Discurso juridico y politico. [Madrid? 1625?]

—Ribera, H. M. de. Por Hernando Matias de Ribera. [Madrid? 1650?]

MEXICO, GULF OF
—Migoen, J. W. Proeve des nu onlangs uyt-ghegheven drooms. [Amsterdam? 1608]

——Eene treffelijcke tzamenspre-kinghe. [Netherlands: ca. 1607?]

MEXICO IN LITERATURE
—Harsdörffer, G. P. Gesprechspiele fünfter Theil. Nuremberg: 1645

Mexico (City). Consulado. Señor. El Prior y consules de la Universidad. [Madrid? 1640?]

MEXICO (CITY)
—Braun, G. Civitates orbis terrarum. Cologne: 1612

—Seville. Casa de la Moneda. El Fiscal de su Magestad. [Seville? 1617?]

MEXICO (CITY)—HISTORY
—Vergara Gaviria, D. de. Nulidades expresas. [Madrid? ca. 1625]

MEXICO (CITY)—STORM, 1630
—Erschröckliche Zeittung wie . . . in der Stadt-Mexico . . . viel tausent seelen . . . ertruncken. Frankfurt a.M.: [1630]

Mey, Aurelio. Norte de la poesia española. Valencia: F. Mey, for J. Ferrer, 1616

——Valencia: F. Mey, for F. Pincinali, 1616

Micalori, Jacomo. Crisis . . . de Erycii Puteani circulo urbiniano. Urbino: M. & A. Ghisoni, 1632

MICHOACAN, MEXICO
—Kornmann, H. Templum naturae historicum. Darmstadt: 1611

Micro-cosmographie. *See* Earle, John, Bp

Microcosmus. *See* Heylyn, Peter

Micrologia. Characters, or essayes. London: T. C[otes]., for M. Sparke, 1629

Middelgeest, Simon van. Discours of t'samensprekinghe. [Amsterdam? 1608?]

—Discurs und Muthmassung. Amsterdam: J. Mucken, 1618

—Droom oft t'samensprekinge. [Amsterdam? 1608]

—Den langh-verwachten donder-slach. [Amsterdam? ca. 1625?]

—Nootwendich discours. [Amsterdam:] 1622

—Ootmoedighe beklagh-redenen. [Amsterdam?] 1622

—Raedtsel. [Amsterdam: 1608]

——[Amsterdam? 1608?] (2)

—Raedtslagh. [Amsterdam? 1608?]

—Het testament ofte wtersten wille. 'Franc end al: Frederijck de Vrije' [i.e., Amsterdam? 1609] (3)

—Tweede noot-wendiger discours. [Amsterdam? 1622]

—Den vervaerlijcken Oost-Indischen eclipsis. [Amsterdam:] 1625

Middleton, Richard. Epigrams and satyres. London: N. Okes, for J. Harrison, 1608

Middleton, Thomas. The blacke booke. London: T. C[reede]., for J. Chorlton, 1604
—A faire quarrell. London: [G. Eld] for J. T[rundle]., & [E. Wright] 1617 (2)
— —London: A M[athewes]., for T. Dewe, 1622
—A mad world. London: H. B[al-lard]., for W. Burre, 1608
— —London: [J. Okes] for J. S[penser]., & J. Becket, 1640
—The phoenix. London: E. A[llde]., for A. J[ohnson]., 1607
— —London: T. H[arper]., for R. Meighen, 1630
—The roaring girle. London: N. Okes, for T. Archer, 1611
Migoen, Jacob Willem. Proeve des nu onlangs uyt-ghegheven drooms. [Amsterdam? 1608]
—Eene treffelijcke tzamenspre-kinghe. [Netherlands: ca. 1607?] (4 variant spellings)
Miguel de la Purificación. Vida evangelica y apostolica. Barcelona: G. Nogues, 1641
Mikrokosmos. *See* Heylyn, Peter
Milagroso successo do Conde de Castel Milhor. *See* Lopes, Francisco
Milles, Thomas, comp. *See* Archaio-ploutos. Containing, ten following bookes. London: 1619
La minera del mondo. *See* Bonardo, Giovanni Maria, conte
MINES AND MINERAL RE-SOURCES
—Aldrovandi, U. Musaeum metallicum. Bologna: 1648
—Apuntamientos para mejor inteligencia. [Madrid? 164–?]
—Elías, J. Señor. Un libelo infamatorio se ha impresso . . . su fecha en Potosí. [Madrid? 1640]
—Montesinos, F. de. Señor. El licenciado D. Fernando de Montesinos. [Madrid? 1645]
—Overbury, Sir T. Sir Thomas Overbury his Observations in his travailes. [London:] 1626
—Plattes, G. A discovery of subterraneall treasure. London: 1639

—Quadro, D. F. de. Todo el pleyto. [Seville? 1640?]
—Rodríguez de Robles, A. Señor. Antonio Rodriguez de Robles dize, que assi como los mineros sacan la plata . . . . [Madrid? 1606?]
—Sandoval, F. de. Advertencia en fabor . . . del arbitrio. [Madrid? ca. 1610?]
—Spain. Laws, statutes, etc., 1556–1598 [Philip II]. Nuevas leyes y ordenanzas, hechas por su Magestad. Madrid: 1625
—Taylor, J. Jack a Lent. [London: 1617?]
— —Superbiae flagellum. London: 1621
MINES AND MINERAL RE-SOURCES—BOLIVIA. *See also* POTOSÍ, BOLIVIA
—Fernández Manjon, L. Por Lucas Fernandez Manjon. [Madrid? ca. 1630?]
— —Señor. Lucas Fernandez Manjon. [Madrid? 1627]
—Fernández Rebolledo, R. Contiene este papel la forma. [Seville? 1650]
—Garavito, G. Cuenta que Geronimo Garavito . . . ha hecho de la mucha plata. [Madrid?: 163–?]
— —Señor. Gerónimo Garavito . . . dize: Que a los 17. de mayo . . . [Madrid? 164–?]
— —Señor. Geronimo Garavito . . . dize: que aviendo presentado muchos memoriales . . . [Madrid? 163–?]
— —Señor. Geronimo Garavito . . . dize: Que de nuevo represento a V. M. los dos capitulos. Madrid: 164–?]
— —Señor. Geronimo Garavito . . . Dize, que tiene suplicado a V. M. . . [Madrid? 162–?]
—Ibarra Gueztaraen, J. de. Señor. Cinco cosas son las que . . . Potosi . . . se sirva de conceder. [Madrid? 1617?]
— —Señor. En el memorial que presento en este Real Consejo. [Madrid? 1618?]
—León, L. P. de. Obras proprias. Madrid: 1631
—Paredes, A. de. Señor. Entre

diversos memoriales. [Madrid: 1639?]
—Potosí, Bolivia. Gremio de los azogueros. El gremio de los azogueros de . . . Potosi . . . suplica. [Madrid? 1636?]
— —Señor. Los azogueros dueños de minas. [Madrid? 1620?]
—Recio de León, J. Señor. El maesse de campo Juan Recio de Leon, dize, Que la riqueza . . . . [Madrid? 1626?]
— —Señor. El maestro de campo Juan Recio de Leon, dize: Que los Indios . . . . [Madrid: 1627]
—Relacion del nuevo descubrimiento de las minas. [Madrid: 163–?]
—Rodríguez Pizarro, J. Señor. Ivan Rodriguez Pizarro. [Madrid? 1650?]
MINES AND MINERAL RE-SOURCES—COLOMBIA
—Spain. Sovereigns, etc., 1621–1665 (Philip IV). El rey. [Madrid: 1634]
MINES AND MINERAL RE-SOURCES—CUBA
—Marín de Armendariz, P. Condiciones que el veedor Pedro Marin de Armendariz . . . tratan de efectuar. [Madrid? 1642]
MINES AND MINERAL RE-SOURCES—GUIANA
—Randolph, T. Poems. Oxford: 1638
MINES AND MINERAL RE-SOURCES—MEXICO
—Baeza, P. de. Este memorial es traslado. [Madrid: 1607?]
— —Traslado del memorial. [Madrid: 1607?]
—Figueroa, A. de. Don Antonio de Figueroa, procurador general. [Madrid? 1640?]
—Medina, B. de. Las poblaciones, assientos y reales de minas. [Madrid? 1620?]
—Rodríguez de Robles, A. Señor. Antonio Rodriguez de Robles dize, que ahora quarenta y cinquenta anos . . . . [Madrid? 1606?]

—Missive van twee Indiaensche coninghen. The Hague: 1621

—Osorio de Erasso, D. Señor. Celebre fue la vitoria. [Madrid? 1630?]

—Pagitt, E. Christianographie. London: 1635

——A relation of the Christians in the world. London: 1639

—Richeome, L. Trois discours. Lyons: 1601

—Scott, T. Vox populi, pt. 2. [London]: 1624

—Torquemada, J. de. Veynte y un libros rituales, pte 1a–3a. Seville: 1615

—Vitoria, P. de. Por el ilustrisimo señor. [Madrid? 1650?]

MISSIONS—CANADA

—Ledesma, D. de. Doctrine chrestienne. Rouen: 1630

—Les veritables motifs [Paris:] 1643

MISSIONS—CHILE

—Ovalle, A. de. Memorial y carta en que el padre . . . representa . . . la necessidad. [Seville? 1642]

—Valdivia, L. de. Sermon en lengua de Chile. [Valladolid: 1621]

MISSIONS—COLOMBIA

—Spain. Sovereigns, etc., 1621–1665 (Philip IV). El rey. [Madrid: 1634]

MISSIONS—LATIN AMERICA

—Spinola, F. A. Vita del p. Carlo Spinola. Rome: 1628

——Vita Caroli Spinolae. Antwerp: 1630

MISSIONS—MEXICO

—Lizana, B. de. Historia de Yucatan. Valladolid: 1633

—Remón, A. La vida del siervo de Dios Gregorio Lopez. Madrid: 1617

——Vida y muerte del siervo de Dios Don Fernando de Cordova. Madrid: 1617

MISSIONS—NEW ENGLAND

—New Englands first fruits. London: 1643

—Shepard, T. The clear sunshine of the Gospel. London: 1648

—Society for Propagation of the Gospel in New-England. An

act for the promoting . . . the gospel . . . in New England. London: 1649

—Wilson, J. The day-breaking . . . of the gospell with the Indians. London: 1647

—Winslow, E. The glorious progress of the Gospel, amongst the Indians. London: 1649

MISSIONS—NEW MEXICO

—Benavides, A. de. Carta. Madrid: 1632

——Memorial. Madrid: 1630

——Relatio quam Philippo iv . . . exhibuit reverendiss. p.f. Joannes de Santander. Salzburg: [1634]

——Relatio, welche Philippo iv. . . . und r.p.f. Joannes de Santander . . . ubergeben lassen. Salzburg: 1634?

——Requeste oft Verhael d'welck den . . . Pater . . . presenteert. Antwerp: 1631

——Requeste remonstrative au Roy. Brussels: 1631

MISSIONS—PANAMA

—Hernández, M. Memorial de Chiriqui. [Madrid? 1620]

MISSIONS—PERU

—Campuzano, B. Planeta catholico. Madrid: [1646]

—Zeiller, M. Das andere Hundert Episteln. Ulm: 1641

MISSIONS—SPANISH AMERICA

—Fuente, G. de la. Historia del capitulo general. Madrid: 1633

MISSIONS—VIRIGINIA

—Canterbury, Eng. (Province). Commissary General. To the minister and church-wardens. [London: 1616]

MISSIONS—WEST INDIES

—Ortiz de Salcedo, F. Curia eclesiastica. Madrid: 1626

MISSIONS—YUCATAN

—Sánchez de Aguilar, P. Informe contra idolorum cultores del obispado de Yucatán. Madrid: 1639

Missive aende Staten vande Provintien. See Holland (Province). Staten

Missive. Daer in kortelijck ende grondigh wert verthoont, hoe-

veel . . . gheleghen is. Amsterdam: B. Janszoon, 1621

—Arnhem: J. Janszoon, 1621

Missive, inhoudende den aerdt vanden treves. [The Hague?] 1630

Missive uyt Middelburg. Middelburg: G. Verdussen, 1647 (4)

Missive van . . . de . . . Staten van Hollandt. See Holland (Province). Staten

Missive van twee Indiaensche coninghen. The Hague: A. Meuris, 1621

Mithridateiotechnia. See Mutoni, Niccolò

Mithridates Gesneri. See Gesner, Konrad

Mitternächtige Schiffarth. See Röslin, Elisaeus

Mnemonica. See Willis, John

Mocquet, Jean. Voyages en Afrique, Asie, Indes. Paris: J. de Heuqueville, 1616

——Paris: J de Heuqueville, 1617

——Rouen: J. Cailloué, 1645

A moderate and safe expedient. [London?] 1646

A modest defence of the caveat. See Herring, Francis

Moerbeeck, Jan Andries. Redenen wâeromme de West-Indische Compagnie dient te trachten . . . Amsterdam: C. L. van der Plasse, 1624

—Spaenschen raedt. The Hague: A. Meuris, 1626 (2)

—Vereenighde Nederlandschen raedt, het eerste deel. The Hague: A. Meuris, 1628 (4)

——The Hague: A. Meuris, 1629

—Vereenighde Nederlandschen raedt, het tweede deel. The Hague: A. Meuris, 1628

——The Hague: A. Meuris, 1629

Moffett, Thomas. Insectorum . . . theatrum. London: T. Cotes, 1634

——London: T. Cotes, & B. Allen, 1634

——London: T. Cotes, & W. Hope, 1634

MOHAWK INDIANS
—Megapolensis, J. Een kort ont-
werp vande Mahakuase In-
dianen. Alkamaar: [1644]
Molina, Cristóbal de. Señor.
Christoval de Molina, regidor
de la ciudad de Mexico . . .
Dize. [Madrid: 1628]
—Señor. Cristoval de Molina
regidor de la ciudad . . . de
Mexico [Madrid: 1628]
—Señor. Cristoval de Molina,
regidor perpetuo. [Madrid:
1629]
Molina, Luis de. De justitia et
jure. Venice: The Sessas, 1611
— —Mainz: B. Lipp, for H. My-
lius, at Cologne, 1614
— —Antwerp: J. van Keerber-
ghen, 1615
— —Lyons: 1622
—De justitia et jure opera omnia.
Venice: The Sessas, 1614
—De justitia et jure tomi duo.
Mainz: B. Lipp, for A. Mylius,
1602
—De justitia, tomus primus.
Venice: Society of Minims,
1602
—Disputationes de contractibus.
Venice: M. Collosini, & B. Ba-
rezzi, 1601
Molina, Tirso de (pseud). *See*
Téllez, Gabriel
Monardes, Nicolás. *See the follow-*
ing:
—L'Ecluse, Charles. Exoticorum
libri decem. [Leyden:] 1605
—Orta, Garcia da. Dell'historia
de i semplici. Venice: 1605
— — —Venice: 1616
— —Histoire des drogues espi-
ceries. Lyons: 1619
—Woodall, John. The surgions
mate. London: 1617
MONARDES, NICOLÁS
—Baricelli, G. C. Hortulus ge-
nialis. Naples: 1617
—Camerarius, P. Les heures des-
robees, ou Meditations histori-
ques. Paris: 1610
—Les meditations historiques.
Lyons: 1610
— —Operae horarum subcisiva-
rum . . . Centuria tertia. Frank-
furt a.M.: 1609
— —Tertia centuria historica,

das ist, Dritter Theil. Leipzig:
1630
—Du Val, G. Phytologia, sive
Philosophia plantarum. Paris:
1647
—Fueldez, A. Observations curieuses, touchant la petite ve-
role. Lyons: 1645
—Gesner, K. Köstlicher Artz-
neyschatz. Zurich: 1608
—Goulart, S. Histoires de nostre
temps, t 2–3. Paris: 1601
—Untzer, M. Tractatus medico-
chymici septem. Halle: 1634
—Villa, E. de. Ramillete de plan-
tas. Burgos: 1637
Monasticon Augustinianum. *See*
Crusenius, Nicolaus
Moncada, Sancho de. Restaura-
cion politica de España. Ma-
drid: L. Sánchez, 1619
Le monde, ou La description
générale. *See* Avity, Pierre d',
sieur de Montmartin
Mondo elementare, et celeste.
See Rosaccio, Giuseppe
Il mondo nuovo. *See* Stigliani,
Tomaso
Monet, Philibert. Invantaire des
deus langues. Lyons: Widow
of C. Rigaud, & P. Borde, 1635
— —Lyons: C. Obert, 1636
— —Lyons: A. Pillehotte, 1636
— —Lyons: Widow of C. Rigaud,
& P. Borde, 1636
—Nouveau et dernier dictio-
naire. Paris: 1628
— —Paris: C. Le Beau, 1645
—*See also* Jesuits. Letters from
missions. Annuae litterae
(1612) 1618. Annuae litterae
. . . anni M.DC.XII. Lyons:
1618
MONEY. *See also* COINAGE
—Cartagena, Colombia (Prov-
ince). A dos cosas se reduze
la pretension de Cartagena.
[Madrid? ca. 1625?]
—González de Mendoza, P. El li-
cenciado Don Pedro Gonçalez
de Mendoça. [Madrid: 1639?]
—Molina, L. de. De justitia et
jure tomi duo. Mainz: 1602
— —Disputationes de contractibus. Venice: 1601
Monita amoris virginei. *See* Cats,
Jacob

La monja alferez, comedia fa-
mosa. *See* Pérez de Montalván,
Juan
Monsalve, Miguel de, friar. Re-
ducion universal de todo el
Piru. [Madrid? 1604]
Monsieur d'Olive. A comedie. *See*
Chapman, George
Monstrorum historia. *See* Aldro-
vandi, Ulisse
Montaigne, Michel Eyquem de.
Les essais. Cologny & Leyden:
J. Doreau, 1602
— —Leyden: J. Doreau, 1602
— —Paris: A. L'Angelier, 1602
— —Paris: A. L'Angelier, 1604
— —Antwerp: A. Maire [1608?]
— —Paris: F. Gueffier, 1608
— —Paris: M. Nivelle, 1608
— —Paris: J. Petit-Pas, 1608
— —Paris: C. Rigaud, 1608
— —Paris: D. Salis, 1608
— —Paris: C. Sevestre, 1608
— —Geneva: J. Can, 1609
— —Leyden: J. Doreau, 1609
— —Paris: F. Gueffier, 1611
— —Paris: M. Nivelle, 1611
— —Paris: J. Petit-Pas, 1611
— —Paris: C. Rigaud, 1611
— —Paris: C. Sevestre, 1611
— —Cologny: P. Aubert, 1616
(2)
— —Geneva: P. Aubert, 1616 (2)
— —[Geneva]: P. Aubert, 1616
— —Geneva & Cologny: [P. Au-
bert] 1616
— —Paris: F. Gueffier, 1617
— —Paris: M. Nivelle, 1617
— —Paris: J. Petit-Pas, 1617
— —Paris: C. Rigaud, 1617
— —Paris: D. Salis, 1617
— —Paris: C. Sevestre, 1617
— —Rouen: N. Angot, 1617
— —Rouen: J. Berthelin, 1617
— —Rouen: J. Besongne, 1617
— —Rouen: T. Daré, 1617
— —Rouen: J. Durand, 1617
— —Rouen: J. Osmont, 1617
— —Rouen: M. de Préaulx, 1617
— —Rouen: R. Valentin, 1617
— —Rouen: Widow of T. Daré,
1619
— —Rouen: J. Durand, for N.
Angot [1619]
— —Rouen: J. Durand, for J.
Berthelin [1619]

————Rouen: J. Durand, for J. Besongne [1619]

————Rouen: J. Osmont, 1619

————Rouen: A. Ouyn, 1619

————Rouen: R. Valentin, 1619

————Rouen: M. de Préaulx, 1620

————Paris: F. Angat, 1625

————Paris: R. Bertault, 1625

————Paris: R. Boutonné, 1625

————Paris: M. Collet, 1625

————Paris: Widow of R. Dallin, 1625

————Paris: C. Hulpeau, 1625

————Paris: T. de La Ruelle, 1625

————Paris: G. Loyson, 1625

————Paris: G. & A. Robinot, 1625

————Paris: P. Rocolet, 1625

————Paris: E. Saucié, 1625

————Paris: F. Targa, 1626

————Rouen: J. Berthelin, 1627

————[Rouen]: J. Besongne, 1627

————Rouen: J. Cailloué, 1627

————Rouen: L. Du Mesnil, 1627

————Rouen: R. Féron, 1627

————Rouen: P. de La Motte, 1627

————Rouen: R. Valentin, 1627

————Paris: P. Chevalier, 1632

————Paris, J. Camusat, 1635

————Paris: T. Du Bray, & P. Rocolet, 1635

————Paris: P. Rocolet, 1635

————Paris: P. Billaine, 1636

————Paris: M. Blageart, 1636

————Paris: L. Boullenger, 1636

————Paris: M. Collet, 1636

————Paris: J. Germont, 1636

————Paris: P. L'Amy, 1636

————Paris: S. de La Fosse, 1636

————Paris: G. Loyson, 1636

————Paris: J. Villery, & J. Guignard, 1636

————Paris: M. Blageart, 1640

————Paris: A. Courbé, 1640 (2)

————Rouen: J. Berthelin, 1641

————Rouen: J. Berthelin [1641?]

————Rouen: J. Besongne the Younger, 1641

————Paris: M. Blageart, 1649

—The essayes. London: V. Simmes, for E. Blount [1603]

——London: M. Bradwood, for E. Blount, & W. Barret, 1613

——London: M. Fletcher, for R. Royston, 1632

—Saggi. Venice: M. Ginammi, 1633

Montalvão, Jorge Mascarenhas, marquez de. Carta, que o Visorrey do Brasil . . . escreveo. Lisbon: J. Rodriguez, for L. de Queiros, 1641

—Cartas que escreveo o marquez de Montalvam. Lisbon: D. Lopes Rosa, for D. Alvarez, 1641

—Copyen van drie missiven. Amsterdam: J. van Hilten, 1641

——Amsterdam: 1642

—Segunda carta. Lisbon: J. Rodriguez, 1641

Montesclaros, Juan de Mendoza y Luna, marques de. *See* Spain. Laws, statutes, etc., 1598–1621 (Philip III). El Rey. Madrid: 1609

Montesinos, Fernando de. Señor. El licenciado D. Fernando de Montesinos. [Madrid? 1645]

MONTEZUMA

—Clercq, N. de. Tooneel der beroemder hertogen. Delft: 1617

—Dickenson, J. Speculum tragicum. Delft: 1601

—Lloyd, D. The legend of captaine Jones. London: 1648

—Wybarne, J. The new age of old names. London: 1609

Montoya, Antonio Ruiz. *See* Ruiz de Montoya, Antonio

Montoya, Juan de. Relacion del descrubimiento del Nuovo Mexico. Rome: B. Bonfadino, 1602

MONTS, PIERRE DE GUAST, SIEUR DE

—Peleus, J. Les questions illustres. Paris: 1608

Montstopping aende vredehaters. Leyden: C. M. van Schie, 1647

Montuval, Marquis de. *See* Montalvão, Jorge Mascarenhas, marquez de

Morales, Juan de. Señor. El capitan don Juan de Morales dize. [Madrid? ca. 1650?]

More, Sir Thomas, Saint. The common-wealth of Utopia.

London: B. Alsop, & T. Fawcet, for W. Sheares, 1639

—De optimo reipublicae statu . . . Beschreibung der . . . Insul Utopia. Leipzig: M. Lantzenberger, for H. Gross the Younger, 1612

—De optimo reipublicae statu, deque nova insula Utopia. Frankfurt a.M.: J. Sauer, for P. Kopff, 1601

——Hanau: H. J. Henne, for P. Kopff, 1613

——*In* Amphitheatrum sapientiae Socraticae. Hanau: 1619

——Milan: G. B. Bidelli, 1620

—Utopia . . . newly corrected. London: B. Alsop, 1624

—De Utopia . . . over-geset. Hoorn: I. Willemszoon, for M. Gerbrantszoon, 1629 [i.e., 1630]

——Hoorn: I. Willemszoon, for M. Gerbrantszoon, 1630

—Utopia à mendis vindicata. Cologne: C. ab Egmondt and Co., 1629

——Amsterdam: J. Janszoon the Younger, 1631

—L'Utopie. Amsterdam: J. Blaeu, 1643

More excellent observations of the estate . . . of Holland. London: E. A[llde]., for N. Bourne, & T. Archer, 1622

More knaves yet? *See* Rowlands, Samuel

Morejon, Pedro. A briefe relation of the persecution . . . in . . . Japonia. [St Omer: English College Press] 1619

Morel, Pierre. Formulae remediorum. Padua: P. Frambotti, 1647, '46

—Methodus praescribendi formulas remediorum. [Geneva:] J. Chouët, 1639

—Systema materiae medicae. *In his* Methodus praescribendi formulas remediorum. [Geneva:] 1639

——*In his* Formulae remediorum. Padua: 1647, '46

—Systema parascevasticum. Geneva: J. Chouët, 1628

Morellas, Cosme Gil. Compendiosa relatio vitae . . . Ludovici

Bertrandi. Cologne: A. Kempen, 1609

Mores, leges, et ritus omnium gentium. *See* Boemus, Johann

Morghen-wecker. *See* Baudart, Willem

Morgues, Matthieu de, sieur de Saint Germain. *See* Arnauld, Antoine (1560–1619). La premiere et seconde Savoisienne. Grenoble: 1630

Moris, Gedeon. Copye. Van 't Journael. Amsterdam: F. Lieshout, 1640 (2)

—Journael. *In* Het naderste ende sekerste journalier verhael . . . uyt Brasyl. The Hague: 1640

Morisot, Claude Barthélemy. Orbis maritimi. Dijon: P. Palliot, 1643

— —Dijon: P. Palliot, 1645

— —Dijon: P. Palliot, 1648

—Peruviana. Dijon: G. A. Guyot, 1645–46

Moro-mastix: Mr John Goodwin whipt. London: T. Underhill, 1647

Morone, Mattia. Directorium medico-practicum. Lyons: J. A. Huguetan, 1647

— —Lyons: J. A. Huguetan, 1648

— —Lyons: J. A. Huguetan, & M. A. Ravaud, 1650

Morovelli de la Puebla, Francisco. Don Francisco Morovelli de Puebla defiende el patronato. Malagá: J. René, 1628

Morrell, William. New-England. or A briefe enarration. London: J. D[awson]., 1625

La mort glorieuse du pere Christophe de Mendoza. *See* Díaz Taño, Francisco

Morton, Thomas. New English Canaan. Amsterdam: J. F. Stam, 1637

— —[Amsterdam: J. F. Stam] for C. Greene, at London [1637?]

— —*See also* A treatise of New England. [London? 1650?]

Moryson, Fynes. An itinerary. London: J. Beale, 1617

Moscherosch, Johann Michael. Les Visiones de don Francesco de Quevedo Villegas, oder

Wunderbare . . . Gesichte. Strassburg: J. P. Mülbe [1640]

—Visiones . . . Wunderliche . . . Gesichte. Strassburg: J. P. Mülbe, 1642–43

— —Strassburg: J. P. Mülbe, 1643

— —Frankfurt a.M.: A. Humm, 1644

— —Frankfurt a.M.: J. G. Schönwetter, 1645

— —[Frankfurt a.M.: J. G. Schönwetter] 1645 [i.e., 1647]

—Les visiones . . . Satyrische Gesichte. Leyden: F. Heger, 1645–46

—Les Visions . . . Wunderliche . . . Gesichte. Leyden: A. Wijngaerden, 1646[–47]

—Wunderliche und warhafftige Gesichte. Strassburg: [1650]

— —Strassburg: J. P. Mülbe, & J. Städel, 1650

—*See also* Les visions de don Queveto Philandri von Sittewaldt Complementum. Frankfurt a.M.: 1648

Moscoso y de Córdoba, Cristóbal de. Alegacion en derecho en competencia de jurisdicion. Madrid: Widow of J. González, 1635

—Discurso juridico y politico. [Madrid? 1625?]

—Discurso legal militar. [Madrid: 1635?]

—El licenciado d. Christoval de Moscoso y Cordova . . . Con Don Juan de Amassa. Madrid: Widow of J. González, 1634

—El licenciado Don Christoval de Moscoso y Cordova . . . con Alonso de Carrion. Madrid: Widow of J. González, 1634

—El licenciado don Christoval de Moscoso y Cordova . . . Con Don Juan de Meneses. Madrid: Widow of J. González, 1634

—El licendiado D. Christoval de Moscoso y Cordova . . . Con el Consulado de Sevilla. Madrid: Widow of J. González, 1634

—El licenciado Don Christoval de Moscoso y Cordova . . . Con el duque del Infantado. [Madrid? 163–?]

—El l[icencia]do Don Christoval de Moscoso y Cordova . . . en defensa de su jurisdiccion. [Madrid: ca. 1635?]

—Señor. La resolucion de V. Magestad. [Madrid: 1635?]

Mosemann, Hermann Fabronius. *See* Fabronius, Hermann

A most delectable . . . discourse. *See* Lithgow, William

The most elegant and wittie epigrams. *See* Harington, Sir John

A most learned and eloquent speech. *See* Corbet, Miles

A most pleasaunt . . . comedie. *See* Shakespeare, William

MOUNTAINS—PERU. *See also* ANDES

—Bodin, J. Universae naturae theatrum. Hanau: 1605

[**Mourning Virginia.** London: H. Grosson, 1622]

Mourt's relation. A relation or journall of the beginning of . . . Plimoth. London: [J. Dawson] for J. Bellamy, 1622

Mr. Blundevil his exercises. *See* Blundeville, Thomas

Mr. Cottons letter . . . examined. *See* Williams, Roger

Mr Grymstons speech in Parliament. *See* Grimston, Sir Harbottle, bart

Müller, Philipp. Miracula chymica et misteria medica. [Wittenberg:] L. Seuberlich, for C. Berger, 1611

—Miracula chymica, et mystica medica. Paris: M. Mondiere, 1644

—Miracula et mysteria chymicomedica. [Wittenberg?] C. Berger, 1614

— —[Wittenberg:] C. Berger, 1616

— —Wittenberg: J. Hake, for C. Berger, 1623

Münster, Sebastian. Cosmographey: das ist Beschreibung aller Länder. Basel: S. Henricpetri, 1614

—Cosmographia, das ist, Ausssführliche . . . beschreibung. Basel: S. Henricpetri, 1615

—Cosmographia. das ist: beschreibung der gantzen Welt.

Basel: Henricpetri Office, 1628

Mundus alter. *See* Hall, Joseph, Bp

Mundus imperiorum. *See* Botero, Giovanni

Munk, Jens. Navigatio septentrionalis. Copenhagen: H. Waldkirch, 1624

—xxvi. Schiff-Fahrt. *See* Le Peyrère, Isaac de. Die xxvi. Schiff-Fahrt. Frankfurt a.M.: 1650

Múñoz, Bernardo. Relacion verdadera, y carta nueva de un traslado embiado del Brasil. Madrid: A. Duplastre, 1639

Munsters discours. [The Hague?] 1646 (2)

Munsters praetie. [Amsterdam?] 1646 (4)

Munsters praetien. [Amsterdam?] 1646 (2)

Munsters praetje. [Amsterdam?] 1646 (4)

Munsters vrede-praetje. [Amsterdam?] 1646

Murcia de la Llana, Francisco. Canciones lugubres. Madrid: Widow of F. Correa, 1622

Murga, Francisco de. Señor. El maestro de campo Francisco de Murga. [Madrid? 1637]

Murner, Thomas. Der Schelmen Zunfft. Frankfurt a.M.: L. Jennis, & J. de Zetter, 1618–25

Murtola, Gasparo. Della creatione del mundo. Venice: E. Deuchino, & G. B. Pulciano, 1608

——Macerata: P. Salvioni, 1618

La Murtoleide. *See* Marino, Giovanni Battista

Musae priores. *See* Leech, John, poet

Musaeum Franc. Calceolarii. *See* Ceruto, Benedetto

Musaeum metallicum. *See* Aldrovandi, Ulisse

La muse chrestienne. *See* Rocquigny, Adrian de

Les muses de la Nouvelle France. *See* Lescarbot, Marc

MUSICIAL INSTRUMENTS

—Praetorius, M. Syntagma musicum. Wittenberg: 1615

MUSK

—Strobelberger, J. S. Tractatus novus. Jena: 1620

Mutoni, Niccolò. Mithridateiotechnia: hoc est; De Mithridatii legitima constructione. Jena: J. Beithmann, for Heirs of J. Eyering, & J. Perfert, 1620

Muy poderoso señor. *See* Barnuevo, Rodrigo

My ladies looking glasse. *See* Rich, Barnabe

Mylius, Arnold, comp. De rebus hispanicis. Cologne: House of Birckmann, 1602

Mylius, Johann Daniel. Antidotarium medico-chymicum reformatum. Frankfurt a.M.: L. Jennis, 1620

Myrothecium spagyricum. *See* Fabre, Pierre Jean

The mysteries of nature and art. *See* Bate, John

The mysteryes of nature and art. *See* Bate, John

N., B. *See* Breton, Nicholas

N., N. *See* Copye van een brief . . . van Sevilien. Amsterdam: 1626

—*See also* Cort verhael vande ordre die sijne Conincklicke Majesteyt van Spagnien . . . gegeven heeft. Amsterdam: [1640]

N., P. E. *See* Den naeckten Spangjaert. [Amsterdam?] 1647

De na-ween vande vrede. 'Poste' [i.e., Amsterdam?] 1650 (4)

Nachrichtung vor alle die jenige welche . . . erbliche gemeinschaft wollen haben. *See* Nederlandsche West-Indische Compagnie

Nader ordre ende reglement. *See* Netherlands (United Provinces, 1581–1795). Staten Generaal

Het naderste ende sekerste journalier verhael . . . uyt Brasyl. The Hague: I. Burchoorn, 1640 (2)

Den naeckten Spagniaerdt. [Amsterdam?] 1647

Den naeckten Spangjaert. [Amsterdam?] 1647

Naerder aenwysinghe der bewinthebbers regieringe. [Amsterdam: 1622]

Naerder bedenckingen over de zee-vaerdt. *See* Usselinx, Willem

Naerder ordre ende reglement . . . over het . . . vry stellen van den handel . . . op de stadt Olinda. *See* Netherlands (United Provinces, 1581–1795). Staten Generaal

Naerdere propositie. *See* Sousa Coutinho, Francisco de

Nájera, Antonio de. Navegacion especulativa. Lisbon: P. Craesbeeck, 1628

NAMES, GEOGRAPHICAL

—Esternod, C. d'. Les desirs amoureux de Dom Phillippe. Paris: 1614

—Megiser. H. Thesaurus polyglottus. Frankfurt a.M.: 1603

—Monet, P. Nouveau et dernier dictionaire. Paris: 1628

NAMES, INDIAN

—Cats, J. Proef-steen van den trou-ringh. [Amsterdam?] 1644

——'s Werelts begin, midden, eynde. Dordrecht: 1637

—Minsheu, J. Ductor in linguas, the guide into tongues. London: 1617

——Minshaei emendatio. London: 1625

Naples (Kingdom). Laws, statutes, etc. Pragmatica circa ilius prohibendi del tabaco. Naples: E. Longo [1650]

Nápoles, Juan de. Señor. El general de toda la Orden. [Madrid? 1645?]

NARRAGANSET INDIANS

—Gorton, S. Simplicities defence. London: 1646

Narratio historica eorum, quae Societas Jesu . . . egit. *See* Ragueneau, Paul

Narratio regionum Indicarum. *See* Casas, Bartolomé de las, Bp

Nash, Thomas. Miscelanea, or, A fourefold way. London: J. Dawson, for T. Slater, 1639

—Quaternio, or A fourefold way. London: J. Dawson, 1633

Nederlandsche West-Indische Compagnie. Acte, waer by een yeder gheaccordeert werdt. [Amsterdam?] 1624

—Advertissement voor allen deen ghenen die sullen willen herideren. The Hague: Widow & Heirs of H. J. van Wouw, 1623

—Aen de . . . Staten Generael. [Amsterdam? 1649]

—Antwoorde vande gedeputeerde. [Amsterdam?] 1647

—Artickel und Satzungen der . . . General Staden. Frankfurt a.M.: J. Schmidlin, 1621

—Articulen, met approbatie . . . over het open ende vry stellen vanden handel. Amsterdam: P. A. van Ravesteyn, 1630

——Middelburg: Widow & Heirs of S. Moulert [1630?]

——Amsterdam: T. Jacobszoon, for M. J. Brandt, 1631

—Bewilligungen bey den Staden General. [The Hague? 1623?]

—Consideratien ende redenen der e. heeren bewind-hebberen. [Amsterdam? 1629?]

——Haarlem: A. Roman, 1629 (4)

—Copye. Van seker articulen. [Amsterdam?] 1623

—Extract uyt de Missive. *See* Nederlandsche West-Indische Compagnie. Hooghe en Secrete Raad. Extract . . . . The Hague: 1648

—Extract uyt de Notulen. [Amsterdam: 1631?]

—Extract uyt den brief vande politijcque raeden in Brasil. The Hague: Widow & Heirs of H. J. van Wouw, 1635

—De gemeene directeurs, ghestelt tottet formeren vande capitalen. [Amsterdam: 1621]

—De ghemeene directeurs. [Amsterdam? 1621]

—Nachrichtung vor alle die jenige welche . . . erbliche gemeinschaft wollen haben. [The Hague? 1623?]

—Nader ordre ende reglement. *See* Netherlands (United Provinces, 1581–1795). Staten

Generaal. Nader ordre ende reglement. The Hague: 1634

—Naerder ordre ende reglement. *See* Netherlands (United Provinces, 1581–1795). Staten Generaal. Naerder ordre ende reglement. Amsterdam: 1638

—Nieuwe in-teyckeninge ende verhooginge der capitalen. [The Hague? 1636]

—Octroy. The Hague: H. J. van Wouw, 1621

——Middelburg: Widow & Heirs of S. Moulert [1623]

——The Hague: Widow & Heirs of H. J. van Wouw, 1623 (3)

——The Hague: Widow & Heirs of H. J. van Wouw, 1624

——The Hague: Widow & Heirs of H. J. van Wouw, 1629 (2)

——The Hague: Widow & Heirs of H. J. van Wouw, 1631

——The Hague: Widow & Heirs of H. J. van Wouw, 1637

——The Hague: Widow & Heirs of H. J. van Wouw, 1642 (3)

—Octroy concédé—par les . . . Estats Generaulx. Amsterdam: J. P. Wachter, 1623

—Orders and articles granted by the . . . States General. [London:] 1621

—Ordonnances, privileges, franchises, et assistances octroyez . . . par les . . . Estats Generaux. Paris: J. A. Joallin, 1623

—Ordonnantien ende articulen beraemt by de . . . Staten Generael. [Amsterdam:] 1621

——[Amsterdam?] 1621 (3)

—Ordonnantien ende articulen voor desen beraemt by de . . . Staten Generael. Arnhem: J. Janszoon, 1623

—Ordre ende Reglement. *See* Nederlandsche West-Indische Compagnie. Kamer Zealand. Ordre ende Reglement op de Comptoiren. Middelburg: [1621?]

—Reglement . . . over het openstellen vanden handel op Brasil. Amsterdam: J. Broerszoon, 1638

——The Hague: Widow & Heirs of H. J. van Wouw, 1638

——The Hague: Widow & Heirs of H. J. van Wouw, 1648

—Reglement . . . over het openstellen vanden handel op S. Paulo de Loanda. The Hague: Widow & Heirs of H. J. van Wouw, 1648

—Remonstrantie ende consideratien aengaende de vereeninghe vande . . . Compagnien. The Hague: [1644]

——The Hague: L. de Langhe, 1644

—De Staten Generael der Vereenichde Nederlanden. [The Hague? 1624]

—Three severall treatises concerning the truce. London: [B. Alsop & T. Fawcet] for N. Butter & N. Bourne, 1630

—Twee deductien, aen-gaende de vereeninge. The Hague: J. Veely, 1644 (3)

——*In* Nederlandsche West-Indische Compagnie. Remonstrantie ende consideratien aengaende de vereeninghe vande . . . Compagnien. The Hague: 1644

—Verhooginge der capitalen . . . voor een derde part. [The Hague? 1629] (2)

—Verhooginghe vande capitalen . . . ghearresteert byde vergaderinghe vande negentiene. [The Hague? 1639]

——The Hague: Widow & Heirs of H. J. van Wouw, 1639

—Voorslack by eenige hooft-participanten. [Amsterdam? 1641]

—Vryheden by de vergaderinghe van de negenthien . . . vergunt aen . . . Nieu-Nederlandt. Amsterdam: M. J. Brandt, 1630

—Vryheden ende exemptien t'accorderen ende toe te staen. [Amsterdam: 1645]

—Vryheden ende exemptien voor de patroonen. Amsterdam: T. Jacobszoon, 1631

——*In* Nederlandsche West-Indische Compagnie. Articulen, met approbatie. Amsterdam: 1631

——*See also* Lampe, Barent. Het

pagie, monture . . . der schepen. The Hague: Widow &
Heirs of H. J. van Wouw, 1627
—Placcaet ordonnantie ende
conditien. The Hague: Widow
& Heirs of H. J. van Wouw,
1625
—Placcaet tegen het: Nootwendich discours. Middelburg:
1622
—Placcaet teghens seecker fameus libel. The Hague: Widow
& Heirs of H. J. van Wouw,
1622
—Poincten der artijckelen, ter
vergaderinghe. Dordrecht:
S. Moulaert, 1647
—Poincten der artijckulen, gear-
resteert. [Dordrecht: S. Mou-
laert, &] J. van Benden [at Am-
sterdam] 1647
—Poincten der artijckulen ter
vergaderinghe. Dordrecht:
S. Moulaert, 1647
—Poincten der artyculen ter ver-
gaderinge. Dordrecht:
S. Moulaert, 1647
—Ses poincten. *See* Ses poincten
welcke by de . . . Staten . . .
zijn vast gestelt. [The Hague?
1649?]
—De Staten Generael . . . . The
Hague: Widow & Heirs of
H. J. van Wouw, 1630
—Vercondinge van de vrede.
The Hague: Widow & Heirs of
H. J. van Wouw, 1648 (2)
NETHERLANDS (UNITED
PROVINCES, 1581–1795).
STATEN GENERAAL.
—Nederlandsche Oost-Indische
Compagnie. Het geam-
plieerde Octroy. [Amster-
dam?] 1623
— —Het out Oost-Indische oc-
troy. [The Hague? 1602?]
—Nederlandsche West-Indische
Compagnie. Artickel und Sat-
zungen der . . . General Sta-
den. Frankfurt a.M.: 1621
— —Bewilligungen bey den Sta-
den General. [The Hague?
1623?]
— —Copye. Van seker articulen.
[Amsterdam?] 1623
— —Nieuwe in-teyckeninge

ende verhooginge der capitalen. [The Hague? 1636]
— —Octroy. The Hague: 1623,
et seq.
— —Octroy concédé—par les
. . . Estats Generaulx. Amster-
dam: 1623
— —Orders and articles granted
by the . . . States General.
[London:] 1621
— —Ordonnances, privileges,
franchises, et assistances oc-
troyez . . . par les . . . Estats
Generaux. Paris: 1623
— —Ordonnantien ende articu-
len beraemt by de . . . Staten
Generael. [Amsterdam:] 1621
— —Ordonnantien ende articu-
len voor desen beraemt by
de . . . Staten Generael. Arn-
hem: 1623
— —Reglement . . . over het
openstellen vanden handel op
Brasil. The Hague: 1638
— —De Staten Generael der
Vereenichde Nederlanden.
[The Hague? 1624]
—Nederlandsche West-Indische
Compagnie. Hooghe en Se-
crete Raad. Extract uyt de Mis-
sive. The Hague: 1648
—Netherlands (United Prov-
inces, 1581–1795). Staatsraad.
Adviis van den Raedt van sta-
ten. The Hague: 1650
—Ontwerp, raeckende het op-
rechten van een Camer. Leeuwarden: 1629

**Netherlands (United Provinces,
1581–1795). Treaties, etc.** Ar-
ticulen, nopende de conditien
des pays. Middelburg: A. P.
van Hagedoorn, 1647 (2)
See also the following:
—Portugal. Treaties, etc., 1640–
1656 (John IV). Accoort ende
articulen. Amsterdam: 1641
— —Tractaet van bestant. The
Hague: 1642
— —Tractatus induciarum. The
Hague: 1642
— —Trattado das tregoas. The
Hague: 1642
—Spain. Treaties, etc., 1621–
1665 (Philip IV). The articles
and conditions. London: 1648

— —Articulen dess Friedens.
[Brussels:] 1647
— —Articulen en conditien.
Ghent: 1648
— —Capitulaciones de la paz.
Madrid: 1648
— —Copia de las cartas y res-
puestas. Barcelona: 1625
— —Tractaet van vrede. The
Hague: 1648
— —Tractatus pacis. Münster:
1648
— —Traicté de la paix. The
Hague: 1648
— —Traicté de paix. Paris: 1649
— —Treatie of peace. The
Hague: [1648]
NETHERLANDS—HISTORY,
NAVAL
—Relacion de la famosa vitoria.
Seville: 1633
—Relacion del sucesso que ha
tenido el marques de Ca-
dreyta. Barcelona: 1633
—Relacion verdadera de la fa-
mosa victoria. Seville: [1633]
—Relacion verdadera, de la
grandiosa vitoria. Granada:
1630
—Relacion verdadera de la re-
friega. Madrid: 1638
— —Seville: 1638
—Relacion verdadera de todos
los sucessos. Madrid: 1641
—Relacion verdadera del viaje
de los galeones. Seville: 1638
—Relatione venuta de Madrid.
Rome: 1630
—Toledo Osorio y Mendoza,
F. de. Relacion embiado . . . de
lo sucedido a la armada. Seville: 1630
— —Relatione venuta de Madrid
a Roma. Rome: 1630
— —Warhaffte Relation, von
dem grossen herrlichen Sig.
Passau: 1630
—Translaet uyt den Spaenschen,
weghens 't gevecht. Amster-
dam: 1639
—A true relation of a late very
famous sea-fight. London:
1640
—Two famous sea-fights. Lon-
don: 1639
—Vera relacion de la famosa vi-

toria. Jerez de la Frontera: 1632

—Vitorias felicissimas. Seville: 1619

Neue Schiffart. *See* Noort, Olivier van

Neuf livres de la dignité . . . des sciences. *See* Bacon, Francis

Neuhaus, Edo. Theatrum ingenii humani. Amsterdam: J. Janszoon the Younger, 1633–34

— —Amsterdam: 1648

—Triumphalia Leowardiana. Groningen: N. Roman, 1629

Neuhusius, Edo. *See* Neuhaus, Edo

Neundter und letzter Theil Americae. *See* Acosta, José de

Die neuntzehende Schiffarth. *See* Braun, Samuel

Neuw vollkommentlich Kreuterbuch. *See* Theodorus, Jacobus

Neuwe Archontologia cosmica. *See* Avity, Pierre d', sieur de Montmartin

Neville, Henry. The ladies parliament. [London: 1647]

—Newes from the New-exchange. London: 1650

—The parliament of ladies. [London:] 1647 (2)

The new age of old names. *See* Wybarne, Joseph

NEW ALBION

—Evelyn, R. A direction for adventurers. [London?] 1641

—Plantagenet, B. A description of the province of New Albion. [London:] 1648

New and choise characters. *See* Overbury, Sir Thomas

Ein new Artzney Buch. *See* Wirsung, Christoph

The new attractive. *See* Norman, Robert

NEW ENGLAND

—Bancroft, T. Two bookes of epigrammes. London: 1639

—The British bell-man. [London:] 1648

—Cotton, J. Gods promise to His plantation. London: 1630

—Great Britain. Laws, statutes, etc., 1649–1660 (Commonwealth). An act for charging of tobacco. [London: 1650]

—Hall, J. A survay of that foolish . . . libell. London: 1641

—Hinc illae lachrymae. London: 1648

—Johnson, E. Good news from New England. London: 1648

—Lechford, T. Plain dealing. London: 1642

—Mather, R. An heart-melting exhortation. London: 1650

—Observations upon Prince Rupert's white dogge. [London: 1643]

—Peacham, H. Coach and sedan. London: 1636

—Ridley, M. A short treatise of magneticall bodies. London: 1613

—Smith, Capt. J. The generall history of Virginia. [London: 1623]

—Taylor, J. A valorous . . . sea-fight. London: 1640

—Walker, C. The history of Independency. [London?] 1648

NEW ENGLAND—CHURCH HISTORY. *See also* PURITANS, *etc.*

—Allin, J. A defence of the answer made unto . . . questions . . . sent from New-England. London: 1648

—Baillie, R. A dissuasive from the errours. London: 1645

—Ball, J. A letter of many ministers. London: 1643

— —A tryall of the new-church way. London: 1644

—Bible. O. T. Psalms. English. Paraphrases. 1647. Bay Psalm Book. The whole book of psalmes. [London?] 1647

—Bulkeley, P. The gospel-covenant. London: 1646

—Cawdry, D. Vindiciae clavium. London: 1645

—Clarke, S. A mirrour. London: 1646

—A coole conference. [London: 1644?]

—Cotton, J. The bloudy tenant, washed. London: 1647

— —The churches resurrection. London: 1642

— —A conference . . . held at Boston. London: 1646

— —A coppy of a letter. [London:] 1641

— —The covenant of Gods free grace. London: 1645

— —A letter . . . to Mr. Williams. London: 1643

— —Of the holinesse of church-members. London: 1650

— —Severall questions. London: 1647

— —Sixteene questions. London: 1644

— —The way of congregational churches cleared. London: 1648

— —The way of the churches . . . in New-England. London: 1645

—Davenport, J. The profession of faith. London: 1642

—Eaton, S. A defence of sundry positions . . . alleged to justifie the Congregationall-way. London: 1645

— —The defence of sundry positions . . . for the Congregational-way. London: 1646

—Edwards, T. Antapologia. London: 1644

— —Gangraena. London: 1646

—Forbes, A. An anatomy of independency. London: 1644

—Gillespie, G. Wholsome severity. London: 1645

—Goodwin, J. M.S. to A.S. London: 1644

—A reply of two of the brethren. London: 1644

—Gorton, S. Simplicities defence. London: 1646

—Hollingworth, R. An examination of sundry scriptures. London: 1645

—Holmes, N. Gospel musick. London: 1644

—Hooke, W. New-Englands sence. London: 1645

— —New Englands teares. London: 1641

—Hooker, T. A survey of . . . church-discipline. London: 1648

—Hudson, S. The essence . . . of the church. London: 1645

— —A vindication. London: 1650

—Independency accused. London: 1645

—Lisle, F. The kingdoms divisions anatomized. London: 1649

—Mather, R. A reply to Mr. Rutherford. London: 1647

—Moro-mastix: Mr John Goodwin whipt. London: 1647

—Norton, J. Responsio ad totam quaestionum syllogen. London: 1648

—Pagitt, E. Heresiography. London: 1645

—Parker, T. The true copy of a letter. London: 1644

—Rathband, W. A briefe narration. London: 1644

—Rutherford, S. The divine right of church-government. London: 1646

——The due right of presbyteries. London: 1644

——A free disputation. London: 1649

——A survey of the spirituall antichrist. London: 1648

—Shepard, T. The clear sunshine of the Gospel. London: 1648

——New Englands lamentation. London: 1645

—Sibelius, C. Of the conversion of five thousand. London: 1650

—Steuart, A. An answer to a libell. London: 1644

——The second part of the duply. London: 1644

——Some observations. London: [1644]

—Taylor, J. A letter sent to London: [Oxford:] 1643

—Twisse, W. A treatise of Mr. Cottons. London: 1646

—Ward, N. The simple cobler of Aggawam. London: 1647

—Weld, T. An answer to W. R. his Narration. London: 1644

——A brief narration . . . of the churches in New-England. London: 1645

—Wheelwright, J. Mercurius Americanus. London: 1645

—Williams, R. The bloudy tenent. [London:] 1644

——Christenings make not Christians. London: [1646]

——Mr. Cottons letter . . . examined. London: 1644

—Winslow, E. The dangers of tolerating levellers. London: 1649

——Hypocrisie unmasked. London: 1646

——New-Englands salamander. London: 1647

—Winthrop, J. Antinomians and Familists. London: 1644

—Workman, G. Private-men no pulpit-men. London: 1646

NEW ENGLAND—COLONIZATION

—Great Britain. Sovereigns, etc., 1625–1649 (Charles I). A proclamation to restraine the transporting of passengers. London: 1638

—A proposition of provisions. London: 1630

—Smith, Capt. J. Advertisements for the unexperienced planters. London: 1631

—White, J. The planters plea. London: 1630

NEW ENGLAND—COMMERCE

—Great Britain. Sovereigns, etc., 1603–1625 (James I). A proclamation prohibiting interloping. London: 1622

—Great Britain. Sovereigns, etc., 1625–1649 (Charles I). A proclamation forbidding the disorderly trading with the salvages in New England. London: 1630

NEW ENGLAND—DESCRIPTION

—Brereton, J. A brief . . . relation of . . . Virginia. London: 1602

—Morrell, W. New-England. London: 1625

—Morton, T. New English Canaan. Amsterdam: 1637

—Smith, Capt. J. A description of New England. London: 1616

——Viertzehende Schiffart oder . . . Beschreibung dess Neuwen Engellandts. Frankfurt a.M.: 1617

—Stirling, W. Alexander, 1st earl of. The mapp and description of New-England. London: 1630

—A treatise of New England. [London? 1650?]

—Wood, W. New Englands prospect. London: 1634

NEW ENGLAND—DRAMA

—Glapthorne, H. Wit in a constable. London: 1640

NEW ENGLAND—HISTORY

—Council for New England. A brief relation of the discovery . . . of New England. London: 1622

——An historicall discoverie . . . of . . . New England. London: 1627

—Edwards, T. Gangraena, pt 2. London: 1646

——Gangraena, pt 3. London: 1646

—Smith, Capt. J. The generall historie of Virginia. London: 1624

——New Englands trials. London: 1620

—Vox veritatis. [The Hague?] 1650

NEW ENGLAND—POETRY

—Bradstreet, A. The tenth muse. London: 1650

New-England. or A briefe enarration. *See* Morrell, William

New-Englands advice. *See* Lechford, Thomas

New Englands first fruits. London: R. O[ulton]., & G. D[exter]., for H. Overton, 1643

New Englands Jonas. *See* Child, John

New Englands lamentation. *See* Shepard, Thomas

New-Englands plantation. *See* Higginson, Francis

New Englands prospect. *See* Wood, William

New-Englands salamander. *See* Winslow, Edward

New-Englands sence. *See* Hooke, William

New Englands teares. *See* Hooke, William

New Englands trials. *See* Smith, Capt. John

drogh. *See* Philopatroös, Erasmus

Het nieuw vermeerde licht. *See* Blaeu, Willem Janszoon

Nieuwe ende warachtighe tijdinghe ghekomen van Sint Lucas de Barrameda. Amsterdam: B. Janszoon, 1616

Nieuwe in-teyckeninge ende verhooginge der capitalen. *See* Nederlandsche West-Indische Compagnie

Het nieuwe licht der zeevaert. *See* Blaeu, Willem Janszoon

Nieuwe tydingen wt den Conseio. *See* Scott, Thomas

Nieuwe Wereldt. *See* Laet, Joannes de

Nieuwe werelt, anders ghenaemt West-Indien. *See* Herrera y Tordesillas, Antonio de

Des nieuwen atlantis aenhang. *See* Jansson, Jan

Nieuwen, klaren astrologenbril. [Amsterdam? 1607?]

Nieuwenborgh, Johann. Het nederlantsche lust-hofken. Amsterdam: G. Joosten, 1647

The night raven. *See* Rowlands, Samuel

Nijkerke, Joost Willemszoon. Klaer-bericht ofte Aenwysinghe. Hoorn: M. Gerbrantszoon, 1630

— —The Hague: A. Meuris, 1630

La niña de los embustes. *See* Castillo Solórzano, Alonso de

The nipping . . . of abuses. *See* Taylor, John, the Water-poet

Nobiliss[imo]rum ac dociss[imo]rum Germaniae medicorum Consilia. *See* Wittich, Johann

The noble cavalier caracterised. *See* Taylor, John, the Water-poet

The noble souldier. *See* Rowley, Samuel

Nodal, Bartolomé García de. Relacion del viaje. Madrid: F. Correa de Montenegro, 1621

Nomenclator aquatilium. *See* Gesner, Konrad

Nomenclator octilinguis. *See* Junius, Hadrianus

Les noms, surnoms et qualitez.

See Compagnie de la Nouvelle France

Nonnius, Ludovicus. Diaeticon, sive De re cibaria. Antwerp: P. & J. Bellère, 1627

— —Antwerp: P. Bellère, 1645

— —Antwerp: P. Bellère, 1646

Noodige aenmerckinge op seeckere propositie. [Amsterdam?] 1650

—'The Hague' [i.e., Amsterdam:] P. Rombouts, 1650

Noodige aenmerckingen op seeckere propositie. Amsterdam: P. Rombouts, 1650 (2)

—'The Hague' [i.e., Amsterdam]: P. Rombouts, 1650

Noodige bedenckingen der trouhertighe Nederlanders. [The Hague? 1643

—[The Hague?] 1644

Noort, Olivier van. Additamentum . . . dess neundten Theils Americae. Frankfurt a.M.: M. Becker, & W. Richter, 1602

—Additamentum nonae partis Americae. Frankfurt a.M.: M. Becker, 1602

—Beschrijvinge van de voyagie om den geheelen werelt-kloot. Amsterdam: M. Colijn, 1618

—Beschryvinghe van de voyagie om den geheelen werelt cloot. Rotterdam: J. van Waesberghe, & C. Claeszoon, at Amsterdam [1601]

— —Rotterdam: J. van Waesberghe, & C. Claeszoon, at Amsterdam, 1602

—Description du penible voyage. Amsterdam: C. Claeszoon, 1602

— —Amsterdam: Widow of C. Claeszoon, 1610

—Eigentliche und warhafftige Beschreibung der wunderbärlichen Schiffarth. Amsterdam: C. Claeszoon, 1602

—Extract oft Kort verhael uit het groote journael. Rotterdam: J. van Waesberghe, 1601

—Neue Schiffart. Frankfurt a.M.: M. Becker, 1602

—Vera et accurata descriptio . . . navigationis. *In* Potgieter, Barent Janszoon. Historiae an-

tipodum sive Novi Orbis. Frankfurt a.M.: 1633

—Wonderlijcke voyagie, by de Hollanders gedaen. Amsterdam: J. Hartgers, 1648

— —Utrecht: L. de Vries, 1649

— —Amsterdam: J. Hartgers, 1650

NOORT, OLIVIER VAN

—Hulsius, L. Achte Schiffart, kurtze Beschreibung. Frankfurt a.M.: 1605

Nootelijcke consideration. *See* Verheiden, Willem

Nootwendich discours. *See* Middelgeest, Simon van

Nootwendige aenmerkinge op een fameus libel. Antwerp: J. van Waesbergen, 1650

Norman, Robert. The new attractive. London: T. C[reede]., for J. Tapp, 1614

NORRIS, SIR JOHN

—Stradling, Sir J. Epigrammatum libri quatuor. London: 1607

Norte de la poesia española. *See* Mey, Aurelio

NORTH, ROGER

—Great Britain. Sovereigns, etc., 1603–1625 (James I). A proclamation declaring his Majesties pleasure concerning Captaine Roger North. London: 1620

NORTH AMERICA— DESCRIPTION

—Castell, W. A short discoverie of the coasts . . . of America. London: 1644

NORTH CAROLINA. *See also* CAROLINA

—Copland, P. Virginia's God be thanked. London: 1622

NORTHMEN. *See* DISCOVERIES—NORSE

North-ward hoe. *See* Dekker, Thomas

North-West Fox. *See* Fox, Luke

NORTHWEST PASSAGE

—Bancroft, T. Two bookes of epigrammes. London: 1639

—Bloys, W. Adam in his innocence. London: 1638

—Donne, J. LXXX sermons. London: 1640

—Fox, L. North-West Fox. London: 1635

—Gerritsz, H. Beschryvinghe van der Samoyeden landt. Amsterdam: 1612

— —Descriptio ac delineatio geographica detectionis freti. Amsterdam: 1612

— —Indiae Orientalis Pars X. Frankfurt a.M.: 1613

— —Zehender Theil der Orientalischen Indien. Frankfurt a.M.: 1613

— —Zwölffte Schiffahrt. Oppenheim: 1614

—James, T. The strange and dangerous voyage. London: 1633

—La Peyrère, I. de. Relation du Groenland. Paris: 1647

— —Die xxvi. Schiff-Fahrt. Frankfurt a.M.: 1650

—Munk, J. Navigatio septentrionalis. Copenhagen: 1624

—Nash, T. Quaternio, or A fourefold way. London: 1633

—Rabelais, F. Oeuvres. Antwerp: 1605

—Röslin, E. Praematurae solis apparitionis. Strassburg: 1612

—Veer, G. de. Verhael van de eerste schip-vaert der Hollandische . . . schepen. Amsterdam: 1648

—Waterhouse, E. A declaration of the state of . . . Virginia. London: 1622

Norton, John. Responsio ad totam quaestionum syllogen. London: R. B[ishop]., for A. Crooke, 1648

Norton, Samuel. Metamorphosis lapidum ignobilium. Frankfurt a.M.: K. Rötel, for W. Fitzer, 1630

Norwood, Richard. The seamans practice. London: [B. Alsop & T. Fawcet for] G. Hurlock, 1637

— —London: T. Fawcet, for G. Hurlock, 1644

—*See also* Prynne, William. A fresh discovery. London: 1645

Nosologia harmonica. *See* Petraeus, Henricus

A notable and wonderfull sea-fight. Amsterdam: J. Veseler, 1621

Notae ad dissertationem Hugonis Grotii. *See* Laet, Joannes de

A note of the shipping, men, and provisions. *See* Virginia Company of London

Noticias historiales de las conquistas. *See* Simón, Pedro

Notitia episcopatuum. *See titles under* Le Mire, Aubert

Notitia patriarchatuum. *See* Le Mire, Aubert

Nouveau chasse peste. *See* Bompart, Marcellin

Nouveau et dernier dictionaire. *See* Monet, Philibert

Le nouveau phalot de la mer. *See* Blaeu, Willem Janszoon

Nouveau théâtre du monde. *See* Avity, Pierre d', sieur de Montmartin; Hondius, Hendrik; Jansson, Jan

Nouvel atlas. *See* Jansson, Jan

Nouvelle histoire des choses plus memorables. *See* Du Jarric, Pierre

La nouvelle histoire du Perou. *See* Torres Bollo, Diego de

Les nouvelles. *See* Cervantes Saavedra, Miguel de

Nouvelles des choses qui se passent. *See* Kerkhove, Jan van

Nova Atlantis. *See* Bacon, Francis

Nova Britannia. *See* Johnson, Robert

Nova et accurata Italiae hodiernae descriptio. *See* Hondius, Jodocus

Nova Francia. *See titles under* Lescarbot, Marc

Nova Gallia delphino. *See* Le Brun, Laurent

Nova iconologia. *See* Ripa, Cesare

Nova reperta sive Rerum memorabilium recens inventarum . . . Liber secundus. *See* Panciroli, Guido

NOVA SCOTIA—HISTORY

—Scotland. Laws, statutes, etc. The acts made in the first parliament. Edinburgh: 1633

—Scotland. Privy Council. [For-

samekle as our soveraine Lordis . . . Edinburgh: 1625]

— —[Our Soverane Lord being formarlie gratiouslie. . . . Edinburgh: 1624]

Nova typis transacta navigatio. Novi orbis. *See* Plautius, Caspar, Abbot

Nova Zemla. *See* Schemering, Daniel

Novae coelestium terrestriumque rerum observationes. *See* Fontana, Francesco

Novae Novi Orbis historiae. *See* Benzoni, Girolamo

Novelas ejemplares. *See* Cervantes Saavedra, Miguel de

Novelas exemplares. *See* Cervantes Saavedra, Miguel de

Novelle. *See* Cervantes Saavedra, Miguel de

Il novelliere. *See* Cervantes Saavedra, Miguel de

Novi Atlantis Anhang. *See* Jansson, Jan

Novi Freti . . . detectio. *See* Schouten, Willem Corneliszoon

Novi Orbis pars duodecima. *See* Herrera y Tordesillas, Antonio de

Novus atlas, das ist Abbildung. *See* Blaeu, Willem Janszoon; *and also* Jansson, Jan

Novus atlas, das ist Weltbeschreibung. *See* Blaeu, Willem Janszoon; *and also* Jansson, Jan

Novus atlas, sive Theatrum orbis terrarum. *See* Jansson, Jan

Novus orbis. Hoc est, Navigationes. *See* Novus orbis regionum

Novus orbis, id est, Navigationes. *See* Novus orbis regionum

Novus orbis regionum. Novus orbis. Hoc est, Navigationes illustriores. Amsterdam: J. Janszoon the Younger, 1623

—Novus orbis, id est, Navigationes primae in Americam. Rotterdam: J. L. Beerwout, 1616

Novus Orbis, seu Descriptionis Indiae Occidentalis. *See* Laet, Joannes de

Novus orbis, sive Descriptio In-

See León Pinelo, Antonio Rodríguez de

Oratio de coeli. *See* Baerle, Kaspar van

Oratio de navigationibus. *See* Slichtenhorst, Arend van

Oratio panegyrica, de illustri victoria. *See* Colonius, Daniel

An oration or speech. *See* Verheiden, Willem

Orationum liber. *See* Baerle, Kaspar van

Orbis maritimi. *See* Morisot, Claude Barthélemy

La orden e instruccion que su Magestad manda dar. *See* Spain. Sovereigns, etc., 1598–1621 (Philip III)

Ordenanças de la Real Audiencia. *See* Spain. Audiencia territorial, Seville

Ordenanças para remedio de los daños. *See* Spain. Laws, statutes, etc., 1556–1598 (Philip II)

Ordenanzas de la Junta de Guerra. *See* Spain. Junta de Guerra de Indias

Ordenanzas del Consejo Real. *See* Spain. Consejo de las Indias

Ordenanzas reales del Consejo. *See* Spain. Consejo de las Indias

Ordenanzas reales para el govierno. *See* Spain. Consejo de las Indias

Ordenanzas reales, para la Casa de la Contratacion. *See* Spain. Casa de Contratación de las Indias

Ordenes, y providencias. *See* Spain. Laws, statutes, etc., 1621–1665 (Philip IV)

An order of Parliament for . . . the observation of the Sabath day. *See* Great Britain. Laws, statutes, etc., 1625–1649 (Charles I)

Orders and articles granted by the . . . States General. *See* Nederlandsche West-Indische Compagnie

Orders and constitutions. *See* Bermuda Islands. Laws, Statutes, etc.

An ordinance . . . *See titles under*

Great Britain. Laws, statutes, etc., 1625–1649 (Charles I)

Ordóñez de Ceballos, Pedro. Beschreibung der West Indianischen Landschafften. *In* Herrera y Tordesillas, Antonio de. Zwölffter Theil der Newen Welt. Frankfurt a.M.: 1623

—Eyghentlijcke beschryvinghe van West-Indien. Amsterdam: M. Colijn, 1621

—Tratado de los relaciones verdaderas . . . de la China. Jaen: P. de la Cuesta, 1628

—Viage del mundo. Madrid: L. Sánchez, 1614

—*See also* Herrera y Tordesillas, Antonio de. Description des Indes Occidentales. Amsterdam: 1622

Ordóñez de Cevallos, Petrus. *See* Ordóñez de Ceballos, Pedro

Ordonnances, privileges, franchises, et assistances. *See* Nederlandsche West-Indische Compagnie

Ordonnantie . . . op . . . tabacco. *See* Utrecht (Province). Laws, statutes, etc.

Ordonnantie, dienende tot versekeringe vande schepen. *See* Netherlands (United Provinces, 1581–1795). Staten Generaal

Ordonnantien ende articulen. *See titles under* Nederlandsche West-Indische Compagnie

Ordre by de . . . Staten Generael . . . ghemaeckt op . . . het sout halen in West-Indien. *See* Netherlands (United Provinces, 1581–1795). Staten Generaal

Ordre ende reglement . . . over het bewoonen. *See* Netherlands (United Provinces, 1581–1795). Staten Generaal

Ordre ende reglement . . . waer naer alle gemonteerde schepen . . . sullen vermogen te varen. *See* Netherlands (United Provinces, 1581–1795). Staten Generaal

Ordre ende Reglement op de Comptoiren. *See* Nederlandsche West-Indische Compagnie. Kamer Zealand

Oré, Luis Jerónimo de, Bp. Relacion de la vida . . . del venerable padre f. Francisco Solano. [Madrid: 1614]

—Rituale. *See* Catholic Church. Liturgy and ritual. Ritual. Peru. Rituale, seu Manuale peruanum. Naples: 1607

ORICHALC

—Guibert, N. De interitu alchymiae. Toul: 1614

Orientalische Indien. *See* Fitzer, William

Origanus, David. *See* Groote schrijf-almanach. Amsterdam: 1641

Origen de los indios. *See* García, Gregorio

Origo et historia Belgicorum tumultuum. *See* Gysius, Johannes

ORINOCO

—Scortia, J. B. De natura et incremento Nili. Lyons: 1617

Orlandini, Nicolò. *See* Jesuits. Historiae Societatis Jesu prima pars. Rome: 1615

Orlando furioso, in English. *See* Ariosto, Lodovico

Orlers, Jan Janszn. Beschrijvinghe ende af-beeldinge van alle de victorien. Leyden: J. J. Orlers, & H. van Haestens, 1610

—Description et representation de toutes de victoires. Leyden: J. J. Orlers, & H. van Haestens, 1612

— —*In his* Généalogie . . . . Leyden: 1615

—Généalogie des . . . comtes de Nassau. Leyden: 1615

— —Leyden: J. J. Orlers, 1615

— —Amsterdam: J. Janszoon the Younger, 1624

—De oorlochs-daden van Maurits. Leyden: 1619

—The triumphs of Nassau. London: A. Islip, 1613

— —London: A. Islip, for R. More, 1620

Ornithologiae . . . libri xii. *See* Aldrovandi, Ulisse

Ornithologiae tomus. *See* Aldrovandi, Ulisse

ORNITHOLOGY. *See* BIRDS

Orozco, Sebastian de Covarrubias. *See* Covarrubias Horozco, Sebastián de

Orta, Garcia da. Dell'historia de i semplici. Venice: Heirs of G. Scoto, 1605

——Venice: G. Salis, 1616

—Histoire des drogues espiceries. Lyons: J. Pillehotte, 1619

——Lyons: J. Pillehotte, 1619

—*See also* L'Ecluse, Charles. Exoticorum libri decem. [Leyden:] 1605

ORTEGA SOTOMAYOR, PEDRO DE, BP

—Reina Maldonado, P. de. Apologia por la santa iglesia de Trujillo. Madrid: 1648

Ortelius, Abraham. Abrégé du Théâtre. Antwerp: [H. Swingen, for] J. B. Vrients, 1601

—— —Antwerp: J. B. Vrients, 1602

—Ausszug auss des Abrahami Ortelÿ Theatro orbis. Frankfurt a.M.: L. Hulsius, & J. van Keerberghen, at Antwerp, 1604

—Breve compendio dal Theatro. Antwerp: J. B. Vrients, 1502 [i.e., 1602]

—L'épitome du théâtre de l'univers. Antwerp: J. van Keerberghen, 1602

—— —Antwerp: J. B. Vrients, 1609

—An epitome of Ortelius his Theatre. [Antwerp:] H. Swingen, for J. Norton, at London [1601?]

—Epitome of the theater of the world. [Antwerp:] for J. Shaw, at London, 1603

—Epitome theatri orbis terrarum. Antwerp: J. van Keerberghen, 1601

—— —Antwerp: J. B. Vrients, 1609

—— —Antwerp: Plantin Office, 1612

—Epitome theatri Orteliani. Antwerp: H. Swingen, for J. B. Vrients, 1601

—Theatro d'el orbe de la tierra. Antwerp: Plantin Office, for J. B. Vrients, 1602

—— —Antwerp: Plantin Office, 1612

—Theatro del mondo. Antwerp: J. B. Vrients, 1608

—— —Antwerp: Plantin Office, 1612

—Theatrum orbis terrarum. Antwerp: Plantin Press, 1601

—— —Antwerp: J. B. Vrients, 1603

—— —Antwerp: J. B. Vrients, 1609

—— —Antwerp: Plantin Office, 1612

—Theatrum orbis terrarum . . . The theatre of the whole world. London: [Eliots Court Press, for] J. Norton, & J. Bill, 1606 [i.e., 1608?]

—Theatrum orbis terrarum . . . Tonneel des aert-bodems. Antwerp: [J. B. Vrients, for] Widow of C. Plantin, & J. Moretus [1610?]

—Thesaurus geographicus. Hanau: Heirs of W. Antonius, 1611

Ortiz de Cervantes, Juan. Informacion en favor del derecho. Madrid: Widow of A. Martín, 1619

—— —Madrid: Widow of A. Martín, 1620

—Memorial . . . a Su Magestad. [Madrid?] 1619

—Memorial que trata de la perpetuydad de los encomenderos. Madrid: J. Sánchez, 1617

—Parabien al Rey D. Felip IIII. [Madrid? 1621?]

—Patrocinium pro eo titulo toto terrarum orbe. [Madrid?] 1621

—Señor. El licenciado Juan Ortiz de Cervantes . . . Dize; que catorze leguas. . . . [Madrid? ca. 1620?]

—Señor. El licenciado Juan Ortiz de Cervantes . . . Dize; que como en este reyno. . . . [Madrid? ca. 1620?]

—Señor. El licenciado Juan Ortiz de Cervantes . . . Dize; que en . . . Cuzco. . . . [Madrid? ca. 1620]

—Señor. El licenciado Juan Ortiz de Cervantes . . . Dize; que en el reyno del Piru. . . . [Madrid? ca. 1620?]

—Señor. El licenciado Juan Ortiz

de Cervantes . . . Dize; que en los pueblos. . . . [Madrid? ca. 1620]

—Señor. El licenciado Juan Ortiz de Cervantes . . . Dize; que una de las mayores causas de la destruycion. . . . [Madrid? ca. 1620]

—Señor. El licenciado Juan Ortiz de Cervantes . . . Dize; que V. Magestad tiene hecha merced . . . . [Madrid? ca. 1620?]

Ortiz de Salcedo, Francisco. Curia eclesiastica. Madrid: Widow of A. Martín, for D. González, 1626

—— —Madrid: F. Martínez, 1634

—— —Madrid: 1642

Ortiz de Valdes, Fernando. Defensa canonica por la dignidad del Obispo. [Madrid: 1648]

Osma, Pierre de. *See* Fueldez, Antoine. Observations curieuses, touchant la petite verole. Lyons: 1645

Osorio de Erasso, Diego. Señor. Celebre fue la vitoria. [Madrid? 1630?]

Ossorio y Guadalfaxara, Juan. Por Lelio imbrea cavallero de la Orden de Santiago. [Seville: 1631?]

Ottsen, Hendrick. Journael oft Daghelijcx-register van de voyagie. Amsterdam: C. Claszoon, 1603

—— —Amsterdam: M. Colijn, 1617

—Warhafftige Beschreibung der unglückhafften Schiffarht. Frankfurt a.M.: W. Richter, 1604

Een oud schipper van Monickendam. [Amsterdam? 1608?]

Our Soverane Lord being formarlie gratiouslie. . . . *See* Scotland. Privy Council

Het out Oost-Indische octroy. *See* Nederlandsche Oost-Indische Compagnie

Outreman, Pierre de. Tableaux des personnages signales. Douai: B. Bellere, 1623

—— —Lyons: C. Rigaud, & C. Obert, 1627

Ovalle, Alonso de. Historica relacion del reyno de Chile.

a.M.: Z. Palthenius, for P. Fischer, 1601

Paredes, Antonio de. Señor. Entre diversos memoriales. [Madrid: 1639?]

—*See also* Elías, Juan, fray. Señor. Un libelo infamatorio se ha impresso . . . su fecha en Potosí. [Madrid? 1640]

Parey, Ambrose. *See* Paré, Ambroise

Le parfaict chirurgien. *See* Chaumette, Antoine

PARIA, BOLIVIA

—Relacion del nuevo descubrimiento de las minas. [Madrid: 163–?]

PARIS. MUSÉUM NATIONAL D'HISTOIRE NATURELLE

—La Brosse, G. de. Catalogue des plantes cultivées. Paris: 1641

Paris. Université. III. [i.e., Troisième] requeste. Paris: University, 1644

Parisi, Antonio. Señor. Don Antonio Parisi, procurador del reyno de Chile. [Madrid? ca. 1620?]

Parker, Thomas. The true copy of a letter. London: R. Cotes, for R. Smith, 1644

Parkinson, John. Paradisi in sole paradisus terrestris. Or a garden. London: H. Lownes, & R. Young, 1629

— —London: T. Cotes, for R. Royston, 1635

—Theatrum botanicum: The theater of plants. London: T. Cotes, 1640

The parliament of ladies. *See* Neville, Henry

Parnaso antarctico, 1a pte. *See* Ovidius Naso, Publius (Two or more works. Spanish)

Parnasso español. *See* Quevedo y Villegas, Francisco Gómez de

Parrot, Henry. The mastive. London: T. Creede, for R. Meighen, & T. Jones, 1615

Part of Du Bartas. *See* Du Bartas, Guillaume de Salluste, seigneur

Parvum theatrum urbium. *See* Romanus, Adrianus

Pascal, Jacques. Discours contenant la conference de la pharmacie. Béziers: J. Martel, 1616

— —Lyons: L. Vivian, 1616

— —Toulouse: D. Bosc, 1616

—Traicté contenant la pharmacie chymique. Lyons: L. Vivian, 1633

Paschetti, Bartolomeo. Del conservare la sanità. Genoa: G. Pavoni, 1602

Pasquier, Etienne. Les lettres. Lyons: P. Frellon, 1607

— —Lyons: J. A. Huguetan, 1607

— —Paris: J. Petit-Pas, 1619

— —Paris: L. Sonnius, 1619

—Les recherches de la France. Paris: L. Sonnius, 1607

— —Paris: L. Sonnius, 1610

— —Paris: L. Sonnius, 1611

— —Paris: L. Sonnius, 1617

— —Paris: J. Petit-Pas, 1621

— —Paris: L. Sonnius, 1621

— —Paris: M. Colet, 1633

— —Paris: P. Ménard, 1633

— —Paris: T. Quinet, 1633

— —Paris: O. de Varennes, 1633

— —Paris: P. Ménard, 1643

Passe, Crispijn van de. Den blomhof. Utrecht: C. van de Passe, 1614

—A garden of flowers. Utrecht: S. de Roy, for C. van de Passe, 1615

—Hortus floridus. Arnhem: J. Janszoon, 1614[–17]

—Jardin de fleurs. Utrecht: C. van de Passe, for J. Janszoon, at Arnhem, [1615?–1617]

PASSIONFLOWER

—Coppie de la fleur de la passion. Paris: 1637

—Donato d'Eremita. Il fiore della granadiglia. Bologna: 1609

—Nieremberg, J. E. Historia naturae. Antwerp: 1635

—Niess, J. Adolescens Europaeus ab Indo moribus christianis informatus. Dillingen: 1629

—Nieuwenborgh, J. Het nederlantsche lust-hofken. Amsterdam: 1647

—Possevino, A. Cultura ingeniorum. Cologne: 1610

—Tanara, V. L'economia del cittadino. Bologna: 1644

The passions of the minde. *See* Wright, Thomas

Pastor, Juan. Señor. Juan Pastor . . . procurador . . . dize, que los Indios del Uruay, y del Parana. [Madrid: 1646?]

—Señor. Juan Pastor . . . procurador general . . . dize: que de seis en seis años [etc.]. [Madrid: 1646?]

—Señor. Juan Pastor . . . procurador general . . . Dize, que los Indios [etc.]. [Madrid: 1646?]

PATAGONIA

—Bachot, G. Erreurs populaires. Lyons: 1626

—Clarke, S. A mirrour. London: 1646

—Topsell, E. The historie of foure-footed beastes. London: 1607

PATAGONIA—FICTION

—Espinel, V. Relaciones de la vida del escudero Marcos de Obregon. Madrid: 1618

Pater, Adrien Janssen. *See* Een cort ende warachtich verhael van de . . . victorie. Middelburg: 1631

Pathologia. *See* Corbeius, Theodorus

Patricius, Philo, pseud. *See* Apologus vanden krijch der gansen. [Amsterdam:] 1622

Patrocinium pro eo titulo toto terrarum orbe. *See* Ortiz de Cervantes, Juan

Pattenson, Matthew. The image of bothe churches. Tournai: A. Quinqué, 1623 (2)

Paulli, Simon. Flora Danica. Copenhagen: M. Martzen, for J. Molikens, & J. Holstis (pt 1); Antwerp: Plantin Office (pt 2), 1648, '47

Paulmier, Julien. *See* Le Paulmier de Grentemesnil, Julien

Paulo do Rosario. Relacam breve, e verdadeira de memoravel victoria. Lisbon: J. Rodriguez, 1632

Paulo Emilio. *See* Emili, Paolo

Pauw, Adriaan. *See* Coignet de la

Thuillerie, Gaspard. Twee propositien. [The Hague:] 1648

Pax Christi. En esta referire a V. R. las nuevas. [Madrid: ca. 1638]

Pax methodicorum. *See* Vege, Petrus de

Pazes entre España, Francia, y otros potentados. Seville: J. de Cabrera [1626]

Peacham, Henry. Coach and sedan. London: R. Raworth, for J. Crouch, 1636

——London: R. Raworth, for J. Crouch, & E. Paxton, 1636

PEARLS

—Cardona, T. de. Señor. El capitan Tomas de Cardona. [Madrid? 1618?]

—Strobelberger, J. S. Tractatus novus. Jena: 1620

—Wonderlicke avontuer van twee goelieven. Leyden: 1624

Pedraza, Julián de. Señor. Julian de Pedraza . . . procurador general de las Indias. [Madrid: 1649]

—Señor. Julian de Pedraza, procurador general de la Compañia de Jesus. [Madrid? 165–?]

Pedrera, Andrés. Andres Pedrera, ensayador mayor, y visitador del oro. [Madrid? ca. 1635?]

Pedro de Osma. *See* Osma, Pierre de

Pedro de Santiago. Relacion del transito. [Madrid: 1631]

Peleus, Julien. Les oeuvres. Paris: M. Guillemot, 1631

——Paris: N. Rousset, 1631

—Les questions illustres. Paris: N. Buon, 1608

——Paris: N. Buon, 1612

—*In his* Oeuvres. Paris: 1631

Peligros del dilitado camino. *See* Recio de León, Juan

Pelletier, Gaspard. *See* Pilletier, Casparus

Pellham, Edward. Gods power and providence: shewed . . . in Green-land. London: R. Y[oung]., for J. Partridge, 1631

Pellier, Gilles. *See* Quarles, Francis. Emblemes. London: 1635

Pels, E. Lof-dicht des vermaerde . . . zee-heldt Pieter Pietersen Heyn. Amsterdam: W. J. Wyngaert, 1629

Pemell, Robert. Ptōchopharmakon, seu Medicamen miseris. London: F. L[each]., for P. Stephens, 1650

Peña, Pierre. Stirpium adversaria nova. *In* L'Obel, Matthias de. In G. Rondelletii . . . Pharmaceuticam . . . animadversiones. London: 1605

——*In* L'Obel, Matthias de. Pharmacopoeia Rondeletti. Leyden: 1618

PENAL COLONIES. *See* PRISONERS, TRANSPORTATION OF

Peñalosa y Mondragón, Benito de. Libro de las cinco excellencias del Español. Pamplona: C. de Labàyen, 1629

De penitentie gegeven aen den Franschen drucker. Amsterdam: J. Nes [i.e., The Hague? J. Veely?] 1648

Penny-wise. *See* Dekker, Thomas

Penot, Bernard Georges. Theophrastisch Vade mecum. Das ist: Etliche . . . Tractat. Magdeburg: J. Franck, 1607

——Magdeburg: J. Franck, 1608

—Tractatus varii. Oberursel: C. Sutor, for J. Rose, 1602

——*In* Theatrum chemicum. Strassburg: 1613–22

——Basel: L. König, 1616

Penotus, Bernardus Georgius. *See* Penot, Bernard Georges

Pensil de principes. *See* Airolo Calar, Gabriel de

PEQUOT WAR

—Underhill, J. Newes from America. London: 1638

—Vincent, P. A true relation of the late battell. London: 1637

Peralta, Pedro de. Señor. El capitan Don Pedro de Peralta contador. [Madrid: 1644?]

Peraza de Ayala y Rojas, Antonio, conde de la Gomera. Señor. Don Antonio Peraça de Ayala y Rojas. [Madrid? 1623?]

Perceval, Richard. A dictionary in Spanish and English. Lon-

don: J. Haviland, For W. Aspley, 1623

——London: J. Haviland, for E. Blount, 1623

——London: J. Haviland, for G. Latham, 1623

——London: J. Haviland, for M. Lownes, 1623

Perdulcis, Bartholomaeus. *See* Pardoux, Barthélemy

Perea, Estevan de. Segunda relacion de la grandiosa conversion. Seville: L. Estupiñán, 1633

—Verdadera relacion, de la grandiosa conversion. Seville: L. Estupiñán, 1632

Perea, Pedro de. Señor. Don Pedro de Perea, governador. [Madrid? 1637?]

Pereira Corte Real, João. Discursos sobre la navegacion. [Madrid? 1622?]

Perez, Antonio, supposed author. Spanish pilgrime. *See* Teixeira, José. The Spanish pilgrime. London: 1625

Pérez, Jacinto. Razon que da de si el padre Jacinto Perez . . . . Madrid: 1646

PEREZ, JACINTO

—Traslados de algunas cartas sacadas de sus proprios originales. [Madrid: 1647]

Pérez de Lara, Alfonso. Compendio de las tres gracias. Madrid: Imprenta Real, 1610

Pérez de Montalván, Juan. [La monja alferez, comedia famosa. Madrid? 1626?]

Pérez de Navarrete, Francisco. Arte de enfrenar. Madrid: J. González, 1626

Pérez de Nueros, Jacinto. Señor. Jacinto Perez de Nueros, religioso. [Madrid: ca. 1620?]

Pérez de Porres, Diego. A Melchor de Castro Macedo, secretario del Rey. [Madrid? 1625]

Pérez de Ribas, Andrés. Historia de los triumphos de nuestra santa fee. Madrid: A. de Paredes, 1645

—Señor. Andres Perez . . . procurador general a esta corte. [Madrid: ca. 1649]

Pérez de Rocha, Antonio. Al Rey nuestro señor. Compendio de medios politicas. [Madrid? 1649?]

—Al Rey nuestro señor. Discurso politico. [Madrid? ca. 1645?]

Pérez Manrique de Lara, Dionisio, marqués de Santiago. Señor. Don Dionisio Perez Manrique. [Madrid? 164–?]

A perfect description of Virginia. London: R. Wodenothe, 1649

The perfect use of silk-wormes. *See* Serres, Olivier de, seigneur du Pradel

Perfuming of tabacco. *See* L'Obel, Matthias de

Periodos. *See* Pindarus. Greek and Latin

Perlinus, Hieronymus. Binae historiae, seu Instructiones medicae. Hanau: Heirs of A. Wechel, for Heirs of J. Aubry, 1613

—De alexiteriis. Rome: 1610

PERNAMBUCO, BRAZIL

—Description de la Brasil. Antwerp: [1625?]

—Extract uyt een brief gheschreven in Maurits-Stadt de Pernambuco. [Amsterdam?] 1649

—Guelen, A. de. Brieve relation de l'estat de Phernambucq. Amsterdam: 1640

— —Kort verhael vanden staet van Fernanbuc. Amsterdam: 1640

—Lampe, B. Het negentiende deel . . . van het Historisch verhael. Amsterdam: 1632

— —Het twintigste deel . . . van het Historisch verhael. Amsterdam: 1633

—Manifest door d'inwoonders van Parnambuco. Antwerp: 1646

—Relacion del lastisomo incendio. Granada: 1631

—Relacion muy verdadera. Barcelona: 1640

—Relacion nueva y verdadera. Madrid: 1640

—Reves, J. de. Biechte des Conincx van Spanien. [Amsterdam? 1630]

—Seeckere tijdinghe vande vlote. Amsterdam: 1630

—Zesen, P. von. Durch-aus vermehrter . . . Helikon. Wittenberg: 1649

PERNAMBUCO, BRAZIL—POETRY

—Veen, J. van der. Schimp-ghedicht. Van Fernabuco. [Haarlem? 1630?]

The perogative of parliaments. *See* Raleigh, Sir Walter

Person, David. Varieties: or, A surveigh. London: R. Badger [& T. Cotes,] for T. Alchorn, 1635

Pertinent bericht. The Hague: L. Breeckevelt, 1634

PERU. As used in the 17th century 'Peru' designates not only the present-day country but also, amorphously, much of Spanish South America as distinct from Brazil, New Granada (Colombia), etc.

—Abreu y Figueroa, F. de. Adiciones al memorial. [Madrid? 1640?]

—Amatus Lusitanus. Curationum medicinalium centuriae septem. Bordeaux: 1620

—Aramburu, G. Memorial. Madrid: 1620

—Aventrote, J. Epistola á los Peruleras. Amsterdam: 1627

— —Sendt-brief aen die van Peru. Amsterdam: 1630

—Avila, E. de. Tratado de domicilio. Madrid: 1609

—Bacon, F. Histoire des vents. Paris: 1649

— —Historia naturalis . . . ad condendam philosophiam. London: 1622

—Bainbridge, J. An astronomicall description. London: 1618

—Barros, J. de. Asia. 4a decada. Madrid: 1615

—Basso, G. Discurso sobre la proposicion. [Madrid?] 1632

—Bauhin, K. De lapidis bezaar. Basel: 1613

—Bickerus, J. Hermes redivivus. Giessen: 1612

—Bustamante y Loyola, S. de. Señor. El licenciado Don Sebastian de Bustamente y Loyola. [Madrid? 1639]

—Campo, G. de, Abp. Copia de un capitulo de una carta. Seville: 1627

—Daniel, S. A panegyricke congratulatorie. London: 1603

—Dekker, T. A knights conjuring. London: 1607

— —Newes from hell. London: 1606

—Del Rio, M. A. Les controverses et recherches magiques. Paris: 1611

— —Disquisitionum magicarum libri sex. Mainz: 1603

—Foreest, P. van. Observationum et curationum medicinalium liber xxxii. Leyden: 1606

—Fueldez, A. Observations curieuses, touchant la petite verole. Lyons: 1645

—Gabelkover, W. Curationum et observationum, centuria V. Tübingen: 1627

—Gough, J. The strange discovery. London: 1640

—Grau y Monfalcón, J. Señor. Don Juan Grau y Monfalcon, procurador general. [Madrid? 164–?]

—Grotius, H. Bewys van den waren godsdienst. [Leyden?] 1622

— —Von der Warheit der christlichen Religion. Brieg: 1631

—Gysius, J. Oorsprong en voortgang der neder-landtscher beroerten. [Leyden?] 1616

— —Origo et historia Belgicorum tumultuum. Leyden: 1619

— —De spaensche tiranije gheschiet in Neder-Lant. Amsterdam: 1621

—Harduin, P. Codex medicamentarius. Paris: 1645

—Hay, J. De rebus Japonicis. Antwerp: 1605

—Inga, A., pseud.? West-Indische Spieghel. Amsterdam: 1624

—King, H. An halfe-penny-worth of wit. London: 1613

—León Pinelo, A. R. de. Velos antiguos i modernos. Madrid: 1641

—Lundorp, M. C. Politische

des voyages dans la riviere de la Plata. Paris: 1632
—Bacci, A. De thermis. Rome: 1622
—Sotomayor, A. de. Señor. Don Alonso de Sotomayor, dize, que las tierras . . . se han reconocido estar muy pobladas de Indios. [Madrid? 1620?]
— —Señor. Don Alonso de Sotomayor, dize que son tan fuertes . . . las razones y causas . . . [Madrid? 1620?]
—Torres Bollo, D. de. Brevis relatio historica in provincia Peruana. Mainz: 1604
— —De rebus Peruanis . . . commentarius. Antwerp: 1604
— —Kurtzer Bericht was Gott . . . in den Peruanischen Ländern aussgericht. Würzburg: 1604
— —La nouvelle histoire du Perou. Paris: 1604
— —O rozszerzeniu wiary . . . w Americe. Cracow: 1603
— —Relatione breve. Rome: 1603
—Victoria, P. G. de. Naufragio y peregrinacio. Seville: 1610
— —Wunderbarliche und seltzame Raiss. Ingolstadt: 1622

PERU—DRAMA
—Ruiz de Alarcón y Mendoza, J. Comedias, pte 1a. Madrid: 1628

PERU—HISTORY
—Calancha, A. de la. Coronica moralizada del orden de San Augustin en el Peru. Barcelona: 1638
—Casos notables, sucedidos en las costas de la ciudad de Lima. Seville: [1625]
—Garavito, G. Señor. Geronimo Garavito . . . Dize, que tiene suplicado a V.M. . . . [Madrid: 162-?]
—Garcilaso de la Vega, el Inca. Le commentaire royal. Paris: 1633
— —Commentarios reales, 1a pte. Lisbon: 1609
— —Histoire des guerres civiles des Espagnols. Paris: 1650
— —Historia general del Peru. Córdoba: 1616

—Insigne victoria que el señor marques de Guadalcazar . . . ha alcançado. [Seville: 1625]
—Matienzo, J. de. Commentaria. Madrid: 1613
—Molina, C. de. Señor. Cristoval de Molina, regidor perpetuo. [Madrid: 1629]
—Monsalve, M. de, friar. Reducion universal de todo el Piru. [Madrid? 1604]
—Ortiz de Cervantes, J. Memorial que trata de la perpetuydad de los encomenderos. Madrid: 1617
— —Parabien al Rey D. Felip IIII. [Madrid? 1621?]
— —Señor. El licenciado Juan Ortiz de Cervantes . . . Dize; que una de las mayores causas de la destruycion . . . . [Madrid? ca. 1620]
— —Señor. El licenciado Juan Ortiz de Cervantes . . . Dize; que V. Magestad tiene hecha merced . . . . [Madrid? ca. 1620?]
—Pizarro y Orellana, F. Discurso en que se muestra la obligacion. [Madrid? ca. 1640?]
—Sandoval, P. de, Bp. Historia de la vida . . . del Emperador Carlos V. Pamplona: 1614
— —Vida y hechos del emperador Carlos Quinto, pte 1a–2a. Valladolid: 1604
—Spain. Laws, statutes, etc., 1598–1621 (Philip III). El Rey. Marques de Montes Claros . . . gouernador . . . del Piru. [Madrid? 1609]
—Spain. Sovereigns, etc., 1598–1621 (Philip III). Instrucion para el virrey del Piru. [Madrid? 1603]
—Traslados de algunas cartas sacadas de sus proprios originales. [Madrid: 1647]
—Ulloa, A. de. Historie . . . van den . . . Keyser Caerle. Dordrecht: [1610]
— —Vita, et fatti dell'invitissimo imperatore Carlo Quinto. Venice: 1606
—Vázquez de Espinosa. A. Confessario general. Madrid: 1623

—Zárate, A. de. Conqueste van Indien. Amsterdam: 1623

PERU—HISTORY, NAVAL
—Este es la verdaderissima relacion de la feliz vitoria que ha tenido Don Fadrique de Toledo. Granada: 1630
—Feliz. vitoria. que ha tenido Don Fadrique de Toledo. Seville: 1630
—Relacion de las cosas notables. [Seville?] 1625
—Translaet uyt den Spaenschen. Vande geluckige victorie. Amsterdam: 1630
—Warachtich verhael vanden slach . . . inde Zuydt Zee. Middelburg: 1617

PERU—POETRY
—Homburg, E. C. Schimpff- und ernsthaffte Clio. Jena: 1642
—Le Moyne, P. Les poesies. Paris: 1650
—Saint-Amant, M. A. de Gérard, sieur de. La Rome ridicule. [Paris: 1643]A

PERU—POLITICS & GOVERNMENT
—Alfaro, F. de. Tractatus de officio fiscalis. Valladolid: 1606
—Carrasco del Saz, F. Initium a Domino. [Madrid? 1616?]
—Escalona y Agüero, G. de. Arcae Limensis gazophilatium regium, Perubicum. Madrid: 1647
—Larrinaga Salazar, J. de. Memorial discursivo sobre el oficio de protector general. Madrid: 1626
—León Pinelo, A. R. de. Libros reales de govierno . . . de la Secretaria del Perù. [Madrid? 1625?]
—Lerma, F. de Sandoval y Rojas, duque de. Señor. Por las razones que en este memorial se refieren. [Valladolid? 1601?]
—Loarte Dávila, ____. Informacion en derecho. [Madrid? 1630?]
—Ribera y Colindres, L. de. Señor. Don Luys de Ribera y Colindres. [Madrid? 1622?]
—Toledo y Leiva, P. de, marqués de Mancera. Relacion del es-

A physicall directory. *See* Culpeper, Nicholas

Physick for the sicknesse. *See* Bradwell, Stephen

La physique reformée. *See* Rochas, Henry de

Phytognomonica. *See* Porta, Giovanni Battista della

Phytologia. *See* Du Val, Guillaume

Piazza universale. *See titles under* Garzoni, Tommaso

Piccino, Giovanni. Il petopiccino, overo Eccellenza . . . del tabacco. Viterbo: The Diotallevi [ca. 1650]

Pick, Jan Cornelisz. Copie eens briefs geschreven uyt West-Indien. Delft: C. J. Timmer, 1624

Pico della Mirandola, Giovanni Francesco. Strix, sive De ludificatione daemonum. Strassburg: P. Ledertz, 1612

A piece of the world. *See* Lenton, Francis

Pierre de Osma. *See* Osma, Pierre de

Pierre de touche politique. *See* Boccalini, Traiano

Pierre de touched. *See* Boccalini, Traiano

Pietra del paragone politico. *See* Boccalini, Traiano

Pifferi, Francesco. *See* Sacro Bosco, Joannes de. Sfera. Siena: 1604

PIGAFETTA, ANTONIO
—Camerarius, J., the Younger. Symbolorum et emblematum . . . centuria quarta. [Nuremberg?] 1604

Pigafetta, Filippo, ed. Regnum Congo. *See under* Lopes, Duarte

Pignoria, Lorenzo. Imagine de gli Indiani Orientali et Occidentali. *In* Cartari, Vincenzo. Le vere e nove imagini. Padua: 1615

——*In* Cartari, Vincenzo. Imagini de gli dei delli antichi. Padua: 1626

——*In* Cartari, Vincenzo. Imagini delli dei de gl'antichi. Venice: 1647

Pigray, Pierre. Chirurgia. Paris: M. Orry, 1609

—La chirurgie. [Paris:] M. Orry, 1604

—Epitome des preceptes de medecine. Paris: M. Orry, 1609

——Rouen: A. Ouyn, 1615

——Lyons: S. Rigaud, 1616

——Rouen: J. Berthelin, 1625

——Lyons: J. A. Candy, 1628

——Rouen: L. Loudet, 1630

——Lyons: P. Bailly, 1637

——Lyons: L. Odain, 1637

——Lyons: Widow of C. Rigaud, & P. Borde, 1637

——Rouen: L. Du Mesnil, 1638

——Rouen: D. Ferrand, 1638

——Rouen: J. Berthelin, 1642

——Rouen: D. Ferrand, 1642

——Rouen: D. Loudet, 1642

——Lyons: J. Huguetan, 1643

——Lyons: C. Prost, 1648

——Rouen: J. Hollant, 1649

—Epitome praeceptorum medicinae. Paris: Widow of M. Orry, 1612

Pilletier, Casparus. Plantarum tum patriarum . . . synonymia. Middelburg: R. Schilders, 1610

Pinax, theatri botanici . . . opera. *See* Bauhin, Kaspar

Pindarus. Greek and Latin. Periodos. [Wittenberg:] Z. Schürer the Elder, 1616

PINEAPPLE
—Besler, B. Continuatio rariorum. [Nuremberg:] 1622

—Cats, J. Maechden-plicht. Middelburg: 1618

——Monita amoris virginei. Amsterdam: 1619

—Taylor, J. Taylors feast. London: 1638

PINEAPPLE—THERAPEUTIC USE
—Bruele, G. Praxis medicinae. Venice: 1602

——Praxis medicinae, or, The physicians practise. London: 1632

Pinon, Jacques. De anno romano carmen. Paris: J. Libert, 1615

——Paris: S. Cramoisy, 1630

Pinto de Moraes, Jorge. Maravillas del Parnaso. Lisbon: L. Craesbeeck, 1637

——Barcelona: S. & J. Matevad, for J. Prats, 1640

Pinto Ribeiro, João. Discurso sobre os fidalgos. Lisbon: P. Craesbeeck, 1632

Piò, Giovanni Michele. Allegatione per confirmare quanto si scrive. 'Antipoli: Stamperia Regia' [i.e., Venice?] 1618

——'Antipoli: Stamperia Regia' [i.e., Venice?] 1621

—Delle vite de gli huomini illustri di S. Domenico. Bologna: G. B. Bellagamba, 1607

——Bologna: S. Bonomi, 1620

—Delle vite de gli huomini illustri di S. Domenico. Seconda parte. Pavia: G. Ardizzoni, & G. B. de Rossi, 1613

Piò, Michele. *See* Piò, Giovanni Michele

PIRATES. *See also* Privateering *and* Seizure of vessels and cargoes

—Relacion del sucesso que tuvo Francisco Diaz Pimienta. Madrid: 1642

—Rijpen raedt. [Antwerp:] 1635

—Verdadera relacion del viage y sucesso de los caravelones. Seville: 1621

—Viage, y sucesso de los caravelones. Madrid: 1621

PIRATES—SANTO DOMINGO
—Baño, P. de. Yo . . . Doy fé y verdadero testimonio. [Granada? 1603?]

Pirma pars Descriptionis itineris navalis. *See* Lodewijcksz, Willem

Pisa, Francisco de. Descripcion de la imperial ciudad de Toledo. Toledo: P. Rodríguez, 1605

——Toledo: D. Rodriguez, 1617

Piso, Willem. Historia naturalis Brasiliae. Leyden: F. Haack, & L. Elsevier, at Amsterdam, 1648

PIZARRO, FRANCISCO, MARQUÉS
—Discours sur l'affaire de la Valteline. Paris: 1625

—Hay, P., sieur du Chastelet. Le mercure d'estat. Geneva: 1634

—Martí, J. J. De la vida del picaro Guzman de Alfarach, 2a pte. Valencia: 1602

—Mylius, A., comp. De rebus hispanicis. Cologne: 1602

—Pizarro y Orellana, F. Discurso en que se muestra la obligacion. [Madrid? ca. 1640?]

—Roca, J. A. Vera Zúñiga y Figueroa, conde de la. Epitome de la vida . . . del . . . emperador Carlos V. Madrid: 1622

— —Histoire de l'empereur Charles V. Paris: 1633

PIZARRO, FRANCISCO, MARQUÉS—DRAMA

—Téllez, G. Comedias, 4a pte. Madrid: 1635

Pizarro y Orellana, Fernando. Discurso en que se muestra la obligacion. [Madrid? ca. 1640?]

—Varones ilustres del Nuevo mundo. Madrid: D. Díaz de la Carrera, 1639

Placaet . . . . *For titles beginning with this word, see under* Netherlands (United Provinces, 1581–1795). Staten Generaal

Placcaet . . . . *For titles beginning with this word, see under* Netherlands (United Provinces, 1581–1795). Staten Generaal

Le plaidoyer de l'Indien hollandois. *See* Walerande, J. B. de

Plain dealing. *See* Lechford, Thomas

A plaine and true relation . . . of a Holland fleete. Rotterdam: M. S[ebastiani?]., 1626

A plaine and true relation of the goodness of God. *See* Hughes, Lewis

A plaine description of the Barmudas. *See* Jourdain, Silvester

A plaine path-way to plantations. *See* Eburne, Richard

Plainte de la Nouvelle France dicte Canada. [Paris? 1620?]

Plancy, Guillaume. *See* Fernel, Jean. Pharmacia. Hanau: 1605

Planeta catholico. *See* Campuzano, Baltasar

Planiglobium coeleste et terrestre. *See* Habrecht, Isaac

Planis Campy, David de. Bouquet composé des plus belles fleurs chimiques. Paris: P. Billaine, 1629

—La chirurgie chimique medicale. Rouen: J. Cailloué, 1642

—Les oeuvres. Paris: E. Danguy, 1646

— —Paris: D. Moreau, 1646

—La petite chirurgie chimique medicale. Paris: J. Périer, & A. Buissart, 1621

—La verolle recogneue. Paris: N. Bourdin, 1623

Plantagenet, Beauchamp. A description of the province of New Albion. [London:] 1648

— —London: J. Moxon, 1650

Plantarum tum patriarum . . . synonymia. *See* Pilletier, Casparus

PLANTATIONS

—Markham, G. Hungers prevention. London: 1621

—Robinson, H. England's safety. London: 1641

—Smith, Capt. J. Advertisements for the unexperienced planters. London: 1631

—Tailor, R. The hogge hath lost his pearle. [London:] 1614

PLANTATIONS—GUIANA

—A publication of Guiana's plantation. London: 1632

PLANTATIONS—NEW ENGLAND

—White, J. The planters plea. London: 1630

Plante, Franciscus. Mauritiados libri xii. Leyden: J. Maire, for J. Blaeu, at Amsterdam, 1647

The planters plea. *See* White, John

Plasse, Cornelis Lodewijckszoon van der, supposed author. Origo et historia. *See under* Gysius, Johannes

—Spaensche tiranije. *See under* Gysius, Johannes

Plater, Felix. *See* Platter, Felix

Platter, Felix. Observationum, in hominis affectibus . . . libri tres. Basel: C. Waldkirch, for L. König, 1614

— —Basel: L. König, 1641

—Praxeos. Basel: C. Waldkirch, 1602–03

— —Basel: C. Waldkirch, 1609, '08

— —Basel: J. Schroeter, for L. König, 1625

Plattes, Gabriel. A discovery of subterraneall treasure. London: J. Oakes, for J. Emery, 1639

Plautius, Caspar, Abbot. Extract und Augsszug . . . . Linz: J. Planck, 1624

—Extract und Ausszug der grossen . . . Schiff-farth Buelij Cataloni. [Linz:] J. Planck, 1623

—Nova typis transacta navigatio. Novi orbis. [Linz:] 1621

Plaza, Juan de la. Por el maestro Juan Baptista del Campo Claro. [Madrid? 165–?]

Plaza universal. *See* Suárez de Figueroa, Cristóbal

The pleasant comodie. *See* Dekker, Thomas

El pleito que se ha començado a ver . . . es sobre tres puntos. *See* Turrillo, Alonso

Plinius Secundus, Caius. Historia natural. Madrid: L. Sánchez, & J. González, 1624[–29]

Plowden, Sir Edmond. *See* Plantagenet, Beauchamp. A description of the province of New Albion. [London:] 1648

Plumptre, Huntingdon. Epigrammatōn opusculum duobus distinctum. London: T. Harper, for R. Allott, 1629

PLYMOUTH, MASSACHUSETTS

—Cushman, R. A sermon preached at Plimmoth. London: 1622

—Higginson, F. New-Englands plantation. London: 1630

—Mourt's relation. A relation . . . of . . . Plimoth. London: 1622

—Winslow, E. Good newes from New-England. London: 1624

Las poblaciones, assientos y reales de minas. *See* Medina, Bartolomé de

A poem on the late massacre in Virginia. *See* Brooke, Christopher

Poemata. *See* Baerle, Kaspar van; *and also* Buchanan, George

Poematum. *See* Baerle, Kaspar van

Poemes lyrick and pastorall. *See* Drayton, Michael

Poems. *See* Donne, John; Drayton, Michael; Randolph, Thomas; Vaughan, Henry; Waller, Edmund

Poesie. *See* Zucchi, Francesco

Les poesies. *See* Le Moyne, Pierre

Poesy . . . Het tweede deel. *See* Vondel, Joost van den

The poetical recreations. *See* Craig, Alexander

Poëtische wercken. *See* Cats, Jacob

Poëzy. *See* Vondel, Joost van den

Poincten der artijckelen. [*and variant spellings*] *See* Netherlands (United Provinces, 1581–1795). Staten Generaal

Poincten van consideratie, raeckende de vrede. Amsterdam: 1648

Poirier, Hélie. Deus harangues panegyriques. Amsterdam: J. Blaeu, 1648

POISONS

—Guyon, L., sieur de la Nauche. Les diverses leçons. Lyons: 1604

Poisson, Jean Baptiste. Animadversio. Paris: 1644

Il Polessandro. *See* Gomberville, Marin Le Roy, sieur du Parc et de

Polexandre. *See* Gomberville, Marin Le Roy, sieur du Parc et de

Politia regia. *See* Botero, Giovanni

Politiae ecclesiasticae. *See* Le Mire, Aubert

Politica indiana. *See* Solórzano Pereira, Juan de

Politiicq discours. *See* Usselinx, Willem

Politijcke redenen. *See* Scott, Thomas

Den politijcken Christen. *See* Teellinck, Willem

Politique redenen. *See* Scott, Thomas

Politische SchatzCammer. *See* Lundorp, Michael Caspar

Politischen Probiersteins . . .

Theil. *See titles under* Boccalini, Traiano

Polo, Gaspar Gil. Casp. Barthi Erotodidascalus. Hanau: D. & E. Aubry, & C. Schleich, 1625

—Diana enamorada. Paris: R. Estienne, 1611

— —Brussels: R. Velpius, & H. Anthoine, 1613

Poly-Olbion. *See* Drayton, Michael

Pompe funebri. *See* Perucci, Francesco

Pona, Francesco. Trattato de' veleni. Verona: B. Merlo, 1643

Pona, Giovanni. Del vero balsamo. Venice: [B. Barezzi, for] R. Miglietti, 1623

Ponce de León, Francisco. Descripcion del reyno de Chile. [Madrid: 1644?]

—Relacion de los servicios. [Madrid? 1632?]

Pontanus, Johannes Isaacus. Discussionum historicarum libri duo. Harderwijk: N. van Wieringen, 1637

—Historische beschrijvinghe der . . . coopstadt Amsterdam. Amsterdam: J. Hondius, 1614

—Rerum et urbis Amstelodamensium historia. Amsterdam: J. Hondius, 1611

Popp, Johann. Chymische Medicin. Frankfurt a.M.: E. Emmel, for S. Schamberger, 1617

— —Frankfurt a.M.: D. & D. Aubry, & C. Schleich, 1625

Por Alonso de Carrion escriuano publico. Madrid: Widow of J. González, 1634

Por Andres de Zavala. *See* González de Ribero, Blas

Por D. Juan Tapia de Vargas. *See* Tapia de Vargas, Juan

Por D. Luis Colon de Toledo. *See* Carranza, Alonso

Por Diego de Vega, vezino del puerto de Buenos-Ayres. *See* León Pinelo, Antonio Rodríguez de

Por Diego de Vergara Gaviria. *See* Vergara Gaviria, Diego de

Por Don Antonio de Cordova de la Vega. *See* Córdoba, Antonio Laso de la Vega de

Por Don Carlos Vazquez Coro-

nado, vezino de Guatimala. *See* Valcarcel, Francisco de

Por Don Juan de Benavides Baçan. *See* Altamirano, Diego

Por Don Juan de Leoz, cavallero. *See* Márquez de Cisneros, ——

Por Don Juan de Palafox y Mendoza, fiscal del Consejo de Indias. *See* Palafox y Mendoza, Juan de, Bp

Por Don Juan Meneses. *See* Rúa, Fernando de

Por Don Lope de Hozes y Cordova. *See* Márquez de Cisneros, ——

Por Don Lope Diez de Aux Armendariz . . . Con el . . . fiscal del Real Consejo. *See* Díez de Auxarmendáriz, Lope, marqués de Cadereyta

Por Don Lope Diez de Auxarmendariz . . . Sobre los cargos de la residencia. *See* Díez de Auxarmendáriz, Lope, marqués de Cadereyta

Por Don Martin y Aldrete. *See* Roco de Córdoba, Francisco

Por el comercio de la ciudad de Sevilla. *See* Seville

Por el Consulado de Sevilla. *See* Márquez de Cisneros, ——; *and also* Seville. Consulado

Por el duque del Infantado. *See* Altamirano, Diego

Por el ilustrissimo señor. *See* Vitoria, Paulo de

Por el licenciado don Iuan de Palafox y Mendoza. *See* Palafox y Mendoza, Juan de, Bp

Por el licenciado Don Juan de Valdes. *See* Valdés, Juan de

Por el licenciado Don Sebastian Zambrana de Villalobos. *See* Olmo, ——

Por el licenciado Don Sebastian Zambrana de Villalobos. *See* Zambrana de Villalobos, Sebastián

Por el maestro Juan Baptista del Campo Claro. *See* Plaza, Juan de la

Por el marques de Zerralvo. *See* Pacheco Ossorio, Rodrigo, marqués de Cerralvo

Por el real fisco. *See* Camargo, Gerónimo de

Por el señor D. Carlos de Ibarra.
See Márquez de Cisneros, ——
Por Fernando de Almonte Veinticuatro de Sevilla. *See* Barriasa, Mateo de
Por Francisco Nuñez Melian, governador . . . que fue . . . de Veneçuela. *See* Prado, Esteban de
Por Fray Geronimo Alonso de la Torre. *See* Vargas, Luis de
Por Hernando Matias de Ribera. *See* Ribera, Hernando Matias de
Por la administracion y prelacia eclesiastica. *See* Rio de Janeiro (Diocese)
Por la iglesia metropolitana de Los Reyes. *See* García de Zurita, Andrés
Por la Junta del Real Almirantazgo. *See* Seville. Junta del Amirantazgo
Por la Real audiencia de Mexico. *See* Altamirano, Diego
Por la Real Universidad . . . de . . . Lima. *See* León Pinelo, Antonio Rodríguez de
Por la villa imperial de Potosi. *See* Potosí, Bolivia
Por la villa imperial de Potossi. *See* Ibarra Gueztaraen, Juan de
Por las religiones de Santo Domingo . . . de Nueva-España. *See* Palma y Freitas, Luis de la
Por Lelio imbrea cavallero de la Orden de Santiago. *See* Ossorio y Guadalfaxara, Juan
Por los herederos del doctor don Marcos Guerrero. *See* Guerrero, Marcos
Por los hijos, y nietos de conquistadores. [Madrid? 1614]
Por los interesados en los quatro generos de mercaderias. [Seville? 1633?]
Por los regidores de la ciudad. *See titles under* Victoria, Francisco de
Por los religiosos de la provincia de san Hipolyto Martyr de Guaxaca. *See* López Solis, Francisco
Por Lucas Fernandez Manjon. *See* Fernández Manjon, Lucas
Por parte de las ciudades de Car-

tagena, y santa Fé. *See* Cartagena, Colombia
Por parte de las ciudades Santa Fé, y Cartagena. *See* Bogotá
Por parte del Dean y cabildo . . . de la ciudad de la Plata. *See* Almansa, Bernardino de
Por Simon Ribero ausente, passagero que fue en la nao S. Pedro. *See* Butron, Juan Alonso de
Porcacchi, Tommaso. L'isole più famose del mondo. Venice: Heirs of S. Galignani, 1603
— —Venice: Heirs of S. Galignani, 1604
— —Venice: Heirs of S. Galignani, 1605
— —Padua: P. & F. Galignani, 1620
Porreño, Baltasar. Dichos i hechos del señor Rei. Seville: Press of the Siete Revueltas, [ca. 1640?]
—Dichos y hechos del Rey. Cuenca: S. de Viader, 1621
—Dichos y hechos del señor Rey. Cuenca: S. de Viader, 1628
— —Madrid: Widow of J. Sánchez, for L. Sánchez, 1639
— —Seville: P. Gómez de Pastrana, 1639
Porta, Giovanni Battista della. Ars destillatoria. Frankfurt a.M.: J. Bringer, for A. Humm, 1611
—De distillatione. Rome: Apostolic Camera, 1608 (4)
— —Strassburg: L. Zetzner, 1609
—Phytognomonica. Frankfurt a.M.: N. Hoffmann, 1608
— —Rouen: J. Berthelin, 1650
Porter y Casanate, Pedro. Relacion de los servicios. [Madrid: ca. 1640?]
—Relacion en que se ciñen los servicios. [Madrid: 1646]
—Señor. El capitan Don Pedro Porter y Cassanate. [Madrid: 1638?]
PORTO BELLO, PANAMA—DESCRIPTION
—Hulsius, L. Die ein und zwantzigste Schifffahrt. Frankfurt a.M.: 1629

De Portogysen goeden buyrman. 'Lisbon' [i.e., The Hague?] 1649
Den Portugaelsen donderslagh. Groningen: Heirs of N. Roman, 1641
Portugal. Sovereigns, etc., 1640–1656 (John IV). Andere declaratie von Jean de Vierde. Amsterdam: C. van de Pas, & J. van Hilten, & B. Janszoon, 1641
—Copye, van een brief van den Koningh. Amsterdam: N. van Ravesteyn, 1649
—Copye vande volmacht. [The Hague? 1647]
—Declaratie van sijn Koninghlijcke Majesteyt. [Amsterdam?] 1649
Portugal. Treaties, etc., 1640–1656 (John IV). Accoort ende articulen. Amsterdam: F. Lieshout, 1641
—Accoort ende artijckelen. Middelburg: Widow & Heirs of S. Moulert [1641]
—Extract uyt d'Articulen van het tractaet van bestant. Amsterdam: F. Lieshout, 1641
— —The Hague: Widow & Heirs of H. J. van Wouw, 1641 (2)
—Tractaet van bestant. The Hague: Widow & Heirs of H. J. van Wouw, 1642
—Tractatus induciarum. The Hague: Widow & Heirs of H. J. van Wouw, 1642
—Trattado das tregoas. The Hague: Widow & Heirs of H. J. van Wouw, 1642
—Tregoas. Lisbon: A. Alvarez, 1642
—Verkondinghe van het bestant. The Hague: Widow & Heirs of H. J. van Wouw, 1641 (2)
PORTUGAL—COLONIES
—Vasconcellos, J. de. Restauração de Portugal prodigiosa. Lisbon: 1643
Portugallia, sive De regis Portugalliae regnis . . . commentarius. *See* Laet, Johannes de
PORTUGUESE IN AMERICA
—Mendoça, L. de, Bp of Rio de Janeiro. Señor. El prelado del

Rio de Janeiro. [Madrid? 1638?]

— —Suplicacion a Su Magestad. Madrid: 1630

—Portugal. Sovereigns, etc., 1640–1656 (John IV). Andere declaratie. Amsterdam: 1641

PORTUGUESE IN BRAZIL

—Amsterdam. Burgemeester. Extract uyttet register der Resolutien. [Amsterdam:] 1650

—Amsterdamsche veerman. [Amsterdam?] 1650

—Barros, J. de. Asia. Lisbon: 1628

—Conestaggio, G. F. di. De Portugalliae conjunctione. Frankfurt a.M.: 1602

— —Dell'unione del regno di Portugallo. Milan: 1616

— —Historia de la union del reyno de Portugal. Barcelona: 1610

— —L'union du royaume de Portugal. Besançon: 1601

—Pastor, J. Señor. Juan Pastor . . . procurador . . . dize, que los Indios del Uruay, y del Parana. [Madrid: 1646?]

—Pinto Ribeiro, J. Discurso sobre os fidalgos. Lisbon: 1632

—De Portogysen goeden buyrman. [The Hague?] 1649

PORTUGUESE IN PARAGUAY

—Ruiz de Montoya, A. Señor. Antonio Ruiz de Montoya . . . procurador general. . . del Paraguay. [Madrid? 1639]

Possevino, Antonio. Biblioteca selecta. Venice: A. Salicato, 1603

—Bibliotheca selecta. Cologne: J. Gymnicus, 1607

—Cultura ingeniorum. Cologne: J. Gymnicus, 1610

POSTAL SERVICE

—Codogno, O. Compendio delle poste. Milan: 1623

— —Nuovo itinerario delle poste. Venice: 1611

POSTAL SERVICE—PERU

—Vargas Carvajal, F. Peticion. [Madrid? 1644]

A poste with a madde packet of letters. *See* Breton, Nicholas

A poste with a packet of . . . let-

ters. *See titles under* Breton, Nicholas

Postel, Guillaume. De cosmographica disciplina. Leyden: J. Maire, 1636

—De universitate libri duo. Leyden: J. Maire, 1635

POTATOES

—Ariosto, L. Orlando furioso, in English. London: 1634

—Dawson, T. The good huswifes jewell. London: 1610

—Greene, R. Theeves falling out. London: 1615

—Jonson, B. The fountaine of selfe-love. London: 1601

—Lauremberg, P. Apparatus plantarius primus. Frankfurt a.M.: [1632]

—Massinger, P. A new way to pay old debts. London: 1633

—Rowlands, S. A terrible battell. London: [1606?]

—Shakespeare, W. A most pleasaunt . . . comedie. London: 1602

—Stephens, J. The errors of men. London: 1627

— —Satyrical essayes. London: 1615

—Taylor, J. Hipp-anthrōpos: or, An ironical expostulation. London: 1648

—Venner, T. Via recta ad vitam longam. London: 1620

—Wither, G. Abuses stript, and whipt. London: 1613

POTATOES—DRAMA

—Jones, J. Adrasta: or, The womans spleene. London: 1635

POTATOES—POETRY

—Harington, Sir J. The most elegant . . . epigrams. London: 1618

—Taylor, J. The sculler. London: 1612

— —Taylors goose. London: 1621

POTATOES IN LITERATURE

—Lenton, F. The puisne gallants progresse. London: 1635

— —The young gallants whirligigg. London: 1629

Potgieter, Barent Janszoon. Historiae antipodum sive Novi Orbis. Frankfurt a.M.: M. Me-

rian, & W. Hoffmann, 1633

—Historisch ende wijdtloopigh verhael. Amsterdam: M. Colijn, 1617

—Historische Relation, oder Eygendtliche . . . Beschreibung. Frankfurt a.M.: M. Becker, 1601

—Relatio historica, sive vera . . . descriptio. Frankfurt a.M.: M. Becker, 1602

—Wijdtloopigh verhael. *In* Neck, Jacob Corneliszoon van. Waerachtigh verhael van de schipvaert op Oost-Indien. Amsterdam: 1648

Poti, Pedro. *See* Poty, Pieter

Potier, Pierre. Insignes curationes. Venice: G. B. Ciotti, 1615

— —Cologne: M. Schmitz, 1616

— —Cologne: M. Schmitz, 1625

— —*In his* Libri duo. Bologna: 1643

—Insignium curationum . . . centuria prima. Bologna: N. Tebaldini, for M. A. Bernia, 1622

—Insignium curationum . . . centuria secunda. Bologna: N. Tebaldini, for M. A. Bernia, 1622

— —Cologne: M. Schmitz, 1623

— —*In his* Pharmacopoea spagirica. Cologne: 1624

— —*In his* Opera omnia. Lyons: 1645

—Libri duo de febribus. Bologna: G. Monti, 1643

—Opera omnia medica et chymica. Lyons: J. A. Huguetan, 1645

—Pharmacopoea spagirica. Cologne: M. Schmitz, 1624

— —Bologna: G. Monti, & C. Zenaro, 1635

— —*In his* Libri duo. Bologna: 1643

Potosí, Bolivia. Por la villa imperial de Potosi. [Madrid: 1634?]

—Señor. Cinco cosas son las que la villa imperial de Potosi suplica. [Madrid? ca. 1613]

Potosí, Bolivia. Gremio de los azogueros. El gremio de los azogueros de . . . Potosi . . . suplica. [Madrid? 1636?] (2)

—Señor. Los azogueros dueños de minas. [Madrid? 1620?]

Practico de morbo gallico. *See* León, Andrés de

Practiicke van den Spaenschen aes-sack. The Hague: 1629

—The Hague: A. J. Tongerloo, 1629

The practise of chymicall . . . physicke. *See* Duchesne, Joseph

Prado, Esteban de. Por Francisco Nuñez Melian, governador . . . que fue . . . de Veneçuela. [Madrid? 1640?]

Prado Beltran, Bernardino de. Razonamiento panegyrico. Madrid: Imprenta Real, 1633

Praelectiones Patavinae. *See* Mercuriale, Girolamo

Praematurae solis apparitionis. *See* Röslin, Elisaeus

Praetorius, Michael. Syntagma musicum. Wittenberg: J. Richter, & E. Holwein, at Wolfenbüttel, 1615–20

Praevotius, Joannes. *See* Prevost, Jean

Pragmatica circa illius prohibendi del tabaco. *See* Naples (Kingdom). Laws, statutes, etc

The praise and vertue of a jayle. *See* Taylor, John, the Water-poet

The praise, antiquity, and commodity, of beggery. *See* Taylor, John, the Water-poet

The praise of hemp-seed. *See* Taylor, John, the Water-poet

Praxeos. *See* Platter, Felix

Praxis alchymiae. *See* Libavius, Andreas

Praxis chymiatrica. *See* Hartmann, Johann

Praxis historiarum. *See* Zacutus, Abraham, Lusitanus

Praxis medica. *See* Mercado, Luis; *and also* Rivière, Lazare

Praxis medica admiranda. *See* Zacutus, Abraham, Lusitanus

Praxis medicinae. *See* Bruele, Gualtherus; *and also* Heurne, Johan van

Praxis medicinae, or, The physicians practise. *See* Bruele, Gualtherus

Praxis medicinae universalis. *See* Wirsung, Christoph

Praxis universae artis medicae. *See* Cesalpino, Andrea

PRECIOUS METALS. *See also* GOLD *and* SILVER

—Alcázar y Zúniga, J. de, conde de la Marquina. Medios politicos. Madrid: 1646

—Avisos de Roma. Valencia: 1620

—Baerle, K. van. Mercator sapiens. Amsterdam: 1632

— —Verstandighe coopman. Enkhuizen: 1641

—Barba, A. A. Arte de los metales. Madrid: 1640

—Benítez Negrete, S. Señor. El aver entrado en estos reynos de España. [Madrid: 1625?]

—Beverwijck, J. van. Autarcheia Bataviae. Leyden: 1644

— —Inleydinge tot de Hollandsche geneesmiddelen. Dordrecht: 1642

—Carranza, A. El ajustamiento i proporcion de las monedas de oro. Madrid: 1629

—Declaracion del valor justo, dela plata. [Madrid? 1640?]

—Memorial de advertencias convenientes para esta monarquia. [Madrid? ca. 1635?]

—Oogh-teecken der inlantsche twisten. The Hague: 1620

—Por los interesados en los quatro generos de mercaderias. [Seville? 1633?]

—Relacion del pleyto, i causa. [Madrid? 1636]

—Romero, G. Señor. Gonzalo Remero. [Madrid? 1625?]

—Sánchez, A. Todo el pleyto que siguen los dueños de barras del Pirù. [Madrid? 1637]

—Sandoval y Guzmán, S. de. El doctor . . . digo, que de pedimiento mio embio V. A. orden. [Madrid? 1635]

— —El doctor . . . digo, que las barras . . . se bolvieron a ensenyar. [Madrid: 1634]

—Seville. Consulado. Por el consulado de Sevilla. Madrid: 1634

—Spain. Sovereigns, etc., 1598–1621 (Philip III). El Rey. Lo que por mi mandado se as-

sienta, y concierta con Juan Nuñez Correa. [Madrid? 1603]

PRECIOUS METALS—LATIN AMERICA

—Coquerel, N. de. Discours de la perte. Paris: 1608

—Lugo y Dávila, F. de. Desenganos y replicas a las proposiciones de Gerardo Basso. Madrid: 1632

PRECIOUS METALS—PERU

—Estaço da Silveira, S. El capitan . . . Dize, que la plata y riquezas del Piru vienen a España conduzidas por tierra a Arica. [Madrid: 1626]

PRECIOUS STONES

—Avisos de Roma. Valencia: 1620

—Silvaticus, J. B. De unicornu. Bergamo: 1605

—Spain. Sovereigns, etc., 1598–1621 (Philip III). El Rey. Lo que por mi mandado se assienta, y concierta con Juan Nuñez Correa. [Madrid? 1603]

—Taylor, J. Superbiae flagellum. London: 1621

Predicacion del Evangelio. *See* García, Gregorio

El predicador delas gentes. *See* Rodríguez de León, Juan

Pregon en que el Rey nuestro señor manda. *See* Spain. Laws, statutes, etc., 1621–1665 (Philip IV)

Preguntas que se propusieron al maese de campo. [Madrid? 1616?]

Prematica . . . . *See items listed under* Spain. Laws, statutes, etc., 1621–1665 (Philip IV)

Premier livre de l'Histoire de la navigation. *See* Lodewijcksz, Willem

La premiere et seconde Savoisienne. *See* Arnauld, Antoine (1560–1619)

Premiere sepmaine. *See* Du Bartas, Guillaume de Salluste, seigneur

I principi . . . con le Aggiunte alla Ragion di stato. *See* Botero, Giovanni

The prerogative of parliaments. *See* Raleigh, Sir Walter

The present estate of Spayne. *See* Wadsworth, James

El presentado fray Christoval de Aguilera. *See* Aguilera, Cristóbal de

Preservatives against sinne. *See* Cole, Nathanael

Pretensiones de la villa imperial de Potosi. *See* Sandoval y Guzmán, Sebastián de

Pretty, Francis. Beschryvinge vande overtreffelijcke . . . zee-vaerdt. Amsterdam: M. Colijn, 1617

— —*In* Journalen van drie voyagien. Amsterdam: 1643

See also the following:

—Le voyage de l'illustre . . . François Drach. Paris: 1613

—Le voyage curieux, faict . . . par François Drach. Paris: 1641

Prevost, Jean. La medecine des pauvres. Paris: G. Clousier, 1646

—Medicina pauperum. Frankfurt a.M.: K. Rötel, for J. Beyer, 1641

— —Lyons: P. Ravaud, 1643

— —Lyons: P. Ravaud, 1644

Price, Daniel. Sauls prohibition staide. London: [J. Windet] for M. Law, 1609

PRICKLY-PEAR

—Satyre Ménippée. Satyre Menippee. [Paris?] 1604

—Satyre Ménippée. English. Englands bright honour. London: 1602

—Theatrum florae. Paris: 1622

Prima parte dell'Historia siciliana. *See* Buonfiglio Costanzo, Giuseppe

Primerose, James. De vulgi erroribus in medicina. Amsterdam: J. Janszoon the Younger, 1639

— —Amsterdam: J. Janszoon the Younger, 1644

— —Amsterdam: J. Janszoon the Younger, 1645

—De vulgi in medicina erroribus. London: B. A[lsop]., & T. F[awcet]., for H. Robinson, 1638

Princelyck cabinet. *See* Clercq, Nikolaas de

Princeps christianus. *See* Rivadeneira, Pedro de

Les principes d'astronomie. *See* Gemma, Reinerus, Frisius

La prise d'un seigneur escossois. *See* Daniel, Charles

La prise de l'isle de Santo Paulo. Lyons: 1631

La prise de la ville d'Ordinguen. Paris: 1625

La prise de la ville de Olinda. *See* Waerdenburgh, Dirk van

PRISONERS, TRANSPORTATION OF

—Great Britain. Sovereigns, etc., 1603–1625 (James I). A proclamation for the better . . . government. London: 1617

— —A proclamation for the due and speedy execution of the statute against rogues. London: 1603

Private-men no pulpit-men. *See* Workman, Giles

PRIVATEERING

—Lof des vrye vaerts. [Amsterdam?] 1629

Le prix et valeur des medicamens. *See* Guibert, Philbert

Problematum medicorum decades. *See* Horst, Gregor

Problemi naturali e morali. *See* Garimberto, Girolamo

Problesmes medicinaux et chirurgicaux. *See* Habicot, Nicolas

A proclamation against the disorderly transporting. *See* Great Britain. Sovereigns, etc., 1625–1649 (Charles I)

A proclamation commanding conformity to his Majesties pleasure. *See* Great Britain. Sovereigns, etc., 1603–1625 (James I)

A proclamation concerning the importation of tobaccoe. *See* Ireland. Lord Deputy, 1633–1641 (Thomas Wentworth, 1st earl of Strafford)

A proclamation concerning the sealing of tobaccoe. *See* Ireland. Lord Deputy, 1633–1641 (Thomas Wentworth, 1st earl of Strafford)

A proclamation concerning the viewing . . . of tobacco. *See*

Great Britain. Sovereigns, etc., 1603–1625 (James I)

A proclamation concerning tobacco. *See* Great Britain. Sovereigns, etc., 1603–1625 (James I); *and also* Great Britain. Sovereigns, etc., 1625–1649 (Charles I)

A proclamation declaring His Majesties gratious pleasure touching sundry grants. *See* Great Britain. Sovereigns, etc., 1625–1649 (Charles I)

A proclamation declaring His Majesties pleasure . . . for licensing retailors of tobacco. *See* Great Britain. Sovereigns, etc., 1625–1649 (Charles I)

A proclamation declaring his Majesties pleasure concerning Captaine Roger North. *See* Great Britain. Sovereigns, etc., 1603–1625 (James I)

A proclamation declaring His Majesties pleasure concerning Sir Walter Rawleigh. *See* Great Britain. Sovereigns, etc., 1603–1625 (James I)

A proclamation for preventing of the abuses . . . of tobacco. *See* Great Britain. Sovereigns, etc., 1625–1649 (Charles I)

A proclamation for restraint of the disordered trading for tobacco. *See* Great Britain. Sovereigns, etc., 1603–1625 (James I)

A proclamation for setling the plantation of Virginia. *See* Great Britain. Sovereigns, etc., 1603–1625 (James I)

A proclamation for the better and more peaceable government. *See* Great Britain. Sovereigns, etc., 1603–1625 (James I)

A proclamation for the due and speedy execution of the statute against rogues. *See* Great Britain. Sovereigns, etc., 1603–1625 (James I)

A proclamation for the ordering of tobacco. *See* Great Britain. Sovereigns, etc., 1625–1649 (Charles I)

A proclamation for the utter prohibiting the importation and use of all tobacco. *See* Great Britain. Sovereigns, etc., 1603–1625 (James I)

A proclamation forbidding the disorderly trading with the salvages in New England. *See* Great Britain. Sovereigns, etc., 1625–1649 (Charles I)

A proclamation prohibiting interloping. *See* Great Britain. Sovereigns, etc., 1603–1625 (James I)

A proclamation prohibiting the buying or disposing of any the lading. *See* Great Britain. Sovereigns, etc., 1625–1649 (Charles I)

A proclamation restraining the abusive venting of tobacco. *See* Great Britain. Sovereigns, etc., 1625–1649 (Charles I)

A proclamation to give assurance . . . in the islands. *See* Great Britain. Sovereigns, etc., 1625–1649 (Charles I)

A proclamation to restraine the planting of tobacco. *See* Great Britain. Sovereigns, etc., 1603–1625 (James I)

A proclamation to restraine the transporting of passengers. *See* Great Britain. Sovereigns, etc., 1625–1649 (Charles I)

A proclamation touching the sealing of tobacco. *See* Great Britain. Sovereigns, etc., 1625–1649 (Charles I)

A proclamation touching tobacco. *See* Great Britain. Sovereigns, etc., 1625–1649 (Charles I)

A proclamation, with articles of directions. *See* Great Britain. Sovereigns, etc., 1603–1625 (James I)

Prodromos Theatri botanici. *See* Bauhin, Kaspar

Proef-steen van den trou-ringh. *See* Cats, Jacob

De proef-stucken. *See* Bacon, Francis

Proeve des nu onlangs uyt-ghegheven drooms. *See* Migoen, Jacob Willem

Proeve, over eenen Rypen-raet. Tholen: C. Speckaert, 1636

The profession of faith. *See* Davenport, John

A profitable and necessarie booke. *See* Clowes, William

Le progrez et avancement aux sciences. *See* Bacon, Francis

Prologo de las constituciones. *See* Lima. Universidad de San Marcos

Proposiciones que haze el Señorio de Vizcaya. *See* Vizcaya, Spain. Señorío

Propositie. *See* Sousa Coutinho, Francisco de

Propositien. *See* Coignet de la Thuillerie, Gaspard

Propositio. *See* Sousa Coutinho, Francisco de

La proposition. *See* Sousa Coutinho, Francisco de

A proposition of provisions. London: F. Clifton, 1630

Propugnaculum chymiatriae. *See* Ruland, Martin

A prospect of the most famous parts. *See* Speed, John

Protest ofte Scherp dreyghement. *See* Kannenburch, Hendrik van

PROTESTANTS IN AMERICA. *See also* PURITANS *and* names of individuals

—Baillie, R. Anabaptism. London: 1647

—Great Britain. Laws, statutes, etc., 1625–1649 (Charles I). Two ordinances of the Lords and Commons. London: [1646]

—Lydius, J. Historie der beroerten van Engelandt. Dordrecht: 1647

Proteus, ofte Minne-beelden. *See* Cats, Jacob

Provechosos adbitrios. *See* Barbón y Castañeda, Guillén

Provintiael advijs van Hollant. *See* Holland (Province). Staten

Provisionele ordre ende reglement. *See* Hoorn, Netherlands. Ordinances, etc.

Prynne, William. A fresh discovery. London: J. Macock, for M. Sparke, 1645

——London: J. Macock, for M. Sparke, 1646

—Histrio-mastix. London: E.

A[llde, A. Mathewes, T. Cotes]. & W. J[ones]., for M. Sparke, 1633 (2)

—*See also* White, Nathaniel. Truth gloriously appearing. London: [1645]

The psalms, hymns, and spiritual songs. *See* Bible. O.T. Psalms. English, Paraphrases. 1648. Bay Psalm Book

Pseudodoxia epidemica: or, Enquiries. *See* Browne, Sir Thomas

Pseudo-martyr. *See* Donne, John

PSEUDONYMS

—Banchieri, A. Von dess Esels Adel. [Strassburg:] 1617

Ptōchopharmakon, seu Medicamen miseris. *See* Pemell, Robert

Ptolemaeus, Claudius. Geografia. Padua: P. & F. Galignani, 1621, '20

—Geographiae libri octo. Amsterdam: [J. Theuniszoon?] for C. Claeszoon, & J. Hondius, 1605

—Geographiae universae. Cologne: P. Keschedt, 1608

——Arnhem: J. Janszoon, 1617

A publication by the Counsell of Virginea. *See* Great Britain, Council for Virginia

A publication of Guiana's plantation. London: W. Jones, for T. Paine, 1632

PUERTO RICO

—Entremeses nuevos. De diversos autores. Alcalá de Henares: 1643

—Khunrath, C. Medulla destillatoria et medica. Hamburg: 1601

—Scholtz, L. Epistolarum philosophicarum . . . volumen. Hanau: 1610

PUERTO RICO—CHURCH HISTORY

—San Juan, Puerto Rico (Diocese). Synod, 1645. Constituciones synodales. Madrid: 1647

PUERTO RICO—HISTORY

—Pazes entre España, Francia, y otros potentados. Seville: [1626]

The puisne gallants progresse.
See Lenton, Francis
Pulgar, Hernando de. Los claros varones de España. Antwerp: J. de Meurs, 1632
Punta del Rey. *See* Araya, Punta de
Purchas, Samuel. Purchas his pilgrim. Microcosmus. London: W. S[tansby]., for H. Fetherstone, 1619
——London: [B. Alsop & T. Fawcet] for T. Alchorn, 1627
—Purchas his pilgrimage. London: W. Stansby, for H. Fetherstone, 1613
——London: W. Stansby, for H. Fetherstone, 1614
——London: W. Stansby, for H. Fetherstone, 1617
——London: W. Stansby, for H. Fetherstone, 1626 (2)
—Purchas his pilgrimes. London: W. Stansby, for H. Fetherstone, 1625
—Purchase his pilgrimage. *See* Purchas his pilgrimage *above*
See also the following:
—Boissard, Jean Jacques. Bibliotheca. Frankfurt a.M.: 1628
—Fotherby, Martin, Bp. Atheomastix clearing foure truthes. London: 1622
—Prynne, William, Histrio-mastix. London: 1633
Purchas his . . . *See titles under* Purchas, Samuel
Purchase his Pilgrimage. *See* Purchas, Samuel
PURITANS
—Canne, A., pseud. A new windmil. [London]: 1643
—Hall, J. A survay of that foolish . . . libell. London: 1641
—Observations upon Prince Rupert's white dogge. [London: 1643]
—Steuart, A. The second part of the duply. London: 1644
—Taylor, J. The devil turn'd Round-head. [London: 1642]
—Walker, C. The history of Independency. [London?] 1648
Puteo, Zacharias. Clavis medica rationalis. Venice: L. Aureati, 1612, '11
—Historia de gumma indica.

Venice: Gioseffo Imberti, 1628
Pym, John. A speech delivered in Parliament. London: R. Lowndes, 1641
——London: R. L[owndes]., 1641
——London: R. Lowndes, 1642
Pyne, John. Epigrammata religiosa. [London: W. Stansby, 1626]
Pyrard, François. Discours du voyage . . . aux Indes. Paris: D. LeClerc, 1611
—Voyage . . . aux Indes. Paris: S. Thiboust, & R. Dallin, 1615
——Paris: S. Thiboust, & Widow of R. Dallin, 1619
Quad, Matthias. Enchiridion cosmographicum. Cologne: W. Lützenkirchen, 1604
—Fasciculus geographicus. Cologne: J. Bussemacher, 1608
Quade, Matthias. *See* Quad, Matthias
Quadro, Diego Felipe de. Todo el pleyto. [Seville? 1640?]
Quadrupedum omnium bisulcorum historia. *See* Aldrovandi, Ulisse
Quadt, Matthias. *See* Quad, Matthias
Quaestio medica . . . in Scholis Medicorum. *See* Bovionier, François
Quaestionarium theologicum. *See* Córdoba, Antonio de
Quaestiones medico-legales. *See titles under* Zacchia, Paolo
Los quarenta libros del Compendio historial. *See* Garibáy y Zamálloa, Esteban de
Quarles, Francis. Emblemes. London: G. M[iller]., for J. Marriott, 1635 (2)
——London: J. Dawson, for F. Eglesfield, 1639
La quarta carta, y verdadera relacion. Valladolid: Widow of F. Fernández de Córdoba, 1625
Quaternio, or A fourefold way. *See* Nash, Thomas
Quatre livres des secrets de medecine. *See* Gesner, Konrad
Le quatriesme des Bigarrures. *See* Tabourot, Estienne
Le quatriesme recueil contenant

l'histoire de la Ligue. *See* Goulart, Simon
Que se dé diferente modo al govierno de la Indias. *See* Gaytán de Torres, Manuel
Quechua language. *See* Kechua language
Queen Anna's new world of words. *See* Florio, John
The queenes arcadia. *See* Daniel, Samuel
Queiros, Pedro Fernandes de. Copia de unos avisos muy notables. Barcelona: G. Graells, & G. Dotil, 1609
—Copie de la requeste. Paris: 1617
—Memoriael. *In* Gerritsz, Hessel. Beschryvinghe van der Samoyeden landt. Amsterdam: 1612
—Memorial. Seville: L. Estupiñán, 1610
—Narratio. *In* Gerritsz, Hessel. Descriptio ac delineatio geographica detectionis freti. Amsterdam: 1612
—Relacion de un memorial. Pamplona: C. de Labayen, 1610
——Seville: L. Estupiñán, 1610
——Valencia: 1611
—Relation von dem . . . vierten Theil der Welt. Augsburg: C. Dabertzhofer, 1611
—Señor . . . con este son ocho los memoriales. [Madrid: 1610?]
—Terra Australis incognita, or A new southerne discoverie. London: J. Hodgetts, 1617 (2)
—Verhael. *In* Journael vande Nassausche vloot. Amsterdam: 1643
Quelen, Augustus van. *See* Guelen, August de
Quercetanus redivivus. *See* Duchesne, Joseph
Quervau, Vincent, sieur du Sollier. Epitome ou brief recueil de l'histoire universelle. Paris: F. Huby, 1613
—Le tableau historiale du monde. Rennes: P. L'Oyselet, 1625

Quesada, Ginés de. Relacion verdadera del martirio. Seville: S. Fajardo, 1633

Question moral. *See* León Pinelo, Antonio Rodríguez de

Les questions illustres. *See* Peleus, Julien

Quevedo y Villegas, Francisco Gómez de. Enseñança entretenida. Madrid: D. Díaz de la Carrera, for P. Coello, 1648

—La fortuna. Saragossa: Heirs of P. Lanaja y Lamarca, for R. de Uport, 1650

——Saragossa: Heirs of P. Lanaja y Lamarca, for R. de Uport, 1650

—El parnasso español. Madrid: D. Díaz de la Carrera, for P. Coello, 1648

——Saragossa: Hospital Real, for P. Escuer, 1649

——Madrid: D. Díaz de la Carrera, 1650

—Todas las obras en prosa. Madrid: D. Díaz de la Carrera, 1650

See also the following:

—Espinosa, Pedro, comp. Flores de poetas ilustres. Valladolid: 1605

—Pinto de Moraes, Jorge. Maravillas del Parnaso. Lisbon: 1637

—Romances varios. De diversos autores. Saragossa: 1640

Quichua language. *See* Kechua language

Quiñones, Diego de. Oracion funebre. Valladolid: A. de Rueda, 1645

Quinta pars Indiae Orientalis. *See* Neck, Jacob Corneliszoon van

Quintanadueñas, Antonio de. Explicacion de la Bula. Seville: S. Fajardo, 1642

El quinto, y sexto punto de la relacion. *See* González de Nájera, Alonso

Quiros, Pedro Fernandez de. *See* Queiros, Pedro Fernandes de

QUITO (CITY)

—Garavito, G. Señor. Geronimo Garavito en nombre de don Juan de Lizaraçu . . . dize, que reconociendo . . . . [Madrid: 163–?]

—Mañozca y Zamora, J. de. Memorial al Rey. Madrid: 1640

—Velasco, D. de. Señor. Descubrimiento del camino. [Madrid? 1620?]

—Vera, e nuova relatione. Florence: [1628?]

QUITO (CITY)—CHURCH HISTORY

—Araujo, L. de. Relacion de las cosas que sucidieron en la ciudad de Quito. [Madrid? 1627?]

—Mañozca, J. de. Señor. El licenciado Juan de Mañozca, inquisidor apostolico. [Madrid? ca. 1630?]

Quodlibets, lately come over from New Britaniola. *See* Hayman, Robert

R., N. *See* Epicedium cum epitaphio . . . Petri Heinii. The Hague: 1629

Rabel, Daniel. *See* Theatrum florae. Paris: 1622

Rabelais, François. Oeuvres. Antwerp: J. Fuet, 1605

Raccolta breve d'alcune cose piu segnalate. *See* Panciroli, Guido

Raedtsel. *See* Middelgeest, Simon van

Raedtslagh. *See* Middelgeest, Simon van

Ragionamenti dottissimi et curiosi. *See* Mexía, Pedro

Ragueneau, Paul. Narratio historica eorum, quae Societas Jesu in Nova Francia fortiter egit. Innsbruck: H. Agricola, 1650

—Relation de ce qui s'est passé dans le pays des Hurons. *In* Lallemant, Jérôme. Relation de ce qui s'est passé . . . ès annees 1647 et 1648. Paris: 1649

—Relation de ce qui s'est passé en la mission . . . aux Hurons. *In* Lallemant, Jérôme. Relation de ce qui s'est passé . . . ès années 1645. et 1646. Paris: 1647

——Lille: Widow of P. de Rache, 1650

——Paris: S. Cramoisy, & G. Cramoisy, 1650 (2)

Raleigh, Sir Walter. Achter Theil Americae. Frankfurt a.M.: K. Rötel, for Heirs of J. T. de Bry, 1624

—Apologie for his voyage to Guiana. London: T. W[arren]., for H. Moseley, 1650

—Die fünffte kurtze wunderbare Beschreibung. Nuremberg: C. Lochner, for L. Hulsius, 1603

——Frankfurt a.M.: E. Kempfer, for Widow of L. Hulsius, 1612 (3)

—The historie of the world. London: [H. Lownes,] for H. Lownes, G. Latham & R. Young, 1628

——London: [R. Young] for G. Latham, & R. Young, 1634

—The history of the world. London: W. Stansby, for W. Burre, 1614

——London: W. Stansby, for W. Burre, 1617

——London: W. Jaggard, for W. Burre, 1621

——London: [W. Jaggard, W. Stansby, & N. Okes] for W. Burre, 1617 [i.e., 1621]

—Judicious and select essayes. London: T. W[arren]., for H. Moseley, 1650

—Kurtze wunderbare Beschreibung dess . . . Königreichs Guianae. Nuremberg: C. Lochner, for L. Hulsius, 1601 (2)

—The perogative of parliaments. [London: T. Cotes] 1640

—The prerogative of parlaments. 'Hamburgh' [i.e., London: T. Cotes] 1628

—The prerogative of parlaments. 'Midelburge' [i.e., London: T. Cotes] 1628 (4)

——[London: T. Cotes?] 1640

—Verclaringe ende verhael. *See* Verclaringe ende verhael hoe de Heere Wouter Raleigh . . . hem ghedreghen heeft. The Hague: 1619

—Warachtighe ende grondighe beschryvinghe van . . . Guiana. Amsterdam: C. Claeszoon, 1605

——Amsterdam: M. Colijn, 1617

Raleigh, Sir Walter, defendant. The arraignment and conviction of Sr Walter Rawleigh.

London: W. Wilson, for A. Roper, 1648
RALEIGH, SIR WALTER
—Baker, Sir Richard. A chronicle of the kings. London: 1643
—Bry, T. de. Americae pars viii. Frankfurt a.M.: 1625
—Camden, W. Annales rerum Anglicarum. Leyden: 1625
— —Annalium rerum Anglicarum, t.2. London: 1627
— —Annals. London: 1635
— —Histoire d'Elizabeth. Paris: 1627
— —The historie of . . . Princesse Elizabeth. London: 1629
— —Rerum Anglicarum . . . annales. Leyden: 1639
—A declaration of the demeanor . . . of Sir Walter Raleigh. London: 1618
—Great Britain. Sovereigns, etc., 1603–1625 (James I). A proclamation declaring His Majesties pleasure concerning Sir Walter Rawleigh. London: 1618
—Hexham, H. A tongue-combat. London: 1623
—Howell, J. Epistolae Ho-elianae. Familiar letters. London: 1645
— —A new volume of letters. London: 1647
—Liceti, F. De monstrorum caussis. Padua: 1616
—Martyn, W. The historie . . . of the kings of England. London: 1638
—Newes of Sr. Walter Rauleigh. London: 1618
—Scott, T. Sir Walter Rawleighs ghost. [London]: 1626
— —Vox populi, pt 2. [London]: 1624
— —Vox regis. [Utrecht: 1624]
— —Vox regis, of De stemme des Conincks. Utrecht: 1624
—Sir Walter Rauleigh his lamentation. London: [1618]
—Stucley, Sir L. To the Kings most excellent majestie. London: 1618
—Taylor, J. The olde, old . . . man. London: 1635
—Verclaringe . . . hoe de Heere Wouter Raleigh . . . hem ghe-

dreghen heeft. The Hague: 1619
Ramillete de plantas. See Villa, Esteban de
Ramón, Tomás. Nueva prematica de reformacion. Saragossa: D. Dormer, 1635
Ramusio, Giovanni Battista. Delle navigationi et viaggi . . . Volume primo. Venice: The Giuntas, 1606
— —Venice: The Giuntas, 1613
—Delle navigationi et viaggi . . . Volume secondo. Venice: The Giuntas, 1606
—Delle navigationi et viaggi . . . Volume terzo. Venice: The Giuntas, 1606
Ranchin, François. Opuscules, ou Traictés divers. Lyons: P. Ravaud, 1640
Ranconet, Aimar de. Thresor de la langue françoyse. Paris: D. Douceur, 1606
Randolph, Thomas. Aristippus, or The jovial philosopher. London: [J. Beale?] for R. Allott, 1630
— —London: T. Harper, for J. Marriott, & R. Myn, 1630 (2)
— —London: [Elizabeth Allde] for R. Allott, 1631
— —Dublin: Society of Stationers [1635?]
— —London: [Elizabeth Purslowe] for R. Allott, 1635
—Poems. Oxford: L. Lichfield, for F. Bowman, 1638
— —Oxford: L. Lichfield, for F. Bowman, 1640
— —Oxford: [L. Lichfield] for F. B[owman]., & L. Chapman [at London] 1640
— —London: 1643
Rapine, Charles. Histoire generale de l'origine . . . des freres mineurs. Paris: 1630
— —Paris: C. Sonnius, 1631
Rapport . . . over 't ver-overen vande silver-vlote. See Willemssz, Salomon
Rapport ghedaen by d'heer van Beaumont. See Beaumont, Simon van
Rariorum plantarum historia. See L'Ecluse, Charles de
The rates of marchandizes. See

Great Britain. Laws, statutes, etc., 1625–1649 (Charles I)
Rathband, William. A brief narration of some courses. London: G. M[iller]., for E. Brewster, 1644
— —See also Weld, Thomas. An answer to W. R. his Narration. London: 1644
RATTLESNAKES
—Peacham, H. Coach and sedan. London: 1636
Rauw, Johann. Weltbeschreibung. Frankfurt a.M.: 1612
Raven, Dirk Albertsz. Journael. In Journael, of Dagh-register gehouden by seven matroosen. Amsterdam: [1650?]
—Journael ofte beschrijvinge vande reyse. In Bontekoe, Willem Ysbrandsz. Journael ofte . . . beschrijvinghe vande Oost-Indische reyse. Hoorn: 1646
— —In the same. Utrecht: 1647
— —In the same. Amsterdam: 1648
— —In the same. Hoorn: 1648
— —In Bontekoe, Willem Ysbrandsz. Die vier und zwantzigste Schiffahrt. Frankfurt a.M.: 1648
— —In Bontekoe, Willem Ysbrandsz. Journael . . . . Utrecht: 1649
— —In the same. Amsterdam: 1650
— —In Bontekoe, Willem Ysbrandsz. Verhael van de avontuerlijke reyse. Amsterdam: 1650
Ravenscroft, Thomas. A briefe discourse of the true . . . use of charact'ring the degrees. London: E. Allde, for T. Adams, 1614
Razon d'estado. See Botero, Giovanni
Razon que da de si el padre Jacinto Perez . . . . See Pérez, Jacinto
Razonamiento panegyrico. See Prado Beltran, Bernardino de
Realis philosophiae epilogisticae partes quatuor. See Campanella, Tommaso

Recentes Novi Orbis historiae.
Geneva: P. de La Rovière,
1612
Recherches curieuses des me-
sures. Paris: M. Collet, 1629
Recherches curieuses sur la di-
versité des langues. *See* Brere-
wood, Edward
Les recherches de la France. *See*
Pasquier, Etienne
Rechignevoisin, Bernard de,
siegneur de Guron. *See* Ar-
nauld, Antoine. La premiere et
seconde Savoisienne. Greno-
ble: 1630
Den rechten konink Midas.
Delft: [1650?]
Recio de León, Juan. Breve rela-
cion de la descripcion . . . de
las tierras. [Madrid? 1623?]
—Peligros del dilitado camino.
[Madrid? 1626?]
—Relation de los servicios . . . de
las provincias de Tipuane.
[Madrid: 1625]
—Señor. El maesse de campo
Juan Recio de Leon. [Madrid?
1625?]
—Señor. El maesse de campo
Juan Recio de Leon . . . pro-
pone. [Madrid: 1626]
—Señor. El maesse de campo
Juan Recio de Leon, dize, Que
la riqueza. . . . [Madrid?
1626?]
—Señor. El maestro de campo
Juan Recio de Leon, dize: Que
los Indios. . . . [Madrid: 1627]
—Señor. Juan Recio de Leon
. . . hace relacion a V[uestra].
M[agestad]. [Madrid? 1625?]
—Señor. Juan Recio de Leon,
masse de campo . . . de las pro-
vincias de Tipuane. [Madrid:
1626?]
—Señor. Quando el nuevo ca-
mino no fuera tan rico prove-
choso. [Madrid: 1626?]
—Señor. Relacion que Juan
Recio de Leon . . . presento a
V. magestad. [Madrid? 1626?]
—Los servicios que refiero a
V[uestra]. M[agestad]. en el
memorial. [Madrid? 1626?]
Recreation for ingenious head-
pieces. *See* Wit's recreations
Recueil de diverses pieces. *See*

Hay, Paul, sieur du Chastelet
Recueil de quelques vers bur-
lesques. *See* Scarron, Paul
Le recueil des excellens . . . dis-
cours. *See* Hurault, Michel,
sieur de Belesbat et du Fay
Recueil des oeuvres burlesques.
See Scarron, Paul
Recuerdos historicos y politicos.
See Salmerón, Marcos
Reden van dat die West-Indische
Compagnie . . . noodtsaecke-
lijck is. [The Hague?] 1636
Redenen, waeromme dat de
Vereenighde Nederlanden
geensints eenighe vrede
. . . konnen mogen . . . te
maecken. The Hague: A. Meu-
ris, 1630
Redenen wâeromme de West-In-
dische Compagnie dient te
trachten. . . . *See* Moerbeeck,
Jan Andries
Redres van de abuysen. *See* Rens-
selaer, Kiliaen van
Reducion universal de toto el
Piru. *See* Monsalve, Miguel de,
friar
Reed-geld over betalinghe.
[Haarlem?] 1630
Reforma de trages. *See* Hernando
de Talavera, Abp
A regiment for the sea. *See*
Bourne, William
Regimento de pilotos. *See* Mariz
Carneiro, Antonio de
Regimiento de navegacion. *See*
García de Céspedes, Andrés
Reglas par el govierno destos
reynos. *See* Gaitan de Torres,
Manuel
Reglement . . . over het open-
stellen vanden handel op Bra-
sil. *See* Nederlandsche West-
Indische Compagnie
Reglement . . . over het open-
stellen vanden handel op. S.
Paulo de Loanda. *See* Neder-
landsche West-Indische Com-
pagnie
Reglement donné par monsei-
gneur le Cardinal de Riche-
lieu. *See* France. Amirauté
Regnum Congo. *See titles under*
Lopes, Duarte
Regole della sanità. *See* Benzi,
Ugo

Regula vitae: das ist, Eine heyl-
same . . . Erinnerung. *See*
Grick, Friedrich
Rei rusticae. *See* Heresbach, Con-
rad
Der reiche Schweden General
Compagnies handlungs con-
tract. *See* Usselinx, Willem
Reidanus, Everardus. *See* Reyd,
Everhard van
Reina Maldonado, Pedro de.
Apologia por la santa iglesia
de Trujillo. Madrid: 1648
Reineccius, Felix. Solon francis-
canus. Innsbruck: M. Wagner,
1650
Reiss-Beschreibung. *See* Wurff-
bain, Johann Sigmund
Relaçam anual das cousas que
fezeram os padres da Compan-
hia de Jesus. *See* Guerreiro,
Fernão
Relacam breve, e verdadeira de
memoravel victoria. *See* Paulo
do Rosario
Relaçam da aclamação. Lisbon:
J. Rodriguez, for D. Alvarez,
1641
Relaçam de varios successos
acontecidos no Maranham. *See*
Figueira, Luiz
Relaçam do dia em que as arma-
das. [Lisbon:] P. Craesbeeck,
1625
Relacam dos procedimentos. *See*
Mascarenhas, Antonio
Relaçam dos successos da ar-
mada. *See* Mello, Francisco
Manuel de
Relaçam universal do que succe-
deo em Portugal. *See* Severim
de Faria, Manuel
Relacam verdadeira de tudo o
succedido na restauraçao da
Bahia. *See* Correa, João de Me-
deiros
Relaçam verdadeira, e breve da
tomada da villa de Olinda. Lis-
bon: M. Rodriguez, 1630
Relação dos procedimentos. *See*
Mascarenhas, Antonio
Relação summaria das cousas do
Maranhão. *See* Estaço da Sil-
veira, Simão
Relação verdadeira dos sucessos.
See Carvalho, Jorge de
Relacino del viaje, y sucesso . . .

Juan Velazquez hizo. *See* Velázquez, Juan

Relacion que en el Consejo real de las Indias hizo el licenciado . . . sobre la pacificacion. *See* León Pinelo, Antonio Rodríguez de

Relacion sumaria . . . del tumulto . . . en Mexico. [Madrid? 1624]

Relacion verdadera . . . de los sucessos, victoria, y batalla que han tenido los galeones de nueva España. *See* Enrique, Pedro

Relacion verdadera de la famosa victoria. Seville: J. Gómez de Blas [1633]

Relacion verdadera de la gran vitoria. Seville: N. Rodríguez, 1638

Relacion verdadera de la grandiosa vitoria. Cadiz: 1625

Relacion verdadera de la grandiosa vitoria. Granada: B. Lorenzana, 1630

Relacion verdadera de la refriega. Madrid: D. Díaz de la Carrera, 1638

—Seville: F. de Lyra, 1638

Relacion verdadera de las grandes hazañas. [Madrid: B. de Guzmán, 1625?]

—Seville: S. Fajardo, 1625

—*See also* [Segunda relacion. . . Dizense en ella cosas admirables. Madrid: 1625?]

Relacion verdadera de las pazes. *See* Ovalle, Alonso de

Relacion verdadera de todos los sucessos. Madrid: J. Sánchez, 1641

Relacion verdadera del felice sucesso. [Madrid? 1641]

Relacion verdadera del martirio. *See* Quesada, Ginés de

Relacion verdadera del viaje de los galeones. Seville: N. Rodríguez, 1638

Relacion verdadera, y carta nueva de un traslado embiado del Brasil. *See* Múñoz, Bernardo

Relacion verdadera y cierta de la desseada . . . de la flota. *See* Fernández de Santiestevan, Blas

Relacion verdadera, y de mucho aprovachamiento para el Christiano. Alcalá de Henares: Heirs of J. Gracián, 1608

Relacion y copia de una carta. Madrid: B. de Guzman, 1625

Relacion, y vista de ojos. *See* Gaytán de Torres, Manuel

Relacione del viaggio, e successo . . . al Brasil. *See* Avendano y Vilela, Francisco de

Relaciones . . . del origen . . . de los reyes de Persia. *See* Teixeira, Pedro

Relaciones de la vida del escudero Marcos de Obregon. *See* Espinel, Vicente

Relaciones universales del mundo. *See* Botero, Giovanni

Relaes ende 't cargo van't silver. Amsterdam: J. F. Stam, for J. van Hilten [1632?]

Relatio historica Habspurgico-Austriaca. *See* Wurfbain, Leonhart

Relatio historica, sive vera . . . descriptio. *See* Potgieter, Barent Janszoon

Relatio quam Philippo iv . . . exhibuit reverendiss. p.f. Joannes de Santander. *See* Benavides, Alonso de

Relatio, welche Philippo iv. . . . und r.p.f. Joannes de Santander . . . ubergeben lassen. *See* Benavides, Alonso de

Relation . . . dess Königreichs Voxu. *See* Amati, Scipione

Relation aus Parnasso. *See* Boccalini, Traiano

Relation d'un voyage aux Indes Orientales. Paris: P. Villéry, & J. Guignard, 1645

Relation de ce qui s'est passé . . . en la Nouvelle France. . . . *For publications treating the years 1645–48 see* Lallemant, Jérôme

Relation de ce qui s'est passé dans le pays des Hurons. *See* Lallemant, Jérôme

Relation de ce qui s'est passé en Espagne. *See* Guidi, Ippolito Camillo

Relation de ce qui s'est passé en la mission . . . aux Hurons. *See* Ragueneau, Paul

Relation de ce qui s'est passé en la Nouvelle France. . . . *For publications treating the years 1633–39 see* Le Jeune, Paul; *for those on the years 1640–45 see* Vimont, Barthélemy; *for those on the years 1645–48 see* Lallemant, Jérôme.

Relation de l'establissement des François . . . en Martinique. *See* Bouton, Jacques

Relation de l'estat de la religion. *See* Sandys, Sir Edwin

[Relation de la mort.] *See* Zoes, Gerardus

Relation de la Nouvelle France. *See* Biard, Pierre

Relation de la prinse. Paris: M. Tavernier, 1624

Relation de los servicios . . . de las provincias de Tipuane. *See* Recio de León, Juan

Relation dell'horrible tremblement. *See* González Chaparro, Juan

Relation derniere. *See* Lescarbot, Marc

Relation des insignes progrez de la religion chrestienne. *See* Jesuits. Letters from missions, (South America)

Relation des voyages dans la riviere de la Plata. *See* Acarete du Biscay

Relation du combat donné par l'armée navale. [Amsterdam?] 1640

—[Paris:] Bureau d'Adresse, 1640

Relation du Groenland. *See* La Peyrère, Isaac de

A relation of a journey. *See* Sandys, George

The relation of a voyage to Guiana. *See* Harcourt, Robert

The relation of a wonderful voiage. *See* Schouten, Willem Corneliszoon

A relation of Maryland. [London:] W. Peasley, & J. Morgan, 1635

A relation of some speciall points. *See* Scott, Thomas

A relation of some yeares travaile. *See* Herbert, Sir Thomas

A relation of sundry particular

Rerum toto orbe gestarum chronica. *See* Le Mire, Aubert

Resende, Garcia de. Choronica . . . do christianissimo . . . Joao o segundo. Lisbon: J. Rodriguez, 1607

—Chronica . . . del rey Dom Joao II. Lisbon: A. Alvarez, 1622, '21

Resolucion y resumen del estado. *See* Núñez Correa, Juan

Responsa varia, ad varias aegritudines. *See* Guarguante, Orazio

Response à un avis. *In* Goulart, Simon. Le quatriesme recueil contenant l'histoire de la Ligue. [Geneva?] 1604

Responsio ad dissertationem secundam Hugonis Grotii, de origine gentium Americanarum. *See* Laet, Joannes de

Responsio ad totam quaestionum syllogen. *See* Norton, John

Responsionum et curationum medicinalium liber unus. *See* Fonteyn, Nicolaus

Respublica Hollandiae. Leyden: J. Maire, 1630 (3)

Respuesta . . . a lo que el Reyno le preguntó acerca de las minas. *See* Ayanz, Gerónimo de

Respuesta al Manifesto. *See* Caramuel Lobkowitz, Juan, Bp

Restauração de Portugal prodigiosa. *See* Vasconcellos, João de

Restauracion de la Bahia. [Lisbon? 1624?]

Restauracion de la ciudad del Salvador. *See* Tamayo de Vargas, Tomás

Restauracion politica de España. *See* Moncada, Sancho de

Return from Parnassus. The returne from Pernassus. London: G. Eld, for J. Wright, 1606 (2)

The returne from Pernassus. *See* Return from Parnassus

Reves, Jacques de. Biechte des Conincx van Spanien. [Amsterdam? 1630]

—Historia pontificorum roma-

norum. Amsterdam: J. Janszoon the Younger, 1632

Revius, Jacobus. *See* Reves, Jacques de

Rex platonicus. *See* Wake, Sir Isaac

El rey. *See* Spain. Sovereigns, etc., 1621–1665 (Philip IV)

El Rey [14 Dec. 1606]. *See* Spain. Sovereigns, etc., 1598–1621 (Philip III)

El Rey [26 May 1609]. *See* Spain. Sovereigns, etc., 1598–1621 (Philip III)

El Rey. Conceio, justicia, veyntiquatros, cavalleros. *See* Spain. Sovereigns, etc., 1621–1665 (Philip IV)

El Rey. Lo que por mi mandado se assienta, y concierta con Juan Nuñez Correa. *See* Spain. Sovereigns, etc., 1598–1621 (Philip III)

El Rey. Marques de Montes Claros . . . gouernador . . . del Piru. *See* Spain. Laws, statutes, etc., 1598–1621 (Philip III)

El Rey. Por quanto de ordinario se han ofrecido y ofrecen dudas. . . . *See* Spain. Laws, statutes, etc., 1598–1621 (Philip III)

El Rey. Por quanto la experiencia y execucion de las ultimas ordenanças. . . . *See* Spain. Laws, statutes, etc., 1598–1621 (Philip III)

El Rey. Por quanto por cedula mia de dos de Otubre del año passado. . . . *See* Spain. Laws, statutes, etc., 1598–1621 (Philip III)

El Rey. Por quanto por cedula mia fecha a dos de Otubre del año passado. . . . *See* Spain. Laws, statutes, etc., 1598–1621 (Philip III)

El Rey. Por quanto por cedula mia fecha en Madrid a catorze de Diziembre del año passado. *See* Spain. Laws, statutes, etc., 1598–1621 (Philip III)

El Rey. Por quanto por diferentes cedulas, leyes y ordenanças. *See* Spain. Laws, statutes, etc., 1598–1621 (Philip III)

Reyd, Everhard van. Belgarum . . . annales. Leyden: J. Maire, 1633

—Historie der Nederlantscher oorlogen. Arnhem: 1626

——Groningen: H. Mucerus, for G. Sybes, at Leeuwarden, 1650

—Oorspronck ende voortganck van de . . . oorloghen. Arnhem: J. van Biesen, 1633

——Amsterdam: Widow of E. Cloppenburg, 1644

—Voornaemste gheschiedenissen. Arnhem: J. Janszoon, 1626

Reyes de Portugal y empresas militares. *See* Coelho de Barbuda, Luiz

Reynolds, John. Vox coeli. 'Elesium' [i.e., London]: 1624

——'Elisium' [i.e., London]: 1624 (3)

——'Elisium' [i.e., London: W. Jones] 1624

Reys-boeck van . . . Brasilien. [Dordrecht?] J. Canin, 1624

Reys-gheschrift. *See* Linschoten, Jan Huygen van

Rezende, Luis Vaz de. Contrato do pao Brasil. Lisbon: P. Craesbeeck, 1631

Rhodologia. *See* Rosenberg, Johann Karl

Ribera, Hernando Matias de. Por Hernando Matias de Ribera. [Madrid? 1650?]

Ribera, Juan de. Lettera annua della v. provincia. Rome: L. Zannetti, 1605

——Venice: G. B. Ciotti, 1605

—Lettre annuelle de la province. Paris: Widow of G. de La Noue, 1605

Ribera, Luis de. *See* Ribera y Colindres, Luis de

Ribera y Colindres, Luis de. Memorial que se dio por parte de Don Luys de Ribera. [Madrid? 1622?]

—Señor. Don Luys de Ribera y Colindres. [Madrid? 1622?]

Le ricchezze della riformata farmacopoea. *See* Duchesne, Joseph

Ricettario Fiorentino. Florence: P. Cecconcelli, 1623

gionis Societatis Jesu catalogus. Antwerp: Plantin Office (J. Moretus), 1608

——Lyons: J. Pillehotte, 1609

—Leben dess seligen p. Ignatii. Ingolstadt: Elisabeth Angermaier, 1614

—Leben Francisci Borgiae. Ingolstadt: A. Angermaier, 1613

—The life of b. Father Ignatius of Loyola. [St Omer: English College Press] 1616

—The life of the holy patriarch. [St Omer: English College Press] 1622

—Las obras. Madrid: L. Sánchez, 1605

—Princeps christianus. Antwerp: J. Trognaesius, 1603

——Mainz: C. Butgen, 1603

——Cologne: B. Wolter, 1604

——Mainz: C. Butgen, 1604

—Traité de la religion. Douai: J. Bogard, 1610

—Tratado de la religion. Madrid: L. Sánchez, 1601

—Trattato della religione. Brescia: Comp. Bresciana, 1609

—Vida di San Ignacio. Madrid: L. Sánchez, 1622

—La vie du b.p. Ignace de Loyola. Paris: C. Chappelet, 1608

——Pont-à-Mousson: M. Bernard, 1608

——Lyons: L. Savine, for P. Rigaud, 1609

—La vie du . . . pere Ignace de Loyola. Tournai: N. Laurent, 1610

——*See also* Maffei, Giovanni Pietro. La vie du bien-heureux p. Ignace de Loyola. Tournai: 1613

—La vie du pere François de Borja. Douai: B. Bellère, 1603

——*In* Maffei, Giovanni Pietro. La vie du . . . p. Ignace de Loyola. Tournai: 1613

—La vie du reverend père François de Borgia. Lyons: L. Savine, for P. Rigaud, 1609

—Les vies des bien-heureux peres. Arras: G. de La Rivière, 1615

—Vies des saints Ignace Xavier et autres . . . pères. Rouen: 1628

—Vita b. Ignatii. Augsburg: C. Mang, 1616

—Vita beati patris Ignatii. Paris: 1612

——Ypres: F. Bellettus, 1612

—Vita del b.p. Ignatio Loiola. Venice: G. B. Ciotti, 1606

——Naples: S. Bonino, for G. B. Sottile, 1607

—Vita del p. Francesco Borgia. Rome: B. Zannetti, 1616

—Vita del p.s. Ignatio Loiola. Milan: G. B. Bidelli, 1622

—Vita Francisci Borgiae. Mainz: B. Lipp, 1603

—Vita p. Ignatii Loiolae. Cologne: House of Birckmann, for A. Mylius, 1602

Rivera, Luis de. *See* Ribera y Colindres, Luis

Riverius, Lazarus. *See* Rivière, Lazare

RIVERS. *See also* names, e.g. AMAZON

—Browne, Sir T. Pseudodoxia epidemica: or, Enquiries. London: 1646

—Ortiz de Cervantes, J. Señor. El licenciado Juan Ortiz de Cervantes . . . Dize; que catorze leguas. . . . [Madrid? ca. 1620?]

Rivière, Lazare. Methodus curandorum febrium. Paris: O. de Varennes, 1640

——Paris: O. de Varennes, 1641

——Paris: O. de Varennes, 1648

——Gouda: W. van der Hoeve, 1649

—Observationes medicae. [London?] 1646

——London: M. Fletcher, 1646

——Paris: S. Piquet, 1646

—Praxis medica. Paris: O. de Varennes, 1640

——Paris: O. de Varennes, 1644–45

——Paris: O. de Varennes, 1647–48

——Gouda: W. van der Hoeve, 1649

The roaring girle. *See* Middleton, Thomas

Robert earle of Essex. *See* Scott, Thomas

Roberts, Lewes. The merchants mappe of commerce. London:

R. O[ulton, Eliot's Court Press?, T. Harper & F. Kingston]., for R. Mabb, 1638

—The treasure of traffike. London: E[lizabeth]. P[urslowe]., for N. Bourne, 1641

Robin, Jean. Enchiridion isagogicum. Paris: P. de Bresche, 1623

——Paris: P. de Bresche, 1624

Robinson, Henry. Briefe considerations concerning . . . trade. London: M. Simmons, 1649 [i.e., 1650]

—England's safety. London: E[lizabeth]. P[urslowe]., for N. Bourne, 1641

—Liberty of conscience. [London:] 1643

Robles, Antonio Rodríguez de. *See* Rodríguez de Robles, Antonio

Roca, Balthasar Juan. Histoire veritable . . . du b.p. S. Luis Bertran. Tournai: A. Quinqué, 1628

—Historia verdadera . . . del . . . padre S. Luys Bertran. Valencia: J. C. Garriz, 1608

Roca, Juan Antonio Vera Zúñiga y Figueroa, conde de la. Epitome de la vida . . . del . . . emperador Carlos V. Madrid: Widow of A. Martín, 1622

——Madrid: Widow of A. Martín, for A. Pérez, 1624

——Valencia: J. B. Marzal, 1625

——Madrid: L. Sánchez, 1627

——Milan: F. Ghisolfi, for G. B. Bidelli, 1645

——Madrid: J. Sánchez, for P. García, 1649

—Histoire de l'empereur Charles V. Paris: 1633

Roca, Juan de la. *See* Catholic church, Liturgy and ritual. Ritual. Brevis forma administrandi apud Indos sacramenta. Madrid: 1617

—*See the same.* Madrid: 1646

Rocaberti, Diego de. Epitome historico. Majorca: G. Guasp, 1626

——Barcelona: S. de Cormellas, 1628

Rochas, Henry de. La physique reformée. Paris: H. Rochas, 1648

Roco de Córdoba, Francisco. Por Don Martin y Aldrete. Madrid: Widow of J. González, 1636

Rocquigny, Adrian de. La muse chrestienne. [London: G. Miller] 1634

Rodríguez Bustamante, Sebastián. Sebastian Rodriguez Bustamante, contador de la real hazienda. [Madrid: 1625]

—Señor. Sebastian Rodriguez Bustamante, vezino de Santa Marta. [Madrid? 1620?]

Rodríguez de Burgos, Bartolomé. Relacion de la jornada del Brasil. Cadiz: J. de Borja, 1625

Rodríguez de Leon, Juan. El predicador delas gentes. Madrid: María de Quiñones, 1638

Rodríguez de Robles, Antonio. Señor. Antonio de Rodriguez de Robles dize, que quando la Nueva España se gano. . . . [Madrid? 1606?]

—Señor. Antonio Rodriguez de Robles dize, que ahora quarenta y cinquenta anos. . . . [Madrid? 1606?]

—Señor. Antonio Rodriguez de Robles dize, que assi como los mineros sacan la plata. . . . [Madrid? 1606?]

—Señor. Antonio Rodriguez de Robles dize, que aunque de algunos años a esta parte. . . . [Madrid? 1606?]

—Señor. Antonio Rodriguez de Robles dize, que como a V. Magestad . . . es notorio. [Madrid? 1606?]

—Señor. Antonio Rodriguez de Robles dize, que de 9. años . . . han residido. [Madrid? 1606?]

Rodríguez Pizarro, Juan. Señor. Ivan Rodriguez Pizarro. [Madrid? 1650?]

Roelofsz, Roelof. Historica descriptio navigationis. *In* Bry, Johann Theodor de. Indiae Orientalis, pars octava. Frankfurt a.M.: 1607

—Historische Beschreibung der Schiffahrt. *In* Bry, Johann Theodor de. Achter Theil der Orientalischen Indien. Frankfurt a.M.: 1606

—Korte ende waerachtig verhael. *In* Noort, Olivier van. Wonderlijcke voyagie. Amsterdam: 1648

——*In the same.* Amsterdam: 1650

—Zwo underschiedliche newe Schiffarten. Frankfurt a.M.: W. Richter, 1605

Röslin, Elisaeus. Mitternächtige Schiffarth. Oppenheim: H. Galler, for J. T. de Bry, 1611

—Praematurae solis apparitionis. Strassburg: K. Kieffer, 1612

Röslin, Helisaeus. See Röslin, Elisaeus

The rogue. See Alemán, Mateo

Romance en alabansa del tabaco. Barcelona: G. Nogues, 1644

Romancero general. Romancero general, en que se contienen todos los romances. Medina del Campo: J. Godínez de Millis, for P. Ossete, & A. Cuello, at Valladolid, 1602

——Madrid: J. de la Cuesta, for F. López, 1604

——Madrid: J. de la Cuesta, for M. Martínez, 1614

Romancero general, 2a pte. See Madrigal, Miguel de, comp

Romances varios. De diversos autores. Saragossa: P. Lanaja, 1640

—Saragossa: P. Lanaja, 1643

—Madrid: Imprenta Real, 1645

—Madrid: Imprenta Real, 1648

Romanus, Adrianus. Parvum theatrum urbium. Frankfurt a.M.: W. Richter, for Heirs of N. Basse, 1608

La Rome ridicule. See Saint-Amant, Marc Antoine de Gérard, sieur de

Romero, Gonzalo. Señor. Gonzalo Remero. [Madrid? 1625?]

Rondelet, Guillaume. Methodus curandorum omnium morborum. Lyons: J. Lertout, 1601

——[Geneva:] J. Stoër, 1609

——*See also his* Opera omnia medica

—Opera omnia medica. Geneva: S. Gamonet, 1619

——Montpellier: P. & J. Chouët, 1620

——[Montpellier:] P. & J. Chouët, 1628

Rosaccio, Giuseppe. Discorso della nobiltà. Florence: V. Tedesco [1615?]

—Il medico. Venice: P. Farri, 1621

—Mondo elementare, et celeste. Treviso: E. Deuchino, for G. B. Ciotti, at Venice, 1604

—Le sei eta del mondo. Venice: 1602

——*In his* Mondo elementare. Treviso: 1604

——Rome: B. Cochi, & in Bologna, 1618

—Teatro del cielo e della terra. *In his* Mondo elementare. Treviso: 1604

——Treviso: G. Righettini, 1642

—Universale discrittione del teatro del cielo. Venice: G. B. Ciotti, 1620

——Venice: The Ciottis, 1629

Rosarium, dat is, Rosen-Garden. See Owen, John

Rosenberg, Johann Karl. Rhodologia. Strassburg: M. von der Heyden, 1628

——Frankfurt a.M.: H. Palthenius, 1631

ROSES

—Rosenberg, J. K. Rhodologia. Strassburg: 1628

ROSICRUCIANS

—Grick, F. Regula vitae: das ist, Eine heylsame . . . Erinnerung. [Nuremberg:] 1619

Rosier, James. A true relation of the most prosperous voyage. London: [Eliot's Court Press] for G. Bishop, 1605

Rossi, Girolamo. De destillatione. Venice: G. B. Ciotti, 1604

Roteiro e navegação das Indias Occidentales. See Figueiredo, Manuel de

Rowlands, Samuel. Democritus, or Doctor Merryman. London:

[W. Jaggard] for J. Deane, 1607

—Doctor Merrie-man. London: [W. White?] for J. Deane, 1609

— —London: [W. White] for S. Rand, 1614

— —London: J. D[awson]., for S. Rand, 1642

—Doctor Merry-man. London: [W. White] for S. Rand, 1616

— —London: [J. White] for S. Rand, 1618

— —London: A. M[athewes]., for S. Rand, 1619

— —London: A. M[athewes]., for S. Rand, 1623

— —London: A. M[athewes]., for S. Rand, 1627

—A fooles bolt is soon shot. London: [E. Allde?] for G. Loftus [& A. Johnson], 1614

—Good newes. London: [G. Purslowe] for H. Bell, 1622

—Humors antique faces. London: [E. Allde] for H. Rocket, 1605

—Humors looking glasse. London: E. Allde, for W. Ferbrand, 1608

—Humors ordinarie. London: W. Ferbrand [1605?]

— —London: E. Allde, for W. Ferbrand, 1607

— —London: [E. Allde] for T. Archer, 1610

—The knave of clubbes. London: [E. Allde] for W. Ferbrand, 1609

— —London: E. A[llde]., 1611

— —London: E. A[llde]., 161[2?]

—The knave of harts. London: [T. Snodham] for J. Bache, 1612

— —London: T. S[nodham]., for G. Loftus, 1612

— —London: [T. Snodham] for J. Bache, 1613

—The letting of humours blood. London: W. White, 1611

— —London: W. W[hite]., 1613

—Looke to it. London: E. Allde, for W. Ferbrand, & G. Loftus, 1604

— —London: W. W[hite]., for W. Ferbrand; sold by W.

F[erbrand]. & G. L[oftus]., 1604

—The melancholie knight. [London:] R. B[lower]., for G. Loftus, 1615

— —London: G. Loftus, 1615

—More knaves yet? London: [E. Allde, for J. Tapp, 1613?]

— —London: [E. Allde] for J. Tapp [1613]

— —See also Olearius, Adam. Lustige Historie. Leipzig: 1635

—The night raven. London: G. Eld, for J. Deane, & T. Bailey, 1620

— —London: W. J[ones]., for T. Bailey, 1634

—A paire of spy-knaves. [London: G. Purslowe, 1620?]

—A terrible battell. London: [W. Jaggard] for J. Deane [1606?]

—Tis merrie when gossips meete. London: W. W[hite]., for G. Loftus, 1602

— —In his A whole crew of kind gossips. London: 1609

— —London: W. W[hite]., for J. Deane [1613?]

— —London: A. Mathewes, for M. Sparke, 1627

—Well met gossip. London: W. W[hite]., for J. Deane, 1619

—A whole crew of kind gossips. London: [W. Jaggard] for J. Deane, 1609

Rowley, Samuel. The noble souldier. London: [J. Beale] for N. Vavasour, 1634

Rowley, William. A new wonder. London: G. P[urslowe]., for F. Constable, 1632

—See also Middleton, Thomas. A faire quarrell. London: 1617

Le Roy continuant le mesme desir. See Compagnie de la Nouvelle France

Le Roy estant en son Conseil. See France. Sovereigns, etc., 1643–1715 (Louis XIV)

Royal College of Physicians of London. Pharmacopoea Londinensis. London: E. Griffin, for J. Marriott, 1618

— —London: [E. Griffin] for J. Marriott, 1618

— —London: [Eliot's Court Press] for J. Marriott, 1627

— —London: J. Marriott, 1632

— —London: J. Marriott, 1639

— —London: W. DuGard, for S. Bowtell, 1650

—See also Culpeper, Nicholas. A physicall directory. London: 1649

La royale chymie. See Croll, Oswald

Rúa, Fernando de. Por Don Juan Meneses. Madrid: A. de Parra, 1934 [i.e., 1634]

Rubeus, Hieronymus. See Rossi, Girolamo

Rubio, Antonio. Commentarii in universam Aristotelis Logicam. Valencia: 1607

—Logica mexicana. Cologne: A. Mylius (House of Birckmann), 1605

— —Lyons: S. Pillehotte, 1611

— —Paris: J. Petit-Pas, 1615

— —Lyons: J. Pillehotte, 1617

— —Lyons: A. Pillehotte, 1620 (2)

— —Lyons: J. Pillehotte, 1625

— —Brescia: L. Britannico, 1626

Rudyerd, Sir Benjamin. A speech concerning a West Indie association. London: 1641

—Two speeches in Parliament. London: B. A[lsop]., for H. Seile, 1642

Ruiters, Dierick. See Ruyters, Dierick

Ruíz de Alarcón y Mendoza, Juan. Comedias, pte 1a. Madrid: J. González, 1628

—Comedias, pte 2a. Barcelona: S. de Cormellas, 1634

—Verdad sospechosa. In Vega Carpio, Lope Félix de. Comedias, pte 22. Saragossa: 1630

— —In the author's Comedias, pte 2a. Barcelona: 1634

Ruiz de Montoya, Antonio. Arte, y bocabulario de la lengua Guarani. Madrid: J. Sánchez, 1640

—Catecismo de la lengua guarani. Madrid: D. Díaz de la Carrera, 1640

—Conquista espiritual. Madrid: Imprenta Real, 1639

—Haseme mandado, que assi

——Rouen: J. Berthelin, 1650

—Ternarius bezoardicorum. Erfurt: Heirs of E. Mechler, 1618

—Ternarius ternariorum. Erfurt: Heirs of E. Mechler, for J. Birckner, 1630

Sala, Gaspar. Secretos publicos. [Barcelona? 1641?]

—Secrets publichs. [Barcelona: 1641]

——[Barcelona: 1641?]

—Secrets publiques. Rouen: J. Berthelin, 1642

—Segredos publicos. Lisbon: L. de Anveres, for L. de Queiros, 1641

Sala y Berart, Gaspar. *See* Sala, Gaspar

Salazar, Ambrosio de. Almoneda general. Paris: A. DuBreuil, 1612

——Paris: T. DuBray, 1615

—Inventaire general. Paris: A. DuBrueil, 1612

——Paris: T. DuBray, 1615

SALAZAR, AMBROSIO DE

—Núñez Correa, J. Resolucion y resumen del estado. [Madrid? 1612?]

Salazar, Pedro de. Coronica y historia de la fundacion. Madrid: J. Flamenco, for Imprenta Real, 1622 [i.e., 1612]

Saldías, Pedro de. Tabla para la reducion de barras de plata. Seville: F. de Lyra, 1637

Salinas y Córdova, Buenaventura de. Memorial del padre. Madrid: 1639

—Memorial, informe, y manifiesto. [Madrid: ca. 1646]

Salmerón, Marcos. Recuerdos historicos y politicos. Valencia: Heirs of C. Garriz, for B. Nogués, 1646

SALT

—Hoorn, Netherlands. Ordinances, etc. Provisionele ordre ende reglement. Hoorn: 1622

—Netherlands (United Provinces, 1581–1795). Staten Generaal. Copia. De Staten Generael. [The Hague? 1627?]

——Ordre by de . . . Staten Generael . . . ghemaeckt op

. . . het sout halen in West-Indien. Amsterdam: 1621

—Waerschouwinghe op de West-Indissche Compagnie. [The Hague? 1622]

SALT MINES & MINING—MEXICO

—Rodríguez de Robles, A. Señor. Antonio Rodriguez de Robles dize, que aunque de algunos años a esta parte . . . . [Madrid? 1606?]

Saltmarsh, John. The smoke in the temple. London: Ruth Raworth, for G. Calvert, 1646

Saltonstall, Charles. The navigator. London: [B. Alsop & T. Fawcet] for G. Hurlock, 1636

——London: [B. Alsop & T. Fawcet?] for G. Hurlock, 1642

SALVADOR, BRAZIL. *See also* BAHIA, BRAZIL

—Beschryvinge van 't in-nemen van . . . Salvador. Amsterdam: 1624

—Relation de la prinse. Paris: 1624

SALVADOR, BRAZIL—CHURCH HISTORY

—Teellinck, W. Davids danckbaerheyt. Middelburg: 1624

SALVADOR, BRAZIL—HISTORY

—Brassillische Relation. inn America gelegen. Augsburg: 1624

—Crosse, W. Belgiaes troubles. London: 1625

—Guerreiro, B. Jornado dos vassalos da coroa de Portugal. Lisbon: 1625

—La quarta carta, y verdadera relacion. Valladolid: 1625

San Antonio, Gabriel Quiroga de. Breve y verdadera relacion. Valladolid: P. Lasso, 1604

San Felipe de Austria, Venezuela. Señor. El cabildo, justicia, y regimiento. [Madrid? 1630?]

San Juan, Puerto Rico (Diocese). Synod, 1645. Constituciones synodales. Madrid: Catalina de Barrio y Angulo, 1647

San Román de Ribadeneyra, Antonio. Historia general de la Yndia Oriental. Valladolid: L. Sánchez, for D. Pérez, 1603

SAN VICENTE STRAIT. *See* LE MAIRE STRAIT

Sánchez, Alfonso. De rebus Hispaniae anacephalaeosis. Alcalá de Henares: A. Duplastre, 1634

Sánchez, Antonio. Todo el pleyto que siguen los dueños de barras del Pirù. [Madrid? 1637]

Sánchez, Francisco. De multum nobili et prima universali scientia quod nihil scitur. Frankfurt a.M.: J. Berner, 1618

—Opera medica. Toulouse: P. Bosc, 1636

—Quod nihil scitur. *In his* De multum nobili et prima universali scientia quod nihil scitur. Frankfurt a.M.: 1618

——*In his* Opera medica. Toulouse: 1636

——*In his* Tractatus philosophici. Rotterdam: 1649

—Tractatus philosophici: Quod nihil scitur. Rotterdam: A. Leers, 1649

Sánchez de Aguilar, Pedro. Informe contra idolorum cultores del obispado de Yucatán. Madrid: Widow of J. González, 1639

Sánchez de Espejo, Andrés. Discurso político del estado. [Granada:] V. Alvarez [1646]

SÁNCHEZ DE HUELVA, ALONSO

—Aldrete, B. J. Varias antiguedades de España. Antwerp: 1614

Sanctius, Alfonsus. *See* Sánchez, Alfonso

Sanctorius, Sanctorius. *See* Santorio, Santorio

Sande, Johan van den. Kort begrijp der Nederlandtsche historien. Amsterdam: J. Hartgers, 1650 (2)

—Nederlandtsche historie. Groningen: H. Mucerus, for G. Sybes, at Leeuwarden, 1650

—Nederlandtsche historie. *In* Reyd, Everhard van. Historie

der Nederlantscher oorlogen. Groningen: 1650

—Trouhertighe vermaninghe. [Amsterdam?] 1605 (2)

— —[Amsterdam? D. C. Troost?] 1605

Sandoval, Francisco de. Advertencia en fabor . . . del arbitrio. [Madrid? ca. 1610?]

—Señor. Por aver entendido quan del servicio. [Madrid? 1610?]

—Señor. Si conviniere al servicio de V. M. [Madrid? 1610?]

Sandoval, Prudencio de, Bp. Historia de la vida . . . del Emperador Carlos V. Pamplona: B. Paris, 1614

— —Barcelona: S. de Cormellas, 1618

— —Barcelona: S. de Cormellas, 1625

— —Pamplona: B. Paris, for P. Escuer, at Saragossa, 1634

—Vida y hechos del emperador Carlos Quinto, pte 1a–2a. Valladolid: S. de Cañas, 1604

— —Valladolid: S. de Cañas, 1606

Sandoval y Guzmán, Sebastián de. El doctor don Sebastian de Sandoval y Guzman . . . digo, que de pedimiento mio embio V. A. orden. [Madrid? 1635]

—El doctor don Sebastian de Sandoval y Guzman . . . digo, que las barras . . . se bolvieron a ensenyar. [Madrid: 1634]

—Epilogo de las pretensiones. [Madrid: 1634?]

—Pretensiones de la villa imperial de Potosi. Madrid: Widow of J. González, 1634

Sandys, Sir Edwin. Europae speculum. The Hague: [for M. Sparke, at London] 1629

— —London: T. Cotes, for M. Sparke, 1632 (2)

— —London: T. Cotes, for M. Sparke, & G. Hutton, 1637

— —London: T. Cotes, for M. Sparke, 1638

—Relation de l'estat de la religion. Geneva: P. Aubert, 1626

— —Amsterdam: L. Elzevier, 1641

—A relation of the state of reli-

gion. London: V. Simmes, for S. Waterson, 1605

— —London: [G. & L. Snowdon] for S. Waterson, 1605

— —London: S. Waterson, 1605 [i.e., W. Stansby? 1622?]

—Relatione dello stato della religione. [Mirandola?] 1625

Sandys, George. A paraphrase upon the divine poems. [London: J. Legat, for A. Hebb] 1638

— —[London:] 1648

— —London: O. D., 1648

—A paraphrase upon the Psalmes of David. London: [A. Hebb] 1636

—A relation of a journey. London: [R. Field] for W. Barrett, 1615

— —London: [R. Field] for W. Barrett, 1621

— —London: [T. Cotes] for R. Allott, 1627

— —London: [G. Miller] for R. Allott, 1632

— —London: [T. Cotes] for A. Crooke, 1637

SANDYS, GEORGE

—Drayton, M. The battaile of Agincourt. London: 1627

Sansovino, Francesco. *See the following:*

—Archaio-ploutos. Containing, ten following bookes. London: 1619

—Mexía, Pedro. Selva di varia lettione. Venice: 1611

— —Selva rinovata di varia lettione. Venice: 1616, '15

— — —Venice: 1626

— — —Venice: 1638

SANTA CATALINA

—Relacion del sucesso que tuvo Francisco Diaz Pimienta. Madrid: 1642

Santa Fé, Colombia. *See* Bogotá

Santa María, Juan de. *See* Juan de Santa María, fray

Santander, Juan de. Señor. Fray Juan de Santander . . . comissario general. [Madrid? 1625?]

See also the following:

—Benavides, Alonso de. Memorial que fray Ivan de Santander . . . presenta. Madrid: 1630

— —Relatio quam Philippo iv . . . exhibuit reverendiss. p. f. Joannes de Santander. Salzburg: 1634

— —Relatio, welche Philippo iv . . . . und r. p. f. Joannes de Santander . . . ubergeben lassen. Salzburg: [1634?]

— — —Requeste oft Verhael d'welck den . . . Pater. . . presenteert. Antwerp: 1631

— — —Requeste remonsrative au Roy. Brussels: 1631

SANTIAGO DE CUBA

—Quiñones, D. de. Oracion funebre. Valladolid: 1645

Santissimo padre. Fray Juan de Silva. *See* Silva, Juan de

SANTO DOMINGO. *See also* HISPANIOLA

—Khunrath, C. Medulla destillatoria et medica. Hamburg: 1601

—Ruland, J. D. Inauguralis de lue . . . venerea disputatio. [Frankfurt a.M.: 1636]

SANTO DOMINGO—HISTORY

—Doglioni, G. N. Compendio historico universale. Venice: 1601

—Victoria, F. de. Por los regidores de la ciudad de la Habana. Madrid: 1633

SANTO DOMINGO—HISTORY, NAVAL

—Cárdenas, A. de. A speech, or complaint. London: 1643

—Great Britain. Sovereigns, etc., 1625–1649 (Charles I). A proclamation prohibiting the buying or disposing of any the lading. [Oxford: 1643]

Santo Tomé, Venezuela. Señor. La ciudad de Santo Tome. [Madrid? ca. 1620?]

Santorio, Santorio. Methodi vitandorum errorum omnium . . . libri quindecim. Venice: F. Bariletti, 1603

— —Geneva: P. Aubert, 1630

— —Venice: M. A. Brogiollo, 1630

— —Geneva: P. Aubert, 1631

SÃO PAULO, BRAZIL

—La prise de l'isle de Santo Paulo. Lyons: 1631

—Rivière, L. Observationes medicae. Paris: 1646

—Rosaccio, G. Il medico. Venice: 1621

—Ruland, M. Curationum empiricarum . . . centuriae decem. Lyons: 1628

—Schenck von Grafenberg, J. Paratērēseōn, sive Observationum medicarum . . . volumen. Frankfurt a.M.: 1609

—Scholtz, L. Consiliorum medicinalium. Hanau: 1610

—Schyron, J. Methodi medendi . . . libri quatuor. Montpellier: 1609

—Severino, M. A. De recondita abscessum natura. Naples: 1632

—Silvaticus, J. B. Controversiae numero centum. Frankfurt a.M.: 1601

—Spinelli, G. P. Lectiones aureae. Bari: 1605

—Vigna, D. Animadversiones. Pisa: 1625

—Wittich, J. Von dem Ligno Guayaco. [Arnstadt:] 1603

—Woodall, J. The surgions mate. London: 1617

—Zecchi, G. Liber primus Consultationum medicinalium. Rome: 1601

—Zimara, M. A. Antrum magicomedicum. Frankfurt a.M.: 1625

SASSAFRAS

—Alonso y de los Ruyses de Fontecha, J. Diez previlegios para mugeres preñadas. Alcalá de Henares: 1606

—Besard, J. B. Antrum philosophicum. Augsburg: 1617

—Brunner, B. Consilia medica. Halle: 1617

—Cortesi, G. B. Pharmacopoeia, seu Antidotarium messanense. Messina: 1629

—Dispensatorium chymicum. Frankfurt a.M.: 1626

—Guidi, G. Ars medicinalis. Venice: 1611

—Guillaumet, T. Traicté de la maladie nouvellement appelee cristaline. Lyons: 1611

—Hobbes, S. Margarita chyrurgica. London: 1610

—Hollings, E. Medicamentorum oeconomia nova. Ingolstadt: 1610

—Libavius, A. Syntagma selectorum. Frankfurt a.M.: 1611

—Loyseau, G. De internorum externorumque ferme omnium curatione libellus. Bordeaux: 1617

—Mérindol, A. Ars medica. Aix-en-Province: 1633

—Messina. Ospedale di Santa Maria della Pietà. Antidotarium speciale. Venice: 1642

—Müller, P. Miracula chymica et misteria medica. [Wittenberg:] 1611

—Pascal, J. Discours contenant la conference de la pharmacie. Béziers: 1616

— —Traicté contenant la pharmacie chymique. Lyons: 1633

—Potier, P. Insignes curationes. Cologne: 1625

— —Insignium curationum . . . centuria secunda. Bologna: 1622

—Scarioni, F. Centuria seconda de' secreti mirabili. Viterbo: 1641

—Schyron, J. Methodi medendi . . . libri quatuor. Montpellier: 1609

—Wittich, J. Von dem Ligno Guayaco. [Arnstadt:] 1603

—Woodall, J. The surgions mate. London: 1617

—Zimara, M. A. Antrum magicomedicum. Frankfurt a.M.: 1625

SASSAFRAS—DRAMA

—Jonson, B. Volpone. London: 1607

Sassonia, Ercole. De lue venerea. *In his* Pantheum medicinae selectum. Frankfurt a.M.: [1603?]

— —*In his* Opera practica. Padua: 1639

—De melancholia tractatus. Venice: A. Polo [& F. Bolzetta], 1620

—Opera practica. Padua: F. Bolzetta, 1639

—Pantheum medicinae selectum. Frankfurt a.M.: Palthenius Office [1603?]

Satiro-mastix. *See* Dekker, Thomas

Saturnalia. *See titles under* Schrijver, Pieter

Saturni ephemerides. *See* Isaacson, Henry

Satyre contre les charlatans. *See* Sonnet, Thomas, sieur de Courval

La satyre d'Euphormion. *See* Barclay, John

Satyre Ménippée. Satyre Menippée. [Paris?] 1604

— —[Paris?] 1612

— —[Paris?] 1632

— —[Leyden?] 1649

Satyre Ménippée. English. Englands bright honour. London: J. Deane, 1602

Les satyres d'Euphormion. *See* Barclay, John

Satyrical essayes. *See* Stephens, John

Satyricon. *See* Barclay, John

Saulnier, Jean. Cosmologie du monde. Paris: M. Daniel, 1618

Sauls prohibition staide. *See* Price, Daniel

Saxonia, Hercules. *See* Sassonia, Ercole

Scaliger, Julius Caesar. Exotericarum exercitationum liber. Frankfurt a.M.: Wechel Office, for C. Marne, & Heirs of J. Aubry, 1601

— —Frankfurt a.M.: [Wechel Office, for] C. Marne, & Heirs of J. Aubry, 1607

— —Frankfurt a.M.: [Wechel Office, for] Heirs of C. Marne (J. & A. Marne), 1612

— —Lyons: Widow of A. Harsy, 1615

— —Hanau: Wechel Office, for D. & D. Aubry, & C. Schleich, 1620

— —Hanau: Wechel Office, for C. Schleich, 1634

Scalona Agüero, Gaspar. *See* Escalona y Agüero, Gaspar de

Scarioni, Francesco. Centuria seconda de' secreti mirabili. Viterbo, Bologna, Verona, Brescia, & Piacenza: G. A. Ardizzoni, 1641

—Vox populi. Or Newes from Spain. [London? 1620] (3)

——[London:] 1620 (5)

—Vox populi. Or News from Spaine. [Utrecht?] 1620 [i.e., 1624]

—Vox populi, pt 2. 'Gorkum: A. Janss' [i.e., London: W. Jones] 1624

——'Gorkum: A. Janss' [i.e., London: N. Okes] 1624 (2)

——'Gorkum: A. Janss' [i.e., London: N. Okes & J. Dawson] 1624

—Vox populi, Vox Dei. Vox regis. [The Netherlands: 1624]

—Vox regis. [Utrecht: A. van Herwijck, 1624] (2)

—Vox regis, of De stemme des Conincks. Utrecht: A. van Herwijck, 1624

—Workes. Utrecht: 1624

—*See also* Boanerges. or The humble supplication. [London:] 1624

—*See also* Hexham, Henry. A tongue-combat. London: 1623

—*See also* Zwey unterschiedliche nohtwendige Bedencken. [The Hague?] 1621

Scotto, Benedetto. Deux cartes maritimes septentrionales. Paris: N. Rousset, 1620

——*In his* Globe maritime. Paris: 1622

—Globe maritime. Paris: J. Bessin, 1622

Scottus, Benedictus. *See* Scotto, Benedetto

The scourge of baseness. *See* Taylor, John, the Water-poet

The scourge of folly. *See* Davies, John

Scribanius, Carolus. L'Apocalipse hollandoise. 'Villeneuve: J. Le Vray' [i.e., The Netherlands?] 1626

—Apocalypsis Holandica. [Strassburg?] 'Parnassus Office', 1626

—Aussführliches wolgegründetes, politisches Bedencken. [Augsburg?] 1629 (2 variant spellings)

—Civilium apud Belgas bellorum initia. [Antwerp: M. Nuyts] 1627

—Copia de un papel. Seville: S. Fajardo, 1626

—Discours d'estat. Brussels: J. Bernard, & J. Pierre, 1628

—Ghereformeerden Hollandschen apocalypsis. *In his* Den vernieuden waer-segger. Amsterdam: [1626?]

—Holländisch apocalypsis. Augsburg: A. Aperger [1625]

——'New Newenstatt: Vielhüppens Warsagern' [i.e., Augsburg?] 1626

—Den Hollantschen apocalypsis. *In his* Veridicus Belgicus. [Antwerp: 1624]

—Den Hollantschen apocalypsis. 'Nieustadt: H. Waerseggher' [i.e., Leyden?] 1625

——'Nieustadt: H. Waerseggher' [i.e., Leyden?] 1626

——[The Netherlands:] 1626

—Den Hollantschen gereformeerden apocalypsis. *In his* Den Neder-landtschen waersegger. [The Netherlands: 1625]

——*In his* Den oor-sprongh . . . Amsterdam: [1625]

—Le manifeste hollandoise. [Amsterdam? 1627?]

—Den Nederlandtschen waerzegger. [The Netherlands: 1625?]

—Den Neder-landtschen waersegger. [The Netherlands: 1625]

—Den oor-sprongh, voortgangh ende gewenscht eynde. Amsterdam: J. Veselaer, & B. Janszoon [1625]

—Reformata apocalypsis Batavica. *In his* Civilium apud Belgas bellorum initia. [Antwerp:] 1627

—Remonstrant hollandois. *In his* Den Nederlandschen waerzegger. [The Netherlands: 1625?]

—Spaenschen raedt. *See* Moerbeeck, Jan Andries. Spaenschen raedt. The Hague: 1626

—Veridicus Belgicus. [Antwerp: M. Nuyts, 1624]

——[Antwerp: M. Nuyts] 1626

—Den vernieuden waer-segger. Amsterdam: J. Veselaer, & B. Janszoon [1626?]

—Weit und tieffsinnig Bedencken. [Augsburg?] 1628

Scriverius, Petrus. *See* Schrijver, Pieter

The sculler. *See* Taylor, John, the Water-poet

The sea-beacon. *See* Blaeu, Willem Janszoon

A sea grammar. *See* Smith, Capt. John

The sea-mirrour. *See* Blaeu, Willem Janszoon

SEA-POWER. *See also* FREEDOM OF THE SEAS

—Hagthorpe, J. England's-exchequer. London: 1625

—Rodríguez Bustamante, S. Sebastian Rodriguez Bustamante, contador de la real hazienda. [Madrid: 1625]

SEAFARING LIFE

—Udemans, G. C. Geestelick compas. Dordrecht: 1637

——Geestelyck roer. Gouda: 1638

The seamans kalendar. *See* Tapp, John

The sea-mans practice. *See* Norwood, Richard

The seamans secrets. *See* Davys, John

Sebastian Rodriquez Bustamante, contador de la real hazienda. *See* Rodríguez Bustamante, Sebastián

La secchia. *See* Tassoni, Alessandro

[Das sechste . . . Hundert Episteln.] *See* Zeiller, Martin

Das sechste Theil Americae. *See* Benzoni, Girolamo

Sechste Theil, Kurtze, warhafftige Relation. *See* Hulsius, Levinus

Sechster Theil der Orientalischen Indien. *See* Marees, Pieter de

Sechster Theil; Kurtze, warhafftige Relation. *See* Hulsius, Levinus

Die xxvi. [i.e., sechsundzwanzigste] Schiff-Fahrt. *See* La Peyrère, Isaac de

Die sechtzehende Schifffahrt. *See* Schouten, Willem Corneliszoon

The second day. *See* Du Bartas,

Señor. Relacion que Juan Recio de Leon . . . presento a V. magestad. *See* Recio de León, Juan

Señor. Rodrigo Barnueuo de la compañia de Jesus. *See* Barnuevo, Rodrigo

Señor. Sebastian Rodriguez Bustamante, vezino de Santa Marta. *See* Rodríguez Bustamante, Sebastián

Señor. Si conviniere al servicio de V. M. *See* Sandoval, Francisco de

Señor. Tomas de Cardona . . . presento . . . la proposicion siguiente. *See* Cardona, Tomás de

Señor. Tres cosas son las que obligan a credito. *See* Suárez de Gamboa, Juan

Señor. Un libelo infamatorio se ha impresso . . . su fecha en Potosí. *See* Elías, Juan, fray

Señor. Un vasallo de V. Magestad . . . que ha estado en las Indias. *See* Spain. Sovereigns, etc., 1621–1665 (Philip IV), addressee

Sensus librorum sex. *See* Grotius, Hugo

Sentencias de revista . . . sobre la paga y consignacion. *See* Spain. Consejo de las Indias

Sepan quantos esta carta vieran. *See* Seville. Consulado

La sepmaine. *See* Du Bartas, Guillaume de Salluste, seigneur

Septentrio novantiquus. *See* Megiser, Hieronymus

Sepúlveda, Juan Ginés de. Apologia. *In his* Opera. Cologne: 1602

—Opera. Cologne: House of Birckmann, for A. Mylius, 1602

SEPÚLVEDA, JUAN GINÉS DE
—Casas, B. de las, Bp. Conquista dell'Indie Occidentali. Venice: 1644

SERICULTURE—MEXICO
—Herrera, G. A. de. Agricultura general. Madrid: 1620

SERICULTURE—VIRGINIA
—Bonoeil, J. His Majesties gracious letter. London: 1622

— —Observations to be followed. London: 1620

—Williams, E. Virginia's discovery of silke-wormes. London: 1650

Sermam que prego o padre frey Gaspar d'Ascenção. *See* Gaspar d'Asenção

Sermam, que pregou . . . Antonio Vieira. *See* Vieira, Antonio

Sermão . . . . *See titles under* Braga, Bernardo de

Sermão da quarta domingo da quaresma. *See* Cristovão de Lisboa

Sermão no procissão de graças. *See* Correa, Simão

Sermão que fez o padre Bartolameu Guerreiro. *See* Guerreiro, Bartholomeu

Sermon at Paules Crosse. *See* King, John, Bp

A sermon at the . . . inauguration of King James. *See* Crakanthorpe, Richard

Sermon en lengua de Chile. *See* Valdivia, Luis de

A sermon preached at Plimmoth. *See* Cushman, Robert

A sermon preached in London. *See* Crashaw, William

A sermon preached to . . . Sir Thomas Warner. *See* Featley, John

Sermon predicado . . . a las obsequias de . . . Pedro de Irramain. *See* Palma Fajardo, Francisco de

A sermon upon the eighth verse. *See* Donne, John

Sermones fideles. *See* Bacon, Francis

The sermons. *See* Hieron, Samuel

Serrano, Martín. Copia de un memorial. [Madrid? 1620?]

Serres, Jean de. A general inventorie of the history of France. London: G. Eld, 1607

—A generall historie of France. London: G. Eld, 1611

— —London: G. Eld, & M. Fletcher, 1624 (2)

—Inventaire general. [Paris:] P. Marceau, 1606

— —Geneva: P. Aubert, 1619

— —Paris: S. Thiboust, 1619

— —Paris: P. Mettayer, 1627

— —Paris: C. Morlot, J. Petrinae, & I. Dedin, 1636

— —Paris: G. Pelé, 1636

— —Paris: A. Alazart, J. Villery, C. Besongne, & J. Promé, 1643

— —Geneva: J. Stoer, 1645

— —Paris: C. Marette, 1647

— —Rouen: L. DuMesnil, 1647

— —Rouen: C. Malassis, 1647

—Le veritable inventaire. Paris: A. Cotinet, & J. Roger, & F. Preuveray, 1648

Serres, Olivier de, seigneur du Pradel. The perfect use of silkwormes. London: F. Kingston, for R. Sergier, & C. Purset, 1607

—Le théatre d'agriculture. Paris: A. Saugrain, 1603

— —Paris: A. Saugrain, 1605

— —Paris: J. Berjon, 1608

— —Paris: A. Saugrain, 1608

— —Geneva: M. Berjon, 1611

— —Paris: A. Saugrain, 1615

— —Paris: A. Saugrain, 1617

— —[Geneva:] P. & J. Chouët, 1619

— —Rouen: J. Osmont, 1623

— —Rouen: R. Valentin, 1635

— —Geneva: P. & J. Chouët, 1639

— —Rouen: J. Berthelin, 1646

Servants on horse-back. *See* Golding, William

Servicios de la Compañia de Jesus. *See* Jesuits

Servicios que . . . hà hecho el capitan. *See* Villagrá, Gaspar Pérez de

Los servicios que refiero a V[uestra]. M[agestad]. en el memorial. *See* Recio de León, Juan

Ses poincten welcke by de . . . Staten . . . zijn vast gestelt. [The Hague? 1649?]

Sesse, Josepe de. Libro de la cosmographia universal. Saragossa: J. de Larumbe, 1619

T'seste deel . . . van het Historisch verhael. *See* Wassenaer, Nicolaes van

Het ses'thiende deel . . . van het Historisch verhael. *See* Wassenaer, Nicolaes van

Settala, Lodovico. Animadversionum . . . libri novem. Dordrecht: V. Caimax, 1650
—Animadversionum . . . libri septem. Milan: G. B. Bidelli, 1614
— —Strassburg: E. Zetzner, 1625
— —Milan: G. B. Bidelli, 1626
— —Naples: L. Scorigio, 1627
— —Padua: G. Tuilio, for P. Frambotti, 1628
The seven champions of Christendome. *See* Kirke, John
Seven verscheyden tsamensprekinghe. *See* Mexía, Pedro. De verscheyden lessen. Amsterdam: 1617
T'sevende-deel . . . van het Historisch verhael. *See* Wassenaer, Nicolaes van
Het seventiende ghedeelt . . . van het Historisch verhael. *See* Wassenaer, Nicolaes van
Severall questions of serious . . . consequence. *See* Cotton, John
Severim de Faria, Manuel. Relaçam universal do que succedeo em Portugal. Lisbon: G. da Vinha, 1626
Severino, Marco Aurelio. De recondita abscessum natura. Naples: O. Baltrano, 1632
— —Frankfurt a.M.: J. Beyer, 1643
Seville. Por el comercio de la ciudad de Sevilia. [Seville? 1650?]
—Señor. La ciudad de Sevilla. [Seville? 1630?]
Seville. Casa de la Moneda. El Fiscal de su Magestad. [Seville? 1617?]
Seville. Consulado. Por el consulado de Sevilla. Madrid: Widow of J. González, 1634
—Sepan quantos esta carta vieran. [Seville? 1618]
Seville. Junta del Almirantazgo. Por la Junta del Real Almirantazgo. [Seville? 164–?]
Sfera. *See* Sacro Bosco, Joannes de
Sgambata, Scipio. Eloge du p. Joseph Anquieta. Paris: S. Cramoisy, 1624
—Elogio del p. Giuseppe An-

chieta. Naples: Il Scoriggio, 1631
Shakespeare, William. Comedies, histories, and tragedies. London: I. Jaggard, & E. Blount, for W. Jaggard, E. Blount, J. Smethwick & W. Aspley, 1623
— —London: T. Cotes, for R. Allott, 1632
—Comedy of errors. *In his* Comedies . . . . London: 1623
—The historie of Henrie the fourth [Pt 1]. London: [J. Windet] for M. Law, 1608
— —London: J. Norton, for W. Sheares, 1632
—The history of Henrie the fourth [Pt 1]. London: V. Simmes, for M. Law, 1604
— —London: W. W[hite]., for M. Law, 1613
— —London: J. Norton, for H. Perry, 1639
—The history of King Henrie the fourth [Pt 1]. London: T. P[urfoot]., for M. Law, 1622
—The merry wives of Windsor. London: T. H[arper]., for R. Meighen, 1630
—A most pleasaunt . . . comedie, of syr John Falstaffe, and the merrie wives of Windsor. London: T. C[reede]., for A. Johnson, 1602
— —London: [W. Jaggard,] for A. Johnson [i.e., T. Pavier] 1619
—Tempest. *In his* Comedies . . . . London: 1623
—Twelfth night. *In his* Comedies . . . . London: 1623
Sharpe, Edward. Britaines busse. London: W. Jaggard, 1615
—England's royall fishing revived. London: [W. Jaggard] for N. Bourne, 1630
Sharpham, Edward. Cupids whirligig. London: E. Allde, for A. Johnson, 1607
— —London: T. C[reede]., for A. Johnson, 1611
— —London: T. Creede, & B. Alsop, for A. Johnson, 1616
— —London: T. H[arper]., for R. Meighen, 1630

—The fleire. London: [E. Allde] for F. B[urton]., 1607
— —London: [T. Purfoot] for N. Butter, 1610
— —London: [T. Snodham] for N. Butter, 1615
— —London: B. A[lsop]., & T. Fawcet, for N. Butter, 1631
Shepard, Thomas. The clear sun-shine of the Gospel. London: R. Cotes, for J. Bellamy, 1648
—The day-breaking . . . of the Gospell. *See* Wilson, John, supposed author
—New Englands lamentation. London: G. Miller, 1645
—The sincere convert. London: T. Paine, for H. Blunden, 1640
— —London: T. Paine, for M. Simmons, 1640
— —London: T. P[aine]., for M. S[immons]., & H. Blunden, 1640
— —London: T. P[aine]., & M. S[immons]., for H. Blunden, 1641
— —London: T. P[aine]., & M. S[immons]., for H. Blunden, 1642
— —London: T. P[aine]., & M. S[immons]., for H. Blunden, 1643
— —London: M. Simmons, for J. Sweeting, 1646
— —Edinburgh: G. Lithgow, 1647
— —London: R. Cotes, for J. Sweeting, 1648
— —London: M. Simmons, for J. Sweeting, 1650
— —London: M. S[immons]., for J. Sweeting, 1650
Sheppard, Samuel. The committee-man curried. [London?] 1647
A shilling, or The travailes. *See* Taylor, John, the Water-poet
Shinkin ap Shone, pseud. The honest Welch-cobler. [London:] 'M. Shinkin', for 'S. Taffie', 1647
SHIPPING
—A letter written to the governours. London: 1603
—Netherlands (United Prov-

inces, 1581–1795). Staten Generaal. Ordonnantie, dienende tot versekeringe vande schepen. The Hague: 1622

——Placcaet ende ordonnantie. The Hague: 1623

——Placcaet ende ordonnantie opte wapeninghe. The Hague: 1607

——Placcaet opte grootte, equippagie, monture . . . der schepen. The Hague: 1627

—Spain. Laws, statutes, etc., 1556–1598 (Philip II). Ordenanças para remedio de los daños . . . de los navios que navegan a las Indias Ocidentales. Madrid: 1619

—Teixeira, J. The true historie. London: 1602

—Velasco, D. de. Señor. Descubrimiento del camino. [Madrid? 1620?]

—Vitoria Baraona, F. de. El capitan Francisco de Vitoria, vezino de la puebla de los Angeles. [Madrid: 1639]

——Señor. El capitan Francisco de Vitoria Baraona dize. [Madrid? 1634?] (634/140)

SHIPPING—LAW. See MARITIME LAW

SHIPS

—Pereira Corte Real, J. Discursos sobre la navegacion. [Madrid? 1622?]

SHIPWRECKS

—Relacion de la gente de mar. [Madrid? 1623?]

—Teixeira Pinto, B. Naufragio que passou Jorge Dalbuquerque Coelho. Lisbon: 1601

Shirley, James. Changes. London: G. P[urslowe]., for W. Cooke, 1632

—The constant maid. London: J. Raworth, for R. Whitaker, 1640

A short discourse of the New-found-land. Dublin: Society of Stationers, 1623

A short discoverie of the coasts . . . of America. See Castell, William

A short discoverie of the unobserved dangers . . . of physicke. See Cotta, John

A short story. See Winthrop, John

A short treatise of magneticall bodies. See Ridley, Mark

Sibbes, Richard. Light from heaven. London: E. Purslowe & R. Badger, for N. Bourne & R. Harford, 1638 (2)

Sibelius, Caspar. Of the conversion of five thousand. London: J. Hammond, for Hannah Allen, 1650

Siebende Schiffahrt in . . . Guineam. See Marees, Pieter de

Siebende Schiffart. See Marees, Pieter de

Siebender Theil der Orientalischen Indien. See Spilbergen, Joris van

Die siebenzehende Schiffart. See Spilbergen, Joris van

Le siege de la ville de Groll. [Paris?] 1627

—Paris: P. Auvray, 1627

Siet den getaanden speck. See Veen, Jan van der

Las siete partidas nuevamente glosadas. See Castile. Laws, statutes, etc., 1252–1284 (Alfonso X)

Siglo de oro. See Valbuena, Bernardo de

Silenus Alcibiadis. See Cats, Jacob

SILK CULTURE. See SERICULTURE

Silva, Antonio Telles da. Successo della guerra de portugueses. [Lisbon? 1647?]

—Sucesso della guerra de' Portoghesi. [Rome? 1647?]

Silva, Juan de. Advertencias importantes. Madrid: Widow of F. Correa Montenegro, 1621

—Santissimo padre. Fray Juan de Silva. [Madrid: 1623]

Silva, Marcos de, Bp. See Marcos da Lisboa, Bp

Silvaticus, Joannes Baptista. Controversiae numero centum. Frankfurt a.M.: Heirs of A. Wechel, for C. de Marne & Heirs of J. Aubry, 1601

—De unicornu. Bergamo: C. Ventura, 1605

Silveira, Simão Estaço da. See Estaço da Silveira, Simão

SILVER

—Advertencias para el papel . . . de la plata. [Madrid? ca. 1635?]

—Brandon, L. Excelmo señor. Siendo la materia del valor de la plata. Madrid: 1621

——Señor. Medios para V. Magestad ahorrar lo mucho. [Madrid: 1622?]

—Cárdenas, A. de. A speech, or complaint. London: 1643

—Collibus, H. à. Fürstliche Tischreden. Frankfurt a.M.: 1614

—Matienzo, J. de. Commentaria. Madrid: 1613

—Pérez de Rocha, A. Al Rey nuestro señor. Compendio de medios politicas. [Madrid? 1649?]

—Saldías, P. de. Tabla para la reducion de barras de plata. Seville: 1637

—Spain. Laws, statutes, etc., 1598–1621 (Philip III). Este en em traslado bien y fielmente sacado . . . para que la plata . . . se labre. [Madrid? 1609?]

—Spain. Laws, statutes, etc., 1621–1665 (Philip IV). Prematica en que su Magestad manda, que toda la moneda . . . labrada en . . . Perù se reduzca. Madrid: 1650

—Vázquez de Serna, J. Libro intitulado Reduciones de oro. Cadiz: 1620

SILVER FLEET, SPANISH

—Allo, P. de. Señor. El desseo del servicio de V. magestad. [Madrid? 164–?]

—Ampzing, S. West-Indische triumph-basuyne. Haarlem: 1629

—Antwooordt op 't Munsters praetie. Dordrecht: 1646

—Antwoordt, op sekeren brief Evlaly. [Amsterdam?] 1629

—Arnauld, A. La premiere et seconde Savoisienne, Grenoble: 1630

—Avellaneda Manrique, J. de. Memorial de la culpa que resulta de la pesquisa. [Madrid? 1629?]

—Aviendo el marques de Cadereyta desalojado al enemigo Olandes . . . [Madrid? 1635?]

—Baardt, P. Loff-en-lijck-gedicht. Leeuwarden: 1633

—Benavides Bazán, J. de. Demas de lo alegado y advertido. [Madrid? 1650?]

— —Señor. Don Juan de Benavides Baçan . . . se postra a los pies de V. Magestad. [Madrid? 1650?]

—Beverwijck, J. van. Spaensche Xerxes. Dordrecht: 1639

—Breve, y ajustada relacion de lo sucedido. Barcelona: 1639

—Cargo de la culpa que resulta contra Juan de Reyna. [Madrid? 1629?]

—Cargo que resulta contra don Feliciano Navarro. [Madrid? 1630?]

—Cayet, P. V. P. Chronologie novenaire. Paris: 1608

—Chappuys, G. Histoire de nostre temps. Paris: 1606

—Colonius, D. Oratio panegyrica, de illustri victoria. Leyden: 1629

—Duircant, A. Rym-vieren. [The Hague: 1629]

—Ens, G. Newer unpartheyischer teutscher Mercurius. Cologne: 1629

—Epicedium cum epitaphio . . . Petri Heinii. The Hague: 1629

—Eroberung der reiche silbervloot inde bay . . . Matancae. [Amsterdam? ca. 1629]

—El estado en que oy se halla el comercio. [Seville? 164–?]

—Fernández de Santiestevan, B. Relacion verdadera y cierta de la desseada . . . de la flota. Granada: 1630

—Grimestone, E. A generall historie of the Netherlands. London: 1627

—Haselbeeck, J. Triumph-dicht. Leeuwarden: 1629

—Hein, P. P. Beschreibung von Eroberung der spanischen Silber Flotta. Amsterdam: 1628

—Heinsius, D. Histoire du siége de Bolduc. Leyden: 1631

— —Rerum ad Sylvam-Ducis . . . historia. Leyden: 1631

—'t Hollandts rommelzootje. [Amsterdam? 1650]

—Jonckheer, M. Teghen-worp op het onwarachtich schrijven. Flushing: 1633

—Kannenburch, H. van. Protest ofte Scherp dreyghement. Middelburg: 1629

—Lampe, B. Het negentiende deel . . . van het Historisch verhael. Amsterdam: 1632

—Laynez, J. Copia de una carta . . . a el . . . fr. Joseph de Sisneros. Malaga: 1639

—Liefs, J. Lof-dicht over de wijt-vermaerde . . . victorie. [The Hague?] 1629

—Lommelin, D. Lof-dicht, ter eeren . . . vanden . . . Generael . . . Heyn. [Amsterdam?] 1629

—López de Guitian Sotomayor, D. Señor. El capitan Diego Lopez de Guitian Sotomayor. [Madrid? 1640?]

—Márquez de Cisneros, ——. Por Don Juan de Leoz, cavallero. [Madrid: 1629]

— —Por Don Lope de Hozes y Cordova. Madrid: 1635

— —Por el Consulado de Sevilla. Madrid: 1634

— —Por el senor D. Carlos de Ibarra. Madrid: 1634

—Martinius, F. Argo-nauta Batavus. Kampen: 1629

—Medina de las Torres, G. de Guzmán y Acevedo, duque de. Relacion. Muerte de Pie de Palo. Madrid: 1638

—Memoria de lo que an de advertir los pilotos de la Carrera de las Indias. [Madrid? 1630?]

—Mendoça, L. de. Memorial a Su Magestad . . . en razon de la seguridad de su plata. [Madrid? 1635?]

—Missive, inhoudende den aerdt vanden treves. [The Hague?] 1630

—Moscoso y de Córdoba, C. de. El licenciado d. Christoval de Moscoso y Cordova . . . Con Don Juan de Amassa. Madrid: 1634

— —El licenciado D. Christoval de Moscoso y Cordova . . . Con

el Consulado de Sevilla. Madrid: 1634

—Nierop, A. van. Loff-dicht, ter eeren . . . Pieter Pietersz. Heyn. Delft: 1629

—Pels, E. Lof-dicht des vermaerde . . . zee-heldt Pieter Pietersen Heyn. Amsterdam: 1629

—Relacion de la gente de mar. [Madrid? 1623?]

—Relacion de la plata y frutos. [Madrid:] 1622

—Relacion verdadera de todos los sucessos. Madrid: 1641

—Relaes ende 't cargo van't silver. Amsterdam: [1632?]

—Reyd, E. van. Voornaemste gheschiedenissen. Arnhem: 1626

—Sánchez de Espejo, A. Discurso político del estado. [Granada: 1646]

—Seville. Señor. La ciudad de Sevilla. [Seville? 1630?]

—Solórzano Pereira, J. de. Discurso i alegacion en derecho. Madrid: 1631

—Souter, D. Eben-ezer. Haarlem: 1630

— —Sené-boher. Haarlem: 1630

—Spaensche vosse-vel. Leeuwarden: 1630

—Spain. Consejo de las Indias. Culpa que resulta contra el licenciado Pedro de Vergara Gaviria. [Madrid? 1639?]

—Spranckhuysen, D. Triumphe van weghen de . . . victorie. Delft: 1629

—Tekel ofte Weech-schale. Middelburg: 1629

—Tijdinge hoe dat . . . Pieter Pietersz. Heyn, ende . . . Loncq, de vlote . . . hebben aenghetast. Amsterdam: 1628

—Translaet uyt den Spaenschen, weghens 't gevecht. Amsterdam: 1639

—Valerius, A. Neder-landtsche gedenck-clanck. Haarlem: 1626

—Veen, J. van der. Siet den getaanden speck. [Haarlem? 1629]

—Verovering vande silver-vloot. Amsterdam: [1629]

Smith, Capt. John. An accidence. London: [N. Okes] for J. Man, & B. Fisher, 1626

——London: [N. Okes] for J. Man, & B. Fisher, 1627

——London: [T. Harper] for B. Fisher, 1636

—Advertisements for the unexperienced planters. London: J. Haviland, for R. Milbourne, 1631

—A description of New England. London: H. Lownes, for R. Clarke, 1616

—The generall historie of Virginia. London: J. D[awson]., & J. H[aviland]., for M. Sparke, 1624

——London: J. D[awson]., & J. H[aviland]., for M. Sparke, 1625

——London: J. D[awson]., & J. H[aviland]., for M. Sparke, 1626

——London: J. D[awson]., & J. H[aviland]., for M. Sparke, 1627

——London: J. D[awson]., & J. H[aviland]., for M. Sparke, 1631

——London: J. D[awson]., & J. H[aviland]., for E. Blackmore, 1632

—The generall history of Virginia. [London: J. Dawson, 1623]

——See also Whitbourne, Sir Richard. Zwantzigste Schifffahrt. Frankfurt a.M.: 1629

—A map of Virginia. Oxford: J. Barnes, 1612

—New Englands trials. London: W. Jones, 1620

——London: W. Jones, 1622

—A sea grammar. London: J. Haviland, 1627

—A true relation of such occurrences . . . in Virginia. London: [E. Allde] for J. Tapp, & W. W[elby]., 1608 (4)

—The true travels, adventures, and observations. London: J. H[aviland]., for T. Slater, [& M. Sparke] 1630

—Vera descriptio Novae Angliae. *In* Vespucci, Amerigo.

Americae pars decima. Oppenheim: 1619

—Viertzehende Schiffart oder . . . Beschreibung dess Neuwen Engellandts. Frankfurt a.M.: H. Palthenius, for The Hulsiuses, 1617

—Vierzehende Schiffart. Frankfurt a.M.: Heirs of L. Hulsius, 1628

—Warhafftige Beschreibung dess Newen Engellands. *In* Vespucci, Amerigo. Zehender Theil Americae. Oppenheim: 1618

SMITH, CAPT. JOHN—POETRY

—Lloyd, D. The legend of captaine Jones. [London:] 1631

The smoke in the temple. *See* Saltmarsh, John

Sobrino, Gaspar. Señor, El padre Gaspar Sobrino. [Madrid? ca. 1615?]

Société de Notre-Dame de Montréal. *See* Les veritables motifs. [Paris:] 1643

Society for Propagation of the Gospel in New-England. An act for the promoting . . . the gospel . . . in New England. London: E. Husband, 1649

SOCIETY FOR PROPAGATION OF THE GOSPEL IN NEW-ENGLAND

—Cambridge. University. To our reverend and deare brethren. [Cambridge? 1649]

—Oxford. University. To our reverend brethren. [Oxford? 1649]

SOCIOLOGY

—Grotius, H. De jure belli ac pacis. Paris: 1625

——Drie boecken . . . nopende het recht des oorloghs, Haarlem: 1635

SÖDER COMPAGNIET

—Oxenstierna, A. G., grefve. Wir Burgermeister und Raht. [Nuremberg: 1633]

—Sweden. Sovereigns, etc., 1611–1632 (Gustaf II Adolf). Ampliatio oder Erweiterung dess Privilegii. Heilbronn: 1633

——Octroy eller privilegium. Stockholm: 1626

——Octroy ofte Privilegie. The Hague: 1627

——Octroy und Privilegium. Stockholm: 1626

—Usselinx, W. Argonautica Gustaviana. Frankfurt a.M.: 1633

——Aussführlicher Bericht. Stockholm: 1626

——Instruction oder Anleitung . . . der newen Süder Compagnie. Heilbronn: 1633

—Kurtzer Extract der vornemsten Hauptpuncten. Heilbronn: 1633

——Manifest und Vertragbrieff der Australischen Companey. [Gothenburg:] 1624

——Der reiche Schweden General Compagnies handlungs contract. Stockholm: 1625

——Sweriges Rijkes General Handels Compagnies contract. Stockholm: 1625

——Uthförligh förklaring. Stockholm: 1626

SOLANO, FRANCISCO, SAINT

—Oré, L. J. de, Bp. Relacion de la vida . . . del venerable padre f. Francisco Solano. [Madrid: 1614]

—Salinas y Córdova, B. de. Memorial del padre. Madrid: 1639

Solanus, Franciscus, Saint. *See* Solano, Francisco, Saint

Soledades. *See* Góngora y Argote, Luis de

A solemne joviall disputation. *See* Brathwaite, Richard

Soler, Vincent Joachin. Brief, et singulier relation d'un lettre. Amsterdam: B. de Preys, 1639

—Cort ende sonderlingh verhael van eenen brief. Amsterdam: B. de Preys, 1639

Solinus, C. Julius. Memorabilia mundi. Frankfurt a.M.: J. Sauer, for T. Schönwetter, 1603

Sologuren, Juan de. Señor. Diferentes ministros han representado a V. Magestad los daños. [Madrid? 1612?]

—Señor. Los sueldos y salarios ordinarios. [Madrid? 1612?]

SOLOGUREN, JUAN DE
—Núñez Correa, J. Resolucion y resumen del estado. [Madrid? 1612?]
Solon franciscanus. *See* Reineccius, Felix
Solórzano Pereira, Juan de. Discurso i alegacion en derecho. Madrid: F. Martínez, 1631
—Disputationem de Indiarum jure . . . tomus primus. Madrid: F. Martínez, 1629
—Disputationum de Indiarum jure . . . tomus alter. Madrid: F. Martínez, 1639
—El doctor Juan de Solorzano Pereira. Madrid: F. Martínez, 1629
—Memorial i discurso de las razones que se ofrecen. Madrid: F. Martínez, 1629
—Memorial, o discurso informativo. Madrid: F. Martínez, 1642
—Politica indiana. Madrid: D. Díaz de la Carrera, 1648
—Traduccion de la dedicatoria real. [Madrid:] F. Martínez, 1639
Some observations. *See* Steuart, Adam
Some yeares travels. *See* Herbert, Sir Thomas
Somma, Agacio di. Dell'America, canti cinque. Rome: B. Zannetti, 1623
Sommaire de l'instance. *See* Compagnie de la Nouvelle France
Sommaire recueil. *See* Usselinx, Willem
Sommario istorico. *See* Zappullo, Michele
La sommation. *See* Spinola, Ambrogio, marchese del Sesto e di Venafro
Sonnet, Thomas, sieur de Courval. Satyre contre les charlatans. Paris: J. Millot, 1610
Sosa, Pedro de. Memorial del peligroso estado . . . de Chile. [Madrid? 1616?]
—Señor. Fray Pedro de Sosa . . . dize . . . de quan nocivos han side los medios. [Madrid? 1617?]
—Señor. Fray Pedro de Sosa . . .

Dize, que ha hecho quanto ha sido de su parte. [Madrid? 1616?]
—Señor. Fray Pedro de Sossa . . . dize, que el dicho reyno le embia a dar quenta. [Madrid? 1614?]
Sostmann, Johann. Indianische Reise. Paderborn: M. Brückner, 1601
Soto, Domingo de. De justitia et jure. Venice: Heirs of G. A. Bertano, 1602
——Venice: P. M. Bertano, 1608
——Douai: P. Boremann, 1613
——Salamanca: 1619
SOTA, HERNANDO DE
—Garcilaso de la Vega, el Inca. La Florida del Ynca. Lisbon: 1605
—Virginia richly valued, by the description of . . . Florida. London: 1609
—The worthye and famous history of . . . Terra Florida. London: 1611
Sotomayor, Alonso de. Señor. Don Alonso de Sotomayor, dize, que las tierras . . . se han reconocido estar muy pobladas de Indios. [Madrid? 1620?]
—Señor. Don Alonso de Sotomayor, dize que son tan fuertes . . . las razones y causas . . . . [Madrid? 1620?]
The soules solace. *See* Jenner, Thomas
Sousa, Antonio de. *See* Sardinha Mimoso, João. Relacion de la real tragicomedia. Lisbon: 1620
Sousa Coutinho, Francisco de. Brevis repetitio omnium quae . . . legatus Portugalliae . . . proposuit. The Hague: L. Breeckevelt, 1647
—Naerdere propositie. [Amsterdam?] 1647
——[The Hague 1647]
——The Hague: 1647
——The Hague: [1647]
——*In* Vertooch aen de . . . Staten Generael . . . nopende de . . . proceduren van Brasil. Amsterdam: 1647

—Propositie. [The Hague?] 1647 (3)
——*In* Vertooch aen de . . . Staten Generael . . . nopende de . . . proceduren van Brasil. Amsterdam: 1647
—Propositio. The Hague: J. Breeckevelt, 1647
—La proposition. The Hague: J. Breeckevelt, 1647
Sousa de Macedo, Antonio de. Flores de España. Lisbon: J. Rodriguez, 1631
Souter, Daniel. Eben-ezer. Haarlem: H. P. van Wesbusch, 1630
—Seer uytmuntende Nederlandtsche victorien. Haarlem: H. P. van Wesbusch, 1630
—Sené-boher. Haarlem: H. P. van Wesbusch, 1630
Souterius, Daniel. *See* Souter, Daniel
SOUTH AMERICA—DESCRIPTION
—Hawkins, Sir R. The observations of Sir Richard Hawkins. London: 1622
SOUTHWEST, NEW. *See also* NEW MEXICO
—Cardona, T. de. Señor. El capitan Tomas de Cardona, por si, y en nombre de los demas participes. [Madrid? 1618?]
—Villagrá, G. P. de. El capitan Gaspar de Villagra, para que su Magestad le haga merced. [Madrid? ca. 1616?]
——Servicios que . . . hà hecho el capitan. [Madrid? 1615?]
Spaensche thriomphe. [Amsterdam?] 1647
De Spaensche tiranije. *See* Baudart, Willem
De Spaensche tiranije gheschiet in Neder-lant. *See* Gysius, JohannesDe Spaensche tirannij in Neder-Lant. *See* Gysius, Johannes
Spaensche triumphe. [Amsterdam?] 1647 (2)
Spaensche tryumphe. *See* Wijnandts, Willem
Spaensche vosse-vel. Leeuwarden: C. Fonteyne, 1630
—Leeuwarden: C. Fonteyne, 1631

gestad . . . que ha estado en las Indias. [Madrid? 1625?]

—Vaughan, W. The golden-grove. London: 1608

—Velázquez, J. Relacion que el licenciado Don Juan Velazquez hizo. [Madrid? 1632?]

—Vergara Gaviria, D. de. Adicion a la informacion. [Madrid? 1639?]

—Vitoria Baraona, F. de. El capitan Francisco de Vitoria, vezino de la puebla de los Angeles. [Madrid? 1639]

—Zambrana de Villalobos, S. Allegatio iuris. [Madrid? 1621]

Spain. Junta de Guerra de Indias. Ordenanzas de la Junta de guerra. Madrid: 1634

——Madrid: Widow of J. González, 1636

Spain. Laws, statutes, etc. Sumarios de la recopilacion general de las leyes. Madrid: J. González, 1628

Spain. Laws, statutes, etc., 1516–1556 (Charles I). Leyes y ordenanças nuevamente hechas por su Magestad. Valladolid: V. de Castro, 1603

Spain. Laws, statutes, etc., 1556–1598 (Philip II). Nuevas leyes y ordenanzas, hechas por su Magestad. Madrid: L. Sánchez, 1625

—Ordenanças para remedio de los daños . . . de los navios que navegan a las Indias Ocidentales. Madrid: Widow of A. Martín, 1619

Spain. Laws, statutes, etc., 1598–1621 (Philip III). Este en em traslado bien y fielmente sacado . . . para que la plata . . . se labre. [Madrid: 1609?]

—Este es un traslado bien y fielmente sacado . . . Para que no se tomen ningun dineros. [Madrid: 1610?]

—Instruccion de la forma que se ha de tener en la provincias. [Madrid: 1609]

—Instrucción de lo que han de observar los governadores, y corregidores . . . de la Nueva España. [Madrid: 1626]

—Lo que se ordena de nuevo. [Madrid? 1609]

—El Rey. Marques de Montes Claros . . . gouernador . . . del Piru. [Madrid? 1609]

—El Rey. Por quanto de ordinario se han ofrecido y ofrecen dudas . . . . [Madrid: 1620]

—El Rey. Por quanto la experiencia y execucion de las ultimas ordenanças . . . . [Madrid: 1618]

—El Rey. Por quanto por cedula mia de dos de Otubre del año passado . . . . [Madrid: 1620?]

—El Rey. Por quanto por cedula mia fecha a dos de Otubre del año passado . . . . [Madrid: 1616]

—El Rey. Por quanto por cedula mia fecha en Madrid a catorze de Diziembre del año passado. [Madrid: 1620]

—El Rey. Por quanto por diferentes cedulas, leyes y ordenanças. [Madrid? 1620]

—Titulo de gran chanciller. [Madrid? 1623]

Spain. Laws, statutes, etc., 1621–1665 (Philip IV). Capitulaciones de el assiento. [Madrid:] 1639

—Ordenes, y providencias. Madrid: A. Bizarron, [ca. 1630]

—Pregon en que el Rey nuestro señor manda. Madrid: D. García Morrás, 1650

—Prematica en que el Rey nuestro señor manda. Madrid: D. García Morrás, 1650

—Prematica en que Su Magestad manda, que . . . no se puede hazer ni escrivir ninguna escritura. [Madrid:] J. Sánchez, for Imprenta Real, 1639

—Prematica en que su Magestad manda, que toda la moneda . . . labrada en . . . Perù se reduzca. Madrid: D. García Morrás, 1650

——Seville: J. Gómez de Blas, 1650

Spain. Sovereigns, etc., 1598–1621 (Philip III). Cedula en que su Magestad da licencia. [Madrid? 1615?]

—Cedula en que su Magestad

reprehende gravemente. [Madrid: 1613]

—Este es un traslado . . . de una cedula de su Magestad . . . para que los . . . maravedis . . . se muden. [Valladolid: 1603]

—Instrucción y memoria de las relaciones. [Madrid: ca.1620]

—Instrucion para el virrey del Piru. [Madrid?] 1603

—Lo que por mi mandado del rey nuestro señor se assienta. [Madrid? 1601?]

—La orden e instruccion que su Magestad manda dar. [Madrid? 1605?]

—El Rey [14 Dec. 1606]. [Madrid: 1606?]

—El Rey [26 May 1609]. [Madrid: 1609] (2 differing memorials)

—El Rey. Lo que por mi mandado se assienta, y concierta con Juan Nuñez Correa. [Madrid? 1603]

Spain. Sovereigns, etc., 1598–1621 (Philip III), addressee. Señor. El agravio que el principe de Esquilache, y el Arçobispo de Lima han intentado. [Madrid? 1620?]

Spain. Sovereigns, etc., 1621–1665 (Philip IV). El rey. [Madrid: 1634]

—El Rey. Conceio, justicia, veyntiquatros, cavalleros. [Madrid? 1622]

Spain. Sovereigns, etc., 1621–1665 (Philip IV), addressee. Señor. Los cargadores interessados. [Madrid? 1630?]

—Señor. Muy notorio es à V. Magestad. [Madrid? 1640?]

—Señor. Un vasallo de V. Magestad . . . que ha estado en las Indias. [Madrid? 1625?]

Spain. Treaties, etc., 1621–1665 (Philip IV). The articles and conditions of the perpetuall peace. London: R. White, 1648

—Articulen dess Friedens. [Brussels: H. A. Velpius] 1647

—Articulen en conditien van den eeuwigen vrede. Dordrecht: S. Moulaert, 1648

——Ghent: S. Manilius, 1648 (2)

912

Speculum tragicum. *See* Dickenson, John

A speech concerning a West Indie association. *See* Rudyerd, Sir Benjamin

A speech delivered in Parliament. *See* Pym, John

A speech made before the Lords. *See* Mervyn, Sir Audley

The speech of a cavaleere. London: 1642

A speech, or complaint. *See* Cárdenas, Alonso de

Speed, John. A prospect of the most famous parts. London: J. Dawson, for G. Humble, 1627

— —London: J. Dawson, for G. Humble, 1631

— —London: M. F[letcher]., for W. Humble, 1646

— —London: J. Legat, for W. Humble, 1646

Het spel van Brasilien. [Amsterdam?] 1638 (2)

Spenser, Edmund. The faerie queene. London: H. L[ownes]., for M. Lownes, 1609

— —London: H. L[ownes]., for M. Lownes, 1611

— —London: H. L[ownes]., for M. Lownes, 1611 [i.e., 1612]

— —London: H. L[ownes]., for M. Lownes, 1611 [i.e., 1613]

— —London: H. L[ownes]., for M. Lownes, 1611 [i.e., 1615?]

— —London: H. L[ownes]., for M. Lownes, 1617

Spes Israelis. *See* Manasseh ben Joseph ben Israel

Sphaera. *See* Du Chevreul, Jacques; *and also* Sacro Bosco, Joannes de

Sphaera mundi, seu Cosmographia. *See* Biancani, Giuseppe

De spiegel der spaense tyrannye, 2de dl. *See* Gysius, Johannes

Den spiegel der Spaensche tierannye-geschiet in Westindien. [*and variant spellings.*] *See* Casas, Bartolomé de las, Bp

Spiegel, Adriaan van de. Isagoges in rem herbariam. Padua: L. Pasquato, for P. Meietti, 1606

— —Leyden: Elsevier Office, 1633

— —*In his* Opera. Amsterdam: 1645

—Opera. Amsterdam: J. Blaeu, 1645

Spieghel der australische navigatie. *See* Le Maire, Jacob

Den spieghel der Spaensche tierannije geschiet in West-indien. [*and variant spellings.*] *See* Casas, Bartolomé de las, Bp. Spiegel . . .

Spieghel der Spaenscher tyrannie, in West-Indien. [*and variant spellings.*] *See* Casas, Bartolomé de las, Bp

De spieghel der Spaense tyrannye, 2de dl. *See* Gysius, Johannes

Den spieghel vande Spaensche tyrannie beeldelijcken afgemaelt. *See* Casas, Bartolomé de las, Bp

Spigelius, Adrianus. *See* Spiegel, Adriaan van de

Spilbergen, Joris van. Americae tomi undecimi appendix. Frankfurt a.M.: J. Hofer, for J. T. de Bry, 1620

—Appendix dess eilfften Theils Americae. Oppenheim: H. Galler, for J. T. de Bry, at Frankfurt a.M., 1620

—Copie van een brief. Delft: J. A. Cloeting, 1617

—Dreyjährige Reise. Frankfurt a.M.: 1625

—'t'Historiael journael. Delft: F. Balthasar, 1601

— —Delft: F. Balthasar, 1605

— —Amsterdam: M. Colijn, 1617

—Historis journael. Amsterdam: J. Hartgers, 1648

—Indiae Orientalis pars septima. Frankfurt a.M.: W. Richter, 1606

—Het journael. Delft: F. Balthasar, 1605 (2)

—Miroir Oost et West-Indical. Amsterdam: J. Janszoon the Younger, 1621

—Newe Schifffahrt einer dreyjährigen Reyse. Frankfurt a.M.: M. Becker, 1605

—Oost- en West-Indische voyagie. Amsterdam: J. Hartgers, 1648

—Oost ende West-Indische spiegel. Leyden: N. van Geelkercken, 1619 (2)

— —Amsterdam: J. Janszoon the Younger, 1621

— —Zutphen: A. J. van Aelst, 1621

—Siebender Theil der Orientalischen Indien. Frankfurt a.M.: M. Becker, 1605 (2)

—Die siebzehende Schiffart. Frankfurt a.M.: J. Hofer, for Hulsius, 1620

—Speculum Orientalis Occidentalisque Indiae navigationum. Leyden: N. van Geelkercken, 1619

— —Leyden: N. van Geelkercken, for J. Hondius [at Amsterdam] 1619

SPILBERGEN, JORIS VAN

—Grimestone, E. A generall historie of the Netherlands. London: 1627

—Nieuwe ende warachtighe tijdinghe ghekomen van Sint Lucas de Barrameda. Amsterdam: 1616

—Een waerachtige beschryvinghe van de schoone victorie. Amsterdam: 1616

—Warachtich verhael vanden slach . . . inde Zuydt Zee. Middelburg: 1617

Spinelli, Giovanni Paolo. Lectiones aureae. Bari: G. C. Ventura, 1605

— —Bari: G. Gudoni, for G. Montini, 1633

Spinola, Ambrogio, marchese del Sesto e di Venafro. La sommation. Paris: J. Martin, 1625

— —Toulouse: J. Boudé [1625]

SPINOLA, CARLO

—Spinola, F. A. Vita del p. Carlo Spinola. Rome: 1628

Spinola, Fabio Ambrosio. Vita Caroli Spinolae. Antwerp: Plantin Press (B. Moretus), 1630

—Vita del p. Carlo Spinola. Rome: F. Corbelletti, 1628

— —Bologna: C. Ferroni, 1629

— —Rome: F. Corbelletti, 1630

— —Rome: F. Corbelletti, 1638

Stratenus, Gulielmus, praeses. Disputationum medicarum . . . secunda. Utrecht: A. Roman, 1542 [i.e., 1642?]

Strix, sive De ludificatione daemonum. *See* Pico della Mirandola, Giovanni Francesco

Strobelberger, Johann Stephan. De dentium podagra. Leipzig: J. Gross, 1630

—Tractatus novus. Jena: J. Beithmann, 1620

Struzzi, Alberto. Dialogo sobre el comercio. [Madrid? L. Sánchez? 1625?]

—Dialogo sobre el commercio. Madrid: L. Sánchez, 1624

Stucken gemencioneert in den Bycorff. *See* Den Nederlandtschen bye-korf

Stucley, Sir Lewis. Aende conincklike majesteyt. *In* Verclaringe ende verhael hoe de Heere Wouter Raleigh . . . hem ghedreghen heeft. The Hague: 1619

—To the Kings most excellent majestie. London: B. Norton, & J. Bill, 1618

STUYVESANT, PETER

—Breeden-raedt. Antwerp: 1649

Suárez de Argüelo, Francisco. Ephemerides generales. Madrid: J. de la Cuesta, 1608

Suárez de Figueroa, Cristóbal. Hechos de Don Garcia Hurtado de Mendoza. Madrid: Imprenta Real, 1613

— —Madrid: Imprenta Real, 1616

—Plaza universal. Madrid: L. Sánchez, 1615

— —Perpignan: L. Roure, 1629

— —Perpignan: L. Roure, 1630

Suárez de Gamboa, Juan. Illustrissimo señor. Advertencias de daños. [Madrid? 1621]

—Señor. Tres cosas son las que obligan a credito. [Madrid? 1621]

Suárez de Salazar, Juan Bautista. Grandezas y antiguedades. Cadiz: C. Hidalgo, 1610

Successi principali . . . di Spagna. *See* Malvezzi, Virgilio, marchese

Successo della guerra de portugueses. *See* Silva, Antonio Telles da

Sucesos principales . . . de España. *See* Malvezzi, Virgilio, marchese

Sucesso della guerra de' Portoghesi. *See* Silva, Antonio Telles da

Sucessos de la armada que fue al Brasil. Seville: N. Rodríguez, 1640

Suchten, Alexander von. Antinomii mysteria gemina. Leipzig: J. Apel, 1604

— —Gera: J. Apel, 1613

— —Leipzig: J. Apel, 1613

Suchtich en trouwhertich discours. [Amsterdam?] 1646

Suchtigh en trouwhertigh discours. [Amsterdam?] 1646

SUCRE, BOLIVIA. UNIVERSIDAD

—León Pinelo, A. R. de. Por la Real Universidad . . . de . . . Lima. [Madrid? 1631?]

SUGAR—BRAZIL

—Beverwijck, J. van. Schat der gesontheyt. [Dordrecht? 1636?]

—Brilleman, J. Collyrium, ofte Costelijcke ooghen-salve. Leeuwarden: 1647

—'t Hollandts rommelzootje. [Amsterdam? 1650]

Suite de l'Histoire de nostre temps. *See* Malingre, Claude

La suite des Oeuvres. *See* Saint-Amant, Marc Antoine de Gérard, sieur de

La suite des oeuvres burlesques . . . Seconde partie. *See* Scarron, Paul

Suitte de l'Histoire des choses . . . advenues en Maragnan. *See* Yves d'Evreux, father

Suma de lo que el licenciado . . . pide. *See* Ibarra Gueztaraen, Juan de

Sumario del concilio provincial. *See* Lima (Ecclesiastical Province). Council, 1567

Sumario en hecho . . . sobre retener los sinodos, ò estipendios que paga en la Indias. *See* Abreu y Figueroa, Fernando de

Sumario, y compendio de lo sucedido en España. [Madrid: 1638]

Sumarios de la recopilacion general de las leyes. *See* Spain. Laws, statutes, etc.

Summarium ad Historiam Hispaniae. *See* Mariana, Juan de

SUNFLOWERS

—Camerarius, J., the Younger. Symbolorum et emblematum . . . centuriae tres. [Leipzig:] 1605

—Duchesne, J. Liber de priscorum philosophorum verae medicinae materia. Saint Gervais: 1603

— —Traicté de la matiere . . . de la medecine balsamique. Paris: 1626

Superbiae flagellum. *See* Taylor, John, the Water-poet

SUPERSTITION

—Vairo, L. De fascino. Venice: 1629

—Valderrama, P. de. Histoire generale. Paris: 1619

— —Teatro de las religiones. Seville: 1612

Suplicacion a Su Magestad. *See* Mendoça, Lourenço de, Bp of Rio de Janeiro

Il supplice schiavo indiano. *See* Casas, Bartolomé de las, Bp

The surgions mate. *See* Woodall, John

A survay of that foolish . . . libell. *See* Hall, Joseph, Bp

A survey of the spirituall antichrist. *See* Rutherford, Samuel

A survey of the summe of church-discipline. *See* Hooker, Thomas

Swan, John. Speculum mundi. Cambridge: T. Buck, & R. Daniel, 1635

— —Cambridge: R. Daniel, 1643

— —Cambridge: R. Daniel [for T. Atkinson] 1643 [i.e., 1644]

— —Cambridge: R. Daniel [for J. Williams, at London] 1643 [i.e., 1644]

Sweden. Sovereigns, etc., 1611–1632 (Gustaf II Adolf). Ampliatio oder Erweiterung dess Privilegii. Heilbronn: C. Krause, 1633

—Octroy eller privilegium. Stockholm: I. Meurer, 1626

—Octroy oder Privilegium. 'Stockholm: I. Meurer' [i.e., Germany?] 1626

—Octroy ofte Privilegie. The Hague: A. Meuris, 1627

—Octroy und Privilegium. Stockholm: I. Meurer, 1626

Sweden. Sovereigns, etc., 1632–1654 (Christina). Förordning huru medh tobaks handelen skal blifwa hällit. [Stockholm: 1641]

SWEDES IN AMERICA

—Wassenaer, N. van. T'achste deel . . . van het Historisch verhael. Amsterdam: [1625]

Sweerts, Emanuel. Florilegium. Frankfurt a.M.: A. Kempner, 1612–14

— —Amsterdam: J. Janszoon the Younger, 1620, '14

— —Amsterdam: J. Janszoon the Younger, 1631, '14

— —Amsterdam: J. Janszoon the Younger, 1641

— —Amsterdam: J. Janszoon the Younger, 1647–54

SWEET POTATOES. *See* PO-TATOES

Sweriges Rijkes General Handels Compagnies contract. *See* Usselinx, Willem

The swords apology. *See* Syms, Christopher

Swymel-klacht des Spaenschen conincks. *See* Eibergen, Rutgerus

Sylva sylvarum. *See titles under* Bacon, Francis

Sylvae lyricae. *See* Balde, Jakob

Sylvester, Joshua. Tobacco battered. [London: H. Lownes, 1617?]

— —*In* Du Bartas, Guillaume de Salluste, seigneur. Bartas his devine weekes. London: 1621

— —*In the same.* London: 1633

— —*In the same.* London: 1641

Symbolorum et emblematum . . . centuria quarta. *See* Camerarius, Joachim, the Younger

Symbolorum et emblematum . . . centuriae tres. *See* Camerarius, Joachim, the Younger

Symmachia: or, A true-loves knot. *See* Scott, Thomas

Symonds, William. Proceedings of the English colonie. *In* Smith, Capt. John. A map of Virginia. Oxford: 1612

—Virginia. A sermon. London: J. Windet, for E. Edgar, & W. Welby, 1609

SYMONSZOON, DIRK

—Cort verhael, hoe den edel. heer admirael . . . vijf schepen . . . heeft verovert. Amsterdam: 1629

—Wassenaer, N. van Het seventiende ghedeelt . . . van het Historisch verhael. Amsterdam: 1630

— —'T vyfthiende deel . . . van het Historisch verhael. Amsterdam: 1629

Syms, Christopher. The swords apology. London: T. Warren, 1644

Synopsis primi saeculi Societatis Jesu. *See* Damiens, Jacques

Syntagma juris universi. *See* Grégoire, Pierre

Syntagma musicum. *See* Praetorius, Michael

Syntagma selectorum. *See* Libavius, Andreas

SYPHILIS—ORIGIN

—Alpherio, H. de. De peste. Naples: 1628

— Beverwijck, J. van. Autarcheia Bataviae. Leyden: 1644

— —Lof der medicine. Dordrecht: 1635

— —Medicinae encomium. Dordrecht: 1633

— —Schat der ongesontheyt . . . Het tweede deel. Dordrecht: 1644

—Calvo, J. Cirugia universal, 1a–2a pte. Madrid: 1626

—Clüver, J. Historiarum totius mundi epitome. Leyden: 1637

—Corbeius, T. Pathologia. Frankfurt a.M.: 1615

—Cotgrave, R. A dictionarie of the French and English tongues. London: 1611

—Crato von Krafftheim, J. Consiliorum et epistolarum medicinalium . . . liber quintus. Hanau: 1619

—Duchesne, J. Conseils de medecine. Paris: 1626

—Dupleix, S. La curiosite naturelle. Paris: 1606

—Ferdinandi, E. Centum historiae. Venice: 1621

—Fernel, J. Traité de . . . la parfaite cure. Paris: 1633

—Fioravanti, L. Corona; oder, Kron der Artzney. Frankfurt a.M.: 1604

— —De' capricci medicinali . . . libri quattro. Venice: 1602

—Fracastoro, G. Operum pars prior. Geneva: 1621

—Guarguante, O. Responsa varia, ad varias aegritudines. Venice: 1613

—Guillaumet, T. Traicté second de la maladie appelee cristaline. Nîmes: 1614

—Héry, T. de. La methode curatoire de la maladie venerienne. Paris: 1634

—Joel, F. Operum medicorum . . . tomus primus[-sextus]. Hamburg: 1616

—Knobloch, T. De lue venerea, von Frantzosen kurtzer Bericht. Giessen: 1620

—Lalli, G. B. Franceide, overo Del mal francese. Foligno: 1629

—Le Paulmier de Grentemesnil, J. De morbis contagiosis libri septem. Frankfurt a.M.: 1601

—Liddel, D. Ars medica. Hamburg: 1608

—Locre, F. de Chronicon Belgicum. Arras: 1616

—Matthieu, P. Della perfetta historia di Francia. Venice: 1624

— —Histoire de France. Paris: 1605

— —Historia di Francia. Venice: 1623

—Mercado, L. Opera omnia. Frankfurt a.M.: 1608

— —Praxis medica. Venice: 1608

— —Tomus secundus Operum. Valladolid: 1605

—Moryson, F. An itinerary. London: 1617

—Pardoux, B. Universa medicina. Paris: 1630

—Pasquier, E. Les recherches de la France. Paris: 1607

—Laugh, and be fat. [London: W. Hall? for H. Gosson? 1612]

—A letter sent to London. [Oxford: H. Hall] 1643

—The needles excellency. London: [T. Harper] for J. Boler, 1631

——London: J. Boler, 1634

——London: J. Boler, 1636

——London: [J. Dawson?] for J. Boler, 1640

—Newes and strange newes. London: J. O[kes]., for F. Coules, 1638

—The nipping . . . of abuses. London: E. Griffin, for N. Butter, 1614

—The noble cavalier caracterised. [Oxford? 1643]

—Odcombs complaint. 'Utopia' [i.e., London: G. Eld, for W. Burre?] 1613

—The olde, old . . . man. London: [A. Mathewes] for H. Gosson, 1635 (3)

—The praise and vertue of a jayle. London: J. H[aviland]., for R. B[adger]., 1623

—The praise, antiquity, and commodity, of beggery. London: E. A[llde]., for H. Gosson, & E. Wright, 1621

—The praise of hemp-seed. London: [E. Allde] for H. Gosson [& E. Wright] 1620

——London: [E. Allde] for H. Gosson [& E. Wright?] 1623 (2)

—St. Hillaries teares. London: 1642

——London: N. V[avasour]., & J. B[ecket?]., 1642

—The scourge of baseness. London: N. O[kes]., for M. Walbanke, 1624

—The sculler. London: E. A[llde]., for [N. Butter] 1612

—A shilling, or The travailes. [London: E. Allde, for H. Gosson, 1621]

—Sir Gregory Nonsence. London: N. O[kes]., 1700 [i.e., 1622]

—Superbiae flagellum. London: G. Eld, 1621

—Taylors feast. London: J. Okes, 1638

—Taylors goose. London: E. Allde, for H. Gosson, & E. Wright, 1621

—Taylor's motto. London: [E. Allde] for J. T[rundle]., & H. G[osson]., 1621 (2)

—Taylors water-worke. London: [T. Snodham?] for N. Butter, 1614

—Three weekes, three daies, and three houres. London: E. Griffin, for G. Gibbs, 1617

—The travels of twelve-pence. London: [A. Mathewes] for H. Gosson, 1635

—A valorous and perillous sea-fight. London: E. P[urslowe]., for E. Wright, 1640

—A verry merry wherry-ferry voyage. London: E. Allde, 1622

——London: E. Allde, 1623

—The water-comorant his complaint. London: G. Eld, 1622

—The watermens suit. [London: G. Eld, 1614?]

—Wit and mirth. London: [M. Fletcher] for H. Gosson [& E. Wright] 1626

——London: [A Mathewes] for H. Gosson, [& E. Wright], 1628

——London: T. C[otes]., for J. Boler, 1629

——London: [T. Cotes] for J. Boler, 1635

—The world runnes on wheeles. London: E. A[llde]., for H. Gosson, 1623

——London: [A. Mathewes] for H. Gosson, 1635

Taylor, Robert. *See* Tailor, Robert

Taylor, Timothy. *See the following:*

—Eaton, Samuel. A defence of sundry positions . . . alledged to justifie the Congregationall-way. London: 1645

——The defence of sundry positions . . . for the Congregational-way. London: 1646

Taylors feast. *See* Taylor, John, the Water-poet

Taylors goose. *See* Taylor, John, the Water-poet

Taylor's motto. *See* Taylor, John, the Water-poet

Taylors water-worke. *See* Taylor, John, the Water-poet

Teatro de las religiones. *See* Valderrama, Pedro de

Teatro del cielo e della terra. *See* Rosaccio, Giuseppe

Teatro eclesiastico de la primitiva iglesia. *See* González Dávila, Gil

Technogamia: or, The marriages of the arts. *See* Holyday, Barten

Teelinck, Ewout. *See* Teeling, Ewoud

Teelinck, Maximiliaan. *See* Teellinck, Maximiliaan

Teelinck, Willem. *See* Teellinck, Willem

Teeling, Ewoud. De derde wachter. The Hague: A. Meuris, 1625

—De tweede wachter. The Hague: A. Meuris, 1625

Teellinck, Maximiliaan. Vrymoedige aenspraeck aen syn hoogheyt. Middelburg: A. de Later, 1650 (4)

——*See also* Bedenkingen en antwoort op de vrymoedige aenspraek. Flushing: 1650

—*See also* Teellinck, Willem. Den politijcken Christen. Middelburg: 1650

Teellinck, Willem. Davids danckbaerheyt. Middelburg: J. van der Hellen, for M. J. Brandt, at Amsterdam, 1624

—Den politijcken Christen. Middelburg: A. de Later, 1650

—Tweede wachter. *See* Teeling, Ewoud. De tweede wachter. The Hague: 1625

Tegen-advys, op de presentatie van Portugal. [The Hague?] 1648

Teghen-worp op het onwarachtich schrijven. *See* Jonckheer, M.

Teixeira, José. Seigneur ofte den groten meester van Castilien. [Amsterdam?] 1641

—The Spanish pilgrime. London: B. A[lsop]., for T. Archer, 1625

—The true historie of . . . Don

Sebastian. London: S. Stafford, for J. Shaw, 1602
Teixeira, Pedro. Relaciones . . . del origen . . . de los reyes de Persia. Antwerp: H. Verdussen, 1610A
Teixeira Pinto, Bento. Naufragio que passou Jorge Dalbuquerque Coelho. Lisbon: A. Alvarez, for A. Ribeiro, 1601
Tekel ofte Weech-schale. Middelburg: J. van der Hellen, for J. vande Vivere, 1629
Téllez, Gabriel. Comedias, 4a pte. Madrid: Maria de Quiñones, for P. Coello, & M. López, 1635
—Deleytar aprovechando. Madrid: Imprenta Real, for D. González, 1635
—Doze comedias nuevas. Seville: F. de Lyra, for M. de Sande, 1627
——Valencia: P. P. Mey, 1631
Tellier, Gilles, See Antwerp. Collegium Societatis Jesu. Typus mundi. Antwerp: 1627
Templum naturae historicum. See Kornmann, Heinrich
The tenth muse. See Bradstreet, Anne (Dudley)
Teorica del globo terrestre. See Nicolosi, Giovanni Battista
Teorica y exercicios de la gineta. See Vargas Machuca, Bernardo de
Termini di mezzo rilievo. See Valori, Filippo
Ternarius bezoardicorum. See Sala, Angelo
Ternarius ternariorum. See Sala, Angelo
Terra Australis incognita. See Queiros, Pedro Fernandes de
A terrible battell. See Rowlands, Samuel
Tertia centuria historica. See Camerarius, Philipp
Tertia pars Indiae Orientalis. See Linschoten, Jan Huygen van
Tesillo, Santiago de. Guerra de Chile. Madrid: Imprenta Real, 1647
Tesoro de la lengua castellana. See Covarrubias Horozco, Sebastián de

Tesoro de la lengua guarani. See Ruiz de Montoya, Antonio
Tesoro de secreti medicinali. See Mazza, Marc' Antonio
Il tesoro della sanità. See Durante, Castore
Il tesoro della vita humana. See Fioravanti, Leonardo
Het testament ofte wtersten wille. See Middelgeest, Simon van
Der teutsche Palmenbaum. See Hille, Carl Gustav von
Thaumatographia naturalis. See Jonstonus, Joannes
Thaumatophylakion, sive Thesaurus . . . Allerley Antiquiteten. See Hofmann, Lorenz
Le théatre d'agriculture. See Serres, Olivier de, seigneur du Pradel
Le théatre de l'univers. See Grenaille, François de, sieur de Chatounières
Le theatre des animaux. See Desprez, Philippe
Theatre des cruautez des hereticques. See Verstegen, Richard
Theatre du monde. See titles under Blaeu, Willem Janszoon
Le théâtre universel des princes. See Doglioni, Giovanni Nicolò
Theatro d'el orbe de la tierra. See Ortelius, Abraham
Theatro de los mayores principes del mundo. See Botero, Giovanni
Theatro del mondo. See Ortelius, Abraham
Theatro del mundo. See Gallucci, Giovanni Paolo
Theatro . . . del mundo. See Gallucci, Giovanni Paolo
Theatrum botanicum: The theater of plants. See Parkinson, John
Theatrum chemicum. Strassburg: L. Zetzner, 1613–22
Theatrum cosmographicum. See Ritter, Stephan
Theatrum crudelitatum haereticorum. See Verstegen, Richard
Theatrum florae. Paris: N. de Mathonière, 1622
—Paris: P. Firens, 1627
—Paris: P. Firens, 1628
—Paris: P. Firens, 1633

—Paris: P. Mariette, 1633
—Paris: 1638
Theatrum historicum. See titles under Helwig, Christoph
Theatrum ingenii humani. See Neuhaus, Edo
Theatrum orbis terrarum. See titles under Blaeu, Willem Janszoon; and also Ortelius, Abraham
Theatrum victoriae, ofte het thoneel der zeeslagen. See Herckmans, Elias
Theeves falling out. See Greene, Robert
Theodorus, Jacobus. Neuw vollkommentlich Kreuterbuch. Frankfurt a.M.: N. Hoffmann, for J. Basse, & J. Dreutel, 1613
—New vollkommentlich Kreuterbuch. Frankfurt a.M.: P. Jacobi, for J. Dreutel, 1625
Theodorus Verax, pseud. See Walker, Clement
Theophilus Anti-Pater. See Anti-Pater, Theophilus
Theophrastisch Vade mecum. Das ist: Etliche . . . Tractat. See Penot, Bernard Georges
Theophrastus. De historia plantarum. Amsterdam: H. Laurenszoon, 1644
La theorie des longitudes. See Duliris, Leonard
La therapeutique. See Fernel, Jean
Thesaurus chirurgiae. See Uffenbach, Peter
Thesaurus chronologiae. See Alsted, Johann Heinrich
Thesaurus geographicus. See Ortelius, Abraham
Thesaurus pharmaceuticus. See Weickard, Arnold
Thesaurus polyglottus. See Megiser, Hieronymus
Thesaurus rerum indicarum. See Du Jarric, Pierre
Thesaurus Rulandinus. See Ruland, Martin
Thevet, André. Singularitez de la France antarctique. See Topsell, Edward. The historie of foure-footed beastes. London: 1607

TOBACCO—DRAMA
—Beaumont, F. Comedies and tragedies. London: 1647
— —The knight of the burning pestle. London: 1613
— —The scornful ladie. London: 1616
—Belchier, D. Hans Beer-pot his invisible comedie. [London:] 1618
—Chapman, G. Al fooles. London: 1605
— —The ball. London: 1639
— —Monsieur d' Olive. London: 1606
—Davenant, Sir W. The triumphs of the Prince d'Amour. London: 1635
—Day, J. Law-trickes. London: 1608
—Dekker, T. The honest whore, pt 2. London: 1630
— —North-ward hoe. London: 1607
— —The pleasant comodie. London: 1603
— —Satiro-mastix. London: 1602
— —West-ward hoe. London: 1607
— —The whore of Babylon. London: 1607
— —The wonder of a kingdome. London: 1636
—Everie woman in her humor. London: 1609
—Field, N. Amends for ladies. London: 1618
—Fletcher, J. Wit without money. London: 1639
—Ford, J. The lovers melancholy. London: 1629
—Gallobelgicus, pseud. Wine, beere, and ale. London: 1629
—Glapthorne, H. Wit in a constable. London: 1640
—Holyday, B. Technogamia: or, The marriages of the arts. London: 1618
—Jack Drum's entertainment. Jacke Drums entertainment. London: 1601
—Jones, J. Adrasta: or, The womans spleene. London: 1635
—Jonson, B. Bartholmew fayre. London: 1631

— —Volpone. London: 1607
— —The workes, v.2–3. London: 1640
—Kirke, J. The seven champions of Christendome. London: 1638
—Marmion, S. A fine companion. London: 1633
— —Hollands leaguer. London: 1632
—Marston, J. The malcontent. London: 1604
— —What you will. London: 1607
—Middleton, T. A faire quarrell. London: 1617
— —The phoenix. London: 1607
—Randolph, T. Aristippus, or The jovial philosopher. London: 1630
—Return from Parnassus. The returne from Pernassus. London: 1606
—Rowley, S. The noble souldier. London: 1634
—Sharpham, E. Cupids whirligig. London: 1607
— —The fleire. London: 1607
—Sheppard, S. The committeeman curried. [London?] 1647
—Shirley, J. The constant maid. London: 1640
—Tailor, R. The hogge hath lost his pearle. [London:] 1614
—Téllez, G. Doze comedias nuevas. Seville: 1627
—Tomkis, T. Albumazar. A comedy. London: 1615
— —Lingua; ofte Strijd. Amsterdam: 1648
— —Lingua, or The combat. London: 1607
—Wilkins, G. The miseries of inforst mariage. London: 1607
TOBACCO—HISPANIOLA
—Lancre, P. de. Tableau de l'inconstance des mauvais anges. Paris: 1612
TOBACCO—LAW AND LEGISLATION
—Great Britain. Sovereigns, etc., 1603–1625 (James I). A proclamation concerning the viewing . . . of tobacco. London: 1619

— —A proclamation concerning tobacco. London: 1624
— —A proclamation for restraint of the disordered trading for tobacco. London: 1620
— —A proclamation for the utter prohibiting the importation and use of all tobacco. London: [1625]
— —A proclamation to restraine the planting of tobacco. [London:] 1619
— —A proclamation, with articles of directions. London: [1619]
—Great Britain. Sovereigns, etc., 1625–1649 (Charles I). A proclamation concerning tobacco. London: [1631]
— — —London: 1634
— — —London: [1638]
— — —London: [1639]
— —A proclamation for the ordering of tobacco. London: 1627
— —A proclamation restraining the abusive venting of tobacco. London: [1634]
— —A proclamation touching the sealing of tobacco. London: 1627
— —A proclamation touching tobacco. London: 1625
—Grimston, Sir H. Mr Grymstons speech in Parliament. [London:] 1641
—Naples (Kingdom). Laws, statutes, etc. Pragmatica circa illius prohibendi del tabaco. Naples: [1650]
—Oxford. University. Statuta selecta. [Oxford:] 1638
TOBACCO—PHYSIOLOGICAL EFFECT
—Leiva y Aguilar, F.de. Desengaño contra el mal uso del tabaco. Córdova: 1634
—Malynes, G.de. The center of the circle of commerce. London: 1623
—Work for chimney-sweepers. London: 1602
TOBACCO—POETRY
—Beaumont, Sir J. The metamorphosis of tabacco. London: 1602

—Brathwaite, R. A strappado for the divell. London: 1615

—Campion, T. Epigrammatum libri ii. London: 1619

—Cooke, J. Epigrames. London: [1604]

—Coryat, T. Coryats crudities. London: 1611

—Craig, A. The poetical recreations. Edinburgh: 1609

—Daniel, S. Certain small works. London: 1607

— —The queens arcadia. London: 1606

—Davies, J. The scourge of folly. London: [1611]

—Dunbar, J. Epigrammaton. London: 1616

—Harington, Sir J. Epigrams. London: 1615

— —The most elegant . . . epigrams. London: 1618

—Harsdörffer, G. P. Gesprachspiele . . . Dritter Theil. Nuremberg: 1643

— —Nathan und Jotham. Nuremberg: 1650

—Heath, J. Two centuries of epigrammes. London: 1610

—Homburg, E. C. Schimpff- und ernsthaffte Clio. Jena: 1642

—Jenner, T. The soules solace. [London:] 1626

—Johnson, J. Schediasmata poetica. London: 1615

—Maluenda, J. A. Cozquilla del gusto. Valencia: 1629

—Martyn, J. New epigrams. London: 1621

—Middleton, R. Epigrams and satyres. London: 1608

—Ovidius Naso, Publius. Amores. English. Ovids elegies. London: [1602]

—Owen, J. Epigrammatum libri tres. London: 1606

—Plumptre, H. Epigrammatōn opusculum duobus distinctum. London: 1629

—Pyne, J. Epigrammata religiosa. [London:] 1626

—Quarles, F. Emblemes. London: 1635

—Rocquigny, A. de. La muse chrestienne. [London:] 1634

—Romance en alabansa del tabaco. Barcelona: 1644

—Rowlands, S. Democritus, or Doctor Merryman. London: 1607

— —Doctor Merrie-man. London: 1609

— —Good newes. London: 1622

— —Humors antique faces. London: 1605

— —Humors looking glasse. London: 1608

— —Humors ordinarie. London: [1605?]

— —The knave of clubbes. London: 1609

— —The knave of harts. London: 1612

— —The letting of humours blood. London: 1611

— —The melancholie knight. [London:] 1615

— —More knaves yet? London: [1613]

— —The night raven. London: 1620

— —A paire of spy-knaves. [London: 1620?]

— —Tis merrie when gossips meete. London: 1602

— —Well met gossip. London: 1619

— —A whole crew of kind gossips. London: 1609

—Saint-Amant, M. A. de Gérard, sieur de. Les oeuvres. Paris: 1629

—Scarron, P. La suite des oeuvres burlesques . . . Seconde partie. Paris: 1647

— —Typhon. Paris: 1644

— —Le Virgile travesty. Paris: 1648

—Schrijver, P. Saturnalia, ofte Poëtisch Vasten-avond-spel. Haarlem: 1630

— —Saturnalia, seu De usu et abusu tabaci. Haarlem: 1628

— —Vasten-avond-spel. Leyden: 1631

—Scot, T. Philomythie. London: 1616

—Sylvester, J. Tobacco battered. [London: 1617?]

—Tabourot, E. Les bigarrures. Paris: 1603

—Tatham, J. The fancies theater. London: 1640

—Taylor, J. An arrant thiefe. London: 1622

— —Beschrijvinge van den ouden . . . man. Delft: 1636

—A common whore. London: 1622

— —The complaint of M. Tenter-hooke. London: 1641

— —Faire and fowle weather. London: 1615

— —The great O Toole. London: 1622

— —A kicksey winsey. London: 1619

— —Laugh, and be fat. [London: 1612]

— —The nipping . . . of abuses. London: 1614

— —The olde, old . . . man. London: 1635

— —The praise . . . of beggery. London: 1621

— —The praise of hemp-seed. London: 1620

— —The sculler. London: 1612

— —Sir Gregory Nonsence. London: [1622]

— —Taylor's motto. London: 1621

— —The water-comorant his complaint. London: 1622

— —The world runnes on wheeles. London: 1623

—Vaughan, H. Poems. London: 1646

—Venne, A. van de. Sinnevonck. The Hague: 1634

— —Tafereel van de belacchende werelt. The Hague: 1635

—Warner, W. A continuance of Albions England. London: 1606

—Weelkes, T. Cantus. Ayeres or phantasticke spirites. London: 1608

—Wit's recreations. Wits recreations. London: 1640

—Wortley, Sir F. Mercurius Britannicus. [London?] 1647

—Zucchi, F. Poesie. Ascoli: 1636

TOBACCO—SONGS AND MUSIC

—Hume, T. Ayres, French, Polish, and others. London: 1605

—Ravenscroft, T. A briefe discourse. London: 1614

in die Orientalische Indien. Nuremberg: 1602

——Historiale beschrijvinghe. Amsterdam: 1619

——Journal was sich von Tag zu Tag . . . . Arnhem: 1601

——The journall. London: 1601

——Le second livre, Journal ou Comptoir. Amsterdam: 1601

——Het tweede boeck, Journael oft Dagh-register. Amsterdam: 1601

—Syms, C. The swords apology. London: 1644

Tobacco battered. *See* Sylvester, Joshua

TOBACCO IN ART

—Sadeler, R. Zodiacus christianus. Munich: 1618

TOBACCO IN LITERATURE

—Jonson, B. Every man in his humor. London: 1601

——Execration against Vulcan. London: 1640

—Randolph, T. Poems. Oxford: 1638

—Rowlands, S. Looke to it. London: 1604

—The speech of a cavaleere. London: 1642

—Taylor, J. Crop-eare curried. [Oxford: 1645]

——The great eater. London: 1630

——A shilling, or The travailes. [London: 1621]

—Vaughan, W. The golden fleece. London: 1626

—Watts, R. The young mans looking-glass. London: 1641

TOBACCO MANUFACTURE AND TRADE

—The armes of the tobachonists. London: 1630

—Dekker, T. Penny-wise. London: 1631

—Earle, J., Bp. Micro-cosmographie. London: 1628

—Great Britain. Sovereigns, etc., 1625–1649 (Charles I). A proclamation declaring His Majesties gratious pleasure touching sundry grants. London: 1639

——A proclamation declaring His Majesties pleasure . . . for

licensing retailers of tobacco. London: 1639

——A proclamation for preventing of the abuses . . . of tobacco. London: 1633

——A proclamation touching tobacco. London: [1627]

—Heywood, T. Machiavel. London: 1641

—Malynes, G. de. Consuetudo, vel, Lex mercatoria. London: 1636

—The man in the moone. London: 1609

—Mervyn, Sir A. A speech made before the Lords. [London?] 1641

—Micrologia. Characters, or essayes. London: 1629

—Middleton, T. A mad world. London: 1608

——The roaring girle. London: 1611

—Nash, T. Quaternio, or A fourefold way. London: 1633

—Scotland. Privy Council. [Forsamekle as it is weill knowin. Edinburgh: 1622]

——[Forsamekle as the Kingis . . . . Edinburgh: 1619]

——[Forsamekle as the Kingis Majestie oute of his princelie . . . . Edinburgh: 1622]

—Strafford, T. Wentworth, 1st earl of, defendant. Depositions and articles against Thomas earle of Strafford. London: [1641]

—Sweden. Sovereigns, etc., 1632–1654 (Christina). Förordning huru medh tobaks handelen skal blifwa hällit. [Stockholm: 1641]

—Tuscany. Laws, statutes, etc. Bando, et ordine da osservarsi per l'appalto . . . del tabacco. Florence: [1645]

—Valdés, J.de. Por el licenciado Don Juan de Valdes. [Seville? 1650?]

Tobacco tortured. *See* Deacon, John

Todas las obras. *See* Góngora y Argote, Luis de

Todas las obras en prosa. *See* Quevedo y Villegas, Francisco Gómez de

Todo el pleyto. *See* Quadro, Diego Felipe de

Todo el pleyto que siguen los dueños de barras del Pirù. *See* Sánchez, Antonio

Toledo Osorio y Mendoza, Fadrique de, marqués de Villanueva de Valdueza. Relacion de la carta . . . del felicissimo sucesso. Seville: S. Fajardo, 1625

—Relacion del sucesso del armada. Cadiz: G. Vezino, 1625

——[Madrid? 1625]

——Naples: Roncallolo, 1625

—Relacion embiado . . . de lo sucedido a la armada. Granada: B. de Lorenzana, 1630

——Seville: F. de Lyra, 1630

—Relation und Eigentliche beschreibung . . . was sich mit der Schiff Armada . . . abgefertigt worden. Augsburg: M. Langenwalter, for J. Keyltz, 1625

—Relatione venuta de Madrid a Roma. Rome: 1630

—Warhaffte Relation, von dem grossen herrlichen Sig. Passau: T. Nenninger, & C. Frosch, 1630

—*See also* Spain. Treaties, etc., 1621–1665 (Philip IV). Copia de las cartas y respuestas. Barcelona: 1625

TOLEDO OSORIO Y MENDOZA, FADRIQUE DE, MARQUÉS DE VILLANUEVA DE VALDUEZA

—Nuevas ciertas y fidedignas de la vitoria que ha alcançado Don Fadrique de Toledo. Barcelona: 1629

—Warhaffte gründliche Relation. Augsburg: 1625

—Wassenaer, N. van. T'neghenste deel . . . van het Historisch verhael. Amsterdam: [1626?]

Toledo y Leiva, Pedro de, marqués de Mancera. Relacion del estado del gobierno del Peru. [Madrid? 1649]

Tomasini, Jacopo Philippo, Bp. Elogia virorum literis et sapientia illustrium. Padua: S. Sardi, 1644

—Illustrium virorum elogio. Padua: D. Pasquardo and Associates, 1630

Tomkis, Thomas. Albumazar. A comedy. London: N. Okes, for W. Burre, 1615 (2)

——London: N. Okes, 1634

——London: N. Okes, 1634 [i.e., 1640]

—Lingua; ofte Strijd. Amsterdam: G.van Goedesberg, 1648

—Lingua, or The combat of the tongue. London: G. Eld, for S. Waterson, 1607

——London: N. Okes, for S. Waterson, [ca. 1615]

——London: N. Okes, for S. Waterson, 1617

——London: N. Okes, for S. Waterson, 1622

——London: A. Mathewes, for S. Waterson, 1632

Tomus alter et idem: or The history. *See* Camden, William. The historie of . . . Princesse Elizabeth

Tomus secundus Operum. *See* Mercado, Luis

A tongue-combat. *See* Hexham, Henry

Tooneel der beroemder hertogen. *See* Clercq, Nikolaas de

Tooneel der keyseren. *See* Clercq, Nikolaas de

Toonneel des aerdriicx. *See* Blaeu, Willem Janszoon

Toonneel des aerdrycx. *See* Blaeu, Willem Janszoon

Toortse der zeevaerdt. *See* Colom, Jacob Aertszoon

Toortse der zee-vaert. *See* Ruyters, Dierick

Topsell, Edward. The historie of foure-footed beastes. London: W. Jaggard, 1607

—The historie of serpents. London: W. Jaggard, 1608

Torquemada, Antonio de. Giardino di fiori curiosi. Venice: G. B. Ciotti, 1604

——Venice: P. Bertano, 1612 (2)

——Venice: G. Alberti, 1620

—Hexameron, ou, Six journees. Rouen: R. de Beauvais, 1610

—Histoires en forme de dialogues. Rouen: J. Roger, 1625

—Jardin de flores curiosas. Barcelona: J. Margarit, 1621

—The Spanish Mandeville of miracles. London: B. Alsop, 1618

Torquemada, Juan de. Veynte y un libros rituales, pte 1a–3a. Seville: M. Clavijo, 1615

Torres, Juan de. Philosophia moral. Burgos: J. B. Varesio, for D. Pérez, 1602

——Lisbon: P. Craesbeeck, 1602

Torres, Marcos de. El licendiado Marcos de Torres . . . contra. Doña Francisca Colon. [Madrid? ca. 1605?]

Torres, Pedro de. Libro que trata de la enfermedad. Alcalá de Henares: Widow of J. Gracían, 1626

Torres Bollo, Diego de. Breve relatione. Venice: G. B. Ciotti, 1604

—Brevis relatio historica in provincia Peruana. Mainz: B. Lipp, 1604

—De rebus Peruanis . . . commentarius. Antwerp: M. Nuyts, 1604

—Kurtzer Bericht was Gott . . . in den Peruanischen Ländern aussgericht. Würzburg: G. Fleischmann, 1604

—La nouvelle histoire du Perou. Paris: J. Richer, 1604

——Paris: [J. Richer] for Catherine Niverd (Widow of Monstr'oeil), 1604

—O rozszerzeniu wiary . . . w Americe. Cracow: A. Piotrkowczyk, 1603

—Relatione breve. Milan: Heirs of P. da Ponte, & G. B. Piccaglia, 1603

——Rome: A. Zannetti, 1603

See also the following:

—Donne, John. Conclave Ignatii. [London: 1611]

——Ignatius his conclave. London: 1611

Torriano, Giovanni. The Italian tutor. London: T. Paine, for H. Robinson, 1640

——London: T. Paine, & H. Robinson, for G. Torriano, 1640

Torsellino, Orazio. Chronicon ab orbe condito. Cologne: Birckmann Office, for H. Mylius, 1631

—Epitomae historiarum libri x. Lyons: J. Cardon, & P. Cavellat, 1620

——Cologne: B. Wolter, 1621

——Lyons: J. Cardon, & P. Cavellat, 1621

——Milan: G. B. Bidelli, 1621

——Lyons: J. Cardon, 1628

—Epitome historiarum ab orbe condito. Cologne: J. A. Kinckius, 1649

—Epitome historiarum libri x. Cologne: Birckmann Office, for H. Mylius, 1622

——Rome: G. Facciotti, for G. B. Brugiotti, 1625

—Histoire générale depuis la création. Paris: R. Chaudière, 1622

—Histoire universelle depuis la création. Paris: T.de La Ruelle, 1633

——Paris: 1647

——Paris: G. Clouzier, 1648, '47

—Historiarum ab origine mundi . . . epitome libri x. Douai: B. Bellère, 1623

——Cologne: B. Wolter, 1624

——Douai: B. Bellère, 1627

——Douai: B. Bellère, 1630

——Rome: G. Facciotti, 1630

——Paris: J. Branchu, 1631

——Paris: M. Hénault, 1631

——Paris: M. Soly, 1631

——Paris: 1637

——Paris: 1640

——Munich: 1641

——Lyons: A. Rigaud, 1643

——Paris: J. Libert, 1645

——Lyons: S. Rigaud, 1647

—Historiarum ab origine mundi . . . libri x. Lyons: J. A. Candy, 1648

—Ristretto dell'historie. Rome: G. Mascardi, for P. Totti, 1634

—Ristretto delle historie. Perugia: P. G. Billi, 1623

——Rome: G. Mascardi, for P. Totti, 1637

——Venice: C. Tomasini, 1642

The totall discourse. *See* Lithgow, William

TOUCANS
—Contant, P. Le jardin et cabinet poétique. Poitiers: 1609
—Gesner, K. Historia animalium. Frankfurt a.M.: 1604
Toutes les oeuvres charitables. *See* Guibert, Philbert
Tractaet . . . van het gebruijck der . . . globe. *See* Hues, Robert
Tractaet tegens pays. The Hague: A. Meuris, 1629
—*See also* Klare aenwijsinge. The Hague: 1630
Tractaet tegens pays, 2de dl. *See* Redenen, waeromme dat de Vereenighde Nederlanden . . . . The Hague: 1630
Tractaet van bestant. *See* Portugal. Treaties, etc., 1640–1656 (John IV)
Tractaet van peys. *See* Spain. Treaties, etc., 1621–1665 (Philip IV)
Tractaet van vrede. *See* Spain. Treaties, etc., 1621–1665 (Philip IV)
Tractaet vande oudtheyt vande Batavische . . . republique. *See* Grotius, Hugo
Tractatus . . . de magnete. *See* Gilbert, William
Tractatus de globis. *See* Hues, Robert
Tractatus de officio fiscalis. *See* Alfaro, Francisco de
Tractatus duo. *See* Botero, Giovanni; *and also* Padovani, Fabrizio
Tractatus duo mathematici. *See* Hues, Robert
Tractatus induciarum. *See* Portugal. Treaties, etc., 1640–1656 (John IV)
Tractatus medico-chymici septem. *See* Untzer, Matthias
Tractatus methodicus . . . de lue venerea. *See* Macchelli, Niccolò
Tractatus nobilis secundus. *See* Amelung, Peter
Tractatus novus. *See* Strobelberger, Johann Stephan
Tractatus pacis. *See* Spain. Treaties, etc., 1621–1665 (Philip IV)
Tractatus philosophici: Quod

nihil scitur. *See* Sánchez, Francisco
Tractatus varii. *See* Penot, Bernard Georges
The trades increase. *See* Kayll, Robert
Traduccion de la dedicatoria real. *See* Solórzano Pereira, Juan de
Tragedies and comedies. *See* Marston, John
Tragicall historie of . . . Doctor Faustus. *See* Marlowe, Christopher. Doctor Faustus
Traicté contenant la pharmacie chymique. *See* Pascal, Jacques
Traicté de la cure generale. *See* Duchesne, Joseph
Traicté de la maladie nouvellement appelee cristaline. *See* Guillaumet, Tannequin
Traicté de la matiere . . . de la medecine balsamique. *See* Duchesne, Joseph
Traicté de la navigation. *See* Bergeron, Pierre
Traicté de la paix. *See* Spain. Treaties, etc., 1621–1665 (Philip IV)
Traicté de la peste. *See* Collège des Maîtres chirurgiens de Paris
Traicté de la verité de la religion chrestienne. *See* Grotius, Hugo
Traicté de paix. *See* Spain. Treaties, etc., 1621–1665 (Philip IV)
Traicté des globes. *See* Hues, Robert
Traicté du tabac. *See* Neander, Johann
Traicté entre le Roy Louis XIII. et Charles roy de la Grand'-Bretagne. *See* France. Treaties, etc., 1610–1643 (Louis XIII)
Traicté second de la maladie appelee cristaline. *See* Guillaumet, Tannequin
Traité de . . . la parfaite cure. *See* Fernel, Jean
Traité de la religion. *See* Rivadeneira, Pedro de
Tranen over den doodt van . . . Heyn. *See* Spranckhuysen, Dionysius
Translaet uyt den Spaenschen.

Vande geluckige victorie. Amsterdam: F. Lieshout, 1630
Translaet uyt den Spaenschen, weghens 't gevecht. Amsterdam: F. Lieshout, 1639
Translaet uyt het Latijn. *See* Portugal. Treaties, etc., 1640–1656 (John IV). Tractaet van bestant. The Hague: 1642
Traslado de una carta, embiada del Brasil. Madrid: Catalina de Barrio y Angulo [1640]
[Traslado del despacho del servicio personal.] *See* Spain. Consejo de las Indias
Traslado del memorial. *See* Baeza, Pedro de
Traslados de algunas cartas sacadas de sus proprios originales. [Madrid: 1647]
Tratado das batalhas . . . do galeão Sanctiago. *See* Amaral, Melchior Estacio do
Tratado de confirmaciones reales de economiendas. *See* León Pinelo, Antonio Rodríguez de
Tratado de domicilio. *See* Avila, Esteban de
Tratado de la immaculada concepcion. *See* Antist, Vincente Justiniano, fray
Tratado de la religion. *See* Rivadeneira, Pedro de
Tratado de las excelencias . . . del tabaco. *See* Ayo, Cristóbal de
Tratado de los relaciones verdaderas . . . de la China. *See* Ordóñez de Ceballos, Pedro
Tratado, relación y discurso . . . de Aragón. *See* Herrera y Tordesillas, Antonio de
Tratado verdadero del viage y navegacion deste año. *See* Vázquez de Espinosa, Antonio
Trattado das tregoas. *See* Portugal. Treaties, etc., 1640–1656 (John IV)
Trattato de' veleni. *See* Pona, Francesco
Trattato della religione. *See* Rivadeneira, Pedro de
The travellers breviat. *See* Botero, Giovanni
Travels in Africa and Asia. *See* Herbert, Sir Thomas.

—Tre navigationi. *In* Ramusio, Giovanni Battista. Delle navigationi et viaggi . . . Volume terzo. Venice: 1606

—Le trois navigations. Paris: N. Buon, 1610

—The true and perfect description of three voyages. London: [W. White] for T. Pavier, 1609

—Verhael van de eerste schip-vaert der Hollandische . . . schepen. Amsterdam: J. Hartgers, 1648

——Amsterdam: A. Roest, for J. Hartgers, 1650

—Vraye description de trois voyages. Amsterdam: C. Claeszoon, 1604

——Amsterdam: C. Claeszoon, 1609

—De waerachtighe beschrijvinge. Enkhuizen: J.L. Meyn, for M. Colijn, at Amsterdam, 1619

—Waerachtighe beschryvinghe van drie seylagien. Amsterdam: C. Claeszoon, 1605

Het veertiende deel . . . van het Historisch verhael. *See* Wassenaer, Nicolaes van

Vega, Garcilaso de la, el Inca. *See* Garcilaso de la Vega, el Inca

Vega Carpio, Lope Félix de. Arcadia. Barcelona: S. de Cormellas, for G. Aleu, 1602

——Madrid: P. Madrigal, 1602

——Madrid: [L. Sánchez] for J.de Montoya, 1602

——Valencia: J. C. Garriz, 1602

——Valencia: J. C. Garriz, for F. Miguel, & R. Sonzonio, 1602

——Madrid: P. Madrigal, for J.de Montoya, 1603

——Madrid: P. Madrigal, for J.de Montoya, 1603

——Antwerp: M. Nuyts, 1605

——Madrid: J.de la Cuesta, for J.de Montoya, 1605

——Madrid: A. Martin, for A. Pérez, 1611

——Lérida: J. Margarit, & L. Menescal, for M. Menescal, 1612

——Barcelona: S.de Cormellas, 1615

——Antwerp: P. & J. Bellère, 1617

——Madrid: F. Correa de Montenegro, for A. Pérez, 1620

——Cadiz: J. de Borja, 1626

——Cadiz: J. de Borja, 1629

——Segovia: D. Flamenco, for A. Pérez [at Madrid], 1629

——Barcelona: J. Margarit, 1630

——Madrid: G. Rodríguez, for R. Lorenzo, 1645

—Comedias . . . quarta parte. Barcelona: S. de Cormellas, 1614

——Barcelona: S. de Cormellas, for J. Bonilla, 1614

—Comedias, pte 20. Madrid: Widow of A. Martín, for A. Pérez, 1625

——Madrid: J. González, for Widow of A. Martín, 1626

——Madrid: J. González, for A. Pérez, 1627

——Madrid: J. González, 1629

——Barcelona: E. Liberòs, for R. Vives, 1630

—Comedias, pte 22. Saragossa: P. Verges, for J. de Ginobart, 1630

—Comedias, pte 21. Madrid: Widow of A. Martín, for D. Logroño, 1635

—Les delices de la vie pastorale. Lyons: P. Rigaud, 1622

——Lyons: P. Rigaud and Associates, 1624

—Doze commedias . . . Quarta parte. Madrid: M. Serrano de Vargas, for M. de Siles, 1614

——Pamplona: N. de Assiayn, 1614

——Pamplona: J. de Oteyza, 1624

—Dragontea. *In his* La hermosura de Angelica. Madrid: 1602

——*In the same.* Barcelona: 1604

——*In the same.* Madrid: 1605

—La hermosura de Angelica. Madrid: P. Madrigal, 1602

——Barcelona: J. Amello, for M. Menescal, 1604

——Madrid: J. de la Cuesta, 1605

—Laurel de Apolo. Madrid: J. González, 1630

Vege, Petrus de. Pax methodicorum. Lyons: B. Vincent, 1620

VEILS
—León Pinelo, A. R. de. Velos antiguos i modernos. Madrid: 1641

Velasco, Diego de. Señor. Advertencias que . . . Diego de Velasco . . . tiene hechas. [Madrid? 1620?]

—Señor. Descubrimiento del camino. [Madrid? 1620?]

Velasco, Pedro de. Señor. Pedro de Velasco . . . procurador general. [Madrid: 1641?]

Velázquez, Baltasar Mateo. El filosofo del aldea. Pamplona: P. Dullort, 1626

——Saragossa: D. Dormer, [ca. 1650]

Velázquez, Juan. Relacion que el licenciado Don Juan Velazquez hizo. [Madrid? 1632?]

Velázquez Minaya, Francisco. Esfera, forma del mundo. Madrid: Widow of L. Sánchez, 1628

Velle, Nicasius Martens van. De oprechte waeg-schaele. Antwerp: P. de Hollander, 1647

—De oprechte waeghschaele. Arnhem: J.T.van Westerloo, 1647

Velos antiguos i modernos. *See* León Pinelo, Antonio Rodríguez de

De veltbouw, ofte Lant-winninghe. *See* Estienne, Charles

De velt-bow. *See* Estienne, Charles

Venero, Alonso. Enchiridion, o Manual de los tiempos. Alcalá de Henares: A. Vázquez, for M. López, 1641

Venetae historiae . . . libri xii. *See* Bembo, Pietro, Cardinal

VENEZUELA
—Rúa, F. de. Por Don Juan Meneses. Madrid: [1634]

—Sumario, y compendio de lo sucedido en España. [Madrid: 1638]

VENEZUELA—CHURCH HISTORY
—Prado, E.de. Por Francisco Nuñez Melian, governador . . . que fue . . . de Veneçuela. [Madrid? 1640?]

VENEZUELA—HISTORY
—Moscoso y de Córdoba, C. de. El licenciado don Christoval de Moscoso y Cordova . . . Con Don Juan de Meneses. Madrid: 1634
—Peralta, P.de. Señor. El capitan Don Pedro de Peralta contador. [Madrid: 1644?]
—Santo Tomé, Venezuela. Señor. La ciudad de Santo Tome. [Madrid? ca. 1620?]
VENEZUELA—HISTORY, NAVAL
—Vera relacion de la famosa vitoria. Jerez de la Frontera: 1632
La venida de Christo. *See* Ojea, Hernando
Venne, Adriaen van de. Sinnevonck op den Hollandtschen turf. The Hague: I. Burchoorn, for A. van de Venne and Heirs, 1634
—Tafereel van de belacchende werelt. The Hague: A. van de Venne, 1635 (2)
Venner, Tobias. A briefe and accurate treatise, concerning . . . tobacco. London: W. J[ones]., for R. More, 1621
—Via recta ad vitam longam. London: E. Griffin, for R. More, 1620
— —London: T. S[nodham]., for R. More, 1622
— —London: F. Kingston, for R. More, 1628
— —London: R. Bishop, for H. Hood, 1637
— —London: R. Bishop, for H. Hood, 1638
— —London: J. Fletcher, for H. Hood, 1650
El venturoso descubrimiento de las insulas. Barcelona: E. Liberòs, 1616
Vera, Diego de. *See* Spain. Laws, statutes, etc., 1621–1665 (Philip IV). Capitulaciones de el assiento. [Madrid:] 1639
VERA CRUZ, MEXICO
—Relacion de lo sucedido a la Armada Real. [Seville? 1638]
—Relaes ende 't cargo van't silver. Amsterdam: [1632?]
—Roco de Córdoba, F. Por Don

Martin y Aldrete. Madrid: 1636
—Tapia de Vargas, J. Por D. Juan Tapia de Vargas. [Madrid? 164–?]
Vera, e nuova relatione. Florence: S. Fantucci [1628?]
Vera et jucunda descriptio . . . Indiae Occidentalis. *See* Schmidel, Ulrich
Vera praxis ad curatione tertianae. *See* Barba, Pedro
Vera relacion de la famosa vitoria. Jerez de la Frontera: F. Rey, 1632
Vera relatione della presa della città d'Olinda. *See* Loncq, Hendrik Cornelis
Vera y Figueroa, Juan Antonio. *See* Roca, Juan Antonio Vera Zúñiga y Figueroa, conde de la
Veracruz. *See* Vera Cruz
VERAGUA. *See* PANAMA
Verax, Theodorus (pseud.) *See* Walker, Clement
Verclaringe ende verhael hoe de Heere Wouter Raleigh . . . hem ghedreghen heeft. The Hague: A. Meuris, 1619
Vercondinge van de vrede. *See* Netherlands (United Provinces, 1581–1795). Staten General
Verdadera relacion de la grandiosa conversion. *See* Perea, Estevan de
Verdadera relacion de la grandiosa vitoria. [Madrid? 1625?]
Verdadera relacion del viage y sucesso de los caravelones. Seville: B. Gómez de Pastrana, 1621
Le vere e nove imagini. *See* Cartari, Vincenzo
Vereenighde Nederlandschen raedt. *See titles under* Moerbeeck, Jan Andries
Veremontanus, Pambonus. *See* Scribanius, Carolus
Vergara Gaviria, Diego de. Adicion a la informacion. [Madrid? 1639?]
—Nulidades expresas. [Madrid? ca. 1625]
—Por Diego de Vergara Gaviria. [Madrid? 1639?]

Vergilius, Polydorus. De rerum inventoribus libri octo. Geneva: J. Stoer, 1604
— —Strassburg: L. Zetzner, 1606
— —Strassburg: L. Zetzner, 1613
— —Cologne: B. Wolter, 1626
Verhael van de avontuerlijke reyse. *See* Bontekoe, Willem Ysbrandsz
Verhael van de eerste schip-vaert der Hollandische . . . schepen. *See* Veer, Gerrit de
Verhael van de Nederlantsche vreede-handeling. *See* Aitzema, Lieuwe van
Verhael van 't ghene den Admirael l'Hermite in . . . Peru verricht. Amsterdam: C Meulemans, 1625
Verheiden, Willem. Nootelijcke consideratien. [Amsterdam?] 1608
—An oration or speech. [Amsterdam: Successors of G. Thorp] 1624
—A second part of Spanish practises. [London: N. Okes] 1624
Verhooginge der capitalen . . . voor een derde part. *See* Nederlandsche West-Indische Compagnie
Verhooginghe vande capitalen. *See* Nederlandsche West-Indische Compagnie
Veridicus Belgicus. *See* Scribanius, Carolus
Verimundima, Pambon, pseud. *See* Scribanius, Carolus
Le veritable inventaire. *See* Serres, Jean de
La veritable response a l'anticipation. [Paris?: 1611]
Les veritables motifs. [Paris:] 1643
La verité de la religion chrestienne. *See* Grotius, Hugo
Verken, Johann. Continuatio oder Ergäntzung dess neundten Theils. Frankfurt a.M.: Widow of M. Becker, for J. T.de Bry, 1613 (2)
Verkondinghe van het bestant. *See* Portugal. Treaties, etc., 1640–1656 (John IV)
Den vermeerderden spieghel der

—Wurffbain, J. S. Reiss-Beschreibung. Nuremberg: 1646

VOYAGES AROUND THE WORLD. *See also names of individual circumnavigators, e.g.* Noort, Olivier van

—Drake, Sir F. The world encompassed. London: 1628

Les voyages avantureux. *See* Alfonce, Jean, i.e., Jean Fonteneau, known as; *and also* Hoyarsabal, Martin de

Les voyages de la Nouvelle France. *See* Champlain, Samuel de

Les voyages du sieur de Champlain. *See* Champlain, Samuel de

Voyages en Afrique, Asie, Indes. *See* Mocquet, Jean

Voyages et descouvertures faites en la Nouvelle France. *See* Champlain, Samuel de

Les voyages fameux. *See* Le Blanc, Vincent

Voyagie, ofte Schip-vaert. *See* Linschoten, Jan Huygen van

Voyasie, ofte Schip-vaert. *See* Linschoten, Jan Huygen van

Vraye description de trois voyages. *See* Veer, Gerrit de

Vreimundima, Pambo. *See* Scribanius, Carolus

De vruchten van't monster van den treves. [Amsterdam?] 1630 (2)

Vrye zeevaert. *See* Grotius, Hugo

Vryheden by de vergaderinghe van de negenthiene . . . vergunt aen . . . Nieu-Nederlandt. *See* Nederlandsche West-Indische Compagnie

Vryheden ende exemptien t'accorderen ende toe te staen. *See* Nederlandsche West-Indische Compagnie

Vryheden ende exemptien voor de patroonen. *See* Nederlandsche West-Indische Compagnie

Vrymoedige aenspraeck aen syn hoogheyt. *See* Teellinck, Maximiliaan

Vrymoedigh discours tusschen twee Paepsche Hollanders. [The Hague?] 1647

T'vyfde-deel . . . van het Histo-

risch verhael. *See* Wassenaer, Nicolaes van

'T vyfthiende deel . . . van het Historisch verhael. *See* Wassenaer, Nicolaes van

Waar-mond, Ymant van. *See* Middelgeest, Simon van

Wadsworth, James. The present estate of Spayne. London: A. M[athewes]., for A. Ritherdon, 1630

— —London: A. M[athewes]., for R. Thrale, & A. Ritherdon, 1630

Waerachtich verhael van de gantsche reyse. Amsterdam: J.van Hilten, 1626

Een waerachtige beschryvinghe van de schoone victorie. Amsterdam: B. Janszoon, 1616

Waerachtigh verhael van de schip-vaert op Oost-Indien. *See* Neck, Jacob Corneliszoon van

Waerachtigh verhael van het succes van de vlote. [Amsterdam?] 1625

De waerachtighe beschrijvinge. *See* Veer, Gerrit de

Waerachtighe beschryvinghe van drie seylagien. *See* Veer, Gerrit de

Waerdenburgh, Dirk van. Copie de la lettre . . . touchant la prise . . . de Olinda. Paris: J. Bessin, 1630 (3)

—Copie eines Schreibens . . . Betreffend die Eroberung der Statt Olinda. [Frankfurt a.M.?] 1630

—Copie vande missive . . . noopende de veroveringhe vande stadt Olinda. The Hague: Widow & Heirs of H. J.van Wouw, 1630

— —Utrecht: L.S.de Vries, 1630

—La prise de la ville de Olinda. [Antwerp?] 1630

—Two memorable relations. London: N. Bourne, 1630

—*See also* Loncq, Hendrik Cornelis. Copia wt de missiven. Amsterdam: [1630?]

WAERDENBURGH, DIRK VAN

—Baers, J. Olinda, ghelegen int landt van Brasil. Amsterdam: 1630

Waerschouwinge over den treves. *See* Usselinx, Willem

Waerschouwinge, verboth, ende toe-latinghe. *See* Rensselaer, Kiliaen van

Waerschouwinghe op de West-Indissche Compagnie. [The Hague? 1622]

Waerschouwinghe over den treves. *See* Usselinx, Willem

Waerschouwinghe van de ghewichtighe redenen. *See* Usselinx, Willem

Wake, Sir Isaac. Rex platonicus. Oxford: J. Barnes, 1607 (2)

— —Oxford: J. Barnes, 1615

— —Oxford: J. Lichfield, 1627

— —Oxford: L. Lichfield, 1635

— —Oxford: L. Lichfield, 1636

Walbeeck, Johannes van, supposed author. *See* Journael vande Nassausche vloot. Amsterdam: 1626

Walerande, J.B.de. Le plaidoyer de l'Indien hollandois. [Antwerp?] 1608 (2)

Walker, Clement. Anarchia anglicana . . . The first part. [London?] 1648 [i.e., 1649?]

—Anarchia anglicana . . . The second part. [London?] 1649 (2)

— —[London?] 1650

—The history of Independency. [London?] 1648

—Relations and observations . . . upon the Parliament. [London?] 1648

— —[London?] 1650

The walking librarie. *See* Camerarius, Philipp

Walkington, Thomas. The optick glasse of humors. London: J. Windet, for M. Clarke, 1607

— —Oxford: W. T[urner]., for M. S[parke, at London, 1631].

— —London: J. D[awson]., & L. B[lacklock]., 1639

Waller, Edmund. Poems. London: J. N[orton]., for H. Moseley, 1645

— —London: T. W[arren]., for H. Moseley, 1645 (2)

—The workes. London: T. W[arren]., for H. Moseley, 1645

— —London: [T. Warren?] for T. Walkley, 1645

The wandering Jew. *See* Gad ben-Arod ben Balaam, pseud.

WAR

—Scott, T. The Belgicke pismire. [Utrecht?] 1622

WAR, COST OF

—Rodríguez de Robles, A. Señor. Antonio Rodriguez de Robles dize, que de 9. años . . . han residido. [Madrid? 1606?]

Warachtich verhael vanden slach . . . inde Zuydt Zee. Middelburg: R. Schilders, 1617

Warachtighe ende grondighe beschryvinghe van . . . Guiana. *See* Raleigh, Sir Walter

Ward, Nathaniel. Discolliminium. London: 1650

—The simple cobler of Aggawam. London: J. Dever, & R. Ibbitson, for S. Bowtell, 1647

——London: J. D[ever]., & R. I[bbitson]., for S. Bowtell, 1647 (3)

——London: J. Dever & R. Ibbitson, for S. Bowtell, 1647

——*See also* Shinkin ap Shone, pseud. The honest Welchcobler. [London:]1647

Wardenburgh, Dirk van. *See* Waerdenburgh, Dirk van

Warhafft Umbständ und gründlicher Bericht. [The Hague?] 1624

Warhaffte Beschreibung der wunderbarlichen Räyse. *See* Schouten, Willem Corneliszoon

Warhaffte Beschreibung dess edelen Krauts Nicotianae. *See* Liébault, Jean

Warhaffte gründliche Relation. Augsburg: A. Aperger, 1625

Warhaffte Relation, von dem grossen herrlichen Sig. *See* Toledo Osorio y Mendoza, Fadrique de, marqués de Villanueva de Valdueza

Warhaffter Bricht welcher Massen die Statt Olinda . . . ist eroberet . . . worden. [The Hague? 1630]

Warhafftige Beschreibung der unglückhafften Schiffarht. *See* Ottsen, Hendrick

Warhafftige und liebliche Beschreibung etlicher . . . Indianischen Landschafften. *See* Schmidel, Ulrich

Warhafftiger und gründlicher Bericht. *See* Casas, Bartolomé de las, Bp

WARNER, SIR THOMAS

—Featley, J. A sermon preached to . . . Sir Thomas Warner. London: 1629

Warner, William. A continuance of Albions England. London: F. Kingston, for G. Potter, 1606

WARWICK, RHODE ISLAND

—Gorton, S. Simplicities defence. London: 1646

Warwick, Robert Rich, 2d earl of. A declaration . . . To the colony. [London: 1644]

Waser, Caspar. *See* Gesner, Konrad. Mithridates Gesneri. Zurich: 1610

Wassenaer, Nicolaes van. T'achste deel . . . van het Historisch verhael. Amsterdam: J. Janszoon the Younger [1625]

—T'derde-deel . . . van het Historischer verhael. Amsterdam: J. E. Cloppenburg, 1623

——Amsterdam: J. E. Cloppenburg, & I. Willemszoon, at Hoorn, 1626

—Het dertiende ghedeelt . . . van het Historisch verhael. Amsterdam: J. Janszoon the Younger, 1628

—Het elfde deel . . . van het Historisch verhael. Amsterdam: J. Janszoon the Younger [1627?]

—Historisch verhael. Amsterdam: J. E. Cloppenburg, 1622. [Individual parts of the *Historisch verhael* are listed here alphabetically under their Dutch titles]

—T'neghenste deel . . . van het Historisch verhael. Amsterdam: J. Janszoon the Younger [1626?]

—T'seste deel . . . van het Historisch verhael. Amsterdam: J. Janszoon the Younger [1624]

—Het ses'thiende deel . . . van het Historisch verhael. Am-

sterdam: J. Janszoon the Younger, 1629

—T'sevende-deel . . . van het Historisch verhael. Amsterdam: J. Janszoon the Younger, 1625

—Het seventiende ghedeelt . . . van het Historisch verhael. Amsterdam: J. Janszoon the Younger, 1630

—'Thiende deel . . . van het Historisch verhael. Amsterdam: J. Janszoon the Younger, 1626

—'Twaelfde deel . . . van het Historisch verhael. Amsterdam: J. Janszoon the Younger [1627]

—Tweede-deel . . . van het Historisch verhael. Amsterdam: J. E. Cloppenburg, 1622

—Het veertiende deel . . . van het Historisch verhael. Amsterdam: J. Janszoon the Younger [1628]

—T'vierde deel . . . van het Historisch verhael. Amsterdam: J. E. Cloppenburg, 1623

—T'vyfde-deel . . . van het Historisch verhael. Amsterdam: J. Hondius, 1624

—'T vyfthiende deel . . . van het Historisch verhael. Amsterdam: J. Janszoon the Younger, 1629

See also the following:

—Lampe, Barent. Het achtiende deel . . . van het Historisch verhael. Amsterdam: [1630?]

——Het eenentwintichste deel . . . van het Historisch verhael. Amsterdam: 1635

——Het negentiende deel . . . van het Historisch verhael. Amsterdam: 1632

——Het twintigste deel . . . van het Historisch verhael. Amsterdam: 1633

A watch-man for the pest. *See* Bradwell, Stephen

The water-comorant his complaint. *See* Taylor, John, the Water-poet

Waterhouse, Edward. A declaration of the state of . . . Virginia. London: G. Eld, for R. Milbourne, 1622

——London: T. S[nodham]., for
F. Burton, 1614
——London: H. Lownes, for F.
Burton, 1615
——London: H. Lownes, for F.
Burton, 1617
——*In his* Juvenilia. London:
1622
—Juvenilia. A collection of those
poemes. London: T. S[nod-
ham]., for J. Budge, 1622
Wits private wealth. *See* Breton,
Nicholas
Wit's recreations. Recreation
for ingenious head-peeces.
London: M. Simmons, for
J. Hancock, 1650
—Recreation for ingenious
head-pieces. London:
R. Cotes, for H. B[lunden].,
1645
—Wits recreations. London:
R. H[odgkinson]., for H. Blun-
den, 1640
—Wit's recreations. London:
T. Cotes, for H. Blunden,
1641
Wittich, Johann. Bericht von
den . . . Bezoardischen
Steinen. [Arnstadt:] Vögelin
Press, 1601
—Nobiliss[imo]rum ac doctis-
s[imo]rum Germaniae medico-
rum Consilia. Leipzig:
H. Gross, 1604
—Von dem Ligno Guayaco.
[Arnstadt:] Vögelin Press,
1603
WOMEN IN SOUTH AMERICA
—Capitulo de una de las cartas
que diversas personas em-
biaron. Seville: 1618
The wonder of a kingdome. *See*
Dekker, Thomas
Wonderbaerlijcken strydt. *See*
Beverwijck, Jan van
The wonderfull year. *See* Dekker,
Thomas
The wonderfull yeare. *See* Dek-
ker, Thomas
Wonderlicke avontuer van twee
goelieven. Leyden: N. Geel-
kercken, 1624
Wonderlijcke historische ende
Journaelsche aenteyckeningh.
See Broeck, Pieter van den

Wonderlijcke voyagie, by de
Hollanders gedaen. *See* Noort,
Olivier van
Wonders worth the hearing. *See*
Breton, Nicholas
Wood, Owen. An alphabeticall
book of physicall secrets. Lon-
don: J. Norton, for W. Ed-
monds, 1639
Wood, William. New Englands
prospect. London: T. Cotes,
for J. Bellamy, 1634
——London: T. Cotes, for J.
Bellamy, 1635
——London: J. Dawson, for J.
Bellamy, 1639
Woodall, John. The surgions
mate. London: E. Griffin, for
L. Lisle, 1617
Work for chimney-sweepers.
London: T. East, for T. Bu-
shell, 1602
Worke for armorours. *See* Dek-
ker, Thomas
Workman, Giles. Private-men
no pulpit-men. London:
F. N[eile]., for T. Langford, at
Gloucester, 1646
——London: F. Neile, for
T. Underhill, 1646
The world encompassed by Sir
Francis Drake. *See* Drake, Sir
Francis
The world runnes on wheeles.
See Taylor, John, the Water-
poet
The worlde. *See* Botero, Gio-
vanni
**The worthye and famous his-
tory** of . . . Terra Florida. Lon-
don: [F. Kingston] for
M. Lownes, 1611
Wortley, Sir Francis. Mercurius
Britannicus. [London?] 1647
Wright, Edward. Certaine errors
in navigation. London:
F. Kingston, 1610
Wright, Thomas. The passions
of the minde. London:
V. S[immes]., for W. B[urre].,
1601
——London: V. Simmes [&
A. Islip], for W. Burre, 1604
——London: A. M[athewes].,
for Anne Helme, 1620
——London: A. M[athewes].,
for Anne Helme, 1621

——London: M. Fletcher, for
R. Dawlman, 1630
Wtenbogaert, Johannes. On-
dersoeck der Amsterdamsche
requesten. [Amsterdam? Rot-
terdam?] 1628
—Tsamen-spraeck over de
. . . gesellen van Treves-krack.
[The Hague?] 1630
—Wtwissinge der schandelicker
blamen. [The Hague?] 1630
Wtwissinge der schandelicker
blamen. *See* Wtenbogaert,
Johannes
Wund Artzney. *See* Paré, Am-
broise
Wunderbarliche . . . Erklärung
von . . . Virginia. *See* Hariot,
Thomas
Wunderbarliche und seltzame
Raiss. *See* Victoria, Pedro
Gobeo de
Wunderliche und warhafftige
Gesichte. *See* Moscherosch,
Johann Michael
Wundt Artzney. *See* Paré, Am-
broise
Wurfbain, Johann Sigmund. *See*
Wurffbain, Johann Sigmund
Wurfbain, Leonhart. Relatio
historica Habspurgico-Austri-
aca. Nuremberg: 1636
—Vier unterschiedliche Rela-
tiones historicae. Nuremberg:
W. Endter, 1636
—*See also* Wurffbain, Johann Sig-
mund. Reiss-Beschreibung.
Nuremberg: 1646
Wurffbain, Johann Sigmund.
Reiss-Beschreibung. Nurem-
berg: M. Endter, 1646
Wurffbain, Leonhart. *See* Wurf-
bain, Leonhart
Wybarne, Joseph. The new age
of old names. London:
[J. Windet] for W. Barret, &
H. Fetherstone, 1609
Wynne, Edward. *See* Winne, Ed-
ward
Wytfliet, Corneille. Descrip-
tionis Ptolemaicae augmen-
tum. Douai: F. Fabri, 1603
(2)
—Descriptionis Ptolemicae aug-
mentum. Arnhem: J. Janszoon,
1615
—Histoire universelle des Indes.

'